天津市志

科学技术志

1991-2005

天津市地方志编修委员会办公室
天津市科学技术委员会
编著

图书在版编目（CIP）数据

天津市志．科学技术志 / 天津市地方志编修委员会办公室，天津市科学技术委员会编著．-- 北京 ：方志出版社，2019.1
ISBN 978-7-5144-3578-8

Ⅰ．①天… Ⅱ．①天… Ⅲ．①天津－地方志 ②科学探究事业－概况－天津 Ⅳ．①K292.1

中国版本图书馆CIP数据核字(2019)第022769号

天津市志·科学技术志

编　　者：天津市地方志编修委员会办公室
　　　　　天津市科学技术委员会
责任编辑：李静
出 版 人：冀祥德
出 版 者：方志出版社
　　　　　地址　北京市朝阳区潘家园东里9号（国家方志馆4层）
　　　　　邮编　100021
　　　　　网址　http://www.fzph.org
发　　行：方志出版社图书经销中心
　　　　　电话（010）67110500
经　　销：各地新华书店
印　　刷：天津中铁物资印业有限公司
开　　本：889×1194　　1/16
印　　张：75印张
字　　数：2227千字
版　　次：2019年1月第1版　　2019年1月第1次印刷
印　　数：0001～1000册
ISBN 978-7-5144-3578-8　　定价：560.00元

天津大学史绍熙（1916 年 8 月～ 2000 年 9 月），工程热物理学家、内燃机燃烧学家，1980 年当选中国科学院技术科学部院士（学部委员）

（天津大学供稿）

南开大学申泮文（1916 年 9 月～ 2017 年 7 月），无机化学和氢化学家，1980 年当选中国科学院化学部院士（学部委员）

（南开大学供稿）

南开大学何炳林(1918 年 8 月 ~ 2007 年 7 月) ,有机化学、高分子化学家，1980 年当选中国科学院化学部院士 (学部委员)

(南开大学供稿)

南开大学陈茹玉 (1919 年 9 月 ~ 2012 年 3 月) ，有机化学家，1980 年当选中国科学院化学部院士 (学部委员)

(南开大学供稿)

南开大学陈荣悌(1919年11月～2001年11月)，化学家，1980年当选中国科学院化学部院士(学部委员)

(南开大学供稿)

徐叙瑢(1922年4月～)，物理学家，1987～1997年受聘于天津理工学院(现天津理工大学)，1980年当选中国科学院数理学部院士(学部委员)

(天津理工大学供稿)

天津大学余国琮（1922 年 11 月 ~ ），化学工程学家，1991 年当选中国科学院化学部院士（学部委员）

（天津大学供稿）

核工业理化工程研究院刘广均（1929 年 7 月 ~ ），同位素分离学家，1991 年当选中国科学院技术科学部院士（学部委员）

（核工业理化工程研究院供稿）

南开大学母国光（1931 年 1 月～2012 年 4 月），应用光学家、教育家，1991 年当选中国科学院技术科学部院士（学部委员）

（南开大学供稿）

天津地质矿产研究所孙大中（1932 年 6 月～1997 年 5 月），地质学家，1991 年当选中国科学院技术科学部院士（学部委员）

（天津地质矿产研究所供稿）

南开大学严志达（1917 年 11 月 ~ 1999 年 4 月），数学家，1993 年当选中国科学院数理学部院士（学部委员）

（南开大学供稿）

天津大学周恒（1929 年 11 月 ~ ），液体力学家，1993 年当选中国科学院数理学部院士（学部委员）

（天津大学供稿）

天津大学彭一刚（1932 年 9 月～），建筑学家，1995 年当选中国科学院技术科学部院士

（天津大学供稿）

天津大学张春霆（1936 年 9 月～），生物信息学家，1995 年当选中国科学院生命科学和医学部院士

（天津大学供稿）

天津大学姚建铨（1939 年 1 月 ~ ），激光技术专家，1997 年当选中国科学院信息技术科学部院士

（天津大学供稿）

南开大学程津培（1948 年 6 月 ~ ），有机化学家，2001 年当选中国科学院化学部院士

（南开大学供稿）

南开大学葛墨林（1938 年 12 月 ~ ），理论物理学家，2003 年当选为中国科学院院士数学物理学部院士

（南开大学供稿）

核工业理化工程研究院钱皋韵（1927 年 3 月 ~ ），核燃料工程、同位素分离专家。1994 年当选中国工程院能源与矿业工程学部院士

（核工业理化工程研究院供稿）

南开大学李正名（1931 年 1 月 ~ ），有机化学家，1995 年当选中国工程院化学、冶金与材料工程学部院士

（南开大学供稿）

中国船舶重工集团公司第七〇七研究所汪顺亭（1935 年 1 月 ~ ），惯性技术与导航设备专家，1995 年当选中国工程院机械与运载工程学部院士

（中国船舶重工集团公司供稿）

天津医科大学吴咸中（1925 年 8 月～），普通外科与中西医结合专家，1996 年当选中国工程院医药卫生学部院士

（天津医科大学供稿）

天津大学沈家祥（1921 年 11 月～ -2015 年 7 月），药物化学家，1999 年当选中国工程院医药卫生学部院士

（天津大学供稿）

天津大学曹楚生（1926 年 6 月 ~ 2017 年 11 月），水利工程设计专家，1999 年当选中国工程院土木、水利与建筑工程学部院士

（天津大学供稿）

天津市黄瓜研究所侯锋（1928 年 2 月 ~ ），蔬菜育种专家，1999 年当选中国工程院农业学部院士

（天津市黄瓜研究所供稿）

交通部第一航务工程勘察设计院谢世楞（1935 年 5 月～），港口和海岸工程专家。1999 年当选中国工程院土木、水利与建筑工程学部院士

（交通部第一航务工程勘察设计院供稿）

天津大学王静康（1938 年 4 月～），工业结晶科学与技术专家，1999 年当选中国工程院化学、冶金与材料工程学部院士

（天津大学供稿）

天津中医药大学第一附属医院石学敏（1938年6月～），中医、针灸学专家。1999年当选中国工程院医药卫生学部院士

（天津中医药大学第一附属医院供稿）

天津华北设计院李猷嘉（1932年11月～），燃气供应专家，2001年当选中国工程院土木、水利与建筑工程学部院士

（天津华北设计院供稿）

天津大学叶声华（1934 年 6 月～），测试计量技术及仪器专家，2003 年当选中国工程院信息与电子工程学部院士

（天津大学供稿）

天津新技术产业园区鼎名密封有限公司王玉明（1941 年 1 月～），机械设计及理论专家，2003 年当选中国工程院机械与运载工程学部院士

（天津新技术产业园区鼎名密封有限公司供稿）

天津药物研究院刘昌孝（1942 年 4 月～），药理学家，药代动力学家。2003 年当选中国工程院医药卫生学部院士

（天津药物研究院供稿）

天津医科大学郝希山（1945 年 9 月～），肿瘤学家。2003 年当选中国工程院医药卫生学部院士

（天津医科大学供稿）

天津大学陈予恕（1931 年 3 月～），工程非线性振动专家，2005 年当选中国工程院机械与运载工程学部院士

（天津大学供稿）

天津大学余贻鑫（1936 年 11 月～），电力系统分析、规划与仿真专家。2005 年当选中国工程院能源与矿业工程学部院士

（天津大学供稿）

核工业理化工程研究院陈念念（1941年10月～），核材料与核燃料专家，2005年当选中国工程院能源与矿业工程学部院士

（核工业理化工程研究院供稿）

天津中医药大学张伯礼（1948年2月～），中医内科专家，2005年当选中国工程院医药卫生学部院士

（天津中医药大学供稿）

陈省身（1911 年 10 月～ 2004 年 12 月），数学家。美国国籍。1984 ～ 1992 年任天津南开数学研究所所长，1994 年当选为中国科学院外籍院士

（南开大学供稿）

2001 年 9 月，陈省身在南开数学研究所与研究生座谈

（南开大学供稿）

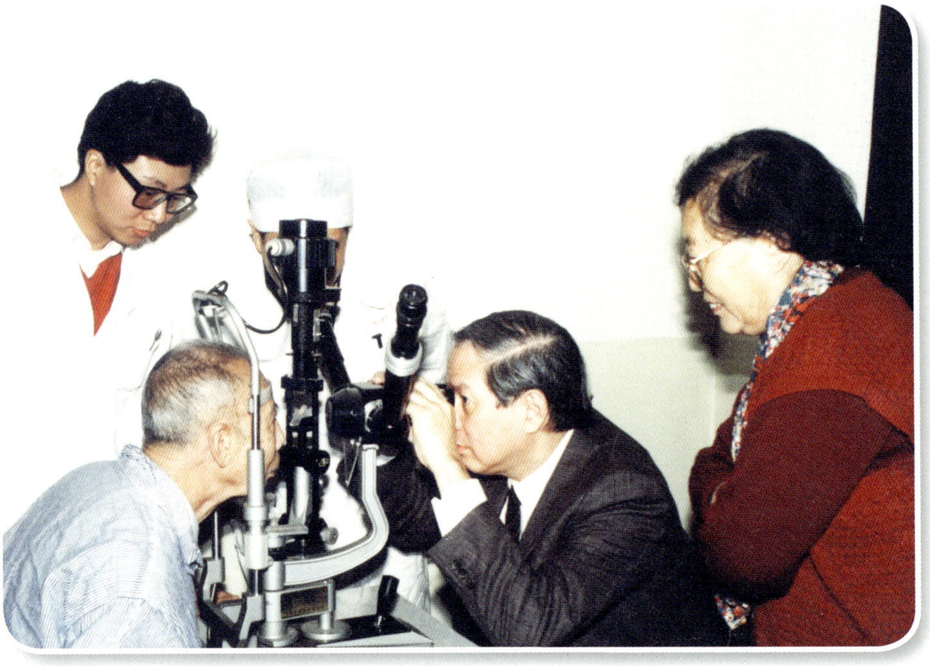

天津医科大学眼科中心眼视光学院名誉院长、新加坡人林少明（右二）获得 1997 年度国家国际科技合作奖

（天津医科大学供稿）

天津力神电池股份有限公司总工程师、加拿大籍华人毛焕宇获得 2000 年度天津市国际科技合作奖和 2001 年度国家国际科技合作奖

（天津力神电池股份有限公司供稿）

天津市燕化新材料有限公司总工程师、法国人 Robert Degeilh（罗伯特·迪盖特）博士获得 2001 年度天津市国际科技合作奖和 2002 年度国家国际科技合作奖

（天津市燕化新材料有限公司供稿）

天津医科大学名誉教授、美国人乔丹·M·菲利普斯（中）医学博士获得 2002 年度天津市国际科技合作奖

（天津医科大学供稿）

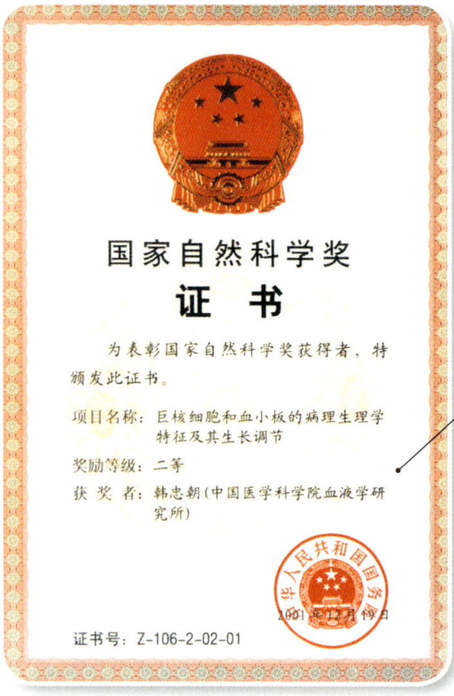
国家自然科学奖
证　书
为表彰国家自然科学奖获得者，特颁发此证书。
项目名称：巨核细胞和血小板的病理生理学特征及其生长调节
奖励等级：二等
获 奖 者：韩忠朝（中国医学科学院血液学研究所）
2001年12月19日
证书号：Z-106-2-02-01

中国医学科学院血液学研究所韩忠朝等完成的“巨核细胞和血小板的病理生理学特征及其生长调节”项目获得2001年度国家自然科学奖二等奖

（中国医学科学院血液学研究所供稿）

南开大学廖代正等完成的“分子磁性的基础研究”获得2003年度国家自然科学奖二等奖

（南开大学供稿）

南开大学陈瑞阳等完成的“中国主要植物染色体研究”获得2003年度国家自然科学奖二等奖

（南开大学供稿）

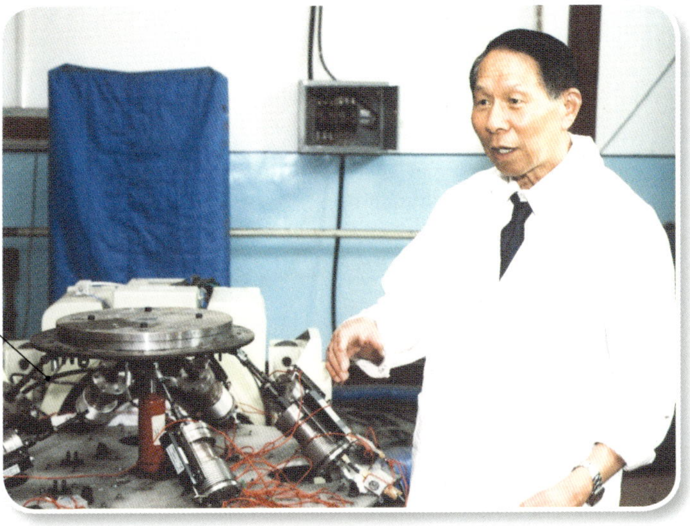

天津大学陈予恕等完成的“复杂非线性系统的动力学理论与应用”获得 2003 年度国家自然科学奖二等奖

（天津大学供稿）

南开大学龙以明等完成的“辛道路的指标理论与在非线性哈密顿系统中的应用”获得 2004 年度国家自然科学奖二等奖

（南开大学供稿）

南开大学张伟平完成的“Atiyah-Singer 指标理论的若干研究”获得 2005 年度国家自然科学奖二等奖

（南开大学供稿）

南开大学许京军等完成的“光折变新效应、机理与器件的研究”获得2005年度国家自然科学奖二等奖

（南开大学供稿）

卢桂章教授负责主持的“面向生物医学工程的微操作机器人系统”，2002年获国家技术发明二等奖。照片为卢桂章教授（第二名持奖状者）在人民大会堂领奖

（南开大学供稿）

天津大学叶声华等完成的“先进制造中空间几何尺寸测量的现场校准方法和装置”获得2004年度国家技术发明奖二等奖

（天津大学供稿）

天津大学王榕树等完成的“新型离子筛的研制及其应用”获得2004年度国家技术发明奖二等奖

（天津大学供稿）

天津鼎名密封公司王玉明完成的“螺旋式浮环密封装置”获得2005年度国家技术发明奖二等奖

（天津鼎名密封公司供稿）

天津工业大学李嘉禄等完成的“三维异型整体编织工艺的研究和三维编织设备及织物的研制”获得2001年度国家科技进步二等奖

（天津工业大学供稿）

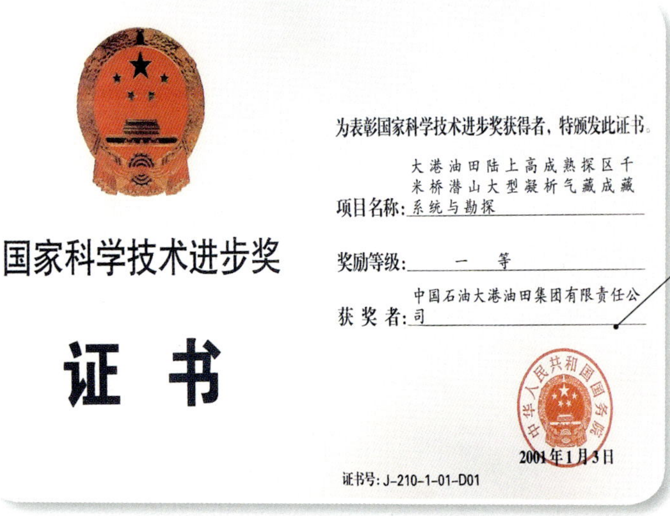
国家科学技术进步奖

证书

为表彰国家科学技术进步奖获得者，特颁发此证书。

项目名称：大港油田陆上高成熟探区千米桥潜山大型凝析气藏成藏系统与勘探

奖励等级：一 等

获 奖 者：中国石油大港油田集团有限责任公司

2001年1月3日

证书号：J-210-1-01-D01

中国石油大港油田集团有限责任公司关于“大港油田陆上高成熟探区千米桥潜山大型凝析气藏成藏系统与勘探”项目研究获得2000年度国家科技进步奖一等奖

（中国石油大港油田集团有限责任公司供稿）

天津大学与天津滨海快速交通发展有限公司合作，李忠献等完成的“天津轻轨工程抗震分析与减震降噪研究”获得2004年度天津科技进步奖一等奖

（天津大学供稿）

天津大学与天津六建建筑工程有限公司陈志华等完成“天津博物馆建筑结构及关键技术研究”获得2004年度天津市科学技术奖一等奖

（天津大学供稿）

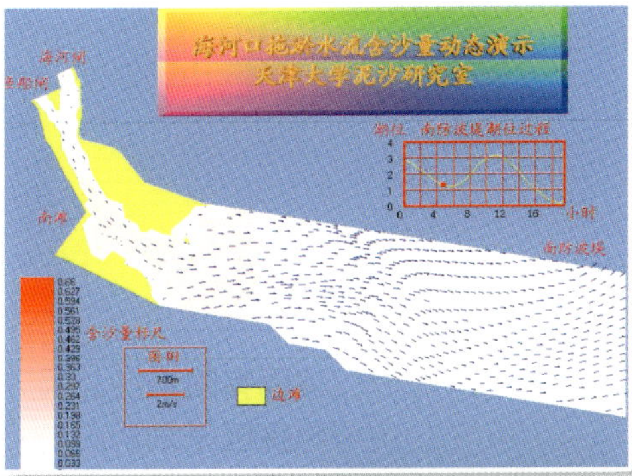

天津大学钟登华等完成“水利工程仿真基础理论与方法研究”获 2004 年度天津市科学技术奖自然科学一等奖

（天津大学供稿）

经陈省身倡议，天津科技馆内建设了数学馆。图为 2002 年 8 月 18 日陈省身（中坐）参观数学馆

（天津科技馆供稿）

天津力神电池股份有限公司于 2000 年开始聚合物电池的研发工作，在国内率先将卷绕式聚合物电池推进到实用性生产阶段。图为聚合物锂离子电池生产线

（天津力神电池股份有限公司供稿）

2002 年 4 月第一辆使用镍氢电池的"幸福使者"纯电动微型客车研制成功

（天津清源电动车辆有限责任公司供稿）

天津赛象科技股份有限公司张芝泉等研制的 TST-LCZ-3-80 全钢载重子午线轮胎三鼓式一次法成型机，获得 2004 年度天津市科技进步一等奖

（天津赛象科技股份有限公司供稿）

1997 年天津药业公司卢彦昌等研制成功地塞米松新工艺。天津大学王静康等开发的高效智能化结晶装置及计算机控制系统，实现了由小试规模直接进行 10 万倍的产业化放大，在天津天药药业股份有限公司建立了年产 60 吨地塞米松磷酸钠结晶生产线，于 2002 年 7 月一次开车成功

（天津药业公司　天津大学供稿）

天津大学与天津天士力集团有限公司合作，王宝光等完成的“复方丹参滴丸自动灌装线”获得2001年度天津科技进步一等奖

（天津天士力集团有限公司供稿）

2002年环欧公司拉制的Φ6″区熔硅单晶

（中环电子集团供稿）

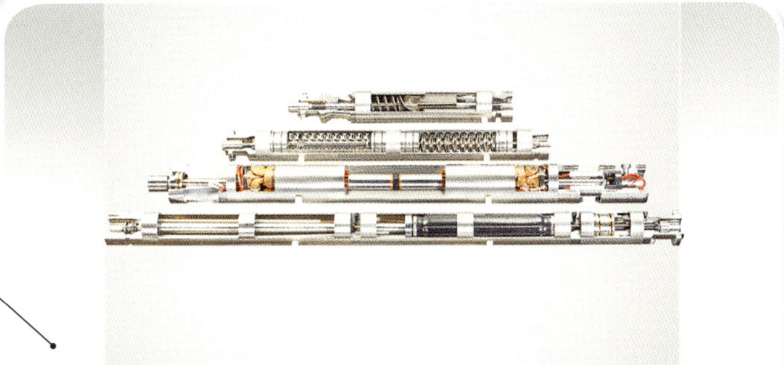

1991年，天津市百利溢通电泵有限公司（原天津电机总厂）自主开发的潜油电泵获得“第二届北京国际博览会金奖”。该厂自主开发的永磁电机，大容量电机，高温、高效电泵等新产品

（天津大港油田集团供稿）

2002 年，中欧表业成功研制开发生产出具有国际先进水平的产品陀飞轮手表

（天津渤海中鸥表业技术有限公司供稿）

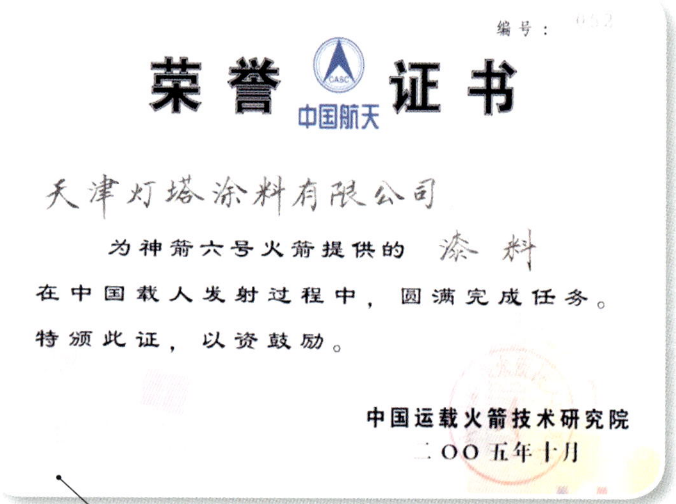

编号：

荣誉证书

中国航天

天津灯塔涂料有限公司

为神箭六号火箭提供的 涂料

在中国载人发射过程中，圆满完成任务。

特颁此证，以资鼓励。

中国运载火箭技术研究院

二ＯＯ五年十月

2003 年，天津灯塔涂料有限公司为中国第一艘载人飞船“神州五号”提供配套产品之后，又为一系列航空、航天及国防重点军工项目提供配套产品

（天津灯塔涂料有限公司供稿）

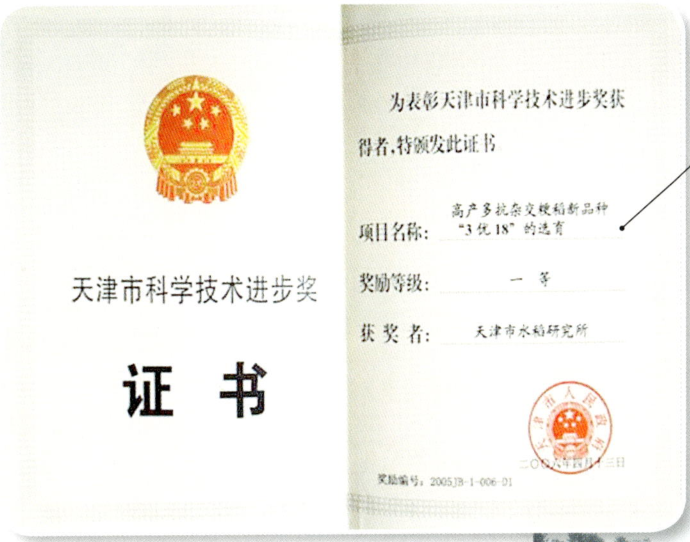
天津市科学技术进步奖

证书

为表彰天津市科学技术进步奖获得者，特颁发此证书

项目名称：高产多抗杂交粳稻新品种"3优18"的选育

奖励等级：一等

获奖者：天津市水稻研究所

奖励编号：2005JB-1-006-01

1998年，天津农业科学院水稻研究所刘学军研制出高产多抗杂交粳稻新品种“3优18”

（天津农业科学院供稿）

1996年，国家科委将“津春四号”黄瓜确定为国家重点科技成果推广计划项目向全国推广并获1995年度天津市科技进步奖一等奖

（天津农业科学院供稿）

从 1993 年始，历经十年攻关，天津农业科学院蔬菜研究所研制出具有国际水平的菜花系列良种。图为“津雪 88”

（天津农业科学院供稿）

2005 年，刚出生的胚胎克隆波尔山羊——津生

（天津农业科学院供稿）

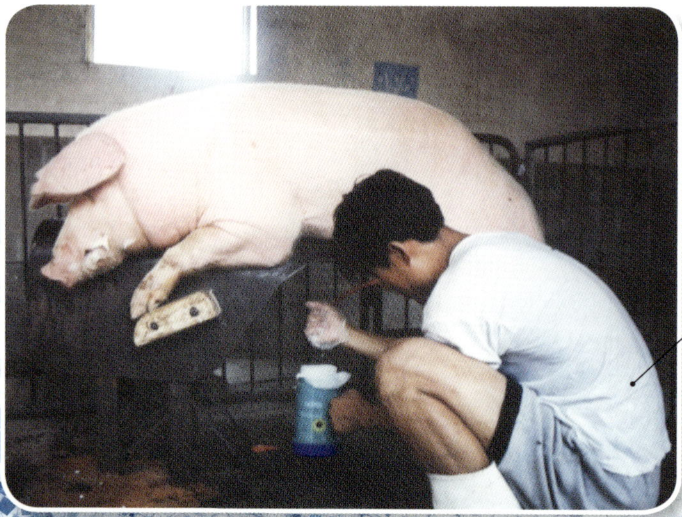

2003 年，天津市畜牧局等单位开展“猪人工授精技术推广”，该成果获 2005 年度天津市科技进步二等奖

（天津市畜牧局供稿）

2001 年天津港成为中国北方第一个亿吨大港

（天津港供稿）

中铁十八局有限公司承担的“李子沟高墩大跨刚构——连续组合梁桥快速施工成套技术”获得天津市 2001 年度科技进步一等奖

（中铁十八局有限公司供稿）

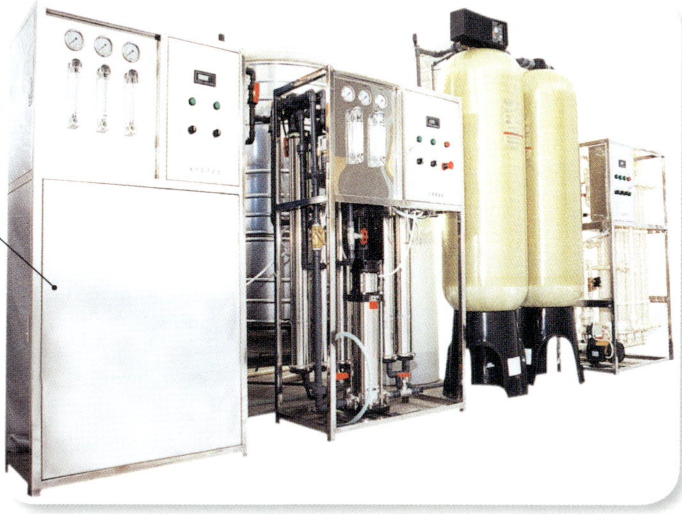

2001 年 3 月，中国军事医学科学院卫生装备研究所龚承元等完成“电去离子技术和反渗透——电去离子高纯水设备的研究”，获 2002 年度天津市科技进步一等奖

（卫生装备研究所供稿）

天津医科大学附属肿瘤医院郝希山等完成的“功能性间置空肠代胃术的临床与基础研究”获得 2001 年度国家科技进步二等奖

（天津医科大学附属肿瘤医院供稿）

由天津城建设计院有限公司承建的不对称斜式钢拱桥——大沽桥，于 2005 年建成

（天津城建设计院有限公司供稿）

天津新技术产业园区是 1991 年 3 月经国务院批准的首批国家高新技术产业开发区

（天津新技术产业园区管委会供稿）

天津市地方志编修委员会组成人员

主　　任　张国清

副 主 任　李　毅　王小宁　高玉葆　孟庆松

委　　员　阎　峰　杨绍启　刘炳刚　王赤涛　胡学明
刘小芃　刘春雷　王　禹　许颖悟　谷云彪
刘东水　徐广宇　薛景山　董玉文　畅志杰
宋称意　刘基智　李伟桥　陈　晖　霍　兵
路　红　张　巍　苗加兴　毛科军　张文波
游庆波　王　浩　梁益铭　刘道刚　苏德芬
褚丽萍　马庆余　侯晓韧　王　洪　杨荣山
李建华　蓝兆琪　鲍培兰　房靖彪　张　莉
李梦林　陈　宇　王云齐　舒令嘉　于学蕴
聂永安　郝树龙　王悦群　严木生　郭振影
王　珂　戴　蕴　谭绪良　张再生

秘 书 长　关树锋

《天津市志·科学技术志》总编审人员

总　　编　关树锋

执行主编　张月光

分志主编　宋铭月　郭天天

分志编辑　陈　颖　沙　洵　徐　钊　王　琳　王中玮
韦　恬　张　轶

评审人员　（以姓氏笔画为序）

马其慧　方兆麟　包英姿　冯　宽　关树锋
李春成　李　群　沙　洵　宋铭月　张月光
罗澍伟　赵淑萍　郭天天　梁　肃　谭汝为
薛景山

《天津市志·科学技术志》编辑委员会

《天津市志·科学技术志》编辑人员

主　　编　马其慧　李树夫

副 主 编　李　群　赵淑萍

编　　辑　（姓氏笔画为序）

仇化庭　刘晏惠　李　红　杨　莉

赵凤珍　程新建

参加前期组稿与编辑人员　（姓氏笔画为序）

吕子林　朱爱荣　赵建军　贾化育

郭红旗　虞志球

序 言

改革开放是中国和世界共同发展进步的伟大历程。习近平总书记强调“改革开放这场中国的第二次革命，不仅深刻改变了中国，也深刻影响了世界”。1978年，以党的十一届三中全会胜利召开为标志，中国开启了改革开放的历史征程。同年召开的全国科学大会，邓小平同志提出“科学技术是生产力”重要论断，我国迎来“科学的春天”，作为改革开放的先导科技改革创新迈入快车道。其后，党中央、国务院先后在1995年、2006年、2012年三次召开全国科学技术大会、全国科技创新大会，确立科教兴国、建设创新型国家为举国发展战略。2016年，习近平总书记在全国科技创新大会上强调把科技创新摆在更加重要位置，深入实施创新驱动发展等重大战略，吹响了“三步走”建设世界科技强国的号角，科技创新迎来了又一个“春天”。

党的十九大胜利召开，标志着中国特色社会主义进入新时代，科技创新肩负起新的历史使命和责任担当。习近平总书记在十九大报告中强调“创新是引领发展的第一动力，是建设现代化经济体系的战略支撑”，对新时代建设世界科技强国发出了新的动员令。在今年两院院士大会上，习近平总书记进一步作出了坚持党对科技事业的领导、坚持建设世界科技强国的奋斗目标、坚持走中国特色自主创新道路、坚持以深化改革激发创新活力、坚持创新驱动实质是人才驱动、坚持融入全球科技创新网络“六个坚持”重要论断，强调“我们比历史上任何时候都更需要建设世界科技强国”“关键核心技术是要不来、买不来、讨不来的”。这“六个坚持”为深入学习领会习近平总书记科技创新思想核心要义，深入学习贯彻党的十九大精神，更好地把握新时代科技工作脉络、掌握科技创新规律、引领科技事业发展提供了根本遵循和行动指南。

与全国科技事业同砥砺、共辉煌，在市委、市政府正确领导和大力支持下，

1978年天津乘全国科学大会的春风，科研工作者振奋精神、发奋图强，科学研究实力强劲增长。进入20世纪90年代，中共中央作出了一系列深化科技体制改革的决定，适时，天津市委、市政府于1992年8月颁布了《关于依靠科技进步，加快经济发展的若干意见》，在国内率先提出"科技兴市"的发展战略，使天津的科技事业在经济发展的大潮中找准了定位。1995年，国家提出实施"科教兴国"战略，市委、市政府坚定不移地响应中共中央号召，提出"吃科技饭，走科技路"的思路，颁布了《关于贯彻全国科技大会精神，加速科学技术进步的实施意见》，全面实施"科教兴市"战略。1999年，中共中央、国务院召开全国技术创新大会，部署和贯彻《关于加强技术创新、发展高科技、实现产业化的决定》，市委、市政府认真贯彻中共中央决定，出台《中共天津市委关于加速科技进步和创新的若干意见》，以面向21世纪的战略眼光和气魄，明确了走自主创新道路，建设创新型城市的科技发展战略。1992年、1995年、1999年这三个重要的历史关节点，在天津科技志中，都得到真实详细的记录。

"科学技术是第一生产力"明确了科技在经济社会发展中的地位，"吃科技饭，走科技路"使科技创新融入了大众视野，这是春风化雨、润物无声的一个发展过程，是艰难探索的一个过程，是天津科技综合实力从全国排位第七跃升到第三名的一个关键历史时期。天津科技事业的发展依靠的是国家和地方的发展战略和顶层设计，依靠的是广大科技人员和各行各业群体的智慧、坚韧和担当。本卷彰显了科技精英献身科技的爱国主义情怀，记录了广大科技人员在各行各业的发明创造，有不少科技成果站在了国内外的前沿，如陈省身院士带领的南大数学研究团队，史绍熙院士带领的天大内燃机研究团队，侯锋院士带领的黄瓜新品种研究团队等等，都应该在历史上大大的书写一笔。科技志全面翔实地记录了这些为祖国的科技事业作出贡献的科技人物和事迹，留下了十分可贵的历史痕迹。

从《天津通志·科学技术志》(首轮)到《天津市志·科学技术志》(二轮)，科技史志办编著的这两部志书，正是对天津科技发展历程全面真实的写照。这两部志书在客观上纵述史实，力求全面、客观、系统地反映天津市科学技术事业发展的脉络，把握大科技的概念，从科技队伍与科技机构、科技管理与服务、基础科学、高新技术及其产业化、工业科技、农业科技、医药卫生科技、城市建设科技、社会发展科技等各个方面，记述全市各行各业的科技事业进展，是一部综合性的资料著述。它着重记载科学技术促进天津经济社会发展的主要成就，囊括天津市的科技大事、要事，科技人物和政策法规。全书以科技创新为主线，坚持以事系人，以人为本，全面系统地反映天津科技发展的历史沿革，内容完整，详略得当，重点突出，表达通顺，是一本值得收藏的科技志书。科技志全面真实地反映了天津科技发展脉络，内容丰富、史料翔实、主题鲜明、精华荟萃，覆盖面广，传承了天津科技文明，发掘了天津智慧，弘扬了科技精神，对借史鉴今，存史育人，启迪未来有着重要的意义，也为天津科技事业留下了珍贵的资料。

在该书即将付梓之际，对该书编纂过程中给予支持的各相关单位，向参与该书编纂的全体工作人员表示感谢。感谢你们一轮接着一轮、一年接着一年，无私忘我、持续奋战、精雕细琢、精益求精，为天津科技发展留下了浓墨重彩的一笔。

今年是改革开放40年周年，是立足新时代、着眼新目标，将改革进行到底，将创新驱动发展作为核心战略置顶，以新应新、创新赢新的新起点。衷心希望科技战线的广大同仁以“志”为镜、以“志”明志，继续弘扬精神、发扬作风，在市委、市政府领导下，坚持以习近平新时代中国特色社会主义思想为指导，以习近平总书记“三个着力”重要要求为元为纲，抢抓京津冀协同发展历史性窗口期，全面深入推进创新驱动发展战略，持续深化科技体制机制改革，努力支撑推动国际影响力创新型城市和产业创新中心建设，为全市高质量发展、加快建成“五个现代化天津”作出更大贡献。

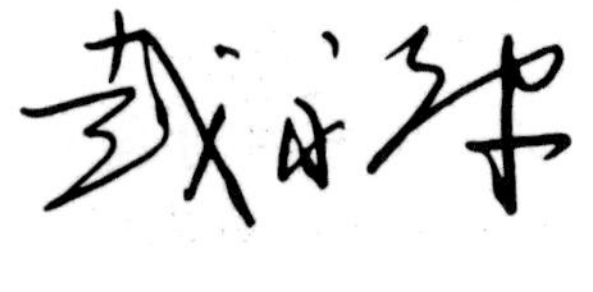

2018年7月

凡　　例

一、本志书坚持以马克思列宁主义、毛泽东思想、邓小平理论、“三个代表”重要思想、科学发展观、习近平新时代中国特色社会主义思想为指导，坚持辩证唯物主义和历史唯物主义的立场、观点、方法，客观、系统地记述天津科技进步的发展规律和特点，全面、真实地反映天津科技发展历史与现状。

二、本志书是第二轮《天津通志·科学技术志》，重点记述1991～2005年天津科学技术事业的发展历程，重要科技事项适当向上追溯，个别重大科技事项适当下延。本志书附录篇设置了补遗栏目，对首轮修志遗漏部分予以补记。

三、本志书是关于天津科学技术发展的资料性文献。对天津市地域内从事科学技术活动的机构、部门、团体和个人的重大科技活动事项均予以选记，内容涉及全市主要行业和学科领域。

四、本志书力求体现时代特点，突出地方特色，做到思想性、科学性和资料性的统一。

五、本志书为述、记、志、传、图、表、录诸体并用的综合体裁，以志为主。述体部分为论述体，夹叙夹议，纵横兼顾，全书设“综述”，各篇设“概述”，部分章、节设“无题序”。志体部分依篇、章、节、目序列编排，部分目下设子目、细目。全书遵循横排竖写，述而不论，详略得当，以事系人的原则。

六、本志书对各种机构、部门、团体和会议等名称的书写，第一次出现时一律用全称，再次出现时可用简称。地名、党派、机构等一律使用记事时名称；名称有变动者，括注2005年底名称。外国的机构名称、人名采用汉文通用译名，必要时在译名后括号内注原名。

七、本志书按《中华人民共和国国家标准-出版物上数字用法的规定》(ICS 01.140.20 A 19 GB/T 15838—1995)书写。

八、本志书中出现的计量单位按1993年国家技术监督局公布的《量和单位》(GB3100-3102-93)标准执行。

九、各单位、各部门的获奖科技成果,统一列在“科技管理篇”中,各章、节不再列表。

十、凡属全市性的数据,以科技统计部门公布的数字为准;各专业细目数字,由各供稿单位提供。

目 录

第三篇 基础科学

第四篇 高新技术及其产业化

第五篇 工业科技

第六篇　农业科技

第七篇　医药卫生科技

第八篇 城市建设科技

第九篇 社会发展科技

第十篇 科技人物

附 录

索　引

CONTENTS

Part III Basic Sciences

Part IV High Technology and Its Industrialization

Part V Industrial Science and Technology

Part VI Agricultural Science and Technology

Part VII Science and Technology of Medicine and Public Health

Part VIII Technology of Urban Construction

Part IX Science and Technology for Social Development

Part X The Lineup of Scientists

Appendixes

Indexes

综　　述

政　策

1991年至2005年，在全国上下深化改革，扩大开放，以科技为先导促进经济结构转型的形势下，天津进入历史上发展较快的时期。中共天津市委（以下简称"市委"）、天津市人民政府（以下简称"市政府"）解放思想、实事求是、开拓进取，面对全市经济和产业结构调整以及企业改制举步维艰，老工业城市改造和民生事项负重前行，财政资金极其紧张的局面，果断确立实施"科教兴市"战略。全市科技界、教育界、产业界和各方面的力量，以坚定不移、一以贯之的努力，协同推进天津的科学技术进步，使得这十五年成为天津市科技综合实力从全国排位第七位跃升为第三位的关键时期。到2005年，全社会R&D（研究与试验发展）支出占GDP（地区生产总值）的比例达到1.97%，是1991年的5.8倍；高新技术产业完成产值2141.4亿元，占工业的比重达到29.9%，是1995年的8倍。2005年，全市年专利申请数量为11657件、专利授权量3045件，分别是1991年的8.56倍和5.02倍；技术市场成交合同金额50.71亿元，是1996年的3.8倍。这个阶段，天津科技发展战略、体制机制改革重大举措相继推出，促进了科技生产力大解放、大发展。继80年代天津在全国率先建立常设技术交易市场，率先出版第一张技术市场报，率先设立青年科技基金和自然科学基金之后，在全国又率先提出"科技兴市"战略，率先颁布实施专业技术人员继续教育法规，率先与国家科委联建国家级技术交易市场，率先建立科技创业孵化器。科技实力的提高，科技与经济融合的加深，科技管理水平的进步，新技术产业园区的孵化和带动，使天津进入一个科技地位和作用更加凸显的新的历史时期。

一、科技发展战略部署

1978年全国科学大会后，"科学技术是生产力""尊重知识，尊重人才"等观念逐步确立，国家发展迎来了"科学的春天"。1985年中共中央发布《关于科学技术体制改革的决定》，在"经济建设必须依靠科学技术，科学技术工作必须面向经济建设"战略方针指导下，天津全面推进科技体制改革，在开辟技术市场、推进科技成果商品化、改革科研院所财政拨款制度、鼓励民营科技企业发展、创建新技术产业园区等方面采取一系列重大举措，科学技术事业步入全新的发展阶段。

进入20世纪90年代，国家不断完善经济和科技发展战略与顶层设计，推出一系列深化科技体制机制改革的重大举措。市委、市政府于1992年8月颁布《关于依靠科技进步，加快经济发展的若干意见》，在国内最早提出"科技兴市"战略，确立天津振兴经济要依靠科技的指导思想，坚决把经济建设转移到依靠科技进步和提高劳动者素质的轨道上。1995年国家作出《关于加速科学技术进步的决定》，提出实施"科教兴国"战略。天津经济正处于调结构、上水平、提高素质的关键时刻，也是经济转型最艰难时期，市委、市政府坚决响应党中央的号召，提出"走科技路，吃科技饭"的发展思路，颁布《关于加速科学技术进步的实施意见》，把"科教兴市"作为一个全局性、先导性和长期性的战略，调整建立由市长任组长的天津市科技领导小组，加强对科技工作的宏观管理和综合协调，把科技工作摆上重要位置。1999年，中共中央、国务院召开全国技术创新大会，颁布《关于加强技术创新、发展高科技、实现产业化的决定》，市委、市政府认真贯彻党中央的决定，出台《关于加速科技进步和技术创新的若干意见》，提出面对跨世纪发展的新形势和新任务，强化企业创新主体，建设技术创新体系，把"发展高技术，实现产业化"作为科技工作的重中之重。1991～2005年，天津以国家发展战略和总体部署为导向，面对新科技革命和产业变革的新要求，结合自身的实际情况，在三个重要的历史节点期间，不断对天津科技发展进行部署和调整，积极开展一系列卓有成效的工作，推动天津经济社会发展一步步走出一条依靠科技进步，提高整体素质，实现加快发展，增强经济实力的新路子。

1991～2005年，天津编制完成"八五""九五""十五"科技发展计划、中长期科学技术发展规划、高新技术产业发展规划等，立足当下，着眼未来，对天津科技发展谋划具有全局性、系统性和综合性的顶层设计和发展路线，成为实现天津科技发展战略和目标的纲领性文件。"八五"期间，按照"科技兴市"战略要求，结合天津的实际和优势，"科技兴市必先科技兴工"，重点围绕"316"（三个带头产业、十个重点行业、六十个重点产品)产业结构调整目标,组织汽车、计算机等10个重大科技攻关项目,推动100项重大科技成果的推广应用。在实施火炬计划的基础上,集中精力组织实施科技百亿工程,促进高新技术成果产业化。扶持和壮大市属科研机构,鼓励他们以各种形式进入经济建设主战场。加快发展技术市场,推动科技成果转化。提高应用基础研究投入,为培育先导产业做技术储备。这个阶段,天津市科技综合实力在全国的排名从1993年的第七位跃升到1995年的第四位。

"九五"期间,面对新技术革命的挑战和经济快速发展的迫切要求,天津市确定重点发展高新技术产业和培育21世纪新兴产业,以新技术产业园区为基地,以科技百亿工程和重大产业化工程等为重点,推动电子信息、新材料、生物技术、先进制造技术、新能源及环保技术等六大高新技术领域的发展。加快高新技术改造传统产业,促进企业逐步成为技术创新和成果转化的主体。改革科研机构体制和运行机制,吸引和鼓励驻津科研院所更多地参与到天津的经济建设中来。加快信息化建设,以天津信息港建设为中心,全面实施"2119工程",把天津建成全国主要的信息产业基地之一。这个阶段,天津市科技进步综合实力保持在全国第三或第四位,高新技术产业开始成为新的经济增长点。

"十五"期间,随着世界经济一体化格局的逐渐形成和知识经济的兴起,天津市迫切需要加快高新技术产业发展,使之成为21世纪新一代支柱产业,努力建设与北方重要经济中心地位相适应的高新技术及产业化基地。为此,天津市将科技工作的重点放在发展电子信息、生物技术与现代医药、新能源三个产业,并积极鼓励和引导光机电一体化、新材料以及环保三个产业的快速发展。同时,安排45个重点应用基础科学研究项目,为高新技术发展提供技术储备;组织30项重大高新技术产业化项目,实行滚动发展,为经济发展培育新的增长点。期间,天津市加快建立和完善科技创新体系和科技投融资体系,提高全市科技创新能力。信息化建设以"1221"计划为主导,信息化水平全面提升。这个阶段,天津综合科技实力继续保持在全国第三位,高新技术产业产值占工业总产值接近三分之一。

在科技发展规划指导下,历经三个五年计划,天津市在面向经济建设主战场、发展高新技术及产业、加强技术储备三个层次上,逐步形成以应用基础研究、科技重大专项、关键技术攻关、科技成果转化、发展战略研究为主体的、相互衔接的天津科技发展计划体系。经过不断调整、充实和提高,使科技计划管理更加科学化、规范化和制度化。

天津市为贯彻落实科技发展战略,重大的改革举措和政策密集出台,以科学技术进步法、促进科技成果转化法、专利法、科学普及法和科学技术奖励条例为内容的科技法律法规体系不断完善;围绕战略规划部署、计划项目管理、科技成果转化、科技奖励、科技评价、人才激励、技术市场和知识产权管理等重大改革和调整的科技政策与管理措施不断推出,为科技事业持续发展提供了体制性的支撑和良好的政策环境。

二、科技创新能力提升

天津市围绕科技发展战略目标,全面推进创新能力建设,在增加科技投入、壮大人才队伍、科技资源合理配置、构建新型科技创新(体系)等方面取得明显成效。

(一)科技投入逐年提高

1991~2005年,天津地方财政对科技发展的经费投入不断增加。2005年,地方财政科技拨款规模达到13.65亿元,占当年地方财政支出比重2.62%。在财政资金的"杠杆"效应带动下,全社会科技投入持续增加,特别是进入新世纪后呈现快速增长的势头。2005年,全市R&D(研究与试验发展)支出72.92亿元,占当年全市GDP(地区生产总值)的比重为1.97%,较1991年约占0.34%的比重有大幅度提高。从资金来源看,2005年企业资金占全市科技活动经费筹集额的比重为73.55%,占全市研究与试验发展经费支出的比重为66.65%,政府引导、企业主体的科技投入格局进一步形成。为拓宽多元化科技投入渠道,启动了科技创业投资工作,逐步构建起科技创业投资体系。2000~2005年,全市科技创业投资企业由10家增加到65家,注册资本总额由9亿元增至42亿元。在市级财政预算中安排天津市创业投资引导资金,先后出资设立创业投资机构7家,用近1.2亿元的引导资金吸引境外及民间资金近10亿元,带动关联资本近100亿元。

（二）科技人才队伍不断壮大

1991～2005年，天津市每万名职工中科技人员数量由1973人增加至2189人，从业人口整体科技素质得到提升。围绕引进科技领军人才、改善科技人员工作生活条件、科技人员奖励、人才职称评聘等制定了一系列政策，科技人才发展环境得到优化。在此期间，天津有12人新当选中国科学院院士，19人新当选中国工程院院士。至2005年，在津两院院士共有42人。1992年，天津市开始选拔自然科学领域学术技术带头人，授予“天津市授衔专家”称号。到2005年，全市获得授衔专家称号的有479人，享受政府特殊津贴的专家有近3000人。他们在全市各学科领域、各行业发挥着引领和带动作用。1989年先后启动的青年科学基金和自然科学基金，为培育学科带头人耕耘播种，一批中青年专家脱颖而出。1994年，启动实施“跨世纪育才工程”（即“131人才工程”），到2005年首批培养期结束时，有40名人选承担国家杰出青年基金、国家“863”和“973”计划、国家自然科学基金等国家级重点项目71项，50名人选完成的90余项科研成果获得国家级、部市级奖励。天津市于2000年建立人才发展基金，主要用于对高层次人才培养、引进和奖励的资助。对“不迁户口、不转关系”、以柔性流动方式到天津工作的人员实行“绿卡”制度。如天津大学集中引进美国在生物制药方面的一个留学生团队，成立了天津大学药学院；南开大学和天津医科大学吸引10多位海外学子担纲天津基因芯片专项的重大攻关项目。海外留学生归国到津创业的人数逐年增多。

（三）科技创新体系建设加快

构建新型科技创新体系是深化科技体制改革，合理资源配置的需要。至2005年，天津市依托各高等院校、科研院所和企业，先后组建以重点实验室、科学研究中心为代表的新型知识创新机构70个，以工程技术中心、企业技术中心为代表的新型技术创新机构191个，以生产力促进中心、科技企业孵化器为代表的成果转移转化与产业化机构（基地）130个。1991～2005年，相继成立天津市科技创业服务中心、北方技术交易市场、天津市创业投资发展中心、天津市科技评价中心等科技服务机构。其中，由市政府与国家科委于1995年联合组建的北方技术交易市场作为国家级唯一的常设技术市场，参考国际惯例和模式运作，实现从单纯技术交易场所向综合性技术转移服务机构的转型。自2001年起，天津市集成利用科技基础条件资源和公共研究服务资源，建立完善科技文献信息平台、大型仪器协作共用平台、技术标准检测平台、科普条件平台、科技发展战略与政策研究中心等服务平台。

传统的科研体制在深化改革中获得新的发展，在贯彻落实中共中央《关于科学技术体制改革的决定》中，出台多项推动科研院所体制改革的政策。1991年，开始对市属科研院所实行分级管理制度，认定骨干研究所，实行全员聘任制。1997年在9个科研院所开展改革试点，2000年对市属72家开发类科研院所实施企业化转制。到2005年，市属科研机构改革取得突破性成果，政府由直接管理转为间接管理，转制院所的市场观念显著增强，更加注重发挥自身科技优势，打造专业技术特长，成为活跃在市场上的一支新生力量。中央驻津科研机构自然科学类有33家，以承担国家重点科研项目为主，同时也为天津经济建设服务，在前沿探索、集成创新方面的骨干和引领作用尤为突出，不断释放创新能量和活力。

（四）企业创新主体逐步到位

在新体系构建过程中，企业的技术创新主体地位逐步增强，“重生产、轻研发”“重引进、轻消化吸收”的通病逐步转变。2005年，天津大中型工业企业科技活动人员占职工总数比重为4.94%，比1991年提高2.02个百分点。企业科技活动经费支出占销售收入的比重从2000年的1.2%增长到2005年的1.8%。其中企业研究与试验发展经费支出占主营业务收入的比重为0.7%，较1991年约占0.3%的水平有明显增长。企业办技术开发机构195个，比2000年增加13个百分点。企业技术开发机构中，从事科技活动人员3.20万人，比2000年增加0.75万人；技术开发经费支出总额93.70亿元，是2000年经费支出总额的4.56倍。2001～2005年，企业每年的专利申请量由不足300件增至2900余件，新产品销售收入由549亿元增至1545亿元，科技创新引领的成果产出和经济效益得到明显提升。高等院校、科研院所与企业进一步深化产学研合作。据统计，2005年全市研究与开发机构、高等院校科技活动经费中，企业资金占比分别达到59.70%和32.56%，与企业间的合作关系不断融合。转制科研院所接受企业委托课题经费收入达38.10亿元。高等院校接受企业委托开展科技活动的资金达到4.68亿元，比2000年增长1.16倍。

（五）民营科技企业快速成长

随着科技体制改革的不断深化，民营科技企业以其“自筹资金、自愿组合、自主经营、自负盈亏”的新型运行机制，成为技术创新中最活跃的群体，涌现出天津赛象科技股份有限公司、天士力制药股份有限公司等领军企业。统计结果显示，1993年天津民营科技企业为2061家，2000年增加到5600家，2005年累计达到8000家，企业资产、收入、净利润、上缴税金等指标持续增长。为促进民营科技企业的发展，先后出台《天津市促进民营科技企业发展的若干规定》《天津市民营科技企业管理办法》等政策，从鼓励申报科技计划项目、企业人员职称、企业孵化、金融工具等多方面予以支持。2005年，天津市设立科技型中小企业技术创新资金，支持民营科技企业100多项技术创新项目，有力地推动了民营科技企业的技术创新活动。

（六）国内外科技资源不断涌入

天津始终以积极开放的态度，拓展国内外科技合作的广度与深度，借以凝聚高端科技资源、增强自身发展实力。国际合作方面，1991～2005年，先后与39个国家和国际组织开展政府间的科技合作，实施合作项目200余项，涉及农业、工业、环保、能源、生物、医药、信息等诸多领域。国内科技合作方面，2005年7月，国家科技部和市政府签署工作会商制度议定书，并举行第一次工作会商会，共同就推进科技体制改革、促进天津滨海新区建设和发展进行协商。同月，中国科学院与市政府签署全面科技合作协议，在项目合作、机构合作、人才交流、院所引进、信息交流等方面建立长效合作机制。部市合作、院市合作机制的建立，为天津带来更多高端科研机构和人才资源，促成一批优秀科技成果在天津转化和产业化，为天津科技发展增添了新的优势。

三、科技引领经济社会发展

随着天津科技创新能力不断提升，科学技术在经济社会发展中的驱动引领作用进一步凸显。这一时期，形成一批有影响的原创性成果和新技术新产品，高新技术产业逐步形成规模，传统产业在科技与信息化支撑下加快转型升级。

2005年，全市年专利申请数量为11657件、专利授权量3045件，其中发明专利申请量4470件，占申请总量的38%，发明专利授权量是763件，占总授权量的25%，所占比重分别是1991年的2倍和2.5倍；在2005年申请的6956件职务发明中，工矿企业5600件，占比80.51%。同年，国内科技论文发表数量9466篇，被SCI、IE、ISTP三大系统收录5527篇；科技成果登记1508项，较1991年的820项增长83.9%。技术成果交易方面，2005年技术市场合同成交数量11295项，成交合同金额50.71亿元，分别是1996的1.4倍和3.8倍，十年间基本上保持每五年翻一番的增长势头。1991～2005年，天津共获得国家科学技术奖励248项。

这期间，在火炬计划、科技百亿工程、重大科技产业化工程等带动下，天津市的高新技术产业得到快速发展，在拉动全市经济快速增长的同时，也从整体上推动产业结构的优化升级，成为全市新的经济增长点。“火炬计划”是面旗帜，催生了高新技术成果转化和高新技术孵化器的建立，培育了一大批科技型中小企业。“科技百亿工程计划”自1994年启动到1998年提前完成，培育出地塞美松、镍氢电池、锂离子电池、中空纤维膜材料、生物制药、环保设备等一批高新技术产业项目。到2005年，重大高新技术产业化项目累计实施100项，其中50个项目建成投产，建成中药现代化、绿色电池、软件出口、环保产品等一批高新技术产品生产基地，一批处于国内领先、国际先进水平的技术实现产业化。2005年，全市高新技术产业完成产值2141.4亿元，占工业总产值的比重由2000年的24.2%增长到29.9%，年均增速24.4%。产值亿元以上的高新技术企业达到180家，其中10亿元以上的28家；高新技术产品实现出口124.7亿美元，名列全国第四位，占全市出口的比重达到45.5%。逐步形成以电子信息产业、先进制造、生物技术与现代医药、新能源等产业为主快速发展的格局。

1994年，市委、市政府作出决定，通过企业改制、引进外资调整结构、技术改造和技术创新等手段，推进国有大中型企业嫁接改造调整，大力发展多种经济成分的高科技企业，同时提出“要把技术创新、技术改造与资产调整重组结合起来，实现产业产品结构的优化升级”。“十五”期间，全市工业加快高新技术及先进适用技术改造传统产业步伐，围绕重点产业、重点产品组织技术创新项目，共实施工业投资项目1829个，将工业投资的70%投在新兴优势产业，其中电子信息、生物技术与现代医药、新能源、新材料、环保等高新技术项目投资占总投资的38.5%。

2001年，天津启动制造业信息化、农业信息化、中药现代化和环保科技等四大科技工程，促进先进技术推广应用。2003年，按照产业方向和技术前沿要求，安排一批对产业升级具有重大突破和带动作用的工业技术创新项目，建设好12个技术含量高的产品基地，推进优势产业升级。在制造业信息化工程支持下，机械、冶金、汽车、模具、轻工、服装等行业一批龙头企业率先推动信息化技术应用示范，进一步带动全市2000多家制造业企业实施信息化，新产品设计能力提高。通过实施中药现代化科技工程，16项中药现代化关键技术在中药企业得到广泛应用，天津医药集团成为全国同行业中的第四大集团，天津中新药业集团公司、天士力制药股份有限公司成为全国最大的中药现代化骨干集团，培育出复方丹参滴丸、速效救心丸等销售收入过5亿元的中药产品。

作为高新技术产业布局的重要基地，天津新技术产业园区、天津经济技术开发区（以下简称“开发区”）也在这一时期加快发展。1991年，天津新技术产业园区（以下简称“高新区”）被国务院批准为首批国家级高新技术产业开发区，1995年《天津新技术产业园区管理条例》颁布，高新区管理体制机制进一步健全，以企业为主体、产学研结合的研发体系建设初具规模，成为天津市集高科技产业、科技开发、成果孵化、技术贸易、科技服务、人才交流、信息集散于一体的科技新城区。2005年，高新区完成技工贸总收入810亿元，工业总产值730亿元，净利润28.5亿元，出口创汇20亿美元，上缴税金43.2亿元，初步形成以绿色能源、软件、生物制药、新材料、先进制造业为代表的优势产业，涌现出天津力神电池股份有限公司、南开创元公司、协和干细胞基因工程有限公司等一批拥有自主知识产权的高新技术企业。

经济开发区自1984年批准建设起，前期以基础建设和招商引资为主，1996年全区第一次科技工作会议提出“科技兴区”，以促进高新技术项目产业化、吸引高级人才到开发区创业、扶持高新技术企业发展为主要抓手，开始进入创新发展的新阶段。到2005年，开发区各类孵化器和科技园区达到8个，包括天津泰达国际创业中心（留学生创业园）、天津大学科技园、泰达华生生物园、国家纳米技术产业化基地、泰达光电园、泰达软件园、开泰企业孵化器、中国绿色包装产业苑，其中天大科技园是国家首批15家大学科技园之一。开发区成功申报国家（天津）通信产业园、国家（天津）片式元件产业园、国家（天津）集成电路产业园等3个国家电子信息产业园，成为全国唯一拥有3个电子信息产业园的区域。2005年，开发区高新技术产品产值达到1425亿元，高新技术产品出口额112.8亿美元。

农业科技方面，1991～1995年，天津共组织实施农业示范工程项目65项，投入科研经费近千万元，在粮食增产、菜篮子工程中大面积推广农业科技成果，使全市农业生产整体水平进一步提高，涌现出一批在全国有影响的科技成果。天津市黄瓜研究所开发的系列黄瓜新产品、天津市蔬菜研究所开发的马铃薯微型脱毒种薯等，在全国得到推广。通过实施农业示范工程，使现代科技与农村经济更加紧密结合。2001～2005年，天津继续实施农产品安全生产、动植物新品种选育、津南农业科技园区等科技专项，启动农业信息化、农产品深加工科技示范工程，总计实施项目102项，投入研发经费3835万元，培育出优质作物、蔬菜等新品种120多个，示范、推广面积近100万亩，繁育良种达200万千克，社会经济效益6亿元以上。

科技促进社会民生方面，社会事业与民生保障领域科技在全市总体科技布局中的地位逐渐加强，在环保科技、气象科技、水运工程、铁路、航空、通讯、广播电视、城市建设、医药卫生等领域取得一批重大科技成果以及多项技术进步，为社会事业与民生保障科技创新提供了强有力的支撑。环境科学领域，取得污水生物除磷脱氮工艺、污泥中温消化技术、污水再生利用示范等10多项国家级科研成果，奠定了天津在全国污水处理技术上的领先地位。气象探测技术由传统的人工方法向应用仪器自动探测转变，在国内首创动态再现或预测城市中暴雨形成的沥涝积水演进过程，对气候变化给出科学预测分析。交通领域，铁道部第三勘测设计院在秦沈客运专线关键技术研究中实现新建铁路一次铺设跨区间无缝线路、桥上无碴轨道，破解在路基、桥涵、通信、信号、接触网设计等方面的关键技术难题，开创客运专线无碴轨道设计和一次铺设跨区间无缝线路之先河，创造中国铁路第一时速321.5千米/小时的试验速度。城建领域，推进"城市数字化"建设，在市政公路工程技术、建筑科学技术、公用事业工程技术、园林绿化等领域取得一系列达到国际先进水平的科研成果，为提高城市建设的整体水平和提升城市形象发挥了积极作用。医药卫生领域，在临床医学、内分泌、外科、肿瘤学、妇科、眼科、药学等学科领域科技水平发展迅速，有力地推动医药卫生事业的可持续发展。

在世纪之交的十五年里，天津科技事业取得长足进步,主要是始终坚持"科学技术是第一生产力"的指导思想，以"科教兴市"作为战略定位；坚持深化科技体制改革，持续推进科技与经济社会发展密切结合；坚持以人为本，把发现、培养和用好人才作为科技工作的根本任务；坚持"有所为，有所不为"的原则，集中力量办大事、抓大项目，力求重点突破，带动全面；坚持政策引导和法规建设，发挥市场机制和政府引导两个积极作用；坚持加大开放力度，优化环境，积极吸引国内外科技资源融入天津科技发展 。

但必须清醒和理性的认识到，天津的科技发展也存在着薄弱环节，科技创新依然面临体制机制上的诸多问题。主要是，多种原因形成的结构性矛盾比较突出，传统产业改造包袱沉重，高新技术对传统产业的技术扩散和辐射力度较小，存在经济"需求"动力不足和科技"供给"能力不强的矛盾，科技还没有成为产业调整的有效载体和突破口；科技资源尤其是人才和资金的缺乏，成为制约科技发展的关键因素，由于缺乏良好的人才发展环境和文化氛围，一定程度上影响高端科技人才的聚集和创新活力的激发；全社会科技投入依然不足，造成原始创新、科技成果转化和科技型中小企业等融资困难，乃至缺少具有相当规模和带动作用的重大创新成果及科技领军人物，科技发展总体环境需要进一步优化。

新一轮科技革命和产业变革为科技发展开辟了新的空间，经济转型、社会变革、民生需求，更加倚重于科技发展。我们必须紧抓这一难得的战略机遇，凝聚共识，科学谋划，不断开拓，使天津科技进一步肩负起支撑和引领经济社会发展的使命，为实施创新驱动发展战略奠定坚实基础。

The years between 1991 and 2005 witnessed Tianjin's rapid development when China deepened reform, expanded opening-up and promoted economic structure transformation with science and technology as the main drivers. The Communist Party of China (CPC) Tianjin Municipal Committee and the Tianjin Municipal People's Government unleashed their minds, sought truth from facts, and implemented the strategy of "invigorating the city through science and education" when faced with the difficulties from tight budget, livelihood provision, enterprises reformation, economic and industrial restructuring, as well as the transformation of Tianjin as an old industrial city.

The science and technology circles, education circles and industry circles in Tianjin made unremitting efforts to promote the city's scientific and technological progress, which helped our rankings of scientific and technological strength in China rise from the 7th to the 3rd in the 15 years. By 2005, Tianjin's R&D expenditure had accounted for 1.97 % of the city's GDP, 5.8 times that of 1991; Hi-tech industry's output value in Tianjin had reached 214.14 billion yuan (roughly 31,5 billion dollars), accounting for 29.9 % of the total value of all industries, which was 8 times that of 1995. The year of 2005 witnessed the city's 11,657 patent applications and 3,045 patent authorizations, 8.56 times and 5.02 times that of 1991 respectively. The contract value in the technology market was 5.071 billion yuan (around 745.6 billion dollars), 3.8 times that of 1996.

Thanks to the science and technology development strategy and mechanism reform in Tianjin, the productivity of science and technology had been growing fast here. Following the first establishment of a permanent technology exchange market in the 1980s, the first technology market newspaper was issued in Tianjin. Tianjin was also the first city to establish a youth science fund and a natural science fund. It took the lead in implementing regulations on continuing education for technical professionals, founding a Sci-tech business incubation center and a national technology exchange market in cooperation with the National Science and Technology Commission (now Ministry of Science and Technology). The rise of scientific and technological strength, the integration between science and technology and economy, the progress of technological management, and the incubation and promotion of new technology industrial parks brought Tianjin into a new stage in which science and technology played a more prominent role.

1. Strategic deployment for scientific and technological development

After the National Science Conference was held in 1978, such concepts as "science and technology are productive forces" and "respect knowledge and talents" gradually gained popularity in China, and science in our country entered a period of rapid growth. In 1985, the CPC Central Committee issued the Decisions on the Reform of Scientific and Technological System, which stressed that "economy growth must rely on science and technology, which must be oriented towards economic development". Under the guidance of the Decisions, Tianjin started to promote the reform on the scientific and technological system and adopted a series of measures in opening up the technology market, commercializing the technologies, reforming the financial allocations system for scientific research institutes, encouraging the private enterprises to advance technology and building new technology industrial parks. Thanks to these efforts, the scientific and technological undertakings in Tianjin entered a new stage of development.

In the 1990s, China continuously optimized the top-level design and national strategies for economy and technological development and launched a scheme to deepen the reform on scientific and technological system. Tianjin government, in August 1992, promulgated the Opinions on Accelerating Economic Development with Scientific and Technological Progress and implemented the strategy of "invigorating Tianjin through science and technology", which was the first such move in the country, and laid out the guidelines of revitalizing the economy by science and technology. The city also embarked on a growth track that relied on scientific and technological progress and improvement of the workers' quality. In 1995, China made the Decisions on Accelerating Scientific and Technological Progress and put forward the strategy of "invigorating the country through science and education". Tianjin's economy, though, was at a critical stage of restructuring, upgrading and improving, government of the city made the development model of "taking the road of science and technology" in response to the call of the CPC central Committee. We also promulgated the Opinions on Accelerating Progress of Science and Technology and made "invigorating the city through science and education" an overall and long-term strategy. Tianjin Science and Technology Leading Group, headed by the Mayor, was established to strengthen the macro-management and coordinate the scientific and technological work.

In response to the Decisions on Strengthening Technological Innovation, High Technology and Industrialization issued by the CPC Central Committee and the State Council in 1999 on the National Technological Innovation Conference, Tianjin government decided to promulgate the Opinions on Accelerating Scientific Progress and Technological Innovation, in which the new situations and new tasks in a new era were proposed. The Opinions also strengthened the main role of enterprises in innovating, introduced a technological innovation system and gave priority to "developing technology and industrialization". From 1991 to 2005, Tianjin, in line with national strategies and the overall plan of China, adjusted continuously the plan on the scientific and technological development and carried out a series of actions, according to our own conditions, and the needs of scientific and technological revolution and industrial transformation. All these efforts helped Tianjin take a new path of relying on scientific and technological progress to improve the overall quality and economic strength.

From 1991 to 2005, Tianjin compiled the eighth, ninth and tenth five-year plans on scientific and technological development, a long and medium-term scientific and technological development plan, and a plan on developing high-tech industries. These systematic, comprehensive plans and top-level designss that were based on our conditions and our goals, had become our development strategies and objectives. During the eighth five-year plan period, we concentrated on three leading industries, 10 key fields and 60 knockout products to adjust our industrial structure. Moreover, 10 major research projects in automobile and IT were also implemented, and the application of 100 technologies were promoted. On the basis of implementing the China Torch Program, a national plan to develop hi-tech industries, the Ten Billion Project, a national plan to develop hi-tech industries, was also launched to promote the industrialization of high-tech achievements. The city's scientific research institutions were also supported and encouraged to enter market to promote economic growth. The technology market was accelerated, and the transformation of scientific results were advanced. The investment in basic applied research rose, making more technological reserves for cultivating leading industries. At this stage, Tianjin's scientific and technological strength rankings in the whole country rose from the 7th in 1993 to the 4th in 1995.

During the ninth five-year plan period, facing the challenges from technological revolution and economic development, Tianjin decided to focus on developing high-tech industries and cultivating emerging industries of the 21st century. With a focus on the Ten Billion Project and industrialization projects, a technological and industrial park was established to promote the development of such six fields as biotechnology, electronic information, new materials, manufacturing technology, new energy and environmental protection technologies. We also accelerated the transformation of traditional industries with high technologies and promoted them to be innovators and transformers of technologies. The system and operating mechanism of research institutes were also reformed to attract more institutes, which were encouraged to participate in Tianjin's economic growth. Informatization in Tianjin were sped up. With the implementation of the "Project 2119" in an all-round way, great efforts were invested in building Tianjin into an information hub and a major IT industry base in China. At this stage, the scientific and technological strength of Tianjin remained at third or fourth position in the country, and its high-tech industry became a new eco-

nomic driver.

During the tenth five-year plan period, as the global economic integration came into shape and the knowledge economy rose, Tianjin sped up the high-tech industries to make them pillar industries of the 21st century. It strove to build itself into a high-tech and industrialization base that was in line with the Tianjin's economic status in northern China. To this end, Tianjin focused on electronic information, new energy, and modern medicine and biotechnology, and encouraged the development of opto-electro mechanics, new materials and environmental protection industries. At the same time, 45 applied and basic science research projects were implemented to provide technologies for the development of high-tech industries. 30 hi-tech industrialization projects were started to promote rolling development and foster new economic drivers. Meanwhile, Tianjin sped up the establishment and improvement of the technological innovation system and the technological investment and financing system to improve the city's innovation capability. Guided by the "Project 1221", informationization in Tianjin had been improved in an all-round way. Tianjin's scientific and technological strength continued to be the third in the country, with the output value of high-tech industries accounting for nearly one third of the city's total industrial output value.

Under the guidance of the Science and Technology Development Plan and through three five-year plans, Tianjin gradually formed a planning system for science and technology development, which was composed of applied and basic researches, major projects of science and technology, key technology researches, transformation of technologies, and researches on development strategies. And these were targeted at such three fields as economic development, high-tech industries, and technology reserves. Tianjin continued to adjust, enrich and improve the planning and managing systems for science and technology to make them more scientific, standard and institutional.

To execute the development strategies for science and technology in Tianjin, reform measures and policies were introduced one after another. Science and technology laws and regulations, such as patent law, law on scientific and technological progress, law on promoting the transformation of technologies, law on science popularization, and regulations on science and technology awards, were refined. Policies and management measures for science and technology that covered strategic planning and deployment, projects management, transformation of technologies, science and technology awards, science and technology evaluation, personnel incentives, technology market and intellectual property management system were promulgated, providing institutional support and a good policy environment for the sustainable development of scientific and technological undertakings.

2. Upgrading of the scientific and technological innovation capacity

To reach our strategic goals for scientific and technological development, Tianjin upgraded the innovation capability, increased investment in science and technology, broadened the talent pool, allocated the scientific and technological resources in a more appropriate way, and constructed a new type of scientific and technological innovation system.

Investment in science and technology increased year by year

From 1991 to 2005, Tianjin continuously increased its investment in science and technology. The city's financial allocation on science and technology reached 1.365 billion yuan (around 199.8 million dollars) in 2005, accounting for 2.62 % of the financial expenditure in that year. Driven by the leverage effect of financial expenditure, the investment from non-public sectors in science and technology continued to increase, especially after the year of 2000, whose growth momentum became more powerful. In 2005, the city's R&D expenditure reached 7.292 billion yuan (about 1.06 billion dollars) accounting for 1.97 % of the city's GDP which was higher than that in 1991—about 0.34 %. As for the capital fund sources for scientific and technological activities, the fund of enterprises accounted for 73.55 % of the total in 2005. The enterprises' R&D expenditure accounted for 66.65 % of the total R&D expenditures in Tianjin. Led by the government, a pattern of scientific and technological investment, in which the enterprises were the main entities, came into shape. To broaden and diversify the channels of scientific and technological investment, a venture capital financing system for scientific and technological firms and an investment system for scientific and technological startups were launched. From 2000 to 2005, the number of investment enterprises for technology startups in Tianjin increased from 10 to 65, and the total registered capital grew from 900 million yuan (around 130 million dollars) to 4.2 billion yuan (roughly 611 million dollars). The venture capital guiding fund and seven venture capital institutions were set up with the city's budget, which attracted nearly 1 billion yuan (around 145 million dollars) of private funds from both home and abroad with nearly 120 million yuan (around 17 million dollars) of guidance funds and spurred the connected capital of nearly 10 billion yuan (around 1,45 billion dollars).

More scientific and technological talents attracted to Tianjin

From 1991 to 2005, the number of technological professionals per 10,000 employees in Tianjin increased from 1,973 to 2,189, an indication that the overall quality of the workforce was improved. Policies were formulated to introduce and award the technological professionals, better the working and living conditions and evaluate on the professional titles of technological personnel. The development environment for the scientific and technological personnel was optimized. Meanwhile, 12 professionals in Tianjin were elected to be members of the Chinese Academy of Sciences (CAS) and 19 were elected to be members of the Chinese Academy of Engineering (CAE). By 2005, 31 academicians of CAS and CAE worked in Tianjin. In 1992, Tianjin started to select academic leaders in the field of natural science and awarded them the title of "Tianjin Recognized Expert". By 2005, 479 people in the city were awarded this title, and nearly 3,000 experts were entitled to special government subsidies, who played a leading role in all disciplines and fields in the city. The Youth Science Foundation and the Natural Science Foundation were launched in 1989 to cultivate future academic leaders. Thanks to the foundation, a group of young and middle-aged experts stood out. In 1994, the "Talent Cultivation Project in 21st Century" (also named as "131 Talent Project") was launched. By 2005, at the end of the first training period, 40 candidates undertook 71 key projects in the state level such as the projects of the National Science Fund for Distinguished Young Scholars, National High-tech R&D Program (Program 863) and National Basic Research Program (Program 973), and the National Natural Science Fund. Moreover, the 90 research projects completed by 50 candidates of them won awards in state-, ministry-and city-level. Tianjin established the Talent Development Fund in 2000, which is mainly used to fund the training, introducing and awarding of high- level talents. A flexible "green card" system was implemented for those who worked in Tianjin but did not transfer their household registration and their relationship to the city. For example, Tianjin University set up the School of Pharmaceutical Science and Technology by introducing a student team in biopharmaceuticals from the United States. The Tianjin-based Nankai University and Tianjin Medical University attracted more than 10 international students to carry out research projects on gene chip. What's more, the number of students who returned to Tianjin after graduation to start their own businesses was also increasing year by year.

Faster development of innovation system

Constructing an innovation system is a need to deepen the reform on the scientific and technological system and to allocate resources rationally. By 2005, Tianjin, relying on universities, enterprises, and research institutes, had established 70 knowledge innovation institutes, including key laboratories and research centers, 191 technology innovation institutes consisting of engineering technology centers and enterprise technology centers, and 130 technology transformation and industrialization bases composed of productivity promotion centers and sci-tech business incubators. From 1991 to 2005, Tianjin established the Tech Startup Service Center, Northern China Technology Exchange Market, Tianjin Venture Capital Center and Tianjin Science and Technology Evaluation Center. Among them, the Northern China Technology Exchange Market was jointly established by Tianjin government and the National Science and Technology Commission (now Ministry of Science and Technology) in 1995, which is the only permanent technology market at the state level. Based on international practices and models, the market transformed itself from a technology exchange marketplace to a comprehensive center providing technology transfer services. Since 2001, Tianjin started to integrate and utilize the scientific and technological resources and research services to establish service platforms such as Science and Technology Literature Platform, Cooperation and Sharing Platform for Instruments, Technology Standard Testing Platform, Science Popularization Platform, and Research Center for Scientific and Technological Development Strategies and Policies.

The traditional science research system also developed in the process of deepening reform. Tianjin promulgated a number of policies to promote the reform on the research institutes in response to the Decisions on the Reform of the Science and Technology System, issued by the CPC Central Committee. In 1991, Tianjin began to carry out a grade management system on the research institutes and recognize the key institutes, in which a full-staff employment system was implemented. In 1997, a pilot reform was carried out in 9 research institutes, and in 2000, all 72 development-oriented research institutes directed by Tianjin government were transformed into enterprises. By 2005, breakthroughs had been made in the reform on municipal research institutes. The role of government transformed from direct management to indirect management, and the market awareness of the institutes were enhanced, which exerted their own technological advantages to build themselves into a professional expertise and an active part in the market. 33 of the research institutes funded by Chinese central government based them in Tianjin, which undertook key research projects in the state level and served for the economic growth in Tianjin. They played a leading role in cutting-edge exploration and integrated innovation, demonstrating their innovative vigor and vitality.

Main position of innovation in enterprises strengthened

In building the new sci-tech innovation system, the main position of technological innovation in enterprises was strengthened, and the common problems of "emphasizing production, neglecting R&D" and "emphasizing import, neglecting absorptive capacity" were overcome. In 2005, the proportion of technological workers in large and medium-sized industrial enterprises in Tianjin was 4.94%, 2.02 % higher than that in 1991; the proportion of enterprise research and experimental expenditures in the core business income was 0.7%, 0.4% higher than that in 1991; enterprises ran 195 technology development institutions, 13% higher than that in 2000; in the enterprises' technological development institutions, the number of personnel engaged in technological activities was 32,000, an increase of 7,500 over 2000; the total expenditures on technology development was 9.37 billion yuan (roughly 1.35 billion dollars), 4.56 times of that in 2000; from 2001 to 2005, the number of patent applications per year increased from less than 300 to more than 2,900, and the sales revenue of new products increased from 54.9 billion yuan (roughly 7.9 billion dollars) to 154.5 billion yuan (roughly 22.3 billion dollars), which showed that the output and economic benefits led by technological innovation were significantly improved. Industry-university-research cooperation was further deepened. In 2005, the proportion of enterprise funds in technological activities of R&D institutions and institutions of higher learning reached 59.70% and 32.56%, respectively, an indication of deepened cooperation with enterprises. The income of the ownership-transferred research institutes from the projects entrusted by enterprises reached 3.81 billion yuan (roughly 0.55 billion dollars). The funds of institutions of higher learning entrusted by enterprises to carry out technological activities reached 468 million yuan (roughly 67 million dollars), an increase of 1.16 times over 2000.

Growing private technology enterprises

As the technological system reform advanced, private technology enterprises, such as Tianjin Saixiang Technology Co., Ltd. and Tasly Pharmaceutical Co., Ltd., had grown into the most active group in technological innovation with their new operating mechanism of "self-raising, self-combining, self-management, and self-financing". According to statistics, the number of private technological enterprises reached 2,061 in 1993, 5,600 in 2000, and 8,

000 in 2,005, and the indicators of enterprise assets, income, net profit and taxes paid continued to grow. In order to promote the development of private technology enterprises, policies such as Regulations on Promoting Tianjin's Private Technology Enterprises Development and Measures on Tianjin's Private Technology Enterprise Management were promulgated as a support for technological plans, professional titles of enterprise personnel, incubation of enterprises, financial instruments, etc. In 2005, Tianjin established the technological innovation funds for small and medium-sized technology enterprises to support more than 100 technological innovation projects of private technology enterprises, effectively stimulating their technological innovation activities.

Influx of technological resources at home and abroad

Tianjin had always expanded its breadth and depth of technological cooperation at home and abroad with a positive and open attitude, so as to pool high-end technological resources and enhance its development strength. In terms of international cooperation, from 1991 to 2005, Tianjin carried out intergovernmental technological cooperation with 39 countries and international organizations, implementing more than 200 cooperation projects in such fields as agriculture, industry, environmental protection, energy, biology, medicine, information, etc. In terms of domestic technological cooperation, in July 2005, the Ministry of Science and Technology of China and Tianjin Municipal Government signed a protocol on a work consultation system and held the first consultation meeting to jointly discuss the promotion of technological system reform and the construction of Tianjin Binhai New Area. In the same month, the Chinese Academy of Sciences (CAS) and Tianjin Municipal Government signed a comprehensive technological cooperation agreement to establish a long-term cooperation mechanism in project cooperation, institutional cooperation, personnel exchange, institute introduction, information exchange, etc. The establishment of the above cooperation mechanisms had brought more high-end research institutions and human resources to Tianjin, promoted the transformation and industrialization of a number of outstanding technological achievements in Tianjin, and added new strength to Tianjin's technological development.

3. Science and technology leading economic and social development

With the improvement of Tianjin's technological innovation capability, the leading role of science and technology in economic and social development was further highlighted. During this period, a batch of influential original achievements and new technologies and products were produced. The high-tech industry gradually formed a scale, and the traditional industries accelerated the transformation and upgrading under the support of technology and informationization.

In 2005, the number of patent applications in Tianjin was 11,657 and the number of patent authorizations was 3,045, of which 4,470 were for invention patents, accounting for 38 % of the total number of applications and 763 were for invention patents, accounting for 25 %, 2 times and 2.5 times of the total number in 1991 respectively. Of the 6,956 on-duty inventions applied in 2005, 5,600 were in industrial and mining enterprises, accounting for 80.51 %. In the same year, the number of domestic technological papers was 9,466, of which 5,527 were included in SCI, IE and ISTP; 1,508 technological achievements were registered, an increase of 83.9% compared with 820 in 1991. In terms of technological achievements trading, the number of contracts concluded in the technological market was 11,295 in 2005 and the amount of contracts concluded was 5.071 billion yuan (roughly 0.7 billion dollars), 1.4 times and 3.8 times of that in 1996 respectively. The number of contracts concluded had doubled every five years in the ten years. From 1991 to 2005, Tianjin received 248 national science and technology awards.

Tianjin's high-tech industry, driven by the China Torch Program, the Ten Billion Project, and the Major Technology Industrialization Project during this period, became a new economic growth point in enhancing the city's economic strength and promoting the optimization and upgrading of the industrial structure. The Torch Program spawned the transformation of high-tech achievements and the establishment of a high-tech incubator and cultivated a large number of small and medium-sized enterprises. The Ten Billion Project, launched in 1994 and completed ahead of schedule in 1998, cultivated a number of high-tech industrial projects such as dexamethasone, nickel-hydrogen batteries, lithium ion batteries, hollow fiber membrane materials, bio-pharmaceuticals and environmental protection equipment. By 2005, a total of 100 major high-tech industrialization projects had been implemented, of which 50 had been completed and put into production. A batch of high-tech product production bases was established, covering the traditional Chinese medicine (TCM) modernization, green batteries, software exports, environmental protection products, etc., and a number of technologies leading in the country at the international advanced level were industrialized. In 2005, the output value of Tianjin's high-tech industries reached 214.14 billion yuan (roughly 31 billion dollars), accounting for 29.9% of the total industrial output value compared with 24.2% in 2000, with an average annual growth rate of 24.4 %.The number of high-tech enterprises with an output value of more than 100 million yuan (roughly 14 million dollars) reached 180, of which 28 were over 1 billion yuan (roughly 0.14 billion dollars). The export of high-tech products reached 12.47 billion dollars, ranking fourth in the country and accounting for 45.5% of the city's exports. Tianjin formed a pattern of rapid development in such industries as electronic information, advanced manufacturing, new energy, and biotechnology and modern medicine.

The Communist Party of China Tianjin Municipal Committee and the Tianjin Municipal People's Government made a decision in 1994 to promote the restructuring of large and medium-sized state-owned enterprises and develop high-tech enterprises with various economic components by means of enterprise restructuring, introduction of foreign capital to adjust structure, technological transformation and technological innovation. Meanwhile, they proposed that technological innovation, technological transformation and asset restructuring should be combined to realize the optimization and upgrading of the industrial product structure. During the 10th Five-Year Plan period (2001-2005), the city's industries accelerated the pace of transforming traditional industries by the high-tech and advanced applicable technologies and set up technological innovation projects in key industries and products. A total of 1,829 industrial investment projects were implemented, and 70% of the industrial investment focused on the emerging advantageous industries, of which high-tech projects covering electronic information, biotechnology and modern medicine, new energy, new materials, and environmental protection accounted for 38.5 % of the total investment.

In 2001, Tianjin launched four major scientific and technological projects, including manufacturing informationization, agricultural informationization, modernization of traditional Chinese medicine (TCM) and environmental protection technology to promote the application of advanced technologies. In 2003, in accordance with the requirements of industrial direction and technical frontier, Tianjin arranged a number of industrial technology innovation projects with major breakthroughs and driving effects on industrial upgrading, built 12 product bases with advanced technology, and promoted the upgrading of advantageous industries. With the support of the informationization project of the manufacturing industry , a group of enterprises in machinery, metallurgy, automobile, mold, light industry, clothing and other industries took the lead in promoting the application and demonstration of informationized technology, further driving more than 2,000 manufacturing enterprises in the city to implement informationization and improve the design capability of new products. Through implementing the technology project of TCM modernization, 16 key technologies were widely used in the TCM enterprises. Tianjin Pharmaceutical Group became the fourth largest group in the medicine industry in the country, and Tianjin Zhongxin Pharmaceutical Group Co., Ltd. and Tasly Pharmaceutical Co., Ltd. became the largest backbone group of TCM modernization in the country, cultivating the TCM products with a sales income of more than 500 million yuan (roughly 72.5 million dollars), such as Fufang Danshen Dripping Pills and Quick-acting Rescue Pills.

As an important base for the layout of high-tech industries, Tianjin Binhai High-Tech Industrial Development

Area (TBHIDA) and Tianjin Economic-technological Development Area (TEDA) also accelerated their development during this period. In 1991, TBHIDA was approved by the State Council as one of the first batch of national high-tech industrial development zones. In 1995, the Tianjin Binhai Hi-Tech Industrial Development Area Management Regulations was promulgated, which further improved the management system and mechanism of TBHIDA. With the R&D system featuring enterprises as the main body and industry-university-research cooperation, TBHIDA became a new technological zone that integrates high-tech industry, technological development, results incubation, technological trade, technological services, talents exchange and information distribution. TBHIDA , with a total revenue of 81 billion yuan (roughly 11.7 billion dollars) in technology, industry and trade, a total industrial output value of 73 billion yuan(roughly 10.5 billion dollars), a net profit of 2.85 billion yuan(roughly 0.41 billion dollars), a foreign exchange earnings of 2 billion US dollars, and a tax payment of 4.32 billion yuan(roughly 0.62 billion dollars) in 2005, initially formed the advantageous industries represented by green energy, software, bio-pharmaceuticals, new materials and advanced manufacturing, and numerous high-tech enterprises with independent intellectual property rights, such as Tianjin Lishen Battery Co., Ltd., Nankai Chuangyuan Co., Ltd. and Xiehe Stem Cell Genetic Engineering Co., Ltd..

Since its establishment in 1984, TEDA focused on infrastructure construction and investment attraction in the early stage. In 1996, TEDA proposed the "Strategy of Developing TEDA by Science and Technology" in its first technological conference to promote the industrialization of high-tech projects, attract high-level talents to start businesses and support the development of high-tech enterprises as the main focus, entering a new stage of innovative development. By 2005, TEDA boasted 8 incubators and technological parks, including TEDA International Entrepreneurship Center (International Student Entrepreneurship Park), Tianjin University Technological Park, TEDA Huasheng Biological Park, National Nanotechnology Industrialization Base, TEDA Photoelectric Park, TEDA Software Park, Kaitai Business Incubator, and China Green Packaging Industry Park, among which Tianjin University Technological Park is one of the first 15 university technological parks in China. TEDA was awarded three national electronic information industrial parks, including the National Communications Industrial Park, National Chip Component Industrial Park, and National Integrated Circuit Industrial Park, becoming the only area in the country with the three parks. In 2005, the output value of high-tech products in TEDA reached 142.5 billion yuan (roughly 20.6 billion dollars), and its export value of high-tech products reached 11.28 billion dollars.

As for agricultural technology, Tianjin, from 1991 to 1995, implemented 65 agricultural demonstration projects, invested nearly 10 million yuan (roughly 1.4 million dollars) in scientific research, and promoted technological achievements of agriculture in grain yield increase and vegetable basket projects, which further improved the city's agricultural production and made a number of influential technological achievements in the country. The cucumber products developed by Tianjin Cucumber Research Institute and the micro-detoxification potato developed by Tianjin Vegetable Research Institute were promoted nationwide. Modern technology was more closely integrated with the rural economy in implementing agricultural demonstration projects. From 2001 to 2005, Tianjin continued to implement technological projects such as safe production of agricultural products, breeding of new varieties of animals and plants, and Jinnan Agricultural Technological Park and launched technology demonstration projects of agricultural informationization and agricultural product deep processing. A total of 102 projects were implemented, with an investment of 38.35 million yuan (roughly 5.5 million dollars) in R&D. More than 120 new varieties of high-quality crops and vegetables were cultivated, the demonstration and promotion area was nearly 1 million mu (roughly 66, 667 hectares), and the breeding of improved varieties reached 2 million kilograms, with social and economic benefits of more than 600 million yuan (roughly 87 million dollars).

In promoting people's livelihood by science and technology, the status of technology in the fields of social undertakings and people's livelihood security had gradually strengthened in the overall technological layout of the whole city. A number of major technological achievements and advances were made in the fields of environmental protection technology, meteorological technology, water transportation engineering, railway, aviation, communications, radio and television, urban construction, medical and health, etc., which provided strong support for the technological innovations in social undertakings and people's livelihood security. In the field of environmental technology, more than 10 national scientific research achievements were obtained, including biological phosphorus and nitrogen removal from sewage, moderate temperature digestion of sludge, and wastewater reuse, which established Tianjin's leading position in the national sewage treatment technology. The technology of weather detection changed from traditional manual methods to automatic detection by instruments. The city was the first in China to dynamically reproduce or predict the evolution of waterlogging caused by torrential rain in cities, and to give scientific prediction and analysis of climate change. In the field of transport, the No. 3 Survey and Design Institute of the Ministry of Railways realized the pioneering one-time laying of cross-section jointless tracks and ballastless tracks on bridges in the key technology research of the Qinhuangdao-shenyang High-speed Railway, solved the key technical problems in the design of subgrade, bridge and culvert, communications, signal, and contact network, and created the "No.1" trial speed of 321.5km/h for. As for urban construction, the Digital City Construction was promoted, and a series of research achievements at the international advanced level were made in the municipal highway engineering technology, architectural technology, public utilities engineering technology, and landscaping, which played an active role in improving the city construction and promoting the image of the city. In the field of medicine and health, the technological level was developed rapidly in clinical medicine, endocrinology, surgery, oncology, gynecology, ophthalmology, and pharmacy, and many technological achievements reached the international leading level, which promoted the sustainable development of medical and public health undertakings.

From 1995 to 2005, the turn of a new century, Tianjin's scientific and technological undertakings witnessed substantial progress thanks to our efforts in adhering to the "Science and Technology are the First Productive Force" and "Developing Tianjin through Science and Education", accelerating reform on the scientific and technological system and the integration of technology with economic and social development, following the people-oriented concept by regarding the discovery, cultivation and use of talents as the fundamental task, focusing on major projects while striving for breakthroughs in key areas to drive the overall development, continuing policy guidance and the construction of laws and regulations while giving full play to the roles of market mechanism and government guidance, and increasing openness and optimizing the environment to attract domestic and foreign technological resources into Tianjin's scientific and technological development.

We must be clear-headed and rationally aware that there are still weaknesses in Tianjin's science and technology development. Technological innovation still faces many problems in the existing system and mechanism. The structural contradictions formed by various reasons are relatively prominent; the burden of transforming traditional industries remains heavy; the technology diffusion and radiation of high-tech industries are relatively small; there is a contradiction between the lack of economic demand power and the weak supply capability of technology, and technology has not yet become an effective carrier and breakthrough for industrial adjustment; the lack of technological resources, especially talents and funds, has become a key factor restricting the development of science and technology; the gathering of high-end technological talents and the stimulation of innovative vitality are affected because of the lack of a good environment and cultural atmosphere for the development of talents; the whole society's investment in science and technology remains insufficient, resulting in financing difficulties of original innovation, transformation of technological achievements, and small and medium-sized technological enterprises, and even the lack of significant innovative achievements and technological leaders with considerable scale and leading role. The overall environment for technological development needs to be further optimized.

The new round of scientific and technological revolution and industrial transformation have opened up new space for the development of science and technology. The economic transition, social transformation and people's livelihood demand rely more on technological development. We must seize this opportunity by achieving a consensus, planning scientifically, and exploring continuously, so that Tianjin's science and technology will further shoulder the mission of supporting and leading economic and social development, and lay a solid foundation for implementing innovation-driven development strategies.

大　事　记

1991年

1月11～14日 国务院总理李鹏到天津考察。他指出：今后10年，天津应发挥老工业基地和港口城市作用，把天津建设成为有自己特色的轻纺、机械、电子工业和原材料工业基地，并使金融、贸易和其他第三产业有更大发展。

1月14日 国家教委和人事部联合对全国310名做出突出贡献的回国留学人员进行表彰。天津市农业科学院(以下简称“市农科院”)副院长路凯旋、天津市蔬菜研究所(以下简称“市蔬菜所”)李卫民名列其中。

同日 天津大沽化工厂年产上万吨环氧丙烷工程通过验收。

2月2日 国家科委副主任朱丽兰、中国科协书记处书记刘恕到天津，出席天津市1991年度青年科学基金与自然科学基金资助项目发布会，并参观天津市科技创业服务中心(以下简称“市科技创业中心”)。

2月6日 国家重点实验室——实验血液学实验室通过国家计委和卫生部的验收。该实验室依托中国医学科学院血液学研究所，实验基地900平方米，承担国家科技攻关课题。

3月6日 天津新技术产业园区(以下简称“天津园区”)被国务院批准为全国26个国家级高新技术产业开发区之一。

3月14～15日 天津市科学技术委员会(以下简称“市科委”)受国家科委和农业部的委托，主持召开全国马铃薯脱毒微型种薯技术推广会。会议决定以市蔬菜所为中心，建立全国马铃薯脱毒微型种薯生产技术推广协作网。

3月21日 天津市人民政府(以下简称“市政府”)召开表彰会，为688项获得国家质量奖、国际金奖、部优、市优的产品颁奖。天津市达仁堂制药厂、天津市仁立毛纺厂等一批先进单位和先进个人受到表彰。

4月16日 天津市召开技术出口工作会议，化工局等6个单位介绍技术出口工作经验，并公布《天津市技术出口管理暂行办法(试行)》。

4月17日 经中国、比利时科技合作第八届委员会北京会议确定，蓟县翠屏科学园(中国天津星火计划培训中心)正式列入中比政府间合作项目。

4月20日～10月15日 市农科院副院长兼天津市黄瓜研究所(以下简称“市黄瓜所”)所长侯锋带领5名科技人员赴美国进行黄瓜试种推广研究。

4月21日 天津市电机总厂生产的潜油电泵机组在第二届北京国际博览会上获金奖。

4月30日 中共天津市委员会(以下简称“市委”)、市政府表彰1990年度市级特等劳动模范38名，其中有8位科技工作者。

5月8日 市科技创业中心正式启用，国家科委常务副主任李绪鄂、市长聂璧初为启用仪式剪彩。

5月9日 在法国巴黎举行的国际发明展览会上，天津市选送的4项发明中，2项获银牌，1项获铜牌，1项获荣誉奖。

5月13日 天津通信广播公司获国家级企业技术进步奖。全国共有108家企业获此奖励。

5月14日 苏联国家科委合作司副司长萨尔谢诺夫和苏驻华使馆科技一秘萨莫林到津，就天津市科技代表团赴苏商定的新材料、生物、冶金、农业等15个合作项目纪要副本签字，并参观市科技创业中心。

5月19日 由国家自然科学基金会数理科学部组织的第二次21世纪中国数学展望学术会议，在南开大学数学研究所开幕。著名数学家陈省身任会议名誉主席，国务委员、国家科委主任宋健，中科院院长周光召等和100多名来自全国各地的数学家出席开幕式。市委常委、市科委主任王成怀等到会祝贺。会议确定了“八五”期间一些数学主要分支的发展规划。

5月20日 国务委员、国家科委主任宋健到市科技创业中心考察并题词:“树立发展高技术产业的战略决心,为形成现代化工业格局而奋斗”,还就发展高新技术产业、形成现代企业格局等问题同部分高校、科研院所负责人进行座谈。

5月30日 市委书记谭绍文接见著名数学家陈省身教授和著名物理学家朱经武教授一行。

6月6日 天津市农药总厂与南大元素所、元素有机化学国家重点实验室举行“长期技术协作议定书”签字仪式。

6月18~22日 全国火炬高新技术及产品展交会召开,天津参展120项,获奖30项,在参展省(市)中均居第二位。

6月24日 国际肿瘤放疗化疗研讨会在天津市肿瘤医院举行。国际乳腺癌研究组织主席、著名肿瘤化疗专家汉斯·耶尔格·森教授等国内外近百名专家学者参加研讨会。

7月3日 美籍华人、高级水资源专家、华盛顿州立大学教授余芸,应国家科委社会发展司和副市长陆焕生邀请,到津考察引滦工程等项目。

8月30日 中央驻津科研单位联络中心成立。该中心提出的宗旨是“联合起来,为天津经济建设作贡献”。

8月31日 天津化工研究院研制开发的世界第一条转化法碳酸钡生产线(年生产量5000吨)在武清县黄庄乡正式开工,化工部部长顾秀莲、副部长贺国强和市委常委、市科委主任王成怀等出席开工仪式。

同日 天津市在东郊区探明一片可采热能相当于5000万吨标准煤的地热田——山岭子地热田。

9月3日 市委副书记、代市长张立昌到市科技创业中心,就进一步组织实施10项科技攻关项目进行现场办公,有关部门负责人参加办公会议。

9月6日 天津市举行国家计量先进单位颁证大会。全市58家企业获“国家计量先进单位”称号。

9月14日 天津市第五届科技周开幕。其主题是“科技进步·经济建设·精神文明”。中国科协副主席、党组书记高潮和市领导谭绍文、张立昌等出席开幕式,并参观中央驻津科研院所及市属先进科研院所成果展览。

9月24日 美国《世界日报》发表标题为《中国黄瓜移植成功,投入美国市场颇受好评》的文章,称赞市黄瓜所侯锋在美国进行黄瓜研究取得的成绩。

10月1日 天津广播电视塔正式开播使用。该塔1988年6月5日破土动工,建设中采用10项科技新成果。同年12月29日,该工程成套技术通过专家鉴定。

10月15日 市农委举办1991年下派科技副乡(镇)长培训班。市委常委王成怀到会,勉励大家把“科技兴农”工作抓实、抓好。

10月31日 国家科委在京召开“七五”科技星火表彰会及科技星火博览会。天津市47名有突出贡献的科技人员、管理人员和星火企业家受到表彰,67项星火成果受到奖励。

11月2日 在西安举行的全国第六届发明展上,天津市参展的25项发明获奖,其中3项金奖、8项银奖、14项铜奖,获奖总数在各展团中居第三位。

11月7日 天津市首批农业示范工程之一“10万亩水稻中低产田变高产配套技术示范工程”通过专家鉴定。该工程实施3年增产稻谷3798万千克,增加经济效益2951万元。

11月11日 天津市科技领导小组召开全市产业(行业)消化吸收国外技术,进行技术成套开发与技术升级对策研究工作动员会。

11月12日 国家科委在天津召开12省市科技创业服务中心工作研讨会。国家科委火炬办公室(中心)主任李肇杰出席会议并讲话,市委常委、市科委主任王成怀等在开幕式上介绍市科技创业中心情况。

11月19日 天津古海岸遗迹(贝壳堤、牡蛎滩)被国家海洋局评为国家级海洋自然保护区。

11月28日 由国内著名放射医学专家、天津医学院附属医院教授吴恩惠主编的《头部CT诊断学》,获1991年度国家教委科技进步一等奖。该书是中国第一部头部CT诊断专著。

11月29日 市政府批转市科委、市计委拟订的《天津市科学技术发展十年规划和"八五"计划纲要》。

12月2日 市科委、市教育局联合宣布从1992年起在全市施行"播种太阳奖",以鼓励传授自然科学知识、为21世纪准备自然科学人才的优秀中小学教师。

12月15日 天津市河东医院宋继昌等研究成功生物型人工乙肝技术,达到国际先进水平。采用该技术可有效治疗高死亡率的急性肝功能衰竭疾病,提高患者的存活率。

12月20日 国家科委政策法规司马左一行到天津审核技术合同仲裁机构,决定将天津市技术合同仲裁机构列为全国首家批准单位。

12月28日 受国务院委托,国家科委正式批准天津园区的区域范围和面积,确定园区建设的各项政策规定。该园区总有效面积22平方千米,其中新建区面积4.1平方千米。

12月30日 南开大学校长母国光等研制的"用黑白胶片作彩色摄影的技术"成果,入选1991年中国十大科技新闻。翌日,市领导聂璧初、王成怀等看望母国光,对入选十大科技新闻一事表示祝贺。该成果获1992年度国家发明二等奖。

1992年

1月10日 天津市轻工业化学研究所孙岩等成功地用农业原料淀粉或葡萄糖合成出多用途新型表面活性剂——烷基葡萄苷(APG),其合成方法和工艺为世界首创。

1月11日 市委、市政府召开部分享受政府特殊津贴专家、学者及有突出贡献中青年专家参加的座谈会,为"科技兴市"出谋划策。市委书记谭绍文、市长聂璧初等出席座谈会。

1月15日 由天津市对外科技交流中心和中国科学会堂共同承办的中国科技成果及实用技术展览会在印度尼西亚举行。

1月16日 市政府与山西省人民政府共同签订《关于进一步发展经济技术合作的商谈记要》。

1月22日 国家科委副主任惠永正到津,听取市科委"京津塘高速公路高新技术产业带"研究课题汇报,并视察武清县新技术开发区和南大元素所。

2月12日 天津水稻育种专家牛景等利用光敏核不育系进行两系杂交稻研究,育成的杂交稻穗大、粒满,平均每穗达200粒,亩产超1000千克。

2月20日 国家专利局局长、党组书记高卢麟就进一步发展知识产权事业到津进行调研。翌日,应市委、市政府邀请,高卢麟作知识产权工作报告。市领导聂璧初、吴振、王成怀及各部委办和区县局有关负责人出席报告会。

2月21日 天津市儿童医院完成一对联体婴儿的分离手术。这是天津市首例成功的联体分离术。

2月23日 南开大学分子生物学研究所教授陈德风等在国际上首次发现识别序列外甲基化对于限制性内切酶活性的抑制作用。

2月25日 天津市畜牧兽医研究所徐直主持完成牛胚胎移植试验，受体黄牛产出1头黑白花奶牛。

2月28日 市政府与中国科学院在北京签订《关于进一步深化改革，扩大开放，加速推进科技与生产紧密结合议定书》。

3月7日 天津市“科技兴市”调查研究工作组召开第一次会议。该工作组由21个部门抽调48名干部组成。市委书记谭绍文要求工作组“讲究方法，注重实效”。

3月16日 天津市中环三津有限公司生产的35厘米高分辨单色管通过美国UL安全认证。这是国内同行业中的首例。

3月24日 天津市“节能消烟炉拱”新技术推广会召开。工业系统225个单位500余人到会，国家科委技术市场办公室和市科委负责人出席会议并讲话。

3月25日 摩托罗拉(中国)电子有限公司经过近4年筹办正式成立。6月9日，在天津经济技术开发区(以下简称“天津开发区”)举行破土典礼。

4月2～3日 国家科委党组副书记、常务副主任朱丽兰到天津，考察天津化工研究院和蓟县翠屏科学园。

4月7日 天津市微型汽车技术引进及技术改造项目全面竣工投产。市计委受国家计委委托，召开该项目的国家级验收会议。

4月9日 天津医学院第二附属医院眼科教授宋国祥等历时17年，首创超声、CT定性、定位诊断以及经眼结膜前路开眶手术，摘除眼眶深部海绵状血管瘤。该成果打破传统的外侧开眶手术方法，经临床193例手术验证，成功率达100%。

4月14日 国际科学园区协会副主席、芬兰科学园区协会主席波奇·胡思肯纳到天津，考察天津园区。

4月16日 天津华立达生物工程有限公司成立。该公司是国内首家与国外生物工程研究机构进行合作生产的科技型企业。

4月18日 市长聂璧初率市政府常务会议成员参观天津园区部分企业及展览，并在市科技创业中心召开市政府第87次常务会议，专题讨论加快天津园区发展问题，批准组建园区管理委员会、园区管理办法与政策规定、园区环境建设等3个实施方案。

4月23日 天津市召开首批卫生、城建系统中青年专家授衔大会，49名中青年科技骨干被授予专家称号。

5月9日 天津市专利局、市司法局和人民艺术剧院联合召开普法宣传知识产权工作会议，国家专利局副局长姜颖、市政法委书记鲁学政出席会议。

5月11日 市长聂璧初同中国科学院院长周光召就“双方开展多种合作，促进天津经济发展”举行座谈，市科委等有关部门负责人参加座谈。

同日 市委组织部、市科委联合召开天津市专业技术人员继续教育经验交流会。人事部副部长蒋冠庄、市委常委王成怀、市人大副主任虞福京、副市长钱其璈出席会议。

5月23～24日 国家科委政法司在天津主持评审会，“天津市现代技术在诉讼过程中的应用”“天津市工业系统技术评价与选择研究”两项软课题研究成果，通过专家鉴定。

5月26日 由南开大学和天津糖精厂合作开发的高效低毒豆田除草剂“豆草除”，通过中试鉴定，达到国内领先水平。

5月28日 市蔬菜所王炳君被评为全国星火计划先进工作者。6月17日,其主持完成的"马铃薯脱毒微型种薯快繁技术"获国家发明专利。

6月2日 市委书记谭绍文会见世界著名物理学家、美籍华人袁家骝。

6月5~9日 第21届理论物理中微分几何方法国际学术会议在南开大学召开。台北研究院院长吴大猷教授专程到津赴会,著名学者杨振宁和陈省身主持会议,23个国家和地区代表100余人到会。

6月9日 国家科委副主任惠永正为天津市区局以上领导干部作《当代国内外高新技术研究与发展》专题报告。

同日 市科委主持召开深化科技体制改革座谈会,38个局领导及科技处处长出席会议。

6月10~14日 中国科学院院长周光召等到天津考察,同市政府洽谈并形成"会谈纪要"。双方同意拓宽合作领域,抓好51个项目的落实,把科学技术真正转化成生产力,推动天津经济发展。

6月23日 国家科委受国务院委托,向天津园区授"国家高新技术产业开发区"标牌,并为天津园区武清开发区破土奠基。

6月27日 天津第一机床总厂研制成功新一代数控机床——YKD2250A曲线锥齿轮铣齿机床。

同日 天津无缝钢管工程项目连铸系统开始热负荷试车一次成功,顺利冶炼出第一炉钢水并连铸成坯。这是国内最大的150吨超高功率电弧炉等成套设备技术热试的成功。7月1日,国家主席江泽民、国务院总理李鹏分别发来贺电。

7月18日 天津市25个项目参展全国科技成果展览交易会,其中获金奖13个,优秀奖1个,天津展团获最佳组团奖。

7月24日 市委书记谭绍文到天津园区考察,并题词"办好新技术产业园区,为振兴天津经济服务"。

8月10~12日 市委、市政府召开科技工作会议,市委书记谭绍文出席并讲话。会上颁布《关于依靠科技进步加快经济发展的若干意见》,提出实施"科技兴市"战略方针和6项具体政策规定。

8月15日 天津市锻压机床总厂研制出具有国际先进水平的新型双重力薄板控伸液压机,填补国内液压机生产的一项空白。

9月10日 市科委代表市政府向4个先进学科教研组、19名优秀中小学教育工作者颁发天津市"播种太阳奖"。

9月14日 天津市第六届科技周活动开幕。

10月3~5日 天津市科学技术协会(以上简称"市科协")第4次代表大会召开。大会选举天津大学校长吴咏诗教授为天津市第四届科协主席。

10月8日 中法合资天津罗素—优克福农药有限公司研制的溴氰菊酯生产技术,通过验收并正式投产,达到国内领先水平。

10月10日 法国国防部顾问、国防基金会副会长夏尔·德利朗应国家科委邀请,偕夫人到津,考察京津塘高速公路高新技术产业带,对在宜兴埠兴办中法合作项目的可能性进行初步探讨。

同日 在北京举办的国际发明展览会上,天津市参展的32个项目中有16项获奖(金牌1枚、银牌6枚、铜牌9枚),其中静海县残疾人李春先发明的转盘式人力收割机获金奖。

同日 中国第一条磁卡电话机生产线在天津电话设备厂磁卡话机分厂建成投产。邮电部确定该磁卡电话机在全国统一使用。

10月10～12日 台湾经济研究院梁荣辉一行4人到天津，考察天津园区。

11月5日 市专利局、市工商局、市出版局联合举办天津市知识产权宣传展示会。国家专利局副局长姜颖、国家工商局副局长李必达等专程到天津参加开幕式。市委副书记李建国等参观展示会。

11月6日 市政府批准天津园区发展规划。规划确定在“2个产业区、4个功能区、1个政策区、1个辐射区”四个层面上全面发展。

11月12日 市科委召开全市情报工作会议，贯彻国家科委决定，将“科技情报”改为“科技信息”，明确科技信息改革发展的总体目标、任务和思路。

11月13日 在第四届中国新技术产品博览会上，天津参展的58项成果中获金奖4项、银奖5项、优秀奖5项，天津展团获最佳组团奖。

11月17日 首届国际中小企业新产品、新技术展览暨合作洽谈会在天津举办。日本、韩国、法国、印度、新加坡、以色列、英国等国家300多家企业及国内1400多家中小企业近万种名优精品和最新技术参加展览和交流。

11月22日 天津市职称改革领导小组办公室提出，企业和企业化管理的事业单位，其专业技术职务不再受指标控制，其聘任全部由企业自主。

11月24日 天津市农业生产最大的科技攻关项目粮食增产示范工程中的2个骨干工程——中低产小麦和中低产玉米技术开发示范工程通过鉴定，总计增产粮食2.67亿千克，纯增效益1.5亿元。

11月25日 中国民航学院三维显示技术研究所研制出中国第一台便携式主体摄像机。

同日 天津无缝钢管工程项目穿孔机热负荷试车一次成功。11月28日连轧管机组热负荷试车一次成功。12月4日，通过定径机进入冷床。

11月27日 蓟县别山乡前楼村农民相宝昶研制成功小麦胚芽油。国家科委将该成果列入国家级重大科研成果，国家计委授予“国家级重大新产品”称号。

1993年

1月4日 天津电气传动研究所研制的水轮发电机转轮实验设备——水力机械通用试验台，通过国家鉴定，达到国际先进水平。

1月8日 市政府批准建立天津园区塘沽海洋高新技术小区。

2月1日 天津铁厂和中国科技大学研制成功电炉炼钢用优质原料——低碳粒铁。天津铁厂建成国内第一条低碳粒铁生产线。

2月18日 市科委、市外经贸委联合召开天津市技术出口座谈会，副市长叶迪生出席。天津市技术出口在全国排名由1991年的第七位上升到1992年的第三位。

2月20日 市政府批准建立天津园区宜兴埠开发小区。

2月26日 天津市召开职称改革工作会议，制定对专业技术人员实行评聘分开、将专业技术职务聘任权下放给事业单位、建立资格制度、实施自主管理等多项深化职称改革制度。

4月16日 市政府召开“科技兴工”总结动员大会，对在“科技兴工”中做出突出贡献的先进企业、优秀新产品及有功人员给予表彰，其中6人获“新品状元”称号，16人获“科技兴工带头人”称号。

4月18日 天津市28名劳动模范、8个先进班组获全国“五一”劳动奖章和全国“五一”劳动奖状，其中天津市锻压机床总厂杨志信、南开大学光电研究所孙仲林、天津大学石油开发中心谈遒、天津医学院任中原等4名科技工作者获此殊荣。

5月5日 市科技创业中心二期工程通过验收。5月8日,该工程举行启用仪式,国家科委有关负责人和在天津出席全国科技创业服务中心研讨会的代表100多人到会祝贺。

5月17日 国际科学园协会秘书长柯卫达访问市科技创业中心,参观进驻企业,称赞该中心已成为一个合格的国际科学园协会成员。市科委副主任梁肃和联合国教科文组织官员吴季松教授及北京开发区副主任赵凤桐陪同访问。

5月20日 国家信息中心和市政府共同组建的天津信息市场开业。

5月24日 天津市首次在蓟县出土一颗长3.6米、直径22厘米、重约100千克的古象牙化石。

5月28日 市长张立昌在市委办公厅《内参》(增37)上批示:“科技口在推动全市科技进步、振兴天津经济工作中,做了大量艰苦的工作。无论是在城市,还是农村,无论是在企业,还是科研院所,都能见到你们的成果。望在‘科技兴市’的工作中再创新业绩。”

6月8日 天津市常设技术市场试开业。当天接待参观者1500余人,洽谈项目260项(次),其中28项达成意向协议,金额达82万元。

6月15日 天津中医药研究院正式成立。它是1987年经国务院批准建立的全国六大中医药研究基地之一。

6月19日 天津中医学院第一附属医院国际康复中心成立。

7月1日 国务院决定,由国家科委牵头进行京沪高速铁路建设论证。以铁道部经济规划研究院院长何璧率领,由国家科委、国家计委、国家经贸委、铁道部等6部委组成的京沪高速铁路重大经济技术问题前期研究课题组到津调研。

7月2日 天津市大中华橡胶厂厂长张振荣在全国首届民营科技型企业工作会议上做《利用民营机制,搞活大中型企业》的典型发言。国家科委主任宋健接见张振荣时讲:“双钱鞋很有名,这样搞下去就有希望了。”

7月14日 国家科委在庆祝火炬计划实施五周年之际,表彰一批实施火炬计划的先进集体、优秀项目和先进个人。市科技创业中心、新星电子公司、清洗润滑防腐公司、津科电子有限公司的“中英文智能电报终端及联网系统”、七〇七所的“微电脑焊机控制箱”等单位或项目以及梁肃、刘俩、袁环、李经建、高孟贤等个人受到国家科委表彰。

7月15日~8月2日 天津碱厂总工程师陈耀汉一行7人,赴俄罗斯巴尔什基尔共和国斯捷尔塔马克制碱联合公司考察碱渣综合利用技术,签订合作意向书,俄方向中方提供用碱渣制取建材的专利和技术诀窍,并向中方提供日产800吨蒸汽和吸氨塔的技术资料。

7月21日 市人大常委会任命梁肃为市科委主任,并兼任天津园区管理委员会主任。

7月30日 市科委召开扩大全方位开放科研院所外向型工作经验交流会,副市长李慧芬出席并讲话。

8月11日 市委书记高德占在市科委召开的科技系统座谈会上强调:“天津要抓住机遇、加快发展,必须不断加深对科技工作重要性的认识。”

8月14日 市科委在常设技术市场正式开设周末科技贸易集市,为企业和科研单位创造广泛接触的机会。

8月19日 副市长李慧芬主持召开首次科技工作联合办公会。市科委、市计委、市经委分别通报3年来科技工作情况。李慧芬指出，三委做了大量工作，今后要明确分工，各有侧重，市科委要牵头把全市科技管理力量组织起来，把科研院所、科技人员的积极性调动起来，推动“科技兴市”。

8月21日　经市政府批准，中华留学生科技创业园在天津塘沽海洋高科技园区成立。

8月23日～9月2日　受人事部、农业部委托，市科委主办，市农科院承办的全国玉米遗传育种及丰产栽培技术高级研究班开班，20个省（市、区）30名专家学者参加，听取7个专题报告，交流22篇学术论文。

8月25日　三峡工程坝区通航水流条件工程模型实验厅在天津水运工程研究所建成。这是国内最大的正态水工模型。

9月1日　市科委和市科协颁发《关于动员科技界积极投入扭亏增盈攻坚战的决定》。9月17日召开的科技界积极投入扭亏增盈攻坚战动员大会上宣读该决定的16条措施。

9月3日　市委书记高德占主持召开发挥高校作用，加速高校科研成果转化座谈会，对加快科技成果转化提出要求。市委有关部门负责人及各高校校长参加座谈。

同日　2.2万用户割入相应程控电话局。天津市最后一批步进制交换机完成历史使命。

9月7～8日　市科委主任梁肃率有关部门负责人分别到天津大学、南开大学就天津市吸收高校科技成果事宜进行洽谈，确定建立市科委与天津大学、南开大学定期接触制度，并汇集12项可供产业化的成果。

9月15日　匈牙利科技报告展示会在天津市科技咨询大厦开幕，匈牙利22家公司和科研院所展出医疗、化学、钢铁等方面的新技术，并举办23项技术交流和专业报告会。

9月25日　京津塘高速公路全线通车。起点为北京市东南四环路，终点在天津塘沽区河北路，全长142.69千米。

10月7日　副市长李慧芬在天津大学主持召开科技成果转化鹊桥会，天津大学校长李光泉、市科委主任梁肃和市经委、市计委负责人及有关工业局总工程师和部分企业负责人出席，天津大学有关专家介绍10项可供转让的新成果。

10月11～16日　天津市金秋科技信息周活动在市科技信息中心开幕。

10月13日　在新加坡举办的国际设计发明、专利技术及产品展览会上，天津市获金狮奖(金牌)6枚、银狮奖5枚。

10月15日　天津市评出首届10大杰出青年，其中有4位科技工作者：大港石油管理局地质研究院总地质师吴永平、南开大学生物系副教授张金忠、天津新星电子公司总经理李经建、市农科院园艺工程研究所副研究员郭富常。

10月28日　《天津市技术市场管理条例》在市人大常委会第3次会议上审议通过，并颁布施行。

10月30日～11月1日　国务院总理李鹏视察天津广播电视塔、天津钢管公司，听取市委、市政府的工作汇报。

11月26日　市人大教科文卫委和市科委联合召开学习贯彻《天津市技术市场管理条例》动员大会，国家科委及市有关领导出席。

11月27日　国家科委副主任韩德乾向大港区中塘乡国家星火技术密集区授匾。

11月28日　市地矿局在蓟县探明一座大型地下水源，总静储量38亿立方米，日采水量可达12万立方米，是天津市探明的最大地下水资源。

11月30日　在中国高新技术产品博览会上，市科委组织30个单位、47个项目参展，获3项金奖、4项银奖、1项优秀奖。

12月15日 天津港东突堤12个万吨级深水泊位码头通过国家验收，正式投入使用，使天津港年增吞吐能力508万吨。

12月24日 全国专利工作会议评出中国专利发明奖10项。天津市林果研究所的“山楂蜜汁的加工方法”、南开大学的“顺返体高效氯氢菊酯制造方法的改革”、市蔬菜所的“马铃薯脱毒微型种薯的生产方法”名列其中。

1994年

1月5~6日 全国人大常委会副委员长倪志福到天津考察期间，观看天津大学机械系正在研制的微机控制“倪志福钻头”多坐标刃磨机床，参观天津园区的金光公司和新星电子公司。

1月12~13日 国务院副总理邹家华到津，视察天津港、核工业理化工程研究院。

1月26日 市人大常委会第5次会议审议通过《天津市实施〈中华人民共和国科学技术进步法〉办法》。

2月8日 天津钢管公司生产的P110钢级139.7毫米石油套管，在中原石油勘探局卫文79156井下井、固井成功。这是此种型号套管在国内的首次使用。

2月16日 天津市建筑材料科学研究所与澳大利亚新南威尔士大学建筑研究中心合作，建立天津市津澳建筑材料研究所。这是天津市第一家中外合作的研究开发机构。

2月23日 天津市科学技术评价中心正式挂牌。该中心挂靠在天津市科技信息中心。

3月1日 由中央驻津高校和科研院所组成的天津市科技协作促进会成立。

3月10日 市委、市政府印发《关于与国家科委联合组建北方技术交易市场及有关问题的通知》，明确北方技术交易市场是自收自支的副局级事业单位，归口市科委。

3月29日 国家外国专家局批准天津市1994年度第一批引进国外智力项目共50项、74人，资助金额148万元。

3月31日 市科委召开百亿工程项目动员会，并与承担单位签订协议书。被市政府列入1994年科技重点工作的科技百亿工程正式启动。

4月1日 第三届天津市青年科技奖评选结果揭晓，南开大学李朝兴等21人获奖。6月7日举行大会，表彰获奖者。

4月6日 天津钢管公司在获得API（美国石油协会）认证的同时，通过中国船级社认证即CCS认证。该公司30%的产品可用于造船业。

4月14日 由市黄瓜所所长侯锋主持培育成的“津春3号”黄瓜新品种，获国家发明专利。该成果在1991~1995年期间累计推广15万亩，使菜农增加收入2.7亿元。

4月29日 市政府举行仪式，向日本专家中村实博士颁发“中国国际奖”，国家科委副主任韩德乾和市委常委、副市长李慧芬向其授奖。

5月10日 市政府召开“科技兴工”工作会议，表彰1993年度“科技兴工”先进集体和先进个人，其中新产品状元8名，“科技兴工”带头人20名，新产品开发先进集体84个，优秀新产品一等奖46项、二等奖74项、三等奖32项。

同日 首届全国优秀发明企业家颁奖大会在北京人民大会堂召开。10名获奖者中，天津新旺达远红外线制品有限公司副董事长、高级工程师李冬绮名列其中。

5月14~17日 市科技创业中心主任袁环在美国布法罗第八届美国企业孵化器年会上作《中国创业中心的管理与发展》演讲。

5月23~24日 市科委主任梁肃出席在北京召开的21世纪亚太地区科技工业园区发展战略研讨会,并作《中国企业孵化器基本经验》的报告。

5月26~29日 国家高新技术开发区立法工作研讨会在天津召开。全国人大法工委主任顾昂然,市委常委、副市长李慧芬及全国43个高新技术产业开发区和部分省市科委负责人出席。会上,天津园区管委会主任梁肃介绍天津市科技立法的体会,园区管委会副主任陈舜琦作典型发言。

5月30日 天津市第七届发明展览会在天津市技术市场召开,展示发明和专利成果近200项。

6月6日 国家海洋局批准天津市设置国家海洋局天津海洋管理办公室。该办公室与天津市海洋管理部门一起,共同负责天津海岛、海岸带及邻近海域的开发协调、保护和管理。

6月16日 市科委主任梁肃与22个中央驻津科研院所负责人共商合作开发、加快发展塘沽海洋高新技术开发区问题。

6月19~21日 天津市举办专利申请量超万项现场展示和咨询会,展出100多项专利产品、400多个专利项目,观看和咨询者达万余人次。

6月21日 国家科委在天津举行全国咨询产业试点城市论证会。9月26日,经国家科委批准,天津市被列为全国发展科技咨询产业4个试点省市之一。

7月2日 市委常委、副市长李慧芬到天津园区管委会调研"一区三制"改革设想。7月5日,李慧芬率领市经委、市体改委、市财政局、中国人民银行天津分行、市政府办公厅等有关部门负责人到天津园区津科公司和新星公司调研股份制改革、流动资金紧缺等问题。

7月6日 市委书记高德占到天津园区视察。在听取园区管委会主任梁肃汇报后指出,天津园区要进入加快发展新阶段,应与天津开发区、保税区并驾齐驱。

7月19日 天津市跨世纪育才工程正式启动,对100名45岁以下自然科学技术领域学术带头人实施重点培养,资助年限4~6年,并对1500名跨世纪青年尖子人才实施培养计划,同时设立21世纪育才工程"伯乐奖"。

7月25日 国家科委、国家外经贸委及有关部门组成的"京津塘高速公路高科技产业带发展研究"课题组一行13人,在市科委有关负责人等陪同下进行全线考察。

8月8日 美国专利申请及科技信息咨询中心主任郑钰博士应邀到津,作关于美国专利法的报告。市专利局事务所与其签订专利代理方面的合作意向书。

8月16日 市科委召开科技体制改革研讨会,总结近年来科技体制改革的基本经验,讨论落实国家科委关于深化科技体制改革要点的具体目标和措施。

8月25日 《天津市专利管理局关于中国专利产品认定办法》开始实行。根据该《办法》,经认定的中国专利产品,可标以天津市专利管理局(以下简称"市专利局")制发的中国专利产品激光全息防伪标记,并由市专利局颁发认定证书。

9月8~17日 在青岛举办的第八届全国发明展上,天津市参展的22个项目中,获金牌2项、银牌7项、铜牌8项。

9月19~28日 全国星火计划科技管理培训班在天津星火计划培训中心(天津翠屏科学园)举行,各省、自治区、直辖市科委及国家星火培训基地负责人52人参加培训。

9月23～24日 中国工程院副院长卢良恕、中国科学院院士庄巧生、国家“863”专家委员会委员贾士荣、国家“863”课题主持人朱裕鼎、总理专项基金课题主持人陈廷伟一行5人参观市农科院，对天津市农业生物工程研究提出建设性意见。

10月10日 香港《大公报》以中英文两种文字发表消息，报道“天津园区发展高新技术产业已成为外商投资的新热点”。

10月14日 天津市第二届技术市场金桥奖大会召开。市委常委、副市长李慧芬，市人大常委会副主任王成怀等出席，并向天津市获全国技术市场金桥奖的10个先进集体和7名先进个人颁奖。

10月18日 市人大常委会第11次会议审议通过《天津市实施〈中华人民共和国农业技术推广法〉办法》，从即日起施行。

10月25日 天津园区和石家庄高新技术开发区建立合作关系，并在市科技创业中心召开合作发展信息发布会。

10月26日 经国务院副总理李岚清提议，中国汽车技术研究中心建设促进会在天津成立，为创建企业与科研院所紧密合作提供一种新形式。

10月27日 全国百强高新技术企业排名揭晓。天津园区5家企业——天津日电电子通信有限公司、天津爱普生有限公司、天津梅兰日兰公司、天津新星电子公司、天津金燕焊接材料有限公司榜上有名。

10月31日 市政府知识产权办公会议制度建立。11月24日，副市长李慧芬主持召开市政府知识产权办公会议第一次会议。

11月1日 国家科委和市政府在京举行新闻发布会，宣布由国家科委和天津市政府联合在天津建设的国家级常设技术交易市场——北方技术交易市场建成。12月27日，北方技术交易市场投入运行。

11月18日 市科委召开天津市科技计划工作会议。市科委主任梁肃作《关于我市今年“科技百亿工程”项目的实施情况及1995年开始全面展开》的动员报告，并发布1995年天津市火炬计划、科技攻关计划及星火计划项目的选题指南。

11月22日 市科委和市财政局联合发文，调整天津市科学技术进步奖奖金数额，一、二、三等奖奖金分别由0.4万元、0.2万元、0.1万元提高到1.5万元、0.6万元、0.3万元。

11月28日 世界首台HNC35－TP高精度9轴数控、4轴联动环面蜗杆磨床在天津开发区华盛昌齿轮有限公司投入使用。该磨床是天津华盛昌齿轮有限公司与德国克林贝尔公司科技人员历经3年努力，合作研制成功。

12月5日 第43届世乒赛重点工程——天津卫星通信地面站竣工，其具备同时传递4路电视节目能力，天津长途通信技术又上了一个新台阶。

12月14日 中共中央总书记江泽民参观天津科技馆并题词。1995年1月1日，天津科技馆正式对社会开放。

12月20日 天津汽车工业总公司生产的TJ7100系列夏利牌轿车、TJ1010系列华利牌微型厢式货车，在全国微型汽车国家级统检活动中获一等奖。

12月22日 市委常委、副市长李慧芬在全国软科学会上作题为《软科学为天津走向21世纪运筹新举措》的发言。市科委主任梁肃当选为中国软科学研究会常务理事。

12月26日 北方技术交易市场管委会举行第一次会议。国家科委副主任韩德乾和副市长李慧芬任管委会主任。北方技术交易市场实行管委会领导下的总裁负责制，王立子为首任总裁。

1995年

1月6日 天津市性科学协会成立，设在天津医科大学内，由石坚、赵玉茹、吴咸中任名誉理事长，崔以泰任理事长。

1月7日 天津津京玻壳股份有限公司实施市级"八五"重大技改项目"黑白电视机玻壳改造工程"，从筑炉施工到点火投产仅用258天，使天津成为世界最大的黑白电视机玻壳生产基地之一。

1月12日 天津石化公司研究所研制出一种新型绝缘薄膜材料——均四甲苯，通过国家级鉴定，生产工艺获国家发明专利。

2月1日 国家科委和市政府联合建设的国家级常设技术市场——北方技术交易市场正式开业。国家科委主任宋健为开业剪彩，市委书记高德占、市长张立昌出席开业仪式。

2月6日 经国家科委批准，塘沽海洋高新技术开发区正式纳入天津园区的区域范围。

2月24日 国家科委批准建立国家黄瓜新品种技术研究推广中心。该中心设在市黄瓜所，是国家在天津建立的第一个全国性农业科技成果研究推广中心。

3月8～13日 在第13届巴拿马万国博览会上，天津市本田摩托车有限公司生产的天虹牌TH90型摩托车获金奖。这是中国摩托车产品首次获得此项荣誉。

3月22日 市政府召开农业科技年动员会，提出用3年时间组织实施5大科技工程，并在5个涉农县各选派一名技术副县长，主管农业技术工作。

4月1日 天津大学物理系教授张春霆当选为国际理论物理研究中心境外研究员，成为生物物理专业获此荣誉的第一名中国学者。同时，美国科学促进会特邀他为该会会员，美国纽约科学院授予他为该院院士。

4月9日 天津地质矿产研究所在蓟县发现17亿年前团山子藻类化石，基本确定是已知的最古老的多细胞藻类化石。

4月18日 在中国专利10年成就展上，天津大学精仪系教授郁道银发明的"NT系列内窥镜图像显示仪"、天津大学化工系教授谌竞清发明的"从等电点结晶母液中回收氨酸的等离子交换工艺"分别获金奖。

5月11日 国际海洋学院中国中心在天津国家海洋信息中心成立。该中心协助发展中国家举办管理好海洋培训班和学术交流活动。

5月24日 市人大常委会第16次会议审议通过《天津新技术产业园区管理条例》。

5月31日 市长张立昌会见杨振宁夫妇一行，并向杨振宁颁发"天津市荣誉市民"证书，赠送天津市金钥匙。

6月5日 市经委、市高教局联合召开天津市"科技兴工"暨产学合作工作会议，表彰9名新产品状元、20名科技兴工带头人、4项产学研联合开发项目、84个新产品开发先进企业或新产品开发带头人、106项优秀新产品。

6月8日 天津市医药卫生新技术新成果展览会开幕。"八五"期间，天津市取得最新医学科研成果567项，其中423项成果获奖，30余项成果居国内领先水平。

6月16日 天津市邮政局从比利时贝尔电话公司引进两套信函自动分拣设备投入使用，结束了百年来手工分拣信函的历史。

6月22日 市政府批准设立的驻津科研院所、高等院校"科技兴市"先进单位奖首次评选揭晓，天津大学、机械工业部第五设计研究院、国家医药局天津药物研究院、电子工业部第46研究所和化学工业部天津化工研究院等5个单位获奖。

6月28日 天津市中心妇产科医院王懿贤、周曰序、刘润环等完成"中期妊娠羊水过少临床治疗研究",达到国际领先水平。

6月29日 市委、市政府召开天津市科学技术大会。副市长庄公惠传达全国科技大会精神,市委书记高德占作重要讲话,市长张立昌作工作报告。会议部署贯彻落实《中共中央、国务院关于加速科学技术进步的决定》,明确提出在天津市实施"科教兴市"战略。

7月5日 由国家海洋局海洋技术研究所研制的中国首台海洋漂移浮标,在中国南海成功布放,其设计性能达到国际同类产品先进水平。

7月19日 由天津新河船厂承担的国家重点科研项目、造价1300万元的海豹3号气枪震源船试航成功,并在新港地区投入使用,标志着中国石油极浅海域勘探告别以炸药为震源的历史,对海洋环境保护起到积极作用。

7月25日 天津市计算机研究所设计开发的"第43届世乒赛计算机系统"通过国家体委和市科委的技术鉴定,在标准化和规范化方面达国际领先水平。

8月2日 中国医学科学院血液学研究所附属医院外科教授瞿全等在国内率先应用紧急脾切除疗法,治疗突发性、血小板减少性紫癜并发脑出血取得成功,并在国内外首创上腹部正中切口同时切除脾脏与胆囊的手术治疗溶血性贫血合并胆石症,疗效达国际先进水平。

8月16日 市委、市政府颁布《关于贯彻全国科学大会精神,加速科学技术进步的实施意见》,全面落实科学技术是第一生产力的思想,把实施"科技兴市"战略落到实处。

9月6日 首届国际头颈肿瘤外科学术会议在天津召开,美国、日本、德国、英国等国内外300多位专家学者出席。

9月7日 天津市科技信息中心向社会推出多功能信息服务网络"联科信息网",正式与国际互联网并网,并开通天津工作站。

9月18日 世界人工晶体中国天津培训中心举行新闻发布会。该中心成立6年来,以先进的人工晶体植入术,使7000余名白内障患者重见光明,其中70%患者术后视力恢复到1.0以上,被世界眼科界列为世界20个著名眼科中心之一。

同日 天津医科大学总医院教授王鹏志主刀的天津市首例、全国第2例小肠移植手术获得成功,标志着天津市在人体器官移植方面取得新突破。

9月20~22日 第五届中日光纤科学与电磁场理论国际会议在天津大学举行,国内外115位专家学者出席,收到论文180多篇。

9月20~27日 天津市第九届科技周举行,主题是"科教兴市,面向21世纪"。

9月21日 联合国开发计划署首次在中国举办的国际创业中心研讨会在天津开幕,24个国家、70余名代表出席,共同探讨创业中心的特点及对支持小企业发展的贡献。

9月22日 国家有关部门批准美国摩托罗拉电子公司增资7.2亿美元,在天津摩托罗拉(中国)电子有限公司建设具有世界一流水平的半导体集成电路芯片厂。

10月2日 天津大学举行建校100周年纪念活动。中共中央总书记江泽民、国务院总理李鹏等为该校百年校庆题词，全国政协主席李瑞环、国务院副总理李岚清等出席庆祝会。

10月5日 天津市第二届“十大青年科技先锋”评选揭晓，孙绪江、何志敏、陈永川、陈秀生、杨池银、赵永坚、修刚、郭义、梁和争、赖振国获此殊荣。

10月7~11日 天津市第四届青年科技成果博览会举行，市领导向获奖者颁发证书和奖牌。博览会接待中外技术洽谈人员7191人次，签订技术成果转让意向书64项，达成技术合作意向443项，新产品成交额63万余元。

10月12日 中国与瑞典环保科技合作项目“海河（天津市区段）污染控制技术研究”通过专家鉴定，达国际先进水平。

11月27~29日 全国政协副主席、中国工程院院长朱光亚到津视察，向天津市领导、有关部门负责人、专家学者作题为《当代工程技术发展态势》的报告，并为市黄瓜所题词“科研攻关和科技体制改革的典范”。

12月3日 天津铁路分局高级工程师魏普钧、钱家寿、白宝曰等发明的铁路车辆双球芯折角塞门，在第44届尤里卡发明博览会上获金奖。

12月8日 天津港海上交通管理中心落成并投入使用。这是国内港口规模最大的塔楼建筑，装备国内最先进的船舶导航系统。

12月10日 国务院批准天津蓟县八仙山自然保护区为国家级自然保护区。

12月12日 国家海洋局海洋技术研究所承担的国家“八五”科技攻关项目“灾害性海冰航空遥感监测实时传输系统”，通过国家海洋局主持的专家鉴定，达到国内领先水平。

12月17日 天津市先导信息网络有限公司建成首家全球信息交互网（Internet）C级工作站，联机一万多个数据库、8个超级计算中心和6000多个图书馆。

12月21日 天津市14万吨乙烯工程4套引进装置流程全部打通，实现一次开车成功。

12月26日 天津市新产品腰椎复位牵引机在美中专利新产品展示暨投资洽谈会上获金鹰奖。该成果由天津中医学院第一附属医院孔令勤研制成功，1993年获国家发明专利。

1996年

2月23日 天津钢管公司生产的抗硫化氢耐腐蚀C90石油套管，达到国内领先水平。

3月19日 天津医科大学第二医院泌尿外科研究所和市橡胶工业研究所，历时6年联合攻关，研制成可控性体内植入人工膀胱，居国际领先水平。

同日 天津大洋电子技术公司研制开发的“用于浑浊海域水下电视系统”，在日内瓦国际发明博览会上获发明金奖。

3月20日 市科委和北方技术交易市场联合举办第一期天津市科技成果信息发布会，80多个单位、150多位代表参加，天津大学、天津工程机械研究所等发布20余项机械行业的新成果。

3月27~28日 国家科委在天津召开13城市专家座谈会，交流发展高新技术产业园区的思路和设想。国家科委副主任徐冠华主持会议，市委常委、副市长曲维枝出席座谈会。

4月2日 大港区中塘镇的中塘国家星火技术密集区通过国家科委和市科委验收。

4月3日 市政府开始实施对蓟县于桥水库库区的科技扶贫工程，市委常委、副市长曲维枝出席仪式并讲话。

4月22日 天津市举办“学绝技、创绝招、争做技术明星”现场动员会。该活动连续开展3年，参加职工累计400万人次，涉及全市340多个重点行业、3900多个主要工种，有数万名职工被评为各级各类技术能手，并从中产生市级技术明星192人。

4月23日 天津市海洋局成立。6月9日正式挂牌办公。

4月24日 中国仪器仪表协会、中国电子协会、天津市电子仪表总公司和市广播电视局等单位联合举办的天津国际仪器仪表、电脑应用、通信设备展览交易会开幕，18个国家和地区、100余家高科技企业参展。

4月29日 天津市自然科学领域跨世纪学术技术带头人座谈会召开，市委常委、副市长曲维枝出席会议并讲话，温和平、何志敏等7位跨世纪培养对象发言。

同日 第四届国际针灸临床研究学术会议在天津中医学院第一附属医院开幕。10余个国家、200多名专家出席，中医针灸专家、该届会议主席石学敏致开幕词。

5月7日 全国医药卫生系统第一个计算机区域网络——天津市医药卫生科技信息计算机网络（津卫网）正式开通。

5月14日 市蔬菜所王炳君研究的“马铃薯脱毒微型种薯快繁技术”，被美国国际农技公司以100万美元买走，首创天津市农业技术出口。

6月2日 中国科协第五次代表大会闭幕。天津代表张道成、母国光当选新一届中国科协常委，吴咏诗、陈惠彬、张天泽当选为委员。

6月16日 天津市胸科医院副主任医师吴建国、裴诚民等开发的“经皮血管镜主视心包活检及介入治疗心包积液”新技术，通过京津两市医学专家评审，达到国内领先水平，具有推广应用价值。

6月21日 天津医院创伤骨科主任医师张铁良应邀在美国亚特兰大市全美骨科学会的大会和专题会上，作《跟骨骨折复位、固定与早期活动》学术报告，引起世界骨科界关注。

同日 天津市河北制药厂研制开发的抗癌新药“培普利欧注射剂”通过卫生部审查，批准生产，达到国内领先水平。

7月3日 天津医科大学总医院杨树源、王明璐等历时3年完成对重型颅脑损伤中弥漫性脑损害的临床及病理生理的研究，通过专家鉴定，达国际先进水平。

7月5日 天津国际康复中心大厦奠基仪式在天津中医学院第一附属医院举行。该中心总投资1.5亿元人民币，成为全国最大的集医疗、科研、康复保健为一体的中医、中西医结合康复基地。

7月9日 天津市召开专家工作会议，向国家批准的1995年度享受政府特殊津贴的115名专家颁发证书。

7月17日 市政府成立信息化领导小组，将天津市金卡工程领导小组和天津市电子振兴办公室并入，由市长张立昌担任组长，办公室设在市科委。

7月 西青区中北镇被批准为国家星火技术密集区。

8月12日 天津市举行科学报告会，中国科学院院长、中国科协主席周光召向区县局以上领导干部、科技工作者作题为《科学技术的发展趋势和它对社会的作用》的报告。

8月24日 南开大学校长、中国科学院院士母国光在韩国大田市召开的国际光学学会第17次学术大会上，再次当选国际光学学会副会长。

8月27日 天津市首家集性病防治、科研、咨询和教学为一体的天津市性病传播疾病医学研究所成立，天津医科大学总医院主任医师、皮肤病学专家傅志宜任所长。

9月11日 以专利权人古春林7项专利为技术入股、西青区上辛口乡投资400万元合作创建的源泉电泵制造有限公司正式开业。

9月13日 国家科委正式同意天津市建立镍氢电池1000万只自动化示范生产线，并将此项目列入国家“九五”重大产业化开发项目。12月21日，天津和平海湾电源集团有限公司年产1000万只镍氢电池示范生产线方案，通过国家科委镍氢电池专家组的评审。

9月18日 中国国际计算机与网络产品展览交易会在天津开幕。市科委主任梁肃主持开幕式，市长张立昌、电子工业部副部长吕新奎、美国国际数据集团公司代表约翰·布莱亚为展览会剪彩，副市长曲维枝致词。

9月18～24日 以“高科技—人才·信息—现代化”为主题的天津市第十届科技周活动全面展开。中国科协主席、中国科学院院长周光召题词“庆祝天津市科技周活动十周年”。

9月20日 世界白内障医师学会第一届国际会议暨天津医科大学世界人工晶体中国天津培训中心第二届国际会议在天津开幕。世界白内障医师学会主席林少明出席开幕式并发表演讲。

同日 市专利局和南开区科委联合举办天津市专利技术展示交易会，35家单位携带1000余项专利技术、40余项专利产品参加展示和展销。

9月23日 全国星火计划工作会议闭幕。天津市25名先进个人和1个先进集体受到国家科委表彰。

9月24日 第四届天津青年科技奖表彰大会召开，20名青年科技工作者获奖。

9月28日 中国中医药学会和天津市天士力联合制药公司举办全国防止心脑血管疾病学术研讨会，全国145位心脑血管医药学专家出席，市政协副主席陆焕生和国家中医药管理局、中国中医药学会负责人参加会议。

9月30日 海水利用技术及防腐技术发展研讨会暨中国高科技产业化研究会海洋分会第三届年会在天津举行，全国30多个科研单位、高等院校和企业的60多名专家出席会议。

10月6日 在全国星火计划成果博览会上，天津市34个项目获奖，天津展团获最佳组织奖。

10月23日 市政府召开会议，批准13项重大科技产业化工程，并批准信息港工程总体框架和规划。

11月6日 在比利时布鲁塞尔举办的第四十五届尤里卡世界发明展览会上，天津市10项发明获奖，其中4枚金奖、1枚银奖、5枚铜奖。

11月21日 第二届天津十大杰出青年颁奖大会召开，南开大学数学研究所教授、博士生导师陈永川代表十大杰出青年发言。

11月26日 天津市肿瘤医院院长郝希山完成第10例胰十二指肠切除术，创该项手术无死亡的国内最高纪录。

12月4～5日 国家科委在天津召开“曙光计算机应用示范（天津）工程”实施方案的综合评审会。该方案通过专家评审，国家科委正式批准实施曙光机应用示范（天津）工程。

12月14日 天津医科大学总医院举行建院50周年庆祝会。该院成为国内临床神经病学和临床内分泌学基地以及环渤海地区临床医学基地。

12月19～20日 国务委员、国家科委主任宋健到津参加全国环保科技工作会议，并视察天津电气传动研究所。

12月27日 1996年度“国家杰出青年科学基金”评审揭晓。南开大学化学系教授刘育、中国医学科学院生物医学工程研究所研究员张其清各获60万元资助。

1997年

1月2日 宝坻县石辛庄生态农业示范村通过市级验收。该村通过鱼饵料喂鸡、鸡粪喂猪、猪粪喂鱼、塘泥肥田的良性循环，既降低生产成本，又改善生态环境，全村树木覆盖率42%，大气环境接近国家一级标准，在全县首先跨入小康村行列。

1月8日 天津信息网(TJnet)正式开通。该网以国家公用信息网为基础，通过中国经济信息网(CEInet)和金桥网(CHINAGBN)，为用户提供国际互联网(Internet)服务，是天津信息港工程的重要构成部分。

1月11日 中国第一艘第五代集装箱船——“鲁河”轮，在天津港集装箱码头顺利首航。全国人大常委会副委员长陈慕华为该轮首航剪彩。

1月13日 大港油田集团有限责任公司整体通过ISO 9000质量体系认证，成为中国第一家通过ISO 9000质量体系认证的陆上石油企业。

1月14日 全球最大的胰岛素和工业酶制剂生产厂——丹麦诺和诺德公司胰岛素工厂，在天津开发区投入生产。

1月16日 天津市科技工作会议召开。会议提出，建设中国北方经济中心，要充分发挥天津技术密集、人才密集、应用研究和技术开发能力较强的优势，依靠科技进步，促进经济增长方式的转变，创造和形成新的发展优势。

2月18日 市蔬菜所被国家科委确定为全国马铃薯脱毒微型种薯技术研究推广中心。

2月 天津邮电本地网最后200多条模拟传输电路全部退网。至此，天津在全国率先实现全网电路的数字化。

3月26日 中宣部、国家科委、国家新闻出版署举行第二届全国优秀科技期刊评比颁奖大会。市科委主办的《科学学与科学技术管理》杂志获一等奖。

3月27日 天津市召开“科技兴海”工作动员会，传达1996年全国海洋厅(局)长会议及“科技兴海”会议的主要精神，副市长曲维枝出席并做总结发言。

4月8日 国务院副总理邹家华为天津信息港工程题词：“统筹规划，联合建设，资源共享，服务经济。”

4月25日 天津国际电脑应用展览会在市体育中心开幕。

同日 国家“九五”重点科技攻关项目——天津港口EDI中心，通过国家交通部验收并开通运行。

5月12日 天津市第三中心医院通过卫生部组织的论证验收，成为卫生部人工细胞工程技术研究中心。

5月15日 天津市召开第八次环境保护会议，落实水、气、声污染治理任务。市长张立昌出席并讲话。

5月21日 市政府批转市财政局和市科委制定的《天津市科技成果推广应用基金管理暂行办法》。

5月23日 南开大学举行原校长、中科院院士杨石先诞辰100周年纪念大会。中共中央政治局常委、全国政协主席李瑞环，中共中央政治局常委、国务院副总理李岚清，国务院副总理邹家华等分别题词。

5月28日 天津市中西医结合医院在南开医院成立。市委教卫工委书记王鸿江、国家中医药管理局副局长于生龙为其挂牌揭幕。

同日 天津市工业系统1997年度合理化建议和技术改进工作会议召开。

5月30日 由德国SEW集团与芬兰圣坦撒罗集团分别投资1亿美元和1500万美元的高科技减速机项目在天津开发区投产。该项目年产15万台减速机，年产值20亿元，是国内最先进、规模最大的减速机厂。

6月16日 《天津市科学技术普及条例》经市人大常委会第33次会议审议通过。

7月9日 由中美两国光学学会首次举办的"固体激光器—材料与应用"国际学术会议在南开大学开幕。国内外专家60余人出席会议。同时,举行中国光学学会首届科技奖颁奖仪式。

7月31日 天津信息港工程第一个应用系统——"天津热线"正式开通。该热线与"上海热线""广东灵通"以及湖南、海南等7个多媒体信息系统联网。

8月5日 天津药业公司总工程师卢彦昌等研制成一项新工艺,使地塞米松原料成本降低30%~40%,所有技术质量指标大幅度提高。

8月9日 经国家环保局批准,天津市开始每周发布城市空气质量情况报告。

8月13日 具有防洪抗旱两种功能的南运河口防洪闸土建工程完工。

8月13~16日 中国(天津)国际计算机与网络产品展览交易会在国际展览中心开幕,市长张立昌,副市长李盛霖、曲维枝等出席开幕式。交易会现场签订合同金额200多万元。展会期间还举办"天津信息港工程国际研讨会",到会中外嘉宾200余人。

8月24日 南开大学在天津体育馆举办杨振宁教授75周岁诞辰庆祝活动。

8月25~28日 "可积模型与杨—巴克斯特系统的物理应用"国际会议在南开大学举行。诺贝尔奖得主杨振宁等70余人知名专家学者出席会议。会议收到论文64篇。

8月28日 天津市信息港工程的重点项目——天津市银行卡网络正式开通运行。

9月8日 天津市环境保护科学研究所经批准更名为天津市环境保护研究院,是从事环境保护科学与技术研究、开发和应用的研究机构。

9月18~24日 天津市第十一届科技周活动全面展开。其主题是"信息连着你我他",共举办全市性的重点活动11项,各区县局和各系统活动近600项,基层单位活动上万项。

9月22日 西门子电力电缆(天津)有限公司引进的德国M85拉丝机等电缆生产先进设备投入生产,开发出高电压、大长度电缆的耐压等级由35千伏增加到110千伏,生产技术居国内领先水平。

10月4日 天津医科大学内分泌研究所通过卫生部组织的专家委员会论证验收,成为卫生部激素与发育重点实验室。

10月7~10日 中国天津国际自动化技术设备展览会在国际展览中心举行。

10月12日 第五届全国脊柱外科学术会议在天津召开,全国480多名专家学者出席会议。

10月13日 国家科委批准市科技创业中心为首批国家级高新技术创业服务中心。该中心被国际科学园协会主席胡思肯尼誉为"最好的孵化器"。10月20日,该中心入选国际企业孵化器试点。

10月18日 在天津市科技进修学院建院35周年之际,中国科学院、中国工程院在天津院士荣誉室在该校落成。中国科协副主席刘恕出席剪彩仪式。市委书记、市长张立昌为荣誉室题词"尊重知识,尊重人才"。

10月18~20日 亚洲青年生化工程协会1997年学术会议在天津大学举行,近80位中外专家学者出席会议。

10月21日 天津市召开CIMS推广应用工作会议。国家863/CIMS主题专家李伯虎,国家科委有关负责人和市委常委、副市长曲维枝等出席会议并讲话。全市各工业总公司和有关企业、科研单位负责人参加会议。

10月27~29日 由国家计委、国家教委、国家科委、电子工业部、中国科学院和国家技术监督局等六部门联合主办的全国软件产业工作座谈会在天津召开。国务委员、国家科委主任宋健出席会议并讲话,戴汝为、杨芙清、倪光南等6位院士出席，并与六部委负责人共商国家软件产业发展大计，国内多家知名软件企业负责人参会。

11月5日 南开大学数学所青年数学家陈永川教授获联合国教科文组织“侯赛因青年科学家奖”。

同日 经市政府批准，《天津信息港规划纲要》正式发布实施。

11月13日 联合国技术信息促进系统中国国家分部天津中心站成立，并开始运行。该站设在市环保局，通过计算机联网与国家分部保持24小时信息互通。

同日 中日（天津）技术交易洽谈会在北方技术交易市场开幕，13家日本企业携80个技术项目到会洽谈。

11月15日 南开大学组合数学研究中心成立，陈永川任主任。市政府向获联合国教科文组织优秀青年科学家奖的陈永川颁发10万元奖金。

同日 市政府批准大港区为全市第一个社会发展综合实验区，标志着天津市可持续发展战略进入分步实施阶段。

11月21日 全国第一所生殖健康技术中心在中国人民解放军二五四医院挂牌。

11月24日 国家科委批准天津市建立“国际企业孵化器”。天津市成为全国8个建立“国际企业孵化器”的试点城市之一。

11月25日 国家“九五”科技成果重点推广项目——“保护地蔬菜二氧化碳增施技术及装置”推广会在北辰区召开。该项技术可使蔬菜增产20%～40%，提前上市10～20天，并可提高抗病能力。

11月30日 经国家科委批准，天津市成为全国5个技术出口试点省（市）之一。

12月2日 市商委柴寿武研制的“废水替代净水冲厕自控装置”，在第46届尤里卡世界发明博览会上获得金奖。该装置可节水20%以上，1996年3月获国家专利。

同日 中国与瑞典两国政府间科技合作项目——中瑞工业废水处理及清洁生产技术研讨会在天津召开。

12月4日 “九五”国家科技成果重点推广洽谈会在天津举行。国家科委副主任李学勇、副市长杨新成、中国工程院院士王涛等出席开幕式和5项技术成果推广的签约仪式。

12月9日 由国家科委生命科技发展中心牵头送审的天津市天士力制药集团有限公司生产的天士力复方丹参滴丸，通过美国食品药物管理局（FDA）评审，成为直接进入美国Ⅰ—Ⅱ期新药临床试验的唯一中药产品，取得中成药进入美国市场的历史性突破。

12月19日 天津市授衔专家增选工作结束。经专家审议，选拔出38名授衔专家，平均年龄49.5岁，最年轻的是南开大学数学所教授陈永川。

12月20～21日 国务院总理李鹏到津考察，提出“天津市是环渤海地区的经济中心，要努力建设成为现代化港口城市和我国北方重要的经济中心。”

12月23日 天津市地震安全性评定委员会成立，国家地震局局长何永年到会并讲话。

12月24日 天津市重点技改项目之一的中国联通天津市话网工程全部竣工。

12月25日 天津力神电池股份有限公司成立。该公司采取技术入股的办法，将天津电源研究所的锂离子电池技术作价折股。

1998年

1月7日 天津地矿研究所女研究员李增慧在蓟县山区常州沟石英岩中，发现大量富集的宇宙尘。经分析推断，17亿年前以蓟县为中心的广大地区曾发生过一次强烈的“石铁陨石雨”。

1月8日 高等院校与企业联合开发项目洽谈会在北方技术交易市场举行。近百家企业就40个在研项目与各有关高校进行洽谈。

1月14日 市政府召开天津园区发展战略研讨会，市委书记、市长张立昌作书面讲话，国家科委副主任徐冠华发来贺信，市委常委、副市长曲维枝，市人大常委会副主任王成怀、钱其璈等出席。市科委主任梁肃作《高新技术产业化的整体推进与加快园区发展》的发言。

1月16日 天津市信息港规划总结表彰会召开。会议发布信息港建设的10个重点项目。

1月20日 市委、市政府召开科技工作会议。市委常委、副市长曲维枝出席并讲话，市科委主任梁肃做工作报告。会议全面总结上年科技工作，确定1998年科技工作的主要任务。

1月23日 天津园区召开落实1998年工作任务动员大会，表彰华苑等4项重点建设项目的有关人员。市委常委、副市长曲维枝到会讲话。

2月8日 天津市第一中心医院、南开医院、天津医院联合成立天津市中西医结合研究院，由吴咸中及三家医院院长组成领导核心。其参照股份制经营模式进行管理。

2月20日 由市信息化工作领导小组办公室与美国SUN公司共同创办的天津JAVA应用研究开发中心成立。

3月2日 市政府召开民营科技企业工作会议。会议总结十几年来民营科技企业发展情况，确定今后5年的任务，并出台《天津市促进民营科技企业发展的若干规定》及其管理办法。

3月27日 市蔬菜所建成全市第一个全自动蔬菜育种加代温室，研制开发的23个蔬菜新品种成为天津地区蔬菜种植的主栽品种，并在宁夏、内蒙古、河北、辽宁、上海、云南、广东等省市建立20多个推广咨询服务站。

4月1日 天津市科研院所体制改革工作会议召开。会议强调按照三个层次和三种类型的基本框架，至2000年，初步建成多层次、多形式，精干、高效、合理配置的新型科技体系。

4月7日 天津市"科技兴农"重要举措——"双十双百"工程启动，组织12个科研院所、教学和推广单位与12个区县对口，选派120名农业技术专家深入100个村开展为期一年的科技下乡活动。

4月8日 天津市分子心脏病学研究中心在市胸科医院成立。市政协副主席、知名心内科专家陈树勋教授任该中心主任。

4月14日 市人大常委会审议通过《天津市促进科技成果转化条例》。

同日 天津市豪升新能源技术研究所陈有孝、胡庸、胡凤祥发明的"电动车用高比能量密闭铅酸蓄电池"，在第26届日内瓦发明与新技术展览会上获金奖。

5月6日 历时3天的中国天津国际针灸暨中医临床学术大会在天津中医学院第一附属医院闭幕，国内外中医界300多名专家学者参加会议。

5月11日 中德(天津)环境技术转移与产业促进中心成立，由市环保局与德国环境技术转移中心、德国奥斯纳布吕克环境技术中心等合作组建。

5月13日 天津市科技百亿工程工作总结大会召开。该工程1994年开始实施，全面完成计划，达到预期效果，把科技和人才优势转化为经济优势方面起到示范、引导和推动作用。

5月19日 天津信息交互网工程启动。市委副书记、常务副市长李盛霖出席新闻发布会并讲话。

5月26日 市科委出台《"九五"期间深化科研院所改革方案》。列入首批试点的9个科研院所在人事制度与分配制度改革、公益型院所改革、院所整体转制为股份合作制科技企业等方面进行深化改革的探索。

6月5日 卫生部临床药理基地在天津市肿瘤医院成立，主要对肿瘤临床药品进行研究开发，拓宽治疗途径，提高防治水平。肿瘤专家郝希山任主任。

6月6日 在北京召开的中国科学院和中国工程院院士大会上，黄瓜育种专家侯锋获第二届中国工程科技奖。

6月10～14日 市政府和国家知识产权局联合主办的第七届中国专利新技术产品博览会在天津举行。全国30个省市和有关部委的70个展团参展，近7万人次参观，技术转让额达3.2亿元。

6月17日 市政府召开《天津市科学技术普及条例》宣传贯彻大会，部署进一步加强科学技术普及工作，表彰65个科普先进集体和194名科普先进个人，授予在天津两院院士科普工作特别奖。

6月25日 天津力神电池股份有限公司的"500万只锂离子电池产业化项目可行性报告"通过专家评审。11月28日，该项目正式开工。

7月7日 天津医科大学代谢病防治中心建成开业。该中心是全国首家以糖尿病预防、诊断、治疗为主的现代化医院。

7月8日 天津市中心妇产科医院试管婴儿妊娠获得成功，为天津市首例。

7月14日 天津市"金桥工程"工作会议召开。3年来天津市实施"金桥工程"项目383项，完成305项，创经济效益6亿元。

7月16日 天津市高新技术产业发展规划编制工作会议召开，市长李盛霖出席并讲话。

同日 天津市快速原型制造技术生产力促进中心在天津内燃机研究所正式运营。这是科技部批准的天津市首家生产力促进中心。

7月18日 中国联通天津市话网与中国电信通信主网实现互联互通，投入试运行。这是中国联通在全国开通的第一个市话网。

7月22日 天津市举行知识经济和"科教兴国"战略辅导报告会，科技部副部长惠永正作专题报告，市领导张立昌、李盛霖等出席。

同日 市政府批准从1998年起建立院士专项工作经费，为在天津两院院士每人每年拨款3万元，用于参加国内外学术交流，出版学术著作，开展科研工作和带培、指导研究生。

7月25日 市科委与北方人才市场共同建立天津市下岗人才供需数据库，对所有下岗科技人员一律实行免费入库登记，并向用人单位积极推荐。

7月31日 市农科院农产品保鲜研究中心被科技部确定为农产品保鲜技术工程研究中心北方分中心。该中心在保鲜片剂、保鲜膜、微型冷库、水果套袋等方面的研究与开发居全国领先水平。

8月2日 天津市地矿局地质环境研究所对蓟县小港乡勘查表明，该地区蕴藏大型紫砂陶土矿，专家预测其潜在经济价值达466亿元以上。

8月3日 国际光学委员会专题学术会议——"信息基础设施中的光学"在南开大学召开，20余个国家200多名光学专家学者出席。

8月9日 市科技创业中心获科技部颁发的首届火炬先进管理奖和火炬先进个人奖。

8月20日 国际华人化学家系列研讨会——第五届国际华人有机化学研讨会在南开大学开幕。世界各地的华裔有机化学家近200人围绕现代有机化学及相关领域的发展前沿进行深入探讨。

8月21日 市委科技工委、市科委召开科技工作座谈会。副市长梁肃同部分科研单位、高新技术企业负责人共同研讨“进一步发挥科技第一生产力作用，为推动经济加快发展做出贡献”。

8月28日 国家火炬计划软件产业基地——天津华苑软件园命名授牌。该园由市科委和天津园区管委会共建，占地500亩，为全国第六个国家火炬计划软件产业基地。

9月16～22日 天津市第十二届科技周开幕式暨现代科技发展趋势与知识经济报告会在天津礼堂举行，其主题是“依靠科技进步，实现跨世纪蓝图”。全国政协副主席、中国科协名誉主席朱光亚出席会议，并做题为《跨世纪科学技术发展趋势简介》报告。

9月18日 中国AO（骨折内固定技术）国际培训中心在天津医院成立，同时首届天津国际AO骨折技术培训班开学。国际著名骨科医学专家、国际AO骨折技术学会主席马特尔出席成立仪式并讲学。

同日 国内首例利用电视胸腔镜技术实施胸膜固定手术，在市胸科医院获得成功。这是治疗结核病的一种全新技术。

9月22日 天津市第五届青年科技奖颁奖大会暨培养跨世纪人才研讨会召开。陈永川等23名优秀科技工作者获青年科技奖。

10月4日 退休工人周殿福经过10年上百次科学实验，研制出适用于流散货物运输的火车自卸货车厢，获国家专利局颁发的实用新型专利证书。

10月7日 天津市外经贸科技工作会议召开，科技部、外经贸部等有关部门负责人专程到天津参加。这是全国首次地方性外经贸科技工作会议。

10月11日 以“21世纪知识经济对继续教育的挑战”为主题，天津市举行专业技术人员继续教育宣传周大型宣传咨询活动。

10月21日 中国环渤海科技博览会在天津国际展览中心开幕。全国近40个城市350多家科研院所、高等院校、技贸机构和企业携带3000多项科技成果参展。科技部副部长李学勇，市委常委、常务副市长杨新成等出席开幕式。

10月23日 由中国科学院北京天文台提出，经国际天文学联合会批准，一颗国际编号为8311号的小行星，以著名中医肾病学专家张大宁的名字命名为“张大宁星”。

10月28～30日 中国（天津）计算机网络与应用国际研讨会暨1998中国（天津）国际计算机与网络产品展览交易会在国际展览中心开幕。信息产业部副部长曲维枝出席开幕式并讲话。

同日 1997年4月投资1亿元建设的天津自然博物馆新馆竣工并开馆。

11月8日 天津大学生命科学与工程研究院成立大会暨首届学术报告会在天津大学举行。全国人大常委会副委员长彭佩云出席并为研究院揭牌，全国人大常委会副委员长吴阶平、成思危分别发来贺信，吴旻、吴咸中、杨胜利、张春霆等院士分别作学术报告。

12月8日 国家经贸委批准的天津市重点技术改造项目——天津化工厂年产8.5万吨离子膜烧碱工程，投入试生产。有42年历史、国内最后一套水银法制造烧碱装置退役。

12月15日 天津大学教授陈予恕被俄罗斯国家应用科学院授予国外院士荣誉称号。同时，天津大学获该院最高奖章——伟大纪念章。

12月16日 天津市科技教育领导小组成立。市长李盛霖任组长，市委副书记刘峰岩，常务副市长杨新成，市委常委、教卫工委书记邢元敏，副市长俞海潮、梁肃任副组长。同日，李盛霖主持领导小组第一次会议，邀请有关专家、学者和企业家共商《天津市高新技术产业发展规划》。

12月28日 北辰区双街镇正式挂牌为国家级星火密集区。该镇3年投入发展资金1.59亿元,形成以双街钢管、德塔、德利得等3个科技型集团和双街房地产、双街生态农业为主的5个龙头产业。

1999年

1月8日 天津大学环境科学与工程研究院成立。全国人大常委会副委员长吴阶平发来贺信,全国人大常委会副委员长丁石孙为研究院成立揭牌并讲话。

1月11日 天津市科技工作会议召开。市委副书记刘峰岩、副市长梁肃出席并讲话。会议宣布246项科技成果获1997年度天津市科技进步奖、4个单位获第二届"科技兴市"先进单位奖。

1月15日 科技部召开星火名牌发展战略研讨会暨中国星火计划产品商标第二批使用单位授权仪式。天津市华威电器公司、星达塑料包装公司、新星兽药厂等3家企业获"星标"使用权。

1月16日 天津市高新技术产业化项目——天津和平海湾电源集团有限公司从日本引进的全自动镍氢电池生产线全线开通。科技部部长朱丽兰、信息产业部副部长曲维枝、科技部副部长李学勇等视察该生产线。经科技部和信息产业部批准,该公司成为国家"863"计划镍氢电池产业化示范基地。

1月18日 国际建筑学会主办的《世界建筑》评选天津市建筑设计院为1998年世界建筑结构工程设计百强企业,名列第16位。

1月19日 曙光计算机应用示范(天津)工程顺利通过以院士汪成为担任组长的专家组验收,科技部副部长惠永正主持验收会,市科委副主任马其慧作项目完成情况汇报。

1月20日 市政府组织有关部门经过一年多的调研和论证,制定《天津市高新技术产业发展规划》。

2月18日 科技部和国家统计局每年一度的科技测评揭晓。天津市综合科技实力在全国各省市区中的排名由1993年的第7位上升到1998年的第4位。

3月19日 天津市企业技术创新工作会议召开,传达全国企业技术创新工作会议精神,部署是年企业技术创新任务。副市长梁肃出席并讲话。

4月6~10日 副市长梁肃率领的市政府代表团出席在西安市举行的中国东西部合作与投资贸易洽谈会。天津代表团签订经济合作项目170项,合作金额15.21亿元,同时实现商品成交额17.1亿元。

4月13日 天津市职工技术协会召开四届五次全委(扩大)会议,百名技术攻关能手和百家工厂技术协会挖潜自救群体受到表彰,40名先进个人和40家先进集体被授予"九五"立功奖章。

4月16日 市科委邀请国家"863"计划自动化领域首席科学家吴澄院士到津做报告,介绍CAD/CIMS/RPM技术的推广应用。

5月12日 城乡建设部1998年度优秀勘察设计评选活动揭晓。平津战役纪念馆、天津华苑居住区安华里小区和居华里小区获优秀设计二等奖,天津电力生产调度综合楼、天津市建筑设计院综合办公楼、天津市金钢桥改造工程获优秀设计三等奖。

5月13日 天津农业信息网正式开通。

5月19日 (天津)国际社会公共安全产品与技术展览会在天津举行,展期4天。国内外200多家厂商参展,展示代表当代世界最高水准的安全防范产品。

5月20日 "津沽环保行"宣传活动开幕,主题是"为了地球上的生命—向大气污染宣战"。该活动持续到6月6日。

5月28日 中国科学院、中国工程院在天津院士史绍熙、吴咸中、母国光、何炳林、陈茹玉、姚建铨、彭一刚、陈荣悌、申泮文、汪顺亭、张春霆等聚集在南开大学，为天津市科普工作献计献策。

6月5日 天津医科大学总医院举行庆祝著名泌尿外科专家虞颂庭教授从医执教60周年座谈会。虞颂庭教授是国内泌尿外科开拓者之一，在泌尿外科领域取得突出成就。

6月7日 市政府主办的中国天津沿海地区农业发展国际研讨会召开。市长李盛霖致开幕词，世界各地的农业技术专家、国家有关部委和天津市有关单位代表共600多人参加研讨。

同日 市政府与中国农业大学、中国农业科学院分别签订农业科技合作协议，副市长孙海麟与中国农业大学校长江树人、中国农科院院长吕飞杰分别在协议书上签字。

同日 市政府召开“政府上网工程”启动动员大会，要求年内市级5大机关和市政府所属各部门、各区县政府等79个单位实现上网。

6月8日 市政府举行仪式，聘请中国工程院前副院长卢良恕院士，两院院士石元春教授，德国霍恩海姆大学前校长艾尔文·莱施教授，美国国际农业、生命科学发展与教育理事会会长左天觉博士为市政府农业科技顾问，聘请中国农科院院长吕飞杰教授、中国农业大学校长江树人教授为市政府农业发展顾问，并向他们颁发聘书。

6月22日 天津石化公司炼油厂80万吨／年加氢裂化装置一次开车成功。该装置完全依靠国内技术自行设计制造，是华北地区最大的航空燃料生产基地。

7月4日 市蔬菜所研究员安志信获英国剑桥国际传记中心授予的20世纪成就奖。他是中国研究地膜栽培技术第一人，撰写专著17部。

7月5日 经市政府批准，确定首批17个重大高新技术产业化项目。其中电子信息产业5项、生物技术与现代医药产业5项、新能源产业2项，总投资27.9亿元。

8月13日 市红十字会、市卫生局召开大会，表彰陈路得、关小瑛、王桂英等3名获得南丁格尔奖章的医务工作者。

8月19日 经市政府第15次常务会议批准，《天津市率先基本实现农业现代化实施规划》正式颁布实施。

同日 经科技部、国家海洋局、国家计委等部门批准成立的塘沽海洋高新技术开发区，为全国唯一一家以海洋精细化工为主攻方向的科技兴海示范基地。

8月23日 市政府决定设立市级农业现代化建设专项引导资金，当年安排3000万元，以后根据财力情况逐年增长。市政府同时要求农业区县分别设立区县农业现代化建设专项资金。

9月2～3日 第二届亚洲乳腺癌学术会议在天津召开，国内外肿瘤医学专家学者400余人参加会议。

9月14日 天津市尊重知识尊重人才经验交流暨表彰大会召开，天津药业有限公司师春生等16名先进个人和中共和平区委等42个先进单位受到表彰，药业公司等6个单位介绍典型经验。

9月15日 天津市第13届科技周开幕，主题是“广泛传播科技知识，加快科教兴市步伐”。经济学家、中国技术经济研究会副理事长傅家骥作“大力推动技术创新，为实现两个根本性转变而努力”报告。

同日 中瑞（天津）环境技术发展中心举行揭牌仪式，市长李盛霖致辞，国家环保总局局长解振华和瑞典王国环境大臣揭牌。该中心由市环保科学研究院与瑞典环境科学研究院合作建立，主要开展环境技术方面的合作研究。

9月16日 天津市首届科技论坛在南开大学开幕。开幕式由中科院院士母国光主持，中科院院士、天津大学教授张春霆,南开大学教授、著名数学家陈永川,市第三中心医院院长宋继昌等作学术报告。科技论坛历时一个月,有6个大型学术研讨会,47场学术研讨和交流活动,3万余名科技人员参加各种学术交流。

9月18日 天津科技名人园在天津科技馆举行揭幕仪式。市委书记张立昌题写园名。市委副书记、科技周组委会名誉主任刘峰岩揭幕,市领导和两院院士及科技界代表1000余人参加揭幕仪式。

10月5日 在深圳市举行的首届中国国际高新技术成果交易会上,天津市45家高新技术企业携带复方丹参滴丸、镍氢电池、膜技术、防伪材料、天财软件等413项高新技术成果参展。

10月6日 市政府聘请英国皇家工程院院士罗杰·费尔科纳博士、德国埃森大学机械工程院院长海尔曼·瓦格纳博士、日本大阪大学环境工程系教授藤田正宪博士为市政府高科技顾问,市长李盛霖向他们颁发聘书。

同日 中国盐碱地绿化造林与可持续发展研讨会在天津举行,全国近百名专家学者出席会议。

10月7日 1999年度中国(天津)国际计算机与网络应用展览交易会暨天津信息港工程成果展示会在国际展览中心开幕。信息产业部副部长曲维枝、副市长梁肃分别致词。国内外70余家计算机与网络厂商参加交易展示活动,天津市42个项目参展。

10月8日 信息产业部副部长曲维枝率计算机2000年问题工作全国检查组到天津检查工作,对天津所做的工作给予充分肯定。

10月9～10日 中共中央总书记江泽民到天津考察工作。他对和平海湾电源公司充分利用国内稀土资源、加快镍氢电池产业化的做法给予充分肯定,亲笔为公司题名,并充分肯定和平区信息港工程重点示范区建设。

10月15～17日 中共中央政治局常委、国务院总理朱镕基到天津考察,听取天津药业、轧钢三厂等企业和市科委的汇报。他充分肯定天津在城市建设、危房改造、环保及加快高新技术产业化等方面的工作,强调天津作为老工业基地必须发挥科教力量雄厚的优势,坚定地走好科教兴市之路,不断调整产业结构。

10月17日 南开大学隆重庆祝建校80周年。全国人大常委会委员长李鹏发来贺电,国务院总理朱镕基接见该校负责人表示祝贺,全国人大常委会副委员长吴阶平等应邀出席庆祝大会。数学家陈省身、著名学者季羡林、北京大学校长陈佳洱、清华大学校长王大中和部分两院院士出席大会。

11月1日 塘沽永定河斜拉输水管桥跨河段主梁顺利吊装成功。该桥为亚洲跨度最大的斜拉输水管桥。

11月10～14日 中国科技网用户研讨会(昆明)上,天津市科技信息研究所被认定为中国科技网天津分中心,成为13个中国科技网地区分中心之一。

12月8日 科技部农村与社会发展司、市科委、市政府农业办公室在北方技术交易市场联合举办中国北方植保与肥料新产品展示研讨会与中国北方秸秆综合利用技术及设备展示会,展示一批新技术、新产品。

12月16日 市委七届五次全会通过并颁布《关于加速科技进步和技术创新的若干意见》,进一步实施"科教兴市"战略,建立知识和技术创新体系,发展高新技术,实现产业化。

12月19日 国家"863"自动化领域首席科学家、中国工程院院士吴澄到天津作《用高新技术改造我国传统产业》的报告。

12月28日 全国政协副主席、中国工程院院长宋健到天津考察。他充分肯定天津大力发展高新科技产业所取得的成就,强调指出这是贯彻执行"科教兴国"战略的中心内容。

同日 科技部和国家经贸委批准在天津建立北方环保科技产业基地。这是国家两部委首次联合批复的国内环保科技产业基地。

12月29日 市委、市政府召开技术创新大会，贯彻落实全国技术创新大会精神，表彰获得国家和市级科技奖励的单位和个人。中国工程院院长宋健作《迎接战略转折，投入发展高技术产业新战役》的报告，科技部副部长李学勇、中国工程院副院长侯云德、中国工程院秘书长常平和市领导张立昌、李盛霖、房凤友、刘峰岩等出席大会。

2000年

1月6日 市政府向首批42个农业现代化实验示范项目挂牌，其中包括列为国家级工程中心的农科院农产品保鲜技术工程中心。

1月10日 由天津园区管委会和科技部共同筹划的“天津技术创新基地”建设方案在京通过论证。该基地在华苑产业区内划出1300亩地，建立一个大型、复合型创业园区，即火炬创业园和大学科技园。

同日 科技部和教育部把天津大学科技园列为国家大学科技园建设的15个试点园之一。天大科技园位于天津开发区，占地33公顷，由开发区投资5亿元人民币，并负责基础设施建设，提供科技发展基金。

1月14日 科技部批准天津市为全国中心城市科普工作试点市。“十五”期间天津市实施“科普示范工程”，形成全市性科普示范体系。

同日 天津市高新技术产业化工作会议召开。1999年全市高新技术产品产值580亿元，比上年增长20%，高新技术产品产值占工业总产值20%。

1月15日 天津市卫生局组建的公共卫生监督所、卫生防病中心、预防医学研究所同时成立。卫生部副部长殷大奎和天津市有关领导出席仪式并揭牌。

1月18日 市公安局举行仪式，授予陈省身等4名对天津经济、科技、教育发展做出贡献的外籍人士永久居留天津的资格。

2月1日 天津市举行院士、专家迎新春座谈会。市委书记张立昌、市长李盛霖等与在天津两院院士史绍熙、申泮文、何炳林等及“国家千百万人才工程”入选专家、国家有突出贡献专家、中青年专家的部分代表进行座谈。

2月15日 全国首家胃肠疾病医疗基地在天津市南开医院挂牌。其以中西医结合、内外科结合诊疗胃肠疾病为特色。

2月17日 天津市第四届“学绝技、创绝招、争做技术明星”活动结束，马守如等9名职工获技术明星标兵称号，张志忠等94名职工获技术明星称号，钢管公司轧管厂电仪作业区传动组等100个班组获明星班组称号。

同日 国家信息化办公室批准天津市列为全国电子商务试点城市。

2月19日 国家环境保护总局授予天津市大港区“国家环境保护模范城区”称号。市长李盛霖、国家环保总局局长解振华等出席授牌仪式。

同日 著名医学专家、全国人大常委会副委员长吴阶平到天津，考察天津天士力集团。

2月20日 天津开发区、天津港保税区、天津园区联合在天津国展中心举办春季人才交流洽谈大会，25000余名求职者到场，当天供需双方达成意向的7000多人。

2月22日 数学大师陈省身偕同哈佛大学数学系教授、华裔科学家萧荫堂参观天津科技馆。

2月23日 应市委、市政府邀请，秦伯益、杨胜利、肖培根、刘耕陶、沈家祥、桑国卫等6位中国工程院院士到天津进行3天考察,为天津市编制"十五"生物技术与现代医药科技专项发展规划献策。

3月1~2日 应市科委邀请,中国工程院化工冶金材料学部殷瑞钰等13位院士到津考察新材料发展情况,为天津市"十五"期间新材料领域科技规划的制定出谋策划。

3月9日 经国家计委、国家环保总局批准,天津碱厂"碱渣治理利用工程"开始启动。此项工程2003年底完成,是继云南滇池治理、山西太钢钢渣治理之后的国内第三大环境治理工程。

3月17日 科技部副部长、中科院院士徐冠华到天津科技馆考察。

3月25~27日 中共中央政治局常委、国务院副总理李岚清到天津,考察滨海新区建设、医药卫生体制改革和教育科技体制改革等情况。

4月6日 科技部和外经贸部认定天津园区等16家高新区为国家第一批高新区高新技术产品出口基地。

4月10日 市政府转发市人事局、市财政局拟定的《天津市人才发展基金管理暂行办法》。

4月11日 市委、市政府举办"生物技术与现代医药学术报告会"。

4月14日 第三届"天津十大杰出青年"评选揭晓。董震、任学锋、孙瑞、王学旺、杨月霞、沈中阳、许京军、王春峰、张家海、翟家华等获此殊荣。

4月28日 天津国际医疗康复中心大厦在天津中医学院第一附属医院落成。该中心以针灸技术和治疗脑血管病的特色优势,为国内外患者提供具有中国特色的康复医疗服务,并进行康复医学技术开发与研究。

5月8~10日 21世纪初期大城市可持续发展水资源保障国际研讨会在天津召开,会议通过《天津宣言》。

6月23日 符合国际标准的天津电子商务运作平台正式开通。天津钢管公司等10家企业获得由天津信息港电子商务有限公司颁发的首批CA认证证书。

6月27日 中(国)西(班牙)农业温室技术示范中心建成,西班牙首相阿斯纳尔与市长李盛霖、副市长梁肃揭幕。该中心占地2.5公顷,建有温室16栋,种植西班牙蔬菜12个品种共32000株。

7月11日 国家"九五"重点建设项目——天津港南疆港区焦炭泊位建成投产。该项目1997年6月开工兴建,投资4.9亿元人民币,全部设备自动控制,计算机全程管理。

7月13日 国内首创的微操作机器人在南开大学机器人与信息自动化研究所诞生。

7月18日 波海航空复合材料部件有限责任公司在塘沽海洋高新技术开发区奠基。这是中美航空领域第一家合资公司,总投资5200万美元,生产用于波音商用飞机内装饰和次受力结构复合材料部件。

7月23日 市政府批准首批72家市属科研院所企业化转制方案,并出台《关于我市科研院所管理体制改革的实施意见》。

7月28日 天津市召开利用高新技术改造传统产业工作会议,市长李盛霖、副市长梁肃出席并讲话。会议要求落实好市政府批准的《天津市利用高新技术改造传统产业三年规划》。

7月31日 天津大学与天津药物研究院签订共建天津大学药物科学与技术学院协议。中国工程院院士沈家祥出任名誉院长。

8月10日 天津市首批按新机制创建的天津市光电子联合科学研究中心、天津市干细胞科学研究中心、天津市新药科学研究中心正式挂牌。市领导李盛霖、刘胜玉、梁肃、周绍熹等为3个中心授牌。市科委分别与3个研究中心签订目标任务书。

8月16日 首届国际音像图形学术会议在天津举行,中国科学院院士、科技部副部长徐冠华出席会议并讲话。

8月18日 市政府出台《关于做好中央及外省市科研院所转制在津属地化和注册工作意见》。

8月21日 市政府与美国摩托罗拉公司在北京举行新闻发布会，宣布对在天津摩托罗拉（中国）电子有限公司增资160亿元人民币，建设世界最大的半导体综合生产中心及亚洲最大的通讯产品生产基地。

8月22日 民航京津塘输油管道工程在天津通过国家计委和国家民航总局的验收。该管线是中国民航系统线路最长、管径最大、自动化水平最高、可顺序输送多品种油品的输油管线。

9月10日 天津纺织工学院、天津市经济管理干部学院合并，组建成立天津工业大学。

9月19日 天津市优秀科技工作者表彰大会召开，王宏等28名科技人员获2000年优秀科技工作者荣誉称号。

9月30日 市政府发布第33号令，颁布《天津市科学技术奖励办法》，同时废止1984年12月16日颁布的《天津市科学技术进步奖励办法》。

10月8日 国家干细胞基因工程产业化基地项目举行签字仪式。该项目技术持有方中国医学科学院，投资方华银控股公司，首期2亿元人民币资金用于在天津园区华苑区内建成国内最大的干细胞库、干细胞移植中心及相关科研用基础设施。中国医学科学院院长巴德年，市领导刘胜玉、梁肃等出席签字仪式。

同日 市政府与中国林业科学院签订科技合作协议，以落实"科技兴林"战略，加快生态环境建设。

10月13日 "代数几何与代数拓扑"国际学术会议在南开大学闭幕，近百名中外著名数学家出席会议。

10月15日 天津津科电子有限公司与美国ADS公司联合研制成功世界上首台"阅读不耗电、无闪烁电子书"。

10月25日 天津大学—ABB等离子体温室气体化学实验室在天津大学揭牌。这是ABB公司在华无偿建造的两个等离子体温室气体化学实验室之一，另一个建在清华大学。

10月30日 经科技部审核、验收，北辰区被批准为"全国科技工作先进区"。

11月1日 天津大学电力系统及自动化专家贺家李教授当选为俄罗斯工程院外籍院士。俄罗斯工程院副院长阿列克谢·费道托夫教授亲临该校，为贺家李颁发证书。

11月3日 天津药物研究院研究员、博士生导师刘昌孝应邀赴香港，出席世界综合医学大会暨紫荆花医学成就奖颁奖典礼，其成为首届紫荆花医学成就奖10名获奖者之一。

11月8日 市人大常委会第20次会议审议通过《天津市促进技术交易条例》。

同日 天津园区国际创业中心经国家审核，被认定为国家高新技术创业服务中心。

11月14日 天津市举行信息产业报告会，邀请两院院士吴澄、童志鹏、邬贺铨、沈家祥、杨芙清做学术报告。副市长梁肃主持报告会，市领导及各有关方面负责人300余人聆听报告。

11月19日 第十一届"中国十大杰出青年"评选活动揭晓。南开大学物理科学学院教授许京军获此称号。

11月30日 南开大学数学所青年数学家张伟平获2000年度第三世界科学院数学奖。

同日 市专利局更名为"天津市知识产权局"，主管全市知识产权工作，并统筹全市涉外知识产权事宜。

12月11日 市政府召开新闻发布会，出台《天津市加速软件产业发展的实施意见》和《关于积极推动我市建立风险投资机制的实施意见》两个文件。市科委负责人就两个《实施意见》作了说明。

同日 天津市器官移植研究中心在市第一中心医院成立。市人大常委会副主任王鸿江、庄公惠，中国器官移植开拓者夏穗生教授等出席成立仪式。

同日 受人事部委托，市第一中心医院在天津举办全国器官移植免疫新进展高级研修班，来自各省

（市、区）的30余名从事器官移植基础与临床研究的知名专家、学者参加研修。

12月19日 科技部和国家经贸委批准在天津建立北方环保产业基地。同时，国家经贸委批准天津市列为全国环保产品10大生产示范城市之一。

12月22日 全国首家肾病专科医院在天津市第一中心医院成立。中国工程院院士、中国人民解放军肾脏病研究所所长黎磊石任名誉院长。

12月23日 科技部批准在天津开发区建立全国首家国家纳米技术产业化基地。该基地由天津开发区与中国科学院、清华大学、北京理工大学等共建。

12月27日 市委书记、市人大常委会主任张立昌接见获2000年度第三世界科学院（TWAS）数学奖获得者、南开大学教授张伟平。市长李盛霖向张伟平颁发“天津市科教兴市杰出人才”证书和20万元奖金。

同日 天津市科技工作会议召开。市委副书记刘胜玉、副市长梁肃出席会议并讲话。会议总结“九五”期间科技工作，颁布1999年度天津市科技进步奖获奖项目，部署“十五”科技发展计划，提出2001年科技战线的工作重点。

2001年

1月3日 曙光计算机应用示范（天津）二期工程在天津通过科技部验收。天津市形成以国产服务器为硬件平台的信息化建设格局。

1月8日 市政府外事办公室首批向在天津开发区外资企业工作的102名外国专家颁发“外国专家证”。

1月9日 天津科技馆为“科技名人园”的国际数学大师陈省身教授半身铜像举行揭幕仪式。

1月12日 全国科技统计工作会议在北京结束。天津市被评为2000年度全国科技统计工作先进单位。

1月15日 全国农业科学技术大会在北京召开，授予217名农业科技人员“全国农业科技先进工作者”称号。市农科院侯锋名列其中。

2月12日 科技部公布2000年度全国科技进步统计监测结果。其中天津市排名：科技进步综合评价第四，科技活动直接产出综合第三，高新技术产品出口额占工业制成品出口额比重第一。

2月24日 天津信息港工程项目2001年工作会议召开，天津市信息化“十五”规划工程正式启动。

3月20日 首届国家最高科学技术奖得主、数学大师、中科院院士吴文俊应陈省身邀请参观天津科技馆，并为天津科技馆拟建的数学区和数学展览馆献计献策。

3月26日 天津市结核病控制中心和国际结核病与肺病联合会合作组建的国内首家结核病与肺病临床研究中心，在天津市结核病控制中心正式成立。

4月2日 天津医科大学二附院马腾骧、宋国祥两位专家被天津医科大学授予终身教授，并给予奖励。

4月8日 市科委、市计委、市经委联合主办并召开中药现代化工程研讨会。天津市中药现代化工程正式启动。

4月27日 应数学大师陈省身和南开大学的邀请，杨振宁教授为该校师生作《美与物理学》的学术报告。

5月11日 全国五大中水利用示范工程之一的天津中水利用示范工程正式启动。这是天津市依靠科技开发污水回用的重大举措。

5月14日 “天津科普网”开通。该网由市科委主办，天津市科技信息研究所承担管理工作。

5月14～20日 以“科技·环境·可持续发展”为主题的天津市第15届科技周暨全国首届科技活动周举行开幕式。经国务院批准，从2001年开始，每年5月的第三周定为全国科技周。

5月15日 在科技部、财政部、国家计委等联合召开的"九五"国家科技攻关计划表彰会上，天津大学教授叶声华被授予"九五"国家科技重点攻关先进个人称号，其主持研制的"夏利汽车车身尺寸激光自动检测站"获全国优秀科技成果。

5月17日 第六届天津青年科技奖表彰大会暨2001年天津青年科技论坛开幕式在天津礼堂举行。马军海、王东江、黄积涛等24人获得奖励。

5月30～31日 科技部、教育部确定的15个国家大学科技园试点单位之一的天津大学科技园正式挂牌。

6月2日 农业部开展无公害农产品(种植业)生产示范基地县创建活动，确定首批100个示范基地县。天津市宁河县、蓟县榜上有名。

6月18日 摩托罗拉公司正式向天津力神电池股份有限公司颁发合格供应商证书。这表明拥有自主知识产权的中国锂离子电池产品得到国际著名跨国公司的认可。

6月25日 中国科协第六届全国代表大会闭幕。天津代表母国光被大会授予荣誉委员，张春霆、张道成、陈永川、吴永平当选为委员。

7月3日 天津力神电池股份有限公司的"方型锂离子蓄电池系列产品产业化" 项目通过国家级验收。该公司成为中国投资规模最大、技术水平最高的锂离子蓄电池生产企业。

7月4日 中国第一块国际电子行业技术含量最高的逻辑芯片(晶片)在摩托罗拉半导体天津集成生产中心成功下线。该中心成为国内逻辑芯片的生产基地。

7月10日 市科委召开区县科技工作会议。12个农业区县科委主任参加会议。市科委介绍天津市"十五"期间农业科技工作的总体思路和重点工作。

7月16日 市科委、市经委联合召开企业信息化工程推动会，天津市四大科技工程之一的企业信息化工程正式启动。

7月28日 天津园区留学生创业园被科技部、人事部、教育部和国务院外国专家局批准为国家留学人员创业园示范建设试点园。

8月10日 《天津市科学技术奖励办法实施细则》公布施行。

8月16日 中国医学科学院血液学研究所与天津开发区管委会共同组建的中国医学科学院血液学研究所泰达生命科学技术研究中心正式成立。

8月20日 国家高技术产业化示范工程建设总结暨授牌大会上，天津天士力制药集团公司的复方丹参滴丸系列中药产业化示范工程等6项高技术工程受到表彰，并获得"国家高技术产业化示范工程"牌匾。

9月8日 天津市津南农业科技园被科技部批准为第一批国家农业科技园区。

9月9日 天津市化妆品研究所与民营企业家赵永良共同组建的天津市化妆品科学技术研究院，在北辰区举行签字仪式。

9月10日 天津天士力制药集团股份有限公司通过ISO 9001-2000版认证。这是国内首家制药企业获得国际质量管理体系最新版本的认证。

9月28日 中国首家肿瘤基因芯片研究中心——天津医科大学太极肿瘤基因芯片中心在天津医科大学附属肿瘤医院成立，并举行揭牌仪式。

10月6日 天津市肿瘤医院在教授郝希山主持下，历时6年攻关，在国内率先研究运用自体外周血干细胞移植并联合大剂量化疗治疗恶性实体瘤获重大突破，无一例移植相关死亡，使近百名患者肿瘤消失。该成果达国际先进水平，获天津市科技进步一等奖。

10月9日 德国柏林工业大学和汉堡大学分别派出专人莅临天津，为数学大师陈省身举行颁奖仪式，授予陈省身德国柏林工业大学名誉博士称号和德国汉堡大学Blaschke奖章。

10月14日 中国首届微侵袭神经外科导航技术研讨会在天津举行。天津市环湖医院神经外科历时5年攻关，在全国率先研究运用神经外科导航高新技术，治疗脑肿瘤、脑血管奇形、脑出血等多种颅内疾患，居国内领先水平。

10月17日 第三届中国国际高新技术成果交易会落幕。天津市40多家企业与国内外客商达成80余项合作协议和意向，总金额14.3亿元。

10月28日 著名数学大师陈省身迎来90华诞。中国科学院14位院士、20多位“求是数学奖”获得者专程到津为其祝寿。南开大学数学学院召开数学报告会，中科院院士、首届国家最高科学技术奖获得者吴文俊作学术报告。

同日 天津市中药现代化工程推动会召开。市科委与市医药集团签订合作协议，并成立天津市中药现代化工程领导推动小组和中药现代化专家组。

10月31日 天津强芯半导体芯片设计有限公司成立，是天津第一家从事集成电路设计的高科技企业。

11月2日 天津市工业系统召开享受政府特殊津贴专家颁证表彰会，表彰经国务院批准享受政府特殊津贴的33位专家。

同日 农业部公布的百亩耕地拥有机械动力、机耕、机收、机播等4项农机水平指标排序中，天津市前两项指标居全国第一，后两项指标列入全国前10名。

11月11日 农业部与市政府联合主办的2001年中国（天津）农产品加工及贮藏保鲜国际研讨会在天津礼堂开幕。

同日 国家海洋技术中心在天津挂牌成立，标志着原国家海洋局海洋技术研究所在技术创新方面迈上一个新台阶。

11月21日 第三届国际（天津）专利、发明及新技术展览会在天津国际展览中心开幕，200余家、1000余个项目参展。

11月28日 在中国国际农业博览会上，天津市参展的汉沽区茶淀玫瑰香葡萄、宁河种猪和天津特精液压股份有限公司生产的液压齿轮泵农产品等3项成果获金奖。

12月18日 南开大学、天津大学联合研究院在南开大学举行揭牌仪式。两校13项科技合作项目同时启动。

12月21日 第二届“牛顿—科学世界”杯科普图书奖揭晓。数学大师陈省身撰写的《九十初度说数学》获2000～2001年度十大科普好书奖。

同日 天津市大港区被科技部批准为国家可持续发展实验区。

2002年

1月6日 东方器官移植研究所在天津市第一中心医院成立。

1月7日 天津市国家干细胞工程技术中心通过国家科技部组织的专家论证。

同日 天津市环境无害化转移技术中心北方分中心正式启动。

1月10日 天津机械进出口有限公司和新港船厂联合，为南非/丹麦船东建造的32500载重吨系列散货船IVS瓦蓝特号在新港船厂顺利下水。这是天津市建造的第一艘3万吨级货轮。

1月15日 天津市信息化工作会议召开。2001年，天津市电子信息产业实现产值751亿元，同比增长20.3%，在全国排名第五，实现利润率在全国名列第一。

1月16日 天津市科技工作会议召开。会议对2001年科技工作做总结，部署2002年科技工作。

1月28日 天津市人大常委会发布第40号公告，公布施行修改的《天津市促进科技成果转化条例》。

2月1日 天津市高新技术产业发展工作会议召开。会议对16个重大高新技术产业化项目授牌，并表彰取得突出成绩的企业。

2月19日 誉为移动通信通往3G最佳解决方案的GPRS网络在天津正式开通。天津市移动客户可得到永远在线、按量计费、快速登录、自如切换、高速传输等增值服务。

2月22日 市科委、市经委、市环保局在咨询大厦联合召开天津市环保科技工程推动会。

3月16日 南开大学化学学科国家基础科学人才培养基地挂牌。这是全国首批挂牌的15个基础科学人才培养基地之一。

3月20日 天津市汉沽区在盐碱地成功栽种4万亩连片经济林，被国家林业局授予全国先进林业示范区称号。

同日 天津市中文图书数据库和中文科技期刊数据库投入使用。两个数据库分别拥有20万册电子版图书和8000种科技书刊。

3月27日 市科委、市经委、市信息化办共同召开制造业信息化工程工作推动会。天津市制造业信息化工程协调领导小组和制造业信息化生产力促进中心同时成立。

3月28日 北方技术交易市场召开第八次会员大会。以北方技术交易市场为依托的技术转移平台，覆盖山东、河北、江苏等5个省(区)，辐射辽宁、山西、浙江等8个省。

4月16日 中国和西班牙政府间的重要合作项目——中西机床技术培训中心在天津正式动工。西班牙驻华大使布雷戈拉特出席该中心的奠基仪式。

同日 天津市数字信息技术研究中心通过专家组验收，并召开成立大会。

4月17日 坐落在天津园区的天津市华苑软件出口基地挂牌成立，是国内首家以软件出口为特色的软件园。

4月24日 天津乳腺癌防治研究中心主体工程封顶。该中心是亚洲最大的乳腺癌防治研究基地，也是国内第一个乳腺癌防治研究中心。

4月26日 中国亚太经合组织(APEC)研究院在南开大学成立。国务院副总理钱其琛出席成立大会并讲话。

同日 科技部批准在天津市建立国内唯一的国家干细胞工程技术研究中心。

5月1日 天津市被科技部批准为首批制造业信息化示范城市。

5月8日 由国家环保总局组建的国家环境保护恶臭污染控制重点实验室，在天津市环境保护科学研究院挂牌成立。

5月14日 经信息产业部评选，天津市中环电子计算机公司、天大天财股份有限公司、南开戈德集团有限公司、环球磁卡股份有限公司等4家企业成为2002年度国家电子信息百强企业。

5月14～17日 市科委和天津园区管委会联合举办中日(天津)软件合作论坛和中日(天津)软件产品展示会。科技部副部长马颂德出席会议并做《中国软件产业发展趋势与国际合作》演讲。近300位中日代表就中日软件领域技术、管理和合作模式进行研讨。

5月16日 天津医科大学眼科中心被全国华侨联合会列为中国12个"科教兴国"示范基地和"科技兴业"示范典型之一。

5月19日 直径130毫米、长度930毫米的区熔硅单晶,在天津环欧半导体材料技术有限公司成功面世。这是国内最长的区熔硅单晶产品,其技术处于国内领先水平。

5月28日 中国首家具有芯片后加工技术的天津高芯电子有限公司成立。

5月30日 泰国国家科学院与天津工业大学膜天膜技术公司就膜技术开发应用项目签署合作协议。

6月12日 台湾晶基生化科技股份有限公司投资的天津晶鼎生物医药技术研究中心奠基。这是台湾在天津投资设立的生物高科技公司。

6月13日 津台生物科技合作研讨会在南开大学举行,就两地生物医药领域的合作进行深入探讨。市科委主任陈超英与台湾晶基生化科技股份有限公司经理赵守宇等出度研讨会。

6月28日 国家高技术产业化示范工程——天津市危险废物处理处置中心兴建。该中心在危险废物的管理和处理方面处于国内领先水平。

7月3日 天津新华中学成为首批全国青少年科普创新示范学校。

7月4日 国际超导科技基地在天津园区动工。该基地的核心产品是填补国内超导市场空白的海泰超导通讯科技(天津)有限公司生产的高温超导滤波器。

7月9日 坐落在宁河县的市级换新水产良种场,通过农业部专家组验收,成为天津市首个国家级水产良种场。

7月10日 华北地区唯一的珍稀苗木基地在蓟县建成。该基地占地200亩,采用由电脑控制的微喷、滴灌等先进栽培技术。

7月15日 科技部主持召开天津市"十五"智能交通系统应用示范工程技术方案专家论证会。

7月16日 市科委召开2002年度科技发展计划项目指南发布会,并在市科委网站上公开项目处理程序和项目评估立项结果。

7月24日 天津市水产研究所、市农学院、制盐工业科学研究院共同组建的天津市现代渔业技术工程中心成立。

8月10～12日 天津市侨联等单位主办海外博士天津科技项目人才交流活动,100多名海外学者和留学人员带着最新研究成果汇集津门,寻找创业良机。会议期间达成合作意向60余项,签订合作协议15项。

8月14日 生物技术药物科学前沿研讨会在天津开发区投资服务中心举行。

8月16～17日 第24届国际数学家大会"微分几何与整体分析"卫星会议在南开大学举行。来自世界各地的60多位专家对20世纪以来微分几何研究进行回顾、总结,并对未来发展进行规划。国际数学大师陈省身出席大会。

8月18日 国内第一座数学馆在天津科技馆建成,并举行揭幕仪式。

8月20日 市科委、市经委、市计委等主办的2002(天津)环保科技工程研讨会在天宇大酒店召开。

8月28日 天津市红十字会、市卫生局在市血液中心举行中国造血干细胞捐献者资料库天津HLA组织配型实验室成立大会暨揭牌仪式。

9月15日 天津华立达生物工程有限公司投资建设的华立达生物园在天津开发区奠基。该生物园是国内率先进入基因工程制药企业之一。

9月17日 天津科技大学教授杜连祥主持的“芽孢乳酸菌粉剂的生产方法”在日内瓦国际专利技术成果博览会上获得金奖。

9月19日 2002年国际中医药博士论坛在天津举行，国内外200余名中医药界专家学者出席。

10月8日 泰达华生生物技术及医药国际研讨会在天津开发区举行，国内外的知名专家学者就生物技术及医药领域的最新研究成果和发展趋势进行研讨。

10月16日 中新药业现代中药产业园在天津开发区开工建设。该园设有中药现代化技术工程中心、中药研究开发中心、制剂中心和植物提取中心。

10月17日 天津市高新技术成果转化中心成立。这是中国北方首家专门推动高新技术成果转化的机构。

10月21日 肿瘤基础与治疗国际研讨会在天津开幕。美国科学院及中国工程院的7名院士和国内外近400名肿瘤专家学者出席。

10月23日 国际微创外科大会在南开医院召开，国内外300余位专家在该院进行20例高难度微创外科手术演示。

11月6日 天津市第一中心医院器官移植中心奠基。这是市委、市政府投资1.3亿元在天津兴建的亚洲最大的器官移植基地。

11月15日 数学大师陈省身获第三届罗巴切夫斯基奖章，成为获此奖项的唯一一位华裔数学家。

11月20日 天津市清源电动车辆有限公司研制出全国第一辆纯电动中巴车。

11月23日 中国民营科技促进会召开全国科技园高峰论坛暨现场交流会。天津市鑫茂民营科技园获全国十佳优秀民营科技园称号。

11月26日 中国农业科学院与天津市玉泰畜牧养殖有限公司合作成立中农玉泰繁育中心。该中心为国内首家奶牛胚胎繁育基地。

11月30日 “天津市脐带血造血干细胞库”通过卫生部组织的验收，并首批获得卫生部颁发的执业许可证。

12月4日 科技部召开全国科技统计工作会议。市科委作为2002年度科技统计工作先进单位受到表彰。

12月19～20日 市科协召开第6次代表大会。大会通过市科协第五届委员会工作报告和修改后的市科协章程，选举产生市科协第六届委员会。

12月24日 天津市高新技术产业化重点推介项目会召开。会议确定2003年高新技术产业发展的总体思路和工作重点。

2003年

1月7日 市蔬菜所科技人员经过5年科技攻关，成功培育出世界首株菜花游离小孢子起源的花粉植株，达到国际先进水平。

1月9日 天津市大港发电厂投资20余万元修建的海水淡化入户工程竣工。大港电厂家属区1000户居民用上高科技生产出的淡化海水。

1月11日 东方器官移植研究所在天津市第一中心医院成立。

1月22日 远程医疗系统在天津市第一中心医院开通。这个中日信息化合作医疗系统示范项目，由天津市一中心医院、北京协和医院、辽宁省金秋医院与日本三菱株式会社共同实施，在国内主要城市间开展超高清晰度远程会诊。

1月29日 在天津的中科院、工程院院士专家迎春座谈会在天津礼堂举行。中共中央政治局委员、市委书记张立昌等市领导和院士、专家代表欢聚一堂，喜迎新春佳节。

2月11日 经市政府批准，天津市2003年蓝天工程规划实施方案正式启动。该方案确定的改善环境空气质量目标是，全市全年环境空气污染指数二级和优于二级天数保证率达到65%以上。

2月18日 国家外国专家局命名国家农产品保鲜工程技术研究中心为葡萄保鲜引进国外智力成果示范推广基地。

2月21～24日 天津市国家农产品保鲜工程技术研究中心、中国蔬菜流通协会等四部门联合举办的首届中国果蔬保鲜与流通研讨会在天津举行。来自全国的300多名蔬菜保鲜、流通专家及有关人士参加研讨会。

3月6日 科技部公布2002年度全国科技进步统计监测结果。天津市2002年度科技进步综合评价在全国31个省（直辖市、自治区）中名列第4位。

3月13日 天津工业大学膜分离工程研发中心落户天津园区海泰火炬创业园，天津工业大学和新技术产业园区合作共建的天津工业大学科技园正式启动。

3月28日 天津市与科技部共建的国家重点实验室——天津药代动力学与药效动力学重点实验室培育基地的建设计划通过专家组论证，成为首批省部共建的29个重点实验室中唯一面向创新药物的实验室。

4月16日 天津中小企业发展园在天津开发区成立。这是国内第一家针对中小企业发展设立的科技园。

4月25日 天津市医药集团所属华立达生物工程有限公司研制的预防“非典”的重组人干扰素α—2b喷雾剂获准上市，第一批3000支喷雾剂用于部分高危人群。

5月6日 中国医学科学院血液学研究所所长、教授韩忠朝主持的抗“非典”科研攻关项目获得国家“863”计划立项，研制开发出防治“非典”的诊断新技术和特效药物。

5月7日 天津金耀集团所属天药药业股份有限公司生产的甲泼尼龙琥珀酸钠注射液及甲泼尼龙片剂投放市场，用于“非典”治疗。

5月11日 天津市知识分子工作领导小组办公室和市人事局联合出台七项政策，激励专业技术人员在防治“非典”中多做贡献。

5月17日 主题为“依靠科学，战胜非典”的2003年全国科技活动周举行网上开幕式，天津市第十七届科技周活动同时拉开序幕。

6月5日 天津市第一批科技抗击“非典”专项中的“汽溶胶喷雾机”，通过市科委组织的专家验收，并生产出120余台，供社会各界进行消毒使用。

6月11日 天津市于桥水库水源保护工程全面启动。

6月20日 天津市科技抗击“非典”专项——呼吸机排气净化机研制成功，并通过市科委组织的专家验收。

6月25日 国家863计划“电动汽车”重大专项“纯电动轿车”项目，通过科技部的验收。该项目由市科委组织，天津市清源电动车辆有限责任公司和中国一汽天津夏利股份有限公司牵头，中国汽车技术研究中心、天津大学、天津和平海湾公司和天津蓝天高科公司等十几个单位共同承担。首批生产出5辆纯电动轿车，并取得12项国家专利。

7月2日 国家海洋局海洋技术中心承担国家“863”计划项目，研制出国内首台极区浮标，打破了日本、美国等发达国家在该领域的技术垄断。

7月3日 天津华立达生物工程有限公司研制开发的高科技新产品预充式重组人干扰素α-2b注射液，被科技部批准为2003年国家火炬计划项目，获国家4000万元贴息贷款支持。

7月5日 天津大学生物信息中心在院士张春霆主持下，率先研究开发出适用于冠状病毒，尤其适用于SARS冠状病毒基因识别的算法与计算机软件。

7月12日 北方医学论坛2003年天津防治非典型肺炎学术研讨会在天津举行。广东、北京、天津等地近400名医学专家、学者出席，中国工程院院士钟南山、侯云德分别作学术报告，中国工程院院士吴咸中主持研讨会。

7月15日 天津大学科技园通过科技部组织的评估验收，是科技部、教育部确定的首批15个国家大学科技园建设试点单位之一。

7月19日 全国防治非典型肺炎优秀科技工作者和先进学会表彰大会在北京召开。天津在防治“非典”斗争中以身殉职的裴鸿烈、马宝璋、赵世勇、孙家华、孙晓荣、刘维宇等6位医务工作者被追授为全国防治非典型肺炎优秀科技工作者称号；任新生、张伯礼、宋诗铎、周静敏等14名医务工作者被授予全国防治非典型肺炎优秀科技工作者，天津市医学会被评为中国科协防治非典型肺炎先进学会。

7月23日 经科技部批准，天津市5个药物研究项目列入国家第二批创新药物与中药现代化重大专项，并获得600万元的经费支持。

7月25日 天津市水利局研制的纳米复合纤维水工闸门在津南区小站湖村双桥河闸通过堆载检测。这种无金属构件闸门属国内首创。

8月5日 第39届南丁格尔奖章颁奖大会在北京人民大会堂召开。梅玉文获南丁格尔奖章，成为天津市继陈路得、关小瑛、王桂英之后的第四位获奖者。

8月7日 国家知识产权局颁发的统计报告显示，2003年上半年天津市专利申请量达3107件，同比增幅39.3%。

8月12日 市政府出台《天津市人民政府特聘专家制度》。

8月14日 市政府举行聘请袁隆平为特聘专家仪式，常务副市长夏宝龙受市长戴相龙的委托，为袁隆平颁发“天津市人民政府特聘专家证书”及铭牌。

8月16日 经科技部批准，国家杂交水稻工程技术研究中心与天津开发区和天津天隆基因工程技术有限公司联合成立国家杂交水稻工程技术研究中心天津分中心。

8月17日 第四届天津十大杰出青年评选揭晓。南开大学数学研究所教授方复全、天津市第三中心医院主治医师展春（女）、天津市第四十二中学高级教师袁滨渤（女）等3位专业技术人员名列其中。

8月29日 天津大学国家大学科技园高新技术产业园区（静海）正式开园。

9月3日 首届天津科技交流学术月开幕式暨海河经济论坛举行。市委常委陈超英出席并致词，在天津两院院士王静康、李猷嘉等专家学者参加开幕式。

同日 市委组织部、市人事局和市科协共同设立并组织实施青年科技奖。青年科技奖每两年评选一次，重点奖励在自然科学研究领域取得重要的、创新性的成就和做出突出贡献的人员等。

9月12日 天津狮子林桥老桥回梁就位，表明重达4200吨的狮子林桥老桥顶升成功完成。这在国内桥梁建设史上尚属首例。

10月9日 中华医学会呼吸病学分会主办、天津医科大学总医院承办的中华医学会全国肺部感染、呼吸衰竭、SARS学术会议暨学习班在天津举行。市委副书记、市长戴相龙，中国工程院院士、中华医学会呼吸病学分会主任委员钟南山出席开幕式并致词。

10月10日 天津水产集团有限公司在保税区空港物流加工区兴建天津市首个海洋科技园——金水海洋生物科技园。

10月14日 天津市召开地热可持续开发利用研讨会。中国工程院、中国科学院的5位院士及中国能源研究会地热专业委员会、国土资源部的专家到津，为天津地热资源的可持续利用与发展出谋划策。

同日 中国首枚自主设计开发的LCOS微显示集成电路芯片在南开大学研制成功。此项成果在IC芯片设计、液晶封装等关键技术上达到国内领先水平。

10月16日 市委、市政府向为“神舟”五号载人飞船工程做出重要贡献的中国电子科技集团公司第十八研究所、中国船舶重工公司第七〇七研究所等单位发出贺信。

10月18日 青年物理学家许京军领衔的泰达应用物理学院成立，中国首个产学研一体化的成长技术型分子束外延（MBE）实验室同时启用。

同日 天津市文化遗产保护中心在蓟县崔店子地区的考古工作中，发现一串距今2000多年的汉代玻璃项链。这是天津地区发现的年代最久远的玻璃制品。

10月23日 由市政府、中国高技术产业发展促进会主办，市科委、市医药集团承办的“天津市中药现代化推动会暨国家中药现代化发展纲要宣传贯彻会”在天津礼堂召开。

10月24日 中国工程院院士、天津中医学院一附院名誉院长石学敏教授潜心研究的石氏中风单元疗法，被国家中医药管理局评为全国中医药十大科技项目之一，并作为中医药科技成果2003年度第一个重点推广项目在全国推广。

10月27日 坐落于天津开发区天大科技园的天津快速成形技术工程中心，是科技部支持成立的国家级快速成形及快速制模技术服务中心。该中心为神舟五号飞船设计了减震坐垫。

10月28日 国家人口和计划生育委员会与市政府签订协议，共同在天津投资成立国家级生殖研发中心和产业化基地。

10月30日 全国城市污水再生利用经验交流和技术研讨会在天津开发区召开。天津开发区污水再生利用工程新水源一厂被评为国家级污水再生利用综合示范项目。

11月3日 南开大学数学研究所教授张伟平获得第九届陈省身数学奖。

11月18～20日 科技部在北京召开全国科技统计工作会议，公布2003年度全国科技进步统计工作评比结果，并对成绩突出的前十名颁发奖状。天津市科委位于第4名受到表彰。

11月24日 国家发改委、商务部、信息产业部和科技部联合批准天津华苑软件出口基地为国家级软件出口基地。12月4日，国务委员吴仪为该基地授牌。

12月17日 11位知名经济学家获“中国诺贝尔经济学奖”第十届孙冶方经济科学奖，其中南开大学两位教授李维安和陈宗胜名列其中。

12月22日 天津市2003年度科技进步监测完成。北辰区连续7年位居12个农业区县科技进步综合评价榜首，南开区、电子仪表工业总公司连续4年分别位居市内6区、15个工业总公司（集团公司）科技进步综合评价榜首。

12月25日 天津市发现一本清朝嘉庆年间修订的天津同仁堂《药目》，从而证实中药老字号企业——天津同仁堂创建于嘉庆元年，即1796年。该成果将原先认定的天津同仁堂创建年代提前了半个世纪。

2004年

1月2日 天津市科技工作会议召开。市委副书记刘胜玉出席会议，市科委主任李家骏做工作报告。

1月6日 国家级奶牛胚胎移植项目启动，总投资5000万元。

1月8日 由市委科技工委、市科委、市科协举办的送科技下乡活动在津南区举行。农业专家组成的科技下乡服务团深入乡镇、农户，开展技术讲座、技术培训、现场指导、咨询服务等活动，为广大农民解决农业生产中遇到的问题。

1月21日 中共中央政治局委员、市委书记张立昌看望著名数学家、中国科学院外籍院士陈省身。

2月18日 天津大有海水资源技术开发公司利用海水日产1000吨纯净饮用水项目正式投入运营。该公司成为全国海水淡化工程示范基地。

2月29日 市委、市政府举行仪式，市委副书记、市长戴相龙向8位特聘专家颁发“天津市人民政府特聘专家证书”和铭牌。

3月16日 天津市科普工作联席会议召开。会议听取2003年科普工作总结和2004年科普工作计划及第十八届科技周活动安排。市领导出席并讲话。

3月24日 工业微生物—高新技术改造传统产业研讨会在天津召开。会议由市科委主办，天津科技大学承办，科技部有关部门负责人应邀出席。

4月1日 第十一届国际机构学与机器科学世界大会在天津开幕。会议由IFTOMM中国委员会和天津大学共同承办，天津大学机械工程学院院长黄田担任大会主席，48个国家和地区近500名专家学者出席。

4月10日 市政府聘请陈竺、孔祥复、王正国、吴祖泽以及法籍专家雅克·康等五位中外院士为特聘专家。

同日 干细胞国际论坛在天津召开，国内外学者就干细胞研究与社会、伦理、法律等关系进行研讨。

4月11日 市政府与国际脱盐协会共同主办的海水淡化及利用技术国际研讨会开幕。国内外230多名专家围绕海水淡化应用技术开发、工程与工艺设计、成套装置研制以及海洋经济综合研究等方面进行专题研讨。

4月17日 天津经济和社会发展战略咨询会在天津举行。中共中央政治局委员、市委书记张立昌会见与会专家。市领导主持会议并讲话，市领导介绍天津经济和社会发展战略构想。国家有关部门负责人和国内知名专家出席会议，为天津经济社会发展献计献策。

4月28日 全国工业节水科技工作交流会在天津召开。会议由科技部高新技术发展及产业司和全国节约用水办公室主办，市科委、市经委、市节水办等部门承办。科技部提出全国工业节水科技试点市的要求，市科委负责人汇报创建工业节水科技试点市的方案，并得到与会专家的肯定。

5月1日 第十一届亚太地区产品优异奖在菲律宾首都马尼拉举行授奖仪式。天津中新药业集团隆顺榕制药厂生产的抗癌新药紫龙金片获得最杰出传统中药奖。

5月4日 中国生物技术产业发展与人才强国战略研讨会在天津开发区召开。全国人大常委会副委员长、民盟中央主席丁石孙，市委副书记、市长戴相龙出席会议。

5月10日 华立达生物园落成典礼在天津开发区泰达工业园区举行，并向中国科学院院士刘新垣、中国工程院院士杨胜利等颁发科学顾问的聘书。

5月11日 首届中国（天津）国际绿色电子制造技术与产业发展研讨会在天津举行。国内外大型企业集团、高校和科研院所的代表100多人参加研讨。

5月12日 天津科技大学主办的2004造纸与环境国际研讨会在天津开幕，来自11个国家和地区的30余位专家学者参加研讨会。

5月17日 天津市第十八届科技活动周开幕式暨全民健康促进行动启动仪式在人民体育馆举行。100名医学专家现场向市民开展健康咨询服务活动，同时举办"人体与健康""依靠科学，关爱健康"科普展览。

5月18日 天津市第二届金桥之友联谊会在天津召开，市长戴相龙、副市长崔津渡、秘书长何荣林出席会议。

5月22日 市科委和北京市科委在北京召开京津科技合作座谈会。天津市与北京市签署京津科技合作协议。

同日 科技部副部长程津培院士到天津，参加由市科委和天津大学共同举办的化工科技发展论坛，并做《基础研究的战略地位与化学的发展机遇》学术报告。

5月23日 天津市第十八届科技活动周活动之一的第七届天津青年科技奖表彰大会暨第四届天津青年科技论坛举行开幕式，向吴文清等21名获奖者颁发荣誉证书和奖金。

5月24日 2004国际扫描探针显微术会议暨第八届全国扫描隧道显微学学术会议在天津举行。国内外600多名纳米技术领域的专家学者汇聚津门，共同"扫描"纳米科学与技术研究领域的最新成果和进展。

6月10日 天津市知识产权工作推动会在天津礼堂召开。

6月16日 人事部、科技部、教育部、国家发改委等6部门联合公布中国新世纪百千万人才工程国家级人选名单，天津市12名优秀人才入选。

7月6日 市科协召开纪念"科普法"颁布两周年专家座谈会，两院院士李正名、吴咸中、王静康、葛墨林、叶声华和科普专家等出席。

7月18日 参加2004北京全球华人生物科学家大会的华人生物科学家访问团到天津，参观中新药业现代中药产业园，并就天津中药现代化和生物医药科研发展趋势进行研讨。

7月20日 天津市集成电路设计产业发展论坛在天津开幕。市委常委、市委科技工委书记陈超英到会致辞并会见与会专家。

7月22日 由京津沪三市高新技术成果转化中心联合发起的全国科技成果转化论坛在上海召开。京津沪三市介绍开展成果转化工作的经验，北京、天津、上海、山西、安徽、武汉、青岛等地代表签署"科技成果转化论坛宣言"。

同日 天津市肿瘤医院与美国癌症研究基金会签订合作协议，共同投资400余万元人民币，计划5年内在天津建成拥有5万例标本的亚洲规模最大的肿瘤组织库。

7月31日 市政府与日本东京大学签署科技与人才交流合作意向书，合作内容包括推进新技术、新产品的研究；推进人员交流；举办学术研讨会、报告会等活动。

8月22日 首届中国青少年科技创新奖颁奖典礼在北京举行。天津大学建筑学院本科生张昕楠、南开大学化学学院本科生易龙、天津医科大学基础医学院本科生孙涛、天津市实验中学高三学生柴恭泉等4名学生获此殊荣。

8月23日 天津市高性能计算中心在南开大学成立。这是继上海之后成立的全国第二个高性能计算中心。

8月27日 全国第二届DSP(数字信号处理)应用学术会议在天津大学召开。来自全国的专家汇集天津,共同探讨数字信号处理技术应用和转化研究。

8月29日 天津市中医药学会心血管病专业委员会在市中医学院第一附属医院挂牌成立,标志着天津市在应用中医药开展治疗心血管疾病临床研究和科研攻关方面迈上新台阶。

9月4日 第二届天津科技交流学术月开幕,主题是"落实科学发展观,促进天津新跨越"。中国科学院院士葛墨林、中国工程院院士刘昌孝出席开幕式。学术月期间开展百余项学术活动。

9月7日 首届邵逸夫奖在中国香港举办颁奖典礼。南开大学数学研究所名誉所长陈省身获数学科学奖。香港特区行政长官董建华及香港著名实业家邵逸夫为陈省身颁奖。

9月14～17日 太平洋电信组织(PTC)2004年中会暨PTC博览会和第九届中国(天津)信息技术博览会在天津举行。美国、日本、韩国等PTC成员国及中国电信、中国移动、中国网通、中国联通等45家知名企业参加展会。会议期间发布电子信息、生物医药等六大类项目51个,项目投资额12亿元。

9月15日 市科委、天津园区管委会主办的中国软件业发展趋势论坛在华苑软件园召开。中外20余名知名专家和天津市60余家软件企业的100多名代表参加论坛。

同日 市科委召开全市科技企业孵化器工作研讨会。全市21家科技企业孵化器负责人参加会议。

9月22日 市政府举行特聘专家聘请仪式,聘请王阳元、时铭显、邹竞等15位中国科学院和中国工程院院士为市政府特聘专家。市领导向受聘专家颁发证书和铭牌。

10月17日 为期6天的第六届中国国际高新技术成果交易会在深圳落下帷幕。天津科技交易团参展的近百项高新技术成果及产品受到关注,签订合作协议和引资入股金额达20.9亿元。

10月20日 教育部、科技部主办的中国大学科技园国际论坛在天津开发区开幕。美、英、日等国学者和国内部分大学校长围绕"大学科技园对推动区域经济和国家经济发展的作用""大学科技园与大学、政府的关系"等进行交流和探讨。

10月23～24日 中国泰达生物论坛在天津开发区召开。海内外知名专家学者汇集天津,围绕全球生物技术与生物经济发展,研讨生物技术最新前沿进展,探讨生物技术为人类服务的新途径。

10月25日 第三届超临界流体技术用于能源与环境国际会议在天津大学召开。

11月2日 经国际天文学联合会下属的小天体命名委员会讨论通过,国际小行星中心发布第52733号《小行星公报》,将一颗编号为1998CS2号小行星命名为"陈省身星",以表彰他对全人类的贡献。

11月3日 农工民主党天津市委会、中华中医药学会、中国中医药研究促进会主办的中国·天津中药现代化国际高层研讨会在天津举行,海内外近百名专家学者就中药现代化的研究成果和今后发展问题进行研讨和交流。

11月4日 第四届移动通信产业(移动应用)国际论坛暨展览会在天津开发区开幕。

11月6日 天津市技术产权交易公司在天津市产权交易中心挂牌运行,为天津及国内外的科技成果转化和技术产权交易提供全方位的服务。

11月23日 天津市医学会器官移植学分会成立。卫生部副部长黄洁夫,中国工程院院士吴咸中、郝希山等参加成立仪式。

12月23日 科技创业、报效祖国—2004海外学人回国创业周活动在天津开发区举行。来自世界各地的200余名海外学子参加此次盛会。现场达成初步合作意向约60个,双方满意率达100%。

2005年

1月3日 第三世界科学院委员会决定,授予南开大学教授龙以明2004年度第三世界科学院数学奖,以表彰其在基础数学研究领域的重大贡献。

1月10日 全国膜分离应用技术研讨会在天津工业大学举行。天津工业大学3项具有完全自主知识产权的膜技术研发技术具有国际先进水平。

1月16日 天津市电动自行车行业锂离子电池应用发展研讨会召开。天津市力神公司先后投资10亿元进行4期工程建设,形成年产2亿只各类小型锂离子蓄电池、聚合物锂电池以及电动车电池的生产能力,成为全国最大规模的绿色能源生产基地。

1月18日 由市委科技工委、市科委、市科协和北辰区委共同举办的天津市科技帮扶行动暨北辰区文化、科技、卫生、法律"四下乡活动",在北辰区双口镇启动。市科委、市科协聘请10名专家与10名种养大户,实行科技帮扶结对子,与农民建立长期帮扶合作关系。

1月19日 市委、市政府召开科技工作会议,全面总结2004年科技工作,部署安排2005年科技工作。

同日 市科委召开编修科技志和科技年鉴工作会议,部署第二轮《天津科学技术志》和2005年科技年鉴的编修工作。

1月23日 在天津市十四届人大三次会议上,市长戴相龙宣布:从2005年开始,天津市设立科技创新专项资金,当年安排资金1亿元,以后每年安排2亿元,到2010年累计达到11亿元。

2月26日 中国北方人才市场与北京、河北、山东、大连、青岛等省市人才服务中心联合举办的2005年环渤海地区人才智力交流洽谈会在天津开幕。洽谈会提供职位4万余个,1500多家企业现场招贤,3万余人入场竞聘,近4000名应聘者与用人单位达成意向。

2月29日 天津市农业科技下乡正式启动。市农业局、市农学会组织100位农业专家和技术人员,深入西青区辛口镇蔬菜生产基地,开展现场咨询活动,接待农民2万多人次,发放农业科技书籍10万册。

3月1日 天津市技术市场发展研讨会暨北方技术交易市场第十次会员大会召开。科技部部长徐冠华发来贺信,科技部原副部长、中国技术市场协会会长韩德乾,市人大常委会副主任梁肃出席并讲话。

3月28日 天津园区被列为国家知识产权试点园区。这是国家知识产权局批准建立的第一家试点园区。

4月5日 天津园区负责人与中国工程院院士、中科院计算所所长李国杰签署联合共建协议,中科院高性能计算机天津产业基地落户天津园区。

4月12日 市政府举行新闻发布会,颁布《关于进一步促进高新技术成果转化的暂行办法》。

4月15日 市科委召开科技型中小企业技术创新工作推动会。市科委首次设立额度为3000万元的天津市科技型中小企业创新资金,用于支持科技型中小企业的技术创新。

4月18日 天津市举办以"加快科技创新,促进天津经济可持续发展"为主题的院士论坛。与会5位院士围绕加快石油化工、现代生物医药、海洋制造业、干细胞生物医学工程发展和滨海新区建设,提出有价值的意见和建议。

4月22日 天津市留学人员联谊会成立。全国人大常委会副委员长、中国留学人员联谊会会长韩启德发来贺信。中国留学人员联谊会副会长朱训专程到会祝贺。

4月23日 中国微生物学会工业微生物专业委员会主办的2005中国工业微生物学术研讨会在天津科技大学召开。中国微生物学会理事长杨胜利等专家出席会议。

4月25日 天津市高校知识产权专题报告会在天津科技大学举行,国家知识产权局副局长田力普做《我国知识产权工作面临的形势和任务》的报告。

4月26日 天津市召开纪念世界知识产权日座谈会,纪念世界知识产权日和《中华人民共和国专利法》颁布实施20周年。

4月29日 环渤海经济区北京、天津、河北、山西、内蒙古、辽宁和山东等两市五省(区)的技术市场管理部门及技术经纪机构共同发起创建的环渤海技术转移联盟宣告成立。

5月8日 国家发改委批准立项,坐落于天津园区的国家干细胞工程产品产业化基地,经过一年多运行通过项目验收,并被市政府确定为市级重大高技术产业化项目。

5月12日 国家环保总局、市信息化办、市环保局、开发区管委会、市科委等联合主办的第二届中国(天津)国际绿色电子制造技术与产业发展研讨会暨配套技术展示会在天津召开,150余名国内外专家学者出席。

5月13日 市科委、科技部共同组织的天津市科技兴贸研讨会暨天津科技兴贸信息网站开通仪式在天津园区举行。科技部中国科技促进发展研究中心主任杨国雄讲话,市科委主任李家俊开通天津科技兴贸信息网。

5月15~21日 以"珍惜资源,建设节约型社会"为主题的天津市第19届科技周开幕式在银河公园广场举行。该届科技周举办五大系列、三个层次、近万项科普活动。

5月17日 市科委召开科技企业孵化器工作推动会。市委常委、市委科技工委书记陈超英,科技部火炬中心主任巫英坚出席会议并讲话。市科委主任李家俊做《科技企业孵化器建设与发展》报告。南开区科委、开发区泰达创业中心等作典型发言。各区县、大学、科研院所近200人出席会议。

5月20日 第三届天津市优秀科技工作者表彰大会暨2005天津科技论坛开幕,向29位天津市优秀科技工作者荣誉称号获得者颁发证书和奖品。

5月23日 天津双港垃圾焚烧发电厂经过近半年的试运行,正式向天津电网供电,标志着天津市实现了城市生活垃圾的科学化处理。

5月29日 国家发改委批准,中国中医研究院、北京同仁堂与天津市中宝科技有限公司共同组建,总投资近6000万元的中药复方新药开发国家工程研究中心中试基地在东丽开发区启动建设。

6月6日 天津市中长期科技发展规划领导小组召开会议。领导小组成员和专家顾问组成员围绕中长期科技发展规划战略研究进行研讨。

7月4日 市政府举行聘请仪式,聘请中国工程院院士、国内著名桥梁及结构工程专家项海帆教授为特聘专家。

同日 首届海河之滨全国心脏病学进展学术会议暨庆祝石毓澍教授从医60周年、天津市心脏病学研究所成立25周年学术报告会开幕。

8月8日 天津市大型科学仪器协作共用网正式启动,面向全社会开放,接受社会各界的科技研发项目和委托实验任务。

8月16日 南开大学国际数学研究中心开始启用,并迎来首批专家。

9月3日 市科协主办的滨海新区建设与发展专家论坛暨天津市2004年科技交流学术月举行开幕式。市委常委、市委科技工委书记陈超英讲话,市政协副主席陆锡蕾和在天津两院院士母国光、李正名、王静康等出席。

9月23日 中国天津绿色能源产业发展论坛暨国家(天津)化学与物理电源产业园成果展在天津园区举行。中国工程院院士杨裕生、"863"项目专家吴锋等专家发表演讲,并围绕当前国内外绿色电源产业的发展现状与趋势等问题进行讨论。

同日 市科委主持召开天津市农民科技培训星火学校培训工作经验交流现场会,25个星火学校、12个农业区县科委和市农口有关局院的负责人参加会议。

10月12日 天津科技代表团赴深圳参加第七届高新技术成果交流会,展出清源电动汽车、废品焚烧发电项目等一批科技含量高的成果。

11月4日 2005国家信息化发展论坛在天津礼堂举办。市政府信息化办公室首次对大会全程进行网上直播。

11月8日 市科委召开2005科技成果转化发展论坛,同时京津沪三地成果转化中心签署高新技术成果转化项目认定绿色通道协议。科技部和京津沪渝四市科委负责人莅临开幕式,国内外专家150余人参加讨论。

11月11日 市科委、中国科学院北京分院主办的2005院市技术项目对接会在滨海新区召开。中科院22个研究所65位专家与天津市103家企业200多位代表就70多个合作项目进行对接洽谈。

11月19~20日 科技部和市科委主办的2005中国科技论坛在天津科技大学举行。国家有关部委和高等院校、科研院所等180余位专家学者,围绕技术标准与国家经济安全进行探讨交流。全国人大常委会副委员长蒋正华应邀出席并做专题报告。

11月21日 2005中韩高新技术展示洽谈会(天津)在天津园区召开。韩国5个科技园的17家企业携20多个项目到津,与近百家中方企业和天津园区的企业代表进行技术洽谈。

12月5日 天津市人才项目合作签约仪式暨科技发展规划咨询座谈会召开。天津市与中国工程院建立开展人才与项目长期整体合作关系,共同构筑企业、研究机构、政府部门协调互动的创新体系。

12月6日 市科委和市信息化办公室联合举办天津市现代物流和电子商务专题讲座。美国前联合包裹服务(UPS)集团国际工程经理查克·杜赫悌、新加坡劲升逻辑有限公司中国区总经理蔡振彬分别就现代物流发展趋势和经验做专题报告。

第一篇

科技队伍与机构

概　述

进入20世纪90年代,随着科技体制改革的深入和科技事业的发展,天津市科技队伍和科技机构发生很大变化。

中共天津市委员会(以下简称“市委”)、天津市人民政府(以下简称“市政府”)认真贯彻落实党的知识分子政策和各项人才政策,大力加强科技人才队伍建设,营造尊重知识、尊重人才的社会环境,科技队伍不断发展壮大,科技队伍的素质得到很大提高,并涌现出一大批优秀科技人才。至2005年,全市各类专业技术人员为42.48万人,每万名职工中专业技术人员含量有所增加,由1991年的1973人增至2189人,特别是专业技术人员中受过高等教育和具有高中级职称(职务)的所占比重大幅提高,其中受过高等教育的人员比重比1995年增加48.51个百分点,具有高中级职称(职务)的人员比重比1995年增加14.47个百分点;在天津工作或曾在天津工作的42名专家、教授先后当选为中国科学院和中国工程院院士,其中1991～2005年新当选两院院士31人;国家有突出贡献的中青年专家179人,享受政府特殊津贴专家2945人,国家“百千万人才工程”一二层入选者33人,国家杰出青年科学基金获得者20人,“长江学者奖励计划”特聘教授31人,同时一大批优秀科技人才得到国家级或省部级的表彰与奖励。经过多年的积累,天津市逐步形成较完备的科学技术与工程学科体系和多层次的科技人才队伍,一些技术领域具备较强的自主创新能力,各类科技人才为促进科技进步和经济社会发展发挥越来越大的作用。

20世纪90年代起,天津市进一步加强知识创新机构和技术创新机构建设,初步形成科技创新体系。通过深化科技体制改革,46个中央驻津科研院所和108个市属科研院所的科技创新与发展能力得到增强,一批驻津科研院所成为国内相关行业设计及工程总承包的龙头单位以及关键技术研发、技术标准制定和质量检测的核心单位,72个市属开发类科研院所完成企业化转制。先后组建一批重点实验室和科学研究中心、工程(技术)研究中心和企业技术开发中心等,并积极组建科技企业孵化器、生产力促进中心、区县特色产业科技园等科技服务机构。至2005年,全市建成新型知识创新机构70个,其中国家级重点实验室5个,国家部局级重点实验室17个,市级重点实验室40个,科学研究中心8个;建成新型技术创新机构191家,其中国家级工程(技术)研究中心11家,市级工程(技术)研究中心18家,国家级企业技术中心12个,市级企业技术中心150个;建立重点成果转移、转化与产业化机构(基地)128个,其中国家级成果推广中心6个,国家级高新技术产业化基地6个,区县特色产业科技园13个,国家级科技创业中心3个,市级和各类科技企业孵化器16个,国家级和市级生产力促进中心21个,创业投资机构65个;建有公共高新技术平台5个,公共科技服务机构15个;大中型工业企业兴办技术开发机构195个,高等院校所属研究与试验发展机构153个,民营科技企业增至8000多家。科技成果转化中心、技术产权交易中心和北方技术交易市场等机构不断探索新的运行机制,加快科技成果转化。全市形成具有自身区域特色的科技创新体系,显著改善了科技创新环境。

全市各级科学技术协会和职工技术协会作为科技工作者和职工的科学技术团体,严格按照社会团体的有关规定顺利完成换届选举,形成自上而下的科学技术协作网络。各级科协和职工技协团结和带领全市广大科技工作者和职工群众以经济建设为中心,在促进科学技术的繁荣和发展,促进科学技术与经济社会的协调发展等方面发挥积极作用。

市委、市政府十分重视对科技工作的领导,在党政机关机构改革中不断加强各级科技管理机构建设,形成自上而下的科技管理体系。市委科学技术工作委员会(以下简称“市委科技工委”)和天津市科学技术委员会(以下简称“市科委”)通过机构改革,职能配置更加明确,内设机构更加合理。经市委批准成立的天津新技术产业园区管理委员会（以下简称“园区管委会”）和市委新技术产业园区工作委员会，积极推动天津新技术产业园区建设的健康发展。先后成立的天津市知识分子工作领导小组、天津市信息化工作领导小组、天津市科技教育领导小组等，进一步加强对全市科技工作的领导与协调。各区县政府不断加强对科技工作的领导，相继成立由区（县）主要负责人担任组长的区（县）科技工作领导小组、科普工作领导小组、知识产权工作领导小组等，并进一步加强和完善各区县科学技术委员会领导班子和职能科室建设，行使对区县科技工作的综合管理。为加强科技管理工作，市政府各有关部门，包括各委、办、局（公司）也都设有科技管理机构或部门。市区各所属局或街道普遍配备分管科技工作的副主任，农业区（县）各乡（镇）也配备有科技副乡（镇）长，为推进科技进步与技术创新提供了组织保障。

经过多年的发展和积累，天津市综合科技实力明显增强，为科技进步和经济社会的协调发展集聚了巨大的能量。2005年，天津市人均国内生产总值（GDP）突破4000美元，经济社会进入依靠科技创新追求更高水平、更加协调发展的新阶段。

第一章 专业技术队伍

据对全市公有制企事业单位各类专业技术人员的统计，1991年专业技术人员为57.53万人，至1995年增加到60.19万人。随着改革的不断深化，部分公有制企业和科研院所实行转制或改制，形成了所有制的多元化，部分专业技术人员流向不同所有制的机构。由于受到管理体制和统计口径的限制，流向非公有制企业的专业技术人员未作统计，造成相关统计数据的缺失。统计数据显示，2000年全市公有制单位各类专业技术人员为59.93万人，2005年全市专业技术人员为42.48万人。

至2005年，全市专业技术人员主要分布在教科文卫系统（占54.4%），制造、建筑、电力、采矿领域（占24.1%），金融、交通、仓储、邮政、信息领域（占13.7%）等，以及科学研究与技术开发机构、高等院校、大中型工业企业等部门。全市各类专业技术人员性别、学历、职称等结构情况变化很大，其中受过高等教育和具有高中级职称（职务）的比重均获得大幅度增长。

第一节 专业技术人员分布

2005年，全市专业技术人员总数为42.48万人，每万名职工中专业技术人员有所增加。全市专业技术人员在国民经济各行业分布的人数不断变化。至2005年，按国民经济行业分布其数量依此为：教育，卫生、社会保障和社会福利业，制造业，建筑业，金融业，科学研究、技术服务和地质勘察业，交通运输、仓储及邮政业，采矿业，农、林、牧、渔业，信息传输、计算机服务和软件业；按部门分布，科学研究与技术开发机构的科技人员总数略有减少，高等院校的科技人员总数有所增加，大中型工业企业科技人员总数波动较大。这个时期，民营科技企业迅速发展，成为科技人员创新、创业的聚集地。

一、类别分布

1991年，全市各类专业技术人员共有57.53万人，每万人中有专业技术人员659人，每万名职工中有专业技术人员1973人。

2005年,全市各类专业技术人员为42.48万人,平均每万人中有专业技术人员407人,每万名职工中有专业技术人员2189人。

(一)自然科学专业技术人员

1991年,全市自然科学专业技术人员29.92万人,占专业技术人员总数的52.0%;平均每万人中有自然科学人员343人,平均每万名职工中有自然科学人员1026人。

至2005年,全市自然科学专业技术人员20.62万人,在专业技术人员中的比重为48.5%,自然科学专业科技人员在每万人中有198人,在每万名职工中有1062人。

(二)社会科学专业技术人员

1991年,全市社会科学专业技术人员27.61万人,占专业技术人员的比重为48.0%;平均每万人拥有社会科学专业科技人员316人,每万名职工拥有社会科学专业科技人员有947人。

至2005年,全市社会科学专业技术人员21.86万人,占专业技术人员比重为51.5%;平均每万人拥有社会科学专业科技人员210人,每万名职工中有社会科学专业科技人员1126人。

1990年和1991年天津专业技术人员情况统计表

表1-1-1-1 单位:人

项目	1990年	1991年
总计	554847	575283
一、自然科学	289612	299214
工程技术人员	160875	169972
农业技术人员	3677	3469
科研人员	12615	12553
卫生技术人员	67784	67844
教学人员	43322	43885
二、社会科学	267935	276069
科研人员	950	1016
教学人员	94105	96862
财会人员	58321	57743
统计人员	15933	15830
编辑、记者、播音员	2291	2280
翻译人员	1916	1920
体育教练人员	731	820
经济人员	81492	85869
文艺人员	2460	2491
其他人员	9736	11238

1995年天津专业技术人员情况统计表

表1-1-1-2 单位:人

项目	总数	高级	中级	市属单位小计	高级	中级	驻津单位小计	高级	中级
总计	601936	43744	160217	467044	29712	118760	134892	14032	41457
一、自然科学	288873	31024	80017	216171	20032	55794	72702	10992	24223
其中:1.高级职称	31024	31024	—	20032	20032	—	10992	10992	—
(正高级)	3229	3229	—	1519	1519	—	1710	1710	—
2.中级职称	80017	—	80017	55794	—	55794	24223	—	24222
工程技术人员	162607	20014	45419	110888	12682	28676	51719	7332	16743
农业技术人员	3417	279	1001	3200	247	939	217	32	62
科研人员	2769	975	1121	1230	317	540	1539	658	581
卫生技术人员	71420	3842	15445	64036	3430	13431	7384	412	2014
教学人员	42384	5772	14540	35468	3325	11804	6916	2447	2736
其他人员	6276	142	2491	1349	31	404	4927	111	2087
二、社会科学	313062	12720	80200	250873	9680	62966	62190	3040	17234
其中:1.高级职称	12720	12720	—	9686	9680	—	3040	3040	—
(正高级)	1131	1131	—	530	530	—	601	601	—
2.中级职称	80200	—	80200	62966	—	62966	17234	—	17234
科研人员	1272	324	602	829	188	356	443	136	246
教学人员	99416	5782	32379	91118	4780	29036	8298	1002	3343
经济人员	87816	1680	16120	64502	951	10265	23314	729	5856
会计人员	60434	601	8220	43006	375	5342	17428	226	2878
统计人员	12695	191	1675	11479	175	1424	1216	16	251
翻译人员	1618	154	596	1171	78	376	447	76	221
新闻人员	2401	447	1007	2135	390	881	266	57	126
体育人员	630	147	322	614	147	319	16	—	3
艺术人员	2468	539	1134	2466	537	1134	2	2	—
其他人员	43654	2830	17944	33547	2058	13827	10089	772	4112

2000年天津专业技术人员情况统计表

表1-1-1-3 单位:人

项目	总数	高级	中级	市属单位小计	高级	中级	驻津单位小计	高级	中级
总计	539334	46075	155591	406818	32771	116847	132516	13303	38741
一、自然科学	252656	29349	74328	180224	19017	51692	72432	10332	22636
其中:1.高级职务	29349	29349	—	19017	19017	—	10332	10332	—
(正高级)	1905	1905	—	1043	1043	—	862	962	—
2.中级职务	74328	—	74328	51692	—	51692	22636	—	22636
工程技术人员	153022	17186	46368	93429	9872	27816	59599	7314	18552
农业技术人员	3221	269	877	2886	229	745	335	40	132
科学研究人员	2506	1069	964	1109	384	439	1397	685	525
卫生技术人员	67124	4218	16565	60018	3774	14482	7106	444	2083
教学人员	36783	6607	9554	22788	4758	8210	3995	1849	1344
二、社会科学	280678	16725	812160	226594	13754	65155	60084	2971	16105
其中:1.高级职务	16725	16725	—	13754	13754	—	2971	2971	—
(正高级)	853	853	—	654	654	—	199	199	—
2.中级职务	81260	—	812450	65155	—	65155	16105	—	16105
科学研究人员	1585	436	747	1196	310	547	389	126	200
教学人员	109619	8314	40109	102139	7338	37279	7480	976	2830
经济人员	68766	1596	114460	44552	969	5895	24214	627	5565
会计人员	50823	700	7068	34765	453	4263	19058	249	21306
统计人员	8490	160	1390	7515	146	1137	975	14	253
翻译人员	1285	252	432	931	147	289	354	105	143
新闻、出版人员	2382	553	952	2091	471	817	291	82	135
图书、文博、档案人员	6978	540	2627	5596	410	2038	1382	130	589
体育人员	538	137	211	526	137	209	12	—	2
工艺美术人员	721	55	213	710	55	210	11	—	3
其他人员	35491	3980	16051	96573	3318	12471	8918	662	3580

2005年天津专业技术人员情况统计表

表1-1-1-4 单位:人

项目	总数	高级	中级	市属单位小计	高级	中级	驻津单位小计	高级	中级
总计	424845	58002	147671	328530	44397	118464	96315	13605	29207
一、自然科学	206222	32642	65795	156138	23067	49244	50084	9575	16551
其中:1.高级职务	32642	32642	—	23067	23067	—	9575	9575	—
(正高级)	3797	3797	—	2401	2401	—	1396	1396	—
2.中级职务	65795	—	65795	49244	—	49244	16551	—	16551
工程技术人员	107745	16493	32481	66036	9769	18756	41709	6724	13725
农业技术人员	2951	413	831	2904	399	814	47	14	17
科学研究人员	3887	1646	1272	2007	779	718	1880	867	554
卫生技术人员	59604	5625	18190	56325	5343	16966	3279	282	1224
教学人员	32035	8465	13021	28866	6777	11990	3169	1688	1031
二、社会科学	218623	25360	81876	172392	21330	69220	46231	4030	12656
其中:1.高级职务	25360	25360	—	21330	21330	—	4030	4030	—
(正高级)	1561	1561	—	1087	1087	—	474	474	—
2.中级职务	81876	—	81876	69220	—	69220	12656	—	12656
科学研究人员	1002	323	430	459	164	151	543	159	279
教学人员	99029	14902	50378	94298	13343	48123	4731	1559	2255
经济人员	43682	1864	7844	23351	827	3152	20331	1037	4692
会计人员	34913	800	6370	21543	504	3889	13370	296	2481
统计人员	3787	205	882	3295	185	720	492	20	162
翻译人员	606	190	216	424	120	146	182	70	70
图书、档案、文博人员	5461	804	2382	4515	654	1930	946	150	452
出版、新闻、播音人员	2656	892	888	2405	803	793	251	89	95
工艺美术人员	295	48	102	289	48	102	6	—	—
体育人员	546	168	168	546	168	168	—	—	—
其他人员	26646	5164	12216	21267	4514	10046	5379	650	2170

1991、1995、2000、2005年天津专业技术人员情况统计表

表1-1-1-5 单位:人

年份	专业技术人员合计	自然科学	社会科学	平均每万人有专业技术人员	平均每万职工有专业技术人员
1991年	575283	299214	276069	659	1973
1995年	601936	288873	313062	639	2079
2000年	539334	252656	280678	549	2726
2005年	424845	206222	218623	407	2189

二、行业分布

1995年，全市专业技术人员在国民经济各行业的分布，按其数量多少依次为：工业，教育、文化艺术和广播电视，卫生、体育、社会福利，商业、饮食、物资和仓储，建筑业，交通运输、邮电通讯，科学研究和综合技术服务，地质普查和勘探，房管、公用和居民咨询服务，农、林、牧、渔、水利，行政机关及其他行业。在各行业中，教科文卫系统专业技术人员数量居第一位，共有229166人，占全市专业技术人员总数的38.07%（其中：自然科学专业技术人员有86524人，社会科学专业技术人员有142642人，分别占总数的33.31%、41.68%）；工业和建筑业专业技术人员数量居第二位，有212113人，占全市专业技术人员总数的35.24%（其中：自然科学专业技术人员有119354人，社会科学专业技术人员有92759人，分别占总数的45.95%、27.11%）；农、林、牧、渔和水利业专业技术人员有11350人，占全市专业技术人员总数的1.89%（其中：自然科学专业技术人员有7488人，社会科学专业技术人员有3862人，分别占总数的2.88%和1.13%）。

至2005年，全市专业技术人员在国民经济各行业中的分布有所变化。在国民经济各行业中，教科文卫系统专业技术人员最多，共有239437人，占专业技术人员总数的56.36%，比1995年上升18.29个百分点（其中：自然科学专业技术人员有115035人，社会科学专业技术人员有124402人，分别占其总数的55.78%、56.90%）；制造业和建筑业专业技术人员共有88444人，占专业技术人员总数的20.82%（其中：自然科学专业技术人员有53833人，社会科学专业技术人员有34611人，分别占其总数的26.10%、15.84%）；农、林、牧、渔和水利业专业技术人员有12650人，仅占专业技术人员总数的2.98%，但比1995年增加1.09个百分点（其中：自然科学专业技术人员有9187人，社会科学专业技术人员有3463人，分别占其总数的4.45%、1.58%）。

1995年天津专业技术人员行业分布情况统计表

表1-1-1-6　　单位：人

项目	合计	自然科学	社会科学
总计	601936	259737	342199
工业	168988	90397	78591
教育、文化艺术和广播电视	153049	19017	134032
卫生、体育、社会福利	55624	50736	4888
商业、饮食、物资和仓储	49514	6937	42577
建筑业	43125	28957	14168
交通运输、邮电通讯	32196	18240	13956
金融、保险	24441	1048	23393
科学研究和综合技术服务	20493	16771	3722
地质普查和勘探	17073	9479	7594
房管、公用和居民咨询服务	13568	5589	7979
农、林、牧、渔、水利	11350	7488	3862
行政机关	7879	3357	4522
其他	4636	1721	2915

2000年天津专业技术人员行业分布情况统计表

表1-1-1-7 单位:人

项目	合计	自然科学	社会科学
总计	549844	292268	257576
教育、文化艺术和广播电影电视业	153104	33988	119116
工业	150325	84062	66263
卫生、体育、社会福利业	56984	51656	5328
建筑业	42566	29838	12728
商业、公共饮食、物资供销和仓储业	36812	6101	30711
交通运输、邮电通讯业	30047	17830	12217
金融、保险业	24587	1076	23511
科学研究和综合技术服务业	15655	12654	3001
房地产管理、公用事业、居民服务和咨询服务业	13928	6589	7339
行政机关	10813	4979	5834
农、林、牧、渔、水利业	8386	5897	2489
其他行业	5803	2303	3500
地质普查和勘察业	834	603	231

2005年天津专业技术人员行业分布情况统计表

表1-1-1-8 单位:人

项目	合计	自然科学	社会、人文科学
总计	424845	206222	218623
教育	146621	39894	106727
卫生、社会保障和社会福利业	61205	55247	5958
制造业	60746	34365	26381
建筑业	27698	19468	8230
金融业	24697	998	23699
科学研究、技术服务和地质勘察业	22707	19139	3568
交通运输、仓储及邮政业	17565	8330	9235
批发和零售业	12400	2639	9761
采矿业	8934	5944	2990
文化、体育和娱乐业	8904	755	8149
水利、环境和公共设施管理业	7404	5356	2048
农、林、牧、渔业	5246	3831	1415
房地产业	5255	2463	2792
电力、燃气及水的生产和供应业	5158	3039	2119
信息传输、计算机服务和软件业	3605	2724	881
租赁和商务服务业	3162	982	2180
居民服务和其他服务业	1878	708	1170
公共管理和社会组织	1044	235	809
住宿和餐饮业	616	105	511

三、部门分布

（一）科学研究与技术开发机构科技人员

1991年，全市县以上全民独立科学研究与开发机构共有154个，职工总数3.12万人，其中从事科技活动人员2.36万人，占职工总数的75.64%；科学家和工程师1.21万人，占科技人员总数的51.27%。在科学研究与开发机构中，自然科学研究与开发机构137个，从事科技活动人员2.19万人，其中科学家和工程师1.12万人，占科技人员总数的51.14%；社会人文科学研究与开发机构6个，从事科技活动人员426人，其中科学家和工程师275人，占科技人员总数的64.55%；科学技术情报和文献机构11个，从事科技活动人员1240人，其中科学家和工程师675人，占科技人员总数的54.44%。

至2005年，全市县以上国有独立科学研究与技术开发机构共有142个，从业人员1.99万人，其中从事科技活动人员1.12万人，占从业人员总数的56.28%；科学家和工程师0.85万人，占科技人员总数的75.89%。在科学研究与开发机构中，自然科学研究与开发机构128个，从事科技活动人员1.03万人，其中科学家和工程师0.77万人，占科技人员总数的74.75%；社会人文科学研究与开发机构3个，从事科技活动人员299人，其中科学家和工程师264人，占科技人员总数的88.29%；科学技术情报和文献机构11个，从事科技活动人员612人，其中科学家和工程师540人，占科技人员总数的88.24%。

（二）高等院校专业技术人员

1991年，天津共有高等院校26个，从事科技活动人员2.45万人，其中教师及其他技术人员2.30万人，占科技活动人员总数的93.88%。在教师及其他技术人员中，高级职称0.51万人，占22.17%；中级职称0.93万人，占40.43%。科技活动人员按隶属关系分，国家教委和其他部委所属高等院校科技活动人员有1.07万人，占科技活动人员总数的43.67%；地方所属高等院校科技活动人员有1.38万人，占科技活动人员总数的56.33%。科技活动人员按不同学科分，从事自然科学活动人员0.34万人，占科技活动人员总数的13.88%；从事工程与技术活动人员0.63万人，占科技活动人员总数的25.71%；从事医学科学活动人员0.54万人，占科技活动人员总数的22.04%；从事农业和其他科学活动人员0.94万人，占科技活动人员总数的38.37%。

至2005年，经调整天津共有高等院校19个，教学与科研人员2.47万人，占从业人员总数的86.6%；其中从事理工农医类学科科技活动人员1.73万人，占教学与科研人员总数的70.04%。在教学与科研人员中，高级职称0.90万人，占其总数的36.44%；中级职称0.81万人，占32.79%。科技活动人员按隶属关系分，教育部和其他部委所属高等院校科技活动人员有0.66万人，占其总数的26.72%；地方所属高等院校科技活动人员有1.81万人，占其总数的73.28%。在理工农医类学科科技活动人员中，从事自然科学活动人员0.23万人，占其总数的13.29%；从事工程与技术活动人员0. 60万人，占总数的34.68%；从事医药科学活动人员0.71万人，占总数的41.04%；从事农业和其他科技活动人员0.19万人，占总数的10.98%。

（三）大中型工业企业科技人员

1991年，全市大中型工业企业有494个，共有职工83.35万人，其中从事技术开发人员2.43万人，占职工总数的2.92%。在技术开发人员中，具有高中级职称人员0.66万人，占其总数的27.16%；工程技术人员1.45万人，占其总数的59.67%。按企业规模分，大型企业从事技术开发人员1.45万人，其中具有高中级职称人员0.40万人，占大型企业技术开发人员总数的27.59%；中型企业从事技术开发人员0.98万人，其中具有高中级职称人员0.26万人，占中型企业技术开发人员总数的26.53%。

至2005年，全市大中型工业企业有549个，共有职工65.22万人，其中科技活动人员3.22万人，占职工总数的4.94%。在科技活动人员中，具有高中级职称人员1.16万人，占科技活动人员总数的36.02%。按企业规模分，大型企业科技活动人员1.49万人，其中具有高中级职称人员0.52万人，占大型企业科技活动人员总数的34.90%；中型企业科技活动人员1.73万人，其中具有高中级职称人员0.64万人，占中型企业科技活动人员总数的36.99%。

第二节 专业技术人员结构

1991～2005年,全市各类专业技术人员结构发生较大变化。专业技术人员中,女性所占比重有所增长,受过高等教育和具有高中级职称的所占比重大幅度增长。

一、性别

1995年,全市各类专业技术人员中女性所占比重为47.00%。其中,自然科学专业技术人员中女性占其总数的40.50%,社会科学专业技术人员中女性占其总数的51.93%。

至2005年,全市各类专业技术人员中女性所占比重49.67%,比1995年上升2.67个百分点。其中,自然科学专业技术人员中女性占其总数的44.73%,社会科学专业技术人员中女性其总数的54.33%,分别比1995年上升4.23和2.4个百分点。

二、文化程度

1995年,全市各类专业技术人员中,受过高等教育的占其总数的20.22%。其中,自然科学专业技术人员中受过高等教育的占其总数的31.62%,社会科学专业技术人员中受过高等教育的占其总数的11.56%。

至2005年,全市各类专业技术人员中受过高等教育人员所占比重增至68.73%,比1995年上升48.51个百分点。其中,自然科学专业技术人员中受过高等教育人员所占比重69.53%,比1995年上升37.91个百分点;社会科学专业技术人员中受过高等教育人员所占比重67.97%,比1995年上升56.41个百分点。

三、职称

1995年,全市各类专业技术人员中,具有高级职称的占其总数的7.26%,具有中级职称的占其总数的26.68%。其中,自然科学专业技术人员中具有高级职称的占其总数的11.13%,具有中级职称的占其总数的27.17%;社会科学专业技术人员中具有高级职称的占其总数的4.33%,具有中级职称的占其总数的26.14%。

至2005年,全市各类专业技术人员中具有高级职称人员所占比例为13.65%,比1995年上升6.39个百分点;具有中级职称人员所占比例为34.76%,比1995年上升8.08个百分点。其中,自然科学技术人员中高级职称人员占其总数的15.83%,比1995年上升4.70个百分点,中级职称人员所占比例31.90%,比1995年上升4.73个百分点;社会科学专业技术人员中高级职称人员占其总数的11.60%,比1995年上升7.27个百分点,中级职称人员所占比例37.45%,比1995年上升11.31个百分点。

1995年天津专业技术人员结构情况统计表

表1-1-2-9　　单位:人

项目	合计	自然科学	社会科学
总计	601936	259737	342199
一、女性	282921	105205	177716
占总计%	47.00	40.50	51.93
二、受过高等教育的	121711	82137	39574
占总计%	20.22	31.62	11.56
三、按职称分			
1、具有高级职称的	43746	28914	14832
占总计%	7.26	11.13	4.33
2、具有中级职称的	160217	70572	89645
占总计%	26.68	27.17	26.14
3、具有初级职称的	355392	142159	213233
占总计%	59.04	54.73	62.31

2000年天津专业技术人员结构情况统计表

表1-1-2-10　　单位:人

项目	合计	自然科学	社会科学
总计	549844	257576	292268
一、女性	259981	107049	152932
占总计%	47.28	41.56	52.33
二、受过高等教育的	287911	154671	133240
占总计%	52.36	60.05	45.59
三、按职称分			
1、具有高级职称的	46910	29784	17126
占总计%	8.53	11.56	5.86
2、具有中级职称的	159539	76093	83446
占总计%	29.01	29.54	28.55
3、具有初级职称的	289014	126383	162631
占总计%	52.56	49.07	55.64

2005年天津专业技术人员结构情况统计表

表1-1-2-11　　单位:人

项目	合计	自然科学	社会科学
总计	424845	206222	218623
一、女性	211026	92240	118786
占总计%	49.67	44.73	54.33
二、受过高等教育的	291987	143385	148602
占总计%	68.73	69.53	67.97

续表1-1-2-11 单位:人

项目	合计	自然科学	社会科学
三、按职称分			
1、具有高级职称的	58002	32642	25360
占总计%	13.65	15.83	11.60
2、具有中级职称的	147671	65795	81876
占总计%	34.76	31.90	37.45
3、具有初级职称的	184656	89740	94916
占总计%	43.46	43.52	43.42

第二章 科技人才队伍建设

1991年起,天津市继续贯彻"尊重知识,尊重人才"的方针,选拔优秀科技人才,向部分高级知识分子发放政府特殊津贴,选拔在自然科学和社会科学领域的授衔专家,遴选和推荐中国科学院和中国工程院院士,大力表彰和奖励在科技工作中做出突出贡献的优秀科技人才。同时,组织实施"跨世纪育才工程",选拔和培养国家级、市级和企事业单位三个层次的专业技术骨干和学术、技术带头人;围绕重点科技攻关、高新技术开发和高新技术产业化,大力引进国外智力和海外留学人员;认真做好专业技术人员的职称评审和继续教育工作,坚持不拘一格选拔人才;建立人才发展基金,推进高级科技人才建设。这些举措,有效地调动起科技人才投身社会主义现代化建设的积极性和创造性,充分发挥科技人员在促进科技和经济社会的协调发展中的主力军作用。

第一节 优秀科技人才的选拔和表彰

天津市贯彻国家关于给部分高级知识分子发放特殊津贴的文件精神,对各学科领域的奠基人、创始人、带头人等继续做好发放政府特殊津贴工作。1992年起,在全市范围内开展自然科学领域授衔专家选拔工作,经过层层选拔推荐,专家委员会评审,市人才工作领导小组认定,市委、市政府批准,授予自然科学领域重点学科和哲学社会科学重点学科的专家为天津市授衔专家称号,并以市政府名义向他们颁发荣誉证书。天津市继续参加中国科学院和中国工程院院士的遴选与推荐工作,其中12人当选中国科学院院士,19人当选中国工程院院士。天津市继续做好人事部组织的选拔有突出贡献中青年科学、技术、管理专家的推荐工作,并参加中共中央组织部、人事部、中国科协等组织的评选优秀科技工作者活动,30余人受到表彰与奖励。同时,天津市组织各种评选先进科技工作者活动,200余人获得各种荣誉称号,受到表彰和奖励。

一、享受政府特殊津贴人员的选拔

1991年，天津市继续贯彻落实《人事部、财政部关于给部分高级知识分子发放特殊津贴的通知》精神，选拔、推荐享受政府特殊津贴人员。经过推荐、评议、审查和天津市知识分子工作领导小组审核，并报请国务院批准，天津市有171名各学科领域奠基人、创始人被批准享受政府特殊津贴，津贴标准与1990年首批14名享受政府特殊津贴人员相同，每人每月100元。1992年，享受政府特殊津贴人员的选拔范围和数量扩大，天津市有798人被批准享受政府特殊津贴，津贴标准调整为每人每月100元和50元两个档次。1993年，天津市有982人被批准享受政府特殊津贴，津贴标准仍为每人每月100元、50元两个档次。1994年，天津市选拔推荐114人享受政府特殊津贴，津贴标准为每人每月100元。同时，根据人事部的要求，对1992年和1993年享受政府特殊津贴人员中享受每月50元津贴标准提高到100元。1995年，天津市将选拔、推荐享受政府特殊津贴人员的范围扩大到45岁以下的中青年，全市共有115人被批准享受政府特殊津贴，其中45岁以下的中青年占人选总数的22%，同时津贴标准改为每人一次性发放5000元。

1996～2000年，天津市享受政府特殊津贴人员分别为116人、115人、116人、104人、110人、津贴标准均为每人一次性发放5000元。

2001年，天津市将享受政府特殊津贴人员选拔的范围扩大到非国有制企事业单位，选拔对象重点为科技、教育、文化、卫生等岗位和在工农业生产第一线做出重大贡献、取得突出业绩的专家、学者、技术人员，并对享受政府特殊津贴人选实行公示制，对2001年享受政府特殊津贴人员一次性发给1万元，还免征个人所得税。经过基层单位推荐，主管部门审核评议，市人事局会同市委组织部、市科委进行综合平衡，市委、市政府审核，2001年、2002年分别确定69人、55人为享受政府特殊津贴人选，上报人事部并获得批准。

自2004年开始，选拔享受政府特殊津贴人员的期限改为每两年选拔一次。2004年，66人上报并被批准享受政府特殊津贴，每人一次性获得政府特殊津贴标准由1万元提高到2万元，并免征个人所得税。至2005年，全市有2945人享受政府特殊津贴。

二、授衔专家的选拔

1992年，市科委在全市范围内开展自然科学领域授衔专家选拔工作，并确定首批授衔专家203人。之后的1994年和1997年分别进行两次增补，分别为140人、38人。至1997年，全市共选拔确定自然科学领域授衔专家381人。

2002年，授衔专家选拔工作由市科委转到天津市人事局。2004年5月，市委、市政府转发市人事局制定的《天津市授衔专家选拔工作的实施意见》，规定每三年进行一次授衔专家的集中评审，同时规定选拔工作要严格把握三点：一是在选拔范围上做到代表性与广泛性结合；二是在人才评价上重在社会和业内认可；三是在选拔程序上突出严肃性和权威性。当年，有98人选拔为天津市授衔专家。他们来自工业、城建、教育、卫生、农业、交通等系统，涉及基础数学、化学工程、凝聚态物理、生物医学工程、材料科学等30多个自然科学领域重点学科和世界经济、实验心理学、中国古代文学等7个哲学社会科学重点学科，其中55人承担天津市重大高新技术产业化项目和重点工程、重点项目。2005年11月22日，市委、市政府召开天津市科学技术奖励暨授衔专家命名大会，市政府作出《关于授予严泽生等98名学术技术带头人"天津市授衔专家"称号的决定》，98人获得"天津市授衔专家"称号。至2005年，全市共有授衔专家479人。

三、两院院士的遴选

1991年起，天津市继续做好中国科学院的遴选与推荐工作。至1995年，9名在天津工作的专家、教授当选为中国科学院院士，其中南开大学数学研究所所长、著名数学家陈省身于1994年当选为中国科学院首批外籍院士。1997年，1名在天津工作的教授当选为中国科学院院士。2001年和2003年，又有2名在天津工作的专家、教授当选为中国科学院院士。至2005年,在天津工作或曾在天津工作的专家教授共有23人当选为中国科学院院士(学部委员),其中1991~2005年有12人当选为中国科学院院士。

1994年起,天津市参加中国工程院院士的遴选与推荐工作。至1999年,10名在天津工作的专家、教授当选为中国工程院院士。2001~2005年,9名专家、教授当选为中国工程院院士。至2005年,在天津工作的专家教授共有19人当选中国工程院院士。

四、优秀科技人才的表彰与奖励

1984年起,天津市参加人事部组织的选拔有突出贡献中青年科学技术管理专家的推荐工作。至1998年,经国家科委或人事部批准,全市共有179人获得国家级有突出贡献中青年科学技术管理专家称号,并享受相关待遇。

1988年起,天津市参加中共中央组织部、人事部和中国科协设立的中国青年科技奖评选活动,评选对象是40岁以下从事自然科学和交叉科学的青年科技工作者。至2005年,天津市有13人获得中国青年科技奖称号。

1990年,市委组织部、市人事局、市科协设立天津青年科技奖,由市科协具体组织实施。该奖项面向全市广大青年科技工作者设立,旨在造就一批进入世界科技前沿的青年学术和技术带头人,表彰奖励在经济发展、社会进步和科技创新中做出突出成就的青年科技人才,激励广大青年科技工作者为加快社会主义现代化建设做出新贡献。至2005年,共举办7届,168名优秀青年科技工作者获此称号。

为充分调动广大中小学教育工作者的积极性、创造性,表彰、奖励为天津市培养21世纪自然科学后备人才做出突出贡献的优秀中小学教育工作者,1991年12月市科委、市教育局决定设立一项特别奖——"播种太阳奖"。此项奖励的范围是中小学从事数学、自然、物理、化学、生物、计算机、语文、外语教学的教师及相应的学科集体(含学校)。该奖项从1992年起在全市施行。

1997年开始,天津市参加由中共中央组织部、人事部和中国科协开展的"全国优秀科技工作者"评选活动。至2005年,天津市有10人获得全国优秀科技工作者称号。同年,市委组织部、市人事局、市科协组织开展"天津市优秀科技工作者"评选、表彰工作,旨在激励广大科技工作者积极投身"科教兴国",为促进科技进步和经济社会发展做出更大贡献。至2005年,共有50人获此奖项。

1999年起,天津市按照人事部的部署和要求,参加"全国杰出专业技术人才"的选拔推荐工作。至2005年,经中共中央组织部、中共中央宣传部、人事部、科技部批准,天津市先后有2人获得此称号。

2000年,天津市设立科学技术重大成就奖。该奖主要授予在当代科学技术前沿取得重大突破,或者在科技发展中卓有建树,以及在科技创新、成果转化和高技术产业化中创造重大经济、社会效益的科技工作者,是天津市科技界的最高奖项。该奖项每年授予人数不超过2名,奖励每名获奖者50万元奖金。至2005年,4人获此殊荣。是年,设立天津市国际科技合作奖,主要奖励对天津科技事业做出突出贡献的外籍科技人员。至2005年,3人获得天津市国际科技合作奖。

2002年起,天津市参加由中华全国妇女联合会、国家知识产权局、中国发明协会共同主办的"新世纪巾帼发明家"评选活动。天津市先后有2人获得这一中国妇女在发明创造领域的最高荣誉。2005年,天津市知识产权局与市妇联开展天津市首届"巾帼发明家"评选活动。经层层评选,最终确定天津市首届"巾帼发明家"5名,提名奖5名。2005年6月,举行天津市首届"巾帼发明家"表彰会,向获奖者颁发荣誉证书。

第二节　职称评审与继续教育

天津市贯彻落实人事部关于职称评审工作的政策规定，在各个专业技术职称系列中开展专业技术职称评审工作，经过各级职称评审委员会评审，并报主管部门批准，评定高级、中级、初级职称。职称评审工作坚持以能力和业绩为导向，落实破格、越级申报职称的政策，不拘一格选拔人才。

1990年1月，天津市颁布实施专业技术人员继续教育法规。之后，天津市对该规定多次进行修订，全市继续教育工作在法制化的道路上健康发展。

一、职称评审

1993年之前，天津市职称评审工作由市科委组织实施。1994年起，此项工作转由市人事局负责。1994~1995年，天津市有27个专业技术职称系列开展职称评审，共批准高级职称22762人（其中正高级1272人），中级职称48666人，初级职称83141人。同时，市人事局组织专业技术人员参加全国专业技术资格考试，其中3613人取得中级职称，5050人取得初级职称。通过职称评审和专业技术资格考试，高、中级职称人员占专业技术人员总数的比例有所上升。

1996年起，天津市专业技术职称评审开始向中青年倾斜。当年评审出45岁以下的高级职称人员所占比例上升到30.5%，35岁以下的中级职称人员所占比例上升到51.92%。1999年，45岁以下的高级职称和中级职称人员分别达到57.1%和65.8%。同年，天津市加强工程技术领域技术带头人队伍建设，为工业、城建、科技等系统评定出501名正高级工程师；为个体、私营企业专业技术人员开展职称评定工作，110人获得相应职称；对专业技术业绩突出、为天津经济建设和社会发展做出重大贡献的人员，对优秀留学回国人员给予越级申报专业技术职称。2000年，2100余名有突出贡献者获破格、越级晋升职称，45岁以下的高级职称人员占比达到59.0%。

1996~2000年，天津市专业技术职称评审工作涉及26个职称系列，共批准高级职称29700人（含正高级职称2584人），中级职称56288人，初级职称81573人。在组织参加全国专业技术资格考试中，有3万余人取得初、中级专业技术职称。2001~2002年，全市评审出高级职称12446人，中级职称27951人，初级职称34601人。

2003年，职称评审工作继续贯彻“重业绩、重贡献”原则，1000多名业绩突出人员被破格晋升高、中级职称。同时，职称评审工作向防治非典型性肺炎（以下简称“非典”）一线专业技术人员倾斜，230名在防治“非典”一线做出突出贡献的卫生、工程技术人员晋升为高、中级职称；对卫生、农业系列10个专业技术职称评审标准进行修订完善，对工程、经济、会计、卫生、农业等24个高级、17个中级职称评审委员会进行调整；推行职业资格制度，制定人才中介人员职业资格认定办法，组织完成执业药师、监理工程师等25项专业考试，报考人数达6万余人，为历年最多。

2004年，市人事局、市交通委员会出台《天津市现代物流专业技术水平考试办法（试行）》，建立全市第一个专业技术水平考试制度。全市有1500多人破格晋升高、中级职称，其中20人越级晋升高级职称，并组织专业技术资格、执业资格、职称外语和职称计算机考试29项。是年，全市取得高级职称6607人（含正高级职称673人）、中级职称15993人、初级职称23676人，其中45岁以下的高级职称人员占比73.7%，比2003年提高7个百分点。

2005年，首次在滨海新区支柱产业和高新技术企业开展职称水平评价试点工作，其中2人取得正高级职称，21人取得副高级职称。同时，出台《天津市引进海内外高层次人才和急需人才职称评审办法》，并有50

余名人才经评审获高级职称。是年，全市共评审出高级职称6423人(其中正高级725人)，中级职称14143人，初级职称23647人，其中45岁以下的高级职称人员占比74.7%；破格晋升中级以上职称1500多人，其中10名越级晋升高级职称；有3924人取得建造师执业资格。

二、继续教育

1991～1994年，天津市继续教育工作由市科委负责。1994年3月，此项工作转入市人事局。1994年，全市各区县、委办局及企事业单位共举办9339期继续教育培训班，约40万人次专业技术人员参加培训；开展继续教育成绩突出的19个区、县、局和48个企事业单位及67名先进工作者受到表彰。1995年，天津市举办继续教育宣传周活动，组织各种宣传活动6000余次，30万人次专业技术人员参加；表彰继续教育先进区县和委办局15个，先进企事业单位49个，先进工作者87名。是年，出台《天津市专业技术人员继续教育登记证书》制度，全市95.18%的企事业单位实行该制度，形成培训、使用、考核、奖励及职称评聘一体化的运行机制。

1996年，继续教育活动强化针对性，组织现代企业管理、涉外企业管理、经营技能、外语和数控技术等10个专业培训班。次年，组织实施继续教育高级研修班51期，近3000名专业技术人员参加研修；举办各区县、委办局、集团公司人事教育部门负责人和继续教育管理干部300余人参加的创造学和无形资产学讲座；为126名教师和培训管理人员举办师资培训班。1998年，开展“21世纪知识经济对继续教育的挑战”主题宣传活动7500余场次，40余万人次参加；各区县、委办局、总公司和11个高等院校免费为1万余人次下岗专业技术人员开展再就业培训，传授计算机应用技术、数控技术、电教制作技术等12大类的知识和技能；1.8万名工程类和1.6万名经济、统计、会计、审计类专业技术人员分别参加创造学和无形资产学培训。1999年，天津市出台《关于专业技术人员继续教育第四周期工作意见》，表彰第3周期86个先进单位和95名先进工作者；组织108名专家，为2万多人次农业技术人员举办265期农业技术培训班；继续免费为4600多人次下岗专业技术人员和管理人员开展再就业培训，传授计算机网络应用、财务软件、服装设计与生产、市场营销、家用电器维修等专业技术知识。2000年，对《天津市专业技术人员继续教育规定》进行修订，形成《天津市专业技术人员和管理人员继续教育条例(草案)》。全年为5000多名高中级专业技术人员组织58期继续教育高级研修班，为68.5万人次举办专题讲座、技术培训、专题研修、考察等继续教育活动共2.4万期(次)。

2001年，天津市为3万余名专业技术人员和企业经营管理人员开展WTO及相关知识培训；为3000多名高中级专业技术人员和管理人员举办47期继续教育高级研修班，为65.4万人次举办专题讲座、技术培训、专题研修等继续教育活动2.8万期(次)。是年，《天津市专业技术人员和管理人员继续教育条例》经天津市人大常委会审议通过，次年2月1日起正式实施。2002年，市人事局出台《关于贯彻〈天津市专业技术人员和管理人员继续教育条例〉有关问题的规定》《天津市专业技术人员和管理人员继续教育证书登记管理办法》《天津市专业技术人员和管理人员继续教育高级研修班管理办法》等，继续教育工作进一步制度化、规范化。是年，为5000余名专业技术人员和管理人员举办各类高级研修班148期。2003年，市人事局、市统计局制定《天津市统计专业技术人员和管理人员继续教育实施办法》。各区县、各委办局采取集中培训、学术讲座、出国(境)研修、技术攻关、远程教育等多种形式开展继续教育，13万人次参加各类继续教育活动4051期(次)，市人事局为2300余人举办高级研修班34期，有效地提高专业技术人员的专业知识和岗位技能。2004年，市人事局为区县、委办局、总公司的继续教育管理人员120余人进行培训，为1200余人举办高级研修班20余期。2005年，市人事局出台《天津市专业技术人员和管理人员继续教育公共科目指南(试行)》，指导各单位采取灵活多样的方式开展公共科目学习。全年为3000余名专业技术人员和管理人员举办公共课程培训班80余期，为2200余人举办继续教育高级研修班40余期，为180余名继续教育管理者开展集中培训与实地考察活动。

第三节　人才工程与人才流动

1994年，天津市开始实施“跨世纪育才工程”，又称“131人才工程”，即选拔100名40岁左右的尖子人才，经过培养成为在国际上具有一定知名度，能够进入世界科技前沿领域或具有国内领先水平，保持学科优势及相当水平的学术、技术权威；选拔300名35岁左右的青年专业技术骨干，经过培养成为在天津市各学科领域具有较高水平、能起骨干作用，居领先地位以及具有相当水平的学术、技术带头人；选拔100名35岁以下青年专业技术人员，经过培养成为各单位专业技术骨干和学术、技术带头人的后备力量。市委、市政府大力实施人才战略，先后制定《关于聚集人才、充分发挥专业技术人员作用的意见》《天津市人才流动条例》《天津市引进国内外优秀人才来津工作的实施办法》等政策规定，引进各类人才特别是高层次人才；建立人才发展基金，对博士后和优秀中青年人才予以经费资助，并带动各用人单位用于人才奖励、人才培养、人才引进的资金投入，促进专业技术人才特别是高级人才建设。同时，加强人才市场建设，做好大中专毕业生就业工作，均收到良好成效。

一、实施跨世纪育才工程

1994年，天津市开始制定并实施“131人才工程”，即跨世纪育才工程。2000年，市人事局、市委组织部、市计委、市科委等出台《天津市“131人才工程”实施方案》，组织实施跨世纪育才工程。当年，经过层层选拔，确定第一层次人选即40岁左右的尖子人才108人，第二、第三层次人选即35岁左右及以下的青年专业技术骨干1236人。2001～2002年，深入实施“131人才工程”，对列入培养计划的各层次人选，通过选送到国外参加中长期培训、做访问学者以及承担重点科研、开发项目等方式进行重点培养。至2002年底，第一层次人选共承担国家级科研课题70多项，市重大科研课题60多项，参加国内外专业培训和学术、技术交流91次，在国内外重要期刊发表论文110多篇，获得国家级科技奖励7项、省部级奖励15项。

2003年，天津市继续深入实施“131人才工程”，并出台“第一层次人选年度考核办法”，结果108名第一层次人选全部通过考核，22名人选考核优秀。至2004年，天津市人才发展基金与各人选单位先后各投入约700万元，重点资助第一层次人选到国外进行中长期培训和参加国内外学术会议。

2005年，天津市首批“131人才工程”3年培养期结束，培养效果显著。一是科研创新能力普遍提高。40名人选承担国家杰出青年基金、国家“863”和“973”计划、国家自然科学基金等国家级重点项目71个；70人承担重大高新技术产业化项目、重大科技攻关等市部级重点研究项目141项；84人承担市部级项目和局级项目215项；50名人选、90余项研究成果获得国家级、部市级奖励。二是学历层次及学术水平提高。其中：7人在职攻读博士学位，5人在职攻读硕士学位；近200余人次参加国内外培训和学术、技术交流活动，其中40人次参加3个月以上中长期培训及合作研究；在国内外学术期刊和学术会议上发表或宣读论文1.1万篇，被国际科学引文索引收录270余篇，被国际工程索引收录30篇，被国际科学技术会议文献索引收录21篇；出版专著40多部，101人在各级学术、技术团体和机构中兼职314个。三是经济社会效益显著。培养人选通过科研开发、技术创新、技术改造、成果转化等方式，创造经济效益超过百万元的有20余人。

二、人才流动与开发

1991年起，天津市先后制定并组织实施一系列促进科技人才流动的政策规定。2000年，经天津市第十三届人大常委会第十八次会议审议通过，颁布《天津市人才流动条例》，对充分发挥人才市场机制的作用，鼓励人才自主流动做出系统规定，进一步完善人才流动的法制环境。是年，又出台“天津市引进国内外优秀人才来津工作实施办法”，围绕经济社会发展需要，大力引进各类人才特别是高层次人才。

2001年，天津市相继出台《关于建立人才柔性流动机制，进一步做好引进国内外优秀人才智力工作的意见》《关于鼓励海外留学人员来津工作或为津服务的若干规定》，建立起方式灵活、渠道畅通、来去自由、待遇平等的人才柔性流动机制，进一步吸引国内外优秀人才和留学生到天津工作或为天津服务。是年，全市共引进各类人才21895人，其中从海外引进589人；办理到天津手续的各类人才5300人，其中4800人具有大学本科以上学历，比2000年增加20%。同时，天津市确定100家高新技术企业和大中型骨干企业，建立为企业服务的直通道，直接受理企业人才引进、人才培养等业务，向企业发布人事人才政策、人才供求信息等各类信息，进一步增强为企业服务的及时性、针对性和有效性。次年，正式办理到天津工作手续的人才6500多人，其中博士后10人，具有博士和硕士学位的167人，具有大学本科以上学历和中级以上职称的6300多人。同时，以短期工作、项目合作等柔性流动方式到天津工作或为天津服务的人才明显增加，进一步提高天津市IT、通信、生物、医药、能源等重点领域、重点产业、重点学科的研发能力和技术实力。

2003年，天津市扩充“直通道”的服务范围，对全国第二届农村优秀人才推荐评选工作做出部署，开展农村优秀人才评选活动。2004年，市委办公厅、市政府办公厅出台《关于实行天津市引进人才居住证制度的意见》，对“不迁户口、不转关系”、以柔性流动方式到天津工作的人员实行“绿卡”制度，进一步增强对周边尤其是北京地区人才的吸引力。是年，为507名优秀专业技术人员办理引进人才居住证，其中具有大学本科学历或中级职称人员504人，另3人则是用人单位急需的特殊技能型人才。

2005年，天津市进一步完善吸引国内优秀人才的政策措施，简化工作程序，大力引进急需人才。全年引进各类人才986人，其中12人为博士后，51人有博士学位，104人有硕士学位；743人具有本科学历；210人具有高级职称，183人有中级职称。

三、人才发展基金

天津市于2000年建立人才发展基金，主要用于对高层次人才培养、引进和奖励的资助。是年，对39名博士后每人资助2万元安家费和租房补贴；对天津大学、南开大学和天津医科大学博士后流动站计划外招收的48名博士后资助68万元；对高新技术重大产业化项目资本运作人员和优秀中青年人才出国培训分别予以50%的经费资助。2001年，246名优秀科技人才获得天津市人才发展基金的资助，资助金额达650余万元。同时，按照有关匹配政策规定，带动各用人单位用于人才奖励、培养、引进的资金达1200余万元。2004年，天津市人才发展基金工作加大对高层次人才培养、引进和奖励的资助力度，全年投入1079.8万元，资助、奖励各类人才323名。2005年，天津市人才发展基金投入1311余万元，资助、奖励各类人才410余人，其中重点支持博士后工作。

四、人才市场建设

2000年起，天津市全面贯彻落实《天津市人才流动条例》，加强对人才市场招聘活动的审批与管理，初步建立起一支人才市场执法人员队伍，规范人才流动秩序，推进人才市场的健康发展。2002年，天津市认真贯彻落实人事部、国家工商总局颁发的“人才市场管理规定”等法规、政策，开展人才流动中介工作执法检查，净化人才交流的环境。同时，加强对举办人才招聘活动的管理，举办人才中介机构从业人员培训，使人才招聘活动安全有序进行。是年，全市共举办各类招聘活动290场，其中全市性大型招聘活动41场，入场招聘单位1.9万家次，入场应聘人员53万人次，达成用人意向16.5万人次，均较往年有大幅度提高。至2002年底，全市设立各类人才中介机构78家。

2003年，天津市按照“政企、政事分开”原则，进一步推动人才中介机构改制，初步实现人才中介机构与原有人才中心在业务上的分离，并举办人才中介员资格认定培训班5期，470余人取得人才中介员资格。是年，共举办各类招聘活动290场，其中全市性大型招聘活动47场，招聘单位2.1万家次，应聘人才55万人次，达成用人意向17.2万人次。同时，进一步加强人才市场执法工作，严格执行市场准入、年检、从业人员执业资格等制度，为人才流动创造良好的市场环境。

2004年，天津市认真落实人事部《关于加快发展人才市场的意见》，开展人才市场执法大检查，规范人才流动秩序，净化人才市场环境。为加强和规范人才市场监管，市人事局先后下发《关于加强全市人才招聘活动管理有关问题的通知》《关于加强天津市人才招聘活动管理的紧急通知》《关于加强人才招聘活动安全工作的通知》《关于加强人才中介机构网站管理的通知》等文件，确保人才招聘活动安全、有序地进行。是年，全市人才中介机构达94家，举办各类招聘活动315场，其中全市性大型招聘活动60场，招聘单位2.5万家次，应聘人才63万人次，达成用人意向19万人次。

2005年，根据《中华人民共和国行政许可法》，天津市第十四届人大常委会对《天津市人才流动条例》进行修订，强化对人才市场的监管，规范人才市场管理行为。为贯彻新的《天津市人才流动条例》，开展广泛、深入的宣传和培训，并召开人才流动工作座谈会，交流人才市场建设的做法和经验，研讨人才市场工作的新举措和新思路。同时，开展联合市场执法，纠正人才中介活动中出现的各类违法违规行为，维护人才交流秩序；举办人才市场执法人员专业法培训考试，增强人才市场执法队伍的整体素质，提高人才市场执法水平；通过自查总结、逐户审查、重点抽查等方式，对全市人才中介机构进行年检，进一步加强人才市场的依法监管，促使中介活动更有序地进行。

五、大中专毕业生就业

天津市一贯重视大中专毕业生的就业问题，并制定一系列相应政策规定，做好大中专毕业生就业工作。1999年，天津市出台《关于放宽非津生源应届大学本科以上毕业生进津条件的通知》，规定凡普通高校非天津市生源的本科以上毕业生，思想品德和学习成绩优秀、身心健康的应届毕业生，在天津有接收单位的，均可经批准进天津就业。此后，2003年出台《关于做好高校毕业生就业工作的十条措施》，2004年颁发《关于做好2004年高校毕业生就业工作的意见》，2005年制定《关于引导和鼓励高校毕业生面向基层就业的实施意见》，切实做好高校毕业生就业服务工作，并组织参加人事部举办的全国人才市场高校毕业生就业服务周活动，均收到很好效果。

第四节　人才引进与博士后工作

天津市大力实施人才引进战略，建立特聘专家制度，聘请一批国家级顶尖人才为天津经济社会发展提供决策咨询。同时，围绕重点科技攻关、高新技术开发和高新技术产业化，做好引进国外技术和管理专家及海外留学人员工作，为促进天津经济、科技、社会发展提供有利的人才智力保障。天津市积极做好博士后工作，博士后科研流动站和科研工作站不断增加，涌现出一批优秀博士后和优秀博士后管理工作者。

一、建立特聘专家制度

2003年，市政府制定《天津市人民政府特聘专家制度》，提出在两院院士和全国著名专家及某一学科领域被同行公认的顶尖人才中挑选一部分人员，聘请为天津市政府特聘专家，为天津经济和社会发展提供决策咨询。是年，先后聘请中国著名杂交水稻专家、中国工程院院士袁隆平，中国科学院院士、中国科学院副院长、国家纳米科技首席科学家白春礼，中国科学院院士、中国科学院物理研究所研究员赵忠贤，中国科学院院士、北京大学教授、中国科学院固体物理研究所所长甘子钊，中国工程院院士、西北有色金属研究院常务副院长周廉，中国科学院院士、中国科学院声学研究所所长李启虎，中国工程院院士、原中国科学院院长巴德年，中国工程院院士、广州医学院院长钟南山，中国工程院院士、中国中医研究院名誉院长王永炎共9人为天津市政府特聘专家。

2004年，天津市为特聘专家制度制定出实施细则、工作程序等配套办法，并聘请陈竺、邬贺铨等30位院士为特聘专家，成为天津市在农业科技、生物医药、基因工程、纳米技术、高温超导等领域顶尖科技领军人才。是年，袁隆平在天津经济技术开发区成立天隆生物基因工程有限公司，建立国家杂交水稻研究中心天津分中心，设立博士后科研工作站，集中人才、技术优势，深入开展杂交粳稻育种与栽培技术研究，精选的30个品种经过在津南国家农业园区进行品比试验，一些优良品种亩产接近800千克；法国干细胞之父、中国科学院外籍院士雅克·冈在天津建立实验室，推动法国科学院与天津市在人才培养、科技交流等方面进行长期合作。据统计，特聘专家与天津市有关单位合作，承担国家"863""973"等研究课题7项，培养研究生19人，作学术报告20场，有效促进了天津市相关领域的科学研究和高层次人才的培养。

2005年，天津市政府首次聘请两位诺贝尔经济学奖获得者，德国科学院院士、欧洲经济学会主席、波恩大学教授莱茵哈德·泽尔滕和英国科学院院士、美国艺术与科学院院士、剑桥大学教授詹姆斯·莫里斯为特聘外籍专家，并聘请中国水产科学研究院黄海水产研究所名誉所长赵法箴、所长唐启升，中国石油化工股份有限公司高级副总裁曹湘洪，国家环保局气候影响研究中心总工程师任阵海，同济大学土木工程学院院长项海帆，国家海洋局杭州水处理技术研究开发中心研究员高从堦等6名中国工程院院士为特聘专家。至此，天津市政府共聘请47位国内外著名专家为特聘专家。特聘专家制度以柔性流动的方式，为农业经济、生物医药、干细胞基因工程、纳米科技、高温超导、石油化工、海洋经济等领域引进一批顶尖科技领军人才，有力推动天津科技进步和高新技术产业化的进程。

二、引进国外智力

1991年，国务院授权国家外国专家局设立中国政府友谊奖，以表彰在中国现代化建设和改革开放事业中作出突出贡献的外国专家。由市科委和新加坡亿智企业集团分别出资775万元于1984年成立的天津国际科技咨询公司，是天津市乃至全国成立最早的中外合资智力型企业之一。该公司与国内外相关机构建立了广泛的合作关系，承接多方面技术交流与技术转移专项任务，为各级政府及国内外企事业单位提供各种重要咨询服务项目达1000余项，并与有关方面合作举办各种学术报告会、专题研讨会和专业知识培训班。其所属的天津科技大厦接待了国内外众多专家学者和八方来客。杜亿春和杜万龄父子两代新加坡籍华裔专家对该公司的建设做出了积极贡献。1988年10月，天津市副市长张立昌向天津国际科技咨询公司副董事长杜亿春颁发了"荣誉市民"证书。1994年9月，国家外国专家局向杜万龄颁发了"友谊奖"。

1991～2000年，天津市围绕重点科技攻关、高新技术开发、高新技术产业化、农业技术现代化、引进技术国产化等方面，引进国外技术、管理专家1638人，派出专业技术人员和管理人员出国（境）培训3961人，为促进经济、科技、社会发展提供人才智力保障。

2001年，引进国外智力工作由市科委转入市人事局。是年，共引进外国专家1311人，其中经济专家242人，文教专家679人，技术、管理专家390人；全市选派各类出国（境）培训团组124个、858人；经中国外国专家局批准，天津市2名外籍专家毛焕宇和罗伯特·迪盖特获得外国人在华最高荣誉奖——国家"友谊奖"，30名在经济建设、社会发展和科技进步中做出突出贡献的外国专家获得天津市"海河奖"称号。

2002年，建立天津市引进国外智力专家咨询委员会，并先后出台《天津市出国（境）培训管理暂行办法》《关于加强对有资格组团赴国（境）外培训的社会团体开展出国（境）培训工作管理的通知》。是年，经市引进国外智力专家咨询委员会评审，引进外国专家1095人，其中经济专家282人，文教专家423人，技术、管理专家390人，资助引进外国专家经费370万元。经中国外国专家局批准，天津市三美电机有限公司总经理田村忠嗣和天津医科大学引进的外国专家乔丹·菲利普斯获得国家"友谊奖"。全年共执行出国（境）培训项目182个、1515人，资助培训经费201.8万元。

2003年，出台《天津市引进国外智力专项经费管理暂行办法》，规范引进国外智力专项经费的管理，推进引进国外智力工作的顺利开展。全年共引进外国专家828人,其中经济专家201人,文教专家310人,技术与管理专家317人;选派各类出国(境)培训团组120个、858人。天津市三星电子有限公司董事长兼总经理李博俊和新华—戴尔特国际商务专修学院教师白瑞经中国外国专家局批准,获得国家"友谊奖"。

2004年,天津市先后举办10余个高水平的国际研讨交流活动,组织30多家项目单位携带引进国外智力需求和引进国外智力成果参加一系列人才交流活动,并举办多期引智工作培训班,推进引进国外智力工作的开展。年内,共实施引智项目215项、引进外国专家519人次,出国(境)培训71项、838人。经层层筛选和认真评比,天津市畜牧兽医研究所等5家单位被命名为天津市引进国外智力成果示范推广基地,华立达生物工程有限公司等8家单位被命名为天津市引进国外智力示范单位。

2005年,共执行引进国外智力项目198项、聘请外国专家431人次,出国(境)培训43项、629人次。同时,举办天津市海外智力引进暨引智成果洽谈会,签订引智合作协议6项,达成引智合作意向41项;与美国休斯敦市签署开展人才智力交流协议,举办第二届意大利—中国(天津)格拉格里奥·卢兹奖男手缝西装设计制作大赛、第八届世界反病毒大会、国家信息化发展论坛等活动,引进国际相关领域的最新研究成果;编印天津市农业引智成果汇编,举办天津市农业引智成果大型推介洽谈会,推动农业引智成果的推广转化;推进引智示范基地和示范单位建设,市畜牧兽医研究所、协和干细胞基因工程有限公司分别被国家外国专家局被命名为"畜禽疫病免疫技术"国家引进国外智力成果示范推广基地和"干细胞工程产品产业化"国家引进国外智力示范单位。同年7月,天津市外国专家局成立,并出台《天津市引智许可工作实施细则(试行)》《天津市办理〈外国专家证〉工作管理办法(试行)》,初步建立天津市引进国外智力许可工作的政策体系。该局举办引进国外智力行政许可工作培训班,培训90余人,并为65位外国专家办理到华工作许可,为260人办理"外国专家证"。摩托罗拉天津总经理委员会主席倪铭声获得2005年度国家"友谊奖"。

三、吸引留学人员到天津工作

1991年起,天津市制定一系列政策规定,积极吸引留学人员到天津工作。2001年,天津市颁布《关于鼓励海外留学人员来津工作或为津服务的若干规定》,对到天津工作或为天津服务的海外留学人员,在政治上高度信任,在报酬、科研、生活等方面十分关心,制定并实施更加优惠的政策。2002年,天津市出台《关于落实〈关于鼓励海外留学人员来津工作或为津服务的若干规定〉有关问题的通知》,成立天津市留学生创业园,组织海外人才招聘团前往美国和加拿大开展招聘活动,300余名留学人员与用人单位达成意向到天津工作或为天津服务,73人当场决定到天津工作。据对全市44个重点单位统计,是年共有347名海外留学人员正式办理在津落户手续。

2003年,天津市采取多种措施,大力吸引海内外人才。一是进一步完善吸引人才的相关政策,出台《关于为已加入外国籍高层次留学人才办理长期多次入境签证、外国人居留证有关问题的通知》,方便外籍高层次留学人才到津工作,增强天津市对高层次人才的吸引力。二是建立海外人才交流工作站,进一步扩大与海外的联系。三是积极主动招聘人才,分别组织赴日本人才招聘团和赴东北人才招聘团。全年办理到津手续的海外留学人才9000余人,其中硕士以上学历1500多人,具有大学本科以上学历或中级职称的7500多人。四是开展评选表彰天津市优秀留学人员和留学回国人员工作先进单位活动。天津市推荐上报的郭治昕、洪浩、陆敏、沈中阳、魏大鹏、赵海山和天津新技术产业园区留学生创业园分别被评为全国留学回国人员先进个人和先进单位。经逐级推荐、评审,选出10名"天津市杰出留学人员"、75名"天津市优秀留学人员"和10个"天津市留学回国人员工作先进单位",市委、市政府予以表彰。

2004年,天津市出台《关于进一步加强留学回国人员工作的意见》,印发《关于对来津高层次留学人才随归子女给予中考加分有关事宜的通知》,并组成天津市海外人才招聘团,携带100多个专业、500多个关键岗位、198项海外合作项目、78项引智需求项目,先后到英国、德国、法国等国开展海外人才招聘和项目合作洽谈,1030余位留学人员和外国专家到场洽谈,与316人达成到天津工作或为天津服务意向,决定到天津工作的留学人员70人,达成经济、科技合作意向29项,引智合作意向34项。为拓宽引进海外人才通道,新建4个海外人才交流工作站。市人事局会同有关部门组织开展“海外学人回国创业周”和“留学回国人员创新创业推动会”“留学生创业园建设交流会”等活动，加强与海外人才的沟通与交流，吸引他们到天津创业。积极申报国家留学回国人员科技活动择优资助项目，全市共有7项获得批准，获资助经费42万元。是年，天津科技大学王硕获得国家首次设立的高层次留学人才回国工作资助经费30万元。在天津市人才工作会议上，市委、市政府表彰75名杰出和优秀的留学回国人员、10个留学回国人员工作先进单位。

2005年8月19日至9月26日，市人事局会同教育部留学服务中心等主办“中国天津海外人才智力网上招聘暨项目合作洽谈会”。10月26日至11月10日，天津市海外人才招聘团参加第六届北美中国留学人才交流洽谈大会，先后与400多位留学人才进行交流洽谈，并与166位高层次人才签订到天津工作或为天津服务的初步意向，达成人才交流和科技合作意向26项。为使回国留学人员增加对天津的了解，并寻找合作机会，分两批组织高等院校、科研院所和企业单位的50多名高层次留学回国人员参加“看津门、寻合作、促发展”活动。市人事局以人事部与天津市共建中国天津留学人员创业园为契机，撰写“加强留学人员创业园建设的对策措施调研报告”，加强留学人员创业园建设研究。

四、博士后工作

1985年，中国开始试行博士后制度，天津大学、南开大学成为全国第一批设立博士后科研流动站的高校。1998年，全国博士后管理委员会下发《关于批准36家企业扩大开展博士后试点工作的通知》，其中包括中国石油天然气股份有限公司大港油田公司、天津药业有限公司分别设立博士后科研工作站。自此，天津市博士后工作的领域从高校延伸到企业。

2001年，人事部和全国博士后管理委员会批准天津市新增博士后流动站7个，包括天津大学3个，南开大学2个，河北工业大学2个；新增中环电子信息集团有限公司、新技术产业园区、天大天财股份有限公司、和平海湾电源集团公司、力神电池股份有限公司等14个企业博士后工作站。至年底，全市博士后流动站增至32个，博士后科研工作站28个，在站博士近200人。

2002年，出台《天津市2003～2005年博士后工作规划》《天津市博士后管理实施细则》，进一步明确博士后工作的发展目标、工作思路和具体措施，并开始每年从天津市人才发展基金中专门划拨200万元，用于支持博士后科研流动站的招收博士后工作。当年各站共招收博士130人，在站总数达230人。“中国博士后（天津）公寓” 项目建设启动，完成投资800万元。是年，中国汽车技术研究中心、中船总公司七〇七研究所等11个单位被批准建站，全市博士后科研流动站和工作站达到71个。

2003年，天津市出台《关于对国内优秀博士到天津市博士后设站单位进行考察、洽谈给予资助的试行办法》《关于资助选派优秀博士后赴欧洲发达国家培训考察及开展合作研究的试行办法》，决定每年选派30名优秀博士后到英、德、法等国家学习前沿科技知识，进一步完善吸引优秀博士到天津做博士后的政策措施。中国（天津）博士后公寓竣工，博士后工作的软硬环境得到进一步改善，从而增强吸引国内外博士的能力。年内，组织60家设博士后流动站、工作站的单位，精心选择100多个专业的合作项目，赴北京大学举办“天津市招收博士后和各类优秀人才洽谈会”，吸引60余名博士达成进站意向。同时，先后组织两次“博士后津门行”活动，并组织天津大学、南开大学部分博士后深入宁河天尊酒厂和宁河种猪场，就企业改制、创立现代营销体制、资本运作等问题，与企业负责人进行深入的探讨与交流。是年，举办“京津两地博士后津门行”活动，组织北京大学、清华大学、天津大学、南开大学等高校61位博士后聚集津门，考察力神电池、天大天财等高新技术企业，就项目合作、人才交流等问题进行深入洽谈，其中10多位博士后当场与相关企业达成合作意向。年内，9所高校获准新建16个博士后科研流动站，18家企业获准建立博士后科研工作站，全市博士后流动站、工作站总数达105个，新进站博士179人，在站博士增至353人。

2004年，天津市组织设博士后流动站和工作站的单位到北京大学、清华大学举办两场洽谈会，与近200名博士达成到天津工作的意向，并先后5次组织设站单位进行业务培训和交流，进一步提高管理水平。天津经济技术开发区和新技术产业园区新增11个博士后科研工作站。至此，全市博士后流动站、工作站总数达

116个，其中工作站达68个，在站博士达到450人。积极选派优秀博士后出国培训，首批选拔的30名博士后获得资助245万元，分赴欧洲8个国家、26所大学进行为期3个月的学习培训或开展合作研究。中国天津博士后公寓入住率达到90%，为博士后学习、科研提供良好生活环境。

2005年，天津市继续扩大博士后科研工作站建站规模，博士后科研流动站、工作站总数达141个，其中博士后科研流动站48个，博士后科研工作站93个。继续选拔博士赴国外深造，30名在站博士分赴欧洲8个国家、29所世界著名大学、科研机构进行为期3个月的考察培训和合作研究。在天津经济技术开发区的国家计算机病毒应急处理中心等5家企业建立首批博士后创新实践基地，为区县和中小企业搭建吸引、聚集高层次人才的平台。博士后工作基础性研究得到加强，其中"天津市企业博士后工作现状、问题及解决途径"课题获人事部优秀调研课题二等奖。至2005年，全市在站博士共承担国家"863"和"973"项目、国家科技攻关项目、国家自然科学基金项目等国家级科研项目186项，承担省部级科研项目318项；在国内核心期刊发表论文1423篇，出版专著140部，其中被EI、CSSCI、SCI等检索收录1170篇。在全国优秀博士后表彰暨博士后工作会议上，天津市5个设站单位分别被授予"全国优秀博士后科研流动站"和"全国优秀博士后科研工作站"称号，4人荣获"全国优秀博士后"和"全国优秀博士后管理工作者"称号。

第三章　科学研究与技术开发机构

1991年起，随着科技体制改革的逐步深入，天津市在不同时期分别对科研机构进行调整和改革，不断完善科研机构布局，积蓄科研力量，充实和调整科研队伍，科研实力不断增强。至2005年，天津市共有县及县以上独立科学研究与技术开发机构167个，大中型工业企业兴办的技术开发机构195个，高等院校属研究与试验发展机构153个；国家有关部门驻津科研机构共有46家；民营科技企业增至8000多个。各类科学研究与技术开发机构的组建与发展，成为推动科技进步和经济社会发展的中坚力量。

第一节　市属与中央驻津科研机构

1991年，市属自然科学技术领域的研究与开发机构有106个，其中市科委属7个；按学科领域分，自然科学1个、工程科学技术89个、医学科学4个、农业科学12个；职工总数17519人，从事科技活动人员13350人，其中科学家和工程师5704人；经费收入2.87亿元，其中政府拨款0.82亿元；经费支出2.78亿元；完成横向技术合同1529项，成交金额0.26亿元。至1995年，市属科研机构仍为106个，职工总数15185人，其中科学家和工程师5914人；经费收入6.03亿元，经费支出5.87亿元；签订技术合同1409项，成交金额1.15亿元。1998年，天津市编制委员会办公室出台《关于科研事业单位机构设置、变更审批有关事项的通知》，对科研机构设置、变更审批作出规定。

至2000年，市属科研机构调整为104个，从业人员9772人，从事科技活动人员6152人，其中科学家和工程师3834人；科技活动经费筹集额6.23亿元，其中政府拨款1.32亿元；科技活动经费内部支出额6.46亿元；承担课题1110个，其中当年开题560个，当年完成655个。

至2005年底，经过机构调整，市属自然科学研究与技术开发机构为108家，其中公益类科研机构41家，开发类科研机构(已企业化转制的科研机构)67家;国家有关部门驻天津科研机构共有46家。科学研究与技术开发机构围绕科技进步和经济建设的需要,承担并完成一批国家和天津市重大科研项目,成为促进科技进步和经济发展的主力军。

一、市属科研机构

(一)市属公益类科研机构

2001年起,天津市进一步加快市属科研院所管理体制改革,将市属科研院所划分为公益类科研机构和开发类科研机构。至2002年,经过机构改革,市属科研机构中划分出41家公益类科研机构,其主要分布于农业、计量、检测、标准、信息服务、医药卫生、环境、环卫、水利、建筑等领域,其中社会公益研究类15家,检测等技术基础类8家、科技信息类3家\农业类15家。公益类科研机构主要承担国家和地方及有关企业委托的产品质量检测、技术标准制定和城市环境、信息服务、农业发展等社会公益任务,为天津的城市可持续发展、产品质量等提供可靠保证。

2002年,41家市属公益类科研机构的人员编制为4153人,在职职工3284人,占总编制数的79.07%;离退休人员1634人;科研机构下属经济实体职工606人,其中科研机构编制内职工362人,占科研机构在职职工总数的11.67%。41家公益类科研机构完成各类课题448项,获得各类科技成果奖励54项,为经济建设提供各类公益性服务1384项。41家公益类科研机构总收入为2.47亿元。其中:政府拨款收入0.89亿元(其中事业费收入0.73亿元),占总收入的36.04%;非政府资金收入1.58亿元,占总收入的63.96%。41家公益类科研机构中,经费自给率超过50%的有21家,有6家科研机构的年收入超过千万元。

至2005年,41家市属公益类科研机构共有从业人员7821人,其中从事科技活动人员5106人,高级职称人员1589人,中级职称人员1502人;离退休人员9198人;固定资产10.23亿元,年技工贸总收入8.61亿元;科技经费筹集额5.62亿元,其中政府资金1.84亿元,非政府资金3.78亿元(其中技术性收入3.69亿元);生产经营活动收入2.37亿元,其中产品销售收入2.04亿元;用于离退休人员的政府拨款为4590万元;出口创汇收入103.8万美元;资产总额19.3亿元,其中流动资产7.14亿元,固定资产10.23亿元;负债总额8.75亿元;承担课题数合计876个,经费内部支出1.99亿元;R&D(research and development,研究与开发)课题数合计343个,经费内部支出1.1亿元;R&D内部支出2.13亿元;发表科技论文798篇;专利申请受理数54件,其中发明专利24件;专利授权26件,拥有发明专利80件;公益类科研机构办经济实体91个,从业人员2641人,全年总收入2.69亿元,全年利税总额3547万元,上缴税金1218万元,出口创汇278万美元。

2005年天津市属公益类科研机构一览表

表1-3-1-12

序号	科研机构名称	主管单位	机构变更情况
1	天津市科学技术信息研究所	市科委	—
2	天津市科学学研究所	市科委	—
3	天津市科技统计与发展研究中心	市科委	2004年由天津市社会发展工程研究所更名
4	天津市农村经济与区划研究所	天津市农业科学院	—
5	天津市土壤肥料研究所	天津市农业科学院	—
6	天津科润农业科技股份有限公司蔬菜研究所	天津市农业科学院	—
7	天津市畜牧兽医研究所	天津市农业科学院	—
8	天津市农作物研究所	天津市农业科学院	—
9	天津市植物保护研究所	天津市农业科学院	—
10	天津市林业果树研究所	天津市农业科学院	—

续表1-3-1-12

序号	科研机构名称	主管单位	机构变更情况
11	天津市农业科学院中心实验室	天津市农业科学院	—
12	天津市农业科学院信息研究所	天津市农业科学院	—
13	天津科润农业科技股份有限公司黄瓜研究所	天津市农业科学院	—
14	天津市农业生物技术研究中心	天津市农业科学院	—
15	天津市园艺工程研究所	天津市农业科学院	—
16	天津市奶牛发展中心	天津市农业科学院	由天津市奶牛研究所更名
17	天津市乳品食品监测中心	天津市农垦集团总公司	—
18	天津市农业机械研究所	天津市农业机械局	—
19	天津市水产研究所	天津市水产集团有限公司	—
20	天津市水利科学研究所	天津市水利局	—
21	天津市电子仪表实验所	天津市电子仪表工业总公司	由天津市电子仪表质量中心试验室更名
22	天津市自行车研究所	天津市一轻集团(控股)有限公司	—
23	天津市轻工标准计量检测所	天津市二轻集团(控股)有限公司	—
24	天津市地毯研究所	天津市二轻集团(控股)有限公司	—
25	天津渤海化工集团公司劳动卫生研究所	天津市渤海化工集团公司	—
26	天津市电工技术科学研究院	天津市机电工业控股集团公司	由天津市电器研究所更名
27	天津市检测技术研究所	天津市机电工业控股集团公司	—
28	天津市市政(公路)工程研究院	天津市市政工程局	—
29	天津市房产住宅科学研究所	天津市住宅建设发展集团有限公司	—
30	天津市园林绿化研究所	天津市园林局	—
31	天津市环境保护科学研究院	天津市环境保护局	—
32	天津市公用事业设计研究所	天津市自来水集团有限公司	—
33	天津市计量技术研究所	天津市质量技术监督局	—
34	天津市市容环境工程设计研究所	天津市市容管理委员会	—
35	天津市劳动卫生职业病研究所	天津市卫生局	—
36	天津市医学科学技术信息研究所	天津市卫生局	—
37	天津市医药科学研究所	天津市卫生局	—
38	天津市刑事科学技术研究所	天津市公安刑侦局	—
39	天津市人防建筑科研设计院	天津市政府人防办公室	—
40	天津市体育科学研究所	天津市体育局	—
41	天津市计划生育研究所	天津市人口与计划生育委员会	—

(二)市属开发类科研机构

2001年起，天津市不断深化科技体制改革，对部分市属科研机构实行企业化转制，将其调整为开发类科研机构。至2005年，市属开发类科研机构共有67家。开发类科研机构中，共有从业人员4460人，其中从事科技活动人员2395人；离退休人员7173人；年收入总额4.26亿元；科技经费筹集额1.92亿元，其中政府资金0.24亿元；非政府资金1.67亿元，其中技术性收入1.66亿元；生产经营活动收入2.17亿元，其中产品销售收入1.89亿元；用于离退休人员的政府拨款为1148万元；出口创汇收入1038万美元；资产总额10.72亿元，其中流动资产4.06亿元，固定资产5.17亿元；负债总额6.54亿元；承担课题数合计313项，经费内部支出4.07亿元；R&D课题数合计102项；R&D经费内部支出0.67亿元；发表科技论文165篇；专利申请受理数26件，其中发明专利8件；专利授权12件，拥有发明专利合计21件；市属开发类科研机构办经济实体62个，从业人员2095人，全年总收入2.08亿元，全年利税总额1828万元，上缴税金857万元，出口创汇278万美元。

2005年天津市属开发类科研机构一览表

表1-3-1-13

序号	机构名称	隶属关系	机构变迁情况
1	天津市制造业信息化生产力促进中心	市科委	由天津市计算中心更名
2	天津市半导体研究所（理化分析中心）	市科委	—
3	天津市技术物理研究所	市科委	—
4	天津市实验动物中心	市科委	—
5	天津市激光技术研究所	市科委	—
6	天津市机械研究设计院	天津市机电工业控股集团公司	—
7	天津市机械研究所	天津市机电工业控股集团公司	—
8	天津市热处理研究所	天津市机电工业控股集团公司	—
9	天津市焊接研究所	天津市机电工业控股集团公司	—
10	天津市石化通用机械研究所	天津市机电工业控股集团公司	—
11	天津市机械涂层研究所	天津市机电工业控股集团公司	—
12	天津市机床研究所	天津市机电工业控股集团公司	—
13	天津市工具研究所	天津市机电工业控股集团公司	—
14	天津市数控及传动技术应用研究所	天津市机电工业控股集团公司	—
15	天津市电材工业研究所	天津市机电工业控股集团公司	—
16	天津市碟桥包装食品机械研究所	天津市机电工业控股集团公司	由天津市包装食品机械研究所更名
17	天津市机电工业科技信息研究所	天津市机电工业控股集团公司	—
18	天津市电子计算机研究所	天津市电子仪表工业总公司	—
19	天津市工业自动化仪表研究所	天津市电子仪表工业总公司	—
20	天津市电视技术研究所	天津市电子仪表工业总公司	—
21	天津市电子仪表信息研究所	天津市电子仪表工业总公司	—
22	天津市电子仪器技术研究所	天津市电子仪表工业总公司	—
23	天津市电子计算机应用技术研究所	天津市电子仪表工业总公司	—
24	天津市化工科技信息研究所	天津市渤海化工集团公司	—
25	天津市合成材料工业研究所	天津市渤海化工集团公司	—
26	天津市橡胶工业研究所	天津市渤海化工集团公司	—
27	天津市染料工业研究所	天津市渤海化工集团公司	—
29	天津市化学试剂研究所	天津市渤海化工集团公司	—
30	天津市第一轻工业局科技信息研究室	天津市一轻集团（控股）有限公司	2003年并入天津市自行车研究所，但仍为独立事业法人机构
31	天津市硅酸盐研究所	天津市一轻集团（控股）有限公司	—
32	天津市硬质合金研究所	天津市一轻集团（控股）有限公司	—
33	天津市轻工业化学研究所	天津市一轻集团（控股）有限公司	—
34	天津市工业微生物研究所	天津市一轻集团（控股）有限公司	—

续表1-3-1-13

序号	机构名称	隶属关系	机构变迁情况
35	天津市界面与胶体科学研究所	天津市一轻集团(控股)有限公司	—
36	天津市玻璃研究所	天津市一轻集团(控股)有限公司	—
37	天津市轻工业造纸技术研究所	天津市环球磁卡集团	—
38	天津市印刷技术研究所	天津市环球磁卡集团	—
39	天津市化妆品科学技术研究院	天津市美伦医药集团	—
40	天津市第二轻工业局技术经济情报研究所	天津市二轻集团(控股)有限公司	—
41	天津市轻工装备研究所	天津市二轻集团(控股)有限公司	—
42	天津市工艺美术研究所	天津市二轻集团(控股)有限公司	与天津市地毯研究所合并,仍为独立事业法人机构
43	天津市五金工具研究所	天津市二轻集团(控股)有限公司	—
44	天津市家具技术研究所	天津市二轻集团(控股)有限公司	—
45	天津市资信家用电器研究所	天津市二轻集团(控股)有限公司	—
46	天津市塑料研究所	天津市塑料集团有限公司	—
47	天津市纺织装饰品研究所	天津市纺织集团(控股)有限公司	—
48	天津市纺织机械器材研究所	天津市纺织集团(控股)有限公司	—
49	天津市服装研究所	天津市纺织集团(控股)有限公司	与天津市纺织服装研究院合并,仍为独立事业法人机构
50	天津市纺织服装研究院	天津市纺织集团(控股)有限公司	由天津市纺织工业研究所更名
51	天津市化学纤维研究所	天津市纺织集团(控股)有限公司	—
52	天津市丝绸技术研究所	天津市纺织集团(控股)有限公司	—
53	天津市针织技术研究所	天津市纺织集团(控股)有限公司	—
54	天津市毛纺织技术研究所	天津市纺织集团(控股)有限公司	—
55	天津市医疗器械研究所	天津市医药集团有限公司	—
56	天津市食品研究所	天津市二商集团有限公司	—
57	天津市调味品研究所	天津市二商集团有限公司	—
58	天津市冶金科技信息研究所	天津市冶金集团(控股)有限公司	—
59	天津市有色金属研究所	天津市有色金属集团有限公司	—
60	天津市粮油科学设计院	天津市粮油集团有限公司	由天津市粮油科学研究所更名
61	天津市农药研究所	南开大学	—
62	天津市建筑科学研究院	天津市建工集团(控股)有限公司	—
63	天津市建筑材料科学研究所	天津市建材集团(控股)有限公司	—
64	天津市交通科学技术研究所	天津市交通局	—
65	天津市汽车研究所	天津市汽车工业集团有限公司	—
66	天津市包装装潢研究所	天津市天马企业集团工业总公司	—
67	天津市光电子显示技术研究中心	天津新技术产业园区管理委员会	—

二、中央驻天津科研机构

1991年,参与天津市科技统计的中央驻津科研机构共有31家,职工总数11766人,其中科学家、工程师5969人,其他科技人员2662人;经费收入2.00亿元,经费支出1.89亿元;签定横向技术合同1347项,成交金额0.93亿元。

1995年,参与天津市科技统计的中央驻津科研机构共有34家,职工总数12095人,其中科学家、工程师6568人,其他科技人员2494人;经费收入5.78亿元,经费支出5.33亿元;签定技术合同907项,成交金额2.07亿元。

2000年,参与天津市科技统计的中央驻津科研机构共有36家,从业人员10752人,其中从事科技活动人员6404人,科学家和工程师4549人;科技活动经费筹集额8.46亿元,其中政府资金积累0.145亿元;科技活动经费内部支出7.56亿元。

至2005年,中央驻津科研机构共有46家,其中参与天津市科技统计的科研机构为33家。中央驻天津科研机构以承担国家重点科研项目为主,同时也为天津经济建设服务。据对33家驻天津科研机构统计,从业人员共计11865人,其中从事科技活动的5952人;离退休人员6434人;年收入总额397亿元;科技经费筹集额1758亿元,其中政府资金339亿元,非政府资金1416亿元,技术性收入3亿元;出口创汇33亿美元;内部支出总额353亿元;总资产合计747亿元,其中流动资产465亿元,固定资产212亿元;R&D人员合计2668人;R&D经费内部支出55亿元;发表科技论文1107篇;专利申请受理数160件,其中发明专利78件;专利授权数63件,其中发明专利18件;拥有发明专利总数166件。33家驻津科研机构创办经济实体43个,从业人员742人;全年总收入283亿元,其中产品销售收入205亿元;全年利润总额166亿元;上缴税金24亿元。33家驻津科研机构内设国家级(重点)实验室2个,国家级工程技术(研究)中心1个,地方重点实验室、工程技术(研究)中心2个,合建研究机构1个。

2005年中央驻天津科研机构一览表

表1-3-1-14

序号	机构名称	隶属关系
1	公安部天津消防科学研究所	公安部
2	农业部环境保护科研监测所	农业部
3	水利部电力工业部机电研究所	水利部
4	中水北方勘测设计研究有限责任公司工程技术研究院	中水北方勘测设计研究有限责任公司
5	中国市政工程华北设计研究院	中国建筑设计研究院
6	地质矿产部天津地质矿产研究所	地质矿产部
7	交通部天津水运工程科学研究所	交通部
8	天津航道勘查设计研究院	中国交通建设集团有限公司天津航道局
9	天津港湾工程研究所	中交第一航务工程局
10	中国医学科学院、中国协和医科大学血液学研究所血液病医院	中国医学科学院、中国协和医科大学
11	中国医学科学院放射医学研究所	中国医学科学院
12	中国医学科学院生物医学工程研究所	中国医学科学院
13	天津市气象科学研究所	天津市气象局
14	国家海洋信息中心	国家海洋局
15	国家海洋技术中心	国家海洋局
16	国家海洋局天津海水淡化与综合利用研究所	国家海洋局
17	中国地震局第一监测中心	中国地震局
18	中华全国供销合作总社天津再生资源研究所	中华全国供销合作总社
19	中国石油天然气集团公司工程技术研究院	中国石油天然气集团公司
20	中国包装科研测试中心	中国包装总公司
21	天津电气传动设计研究所	机械工业部

续表 1-3-1-14

序号	机构名称	隶属关系
22	天津工程机械研究院	中国机械工业集团公司
23	天津复印技术研究所	中国纺织机械(集团)有限公司
24	中国汽车技术研究中心	国务院国有资产监督管理委员会
25	机械工业部第五设计研究院	机械工业部
26	中钢集团天津地质研究院	中国中钢集团公司
27	天津化工研究设计院	中国化工建设总公司
28	中盐制盐工程技术研究院	中国盐业总公司
29	天津水泥工业设计研究院	中国非金属材料总公司
30	天津市电力科学研究院	天津市电力公司
31	天津药物研究院	天津市医药集团有限公司
32	天津市地质矿产测试中心	天津市地质矿产勘查开发局
33	核工业理化工程研究院	中国核工业集团公司
34	信息产业部电子第46研究所	信息产业部
35	信息产业部电子第18研究所	信息产业部
36	中国航天工业总公司三院8357所	中国航天工业总公司
37	中国航天工业总公司三院第8358研究所	中国航天工业总公司
38	中船重工集团第七研究院第707研究所	中船重工集团
39	国家教委天津内燃机研究所	国家教委
40	大港油田集团钻采工艺研究院	大港油田集团
41	渤海石油研究院	中国海洋石油渤海公司
42	中交第一航务工程勘察设计院	中交第一航务工程局
43	铁道第三勘测设计院	铁道部
44	天辰工程公司	中国化学工程集团公司
45	天津华北地质勘察局	天津市人民政府
46	天津修船技术研究所	中国船舶重工集团公司

第二节　高等院校

1991年起，特别是1995年以后，随着教育体制改革的不断深化，在天津高等院校发生较大变化。由于院校合并和隶属关系变更等原因，在天津的高等院校总数有所减少，但高等院校科技经费投入额和发表科技论文数量却有较大幅度提高。

1991年，在天津高等院校共有26个，其中国家教育委员会所属2个，国家其他部委所属6个，天津市所属18个。按学校类型划分，综合大学1个，理工学科院校10个，农林学科院校1个，医药学科院校3个，师范类院校4个，其他院校7个。高等院校中，科技活动人员24532人，其中高级职称人员5086人，中级职称人员8609人；研究与发展全时人员4114人年，其中高级职称人员1550人年，中级职称人员1677人年。理工农医学科研究与开发经费收入总额4787万元，其中科研事业费648万元，主管部门专项费562万元，国家计委、国家科委专项费235万元，国家自然科学基金308万元，国务院其他部门专项费602万元，省、市、自治区专项费820万元，企事业单位委托经费1377万元。理工农医学科研究与开发经费支出总额4082万元，内部支出经费3944万元。

至2005年，在天津高等院校共有19个，其中教育部所属2个，国家其他部委所属1个，天津市所属16个。高等院校中，科技活动人员12433人，其中科学家和工程师10506人；理工农医类学科科技活动人员8442人，其中科学家和工程师6534人；高等学校属科技活动机构153个，其中理工农医类学科科技活动机构103个，人文、社会科学类学科科技活动机构50个。理工农医类学科R&D人员全时当量3795人年，其中科学家和工程师3719人年。科技活动经费筹集额14.36亿元，其中理工农医类学科科技活动经费筹集额13.45亿元；理工农医类学科科技活动经费内部支出4.10亿元。

统计数据显示，在天津高等院校发表科技论文数量呈快速增长的态势。1996～2000年，在天津高等院校在国内发表科技论文19540篇，三系统（SCI、EI、ISTP）收录科技论文4255篇，其中：SCI发表论文2115篇、EI发表论文1284篇、ISTP发表论文856篇。

2001～2005年，在天津高等院校在国内发表科技论文37179篇，是前5年的1.90倍；三系统收录科技论文15162篇，是前5年的3.56倍；SCI发表论文6766篇，是前5年的3.20倍；EI发表论文5478篇，是前5年的4.27倍；ISTP发表论文2918篇，是前5年的3.41倍。

1991年、1995～2005年天津高等院校科技工作情况统计表

表1-3-2-15

年份	学校数	从事科技活动人员（人）	研究与开发经费拨入额（千元）	研究与开发经费支出额（千元）	研究与开发课题数（项）
1991	26	24532	49699	42348	2491
1995	24	24558	225149	169588	3760
1996	20	24578	210304	196845	3608
1997	20	25080	312304	320424	3485
1998	20	24078	293982	284094	3846
1999	20	25402	398961	341903	4105
2000	20	24671	506385	438001	4167
2001	19	10277	583807	490784	4689
2002	19	10920	654897	532889	5210
2003	19	11348	776259	645543	6423
2004	19	11713	1099727	736031	7348
2005	19	12433	1436371	1078138	8258

1996～2005年天津高等院校发表论文情况统计表

表1-3-2-16　　单位：篇

项目＼年份	1996	1997	1998	1999	2000	2001	2002	2003	2004	2005
国内发表科技论文数	3229	3280	3522	4570	4939	5433	6397	7541	8342	9466
三系统收录科技论文数	699	725	719	934	1178	1440	2070	2686	3439	5527
SCI	304	303	395	442	671	795	990	1277	1509	2195
EI	304	276	247	330	127	418	486	881	1302	2391
ISTP	91	146	77	162	380	227	594	528	628	941

第三节　企业技术开发机构

1991年，天津市共有规模以上大中型工业企业494个，其中有技术开发机构的企业280个，占企业总数的56.68%。企业创办技术开发机构304个，从事技术开发活动人员2.43万人，其中高级职称1863人，中级职称4759人；完成技术开发项目1093项。

1995年，全市有大中型工业企业770个，其中有研究与发展活动的企业117个，占企业总数的15.2%。企业办技术开发机构371个，从事技术开发活动人员2.94万人，其中具有高中级职称或大学本科以上学历人员5795人。

2000年，全市有大中型工业企业694个，其中有科技活动的企业311个，占企业总数的44.81%。企业办技术开发机构154个，占企业总数的22.19%；从事技术开发活动人员2.45万人，其中科学家和工程师5593人；技术开发经费内部支出总额20.54亿。1996～2000年，企业技术开发机构共完成技术开发项目12571项。

2005年，全市有大中型工业企业549个，企业办技术开发机构195个，占企业总数的35.52%，比2000年增加13个百分点。企业技术开发机构中，从事科技活动人员3.20万人，比2000年增加0.75万人；技术开发经费内部支出总额93.70亿元，是2000年经费支出总额的4.56倍。2001～2005年，企业技术开发机构共完成技术开发项目12062项。

1991年、1995～2005年天津市大中型工业企业技术开发机构情况统计表

表1-3-3-17

年份	企业办技术开发机构个数（个）	从事技术开发活动人员（万人）	技术开发经费支出总额（亿元）	技术开发项目数（项）
1991	304	2.43	3.47	1093
1995	371	2.94	10.60	1000
1996	278	3.52	10.89	1878
1997	258	3.49	12.37	2584
1998	274	3.51	12.49	2699
1999	234	3.26	11.43	2489
2000	154	2.45	20.54	2921
2001	174	2.30	24.00	2718
2002	185	2.30	29.20	2898
2003	148	2.70	42.70	3219
2004	198	2.70	67.40	1548
2005	195	3.20	93.70	1679

第四节　民营科技机构

1991年起，天津市不断研究和制定促进民营科技企业发展的政策，民营科技企业得到迅速发展。同时，积极探索促进试用于难以发挥作用的企业内技术开发机构的机制和政策。在化工局支持下，天津市大中华橡胶厂和几个化工厂进行试验，在开发新产品、发挥技术人员作用、增加效益方面取得效果，该厂开发的新鞋被国家乒乓球队选用。在全国民营科技企业大会上天津市大中华橡胶厂介绍了经验，国家科委主任宋健称赞“我小时候就穿这个牌子的鞋，真是老牌子新创造”。

1992年，市人事局、市科委紧跟国家科技体制改革的步伐，联合下发《关于集体、个体科研机构人事管理若干问题的暂行办法》，推动民营科技机构的健康发展。同时，市科委转发市职称改革办公室《关于企业考评专业技术职务工作的有关意见》，推进民办科技机构职称改革工作。至1992年底，全市民营科技机构发展到1283家，技工贸总收入实现14.7亿元。1993年，天津市科委转发国家科委、国家体改委《关于大力发展民营科技型企业若干问题的决定》等一系列政策文件，进一步促进民营科技企业的发展。

至1993年底，民营科技企业为2061家，比1992年增长2.2倍，其中高新技术企业1052家；集体企业1386家、占67.1%，私营企业201家、占9.8%，个体企业102家、占5%，国有民营企业292家、占14.2%，三资企业80家、占3.9%；民营科技企业中固定资产原值8.9亿元，比1992年增加10.2倍，流动资金4.2亿元，比1992年增加17.9倍；职工总数34031人，其中科技人员17618人、占52%，高中级科技人员10925人，占科技人员总数的62%；全年技工贸总收入27.8亿元，技术性收入3.5亿元，占技工贸总收入的12.4%，年度利税4.3亿元，人均利税1.3万元；在研科技项目2131项，当年完成1435项，获国家级奖励3项，省部级奖7项，地市级奖7项，专利104项；研究开发费用2.73亿元。

1994年，市科委下发《1993年度天津市民营科技企业基本情况的通知》，通报天津市民营科技企业发展的状况。此后，市科委每年均以文件的形式，下发当年民营科技企业工作要点，明确民营科技企业发展方向和目标，并对民营科技企业中科技人员的专业技术职称评定进行规范，促进民营科技企业的健康发展。1994年，天津市民营科技企业数增至2215家，居全国各省市的第八位。

1996～2000年，天津市认真贯彻落实全国民营科技企业工作会议精神，先后出台《天津市促进民营科技企业发展的若干规定》《天津市民营科技企业管理办法》等政策规定，支持和促进民营科技企业的发展。全市新增民营科技企业2031家，累计达到5600家；技工贸总收入累计965.41亿元，利税累计92.14亿元，分别比1991～2000年的170.09亿元和21.77亿元，提高4.68倍和3.23倍。

2001～2005年，市政府先后出台《关于鼓励支持和引导个体私营等非公有制经济发展若干问题的意见》《批转市科委关于促进天津市科技企业孵化器建设与发展意见的通知》《批转市科委关于加强天津市区县科技工作若干意见的通知》等一系列促进民营经济发展的政策法规，民营科技企业取得长足的发展。为提高民营科技企业整体创新能力，市科委积极鼓励更多的民营科技企业参与或申报天津市各类科技发展计划、国家科技型中小企业创新基金及国家重点新产品计划等项目，多渠道争取资金，加大研究开发投入，吸引区县政府和社会力量的投资，逐步形成以企业为主体的多元化投资体系。2005年，天津市设立科技型中小企业技术创新资金。当年支持100多个民营科技企业的技术创新项目，有力地支持天津市民营科技企业的技术创新活动。同时，市科委还积极组织民营科技企业申报国家中小企业创新基金项目。从2003年开始，市政府每年组织召开由企业、银行和科研单位参加的“金桥之友”联谊会，与农业银行天津市分行签订科技与金融合作促进科技成果转化的协议，建立向成长性好的科技型中小企业授信和专利抵押贷款等新型金融制度。

至2005年底，天津市民营科技企业累计建立8000多家，其中高新技术产业园区以外的民营科技企业为2377家。据对2377家民营科技企业统计，2005年其资产总额为474.78亿元，年总收入436.23亿元，净利润28.36亿元，上缴税金21.34亿元，分别是2001年的1.03倍、3.07倍、4.20倍、4.26倍和1.18倍；其中固定资产168.48亿元，流动资产267.99亿元；长期在职职工近11万人；人均总收入41.20万元，是2001年人均总收入的2.55倍；其中全年技术性收入32.60亿元，产品销售收入313.12亿元；出口创汇2.85亿美元。民营科技企业逐渐成为天津市新的经济增长点，其在天津区域经济中的地位和作用得到不断巩固和提升。

第四章　新型科技研发和服务机构

1991年起，天津市进一步加强重点实验室和科学研究中心建设，建立一批新型知识创新机构。1991年，天津市科技创业服务中心成立，成为天津市第一家科技企业孵化器。1994年成立北方技术交易市场。同年组建的国家工业水处理工程技术研究中心，成为天津市第一家国家级工程（技术）研究中心。此后，天津市先后启动企业技术开发中心和生产力促进中心建设。2001年起，天津市依托企业、高校和科研院所，通过认定、新建、升级等形式，按照新的体制和机制组建一批新型技术创新与服务机构。2003年，成立国家软件出口基地。至2005年，天津市共组建新型知识创新机构70个，新型技术创新机构191个，重点成果转移、转化与产业化机构（基地）128个，公共高新技术平台和公共科技服务机构20个。新型知识创新和技术创新机构的建立和发展，对相关行业和领域发挥重要作用。科技企业孵化器、生产力促进中心和区县特色产业科技园，聚集科技资源，实施重点攻关，加快科技成果转化，以科技引领科技型中小企业和区县特色产业发展。科技服务与中介机构以服务科技为宗旨，以科技网为纽带，推动科技基础条件资源共享，优化科技条件布局，对营造合理、有序的科技公共条件平台和社会公益研发平台起到重要作用。

第一节　新型知识创新机构

1991年，天津市在原有国家级重点实验室基础上，先后开放一批国家级重点实验室和国家部局级重点实验室，并于20世纪90年代末开始组建科学研究中心。2004年，天津市又开放40个市级重点实验室。至2005年，天津市共组建新型知识创新机构70个，其中国家级重点实验室5个，国家部局级重点实验室17个，市级重点实验室40个，科学研究中心8个。重点实验室和科学研究中心聚集一批高水平的科技人才，承担和完成大量高水平的基础研究、前瞻性高技术研究和公益性研究，为提高天津科技创新水平做出贡献。

一、重点实验室

（一）国家级重点实验室

1991年，天津市在元素有机化学国家重点实验室和内燃机燃烧学国家重点实验室对外开放的基础上，又先后开放化学工程联合国家重点实验室、实验血液学国家重点实验室。1995年，精密测试技术及仪器国家重点实验室开放。至2005年，天津市共开放5个国家级重点实验室。

天津国家级重点实验室一览表

表1-4-1-18

序号	名称	依托单位	开放时间（年）	主管部门
1	元素有机化学国家重点实验室	南开大学	1988	教育部
2	内燃机燃烧学国家重点实验室	天津大学	1989	教育部
3	化学工程联合国家重点实验室（精馏分离）	清华大学、天津大学、华东理工大学、浙江大学	1991	教育部

续表1-4-1-18

序号	名称	依托单位	开放时间(年)	主管部门
4	实验血液学国家重点实验室	中国医学科学院血液学研究所	1991	卫生部
5	精密测试技术及仪器国家重点实验室	天津大学、清华大学	1995	教育部

（二）国家部局级重点实验室

1994年，国家部局级重点实验室——天津大学先进陶瓷与加工技术重点实验室、南开大学生物活性材料重点实验室对外开放。此后的1995年、1996年、1997年，天津市分别开放2个、2个、3个国家部局级重点实验室。2000年以后，天津市又有8个国家部局级重点实验室对外开放，其中：2002年开放1个、2004年开放5个、2005年开放2个。至2005年，坐落在天津的17个国家部局级重点实验室开放。

天津国家部局级重点实验室一览表

表1-4-1-19

序号	名称	依托单位	开放时间(年)	主管部门
1	先进陶瓷与加工技术重点实验室	天津大学	1994	教育部
2	生物活性材料重点实验室	南开大学	1994	教育部
3	吸附分离功能高分子材料重点实验室	南开大学	1995	教育部
4	一碳化学与化工重点实验室	天津大学	1995	教育部
5	核心数学与组合数学重点实验室	南开大学	1996	教育部
6	农业环境与农产品安全重点开放实验室	农业部环境保护科研监测所	1996	农业部
7	光电信息技术科学重点实验室	天津大学、南开大学	1997	科技部
8	激素与发育重点实验室	天津医科大学	1997	卫生部
9	危重病急救医学重点实验室	天津市第一中心医院	1997	卫生部
10	国家环境保护恶臭污染防治重点实验室	天津市环境保护科学研究院	2002	国家环境保护总局
11	药代动力学与药效动力学重点实验室	天津药物研究院	2004	教育部
12	弱光非线性光子学材料及其先进制备技术重点实验室	南开大学	2004	教育部
13	电力系统仿真控制重点实验室	天津大学	2004	教育部
14	中空纤维膜材料与膜过程重点实验室	天津工业大学	2004	教育部
15	乳腺癌防治重点实验室	天津医科大学	2004	教育部
16	方剂学重点实验室	天津中医学院	2005	教育部
17	先进纺织复合材料重点实验室	天津工业大学	2005	教育部

（三）市级重点实验室

2004年，天津市共开放40个市级重点实验室，其中大多数重点实验室依托在高等院校。40个市级重点实验室中，共有科技人员1638人，其中高级职称1124人，中级职称269人；留学回国人员303人；总资产11.24亿元。

天津市级重点实验室一览表

表1-4-1-20

序号	实验室名称	依托单位	开放时间(年)
1	天津市信息光子材料与技术重点实验室	南开大学	2004
2	天津市农药科学重点实验室	南开大学	2004
3	天津市金属与分子基材料化学重点实验室	南开大学	2004
4	天津市微生物功能基因组学重点实验室	南开大学	2004

续表1-4-1-20

序号	实验室名称	依托单位	开放时间(年)
5	天津市城市生态环境修复与污染防治重点实验室	南开大学	2004
6	天津市光电子薄膜器件与技术重点实验室	南开大学	2004
7	天津市组合数学重点实验室	南开大学	2004
8	天津市生物与制药工程重点实验室	天津大学	2004
9	天津市先进制造技术与装备重点实验室	天津大学	2004
10	天津市港口与海洋工程重点实验室	天津大学	2004
11	天津市应用催化科学与工程重点实验室	天津大学	2004
12	天津市现代工程力学重点实验室	天津大学	2004
13	天津市低维功能材料物理制备技术重点实验室	天津大学	2004
14	天津市过程检测与控制重点实验室	天津大学	2004
15	天津市生物医学检测技术与仪器重点实验室	天津大学	2004
16	天津市建筑物理环境与生态技术重点实验室	天津大学	2004
17	天津市电力系统仿真控制重点实验室	天津大学	2004
18	天津市神经损伤变异与再生重点实验室	天津医科大学	2004
19	天津市肿瘤防治重点实验室	天津医科大学	2004
20	天津市泌尿外科基础医学重点实验室	天津医科大学	2004
21	天津市激素与发育重点实验室	天津医科大学	2004
22	天津市中药药理学重点实验室	天津中医学院	2004
23	天津市针灸学重点实验室	天津中医学院	2004
24	天津市食品营养与安全重点实验室	天津科技大学	2004
25	天津市工业微生物重点实验室	天津科技大学	2004
26	天津市制浆造纸重点实验室	天津科技大学	2004
27	天津市薄膜电子与通信器件重点实验室	天津理工大学	2004
28	天津市光电显示材料与器件重点实验室	天津理工大学	2004
29	天津市先进纺织复合材料重点实验室	天津工业大学	2004
30	天津市改性与功能纤维重点实验室	天津工业大学	2004
31	天津市中空纤维膜材料与膜过程重点实验室	天津工业大学	2004
32	天津市水产生态及养殖重点实验室	天津农学院	2004
33	天津市食品生物技术重点实验室	天津商学院	2004
34	天津市智能信号与图像处理重点实验室	中国民航学院	2004
35	天津市药代动力学与药效动力学重点实验室	天津药物研究院	2004
36	天津市农产品采后生理与贮藏保鲜重点实验室	天津市农业科学院	2004
37	天津市生物医学材料重点实验室	中国医学科学院生物医学工程研究所	2004
38	天津市农业环境与农产品安全重点实验室	农业部环境保护科研监测所	2004
39	天津市分子核医学重点实验室	中国医学科学院放射医学研究所	2004
40	天津市人工细胞重点实验室	天津市卫生局	2004

二、科学研究中心

1999年，天津市光电子联合科学研究中心成立，成为天津市组建的第一个科学研究中心。2000年，天津市又组建天津市干细胞科学研究中心、天津新药科学研究中心、天津市数字信息技术研究中心等3个科学研究中心。2001～2005年，又组建天津市中医药研究中心、天津市电动车辆研究中心、天津市农业生物技术研究中心、天津市功能基因组与生物芯片研究中心等4个科学研究中心。至2005年底，天津市共组建科学研究中心8个，有科技人员610人，其中高级职称268人；拥有总资产4.35亿元。大多数科学研究中心依托在高等院校和科研机构，充分发挥其应用基础研究的学科优势，聚集、培养一批国内外的优秀人才，开展未来经济和社会发展需要的应用基础性研究和重大科技攻关项目，为天津经济社会发展提供技术储备和后劲支撑。

天津科学研究中心一览表

表1-4-1-21

序号	研究中心名称	依托单位	组建时间（年）
1	天津市光电子联合科学研究中心	天津大学、南开大学	1999
2	天津市干细胞科学研究中心	中国医学科学院血液学研究所、天津医科大学附属肿瘤医院	2000
3	天津新药科学研究中心	天津药物研究院	2000
4	天津市数字信息技术研究中心	天津大学、天津津科电子有限公司	2000
5	天津市中医药研究中心	天津中医学院	2001
6	天津市电动车辆研究中心	天津市清源电动车辆有限公司	2001
7	天津市农业生物技术研究中心	天津市农科院、南开大学	2002
8	天津市功能基因组与生物芯片研究中心	天津生物芯片技术有限公司	2005

第二节　新型技术创新机构

1994年起，天津市开始组建工程（技术）研究中心和企业技术开发中心，并获得较快发展。至2005年，天津市共建成新型技术创新机构191家，其中国家级工程（技术）研究中心11家，市级工程（技术）研究中心18家；国家级企业技术中心12个，市级企业技术中心150个。工程（技术）研究中心作为技术创新体系的重要组成部分，以具有行业优势的转制科研院所、高等院校和骨干企业为依托，具有较强的科研开发实力和较高的技术水平，在相关行业、领域发挥重要的技术辐射和技术扩散作用。企业技术开发中心围绕工业企业在生产中遇到的重大技术和工艺问题开展研究，促进企业的科技进步和发展。

一、工程技术中心

（一）国家级工程（技术）研究中心

1994年，国家工业水处理工程技术研究中心成立，成为天津市第一家国家级工程（技术）研究中心。此后的1995～1997年，天津市相继组建国家城市给排水工程技术研究中心、农药国家工程研究中心、新型电源国家工程研究中心、国家消防工程技术研究中心等4家国家级工程（技术）研究中心。2002～2005年，天津市又先后组建国家干细胞工程技术研究中心、精馏技术国家工程研究中心、电气传动国家工程研究中心、国家农产品保鲜工程技术研究中心、计算机防病毒技术国家工程研究中心、重型技术装备国家工程研究中心等6

家国家级工程(技术)研究中心。至2005年,天津市共建成国家级工程(技术)研究中心11家。

天津国家级工程(技术)研究中心一览表

表1-4-2-22

序号	名　称	依托单位	组建年份	主管部门
1	国家工业水处理工程技术研究中心	天津化工研究设计院	1994	科技部
2	国家城市给排水工程技术研究中心	中国市政工程华北设计研究院	1995	科技部
3	农药国家工程研究中心	南开大学	1995	国家发改委
4	新型电源国家工程研究中心	中国电子科技集团公司第十八研究所	1996	国家发改委
5	国家消防工程技术研究中心	公安部天津消防科学研究所	1997	科技部
6	国家干细胞工程技术研究中心	中国医学科学院血液学研究所	2002	科技部
7	精馏技术国家工程研究中心	天津大学	2003	国家发改委
8	电气传动国家工程研究中心	天津电气传动设计研究所	2003	国家发改委
9	国家农产品保鲜工程技术研究中心	天津市农业科学院	2003	科技部
10	计算机防病毒技术国家工程研究中心	国家计算机防病毒应急处理中心	2004	国家发改委
11	重型技术装备国家工程研究中心	天津重型装备工程研究有限公司	2005	国家发改委

(二)市级工程(技术)研究中心

2000年,天津市开始组建市级工程(技术)研究中心。其中,2000年建成市级工程(技术)研究中心8家,2001年建成5家,2002年1家,2004年3家,2005年1家。至2005年,市级工程(技术)研究中心共有18家。

18家市级工程(技术)研究中心主要分布在装备制造业、现代农业、资源与环保、生物技术与现代医药、新能源与节能技术、石油化工与精细化工等领域,其全部采取企业化运作模式,其中独立一级企业法人型机构16家,独立二级企业法人型机构2家;17家工程(技术)研究中心在财务上独立核算。工程(技术)研究中心的经营形式多样化,其中以技术开发、推广和服务为主的工程中心8家,以产品研制、生产和销售为主的工程中心8家,以工程设计与承包为主的工程中心各1家。参与工程中心建设人员累计1004人,其中高级职称200人,中级职称149人;博士57人,硕士101人。2001～2005年,工程(技术)研究中心总投资2.54亿元,其中市财政投入0.34亿元;工程中心总资产5.67亿元;工程中心研发投入1.23亿元;工程中心承担国家级项目34项,市级项目85项,区县级、企业委托和自选项目545项;其中国家级项目资金0.24亿元,市级项目资金0.21亿元;获奖科技成果42项,发表论文384篇、专著30部;取得营业收入7.43亿元,净利润1.15亿元,上缴税金540万元,出口创汇75万美元;技术推广及转让辐射单位26861家,开展技术培训1062班(次)。

天津市级工程(技术)研究中心一览表

表1-4-2-23

序号	名称	依托单位	开放年份
1	天津市快速成型技术工程中心	天津市天大银泰科技有限公司	2000
2	天津市现代集成制造技术工程中心	天津市鼎成现代集成制造技术工程有限公司	2000
3	天津市农产品保鲜技术工程中心	天津绿达保鲜工程技术有限公司	2000
4	天津市蔬菜育种技术工程中心	天津科润农业科技股份有限公司	2000
5	天津市现代畜牧技术工程中心	天津市博仁畜牧技术有限责任公司	2000
6	天津市盐碱地生态绿化工程中心	天津市海岸盐碱地生态绿化工程有限公司	2000
7	天津市膜技术工程中心	天津膜天膜过滤工程有限公司	2000
8	天津市新型储能材料工程中心	天津和平海湾电源集团有限公司	2000
9	天津市工程机械传动工程中心	天津市精研工程机械传动有限公司	2001
10	天津市留学生应用生物工程中心	天津博实生物技术有限公司	2001

续表1-4-2-23

序号	名称	依托单位	开放年份
11	天津市机动车尾气催化净化工程中心	天津市环科机动车尾气催化净化技术有限公司	2001
12	天津市现代渔业技术工程中心	天津市海发珍品实业发展有限公司	2001
13	天津市中药现代化工程中心	天津中新药业集团股份有限公司	2001
14	天津市工业自动化及装备工程中心	天津七所机电一体化装备有限公司	2002
15	天津市食品加工工程中心	天津市食品加工工程中心	2004
16	天津市水稻技术工程中心	天津天隆农业科技有限公司	2004
17	天津市配电自动化工程中心	天津天传电控配电有限公司	2004
18	天津市高档有机颜料技术工程中心	天津理工产业股份有限公司	2005

二、企业技术中心

(一)国家级企业技术中心

20世纪90年代末,天津市开始组建国家级企业技术开发中心,以帮助企业解决生产中的重大技术和工艺问题。至2005年,天津市共建成国家级企业技术中心12家。

天津国家级企业技术中心一览表

表1-4-2-24

序号	名称	序号	名称
1	天津渤海化工集团公司技术中心	7	天津汽车工业(集团)有限公司技术中心
2	天津天士力集团技术中心	8	中国石化集团天津石油化工公司技术中心
3	天津药业研究院有限公司技术中心	9	天津灯塔涂料有限公司技术中心
4	乐金电子(天津)电器有限公司技术中心	10	天津中新药业集团股份有限公司技术中心
5	鼎盛工程机械有限公司技术中心	11	中法合营王朝葡萄酿酒有限公司技术中心
6	天津钢管集团有限公司技术中心	12	天津赛象科技股份有限公司技术中心

(二)市级企业技术中心

1999年,天津市开始创建市级企业技术开发中心。至2005年,天津市共建成市级企业技术中心150个。

天津市级企业技术中心一览表

表1-4-2-25

序号	企业技术中心名称	序号	企业技术中心名称
1	天津市天锻压力机有限公司技术中心	14	特变电工变压器有限公司技术中心
2	泵业机械集团技术中心	15	帕金斯动力(天津)有限公司技术中心
3	特精液压股份有限公司技术中心	16	天津市天发重型水电设备制造有限公司技术中心
4	天津第一机床总厂技术中心	17	天津光电通信技术有限公司技术中心
5	天津减速机股份有限公司技术中心	18	天津仪表集团有限公司技术中心
6	鼎盛工程机械有限公司技术中心	19	天津通信广播集团有限公司技术中心
7	天津动力机厂技术中心	20	天津六O九厂电缆有限公司技术中心
8	天津金山电线电缆股份有限公司技术中心	21	天津广播器材公司技术中心
9	天津机电控股集团技术中心	22	天津市中环半导体股份有限公司技术中心
10	天津起重设备有限公司技术中心	23	天津市中环电子计算机公司技术中心
11	天津市鼓风机总厂技术中心	24	天津中环三津有限公司技术中心
12	百利环保装备集团有限公司技术中心	25	天津市天佳电子有限责任公司技术中心
13	天津市百利电气有限公司技术中心	26	天津三星电机有限公司技术中心

续表1-4-2-25

序号	企业技术中心名称	序号	企业技术中心名称
27	天津真美电声器材有限责任公司技术中心	69	天津诺曼地橡胶有限公司技术中心
28	天津三星视界有限公司技术中心	70	天津长芦汉沽盐场有限责任公司技术中心
29	天津实发集团有限公司技术中心	71	天津药业集团有限公司技术中心
30	天津华一有限责任公司技术中心	72	天津天士力集团技术中心
31	天津蓝天集团股份有限公司技术中心	73	天津中新药业集团股份有限公司技术中心
32	天津天女化工集团股份有限公司技术中心	74	天津市中央药业有限公司技术中心
33	天津津酒集团有限公司技术中心	75	天津华立达生物工程有限公司技术中心
34	天津中鸥表业(集团)有限公司技术中心	76	天津同仁堂股份有限公司技术中心
35	天津郁美净集团有限公司技术中心	77	中美天津史克制药有限公司技术中心
36	华润雪花啤酒(中国)有限公司技术中心	78	天津新新制药厂技术中心
37	天津市隆庆集团轻工控股有限公司技术中心	79	中新药业集团股份有p蜙司第六中药厂技术中心
38	乐金电子(天津)电器有限公司技术中心	80	中国大冢制药有限公司技术中心
39	天津福亚实业有限公司技术中心	81	天津东亚毛纺厂集团有限公司技术中心
40	天津环球磁卡公司技术中心	82	天津纺织集团天一有限公司技术中心
41	天津万华股份有限公司技术中心	83	天津纺织集团有限公司技术中心
42	天津塑料集团技术中心	84	天津市北洋纺织有限公司技术中心
43	天津汽车工业(集团)有限公司技术中心	85	天津市赛远保健品有限公司技术中心
44	天津汽车模具有限公司技术中心	86	天津市健龙保健品有限公司技术中心
45	天津市汽车灯厂技术中心	87	中法合营王朝葡萄酿酒有限公司技术中心
46	天津天德减震器有限公司技术中心	88	天津海河乳业有限公司技术中心
47	天津市轧三制钢有限公司技术中心	89	天津红港绿茵花草有限公司技术中心
48	天津市轧一制钢有限公司技术中心	90	天津远洋龙达玻璃制品有限公司技术中心
49	天津钢线钢缆集团有限公司技术中心	91	上海烟草(集团)天津卷烟厂技术中心
50	天津市冶金集团(控股)有限公司技术中心	92	天津灯塔涂料有限公司技术中心
51	天津钢管集团有限公司技术中心	93	凯莱英医药化学(天津)有限公司技术中心
52	天津天铁冶金集团有限公司技术中心	94	天津中集北洋集装箱有限公司技术中心
53	天津钢铁集团有限公司技术中心	95	天津斯坦雷电气有限公司技术中心
54	天津有色金属集团有限公司技术中心	96	天津市金桥焊材有限公司技术中心
55	大港油田集团有限责任公司技术中心	97	天津南开戈德集团有限公司技术中心
56	大港油田集团中成机械制造有限公司技术中心	98	天大天财股份有限公司技术中心
57	大港油田集团新世纪机械制造有限公司技术中心	99	天津力神电池股份有限公司技术中心
58	天津市华孚油田化学有限公司技术中心	100	天津赛象科技股份有限公司技术中心
59	天津石油化工公司技术中心	101	天津赛恩投资集团有限公司技术中心
60	天津渤海化工集团公司技术中心	102	海泰数码科技有限公司技术中心
61	天津海豚炭黑有限公司技术中心	103	中海油田服务股份有限公司技术中心
62	天津海豚橡胶集团公司技术中心	104	天津塑力线缆集团有限公司技术中心
63	天津长芦海晶集团有限公司技术中心	105	天津勤美达工业有限公司技术中心
64	天津有机化学工业总公司技术中心	106	天津市三源电力设备制造有限公司技术中心
65	天津市乳胶厂技术中心	107	天津美伦医药集团有限公司技术中心
66	天津化学试剂有限公司技术中心	108	天津市中重科技工程有限公司技术中心
67	天津大沽化工股份有限公司技术中心	109	天津巴莫科技股份有限公司技术中心
68	天津渤海化工公司天津碱厂技术中心	110	天津红日药业股份有限公司技术中心

续表1-4-2-25

序号	企业技术中心名称	序号	企业技术中心名称
111	协和干细胞基因工程有限公司技术中心	131	天津市新星兽药厂技术中心
112	天津天大天久股份有限公司技术中心	132	天津斯必得服装集团有限公司技术中心
113	天津市生机生物集团有限公司技术中心	133	德塔科技集团有限公司技术中心
114	天津港务局技术中心	134	天津施普乐农药技术发展有限公司技术中心
115	亨特尔机电发展有限公司技术中心	135	天津天狮集团技术中心
116	天津新港船厂技术中心	136	天津田歌纺织有限公司技术中心
117	天津塘沽瓦特斯阀门有限公司技术中心	137	天津金轮自行车集团有限公司技术中心
118	天津市大港区天成化工厂技术中心	138	天津市津宝乐器有限公司技术中心
119	天津天海同步器有限公司技术中心	139	天津久安集团有限公司技术中心
120	天津市津海真空开关厂技术中心	140	天津荣亨集团股份有限公司技术中心
121	天津多福源实业有限公司技术中心	141	天津有容蒂康通讯技术有限公司技术中心
122	天津金世集团技术中心	142	天津富士达集团技术中心
123	天津太平洋制药有限公司技术中心	143	天津春发食品配料有限公司技术中心
124	天津大桥焊材集团有限公司技术中心	144	天津宝成机械集团有限公司技术中心
125	天津巨能药业有限公司技术中心	145	天津甘泉集团有限公司技术中心
126	天津市津津药业有限公司技术中心	146	天津立林集团有限公司技术中心
127	天津挂月集团有限公司技术中心	147	天津市华爱集团技术中心
128	天津吉华化工有限公司技术中心	148	天津市津南化肥实验有限公司技术中心
129	天津华能集团能源设备有限公司技术中心	149	天津市企美科技发展有限公司技术中心
130	天津双街钢管集团有限公司技术中心	150	天津渤海阀门制造有限公司技术中心

第三节 成果转化与产业化机构

1991年，天津市科技创业服务中心成立，为中小企业发展和科技人员创业提供优化环境。1996年，天津泰达生产力促进中心成立。之后，一批科技企业孵化器和生产力促进中心逐步建立起来。科技企业孵化器逐步从为进驻企业提供简单的初期创业服务转向为进驻企业提供网络化、信息化、专业化、社会化服务，加速科技成果转化和产业化。生产力促进中心作为联系政府、科研院所和中小企业的桥梁，在咨询服务、技术服务、信息服务、培训服务、人才和技术中介、培育科技企业、融资担保、对外合作、展览展销和法律咨询等方面发挥重要作用。

2003年，天津市开始组建区县特色产业科技园，大力推动区县科技创新，以科技进步引领区县特色产业发展。至2005年，天津市共建有重点成果转移、转化与产业化机构（基地）128个，其中国家级成果推广中心6个，国家级高新技术产业化基地6个，区县特色产业科技园13个，国家级科技创业中心1个，市级或其他各类科技企业孵化器16个，国家级（示范）生产力促进中心1个，市级生产力促进中心20个，科技创业投资机构65个。

一、科技企业孵化器

1991年起，天津市政府和市科委将天津市科技创业服务中心作为火炬计划的重要组成部分和高新技术成果转化基地，无偿提供建设用地，并投入700余万元，积极支持和大力扶植天津市科技创业服务中心建设。1991年5月8日，天津市科技创业服务中心举行正式启用仪式，国家科委常务副主任李绪鄂和天津市市长聂璧初为该中心正式开业剪彩，并决定在一期5000平方米基建工程完成的基础上实施二期增建6000平方米工程。1994年5月，天津市科技创业服务中心出席国际孵化器专业论坛——美国企业孵化协会（NBIA）年会，并发表演讲，向26个国家的代表报告中国科技创业中心的发展情况。

1996～2000年，天津市科技企业孵化器建设进一步发展，先后成立天津泰达国际创业中心、天津塘沽海洋高新技术开发区创业服务中心、天津新技术产业园区国际创业中心和国家纳米技术产业化基地。2000年1月28日，天津市副市长梁肃在《人民日报》发表"建立创新孵育体系，发展新兴产业"，阐述天津市发展科技企业孵化器的思路和经验。1997年，天津市科技创业服务中心在西安成立的中国国际企业孵化器网络上成为首任主席单位，并在1998年主持召开中国国际企业孵化器网络年会。天津市科技创业服务中心成为国家级创业中心。

2001～2005年，天津市科技企业孵化器建设得到蓬勃发展，先后成立14家科技企业孵化器，是前10年的近3倍。其特点：一是向区域性发展，其中天津新技术产业园区的孵化器达10家，天津经济技术开发区的孵化器有5家；二是大学科技园开始布局，建起天津大学、南开大学大学科技园；三是投资主体向多元化方向发展，建起天津火炬鑫茂创业服务中心、天津开泰企业孵化器有限公司等民营企业孵化器；四是孵化器发展水平不断提高，从为进驻企业提供简单的初期创业服务转向服务的网络化、信息化、专业化、社会化和管理的规范化；五是向形式多样化和国际化的方向发展，综合技术孵化器、专业技术孵化器、大学科技园、归国留学人员创业园、华侨创业园和国际企业孵化器等相继产生，软件园、转制院所创业园等发展迅速。2005年2月，市政府批转市科委《关于促进天津市科技企业孵化器建设与发展意见的通知》，提出科技企业孵化器建设的指导思想、总体目标和孵化器建设的原则，明确孵化器的主要任务，并制定鼓励孵化器发展的相关政策措施，促进科技企业孵化器的发展。同年3月，市科委出台《天津市科技企业孵化器管理办法》，对管理、建立、认定和审核市级科技企业孵化器制定规范的标准。2005年5月，召开"天津市科技企业孵化器工作推动会"，围绕贯彻落实《关于促进天津市科技企业孵化器建设与发展意见的通知》，引导全社会积极投入科技企业孵化器建设，进一步为中小企业发展和科技人员创业提供优化环境，激发全社会创新创业活力，加快科技成果转化和产业化。

至2005年，天津市共建有19家科技企业孵化器，其中国家级创业中心1家，市级或其他各类科技企业孵化器18家；资金总额3.83亿元，其中自有资金1.87亿元，政府拨款0.33亿元，贷款1.08亿元，其他来源0.55亿元。2001～2005年，19家科技企业孵化器孵化面积共计56.84万平方米，在孵企业1521家，在孵企业就业人员21491人，在孵企业收入120.16亿元，净利润3.86亿元，上缴税金2.86亿元；孵化器收入0.52亿元，其中综合服务收入0.38亿元，投资收入0.03亿元，其他收入0.11亿元，上缴税金0.03亿元；孵化器累计毕业企业866家，累计毕业企业就业人员15689人，累计毕业企业收入24.14亿元，出口创汇1.69亿美元。

天津科技企业孵化器一览表

表1-4-3-26

序号	孵化器名称	依托单位	成立年份
1	天津市科技创业服务中心	天津市科技创业服务中心	1991
2	天津泰达国际创业中心	开发区管委会	1996
3	天津新技术产业园区国际创业中心（海外留学生创业园）	天津新技术产业园区管委会	1998
4	天津市塘沽海洋高新区创业服务中心	塘沽区海洋高新区管委会	1998

续表1-4-3-26

序号	孵化器名称	依托单位	成立年份
5	国家纳米技术产业化基地	国家纳米技术与工程研究院	2000
6	天津大学国家大学科技园	天津大学	2001
7	天津海泰企业孵化器	天津海泰科技发展股份有限公司	2001
8	天津泰达华生生物园	天津泰达华生生物园发展有限公司	2001
9	津滨科技园	天津滨海生产力促进中心	2001
10	天津火炬鑫茂创业服务中心	天津市高新区火炬创业园协调服务中心 天津鑫茂科技投资集团有限公司	2002
11	天津开泰企业孵化器有限公司	天津开发区科技局	2002
12	天津天保科技发展有限公司	保税区管委会、天保控股有限公司	2002
13	南开大学国家大学科技园	南开大学	2003
14	和平区电子信息孵化器	和平区科委	2003
15	河北区光机电一体化科技企业孵化器	河北区科委、天津动力机厂	2003
16	天津市帅超科技园	天津天传电气节能产业孵化器有限公司	2004
17	中国民航国家大学科技园	中国民航大学	2004
18	天津市光电子专业孵化器	天津市激光技术研究所	2005
19	天津市金虹桥电气企业孵化器有限公司	红桥区科委	2005

二、生产力促进中心

1996年，天津市组建第一家生产力促进中心。至2000年，天津市又先后组建天津市食品工业生产力促进中心、天津市勘察设计生产力促进中心、天津市制造业生产力促进中心、天津市工程机械生产力促进中心等4家生产力促进中心。

2001～2005年，天津市生产力促进中心建设快速发展，共建成各领域、各行业或区域性生产力促进中心15家。至2005年，全市生产力促进中心发展到20家，其中国家级生产力促进示范中心1家。生产力促进中心主要分布食品、纺织、机械、电子、冶金等领域，其业务包括咨询、信息、技术培训、人才培训与交流、科技中介及培育科技型企业等。2001～2005年，天津市生产力促进中心累计参与人员304人，其中高级职称122人，中级职称89人；总资产81802万元，总投资2756万元，其中政府投入435万元。

天津生产力促进中心一览表

表1-4-3-27

序号	机构名称	依托单位	成立年份
1	天津泰达生产力促进中心	天津泰达国际创业中心	1996
2	天津市食品工业生产力促进中心	天津市食品研究所	1998
3	天津市勘察设计生产力促进中心	天津市土木工程学会	1999
4	天津市制造业生产力促进中心	天津市冶金工业总公司	2000
5	天津市工程机械生产力促进中心	天津市工程机械设计院	2000
6	天津市制造业信息化生产力促进中心	天津市计算中心	2001
7	天津滨海生产力促进中心	天津市塘沽区科学技术委员会	2001
8	天津市快速成形制造技术生产力促进中心	天津市天大银泰科技有限公司	2001

续表1-4-3-27

序号	机构名称	依托单位	成立年份
9	天津市津南区生产力促进中心	天津市津南区科学技术委员会	2001
10	天津市二轻企业信息化生产力促进中心	天津市二轻集团(控股)有限公司	2002
11	天津市服装信息化生产力促进中心	天津科技大学	2002
12	天津市西青区制造业信息化生产力促进中心	天津市西青区科学技术委员会	2003
13	天津市模具行业信息化生产力促进中心	天津理工大学	2003
14	天津自行车行业生产力促进中心	天津市华轮展览有限公司	2004
15	天津市北辰区制造业生产力促进中心	天津市实效企业管理咨询服务有限公司	2004
16	中国对虾特色产业技术促进中心	天津市汉沽区水产局	2004
17	天津市静海县枣产业生产力促进中心	静海县科学技术委员会	2004
18	天津市汽车零部件国际化生产力促进中心	中国汽车技术研究中心	2004
19	天津市汽车行业生产力促进中心	天津汽车(集团)工业有限公司	2005
20	天津市东丽区生产力促进中心	天津市东丽区科学技术委员会	2005

三、区县特色产业科技园

2003年开始，天津市科委以各区县特色工业、特色农业为重点，帮助各区县建立产业孵化器、生产力促进中心和农业科技服务中心，聚集科技资源，实施重点攻关，大力推动区县科技创新，加快科技成果转化，实现以科技引领区县特色产业发展。至2005年，天津市建设各类区县特色产业科技园13家，其中5个技术促进中心、8个产业孵化器。13家区县特色产业科技园分布在各个技术领域，其中现代农业领域5家，装备制造业领域2家，材料技术、电气制造、港口服务、生物制药、现代服务业、电子信息等领域各1家。区县特色产业科技园依托区县科委组建的4家，依托行业主管局组建的3家，依托区县科技园组建的2家，依托生产力促进中心和有限责任公司组建的各1家，无依托单位直接组建的2家。

至2005年，区县特色产业科技园参与人员204人，其中高级职称80人，中级职称67人；总资产4823万元，经营面积4013.2平方米，实验室面积751.43平方米；市科委累计投入100万元，带动13个区县投入配套资金730万元，分别建立特色鲜明的产业孵化器和生产力促进中心，实施科技攻关项目21项，有力地促进区县特色产业的发展，实现企业增效，职工和农民增收。据统计，至2005年，5个区县特色产业生产力促进中心的特色产业总产值达18亿元，实现利税12亿元；8个区县特色产业孵化器孵化面积20.42万平方米，入驻企业321家，在孵企业年产值8.6亿元，实现利税8450万元，解决就业4142人。

天津区县特色产业科技园一览表

表1-4-3-28

序号	机构名称	依托单位	成立年份
1	科丽泰科技企业孵化器	东丽区科学技术委员会	2003
2	和平区电子信息孵化器	和平区科技创业中心	2003
3	河北区光机电一体化孵化器	河北区科学技术委员会	2003
4	塘沽港口服务科技企业孵化器	天津滨海生产力促进中心	2003
5	汉沽区中国对虾特色产业技术促进中心	汉沽区水产局	2004
6	静海县枣产业生产力促进中心	静海县科学技术委员会	2004
7	宁河县肉猪生产力促进中心	宁河原种猪场和宁河县畜牧水产局	2004
8	天津天传电气节能产业孵化器	天津市帅超科技园	2004

续表1-4-3-28

序号	机构名称	依托单位	成立年份
9	武清区奶业生产力促进中心	武清区畜牧水产局	2004
10	西青区生物医药产业孵化器	天津太平洋制药有限公司	2004
11	宝坻区"三辣"生产力促进中心	宝坻区科学技术委员会	2005
12	金虹桥电气企业孵化器	虹桥创业投资有限公司	2005
13	津天感数码影像产业孵化器	河西区天感科技园	2005

第四节　科技服务与中介机构

2001年起，天津市不断加强科技条件服务平台建设，在科技网络信息平台、公共科技条件平台、社会发展公共研究服务平台等建设方面取得较大进展。至2005年，天津市建有公共高新技术平台5个，公共科技服务机构15个。天津市科技条件服务和中介机构以政府为主导，以服务科技为宗旨，以科技网为纽带，突出制度创新和运行机制创新，积极推动科技基础条件资源共享，优化科技条件布局，营造合理、有序的科技公共条件平台和社会公益研发平台。

一、科技网络信息机构

2001年起，天津市科技信息中心通过天津科技网顶层架构的重新设计，建立提供科技信息网络中心。该中心连接国内外数字图书馆，发布包括中外文科技期刊、重点科技数据库、科技基础数据等公用电子科技信息资源，重点开发专利等特色信息服务资源，使天津科技网形成较强的自我发展能力和社会化服务能力。

二、公共科技条件机构

2001年起，市科委通过集成利用天津及北京等相邻地区的科技基础条件资源，不断增强公共科技条件共用共享功能，建立和完善天津市科技文献信息平台、大型仪器协作共用平台、技术标准检测平台、实验动物平台、化学试剂与同位素平台、软件测试服务平台、科普条件平台等，为全市提供公共科技条件服务。

三、社会发展公共研究服务机构

2001年起，市科委针对制约可持续发展的关键领域和科技发展战略研究的薄弱环节，结合社会公益科研院所改革，组建或整合建立一批关系社会发展的公共研究服务机构，包括天津市科技发展战略与政策研究中心、天津市科技统计与发展研究中心、天津市星火科技发展中心、天津市科普中心、环境无害化技术转移中心北方分中心等，为社会发展提供公共研究服务。

四、科技系统科技条件服务机构

天津市科技系统成立最早的科技条件服务机构是天津市理化分析中心和天津市翠屏湖科学园。1991年起，先后成立天津市科技创业服务中心、天津市科学技术评价中心、北方技术交易市场、天津市创业投资发展中心等4家科技条件服务机构。其中，天津市科学技术评价中心于1994年2月组建，是国内率先成立的省市级专业科技评估机构。该中心着眼于服务政府部门、服务社会、服务企业的理念，客户从成立之初的市科委延伸到科技部和市发改委、市工信委、市财政局、市商务委等政府部门以及大学和科研机构、各类企业；

业务也由科技计划项目立项评估延伸到科技计划项目中期和后期评估、科技成果评估、无形资产评估、科技政策评估、各类科技项目咨询等。

1995年3月，由市政府和国家科委联合组建的北方技术交易市场，是国家级常设技术市场。经过几年的发展，成为中国北方重要的区域技术交易中心。2000年12月成立的天津市科技创业投资发展中心，作为创业投资联席会的日常办事机构，在创业投资管理方面发挥重要作用。

2001～2005年，天津市科技系统先后成立环境无害化技术转移中心北方分中心、天津市高新技术成果转化中心、天津市星火科技开发中心、天津市科技统计与发展研究中心、天津市科普中心、天津市科技发展战略与政策研究中心、天津市科技信息网络中心、天津市现代中药质量检验中心等8家科技服务机构，是前10年的2倍。

至2005年，天津市科技系统共建立14家科技条件服务机构，主要分布在网络服务、软科学研究、资源共享、技术转移、农业科技、技术培训与科学普及、创业投资、质量检验、科技统计等领域。14家科技条件服务机构共有管理、研究与工作人员307人，其中高、中级职称人员203人；资产总值超过1亿元，仪器设备819台（套），办公场所面积5万多平方米。14家科技条件服务机构共实施国家级星火计划和建设项目150余项，承担国家软科学研究课题40余项，承担市级软科学研究120余项，获得国家级奖励和成果表彰12项，天津市科技进步奖和市委优秀调研成果奖等80余项。同时，14家科技条件服务机构网络一批致力于科技条件平台建设的人才队伍，承担并完成大量基础条件平台的建设任务和科技发展中长期规划的调研、编制工作，充分体现出其公益性和开放性的特点，服务于天津科技和经济、社会发展。

天津科技系统科技条件服务机构一览表

表1-4-4-29

序号	机构名称	依托单位	成立年份
1	天津市理化分析中心	天津市理化分析中心	1983
2	天津市翠屏湖科学园	天津市翠屏湖科学园	1984
3	天津市科技创业服务中心	天津市科技创业服务中心	1991
4	天津市科学技术评价中心	天津市科学技术信息研究所	1994
5	北方技术交易市场	北方技术交易市场	1995
6	天津市创业投资发展中心	天津市创业投资发展中心	2000
7	环境无害化技术转移中心北方分中心	环境无害化技术转移中心北方分中心	2001
8	天津市高新技术成果转化中心	天津市高新技术成果转化中心	2002
9	天津市星火科技开发中心	天津市星火科技开发中心	2002
10	天津市科技统计与发展研究中心	天津市科学学研究所	2003
11	天津市科普中心	天津市科学技术信息研究所	2003
12	天津市科技发展战略与政策研究中心	天津市科学学研究所	2004
13	天津市科技信息网络中心	天津市科学技术信息研究所	2005
14	天津市现代中药质量检验中心	天津海世达检测技术有限公司	2005

第五章 科学技术团体

天津市科学技术协会(以下简称“市科协”)和天津市职工技术协会(以下简称“市职工技协”)作为全市科技工作者和职工的科学技术团体,严格执行社会团体的有关规定,依靠各级科协和职工技协组织,团结和动员科技人员和职工以经济建设为中心,在促进科学技术的繁荣和发展,促进科学技术与经济、社会的紧密结合和发展等方面发挥重要的桥梁和纽带作用。

第一节 科学技术协会

市科协严格按照社会团体选举产生的有关规定,分别于1992年、1997年、2002年召开代表大会,选举产生第四届、第五届、第六届委员会,并选举产生市科协主席、副主席等。至2005年,市科协内部机构和所属事业单位几经调整,逐步趋于稳定。

1991年起,全市各区县和主要工业局或公司、企业以及各街道、乡(镇),均先后设立科学技术协会,形成自上而下的科学技术协作网络。随着经济建设和科学技术事业的发展,市科协所属各学会、协会、研究会得到不断巩固和发展。

一、市科协

(一)领导机构

1992年10月3~5日,市科协召开第四次代表大会,选举产生第四届委员会。第四届委员会由159人组成,主席:吴咏诗,副主席(以拼音字母为序):毕福春、黄其兴、金桂玉(女)、李光泉、娄肇昆、陆焕生、吴咸中、武玖玲(女)、张道成、张淑华(女)、赵友华,名誉主席:胡国定、陈茹玉。1993年10月16日,在市科协召开的第四届五次常委会会议上,增补陈树春、李金亮为副主席。1996年1月15日,市科协第四届五次全委(扩大)会议决定,增补母国光院士为市科协四届委员会副主席。

1997年11月11~12日,市科协召开第五次代表大会,选举产生第五届委员会。第五届委员会由153人组成,主席:母国光,专职副主席:张道成、宣栋生、陈树春、董天祺,兼职副主席:刘广均、张春霆、李正名、黄其兴、陆焕生、陈永川,吴咏诗、吴咸中为名誉主席。

2002年12月19~20日,市科协召开第六次代表大会,选举产生第六届委员会。第六届委员会由160人组成,主席:母国光,常务副主席:宣栋生,专职副主席:洪解亮、姜沂,兼职副主席(按姓氏笔划为序):王静康、李正名、李朝兴、何志敏、汪顺亭、陈永川、姚建铨,黄其兴、刘广均为名誉主席。2004年3月25日,市科协召开六届六次常委会会议,同意增补白景美为市科协委员、常委、专职副主席,并于会后电话征求确认市科协全体委员的意见。2005年11月5日,市科协召开六届十次常委会会议,同意增补王运洪为市科协委员、常委、专职副主席,并于会后电话征求确认市科协全体委员的意见。

(二)内设机构

1997年8月22日,市科协内部机构调整为9个职能部门,即:办公室、学会工作部、科学技术普及工作部、工业企业工作部、国际交流工作部、组织人事处(老干部处)、综合计划处、审计处(事业发展处)、研究室(培训部)。2001年4月3日,市科协增设反邪教协会办公室。

2002年4月28日,市科协内设机构再次调整,设8个处级机构,即:办公室(调研部)、学会工作部、科学技术普及工作部、反邪教协会办公室、工业企业工作部、国际交流工作部、组织人事部(老干部处)、综合计划部。市科协设主席1名,党组书记兼常务副主席1名,副主席4名,纪检组长1名。

(三)所属事业单位

1991~2005年,市科协所属事业单位减少2个,包括《中国技术市场报》和开发报社。至2005年底,市科协所属事业单位共有15个,包括:市科学技术进修学院、市青少年科技中心、市留学人员联谊会秘书处、科普杂志社、智力杂志社、科学会堂、科学技术咨询公司、科技团体联合技术服务中心、对外应用技术交流促进会(国际科技会议中心)、声像资料服务中心、水产生物技术开发中心、国际海洋信息研究中心、津科设计所、科协机关印刷车间。

二、区县及基层科协

(一)区县科协

至2005年,全市18个区、县均设有科协组织。

2005年天津各区县科协组织一览表

表1-5-1-30

序号	单　位	序号	单　位
1	和平区科协	10	北辰区科协
2	南开区科协	11	塘沽区科协
3	河西区科协	12	汉沽区科协
4	河东区科协	13	大港区科协
5	红桥区科协	14	蓟县科协
6	河北区科协	15	宝坻区科协
7	东丽区科协	16	武清区科协
8	西青区科协	17	宁河县科协
9	津南区科协	18	静海县科协

(二)局(公司)科协

1991年起,石油化工公司、钢管工业公司、港务局、中石化第四建设公司、渤海化工集团和天津经济技术开发区及新技术产业园区先后成立科协组织,天津铁路分局、服装工业公司和丝绸工业公司由于体制改革取消科协组织。至2005年,全市有17个工业局(公司)设有科协组织。

2005年天津有关局(公司)科协一览表

表1-5-1-31

序号	单位名称
1	天津经济技术开发区科协
2	天津新技术产业园区科协
3	天津市中环电子信息集团有限公司科协
4	天津市电力公司科协

续表1-5-1-31

序号	单位名称
5	天津市二轻集团(控股)有限公司科协
6	天津港(集团)有限公司科协
7	天津市粮油集团有限公司科协
8	天津长芦盐务管理局科协
9	天津市一轻集团(控股)有限公司科协
10	天津市冶金集团有限公司科协
11	天津市机电工业控股集团公司科协
12	中国海洋石油渤海公司科协
13	中国石化第四建设公司科协
14	中国石油化工股份有限公司天津分公司科协
15	天津市飞鸽集团有限公司科协
16	天津钢管集团有限公司科协
17	天津市渤海化工集团公司科协

（三）基层科协

1991年起，全市各区、县不断加强街道科协和镇、乡科协组织建设。至2005年，全市共建成街道科协94个，镇科协121个，乡科协18个。

2005年天津各区县的街、镇、乡成立科协组织情况统计表

表1-5-1-32　　单位：个

单　位	街道	镇	乡	合计
和平区	6	0	0	6
南开区	12	0	0	12
河西区	12	0	0	12
河东区	12	0	0	12
红桥区	9	0	0	9
河北区	10	0	0	10
东丽区	5	3	1	9
西青区	2	7	0	9
津南区	1	8	0	9
北辰区	0	9	0	9
塘沽区	8	1	0	9
汉沽区	4	4	0	8
大港区	5	3	0	8
蓟　县	0	22	4	26
宝坻区	3	18	3	24
武清区	5	19	5	29
宁河县	0	11	3	14
静海县	0	16	2	18
合计	94	121	18	233

（四）企业科协

1991～1996年，全市共成立企业科协618个，会员达到7万余人。1997年起，对企业科协组织进行较大调整。至2005年，全市企业科协组织共有307个，其中非国有企业科协191个，会员5.42万人。

三、市级学会、协会、研究会

1991年起，市科协所属各学会、协会、研究会按自然科学、技术科学及其相关学科或科普业务得到不断巩固和发展。随着经济建设和科学技术事业的发展，各学科间不断交叉融合，新兴学科不断建立，相继建立一些新的学会、协会、研究会，而一些已经不适应现代社会生产、生活需要或长期不能开展活动、处于瘫痪状态的学会、协会、研究会逐步被淘汰或撤销。

1997年9月，市科协贯彻落实中共中央办公厅、国务院办公厅和天津市人民政府办公厅《关于加强社会团体和民办非企业单位管理工作》的文件精神，成立天津市科协学会清理整顿工作领导小组，并下发《关于认真做好天津市科协所属学会清理整顿工作的通知》和《天津市科协清理整顿学会工作的实施办法》。参加清理整顿的159个学会、协会、研究会按照文件精神，积极组织落实清整工作。经过各学会、协会、研究会的自查和市科协的严格审查，没有发现非法团体和违法违纪团体。经1997年12月30日市科协五届一次常委会议批准，市社会团体办公室审核批准，保留152个科技团体，撤销7个科技团体。

至2005年，市科协所属学会、协会、研究会共有151个，其中理科学会20个，工科学会62个，农科学会7个，医科学会25个，综合学科学会37个；会员有13.33万人，团体会员8736个。

2005年天津市科协所属学会、协会、研究会一览表

表1-5-1-33

序号	团体名称	成立时间	理事会届别	上次换届时间	理事长姓名（2005年）
1	数学会	1950.6	7	2002.5	龙以明
2	电机工程学会	1951.2	8	2002.1	张文利
3	化学会	1951.3	7	2005.3	关乃佳
4	医学会	1951.4	6	2003.8	赵克正
5	药学会	1951.5	5	1997.12	叶咏年
6	机械工程学会	1951.5	6	2002.6	杨力恒
7	心理学会	1951.12	8	2003.12	沈德立
8	纺织工程学会	1952.10	4	1998	于广才
9	化工学会	1952.12	5	1998.12	曹柏林
10	生理科学学会	1953.1	7	2005.7	徐淑梅
11	解剖学会	1953.4	7	2004.11	李云生
12	土木工程学会	1953.5	8	2005.12	孙增印
13	建筑学会	1953.5	11	2003.9	刘文藩
14	水利学会	1953.5	7	2002.7	刘振邦
15	地理学会	1953.6	5	2005.6	靳润成
16	微生物学会	1953.8	6	2004.1	刘　方
17	中医药学会(中医学会)	1954	5	2005.2	张大宁
18	护理学会	1955.4	6	2001.12	曹文媚
19	防痨协会	1955.9	5	1996.12	王撷秀
20	金属学会	1956.5	6	1997.3	王克昌
21	物理学会	1956.6	5	2003.7	许京军

续表1-5-1-33

序号	团体名称	成立时间(年月)	理事会届别	上次换届时间(年月)	理事长姓名(2005年)
22	电子学会	1956.11	5	2000.1	张旭光
23	农学会	1957.5	4	2003.10	张树明
24	硅酸盐学会	1957.5	5	2004.10	刘志江
25	造船工程学会	1957.7	8	2005.11	高学虎
26	力学学会	1958.11	8	2001.09	佟景伟
27	畜牧兽医学会	1959.10	6	2003.11	傅润亭
28	水产学会	1959.11	5	1997.12	蔡明玉
29	食品学会	1959.11	6	2004.1	汪恩华
30	仪器仪表学会	1960.1	5	1999.0	李　军
31	水运工程学会	1960.4	6	1999.3	魏兴华
32	电镀工程学会	1960.9	7	2003.2	唐致远
33	皮革学会	1962.2	5	2004.12	李明海
34	气象学会	1962.3	7	2005.10	王宗信
35	电力学会	1962.4	7	2003.12	薛　锦
36	林学会	1962.5	5	2000.11	赵万明
37	农业机械学会	1963.9	6	2005.3	胡　伟
38	造纸学会	1964.2	8	2005.09	谭国民
39	环境科学学会	1978.2	4	2005.5	邢振纲
40	地震学会	1978.4	6	2005.12	赵国敏
41	激光技术学会	1978.4	4	2003.4	杨洗陈
42	印刷技术协会	1978.4	8	1999.10	张德旺
43	铁道学会	1978.10	6	2002.10	郑　健
44	计量测试学会	1978.10	6	2005.1	杨振林
45	自然辩证法研究会	1978.10	4	1997	甄建民
46	科普作家协会(科普创作协会)	1978.11	3	1997	尹怀勤
47	电视技术研究会	1978.12	6	2004.3	王东江
48	中文信息研究会	1978.12	3	1993.8	许家梁
49	太阳能技术研究会	1978.12	4	2004.12	马一太
50	地质学会	1979.2	6	2005.1	廉敬民
51	标准化协会	1979.2	6	2004.10	马伯禄
52	图书馆学会	1979.3	5	2002.5	陆行素
53	科学技术情报学会	1979.3	5	2005.4	姚　学
54	科教电影电视协会	1979.3	4	1996.9	游泽清
55	自动化技术应用研究会	1979.4	5	1999.8	柴仲铨
56	色谱技术研究会	1979.5	6	2002.6	寇登民
57	科学学研究会	1979.6	8	2004.11	锦　聚
58	电子计算机应用技术研究会	1979.8	6	1999.9	戴居丰
59	自动化学会	1979.9	7	2005.4	赵海山
60	石油学会	1979.10	4	1998.11	周守为

续表1-5-1-33

序号	团体名称	成立时间(年月)	理事会届别	上次换届时间(年月)	理事长姓名(2005年)
61	能源研究会	1979.10	2	1998.8	林鸿增
62	锅炉、压力容器学会	1979.10	4	1997.3	花绍增
63	技术经济和管理现代化研究会	1979.11	5	2003.1	魏大鹏
64	航海学会	1979.12	5	2002.9	张　良
65	塑料工程学会	1980.2	5	2000.9	强　越
66	珠算协会	1980.5	5	1998.6	周时悌
67	乐器学会	1980.5	2	1992	刘作人
68	照明学会	1980.6	7	2004.10	范世福
69	制冷学会	1980.6	6	2002.9	何绍书
70	生物医学工程学会	1980.7	8	2003.9	宋继昌
71	电源技术研究会	1980.8	6	2005.1	王　萍
72	通信学会	1980.9	5	2003.12	段玉奎
73	青少年科技教育协会 (青少年科技辅导员协会)	1980.12	5	2003.1	朱　坦
74	X射线分析技术研究会	1981.2	6	2003.1	姚心侃
75	胶粘剂研究会	1981.2	6	2005.1	王永红
76	中西医结合学会	1981.12	4	1998.12	吴咸中
77	工业产权与技术转让研究会	1982.4	2	1990	张国玉
78	未来与预测科学研究会	1982.10	5	2004.12	荣长海
79	节水、水处理技术研究会	1984.1	2	1990.1	张　准
80	生物化学与分子生物学会	1984.5	7	2001.12	耿运琪
81	遗传学会	1984.5	6	2005.8	李明刚
82	动物学会	1984.5	7	2002.6	杨竹舫
83	植物学会	1984.5	6	2002.9	高元泰
84	内燃机学会	1984.5	5	2005.1	刘　宁
85	生态学会	1984.5	4	2004.3	朱　坦
86	工程图学学会	1984.5	7	2004.6	蒋秀明
87	园林学会	1984.9	4	1996.11	高国华
88	城市科学研究会	1984.9	5	2004.12	刘玉麟
89	工艺美术学会	1984.9	4	1994	张国华
90	体育科学学会	1984.10	4	2005.3	谢德龙
91	抗癌协会	1984.11	4	2005.11	李　强
92	基本建设经济研究会	1984.11	3	2000.12	赵铁生
93	汽车工程学会	1984.11	4	1998.12	张应吉
94	烹饪协会	1985.1	4	1999.1	杨春生
95	计算机辅助设计研究会	1985.1	3	1998.4	胡小唐
96	热喷涂技术研究会	1985.1	3	1998.12	张文利
97	现场统计研究会	1985.2	4	1999.1	沈世镒
98	园艺学会	1985.3	6	2004.12	蒋如生

续表1-5-1-33

序号	团体名称	成立时间(年月)	理事会届别	上次换届时间(年月)	理事长姓名(2005年)
99	继续工程教育协会	1985.3	3	1997.1	沙小泉
100	消防协会	1985.10	4	2001.7	葛 毅
101	模具技术研究会	1985.12	5	2002.1	安庆骅
102	光学学会	1985.12	3	2002.1	郁道银
103	核学会	1987.2	3	2004.5	姚 学
104	中小企业技术与开发协会	1987.2	5	2005.4	齐茂忠
105	卫生保健协会	1987.3	4	2004.1	曲学申
106	康复医学会	1987.4	4	2004.11	曲学申
107	归国科技工作者协会	1987.4	2	1990.12	孙履厚
108	学会学研究会	1987.4	3	2004.12	宣栋生
109	技术市场协会	1987.9	3	2000.11	毕福春
110	民办科技实业家协会	1987.12	2	1996	李长兴
111	针灸学会	1987.12	4	2000.12	石学敏
112	测绘学会	1988.1	5	2005.3	韩振镖
113	工厂科协研究会	1988.4	2	1996.11	毕福春
114	预防医学会	1988.5	3	2003.12	张柏捷
115	系统工程学会	1988.5	4	2000.12	李光泉
116	分析测试协会	1988.5	4	2003.9	姚心侃
117	振动工程学会	1988.6	3	2000.2	王洪礼
118	化工过程及设备技术研究会	1988.6	4	2003.12	柴诚敬
119	计算机学会	1988.7	3	1999.7	张振铎
120	科学技术期刊编辑学会	1989.4	4	2003.1	杨旭才
121	劳动保护科学技术学会	1989.5	2	1996.12	花绍增
122	输血协会	1989.6	3	2002.12	李 研
123	声学学会	1989.9	3	1999.4	王以真
124	轻工工程学会 (轻工设备工程学会)	1989.9	2	2005.4	王学魁
125	医学辩证法研究会	1989.11	3	1994.4	孙福泉
126	腐蚀与防护学会	1990.3	2	1993.12	陆焕生
127	神经科学学会	1990.3	3	2005.7	只石达
128	真空学会	1990.5	3	2003.11	孙 云
129	灾害防御协会	1991.9	3	2005.9	孙海麟
130	健康教育协会	1991	1	1991	钱其敖
131	农村专业技术协会	1992	1	1992	王隆清
132	城市规划学会	1992	3	2004.9	郝寿义
133	公路学会	1992	2	1997.3	孙增印
134	土地学会	1992	2	1997.4	赵友华
135	粮油学会	1992	3	2005.4	孙 瑞
136	水力发电工程学会	1992	3	2001.12	刘德堂

续表1-5-1-33

序号	团体名称	成立时间(年月)	理事会届别	上次换届时间(年月)	理事长姓名(2005年)
137	科技成果转化协会	1992	2	2003.3	马其慧
138	药理学会	1993.1	4	2004.12	刘昌孝
139	营养学会	1993.1	3	2003.9	傅金茹
140	材料研究学会	1993.1	2	2000.12	袁启明
141	图象图形学学会	1995.1	2	2001.10	戴威岭
142	抗衰老学会	1993.4	2	2000.12	邢克浩
143	体视学学会	1994.4	2	2001.6	吕少文
144	电磁兼容研究会	1994.9	1	1994.9	李健雄
145	老科技工作者协会(退休工程师协会)	1998	3	2001.10	陆焕生
146	天文学会	2000.2	2	2003.9	苏　宜
147	反邪教协会	2001.5	1	2001.5	刘广均
148	微量元素学会	2003	1	2003	孙大泽
149	工业工程学会	2004	1	2004	齐二石
150	运筹学学会	2005.3	1	2005.3	吴育华
151	空间结构研究会	2005.10	1	2005.10	刘锡良

第二节 职工技术协会

天津市职工技术研究总会成立于1950年4月。1963年11月,在天津市职工技术研究总会的基础上,成立天津市职工技术协作委员会。1966年“文化大革命”开始后,天津市职工技术协作委员会活动受到冲击。1979年,经市委批准,成立天津市群众技术协作委员会,后改称为天津市职工技术协作委员会,成为中华全国总工会领导下的中国职工技术协作委员会的地方组织。

1983年5月30日,召开天津市职工技术协作委员会第二届会员代表大会。大会聘请市长李瑞环任该委员会名誉主任,选举单书任该委员会主任。在市总工会领导下,基层职工技术协作组织得到快速发展,由1983年的1232个发展到1989年的1800个,职工技术协会会员由1983年的4.8万人发展到1989年的17万人。

1989年11月11日,天津市职工技术协作委员会第三次代表大会召开。会议根据中国职工技术协会章程,将天津市职工技术协作委员会更名为天津市职工技术协会。会议聘请市长聂璧初担任市职工技协的名誉会长,选举单书任会长,苏兰洲等10人任副会长。

1994年12月16日,市职工技协第四届委员会召开第一次全体会议。大会聘请张立昌、李慧芬、潘义清、单书为名誉会长,选举苏兰洲为新一届会长,吴凡等12人为副会长。1999年4月13日,市职工技协召开四届五次全委(扩大)会议,市委副书记、市长李盛霖,市委常委、市总工会主席孙宝树出席会议并讲话。会议充分肯定职工技协对深化改革、促进发展、保持稳定做出的贡献。

2006年2月28日,市职工技协召开第五次代表大会,并举行五届一次委员会议,有14人当选名誉会长、会长及副会长。在新当选的副会长中,孔祥瑞、刘超英、苗起瑞、陈乃克是来自生产第一线的劳动模范和技术专家。

第六章 科技管理机构

1991～2005年，为加强对全市科技工作的领导，市委、市政府在党政机关机构改革中不断加强各级科技管理机构建设。市委科技工委和市科委经过机构改革，内设机构更加合理，职能更加明确。经市委批准成立的天津园区工委和天津园区管委会，对天津新技术产业园区实行领导和管理。其间，先后成立的天津市知识分子工作领导小组、北方技术交易市场管理委员会、天津市信息化工作领导小组、天津市科技教育领导小组、天津市科技创新专项资金领导小组等市级科技管理机构，进一步增强对全市科技工作的领导与协调。

各区县政府为推进区县科技进步，不断加强对科技工作的领导，相继成立由区（县）主要负责人担任组长的区（县）科技工作领导小组、科普工作领导小组、知识产权工作领导小组等机构。各区县科学技术委员会作为区县科技工作的行政主管部门，在机构改革中领导班子建设得到进一步加强，职能科室配置更加完善，并在区委、区政府领导和市科委指导下，通过规划指导、组织调控、协调服务、宣传培训，行使对全区（县）科技工作的综合管理职能，在推动区域科技事业发展的过程中发挥重要作用。同时，市区各所属局或街道普遍配备分管科技工作的副主任，农业区（县）各乡（镇）也配备有科技副乡（镇）长，为推进科技进步与技术创新提供强有力的组织保障。

天津市在加强市级和各区县科技管理机构建设的同时，为加强对科技工作的领导，市政府各有关部门，包括各委、办、局也都设置有科技管理机构或部门，从而形成自上而下的科技管理体系。

第一节 市级科技管理机构

1991年4月，市委决定成立天津市知识分子工作领导小组，加强和改进知识分子工作。1992年6月，经市委批准，成立天津园区管委会，负责天津新技术产业园区管理工作。1994年11月，国家科委和市政府联合成立北方技术交易市场管理委员会，促进北方技术交易市场的健康发展。1995年，市委、市政府贯彻党和国家提出的“科教兴国”战略，调整并加强了天津市科技领导小组。1996年7月，市政府决定成立天津市信息化工作领导小组，组织、推动全市信息化建设。1998年12月，市政府决定成立天津市科技教育领导小组，进一步加强对全市科技、教育工作的领导与协调。2004年7月，市委批准成立的天津园区工委，为市委的派出机构，负责科技系统党的工作，保证党的路线、方针、政策和市委的工作部署在科技口的贯彻执行。市科委作为市政府综合管理全市科技工作的职能部门，机构设置几经调整，职能更加明确。2005年5月，成立天津市科技创新专项资金领导小组，加强对科技创新专项资金的管理。市级科技管理机构的建立，进一步加强了对全市科技工作的领导与协调，为推动全市科技工作的健康发展提供了组织保障。

一、市委科技工委

（一）职能与机构设置

1986年7月，根据《中共天津市委、天津市政府关于调整市委科学技术工作部、市科学技术委员会机构体制方案的通知》精神，在撤销市委科学技术工作部、市科学技术委员会党组的基础上，成立市委科技工委。市委科技工委作为市委的派出机构，在市委领导下负责科技系统党的工作，讨论决定科技系统的重大问题。其主要任务是：贯彻执行党和国家有关方针、政策、法规；研究决定全市科技发展战略，宏观管理科技体制改革等重大问题；负责归口单位党的建设，干部工作和思想政治工作以及科学技术团体工作。市委科技工委定编39人，内设办公室、组织处、干部处、宣传处、纪检组、研究室。此后，经征得天津市总工会和共青团天津市委同意，市委科技工委增设科技工会和科技团工委。

1996年4月30日市委发出通知，同意《中共天津市委科学技术工作委员会职能配置、内设机构和人员编制方案》，明确指出："市委科技工委是市委的派出机构，在市委的统一领导下，归口管理科技口党的工作，保证党的路线、方针、政策和市委的工作部署在科技口的贯彻执行。"其主要职责是：贯彻中央的路线、方针、政策和市委的指示、工作部署，并督促检查在科技口的实施；负责科技口党组织的思想建设、组织建设、作风建设，指导推动基层党建工作；同市政府有关部门共同研究决定科技发展战略、宏观管理和科技体制改革等重大问题；按照市委授权和干部管理权限，负责归口管理单位领导班子建设，负责中央驻津单位局级干部的协管工作，指导推动基层领导班子建设，负责干部管理、培训工作和老干部工作，负责后备干部队伍建设；负责科技口的思想政治工作和精神文明建设；负责科技口党的纪律检查、监察工作和党风廉政建设；负责科技口的统战工作；负责科技口维护社会政治稳定工作；领导科技口工会、共青团工作；完成市委交办的其他工作。根据上述职责，市委科技工委设有办公室、干部处（统战处与干部处合署办公）、组织处、宣传处、研究室等5个职能处室及纪检组。市委科技工委行政编制为38人，其中书记1名、专职副书记1～2名、纪检组长1名、正副处长15名、工勤人员2名。

2001年9月12日，根据《中共天津市委关于市委机构改革的实施意见》，市委办公厅发出通知，同意《中共天津市委科学技术工作委员会职能配置、内设机构和人员规定》，明确提出：市委科技工委为市委的派出机构，与市科委实行合属办公，其主要职责与1996年4月30日市委通知精神基本一致，内设机构增加老干部处，行政编制由38人缩减为30人，工勤人员改为事业编制。

（二）主要负责人更迭情况

书记：

杨竞衡（1986年8月～1988年5月）

王成怀（1988年5月～1993年6月）

武耀贤（1994年4月～1996年11月）

张道成（1996年11月～2000年8月）

陈超英（2000年8月～2005年12月）

副书记：

王成怀（1986年8月～1988年5月）

孙焕时（1986年8月～1994年3月）

王保忠（1990年7月～1995年10月）

梁　肃（1993年6月～1999年10月）

张道成（1993年10月～1996年11月）

李　平（女）（1995年10月～2005年12月）

陈超英（1999年10月～2000年8月）

陈巧林（2001年4月～2005年12月）

李家俊（2003年2月～2005年12月）

至2005年12月，担任市委科技工委委员的还有：甄建民、徐润达、沙小泉、郭宏勤、陈卫、陈罗云、顾毅然、于文海、李之珍、唐顺善、张纬、马其慧、李群、魏宗海等。

二、市科委

(一)职能与机构设置

1、1991年1月～1996年4月

主要职责:贯彻执行党和国家有关科学技术的方针、政策、法规,推进和完善科技体制改革;进行科技发展预测,提出相应的对策,编制科技发展规划与年度计划,并组织实施;组织重大科技攻关,开展国内外科技交流与合作,会同有关部门组织对重大的引进技术进行消化吸收;提供科研条件服务,负责科研经费的分配与管理;负责科技保密工作,组织科技信息交流,科技成果管理与推广,技术市场管理,发展科技服务事业;负责科技干部管理工作。

内设机构:办公室、规划预测处、综合计划处、科技体制改革处、农村科技处、社会发展科技处、科技人才处、条件财务处、审计处、科技政策法规处、科技体制改革处、科技成果处、科技保密处、技术市场处、国际科技合作处、直属事业管理处(保卫处)、人事教育处、老干部处等职能部门。

2、1996年4月～2001年1月

1996年4月23日,中共天津市委、市政府印发《天津市科学技术委员会职能配置、内设机构和人员编制方案的通知》,对市科委职能配置、内设机构和人员编制做出具体规定。

下放和转移的职能:具有技术标准的应用科技成果的鉴定,转移给行业检测鉴定机构负责;职称改革工作转移给市人事局;国务院特殊津贴、有突出贡献的专家选拔、吸引留学人员出国、高级专家离退休、来华定居专家、博士后流动站和专业技术人员农转非等管理工作转移给市人事局。

加强的职能:进一步把工作重点集中到全市科技发展战略和中长期规划的研究与制定上,加强科技进步方针政策的研究,科技工作的综合协调、督促检查和指导服务;加大对国民经济和社会发展中有重大影响,跨部门、多学科、综合性强的科技工作的宏观调控力度;加强对产业结构、产品结构调整具有重大影响的科技转化和高新技术及产业化的研究与开发;加大科技体制改革力度,强化科技领域国有资产管理;加强跨世纪科技人才队伍建设;加强国际科技合作、交流和智力引进;加速信息化建设;加强社会发展科技和科学技术普及工作。

主要职责:组织制定全市科技发展战略、方针和政策,拟定有关法规;研究制定科技体制改革的方针、政策、总体规划和措施并组织实施,宏观管理全市科技机构;归口负责科教兴市的有关综合工作;研究确定科技优先发展领域,研究分析科技促进经济、社会发展的重大问题,组织制定全市科技发展规划、计划,合理配置科研经费;制定应用基础研究、高新技术开发和科技成果商品化、产业化、国际化的政策和措施,负责组织重点科技攻关项目及高新技术产业化重点工程;负责科技进步重大奖励、市级重大科技成果推广和科技保密工作;研究制定技术市场的有关政策和法规,监督检查技术合同法实施工作,宏观指导技术贸易活动;归口管理全市科技外事和引进智力工作;负责自然科学技术领域学术(技术)带头人的选拔授衔工作,负责组织科技人员培训;负责软科学研究和科技信息工作,制定科技信息工作发展规划和计划,指导科技第三产业发展;组织制定农业科研规划、计划;指导农村重大支柱产业的科技示范;负责星火计划的制定及管理工作;负责科普工作,组织制定全市科普工作的规划、计划,并推动实施;负责拟定全市信息化建设规划、计划,促进全市电子信息技术的推广应用,组织协调国民经济信息化的实施;负责办理市人民政府知识产权办公会议议定的事项及其他有关知识产权方面的工作;归口管理新技术产业园区;负责全市科技统计、科技档案工作;管理直属单位;管理全市实验动物、大型仪器设备、同位素、自然科学期刊等办公室工作;协调、指导各部门、各区县的科技管理工作;承办市政府交办的其他工作。

内设机构:办公室、综合计划处、工业科技处(火炬计划办公室)、农村科技处(星火计划办公室)、社会发展科技处、科技人才处、条件财务处(审计处与条件财务处合署办公)、科技政策法规处(市政府知识产权办公会议办公室)、科技体制改革处、科技成果处、科技保密处(市国家科技保密办公室)、技术市场处、国际科技合作处、引进国外智力处(市政府引进国外智力办公室)、信息化办公室、直属事业管理处(保卫处)、人事教育处、监察室、老干部处(市委科技工委老干部处)等19个职能处(室)。

3、2001年1月～2005年12月

2001年1月11日,中共天津市委办公厅、市政府办公厅印发《天津市科学技术委员会职能配置、内设机构和人员编制规定的通知》,对市科委的主要职能、内设机构做出具体规定,并对原有职能作出调整:将引进国外智力的工作交给市人事局;将拟定全市信息化建设规划、组织协调国民经济信息化实施工作交给市信息化办公室;将办理市政府知识产权办公会议议定的事项及其他有关知识产权方面的工作交给市知识产权局;将市海洋局及其相关职能划给市规划和国土资源局;划入编制重大科技攻关和重点实验室项目的计划及相关经费安排的职能。

主要职能:贯彻落实国家科技工作的方针、政策和法律、法规,组织制定天津市科技发展战略、方针、政策;拟定地方性科技法规、规章,并组织实施;组织编制天津市科技发展中长期规划、年度计划;研究确定天津市科技发展的布局和优先领域,研究分析科技促进经济、社会发展的重大问题,推动科技创新体系的建设;组织制定应用基础研究、高新技术发展的政策措施,负责制定应用基础研究计划、高新技术研究发展计划、科技攻关计划、科技创新工程和社会发展科技计划,并组织实施,负责软件产业的规划、组织和协调工作;参与制定信息化发展计划;强化高新技术产业化及应用技术的开发与推广工作,负责制定火炬计划、星火计划、成果推广计划等科技开发计划指南,并指导实施,推动用高新技术改造传统产业、指导农村重大科技产业的示范和可持续发展综合实验区的科技工作;研究多渠道增加科技投入的措施,优化科技资源配置,归口管理全市科学事业费、科技"三项费"、科技专项经费等有关经费的预决算;研究制定全市科技体制改革的政策和措施,并组织实施,推动建立适应社会主义市场经济和科技自身发展规律的科技创新体制和机制,推动科技创新体系和科技服务体系的建设,会同有关部门做好对全市民营科技企业的统筹规划、指导、协调和服务等工作;负责管理全市科技成果、科技奖励、科技保密、技术市场等工作,制定科技普及工作的规划、计划,推动全市科普工作发展,促进科技咨询、招标、评估等社会中介组织的发展;研究制定对外科技合作与交流的方针、政策,负责科技外事工作和对香港、澳门特别行政区及台湾地区科技事务工作;研究科技人才资源的合理配置,会同有关部门做好科技人才的培养、选拔和两院院士候选人的提名、遴选工作;负责软科学研究;负责全市科技信息、科技统计、科技档案、科技期刊的管理工作;协调、指导区县科技工作;承办市委、市政府交办的其他事项。

内设机构:办公室、综合计划处、高新技术及产业化处(火炬计划办公室、市软件园管理办公室)、生物医药与环保科技处、农村科技处(星火计划办公室)、社会发展科技处、基础研究处、政策法规与体制改革处、科技成果与技术市场处(市技术市场管理办公室、市国家科技保密办公室)、国际科技合作处、条件财务处(审计处)、科技企事业管理处(保卫处)、人事教育处等13个职能处(室)。

(二)主要负责人更迭情况

1、1988年6月～1993年7月

主任:

王成怀(1988年6月～1993年7月)(兼)

副主任:

沙小泉(女)(1988年6月～1993年7月)

徐润达(1988年6月～1993年4月)

郭宏勤(1988年6月～1993年7月)

李之珍(1988年6月～1993年7月)

梁　肃(1988年6月～1993年7月)

张道成(1988年6月～1993年7月)

雷世钧(1993年4月～1993年7月)

王保忠(1993年4月～1993年7月)

秘书长：

王绳兮(女)(1988年9月～1989年11月)

于广明(1993年4月～1993年7月)

副秘书长：

张洪涛(1988年6月～1990年11月)

张 洪(1988年6月～1988年12月)

鲁智远(1988年9月～1989年11月)

于广明(1990年11月～1993年4月)

陈舜琦(1990年11月～1993年4月)(兼)

孙贤德(1993年4月～1993年7月)

唐顺善(1993年4月～1993年7月)

副局级巡视员：

修正奇(1988年4月～1991年2月)

苏 澄(1988年4月～1991年2月)

于广明(1993年4月～1993年7月)

2、1993年7月～1999年11月

主任：

梁 肃(1993年7月～1998年12月)

副主任：

李之珍(1993年7月～1996年11月)

雷世钧(1993年7月～1999年11月)

王保忠(1993年7月～1995年10月)(兼)

马其慧(女)(1995年7月～1999年11月)

杨应敏(1995年7月～1999年11月)

李 平(女)(1995年12月～1999年11月)

姚 学(1996年9月～1999年11月)

余学林(1996年10月～1998年6月挂职),(1998年6月～1999年11月副主任)

秘书长：

于广明(1993年7月～1996年5月)

孙贤德(1996年5月～1997年3月)

张海河(1998年3月～1999年11月)

副秘书长：

马其慧(女)(1993年7月～1995年7月)

唐顺善(1993年7月～1999年11月)

万慎青(女)(1996年5月～1999年11月)

王士禧(1998年12月～2002年4月)

副局级巡视员：

于广明(1993年7月～1996年11月)

3、1999年11月～2003年2月

主任：

陈超英(1999年11月～2003年2月)

副主任：

马其慧(女)(1999年11月～2003年2月)

雷世钧(1999年11月～2000年1月)
杨应敏(1999年11月～2000年1月)
李　平(女)(1999年11月～2000年7月)
姚　学(1999年11月～2003年2月)
余学林(1999年11月～2000年6月)
赵海山(2000年1月～2003年2月)
何志敏(2000年7月～2003年2月)
总工程师:
陈养发(2001年11月～2003年2月)
助理巡视员:
杨旭才(2002年3月～2003年2月)
4、2003年2月～2005年12月
主任:
李家俊(2003年2月～2005年12月)
副主任:
姚　学(2003年2月～2005年12月)
赵海山(2003年2月～2005年12月)
何志敏(2003年2月～2005年12月)
李宝纯(女)(2005年9月～2005年12月)
总工程师:
陈养发(2003年2月～2005年12月)
助理巡视员:
杨旭才(2003年2月～2005年12月)

三、天津园区工委

1992年6月17日,经市委批准,成立天津园区管委会党组,王成怀、梁肃、庞金华等先后担任党组书记。

2004年7月9日,市委发出通知,批准成立市委园区工委。其为市委派出机构,领导职务列入市委管理,由市委决定任免,同时撤销天津新技术产业园区管委会党组。同日,市委决定周思纯担任天津园区工委委员、书记;庞金华担任天津园区工委委员、副书记。

2004年7月12日,市委组织部下发通知,市委同意:刘津元、宗国英、刘力、张世军、高晓英、任民谊担任天津园区工委委员。同日,市委组织部下发通知,市委同意建立中共天津新技术产业园区纪律检查工作委员会,撤销中共天津市纪委驻天津新技术产业园区纪律检查组。高晓英任中共天津新技术产业园区纪律检查工作委员会书记。

2004年10月26日,市委办公厅下发《中共天津市委新技术产业园区工作委员会职能配置、内设机构和人员编制的规定》。其主要职责是:贯彻执行中央的路线、方针、政策和市委决定的工作部署,并指导推动和督促检查在新技术产业园区的实施;会同市委、市政府有关部门共同研究决定新技术产业园区改革发展稳定的重大问题,并对实施过程进行督促检查;负责新技术产业园区党的建设和精神文明建设,民主法制建设;做好党的宣传工作和思想政治工作;按照市委的授权和干部管理权限,负责新技术产业园区机关及直属企、事业单位的干部管理和领导班子建设,协助市委组织部做好市管干部的有关管理工作;负责干部教育、培训、管理和老干部工作;负责指导推动新技术产业园区的干部人事制度改革,各类人才队伍建设以及后备干部队伍建设;负责新技术产业园区基层党组织建设工作,做好培训、教育、管理和发展工作;负责新技术产业园区的纪律检查、行政监察和党风廉政建设工作;负责新技术产业园区的统战、对台工作;领导新技术产业园区工会、共青团等工作;负责新技术产业园区维护稳定和社会治安综合治理工作;完成市委交办的其他工作。天津园区工委设有办公室、组织部、企业工作部、宣传部、研究室等5个职能部门。同时,市委任命周思纯为天津园区工委书记,庞金华为副书记,刘津元(女)、宗国英、刘力(女)、张世军、高晓英(女)、任民谊为委员。

四、天津园区管委会

(一)机构沿革与内设机构

1991年3月6日,国务院批准建立天津新技术产业园区。1992年6月17日,经市委批准,撤销设在市科委的天津新技术产业园区办公室,成立天津园区管委会,为正局级行政机构,负责园区管理工作。天津园区管委会内设机构有综合办公室、业务管理处和规划发展处。1992年7月15日,天津园区管委会正式对外办公,科技工作由业务管理处负责。天津园区管委会的职责是:贯彻实施国家和天津市发展高新技术产业的法律、法规和有关规定,为高新技术产业的发展创造良好环境;制订园区高新技术产业发展规划,经市人民政府批准后,组织实施;制订园区的行政管理规定,并组织实施;初审和认定园区内高新技术企业;依法管理园区的财政、税务、工商、劳动和人事等事务;管理园区有关地域内土地和规划建设事务,并按照市政府规定的权限,审核、批准和管理相应地域内固定资产投资项目;负责园区内火炬计划项目和新产品项目的申报;审核园区内高新技术企业进出口货物免税的申请,并报有关部门批准;审核园区内高新技术企业因公出国人员的申请,并报有关部门批准;市政府授予的其他职权。

1993年10月22日,市政府主持召开会议,同意天津园区管委会关于健全管理服务机构的方案,编制由25人增至50人,机构设置为8个部门,即党组办公室、办公室、政策研究室、企业管理处、外经外事处、建设发展处、劳动人事局、财政局,并先后建立人才交流中心、人才培训中心、高新技术企业协会等支撑服务机构。此期间,天津园区科技工作由企业管理处负责。

1994年11月22日,召开市政府办公会议,决定在天津园区实行"一区三制"管理办法,即天津园区、华苑产业区和南开区所有高新技术企业的各项税收均由国家税务局园区分局负责征管,同时北辰科技工业园和塘沽海洋科技工业园为天津园区的辐射区。

1999年9月28日,天津市机构编制委员会批准园区管委会内设9个处室(局),即党组办公室、办公室(社会发展局)、经济发展局(招商局、统计局)、建设发展与环境保护局、城区管理局(房地产管理局)、劳动人事局、财政局(物价局)、政策法规处、市工商行政管理局天津园区分局。此期间,天津园区的科技工作由天津园区经济发展局负责。

2003年,天津市编制委员会批复天津园区管委会内设机构的调整方案。其设有12个处室(局),即党组办公室、办公室、社会发展局、经济发展局(统计局)、招商局、建设发展与环境保护局、城区管理局(房地产管理局)、劳动人事局、财政局(物价局)、政策法规处、市工商行政管理局天津园区分局、科技局。

2004年7月,天津园区管委会内部机构调整为13个部门,即监察室、办公室、社会发展局、经济发展局(统计局)、招商局、建设发展与环境保护局、城区管理局(房地产管理局)、劳动人事局、财政局(物价局)、政策法规处、市工商行政管理局天津园区分局、科技局、行政执法局。此间,科技工作由园区科技局负责,主要职责有高新技术企业认定、科技成果鉴定、火炬计划申报、创新基金申报等。

(二)主要负责人更迭情况

主任:

王成怀(1992年6月~1993年7月)(兼)

梁　肃(1993年7月~1997年5月)(兼)

庞金华(1997年6月~2005年12月)

副主任:

宣栋生(1993年7月~1998年7月)

陈舜琦(1993年10月~2002年6月)

李大亚(1996年5月~2002年5月,其中1997年6月起任常务副主任)
刘津元(女)(1999年8月~2005年12月)
任学锋(2002年6月~2004年7月)
宗国英(2002年6月~2005年12月)
刘 力(女)(2002年6月~2005年12月)
张世军(2003年11月~2005年12月)

五、天津市知识分子工作领导小组

为贯彻中央关于进一步加强和改进知识分子工作的通知精神,1991年4月市委发出通知,决定成立天津市知识分子工作领导小组。该领导小组由王旭东、王成怀、钱其鳌3人组成,王旭东牵头。领导小组下设办公室,负责日常工作。领导小组办公室由市委组织部、市科委和市人事局的职能处室组成(不另设机构)。市委组织部副部长武耀贤兼任办公室主任,市科委副主任郭宏勤、市人事局副局长倪平兼任办公室副主任。

1994年2月,市委根据工作需要,决定调整天津市知识分子工作领导小组成员。李建国任领导小组组长,房凤友、李慧芬、罗远鹏、庄公惠任副组长,市委组织部、市委宣传部、市委统战部、市科委、市人事局为成员单位。武耀贤兼任领导小组办公室主任。办公室的日常工作由市委组织部、宣传部、统战部和市科委、市人事局的职能处室承担,不另设机构。

天津市知识分子工作领导小组自成立之日起,围绕选报和考核享受政府特殊津贴人员、筹建专家公寓和青年科技公寓、建立高级专家人才库、编撰当代专家名人录等多方面开展工作,并在全市范围内开展爱国爱市创业成才活动和为特困专家雪中送炭活动,还为部分高级知识分子解决医疗保健问题。

六、北方技术交易市场管理委员会

为加强对北方技术交易市场的领导,促进技术交易健康、快速发展,1994年11月,市政府和国家科委做出决定,成立北方技术交易市场管理委员会。该管委会主任由副市长李慧芬、国家科委副主任韩德乾兼任,副主任由市政府卢金发、市科委梁肃、国家科委技术市场管理办公室刘东升、市科委李之珍兼任,市计委、市经委、市外经贸委、市体改委等12个部门负责人为管委会委员。

1996年3月,鉴于人事变动,决定调整北方技术交易市场管理委员会成员。调整后的管理委员会主任由副市长曲维枝、国家科委副主任韩德乾兼任,副主任由市政府周思纯、市科委梁肃、国家科委技术市场管理办公室刘庆辉、市科委李之珍兼任,部分管委会委员也做出调整。

七、天津市科技领导小组

1995年8月,市委、市政府根据《中共中央、国务院关于加速科学技术进步的决定》和全国科学大会精神,为认真贯彻落实党和国家提出的“科教兴国”战略,决定调整并加强天津市科技领导小组。科技领导小组组长由市长兼任。其办公室设在市科委,主要负责政策研究和日常工作。

八、天津市信息化工作领导小组

1996年7月,市政府发出通知,决定将天津市金卡工程领导小组、天津市电子振兴领导小组合并,合并后的领导小组更名为天津市信息化工作领导小组。张立昌兼任领导小组组长,李盛霖、曲维枝兼任副组长,成员由各有关委、办、局的主管领导组成,杨竞衡、杨天行、谢麟振、叶培大等11人为领导小组顾问组成员。领导小组下设办公室,承担领导小组交办的各项日常工作。办公室工作由电子振兴办公室承担。市科委副主任马其慧兼任办公室主任。

领导小组的主要职责是:研究制定天津市信息化工作的方针、政策,组织制定相关法规和制度;组织拟订天津市信息化的发展战略、总体规划以及分阶段实施方案，监督检查规划、方案的实施；组织协调跨部门、跨行业、关系国民经济和社会发展的重大信息化工程项目，协调、指导重点行业的信息化建设，在统筹规划下对重大信息化工程项目的立项、投资、可行性研究、引进技术和开工建设等提出意见；协调解决天津市大型计算机信息网络及有关国际联网工作中的重大问题；组织研究信息化建设中关键技术、装备及有关共性的技术、应用接口、标准、规范、协议；协调各系统、各部门的电子信息技术与系统的推广应用工作；国务院信息化工作领导小组交办的有关工作。

1997年9月，天津市信息化工作领导小组办公室发出通知：随着信息化工作的扩展和深入，领导小组成员需要进行增补。经信息化工作领导小组第二次工作会议研究同意，增补市政府办公厅等部门负责人为领导小组成员。

九、天津市科技教育领导小组

为进一步推动科教兴市战略的实施，加强对全市科技、教育工作的领导与协调，1998年12月市政府发出通知，决定成立天津市科技教育领导小组。该领导小组组长为李盛霖，副组长有刘峰岩、杨新成、邢元敏、俞海潮、梁肃，成员由市政府办公厅、市计委、市经委、市建委、市农委等18个部门负责人组成。市科技教育领导小组下设办公室，负责日常工作。办公室设在市政府办公厅，办公室主任由周思纯兼任，副主任由市科委张海河、市教委李家俊兼任。通知还明确提出，1988年10月成立的天津市科技领导小组自行撤销。

2000年8月，鉴于人事变动，市政府决定对市科技教育领导小组成员进行调整。调整后的领导小组组长由李盛霖兼任，刘胜玉、杨新成、邢元敏、俞海潮、梁肃兼任副组长，领导小组成员由市委宣传部、市政府办公厅、市委科技工委、市委教卫工委等市委、市政府有关部门负责人组成。领导小组办公室主任由董迎科兼任，副主任由市科委何志敏、市教委李家俊兼任。

十、天津市科技创新专项资金领导小组

2005年5月12日，市政府决定成立天津市科技创新专项资金领导小组，以进一步加强对科技创新专项资金的管理。市政府分管科技工作的副市长兼任领导小组组长和副组长，市发改委、市经委、市教委、市科委等部门负责人兼任领导小组成员。领导小组下设办公室，办公室设在市科委。

第二节 区县科技管理机构

20世纪90年代开始，各区（县）为加强对科技工作的领导，相继成立由区（县）主要负责人担任组长、主管科技工作的副区（县）长任副组长的区（县）科技工作领导小组、科普工作领导小组等机构，并不断健全和完善区（县）科委领导班子和职能科室，且大多数区（县）科委与区（县）科协实行合署办公，将行政管理与科技团体活动紧密结合起来。涉农区（县）各乡（镇）普遍配备科技副乡（镇）长，有的乡（镇）还建有乡（镇）科委（科技办），在各村配备分管科技工作的副主任，把科技工作纳入对区、镇、村三级科技工作任期目标责任制考核内容，为推进科技进步与创新提供组织保障。各区（县）政府依据区位优势和特点，相继制定“科技兴区（县）”发展战略，积极推进科技进步工作。2003年起，各区（县）政府从加强专利管理工作规范化、制度化建设入手，做好知识产权保护工作体系建设，普遍成立由主管区（县）长负责、各有关部门为成员单位的知识产权工作领导小组，并设立知识产权管理办公室，打击侵犯专利权的行为，维护市场经济秩序。

一、区(县)科委主要职责

1991年起,各区县科委作为区县政府分管科技工作的行政主管部门,在机构改革中其主要职责虽几经调整,但更加趋于明确和具体。主要职责是:贯彻执行国家和天津市制定的有关科技发展的法律、法规和方针、政策;组织制定该区县科技发展战略、规划、计划,并组织实施;宏观管理该区县科技机构,推进科技体制改革工作;负责"科教兴区(县)"的综合工作;组织各类科技计划项目和各类基金项目的申报和实施,管理使用好该区县科技发展基金和科技奖励基金;组织专家对重大科技、经济项目进行咨询、论证、评估,为科学决策提供依据;负责科技成果的培育、认定、登记、奖励和推广应用工作;负责该区县专利技术的申报、实施等项管理工作;负责科技信息的收集、整理和信息技术的推广与应用;负责该区县民营科技企业和技术贸易机构审核及归口管理;负责该区县技术交易合同的认证、登记等管理工作;会同有关部门拟订科技人才队伍建设规划,提出相关政策建议,做好科学技术领域学术、技术带头人的培养、选拔工作,做好引进高级技术人才工作;负责科技进步考核、科技进步监测、科技统计、科技培训及科技保密工作;承办区政府交办的其他事项等。其中,大部分区(县)科委与区(县)科学技术协会实行合署办公,会同区(县)科协负责科学普及工作,指导区属学会、协会、研究会和工厂科协的各项工作,抓好青少年科技活动等。部分区县科委还负责该区县地震监视、分析预报管理及防震减灾工作。有农业的区县科委还负责健全和完善农业科技管理服务体系,会同有关部门做好该区县种植业和养殖业的新品种引进、筛选、培育、提纯、复壮、试验、示范、推广应用和管理,推动科技示范镇、村、户的发展。

各区县科技管理机构在区(县)委、区(县)政府的领导下,结合各地区的实际,认真贯彻执行党中央、国务院一系列科技工作的方针政策,积极推进"科教兴区(县)"战略的实施,不断发展改革开放的大好形势,努力促进区域经济发展,为推动科技进步和经济发展做出积极贡献。1996年,经天津市科技教育工作领导小组批准,各区县科委开始实施科技进步监测,客观、全面地反映各区县科技工作状况,以科技进步监测为鉴,推动科技进步。1996~2000年度,天津市科技进步监测采取市区、农口区县、工业公司同步考核,科技进步监测各自排序的方法。2001年起,天津市科技进步监测排序由市内六区、农口区县各自排序,改为全市18个区县共同排序的办法进行,科技进步监测在不断充实完善中进一步走向科学化、规范化,各区县相互间的竞争力不断增强。2003年,市政府决定在全市18个区县范围内开展科技进步考核,不仅考核一个地区的科技进步情况,而且重点考核区域科技、经济和社会发展的整体水平。至2005年,全市18个区县全部通过科技进步考核。

二、区(县)科委基本情况

1991~2005年,各区(县)科委在机构改革中内设机构、人员编制、主要负责人几经调整和变更,领导班子建设得到加强,内设机构更加合理,其中大部分区(县)科委与区(县)科协实行合署办公。

1991~2005年天津市各区(县)科委基本情况一览表

表1-6-2-34

项目 区县 科委名称	内设机构(2005年)	人员编制(2005年)	科委主任变更(1991~2005年)	备注
和平区科委	办公室,科技兴区办公室,科技管理科,科普培训科,基层协会科。	行政编制8人, 事业编制8人, 工勤事业编2人	马兴顺(1988年7月~1995年7月),王毅(1995年7月~2003年1月),岳和平(2003年1月~2005年9月),赵光普(2005年9月~2005年12月)	与区科协合署办公
河西区科委	办公室,综合科技管理科,科技企业管理科,科协工作科	行政编制5人, 事业编制8人	刘凤山(1986年6月~1996年9月),徐景瑞(1996年11月~1998年8月),高志达(1998年8月~2002年10月),宋连生(2002年10月~2005年12月)	与区科协合署办公

续表1-6-2-34

区县科委名称 \ 项目	内设机构(2005年)	人员编制(2005年)	科委主任变更(1991～2005年)	备注
河东区科委	办公室,科技管理科,科教兴区工作科,科协工作科	行政编制5人,事业编制6人	宋进发(1991年～1994年4月),白树栋(1994年5月～2005年12月)	与区科协合署办公
南开区科委	办公室,科技管理科,科教兴区科,专利管理办公室	行政编制8人	刘桂星(1986年11月～1998年2月),董法源(1998年2月～2004年12月),赵元(2004年12月～2005年12月)	与区科协合署办公
河北区科委	办公室,科技管理科,科教兴区管理科,市科技进修学院河北分院,科普工作科,河北科贸街和河北科技园区管理办公室	行政编制7人,事业编制15人	岳琪(1987年8月～2001年12月),吕勋(2002年1月～2005年12月)	与区科协合署办公
红桥区科委	办公室,科技兴区工作科,科技管理科,信息化建设工作科,科学普及部,学会基层部,天津市科技进修学院红桥分院,知识产权办公室	行政编制10人,事业编制23人	孙家本(1984年2月～1993年4月),梁成宝(1993年4月～2002年2月),马静茹(2002年2月～2005年12月)	与区科协合署办公
塘沽区科委	办公室,综合计划科,科技管理科,科技信息科,基层科,科普科	行政编制14人,事业编制9人	王玉琪(1988年6月～1992年11月),姜承来(1992年12月～1997年11月),刘振禄(1997年12月～2004年6月),张玉民(2004年7月～2005年12月)	与区科协合署办公
汉沽区科委	办公室,综合计划科,科技管理科,科学普及科,基层工作科	行政编制9人,事业编制8人	王力行(1991年～1993年1月),陈贵友(1993年2月～1995年3月),付有明(1995年4月～2005年7月),苗雨状(2005年8月～2005年12月)	与区科协合署办公
大港区科委	办公室,科技管理科,农业科技科,工业科技科,社会发展科技科	行政编制11人	李筱纯(1991～1999年),宁培楼(1999年8月～2005年7月),阚永才(2005年7月～2005年12月)	与区科协合署办公
东丽区科委	办公室,综合计划科,成果管理科,知识产权科	行政编制9人	王海广(1985～1993年),王天春(1994～2001年),田先钰(2002年12月～2005年12月)	与区科协合署办公
西青区科委	办公室,工业科技与知识产权科,农业与社会发展科技科,科普科	行政编制14人	王怀义(1991年1月～1993年4月),林锡福(1991年1月～1995年3月,副主任主持工作),王锋(1995年3月～2003年10月),毛玉虎(2003年10月～2005年12月)	与区科协合署办公
津南区科委	办公室,计划科,技术市场科,信息科,地震工作管理科,生产力促进中心	行政编制19人	赵树源(1983年11月～1992年9月),陶长才(1984年5月～1991年4月),于庆生(1994年～1998年),孙宝顺(1998年～2001年),时玉成(2001年～2005年12月)	
北辰区科委	工业科,农业与社会发展科,信息化办公室,办公室	行政编制6人,事业编制10人	王教普(1990年1月～1994年5月),乔立元(1994年5月～1995年5月任副主任并主持工作,1995年5月～2004年3月任主任),骆守佶(2004年3月～2005年12月)	与区科协合署办公
武清区科委	办公室,科技计划科,技术市场科,综合科	编制19人	甄玉鑫(1983年10月～1998年1月),解华(1998年1月～2005年12月)	
宝坻区科委	办公室,科技发展与计划科,法规与专利科,防震减灾科,科学技术普及科	行政编制17人,事业编制8人,工勤人员4人	韩洁生(1990年5月～1994年8月),宋子洪(1994年8月～1995年12月),芮岐任(1995年12月～1998年4月),朱兆平(1998年4月～2001年4月),崔文学(2001年4月～2005年12月)	与区科协合署办公
宁河县科委	办公室,科技管理科,科技普及科,知识产权科,科技培训科,地震办公室,财务科	行政编制12人,事业编制6人,工勤人员6人	李太昌(1982～1991年),李连增(1991～1998年),孙学力(1998年～2005年12月)	与区科协合署办公
静海县科委	办公室,科技兴农科,科技综合科,科协、地震办公室	行政编制19人,事业编制8人,工勤人员3人	刘忠义(1987年3月～1994年10月),李松林(1994年10月～2003年3月),于传利(2003年3月～2005年12月)	与区科协合署办公
蓟县科委	办公室,计划科,技术市场办公室,科普科,县院合作办公室	行政编制10人	刘会春(1990～1992年),赵春生(1992～2001年),乔金生(2001～2003年),王建业(2003～2005年)	与县科协合署办公

第二篇

科技管理与服务

概　述

进入20世纪80年代，随着改革开放的推进，经济对科技的需求日益突显。特别是1985年3月中共中央颁发《关于科学技术体制改革的决定》，天津市认真贯彻党中央关于“经济建设必须依靠科学技术，科学技术工作必须面向经济建设”的方针，深入进行科技管理体制方面的改革，并从改革科研院所拨款制度入手，对市属科研院所实行分级管理和考评制度。在“放活科研机构，放活科技人员”政策的推动下，科研院所面向企业和基层积极开展技术咨询、技术转让和技术服务，寻求新的发展途径。1989年，在中共天津市委员会（以下简称“市委”）的统一领导下，由天津市人民政府（以下简称“市政府”）研究室牵头，天津市科学技术委员会（以下简称“市科委”）、天津市经济委员会（以下简称“市经委”）、天津市体制改革委员会（以下简称“市体改委”）等部门联合对全市工业企业依靠技术进步的现状、条件、机制及体制等问题进行深入的调查研究，并对科技进步的主体做出全面剖析，为进一步研究制定科技发展战略做好思想和理论准备。

1992年，天津市认真贯彻“邓小平视察南方谈话”精神，提出“科技兴市”战略，并集中时间和人力进行专题调研。在对一些重大问题取得统一认识后，市委、市政府发布《关于依靠科技进步，加快经济发展的若干意见》，第一次以党的文件形式，把科技优先发展的战略地位作为全市的共识确定下来。该文件在内容上体现了一条主线，即进一步解放和发展第一生产力，把科学技术发展摆在全市发展的先导地位，加速经济建设向依靠科技进步和提高劳动者素质的轨道转移，全面振兴天津经济。文件明确提出“科技兴市”的重点是“科技兴工”和“科技与经济的结合”。1993年10月，国家颁布《中华人民共和国科学技术进步法》。由于天津市早有准备，很快起草相应的地方法规——《天津市实施〈中华人民共和国科学技术进步法〉办法》，并于1994年1月经天津市人民代表大会常务委员会（以下简称“市人大常委会”）审议通过，以立法的形式把“科技兴市”的具体内容纳入法制轨道，成为天津市依法推动经济发展方式转变和经济结构调整、推进科技进步和自主创新的一项重要举措。为营造“科技兴市”的环境氛围，召开了天津市科技宣传工作会议，动员全市各个方面提高认识，推动“科技兴市”战略的实施。之后科技兴工、兴教、兴企、兴农、兴商相继展开，公检法、工商、财政、金融、税务等部门纷纷为“科技兴市”献计献策，支持科技进步各项举措的实施。天津市“科技兴市”战略的实施，为1995年贯彻党中央、国务院的部署，实施“科教兴国”战略打下了良好的舆论和实践基础。1994年，市委、市政府批准实施科技“百亿工程”，就是集成全市的科技优势，集中有限资金，用5年左右的时间，培育一批有发展潜力的高新技术产品，带动全市高新技术产业的发展。在市委、市政府及有关部门的支持下，市科委全力推动，支持一批成长性好的项目，帮助企业解决资金、场地、能源、配套、销售等诸多问题，在培育、引导和带动全市高新技术产业的发展中起到重要推动作用。

1995年党中央确立“科教兴国”战略方针，市委、市政府对“科技兴市”战略做出进一步的拓展和深化，提出实施“科教兴市”战略，把经济建设切实转移到依靠科技进步的轨道上来。同年，市委、市政府召开全市科学技术大会，并制定《关于贯彻全国科学技术大会精神，加速科技进步的实施意见》，明确提出天津经济建设从根本上“必须走出一条依靠科技进步，提高整体素质，实现加快发展，增强经济实力的路子”。这标志着天津进入全面追求科技进步的年代，经济发展必须要走科技路，吃科技饭。1996年，市政府确定集中全市的人力、物力、财力，实施重大科技产业化工程，市科委会同天津市计划委员会（以下简称“市计委”）、市经委共同组织推动，筛选出技术含量高、生命周期长、竞争能力强的干细胞、干扰素、镍氢电池、锂离子电池、工程机械、轮胎设备等13个项目首批先行，对高新技术产业化起到示范带动作用。1998年，市政府组织制定《天津市高新技术产业发展规划》，确定了高新技术产业发展战略、重大对策和发展重点，并实施“重大高新技术产业化工程”计划,每年确定10~20个项目,加大高新技术产业化的力度,许多重大项目形成具有自主知识产权、跨世纪的创新产品,培育了带动经济发展的产业群体,成为天津市的品牌产品,使高新技术产业规模迅速扩大。

1999年全国技术创新大会做出《加强技术创新,发展高科技,实现产业化的决定》,年底市委颁布《关于加速科技进步和技术创新的若干意见》。市科委以技术创新为突破口,调整科技布局,改革管理体制,加大研发力度,不断培育技术与项目资源,强调有限目标、集中资源、重点突破,到1998年“百亿工程”突破百亿,“重大科技产业化工程”初见成效。

天津市对科技计划的管理,分为三个层次。第一层次是应用基础研究,分为重点项目和面上项目;第二层次是面向经济建设主战场,开展技术开发与创新,重点抓企业包括民营科技型企业技术创新以及科研院所与高校的成果转化;第三层次是培育面向21世纪的高新技术产业,如新能源、环保、电动汽车、设施农业等。同时,市科委还提出依托整合现有资源,在全市建立10个科学研究中心、20个工程技术中心、50个企业技术开发中心,并建立完善科技服务体系的举措。与三个层次的管理相互对应,形成以大院大所为依托,以企业为主体的新型科技创新体系,以信息咨询、技术市场、创业服务中心、生产力促进中心等骨干机构为依托的科技服务体系。市科委还调整机构,成立了综合计划处,其他各部门的职能也相应作出调整和划分。

据国家科委和国家统计局每年一度的科技进步测评显示,天津市综合科技实力在全国各省市区中的排名连续跃升,从1993年的第七位,到1995年、1996年、1997年、1998年分别上升至第四位,1999年跃升至全国第三位,以后几年在全国一直保持在第三、第四位的水平。同时,天津市的全社会研究与开发经费(R&D)投入总量持续增加。据统计,1999年天津市R&D投入总量为15.95亿元,是1995年R&D总量的2.89倍,与1995年相比年均增长29.15%,R&D占GDP(国内生产总值)的比重由1995年的0.6%提高到1999年的1.1%。在1999年R&D总量中,约有44%经费来自政府,其中中央政府投入约5亿元,地方财政科技拨款用于R&D约为2亿元;企业R&D投入8.45亿元,占总量的53%,其中民营科技企业R&D投入3.05亿元,占企业投入的36.1%。科技投入的增加和科研条件的改善,促进科技活动直接产出的迅速增长,科技成果数量及专利授权量显著增加,科技进步贡献率由90年代初的30%增长到90年代末的43%,科技成为经济和社会发展的重要推动力量。

进入21世纪,市委、市政府坚持将科技工作摆在优先发展的位置,围绕实施“科技兴市”战略和大力推动科技进步,制定并实施一系列重要的科技法规与政策,推动科技管理工作的规范化、制度化、科学化。科技体制改革不断深化,特别是转制科研院所通过产权制度改革建立现代企业制度,形成有利于科技创新和科技成果产业化的体制和机制,科技创新创业环境不断优化。至2005年,天津市面向经济社会发展的需求,组织实施33个科技专项和6个科技工程,加快科技创新、成果转化与产业化步伐,推动产业技术和结构的升级,促进高新技术产业发展,圆满完成“十五”科技发展规划确定的各项任务。全市专利申请量由2000年的2789件增加到2005年的11657件,专利授权量由2000年的1611件增加到2005年的3045件。2001~2005年,全市共获得国家级科学技术奖励60项,取得市级重大科技成果6339项,技术交易额累计达到204.67亿元。2005年,天津市设立科技型中小企业技术创新资金,支持民营科技企业的技术创新活动。至此,全市科技投入形成多渠道,增加了新来源。全市财政科技拨款由2000年的5.05亿元增加到2005年的13.65亿元,有力地支持了科技成果转化为生产力。围绕“科教兴市”战略的实施,国际间科技合作日趋加强,在重点高新技术领域以及城市建设、水资源、环保等方面与美、英、澳等国家和地区开展国际科技合作与民间学术交流,并实施国外智力引进项目,聘请近万名外籍专家到津工作,使天津市在基因芯片、生物新药、软件、集成电路设计等领域的研发从无到有、从弱到强,达到国内领先水平和国际先进水平。天津新技术产业园区和经济技术开发区成为高新技术产业发展的重要基地,在促进高新技术项目产业化、扶持高新技术企业发展等方面发挥重要作用。自1987年起,天津市每年9月组织一次科技周活动持续不断,向社会公众特别是青少年宣传普及科学知识,逐步形成政府引导、全社会共同参与的科普工作的良好局面,特别是1997年6月市人大常委会颁布实施《天津市科学技术普及条例》,将科学技术普及工作纳入法制化的轨道。2005年,天津市与科技部、中国科学院、军事医学科学院和北京市建立科技工作会商制度和科技合作关系,促进国家科技力量聚焦天津发展和京津两地科技资源的共享。

第一章　科技条件

1991年起，天津市在不断加大科技投入的同时，进一步加强科技基础条件平台建设，科研工作条件得到不断改善。天津市地方财政对科学技术的经费投入不断增加，其中1996~2000年科技投入总额是1991~1995年的2.32倍，2001~2005年科技投入总额是1996~2000年的3.12倍。2000年，天津市开展科技创业投资工作，并不断加强组织推动、政策制度、骨干机构和人才队伍等方面的建设，逐步实现创业投资行业的跨越式发展。

同时，天津市不断加强科技基础平台建设。开展科技网建设，建立一个高速宽带的科技网络，向社会提供全方位的科技信息服务与技术支撑。建立科技文献平台，实现科技文献信息检索与查询的计算机化与网络化。研究并解决科技期刊发展中的问题，科技期刊的编辑出版水平不断提高。构建并开通天津科研条件信息网、大型科学仪器协作共用网和实验动物网，促进科技资源的共用共享和优化配置，为科技和经济社会发展创造有利的科研条件和基础环境，为科技进步和发展提供优质服务。

第一节　科技经费

天津市地方财政科技拨款逐年增加。1991~1995年，天津市地方财政科技拨款7.03亿元，占全市地方财政支出的比重为2.29%。1996~2000年，地方财政科技拨款16.32亿元，占全市地方财政支出的比重为2.06%。2001~2005年，地方财政科技拨款50.85亿元，占全市地方财政支出的比重为2.73%，科技投入比例比1996~2000年上升0.67个百分点。

一、科学事业费

1991~1995年，天津市财政科学事业费拨款逐年增加，其中1995年是1991年的2.4倍；科学事业费拨款总额为2.09亿元，占全市地方财政科技拨款总额的29.73%。在全市科学事业费拨款中，市科委归口管理的事业单位科学事业费为1.74亿元，占全市科学事业费的83.3%。

1996~2000年，天津市财政科学事业费拨款不断递增，其中2000年是1996年的1.6倍；科学事业费拨款总额为5.24亿元，占全市地方财政科技拨款总额的32.11%，比1991~1995年占全市地方财政科技拨款总额的比例上升2.38个百分点。市科委归口管理的科学事业费累计3.72亿元，占全市科学事业费总额的71.0%，比1991~1995年科学事业费增加1.98亿元。其中，2000年市科委归口管理的事业费拨款为0.76亿元，比1995年增加0.24亿元，增长率为47%。1996~2000年，市科委归口管理的科学事业费年平均增长率为8%。

2001~2005年，天津市科学事业费的投入有较大幅度增长。全市科学事业费累计投入总量达10.01亿元，比1996~2000年投入总量增加4.77亿元；占全市地方财政科技拨款总额的19.69%，比1996~2000年占全市地方财政科技拨款总额的比例下降12.42个百分点。市科委归口管理的科学事业费累计达4.60亿元，占全市科学事业费总量的46.0%，比1996~2000年增加0.88亿元，增长24%。其中，2005年市科委归口管理的科学事业费为1.10亿元，比2000年增加0.34亿元，增长45%。2001~2005年，市科委归口管理的科学事业费年均增长率为11%。

二、科技三项费

1991～1995年，天津市财政科技三项费拨款总额为4.48亿元，占全市地方财政科技拨款总额的63.73%。其中市科委归口管理的科技三项费财政拨款为2.34亿元，占科技三项费拨款总额的52.23%。

1996～2000年，天津市财政科技三项费拨款总额为9.99亿元，占全市地方财政科技拨款总额的62.21%，是1991～1995年科技三项费拨款总额的2.23倍。其中，市科委归口管理的科技三项费累计5.15亿元，比1991～1995年增加2.81亿元，增长率为192%。1996～2000年，市科委归口管理的科技三项费年均增长率为12%。

2001～2005年，天津市财政科技三项费拨款总额为40.6亿元，占全市地方财政科技拨款总额的79.84%，是1996～2000年科技三项费拨款总额的4.06倍。其中，市科委归口管理的科技三项费累计达8.4亿元，比1996～2000年增加3.25亿元，增长率为157%。2001～2005年，市科委归口管理的科技三项费年均增长率为14.5%，比1996～2000年上升2.5%。

三、科技基建费

1991～1995年，天津市财政科技基建费拨款总额为0.46亿元，占全市地方财政科技拨款总额的6.54%。1996～2000年，财政科技基建费拨款总额为0.24亿元，占全市地方财政科技拨款总额的1.47%，比1991～1995年下降5.07个百分点。2001～2005年，财政科技基建费拨款总额为0.05亿元，占全市地方财政科技拨款总额的0.10%，比1996～2000年下降1.37个百分点。天津市财政科技基建费拨款呈现逐步递减趋势。

1991～2005年天津市地方财政科技拨款情况统计表

表2-1-1-35 单位：亿元

年份	天津市地方财政支出	天津市地方财政科技拨款					地方财政科技拨款占地方财政支出的比重(%)
		合计	科学事业费	科技三项费	科技基建费	其他	
1991	47.47	1.19	0.29	0.90	0.00	0.00	2.51
1992	46.52	1.59	0.33	0.90	0.36	0.00	3.41
1993	51.27	1.21	0.30	0.89	0.02	0.00	2.36
1994	69.00	1.29	0.47	0.80	0.02	0.00	1.87
1995	93.30	1.75	0.70	0.99	0.06	0.00	1.88
5年小计	**307.56**	**7.03**	**2.09**	**4.48**	**0.46**	**0.00**	**2.29**
1996	110.19	2.48	0.82	1.17	0.04	0.45	2.25
1997	140.08	2.52	1.02	1.43	0.05	0.02	1.80
1998	155.15	2.78	1.07	1.58	0.05	0.08	1.79
1999	177.62	3.49	1.02	2.11	0.06	0.30	1.90
2000	209.57	5.05	1.31	3.70	0.04	0.00	2.41
5年小计	**792.61**	**16.32**	**5.24**	**9.99**	**0.24**	**0.85**	**2.06**
2001	259.78	7.52	1.42	6.06	0.04	0.00	2.89
2002	300.07	8.45	1.56	6.68	0.01	0.20	2.82

续表 2-1-1-35　单位：亿元

年　份	天津市地方财政支出	天津市地方财政科技拨款					地方财政科技拨款占地方财政支出的比重(%)
		合计	科学事业费	科技三项费	科技基建费	其他	
2003	350.63	9.74	1.94	7.80	0.00	0.00	2.78
2004	431.49	11.49	2.29	9.20	0.00	0.00	2.66
2005	520.28	13.65	2.80	10.86	0.00	0.00	2.62
5年小计	**1862.25**	**50.85**	**10.01**	**40.60**	**0.05**	**0.00**	**2.73**

注：科技三项费用是指国家为支持科技事业发展而设立的新产品试制费、中间试验费和重大科研项目补助费。科技三项费用是国家财政科技拨款的重要组成部分，是实施中央和地方各级重点科技计划项目的重要资金来源

第二节　科技创业投资

2000年，天津市启动科技创业投资工作，并逐步构建起科技创业投资的组织推动体系、政策制度体系、骨干机构体系和人才队伍体系，探索民营化、商业化、国际化和专业化的创业投资发展模式，实现创业投资行业的跨越式发展。全市科技创业投资企业由2000年的10家增加到2005年的65家，科技创业投资企业的注册资本总额由2000年的9亿元增加到2005年的42亿元。

一、组织建设

2000年12月，天津市创业投资发展中心成立。该中心作为天津市创业投资工作联席会的日常办事机构，为正处级、自收自支事业单位，在全市创业投资行业的综合管理和创业投资引导资金的经营管理方面发挥重要作用。

2002年6月，成立天津市创业投资工作联席会，负责组织协调全市创业投资工作。该联席会主任由主管科技工作的副市长担任，成员由市科委、市财政局、市发改委、市经委、市商委、市人事局、市国税局、市工商局、市证监局、中国人民银行天津分行等部门负责人组成。

2002年9月，在原天津市风险投资促进会的基础上，改组成立天津市创业投资协会。该协会是全市创业投资行业的自律组织，在创业投资专业资格认证、行业培训和业务交流等方面积极开展工作。

二、政策制度建设

2000年9月，市政府印发《关于积极推动天津市建立风险投资机制的意见》，形成启动创业投资工作的总体方案，成为推进全市创业投资工作的基本政策。2002年4月，市政府印发《天津市促进创业投资业发展的暂行规定》，对设立创业投资企业的条件及优惠政策做出规定，为吸引境内外各类创业资本在天津投资制定具体的优惠政策。2004年，市科委、市财政局联合制订《天津市创业投资机构财税优惠政策的实施办法》，天津经济技术开发区出台《鼓励风险（创业）投资的暂行规定》，天津新技术产业园区出台《鼓励风险投资机构及中介服务机构进驻火炬创业园的暂行规定》，进一步落实市政府促进创业投资发展的意见。天津市创业投资的政策制度建设逐步得到完善。

三、骨干机构建设

2001年，市财政局在市级财政预算中安排天津市创业投资引导资金总额度5亿元，用于吸引境内外民营

机构在天津合资设立商业性创业投资基金及其管理公司，培育天津市创业投资骨干机构。市科委与市财政局联合制订《天津市创业投资资金管理暂行办法》，并成立创业投资决策与风险控制委员会。

至2005年，市财政共投入创业投资引导资金2.2亿元，先后出资设立诚信（天津）创业投资基金、天士力生物技术创业投资基金及其管理公司、赛富成长（天津）创业投资基金及其管理公司、天津创业投资担保公司、天津创业投资管理公司等7家创业投资企业，用近1.2亿元的引导资金吸引境外及民间资金近10亿元，带动关联资本近100亿元，形成支持天津高新技术产业发展的创业投资平台。赛富成长（天津）创业投资基金先后投资顺驰（中国）不动产网络公司、北京数字太和科技公司、北京冠图通讯科技公司、广东惠州雷士照明公司、天津汽车模具公司等，累计投资额达1200万美元，带动软银亚洲、凯雷投资等世界级创业投资基金的联合投资7450万美元，其中在天津投资6300万美元，是天津市引导基金实际出资额的10倍。其中，天士力生物技术创业投资基金向北京迪威华宇公司的抗乳腺癌一类生物新药项目“热休克蛋白联合阻断抑制剂”投资1000万元人民币。

四、队伍建设

2000～2005年，天津市本着“人才为本”的思想，大力加强创业投资人才队伍建设，通过资格培训、交流研讨、研究宣传等活动，提高创业投资管理人员的素质和技能，涌现出一批创业投资专业人才。天津创业投资有限公司（以下简称“天津创投公司”）通过公开招聘、加强培训、优胜劣汰，特别是与境外创业投资机构开展合作，成为天津市具有国际化能力的特色团队，受到软银亚洲、美国博乐、新加坡祥峰等合作伙伴的高度评价。

天津创投公司创立“基金的基金”的特色业务模式，即采取“母基金”运作模式，吸引境外及民间机构，发起设立若干商业性子基金，实行委托管理，建立有效的决策、激励与约束机制，调动其他出资方的积极性，实现政府资金的二次放大，发挥对社会资金的杠杆作用。该公司通过业务实践、人才引进、加强培训、业绩考核、优胜劣汰等方法，不断提升团队质量，形成一整套运作规范的商业化管理模式。天津创投公司作为天津市创业投资协会的理事长单位，积极探索并建立管理人个人“跟投”的新机制，即通过重组天津创投管理公司，管理团队获得管理公司60%的股权，并将其作为“跟投”平台，通过管理公司向受托管理的基金按照1%的比例对具体项目进行“跟投”，实现管理人与基金利益的有效捆绑，建立具有特色且有效的激励与约束机制。

五、发展模式

天津市积极探索创业投资工作的民营化、商业化、专业化和国际化发展模式。天津市科技创业投资坚持以社会力量为主开展创业投资，政府主要制定规则和创造环境。在创业投资业起步初期，政府以一定量的资金（一般不超过30%）进行引导，重点放在吸引境外和民间资本上，以此优化子基金的股权结构，防止政府干预，落实商业化决策机制。天津创投公司所投资的子基金以投资收益最大化为经营目标，资本、人才、项目等要素靠市场机制进行调节和配置，按商业化原则落实子基金的决策、激励及约束机制，如管理人只出资1%，可以获得20%的投资收益奖励。天津创投公司按照国际通行的创业投资委托管理模式，明确出资人与管理人的权利和责任，固定管理成本，建立激励与约束机制，并根据高新科技产业不断细分的特点，建立专业化创业投资基金，以提高投资效率，降低管理风险。至2005年，设立信息技术、生物技术、新材料技术等专业创业投资基金，并在环境保护、新能源等专业领域继续拓展。天津市积极引进国际创业投资管理技术及资本、人才、项目等资源，以实现天津创业投资业的跨越式发展。至2005年，天津市创业投资中心与境外100多家创业投资机构建立联系，并邀请美国、新加坡、日本、加拿大等国家和中国台湾地区的50多家创业投资机构的代表到天津考察，吸引一些国际大型创业投资机构进入天津，并引入国际通行的创业投资理念、管理技术和资本、人才及项目资源，推进天津创业投资的国际化进程。天津市的做法得到科技部的充分肯定，多次在全国性会议上介绍经验，许多省市创业投资企业纷纷到津学习。在全国火炬计划“十五”总结表彰大会上，天津市创业投资中心被科技部授予“全国优秀创业投资机构”称号。

第三节　科技基础条件建设

1991～2005年，天津市不断加强科技基础条件建设，科研工作条件得到不断改善。开展科技网建设与服务，集中科技网的资源、技术和人才优势，向社会提供全方位、多功能的综合信息服务。开展科技文献平台建设，从单一的阵地信息服务发展成为印刷型文献、电子型文献、网络数字型文献相结合的现代化科技文献信息服务平台。不断提高科技期刊的编辑出版水平，研究并解决科技期刊发展中的问题。2004年起，天津市贯彻落实“国家科技基础条件平台建设纲要”，搭建公益性、基础性的科技基础条件平台。2005年，开通天津科研条件信息网和大型科学仪器协作共用网及实验动物网，促进科技资源的共用共享和优化配置，提高国有资产的使用效率和管理水平，为科技发展创造有利的科研基础条件和服务。

一、科技信息平台

1991年起，天津市逐步开展科技网络建设。至1992年，天津市科技信息研究所投入安全宽带路由器（VS-80）、微机设备，并自建和购买10个数据库，实现内部资源共享。1993年，天津科技信息网络中心与中国分组交换网CNPAC联网，直接访问国内外信息资源，开展“信息快餐”形式的信息服务，并建成将科技、经济、商贸、金融、物资、市场商情等类信息融为一体的联科（LINK）信息网。1995年9月，联科信息网与国际互联网正式互联，开通天津工作站，为用户提供包括电子邮件、远程登录、文件传输、客户机/服务器模式等各种服务，并为用户代检网上信息。同时，通过该互联网将市科委百项工程向全世界发布。

1996年起，天津市科技信息研究所在购进先进设备的基础上，建立9个科技子网，并开通天津科技网，丰富网上资源，提升网络服务功能；完成TRIP Web接口软件，实现网上用户直接浏览数据库功能。1998年，该所承担天津科技网曙光机示范工程，并于1999年1月通过科技部组织的验收，获得1998年度中国互联网络信息中心域名注册申请授权代理单位。至2000年，该所为提升网络使用效率，对原线路进行扩容改造，实现天津—北京（中科院国际出口）之间直通，并在31种数据库的基础上，自主建立“天津科技成果库”和“天津科技及经贸动态数据库”。

2001年起，天津科技网重点实施“一二五工程”，即建设一个高速宽带的科技网络，强化提升两大平台功能，重点实施5项工作。天津科技网对服务器、交换机、路由器、磁盘阵列等设备进行升级改造，全面提高网络传输速率，成为天津信息港工程的标志性网络。2002年，市科委建立科技工作管理与决策支撑平台，向上连接国家各部委和各省市科委等政府部门500家，向下沟通天津市各级政府科技主管部门、各企事业单位和基层科研机构等1000家，实现科技管理工作的现代化。2003年，市科委建成电子政务外网并投入使用，实现政府网络上的科技管理信息发布、科技工作宏观指导、业务服务、信息交流等社会服务功能。同时，建立科技创新服务体系的信息共享平台，为全市各科学研究中心、工程技术中心和企业技术开发中心提供系统集成、软件开发等技术和信息服务，发展科技服务体系，为高新技术企业发展提供服务。天津科技网充分发挥网络优势，为企业信息化、农业信息化、中药现代化、环保科技提供全方位、多功能的综合信息服务与技术支撑。至2005年，将企业信息化建设的经验推广到500家工业企业，推动和发展工业企业的网络化与信息化。全市5000多家企业的主页上网率达到80%，实现网上交易活动的企业超过50%。天津科技网于2001年开通科普网。至2005年，天津科普网站设有25～30个栏目，网上读者突破100万人次/年。天津科技网在链接各高等院校、科研院所及企事业单位的同时，与国内外有关行业专业网络、门户网站实现链接，使其成为覆盖全市、遍及国内外的国际知名的专业网。天津科技网向社会各界提供网络技术咨询与服务、网络系统集成和软件开发、网站建设等服务，并利用网络孵化中小型企业，为中小型企业科技创新提供服务，还定期开设专业课程，聘请国内外知名专家、学者，举办专题学术报告会和研讨会，办好专业化继续教育。

2001～2005年，天津科技网每年访问量达到12万人次，联科信息网访问量达到26万人次，访问者涉及美国、英国、日本、比利时、瑞典、加拿大等国家和中国香港、台湾等地区及全国各省、市、自治区，联科信息集团用户7个，直接注册用户230多个，注册用户总数1000余个。

二、科技文献平台

1991～1995年，天津市科技信息研究所文献馆（以下简称"文献馆"）充分发挥其馆藏文献体系完整、品种齐全、数量充裕的特点，以印刷型、缩微型的文献信息为广大科技工作者提供服务，年接待读者量均在6万人次左右。随着计算机技术的发展，文献馆大力开展科技文献资源建设及服务的软课题研究，其中"多文种、多类型国外文献管理系统"和"中文会议文献数据库"两项研究成果分别获得国家科技进步三等奖和天津市科技进步奖。文献馆开始向科学化、信息化、网络化方向迈进。

1996～2000年，文献馆对科技文献结构进行较大规模的调整，完成从印刷型、缩微型向光盘数字型和网络化方向的转变。该馆相继引进中文期刊篇名数据库、中国专利数据库及中国化工数据库等3个中文光盘数据库，将中外文专利全文的载体全部由缩微型转为光盘，并配备光盘塔、光盘库等硬件设备，使科技文献信息检索和读者需求查询实现计算机化，提高文献检索的速度和质量，受到广大科技工作者的欢迎。以往文献馆的业务管理一直沿用手工卡片形式，无论工作人员的管理工作，还是读者在阅览室的查询，都要通过卡片实现。文献馆开展并完成"科技文献集成管理系统的研究及建设"课题，从根本上解决了文献采购、编目、流通、检索、咨询、读者服务等落后的管理模式，摈弃手工操作，全面实现计算机化与网络化，使文献馆的工作水平迅速达到国内先进水平。1998年，建成电子阅览室并对外开放，读者可根据不同需求，在互联网、光盘库局域网区和单机区3个区域内查询所需信息。同时，该馆开发出有别于公共图书馆的子系统——中国标准文献子库，并获得天津市最佳科技信息成果奖。

2001～2005年，文献馆建立天津科技文献信息网，将该馆文献资源及与天津经济、科技发展有关的信息资源定期在网上发布和定期更新，并与各公共图书文献机构和各专业图书文献机构实现联网，还与北方网、北方教育网等联合，集成文献资料和技术信息，建成网上虚拟科技图书与文献资料中心，实现资源共享。同时，该馆引进中外文光盘数据库25种，光盘近2000张，加上原有的中文期刊及国内外专利文献光盘数据库等，数字型文献的比例占文献总量的一半以上。文献馆还以文献资源为依托，充分利用网络资源，出版《国内外科技动态》《互联网科技速报》等内部刊物，为市委和市政府及有关部门提供文献信息服务。至2005年，天津文献馆逐步从单一的阵地信息服务发展成为印刷型文献、电子型文献、网络数字型文献相结合的现代化科技文献信息服务机构，成为天津市科技文献信息资源的采集、服务中心，科技文献的种类及数量均达到历史最好水平。

三、科技期刊

在天津市主办的科技期刊中，以科研机构、高等院校和学术团体主办的科技期刊为主体。至2005年，天津科技期刊共有139种（其中英文版期刊6种），包括学术类、技术类、综合指导类、检索类、科普类等5种类型，其中学术类、技术类占科技期刊总数的81.3%。天津科技期刊通过适当缩短刊期、增加页码、扩大论文载容量等方式，缩短论文发表周期，建立科技期刊的快速反应机制，取得较好效果。其中，周刊、半月刊有3种（占2.1%），月刊和双月刊有105种（占75.6%），季刊、半年刊有31种（占22.3%）；平均每期刊物页码为113页，其中61.1%的科技期刊页码在64～128页；期刊平均载文215篇/年；63.7%的科技期刊论文发表周期在7～12个月。

1991年，天津科技期刊的科技论文被国内重要检索机构收录2336篇，被国际重要检索机构收录292篇。至2005年，分别增至9466篇和5507篇；121种科技期刊被《中国刊引证报告(2006)》收录，总被引频次平均值为548次；15种期刊的总被引频次≥1000次，其中《中草药》总被引频次为6622次。据统计，2005年度天津科技期刊被“科学引文索引”（SCI）核心版收录2195篇，增长92.2%；被“美国工程索引”（EI）收录2391篇，增长96.4%。天津科技期刊在国内外的影响逐渐扩大，科技论文的数量和质量有很大提高，在国际著名学术检索系统中被收录的比例逐步提升。

至2005年，天津科技期刊中，约有70%的编辑部聘请国内知名专家担任编委，有的期刊还聘请国际知名专家担任编委，一批高学历、懂专业、善经营的中青年编辑出版人员成为工作的骨干，逐步形成新型的编辑出版队伍。据统计，全市有833人从事科技期刊编辑工作（平均每刊5.9人），其中50岁以下的编辑出版人员占66.7%；硕士和博士占18.8%；具有高级职称的编辑所占比例由20世纪90年代初的27.8%增至49.6%。各类科技期刊为吸纳高水平、高质量的论文，采取参加各种学术研讨会、组织选题策划、跟踪课题研究等方式，主动约稿，不断提高期刊的论文水平。随着信息技术的发展，越来越多的科技期刊利用计算机技术及网络技术，进行内容传播和编辑出版。至2005年，有80%的科技期刊使用电子邮件，有35.7%的科技期刊使用网络远程投稿系统，有40.9%的科技期刊建立独立网站，有的还具有在线出版功能和提供网上免费论文的下载。天津各类科技期刊逐步建立并完善编委会和审稿队伍，引进和培养一批高素质的编辑出版人员。

天津科技期刊不断在经营管理体制、运行机制及强化市场经营等方面进行探索，并取得进展。至2005年，天津科技期刊的经费来源与经营运行机制主要有4种方式：全额拨款、实报实销的有15种，占期刊总数的10.79%；定额拨款、不足部分自筹的有50种，占期刊总数的35.97%；内部承包、自负盈亏的有52种，占期刊总数的37.41%；法人实体、独立核算、自主经营的有22种，占期刊总数的15.82%。

2001～2005年，市科委制定并实施精品科技期刊工程示范计划，重点支持一批科技期刊（特别是英文科技期刊）直接面向国际，参与国际学术交流，为国际同行所接纳和认同，并逐步成为同学科领域的知名科技期刊。在2004年第三届国家期刊奖评选活动中，天津天和医院主办的《中国危重病急救医学杂志》获国家期刊奖，天津药物研究院主办的《中草药》获提名奖，天津大学主办的《天津大学学报》、天津工程机械研究所主办的《工程机械》被评为百种重点期刊。在天津市第八届（2005年度）优秀期刊奖评选中，3种期刊获特别荣誉奖，19种科技期刊获优秀期刊奖。

四、大型科学仪器协作共用

天津市贯彻执行国家有关科学仪器方面的政策与条例，组织科学仪器设备的协作共用，积极构建科学仪器共享服务网络，促进科技资源共享建设，同时组织科学仪器设备的维护和升级改造，为科研机构和科技型企业提供支撑性服务。1988年开始，天津市大型仪器管理办公室每年都要组织5～10次大型仪器分析检测专业技术培训班或大型仪器新技术新方法报告会，邀请国内外知名仪器厂商和分析检测专家作学术报告，参加人数在50～300人规模不等，受到大型仪器使用者和专业技术人员的欢迎。

1993年，天津市大型仪器管理办公室与天津市分析测试协会开展“天津市大型精密仪器现状及管理对策研究”，对全市大型仪器资源进行普查与信息收集，调查大型仪器分布与使用情况及存在的问题，探讨大型仪器资源共享方式。此后的2001年和2005年，又分别进行两次大型仪器信息的大规模收集、整理和普查，全面更新大型仪器资源信息，探讨大型仪器资源共享机制。1996年，天津市大型仪器管理办公室与天津市分析测试协会开始编印《仪器管理与分析测试信息》，使分析测试技术人员及时了解国内外大型精密仪器的发展动态，促进大型仪器使用和分析测试水平的提高。

1994年，天津市大型仪器管理办公室组建大型精密仪器维修站，把现有仪器资源的维修、改造和升级作为重点工作，发挥现有科技资源的最大效用。同时，制定《天津市大型精密仪器维修管理办法》，招聘兼职维修员，举办仪器维修培训班，提高维修人员的技术水平。1995年，针对日本岛津仪器公司在天津分析仪器较多的实际情况，成立日本岛津分析仪器天津维修站，接受用户请求30余宗，为用户维修好14台分析仪器，并逐步形成一般通用分析仪器的维修网络。至1997年，初步形成大型精密仪器零部件供应网，解决了国外分析仪器维修费用高昂、零配件少、维修时间长等问题。

1995年,天津市大型仪器管理办公室开始尝试科学仪器的调剂和升级换代。至2000年,调剂使用41台(套)大型科学仪器,21台(套)科学仪器得到升级,其中ICP等离子体光谱仪、离子探针、气液相色谱仪、X荧光光谱仪等一批最早进入国内的大型仪器,经过升级改造,加入外置电脑和软件控制,仪器功能和性能均有不同程度的提高,延长了仪器的使用年限,科学仪器的检测精度和自动化水平得到提高,科学仪器存量资源得到充分利用和开发。

2004年,天津市贯彻国务院办公厅转发科技部、发改委、财政部、教育部联合制定的《2004～2010年国家科技基础条件平台建设纲要》,全面启动大型科学仪器协作共用平台建设。天津市大型仪器管理办公室以新的理念对大型科学仪器协作共用机制进行积极的探索。在运行上,引入优胜劣汰机制,实施动态管理,对服务质量不好、运行效果欠佳、分析测试数据不准确和仪器故障频繁、无法向社会服务的仪器予以淘汰,并不断吸纳型号更新、功能更广的科学仪器设备入网,为各行各业提供高水平、高信誉、高质量的分析测试和质量监督等社会化服务。在管理上,采取政府激励与市场机制下的服务承诺相结合的模式,通过大型科学仪器协作共用网开展科技服务,促进科技资源的共用、共享和优化配置,并逐步发展成为适应市场经济运行机制的社会化科技网络服务机构。在服务上,突出政府的主导作用,为高新技术开发与技术创新提供更好的协作共用服务。2005年8月10日,大型科学仪器协作共用平台——天津市大型科学仪器协作共用网正式启动,实现津、京、冀三地大型科学仪器、化学试剂、试验室等资源共享,带动相关产业的发展。

五、实验动物管理

天津市实验动物管理委员会及其常设办事机构——天津市实验动物管理委员会办公室(以下简称“实验动物办”)自1986年成立起,积极开展实验动物管理工作。1994年9～11月,天津市开始颁发实验动物质量合格证,并制定“卫生防疫制度”“高压锅安全操作规程”“实验动物室工作制度”“保种制度”等规章制度,从而保证全市实验动物管理工作的顺利进行。

1996～2000年,实验动物办认真做好实验动物设施的咨询和服务工作,先后为天津市及外省市的17个科研和生产单位提供改建和新建实验动物设施的咨询服务,并在人手少、任务多的情况下,千方百计从外地调入合格的实验用大、小鼠,为基层单位分忧解难。1997年,组建天津市实验动物质量监测站,先后对全市实验动物生产单位和部门的实验动物进行全面的质量检测,为提高实验动物的质量和全面推行实验动物合格认证工作打下基础。同时,实验动物办按照天津市法制办公室的要求,完成对原天津市实验动物地方法规——《天津市实施〈实验动物管理条例〉的办法》的修订,并起草《天津市“九五”期间实验动物发展计划》。1998年,《天津市实施〈实验动物管理条例〉的办法》作为天津市实验动物管理的地方法规,由市政府以第140号令予以颁布执行。

2001年,天津市爆发实验动物流行性出血热传染病,疫源系由外地购入的实验动物引起。为控制疫情,实验动物办协同实验动物质量监测站技术人员到21个实验动物工作单位,现场抽检大鼠168只、小鼠571只,并进行85批次、4103个样品检测。在被检的21个单位中,发现感染流行性出血热的单位20个,占检测单位总数的95%。据统计,此次疫情造成直接经济损失上百万元。为贯彻落实国家七部委《关于实行实验动物许可证管理工作通知》精神,实现实验动物设施合格证管理到实验动物许可证管理的平稳过渡,2004年5月举办“实验动物国内外现状和发展趋势专题报告会”,聘请知名专家作报告,受到与会者的欢迎与好评。2004年6月,对《天津市实施〈实验动物管理条例〉的办法》进行修订,并以市政府30号令颁布。同年10月28日,天津科研条件网正式开通,其中实验动物网页布局在新的管理模式下得到重新调整。为全面推行实验动物许可证的认证工作,实验动物办从50多个与实验动物相关的单位和部门推选的100多名的科研人员中,筛选出40人组成天津市实验动物专家库。2005年6月25日,市科委印发《关于发布〈天津市实验动物许可证管理办法(试行)〉的通知》,标志着天津市实行实验动物许可证管理工作的时机已经成熟。与此同时,实验动物办对首批20个单位114名从事实验动物工作的科技人员进行岗位培训,经过考核全部取得“天津市实验动物从业人员岗位证书”。同年7月,实验动物办应邀出席由科技部举办的“中国北方八省市实验动物许可证验收工作经验研讨会”,并作大会交流发言。

第二章　科技发展规划与计划

1991～2005年，是天津市科技发展规划和科技计划管理逐步走向规范化、制度化的过程。继国家提出“科学技术是第一生产力”和“面向、依靠”一系列科学技术发展方针，天津在三个五年计划和中长期发展规划制定中认真贯彻执行，把“科教兴市”和发展高新技术、加强技术创新作为科技发展的战略目标。科技计划根据科技发展规划确定的奋斗目标、主要任务和发展重点，制定规划期内各年度的科技发展计划。1995年起，市科委对科技发展计划管理进行改革，各类科技计划依照规划目标，预先发布立项指南，并组织专家对申报项目进行论证和评选，做到立项过程公开、透明。至2005年，市科委共发布20多个与科技计划相关的管理规章制度，文件涵盖计划管理、项目管理、经费管理、机构管理、成果管理等方面。天津市基本确立和完善了科技计划框架和管理体系，建立起以项目单位、主管部门和市科委三级管理体系，组建科技项目咨询专家库和科技项目第三方评价体系，建成推动科技成果转化与产业化的各类服务机构，基本适应了各阶段经济和社会发展对科技计划管理的需求，成为优化全市科技资源配置，引导和促进科技发展的重要支撑。

1991～1995年，“八五”科技规划确立了科技工作的战略地位和部署，加快构建科技经济一体化新格局。科技计划按照近期计划和中长期规划的部署，主要包括科技攻关计划、自然科学基金与21世纪青年科学基金项目、火炬计划、星火和农业示范工程计划、成果推广计划和软科学计划等。

1996～2000年，“九五”科技规划全面实施“科教兴市”战略，确立高新技术及产业发展的地位和重点，培育新的经济增长点，走出一条依靠科技进步加快经济发展的路子，重点实施50项重大科技产业化和重大科技攻关（含导向性科技攻关）项目。科技发展计划主要包含8个专项计划，即：科技攻关计划、科技重大产业化项目计划、基础研究计划（即自然科学基金和青年科学基金）、软科学研究计划、成果推广计划、星火计划、火炬计划、重点武装科研院所计划。同时，根据经济和社会的发展需求，又新设立国际科技合作计划、科技型中小企业技术创新资金、科技创新专项资金。

2001～2005年，“十五”科技规划旨在优选天津高新技术发展领域和重点，提高投资强度加快发展，大力推进科技创新体系建设。设计实施了“3+1”科技计划体系，即包括：科技发展战略研究计划、应用基础研究计划、科技发展专项研究开发计划及研究开发条件建设计划，并增设重点新产品计划和社会发展科技计划等。

第一节　科技发展规划

1991年起，天津市紧密结合科技和经济社会发展的需要，先后组织专家学者编制完成各个时期科技发展规划，包括天津市科学技术发展十年规划和“八五”计划纲要、天津市科学技术发展“九五”计划和2010年长期规划纲要、天津市高新技术产业发展规划、天津市科技发展“十五”规划、天津市中长期科学和技术发展规划纲要（2006～2020年）和天津市科技发展“十一五”规划等。这些科技发展规划分别提出各个时期科技发展的指导思想和奋斗目标、发展重点及保证措施等，并积极组织实施。

一、科技发展十年规划和“八五”计划纲要

1991年12月，市科委根据国务院批准实施的天津城市总体规划方案和《天津市国民经济和社会发展十

年（1991～2000年）规划与“八五”计划纲要》，制定出《天津市科学技术发展十年（1991～2000年）规划和“八五”（1991～1995年）计划纲要》。

该“纲要”的指导思想：1991～2000年，天津市继续认真贯彻中共中央关于科技工作的指导方针，发挥“第一生产力”的作用，全面深化科技体制改革，在面向经济建设主战场、跟踪和发展高新技术、加强基础研究三个层次的总体部署中，结合天津市的优势和实际，一是集中精力解决工农业适度规模经济的关键技术和装备现代化问题，促进技术引进—消化吸收—进口替代—技术出口的外向型经济发展的良性循环，加速技术成熟、效益显著、量大面广的重大科技成果的推广应用；二是积极推动高新技术向产业化、国际化发展；三是安排好储备技术的应用基础研究，为在21世纪天津市经济发展和科技振兴打下基础。

该纲要提出的主要发展目标是：“八五”末，全市重点行业技术水平达到70年代末或80年代初发达国家水平，“九五”末，争取达到80年代末或90年代初水平。工业新产品率“八五”达到15%以上；主要产品引进消化吸收国产化率达到50%~80%；高新技术产业产值占工业总产值“八五”末达到4%；技术合同成交额“八五”期间达到15亿元。国家授权专利总数达到四千件以上。到2000年科技综合实力走在全国前列。

该“纲要”提出的发展重点是：围绕天津市“316”（3个带头产业，10个重点行业，60个重点产品）产业结构，合理配置科技资源，精心组织汽车、计算机等10个重大科技攻关项目；抓好100项重大科技成果的推广应用；重点预研30类产品和技术。高新技术重点发展领域有电子信息技术、机电一体化技术、生物技术、新能源、新材料和环境保护技术。加强应用基础科学研究，增强科技资源储备。推动“科技兴农”，发展城郊型农业，加快农业现代化进程；深化体制改革，加速科技事业发展。

该“纲要”提出的保证措施有：稳定和完善促进科技进步的政策法规；拓宽投资渠道，调整资金使用结构，提高科技投入额度；加强宏观管理，发挥大科技计划体系和市场调节机制相结合的综合优势；加强科技队伍建设，提高劳动者素质；强化科技成果推广的意识，建立、健全科技成果推广服务体系；提高自我发展能力，推动企业技术进步；鼓励天津市科技力量参与国际竞争，加强国际合作、交流及国外智力引进。

二、科技发展“九五”规划和2010年规划纲要

1996年初，市科委根据《中共中央、国务院关于加速科学技术进步的决定》，紧密围绕天津市国民经济和社会发展的总体目标，编制《天津市科学技术发展“九五”计划和2010年长期规划纲要》（以下简称“纲要”）。同年11月26日，市政府将该纲要转发全市各区县政府和各委、局及直属单位，要求遵照执行。

该纲要提出的指导思想是：坚持科学技术是第一生产力的战略思想，继续贯彻经济建设必须依靠科学技术、科学技术工作必须面向经济建设、努力攀登科学技术高峰的基本方针，从切实转变天津市经济增长方式出发，坚定不移地走“科教兴市”之路，进一步解放思想，更新观念，大胆实践，为21世纪科技腾飞打下基础。

该纲提出天津科技发展战略是：坚持实施“科教兴市”战略，建立科技经济一体化新格局。面向经济建设主战场，主要围绕天津汽车和机械、电子、化工、冶金四大支柱产业，集中抓好关键技术攻关，运用高新技术嫁接改造传统产业，促进引进技术消化吸收，提高产业自主创新能力，加速科技成果转化；面向新技术革命挑战，大力推动高新技术及其产业化发展，围绕电子信息、生物技术、先进制造技术、新材料、新能源和环保技术六大高新技术领域，培育21世纪主导产业；安排好应用基础研究，加强科技自身建设，增强技术储备和科技发展后劲。到21世纪初，形成结构优化、布局合理、精干高效的科研开发体系；具有自主开发和设计能力的工业技术创新体系；开放、灵活、完善的科技服务体系；以及多渠道、多层次的全社会科技投入体系。

该纲要提出的主要发展目标是：科技进步对经济增长的贡献率大幅度提高，到2000年提高到50%，到2010年提高到60%；大力发展高新技术及其产业，到2000年，高新技术产业产值占工业总产值的比重达20%，到2010年提高到30%；加速科技成果转化为现实生产力，推广应用率达80%，工业系统新产品产值率达25%；到2000年，科技进步对农业增长的贡献率达到55%，农业先进技术的覆盖率达80%，主要农作物良种普及率达95%；实施《中国21世纪议程》，促进经济和社会可持续发展；培养一批跨世纪的优秀人才；加强科技投入强度，形成多元化投入格局；科技综合实力要达到全国前列水平。

该纲要提出1996～2000年的主要任务是，以提高天津市国民经济运行素质为中心，以发展高新技术为先导，为天津经济社会发展提供技术支撑。发展高新技术及其产业，以“科技百亿工程”为示范和引导，带动一批高新技术产品，最终形成100亿元产值规模的高新技术产业群体，成为全市新的经济增长点。加快培育现代通信、新医药、计算机技术和应用及环境工程等一批高新技术新产业，为塑造21世纪的先导产业夯实基础。以高新技术产业园区为全市发展高新技术的孵化器和产业化基地，加快建设与发展。利用高新技术改造传统产业，工业以四大支柱产业为重点，攻克一批技术难点热点问题，加强关键技术的工程化和产业化开发，加强新产品开发和培养名牌拳头产品，形成技术先进、结构合理、高附加值的工业体系。农业以丰富“米袋子”和“菜蓝子”为重点，积极发展两高一优农业和生态农业。推进城市农业产业化进程。该纲要还在社会发展、应用基础研究、科技事业和软科学研究等方面确定了发展重点任务。

该纲要提出的保证条件和措施是：坚持实施“科教兴市”战略，加强对科教兴市工作的领导；切实加大科技投入力度，形成以企业为主体，各级政府、各类金融机构以及全社会构成的多层次、多渠道的科技投入体系。到2000年，全社会研究与发展（R&D）经费占国内生产总值（GDP）的比重要达到1.5%以上。市财政每年对科技投入的增长幅度要高于财政收入的增长幅度，企业科技开发投入占销售额的比例不低于1%，多方筹集资金发展科技风险投资业，积极吸纳国内外各类资金，支持科技事业发展；改革和完善科技计划管理体系，实施科技重点工程；加强科研基础设施建设，努力为推动科技成果转化创造物质条件；增强企业技术创新实力，确立企业技术开发主体地位；合理利用和开发人力资源，优化尊重知识、尊重人才的社会环境，发展天津市科技人才优势；建立健全科技服务体系；利用国外科技资源，提高科学和技术水平；健全科技法规体系，以实施科技进步法为重点，形成配套的科技法规体系。

三、高新技术产业发展规划

随着世界经济一体化格局的逐渐形成和知识经济的兴起，天津市迫切需要加快高新技术产业发展，使之成为21世纪新一代支柱产业，努力建设与北方重要经济中心地位相适应的高新技术及产业化基地。从1998年下半年开始，由市计委会同市科委、市经委、市统计局、市财政局等部门，组织全市几百名专家学者，编制完成《天津市高新技术产业发展规划》，经市政府批准发布实施。

该“规划”提出的指导思想是：以“科学技术是第一生产力”为指针，坚持以市场需求为导向，以改革开放为动力，加快实施“科教兴市”战略，突出重点，锐意创新，大力发展高新技术产业，积极利用高新技术改造传统产业，带动产业结构升级，走出一条依靠科技进步、提高整体素质、实现加快发展、增强经济实力的路子，使高新技术产业成为天津市经济增长的重要支撑，为实现跨世纪奋斗目标发挥重要作用。

高新技术产业发展的战略目标是：到2020年，建立起比较完善的适应高新技术产业发展特点与规律的经济体制和运行机制；发展壮大一批在国内外具有重大影响的企业和企业集团，形成一批具有较高市场竞争力的名牌拳头产品；把天津新技术产业园区和经济技术开发区建成全国一流的高新技术产业化基地；高新技术产业实现产值占全市工业总产值的比重达到30%以上，成为国民经济的主导产业，使天津成为中国北方重要的高新技术科研开发和产业基地之一。

高新技术产业发展的具体目标是：到2020年，高新技术产业产值达到1100亿元，年均增长19%，占全市工业总产值的比重达到22%；高新技术产品出口额达到18亿美元以上，年均增长15%，占全市出口额的比重达到20%；建设10个应用基础科学研究中心，20个工程技术研究中心，50个企业技术开发中心；培育和发展一批销售额达到10亿元以上的企业，力争形成2至3个销售额超过50亿元的大型企业或企业集团；新技术产业园区和经济技术开发区高新技术产品产值分别达到320亿元和540亿元，年均分别增长21%和18%，占全市高新技术产品产值的比重达到29%和49%。

高新技术产业发展的重点任务是：重点发展电子信息、生物技术与现代医药、新能源三个产业，使其产值规模到2020年达到860亿元，占全市工业总产值的17.2%；积极鼓励和引导光机电一体化、新材料以及环保三个产业快速发展，提高产品的水平和市场竞争能力，到2020年形成240亿元的产值规模，占全市工业总产值的4.8%。

该"规划"提出的要求是:按照天津市高新技术产业发展方向,选择与其关联程度大的45个重点应用基础科学研究项目,组织全市乃至聘请国内外专家学者开展科学研究,为高新技术发展提供技术储备;围绕高新技术产业发展重点,组织30项重大科技攻关项目,实行滚动发展;在已启动的13项重大科技产业化项目的基础上,调整补充和重点实施20项重大高新技术产业化项目;加快建设高新技术产业化基地,为经济发展培育新的增长点。

该"规划"提出的主要措施是:抓紧制定促进高新技术产业发展的有关政策,增强政策竞争力;建立多元化投资机制,加大对高新技术产业的投入资金,扩大对高新技术产业的投入;完善激励机制,大力引进高新技术人才;深化科技体制改革,健全高新技术开发体系;加大扶持力度,促进新技术产业园区加快发展;积极利用高新技术,加快传统产业的改造步伐;加强领导,搞好规划的组织实施。

1999年,市政府向全市印发《天津市高新技术产业发展规划》,并转发市计委等13个部门制定的《关于促进高新技术产业化的意见》。同时,由市计委牵头,市科委、市经委、市建委、市外经贸委、市农委、市教委、市商委、市财政局、市人事局、市统计局参加,成立天津市高新技术产业发展规划实施办公室,负责组织推动《天津市高新技术产业发展规划》的实施,并建立《天津市重大高新技术产业化项目计划》。配合重大高新技术产业化项目计划的实施,设立天津市科技发展资金,市财政局、市计委、市科委制定《天津市科技发展资金管理办法》。1999年和2000年,市财政每年安排5000万元资金,主要用于重大高新技术产业化项目的补助及贷款贴息,并从税收、减免建设费用、投融资、吸引人才等方面对重大高新技术产业化项目予以扶持。

《天津市高新技术产业发展规划》构筑起高新技术及产业发展的总体框架,举全市之力,加强技术创新,发展高科技,实现产业化。

四、科技发展"十五"规划

2001年7月,市科委编制完成《天津市科学技术发展第十个五年计划》。同年8月,市政府批转发布实施。该规划提出的指导思想是:面对国内国际经济与科技发展的新形势,充分发挥社会主义市场经济对科技进步的推动作用,坚持"以人为本,以改革开放为动力,全面实施科教兴市战略,加速科技创新,发展高科技,实现产业化,推动产业结构升级,促进科技、教育、经济、社会协调发展"的方针,创建国内一流的科技强市。21世纪初期,建成支撑天津市科技和经济发展的科技创新体系,形成完善的适应社会主义市场经济发展的科技创新机制,基本实现科学技术现代化。

该规划提出的具体发展目标是:"十五"期间,科技综合实力继续保持在全国前列,科技进步对经济增长的贡献率达55%;高新技术产品产值占工业总产值的比重达35%,工业新产品产值率达30%以上,农业先进技术覆盖率达90%;全社会R&D占GDP比重达2%;社会可持续发展综合水平保持国内前列;提高产业技术开发能力,基本建成支撑重点科技领域和重点产业发展的科技创新体系。

该规划提出的主要任务与重点:加快建立和完善科技创新体系和科技投融资体系,提高全市科技创新能力;积极抢占科技制高点,以建立有自主知识产权的产业核心技术为目标,创建数字技术、光电子技术、高能电池技术、生物技术及中药现代化技术、软件开发、环保科技等6个研发基地,带动相应新兴产业的发展,实现高新技术成果从量的增加到技术上的跨越;集中力量抓好留学生科技园、科技创业广场、国际科技交流中心、生产力促进中心、科技风险投资服务中心等5个21世纪科技形象工程,推动高新技术和各类高级科技人才的聚集与培养;积极采用高新技术改造、提升传统产业,不断提高拳头和名牌产品的技术水平;积极引导农业走集约化、工厂化可持续发展之路,加快实现农业现代化;积极实施《天津市21世纪议程》,增强社会可持续发展能力。

该规划提出的具体措施是:加强科技法制建设,营造良好的科技创新和高新技术产业发展的政策环境;建立健全多渠道、社会化、高效率的科技投入体系,加大科技投入力度;深化科技体制改革,加快科技型企业的发展,推动企业成为技术创新主体;广泛开展国内外科技合作,大力吸纳国内外科技资源,加速科技和高新技术产业国际化发展步伐;大力吸纳国内外人才资源,发展壮大重点科技领域学术(技术)带头人队伍;提高全社会科技进步意识,进一步加强对全市科技工作的领导。

五、中长期科技发展规划纲要

为落实科学发展观,贯彻《国务院关于印发国家中长期科学和技术发展规划纲要(2006~2020年)的通知》精神和要求,支撑和引领天津市经济社会全面协调可持续发展,按照市委、市政府和科技部的部署和要求,天津市于2003年12月启动制定中长期科技发展规划纲要和编制科技发展"十一五"规划的工作,并成立以市长戴相龙为组长的规划领导小组。该规划纲要的编制分为两个阶段。2003年11月至2005年5月为战略研究阶段,组建了精干和有代表性的战略研究专家队伍,分别由有关领导和知名专家主持,参加规划战略研究的科技、经济、管理等方面研究人员有450人。经过一年多的努力,中长期科技规划战略研究的12个专题、45个课题研究工作全部通过专家研究,取得重要成果。在战略研究取得初步成果的基础上,2005年6月开始进入该规划纲要的编制阶段,并成立专门起草小组。在编制过程中,先后征求科技部、部分参与国家纲要起草的北京专家和天津市有关专家等各方面的意见,并先后召开10余次综合性征求意见会、20余次分领域的技术专家征求意见会。经过近两年的工作,十易其稿,2006年1月4日经市政府第63次常务会议审议通过,形成《天津市中长期科学和技术发展规划纲要(2006~2020年)》。2006年4月21日,市政府向全市各区县局及有关单位印发该规划,以指导全市未来15年科技发展和创新。该规划纲要的编制过程中,注重把握以下方面:一是坚持以邓小平理论和"三个代表"重要思想为指导,坚持用科学发展观统领规划编制工作;二是坚持从天津的城市定位和未来发展需求来规划科技发展,切实发挥科技对天津市经济和社会发展的支撑引领作用;三是认真把握科技发展的前沿,注重规划的落实;四是强化地方规划与国家规划的有机衔接。

该规划纲要设有6章。第一章明确提出,天津市未来15年科技发展的指导思想、发展目标、总体部署和远景展望。第二章主要是按照中长期科技发展总体目标的要求,对未来重点发展领域及优先发展技术进行规划和布局,确定10个重点发展领域和46种优先发展技术,其中10个重点发展领域是:电子信息,生物与现代医药,能源,石油化工与精细化工,装备制造业,都市农业,现代服务业,资源与环境,人口与健康,城市建设与交通。第三章提出,天津市应用基础研究和前沿技术的开发要以培养高素质创新人才为使命,以增强原始创新能力为目标,鼓励科研人员和创新团队自由探索,围绕国家与天津市经济社会发展的重大战略需求,追求科技发展的前沿与热点,为高技术产业发展提供技术源泉,形成面向重点产业、兼顾国家需求、体现区域特色的应用基础研究格局。第四章指出,按照增强主体、注重制度、促进互动、培养集群、聚拢人才、优化环境的思路,以建设企业为主体的技术创新体系为突破口,进一步发挥市场在科技资源配置中的基础作用和政府的主导作用,深化科技体制改革,加强科技服务体系和知识创新体系建设,建设一批高水平的科技创新机构,构建有利于各类创新主体有机联系的创新网络,加快提升优势产业、重点领域科技创新能力,形成功能完善、特色鲜明、创新效率高、充满生机和活力的区域创新体系。第五章提出,以滨海新区研发转化基地为核心,以津西知识创新与孵化基地、京津塘高新技术产业带为重点,形成资源配置合理、功能明确、相互衔接的"两基一带"(滨海新区研发转化基地、津西知识创新与孵化基地,京津塘高新技术产业带)科技发展布局。同时,加强国内外科技合作与交流,充分利用国内国外两个市场和两种资源,以大开放促进大发展。第六章提出的政策和措施是:制定落实鼓励企业技术创新的政策措施,建立科技投入稳定增长机制,加强科技人才队伍和创新文化建设,实施知识产权和技术标准战略,加强科技法规体系建设,加强科技发展的决策和组织协调。

该规划纲要顺应经济全球化和科技发展的潮流和趋势,体现社会主义市场经济条件下科技发展的规律,把握区域和地方科技发展的特点,满足天津市经济社会发展的战略需求,着重突出以下特点:一是以"提高自主创新能力"作为科技发展的主线;二是强调科技的支撑与引领作用并重,处理好近期与中长期发展的关系;三是突出滨海新区的战略地位,把支撑和引领滨海新区的开发开放作为科技发展的最大机遇和重大任务;四是更加突出企业技术创新的主体地位,把尽快建成以企业为主体、产学研有机结合的技术创新体系作为创新体系建设的突破口；五是注重在战略部署、发展重点、政策方向等方面与国家层面进行全面对接，既充分发挥天津市的优势，又能争取更多国家的支持。

六、科技发展“十一五”规划

“十一五”(2006～2010年)期间，是加快实施科技兴市战略、构建社会主义和谐社会和全面加快建设滨海新区的关键时期。天津市科技发展紧紧抓住经济社会发展的重大战略机遇期，把握当代科学技术发展的特点与趋势，加强自主创新，进一步加强科学技术对经济社会的支撑和引领作用。2003年11月，天津市在制定中长期科技发展规划纲要的同时，开始编制科技发展“十一五”规划。在编制该科技发展规划过程中，体现了新的规划理念与规划内容。主要表现有如下特点：一是与中长期科技发展规划纲要紧密衔接。“十一五”规划是在中长期科技规划纲要的基础上制定的，围绕纲要提出的长期科技战略方向提出了近五年的科技战略目标和任务。二是突出自主创新战略。明确了走自主创新道路，建设创新型城市的科技发展战略。三是突出提升产业自主创新能力。强调提高优势产业的核心竞争力能力，培育新兴科技产业。四是突出滨海新区带动作用。抓住滨海新区开发开放难得的历史机遇，全力推动滨海新区研发转化基地建设。五是突出企业的主体地位。要建立企业为主体、市场为导向、产学研结合的技术创新体系，并作为创新体系建设的突破口。六是突出体制机制创新。围绕滨海新区综合配套改革试验区的建设，创新科技体制和机制。2006年1月4日，经市政府第63次常务会议审议通过《天津市科技发展“十一五”规划》，并于同年4月印发到全市各区县局及有关单位贯彻执行。

该规划在回顾“十五”科技发展情况的基础上，提出“十一五”科技发展的指导思想、基本原则、发展目标。其指导思想是：贯彻国家“自主创新、重点跨越、支撑发展、引领未来”的科技发展指导方针，大力实施科教兴市、人才强市和可持续发展战略，按照率先建成创新型城市的总体要求，以“提高自主创新能力”作为科技发展的主线，坚持以人为本，创新体系机制，广泛集聚创新资源，着力培育行业主体，突出集成创新和消化吸收再创新，加强原始创新，支撑和引领经济社会全面协调可持续发展。其基本原则是：坚持以人为本；坚持体制机制优先；坚持对内对外开放；坚持突出发展重点；坚持突出培育创新主体。该规划根据天津市中长期科学和技术发展规划纲要确定的战略目标和总体部署，突出产业自主创新，提高优势产业的核心技术开发和新兴科技产业化能力；支持社会发展领域的科技创新，增强科技对社会发展的支撑能力；加强应用技术研究和前沿技术开发，提高科技持续创新能力；优化科技创新环境，强化科技资源整合，提高吸纳利用科技资源的能力；建设国内一流的科技创新体系，夯实创新的制度基础，激发创新创业活力，科技综合实力继续保持各省市前列，为率先建成创新型城市打下坚实的基础，使天津市成为国内重要的高新技术的原创地、聚集地和先进技术引进消化吸收的承接地与扩散地之一。

该规划确定的科技发展重点任务是：围绕电子信息、生物与现代医药、能源、石油化工与精细化工、装备制造业、都市农业、现代服务业、资源与环境、城市建设与交通等10个重点领域、软件技术、微电子技术、光电子与激光佳话、数字技术、医药生物技术等46种优先发展技术，攻克一批关键技术；实施半导体照明、基础应用软件及高端通用芯片、节能环保汽车膜技术及产品等12项重大科技项目，实现信息、生物等领域的技术跨越；培育壮大软件产业、生物产业、现代中药产业、绿色能源产业、环保科技产业、水资源产业、纳米与新材料产业、海洋科技产业、民航科技产业、科技服务业等10个新兴科技产业；加强应用基础研究，突破一批前沿技术；完善科技投融资体系，建设科技基础条件平台；构建一流的科技创新体系；以滨海新区研发转化基地为核心，以津西知识创新与孵化基地、京津塘高新技术产业带为重点，形成资源配置合理、功能明确、相互衔接的“两基一带”的科技发展布局，营造有利于科技创新的开放环境，显著提高天津市整体自主创新能力。

该规划提出的政策和措施是：制定落实鼓励企业技术创新的政策措施；进一步完善多渠道、社会化科技投入体系；加强科技人才队伍和创新文化建设；加强科技法规体系建设；实施知识产权和技术标准战略；加强科技发展的领导和组织协调。

第二节 科技发展计划

从1983～1990年国家科技计划体系初步形成，到1991～2000年对科技计划体系进行补充和调整，再到2001～2005年又经过进一步的补充和调整，逐步形成国家科技计划体系，包括国家科技重大专项、“973”计划（基础研究发展计划）、“863”计划（高新技术研究发展计划）、国家科技攻关计划、政策引导类计划（包括星火计划、火炬计划、重点新产品计划、软科学计划）、国家科技合作计划、重大科技创新基地建设（包括国家实验室、国家技术基础条件平台、国家工程技术研究中心）和科技型中小企业技术创新基金等基本计划管理框架。

天津市对应国家科技发展规划和计划，结合区域经济发展需求和实际情况，从“八五”计划开始，历经三个五年计划，在面向经济建设主战场、发展高新技术及产业、加强技术储备三个层次上逐步形成天津科技发展计划体系。部署和制定的天津科技发展计划包括：应用基础研究计划，1989年和1990年先后实施21世纪青年科学基金和自然科学基金，2001年起，逐步分成面上应用基础研究项目和重点应用基础研究项目；科技发展专项计划，分为重大科技攻关计划和重点科技攻关计划，重点支持高新技术及产业化项目，经济建设重大工程和重大装备的技术攻关项目，企业技术创新项目；科技产业化推动计划，包括星火计划、火炬计划、科技成果推广计划、新产品计划、农业科技示范工程、科技型中小企业技术创新基金等，属指导性计划；社会发展科技计划，重点支持人口健康、生态环境、资源综合利用、防灾减灾等专项；国际科技合作计划，开展政府间合作项目，针对天津重大科技攻关需求引进人才和科技资源；科技发展战略研究计划，围绕天津科技发展战略与对策、科技政策、科技体制改革、科技创新能力建设等重大问题实施软科学与科技发展战略研究计划；研究开发条件建设计划，重点支持科研中心、实验室、工程研究中心、科技信息服务等科技能力建设。

根据发展需求，基于科技计划体系，在实施过程中为突出重点、聚集资源，先后安排系列“冠名”专项计划，均在计划体系的基本框架之中。

一、应用基础研究计划

为加强基础研究，增加科技资源和储备，强化科技人才和青年科技人员的培养工作，市科委于1989年和1990年先后设立“天津市21世纪青年科学基金”和“天津市自然科学基金”。每年投入不低于“科技三项经费”的10%，并逐年增加。

1991～1995年，天津市安排自然科学基金和青年科学基金资助项目共计1109项，资助经费2327.15万元。1996～2000年，天津市安排自然科学基金和青年科学基金资助项目951项，资助经费4185.5万元。“八五”和“九五”期间，两项科学基金项目涉及工业、农业和社会发展领域，具有项目覆盖面大、支持面广的特点，作为地方性科技计划项目，本着“有所为，有所不为”的原则，突出重点，优先支持具有地区传统优势的医学、化学与化工、机械等学科领域，以及天津市高新技术发展规划中确定的电子信息、生物技术和现代医药、新能源、光机电一体化、新材料和环保等六大高新技术产业的相关学科领域，充分体现出其服务于天津地区经济和社会发展这一地方特色。通过不断地优化基金配置，资助经费总量和项目投资力度逐年增长，有力地促进了天津市基础研究事业的发展。同时，促进了全市各领域自主开发创新能力的提高，造就了一支年龄结构合理，愈来愈年轻化，学历、知识层次更高，充满活力，勇于开拓创新的科技专业人才队伍，为天津市社会和经济的跨越式发展打下了基础。科学基金项目的实施，产生一批具有创新性和应用前景的研究成果，包括实用技术或产品、专利、研究论文等，其中部分项目分别在国际、国内获奖，高水平论文被SCI、EI和ISTP等收录并多次引用。这些成果的取得，有力地推动源头技术创新，促进了全市自主知识产权成果总量的增长，促进了学科建设和国际科技合作和交流，为实施科技攻关、科技产业化等计划项目提供强有力的支撑，对提高天津市科技综合实力和引导促进高新技术产业的可持续发展起到重要作用。

2001年起，天津市将自然科学基金和青年科学基金按照重点应用基础研究和一般应用基础研究两个层面进行安排。至2005年共安排应用基础研究计划项目934项，其中一般项目723项、重点项目211项，资助资金7220万元，涉及信息科学、材料科学、环境科学、化学与化工科学、生物技术与医药科学等多领域。应用基础研究计划项目立足于解决制约天津市经济和社会发展的关键科学问题，注重人才培养和项目培育相结合，为天津市吸引、凝聚和稳定了大量优秀科技人才，涌现出一批杰出的学术带头人，为获得国家级科技计划项目奠定了基础，取得一批具有创新性和应用前景的研究成果。

二、科技发展专项计划

在三个五年计划中，市科委先后安排了系列"冠名"专项计划。

1991年，市科委会同市计委、市经委组织"十项科技攻关会战"，调动全市大学、科研院所和企业的科技力量，集中三委资源，以产业关联度大、带动作用强的关键技术为重点，对数控机床及加工中心、夏利汽车改型和轻型汽车发动机、医疗电子仪器、化工设备、精密制造技术以及环保、能源、新材料等十个关键技术项目组织联合攻关，实现了产学研的紧密结合。通过攻关，自主研发的夏利三厢式轿车当年试产3000辆，并很快进入年产5万辆的技术改造；研发设计了轻型车491Q发动机，替代进口；中空纤维、药芯焊丝、新型能源、中药制剂等项目在一系列关键技术上取得重大突破，成功实现了成果转化。之后，市科委每年都安排科技攻关计划项目。至2005年，市科委积极组织实施科技攻关计划，通过整合资源、聚集人才、集中目标对优势领域和项目加大支持力度，加快技术创新，大力培育新的经济增长点，取得一批具有自主知识产权的高新技术成果。

1992年，市科委设立"天津市高新技术成套设备计划"和"天津市高新技术吸收创新计划"两个专项。当年安排18项"技术成套设备计划"，投资4605万元；安排13项"吸收创新计划"，投资1360万元。两个专项计划的实施，促进传统产业的技术更新，带动企业产品结构的优化升级。

1994年3月，天津市启动"科技百亿工程计划"，旨在用5年时间建成10个年产值在5亿元以上的高新技术产业，带动一批高新技术产品，最终形成100亿元产值规模的经济增长点，使若干高新技术产业走在全国前列，形成经济发展的新优势。是年，组织实施游戏学习机、皮质激素、镍氢电池、新型农药和数控机床5个产业项目和膜技术、铁基记忆合金、系列新药、药芯焊丝及成套设备4个培育项目，实现工业总产值9.5亿元，同时带动一批相关行业的发展，为全市经济发展增添后劲。

1995年，天津市围绕全市经济发展支柱产业和培育新兴产业，以"科技百亿工程"为重点，全面推进高新技术产业化取得显著成绩。其中，皮质激素、新型农药、游戏机、膜技术、生物制药、数控机床、环保产品等一批项目初具规模，走出一条低投入、高产出、高效益的经济发展之路，为国有大中型企业依靠科技进步、提高技术创新能力提供示范。1996年，科技百亿工程实现产值突破40亿元。至1998年科技百亿工程提前完成5年发展计划，实现产值突破100亿元，达到117亿元。

1996年，天津市启动"重大科技产业化计划"，在科技"百亿工程"的基础上，市科委会同市计委、市经委首批筛选13项重大产业化项目，涉及电子信息技术、生物技术、先进制造技术、新材料和环保技术等重点领域的高新技术产业化。该项计划的实施，既促进了绿色电池、新医药、新材料和软件等产业上经济规模，逐步成为新的经济增长点，又促进了产学研结合，催生一批高新技术企业集团。

1998年，市政府组织制定《天津市高新技术产业发展规划》，确定高新技术产业发展战略、发展重点和重大对策。1999年，由市计委牵头，会同市科委、市经委和市财政局等部门共同筛选，先后实施了多批重大产业化项目，从原重大科技产业化计划13项，调整补充到20～30个项目，并增加5000万元的投资，举全市之力加以推动。这些重大项目，如锂离子电池、地塞美松、膜技术、干细胞和曙光服务器应用等项目覆盖了全市重点发展的六大高新技术领域，使全市形成了一批具有自主知识产权的跨世纪先导产品，对未来经济发展具有重要带动作用的产业群体。到2000年，全市高新技术产品产值达744.6亿元，占工业总产值的23%，高新技术产品出口额从1990年不足1亿元增到2000年的20亿元。天津市高新技术产业化走出了一条优势集成、多方配合、重点突破、全力推进的发展新路，高新技术产业规模迅速扩大，成为全市新的经济增长点。

2001年，天津市启动“科技专项计划”，为占领科技制高点和培育经济增长点，在信息技术、生物技术与新药、新能源、新材料和环保技术领域，建立新药专项、纳米专项、集成电路设计专项、基因芯片专项、高能电池专项、电动汽车专项 、软件专项等10个重点科技专项，取得一批具有自主知识产权的科技成果与产品。科技专项的实施，形成了创新的集群效应，如新药专项，开发出新一代抗生素—头孢地尼、抗肿瘤药物—紫金龙片等10余个新药；纳米专项，开发出负载型纳米催化剂、药用树脂、汽车漆等6大类纳米材料新产品。还有微操作机器人、0.25微米SOC系统芯片等项目是具有国际先进水平的科研成果。科技专项的实施，产生了人才聚集效应，在生物技术领域，有60多位来自海外的博士、留学生活跃在生物芯片、生物医药重点专项上。纳米专项集结了清华、北大、中科院、南大、天大等十几个研发团队，仅博士就有40余位，形成了科技资源的凝聚效应。

2001年，天津市启动“制造业信息化、农业信息化、中药现代化和环保科技”四大科技工程，促进了先进技术在传统产业上的推广应用，促进了科技与经济的结合。制造业信息化工程的实施，使CAD、CIMS等项技术在冶金、机电、汽车、医药、纺织、轻工等9大行业400余家企业得到推广应用，机电行业CAD普及率由原来不足40%，提高到80%以上，企业的新产品创新设计和开发能力有很大提高。锻压机床厂、液压集团通过应用CAD模板、模块化设计软件，在机电产品竞标中，连续中标20多个项目，其中有设备中标出口。信息化盘活了传统产业的存量，大大提高了企业在国内外市场的竞争力。天津市成为国家首批制造业信息化示范城市。农业信息化工程遍及12个区县的30个乡镇，500个示范点（村、企业、农行），成为农业新技术普及推广的重要途径。通过农业信息化工程，网上交易产品达2000多个，销售收入达数亿元，为提高农民收入助力。在中药现代化工程上，推动了十几项关键应用技术的应用。如澄清技术、树脂吸附纯化技术等在天津中药产业上得到应用。一些前瞻性高新技术，如超临界萃取技术、纳米技术、三相流化床技术、分子蒸馏技术等在中药产业开展了示范工程研究。丹芪偏瘫、霍香正气软胶囊、京万红等药物加快二次开发，GAP、GLP等规范建设进入程序。四项工程的实施，用高新技术提升改造传统产业取得明显成效。

2005年，天津市重大高新技术产业化项目累计100项，其中有50个项目建成投产，涌现出天津天士力制药股份有限公司、天津药业集团有限公司、天津力神电池股份有限公司、天津赛象科技股份有限公司等一批重点龙头高新技术企业，建成中药现代化、绿色电池、软件出口等一批高新技术产品生产基地。2005年，纳入统计的天津市重大高新技术产业化项目实现产值占自主研发高新技术产值的76.1%，成为支撑自主研发高新技术产业发展的重要力量。同时，组织实施采用连续式无介质焊接新工艺生产建材型纯铜芯高温太阳能集热板高技术产业化示范工程、新型畜禽疫苗高技术产业化示范工程等7个国家高新技术产业化项目，争取国家补助资金4200万元。这些项目拥有自主知识产权，具有较高的技术水平和良好的市场前景，有力地发挥了示范带动作用。

三、科技产业化推动计划

国家科委于1985年启动面向农村经济主战场的“星火计划”，1988年启动加速高新技术发展的“火炬计划”，1991年推出“国家科技成果推广计划”，1997年实行“国家重点新产品计划”。以上计划是指导性计划，实行国家、地方两级管理，资金筹措以企业为主、贷款为主，国家和地方适度引导的办法。天津设立了各项对应计划。

（一）星火计划与农业示范工程

市科委于1986年开始编制并组织实施“星火计划”。1991～1995年，实施星火计划367项，覆盖全市50%以上的乡镇，产生良好的经济和社会效益。一批依靠科技进步振兴农村经济的先进集体和个人脱颖而出，其中大港区中塘乡1993年被国家科委批准为国家级星火技术密集区。1996~2000年，天津市实施星火计划514项，星火计划向规模化、集约化、产业化方向发展，西青区中北斜乡和北辰区双街镇被批准为国家级星火技术密集区。1998年9月，成立国家农产品保鲜工程技术中心。2001~2005年，天津市实施星火计划170项。星火计划主要涉及农副产品加工、农村资源综合利用与环境保护、农业高效种植和养殖、农用化工、农业机械与设备、农村建材和区域特色产业等领域。星火计划以形成区域化布局、专业化生产、产业化经营和社会化服务为主，开创农村科技服务体系新模式，促进农村科技服务体系的初步形成。市科委在组织实施市级星火计划的同时，争取到一批国家级星火计划项目和各类农业计划项目，得到国家用于农业方面的资金支持。通过星火计划项目的实施，发挥区域性支柱产业优势，培育星火技术密集区，促进水产养殖业的发展，带动农村科技和经济的发展。至2005年，大港区中塘乡、西青区中北镇、北辰区双街镇3个国家级星火技术密集区建设初具规模，产值达到70.1亿元，利税11亿元，年人均收入超过万元。

为在全市农业生产中大面积推广配套的农业先进技术成果，市科委于1989年开始实施农业示范工程项目。1991~1995年，实施农业示范工程项目65项，投入科研经费近千万元，在粮食增产、菜篮子工程建设等方面通过大面积推广农业科技成果，使全市农业生产整体水平进一步提高，涌现出一批在全国有影响的科技成果。黄瓜研究所开发的系列黄瓜新产品、蔬菜研究所开发的马铃薯微型脱毒种薯在全国得到推广；“蓟县农业高产高效益综合技术示范工程项目”，为在一个县范围内进行高效农业建设起到示范作用；武清县“双千田”（亩产粮食千斤以上，亩效益千元以上）综合栽培技术示范工程和静海县10万亩旱作农业技术示范工程等粮食增产示范工程项目的实施，取得显著成效。1996年起，天津市开展工厂化农业技术与示范研究，为农业现代化提供技术储备和示范窗口。列入市级重大科技攻关项目的“工厂化农业技术研究与示范区建设”，按计划要求建成示范区1333亩，累计投入60001万元，辐射带动全市21个示范区的建设，辐射面积达到6000亩。该项目于2000年5月通过验收。农业示范工程的实施，使现代科技与农村经济更加紧密结合，科技促进农业的发展。

2001~2005年，天津市实施农产品安全生产、动植物新品种选育、津南农业科技园区等3个科技专项以及农业信息化、农产品深加工科技示范工程，总计实施项目102项，投入研发经费3835万元。通过这些科技专项和示范工程的实施，培育出优质作物、蔬菜等新品种120多个，其中通过国家品种审定的作物品种9个，通过天津市品种审定的品种50个，共引进蔬菜、农作物等资源材料近3000份，筛选优良资源材料600多份，示范、推广面积近100万亩，繁育良种达200万千克，社会经济效益6亿元以上。津南国家农业科技园区累计吸引资金协议额近20亿元，到位额近10亿元，引进涉农企业40余家，先后与日本东京大学、法国昂热大学、丹麦奥胡市农业职业学院、美国西部种业公司等8家国外机构和南京农业大学、中国水产科学院等15家国内科研机构建立全面合作关系，共同实施各类科技项目40余项，开发科技产品50多种，并建成电子商务网站——欣农网；培训人数1000余人次；龙头企业带动农户7800户，创造1800余个就业岗位，实现年产值3.5亿元，成为天津市农业科技的示范窗口和农业科技成果转化基地。全市通过农业信息化工程的实施，建立了完善的市—区（县）—乡（镇）—行政村四级网络服务体系，推广应用一批先进、实用的农业科学技术，在4.65万亩的种植对象、3.68亿尾的对虾、6.05万头的畜牧养殖对象上示范应用了专家决策咨询系统，新增效益2.75亿元，受益农民7万余人。

（二）火炬计划

为贯彻实施中共中央提出的“发展高科技，实现产业化”的战略方针，1988年9月市科委组织专家编制“天津市火炬计划”，将技术水平处于国内领先地位、发展前景好、能够形成规模经济，且投入少、周期短、效益高的项目列入该计划。1991~1995年，天津市实施火炬计划339项，其中国家级50项，累计投入5亿元，实现新增产值24亿元，新增利税7亿元。1996~2000年，天津市安排火炬计划项目313项；2001~2005年，安排火炬计划179项。各高校和科研院所十分重视科技成果的转化工作，筛选出一批好的高新技术成果，分别列入国家级和市级火炬计划。火炬计划涉及电子信息、先进制造技术、新材料、新能源与高效节能、生物医药、环保等高新技术领域。在火炬计划的支持下，天津市高新技术产品的开发研究和产业化得到迅速发展，形成一批拥有自主知识产权的高新技术产品，如复方丹参滴丸、养血醒脑颗粒、柴胡滴丸等产品，在国内外市场具有很强的竞争优势。火炬计划的实施，培育并形成一批高新技术企业，加速用高新技术改造传统产业的步伐，企业产品的技术含量得到提高，并为“科技百亿工程”和“重大科技产业化计划”实施打下基础。

（三）科技成果推广计划

1990年，天津市开始制定并组织实施科技成果推广计划，其中具有明显效益、覆盖面广的市级科技成果推广计划项目，逐步滚动进入国家级科技成果推广计划。1991～1995年，制定并组织实施市级科技成果推广计划38项，同时实施国家级重点推广计划25项，争取到国家科技成果推广贷款3580万元，取得社会经济效益近10亿元。为加快科技成果转化步伐，市科委、市计委、市经委、市高教局等部门分别制定并组织实施各自的成果推广计划，其中市经委每年都要制定新产品开发计划、倍增计划，把科技成果的推广应用与产业、产品结构调整结合起来，一大批高水平的科技成果在工业生产中得到应用，促进全市支柱产业的发展和经济增长向集约型方向的转变。1995年2月，天津市5个单位入选国家科委确定的重点科技成果推广中心，分别是化工部天津化工研究院的国家工业水处理技术研究推广中心，天津大学的国家工业结晶技术研究推广中心、国家化工填料塔及内件技术研究推广中心，农科院黄瓜新品种技术研究推广中心和马铃薯微型种薯技术研究推广中心。

1996～2000年，天津市承担国家级科技成果推广计划40项；实施市级科技成果推广计划69项，其中工业方面40项，农业方面24项，其他方面5项。2000年，市科委、市农委出台《天津市科技成果推广示范乡（镇）建设暂行管理办法》。当年，评选津南区双港镇、大港区中塘镇、蓟县罗庄子乡、西青区辛口镇、东丽区万新庄街（镇）、宁河县板桥镇等6个乡镇为科技成果推广示范乡（镇）。

2001～2005年，天津市承担国家级科技成果推广计划70项；实施市级科技成果推广计划59项，其中工业方面35项，农业方面14项，其他方面10项。科技成果推广计划的实施，有力地促进科技成果的推广应用，并产生明显的经济和社会效益。

2003年起，天津市进一步加强科技成果技术推广中心建设。其中：2003年批准建设天津市配电系统规划及自动化技术推广中心、天津市城市环境空气污染防治技术推广中心、天津市纺织品应用化学技术推广中心；2004年批准建设天津市主要粮食作物新品种及技术推广中心、天津市工业智能控制技术推广中心、天津市微创外科技术推广中心；2005年批准建设天津市畜禽营养与饲料配制技术推广中心、天津市家畜繁育技术推广中心、天津市器官移植技术推广中心。

（四）重点新产品计划

2001年，天津市设立重点新产品计划，旨在以宏观政策引导，加速推进科研机构科技成果转化，推动企业技术创新与产品创新，为进一步促进产业结构优化和产品结构调整，提高企业自主创新能力做出贡献。至2005年，天津市共实施市级重点新产品计划项目89项。这些项目涉及电子信息、航天航空及交通、光机电一体化、生物技术、新型材料、新能源及高效节能、环境保护、医学与医药工程、农业等领域，其中电子信息、光机电一体化、新型材料3个领域的项目数占计划项目总数的70.8%；累计投入总经费1.80亿元，其中财政经费1715万元，吸引社会资金1.63亿元；承担单位89家，其中企业80家，科研院所6家，高等学校3家；项目参加人数791人，其中科技人员占82.3%。

天津市新产品计划重点支持原创型新产品的项目。按照技术创新程度统计，国内首创项目64项，占项目总数的71.9%；重大改进项目22项，占项目总数的24.7%；新产品计划自主研发的产品有74项，占项目总数的83.1%；具有自主知识产权或专利的项目有50项，占项目总数的56.2%。按照技术水平统计，达到国际领先水平的项目5项，占项目总数的5.6%；达到国际先进水平的项目13项，占项目总数的14.6%；达到国内领先水平的项目47项，占项目总数的52.8%；达到国内先进水平的项目24项，占项目总数的27.0%。这些新产品计划项目的实施，在促进新产品开发、增强新产品在国际、国内市场的竞争力等方面取得成效。

天津市在组织实施市级重点新产品计划的同时，认真落实国家级新产品计划。2001～2005年，天津市列入国家级新产品计划的项目累计187项，获得经费支持1670万元，累计实现产品销售收入约67亿元，实现利税约17亿元，出口额约5000万美元。

四、社会发展科技计划

2001年，市科委从科技发展专项计划中分列出社会发展科技计划。至2005年，天津市在社会发展科技领域共支持118个项目，涉及城建、环保、医学、生物医学工程、资源综合利用、减灾防灾、可持续发展等领域，共投入资金15986.5万元，其中财政支持4534万元，吸引社会资金11452.5万元。这些社会发展科技计划的实施和资金的投入，使社会发展领域的科技水平得到提升，同时促进全市社会发展总体水平的提高。

（一）环境保护领域

2001～2005年，天津市环境保护科技工作依靠科技进步，坚持污染防治与生态保护并重，突出重点领域和重点区域，重点针对控制大气污染、改善城市水源水质和城市污水的处理与再利用等方面，先后实施蓝天工程、碧水工程和生态工程，开展创建环保模范城区等工作。为创建环保模范城市，天津市社会发展科技工作支持一批示范性很强的项目，取得显著成效，使城市环境质量得到明显的改善，为“创建模范城市”工作提供有力的支撑。天津市环境保护科技领域共有23个项目获得国家级和市级科技进步奖。

（二）城市建设领域

2001～2005年，天津市实施平房改造、海河开发、老城厢改造、道路拓宽、路口改造等重点工程，完成津滨轻轨、津蓟和唐津等多条高速路及地铁一号线、快速路建设等重大交通工程项目，城市建设力度空前加大，市政建设规模、建筑竣工面积、供热面积、绿化面积都创历史最好水平。加大对地铁、轻轨等重要城市基础设施的科技投入，提高城市交通的科技含量，使天津市重大建设工程项目的技术水平不断提高，推动城建行业整体水平的提高。至2005年，天津市城市建设领域共完成科技成果122项，其中实现应用转化的32项，25项达到国际先进水平，52项达到国内领先水平，32项获国家级和市级科技进步奖。

（三）医学领域

2001～2005年，天津市按照“依托优势领域，确定科研方向，选择重点项目，培育优秀人才，促进学科发展”的思路，在中西医结合治疗急腹症的研究、泌尿医学研究、血液病研究、造血干细胞移植治疗恶性肿瘤的研究、肝脏移植技术的研究、介入治疗技术的研究等方面取得丰硕成果。在此基础上，2005年启动“重中之重”重点学科建设工程，确立神经外科学、内分泌学、泌尿外科学、中西医结合学科、针灸学、中医内科学、运动生理学等7个学科作为天津市医学领域的标志性学科，在人才培养、科研开发和实验室建设等方面重点投入，力争用3年时间进入国家级重点学科行列。至2005年，高新技术在医学诊疗方面发挥重要作用，放射介入、器官移植、腔镜治疗、生物技术和血液净化等高新技术的应用，从引进阶段进入快速发展和创新阶段，为临床诊断和治疗水平的提高奠定坚实基础。

（四）生物医学工程领域

2001～2005年，天津市投入280万元用于生物医学工程领域的科学研究，促进生物医学工程领域科研能力和科研水平的提升，其中眼科B超形成产品优势，占国内市场份额达60%。天津市的“眼科超声显微镜的研制”“生物功能材料及表面修饰、改性技术”“医用电子内窥镜”“无创人体血糖监测技术研究”“眼内人工晶体表面梯队修饰研究”等5个项目成功申报国家科技攻关项目，获拨款210万元，中期项目追加200万元，反映出天津市在该领域的科研实力。

（五）可持续发展战略领域

2001年，天津市制定并颁布《天津市21世纪议程》，同年12月天津市大港区被科技部评为全国可持续发展实验区。2005年，天津市河西区成为市级可持续发展试验区。同时，南开区、塘沽区、西青区和东丽区等区县也积极创办可持续发展试验区。

（六）减灾防灾领域

2001～2005年，天津市在减灾防灾领域的社会发展科技计划中，重点安排和支持生产安全、地震、气象、赤潮、公共安全、火灾与爆炸、出入境检验与检疫等方面的项目，并取得一批成果。

五、国际科技合作计划

1999年，天津市设立国际科技合作计划，从资金上对国际科技合作研究项目给予相应的补贴。至2005年，天津市国际科技合作计划项目共安排109项，获得财政拨款874万元。国际科技合作研究成果中，申请专利165项，其中发明专利22项，实用专利143项；培养博士后21人，博士136人，硕士252人。国际科技合作计划的实施，对重点课题及政府间科技合作的开展起到良好的推动作用。

六、软科学与科技发展战略研究计划

市科委于1981年开始组织实施软科学研究计划。1991～1995年，全市安排软科学研究计划384项，主要围绕为重大决策服务、为社会需求服务和加强软科学自身建设三个层次深入开展研究，尤其是面向市场进行咨询服务的尝试，使软科学研究更加贴近社会主义市场经济，并取得显著成效。软科学研究主要有：科技兴市战略研究；科技体制改革研究；民办科技机构发展研究；京津塘高新技术产业带研究；新技术产业园区发展研究；高新技术产品出口研究；人口、资源、环境与经济协调发展问题研究；南水北调、引滦入津等水资源问题研究；科技咨询业发展问题研究；环渤海区域经济发展问题研究等。全市百余家研究机构近3000名研究人员从事软科学研究，完成市级软科学研究项目240项，其中33项研究成果获天津市科技进步奖。

1996～2000年，天津市软科学研究在为市政府重大决策服务的同时，更加注重为科技进步促进经济、社会发展服务。这一时期，市委、市政府大力实施科教兴市、滨海新区开发、工业东移等战略，软科学研究重点关注的问题有：跨世纪经济科技与人才问题；滨海新区开发开放研究；深化科教兴市战略相关问题；推动知识经济发展问题；若干大企业集团发展战略研究；高新技术产业规模化问题等。5年间，共立项236项，完成研究项目228项，其中直接服务于经济发展的项目占80%以上；有45项成果获得天津市科技进步奖，其中二等奖9项、三等奖36项。至2000年，全市从事软科学研究和咨询工作的有1万余人，各类咨询机构发展到4000余家，咨询服务收入总额达2亿元。

2001年，天津市对软科学研究工作进行重大改革，将软科学研究计划改为科技发展战略研究计划，并将其作为整个科技计划体系决策支持系统的核心部分，重点围绕天津市科技发展战略与对策、科技政策与产业技术政策、科技发展重点领域的选择、重点科技领域的发展预测、科技创新能力建设、科技投融资体系与机制建设和科技队伍建设等方面的重大问题进行研究，为天津市科技发展提供前瞻性、创新性和可行性咨询服务，使软科学研究内容更注重全局性、战略性和前瞻性，为领导科学决策提供有效服务。至2005年，安排市级科技发展战略研究计划项目256项，资助金额2041万元，是1991～1995年资助金额的6.6倍；全市百余家研究机构，近4000名研究人员从事此项研究工作，并取得一批学术水平高、可操作性强的研究成果，为有效提高政府的执政能力和决策水平发挥积极作用。

七、研究开发条件建设计划

为推动区域科技创新体系建设，1999年天津市提出“121”工程计划，即重点组建10个科学研究中心、20个工程技术中心和100个企业技术中心，带动新型科技研发和服务体系建设。“十五”期间，天津市全面启动“121”工程。至2005年，天津市共组建新型知识创新机构70个，新型技术创新机构191个，重点成果转移、转化与产业化机构（基地）130个，公共高新技术平台和公共科技服务机构20个。全市建立起由国家级和市级重点实验室、跨学科的科学研究中心为骨干的知识创新体系；由国家级和市级工程研究中心和企业技术中心为骨干的技术创新体系；由孵化器、生产力促进中心、大学科技园区、区县特色产业园、产业化基地和公共科技平台为主要载体的科技服务体系；具有自身区域特色的科技创新体系，显著改善了科技创新环境。

八、科技型中小企业技术创新基金

1999年,经国务院批准,科技部、财政部共同设立科技型中小企业技术创新基金,是专门用于促进科技成果转化、引导社会支持企业技术创新的政府专项基金。天津市组织实施该项基金的主要方式是:根据科技部发布的年度指南和项目申报须知,在全市范围内征集和组织符合要求的项目,向国家申报,待获得该项基金立项支持后予以配套。

至2005年底,全市共组织申报科技型中小企业技术创新基金项目375项,获得资助83项,资助金额为5434万元(其中获得无偿资助4120万元,贷款贴息1043万元,小额资助270万元),占全国该项基金资助总金额的1.58%,申报立项率为22.9%,每个项目平均获得资助65万元。

至2005年,市科委共完成230余项科技型中小企业技术创新基金项目的监理工作。统计数据显示,天津市科技型中小企业技术创新基金项目共实现销售收入102462.3万元,净利润17644.1万元,缴税10313.4万元,提供就业岗位2217个。在该项基金的支持下,天津市许多立项项目不仅顺利完成研发阶段,而且成功地抢占市场,促成快速发展。

科技型中小企业技术创新基金项目的实施,推动科技型中小企业的迅速发展壮大;促进创新创业氛围的形成;加快成果转化速度与水平;促进企业机制创新,实现新的跨越;促进科研院所改制工作,发挥科研带动产业发展的龙头作用;促进科技中介机构的规范发展。科技型中小企业技术创新基金成为科技型中小企业实施技术创新工程的重要推动力,通过实施一批创新基金项目,为科技型中小企业培育造就一支懂市场、善管理、会经营的企业家队伍,培育造就一支从单纯科研型转为科研开发型的科技人才队伍,培育造就一支科技中介人才和项目管理人才队伍。

第三章 科技成果与技术市场

1991~2005年,天津市贯彻执行国家有关科技成果鉴定与登记的政策规定,认真做好科技成果鉴定与登记工作。同时,天津市贯彻执行国家科学技术奖励的有关政策规定,表彰和奖励优秀科技工作者和优秀科技成果,激励科技人员投身技术发明、技术创造的积极性。各级技术市场管理机构贯彻国家有关技术市场的法律、法规,组织技术交易活动,引导技术市场健康发展。

第一节 科技成果鉴定与登记

天津市贯彻执行国家科委颁布的《科学技术成果鉴定办法》,认真组织科技成果鉴定,为促进科技成果水平的提高、加速科技成果的推广应用起到重要作用。同时,天津市设有5个科技成果登记点,加强科技成果登记工作。

一、成果鉴定

1991~1994年,天津市科技成果鉴定工作依据1990年市科委颁发的《天津市科学技术成果鉴定实施细则》和《天津市科技成果升格鉴定管理办法》执行。

1995年1月1日起，天津市认真贯彻执行国家科委颁布的《科学技术成果鉴定办法》，组织科技成果鉴定，为正确评价科技成果的质量和水平，促进科技成果水平的提高，加速科技成果的推广应用起到重要作用。1996年，出台《天津市实施国家科委〈关于科学技术研究成果管理的规定〉细则》，将科技成果鉴定按照科技计划内成果、科技计划外重大成果和科技计划外授权成果3种类型组织鉴定，科学技术成果鉴定的可操作性得到提高。

2005年，天津市贯彻科技部提出的“科技成果鉴定组织工作由政府部门组织鉴定向科技中介机构组织鉴定转变”精神，将一部分科技成果鉴定工作委托给科技中介机构组织鉴定，并制定科技成果鉴定评价指标体系，为科技成果鉴定组织方式的转变打下基础。

二、成果登记

1991年起，天津市科技成果登记继续贯彻市科委有关科技成果登记的规定，凡计划内项目鉴定后两周内上报登记，计划外项目鉴定后1个月内上报登记，未登记的科技成果不予受理国家级、市级科技成果奖励的申报。1996年8月8日，市科委颁布《关于加强科技成果登记工作的通知》，规定自1996年8月1日起凡是已进行登记的科技成果，由市科委统一颁发《天津市科技成果证书》。进行科技成果登记时，各有关单位根据不同类型的成果提供相应的材料，办理完科技成果登记的成果，在《天津科技》期刊上公布征求异议，期限为2个月，期限内无异议的方可办理科技成果证书。2003年，科技成果公示方式改为在天津市科委网站进行公示，公示期限为1个月。

天津市科技成果登记数量不断增加。1991～1995年，登记科技成果3681项；1996～2000年，登记科技成果5591项，比前5年增加1910项；2001～2005年，登记科技成果6339项，比前5年增加748项。

天津市科技成果水平不断提高。1996～2000年，具有国际领先水平的科技成果197项，具有国际先进水平的903项，具有国内领先水平的1991项，具有国内先进水平的2500项。2001～2005年，具有国际领先水平的科技成果284项，比前5年增加87项；具有国际先进水平的1320项，比前5年增加417项；具有国内领先水平的2856项，比前5年增加865项；具有国内先进水平的1299项，比前5年减少1201项。

1991～2005年天津市科技成果登记情况统计表

表2-3-1-36　　单位：项

年度/项目	1991	1992	1993	1994	1995	1996	1997	1998	1999	2000	2001	2002	2003	2004	2005	15年合计
科技成果登记数	820	942	694	673	552	936	1085	1105	1202	1263	1200	1020	1203	1408	1508	15611

1996～2005年天津市科技成果水平情况统计表

表2-3-1-37　　单位：项

年度/项目	1996	1997	1998	1999	2000	2001	2002	2003	2004	2005
合计	936	1085	1105	1202	1263	1200	1020	1203	1408	1508
国际领先	40	42	37	39	39	43	32	59	75	75
国际先进	170	180	182	184	187	209	197	311	282	321
国内领先	354	402	390	420	425	455	413	559	697	732
国内先进	372	461	496	559	612	254	182	236	306	321
其他	—	—	—	—	—	239	196	38	48	59

注：1991～1995年天津市科技成果水平情况未作统计

第二节 科技奖励

天津市将科学技术奖励制度作为科技政策的重要组成部分，认真贯彻“尊重知识、尊重人才”的方针，鼓励团结协作、联合攻关和自主创新，表彰和奖励优秀科技成果和优秀科技工作者。1991～2005年，天津市共有248项科技成果获得国家级科技奖励，3493项科技成果获市级科技奖励，并有4人获天津市科技重大成就奖，3人获天津市国际科技合作奖。

一、国家级科学技术奖励

1991～1999年，国家科学技术奖分为一等奖、二等奖、三等奖和四等奖4个级别。1999年，国务院颁发《国家科学技术奖励条例》，规定设立国家最高科学技术奖、国家自然科学奖、国家技术发明奖、国家科学技术进步奖和国际科学技术合作奖等5类科学技术奖，其中自然科学奖、技术发明奖和科学技术进步奖分为一等奖、二等奖、三等奖。

1991～1995年，天津市独立承担或参与完成并获得国家级奖励的科技成果共有93项；1996～2000年，获得国家级奖励的科技成果有95项；2001～2005年，获得国家级奖励的科技成果60项。

根据国家科技奖励办公室编印的《1999年度国家科技奖励公报》公布的数据显示，该年度天津市获得国家科技奖励共有27项，获奖数在全国30个省、直辖市、自治区中仅次于山东省，与北京省、上海市并列第2名。这是自国家设立科技奖励办法起，天津市获得国家科技奖励的最好记录。

1991～2005年天津市获国家级科学技术奖励情况统计表

表2-3-2-38 单位：项

项目＼年度	1991	1992	1993	1994	1995	1996	1997	1998	1999	2000	2001	2002	2003	2004	2005	15年合计
获奖项数	32	25	19	—	17	16	20	19	27	13	9	13	14	10	14	248

注：1994年未评国家科学技术奖

1996～2005年天津市获国家级科学技术奖励情况统计表

表2-3-2-39 单位：项

项目＼年份	1996	1997	1998	1999	2000	2001	2002	2003	2004	2005	10年合计
国家自然科学奖	—	1	—	2	—	1	—	3	1	2	10
国家技术发明奖	5	2	3	2	—	—	1	—	2	1	16
国家科技进步奖	11	16	16	23	13	7	11	11	7	11	126
国际科学技术合作奖	—	1	—	—	—	1	1	—	—	—	3
合计	16	20	19	27	13	9	13	14	10	14	155

注：1991～1995年天津市获国家科学技术奖励情况未作统计

二、天津市科学技术奖励

1991～1999年，天津市设立"天津市科学技术进步奖"，奖励等级分为一等奖、二等奖和三等奖。1994～1998年，天津市每两年评选一次"科技兴市"突出贡献奖，其中1994年5项，1996年9项，1998年11项。

2000年，市政府颁布《天津市科学技术奖励办法》和《天津市科学技术奖励办法实施细则》。该办法和实施细则规定，天津市设立天津市科学技术奖，包括科技重大成就奖、自然科学奖、技术发明奖、科学技术进步奖和国际科技合作奖5个类别，其中自然科学奖、技术发明奖和科学技术进步奖分为一等奖、二等奖和三等奖3个级别，科技重大成就奖和国际科技合作奖不分级别。同时，该办法和实施细则就科技奖励的范围、条件，评审标准，评审机构，推荐、评审、异议、处理程序及授奖等做出明确规定。全市奖励经费增加到400～500万元，其中天津市科技重大成就奖每年评选1～2项，每项奖金50万元。

2005年，市政府颁布《关于修改〈天津市科学技术奖励办法实施细则〉的通知》，对原实施细则中的有关内容进行修订，其中明确规定科技重大成就奖的获奖条件，将科普著作作为科学技术进步奖奖励范围，将一等奖、二等奖的奖金由原来的5万元、2万元提高到8万元、3万元，三等奖的奖金维持原来的1万元不变，并明确科学技术奖确定初评结果的基本原则等。

1991～1999年度，2098项科技成果获天津市科学技术进步奖。2000～2005年度，1402项科技成果获天津市科学技术奖励，其中科技重大成就奖4项，国际科技合作奖3项，自然科学奖、技术发明奖和科学技术进步奖中的一等奖81项、二等奖391项、三等奖923项。期间，侯锋、张芝泉、余国琮、何炳林共四人获得天津市科技重大成就奖。

1991～1999年度天津市科学技术奖励情况统计表

表2-3-2-40 单位：项

项目 年度	获奖数			
	小计	一等奖	二等奖	三等奖
1991	232	5	57	170
1992	220	4	54	162
1993	204	6	61	137
1994	205	5	38	162
1995	198	3	43	152
1996	244	4	51	189
1997	246	4	58	184
1998	253	7	72	174
1999	296	9	72	215
合计	2098	47	506	1545

2000～2005年度天津市科学技术奖励情况统计表

表2-3-2-41 单位：项

项目 年度	科技重大成就奖	自然科学奖、技术发明奖、科学技术进步奖			国际科技合作奖
		一等奖	二等奖	三等奖	
2000	1	11	48	204	1
2001	—	14	67	166	1
2002	1	13	64	167	1
2003	1	14	62	141	—

续表2-3-2-41 单位:项

年度\项目	科技重大成就奖	自然科学奖、技术发明奖、科学技术进步奖			国际科技合作奖
		一等奖	二等奖	三等奖	
2004	1	15	70	129	—
2005	—	14	80	116	—
合计	4	81	391	923	3

第三节 技术市场

天津市技术市场是20世纪80年代初在全国率先建立和发展起来的。1991年起,天津市通过举办或参加各种类型的高新技术成果展示会、交易会、洽谈会等大型科技交流活动,展示天津市的科技成果,活跃了技术市场,促进了科技成果的转化。至2005年,天津市技术市场保持较好的发展势头。特别是2001~2005年,天津市技术交易额每年以14.25%的速度持续增长。据统计,1991年1月~2005年12月,天津市共登记、统计技术合同128334项,技术合同成交总金额338.61亿元,技术合同流向遍及除台湾省以外的全国各省、自治区、直辖市。2005年,天津市技术合同交易额位居全国第六位。

1995年3月1日,由天津市政府与国家科委联合组建的国家级常设技术市场——北方技术交易市场正式开业。该市场在"上水平,增效益,培育核心竞争优势,打造服务品牌,努力建设成为跻身国内一流水平中介机构"的工作方针指导下,构建起国内最大的技术供、需两大网络,至2003年与国内17个省市的94个县(市)建立129个联络站和技术转移分公司,在汇集科技资源与市场资源上形成长期、稳定的渠道和合作伙伴,在运作水平、发展规模和速度上成为重要的区域技术转移中心。

一、技术市场交易

1991年起,天津市技术市场的技术交易活跃,签订的技术合同及技术合同成交金额呈现逐年上升趋势。统计数据显示,1996~2000年全市签订技术合同为35324项,合同成交金额为96.67亿元;2001~2005年签订技术合同为40799项,合同成交金额为204.66亿元,分别比前5年增加5475项、107.99亿元。其中1996年合同成交金额为13.35亿元,2000年上升至26.26亿元,是1996年的1.97倍;2005年合同成交金额为50.71亿元,是2000年的1.93倍。

1996~2005年天津市技术市场签订合同数及合同成交金额统计表

表2-3-3-42

项目\年份	1996	1997	1998	1999	2000	2001	2002	2003	2004	2005
一、签订合同数(项)	8348	7573	7416	5572	6415	7335	6889	7278	8002	11295
技术开发	1710	1974	1539	1317	1716	1699	1642	2349	2746	2942
技术转让	595	450	424	569	446	613	508	398	353	213
技术咨询	1181	935	1116	948	1145	1386	1387	1462	1658	2100
技术服务	4862	4214	4337	2738	3108	3637	3352	3069	3245	6040

续表2-3-3-42

项目＼年份	1996	1997	1998	1999	2000	2001	2002	2003	2004	2005
二、合同成交金额(万元)	133475	150074	200298	220296	262581	306009	363262	420008	450276	507093
技术开发	67586	80907	117608	148991	165005	187013	164723	278607	298502	269098
技术转让	14169	15014	14597	17967	26026	37424	132474	50416	20516	29957
技术咨询	8578	6728	9615	7044	11403	14229	13996	17579	28167	55816
技术服务	43142	47425	58478	46294	60147	67343	52069	73406	103091	152222

注：1991～1995年天津市技术市场签订合同数及合同成交金额情况未作统计。

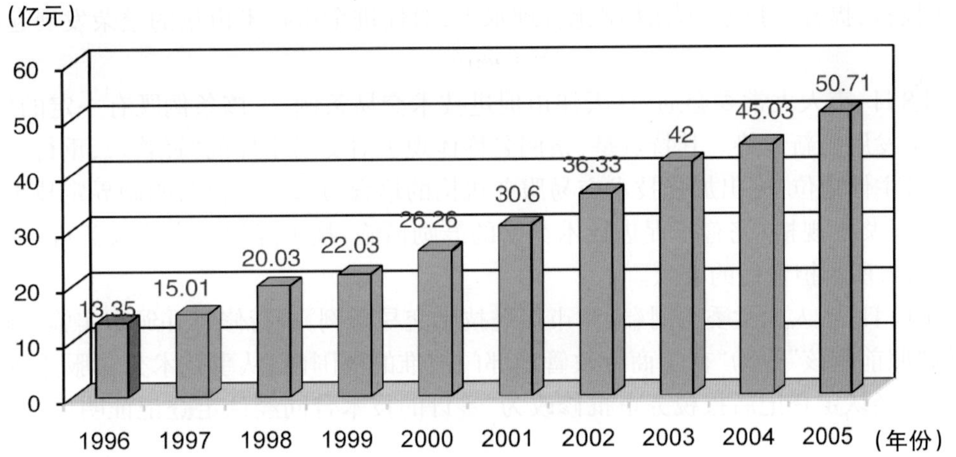

图2-3-3-1　1996～2005年天津市技术交易额趋势图

二、技术市场体系

(一)管理体系

天津市技术市场管理采取市级和区县级两级管理模式。市级技术市场管理机构为天津市技术市场管理办公室(以下简称“市场办”)，负责指导全市技术市场管理工作。18个区县和开发区、保税区及新技术产业园区的科技管理部门为二级技术市场管理机构，负责所属地区的技术市场管理工作。同时，经市场办认定，在全市设立30个技术合同认定登记站，负责技术合同认定登记、技术市场统计分析、技术市场法律培训等项管理工作。各级技术市场管理机构在宣传贯彻有关技术市场法律法规和优惠政策、培训管理经营人员、组织全国性和地区性技术交易活动、技术合同管理、表彰先进、引导技术市场发展及规范市场行为等方面发挥重要作用。

(二)经营服务体系

天津市技术市场经营服务体系由技贸机构(含民营机构)、技术中介机构、评估机构、技术交易市场等组成。技术市场经营机构的服务功能逐步由单一的技术中介咨询、代理服务向新技术新产品开发、技术信息传递、产品联销、技术咨询与市场调查、人才培训与交流、技术评估与作价等配套功能发展，其服务手段开始使用现代网络和通讯技术。各区县普遍建立该地区的技术交易服务机构，为发展区域经济、促进区域科技与经济的结合发挥一定作用。

1994年11月1日，国家科委和天津市人民政府在北京举行新闻发布会，宣布由国家科委和天津市政府联合在天津建立国家级常设技术交易市场——北方技术交易市场。同年12月26日，北方技术交易市场管委会举行第一次会议，选举国家科委副主任韩德乾和天津市副市长李惠芬为该管委会主任。北方技术交易市场实行管委会领导下的总裁负责制，王立子为首任总裁。12月27日，北方技术交易市场投入试运行。1995年3月1日，北方技术交易市场正式开业，国家科委主任宋健为开业剪彩，中共天津市委书记高德占、市长张立昌出席开业仪式。该市场采用国际惯例运作，参照国际模式实行会员制。7层的交易大厦建筑面积7000平方米，设有1000平方米的展厅、30多个洽谈室，90多个写字间，可为进场会员提供与国际、国内信息网络联网的计算机信息系统及大屏和分屏显示、多媒体制作演播、程控通讯等全方位开放型服务。2001年，刘友林任北方技术交易市场总裁。至2005年，该市场经历了从规模做大到功能做强、从技术单一服务向集成服务的跨越，从单纯技术交易场所向综合性技术转移服务机构的转型，探索出一条从网络化到集成化再到国际化的发展路子。

（三）法律保障体系

1993年10月28日，天津市人大常委会颁布《天津市技术市场管理条例》，规范技术市场管理，保障技术交易各方的合法权益，提升了技术市场法制化管理水平，对促进全市技术市场的繁荣发展起到重要的推动作用。

2000年11月8日，市人大常委会通过《天津市促进技术交易条例》。该条例既有一定的延续性，又更好地适应了市场经济发展的新形势。其特点是：条例名称体现了对交易主体的“轻管理，重行为规范”；明确科技行政部门的监管主体地位；突出加强技术交易服务机构的培育、建设和管理；明确界定技术交易和技术交易服务范围；提升了奖励规格；完善了促进技术交易的鼓励措施；技术经纪人合法权益得到依法保护；增加了执法依据和行为人所承担责任的条款。

2004年11月12日，市人大常委会对《天津市促进技术交易条例》进行修订并颁布实施。修订内容：将技术交易服务机构“照前审核”改为“在工商行政管理部门核准的范围内，从事技术交易服务活动”；将免税审批手续由技术合同经认定登记后报税务审批修改为“签订的技术合同经认定登记证明后，可以享受国家规定的税收优惠”。

天津市在不断完善技术市场法律法规体系的同时，制定一系列的政策措施，保证技术市场在制度化、规范化的道路上健康发展。

三、技术市场奖励

1991年1月14日，市科委颁发《关于做好天津市技术市场表彰工作的通知》，决定设立天津市技术市场金桥奖，表彰在技术市场和技术贸易工作中做出突出贡献的集体和个人。1991年，天津市首次开展“技术市场金桥奖”评选。之后，分别于1993年和1995年进行第二届和第三届“技术市场金桥奖”的评选。1996年1月18日，市科委、市人事局下发《关于印发“天津市技术市场金桥奖评奖办法”的通知》，明确了表彰奖励的范围、申报金桥奖的条件以及评奖领导小组的构成和职责，并规定技术市场金桥奖属天津市科技进步奖励范畴，其集体奖的奖金额度依照天津市科技进步奖二等奖的标准执行，个人奖的奖金额度按集体奖10%～30%执行，奖金由获奖单位从技术贸易收入或预算外收入中列支，个人奖可作为评定职称实行奖励等的重要参考依据，并记入个人考核档案。从2004年起，每年评选技术交易先进单位10名（技术合同交易额最高的前10名）、技术市场管理先进单位20名和技术合同认定登记工作先进个人20～30名，由市科委发出表彰通知。

四、技术合同认定登记

（一）机构

根据《天津市促进技术交易条例》规定，市科委对技术合同认定登记机构进行多次调整。1992年7月3日，市科委认定24个技术合同认定登记机构。1994年10月26日，市科委将认定登记机构调整为28个。1996年2月26日，市科委重新认定35个技术合同认定登记机构。2002年5月24日，天津市取消3个具有企业性质的技术合同认定登记机构。同年6月5日，在天津新技术产业园区管理委员会和天津港保税区管理委员会增设技术合同认定登记机构。2005年4月22日，市科委取消4家技术合同认定登记机构。至此，天津市共设30个技术合同认定登记机构。

(二)收费

1991年10月8日,市科委印发《关于调整技术合同认定登记费的通知》,技术合同认定登记费按技术合同成交额的0.1%~0.2%计收。2001年4月30日,市科委印发《关于调整技术合同登记费的通知》,将原技术合同认定登记收费标准由原来的0.2%调整为0.1%,最高收费限额为1万元,最低收费由10元调整为100元。2005年1月1日,市财政局发出通知,停止技术合同认定登记收费。从这年开始,市财政局根据收取登记费情况,每年给天津市技术市场管理办公室的账号拨付一定的经费,用于技术市场工作的开展和技术合同登记机构及登记人员的奖励。

第四章　知识产权

1991~2005年,天津市专利及知识产权事业取得显著成绩。全市专利申请量大幅度上升,专利申请质量明显提高,一批运用知识产权制度较好、专利申请量较多的企事业单位脱颖而出。2000年,天津市专利管理局更名为天津市知识产权局,成为组织协调全市保护知识产权和主管专利工作的市政府直属机构。该局认真贯彻国家有关知识产权方面的政策法规,与各相关部门密切配合积极开展专利及知识产权工作,专利管理与服务体系日趋完善,社会公众的专利意识明显提高,专利政策法规建设取得进展。同时,天津市积极扶持和推广优秀专利技术,推动专利技术的实施和产业化进程,专利行政保护和司法保护进一步加强,专利创造、管理和保护水平显著提高。

第一节　管理与服务

天津市经过各方面的积极努力,逐步建立知识产权管理体系,建立由市政府主管领导主持的知识产权办公会议制度,成立天津市保护知识产权工作领导小组,天津市知识产权局成为组织协调全市保护知识产权和主管专利工作的市政府直属机构,全市18个区县和经济技术开发区、新技术产业园区都设立知识产权管理机构,企业知识产权管理网络初步形成。同时,天津市基本建立知识产权服务体系,形成"一处"(国家知识产权局天津专利代办处)、"一网"(天津知识产权网)、"两会"(天津市发明协会、天津市知识产权保护协会)、"两平台"(天津市知识产权服务平台、天津市知识产权交易平台)、"三中心"(天津市知识产权服务中心、天津市知识产权交易中心、天津市知识产权司法鉴定中心)的服务网络,具备从专利信息获取、相关法律咨询、业务服务受理、司法鉴定等多方位为社会公众提供服务的能力,服务功能日趋完善。

一、管理体系

(一)天津市人民政府知识产权办公会议

1994年10月,市政府印发《关于建立天津市人民政府知识产权办公会议制度的通知》,建立由市政府主管领导主持的知识产权办公会议制度,同时明确知识产权办公会议办公室设在市科委。2000年,知识产权办公会议办公室的职能由市科委转到市知识产权局。2004年6月14日,市政府印发《关于明确天津市知识产权办公会议制度组成单位成员的通知》。调整后的办公会议成员由知识产权行政管理、执法、司法机关以及其他与知识产权工作有关的政府部门共24个单位组成,办公会议由主管知识产权工作的副市长主持。办公会议下设办公室,办公室成员由市知识产权局、市工商局、市新闻出版局、市广播电视局、市文化局和天津海关等单位的主管领导组成,办公室设在市知识产权局。2004年11月19日,召开市政府知识产权办公会议第一次全体会议,布置知识产权办公会议近期主要工作,审议、通报知识产权办公会议有关文件。2005年2月和9月,先后召开两次知识产权办公会议,总结2004年知识产权工作,部署2005年的重点工作,并审议通过《天津市知识产权"十一五"发展规划》等。

(二)天津市保护知识产权工作领导小组

2005年11月,市政府颁发《关于成立天津市保护知识产权工作领导小组的通知》,成立天津市保护知识产权工作领导小组,由分管科技工作的副市长兼任组长。领导小组成员由市知识产权局、市整顿办、市公安局、市商务委等13个部门的负责人组成。领导小组办公室设在市知识产权局,负责日常工作。为进一步加强对知识产权保护工作的领导,充分发挥领导小组各成员单位的作用,制定了《天津市保护知识产权工作领导小组工作机制》和《天津市保护知识产权工作领导小组成员单位职责》。

(三)天津市知识产权局

2000年11月2日,市委办公厅、市政府办公厅颁发《关于印发〈天津市知识产权局职能配制、内设机构和人员编制规定〉的通知》,天津市专利管理局更名为天津市知识产权局。该局作为组织协调全市保护知识产权和主管专利工作的市政府直属机构,主要职责是:贯彻国家知识产权战略纲要,研究制订天津市知识产权战略纲要和发展规划,并组织实施;贯彻实施国家专利和知识产权方面的法律、法规和政策,研究制定并组织实施地方性法规、规章和政策措施;组织协调全市保护知识产权工作,建立知识产权执法协作机制,开展专利行政执法;组织开展专利的法律法规、政策的宣传和培训;组织推动重大专利技术的实施;承担国家知识产权局专利局授权和委托的专利代办相关工作等。至2005年,该局设有办公室(人事处)、发展规划处、专利管理处、条件法规处、专利实施处(专利信息处)、国家知识产权局天津专利代办处等6个职能处(室)。

1993年10月20日,市政府批准王建英任天津市专利管理局局长,免去李之珍天津市专利管理局局长职务。1998年8月20日,市政府免去王建英天津市专利管理局局长职务。2002年4月3日,市政府任命张盛如为天津市知识产权局局长。

(四)区县知识产权机构

1999年6月21日,宁河县在全市第一个成立专利管理办公室。此后,全市各区县陆续成立专利管理办公室。至2005年底,全市18个区县和开发区都设有知识产权管理机构,其中南开、河西、河东、红桥、津南、北辰、汉沽、大港、宝坻等9个区县和天津开发区、新技术产业园区建立知识产权办公会议制度,河西、津南、北辰、汉沽、宝坻、蓟县等6个区县和经济技术开发区建立保护知识产权工作领导小组,组织推动区域知识产权工作。

(五)企业知识产权管理网络

1991~2005年,全市大多数企业逐步建立知识产权管理制度,并涌现出一批管理完善、熟练运用知识产权制度的企业,企业知识产权管理网络初步形成。

二、服务体系

(一)国家知识产权局天津专利代办处

2002年9月20日,经国家知识产权局批准,设立国家知识产权局天津专利代办处。天津专利代办处依据国家知识产权局专利局的授权和委托,负责办理国家知识产权局专利局在天津业务。具体职责为:受理专利申请;审批费用减缓请求,代收专利申请费、专利年费及年费滞纳金;开展专利相关事务的查询和咨询,办理专利权转让、许可备案和专利法律状态出证等。至2005年底,天津专利代办处共受理专利申请25719件,收缴专利费用2280万元。

（二）天津市知识产权服务中心

2003年3月13日，经天津市编制委员会批准，天津市专利技术服务中心更名为天津市知识产权服务中心。其主要职责是：提供知识产权的培训、研究、评估、鉴定等技术咨询；提供专利技术及产品的技术开发和服务；提供知识产权法律、知识产权信息网络化及信息服务；承办知识产权成果展示和技术交流会议。2005年2月23日，经天津市编制委员会批准，天津市知识产权服务中心加挂天津市知识产权交易中心牌子。天津市知识产权服务中心在专利文献信息利用方面取得成果，其中2004年开发出“中国失效专利数据库”，2005年研发出企业专利文献信息系统。

（三）天津市知识产权司法鉴定中心

2003年7月24日，经天津市司法局批准，成立天津市知识产权司法鉴定中心。该中心依托天津市知识产权服务中心，主要从事知识产权司法鉴定工作。2005年10月，天津市知识产权司法鉴定中心通过国家司法部验收，知识产权司法鉴定专家由12人增至14人。

（四）天津市发明协会

天津市发明协会成立于1985年9月。至2005年，该协会以市场为导向，不断扩大与企业的横向联合，大力宣传、推广新技术、新产品，推动专利技术的实施，并取得成效。

（五）天津市知识产权保护协会

2005年4月27日，召开天津市知识产权保护协会第一次代表大会，讨论通过《天津市知识产权保护协会章程》，选举产生协会理事会成员，并召开第一次理事会议，选举产生会长、副会长、秘书长及常务理事，通过《天津市知识产权保护协会财务管理制度》。同年5月，天津市社会团体管理局批准成立天津市知识产权保护协会。该协会先后举办企事业单位专利工作者参加的培训班，出版《天津市知识产权保护协会会刊》。

（六）专利代理机构

自实施“专利法”起，天津市先后成立一批专利代理机构。至2000年，天津市专利代理机构增至20家。2001年，市知识产权局对20家专利代理机构实施脱钩改制，专利代理机构调整为12家，全部为有限责任制或合伙制。2003年，市知识产权局发布《关于印发〈天津市专利代理机构管理办法（试行）〉通知》，并成立天津市专利代理惩戒委员会，制定《天津市专利代理惩戒委员会工作规程》，加强对专利代理机构和代理人的执业监督，维护专利代理行业的正常秩序。同年7月，市知识产权局出台《关于印发〈天津市专利代理机构设立办事机构办法（试行）〉的通知》，对专利代理机构在外设立办事机构的条件和程序做出明确规定。

第二节 宣传与培训

天津市以宣传、普及专利法为先导，努力提高公众的知识产权保护意识，卓有成效地开展知识产权宣传与培训工作，为知识产权事业的发展提供有力支撑。

一、宣传工作

1991年8月，天津市专利局编辑出版《专利纠纷案例》《知识产权概述》。同年4月23日，市专利局创办内部刊物《天津专利》。2003年，该刊更名为《天津知识产权》，成为宣传知识产权工作的主要阵地之一。1992年4月21日，天津电视台播出由天津市专利管理局与市司法局、天津市人民艺术剧院共同创作的普及专利法知识的系列电视剧《助燃》。

1992年，市专利局与市工商局、市版权局举办知识产权宣传展示会，展示天津市148项专利技术，参观者7.2万人次，技贸成交额446.1万元，评出金奖15项、银奖35项。2002年，市知识产权局多次邀请国家知识产权局领导和专家到天津做报告，其中6月邀请国家知识产权局副局长田力普做题为《入世后知识产权保护与区域经济发展》的报告。2003年，市知识产权局举办多场领导干部知识产权专题讲座，在领导干部中普及知识产权知识。2005年2月23日，国家知识产权局在天津召开全国知识产权宣传培训工作会议，全国各省、市、自治区和专利试点城市知识产权局负责人80余人参加会议，国家知识产权局局长王景川发表重要讲话。

自2001年开始，天津市在每年4月26日的世界知识产权日期间，都要开展丰富多彩的宣传活动。2002年，天津市以庆祝世界知识产权日为契机，以“鼓励创新”为主题，在《今晚报》刊登两期专版，与天津电视台联合制作知识产权专题宣传片10部，在《天津日报》开设知识产权战略对话栏目，在天津人民广播电台将知识产权保护话题走进直播间，并在各类媒体上宣传知识产权及专利达200余篇文章。2003年，天津市将4月份定为知识产权宣传月，在全市范围内掀起宣传知识产权的新高潮，编印发放数千份宣传材料，向有关单位赠送500余张视盘和近200套挂图，在各类媒体刊登知识产权报道200余篇。2004年，天津市以多种形式大张旗鼓地宣传知识产权，成功举办一系列、大型的宣传活动。多次邀请国家知识产权局的领导和专家，以专题报告会、理论研讨会的形式，为各级领导干部宣讲知识产权知识；先后编印《天津市知识产权局2003年年报》《2003年天津市知识产权保护状况》等，并在《中国知识产权报》《天津日报》、天津电视台等媒体刊发知识产权宣传报道200余篇（次）。2005年，天津市组织开展形式多样的知识产权法制宣传，形成从中央新闻、国家知识产权报刊、网站到天津地方各媒体广泛开展知识产权知识的宣传普及活动，为全面提高全社会的知识产权意识起到积极作用。市知识产权局开展知识产权讲座、座谈会近百场，发送各种知识产权宣传资料约10万份，《天津日报》《今晚报》、天津电视台、广播电台等媒体刊发各类知识产权报道500余篇。2005年11月，中央电视台在新闻联播节目中两次报道天津市知识产权保护的情况。

2005年6月18～20日，人民日报、经济日报、中央人民广播电台、人民网、中国经营报、中国广播网、中国知识产权报等30余家媒体记者，组成“保护知识产权—我们在行动”联合采访团共34人，在天津进行3天的采访，天津市主要媒体与驻天津媒体记者随队采访。知识产权专家顾问团与采访报道队伍通过举办论坛、召开座谈会、开展咨询等活动，从知识产权战略的高度为天津经济发展出谋划策，对促进天津知识产权工作产生重要影响。

二、培训

天津市历来重视知识产权人才培训工作。2001～2005年，天津市实施“双百万”知识产权人才培训计划，即用2～3年时间培训100名专利管理人才和100名专利代理人员，培训1万名适应企事业单位开展专利工作所需要的“专利明白人”。2003年，市知识产权局印发《天津市专利工作者培训暂行办法》，对专利工作者的培训内容、时间、组织实施等工作做出规定，以保证培训质量。至2005年，天津市在领导干部、区县或行业、专利工作者和知识产权学历教育4个层面上，开展形式多样的知识产权培训，举办或参与举办各类知识产权培训班1164期，48525人次接受知识产权基础知识、基本业务的培训。

第三节 专利申请和授权及实施

1991～2005年，天津市专利申请量和授权量逐年增长，专利申请质量显著提高，拥有自主知识产权的技术和产品不断增加，核心竞争力逐步增强。

同时，天津市通过政策引导和扶持服务，专利技术的产业化和规模化效果显著。1991～1995年，全市累计实施专利技术1041项，累计新增产值38.21亿元，新增利税5.37亿元。1996～2000年，全市累计实施专利技术1056项，累计新增产值23.08亿元，新增利税6.19亿元。2001～2005年，全市累计实施专利技术6248

项，累计新增产值428.70亿元，新增利税52.20亿元；其中2005年实施专利项目2240项，实现新增产值178.71亿元，新增利税229627万元。同时，天津市实施专利产业化扶持计划，重点扶持50项优秀专利产品，推动专利技术的产业化、规模化和国际化。

一、专利申请

1991年，天津市专利申请量首次突破千件，1999年超过2000件，2001年超过3000件，2005年突破万件。1991～2005年，专利申请量年均增长率达到18%。其中，20世纪最后10年的年均增长率为11%；21世纪头5年的年均增长率达33%。至2005年底，全市累计专利申请量达到53057件，其中“十五”期间专利申请量比“九五”期间增长3.7倍。

天津市专利申请量在全国各省、市、自治区的排名不断提升。其中，2000年以前，天津市专利申请量在全国处于中游水平；2001年排在第16位，2002年、2003年分别排在第12、11位；2004年起跻身前十名行列，连续两年排在第9位。

专利申请的类型结构明显优化，特别是发明专利在当年专利申请总量中所占比例明显提升。1991～2000年，全市发明专利申请共有2812件，占同期专利申请总量的16%。2001～2005年，发明专利申请共14665件，所占比例提升到42%，比20世纪90年代增加26个百分点。其中，2005年发明专利申请量居全国第8位。

1991～2005年天津市专利申请情况统计表

表2-4-3-43　　单位：项

年份	当年申请量	按申请类型划分			按申请人划分		职务发明构成			
		发明	实用新型	外观设计	非职务发明	职务发明	高等院校	科研单位	企业	机关
1991年	1362	258	1023	81	894	468	109	85	188	86
1992年	1767	282	1362	123	1201	566	121	79	202	164
1993年	1850	308	1356	186	1270	580	85	88	201	206
1994年	1541	269	1067	205	1095	446	65	71	119	191
1995年	1648	239	1151	258	1169	479	63	61	234	121
1996年	1743	285	1111	347	1208	535	70	52	388	25
1997年	1540	257	1011	272	1047	493	53	62	370	8
1998年	1485	204	925	356	1034	451	59	41	322	29
1999年	2016	240	1205	571	1255	761	99	73	565	24
2000年	2789	470	1492	827	1815	974	118	95	744	17
2001年	3081	784	1707	590	1913	1168	162	102	881	23
2002年	5360	2070	2361	929	2981	2379	363	116	1876	24
2003年	6812	3328	2713	771	3358	3454	436	193	2791	34
2004年	8406	4013	3142	1251	3703	4703	674	183	3812	34
2005年	11657	4470	4690	2497	4701	6956	1008	303	5600	45
总　计	53057	17477	26316	9264	28644	24413	3485	1604	18293	1031

二、专利授权

1991~2005年，天津市专利授权量逐年增长。其中，1993年首次突破1000件，2003年超过2000件，2005年超过3000件。至2005年底，全市累计专利授权量为23084件。15年间，全市专利授权量年均增长率为11%，其中1991～2000年年均增长率为9.7%，2001～2005年年均增长率为14%。获得授权的专利中，发明专利平均占10%，实用新型专利平均占68%，外观设计专利平均占21%。15年中，发明专利授权量年均增长率为20%，实用新型专利授权量年均增长率为7.1%。2005年,发明专利授权量在当年专利授权量中所占比例达25%,比1991年提升15个百分点。以上数据表明,天津市科技研发能力的提高和自有知识产权含量的稳步上升。

1991～2005年天津市专利授权情况统计表

表2-4-3-44 单位:项

年份	当年授权量	按申请类型划分			按申请人划分		职务发明构成			
		发明	实用新型	外观设计	非职务发明	职务发明	高等院校	科研单位	企业	机关
1991年	607	63	488	56	336	271	50	63	110	48
1992年	897	58	778	61	568	329	57	63	142	67
1993年	1698	106	1447	145	1097	601	121	78	258	144
1994年	1064	72	891	101	712	352	58	51	109	134
1995年	1034	63	785	186	711	323	41	46	99	137
1996年	899	51	666	182	584	315	45	41	161	68
1997年	940	56	634	250	591	349	32	39	254	24
1998年	1042	43	706	293	664	378	39	38	286	15
1999年	1508	95	1039	374	943	565	70	56	401	38
2000年	1611	163	994	454	960	651	69	71	486	25
2001年	1829	96	1214	519	1190	639	49	61	505	24
2002年	1827	102	1163	562	1154	673	77	68	513	15
2003年	2505	241	1547	717	1536	969	175	97	675	22
2004年	2578	432	1587	559	1365	1213	267	105	810	31
2005年	3045	763	1543	739	1370	1675	317	103	1240	15
总 计	23084	2404	15482	5198	13781	9303	1467	980	6049	807

三、专利实施

(一)政策引导

1997年10月,市专利局、市国资局联合转发《中国专利局、国家国有资产管理局关于印发〈专利资产评估管理暂行办法〉的通知》,并提出加强专利资产评估的若干意见。2003年9月16日,市知识产权局与农业银行天津市分行签订《专利权质押担保银政合作框架协议》,专利权质押贷款的模式引起众多企事业单位的关注,在全国影响广泛。2004年9月,市科技兴贸联合工作机制领导小组办公室增加市知识产权局为该领导小组成员单位。同年,市知识产权局与市发改委制定《关于加强天津市重大高新技术产业化项目知识产权保护和管理工作的指导意见》,对天津市重大高新技术产业化项目提出具体指导性意见。是年,市知识产权局选出20项市场前景好、基本实现产业化的专利项目从推广、资助、信贷服务等8个方面进行重点扶持,以点带面,拉动经济的快速增长。至2003年,20项重点扶持服务专利项目创产值26.8亿元,利税7.4亿元。2005年,市知识产权局开始实施专利产业化扶持计划,确定50项市场前景好、竞争能力强的专利产品作为首批重点扶持专利产品,从专利申请资助、宣传推广等方面给予重点扶持服务,推动专利技术的产业化、规模化。

(二)项目推介

1995年3月,市专利局在北方技术交易市场举办"天津市专利十年成就展暨天津市第八届发明展览会"。1995年11月,市专利局组织专利项目和产品参加在马来西亚吉隆坡举办的"国际科技与新产品贸工展",天津有4项获金奖。1996年10月,市专利局举办"夹筋水泥袋纸专利技术及产品新闻发布会",推广优秀专利技术。1998年,受市政府和国家知识产权局委托,市专利局与中国专利报社在天津国际经济贸易展览中心举办“第七届中国专利新技术、新产品博览会”。全国各省、市、自治区和有关部委76个展团、2000余项专利技术和科技新成果、新产品参展，参观人数7万人次，交易总额11.8392亿元。2000年4月，市知识产权局参加国家知识产权局在北京举办的“中国专利十五年成就展”，天津参展的7项专利技术获最佳参展项目、4项获优秀参展项目。2001年1月，市知识产权局与市科协等联合召开“开展发明创新保护知识产权科技传播启动大会”。会上，宣读国务院总理温家宝的复信和天津市青少年的倡议书，国家知识产权局、中国科协和市领导发表重要讲话，世界知识产权组织总干事加米尔·伊德里斯博士出席大会并讲话。同年11月，市知识产权局和市发明协会等在天津国际展览中心举办“第三届国际（天津）发明专利及新技术新产品博览会”，其中天津市优秀专利项目“多燃式蒸汽汽燃机”先后与北京市、吉林省、河北省、辽宁省280家企事业单位和个人达成合作意向。2003年，市知识产权局与河东区政府联合举办“专利项目推介洽谈大会”，组织90个展位、1000多个专利项目，参加洽谈、咨询的有千余人次，达成意向协议100多项。同年，市知识产权局组织优秀专利项目参加国家知识产权局组织的“2003中国国际专利技术与产品交易会”金奖展，天津的“螺环类光致变色化合物及其制造方法”等3个专利金奖、优秀奖项目和“多燃式四温热水机”等8个专利项目受到厂商的关注，签订专利技术合作意向的合同额近亿元。2004年2月，国家知识产权局与欧洲专利局主办，市知识产权局承办的“知识产权与企业发展国际研讨会”在天津召开。2004年，市知识产权局与河东区政府联合举办“专利项目交易洽谈大会”，组织120多个展位，参展专利项目千余项，两千余人次参加洽谈、咨询。2005年5月，在国家知识产权局等单位举办的第五届中国·北京国际科技产业博览会上，天津市2项专利项目获金奖。同年8月，市知识产权局组织9家企业百余项专利项目参加“中国国际专利技术与产品交易会”，天津展团获优秀组团奖。同年11月，市知识产权局组织数项优秀专利项目参加第十二届中国杨凌农业高新科技成果博览会，天津市富康农业开发公司获得博览会优秀展示奖。

（三）专利奖评选

2000年起，天津市开展中国专利优秀奖的推荐活动。经国家知识产权局批准，2001年和2003年天津市有5项专利获中国专利优秀奖。

2003年，天津市政府决定每两年组织一次“天津市专利奖”评选活动。在层层筛选、专家组评审的基础上，2003年和2005年，评选出天津市专利金奖11项、天津市专利优秀奖20项。

2001～2003年天津获中国专利优秀奖项目一览表

表2-4-3-45

年度	专利号	发明创造名称	专利权人
2001	93105858	弱酸性阳离子交换树脂	南开大学高分子化学研究所
2001	97120274	螺环类光致变色化合物及其制备方法	南开大学戈德防伪技术公司
2003	94119090	屏膜控制电缆及其制造工艺	天津六〇九电缆有限公司
2003	95207057	具有精馏塔段的精馏结晶装置	天津大学
2003	01201816	危险品遇水放出易燃气体物质实验仪	中华人民共和国天津出入境检验检疫局

2003～2005年获天津市专利金奖项目一览表

表2-4-3-46

年度	专利号	发明创造名称	专利权人
2003	94118793.4	磺酰脲类化合物及其除草用途	南开大学
2003	97230876.8	全钢丝载重子午线轮胎一次法成型机	天津市橡塑机械联合有限公司张芝泉
2003	00105518.6	生产硅单晶的直拉区熔法	天津市环欧半导体材料技术有限公司
2003	02257108.6	可360度旋转书皮的电子书	天津津科电子有限公司
2003	97116662.5	连续间歇曝气序批式活性污泥污水处理方法	天津市市政工程设计研究院、天津水工业工程设备有限公司等

续表2-4-3-46

年度	专利号	发明创造名称	专利权人
2005	99125582.8	一种稳定的干扰素水溶液	天津华立达生物工程有限公司
2005	02116759.1	超大规模集成电路多层铜布线用化学机械全局平面化抛光液	河北工业大学
2005	00100635.5	超稠油热采井用高强度石油套管及其生产方法	天津钢管公司
2005	01136502.1	大尺寸三维空间测量的现场标定装置及测量方法	天津大学
2005	94118836.1	组织引导再生胶原膜及其制造方法	中国医学科学院生物医学工程研究所

2003～2005年获天津市专利优秀奖项目一览表

表2-4-3-47

年度	专利号	发明创造名称	专利权人
2003	94119090.0	屏膜控制电缆及其制造工艺	天津六〇九电缆有限公司
2003	97103901.1	一种苦卤综合利用的方法	中国石油天然气总公司工程技术研究院
2003	98121576.9	一种复合锂钙基润滑脂组成物及其制造工艺	燕化集团天津润滑油脂有限公司、中国人民解放军总装备部军械技术研究所
2003	97100652.0	低位真空预压软土地基加固法	天津市水利科学研究所
2003	99103300.0	打火机持续燃烧试验仪	中华人民共和国天津出入境检验检疫局
2003	00267647.8	管道全位置自动焊装置	中国石油天然气集团公司
2003	01260511.5	带有四角调平装置的玻璃钢制品液压机	天津市锻压机床总厂
2003	00231363.4	锂离子蓄电池半自动卷绕机	信息产业部电子第十八研究所
2003	00267570.6	双轴向多层衬纱纬编织物	天津工业大学
2003	01301419.6	针灸针	石学敏
2005	00134156.1	甲氰菊酯的制备方法	南开大学
2005	95117497.5	聚偏氟乙烯中空纤维多孔膜及制膜方法	天津纺织工学院膜天膜技术工程公司
2005	01136155.7	一种预防和治疗冠心病心绞痛的药物及其制备方法和其他用途	天津天士力制药股份有限公司
2005	97100641.5	多层框架式线路阻波器	水利部电力工业部机电研究所
2005	01119851.6	光稳定剂中间体2,2,6,6-四甲基-4-哌啶胺类化合物的制备方法	天津大学
2005	01134887.9	空气净化器	乐金电子(天津)电器有限公司
2005	01145167.X	天然石墨改性方法	信息产业部电子第十八研究所
2005	02294921.6	制碱用的结晶器	天津渤海化工有限责任公司天津碱厂
2005	02285064.3	软卸料转接塔	天津港(集团)股份有限公司焦炭码头分公司
2005	03257649.8	可异地通讯数控液压机	天津市天锻压力机有限公司

第四节 行政执法与政策法规

天津市认真贯彻《中华人民共和国专利法》和《中华人民共和国专利法实施细则》,并结合实际制定了一系列加强专利市场管理、查处冒充专利行为的政策规定。同时,各有关部门加强协调与配合,共同推进知识产权保护工作,认真做好专利行政执法,调处专利纠纷和查处假冒他人专利、冒充专利行为。1991～2000年,全市共受理专利纠纷54件,结案51件;查处假冒、冒充专利行为186件。2001～2005年,全市共受理专利纠纷63件,结案40件;查处假冒、冒充专利行为155件。

同时,天津市知识产权政策法规建设不断得到完善,相继出台一系列知识产权保护和管理方面的政策法规或规定,基本建立起符合经济、社会发展的知识产权政策法规体系,对发展天津知识产权事业,促进全市经济和社会全面、协调、可持续发展起到重要作用。

一、行政执法

1998年12月,市专利局与市商业委员会联合制定《关于加强天津市场专利商品管理的通知》,并于1999年5月召开"天津市查处冒充专利商品监督网络成立大会",推进查处冒充专利工作。1999年8月,市专利局与市商业委员会制定《天津市场专利商品监督管理暂行办法》。2000年,市知识产权局与市商业委员会联合召开"天津市督查冒充专利现场交流会",天津华联商厦做"加强商品管理,净化专利市场"的经验介绍,促进查处冒充专利工作的开展。

2001年4月26日,市知识产权局与市版权局、市打假办、市商委、市公安局等开展联合执法行动,对有关商场进行联合执法检查,打击假冒、冒充专利行为,净化专利商品市场。2002年8月28日,市知识产权局与天津海关签订《关于加强实施专利权海关保护的合作办法》,加强在进出口货物中有关知识产权侵害行为的查扣、处罚等方面的协调与配合,打击进出口过程中的知识产权侵权行为。2003年4月,市知识产权局与市公安局、市工商局、市技术监督局、市版权局签发《关于印发〈关于打击侵犯知识产权违法犯罪活动,保护公民法人和其他组织合法权益的实施意见〉的通知》,并召开打击侵犯知识产权违法犯罪活动动员大会,开展联合执法活动。国家知识产权局将天津市联合打击侵犯知识产权违法犯罪活动的工作方式向全国推广。同时,在国家知识产权局主持下,天津市知识产权局与北京、上海、江苏等16个省、市、自治区知识产权管理部门签订《省际间专利行政执法协作协议》,并查处省际间专利行政执法案件3起。同年11月,市知识产权局为24名区县专利行政执法人员颁发"专利行政执法证",加强专利行政执法队伍建设。同年,市知识产权局联合工商、版权、公安、海关、法院等部门,编制中英文双版《2003年天津市知识产权保护状况》白皮书,向社会公布天津市知识产权保护状况。其后,连续3年编制并公布《天津市知识产权保护状况》。2004年和2005年,市知识产权局利用"3·15"消费者权益日和"4·26"世界知识产权日,分别与市公安局等部门联合开展专项执法集中大检查,并多次组织对食品、药品和建材等市场的检查,收到良好效果。2004年,天津市整顿和规范市场经济秩序领导小组办公室、市知识产权局出台《天津市保护知识产权专项行动工作方案》,在全市范围内重点对食品、药品领域开展专项整治活动,打击假冒国际知识产权组织或其他合法组织、欺骗公众谋取非法利益的违法犯罪活动,并与公安机关建立打击知识产权违法犯罪活动的长效机制,有效地保护专利权,营造良好的法制环境。2005年6月,市知识产权局与市公安局制定《联合打击侵犯知识产权违法犯罪活动工作制度》,为依法严厉打击知识产权违法犯罪活动,整顿和规范市场经济秩序,提供有效的措施保障。2005年12月5～7日,海关总署副署长龚正率领国务院保护知识产权专项行动第六督查组对天津市开展保护知识产权专项行动进行督查,并给予充分肯定。

二、政策法规

1994年，市专利局印发《关于中国专利产品认定办法的通知》，对全市范围内“中国专利产品”的认定保护工作做出规定。1996年，市专利局制定《关于加强专利管理工作的通知》，对各区县、委办局、工业总公司的专利管理机构、人员、制度等事项提出具体要求。1997年，市政府发布《天津市加强专利法律状态检索的规定》，对科研项目立项、新产品开发、产品出口、专利广告、企业合资合作等事项前的专利法律状态检索工作做出明确规定。同时，市专利局出台《天津市加强专利法律状态检索的规定实施办法》，对专利法律状态检索的项目、相关事项前的检索程序做出具体规定。同年，市经委、市专利局印发《天津市企业专利工作办法》，对企业专利工作的任务、管理和专利的申请、实施、保护等做出规定，为加强企业专利工作，提高企业技术开发能力提供政策保证。1998年，市专利局出台《关于贯彻国家知识产权局〈关于做好专利广告出证管理工作的通知有关问题〉的通知》，对涉及专利广告的事项做出具体规定，规范专利广告市场。同年，市商委、市专利局印发《关于加强天津市市场专利商品管理的通知》和《天津市专利商品监督管理暂行办法》，对专利商品的进货确认制度、商场和各经销单位的专利管理工作提出要求。2000年，为贯彻《中共天津市委关于加速科技进步和技术创新的若干意见》，市政府办公厅转发市科委、市财政局、市专利局拟定的《天津市加强知识产权管理和保护，促进技术创新的实施意见》，对各级政府、企事业单位的知识产权管理、信息利用、自主知识产权开发和利用的财税政策等做出规定并提出要求。同年，市经委、市专利局下发《关于建立健全天津市重点企业专利工作制度的通知》，对重点企业的专利管理机构、人员、制度建设等提出要求，推动企业建立健全专利工作制度。

2001年，市财政局、市科委、市知识产权局印发《天津市知识产权专项资金管理暂行办法》，对知识产权专项资金的来源、范围、资助方式、审批程序、具备条件等做出规定。2002年，市知识产权局印发《天津市专利申请资助办法》，对专利申请资助的范围、条件、标准、程序做出规定。同年，市科委、市知识产权局出台《关于进一步加强专利技术合同认定登记和备案工作的通知》，对专利技术合同的认定登记和备案工作做出规定，提出要求。2003年，市知识产权局印发《天津市专利权质押贷款操作暂行办法》，规范专利权质押贷款工作。2004年，为贯彻中共中央、国务院《关于加强技术创新，发展高科技，实现产业化的决定》，市知识产权局、市发展改革委员会出台《关于加强天津市重大高新技术产业化项目知识产权保护和管理工作的指导意见》，在增强知识产权意识，推进高新技术产业化进程，创建良好的知识产权法制环境，完善各项工作机制等方面做出规定，提出要求。

2005年，市教委、市知识产权局印发《关于贯彻落实教育部、国家知识产权局〈关于进一步加强高等学校知识产权工作的若干意见〉的意见》，全面推动高等学校知识产权工作。同年，市知识产权局、市公安局出台《天津市联合打击侵犯知识产权违法犯罪活动工作制度》，对打击专利违法犯罪活动的工作制度、案件移送等事项做出规定。同年10月31日，市政府第58次常务会议讨论通过《天津市专利保护和管理办法》，并颁布实施，知识产权保护和管理在法制化的道路上迈出新步伐。

第五章 科技体制改革与科技政策法规

天津市科技体制改革工作，按照中共中央文件的要求，执行市委、市政府的部署，从1983年的机构整顿、1985年的削减事业费、1988年发展民营科技企业、1989年号召开发型院所进入企业、1990年实行分级管理、1993年建立骨干研究所、1994年实行全面绩效考核、1995年公布民主管理文件、1997年制定《天津市“九五”期间深化科研体制改革的若干意见》等等，并结合天津市开发型科研院所多、科研实力弱的实际，做到分类指导、因所制宜，始终围绕“增强实力、择优支持、服务行业、服务社会”为目标，不断深化科研体制改革。在工作层面，进行计划、经费、机制、服务和院所结构等方面改革；在内容方面，从地方院所扩大到中央院所、民营科技企业、企业内部科技机构；在政策环境方面，从领导体制、财税政策、技术市场、人才队伍、国际合作等方面提供帮助，在政策制定前坚持软课题可行性研究先行，广泛征求意见，推进科技体制改革逐步深入。天津市科技体制改革工作力图逐步建立符合市场发展和科技发展规律新的创新体系、保障体系、政策环境，为天津和全国的全面发展做出贡献。2001年起，天津市进一步加快市属科研院所管理体制改革步伐，对市属开发类科研院所实施企业化转制。同时，认真做好部分中央驻津科研院所属地化和注册工作。

天津市在不断深化科技体制改革的同时，围绕实施“科技兴市”战略和大力推动科技进步，制定并实施一系列重要的科技法规与政策，推动科技管理工作的规范化、制度化、科学化进程。

第一节　科技体制改革

在1983年开始的科研机构的整顿工作中，针对“文革”期间地方科研院所的混乱情况进行了恢复机构、重组队伍和建立秩序，是天津市科技力量的恢复和重组过程，为后来的科技体制改革奠定了基础。“八五”末期，中共中央科技方针从“经济建设必须依靠科学技术，科技工作必须面向经济建设”提升为“面向、依靠、攀高峰”；加之当时天津经济社会发展对科技提出了更高要求，科研院所的结构、机制、能力等不能满足需要，市财力、政策的实力有所增强，外地和天津一些科研院所已经创造、摸索出一些经验可以借鉴，科研院所以及主管局希望加速改革。面对新形势，市领导提出“抓住机遇，深化改革”。通过十多年的实践，市科委也深感到需要顶层设计、全盘考虑。经过软课题研究和征求多方意见，出台了《天津市“九五”期间深化科研院所体制改革的若干意见》。按照国务院文件要求“到本世纪末，初步建立适应社会主义市场经济体制和科技自身发展规律的新科技体制”，天津市把科研院所按科技层次分成科研类、开发类和推广类等三类；按与市场关联程度分为政府主导型、政府与行业共建型和市场主导型等三种类型，并根据多年的统计和绩效考核数据，用“横的三层”和“竖的三类”给每个科研院所定位，实施不同走向和政策。科技部部长朱丽兰在华北地区科委联席会上说：“天津找到了深化改革的新模式”。《科技日报》在头版介绍了天津市的做法，科技部发文向全国推荐。

2000年，天津市完成对市属72家开发类科研院所实施企业化转制。2003年起，通过产权制度改革在转制科研院所中建立现代企业制度，形成有利于科技创新和科技成果产业化的体制和机制。至2005年，市属科研机构全部实行全员聘任制，并建立科技人员业绩考核制度，促进人才培养和分流，科研机构活力进一步增强。同时，市属科研机构创办经济实体200余个，从总体上对政府的依赖程度明显降低，面向市场获得收入的能力显著提高。

2000年起，天津市贯彻国务院和科技部有关文件精神，认真做好中央驻津科研院所在天津的属地化和注册工作，顺利完成天津药物研究院的属地化管理。

一、拨款制度改革

1983年，市政府批转市科委《关于天津市科研机构整顿工作意见的报告》。市科委贯彻该文件精神，与各委、办、局协调着手调整市属科研院所的领导班子、科研方向和科研队伍、机构等，进一步规范对科研机构的管理，促进科研机构多出成果、多出人才，以适应经济社会发展的需要。同时，市科委确定天津市合成材料研究所、天津市工业微生物研究所等22个科研机构作为科技体制改革的试点单位，试行科研机构新产品免税申报制度，免征其新产品税。

1985年初，根据国家科委、国家体改委《关于开发研究单位由事业费开支改为有偿合同制的改革试点意见》精神，天津市加大市属科研机构拨款制度改革的力度。1986年，市政府印发《天津市关于独立科研单位体制改革若干问题的补充意见》，对科研院所在体制改革中建立科研发展基金、改革拨款制度、促进技术成果商品化、扩大科研单位自主权、改革和完善奖励制度等8个方面的问题做出明确规定。同年，为鼓励科研院所贯彻中共中央关于科技体制改革的决定，市科委制定《关于科研改革试点单位的性质和对做出贡献的人员实行晋级奖励的通知》，明确界定改革试点科研院所的性质，并对相关优秀科研人员进行晋级奖励。1987年，市委、市政府贯彻国务院出台的《关于进一步推进科技体制改革的若干规定》和《关于推进科研设计单位进入大中型工业企业的规定》，并结合天津实际，制定《关于实施国务院推进科技体制改革两个规定的若干办法》，将科技体制改革推向深入。1989年，市科委印发《关于天津市独立科研单位1989年削减事业费的通知》和《关于继续稳步推进科学事业费拨款制度改革的几点意见》，分步实施核减市属独立科研单位科学事业费，建立天津市科技发展事业基金，加强科研院所与企业的结合。一批科研院所加快科技体制改革的步伐，积极进入企业，寻求新的发展途径。其中，市电视技术研究所进入长城电子公司，市标准件研究所进入机械配件公司，市液压气动工程技术研究所进入液压密封件公司，市电机研究所进入大明电机公司，市工程机械公司研究所进入叉车总厂，市电材工业研究所进入电线电缆集团公司，市机床研究所进入数控机床公司，市工业自动化仪表研究所进入中环自动化仪表公司，市工具研究所进入工具工业公司，市计时研究所和轻工业机械设计研究所也分别进入企业。同时，市冶金材料所和市造纸技术研究所试点进行科技承包责任制改革。1993年，市科委削减市电子计算机研究所、市建筑材料研究所的科学事业费。1994年，市电子计算机研究所并入市缩微技术公司。1996年，市环保设备技术研究所并入市银箭表业公司。1997年，市标准件研究所并入市紧固件公司；市无机化工研究所、市电材工业研究所由全额拨款改为自收自支。至此，天津市完成市属开发类科研机构科学事业费拨款制度改革。

二、市属科研机构改革

1990年，市科委出台《本市独立自然科学研究机构试行分级管理办法》，对市属科研院所开始实行分级管理制度。1991年，市科委印发《关于市科委表彰"为经济建设服务先进科研所"的通知》，表彰市化工局所属合成材料研究所，农科院所属黄瓜研究所、蔬菜研究所，一轻局所属轻工业化学研究所、工业微生物研究所，纺织局所属纺织机械器材研究所，建工局所属建筑科学研究所，机械工业局所属焊接技术研究所，电子仪表局所属电视技术研究所，市科委所属科学技术情报研究所、技术物理所，环保局所属环境保护科学研究所等12个研究所。1993年，市科委将市黄瓜研究所等10个科研机构认定为天津市骨干研究所。同年，市科委、市人事局联合印发《天津市市属科研院所全员聘任制的暂行办法》，明确规定市属科研院所实行全员聘任制，聘任对象包括除上级任命的院所党政主要负责人以外的管理人员和专业技术人员；实行全员聘任制，要坚持公开、公平、公正和竞争、择优的原则，逐步实现上岗靠竞争，收入靠贡献；打破干部、工人的身份界限，做到能上能下。全市各科研院所逐步实行全员聘任制。1994年，市科委颁布《关于市属独立科研院所实行业绩考评的若干规定》，明确规定连续3年被评为一级所的科研院所由市政府命名为"天津市骨干研究所"，颁发荣誉证书；市骨干研究所和连续两年保持一级所的科研院所，市政府给予重点扶持，进一步细化和规范市属独立科研院所业绩考评分级管理工作。1995年，市总工会印发《关于完善科研院所职工民主管理工作的若干意见》，各科研机构进一步推进落实民主管理制度。

1997年，市政府印发《天津市"九五"期间深化科研院所体制改革的若干意见》，明确深化科研院所体制改革的指导思想、原则、目标及相关政策措施，提出科研院所运行机制、领导体制、用人制度、分配制度等项改革的具体内容和要求。同时，市科委确定首批市属科研院所深化体制改革试点单位名单，并积极组织落实。各科研院所对改革试点方案经职工代表大会讨论通过后，由主管部门申报，经市科委、市体改委审核，最后确定在9个科研院所开展改革试点。市化妆品研究所全体职工全资买断国有资产，整体转制成为股份合作制科技型企业。市技术物理研究所、市工业微生物研究所、市合成材料研究所通过建立新型机制，与企业进行跨地区、跨部门、跨行业、跨所有制的联合，组建市级工程技术研究中心。市橡胶研究所以自身为主体，以名牌产品为龙头，通过兼并、联合等形式，建立科技集团公司。市环境保护科学研究院、市自行车研究所等通过发展科技产业，逐步实现自我发展。各试点单位通过科技体制改革试点，发挥试点单位以点带面的作用，促进全市科研院所的全面健康发展。至1998年，9个试点单位技工贸总收入达1.3亿元，完成课题124项，登记成果59项，发表论文74篇，获得专利2项，获奖成果11项；成交技术合同299项，技术合同成交额3527万元；其中在天津市成交190项，成交额1874万元；成果转让产生经济社会效益2.32亿元，成果应用产生经济社会效益19.51亿元。1998年4月1日，市科委召开天津市科研院所体制改革工作会议，总结市属科研院所体制改革工作10余年取得的效果和存在的不足，将科研院所体制改革推向深入。1998年10月9日，科技部转发《天津市深化科研院所体制改革的思路与作法》，介绍并推广天津市科技体制改革的经验。1998年，市科委命名天津市技术物理所、市化妆品研究所、市工业微生物研究所、市合成材料研究所、市橡胶研究所等9个科研院所为"天津市骨干研究所"，并确认市自行车研究所、市环境科学研究院、市化学试剂研究所、市建筑科学研究所、市冶金材料研究所等14个科研院所有经营进出口业务。

2000年4月，市政府颁发《批转市科委等16个部门〈关于天津市科研院所管理体制改革实施意见〉的通知》，对市属72家开发类科研院所实施企业化转制，并提出转制科研院所实行企业职工基本养老保险制度，其退休人员基本养老金均按企业基本养老金计发办法执行，并按转制前、转制过渡期、转制后3个阶段分别享受不同的政策。市科委等政府部门积极推进科技体制改革，加强思想政治工作，提高科研机构改革意识，认清改革的紧迫性和必要性，强化科研院所考核工作，对市属科研机构进行择优支持，重点装备科研开发实力强、技术优势明显的科研院所，增强各单位科研与中试能力。至2000年，天津市投入3200余万元装备重点科研机构，使科研机构硬件环境得到大幅改善，科研与中试能力显著提高，为开发类科研机构顺利实施企业化转制奠定了基础。

至2001年，各开发类科研机构企业化转制后，呈现三种不同类型。第一种类型是完全或基本适应转制。市橡胶工业研究所、市工业微生物研究所、市焊接技术研究所、市塑料研究所等单位有较好的改革基础，进入市场较早，以转制为契机，通过资源重组、转换机制和制度创新，由原来的事业单位直接转变为科技型企业，走出一条"靠改革促进发展，以发展推动改革"的道路。这类开发类科研机构约占转制科研机构总数的60%。第二种类型是尚未完全适应转制。这类科研机构有3种情况：一种是有一定的科技实力，可以开发一些"短、平、快"的科研项目和科技含量较低的产品，以维持生计，但在发展高新技术产业方面则显得力不从心；另一种是领导决策层的主要精力集中在解决单位职工的"吃饭问题"上，无暇顾及深化改革和长远发展问题；再一种是领导的思想观念没有完全转变，仍依恋过去事业单位的种种好处，甚至希望再回到原来的体制。这类科研机构普遍缺乏开拓创新精神，科研院所的优势和潜力未能充分发挥，约占转制科研机构总数的20%。第三种类型是基本不适应转制。这类科研机构大多观念陈旧，基础较差，人才、技术和资金缺乏，产品没有市场；转制前完全依靠事业费吃饭，转制以后缺乏进入市场的充分心理准备，领导班子缺乏市场观念，成果匮乏，人才流失严重，人员老化，在同行业中缺乏竞争力。这类科研机构约占转制科研机构总数的20%。2001年，市政府和市科委围绕开发类科研机构转制为企业后出现的种种情况和问题，先后出台一系列政策性文件和配套措施，及时解决科技体制改革过程中出现的问题，保证科技体制改革的顺利进行。

至2002年，市属72家开发类科研院所实行企业化转制后，虽然从业人员总数较转制前减少2910人，但从事科技活动的人员占从业人员总数的比率上升到57%；拥有资产合计11.6亿元，其中固定资产6.2亿元，比转制前的5.87亿元增长5.6%，科研仪器设备总额2亿元；年技工贸总收入3.9亿元，比转制前的3.2亿元增长21.87%，通过市场获得收入与政府资金投入比约为14∶1；拥有发明专利总数21件，年转让科技成果275项，比转制前增长2倍；技术开发收入占技术性收入的64%左右，科研成果应用实现利税20亿元，比转制前提高23%。开发类科研院所转制后，技术力量和科研开发能力增强，并具备面向市场的发展能力。同时，转制后的科研机构积极进入经济建设主战场，与经济的结合日趋紧密，成为环保、种子、新材料、发酵、水处理、新农药等领域技术支撑的核心，在传统产业的技术改造、技术监督、技术服务及社会发展科技进步中发挥越来越大的作用。转制科研机构的技术创新能力不断提高，科技成果转化能力进一步增强，初步形成面向市场需求、自觉增加研发投入的良性循环。其中，约60%的科研机构转制以后，研发经费投入提高，横向课题数量增加，市场竞争能力增强，经济效益有所提高，并在科研成果产业化方面进行有益探索；相当一部分转制的科研机构步入二次创业的发展时期，开始探索向投资主体多元化方向发展。

2003年起，天津市贯彻《国务院办公厅转发国务院体改办等部门〈关于深化转制科研机构产权制度改革若干意见〉的通知》精神，以深化转制科研院所产权制度改革为突破口，建立产权明晰、投资主体多元化、适应市场经济规律的现代企业制度，出台《天津市转制科研院所产权制度改革实施意见》，通过产权制度改革在转制科研院所中建立现代企业制度，最大限度地调动科技人员的积极性和创造性，形成有利于科技创新和科技成果产业化的体制和机制。同时，按照科技部"以部门为单位整体推进，成熟一个，启动一个，示范引导，逐步推开"的原则，以《批转市科委等16个部门〈关于天津市科研院所管理体制改革实施意见〉的通知》为政策依据，采取"先易后难，试点先行"的工作方针，加快社会公益类科研院所的试点改革，建立符合天津市创新体系建设需要的公益研究队伍，进而实现体制和机制的创新，促进科技成果的转化，增强技术创新能力，加快科研院所改革和产业化进程。

至2005年，市属科研机构创办经济实体201个，实现人员分流近4000人，占在职职工总数的27.6%，年总收入达3.1亿元，从总体上对政府的依赖程度明显降低，面向市场获得收入的能力显著提高。市属科研机构内部机制改革进一步深化，在事业单位中率先实行全员聘任制，建立科技人员业绩考核制度，促进人才培养和分流，机构活力进一步增强。各转制科研机构的市场观念显著增强，注重发挥科研技术上的优势，努力保持在该行业某一领域的技术先进性，并以此为基础进入市场，寻求更大发展。科研机构宏观管理体制逐步健全，政府宏观管理已经由直接管理转为间接管理。市科委对科研机构的管理主要为政策调控，坚持对市属科研机构进行统一考评、分类指导，优先支持科研实力强的机构，对不具备科研开发实力或不再从事科研活动的机构限期整改或撤销。

市科委不仅通过计划项目、重点武装、国际合作等多方面的努力，不断增强科研院所的科技能力，更在管理、机制方面进行了多方面积极探索。市科委和市总工会一起发布了关于科研院所发挥职工代表大会作用的文件，探讨党委领导、行政负责和职工民主监督的关系。同时，市科委举办了三期科研院所所长培训班，大部分院所所长参加了培训。通过培训，学习中央和市委、市政府关于深化科技体制改革文件、"社会主义商品经济"理论、有关财税制度和科技管理知识等，为推动科研院所深化改革、进入市场打好思想基础，掌握过去不熟悉的财税政策和可以享受的优惠政策，收到较好效果。

三、中央驻津科研机构属地化

天津市始终重视发挥中央驻津科研院所的作用。市科委主任王成怀参加天津第一个整顿验收的一机部天津电气传动设计研究所验收大会，让该所给全市市属科研院所介绍一机部科研院所整顿的目的、流程和意义，推动市属科研院所的整顿工作。在全市学大庆大会上，推荐天津市焊接研究所作"服务行业"和一机部天津电气传动设计研究所作"立足天津面向全国"的典型发言。为促进中央驻津科研机构与天津市的科技交流，充分发挥中央驻津科研院所的作用，推动天津经济社会发展，1991年9月市科委举办了中央驻津科研院所和市属先进科研所成果展览，推广介绍驻津科研院所与天津企业相结合的成果。市委书记谭绍文仔细观看每个展位，详细了解驻津科研院所涉及的科技领域和行业作用。经济部门领导反映，该成果展对了解驻津科研院所起了很好的作用。

中央驻津科研院所不断探索中央与地方共建的组织形式和管理方式，促进与地方科技、经济的紧密结合。1994年，由市科委牵头成立天津市科技协作促进会，吸收核工业理化工程研究院、天津化工研究设计院、天津大学、南开大学等45家中央驻津科研机构和高等院校为成员单位，进一步促进中央驻津科研机构与天津市的科技合作与交流。

2000年,根据《国务院办公厅转发科技部等部门〈关于国家经贸委管理的10个国家局所属科研机构管理体制改革意见〉的通知》和科技部等12个部门《关于印发〈关于国家经贸委管理的10个国家局所属科研机构管理体制改革的实施意见〉的通知》文件精神,天津市政府印发《批转市科委〈关于做好中央及外省市科研院所转制在津属地化和注册工作意见〉的通知》,鼓励和吸引国家有关部门和外省市所属科研院所在天津的属地化和注册。至2005年,实施属地化管理的中央驻津科研院所仅有天津药物研究院。天津药物研究院在各有关部门的支持下,坚持科技创新,密切产研结合,在推进科技成果产业化方面取得成效。

第二节　科技政策法规

1991~2005年,经市人大常委会讨论通过,先后颁布实施《天津市技术市场管理条例》《天津市实施〈中华人民共和国科学技术进步法〉办法》《天津市科学技术普及条例》《天津市促进科技成果转化条例》《天津市促进技术交易条例》等地方性科技法规。

1991~1996年,天津市围绕全面实施市委确定的"科教兴市"战略方针,在大力推动科技进步、促进科研机构改革、建立对科技人员的激励机制、促进科技管理的规范化、科学化等方面制定并实施一系列政策。大力吸引和扶持外资和民营科技企业、建设一支高素质的专业技术人才队伍、推进科研院所体制改革,是1996~2000年科技政策的重要内容。2001~2005年,天津市进一步完善促进科技服务业发展的政策,并在促进区域经济发展和高新技术成果转化、扶持软件人才与软件企业建设以及规范科技管理等方面制定并实施一系列科技政策。

一、科技立法

1991~1995年,天津市加强科技立法工作。1993年10月28日,市人大常委会讨论通过《天津市技术市场管理条例》。1994年1月26日,市人大常委会讨论通过《天津市实施〈中华人民共和国科学技术进步法〉办法》。该"办法"明确规定:各级政府应当鼓励科学探索和技术创新,鼓励自然科学研究与社会科学研究相结合,保护知识产权,促进科技成果转化为现实生产力;全社会都应当尊重知识,尊重人才,增强科学技术意识,注重普及科学技术知识,切实提高公民的科学文化水平,推动科学技术进步。该"办法"共45条,第一次用立法的形式对编制科技发展规划与技术政策、科技计划管理、科技成果转化与推广、科技奖励、科技人才激励与流动、科技投入和风险基金、技术市场、知识产权、新技术产业园区建设和民营科技等重要科技发展问题做出明确规定,并明确要求各级政府在财政预算中用于科学技术的经费应当逐年有所增加,其增长幅度应当高于财政经常性收入的增长幅度。全市科学技术研究开发的经费与国民生产总值的比例应当逐年提高,并逐步达到全国先进水平。

1996~2000年,天津市科技立法工作迈出新步伐。1996年,市人大常委会教科文卫委员会组织市科委、市科协以及南开大学和部分科研院所的专家学者进行科普立法工作的调研,并起草《天津市科学技术普及条例(草案)》。1997年6月18日,市人大常委会讨论通过《天津市科学技术普及条例》。该"条例"对科普工作的重点、形式和内容、组织和管理、社会责任、科普组织和场所、科普工作者、保障措施、奖励与处罚等方面做出规定。为促进科技成果向现实生产力转化,依法维护科技成果转化各方的合法权益,加速科技进步,推动经济建设和社会发展,根据《中华人民共和国促进科技成果转化法》和有关法律、法规,结合天津市实际情况,制定《天津市促进科技成果转化条例》,并于1998年4月14日由市人大常委会讨论通过。该"条例"对科技成果转化的组织管理、转化实施、促进措施、技术权益保护、法律责任作出明确规定:科技成果转化活动应当注重经济效益和社会效益，遵循自愿、互利、公平、诚实信用的原则，依法维护从事转化活动当事人的合法权益，维护国家和社会公共利益。随着科技事业与社会主义市场经济发展的需要，为保障技术交易当事人的合法权益，促进技术交易，加速科技成果转化，促进科技进步和经济发展，根据国家有关法律、法规，结合天津市实际，对1993年市人大常委会通过的《天津市技术市场管理条例》进行修订，形成《天津市促进技术交易条例》，并于2000年11月8日由市人大常委会讨论通过。该"条例"对技术交易、技术交易服务、技术交易鼓励措施、法律责任等，均做出明确的规定。2000年，市政府以第33号令颁布《天津市科学技术奖励办法》，明确规定天津市设立科学技术奖，其中包括科学技术重大成就奖、自然科学奖、技术发明奖、科学技术进步奖、国际科学技术合作奖5个类别；天津市科学技术奖的推荐、评审、授予，实行公开、公平、公正的原则，不受任何组织或个人的干涉。

2001～2005年，天津市科技立法呈现新的特点。一是按照国家"行政许可法"，对地方性科技法规与政府规章进行修订。经过对24件市政府规范性文件和42件市科委规范性文件的清理，对其中3件市政府规范性文件，即《转发市科委、市财政局拟定的〈天津市科技三项费用管理暂行办法〉的通知》《关于发布〈天津市促进民营科技企业发展的若干规定〉的通知》《批转市科委拟定的〈天津市科学技术奖励办法实施细则〉的通知》进行修订，废止1件市政府文件，即《关于发布〈天津市"九五"期间深化科研院所体制改革的若干意见〉的通知》；修订7件市科委规范性文件，废止2件市科委规范性文件，即《印发〈天津市市属科研院所全员聘任制暂行办法〉的通知》《关于印发〈关于加强全市民营科技企业技术经营资格认定工作的意见〉》。二是加强科技立法调研，分别由市人大教科文卫委员会和市政府法制办公室牵头，先后开展"天津市科技投入立法研究""加强科技法规环境建设的对策研究"，分析全市科技进步与技术创新对科技立法的需求，明确近期科技立法的主要任务与工作重点。

二、科技政策

（一）1991～1995年科技政策

1991年起，天津市围绕全面实施市委五届八次会议确定的"科技兴市"战略方针，制定并实施大力推动科技进步的一系列政策。1992年8月，市委、市政府颁发《关于依靠科技进步，加快经济发展的若干意见》，市政府有关部门相继制定《关于推进工业企业技术进步的暂行规定》《关于进一步加快技术引进和国产化的暂行规定》《关于增强科研院所科技实力与活力的暂行规定》《关于充分发挥科技人员作用的暂行规定》《关于吸引国内外优秀科技人才来津工作的暂行规定》《关于提高天津市城乡劳动者素质的暂行规定》等6个政策性文件，为"科技兴市"战略方针的实施起到推动作用。1995年8月，市委、市政府颁布《关于贯彻全国科技大会精神，加速科学技术进步的实施意见》，进一步明确实施"科教兴市"战略的政策，为科技进步营造良好的政策环境。同时，天津市围绕全面实施"科教兴市"战略，制定了一系列鼓励或奖励科技进步的政策。其中，市政府批转市科委拟定的《天津市"科技兴市"突出贡献奖颁发暂行办法》，市科委先后印发《关于颁发天津市鼓励技术出口的暂行规定》《关于动员科技人员积极投入扭亏增盈攻坚战的决定》《关于鼓励驻津科研院所和高等院校为科技兴市做出贡献的若干规定》《关于鼓励企业加速科技成果转化为生产力的若干规定》等政策规定。

1991～1995年，天津市在促进科研机构转变运行机制、建立科学的科研院所管理制度方面制定一系列政策。1993年，市科委、市人事局联合印发《天津市市属科研院所全员聘任制的暂行办法》。该办法明确规定：市属科研院所实行全员聘任制，聘任对象包括除上级任命的院所党政主要负责人以外的管理人员和专业技术人员；实行全员聘任制，要坚持公开、公平、公正和竞争、择优的原则，逐步实现上岗靠竞争，收入靠贡献；打破干部、工人的身份界限，做到能上能下。为实现科技与经济一体化，建立激励和竞争机制，促进全市独立科研院所上水平、出成果、创效益，市科委颁布《关于市属独立科研院所实行业绩考评的若干规定》。其中明确规定：对连续3年被评为一级所的科研院所，由市政府命名为"天津市骨干研究所"，颁发荣誉证书；市骨干研究所和连续两年保持一级所的科研院所，市政府给予重点扶持。

发展壮大科技带头人队伍，不断改善科技人员的工作和生活条件，建立对科技人员的激励机制，是1991～1995年天津市制定科技政策的一个重要方面。市委科技工委和市科委颁发《关于充分发挥自然科学技术领域中青年授衔专家在重大科技活动中科技带头人作用的通知》，提出要为中青年授衔专家发挥科技带头人作用积极创造条件。同时，颁发《关于继续做好科技领域跨世纪育才工程实施工作的通知》，明确对跨世纪科技带头人加大资助培养力度；颁发《关于培养造就科技领域跨世纪学术、技术带头人的若干意见》，明确规定："制定总体规划、目标、措施和年度计划，有领导、有组织的实施；建立、健全培养造就科技领域跨世纪学术、技术带头人的有关制度，形成加速其成长、促其脱颖而出的机制。"市委、市政府在《关于贯彻全国科技大会精神，加速科学技术进步的实施意见》中，围绕充分发挥科技人才优势，进一步完善了相关政策，加大政策扶持力度。

同时，天津市在促进科技管理的规范化、科学化方面制定多项政策。其中，市科委与天津市国家保密局联合印发《关于认真贯彻〈科学技术保密规定〉进一步加强科技保密工作的几点意见》，为科技保密工作逐步走向科学化、规范化、标准化做出相关规定。为更好地贯彻执行国家科委新的《科技成果鉴定办法》，市科委颁布《天津市关于贯彻执行国家科委新的〈科学技术成果鉴定办法〉及〈科技成果鉴定规程（试行）〉的意见》。1994年，市科委颁布《天津市科技百亿工程管理暂行办法》《关于科技项目实行管理责任制的有关规定》《天津市火炬计划项目管理暂行办法》等规定，从政策上保证科技项目的顺利完成。

（二）1996～2000年科技政策

1996～2000年，天津市围绕加速科技进步和创新、推进科技体制改革和发挥专业技术人员作用等方面制定一系列科技政策。

推动高新技术和民营企业发展，加速科技进步和创新，是这一时期制定科技政策的一个重要方面。1996年，为贯彻实施"科教兴市"战略，积极引导和鼓励外商投资发展知识密集型、技术密集型产业即高新技术产业，加速产业结构、产品结构调整步伐，推动全市高新技术产业发展，市科委、市国税局联合印发《天津外商投资知识密集型技术密集型企业的认定办法》。该办法规定：市科委认定的外商"双密"（知识密集型、技术密集型）企业，经市国税局核实报批后，可享受按15%的税率缴纳企业所得税，并自企业获利年度起免征2年，减半征收3年企业所得税。1997年，为贯彻市委、市政府加速实施信息港工程，大力推动以计算机和通信为核心的信息产业发展的战略部署，天津市信息化工作领导小组办公室和市科委等7部门联合印发《天津信息港工程项目的采购办法》，明确规定凡列入天津信息港工程的项目单位，采购设备时在质量、价格、服务同等条件下优先采购中国自有品牌、自主版权的产品，列入市政府采购清单的天津市产品可享受优先列入科技计划、技改计划、重大科技产业化工程项目及流动奖金贷款利率优惠等方面的扶持政策。同年，市信息化工作领导小组办公室、市计委等5部门联合印发《天津信息港工程项目管理暂行规定》。1998年，市政府颁布《天津市促进民营科技企业发展的若干规定》，明确规定：支持并鼓励优秀民营科技企业通过平等竞争，承担市级及以上的技术开发和新产品试制项目，在科研项目立项、贷款、科技三项费使用、科技成果鉴定、开展国际科技合作等方面可享受国有科研单位的同等政策；从文件下发之日起，天津新技术产业园区以外新开办、注册的民营科技企业，其所得税实行5年内先征后返政策，前两年100%返还，后3年50%返还。1999年，市委、市政府贯彻全国技术创新大会精神，围绕加快实施"科教兴市"战略，走好依靠科技进步的发展道路，对促进高新技术产业化制定新的举措。1999年1月，市政府印发《天津市高新技术产业发展规划》的通知。1999年12月16日，市委七届五次全体会议通过《中共天津市委关于加速科技进步和创新的若干意见》，围绕加速技术创新，大力促进结构优化和产业升级；深化改革，扩大开放，促进科技成果产业化；高度重视人才工作，健全和完善人才激励机制；加大政策扶持力度，营造技术创新的良好环境；切实加强领导，为技术创新提供强有力保证等方面，对加速科技进步和技术创新进行全面部署，制定一系列的政策措施。为确保这些部署和措施的落实，市政府有关部门在调查研究的基础上，相继制定一系列更具体、更具可操作性的实施细则。这些实施细则，涉及科技进步和技术创新的诸多方面，包括《天津市鼓励外商投资高新技术研究开发和产业化项目的暂行规定》《关于做好中央及外省市科研院所转制在津属地化和注册工作的意见》《天津市加强知识产权管理和保护，促进技术创新的实施意见》《关于积极推动天津市建立风险投资机制的意见》等。2000年，为贯彻落实《国务院关于印发鼓励软件产业和集成电路产业发展若干政策的通知》精神，推动软件产业的发展，市政府颁发《批转市科委〈关于加快天津市软件产业发展实施意见〉的通知》。该文件进一步明确加快天津市软件产业发展的指导思想、发展目标，并从投融资、税收、人才吸引、人员培养、营造环境等方面做出较为全面的政策规定。

这一时期，制定科技政策的一个重要方面是促进科研院所体制改革。1997年，市科委根据《国务院关于“九五”期间深化科技体制改革的决定》和国家科委《关于加快深化地方科技体制改革实施工作若干意见》，制定《天津市“九五”期间深化科研院所体制改革的若干意见》。其中，围绕完善科研院所体制改革的外部环境提出7项政策性措施：多渠道增加科技投入，加强对科研院所改革的支持；加速培养中青年科技骨干队伍；鼓励大部分开发型院所逐步向科技企业过渡或进入企业，推动科技成果产业化；坚持和完善科研院所绩效考评制度，加强科研院所宏观管理；建立社会保障和科技服务体系；建立科研院所发展的政策法规体系；坚持对外开放，积极参与国际交流与合作。2000年，参照国务院及科技部关于科研机构管理体制改革的相关政策，市政府颁布《批转市科委等16个部门〈关于天津市科研院所管理体制改革实施意见〉的通知》，明确规定转制科研院所的范围：市属开发型院所和总公司（集团公司）所属信息类研究院所，并提出转制科研院所实行企业职工基本养老保险制度，其退休人员基本养老金均按企业基本养老金计发办法执行，并按转制前、转制过渡期、转制后3个阶段，分别享受不同的政策，即转制前退休人员待遇标准不变，其基本养老金调整按企业基本养老金计发办法执行；5年过渡期内退休人员（2000年7月1日至2005年6月30日）其低于原事业单位退休金计发办法的部分，采用加发补贴的办法解决，补贴比例按“9、7、5、3、1”逐年递减；2005年6月30日后退休的不再发放该项补贴。

聚集人才、充分发挥专业技术人员作用，是这一时期科技政策的一个重要特点。1999年9月，为全面实施“科教兴市”战略，大力推进科技进步，加强科技创新，实现天津市跨世纪发展的宏伟目标，围绕聚集人才、充分发挥专业技术人员的作用，努力建设一支高素质的专业技术人才队伍，市委、市政府颁布《关于聚集人才、充分发挥专业技术人员作用的意见》，从大力培养造就高级人才、积极引导各类专业技术人才、鼓励专业技术人才在科技成果转化中发挥作用、对有突出贡献的专业技术人才实施重奖、努力提高高级人才待遇、营造有利于优秀人才脱颖而出的环境等6个方面做出较为全面的政策规定。

（三）2001～2005年科技政策

2001～2005年，天津市在促进科技服务业和高新技术发展、规范科技管理等方面制定多项政策。

为进一步促进科技服务业的发展，2002年市政府颁发《天津市促进创业投资业发展的暂行规定》，为吸引境内外各类创业资本在天津投资制定多项具体的优惠政策。2004年，市政府发布《关于进一步实施科技兴贸战略的意见》。同年，市科委、市财政局印发《天津市创业投资机构财税优惠政策的实施办法》。2005年，市政府批转市科委《关于促进天津市科技企业孵化器建设与发展的意见》，明确了对科技企业孵化器的扶持政策，促进科技企业孵化器的发展。

为促进区域经济的发展，2003年市政府发布《关于加强天津市区县科技工作的若干意见》，明确提出：市科委要加强对区县科技工作的指导与支持；为区县科技管理部门创造更大的工作空间；市科委设立区县科技创新引导专项资金；积极帮助区县开展国际科技交流与合作。

为促进高新技术成果转化，2005年市政府批转市科委《关于进一步促进高新技术成果转化的暂行办法》。该文件明确规定：实行高新技术成果转化项目认定制度；市政府设立高新技术成果转化专项资金，并给予贷款等扶持，促进高新技术成果项目转化；鼓励科技人员兼职办科技企业，兼职从事高新技术成果的转化工作；鼓励外商在天津市投资创业，转化高新技术成果。为做好高新技术成果转化项目认定工作，市科委还制定了《天津市高新技术成果转化项目认定管理办法》等。

为扶持软件人才与软件企业的发展，2005年市政府批转市科委等12部门《关于加快天津市软件人才培养和队伍建设的实施意见》，较系统地规定了关于加快软件人才培养和队伍建设的投融资、税收优惠、人才吸引、人才培养与培训、人才环境等方面的政策。同时,市科委先后制定《天津市软件企业和集成电路企业认定管理办法》《天津市鼓励软件企业CMM认证工作的管理办法》,并与市财政局、市人事局联合制定《天津市软件企业和集成电路设计及生产企业高级人才专项奖励的暂行办法》,对软件高级人才进行专项奖励作出具体规定。

为规范科技管理,2001~2005年市科委和有关部门围绕规范科技管理工作制定了一系列规范性文件,其中包括《〈天津市科学技术奖励办法〉实施细则》《关于国家科研计划实施课题制管理的意见》《天津市自然科学基金管理办法》《天津市科研院所技术开发工作扶持经费暂行管理办法》《天津市科技创新专项资金管理办法》《天津市科技计划项目奖金管理办法》《天津市实验动物许可证管理办法》《天津市重点实验室管理办法》《天津市软件企业和集成电路企业认定管理办法》《天津市外商投资技术密集知识密集型企业认定管理办法》以及《天津市科普税收优惠政策实施细则》等若干政策规定。

第六章 科技合作与交流

1991~2005年,天津市抓住机遇,围绕经济社会发展、科技进步和对外开放的需要,先后与39个国家和国际组织开展政府间的科技合作,实施合作项目200余项,涉及农业、工业、水利、交通、环保、能源、生物、医药、信息、水资源、新材料、核辐射、职业技术教育、企业管理等诸多领域。同时,通过组织科技人员出国考察培训、参加学术会议,参加或举办境内外的国际学术会议和国际展览,以及对外开展共同研究等方式,广泛开展民间国际科技交流活动,对促进天津科技与经济社会的协调发展产生积极作用。

天津市科学技术协会与职工技术协会作为社会科技团体,围绕科技、经济、社会发展亟待解决的重大问题,组织广大职工和科技工作者开展形式多样的科技交流活动,大力推广新技术、新成果,为企业和农村提供技术服务,为促进科技进步和经济社会发展起到纽带和桥梁作用。

市委、市政府高度重视与中科院的科技合作,将其作为聚集国内外科技资源,推进全市尤其是滨海新区开发开放的重要举措,在项目合作、机构合作、人才交流、院所引进、信息交流等方面建立长效合作机制。2005年7月,天津市与中科院签订全面科技合作协议。通过院市合作,聚集中科院优质项目和科技资源落户天津,大大提升了天津自主创新能力和水平,为天津市增添了一批新的科技优势,为天津经济社会发展提供了强有力的科技支撑。

第一节 国际科技合作与交流

1991~2005年,天津市通过科学考察、技术交流、科技培训、专家或志愿者派遣、开发调查、单项器材提供、专项及合作研究等形式,与日本、韩国等亚非拉国家开展政府间的科技合作,完成106个项目;通过互相考察、访问和交换种子资源等方式,与俄罗斯、捷克等东欧国家开展政府间科技合作项目共58项;通过合作研究、合作建实验室、合作建培训中心、合作建示范中心、赴国外培训和考察等形式,与欧洲国家开展政府间科技合作项目30项;与欧盟的科技合作有6项,其中能源技术方面的合作2项;与澳大利亚的科技合作1项。同时,天津市本着“政府与民间并举,以政府为主”的方针,组织科技人员出国考察培训、参加学术会议,支持高等院校、科研机构和高新技术企业通过参加或举办境内外的国际学术会议和国际展览，开展共同研究等方式，不断拓展国际科技交流渠道，积极开展民间国际科技交流。

1994年，国务院设立国际科技合作奖，1995年开始评奖。该奖项是授予在双边或者多边国际科技合作中对中国科学技术事业做出重要贡献的外国科学家、工程技术人员、科技管理人员和科学技术研究、开发、管理等组织，是中国政府设立的五大科技奖项中授予外国人或者外国组织的奖项，每年授奖数额不超过10人。1995年，在天津工作的外籍数学家陈省身获得国家级国际科技合作奖。1997年，在天津工作的新加坡籍眼科专家林少明获得国家级国际科技合作奖。此后，2001年在天津工作的外籍专家毛焕宇、2002年外籍专家罗伯特·迪盖特分别获得国家级国际科技合作奖。至2005年，4名在天津工作的外籍专家获得国家级国际科技合作奖。

一、政府间科技合作

（一）与亚洲国家的科技合作

1、中日科技合作

为解决现代奶业技术和管理水平相对落后，牛奶及奶制品供应跟不上需求的问题，1990年3月至1997年2月，天津市通过JICA渠道与日本开展政府间“中国天津奶业发展项目”的科技合作，天津市奶类发展项目办公室和日本荷斯坦登陆协会为项目实施机构。日方在试管式冷冻精液制造技术、奶牛品种改良方法、奶牛饲养管理技术、奶牛胚胎技术、国营农场饲养管理技术及饲料作物生产技术等5个方面对中方技术人员给予指导和培训，使天津市奶业技术和管理水平得到提高。天津市奶牛育种中心成为全国首家能鉴定奶牛泌乳能力的单位；天津市奶业试管精液使用普及率达到100%；奶牛的非传染性繁殖障碍的防治技术得到普及与提高；奶牛的移植胚胎技术得到提高，移植成功率达到60%；奶牛场的饲养管理技术及饲料作物生产技术得到改善和提高，奶牛的泌乳能力和犊牛成活率得到提高。

1993年，天津市通过JICA渠道获得日本单项器材项目，日方向天津市提供1辆价值0.6亿日元的广播电视质量检测车。该检测车可对广播电视质量进行检测，并及时反映播送质量状况，进一步保证了广播电视的质量。

1993年11月至1998年10月，天津市通过JICA渠道与日本开展药品检验技术的合作研究，天津市药品检验所和日本国立卫生实验所（后更名为日本国立药品食品卫生研究所）为实施机构。该项目围绕提高药检技术、培养人才、改善实验环境等方面具体实施。天津市药品检验所相继派出28名专业技术人员赴日进修，并先后邀请日本专家81人次到津进行短期或长期技术指导和传授技术，使该所药品检验能力和水平得到提高，并涌现出一批年轻的技术骨干。项目实施中，通过每年在天津召开全国性的中日药品分析技术研讨会，赴河北、内蒙古、上海、广州等省市进行学术演讲或举办伪劣药品快速检验培训班，接收外单位人员到该所进修等方式，将先进的药品检验技术辐射到许多省市。

1994年11月至1999年10月，经中日两国政府签约，在天津实施“中国劳动和社会保障职业培训指导教师进修中心”项目。天津职业技术师范学院和日本劳动省职业能力开发局为项目实施机构。1994年11月1日，开始在生产技术、控制技术、电子技术、信息技术及汽车技术等领域实施技术合作。至1999年，该中心共招收4届学员计774人，培养毕业生392人，其中218人作为指导教师分别到技工学校、中等职业技术学校和大学就职。由于该中心设备充实，促进教学专业理论和实际操作技能一体化教育，为制造业和现代服务业培养大批高级“蓝领”人才创造了有利条件。该中心除完成教学任务外，还接受国家劳动和社会保障部委托，编制完成数控机床操作技术等级标准，并出版相关教材。

2002年，在天津举办首届中日（天津）软件合作论坛和软件产品展示会，科技部负责人出席。2003年，继续在天津举行第二届软件合作论坛和软件产品展示会。2004年6月，第三届“中日（天津）软件合作论坛”在东京举行。

2003年，中日双方在生物技术领域开展科技合作。天津科技大学与日本大藏省酿造研究所承担“酵母菌乳酸耐性机理研究”项目，对抗酸酵母进行选育，并对其进行生理学、遗传学等方面的分析、研究，阐明其机理，为在酒类酿造、酒精发酵、特种面包生产的应用奠定了基础。同年，中日双方开展发菜多糖替代发菜的合作研究与开发。至2004年，获得2升容积规模发菜多糖的培养技术，对降低药品、保健品成本和原料的供给有着重要意义。天津科技大学与日方开展的科技合作项目“新型生物产业开发”，对降低乳酸生产成本进行研究，以L-乳酸为原料合成的聚乳酸可用于生产可降解塑料，可降解塑料的生产成本降低，同时可有效改善对环境的污染。

2、中韩科技合作

1991～2005年，天津市与韩国开展的政府间科技合作项目，主要通过韩国科技厅和KOICA渠道实施，共实施12个项目，其中合作研究1项、科技专项1项、专家到津工作5项、培训项目5项。

1996～1997年，为解决工业化和经济快速发展过程中带来的环境污染问题，天津市与韩国合作开展“近海地区有毒金属有机化合物和城市大气颗粒物的研究”项目。南开大学环境科学系为中方项目的实施单位。中韩双方专家密切配合，完成研究报告，并在国际会议上合作发表论文1篇。该项目对天津市治理环境污染问题具有一定的指导意义。

3、中泰科技合作

1998年，中泰两国将膜技术研究和开发列入政府间的科技合作项目。项目执行单位是天津膜天膜工程技术有限公司和泰国科学技术研究院。根据中泰两国科技合作议定书，天津膜天膜工程技术有限公司组团赴泰国进行短期技术考察和交流，泰国科学技术研究院专家团回访天津膜天膜工程技术有限公司。双方在相互了解的基础上签署合作协议书。中泰双方密切配合，对中方原开发的净化装置进行多次技术改进和实验，研制出适用于泰国高含盐地下水的微滤+反渗透装置和适用于地表水除菌、排异味、可直接饮用的超滤、微滤净水成套装置，为推动膜技术进入泰国等东南亚市场打下基础。

2003年，“黄瓜品种选育及推广合作研究”列入中泰政府间科技合作项目，中方承担单位是天津科润黄瓜研究所，泰方承担单位是Almatha种子公司。双方在考察黄瓜的种植与市场的基础上，在泰国进行中国黄瓜的试种，材料纯化、筛选、形状考察和分析，抗性鉴定及分析等，并对中国黄瓜栽培环境等进行研究，为享誉全国的天津黄瓜品种向泰国推广和输出奠定基础。

（二）与欧洲国家的科技合作

1、中英科技合作

1993年，为进一步提高天津市工业污水处理技术，天津市通过英国海外开发署开展天津市工业污水改进项目研究。项目实施机构为天津市环境保护科学研究所、天津市市政排水管理处、天津市世行办污染控制基金办公室和英国吉布公司。中英双方围绕化工、香料、染料、油墨、香皂、造纸、电镀等行业的污水治理方案，天津市污水处理厂布局，市政工程局排水管理处企业化改造以及污染控制基金合理使用等问题进行研究。2000年，天津市对原排水管理处实施企业化改造，筹建数个排水管理公司，其行使排水管理处的部分职能。按该项目研究报告所提建议，2001年天津市开始筹建咸阳路污水处理厂，并于2004年完成日处理污水45万吨的一期工程。中方技术人员利用该项目中试设计方案，在天津东洋油墨厂的污水处理工程中采用物化、生化联合处理技术，使工程在低投入、低运行的条件下，污水排放达到国家标准，成为国内外首例成功运转、达标的油墨废水处理工程。1998年，天津市东洋油墨厂污水处理工程设计技术获国家环保局科技进步三等奖。

2、中法科技合作

1994年，通过中法两国政府间科技合作渠道，中国医学科学院血液学研究所和试验血液学国家重点实验室与法国巴黎血液血管研究所共同在天津创办中法合作实验室。该实验室围绕趋化因子与造血，造血干细胞的扩增与移植，血管内皮细胞、血管新生和血管生长因子，巨核细胞和血小板生成及其功能调节等课题开展合作研究，双方各投入科研经费40万元人民币。2000年第一期协议到期后，又续签第二期合作协议。通过合作，双方共同在国际学术刊物发表研究论文20余篇，共同申请发明专利2项，其中合作研究课题——“趋化因子PF4调节造血和血管内皮细胞增殖以及放化疗反应的研究”于2000年获天津市自然科学一等奖。

3、中意科技合作

2004年，为更好地利用天津市丰富的地热资源，解决地热开采造成的地面下沉问题，中意两国开展“地热回灌”政府间科技合作项目。项目承担单位为天津奥德可再生能源研究所和意大利地球科学与地球资源研究所。中意双方围绕地热种植、地热养殖、地热采暖等问题，对异层回灌技术及浅层回灌技术进行示范，为天津市进一步开采地热资源打下基础。

4、中瑞科技合作

1993~1997年，天津市通过中瑞两国政府间科技合作渠道，实施“天津市经济发展的环境保护与污染控制技术”合作研究，实施机构为天津市环境保护科学研究所和瑞典环境科学研究院。瑞方赠予的设备可完成几乎所有的常规污水处理试验，在实际条件下模拟不同的工业污水处理工艺，从中获得大量可靠的试验与设计数据，可最大程度上提高工业污水处理工程设计的可靠性，加之它可以移动，具有较高的实用性。中瑞双方专家利用该设备对天津市工业水污染存在的主要问题进行大量实验，解决一批难题。通过开展科技合作，为天津市环境保护科学研究所培养一批具有较高研究水平的专业技术人员，承担并完成一批国家及天津市科技攻关项目。该所在与瑞典环境科学研究院开展科技合作中建立良好关系，1999年共同组建中瑞（天津）环境技术发展中心，在两国间搭建一座开展环境技术交流与合作的桥梁。

5、中荷科技合作

1994年，天津市通过中荷两国政府间科技合作渠道，开展“职业暴露二恶英引起的氯痤疮发病条件和机制”合作研究。项目实施单位为天津医学院和荷兰国立格罗宁根大学职业与环境皮肤病研究所。经过双方多年研究，至2000年，发现二恶英引起的职业性氯痤疮可能与皮肤维生素代谢障碍有关，并发现引起氯痤疮的血脂TEQs值为650~1200皮克/克，为攻克氯痤疮发病机制打下基础。

6、中芬科技合作

1994年，为提高天津市防汛抗洪和消灾抗灾能力以及水务行政主管部门现代化管理水平，特别是提高天津市防洪减灾的决策调度和管理水平，通过中芬两国政府科技合作渠道，进行“天津市防洪输水信息系统的技术分析与可行性研究”的科技合作。项目实施单位为天津市水利局和芬兰阿特利—雷彼特工程公司。在双方通力合作下，1995年完成防洪输水信息系统工程的技术分析和可行性研究，为天津市城市防洪信息系统工程建设奠定基础。

2003年，“食用真菌疏水蛋白的分离纯化性质与应用”项目列入中芬两国政府间科技合作计划。项目承担单位为南开大学生命科学学院和芬兰赫尔辛基大学。真菌疏水蛋白广泛存在于真菌菌丝表面可分泌的小分子蛋白，具有膜表面活性，在两相界面可自我装配，改变表面亲水性和疏水性，在食品、医药、化工等领域有较高的应用价值。中芬双方技术人员采取互访、信息互换、成果分享等方式进行合作研究，推动这一国际前沿研究领域的进展，带动食品、医药、日用化工等工业的科技创新。

7、中西科技合作

为使中国加碘盐生产技术接近或达到国际先进水平，中国和西班牙两国政府签约在天津进行食盐加工加碘技术及装备的研究并在中国建立加碘盐生产样板厂项目合作。经中西双方多次协商和谈判，1997年3月签署项目实施协议。该项目实施机构为中盐制盐工程技术研究院和西班牙食品包装机械集团。双方通力合作，精心设计，确立总体技术方案和工艺路线，对重点设备及供货商进行考察，制造和选购89台套设备，完成厂房建筑3200平方米。样板厂建成后，1998年10月进行试生产，1999年3月通过验收。项目实施期间，接待来自上海、北京和内蒙古、河北、山东、山西、安徽等省市碘盐生产企业技术人员的参观学习，了解和学习国际上粉洗精制盐的先进技术。中方实施单位在学习外国先进技术的同时，结合中国的技术和经验，总结出一套具有中国特色的先进的粉洗精制加碘盐技术，并利用该技术为埃及设计建造一条年产10万吨粉洗盐加工生产线，使中国制盐技术走向世界。

1999年，通过中国和西班牙两国政府间科技合作渠道，实施天津中西农业温室技术示范中心项目。项目实施机构为天津市蔬菜研究所和西班牙农业技术产业集团。双方通过利用农用塑料新技术、滴灌技术以及植物新品种，研究开发适合中国国情的温室，进而提高中国农业现代化生产技术。至2000年，农业温室技术示范中心相继建成总面积1.1万平方米的9座配有肥水滴灌系统的不同类型的西班牙温室，并进行试种和比较。项目实施期间，通过举办各种培训班、研讨会以及同行对该示范中心的参观访问，使先进的温室技术得到推广。

8、中比科技合作

1997年1月至1999年12月，针对渤海湾地区水产养殖所需的卤虫耐寒、耐盐性能差，卤虫的年产量相对较低的状况，为选择卤虫的优良品种，更好地用于水产养殖业，通过中比政府间科技合作渠道，进行中国特殊卤虫品系的研究及进一步开发利用项目。项目实施机构为中盐制盐工程技术研究院和比利时根特大学水产养殖与卤虫参考中心、比利时鲁文大学、比利时皇家自然科学研究所。该项目通过进行中国内陆盐湖和沿海盐场卤虫的鉴定、生态环境特征的研究，卤虫卵和无节幼体的休眠、孵化特性、营养组成及水产养殖业适用性的研究，发现一个卤虫新品种，丰富了中国卤虫基因库资源。同时，该项目还对9种内蒙古卤虫品系、2种西藏卤虫品系及1种美国旧金山卤虫品系进行品系特征、遗传特性等方面的深入研究，选择出一个优良卤虫品种，将其引种至盐池，其耐寒、耐盐性得到很大提高，同渤海湾地区原品种比较，卤虫卵产量提高50%，卤虫卵孵化率大于85%，杂质率小于1%，具有较高的商业价值，可广泛推广到整个渤海湾地区。同时，通过该项目的合作研究，扩大了中盐制盐工程技术研究院在国外的影响，该院先后又与比利时、希腊等国和欧盟组织进行相关项目的科技合作。

（三）与东欧国家的科技合作

1、中俄科技合作

1992年，天津碱厂在进行技术改造中，考虑到碱碴处理、综合利用技术和蒸吸氨技术的落后将严重制约生产发展，科技人员获悉俄罗斯斯捷尔利塔马制碱联合公司在碱碴处理及综合利用技术方面有独到之处。在中国驻俄大使馆科技处的帮助下，开通与俄方开展政府间科技合作的渠道。1994年4月，双方签署《科学技术产品交换合同》，并按合同条款交换技术资料。俄方的蒸氨塔技术耗能低，生产能力大，运转周期长，具有国际先进水平。天津碱厂采用俄方蒸氨塔技术，于1998年完成蒸吸氨工序的技术改造，每年可节约乏汽19万吨、石灰石5万吨、煤5700吨，加之其运行周期长等因素，直接经济效益850万元。

2、中捷科技合作

1998年1月，通过中捷两国政府间科技合作渠道，开始进行“X射线粉末衍射法物相定性分析项目”合作研究，以合成出新型铁基纳米合金材料。项目实施机构为南开大学化学学院中心实验室和捷克科学院材料物理研究所。中捷双方围绕铁基纳米材料的制备、纳米材料最佳合成条件、纳米材料有关性能特征精确测定、纳米合金材料的结构—性能关系以及纳米合金材料的结构精修等问题进行合作研究，合成出7种新型铁基纳米材料，并在有关国际会议及杂志发表相关论文，研究成果具有国际先进水平。

（四）与欧盟的科技合作

中国—欧盟天津电能及热能培训中心成立于1986年。至1995年，该中心以普及能源管理的基本原理、方法及实用节能技术为主。1995～1999年，该中心根据中国市场及中国工业企业的需求，进行天然气在工业领域中的应用等培训，并派学员赴欧洲进行实地考察，亲身感受欧盟能源管理的实际运作。至1999年，该中心先后举办13期不同类型的培训班，培训能源管理人员及厂长、经理470人。该项目的实施，使培训人员获得国际在能源领域的最新信息和发展动态，了解到欧盟国家在节能降耗、提高能源利用率等方面的成功经验及有关能源、节能方面的法规、政策、标准及其实施方案，并在学习国际先进节能技术的基础上，经过实践和努力，将欧盟国家在能源领域和节能方面的新技术、新材料、新设备、新工艺广泛应用于国内工业生产中。

2003年，在天津开展“中国—欧盟中国天津铸造行业清洁生产”合作项目。至2005年，共举办4期培训班，培训企业32家，培训人员160余人次。在项目实施过程中，除集中培训外，60余人还接受现场培训，并建立清洁生产网站，组织10余家铸造企业撰写清洁生产技术评估报告，实施清洁生产整改措施60余项。该项目的实施，使天津10余家铸造企业不但改善了工人的劳动环境和操作条件，而且每年可节约2000多万元。

（五）与澳大利亚的科技合作

2002年，中国与澳大利亚将“动态上地理信息系统（DGIS）”项目列入两国政府间科技合作项目。中方承担单位是美天网络（天津）公司，澳方承担单位是Clismap。通过开展合作研究，开发出新的地理信息系统（DGIS）软件，并出口到澳大利亚，受到当地用户的欢迎。

二、民间科技交流

（一）出国考察培训或参加学术会议

1991～2005年，天津市科委先后组织约6500人次分赴78个国家和地区，进行科技考察与培训、开展科技合作研究、参加国际科技学术会议等，其中约有3200人次分赴国外参加各种学术会议并发表论文。民间科技交流涉及汽车、机械、电子、信息、通讯、医药、农业、环保、能源、新材料、生物技术、城市建设等诸多领域。通过民间科技交流活动，科技人员广交朋友，并向世界宣传天津、介绍天津。

同时，市科协围绕天津经济建设的重点项目，每年派出科技团组出访。至2005年，市科协所属团体先后派出交流团组1300余人，并通过中国科协的国际交流渠道和自行开辟的渠道向日本、德国、英国派遣研修生70余次，500余人。市科协还通过科技团体渠道组织参加国际学术会议。1998年，市科协组团出访首届世界工程师大会主办单位之一的德国工程师学会。该学会主席兼首届世界工程师大会主席麦德母邀请市科协副主席张道成作为地方性科技组织代表，担任首届世界工程师大会顾问委员会委员。此后，张道成多次代表天津出席世界工程师大会筹备工作会议，并与很多世界级和国家级的科技组织建立联系。2000年6月19日，市科协组织工程界代表参加在德国汉诺威召开的首届世界工程师大会，并在会上交流11篇论文，受到与会人士的高度评价。2004年9月，市科协携带《2004年世界工程师大会天津地区论文专集》并派出代表出席在上海举行的世界工程师大会。

（二）在天津举办国际学术会议

1991～2005年，市科委在天津举办各种国际学术会议89个，约有60余万人次参加在天津举办的国际学术会议或与外国朋友进行技术交流和洽谈；约有2万人次外国友人到津进行科技交流、洽谈。市科协先后接待英国、美国、日本、德国、法国、荷兰、瑞典、新加坡、俄罗斯、印尼、越南、朝鲜等20多个国家访问团组的1800余人。

1992年，市科协与市中医学会等在天津举办第二届国际针灸临床学术会议，宣读论文90篇，作报告7场，120位外方代表出席会议。同年11月4～6日，市科协与加拿大国家水研究所在天津召开国际环境水化学会议，发表论文70篇，中外专家近100人参加会议，其中外籍专家约20人。1993年11月，市科协与电子学会在天津举办多国元器件会议及展示会。1995年10月24～26日，市科协、市国际科技会议中心、中国植物学会、市植物学会、国际木材解剖学家协会在天津共同举办国际树木解剖及木材形成学术会议。参加会议的中外代表近80人，其中美、德、日等十几个国家的外方代表约30人。这是首次在中国举行的国际性林业和木材专业科技会议，收到论文90篇，并出版论文集。1999年，市科协取得科技部颁发的举办国际会议资格认证。此后，承办第三届国际IIGSS会议、国际自控联“经济、金融及工程经济系统电算化”会议、中国沿海地区农业现代化国际研讨会、中日CAD技术研讨会等，推动天津乃至全国相关行业和领域与国际同行的交流与合作。

2000年，天津市知识产权局与日本国际贸易促进会中国专利协力会访华团在天津联合举办2000’天津中日专利实务研讨会，对中日两国专利申请、审查等业务进行工作研究和探讨，从而增强两国专利界的了解与沟通。

2002年10月25～26日，在天津举办2002’（天津）技术转移与知识产权战略国际研讨会，北京、上海、重庆、广东等20多个省市的代表参加会议。研讨会上，美国大学技术管理者协会会长泰瑞·扬、德国史太白基金会国际事务部部长乌韦豪、日本产业规划中心技术市场部部长村上武志和科技部、中国技术市场管理促进中心、清华大学及有关省市代表分别发表演讲。这次研讨会的举办，进一步促进天津科技服务业的发展，并宣传了天津经济与科技发展的新成就。

2004年2月，天津市知识产权局与欧盟组织在天津召开中国—欧盟知识产权国际研讨会，国家知识产权局和国内外知识产权界知名专家出席研讨会。该研讨会进一步加强中国与欧洲在知识产权领域的合作与交流，促进天津市自主创新水平和运用知识产权制度能力的提高。

2004年4月1～4日，在天津召开由国际机构学与机器科学联合会（IFToMM）主办、天津大学和IFToMM中国委员会承办的第11届机器与机构学世界大会，是中国第一次举办。来自美、英、德、法、俄罗斯、意大利、加拿大等44个国家和地区的400余名专家学者，就计算运动学、齿轮与传动、人机系统、连杆与凸轮、机电一体化、微型机构、非线性振动、机器人学、生物力学、机器与机构的可靠性等17个领域的学术前沿问题进行广泛深入的交流和研讨。美国斯坦福大学Kenneth J Waldron教授、加拿大麦吉尔大学Jorge Angeles教授、法国巴黎机器人实验主任Philippe Bidaud教授等参加会议。大会收集论文491篇，覆盖机构学与机器科学研究与工程实践的诸多领域。此次大会的成功召开，对提升天津机械工程领域的国际学术地位，宣传和扩大天津的对外影响起到积极作用。

2004年10月25日，市知识产权局在华苑产业区海泰大厦召开美国知识产权保护和中国企业如何应对美国关税法337条款调查和反倾销调查报告会，邀请美国博达律师事务所霍瓦纳博士和斯鲁特博士做专题报告，受到与会者的欢迎。

（三）在天津举办国际科技展览

1996年9月18～21日，在天津举办中国国际计算机与网络产品展览交易会。展览共设108个标准摊位，面积3500平方米，国内外知名计算机和网络工程厂商共60余家参加展览。交易会汇集各类计算机网络工程、软件开发、应用系统及外部设备等400多个展品，参观人数达4万余人次，成交额400余万元。由于此次展览效果显著，1997～2000年天津市又先后4次举办此类展览。其中，1997年举办的展览，标准展台增至144个，比1996年增加33%，国际知名厂商微软公司、IBM公司、西门子等参加展览。在为期4天的展览中，有6万人次到场参观。1999年，市科协取得科技部颁发的举办科技展览的资格认证。之后，先后主办或协办国际科技展览20个。1999年，印度软件代表团参观中国国际计算机和网络产品展览交易会，并在天津举办中国（天津）—印度软件项目合作与出口研讨会，为中印两国在软件领域的交流与合作奠定基础。2000年，为配合信息港工程的实施，展览将主题定为电子商务，展出产品的技术水平均超过以往各届，各省市赴津参观展览者约千余人。连续5年在天津举办的计算机网络及产品展览交易会，为天津学习、吸收国内外信息领域的先进技术提供一个有效平台，也为天津展示自身技术提供了机会。

（四）在境外举办或参加国际展览

1991年，天津市组织有关企业参加由中国科技交流中心赴加拿大举办的中国新技术产品展览会。天津展团接待参观人员2万余人次，成交额140万美元（占展览会成交总额的82%），意向成交额200多万美元。此次展览，促进了天津科技产品的出口，也增进了加拿大有关企业和商家对天津及天津科技产品的进一步了解。

1992年，为促进大中型企业和科研机构的对外合作和贸易，天津市组织55个单位赴印度尼西亚首都雅加达参加中国科技成果及实用技术展览会。天津展团展出的项目涉及机械、电子、轻工、化工、医药、卫生、冶金、汽车、环卫等领域。展览期间，签署销售合同金额70万美元，签署合作协议40份，协议金额500余万元。此次展览会，开辟了印度尼西亚的技术、贸易市场，推动了天津市的技术出口。

1994年7月，天津市专利局组织110项专利项目和120多种专利产品参加在新加坡举办的世界贸易和科技博览会。天津展团与20多个国家、100多家客商进行商贸洽谈，签订合同4项，合同金额2300万元；达成意向协议30多项，协议金额1.225亿元。

1995年，天津市专利局组织优秀专利项目和产品参加在吉隆坡举办的国际新科技与新产品贸工展览会。天津展团参展的10项专利技术和25种专利产品受到评委会及参观者的好评,其中螺旋关节锁等4个项目获金奖。通过洽谈,与外商达成意向协议18项。1996年,天津市专利局组织参加在新加坡举办的第一届国际企业及创新科技专利产品展览会,取得良好效果。

1997年,为进一步开拓国际科技交流与合作渠道,促进天津技术与产品的出口,天津市组织参加由联合国工业发展组织、印度政府工业部、印度南方各邦政府共同主办的国际技术市场展览会。针对印度及其周边国家与地区的技术市场特点和需求,天津市组织医药、轻工、纺织、化工、冶金、环保、农业等领域近百项技术和产品赴会展出。天津展团的展位规模在外国展团中名列第一,吸引大批客商前来洽谈,其中列入天津市重大科技产业化工程的复方丹参滴丸、皮质激素、镍氢电池、电脑电话等产品技术受到外方各界的欢迎。展览期间,天津科技交易团与印度及其他国家和地区签订合资、合作、技术转让等方面的意向书、备忘录、协议书共27份,总成交额400多万美元。

(五)开展合作研究

随着与国外科技交流的逐步增多,开展民间国际科技合作研究的项目逐年增加。特别是进入21世纪初,天津市将开展民间国际科技合作研究的重点逐渐转移到围绕重点科技攻关、应用基础研究等项目中,其中仅2003年分别与美、英、法、德等14个国家和地区开展民间国际科技合作研究项目有68项。

2002~2004年,南开大学与美国MVSystems公司进行"新型硅基薄膜太阳能电池大面积低成本技术研究"合作项目。双方本着共同设计、共同研究、共享成果的原则,建成具有国际先进水平、能制备大面积、均匀硅基薄膜材料与太阳能电池的薄膜沉积技术研究平台,属国内首创。利用该平台研制的非晶硅薄膜成膜率达53.6埃/秒,比原1.8埃/秒的成膜率提高近30倍,为大幅度缩短电池制造周期奠定技术基础。由于该系统衬底温度低于200℃,能获得优质的非晶硅薄膜,使太阳光谱能的利用从46.5%提高到79.7%,提高了太阳能电池的性能。

2003年,天津科技大学与日本北海道大学进行"活性速溶骨复合物制备技术的开发"合作项目,成功地将坚硬的骨材料制成可溶性的全骨复合物。该活性速溶骨既保持骨中所有有机、无机成分均处于游离、可溶解和可吸收状态,又保持全部生理活性物质的生理活性,其所含的骨胶原蛋白及蛋白多糖能起到降低胆固醇、延缓衰老作用,其生理活性物质和离子化矿物质能对骨代谢起到调节作用,提高了骨材料的附加值。

第二节 国内科技合作与交流

天津市组织科技交易团先后出访新疆、甘肃、云南、贵州、广西、重庆、北京、西安、深圳等省市,并通过举办或参加各种类型的高新技术成果展示会、交易会、洽谈会等大型科技交流活动,展示天津市的科技成果,加强地域间的科技合作与交流,带动技术交易活动的发展。特别是北方技术交易市场通过技术供需网络,为供需双方牵线搭桥,并与国内近20个省市建立联络站或技术转移分公司,在汇集科技资源与市场资源上形成长期、稳定的渠道和合作伙伴,在运作水平、发展规模和速度上成为重要的区域技术转移中心。2000年起,天津市贯彻落实中共中央、国务院提出的西部大开发战略,市科委主要负责人多次随市政府代表团或组织科技代表团出访甘肃、内蒙古、青海、四川、重庆、新疆等省市,与上述地区科技部门签订科技合作协议,并组织实施。特别是2005年7月与中科院签订科技合作协议,通过院市合作,促进中科院一批优秀科技成果在天津的转化和产业化,从而大大提升了天津市的自主创新能力和水平。

市科协及其所属学会、协会、研究会采取多种方式,通过各种渠道,举办不同类型的学术研讨会或学术年会,开展学术交流与研讨,为经济、科技、社会发展提出意见和建议,其中有些意见被市委、市政府采纳。同时,市科协紧密围绕市委、市政府确定的中心工作,针对天津科技、经济、社会发展亟待解决的重大课题,组织科技团体和广大科技工作者开展调研论证、决策咨询,并围绕工农业生产和城市建设中的问题,大力推广新技术、新成果,开展技术协作和讲比竞赛活动,为科技进步与经济发展服务,较好地发挥"科技智囊团"的作用。天津市科技进修学院和各区县科技进修学院分院通过举办各种类型、各种专业的培训班,积极开展包括成人学历教育、职称培训、单科培训、星火培训等在内的科技培训,为提高科技队伍素质做出积极贡献。天津市职工技术协会通过举办技术培训班、技术讲座和开展岗位练兵、技术比武、提合理化建议等活动,不断提高职工的文化和科技素质,并组织广大职工开展技术攻关和发明创造活动,开发和推广具有市场前景的新技术、新产品,在推动企业技术进步和提高经济效益上发挥重要作用。

一、国内科技合作

(一)与中西部地区的科技合作

1995年起,北方技术交易市场积极开展与中西部地区的科技合作,先后出访河北、内蒙、甘肃、新疆等省市,与当地签订各类科技合作协议,同国内240多家科研机构建立合作科技关系。1997年起,天津市加快实施内联战略,增强区域间的技术合作与交流,组织科技代表团先后赴宁夏、河北、北京、陕西、青海、甘肃、新疆等省市,进行技术需求和科技合作项目洽谈,与其科技部门签订长期科技合作协议,并组织科研单位参加中国东西部合作与投资贸易洽谈会、乌鲁木齐经贸洽谈会等,参加项目展示、发布和洽谈,签订各种技术合同和合作协议等,促进科技成果转化。

2000年6月,中共中央、国务院提出西部大开发战略。同年,天津市政府出台《关于天津市服务参与西部大开发的实施意见》。为贯彻落实市政府服务参与西部大开发的战略部署,市科委确定了参与西部大开发的工作重点。市科委主要负责人多次随市政府代表团或组织科技代表团出访甘肃、内蒙古、青海、四川、重庆、新疆等地区,并与上述地区的科技部门签订科技合作协议,为双边进行科技合作制定总体框架。同时,积极组织参加在西部地区举办的东西部经济贸易洽谈会、重庆高新技术成果交易会、兰州高新技术成果交易交会、乌鲁木齐高新技术洽谈会等大型科技交流活动,取得很好效果。

(二)对口支援

1999年,市政府确定市科委对口支援重庆市龙宝区科委。2000年,天津市科委向龙宝区科委捐赠价值5万元8台(套)计算机及设备,帮助龙宝区科委建立信息网站,改善办公条件,并与北方技术交易市场建立网员关系。2000年,市科委向西藏自治区昌都地区捐赠10万元,用于信息中心网络建设。2003年11月,市科委再次支援龙宝区科委价值5万元10台(套)计算机及设备。

(三)院市合作

2005年7月21日,科技部部长徐冠华和天津市市长戴相龙分别代表双方签署《天津市人民政府和中国科学院院市科技合作协议》和工作会商制度议定书,同时举行第一次部市工作会商会。按照该议定书的规定,科技部和天津市政府要围绕国家科技创新体系建设目标,共同就推进科技体制改革、提高科技自主创新能力、建设区域创新体系、促进滨海新区的建设和发展进行协商。科技部按照该议定书的规定,对做好滨海新区中长期科技发展规划进行帮助指导,推进天津高新技术产业开发区的发展,共同推进重大科技项目的实施,加速科技成果转化。

同月,天津市分别与中国科学院、中国人民解放军军事医学科学院签署科技合作协议。天津市与军事医学科学院签署合作协议的主要内容有:天津市政府支持军事医学科学院在天津滨海新区建立军事医学科学院天津新药研究中心,并在资源配置及政策上给予一定优惠;军事医学科学院天津新药研究中心作为创新药物的研发及产业化基地,积极配合天津市政府在该中心实现成果的产业化。

同年10月16日,天津市与中国民航总局签署共建国家民航科技产业化基地协议。签字仪式前,双方举行中国民航产业化基地领导小组第一次会议,就进一步加强天津市与国家民航总局的科技合作,共同建设国际遗留的航空产业化基地,服务和带动区域经济发展达成一致。

2005年12月5日,举行中国工程院与天津市人民政府人才与项目合作协议签约仪式暨科技发展规划咨询座谈会。全国政协副主席、中国工程院院士徐匡迪和天津市委副书记、市长戴相龙分别代表双方在协议上签字。

二、科技交流

(一)科学技术协会交流活动

1、学术研讨

(1)两科联盟活动 1987年,市科协与市社联、市社科院签署两科联盟协议书。此后,两科联盟活动由三方轮流承办,持续不断,每年确定一个主题,组织全市自然科学工作者和社会科学工作者开展多种形式的学术研讨和专题论证活动,为促进天津经济、科技发展做出贡献。1991年1月30日,市科协承办两科联盟年会,主题是“两科联盟为科学决策、振兴经济服务”,展出照片106张、专著131本、论文集10册、优秀论文45篇、刊物12本、录像带2盘、心理测试仪器13台。8月,两科联盟从科学技术、人口等5个方面开展与经济社会发展关系的系列研讨。1993年12月18~20日,由市科协、市社联、市社科院共同发起,联合4省4市(北京市、辽宁省、河北省、山东省、山西省、沈阳市、大连市、青岛市)科协、社联、社科院共同组织召开环渤海地区科技与经济发展研讨会。国家有关部门领导和专家于光远、马洪、高潮,市领导李建国、李盛霖、杨竞衡等出席,环渤海地区和吉林、黑龙江等省市科技与经济工作者等近400人参加会议。会议围绕战略与规划、地区发展与国际合作、城市服务体系、产业结构与发展布局、科技与人才、资源与开发、环境保护与灾害防治等问题进行研讨,收到论文115篇,93篇入选论文集。1994年12月6~9日,市科协配合市社联召开京津冀联合与发展研讨会,出席代表约200人,收到论文48篇,巩固和扩大1993年度研讨会的成果。

1996年11月,市科协承办两科联盟活动,主题是“贯彻科教兴市方针,转变经济增长方式,促进天津经济可持续发展”。大会交流94篇论文,其中59篇选入《经济增长方式转变与可持续发展论文集》。1998年9月16日,市科协、市社联、市社科院联合举办知识经济与天津跨世纪发展研讨会,市领导黄其兴、朱连康等出席。会议收到论文24篇。

2001年,市科协、市社联、市社科院以“城市信息化”为主题,开展系列学术研讨活动,重点活动之一是“数字天津与国内数字化城市的比较研究”。2002年,市科协、市社联、市社科院联合举办天津市应对入世学术研讨会和天津市企业创新论坛,针对入世后天津传统工业改造、政府职能调整、城市功能提升、企业制度与技术创新等进行探讨,并提出建议。工程院院士王静康就发展天津化学工业提出建议,著名经济学家陈清泰作《中国加入WTO—战略与改革》专题报告。2005年,两科联盟开展“服务业扩大总量、优化结构、拓展领域、提高水平的研究”课题,50名专家通过对国际贸易、区域金融、现代物流、旅游休闲、科技中介、电子商务等6个方面的调研,提出加快天津现代服务业发展、缓解就业压力、增强城市竞争力的对策建议。

(2)青年科技论坛 1995年11月,举办天津市首届青年学术年会(后改称青年学术论坛),主题是“科技振兴天津,青年开创未来”。这是全国第二届青年学术年会的卫星会议。论坛由市科协主办,共收到论文300多篇,有280篇编入《天津青年学术研讨会精粹》。朱光亚、高德占、张立昌等为论文集题词。中国科协党组书记张玉台、市委副书记李建国出席会议并讲话。参加会议的400多名青年科技工作者围绕8大学科领域,对天津科技发展中的重要问题提出对策建议,并向全市青年科技工作者发出倡议书。

1998年5月18日,举办第二届天津青年科技论坛,主题为“科技振兴天津,青年开创未来—高新技术与经济发展”。此次论坛是中国科协第三届青年学学术年会卫星会议,围绕生物工程、化学化工及制药、材料科学与工程、电子信息、农业与环境等五大学科领域开展研讨。其论文集《跨世纪的科学与技术》收录176篇论文,两院院士母国光、余国琮、吴咸中等为论文集题词。中国科协书记处书记宋南平及市领导王成怀、黄其兴等出席会议并讲话,全市300余位青年科技工作者参加会议。

2001年,举办以“21世纪天津信息—环境”为主题的第三届天津青年科技论坛,也是中国科协第四届青年学术年会的卫星会议。论坛设一个主会场,即“第六届天津青年科技奖表彰大会暨2001年天津青年科技论坛开幕式”,设“信息技术研讨会”“环境与生态研讨会”“材料科学研讨会”“工厂化农业研讨会”4个专题研讨会和21个分会场。在天津两院院士吴咸中、刘广均、李正名等出席开幕式。论坛编辑出版《2001年天津青年科技论坛集萃》,收录论文240篇。全国人大常委会副委员长、中国科协主席周光召,全国政协副主席、中国科协名誉主席朱光亚,市委书记张立昌,在天津两院院士母国光、吴咸中、刘广均等为论坛集题词,市委副书记刘胜玉作序。

2004年5月23日,第七届天津青年科技奖表彰大会暨第四届天津青年科技论坛举行开幕式,市委常委、市委组织部部长史莲喜,市人大常委会副主任梁肃等出席。论坛编辑出版《第四届天津青年科技论坛集萃》,收录论文206篇。中共中央政治局委员、市委书记张立昌,中国科协主席周光召,市科协主席母国光及在天津两院院士石学敏、葛墨林、郝希山等为论坛集题词,市委副书记邢元敏作序。

(3)科技论坛 1999年9月,市科协举办天津首届科技论坛,主题是“21世纪的天津科技与经济”。论坛设主会场和47个分会场,市科协所属100多个学会、协会、研究会近2万名科技人员参加活动。《天津首届科技论坛集萃》收录论文333篇,全国人大常委会副委员长、中国科协主席周光召,全国政协副主席、中国工程院院长朱光亚,天津市委书记张立昌等为论文集题词。

2000年9～11月,举办第二届天津科技论坛,主题是“天津技术创新与经济增长”。论坛设8个专场和63场相关专业科技研讨会,共收到千余篇论文,选编的《专家建言集》供市领导和有关部门参考。

2002年9月,市科协与市社联等联合举办第三届天津科技论坛,即天津市企业创新论坛,著名经济学家陈清泰教授作《中国加入WTO—战略与改革》报告。

2003年9月,市科协举办第四届天津科技论坛,即海河经济论坛。中国工程院院士王静康等专家就海河综合开发中的生态、建筑、环境、经济规划、水资源开发利用、地质构造等问题做专题发言,对海河的规划、开发和建设提出建议。

2005年9月,市科协与滨海新区管委会联合举办第五届天津科技论坛,即滨海新区建设与发展专家论坛。天津大学化工学院国家工业结晶技术研究推广中心主任、中科院院士王静康,天津师范大学党委书记、博士生导师李家祥等分别就滨海新区开发建设、国际航运、现代物流、国内发展与对外开放、海水淡化、滨海新区石油化工产业发展等提出建议。

2001年9月,市科委联合市卫生局和天津医科大学等共同创办并连续3年举办北方医学科技论坛。2001年,成功举办“干细胞——生命科学”“健康与安全”等专题研讨,在医学界产生强烈反响。2002年,“21世纪公共卫生面临的挑战与对策”和“干细胞与血管新生”等专题论坛,吸引大批专家和专业技术人员的积极参与。2003年,在抗击“非典”疫情中,“天津市SARS患者流行病学回顾性调查和健康随访与干预试验研究”取得成功,其研究成果得到进一步应用,获得2005年度天津市科技进步一等奖。武警医学院附属医院应用该项研究成果,承担“综合医院SARS爆发流行临床救治与流行病学研究”,并获2005年度武警部队科技进步一等奖。2003年,中国工程院院士、天津市急腹症研究所所长吴咸中主持北方医学论坛2003年天津防治传染性非典型肺炎学术研讨会,总结防控“非典”的经验,并加强协作,推动防控“非典”的科学研究取得新突破。

(4)科技交流学术月 2003年起,市科协每年9月联合全市自然科学学术团体举办天津科技交流学术月,每届开展活动近百项,近万名科技工作者参与,形成年度学术交流的高潮。2003年9月,举办首届天津科技交流学术月,主题是“科技进步与三步走战略”。同时,市图像图形学会等承办第四届虚拟现实及其在工业中的应用国际会议,中国科协副主席赵忠贤院士作《21世纪科技发展趋势》报告等。首届学术月印发《科技进步与“三步走”战略论文集》,收录论文75篇,在天津两院院士母国光、刘广均、吴咸中等为论文集题词。

2004年9月,举办第二届天津科技交流学术月,主题是“落实科学发展观,促进天津新跨越”,集中开展各种学术活动113项,重点活动有市医学会举办的第二届内镜腹腔镜国际学术研讨会、市电子仪表学会承办的中国信息技术电子仪表创新学术会议等。国际数学大师陈省身和在天津两院院士吴咸中、姚建铨、葛墨林等众多海内外专家、学者参加相关活动。

2005年9月,举办第三届天津科技交流学术月,主题是“以人为本,协调发展”,举办中国·天津风力发电产业论坛、现代化造船发展论坛等学术会议5场，学术年会6场，科技报告会、专题研讨会40余场，科技培训等20余场。其中，9月8～12日在天津宾馆召开第十届全国眼科大会，组织120场专题报告会，并直播眼科手术实况，举办大型眼科医疗器械展览，60多位国际眼科著名专家和3000余名全国各地眼科界代表参加会议。

2、科技咨询

1991年，市科协组织电子、机械等16个学科的专家对《天津市科学技术发展十年规划和"八五"计划纲要》及《天津市"八五"科技发展计划》两个文件进行审议，提出修改意见89条，其中67条被采纳。同时，组织塑料、电镀、家电等15个学会参与行业评估，并纳入市科委"天津市工业技术发展分析与对策"主课题。1992年，市科协完成"关于新材料技术政策调研"课题，提出天津市电子信息材料、功能材料和结构材料3种材料的发展战略。1993年，组织汽车、机械、金属等十几个学会开展"机械、电子、化工、冶金4个支柱产业以及城市基础设施调研"，提出"依靠科技进步，加大投资力度，调动各方面积极因素加快汽车工业发展""对天津市汽车工业经济规模、产品更新换代、零部件工业与国产化、技术开发能力的建设""发挥整体优势，加速发展石油化工、海洋化工和精细化工"等建议，市领导听取专家的意见和建议。1994年，市科协组织开展天津30万辆轿车发展论证，经过半年调研，向市委、市政府提交"天津30万辆轿车市场预测""天津市30万辆轿车发展车型分析""天津市30万辆轿车发动机选型及分析""天津市15万辆新经济型轿车发展规划""天津市30万辆轿车零部件规划"和"天津市30万辆轿车发展战略总论"等6份11万字的专题报告，主要建议被主管部门及汽车公司采纳，其中"天津市30万辆轿车发展研究论证"获天津市优秀调研成果一等奖。1995年7月11～13日，市科协召开"天津市'九五'及2010年工业规划"专题论证会，组织60余名专家分别就汽车、机械、电子、冶金、化工、轻纺等行业发展规划的思路、目标、重点及政策措施进行论证，市有关部门负责人听取专家们的建议。

1996年10月7日和11月23日，市科协分别组织召开"九五"科技产业化和重大科技攻关项目论证会，30多名专家从项目的技术、效益、市场及实施基础等方面进行评估，提出重点支持有机光导(OPC)产业化研究、微生物强化采油技术等22个项目。1997年10月，完成"天津市通信与电子信息产业发展战略研究"报告，撰写出"天津发展光纤通信产业战略研究""天津发展程控交换机产业战略研究""天津发展信息产业总论"等5个报告、10万余字。该课题获天津市科技进步二等奖和优秀调研成果一等奖，2001年获中国科协第四届优秀建议二等奖。1998年，市科协开展软件产业和系统集成产业发展战略论证，并提交"天津发展软件与系统集成产业战略研究"报告，其主要建议纳入天津市高新技术产业发展规划。1999年，市科协组织专家分别就机电行业抓住电网改造契机、促进产品的升级换代，推广应用化学建筑材料、形成新的经济增长点，重点发展的产品种类及具体操作方法等提出建议，并通过集萃形式上报市政府。2000年，市科协开展天津市生物医学工程(BME)论证和天津市精细化工产业论证，提交"生物医学工程产业能成为天津21世纪经济支柱产业"报告。市委书记张立昌高度重视并先后3次做出批示，要求有关部门加强调研，制定方案，大力发展生物医学材料产业，并据此成立天津市催化净化技术工程中心。

2001年，市科协开展天津新能源产业规划课题研究，完成"天津市新能源产业发展研究"报告。2002年，市科协邀请化工行业的专家学者，对市计委起草的"天津石化与化学工业发展规划"进行论证，并提出修改建议。2003年11月28日，市科协、市政府研究室联合举办天津石化产业发展论坛，对启动天津石化公司百万吨乙烯和千万吨炼油工程进行论证，促使投资数百亿元的两个项目的正式立项。同年，市城市科学研究会牵头承担"海河两岸综合开发改造若干问题的研究"课题，对海河两岸开发改造中的功能定位、经济发展、环境保护、建筑风貌与景观效果等问题提出对策建议，被市建委采纳。此课题于2005年获中国科协第五届优秀建议二等奖。2004年，市科协组织19个主要产业的180名专家开展"天津市产业技术进步政策研究"，历时一年半，提交7万字的课题总报告和47万字的包括农业、冶金、石化、电子信息、海洋等19个产业的子课题报告，形成《天津市产业技术进步指导目录(2005~2010年)》。该目录于2005年经市政府第55次常务会讨论通过并批转实施，并获天津市第九届优秀调研成果一等奖。同年，市科协承担"解决天津市经济社会发展制约因素问题的研究"课题，围绕水资源、电力资源、土地资源、市内交通和地下管网设施等5个主要制约因素，提交1个总报告和5个子报告。此课题获天津市第九届优秀调研成果三等奖。2005年初，市科协与市发改委、大港区政府联合举办建设大港国家级生态石化基地论坛，就滨海新区建设国家级生态石化基地展开研讨，形成一套系统的决策咨询意见。下半年又在市科委立项，组织专家开展“天津滨海新区石油化工产业布局及生态保障措施研究”，为将滨海新区建成集约型、节约型、生态型的国家级石化产业基地献计献策。

3、技术服务

(1)技术推广活动　1991年起，市科协及其所属学会、协会、研究会围绕天津工业、农业和城市建设中的重大问题，大力推广新技术、新成果，为企业和农村提供技术服务，帮助他们解决技术难题，为促进经济、社会发展起到纽带和桥梁作用。

(2)厂会协作行动　1998年起，市科协组织开展“千厂千会”行动，即组织1000个学会、协会、研究会与其对口的1000个工厂结成对子，开展厂会技术协作，组织科技攻关和技术开发，取得成效。

(3)讲比竞赛活动　1991年起，在全市工厂企业中开展“万、千、百、十讲比竞赛活动”，即提万条科技建议，搞千项技术攻关，区、局科协抓百项重点项目，市科协抓十项重点项目，并号召每个科协会员全年贡献3千元，全市工厂企业年创经济效益两亿元。此后，每年都要开展“讲比竞赛活动”。至2005年，市科协设立市级讲比竞赛项目3000余项，其中2000余项被市科协评为优秀项目，创造经济效益近10亿元。

4、科技培训

1991～1993年，天津市科技进修学院作为在职科技人员继续教育培训阵地，开展成人学历教育、职称培训、单科培训、星火培训等继续教育培训，培训人员17523人。1993年4月5日，天津市科技进修学院获得社会力量办学许可证。1994年8月，市科技进修学院恢复对各区科技进修学院分院的业务指导。至2002年，全市除东丽区以外的17个区、县都成立科技进修分院，开展继续教育培训。2004年，市科技进修学院投资1700万元，购置天津工业学校河东校区，占地35亩，包括综合楼、教学楼等建筑12800余平方米，为开展继续教育培训提供场所。1994～2001年，市科技进修学院开展包括成人学历教育、职称改革培训、单科培训、高等自学考试助学培养、中央党校研究生班等各类科技培训，共培训30911人。2002～2005年，市科技进修学院共培训23811人，包括成人学历教育、职称培训、单科培训、中央党校研究生班、“351”工程培训等。

(二)职工技术协会交流活动

自1989年11月天津市职工技术协作委员会更名为天津市职工技术协会(以下简称“市职工技协”)起，各级职工技术协会积极开展包括成人学历教育、职称培训、单科培训、星火培训等在内的各种培训班，并为企业开发出一大批具有市场前景的新技术、新产品。至1991年，共研发出创新科技成果1150项，其中10项受到全国总工会的嘉奖，2项在新加坡举办的国际发明展上获金狮奖，1项获银奖。1991年10月24日，在北京举行的庆祝职工技协活动兴起30周年暨表彰大会上，天津市职工技协焊接应用技术协会等6个单位获得全国职工技协先进集体称号，王恩文等13人获得全国职工技协先进个人称号，天津冶金局职工技协的“电炉炼钢降低用电和电极消耗技术攻关”等6项成果被评为全国职工技协优秀技术成果，单书、赵德俊等参加技协活动近30年的积极分子受到中华全国总工会的表彰。

至1994年，天津市各级职工技术协会共攻克技术关键27486项，推广新技术5358项，创经济效益5.8亿元；建立1800多个基层组织，发展会员近20万人；涌现出全国职工技协先进集体11个、全国职工技协先进个人28名；78名会员获得“七五”“八五”立功奖章。市职工技协组建技术革新、技术推广服务部802个，兴办科技实体136家，签订技术合同29861项，合同金额4.18亿元，为国家上缴利润6689万元。市职工技协连续两届被评为全国技术市场金桥奖先进集体，并被市民政局授予先进社团称号。

1994年12月16日，市职工技协第四届委员会召开第一次全体会议。市职工技协按照全国总工会和市总工会的工作部署，抓住为企业“解难增效，帮扶扭亏”这条主线，动员和组织以职工技协为骨干的广大职工，开展技术攻关和发明创造活动，开发新产品，推广新工艺，采用新材料，应用新技术，形成“管理干部擎大旗，技术人员拿主意，能工巧匠唱大戏”的为企业办实事的群众性科技团体。至1996年，为企业实施合理化建议41.3万项，为企业解决技术难题、搞技术攻关近4万项，创经济效益12亿多元，并涌现近百名劳动模范、技术明星，近千名技术能手，上万名先进个人，成为天津市“科技兴市”“科技兴厂”的一支重要力量。1997

年，全市职工技协共实施合理化建议15万件，开展技术攻关3500多项，其中10万元以上重大项目130多项，创经济效益5.2亿元；举办技术讲座1130次，传授技术经验和技术诀窍2000多条，培训下岗职工近万人；技术合同成交额达1亿元；科技实体营业额1.3亿元，安置下岗职工1300余人。同年，市职工技协和天津市邮电管理局、市规划局、市电力局等单位的职工技术协会获得天津市第四届技术市场金桥奖先进集体奖，孙复凯、张晓峰、王春发、周锦永、董建国、郭宜荣获得天津市第四届技术市场金桥奖先进个人奖。

1998年5月13日，市总工会召开职工技协第三届为企业"解难增效"成果发布会，从7000多个较大技术攻关项目中，经过各系统、各单位层层推荐和专家评审小组认真审定，筛选出191个项目进行表彰，天津减速机总厂五车间技协分会和第二轻工业总公司技协等5个单位介绍经验。1998年，全市各级职工技协组织共实施合理化建议11.6万件；完成技术攻关3230项，其中创造经济效益10万元以上的212项；创自救群体100多个；安置下岗职工3000多人。1998年12月，在全国职工技协优秀技术成果评选活动中，天津市职工技协选送的天津市减速机总厂五车间技协分会研制的数控针齿孔钻铰机床等7项优秀成果获奖。

1999年11月2日，天津市总工会在天津钢管公司召开职工技协为企业"解难增效"现场会，各工业总公司和部分区、县、局工会主席百余人出席会议。钢管公司、第一轻工业总公司印刷制版厂工会等介绍为企业"解难增效"的经验。在1999年11月11日召开的中国职工技术协会四届一次会议上，市职工技协等8个先进集体、13名先进个人、5项优秀科技成果受到表彰。

2000年开始，市总工会和市职工技协组织开展百万职工技术创新活动。全市170多万名职工广泛参与，提出并实施合理化建议120多万件，完成技术攻关9600多项，开展多层次、多形式、多门类的岗位练兵、技术比武活动1.1万场次，"精一门、会两门、学三门"的复合型人才比例不断上升，形成"党委统一领导，行政全力支持，工会组织实施，职工踊跃投入"的创新热潮，涌现出一大批先进操作法和技术明星，促进职工整体素质的提升和企业竞争力的提高。

2001年，在全市百万职工技术创新活动中，市职工技协先后召开两次成果发布会，完成技术攻关144项，其中13个重大项目全部完成，创经济效益1.08亿元；开办职工专业技术技能讲座29期，培训职工2000人。经全国总工会推荐，市总工会技协办公室副主任、市职工技协常务秘书长董建国获国家经贸委"九五国家技术创新先进管理者"称号。

2003年10月20～24日，天津代表团8名选手参加全国职工职业技能大赛，其中天津职业技术师范学院王启祥、张国刚分别获得全国劳动和社会保障部授予的全国技术能手称号，天津钳工代表队获团体总分第5名，其他选手均获优秀选手奖，天津代表团的总成绩在全国4个直辖市中名列第一。

2000～2005年，全市各级职工技协通过开展技术攻关取得技术创新成果1423项，为企业创造经济效益30.69亿元，其中509项被评为市级优秀成果，近百项科技成果获得天津市科技成果证书或科技进步奖，在推动企业技术进步和提高经济效益上发挥重要作用。在此期间，全市职工技协系统共认定技术合同5777份，实现技术合同成交额4.45亿元，上缴国家税金2670万元，建立科技型企业和经济实体160多家，实现营业收入20亿元，上缴利税2.5亿元。市职工技协先后三次获得全国和天津市技术市场金桥奖，被国家科技部评为全国技术市场工作先进集体。

市职工技协所属的锅炉、制冷、焊接、金切等16个专业技术协会，汇集一大批能工巧匠和专业技术人员，在所属行业中具有很大的影响力。这些专业技术协会经常应基层单位的邀请，组织专家深入企业，协助企业技术攻关，解决大量的技术难题，多次受到市领导的表扬。2005年，市技协发动各专业协会积极投身全市节能减排工作，全年召开节能减排新技术推广会21次，推广新技术新产品44项。制冷协会深入企业，为空调制冷设备诊病断脉，提出有效的改进方案。焊接协会通过组织技术培训、技术推广活动，推广焊接节能设备和节能技术。锅炉应用技术协会开发"中拱强化燃烧技术"，在天津乃至全国锅炉节能改造中产生积极推动作用，受到市政府多次表彰，并获得科技进步一等奖。该协会先后推出"高温水采暖技术""蒸汽锅炉改造为热水锅炉或水、汽两用锅炉技术""板式换热器在水采暖上的应用"等多项技术成果，为落实"蓝天工程"、集中供热等重点工程做出贡献。

2005年12月8～13日，市总工会举办天津市职工建设节约型社会技术创新成果展示会，对最能反映广大职工创新水平的100项科技成果进行展示。全国总工会、中国职工技术协会和天津市领导及市科委、市科协等部门负责人200余人出席开幕式并参观展览。同年12月9～10日，全国总工会经济技术部和中国职工技术协会在天津举办环渤海地区工会经济技术工作研讨会。中国职工技术协会副会长李永安出席会议并讲话，北京、天津、河北、辽宁、山东等省市及环渤海地区7个城市的总工会和职工技协负责人30余人出席会议，并参观、考察天津市职工建设节约型社会技术创新成果展和天津经济技术开发区。会议紧紧围绕国家区域经济协调发展战略，就如何加强环渤海地区工会技术项目、技术人才和信息的交流及开展跨地区经济技术协作等问题进行研讨。与会代表亲眼目睹天津滨海新区的迅速发展态势，感受到中央关于加快环渤海区域建设的战略意义，并就一些协作事宜达成共识。

2006年2月28日，天津市职工技术协会召开第五次代表大会，总结市职工技协四届五次会议以来工作和经验，授予孔祥瑞等7人"天津市职工岗位创新标兵"称号，授予窦德生"侧芯绕包操作法"等10个操作(工作)法为天津市职工十大先进操作法，授予天津钢管公司炼钢厂"四流变六流连铸机技术改造"等10个项目为天津市职工十大技术创新成果，并对取得突出成绩的天津减速机股份有限公司职工技协等83个先进集体和孔祥瑞等151名先进个人进行表彰。

第七章 科学技术普及

1991年起，天津市社会各界积极开展科学技术普及宣传活动，科普工作不断得到加强。特别是1996年起，天津市贯彻落实《中华人民共和国科学技术普及法》，建立科普工作体系和管理网络，切实加强政府对科普工作的领导和管理。1997年6月，市人大常委会颁布《天津市科学技术普及条例》，将科学技术普及工作纳入法制化的轨道。同时，天津市不断加大对科普工作的经费投入和科普能力建设，建成天津科技馆和天津自然博物馆等科普宣传与教育基地，为社会公众特别是青少年提供广阔的科普教育活动阵地。通过开展科技活动周、科普宣传、青少年科技活动、科教进社区和科技下乡活动，实施科普示范工程和"351"培训工程，以及创建农业科技直通车、选派科技特派员等一系列各具特色又行之有效的科普活动，向社会公众特别是青少年宣传普及科学知识，逐步形成政府引导、全社会共同参与的科普工作的良好局面。

第一节 科普工作体系和管理网络

市委、市政府历来十分重视科学普及工作，特别是1996年建立由主管科技工作的副市长为召集人、有关部门负责人参加的科普工作联席会议制度，并建立科普联络员制度，形成一个新的科普工作组织管理机制。2002年，开通"天津科普网"，成为科普工作的重要载体。2003年，天津市在全国率先成立科普中心。科普工作体系和管理网络的建立与形成，为科普工作的开展提供了有利的组织保证。

一、科普工作联席会议

1996年，市委、市政府颁发《关于加强科学技术普及工作的意见》。同年，建立天津市科普工作联席会议制度，由主管科技工作的副市长为召集人，市委组织部、市委科技工委、市科委、市科协等29个部、委、办、局和人民团体负责人参加。联席会议每年定期召开工作会议和专题会议，对全市科普工作进行决策、规划、协调、督促和检查，审定重点科普工作，在充分整合各级政府部门、各社会团体科普资源的基础上，构筑起一个上下联动、分工协作、资源共享的科普网络，初步形成科普工作的长效管理机制。同时，天津市建立科普联络员制度，负责日常科普工作的协调、联络和沟通。从此，全市科普工作建立一个新的组织管理机制。1996年5月，召开天津市第一次科普工作会议，明确全市各有关部门科技或宣传教育部门负责科普工作。1997年6月18日，市人大常委会颁布《天津市科学技术普及条例》，将科学技术普及工作纳入法制化的轨道。1997年12月，市政府转发《天津市科学技术普及工作"九五"计划纲要》，使科普工作有计划地进行。1998年8月，天津市科普工作联席会议办公室印发《关于在全市开展创建科普教育基地工作的通知》，在全市范围内开展创建科普教育基地活动。1999年12月，科技部批准天津市为全国中心城市科普工作试点市，全市科普工作进入新阶段。至2000年，天津市科普工作行政管理网络基本形成，为科普工作的开展奠定了良好基础。

至2005年，全市各区县按照《天津市科学技术普及条例》要求，普遍建立联席会议制度或成立科普工作领导小组，并结合自身实际，积极探索科普工作的奖励、评价机制，将科普工作纳入区县考核体系。其中，东丽区制订《东丽区科学技术普及奖奖励办法》和《东丽区科学技术普及奖励实施细则》；南开区建立党政领导干部科技进步目标责任制考核评估制度，把加强领导、科普进社区、网络设施建设、开展科普活动等工作列为科技进步目标责任制考核的重要内容，并请人大代表、政协委员和专家学者对各部门工作进行评议，均取得较好效果。

二、科普网络

2002年，"天津科普网"正式开通。该网作为政府网站之一，集科技工作宣传、科普工作指导、科技知识传播为一体，覆盖面广，信息量大，内容丰富，为提高全市科普工作水平，展示科普工作成就发挥独特作用。和平区、南开区等也先后开通社区科普网、健康卫生服务网，红桥区、河西区、蓟县等有线电视台制作的科普专题节目，使公众了解相关知识，树立科学意识。2003年，天津电视台科技教育频道正式开播。该频道以"服务教育、传播知识、普及科学、树人育人"为宗旨，报道科教事业最新动态，提供电视教育服务，展示国内外最新的科教、文化成果，成为科学普及的又一媒介。市科协与天津电视台合作举办《科普示范行》专题节目，专题采访报道典型示范单位的成果和经验。市科协与天津电台联合举办科技专家系列讲座，产生广泛的影响。

2003年，市科委将科普工作引入项目化管理，编写《天津市科普计划项目指南》，围绕市政府每年的中心工作，对全市科普工作进行宏观指导。经组织专家评审，确定30个基础较好、工作思路新颖、具有示范性和带动性的科普计划项目并予以重点资助，调动社会各界投入科普工作的积极性，促进全市科普工作的发展和整体水平的提高。

三、科普中心

2003年，成立天津市科普中心。该中心是从事科普工作的专职机构，负责协助有关部门组织协调社会各界共同推进科普工作；承担社会各界委托的科普工作，以及开展国内外科普工作的交流与合作等任务。该中心为深入落实"科普法"，开展大量基础性工作并进行多项基础调查，较全面地掌握公民科学素养水平和全市科普工作现状，为制定科普政策及中长期科普工作发展规划提供科学的决策依据。

第二节　科普经费与科普能力建设

1996年起，天津市设立市级和区县级科普专项经费，并积极争取科技部和社会各界对科普工作的经费投入，以加强对科普工作的支持。科普经费的不断增加，使科普工作得到保证。同时，天津市十分重视科普能力建设，建成全国一流的天津科技馆和天津自然博物馆等科普宣传阵地，科普教育基地由最初的10家增加到80家，并通过建立电子科普（科技）宣传屏、科普长廊、社区科普活动室和农村科普活动场地等科普基础设施，为社会公众特别是青少年提供广阔的科普教育活动阵地，科普工作能力得到提高。

一、科普经费投入

1996年，市委、市政府在《关于加强科学技术普及工作的意见》中做出决定，设立市级和区县级两级科学技术普及工作专项经费。1996年和1997年，市级科普经费均为90万元。1998～2002年，市级科普经费均为120万元。2003年起，市级科普经费增至200万元。按照市委、市政府的文件要求，各区县政府也分别设立科普工作专项经费，使各区县科学技术普及工作得到经费支持。同时，天津市十分注意吸引社会资金对科普工作的投入，仅1998年有关企业对科普工作投入经费达65.9万元。此外，2001年和2002年从科技部争取到科普经费共计60万元。这些科普经费的投入，对保障科普工作的开展起到支撑作用。

二、科普能力建设

市委、市政府一贯非常重视科普能力建设，把它作为科普形象工程的重要组成部分。1997年，市政府转发的《天津市科学技术普及工作"九五"计划纲要》中，确定到2000年基本建成全国一流的天津科技馆和天津自然博物馆，成为科普形象工程的重要组成部分，科普工作的载体资源更加丰富。从此，天津市从科普阵地、科普网络、科普队伍到日常性科普工作得到加强，科普事业蓬勃发展。1999年，在第二次全国科普工作会议公布的首批100个全国青少年科技教育基地中，天津科技馆、天津自然博物馆、蓟县中上远古界国家级自然保护区、天津青少年科技中心等4个单位榜上有名。

（一）科普宣传阵地

天津科技馆作为天津市科普宣传阵地的重要组成部分，于1992年开始兴建，1994年9月一期工程竣工，1995年元旦正式向社会开放。天津科技馆占地4万平方米，建筑面积2.1万平方米，其中常设展厅面积1万平方米。其建筑规模、展品数量和服务功能具有国际先进水平，是一座现代化的综合性科普设施。该馆的造型风格独特，寓意深刻，主体建筑为桥型，其上方为30米直径大户球型建筑，宛如一轮蓬勃欲出的朝阳，象征青年一代是科技事业的未来和希望。普及科学知识，树立科学思想，培养科学方法，是天津科技馆的主要功能。展示厅是科技馆的主体部分，分上、下两层，按不同学科和专业技术门类设立展区，共有300多件（套）展品。展示厅布局气势恢宏，分区布展又各具特色，使参观者进入展厅尤如置身于科学殿堂之中。科技馆的展品集科学性、知识性、趣味性、参与性、艺术性于一体，借助声、光、电、计算机等现代化展示手段，生动形象地向公众普及科学技术知识，参观者在直接参与操作展品的过程中，通过视觉、听觉、触觉等感觉系统，亲身体验到科学技术带来的乐趣，大开眼界，受益无穷。全馆共分14个展区，即力学世界，天地万象，通讯与信息，交通与航天，食品与营养，磁电奥秘，测试区，电脑与机械，声学探秘，生活与科学，人体与科学，数学漫游，光学奇观，能源与材料，还有一个宇宙剧场。天津科技馆自1995年对外开放，党和国家领导人多次到此视察，很多国内外朋友也纷纷前往参观，受到社会各界的广泛赞誉。1999年起，天津科技馆每月都举办科普报告会，先后有37位科学家和科技工作者为公众举办科普报告会35场，内容涉及气象、天文、水资源保护、防震减灾、环保及可持续发展、城市规划、核能、绿色能源、生物、医药、信息技术等领域，收到良好效果，为提高国民的科学文化素质起到重要作用。

天津自然博物馆始建于1914年，原名北疆博物院，其馆藏的生物、地质、化石标本，来源广泛，门类齐全，珍品荟萃，享誉国内外。为保护和弘扬这一自然科学文化遗产，1997年市委、市政府决定投资建设天津自然博物馆。新展馆占地2万平方米，主体建筑1.2万平方米，于1998年10月1日建成并对外开放。展览馆共分8个厅：以地球与生命为主题的序厅，以展示恐龙风貌为主的古生物一厅，展出距今1000万年到1万年间的古生物二厅，展出五彩缤纷的水生物厅，展示珍贵稀少的两栖爬行厅，以生态地理形式陈列的爬行、鸟兽动物生态厅，展示千姿百态昆虫大世界的昆虫厅，展现海洋贝类资源的海洋贝类厅。至2005年，该馆共接待参观者60万人次，并开展"可持续发展""保护生态环境"为主题的征文、竞赛等青少年科学普及活动，均收到良好效果。

（二）科普教育基地

1998年8月，天津市科普工作联席会议做出决定，在全市范围内开展创建科普教育基地活动。各科普场馆、科研院所、高等院校、自然保护区、风景名胜区、工厂化农业示范基地等20多种类型的科普场所，充分调动科普资源的利用与开发，开展形式多样的科普活动，208个单位和部门参与申报创建科普教育基地活动。通过5年的培育，全市科普教育基地建设取得较快发展，科普教育基地由最初的10家增加到80家。其中，天津科技馆、天津自然博物馆、蓟县中上元古界国家自然保护区、天津市青少年科技中心、消防局红领巾消防警校等7家单位成为国家级科普教育基地。遍布全市的科普教育基地，为公众特别是青少年提供广阔的科普教育活动阵地。据不完全统计，各类科普教育基地每年接待公众达230万人次，成为全市科普工作的重要力量。

同时，各大中型企业积极开展科学普及活动，并取得明显进展。天津海河乳业集团有限公司、天津宝成机械集团有限公司、天津天士力集团有限公司、天津市双港垃圾焚烧发电厂等高新技术企业定期向公众开放，集中展示高新技术产品技术知识和工艺知识，宣传高新技术成果产业化的最新进展；天津红光农场、天津市农业高新技术产业示范园区等农业示范基地积极开发科普设施，开展丰富的科普活动，宣传现代科技农业知识、农业技术示范和现代化农业生产知识，均取得较好效果。

（三）科普基础设施

1991年起，天津市不断加强科普基础设施建设。至2005年，全市建立21个电子科普（科技）宣传屏和2612.5延米科普长廊，其中包括5个百米科普长廊；建立723个社区科普（技）活动室，70个农村科技大院、农村科技活动站、农村科技活动室等农村科普（技）活动场地，其中大多数活动场地配有电视、VCD、计算机等，具备较好的开展科普活动的条件。同时，天津市开展科普长廊和科普名人园建设，建成5个百米科普长廊和一个科技名人园，成为进行科普宣传的重要阵地。天津经济技术开发区微电子工业区总公司结合21世纪微电子行业的发展特点，建成全市第一座以世界科学家群像为主要内容的绿化带状公园，成为进行科普宣传的一道风景线。

第三节 科普特色活动

天津市在政府科普经费投入的引导下，各科普工作联席会议成员单位和各区县及科普教育基地等结合自身实际情况，围绕公共安全、减灾防灾、节能减排、建设节约型社会、自主创新等重大主题，面向全社会，针对青少年等重点科普人群，探索科普活动内容和形式的创新，策划和开展一系列高水平、有影响的特色科普主题活动，收效显著，年受益人数超过230万人次。天津市科技活动周围绕社会热点问题，组织丰富多样的报告会、研讨会、知识竞赛、展览、科教影片展映等活动，吸引广大市民的广泛参与，收到明显成效。市、区、街三级政府和科协组织通过举办科普展览、科普讲座、知识竞赛等多种形式，广泛深入地开展丰富多彩又各具特色的科学普及活动。在城市科普活动中，开展科技活动周、全国科普日、“科教进社区”等多项活动，组织实施“科普示范工程”；组织并参加全国青少年科技创新大赛，设立并颁发天津市青少年科技创新市长奖，激发青少年科技创新热情；企业科协开展创建优秀科普车间活动；市反邪教协会联合有关单位开展反对邪教科普宣传活动。在农村科普中，组织1万余名农业专家、科技人员深入开展“科技下乡”活动，并通过举办科普大集、科普一条街市和开展各类农业适用技术培训，普及农业科技知识，不断提高农民的科技意识和文化素质。

一、科技周和科普日活动

1987年起，天津市每年9月份的第3周都要围绕不同的主题，开展形式多样的科学普及活动。1994年9月第八届科技周期间，恰逢天津科技馆落成，中国科协在天津科技馆举行首届全国城市科技周开幕式。全国政协副主席、中国科协主席朱光亚亲临开幕式并发表讲话，市长张立昌主持大会，中国科协党组书记高潮和中外来宾及各界群众1000多人出席开幕式。天津科技活动周在全国引起强烈反响。

2000年，国务院发出通知，决定每年5月份的第3周为全国科技活动周。从此，科技活动周成为遍及全国的联合大行动。2001年，天津市作为全国第一届科技活动周的分会场之一，以“科技·环境·可持续发展”为主题，举办第十五届科技活动周。2002年全国第二届科技活动周期间，天津市承担全国科技活动周分会场工作的同时，举办第十六届科技活动周，广泛开展世界贸易组织规则和知识的宣传普及，开展应对入世研讨、科技交流、群众性的科普活动、表彰宣传优秀科技工作者、为科技工作者办实事等五大系列活动。

2003年开始，根据中国科协的决定，天津市每年9月第3周的公休日举办科普日活动。当年，面对突发“非典”疫情，按照党和国家有关部门的统一部署，天津市及时调整科技活动周的内容，以“依靠科学，战胜非典”为主题，成功举办第十七届科技活动周，在全社会形成依靠科学、抗击“非典”的良好氛围。2004年，第十八届科技活动周期间，围绕“科学·文明·健康”主题，在天津科技馆举办“崇尚科学，关爱生命，维护人权，反对邪教展览”，中共中央政治局常委李长春、市委副书记刘胜玉等与群众一起参观展览，并分别参加科技周活动。同时，举办科普宣传、健康咨询、科普展览、文艺体育表演等大型活动89场，科普报告会百余场；组织7大专题健康知识展览，在18个区县巡回展出；开展全民健康促进行动，在城区广泛开展义诊咨询活动，在农村为380万农民检查身体等，全市各单位共举办各类活动3000多项。2005年，天津市举办以“珍惜资源，建设节约型社会”为主题的第十九届科技活动周期间，组织开展资源形势宣传、资源节约知识普及、资源节约研讨、“珍惜资源，从我做起”宣传咨询联合行动、表彰宣传优秀科技工作者等五大系列活动。各区县局(集团公司)共组织617项主要活动，其下属基层单位组织“珍惜资源，建设节约型社会”主题活动近万项。

至2005年，天津市连续组织19届科技周活动，成为持续开展大型科普活动时间最长的省市之一，有力地推动“科教兴市”战略的实施。

1991～2005年天津市科技活动周主题一览表

表2-7-3-48

时　间	届　别	主　题
1991年9月	第五届科技周	科技进步，经济建设，精神文明
1992年9月	第六届科技周	依靠科技进步，提高劳动者素质，加快改革开放，促进经济发展
1993年9月	第七届科技周	抓住机遇，加快发展，科技兴市，振兴天津
1994年9月	第八届科技周	科学技术——天津辉煌的金钥匙
1995年9月	第九届科技周	科教兴市——二十一世纪
1996年9月	第十届科技周	高科技—人才、信息—现代化
1997年9月	第十一届科技周	信息连着你我他

续表2-7-3-48

时间	届别	主题
1998年9月16～22日	第十二届科技周	依靠科技进步，实现跨世纪蓝图
1999年9月15～21日	第十三届科技周	科技·创新·新世纪
2000年9月13～19日	第十四届科技周	科技创新与跨世纪发展
2001年5月14～20日	第十五届科技周	科技·环境·可持续发展
2002年5月18～25日	第十六届科技周	科技·入世·发展
2003年5月17～23日	第十七届科技周	依靠科学，战胜非典。
2004年5月17～23日	第十八届科技周	科学·文明·健康
2005年5月16～22日	第十九届科技周	珍惜资源—建设节约型社会

二、青少年科技活动

1990年起，天津市面向青少年，每年都要举办数学、物理、化学、生物学、信息学等奥林匹克竞赛；每两年举办一届青少年发明创造比赛和科学讨论会、青少年生物百项活动评选、青少年科技活动成果展览、青少年科技摄影展览、科学幻想绘画展览等多项活动。在每两年组织一次的全国“挑战杯”大学生课外学术科技作品竞赛中，天津市总成绩和获奖作品多次名列前茅，其中多项科技作品实现成果转化，产生良好的社会和经济效益。市科协面向青少年开展的小发明、小创造、生物百项、少年电子技师、航模制作、科幻绘画、计算机应用等各种科普竞赛活动，内容丰富，形式多样，吸引广大青少年的踊跃参与。

2002年，在全国优秀青少年科技活动方案评审活动中，天津市获得11项一等奖、7项二等奖、6项三等奖。2003年，经市政府批准，设立天津市青少年科技创新市长奖，每两年评选一次，表彰、奖励在科学实践、技术创新方面取得卓越成绩的青少年。同年，天津市在百所中小学校推广优秀青少年科技活动方案，并实施近百项科普活动，组织专家对全市百所中小学校的科技教师、科技辅导员进行培训，全市10余万名青少年参与活动，推动青少年科普活动的开展。同时，科普工作联席会议各成员单位充分发挥各自优势，积极支持和投入科普事业；各区县和科普教育基地、科技团体、科研院所、高校、企业等发挥自身优势，开展各具特色的科普活动；各有关单位结合世界水日、世界气象日、世界地球日、世界环境日、地震宣传日等科普宣传日，开展专题宣传活动，均收到较好效果。2005年6月30日，举行首届“天津市青少年科技创新市长奖”颁奖仪式，向3名获奖者颁发由市长戴相龙签名的证书和奖品。

三、科普宣传

1991年起，天津市社会各界积极开展科普宣传活动。市环保局围绕地球日和世界环境日，在全市范围内开展以“可持续发展战略”为主题的科普宣传活动。1994年，天津电视台设立科普专题节目《科技长河》，并设立《健康家园》《今晨相会》等栏目，普及医疗卫生知识。1998年，市水利局在《天津日报》开办“节约一滴水”专栏，进行可持续发展战略科普宣传。1999年，市委组织部在揭批法轮功斗争中，与市科委、市科协等部门联合举办一系列科普宣传活动，并与人事局共同成立专家服务中心，将100多位专家组织起来，面向社会开展科普知识讲座和咨询服务等活动，均收到良好效果。

2000年，市环保局面向中小学开展“绿色学校”创建活动，编辑出版中小学生的科普读本，组织中小学生环境保护夏令营，举办“绿色征文”评比、中学生环保知识演讲比赛等活动，提高广大青少年的环保意识。同年，市科协和河北工业大学建立科学家讲师团，面向社会开展科普宣传；大港区等区县建立科普宣传员制度；市农委、市经委、市建委、市地震局、市环保局、市气象局、市卫生局、市水利局等部门利用宣传教育网络，大力加强日常性科普工作，开展丰富多彩的科普活动；市旅游局推出包括普及科学知识为主要内容的“博物馆之旅”和“自然生态旅游路线”；市妇联组织女科技工作者与农村女技术能手结成对子，将科普工作融入“双学双比”活动中，对提高妇女的科学文化素质起到重要作用；团市委组建50支面向农村的青年科普志愿者队伍，建立200多个农村青年科技图书服务站；各高校通过举办“挑战杯”大学生科技发明创造比赛，组织大学生开展科技活动，天津医科大学、南开大学、天津师范大学等高校面向公众和青少年举办扎扎实实、丰富多彩的科普活动，天津医科大学还面向糖尿病患者和家属开办“周日快车”讲座，免费普及有关糖尿病防治知识。

2001年9月11日，天津市反邪教协会与有关单位共同举办“崇尚科学、破除迷信、清除邪教”漫画大赛，同时出版《全国崇尚科学、破除迷信、清除邪教漫画大赛作品选》和宣传挂图。同年，天津市环境保护科学院等科研院所面向青少年开放，开展可持续发展战略宣传普及活动，组织中小学生参观实验室、示范工程，组织专家举办科普讲座；南开大学等高校在世界地球日和世界环境日，组织研究生和大学生撰写科普文章，面向公众发放科普资料和开展科普知识有奖答卷。2002年5月，市反邪教协会将800册《崇尚科学、破除迷信、清除邪教漫画大赛作品选》和134400幅图片分发给各区县、街道、乡镇。2003年上半年，市反邪教协会组织天津市著名画家创作一套6幅“崇尚科学，反对邪教”系列宣传画，印制2000套，发放到基层张贴。2004年5月19日至6月21日，市反邪教协会在市科技馆举办“崇尚科学，关爱生命，维护人权，反对邪教”大型展览，中共中央政治局常委李长春参观展览，360个单位、近4万人次参观展览。2004年12月14日，开展大型展览进大墙活动，在位于大港区的天津女子劳教所举办“崇尚科学，关爱生命，维护人权，反对邪教”展览。市反邪教协会将科普宣传工作作为协会工作的重要内容，组织专家撰写科普文章并在新闻媒体发表，与新闻媒体开办“崇尚文明，反对迷信”专栏，组织专家深入高等院校和社区街道作科普报告，组织医学专家赴农村进行健康咨询活动，均收到良好效果。

四、科教进社区活动

1992年起，天津市按照市、区、街三个层面展开“科教进社区”活动。每年“科教进社区”活动中，市、区、街三级政府和科协组织通过举办科普报告会、科普知识展览和各种培训班等活动，发放各种科普宣传资料，组织丰富多彩的科普活动。据统计，2002～2005年，参与“科教进社区”活动的居民群众达392万余人次，其中各城区举办科普讲座2540次，科普报告会1032场，参与活动的干部群众116万人次；举办科普培训、竞赛4000余场，参加人数28万余人次；举办科普展览1968场次，参观者达132万人次；举办青少年课外科技活动3748项。

五、科技下乡活动

1994年开始，市委组织部、市委科技工委、市科协、市科委贯彻中宣部、中国科协等12个部委关于深入开展文化、科技、卫生“三下乡”活动的指示精神，组织有关科技和农业部门及科研院所、高等院校等方面的专家组成专家服务团，深入涉农区县的乡镇、村，开展科技下乡活动。2002年起，每年科技下乡活动都有相应的主题，其中2002年主题是“崇尚科学、移风易俗”，2003年主题是“搭科技成果转化平台，送适用技术下乡”，2004年主题是“送技术，解难题，促转化，增效益”，2005年主题是“科技帮扶行动”暨北辰区文化、科技、卫生、法律“四下乡”活动。至2005年，全市组织开展科技下乡活动1806次，参加科技下乡活动的农业专家、科技人员10357人次，组织科普大集、科普一条街市共395场，举办各类农业适用技术培训班1625次，农民及种养殖大户111616人次参加学习和讲座，发放各种科普宣传资料548414份，发放各类农业新技术、新成果、新品种的科普资料光盘和录像带1623盘，在市级电视台、电台和涉农区县有线电视台反复进行播放。

六、农业科技直通车

1996年起，天津市农村工作委员会（以下简称“市农委”）与天津人民广播电台利用现代通讯手段，创建津沽大地农业科技直通车，在广播电台设立农业110咨询电话系统，组织农业技术专家下乡进行现场技术咨询和服务。同时，市地震局在全市18个区县举办“防震减灾科普知识巡回展”，直接受益人数达35万人次，并编印“防震减灾明白纸”300万份，在青少年中举行防震演习，举办“家庭防震减灾知识竞赛”，数万人参加，还举办几十场大型专家报告会，普及防震减灾知识。1997年，蓟县开展“科普之冬”活动，深入山村和农户传播科技知识、科学思想和科学方法。1999年，宝坻县启动科技入户工程，通过多种形式调动全县各有关部门面向农村广大干部群众开展科普工作，切实让科学知识深入到农户。

七、科普示范工程

1999年起，在全市范围内组织实施"科普示范工程"，旨在充分利用社会科普资源，构建科协科普工作网络，通过在社会不同层面创建的一批科普示范单位和家庭的示范作用，形成从区县到家庭的科普示范体系，并以此为龙头带动全市科普工作的深入开展。至2005年，全市创建全国科普教育基地13个，在城区创建全国科普示范城区3个，科普示范街道23个，科普示范小区199个，科普示范家庭(科普文明家庭)309户；在农村创建全国科普示范县(区)3个，科普示范乡镇58个，科普示范基地59个，科普示范农户307户(种养状元24名，种养能手283名)；在企业创建科普示范车间74个，在中小学创建科普示范学校100个。

八、"351"培训工程

2001年起，市农委实施天津市农村劳动力"351"培训工程，即在3年的时间内，组织全市农村科技教育资源，实施"红色证书、绿色证书、蓝色证书、村干部培训、农村经纪人培训"五大工程，对农村100万名各类劳动力进行专项技术培训。2003年，市农委与市农业科技图书馆以服务"三农"、方便群众为宗旨，在全市开展"科普知识到农家"项目，在静海县、西青区建立农业科技图书分馆，在津南区、宝坻区建成4个农民科技书屋，向农民借阅农业科技图书，播放种植、养殖技术光盘，编发各种信息资料，提供农业科技信息网上查询等多项服务。2004年，市农委与市农业局联合开展"普及新技术，施惠到农家"项目，面向农村基层干部和技术人员，组织开展专题讲座、先进适用农业技术推广、送科技图书下乡、建立县乡镇农业图书文献共享网络、科普知识培训等多项活动，提高农业技术干部的业务水平，促进农业增效和农民增收。同时，在农村开展"文化、科技、卫生三下乡"活动，深入村镇开展咨询服务，为农民带去科普宣传资料，受到群众欢迎。津南区、蓟县、静海县等连续举办"科普文明百日大下乡""科普之冬""科技下乡服务团"等活动，北辰区支持有关部门与经济薄弱村、贫困农户结成帮扶对子，宝坻区在各乡镇普遍开展科技入村、入户活动，把科技送到田间地头。"351培训工程"为农民科技致富、增收增效搭建桥梁，为在广大农村全面建设小康社会提供了强有力的智力支持。通过不断传播科学思想，倡导科学方法，普及农业科技知识，提升广大农民的科技文化素质，提高农民的就业能力和生产水平，增加农民的收入，并涌现出一大批先进典型，对周边群众发挥带头作用。

九、选派科技特派员

2004年，蓟县在全市率先启动实施科技特派员行动计划，探索和实践科技与农村、农民和农业相结合的有效形式和有效机制。至2005年，蓟县从有关高等院校、科研院所及蓟县科技人员中选派两批共20名科技特派员，其中12名来自天津市农学院、市农科院和天津师范大学的专家、教授。这些科技特派员分别派往乡镇、村庄和种养殖场(站)等20个基层单位，涉及农业、林业、畜牧、果树、生态建设、科普旅游、农业信息化、设施农业等8个行业。他们向农民推广农村实用新技术126项，向乡镇、村和企业推广新品种68个，举办技术培训162期，累计12900余人次接受各种培训，帮助派驻地创造经济效益超过2000万元。

第八章　软科学研究

1991～2005年，天津市紧密围绕市委、市政府的各项重大战略部署，针对经济建设、社会发展、科技进步和科学管理等方面的重大决策和管理问题，发挥有关高等院校、科研院所、民间咨询机构的作用，开展有组织、有计划的软科学研究，累计完成软科学研究计划课题561项，取得一大批研究咨询成果。同时，从事软科学研究与咨询的队伍不断壮大，软科学研究对促进决策的科学化、民主化、程序化发挥积极作用和广泛影响。

第一节　经济建设研究

1991～2005年，是天津市经济持续、快速发展的时期。软科学研究工作以经济建设为中心，围绕工业、农业、服务业、综合性经济发展问题的软科学计划项目达185项，占立项总数的33%。在工业重点行业及技术发展、传统产业技术改造、工业产业布局、农业发展战略、科技兴农与农业结构调整、现代服务业等方面，取得一大批决策研究成果。

一、促进工业发展研究

（一）重点工业行业和骨干产业研究

1991年4月，市科委立项、天津市科技情报研究所（以下简称“情报所”）牵头开展“天津市工业技术发展分析与对策研究”重点软课题研究。该课题组织动员14个工业局（公司）及其所属骨干企业、高等院校、科研院所等部门的领导、管理人员和专家学者，共400多人参与调查研究和咨询论证，历经两年的时间完成36个行业的38份技术发展分析对策研究子报告，对36个行业进行技术评估，比较国内外差距，预测行业发展前景，并提出对策建议。这是天津市首次大规模地进行的工业技术经济水平系统分析与调查研究工作。

1994～1997年，天津市科学技术评价中心（以下简称“评价中心”）牵头，组织大批行业专家开展工业重点行业及技术发展系列跟踪研究。1994～1995年开展的“天津市工业重点行业和科技发展跟踪研究”课题，对全市汽车、机床、工程机械、计算机、金属制品、化纤、化学制药、中药、农药和墙体材料等10个行业的技术发展现状、实力地位变化、国内外技术发展趋势、行业发展前景进行综合评价分析和预测，并从技术发展的高度对行业技术发展的方向和产品开发重点、技改、引进、攻关项目重点和技术政策、行业管理等方面提出对策建议。课题还参照国际通行的评价指标体系和国内的实际情况设计出以行业生产经营情况指标、主要产品技术经济指标、关键技术评价指标、综合实力地位、评价指标和发展前景指标为构架的指标体系，并采用模糊综合评价方法、比较研究方法、定性和定量相结合的方法，对行业进行全面的分析研究。1995～1996年开展的“天津市工业重点行业（主导产品）技术发展跟踪研究”课题，对全市汽车、水力发电设备、通信、广播电视、特殊钢、石油化工、涂料、洗涤剂、包装食品机械和塑料制品等10个行业的主导产品技术发展进行跟踪研究，内容包括行业的生产经验现状分析、关键技术水平、综合实力地位分析、行业发展前景和技术发展对策等方面。1996～1997年开展的“天津市工业重点行业技术发展跟踪研究”课题，选择电子元件行业、自动化仪表行业、纯碱行业、烧碱行业、染料行业、感光材料行业、医疗器械行业、普通钢行业、家用电器行业、绵纺织行业等作为重点研究对象，对行业的基本状况、主导产品的技术水平、工业装备水平、经济效益水平等与国内外同行业进行比较研究，并根据综合评价研究、行业技术发展趋势、国家产业政策、市场需求等方面的研究，提出行业技术发展方向、产品开发重点、技改、引进、攻关重点、技术政策、行业管理等方面的对策建议和方案。

2001年，天津市发展计划委员会工业经济发展处、天津市科学学研究所（以下简称“科学学所”）联合开展“天津市骨干产业发展模式分析与对策研究”。课题针对工业“十五”规划中提出的五大骨干产业，对天津市电子信息、汽车、生物技术和现代医药、化学工业、钢铁工业等五大产业进行发展回顾，对产业竞争优势作出分析，总结国内外相关产业发展模式，并结合全市面临的形势，提出五大产业在新世纪前10年的发展模式以及对策建议。

（二）传统产业技术改造研究

1993～1994年，天津市社会发展工程研究所承担“天津市部分乡镇工业企业技术状况和发展的研究”，用宏观统计数据与微观抽象调查相结合的方法，全面分析和总结15年来全市乡镇工业企业发展的技术现状，分析全市乡镇工业企业在总体及人员素质、生产装备、制造工艺、检测水平等方面与国内其他沿海省市的差异，并提出转变观念、调整乡镇工业企业结构、发展规模经济、培训人才、建立现代企业管理机制、建立企业技术进步促进机制等对策建议。

2000年，南开大学经济学系承担的“天津市加快利用高新技术改造传统产业政策选择研究”课题，在调研天津市传统产业发展和技术改造的现状、问题和优势的基础上，提出了用高新技术改造传统产业的目标、重点、途径和机制，以及相应的政策建议，并就电子信息、生物医药、石油化工等重点行业技术升级改造开展了可行性方案研究。

2002～2004年，评价中心围绕传统产业技术提升与改造完成多项研究课题，其中相继完成“天津市制造业信息化对策研究”“实施新一轮嫁接改造调整，加快优势产业的研究”“天津市传统制造业的提升关键科技问题研究”等项目。

2003年，科学学所完成“用高新技术提升本市装备制造业的对策研究”。课题研究提出天津市发展装备制造业的战略思路，并提出建设技术支撑服务平台、推广一批关键技术、加快形成产业增长源、培育有知名度的大型装备制造企业、孵化科技型中小装备制造企业等方面的具体对策，基本形成成套装备制造能力、综合配套能力与技术创新能力的装备制造产业链。课题还在组织领导、整合重组、技术和体制创新、人才培养等方面提出加快装备制造业新型工业化步伐的战略措施。

（三）工业产业布局等问题研究

1994～1995年，天津市总工程师联谊会承担“促进轿车进入家庭的系统研究”课题。该课题开展了轿车进入家庭的宏观环境研究、中国轿车工业内部因素研究和中国汽车工业外部环境研究等，并在系统研究的基础上提出相应的综合性对策。

1999～2000年，评价中心承担“天津市实施工业战略东移的对策研究”课题。该课题从天津市建设环渤海经济中心、北方重要经济中心和现代化国际港口大都市的总体要求出发，研究实施天津市工业战略东移的具体对策，实现国务院对天津市的战略定位，为加快天津经济起飞和可持续发展提供决策依据。该课题研究还提出实施战略东移中的工业结构优化、工业布局、相关科技服务体系建设、投资体系、政策措施及实施方案。

2003～2005年，环境无害化技术转移中心北方分中心承担“天津市水工业产业发展对策研究”项目。该课题在充分调研国内外水工业发展动态与趋势的基础上，围绕天津市水工业发展现状，按照战略与规划、政策与法规、科技与产业三个层次综合研究天津市水工业发展问题，结合城市发展急需，提出对水工业产业进行整体规划、多方协作、多层次推进水工业市场化进程的观点。课题成果还有针对性编制了实施科技工程，以及海水淡化、污水处理等多项水工业关键领域的工业化实施方案。

二、促进农业与农村发展研究

（一）农业发展战略与总体思路

1992～1994年，情报所承担"九十年代天津农业发展的基本思路与对策研究"课题。该课题通过对天津农业发展问题的深入调研，认为天津市农业在长期计划经济体制下，沿着传统思想与方式建立起来的数量型产业和产品结构与天津经济发展、经济转轨和不断深化的改革开放形势不相适应，面临着严峻的挑战和诸多问题。课题结合进入20世纪以来发达国家发展农业的经验，提出走向21世纪天津农业发展的基本思路与对策：90年代天津市要努力实现传统农业向现代科学技术和现代管理的转变；实现农村劳动力一半真正转移到城镇二、三产业。该课题获1994年度天津市科技进步二等奖。

2000～2001年，天津市农村工作委员会（以下简称"市农委"）政研室完成的"天津市沿海都市型农业发展研究"课题，从把握天津沿海都市型农业发展战略的背景和依据入手，提出天津沿海都市型农业建设的思路、目标、基本框架和对策措施。课题设计出天津沿海都市型农业的评价指标体系，并提出了新的建设思路。

2002～2003年，天津大学管理学院和南开大学合作承担的"我国农村经济社会系统研究"，运用系统科学理论和方法，研究农村经济社会系统的运行规律，分析农村经济社会系统可持续发展途径，并以经济、生态、社会和城乡协调发展为切入点，详细分析农村经济社会系统，提出以经济GDP、绿色GDP和人文GDP进行总量衡量，以熵衡量系统效益和结构等新思想，建立指导农村经济社会协调发展的理论。

（二）科技兴农

1991～1992年，市科委星火计划办公室、天津市农村经济与区划研究所（以下简称"区划所"）共同承担的"天津市科技兴农推动机制及对策研究"，通过理论探讨、实证调查与经验总结，提出建立天津市科技兴农推动机制的方法和途径，为推动全市科技兴农的深入发展提出合理、配套的实施对策。

1996～1997年，市农科院科研处、天津市种子管理站承担的"天津市农作物良种产业化技术对策的研究"，采取比较、分析、综合、归纳的研究方法，遵照国家有关条例、法规和政策以及产业发展规划，密切结合天津现状和优势与不足，对良种产业化主要环节进行全面深入研究，提出技术对策与科技项目题录，对领导决策、主管部门实施以及种子科技人员工作方向具有重要指导价值。

1999～2000年，区划所、市农委科教处共同开展"天津市农业科技进步贡献率测算及增长对策研究"。该项研究坚持定量与定性相结合、研究与应用相结合，综合运用国际、国内通用的经济学理论和增长速度测算模型，并通过建立全市总合生产函数回归方程，对资金、劳动力、土地等各投入要素的回归系数（弹性系数）进行模拟测算，测算出天津市"八五"期间农业科技进步贡献率为47.1%，1995～1999年农业科技进步贡献率为53.1%。

2001年，市农学院、区划所承担的"天津市农产品深加工技术发展对策研究"，通过对天津市与国内外农产品加工业发展比较研究，并采用数学、统计学与经济学相结合的方法进行系统地分析，全面阐述今后农产品深加工科技发展重点领域，提出发展具有天津特色的农产品深加工的对策措施，为决策部门选择重点科技项目和产业项目、推动农产品深加工产业发展提供决策依据。

2004年，市农科院、区划所根据《天津市中长期科学和技术发展规划（2006～2020年）》要求，开展"天津都市农业发展重大科技问题研究"。该项研究着眼于未来5～15年天津都市农业发展对科技的需求，提出农业功能转化、产业升级、优势突破、开放合作等创新型科技发展的战略思路，对天津都市农业科技2010年和2020年发展目标进行科学预测，并经过筛选和论证，提出未来15年特别是"十一五"期间，应优先研究的动植物新品种选育、农产品质量安全、资源高效利用与可持续发展、产后农业、农业信息技术等五大科技领域的关键技术，并筛选出科技攻关专项、科技示范工程、重点科技平台和重大科技项目。

（三）农业结构调整研究

1992～1994年，市农委农业处、区划所共同承担的“天津市种植业结构调整及高效对策研究”，综合运用实证分析、比较分析和数量经济分析相结合的研究方法，揭示津郊种植业的现状特点，以及在市场经济新形势下所面临的机遇和挑战，确立在市场经济体制下津郊种植业结构调整及高效的基本思路和综合性对策措施。

1998～1999年，天津市园艺工程研究所承担的“天津市农业设施产业化对策研究”，通过对国内外农业设施产业发展及其在园艺上的应用现状进行综合调研，提出天津市农业设施产业发展对策，确定天津市目前应发展农业设施产业的方向、规模，并提出一整套具体的实施思路。

2000～2001年，天津市蓟县山区综合开发办公室承担的“天津市山区综合开发持续发展模式研究与实践”课题，按照市委、市政府对蓟县山区综合开发确定的城郊型山区综合开发定位要求，重点对城郊型山区综合开发指导思想与基本原则、城郊型山区农业产业化、城郊型山区县精品农业建设、山区开发与生态环境关系等方面开展研究，提出城郊型山区建设与发展的理论和对策措施，为探索城郊型特色山区综合开发之路提供决策依据。

2000～2001年，区划所完成的“天津市无公害蔬菜产业发展研究”，对国内外绿色食品与无公害农产品的发展状况及天津市蔬菜产业的现状、发展趋势进行预测研究，制定出“十五”期间天津市蔬菜产业发展规划，并通过对无公害蔬菜标准体系与监测管理、产业营销对策、产业组织创新、产业化经营模式进行研究，提出天津市蔬菜产业发展战略及对策研究。

三、促进服务业发展研究

（一）服务业总体问题研究

1991～1993年，市政府研究室承担完成“天津市发展第三产业的战略和对策研究”课题。课题全面、深入地研究天津市第三产业发展的现状、问题、有利条件以及90年代加快第三产业发展的紧迫性，同时采用定量与定性相结合的方法，建立天津市第三产业2000年发展规划的经济预测模型，为市领导决策提供重要的科学依据。

（二）现代服务业研究

1993～1994年，天津市工业设计培训中心完成的“天津市工业设计现状调研及对策研究”课题，在借鉴国内外工业设计发展经验的基础上，结合天津市相关行业的具体情况提出发展天津市工业设计的对策和建议。课题成果包括：国内外工业设计发展源述；天津市工业设计现状分析；发展工业设计的支持系统；发展工业设计的总体规划；发展工业设计的基本措施等。依据该课题研究成果，为宣传普及工业设计知识，编制出《工业设计理论与方法》宣传手册。

1991～1993年，科学学所承担完成“天津市咨询业发展构想与建议”。该课题对国外咨询业发展的基本规律和主要经验进行研究，采用多种研究方法，对咨询业的定义、性质、分类进行科学界定，对天津市咨询业的现状，包括系统规模、发展阶段及特征、重要作用、管理体制、经营方式、支撑条件与政策环境进行研究和评价。在此基础上，参照国内外咨询业发展经验，提出天津市咨询业发展的思路和任务、咨询业发展的主要目标和可能模式、市场发育和支撑环境以及运行体制、加快天津市咨询业产业化和国际化发展的政策措施等建议。

此外，科学学所于1994～1995年承担完成“天津市科技咨询产业试点实施方案研究”、1996年承担完成“推动天津市科技咨询产业发展的政策研究”等两项咨询产业发展课题。

2000～2001年，南开大学承担完成的“天津市现代化物流发展纲要研究”，是国内率先进行的城市现代化物流规划理论及方法研究课题，在全国处于领先水平。课题通过大量的调研和分析研究，对天津市现代物流发展现状进行全面、客观地分析，并采用定性和定量相结合的分析方法，对全市物流的发展做出需求分析和未来发展预测，同时结合中国现代物流发展特点及现状，率先在国内进行现代物流核算体系及指标评价体系的开创性研究。课题还从现代物流与经济发展的互动关系的角度，从行业与区域两个方面，全面论述天津市发展现代物流的战略构想，系统设计出天津市现代物流体系的规划构架。

四、综合经济与产业问题研究

（一）综合性经济发展研究

1992～1993年，天津市计划经济研究所完成"关于天津市经济运行中制约因素分析和对策研究"。该课题以建设有中国特色的社会主义理论为指导，通过对上百个经济指标的分析对比，对天津市经济运作15年来的状况进行定量定性分析，综合提出天津经济发展中的主要制约因素，并对制约因素的内含和形成，提出了"治老、聚财、转机制"三大对策建议，同时对制约因素的理论问题和发展的新路径进行了探索。

1995年，南开大学经济研究所承担的"积极利用外资，促进天津经济发展"课题，运用国际投资学和利用外资学原理，采用理论研究和实证分析相结合的方法，对90年代后半期天津市如何积极、合理、有效利用外资，促进天津经济发展进行对策性研究。课题成果包括：天津市利用外资与经济发展的总体评价；90年代后半期天津市利用外资的国际国内环境分析；天津市自身利用外资环境考察和判断；90年代后半期天津市利用外资的任务、思路和实施策略。该课题为天津市利用外资的基本政策提供理论依据，并为实际工作提供利用外资的新方式、新方法。

1998～1999年，科学学所完成"知识经济与天津市产业发展的对策研究"课题。为迎接21世纪的到来，天津市作为直辖市和中国北方重要的经济中心，面向21世纪的发展必须走依靠知识经济之路。课题研究提出依靠知识经济发展天津市高新技术产业、依靠知识经济改造天津市传统产业等两大战略方向，并研究分析发展知识经济与培养和吸纳人才、造就职业企业家的内在关系，还就天津市高新技术产业和传统产业发展以及人才队伍培养提出一整套有针对性、操作性的对策措施。

2005年，南开大学环境与社会发展研究中心完成的"天津市循环经济发展战略研究"课题，在对国内外循环经济理论和实践进行比较研究以及对天津市循环经济发展状况进行深入调研的基础上，结合天津实际，为天津市发展循环经济提出既具前瞻性又切实可行的战略思路和战略措施。

（二）综合性产业发展研究

1995年，由天津市经济发展研究所、评价中心、南开大学经济研究所协作完成的"天津市跨世纪战略产业选择研究"，以产业结构演进理论为根据，重点分析天津市产业结构特别是支柱产业的现状，研究提出选择战略产业的依据、标准及指标体系，跨世纪战略产业的目标选择以及培育和发展战略产业的主要对策等。课题以建成北方经济中心为目标，对天津市现有产业结构和支柱产业的综合评价，指出已有支柱产业的局限性和不完善性，提出在三次产业中均衡地选择战略产业及其意义，阐明发展跨世纪战略产业需要统一认识等方面问题，强调支柱产业的更替和连续性问题。

1995～1996年，国家海洋信息中心承担的"天津市海洋产业发展及其关键技术研究"，综合分析评价天津海洋资源开发潜力和天津海洋产业及其技术发展现状，指出天津海洋产业在天津经济发展中的地位作用、产业结构变化及存在的主要问题，提出天津海洋产业发展战备目标和港口海运业、海洋油气业、海洋渔业等应采用的关键技术。课题提出建立健全管理机构体系、制定海洋综合开发利用规划和有关海洋法规政策、依靠科技进步加快海洋产业发展、建立适宜的产业组织结构、大力培养各类适用人才等对策和建议。

1998～1999年，天津大学承担"加快天津市海洋产业开发的对策研究"课题。该课题对天津市海洋渔业、海洋盐业、海洋油气业、海洋造船业、海洋交通运输业、海洋旅游业等产业现状作出全面分析，并与沿海其他省市海洋产业进行优势对比，探讨天津市海洋产业发展途径。该项目设计并编制出1997年天津市海洋产业投入产出表，从优势性、效益性、关联性、技术水平和重要度等方面建立海洋产业综合优势评价指标体系，通过综合评价确定天津市海洋产业中的海洋油气开采、海洋石油化工、制碱业、海洋货运及采盐业和港口辅助业等主导产业及一般产业。

（三）开放型经济问题研究

1993～1994年，天津财经学院完成“天津市出口商品结构研究”课题。该课题在深入调查的基础上，对天津出口商品结构的现状进行全面、系统分析，运用预测模型的科学方法分析世界市场出口商品结构的变化趋势，从宏观上提出对实际工作具有可操作性和参考价值的措施和对策建议。

1996～1997年，南开大学完成“利用跨国公司投资加快天津支柱产业发展研究”课题。该课题重点开展以下研究：利用跨国公司投资加快天津市汽车、机械、电子、化工、冶金、家电等制造业支柱产业发展的必要性、可行性分析，着重讨论这些行业利用跨国公司的目标和方式及应注意的问题；近年来跨国公司对外投资及对华投资的动向分析，天津市在利用制造业跨国公司投资方面的优势探讨与所面临的主要竞争，并提出天津市今后在进一步扩大利用跨国公司投资方面应采取的政策和措施。

1996～1997年，科学学所承担的“天津市高技术产品出口状况分析研究”课题，参照国际通行做法对出口的高技术产品做出界定。该课题从海关出口清单中分离出天津市高技术产品的出口清单，对1996年天津市高技术产品出口进行统计分析，并对1993～1996年天津市高技术产品出口状况进行对比研究。

2001年，南开大学经济学院完成“提高天津市国际竞争力对策研究”项目。该课题以实现天津产业升级、提高其综合竞争力为主线，在大量调研和统计分析的基础上，探索“提升天津新兴产业竞争力的对策”“天津高技术产业竞争力的战略选择”“增强天津金融体系竞争力对策”“天津新一轮国企改革取向”“以自行车产业为例的传统产业改造与升级”等问题，并提出相应的对策。

第二节 社会协调发展研究

1991～2005年，天津市在促进社会协调发展方面的软科学计划项目共有85项，占立项总数的15%，其中重点开展科技兴市、城市规划与布局、城市建设与管理、资源环境等可持续发展问题。天津软科学界在国内较早开展“科技兴市”战略研究，完成的相关研究成果与对策建议得到市委、市政府的关注。

一、城市发展战略与城市建设研究

（一）城市发展战略与规划

1992～1993年，市委研究室承担的“实施‘科技兴市’战略方针研究”课题，重点对推进工业企业技术进步、进一步加快技术引进和国产化、增强科研院所科技实力与活力、充分发挥科技人员作用、吸引国内外优秀科技人才到津工作、提高天津市城乡劳动者素质等方面进行专题研究。该项研究为“科技兴市”战略成为天津市委、市政府的战略决策提供了前期准备。

2001年，市政府外事办公室、中国社会科学院世界经济与政治研究所承担的“港口型国际大都市特征及对策研究”课题，借鉴世界主要国际化港口大都市的实践经验，在大都市的衡量标准、应具备的基本内涵和功能、环境建设及基础设施、政府发展战略和政策所起的作用等方面开展国际比较研究，并根据天津实际情况，分析天津的资源、产业结构、地理位置、应具备的内涵和功能等，提出建设港口型国际大都市的战略与措施。

2000年初，在建设部的直接领导下，北京市、天津市和河北省的100余名专家、学者开展“京津冀北地区城乡空间发展规划研究”课题，为实现天津与京冀地区的相互协调、共同发展提供了难得的机遇。在此研究基础上，按照建设部的要求，2001年，天津市规划和国土资源局、天津市城市规划设计研究院完成“天津城乡发展空间规划研究”课题。该课题从区域角度出发,从可持续发展和人居环境的战略高度,以整体的观念,探讨天津城乡空间发展中的问题,为天津制定城市发展政策提供实践基础,同时为城市总体规划的深化调整做好理论准备。

2005年,科学学所承担的“天津市建设国际创新型城市路线图研究”课题,是在中共中央将建设创新型国家作为面向未来的战略选择的背景下开展的。该课题综述了学术界对创新型城市研究的相关理论、各个创新国家或地区的实践;构建了创新型城市的理论体系,涉及创新型城市的概念、特征、发展模式、系统要素、评价指标等;着重在对天津城市经济社会发展的基本特征判断基础上,研究提出天津创新型城市的模式选择、目标路线图、基本要素构成路线图、基本指标路线图和相关政策导向。

(二)城市建设与管理研究

1996~1997年,天津市电子振兴领导小组办公室承担的“天津市城市信息基础设施建设规划研究”课题,以建设国际化大都市为标准,就如何规划和实施天津市的信息化进程、搞好信息基础设施建设开展深入研究。课题通过深入调查研究和专家审议,提出天津市信息基础设施建设规划,包括通信网络、计算机及应用系统、数据库、图像库及信息资源库等方面的统筹规划。

2001年,天津社会科学研究院、南开大学协作开展“数字天津与国内数字化城市的比较研究”课题。该项目以天津市的信息化建设为背景,通过对城市信息化建设指标体系的对比研究以及建设规划、建设思路和特色的对比,对“数字城市”的功能组成、发展阶段以及中国数字城市建设中普遍存在的利弊问题进行分析,研究归纳和总结数字城市建设的要点,为数字天津建设提出相应的对策和建议。

(三)重点区域规划与布局

1996年,天津开益国际咨询研究中心承担完成“天津市开发区跨世纪发展战略研究”项目。天津开发区自1984年起,各项事业取得快速发展,成为天津市最大、最强有力的新的经济增长点,而且在全国发展中居于前列。该课题通过开展完善天津开发区的功能等问题的咨询研究,为天津开发区今后10年发展战略提供科学依据和切实可行的咨询方案。

1996年,天津市滨海新区办公室组织承担“中外合作研制滨海新区战略发展规划”项目。该课题采用国际上先进的技术手段,对滨海新区不同发展模式进行的比较研究;滨海新区2000年及2010年发展前景的分析、预测;从战略的高度对滨海新区的土地利用、产业布局、基础设施、人口状况、环境保护等方面进行政策研究,为领导决策提供参考性意见。

2005年,天津工业大学承担“滨海新区研发与转化基地建设及与环渤海区域互动战略的研究”课题。同年,天津市科学技术信息研究所完成“加快‘三区一带’建设的思路研究”课题。

二、可持续发展问题研究

(一)人口、资源、环境与经济协调发展

1991年,天津市海岸带公司完成“天津市资源、环境、经济和技术数据手册”研究与编制。该课题通过汇集整理沿海社会科学、自然科学的经济及技术的真实数据与资料,研究指标的分类汇总,补充现状调查并进行筛选、核实,在此基础上进行必要的分析,为领导决策提供及时而可靠的依据,同时为适应海洋数据库建设需要打下基础。编辑出版的《天津市海洋与海岸经济技术的数据手册》,融自然、经济、科技于一体,是第一本独具海洋特色的综合性统计资料实用工具书,对天津经济发展与城市建设具有参考价值。

1992~1993年,天津市人口普查办公室、南开大学数学研究所承担的“天津市未来50年人口发展趋势及其对社会经济的影响”课题,立足天津市跨世纪之际的人口发展趋势及其对社会经济影响,分析预示未来50年人口结构的变化过程,依据人力资源理论和生产函数理论,建立人口—经济计量经济学模型和人口—经济流动力学模型,从而形成以人口与经济发展、人口增长对经济发展的影响,促进人口与经济协调发展的对策为核心的分析成果。该课题论证了天津市实现“经济起飞”的可能性及其人力资源的保证程度,说明了人口问题对未来经济发展的相对制约作用和未雨绸缪的对策。

1994年，科学学所完成“人口、资源、环境与经济发展问题研究”课题。该课题重点分析天津市实现经济可持续发展的人口、资源、环境现状和趋势，提出天津市实现可持续发展主要战略目标、规划思路和政策措施。同时，分别研究提出了人口流动与人才、资源合理开发与保护，环境治理与改善等方面的专项对策。课题强调要依靠科技进步的整体优势，发挥软硬科技的作用，辩证地、积极地对待人口、资源、环境与经济发展的关系，趋利避害，为天津经济发展提供支撑和保障。

（二）人口、资源、环境专项问题研究

2000年，评价中心完成“天津市开发利用清洁能源的战略研究”课题。该课题从天津市现有的能源结构和近中期能源建设工程（项目）入手，分析及预测天津市能源利用的现状和前景，提出以开发利用好天然气和地热等清洁能源为主线，逐步调整和优化天津传统能源结构，不断增加清洁能源利用的比例的优化天津能源的总体设想，在此基础上针对天津市经济和能源协调发展提出若干具有可操作性的对策建议。

同年，天津市环境保护科学研究院完成“实施环境无害化技术转移的对策研究”项目。该课题通过对环境无害化技术的需求、实施无害化技术的障碍及问题、开展环境无害化技术转移的有利条件等现状进行分析，提出环境无害化技术转移的对策，同时建立“天津市环境无害化技术信息库”。

2004～2005年，天津市医学信息研究所承担“天津市卫生与人口健康中的重大科技问题研究”课题。该课题为天津市中长期科技发展规划战略课题之一，对天津市公共卫生突发事件应急处理体系建设；重大疾病以及伤害预防、控制技术；天津市公共卫生信息体系建设；建设小康社会，健康城市的健康指标及其评价体系；生物安全与病原生物监测体系建设等方面开展系统研究，其成果纳入天津市中长期科技发展规划纲要中。

第三节 高新技术及产业发展研究

在促进高新技术及产业发展方面，天津市软科学计划项目重点从技术、产品、企业、产业化等不同层面开展开拓性研究，促进高新技术产业的发展。主要研究的问题包括：高新技术产品调查及其跟踪研究、高新技术企业规模化发展研究、高新技术产业带与科技园区研究、重点领域高新技术产业化研究等。

一、促进高新技术与高新技术企业发展研究

（一）高新技术与产品研究

1993年，科学学所承担“天津市高新技术产品现状调查与发展对策研究”课题，对全市1009个企业、1489项高新技术产品的17项相关指标进行系统调查和分析，在此基础上总结归纳出天津市高新技术产业发展特点及存在的主要问题，并提出天津高新技术产业发展战略与措施。

1994～1995年，评价中心承担“天津市跨世纪经济发展的关键技术”课题。该课题对20世纪90年代以来世界各国把产业技术的发展作为国家科技政策的焦点和核心这一国际趋势进行深入的分析，阐明开展地区性跨世纪经济发展关键技术选择的战略意义及其紧迫性；对天津市关键技术的含义作出界定，从地区性、实用性、相关性、时间性与网络性等方面提出天津市关键技术的特点和选择准则，建立筛选关键技术的评价指标体系和综合评价方法；对天津市众多学科、技术门类的产业技术的发展现状进行深入调研，在此基础上建立技术项目备选库；参照国际上通用的方法，设计出严谨的初选和复选程序，在200多名高层次专家的广泛、反复参与下，采用专家辅助决策综合评价等科学方法和手段，进行数据综合处理，筛选出作为近期重点开发的领域及其关键技术。该课题获得1995年度天津市科技进步二等奖。

2002年，科学学所承担系列高新技术产业领域的发展动态跟踪研究项目，涉及电子信息产业、环保产

业、光机电一体化产业、新材料与新能源产业等。

2005年，科学学所、天津大学化工学院，天津农学院联合开展“生物技术领域技术预见研究”课题。天津市开展生物技术领域的技术预见工作是组织、方法上的一种有效探索。课题详细阐述技术预见和生物技术相关概念及其发展情况，结合天津生物产业发展的现状和需求，揭示天津市开展生物技术预见的重要性和必要性。课题主要采用情景分析与专家访谈相结合的方法，对天津市生物技术领域未来10年的发展方向作出基本判断，研究出较详细的可供选择的技术项目清单。

（二）高新技术企业发展研究

1997年，科学学所完成的“天津市高新技术企业规模化发展思路研究”课题，调查天津市高新技术企业发展现状，剖析规模化发展前景、优势和影响天津市高新技术企业规模化发展的制约因素，总结了发达国家高新技术企业规模化发展的基本规律。在以上研究的基础上，按照天津市有优势的高新技术领域，筛选重点扶植的高新技术企业，提出重点扶植高新技术企业和当前推动高新技术企业规模化的举措与对策。

1999～2000年，天津大学承担“关于促进高新技术企业进入资本市场的对策研究”课题。该课题从高新技术企业和资本市场发展的现状出发，提出促进天津市的高新技术企业与资本市场的有效结合并实现高新技术产业化的总体思路，并通过案例对比分析，找出高新技术企业进入资本市场所面临的困难和瓶颈问题，提出对策与具体可行的实施办法。

2000年，评价中心承担的“天津市利用科技型中小企业创新基金现状及对策研究”课题，总结从国家创立基金以来天津市中小企业获得该基金支持的情况，分析创新基金在天津市中小企业创建及成长过程中起到的重要作用，并就今后如何获得基金支持提供对策建议。

2002年，天津市科技信息研究所（以下简称“信息所”）、市政府经济体制改革办公室共同承担的“高新技术企业实施股权激励机制的对策研究”课题，围绕产权制度的创新；把按劳分配和要素按贡献分配结合起来，实施股票期权等多种分配方式；建立有效激励和约束机制等问题开展深入研究。课题提出高新技术企业实施股权激励机制应处理好的若干关系。

二、促进高新技术产业发展研究

（一）高新技术产业基地建设研究

1992～1993年，市科委规划预测处牵头，组织有关单位及专家开展“京津塘高速公路高新技术产业带（天津段）发展研究”课题，对产业带建设的发展条件、发展规模、基础设施建设、总体规划及配套政策等进行系统、深入的研究，为高新技术产业带的高起步、高起点建设提供总体方案和实际措施，论证产业带的必要性和可行性，为国家和天津市有关决策提供科学的依据。该课题依据区域经济学、产业经济学、技术经济学等基础原理，提出实现产业带建设的重要途径、基本步骤、阶段目标。在管理模式上，提出建立产业带京津冀联合管理新体制和运行机制，对产业带建设中政府的作用，产业带的经营主体，产业带的企业环境，产业带建设的财政、金融支持，产业带的人力资本投资，产业带的法规体系设计等方面进行深入的研究，提出许多可操作性的对策建议。研究成果引起社会各界的重视，《光明日报》《科技日报》《瞭望周刊》和中央电视台等进行了专题报道。该课题获得1994年度天津市科技进步一等奖。

1997年，市委研究室完成的“天津市新技术产业园区发展战略研究”课题，通过广泛深入的调查研究，进一步明确了天津新技术产业园区今后一个时期的主要奋斗目标、总体发展战略和基本工作思路，以及应采取的方针、政策和主要举措。课题还下设子课题开展了专题深入调研。该课题获得1998年度天津市科技进步二等奖。

2005年，科学学所、天津大学共同完成北京市招标项目“京津软件产业共同体发展规划”课题。该课题分析了建立京津软件产业共同体的背景与意义，并在调查研究的基础上，总结了京津软件产业各自的优势和不足，提出京津软件产业发展规划思路，给出京津软件产业共同体建设的重点任务。

（二）高新技术产业发展研究

1999年，科学学所完成"天津市高新技术产业发展的若干重大问题研究"课题。该课题通过对影响高新技术产业化的若干重大问题的调查研究，找出主要问题及其症结，提出跨世纪高新技术产业发展相关对策及措施。课题阐明天津市高新技术产业发展要重点关注重点产业与一般产业、制造业与高智力服务业、政府与民间、高新技术产业与传统产业改造、引进型与自主型产业关系等战略关系，详细研究了高新技术产业发展的人才保障、资金筹集、基地建设和规模化、国际化、政策环境等问题。

1999～2002年，天津市软科学研究计划还支持开展了一批高新技术产业的重点行业的发展战略研究。其中主要有：1999～2000年，评价中心承担完成"天津市HDTV发展模式和实施方案研究"课题；2000年，科学学所、天津工业大学共同承担完成"天津市高性能绿色电池产业化发展战略研究"；2000～2001年，国家药品监督管理局、天津药物研究院承担完成"天津市中药现代化发展的对策研究"课题；2002年，天津市专家协会、天津市光电子联合科学研究中心完成"天津市光电子产业发展的战略研究"课题；同年，中国汽车技术研究中心、信息产业部第十八研究所、评价中心联合开展了"加快天津市电动汽车和动力电池发展对策研究"课题。

第四节 科技管理与体制改革研究

科技管理与科技体制改革研究是天津市软科学计划项目重点支持的内容之一，研究的主要内容包括：科技发展战略，科技发展规划编制，科技政策与法规，科技基础能力建设，科技创新体系建设，科技体制改革，科技人才队伍建设和知识产权战略等。

一、科技发展规划与科学管理研究

（一）科技发展规划与计划研究

1999～2000年，科学学所承担完成"天津市科技发展'十五'计划和15年规划思路研究"课题。该课题根据科技部和市政府编制天津市科技发展"十五"计划和2015年长远规划纲要的部署和要求，回顾总结"九五"计划执行情况和过去10年科技发展成就与面临的问题与挑战；提出今后科技工作的指导思想，依照国际科技竞争力指标体系、实现科学技术现代化目标的要求和科技发展趋势，并提出今后15年和"十五"期间的科技发展奋斗目标；提出"十五"期间重点科技任务，以及相应的保障措施与条件。研究成果对编制《天津市科技发展"十五"计划与2015年长远规划纲要》起到支撑作用。

2001年，天津财经学院完成的"天津市科技计划项目资金预算评估制度研究"课题，对天津市科技计划项目资金预算评估系统存在的主要问题进行分析，确定评估原则和预算评估内容，分析各种评估方法实行的成本、潜在困难和预期效果，对预算评估组织体系、评估流程、预算评估数据文件进行设计，并根据预算评估的具体需要和在实际评估中所发现的问题构建专家数据库，开发出一套可行、简便、高效的预算评估专家数据库管理软件。

（二）科技政策与法规研究

1994～1995年，天津科技风险投资公司、天津大学管理系承担完成"科技风险投资运作的研究"课题。该课题对国内外科技风险投资的现状及发展趋势和天津科技风险投资的环境条件、运行机制与相关政策、资金来源构成、体制与运行机制、项目来源与信息网络的建设等开展全面研究与方案设计，从理论和实践上探索一套适应中国国情的科技风险投资运作模式，对指导天津市风险投资行业的起步与发展，推动科技成果的商品化、产业化具有积极意义。

1996～1997年，科学学所承担“天津市促进科技成果转化立法研究”课题。为落实1996年5月全国人大颁布的《促进科技成果转化法》，进一步全面规范科技成果转化的行为，该课题调研分析天津市科技成果转化政策法规的现状、国内有关省市科技成果转化地方法规制定情况和国外技术转移、技术创新法规可借鉴经验，以成果转化的重点环节为主线，进行促进成果转化为突破性政策法规研究，起草《天津市实施〈促进科技成果转化法〉办法》。

2000～2001年，南开大学、天津市人事局联合开展的“关于鼓励管理和技术要素参与收益分配的实施方案研究”课题，在对天津市企事业单位的专业技术人员和高级管理人员的收入分配现状进行调查分析的基础上，以现代经济理论和管理理论为指导，参照国内外的相关做法，为天津市这两类人员的管理和技术才能等要素参与收益分配，设计出实施方案。

（三）科学管理与方法研究

1992年，科学学所完成“天津市软科学研究的现状分析和预测研究”课题。该课题研究采用资料调查、统计调查、专家咨询等方法，并将其有机结合建立一套较为简便易行的软科学研究项目预测方法，在对大量的信息资料进行分析与研究的基础上，摸清了天津市1980～1992年的软科学研究的发展与现状，并做出客观分析与评价；拟定了切实可行的促进天津市软科学研究工作向更高层次发展的若干具有可操作性的对策建议。

1994年，天津大学完成“应用工业工程提高企业效益模式的研究”课题。课题主要成果包括：提出应用工业工程提高企业效益模式，从企业宏观战略决策分析和企业内部效率两方面研究提示企业效益的具体内容和方法；提出基于模糊影像图原理的企业战略决策分析方法，可以迅速判明所研究企业在战略上的焦点问题，并为制定正确的企业战略经营领域提供科学的评价；开展天津自行车厂降低财务费用的案例研究，包括“降价压库”的可行性分析与天津自行车厂生产系统管理与改造方案—冲压车间JIT生产管理系统的开发与设计两部分内容。该项目还针对“应用工业工程提示企业效益模式”在示范企业的研究结果，从该企业的战略目标、战略经营领域和战略措施与改进意见三个方面进行系统总结。

2001年，天津大学、天津财经学院、天津新技术产业园区海泰控股集团公司联合开展“天津市科技风险投资机制的研究”。该课题研究天津市风险投资机制建设构想，描述这一系统内各个元素（组织机构）的设计、基本功能、基本活动及其相互关系，以及系统运行所需要的资源及其计划、分阶段建设计划及其目标，为启动天津市风险投资机制建设提供可操作的方案。

二、提高科技自身发展能力研究

（一）提升科技发展实力的研究

1997～1998年，天津市经济发展研究所、天津市计委科技处承担“加强科研基础设施建设的对策研究”课题。课题组在摸清中央驻津科研院所、市属科研院所、高等院校、大型企业集团科研开发机构以及天津新技术产业园区等单位科研基础设施的基本概况和存在问题的基础上，研究国民经济和科技发展对科研基础设施建设的需要和重点，探讨增加投资和多种方式、多渠道筹措资金的可能性和可行性，提出科研基础设施建设的投资体制和管理模式的建议。

2001年，信息所、天津财经学院共同开展“提高天津市科技综合实力的对策研究”课题。该课题以全国科技综合实力监测结果为依据，剖析天津科技综合实力的优势和劣势，以及影响天津科技综合实力提高的制约因素和深层次的原因，从机制、体制和政策等方面提出切实可行的措施。

（二）科技创新体系研究

1994年，天津市技术市场课题组承担“北方技术交易市场建立与运作研究”课题。该课题根据国家科委同天津市政府联建中国北方技术交易市场的需要，通过调查研究，借鉴国际经验，着眼中国实际，深入研究探索技术市场建立与运作中的一些关键问题，包括市场模式、运作机制、组织分工与协调、人员配备、硬设施优化配置及软环境设想等。该课题获得1995年度天津市科技进步二等奖。

1995～1996年，科学学所承担完成“天津市工程技术研究中心建设规划方案研究”课题。该课题对国内外工程技术研究中心建设的理论与实践进行系统的分析和比较研究，对工程中心产生的背景、原因和工程中心的概念、性质、功能、组织模式、管理体制、运行机制进行理论概括；分析天津市工程中心未来建设的优势、基础和条件；从规划的基本依据、指导思想、基本原则、目标及领域选择等方案设计、建设措施方面提出建议；草拟了《天津工程技术研究中心暂行管理办法》。

1997年，天津市经济委员会开展“天津市支柱产业技术中心建设研究”课题，对国外企业技术中心的发展特点、运行机制进行深入的研究，介绍国内企业技术中心建设的发展状况、组建方式以及建设经验；分析天津市企业技术中心建设过程中的主要成绩及存在的问题，并对天津市支柱产业组建企业技术中心的需求、具备的条件做了抽样调查和统计分析，提出天津市企业技术中心建设的发展思路、规划目标、布局优选范围和分步实施方案。

2001年，科学学所承担完成“天津市科技创新服务体系建设总体框架与实施方案研究”课题。该课题重点研究国内部分地区科技服务体系建设的经验，分析科技创新服务体系发展的趋势，对天津市科技创新服务体系现状进行剖析，提出“十五”期间天津市科技创新服务体系建设的总体思路，特别是对如何加强各种科技服务机构的优势整合，更好地发挥科技服务功能开展重点研究，提出整合方案。同年，天津市科学学研究所还完成“天津市科研中心与工程中心运行机制的研究”课题。

三、深化科技体制改革研究

（一）总体科技体制改革研究

1992～1994年，科学学所开展“天津市研究与开发机构体系结构调整的原则与对策研究”。该课题提出，在社会主义市场经济体制条件下，天津市研究开发机构组织体系结构调整的必要性、指导思想和基本原则；通过对现有科研机构的认证、分类，依据各类机构的不同功能和特点，提出天津科研机构体系结构近期、远期的可能模式和初步方案。

1994～1995年，科学学所完成“天津市科技体制改革十年评价与深化发展研究”课题。该项研究提出，从1978年以来，天津市科技体制改革历程可划分为酝酿探索、全面推进、深化发展三个阶段，改革实践围绕思想观念转变、放活科技人员、科技与经济结合三大突破口逐渐展开，并取得明显成就。该课题还全面分析了改革和发展面临的形势和环境，指出科技体制改革与发展的新动向，并从战略高度提出构建新型科技体制的基本思路、策略、措施和工作重点。

（二）科研院所改革与发展研究

1991～1992年，科学学所完成“天津市科研机构外向型发展的研究与对策”课题。该课题通过调查天津市科研机构外向型工作现状，概述1986～1991年天津市科研机构外向型工作的现状和特点、趋势和问题，提出促进科研机构外向型发展的对策建议。

2000～2001年，科学学所承担“天津市社会公益类科研院所改革模式及配套政策的研究”课题。该课题针对社会公益类科研机构类别复杂、界定不明确等问题，进一步理清了全市公益型科研院所现状，总结出公益类科研院所在改革中的经验和存在的问题，并提出天津市公益型科研院所的改革方案以及有关发展措施，促进全市公益类科研院所改革积极、稳定地进行。

（三）民营科技企业发展研究

1992～1994年，科学学所开展“天津市民办科技机构发展对策研究”。该课题采用定量与定性相结合的方法，对全市民办科技企业的人员、经费收支结构、科研水平和管理状况等进行全面调查，在此基础上对全市民办科技企业的发展现状及相关的政策法规做出较为全面的分析，并深入探讨与研究天津市民办科技企业的管理体制，提出促进全市民办科技企业发展的对策及政策建议。

1998～1999年，天津市经济体制改革委员会开展“推动本市民营科技企业发展的对策研究”课题。该课题通过对全市民营科技企业的调查、研究，利用大量的统计资料和有关数据，分析全市民营科技企业所处的地位、现状、存在的问题以及发展态势，并从理论和实践的结合上提出推动、发展民营科技企业的战略性措施。课题成果制定的民营科技企业发展规划、政策法规等具有参考价值。

四、科技人才与知识产权战略研究

（一）科技人才研究

1993～1994年，科学学所承担完成"关于天津市专业技术人员流动的有关地方性法规研究"课题。该课题通过分析天津市专业技术人员流动的现状，对天津市专业技术人员流动立法的必要性与可行性进行深入论证，设计了专业技术人员流动的地方性法规体系框架。课题还重点研究草拟了《天津市专业技术人员聘任合同条例》，并提出天津市专业技术人员流动立法的实施步骤、对策和措施。该课题系在国内首次研究专业技术人员流动立法问题。

1994～1995年，中国民盟天津市委员会承担完成"培养社会主义市场经济急需人才的研究"课题。该课题在对天津市人才资源现状以及社会主义市场经济条件下人才需求和开发的新特点、新趋势进行分析，对重点领域急需人才的状况进行调查研究的基础上，采用定性与定量相结合的系统分析预测技术和人才预测方法，对到2000年和2010年天津市人才需求的总量和结构进行预测，在借鉴国内外培养市场经济急需人才有益经验的基础上，提出天津市加快培养社会主义市场经济急需人才的实施战略、目标评价、重点领域及对策建议。

1996～1997年，科学学所开展"关于培养造就天津市跨世纪学术和技术带头人对策研究"。该课题站在全国和天津市经济、社会发展的战略高度，对近几年有关部门、不同行业实施的一系列人才工程进行深入的调查研究，特别对世界范围内人才争夺的焦点、学术和技术带头人的基本特征和成才的基本规律进行研究，提出培养造就天津市学术和技术带头人的可操作性对策建议。

1998年，科学学所开展"天津市两院院士人才基础及产生机制研究"。该课题分析了天津市两院院士的现状；研究了院士级顶尖科技人才产生规律和机制，包括两院院士等顶尖科技人才产生的一般规律和机制、特殊规律和机制、时代特征等；对天津市两院院士后备人才基础开展调查和分析；按两院院士等顶尖科技人才成长的基本要求，提出天津市未来10年院士新增目标及相关政策措施。

（二）知识产权战略研究

1991～1992年，天津市专利局承担"天津市专利权属及专利实施对策研究"。该课题调查和分析了有关权属和实施的现状，开展了有关解决权属问题的对策，以及关于对职务发明的发明人和设计人的奖励的对策研究。课题还汇集全国部分地区法院和地方专利管理局结案的专利纠纷30余例，编辑了《专利纠纷案例》；汇集近500个专利项目，编辑了《最新国内外专利技术项目汇编》。

1998～1999年，科学学所开展"天津百种名牌和高新技术知识产权保护现状研究"课题。该课题组会同天津市高级法院、市专利局、市版权局、市工商局和有关高校的专家，集中围绕天津市百种名牌产品及高新技术产业中生物、信息、环保、绿色电源等领域，分析研究知识产权保护现状，并结合国内外知识产权保护方面的先进经验和教训，提出相应的政策建议。

2000～2001年，科学学所承担"天津市若干高新技术领域自主知识产权开发和利用研究"课题。该课题从全球视野研究探寻知识产权保护对高新技术发展的推动作用及其机制；深入调研并剖析天津市高新技术领域知识产权开发利用状况，包括高新技术领域知识产权的总体状况、高新技术领域知识产权开发利用状况、存在的主要问题和差距等；提出进一步提高全社会知识产权保护意识、建立激励机制、制定扶持政策等加强高新技术领域自主知识产权开发和利用的对策措施。

2005年，天津市国资委开展"天津市国有工业企业坚持科技创新实施品牌战略的思路研究"课题。该课题在坚持科技创新实施品牌战略方面，比较和吸收国内外尤其是发达国家及地区的成熟经验，分析天津工业企业实施品牌战略的现状，开展大量实地调查，提出天津市国有工业企业坚持科技创新实施品牌战略的思路和具体措施，为领导决策提供依据，为推动天津市国有企业开展科技创新和振兴品牌提供良好的借鉴。

第九章　高新区建设

1991年3月6日，国务院批准天津新技术产业园区（以下简称“天津高新区”）为首批国家级高新技术开发区之一，由服务基地、科研基地、北草坝工业区和科技贸易街四个功能区在内的政策区和华苑产业区、武清开发区两个产业区组成。天津高新区创建初期，从鞍山西道科技贸易街起步，重点发展包括创业服务中心在内的科研基地、鞍山西道科技贸易街和南开区大部分统称政策区。至1991年底，天津高新区高新技术企业发展到228家，技工贸总收入达到4.74亿元，上缴税金2416万元。

1992～1995年，是天津高新区构筑管理体制，不断改革和建立创新机制的阶段。此阶段，市政府把高新区发展列入天津市总体发展布局，作为全市加快发展的战略重点之一，特别是1995年5月天津市人大常委会第16次会议通过《天津新技术产业园区管理条例》，成为天津高新区发展历史上的里程碑。

1996年起，天津高新区将工作重点转移到华苑产业区建设上。华苑产业区作为天津高新区的核心区，是市区内唯一成片开发的高新技术区域，在电子信息、绿色能源、生物技术与现代医药、新材料和先进制造业等领域形成具有较强创新能力的产业集群，一批具有自主知识产权的高新技术龙头企业迅速成长。其科技服务业快速发展，科技服务机构有近百家，涉及科技孵化、投融资服务、专业技术服务、科技中介和科技咨询5个重点领域，从业人员近3000人，资产超过30亿元。2000年，天津高新区完成国内生产总值和技工贸总收入均比1995年翻了两番。

2001～2005年，天津高新区进入“二次创业”阶段。天津高新区成为全国第一家“国家知识产权试点园区”，企业专利申请量年均占天津市企业专利申请量的60%以上。天津高新区以企业为主体、产学研结合的研发体系建设初具规模，拥有企业研发机构60余家，其中包括数家国家级工程研究中心和国家级企业技术中心，30余家市级企业技术中心，13家博士后工作站。天津高新区通过研发合作、引进专家、人才培养等多种方式，建立一批与中国科学院、军事医学科学院和清华大学、天津大学、南开大学等有紧密合作关系的高水平研发机构。一大批具有自主知识产权的高新技术中小企业在孵化器中茁壮成长，源源不断地为高新区输送“新鲜血液”，逐步成为支撑高新区快速发展的中坚力量，使该区逐步成为天津市集高科技产业、科技开发、成果孵化、技术贸易、科技服务、人才交流、信息集散于一体的科技新城区。此阶段，天津高新区继续保持经济快速增长的好势头，其中2003～2005年经济增长幅度超过35%，特别是华苑产业区经济增长幅度超过45%。

天津滨海高新区作为天津高新区的扩展区，于2006年由科技部与天津市政府共同启动筹建工作。该区规划面积36平方千米，分为集中新建区和政策区，即渤海石油25平方千米生活基地和空港物流加工区内11平方千米的中国民航科技产业化基地。滨海高新区作为滨海新区的经济功能区之一，以生物医药、高端信息技术、纳米及新材料、新能源、民航科技等五大高新技术为重点，以增强自主创新能力为核心，努力构建与国际接轨的研发转化环境以及高效并充满活力的科技创新体系，建立健全高水平的研发支撑体系、高层次的人才支撑体系、一流的创新创业服务支撑体系、多元化的投融资支撑体系、优良的制度与政策支撑体系等五大支撑体系，成为带动滨海新区发展的领航区。

第一节 创建新技术产业园区

1991年3月，经国务院批准，天津高新区成为国家级高新技术产业开发区。天津高新区规划面积55.24平方千米，按照“因地制宜，就地起步，分期发展，远近结合”的方针，重点发展已经成熟的高新技术成果转化。经过几年的建设，天津高新区初步形成电子信息、机电一体化、生物工程、新材料和新能源等几大门类高新技术产业的雏型，并逐步建立较完善的政策软环境。至1991年，天津高新区高新技术企业由1988年的36家发展到228家，技工贸总收入由1988年的31万元增加到4.74亿元，上缴税金由1988年的1.2万元增加到2416万元。

1992年起，市政府把天津高新区建设列入全市总体发展布局，作为加快发展的战略重点之一，从政策和经费上不断加大支持力度。天津高新区科技管理体制得到完善，并不断改革和建立科技创新机制。1995年5月22日，天津市人大常委会第16次会议通过《天津新技术产业园区管理条例》，以地方法规的形式确立天津高新区的优惠政策、高新技术企业的范围，更重要的是把各项行政规定从法律的高度统一起来。这一阶段，政策区经济主要依靠国有企业、科研院所和高等院校创办的企业为依托，产业区发展完全依靠武清开发区，以引进外资为主。其间，天津高新区经济的主要特点是：内资企业所有制性质以国有和集体所有制为主，企业规模普遍较小，抗风险能力差；外资企业以加工型为主；园区管委会职能尚不健全，缺少投融资平台，对企业的扶持以落实优惠政策为主。到1995年，高新区的高新技术企业增加到2222家，技工贸总收入实现67.05亿元，上缴税金2.06亿元，出口创汇3.82亿美元。

1996年开始，天津高新区建设实行战略转移，把工作重点放到华苑产业区开发和建设上。天津高新区步入稳定、持续、健康、快速发展，特别是华苑产业区实现跨越式发展。2000年，天津高新区完成国内生产总值61.58亿元，完成技工贸总收入296亿元，上缴税金14.13亿元，出口创汇9.12亿美元。

2001～2005年，天津高新区继续保持经济快速增长。至2005年，天津高新区完成技工贸总收入810亿元，是2000年的3.11倍，年均增长25.5%；工业总产值730亿元，是2000年的2.96倍，年均增长24.3%，占全市高新技术产业产值的32.6%；净利润28.5亿元，是2000年的1.75倍，年均增长11.8%；出口创汇20亿美元，是2000年的2.2倍，年均增长17.1%；上缴税金43.2亿元，是2000年的2.94倍，年均增长24.1%；生产总值208亿元，是2000年的3.37倍，年均增长27.5%。

一、管理体制

1992年，经市政府批准，成立天津新技术产业园区管理委员会(以下简称“园区管委会”)。其作为市政府的派出机构，对天津高新区实行统一管理，内设机构从3个部门发展到8个部门，服务职能不断充实完善。随着形势的不断发展，天津高新区的人才交流中心、人才培训中心、高新技术企业协会、园区报社(科技先导报社)以及会计师事务所、律师事务所、公证处、保险所等和工商、税务、金融等支撑服务机构先后建立，逐步形成科技管理与科技服务体系。1994年11月22日，市政府召开办公会议，决定天津高新区、华苑产业区和南开区所有高新技术企业的各项税收均由国家税务局园区分局负责征管。1994年12月27日，天津市财政局发布文件，确立天津高新区的财政问题：政策区内区级财政收入中，以1990年基数之内的作为南开区收入，比1990年基数增长部分作为园区和南开区共享收入，还确定天津高新区与南开区45∶55的财政分成比例；产业带辐射区财政纳入所在区县财政预算，按照适当比例上缴园区管委会。但是，园区管委会考虑到各个区县的积极性，一直未收取辐射区的管理费用。

1995年，国家科委发布《关于调整部分高新技术产业开发区区域范围和面积的函》，同意天津高新区实行“一区三制”管理体制，其区域范围调整为：华苑产业区起步区2平方千米，北辰科技工业园起步区2.35平方千米，塘沽海洋科技工业园起步区2.28平方千米，共计6.63平方千米，天津高新区总面积调整为21.85平方千米。同时，该文件还明确天津高新区调整的区域范围，北辰科技工业园和塘沽海洋科技工业园成为天津高新区的辐射区。

2002年，市政府作出决定，天津高新区政策区和产业区剥离，并将政策区移交南开区政府管理，进一步理顺了管理体制。同时，南开区政府撤销北草坝工业区管委会和科技贸易街管委会，统一成立南开区科技园管理委员会。至2003年3月，园区管委会将2094家高新技术企业移交南开区科技园管理委员会，以充分发挥南开区政府发展高科技产业的积极性。2005年，市政府对天津高新区的考核口径由过去的大园区调整为华苑产业区，从此华苑产业区的建设和管理走上规范化、系统化、科学化轨道。

二、建设主体

1992年，经市委批准，成立天津新技术产业园区开发总公司，为副局级单位。1994年4月，经市委科技工委批准，正式建立园区开发总公司党委。1996年3月，经市委、市政府批准，华苑科技开发建设有限公司的党政正职领导干部由市委、市政府任命和管理。1997年7月，经市委批准，正式建立中共天津华苑科技开发建设有限公司委员会。

2000年6月，天津海泰控股集团有限公司(以下简称“海泰集团”)成立，是园区管委会投资建设的国有直属企业，其前身是园区开发总公司和华苑科技开发建设有限公司、政通公司等重新组合而建立的集团公司。海泰集团依托天津高新区的自身优势，对华苑科技园12平方千米的土地进行统一的开发建设和招商引资，承担滨海高新区开发建设任务，对高新技术的研发和产业化进行风险投资和全程孵化服务，培育具有自主知识产权和国际竞争力的高新技术企业及产品，为高新区创建优越的投资环境和服务体系，在华苑产业区的开发建设中发挥重要作用。

第二节 增建华苑产业区

华苑产业区是天津高新区的主体产业区和中心区，规划面积11.58平方千米，其中环内2平方千米，环外9.58平方千米。其坐落在天津市区西南部，地处京、津发展轴，距北京100千米，距天津滨海国际机场18千米，距天津港50千米，紧靠京沪、津保、京塘高速公路，毗邻京沪高速铁路，周边有南开大学、天津大学等13所高等院校，拥有雄厚的科技教学力量。园区管委会依法对华苑产业区实行全面行政管理。

1994年，天津高新区开始筹备华苑产业区环内基础设施建设。1996年，园区管委会将工作重点转向华苑产业区开发和建设上，并坚持高标准规划，多层次融资，高层次招商，全面完成华苑产业区规划征地、融资、招商引资、基础设施建设等任务。至2004年，顺利完成华苑产业区环内、环外基础设施建设，为进驻高新技术企业提供良好条件。

天津高新区在加强基础设施建设的同时，十分重视环境建设。2002年12月，华苑产业区ISO 14001环境管理体系通过中国环境科学研究院环境管理体系认证中心认证。2005年11月，华苑产业区通过ISO 14000国家示范区现场验收，生态华苑产业区凸显特色。

至2005年底，华苑产业区进驻企业2600家。2005年，华苑产业区实现工业总产值266亿元，是2000年的5倍，年均增长37.7%，占全市高新技术产业产值的11.9%；净利润7.8亿元，是2000年的3.2倍，年均增长25.8%；出口创汇7.2亿美元，是2000年的2.9倍，年均增长23.9%；上缴税收10.1亿元，是2000年的3.3倍，年均增长27.0 %；生产总值58亿元，是2000年的5.6倍，年均增长39.4%；财政收入13.2亿元，实现大幅增长；主要经济指标增长速度均比全区增长速度快10个百分点。

一、基础设施建设

（一）环内基础设施

1994年，天津高新区开始华苑产业区开发建设的筹备工作。1996年下半年，园区管委会实行战略转移，把工作重点放在华苑产业区的筹资、征地、规划、建设和招商上。是年7月30日，园区管委会召开加快华苑产业区建设动员大会，市委常委、副市长曲维枝，市政府副秘书长周思纯，市委科技工委书记武耀贤等出席。曲维枝在讲话中强调“要认清形势，落实责任，打好华苑建设这场硬仗。”当年，华苑产业区完成环内83.59公顷征地手续并办理土地证，完成环内2平方千米总体规划调整和环外8平方千米总体规划；实现融资1.4亿元，完成66.67公顷土地的“五通一平”建设；签订土地出让协议和意向11份，占地26.87公顷，回收资金1250万元。

1997年3月，园区管委会再次召开加快华苑产业区建设动员大会暨1997年目标责任书签订仪式，融资、征地、建设、招商等部门负责人分别与管委会签订1997年任务责任书，推动华苑产业区的开发建设。园区管委会坚持高标准规划，多层次融资，高层次招商，全面完成华苑产业区规划征地、融资、招商引资、基础设施建设等4项任务。全年融资3.36亿元，完成52.93公顷的征地和57.12公顷基础设施建设，签订18宗土地出让协议，出让土地42.04公顷，回收资金1.5亿元。

1997年11月，市政府批准华苑产业区环内街道名称命名方案。东西向为道，以“天、工、开、物”为头，分别加上“华”字组成道名。由于天津市已有天华道，所以不能以“天”字开头配以“华”为路名，只能成为“华天道”。南北向为路，以“桑、梓、榕、桂、梅、兰、竹、菊”为字头，分别加上“苑”字组成路名。

1998～2000年，华苑产业区环内绿化面积达21万平方米，并建成半径为21米的陆地喷泉工程。2001～2005年，完成环内主要街道的绿化工程，绿化面积115万平方米。

1998～2000年，华苑产业区完成梅苑路、开华道、物华道和榕苑路等绿化工程，绿化总面积21万平方米。同时，筹资建设环内半径为21米的陆地喷泉工程，成为当时全市最大的陆地喷泉。

2001～2005年，华苑产业区环内环外总计完成绿化面积115万平方米，其中环内绿化景观建设获天津市“街景绿化”优胜杯。

（二）环外基础设施

海泰集团负责华苑产业区环外起步区的开发建设。1999年12月，华苑产业区环外部分起步区第一座桥梁——华拓桥工程开工并完工，标志着华苑产业区环外基础设施工程建设的正式启动。2000年9月18日，历时15个月的白堤路（南段）道路工程全线完工，其全长1768米，宽30米，施工总面积达53957平方米，总投资3860万元。该项目由园区管委会出资建设，是天津高新区支援区县政府发展高科技产业的重要举措，为第二科贸街的发展打下良好基础，也为改善南开区的投资环境提供有利条件。

2001年，全面启动华苑产业区环外部分基础设施建设，并对华苑产业区环外部分进行规划调整，将原规划南北两侧备用地纳入规划范围，规划面积由7.8平方千米增至9.58平方千米，并委托天津市规划设计院进行详细规划。2001年6月，华苑产业区办理环外起步区246公顷征用手续。2002年7月，园区管委会分别与农垦集团、华庄村、杨伍庄等签订558.8公顷土地协议，并落实开垦方案，完成土地勘测定界，10月初上报国土资源部，11月底土地征用报批材料通过国土资源部审查。2003年6月15日，经国务院总理办公会通过，华苑产业区征用土地被正式批准转为建设用地。

2004年12月10日，市政府批准华苑产业区环外的地名方案，均以海泰为头，分别加上华科、创新和发展等组成路名。华苑产业区环外基础设施建设，为进驻高新技术企业提供良好的外部环境。

二、环境建设

2002年12月28日，华苑产业区ISO 14001环境管理体系通过中国环境科学研究院环境管理体系认证中心认证。至2005年6月底,华苑产业区连续3次通过外部审核。2005年11月,华苑产业区通过ISO 14000国家示范区现场验收。天津高新区提出"节约每一分土地,建设绿色华苑"的目标,要求进驻企业3年内达到每10亩土地实现产值1.5亿元、纳税500万元的标准。按照此标准,美国微软公司、美国波音公司、德国西门子集团、法国施耐德电器有限公司、日本丰田汽车公司、韩国LG电子株式会社等11家世界500强企业和中国海洋石油工程股份有限公司、海泰科技发展股份有限公司、天津大学天财股份有限公司、天津特精液压股份有限公司等国内8家上市公司先后进驻天津高新区投资发展。

在能源利用效率上,华苑产业区的产业结构是一种绿色的结构,其通信设备、计算机及其他电子设备制造业、医药制造业、专用设备制造业、电气机械及器材制造业万元产值消耗能源分别为57.8千克、306.1千克、210.7千克和173.8千克标准煤,能耗都有降低,具有可持续发展的优势。

在基础设施建设上,华苑产业区充分调动社会力量,环内部分2000年引进热源并于2001年拆除所有锅炉房,环外部分2003年开始引进热源,既节约了土地,又发挥了周边地区集中供热的作用。华苑产业区成为全市第一个没有烟筒的区域。

2004年12月8日,市政府批准华苑产业区环外322.899万平方米土地以国有土地使用权作价入股形式注入海泰集团。2005年6月,经国务院批准,天津高新区规划用地范围正式通过国家审核。经审核,天津高新区确定的总面积为5524公顷,集中新建区面积为4421公顷。

第三节　构建技术创新体系

2001年起,天津高新区加强高新技术产业创新体系建设,建立科技企业孵化器与火炬创业园,并开展三级孵化体系建设,制定实施技术创新3年规划,创建国家级知识产权试点园区,为促进高新技术产业的发展提供有力的技术支撑。

一、创新体系建设

(一)政策体系

2001~2005年,园区管委会为鼓励企业自主创新,优化创新创业环境,先后出台《天津新技术产业园区火炬创业园孵化基金管理办法》《天津新技术产业园区技术创新专项资金管理办法》《天津新技术产业园区鼓励高新技术企业申请国家专利的资助办法》《天津新技术产业园区创新基金匹配资金申请受理办法(试行)》《天津新技术产业园区鼓励风险投资机构和中介服务机构进驻天津火炬创业园的暂行办法》等一系列支持高新技术企业发展的政策,并设立火炬创业园孵化事业基金。为支持孵化体系建设,每年按照火炬创业园入驻企业纳税总额高新区留成部分3%的比例从该项基金中支出,用于扶持火炬创业园内各科技园开展企业孵化工作。2003~2005年,共拨款638万元,有力地支持孵化器的发展,为高新技术企业创新创业提供良好环境。

(二)研发体系

为推动技术创新体系建设,提高入区企业的创新能力与核心竞争力,天津高新区积极引导、协助高新技术企业建立研发机构,形成以企业为主体、产学研结合的研发体系。至2005年,天津高新区拥有企业研发机构60余家,其中包括农药(天津)国家工程研究中心、新型电源国家工程研究中心、电气传动国家工程技术研究中心、国家农产品保鲜工程研究中心等4家国家级工程研究中心,天津药业有限公司技术中心、天津天士力集团有限公司技术中心、天津鼎盛工程机械有限公司技术中心、乐金电子(天津)电器有限公司等4家国家级企业技术中心,还有30多家市级企业技术中心和工程技术研究中心及13个博士后工作站。这些研发机构每年都要承担国家和市级重点科技(计划)项目200多项,成为主导高新技术产业发展的骨干力量。

(三)服务体系

天津高新区按照面向社会、整合资源、集成优势、强化功能的思路,采用组建服务机构与引进服务机构相结合、服务机构入区与服务业务入区相结合的方式,加快创新服务体系建设,创造最优的创业、创新环境,引导企业加强产学研结合,加快科技成果产业化,促进科技型企业做强、做大。至2005年,华苑产业区科技服务中介机构增至近百家,基本形成以投融资服务、信息网络服务、咨询与培训服务、人力资源开发服务、技术产权交易服务、技术贸易服务、产品营销服务、知识产权服务、留学人员服务等八大服务体系为支撑的创新服务平台。

(四)信用体系

2004年3月,天津高新区成立第一家政策性信用担保机构——天津海泰投资担保有限责任公司,为有良好信用记录的国有、民营科技型中小企业的技术改造、技术创新、扩大再生产规模的贷款提供担保。至2005年6月,该公司为38家企业提供融资服务,贷款担保额突破3亿元,为高新区企业的发展搭建一个坚实的融资担保平台。2004年12月28日,天津高新区企业信用促进会成立,配合融资信用评估机构对25家会员企业进行企业信用评级,为园区各企业搭建一个良好的信用平台。2005年3月,天津高新区推行企业信用报告,为园区企业办理贷款、融资担保、争取各种政府资源、申请科技型中小企业创新基金等政府性资助和企业商务往来等提供一个高效的信用评估和信用服务的辅助平台。华正信用服务公司作为天津高新区唯一一家国有控股、多元投资主体的信用服务有限公司,通过引入国内信用管理的先进理念和科学方法,整合园区信用信息资源,开展客户资信调查和信用评价等信用服务业务。

二、孵化体系建设

(一)孵化器与火炬创业园

天津高新区创建初期,仅有一家企业孵化器,即由天津市政府和国家科委投资建设的天津市科技创业服务中心,孵化面积1.1万平方米。随着形势的发展,其孵化面积远远不能满足企业发展的需求。为进一步加大孵化力度,1998年天津高新区投资4300万元建设的国际创业中心投入使用。该中心是由园区管委会创办的公益性创业服务机构,孵化面积近2万平方米,初步形成以归国留学人员为重点孵化对象,以具有自主知识产权项目为重点孵化项目,以推动孵化器网络化、信息化、国际化为发展方向的孵化器。至2005年,该中心累计孵化企业274家,毕业企业102家。据统计,该中心有6项指标名列全国第一,即每万平方米孵化面积所创造的产值、利润和税收名列第一,每万平方米孵化面积的在孵企业项目立项数和专利持有量名列第一,每万平方米孵化面积获中小企业创新基金项目资助金额名列第一,每万平方米孵化面积实现的毕业企业数量名列第一,每万平方米孵化面积中建立产业化基地、购地及安排就业人员数量名列第一,每万平方米孵化面积中实现企业融资额度名列第一。

1998年6月,华苑软件园成立。该园是软件企业的专业孵化器,承担“天津国家软件出口基地”和“天津国家863软件专业孵化器”两个国家级项目的实施。华苑软件园坚持以“产业招商和重点企业培育”两项工作为重点,为软件企业提供“管理服务、公共技术、人才和资金”等4个支撑的工作思路,推动天津高新区乃至全市软件产业规模的增长。至2005年,华苑软件园累计通过认定的软件企业150家,占全市总数的65%;计算机软件著作权登记新增125件,占全市总数的58%;软件产品认定新增86个,占全市总数的72%。这一时期,天津高新区的孵化器建设以政府投资为主,以培育初创期科技型小企业为主的经典孵化器为主要特征。2000年5月,天津海泰科技发展股份有限公司投资建设海泰火炬创业园。2002年1月,该创业园投入运营,成为全国第一家由上市公司经营的科技园。至2005年,该创业园累计投资8.2亿元,孵化器建筑面积达34万平方米,入驻企业400多家。

同时期建设的还有3家企业孵化器。一是由天津高新区华苑开发总公司投资、2001年底投入运营的华科科技园。该园由厂房区、别墅区、办公区以及服务区组成,本着“立足高新区、服务企业、创新发展”的精神，为入驻企业提供服务。为进一步拓展科技园的发展潜力，又兴建华科创业中心，总投资1.404亿元，对厂房进行改造，建设规模7.8万平方米。二是由鑫茂科技投资集团2000年7月底投资建设的鑫茂民营科技园，2001年11月建成并投入运营，总建筑面积13.8万平方米。该园整合各种有效资源，为入驻企业提供管理咨询、投资与担保、科技项目申报等多项服务，并建立“企业信用共同体”，有100余家企业经过信用评估加入该共同体，24家企业获得2400万元银行信用贷款。这一举措引起科技部和天津市有关部门的高度重视，并被中国民营科技促进会评为“全国十佳民营科技园”。三是由南开大学允公集团2000年10月开始投资建设的南开大学科技园。该园作为国家级的大学科技园，充分发挥其整合园、服务园、信息园和虚拟园的功能，以培养和发展在全球化竞争中有持久竞争力和持续自我成长能力的高新技术企业，培养创新、创业人才，促进产学研相结合，推动区域经济发展为目标，采取“一园多址，多校一园”的多元化投资共建和功能呼应的办园模式，形成以IT产业为主的综合科技园、以新疆大学为主的西部地区大学虚拟科技园、以戈德集团为主的新型材料与防伪技术园以及生物信息科学园、环境与资源科技园和人才培训与孵化园。

2000年5月31日，科技部火炬中心与天津高新区合作建设天津火炬创业园的签字仪式在北京举行，科技部副部长徐冠华和天津市副市长梁肃出席签字仪式。至2005年，该园总孵化面积超过120万平方米，入孵企业1500多家，累计毕业企业145家；在孵企业中年收入超5000万元的企业4家，3000万～5000万元的企业11家，1000万～3000万元的企业48家，纳税100万元以上的企业57家，基本实现产业化的企业占在孵企业总数的5%，成为天津高新区发展的生力军。

（二）三级孵化体系

2001年起，天津高新区开始“三级孵化体系”建设，强调打造孵化器簇群和产业链，扩大传统孵化器的孵化范围，并以三级孵化服务为手段，以创业的初创期企业、成长期企业和规模化的成熟期企业为三级孵化对象，从企业初创期开始进行持续追踪，培育其进入二级、三级孵化，在孵化企业的同时，筛选优秀项目，进行产业投资，培育核心产业，通过核心产业带动中小企业成长，从而拉动区域经济的增长。一级孵化的重点是科技成果转化和小企业创业培育，主要提供基础层面的服务，将创业者的各种创业成本降到最低，进入创业园的企业不仅可享用这里创造的硬件条件，还可为企业起草章程，代办工商注册、税务登记、银行开户手续，以缩短企业创办所耗费的时间。二级孵化的重点是为一级孵化毕业的企业提供全方位的产业孵化服务及各种增值服务，包括专业技术、管理咨询、风险投资、人力资源开发、企业培训、产权交易等多项服务。三级孵化的重点是帮助具有中型规模的企业建立核心产业，形成产业簇群，由核心产业带动周边企业发展，提高区域经济的核心竞争力，实现项目的产业化聚集，为企业提供符合个性化需求的硬件设施，并为企业提供发展层面的投融资服务，实现巨量资金的融通。

三、制定并实施技术创新规划

2001年起，天津高新区先后制订《2003～2007年天津新技术产业园区科技服务业发展实施计划》和《天津新技术产业园区技术创新三年规划（2003～2005年）》。华苑产业区通过实施“技术创新三年规划”，重点推进孵化体系、服务体系和研发体系建设，为经济发展提供有力的技术支撑。至2005年，华苑产业区累计申请专利超过万项，科技创新使经济的运行质量得到提高，科技进步贡献率达到55%，万元工业产值能耗0.1吨标准煤，万元产值用水量2.16吨，节能降耗均处于全市较低水平。

四、创建国家知识产权试点园区

2005年，国家知识产权局正式批准天津高新区为“国家知识产权试点园区”。在天津市知识产权局的指导下，天津高新区制定《国家知识产权试点园区工作方案》，经国家知识产权局和天津市政府批准正式实施。2005年，天津高新区约5000人次参加知识产权培训，24家企业列入天津市重点企事业单位专利申请计划，7项专利列入天津市重点扶持专利产品名录；园区内资企业专利申请量比2004年增长67.7%；华苑产业区内获专利申请资助的企业专利831项，专利资助款43万元，分别是2004年的4倍和6倍。2005年，天津高新区拥有知识产权的项目共获得上亿元的各类科技立项支持。

天津高新区知识产权试点工作开展仅一年,产生两个变化。一是知识产权申请量快速增长。2002年高新区企业知识产权申请量1182项,2003年为1793项,2004年为2946项,2005年达到3353项,其中内资企业专利申请量达1426项,比2004年增长117%。二是企业申请专利的积极性和知识产权保护意识明显提高。2005年,华苑产业区24家企业列入天津市重点企事业单位专利申请计划,7项专利项目列入天津市重点扶持专利产品名录。

第四节 发展高新技术产业

为加快高新技术产业发展,天津高新区采取一系列措施,并从1993年起开展明星企业评选活动。在扶持、发展高新技术企业的同时,注重加强对国有老企业的改造,高科技产品生产规模不断扩大,初步形成以绿色能源、软件、生物制药、新材料、先进制造业为代表的优势产业和具有天津地方特色的计算机软硬件、通讯设备、电子元器件、家用电子电器、新药、绿色能源、特种电缆、精细化工、电子屏幕等10大系列产品,涌现出天津力神电池股份有限公司、天津赛象科技股份有限公司、鼎盛天工工程机械股份有限公司等一批高新技术企业,高新技术产业得到快速发展。

一、发展概况

1995年,天津高新区高新技术产品出口创汇仅为3.82亿美元。到2000年,高新技术产品出口创汇达9.12亿美元,是1995年的2.38倍。1996年,天津高新区技工贸总收入500万元以上的企业有198家,千万元以上的企业有111家,其中天津三美电机有限公司、中环电子计算机公司、德塔科技集团有限公司等15家企业年技工贸总收入超过亿元。1995~1997年,天津高新区连续3年获市政府颁发的内联引资先进单位。

至2000年,天津高新区入驻企业达4070家,其中国内投资企业3509家,注册资金42.1亿元;外商投资企业561家,总投资29.83亿美元;产值在亿元以上的企业有35家,年产值超过千万元以上的企业有200家;高新技术产品超过6000种,逐步形成具有天津地方特色的计算机软硬件、通讯设备、电子元器件、家用电子电器、新药、绿色能源、特种电缆、精细化工、电子屏幕等10大系列产品,其中年销售收入超亿元的有31项产品。天津三美电机有限公司的光盘驱动器和调幅器系列产品、天津日电电子通信工业有限公司的电子数字程控交换机、天津爱普生有限公司的计算机打印头、天津杰普智能卡有限公司的智能IC卡、天士力制药股份有限公司的复方丹参滴丸、天津兰吉尔通讯设备有限公司的IC卡电话机、天津金普斯新技术有限公司的IC卡加密技术、西门子电器传动有限公司的全数字直流调速产品、天津中新药业集团股份有限公司的新型中药制剂和天津大真空有限公司的音叉型水晶振荡子等产品,均跨入亿元产品之列。此外,年收入达千万元的产品有116个。外资企业投资者来自日本、美国、韩国、瑞典、新加坡等22个国家和中国台湾、香港等地区,其中法国益普生制药公司、日本电器株式会社、德国西门子公司、丹麦丹佛斯国际有限公司等一批跨国公司纷纷到天津高新区投资建厂,投资额均在千万美元以上。

2001~2005年,华苑产业区高新技术产品生产规模不断扩大,显示出很强的竞争能力。天津新巨升电子有限责任公司的能源信息自动集成管理系统及智能仪表产品处于国内领先水平。天津蓝天高科电源股份有限公司为"神舟"四号、"神舟"五号生产机载测控设备供电系统的配套电源产品,为"神舟"发射升空及返回过程的数据采集监控系统提供可靠的能源保障,为中国的航天事业做出贡献。天津南开创元信息技术有限公司的目录服务系统ITEC-iDS,是国内首套具有完全自主知识产权的LDAP目录服务系统,打破国外厂商在目录服务领域的垄断地位。天津中环半导体股份有限公司的高压硅堆产品产销量居世界第二,国内第一，国际市场占有率达17%，国内市场占有率达43%。天津宏大纺织机械有限公司是国内生产时间最早、品种规格最齐、市场占有率最高的企业，研制和生产各类粗纱机和络筒机两大系列产品，技术水平和市场占有率全国第一。天津市企之星信息技术有限公司开发的大型企业管理软件“企星MRP_II”“企星ERP”，在国内有很大知名度，被国家五部委评为国家级重点新产品，是科技部测评通过的六大ERP产品软件之一。天津南开和成科技有限公司开发的固相合成载体树脂和药用吸附树脂两大系列产品，占国际市场的绝大部分份额，同时向国内50多家厂商供货。天津绿达保鲜工程技术有限公司的微型节能保鲜库、系列果蔬保鲜膜、保鲜剂、果实袋等四大类产品，辐射到全国各省、市、自治区，葡萄保鲜剂在国内市场占60%以上的份额。天津市海量科技发展有限公司的核心产品“中文分词软件包”“中文全文检索软件包”，在市场得到客户的高度评价，与微软中国公司、北大方正等著名公司签订长期合作协议。天津津科电子公司的阅读不耗电的类纸电子书等多个项目，获得市级科学技术奖励；天津赛象科技有限公司总经理张之泉研制的轮胎子午线项目，获得天津市技术发明奖；天津鼎名密封有限公司王玉明研制的高参数离心机密封技术，获得4项国家专利和2项美国注册专利，其领衔研究的“干式气体密封”和“组合式螺旋浮环密封”两项成果为国内首创，分别获得国家科技进步二等奖和天津市技术发明二等奖。

高科技产品生产规模的不断扩大，使越来越多的企业跨入纳税超过100万元的行列，成为纳税大户。2002年，在华苑产业区经营的纳税大户为42家，2003年为48家，2004年为83家，2004年是2002年的近2倍。纳税大户为天津高新区所作的贡献越来越大。

二、优势产业

2001～2005年，华苑产业区优势产业得到快速发展，初步形成以绿色能源、软件、生物制药、新材料、先进制造业为代表的优势产业群的特点。绿色能源产业基本连接成相对完整合理的产业链，形成天津力神电池有限公司、和平海湾电源集团等龙头企业，绿色能源产业的可持续创新能力较强，其技术水平、产品门类、投资强度、市场占有率均在国内处于领先地位。软件产业蓬勃发展，特别是软件出口处于国内领先地位，华苑软件园被国家发改委、商务部等部委联合授予“国家软件出口基地”。该基地汇聚全市51%的软件企业，销售收入超过全市软件出口的50%，在对美、日软件出口上具有较强的优势。生物制药和生物工程产业不断发展，干细胞技术在国内处于领先地位，国家干细胞基因工程产业化基地为国内唯一。新材料产业中，海泰超导通讯科技（天津）有限公司的高温超导滤波器产品制造技术达到国际先进水平，麦格昆磁（天津）有限公司成为世界上最大的粘结钕铁硼磁粉生产商。先进制造业在华苑产业区产业中占有较大的比重，其中天津工程机械研究院、天津宏大纺织集团公司等企业优势突出，德国西门子公司决定在华苑产业区建设其在全球的第二大生产基地。

三、重要举措

（一）主要措施

1991年起，天津高新区采取一系列措施，加快高新技术产业发展。包括：依靠优惠政策与创造良好环境并举，扩大吸引人才、项目、资金的数量和质量，营造创业氛围，为高新技术产业发展提供良好条件，在区域政策优势逐步弱化的同时，在强化创造园区良好的软、硬环境上下功夫，依法治区，与国际接轨。孵化企业与造就企业家并举，在扶持中小型科技企业的同时，制定相关政策，落实并保护创业者权益，激励科技人员、企业家创业，进一步增强高新区的技术创新能力，鼓励企业做大、做强，形成高新区品牌。政府扶持与风险机制并举，一方面依靠政府和高新区财政支持，多方筹集资金，建立以创业投资资金、科技型中小企业创新资金、创业孵化资金和担保资金等为内容的创业资本市场；另一方面与市场和国际接轨，在发挥高新区新纪元风险投资公司作用的同时，积极引进国际风险投资公司，在投资资本市场方面率先实现市场化和国际化，解决制约高新技术企业发展资金的瓶颈问题。扩大经济规模与提高质量效益并举,实现由注重招商引资和基本建设向注重创新质量和优化配置科技资源转移,由扩大建设项目向优化产业、创新环境转移,由产业分散向集中优势、发展特色产业转移。实现招商引资上水平,开发建设上水平,优质服务上水平,科学管理上水平,政企互动上水平,进而推动高新区整体上水平。构建和完善多层面、交叉型的政策体系,逐步制定并出台相关配套政策。建立、健全配套的支撑服务体系,形成面向高新技术企业的社会、科技、中介三大服务体系,完善建立投融资服务、人才交流与培训服务、信息网络服务、技术产权交易服务、留学人员交流服务、科技咨询服务、社会咨询服务、政府采购支持服务等8个服务系统。加大人才培养的工作力度,建立一套有利于人才培养和使用的激励机制,培养高新技术产业化需要的多元化人才和复合型人才,促进高新区科技队伍的不断发展壮大。增强企业的竞争能力,扶植一批能够完全溶于国际市场体系,按照国际惯例运作的高科技企业群体,进一步加强高新区信息网络建设,实现电子商务,为企业的国际化提供更广阔的空间。创建全国一流的基础设施和宽松环境,形成高品位的符合高新技术产业发展需要的生产、生活环境和与市场经济、国际惯例接轨的投资环境,形成对创业者具有吸引力的适宜技术创新的宽松的人文生态氛围。

(二)评选明星企业

1993年,园区管委会为加快高新技术产业化进程,决定开展明星企业评选活动。明星企业评选条件以企业技工贸总收入不低于500万元,技术性收入和高新技术产品销售收入之和大于技工贸总收入的50%。天津新星电子公司、天津爱普生有限公司、天津普辰电子工程有限公司、天津津科电子有限公司、天津铝合金电力电子开发公司、天津爱德计算机系统公司、天津大学制药厂、天津大学填料塔新技术公司、天津市华核新技术开发公司、天津市医学影像电子公司等10家企业成为天津高新区第一批明星企业。园区管委会奖励明星企业的总经理每人1万元。1994年,天津日电电子公司等3家企业技工贸总收入超过亿元,成为全国百强高新技术明星企业。

(三)改造老企业

天津高新区内共有市属工业企业172家,其中列为市政府改造国有大中型企业33家,中小型国有企业47家,其他类型企业92家。园区管委会在扶持、发展高新技术企业的同时,注重加强对老企业的改造,采取帮助企业利用存量嫁接外资、引导企业"一转机制、二找技术"、以"一厂两制"和"厂内特区"等形式创办高新技术企业等多种措施,历时4年将国有企业改造一遍。天津市中环计算机公司、天津市第八电子仪表厂、天津市显示器厂、天津中环半导体公司(原天津市第三半导体厂)、天津市第二半导体器械厂等8家老企业充分享受到园区的优惠政策,另外政策区内52家重点企业中有三分之一是老企业创办或参股的。1993年11月20日,园区管委会批准天津市第一轻工业局科技企业管理办公室为天津高新区工业系统二级管理机构。此后,天津市第二轻工业局、电子仪表局、冶金工业局、化学工业局、医药管理局、第一机械局、建材局和河北区科技贸易街等纷纷派出科技企业管理办公室进驻天津高新区。这些派出机构充分利用高新区发展高新科技产业的优惠政策和园区企业的新技术创办高新技术企业,衔接于工业局与高新区之间,为国有企业的改制、改造和技术进步做出贡献,也为天津高新区的招商引资扩展新渠道。

四、高新技术产业成果

(一)力神高能锂离子蓄电池

1997年12月,天津力神电池股份有限公司成立。其位于华苑产业区,占地8.5万多平方米,注册资本6亿元,主要从事绿色高能锂离子蓄电池的研发和生产经营。该公司以自身具有的自主知识产权和创新机制为依托,引进国外先进的自动化生产设备建立生产线,生产规模不断扩大。至2004年,形成2亿只锂离子电池的年产能力,具有圆柱型、方型、聚合物和软包装、动力电池四大系列100多个型号的产品群。2005年,生产电池9700万只,实现销售收入11.4亿元,同比增长144%;上缴税金4236万元,同比增长325%;全球市场份额为5%,国内市场份额超过30%,其50%以上的产品出口。该公司通过ISO 9002国际质量体系认证、ISO 14001环境管理体系认证以及CE认证、UL认证;2001年获得摩托罗拉、三星电子等认证证书,成为全国移动通信配套专项中第一家与跨国大公司实现合作的企业，并在北美、欧洲、亚洲等国家和地区设立分支机构，建立起覆盖国内和国际的营销网络。该公司建立具有国内一流水平的研发中心和测试中心，有科技人员近200人，并依托博士后流动工作站，与高等院校和科研院所建立长期稳定的合作关系，实现在自主研发基础上的持续技术进步。2005年1月，世界著名财经杂志《福布斯》公布的“2005年中国潜力100”上，天津力神电池股份有限公司名列第10位，成为天津唯一一家上榜企业。

（二）赛象子午线轮胎系列制造设备

天津赛象科技股份有限公司是一家从事高等级子午线轮胎制造设备研制开发的高新技术企业，研发生产的子午线轮胎系列设备达到国际先进水平。2004～2005年，该公司主要经济指标均居全国同行业第一，2005年销售收入名列世界橡胶机械行业第5位。其应用光机电一体化以及超声波、激光、伺服、阀岛等一系列高新技术，改造和提升传统橡胶机械制造业的水平，自主开发和研制20多个系列、80余种规格的子午线轮胎系列设备，年产多种子午线轮胎系列设备200余套，半数产品为国内首创，并取得40项实用新型专利和11项发明专利，技术和质量处于国际先进水平，整体技术水平在国内橡胶机械行业具有领先水平。该系列产品注册“赛象”和“TST”两个商标，其中“赛象”商标于2005年被评为天津市著名商标。“赛象”品牌的橡胶机械产品遍及全国，并出口到欧美和日本等世界著名轮胎制造公司，在橡胶机械行业和轮胎行业具有较高的知名度。

该公司拥有国家级企业技术中心、博士后科研工作站和191名高级科技人才组成的研发团队，每年都拿出年销售收入的10%左右的经费用于技术开发，使企业获得持久发展。公司相继承担30余项国家重大装备科技攻关项目，其中“轮胎胎面复合挤出联动生产线”和“全钢丝载重子午线轮胎一次法成型机”于1997年和2000年分别获得国家科技进步二等奖，并获得国家经贸委批准的国家级新产品1项，科技部等5部门联合授予的国家重点新产品6项，获得2005年科技部科技兴贸行动计划项目立项1项，获得天津市科学技术进步一等奖1项，取得发明专利4项、实用新型专利26项，取得计算机软件著作权12项。2005年，该公司开发成功全钢工程子午线轮胎一次法成型机等9个新产品，打破国外对中国的垄断，抑制进口设备对民族工业的冲击，并打入美、法、英等国市场，新产品产值超过1亿元人民币。2005年，实现销售收入5亿多元，出口创汇117万美元。

（三）鼎盛天工工程机械

鼎盛天工工程机械股份有限公司是天津工程机械研究院通过划转、收购中外建发展股份有限公司、天津鼎盛工程机械有限公司的控股权，更名成立的高科技产业化上市公司。该公司重组之后，集合“天工”与“鼎盛”两个著名品牌，总资产达到15亿元，产品涵盖铲运机械、筑养路机械、路面机械、混凝土机械等多种工程机械产品门类，具备为国内外公路建设提供成套施工机械的综合能力。其中，“天工”牌平地机，以系列全、档次高、配置多、具有自主知识产权的优势，成为中国平地机的第一品牌，引领中国平地机的发展方向与潮流；“鼎盛”牌摊铺机综合现代机电液高新技术，采用最优化配置，以卓越的性能、可靠的品质成为行业前3位的强势品牌；其他产品也在符合优良性价比要求的基础上，以高技术含量和附加值的特性全面进入市场，成为该公司重要的经济增长点。其产品的技术水平和价格在国内名列前茅，市场占有率达50%左右，还有大量产品出口。

该公司长期从事工程机械的科研开发和生产制造，积累丰富的设计实践经验，新产品、新技术开发项目运用CAD、CAM系统软件，采用三维设计进行模拟及相关分析研究，使产品始终处于国内领先水平。公司承担国家“863”计划重点项目——机群智能化工程机械、路面施工机械智能化和制造信息化、工程机械工况监测和质量管理技术研究等项目，研制的数控切割机、数控折弯机、数控加工中心、瑞士362数控齿轮磨、ABB焊接机器人工作站等设备投入使用，不仅有利于零部件加工精度、生产效率和可靠性的提高，而且实现制造体系的历史性跨越，从备料到总装的全部生产过程达到国际先进水平。

（四）获奖科技成果

1、获国家级科技成果奖励

1997年，天津市橡塑机械联合有限公司完成的“LM-X850，600轮胎胎面复合挤出联动生产线”，获国家科技进步二等奖。2000年，天津天大天财股份有限公司等7单位承担的“曙光计算机应用示范（天津）工程”、天津市橡塑机械联合有限公司完成的“全钢丝载重子午线轮胎一次法成型机”，获国家科技进步二等奖。2002年，天津鼎名密封有限公司“干式气体密封”项目，获国家科技进步二等奖；南开大学、天津市南开太阳高技术发展有限公司完成的“面向生物医学工程的微操作机器人系统”，获国家技术发明二等奖。2005年，天津鼎名密封公司完成的“螺旋式浮环密封装置”，获国家技术发明二等奖。

图2-9-4-2 干式气体密封圈

2、获天津市科技成果奖励

2000年，天津鼎名密封有限公司完成的“干式气体密封”项目，获天津市科技进步一等奖。2001年，天津大学、天津天士力集团有限公司完成的“复方丹参滴丸自动灌装线”项目，获天津市科技进步一等奖。2002年，天津津科电子有限公司承担的“阅读不耗电类纸显示电子书”项目，获天津市技术发明一等奖。2002年，国家（天津）农产品保鲜工程技术研究中心的“果蔬保鲜新技术推广”项目，获天津市科技进步一等奖。2004年，天津赛象科技股份有限公司的“TST—LCZ—3—80全钢载重子午线轮胎三鼓式一次法成型机”项目，获天津市科技进步一等奖。2005年，天津理工大学、天津理工产业股份有限公司的“高档有机着色材料的工艺研究与产业化”项目和天津大学、天津市天大泰和自控仪表技术有限公司的“数字式金属浮子流量计的研制”项目，获天津市科技进步一等奖。

第五节 培养和引进人才

天津高新区把培养造就大批科技人才作为推进自主创新的最根本任务来抓，为各类高新技术人才提供交流和服务的平台，努力打造高新技术人才的聚集地。天津高新区大力加强人才培养与开发的工作力度，建立一套有利于人才培养和使用的激励机制，拓宽人才培养渠道，形成多元化、多层次、合理多样的人才培育体系，鼓励有条件的高新技术企业与高等院校、科研院所联合培养研究生，鼓励高校到园区发展教育培训和职业教育的产业，鼓励建立博士生流动站，在高新区建立社会化的专业技术职称评审制度和人才成长与企业发展互动的双赢模式。天津高新区注重培养高新技术产业化需要的多元化人才和复合型人才，使高新区在推进高新技术产业化进程中，既有能进入国内外科技前沿的科学家，又有具有技术创新能力的发明家，还要有既掌握现代技术，又懂得经营管理的复合型人才，使创业者和正在创业的科技人员尽快成为一个合格的企业家，使高新区的人才队伍不断扩展、增大、成熟。

同时，天津高新区按照科学、创新的原则，加强行政管理队伍建设，不断提高人才资源的管理水平，建设高素质的行政管理队伍，再造天津高新区以人为本的区位优势，并以全新的模式进行运作，形成强大的吸引力和全新的品牌。

一、建立人才流动平台

1994年12月，为促进人才的合理流动，为天津高新区企业提供人才服务和人才需求信息的平台，经园区管委会批准，成立天津新技术产业园区人才市场，与园区人才交流中心合署办公。1995年1月，天津高新区举办首届人才招聘会。至1998年，天津高新区共举办30期人才招聘会，建立人才流动平台，为企业提供人才服务和人才需求信息。

2001年9月，经市人事局批准，在天津高新区成立天津市高新技术人才市场。该市场立足天津高新区，面向全市，为各类高新技术人才提供交流和服务的平台，努力将天津高新区打造成高新技术人才的聚集地。

二、人才引进

1997年起，天津高新区开展智力引进工作，先后组织企业经营管理人才和专业技术人才的出国团组10余批，分赴美国、德国、澳大利亚等国家学习先进经验和先进技术。1999年，天津高新区劳动人事局与开发区劳动人事局、保税区劳动人事局联合举办"首届三区大型人才智力交流洽谈会"，400家企业进场招聘高级科技人才。此后，每年举办一次，成为天津市具有品牌效应的大型科技人才招聘会。

2000年10月，为吸引和鼓励更多的高级人才到天津高新区创业、工作，制定《天津新技术产业园区鼓励高级人才入区创业的暂行办法》，为入区工作的高级人才提供住房、配偶就业、子女入学、创办企业和社会保险等方面的奖励、优惠政策。

2003年，在认真总结经验的基础上，天津高新区在"3年技术创新规划"中明确提出"人本智源"战略，把落实"以人为本"科学发展观及"人才是第一资源"的理念，提升为天津高新区"二次创业"重要战略的认识高度，重点加快建立与国际惯例接轨的高级人才引进、使用和培养制度，在高新技术产业、重点行业、重点技术领域、重点学科积极引进高层次的科学家、学科带头人、高技术产品开发人员、高级企业家和经营管理人才，并建立健全外国专家以知识、技术、管理入股参与分配的机制，积极引进海外高层次人才和团队到天津高新区创业，形成多层次的人才梯次结构。

2004年起，为促进高新区重点产业的发展，园区管委会先后聘请赵忠贤、甘子钊、周廉、陈竺等10名国内知名的两院院士和1名外籍院士为特聘专家，为天津高新区的发展建设献计出力。其中，聘请中国科学院、中国工程院院士陈竺、王正国、孔祥复、吴祖泽及外籍院士 Jacques p.Caen 等5位血液学及干细胞领域专家为特聘专家，支持协和干细胞基因工程有限公司的发展；聘请中国科学院院士赵忠贤、甘子钊、周廉等3位超导领域专家，支持天津海泰超导公司的发展。在天津两院院士何炳林、余国琮、李正名、王玉明等分别到天津高新区创办高新技术企业，成为高新技术产业发展的领军人物。

三、建立博士后科研工作站

2001年4月，经人事部、全国博士后管委会批准，建立天津高新区博士后科研工作站，同时批准天津大学天财股份有限公司、天津力神电池公司、和平海湾电源公司、园区开发总公司等企业在园区建立博士后科研工作分站。2003年4月，为加快高新区博士后工作的开展，加强对企业博士后科研工作站设站单位及在站博士后的管理，成立天津高新区企业博士后科研工作领导小组及博士后工作办公室，园区管委会主任庞金华担任领导小组组长，园区管委会副主任任学锋担任领导小组副组长，博士后管理办公室设在园区劳动人事局。至2005年，企业博士后科研工作站有13家，累计进站博士后18名，形成生物技术、电子信息、绿色能源和机械制造等产业特色的科研集群。

四、选拔优秀人才

2003年10月，经园区管委会推荐，天津高新区鼎名密封公司总经理王玉明当选中国工程院院士，成为在天津高新区成长起来的第一位院士。2005年9月，聘任王玉明为园区管委会总工程师。

同时，园区管委会认真做好选拔和培养创新型人才工作。2004年，任学锋入选"天津市131创新型人才培养工程"第一层次人选。2005年，经过严格筛选，天津高新区赛象科技公司张建浩、协和干细胞基因工程公司方健、巴莫科技公司黄来和等3位企业科研项目的领军人物，被市政府授予"享受政府特殊津贴专家"称号。

第十章　开发区科技

天津经济技术开发区(以下简称“天津开发区”)于1984年12月6日经国务院批准成立,1985年正式开发建设。1985～1995年,是天津开发区打基础的十年,以基础设施建设和招商引资工作为主。1994年,天津开发区设立科技局,1996年召开全区第一次科技工作会议,提出“科技兴区”战略,并建立泰达国际创业中心和留学生创业园。随着“科技兴区”战略的深入实施,天津开发区科技工作在全市科技创新体系中的重要地位逐渐显现。

1996～2005年,天津开发区在促进高新技术项目产业化、吸引高级人才到开发区创业、扶持高新技术企业发展等方面开展大量工作,设置机构,制定政策,建立载体,明确理念,形成声势。1999年,天津开发区成立高新技术指导委员会,并与天津大学合作建立天大科技园,成为国家首批15家大学科技园之一。2000年,天津开发区与南开大学合作建立泰达学院,开始建设国家纳米技术产业化基地。同时,出台《天津开发区促进高新技术产业发展的暂行规定》和《天津开发区鼓励高级人才入区的暂行规定》两项规定,建立泰达科技发展基金和泰达科技风险基金,组建泰达科技风险投资公司,为到开发区的创业者提供市场化的融资渠道。2001年,天津开发区修订并重新颁布《天津开发区促进高新技术产业发展的规定》《天津开发区鼓励高级人才入区的规定》《天津开发区鼓励风险(创业)投资的暂行规定》和《天津开发区鼓励企业孵化器发展的暂行规定》等政策规定。2002年,建立天津泰达小企业信用担保中心和天津泰达生产力促进中心。2004年,天津开发区继续完善科技政策体系,颁布实施《国家及天津市重点科技项目开发区匹配专项资金管理暂行办法》,形成以市场为导向,以大学、科研机构为支撑,以企业为主体的科技产业化创新体系。2005年,天津开发区高新技术产品产值达到1425亿元,高新技术产品出口额112.8亿美元。天津开发区高新技术产业连续十年保持快速、稳定增长。

第一节　科技机构

天津开发区初创时期,就设立分管科技工作的科技管理机构。其后,科技管理机构得到不断加强。随着“科技兴区”战略的实施,一批科学研究机构相继进驻天津开发区,形成一个由高校、科研机构以及高新技术企业组成的科技创新群体。这些科学研究机构承担大量国家及天津市的各类科技计划项目,为加快形成自主创新型区域做出贡献。

一、科技管理机构

天津开发区创建初期,科技管理工作由开发区管委会企业室负责。1988年,开发区管委会成立科技处。1994年,科技处更名为科技局,主管全区科技工作,下设办公室、科技管理科和专利管理科,与质量技术监督局合署办公,编制10人。其主要职责是:贯彻执行党和国家有关科技工作的方针、政策;拟定科技发展的有关政策和管理办法;制定科技发展战略和中、长期科技发展规划及年度计划;组织实施国家、天津市下达的各类科技计划；管理泰达科技发展金，审核各种科技扶持资金申请；认定高新技术企业和先进技术企业；管理科学技术成果，对重大科技成果组织推广应用；组织科技培训、科技信息归档和科技进步统计；管理技术市场，进行技术合同登记，组织和协调技术贸易活动；负责全区的知识产权保护工作，协助专利技术成果实施产业化。1993年，天津开发区在北京中关村设立联络处，联络科技部、教育部、信息产业部、卫生部等部门，为开发区引进高级人才和高新技术项目提供快速准确的信息。

为实现开发区管委会提出的将开发区建设成为全国一流的高新技术产业化基地的战略目标，1999年7月28日成立天津开发区高新技术指导委员会，其办公室设在科技局。高新技术指导委员会的主要职责是：对开发区高新技术发展战略与规划进行研究并提出建议；对开发区高新技术产业政策与人才政策进行研究并提出建议；对开发区拟投资的高新技术项目进行评估并提出决策建议等。

为加快信息化建设，1999年天津开发区组建信息化工作领导小组，并成立信息化工作领导小组办公室，负责全区信息化建设的日常事务。2000年3月，科技局增设信息化发展科，主要负责研究、制定促进开发区信息化发展的有关政策；进行开发区信息化水平调查、分析；组织编制开发区信息化发展战略和总体规划；管理开发区重大信息化工程等。2001年，天津开发区管委会进行机构改革，科技局更名为科技发展局，并重新调整科室，设立高新技术产业促进科、信息化发展科和质量计量与标准化科，人员编制为18人。

二、科学研究机构

随着“科技兴区”战略的实施，一批科学研究机构相继进驻天津开发区。这些机构集中开发区主要研发力量，承担大量国家及天津市的各类科技计划项目，促进自主创新型区域建设。至2005年，天津开发区拥有23家工程技术研究中心、11家企业技术中心和37家跨国公司研发中心。

（一）国家纳米技术与工程研究院

2000年12月6日，经科技部批准，国家纳米技术产业化基地在天津开发区正式成立。该基地通过建立人才、资金、技术和信息平台，与清华大学、北京大学、军事医学科学院、天津大学、南开大学等高校和科研机构、企业形成联合攻关、动态联盟的科研新体制，建立有利于纳米技术发展的创新机制，以体制创新推动技术创新，依托纳米技术成果，孵化和培育科技型企业，促进中国纳米技术及相关产业的迅速发展。在科技部、中科院、财政部、发改委等有关部门的大力支持下，2005年5月13日由国家编制委员会正式批准成立国家纳米技术与工程研究院。至2005年底，该院建成近2万平方米的研发平台，共投入1.5亿元人民币，配置400余台（套）世界最先进、最新型的纳米技术分析、检测和制备设备，财政部还提供3800万元的项目启动经费，支持国家纳米技术与工程研究院的科技创新。

（二）国家计算机病毒应急处理中心

2001年7月25日，经国家信息化工作领导小组和公安部批准，在天津开发区建立国家计算机病毒应急处理中心。该中心成立后，连续3年成功地进行3次全国计算机病毒疫情网上调查活动，发布3期中国计算机病毒疫情报告，引起国内外计算机病毒防治领域专家的高度重视。该中心完成国家“863”计划和“国家信息关防与网络安全保障持续发展计划”科研项目5项，发布重大病毒疫情通报数十次，病毒预报和病毒监控周报数百期，在中央电视台一套建立每周病毒预报专栏，在各种国内外学术交流会或刊物上发表论文30余篇。

（三）泰达生命科学技术研究中心

2001年8月，泰达生命科学技术研究中心在天津开发区成立。该中心由中国医学科学院血液学研究所与天津开发区管委会组建，主要从事干细胞应用基础研究（包括干细胞扩增、干细胞分离纯化和鉴别、干细胞相关基因调控等）、干细胞相关治疗产品研制、基因工程药物研制等。2002年4月12日，经科技部批准，正式成立国家干细胞工程技术研究中心。

（四）天津市电动车辆研究中心

2001年12月4日，经市科委批准，在天津清源电动车辆有限责任公司的基础上，在天津开发区组建天津市电动车辆研究中心。该中心集成和优化天津市在汽车、发动机、电池、电机等各方面的优势力量，吸引国家、地方及企业等多方面资金，引进国内外人力、技术和产品等资源，科研方向重点围绕纯电动汽车、混合动力汽车等领域，承担天津市"十五"重大科技攻关计划项目和科技部"863"计划——纯电动轿车整车项目。2005年，纯电动轿车整车项目顺利实现产业化，生产的112辆电动轿车出口美国。该中心秉承服务天津、面向全国、放眼世界的宗旨，致力于中国新一代绿色环保的电动车辆的研发和生产，为促进中国电动汽车工业的技术进步和快速健康发展发挥重要作用。

三、博士后科研工作站

1999年，经人事部批准，天津开发区企业博士后科研工作站成立。该站是首批在国家级开发区设立的博士后工作站之一，其采取总站下设分站的管理模式，分站建立在各个企业，主要集中在大型跨国公司和高新技术企业。天津开发区博士后工作发展迅速，分站数量以每年20%的速度增长。至2005年底，建立分站43家，建站领域与开发区产业结构紧密相连，覆盖天津开发区主要的支柱产业。天津开发区博士后工作站共聘请7名院士、10名国外专家和大批国内高校、科研院所专家，担任博士后导师。至2005年，天津开发区博士后工作站累计进站博士70名，其中在站博士后47名，培养出站博士后23名，出站后继续留在开发区工作的博士后占80%左右，同时还培养200多名硕士生、本科生等科研助手和后备人才，形成高水平、可持续发展的人才梯队；博士后共完成科研课题59项，其中国家级课题3项，省部级课题13项；企业承担的科研课题达到国际先进水平的15项，达到国内先进水平的26项；获得授权专利28项；5位博士后获得国家博士后科研基金。

第二节 科技成果与知识产权

经过20年余的发展，天津开发区形成一个由高等院校、科研院所以及高新技术企业组成的强大的科技创新群体，并涌现出一大批具有自主知识产权的高新技术成果。

一、科技成果

1990~2005年，天津开发区科技局组织鉴定科技成果120项，其中多项科技成果获得国家或天津市科技进步奖励。天津南大强芯公司在深亚微米的集成电路设计上突破90纳米SOC(系统级)芯片设计，抢占国内IC设计领域的最高水平，被信息产业部列入基础元器件的10件大事之一。天津市电动车辆研究中心承担4项国家"863"计划课题，开发出具有自主知识产权的纯电动轿车和客车，在国内率先实现电动车产业化生产。天津生物芯片公司搭建起生物信息学、基因组学、功能基因组学等具有国际先进水平的高端微生物检测平台，其中"重要致病菌检测芯片"成为国内第一个进入产业化阶段的具有国际先进水平的微生物芯片。天津膜天膜科技有限公司完成的"年产100万平方米中空纤维膜系列产业化示范工程"项目，顺利通过国家发改委组织的专家验收。博益(天津)气动技术研究有限公司研制的"汽车燃油供给系统测漏仪"，成为国内汽车生产厂家首选的检测设备，国内市场占有率达90%以上。

二、知识产权

天津开发区自1996年提出"科技兴区"口号起，知识产权工作不断得到加强。2003年5月28日，天津开发区在全市各区县中第一个成立知识产权局。该局与科技发展局合署办公，逐步形成知识产权管理体系，不断加大知识产权保护力度。天津开发区成为全市知识产权保护示范区。同时，天津开发区加快知识产权中介服务体系建设，成立开发区知识产权服务中心，开通开发区知识产权网站，建立专利信息检索查询系统,为区内企业专利的创造、管理和转化提供有力支持。在知识产权工作的推动下,天津开发区科技型企业数量迅速增加,科研活动广泛开展,知识产权意识不断增强,拥有自主知识产权的企业和产品越来越多。至2005年,全区企业共拥有专利1230件,其中发明专利434件;内资企业拥有专利898件,其中拥有10项以上专利的企业达到10家。天津生物芯片公司累计申请国内外专利105项;天津电动车辆研究中心开发出具有自主知识产权的纯电动汽车,取得14项专利,处于国内电动汽车技术的领先地位。天津开发区知识产权优惠扶持政策和法规体系建设日益完善,知识产权保护的力度不断加大,司法和行政两条途径协调运作,知识产权局、工商局、法院、海关等部门紧密配合,有效地遏制和打击知识产权侵权行为,知识产权所有者的合法权益得到保护。

第三节 科技园区建设与技术市场

天津开发区认真执行国家和天津市有关科技政策规定,推进科技园区建设和技术市场的健康发展。

一、科技园区建设

天津开发区自1996年投资设立天津泰达国际创业中心起,经过十年的发展,通过“双高”政策的引导和扶持,先后采取引进、合作、吸引社会力量投资等多种形式,建立不同形式和不同投资主体的各类孵化器和科技园区。至2005年,天津开发区各类孵化器和科技园区达到8个,包括天津泰达国际创业中心(留学生创业园)、天津大学科技园、泰达华生生物园、国家纳米技术产业化基地、泰达光电园、泰达软件园、开泰企业孵化器、中国绿色包装产业苑,其中泰达华生生物园于2005年被认定为天津开发区首家科技企业孵化器。此外,2001年,天津开发区与北京清华工业开发研究院合作建立化工产品研发、生产基地——清华工业园;2002年,南开大学所属的化工类产品研发基地、精细化工企业的孵化基地和产业化基地——南开大学化工产业园开始建立。2005年,天津开发区与中新药业集团合作的现代中药产业园正式建成启用,与金耀集团合作的生物工程工业园在开发区西区开始建设。同年,天津开发区成功申报国家(天津)通信产业园、国家(天津)片式元件产业园、国家(天津)集成电路产业园等3个国家电子信息产业园,成为全国唯一拥有3个电子信息产业园的区域。2005年,中国石油化工协会为天津开发区授牌“中国精细化工(天津)园区”。

为促进天津开发区各类科技企业孵化器的发展,自2000年出台“双高”政策之后,不断完善产业促进政策和科技创新支撑体系,先后成立天津泰达科技风险投资有限公司、泰达小企业信用担保中心、天津泰达生产力促进中心。2004年,天津开发区成立生物技术产业发展推动小组,并出台《天津开发区生物医药产业发展纲要》。2005年,天津开发区召开第二届科技工作会议,进一步推进科技园区的健康发展。

(一)天津泰达国际创业中心

1996年8月5日,天津泰达国际创业中心成立。该中心作为天津开发区技术创新链中的重要载体之一,致力于帮助新兴中小企业迅速发展,成功建立生物、IC设计和光电等3个专业孵化器,涵盖生物医药、信息技术、光电等高科技领域的尖端行业,为天津开发区培育一批颇具竞争潜力的高新技术企业。经过10年的积极工作,该中心成为转化科技成果、凝聚科技人才、培育企业成熟的高新技术产业的孵化器。2003年,天津泰达国际创业中心被评为“国家级创业中心”。

(二)天津大学科技园

1999年10月11日,天津大学科技园成立。该科技园是天津开发区和天津大学共同建设的国家级大学科技园。1999年12月3日,经科技部和教育部批准,天津大学科技园成为国家首批15个大学科技园试点单位之一,同时也是天津市第一家国家级大学科技园。该园占地13万平方米,建筑面积11万平方米,包括7万平方米的产业区、3万平方米的中心区和1万平方米的会议区，绿化率达到45%。2001年12月28日，天大科技园正式投入使用。经过近5年的发展，天大科技园建成一流的技术创新基地、高新技术企业孵化基地、创新创业人才聚集培养基地和高新技术辐射基地。天大科技园的建设和发展，得到各级领导的关心和支持。国务院副总理李岚清于2002年5月8日和10月13日先后两次到科技园视察，国务委员、教育部部长陈致立，市委书记张立昌等多次到此视察并指导工作。

在天津开发区良好的产业环境、政策环境、管理环境支持下，天大科技园以其优越的创业条件吸引大批项目，一批高水平的研发中心、工程技术中心和科技型企业纷纷进驻，使其迅速成为天津开发区最大的高新技术产业聚集地。至2005年，有近70个项目进驻该园，其中国家和省市级的研发机构12家，专业孵化器4个，高新技术企业30多家。园内工程中心和高新技术企业累计有100多个项目列入国家级和市级科技计划。至2005年，园内有博士后工作站近20个，进站博士30多人，累计引进各类高级人才300多人，其中两院院士10余人，长江学者2人，具有中高级职称的200多人。

(三)国家纳米技术产业化基地

2000年12月6日，科技部正式批准成立国家纳米技术产业化基地。该基地坐落在天大科技园内，建筑面积2万平方米，投入1.5亿元人民币，配置400余台(套)世界最先进的纳米技术分析、检测和制备设备，在纳米技术应用研发领域建立具有开放、流动、联合等新模式的10多个实验室，建成功能强大的公共检测平台和专业研发平台，并采用先进的LIMS系统——实验室管理系统进行信息化的实验室管理。该基地拥有研发及产业人员200余人，其中博士和博士后19人，归国专家5人，并启动国家“双百学者计划”，吸引国内外优秀专家加盟。该基地在科研体制上运用新的模式，形成“中央政府＋地方政府＋大学群＋国家工程研究院＋企业群”的全新模式。至2005年，该基地与中科院、清华大学、北京大学、军事医学科学院、北京航空航天大学、南开大学、天津大学等高校和科研院所合作，在电子信息、生物、医药、机械等领域搭建起纳米技术研发和应用平台，形成动态联盟、联合攻关、系统集成的科技产业发展新模式，其中2005年开展的在研项目20个，中试项目5个。

(四)泰达软件园

泰达软件园于2003年开始建设，2004年正式启用，是天津市软件园的重要组成部分。其坐落在天津大学科技园内，具备培育大型骨干软件企业和孵化中、小软件企业的条件，建筑面积3万多平方米。至2005年，有20余家软件和集成电路设计企业入驻泰达软件园，包括美国IBM、联盟计算机(ACS)、思捷思电脑(CSC)和国家计算机病毒应急处理中心等国内外知名企业，在计算机信息安全、数据库、电子政务、电子商务、外包服务、集成电路设计和IT服务等领域形成聚集优势。天津开发区互联网数据中心(IDC)坐落在泰达软件园内，由IBM公司负责运营和维护，可以为用户提供涵盖应用解决方案和应用维护管理的全方位服务。经过两年多的发展，泰达软件园初具规模，并形成良好的发展态势。2005年，园内企业实现收入总额5亿元，出口金额500万美元。

二、技术市场

1996年，天津开发区被市科委确定为天津市31家技术合同认定管理单位之一，开始建立技术合同登记、统计制度。同年12月20日，天津开发区召开首届技术市场工作会议。至2005年，天津开发区从事技术开发和服务的机构发展到1000多家，形成多层次、多形式的技术市场体系，技术贸易机构的从业人员发展到近万人。技术贸易机构逐渐由单纯技术中介服务向技工贸综合经营发展，技术含量从一般技术商品向高新技术产品发展，技术合同由技术咨询、技术服务向技术开发、技术转让等高科技领域发展。

天津开发区技术合同成交额逐年增长。其中，1995～1999年技术合同成交额共计1728.91万元，到2000年增至2172.52万元，比前5年的总和还要多400多万元；2001～2005年，技术合同成交额共18946.18万元，是前6年的4.86倍。

1995～2005年天津开发区技术合同成交金额统计表

表2-10-3-49

年度	1995	1996	1997	1998	1999	2000
技术合同交易额（万元）	220.14	300.89	300.4	405.58	501.9	2172.52
年度	2001	2002	2003	2004	2005	11年合计
技术合同交易额（万元）	2300.0	2200.0	3500.0	4000.0	6946.18	22847.61

第四节　信息化建设与科学普及

天津开发区积极推进信息化建设，建立并完善光纤传输系统及与电子政务、电子商务和数字化社区综合服务相关的各种配套设施，为建设数字化开发区做出贡献。同时，天津开发区依靠各级科协组织积极开展科学技术普及活动，取得卓有成效的成绩。

一、信息化建设

天津开发区管委会将经济社会的信息化作为覆盖现代化全局的战略举措，为加速信息化建设进程，提出“数字化开发区”的概念，通过建设和完善光纤传输系统以及与电子政务、电子商务和数字化社区综合服务相关的各种配套设施，建设数字化开发区。

2001年，泰达城市宽带信息网络正式开通。2002年，建成拥有308个机架、可容纳1500台服务器的华北地区最先进互联网数据中心——泰达互联网数据中心（IDC）项目，并启用泰达呼叫中心。2003年，泰达投资网、泰达企业在线网等网站相继开通。2004年，天津市电子政务专网滨海新区核心节点落户天津开发区。2005年，天津开发区成功开通数字电视，完成数字电视用户改造1.28万户。

至2005年，天津开发区的光纤网络建设实现光纤到路边，光纤到小区，光纤到大厦，宽带网覆盖全区，可提供光纤、局域网、ADSL和VDSL等多种宽带网接入方式，宽带网接入能力达到千兆到小区、百兆到企业、十兆到家庭。至2005年，天津开发区光纤长度3.05万芯·千米，通信管道3460孔·千米，城域互联网出口带宽突破40G，城域网主干速率达43G，接入宽带家庭1.17万户，接入宽带企业3270家。

2005年，天津开发区政府门户网、企业在线、投资网、人才热线等政府服务网站全年累计访问量达1592.83万人次，国际手机采购网、贸促网等电子商务网站全年点击量达306.60万人次，呼叫中心全年共接听电话31万人次。

二、科学普及

1992年，天津开发区科学技术协会正式成立，与开发区科技局合署办公。至2005年，天津开发区内的国有企业、民营企业、事业单位、中外合资企业以及跨国公司设立的外资独资企业等共100多家企事业单位建立基层科协组织。2003年，在中国科协召开的非国有企业科协工作交流会上，摩托罗拉科协做典型发言。在摩托罗拉的带动下，天津开发区很多外资企业相继成立科协组织。

天津开发区科协每年都举办一系列的科普讲座和技术培训。自2002年开始，天津开发区科协引导和协助区内企业建立科普教育基地，包括滨海新区气象预警中心的“气象基地”、泰达生态园林公司的“绿化基地”、泰达热电公司的“节水节能示范基地”、诺维信公司的“可持续发展基地”、微电子工业区的“科学家世纪园”、泰达环保公司的“循环经济示范基地”和中新药业研究中心的“自然人文教育基地”等。至2005年底，建成7个市级科普教育基地、3个市级科普车间和2个“科技工作者之家”。天津开发区科协为科技人员增进交流搭建平台，每年出版《科技论文集》，累计出版16辑，收录论文533篇。

2001年开始，天津开发区科协参与天津市科技周活动，并积极举办区内的科技周活动，累计达100多项。2002年起，天津开发区科协每年组织科技人员和居民参观天津科技馆和天津自然博物馆，参观人数累计3000人次。天津开发区科协还先后组织中国生物工程学会第四届代表大会暨学术研讨会、第四届生物医学光电子学和成像技术国际会议、第十三届国际先进激光会议、首届中国生物经济论坛农业生物分论坛、图像图形学学会成立十周年纪念暨全国立体图像技术及其应用研讨会等一系列大型国际、国内学术会议，并配合市科协在开发区组织举办全国奥林匹克信息竞赛，均收到良好效果。

第三篇

基 础 科 学

概　述

天津市的基础研究具有历史渊源的优势。天津大学与南开大学是天津市从事基础研究的两个最重要的基地，两所大学在长期发展过程中，杰出人才不断聚集，学科特色逐渐形成，在数学、化学、化工、物理、力学等学科领域科研实力雄厚，位居全国一流水平，以杨石先、申泮文、何炳棣、严志达、母国光和张国藩等为学术带头人的科研团队于“文化大革命”以前在有机磷化学、金属氢化物、离子交换树脂、“李群和李代数”和湍流机理与规律等项的研究工作中取得突出成果。苯乙烯强碱性阴交换树脂则用于提取国家急需的核燃料铀，为中国第一颗原子弹实验成功做出贡献。

1978年全国科学大会胜利召开，在国家百废待兴的形势下，解放思想，拨乱反正，打开“文化大革命”中禁锢科技界的桎梏，迎来了科学的春天。

1986年国务院批准建立国家自然科学基金，旨在资助基础研究和应用基础研究。1991年国家科委推出国家基础性研究重大关键项目计划（攀登计划）。1997年开始实施国家重点基础研究发展计划（“973”计划），支持具有全局性和带动性的重点基础研究项目。

天津市十分重视加强基础研究和科技人才，特别是青年科技人员的培养工作，于1989年和1990年先后在全国率先设立“天津市21世纪青年科学基金”和“天津市自然科学基金”。两项科学基金项目本着“有所为，有所不为”的原则，突出重点，优先支持天津优势学科，资助经费总量和项目投资力度逐年增长，有力地促进天津市基础研究事业的发展。

2001年起，天津市将自然科学基金和青年科学基金按照重点应用基础研究和一般应用基础研究两个层面进行安排，至2005年共安排应用基础研究计划项目934项，资助资金7220万元，涉及信息科学、材料科学、环境科学、化学与化工、生物技术与医药科学等多个领域。两个科学基金的设立与实施为缓解“文化大革命”十年人才断层，为天津市培养、凝聚和稳定优秀科技人才，为获得国家级科技计划项目奠定基础，取得一批具有创新性和应用前景的研究成果。

1994年，天津市开始实施“跨世纪育才工程”，又称“131人才工程”，即选拔100名40岁左右的尖子人才，经过培养成为在国际上具有一定知名度，能够进入世界科技前沿领域或具有国内领先水平，保持学科优势及相当水平的学术、技术权威；选拔300名35岁左右的青年专业技术骨干，经过培养成为在天津市各学科领域具有较高水平、能起骨干作用，居领先地位以及具有相当水平的学术、技术带头人；选拔100名35岁以下青年专业技术人员，经过培养成为各单位专业技术骨干和学术、技术带头人的后备力量。天津市首批“131人才工程”效果显著：科研创新能力普遍提高，学历层次及学术水平提高，经济、社会效益显著。

1991~2005年，坐落在天津市的国家级重点实验室由2个增至5个。坐落在天津市的国家部（局）级重点实验室于1994年始创，至2005年计有17个。市级重点实验室由无到有，至2004年共40个开放，其中大多数重点实验室依托在高等院校。1999年，天津市光电子联合科学研究中心成立，成为天津市组建的第一个科学研究中心。至2005年底，天津市共组建科学研究中心8个。

作为基础科学主体的天津市高等院校，1991年与2005年，研究与开发经费拨入额（或筹集额）分别为4970万元和143637万元；研究与开发经费支出额4235万元和107814万元。研究与开发课题数分别为2491项和8258项。

1991年至2005年期间，天津市高等院校发表的自然科学论文数呈快速增长态势。以自1996年开始的具有相同统计口径的数据和2005年比较，国内发表的篇数分别为3229篇，9466篇；国外三大系统（SLI EI

ISTP)收录的论文分别699篇和5527篇。

1991年至2005年,天津市的基础研究在不同学科取得十分可贵的成果。南开大学龙以明关于哈密顿动力系统与辛几何的研究进展引起国际数学届瞩目,张伟平在阿蒂亚-辛格指标理论及其应用的研究成果被国际数学界公认为是20世纪最辉煌的数学成就之一。天津大学陈予恕领导研究团队将非线性动力学理论引入到振动研究中,形成基础理论与工程应用研究相结合的交叉学科——工程非线性动力学,成为这个研究领域的一面旗帜。南开大学许京军、孙骞、张光寅等完成三维光折变存储材料及其存储器的研究,首次在国际上发现光折变光散射光强阈值效应,成果得到国际同行的高度评价。河北工业大学刘玉岭所从事的FA/O半导体材料切削液及技术和超大规模集成电路纳米磨料化学机械全局平面化新技术的研究,均为国际领先水平的成果。南开大学程津培在物理化学领域关于化学键能量的研究,对一些现存化学理论做出重要发展或修正。南开大学廖代正等在配位化学领域主持完成的分子磁性的基础研究项目获国家自然科学二等奖。南开大学李正名开展对环境友好的超高效除草剂的创制和开发研究成果丰硕,单嘧磺隆是中国第一个具有自主知识产权的创制除草剂,单嘧磺酯为第二个具有自主知识产权的创制超高效绿色除草剂。天津大学在化学分离工程领域占居全国领先地位,余国琮主持完成的高效精馏塔技术及其应用的研究项目、天津大学王静康主持完成的青霉素结晶新型技术与设备研究项目,均创造重大经济效益和社会效益。天津大学王榕树等共同完成新型离子筛的研制,开发出对水体具有直接净化和修复功能的新型环境材料。南开大学陈瑞阳带领的科研团队对中国95科331属2834种(含种下分类单位)植物染色体数目进行报道,完成1045种植物核型分析,出版世界上第一部植物基因组染色体图谱(共五册),填补世界植物染色体图谱的空白。

第一章 数 学

自1985年国际数学大师陈省身创办南开数学研究所起,天津数学领域的研究工作蓬勃发展,硕果累累。一批年轻有为的学者和数学家脱颖而出,跻身于国际数学研究的前沿,南开大学张伟平的微分几何阿提耶-辛格指标理论的研究,龙以明领导的动力系统与非线性分析课题组的哈密顿动力系统与辛几何的研究,陈永川创建的南开大学组合数学中心的组合数学研究等多项研究成果达到国际领先水平,得到国内外同行赞誉。1995年,陈省身当选中国科学院首批外籍院士。2001年,张伟平被第三世界科学院授予2000年度第三世界科学院数学奖,并当选第三世界科学院院士。在2002年第24届国际数学家大会上,陈省身被推举为大会名誉主席,张伟平和龙以明应邀做45分钟特邀报告。2003年,南开大学数学研究所副所长葛墨林当选中国科学院数学物理学部院士。2004年,南开科学计算研究所研发出超级计算集群系统"南开之星",其计算速度达到5万亿次/秒,名列2005年11月世界HPC(High Porformance Computing,高性能计机群)500强第46位。

第一节 函数论

1991~2005年,天津函数论研究主要集中于巴拿赫(Banach)空间理论、泛函分析与控制论、函数空间与算子理论等方面。

一、巴拿赫空间理论

1991年,南开大学定光桂等开展在等距逼近和等距延拓问题研究。1992年,定光桂等构造一列从 $L^1(\mu)$ 到 $L^\infty(\nu)$ 的 $\frac{1}{2^k}$ -等距算子 $\{T_k\}$,使其均不能用等距算子来逼近;1995年,其在研究等距逼近问题中提出,当 (A,μ) 是 σ -有限测度空间时,从 $L^\infty(A,\mu)$ 到 $L^\infty(A,\mu)$ 上的最小内同构,一定可以用等距算子来逼近;2000年,其进一步证明上述结论对于任意测度空间 (A,μ) 均是成立的。

2002年和2004年,定光桂在《中国科学》等期刊上发表3篇论文,分别给出 $l^p(\Gamma)(1\leqslant p\leqslant\infty)$ 的单位球面之间满等距算子的表现定理,从而肯定回答其上述的等距延拓问题。

2002年,定光桂研究非满映射的等距延拓,证明希尔伯特(Hilbert)空间单位球面之间的任何等距算子均可实线性等距延拓到全空间。2003年,他首次研究不同类型巴拿赫空间上的等距延拓问题,给出充分条件,使得 $C(\Omega)$ 的单位球面到任何巴拿赫空间单位球面的满等距算子,都可线性等距延拓至全空间。

1991年,南开大学王日生给出复 $B(l^1,m)$ 和 $B(l^1,C[0,1])$ 中等距逼近问题的否定回答。1994年,他得到从 $C_0(X)$ 的单位球面到 $C_0(Y)$ 的单位球面上的满等距算子的表现定理,推广泛函分析理论中著名的巴拿赫-斯顿(Banach-Stone)定理。1995~1996年,他在研究 $C_0(X,\sigma)$ 和 $C_0^{(m)}(X)$ 上等距延拓问题的同时,研究 $C_0(\Omega,E)$ 的 l^p -和($1\leqslant p<\infty$)上的等距延拓问题,均给出肯定回答。

二、泛函分析

1994~1997年,曾致力研究凸分析及非光滑分析等的南开大学史树中,在泛函分析与控制论方面取得成果,先后与他人合作发表《集值鲁棒映射和逼近映射》等多篇论文。

2000~2005年,天津工业大学苏永福提出随机结构空间的概念,用泛函分析和概率论的基本理论对随机结构空间进行研究。成果包括:给出随机结构空间的公理化定义;随机拓扑空间、随机度量空间、随机赋范空间和随机内积空间定义;随机结构空间与概率度量空间的关系;随机结构空间中的基本定理;随机结构空间理论的应用等。

2001年,南开大学王日生对泛函分析中著名的亚历山德罗夫(Aleksandrov)问题展开研究,构造出非连续的或非一一的或非满的保1映射。2003年,王日生构造出亚历山德罗夫问题实数域上的保无穷多个距离值的非等距映射。

2004年,南开大学吴志强和香港中文大学梁子威合作研究C*-unique局部紧群在一些构造之下的封闭性,证明每个经得起检验的线性群和离散群,都是一个C*-unique群的收缩核,成果发表在《泛函分析》上。2005年,吴志强研究有单位元的霍普夫(Hopf) C^* -代数的右上模的范畴及其扩展函子,以及该范畴的一些单对象。研究结果发表在《国际数学》上。

2004~2005年,天津工业大学数学研究所陈汝栋、苏永福等研究非线性泛函分析领域中的迭代逼近。他们改进和推广了一系列前人的结果,关于"有限连续伪压缩映像族的隐迭代过程的收敛定理""严格伪压缩的逼近方法""非扩张非自映像的粘滞逼近方法""有限严格伪压缩公共不动点的复合引迭代格式""连续伪压缩映像族""强伪压缩映像族和严格伪压缩映像族的公共不动点的隐式、显式迭代的强、弱收敛定理"等研究论文发表在《数学分析与应用》《非线性分析》等刊物上。

三、函数空间与算子理论

1995~1999年,天津大学周泽华开展多复变双全纯映照的边界开拓问题、多复变函数值分布及德贝尔(dbar)方程的研究,给出多元K拟共形映照族的正规定则。2000~2005年,周泽华进行多复变函数空间与算子理论及布雷金(Berezin)量子化问题等方面的研究,系统地讨论多圆柱、超球、有界对称域上各种函数空间上的复合算子、特普利茨(Toeplitz)算子、切萨罗(Cesaro)算子的有界性与紧性问题,并给出一些算子的本性模估计及谱特征。其研究成果发表在《密歇根数学期刊》《国际数学》《中国科学 A》等中外著名数学杂志上。

1991～2000年,天津大学熊洪允进行里兹(Riesz)乘积空间及表示定理的研究,相关结果发表在英文版《中国数学学报》上。2001～2005年,熊洪允有关里兹代数的研究成果发表在《数学分析与应用》期刊上。

2005年,天津科技大学李伟研究函数空间,在不加任何条件限制的情况下给出如下结论:设f是复平面上的超越亚纯函数, $a_j(j=1,2,L,m)$ 为亚纯函数,且是f的小函数,则当 m≥2 时, $fP^n[f]$ 取任意非零复数无穷多次;当 $n_0>2$ 时, $F=f^{n_0}(f^{'})^{n_1}L(f^{(k)})^{n_k}$ 可以取任意复数无穷多次。

第二节　概率论与数理统计

1991～2005年,天津在概率理论的研究中主要集中于对与马尔可夫过程理论密切相关的特殊过程类,包括莱维(Levy)过程、O—U过程、超过程、分支过程、风险过程以及随机偏微分方程的理论方面。由于在国内外的影响,南开概率学术团队被公认为国内风险理论研究领域的带头者,他们在国际概率论领域的主流学术刊物上发表论文30余篇。吴荣被多次邀请在国际保险金融学术会议上做报告,并且在2004年被世界华人数学家大会邀请做45分钟大会报告。

一、概率论

(一)马氏过程理论及其应用

20世纪90年代初,南开大学吴荣与其合作者在马氏过程理论研究中,解决多维布朗运动理论研究中提出的一系列布朗运动与球面之间关系的长期未决的重要问题,对一类扩散过程的轨道理论和O-U型过程单点击中概率及局部时问题均给出很好的结论。南开大学张春生对多指标布朗运动和多指标O-U过程的常返性给出完整结论,并证明无穷维布朗运动和O-U过程的连续修正的存在性。南开大学朱成熹与合作者证明非齐次柯尔莫哥洛夫(Колмогоров)方程组解存在的唯一性,并研究多指标过程的0-1律,于1994年发表研究结果。

同期,河北工业大学刘文在研究概率论强极限定理中提出新分析方法,开创一类强偏差定理的研究。在无平稳性及遍及性假说的条件下,研究信息论中香农-麦克米伦(Shannon-McMillan)定理(即熵定理)得到一系列结果;在实函数的构造和博策略的研究方面也取得成果。其主持完成《关于相对熵密度与强大数定律的若干研究》在研究方向、所用方法和应用前景诸方面都具有重要意义;《熵密度与概率论极限定理》在关于非齐次马氏链、香农-麦克米伦定理及其分析方法等方面取得重要研究成果。

(二)超过程

1991-1998年,吴荣建立超过程的调和函数,并深入研究它的性质以及与非线性偏微分方程之间的关系。1995～1998年,南开大学博士生任艳霞深入研究了超过程与几类偏微分方程之间,用超过程这一概率模型给出了一些相关非线性微分方程边值问题解的表达式,同时通过对非线性微分方程的研究得到超过程的绝对连续性条件、超过程的灭绝性条件等。

1994-1998年,南开大学王永进广泛研究超过程在球域内的负荷问题、绝对连续性问题,并用独特的方法给出超过程长时间的极限准则;从分支粒子系统建立有较强背景意义的随机偏微分方程,进而集中讨论带分支噪声和莱维时空噪声的随机偏微分方程的解的存在性、唯一性,以及解的性质。1997年,南开大学郭军义对具有一般分支特征的超布朗运动进行研究,证明其临近灭绝时样本支撑的直径几乎处处收敛到零。

(三)风险理论

1991～2005年,南开大学在风险过程研究中应用马尔可夫过程、随机分析等现代数学分支的理论,在与现代保险业密切相关的风险理论中若干重要研究论题上获得突破性的进展和创新性成果。

2002年,吴荣在研究具有马尔可夫性的风险模型时,灵活运用首中时与末离时之间对偶关系解决问题的思路,巧妙解决多个重要精算量的联合分布问题,国外审稿专家对此称赞"非常杰出"。

2003年,吴荣提出构造更新测度的方法,给出若干重要风险模型的首中时和负持续时间分布的解析表达,并运用到古典风险模型的盖伯-休(Gerber-Shiu)函数的表达上,对其中待定因子首次给出显式,得到其完全的明确表达式。

2003年,在研究与盖伯-休函数等价但表达更具难度的三者联合分布问题上,吴荣和张春生分别运用离散化技巧、莱维过程中的对偶原理,解决对带常利率古典风险模型和带干扰古典风险模型的联合分布表达问题。

2002年,郭军义研究一类相依保险风险模型,其中副索赔发生的时刻在主索赔之后,即延迟风险模型。对连续时间参数情形,通过鞅方法,给出了破产概率估计和兰德伯格(Lundberg)指数,对于离散事件模型,给出了生存概率以及盖伯-休(Gerber-Shiu)函数的递推计算公式。

二、数理统计

(一)试验设计

1991~2005年,南开大学数学学院张润楚等在试验设计的许多方向(特别是在正交设计、超饱和设计、均匀设计、区组设计等)上和各类设计的优良性准则、构造方法及数据分析方面,做出多项具有国际先进水平的研究成果,大量论文发表在国际著名期刊上。

张润楚与其合作者于1992年发展一种构造非对称(混合水平)正交设计的集群(grouping)方法,该法构造出的正交表,优于用其他方法构造的同类正交表。

1993年,张润楚与吴建福(C.F.J.Wu)合作,首次提出二和四混合水平最小偏差(MA,Minimum Aberration)设计理论,开创该类设计选优的途径,为后来的研究打下基础。其后,他与邵琴合作研究任意素数幂和素数幂方次混水平MA设计。2000年,他又与朴(Park)合作对正规设计最优分组提出在MA原则下的一种最优准则和构造方法,为其后来提出MA准则的一种新理论和一般最小低阶混杂准则奠定基础。

1995~1997年,南开大学数学学院王兆军与张润楚提出可以避免多个不可实施组合的正交表的充要条件,给出相应构造方法,同时给出可以避免某些组合的MA设计构造方法。

1997~2004年,南开大学数学学院马长兴与其合作者首次建立起正交设计与均匀设计的联系,给出这些设计的多种构造方法,并利用编码理论定义因析设计的广义最小低阶混杂准则。

1997~2005年,南开大学数学学院刘民千与其合作者发展超饱和设计的一系列最优性理论和构造方法,包括:提出E(fNOD)最优准则以及构造设计的组合设计法和饱和正交表拆分法等;提出离散偏差和最小低阶投影均匀性准则,并利用它们深入刻画各种设计的优良性,给出利用组合设计等构造均匀设计的理论和方法;给出纯净效应准则和MA准则下最优部分因析设计的理论及构造,所得结果很好地补充已有的研究成果。

张润楚、王兆军、马长兴等关于试验设计的最优性理论和构造的研究成果,得到国内外同行好评并被广泛引用。

(二)极值理论及其应用

1991~2001年,天津大学理学院史道济研究二元及多元极值参数模型、二元指数分布的唐顿(Downton)模型,给出随机表示,并在此基础上得到模型的菲舍尔(Fisher)信息阵元素及各阶矩的解析表达式,进而得到模型参数的矩估计量,并研究其统计性质。该系列研究成果总结在专著《实用极值统计方法》中,相应论文发表在国际顶级统计期刊《生物统计学》和其他重要期刊上,多次被极值统计专著、期刊引用。

(三)统计诊断与统计过程控制图

2004年8月,在美国纽约州立大学石溪分校邓越凡教授的指导下,梁科领导的南开科学计算研究所研发的“南开之星”在南开大学建设完成。该超级计算集群系统计算速度达5万亿次每秒，在2005年11月世界HPC500强中排名第46位，为天津市各科研单位、高等院校和企业提供高水平并行计算平台。至2005年底，“南开之星”承担了1000万元高性能计算专项课题，为近300余课题提供并行计算服务，总使用有效机时超过了1500万CPU/时。

20世纪90年代初期，天津市中心妇产科医院王淑雯、岳琏等与南开大学数学院吴荣、王公恕、左义欣合作开展对产科生理常数的研究。用统计聚类法等数学方法测量和分析处理女性生理常数，以解决分娩中有关盆头关系、盆头不称、难产等的诊断与处理。

1994年，南开大学数学系吴喜之和罗震研究统计诊断，提出基于二阶导数的局部影响分析方法，结果发表于《皇家统计学报》上。

2005年，王兆军、赵毅、吴纯杰研究统计过程控制图，提出针对区间飘移的检测准则、双CUSUM控制图，并研究7种总体方差估计方法对休哈特(Shewhart)控制图的影响问题。

第三节　几何学

国际数学大师、微分几何之父陈省身在其人生最后阶段，大力倡导和推动关于芬斯勒(Finsler)几何的研究，先后出版和发表一系列有关芬斯勒几何研究的专著和论文，为国际数学界在该研究领域的进一步发展奠定基础，指明方向。张伟平的阿蒂亚-辛格指标理论及其应用的研究成果，被国际数学界公认为20世纪最辉煌的数学成就之一。他的叙述和证明涉及几何、拓扑、分析等众多数学领域，包含大量创新思想，其成果统一并推广数学中的一系列大定理，为数学的各个领域之间架起一座桥梁。

一、芬斯勒几何

1991～2004年，陈省身向国内外数学界大力倡导和推动关于芬斯勒(Finsler)几何的研究。他身体力行，先后在《法国科学院院刊》《数学年鉴》《中国数学年鉴》以及施普林格(Springer)的研究生丛书和世界科学出版社出版的南开数学系列丛书上，发表一系列有关芬斯勒几何的研究论文和专著。

2002年，陈省身在《中国数学年鉴》发表《论芬斯勒空间联络》，对其早在1943年提出的芬斯勒空间一个联络(文献中被称为陈(Chern)联络)，给出一个新的、精练的定义，并由此出发给出芬斯勒空间局部等价问题的一个解。其中陈联络具有突出的性质，使得黎曼(Riemann)几何成为芬斯勒几何的特殊情形。黎曼的几何基础包含芬斯勒几何，陈省身新的研究工作把黎曼几何的发展，局部的和整体的完全推广到芬斯勒几何，而且很简单。2005年，陈省身与沈忠民合作的专著《黎曼-芬斯勒几何》在世界科学出版社出版。该书涉及芬斯勒几何最基本的概念、定理，直至该领域最前沿的热点研究问题，是从事芬斯勒几何研究的研究生及年轻数学家们极其重要的参考文献。

2004年，陈省身荣获首届邵逸夫奖数学科学奖，以表彰他的“开辟整体微分几何学的成就，以及他对这个数学范畴一直以来的领导”。

二、阿蒂亚-辛格指标理论及应用

1991～2005年，南开大学数学研究所张伟平在微分几何阿蒂亚-辛格(Atiyah-Singer)指标理论及其应用的研究中，取得一系列有重要国际影响的系统性研究成果。

1991年，张伟平与比斯姆(Bismut)合作首次成功地把物理学家维滕(Witten)对德拉姆(De Rham)复形引

图 3-1-3-3 南开大学数学研究所张伟平

进的形变，应用于研究解析挠率和拓扑挠率之间的关系，将著名的奇格-穆勒(Cheeger-Mueller)定理推广到一般情形，并给出一个解析的证明。该结果被通称为比斯姆-张定理，并成为后来该研究领域中许多工作的出发点。

1994年，张伟平计算圆周丛上的迪拉克(Dirac)算子的埃塔(eta)不变量的绝热(adiabatic)极限，推广著名的(阿蒂亚—希策布鲁赫 Atiyah-Hirzebruch)整除性定理。美国科学院院士奇格称该结果“大大超越了先前已有的所有结果”。在此基础上，2004年张伟平与其学生韩飞合作进行奥沙宁-菲内欣(Ochanine-Finashin)同余式的研究，有关结果发表在《微分几何》上。

1994～2002年，张伟平与戴先哲开展带边流形指标定理和谱流方面的研究，获得一系列成果。他们提出“广义谱截影”的概念，将阿蒂亚-帕图迪-辛格(Atiyah-Patodi-Singer)关于单个算子的经典结果推广到算子簇情形；将阿蒂亚-帕图迪-辛格的谱流概念推广到算子簇情形，引进“高维谱流”的概念；给出著名的阿提耶-帕图迪-辛格带边流形指标定理的一个K-理论证明。他们还成功地建立奇数维带边流形的一个指标定理，该定理可以看成是阿蒂亚-帕图迪-辛格带边流形指标定理的奇数维类比，解决该领域一个长期未能解决的问题，并成为张伟平在2002年国际数学家大会45分钟报告的主要内容。

1995～2001年，张伟平与田有亮合作在几何量子化猜测方面进行一系列研究。在其1998年发表于《数学发现》的一篇文章中，通过对迪拉克算子引进一个新的形变，给出辛几何中著名的圭利闵-施特恩贝格(Guillemin-Sternberg)几何量子化猜测的一个全新解析证明。之后，张伟平独立或与他人合作，得到该结果的若干推广。值得强调的是，张伟平和田有亮发展起来的解析方法是唯一能够用来统一证明所有上述结果的方法。

同期，张伟平就流形上的向量场零点集与流形的内在不变量之间的关系展开研究，对4q+1维流形构造了一类新的椭圆算子，从而给出著名的柯威尔(Kervaire)半示性数的一个新的解析解释。他对该算子还引入一个维滕型的形变，并由此给出柯威尔半示性数的一个普遍有效的计数公式。相关研究成果及论文发表于2000年《拓扑学》期刊上，被审稿人认为是“惊人的，显然是新的”。张伟平在世界科学出版社出版的专著《陈-韦伊理论和维滕形变讲义》中，简化最新发展起来的解析局部化技术，对数学中若干个著名的大定理诸如莫尔斯(Morse)不等式、彭加莱-霍普夫(Poincare-Hopf)定理、高斯-邦内特-陈(Gauss-Bonnet-Chern)定理等，给出一个简洁、漂亮、统一的处理，同时也对叙述和证明这些定理所依赖的概念、理论等，给出与当前数学文献相衔接的简明的处理。该专著的创造性不但填补中国在该领域研究生教育中的一项空白，而且大大缩短初入门的研究者进入到指标理论前沿热点问题研究的距离。陈省身高度评价该书，认定其“内容丰富，当为一部名著”。同时，张伟平独立或与他人合作在椭圆亏格的刚性定理及消灭定理、叶状结构等方面进行的研究，同样获得许多具有重要影响的研究成果。

同期，南开大学数学研究所冯惠涛利用维滕的形变思想以及由比斯姆和勒布(Lebeau)系统发展起来的解析局部化技术，对流形上的某些拓扑不变量进行研究。如：他与郭恩力合作构造出一个所谓的“超扭化迪拉克算子”，由此出发给出联系于实向量丛截面的彭加莱-霍普夫定理一个解析的证明；在《国际数学》发表的一篇论文中，冯惠涛研究复流形上的等变上同调，一定程度上推广比斯姆的一个定理，并给出其解析证明。在此基础上，冯惠涛与麻小南合作给出某种解析挠率的一个局部化公式，相关结果发表在《太平洋数学》上；冯惠涛还研究联系于向量场的诺维科夫(Novikov)型不等式、非交换陈特征、复射影空间中超曲面的完全交上具有正数量曲率的黎曼度量的存在性等问题。

三、微分几何、算术代数几何

1991～2004年，陈省身在微分几何领域的许多其他研究方向，如杜潘(Dupin)子流形(1991年)、欧氏空间中的超曲面(1995年)、示性形式、示性类及超度(1991年,1993年)等方面的研究中,同样做出重要贡献。他研究获得的著名黎曼映照定理的一个推广,发表在1996年《数学年鉴》上。

同期,南开大学数学研究所扶磊研究特殊拉格朗日(Lagrange)子流形的几何,讨论什么样的子流形是特殊拉格朗日子流形的边界,得到特殊拉格朗日子流形上函数的拉普拉斯算子的公式,找到在所有特殊拉格朗日子流形上调和的函数,并研究特殊拉格朗日方程的波恩斯坦问题。其研究成果被国际数学杂志引用达11次。

图3-1-3-4 1992年6月5~9日,第21届理论物理中微分几何方法国际学术会议召开,著名数学家陈省身(右一)和著名物理学家杨振宁(左一)主持学术会议。出席会议的还有中国台湾的吴大猷和俄罗斯的法捷耶夫等著名科学家

1998年起,扶磊对代数几何和数论开展研究,得到l-adic层的半单性判定准则,并用于研究代数几何中的塞尔—格拉腾迪克猜想,即有限生成域上光滑投影代数簇的l-adic上同调群所给出的域的伽罗华表示是半单的。他与万大庆合作研究一类非完整三角和与分完整L-函数,确定克罗斯特曼(Kloosterman)表示在无穷远处的性质,计算克罗斯特曼表示的对称积的L-函数的欧拉因子。他还与刘春雷合作研究高斯和与克罗斯特曼和的一致分布问题。

第四节 拓扑学

南开大学数学学院周学光研究代数拓扑的理论,特别是在同伦论研究中取得进展,发表大量水平高、影响力大的论文。在他带领下,天津在拓扑学研究方面取得长足进展。

一、微分拓扑和几何拓扑

1994年,南开大学数学研究所方复全的研究彻底解决"四维流形到七维欧式空间中的嵌入问题",成果填补惠特尼(Whitney)嵌入理论的空白。为展示其成果,拓扑学权威杂志《Topology》连续发表他3篇相关的论文。

1997年,方复全将赛贝尔—维滕(Seiberg-Witten)理论与拓扑K-理论结合起来,并研究有一定对称性四维流形的赛贝尔—维滕理论,由此证明后来被他人广泛称之为"赛贝尔—维滕不变量的模p消灭定理"。该定理在辛几何等重要领域得到应用,在中村(Nakamura)、陈为明等的后续工作中起到关键作用,并被日本数学家古田(Furuta)在2002年国际数学家大会45分钟特邀报告中引用。

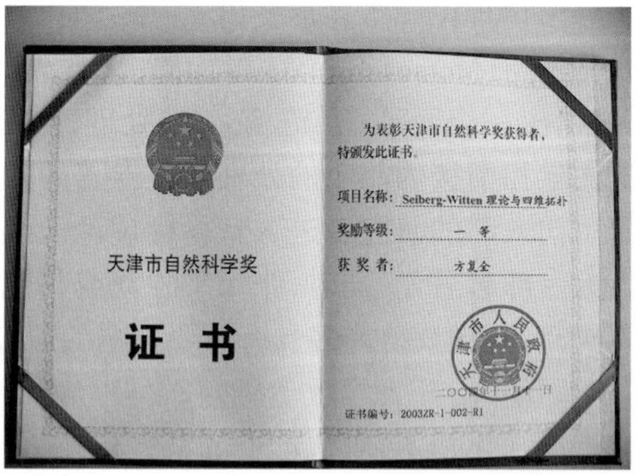

图3-1-4-5 南开大学方复全学术成果获奖证书

在四维拓扑方面,方复全还系统地研究四维流形的光滑结构问题,并将它与三维流形的嵌入问题联系起来,证明一大类非紧四维流形上,比如乘积流形M×R,存在有不可数多个光滑结构。其特例推广菲尔兹奖获得者弗雷德曼(Freedman)在1979年证明的定理:"$S^3 \times R$上有无限多个光滑结构"。特别是由此发现三维流形到四维正定流形中嵌入问题的一个新的阻碍。该研究工作被贡普夫—什蒂普希茨(Gompf-Stipsicz)写入美国数学会研究生教材,并启发王诗宬、埃德蒙兹(Edmonds)等的多项后续研究。

20世纪90年代后期,方复全与戎小春合作研究证明:"对每个正数δ,2-连通δ-扭的黎曼流形的单射半径有一个只依赖于常数 δ 及维数n的正下界"。作为直接推论,2-连通流形的丘成桐猜想、克林根贝里-界(Klingenberg-Sakai)完全得到解决;并且得到2-连通的 δ -扭的流形的拓扑型有限性定理,即:在每个维数,只存在有限多个2-连通的 δ -扭的流形的拓扑型。相关论文发表于顶尖数学杂志《数学研究》。该研究成果被法国科学院院士、美国科学院外籍院士格罗莫夫(Gromov)的重要专著《黎曼和非黎曼空间的度量构造》引用,成为2002年国际数学家大会中两个45分钟特邀报告的主要内容之一,并被写入法国科学院通讯院士贝格尔(Berger)的数学史报告《20世纪后半叶的黎曼几何》中,该报告由美国数学会出版。

2002~2005年,方复全与戎小春合作证明:"如维数n不等于6,7的正曲率流形有[(n-1)/2]可交换的基林(Killing)向量场,则必同胚于一个标准的秩一对称空间"。利用方复全、戎小春、门东萨(Mendonca)合作研究发展的连通性原理,方复全与戎小春进一步合作研究只有有限对称性的正曲率流形的拓扑,给出只有离散对称性的正曲率流形的拓扑分类。特别要指出的是,该连通性原理与代数几何中的莱夫谢茨(Lefschetz)型连通性原理极为相似,并有本质的联系。此外,方复全还独立发展了四维凯勒(quaternionic Kaehler)流形的莱夫谢茨型连通原理,并应用于四维凯勒流形几何分类。上述研究成果分别发表于《数学年报》《美国数学志》等一系列重要数学杂志。

同期,方复全与张振雷、张宇光合作,研究证明"四维流形上里奇(Ricci)流长期解存在,则流形的欧拉示性数非负"。这是在Ricci流方向发现的第一个拓扑障碍,有关成果被称之为方-张-张不等式,相关论文发表在《数学年报》《数学物理通讯》。

二、球面稳定同伦群与代数拓扑

1991年,南开大学数学学院林金坤在球面稳定同伦群新元素族的发掘方面取得进展,证明莫尔(Moore)谱同伦群中一些高阶 β 族元素乘积的平凡性和非平凡性,其论文《在稳定莫尔空间同伦群中 β 元素族非开裂环谱与乘积》发表在1992年的《太平洋数学》上。1994年,他在《美国数学会会刊》发表《莫尔空间诸维科夫 E_2 -项中一些 β 元素族的乘积》,证明莫尔谱的诺维科夫 E_2 -项中另一些高阶 β 族元素的乘积的平凡性或非平凡性。2001年,他在日本《广岛数学杂志》发表《球面稳定同伦群新元素族》,证明 $b_0h_n+h_1b_{n-1}$ 的收敛性。

1991年,南开大学陈吉象在研究代数拓扑中讨论同伦偶范畴HPM中的同伦性质:CHP,WCHP,HEP与WHEP等;在链复形与链映射范畴中证明各种同伦扩张性质(HEP,WHEP,RWHEP与VWHEP)的等价性,及约化奇异链函子保持普珀(Puppe)序列的右正合性。1994年,陈吉象与比利时布鲁塞尔自由大学教授基博姆(R. W. Kieboom)合作证明FWHEP严格介于WHEP与RWHEP之间,并发现一种严格介于形变收缩核与强形变收缩核之间的新形变收缩核。1997年,陈吉象引进严格介于同伦单态与同伦等价之间的同伦正则单态的概念。该概念在某种意义下刻划了同伦等价的一个特征。1997~1998年,陈吉象研究迹同伦范畴,引进分裂的范畴纤维化并得到若干对伴随函子。

1996~1998年,南开大学郑弃冰研究证明两个交换上结合的霍普夫代数的扭曲张量积的上同调群,是两个霍普夫代数的科巴尔(Cobar)复形的扭曲张量积,进而发现霍普夫代数的埃克斯特(Ext)群上的一种新的马西(Massey)积,并且证明该马西积的同伦交换性和同伦结合性;发现经典亚当斯(Adams)谱序列的E2项中的一类新的上同调类,对应了希腊字母元素类的表示。此后,他与王向军合作证明 $\tilde{\alpha}_s^{(n)}h_0h_n$ 的收敛性。

2000年,南开大学王向军开始在亚当斯—诺维科夫谱序列方面开展研究工作。2002年,他与日本高知大学教授下村(K.Shimomura)合作计算出 $\pi_*(L_2S^0)$ 的3分量群,并计算出收敛到 $\pi_*(L_2S^0)$ 的2分量群的亚当斯-诺维科夫谱序列的 E_2 -项。

第五节 微分方程与动力系统

1991～2005年，由龙以明领导的南开大学动力系统与非线性分析课题组，在哈密顿动力系统与辛几何研究中取得令人瞩目的进展。至2005年，龙以明等在国际重要学术刊物发表论文50多篇，其中大多被SCI收录，被SCI收录论文他引200多次。其成就被国外数学家誉为“哈密顿系统领域过去15年来的里程碑”，并称“这些工作建立了龙以明作为世界上关于马斯洛夫指标理论方法的首席科学家的地位”。龙以明先后获得1997年度中国数学会陈省身数学奖、2004年度第三世界科学院数学奖等奖项。

一、哈密顿系统与非线性分析

（一）一般辛道路的指标理论

1990～1991年，南开大学数学研究所龙以明在《中国科学》发表论文，对退化线性哈密顿系统的基本解定义马斯洛夫型指标，使它可以应用于任意非线性哈密顿系统的周期解。1993年，龙以明在科学出版社出版专著《哈密顿系统的指标理论及其应用》，介绍该指标理论与其应用。1997年，龙以明在《非线性分析拓扑方法》上发表论文，将上述马斯洛夫型指标理论推广到辛群Sp(2n)中的任意连续道路上。该指标理论被国内外数学家多次引用并应用于研究中。

（二）一般辛道路指标迭代理论

图3-1-5-6 龙以明为京津几何工作营作报告

1997年，董堤与龙以明在《美国数学会汇刊》上发表论文，研究辛道路的马斯洛夫型指标的迭代性质，建立迭代指标的估计。1999年，龙以明在《太平洋数学杂志》发表论文，引进辛矩阵的基本标准型，定义辛矩阵的同伦成分和最终型数；对任意辛道路建立以单位圆周上的点为参数的ω指标理论和鲍特(Bott)型指标迭代公式。1997～2000年，刘春根与龙以明合作，分别在英文版《中国科学通报》和《微分方程杂志》发表论文，建立辛道路的多种指标迭代不等式。2000年，龙以明在美国《数学进展》上发表论文，建立辛群Sp(2n)中任意辛道路的精确指标迭代公式，解决指标迭代理论中的基本问题，即根据初始指标和迭代次数精确计算任意次迭代指标的问题。该论文于2001年被美国《数学评论》重点评述。2002年，龙以明与朱朝锋在美国《数学年刊》发表论文建立有限辛道路族的公共指标跳跃定理。第三世界科学院网页评价称“龙的辛道路指标迭代理论是一个极其有力和有用的工具，它已给出了许多有趣和基本的应用”。美国《数学评论》评价称“龙与其合作者在1990年代的一系列文章中对此指标的发展做出了决定性的贡献”。

（三）紧凸超曲面上闭特征猜想

哈密顿系统中长期未解决的多重性和稳定性猜想是：2n维实空间中的任意紧凸超曲面上总存在至少n条几何相异的闭特征和1条椭圆闭特征。1998年，龙以明在《微分方程杂志》发表论文，证明2n维实空间R^{2n}中的紧凸超曲面上的闭特征有限蕴涵非双曲闭特征的存在。1999年，刘春根与龙以明合作在《AIHP.非线性分析年刊》发表论文，证明上述结果对某类星形超曲面也成立。2000年，龙以明在美国《数学进展》上发表的论文中，证明4维实空间中的任意紧凸超曲面上若恰有二闭特征，则它们必为椭圆的。蒿缶(H.Hofer)等在其2002年综述文章中指出，此结果证明了“双曲闭特征的存在性蕴涵无穷多条闭特征的存在性”。

2002年，龙以明与朱朝锋在美国《数学年刊》发表论文，证明R^{2n}中的任意紧凸超曲面上总存在至少[n/2]+1条几何相异的闭特征；而且若所有闭特征均非退化，则总存在至少n条几何相异的闭特征。他们还证明紧凸超曲面上闭特征条数有限蕴涵存在至少一条椭圆闭特征和至少[n/2]条具有无理平均指标的几何相异的闭特征等结果。该论文于2003年被美国《数学评论》重点评论。2002年，刘春根、龙以明与朱朝锋合作在德国《数学年刊》发表论文，证明R^{2n}中的任意对称紧凸超曲面上总存在至少n条几何相异的闭特征。2002年，胡锡俊与龙以明在英文版《中国科学》发表论文，证明R^{2n}中的任意非退化紧星形超曲面上，总存在至少2条几何相异的闭特征。2002年，埃克朗（I. Ekeland）和葛苏卜（N. Ghoussoub）在《美国数学会通报》发表的综述文章中，指出在闭特征研究中"迄今最好的结果属于龙以明和他的学生"。是年，龙以明在德国博克霍伊泽（Birkhäuser）出版社出版专著《辛道路指标迭代理论与应用》，介绍指标迭代理论及其应用。美国《数学评论》评价此书"是关于哈密顿动力理论的重要贡献并将必然引起进一步的研究""对此领域有兴趣的任何人都是不可或缺的"。

（四）其他课题研究

1991年，龙以明在英文版《中国数学学刊》发表论文构造出一族具有无界解的带有间断强迫外力项的超线性达芬（Duffin）方程。莱维（M.Levi）在其发表的论文中提到"龙首先指出了利特尔伍德论文中的错误"。

1993～1997年，龙以明先后在《AIHP.非线性分析年刊》《微分方程杂志》等发表论文，研究伦比诺维茨（P.Rabinowitz）提出的哈密顿系统的最小周期解猜想。1997年，董堤与龙以明在《美国数学会汇刊》发表论文，进一步证明关于凸哈密顿系统的最小周期解猜想，推广埃克朗和蔼缶的相应成果。美国《数学评论》称此文"发展了一个非常有启发性的关于最小周期问题的分析方法"。

2000年，龙以明在德国《数学杂志》发表论文证明环面上的拉格朗日（Lagrange）系统的彭卡雷映射必有无穷多个由可缩解产生的周期点，对拉格朗日系统的特殊情形证明康莱（C. Conley）关于环面上的哈密顿系统的猜想。2003年龙以明和卢广存在《泛函分析杂志》发表论文将此结果推广到自治二阶哈密顿系统。

2000年，龙以明与张世清合作在英文版中国《数学学报》和《微分方程杂志》发表两篇论文，证明3维或2维实空间中的3体问题的变分最小解必为拉格朗日平面等边三角形圆周运动解。2002～2004年，龙以明与孙善忠合作研究中心构型，在《理性力学与分析杂志》（*Arch. Rational Mech. Anal.*）发表论文，特别证明非共线凸四体中心构型对顶质量相等。而且，较重质量对应的对角线较短时，必为风筝形。对于非共线凹四体中心构型，若其3个质量相等，则它必为一等腰三角形。

2005年，南开大学刘春根在《微分方程杂志》发表论文，证明在某个条件下辛流形的拉格朗日子流形与其哈密顿微分同胚之相交数的下界至少是此拉格朗日子流形的上积长，就此情形部分正面回答著名的阿诺德（Arnold）猜想。

二、动力系统

（一）弱希尔伯特第16问题等

20世纪90年代，天津师范大学李宝毅利用无穷小分析的方法和鞍点附近的正规形理论，研究弱希尔伯特（Hilbert）第16问题和余维3的奇异环的环性，结果彻底解决"Kotova动物园"中所遗留的问题。在北京大学动力系统国际研讨会、武汉分歧理论和控制论国际研讨会、全国常微分方程青年学术研讨会等国内外学术会议上，多次宣读、交流其研究论文，并多次被同行专家引用。其在《理论与应用数学纪事》（意大利）、《数学分析与应用》（美国）、《中国科学》《应用数学学报》《数学进展》《北京大学学报》等国内外学术刊物上发表的多篇高水平论文，得到国内外同行专家的重视。

（二）超线性系统吸引子存在性

1996～1998年，南开大学李德生与合作者研究建立超线性卡恩–伊尔李雅德（Cahn–Hilliard）系统吸引子的存在性，证明著名数学家泰曼（R.Temam）的有关猜想，相关论文被全文录入专著《抽象抛物线状的地球引力》（J.W. Cholewa，T. Dlotko著，剑桥大学出版社，2000），并被著名数学家塞尔（G.R. Sell）和Y.C. You等人的专著所收录。1999～2001年，李德生研究隐式微分方程，完整地建立隐方程的皮亚诺（Peano）定理和延拓定理，为隐方程研究奠定基础。2002～2007年，李德生和国际著名数学家克勒登（P.E. Kloeden）合作，首次从微分包含的动力学角度证明反馈控制系统的渐近能控性关于小时间滞后的鲁棒性。同时，李德生还独立地建立微分包含的莫尔斯分解理论，并给出非线性开环系统控制集的莫尔斯分解刻划。

（三）微分方程的反问题

1990～2000年，天津大学喻文焕主要从事微分方程的反问题的研究，工作涉及到反问题适定性及求解反问题的计算方法，先后在国内外学术期刊及学术会议发表论文近20篇。

（四）偏微分方程数值解

1997～1999年，中国民航大学何松年在偏微分方程数值解研究方面，对于非周期不可压粘性流问题提出车贝雪夫（Chebyshev）谱-有限元混合方法和勒让德（Legendre）谱-有限元混合方法，充分结合谱方法精度高和有限元方法便于处理复杂区域的优势，建立起这类混合方法数值分析的一般性框架，数值模拟试验显示出该方法的优越性。

第六节 代数学

天津在代数学方面的基础性研究成果，突出表现在李（Lie）群、李代数的研究上，南开大学严志达、侯自新、孟道骥等都有卓著贡献。严志达长期从事李群、李代数的研究，在特殊李群的拓扑、实半单李代数的分类理论等方面获重要成果，并在微分几何理论应用于研究齿轮啮合问题方面颇有建树。1993年，严志达当选中国科学院数学物理学部院士，成为天津市第一位数学领域的中科院院士。

一、李群和齐性空间

1991～2005年，南开大学侯自新领导的课题组承担3个国家自然科学基金重点项目研究，包括李代数的双极化与齐性仿凯勒流形、李群与芬斯勒几何、李群表示理论等领域3个项目，属于李群及其应用的核心领域之一。该课题组在著名学术期刊《太平洋数学》《中国科学》等发表学术论文35篇，其中14篇论文被SCI收录，被他人23篇次SCI收录论文引用。其所建立的李群与芬斯勒几何的理论被国际数学同行使用和进一步研究。

侯自新课题组主要成果包括：给出半单李代数双极化的分类及半单型齐性仿凯勒流形的分类；证明任何芬斯勒流形的等距变换群必定是李群；给出轨道覆盖抛物诱导概念，并利用轨道抛物诱导给出轨道数据一个几何解释，对约化李群证明了几何轨道数据的抛物诱导与抛物子群选取无关，并且几何轨道数据的片层（Sheets）是不相交的，部分证明了沃甘（Vogan）的两个猜想；给出最小K-型正则迪拉克上同调非零的酉表示的分类。

其中，邓少强与侯自新于2002年在《太平洋数学》发表论文证明任何芬斯勒流形的等距变换群必定是李群，被美国《数学评论》评价为“为利用李群理论研究芬斯勒几何开辟了一个新的方向”。

二、李代数和左对称代数

1998年，严志达的专著《实半单李代数》在南开大学出版社出版。该书总结他从20世纪50年代开始在实半单李代数方面研究的系列成果，被国内外许多学者引用，或被相关专著列入参考文献中。

同期，南开大学孟道骥、姜翠波与朱林生研究无限维李代数的结构、表示及二次李代数等。

同期，孟道骥及其博士生杨明升、高永存、任斌等合作研究李代数的双极化及其几何性质、无限维李代数的表示、顶点算子代数、幂零李代数，尤其是二步李代数、完备李超代数、李三系、多元李代数、限制李超代数、左对称代数及诺维科夫（Novikov）代数等。其中，孟道骥与白承铭合作研究的可递Novikov代数的实现，被著名数学家、菲尔兹奖获得者Novikov称为“在现代代数学和现代数学物理交叉的领域中有趣的结果”，而“费米型Novikov代数”等工作，则被其称为“高质量的、原创的和有国际竞争力的……它对整个领域做出了贡献。”

图3-1-6-7 南开大学严志达在查阅资料

2001年，孟道骥与朱林生、姜翠波合作的《完备李代数》专著在科学出版社出版。陈省身与王叔平曾称孟道骥等工作“首先对完备李代数完成了系统化的讨论，使完备李代数的研究在国内外活跃起来”。

三、有限典型群

1999～2003年，中国民航大学高有在有限典型群的结构与应用方面，研究有限域上典型群的二元生成问题；确定出有限交换环上典型群的卡特（Carter）子群的结构；研究有限域上典型群作用下子空间轨道生成的格，刻划给定的子空间轨道生成的格中所含元素的特征；给出奇异典型群作用下子空间轨道生成的格的几何性；利用偏序集上的默比乌斯（Mobius）反演公式，计算出奇异典型群作用下子空间轨道生成的格的特征多项式。其部分研究成果发表在《代数通讯》和《线性代数与应用》《数学学报》上。

第七节 计算数学与运筹学

1991～2005年，天津计算数学与运筹学领域在微分方程数值方法、金融数学等方面取得令业界瞩目的成果。

一、微分方程数值解

20世纪90年代，天津财经学院（2004年5月更名天津财经大学）张书华等在积分方程与积分—微分方程的有限元与混合有限元高精度算法的研究中。利用超逼近分析技术，得到沃尔泰拉（Volterra）型积分方程有限元的最优收敛率及超收敛结果；首次引进混合型里茨—沃尔泰拉（Ritz–Volterra）投影算子与混合型正则格林（Green）函数，得到某类多孔介质流体混合有限元方法的最优L^2估计及局部超收敛与整体超收敛结果；同时，利用最优剖分等技术，得到某类热传导问题有限元方法的误差估计外推。

1991～2003年，南开大学孙澈等合作研究流占优扩散方程及一阶双曲型（纯对流）方程的新型有限元方法，对国外学者提出的有关计算方法进行改造与发展，对上述两类方程提出多种新型有限元算法，并阐明其机理。新方法的计算工作量较少、稳定性能好、计算精度高，可应用于高维及非线性问题的新型有限元算法。

同期，南开大学胡健伟等在对流—扩散问题的伽辽金（Galerkin）迎风有限元方法的研究中，提出部分迎风格式，并将该方法应用于比格尔斯（Burgers）方程和其他非线性方程。同时将该方法与区域分解方法和自适应方法的结合。

2002年，天津财经学院刘棠利用椭圆逆算子和积分恒等式技术，获得索伯列夫(Sobolev)方程半离散有限元方法的一种新型最优误差估计和超收敛估计；建立索伯列夫方程一种时间高阶的新型全离散格式，获得整体超收敛与后验误差估计量。

二、应用数学

1995年，南开大学史树中与山东大学彭实戈等向国家自然科学基金委提出开展金融数学研究的建议，并很快促成设立跨学部重大课题、国家"九五"重大项目《金融数学、金融工程与金融管理》。1996年，在史树中倡导下，南开大学设立金融数学专业；转年建立金融信息技术系，史树中为该专业方向研究生开设多门课程；先后出版《数学与经济》《凸分析》《凸性》《金融经济学十年》等专著，其中《数学与经济》一书，在2000年被评为"科学家推介的20年来100部科普佳作"之一；其先后发表《一般经济均衡的数学问题》《微分包含与经济均衡》《凸分析及其在微观经济学中的应用》《纯交换经济的单调轨线》《生存理论与价格调整》等论文。

同期，天津大学荣喜民，在国内率先提出将保险定价与保险基金投资同时进行考虑，以投资确定保险价格、以价格影响投资动态定价模式，并将倒向随机微分方程等用于保险投资与定价研究。他先后在著名学术期刊上发表《投资对保险价格的影响研究》《保险费调节时间研究》《保险定价的方法》等。

1999～2003年，天津职业技术师范学院姬振豫参加产品稳健设计的课题研究，通过研究成果，撰写出版《正交设计的方法与理论》专著1部。

2002～2004年，天津工程师范学院吴爱弟与何文章等承担多小波理论及其在图像压缩中的应用课题，利用多小波变换理论，结合图像数据的特点，在图像去噪、增强、压缩和数字水印等方面取得研究成果。在此基础上，何文章、吴爱弟等于2004～2005年从事多小波变换理论及其在地震数据处理中的应用研究。同时，他们也分别研究石油开发中的油田年综合含水率和油田年产量发展趋势预测等问题。

三、控制理论与应用

1985～1996年，天津大学许跟起研究中子迁移方程解以及算子双半群理论。他给出扰动后半群本质谱半径的估计，研究算子双半群的扰动与积分双半群的生成问题。于1997～2005年研究分布参数系统控制理论。以季莫申科(Timoshenko)梁为主要研究对象，他给出系统本征值的渐近表达式，并给出系统本征值和广义本征向量构成能量空间的里斯基。根据弹性系统镇定问题的研究，其本征函数都与指数函数以及线性组合有关，许跟起研究指数函数族与算子本征函数的完整性与基性质的联系。在抽象空间的度量下，假定算子A生成半群，可以证明：如果A的本征值是简单的，且本征值的对应函数族，构成空间$L^2[0,T]$的里斯基序列，则算子A的本征向量也构成空间的一个里斯基。该研究成果于2003年在美国工业与应用数学学会的《最优控制》期刊发表。继而，他将该成果推广到每个本征值可以附加一个重数的情况，此时A的本征向量和广义本征向量也构成空间的里斯基，该研究结果于2005年发表在《微分方程》上。

1992～2004年，天津大学毛云英从事线性系统最优控制理论及其应用的研究。对于具有状态和控制不等式约束的线性二次型系统的最优控制问题给出最优反馈控制律，并探讨几类带有约束的动态投入产出最优控制模型，导出最优反馈控制律。

2000～2005年，天津财经大学亢京力在迭代学习控制、2-D系统理论、智能控制等方面开展一系列研究，并主持非线性系统的迭代学习控制算法理论与应用研究。南开大学王红利用整体微分几何方法研究力学非线性控制系统的结构、反馈控制与状态空间(微分流形)的几何结构之间的相互关系和影响，并应用于力学、工程中的机器人系统和航天飞行器系统的稳定性和优化设计问题研究。该课题对于促进力学、现代控制论和整体微分几何学的结合和发展具有重要的意义。王红的研究结果分别发表在《控制理论与应用》《自动化学报》《应用数学与力学》《IEEE系统控制技术》等国内外学术刊物上，部分论文被SCI和EI引用。

四、最优化理论、方法与应用

1990～2003年，天津大学喻文焕及其合作者针对分布参数系统辨识以及一般非线性系统的非参数辨识等，开展理论与实际应用研究工作。他们先后涉及参数能辨识性、带约束参数辨识、一般非线性系统的非参数辨识、以及辨识算法等问题。

1995～2003年，解放军军事交通学院卢占禹从事无穷维空间向量优化理论的研究工作，分别讨论最优性条件、解的结构与解的存在性等问题，给出广义的阿罗-巴兰金-布莱克韦尔定理和集映射向量极值问题的拉格朗日乘子定理。发表论文10余篇。

2001～2004年，天津大学黄正海利用度理论和同伦不变定理，给出几个变分不等式问题解的存在性定理。2003～2005年，黄正海探讨求解各种最优化问题的光滑型算法，并在较弱的条件下讨论算法的各种收敛性质。有关结果发表在《数学规划》《数值分析》等学术刊物上。

2003～2005年，天津大学边馥萍研究含有非期望输出的DEA理论、DEA随机生产前沿函数、DEA技术有效度量、随机DEA预测模型与综合模型等。并探讨代谢网络结构优化问题，研究AIDS/HIV免疫系统优化防治等问题。

2003～2005年，南开大学叶培新运用多元多项式逼近方法，确定出某些如各向异性索伯列夫类与赫尔德-尼可尔斯基(Holder-Nikolskii)类等光滑函数类的随机、量子框架下的数值积分的最优误差。

2004～2005年，南开大学杨庆之研究求解分裂可行问题和变分不等式问题的理论及算法。他对求解分裂可行问题的一种方法做出改进，并与合作者提出分裂可行问题的其他几种方法，有关结果发表在《反问题》等杂志上；在对变分不等式两个经典算法的研究中，杨庆之提出一种便于实现的松弛投影算法，并证明算法的收敛性，有关结果发表在《数学分析与应用》杂志上。

第八节　组合数学

1997年，陈永川创建南开大学组合数学研究中心，并出任主任，著名数学家、中国科学院院士万哲先任学术委员会主任。研究中心成员有李学良、克里斯蒂安·利迪(Christian Reidys)、高维东、向开南等教授。至2005年，研究中心在国际著名杂志上发表200余篇相关论文，出版专著1部，开发软件4套，并形成系列《中国城市竞争力报告》。

一、构造组合学

图3-1-8-8　陈永川(左一)与同行进行学术交流

2001年，陈永川、郭军伟合作研究，用构造的技巧解决1998年国际数学家大会1小时报告人、1998年奈望林纳奖和1999年麦克阿瑟奖获得者、美国科学院院士肖(P. Shor)提出的一个关于树的凯莱(Cayley)公式和印度传奇数学家拉玛努金(Ramanujan)的一个多项式的公开问题，揭示出拉玛努金多项式的组合内涵。该研究成果发表在《应用数学进展》第27卷上。2003年，陈永川与邓玉平、杨丽敏合作在《电子组合期刊》第9卷上发表文章，利用标准约合分解刻画一类禁止模式的排列，构造该类禁止模式的排列和莫茨金(Motzkin)路之间的双射,并类似地刻画出另一类禁止模式的排列。审稿者评价该文为"原创性的结果"。2005年,陈永川与邓玉平、杜若霞合作,在《欧洲组合期刊》第26卷上发表文章,通过用有向图来表示分拆给出分拆的约简算法,从而巧妙地证明关于m正则分拆以及m正则不交分拆计数的两个等式,并同时给出推广的RNA二级结构的计数以及拿拉央(Narayana)数和卡塔兰(Catalan)数之间关系的一个恒等式。其研究成果被评价为"独创性的工作""强有力的工具"。

2005年,由陈永川和美国科学院院士斯坦利(R.Stanley)等合作完成的论文《匹配与划分的交叉和嵌套》(Crossings and nestings of matchings and partitions),发表在《美国数学会汇刊》上。该文解决一个经典计数理论中的重要问题,在正式发表前便被世界著名计算机学家、图灵奖获得者、美国科学院院士克努斯(Donald E. Knuth)收录在经典名著《计算机程序设计技巧》的第四卷中,并在书中称赞其"重要且令人惊奇"的工作。

二、代数组合学

代数学中的组合方法被美国数学会列入21世纪纯数学中最具挑战性的方向之一。1995年至2001年,陈永川与美国洛斯阿拉莫斯国家实验室著名理论物理学家劳克(James D.Louck)合作,最先将组合数学的经典理论应用于量子角动量的研究,研究内容涉及对称函数、特殊函数、群表示理论和代数几何。其研究取得出人意料的成果,在组合数学界产生了重要影响。对此,美国数学会1998年斯蒂尔(Steele)奖获得者泽尔贝格尔(D.Zeilberger)在《电子组合期刊》(3 (1996) R13)上评价陈永川在构造组合学领域"做出了令人惊叹的工作"。1996年,他们发表在《数学进展》117卷上的文章,得到对称函数的基本插值公式,推出李斯特伍德(D.E. Littlewood)的一个重要定理,被巴特纳格尔(G.Bhatngar)在其发表于《国际数学与数学科学》(22 (1999) 431-435)上的论文中评价为"深远的推广"。

1998年,陈永川在《欧洲组合期刊》上发表文章,解决格塞尔(Gessel)等在《图论杂志》(19 (1995), no.4, 435~459)中提出的公开问题。对此,皮珀特(R.E. Pippert)与恩特林格(R.C.Entringer)分别在《数学评论》(99g: 05103)等学术期刊上提到。是年,陈永川与劳克(James D.Louck)合作,发现1965年诺贝尔物理奖得主施温格尔(Schwinger)的一个经典公式与组合数学中麦克马洪(MacMahon)定理的联系,给出施温格尔公式一般形式的严格数学证明。其论文在《线性代数应用》上发表后,被国际数学大师、1978年首届沃尔夫奖获得者盖尔芬德(I.M.Gelfand)引用;被布雷松德(D.M.Bressound)评价为"正是我们所需要的严格的数学方法";被皮珀特(R.E. Pippert)评论为"给出一个新的搜索方法"。是年,陈永川等发表论文,提出研究超几何级数的参数扩充方法。美国科学院院士安德鲁斯(George E.Andrews)对此在《数学评论》(99f: 33020)评价:"精巧而优美地证明大量重要的经典定理,但该方法为什么会与这些经典技巧产生联系却仍然是个谜"。

2002年,陈永川与合作者一起在《代数组合》第15卷上发表论文,从另一个独特的角度对"格路径(lattice path)"给予应用,给出与陈省身类有密切联系的"双舒尔(Schur)函数"的组合解释,得到辛群和正交群特征标更简单的行列式公式,对揭示对称函数的本质和性质起到重要的作用。英国著名数学物理学家金(R. C. King)在《代数组合》第16卷上发表的论文中评价该文为"引人注目"。

由于上述代表性的研究成果,陈永川团队以"组合数学及其应用"项目荣获1997年度国家教委科技进步一等奖,其"代数组合学中的组合变换"荣获2005年度天津市自然科学一等奖。陈永川荣获:1994年美国李氏基金学术成就奖,1995年首届国家杰出青年科学基金,1997年联合国教科文组织"侯赛因"青年科学家奖,1998年国家教委霍英东教育基金会青年奖,1998年中国青年科技奖,1999年香港"求是"基金杰出青年科技奖,1999年首届长江学者特聘教授。

三、图论

通过用图论的方法研究化学分子图形的结构与指标,可为新材料研究提供理论依据。2001年至2005年,南开大学组合数学研究中心在化学图论方面有建树,李学良对在化学、生物制药领域有重要应用的维纳(Wiener)指标和广义兰迪奇(Randic)指标进行系统研究,建立起一套研究体系,在美国工业与应用数学会的

《离散数学》《计算机生物学》等国际重要杂志发表多篇论文,并出版专著1部。2004年,李学良等巧妙利用哈迪、利特尔伍德和玻利亚(Polya)关于置换二次型极值的经典不等式,解决美国工业与应用数学学会和计算机协会共同举办的、离散算法研讨会论文集(Proc. SIAM-ACM Symp. on Discrete Algorithms)中提出的、两个关于维纳指标的猜想。李学良等还在兰迪奇指标研究方面解决一些理论难题,被国际数学化学领袖人物古特曼评价为“杰出的成果”,并因此应邀编写一部关于兰迪奇指标方面的专著《分子结构的兰迪奇型指数的数学概论》(MATHMATICAL ASPECTS OF RANDIC-TYPE MOLECULAR STRUCTURE DESCRIPTORS)。该专著由*KRAGVJEVAC*出版社于2006年出版。

图的塔特(Tutte)多项式是塔特于1954年提出的,其应用覆盖到图论、结理论(knot theory)和统计物理等各方面,染色多项式与流多项式都是塔特多项式的特殊形式。南开大学组合数学研究中心在新世纪开展图的塔特多项式研究。2001~2005年,李学良等利用戈兹尔(Godsil)的道路-树(Path-Tree)方法,非常简洁地解决了古特曼等提出并一直力图解决的关于贝塔(beta)多项式的实性猜想,该猜想历经十余年未获解决;解决了国际重要期刊关于色唯一和色等价方面的多个公开疑难问题和猜想。他们完成的一系列深刻结果,被新加坡国立大学许其明(Koh KM)教授等以几个章节的篇幅编入专著中。2004年起,于青林研究几类图的塔特唯一性,支持巴洛巴斯(Ballobas)给出的、几乎所有图都是塔特唯一的猜想。同期,于青林在图的匹配和因子可扩方面开展系统深入研究,解决多个国际重要杂志上提出的公开问题和猜想,如给出关于因子临界图健壮性猜想的一个简洁证明,解决法瓦龙(Favaron)关于因子临界图中可传递性的一个公开问题。此外,于青林与合作者研究得到若干有关笼结构的定理、如度递归性定理和范因子定理等,其成果在笼理论研究中具有很重要意义。于青林对于阿南钦(Ananchuen)和普卢默(Plummer)提出一个关于临界因子的猜想,证明在除两个反例之外的情况下猜想成立;同时对于“在普卢默的关于3边临界的图在一定假设下是k因子临界的猜想”的研究,亦取得一定进展。

2004年起,天津科技大学邢化明在图的控制数、负控制数、符号控制数、罗马控制数和边控制数等方面都获得新的研究结果,已在《离散数学》《图与组合》等多种国际著名数学刊物上发表。

2001~2005年,李学良在组合优化方面解决了20世纪80年代由国际著名运筹学家南木豪瑟(Nemhauser)提出的关于寻找无爪完美图的最小加权着色问题的多项式时间组合算法的问题。而2002年国际数学家大会45分钟特邀报告人瑞德(B.Reed)也试图解决该问题,只是在他们的一篇文章中称,看不出他们自己的结果对这一问题的解决有何帮助。一般图的最小全一问题是NP-完备的,2004年,陈永川与李学良等在《美国工业与应用数学会计算杂志》发表文章,对树的最小全一问题得到线性时间算法,并给出树的全一问题的解的计数,该算法可进一步用于单双圈图的最小全一问题。

应用图来研究群及应用群来研究图,始于20世纪30年代后,但研究趋向广泛已是60年代后了。因此其仍属新的数学领域。在此领域,南开大学组合数学研究中心路在平做出贡献。他于2004年给出素数度半对称图的群论刻画和给定阶的三度半对称图的分类,得到三度边正则图的群论刻画和构造方法。同时,他给出特定阶或特定度数边传递凯莱图的刻画,构造出具有特殊性质的图类;并发现两类CI-群以及从原有的可能CI-群列表中排除了一类群等。

四、组合数论

南开大学组合数学研究中心高维东在组合数论领域取得一系列重要研究成果,得到以色列著名组合数学家、2002年世界数学家大会一小时邀请报告人阿隆(Noga Alon)的高度评价,其成果被认为有“极强的原创性、独创性和高超的技巧性”。在零和理论研究方面,高维东的数个结论和若干方法技巧,已为同行广泛熟知和引用,而且其中的一些结论还被应用于代数数域的算术性质和算法研究中。

2004年起,高维东致力于将群环理论应用于组合问题的研究中,发展出一套系统的群环理论。新发展的理论是由于研究组合问题的需要产生的,难以从代数学本身提出来。所以,研究成果除了其自身重要的代数意义外,更重要的是应用在若干组合问题研究,获得数个深刻的结论。

五、组合数学应用开发

1999年,陈永川与侯庆虎等完成金融风险预警研究课题,开发出系列金融风险分析软件。该软件成功地将国外最新VaR方法引入中国市场,结合中国国情进行合理改进,为金融管理部门和投资机构及个人提供风险管理和决策指导。2000年,陈永川与杨立波等开发的二十五史全文检索系统,使用组合中的倒排文件算法建立全文索引,采用改进的二叉树遍历算法进行检索。该系统被用于对中国历史研究中各种资料的查询、引用。

2001年,陈永川与其学生王超等合作,综合运用图像处理、模式识别、数理统计和模糊数学理论,开发出骨龄智能测试系统。该测试系统对彩色图像采集卡读入的青少年儿童手掌X光片图像数据进行分析,结合少年儿童手掌骨骼发育状况、形状、大小比率等特点,快速简捷地判断出被测青少年儿童的骨龄,并结合其他情况预测其成年后的身高,显示其将来从事何种运动项目更有利于身体发展。该测试系统填补国内空白。

2004年,南开大学组合数学研究中心马万宝等研发中国药物专利数据库,提供中西药专利信息的全文检索和高级检索,中药方剂相似检索,化学物质结构检索,中药词典检索,化学物质信息检索,同义词检索,扩词检索以及历史组配检索等入口检索。

2005年,南开大学组合数学研究中心侯庆虎和天津社会科学院合作,将最先进的数据分析技术应用到经济领域,形成系列《中国城市竞争力报告》,成为国内最权威的城市竞争力分析报告之一。

第九节 理论计算机 信息论 数学史 数学教材

在1991～2005年期间,天津其他数学分支,如理论计算机、信息论、数学史等领域的研究工作,在承袭传统的基础上开创出新的局面。

一、理论计算机

1991～1993年,南开大学胡国定对并行计算的数学理论进行研究,先后发表《模拟序列计算的并行计算》《面向对象并发程序设计的基础理论》等论文。

1988～1992年,南开大学数学研究所徐书润的论文"Petri网一类语言"(发表在亚洲逻辑会会议录—东京)是为研制有效的并行计算机语言所作的基础工作。王永革,赵杰,周志东参与该研究工作。

1994年,针对布卢姆(Blum)的"任意"加速定理,对计算复杂性定义的合理性提出质疑,且20多年中不少研究者对此进行各种专门性的研究,王永革,徐书润在《软件学报》第4卷第4期发表论文《加速定理和函数分层》,证明在某种意义上,这种复杂性定义的合理性。

已故数理逻辑学家王浩在他的《数理逻辑通俗讲话》中说:忙海狸(Busy Beaver)问题是组合练习的取之不尽的源泉。1995年,王克文和徐书润发表在期刊《中国高级软件研究》(Vol 2(2))上的论文《移位函数与忙海狸函数之间的新关系》,对此大大改进了朱尔斯特罗姆(Julstrom)的结果。1997年,丁龙云,杨瑞光和徐书润则将几种忙海狸函数进行综合考察和研究,得到几乎是最好的结果。

二、小波分析与信号处理

1993～2005年,南开大学周性伟课题组从事小波分析与信号处理研究。课题组周性伟、孙文昌等针对该国际数学界热点，在著名学术期刊等发表学术论文50多篇（含SCI收录论文40多篇），陆续报告其研究成果，包括：(1)给出不规则小波和加博尔（Gabor）系统构成框架及其稳定性的条件。该结果在比克霍伊泽出版的小波分析专著中被认为是“重要、最早、最终解决、不同寻常”的；(2)给出不规则采样定理成立的一个条件，在Chapman &Hall/CRC出版的专著中认为该结果是“最全面的”。经查证，他们的成果已被他人的SCI收录论文引用100多篇次。

同期，天津大学宋占杰在信号采样与逼近、随机过程反演与重构方面展开研究。他率先采用随机积分平均采样，证明小波框架重构频谱有限随机过程的采样定理，并给出明确的误差上界估计。相关研究成果发表在《美国电气学工程师学会—信息论汇刊》、英文版《中国科学（数学卷）》、英国《应用数学快报》等学术期刊上。

三、信息论

1998～2002年，南开大学胡国定致力于新的信息论研究，2000年发表论文《在自动测不准推理中的置信度》（The degree of certainty in automated uncertainty reasoning）。传统香农（Shannon）信息论中只有信息量（熵）的数学定义，且主要用于通信的领域。胡国定在其新研究论文中给出事件的信息与信息量的数学定义，并使用公理化方法得到信息与信息量表示的存在性与唯一性，在此基础上建立起信息推理的数学理论，能广泛有效地应用于人工智能的各个方向，进一步扩展信息论的应用领域。在神经网络方面，南开大学沈世镒等于1998年对感知器理论与霍普菲尔德（Hopfield）神经网络系统中的几种模型给出新的算法，并证明这些算法在一定条件下的收敛性。在生物信息学方面，沈世镒等于2002年给出生物序列比对列线的（Alignment）快速算法——SPA（Super Pairwise Alignment，超级比对列线），该算法利用统计判决理论改进了史密斯-沃特曼（Smith-Waterman）的动态规划算法，使序列比对的计算复杂度从O(n*n)降低到O(n)。

同期，南开大学杨恩辉等在信息论与编码方面做出重要贡献。其研究成果包括：(1)在通用有损编码的理论、算法和实践方面，设计出低编码复杂度的有损编码算法，得到的变码率格子结构（trellis）信源编码是在低码率编码里非常有效的。并成功开发出用于连接量化优化、游程编码等方面一系列有损编码算法。其理论和算法已被通信领域著名国际标准：JPEG、MPEG、MP3及H.264所采用，并被转化成数据处理和通信产品，为全球数千万人每天使用。评论家们认为这些研究成果是压缩系统的理论和设计中的重大贡献。(2)在率失真理论与冗余分析方面，解决在一个信息论中长期的开放问题——关于渐进最优率失真有损压缩算法的性能。并解决余（Yu）和斯皮德（Speed）的一个猜想。该研究成果被推荐为IEEE信息论协会1998、2003年最优秀论文奖。杨恩辉在国际顶级刊物和会议上发表论文100多篇，持有14项专利申请文件，开发出8项用于信息技术产业的编解码器软件包，应邀在40多个国际讲座和研讨会上发表演讲。他不仅为加拿大滑铁卢大学第一个获得加拿大专业领域研究主席（Canada Research Chair）殊荣，还被聘为该校的终身教授；他是5个科研奖的获奖者，一些最新、最流行的在线无损和有损数据压缩算法的发明者，IEEE信息论国际研讨会长时间报告的报告人。

同期，南开大学符方伟等在编码方面获得重要研究成果，包括：(1)1998年，符方伟等给出等重码的两种构造方法，并且产生一系列最优等重码。转年，给出q元码的一个上界。该上界被国际上一些编码学者称为FKS界。2003年，给出等成分码的一个上界和新的构造方法。国际上一些编码学者称该上界为卢-符-万克-陈（Luo-Fu-Vinck-Chen）界。(2)1999年，提出一般一次写入记忆介质编码问题的信息论模型，利用信息论方法确定它的容量区域，并且给出计算一般一次写入记忆介质上可存储的最大信息量的公式。(3)信源的多描述编码问题是多用户信息论中一个著名难题。2002年，符方伟等针对该难题给出信源的多描述编码问题的率失真区域的一个新的外界，该外界要好于怀纳（Wyner）和齐夫（Ziv）等人所给出的外界，并且确定出某种重要情形下信源的多描述编码问题的率失真区域。(4)码的不可检错误概率是重传反馈通信系统中码的重要的性能指标。1998年，符方伟等研究等重码的检错性能，给出二元等重码成为检错好码的很一般的必要条件，在二元等重码中发现一些新的检错好码。2000年，符方伟等研究n中取m码的检错阈值，得到检错阈值的很好的上界和下界，从而确定出检错阈值的精确渐进值。2003年，符方伟等研究二元码和二元等重码的不可检错误概率，得到一些重要的性质和优良的性能界，并且在某个区间内完全确定出二元等重码的不可检错误概率的渐进指数。(5)2000年，符方伟等给出序列深度的一种新的快速计算方法，推导出一般线性码深度分布的计算公式，确定出雷德-米勒(Reed-Muller)码的深度分布和三元戈莱(Golay)码的所有深度分布等价类。

同期，南开大学陈鲁生、沈世镒、符方伟等在密码学研究领域也取得许多成果，给出一些安全性能良好的密码函数的构造方法，提出一些数字签名方案以及一些密码协议。同时，由陈鲁生编写的《现代密码学》被纳入"十一五"国家级规划教材，于2002年由科学出版社出初版，以后又再版，为国内高校广泛采用。

四、数学史研究和数学教材

天津师范大学李兆华通过深入考证与推算，证实汪莱(1768-1813)《衡斋算学》的原文完整无缺，数学内容正确无误，改正前人相关研究中的错误。在此工作的基础上，完成《衡斋算学校证》一书(陕西科学技术出版社，1998)。作为"中国科学院知识创新工程"项目子课题、由李兆华主编的《中国近代数学教育史稿》2005年由山东教育出版社出版问世。由吴文俊主编、李兆华任执行主编的第八卷《中国数学史大系》于2000年由北京师范大学出版社出版问世。

20世纪末，南开大学数学科学学院组织编写南开大学数学试点班数学教学丛书。该套丛书共七种九册，由科学出版社出版，包括李成章、黄玉民的《数学分析》(上下册)，孟道骥的《高等代数与解析几何》(上下册)，杨振明的《概率论》，周性伟的《实变函数》，刘炳初的《泛函分析》，孟道骥、梁科的《微分几何》和林金坤的《拓朴学基础》。丛书在全国产生了很大的影响，被列为科学出版社教材目录首页推荐，被教育部审定为"十一五"国家级规划教材。

2001～2002年，由天津工程师范学院李金诚、王璞杰、黄春生等受劳动和社会保障部就业司委托编写高级技工学校数学教材。2002年，该教材由中国劳动社会保障出版社出版，在全国高级技工学校推广使用。

第二章　力　学

天津的力学研究始于19世纪末，自国外传入，经百年之积淀，形成较强的基础与实力。以天津大学为代表，具有一支高水平的队伍，位于国内前列。

1997年，天津大学力学学科获准具有一级学科博士学位授予权，覆盖4个博士学位二级学科，包括一般力学、流体力学、固体力学(含实验力学)和工程力学。周恒1993年当选为中国科学院院士，陈予恕1998年当选为俄国应用科学院外籍院士、2005年当选为中国工程院院士。

1991~2005年，天津的力学研究在流体力学、非线性动力学、实验力学，以及结构力学与水动力学等领域取得多项出色成果。其中，湍流及其控制等研究居国内先进水平，关于非线性动力学的理论与应用的研究均居国际先进水平。

第一节　一般力学

天津一般力学的研究在国内起步较早，20世纪50年代，天津大学主编出版《理论力学》，1962年成立理论力学教研室。20世纪80年代，周恒在流体力学领域的研究取得突出成果。

1991~2005年，天津一般力学的研究取得新成就。周恒领导的团队在流体力学的研究上，科研方向由关于流动稳定性和转捩问题转向湍流及其控制、分叉与混沌理论等，继续取得新的成果，成为国内最有优势的团队之一。

一、理论力学

2002年，天津大学王树新、章青、张大钧等完成计及柔性的机械多体系统动力学理论与应用研究，将多体系统动力学方法与有限元方法有机结合，采用综合模态分析方法描述弹性特征，引入单元耦合行程函数将变形场表示为广义坐标的二阶小量形式，首次提出动力刚化向的动力学本质及其数值解算量化依据，建立面向复杂机械结构的柔性多体系统动力学理论体系。该理论成功应用于柔性机机械臂振动控制，使柔性机械臂端点振动幅值减少一个量级；成功解算中继卫星太阳帆板与抛物面天线展开过程以及汽车碰撞过程人体动力学响应，在数控机床几何误差补偿方面取得明显效果。

2002年，天津大学张策、马文贵、宋轶民等完成改善动力学特性的智能化机构的理论与实验研究。项目对改善动力学品质的智能化机构开展系统、深入的理论研究，表明这种具有传感器、动作器与控制器的智能化机构可以改善机构多方面的动力学性能，如降低弹性连杆机构的构件动应力，提高弹性连杆机构的创成轨迹精度，抑制凸轮机构的残余振动、提高分度定位精度等。同时，与理论研究并行地开展相应的实验研究，建立弹性连杆机构的实验装置及其控制系统；建立伺服电机驱动的凸轮机构实验装置及其主动控制系统；对含间隙的弧面分度凸轮机构的动力学行为进行深入的实验研究。研究成果初步形成以改善动力学品质为目标的智能化机构的理论体系。在国内外核心期刊及重要学术会议上发表科技论文42篇，他引44次。

二、流体力学

（一）湍流及其控制

2002年10月，天津大学周恒、罗纪生、姜楠等完成湍流及其控制的研究，以平板边界层近壁区为研究对象，提出相干结构的不稳定波模型、单个相干结构的模型、以及外区扰动激发近壁区单个相干结构的模型，从而给出边界层近壁区相干结构的基本完整的动力学模型，这一套模型合理地解释很多由实验和直接数值模拟发现的重要现象，并能用于湍流中标量输运的计算。在实验研究方面，在国内第一个将子波分析方法用于湍流实测信号分析和湍流大尺度相干结构的识别，提出用不同尺度的"子波"分解湍流中不同尺度局部"涡"的思想。发展湍流相干结构检测方法，提出用子波分析识别壁湍流相干结构的能量最大准则。该课题具有完整、系统的理论体系，在研究方法上注意理论与实验相结合，技术路线在国内外都有其独创性，理论结果有实验的可

图3-2-1-9　天津大学周恒作学术报告

靠验证。

(二)分叉、混沌理论及其应用

1996年1月至2003年6月,天津大学、北京工业大学和石家庄铁道学院共同完成分叉、混沌理论及其应用的研究,参与研究的有王洪礼、张伟、杨绍普、张琪昌等。项目在理论与应用方面分别获得创新成果:理论上,对于高维非线性系统的全局分叉和混沌动力学,高维非线性系统的全局摄动发,机械柔性结构的非线性动力学,参数激励非线性系统的分叉和混沌,高维非线性系统规范形和最简规范形的计算和应用,高余维退化分叉,滞后分线性系统分叉动力学,柔索的混沌动力学等方面进行深入和广泛的研究。应用研究上,运用现代非线性动力学理论,分叉与混沌理论,结合强非线性理论、时变控制理论、鲁棒自适应控制理论和神经网络控制理论等,对汽车四轮转向系统,滞后非线性运载机械系统,高速机车车辆运行稳定性,高速机车车辆悬架系统,非线性转子—形状记忆合金轴承系统,柔性机械臂的非线性振动与控制,藻类生态系统和社会经济等领域中的非线性动力学问题进行广泛、全面和深入的研究。在国内外重要刊物和国际学术会议上发表论文62篇,出版专著一部。

第二节 非线性动力学及其应用

自20世纪60年代开始,天津的非线性动力学研究,以陈予恕为代表取得一系列突出成果。

1991~2005年,天津关于非线性动力学的研究,既重视理论又重视与生产实际的密切结合,将非线性动力学理论引入到振动研究中,形成具有基础理论和工程应用研究相结合特色的交叉学科:工程非线性动力学。并将非线性动力学理论引入到机电耦联系统、大型旋转机械系统和大型火电机组之中,解决复杂的动力学问题,取得突出成果,在指导旋转机械振动故障治理中发挥显著作用,是这个方向理论及应用相关研究的一面旗帜。陈予恕领导研究团队,其理论成果和应用成果分别荣获国家自然科学二等奖和科技进步二等奖。

一、非线性动力学理论研究

1994年1月至2000年12月,天津大学陈予恕、吴志强、丁千等与北京航空航天大学、清华大学、西安交通大学众多学者合作完成复杂非线性系统的动力学理论与方法的研究。将LS降维约化和分岔奇异性理论结合,首次引入非线性振动系统的研究,创建C-L(Chen-Langford)方法,将非线性振动理论推进到新的阶段,为动力学结构设计、参数控制和某些重大故障治理奠定理论基础;在高余维分岔理论方面,对参数激励广义von der Pol-Duffing系统,对其Z_2余维数≥3的分岔行为进行普适分类;对力学系统中广泛存在的一类余维5分岔,导出其普适开折所有形式,计算所有双参数开折的分岔图;提出计算非线性自治系统的正规形的直接方法以及计算非自治系统正规形的复内积平均法,建立用切比雪夫多项式形式求解高维系统周期解方法;进行复杂动力学研究;研究转子的碰摩机理、旋转机械非线性振动的突发低频失稳非线性机制等,进行非线性转子动力学研究;发展转子振动故障综合控制治理技术。发表论著影响广泛,被SCI、EI分别收录73、79篇,共被引用251次,大大促进国内非线性动力学理论及应用研究,开创中国非线性振动学科新的研究领域。

图3-2-2-10 天津大学陈予恕

2004年6月，天津大学陈予恕、吴志强、唐友刚等研究非线性系统分岔控制及应用，提出的复杂非线性系统参数动力学控制的思想，将引起故障的原因消除在设计阶段，与传统的故障控制路线相比，能使产品性能更优越。在解决转子动力学、舰船运动工程方面的问题得到较普遍的应用。该项成果开创分岔控制理论的新方向——分岔参数鲁棒性控制，达到国际先进水平。有关学术论文，发表在同领域国内外最高水平杂志上，被SCI、EI、ISTP等收录34篇次。

二、非线性动力学应用研究

（一）工程非线性动力学

1994年4月至1999年12月，天津大学王洪礼、元英进、张琪昌等共同完成生化反应系统中的非线性动力学研究，内容包括：生化反应的非线性动力学理论研究；细胞分化与分化细胞反应器的非线性特性研究；生化反应过程中的非线性动力学研究。在国内外重要刊物上发表论文30多篇，完成专著1部。

1997年12月，天津大学陈予恕、徐鉴、吴志强等完成工程非线性动力学关于基础理论与应用的研究，项目在奇异性理论基础上发展C-L方法，首次推广Liapunov-Schmidt方法并完成复杂非自治动力系统的研究，同时将几何方法引入非线性振动的研究中。项目的理论研究始终以工程应用为最终目的，既发展理论，也紧密结合重大工程应用，形成具有交叉学科特色的工程非线性动力学，受到多领域的重视，同时在实际应用中取得较大的经济效益和社会效益。发表论文百余篇，被SCI、EI、国内中心刊物等收录多篇，并被多次引用。

2001年12月，天津大学陈予恕、陆启韶、褚福磊等开展复杂非线性系统的动力学理论与应用的研究，系统研究复杂非线性系统的动力学、控制及其在大型旋转机械非线性动力学问题方面的应用，促成并发展新的学科方向——工程非线性动力学。理论用于非线性转子动力学，对转子的碰摩机理及碰摩位置判断的研究、旋转机械非线性振动的突发低频失稳机理的研究，发展现代非线性转子动力学理论，由此提出大型高速转子重大振动故障综合控制治理技术，在实践中取得显著的经济效益。项目研究学术思想新颖独特，具有科学的系统性、理论的先进性和解决工程问题的良好经济性。成果在整体上达到国际先进水平，部分成果达到国际领先水平，突破传统非线性振动理论发展的瓶颈，形成新的学科方向。发表的论著影响广泛，被SCI、EI、ISTP等收录407篇次，且被多次引用。

（二）机电耦联非线性振动学

1996年3月，天津大学邱家俊、王洪礼、张琪昌等开展机电耦联系统的非线性振动理论及应用的研究，针对机电分析动力学、电机电磁激发的参数共振、电磁激发的非线性多重共振、电机的机电耦联非线性振动在电磁激发的非线性振动、磁力轴承的非线性振动、非线性振动理论方法、内燃机气门机械及减振器的分岔混沌和参数强迫联合激励的局部分岔、全局分岔、同宿及异宿分岔方面进行研究。把力学（一般力学、非线性振动）与电磁学（电磁场理论、电机理论）有机结合与统一起来，开辟出电磁激发振动与机电耦联非线性振动新的研究领域。不仅在理论及实验研究方面取得深入系统的研究成果，并且有重大的工程应用价值。发表论文60余篇，10余篇被EI、PA、CCA等国际检索刊物收录。

2002年，天津大学张策、马文贵、宋轶民等完成改善动力学特性的智能化机构的理论与实验研究。项目对工程中广泛应用的连杆机构、凸轮机构，设计具有传感器、作动器与控制器的智能化机构，并基于最优控制、神经网络控制等先进的控制理论，获得了系统的控制输入，显著地改善机构的动力学性能。对智能化机构的分类、计算及设计原理等进行了深入研究，初步形成以改善动力学品质为目标的智能化机构的理论体系。成果在国内外核心期刊及学术会议发表论文42篇，其中SCI收录3篇、EI收录9篇。

（三）机械系统非线性振动学

1991年1月至2000年10月，天津大学王洪礼、张琪昌、孙景等与北京工业大学张伟合作完成现代非线性动力学理论及在机械系统中的应用研究课题，首次研究参数与强迫振动激励联合作用下非线性系统的高余维退化分叉，填补国内外在该领域的空白，解决当平均系统具有双零特征值时解的稳定性问题；在国际上首创用计算机符号运算的方法推导和计算Normal Form，开辟用非线性动力系统理论研究高维非线性机械系统的复杂动力学行为新方法。研究成果为磁力轴承、磁悬浮列车和汽车四轮转向系统及悬架系统的新型设计打下良好的基础。

1994年1月至2003年2月，天津大学、哈尔滨工业大学、西南交通大学、东北大学、北京大学、大连理工大学、天津市电力公司，复旦大学、国家电网公司国电自动化研究所共同参与完成大型旋转机械和振动机械重大振动故障治理与非线性动力学设计技术研究项目，研究团队成员有：陈予恕、黄文虎、闻邦椿、朱均、武际可、薛禹胜、张文、曹树谦、吕和祥、虞烈、刘树英等。课题围绕大型旋转机械重大非线性振动故障机理，开展理论、计算、实验及工程应用等方面的学术前沿研究，成果包括：应用高维非线性动力学理论、方法，研究复杂转子系统的稳定性、分岔和混沌现象，揭示重大振动故障的机理；提出非线性转子系统稳定性量化分析方法；给出能反映大型旋转机械系统典型振动故障特征的新的计算方法；从理论和实验两方面，揭示旋转机械典型微小间隙约束激励源的非线性机理，完成理论和数值建模；完成国产主力火电机组非线性动力学计算，验证某些重要理论结果；发展并提出转子系统疑难振动故障治理技术，开展大型旋转机械非线性动力学设计的初步研究工作。其应用研究产生显著经济效益。发表期刊论文492篇（其中核心期刊和国外刊物论文430篇），会议论文102篇，出版中英文专著6部。该成果荣获2005年度国家科技进步二等奖。

1994年1月至2003年12月，天津大学和平顶山天安煤业（集团）田庄选煤厂合作，由陈予恕、高亚平、曹树谦、林建等共同完成共振筛动力学性能分析与调整技术项目，针对大型振动筛分机械，在动力学元件参数优化设计、模态选型、动态响应和应力测试、强度分析、结构安装与参数调整等方面开展一系列研究工作，提出一套参数与结构优化的设计理论技术及现场调整方法。所用非光滑系统的非线性振动理论成果得到国内外同行专家的广泛认可，根据该理论给出的设计计算方法研制的大型共振筛结构参数合理，模态选型和动应力分析准确可靠，产品性能达到国际先进水平。

（四）大型火电机组非线性振动分析

1992年4月至1996年3月，天津大学与天津市电力科学研究院、天津军粮城发电厂合作，陈予恕、金宗武、田家玉等共同完成大型火电机组非线性振动事故机理分析及应用研究。在理论研究方面，发现在油膜力、密封力、材料内阻尼力和碰磨等主要激励因素作用下，汽轮机组产生振幅多解、跳跃、分岔、亚谐共振、混沌运动等现象，解释过去用线性理论无法解释的低频振动分量问题，揭示一些新的动力学现象与系统参数的关系。同时，大型汽轮发电机组非线性振动数据库与故障诊断软件的建立与研制成功，对于机组振动故障的诊断与查找具有极大的实用价值，在实际应用中获得显著的经济效益和社会效益。

1992年4月至1996年3月，天津大学、天津电力科学研究院和天津军粮城发电厂陈予恕、王文永、田家玉、丁千、张宁等合作完成非线性转子动力学数据库与软件研究及其在大型火电机组中的应用项目，应用非线性动力学力学理论研究大型高速转子系统的非线性动力学机理。建立国内第一个大型汽轮发电机组非线性振动数据库，首次研制出转子非线性振动故障诊断分析软件，并应用于大型汽轮发电机组振动监测、分析和诊断。项目在基础理论研究方面取得较全面的成果，丰富非线性转子动力学理论。大型汽轮发电机组非线性振动数据库与故障诊断软件的建立与研制成功，对于机组振动故障的诊断与查找极具有实用价值。

第三节　实验力学

天津在全国最早开始光测和电测技术的研究，创建实验力学。20世纪80年代，天津的实验力学在多个方面居国内领先水平。1991~2005年，天津在实验力学研究领域继续取得可喜成果。天津大学在细观、纳微观尺度力学行为的表征及机理、光测力学中的瞬态图像采集技术研究与测量等方面开展具有原创性的研究。

1994年1月至1996年12月,天津大学亢一澜、贾有权、王燕群等完成实验界面力学若干问题研究。项目在现代光测实验技术研究的基础上,对几种高灵敏光测力学实验技术、实验与数值计算的混合法研究与应用、界面层力学行为、界面端部应力集中和界面断裂力学问题进行科学研究。首次用实验的方法检验著名的Bogy楔形尖端奇异性的特征方程,证实方程中较大实根与实验应力奇异性对应,并且根据实验位移场对垂直界面裂纹裂尖区域应力奇异性、角位移分布、应力强度因子进行全面的分析,讨论D.H.Chen理论位移解的适用范围。在光测细观力学实验技术方面和界面力学问题实验分析的研究上均有所发现和创新,达到国内外先进水平。发表论文多篇,被EI收录2篇,美国科学文献收录4篇,ESTP收录4篇。

1992年1月至1997年6月,天津大学佟景伟、李鸿琦、张东升等完成光测力学中的瞬态图像采集技术研究及其应用项目,巧妙利用电荷耦合摄像机(CCD)的短暂存储效应和红宝石脉冲激光光脉冲宽度极短的特点,配以精密的同步控制系统,实现利用普通图像采集卡和CCD摄像机捕捉相当于200万次/秒高速照相机才能记录的瞬态图像。在动态光测力学中,在明光下使用瞬态光学图像采集系统可以将数字化的图像存储在图像采集卡的帧存体中,进行图像处理。采用瞬态光学图像采集系统还可以实现撞击载荷下数字散斑干涉的计量,对物体动态面内位移和离面位移场进行定量分析,在交变应力过程中使用新光学方法不停机测量物体表面的位移场和应变场,并进行材料损伤过程观测。研制的瞬态图像采集系统是一项具有创造性的研究工作,在研究构件的动态响应、动态中材料损伤的发生与发展和国防工业中有广阔的推广和应用价值。

第四节 结构力学与水动力学

1991~2005年,天津大学在结构力学研究领域取得的成果具有重要应用价值,关于水动力学的研究也极具社会、环境和经济效益。

一、结构力学

1994年6月,天津大学严宗达、卜小明、钱民刚等完成建筑结构分析中正交函数系级数展开法的理论和应用研究,建立对Fourier-Bessel级数和Legendre级数逐项求导的系列定理和若干有用的和式,奠定通用解法的重要理论基础,完善建筑结构分析中的级数解法的理论基础。项目成果汇总专著《结构力学中的傅里叶级数解法》在国内外独树一帜,有重要理论和应用价值,在建筑结构设计中推广亦获得提高设计精度、节省机时等显著效益。

二、水动力学

2001年8月至2003年8月,天津大学陶建华,袁德奎,刘长根等开展河流、海洋和水环境数值模拟技术及其应用研究,包含四套软件系统的集成,建立一个可靠的能够直接用于波浪潮流洪水和水质等问题研究的平台,为相关研究提供重要的技术支持。首次提出缓坡浅海污染物的迁移扩散规律;建立渤海湾的生态水动力学模型;将能模拟波浪破碎的"roller"破碎模型和"波浪多次破碎模型"引入到大面积波浪场的数学模型中。该研究平台在天津近岸海域的规划和管理中得到充分的应用,为其提供十分重要的技术支持。同时,在近岸海域区域评价及环境-经济规划中得到应用,取得良好的社会、环境和经济效益。

第三章 物理学

20世纪70～80年代，天津的物理学研究在光学、电子物理学、凝聚态物理学以及半导体物理学和核物理学等领域，开展一系列工作并取得可贵成果。

1991～2005年，天津的物理学研究继续深入、不断拓展，在理论物理、光谱学与非线性光学、凝聚态物理、激光物理与激光器、发光材料与薄膜以及电磁学等领域，辛勤努力，积极探索，取得大量新的成果。南开大学关于光折变非线性光学和凝聚态物理和天津大学关于激光物理与激光器的研究工作，所取得的成就尤为突出。2005年，许京军、张光寅、刘思敏等以项目“光折变新效应、机理与器件的研究”获国家自然科学奖二等奖，王清月、邢岐荣、张伟力等开展飞秒激光技术的研究，获1999年度国家科技进步二等奖。

第一节 光 学

20世纪80年代起，南开大学在国内率先开展非线性光学的研究工作，发现大量新现象、新效应。20世纪90年代后南开大学拓展研究，在光折变非线性光学和弱光非线性研究两个不同分支领域，取得一系列新成果。1991～2005年，天津的光谱学研究在20世纪80年代工作的基础上取得新的突出成果。

一、光谱学

1991年，南开大学张光寅、蓝国祥撰写出版《晶格振动光谱学》，较系统地阐述晶格振动光谱的原理与实验，介绍晶格振动的红外光谱、拉曼光谱和布里渊谱。2000年被教育部研究生工作办公室遴选、推荐为研究生教学用书。

1998年，南开大学蓝国祥、扈士芬、李玉栋等持续十余年关注国际高压物理领域的研究热点，研究晶体的高压拉曼光谱和压致非晶化现象，发现一些压致晶态到晶态和晶态到非晶的相变，并研究压致非晶态的结构、机制以及退火时的重新晶化过程。发表论文27篇。

1999年，南开大学蓝国祥、李冠告、王玉芳等开展对非线性光学晶体的晶格振动光谱的研究，包括LiNbO等无机晶体和DGSe等有机晶体的拉曼光谱和红外反射光谱。对其中一些晶体测定异常声子的方向色散以及电磁激元色散，采用C-F矩阵方法计算正则振动频率，对红外反射光谱进行K-K分析，对晶格振动光谱进行认定。其中，有些非线性光学晶体是国内研制的新晶体，研究成果提供这些晶体的声子谱数据和结构信息，在国际上受到广泛重视与应用。

2000年，南开大学蓝国祥、王玉芳、刘友婴等经对新型碳材料的多年研究，发现高氯酸石墨层间化合物的共振增强拉曼散射效应，成功研制出稀土-碳60(C_{60})插入化合物，其中镱3碳60和钐3碳60具有超导电性。利用X射线衍射确定插入化合物的结构，利用拉曼光谱获得C_{60}分子遭到严重畸变的证据。采用激光蒸发法和电弧放电法制备出单壁碳纳米管，建立起识别单壁碳纳米管特征振动拉曼谱线的图表法，将单壁碳纳米管拉曼光谱研究推进一步。在国内外学术刊物上共发表论文17篇。

2000~2003年，南开大学母国光开展基于白光信息处理的历史文物彩色恢复及存储技术和设备的研究，创造性地提出白光图像处理的加、减、消卷积、微分、相关等运算和褪色胶片的彩色恢复、彩色档案存储、立体显示、菲涅尔全息滤波、光学傅立叶变换光谱以及相型图像假彩色等技术，扩展和发展白光光学信息处理技术。

二、非线性光学

(一)光折变非线性光学

1991年，南开大学张光寅、刘思敏、许京军等从事$LiNbO_3$:Fe晶体的光谱特性与光折变非线性研究。1992年，刘思敏、郭儒、凌振芳编著出版该领域在国内的第一部专著《光折变非线性光学》，受到国内同行的好评，促进中国开展光折变非线性光学领域的研究工作。2004年，刘思敏、许京军、郭儒根据多年来科研工作的积累，丰富国内外该领域的研究动态，又编著出版《光折变非线性光学及其应用》。

1994年开始，张光寅、刘思敏、张国权等人利用光折变空间孤子在$LiNbO_3$:Fe晶体中实时写入并存储一维和二维波导，为实时光导向光、传播空间信息和集成光学的小型化探索一条高效益、低成本的新路。而以往的波导多是在介质衬底上通过扩散或离子交换等方法得到，工艺复杂、成本高、周期长。张光寅等的这一工作是与美国斯坦福大学、普林斯顿大学几乎同时分别独立完成的。

2001年，刘思敏首次提出"变折射率光学工程"的基本思想，这是利用光折变非线性光学效应，分别运用模拟记录和数字记录方式，使用光学傅立叶变换方法，干涉法和成像法等，通过入射光强的空间分布直接实现并控制介质中的折射率的空间分布的全光学方法。刘思敏、温海东、陈晓虎等由光折变空间孤子成功制作光折变位相图，位相波带片和达曼光栅，透镜阵列，波导和波导阵列等光学器件，为二元光学和集成光学器件的制作提供新思路。

自2002年起，刘思敏、郭儒、杨立森等人在$LiNbO_3$:Fe晶体中，利用光折变效应和成像方法首次实时写入阵列波导。与连续、均匀介质不同，在阵列波导中的分立衍射和分立孤子具有明显的反常性。通过改变入射光方向和阵列波导的参数可以操纵和控制分立衍射的符号和数值，在同一种材料的阵列波导中观察到亮和暗的分立孤子。宋涛、齐新元、曲迪等人利用相干光在$LiNbO_3$:Fe晶体中分别制作一维和二维阵列波导，实验研究在阵列波导中的分立孤子及其相互作用，布拉格带隙分立孤子及其缺陷孤子等。

美国普林斯顿大学的研究者们于1996年首先证明部分非相干光空间孤子和白光亮空间孤子的存在，表明相干光并不是研究非线性光学的必要条件。南开大学刘思敏、郭儒、高垣梅等和天津理工大学陆猗从2003年以来，首次报道白光一维光生伏打暗空间孤子以及由它们感应的波导和定向耦合器，圆形和椭圆形白光暗空间孤子、二维白光光子晶格和白光暗空间孤子在数字图像传输中的应用。数值模拟在饱和对数非线性介质中的两个及多个部分非相干亮空间孤子、白光亮空间孤子对之间的相互作用。理论和实验结果表明，在自散焦的各向异性光折变非线性介质中，一维、二维白光暗空间孤子之间的相互作用总是吸引。白光的衍射不依赖于波长，白光孤子是它所包含的所有波长的光共同参加的集体行为。

(二)弱光非线性研究

1998年，南开大学田建国、张春平、张光寅等完成"弱光非线性的机理、测量及应用"项目。项目组对一些光学非线性材料如茶溶液、细菌视紫红质(bR)、无机晶体及有机分子等材料的弱光非线性的机理及性质进行较系统的研究。发展Z扫描方法，首次成功地区分热光非线性与其他机制的光学非线性，正确地分析茶溶液光学非线性起源，对自聚焦、自散焦现象和概念进行深入地分析和概括；首次提出两种改进的Z扫描方法，可简便地测量光学非线性系数，与原方法相比，灵敏度提高一个数量级；发展两种光束在厚非线性光学介质中传播的分析方法，首次获得测量量与非线性系数之间由解析表达的直接联系；首次发现bR膜和铌酸锂晶体存在双光强区不同光学非线性机制，并阐述其产生机理；利用光束在厚非线性光学介质中的传播分析法和自洽方程，首次获得克尔透镜锁模输出功率、脉冲宽及增益的解析解；对铌酸锂和掺铁铌酸锂晶体中的各种散射做测量和分析，将过去一些模糊或有争论的说法给出明确的解释；在染料掺杂PMMA高分子薄膜中，利用类光析变光栅的高阶衍射光的多波耦合过程，首次在材料的共振和非共振区分别实现类光折光放大，其增益高出光析变聚合物一个数量级。

2004年2月，由南开大学承担，张春平、陈桂英、富光华等完成的“细菌视紫红质的特异性质及其新应用研究”项目通过评审。该成果首次提出“光偏置光子晶体管”的新模型，这种全光学器件具有操作简便、实时、成本低、无相干噪声等优点。其基本原理是建立bR分子的基态和最稳中间态之间的两能级系统和速率方程。当蓝光和黄光同时照射bR膜时，可实现双光束互补抑制透射。利用此方案实现亮背景滤除、图像翻转、新事物滤波以及数字计算，并对亮背景滤除和新事物滤波应用中bR膜参量的影响做分析。利用高斯光束照射bR膜时产生的折射率和透过率变化的非线性，实现高斯光束的整形和束腰位置的测量。对由非线性折射率变化引起的高阶衍射和自衍射的特性做实验研究并给出理论解释。利用bR紫膜去质子化处理后得到的bR蓝膜，实现重复使用的用于信息存储的生物膜片。测量偶氮聚合物薄膜的光致双折射特性；获得双硫腙汞聚合物薄膜的非线性折射系数及其折射率与波长的关系，研究其自衍射现象及在光限幅方面的应用；从理论上分析毛细管测量样品折射率的方法，得到650纳米连续激光入射到生物组织模拟液中不同方向散射光沿空间分布的实验结果；分别用光纤和CCD测量几种动物组织的表面漫反射光和透射光的分布，与Monte Carlo模拟结果相符合。对光在散射介质中分布的实验结果作合理的解释。

第二节 凝聚态物理

1991～2005年，南开大学在凝聚态物理领域的研究，成果丰硕，成绩突出，引起国内外同行关注。以南开大学为第一完成单位，许京军、张光寅、刘思敏等从事的“光折变新效应、机理与器件的研究”，获2005年度国家自然科学奖二等奖。2005年，南开大学作为大会组织单位，许京军作为大会主席，主办美国光学学会系列学术会议之一的“10th International Conference on Photorefractive Effects, Materials, and Device”国际会议，作为主编之一组织编辑美国光学学会会刊“Trend of Optics and Photonics, American Optical Society, Vol.99”。

一、人工晶体

2002年，天津市环欧半导体材料技术有限公司沈浩平、李翔、汪雨田等研究开发出CFZ硅单晶新材料，其性能、生产技术和生产成本等各方面介于直拉硅单晶和区熔硅单晶之间，具有地氧含量、电阻率稳定性好、生产周期短、并易于规模化生产等多种优点，推动行业技术进步。2004年，致力于半导体材料Φ6〃区熔硅单晶的研制，并实现产业化生产。

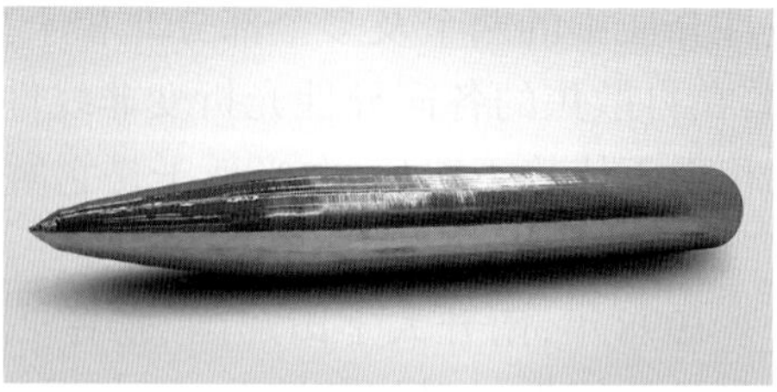

图3-3-2-11 天津环欧半导体材料技术公司研制的区熔硅单晶

2003年11月，南开大学孔勇发等完成的大尺寸光学级铌酸锂晶体生长技术的开发项目通过鉴定。研究成果包括：研制出大尺寸单晶生长炉，可同时采用上称重和下称重的控制技术；改造原有单晶炉的提拉系统，大幅度降低提拉过程中的振动和爬行；改进传统的固相反应烧料方法，减少原材料的团聚，有效降低小角晶界缺陷；采用计算机程序控制，获得比较理想的等径控制；成功生长出直径≧3英寸（76毫米）的光学级铌酸锂晶体，晶体整体双折射梯度优于3×10^{-5}；利用正交偏光干涉法，建立光学均匀性检测系统，精确测量大尺寸铌酸锂晶体的双折射梯度；获得76毫米近化学计量比铌酸锂晶片和高抗光折变性能的近化学计量比掺镁铌酸锂晶片。

2004年3月,天津大学完成多孔阵列光子晶体制备技术研究。成果包括项目建立粒径均一分布聚苯乙烯、二氧化硅乳胶粒子及复合粒子的制备技术;探索几种不同制备蛋白石结构光子晶体的制备技术,在此基础上构制CdS量子点蛋白石结构光子晶体和CdS反蛋白石结构光子晶体;首次制备出钛酸钡/二氧化钛杂化反蛋白石结构光子晶体及钛酸钡光子晶体,并对蛋白石结构光子晶体光学特性进行测试。专家鉴定达到国际先进水平。

2005年,中国电子科技集团公司第46研究所赖占平、周春锋、赵权等研究直径Φ6英寸半绝缘砷化镓单晶晶片制备技术,突破Φ6英寸半绝缘砷化镓单晶生长关键工艺技术,完成晶片精细加工工作,达到开盒即用水平,形成Φ6英寸半绝缘砷化镓单晶材料批量研制生产能力;开展主要分析测试技术的研究,建立Φ6英寸半绝缘砷化镓单晶抛光片各项指标的测试范围。研制出一台6英寸半绝缘砷化镓常压LEC单晶炉,性能可靠、功能先进。

二、光折变新效应、机理与器件

(一)新效应与机理

1993~2000年间,许京军等在共掺Mg或In的LN:Fe晶体中,发现光折变光散射光强阈值效应,打破人们普遍认为的光折变非线性与光强无关的传统概念。这一效应使这些双掺LN晶体成为更为理想的光折变体全息存储材料,为彻底解决光折变三维存储器中的光散射噪音提供新的有效可行途径。

1996年开始,许京军等相继开展三维全息光折变存储材料及其应用、α-$LiIO_3$晶体弱光光学非线性与弱光非线性光学中的新机制新材料新器件的研究。1999年,南开大学张光寅、许京军、刘思敏完成的新型高性能掺杂KNSBN晶体自泵浦相位共轭器的研究。首次发现"无回路背向散射光放大自弯曲相继四波混频"产生相位共轭波的新机制,并将该器件的反射率从国际上已报导的29%突破性地提高到68%的高指标,并在研究中还发现单光束作用下的光折变自弯曲、自聚焦和自反射等新效应,使得该自泵浦相位共轭器综合指标好于国际上被认为最优的"猫式"自泵浦相位共轭器。同时,课题组实现图像复原、图像反转、双泵浦相位共轭器、相位共轭激光输出(减少纵模、压窄频宽、抑制高阶行模、提高输出稳定性等)等实验操作,实验表明:这种新型自泵浦相位共轭器性能好、易加工、尺寸小、成本低、使用方便,是一种很有竞争力的光折变器件,为光折变自泵浦相位共轭器在光学信息与图像处理、激光器等领域的实际应用奠定基础。在国内外一流刊物发表相关论文20余篇。这一机制被广泛用于其他晶体的自泵浦相位共轭器上及其激光应用和图像处理领域中。同期,张光寅等从事紧凑可调谐光子源及其光谱传感应用基础的研究。

图3-3-2-12 南开大学许京军在做实验

2000年,许京军等首次实验发现在铌酸锂晶体中随着掺镁浓度的增加,紫外波段的光折变效应增强的效应,这是与锌或镁的掺入使晶体中的光折变敏感中心如Fe、Cu等从Li位向Nb位的转移,引起光折变敏感吸收带从可见波段向紫外波段的变化直接相关。此前,国际上通常认为镁或锌元素是绝对的抗光折变元素,而该研究表明:这只局限在可见波段,在紫外波段这个结论恰恰相反。这一结果不仅突破掺镁抗光折变非线性的传统认识,而且,发现高掺镁晶体为优良的紫外光存储与光放大材料,为紫外光存储提供新的途径,进而,他们采用这一效应与材料,与法国科学家合作研制成功二维可编程激光打标设备原型。

2003~2004年,许京军与合作者提出相位耦合导致光速减慢的新机制,在室温下通过固体材料的某种非线性过程控制光单位传播距离内光波相位改变量的色散特性,成功地在室温下固体中实现对光速的大范围调控,并成功地在室温下固体中实现光速减慢到0.05米/秒,同时在实验中发现光耦合放大增强等弱光非线性光学效应。成果发表于美国《物理评论快报》。

2004年,许京军等在光折变空间孤子与波导及其光子学晶格的研究基础上,利用光电光致波导成功地实现飞秒脉冲信号的二次谐波增强效应，为光控光操作提供新的途径。

2005年，南开大学张光寅、陈云琳、孔勇发等完成抗光损伤近化学计量比铌酸锂晶体与全光微结构研究。基于对掺镁铌酸锂晶体中缺陷微结构及其相应光谱的研究，提出“中国之星－Ⅱ”的新概念，并在实验上得以实现。使铌酸锂晶体的抗光损伤能力又提高约2个数量级。利用双坩埚技术成功地制备大尺寸近化学比铌酸锂（NSLN）晶体。还为实现短波准相位匹配倍频输出提供条件，简化利用电场极化方法制作光子学微结构PPLN的方法，具有很大的实际意义。

2005年，南开大学张桂兰、陈文驹、汤国庆等完成新型激发态质子转移有机材料及皮秒全光光开关应用研究。首次研究激发态质子转移有机分子的光开关效应。用吸收光谱和荧光光谱研究不同溶剂对激发态质子转换的影响及质子转移的机制；用Z-Scan技术测量这些分子在不同溶剂中的三阶非线性极化系数；用泵浦探测方法观测它们在不同溶剂中的光开关效应。实验结果发现，激发态质子转移效率高者，其三阶非线性极化系数亦大，其光开关效应就强。探讨分子的光开关效应与其三阶非线性极化率及其激发态质子转移效率的关系。实验结果为开发应用这些有机分子提供实验依据和理论分析。

2005年，孔勇发、许京军、陈云琳等完成近完美铌酸锂晶体及其光性能的优化研究。该项目在国内首先成功生长出一种近化学计量比铌酸锂晶体。与通常的同成分（Li / Nb = 48.5∶51.5）晶体相比，近化学计量比晶体的电光系数更大，光折变灵敏度和光致折射率变化提高一个量级，周期化反转电压下降，在掺入1.8 mol.% MgO后抗光伤能力提高4个量级以上，非挥发性全息存储的响应时间缩短2个量级。该项目开展的近完美铌酸锂晶体研究工作，大幅减少晶体中各种点缺陷及生长缺陷的数量，提高它在抗光折变、全息光栅的响应速度及寿命、期极化、发光效率等方面的电光性能；研究晶体完美系数与晶体各项性能指标的关系，及其对电子输运过程及光折变动力学的影响，建立与实验结果相符合的物理模型，为设计、开发各种铌酸锂光电子器件打下坚实的物理基础。该项目首次明确提出一个重要思想，即要彻底扭转铌酸锂晶体在电光性能与应用上的不利局面，必须尽量减少晶体的各种缺陷，走近完美晶体的路子；首次提出近完美铌酸锂晶体的概念，是一次质的飞跃。该项目从原料提纯、缺陷控制、近化学计量比、均匀组分到性能优化，给出一整套制备近完美铌酸锂晶体的方法，这种新的尝试，对铌酸锂晶体及其他非完美光学晶体的生长及制备技术产生很大影响。

（二）器件

2000年，南开大学许京军等开展三维数字存储器与图像数字编码技术及高性能光学存储材料的研究。2001年，许京军、孙骞、张光寅等完成三维光折变存储材料及其存储器的研究，首次在国际上发现光折变光散射光强阈值效应，提出最佳写入光强；开发出高性能双掺铌酸锂晶体，在国内首次生长出近化学比铌酸锂晶体；采用小型半导体激光器，利于系统的小型化，提高图象信噪比，实现清晰图像再现；研制成相位失配调整器，大面积无畸变复现图像；建立国际上较为完善的晶体本征与非本征缺陷结构模型；在国际上首次发现高掺镁晶体紫外光折变增强效应；建立动态差分编解码技术，大大降低误码率。在国际上一流刊物发表论文30余篇，研究工作得到国际同行的高度评价。同期，许京军等首次提出铌酸锂晶体多功能集成芯片的概念，并实验上在一片铌酸锂中实现光束分束、偏转、全息记录和自相干等功能的协作效应，这一概念的实现为光折变器件，尤其是三维光折变存储器的小型化、低成本、实用化奠定基础。国外评审人评价成果是“对整个光学社会有兴趣的工作”。2005年，许京军、张光寅、刘思敏等以项目“光折变新效应、机理与器件的研究”获国家自然科学奖二等奖，南开大学为第一完成单位。该项目发表SCI收录刊物论文104篇，著作3部，其主要成果被他引554篇次（中SCI论文引用309篇次），并获得中国发明专利8项，美国专利2项。

2005年，南开大学陈云琳、孔勇发、陈绍林等完成准相位匹配掺镁化学计量比铌酸锂波导全光开关的研究。项目以成熟的铌酸锂晶体制备工艺为基础，生长出不同掺镁浓度的铌酸锂晶体，将掺镁铌酸锂晶片放入到富锂气氛中对其进行气相平衡扩散输运，制备出化学比铌酸锂晶体，对掺镁浓度和气相平衡扩散过程进行系统的实验与理论研究，并对所研制的晶体进行系统的光学测试，获得光学性能优异的掺镁化学计量比铌酸锂集成光学基片；优化原有极化工艺，对不同组分和掺镁浓度的化学计量比铌酸锂晶体的极化过程及工艺进行系统的研究，进一步降低制备准相位匹配铌酸锂全光微结构的开关电场，制作出高质量掺镁不同组分铌酸锂准相位匹配全光微结构；在国内外率先就改变铌酸锂晶体中锂离子浓度对周期极化开关电场的影响进行系统的研究，解决制备周期极化铌酸锂全光微结构所需高外加极化电场这一困扰多年的难题。研究成果具有鲜明的创新性学术和实用价值；初步研制出准相位匹配掺镁化学比铌酸锂波导全光开关，并对全光开关运行过程进行研究，分析进一步提高全光开关性能的途径，为此类全光开关的实用化提供理论和技术依据。该课题发表论文15篇，其中9篇被SCI收录，14篇被EI收录。

第三节　激光物理与激光器

关于激光物理与激光器的研究，20世纪70年代起，天津大学姚建铨、南开大学张光寅等做过有益的探索。1991～2005年，这个方向的科研工作更加活跃，天津大学、南开大学取得新的出色成果，天津师范大学也做出可贵成果。

一、激光物理

1983~1992年，天津大学姚建铨、生卫东等开展双轴晶体最佳相位匹配参量计算的研究，提出计算、分析双轴晶体中三波互作用的最佳相位匹配参量完整、系统的理论方法，为双轴晶体的实际应用奠定理论基础。1995年3月，天津大学姚建铨编著的《非线性光学频率变换及激光调谐技术》由科学出版社出版。该书论述非线性光学晶体中三波互作用的理论及计算方法、非线性光学混频理论、倍频激光器理论及有关技术，超短脉冲的混频、光学参量振荡器、染料可调谐激光器、染料激光器调谐技术、固体可调谐激光器、掺钛蓝宝石激光调谐技术及其他调谐技术。专著包括非线性光学频率变换及激光调谐技术领域的国内外最新研究成果及进展，收集有关资料，并作系统分析综合；专著理论与实际结合好，实用性高。被从事激光科技的高等院校，研究机构及工程技术界所接受及广泛使用。

图3-3-3-13　天津大学姚建铨给学生授课

2002年3月，天津师范大学王永晨完成用于可调谐InGaAs/InP激光器的量子阱后置无序技术研究。该项目对1.55艴光通讯——InGaAsP/InP多量子阱材料，采用新的互扩方法，带隙改变224meV的最大移动量。创新之处在于采用含磷组份新的电介质膜SiOP，替代国际上传统的电介质膜（SiO_2，Si_3N_4……）获得突破的数据，达到目前国际上有关此项目研究的最高数据（据文献报导美、德、英、加、日等国为10～150meV）。同时也为光集成组件和超大规模集成电路找到新的低介电常数的电介质薄膜。

2002年6月，南开大学张光寅、沙作金、张潮波等完成V-型固体激光腔设计研究。项目利用谐振腔变换圆理论，对热透镜对固体激光器的影响作系统的动力学分析，提出以短曲率半径的M1镜代替通用V-型腔的M1平面镜；同时，除去通用V-型腔中的折叠镜与平面反射镜，取而代之的是相应曲率半径的凹面镜，从而大大缩短与简化腔结构。可将KTP等倍频晶体置于热透镜，对该凹面镜的"像"点上，使得倍频晶体处的光斑尺寸受热透镜大小变化影响很小，进一步折叠此腔，从而形成一个全新的V-型腔。在激光介质与倍频晶体间用一个平面镜做折叠输出镜，可以防止绿光返回激光介质，引起激光介质附加吸收，加剧热效应。该腔型设计使得固体激光器结构更为紧凑，极大压缩激光器体积，而且腔内无象散元件，可保证光束具有更好的质量。

2003年12月，南开大学承担，张光寅、宋峰、颜彩繁等完成自适应动力稳定腔的研究。项目成果提出固体激光谐振腔设计的一种新概念，即自适应动力稳定腔。在其中通过轴向移动腔内一二个元件，使腔的双“U”曲线随动力因子的增大，同步地向横坐标的增量方向移动，使激光器总保持在动力稳定区内运行，并使激光介质处的基模光斑尺寸保持不变；或在腔内引入一个具有负热透镜效应的介质元件，其负热透镜的光焦度随光泵浦功率的增大相应地增大，以达到完全补偿激光介质的动力因子的影响作用，使谐振腔运行的动力状态不随泵浦功率的变化而改变，从而使固体激光器的输出功率随光泵浦功率的增大，可持续地增高，并使激光介质处的基模光斑尺寸保持不变。成果是解决高功率固体激光器输出功率继续提高的一条重要途径。

2005年，南开大学朱晓农、张铁群、王明伟等完成超短脉冲激光超微细加工中临界脉冲宽度问题的研究。该项目建立有着多参数计算机控制和实时监测能力的飞秒激光超微细加工系统，通过研究铝、铜、玻璃等金属和非金属材料在不同加工条件下烧蚀深度和粉尘分布的变化特性，比较在临近材料损伤阈值和在高出材料损伤阈值情况下所确定的临界脉冲宽度，深化对超短脉冲激光作用下“冷加工”与“热加工”的界定和控制的认识，前者主要起源于超热电子温度梯度力引发的局域爆炸，而后者则主要与材料的超热熔化即所谓“相爆炸”相联系。研究成果为实际超微细激光加工中如何正确选取超短脉冲激光的脉冲宽度和其他工艺技术参数提供科学依据。结合激光超微细加工研究的需要，项目对所用飞秒激光放大系统的各项技术参数，包括光束质量特性进行仔细的分析测定。

二、飞秒激光技术

1991年，天津大学王清月、邢岐荣、章若冰等完成飞秒激光脉冲的产生、传输及其孤子效应的研究。项目在飞秒激光脉冲的产生、传输及其孤子效应等方面进行系统的理论和实验研究，首次得到谐振腔的严格的解析解，为CPM激光器的稳定运转提供理论指导和设计依据；首次对CPM激光器的脉冲特性进行定量研究。研究成果受到国际著名超短脉冲激光专家的好评和重视。

图3-3-3-14 天津大学精密仪器学院的飞秒激光研究

1997年12月，王清月、邢岐荣、张伟力等开展飞秒激光技术的研究，得到CPM染料飞秒激光器谐振腔的解析解，提出增大稳定区域新的谐振腔方案；计算并设计可以获得负色散特性的双膜系介质镜，在CPM染料激光器中获得25飞秒脉冲宽度的锁模运行；建立一种自相位调制和群速色散相分离的计算方法，获得飞秒激光在光纤中一、二、三阶孤子解和在飞秒激光器中的孤子解。实现在同一谐振腔内两种不同介质和波长的双锁模；研制CPM染料飞秒激光器样机；发现掺钛蓝宝石的自调Q自锁模现象及其运转条件；设计新型谐振腔，发现脉冲序列调制可增宽光谱，给出压缩脉冲的新途径；实现钛宝石飞秒激光器的低泵浦、窄脉宽运转，并研制出样机；研制脉宽为40飞秒的太瓦激光系统，并发现self-trapping和具有平台效应的超连续飞秒白光；研制具有飞秒精度的实时显示干涉(8:1)自相关器。该成果荣获1999年度国家科技进步二等奖。

1991~1997年，王清月、邢岐荣、张伟力等开展固体飞秒激光机理及技术研究，对以掺钛蓝宝石为增益介质的飞秒固体激光器kerr-lens锁模动力学过程和运转特性进行全面系统的研究；对峰值功率为太瓦(W)级飞秒钛宝石固体激光系统及高功率飞秒激光作用下超连续飞秒激光光谱研究；设计和研制飞秒激光系统和相关器测量系统的实验装置和样机，包括固体飞秒激光器、太瓦飞秒激光放大系统等。研制的实时显示干涉(8:1)自相关器已经分别用于中科院半导体所超晶格研究、北方交通大学文理学院物理系和天津大学精仪学院超快激光研究室的研究工作中。

1998~2002年，王清月、张志刚、柴路等开展自启动飞秒激光系统的研究，发现固体飞秒激光器自启动机制是固体自锁模激光器运转技术应用的关键。该研究重点分析半导体可饱和吸收镜SESAM结构及性能，启动自锁模的动力学过程，最佳运转参数，并研制出自启动飞秒激光器及放大系统的试验样机，取得良好的效果。王清月等在国际上首次研制成功宽带低损耗半导体可饱和吸收反射镜；首次发现并界定SESAM启动锁模的三个不同物理阶段；将SESAM用于固体飞秒激光器，实现两种激光器的国际最高纪录。在国际利用SESAM首次实现飞秒太瓦激光系统的自启动运转。该研究成果是固体自锁模激光器运转技术应用的关键。在研究成果基础上，国内首次研制出自启动飞秒激光器及放大系统的试验样机。

三、激光器

1987 ~ 1991年，天津大学姚建铨、邓家诚、韩汝聪等采用准连续泵浦的高功率倍频激光器，研制完成激光三维扫描系统，用于三维遥感扫描系统获得成功。

1991~1998年，天津大学张伟力、柴路、邢歧荣等研究掺钛蓝宝石飞秒激光器及自相关器，设计研制中国第一代自锁模掺钛蓝宝石飞秒激光器样机；设计研制实时显示干涉自相关器样机，用于飞秒光脉冲宽度的实时精密测量。研究成果结束西方国家产品独占中国市场的局面。

20世纪90年代以来，南开大学张光寅、宋峰、颜彩繁等开展固体激光器及其谐振腔研究，课题组利用变换圈图解方法得出固体激光器的动力稳定性双“U”曲线，提出稳功率稳定腔不同于稳模式稳定腔的概念，进行实验证明；提出调控固体激光器动力学稳定性的若干方法，建立“自适应固体激光器”研究的新途径；首先提出“光学镇定器”的新概念，并在实验上加以证实；分析研究上转换对激光的影响。该项目提出光学谐振腔设计的一种新的方法，具有直观、形象、易于计算的优点，对激光器的生产和实际应用很有意义。编著《光学谐振腔的图解分析与设计方法》一书。成果在国内外许多重要学术刊物上发表。10篇论文被SCI收录，7篇论文被EI收录，出版专著1部。

1995 ~ 2001年，南开大学董孝义、袁树忠、开桂云等合作完成光纤光栅、全光纤集成光子器件与系统，提出“光纤集成”的新概念、新思想，以及因此而形成的“全光纤光子器件、全光纤光子系统”技术，创新性地开发出多种光纤光栅及无源光子器件。项目组发现和确定光纤光栅的写入规律，进而建立光纤光栅的写入平台，研制出Bragg光纤光栅、Tapped光纤光栅、Comb光纤光栅等多种特种光纤光栅；利用自行研制的光纤光栅，成功研制出用于光通信系统的光频滤波器、OADM以及多种新颖的光纤光栅传感器等；成功地开发出多种新颖的全光纤光子激光器件，包括可调谐光纤激光器、偏振光激光器、窄线宽单频光纤激光器、可编程波长扫描光纤激光器、双波长多波长光纤激光器、调Q光纤激光器、锁模（超短）脉冲光纤激光器、双包层光纤激光器、增益平坦光纤放大器和Raman光纤放大器等；成功研究出具有多功能、多参数、分布式、灵巧型的全光纤光栅传感器网络系统，开发出一种具有创新性的全光纤WDM通信实验系统。

2001年6月，天津大学张德龙、陈才和、丁桂兰等完成天Er–Nd:$LiTaO_3$连续波导激光器的研究，成果包括：Er:$LiTaO_3$晶体的吸收光谱和荧光光谱特性；钛扩散和质子交换光波导的光学性质；Er–Nd:$LiTaO_3$波导荧光光谱和吸收光谱特性，Nd3+→Er3+之间的能量转换机制；高质量、低损耗钛扩散和质子交换条形波导基片的参数设计和制备工艺；谐振腔镜的膜系设计与制备工艺；详细的激光振荡理论，解决低损耗、高质量单模条形波，为研制成器件奠定良好的理论和实验基础。在国内外高水平杂志上发表学术论文近20篇。

2002年11月，由天津大学精仪学院姚建铨主持的激光器研究项目：“高功率、高重复频率全固态绿光激光器样机研制”和“准连续660nm红光激光器研究”通过专家鉴定，前者达到国际先进水平，后者达到国内领先水平。

2002年12月，南开大学研制开发的包层泵浦调Q光纤激光器，进行双包层、掺Yb3+单模光纤的设计和制造，通过采用包层泵浦技术和普通单模或多模光纤中的受激布里渊散射效应，实现脉宽5纳秒、峰值功率100千瓦、单脉冲能量0.5毫焦耳的调Q脉冲。双包层光纤激光器的斜率效率接近80%，最大输出功率6.8瓦。成果属国内首创，主要性能指标接近国际先进水平，具有效率高、阈值低、可调谐、紧凑小巧、性能价格比高等特点，且不需要水冷和电制冷，大有替代固体激光器之势。

第四节 发光材料与薄膜

20世纪80年代,天津理工大学徐叙瑢院士带领的科研团队在发光材料研究领域取得系列成果。1991～2005年,天津在这方面的研究工作再接再厉,取得新成果。薄膜是一种二维新型材料,由原子、分子或离子在基片表面沉积而成。这个时期天津在这个领域也开展有益的探索,并取得可喜成果。

一、发光材料

(一)光致变色防伪材料

1996年开始,南开大学戈德集团李明智、孟继本、王淑芳等研制开发螺旋类光致变色防伪材料获得成功。光致变色防伪技术合成两大系列新的光致变色化合物,其化学结构可在光照情况由螺环形变成双性离子型,从而由无色变为有色;当避光或加热时,分子又由双性离子型变为螺环形,从而由有色恢复到无色状态。还采用特殊的配方和制作工艺,研制成功光致变色丝网印刷油墨、凹版印刷油墨和凸胶印油墨,实现光致变色防伪材料和产品的规模化生产和在多个领域的应用。

(二)荧光材料

2001年3月,天津理工大学李岚、王世铭、徐力等完成场发射显示荧光材料发光性能机理研究。该项目采用固相合成法,分别研制出ZnS:Zn,Pb;$Y_3(Al,Ga)_5O_{12}$:Tb,Gd(绿);$Sr_5(PO_4)^3Cl$:Eu(蓝)和Gd_2O_3:Eu(红)几种荧光材料。自行研制一台阴极射线发光测试仪,可以对荧光材料进行发光亮度的相对测量。利用X射线衍射方法,对制备的荧光材料、被电子轰击过的材料以及经过处理后的材料,进行结构分析,材料结构的定态性、杂质等分析,并与发光测量结合,确定不同制备工艺下发光与结构的关系。利用扫描电镜对荧光材料表面进行观察分析,结合发光性能研究,确定不同处理方法对材料的粒度、表面定态性的影响以及与发光的关系。利用分光光度计对材料的发光光谱和基本发光机制进行研究,比较新材料与传统材料在阴极射线激发下发光的优劣。为降低材料发光阈值,通过与导电材料如In_2O_3混合对荧光粉表面进行处理,使ZnS:Zn,Pb和$Y_3(Al,Ga)_5O_{12}$Tb,Gd的阈值电压达到可用于FED的水平。该课题成果首次研制出ZnS:Zn,Pb蓝粉,亮度超过国际上现有的商用荧光粉水平。改进后的YAGG:Tb,Gd绿粉,首次被应用于FED中,有极好的稳定性。对器件中硫污染和阳极电荷积累等问题,采用材料表面加工的方法克服,从而在FED荧光材料的研制方面取得明显进展,某些性能指标达到或超过国际同类产品的水平。

2001年8月,天津理工大学李岚、熊光楠、王世铭等承担高清晰投影电视用荧光粉的亮度研究项目,内容包括研制三基色荧光材料;研究三种材料的阴极射线发光性能;分析效率的影响机理,退化机理,并依此进行材料的改善,制备出高清晰投影电视用三色荧光材料。该成果对于制约显示器整体效果的蓝色荧光粉,研制获得ZnS:Zn,Pb,结果显示它的发光亮度高于现有商用品的5倍以上;在绿色荧光材料方面,改善原有材料的色纯度,提高亮度。

(三)光激励发光研究

2004年,天津理工大学熊光楠、娄素云等完成影像板用新型光激励发光研究。课题组通过对光激励发光材料的激发、能量输运、信息存储、色心结构、光释光动力学过程等问题的基础性研究,提出新的物理机制,建立新的模型、新的配方和工艺。在不改变基质材料、保持其优异理化性能的前提下,可使光激励发光材料的工作波段红移到半导体激光工作波段。用光激励发光材料制成影像板,与数字化影像仪一起构成数字影像系统,其图像更为清晰,且可图像处理,X线曝光剂量可以减少,可以用于远程诊断、安全检测及射线仪器检测。

二、薄膜

(一)功能金属薄膜

1992～2001年,南开大学阎少林先后开展Te系高温超导薄膜及其应用的研究、Ti系薄膜和Hg系薄膜技术的研究,以及铊膜及外延铊膜台阶结、铊系外延超导薄膜与铊系高温超导薄膜与结技术的研究。2003年,南开大学的大面积实用高温超导薄膜研究开发项目,进一步提高和完善高质量、大面积、双面铊系高温超导薄膜的制作技术,使薄膜的各项技术指标达到实际应用水平,为铊系超导薄膜在移动通信用滤波器和其他超导器件方面的应用提供技术支撑。

1994～1996年,南开大学张允什从事功能合金薄膜的制备及电化学性能的研究。

1994~2000年,天津大学姜恩永、白海力、王存达等完成新型化合物软X射线光学多层膜的制备及其结构稳定性研究。课题针对1~3纳米软X射线系统,建立物理模型,为之提出某型号可应用的新的多层膜设计思路和模型。还研究成功多层膜结构评价方法和计算拟合程序,并用其对超薄多层膜和多层膜的界面糙度、界面过渡区、层厚漂移等不完美因素对软X射线光学多层膜的镜向反射率的影响极其微观机理进行表征和评价。同时用对向靶溅射法制备出高质量的Co/C和CoN/CN新型软X射线光学多层膜系统,研究其在非常高温环境下的结构热稳定性。首次利用N掺杂使Co/C软X射线光学多层膜得结构热稳定性提高200℃达到国际领先水平。研究成果在*J. Phys*、*J. Appl. Phys*、《中国科学》《物理学报》等刊物上发表论文32篇,均被SCI收录。

1994~2000年,天津大学徐明霞、徐廷献、杨兆选等完成轿车发动机电控燃料喷射系统传感器用氧敏薄膜材料的开发项目,研制成功新型氧敏材料,并进而研制出结构简单新型空燃比传感器。所研制的新材料La_1-xSrxNiO_3、TiOx、La_2NiO_4均含有类金属相,即准自由电子浓度高,导电活化能低。与目前空燃比传感器通用的氧敏材料相比,电阻-温度系数小,温度稳定性好;材料为超微粒薄膜形态,对气体敏感度高,响应速度快。该材料在温度400~800℃范围,具有高的测氧灵敏度;新材料的制造采用ISG新工艺,即无机盐溶胶—凝胶工艺,选用数种特定的络合稳定剂大大拓宽溶胶—凝胶工艺中原料来源,降低成本。

1995~1997年,天津大学姜恩永、王忠杰、孙多春等针对国内外为实现超高密度磁光和磁性存储,创造新型高性能磁性薄膜材料合作开展新型铁基磁性薄膜的结构与磁性研究,在国际上首先制备出取代自然界蕴藏很少、价格昂贵的铽元素新型Dy系垂直磁化薄膜材料,用于磁和磁光存储使用。参考块体梯度材料,首先提出"梯度薄膜"的概念,并成功制备出铁氮梯度薄膜。在国际上首次观察到并获得处于亚稳态的薄膜晶体沿六个晶带轴方向的具有完美对称性的电子衍射谱图。首次发现在基片上,薄膜有三种生长模式,并从晶体学角度给出解释。用VSM(振动样品磁强计)测量得到具有280Wb/m^3的高饱和磁化强度,约高于纯铁的34%,制备成一种新的高性能的磁性薄膜材料。理论上研究发现以前被人们广泛使用的作为存在的判断错误之处。研究成果在*J.Phys*(英)、*J.Magn.Magn.Matter*(荷兰)、*J.Appl.Phys*(美)、*Thin Solid Films*(欧)、《科学通报》等重要刊物上发表40余篇基础性学术研究论文,均被SCI收录。

1999年,天津大学姜恩永、吕旗、王忠杰在国际上率先研制出含铋系非晶态磁性薄带材料,并发现两种新的结构弛予现象。用Dy取代价格昂贵的Tb元素,制成新型非晶磁光薄膜。成果在*J.Appl.Phys*、《金属学报》等刊物上发论文20余篇,多篇被SCI收录。

2003年7月,天津理工大学承担NiTi/PZT多层薄膜复合工艺及智能阻尼功能研究,项目组将NiTi形状记忆合金的阻尼特性与压电陶瓷锆钛酸铅(Pb(ZrxTil-x)O_3,即PZT)的阻尼及其机电耦合特性有机地结合起来,在制备具有高效、智能阻尼特性的NiTi/PZT多层薄膜复合材料的研究上取得突破性进展。项目组借助电子显微镜观察及热机械动态分析等技术方法,研究NiTi记忆合金与PZT陶瓷薄膜异质间的复合制备工艺及材料的阻尼性能。通过采用Sol-Gel法及控制热处理加热温度,在NiTi形状记忆合金基体与PZT陶瓷薄膜异质间形成TiO_2+富Ni区过渡结构,进而制备出NiTi/PZT多层薄膜复合材料,NiTiSMA基体与PZT陶瓷之间具有良好的结合。相对于自由态NiTi形状记忆合金,阻尼性能复合效应显著。

2005年，南开大学石可瑜、张保龙、何尚锦等完成磁性诱导高取向度液晶环氧热固性材料的制备及性能研究。课题组以(甲基)丙烯酸酯为主链，通过改变侧链中柔性间隔基的长度，合成出一系列含有两个手性中心的侧链液晶高分子；采用红外、核磁和GPC对各中间体、单体及聚合物的结构和分子量进行表征；通过DSC和热台偏光显微镜，系统地研究单体和聚合物的液晶态织构。结果表明，含有6个碳的柔性间隔基的丙烯酸酯类聚合物表现为近晶SA和手性近晶S*C液晶相。在此基础上合成出一种侧链上同时含有液晶基元、柔性间隔基和肉桂酰感光基团的新型液晶聚合物，用核磁共振确定该中间体结构，经线性偏振紫外光聚合技术处理聚合物膜，通过检测照射前后聚合物薄膜透光率变化表明，其取向薄膜具有良好的定向能力，是一类具有潜在应用价值的新型液晶光取向薄膜材料。

(二)LB薄膜

1993年12月，天津理工学院华玉林、蒋大鹏、彭俊彪等完成高质量LB薄膜及其在光电器件中的应用研究，将硅取代酞菁LB薄膜作为功能膜应用于MS结及MIS结的有机太阳能电池中，大大节省材料，仅为传统蒸发及涂敷方法的1/20，而效率至少提高1倍；将该LB薄膜作为I层，引入Au / LB薄膜 / ZnSe(MOCVD法制得)的MIS结构中，有效地提高少数载流子注入速率，首次得到用一般方法无法得到的ZnSe单晶薄膜的蓝色电致发光；将该材料的LB薄膜作为功能层应用于平面电导型的气敏传感器中，膜厚为30层时，在NO_2(200ppm)中，其电导增加100倍。

(三)稀土镧系薄膜

1995年，南开大学邵淑敏、席光康、李胜林等用俄歇谱与分子束技术就地(薄膜制备与分析处于同一真空室)与非就地(薄膜制备后暴露空气后再送人另一真空室分析)研究稀土镧系薄膜的特性，结果表明两种薄膜的表面成分有根本区别，前者为La，后者为$La(OH)_3$。经过热处理后两种薄膜都变成La_2O_3，然而催化特性不同。用非常态分子束作用后的表面化学解离吸附实验表明，后者的吸附势垒较低，具有更好的催化特性。该成果对稀土材料的应用与开发具有指导意义。

(四)金刚石膜

1996年，南开大学席光康、邵淑敏、贺天喜等开展金刚石膜的研制、生长特性与应用研究，应用化学气相沉积(CVD)方法，模索出一套膜制备工艺，在Si(111)面上制备出高质量的金刚石膜，并运用扫描电镜、激光拉曼光谱、光电子谱、俄歇电子谱及X射线谱等对其表面进行分析研究。在此基础上开展应用研究，在硬质合金WC刀具上，提高刀具的硬度与耐磨度。

1997年，天津理工大学常明、杨保和、曲长庆等研制出金刚石薄膜压力和温度传感器。课题组依据CVD金刚石薄膜热敏特性和压阻效应，利用化学气相沉积(CVD)技术，研制出高温平衡电桥式自补偿温度和压力传感器，完成最佳设计方案与最佳工艺方案。该项目提出无籽晶无偏压金刚石准单晶膜的沉积方法，使承载膜片应力分布均匀，提高传感器稳定性和一致性。金刚石薄膜片状温度电阻器获专利。把金刚石薄膜制成惠茨通(wheatstone)电桥直接沉积在超高阻硅衬底制作压力和温度传感器，国内外未见报道。用数值计算中的有限元理论和ANSYS程序，提出电阻条圆角设计方案，从而优化电阻条形状及长、宽、厚尺寸设计。金刚石薄膜传感器耐高温性能好、工作频率高、输出功率大、易于集成化。

第五节 半导体物理与金属物理

1991~2005年，在半导体物理与金属物理研究领域，河北工业大学显示出独特优势，取得多项突出成果。其中，刘玉岭在半导体切削液与切削技术的研究成果和谷南驹等关于马氏体相变晶体学、形态学研究及应用的研究是具有创新意义的成果，均引起国际同行关注。

一、半导体物理

(一)半导体研究

1991年,天津大学与天津市第四半导体器件厂合作,由郭维廉、郑丽滋、杜长景等共同完成变容二极管击穿电压机理的研究。

2000年,天津大学郭维廉、郑丽滋、宋永淳完成P-N结电压蠕变理论新发展的研究项目。该研究建立P-N结击穿电压蠕变理论转模型,克服关于P-N结击穿电压蠕变两大传统理论模型各自的不足,建立的新理论模型能更为普遍的说明更多实验事实,且与实验数据更为吻合。模型首次定义出能定量描述击穿电压蠕变特性的三个基本参数,以量度蠕变现象的强度和时间相应特性,使击穿电压蠕变理论趋于系统化和完整化。并以该模型为指导解决许多实际问题。

(二)半导体技术

1997年,河北工业大学鞠玉林等研究开发出5μm IC 质量工艺控制技术,针对5μm IC生产中出现的埋层图形畸变和飘移问题进行深入研究,通过分析和改变外延生长中的各项影响因素及工艺参数,获得优化的外延生长工艺,使图形畸变和飘移问题大大降低,并揭示外延埋层图形畸变和飘移的形成机理。成果应用到生产企业,提高产品质量,推动行业科技进步。

1997年,河北工业大学徐岳生等完成NTD硅片辐照施主的形成与消除研究,成果在国内外首次发现并报导NTDCZSi中的辐照施主现象,揭示辐照施主的特征、结构、产生条件与退火行为,提出消除辐照施主获得准确真实电参数的退火工艺。首次提出通过引入缺陷,达到控制缺陷、利用缺陷的学术思想,并实现直拉硅片在集成电路制造工艺中缺陷的控制与利用,为半导体缺陷工程增添新内容,对发展中国超大规模集成电路,具有重要学术价值和实用意义。成果应用到生产企业,推动行业科技进步。

1999年,河北工业大学任丙彦教授等完成直拉硅中子辐照与内吸除技术的结合在压敏传感器中的应用研究项目。项目组结合中子辐照直拉硅和半导体内吸杂工艺,将成果应用到压敏传感器领域。在此基础上通过对内吸杂工艺的深入研究,将吸杂工艺应用到太阳能电池制造工艺中,使硅片表层杂质含量和缺陷水平大幅度下降,光子寿命显著提高,光电转换效率大大提高,研发成功新型高效太阳电池。

2001年6月,河北工业大学刘玉岭、张楷亮、张志刚等完成FA/O半导体材料切削液及技术的研究项目。切削剂是半导体材料切削加工的重要配套材料。课题组根据微电子业发展需要及国内外存在的问题,成功研制出新型FA/O切削剂,具有降低损伤和微裂、效率高、成本低等特点。成果的创新点在于:选用无金属离子的高效渗透剂,提高效率,保护刀具;利用复合活性剂,降低表面张力,减少摩擦,减少切割面的应力与微裂;利用羟胺,减少由于切、倒处温度高引起的离子沾污,防止锈蚀,提高切削速率。该成果经对硅单晶切片、倒角使用效果表明:刀具寿命延长20%以上;切割稳定,切割速度提高15%~20%;表面光洁,磨轮寿命、晶片质量均显著提高。

(三)半导体检测方法

1994年4月,南开大学李增发、王宏杰、颜彩繁等研制完成硅片及硅片外延表面缺陷魔镜检测仪和表面缺陷检测方法,被认定具有国际领先水平,填补国内半导体表面缺陷光学无损检测的空白。该成果无需对样品作任何化学和物理处理,即能对各种尺寸的半导体晶片表面30余种缺陷进行大面积(φ152毫米)的图示观测,并编制成图谱。其检测分辨率为0.5微米,具有直观、灵敏、快速、无损等优点。可用于半导体单晶生长,晶片加工,外延生长等各工艺流程的在线检测,也可对各种镜状表面器件进行质量检测和现场产品认证。1995年该成果获国家级科技成果证书,并被国家技术监督局采纳,确定为国家标准。

二、金属物理

1999年,河北工业大学谷南驹等完成马氏体相变晶体学、形态学研究及应用项目,是有关马氏体相变的基础理论及其应用的研究成果,谷南驹等发现占有统治地位的马氏体相变晶体学表象理论的局限性和不足，针对该理论不能解释的现象建立新的模型，并做出修正和补充。率先导出马氏体相变的位移矢量，并成为定量分析相变引起的形状改变、形状记忆效应以及相变晶体学特征的有力武器。对马氏体形态转化规律提出以母相塑性协作和马氏体变体间自协作之间的竞争决定马氏体形态的新观点，从而可解释“以母相强度来确定马氏体形态”的观点所不能解释的实验现象。将上述理论用于指导先进钢铁材料的研究，使开发的超淬透性耐磨钢技术出口印尼，研制的微合金热轧双相钢线棒材已在唐山钢铁公司的高速线材生产线上批量生产，推动钢铁企业的技术进步和产品升级。该成果在国内外产生较大影响，许多学者纷纷来函索取论文，作者三次赴日本大阪大学、筑波大学等讲学，1993年出任国际MRS会议执行主席。在1998年捷克布拉格召开的第18届欧洲晶体学会议上作为唯一的引导性特邀报告。

同期，谷南驹等完成马氏体相变及形状记忆合金研究，是马氏体相变及其在新材料研制中的应用研究成果，率先导出马氏体相变的位移矢量，并成为定量分析相变引起的形状改变、形状记忆效应以及相变晶体学特征的有力武器。在此基础上，研制出CuZnAl系和FeMnSi系两类形状记忆合金，创新铜基形状记忆合金的最佳训练工艺和时效稳定化范围，对该合金相变点漂移问题有较大突破。该成果在国内外产生较大影响，研制的相关器件获得多项国家专利。

2001年，河北工业大学林成新等人完成铁锰硅系记忆合金低温松弛研究，发现铁锰硅系记忆合金的低温松弛程度随温度降低而增大；温度降低，马氏体相变的化学驱动力增大，促使合金在恢复力的作用下发生应力诱发ε和 马氏体相变是导致低温松弛的根本原因，应力诱发的ε和 马氏体数量越多，合金的松弛程度就越高。在铁锰硅系记忆合金中加入Zr、Nb、Ti、V等强碳化物形成元素、合理选择预变形量等均可达到降低合金低温应力松弛的目的。在管接头实际应用中可以通过改变其结构提高管接头连接组件的耐压密封性，降低合金低温松弛的影响。发表学术论文多篇，刊登于《金属学报》和《材料科学论坛》上。

第六节 电磁学

1991～2005年，天津在电磁理论与电磁技术的研究，以河北工业大学为主力军取得新的成果。

1998年，河北工业大学杨庆新、汪友华等完成电磁场耦合问题与逆问题的数值问题的研究。研究内容涉及神经网络的自适应最佳场域网格生成技术、三维电磁场(恒定磁场、永磁场和涡流场)数值计算、三维电磁场并行算法和交流电磁铁吸力计算等。在国际上首先提出自适应模拟退火法，该方法在获得全局最优解的前提下，具有较高的收敛速度。将模拟进化法与模拟退火法的优点结合应用于电磁场逆问题的求解，达到良好的全局优化效果。以上理论成果成功应用于真空组合电器、真空接触器、制动电磁铁和交流接触器的优化设计。

2000年，河北工业大学徐桂芝、杨庆新等完成永久磁铁磁场数值计算方法软件及应用研究，该成果围绕着永磁磁场中的磁块具有任意充磁方向、形状各异且媒介质分布复杂和磁场的非线性等特点，对永磁磁场的有限元计算方法、软件及应用做出具有创新性的工作。建立具有任意充磁方向的二维永磁磁场的有限元离散格式；分别给出具有任意充磁方向的三维永磁磁场的磁矢量位A方法和磁标量位Ψ方法的有限元离散格式；提出并实现磁矢量位与磁标量位相结合的具有任意充磁方向的三维永磁磁场的A-Ψ有限元法；根据上述各方法研制成功电永磁磁场有限元数值计算软件包FEPM。该成果在磁共振成像(MRI)系统中的高均匀度永磁磁体、硅单晶生长炉用永磁磁体及其他几种电永磁产品的开发设计中得到成功应用，均取得较好的经济效益和社会效益。

2001年，天津大学自动化学院徐苓安、徐立军、熊汉亮等完成基于电学敏感原理的过程层析成象技术的研究,以自行研制的透射模式超声层析成象系统、多激励模式电磁感应成像系统和电阻层析成象系统等为具体研究对象,对基于电学敏感原理的过程层析成象系统的理论进行了深入探讨。研制的超声成像系统和电磁成像系统具有创造性,电阻成像系统的实时性能达到国际先进水平,在气/液两相管流流型识别和流动参数检测的研究方面也取得具有实际应用价值的成果。

第七节 原子核物理与天体物理

20世纪80年代,天津开展原子核物理及天体物理研究,取得可喜成果。1991~2005年,天津继续探索原子奥秘与天体奥秘,取得新的成果。其中,南开大学宁平治与中国科学院有关研究所合作完成的奇异性系统与核多体系统的若干研究较为突出。

一、原子核物理

1992~1994年,天津大学李希曾、苏保霞与东北大学单莹、东南大学王俊合作,完成双模量子电磁场高阶压缩与广义测不准关系的理论研究。项目组将1985年Hong与Mandel提出的单模压缩态中量子场的高阶压缩的概念进行推广,建立起双模式声高阶压缩理论,并应用于非简并参量下转换和四波混频过程,提出一个双模压缩态中量子电磁场的压缩的理论,研究高阶压缩产生的条件、性质并计算高阶压缩参数和固有高阶压缩;计算和讨论非简并参量下转换过程中量子场的高阶压缩效应;计算和讨论并四波混频过程中量子场的高阶压缩效应;提出一个量子电磁场在单模压缩态和双模压缩态中高阶广义测不准关系式,此外,通过研究正交偶相干叠加态的高阶压缩,发现该态中两个正交分量的涨落,同时存在阶数N>4的高阶压缩,并探讨其根源和机理。成果在*Physicsw A*、*Coherence and Quantum Optics*等国内外刊物上发表论文10篇。

2001年,南开大学宁平治等与中国科学院高能物理研究所、中国科学院理论物理研究所共同完成奇异性系统与核多体系统的若干研究,对奇异性核物理系统和核多体系统的结构和性质、可靠地提取原子核内信息、有关散射和反应的机制以及若干动力学和运动学问题进行探索。研究成果被一些权威刊物评价为新的理论进展,成为若干新理论研究的起点和佐证,被国际核数据机构作为关于核性质的新信息、新知识载入汇编,还被一些国际核物理实验中心作为设计新实验的理论依据。在SCI检索的杂志上发表论文46篇。

2002年,南开大学高成群完成α-组态核碰撞粗共振结构的核分子轨道深势模型的研究,项目基于α-组态核重离子碰撞激发函数和熔合激发函数中呈现出的粗共振结构是属于主量子数为N=2n+L的共振转动带的思想,建立核分子轨道深势模型。成果在国际重离子碰撞研究领域处于先进水平,在α-组态核碰撞粗共振特性的研究方面处于领先地位。

二、天体物理

2003年12月,南开大学申虹、宁平治、李磊等合作完成夸克层次上的核多体方法及其在天体物理中的应用研究。项目在夸克层次研究核多体系统,研究现代核物理在天体物理中的应用。从组分夸克模型出发,提出夸克平均场模型,采用该模型研究无限大核物质和有限核系统的性质,研究核子性质在核介质中的改变;推广该模型至包含奇异夸克的系统,研究超核的性质。结果能够很好地符合核物质、有限核及超核的实验结果,为在夸克层次研究核多体系统开拓出一条重要并切实可行的途径。相关的两篇论文被国际同行引用100余次。项目在此基础上进一步研究奇异强子自由度对高密度区状态方程的影响,构造中子星物质的状态方程,并研究中子星的结构和性质。成果的论文发表在*Phys.Rev.C*和*Nucl.Phys.A*。

第四章 化 学

在化学研究领域，天津的实力优势突出，位居全国前列。天津关于无机化学、有机化学、物理化学、分析化学、高分子化学、农药化学和化学工程的研究具有深厚的历史积淀和突出的创新能力。

1991～2005年，天津在化学研究的多个领域取得丰硕成果，南开大学对于无机合成、功能有机化合、物理化学、合成受体、新型过渡金属有机化合物和生物医学高分子的研究，以及对环境友好的农药的创制与开发，尤为突出，居国内领先或先进水平。天津大学在化学工程领域关于精馏的研究，居国内国际先进水平。南开大学关于物理化学的研究居世界领先水平。

第一节 无机化学

20世纪50年代至60年代，天津的无机化学研究以金属氢化物为重点。20世纪80年代开始，南开大学王耕霖、廖代正等以其有关桥联偶合体的研究，丰富了配位化学学科内容。

1991～2005年，天津关于无机化学的研究取得多项可喜成果。南开大学程鹏等在无机合成领域关于新型发光配合物的研究成为亮点。廖代正等在配位化学领域持续开拓，获得新成果，关于磁性配合物的研究居国内先进水平。

一、无机合成化学

1998年，南开大学化学系李赫咺、袁忠勇、陈铁红等完成中孔分子筛材料的合成与表征研究，对中孔分子的筛的合成、表征、形成机理和催化性能进行较系统的研究。为开发选择氧化和双功能的催化材料，合成10多种新型中孔杂原子分子筛，首次报道分别含Fe，Cr，Cd，V-Ti等的MCM-41分子筛的合成与表征，首次采用廉价的新模板剂合成出分别含V，Cr，V-Cr等MCM-41分子筛，并用混合模板剂合成出新型的双中孔分子筛（孔径2.6nm和3.8nm）。在系统考察合成条件和影响因素时，发现MCM-41分子筛由于体系和合成条件的不同，其形成机制亦不同；通过核磁共振对溶胶体系的考察，发现“局部浓缩效应”的作用机制，进一步从实验上说明液晶模板机理。将L酸量大和适度酸强度的MCM-41分子筛催化剂应用于芳樟醇乙酰化制备乙酸芳樟酯反应，得到比其他固体催化剂收率和选择性都好的结果。

2003年起，南开大学程鹏等进行新型发光配合物的设计、合成以及性质的研究，首次合成稀土-过渡混合金属的高对称性和高级有序结构的纳米管状聚合物。该系列产物热稳定性高、吸附性能良好、骨架结构稳定，为发光微孔材料的发展和稀土基高性能材料的探索开辟一条新途径；采用高温法调控配位水分子数目，首次实现从一维分子梯状结构到三维纳米管状结构的转变，从而为合成稀土—过渡混合金属微孔聚合物发光材料提供新方法；实现通过改变微孔结构中的客体小分子的数目，实现对其在紫外和可见区发光的调控，为先进变频发光材料研究提供实验和理论支持；在国际上首次甄选出基于稀土—过渡异金属微孔聚合物的Zn(II)、Mg(II)离子荧光探针，在生命科学领域具有广泛应用价值。在国际著名刊物上发表论文50

篇，被他人正面引用500余篇次，获得授权中国发明专利3项。该项研究工作深受国际同行(包括国际著名化学杂志JACS副主编Hupp教授等)的好评。

2003年，南开大学赵学庄、尚贞峰、潘荫明开展富勒烯化学的理论研究，系统研究C_{36}、C_{40}、C_{50}、C_{60}和C_{70}等富勒烯及其衍生物的光谱和稳定性规律性，为设计合成新的富勒烯衍生物提供一定的理论基础。对富勒烯一些典型的氧化、加成反应机理进行深入的量子化学研究，合理解释一些实验现象。对异质富勒烯的杂原子分布、结构与性质的变化进行系统研究，得到一系列规律。发表论文60篇，被SCI收录45篇。

2004年，南开大学关乃佳、章福祥、陈继新等完成纳米新催化材料的制备及其在环保中的应用基础研究，通过简单的光催化过程实现纳米TiO_2上负载Ag、Pt、Pd、Pd-Cu等过渡金属形貌的人为控制，使负载金属的分散性和尺寸分布均优于传统方法制备的催化剂，并发现TiO_2的稳定性和沉积金属速率是实现负载金属形貌控制的决定性因素；创造性地将原位技术用于MeZSM-5和MeTS-1分子筛/堇青石等纳米复合材料的制备，研究活性组分和载体间的主客体相互作用，将其应用于稀燃发动机，取得优异净化效果；系统考察MeZSM-5和MeTS-1分子筛/堇青石等复合材料在稀燃条件下，对NOX的还原性能和这种整体式分子筛催化剂的水热稳定性、抗中毒能力和寿命，应用于准均质混合气下点燃式稀薄燃烧发动机，有效控制稀燃汽油机氮氧化物的排放；系统考察TS-1/堇青石整体式催化剂，其他含钛的分子筛催化剂，TiO_2或TS-1载体上分子单金属或双金属催化剂等催化脱除饮用水中硝酸根和亚硝酸根反应活性，在Al/ TiO_2上取得光催化还原硝酸根的转化率98.4%和生成理想产物N_2的选择性99.9%，具有重要的应用前景。发表论文50余篇，被SCI收录23篇。

二、配位化学

1998年，南开大学廖代正、姜宗慧、阎世平等完成磁性配合物功能材料的基础研究，合成600多个新型多核配合物，解析50多个单晶结构，总结出一套评价分子磁性的理论处理和实验方法。利用非正规自旋态理论设计，合成一系列罕见的高自旋基态的ABA型三核配合物，并推广到高自旋基态的自由态—多金属配合物的合成。设计合成多种类型，具有铁磁偶合的多核配合物，得到二个具有一定相转变温度的分子磁体。系统开展以扩展桥基相联的稀土之间和稀土—过渡金属间配合物磁性的研究，合成出以扩展桥基联的双、三、四核配合物均为这类配合物首例，证实长距离相隔下有磁相互作用。运用量子化学、分子力学计算、单晶解析，归纳出某些结构与磁性的相关性，首次发现侧链为醇式的双核配合物其反铁磁偶合作用大于侧链为酮式的配合物。共发表论文400余篇，被SCI收录近100篇。其后，廖代正与杨光明、王文珍等开展多金属分子磁体的组装及有序结构研究，选用多种有效金属断片(如含CN- 的配合物桥基、含草酰胺基的大环配合物配体)，多种桥基以及不同自旋载体的组合，设计、合成多系列的含不同桥基、不同自旋载体、不同核数及不同维数结构的新型磁性多金属配合物。解析70多个单晶结构，进行波谱分析和磁性表征，提出某些文献未见报道的理论处理方法，评估复杂体系的磁相互作用的本质和大小；归纳出某些磁和结构的相关性。获得17个具有铁磁偶合或高自旋基态的分子；研制出4个具有Tc温度的配合物分子基磁体。在国内外重要刊物上发表论文56篇，52篇被SCI收录。

图3-4-1-15　南开大学廖代正(后中)与他的同事们

2002年，南开大学姜宗慧、阎世平、赵琦华完成“自由基—金属”配合物及多自旋体系的基础研究，设计合成各种预期磁性的单、双、三、四和六核“自由基-金属”配合物，丰富“自由基—金属”配位化学的内容；在磁性研究中归纳出某些新规律，为磁功能“自由基—金属”配合物的设计与合成提供指导性信息；将分子力学和量化计算方法应用于含自由基的多自旋偶合体系中，并将处理异核多自旋体系的磁交换作用的理论方法用于自由基的异核多自旋体系，为诠释自由基的异核多自旋体系的磁交换作用本质提供一种可行的手段；建立研究磁不对称的“杂自旋”体系中自旋载体间磁相互作用的近似理论模型，丰富磁化学的研究方法；合成出一系列结构新颖、性质独特的一维、二维及三维新型配合物和铁磁、反铁磁交替排布的一维链配合物，为分子的组装提供有用的基块。发表论文95篇，被SCI收录88篇。

第二节 有机化学

20世纪80年代，天津在有机化学领域的研究成果突出。南开大学杨石先、陈茹玉关于有机磷化学和宋礼成等关于多核金属有机物的研究获得国家级成果奖。

1991~2005年，天津的有机化学研究，涉及领域更加广阔、十分活跃、新人辈出、硕果累累。在金属有机化学领域，宋礼成继续奋力探索，成果叠出；在有机合成领域，天津大学何志敏等关于酶的研究、南开大学周其林等关于手性催化的研究，成果令人瞩目；在有机功能化合领域，南开大学程鹏与卜显和带领的科研团队成绩斐然；而南开大学刘育关于合成受体的研究成果尤其突出。

一、有机合成化学

（一）酶及酶模拟

1991~2000年，天津大学何志敏、张子丁、吴金川等完成酶的结构、稳定性及应用基础研究，从分子水平研究酶分子的二级结构类预测和三级结构计算机模拟方法，着力于改进预测精度，将三级结构模拟方法用于揭示酶热稳定性机理。用化学修饰法从分子水平改造酶分子，提高酶的热稳定性；合成若干新的表面活性剂，构建出新的反胶团体系；采用酶膜耦合反应器和色谱反应器等先进酶催化反应技术，重点解决其面向工业生产的应用基础理论，从而形成比较完整的酶学应用基础理论体系。所采用的研究方法和研究成果丰富酶学应用基础理论，有助于推动酶工程及其相关学科的发展，特别是对酶分子结构的预测和利用蛋白质结构计算机模拟技术研究酶的热稳定性机理，有助于深刻理解酶的内在催化机制。在国内外著名学术刊物发表论文40篇，被SCI收录13篇、被EI收录7篇；在世界化工大会、亚太生物工程会议、中国生物工程年会等学术会议上报告论文36篇。

1991年开始，南开大学周秀中、徐善生、王佰全等对硅桥连环戊二烯基单核及双核过渡金属化合物进行较系统的研究，特别是在研究四甲基二硅桥连双环戊二烯与五羰基二铁的反应过程中，发现一个新颖的重排反应，生成具有新奇环状结构的重排产物。经过近10年深入研究，课题组弄清该反应是一立体专一性的分子内重排反应。并且根据大量实验事实，提出相应的反应机理。同时对该反应适用范围进行探索，发现引入各种取代基后以及用茚代替环戊二烯，用锗代替硅，用钌代替铁，用膦配体或异腈取代羰基，都能发生类似的重排反应，而且反应也遵循同样的重排规律。表明这一重排反应具有普遍性，是金属有机化学中一个的很有意义的新反应。这一新颖重排反应的发现，及对其重排机理的深入研究，具有很高的学术价值，丰富和充实金属有机化学的内容。成果在国际权威杂志*Organometallics*上系列发表后，引起国际同行的广泛关注。

1998年，天津商学院马书林、高健、孟宪坊等开展酶模型化合物的合成、性能与结构研究，设计与合成以不同扩展桥为桥基配体的新型双核、叁核配合物，均属国内外首次合成。同时对模型化合物的光谱和磁性进行表征，通过研究比较，就桥基的性质、长度、金属离子的组态、能量、对称性等因素对模型化合物的影响有更进一步的阐明。结果对生物电子传递链中电子转移途径的解提供重要的理论依据。首次设计合成以联苯二甲酸、萘二甲酸根为拓展桥的同双核配合物。研究结果表明，顺磁中心在较远的情况下，超交换作用明显降低。

1998年，天津理工大学黄积涛、郑嗣华、张嘉琪等完成高效酰化催化剂：超亲核催化剂的高分子化及酶模拟的研究，将对酰化、水解、烷基化等许多有机反应具有极高催化活性的吡啶胺类超亲核功能基团进行高分子化和人工酶模拟。制备出1种新型催化剂，10种新型单体；合成出5大类28种新型高分子催化剂；把超亲核基团键接到大空树脂、溪水树脂和具有超分子包络功能的环糊精上；借鉴酶固定和微生物固定技术，将线型高分子超亲核催化剂进行包埋及微胶囊固定。在合成物中，线型高分子催化剂具有比DMAP更高的催化活性，交联型高分子催化剂具有可反复使用的特点，模拟酶的研究则对分子的专一性识别进行探索，其遴选产物在药物及香料的出合成中取得令人满意的结果。发表论文16篇，5篇被SCI收录。

2003年12月，南开大学刘育、张衡益、韩宝航等共同承担含硒人工酶及紫杉醇复合新药应用基础研究。课题组设计与合成功能化环糊精衍生物（一类由D型吡喃葡萄糖单元形成的环聚多糖），采用现代谱学等先进技术研究一系列功能性硒和氮杂等修饰环糊精的分子识别，尤其是研究作为谷胱甘肽过氧化物酶和超氧化物歧化酶的活性，探讨结构与活性之间的关系，为进一步研究抗衰老等类酶作用机理奠定基础。采用超分子技术制备并分离得到含有两个环糊精空腔的多胺桥联双环糊精和紫杉醇复合物固体，将紫杉醇的水溶性提高到大约2.0毫克/毫升，大大提高该药物在水中的溶解性。体外试验表明，该紫杉醇复合物对K562白血病癌细胞的抑制能力高于紫杉醇自身。该发现为紫杉醇的替代品应用于临床，提供新的潜在的水溶性缓释复合物，也为开发紫杉醇复合新药奠定坚实的基础。在《美国药物化学杂志》《美国有机化学杂志》等国内外重要刊物上发表论文26篇，SCI收录25篇。

（二）不对称催化

1997年开始，南开大学周其林等开展金属介入的高选择性有机合成新方法和生物活性寿星环丙烷化合物的不对称催化合成的研究。1999年，开展手性催化的研究，设计全新的手性螺环配体骨架，合成200多个手性螺环双磷配体、单齿磷配体、磷—氮配体、双氮配体及其手性催化剂，这些手性磷配体和催化剂都是首次被合成，在许多不对称催化反应中表现出优秀的手性诱导效果，在新型手性催化剂的研究上处于国际领先地位。其中12个手性配体由国际著名试剂公司实现商品化生产和销售，这是中国大陆地区具有自主知识产权的手性配体和催化剂首次在国际上销售。应邀在第七届IUPAC国际杂原子化学大会（2004）、泛太平洋国际化学大会（2005）和四面体大会（2006）等重要国际学术会议上作邀请报告。

图3-4-2-16 南开大学周其林

2000年，周其林等从事螺旋型手性催化剂的设计合成及其应用的研究以及新型手性配体和催化剂的合成与开发。2002年，周其林等开展不对称催化氢化反应研究，发展多个高活性、高对映选择性的催化剂体系。在简单酮和环状酮化合物的不对称氢化反应研究中发展的手性螺二氢茚双膦配体钌络合物催化剂是最有效的手性催化剂之一。在共轭羧酸化合物的不对称氢化反应中发展手性螺二芴双膦配体钌络合物催化剂，为光学活性手性羧酸化合物提供高效、高对映选择性的合成方法。在烯酰胺化合物的不对称氢化反应研究中首次发现手性单齿磷配体能够高选择性地催化氢化-脱氢氨基酸酯和烯酰胺化合物，得到光学活性的手性-氨基酸和手性胺化合物。在亚胺化合物的不对称氢化反应研究中发展高效的手性螺环膦—氮配体铱络合物催化剂，为光学活性手性胺化合物的合成提出新方法。

2004年，周其林等开展不对称催化碳—碳键形成反应研究，应用单齿磷配体研究多个不对称碳—碳键形成反应。在铜催化的环氧化合物不对称开环反应研究中，首次采用格氏试剂作为开环试剂，取得很高的选择性，为多手性中心环醇化合物的合成提供新方法。在铑催化的有机硼酸试剂对醛的不对称加成反应中取得该反应的最高对映选择性，还实现有机硼酸试剂对酮酸酯化合物的不对称加成反应，发展手性叔醇化合物的合成新方法。首次采用镍催化不对称烯氢化反应构筑手性季碳中心，发展一个合成含季碳手性中心化合物的全新方法。在镍催化的双烯化合物与醛的还原偶联反应研究中，采用手性螺环单齿磷配体实现不对称催化，为光学活性的手性双高烯丙醇化合物提供有效合成方法。研究论文发表在《美国化学会志》和《德国应用化学》等国际权威化学期刊上。

（三）CO_2活化

2002年，天津大学钟顺和、王建伟、高健等完成CO_2活化与反应固体催化剂分子设计的项目，以多相催化CO_2活化及其与CH_3OH、环氧乙烷、C_2H_6及H_2反应合成DMC、EC、$CH_2=CH_2$及CH_3OH为应用背景；探求CO_2多相活化的基本理论和方法以及与其化学利用相关的固体催化剂分子设计原则和制取这类催化剂的技术原理。设计和制得的固体催化剂分别应用于该研究相关反应体系。

（四）超分子

1990年1月～1996年12月，南开大学与中科院兰州化学物理研究所合作，刘育、韩宝航、童林荟等共同完成超分子体系中的分子识别的基础研究，设计和合成一系列高选择性的功能主体化合物，研究主体识别客体形成超分子配合物的构效关系，探讨高选择性的热力学起源。研究发现，改变冠状化合物的分子对称性，是设计高选择性的功能主体化合物是一个非常方便和有效的工具；环糊精作为分子受体不仅可以定向包结客体分子，而且还可以识别分子异构体；修饰环糊精在光的作用下通过手性微环境可以进行异构体的定向合成，对于光的绝对不对称合成具有重要意义；离子客体受体和分子客体受体在分子识别过程中具有广泛的焓-熵补偿线性关系，大的斜率和截距是三维配位作用的重要标志，表明在分子识别过程中经历较大的构型变化和广泛的脱溶剂效应。这些分子识别机理的研究对于设计合成高选择性的主体化合物具有重要的指导意义。

2000~2005年，南开大学何家骐等先后开展环肽超分子化学和一氧化氮生理功能的化学本质问题研究和以环肽为基础的新型超分子化学的研究。

2005年，南开大学张正之、徐凤波、曾宪顺等从事超分子化学基础——识别、组装和化学传感的研究。该项目开展荧光有机配体和金属化合物通过分子识别、自组装形成单、双金属大环或多金属环番，可识别客体金属离子和中性分子，构成新型分子基荧光化学传感器的研究。为具有特定识别基团荧光N—杂环卡宾金属络合物或聚合物的合成为新型荧光化学传感器的研究开辟道路。合成一系列新型有机杯芳烃受体，它们可作为银离子选择膜电极材料。发表SCI收录论文40篇，被他引112次。有关荧光化学传感器的工作被编入到《光化学和光生物学手册》（Handbook I Photochemistry and Photobiology，2003），某些杯芳烃材料方面的工作被编入到纳米科和纳米技术大全（Encyclopedia of Nanoscience and Nanotechnology，2004）。

二、功能有机化合

南开大学卜显和等自1990年代初开始进行具有催化和生物活性的新型功能性大环化合物的研究。1997～2000年，开展具有药物活性的新型大环化合物研究。1998年，南开大学卜显和、张智慧、张若桦等进而研究具有抗艾滋病病毒药物功能新型大环多胺化合物，通过在二氧四胺十三员和十四员大环骨架上引入系列功能性侧臂，制备出系列金属配合物单晶，并解析配合物的单晶结构，通过对其功能进行系统研究，发现新型大环配体具有稳定高价态金属离子的功能。把具有光敏性能的基团与具有催化活性的大环金属配合物“组装”在同一分子中，制备出具有能够利用太阳能催化活化CO_2的功能性催化剂。利用琼脂糖凝胶电泳，薄层扫描等方法研究大环金属配合物对DNA识别与断裂作用，发现Ru-Ni大环配合物在光照下有断裂DNA的功能，利用体外细胞筛选的方法，研究并发现此类化合物的抗艾滋病毒活性。2000~2002年，卜显和等进行以核酸等为模板的新型多功能高级有序结构的创造研究。

1998年，南开大学金桂玉开展定向分子设计与结构活性关系的研究。1999~2004年，南开大学史林启等从事依据嵌段共聚物形态制备纳米结构功能材料和规整纳米材料的制备与联复合用于血液净化的研究。

2001年，南开大学程鹏、杨光明、刘欣等完成功能性有机—无机杂化材料的组装与性质研究，采用新的合成方法，使设计具有预期功能性有机—无机杂化材料能快速方便地实现；为分子设计和晶体组装提供某些指导性信息;合成出一批结构新颖、性质独特的新型功能配合物;在国内首次获得分子铁磁体和转换温度接近室温并伴有滞后和热致变色现象的自旋转换体系。发展合成有机—无机杂化材料的新方法;在国际上首次提出磁交换作用的一些新规律;率先报道铁磁—反铁磁交替链体系、多维大孔结构的超分子体系等。发表论文160多篇,其中被SCI收录128篇,被引用231篇次。主要完成者多次应邀在国际性学术会议作大会报告

2002年,南开大学卜显和、杜淼、张若桦等完成功能高级有序结构分子聚集体研究,以双亚砜为桥联配体,获得系列多维配聚物,开创配聚物研究新方向;从非手性配体构筑手性分子箱及多维配聚物,成为标志性成果;研究多吡啶配合物的合成、结构性能,发现部分配合物的光、电及抗肿瘤活性等;研究二氮环功能化及其配合物的结构和性能,获得结构独特的系列多核及配聚物,开创二氮环配位化学的新局面。首次系统研究双亚砜的配位化学并阐明其配位选择性,获得结构及性能独特的配聚物,发现改变配体链长能控制配聚物维数和空穴大小,开拓双亚砜配位化学新领域;对二氮环系首次进行系统结构改造,设计数十个新配体及其系列配合物,阐明性能,发现二氮环的独特性质;从非手性配体构筑多个手性分子聚集体。发现一些新型多吡啶配合物的重要光、电、磁性能及抗肿瘤活性等及构效关系,为设计新功能配合物提供一定理论基础。成果多次在国内外重要学术会议上作特邀报告,发表相关论文80多篇,SCI收录64篇。

2003年12月,南开大学黄文强、罗君涛、孙维敏等完成组合化学中新型聚合物载体研究(固相合成化学)项目。通过设计和合成新的连接基团,增加反应基团与聚合物骨架之间连接臂的长度,开发载体的新合成应用等方法,研究合成聚苯乙烯基磺酰氯树脂、聚苯乙烯基磺酰胺树脂等系列树脂,并研究这些树脂在固相合成中的性能和应用。利用磺酰胺树脂的反应活性,采用Zn/$TiCl_4$自由基直接还原裂解磺酰胺基的S-N键的新方法,开发一条合成酰胺库的新途径;利用酰基磺酰胺上的酰基反应活性,开发酰基转移的方法合成酰胺库的途径。聚苯乙烯磺酰胺基乙醇树脂、聚苯乙烯磺酰基乙醇树脂和聚苯乙烯磺酰基丙醇树脂,被成功地应用于固相合成海因、异恶唑和脲化合物。

2003年12月,南开大学孙平川、陈铁红、金庆华等开展软态核磁共振波谱研究智能高分子凝胶结构与相转变的研究,建立表征溶胀态高分子凝胶结构的软态NMR理论及相应的实验新技术;建立监测凝胶相转变时聚集态结构变化的NMR实验新方法,进一步阐明智能高分子凝胶的相转变机理,为设计新型智能高分子凝胶提供理论依据。建立的研究方法丰富和发展液态和固态高分辨NMR理论和实验技术。

2005年,南开大学孟继本、李金亮、徐黎立等完成的新型有机功能化合物设计、合成及性能研究,首次合成光信息基因化合物、茚满类可逆光致磁性变色化合物、Nobin树枝状手性催化剂、磷硒大环化合物和同金属配合物。发现光基因化合物有双重海量信息存储功能,茚满类化合物固态光致变色有磁性,去光恢复原状。磁性消失的可逆功能,阐明合成反应和光致磁性变色机理。磷硒大环化合物是有杀菌除草活性、同金属有很强配位能力的新型催化剂。发现NOBIN树枝状催化剂催化反应得到高收率、高ee值手性产物,提出催化机理模型。首次从理论上阐明微反应器中硒醚反应机理。这些研究的发展和突破,促进有机理论和方法的发展,对分子材料、材料科学等也有直接的推动作用。在*Chem.Eur.J Chem.Comun*等刊物发表110篇论文,被SCI收录84篇,被EI收录38篇,他引143次。*Chem.Comun*审稿人对该成果论文的评价是"非常有意义的对分子筛化学有很大贡献的"。

2005年12月,南开大学何良年、杜亚、蔡飞等人完成从二氧化碳直接合成碳酸酯及其衍生物的研究项目。项目在超临界流体条件下通过运用分子催化活化二氧化碳的原理,将二氧化碳有效地转化为具有重要应用价值的基本化工原料碳酸酯,为二氧化碳资源化利用提供一个有效方法,取得重要创新成果。设计并合成功能化的PEG均相催化剂,解决催化剂的活性不高、稳定性不足的问题,实现制备环状碳酸酯工艺过程的绿色化。使用金属锡化合物催化邻二醇与二氧化碳反应,成功地制得环状碳酸酯。这一方法拓宽以二氧化碳为原料合成环状碳酸酯的范围,包括高收率地制备那些难于从环氧化物合成的各类环状碳酸酯。发表论文12篇,5篇发表在国外高水平学术刊物上,特别是其中一篇作为国际知名刊物《绿色化学》2005年第七期的封面论文。

2005年,南开大学何锡文、陈朗星、李文友等开展分子模板–分子识别联用的基础研究和应用研究,应用

新型杯芳烃衍生物研制成多种化学传感器包括离子选择性电极、固态化学修饰电极、石英压电传感器阵列，结合化学计量学，成功建立识别金属离子、生物活性分子、有机气体分子的方法。合成一批金属、药物、农药、手性分子模板体系，结合液相色谱和固相萃取技术，实现药物分子的纯制和标准品的精制，建立复杂体系中药物分子的分离和检测方法。建立在水相合成分子模板聚合物微球或纳米球或膜的方法。选择有代表性的分子模板体系制成微球、分子模板膜，运用于色谱柱、固相萃取剂、萃取分离膜和传感器敏感膜、合成新型分子模板功能单体并用于分子识别。将分子模板体系扩展到中药领域，在实验室规模上将丹参活性成分纯制的产率提高3个百分点以上。发表论文144篇，被SCI收录108篇。

2005年，南开大学左榘、李鑫、罗亮等完成离子多糖热可逆凝胶化及结构性能关系研究，摸索出试剂级KC进一步纯化及光学净化的方法，为KC研究奠定基础。用溶胀动力及激光散射方法，分别得到凝胶力学性能，溶胀行为及非遍历行为数据。该项目不仅触及该研究领域最敏感、最有争议的核心问题，而且引入高分子物理方法，在"高度""方法""水平"方面提高多糖研究的整体水平，既有理论意义又有应用价值，在该热门领域占得一席之地。

三、合成受体

1997年1月~1999年12月，南开大学刘育、尤长城、厉斌等完成合成受体分子识别的基础研究。在国际上首次构筑有机硒-环糊精高选择性超分子体系，开创有机硒修饰环糊精分子识别的新路线；研究具有生色功能基的修饰环糊精的分子识别和多重识别机理，发现功能取代基不仅可以作为光谱上的一种分子探针，而且可以对客体分子具有诱导楔合和几何互补作用，实现协同键合；系统地研究冠状化合物离子识别的热力学起源，发现配合物的稳定性通常来自于焓的贡献，而其选择性是由熵控制的；在国际上率先系统地研究化学修饰环糊精分子识别的热力学起源，发现修饰环糊精大的构型变化是修饰环糊精分子识别的一个重要特征。研究成果对超分子化学的发展具有重大的理论意义，对于高选择性的功能体系设计及合成受体的分子识别具有实际的指导意义。发表论文20余篇，均被SCI收录。

图3-4-2-17 南开大学刘育在实验室

2000年1月~2001年12月，南开大学刘育、张衡益、陈湧等完成基于合成受体的分子识别及其纳米超分子体系的构筑研究。实现多种含杂原子的功能性冠醚、杯芳烃、环糊精等衍生物的高效、高选择性反应，系统研究这些功能受体选择性键合客体的热力学起源和修饰环糊精和桥连双环糊精的键合模式、光物理性能、分子识别机理。发现桥连双环糊精具有键合金属离子和包结客体分子等多功能特征，键合的金属离子对形成超分子配合物的稳定性起重要作用，可以产生特殊的理化性能。尤其是构筑杯芳烃连接环糊精等多种键合模式的功能超分子体系，使简单的有机化合物向复杂的功能超分子体系方向发展，对于当代化学的发展具有重要意义。进而通过简单修饰环糊精组装具有类螺旋的有序高级结构和通过杯芳烃衍生物自组装形成的锁链状有序高级结构，开拓含金属离子配位的双分子管道合成新路线，成功地构筑含硒-铂配位的双纳米管以及基于环糊精-杯芳烃的纳米线，尤其是研究这些弱相互作用的协同性和自组织性对于形成纳米超分子材料的贡献，对于该领域的研究具有重大理论意义和应用价值。发表论文71篇，均为SCI收录。

四、金属有机

1995年1月~2001年12月，南开大学宋礼成主持的课题组先后完成等瓣置换反应及新颖金属有机簇合物的合成、官能团过渡金属双核及多核有机物的化学研究及新型金属有机应答大环的合成及其超分子化学行为的研究等项目，通过研究第6族金属的单核有机物与汞单核有机物的[1 1]反应，意外地发现M-Hg键对称化反应，高产率地合成含M-Hg-M（M = Cr, Mo, W）线型簇核的开链及大环金属有机物。研究成果被编入国际著名COC大全，有两个化合物被编入国际著名DOC辞典。在对双核$Co_2(CO)_8$与双核M-M（M = Mo, W）金属键化合物的[2 2]反应研究中，提出合成MCo3四面体簇核的新方法及簇核形成的机理。在原子簇核转化反应的研究中，发现一种双等瓣置换反应，并基于这一反应合成难以用其他方法合成的桥连双簇物。还发现伴随加合的等瓣置换及环化等瓣置换反应，并利用后一反应合成具有一定离子传输功能的四面体原子簇大环冠醚。率先将有机官能团环戊二烯基配体引入簇核体系，实现一系列有意义的官能团转化反应，合成醇、酮、酯、腙等四面体原子簇金属有机衍生物。

图3-4-2-18　南开大学宋礼成在查资料

1998年1月~2004年12月，宋礼成等完成富勒烯C_{60}过渡金属有机化学的研究及含金属有机双磷配体的C_{60}及C_{70}富勒烯衍生物的化学研究。项目组研究C_{60}双负离子与金属有机卤化物的亲核取代反应，合成鉴定首批C_{60}以σ-键与过渡金属 Cr, Mo, W 相连的金属有机衍生物，有6篇他人论文引述他发表的相关论文，指出这类σ-键络合物非常重要和少见。提出适合于合成富勒烯金属有机物单一异构体的“松散”配体交换法，合成首批含dppb双膦配体的单一异构体富勒烯Mo/W衍生物。设计合成首批含二茂钌双膦、二茂钴双膦及二茂铁双胂配体的Pt/Pd富勒烯双金属衍生物，以及含反式-乙烯基双膦配体的双金属双C_{60}衍生物，研究某些富勒烯衍生物的电化学和非线性光学性质。尽管富勒烯金属衍生物由于溶解度太小和碳球的易旋性，其单晶很难培养和测定，项目组成功地测得17个富勒烯金属衍生物的单晶结构，丰富富勒烯金属有机化学的内容。

2000年1月，宋礼成等开展线性多蝶状铁硫簇合物的逐步合成及自组装研究、一类新奇的蝶状桥羰基铁硫簇合物的合成及反应研究，系统地研究单桥羰基单蝶状Fe/E络盐（E=S, Se, Te）的反应活性，例如，单桥羰基单蝶状铁硫硒碲络盐同联硫六羰基二铁可发生S-S键还原断裂反应，这一反应在新型双蝶状和多蝶状簇合物的合成中得到广泛应用。设计合成一类双桥羰基双蝶状铁硫络盐，并系统研究它的双官能团特性，合成结构和性质新颖的线型和大环蝶状化合物，成果发表在国际著名刊物JACS上。还设计合成另一类三桥羰基三蝶状铁硫络盐，并利用它的三官能团特性，合成含三个蝶状簇核的星状分子。系列成果应邀在中日原子簇会议及全国金属有机等学术会议上作报告。

其后，宋礼成与胡青眉、范洪涛等合作，完成新型过渡金属有机化合物的合成、反应、结构和性质研究，开展蝶状过渡金属Fe/E（E=S，Se，Te）化合物的合成、反应、结构和性质合成研究，表征一系列新型单蝶状、双蝶状及多蝶状Fe/E（E=S，Se，Te）过渡金属有机化合物。发现四面体过渡金属有机化合物所发生的伴随加合的单等瓣置换、双等瓣置换及环化等瓣置换三种新反应，揭示四面体金属有机物与异腈的选择性亲核取代反应规律，提出反应机理，合成表征一系列新的桥连四面体、大环四面体及含醇、醛、酮、酸、酯、腙等有机官能团的过渡金属研究化合物。提出适于合成富勒烯过渡金属衍生物的“松散”配体交换法，合成出σ-键Cr/Mo/W富勒烯衍生物及含砷配体的Pd/Pt富勒烯衍生物。供合成表征700多个新过渡金属研究化合物，对其中130多个化合物进行X-射线单晶结构分析。发表论文94篇，被SCI收录90篇。被特邀在国际学术会议上作报告4次。

2001年，南开大学张正之、麦松威、支志明等从事超分子金属有机化学研究项目，合成大量金属有机多齿配体，研究此类配体与过渡金属化合物反应形成大量双及多金属化合物的结构和成键规律以及特异物理化学性能。首次引入中性有机多齿配体及其配位化学的概念，对金属有机化学的发展具有重要意义，合成的双金属化合物具有特异的分子识别性能和发光性能，其中Cu、Ag的化合物可作为潜在的金属导体或发光材料。成果被国外几十位科学家上百次的引用，其中所合成的新型双金属化合物在催化性能及光物理性能及物理性质研究上受到国际同行的广泛关注和多次引用，在国际水平杂志上发表论文40余篇。

2002年，南开大学谢庆兰、李靖、徐效华等开展有机锡化合物的合成、结构及其应用的研究，通过分子力学和疏水性参数的计算，有机锡原子上取代基对杀螨活性的影响，由此能够有效地寻找到高杀螨活性的有机锡化合物结构类型。研究二烃基锡衍生物及其锡氧簇合物四烃基二锡氧烷的合成、结构及其在酯化、缩醛比等反应中的催化作用，实验表明该类化合物是一类新颖的二聚层状结构的锡氧簇合物。研究不对称锡氧簇合物对结构的影响，该类化合物能很好地催化缩醛比和酯化反应，催化活性和选择性高，能溶于包括脂肪烃在内的多数溶剂，催化剂对空气稳定，对设备没有腐蚀等。发表论文90篇，被SCI收录40篇。

2003年12月，南开大学王维、段学欣、翟雪梅完成刚性共轭键大分子物理结构和功能相关性研究。在研究聚噻吩的物理结构时发现，从溶液浇铸成膜时，这种聚噻吩能够形成球晶，通过SEM和TEM观察，发现球晶内部存在几十到几百纳米长、直径在20到30纳米范围内的"微纤维"结构，合成树枝状聚苄醚—线形聚乙二醇嵌段共聚物。在研究聚乙二醇嵌的结晶行为时，发现熔点变低，结晶速率变慢。观察到结晶导致的微相分离，微区结构由结晶和非结晶层交替排列而成。由于聚苄醚不具有线形大分子的特性，已有的描述结晶和非结晶嵌段共聚物的交替层厚与聚合度的标度关系不适用于该体系。研究成果加深对刚性的共轭键大分子物理结构与性能相关性的理解，对于提高这些高分子材料的性能有较大的帮助。

2005年，南开大学程鹏、张敏、王红梅等完成具有信息存储功能的高分子金属配合物研究，以设计合成具有铁磁性和自旋转换性质的配位聚合物和高分子金属聚合物，研究具有信息存储功能的分子材料为目标，取得主要进展：以1,2,4-三氮唑及其衍生物和亚铁盐为原料合成出几个系列的含Fe(II)一维自旋转换聚合物，这些聚合物纯度高，热稳定性好，具有热致变色现象，自旋转换温度均在100开尔文以上。其中2个聚合物最高转变温度在室温附近(Tc = 270 ~ 280开尔文)，且滞后温度大于10开尔文；在自旋转换理论方面的深入研究，揭示出滞后效应是信息读写的关键因素；利用水热合成方法，得到一系列含有稀土和过渡混合金属的纳米管状聚合物，具有高对称性(C6)和热稳定性，某些体系具有良好的发光性能和铁磁性质；在一维含铜聚合物结构与磁性研究中，发现桥基对磁交换性质和大小的影响规律。该项目发表SCI论文39篇，其中3篇论文的SCI影响因子大于6.0。

第三节 物理化学

南开大学以程津培为学术带头人的课题组长期从事物理化学关于化学键能量的研究，创新键能研究的方法学，在对键能数据进行系统的实验测定和定量分析的基础上，揭示具有重要理论和应用意义的化学过程和生命模拟过程的未知规律，从而对物质的性质和变化进行理论解释和预期。对一些现存化学理论做出重要发展或修正。

程津培于2001年当选中科院院士，同年当选第三世界科学院院士，2005年获何梁何利科学与技术进步奖。

图3-4-3-19 南开大学程津培

一、溶液态均裂键能数据库

1988~2000年期间，南开大学程津培课题组建立实验测定有机化合物在溶液中的C-H键绝对均裂键能(BDE)的方法，据此构建当时最大的溶液态均裂键能数据库。该项工作是通过系统测定化合物在特定溶剂中的pKa参数(即C-H键的异裂自由能)和负离子的氧化电位，利用巧妙设计的热力学循环实现的。该方法的建立为解决有机物中占主体的这部分键的键能测定提供有效途径，而且使测定效率和精度显著提高。在此基础上，课题组还发展估测自由基离子键能的实验方法。自由基离子是中性化合物失去或者得到一个电子所形成的活泼中间体，也在许多反应中产生，其键能对有机反应机理和速率的研究具有重要意义。上述各类方法，在有机键能领域获得普遍应用。

二、自由基热力学稳定性

上世纪90年代，南开大学程津培课题组证实Class O自由基的存在及其普遍性，建立按取代基对自由基热力学稳定性的影响模式分类（即Class S/Class O）的原则及判据，揭示决定自由基取代基效应的方向和强度的结构基础。基于键能的系统研究，课题组发现拉电子基团对一些自由基可使其热力学稳定性增加，而对另一些自由基则体现为降低，这与文献普遍报道的无论取代基是拉电子还是供电子，均会使自由基稳定性提升的现象不同。进一步的研究发现，拉电子基究竟是增加还是降低自由基的稳定性，以及取代基效应的强度大小，实际上取决于自由基中心原子的表观电负性，而表观电负性既与该中心原子的本征电负性有关，又受其他结构基团的影响而变化。课题组通过对各结构因素的归纳，建立判断自由基取代基效应的类型和程度的判据，为判断自由基行为提供新的理论基础。

三、键能系统测定

1998~2005年，南开大学程津培课题组完成溶液中Y-NO键（Y= N、S、O、C、M等）键能的首次系统测定，为理解和分析NO的重要生理作用提供理论依据。一氧化氮（NO）是体内最重要的生物信号分子之一，但NO既可以作为自由基又可作为正离子发挥生理作用，其载体究竟会以何种方式发生Y-NO键的断裂及转移，其化学基础并不清楚。课题组通过建立相应方法，系统研究相关的键能和NO转移机理，从化学驱动力角度，提出理解其生理行为的定量解析思路。二氧化氮（NO_2）也具有重要生理功能。2008年该课题组还首次完成Y- NO_2键的键能测定，为研究相关生命过程以及硝化反应提供基础数据。

程津培与合作者在国内外重要刊物发表论文200余篇，他引四千余次，形成较大的学术影响力，并建成具有重要国际影响和中国优势及特色的物理有机化学研究梯队。

第四节 分析化学

1990年以后，分析化学从传统和经典的化学分析进入到生物、环境、能源、材料、药物等新型学科，并密切结合，形成具有新意义的“分析化学”。1991 ~ 2005年，在传统意义分析化学上素有基础的南开大学积极调整，先后开拓一系列新的学科研究方向，得到可贵发现并取得成果。

图3-4-4-20 南开大学沈含熙在讲学

1995 ~ 1997年，南开大学沈含熙等在流动注射分析领域，对气体流动注射分析体系以及金属-有机配合物显色体系进行深入研究。建立大气体系中氮氧化物及二氧化硫气体的新的自动化在线监测方法。

1995 ~ 1998年，沈含熙等开展超分子配合物在分析化学中的应用研究，以超分子大环配合物为主要对象，开展以环糊精聚合物为受体的超分子配合物的分析应用。提出用有机客体修饰β-环糊精交联聚合物树脂作为固定相光度分析法测定痕量物质的新方法。研究环糊精包结物作为超分子受体在酶法分析中应用的可能性，建立以金属卟啉固相超分子在催化动力学分析中应用的新方法。

1996～1999年，沈含熙等对仿生生物分析及分子组装体在生化分析中的应用开展研究。系统地研究辣根过氧化物酶及其模型物催化底物的开发。建立多种不需要进行偶联反应的，以偶氮染料、隐性三苯甲烷染料、席夫碱以及咕吨酮等有机试剂作为高灵敏底物的新的酶分析方法。通过酶催化反应研究非氨基偶氮染料的致癌机理。1998～2001年，在分子自组装形成的液晶型脂质体基础上，分别研究药物吸收的新模型以及有关双层类脂膜的电化学行为，以及开发生物电化学传感器的可能性。1999～2003年，开展多种包括自组装荧光二聚体染料、金属配合物和高灵敏有机配体作为生物大分子探针的研究，建立多种可用于核酸及蛋白质测定的荧光光谱、分子吸收光谱和共振瑞利散射光谱的新分析方法。

1999～2005年，沈含熙等展开生物电化学传感器的研制。系统研究各种生物物质，包括天然物质的电化学行为，进一步建立各种生物材料以及药物的电化学分析传感器究许多生物膜修饰电极，试用于多种微量生物物质及药物的检测，取得很好的效果。

2002年，沈含熙等开始对检测病原体病毒以及重大疾病预警标志物的新型荧光基因探针的研究。经过5年的探索和努力，课题组在乙肝病毒HBV以及对恶性肿瘤早期诊断的预警标志物—端粒酶活性检测方面，取得突破性的进展。设计并合成多枚检测乙肝病毒基因的新型萤光探针。成功地实现对全国人民健康危害极大的乙型肝炎病毒的基因检测。针对端粒酶延伸产物序列的特殊性，设计合成若干个复合式和发夹型引物。初步实现对一系列恶性肿瘤细胞中的端粒酶活性进行快速定量检测。方法允许检测10-10000拷贝数的目标物。研究成果达到国际先进水平。所建立的检测方法均具有较好的临床应用价值。

第五节　高分子化学

在高分子化学领域，南开大学以何炳林院士为代表，聚集着一批杰出人才。1958年，何炳林开始研究和生产离子交换树脂，开创并发展中国的离子交换树脂工业，为中国的功能高分子研究做出巨大贡献。

1991～2005年，何炳林等在医学高分子领域开展卓有成效的研究，开发成功多种血液灌流吸附剂用于不同病症的治疗，史作清等研究多种树脂用于药物提取。同时，南开大学在无机高分子、有机高分子不同分支领域的研究做出突出贡献。

一、医学与药用高分子

20世纪80年代中期开始，南开大学何炳林与北京大学、武汉大学、南京大学的冯新德、卓仁禧、林思聪等在生物医学高分子领域开展卓有成效的研究。提出和发展一系列生物医学高分子的结构设计思想，并成功地实现新型生物医学高分子的设计与合成；开创和发展多种生物医学高分子合成新方法，实现新品种生物医学高分子与生物体之间相互作用的认识；发明一批生物医学高分子新品种，产生一定的经济效益和良好的社会效益；通过联合开展生物医学高分子研究与组织学术交流，系统地建立和发展国内生物医学高分子领域。何炳林在血液净化高分子材料方面，在国内最早系统研究用于血液灌流的吸附剂：开发出安眠药、农药中毒血液灌流吸附剂，用于临床，挽救无数患者的生命。研制的全新型尿毒症中分子毒性物质吸附剂的临床应用表明，对中分子毒性物质的清除率明显优于血液透析。用于治疗系统性红斑狼疮的免疫吸附剂在临床试验中，患者体内免疫复合物由阳性变为阴性。开发多种用于治疗高脂血症的低密度脂蛋白亲和吸附剂，可以高选择地清除低密度脂蛋白。

20世纪80年代开始，陈长治等从事可再生高吸附量胆红素吸附树脂的研究和特异活性材料-类风湿因子免疫吸附剂的研制。20世纪90年代初开始至2000年，俞耀庭等开展特异性活性材料-免疫吸附剂、EBB

类化合物对恶性肿瘤病细胞的抑制作用、高强度纤维素树脂键联DNA制备新型免疫吸附剂的研究、“DNA”抗体及免疫复合物吸附树脂治疗SLE的研究、以及哮喘病血液灌流用免疫吸附剂的制备研究。俞耀庭科研团队从理论上研究生物材料选择性识别患者体内致病毒素的机制，成功制成具有自主知识产权的固定化DNA碳化树脂和大孔径、高比表面选择性吸附树脂等，通过血液净化装置治疗疑难性免疫疾病，如系统性红斑狼疮，类风湿关节炎，重症肌无力，重症黄疸性肝炎，药物及农药急性中毒及内毒素血症等。同时，俞耀庭等还开展免疫吸附治疗类风湿关节炎血凝净化装置、肝细胞聚集体的培养系统和生物人工肝反应器的构建与材料表面分子识别及其评估方法的研究。

1992～1994年，南开大学史作清分别进行均孔吸附树脂的合成及其对气体有机物吸附分离性能研究和弱碱阴树脂的合成。自1994年开始，史作清，施荣富，路延龄等开展氢键吸附剂合成、结构和吸附性能研究，首次提出氢键型吸附树脂的概念，先后合成三种类型的以形成氢键为吸附机理的选择性吸附树脂，即给体型（提供形成氢键的质子）、受体型（接受形成氢键的质子）和混合型。此类吸附树脂的功能基团能与黄酮类、生物碱类、多酚类等天然产物成分形成氢键，具备显著的选择性吸附性能和较强的吸附力，并且吸附热的大小适中，也能用一般有机溶剂进行洗脱，用于天然产物的提取可明显提高吸附量，得到纯度较高的提取物，在中药成分提取方面具有广泛的用途。该项研究丰富功能高分子材料的内容，成为吸附分离材料的新发展，改变以往国内外对吸附树脂按功能基的极性分类的传统。以氢键吸附树脂为核心的药用功能高分子材料在医药工业中的应用被列为国家科技成果重点推广计划。

同期，史作清、路延龄、施荣富等开展选择性树脂吸附法银杏叶提取物及生产工艺研究，成功地研制出受体型氢键吸附树脂，并将其用于银杏叶提取物的生产。银杏叶提取物首先由德国开发，成为世界范围的治疗心脑血管病的植物药。国外的生成工艺系采用复杂的溶剂萃取法，成本高，环境污染大。国内则采用普通吸附树脂提取法，但提取物的黄酮含量达不到要求，白果内酯损失大，质量达不到国际公认标准。选择性树脂吸附法的应用不仅克服溶剂萃取工艺的缺点，还大大提高提取物的黄酮和萜内酯的含量，成为国内外最先进的生成工艺，使国内生产的银杏叶提取物在质量上和成本上具有明显的国际竞争力，不仅使中国成为银杏叶提取物生产、出口大国，也成为其他中药成分的提取分离的典范。研究成果于1997年首先在天津成功实现产业化。

1996年，史作清、路延龄、范云鸽等开始固相有机合成载体树脂的研究，至1999年陆续合成出几个重要品种。此类产品属精细功能高分子材料，结构为在交联聚苯乙烯骨架上键合上不同的反应性化学基团，用于多肽药物的合成。其创新点在于在高聚物上引入功能基团的高分子反应的定量控制技术和窄分布微球的工业化制备方法。1999～2001年，南开大学史作清等进行树脂吸附分离法研究沙棘叶有效成分研究，2000～2002年，史作清等进行非水体系中的氢键吸附和氢键吸附剂的研制。2002年，项目组按期完成MBHA、三苯基和Rink三个主要载体树脂的放大试验，并在和成科技发展公司投产，质量达到国际先进水平，成为国际主流产品之一，销售到欧美等发达国家。其后，南开大学史作清、徐满才、施荣富等完成多功能吸附树脂及其对中药有效成分的吸附性能研究，合成出4类多功能吸附树脂，即单功能基吸附树脂、双功能基吸附树脂、纳米网孔筛分吸附树脂、色谱分离树脂。这些吸附树脂可以不同的机理进行物质分离，为实现中药现代化提供效果突出的分离纯化方法。对多功能树脂热力学的研究表明，其吸附焓远高于范德华力吸附和氢键吸附。在吸附的初始阶段，吸附焓可高达100千焦/摩尔左右，明显地说明对同一个分子的多重吸附作用，与分离实验的结果相符。课题组对几种中药成分的分离进行初步探索，取得良好效果。

2001年2月，南开大学何炳林、袁直、王虹等研制血液灌流用高分子吸附材料，建立从正常人尿液内分离、提取尿毒症中分子物质的方法，克服由于患者血液紧张而对中分子物质深入研究的限制。通过先进的分析测试手段，证明A-3中分子物质是患者难以通过尿液排出而在体内累积的代谢废物，其中含有分子量为1007.94和2015的8肽和16肽，并确定他们的一级结构。通过初步动物实验，证实它们的毒性作用。在此基础上，进行吸附剂的结构设计和制备。成功地研制出以壳聚糖为载体的中分子物质吸附剂，对尿毒症血清中分子物质的吸附量达到14毫克/克，吸附平衡时间在2小时之内，对牛血清白蛋白几乎不吸附。材料的血液相容性指标符合临床应用标准，适合用作血液灌流吸附材料。

二、无机高分子

1996年，南开大学范云鸽、史作清和海军司令部防化研究所陈茂华、陈兆礼等共同进行二氧化碳固体吸收剂研制，研究封闭舱室（如载人宇宙飞船、潜艇以及现代建筑）中，不能与大气中的空气进行交换的条件下，有效去除舱室中有害杂质（如二氧化碳），维持必需的气体成分和纯净度的空气调节与再生装置。致力于研究合成交换容量高、对二氧化碳具有良好吸附—解吸性能的弱碱性阴离子交换树脂。项目组对聚苯乙烯型、聚丙烯酸型、互贯型、后交联型和聚丙烯酸缩水甘油酯型5个系列上百个弱碱性阴离子交换树脂的合成设计、工艺研究、制备条件优化进行较为系统的研究，在此基础上进行二氧化碳吸附筛选、二氧化碳吸附条件试验、二氧化碳吸附剂再生方法、毒性评价、使用寿命及稳定性、二氧化碳共存环境组分干扰条件试验研究。项目组研制成功固态胺二氧化碳吸收剂，结果表明该交换树脂吸附清除空气中的二氧化碳在技术上可行，具有耗能少、装置体积小、安全、无污染优点。

三、有机高分子

1993年，天津化工厂戈文章、宗永兴、廖世铿等研制成功TH-4000系列高聚合度PVC树脂，采用复合引发剂配方，解决聚合反应后期出现的放热高峰现象，使整个聚合反应放热平衡，易操作、控制，采用后加引发新工艺，使产品质量稳定可靠。还采用高聚合度的PVA分散剂，使产品的表观密度在0.44%/毫升以上。产品质量达到国际相同牌号PVC树脂质量水平。

1993年，南开大学张政朴、李贺先、张华等开展离子膜法制烧碱用螯合树脂生产应用技术的研究。离子膜法制烧碱技术是20世纪80年代由国外引进的电解食盐水制烧碱新技术，优点是污染小、能耗低、产品质量好，其中氨基磷酸型螯合树脂的生产是关键技术之一。该树脂的作用是纯化一次盐水，使其中Ca^{2+}，Mg^{2+}，Fe^{2+}，Fe^{3+}等离子含量小于5×10^{-8}克/升，以便保护离子膜，延长其使用寿命。为各氯碱厂所急需的氨基磷酸型螯合树脂的生产在国内是空白。项目组完成的螯合树脂生产应用技术，使中国有更多的氯碱厂采用离子膜法制烧碱新技术，达到国际先进水平，解决依赖进口的问题。

1998年，天津大学姚康德、尹玉姬、成国祥完成刺激响应性高分子材料的研究，以生物相容性良好、且能生物降解、资源丰富的壳聚糖为基础，分别与聚醚、明胶和果胶形成互穿、杂混、配合物网络，利用氢键的形成与解离，构成pH刺激响应性凝胶，对其形成机理、pH响应溶胀特性、网络中水的状态以及药物释放行为进行系统研究。项目组更利用多组分柔性聚合物表面的环境响应性设计与合成适于极性与非极性基材的智能粘合剂。该工作拓宽刺激响应高分子材料的应用领域。相关论文为SCI引用2次。

第六节 农药化学

1965年，国家科委确定，南开大学元素有机化学研究所以元素有机化学及农药化学为主要科研方向，李正名积极投身有机磷化学和有机磷农药的研究；1995年底，原国家计划委员会正式批准南开大学成立农药国家工程研究中心，李正名任中心主任。1992年李正名主持“创制新农药研究”获国家“七五”科技攻关重大成果奖，1999年经过大量合成和筛选研究发现中国特色作物谷子专用超高效除草剂单嘧磺隆，是中国获得国家正式登记的第一个具有自主知识产权的创制除草剂；2004年又开发出小麦专用除草剂单嘧磺酯，为第创制超高效绿色除草剂。此创新成果获天津市技术发明一等奖、国家技术发明二等奖。

1990年起，南开大学李正名主持的课题组对新型磺酰脲和构效关系进行研究，开展对环境友好的超高效除草剂的创制和开发研究，1993年首次发现含有单取代嘧啶环结构的磺酰脲分子同样具有超高效除草活性，2001年，李正名与澳大利亚Duggleby教授合作，发现此磺酰脲除草剂抑制已提纯ALS靶酶的Ki值与其在植物体内生物活性IC50有良好的相关性，并合作获得单嘧磺隆和单嘧磺酯与ALS酶复合物晶体，从分子水平阐明这类除草剂的作用机制。同年，作为杰出科研成果在《有机化学》杂志上发表论文报告"新磺酰脲类除草剂活性构效关系的研究"，从理论上总结磺酰脲分子除草活性三要素，修正和发展国际上公认的磺酰脲构效关系的理论。单嘧磺隆和单嘧磺酯分别于1999年和2004年开发成为具有中国自主知识产权的创制新品种绿色除草剂：单嘧磺隆为谷田专用除草剂，单嘧磺酯为小麦专用除草剂。由于它们的使用量很低（比传统品种低1-2个数量级）、基本无毒，按国家新农药规定进行了38~41项各类种环境生态试验均顺利通过，最后得到国家新农药三证并批准进入市场。2004年获天津发明专利金奖。国家"十五"科技攻关项目验收专家评价："具有自主知识产权的单嘧磺隆产业化的成功，标志着我国磺酰脲类除草剂已经进入理论指导下的创制"

图3-4-6-21 南开大学李正名在除草剂试验田

1996年6月~2000年3月，天津大学闻建平、黄琳、朱智勇等研究成功啶虫脒农药合成的新工艺，致力于3-甲基吡啶氧化法四步法合成吡虫啉、啶虫脒原药的新工艺、新技术的研制与开发工作，开发出基于2-氯-5-氯甲基吡啶与N-氰基-N-甲基乙脒一步法合成啶虫脒中的吸酸剂，采用安全性能好的无水碳酸钾代替毒性大、易燃易爆的氢化钠作为啶虫脒缩合过程吸酸剂，有效解决生产过程中的安全隐患。筛选优化基于2-氯-5-氯甲基吡啶与N-氰基-N-甲基乙脒一步法合成啶虫脒中的高效催化剂，并优化啶虫脒生产的合成工艺，新工艺的技术达到国际先进水平。

1996年，南开大学杨华铮等开展新型抑制光合作用除草剂的研究。1998年起，杨华铮等先后从事膦酰基杂环化合成方法及生物活性、生物合理方法设计合成新农药及其构效关系以及具有生物活性的杂环化合物库的组合合成研究。开展光合作用抑制剂、ALS酶抑制剂以及具有生物活性的含磷化合物等方面的研究，从生物合理的角度，开展新农药的设计、合成及构效关系研究，创制出一新型水旱两用除草剂新品种H-9201。2005年，杨华铮、陈凯、程永浩完成基于药效团模型的新型除草剂合成及生物活性研究，总结先导化合物的结构与活性的关系，研究各自的药效团特征，分别设计出不同结构的多种含氮杂环化合物和稠杂环化合物，研究设计化合物的合成方法，包括固相组合合成及液相平行合成的方法。建立ALS及PPO酶的测定方法，同时用传统的小杯法，平皿法及盆栽试验等活性测定法，测定所合成化合物的除草活性。在计算机辅助下，通过不断优化结构，共合成出数十种类型、数百个化合物，发现其中一些未见文献报导的新型结构，它们具有很好的除草活性，有望从中找出具有自主知识产权的新型高效除草剂。

2002年，南开大学徐凤波、张正之、解放等研究甲氨基阿维菌素苯甲酸盐合成技术，产品甲氨基阿维菌素盐是抗生素类绿色杀虫剂，具有独到的广谱、高效、微毒杀虫杀螨特征，杀灭鳞翅目害虫的活性和安全性为其他农药无法比拟，是高度农药的理想替代品种。合成技术填补国内空白，推动着绿色农业发展。研究成果引起农药界的广泛关注和好评。

第七节 医药化工

天津大学和天津理工大学从事的医药化工研究项目，或弥补国内空白或获得独立知识产权，技术路线先进，产品质量优秀。

2000年5月~2003年12月，天津大学冯亚青、张尚湖、周立山等共同完成2-氰基吡嗪的开发与应用研究项目。项目从廉价原料乙二胺、1,2-丙二醇或环氧丙烷出发，制备高效催化剂、经气固接触固体床连续反应器两部反应制备高质量、低成本的2-氰基吡嗪的新技术。开发出高效环合催化剂——Zn/Cu/Cr/Al复合型催化剂，用于合成2-甲基吡嗪；研制出杂环用高效氨氧化催化剂——VmoOP催化剂，用于合成2-氰基吡嗪；完成由乙二胺与1,2-丙二醇，以及乙二胺与环氧丙烷为原料经环合脱水脱氢制备2-甲基吡嗪，再经氨氧化制备2-氰基吡嗪的工艺。将小试技术应用于工业生产。该项目弥补国内空白，为国家医药生产节约大量资金，具有显著经济与社会效益。发表论文8篇。

2004年，天津理工大学卢俊瑞、张桂芝、吕振波等研究氯代羟基二苯醚类化合物的化工生产工艺。以三氯生为模板化合物，设计选定制备路线、中间体和产品的处理与控制方法，建立完善的高品质三氯生生产工艺技术，系统研究系列氯代羟基二苯醚制备的类型反应动力学、机理、催化剂、分子结构与反应活性的关系，优化工艺条件，设计多项通用后处理技术，完善相关理论。建立适用于氯代硝基二苯醚、氯代氨基二苯醚和氯代羟基二苯醚三类化合物制备的平台技术，将相转移催化剂应用于氯代酚与氯代硝基苯的缩合反应，发现取代基和金属离子对邻氨基二苯醚类重氮盐的分子内闭环反应的影响规律，推证反应机理，提出"组合纯技术"，创造性地将分子精馏、重金属离子络合萃取和沉降去除等技术应用于产品处理，形成多项先进理论突破和创新技术。在国内率先精馏三氯生在线全检系统，具有多项自主知识产权，适用于高品质氯代羟基二苯醚产品的生产。建成年产30和100吨的两套三氯生生产线和一套应用系统，三氯生总收率大39.5%，含量达99.9%，产品质量符合美国药典USP26的要求。

第八节 化学工程基础参数研究

以天津大学为主完成的若干化学工程基础参数研究，一定程度上补充国内缺乏化工数据中心的不足，对工程设计或计算具有很大实用价值。

1993年1月~2001年12月，天津大学、河北理工大学、美国Aspen软件公司三方合作，由马沛生、梁英华、夏淑倩、李平、刘粘畦等共同完成临界参数及其他化工数据测定与研究。该项目研究多项物性，包括临界参数、溶解度（多种相平衡）、液体扩散系数、极微蒸汽压、表面张力、蒸发焓、高压PVT、高压粘度。主要特点：系统性强，全方位从事有关化工数据的研究工作，从测定至估算有配套性；有直接实用背景，所得数据为化工计算所必须；研究工作注意理论创新；在实验技术上有独特的创新，多项设计中有独特的测定装置及技术。该项目是国内唯一系统进行化工数据全方位工作的单位，在一定程度上补充国内缺乏化工数据中心的不足。

2002年8月~2004年9月，天津大学马沛生、夏淑倩共同完成热力学性质和传递性质的测定和计算，研究成果包括临界性质、极微蒸气压、加压液相扩散系数等方面处于国内领先地位，并在多方面提出创新方法。当缺乏实验性质时，提出多种估算方法，包括临界性质、蒸气压、液相扩散系数、表面张力、液体黏度等多个热力学或传递性质，对工程设计或计算有很大实用价值。发表SCI论文22篇，EI论文22篇。

第九节 化学分离工程

化学分离工程，包括精馏、蒸发与结晶、膜分离、吸附与离子交换等，是化工的传统研究领域，天津大学在该领域占居全国领先的地位。1991~2005年，余国琮的高效精馏塔技术及其应用、王静康的新型工业结晶技术与设备的研究、青霉素结晶新型技术与设备研究和粒子过程晶体产品分子组装与形态优化技术以及王榕树的新型离子筛的研制及其应用，荣获国家科技进步二等奖和国家技术发明二等奖。

一、精馏

1989年1月~1997年7月，由天津大学余国琮主持，袁希钢、黄洁、张敏卿等共同完成精馏塔气液两相流的流动特性及计算流体力学研究，采用k-ε方程对Raynold方程进行封闭，在动量方程中增加气相阻力项，从而提出适合于精馏塔版气液两相错流流动的计算流体力学模型和方法，同时，通过实验测量，获得塔板上液相流动的二维速度分布；通过实验测量，获得精馏塔板上、填料床层内液相停留时间分布，建立通过停留时间分布计算液相流速分布等有关参数的方法，并提出塔板上液相流动的二维涡流扩散系数计算方法；建立考虑液相流速分布的塔板分区模型及计算塔板效率方法；研究精馏塔板雾沫夹带、漏液的不均匀分布以及塔板沟流对塔板效率的影响，建立相应的塔板效率计算模型和方法。研究成果为从实验室小型实验的数据直接放大到大型工业精馏塔提供必要的理论依据。发表论文22篇。

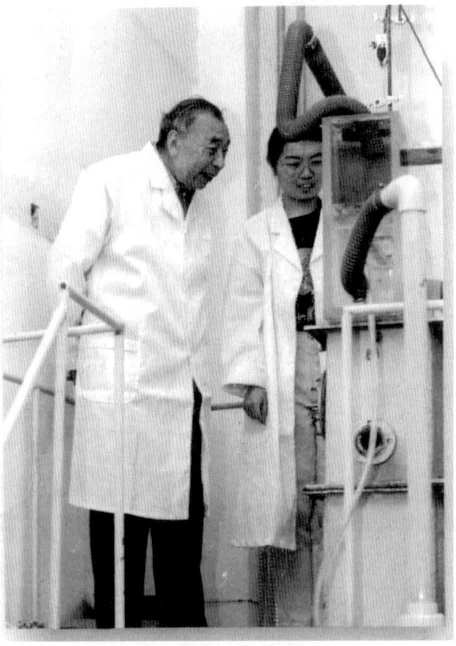
图3-4-9-22 余国琮（左一）在进行实验观察

1990年1月~2000年12月，天津大学余国琮、袁希钢、杨志才等共同完成精馏过程中若干基础理论问题研究，首次提出在精馏塔板上气液两相流动的二维分布对分离效率影响的研究命题，并提出塔板上流速场的分区理论以及对分区流速的描述方法；提出考虑气相影响的塔板以及填料中的气液两相流流速分布计算流体力学模型，建立采用热线测速技术对气液两相流进行测量的方法；在精馏塔板分区理论基础上分别提出对沟流及不均匀漏液对分离效率的影响进行描述的新方法；建立板式精馏塔以及填料塔的三维非平衡传质模型，实现对精馏过程更加精确的模拟，初步奠定计算机传质学这一新研究领域的基础；观测近气液相界面流动及传质行为，揭示运动气泡近界面浓度场分布、传质特性以及湍流结构等特性，发现近界面处气液两相浓度分别远离平衡浓度。为发展非平衡级模拟理论提供依据，同时为多相非平衡热力学的基础研究开辟新的领域并提供实验依据；提出新的特殊精馏过程操作策略以及对精馏操作过程中的持液量对过程影响评价的分析方法，从而为精馏过程在热敏物系等特殊物系的分离上的应用提供理论依据。该成果构成对精馏过程中多相流的流动、界面现象以及操作策略重要基础问题进行理论研究的较为完整的方法体系。发表论文58篇，其中被SCI及EI收录25篇。

1997年1月~2003年8月，天津大学余国琮主持，张鹏飞、许春建、朱慧铭等共同完成高效精馏塔技术及其应用的研究项目，进行精馏过程与设备的设计、操作方式、塔内构件设计与制造的研究与开发，进一步解释并掌握精馏塔在多种工艺与操作条件下的流体力学及传质过程的特性和规律。研究的新型高效精馏塔技术建立规整填料精馏塔非平衡离散模型，结合流体力学性能，提出精馏塔整体优化设计的新方法；针对热敏物料等特殊要求，提出多种新流程，包括可有效提高收率的分批精馏过程及其操作方法和有效消除瓶颈的冷回流工艺等；开发JZF型折峰规整填料。与相同比表面积的常规规整填料相比，提高传质效率，降低阻力；开发塔填料加工整体预组装新工艺以及采用先进的自动生产线，有效保证加工精度与质量。应用该技术的精馏装置可提高处理能力20%~30%，降低蒸汽用量30%~50%，并明显提高产品纯度。

2001年9月~2002年10月，天津大学李鑫钢、姜斌、孙津生等共同完成精馏过程大型化关键技术的开发与应用项目，综合应用现代传质理论、流体力学与计算流体力学和系统分析优化等化工过程领域的最新研究成果和方法，针对炼油厂润滑油型减压蒸馏过程，深入探讨大型装置的运行特点和设备要求，开发大型蒸馏塔内件集成新技术，提出中国石化上海高桥分公司800万吨/年大型润滑油型减压塔成套塔内件集成技术总体方案。该方案在结构上采用ZUPAC规整填料、槽盘式气液分布器、多级组合槽式液体分布器、具有捕液吸能作用的双切向挡板进料分布器、埋藏梁支撑及桁架梁支撑等多项专利和专有技术，该装置于2002年一次开车成功，润滑油基础油料收率和拔出率大大提高，各侧线产品质量合格并降低能耗，设计工艺完全满足润滑油生产的需要，各项技术指标均达到或超过设计要求。获得效益10265.4万元，润滑油型常减压蒸馏装置减压塔突破500万吨/年处理能力，首次达到800万吨/年的规模。减压塔直径也突破茂名国内最大直径塔（8.4米），达到10.2米，为国内目前最大减压蒸馏塔和世界上目前最大润滑油型减压蒸馏塔之一。

二、结晶

1987年6月~1998年11月，由天津大学王静康主持，薛履中、张美景、王玉德等共同完成新型工业结晶技术与设备的研究，项目实现由小试研究、结晶热力学机动力学研究、工业放大直至生产成功的系列化研究。主要成果包括：开发能严格控制结晶过程的物理环境和新型蒸馏结晶器，能有效控制结晶母液的温度场、流体力学场及密度场；发明液膜熔融结晶机电一体化塔式结晶装置，实现难分离物系的超纯分离，建立液膜结晶数学模型；自主研发新型反应结晶装置，可用于超细反应结晶生产过程；开发先进的结晶工艺，可控制结晶成核速率和成长速率，提高结晶产品的纯度；研究多种物系的结晶热力学、动力学等基础数据，进行结晶器流体力学的规律研究；实现结晶过程的计算机辅助与操作，保证最佳操作时间表的成功实现，解决结晶产品批间差异问题；建立新型结晶器、新型工艺与计算机辅助控制三位一体的新型技术运作模式。研究成果提高收率、容时生产能力、降低消耗和成本，并显著提高产品质量。

图3-4-9-23 天津大学王静康

1991年1月~1993年8月，由天津大学王静康主持，韩贵安、薛履中、平志存等共同完成青霉素结晶新型技术与设备研究项目，严格测取青霉素结晶的热力学、动力学及流体力学基本数据，一步建成新型的结晶生产装置，一次开车成功。蒸馏结晶装置与高悬浮密度结晶工艺条件是此项成果的创造点，体现在首先研究测定青霉素结晶热力学及青霉素结晶动力学等基本数据，并进行结晶器的流体力学放大准则研究；开发的新型蒸馏结晶器能严格控制结晶过程的物理环境；开发的新型结晶工艺，达到结晶成核速率尽可能小，结晶成长速率尽可能大的效果，解决结晶粒度分布不均匀结晶多的问题，保证结晶形成完美晶形，提高产品纯度，并避免在过滤过程中细晶通过滤网而流失或洗涤再溶解造成结晶收率的损失的问题；用计算机精确控制操作条件，即实现最佳操作时间表，保证生产装置一次开车成功，全面达到并超过攻关规定的指标。成果列为“九五”国家重大科技成果推广项目。

2001年1月~2005年12月，天津大学王静康、尹秋响、王永莉等完成粒子过程晶体产品分子组装与形态优化技术研究，系统研究不同类别医药等功能产品形态学特征，发明其分子组装与晶型优化技术，进而建立晶体形态优化方法学，解决产品中晶形不唯一的国际难题；开拓耦合结晶新技术，实现分子有序组装与规则排列和智能化调控的过程；完成发明成果的产业转化，达到由分子层次研究直至产业化集成创新的多尺度研发目标，实现该共性技术的突破。该专利核心技术成功应用于药用氨基酸、盐酸大观霉素、头孢曲松钠等十余种产品，质量及技术经济指标（节能、降耗、减排）达到并部分超过国际先进水平。直接经济效益显著，新增产值12.44亿元，新增利税2.86亿元，创收外汇3171万美元；社会效益突出，如地塞米松磷酸钠产品击败国际竞争对手，占有50%海外市场和60%国内市场。获5项发明专利。

2002年9月~2005年，天津大学和深圳九新药业有限公司合作，王静康、钱昱昕、张美景、武洁花等发明的五水头孢唑林钠晶体结构及晶体分子组装制备方法获国家专利，研究通过特定的结晶工艺，得到具有自主知识产权的国家级新药——五水头孢唑林钠原料及制剂。该产品粒度分布集中，产品流动性好、表面光洁、结晶度高、稳定性好、溶解速度快。对光和热的稳定性明显提高，解决普通头孢唑林钠澄清度和稳定性较差的问题，有效期也延长半年。创新的制备方法与生产成为解决细菌耐药性、不良反应增高问题的重要途径，对抗感染药物产业的发展起到很好的示范作用，也对抗感染药物的研发与生产产生持续而深远的影响。

三、蒸发

1995年8月~2000年6月，天津大学与天津长芦汉沽盐场有限责任公司合作，由李修伦、林瑞泰等人共同完成万吨级汽液固三相流化床卤水蒸发装置的关键技术研究，项目研究在实施能源利用的众多工业与民用换热设备中换热壁面结垢问题。该技术将三相流化床与卤水蒸发装置相结合，形成汽液固三相流化床阵法装置，该流化床蒸发装置具有防除壁垢、强化沸腾换热、降低壁温、减轻壁面腐蚀、节能、节水、降耗、减少环境污染、增加蒸发量等多种功能，且设备构造简单、操作方便、运行可靠、适应性好。成果包括三相流化床蒸发装置防除垢和强化传热机理和模型、工业化中的技术关键、最佳运行参数和操作方法。项目具有新颖性、先进性和实用性。

四、离子筛

1991年1月~2002年12月，天津大学王榕树、王林双、那平等共同完成新型离子筛的研制及其应用项目，着力研究与开发对水体具有直接净化和修复功能的一类新型环境材料，其中包括重金属离子筛（如脱铅离子筛）、阴离子筛（如降氟离子筛）、乏燃料专属离子筛（如固镭离子筛、提铯离子筛、提鉬离子筛等）、中药专用离子筛（如脱砷离子筛）、离子筛膜反应器（如γ-MnO_2纳米筛膜反应器）和特种水分子簇-六环水的研制。创新点包括开发多种具有坚稳三维骨格的、非整比的新型无机复合物，并用化学制筛手段赋予对特定离子的筛效应与键合能力，使之能够高效地捕获待净化地有害离子，分离或回收贵金属离子；利用大孔分子筛高度发达的比表面，在其内外孔道构铸离子筛膜，制备出离子筛膜反应器。并且，以专用离子筛和离子筛膜为关键技术，研制出一类具有渗透力强、表面张力小的特种水分子簇即六环水。成果在实际中地应用也获得显著地成效。在《中国科学》《自然科学进展》*J.Colloid & Interface Science* 和 *J.Radioanal. &Nucl.Chen* 等学报上发表论文80余篇。

图3-4-9-24　天津大学王榕树（左）与同事在实验室

五、膜分离

1996年，天津大学王静康、杨志勇、薛履中等共同完成液膜结晶技术分离高纯对二氯苯研究项目，开发具有填料管板的塔式液膜结晶装置。根据熔融混合物系中各组分构成的低共熔体或固体溶液熔点的差异，在一塔式液膜结晶器中完成不同组分的多级固-液传质过程，提取出高纯（或超纯）的单一组分。创新点包括：发明液膜熔融结晶机电一体化塔式装置，实现难分离物系的高纯或超纯分离；发明液膜结晶过程数学模型及模拟、分析优化软件，可计算出不同分离物系的最佳操作时间表，指导完成不同品种物系的分离提纯，使设备具有较大的操作弹性；建立液膜结晶过程动力学、热力学及流体力学参数通用测用方法；开发计算机辅助操作与控制软件，保证准确实现高纯或超纯分离，可进行人机对话，完成不同品种物系的高纯分离任务。实现攻关成果的工业转化，具有良好的经济与社会效益。

2004年，天津大学王世昌、王志、王宇新等完成膜与膜过程基础研究，成果包括：发现铸液膜的流体力学不稳定性是形成膜表面缺陷的重要原因，而膜厚是影响该不稳定性的主要参数，由此得出最佳膜厚并研制出高性能反渗透膜；建立具有普适性的膜孔径分布模型，揭示膜蒸馏过程气态膜传递边界层影响和脱NH3阻力分配规律，研究冷侧盐水循环膜蒸馏，发现引起同样水渗透通量的浓度差与温度差存在当量关系；研制成功系列脱酸气（CO_2）的气体分离膜和膜材料；研制出多种具有高质子电导率及阻纯性能的燃料电池膜，制备成功聚吡咯纳米纤维膜材料，将多孔壳聚糖膜用于非水介质中有机酸和醛类的去除。成果对膜技术的应用产生重要指导作用，已用于膜法丙烯脱水，膜法回收氢气和有机蒸汽，反渗透/电去离子生产高纯水以及制药关于废水深度处理等。发表论文71篇，被SCI收录35篇，被EI收录33篇。

2005年，天津工业大学和天津膜天膜工程技术有限公司肖长发、安树林、贾广霞、林严等合作完成智能中空纤维分离膜及其应用研究，项目根据聚合物共混物界面相分离原理，发明一种全新成孔之末方法，开发出具有界面微孔结构特征，对分离体系压力及温度变化有明显响应性的智能中空纤维分离膜及其分离技术，即以具有显著形状记忆特征的聚氨酯为基质相，以与聚氨酯部分相容或不相容有机聚合物或无机物微粒为分散相，根据共混物界面相分离原理，控制分散相相畴尺寸，纺丝成形、拉伸及必要的后处理，制备具有界面微孔结构特征，对分离体系压力及温度变化等有明显响应性的智能中空纤维分离膜，研究界面微孔结构的控制问题和相应的膜分离技术及其应用，开发具有自主知识产权的中空纤维分离膜新品种及其分离技术。

第五章　天文学和地球科学

1957年4月，中国科学院紫金山天文台在天津建立天津纬度站，是为天津现代意义天文学的发端，该纬度站于1989年撤销。1991~2005年，天津的天文学事业在发展，并取得新成绩，而以天津师范大学关于星系相互作用和并和作用的多波段观测与研究较为突出。

1991~2005年，天津关于地质学的研究以天津地质矿产研究所为主要队伍，在基础地质与矿床地质、区域地质调查与环境地质研究四个方面均取得极为丰硕的成果，区域地质调查与环境地质研究贯彻为经济建设和社会发展服务方针，为政府领导机关制订区域规划和规避地质风险提供可靠依据。而以天津地矿所作为主要参加者，与地质矿产部等国内多家相关单位合作完成的《中华人民共和国及其毗邻海区第四纪地质图（1∶250万）及说明书》项目最为突出，获国家自然科学二等奖。

1991~2005年，作为地球科学一个重要组成部分的海洋科学研究，在天津得到进一步的重视，重点围绕着海洋、海域、海岸的变化与保护展开，取得多项成果，对于环境保护具有重要意义。

第一节 天文学

一、天文视宁度研究

2001年3月,天津理工大学黄寅亮、付元芬、李建国等完成中国天文视宁度研究。Fried参数r0在时间和空间上的分布数据是湍流大气的基本参数,在天文选址以及各种大气中的激光、光学工程中是首先要考虑的重要因素。课题组在塔塔斯基的理论框架下,首先利用云南天文台和北京天文台实测的r0与对应地区气象站的常规气象探空资料,采用独特的统计方法,确定Cn2中的数值常数,然后把它推广到全国,从理论上计算出全国81个气象测站上空的r0分布。计算结果表明,各地r0分布存在着明显的空间差异性和时间变化,发现冬季和夏季r0的最大分布区域。在冬季1月r0平均值20点在3千米上空的极大值在丽江(13.05厘米),仅稍低于海拔4301米的定日(13.37厘米);在夏季7月3千米上空的极大值在哈密(12.35厘米)、酒泉(12.17厘米)一带,高于丽江(9.64)及定日(10.96厘米)。该项目在如此大的面积上进行r0统计工作,在国内外还是首次。研究结果在天文和军事方面都有一定的参考价值。

二、星系的多波段观测和研究

2002年,天津师范大学、中国科学院国家天文台、中国科学院研究生院夏晓阳、吴宏、邓祖淦、邹振隆、薛随建合作完成星系相互作用和并合过程与星系形成和演化关系的多波段观测和研究。

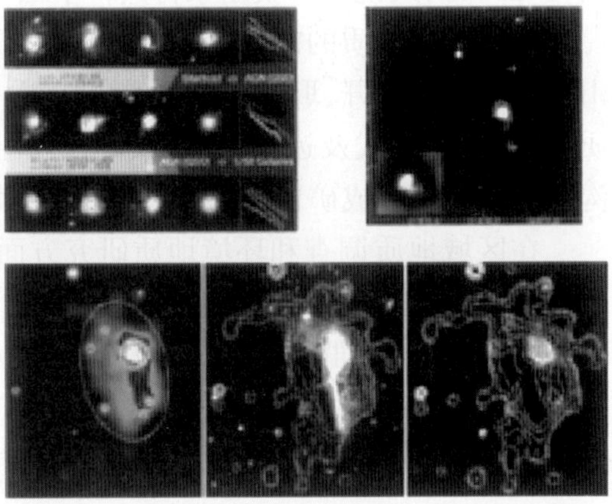

图3-5-1-25 关于星系形成和演化过程研究的观测照片

该项目充分利用国外巡天资料和一流设备的归档数据并与国内设备相结合,对星系的大尺度结构研究揭示星系的空间分布存在超大尺度结构;对极亮红外星系的形态和光谱进行分类,在国际上首次提出部分极亮红外星系可能是星系群多重并合的产物;Chandra对Mrk273的观测首次发现极亮红外星系有非常大的低金属丰度热气体晕。按最流行的结构形成理论星系是等级成团的,星系形成是由小到大的一个过程;对低红移星系的高分辩观测发现,相当一批椭球星系有并合的痕迹。因此,星系的环境、星系之间的相互作用和并合过程对星系形成起着非常重要的作用。项目组从多波段对低红移的并合星系样本作详尽的观测研究,对星系的形成和演化过程提供了重要的观测证据。

共发表论文70余篇,其中SCI论文39篇,最有代表性的16篇被引用159次,他引121次。

三、微大气物理学

1999年,南开大学温景嵩完成“微尺度大气运动中气溶胶物理等过程的研究”,极大地丰富人类对微尺度大气运动的研究。该成果突破斯莫鲁霍夫斯基(Smoluchowski)的悬浮粒子对流碰并的轨迹分析法限制,建立悬浮粒子对流碰并的统计理论;突破斯莫鲁霍夫斯基的悬浮粒子两种极限碰并理论限制,建立悬浮粒子重力对流和布朗运动耦合碰并的统计理论;突破巴切勒(Batchelor)1972单分散悬浮粒子沉降的统计理论限制,建立多分散悬浮粒子沉降的统计理论(1982);出版一本英文专著:*The Fundamentals of Aerosol Dynam-*

ics, *World Scientific*, Singapore, 1996(气溶胶动力学基础,世界科学出版社,新加坡,1996)。标志着气溶胶力学从经典的富克斯(Fuchs)孤粒子动力学到现在多粒子相互作用下的动力学的新进展;澄清对流暖云中湍流起伏场对云滴增长的作用,建立对流暖云大云滴随机增长的马尔柯夫(Markov)过程理论;发现湍流的不连续性,揭示出它和国际公认的柯尔莫果洛夫(Kolmogorov)湍流理论中的物理模型有矛盾;建立中国整层大气湍流强度分布的一个模型,并发现在一定条件下,它对中国远程激光工程会有严重影响;出版专著《微大气物理学导论》(科学出版社,北京,1989)和《概率论和微大气物理学》(气象出版社,北京,1995),标志着对微尺度大气运动的研究,从经典的萨顿(Sutton)的微气象学,发展到现在的微大气物理学的新阶段。

第二节 地质学

1991~2005年,天津关于地质学的研究以天津地质矿产研究所(以下简称天津地矿所)为主体,关注于基础地质、矿床地质、区域地质调查和环境地质研究四个方面,取得丰硕成果。

关于基础地质的研究,在前寒武纪大陆地壳演化示踪、中国北方元古宙沉积—构造环境及对大型超大型矿床的制约研究和秦岭中-新元古代造山带与Rodinia大陆再造等研究方向上取得出色成果,中国前寒武纪陆壳的拼接和生长研究达到国际同类研究的领先水平。1993年,天津地质矿产研究所作为主要参加者,与地矿部水文地质工程地质研究所等国内多家单位共同完成的中华人民共和国及其毗邻海区第四纪地质图(1:250万)及说明书获国家自然科学二等奖。

关于矿床地质的研究,以探查金矿及研究金矿的成矿条件为重点,在东北、华北的熊耳山、五台山、中条山等多个地点展开,取得一系列突出成果。以天津地矿所为牵头单位完成的中国花岗岩—绿岩地体金矿地质特征、矿床模式及远景预测,取得开创性成果。天津地矿所和夹皮沟黄金矿业公司合作完成的吉林夹皮沟地区金矿深部成矿预测,提供较充足的黄金资源依据,经济效益显著。

在区域地质调查和环境地质研究方面,查明的地质资源信息,为当地政府制定长远经济发展与社会发展规划和规避地质风险提供科学根据,尤其是为天津的发展做出宝贵贡献。关于燕山长城系(1800-1400 Ma)的多细胞生物群的研究成果发表在*Science*和《科学通报》上。

一、基础地质研究

1991年,天津地矿所高凡撰写的专著《燕山早前寒武纪岩石退变质作用的研究》出版。该项工作利用现代微区分析技术,采用多学科综合研究方法,以创立退变质作用的独立分支为特色,对冀东迁西群、北京密云群、张家口—宣桑干群典型剖面的古老变质岩石,进行退变系列演化、退变质岩相、退变地球化学特征以及退变改造含铁建造等方面的研究,填补该学科领域空白。

1991年,天津地矿所朱士兴、地科院地质研究张鹏远、邢裕盛等合作完成华北地台中、上元古代生物地层序列的研究。项目组在总结前人研究工作的基础上,开展整个华北区晚前寒武纪生物地层学及相关含矿层位对比的研究,同时,对晚前寒武纪各门类化石、古生态及古地理等方面的问题进行全面和较高层次的总结和回顾。成果为建立全球性的晚前寒武纪生物地层层型剖面奠定基础。专著于1995年出版。

1991~1995年,天津地矿所赵风清、孙大中承担华南北区深部地壳结构及演化研究,厘定华南地区变质基底(以群为单位)大套地层的层群为成层有序的沉积盖层,并非中生代的“构造混杂岩”。使用锆石测年技术,厘定华南重要的火成事件、变质事件年龄。将华南划分扬子地块两大构造单元,提出夹持于两地块之间的赣湘粤桂海盆属于陆性质,同时指出华南元古宙不存在古岛弧和古洋壳,基本上为陆内、陆地环境。建立宁德—湖口、衡阳—凤凰两条断面有时间维的地壳结构。该项目所建立的有时间维标志的地壳结构模式等研究成果总体上达到国内同类研究的领先水平。

1992~1996年，天津地矿所白瑾完成华北地台早元古代地壳破裂、焊接和增生的研究。确定华北原始构造方位是近南北向的，其基底与西伯利亚地台可能连为一体，推北缘早元古代岛弧和裂陷槽，可能分别同原地台内部青滦活动带、晋冀再造华北原地台早元古代的沉积-构造格架。强调中条群构造环境和地球化学特征动大陆边缘性质，推测它们应属于华北原地台南缘活动带近大陆一侧，提出华北和塔里木原地台存在碰撞焊接的过程。首次提出早元古代不同阶段积盆地和造山带交替出现的规律和周期性，即大致300百万年为一周期，提出造山带叠加变形变位的新思想。从早元古代华北原地台变形、应力场变化、造山带叠加变形变位等资料出发，将它们归因于地变化，将地壳演化与行星运动相联系，是一新的见解。

1992~1995年，天津地矿所陆松年承担前寒武纪大陆地壳演化示踪课题，全面系统地探索国内前寒武纪陆块活动带及地壳慢分离和地壳活化再造的标志、形成峰期和特点；探讨塔里木、华北、扬子陆块和南华、秦岭、兴安活动带的大地构造特征和相互关系。指出当代各种测年方法确定大陆地壳演化时间维的局限性和应用上的多解性，同时有针对性地提出应着重解决的研究课题。重点探索钕同位素地质信息，同时也研究铅同位素的示踪结果。通过晋冀蒙、冀东和鲁东岩块的大量同位素年代学、地球化学和P-T-t轨迹研究的实际资料，提出华北前寒武纪大陆地壳生长经历四个重要发展阶段。根据地壳物质来源和形成方式，将地壳分为初始地壳、活化再造地壳、沉积再造地壳和沉积自生地壳等4个端元类型。着重探讨初始地壳和活化再造地壳的TDM等时线年龄和U-Pb年代之间的关系。在分析中国各地质单元造壳峰期的基础上，同时指出中国大陆前寒武时期地壳活化再造的重要性，突出中国大陆地壳演化过程中多旋回发展的同位素示踪特点。成果著作于1996年出版。

1993年，天津地矿所孙大中等完成中条山前寒武纪年代构造格架和年代地壳结构研究。项目使用6种测年方法，厘定中条山区前寒武纪地层系统并取得华北克拉通盖层最可靠的最老年龄1840百万年；发现深部有2800~2700百万年和2600~2450百万年的长英质岩石以及近于3000百万年和2700百万年的基性岩石。提出该区早、中元古代的四层结构的年代地壳结构模式；首次在该区探索区域变质的P-T-t轨迹，指出早元古代的区域变质作用主要表现在中条运动Ⅰ、Ⅱ幕；运用底板垫托或岩浆柱运移理论推演提出一个新的地壳深化和成矿作用演化的图式，指出新的找矿条件和线索。首次建立中条山前寒武纪年代构造格架，提出中条山年代地壳结构的模式，在国内开创以火山岩年代地球化学为岩石圈探针研究深部地壳结构的先例。成果专著于1993年出版。

1993年，地矿部水文地质工程地质研究所、天津地矿所、地矿部地质研究所、中国地质大学（武汉）、甘肃省地矿局、地矿部地质遥感中心、四川省地矿局和安徽省地矿局等12个科研、勘查、教学等单位共同协作完成中华人民共和国及其毗邻海区第四纪地质图（1:250万）及说明书获国家自然科学二等奖，天津地质矿产研究所为主要参加者。该图范围覆盖中国全部领域，并包括毗邻海区，主要成果包括：中国海陆第四纪堆积物的成因类型、岩性、时代、新构造运动形迹、物理地质现象、第四纪火山活动、前第四纪基岩以及某些堆积物的成因地貌形态，并附有重要第四纪地质点、古人类化石等研究资料；首次对海区第四纪沉积物进行统一的岩性命名，建立海区的成因类型系列；建立《中国第四纪地层对层表》；综合反映第四纪地质基本规律和特点，反映第四纪时期的主要地质事件，如多期的新构造运动、火山活动、冰川活动、海面变化、不同气候条件下形成的堆积物以及古人类活动遗迹等，对于第四纪时期形成的多种堆积物，从其成因上进行分类，并建立中国第四纪沉积物成因类型表，特别是对其中的“残坡积类型”，按其形成的气候条件的不同作更细地划分，以反映气候因素对第四纪沉积物的影响。该图有别于国外同类同期图件的特点为：对从海到陆、中国全域的地层对比和成因类型建立系统的分类，特别是首次对一千万平方千米毗邻海区的第四纪成因、地貌和底质作统一分类和岩性命名，基岩区表示岩石类型和高程分区，沙漠区反映沙丘的活动性质。

1993~1995年，天津地矿所白瑾开展中国前寒武纪陆壳的拼接和生长研究，首次提出“涡旋构造”假说，作为太古宙大陆形成的动力学机制，并探讨它与地幔柱构造的联系及不同于板块构造的运动学、动力学特征，是理论上的一个重要创新。提出华北原地台可能是在1600百万年以后裂解的，古代华北原地台南缘活动带的北界应向北推移约180千米，论证元古宙时期中国几个主要陆块破裂、增生、碰撞、拼接的历史。论述各陆块之间主要造山带的发育过程及特征，并提出在中新元古代，华北、扬子和塔里木三个原地台上发育一系裂陷槽、拗拉槽、裂谷和地斜构造，并以华北原地台为例，进行解剖。在理论及方法上，首次提出造山带变形变位的新思路，用以探讨前寒武纪陆壳的形成和演化规律，为正确恢复、确定地壳变形及横向结构边界开辟新途径。该研究成果总体达到国际先进水平，其中有关太古宙原始大陆形成的动力学机制（涡旋构造假说）研究达到国际同类研究的领先水平。

1996~2000年，天津地矿所陆松年完成中国北方元古宙地质演化及与成矿作用耦合性研究，探讨元古时期沉积—构造信息，并重溯古大地构造桁架；研究大陆地壳演化过程，特别是元古宙地质演化与矿集区之间的成因联系；研究元古宙大型、超大型矿床形成的地质条件与元古宙特殊地质事件的耦合关系。在阿尔金山阿克塔什培格原划为“米兰群”的花岗片麻岩中测得3605±43百万年颗粒锆石的U-Pb年龄数据；首次在甘肃北山柳园茵的古堡泉发现榴辉岩，对该地的榴辉岩及围岩—眼球状花岗片麻岩进行深入的研究，获得精确的新元古代早期的年代学信息；以柴达木盆地北缘的研究资料为依据，初步建立新元古代早期汇聚和新元古代晚期裂解事件群的特点和时间序列；初步建立研究区内前寒武纪地层和地质事件的年代格架，显示出新元古代地质事件在该区地质演化和构造分区中的重大意义，其成果明显提高青藏高原北部前寒武纪地质的研究水平，同时也促进国内相同领域内的研究工作；探讨阿尔金两侧前寒武纪变质基底的可比性问题，提出新元古代构造分区可能的工作模式，讨论这种可能的分区模式对找矿战略布局的影响。成果专著《青藏高原北部前寒武纪地质初探》于2002年出版。

2000年，天津地矿所朱士兴等完成微生物岩形成环境的研究，通过对蓟县层型剖面、迁西陡岭子剖面、宽城崖门子剖面，以及兴隆有关剖面的微生物岩与沉积环境关系问题的研究，结果表明其各种代表性的微生物岩类型及其组合不仅在全区具有明显的地层对比意义，而且还是研究碳酸盐地层沉积相的良好指相标志。在碳酸岩盐地层中，不同形态类型的叠层石在地层剖面（纵向）上的规律变化称为叠层石旋回，它们是沉积环境随时间旋回性变化在叠层石形态上的反映。叠层石旋回与地层层序或旋回相耦合，因此不同级别的叠层石旋回及其主要组成可分别成为在碳酸盐岩地层中划分不同级别的地层层序或旋回，以及它的不同体系域的可靠标志，甚至是最主要的标志。微生物岩碳氧稳定同位素确定叠层石生成时的古海水温度和盐度，借以恢复古地理沉积环境，是该项目另一个主要成果和创新点。用叠层石的生长节律来探讨古天体动力学是叠层石研究中的一大创新。初步揭示中元古代每月约有42天以上，亦即地球自转的速率每月要比现代快12天以上；每年有546天以上，即绕太阳一次公转，地球自转546圈以上。

2000~2002年，天津地矿所李惠民等开展大别—苏鲁超高压变质带变质矿物的铀-铅同位素年代学研究，主要是对中国大别—苏鲁地替超高压变质岩石中的金红石、石榴子石、独居石、榍石等变质成因矿物进行系统的铀-铅同位素地质年代学研究。

2000~2003年，天津地矿所陆松年完成秦岭中—新元古代造山带与Rodinia大陆再造研究，探讨中国主要陆块在全球Rodinia超大陆复原中的配置关系，得出具有中国特色的Rodinia超大陆研究成果。项目确认并厘定秦岭造山带中—新元古代热—构造事件的性质、序列和年代格架；依据区域地质及最新的测年资料，强调研究区南华纪大裂解的标志及其重要意义；通过对二郎坪群火山岩、富水杂岩、秦岭岩群中淡色脉体及花岗岩的深入研究，获得有关古生代早期热-构造事件性质、特征和精确的时代证据，为秦岭造山带加里东期造山作用的存在提供更丰富的地质事实和数据；修正前人认为龙王幢碱性花岗岩形成于新元古代的认识。进一步提供华北在1.8~1.6镓存在裂解的证据，为厘定华北演化过程中特征的地质事件群以及华北与其他陆块的对比增加新的科学证据；对秦岭造山带的时、空结构划分进行新的尝试。对中-新元古时期的中国大地构造格架及其在Rodinia超大陆构造中的位置的认识取得重要进展，提出新元古代时期扬子与塔里木陆块连接或相邻，认为华北陆块没有与Rodinia汇聚和裂解有关的强烈的热-构造活动，因此也不存在晋宁期华北陆块与扬子陆块的拼合。

2001年，天津地矿所朱士兴、孙淑芬等完成燕山长城系（1800~1400百万年）的多细胞生物群的研究，进一步丰富长城系碳质宏观化石的层位、种类和数量。继在蓟县17亿年团山子组发现大量叶状的宏观藻类化石以后，又在其邻区的常州沟组（18亿年）发现以*Chuaria-Shoushihnia- Tawuia*组合为特征的碳质宏观化石。进一步肯定它们为碳质压型化石的性质。进一步发现长城系多细胞藻类植物的新证据。首次在长城系发现动物化石的重要线索。初步确定含化石层位的古生态条件。研究成果分别发表在《科学》《科学通报》《古生物学报》《微体古生物学报》。

2001~2004年，以天津地矿所陆松年为项目负责人与中国地质科学院地质研究所和西北大学合作完成中国中新元古代重大地质事件及与超大陆事件的对比研究。项目针对中国大陆在新元古代Rodinia超大陆事件中的聚合与裂解的科学问题，获得许多新的地质学以及同位素年代学和古地磁学证据，提出中国古陆块在新元古代时期的演化模式。以翔实的野外地质资料和一批高精度测试数据为研究Rodinia超大陆最终汇聚时代、破裂的启动时代、古大陆重建和动力学机制提供坚实的科学基础，为全球Rodinia超大陆的研究作出重要贡献。

2003~2005年，天津地矿所陆松年为项目负责人和南京地质矿产研究所合作开展中央造山带变质基底构造分区与时序研究。确定中央造山带的基本构造格架形成于早古生代时期，在研究区范围内，存在6条重要的早古生代缝合带，对每条缝合带的物质组成、特点及时代进行系统的研究和总结，以丰富和翔实的资料证明中央造山带内早古生代造山作用的重要性，并指出该时期造山作用对中国及亚洲大陆早期增生的重要性。深入研究并系统总结早古生代缝合带所围限的前寒武纪地块或变质地体的组成及基本特征，将中央造山带内的原位地块和变质地质体划分为中阿尔金-祁连-全吉、柴达木、北秦岭等三个地块及东、西昆仑两个变质地体及卷进造山带中的扬子陆台北缘-南秦岭。将区内前寒武纪地块或变质地体划分为全吉型、柴达木型和西昆仑型，系统阐述每种类型的特点和彼此之间的差异。在对研究区内前寒武纪重大地质事件研究的基础上，对它们的全球构造意义进行探索。指出新太古代大规模地壳增生和2500 ~ 2300百万年发生的双峰式岩浆侵入事件具有超级大陆事件的性质，可能预示前哥伦比亚超大陆的存在。针对前期工作中遗留的疑难问题进一步开展深入研究，对中央造山带内前寒武纪构造地层系统进行重新厘定和清理。其中重要的进展为：前人所划古元古代秦岭岩群、金水口岩群、北大河岩群中的副变质岩沉积时代应为中元古代；西昆仑地块中的布伦阔勒群、桑珠塔格群则为新元古代晚期至早古生代，而北秦岭的宽坪群应为早古生代奥陶纪的产物。新获得一批与早古生代造山过程有关的关键地质事件的野外证据和年代及地球化学数据，进一步丰富泛华夏造山作用的证据，为探讨泛华夏造山作用的科学意义及早古生代全球构造格架起重要作用。编制完成1:250万中国中央造山带前寒武纪变质基底地质图，并建立相关数据库。

2005年，天津地矿所朱士兴等开展冀北前寒武纪微体化石研究，提出将原长城系解体为下部长城群和上部高于庄群的新建议。在总结长城系各“组合带”微古植物的基础上，对长城系微古植物的总体特征进行新的总结，并在其中初步鉴别出21属32种的真核藻类化石，从而将长城系微古植物的研究提升到同类研究的新水平。在常州沟组多细胞生物细胞学的研究方面取得新突破，从而确证早在常州沟组（约1800百万年）就有多种多细胞藻类生物的存在，不仅对地球早期多细胞生物的起源和早期演化的研究提供宝贵的新资料，也为将长城系划归中元古界的方案提供新根据。

二、矿床地质研究

1991~1993年，天津地矿所任富根等运用国际上研究的板块理论及其他技术开展熊耳山南坡金矿成矿地质条件和找矿靶区研究，分析熊耳山—崤山地区金矿的成矿地质背景，研究成矿地质条件，总结矿床成因类型、成矿系列和成矿模式；提出金矿靶区综合评价模型，并对区内金矿进行预测。专著《熊耳山-崤山地区金矿成矿地质条件和找矿综合评价模型》于1996年正式出版。

1991~1993年，天津地矿所王官福等承担熊耳山地区前寒武纪地层及典型金矿床的古地磁研究，运用国际研究板块理论及古地磁技术方法，对熊耳山地区前寒武纪地层及典型金矿床的古地磁研究。

1991~1994年，天津地矿所和山西省地质科学研究所合作开展五台山地区条带状铁建造金矿地质及成矿预测。天津地矿所骆辉为项目负责人。项目以五台山西部条带状铁建造金矿为重点，研究总结条带状建造金矿区域成矿规律，评价成矿远景。预测5个成矿远景区（带），圈定5个找矿靶区，提出地球化学勘查最佳元素金、银、铜、铋、砷组合。成果专著于2002年出版。

1991~1994年，天津地矿所李俊建等研究清原–夹皮沟绿岩带地质及金的成矿作用，首次测得区内高级区表壳岩的最古老的年龄；首次论证中国绿岩带地质特征、地球化学、同位素年代、变质作用、成矿作用及形成构造环境特点和绿岩带有关三类金矿"一老""一新"的成矿规律和成矿格局；提出金成矿的地球化学背景，变质矿物及其共生组合和变质作用温压条件，高级区的产状、分布、形成时代及与绿岩带的关系，典型金矿床的地质特征、控矿因素和成矿作用；探讨该区地壳的形成和演化；应用综合找矿方法和信息分析，对夹皮沟金矿盲矿体深部进行预测、提出七个成矿远景预测区。经钻探验证、在夹皮沟地区探获D级储量约2.5吨。该成果专著于1993年出版。

1991~1995年，天津地矿所、天津冶金地质研究院与吉林省有色金属地质勘查局合作完成中国花岗岩–绿岩地体金矿地质特征、矿床模式及远景预测，课题负责人为沈保丰（天津地矿所）、杨敏之（天津冶金地质研究院）、程玉明（吉林有色地勘局），该项目反映中国花岗岩–绿岩地体及其金成矿作用理论研究取得新的进展，总结成矿规律，建立矿床和区域成矿模式和找矿模式，为区域找矿战略部署、矿田和矿床地质找矿提供地质理论依据，并取得明显的经济效益。完成的项目报告具有一系列开创性的成果。

1991~1995年，由天津地矿所沈保丰主持完成华北地台北缘太古宙绿岩带形成、演化及对金矿的成矿控制作用和成矿预测，开展3个专题研究：吉林省穷棒子沟一带太古宙金矿床成矿条件和远景预测；冀东地区太古宙地质特征、金矿控矿条件及成矿预测；辽西太古宙地质特征、金矿成矿控制因素及成矿预测。该项目在理论上有剖析，在成矿预测方面成果显著。

1992~1996年，由天津地矿所沈保丰牵头，夹皮沟黄金矿业公司协作，合作完成吉林夹皮沟地区二道沟、庙岭及该区金矿深部成矿预测。项目组对夹皮沟地区二道沟、庙岭及该地区金矿进行综合信息深部成矿预测，建立综合信息找矿模型、圈定靶区、进行定性定量预测，以供生产验证。项目组应用国际绿岩带金矿成矿找矿的最新理论，引进先进的地、物、化、遥综合找矿新技术、新方法，在金矿成矿地质背景、成矿时代、成矿作用和定性、定量成矿预测等方面均取得重大突破，预测金储量17.2吨，为促进夹皮沟黄金工业的发展，提供较充足的黄金资源依据。成果《吉林夹皮沟金矿地质与成矿预测》于1998年出版。

1993~1995年，天津地矿所陆松年等完成小秦岭、冀北和胶北金矿城基底特征及成矿作用主要特征对比，分析上述地区形成金矿密集区的深层次内因研究，发现前寒武纪变质基底与金矿化存在密切的成生联系，小秦岭等三个地区的前寒武纪变质基底存在双层结构特点，下层变质结晶基底与金矿有密切成生联系，但发育下层基底的地区未必都能够形成金矿密集区；对金矿成矿时代进行深入研究，在剖析当代测年方法适用性和局限性基础上，强调对锆石进行成因矿物学研究和对等时线年龄进行合理性判别的重要性；揭示小秦岭等三个地区地质历史演化过程中造壳和地壳活化再造的时间及特点，从地史演化的角度阐述热—构造事件与成矿作用的耦合关系；从区域研究角度，提出发现区域地质异常的五条准则。其成果专著《金矿密集区的基底特征与成矿作用研究——以小秦岭、冀北和胶北金矿密集区为例》于1997年出版。

1994年11月~1998年6月，天津地矿所沈保丰和陆松年主持开展矿床密集区预测的理论和方法研究。专题以地壳形成演化与成矿作用最佳耦合为主线，选择胶东、小秦岭、夹皮沟、张宣等金矿床密集区为研究重点，并对前景不明的鲁西、太行山北段和冀北地区进行成矿预测与示范。提出区域地质构造、地质年代、区域地球化学、岩浆活动、矿田构造等五项成矿预测准则。

1995年，天津地矿所沈保丰等开展华北陆台太古宙花岗岩—绿岩带地质特征成矿条件及找矿预测研究，运用国外金矿床成矿理论及技术，系统总结华北陆台太古宙绿岩带的空间分布、地层、变质岩、构造变型、花岗质岩石、同位素年代和有关的金矿、铁矿、块状硫化物矿床的类型、地球化学、成矿作用等。论证华北陆台太古宙绿岩带地质及找矿。

1996年10月~2000年12月，天津地矿所李俊建等完成内蒙古阿拉善地区矿产资源潜力评价综合研究，以野外地质调查为基础，从该区实际出发，重点开展工作区已知矿点和重要物化探异常区的野外地质调查；开展区域地球化学背景、层控型朱拉扎嘎式金矿、火山岩型铜金矿和与花岗岩有关的金矿床等的研究工作，进一步厘定各类矿床的成矿地质条件和控矿因素，明确找矿标志，归纳区域成矿规律，筛选物化遥异常，并在此基础上圈定找矿有利的预测区，编制出阿拉善地区1∶50万区域成矿预测图。

2000~2003年，天津地矿所与中国地质科学院矿产资源研究所合作开展前寒武纪成矿作用研究，负责人为天津地矿所沈保丰。项目研究中国前寒武纪成矿地质构造背景，总结中国前寒武纪成矿作用的特色和前寒武纪大规模成矿作用、成矿系列和地壳演化的时空结构关系，开展以辽吉成矿带等为重点的地质调查和综合研究，编制出1∶500万前寒武纪矿床成矿系列图。成果专著于2006年1月出版，部分成果发表在《矿床地质》《地质调查与研究》等杂志上。

2000~2003年，由天津地矿所负责，新疆地调院、青海地调院、青海有色地勘局协作，共同完成新疆阿尔金成矿带成矿规律和找矿方向综合研究，天津地矿所毛德宝为项目负责人。该项目建立阿尔金成矿带地质矿产图数据库、重力数据库、化探数据库、航磁数据库、矿产地数据库和遥感数据库。系统研究地层、岩浆、构造及变质作用及其对成矿的控制作用；阐明矿床在区域地球物理场中的分布位置，划分成矿系列，分出5个成矿亚带，8个成矿系列和13个亚系列。新发现Au、Cu、Fe、Pb、Zn等矿化点10处。划分11个找矿远景区，25个找矿预测区。

2001~ 2003年，天津地矿所李俊建等开展华北地台成矿规律和找矿方向综合研究，系统总结区内地层、构造、岩浆岩、同位素年代和物化遥特征，建立区域地质构造格架；编制完成成矿规律和成矿预测系列图件百余张，建立区域地理、地质、矿产地、化探和重力等基础数据库；总结区域成矿条件成矿时代成矿规律，划分各级成矿区带，建立区域成矿找矿模式；总结豫西南小秦岭太行山北段辽吉东部中条山胶东鲁西夹皮沟和阿拉善及华北陆块铁矿区的成矿规律，明确主攻矿种、矿床类型，圈定找矿靶区119处，提出工作部署建议37项；系统论述小岩体成矿和岩浆岩成矿专属性，讨论铁铜铅锌钼金银等的成矿时代，首次获得迭布斯格岩群形成年龄，在豫西南新发现新元古界热水沉积、热水交代型铅锌矿，采用最新测年法获得朱拉扎嘎金矿等20余处矿床形成年龄，获得华北陆块北缘存在印支期贵金属矿床的新认识等。

2003~2005年，天津地矿所李俊建等承担内蒙古二连—东乌旗成矿带铜矿找矿方向研究，以板块构造、边缘成矿和成矿系统理论为指导，以野外地质调查为基础，建立该区矿产地、化探、遥感等基础空间数据库。在该区划分3个地球化学异常带，提出23处重点工作的化探异常区。与南蒙古斑岩型铜金成矿区进行对比研究，进一步厘定各类矿床的成矿地质条件、控矿因素和找矿标志，总结控矿因素、成矿规律和找矿模式，明确区内主攻矿种、主攻矿床类型，筛选地物化遥异常，圈定有利的找矿远景区，圈定找矿远景区7个，提出该区下一步工作部署立项建议，提出二连—东乌旗成矿带在阿巴嘎断裂以西钨、钼多金属矿床成矿时代主要为华力西期，以东铜多金属矿床成矿时代主要为燕山期的新认识。新发现海墨塞格呼和敖包、塔尔巴格特等3处矿点。

三、区域地质调查

1991年，天津地矿所李凤林、王强、蒋明媚等完成渤海沿岸现代海蚀研究，经过三年野外调查和对所收集的国内外大量有关资料的分析整理，基本查清环渤海地区现代海蚀形成机制、危害程度，并针对要害提出切实可行的防治对策与建议。研究表明引起海蚀原因不下10余种，但起主导作用的不过2～3种，其中各河入海水沙量明显减少具有决定性的作用；水动因素对海岸有侵蚀，只是局部反映，不能把大面积长时期的海岸侵蚀归咎于水动因素；地动因素无广泛的动能效应，全岸性海蚀也不是由地动所形成的；渤海沿岸现代海蚀的主要原因是修库、建闸使河流入海水沙量大量减少，引起渤海水沙运动失衡。沿岸居民盲目在海岸、海底、河床及其两岸等地挖沙掘砾开采贝壳（堤）等活动引起浅滩下滑，也是加剧渤海沿岸现代海蚀发生的原因。成果专著于1996年出版。

1994年，天津地矿所完成天津市岩石地层的调查研究工作，应用现代地层学和沉积学的新理论、新方法，对天津市以往所建立的中元古代~第三纪岩石地层单位进行研究(清理),追溯地层单位创立的沿革,重新厘定单位含义、层型类型与特征、区域延伸与对比,消除同物异名,查清同名异物,在大范围内建立若干断代岩石地层单位的时空格架,编制符合现代地层学含义的新一代区域地层序列表,创建地层数据库。

1995年,以天津地矿所为第一完成单位承担的京津塘地区国土整治中的环境地质条件综合评价项目通过评审,项目第一负责人为天津地矿所陈明、王强。该项目在基础地质研究中,突出地球四大圈的相互作用,发现甚至在现代环境变化动态中也存在海-气、海-陆、侵蚀-堆积这样的相互作用问题,为地质科学介入环境监测的必要性提供科学依据;首次在华北平原提出井下上新统以厚层浅棕红色沉稳物为岩石地层学特征,并提出水平化学分带问题,建议在灰绿色厚层沉寂中补做古地磁,再用时限卡住N/Q界限,这是指导以后地层划分、利于相邻学科利用地层划分开展工作的基础;首次提出滦河三角洲晚第四纪海侵受制于河流沉积物供给量及山区抬升、掀斜作用,进而从地质背景上提出渤海西岸需警惕海面上升危险;对现代相对海面上升的危险提出泥质海岸沉积物的物质平衡问题及补充海岸沉积物源问题,为防止海面上升的减灾提出新理论和技术措施;首次提出未来50~100年研究区地震区划。

1996年1月~1999年12月,天津地矿所王惠初等承担内蒙古固阳下湿壕地区1:5万下湿壕幅、石兰哈达幅区域地质调查。通过对测区内早前寒武纪变质岩的重新划分,在测区内建立兴和岩群,确认其为测区内主要的含铁建造(BIF);并在地质图上较详细标出含铁建造的分布和变形特征,促进区内的铁矿找矿工作;通过对下湿壕大型近东西向构造带的研究,认为它是两个不同大地构造单元的分界线。该认识为此后国内外学者研究成果所证实,有重要的科学意义;通过对测区的铁矿和金矿(矿化)点总结和分析,指出测区金矿(矿化)点明显受测区南部的两条构造带的控制,即下湿壕大型东西向韧性剪切构造带和石报兔-大英兔断裂构造带的控制。

1999年,天津市勘察院完成天津市深层地基土工程地质特性及桩基工程地质图系编制研究。该项工作以已有的工程地质勘察资料为依据,以地质分析和数理统计的方法,分析研究天津市区(外环线以内)全新统底界~埋深80米段深层地基土——即第四系更新统地层的土质特征、分布和变化规律及其桩基工程特征。在此基础上,进行地基土层划分;按地基土层单位编制砂性土分布图;分析研究并提供最佳桩端持力层;研究并提供与最佳桩端持力层相应的单桩极限承载力及其分布图。成果为指导天津市城市规划及工程选址以及高层或超高层建筑物、高耸构筑物桩基础初步设计提供依据。

1996~2000年,天津地矿所王惠初等承担大青山地区石兰哈达幅、下湿壕幅区域地质调查。对幅内变质岩、岩浆岩、地层和构造进行系统的调查,查明各地质体的分布与物质组成,探讨变质岩系的原岩建造、变质变形特点和形成构造背景,研究不同时期岩浆岩的形成和演化,对中生代沉积岩的研究也取得新进展。在测区内对前寒武纪变质建造进行重新划分,解体朱拉沟杂岩,建立兴和岩群和色尔腾山岩群,并确认兴和岩群是测区的主要含铁建造。确认测区下湿壕大型近东西向韧性剪切带是两个大地构造单元的分界线,并对金矿的形成有控制作用。重新厘定和建立测区中生代四个组级单位的岩石组合和地层层序。对测区内显生宙的花岗质侵入体按岩石谱系单位原则进行重新划分。

1998~2001年,天津地矿所王宏等完成淮淀乡幅1:5万区域地质调查。该项目以渤海湾晚全新世末期以来的海陆交互作用为主要研究对象,首次在国内引入、确立浅表地层的Eijkelkamp全取心钻探与地质点高程水准测量的调查方法,结合GPS定位和多学科研究(^{14}C和OSL测年、高精度古地磁测量、有孔虫和介形虫鉴定等),对全新世进行高精度时空研究:时间上达到千年分辨率、空间上绘制中全新世6米以浅地层的6张古地理图,进而开展假三维古环境重建。在提交区调报告的同时,还完成两份专题报告(《淮淀乡幅浅表地层沉积特征及其沉积环境演变》和《渤海湾牡蛎礁平原牡蛎礁的形成与灭绝》)。该项目的实施是在国土资源部系统形成"泥质海岸带近现代地质环境变化"研究方向的开端。

1999年1月~2001年12月,天津地矿所王宏等完成岐口镇幅、白水头幅(1 J50E008015)1:5万地质图说明书。测区位于渤海湾西岸,实际调查面积400平方千米,完成地质点182个。通过使用槽型人工钻配合地表地质点观察,详细揭露上全新统地层分布及特征,查明区内全新世、特别是中晚全新世以来地层特征及空间结构。通过多种测试样品分析及多重地层划分，对浅表地层及沉积环境进行系统的划分。收集利用区内基岩地质、物化探、钻孔等资料，编制基岩地质图，探讨新生代地质构造演化及其对地层的控制作用。对天津市所在的渤海西岸近130年以来的海岸线和潮间带的地质环境变化进行详细研究，提出可能影响天津市安全的重大基础地学问题及对策建议。

2000~2002年，天津地矿所王惠初等完成青海绿梁山地区1:5万鱼卡沟幅、西泉幅区域地质调查，对测区原大肯大坂岩群进行解体，按照岩石自然组合与变形变质特点，结合同位素测年数据，重新厘定大肯大坂岩群，新建立含高压—超高压变质岩的鱼卡河岩群；通过对滩间山岩群时代，成岩环境及与同期超镁铁质岩等关系研究，初步确认柴北缘存在早古生代蛇绿混杂岩带，为区域构造演化和早古生代构造环境重塑增添新资料；经野外宏观调查、室内镜下观察和大量电子探针与SEM测试，对该区基底地质体的变形、变质作用，特别是鱼卡河岩群中榴辉岩的分布、矿产组合、成岩环境等进行较为深入的研究和总结；针对该区地质体变质、变形强烈，岩浆岩发育的特点，利用锆石U-Pb等方法取得大量同位素测年数据，对该地区古板块裂解汇聚、变质、变形作用、岩浆作用等构造—热事件时代的确认提供直接的年代学支持；编写绿梁山地区榴辉岩的产状、成因及其形成时代研究专题报告。高压-超高压变质榴辉岩带、滩间山蛇绿混杂岩带和早古生代侵入岩的确认，为柴北缘早古生代大地构造格架（早古生代碰撞造山带）的研究奠定基础，鱼卡沟幅地质图为多个研究项目所利用。

2000~2002年，天津地矿所王宏等承担白水头-歧口镇幅（西半幅）1:5万区域地质调查。对BQ1孔岩心的沉积学、岩石矿物学（石膏晶粒、黄铁矿晶簇等）、软体动物、有孔虫、介形虫、AMS 14和OSL测年和古地磁研究，将全新统划分为17层，存在9次海水影响的强弱变化、其中中全新世的海水影响减弱最为明显；将中上全新统划分为两个沉积单元、11个亚单元，绘制各个单元地层的三维埋深图，并在渤海湾西岸湾顶处尝试对近4000cal BP以来的11个亚单元进行假三维表达；潮间带-泻湖-盐沼泥质沉积物与作为古岸线的贝壳堤的关系蕴含的沿海平原形成机制信息；发现障壁岛-泻湖沉积体系的初步证据。

2001~2003年，天津地矿所与辽宁、河北、天津、山东四省（市）地调院共同完成环渤海地区地下水资源与环境地质调查评价。基本查明辽东湾、渤海湾、莱州湾泥质海岸带全新世以来三个不同尺度地质环境演化规律和近30年以来环渤海地区海岸侵蚀与淤积速率，为环渤海海岸带开发利用、灾害防治等规划提供警示性资料；建立环渤海平原区第四纪地层岩相分析方法。厘定第四系及上第三系的几个重要地层单位，理顺环渤海地区第四纪地层层序，建立环渤海地区第四纪地层结构研究的统一平台；采用多因子模糊数学评判法对环渤海地区区域地壳稳定性进行分区评价；查明环渤海地区地下水资源潜力，提出地下水资源优化开发调整方案建议，为环渤海地区地下水资源合理开发利用提供依据；查明区内主要环境地质问题及其变化特征，提出地质环境可持续利用的综合性对策建议和重点环境地质问题的防治对策建议，为区域国土规划、城市与港口建设布局提供依据；建立环渤海地区地下水资源与环境地质空间数据库，实现跨行政区、跨水文地质单元的水文地质、环境地质信息的综合管理和应用。

2001~2003年，天津地矿所辛后田、韩英善、郝国杰等完成青海省1:25万都兰县福区域地质调查。查明柴北缘主体构造格架——沙柳河新元古代花岗片麻岩焊接柴达木盆地南、北缘前寒武纪基底，柴达木地块通过加里东期碰撞造山带与欧龙布鲁克微陆块碰撞。首次识别出两期古元古代变质深成体和吕梁期（1939±21百万年）地质事件的存在；明确沙柳河花岗片麻岩的性质、时代及其Rodinia超大陆汇聚的响应。查明榴辉岩的赋存状态及其超高压成因、485百万年UHP变质年龄和450百万年折返年龄。明确加里东期蛇绿岩套及450Ma俯冲花岗岩、D1板内伸展事件的存在，重塑柴北缘加里东期的造山过程；之后进入克拉通盆地演化阶段。首次在东昆仑识别出250~235百万年和230~225百万年两期花岗岩，明确前者的浆混成因，以及与巴颜喀拉洋向北俯冲有关的性质。

2002~2003年，天津地矿所李俊建等完成环渤海地区海洋及陆地矿产资源图集整编。全面收集1949年以来环渤海地区海洋及陆地矿产资源勘查及科研成果资料，进行系统整理和综合研究，形成一套系统完整的资料。编制环渤海地区1:250万贵金属、有色金属、非金属、固体燃料、油气田矿产资源数字化矿产图和修编地质图，并分省(市、自治区1:600万)编制1:200万贵金属、有色金属、非金属、固体燃料、油气田矿产图集，为每张图件分别编制简要说明。总结黑色金属、贵金属、有色金属、非金属、固体燃料和油气矿产资源的成矿地质特征、控矿地质条件及时空分布规律，根据编图要求提出主要矿床的类型划分，厘定区内一些重要矿床的成矿时代，确定不同矿种的分布规律，提出油气藏的划分方案。整理并填制超大型、大型、中型和小型矿床系列卡片4278张，涵盖环渤海地区所有矿种小型以上(包括小型)矿床。同时，还获得一批高精度的同位素地质年代学数据，极大地丰富该地区矿产资源研究资料和成矿学理论的研究内容。该项目首次系统地编制环渤海地区矿产资源图集，充分和准确地反映该地区矿产资源现状，对该地区矿产资源的勘查、评价、科学研究和政府决策有重要参考价值。

2003~2005年，天津地矿所王强、袁桂邦等完成天津1:5万官庄乡、黄骅市、南排河镇泥镇幅海岸带生态环境填图，调查面积1140.9平方公里。针对全新世、特别是中晚全新世地质环境变化的时、空特征及原因，进行沉积地层、沉积相、微体生物与古环境、孢粉与古生态、年代地层和地球化学等多学科综合研究，查明全新世以来地层结构，相当深海氧同位素3阶段约三万余年来古河道、古湖泊的分布和海岸线、潮间带的位置和变化、古地貌和现代地貌的类型及其成因，总结地质环境演变对生态环境、沉积物、古代与现代地貌、现代土壤类型及工程地质条件的影响；对区内工程地质、水资源与地表水污染、地质灾害等环境地质问题进行初步评述，提出对策建议，为相关行业提供可利用的基础地质资料。

四、环境地质研究

1991~1993年，天津地矿所王强等完成天津市第四系沉积结构与地下水赋存条件分析，项目组收集整理200余个深孔钻探、投入古地磁样品测试620块、微生物分析500块、碳14测年样品61块、重新整理400余个粒度分析结果。采用多学科研究方法，对天津市第四系地质进行全面研究。把第四系沉积结构与地下水赋存条件结合起来分析；把土壤学概念引入第四系地质研究；把重矿物分析应用于恢复水动力条件；首次在沿海第四纪地质研究中，大量使用物探测井资料；这些新思路和新方法对促进第四纪地质研究具有重要意义。

1992年，天津地矿所卢伟等完成个旧地区致癌氡的环境地质迁移模式及防治研究。课题组将放射化学、核物理先进方法与地质、医学研究相结合，在中国地质界首次应用SSNTD方法研究室内氡，成功地探讨氡的地质来源问题；系统研究个旧地区环境中氡含量分布、迁移机制和肺癌患病的关系；经过对个旧地区氡的来源途径与断裂构造系统、喀斯特等因素的关系和氡在断裂带上居民室内含量季节变化、楼层高低变化以及矿山通风实验、氡的监测等工作，对氡的迁移机制有新的认识，研究表明，该区氡的迁移、运行主要是高原风力压差抽吸作用的结果，由此提出氡的防治途径和措施。

1996年2月~2000年12月，天津地矿所承担泥质海岸带现代地质作用(沉积、剥蚀及岸线变迁)与精细测年的研究，大幅度提高渤海湾西岸(近现代)泥质岸带地质作用的认识程度，为研究沿海同类地区地质环境变迁提供一个范例。对泥质海岸带的晚全新世-现代沉积的地质作用、地质环境等进行系统研究和精细测年，并据沉积速率初步估算划分不同亚区，为预测今后的海岸带地质环境变化提供科学依据。通过对不同年代地形图、航片、卫片的对比研究和实地验证，查明研究区近百年来的海岸带地质变化，揭示近百年来海岸带地表形态及微地貌的变化和数千年来地质环境的变化，建立该地区海岸带演化模式。获得近百年来的沉积速率，依沉积速率将海岸带划分为有阻挡的堤后盐沼——沿海低地型、堤后盐沼型、开放潮坪型、三角洲前缘型、浅海型五个亚区。气温升高致海面上升，长期、缓慢的地面下沉，是沿海地区面临的两大地质环境问题，基于对上述问题的综合研究，预测到2050年时，不同亚区地质环境演化的20种可能趋势及安全程度。提出防治水患和增加新生国土资源的对策与措施，对该类地区社会发展和经济建设具有参考意义。

2004~2005年，天津地矿所马震等承担华北地区不同类型矿产开发环境地质研究，查明华北地区矿产开发现状，分析矿山环境地质问题及其危害性，研究不同类型矿产开发对地质环境的影响，综合分析不同类型矿产开发环境地质问题特征，进行矿山地质环境质量评估，划分出环境保护治理分区，提出保护和恢复治理对策，建立华北矿山地质环境信息系统，编制250万华北地区矿山分布图、华北地区矿山地质灾害分布图、华北地区矿山地质环境综合评估分区图、华北地区环境保护与恢复治理分区图，为矿山地质环境保护及恢复治理规划提供基础资料。

2004~2005年，天津地矿所裴艳东完成天津沿海地区近现代重大地质环境演变的研究，经过对几期地形图和卫星遥感影像进行对比研究，总结天津市沿海地区自1870年至20世纪末期的地表环境变迁。根据天津市沿海平原地区的人工浅钻所揭示的近4000年来古潮滩的物质组成，将浅表地层中的沉积环境进行详细划分和深入研究；依据年轻沉积物测年结果，按照沉积速率特征，将该地区初步划分为不同的沉积亚区；以2030年为时限，对渤海湾西岸地区地表形态未来发展趋势做出预测。

第三节　海洋科学

1991~2005年，天津地质工作者在海洋科学领域开展多个角度的调查研究工作，取得多项可贵成果，对社会发展和经济建设，特别是环境保护具有重要意义。针对百年尺度气温上升与海面上升的耦合与非耦合关系的研究，以及环渤海海岸带近代沉积环境所展开的研究对底层下的秘密获得新认识。

1992~1997年，天津大学、天津市环境保护局海洋环境保护办公室和天津市环境监测中心陶建华、王德龙、辛志伟和张亦泳等合作完成天津海域污水海洋处置和环境管理信息系统研究。首次对渤海湾应用多种科学手段和方法，进行8个潮周期的观测和监测，取得大量有价值且较完整的资料、数据，完成天津近海岸海域主要污染物总量和浓度分布，并通过对9种污水排海方案和莱州湾7种污水排海方案的分析，提出污水海洋处置可行性优选方案。用"窄缝法"处理天津近海缓坡潮间带上水边线不断变化的动边界问题是水质模型的一项关键技术，这一方法由陶建华于1982年在丹麦首次提出并应用在海湾污染物输移扩散的数学模型中，属国际首创，并首次在实验室得出天津近海有机物COD降解动力学公式。水质模型的信息化系统被用于政府决策和日常海洋管理。

1997~1999年，天津地矿所王宏等承担百年尺度气温上升与海面上升的耦合与非耦合关系的研究，建立渤海湾西岸老狼坨子潮间带表层现代活体有孔虫种群分带、订正年轻贝壳堤形成时代、提出障壁岛–潟湖体系参与渤海湾西岸贝壳堤平原形成的假说等；发现在1550 cal BP（AD400）时，渤海湾西岸海平面较今约低70厘米；自那时以来，该地区经历中盐沼→高盐沼→中、高盐沼→沼泽低地→中、高盐沼→滨海平原的环境转换过程，并有数次海洋影响增强的时段，波动幅度均不超过现今海平面高度；1550 cal BP时气温与现代近似，自那时以来的3次波动，幅度均在1°C左右；气温升高与海面上升在地层中不具同相位的耦合关系，海面上升层段滞后于气温上升层段；受风暴潮或持续向岸风控制的海水影响增强期，可能是此种非耦合关系的原因。

1998年，天津古海岸与湿地国家级自然保护区管理处组织南开大学、天津师范大学、地矿部天津地矿所等单位，开展天津古海岸与湿地国家级自然保护区湿地生态系统综合评价指标体系的研究，南开大学朱坦担任课题负责人。课题组以PSR模型作为评价基础框架，运用生态学理论、生态监测技术、层次分析法等构建天津七里海湿地生态系统健康评价体系，通过实践验证，该评价体系客观地反映出七里海湿地生态系统健康水平，为保护区管理部门科学决策七里海湿地的可持续发展提供技术支持。

1999年6月，天津大学李清雪、陶建华完成天津近岸海域浮游植物生态性的研究，项目组开展天津近岸海域的浮游植物种类组成、生态类群及分布状况研究，结果表明：各季节硅藻门占绝对优势，种类组成以广温广盐近岸种为主；浮游植物的平均细胞丰度以8月份最高，5月份次之，再次之为10月份；浮游植物的种类组成和丰度具有明显的季节性和空间分布特征，其变化与温度、氮营养盐含量密切相关。

2001~2003年，天津地质矿产研究所王宏、李建芬等承担环渤海海岸带近代沉积环境的研究，通过岩石地层学、年代学、微体古生物学、地球化学多学科的综合研究和遥感解译等方法，对渤海湾、辽东湾和莱州湾泥质海岸带近现地质环境变化进行详细调查和研究，完善在泥质海岸带开展近现代地质环境变化调查研究并与先进水平国际接轨的一套工作方法。建立3个湾区不同尺度（万年、千年和百年）的沉积环境演化模式，细化全新世地层结构；利用^{210}Pb和^{137}Cs示踪与测年技术，详细研究泥质海岸带的现代沉积速率，将3个湾区划分为6个不同沉积速率区；基本查明近30年来研究区地表环境在人类活动影响下的变化程度、海岸带湿地现状及其面积变化数量；对研究区今后30年地质环境变化趋势进行警示性预测，为海岸带灾害防治、规划等提供警示资料。

2005年12月，天津大学陶建华、李清雪、姜国强等完成天津近岸海域生态环境特性研究，项目组采用现场监测、实验室试验、环境评价和数值模拟等方法，确定主要评价因子，对渤海湾天津近岸海域生态环境的水质污染及富营养化状态进行评价；建立灰关联评价方法，首次对渤海湾近岸海域水环境进行综合评价；建立空间变异模型，在大量渤海湾水质监测数据的基础上分析渤海湾天津近岸海域的水质分布特性；研究并得到渤海湾营养盐限制特性及浮游细菌在渤海湾分布及和环境因子的关系；建立基于浮游生态系统的模拟和预测渤海湾海域营养水平的生态水动力学模型；研究排污和海岸带开发对生态环境和经济发展的影响和对策，为海洋经济可持续发展提供依据。成果对天津市海岸带综合开发管理具有很大的现实意义。

第六章 生物学

1991~2005年，天津生命科学领域的研究人员潜心于基础研究，在动物资源调查与研究、生物生理学、细胞遗传学取得多项突出成果。其中，中国织蛾科昆虫和中印区摇蚊科昆虫学等方面的研究为国内领先；陈瑞阳等主持完成的中国主要植物染色体研究居国际一流，编制出版的出版植物基因组染色体图谱填补世界空白。

1995年，天津大学张春霆当选为中国科学院生命科学与医学部院士，成为天津首位该领域的中科院院士。

第一节 动物学与植物学

1991~2005年，天津在动物学的基础研究中，南开大学关于中国半翅目昆虫卵的研究、中国织蛾科昆虫的研究和中印区摇蚊科昆虫学的研究，是具有代表性的成果。关于植物与动物的资源调查，与生产实际密切结合，服务区域经济建设。天津的实验动物繁育与利用有多年基础，1991年后适应科研工作需要，获得更大发展。

一、动物资源调查与研究

（一）动物资源调查

1995年，天津师范大学李海峰、孙易、郝泗城等完成天津两栖爬行动物调查及分布聚类研究，对天津地区两栖爬行类进行调查，记录动物5目11科16属28种，其中黄纹石龙子EumecesxanthiGuenther为天津爬行类新记录，用系统聚类法进行分析，将天津划分为滨海，平原，山地三个两栖爬行动物分布区。平原和山地分布区中的两栖爬行动物组成有明显的不同。爬行类中山地分布的种占61%。物种分析表明天津属古北界华北区。

1998年，南开大学李后魂、郑永怡发表论文中国鞘蛾研究（鳞翅目：鞘蛾科）：线鞘蛾组研究及二新种记述（英文）。报道鞘蛾科线鞘蛾组（Coleophoraamellivoragroup）分布于中国的4个种，其中包括2个新种1个中国新记录种：齿线鞘蛾（新种）Coleophoraapicidentatasp. nov. 分布新疆（乌鲁木齐）；长刺线鞘蛾（新种）Coleophoralongispinasp. nov. 分布内蒙古（锡林浩特）；弯茎线鞘蛾ColeophorapandionellaBaldizzone新记录于内蒙古（锡林浩特、赤峰）和黑龙江（黑河），国外分布俄罗斯（东西伯利亚）；云南线鞘蛾ColeophorayunnanicaBaldizzone分布于云南（丽江）。文中并提供线鞘蛾组中国已知种检索表和新种的外生殖器特征图。模式标本保存在南开大学生物系。

（二）半翅目昆虫卵研究

2001年，南开大学任树芝著《中国半翅目昆虫卵图志》出版，是该领域研究工作的结晶。任树芝带领的科研团队经过近30年在国内各地采集、观察和饲养，收集大量异翅亚目昆虫卵的标本，并做生物学记录，积累详实的材料。图志全面、系统地记述中国的35科，计236种半翅目昆虫卵，详细描述各种卵的外部形态、细微结构、生态习性等。图志中90%以上种类卵的细微结构特征构造属世界首次在扫描电镜下揭示出来，特别是发现若干新的形态特征和新的细微结构。在世界半翅目昆虫卵的研究领域中，该图志对卵的描述最为全面系统，细微结构特征清晰、制图及图片精制、记述的半翅目昆虫卵种类最多、学术性强。图志不仅为昆虫经典分类学研究提供一种新的手段，也为昆虫系统发育、害虫的防治、益虫的利用开创新的研究领域，还为半翅目昆虫卵的系统研究及教学、植保与森林工作、特别是对昆虫学的研究提供新的有价值的资料。

（三）中国织蛾科昆虫的研究

2004年，南开大学王淑霞、李后魂、尤平等完成中国织蛾科分类修订和系统发育研究，这是一项关于国家生物资源及其多样性的基础性研究。成果包括：修订隐织蛾属Cryptolechia，这是以中国中、南部为分布中心的一类重要种实害虫，使中国种类由18种上升到60种，约占古北区和东洋区已知种的66%，其中记述27个新种；发表锦织蛾属Promalactis新种15个，使中国种类达到59种，约占世界已知种的50%，初步完成该属的修订研究，为进行相关属群的系统发育研究、准确判断它们的亲缘关系和分类地位奠定基础；进行伪带织蛾属的厘定，涉及到14种（包括5个新种），使中国种类占到世界已知种的69%。同时，该研究对广义织蛾中系统学地位很重要的列蛾属Autosticha进行修订，首次报道中国33种，其中有23新种和3新纪录种，约占世界已知种的36%。共发现中国新纪录属1个及一些中国新纪录种，建立科学上的新属1个，新种78个，其中发表新种56个。对查清国家物种资源、澄清重要害虫的学名和分类地位、为害虫的综合治理提供基本依据有重要意义。发表学术论文6篇，1篇被SCI收录。发表的物种均被国际重要刊物*Zoological Record*和*BIOSIS Preview*等收录。

（四）中印区摇蚊科生物研究

2005年，南开大学王新华、纪炳纯和Chaudhuri等通过国际合作，采用比较形态学方法，对世界生物多样性最丰富地区之一的中印区开展摇蚊科昆虫生物多样性和生物地理学研究。生物地理学研究采用区系成分分析和BPA支序生物地理学及Bremer祖先分布区估算方法。共完成20余属的系统学修订工作。鉴定描述中印区摇蚊种类200余种，建立1新属和20余属的120余个新种及大批中国新记录；核定纠正一大批旧有记录种属的错误鉴定与不当安置；新增研究标本万余号；找到中印区摇蚊生物地理学分布格局和特点。进一步证实中印区，特别是中国“东洋区部分”是世界物种分化的热点地区和重要的起源中心；Banarescu世界淡水动物地理区划的合理性得到进一步求证和支持。研究结果同时对Banarescu区划中南亚区有关中国地区的区划进行修订，同时为水环境生物监测和水产养殖等领域的相关研究和生产实践提供有价值的资料。发表论文20篇，参编专著4本。

（五）实验动物

实验动物是生物科学和生命科学的物质基础。自20世纪50年代后期，天津就是全国屈指可数的几个最先跨入实验动物科学领域的城市之一。1991~2005年，天津实验动物科学不断发展进步。

图3-6-1-26 供作肿瘤细胞研究的实验鼠

进入20世纪90年代，天津中医学院第一附属医院为配合老年病的研究，从日本引进新品系，包括SAMR1、SAMP6、SAMP8、SAMP10等品种。从而丰富和提高天津的实验动物种质资源商品数量和品质。

1997年年底，中国医学科学院放射医学研究所实验动物中心开始针对肿瘤癌细胞研究的创新种质资源KM—HM无毛鼠的培育研究，进一步扩大在医学研究种质的应用领域，使其具有更大的开发价值。这一项目取得重大突破，在基因水平上进行生物遗传学研究和鉴定，加速其在医药领域中应用的进程，对肝癌、淋巴癌、白血病等癌细胞的研究具有深远的意义。

进入21世纪，中国医学科学院放射医学研究所实验动物中心和天津实验动物中心合作改造建立的600平方米屏障级实验动物饲养实验系统，年均可提供屏障级WISTER商品大鼠3万只、屏障级ICR商品小鼠3万只、屏障级BALB/C商品小鼠2万只，大大提高天津地区实验动物商品的自给率。

二、植物资源调查与研究

1989年9月~1992年9月，蓟县政府农业区办公室和南开大学合作，由唐廷贵主持，张国兴、张銮光、郑乐怡等参加，共同完成天津蓟县山区野生动植物的资源调查研究。项目调查山区自然生态环境、动植物区系、植被特点，绘制植被图。报导山区野生动植物种类共1524种，隶属96个目304个科968个属，其中包括鸟类190种，被子植物744种。提出利于发展山区经济，合理开发和保护生物资源的措施。项目为成功申报“国家八仙山自然科学保护区”提供重要生物资源数据依据。

2000年9月，中国盐业总公司制盐工程技术研究院郭连城、季奎武、高清潭等完成盐藻多糖复合物的研究，通过室内不同条件盐藻培养试验，确定藻体富含多糖复合物的培养液的盐度、pH和氮、磷的合理配比，并在300平方米培养池中进行完善、验证；确定提取液组成、固液比、提取温度、提取时间和提取次数等技术参数，确定纯化、分级条件；研究确定盐藻多糖复合物的理化特性、化学组成及其结构，盐藻多糖复合物的有效组成及其测定方法；对盐藻多糖复合物进行新药临床前的急毒、药效和药理试验，以及小鼠急性毒理试验（LD50）；进行盐藻多糖复合物的主要药效学试验，包括抗肿瘤作用和对免疫功能的影响。

2001年10月，中国盐业总公司制盐工业科学研究院和中纬集团共同完成盐藻生物资源综合开发与产业化研究，对已知植物中含天然胡罗卜素最高的盐藻进行开发，填补国内空白。

2005年，天津药物研究院张铁军、刘昌孝、岳南等，历时20余年完成中国半边莲属等八个类群药用植物资源的系统研究，内容包括中国半边莲属、石竹属、萱草属、三棱类、决明子类、刘寄奴类、冬葵子类以及三棵针等八个类群。项目对中国半边莲属山梗菜亚属进行分类修订；对萱草属和冬葵属6个植物学名进行修订；发现一个新化合物、发现5个新有效成分，首次分得13个成分；首次对中药刘寄奴、萱草根、冬葵子瞿麦、三棱、决明子等6个多基元的中药材进行系统、全面地品种整理和质量评价，具有多项原创性成果；对半边莲属、石竹属、萱草属等地分类修订广泛在分类学及相关的研究中应用；对中药刘寄奴等6个多基元的中药材进行系统的品种整理和质量评价，澄清古今用药历史沿革及品种混乱情况，确定药材正品，为《中国药典》修订提出建议稿。获3项发明专利，研制3个中药新药和5个保健食品。

三、动植物资源调查与研究

1992年，蓟县政府农业区办公室和南开大学张国兴、唐廷贵、张釜光、郑乐怡等完成蓟县山区野生动植物资源调查研究，第一次全面调查蓟县山区野生动植物资源的种类、数量、分布及经济用途；划分植被分类系统、绘制植被图、量算各植被面积；科学评价山区生物资源，确定名特优稀品种；提出合理开发和保护生物资源的措施和建议。

1999年前，天津市农林局、林业局两次共用时7年，开展天津八仙山国家级自然保护区动植物种质资源保护与开发应用的研究，进行动物种质资源的调查，分别对昆虫、鱼类、两栖类、爬行类鸟类与哺乳类动物做种类、数量、分布、演替规律、生境特征和经济价值的研究；进行植物种质资源的调查，对种类、特点、植被分布及植被类型进行研究，获知有植物种类545种，发现大量属于国家和世界级保护的物种，对植被划分五大类型。并对植被与生境的关系以及经济价值进行研究，同时进行开发应用的研究，对区域的科学管理提出建议。

第二节　生理学

1991～2005年，天津市从事生命科学研究的科研工作者在微生物学、基因学等领域的积极探索，多项工作取得成果。

一、微生物学

1998年，南开大学张金红、张秀明、陈长治等研究有机相中梨头霉菌催化11-脱氧皮质醇转化成氢化可的松的过程中，有机相中底物浓度、转化环境、菌体成熟状态以及有机相所占比例等因素对转化反应的影响。实验结果表明，收集pH3.8～4.1的发酵液，在12.5%的丙二醇转化体系中，将底物浓度由2.8‰提高到4.5‰，底物仍能被完全转化且目的产物（β—异构体）的生成与低浓度时相近。

2000年，南开大学梁凤来、刁虎欣、张心平等进行假单胞菌GD-23对石油乳化降解作用的研究。从大港油田生产井中分离到一株PseudomonasGD-23。该菌株为兼性厌氧菌，在以原油烃为碳源的矿质盐培养基中，50℃缺氧条件下，可分解原油产生表面活性剂、有机酸及气体，并可使原油粘度、蜡含量、胶质沥青含量和凝固点分别降低48%、17.7%、8.3%、和3.5C. 经气相色谱分析，Pr/C17Ph/C1s、和（C21+C22）/（C28+C29）的峰面积比值均有明显的增大，原油组分主峰由C24前移至C20。

2003年12月，南开大学高玉葆、任安芝、何兴东等共同完成内真菌转接对可相容宿主植物干旱适应性的影响的项目。项目组筛选具有干旱胁迫抗性但并不引起草食家畜中毒现象的内生真菌菌种或菌株，将它们转接到可相容的宿主植物中形成稳定的互惠共生体，建立可持续的草地生态系统。项目组从黑麦草和高羊茅的带菌植株中分离出内生真菌菌株61株，按照形态观察和分子生物学标记的方法将其划分为3个形态群；在所调查的内蒙古中东部草原的9种禾本科植物中，只发现羽茅体内含有内生真菌；从分离到的内生真菌菌株中提取生物碱麦角固醇和麦角结氨酸，建立起菌丝生物量与特定生物碱的定量关系，选择愈伤组织培养法进行人工转接。

2004年12月，天津科技大学贾士儒完成超临界相态下微生物反应过程的基础研究，结果表明：一定压力下影响微生物活性的主要原因是升降压速度和加压介质的性质，其次是厌氧环境。当选择高纯空气为加压介质，控制合适的条件，微生物活细胞率不会损失。由于一定压力的影响，微生物的代谢通量和相应的酶活性发生变化。温和压力下有的酵母菌的海藻糖合成酶活力较常压下提高1倍，相应的酵母菌海藻糖生物合成能力最高提高200%。酵母菌代谢过程分析表明，一定压力下与海藻糖生物合成相关的代谢分枝的获得加强。利用蓝色梨头霉进行氢化可的松生物转化的过程中，若采用加压生物转化，可提高氢化可的松生物转化率15%左右，酶学研究同样表明此时相应的酶活力大幅度提高。

2004年12月，天津科技大学王昌禄主持完成微生物过量转化目的产物的条件及其代谢通量分析的研究。项目以低能离子生物学、代谢工程、发酵工程等理论为基础，以D-核糖为微生物代谢产物代表，以短小芽孢杆菌为菌株，采用离子注入等诱变方法，定向、推理选育带有转酮酶缺陷等遗传标记的D-核糖高产突变株；通过注入不同剂量离子，研究离子注入对D-核糖高产菌生物学效应及突变株的遗传特性；比较发酵过程中菌体形态、D-核糖转化关键酶系的酶活力变化等因素与D-核糖产量的关系；解析该微生物过量转化D-核糖的机制、条件；构建该微生物进行D-核糖转化的代谢网络并进行代谢通量分析，为离子注入定向、推理育种和利用代谢工程等技术平台研究微生物过量转化不同目的产物的机制和条件奠定基础。

二、基因学

1999年，南开大学陈月华、关海山、曾林等对中国Btken-Agcry1Ac杀虫毒素基因核心片段的克隆及核苷酸序列进行测定。并与已发表的肯尼亚亚种HD588-2菌株、库斯塔克亚种的HD-1和HD-73菌株的cry1Ac基因序列进行比较。

1999年，南开大学李明春、岳慧琴、邢来君进行深黄被孢霉染色体数目及基因组大小的研究。利用钳位均匀电场凝胶电泳技术分离γ-亚麻酸，生产菌深黄被孢霉AS3.3410的染色体DNA，电泳核型显示出其具有15条明显的带型，分离的染色体DNA带范围大约为390～2660千碱基对，基因组大小约为21640碱基对。

2000年，南开大学和天津市卫生防病中心的牛淑敏、洪伟、刘方、朱颂华等研究大鼠CuZn-SOD cDNA的克隆及高效表达问题，采用PCR技术扩增大鼠CuZnSODcDNA，双酶切后与表达载体pBV220连接，构建出表达质粒pBV-RCS，并转化大肠杆菌DHSα。经金属离子和42℃诱导，pBVRCS得到高表达，经SDS-PAGE及薄层扫描测定表达蛋白占菌体总蛋白的49%，是目前国内外SOD高表达菌株之一。表达蛋白以包涵体形式存在于菌体内。经超声波破壁后，再经透析复性和稀释复性，表达蛋白具有特异性SOD酶活性（1298单位/毫升）。

2004年7月，天津师范大学刘丽丽完成植酸酶基因工程菌株的构建及应用技术项目，筛选出属于原核生物的植酸酶基因供体菌株，以基因克隆的方法获得植酸酶基因，以分子生物学的方法进行植酸酶基因的转化和表达。受体菌经转化植酸酶基因后，可以降解植酸及其盐类，释放无机磷酸营养，促进植物生长。为创建新型基因工程菌种的微生物肥料奠定基础。并可减轻畜禽粪便中磷的排出对江河、水域、土壤等环境的污染。

2005年，天津大学元英进、马红武、葛志强等完成细胞代谢信息与次生产物合成的基础研究。项目从细胞培养过程中细胞与代谢产物合成的信息系统的微观人手，针对细胞培养中细胞与细胞之间、细胞与周围环境之间信息物质的释放与识别、信息的跨膜传递以及与次生代谢产物合成的关系方面进行了研究，并在非线性条件下研究了基因网络和代谢网络之间的相互作用。研究内容和取得的结果受到了国内外同行的关注，并给予肯定。成果在国内外重要刊物上发表论文77篇，其中被SCI收录50篇。

第三节　细胞遗传学

1991～2005年，天津在细胞生物学和遗传学研究方面，科研工作者积极探索，取得多项成果。其中，南开大学陈瑞阳等主持完成的中国主要植物染色体研究荣获2003年度国家自然科学奖二等奖，专著《中国主要植物基因组染色体图谱》（共五册），填补世界植物染色体图谱的空白。

一、染色体研究

(一)细菌

2005年12月,由南开大学王磊、冯露、郭宏杰等人完成的细菌表面多糖抗原多样性的遗传学基础的研究结题。致病菌的快速检测是世界性的难题和研究热点。该课题以22种细菌表面多糖抗原(包括大量致病性较强,进化位置特殊的菌种)为研究对象,通过O抗原基因簇的破译、生物信息学分析等手段,对细菌表面多糖抗原的进化和形成机制进行系统的研究,发现大量O抗原多样性扩散的直接证据,进一步丰富对不同种、属之间抗原基因簇的横向转移、DNA重排和转座子引起的重组在表面抗原多样性形成和进化过程中的作用的认识。在世界上首次发现ABC转运系统在大肠杆菌中负责异多糖O抗原的转运。鉴定出22种革兰氏阴性菌以及90种肺炎链球菌中针对细菌表面抗原的特异分子标识,在此基础上建立分子分型方法。通过大量环境样品的检测,证明该方法可应用于临床、环境、食品等多方面,具有很高的特异性和灵敏性。

(二)植物与作物

1989~1991年,南开大学张自立主持完成植物染色体分带及其机理研究,项目系统研究10种作物染色体的C、N、Q、Ag分带技术及其机理,成果在国内外学术刊物发表30多篇论文,其中在国外《遗传》(*Hereditas*)发表的"黑麦染色体G带分带和染色体大螺旋"具有首创性。1993~1995年,张自立主持完成植物姊妹染色体单体交换(SCE)研究项目,张自立等证明:很多非有害物质如营养物糖、盐、维生素、氨基酸等在超过人体所需的浓度下同样诱发SCE大大提高。研究结果提醒使用SCE技术检测有害物质要谨慎,作者对广泛使用SCE检测诱变因子提出质疑。论文发表在《突变研究》(*Mutation Research*)杂志后,受到学术界关注。

1995年,南开大学和天津卫生环境医学研究所吕宪禹、云希勤、寇登民、葛伟文进行6种食用豆脂肪酸组成的研究和比较。对收集自全国各地的豌豆、菜豆、绿豆、豇豆、小豆和蚕豆进行脂肪酸组成和含量的分析,发现这六种食用豆中,普遍含有亚油酸、软脂酸、亚麻酸、油酸、硬脂酸和花生酸,除花生酸在6种食用豆中的相对含量很低没有差异性外($P>0.05$),脂肪酸的组成存在种的差异性($P<0.01$),并且多烯不饱和脂肪酸与饱和脂肪酸的比例(PUFA/SF)也存在极显著差异($P<0.01$),硬脂酸$F=14.980$,花生酸$F=2.271$,油酸$F=36.325$,亚油酸$F=87.568$,亚麻酸$F=101.090$。在所分析6种食用豆中,除花生酸($F=2.271$,$P>0.05$)外,其他脂肪酸的相对含量种间存在显著性差异($P<0.01$)。总的来说,不同的食用豆具有各不相同的脂肪酸组成,似乎受各自基因的控制;而花生酸的相对含量在种间却无差异性,似乎受着食用豆共同基因的控制。同种食用豆总脂肪酸组成的不平衡性对同种食用豆的总脂肪酸组成作方差分析,结果如下:碗豆$F=285.350$,菜豆$F=67.007$,绿豆$F=416.200$,豇豆$F=123.548$,小豆$F=1090.928$,蚕豆$F=101.090$。由此可见,在同种食用豆中,脂肪酸组成极不平衡。

1997年,南开大学王勇、王宁宁、王淑芳等研究大豆叶片衰老过程中半胱氨酸蛋白酶基因的特异性表达,用反转录和多聚酶链式反应(RT-PCR)和琼脂糖凝胶电泳方法对大豆叶片衰老过程中半胱氨酸蛋白酶基因的表达情况进行研究,发现PCR扩增出的CDNA带谱会随着叶片的不断衰老而发生较明显的改变。证明:至少有一条cDNA带为绿叶样品所特有,另外两条cDNA带则为衰老叶片样品所特有,实验结果为进一步分离大豆叶片衰老时特异表达基因及其启动子和最终实施转基因工程奠定基础。

1999年,南开大学宋文芹、李秀兰、祁仲夏等研究水稻染色体的显微分离与克隆问题。对水稻染色体识别、显微分离与切割、PCR体外扩增和微克隆进行研究,利用改进的显微切割装置,在100×油镜下进行染色体分离与微切割,不仅解决水稻染色体的识别和显微分离的困难,而且使染色体特定区微切片段缩小到7Mb级;利用SUP-PCR可使fg级水稻染色体DNA扩增到μg级.电泳检测结果表明,扩增片断在80~600基底左右,经与pUC19连接,转化大肠杆菌DH5a,一次分离的单条水稻染色体可以获得9×10^4克隆,一个7Mb级片段可以获得3×10^4克隆,经分析,插入片段大小在80~500基底范围。该方法为直接从水稻单条染色体或染色体特定区DNA文库中筛选分子标记奠定基础。

2001年,南开大学白艳玲、杨之龙、于国武等研究黄瓜线粒体中DNA类质粒的分离与鉴定。应用琼酯糖凝胶电泳、S1酶处理及电镜技术，从黄瓜线粒体中分离并鉴定三种环形DNA类质粒，依其分子由大到小，分别称之为pC1、pC2和pC3。以类质粒凝胶电泳带的荧光扫描值与DNA类质粒的分子长度之比作为类质粒拷贝数的参照值，对3种类质粒进行荧光扫描分析，结果表明pC3拷贝数明显高于pC1和pC2；pC2的拷贝数略高于pC1。其后，白艳玲、杨之龙、陈延辉等研究生长条件对黄瓜线粒体类质粒稳定性的影响，"津新密刺"等一些黄瓜品种的线粒体中存在主基因组以外的3种环形DNA类质粒pC1、pC2和pC3。改变植株生长的温度、pH或以蔗糖溶液代替无菌水培养黄瓜植株，电泳均能检测到上述3种类质粒。应用ImageMaster VDS系统对各类质粒电泳带的密度进行扫描，通过计算3种类质粒的相对拷贝数及类质粒之间的拷贝数比值，分析不同生长条件对黄瓜类质粒稳定性的影响，结果表明，上述3种培养条件均对黄瓜线粒体类质粒的拷贝数有影响，其影响的程度因类质粒而异，pC3与pC1和pC2相比对环境改变更敏感，提示类质粒间的这种差异可能是类质粒复制方式不同引起的。

2004年7月，天津师范大学王振英、彭永康、陈宏等完成小麦白粉病主要抗原的分子标记与产业化应用研究及小麦抗白粉病基因的克隆与分子标记育种和小麦抗白粉病相关特异DNA片段的克隆与测序。项目组以抗病栽培小麦Brock、近等基因系Brock/015//京4117、轮回亲本京411及抗性单株为材料，利用分子标记方法，筛选与抗白粉病基因紧密连锁的分子标记，完成连锁性分析及遗传距离测定，分子标记的克隆、测序、SCAR标记转换，利用分子标记选择出抗病、农艺性状良好的高产小麦新品系。研究确定抗病栽培小麦Brock中存在一个未知的强抗白粉病基因；以Brock为抗性基因供体，配制近等基因系Brock/015//京4117；从Brock和近等基因系中筛选出与未知抗性基因紧密连锁的分子标记两个。根据分子标记选择出2个具有抗病、农艺性状优良、高产的小麦新品系。

2005年，南开大学邢来君、李明春、卜云萍等人完成产生高γ—亚麻酸含量的转基因大豆的方法的研究，从高产γ—亚麻酸的低等真菌菌株中，克隆△6—脂肪酸脱氢酶基因的核酸序列，采用异源的调节性功能单元构建表达载体，选用中国东北大豆品种，以农杆菌介导的转化方法，将△6—脂肪酸脱氢酶基因转入大豆中，获得转化植株，从中选育出富含γ—亚麻酸的转基因大豆植株。项目采用农杆菌介导的大豆子叶节转化系统，首次成功地将来源于深黄被孢霉的△6—脂肪酸脱氢酶基因导入东北栽培大豆的6个品种中，并在转录水平mRNA上得到表达，获得T1代转基因种子。这是首次将△6—脂肪酸脱氢酶基因成功导入国内栽培大豆品种产生γ—亚麻酸；在大豆再生系统的基础上，对大豆遗传转化受体系统进行相应的调整和改良，建立一套特有的简便实用的大豆子叶节转化系统。

(三)人与动物

1995年，天津师范大学和天津中医学院郝泗城、夏文、毕平、宇克莉等进行澳洲蟾酥三氯甲烷提取物抑瘤作用的研究，用澳洲蟾蜍(Bufomarinus)皮脂腺分泌物(蟾酥)的三氯甲烷提取物(O.R)进行的抗肿瘤实验表明，其可以延长载有腹水肝癌(Hca)细胞的津白Ⅰ号(TA-1)小鼠的生存期，并对TA-1小鼠移植性子宫颈癌(U(14))实体瘤的生长有一定抑制作用。该项研究为该药物资源的开发利用提供依据。

1995年，南开大学陈荷新、刘淑红、纪永刚等研究对BIV-Gag和Env抗原特异性抗体的免疫检测问题。用高效表达载体表达出的融合BIV核心蛋白(TrpE-Gag)和外膜蛋白(TrpE-Env)作为WesternBlot检测的抗原，分别对Ⅰ、Ⅱ两口岸进口奶牛及后代进行流行病学调查，发现用外膜蛋白检测阳性率比核心蛋白阳性率略高，进一步的追踪调查表明核心蛋白的抗体水平在减弱的同时外膜蛋白的抗体有加强的趋势。

1997年，南开大学和天津教育学院蔡宝立、张富国、王淑芳、朱祚铭进行谷胱甘肽S-转移酶5-5和细菌二氯甲烷脱卤素酶的性质比较研究。通过简便的两步阴离子交换色谱，从遗传工程菌株大肠杆菌JM105中纯化出哺乳动物的谷胱甘肽S-转移酶5-5(GST5-5)。GST5-5以二卤甲烷为底物时的动力学常数、热稳定性和最适pH被测定，并与细菌二氯甲烷脱卤素酶(DM11脱卤素酶)的上述性质进行比较。

2000年，南开大学、山东省莒南县皮肤病防治站和军事医学科学院放射研究所张金红、徐畅、张凤川、张津辉、侯奕等进行邻苯二甲酸二丁酯(DBP)诱导肿瘤细胞凋亡机制的初步研究。证明DBP在体外对肺巨细胞癌细胞(PG)和人早幼粒白血病细胞(HL-60)的增殖有明显的抑制作用。经DBP处理过的PG细胞，DNA

断裂，在琼脂糖凝胶电泳上呈现出特异的断裂带。流式细胞术分析表明，DBP能提高PG细胞的凋亡率，并且随作用时间的延长而增大。斑点杂交的结果显示，被DBP处理过的HL-60细胞中某些原癌基因、抑癌基因和肿瘤抑制基因的mRNA表达水平都有所下降，提示DBP对HL-60细胞增殖抑制作用的机制之一可能通过抑制这些癌基因和突变的抑癌基因的表达来实现。

2003年，南开大学程勇、石建党、张琚等研究含有肌球蛋白重链启动子的p-EGFP1质粒的构建，从前列腺组织中提取总DNA，以其为模板经PCR扩增得到肌球蛋白启动子，将扩增片段和处理好的p-EGFP1载体相连，连接产物转入到大肠杆菌HB101中，经筛选得到连有myosin启动子的p-EGFP1重组质粒.用酶切和PCR的方法对重组质粒进行鉴定.成功构建的质粒可用于前列腺平滑肌细胞和成纤维细胞的分离，这将对于阐明前列腺基质增生的机理起到重要作用。

（四）显微切割技术

1998年，南开大学李秀兰、宋文芹、许文胜等研究一种改进的染色体显微切割方法。利用普通光学显微镜进行染色体显微切割的方法，先使显微镜物镜焦点平面升高约7毫米，将制在盖玻片上的染色体标本反扣在自制的玻璃台架上，从物镜下方进行染色体切割，成功解决在100×油浸物镜下不能切割染色体的困难，实现在高放大倍数（放大率1000～1500×）条件下进行染色体显微切割的问题，大大提高显微切割的精度和准确度。

二、去壁低渗法及其应用

2001年，南开大学陈瑞阳主持，宋文芹、李秀兰、安祝平等参与完成去壁低渗法（WDH法）及其在中国植物染色体研究中的应用课题。2003年，陈瑞阳主持完成“中国主要植物染色体研究”获国家自然科学奖二等奖，合作单位是北京大学、中国农业科学院兴城果树研究所与西南大学，参加者有宋文芹、李秀兰、李懋学、林盛华和梁国鲁等。

图3-6-3-27 南开大学陈瑞阳（左一）和他的同事们

1970年代末，陈瑞阳等首次建立植物染色体标本制备与研究的去壁低渗新方法（简称WDH法），对植物染色体Giemsa C-带、N-带、G-带、Ag-染、微切微克隆、FISH等研究技术进行一系列改革与创新，制定出中国植物核型分析标准化，摒弃植物染色体研究一直沿用的落后的压片法，使该领域研究达到国际先进水平。此后，项目组用WDH法对国内原产和土著经济植物染色体进行长期系统研究，通过所积累的大量、科学的染色体数据，总结出中国主要栽培植物分类、起源进化方面的规律；并对中国2130种植物染色体数目、754种植物核型进行定和分析，其中85%为首次报道。新发现103种果树多倍体，出版世界第一部植物染色体图谱。为推广应用WDH新方法，举办3次共300多个单位技术人员参加的全国植物染色体技术培训班，组织召开两次“中日植物染色体学术讨论会”和两次国内植物染色体学术讨论会，对中国植物染色体研究的发展做出开创性和奠基性的贡献，获得国际上的承认，带动植物染色体及其相关领域的发展。

多年来，陈瑞阳带领的科研团队对中国95科331属2834种（含种下分类单位）植物染色体数目进行报道，完成1045种植物核型分析，从细胞水平对中国苹果属、梨属、柑桔属、茶属、大豆属、小麦属、大麦属、玉蜀黍属、绵属、狗尾草属、菊属等主要栽培植物的分类、起源、进化提出新的认识，新发现191种具有重要经济价值和科学意义的多倍体、多倍体复合体和细胞型，首次报道中国银杏、芦笋的性别机制为ZW型和XY型。该项目研究共发表论文256篇，在国内外被引用1355次，染色体资料已被《中国果树志》等10部专著和教科书引用。该项目出版世界上第一部植物基因组染色体图谱（共五册），填补世界植物染色体图谱的空白。20世纪90年代末，陈瑞阳等研究水稻基因组第4号染色体DNA文库的构建及其克隆定位。

第四篇

高新技术及其产业化

概　述

发展高科技、实现产业化，是带动产业结构优化、大幅度提高劳动生产率和经济效益的根本途径。20世纪90年代以来，天津市的经济处于调整结构、上水平、全面提高素质的关键时期，高新技术及其产业化面临不可多得的发展机遇。坚持用高新技术改造传统产业，形成一批面向21世纪的先导产业，抢占战略制高点，是科技工作的重中之重。天津市通过实施“火炬计划”“科技百亿工程计划”“重大科技产业化计划”“科技专项计划”“重大高新技术产业化项目”等国家和地方计划，引导和推动高新技术及其产业取得较大发展。据统计，1990年天津高新技术产业产值13.7亿，占全市工业总产值的2%，高新技术产品出口创汇额1.2亿美元。1995年高新技术产值达到266亿元，占工业总产值的12%。2000年高新技术产值达到744.6亿，占工业的比重达到24.2%。到2005年高新技术产业完成产值2141.4亿元，占工业比重达到29.9%，出口124.7亿美元，产值亿元以上的高新技术企业达到180家，其中10亿元以上的28家。按可比口径，从1995年到2005年，天津市高新技术产业，年均增长率保持在20%以上，产值增长8倍，在整个工业中占有举足轻重的地位。截至2005年，天津市建成国家和省部级重点实验室20个、工程技术研究中心25个、企业技术中心150个，部分三资企业在津设立研发中心，高新技术产业创新体系初步建立。1991～2005年，天津市既是高新技术产业的起步时期，也是夯实基础快速发展的时期。经过这十五年的发展，概括说来，天津市高新技术及其产业在如下三个方面取得明显进展。

一、取得一批高新技术及产业化成果。从科技“百亿工程”到“重大科技产业化工程项目”，天津市高新技术产业走出一条优势集成、多方联动、重点突破、整体推进的发展新路，举全市之力取得显著效果，如镍氢电池、锂离子电池、地塞美松、复方丹参滴丸、中空纤维膜材料和组件、干细胞和曙光服务器应用工程等项目，成为天津新一代标志性产品。进入2000年，通过设立“重大科技专项”，实现技术、人才和资金的再次集成，在信息技术、生物技术与新药、新能源、新材料和环保技术等重点领域取得重大突破，如具有国际先进水平的原创性科研成果“微操作机器人”、被誉为“世界首创阅读不耗电”的电子书、国内首枚用于硅上液晶(LCOS)微显示的集成电路芯片，开发出0.25微米~0.18微米具有国际一流水平的SOC系统芯片、申请多项专利的用于病原微生物检测的生物芯片、新一代抗生素头孢地尼、抗肿瘤药物紫金龙片等新药。开发出居国内领先水平的聚合物锂离子电池和锂离子、镍氢动力电池与形成12.5兆瓦的产业规模的多晶硅、非晶硅等太阳能电池，以及光电转换效率达到国际先进水平的铜铟硒化合物薄膜太阳能电池。还有中巴型纯电动车、混合动力轿车样车、实现产业化的负载型纳米催化剂、药用树脂、汽车漆等纳米材料新产品等等，以及应用数字化设计和快速成型制造技术研制的成功用于“神舟五号”载人航天工程的宇航员赋型座垫。形成一批具有自主知识产权、具有产业化前景的跨世纪先导产品。

二、用高新技术改造传统产业成效显著。通过实施制造业信息化、农业信息化、中药现代化和环保科技“四大工程”，促进先进共性技术和先进科技成果在传统产业上的推广应用，增强企业的活力和市场应变能力，提高产品的竞争力。实施制造业信息化科技工程，累计带动全市2000多家制造业企业实现信息化，新品开发周期平均由131天缩短为86天，全市80%以上的重点企业采用计算机辅助设计(CAD)、辅助制造(CAM)，有效提升企业的新产品设计能力，获全国制造业信息化优秀示范省市奖。通过实施中药现代化科技工程，加快中药企业的规范化和现代化建设，推动超临界萃取、分子蒸馏、三相流化床、薄膜包衣、膜分离等16项中药现代化关键技术在中药企业中的广泛应用，复方丹参滴丸、速效救心丸居全国中药单品种销售量的第一和第二，培育中药大品种、大企业战略取得显著成效，成为国家中药现代化科技产业基地。在农业信息化工程中，开发完成农业专家决策系统7个，建立西青、北辰等12个农业区县的30个乡镇、500个示范点（村、企业、农户），成为农业新技术普及推广、咨询和培训的重要渠道，数十万农户受益。通过网上交易农产品达2000多个，销售收入数亿元，在提高农民收入上发挥重要作用。通过环保科技工程，实现污水处理专用设备、新型水处理药剂、中空纤维膜、汽车尾气净化、工业有毒有害废物处理等一批项目的产业化。建立海水淡化、污水资源化、工业节水等一批科技示范工程。建成国内技术水平最高、规模最大的中空纤维膜产业化基地。重点扶持天津化工研究设计院等3家先进单位，并促进传统机电企业转型为环保设备制造商。

三、建成国家重要的研发与创新基地。天津新技术产业园区和天津经济开发区作为发展高新技术产业的基地，其功能不断增强，发挥孵化、引导和示范作用。一批科技创新与产业化项目进入国家层面，建成国家级软件、新能源、纳米技术、通信技术、生物技术和环保科技、农业科技等产业化基地和大学科技园。天津成为国家首批制造业信息化示范城市、首批智能交通系统应用示范工程试点城市、清洁汽车试点示范城市、电动汽车示范运行城市、干细胞产业化基地、海水淡化示范城市和电子商务与现代物流示范城市。天津成为国家科技创新、高新技术产业化和科技示范应用的重要基地。

第一章　信息科学与技术

进入20世纪90年代，以计算机技术、微电子技术和通信技术为主的现代信息技术成为带动地区经济增长的战略性产业。1991～2005年，天津形成三个具有特色、生产相对集中的信息产业密集区，即：移动通信设备及终端密集区、加工配套产业密集区、软件及系统集成业密集区，是信息产业部认定的9个国家信息产业基地之一。1998年科技部批准天津国家级的华苑软件园，2003年国家发改委等几部委联合批准天津软件出口基地，2004年信息产业部批准天津建立包括通讯产业园、集成电路产业园、化学与物理电源产业园和片式元件产业园的国家电子信息产业园，这在全国是第一批。

2000～2005年，天津市电子信息产业产值由676.46亿元迅速增长至1959亿元，年均增长24%，电子信息产业综合经济效益持续名列全国第二，是全国IT业回报率最高的地区之一，成为天津第一大支柱产业。1996年天津市金卡工程领导小组与天津市电子振兴领导小组合并，成立天津信息化工作领导小组。同年信息化办组织专家和有关部门编制《天津市信息港工程规划纲要》，到2000年，天津市顺利完成规划纲要确定的第一阶段任务：基础通讯网络设施建设有显著提高；全市综合信息交互平台先后开通；各类信息资源相继上网；计算机及网络的应用飞跃性的提高；“三金工程”特别是金关、金卡实施成效显著。天津承担的国家863高新技术产业化项目——曙光机应用（天津）示范工程，加快全市税收、商业、科教、外贸四个系统的信息化建设步伐。

2000～2005年，天津市信息基础设施建设投入约190亿元，一大批信息基础功能平台相继投入使用，提升面向社会和公众的信息服务能力。互联网数据中心在天津通信公司和开发区相继建成运营；电子政务专网（一期）正式投入运行；电子商务平台的数字密钥中心正式投入使用；国家防病毒中心成为国内重要的计算机与网络防病毒测试、研发、预报发布中心；制造业信息化工程和农业信息化工程取得明显成效。2004年建成的“南开之星”超级计算机为生物医药、化工、气象、海洋等系统服务，提高科研与生产水平。据国家有关部门测评，天津城市信息化综合指标位居全国第三。

第一节　集成电路

20世纪60年代初期，天津大学开始半导体材料和器件研究，成功设计制造并批量生产半导体大功率三极管。70年代后期，天津大学和南开大学陆续开始集成电路设计的研究。80年代初，天津大学在601半导体器件厂改建成一条2微米的半导体超净生产线，是当年先进的半导体工艺生产线，藉此开展各种半导体器件和CMOS集成电路工艺研究。该项目由道克刚主持，并在M6800 MPU版图逻辑纠错中做出成绩。进入90年代，南开大学秦世才主持开展模拟集成电路设计研究和人才培养，孙钟林课题组开展Lcos显示芯片研究。跨入21世纪，在原副市长叶迪生积极组织推动下，成立天津强芯半导体芯片设计有限公司，实现天津芯片设计企业零的突破，带动天津芯片设计产业的发展。

一、集成电路设计

南开大学秦世才多年从事集成电路基础性研究。1991年完成集成系统中MOS模拟基础电路研究，1994年开展高分辨率VLSI/AMLCD天屏显示技术研究，1995年完成高分辨率VLSL/AMLCD无屏显示技术的研究，1997年完成RC有源滤波器的全过程辅助设计与仿真研究，2000~2001年开展VLSI工艺流程演示软件研究。

2001年，在市科委的支持下，天津大学成立由姚素瑛主持的专用集成电路（ASIC）设计中心。该中心建设起全流程超大规模集成电路设计和测试环境（包括各种高端硬件设备和最新版本的EDA设计与验证工具），能同时容纳50人上机实践设计。中心逐渐形成一支以海外归国学者为骨干的优秀IC设计队伍，每年为国家培养出一批优秀设计人才。截止到2005年，设计中心完成天津市重大攻关项目“RISC结构8位MCU IP核的研发”和“高性能大动态范围CMOS图像传感器研发”两款芯片的设计和工艺制造项目。这两款芯片的流片及测试结果，表明天津大学ASIC设计中心拥有超大规模数字集成电路设计和极具挑战性的大规模数模混合集成电路的设计能力。

2001年10月，天津强芯半导体芯片设计有限公司成立。2002年9月，天津强芯半导体芯片设计有限公司与摩托罗拉公司半导体部门合作，成立摩托罗拉强芯（天津）集成电路设计有限公司，该公司利用最尖端的电子设计自动化工具，在摩托罗拉全球领先的8位单片机芯技术的基础上，研制出具有国际领先水准的新产品；2003年4月，该公司通过国家信息产业部的考核，被认定为中国第一批集成电路设计企业；2003年7月，该公司成功推出第一款产品——8位微控制器HC08GZ32，是低成本GZ系列产品的首款只读存储器产品，主要面向低成本、高可靠性和能进行高速通信的CAN总线执行系统的汽车电子和工业界用户。2004年8月，公司采用0.5微米工艺，推出名为MC68HC908JL16的8位微控器产品，该产品作为低成本、高性能的MC68HC08系列产品的重要一员，采用增强型的中央处理器（CPU08），提供多种模块、内存大小和不同封装类型的选择，用于工业控制及家用电器中。2004年12月，摩托罗拉公司将半导体部门独立分拆出来，摩托罗拉强芯（天津）集成电路设计有限公司更名为飞思卡尔强芯（天津）集成电路设计有限公司。2005年4月，该公司推出名为MCF5207/08的产品，是公司的第一款32位MCU产品，采用0.13微米工艺，主要面向低成本、低功耗市场。该产品包括一个可选择的DDR/SDR SDRAM和一个电源管理模块，处理速度在133MHZ时达到127MIPS，用于POS机及手持医疗设备中。

2002年10月，南大强芯公司成立，以戴宇杰等三位留学生为主从事专用大规模集成电路的设计和开发。该公司完成日本东芝公司的手机电源系统芯片、软盘驱动系统芯片及90纳米SOC芯片等多项委托设计，其中“90纳米CMOS工艺的SOC芯片设计”被《中国电子报》评为基础电子业十件大事之一，并获得东芝微电子株式会社两项大奖。公司科技攻关项目“SOC用锁相环IP的开发”流片验收结项，产品IP核被日本OKI公司采购使用，还完成模拟视频信号前端处理器芯片设计、条形码驱动系统芯片设计、锂电池保护芯片、移动端末电池管理芯片等设计项目。

二、集成电路器件

1990年起，南开大学熊绍珍、赵颖、吴春亚等合作开始非晶硅（a-Si）基薄膜功能集成器件和技术的研究，至2004年取得多方面成果。在a-Si TFT-LCD方面：最早用高换气率改善界面，使TFT的Ion/Ioff比达7个数量级；在国内首次用磁悬浮等离子刻蚀法改善界面；首次用阳极氧化Ta、Al形成双绝缘层的冗错技术，提高器件稳定性和成品率；提出电荷收集法进行TFT矩阵的有效、动态检测技术；提出一种显示工作点选择的VgL的概念和驱动方法，提高显示均匀性；首次将无源液晶显示的控制电路用于有源选址之中，以数/模混合技术用于液晶显示，达到良好显示效果。在a-Si TFT/PIN方面：首次提出TFT/PIN耦合对模拟计算物理模型，概念新颖，获深入认识；移植非晶电池技术，SiNx和a-Si界面的氢处理，提高迁移率两倍；提出Al:Ti合金电极材料，减少小丘，改善信号延迟，提高稳定性；独立发现Mo和Si室温下能互作用形成Mo:Si作用层，使TFT的Ion/Ioff比达8个数量级，迁移率为0.86cm²/V.s；提出一种低温固化PI内联绝缘层的概念和工艺方法，改善PIN和TFT有效隔离，提高工艺相容性，使a-Si PIN在100勒低光强下，光/暗电流比仍有4个量级。在a-Si PIN/OLED方面：提出一种新型的薄膜PIN/PLED耦合面阵，PIN接受来自信号源的光信号，直接以光生电流形式传递给有机发光元件发光，集图像传感与显示功能于一身，可实现普段转换、光-光信号的转换；移植、改造无几LED驱动电路用于OLED，获得良好显示效果。发表论文54篇，其中多篇被SCI或EI收录。

天津中环半导体股份有限公司生产的塑封高压硅堆、高压二极管、硅整流二极管和硅桥式整流器见本卷第五篇第八章第一节。

三、集成电路的封装与测试

1992年，摩托罗拉公司在天津开发区投资建立半导体封装测试厂。1994年5月通过ISO 9002国际质量体系认证。1995年9月22日国家有关部门批准美国摩托罗拉电子公司增资7.2亿美元，在天津摩托罗拉（中国）电子有限公司建设具有世界一流水平的半导体集成电路芯片厂。1997年11月，通过QS 9000质量体系稽核，1998年1月通过ISO 14001，环境管理管理体系审核，成为天津市获得该项认证的首家企业。2000年8月21日 市政府与美国摩托罗拉公司在北京举行新闻发布会，宣布对在津摩托罗拉（中国）电子有限公司增资160亿元人民币，建设世界最大的半导体综合生产中心及亚洲最大的通讯产品生产基地。

摩托罗拉公司所属天津半导体集成生产中心，集半导体前工序芯片厂和后工序封装测试厂于一身，具有完整的生产流程。封装测试厂简称“BAT111”，引入0.25/0.35微米级八英寸芯片生产技术，使中国进入微电子技术国际先进行列。2001年7月4日 中国第一块国际电子行业技术含量最高的逻辑芯片（晶片）在摩托罗拉半导体天津集成生产中心成功下线。该中心成为国内逻辑芯片的生产基地。

四、集成电路制造辅助技术

2001年6月，河北工业大学刘玉岭、王新、王弘英等完成对超大规模集成电路（ULSI）表面状态的研究，在超大规模集成电路表面状态的理论与工程技术上取得重大突破，获得具有工业规模应用前景的CMP抛光剂。这种抛光剂，能有效控制铜离子沾污，具有无金属杂质沾污、高速率、低粒径、低损伤、高选择，高洁净诸特点，为微电子第三代布线做出创造性贡献。同年，刘玉岭、王新、檀柏梅完成超大

图4-1-1-28 河北工业大学刘玉岭在办公室

规模集成电路纳米磨料化学机械全局平面化新技术的研究，该成果对国际上微电子技术发展亟待解决的关键技术衬底与立体结构多层布线的高平整、低损伤、高光洁、低沾污要求进行理论及试验研究，分别获得关键理论与技术的突破。成果揭示ULSI多层Cu布线化学机械全局平整化动力学过程，确立"强络合、弱氧化；高速率、高选择；小粒径、高浓度；低损伤、高平整"的新机理模型。发明纳米磨料CMP抛光液；磨料选用粒径为15~20纳米、浓度高达40%的硬度低的SiO_2水溶胶，代替美日的粒径>40纳米，浓度为5%~10%的Al_2O_3磨料；发明由渗透力很强的表面活性剂和羟胺组成的能生物降解的环保清洗剂。该技术使IC衬底片抛光后存放时间由正常不足两小时增至(100)硅片120小时、(111)硅片168小时；取代效率低、造成损伤、返修率高、价格昂贵(40多万美元/台)、工艺复杂的双面刷片机工艺。且抛光返修率低，一次合格率达85%以上，其指标超过SEMI国际标准。

第二节 光电子

光电子领域中，显示、传感和存储三大技术的研究是信息科学与技术的基础。1991~2005年，南开大学在这三个领域的研究工作中，取得丰硕而突出的成果：研制出国内第一个TFT-LCD具有视频显示能力的液晶显示模块及其投影系统，在LCoS芯片设计、驱动电路设计和液晶显示模式设计等方面，制备出中国第一块彩色AMOLED屏。

一、显示技术与显示器

(一)显示技术

1、TFT-LCD与TFT-OLED

1992年初，以南开大学牵头的"a-Si-TFT-LCD投影显示"的攻关项目正式启动。经熊绍珍、孟志国、代永平等精心研究，并与北京大学、清华大学紧密合作，最终在天津由南开大学研制出国内第一个TFT-LCD具有视频显示能力的液晶显示模块及其投影系统的自有知识产权的全套技术。

1995年，南开大学开展适于作OLED有源驱动基板的高迁移率多晶硅材料及其TFT的研究。1996年起开始进行全方位器件性能测试与模拟分析。随后于1999年起连续就OLED的稳定性、PIN/OLED、倒置TFT/OLED矩阵等继续进行深入。2003年底，以南开大学熊绍珍、孟志国、吴春亚等为主力的OLED有源基板研究团队，与香港科技大学、清华维信诺、华中科大等单位合作，利用成熟的光刻技术，采用白光分色的思路，良好地解决需精细制备红绿蓝三色OLED的彩色化难度，成功研制出中国第一个多晶硅TFT的彩色AM-OLED显示模块，显示屏尺寸为2.1英寸，是当时除日、韩之外的第三个独立开发出多晶硅TFT彩色AM-OLED显示屏的国家，表明中国彩色AM-OLED的多晶硅TFT有源驱动技术研究跻身于国际先进行列。此后，在研制的多晶硅TFT矩阵基板上，与汕尾信利公司合作，研制出5英寸AM-OLED显示模块。成果在国内外重要学术杂志发表文章百余篇，多数被SCI、EI收录，获国家发明专利19项。

2、LCoS

1998年，南开大学孙钟林主持军民两用头盔式显示系统研究项目，开国内LCoS(硅晶光)技术研究的先河。2000年，在此基础上，耿卫东作为负责人，承担LCoS微型显示器件关键件及系统的研究，于2003年4月，研制成功国内首枚LCoS显示芯片(在北京NEC流片)，

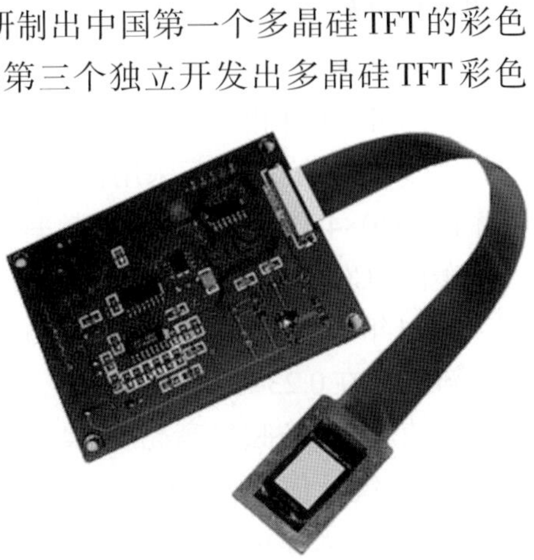

图4-1-2-29 LCoS模块与驱动电路

该芯片的分辨率为SVGA(800×600),芯片尺寸为17.1毫米×12.5毫米,像素截距为15.99微米×15.99微米,课题组利用该芯片完成50英寸三片LCoS投影样机。2003年,代永平作为课题负责人,承担头盔显示LCoS芯片和系统的研究,于2005年开发出单片彩色头盔显示LCoS微显示芯片,该芯片的分辨率为VGA(640×480),芯片尺寸为尺寸15.0毫米×14.0毫米,像素截距为16微米×16微米。该显示器采用自主设计的时序彩色像素单元和场序化彩色控制,在中芯国际(上海)流片,是国内首枚单片彩色LCOS显示模块。南开大学在LCoS芯片设计、驱动电路设计和液晶显示模式设计等方面,这段时期一直处于国内领先水平。

2002年,南开大学在国内开展LCoS新型显示器件关键件及系统研究,2003年6月,南开大学光电子研究所承担LCoS新型显示器件中的关键件及系统研究,研制出国内首枚LCoS微显示模块。模块为南开大学自主设计,由首钢NEC代工、天大天财液晶封装,采用0.6微米CMOS工艺,分辨率为SVGA(800×600),尺寸0.7英寸(18毫米),像素截距12微米×12微米。模块在测试中成功地实现动态视频图像显示,表明天津市在IC设计、代工适配、液晶封装等关键技术上占据国内领先水平。同年10月,研制出国内首枚LCoS微显示集成电路芯片,其对角线0.63英寸(16毫米),连接VCD机通过放大镜观看,芯片显示的播放画面十分清晰;其分辨率为800×600,亮度为300尼特,寿命可达1万多小时。并具备从芯片设计、流片、液晶封装、形成相关产业链的基础。此项成果在IC芯片设计、液晶封装等关键技术上填补国内空白。

3、LCD和OLED MIUC

2004年1月,南开大学孟志国、吴春亚、熊绍珍等完成高性能金属诱导横向晶化多晶硅薄膜晶体管技术的研究。项目组获得高迁移率、高开关比、低阈值电压、低亚阈值幅摆、低漏电流的单栅结构多晶硅薄膜晶体管;通过采用超薄沟道使得阈值电压和开关比得到进一步改善;采用多栅结构使关态电流得到进一步降低。同年,孟志国、吴春亚、熊绍珍等完成适用于彩色有机发光显示器的MIUC poly-Si TFT有源选址基板的研究,制备出中国第一块彩色AMOLED屏,具有象素单元电路简单、开口率高、功耗低、信息容量高等优点。

与此同时,吴春亚、孟志国、熊绍珍等还完成适用于LCD和OLED平板显示的彩色膜上室温直接沉积ITO透明导电膜及微细加工技术的研究。该技术成果使用直流磁控溅射方法,在室温下直接在已光刻成微小图形的彩色膜上沉积出粘附性良好的ITO透明导电薄膜。经查新检索国内外的23个数据库和专业网站,均未发现有相同的专利文献报导。

2004年1月,南开大学吴春亚、孟志国、熊绍珍等共同完成玻璃衬底上LCD和OLED MIUC poly-Si TFT显示驱动电路的设计和制备研究,利用该技术成果,与LCD或OLED MIUC poly-Si TFT象素单元电路相结合,制备出外围驱动电路一体化的全集成型有源选址基板,从而大幅度降低外围引线的数量和烦杂程度,提高显示屏与外围其他部分连接的可靠性。

2005年9月,天津工业大学牛萍娟等完成白色大尺寸GaN基LED器件研究,在大功率器件倒装焊接工艺方面取得突破,有效地提高器件出光效率,改善散热性能,获得瓦级功率的LED发光芯片,其一致性测试表明效果良好。

(二)显示器

1993年,天津市显示器厂王永安、曹玉瑛、薛来平等研制出SM1418平面直角单色显示器。SM1418采用分离同步信号输入,视频采用模拟通道。水平扫描频率为31.5千赫兹,垂直刷新频率为50~70赫兹。具有分辨率高(640×480)、较高的刷新频率(保护视力)、灰度等级丰富等特点,且结构精巧、外观别致,于1992年底通过美国FCC-B级认证,销往美国市场。

1994年,天津中环三津有限公司张文铭、冯志存、胡小试等研究成功C14MP55P-系列单色显示管,电子枪分辨能力在0.23~0.24毫米左右,处于国内先进水平。自行配置单色粉以提高CRT的亮度和分辨能力。具有平面直角形、防眩目高亮度、高对比度等特点,减少操作者长期工作状态下眼睛的疲劳,分辨率的提高更利于图表,统计信息中使用。

1995年,天津市电视技术研究所李月国、王东江、周秀云等研制成功SGB高温工业电视系统保护装置系列产品,包括SGB-101探头式高温工业电视、SGB-102炉壁式高温工业电视、SGB-103水冷式高温工业电视和SGB-104风冷式高温工业电视系统保护装置。分别适用于100°C~2000°C的高温、多水汽尘埃、腐蚀性气体等恶劣条件下,保护电视摄像系统正常工作,实时观察监控,极大地提高生产自动化程度。

2002年,天津光电星球公司开发成功国内最大型LED全彩电子大屏幕,支持多种视频及图文播放方式,高保真转播闭路电视、卫星电视节目,实现现场实时摄录转播、精彩回放等功能,图象显示逼真,做到画面显示色彩与摄录现场色调一致,不变色、不失真,完全达到彩色显示效果。

二、传感技术与传感器

2003年6月,南开大学董孝义主持完成AFSN-1型光纤光栅传感网络系统的研制,将光纤光栅与多种通信复用技术集成起来,提出一种新型光纤光栅调谐解调技术,研制成功一种多功能、分布式光纤传感网络系统,能够同时对32个点的多个物理量(例如温度、应变等)进行测量,可检测最大应变20000$\mu\varepsilon$,应变分辨率1$\mu\varepsilon$,可检测温度范围为-30℃~200℃,温度分辨率0.03℃,并可给出相关物理量的分布曲线。成果在反射解调原理及传感网络解调系统和数据快速处理等方面具有创新性,实现对其诸多特性(如温度、压力、应变等)进行实时的多点监测。

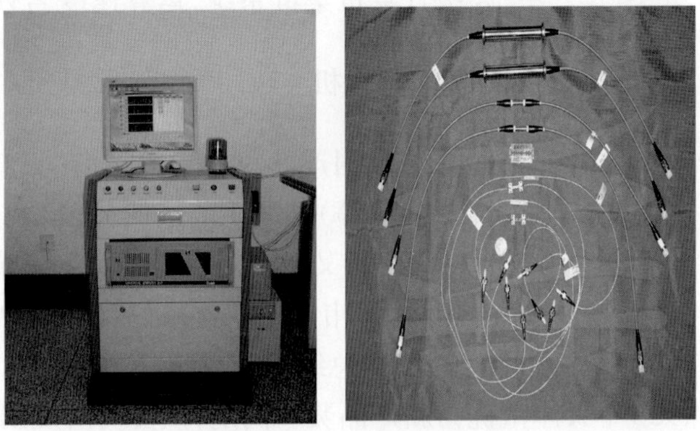
图4-1-2-30 光纤光栅传感技术与应用

2003年,南开大学董孝义、开桂云、袁树忠等完成光纤光栅传感技术与应用的研究。项目组利用光纤的光折变效应,自行设计并研制出多种新颖光纤光栅;利用折射率调制与编码效应,研制出应变、温度等多种新型光纤传感器件。通过进一步与光纤通信技术中的波分复用、时分复用、空分复用等巧妙结合,研制出光纤光栅传感网络与系统,促成光纤传感的多功能化、分布式多点化与多维化,扩大光纤光栅传感技术的应用领域。成果利用自行研制的光纤光栅写入系统,研制出Chirped、Tapped等多种光纤光栅;提出多种光纤光栅敏化技术,并研制出基于多种新颖力敏、温敏传感机制的传感器件;设计和研制出力学量、电磁量等系列性光纤光栅传感器件;首次提出光纤光栅传感解调模型,并建立关联理论;首次研制出多参数、多功能、分布式光纤光栅传感网络系统;首次研制出微震动光纤光栅传感技术。该成果受到国内外同行关注。

三、存储技术、存储器与放大器

(一)存储技术与存储器

1993年开始,南开大学许京军等从事共掺Mg或In的LN:Fe晶体研究,发现光折变光散射光强阈值效应,这一效应使这些双掺LN晶体成为更为理想的光折变体全息存储材料。1996年起,许京军等相继开展三维全息光折变存储材料及其应用、α-LiIO$_3$晶体弱光光学非线性与弱光非线性光学中的新机制新材料新器件的研究。研制成功具有自主知识产权的固定式三维全息光子存储器实验样机,成果达到国际先进水平,部分指标具有国际领先水平。项目相关成果获中国发明专利5项,美国专利2项。

2004年10月,南开大学卢桂章、安刚、黄大刚等研制成功实用化三维光学数据存储器。该成果提交一套体全息数字数据存储器的样机,它采用空间-角度复用方式,能读可写,机械部件自制,整机35×35×35厘米,在机械结构、光路以及读取方式方面具有明显特点,为进一步减小体积并使之成为实用的装置奠定基础。

(二)放大器

1995年至2001年,南开大学袁树忠、刘艳格、董孝义等共同研制成功增益平坦的超宽带光纤放大器,用980纳米的LD做泵源,利用长周期光纤光栅加吸收光纤做平坦元,消耗1532纳米附近的增益峰,使EDFA的3分贝增益带宽达到40纳米,其中不平坦度为+0.5分贝的增益带宽达到31纳米。

第三节 计算机

天津是开展计算机研究和生产起步较早的城市。20世纪70～80年代天津电子计算机研究所和天津电子仪器厂开始小型机的研究与生产。至90年代,国有企业通过嫁接、改造和调整,引进国外技术,形成以微小型计算机、显示器、专用计算机和网络产品为主的计算机产业。2004年南开大学联手IBM研制成功"南开之星"超级计算机集群系统,运算速度名列2005年11月世界Top500强第42位,国内排名第3位。

一、小型计算机和微机

1974年8月第一台国产小型机DJS130在天津电子计算机研究所诞生,继而1975～1983年DJS系列(120、110、132、153、162等)小型机陆续研制成功。期间,还研制成功军用小型机DJS135和DJS155。1984年天津电子计算机研究所又研制成功天鹰汉字终端与1000系列汉字信息处理系统。

1987～1988年,天津市电子仪器厂(后天津市中环电子计算机公司,下简称中环计算机公司)组织研发0504系列(STD标准工业总线)工业控制机,开发出由14块模块组成的0505系列工业控制机,连续获1987与1988年天津市优秀新产品奖。同期,该公司研发出0530微型计算机,获1988年天津市优秀新产品奖。1990年,该公司开发出中环386—25B微机系统。

1989～1991年,中环计算机公司先后研制开发出中环CT-400中英文终端机(字符终端)、中环CT-100D中英文终端机(图形终端),产品主要应用在银行终端。其中,中环CT-100D项目被列为天津市10项重点开发项目之一"计算机及外设"项目的子项。

二、超级计算机

2004年8月,在美国纽约州立大学石溪分校邓越凡教授的指导下,梁科领导的南开科学计算研究所研制成功"南开之星"超级计算机集群系统。"南开之星"的由400台双CPU服务器共800个节点、三台网络交换机和54T硬盘存储组成。设计理论速度5万亿次/秒,实测峰值达到3.231万亿次、实测效率达到68.74%,在2005年11月世界HPC500强中排名第46位。"南开之星"构建天津市高性能计算平台。

2005年,天津市科委利用"南开之星"提供500万CPU小时的计算服务,启动大规模并行技术及推广课题,设立24个子课题项目,涉及海洋、气象、港口物流、化工、医药、生物制药、汽车尾气等多项学科。该课题首次在分布式大规模高性能计算机上,实现面向天津地区灾害性天气预报、海洋污染和地震分析预测的准业务运行,积累高性能计算机的应用经验;在生物医药、农药工程、石油化工、区域物流领域的高性能计算方面为天津地区的科研工作做出实质性贡献。首次在天津市分布式大规模高性能计算机的管理、维护、研究、应用和算法研究上,取得实质性的进展。该项工作推动全国高性能计算应用水平的提高,同时高性能计算培养一批并行技术人才。

图4-1-3-31 2004年"南开之星"在HPC500强中的排名证书

三、专用计算机

2003年,由中国船舶重工集团公司第七〇七研究所张军、曹晖、严丽峰等研制成功防水式坚固型计算机。该型计算机总体设计合理、技术先进、配置灵活、兼容性好。首创在同一台便携计算机上成功解决整机防水、防信息泄漏、防整机振动和高低温工作等关键技术，填补国内空白，特别适于在环境恶劣、电磁场复杂和移动中等工作条件下使用。

四、计算机及图文终端设备

1992年，中环计算机公司先后研制出WL—1000C和WL—2000系列中英文字处理机，产品突出超扭曲、大屏幕液晶显示等特性。

1998～1999年，相继开发出基于IP的Ⅰ型、Ⅱ型机顶盒。2000年，开发出可进行MPEG2视频流式解压的机顶盒。2001～2002年，中环计算机公司推出"中环宽带多媒体网络综合服务系统"，适用于从服务提供、主干网、用户接入方式到用户接入工具等方面的宽带多媒体网络。2004～2005年，研制出中环TC518A税控收款机和中环TC168A税控收款器。2005年6月，这一成果通过国家信息产业部企业资质审查；同年9月，通过国家技术监督局生产许可证工厂审查。

五、电子书

1999年，天津津科公司李庆诚、刘全礼、王计会研制出手机伴侣，成功解决多机信息终端的互通兼容问题，同年研制出类纸电子书阅读器。该成果采用津科公司自主开发的WOLF OS嵌入式操作系统，具有电子书阅读器、电子书籍、操作系统整体合一的特点。相关技术申报10项国家发明、实用新型专利及多项软件著作权。公司以行业创新精神和专业专注能力引领全球范围内类纸阅读电子书产业。

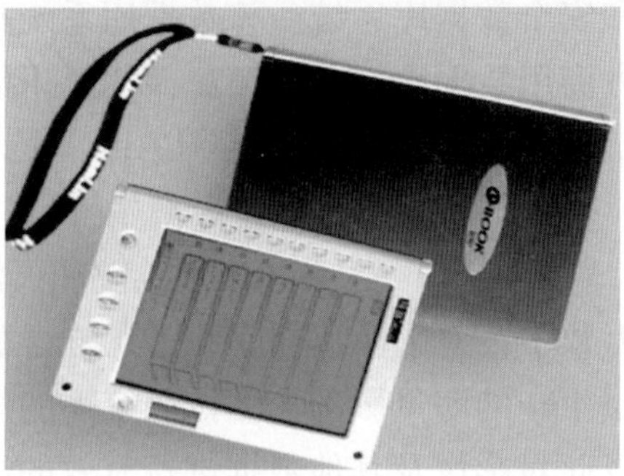

图4-1-3-32　天津津科电子公司研制的类纸电子阅读器

第四节　计算机软件

天津的计算机软件起步于上世纪80年代改革开放之初，随着计算机技术的引进和快速发展，天津大学、南开大学等高等院校建立、调整和充实计算机专业，开展软件科研和人才培养。1980年电子部在天津计算机研究所建立1000系列软件中心。与此同时，天津计算中心等单位也加强软件技术的开发应用研究。进入90年代，计算机的广泛应用，催生一批独立的软件企业服务于办公、金融、校园、商业和工业企业等领域。1996年天津市政府发布《天津市信息港工程发展纲要》，实施"2119"信息港工程和"曙光机应用示范工程"，为天津软件产业提供加快发展的机遇与平台。1998年8月，原国家科委批准成立"国家火炬计划软件产业基地——天津华苑软件园"，以新技术产业园国际创业孵化器大楼为中心，形成包括天大天财软件公司和大宇宙软件公司等为骨干的一批软件企业聚集地。2000年6月24日国务院颁布"鼓励软件产业和集成电路产业发展的若干政策"，同年11月30日天津市政府出台"关于加快软件产业发展实施意见"。自此，天津软件产业发展步入快速发展的时期。2000年的销售收入为21.2亿元，到2005年增长到108亿元，平均年增长速度为31.24%。

一、数据库

(一)目录服务系统ITEC-iDS

2001年,南开创元公司研发出目录服务系统ITEC-iDS,该系统具有通用性、高效性、安全性、可扩展性与可扩充性,以及易用性等突出特点,支持遵循LDAP协议标准的所有应用,在数据库容量、同时访问数目、应答时间等性能指标上达到国际同类产品水平。采用数字证书的身份认证和SSL的安全机制,对目录数据的访问限制可以做到目录条目的属性级。对受控应用身份信息的存储、缓存、传输、调用均采用不同手段进行安全保护。API接口支持应用系统的嵌入,支持元目录功能。通过增加应用代理,模块化地扩充功能。受控应用不需修改受控应用的源程序,用户登录受控应用的过程透明。这是国内第一套具有完全自主知识产权的LDAP目录服务系统,是中国自主研发的安全数据库产品。

(二)安全数据库系统

2001~2005年,南开创元公司研发出电子签章系统ITEC-iES,电子签章安全控件产品、通用数据库系统和安全数据库系统。该数据库系统具有防止越权访问数据和篡改数据、完善的系统审计功能、提供对第三方商用数据库的安全保密、高度的网络安全、自动防范非法用户侵入、透明性等强大功能。该系统获得中国信息安全认证中心颁发的CCIS认证证书,成为国内安全等级最高数据库。

(三)数字正射影像数据库

2005年6月,天津市测绘院和天津金宇信息技术有限公司韩振标、胡珂、贾有良、周奎等完成天津市1:1万数字正射影像数据库的研究与建立。该项目采用最先进的图像压缩技术和海量数据存储技术,将分幅分层生产的海量影像数据按照统一的规范和标准进行整理入库,将分幅的数据组织成为逻辑上无缝的整体,以此对影像及其他数据进行有效的组织和管理。为用户提供由全貌到细节、由整体到局部、由低分辨率到高分辨率快速、无缝的影像漫游、浏览、查询及其他应用。系统遵循先进性、标准化、系统性、实用性、经济性、开放性、可扩充性和安全性等原则,为宏观管理提供科学有效的依据,为政府、企业和社会提供优质服务。该课题的影像建库技术应用到天津市1:1万数字正射影像数据库、以及天津、北京、成都、苏州等多个城市的0.2米真彩色数字影像数据库。

二、应用软件

(一)公共安全

1994年,公安局人像数据库管理系统由天津市创远电脑系统发展公司和天津市公安局人口信息计算机管理系统工程领导小组办公室及天津市国安局谢睦南、甘建仁、刘文胜、曹新国等合作开发成功。该系统利用最新的图像处理技术在公安派出所人口信息管理系统中建立人口人像处理系统,提供人像的输入、变换、压缩、存贮和查询等多种功能,为公安部门维护社会治安,提高户籍管理工作水平提供服务。该系统率先采用JPEG静态图像压缩技术,压缩存储大规模大容量的人像信息并可同时处理灰度和彩色图片,在CVGA显示卡上实现图象与文字快速叠加显示,使整个系统图文合一,图像显示高速高效。图象查询接口模块使图象数据库可以与任意的系统相联接,构成各种图像应用系统。该系统的使用大大地提高公安部门办案、破案的能力和速度,为维护社会治安发挥重要作用。

1999年,天津市公安消防局与北方信息产业(天津)有限公司张学伟、莫秀忠、王文俊、王亚森等研制成功智能型"119"调度指挥系统。该系统以"SS"为模式,集计算机、网络、数据库技术,有线、无线、数据通讯技术及GPS技术于一体,实时性强、集成度高、功能完备、信息齐全、操作简便、具有较强的可推广性。系统开发严格从实战需要出发,实现尽可能降低消防一线指挥员的劳动强度,尽量减小因火警处理延迟造成国家和人民生命财产损失。

2000年,天津市交通工程科学研究所吕克逊、田建坤等运用系统工程、交通工程理论、综合计算机网络、电视监视、通讯等技术，并结合天津市道路交通特点，提出适合天津市道路和交通条件的控制战略，对自行车行车规律、绿波带控制技术、多相位控制技术、电视监控技术、通讯技术等诸多技术领域进行研究，开发成功交通控制信息管理系统。建成集交通信号控制、交通监视、交通诱导、无线指挥调度等于一体的交通控制指挥系统。

(二)南大阳光校园卡

1995年，南开大学太阳能高技术发展有限公司研发出太阳食堂自动售饭结算系统(阳光校园卡)。1996年9月天津师范大学开始使用该系统，成为天津市高校最早启用售饭自动结算系统的单位之一。阳光校园卡的使用一举解决食堂售饭使用饭菜票速度慢、不卫生以及费时费力等种种弊端。

2001年2月，南开太阳能高技术发展有限公司将该系统的信息介质改进为加密光电卡，克服IC卡、磁卡存在可读写次数低、抗磁干扰差等缺点，具有不受油、水、汽、电磁场、静电等环境影响的特点。它采用独具特色的加密技术，可以挂失或者设置违章报警。并具有DOS自主内嵌汉字系统和图形式风格的用户界面，单机联网能力可达256台窗口结算机，实时结算的联网半径达2.5千米。该软件在全国100多所高等院校、企业、国家机关等单位成功使用。

(三)"创优100+"医院信息管理系统

首佳系统工程技术有限公司成立于1998年3月，致力于医疗信息化软件的开发，开发出"创优100医院信息系统普及版"，系统采用Foxpro作为前端开发工具，服务器采用Novell 3.12网络系统。系统涵盖HIS系统的基本功能包括门诊管理、住院管理、药库管理、药房管理、病区管理、医技科室管理、手术麻醉管理、财务查询、院长查询。1999年，公司开发"创优100专业版"，功能比普及版有大幅度扩展，增加病案管理、物资管理、设备管理、人事管理、门诊部管理、护理部管理、医政管理。同时推出了门诊医生站系统。2000年，公司升级原有的系统，命名为"天卫2000"，前端工具采用第4代(4GL)开发工具PowerBuilder 6.5，后台为Windows NT 4.0，数据库采用SQL Server 6.0，全部Windows界面。并升级"创优100专业版"的所有系统，同时增加固定资产管理、供应管理等模块。2001年，公司在"天卫2000"的基础上推出"创优100+"系列产品，数据库升级到SQL Server2000，并开发出"创优100+"一日清单系统。2002年，对原有系统进行全面升级，前台开发工具由PowerBuilde 6.5升级到PowerBuilde 8.0，升级后的系统更稳定，运行速度更快。同年推出住院医生站系统和住院护士站系统。2003年，开发社保中心与HIS系统的接口，在"创优100+" 医院管理信息系统内核中为医保接口做充分准备，结合当地医保结算政策开发出不同的医保接口模式，使医院与当地的医保结算中心做到无缝结合。2004年，首佳公司引进日本龟田医疗信息研究所的国际先进技术，遵循《医院信息系统基本功能规范》等文件中对电子病历的标准规范，开发出一套真正意义完善的数据库式的电子病历。2005年，开发工具升级到PowerBuilde 10.0，数据库支持SQL Server 2005和Oracle 9i。

"创优100+"医院信息管理系统设计结构合理，功能齐全，核算清楚，运行稳定可靠、安全实用。对规范医院管理，提高医院管理水平产生重要作用。

(四)档案管理

2004年，天津市档案馆和天津七所信息技术有限公司完成网络数字化视听档案馆的研究，将现有的传统模拟音视频资源信息和卫星广播电视节目转换成数字信息，实现在网络上存储、编辑、发布、直播和应用，使档案馆在资源开发和利用上能够多方位、多角度地将多种电子档案信息在专用网甚至互联网上直播，将档案馆的概念扩展到整个城市和世界的每一个角落，同时将所有内容存储在服务器中，利用者可以在任意时间点播利用。

2005年，天津市档案局和北京北大方正电子有限公司合作开发出电子公文文档格式转换及软件，该软件基于页面描述语言的CEB版式文件技术，不仅可以描述文字、图形、图象等各种复杂的版面，还支持各种语言文字，包括蒙文、藏文等少数民族文字，适合各种版式的公文版面处理；各种文件格式转换为CEB文件后，通过同一种阅读软件即可阅读所有文件，无需配备各种编辑与阅读软件；CEB文件经加密处理，采用版面对象级的加密方法，其加密粒度小，从其他文件转换后，保持其原有版式与内容完全保真、不可篡改，满足档案“保真、保密、保存”的本质要求；CEB与XML的双向转换，存档格式CEB，对应流转格式采用XML以一种开放的、自我描述的方式定义数据结构。在描述数据内容的同时能突出对结构的描述，从而体现出数据之间的关系，与其他系统集成或对接更便捷。

（五）自动控制软件

自20世纪90年代初，南开大学袁著祉从开展发酵罐数学模型、优化操作条件与计算机控制系统研究开始，进行工业控制与管理结合的新模式的系列研究，进而实现神经网络实时控制研究。

2004年3月，南开大学陈增强、孙青林、袁著祉等完成计算机软件智能预测自适应控制器及其实现的研制，将多变量预测控制算法进行简化和解耦等处理，使得算法在所占存储空间及运算速度上均达到能在单片机上实现运行的要求，研制出多变量GPC、多变量β-GPC、多变量模糊GPC、多变量神经网络GPC等多种预测控制器的快速算法，制成软件模块，在基于单片机的嵌入式控制系统中实现。研究成果发表论文26篇，其中3篇被SCI检索、8篇被EI检索。此外，该项目还研制开发出“神经网络非线性预测控制仿真”软件包，形成自动控制算法教学和研究的实验平台，获得两项国家软件著作权登记。

（六）建筑类应用

1999年，天津大学孙济州、邢昌玉、车明等研究成功分布式虚拟现实系统技术与建筑设计应用系统，在深入研究国际最新成果的基础上，提出新的或改进的技术方案与实现算法，成果在增强生成图形、声音的真实感和加快显示与再现速度、满足虚拟场景的实时性交互以及现实虚拟环境的浸入感上起关键作用。

2001年5月，天津大学王依群、严士超、赵艳静等完成钢筋混凝土异形柱结构计算及配筋软件（CRSC）研究课题，CRSC软件输出的配筋信息完全符合《大开间住宅钢筋混凝土异形柱框轻结构技术规程》关于异形柱截面设计及结构构造各条款的要求。CRSC软件在数十个工程中采用，性能稳定、实用性强、计算速度快、用户反映良好，符合建筑结构设计软件开发要求；LCRSC软件可以与TAT、SATWE等国内主要结构空间分析软件接力运行，直接计算异形柱整体配筋，计算结果正确，配筋构造合理。

（七）体育赛事软件

1995年，天津市电子计算机研究所郑平、沈大龙、蔡连忠等开发成功第43届世乒赛计算机系统。该系统由比赛成绩处理、电子信息查询、人员注册等子系统组成。采用计算机网络与通讯技术，实现国际上先进的分布式网络体系结构。在第43届世乒赛期间，系统为人员注册、比赛抽签、场次编排、现场成绩处理、记时记分、文印、大屏幕显示、电视字幕及电子要查询等提供全面、系统的技术支持和服务，大大地提高竞赛组织、准备与现场比赛工作的效率。实现比赛成绩的动态实时传输，通过覆盖天津市的网络系统与天津和北京的远程通讯，及时地向外界发布比赛最新成绩与进展情况。第43届世乒赛组委会对该系统的可靠运行给予肯定。

三、软件出口

进入21世纪，随着留学生归国创业增多，软件出口和信息服务外包异军突起，ITO/BPO快速发展，以呼叫中心、移动通讯增值服务以及现代服务业共性服务，如人力资源外包、财务外包、IT数据管理外包等信息服务为主，逐步扩大业务流程外包（BPO）的领域和范围。2001年天津市软件园在美国硅谷和日本神户设立办事处，拉开天津软件进入国际软件市场的序幕。2002年4月天津建立华苑软件出口基地，是国内最早组建软件出口基地的城市。该基地于2003年11月14日被国家发改委、商务部和信息产业部联合批准为国家六大国家软件出口基地之一。2004年1月6日，国务院副总理吴仪向天津基地负责人马其慧授牌。同时，经科技部863专家组评审，批准天津建设国家863软件专业孵化器。在华苑软件园的发展基础上，叠加国家软件出口基地和863软件专业孵化器，三套平台无缝衔接、协同运行，标志着天津软件产业进入国家重点布局，促进天津市软件产业发展、推动软件出口、聚集软件人才，实现软件产业跨越式发展迈上一个新台阶。

自2004年初天津国家软件出口基地挂牌运作以来，在公共技术平台建设、引进人才、技术培训、举办软件国际合作论坛、以及组织企业参展参会、招商引资等方面开展大量公益性工作。同时，也为国家有关部委和天津市有关政府部门在规划研究、企业调研、出口统计等方面提供相应的服务。2000～2005年，天津软件出口从3100万美元增长到6.8亿美元，平均增长速度为49.7%，累计实现出口11.5亿美元。软件产品出口以嵌入式软件和外包加工为主，产品包括企业资源计划（ERP）、金融软件、光学字符识别（OCR）、IC设计、计算机直接制版（CTP）、游戏软件、BPO等数十种，涉及日、美、加、意、韩、新加坡、港、澳、台等国家和地区。1999～2005年，从事软件出口的企业从最初的12家增长到近百家，其中大宇宙、英业达、南开创元、飞思卡尔强芯是出口骨干企业。

图4-1-4-33　天津国家软件出口基地

2004年，市财政连续三年拨出专款，与相关部门一起建立市软件产业发展专项资金。三年中，各部门用于软件产业发展资金共1.465亿元，其中市财政6000万元，重点支持国家软件出口基地、国家“863”软件专业孵化器和软件园的公共技术与服务平台建设、科技攻关与产业化项目、信息化工程与软件产业互动、人才培养、软件出口及政策性补贴等，取得显著成效。

第五节　通信技术

1991～2005年，天津市的高水平通信技术在移动通信设备与终端方面体现在摩托罗拉公司产品上，在程控机上体现为天芝-敏迪通讯有限公司和天津日电电子通信工业有限公司（NEC）的产品上。

一、移动通信设备与终端

1992年，坐落在天津开发区的摩托罗拉公司亚洲通讯产品生产基地建成投产，是为亚洲最大的通信产品生产基地。至2000年，公司下设有手机厂、基站厂、对讲机厂和能源电子产品厂四家工厂，该生产基地成为摩托罗拉全球最先进、产量最高的通信设备和产品生产基地之一，其产品不仅供应国内市场，还远销亚太及欧美地区。

（一）手机厂

主要生产寻呼机和蜂窝电话。寻呼机有数字寻呼机、汉字寻呼机及个人信息机等，质量达世界一流水平。蜂窝电话产品由模拟到数字，有双屏到三屏，直到WAP、CDMA产品问世，生产技术及开发设计能力始终处于世界前列，产品不断推陈出新，以科技追求型、时间管理型、形象追求型及个人交往型四种不断开发新产品。

2000年12月，公司推出集手机、掌上电脑集WAP于一体的“天拓A6188”产品，具有发送图文传真，实现中英文手写识别，快速书写及级超大触摸屏、编辑修改传真等功能。此后又陆续推出A6288、A388、C289-330、V60-V70、V730、A760、MOTO RAZR V3等新产品。

（二）基站厂

是为中国地区GSM系统和CDMA系统的重要生产企业，GSM方面主要包括MCELL-61800MHZ、HORIZON900MHZ和HORIZON1800MHZ基站产品；CDMA系统主要包括CDMA基站、及CDMA基站中的BBX和MCC两类产品。

（三）对讲机厂

该厂引进世界上最先进的生产设备和管理经验，具有独立生产无线电对讲机产品及配件的能力，是生产常规和集群手持对讲机的基地。产品包括GP68、GP88S、GP300、PMUE1623A、WARIS、KARSMA等,广泛应用于铁路、公安、交通运输、旅游等行业与部门,产品质量与水平在世界居领先地位。

GP88S型无线电对讲机,为无线操作平台,其选边选件板接口允许改装,常根据行业和用户需求进行改装,复制功能是GP88S的突出特点,使工作人员现场编程成为可能,同时确保通话频率不被盗录。GP88S对讲机分为无键盘和带键盘两种机型,均拥有16信道,允许用户使用多个信道,保证多个不同场所的谈话组分别保持私密性通话。键盘型对讲机允许用户直接与固定电话网通讯。X-PAND语音压扩技术和低水平扩张功能,可降低对话噪音,使声音更清晰,更宽的覆盖频段与信道间隔调整功能,可满足各行业用户对不同频段需求,用户可根据通讯距离长短,在高/低频率发射之间,联网/中继通话之间进行转换,使用户在特殊情况下继续保持通话状态。

(四)能源电子产品厂

主要从事移动通信设备的各种充电器、电池和电源产品的设计与生产。电池产品包括95、96镍铬电池,96、97镍氢电池,99、2000锂离子电池,及新一代容量大、体积小、重量轻的锂聚合物电池。

2006年,天津摩托罗拉走到历史巅峰,销售额达到100亿美元左右,极大地提升天津电子产业的发展水平,使天津成为中国乃至世界最大的手机生产基地之一。摩托罗拉通过本地采购,促进一大批天津企业的发展,发挥产业链的聚集效应,推动天津手机产业走在全国前列,以及由此带来的出口、税收、就业的全面增长。摩托罗拉落户开发区后,形成一系列的蝴蝶效应。

二、数字程控交换机

(一)用户交换机

天津天芝-敏迪通讯有限公司,其前身天津天芝通讯有限公司于1986年7月注册成立,是专门生产数字程控用户交换机的企业,1986年被中国电子部和邮电部共同认定为引进和生产数字程控交换机的十家定点企业之一。

1986年,天芝通讯有限公司引进美国Cyber Digital公司设计生产的MSX数字时分用户程控交换机,属于第四代产品。由于技术引进消化吸收得好,天芝公司被天津市科委评为高新技术企业。1993年获得“天津市百强企业最佳经济效益第35名”。

1994年,天津天芝通讯有限公司中的美方股份被加拿大敏迪公司收购,公司更名为“天津天芝-敏迪通讯有限公司”。

天芝-敏迪从加拿大敏迪公司引进MSX-2000(Mitel SX2000)系列数字程控用户交换机和MSX-50(Mitel SX50)墙挂式数字程控用户交换机,被评为邮电部优选机型,并获得邮电部进网许可证。这两种机型在中国市场具有广泛的适用性,应用于电力、军队、武警、公安、水利、煤炭、石油、宾馆、医院、银行、厂矿、机关、学校等各行各业。

MSX-2000数字时分程控交换机也属于第四代产品,其先进性时列世界前五名。该用户交换机在世界上首次采用服务器-客户机模式的模块化全分散分布式控制结构以及光纤总线技术,功能强大、接口丰富、组网功能透明,为网络化的语音、数据、图像的综合业务通讯提供全面解决方案,单机容量2112端口,可扩展到4224端口,组网后可达到65000端口。主要功能板有主机板(Main Control),时分控制板(Peripheral Switch Control),ONS用户板 ,LS环路中继板,DNI数字用户板,E&M中继板,PRI E1,R2中国1号板。

软件基本服务功能达200余种,如呼叫转移、呼叫保持、会议电话、回叫、强插、呼叫信息显示、文字留言,并有30余种选加服务功能根据用户需要进行配置,如宾馆酒店功能、自动呼叫分配、留言信息中心、语音信箱、自动话务台、高级数据通信等功能。并具有计算机电话集成(CTI)提供计算机局域网与电话网的交互控制。

天芝敏迪公司生产国产化率较高,曾受到电子工业部和邮电部的表扬。

2002年7月,天芝-敏迪公司通过ISO 9001标准认证,并获得国家邮电通信质量体系认证中心授予的质量体系认证证书。

此后，随着通信技术的进步，用户交换机落伍，而被其他更为先进的技术产品所替代。

(二)NEC大程控交换机

1992年，中日合资的天津日电电子通信工业有限公司(NEC)成立。公司坐落在天津计算机工业小区内，主要产品：NEAX61E。日电的技术水平在当时全球市场上与西门子、贝尔公司水平相当，是三大国际品牌。NEAX61E系统有四个基本子系统组成，即应用子系统、交换子系统、处理机子系统和操作维护子系统。NEAX61E系统的结构特点是：多处理机负荷分担的分散控制、PCM时分复用的TSST交换网络、硬件和软件均采用模块化结构、全数字化的用户集线器以及符合CCITT要求的CEPT结构。公司生产规模达100万线，销售收入6~7亿元人民币，1996年实现利润过亿元。公司还开设应用软件培训基地，为用户进行系统应用的培训。1998年产品升级为NEAX61，增加带宽，可实现VOD点播。随着国产化进度加快，逐步有40%以上的零部件在本地采购，带动天津市相关产业的发展。

第六节　图像处理

1991~2005年，天津市在信息科技领域的图像处理方面深入开展探索。图像显示的基础性研究以天津大学为主，围绕高清晰彩色电视的机理展开，取得系列成果；图像显示的应用性研究以南开大学为主，取得丰富成果，而以母国光研制出用于航空侦察彩色摄影的编码系统和光学解码仪及计算机数字解码系统最为突出。

一、图像显示的基础性研究

1992~1993年，天津大学李华、滕建辅、赵宇、俞斯乐研究用于HDTV的非递归正交镜像滤波器设计。课题组提出一种用窗函数进行QMF优化设计方法，并给出两个具体QMF设计例子。

1998年，天津大学王少勇、王金刚、王兆华开展HDTV视频解码器中系统控制的分析与实现研究，详细分析为实现高性能的系统控制功能所采用的一系列先进技术，包括拆包处理、码率缓存器管理、音视频同步和视频显示缓存控制等，最后给出一套完整的硬件实现方案及其相应的调试、验证方法。

1997~1999年，天津大学李桂苓、郑荣林、程宇新等开展对HDTV(高清晰度电视)测试码流发生系统的研究，实现将存于计算机硬盘的软件编码HDTV数据流转换成串行码流、码率范围可程控、有顺序和循环工作方式、硬件为计算机插卡，在TCL等单位得到应用。

1998~1999年，天津大学国狄非、国澄明、赵宇航等研制完成在TMS320C80上实现H.263编解码器，通过改进，并结合TMS320C80的软硬件特性对具体模块进行优化。通过在TMS320C80软件开发板上进行仿真实验表明，该方案完成H.263全双工实时视频编解码的要求。

1999年，天津大学刘开华、国澄明、秦好亮研究HDTV图像数据结构变换的数学模型与电路实现。课题组开发出一种适用于MPEG-2标准MP@H-1440级数字HDTV图像的数据结构变换数学模型及电路的实现方法。该模型与电路被成功地应用于国内第一台数字高清晰度电视功能样机系统的开路演示，表明模型建立正确、电路工作稳定，各项性能指标均达到要求。该模型与电路的设计思想对其他格式的图像数据结构变换有重要参考价值。

1998~2000年，天津大学李桂苓、王楠楠、徐岩等开展MPEG-2系统运动图像质量评价技术的研究，结合MPEG-2系统特点和人的视觉特性，在三维加权信噪比和三维加权块效应等方面取得理论和实用价值的成果。实验表明，加权处理后的客观测试指标比常用的物理峰值信噪比与主观评价结果的相关性更高。

二、图像显示的应用性研究

图 4-1-6-34 南开大学母国光(中)在实验室工作

1992~2000年,南开大学母国光、方志良、翁志成等开展白光信息处理用于航空侦察彩色摄影的光学/数字技术及其设备的研究和开发,以白光富里叶光学信息处理的彩色编码与解码技术为基础,研制用于航空侦察彩色摄影的编码相机和光学解码仪及计算机数字解码系统。研制的航空编码相机,通过三色光栅彩色编码器将拍摄的彩色图象编码记录在黑白底片上,将黑白编码片置于大幅面彩色图象光学解码仪中,经富里叶变换及频谱彩色滤波,解码再现彩色图象,亦可将黑白编码片数字化输入计算机,经数字运算解码再现彩色图象,由电视监视器显示,并打印出彩色相片。这项技术利用黑白胶片幅面大、分辨率高、信息量大和无褪色问题的优点,又能记录和再现彩色信息,提高对目标分辨能力,达到数字化图象处理,便于图象的传输和网络化。

2003年,中国船舶重工集团公司第七〇七研究所杨功流、陈超英、何河通等开发出一套能直接使用标准格式数字海图的电子海图显示信息系统,可以直接调用中国标准的MVCF格式的数字海图,无须进行格式转换,符合中国电子海图的相关标准,系统广泛装备于多种舰船上。

2004年8月,南开大学王庆人、靳简明、史广顺完成数学公式图像识别与理解的研究项目。该项目在世界上率先实现完整演示数学公式处理功能的系统,在处理上首次提出采用Parzen窗定位独立公式以及通过检测二维结构定位内嵌公式的方法;采用统计特征与结构特征相结合,先识别再验证的一般符号识别方法,取得比单一方法更高的识别率;提出识别公式类型,并分解其为一系列子表达式的公式版式识别方法,为此定义11种基本公式类型,并用产生式规则限定每类公式的唯一分解方法,该方法能够分析的公式类型,比以往方法都丰富;实现公式分析结果的LATEX格式输出;提出基于树匹配的公式处理自动性能评估方法,是唯一能够发现公式符号切割、识别以及公式分析中产生的任意错误的评估方法。研究成果建立300页样本库,完成Page级数学公式自动处理原型系统的研发,建立产品级应用的基础。

2005年,南开大学翟宏琛、梁艳梅、王熠等完成智能化复杂彩色形态信息的整体提取和识别的研究。该项目采用彩色直方图作为彩色图像特征参数,将模糊相关计算方法应用于对彩色图像进行的检索和识别中,提出在计算相关的求和过程中引进非线性加权因子的算法,对感兴趣的特征色赋予特定的求和权重,使检索能针对检索目的或待检索图像的内容得到优化,大大提高检索系统的色彩畸变不变的检索能力及对具有局部色彩特征的图像的检索能力。此外,还提出表达图像中特定区域内点分布信息的形态描述矩阵方法,提出基于形态描述矩阵和彩色直方图的整体描述彩色图像色彩内容及位置匹配程度的广义彩色直方图方法,能够更有效地进行彩色图像的检索和识别。研究成果应用于智能化自动图像识别、检索、跟踪、过滤及其分析等方面。

第七节 信息安全

1991~2005年,天津市关于信息安全的研究,在编码技术、计算机病毒防治、加密技术与档案中的数字签名分别取得有价值的系列成果。以南开大学完成的多项关于商务安全支撑平台和电子商务加密交易系统为突出。

2005年,为适应严峻的信息安全的需要,由国家计算机病毒应急中心牵头,联合包括南开大学、天津大学在内的多家京津相关单位在天津成立计算机病毒防治技术国家工程研究中心。

一、编码技术研究

1999年6月,天津师范大学武金木申请的专利“排列码加密解密方法及其排列码加密解密器”获得专利授权。该专利系由一种排列码加密解密方法及其排列码加密解密器,排列码加密解密器由排列码加密器和排列码解密器构成,其中密钥处理器相同。排列码加密解密的方法是在密钥寄存器RS的输入端输入密钥Key后,通过运算器ALU的运算,密码Key与译码控制寄存器的输出构成排列码;在加密处理器中,其排列码控制译码器使D11′、D12′…、D1n′是D11、D12…、D1 n ′的一个排列;在解密处理器中,其排列码也控制译码器使D21′、D 22、…、D 2 n是D21′、D22′…、D2n′的一个排列。该发明加密强度高、速度快、密钥更换容易、破译难、成本低,可用于任何数字数据传输和存储的地方。2004年7月后,武金木申请的“一种快速除法器”“第一种除数是15×2n的快速除法器”“第二种除数是15×2n的快速除法器”等6种专利获批准公开。该除法器结构简单,使用的元器件少、造价低。在某些特殊场合下有不可替代的作用,广泛运用于数字信号处理系统中。

2005年,南开大学符方伟、沈世镒、陈鲁生等完成等重码在信息传输和存储系统中的应用与性能分析项目。课题研究包括设A(n,d,w)码,n、d、w为码长、码距和码重,研究极小距离不小于d的二元等重码的最大码字数目;确定A(n,d,w)的精确值或推导好的上下界,并且构造相应的最优等重码;研究等重码的不可检错误概率,并且寻找最佳检错等重码,确定等重码的检错阈值;研究具有某种特殊结构的等重码(特别是平衡码)的构造,快速编译码方法的设计,并且要求所设计的等重码具有一定的检错和纠错能力。

二、计算机病毒防治技术研究

1996年,天津市公安局与天津市技术监督局在国内建立唯一的计算机病毒防治产品检验中心(天津市质量检验站第70站),承担对在国内销售的计算机病毒防治产品的质量检验认证工作。该中心建立以来,对国内外十多个病毒防治产品进行质量检验工作,并建立国内计算机病毒标准样本库,填补一项空白。在检验工作中,该中心积累大量的计算机病毒的技术资料,在对流行的计算机病毒深入了解的基础上,先后编制起草公安部公共安全行业标准《DOS操作系统环境下计算机病毒检测方法》《计算机病毒防治产品评级准则》和《计算机病毒库建立准则》。1997年,参加公安部全国计算机安全培训教材的编写工作,于1998年由群众出版社出版发行。

2000年到来之际,国外黑客组织宣称要在新世纪交替之时,通过国际互联网释放大量病毒和有害程序,干扰、破坏世界的计算机网络。该检验中心通过监控获知这种情况,及时上报公安部,建议组织国内所有计算机病毒防治产品生产厂家,组建中国2000年计算机病毒应急中心,该建议得到批准,从而开展对国内的计算机网络和信息系统的运行情况进行24小时的监控,保障2000年的顺利过渡。

2000年8月,国家信息化工作领导小组计算机网络与信息安全管理办公室和公安部公共信息网络安全监察局的领导对天津计算机病毒防治产品检验中心进行考察后决定,在该中心的基础上,建立国家计算机病毒应急处理中心。该中心的主要工作任务是充分调动国内防病毒力量,快速发现病毒疫情、快速发应、快速处置,防止计算机病毒对全国的计算机网络和信息系统造成重大破坏。

2005年2月,由国家计算机病毒应急处理中心为牵头单位,联合南开大学、天津大学和北京瑞星科技股份有限公司、北京启明星辰信息技术有限公司共同组建计算机病毒防治技术国家工程研究中心。该中心负责对计算机病毒入侵事件进行预警,提高国内对计算机病毒的防范能力;为国内计算机网络提供主动控制与管理技术,遏制计算机病毒在网络中的蔓延,保障国家信息化基础设施的安全运行;加强计算机病毒防治关键技术的研究,研发计算机病毒防治高端产品和新产品,促进全国计算机病毒防治产品的产业化;提供计算机病毒防治培训、系统评估等服务,推进国际技术交流与合作。

三、加密技术

2002年9月,天津南开戈德集团有限公司完成二维码加密识别技术及其应用研究,该数据加密技术采用分组加密体制,引进多种密码技术,形成难以破解的独特算法。所开发的应用系统包括通用证卡制作平台系统、货币二维码信息管理系统两个子项目。该项研究还开发出适用于不同行业的基于二维码识别的应用系统,以满足不同用户需求。

2002年12月,天津大学研发成功用于多媒体信息认证的脆弱数字水印技术。该技术包括空间域数字图像真实性、完整性认证算法;适应JPEG压缩标准的DCT(离散余弦变换)数字图像真实性、完整性认证算法;适应JPEG2000压缩标准的小波域数字图像真实性、完整性认证算法。课题组还开发出用于中文PDF文档真实性、完整性认证的数字水印算法。

2003年,南开大学和戈德防伪技术有限公司合作完成商务安全支撑平台的研究。该项目提出任务处理单元的新概念,以此构造通用CSCW系统体系结构,建立Petri网协作模型,推进CSCW研究;提出以欧氏弹性距离为选择伙伴的多目标遗传算法的适应函数的新算法;改进工作流Petri网模型,实现工作流仿真和诊断、冗余检验、预估性能的算法,创新实现工作流动态调整和配置;在工作流仿真中引入蚂蚁算法,开辟新研究方法,使工作流系统具有自学习和自修整的功能,填补工作流仿真的空白。该项目取得一系列的原创成果,对CSCW的理论研究有重大推进意义。对协作系统的体系结构设计、安全访问信息、工作流仿真、诊断等的实现具有指导意义,尤其是实现工作流的配置、修改、工作流仿真等,为应用系统的用户提供工作流故障诊断和冗余检测的方法。

2003年11月,南开大学辛运帏、卢桂章、刘景泰等共同研究完成应用于电子商务的加密交易系统研究。成果包括提出包含身份认证中心、交易中心及加密模块在内的加密交易系统的系统架构,并在Windows平台下开发出一个加密交易平台,为电子商务中的双方提供在网上自由安全地进行贸易谈判的环境;基于Windows平台、使用面向对象技术开发的加密模块,采用混合加密机制,配合身份认证中心,可以完成网上信息的加密、解密及数字签名和验证操作;按照国际标准化组织制订的X.509标准,开发CA中心,负责为用户发放数字身份证书,认证中心证书数据库采用商用数据库软件,数据记录容量仅受机器配置及运行环境的限制;交易中心采用目录管理方式,用户可以在交易中心内发布信息、选择交易对象、进行加密交易谈判,直到最终签订电子合同。项目完成的加密交易系统实现城市流通领域、政府办公系统等涉及信息加密传送的应用。

2004年6月,天津大学孙济洲、李明楚、车明等共同研究完成大规模网络入侵检测与战略预警系统。该成果提出新的二维总体模型的设计方案;提出自适应重组的实现方法和用分布式并行计算提高系统性能的策略;提出虚拟分布式“蜜罐”(Honey Pot)欺骗技术的思想;提出分布式入侵攻击源反向追踪的解决方案;提出分布式互动代理的概念并在此基础上提出使用手持无线移动设备实时控制NIDS的设计方案;将智能分词技术应用于入侵日志数据检索,提高检索的速度和准确度;提出NIDS可视化的概念并构建NIDS可视化模型。

2005年1月,南开大学刁成嘉、邵秀丽、白刚等完成具有反攻击能力的双向指纹校验密钥系统的研究。该系统具有反攻击能力的双向指纹校验密钥系统使网络间传送的信息(如电子邮件),能够执行双向指纹校验。这样不仅可以有效地保护被传送的信息本身不被攻击,而且还可以有效地检测出入侵攻击者通过某种方法控制信息的发送端或接收端。双向指纹校验技术实现防止攻击者修改用户接收程序的执行代码,大大提高网络信息安全水平。

四、数字签名

2004年,天津市档案局与天津工程机械研究院、天津商学院合作完成数字签名和工程图纸整合技术在CAD图纸档案管理中的应用研究。项目形成两项成果:一是一个具有128位密钥长度的数字签名系统,可以完成公钥和私钥的生成、数字签名及认证,并将数字签名技术与工程设计的电子文档进行整合,实现电子档案管理的安全目的;二是开发基于STEP标准的工程图纸明细表管理系统软件,可以对CAD电子文档进行有效的数据筛选、材料汇总、图纸查询和项目管理。项目在AUTOCAD软件平台上，开发工程图纸明细表汇总系统，对CAD电子文档的工程信息进行筛选和图纸查询，有效地完成产品的材料汇总、项目和图纸管理。

2005年，天津市档案局和铁道部第三勘察设计院联合开发出电子CAD文档网络数字认证和多重签名系统，包括签名模板生成及管理系统、CAD图纸签名系统、CAD图纸临时签名系统三个应用软件，成功地解决工程图档CAD文件按国家档案法的要求直接归档和电子文件作为档案进行管理与使用所必须解决的关键技术问题，对逐步甩掉纸介质图库，实现档案管理现代化和电子签名技术在生产和管理中广泛应用具有重要意义。

第八节 信息网络系统

天津大学在天津市最早开展Internet（互联网）接入和相关服务。1995年3月，天津大学校园网连接到北京大学网络中心，实现与Cernet和Internet的全业务连接，在全国大学之中是第五个，在天津市是第一个。此前，天津大学舒炎泰、来可伟教授等组建天津大学网络中心，服务于天津大学的师生员工，并为天津市的其他高校和单位提供网络技术服务。

一、网络互联技术

1992年，天津市公安局和天津大学徐汉申、许林英、李建、滑建忠等合作完成异种网互联涉外信息网络系统。项目在已有的全国公安远程网与各宾馆中互不相同的网络系统及异型机间建立互联网络，实现天津市涉外暂住人员信息管理现代化。系统符合国家标准及国际网络发展趋势、完全汉化的开放互联系统；各子系统具备可相互任意互联的通用接口，各子系统间连接方式灵活，采用动态网络服务技术，不需要附加专门网络服务器和网络板卡等任何网络硬件，采用全软件方式互联，节省开支。网络互连功能齐全，具有双向拷贝文件、虚拟远程终端、远程系统命令、本地系统命令、邮包发送、为远程的互联要求提供动态服务器功能，并在任何符合国际标准的系统上移植。

1997年，天津中环电子计算机公司在第一代机顶盒的设计工作的基础上，完成第二代机顶盒的研究，该产品定位于家庭普及型的新一代产品，从印刷线路板到电源等设计上和原件的选型上，都突出先进性、可靠性，易操作。

2003年，天津大学井文才、张以谟、周革等完成光纤互连及其检测技术的理论与实验研究。该项目通过采用时分复用和硬件路由技术，实现计算机PCI总线间峰值速率下的虚拟并行光纤互连；采用时分复用和波分复用相结合的方法，设计完成硬件路由和波长路由相结合的分层光互连网络结构，提高网络的数据吞吐率，扩展网络的规模；提出并设计完成多种光互连相关器件方案；采用联合变换相关技术及白光干涉技术，对光纤内部缺陷进行高精度检测，提出相应的高精度检测算法并设计完成检测系统。发表论文被SCI收录22篇、被EI收录46篇。

二、局域网的建设

1995年，南开大学吴功宜、曹勇、徐敬东等研究智能局域网，在研究方向上，开辟一个新的领域。成果对该领域中的重要概念进行严格的科学定义，提出相应的实现方法。在局域网智能化管理问题上提出分层的体系结构模型，指出智能化局域网管理系统应由三部分组成：网络管理实体层、集成网络管理层、网络管理决策层。研究网络设计、网络规划、性能监控与故障诊断等专家系统的设计方法。并独立设计完成NKNet-

Watch V1.0网络监控软件包的研制与应用。

2001年,数字化天津开发区建设取得成效,企事业信息化工程获突破性进展。宽带网建设基本完工,形成区内环路,政府、企业、教育机构、各居民小区相继铺设宽带网,使开发区拥有一流的信息化基础设施。电子政务项目取得突破性进展。电子政务网(Teda. gov. cn)的投入使用,提高泰达机关的服务质量。并顺利建成地理信息系统(GIS)客户管理系统(CRM)等重要项目互联网数据中心(IDC)。

2001年6月,天津市电信公司建成天津滨海宽带网。在天津市率先实现千兆到小区、百兆到企业和楼栋、十兆到用户桌面的目标,采用IP接入方式,出口带宽达到310兆字节,于年底达到2.5千兆字节带宽,是天津第一家直接登录国家骨干网的网络。该宽带网覆盖整个滨海新区,接入网进入9个住宅小区。滨海新区管委会、开发区管委会、滨海石油、泰达学院等7个单位的局域网和200多户个人用户均接入滨海宽带网。用户通过宽带网,不但大大提高上网速度,而且可以进行互动式的可视业务,如网络会议、网络远程医疗、网络教学、视频点播等等。电信公司利用宽带网对环境监控、网上银行、网上报税、虚拟泰达、网上电视等项目的尝试也获得成功。

第九节 计算机应用系统工程

信息技术代表着当今先进生产力的发展方向,深刻地影响着经济社会发展的变革。1991~2005年,为推广应用信息技术,天津先后启动"三金工程"、信息港工程、曙光机应用示范工程、制造业信息化工程、智能化小区示范工程等,采取政府搭台市场运作的方式,集中资源,在政务、金融、港口、税务、商业、科教、工业企业等有关部门和单位推动信息化建设,取得显著成效。

一、三金(金卡、金桥、金关)工程

1997年8月28日天津市银行卡交换中心开通运行。按照国务院"金卡办"和中国人民银行总行的要求,天津市信息化办公室会同中国人民银行天津分行协调组织工商银行、建设银行、农业银行和交通银行等行的天津分行,共同出资组建成立"天津市银行卡交换中心"。该中心的建立为广大信用卡用户提供异行使用的环境,使不同行的信用卡,可在同一POS机、ATM机及其他机具上实现提取现金、持卡消费和转账等应用,并通过与国家银联中心联网,可使天津市的信用卡用户实现在全国各地跨行跨省的各种消费,为实现"一卡在手,走遍全国"奠定基础。

金桥工程是以建设中国重要的信息化基础设施为目的的跨世纪重大工程,是"天地一体化"的网络结构,天网(卫星网)和地网(光纤网)在统一网管系统下实行互联互通,具有互操作性、互为补充、互为备用,是中国的信息通道。金桥工程包括金桥地面骨干网项目、金桥卫星通信网项目、金桥无线移动数据用户接入网项目、金桥光纤城域用户接入网项目、金桥网络电话/传真项目、金桥Internet信息服务项目、国有大型企业综合信息网技术改造项目等。天津是国家确定的首批建设金桥网络分中心的24个省(市)之一。

1995年,天津市信息中心与国家吉通通讯公司共同组建天津市金桥网络工程公司,全面负责天津金桥工程建设工作。该工程于1998年全面完成,建成天津市金桥区域网络分中心,实现与国家信息中心联网,与中央部委专用网互联,与国内30个省、自治区、直辖市和500个中心城市、12000个大中型企业连接,并与Internet联通。金桥工程为经济和社会信息资源共享以及建设电子信息市场创造条件,金桥工程中建立的信息交换平台,为实现网络增值服务提供条件,推动全国电子信息产业加快发展。

1998年7月14日 天津市"金桥工程"工作会议召开。三年来天津市实施"金桥工程"项目383项,完成305项,创经济效益6亿元。

2001~2002年，天津港务局的信息化建设取得突破性进展。天津港坚持“统一规划、面向应用、重点突出、联合开发、统一标准、资源共享”的信息化建设指导方针，完成“办公自动化”“光缆基础网络”“集装箱码头管理现代化”“物资信息管理系统”等重点建设项目。船舶调度系统、货源系统、煤炭系统、焦碳系统，生产统计、海关电子舱单报关系统、海关放行核销系统、EDI标准报文传输等的相关应用系统切换到光缆网正式运行。EDI示范工程的实施，实现舱单、船图的电子数据在船代、码头、理货、海关等单位间的多向流转，提高各单位的业务处理效率；开通与外国船舶公司的EDI业务，增加对船舶公司的多项增值服务，实现集装箱运输业务与国际接轨；统一、规范集装箱EDI报文标准，完成部标报文与国际标准报文之间的相互转换，大大地改善口岸软环境。集装箱公司引进国际先进的集装箱码头操作管理软件和具有世界先进水平、功能强大的计算机服务器群、千兆有线网络和无线网络系统，加快与国际集装箱运输体系接轨的步伐，大大增强在国内港口群中的竞争力，确保天津港集装箱枢纽港的地位。一公司、二公司完成集装箱码头实时管理系统，在生产中产生效益；箱货公司实现集装箱堆场、计费、仓储管理等无纸化，车载控制管理实现堆场集装箱作业的实时控制，加快集装箱的周转，提高集装箱堆场的利用率；储运公司集装箱堆场管理系统中引进箱号和车号的自动识别技术，大大提高集装箱运输的管理水平；GPS定位车辆监控调度系统的运行，实现集装箱运输的全程跟踪。

2003年1月，由天津海关和天津移动通信公司共同建设的天津数字化海关工程，开通海关系统内的移动虚拟网，实现诸多移动办公功能的短信手段开始应用。天津数字化海关工程以涵盖数据通信、信息服务、增值业务的全数据观念为基础，利用天津移动通信公司的移动通信网络、移动智能网及移动互联网，实现海关的要求提供IP话音业务、数据业务、互联网接入及其他特定的应用一体化的技术目标。天津数字化海关将现代化移动通信的最新技术和移动互联网资源应用于管理，实现海关内部办公和对外服务的信息化，提高对外服务质量，树立天津海关服务领先、技术领先的优势，该工程的建设为天津海关建成国内最好的海关、带动天津及周边地区的经济发展、实现经济效益和社会效益的多赢打下良好的基础。

二、信息港工程

1996年6月，天津市成立市信息化领导小组，办公室设在科委。同年，信息化办组织专家和有关部门编制《天津市信息港工程规划纲要》，总体目标是要用15年时间，把天津市建设成为中国北方信息港，国内主要的信息中心和重要的信息制造业基地，使天津市成为具有较高信息化水平的国际大都市。这是天津市第一个全面提高经济和社会信息化程度的规划，并启动带有标志性的信息港“2119”工程建设，即建设公共通信和信息交互两个网；以曙光机推广应用起步，全面推动经济、政务、税收征管等11个计算机应用系统建设；开发科教、金融、人才等9类信息资源库。到2000年信息港工程总体框架基本筑就：全市光缆干线达7000多公里，比1996年增加75%，网络总流量增长达到4500千兆字节；市装机容量305万门、移动电话200万门、有线电视用户近130万户；建成天线直径16米的国际A类和B类通信卫星地面站；全市计算机拥有量达84万台，城市居民每百户拥有个人计算机15.2台；全市信息交互网建成，初步实现“同城信息，本地交换”，因特网用户超过57万户。11个应用系统全部实施，其中政务、金融、科教等9个系统实现开通；发布天津电子商务发展总体框架；一批电子商务网站开通并投入运营。9类信息资源库建设初步实现网上共享，信息港工程的实施带动全市信息化的快速发展。2001年4月，原隶属科委的信息化办公室改组为天津市政府直属信息化办公室，标志着天津信息化建设迈上一个新台阶。“十五”期间，信息化建设全面发展，圆满完成“1221”计划(即一个通讯网络平台、电子政务与电子商务两个平台、以及包括政务、金盾、金农、金卡等金字号工程和其他面向企业和社会的总计21个应用系统)，信息基础设施建设快速发展，以光纤为主、无线为辅、立体交叉的城市宽带王建成，光纤达68.2万千米，通信能力城乡覆盖达到100%。与2000年相比，宽带城域网核心交换能力从20G增长到2000G，城市出口带宽从955兆字节增长到121千兆字节，互联网用户从56.9万户增长到340万户其中，宽带用户从无到90万户。固定电话用户从247万户增长到437.2万户；移动电话用户从122.8万户增长到502万户。信息基础设施的发展，为经济和社会加快发提供技术支持和更高的平台。

同期，天津市关于信息化的软科学研究十分活跃。

1997年，天津市科学技术信息研究所余学林、刘文成、万家泰等开展天津联科信息网络系统研究。课题组对全市信息需求和发展的实际需要进行研究，提出网络系统的建设原则、功能、目标结构和服务方式，筛选出天津市需要并可能获取的信息资源，提出网络系统中心——计算机的选型和配置，提出建设“联科LINK信息网”的实施方案，启动网络建设、开展服务，为与国际信息网络接轨创造奠定基础。

1998年，由张峻屹牵头，天津市科学技术评价中心、天津市人民政府研究室、天津市信息化工作领导小组办公室和天津市发展计划委员会合作完成天津市启动信息港建设的思路与对策研究。课题对信息港建设的战略目标、总体思路、实施方案、技术路线、支撑环境及配套政策等方面进行全面系统的研究，阐述信息港建设带动天津信息产业发展、推动传统产业技术改造、加快全市信息化进程的战略与策略，并从加快宏观调控、建立和健全运行机制、抓关键技术开发带动产业发展、人才队伍建设及营造环境等五个主要问题提出具体的对策建议。

2000年，天津市南开区信息网络中心韩树森、刘秋平、王建国等开发成功宽带多媒体城域网分配与接入技术。南开示范区建设是天津信息港工程的重点示范项目，其主要内容是建成宽带多媒体综合信息网络和网管中心，建设小区社区服务接入网和应用系统。建成一条能够覆盖全区20多万用户的宽带多媒体综合信息网，连接100多个居民小区，并为市政府和和平区提供接口。建立几十个web站点，基本建成政务公开、民政服务、寻医问药、应急服务等16个社区服务的应用系统。通过VSAT（甚小天线地球站）接入中国科技网成为中国科技网的分中心；用光纤实现与天津交互网、天津联通网和中国教育科研网等网络的互连互通，为用户提供互联网、DNS（域名系统）、电子邮件和VPN（虚拟专用网络）及视频服务等。

2005年，由徐梦苏主持，天津市电子计算机研究所与天津市政府办公厅共同编制完成协同办公、目录服务及资源应用平台软件包。该项目参照LDAP（轻量目录访问）协议，完成信息模型、命名模型、功能模型、安全模型设计，自主研发邮件地址目录服务和应用目录服务；自主研发的中间件，能提供完整的软件平台的支撑功能；自主研发的“手迹留痕处理”技术，具有创新性，且符合国家相关的信息安全规定。该成果在应用层的开发与国务院规定的防火墙安全策略相匹配，专用文件传输协议字迹留痕平滑流畅，保持原形，防伪，防粘贴，能缩放和打印。该系统是全国首批投入实际使用的可发布、发现、控制和管理的目录服务系统之一。

三、曙光机工程

曙光计算机是中国高技术研究发展计划信息领域“863”的重大成果，是具有自主知识产权的高性能计算机。面对国内高性能计算机市场被外国品牌一统天下的局面，为推动国产服务器产业化，1996年12月原国家科委将曙光计算机应用示范（天津）工程列为国家六个重大科技产业工程计划项目之一，委托天津市科委组织实施。过两年努力，天津市全面完成一期工程的各项任务，在税务、商业、科教、外经贸四个信息港工程系统中共应用曙光机222台，开发基于曙光计算机的应用软件模块61种，在近百个企事业单位使用中，曙光机运行情况良好，各项技术指标及机器性能均满足用户要求，与国外同类产品相比具有较好的性能价格比。该项目荣获2000年度国家科技进步二等奖，获奖人：寇纪淞、马其慧、韩维恒等。

天津市税务系统由天大天财公司承担，按照国家税务总局提出的整体规划，配合国家“金税工程“，以曙光计算机为服务器的网络系统下，采用先进的客户机/服务器结构，开发同时满足国税、地税要求的税收征管系统，项目包括数据采集、管理服务、发票管理、征收管理、滞补罚管理、综合查询、稽查、统计、税法宣传和法规档案管理9个子系统，选用MS Windows NT Server 3.51和MS SQL Server6.0系统软件，采用基于精减指令集（RISC）技术的PCower PC中央处理器和具有磁盘阵列的双机容错系统，以纳税申报和优质服务为基础，集中征收，重点稽查，实现税收管理各个环节的计算机化，并保证系统的运算速度、安全性和可靠性。实

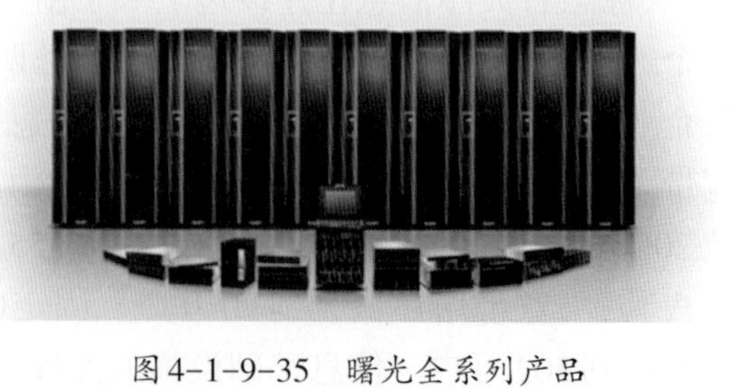

图4-1-9-35 曙光全系列产品

现电子化申报后，使纳税时间由原来的20分钟缩短到1分钟以内，提高税收征收统计的及时性和准确性，并遏制个别不法企业欠税以及加强依法办事、依率稽征，同时节省50%的税务干部，用以加强稽查等环节。天津税务系统在国内率先实现统一硬件平台、统一软件、统一国地税软硬件支持的“三统一”目标。

商贸自动化系统的建设由天津计算中心和天津计算所承担，建立基于曙光计算机的商贸自动化系统开发环境，完成12个大中型商场、连锁超市、酒店和区县商委系统的4个专题的应用软件开发，包括前台POS机收款、商品编码、进货管理、物价管理、销售统计、库存管理、财务管理和人事管理等子系统，实现商业物流、资金流、信息流和人力资源的计算机管理。商业电子化规范商业企业的内部管理，有效地杜绝货款流失，还大大提高劳动效率和人员素质，增强企业的声誉，提高市场竞争力，为商业发展注入新的活力。

天津科研教育网由南开大学、天津大学和天津科技信息所承担，建成基于曙光机的“同城信息，本地交换”交互网。网上信息资源包括4类静态科技数据库、8类动态科技数据库、31万条图书书目库和200条期刊库，此外还有8000多种西文科技人文期刊，与全市20多所科研机构和大专院校连通，实现全天候使用。

外经贸EDI（电子数据交换）服务系统由外经贸委信息中心承担，建成基于曙光机的EDI网络系统环境和数据库，包括用户认证、信息发布、信息查询、国际国内信息资源库、外经贸法律法规库和电子商务日志处理，系统采用Web/Broser方式，实现上与国家外经贸委相联，下与全市各外贸公司互连互通，为用户提供各种有关外经贸信息服务，为进一步实现电子商务打下基础。

1999年1月19日科技部副部长惠永正带专家组到津验收，对天津示范工程给予很高评价，专家组认为天津市在曙光计算机应用上成功探索出一条国产高性能计算机硬件与国产软件捆绑发展民族信息产业之路。

曙光计算机应用示范（天津）二期工程在邮政电子化和农村信息化方面继续推广应用曙光计算机机，也取得明显的应用效果。

第十节 制造业信息化工程

天津市作为工业城市在国内较早启动计算机在制造业应用。1985年成立CAD研究会，开展计算机辅助设计（CAD）、计算机集成制造系统（CIMS）相关技术的应用研究。1995年“轧钢三厂型钢一分厂CIMS工程”在市科委立项，是天津市第一个企业实施的CIMS项目。1996年后，天津市加大企业应用CAD、CIMS、RPM等共性关键技术的支持力度，相继启动天津市CAD应用工程、天津市CIMS应用示范工程和建立快速原型生产力促进中心（天津）。1997年国家科技部批准天津市成为国内首批CIMS应用示范省市。1998年天津汽车暖风机CIMS工程荣获科技部颁发的“863计划CIMS主题先进集体”的优秀工程荣誉。示范工程在天津企业信息化中起到积极推动作用。

1997~2000年，天津市CAD、CIMS应用示范工程，带动示范企业实现工业增加值20多亿元。企业应用促进国内相关软件开发、系统集成以及咨询服务产业化的发展，催生10余家专业软件服务企业。全市企业装机国内正版CAD软件2000余套、自主开发的ERP、PDM等软件在国内50余家企业得到应用，还进入OTIS公司、NEC公司等一些国际著名企业做技术开发与服务。CIMS咨询服务辐射广东科龙、兰州石化等众多家国内著名企业。

2001~2005年，天津市在企业基础信息化示范的基础上，进一步完善技术服务体系，拓展企业应用示范和开展具有前瞻性技术开发与应用示范三个层面上开展工作。2001年天津市科委、经委和信息化办联合发文《关于制造业信息化工程的实施意见》，为制造业信息化工作创造良好环境，并提供政策支持。2002年成立全国第一家制造业信息化生产力促进中心，加强制造业信息化发展战略研究和工程项目的咨询、监理、培训和技术服务。300家企业实施信息化应用示范，国产软件的应用率达到50%以上，推动企业新产品率达到

30%以上，培训各种层次的企业信息化人才5万人次以上。2002年5月国家科技部批准天津市为全国首批制造业信息化示范城市。

一、计算机辅助设计（CAD）

1996年，天津11家CAD示范企业覆盖汽车、电子、化工、机械和工程建设等重点行业，其企业劳动生产率平均提高170%；新产品设计周期缩短45%；设计创产值平均提高97%，经济综合效益显著。

2000年，重点推动机电、汽车行业100家企业开展三维CAD应用开发，并在其中遴选20家重点示范企业，向集成应用发展。天津汽车模具有限公司全面推广三维CAD设计，完善基于主流设计平台的模板化模具设计标准件数据库，实现拉延、修边、翻边模具快速模板化设计，不仅提升设计手段，而且减少结构设计和铸件制造中的失误。通过无图化生产的实现，生产能力2002年新增产值比2001年增长46%；合同额增长18%；生产计划制定时间由2天缩短为2小时；采购计划制订时间由2天缩短为1小时；产品设计正确率，主要是模具明细表的正确率提高到95%，交货率提高到85%，模具设计制造周期由8个月缩短为7个月，减少资金占用500万左右。

2001年，继续推动轻工、模具、服装等行业100家企业的CAD应用工程。一些传统企业通过改组、改造，形成良好的运行机制，CAD的应用提高企业响应市场的能力。隆庆集团是天津市轻工行业传统企业改造而成，其CAD应用工程促进企业技术创新能力，CAD普及率由原来的35%上升为85%。2000年共用CAD设计新产品109种，企业经济效益显著提高。

到2002年，机电行业的CAD普及率由原来不足40%提高至88%。天津锻压机床厂与天津大学合作开发CAD设计模块软件，设计一台世界最大吨位——万吨级锻压机，由原来需要4个月，缩短到20天，不仅中标国内万吨级锻压设备的设计与生产，产品还出口美国。

2001～2005年，天津市依托制造业信息化生产力中心等服务机构，推动124家示范企业建立CAD/CAE/CAPP/PDM集成化的信息系统，提高产品创新能力和企业核心竞争力，新产品贡献率全部在30%以上，其中锻压、华一、蓝天（待规范）等企业新品贡献率达到70%。开发新产品1505种，取得专利1079项。

二、快速原型制造技术（RPM）

1998年，天津市快速原型制造技术（RPM）服务中心是国家首批专业性生产力促进中心。该中心引进多种先进的快速成形和快速制模设备，面向制造业企业的新产品开发提供快速成形、快速制模、快速反求、快速铸造以及工业设计等技术服务。1996~2000年，为100多家客户提供RP制件服务1300余件，支持企业开发新产品150多项。用户包括环球磁卡、天津夏利、长安汽车公司等国内企业，也包括一些知名跨国公司，如惠普、摩托罗拉。

2001年，天津快速原型制造（RPM）技术服务中心的服务项目比2000年翻了一番，在原天津快速原型制造（RPM）技术服务中心的基础上，以天津大学和河北工业大学为主体，扩展建立天津市快速成形技术工程中心，具备立体光固化成形（SLA Stereolithography）、SLS（选择性激光烧结Selective Laser Sintering）、分层实体制造（LOM Laminated Object Manufacturing）和熔融沉积成形（FDM Fused Deposition Modeling）等多种激光快速成形及其应用工艺、以及CAD建模、快速制模、反求工程和快速铸造等技术。2002年在天津经济开发区设立分部，中心在建设规模和技术服务能力上处于国内领先水平。

至2005年，中心已经与百余家企业建立技术合作关系，为企业提升新产品开发能力，缩短开发周期，快速响应市场提供有力的技术支持。中心承担为中国载人航天飞船研制航天员专用的赋形缓冲减振坐垫设计及其制造模具研制任务，自主开发完成由产品分析、工业造型设计、快速取模、三维非接触式光学测量、CAD/CAM、CAE动态仿真，虚拟设计验证和激光快速成形等技术构成的赋形产品研制工艺的新产品快速设计制造技术，成功应用到中国“神舟”载人航天飞船，为中国的航天事业做出重要贡献。

三、计算机集成制造系统(CIMS)

天津大学、南开大学和天津计算中心与天津计算机应用研究所等单位在国内较早开展计算机集成制造系统的研究和应用推广工作。

(一)计算机集成制造系统的研究

南开大学以涂莘生为核心的科研团队,在1991至2000年的10年间,前后承担多项CIMS主题研究项目。对新的经济环境下制造系统中新出现的若干关键问题,包括机器调度理论、生产线参数优化以及优化方法进行深入的研究。

1991年3月,南开大学涂莘生、王秀峰等开展CIMS调度方法研究,开发出4个软件包,可直接用于寻求最优或次优调度,使得仿真计算量大大减少,从而奠定生产线参数优化设计的理论基础。1993年3月,涂莘生、陈秋双、王厦生等从事CIMS中在线与优化调度的研究,开发出在线调度软件。同年7月,涂莘生,王秀峰,乞敬换等完成DED的扰动分析及其在优化设计中的应用项目,对随机生产线的参数优化设计进行研究,给出有效的计算方法和设计步骤,编制相应的仿真与优化软件。1993年,涂莘生,王秀峰,乞敬换等还完成离散事件动态系统与调度理论及其在CIMS中的应用的研究。1995年6月,涂莘生,刘瑞华、陈秋双等从事的CIMS优化方法及智能调度的研究,在CIMS优化方面,给出生产线(包括串行、装配、拆散、反馈以及Fork-Join网络等类型生产线系统)的最优设计,对不可靠制造系统,根据需求,给出最优控制的设计,对拉动式看板系统给出适用于CIMS的扰动分析法、遗传算法、以及积分全局寻优法等诸种寻优方法,并开发出相应软件。1997年6月,由涂莘生,陈秋双主持完成的轧管过程的生产计划与优化调度的计算机集成系统,该系统以天津钢管公司为背景,研制的软件可以根据公司下达的月计划生成轧管分厂的日计划,可根据生产现场的实际情况以及新的需求,及时调整每日的日计划;根据日计划生成装炉顺序表,并生成管加工所需的工具计划。它解决上层计划与底层生产脱节的矛盾,具有实用性。2001年,涂莘生、陈秋双、贾春福完成制造系统理论与优化方法的研究,对新的经济环境下制造系统中新出现的若干关键问题进行深入的研究,主要内容包括机器调度理论、生产线理论、优化方法的研究,这些结果具有很好的应用前景和重要的理论价值。

2000年10月,南开大学陈秋双完成CIMS环境下营销策略与营销管理信息系统的研究。该项目对市场营销管理与决策信息系统(MMDIS)进行研究,提出帮助企业实现主动竞争、解决决策滞后、注重系统的系统性和协调性等MMDIS的建模指导思想,并探讨解决方案。研究市场营销情报系统和营销预警系统的模型,提出顾客满意边界和客户分级服务体系,研究定性与定量相结合的目标市场研究和选择方法。开发出市场营销管理与决策信息系统,基于数据仓库的客户分析系统,并进行应用企业研究。

2003年12月,天津大学完成制造业连续质量改进的方法与应用研究。课题组开发的集成质量管理系统(IQMS),帮助企业从产品生命周期角度,将质量工程的各种工具和方法实现有效的集成,达到客户驱动的质量改进,提高产品/过程的质量水平,从而在激烈的市场竞争中保持质量优势。IQMS应用于天津起重设备有限公司,并取得效果。该成果具有自主知识产权的和较高的应用转化效益。

(二)计算机集成制造系统的推广应用

早在1992年,天津大学舒炎泰负责建设国内第一个863/CIMS的流程CIMS应用示范工程——兰化化纤厂CIMS应用工程,该项目第1期和第2期分别于1995年和1998年通过国家863/CIMS专家组验收,为该厂产生几千万元经济效益,1999年国家科技部授于该厂"CIMS应用工程示范企业"。

1995年,天津轧钢三厂型钢一分厂在天津市第一个实施企业CIMS项目。1998年,天津汽车暖风机CIMS工程被科技部评为"863计划CIMS主题先进集体"。此外,三源电力成套

图4-1-10-36　被列为国家"863"计划、CIMS工程的天津汽车暖风机有限公司

设备公司以及天津外贸纸箱厂、亿利达集团公司、真美电声器材集团公司的CIMS应用示范工程相继通过国家科技部和天津市科委验收，上述示范企业均取得明显的经济效益，成为天津市制造业信息化的典范。如天津暖风机厂产品设计周期缩短60%，开发设计费用降低64%，库存资金占用率减少21%。

1996~2000年，天津市通过开展CIMS应用示范工程研究开发实施、十大企业集团CIMS应用工程研究开发和集团化CIMS工程与CIMS技术应用等攻关项目，实施百余家示范工程企业。

2001年，天津市以十大企业集团CIMS工程为重点，又相继启动20家集团化企业CIMS应用示范工程，涉及机械、汽车、电子、化工、冶金、轻工、纺织、医药、能源和建材等行业，实现企业基础信息化，并在产品设计与生产经营管理业务流程中实现信息集成；在50家企业完成CIMS核心技术应用；在100家企业开展CIMS单元技术的推广应用。

至2005年，天津市实施CIMS工程深入发展，效益更加突出。天津天铁冶金集团有限公司CIMS工程以天津市华钢科技有限公司为技术依托，规范工程设计、改善企业管理，完成集团公司CIMS工程总体方案设计；实现运销管理、设材管理、原料管理、客户关系管理、财务管理、计量管理和质量检验系统的上线运行；完成生产制造执行层初步设计；完成过程控制层对PLC、DCS系统的升级改造工作；完成生产管理层炼铁、烧结等生产厂管控一体化工作。天津天铁冶金集团有限公司实施CIMS工程，促进企业管理面貌的转变，取得看得见、摸得着的经济效益，也增加企业无形资产，增强企业可持续发展的后劲。

此期间，随着企业对信息化需求的增强，天津金驰、大象、企之星等10余家技术服务企业应运而生，2001年成立以天津计算中心、天津大学、南开大学为主的“天津市CIMS工程中心”，2002年在整合CAD技术服务中心、RPM工程中心、CIMS工程中心和培训中心的基础上，成立天津市制造业信息化生产力促进中心，依托专家委员会开展制造业信息化的发展战略研究；组织制造业信息化共性关键技术研究开发；发展中介技术服务队伍；进行示范工程项目评审和监理。

2001~2005年，天津市作为国家制造业信息化首批试点城市，全面开展制造业信息化工程，CAD、CIMS典型示范企业已覆盖全市大中型企业的三分之一，到2004年底，实施市、区两级示范企业达596家，发挥示范企业的辐射作用，并创建和完善技术服务体系。市政府投入企业示范引导资金2045万元，拉动企业投入34562万元。信息化工程促进示范企业的产品创新，实现专利1084项。2004年已验收的示范企业实现销售收入921572万元，实现利税93758万元，实现较好的投入产出成果。

第二章 生物技术

20世纪80年代，生物技术的蓬勃兴起成为新技术革命的重要标志。1991～2005年，天津生物技术领域的科研工作者密切联系实际，既致力于应用基础研究，也致力于将科研成果转化为实际产品，取得食用黄原胶研制、采油微生物产品应用、现代酿造技术推广、提高氢化可的松转化率、血液净化生物材料、生物芯片研制等一系列成果。

天津大学张春霆在对DNA双螺旋结构、DNA动力学理论和用几何学方法探索、分析DNA序列的研究中，取得重大突破，荣获1997年度国家自然科学奖二等奖。

第一节　微生物工程

1991～2005年,天津的微生物学的应用基础和应用研究,取得多项成果。这一时期,微生物工程在生产实际中,应用于酿酒行业,推动国内食品发酵酿造技术迈上一个新台阶;应用于制药行业,提高氢化可的松转化率,技术水平达到国内领先。在高新技术领域,研发出抗艾滋病膜融合抑制剂"扶素康",拥有自主知识产权。

一、食品微生物

1991年,南开大学赵大健、刁虎欣、张燕珠等与山东省食品发酵研究设计院完成新型食品添加剂黄原胶的应用研究项目,用新技术系统地对食品级黄原胶化学组成、理化特性等开展基础研究,测定分子形貌、分子量,在透射电镜观察中获得新发现,观察到细胞分泌丝状黄原胶,为对黄原胶在食品中开发应用提供理论指导。在国内首次用蛋白酶酶解技术去除发酵醪中大部分菌体细胞并降低氮含量,用平板膜超滤机进行黄原胶微滤浓缩与纯化,其食品级黄原胶生产工艺先进。参考WHO/FAO国际标准,制定出国内第一部食品添加剂黄原胶国家质量标准。将国产食品级黄原胶成功用于饮料、肉制品、冷饮、调味品、方便面、奶油等食品,取得较好经济效益和社会效益。研究成果填补食品级黄原胶工业规模生产的国内空白。

1993年,天津科技大学杜连祥开展乳酸芽孢杆菌的研究,从脱脂奶粉中分离到一株能形成芽孢的乳酸菌——凝结芽孢杆菌。该菌具有耐胃酸、抗高温、抗干燥等优点,其制剂稳定性高,安全无毒,能够促进肠道蠕动和改善肠道功能,并具有降血糖、降血脂和提高机体免疫能力等功能。制剂经人体服用试验证明,对便秘、慢性结肠炎有独特疗效。2003年3月,杜连祥完成乳酸芽孢杆菌粉剂中试与开发,采用乳酸芽孢杆菌粉剂,确定1吨发酵罐的发酵工艺和粉剂制备工艺。与同类产品的生产过程相比,工艺简单、设备低廉、能耗小和成本低。乳酸芽孢杆菌粉剂中试产品经天津市畜牧兽医研究所对鸡和猪的饲喂实验证明,与饲料添加剂普遍使用的抗生素相比,抗病和增重效果明显、且无残留、不引起抗药性。以乳酸菌等有益菌制成的活菌制剂,被广泛应用于医疗、保健、食品、畜牧业和水产等行业。其后,由天津科技大学和天津市新星兽药厂合作,杜连祥、戚薇、陈莹、路福平等共同开展乳酸芽孢杆菌粉剂的生产方法与应用研究,在国内首次生产芽孢乳酸菌制剂。工艺上采用流加NaOH溶液,以严格控制pH值的好氧法培养菌体,用喷雾干燥法制备菌粉。产品为耐热性芽孢,具有耐热与耐酸性强、保存期长等优点,成果获国家发明专利。

图4-2-1-37　天津科技大学杜连祥(右三)指导学生做实验

图4-2-1-38　天津科技大学率先在国内开展酿酒行业生产模式改革研究

自20世纪80年代始,天津科技大学邹海晏、肖冬光等所在现代酿造技术研究室率先在国内开展酿酒行业生产模式改革研究。该室实行产学研结合,先后到全国几十家(酒精、、葡萄酒、黄酒和食醋等)酿造厂,进行用活性干酵母代替传统自培酒母,用酶制剂、活性根霉曲等全部或部分代替传统酒曲的研究开发，在酿造工业中引发应用研究和生产实践的高潮。1992~1997年，该室同全国数十位酿酒专家一起，进行耐高温酿酒活性干酵母应用技术的开发研究与推广，在国内正式形成酿酒活性干酵母的工业生产。1995年该项目被列为国家科委成果重点推广项目后，三年累计创经济效益33亿元，节约粮食172.8万吨。

1989～2002年，天津科技大学高年发、杨枫等历经10余年研发吸交法提取柠檬酸新工艺工业化生产新技术。2005年，新技术应用于黑龙江富华集团总公司年产3万吨的柠檬酸项目中，验证新技术的优越性、成熟性和稳定性，受到国内柠檬酸行业及发酵行业的高度评价和赞扬。该成果工艺路线新颖、工艺过程科学合理，技术经济指标突破国内纪录。

2001～2004年，天津科技大学贾士儒主持加压发酵提高生物反应的生产能力研究项目，提高酵母胞内海藻糖的生成能力20%以上，提高蓝色梨头霉生物转化率10%以上，并在大肠杆菌工程菌、鸟苷和谷氨酸加压发酵中得到印证，为国内外首创。同期，贾士儒承担的“医药发酵工程关键技术与重大产品开发”和“生物防腐剂ε-聚赖氨酸研制”两个项目，通过紫外、硫酸二乙酯和离子注入等诱变方法，获得一株ε-聚赖氨酸高产菌株，经过发酵过程优化和提取技术的研究，取得中试平均产量为21.3%，平均收率67.5%的好成绩。

2001年8月，南开大学张秀明、乔明强、高才昌等开展乳酸链球菌素（NISIN）的中试发酵研究，证明是一种可以取代化学合成防腐剂的天然食品防腐剂。课题组通过对发酵培养基配方的筛选及发酵工艺的改进，研究工业原料、乳酸乳球菌种龄、接种量、搅拌速度、温度和pH值等对NISIN发酵效价和发酵周期的影响，观察发酵过程中菌浓度、pH、NISIN效价和残糖的变化规律。在实验室使NISIN的发酵效价达到5000IU/ml（国际单位/毫升）以上，4批6升自动化发酵罐发酵实验NISIN的效价均达到6000IU/ml以上，100升罐连续发酵3批发酵效价达到7300IU/ml以上，1吨罐连续发酵3批发酵效价达到8000 IU/ml以上。

2004年7月，天津师范大学与天津科技大学共同承担，孙建华主持完成总状共头霉（Srl8）杀虫活性物质工艺放大及分离纯化研究。确定筛选到的Srl8代谢产物具有杀线虫活性，其作用方式为触杀型，并具有耐热、水溶性、杀线虫谱广等特点；确定Srl8菌摇瓶发酵的优化条件以及5L罐发酵放大的工艺参数，发酵液1/2浓度的室内杀线虫活性超过95%；确定菌液分离的工艺以及制备高活性杀线虫制剂的方法，制得的浓缩剂在3小时内可将线虫全部杀死；通过重结晶和色谱层析等技术确定杀虫活性组分中含包括有机酸在内的多种活性组分；药效试验证实，其发酵制剂对番茄和黄瓜根结线虫病害有较好的防治效果，大大降低病情指数，对番茄根结线虫病和黄瓜根结线虫病害的防效，分别相当或部分优于化学杀线剂（甲萘威、灭线磷）及生物杀线剂（阿维菌素）的效果。研制的发酵制剂经天津市化学品毒性检定所进行的毒理学评价试验，证明其对大鼠急性经口、经皮吸入毒性属低毒；眼、皮肤刺激实验属无刺激性级。成果填补线虫生物防治剂的国内空白。

二、医药微生物

1992~1996年，南开大学耿运琪带领科研团队进行牛免疫缺陷病毒（BIV）检疫系统的建立、流行病学调查和病毒分离的研究，主要完成人有秦贞奎、陈启民、赵祥平、刘淑红等，合作完成单位是天津市动植物检疫局。耿运琪等利用分子生物学技术，克隆牛免疫缺陷病毒（BIV）的核心抗原基因，并获得高表达；通过免疫方法在牛群中检测BIV的感染，开发成检测试剂盒；通过对中国北方地区30万头牛随机采样进行的流行病学调查，首次确定在中国牛群中存在BIV自发感染，为BIV在世界范围内的流行提供新的证据；分离到BIV中国毒株（BIV92044），为动物慢病毒（Lentivirus）的分子生物学研究和HIV的动物病毒模型研究提供新的材料。BIV与人免疫缺陷病毒（HIV）基因组结构、复制方式、生活周期、表达调控和致病机理十分相似，是HIV研究的动物病毒模型之一。该项目提供的检测方法为中国BIV研究和检疫提供技术手段。同期，耿运琪、陈启民、刘淑红等进行抗AIDS药物筛选新模型的研究，协作单位是国家医药管理局天津药物研究院。项目组利用牛免疫缺陷病毒（BIV）系统，通过重组DNA技术建立抗艾滋药物筛选新模型。项目的创新之处在于使用BIV系统，不感染人，操作安全，可在生物安全二级实验室进行抗艾滋药物的大规模初筛；根据慢病毒

(Lentivirus)基因表达调控的分子生物学原理，选择luc报告基因，以该基因表达水平判断药物对病毒的抑制作用，思路和设计新颖独特；操作过程中不使用同位素，luc测定灵敏度高，使筛选过程简单、微量，周期短、成本低。

1992年，天津科技大学杜连祥等完成高转化率醋酸泼尼松生产菌株BY-2-13-51的选育及应用的研究，技术水平达到国内领先。其后，杜连祥等承担天津市科技攻关计划项目提高氢化可的松转化率的中试。研究出以RSA为底物生产氢化可的松的新工艺，即细胞稀释法转化工艺。经逐级放大并在15吨发酵罐上进行试验，确定出工艺路线，优化工艺参数，具有11β-羟基化反应专一性高、副产物生成少、产物收率高、易于操作和控制等优点。应用于生产后，在原5吨生产规模条件下，净增产量375千克，经济效益显著。

2003～2004年，杜连祥等和天津市津津药业有限公司共同研究高转化率氢化可的松生产菌株蓝色犁头霉JY-2＃的选育与应用，通过原生质体紫外诱变，选育出高转化率氢化可的松生产新菌株，生长速度较快，生产周期短。经过发酵过程优化和提取技术的研究，氢化可的松平均转化率达86.6%，对化合物RSA的吸收率达48.3%，生产成本下降12.7%。

2003年2月，扶素生物技术有限公司研发出生物工程药物抗艾滋病膜融合抑制剂“扶素康”，拥有自主知识产权，获得国家专利。“扶素康”根据HIV膜蛋白GP41的结构，利用分子生物学、蛋白质化学、结构生物学和先进的计算机技术设计，填补中国医药行业的一项空白。体外实验表明，“扶素康”比T20(美国一家制药企业开发的抗艾滋病膜融合抑制剂，在美国和欧洲上市)的有效性高20倍，且与GP41的结合更稳定。“扶素康”使该公司成为国内首家运用生物技术研发抗艾滋病药物的企业。

三、微生物农药

1998年，天津市米都利科技发展有限公司蒋如璋、郭金昌、张政等完成生物转基因工程防治害虫研究，利用基因工程的方法，成功地将苏云金芽孢杆菌以色列亚种(简称Bti)的杀虫晶体蛋白(简称ICP))串联双基因CryVIA、CryVIB，导入荧光假单胞菌中，获得ICP高表达的系列工程菌株。经两年多的田间试验，成功地开发出有效控制韭蛆的转基因荧光假单胞工程菌悬浮剂OAX1(杀虫率78%～93%)。将对植物有益菌荧光假单胞菌及其转基因技术进行研究和开发，应用于韭菜上，有效避免大量使用剧毒或高毒化学农药，或使用低毒农药未达安全期就收割，致使韭菜中毒事件的发生，成果填补国内空白。

2001年9月，南开大学任改新、陈月华、刘春勇等完成新型遗传改良BtKen-Ag微生物农药研究，通过基因重组手段，首次将对绵铃虫及甜菜夜蛾特效、且具有延缓抗性发生的不同基因cryIAc、cryIC和cyt等导入对蚊、蚋等双翅目高效的苏云金芽孢杆菌以色列亚种(Bti)野生株及其消质粒株4Q8，并得到表达。构建对双翅目和鳞翅目害虫均有活性的工程菌株3株，且在工程菌的构建、抗虫植物基因工程及Bt的抗性治理等方面丰富可供应用的基因源。其中对韭菜蛆病原菌Bt-189株cyt基因的克隆及表达，为进一步阐明cyt基因的协同作用具有重要的理论及实用意义。

2002年，南开大学徐凤波、张正之、解放等完成甲氨基阿维菌素苯甲酸盐合成技术的研究，甲氨基阿维菌素(甲维)是从生物发酵药物阿维菌素开始的一种半合成杀虫剂农药，具有光谱、高效、低毒、无公害等优点。项目组将国际专利与国内具体情况相结合，完成甲维合成技术。以阿维菌素为原料经基团保护、羟基氧化、还原氨化、脱保护、成盐，五步总收率大于45%，部分产品纯度大于90%，技术原料立足国内，基本没有三废，工业化获得成功。经查新，合成工艺属国内首创。

四、石油微生物

1994年，以南开大学刘如林为首的四位教授建立起全国高校唯一的“石油微生物实验室”，在国内率先开展微生物采油技术研究。与大港油田合作，刘如林主持筛选以烃类为碳源、能在油藏极端环境条件下生长并代谢、产酸、产气、产表面活性物质的微生物菌种，经发酵工艺制成产品，以“单井吞吐”或“微生物驱油”

等方式在油田应用，提高原油产量或提高原油采油率。筛选出以烃类为碳源、适合不同油藏条件的系列采油微生物菌种，建成采油微生物菌种库；确定嗜热菌的选育、评价和培养方法，利用现代发酵技术确定出逐级扩大的高温、高密度发酵工艺；用遗传操作手段，在国内首次构建采油微生物工程菌种；在国内外首次在聚合物驱油后油藏开展微生物驱油矿场试验并获得成功；在国内率先在高温、高含水、高采出程度油藏开展以烃为碳源的微生物驱油试验，并获得成功。研制的采油微生物产品在大港、辽河、吉林、新疆等多个油田推广应用，增产效果明显，经济效益、社会效益显著。

1998年后，南开大学与大港油田、辽河油田等合作，刘如林、梁凤来、张心平、刁虎欣等参加，完成微生物提高石油采收率项目，经多年攻关，取得多项技术创新成果：确立从菌种选育—性能评价—菌剂生产—矿场试验方案设计—施工工艺—跟踪检测—效果评价等一整套技术；建成采油微生物菌种库和菌剂制备实验厂；建立菌剂质检方法和企业质量标准；研制成功微生物活动注入装置。成果用于国内稠油油藏、聚合物驱后油藏、高温油藏、高含水高采出程度油藏，均获得成功和突破。1995～1998年，应用该技术共增产原油50868吨。巨大的应用潜力，使其成为国内各老油田可持续发展的有力支撑。

第二节 生物工程

1991～2005年，天津生物技术的研究与开发呈现前所未有的活跃局面，以归国留学生为主体的创新团队开展关于细菌表面多糖抗原多样性的遗传学基础的研究，以及生物芯片制造新技术——基因多态性测定技术和生物芯片技术基础研究与应用开发研究，达到先进水平。天津大学张春霆在对DNA双螺旋结构、DNA动力学理论和用几何学方法探索、分析DNA序列的研究中，取得重大突破。

一、基因表达

1991年初，南开大学陈德风等在国际上首次发现识别序列外甲基化对限制性内切酶活性的抑制作用，被权威人士认为是分子生物学研究领域内取得的突破性进展，给内切酶领域引入一个重要的DNA结构参数，为从新角度理解和研究基因表达，特别是为研究甲基化作用与基因表达调控的关系，提供一条新途径。

1991年9月~1993年7月，天津医科大学与南开大学陈昆明、李建民、张墨玲、孙贵连等合作完成人血清降钙素cDNA重组及在大肠杆菌(E.coli)中的表达项目。降钙素(Calcitonin)是将人体血液中的钙调控到骨骼上去的重要激素，可抑制骨钙流失，主要用于治疗骨代谢病。由于降钙素从猪甲状腺中提取，所以其来源受限制。为摆脱材料来源限制，项目组采用基因工程技术，将人血清降钙素cDNA重组并在大肠菌(E.coli)进行表达，制备基因工程降钙素。

1995～1999年，南开大学李建民先后进行真核细胞中人生长激素基因工程研究和真核细胞中基因工程人生长激素产业化研究。

1995年12月，天津大学张春霆开展DNA双螺旋结构、DNA动力学理论和用几何学方法探索，分析DNA序列的研究，历时9年，取得重大突破。此前张春霆提出完整的DNA碱基运动的动力学方程组即DNA双螺旋碱基运动是一组耦合的双变量非线性偏微分方程组，适合于用数学方法进行解析研究，其解较合理地解释转录和复制过程中碱基的运动变化情况。项目组根据Dickerson求和规则，计算出DNA双螺旋中四种螺旋参数随序列变更的上限，并为实验结果所证实；计算出各种序列螺旋参数岁序列的变化，发现对TATAAT和TATAAA等序列，其螺旋扭角的变化几乎达到最大，指出这与RNA聚合酶识别启动子有关；根据对DNA双螺旋碱基堆积能的计算提出，在转录时DNA双螺旋可能经历B-A-B的构象变化。而后系统地开拓DNA序列分析的几何学研究新领域，发现在几乎所有的编码序列中，四种碱基出现的频率的平方和恒小于1/3。

把这一规则推广到整个基因组，计算出各物种基因组DNA中的G C含量应介于78.9%与21.1%之间。结论为实测结果所证实。证明任一DNA序列，均存在唯一的一条三维空间曲线与之对应，研究曲线的几何学方法被系统地引入到DNA序列研究中来。这种方法特别适合于探索隐藏在一维DNA序列中的高维信息。根据美国科学引文索引SCI统计，从1987年1月至1995年12月，张春霆相关研究论文被引用达83次。

1990年代初，南开大学元素所陈茹玉等开始进行生物体内活性物质糖核苷酸白藓碱等磷酸衍生物的研究。1996～1999年，陈茹玉、戴庆、周嘉等完成新型抗癌抗病毒活性磷脂—核苷缀合物及α—氨基膦酸衍生物研究，以生物膜的基本组分——磷脂与已有抗癌药物分子以共价键连接成脂核苷酸化合物，以降低其毒性提高抗癌活性为目的，设计并合成几个系列百余种新型磷脂缀合物，研究有关化合物的反应、结构和性质，先经体外筛选出高效低毒具有抗癌活性的化合物3个，后经体内小鼠抗癌试验筛选出CPLT抗癌化合物。将锗、硒、核苷、氮芥、磺酰基、磺酰脲基、磷酰基等活性基团引入到a-氨基膦酸的母体结构中，合成一系列功能a-氨基膦酸化合物，发现某些新化合物具有较好的抗癌、抗病毒或除草活性。还设计合成一些高活性的除草剂先导化合物，筛选出具有高效低毒的抗癌化合物CPLT，为新农药及医药的创制做出示范，为国内药物化学工业做出贡献。发表论文54篇，得到国内外同行的高度肯定，国际著名的《杂原子化学》主编William E.McEwen来信说：研究水平处于世界领先地位。

1997年3月~1999年10月，天津市中医学院第一附属医院黄铁石主持、南开大学牛淑敏合作完成针刺对快速老化脑萎缩模型小鼠SAM-P/10脑、肝抗氧化酶活性及其基因表达水平影响的实验，以快速老化模型鼠SAM-P/10作为研究对象，通过对实验鼠进行穴位针刺，然后应用现代分子生物学技术和方法检测脑、肝组织中抗氧化酶活性及其基因表达水平变化与衰老的关系，发现机体穴位针刺能提高其体内抗氧化酶活性；通过PCR扩增以及斑点杂交以及Northern杂交，结果显示穴位针刺增加CuZn-SOD mRNA基因的表达量。项目以现代化的技术手段从理论和实践的结合上对传统针刺疗法进行探索和尝试。

2002年2月，南开大学黄熙泰、徐建国、张臻峰等完成DNA超螺旋对大肠杆菌CFA/I基因表达的调节研究，取得成果：CFA/I基因的表达水平与质粒DNA的超螺旋水平有负相关性，结果与传统认识相悖；当CFA/I基因去掉启动子区后插入tetr基因下游，其高表达不需要正调节因子cfaR；CFA/I菌毛的表达依赖于cfaA、cfaC和cfaE基因，这些基因的突变可导致菌毛低水平表达；拓扑酶I基因缺失不是导致细胞内质粒DNA高度负超螺旋的唯一原因；topA基因缺陷导致两种特殊DNA结构实体“拓扑连系数不定cccDNA”和“低迁移率cccDNA”的产生，这是前人未曾发现的两种DNA结构；获得一株CFA/I菌毛高表达克隆；证实质粒DNA的螺旋管型结构。CFA/I菌毛是致泻大肠杆菌的致病因子之一，国内外学者对开发菌毛蛋白作为保护性抗原积极性很高，但对该基因操纵子的调节机制解很少。研究DNA超螺旋对CFA/I基因表达的调节作用，增加对原核生物基因表达调节的了解，也有利于CFA/I菌毛的保护性抗原和DNA疫苗的开发研究。

2005年，天津大学元英进、马红武、葛志强等人完成细胞代谢信息与次生产物合成的基础研究。项目组从细胞培养过程中细胞与代谢产物合成的信息系统的微观入手，在细胞培养中细胞与细胞之间、细胞与周围环境之间信息物质的释放与识别、信息的跨膜传递以及与次生代谢产物合成的关系方面进行研究，并在非线性条件下研究基因网络和代谢网络之间的相互作用。发现真菌寡聚糖诱导氧迸发信号强度与紫杉醇合成存在二次激励关系，确定环境信息（诱导子和剪切）转导的关键控制点和信息流波形。基于基因组信息重构100多种生物的代谢网络，提出一种更具有生物学意义的途径长度的定义，揭示一个由4个子系统组成的蝴蝶结结构的代谢网络组织原理。提出一种新的代谢网络解耦方法，并以此为基础建立一种针对大规模代谢网络的基元模式的计算理论。发表论文77篇，其中被SCI收录50篇，被EI收录27篇，被他引97次。

二、基因工程

1998年，天津师范大学刘东华、蒋悟生、王威等研究金属离子对植物根细胞毒害作用，完成不同金属离子（主要为重金属）对植物根细胞毒害效应的研究，完成不同金属离子毒害的临界浓度以及相关的细胞学特征的研究。工作开展以植物为材料，对金属离子的毒害进行监测，并对其毒害的细胞学机理进行理论研究，方法简易并具有可操作性，得到国内外同行的肯定与应用。在国外主要是瑞典学者G.Fiskesjo博士开展一些工作。在国内该领域则仍属空白。

2003年12月，南开大学阎世平、王庆伦、顾文等完成人工限制酶分子设计和DNA切割机制研究，人工限制酶的分子设计，从配体的设计为出发点，设计出3大系列的配体，分别是Schiff base配体、大环配体以及多齿非环配体，以其与过渡金属组装，研究其结构、光谱等特征；研究上述配合物与生物大分子DNA或RNA相互识别和作用；研究上述识别和作用中的机制，探讨外部环境对与DNA作用机理的影响，研究DNA断裂机理，重点是以水解方式切割DNA的机理，从而筛选出部分人工核酸酶化合物。筛选出几个具有生物活性、即可以以水解方式断裂DNA的金属配合物，均是文献未报道的。

2004年1月，南开大学邢来君、李明春、胡国武等共同完成Δ6-脂肪酸脱氢酶转基因大豆的研究，创新点在于：采用农杆菌介导的大豆子叶节转化系统，首次成功地将来源于深黄被孢霉的Δ6-脂肪酸脱氢酶基因导入东北栽培大豆的6个品种中，并在转录水平mRNA上得到表达，获得一批转基因植株和种子；在大豆再生系统的基础上，对大豆遗传转化受体系统进行相应的调整和改良，建立一套大豆子叶节转化系统；成功克隆大豆β-伴球蛋白α′-亚基基因启动子；从少根根霉（Rhizopus arrhizus）中成功克隆Δ6-脂肪酸脱氢酶基因，并完成该基因在啤酒酵母和毕赤酵母中的表达。

2004年7月，天津师范大学王振英、彭永康、陈宏等完成小麦白粉病主要抗原的分子标记与产业化应用研究、小麦抗白粉病基因的克隆与分子标记育种和小麦抗白粉病相关特异DNA片段的克隆与测序。项目组以抗病栽培小麦Brock、近等基因系Brock/015//京4117、轮回亲本京411及抗性单株为材料，利用分子标记方法，筛选与抗白粉病基因紧密连锁的分子标记，完成连锁性分析及遗传距离测定，分子标记的克隆、测序、SCAR标记转换，利用分子标记选择出抗病、农艺性状良好的高产小麦新品系。研究确定抗病栽培小麦Brock中存在一个未知的强抗白粉病基因；以Brock为抗性基因供体，配制近等基因系Brock/015//京4117；从Brock和近等基因系中筛选出与未知抗性基因紧密连锁的分子标记两个。根据分子标记选择出2个具有抗病、农艺性状优良、高产的小麦新品系以及分子育种的特点。

2005年12月，南开大学王磊、冯露、郭宏杰等人完成细菌表面多糖抗原多样性的遗传学基础的研究。该课题以22种细菌表面多糖抗原（包括大量致病性较强，进化位置特殊的菌种）为研究对象，通过O抗原基因簇的破译、生物信息学分析等手段，对细菌表面多糖抗原的进化和形成机制进行系统的研究，发现大量O抗原多样性扩散的直接证据，进一步丰富对不同种、属之间抗原基因簇的横向转移、DNA重排和转座子引起的重组在表面抗原多样性形成和进化过程中的作用的认识。在世界上首次发现ABC转运系统在大肠杆菌中负责异多糖O抗原的转运。鉴定出22种革兰氏阴性菌以及90种肺炎链球菌中针对细菌表面抗原的特异分子标识，并在此基础上建立分子分型方法。通过大量环境样品的检测，证明该方法可应用于临床、环境、食品等多方面，具有很高的特异性和灵敏性。

图4-2-2-39　南开大学王磊带领的科研团队研制出基因芯片检测试剂盒

三、基因芯片

2001年2月，由天津籍旅美学者张佳与旅美学者李凯、南开大学教授张允什、天津再生资源研究所张旭共同发明的生物芯片制造新技术——基因多态性测定技术通过鉴定。传统的基因检测有杂交法和酶解法，精确度较高，但效率低下；基因芯片技术问世后解决低效率，但失之精确。新发明既利用经典方法中的酶解步骤，又实现直接测定RNA（核糖核酸），避免芯片技术间接引起的检测误差，从而实现准确而又快速。发明的基因多态性测定技术，完全消除美国Affymetrix公司高达20%的假阳性，基本消除10%的假阴性，为进一步开拓生物芯片作为一类快速高效的基因测定技术奠定基础。

2001年，从海外归国受聘于南开大学的王磊致力生物芯片技术基础研究与应用开发研究，组建天津生物芯片技术有限责任公司，拥有具有“海归”背景的112人创新团队。凭籍基因组学、功能基因组学研究和微生物检测芯片研发3个领域的优势，王磊的团队与公司成为由科技部专项资助的全国5个生物芯片研发的产业化基地之一。截至2005年，先后申请国内发明专利104项，其中14项已获得授权；申请国际发明专利4项，在国际微生物学权威刊物发表论文18篇，全部被SCI收录，总影响因子46。研究经实验数据证明，不同种类或亚种的细菌间，其表面多糖分子的差异性极大，深入到分子水平，其负责合成表面多糖的基因也具有差异性。选择不同菌株的特异基因序列，设计特异的DNA探针，再将其按一定的阵列固定于一片经特殊处理玻璃片上，就可制成一片用于致病菌检测的生物芯片。基于细菌表面多糖分子的多样性研发出的生物芯片、特别是DNA芯片，用于病原菌鉴别，具有大通量、高速度的优点，仅一次反应就可以对感染菌进行全面检测。整个过程只需数小时，而传统血清学方法则要耗时6天左右。血液重要致病菌基因芯片检测试剂盒申报国家Ⅰ类新药。BactaarayTM血液重要致病菌基因芯片检测试剂盒、BactaarayTM肠道重要致病菌基因芯片检测试剂盒和BactaarayTM志贺氏菌基因芯片检测试剂盒进入中试。

2001年4月，南开大学研制成功乙肝病毒突变类型基因芯片。芯片上有450个点，记录着21个质量控制信息和429种肝炎病毒基因类型，每个点对应一段病毒基因序列，通过多种反应方式，可以检测出患者的病毒类型和变异情况。利用这种芯片，只需一滴血液，不仅可检测出是否患有乙肝，还可以确定是属于乙肝的哪种突变类型，进而确定有针对性和疗效的药物。

2001年，军事医学科学院卫生学环境医学研究所的李君文开展基因芯片检测环境中常见致病菌的应用基础研究。项目组利用分子生物学和生物信息学技术，以细菌16SrRNA基因和部分致病基因为检测的靶基因，建立环境中常见致病菌的基因芯片检测技术，可以对环境中常见的13属14种115株致病菌进行全面、快速检测。在扩曾靶基因时利用细菌16S rRNA基因可变区与保守区交替排列的特点巧妙设计PCR引物，实现一次PCR可扩曾全部待检细菌模板的目的，大大减化操作步骤、缩短检测时间、降低检测成本。该技术主要用于环境（各种水体、公共场所空气等）中常见致病菌的快速检测与鉴定，对未知菌株的检测可在4小时内完成，敏感性优于其他传统及现代技术。天津市商检局等单位提供的50余株分离菌株对芯片进行的试用结果表明，芯片的检测鉴定结果与根据标准方法或仪器鉴定的结果基本一致。北京博奥生物芯片有限责任公司等多家单位试用，结果可靠。

2003年4月，南开大学陈力主持应用cDNA芯片技术筛选抗癌中药，利用cDNA微阵列芯片构建起抗癌中药筛选平台，提纯中药复方的经验方剂，为国内中药现代化和中药筛选提供分子生物学的研究手段。

四、蛋白质工程

2002年，天津大学姚康德、刘文广、尹玉姬等完成壳聚糖基仿生高分子凝胶的研究，将多重生物活性的壳聚糖为基础创建pH响应性水凝胶，通过不同类型壳聚糖基水凝胶对比研究，阐明它们的pH响应性机理。对网络的自由体积和其中水的动态行为进行研究，并以壳聚糖基凝胶网络构筑渗透特性可控的pH敏感药物释放体系。将壳聚糖和明胶复合创建组织工程支架，并以壳聚糖及其衍生物和明胶作为合成生物材料的表面修饰物；以N-烷基化壳聚糖作为非病毒DNA控制释放载体。在国内外SCI收录刊物发表论文20篇，出版专著一册。

2003年，天津大学孙彦、董晓燕、白姝等完成蛋白质分离复性方法和理论研究，在蛋白质的亲和沉淀及亲和反胶团萃取方面取得突破。项目组首次合成离子强度响应性的可逆沉淀聚合脂质体，实现蛋白质的快速亲和沉淀化，分离容量达多糖凝胶的3倍以上；发现生物相容性表面活性剂，研制成功色素为配基的亲和反胶团系统，并系统研究萃取和反萃取过程动力学。该亲和反胶团系统萃取选择性高，酶的活性收率达100%。将该亲和反胶团系统与中空纤维膜设备相结合，开发成功中空纤维膜亲和反胶团分配色谱装置。利用该装置亲和分离溶菌酶的纯化倍数达47，收率达98%。发表论文51篇，其中SCI收录26篇，EI收录13

篇。出版专著1部。

2005年4月,天津师范大学杜奇石完成用计算化学方法预测蛋白质的三维结构与功能项目。项目研究分析20个天然氨基酸的亲水和亲脂性,找出其关联和制约关系,发展预测蛋白质三维结构的方法。发现β型蛋白质的氨基酸D和I之间有很强的正相关,在β型的艾滋病毒的HIV-1 GP120 蛋白质(1acyL)中找到4个D和I紧密相连处,都出现在β带发生折叠的地方,由于D是强亲水性氨基酸,而I是强疏水性氨基酸,经常成对出现在β带拐角处,由此造成D与I的强正相关。氨基酸主成分分析法克服原始数据中可能的实验误差和分类上的模糊性带来的不确定因素,从而提高预测准确率,蛋白质结构类型预测的整体准确率达到85%,远高于一般预测方法的60%～70%的水平。

2005年,南开大学宓怀风、张万起、王亦农等完成白介素-4启动子中衰减子结合蛋白的研究,发现由B细胞激活因子白介素-4通过诱导抗体组向生成IgE转换,对过敏性炎症病原起关键作用。在毗邻与增强子PRE-I的DNA顺序(-225到-201)是一个衰减PRE-I的部位,并存在与该处DNA顺序CTTTGTAG特异性结合蛋白质因子。项目组采用电泳淌度迁移法在Jurkat细胞核提取物中确认这一蛋白质因子。同时证实这些蛋白因子分别为TCF-1、LEF-1和b-catenin,发现LEF-1会优先在Th1细胞内表达,TCF-1/LEF-1能够结合在IL-4启动子上,活化的T细胞能够下调TCF-1/LEF-1的表达以及TCF-1/LEF-1的表达会被IL-4下调。还对抗过敏的免疫抑制剂FK506在细胞内的受体蛋白内质网体中FKBP进行研究,第一次阐明这个肽脯氨酰顺反异构酶分子(mFKBP23)能够与Hsp70家族的分子伴侣(mBiP)相结合,并且还发现这种结合受到Ca2+浓度的调控。成果对研究机体的超敏反应以及器官移植中的免疫抑制具有指导意义。

五、生物传感器

1991年2月~2003年6月,南开大学陈强主持完成光、电化学生物传感器技术理论研究,主要参加人有史海滨、吴宝艳、李静等。项目组成功地利用同一技术体系将两种结构和性质存在很大差异、催化连续反应的酶高效稳定地固定在电极表面,并首次提出由偶氮苯聚合体(Az-PAH)和聚阴离子环式糊精(CyD)结合层层累积技术制备包含偶氮苯发色团的光致异构化PEM膜的新方法。提出由高分子聚电解质、壳聚糖和纳米碳管(CNTs)分别构建纳米级结构葡萄糖氧化酶电极的研究方案,提高传感器的整体性能并首次成功地将亲和型生物传感技术应用于赤芍801和丹参作用机理的研究,发现内皮素-1、白细胞介素-1、肿瘤坏死因子是赤芍801和丹参在体内的一条作用靶点。首次成功地将亲和型生物传感技术应用于实时监测亲和素对低密度脂蛋白的吸附研究,发现Avidin与LDL之间存在着特异性的吸附作用。共发表论文47篇,多篇发表在中医药权威杂志《中国中西医结合杂志》,应邀在国际学术会议上作特邀报告1次,大会报告2次。

2003年10月,南开大学研究高性能纳米水平光电化学生物传感器的开发,研制出的光电化学生物传感器具有小型化、测试精度高、响应时间短、样品无需标记、分析物无需纯化、测定快速、分析过程全自动化、可进入生物体组织甚至细胞内监测反应动态及生物体动态过程等优点,成果达国际先进水平。

2005年,南开大学研究SPR生物传感器及其对DNA的检测分析,研制出一套完整的光、机、电一体化、自动化、智能化的SPR生物传感系统,用于DNA分子及其相互作用的检测分析,得到理想的检测结果。为SPR检测分析技术的产业化进程,即开发具有自主知识产权的生物医学检测分析仪器奠定坚实基础。

2005年,南开大学陈强、史海滨、吴宝艳等完成光、电化学生物传感技术理论研究。项目开展生物酶单分子定向排列累积膜高效纳米水平生物传感器的研究;高性能纳米水平光、电化学生物传感器的研究;复合纳米材料增效生物传感器的研究;生物材料与机体蛋白质、细胞之间相互作用和识别机制的研究;LDL血液灌流吸附剂治疗高血脂症及吸附剂评价方法的研究,特异选择性生物传感技术对活血化瘀中药作用机理的研究。研究成果促进生物传感技术、生物活性材料、中药药理学相关学科的发展。发表相关学术论文47篇,SCI收录10篇,EI收录6篇,9篇论文被SCI收录的论文引用108次(他引97次)。

第三章　材料科学

1991～2005年，天津材料科学的研究获得丰硕成果，南开大学、天津大学、天津工业大学、河北工业大学等研究领域各有侧重，优势各有专长，在金属材料、无机非金属材料、有机高分子材料、复合材料以及焊接材料等领域积极探索。

第一节　金属材料

金属是传统意义的材料，新型金属材料不断涌现，并向功能金属材料延伸，更拓展到功能金属涂层和非晶金属材料与纳米材料。1991～2005年，天津关于新金属材料的研究取得多项成果。

一、金属合金材料

1992年10月，天津理工大学彭日升完成新型高耐磨锌合金及其应用研究，在研制出锌铝铜镁锑（ZnAlCuMgSb）新型锌基合金基础上，通过调整合金中A1、Cu配比，得到组织组成及形貌不同于ZA27的锌合金。合金中添加适量Sb，达到细化组织、细化晶粒及共晶化合物变细小、分布均匀，分散度增大的效果，提高合金的综合性能指标。该合金耐磨性为ZA27的3倍，其抗蚀性、抗老化性、尺寸稳定性及铸造性均优于ZA27锌合金，合金的热锻性好。新型锌合金为国内外首创，性能指标达到国际领先水平。

2001年5月，天津大学刘文西、王德法、董治中等研制成功铁基形状记忆合金材料和管接头，课题组进而开展高耐蚀不锈钢与铁基形状记忆合金研制、难变形铁基形状记忆合金管成型工艺、训练记忆不衰退工艺研究，抗低温弛豫记忆管连接结构设计和耐高压记忆管连接结构设计，成果达到国际领先水平。

2003年12月，南开大学王一菁、袁华堂、曹建胜等开展新型镁基储氢合金材料制备及性能研究，课题组研究镁基合金的成份与制备条件等对新相的影响，新相的结构与性能的关系，以及吸放氢过程中的结构转化等问题。采用掺杂形式，合成新型、具有新相结构的多元镁基合金，探讨镁基储氢合金结构与性能间的规律，寻找一种容量高、循环寿命好的多元镁基储氢合金。利用正电子湮灭技术，研究储氢合金的缺陷、界面等对氢在合金相中的传输占位等性能的影响。

二、金属涂层

1997年，河北工业大学曹晓明等完成耐锌液腐蚀金属间化合物的研究及应用项目，提出液体金属腐蚀新机制，证明锌液对与之不互溶的材料的腐蚀主要是材料表面的缺陷和材料本身的脆性所致。提出难熔合金和金属间化合物的脆性通过稀土元素微合金化得以改善，为开发利用这类性能独特的材料提供新的途径。研制出具有良好耐锌蚀性和成型性的稀土—硼化铁新型韧性金属间化合物和在普通碳钢表面的复合技术，制成钢基表面复合稀土—硼化铁耐锌蚀层的新型复合材料，成功解决工业热镀锌的腐蚀问题。

1998年，河北工业大学和天津开发区特种涂层技术有限公司阎殿然、何继宁、李香芝、武建军等完成金属表面耐蚀涂层的研究，较好解决在温度较高，磨、蚀共存的条件下，金属材料、有机材料所不能承受的严重磨蚀问题。

2001年，河北工业大学阎殿然等开展金属表面耐磨蚀陶瓷梯度材料研究，研究用等离子喷涂方法在金属表面制备耐磨腐蚀梯度陶瓷涂层的材料、涂层结构及制备工艺；研究梯度陶瓷涂层的结构与涂层通孔率、与基体的结合强度间的关系及对涂层耐蚀性的影响。解决在较高温度磨蚀共存条件下服役部件的耐磨蚀陶瓷涂层的材料问题。为工程上解决耐磨蚀材料问题开辟新的途径，提供可靠的制备工艺。成果在油田用螺杆泵的轴封、螺旋套及衬套上应用，在化工行业的齿轮泵的端盖及火力发电厂用于管道输送炉渣的大口径弯头上应用，使用寿命较原材料提高一倍以上，高的达数十倍，效果十分明显。

2005年，河北工业大学阎殿然等完成焰流控制自反应合成陶瓷/金属复合涂层的研究，针对陶瓷材料的脆性问题，采用微米级粉为原料，通过反应等离子喷涂的方法在国内外首次合成尖晶石/金属纳米复合涂层。为纳米及纳米复合涂层的制备提供新的途径，为深入开展陶瓷材料的韧化机理的研究提供可靠保证，为纳米陶瓷材料在工程上的广泛应用奠定理论基础。所制备的具有纳米结构的尖晶石陶瓷/金属复合涂层的韧性约是Al_2O_3涂层的10倍；无润滑磨损是Al_2O_3涂层的4.7倍，摩擦系数仅是Al_2O_3涂层的60 %。应用此涂层前后比较，双螺杆泵轴的寿命较原镀铬提高8倍，舰艇用消防水泵叶轮的寿命提高4倍，冶金行业的轧制角钢用整型模具提高4～5倍。具有明显的经济效益及社会效益。

三、非晶金属材料与纳米材料

（一）非晶金属材料

2003年12月，南开大学李伟、陶克毅、张明慧等完成二氧化钛载体负载非晶钛合金新型催化剂的设计项目，首次将“化学镀”原理与技术引入到催化剂制备中，开发出非晶态合金催化剂的制备新技术——金属诱导催化粉末化学镀。新制备方法在简单、可控条件下，制备出负载型纳米非晶态合金催化剂，实现非晶态合金的高分散、高比表面积和高催化活性，克服在制备中传统骨架镍催化剂对环境的污染，在环丁烯加氢反应中达到骨架镍的催化活性，并且克服骨架镍的不安全性。用于环丁烯加氢制重要溶剂环丁砜反应，其催化剂成本可下降30%，显著低于骨架镍。

（二）金属纳米材料

2004年，天津理工大学王治、何开元、张雅静等开展非晶与纳米软磁材料的研究，从合金的成分、非晶合金的纳米晶化过程与材料软磁特性的关系入手，探明获得优异软磁性能的根源及方法；从合金的软磁性能随温度的变化入手，探明纳米晶软磁合金的一些新的特征及其与微观结构的关系。

2005年1月，天津大学高后秀、杨渝钦、李松林等研究材料的纳米化机理及设计技术，证明常温常压下Cu-Zn-Al合金在某些微区中存在具有活性原子区的类流态，会导致纳米结构的出现。成果展现出一种制备一维纳米结构的新方法，为一维纳米结构生长机制研究提供新的数据，提出两种一维纳米结构的生长机制。发表论文9篇，其中SCI检索1篇，EI检索4篇。获2项发明专利。

2005年，南开大学唐祥海、王敬中、马延风等完成新型钛硅氧化物基纳米结构复合材料设计及超声辅助合成研究。成果表明：辅以高能超声辐射，以部分准晶态分子筛为起始原料之一，可快速合成钛硅氧化物复合材料，并可在中孔结构骨架中有效保持准晶态结构；而单纯用常规水热法处理则导致生成晶相分离的混合物或微孔分子筛。在超声辐射辅助下，合成出中孔氧化钛和负载纳米氧化钛及铁/氧化铁的中孔氧化硅，经适当处理后分别呈现出超强酸性或超顺磁性；在苯酚叔丁基化催化反应中，与微孔分子筛相比，部分复合材料具备大孔径、高比表面积和理化性质的高度可调变性。

（三）新型催化剂

1991~1993年，南开大学陶克毅从事甲苯歧化与C9芳烃转烷基分子筛催化剂、合成甲基异丁基酮新型催化剂及相关技术的研究。其后，开展丙酮水和制异丙酮新型催化作用和催化剂的研究。1999~2002年，陶克毅又开展TiO_2载体性能调控和油品加氢精制新型催化剂、TiO_2载体新型催化剂制备科学的基础研究，以及活性炭纤维催化剂的制备与性能研究。

1998~2001年，南开大学周秀中等开展茂金属催化剂聚合反应的研究。

2004年，南开大学关乃佳、章福祥、陈继新等完成纳米新催化材料的制备及其在环保中的应用基础研究，首次原位合成出分子筛/堇青石新型催化材料和光催化合成出高分散和窄尺寸分布的金属催化剂；验证分子筛/堇青石整体式催化剂具有文献报道最好的汽车尾气净化效果。发表论文50余篇，被SCI收录23篇。

第二节 无机非金属材料

1991~2005年，在无机非金属材料的研究中，天津大学在先进结构陶瓷与先进功能陶瓷的研究上，面向汽车、石油工业需求，致力于产业化，成果丰硕。河北工业大学开展的保健抗菌建筑材料研究成果成功应用到日用陶瓷、环保陶瓷等行业的生产实际，取得显著的经济效益和社会效益，荣获2004年度国家技术发明二等奖。

一、玻璃

2003年11月，天津市硅酸盐研究所聂春生、李宝璋、王长虹研制成功口径高性能法拉第旋光玻璃，采用铂金坩埚及特制原料，围绕配方设计配制、稀粘度浇注、精密退火及特殊除铂熔炼诸工艺开展研究，成功地制出Tb_2O_3-Al_2O_3-SiO_2-B_2O_3系统的大口径高性能法拉第旋光玻璃，尺寸达Φ100×4000毫米，旋光系数高达0.34分/奥·厘米，性能优于国外同类产品。

二、陶瓷

（一）先进结构陶瓷

1991~1995年，天津大学袁启明、谈家琪、杨正方等承担多项先进结构陶瓷方面的国家重点科技攻关项目。关于汽车发动机陶瓷缸套上圈的研究和陶瓷缸盖底板的研制，构件通过断水增压下逾千公里的上机考核，达到国际先进水平；关于陶瓷组合缸套、陶瓷气门座、石油钻井高压泵陶瓷缸套、石油钻井泵用陶瓷缸套等研制的相关基础材料氧化锆、莫来石基陶瓷的研究，在改善氧化锆陶瓷高温性能和提高莫来石陶瓷低温强度方面取得多项突破，赢得国际同行的赞誉，奠定中国在此领域的国际领先地位。同期，天津大学沈继耀等承担板状氧化铝的研究和莫来石及莫来石刚玉质窑具的研究，在高温抗热震陶瓷材料的研究方面，从制备到应用为中国耐火材料行业提供典范。

1993~1995年，天津大学李志宏、朱玉梅等承担新型陶瓷氧化铝磨料的研制，对新型陶瓷刚玉磨料的制备方法、工艺、烧结、结构、添加剂及作用机理进行详细研究，所研制的新型陶瓷刚玉磨料硬度与普通电熔刚玉磨料硬度相当，韧性达到普通电熔刚玉韧性的1.5倍左右，晶粒尺寸≤500纳米，制备技术和产品性能达到国际先进水平。1995~1997年，承担CBN磨具用低温陶瓷结合剂的研制及应用研究，对立方氮化硼(CBN)磨具用陶瓷结合剂的组成、烧结温度及物理化学性能进行较为系统的研究，研制成功烧结温度低于800℃，性能满足CBN磨具制备需要的低温陶瓷结合剂。1996~1999年，承担磨汽车液压挺杆CBN砂轮的研制及应用，对汽车液压挺杆用陶瓷结合剂CBN磨具的制备和磨削应用进行研究，产品应用效果超过国外进口同类产品。1999~2005年，承担磨凸轮轴CBN磨具的制备研究及陶瓷结合剂CBN磨具的开发及应用研究，对陶瓷结合剂CBN磨具的制备及磨削应用进行系统研究。2003~2005年，承担陶瓷结合剂CBN磨具制备技术的研究，产品使用性能达到或超过国外进口的同类产品水平，使这类先进产品在国内成功产业化推广应用，为磨具生产企业创造显著的经济效益，为应用企业降低生产成本，节约进口CBN磨具的大量外汇开支。

1996~2000年，天津大学杨正方等承担石油钻井高压泵陶瓷缸套的研究，对氧化锆陶瓷体系进行适合规模化生产的配方和工艺调整的系列研究，开发多类氧化锆类陶瓷构件，为推进国内氧化锆陶瓷的产业化进程做出贡献。

1997~2002年，天津大学徐廷献等承担陶瓷纤维复合技术及电连接器工艺研究。1998~2002年先后与丰田汽车、福特汽车公司合作，分别开展汽车电喷系统用氧敏薄膜的化学镀膜和微波等离子体镀膜的研究。2001~2005承担新型功能陶瓷材料的制备科学及其关键基础问题研究，采用液相化学法和气相化学法，在各类基底上沉积形成纳米结构的导电薄膜、介电薄膜、铁电薄膜等，重点研究材料组成、结构、工艺与性能的关系，为多种薄膜材料与器件研制与应用提供基础研究。

2000~2002年，天津大学郭瑞松、赵丹、齐海涛对反相微乳液法非水相ZrO_2陶瓷墨水的制备与性能展开研究。课题组采用脂肪醇聚氧乙烯九醚（AEO9）/正丁醇/正辛烷/乙醇体系，研究体系的组成设计，其最佳组成的质量分数为：AEO9：正丁醇：正辛烷=29.1：19.4：51.5；温度控制在30℃，制备出$ZrOCl_2·8H_2O$和$NH_3·H_2O$两种非水微乳液，将二者搅拌混合、反应，制得ZrO_2陶瓷墨水；从喷射打印成型的技术要求出发，考察陶瓷墨水的物理化学性能及变化规律。结果表明，陶瓷墨水透明稳定，质量浓度达1.4%，粒度20nm左右，高度分散、表面张力、粘度等指标均满足间歇式喷墨打印机的技术要求。该成果有12篇论文发表在国内外权威刊物上。

2000~2003年，天津大学刘家臣等承担可加工陶瓷设计及其机理研究项目，研究稀土磷酸盐对氧化物陶瓷可加工性能影响，研制出多类氧化物/稀土磷酸盐可加工陶瓷体系，并对相关的可加工机理进行分析，达到国内领先水平。同期，负责结构陶瓷及其复合材料的应用项目，研制出包括陶瓷阀门、弯头、机床导轨、金属熔炼坩埚等多类实际应用构件，对其中陶瓷加工和连接使用技术的相关原理开展大量研究，收到良好效果。

2001年，天津大学徐燕申、林彬、肖学福等承担轿车用陶瓷摇臂量产化关键技术研究与开发项目，课题组选用铝合金和氮化硅陶瓷两种具有不同性能特点的材料，分别作为摇臂基体和工作圆弧面镶块，通过科学合理的结构设计和压铸包容连接的制造工艺，将它们组合在一起，发挥两种材料各自的性能优势，达到提高部件综合性能、降低部件制造成本的目的。研制的I型陶瓷摇臂通过天津市汽车研究所300小时全速、全负荷台架试验，技术数据完全达到预定指标。

2002~2004年，天津大学蔡舒等承担稠油蒸汽驱开采用大尺寸氧化物复相陶瓷柱塞的研制和开发项目，课题组在天津大学既有的研究成果基础上，加快对已开发产品产业化进程，研究大尺寸陶瓷柱塞的制备技术。根据不同采油工况、使用寿命和性能/价格比，开发出氧化锆增韧莫来石（ZTM）、氧化锆增韧氧化铝（ZTA）、ZTM、ZTM/Al_2O_3、多元系氧化锆陶瓷〔（Ce，Y）-TZP/Al_2O_3〕等系列材料体系；通过复合陶瓷粉末批量化生产的质量保证控制和解决大尺寸部件烧结过程的变形和开裂等关键技术，实现陶瓷柱塞的高效生产，产品合格率达90%以上。经现场考核，陶瓷柱塞正常使用寿命已超过6个月，延长检泵周期。产品在国内外多个油田试用，开发出系列型号的陶瓷柱塞。结合陶瓷柱塞的特点，改进现有管式抽油泵的结构，研制出与陶瓷柱塞配套的新型抽油泵。该项目的实施，延长石油开采设备中重要部件的使用寿命，有效减少停机和检泵作业次数，提高采收效率，降低成本，产生巨大的经济效益与社会效益。研究成果获2项发明专利、1项实用新型专利。

（二）先进功能陶瓷

1991~1993年，天津大学徐明霞等承担超细陶瓷粉体表面处理改性新技术的研究，项目组采用表面处理改性替代无水乙醇脱水技术，控制粉体团聚状态，成本低、过程清洁、环保。2001~2003年承担功能陶瓷粉体与薄膜纳—微米粒子尺寸与形态控制项目，研究粉体与薄膜粒子的形成过程、薄膜应力、结晶取向等控制因素及其控制原理及措施，归纳湿化学工艺粒子形成的结晶学规律，确立粒径形态与材料结构功能特性间的关系，成果达到国内领先水平。1998~2000年承担轿车发动机电控喷射系统用新型传感器的开发研究，采用新颖气敏多孔、超微粒薄膜材料，灵敏度高、响应快、器件结构设计简单，不需要参比气体，制造成本低，新型A/F传感器可调整变送器参数，提高新传感器与不同车型的ECU匹配性，器件整体技术水平达到国际先进水平。2000~2002年承担轿车用A/F传感器及变送器的研制与开发，通过传感器及相匹配的变送器、零部件结构参数的改进，研制出具有独立知识产权的轿车用A/F传感器。

1995~1996年，天津大学曲远方开展高效节能荧光灯自动限流保护电阻瓷料的研究，采用复合施主和受主掺杂的方法，控制瓷料配方和配套工艺使$BaBaTiO_3$基的陶瓷半导化，以及加入少量其他掺杂加入物，保证限流保护电阻的温度在高于居里温度200℃左右的情况下，使其高电阻值保持几乎不变，工作稳定可靠。该自动限流保护电阻与节能灯的灯丝串联，既能使节能灯完成预热、延时和启辉的功能，又自动限制和防止灯丝电流过大导致灯丝过热造成的节能灯寿命低的问题，提高节能灯使用寿命3~10倍以上。节能灯寿命的提高，相当于国家可少建立若干个节能灯厂和发电厂，节省能耗、经费和资源，对改善环境意义重大。

1996~1998年，天津大学曲远方开展"…PTC材料研制"，采用复合多施主与受主掺杂的方法，有效地控制并提高材料的特性，向用户提供合格样品，配方和工艺的性能稳定，重复性好，达到国际领先水平。1997~2002年承担汽车用系列节能型自控温PTC加热器、过电流保护器的应用研究和产业化研究，采用系列复合多施主和受主掺杂的方法、金属（石墨）/$BaTiO_3$复合系统等方法和改进工艺条件等措施，有效地控制并提高材料的特性，解决国内外都在攻关的PTC材料低阻化这一关键问题，显著降低PTC材料的室温电阻率，在高于居里温度约250℃的较宽温度区间其高电阻率仍保持几乎不降低，避免一般PTC材料在高于居里温度几十度时因电阻率突然下降引起的材料热击穿和失效，提高PTC材料的升阻比、耐电压性、使用性能和可靠性，在PTC材料的基础理论研究、无铅化和提高材料的性能方面取得很好的研究成果，达到国际领先水平。2001~2003年，承担节能型PTC热敏陶瓷电暖器研制，完成样机的研制和检测，获得国家专利，这种电暖器结构简单、节能效果突出。2004年，承担金属/石墨/聚合物/$BaTiO_3$复合PTC材料的研究，首次进行金属、树脂、石墨与BaTiO3基PTC材料的复合研究，开辟PTC材料低电阻率、高升阻比、高耐压研究的新途径和基础理论研究的创新，研究成果突破目前传统PTC材料室温电阻率高，限制该材料在低电压和超低电压条件下应用的现状。

20世纪90年代后期，天津大学侯峰、阴育新、徐廷献开展对镍酸镧（$LaNiO_3$）纳米陶瓷薄膜氧敏特性的研究。课题组以$La(NO_3)_3\cdot 6H_2O$和$Ni(NO_3)_2\cdot 6H_2O$为原料，采用柠檬酸为螯合剂，利用溶胶-凝胶法合成出钙钛矿型稀土复合氧化物LaNiO3纳米陶瓷薄膜，研究结果揭示：$LaNiO_3$纳米陶瓷薄膜具有良好的氧敏特性和重复性；适当的烧成温度和保温时间能获得具有高灵敏度的薄膜材料，烧成温度过高，材料灵敏度下降；掺杂能够明显改善$LaNiO_3$纳米陶瓷薄膜的氧敏特性。徐明霞、徐廷献、季惠明等结合国内外氧传感器及其氧敏材料特点，研制开发新型氧敏材料及传感器，针对轿车发动机电控喷射系统用传感器，研制开发出一种新型的氧化物薄膜状电阻型氧敏传感器，在夏利车、一汽集团发动机上，进行极端环境的排放控制试验，研发出的新型氧敏薄膜材料及其制备工艺都具创新性，处于国内外领先水平；其传感器的控制性能达到进口件水平，灵敏度和反应速度比进口件高，成本估计约为进口的1/2 ~ 1/3。该项研究成果从材料到器件结构，获得4项国家专利。

1999年，河北工业大学梁金生等与中国建筑材料科学研究院合作开展稀土激活保健抗菌材料的研制与应用开发，研究涉及无机保健抗菌材料研究与应用技术基础、稀土激活保健抗菌材料的化学组成设计与性能优化技术、工艺优化技术及性能评价技术与评价方法。成果成功应用到建筑卫生陶瓷、建筑涂料等行业。2003年，梁金生等与淄博博纳科技发展有限公司合作完成多功能健康陶瓷材料的制备及其功能制品的开发，成果应用到日用陶瓷、环保陶瓷等行业的骨干生产企业，取得显著的经济效益和社会效益。其后，梁金生等又与中国建筑材料科学研究院继续合作，完成具有抗菌、净化空气及产生负离子的功能材料的研究，内容包括具有抗

图4-3-2-40 河北工业大学梁金生检查研制产品的质量

菌、净化空气及产生负离子的功能材料的化学组成设计与性能优化理论、制备工艺过程中的若干材料物理化学问题，以及性能评价理论方法，奠定中国具有健康环保材料研究理论基础与应用技术基础。成果推动卫生陶瓷、日用陶瓷、化学建材等行业的科技进步，对提高国内建材行业产品附加值与环保功能化技术水平、增强中国建材产品在国际上的竞争力、取得较为显著的经济效益和社会效益。

1999~2001年，天津大学徐明霞等承担新型高稳定氧敏陶瓷超微粒薄膜的制备研究项目，以可溶性的无机盐为原料，利用液相化学法在基片上合成氧化物超微粒子薄膜，达到国内领先水平。2001~2003年承担掺杂纳米粒子膜的新工艺及污水回用性能优化研究，以TiO_2、TiO_2-SrO、TiO_2-Fe_2O_3等为主要研究对象，制备的薄膜光催化-氧化性能高，在阳光下具有较高的光催化-氧化效果，属于国内首创。2004年研制成功单分散纳米ZrO_2粉体及纳米结构化光纤陶瓷器。2001~2004年承担多功能复合粉体的应用开发，采用包覆法复合其他氧化物，以适应不同的复合条件和复合粉体的用途，在昆明建成20吨/年的中试线。2003年承担钛—氧系纳米粒子膜微结构设计、制备原理与性能研究，所设计的新结构材料在气敏性、光催化活性上有突破性提高。

2002~2004年，天津大学季惠明承担低压压敏电阻材料及相关电子陶瓷材料的开发，通过在原有固相法中引入液相纳米制备技术，实现TiO_2、$SrTiO_3$材料的低压压敏化与高电容量双功能材料设计，新合成的材料在集成电路、互联网等防浪涌领域有重要应用价值。2003~2004年与企业合作开展长余辉光致发光材料的研究，采用高温固相反应法和溶胶—凝胶法制备出硅酸盐系与铝酸盐系长余辉发光材料，具有良好的化学稳定性和热稳定性，其发光颜色主要涉及黄绿光、蓝光与红光等，达到国内领先水平。

2004～2005年，天津大学季惠明承担氧化物半导体薄膜气敏材料在医学检测中的应用研究，通过检测人体呼吸中标志物气体的组成与含量，定性或定量地预测人体的某些疾病，达到早预防、早发现病症的目的。该技术将敏感材料与纳米技术相结合，在快速简捷，特别是无损检测方面具有重要意义。

2005年，天津大学刘永长承担快速凝固大尺寸超导化合物MgB_2形成机理与单晶制备项目。该研究对于高品质块体二硼化镁（MgB_2）低温快速制备技术取得重要进展：一是通过结合晶化过程分析，确定深过冷快速定向凝固技术制备MgB_2单晶的镁-铜-硼（Mg-Cu-B）合金成分，通过熔配共晶Mg-Cu和Cu-B中间合金降低了Mg-Cu-B合金的熔炼温度，采用悬浮熔炼和循环过热方法稳定实现合金深过冷，系统研究过冷合金熔体中的相选择规律，确定MgB_2相稳定析出的过冷度范围，发展熔体法制备单晶的新技术；二是结合国际上对提高MgB_2临界电流密度的新要求，发展低温快速原位制备MgB_2纳米相、晶须和块体的新方法，原位掺杂碳和铜后，有效磁通钉扎中心大大增加，临界电流密度显著提高，极大地推进MgB_2低温快速合成技术。研究成果发表论文40余篇。

三、非金属纳米材料

2002年，河北工业大学梁金生等与中国建筑材料科学研究院合作研制成功空气净化功能纳米复相涂覆材料，开辟国内建筑内墙涂料健康环保功能化研究与应用技术的理论基础。成果应用到建筑涂料行业的骨干生产企业，取得较为显著的社会经济效益和环保效益。

2002年11月，天津大学常津、常青、姚康德等完成纳米生物材料与技术在药物治疗和医学诊断方面的应用研究，成果具有双重靶向性、控释性、非免疫原性和高效性。

第三节 有机高分子材料

1991~2005年，天津工业大学在纤维材料的研究成果令人瞩目，一些成果获国家专利授权并应用于生产实际，取得明显经济效益。

一、纤维材料

（一）纤维结构与性能研究

2002年12月，天津工业大学肖长发、张宇峰、安树林等开展高性能纤维结构与性能研究，以柔性超高相对分子质量聚乙烯纤维和刚性芳香族共聚酯纤维，进行高性能纤维结构与性能关系的基础研究，为合理开发和使用新型高性能纤维提供科学和实践依据。研究阐述和解释超高相对分子质量聚乙烯和芳香族共聚酯两类有代表性高性能纤维成形原理、结构与性能关系等基本问题和现象，填补该领域基础研究某些空白。

2005年6月，天津工业大学程博闻完成产业用熔喷细旦聚丙烯纤维的研制与应用研究，选择自极化效应强的特种电气石超细微粒作为驻极熔喷聚丙烯超细纤维非制造布的改性添加剂，通过表面修饰均匀分散到熔喷丙烯切片中，制得可纺性良好的驻极体聚丙烯母粒。

2005年8月，天津工业大学王瑞研究亚麻纤维非织造物增强复合材料，采用工艺流程短、加工成本低的非织造物生产方法制作亚麻/低熔点混合纤维预成型材料，并通过模压方法优化制成热塑性复合材料板材及异型件样品，制作方法与工艺路线便于实际操作和工业化生产，制品性能优良，优化的复合材料力学性能超过同类天然增强热固性复合材料及普通工程塑料的水平。

（二）异形短纤维

2004年，中国石油化工股份有限公司天津分公司化纤厂与东华大学王建中、王华平、张勇等研制异性涤纶短纤维，对异性纤维的纺丝动力学模拟研究，结合能量平衡、质量守恒及材料力学纺程，对异形纤维进行纺丝过程的计算机模拟。研究纤维截面及异形度的变化对纺丝张力、速度梯度、温度分布等的影响。

（三）功能纤维材料

1. 远红外纤维材料

1993年，天津工业大学段谨源等利用其在防中子辐射纤维和防X射线纤维研究方面取得成果，将金属和非金属的氧化物、碳化物等加工成直径在3微米以下的微粉，经偶联剂处理后与聚丙烯混合、熔融挤出制成切粒，纺丝制成远红外纤维。该远红外纤维中含有5 wt%（重量百分比）左右的无机功能材料，纤维的物理力学性能与常规丙纶相当，远红外辐射率达到85%以上，而常规丙纶的远红外辐射率仅为70%左右。随后，与天津市华林医疗保健用品公司合作将远红外丙纶纤维开发出保健护膝，委托中国医学科学院血液学研究所进行测试，结果表明：使用远红外丙纶护膝20分钟后，小腿血流量增加42.0%，微循环增加114.2%，而同结构和厚度的绵纤维护膝，血流量增加仅为4.9%，微循环增加1.3%。采用远红外丙纶和绵纤维加工成的绒衣，经总后勤部军需装备研究所在人工气候舱内测试，胸前和后背保暖率提高8%，皮肤表面温度提高0.5℃左右。远红外丙纶短纤维工业化生产技术获专家肯定，一种可纺性良好的远红外纤维获得国家发明专利授权。1994年，远红外丙纶母粒生产技术与开发被列入天津市“火炬计划”和“百亿工程”，在天津市麻纺织厂投入工业化生产。至1997年，远红外丙纶的产量达到1000吨/年，天津成为远红外纤维制品主要研究生产基地。

1999年，天津市麻纺织厂孙治、栾凤祥、张金凤等开发研制成功远红外功能母粒、纤维及制品，属国内首创，达到国内领先水平。产品销往北京、河北等省市自治区，并有部分产品远销日本、俄罗斯等国家和中国台湾地区。还利用功能母粒试制生产功能性非织造布及功能性塑料制品。

2. 蓄热调温纤维材料

1993年，天津工业大学张兴祥设想，将具有热能吸收、储存和释放功能的相变材料与纤维的制造过程相结合，制备在常温下具有热能吸收、储存和释放功能的智能化调温纤维。他采用熔融缩聚工艺合成制备聚对苯二甲酸乙二酯—聚乙二醇嵌段共聚物，并测试该样品的低温热能吸收和释放功能。研究发现，这种聚合物的热稳定性较差，不能满足熔融纺丝工艺要求。1995年，张兴祥等开展碳原子数为2~8的二元脂肪酸和二元脂肪醇的聚合反应研究，得到在常温下有明显吸热和放热功能的脂肪族聚酯，其吸、放热量达到70焦/克。进一步研究发现，该类聚合物的熔融温度可以满足服装保温需要，而结晶温度则较低，通常在10℃以下，不能满足服装保温需要。1997年，张兴祥等系统研究不同分子量的聚乙二醇和聚丁二醇的性能特点，发现聚乙二醇的熔融和结晶行为具有分子量依存性，分子量为800~2000的聚乙二醇适宜用于调温纤维，但聚丁二醇的结晶温度较低不适宜用于调温纤维。随后进行的熔融复合纺丝实验证实，只有分子量在10000以上的聚乙二醇才具有可纺性，而分子量在10000以上的聚乙二醇不适用于调温纤维。研究人员将聚乙二醇与可以增加熔体粘度的乙烯类共聚物混合，制成形状稳定的切粒，以该切粒为纤维芯成分，以聚丙烯为鞘成分，采用熔融复合纺丝工艺制成调温复合纤维。该纤维的物理力学性能可以满足一般纺织加工需要，制成的服装具有比一般纤维服装更好的舒适性。该项研究于2000年通过国家"九五"重点科研计划项目验收，由中国工程院院士梅志强等组成的验收专家组认为：工艺技术路线新颖、先进，成果填补国内空白，整体达到国际先进水平。2001年，研究人员在系统研究多种相变材料性能特点的基础上，实现相变材料的纳胶囊化和微胶囊化，制备出调温丙纶和阻燃调温腈氯纶，并采用多种实验手段测试调温纺织品的保温和调温性能。调温纺织品与同规格的普通纺织品具有等同的保温性能，并且在升温和降温过程中其内部温度较普通纺织品低或高3℃以上，持续时间可达30分钟。2005年，该纤维织物已由天津工业大学功能纤维材料开发中心小规模生产，并用于新型军用服装的开发中。获发明专利3项，实用新型专利2项。

3. 抗菌纤维

2001年1月，天津大学管云林、刘晓非、李治等完成仿生抗菌纤维的应用基础研究，选用微晶壳聚糖水分散体，代替壳聚糖粉末，作为抗菌添加剂，并在纺丝液中添加N，O-羧甲基壳聚糖为增容剂；采用辐照降解后的壳聚糖制备微晶壳聚糖水分散体、N，O-羧甲基壳聚糖、O-羧甲基壳聚糖、壳聚糖碘季铵盐和壳聚糖季铵盐酸盐，研究这些聚合物的抗菌性，探讨壳聚糖抗菌性的影响因素及其可能的抗菌机理；在此基础上，以微细壳聚糖水分散体、O-羧甲基壳聚糖和壳聚糖季铵盐的混合物为抗菌剂，以N，O-羧甲基壳聚糖为增容剂，加入到粘胶长丝纺丝液中，共混液脱泡后在50℃的酸浴中纺丝，牵伸比为1.25∶1，成型的纤维经水洗、脱硫、漂白等系列后处理后，即成为外观理想、抗菌型优异的壳聚糖/粘胶抗菌纤维。

2005年1月，天津工业大学程博闻与天津大学共同承担壳聚糖/纤维素抗菌纤维的应用基础研究，项目制备两种在NMMO/H_2O溶剂中溶解性能很好的壳聚糖衍生物-乙醚胺壳聚糖和乙酸钠壳聚糖，与壳聚糖相比，二者的抗菌性能和溶解性能均有明显提高。

4. 吸水性功能纤维

2005年1月，天津工业大学邓新华完成超强吸水性功能纤维的研究，研制出四种丙烯酸类高吸水纤维和三种高吸水树脂，纤维最高吸水倍率达246倍，最高吸生理盐水倍率达58倍，最大吸水速率达71%每30秒，最大抗拉强度为0.212CN/Tdex，断裂伸长率约为31.8%；有机—无机物复合型高吸水树脂最高吸水倍率达4402倍，最高吸生理盐水倍率达357倍，吸水速率大于74.5%每30秒。

2005年6月，天津工业大学肖长发完成多孔超吸水吸湿纤维的研究与开发，开发两条工艺技术路线研制高吸水纤维，即后交联-水解型共聚丙烯腈纤维和丙烯酰胺共聚物/聚乙烯醇共混纤维，均取得良好效果。试制的后开交联-水解型高吸水纤维填补国内空白。

5. 紫外荧光防伪纤维

2005年，天津南开戈德集团有限公司、天津南开大学戈德防伪技术有限公司李伯平、王淑芳、董轶望、王旭研制成功紫外荧光防伪纤维，采用创新的"复合溶剂渗透染色法"解决常规纤维难于渗染紫外荧光防伪物质的大难题，通过建立灵活、简便、稳定、高效的生产新工艺，内含防伪纤维的防伪纸比激光全息标志、荧光防伪油墨等传统防伪产品具有更优异的防伪可靠性。在国内外率先实现紫外荧光纤维的小批量、多品种、低成本的产业化生产，并进一步开发出含有紫外荧光纤维的防伪纸。

6. 多功能纤维

1996年，天津工业大学开始研究负离子纤维和纺织品，对多种天然或人工合成热释电、压电材料的组成、结构、粒度、添加量、实验工艺条件等展开系统研究，得到性能最佳的多功能微粉，而后采用熔融纺丝技术制得多功能纤维，其强度和伸度等指标均可满足纺织加工生产要求，用于非织造布、针织布和机织布等多种用途。2000年，天津工业大学与天津市华林医疗保健用品公司合作开发出负离子织物，实现产业化生产，织物的负离子数高于3500个每立方厘米,远红外辐射率在87%以上,对金黄葡萄球菌和大肠杆菌具有抑制作用,其负离子纤维技术获得发明专利授权。

2003年6月,天津工业大学张华等研究具有压电和热释电性的PVDF纤维。聚偏氟乙烯(PVDF)压电材料具有独特的热释电效应和压电效应,与目前常用的无机物压电材料相比(如石英、压电陶瓷类),具有声阻抗小、频率响应宽、介电常数小、耐冲击性强、便于加工等优点,是一种新型高分子换能材料,在电声超声、红外及生物医学工程领域都受到广泛重视。该课题在研究PVDF压电和热释电性能的基础上,开拓材料的应用,开发出具有一定纤度和强度同时具有压电性和热释电性的PVDF纤维材料。研究成果在PVDF纺丝、PVDF/Nylon11共混纺丝方面有创造性突破,在PVDF纤维的晶态结构研究方面有新的发现。

2005年7月,天津工业大学郑帼研制成功丙纶拒水拒油纤维。项目对含氟、含硅的拒水拒油油剂进行基础及应用基础研究,通过光散射仪研究拒水拒油剂粒径,并以电子扫描显微镜对油剂在纤维表面的形貌进行表征,首次研制出具有优异拒水拒油性的氟烷基改性氨基硅油。并以此为主体,开发出TFSF-10型拒水拒油助剂。在丙纶纤维现有生产工艺条件下,以该助剂替代常规纺丝油剂,制得拒水拒油纤维,成果达到国际先进水平。

2005年9月,天津工业大学齐鲁研制多功能防护纤维,采用在聚合物(PP和PA6)中添加无机粉料的方法,通过共混和皮芯复合纺丝研制出多功能防护纤维。研究添加改性助剂改善无机粉料与聚合物的相容性,较好的解决高含量无机粉料(30重量百分比~50重量百分比)分散性、混和物的流动性和可纺性。

二、纤维膜材料

(一)中空纤维膜

1993年1月,创建于1974年7月的中国第一家膜研究单位——天津纺织工学院膜分离技术研究所,继在国内率先第一支聚砜中空纤维超滤膜组件、第一支醋酸纤维素中空纤维反渗透膜组件之后,该所组建的膜技术公司又研制出中国第一支聚偏氟乙烯中空纤维微滤膜。2004年,天津膜天膜工程技术有限公司在天津滨海新区建成中国最大的中空纤维膜产业化生产基地,其产能达到300万平方米每年,标志着一个新产业崛起。

图4-3-3-41　天津纺织工学院(现天津工业大学)膜分离技术研究所

2003年8月,天津工业大学膜天膜公司吕晓龙等开发出用于发酵液分离与精制的中空纤维膜双向流技术。针对发酵行业发酵液菌体分离的特点,设计中空纤维膜装置TWF双向流工艺流程,将发酵液流向周期性倒向,即发酵液流向按通常的下进上出方式运行一定时间后,通过阀门切换,将发酵液流向反转为上进下出方式,运行一定时间后再次换向,依此循环进行。由此循环交替,同一支中空纤维膜组件始终同时处于高效的工作与清洗状态。该工艺尤其适用于发酵液等较粘稠液体的过滤与精制,改变以往中空纤维膜不能用于浓粘液体的过滤分离的情况,拓展中空纤维膜的应用领域。

2003年12月,天津工业大学完成聚丙烯腈碳中空纤维膜研究,项目围绕中空碳纤维液相分离膜展开研制工作,合成高分子量聚丙烯腈(PAN),适合制备碳中空纤维膜的基膜,在加入一定含量的聚甲基丙烯酸甲酯(PMMA)和聚酰亚胺(YJ-16)后,形成规则的指状孔,制备出合格的聚丙烯腈碳中空纤维膜。聚丙烯腈碳中空纤维膜应用于石油开采、化工、制药、发酵、环保等行业,促进这些行业的技术进步。

2004年5月,国家海洋局天津海水淡化与综合利用研究所完成聚丙烯中空纤维微孔膜研发及应用研究项目,利用国产原料和自主配套设备,采用熔纺纺丝、拉伸法制膜工艺,成功研制出聚丙烯中空纤维微滤膜。实现清洁生产(无公害和污染),具有优良的耐化学药剂、耐细菌侵蚀性、生物相容性和疏水性等;同时,可亲水化、并具有良好的耐热性、耐折绕性,机械强度高,便于装配、使用及清洗。液体充氧(或CO_2)技术及装置属国内首创,可以部分取代传统气体吸收与解吸工艺过程。建成年产40万平方米的微孔膜工业化生产线,产品大批量销往国内市场,并销往韩国、新加坡等海外市场,用户反映良好,经济效益和社会效益显著。

2005年,天津工业大学、天津膜天膜工程技术有限公司吕晓龙、郭振友、马世虎、李先锋用fi-发酵液分离与精制的中空纤维膜。该项目改变以往中空纤维膜不能用于浓粘液体的过滤分离的情况,拓展中空纤维膜的应用领域,尤其适用于发酵液等较浓稠液体的过滤与精制。与板式膜和管式膜相比,中空纤维膜装置具有设备占地少、造价低、浓缩液回收率高等优点,尤其适用于大型发酵液处理,具有良好的社会和经济效益。

(二)纤维素农膜

2005年4月,天津工业大学程博闻完成环境友好型纤维素纤维及纤维素农膜的开发。项目组采用电子束辐射、超声波、蒸汽闪爆一系列现代加工技术,对纤维素进行活化;定量讨论各种活化条件与纤维素聚合度的关系;分析纤维素经活化后结构的变化及反应性能变化;围绕新的纤维素衍生物氨基甲酸酯的合成、共混溶液纺丝成形及其性能等方面,开展富有特色的工作。

三、凝胶与聚醚

(一)凝胶

2003年5月,天津工业大学陈莉、刘文广、赵义平等完成防止海洋生物附着的智能凝胶研究,发现离子型凝胶比非离子型凝胶具有更好的防附着能力,其中聚3-丙烯酰胺基丙基三甲基氯化铵凝胶和聚丙烯酸凝胶表面的防附着能力最好,适合作为防附着材料;确认凝胶的交联密度可影响离子型凝胶表面孢子的附着量,而对配子体数、排卵量以及发芽率等没有影响;提出一种可提高凝胶力学强度的方法。

2005年7月,陈莉开展智能凝胶微机器及其在生物分离中的应用研究,设计并合成新型热、电和光响应凝胶,研究合成条件、聚合比例等因素对凝胶溶胀性能的影响以及外界环境刺激下凝胶的溶胀、吸附行为。特别是所合成的温敏葡聚糖共聚凝胶显示出较聚(N-异丙基丙烯酰胺)凝胶更优越的温度敏感性、溶胀性能和力学性能,从而为进一步研究凝胶在生物分离方面的应用奠定基础。

2005年,陈莉、赵义平、董晶等完成聚电解质凝胶的协同作用及其环境响应性研究,通过将PDMAPS两性聚电解质溶液互穿于阴离子聚合物PAMPS凝胶中,制备出一种新型的温度敏感的显示相转变行为而无体积变化的IPN凝胶;首次合成出导电聚噻吩水凝胶;用碘和高氯酸水溶液作掺杂剂,研究水溶性的聚噻吩及其水凝胶的掺杂行为;提出一种可以提高凝胶力学性能的新方法。首次提出聚电解质对相反电荷表面活性剂的吸附分两个阶段进行:第一阶段,形成等化学量的1∶1不溶复合物;第二阶段,过剩的表面活性剂进一步吸附到高分子链上,使高分子带电荷从而形成非等化学量的可溶的复合物。首次阐述复合行为的不同不只是静电作用,而且与它们的化学结构有关。研究成果发表在多种中外学术刊物上,被SCI收录12篇;部分内容写入论著《智能高分子材料》中。

(二)聚醚

2000年,天津工业大学郑帼承担功能性聚醚的研制与开发,研制出功能性聚醚,并建成国内第一套外循环直冷式高价澄碧的物化反应精制系统,成功实现低沸点起始剂合成聚醚,以及从小试到大生产的技术转换,其专利产品填补国内空白。

2004年,天津工业大学张继梅完成生物酶催化特种聚醚研究,对生物酶、镁铝复合金属氧化物和改性镁铝复合金属氧化物催化剂制备、结构、组成及合成窄分布聚醚反应工艺等进行系统研究。

2005年7月,天津工业大学魏俊富等开展环境友好可降解双烷基聚醚的研究,研究可降解缩醛化双烷基聚醚表面活性剂的合成、水解和生物降解性,首次采用辐射接枝法合成出具有超强酸性和强酸性的聚四氟乙烯基纤维催化剂。开发出合成可降解缩醛化双烷基聚醚的新方法,其最高转化率可以达到88.6%。

四、功能高分子材料

2003年12月，南开大学李贺先、王国昌、斯志怀等研究分子组装制备高分子纳米结构复合材料，研究小分子自组装形成高分子纳米球体、嵌段共聚物自组装形成纳米结构以及磁性杂化纳米纤维自组装形成超晶格有序结构的机理和方法；发明磁性杂化纳米纤维自组装超晶格结构材料及其制备方法和高分子纳米球体及其准临界聚合制备方法。制备的超晶格结构材料具有有序介观结构、不同几何结构形态（如四楞锥形）并达到微米尺度，在显示技术和高密度存储器等方面具有重要的应用前景。

第四节　复合材料

1991~2005年，天津在复合材料研究领域取得一系列可喜成果。关于金属基复合材料与医学功能材料的探索极具实际应用价值。

一、金属基复合材料

2003年3月，天津理工大学完成颗粒增强金属基复合材料喷射成型技术的研究，自行设计研制喷射成型装置，确定最佳复合材料喷射工艺路线与工艺参数，开展沉积材料组织结构分析和材料性能实验，并采用计算机模拟技术顺利完成喷射沉积过程的坯料温度场及热应力场演变及发展过程的模拟。其中Zn27Al+SiC沉积坯料拉伸强度比基体强度提高2.6倍以上，沉积坯料晶粒尺度达到均匀、细小，平均晶粒尺度3~5微米以下，制备出的材料具有微观组织均匀细化、消除成分宏观偏析，形成亚稳结构，减少脆性相的特性。成果达到国际先进水平。

2004年11月，天津大学刘东志、周雪琴等完成新型电荷传输材料的合成及其与电荷产生材料物质的复配效应研究。该项目以新型功能材料为根本，合成出两大系列共9种偶氮电荷产生材料，两类共8种芳乙烯基三苯基胺类电荷传输材料以及3种新型的均三嗪基修饰1，3，4-噁二唑类小分子化合物；并研究这些新型材料的结构与性能关系。所制备的偶氮化合物与偶氮复合物具有良好的内光电效应，是性能优良的电荷产生材料；合成的系列芳乙烯基三芳胺类化合物和1，3，4-噁二唑类基团修饰的不对称均三嗪化合物，不仅是传输性能优良的载流子传输材料，也是一类性能稳定的有机电致发光材料。

二、医学功能材料

2000~2003年，河北工业大学崔春翔、申玉田等研制钛酸钾颗粒表面增强钛合金梯度生物医学材料，该复合材料具有很高的结合强度，克服现有羟基磷灰石涂层脆性大、强度低、与Ti合金基体间结合强度差的不足。课题组首次研究该类材料的生物医学特性，开发出高结合强度的诱导生物活性的钛酸钾原位自生层/Ti合金生物医学材料，比国内外临床中广泛应用的316L不锈钢、Co-Cr合金和Ti_6Al_4V等钛合金具有更加优越的生物相容性和生物活性。

2003年8月，天津大学成功研制出中药纳米透皮吸收制剂高分子辅料，开发出4种不同类型的亲水性高分子药用压敏胶材料，在皮肤相容性、促进经皮释放等方面优于橡胶类压敏胶，且工艺简单、无环境污染，为解决现有中药橡胶膏剂存在的皮肤过敏、粘贴过牢、透皮吸收率低等问题提供新的途径，填补国内药用亲水压敏胶的空白。还开发5种具有自主知识产权的纳米药物载体和疏水性药物纳米化工艺技术，为中药透皮吸收和纳米药物的开发奠定技术和材料基础。该项目具有实用性、创新性和先进性。

2004年9月，中国医学科学院生物医学工程研究所张其清、刘玲蓉、张立海等研制成功胶原基骨组织工程支架材料，项目组模拟天然骨组织细胞外基质成分，以胶原、羟基磷灰石（HA）、粘多糖-硫酸软骨素（CS）、细胞生长因子-骨形态发生蛋白（BMP）为主要原料，构建成胶原基骨组织工程支架材料。支架材料具有良好的理化和生物学性能。种植实验和动物实验表明，成骨细胞在支架材料上生长状况良好并分泌大量细胞外基质，能诱导新骨形成。

2005年，河北工业大学开展生物及结构复合材料原位自主复合机制的基础研究，从理论上阐明钛酸锂/钛合金、TiC-AIN/AI和TiN-AIN/AI、双相纳米磁性材料和Al_2O_3Cu复合材料的原位生长机制；建立增强相颗粒在基体快速凝固时的固/液界面交互作用机制模型，并用来确定一定凝固条件下，陶瓷颗粒能被基体的固/液界面吞噬而实现晶内增强的尺寸。还从理论上阐明自生增强相的生成机制；复合材料的显微组织与力学性能和生物、导电功能的关系与规律；自生相对材料的强化机制及增韧机制以及不同凝固过程对组织形态的影响。

第五节 焊接材料

焊接是两种或两种以上同种或异种材料通过原子或分子之间的结合和扩散连接成一体的工艺过程，属于材料科学中的一个分支。1991~2005年，天津关于焊接材料有可贵发现，处国内先进水平。

1993年12月~1999年12月，天津大学与天津市电焊条公司合作，张韵慧、尹淑梅、李之唐等人共同完成药芯焊丝工艺润滑剂研究及开发项目，采用的基础原料立足国内，研制出碳钢自保护药芯焊丝、碳钢气体保护药芯焊丝和不锈钢药芯焊丝三种固体润滑剂，统称为TYH940型药芯焊丝固体润滑剂，广泛适用于不同种类药芯焊丝生产全过程，满足生产过程对润滑材料的要求，填补国内空白。

2001年3月~2003年6月，天津大学李午申完成超高硬度抗裂堆焊材料的强韧化设计，项目采用试验优化技术建立超高硬度堆敷金属性能和因子之间的数学模型，利用最优化技术求取堆敷药芯焊丝的最优配方，使超高硬度堆焊材料设计，实现由定型到定量、经验到科学的发展。项目研究微量元素对堆敷金属强韧性的影响规律：适量加入钇基重稀土、微量钛和金属镍，可提高堆敷金属的强韧性；利用电磁搅拌技术，可促使堆敷金属细化晶粒、减少夹杂物和成分偏析、打碎网状共晶碳化物，改善共晶碳化物及夹杂物颗粒的大小及分布形态；用组织工程和热处理等方法，可控制堆敷金属硬度的均匀性。项目研究成果为超高硬度堆焊材料在冷轧工作辊上的应用，奠定坚实的研究开发基础。

第四章 新能源

20世纪80年代初南开大学即开展化学储能技术研究，是国内最早开展新能源技术研究的单位。天津关于新能源技术的研究与开发及其产业化以南开大学、中国电子科技集团公司第十八研究所和天津大学为主要代表。1991~2005年，关于太阳能电池和储氢电池的基础研究，南开大学取得多项创新成果，其中低温晶化硅薄膜材料及非晶硅/低温晶化硅叠层电池的研究达到国际先进水平。中国电子科技集团公司第十八研究所也一直致力于太阳能和化学储能技术的研究工作，成果应用于航天与深潜领域，达到国际先进水平。

早在20世纪80年代，天津市就开展新能源科研成果的产业化工作，并逐渐发展成为国内最大的绿色新能源基地。国家科学技术委员会在“九五”计划期间抓好的全国15个“重中之重”项目，天津市的“镍氢电池产业化”建设项目列为其中之一。1991~2005年期间，天津涌现出一批新能源企业。

第一节 太阳能电池及产业化研究

天津关于太阳能利用的研究与开发技术以南开大学、中国电子科技集团公司第十八研究所和天津大学为主要代表。1991~2005年，南开大学以晶化硅、非晶硅、微晶硅、铜铟镓硒为材料的太阳能电池研究取得多项创新成果，其中大面积ZnO透明导电薄膜MOCVD制备系统的研制成功和低温晶化硅薄膜材料及非晶硅/低温晶化硅叠层电池的多项研究成果达到国际先进水平。中国电子科技集团公司第十八研究所研制的带通滤光器高效硅太阳电池为神舟飞船二期工程配套。

一、硅基材料的太阳能电池

1990年末，南开大学孟志国、耿新华、孙云等在非晶硅薄膜太阳电池的研究中取得突出成绩，但稳定性较差。1992年1月，南开大学耿新华、孙云承担大面积高效高稳定非晶硅太阳电池的研究与应用项目，至1995年10月，耿新华等研制出低温p型微晶硅碳(p-μc-SiC·H)材料，其带隙(2.2eV)比常规非晶硅碳(p-a-SiC:H，Eg=1.9eV)高，而其电特性(暗电导率达0.2S/cm)提高几个数量级。耿新华、孙云、刘世国等采用p-μc-Si:H/p-a-SiC:H复合窗口层、氢稀释本征非晶硅材料、n-μc-Si:H/p- SiC:H隧穿结，以及氢处理技术，使用全部国产化原材料和适合工业化生产的电池结构与互联技术，在没有背反射电极情况下，使20厘米×20厘米非晶硅/非晶硅(a-Si/a-Si)叠层集成型电池效率达到8.28%(Voc=36.4伏，FF=73.4%，Isc=111.63毫安)，室外光照一年后的稳定效率为7.35%，为国际先进水平。同期，王广才、耿新华、李洪波等研制的20厘米×20厘米非晶硅/非晶硅锗/非晶硅锗(a-Si/a-SiGe/a-SiGe)不同带隙三结叠层电池的效率达到6.74%，10厘米×10厘米非晶硅/非晶硅锗(a-Si/a-SiGe)双结叠层电池的效率达到7.524%，为国内领先水平。

1995年2月，南开大学刘世国、耿新华等研制的非晶硅/非晶硅双结内联式弱光电池系列，荧光照度200勒下，开路电压1.3伏，短路电流密度6微安培/平方厘米，产品合格率达85%以上。王宗畔、耿新华等研制的非晶硅太阳电池荧光特性测试系统照度不均匀性小于1%，测试重复性达98%以上。

2000年10月，南开大学耿新华和赵颖分别牵头承担的稳定获得大面积高稳定非晶硅电池及其实用化技术基础研究和器件质量级低温晶化硅薄膜材料及稳定非晶硅/低温晶化硅叠层电池的研究正式启动，2005年通过鉴定。两个项目在大面积非晶硅、微晶硅及其叠层电池、大面积染料敏化纳米薄膜电池的研究等方面均达到国际先进水平，并分别建立600瓦非晶硅电池和500瓦染料敏化纳米薄膜电池自动跟踪测试电站，以考核研制电池的长期寿命。项目组在南开大学和新疆首次建立4千瓦和百千瓦级非晶硅、晶硅混合并网发电示范电站，进行对比发电试验。建立国内唯一的年产5兆瓦非晶硅/非晶硅叠层太阳电池生产线。中国科学院院士霍裕平以“走出了相当大的一步”评价该项目的工作。

2001年，南开大学赵颖等承担低温晶化硅薄膜材料及非晶硅/低温晶化硅叠层电池的研究项目，2003年2月，该项目首次在高TCO绒度衬底上，获得高性能晶化硅电池，为实现低价长寿命电池的理念提供有益的途径。微晶硅薄膜材料相对于非晶硅材料有很高的有序性，是解决硅基薄膜光伏电池稳定性的有效办法。薄膜微晶硅电池既具有晶体硅电池高效、高稳定的优势，又具有薄膜电池工艺简单、节省材料的优点，有大幅度降低成本的潜力。

2004年9月,中国电子科技集团公司第十八研究所研制的带通滤光器高效硅太阳电池实现批量生产,为圆满完成神舟飞船二期工程任务奠定基础。该电池平均光电转换效率达到16.8%以上,为国内批量生产光电转换效率最高的单晶硅太阳电池。神舟飞船二期工程对太阳电池方阵提出比神舟飞船一期工程更高的要求:重量更轻,功率更大,寿命更长。该太阳电池的带通滤光器达到450纳米~1050纳米波段时,平均透过率T不小于92%、紫外光反射峰值大于80%、红外光反射峰值大于85%,均达国际先进水平。带通滤光器太阳电池平均光电转换效率16.8%以上,电池厚度0.15毫米以下、吸收系数低于0.78。同时还具有较高的抗高能粒子辐射能力。它的批量生产使中国空间用薄型高效硅太阳电池的研制生产跻身世界先进行列。

2005年5月,南开大学赵颖、薛俊明、耿新华等研制成功大面积ZnO透明导电薄膜MOCVD制备系统,在国际上首次自主开发建成大面积(218×218平方毫米)ZnO透明导电薄膜MOCVD制备系统,解决大面积太阳电池的ZnO成膜,对薄膜电池的研发起到重要作用,成为新一代薄膜电池专用装备。该系统于2004年7月开始用于研究大面积非晶硅太阳电池、微晶硅电池和非晶硅/微晶硅叠层电池的背电极,使硅基薄膜电池性能指标达到国际先进水平。同期,耿新华、赵颖、魏长春等研制成功辐射型多功能薄膜自动沉积系统。该系统为新一代非标CVD设备,具有故障率低和线列式无交叉污染的优点,并克服只能制备单一结构器件的局限性。该系统于2004年7月用于研究新型微晶硅电池和非晶硅/微晶硅叠层电池研究,使新型电池性能指标达到国际先进水平。对于高速沉积稳定非晶硅材料和电池的研究,也取得较好结果,提高国内在光电子领域设备设计及自动化控制等硬件方面的技术水平,提升国家在薄膜光伏领域的国际竞争力。

图4-4-1-42 南开大学用MOCVD技术研制薄膜太阳电池

2005年7月,南开大学赵颖、耿新华、薛俊明等完成用MOCVD技术研制硅薄膜太阳电池的ZnO/Al复合背反射电极项目,该成果采用MOCVD技术制备硅基薄膜太阳电池复合背反射电极的ZnO薄膜,成功解决其他制备技术对电池造成的损伤,使电池性能显著提高。在面积20×20平方厘米内,薄膜厚度为500纳米时,采用MOCVD方法制备的透明导电ZnO薄膜,方块电阻38Ω,霍尔迁移率17.8平方厘米/Vs,透过率>85%(400~1100纳米),薄膜不均匀性低于±5%。同时使0.253平方厘米非晶硅/微晶硅叠层太阳电池短路电流密度增加1.8毫安/平方厘米,效率增加1.44个百分点,达到11.8%。(10厘米×10厘米)非晶硅/微晶硅叠层太阳电池组件效率9.7%。大面积(20厘米×20厘米)非晶硅电池组件的短路电流密度增加0.6毫安/平方厘米,效率增加0.59个百分点,达到9.10%。电池性能达到国际先进水平。同一时期,耿新华、任慧志、薛俊明等还从事大面积高效稳定非晶硅/非晶硅叠层太阳电池的研究工作,制成高效稳定太阳电池,在没有背反射电极的情况下,400平方厘米非晶硅/非晶硅叠层电池,沉积速率3安培/秒,最高效率达到9.2%;连续10批(片),平均效率为8.76%;连续光照1000小时,效率衰退率小于12%。即最高稳定效率8.1%,平均稳定效率7.7%。该项目通过国际薄膜电池老化标准-IEC1646中高低温、高湿循环老化等最严酷条件的考核,寿命达到20年。该成果在多方面具有创造性和先进性,为提高该类产品水平、降低制造成本,奠定理论和技术基础。与此同时,耿新华、赵颖、张晓丹等开展高效非晶硅/微晶硅叠层太阳电池的研究,以非晶硅为顶电池、以微晶硅为底电池的叠层电池,组成非晶硅/微晶硅叠层太阳电池,采用VHF-PECVD技术制备微晶硅p材料,该优质P层微晶硅材料在厚度为20~30纳米情况下,材料电导达10~1秒/厘米量级,晶化率在40%~50%;实验中发现p层晶化率对微晶硅电池本征层晶化率调制作用不大,但对孵化层的影响较大,为此,首次提出通过调制p层晶化率,优化叠层电池的填充因子和开路电压,从而获得提高叠层电池效率的新途径;通过非晶硅顶电池和微晶硅底电池的厚度匹配,使非晶硅/微晶硅叠层太阳电池的效率达11.8%,对应电池的短路电流为14.5毫安/平方厘米,开路电压1.33伏,填充因子为61%。成果达到国际先进水平。耿新华、赵颖、薛俊明等还采用甚高频等离子体增强化学气相沉积(VHF-PECVD)方法,从事"低温晶化硅薄膜太阳电池"的研究,根据需要引入各种不同气体，并控制相互之间的比例关系和总量，在一定的衬底温度和功率条件下，在特定的衬底上沉积完成具有各种光电性能的硅基薄膜，特别是器件质量级本征微晶硅薄膜，进而制成微晶硅薄膜太阳电池。2005年9月，赵颖、耿新华、张晓丹等完成低温晶化硅薄膜材料及非晶硅/低温晶化硅叠层电池的研究，该项目在TCO绒度8%~80%范围内，生长微晶硅电池，具有更佳的陷光结构。在42%绒度的TCO衬底上，采用光-CVD方法沉积微晶硅电池，Jsc达到22毫安/平方厘米，电池效率可提高1%~2%。由MOCVD方法制备的ZnO与金属银/铝组成复合背反射电极，并与前电极形成优化的陷光结构，使硅薄膜电池效率大幅提高。通过对不同沉积条件下制备的微晶硅薄膜的特性研究，总结出器件质量级微晶硅材料完整的表征体系。研究成果首次提出高效太阳电池用、器件质量级微晶硅材料应具有的特性，以及获得器件质量级微晶硅薄膜所对应沉积条件的三维立体趋势图。采用VHF-PECVD技术，在170℃低温下所制备的双层p型窗口材料，在厚度为20~30纳米情况下，材料电导率达1~10秒/厘米量级，晶化率达40%~50%。制备的单结微晶硅太阳电池效率为9.2%(0.253平方厘米)；小面积非晶硅/微晶硅叠层太阳电池效率11.8%(0.253平方厘米)；100平方厘米集成型非晶硅/微晶硅太阳电池组件效率9.7%。这些结果标志低价长寿命薄膜太阳电池研制取得一个重大进步。

2005年7月，南开大学赵颖、张晓丹、耿新华等完成高效大面积集成型非晶硅/微晶硅叠层太阳电池组件项目。该项目采用甚高频等离子体增强化学气相沉积(VHF-PECVD)方法，根据需要引入各种不同气体，并控制相互之间的比例关系和总量，在一定的衬底温度和功率条件下，在特定的衬底上沉积完成具有各种光电性能的硅基薄膜，最终研制成高效大面积集成型非晶硅/微晶硅叠层太阳电池组件。太阳电池组件主要性能指标均达到设计要求。国内未见有电池面积大于100平方厘米、电池效率大于9%的薄膜非晶/微晶集成型太阳能电池组件的文献报道。赵颖、张晓丹、耿新华等还开展高效单结pin型微晶硅薄膜太阳电池的研制，采用VHF-PECVD技术系统研究硅烷浓度、反应气压、辉光功率、衬底温度和衬底材料对沉积速率、结构特性和光电特性的影响，建立比较完整的器件质量级微晶硅材料的表征体系以及达到器件质量级微晶硅材料的制备参数；用SnO_2/ZnO和溅射后湿法腐蚀ZnO两种不同衬底制备电池，结果发现衬底的结构对电池的性能参数有很大影响，这对制备高效率微晶硅太阳电池具有重要意义；采用VHF-PECVD技术(激发频率60兆赫兹)，制备面积0.253平方厘米、结构为Glass/ZnO/p-μc-Si:H/i-μc-Si:H/n-a-Si:H/ZnO/Ag/Al的单结微晶硅薄膜太阳电池，其开路电压0.55伏，短路电流密度26.5毫安/平方厘米，填充因子63%，电池的转换效率9.2%。该项目采用的技术路线，与硅薄膜生产线工艺技术兼容，通过技术放大可直接服务于生产，较快产生经济效益，使硅薄膜电池产品质量大幅提高，制造成本大幅降低。同期，南开大学薛俊明、侯国付、孙建等完成用VHF-PECVD技术研制大面积硅基薄膜项目，采用中心点馈入法，在反应室外采用同轴电缆，在真空反应室内采用矩形不锈钢导槽不接触式包裹VHF铜板导线，实现VHF信号的良好屏蔽；采用中心点馈入法很好地消除电极表面的驻波(TEM波)和损耗波(TE波)造成的电场不均匀性问题；在VHF-PECVD的辉光区保持两个平行板电极绝对平行，没有任何的金属突起，以获得均匀的薄膜材料；VHF信号在电极馈入点的连接结构，选择特殊设计；通过改变流量、激发功率、工作压力等工作参数来分析比较a-Si:H薄膜的均匀性。

2005年12月，中国电子科技集团公司第十八研究所研制的空间用TDJ25.5×51、TDJ23.2×51单晶硅太阳电池，通过信息产业部的设计定型。该产品是国内首次采用氧化钛/氧化钇双层减反射膜系的太阳电池。在产品研制过程中，采用钛-钯-银金属电极、铝背反射器、氧化钛/氧化钇双层减反射膜结构设计，电池实际平均光电转换效率达到12.68%，经1MeV、7×10^{14}当量/平方厘米电子辐照后，平均光电转换效率衰降仅20.32%；其环境适应性好，可靠性高，适合空间应用，产品主要性能指标达到国际先进水平。

二、铜铟硒(CIS)薄膜和砷化镓太阳电池

(一)铜铟硒(CIS)薄膜太阳电池

1989年初，南开大学李长健开始新型化合物半导体铜铟硒($CuInSe_2$，简称CIS)薄膜太阳电池的研究，于1991年底制出一批CIS/CdS薄膜太阳电池。1991年李长健开始研究高效4端薄膜太阳电池，使CIS电池的

研制工作日渐成形。1992年李长健承担的CIS薄膜太阳电池研究列入国家"八五"科技攻关计划，1995年，1平方厘米的CIS/CdS薄膜太阳电池效率为7.28%，5×6平方厘米面积上9个单体子电池，平均效率为6.67%，表明具有较好地均匀性，超额完成合同任务。

1996年，孙云与李长健合作承担$CuInSe_2$薄膜太阳电池开发研究，首次开始研究铜铟硒（$CuInSe_2$）掺Ga（镓）制备铜铟镓硒（CIGS）薄膜太阳电池。1997年11月CIS/CdS电池效率达到8.34%。1998年，探索制备出5×6平方厘米面积集成型CIS/CdS薄膜太阳电池，转换效率为3.1%。1999年研制1平方厘米面积铜铟镓硒异质结CIGS/CdS薄膜太阳电池转换效率达到9.13%，专家认为，电池技术水平较高，在研制过程中解决一些技术关键问题，为后续工作打下基础。此后，南开大学于2000年底初步建立CIS和CIGS薄膜太阳电池的试验线，居于国内领先地位。2001年，南开大学承担国家"十五"计划"863"重点课题铜铟硒太阳薄膜电池试验平台与中试线。2001年7月，孙云开始"固态源光硒化法研制铜硒薄膜太阳电池"的研究工作，完成设备改造，在关键技术取得多项突破，电池效率在6%～9%基础上达到10.4%。

（二）砷化镓太阳电池

2004年12月，中国电子科技集团公司第十八研究所研制的三结$InGaP_2$/GaInAs/Ge太阳电池平均光电转换效率达到26%，开始小批量生产。这是国内达到批量生产光电转换效率最高的太阳电池。GaAs/Ge单结太阳电池平均转换效率约19.5%，是用不同禁带宽度的Ⅲ－Ⅴ族元素作材料，按禁带宽度大小叠合制备的多结太阳电池，分别选择吸收并转换太阳光谱的不同子域，提高太阳电池的光电转换效率。它在航天器上使用，对于减小太阳电池方阵的面积，简化卫星的姿控设计，减轻卫星重量，具有极其重要意义，是较好适用于超大功率卫星的太阳电池品种。十八所开发的三结$InGaP_2$/GaInAs/Ge太阳电池采用MOCVD技术制造，产品以锗单晶为衬底，外延过程中在锗衬底上形成锗电池，依次外延生长GaInAs电池和$InGaP_2$电池，并在三个p-n结之间用隧穿结相联接，电池极性与单结GaAs/Ge太阳电池相同，三结电池的典型参数为：开路电压2.6435伏，短路电流16.1毫安/平方厘米，填充因子0.8364，平均光电转换效率26%。三结电池不仅效率高，还具有高于单结电池的抗高能粒子辐射能力。该产品在长寿命、大功率卫星上使用，即使运行到卫星设计寿命末期仍能保持比其他电池更高的转换效率。三结电池进入实用化批量生产是中国空间电源技术的一次飞跃。

三、太阳能电池阵

2005年1月TC-1、TC-2卫星太阳能电池阵项目由中国电子科技集团公司第十八研究所金海雯、孙彦铮、高剑峰等完成。该项目所研制的太阳能电池阵是TC-1、TC-2卫星在轨运行期间电源分系统的主发电设备。该系统采用体装式的外形结构，包括上、下两个太阳电池壳，单体电池选用BSFR型硅太阳电池，平均光电转换效率达到14.8%，太阳阵输出功率280瓦以上。在太阳电池玻璃盖片上蒸镀一层ITO透明导电膜，并将每片盖片上的导电膜有效地连接组成网络，与卫星的"结构地"相连，使太阳电池阵表面等电位。经中国、欧空局专家双方地面联试，证明太阳电池阵ITO膜表面最大电位差不超过±1伏。这是国内首次将这项技术应用于卫星工程中。太阳电池阵的剩磁小，卫星剩磁在距离星体表面2.9米处，不超过0.5nT，优于设计指标要求。TC-1、TC-2卫星太阳电池阵技术处于国际先进水平，可靠性高。TC-1、TC-2卫星分别于2003年12月30日和2004年7月25日发射成功，太阳电池阵遥测数据正常，特别是在剩磁和静电洁净度的控制上，欧空局的专家也给予很高评价。

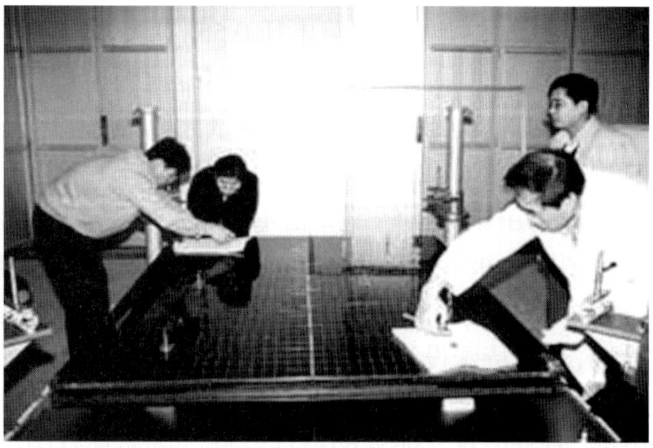
图4-4-1-43 科研人员在组装太阳电池方阵

四、太阳能利用的产业化

2001年9月8日，南开大学耿新华、王庆章、王宗畔等完成非晶硅弱光型太阳电池产业化技术及应用通过专家鉴定。项目采用国产化元部件，自行设计研制成功适用于产业化的非晶硅关键设备，分别在内蒙古、西藏进行应用示范，在研究产业化关键技术基础上，推动非晶硅电池产业化进程。南开大学与天津津能投资公司、天津机械进出口集团有限公司合作，建设5千瓦非晶硅太阳电池生产线，获得国家计委立项，该项目的实施，使中国非晶硅太阳电池产业跨入国际先进行列。王宗畔、薛俊明、耿新华等研制的非晶硅太阳电池产业化基本单元为国内最大型非晶硅沉积设备（沉积面积达730×1110平方毫米），并解决大面积成膜技术中温度、气流分布和电场分布均匀性等技术问题，填补国内在该领域的空白，为非晶硅太阳电池沉积设备国产化积累技术与经验。王庆章、王宗畔、耿卫东等研制的弱光型非晶硅太阳电池修复技术与设备，对弱光型非晶硅太阳电池的治疗修复率达50%以上，属国内领先水平。王庆章、耿卫东、王宗畔等完成的双结叠层非晶硅太阳电池示范电站，1999年4月在内蒙古阿拉善左旗银根苏木民族小学建成1300瓦风光互补型叠层非晶硅太阳电池示范电站，为学校照明、计算机教学、广播电视等供电，电站运行2年发电6831度，太阳电池方阵衰退率＜14%；2000年7月份在西藏组建2000瓦叠层非晶硅太阳电池示范电站。

2004年2月，列入国家和天津市高新技术产业化项目的年产5兆瓦非晶硅薄膜太阳电池生产线在天津市津能电池科技有限公司建成并投入生产，这标志着代表当前世界先进水平的单室、大容量薄膜太阳电池制造产业化技术落户天津，大大提升中国薄膜太阳电池产业化的制造水平。该项目是在天津市科委重大攻关计划支持并取得成果的基础上，以南开大学的技术为支撑，由天津市津能投资公司、国家开发投资公司所属国投创业公司、天津机电国际贸易集团公司和南开大学共同出资组建。一期工程引进美国EPV公司先进的单室沉积、大容量生产设备，年产5兆瓦双结非晶硅薄膜太阳电池，产品销往国内西部地区。同时建成一条年产3兆瓦单晶硅、多晶硅太阳电池组装线，该生产线主导产品为10瓦、20瓦、30瓦户用电源组件和58瓦、85瓦、120瓦电站用电池组件，也可以根据客户特殊需要设计、生产定制电池组件。

2004年4月，天津大学承担的用条形平面镜聚光获取高温太阳热的中试研究及示范工程项目，通过专家鉴定，认为达到国际领先水平。该成果研究开发的采用条形平面镜聚光、太阳方位角自动跟踪、选择性吸光液体获取高温太阳热能技术，可以有效、经济地获得高质量的太阳热能。课题组在天津市建成72平方米、500平方米、308平方米等3个中试示范工程，经实际应用与测试表明：反光镜反射率为0.92，方位角跟踪太阳精度优于0.5度，高角度跟踪太阳精度优于0.8度；对直射阳光的光热转化效率达60%以上，获得高于306℃的高温液体；在集光比为1∶20的情况下，集光系统的综合造价低于300元/平方米。该成果在条形平面反光镜线聚焦技术方面具有原创性。使利用太阳在资源环境和可持续发展方面有着非常巨大的意义，使仅限于提供生活用热水的太阳利用局面一举打破，形成新的以太阳能空调、热发电、工业用热、光伏发电、海水淡化、新法制盐及污水浓缩等工业为背景的太阳能应用产业。

2005年9月，南开大学与天津港保税区签署协议，在保税区建设中国第一条铜铟硒薄膜太阳电池中试线，形成具备自有知识产权的铜铟硒薄膜太阳电池产业，使中国成为继德、美、日之后的第四个开展该类电池中试开发的国家。以孙云为组长的课题组自主开发一系列薄膜沉积设备，攻克多项技术难关，建立国际水准的试验平台。研制开发的电池光电转换效率达到14%，填补国内空白，接近国际先进水平。铜铟硒薄膜太阳电池中试线的建立，标志着国内该项技术自主创新能力达到实现产业化的程度。

2005年9月，南开大学耿新华、赵颖、薛俊明等完成稳定获得大面积高稳定非晶硅电池及其实用化技术基础研究项目。该研究获得不同带隙a-Si:H材料，拓宽光谱响应范围；获得过渡区稳定非晶硅，特殊设计变梯度碳缓冲层，采用顶电池电流限制叠层电池设计等，提高稳定性；采用简单的glass/SnO_2/a-Si/a-Si/Al结构，实现沉积速率(3~4)安/秒，400平方厘米叠层电池组件效率达到9.2%，连续10批，平均效率8.76%，最高稳定效率8.1%，平均稳定效率7.7%，寿命20年，达到国际先进水平。研究的电池结构和制造技术路线与实际生产线相同，经过放大直接应用于生产线，提高产品效率，降低成本。自主设计，国内首创研制成功制备ZnO膜的MOCVD新装备，获得20厘米×20厘米均匀ZnO膜，实现陷光结构，使电池效率提高1～2个百分点。设备设计方案在国内推广应用，陷光结构技术移植到天津非晶硅电池生产线，提高产品效率。自主设计研制兼有三大高速沉积技术、性能指标国际一流的国内第一台新一代多功能薄膜沉积系统，于2004年7月用于研究新型微晶硅电池和非晶硅/微晶硅叠层电池研究，使新型电池性能指标达到国际先进水平。在研究大面积硅基薄膜材料和大面积电池组件的基础上，开发出国内首台73厘米×120厘米4片共沉积PECVD系统，大面积薄膜均匀性达到国际先进水平。以南开技术为依托，建成的5千瓦a-Si/a-Si叠层电池生产线，90%产品出口欧洲和东南亚。

第二节 化学储能技术及产业化研究

南开大学是全国最早开展化学储能技术研究的单位，申泮文院士是提倡者和发起人，是国家“973”计划“绿色二次电池新体系相关基础研究”项目的推荐人和参加人。1991~2005年，南开大学化学储能技术的研究取得丰硕成果，中国电子科技集团公司第十八研究所多年来也一直致力于化学储能技术的研究工作，成果应用于航天与深潜领域，达到国际先进水平。这一时期涌现出以和平海湾电源(集团)公司、天津力神公司、蓝天高科电源股份有限公司等一批从事新能源研发和产业化的新型企业。

一、化学储能技术研究

20世纪80年代开始，南开大学袁华堂带领的科研团队开展镁基储氢合金及镁基合金复合材料的相关研究工作，自1997年至2005年，袁华堂等相继承担天津自然科学基金、天津科技发展计划、国家自然科学基金、国家“973”计划等一系列镁基化学储能材料与储能技术的研究项目。研究发现镁基合金立方结构新相改变镁基合金的原有结构，大大提高镁基合金储氢性能，过渡金属硼化物的添加，大大降低镁基合金吸放氢温度，提高合金材料的可逆电化学容量和循环寿命，使得镁基合金的研究取得重大突破。袁华堂等在国内率先开展可充电镁电池的研究，特别是在正极材料、电解液方面取得重大进展，并获首项中国发明专利。该新型电池的成功研制，以廉价、资源丰富的镁替代锂，是二次电池发展史上的新革命。袁华堂还对锂离子电池正极材料进行深入研究，制备高比容量、高倍率性能的磷酸铁锂材料，促进高功率动力电池的发展。

在此期间，1997 ~ 2000年，南开大学杨小明进行锂离子二次电池正极材料的研究。1993 ~ 1996年，张允什、宋德瑛开展Ti-Fe-Mn-V系Laves相储氢电极材料研究。

1998年，南开大学申泮文院士承担复合储氢材料化学合成、结构与性能研究项目。该项目涉及碳纳米管及其复合储氢材料制备与电化学储氢性能研究，复合储氢材料主要为稀土镍系AB5型储氢合金和镁基储氢合金。该项目的研究成果主要体现在优化设计并制备纳米管和纳米纤维，并对纳米管进行管内填充金属镍纳米丝和表面修饰金属纳米粒子，探索纳米管与多种储氢合金的复合储氢电极材料的高温冶炼制备和机械球磨制备技术，研究相应的复合材料的电化学储氢性能和相关作用机制。研究发现，低温处理合金有利于碳纳米管的形成，高温处理导致大量碳纳米纤维生成。碳纳米管管内填充和表面修饰金属镍可以改善其电化学储氢性能，镁基储氢合金与碳纳米管复合后可以提高储氢容量，稀土储氢合金与纳米管机械球磨复合可以改善复合材料的高倍率放电性能。2002年，申泮文院士作为推荐人，并亲自参与“973”计划绿色二次电池新体系相关基础研究项目的研究工作。该项目设置7个课题，南开大学是该项目中一个课题的承担单位。该课题立足于国内在此领域相关材料的资源优势，主要解决绿色二次电池发展的基础性和前沿性问题，创立具有自主知识产权的绿色二次电池新体系，提升中国在此领域的创新能力，并重点解决绿色二次电池能量密度、功率密度、安全性、性价比等问题，以推动国内相关产业的快速发展。该项目的主要研究内容是进行电池新体系的探索，以及作为电池应用的新材料，研究其应用基础问题；建立材料的电化学性能与其物理化学参数之间的联系，对材料的电化学行为进行合理预测。在研究几类典型电池反应过程的基础上，建立电池参数与状态的相应数理模型，建立电池性能的快速诊断方法，研究非常规条件下电池中化学与电化学反应的特殊性。

2000年，南开大学阎杰从事镍氢电池正极材料的开发研究。

2001年，南开大学吴锋、宋德瑛、袁华堂等完成新型稀土镍基储氢合金(AB5)电极材料及其制备方法的研究。项目突破国外专利组分覆盖范围，发明新的储氢合金MmB5(Li)；从电化学原理和实践预测，电池使用中锂的作用，能提高电池电催化活性和循环寿命；第一次用中间合金，熔炼MmB5(Li)样品，并用近代仪器进行测定，证实它具有新的特性；发明LiH扩散、LiH和Li机械合金化法制备MmB5(Li)，彻底解决锂易挥发问题，使产业化成为可能。

2003年，高学平、阎杰、王光友等完成金属氢化物-镍电池关键材料研究，就Laves相储氢电极材料，提出新的储氢合金电极表面的反应机理，即氢的表面点催化、吸附和传输机理。研究碳纳米管及其复合储氢，采用净表面处理后的LaNi5储氢合金为催化剂制备碳纳米管，直接制备出储氢合金和碳纳米管的复合储氢材料，开展多壁碳纳米管及其复合储氢电极材料研究。研究氢氧化镍电极材料，为改善电极性能和增加电池能量密度，采用金属钴及CoOOH对球型氢氧化镍进行表面修饰，发现修饰后的球型氢氧化镍电极具有高的氧化还原可逆性和更大的放电容量。研究纳米氢氧化镍，发现其性能优于微米级氢氧化镍。

2003年3月，南开大学为参加单位之一参加高效金属氢化物储氢装置与技术项目的研究工作，主要研究内容有：高效金属氢化物储氢罐体的研制、金属氢化物储氢工程技术研究、新型高容量镁基储氢合金以及钛系储氢合金的研究，取得创新性成果。先后共发表学术论文8篇，申请发明专利3项。

2003年10月，南开大学杨化滨、周作祥完成的新型高效锌镍二次电池的研究与开发项目通过验收鉴定。锌镍电池是以锌作负极，氧化镍为正极的碱性二次电池，以其比能量大、比功率高、成本低和无污染等优点，被视为电动车辆所用动力电池的候选者之一，但存在电池循环充放电寿命短、使用过程中易产生大量气体等缺点而未被实际使用。课题组围绕这些问题，展开应用基础研究，获得成果：研制在碱性溶液中的氢超电压、腐蚀电流等参数与贵金属Ag相近的合金，做成泡沫状集流体并制成高比容量的锌电极；采用高能球磨法合成锌酸钙作为锌电极活性物质，从而防止锌酸根离子进入电解液，产生充电时的电极"形变"和"锌枝晶"，缩短电池寿命；在锌酸钙中添加纳米氧化物，显著改善锌电极的性能，以添加TiO_2为例，设计容量为500毫安时的锌镍电池，0.3C率充电、0.5C率放电，300周期充放电的容量仍稳定在271毫安时(100%DOD)。

图4-4-2-44 南开大学研制的新型高效锌镍二次电池

2004年1月，中国电子科技集团公司第十八研究所研制的直径115毫米的高压氢镍电池通过成果鉴定。其代表产品106安时高压氢镍电池采用背靠背-菠萝片大中心孔极组，单极组单焊接环，干法镍正极，PTFE化P铂黑负极，F115mmd0.8mm压力容器。该电池创新引入单极柱绝缘设计，正极采用金属—陶瓷封接极柱，负极采用全金属极柱，使电池漏液和氢气泄漏的可能性降低一半。单体电池的最大工作压力为6.0兆帕，压力容器的爆破压力超过18兆帕，安全系数达到3.0。单体电池的容量、重量、放电中点电压的平均值分别为118.2安时、2172克、1.298伏，实际重量比能量达到70.6瓦时/千克。研制过程中攻克F115毫米压力容器引伸和焊接及安全检验技术、金属陶瓷密封极柱制造技术、高孔率高强度正电极制造技术和电液回流加速技术等，实现轻量化目标。

2004年7月，天津大学唐致远、马聪、郑广泉等承担的新型针管式锂锰电池项目通过鉴定。课题组研制出国内第一批合格的CR435电池，并实现小批量生产。经信息产业部化学物理电源产品质量监督检验中心检测，容量达到69毫安时，工作电压平台为2.75伏，超过日本松下产品指标，填补国内研发针管式锂锰电池的技术空白。该成果首次采用灌浆技术制备出直径为4毫米的针管式锂锰电池(CR435)，从而彻底解决针管式锂锰电池在生产中遇到的各种难题，有利于实现批量化工业生产；在锂锰电池正极制备工艺中明显增加石墨的含量，并大大减少粘合剂的使用量，既提高电池的容量，又增加电极材料的导电性，减少电池的内阻,提高电池的工作电压平台;新型的正极制造技术,可在直径为2~5毫米的电池壳内制造正极,并且深度可达80毫米。可以制造外径Φ2.0~Φ5.0毫米、全高10~80毫米的各类细长形针管式锂锰电池。在小试成功的基础上,实现班产量800~1000只CR435锂锰电池的小批量生产,合格品率为95%~98%,产品经用户检测和试用,符合要求。

2004年,天津巴莫科技股份有限公司开发生产的出绿色电池材料—正极前驱体四氧化三钴、锂离子电池正极氧化钴锂,氧化钴锂的振实密度大于2.5克/立方厘米,提高锂电池有效物质的填充量,增加电池容量。其产品形貌好,生产锂离子电池正极片时加工性能好,特别是,安全性能是在不加安全添加剂的情况下,锂离子电池安全测试通过2C/5V、1C/12V和150℃热箱测试。

2004年10月,天津大学王成扬研制成功锂离子电池负极材料中间相炭微球,将煤焦油中温沥青与较为纯净和较高反应活性的乙烯裂解焦油混合,经共缩聚反应制备出中间相炭微球。这种方法既调整煤焦油沥青中影响中间相成核喹啉不溶物的含量,又增加沥青原料的反应性,其原料选择和工艺路线具有创新性。与原有工艺相比,该工艺过程简单合理,产品粒径均匀,产品质量容易控制。该成果在中间相炭微球生产中减少原料预处理步骤,达到24%~25%的较高收率,生产成本明显降低,具有较高的技术先进性和实用性。该技术及设备获得中国发明专利和中国实用新型专利各一项。该成果技术可靠,生产装置运行良好,所得中间相炭微球产品性能优异,质量稳定,销往多家大型锂离子电池厂。

2005年,南开大学陈军、袁华堂、王一菁等完成-MnO_2纳米管/线电极材料应用于Zn-MO_2电池领域的研究,从结构方面对-MnO_2纳米管|线提高电池性能做完整阐释;合成$Ni(OH)_2$系列纳米管,并研究其电极电化学性能;开展Fe_2O_3、$LiCO_2$、$LiMn_2O_4$等纳米管制备及电化学嵌锂研究;开展TiS_2和MoS_2纳米管储氢、储锂、储镁及催化CO加氢研究;开展无Co的AB5型、新型Mg基合金的制备及储氢性能研究。在国际杂志上发表SCI收录论文60篇,被他引301次。

2005年1月,中国电子科技集团公司第十八研究所研制的深潜器用锌银蓄电池通过成果鉴定。该电池是为国家重大工程专项7000米载人潜水器研制的动力及仪表电源,是国内首次在载人深海潜水器上以充油压力补偿的方式使用的锌银蓄电池。电池在7000米海底工作,承受71兆帕的高压,为防因壳体破裂和变形而导致电池短路失效,采用充油压力补偿方式的耐压结构设计;电池放电过程中产生的气体,逸出时会将电解液带出,并进入电池箱的绝缘油中,进而引起电池短路失效,对此,创新性采用液体膜作为气液分离膜,选用耐强碱的绝缘油,确定合适的气液分离装置,满足电池使用要求;解决电池长寿命问题,提高后期容量。通过采用对银迁移具有高阻力的隔膜和装配工艺改进,减缓电池的锌下沉和正极容量损失,防止锌枝晶的产生,锌银蓄电池循环寿命达到30次,荷电寿命达到30天,湿寿命达到1年。

2005年1月,中国电子科技集团公司第十八研究所先后开发聚合物电解质膜、高性能电极、提高电池安全可靠性等方面的技术,研制成功高比能量、低温型聚合物锂离子电池,并通过设计定型。该电池单体比能量大于180瓦时/千克、工作温度范围-40℃~+60℃、循环寿命大于500次。组合电池在充分保持比能量高的前提下,安全性能、力学性能及环境适应性满足GJB4477的有关规定。单体电池的容量范围为80毫安/时~20安/时,在多种便携式电子装置中进行试用,取得良好效果。同期,中国电子科技集团公司第十八研究所的创新产品高功率型软包装锂-二氧化锰电池通过设计定型,产品性能居国际先进水平。锂-二氧化锰电池是以金属锂为负极、二氧化锰为正极、采用有机溶剂电解质的一次电池。软包装锂-二氧化锰电池利用锂-二氧化锰电池内部压力小的特点,突破传统金属壳体的束缚,采用软包装结构,即采用铝复合膜代替传统金属外壳,不但减小电池的重量和体积,而且电池可以做成任意尺寸和形状,使组合电池的体积效率达到最佳;其次通过采用多种物理方法处理活性物质,改善高功率薄型电极的工艺性;用涂布式正极制备工艺取代原有粉末式或碾压式制备工艺,将电极厚度从毫米级降到微米级。该电池比功率达到575瓦/千克、644瓦/升,是该体系原有电池的4倍,最大输出电流密度达到14毫安/平方厘米。这项研究大大提高锂-二氧化锰电池输出功率,改善低温性能。

2005年7月,天津蓝天双环科技有限公司张泽波、陈洪枫、李恩花等完成的ICR50/300锂离子蓄电池项目通过鉴定。该电池选择具有高安全性的高容量活性物质,采用多元复合有机电解液+功能添加剂的电解液体系,优化正负极匹配设计,改进电极加工工艺和电池组装技术而研制成功。

2005年12月,中国电子科技集团公司第十八研究所研制的卫星用锂离子蓄电池通过国家信息产业部的成果鉴定。该产品是针对卫星使用的特殊要求设计开发的高比能、长寿命和高可靠蓄电池。研制过程中,通过新型可靠的全密封设计,保证电池在空间高真空环境下使用的密封需要;通过优选新材料、优化电极制造技术、优选电解液和隔膜材料,改进电池卷绕和装配技术,严格单体电池筛选匹配,保证电池的长寿命工作要求。单体电池的比能量达到120瓦时/千克~130瓦时/千克,组合电池比能量达到90瓦时/千克,电池的低轨循环寿命积累达到1.2万次以上的寿命数据,电池组高轨寿命积累2000次以上的数据,电池的漏气率小于10-10帕立方米/秒。该项技术达到国际先进水平,产品经中国航天科技集团公司地面模拟试验,电性能满足要求,该电池应用于月面巡视探测器用原理样车电源子系统中。同期,中国电子科技集团公司第十八研究所承担的高性能温差电材料及级联温差电池的研究项目通过国家信息产业部的鉴定。该项目通过深入研究,提高高性能温差电材料热电性能的机理和材料制备工艺技术,合成BiTe基材料、填充式Skutterudites化合物、PbTe基材料等多种高性能的温差电材料。在深入研究级联温差电池设计理论基础上,进行级联温差电池的设计,并突破级联温差电池集成工艺,制备级联温差电池样品。经测试级联温差电池样品的热电性能,热电转换效率达到了8.45%。

二、化学能利用的产业化

2000年,天津力神电池有限公司开始聚合物电池的研发工作,在国内率先将卷绕式聚合物电池推进到实用性生产阶段,研究开发成果于2001年7月通过技术鉴定。胶体聚合物锂离子电池的极组采用卷绕方式,正负极之间有一层PE或PP的隔膜,电液是胶体聚合物电解质,电解液被三维网状交联的聚合物所固定,电池内没有多余的液态电液,是一种真正的聚合物电解质。电池的外观坚硬,抗冲击能力较高,有高温闭孔特性,安全性更高。该技术的优点是能够利用目前的方型液态锂离子电池的某些技术和工艺装备进行大规模生产。该种新型聚合物电池,在0.5C放电条件下容量达到550毫安小时,其中重量比容量为160瓦小时/千克,体积比容量为400瓦小时/升,两项指标均达到国际先进水平,与日本同类产品相比,体积更小、重量更轻、厚度更薄,具有自主知识产权,高倍率放电性能等关键指标达到国际先进水平。2002年8月,天津力神电池股份有限公司卷绕式聚合物电池产业化项目经国家计委审批,入选新型电子元器件项目2002年国家示范工程,率先在国内进入实用生产阶段。2004年,力神电池股份有限公司开发出的大容量聚合物锂离子电池,该电池具有质地轻薄、体积小、容量高、安全性好等特点,电池容量达到3.5安小时,是国际电池容量最大的聚合物锂离子电池(日本最高容量为2安小时),循环寿命达到400次,电池一致性由80%提高到85%,主要技术性能指标居世界领先水平。

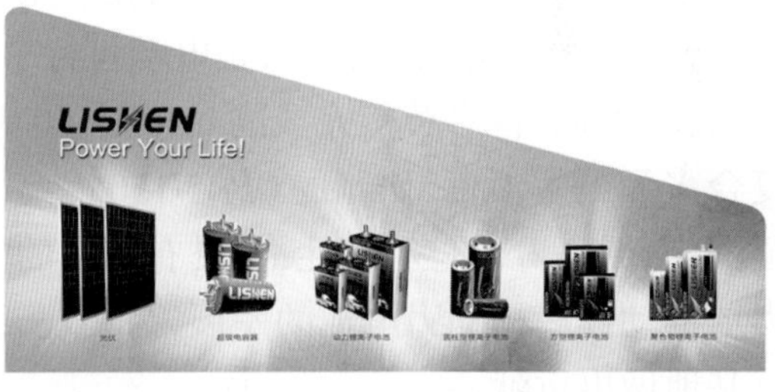

图4-4-2-45 天津力神电池有限公司研制的产品

2003年,天津和平海湾电源集团有限公司闫德意、王兴贺、刘莉等完成700AAA镍氢电池的研制及其产业化项目的研究工作。该项目在消化吸收引进东芝生产线的基础上进行高容量镍氢电池的开发,在不降低电池的其他综合性能的前提下,使AAA型电池容量提升到700毫安小时,达到国内领先、国际先进水平。项目实现电池在1C率、100%DOD下寿命达500次以上,找出少数电池短期失效的本质原因和解决这一问题的根本途径;解决电池充电后期电压偏高问题,有效提高电池的电化学性能综合指标;建立新型正极片制造工艺;建立新型密封工艺;建立电池处理新工艺;成功研制出AAA800毫安小时镍氢电池。该项目的成功,提高公司产品的国内市场占有率和出口创汇能力,带动国内镍氢电池技术和产业发展到一个新水平。

2003年12月,天津蓝天高科电源股份有限公司谭逸雄等承担的ICR3265锂离子蓄电池项目通过鉴定。该电池容量超过5安小时,重量比能量达到145瓦小时/千克,体积比能量380瓦小时/升。正极采用$LiCoO_2$,

负极采用石墨，隔膜采用聚丙烯/聚乙烯复合膜，电解液为LiPF6的多元有机体系。该产品具有使用温度范围广（-40℃～+60℃），倍率放电特性好（可1C、2C放电），使用安全（短路、过充电、热冲击等滥用条件下安全），循环寿命长，无污染等特点。该电池结构设计、配方、制造工艺拥有完全知识产权；电池尺寸选用D型，有广泛的应用价值，为国内首创；电池盖为专门设计，属关键技术；专门设计制造两种型号的半自动卷绕机，解决长电极极芯卷绕技术难题。ICR3265锂离子蓄电池是为满足特种装置用电源的需求，为跟踪国际上锂离子蓄电池的最新发展趋势而开发的新型号产品。该产品成功应用于通讯对抗干扰机、军用加固计算机、空降兵夜视望远镜、装备用大容量侦察设备等多项国家重点军事装备中。该型电池的使用带来整机更新换代，大大提高整机性能。成果为国内首创，达到国际先进水平。2004年10月，该公司张健完成高容量金属氢化物镍蓄电池关键技术研究及产品开发课题的研究工作，研制的SC型电池容量达到3500毫安时，体积比能量达到256瓦时／升，达到国内先进水平。该成果采用优化电池结构设计，采用薄壁电池壳和薄型电池盖，提高电池内部的有效容积，并完善相应的电池滚槽和封口技术。该成果着力于高容量泡沫镍正极的研制，进行大量基础性工作，包括对泡沫镍基体、胶量、钴含量、正极密度、隔膜等因素对电池性能的影响等研究，总结出一整套对实际生产具有指导意义的研究成果。在主攻电池高容量的同时，高倍率放电方面也取得进展。该项目的成功提高中国电池档次和生产技术能力，打破外国电池在高端市场的垄断。

2004年9月，天津蓝天双环科技有限公司杨清欣等完成电动自行车用锂离子电池组的研制。该项目优化电极的加工技术、单体电池电化学体系设计和单体电池的安全设计，使电池的大电流放电和低温性能等均达到或超过企业标准规定的技术指标，重量比能量达到140瓦时/千克，体积比能量达到350瓦时/升。电池组中专用的保护电路确保电池组在使用过程中出现过充、过放及过电流的情况下安全可靠。该电池组重量轻、体积小、放电性能优良，是电动自行车用铅酸电池和氢镍电池的更新换代产品。2005年7月，该公司张泽波、陈洪枫、肖彩英等完成的ICR45/150锂离子蓄电池项目通过鉴定，研究成果采用优选的正负极材料和复合多元电解液；所研制的CR45/150锂离子蓄电池比功率大于800瓦时/千克，具有工作电压高、工作温度范围广、循环寿命长等特性；且具有优越的安全性能，综合性能居于国内外同类产品领先地位。研究成果有力地推动锂离子动力电池的发展，为实现天津市电动汽车工业快速发展和建立国内第一个电动汽车示范运行基地做出贡献。

2004年11月，海蓝德公司完成燃料电池专用储氢罐的研制开发，针对燃料电池要求储氢合金低温放氢的性能开展低温储氢合金的开发，研制出可在0℃～10℃具有良好放氢性能的AB2和AB5系列合金，在此基础上，开发出可在环境温度下无需外部加热的储氢罐。该储氢罐，其储氢量、放氢速率等主要技术指标均优于ERGENICS公司同类产品，达到国际同类产品的先进水平，在罐体氢气残余量测定方法、储氢罐结构设计和活化技术方面获得2项发明专利、2项实用新型专利授权。该型产品主要用于小型电动两轮车、高尔夫球车、备用电源、氢气存储等小型移动设备。海蓝德公司形成从20升到6立方米的系列储氢罐生产线，在国内率先实现小批量生产和销售，产品销往美国、德国、新加坡、葡萄牙等国及中国香港地区。

2004年，天津巴莫科技股份有限公司开发的镍钴锰三元正极材料列入天津市新能源新材料产业技术创新重点项目。该材料具有高功率、高容量、高安全性、延长电池寿命等特点。与钴系列材料相比，采用三元正极材料的锂离子电池的安全性、高温容量指标明显提高，三元正极材料的比容量指标达到150毫安时/克～155毫安时/克，比氧化钴锂正极材料提高10毫安时/克～15毫安时/克，可满足高功率放电和动力电池的要求，达到国际先进水平。利用该材料可生产高性能电池。镍钴锰三元正极材料的生产成本比钴系列材料下降30%～40%，每吨可下降4万元～5万元。

2005年12月，中国电子科技集团公司第十八研究所研制的XXX鱼雷用锌银一次电池段通过信息产业部的设计定型。该项目在研制过程中，围绕提高电池段输出功率、比能量和电池段的安全性等重大技术难题开展技术攻关，解决紧凑的电池段（含独立的仪表电池）总体设计、单体电池、单体电池间的连接结构、贮液器的轻型化、可靠的激活系统及加热系统和安全排气系统等一系列技术关键。电池段在850安的电流下工作，电压稳定在250伏～263伏，时间超过15.5分钟，实际比能量达到100瓦时/千克。电池段湿贮存寿命达到4小时，激活放电后排气系统工作正常，使用后6小时安全回收。该电池段的自主创新性鲜明，如薄壁单体电池和穿壁连接、轻质异型钛贮液器、共贮液器独立分配仪表电池以及可靠的密闭激活机构与延时放气装置等，这些创新技术的应用确保电池段的优异性能。

截至2005年1月，天津力神公司共投资10亿元、分4期进行工程建设，形成全国最大规模的绿色电池能源基地，形成年产2亿支各类小型锂离子蓄电池、聚合物锂电池以及电动车电池的生产能力，产品大批量销往美国、韩国、德国、澳大利亚等国家和中国香港地区。

截至2005年，天津市作为国内自行车及电动自行车重要生产基地，年产销电动自行车突破200万辆，其中大多出口美国、日本、加拿大等市场。绿色电池能源基地的建设，对加强电动自行车与锂离子电池的联合，发展天津电动自行车产业配套，造就新的产业优势，做大做强天津电动自行车产业，形成新的经济增长点。

第五章　地　热

2005年世界地热大会上发布的统计数据显示，全球地热直接利用最多的国家是中国，而中国地热直接利用最多的城市是天津。1991~2005年，天津以地热勘探程度高、探明储量多、利用规模大、管理秩序好、技术水平高、产业化程度完善，成为中国地热资源勘查、开发和管理工作领先的大城市。在地热学研究领域也取得显著成果，有两项研究成果获国家级大奖，是迄今为止中国地热界所获得的最高科研奖项。

第一节　地热勘查

天津地热资源勘查始于20世纪70年代初，截至2005年，通过科学勘查，天津已圈定出10个地热异常区，北至宝坻的周良庄、南到大港的沙井子，西从武清的王庆坨、东到汉沽的看才庄，以及王庆坨、万家码头、王兰庄、山岭子、唐官屯、桥沽异常区。地热异常区总面积约3000平方千米。其中宁河-宝坻断裂以南、4000米以内热资源总量：1497.266×1014千卡，可开采量：290.123×1014千卡，相当于41.45亿吨标准煤、29亿吨原油或337409.891亿度电能。

图4-5-1-46　天津市开展地热田勘探

一、天津市及王兰庄的地热田勘探

天津市区及王兰庄地热田勘探项目由天津地热勘查开发设计院承担，自1982年10月始至1987年10月提交报告止，历时5年。第一期勘探主要参加人员有卢润、杜宝金、蔡冠英等。此次勘探采取钻探、物探、水文地质试验、化探、岩样和水样分析、热储计算等工作方法。经勘探查明热田内有以第三系碎屑岩为主的孔隙型热储层2个和以碳酸盐岩为主的基岩岩溶裂隙热储层3个。

1990年，在王兰庄一期野外勘探完成之后，地矿部要求天津地矿局整理钻井资料，开展天津市区及王兰庄地热田二期勘探工作，仍由天津地热勘查开发设计院承担，主要参加人员有卢润、高维勤、安逸仙等。该次勘查项目投入的主要实物工作量有：钻井7眼，总进尺9098.64米；井下物探包括视电阻率、自然电位、声波、测温、测压等共计34880米；抽水试验4组；水质全分析52组、岩样分析48个。该项目首次利用地球化学、热力学和质量与能量平衡理论，探讨天津地区水岩均衡动态特征，计算热储层的热水化学组分与溶解矿物之间的平衡关系，研究地下热水径流和滞留过程，以及在开采中脱气修和热水运行的关系。分析起泡点的原因和危害，提出控制举措。《天津市区及王兰庄地热田二期勘探报告》借鉴国外经验，结合华北油田注水实践，指出对井开发的优势，开启天津地热对井开发利用模式之先河。

二、天津市山岭子地热田普查

1991年，天津地热勘查开发设计院陈振霞、蔡冠英、陈双海等完成天津市山岭子地热田普查工作，整个项目历时5年。该项目普查面积1190平方公里、勘查面积840平方公里，其中主要工作量包括：开凿勘探孔6个，总进尺9005.7米，其中基岩孔4个；1∶5万重力勘探面积500平方公里，重力勘测剖面11.20公里；井温测量127眼，其中稳态测温5眼；岩样的岩矿鉴定、古生物鉴定、岩石热物理性质测试、土样物理性质试验共计89样；水样全分析155组；此外还进行水文地质抽水试验、热水动态观测、地球物理测井等工作。建立热储地质模型，应用体积法对地热资源和地热流体资源进行计算，首次获得普查区840平方公里范围内3000米以浅的孔隙型热储及基岩热储的地热资源量20.3×10^{18}焦耳（基准温度13.5℃）、地热流体总静储量（573×10^{8}立方米），预测出按当时开采规模30年后各热储层的水位埋深。该次普查工作加深对天津地势地质条件的认识，开辟新的找热领域，对天津地区乃至华北平原区的地热地质勘查研究和地热开发利用具有标志意义。

三、天津市滨海地区地热资源普查

1995年12月，天津地热勘查开发设计院张素凤、林黎、张淑清等完成天津市滨海地区地热资源普查工作，项目从1991年3月开始，历时近4年。该项普查工作涵盖塘沽、大港、汉沽即现在的滨海新区的大部分范围，实际完成普查面积2000多平方公里、超过任务下达的1500平方公里。完成的主要实物工作量包括：开凿勘探孔15个，总进尺30000米；井温测量148眼，其中稳态测温4眼；电测井9组；水文地质抽水试验8组；岩样的热物理性质及放射性测试共计24样；水样简分析61组、全分析54组、同位素7组；建立水位、水质、水温等长观井28眼；此外还调查大量的机井利用情况、收集大量的地震测线资料、石油钻孔资料等。建立热储地质模型，应用体积法对普查区新近系馆陶组的地热资源和地热流体资源进行计算，首次获得普查区2000平方公里范围内馆陶组的地热资源总量为5.5168×10^{18}焦耳（基准温度13.5℃）、地热流体总静储量（11.334×10^{10}立方米）。采用LUMPFEIT软件对该区地热开采现状进行模拟，并对不同开采方案下的水位动态进行远期预测。

该次普查工作对上第三系馆陶组热储层进行深入细致的分析研究，其工作程度超过普查阶段的要求。完成《天津市滨海地区地热普查报告》，内容丰富，论述充分，可作为进一步勘查和某些地段开发利用的依据，滨海地区的地热资源开发利用由此展开。

四、天津市武清县地热资源普查报告

1999年，天津地热勘查开发设计院林建旺、林黎、王坤等完成天津市武清县地热资源普查项目。项目从1997年5月开始，于1999年7月提交报告。该项普查面积为100平方公里，勘探深度2000～3000米，重点控制新近系馆陶组热储层，投入勘探孔4个，总进尺9702.96米。投入物化探工作、抽水试验、地温测量、地热流体化学分析等。首次对普查区100平方公里范围内新近系热储层的岩性、结构和水文地质特征、水质进行全面的评价；对热流体的成因和运移规律进行分析。报告建立简单的热储概念模型，采用体积法及水文地质方法计算馆陶组地热资源总量为2.57×10^{18}焦耳（基准温度13.5℃）；地热流体总静储量为132.8×10^{10}立方米。根据当时的地热井开采动态，利用VARFLOW程序进行按拟合并对未来30年武清地区馆下热储层的开采进行分析预测。该项勘查工作全面完成普查任务，精度充分满足国家标准（GB11615-89）对普查的要求；资源评价方法符合《地热资源评价方法(DZ40-85)》要求，勘探精度达到规范对C级资源的要求，为武清大规模地热开发提供科学依据。

五、天津市深部地热资源普查

2000年，天津地热勘查开发设计院林黎、王坤、林建旺等承担天津市深部地热资源普查工作，项目从1997年开始，于2000年底提交报告。该项目工作面积为640平方公里，投入勘探孔8个，总进尺23833.48米。投入物化探工作、水文地质试验、地温测量、地热流体化学分析等，建立地质概念模型，应用体积法及水文地质方法对地热资源和地热流体资源进行计算，首次获得普查区640平方公里范围内深部基岩热储层的地热资源量199.7432×10^{18}焦耳(基准温度25℃)、地热流体总静储量(337.1742×10^{10}立方米)，预测出按目前开采规模30年后各热储层的水位埋深。该次深部地热普查对超过2000米的深部基岩热储结构特征、边界条件、物性参数分布进行全面了解和掌握，并在地热规模化回灌开采方面做出开拓性工作。该项目深部基岩地热资源普查，无论从钻进施工技术还是野外调查，在天津乃至全国都是首次，国际上这样深度和规模的中低温地热资源普查也尚无先例，成果国际先进水平。

2000年，天津市地质矿产局完成天津市深部基岩热资源开发潜力研究。该项目对天津市区埋深4000米以浅的基岩地热水储层进行勘探、试验研究，评价其地热资源潜力，预测深部地热资源开发可能产生的环境地质问题，并提出防治对策，为天津市科学开发利用地热资源提供依据。

六、天津市万家码头地热田普查

2000年1月~2002年12月，天津地热勘查开发设计院林建旺、李俊、马锋等完成天津市万家码头地热田普查项目。该项目的普查范围位于天津市东南部，津南区的咸水沽-小韩庄-大洪区万家码头一带，面积240平方公里。投入的主要实物工作量有：地热勘探孔2个，总进尺5694米，井下物探测井6孔次；井口测温72点次、全孔测温3眼；大地电磁测深6条剖面共47点；单孔及多孔抽水试验6组；水质全分析64组、同位素10组、气体分析4组；动态长观孔6个；收集大量的人工地震剖面、石油钻孔及水文井等资料。建立地热地质模型，首次获得普查区240平方公里范围内新近系热储层和基岩热储层的地热资源，总量为110.7214×10^{18}焦耳(基准温度13.5℃)、地热流体总静储量为584.6643×10^{8}立方米。

该项目运用物探、钻探、地球化学、综合分析等方法，查明区内的沧东断裂、白塘口断裂、海河断裂、增福台断裂、小营盘断裂、独流减河断裂、咸水沽断裂的埋深、位置、产状、性质、活动史等时空分布特征以及地层层序和空间展布特征。编制的各类因条件限制基本建立起地热田的三维地质结构，对该区地热的开发利用具有重要的实践指导意义。

七、天津宁河—汉沽地热资源普查

2000年~2002年2月，天津地热勘查开发设计院李俊峰、靳宝珍、胡燕等完成天津市宁河—汉沽地热资源普查项目。该项目在充分收集地震、重力、航磁等资料的基础上采取探采结合的方式，共投入野外调查700平方千米，地热勘探孔2个，钻探进尺2806米，大地电磁测深剖面4条共计16点，井口测温106点，抽水试验3组，水样测试34件，开展热流体动态监测和开采量调查。所提交的勘察报告阐述普查区地温场特征，指出基岩埋深与断裂构造对热异常的分布起控制作用。区内热异常主要沿北北东向的沧东断裂方向展布，最高地温梯度达5.5℃/100米，南部凹陷区温度相对较低。根据水质分析测试资料，报告在阐述馆陶组和明化镇组地热流体化学特征的基础上，对馆陶组和明化镇组地热流体水质参照相关国家标准，针对多种用途进行初步评价，为开发利用地热资源提供水质依据。

报告在分析热源、水源、储层、盖层和边界条件的基础上确立热储地质模型，应用热储法计算馆陶组和明化镇组的地热资源量，区内地热资源总量为82.15×10^{14}千卡(按基准温度13.5℃计算)，可采热资源量为

7.26×10^{14}千卡，地热流体资源总量439×10^{8}立方米，计算方法符合《地热资源评价方法(DZ40-85)》的要求，计算参数选择基本得当。报告分三种不同开采方案采用泰斯公式对地热流体水位动态进行预测，预测结果为今后合理开发地热资源提供参考。报告对开发利用地热资源的经济效益、社会效益进行综述，对地热开发利用中的环境影响进行概略评价，并提出统一规划、建立地热流体动态监测系统、加强回灌研究等建议，对地热管理部门具有参考价值。

八、天津市宝坻地区地热资源调查

2003年1月~2003年12月，天津地热勘查开发设计院李丹、李俊、程万庆等完成天津市宝坻地区地热资源调查项目。该项目野外调查面积约120平方公里，报告在充分收集并综合分析已有地质、地球物理、石油探井和地热开采等资料的基础上，成功布置勘探孔1个，总进尺2700米；投入物化探工作、水文地质试验、地温测量、地热流体化学及同位素分析等。建立地质概念模型，依据国家标准(GB11615-89)《地热资源地质勘查规范》和地矿部DZ40-85《地热资源评价方法》，初步估算和评价调查区第三系和基岩热储(4000米以浅)地热资源总量为24.4355×10^{18}焦耳(基准温度13.5℃)，其中第三系热储量为5.4973×10^{18}焦耳、基岩热储量为18.9382×10^{18}焦耳；地热流体总静储量为135.27×10^{8}立方米分别，其中第三系静储量为118.72×10^{8}立方米、基岩静储量为16.55×10^{8}立方米。该项目圆满完成任务书规定的各项工作，并在该区地热地质条件调查方面有新的突破，发现高温高压热储层。

九、天津市潘庄—芦台地热资源普查

2003年12月，天津地热勘查开发设计院李俊峰、靳宝珍、胡燕等承担天津市潘庄—芦台地热资源普查项目。该项目在充分收集地震、重力、航磁等资料的基础上，共完成野外调查850平方千米，地热勘探孔2个，钻探进尺2806米，大地电磁测深剖面12条共计85个测点，井口测温106点，抽水试验4组，水样测试40件，此外还开展热流体动态监测和开采量调查。报告从地球地温场、重力场、磁场、电磁特征等方面详细论述地热异常的分布、形成条件，指出基岩埋深与断裂构造对热异常的分布起控制作用。区内热异常主要分布于潘庄凸起和宁河凸起，最高地温梯度分别达6.7℃/100米和5.5℃/100米；根据水文地质条件和地球水化学特征，论述明化镇组、馆陶组地热流体的补径排条件及成因，为全面掌握区内热储特征和资源计算提供保征。

应用热储法计算区内馆陶组和明化镇组地热资源总量为12.456×10^{15}千卡(按基准温度13.5℃计算)，可采热资源量为14.447×10^{14}千卡，地热流体资源总量657.14×10^{8}立方米，计算方法符合《地热资源评价方法(DZ40-85)》的要求，计算参数选择基本得当。报告结合开采井布局，采用泰斯公式计算明化镇组在给定降深与开采年限条件下的地热流体可采资源量，并预测三种不同开采方案下地热流体水位动态下降趋势，计算结果为今后合理开发利用地热资源提供依据。

十、天津市西南部地热资源调查

2004年12月，天津地热勘查开发设计院完成天津市西南部地热资源调查项目，主要参加人员有靳宝珍、张淑清、高宝珠等。该项目在充分收集人工地震、重力、航磁及以往地热勘查成果等资料的基础上，完成野外地面综合调查736平方公里，地热探采结合孔1个，钻探进尺1500米，大地电磁测探100点，全孔测温1个，井口测温65个，抽水试验1组，水样测试55件，还开展热流体动态监测和开采量调查。该报告从区域地质构造、区域地层和区域地质发展史等方面阐述区域地质背景，重点分析调查区的基本构造特征和对热储起控制作用的各条断裂的分布与产状，并发现新的断裂。阐述该区地层空间分布和岩性特征。系统划分该区的热储层，基本查明各热储特征。在分析热源、水源、储层、盖层和边界条件的基础上客观确立热储地质模型，应用热储法计算地热资源总量为539.27×10^{14}千卡(按基准温度13.5℃)，可采地热资源为39.64×10^{14}千卡，地热资源总量为827.41×10^{8}立方米，预可采资源量53334立方米/日，其中新增储量267.72×10^{14}千卡。此次通过地温场的调查分析，新圈定三个小型地热异常区，为进一步地热勘探和开发提供靶区。

十一、天津市静海县地热资源普查

2005年12月，天津地热勘查开发设计院靳宝珍、曾梅香、高宝珠等完成天津市静海县地热资源普查，项目从2003年开始，历时3年。该项目在充分收集钻探、物探（包括人工地震、重力、航磁）、化探、煤层气勘探及以往地热勘查成果等资料的基础上，完成野外地面综合调查700多平方公里，大地电磁测深100点，井口测温65个，GPS坐标定位60个，抽水试验1组，水样测试50个，同位素分析2组，气体分析1组，动态监测90点次，还开展地热井开采量及开发利用情况调查。从区域地质构造、区域地质发展史等方面阐述区域地质背景，重点分析普查区的地质构造特征。分析该区地层（尤其是热储层）的空间分布和岩性特征，划分该区的热储层，为地热资源的进一步勘探和开发奠定基础。根据水质分析测试资料，阐述各热储层地热流体的化学组分特征及空间变化规律，采用同位素法研究地热流体的起源，对地热流体水质参照相关国家标准，针对多种用途进行初步评价，为合理开发利用地热资源提供水质要求。通过温度场的调查分析，圈定该区地热异常范围，分析该区地热开发的有利地段，为进一步地热开发提供可靠的依据。分析热源、水源、储层、盖层和边界条件的基础上，建立三维立体热储地质模型，客观地反映该区地热的形成情况，应用热储计算普查区内86平方公里的地热资源总量和地热流体可采量。应用热储法计算新近系总的地热资源量334.25×10^{13}千焦（按基准温度13.5℃），新近系热流体总可采量为341.275×10^{6}立方米，总产热量为3.228×10^{12}千焦，总可开采电能为11.055兆瓦，大于10兆瓦。对该区地热资源开发的经济、社会及环境效益进行分析，并对开发利用的可行性进行初步评价，对地热开发方向和利用方式进行分析，结合区域地热开发现状提出合理的保护意见。

第二节　地热钻井技术

1990~2005年，天津的地热开发范围由市区向外围扩展，钻井深度逐渐增加，基岩热储层开采逐步取替孔隙型热储而占主导地位。地热钻井技术在学习石油钻井经验的基础上，对超深对井采/灌技术、定向井施工技术、酸化压裂技术、可降解钻井液利用等技术引进、消化、吸收。通过不断研究、探索，特别是在安全钻井、热储层保护、完井方式、洗井作业、随钻分析、判断等方面都加强研究与改进，具备钻进4000米孔深的施工能力，在国内处于领先水平。

1992年，天津地热勘查开发设计院在河西区紫金新里施工中国第一眼基岩定向井，该井孔深2010米、水温达92℃、水量150立方米/时。1996年，天津地热勘查开发设计院在河西一商储运公司完成中国第一眼基岩定向对井的施工，并被作为示范工程。

2002年2月，天津地热勘查开发设计院在宝坻周良庄成功钻探一眼优质高产地热井（井深2695.80米，温度为103℃，静水头高出地面68米，涌水量在300立方米/时以上的高温自喷地热井，被称为“华北第一井”，丰富的地热资源成为地区招商引资，发展经济的有利条件，成为新的经济增长点，吸引港商数十亿元的投资，直接促进宝坻珠江温泉城的开发建设。

第三节 地热利用

20世纪80年代末,随着经济的发展,人民生活水平的提高,天津所拥有的地热这一得天独厚的绿色环保型能源得以进入一个快速的开发发展时期。开采的地热主要用于建筑供暖、居民生活热水、温泉游泳、理疗等。

至2005年,天津市地热开发利用进入新阶段,形成以地热采暖为主体,集工农业生产、温泉康乐、旅游度假、生活洗浴、饮用矿泉水生产等多领域的地热利用格局。

一、居民供热

至2005年,天津市有近140个单位利用地热水进行居民采暖,供暖面积1000万平方米,约占国内地热供暖面积的77%,是国内利用地热供暖规模最大的城市。地热资源在市区用于供暖取代昔日的锅炉,推动天津市"蓝天碧水"现代化生态型城市的进程。以2004年地热采暖总面积为900万平方米为例,每年可节约原煤21.56万吨,减少向大气中排放SO_2、NO_x、CO_2总量分别为:6653吨、1996.3吨、17.14万立方米;减少煤尘排放量为1552吨。

二、生活用水

至2005年,天津市有11.16万户居民用上地热温泉,职工和学生洗浴达1000万人次/年。

温泉娱乐及游泳设施:有18个单位利用地热资源建成温泉娱乐设施,如宝坻珠江温泉度假村、塘沽温泉娱乐中心等。有21个单位修建温泉游泳池,面积达19644.5平方米。

矿泉水开发:天津市有6个单位利用地热水生产矿泉水,年生产能力达37570立方米。

三、工农业上的应用

天津市有16个单位将地热水用于工业生产,如洗涤、印染、空调生产等。

有3个比较大型的农业基地利用地热水进行农业养殖,种植面积达243.16亩,品种有黄瓜、西红柿、茄子和各种花卉等。

有7个单位利用地热水进行水产养殖,养殖面积达243.16亩,品种有左口鱼、石斑鱼、罗非鱼、甲鱼、河蟹、对虾等。

第四节 地热开发技术

天津的地热开发技术处于国际先进、国内领先地位,由天津大学与中国地质大学(北京)、以及天津市地热管理处、天津地热勘查开发设计院等单位参与的"中低焓地热工程建设技术"和"天津市地热资源开发利用集约化技术及工程应用"两个项目同时获得2003年度国家科技进步二等奖。

1992年,天津大学蔡义汉等人完成地热开发利用研究,该项目以天津静海团泊村为中试点,设计出一种实用型地热半坡式温室,结构合理,具有良好的抗风性、承压性、保温性,热耗<100大卡/平方米小时;提出

一组描述温室微气候模型的方程，编制较高精度的计算机软件；研制出两用型地热井口装置，解决泵轴与自流转换时漏水、腐蚀的关键技术，使自流井起到有效的调峰作用；项目还对中试点地热系统各种水质土壤进行调查分析，提出尾水治理与环境保护建议等。经济和社会效益显著。

1994年，天津大学张启、齐金生、梁军合作研制成功地热深井潜水电泵，该型水泵适用于70℃~85℃并机时地热水腐蚀的地热深井潜水，这是开发利用地热能的关键设备，成功解决国内深井潜水电泵不耐高温、不耐腐蚀等问题，产品填补国内空白。

1997年5月~2001年10月，天津大学与中国地质大学(北京)、天津市地热管理处、天津地热勘查开发设计院、黑龙江科技学院单位合作，由何满潮，李春华，朱家玲等人牵头共同研究成功"中低焓地热工程建设技术"，该项目攻克二维信息与三维信息相互转换问题，开发中低焓地热工程信息系统。并在此基础上深入分析研究地热供暖工程设计与地热井设计的特征，创建供暖工程与地热井建设工程一体化设计系统。该项目研究地热资源梯级开发循环利用新工艺与混合热源联动运行空调新工艺，解决富热地区地热尾水排放温度过高造成的环境热污染与资源浪费以及贫热地区单一热源和建设工程需要不相匹配等问题。同时，该项目还研究地热农业生产新工艺，实现生物对温度的不同需求与地热梯级利用的耦合，充分利用地热资源的热、矿与水的复合特性，形成热农业生产新工艺。该项目还针对利用地热进行供热所带来的热污染、地表沉降等问题，建立地热回灌井的分类体系，形成以三种回灌模式为主的中低焓地热回灌技术，有效地保护资源与环境。该项目研究成果在天津、北京、河北、黑龙江、陕西、吉林、内蒙古、山东等8个具有中低焓地热资源的省市得到应用，覆盖率达66.7%。该项目研究成果的应用可有效减少污染源排放，减少城市运输量，社会效益显著。

1997~2002年，天津地热勘查开发设计院曾梅香、张百鸣、李春华等承担天津市基岩岩溶裂隙热储层回灌研究项目。项目全面总结天津市热储回灌开采的实践经验，并采用多种回灌方式开展有针对性的基岩热储回灌试验工作。这是国内首次进行的大范围热水回灌开采实践，取得大量宝贵的实验数据，为深入开展回灌研究工作奠定基础。该项目历时5年，共建成各种类型的地热回灌对井15对，运行效果良好，补给大量资源开采量，回灌总量已达500多万立方米，总收益在1000万元以上，实现巨大的经济效益和社会环境效益。项目研究报告认为回灌主要控制因素是区域构造和断裂，并指出岩溶裂隙中地热流体以管道流、裂隙流的形式运移，存在明显的非均质性和各向异性，为对井回灌提供介质特征方面的依据；通过不同模式的回灌试验，对回灌水的运移方式和机理以及对影响热储层回灌效果的因素进行系统的研究，对灌量、灌压与时间之间的关系进行深入的探讨；同时提出采用热储条件分析、抽水试验曲线水流性质分析和示踪剂试验相结合方法，进行回灌井位合理选择和方案布署；重点对采灌条件下热储温度场、压力场、水化学场进行分析研究，提出回灌开采是地热资源可持续利用的最佳方式之一，对缓解热储压力下降、延长热田开发年限具有良好的效果。

该项目内容丰富、信息量大、研究方法全面多样，手段先进。开展如此大规模和系统的热储回灌研究，其水平不仅在国内居于领先地位，在国际上也是不多见的。研究成果具有较强的利用和推广价值，对贯彻落实"在保护中开发"和"资源与环境并重"的矿产资源开发指导思想有着重要的理论和现实意义。

1998年8月~2001年8月，天津大学与中国地质大学(北京)、天津市地热管理处、天津地热勘查开发设计院等单位共同完成"天津市地热资源开发利用集约化技术及工程应用"项目。该项目运用信息技术，开发由地热工程分析、设计及数据库等集成的地热工程分析设计系统，建立地热井辅助设计子系统，形成地热井参数及结构设计新方法，提出回灌井分类方法，形成分析与预测渗流场、温度场变化新的理论框架，形成供热基本参数与地面配套设备的优化设计新方法、地热供暖设备与基该技术参数的优化设计系统。有效解决地热数据以文档保存，丢失严重，利用不便；结合地热井的设计落后，没有计算机辅助设计系统；缺乏成熟的地热回灌技术、配套设备和先进的工程设计方法等问题。项目组从地热信息技术、回灌技术、地热井与地面设计技术四方面进行研究，形成地热资源开发利用集约化技术体系。该项目获得2003年度国家科技进步二等奖，这是迄今为止中国地热界所获得的最高科技奖项，成为天津市地热开发利用综合技术处于国际先进、国内领先地位的标志。

第六章 电力工程与电工技术

天津关于电力工程与电工技术的科研实力与成就分别以天津大学和河北工业大学为主要代表。1991~2005年，天津大学余贻鑫院士在电力系统规划和电力系统安全稳定性方面获得高水平成果，城市电网规划计算机辅助决策系统荣获2004年度国家科技进步二等奖。贺家李作为中国电力系统继电保护研究的奠基人之一，在电力系统保护方面，做出突出贡献。河北工业大学陆俭国开展电器设计理论研究和低压电器的可靠性检测技术的研究，创新成果多，作为负责单位参与制订多项机械行业电工领域可靠性考核的行业标准，其中，关于低压可靠性理论的研究和低压电器检测技术与测试技术的研究分别荣获2000和2002年度国家科技进步二等奖。

第一节 电力工程

关于电力工程的研究，以天津大学为代表，历史悠久、实力雄厚、成果丰硕。余贻鑫院士等在城市电力系统规划、评估与优化方面，研发出一套具有自主知识产权、完整的城市电网规划计算机辅助决策系统，为国内城网改造的实施提供有效的辅助决策手段，经济效益社会效益极大。在电力系统安全稳定性方面，余贻鑫院士等在国内率先提出电力系统安全稳定分析中的安全域方法学，1993年获教育部科技进步一等奖，并在后来的研究中不断深化完善，2009获教育部技术发明一等奖。在电力系统保护方面，贺家李主编的《电力系统继电保护原理》一书是国内该领域的第一部本科生教材，获国家教委优秀教材一等奖，所研制的500千伏超高压线路保护装置获国家科技进步三等奖。

一、电力系统安全稳定性

1991年9月，天津大学余贻鑫、黄纯华、冯飞等共同完成电力系统静态和动态安全域的研究，项目在静态安全域方面，建立使用有功和无功静态安全域研究之用的数学模型，在该模型的基础上，得到事故前注入功率空间上静态安全域的几何性质；给出两个超长方体形式的实用静态安全域：全域和响应域；提出寻找最大全域和响应域的扩展算法及直接算法；以超长方体近似表达静态安全域。在动态安全域方面，利用动力系统和微分拓扑理论，证明动态安全域的连通性、稠密性和紧致性等一些重要性质；发现动态安全域边界可用超平面近似这一启发式结论。提出识别失稳模态的综合指标法，该方法具有简单、快速和精度高等特点，结果很具有启发性。该成果在理论上有多方面的重大创新，并为其实用化打下很好的基础。

图4-6-1-47 天津大学余贻鑫

1996~2000年，天津大学房大中、宋文南、孙景强等与天津市电力公司调度通信中心合作完成电力系统暂态稳定性裕度分析新算法研究及其应用系统开发。项目研究电力系统暂态稳定分析中所存在的问题，提出修正的暂态能量函数(CTEF)和修正的势能界面(CPEBS)的概念。在实际电力系统上验证修正的暂态能量函数(CTEF)沿故障后轨迹的守恒性。并以CTEF的理论为基础提出系统稳定安全分析的改进的混合算法。改进的混合算法克服传统混合算法缺点，其良好的有效性和可靠性在实际电力系统稳定性分析中得到验证。针对天津电网稳定性分析的现状，实现与美国电力系统分析软件BPA接口。开发的软件具有很强的自动计算功能并配有强大的输出结果数据库系统，交付天津电网使用以来，在电网安全性评价中发挥重要作用，为排除故障隐患、改造电网薄弱环节做出贡献。

二、电力系统保护

1991年12月，天津大学、南京电力自动化设备厂、能源部西北电力设计院三方合作，宋从矩、贺家李、王笑然、张艳霞、张荣华等共同完成500千伏~110千伏输电线及电铁线路系列配套集成电路型继电保护新技术与装置的研究。项目完成基本电路的实验研究和数字仿真工作及相关配套保护装置；完成集成电路继电保护新技术的理论分析，涉及的原理具有独创性，性能和主要技术指标处于国内首创，国际领先水平。保护装置适用于作为500~330千伏高压输电线及电气化铁路供电线路的主保护和后备保护，具有快速切除故障的功能，在国家华中电网，华北电网等投入使用，保证电气化铁路的通畅运行，具有巨大的经济效益和社会效益。

1993年7月，天津大学与电力工业部南京电力自动化设备总厂合作，贺家李、王钢、刘志祥等共同完成微机高压、超高压输电线路继电保护的技术与装置。项目完成微机高压、超高压输电线路继电保护的新技术的理论研究、数字仿真和试验研究，完成WXB-91型微机高压线路保护装置。该保护装置由多个微处理器并行处理构成微机成套线路保护，适用于110千伏~500千伏电压等级的各种距离的输电线路。成果经过严格合理理论分析、数字仿真、科学实验和多年现场实际运行的考验；对工农业安全生产、社会正常运转、人民生活用电起着重要保障作用，同时可避免由于扩大停电范围、延长停电时间以及电力系统一次设备因长时间遭受故障电流而损坏带来的重大损失。

三、电力系统规划

1990~1998年，天津大学余贻鑫、王成山、肖峻等完成配电网运行与改造决策支持系统电力系统规划电力系统安全稳定性项目。配电网是电力系统的重要组成部分，目前国内的配电网结构普遍薄弱且运行水平低，迫切需要改变传统配电方式，该项目深入开展配电网安全分析与经济运行模型与算法的研究，并开发出一套配电网运行与改造决策支持系统。该课题研究的配电网运行与改造决策支持系统(DDMSS)由两个子系统组成：配电网管理系统和配电网分析系统，其功能十分完善。该项目提出的系统较为先进，成果对于提高配电网改造的投资效益，保证电网安全、经济运行具有十分重要的意义。

1990~2003年，天津大学余贻鑫主持完成城市电网规划理论、模型、方法的研究与工程应用电力系统规划研究，研究团队成员包括王成山、黄纯华、葛少云等。该项成果将理论与实际深入结合、数值计算与规划人员经验密切结合，系统解决城市电网情况复杂，存在大量不确定数据和难量化因素的这一难题。研究在理论上有重要创新，开发具有空间负荷预测、变电站优化、配电系统网络优化规划、无功电源优化规划和可靠性计算等功能的计算机辅助决策系统软件。首次将认知科学与数学优化理论紧密结合，发明"认知反馈""认知遗传算法"与"高效全局数学优化计算"相结合的配电网优化规划系统算法和决策支持系统；提出"多层分解模糊多属性空间电力负荷预测"、无需预置待选变电站站址、容量和供电范围的"平面多中位优化"等一系列基本算法；研发一整套完整的城市电网规划计算机辅助决策系统，其整体水平超过法国EDF公司和德国SIEMENS公司的电网规划软件包。在国外学术刊物发表论文60余篇。研究成果在全国数十个城市推广，取得重大经济和社会效益，为全国电网规划的标准化和科学化发挥巨大推动作用。

1993年7月，天津大学与天津电力工业局合作，余贻鑫、肖健、黄纯华、周义、王成山等共同完成城市电网规划计算机辅助决策系统，包括独具特色的三个子系统，即负荷预测、变电站站址自动化优化选择、和供电网络规划优化，每一部分均有自己的数据库系统和图形库，可单独使用，同时三个子系统间信息相互交换，连续的进行负荷预测，变电站站址站容选择和供电网络规划，完成城市电网规划的全部任务。在确保供电安全的基础上可以大量节省投资与运行费用，社会与经济效益巨大。

2001年12月，天津大学自动化学院余贻鑫、王成山、贾宏杰等人合作开展电力大系统安全性与稳定性的理论与方法的研究。电力系统规划电力系统安全稳定性，该项目开创并显著推进电力系统安全性与稳定性分析与控制中域的方法学研究，通过理论与实用化研究工作系统深入，解决把域推向应用的重大难题。显著推进电力系统安全性与稳定性分析与控制中域的方法学、概率分析和逐点法的改进等方面的研究，带动非线性数学的应用研究，在世界上首次把保证暂态稳定性的注入空间上的动态安全域和保证小扰动电压稳定性的割集空间上的静态安全域的研究用于实际电力大系统。

第二节 电工技术

1991~2005年，河北工业大学陆俭国带领的研究团队，在低压电器的可靠性设计理论和低压电器的可靠性检测技术与测试技术两个方向的研究中，不断探索，获得丰硕成果，作为负责单位参与制订多项机械行业电工领域可靠性考核的行业标准。其中，关于低压电器可靠性理论和低压电器检测技术与测试技术的研究成果尤为突出。

一、电器设计理论研究

1999年，河北工业大学陆俭国等完成电器现代设计方法研究，内容涉及电器电磁系统的吸合可靠性理论、电器电磁系统可靠性优化设计、电器触头的可靠性设计方法、电器弹簧的可靠性优化设计方法等关键技术研究，丰富电器电磁系统的吸合可靠性理论。项目研究电磁系统动态可靠性优化设计方法并建立其数学模型，提出采用冗余设计技术的电器触头的可靠性设计方法，基于应力—强度干涉模型研究弹簧在静载荷及交变载荷作用下的可靠性优化设计方法，编制快速、实用的电磁系统及弹簧的可靠性优化设计软件。该研究成果对保证产品质量、提高产品可靠性、达到产品设计结果的经济性、缩短设计周期均有重要作用。

图4-6-2-48 河北工业大学陆俭国

2000年，河北工业大学陆俭国等完成低压电器可靠性设计及其应用研究，内容涉及电接触理论、可靠性理论、现代设计理论、计算机和电工测量技术。主要成果包括对电工产品的可靠性理论进行深入研究，发表大量学术论文，并出版国内电工产品可靠性领域第一本专著《低压保护电器可靠性理论及其应用》；将可靠性设计理论与优化设计理论相结合，在国内外首次提出交流和直流电磁系统的可靠性优化设计方法及软件包；提出控制继电器的失效判据、可靠性试验方法及抽样方案，作为负责单位制订国家继电器可靠性方面的第一个国家标准《控制用电磁继电器可靠性试验通则》，并研制成功实施上述国家标准的具有国际先进水平的继电器可靠性试验装置，该装置功能完善、自动化水平高，不仅适用于继电器，也适用于接触器可靠性试验。该项目的理论研究成果和可靠性试验装置应用到国内十几家主要电器检测中心、试验站和机械工业系统、信息产业系统和航天工业系统的大型企业，为其开展电器产品可靠性评定工作提供有效手段，对改进电器产品的设计、提高产品质量与可靠性起到重要作用，取得显著的经济效益和重大的社会效益。

2002年，河北工业大学陆俭国等完成小型断路器可靠性技术的研究，内容涉及小型断路器的可靠性抽样理论、可靠性试验方法与程序、微机控制与检测技术、自动控制技术。主要成果包括制订小型断路器的可靠性指标体系；运用可靠性抽样理论，确定小型断路器的可靠性试验方法与失效判据；研制出符合上述方法的小型断路器可靠性试验装置；研究小型断路器的失效机理，提出提高其可靠性的措施；作为负责单位制订出小型断路器可靠性考核的行业标准《小型断路器可靠性试验方法（送审稿）》；实现小型断路器手柄的自动操作，其操作机构已申请国家专利小型断路器手柄电动分合器，取得显著的经济效益和重大的社会效益。在国内外学术会议及刊物上发表7篇论文。

2003年，河北工业大学陆俭国教授等完成漏电保护器的失效机理及其可靠性研究，内容涉及漏电保护器可靠性抽样理论、可靠性试验方法与试验程序、微机控制与检测技术、自动控制技术。主要成果包括制订漏电保护器的可靠性指标体系；运用可靠性抽样理论，确定漏电保护器的可靠性试验方法与失效判据；研制出符合上述方法的漏电保护器的可靠性试验装置；研究漏电保护器的失效机理，提出提高其可靠性的措施；作为主要参加单位制订机械行业标准《家用和类似用途的剩余电流动作断路器的可靠性试验方法（送审稿）》；实现漏电保护器试验按钮及复位按钮等手动操作部分的电动操作，其操作机构获得国家专利。项目成果应用到国内漏电保护器的主要大型生产厂及检测机构，对提高产品质量、产品打入国际市场有重要意义，取得显著的经济效益和重大的社会效益。在国内外学术会议及刊物上发表8篇论文。

二、低压电器的可靠性检测技术

1999年，河北工业大学陆俭国等完成继电器、接触器可靠性检测技术的研究，提出继电器、接触器两种产品的失效判据，确定采用测试触点接触压降的考核方法来判定触点是否接触良好及采用筛选方法来剔除早期失效的试品，又根据失效判据提出一套完整的可靠性试验方法。研制出继电器、接触器可靠性试验装置，该装置既能控制带直流线圈的继电器又能控制带交流线圈的接触器，既能在直流负载条件下监测触点的状态又能在交流负载条件下监测触点的状态，解决交直流兼容问题，设备性能价格比高，各项功能完善，使用方便。该成果提出的可靠性试验方法和研制的继电器、接触器可靠性试验装置得到广泛的应用，对提高国内继电器、接触器产品质量与可靠性有重要作用，取得显著的经济效益和社会效益。

2000年，河北工业大学陆俭国等研究成功电器试验数据高速采集与处理技术，该成果的数据采集与处理系统，具有高速、大容量、多通道、在线处理与显示电器试验参数等特点，在性能和价格等方面大大优于国内外同类产品。

2002年，河北工业大学陆俭国等完成低压电器检测技术与测试技术的研究，主要内容包含提出低压电器试验的基本理论、试验方法及抽样方案，研究电器试验的数字化处理技术，包括电器试验参数的高速采集、处理和分析方法。出版全国低压电器测试技术领域专著《低压电器试验技术与试验方法》，发表大量论文。在以上理论研究的基础上发展三个应用研究方向：电器试验数据的高速采集与处理技术，实现电器试验参数的实时测量、分析和在线显示；电器电弧图像的高速采集与处理技术，首次将高帧频CCD用于电器电弧图象的动态拍摄，设计独特的直管纤维镜、目镜和析光镜的结构，为研究电器中电弧的运动规律提供有效手段；电器试验的测控技术，实现继电器、接触器、断路器和剩余电流动作保护器（漏电开关）等典型电器产品试验的自动控制与检测。该项目将传统电器试验与检测技术向电器智能化测试技术发展，成果应用到国内主要电器检测中心、试验站和机械工业及信息产业系统众多大型企业，对改进电器产品设计、提高产品质量、产品打入国际市场具有重要意义，取得显著的经济效益和社会效益。

2004年，河北工业大学陆俭国教授等完成塑壳断路器瞬动特性调试技术研究，涉及数据采集与数据处理技术、塑壳断路器实验技术、微机控制与检测技术、自动控制技术。研究内容包括分析目前塑壳断路器瞬动特性试验装置存在的主要问题，即塑壳断路器瞬动特性试验中，试验电流非周期分量影响瞬动特性的调试，难以获得准确的试验结果；应用先进的快速傅立叶变换方法计算电网的频率、电路功率因数以及合闸相角，并采用选相合闸方法，从根本上消除塑壳断路器瞬动特性试验中试验电流非周期分量的影响，解决国内外电器行业中存在的技术难题；研究并采用自动调压与计算机控制检测技术，保证试验电流的精度，解决电器行业中目前普遍存在的调节精度不高、调节电流受室温变化及回路电阻变化而波动的技术难题。所研制的塑壳断路器瞬动特性调试装置设计先进、使用方便、抗干扰能力强，性能价格比高，其性能优于国内外同类装置。该成果对提高全国电器试验技术水平、推动学科发展有重要作用。

第七章 先进制造技术

天津关于先进制造技术的研究，以天津大学为主力军，历史悠久、实力雄厚，在国内占有重要的一席之地。天津大学机械工程系的建立可追溯到19世纪末的北洋大学时期，为国内最早。精密仪器仪表、内燃机也是国内最早建立的专业，均具有国内一流的学科和学术地位。

1991~2005年，天津在先进制造技术研究的多个领域取得丰硕成果。其中，叶声华院士率领的科研团队完成的精密测量技术，胡小唐等完成的动态检测技术达到国际先进水平。

第一节 机械工程

1991~2005年，天津大学在机械工程的基础与应用基础研究方面的成果十分突出，理论联系实际，获得可观经济效益，获省部委级科技进步奖、发明奖50多项，发表SCI检索论文250余篇，多项成果达到国际先进水平。天津新技术产业园区鼎名密封有限公司王玉明等研究的螺旋槽端面密封技术获2002年度国家科技进步二等奖。

一、机械理论研究

1991年，天津大学刘又午教授主持完成机械多体系统理论方法和应用的研究。该项目在开环树形多体系统动力学分析程序基础上，针对一般多体系统（开环和闭环、完整和非完整、刚体和柔性体、时域和频域）动力学问题，开展理论分析、计算方法和计算程序编制等方面研究，并针对典型系统进行具体计算和实验验证。项目采用凯恩方程，形式最简单、计算量最少、合理选定广义速率时，可使接点力解耦，且最适于数值分析程序编制；采用休斯敦方法，用低序体阵列描述系统的拓扑结构、偏角速度和偏速度标分量及其导数为主要参数；研究具有闭环和运动约束多体系统的解法，利用正交补矩阵构造具有待定乘子和简约的凯恩方程，以消去非完整约束所对应的无功约束力；研究柔性体的有限段计算方法和建模策略；应用实验模态分析技术，开发出一种体间联接点动态特性参数的确定方法。该成果初步建成一个完整的理论体系，开发出一套多功能通用程序，适用面广、使用方便、属国内首创。

1991年，天津大学徐燕申、黄田、李立等完成机械动态分析技术的应用研究。该项目对天津第一机床厂YM5150紧密插齿机进行动力分析和结构改进，通过对让刀系统建模、计算机仿真，提出改善系统动态性能的结构改进措施，把机械动力学、模态分析和故障诊断的理论和技术应用于解决工程实际问题，经改进后的插刀冲程数由原来538次/分提高到800次/分。该项目的研究成果YM5150精密插齿机，不但解决原机床的振动、噪声和加工表面质量问题,而且调高插齿的速度。应用模态分析和故障诊断的理论和技术,对进口集装箱桥吊370千瓦直流电机升高片断裂进行动力分析和故障诊断,以此作为索赔谈判的技术后盾,使索赔谈判获得成功。风机振动状态监测及故障诊断系统在天津重型机械厂成功运行,具有显著的社会效益。

1999年,天津大学王树人、程福安、孙月海等组成的齿轮蜗杆传动科研组完成ZC1蜗杆传动全新技术的理论研究,并参与编订《GB9147-88,JB5558-91圆弧圆柱蜗杆减速器系列标准》。该项目研究主要包括ZC1啮合理论、参数优化理论、可控修形理论以及蜗轮滚刀铲磨理论等22项内容,涵盖200多个公式的建立、推导及其计算程序和绘图软件。齿轮蜗杆传动科研组与天津万新减速机厂联合,试制出国内首创的ZC1蜗杆减速机,达到80年代中期国际先进水平。从1990年至1999年,仅天津万新减速机厂生产的ZC1系列蜗杆减速机近万台,累计产值超过5000万元。ZC1蜗杆减速机被原机电部指定为更新换代新产品,并用于替代同类型进口的蜗杆减速机。该产品1992年列入国家级火炬计划项目,两次获国际新产品新技术专利发明展览会金奖。

2000年4月,天津大学彭商贤、张平、孟庆刚等共同完成智能柔性装配系统设计理论及其关键技术的研究。该项目属于开发研究智能柔性装配系统相关理论及其工程技术,具体内容包括柔性装配系统设计理论及技术;数字化装配与CAD集成理论及技术;智能装配及其控制策略的研究;智能装配机器人开放式控制系统;装配体物流传输小车反应导航的研究;主、被动柔顺装配理论及技术;新型六维腕力传感器理论及技术;机器人视觉技术;装配机器人精度分析与误差补偿理论及技术。发表论文50余篇,开发各类软件6套。

二、机床与机械研制技术

(一)机床研制技术

1994年12月,天津大学与天津第一机床总厂、天津市天动数控专用设备技术开发公司合作,刘又午、王树新和吴建华等人合作完成基于动态特性的数控机床研究与开发。该项目采用动态性能综合实验、整机模态分析以及有限元分析等现代实验和设计方法,完成样机研制和定型生产。其关键技术在于提出采用非惯性坐标系判别机床优势模态,将动力减振原理用于数控机床结构设计,并提出一系列特别是空气泵构造阻尼原理的构造阻尼方案,提高机床在优势模态下的整体阻尼。还进行整机动态特性的综合分析,提出改进设计方案。研究成果达到国内外同类研究的先进水平,在生产实际中得到验证和应用,取得良好的经济效益。

1999年12月,天津大学与天津第一机床总厂合作,黄田、倪雁冰、张大卫、曾子平共同完成3-HSS并联机床关键技术的研究与产品开发。该项目采用3-HSS并联机构作为传动进给机构,由底座、动平台和三对立柱—滑鞍—支链组成。每条支链中含三根平行定长杆件,各杆件一端与滑鞍,另端与动平台用球铰链接,滑鞍由伺服电机和滚珠丝杠螺母副驱动,沿安装在立柱上的滚动导轨作上下移动。样机采用3-HSS构型,属国内首创,设计理论与关键技术达到国际领先水平。样机的几何运动和工作精度达到或接近加工中心相当水平,刚度/重量明显高于传统机床,达到实用化程度,能够用于开发用户需求的各种变形产品。

(二)机械研制技术

1991年,天津大学与青岛第四铸造机械厂合作,刘树藩、沈以心、孙学忠和孙京豪等研制成功新型转子混砂机。该项发明是一个混砂机构,选用中速转动的叶片与低速转动的刮板作为混砂工具,使叶片对型砂施以冲击力,同时使叶片与刮板配合对型砂施以剪切力。两种力共同迫使砂粒相互迅速穿插,强烈摩擦,达到优质、快速的混砂目的。在该发明中,转子设置多层叶片,将上抛式叶片与下压式叶片组合,使各种材料在混砂机内作由内向外、由上向下,及水平环流运动,使砂粒与空气形成两相流,砂层蓬松,有利于砂粒间的穿插、混合与相互摩擦。根据正交实验选出叶片与刮板的最佳参数组合,采用叶片与刮板同向转动的顺流方案,在实际应用中获得满意的结果。该发明新颖独特,一次加料量大、混砂周期短、节能显著、运行平稳、噪声低,且结构简单、维修方便、适用范围广,为国内外首创,获得国家专利,取得明显的经济和社会效益。

1991年,天津大学傅佑同、姜培兰、林彬等完成的陶瓷冷加工技术研究。课题组创造性地开发一系列加工技术与工艺,完成陶瓷气门、陶瓷气门导管、陶瓷针阀、陶瓷气缸盖板、陶瓷活塞顶、陶瓷缸套以及陶瓷气门座圈等陶瓷发动机零部件的研制。其中采用普通磨料砂轮对Sialon、Si_3N_4、PSZ、ZrO_2陶瓷零件超细加工后，表面粗糙度最小可达5纳米；采用的高效低成本车磨法加工技术可以实现切深达5毫米的陶瓷材料高效率加工。镜面加工技术和曲线高效率加工方法达到同期国际先进水平。开创中国陶瓷及硬脆材料加工技术的新领域，研究成果在国内的国民经济各个领域获得广泛应用。

1991年10月，天津大学与天津市计算中心、天津长城电子公司、塑料制品模具厂合作，薛大中、陈亿、崔文林、李洪林、杜君文等共同完成21英寸平面直角彩电外壳模具CAD/CAM的研制工作。该项目在计算机系统上设计产品的结构、美工和模具，进行产品应力分析、流动分析和冷却分析，提出优化设计方案，试模一次成功。采用CAD/CAM技术，为用户设计完成21英寸彩电外壳模具，依靠地方技术设备优势，采用特殊设计方法和加工工艺，解决引进设备不配套的矛盾，使用自己研制软硬件完成从计算分析到加工组装过程中的诸多难题。

1998年6月，天津大学黄田、张大卫、杨志永等完成轿车车身高速静电喷涂涡轮维修与零部件制造关键技术研究。项目组应天津汽车夏利股份有限公司的紧急要求，自1997年1月开展高速喷漆涡轮故障诊断、修复和再制造关键技术攻关，攻克英国BINKS引进涡轮的高速轴承寿命预估、关键零部件的制造和整机装配技术。上线运行结果表明，自行修复和制造涡轮各项性能指标及使用寿命达到或超过进口设备的相应水平，同时确保新型夏利轿车静电涂装生产线的正常运行。研究成果打破国外技术和产品垄断，降低国产轿车的生产成本，促进静电涂装设备国产化，取得重大的社会效益和经济效益。

1999年，天津大学郝志勇、黎家玲、舒歌群等完成电磁式扭振实验台。该实验台由激励系统、模拟轴系、旋转驱动系统和测量分析系统组成。变频电源控制下的扭振电机输出交变扭矩的幅值和频率连续可调、模拟轴系的惯量和刚度连续可调；扭振电机的定子磁极与磁轭用矽钢片叠压而成，电刷置于磁极的几何中性线位置，并串联平波点抗器和整流二极管；变频电源提供连续可调的交励磁电流；转子符合模拟轴系的设计要求等。其总体设计构思完全创新，根据用户的需要先后有3种不同型号的扭振实验台在8个企业和研究机构推广应用，取得理想的效果。

2002年，天津新技术产业园区鼎名密封有限公司进行的“螺旋槽端面密封”技术研究，王玉明、李德刚、杨桦等完成的“干式气体密封”项目实现密封端面的非接触、微磨损、高可靠性和长寿命。技术创新水平为“国际首创”。拥有自主知识产权，打破外国公司对中国的行业垄断，使国内石化行业受益；产品的高可靠性和及时的售后服务减少石化行业的停机损失；高密封性能防有毒危险气体的泄漏，减少污染有利于环保；高效节能节省用户的运行维护费用。

图4-7-1-49 王玉明(右一)在试验室与外国专家讨论技术问题

（三）焊接技术

1995年12月，天津大学张文钺、陈邦固、许玉环等完成焊接冶金质量的控制因子的研究，结束长期以来一直沿用国外判据公式的局面，在国内首次建立焊接冶金质量控制因子优化系统，正确制定焊接工艺，有效预测焊接质量，提高焊接结构的安全可靠性。成果具有理论意义和工程实用价值。

1996年1月~1999年12月，天津大学霍立兴、王东坡、张玉凤、荆洪阳、杨新岐共同研究成功改善焊接结构疲劳强度的超声冲击方法及其装置。项目组研制成功一台HJ-I型超声冲击样机，并在此基础上进行多种钢材及铝合金的原始焊态与超声冲击处理态的大量疲劳对比试验，研究超声冲击提高接头疲劳强度、延长其使用寿命的效果。此外，对此超声冲击处理技术的使用方法和相关工艺参数进行研究，为普及推广超声冲击技术奠定基础。该超声冲击处理大幅度提高焊接接头的疲劳强度。

1996年1月~2004年6月，天津大学霍立兴、王东坡、王文先等研究焊接结构延寿中的超声波及相变应力作用，利用超声波冲击焊趾部位产生局部压缩应力并改善应力集中状态，利用相变应力焊条使焊缝金属冷却中产生的相变应力获得压缩应力，进而解决焊趾部位的应力集中，延缓疲劳裂纹的产生。成果使焊趾部位疲劳强度提高60%～70%，使其疲劳寿命延长几倍到几十倍。在国内外重要期刊发表论文32篇，多篇被EI、SCI、ISTP收录。

2001年3月~2003年6月，天津大学李午申完成超高硬度抗裂堆焊材料的强韧化设计，项目组采用试验优化技术建立超高硬度堆敷金属性能和因子之间的数学模型，利用最优化技术求取堆敷药芯焊丝的最优配方，使超高硬度堆焊材料设计实现由定型到定量、经验到科学的发展。项目研究微量元素对堆敷金属强韧性的影响规律：适量加入钇基重稀土、微量钛和金属镍，提高堆敷金属的强韧性；利用电磁搅拌技术，促使堆敷金属细化晶粒、减少夹杂物和成分偏析、打碎网状共晶碳化物，改善共晶碳化物及夹杂物颗粒的大小及分布形态；用组织工程和热处理等方法，控制堆敷金属硬度的均匀性。研究成果为超高硬度堆焊材料在冷轧工作辊上的应用，奠定坚实的研究开发基础。

（四）激光热处理技术

1991~1995年，天津工业大学杨洗陈承担10KW激光宽带涂敷扫描转镜及激光宽带涂敷自动喷粉机研究，利用中科院上海光机所的10千瓦 二氧化碳激光器，在国内首次开展冶金轧辊的激光熔敷，成为国内冶金轧辊激光表面强化与修复的工业应用先导工作。1994~1996年，杨洗陈承担激光热处理新型光束优化技术研究，1996~2000年，完成大面积激光涂敷关键单元技术。后者的大面积激光涂敷系统在国内广泛应用，并从1998年开始出口俄罗斯、韩国等国家及中国台湾地区。

2001年8月~2003年8月，天津大学张国顺、李荷芬、孙攀峰等共同研制成功数控YAG激光焊接机，成果达到国内领先水平，批量生产，供应全国各地，实现科研成果产业化，主要用于航空、航天、国防工业、移动电器、电池制造、石油工业等领域，获得由国家科技部等五部委颁发的国家重点新产品证书，被天津市科委列入高新技术重点推进化项目。国家计委列入高新技术产业化推广项目。

三、机械系统的测试与监控

1991年，天津大学与唐山冶金锯片厂、天津无缝钢管厂合作，张策、朱梦周、张纪锁、王太勇、汤和等共同完成机械噪声及其控制研究。该成果开展自动车床低噪声料管的研究，采用内衬弹簧，外注橡胶的分段式双层内料管，较原有的噪声降低20分贝（A）左右；对双槽洗衣机隔振减噪的试验研究，研制出同时具备多方向隔振减噪功能的GZ-1型隔振减噪元件，使得洗衣机噪声从60分贝（A）降至51.5分贝（A）以下；关于齿轮装置噪声评价参量的研究，提出以功噪比节圆圆周速度之和作为评价参量，为制定国家标准提供依据；切削加工噪声及其控制，圆锯机床身设计成高效隔声系统，夹紧机构本身作为一个隔声盖板，该锯机较原有锯机的锯切噪声降低22分贝（A），具有国际先进水平；降低圆锯片噪声的研究，分层锯片有效地增大结构阻尼，使振动响应减至原有的数十分之一，阻尼比也增大几倍到数十倍；车削噪声的发射机理及降噪研究，对称布局的阻尼刀杆具有明显的减振降噪作用，为寻找经济而有效的降噪措施奠定理论基础；齿轮噪声信号的分析识别与诊断的专家系统，建立噪声振动信号的分析系统，开发多种实用软件和仿真软件，实现利用噪声振动信号对齿轮多种故障的自动诊断。研究成果推动国内关于机械噪声，机械动态性能等研究工作的开展，取得显著的社会效益。

1996年12月，天津大学王太勇、郭红旗、张纪锁等完成机械加工系统的声振识别与动态测控技术的研究。该项目对机械加工过程及其设备的噪声与振动识别及其动态测控等进行深入系统研究。对机械噪声的识别及其控制，提出圆板结构模态参数的新方法，实现噪声源的计算机辅助自动识别与控制，创新性地研究齿轮减振降噪阻尼环的理论分析与优化问题，并在铣床、车床上得到成功应用和验证。研制多用途模块化设计的保真消噪传声套筒，使得复杂背景下的噪声源识别与声学测量成为可能，并在车削过程监控及玉柴的故障诊断项目中得到有效的验证。基于有限元理论分析、脉冲相应实验模态分析及砂型激振分析等多种方法的各有特色而又互为补充的综合协调运用，建立规范的动态特性理论估算和实测分析方法。该技术应用于冶金工业的钢锭锯切，取得12～15分贝（A）的显著降噪效果。研究在线自动报警与保护系统，提出多级在线监测策略的模式构建问题，并进一步应用于玉柴设备诊断及天津钢管公司的钢管在线检测等项目，成功地取得实用性进展，获得较大的经济效益。

1998年9月，天津大学黄田、张大卫、倪雁冰等研究夏利轿车引进自动喷漆生产线关键设备的故障诊断与自行维修技术，该成果应用现代信号分析方法、结构动力学理论和相关实验技术与现代先进制造技术，解决国内轿车引进自动喷漆生产线关键设备—喷漆涡轮的故障诊断和修复问题。项目组利用模态分析与频谱分析技术，对高速喷漆涡轮进行结构动态特性研究，进行绝对温升和噪声试验，摸清轴承预紧量、最佳装配状态、配合精度、润滑脂填充量对系统动态特性的影响规律；对涡轮转子轴的选材、机械加工和热处理工艺进行大量实验，最终掌握该零件制造的关键技术，替代进口备件；在国内率先掌握进口高速涡轮的自行维修技术，并制定出一套质量检测标准，成功维修一批涡轮；对自行维修涡轮实际使用寿命进行跟踪统计，提出一种震动烈度和灰色系统理论预测涡轮寿命和突发性故障的方法，取得良好效果。在高速转子轴承寿命预测和突发性故障诊断、喷漆涡轮系统动态性能分析与设计、喷漆涡轮装配和检测、高速转子轴承制造是创新性的研究成果。

第二节 精密测试原理与方法

天津大学于1952年在国内高等院校中最早设置仪器仪表类专业，拥有实力雄厚的科学研究队伍和国家级研究基地。天津的仪器科学研究在国内具有一流的学科和学术地位。

1991~2005年，天津在精密测试的研究方面积极探索，取得可贵的成果，具有重要的学术价值和应用价值。天津大学叶声华院士将激光技术引入精密测试领域，研究出一系列新测量原理和方法，由其率领的科研团队完成的视觉检测技术及应用和先进制造中空间几何尺寸测量的现场校准方法和装置两项工作，成果荣获2004年度国家技术发明二等奖。胡小唐等井下采油工具动态检测技术及系统达到国际先进水平，获2005年度国家技术发明二等奖。靳世久等完成原油管道泄漏检测与定位技术获得2005年度中国仪器仪表学会科学技术奖(最高奖)。

一、光电测试原理和方法

(一)在线测试

1992年，天津大学叶声华、冯克献、王春和等研究标准金属筛网孔尺寸及缺陷在线检测系统，利用光学付利叶变换原理，采用激光、光电变换、高速数据采集及处理、空间滤波等先进技术，解决金属筛(特别是高目数密网)网孔尺寸及缺陷的非接触在线测量问题。精度指标符合国家标准对金属筛网检测的要求，填补国内空白。

1992年5月，天津大学叶声华、郸继贵、段发阶等研究几何量光电在线测量新原理方法。项目系统规范结构光传感原理、统一测量模型，提出简便、精确的标定原理，建立多种几何参数中形位误差的测量新方法；全面阐述微小几何参数的光学衍射测量原理，明确提出一维衍射测量、二维衍射测量和统计衍射测量的概念和计算式；深入研究动态测量中误差理论，阐明动态测量误差的组成成分，以及动态误差与静态测量误差的区别；提出应以均方误差来表述动态测量误差及其不确定度。项目原理具有普遍意义，共同特点是非接触、在线、动态、快速、自动化，易于数字化、智能化，从而满足先进制造业的要求。

1993年，天津大学与太原钢铁公司一轧厂合作，由陈林才、蒋诚志、金篆芷等共同完成中型热轧圆钢直径在线检测的研究，以投影法双光路测量原理，有效地克服各种恶劣条件对测试的影响。仪器的测量结果同时以大屏幕显示器、仪器控制柜显示窗及打印机等形式输出，便于及时调整轧机。仪器可用于对Φ60~

130毫米热轧圆钢直径的在线检测和多种钢材的在线测量，减轻工人的劳动强度、消除安全隐患、减少或防止产出废品、实现负公差轧制，技术先进。

1997年，天津大学与第一汽车集团公司二轿厂合作，由叶声华、王春和、邹定海等共同研究开发成功轿车白车身激光视觉检测系统。该项目研究计算机视觉在工业在线检测中的应用，开发用于汽车自动化生产线中的产品质量自动检测与控制的计算机视觉检测技术，实现车身关键尺寸的100%在线检测，并实现数据采集、数据处理、显示及预报自动化。成果为全国轿车工业提供先进在线检测设备，用于车身、车身各部件及其他大型工件的三维轮廓尺寸的在线检测，填补国内空白。

（二）非在线测试

1991年1月，天津大学与天津市公安局车辆管理所王春和、王向军、叶声华、梁和争等共同完成汽车位置光电自动测量系统。该系统采用CCD光电摄像器件，通过光电转换，测量汽车轮廓的坐标，有效避免采用国外设备（主观摆正车位）导致的前照灯水平偏转角的测量误差。该成果是国内首创的汽车位置光电自动测量系统，大大提高调修效率，实现一次检测成功，实用价值很高。

1996年10月，叶声华、朱鸿锡、蒋诚志等完成准直技术及应用研究，提出减少漂移、提高准直精度的有效方法，研制成功多项探测仪器，用于船舶轴系的准直安装、用于高层电梯导轨的准直测量与安装、用于“857”工程中重型零部件同轴度高精度测量与摇摆台安装同轴度基准的给定、用于轻工部“八五”重点科技攻关项目等。

1998年3月，天津大学叶声华、王仲、杨学友等完成视觉检测技术及应用的研究。项目建立通用摄像机数学模型，提出高精度摄像机参数标定方法和多种靶标，达到快速、高精度、简便标定的目的；研究物体表面散射特性对测量结果的影响，进一步提高测量精度；提出以摄像机坐标系为中介实现视觉检测系统全局标定的新方法；建立机械定位误差的测量及补偿模型，降低该误差对测量结果的影响；把CAN总线控制网络技术引入视觉检测系统；在国内率先开展单个视觉传感器、三维视觉监测系统的应用。

1999年，天津理工大学龚正烈、程晓曼、蒋振平等完成单光束激光轴对中测量计算机数据处理模型研究，针对国内花费昂贵外汇引进的激光对中仪国产化所存在的问题，提出单光束激光对中测量方案，研究两个数学模型。利用虚拟现实技术解决人们在直观条件不易解决的问题。研制具有单光束一个探测器的激光对中仪，灵敏度为0.005毫米，其结构简化，具有激光对中和准直测量的两种功能，扩大仪器使用范围，提高性价比。

二、动态测量原理和方法

（一）同轴度测量

1991年，天津大学与青海重型机床厂合作，由张国雄、何晓葵、李敬杰、朱乃彬等共同研制成功的重型机床箱体孔同轴度测量仪。重型机床箱体孔同轴度一直是困绕青海重型机床厂大型机床质量的一个关键问题，该项目创造性地提出误差补偿的方法，在测量系统中采用2个标准环，同时监测心轴的径向、轴向运动误差与角摆，并用等量配重的方法测出心轴在自重下的变形，进行误差补偿，大大提高测量精度。经鉴定与长期使用表明，所研制的测量仪重复性误差小于0.005毫米，包括转位、卸装带来的误差在内的长期稳定性误差不超过0.010毫米，大幅度提高重型机床加工精度。成果填补国内空白、经济效益显著。

1995年6月，天津大学与天津工程机械研究院合作，叶声华、朱鸿锡、孟青伟等完成H/YB-1型摇摆台台体同轴度误差测量及安装基准给定系统的研究。项目以钢丝准直为基础，辅以误差修正技术，用新型高精度、高灵敏度的电容和电感传感器，提高灵敏度，保证测量的稳定和可靠性。项目成果是中国重大现代化军事训练装备的关键组成部分，有效地保证机件加工及部件和整机的安装精度。该仪器为国内首创。

（二）自标定技术

2000年10月，天津大学与军事交通学院合作，叶声华、曲兴华、郏继贵、付敬业合作完成几何量计量仪器自标定、现场标定新技术的开发研究。项目研究自标定原理和方法，推导自标定解析表达式；研究设计电容测微仪自标定装置；分析自标定误差；编制自标定软件、研制外围硬件电路，实现电容测微仪的直接溯源。该技术能够应用于其他有效测量面积型或点型的精密测微仪中，特别是在没有更高等级的传递基准或常规无法比对的特殊仪器现场标定中；能够应用于各种大型空间三维尺寸测量仪器的标定过程，特别是在线测量装置的现场标定；还可以作为独立的三维尺寸测量仪器使用。其特点是可以现场组件、测量范围大、精度高。

2001年6月，天津大学曲兴华、付敬业、叶声华等完成精密测微仪自标定技术与电容测微仪自标定装置的研究。该课题针对具有有效测量面积型的精密电容测微仪设计研制的电容测微仪自标定装置，对自校正原理进行分析推导，给出基本公式，分析采用自校正方法引起的误差，推导计算式。通过多次反复试验，利用该装置可以对精密电容测微仪进行精确的自标定。该装置的非线性达到70纳米，稳定性达到2毫伏。

2005年，由天津大学叶声华、郏继贵发明的专利“大尺寸三维空间测量的现场标定装置及测量方法”获天津市专利金奖，第九届中国专利优秀奖，该专利支持“白车身三维尺寸视觉测量系统”“柔性在线自动测量方法”等多项大尺寸测量项目。

（三）井下工具检测技术

1999年12月，天津大学与大庆油田公司采油工艺研究所胡小唐、徐世民、刘合、傅星等合作，共同研究成功井下采油工具动态检测技术及系统。该系统集测控、机械、自动化、计算机等技术于一体，主机系统高17米，自重52吨。液压系统额定工作压力22兆帕，最大工作压力40兆帕。测控系统完成多参数、高精度、动态检测和控制。利用该系统，在井下采油工具下井之前即对其机械性能和工艺性能进行检测，使质量和性能有可靠保证。在地面上建立仿真的实验系统，采用动态检测技术，对下井工具的优化、采油工艺理论与技术的基础研究和应用研究有重要意义。

2000年12月，天津大学与大庆油田采油工程研究所、中国石油辽河油田分公司的胡小唐、刘合、刘喜林等共同完成井下工具检测技术及试验平台的研究与开发项目。研究开发采油工具检测技术，并建设适于复杂工艺工况的采油工艺工具综合研究试验平台，其中共包括井下工具综合模拟试验系统、细分开采工艺模拟试验系统、稠油热采工艺工具试验系统、稠油防砂试验系统、斜直井工艺工具试验系统。研究平台解决四柱框架结构下的大量程载荷精确施压、非牛顿流体层间分布控制与检测、多细分支路压力、流量之间扰动耦合、不同角度斜直井温度梯度的测量与控制、承受不同地层压力条件下各种工具在套管内运动及机械力学特性的测量与控制等关键技术，为中国石油开采可持续发展提供保障。给企业带来较大的经济效益和社会效益。

（四）MEMS动态测试系统

2004年8月，天津大学胡小唐等完成基于计算机视觉和显微干涉技术的MEMS动态测试系统的研究。该课题站在国内外相关研究方向的最前沿，研制出具有自主知识产权的基于计算机视觉和显微干涉技术的MEMS动态测试系统样机。课题利用纳米级平面栅格和台阶对MEMS动态测试系统功能样机进行标定，并结合MEMS器件动态测试的需求进行MEMS谐振器、扭镜等器件的几何形貌、运动参数、表面变形及谐振频率等参数的测试工作，并在工艺平台进行应用，为产品化的MEMS测试系统提供理论基础和技术储备。该课题将计算机微视觉测量技术、显微干涉测量技术、频闪成像技术及激光多普勒测量技术充分融合，实现MEMS微结构三维静态几何量参数、周期运动特性和瞬时运动特性的综合测量，在系统的整体构思、模块化和虚拟仪器的设计思想、时间平均法的快速测试及三维运动参数重构等方面具有创新性。

（五）定位与校准

2000年5月，天津大学、天津天士力制药集团有限公司王宝光、柴天达、门大春、张国雄等开发成功复方丹参滴丸自动灌装线。该灌装线采用三级主从分布式微机控制与管理系统，设备选材、电器安全性、易于拆卸、清洗和维修及设备运转过程中不产生污染等所有环节均符合GMP国际通用管理标准，自动化程度高、性能稳定、效率高，攻克中药滴丸自动灌装的6项关键技术，包括滴丸的静电干扰强，滴丸的黏度大、滴丸易碎、灌装量大而瓶口较小、瓶盖极轻以及小异性瓶的夹持与定位难等问题。灌装线的研制成功填补国内外中药滴丸自动灌装线的空白，为中药产业化与自动化的发展开创道路。

2003年10月，天津大学与清华大学合作，叶声华、殷纯永、郗继贵、曲兴华等共同研究成功先进制造中空间几何尺寸测量的现场校准方法和装置，解决现场条件下高精度标准量值现场溯源与传递。由多台经纬仪、精密靶标和标定软件构成的大尺寸三维空间测量的现场标定装置及测量方法，适用现场大型三维尺寸监测系统的现场校准。电容测微仪互易回归非线性现场校准方法和装置，由滑块平移放大机构组成装置，借助易位，使两个同样类型的有效测量面积型测微仪多次相互校准，并对测量结果进行回归，发现各自测量的非线性。为远程相互位置（同轴度、直线度、直角度）现场校准的方法和装置。该测量模型先进，精度达到世界先进水平。

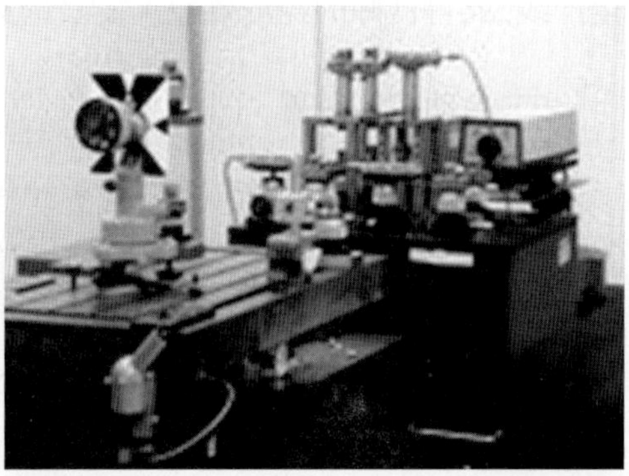
图4-7-2-50 先进制造中空间几何尺寸测量的现场校准方法和装置

2004年5月，天津大学靳世久、李健、王立坤等完成原油管道泄漏检测与定位技术研究，针对中国原油高粘度、高含蜡、高凝点必须加热输送的特点，提出相应的泄漏定位方法，大大提高定位精度。该研究提出一系列检测方法，提高检测的灵敏度和精定位的精度，适用于中国石油管道。成果在中国原油管道上安装使用，开创油管泄漏检测与定位的新局面，效果显著，产生巨大的经济效益和社会效益。

第三节 机械自动化

1991~2005年，天津大学、南开大学、河北工业大学等多所高校紧密结合经济发展和社会生活的需要，开展机械自动化研究，研制自动控制装置和机器人，取得丰硕而可贵成果。天津大学基于模糊小生境遗传算法优化的电机设计技术研究与应用研究和全景式（SJ-2）水井检测彩色电视系统的研究、南开大学关于网络遥操作机器人系统和基于虚拟现实技术的MEMS设计方法的研究，均为国际先进水平的成果。

一、自动控制理论研究

1994年8月，南开大学卢桂章、黄亚楼、刘景泰等完成机器人控制理论与方法研究。该工作基于传感信息的控制提出基于参考模型的自适应控制方案，并在机器人系统上进行验证；冗余机器人系统的研究针对一特定情形，六自由度机器人安装在一移动导轨上进行，提出一种笛卡尔空间运动分解控制方案；对多机器人协调运动提出基于时间同步约束和空间几何约束的运动分类，探讨面向被操作物体的运动描述方法；提出系统的可协调性概念并加以量化，用以规划多机器人的运动，尤其是冗余自由度的优化。

2000年，南开大学涂菶生、陈秋霜、贾春福完成制造系统理论与优化方法的研究。该项目对新的经济环境下制造系统中出现的若干关键问题进行深入研究，内容包括机器调度理论、生产线理论和优化方法的研究，提出新的调度问题、最优调度的性质以及最优调度的寻优算法等。深入研究考虑多种不确定因素的随机生产的模型和优化方法，建立起一般生产的极大代数上的随机线性系统模型，给出随机生产线的自适应综合寻优算法。对相当广泛的一类具有偏序结构的离散事件动态系统，给出采样道路的关键路径，给出性能函数在参数点邻域的解析表达式，从而得到性能函数的各阶导数，较好地改进随机梯度寻优算法，这些结果具有很好的应用前景和重要的理论价值。多篇论文被SCI、EI和ISTP等权威检索刊物收录，在国际和国内产生一定影响。

2004年，南开大学、天津工程师范学院陈增强、袁著祉、孙青林、张兴会等完成智能预测自适应控制理论与应用研究，将自适应控制、预测控制、智能控制、非线性控制等多种控制理论进行有机结合形成新的智能预测自适应控制理论，具有很强的理论创新性。成果应用于钢坯加热炉、工业锅炉和油田钻杆对焊热处理生产线，取得良好的经济效益。发表论文被SCI收录8篇，被EI收录42篇。

二、自动控制装置

1991年，天津大学郝久玉、陈金亭、侯秀卿等研制成功SRB-7型微机控制组合湿热实验室，装置首次将人工智能(AI)方法用于温湿度控制，控制精度好，调试时间极大缩短；设计新型的浅槽电热加湿器，用电子电路精确控制水位，加湿效率提高，器材体积减小；综合运用微机控制技术、电子电路控制技术、抗干扰技术等，精心设计接口和软件，实现检测的全自动化，提高控制精度和效率。用于对电工电子产品进行环境适应性检测试验，其控制系统具有控制和巡检分时复用功能，实现湿热室控制和检测的全自动化，属于国内首创。仪器系统控制能力强，精度高，重复性好，抗干扰性能好，自动化程度高，操作简便，有多种预报警功能，运行可靠。1994~1995年，天津大学郝久玉、李惠敏、许中昌等研究完成交变湿热室智能控制及试验系统，项目成果用于自动控制大型交变湿热室(＞5立方厘米)的温、湿度变化及试验流程，是一个由软件、硬件组成的大型湿热控制和试验系统。提出模糊规则的工程建立法和多变量模糊控制的前馈解耦法，并基于以上方法研制成功软件系统。其配套的硬件是一种新型数字触发器、控制和巡检的分时复用、四成监控式水位自动调节装置。首创专家技术和模糊技术相结合控制交变湿热室的方案，明显提高控制指标和自适应性；提出模糊规则的工程建立法，有利于模糊控制技术在工程应用中的推广；提出多变量模糊控制的前馈解耦法；交变湿热室控制和巡检分时复用功能，便于用户的自诊断和自维护；四成监控式水位自动调节装置，提高加湿系统的可靠性。

1993年11月，天津大学于景良、王德福、孙鼎俊等完成全景式(SJ-2)水井检测彩色电视系统的研究。该设备为全景式观测、无需调焦、图像清晰、具有直观性，测量深度可达400米，在最佳条件下观测精度可达0.1毫米。设备用于测量水井结构，检查水井故障，指导打捞水中掉落物及验收水井质量等，具有新颖性，是当代电子新技术高度密集的光机电一体化系统，成功解决困扰国内水文地质工作者几十年的一大难题，填补国内水文地质检测仪器的一项空白。

2004年9月，天津市工业自动化仪表研究所、天津市天派工业自动化技术有限公司与天津一汽夏利汽车股份有限公司变速器分公司合作，陈宝奎、徐滨宽、孟繁中、秦克景、史小贤等共同完成汽车电控液力自动变速器(AT)电控单元ECU及AT关键技术研究。汽车电控液力自动变速器的核心部件—电子控制单元ECU为国内首创。项目研究从汽车电控液力自动变速器(AT)关键部件的关键技术研究开发入手，通过研究AT的动力匹配搭载技术研制而成。该变速器满足汽车在恶劣工作环境下能够正常工作，实现车辆行驶的最佳动力性、最佳舒适性、最佳经济型的要求，具有很高的技术附加值，达到国外同类产品的技术水平。同时研制出一系列汽车自动变速器总成及关键零部件性能试验和出厂检测自动化设备，已形成3个试验基地和一条中试生产线。

三、机械手

2003年12月，天津大学黄田主持研制钻石600高速轻型混联机械手，采用当今国际领先技术，使机器人并联电机带动两只手臂在一条轨道上纵向运动，更适合较短和较长距离的抓取，具有造型独特、成本低、抓取速度快等特点，其抓取的速度和精确度达世界一流，是中国首台出口国外的整机机器人。该“抓取”机器人具有独立知识产权，在英国著名的华威大学机械专业教学与科研中投入使用，达到设计要求，运行状况良好。

2004年9月，天津大学黄田主持，天津大学和天津市力神电池股份有限公司合作完成的高速、轻型、低成本并(混)联机械手及其示范工程通过验收。该课题针对医药、轻工、电子、食品等行业中急需高速抓取装备的需求，研发出一种具有自主知识产权、可实现2个平动自由度的高速、轻型、低成本全铰接并联结构机械手。获得国家发明专利和实用新型专利各1项,在国际学术刊物和会议上发表论文6篇。

四、机器人

1992年7月,南开大学黄亚楼、刘景泰等主持完成机器人快速力控制系统,以PUMA-760机器人为本体,配置JR3力/力矩传感系统和CA5300图像采集系统,以机器人控制器NKRC-04为底层控制器,以AT-286微机为远程控制机,形成一个手、眼配合的两极控制系统。

1992年12月,南开大学卢桂章教授主持开展微驱动机器人系统及其应用研究,研制用于生物工程的微操作机器人系统。1996年研制成功中国第一台用于显微操作的机器人系统,建立一套用于显微操作的微驱动机器人系统。该系统以生物显微镜为基座,配置三自由度机器人操作手、二自由度电动载物平台、显微视觉及激光测距系统。显微镜、机器人、载物台及CCD摄像机集成为一体,由计算机统一管理。该系统具有自动标定、校准、运动规划和基于视觉的运动伺服能力。

1994年8月,南开大学黄亚楼、王孝喜、卢桂章等完成机器人双臂协调控制系统的研究。该课题建立PUMA 760和PUMA 562双机器人协调系统,具有分层递阶结构,三个层次分别负责关节伺服、运动协调和作业规划。PUMA 562机器人安装在一个线性伺服导轨上,实现导轨与两机器人协调联动;提出可协调性概念并加以量化,用以指导多机器人运动规划与抓取模式选择;探讨载荷分配中的内力不变性问题,提出实用的分配准则;采用机器人测量位置和三维视觉实现系统标定;实现主从控制和基于约束偏差观测器的动态补偿控制;完成包括双手搬运物体、复杂装配、双手自由运动避碰、双手协调运动时的避障在内的多种协调作业;设计开发一面向被操作物的多臂机器人语言OMARL及任务级的编程环境TOPE。1997年10月,刘景泰、安刚等完成双臂机器人协调集成技术及其复杂作业的研究,在国内首次研制出PUMA760、PUMA562和导轨的开放性协调控制系统,提出双机器人协调进行复杂作业的运动规划与控制的方法,并在其上完成大范围表面喷涂,多轴孔互锁装配,柔性物体操作等复杂作业演示。研究成果为机器人学和机器人技术的研究提供一个功能完备的实验环境,同时也为工程应用提供大量可以借鉴的技术和经验。

2000年,南开大学刘景泰完成基于远程网开放的机器人实验平台研究课题,包含宽带网和窄带网两种情况内容。宽带网情况的研究包括增加遥操作的人机交互能力,由传统遥操作的监控型提升到实时干预和实时改变控制策略;为远程操作者提供虚拟现实的操作环境,其中包括高保真视频流、图形仿真预览和实时的线框图形到视频流的叠加;软件系统的结构化设计,建立可扩充的软件支撑环境;对专业级操作者提供客户端的机器人编程语言环境,对通用级操作者提供演示示例;在双臂系统的基础上构建基于远程网的机器人遥操作开放实验平台;作业型的机器人遥操作研究,完成带现场力反馈的双臂复杂作业。窄带网情况的研究包括:结合多线程的通信机制优化技术的研究;基于互联网的命令和图像综合传输系统的实现。

2002年11月,河北工业大学岳宏教授主持完成基于小波变换机器人视觉处理跟踪系统研究。项目充分发挥光学信息处理的实时性、快速性、高度并行性的特点,并考虑小波函数的特点,提出光学小波空间匹配滤波法,实现物体的形状特征提取,图像处理时间达到50 ms以内。该研究成果除用于机器人系统外,还可以针对不同应用目的要求进行二次开发,拓宽其应用范围,例如,用于公安、海关、军事等领域中目标图像的实时特征提取及识别。

图4-7-3-51 基于小波变换机器人视觉处理跟踪系统

2002年12月,河北工业大学高峰、张建军、金振林等完成结构解耦并联微操作机器人研究。该项目研究并联微动机器人机构的构型理论,提出多种3～6自由度结构解耦的并联微动机器人机构;提出并联微动机器人分析与设计用的性能评价指标,包括微位移传递性、力传递性、微位移传递各向同性、力传递各向同性等;提出并联微动机器人的空间模型理论,研究机构尺寸与各性能关系，为微动并联机器人参数选择提供有效工具，提出一体化整体结构设计思想；设计并制造结构简单紧凑的6-PSS并联微动机器人样机，并进行有限元仿真与实验验证；利用自制的六维鼠标实现微动并联机器人的人机交互控制。该项目获4项国家发明专利。

2002年12月，河北工业大学机械学院张明路等完成面向复杂任务移动机器人系统技术研究。研制成功的移动机器人采用CCD摄像机和超声波传感器感知周围的环境，经过基于模糊神经网络的信息融合，获得环境特征，为移动机器人行走、避障、环境识别等决策提供信息，进而实现自主决策和自主导航。整个车体结构呈圆柱形，最高时速2.4千米每小时，最小转弯半径40厘米。该成果为石油化工的相关设备的泄漏自主监测和自主修补提供应用平台，为核废料存储场合和设施提供自主检测和修补技术平台，还为传染病人的日常用品和生活垃圾的传输与处理提供平台。

五、网络遥操作机器人系统

1998年，南开大学刘景泰主持完成利用远程网络技术的机器人遥操作研究，实现基于远程网的机器人遥操作；初步建立基于远程网络的包括有图像、图形和机器人控制信息的数据压缩及传输机制。课题充分利用互联网的通用性和交互性，构建一个集研究和实验为一体的机器人遥操作平台，提高机器人设备的资源共享率，推进机器人技术在科研和工程领域的应用范围和深度。

2001年，南开大学刘景泰主持基于远程网开放的机器人遥操作作业模式的研究，构建一套基于远程网开放的机器人实验平台（TTRP: Telegame/Teleoperation Robot Platform）。项目利用网络技术实现对机器人实时、灵活的控制；采用包容体系结构，使得系统可以执行从机器人动作级到任务级的各级别控制命令，提高本地控制系统的实时性、灵活性和可扩展性。远程控制系统充分运用实时视频反馈、机器人运动仿真、基于虚拟力势场的游戏杆操作控制等技术，显著提高操作者的临场感，便于远端操作者对机器人进行控制，完成遥操作作业任务。在TTRP上设计一种基于多维视觉伺服的人工辅助机器人遥操作精密装配作业，并在远程网上实现配合公差小于0.05毫米的轴孔互锁实验。同时，为了研究机器人遥操作系统深层次的理论问题，特别是探索网络环境和机器人遥操作作业能力之间的关系，指导各种遥操作实验平台的构建，项目组设计实现一个难度可调的强交互遥操作机器人对弈系统。通过调节对弈游戏的难度，改变系统对远端操作者和本地机器人系统的实时性、交互性的要求，从而达到在不同环境下，测试各种遥操作控制策略和算法的目的。

2003年5月，南开大学刘景泰进一步推动基于远程网开放的机器人遥操作作业模式的研究，根据作业要求，分别针对协作型和竞争型机器人遥操作作业特点对现有平台的软硬件系统进行适度改进。同时，引入“智慧空间”提升机器人遥操作实验平台在动态复杂下的作业能力，为课题的研究提供良好的实验平台。构建包括本地多机器人控制系统、远程控制系统、网络通信系统的软件系统，并通过实验验证。在了解国内外相关研究方向的最新进展的基础上，引入机器人遥操作机理的概念，并在该理论体系的指导下，从作业模式和作业机理的角度出发，提出竞争型机器人遥操作的概念，同时结合已有协作型机器人遥操作系统的研究成果，根据各种多操作者多机器人遥操作系统特点进行分类研究。

2004年10月，南开大学刘景泰完成的上述多项课题通过专家鉴定，结论认为：该项目构建一个完整的关于机器人遥操作机理的理论体系；在竞争型遥操作研究领域做出奠基性工作，在该项目提出的新的理论体系的指导下，将机器人遥操作系统分为竞争型和协作型，通过这种系统化和量化的研究，使机器人遥操作的研究对象更明确，研究目标更为精准；针对机器人遥操作精密装配作业特点，提出在人工辅助下的基于视觉的精密装配技术；引入以人为中心的系统设计理念，通过对人机功能的恰当划分，有效地提升系统对于环境的适应性和装配作业的成功率；通过对Telegame的研究，首次引入竞争型机器人遥操作的概念，并在此基础上与传统的协作型的机器人遥操作机理进行比较和分析，为今后远程服务机器人、军事和反恐等领域的机器人遥操作的设计与研究提供一些有益的指导。

六、基于虚拟现实技术的MEMS设计方法

1995年1月，南开大学卢桂章主持微电子机械系统项目中微机械的结构学、运动学和动力学研究课题。初步建立微机械的机构学、运动学和动力学的基础理论和方法，并利用这些原理与方法对微电子机械系统进行有关机构学、运动学和动力学分析，利用虚拟现实技术队微电子机械系统进行仿真研究，为实用的微电子机械系统的设计提供理论依据。

1998年12月，南开大学卢桂章、赵新完成基于虚拟现实技术的微机械快速原型设计系统。项目针对微电子机械系统的尺度效应（微米至毫米量级），传统的基于原型机的快速原型设计不能满足MEMS器件设计需要的情况，提出用虚拟现实技术实现MEMS器件的快速原型设计思想，进行基于虚拟现实的微电子机械系统快速原型设计的研究。该课题的中心问题就是在虚拟环境中实现微机械的虚拟组装、虚拟运行，以此来提供快速原型设计所需的观测、判定、重复开发、优化等用途。

2003年11月，南开大学赵新、卢桂章完成虚拟MEMS加工工艺原型系统的研究。该系统用于MEMS设计过程，在MEMS设计与加工之间架起桥梁，较好地解决目前MEMS器件研制过程中设计与加工脱机的问题；从而大大提高MEMS器件的设计效率，缩短整个开发周期；最终促进微电子机械系统技术的发展。

2004年12月，南开大学卢桂章、赵新完成基于虚拟现实技术的MEMS设计环境的研究。该项目在已有的静态分析基础上，研究对所设计的MEMS器件建立动态模型；利用这一模型进行虚拟运行；针对特定工艺过程，提取专家知识，建立虚拟工艺；建立MEMS部件库的整件框架。以部件库为核心，建立包括结构拓扑设计，虚拟组装，建模，虚拟运行。建立虚拟显微镜仿真模块。

第四节 内燃机燃烧理论与技术

天津关于内燃机燃烧学的研究，历史长、基础厚。天津大学内燃机专业始建于20世纪50年代初，是国内最早建立的内燃机专业之一。学科创始人史绍熙推动建立的天津大学内燃机研究所，在20世纪60年代与上海内燃机研究所并称南北呼应的两大内燃机研究基地。以内燃机节能和净化为主要研究目标的内燃机燃烧学研究室，1985年被国家科委批准为首批“博士后”科研流动站，1986年被国家计委首批批准建设内燃机燃烧学国家重点实验室。

1991~2005年，天津在内燃机理论与技术两个领域的研究都取得丰硕成果。

一、内燃机燃烧理论

图4-7-4-52 天津大学苏万华作学术报告

1999年，天津大学机械学院史绍熙、苏万华、汪洋等完成直喷式柴油机燃烧室内近壁混合气浓度分布及紊流过程的研究，对柴油机近壁区燃油与空气流动及混合过程进行深入的研究与探索，创造性的提出两种先进的试验技术。通过对湍流结构、湍流混合率等物理量的理论研究，提出两种能有效防止壁面浓混合气堆积，大幅度提高混合气浓度耗散率的方法，并开发成功一种新型的燃烧系统与样机。

1999年，天津大学史绍熙、刘书亮、李玉峰等完成火花点燃式发动机缸内横轴涡流及期对燃烧过程影响的研究。运用

LDA和多维数值模拟技术，对汽油机缸内涡流生成发展和破碎过程进行系统研究，探明其转变为湍动能的机理；建立涡流比预测物理模型和计算公式；将电喷、多气门和涡流控制阀技术结合起来，研究多种稀燃方案发动机的性能，为中国发展高性能汽油机提供理论依据。

二、内燃机燃烧技术

1991年，天津大学史绍熙、傅茂林、杨景云等完成柴油机燃用纯甲醇的研究，在采用复合式燃系统的X 1105型柴油机上进行燃料喷射系统改进，使发动机燃用纯甲醇时获得满意的性能，运转平稳，功率和扭矩达到原机水平，在中、高负荷时有效热效率高于原机。试验结果表明，热面点火系统的设计对发动机性能有着极为重要的影响，是在直喷式柴油机上用热面点火法燃用纯甲醇方面的研究成果。

1997年，天津大学刘友均、尚秀镜、李志雄完成汽油机射流燃烧技术的研究，采用新发明的带有射流燃烧室的汽缸盖，对原有供油系进行调整，使之提供稀混合气；对原有点火系进行调节，使之延迟点火角度。独特的燃烧室结构设计可以保证稀混合气的着火和快速燃烧，有很强的抑制爆燃能力，在汽油标号一定时，可以大幅度地提高机器的压缩比，稀燃可以节油和减少排气中CO和HC有害物，速燃可以延迟点火角，提高热能转换效率和减少排气中由于稀燃产生的NOX有害物的排放量。该(射流)燃烧系统打破传统的汽油机燃烧室的设计概念，创建利用微涡流促进燃烧理论，最低比油耗达180克/马力小时以下，具有国际先进水平，怠速排放也有显著改善，达到国外同类型汽油机水平。获得中、美、英、法、德、意、日七国发明专利。

2000年，天津大学与无锡威孚集团公司、潍坊柴油机厂合作，苏万华、汪洋、谢辉、李绍安等共同完成柴油机高压共轨式电控燃油系统及相关应用技术的研究。项目成功地解决一整套电控燃油系统的关键技术，完成电控单元ECU的开发；完成内燃机电控开发系统的研制；完成蓄压共轨式和高压共轨式两种电控燃油系统的开发；完成电控单元优化标定技术的开发；完成基于共轨式电控燃油系统多脉冲复合喷射控制模式和BUMP燃烧室的清洁燃烧系统的开发。项目采用国际上最先进的32位微处理器，研制出结构紧凑，可靠性高，抗干扰能力强的电控单元；独立解决超快速响应电磁阀的设计与制造、液力系统参数的选择与设计等关键技术，开发成功具有国家先进水平的柴油机高压共轨式电控喷油器；开发出一整套电控柴油机优化的硬件和软件技术，为提高国内电控柴油机的自主开发能力，积累有益的经验。该成果填补国内空白。

2005年，天津大学、重庆宗申汽车进气系统制造有限公司刘德新、蒋中林、王天友、刘书亮等合作完成汽油机塑料进气歧管的开发研究。该项目采用先进的融芯法制造技术，在国内首次研制成功有进气歧管和冷却水道的465/462汽车发动机用塑料进气管。该塑料进气歧管气流阻力小，进气温度较低，充气效率明显提高，重量大大降低。发动机使用塑料进气歧管后，动力性、经济性、排放特性都有明显改善。该塑料进气歧管具有加工简单、流动性能好、热惰性低等优点，而且无需重新匹配电控系统。批量生产后，取得数千万元的经济效益。

三、内燃机工程技术研究

2002年，天津大学与天津军粮城发电厂合作，郝志勇、张俊红、高文志、张其显等共同完成大型汽轮发电机组轴系扭振危害及其控制的研究。项目组根据大型汽轮发电机组扭振产生的原因和特点，通过建立数学模型、进行计算机模拟计算和模拟试验，首次提出在大型汽轮发电机组上应用扭振主动控制技术，并进行开拓性的大型汽轮发电机组轴系扭振控制理论和试验研究。研究工作建立汽轮发电机组转子轴系的阶梯轴弹性连续体模型，求解弹性连续体扭振波动方程，提出求解复杂阶梯轴系扭振响应的解析方法；对转子轴系在外部载荷作用下的扭振响应进行计算机模拟，开发轴系扭振计算的通用软件；对轴系扭振产生的原因进行全面系统的分析，剖析各种故障对轴系的危害性，并对汽轮发电机组轴系扭振主动控制进行可行性的分析，提出汽轮发电机组轴系扭振主动控制的部分施控和全局控制新策略，建立轴系扭振主动控制离散系统和弹性连续系统两种数学模型；通过轴系在各种电网激励下的主动控制计算机模拟分析和比较，建立大型汽轮发电机转子轴系扭振主动控制模拟试验台，完成轴系扭振主动控制模拟实验研究。该课题在主动控制策略的理论研究、方案实施及可行性研究方面具有创新性，在汽轮发电机组的扭振主动控制方法的研究上，技术先进。

2002年，天津大学、东风朝阳柴油机有限责任公司宋崇林、王守元、高文志等合作完成4102增压中冷车用柴油机关键技术的研究及应用研究，在4102BZQ型增压柴油机基础上，开发出CY4102BZLQ型增压中冷柴油机，应用零部件优化设计、正交试验、燃烧室优化、有限元可靠性计算、供油系统优化匹配、冷却系统设计计算等现代手段和方法，对整机和主要零部件进行设计和考核。在动力负荷、热负荷提高的情况下，成功解决性能和可靠性存在的问题，同时采用带放气阀的增压器，使柴油机低速性能提高；采用模拟计算和试验相结合的现代内燃机设计理论和方法，优化4102增压中冷柴油机的整体结构。改进后的柴油机体积小、质量轻、动力性能好、燃油消耗率低，噪声排气污染小且启动性能好，其综合性能指标居国内领先地位，应用于生产实际，获得良好的经济效益。

2003年，天津大学机械学院舒歌群、郝志勇、薛远等完成内燃机声振信号测量及其对工作过程识别的研究，利用表面振动信号和近场声压信号测量声强的技术与方法，开展激励源的识别研究，揭示燃烧压力高频振荡对燃烧噪声的激励机理，揭示气缸压力激励与缸盖表面振动之间的传递关系，提出动态传递函数的概念，设计反相滤波器的数字处理方法，并利用数字滤波技术成功地由缸盖表面振动信号恢复内燃机气缸压力。该工作在国内首先开展由缸盖表面振动识别气缸压力的研究，推动国内在该领域的研究。

2005年，天津大学刘书亮、王天友、李玉峰等完成内燃机气道稳流试验评价方法的理论与应用研究，提出新型的气道稳流试验综合评价方法，提出在稳流试验台上评价滚流强度的评价方法，在两种机型上用激光多普勒测速仪（LDA）试验测量中得到验证，证实能够更精确地预测内燃机缸内的涡流和滚流强度。针对工业企业的需要，对国际著名的气道稳流评价方法进行重大改进和发展，提出可变压差的试验方法，使气道稳流试验效率提高10倍，在试验方法中首次考虑气体的可压缩性，提高测试精度。并研制出一系列气道稳流试验台，不仅可用在实验室进行发动机进、排气道的开发，研制及试验；而且也可用在缸盖生产现场检测和评价成品缸盖的气道性能；同时还可测量进气管和滤清器的流量特性。气道试验台在各大发动机生产企业、研究所、高校得到广泛的应用，创造巨大的经济效益和社会效益。

四、柴油机损坏诊断与监测研究

1991年，天津大学文世骐、何万祥、程熙等完成日本三井30.5吨集装箱起重机用柴油机损坏诊断与原因研究。该项目针对天津市集装箱港进口的十二台日本三井30.5吨集装箱轮式起重机，在运转不到一年时间里，有七台车连续发生柴油机活塞严重烧蚀、环岸断裂、活塞环折断等严重损坏问题进行探究。在无设计原始资料的条件下，项目组经文献调研、现场动态数据采集，对整套设备按系统工程理论作理论计算分析，并通过试验室实验，在经对损坏实物的断口及微观组织状态实验与分析，对起重机的现场动态数据采集及处理，找出问题。论证出日方柴油机零件制造上有明显缺陷：动力系统的各分系统间匹配不合理；增压柴油机计与从动机（发电机）间不匹配；柴油机后备功率计算方法有误，后备功率不足；进口机活塞铸造缺陷；活塞环镀铬质量不合格；活塞环锒槽制造不合格，存在严重问题。天津港依据项目组研究成果向日方索赔成功，保障集装箱起重机的正常运转，取得较大的经济和社会效益，使中国的技术水平得到国际上的承认。

1991年，天津大学与天津远洋运输公司合作，郝志勇、王永福、舒歌群、李正国等共同完成船舶柴油机运行状态连续无孔监测仪研制工作。项目以缸盖表面振动信号作为信号源，以动态测试技术和数字信号处理技术为基础，提出利用动态传递函数和自适应滤波技术辨识内燃机的工作状态，提出反映发动机工作状态的特征参量和基于动态传递函数设计反相滤波器的自适应滤波识别发动机工作状态的新方法，开发出由计算机控制的以TMS320C25高速数据处理系统为核心的发动机运行状态的实时监测系统。利用该方法测试的精度较高，实用性较好，属国内首创。

第五节 电机与电器

1991~2005年，天津关于电机与电器的研究，以天津大学行波型超声电波电机及其控制系统的研究最为突出，多年持续努力，取得可贵成果，应用于生产实际，创造出较好的经济效益。

一、电机及控制系统研究

1999年，天津理工大学赵辉、王红君、赵刚等成功研究全数字控制同步发电机可控硅励磁系统，该项工作采用模糊控制技术，设计模糊参数自适应励磁控制器，很好地解决抗外部干扰和内部参数变化的鲁棒性往往较差、难适应各种运行状况的问题。该系统技术先进、控制效果好、可靠性高，深受各类电站欢迎。

2001年，天津大学夏长亮、史婷娜、王太勇等开展行波型超声波电机及其控制系统研究与应用项目。该项目利用铁摩辛柯梁振动理论，建立行波型超声波电机定子振动的数学模型，通过转子接触面上高频振动和外部负载引起接触面的弹性变形，研究定子振动对电机转矩、效率及转子速度的影响；从压电振子等效电路出发，研究行波型超声波电机定子环及至整个电动机的等效电路，为电机控制系统的建立打下基础；探讨定子振动和转子运动之间的内在联系，建立行波型超声波电机设计理论及实用设计方法。建立行波型超声波电机控制模型，进行控制灵敏度解析，确定系统状态可控性、可观测性和输出可控性评价指标，对电机控制相应特性规律进行研究；结合试验研究行波型超声波电机各种控制策略和控制方法，研究控制模型与控制策略、控制方法之间的内在联系；考虑定子环沿径向厚度变化以及内、外边界约束条件的基础上，利用有限元法对行波型超声波电机进行定子模态和强迫振动相应分析，此研究成果居国际先进水平。项目建立行波型超声波电机及理论体系，得到电机最佳控制策略和控制方法，完善电机控制系统；建立一套行波型超声波电机样机及控制系统，对超声波电机在中国的推广应用具有重要意义。

2002年，夏长亮、史婷娜、王太勇等完成无位置传感器永磁无刷直流电机及其微机控制系统。该项目开展对定子裂比对转矩密度和磁钢抗电枢退磁能力的影响的研究；引入区域函数的概念计算气隙及泛磁钢区中的磁密，计算有效的电磁转矩和齿槽定位转矩，对电机结构参数对齿槽定位转矩的影响分析，提出有效削弱齿槽定位转矩的措施；对无位置传感器控制技术的深入研究，分析负载转矩、转动惯量、转子定位位置等参数对电机加速过程的影响，提出加速过程中电机不失步的必要条件，并利用设计的优化加速曲线，实施软起动；提出正确切换的前提条件及实现方法；对电枢反应对转子位置检测误差的影响定量分析，并提出误差补偿措施；采用单片机控制，实现无刷电机系统速度、电流双闭环控制方式下的运行；开发出一套无位置传感器永磁无刷直流电机及其危机控制系统样机；提出一种基于自适应人工神经网络控制的转矩波动抑制新方法和一种基于径向基函数神经网络的无位置传感器控制方法。发表相关论文13篇，项目成果是一种典型的环保型机电一体化产品。

2004年，夏长亮、史婷娜、王太勇等研究成功行波型超声波电机及其控制系统，在考虑定子环沿径向厚度变化及内外边界约束条件的基础上，利用有限元法进行定子模态和强迫振动响应分析；研究超声波电机速度优化控制方法；建立适合行波型超声波电机的PWM驱动控制系统，实现该电机的快速响应、稳定运行、正反转控制、变频调速以及过流保护等，完善电机控制系统。

2004年，河北工业大学刘子胥等完成KZJ—系列全数字型交流电动机软启动项目，该技术采用工业级MCU为主控核心，晶闸管为主功率元件，具有液晶汉字显示、RS485工业标准通信、负载电流、电压动态显示、故障诊断、全功能保护等功能，并解决高压电场以及动态大电流形成的突变磁场交织在一起形成的干扰问题,使控制电压等级达到10千伏级。主要适用于工矿、港口、造纸、石油、化工、水利、换热等场所的交流50赫兹、电压10千伏及以下、功率7.5千瓦~10000千瓦的三相交流电动机的软起动控制。由于该技术具有无触点、无火花、起动平稳、冲击电流小等特点,提高控制系统以及煤矿井下采煤,排水系统的稳定性和设备寿命,极大地降低供电系统的故障隐患,提高安全生产。在电机控制领域的高端控制技术拥有自主知识产权,推广应用到天津、河北、上海省市多家企业,经济效益,社会效益显著。

2005年,天津大学、扎努西电气机械天津压缩机有限公司夏长亮、史婷娜、陈炜、王太勇等完成基于模糊小生境遗传算法优化的电机设计技术研究与应用研究,在国际上首次提出基于模糊小生境遗传算法优化的电机设计新技术,解决电机优化设计中存在的收敛速度慢、参数设定难等问题,算法具有更高的鲁棒性、全局最优性和更快的收敛速度,经鉴定为国际领先水平。新技术应用于115伏/60赫兹压缩机感应电机设计中,有效解决115伏/60赫兹压缩机电机存在的制冷系数低的问题,很大程度地改善电机的性能指标。成果应用于扎努西电气机械天津压缩机有限公司,自2002年至2004年三年累计生产销售新产品137万台,新增产值23190万元。

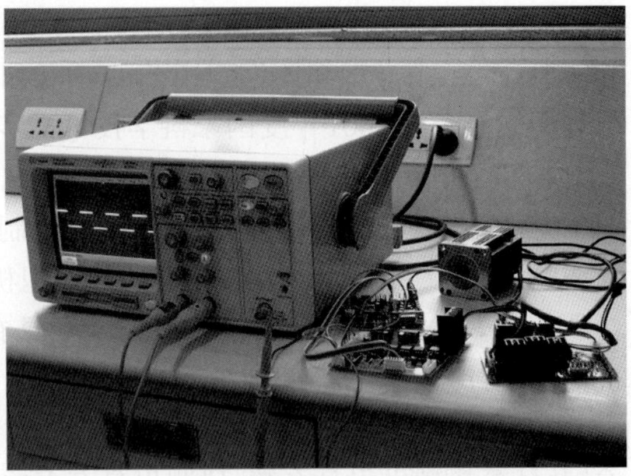

图4-7-5-53 进行基于模糊小生境遗传算法优化的电机设计技术研究与应用研究装置

二、检测技术与自动化装置

1999年12月,天津大学与中国石油天然气股份有限公司华北石化分公司合作,刘宝坤、张景涛、童刚、杨立峰等设计完成成品油销售及测控系统。该系统采用信息网络系统与自动控制系统双层结构的有机结合,杜绝管理漏洞;在测控系统中采用质量流量计以及高性能的自动控制系统,减少计量误差,提高测控精度。系统设置可支持TCP/IP协议和其他通信协议,采用星形以太网络,将操作站和控制站模块化按需配置,对于不同操作任务采用不同操作级别。系统服务器采用双击热备份,进一步完善系统安全保护功能,提高系统的可靠性。该项目开发系统基于C/S结构的石油产品销售管理系统与装车异构网络集成,实现管理控制一体化网络销售系统,其检测系统采用基于专家预估技术的高性能自动控制系统,减少销售计量误差。该系统配置灵活、可扩展、实用性强、可靠性高,有完善的安全保护功能,建立石化企业成品油销售运营利润的数学模型,从而加强对市场的应变能力。

1999年,天津大学徐苓安、徐立军、熊汉亮等完成基于电学敏感原理的过程层析成象技术的研究,该项目以自行研制的透射模式超声层析成象系统、多激励模式电磁感应成像系统和电阻层析成象系统等为具体研究对象对基于电学敏感原理的过程层析成象系统的理论进行深入探讨。研制的超声成像系统和电磁成像系统具有创造性,处于国际领先水平。其中电磁成像系统获得中国发明专利一项。

第六节 三维异型整体编织与设备

三维异型整体编织技术是国外20世纪80年代初发展起来的一种新型纺织技术,由此种技术编织出的三维异型整体编织件是制作航天、航空等部门所急需的高级复合材料的理想增强体。天津工业大学李嘉禄带领的研究团队所取得的成果尤为突出。

1991~2005年,天津工业大学李嘉禄和他的同事们承担多项国家和部委下达的科研课题,研制出国内最大的由计算机控制的挂编织纱2万根、轴纱2万根的三维整体编织机和多台组合式三维异型编织机;开展多种三维编织工艺的研究和三维编织计算机辅助设计的研究;开发出三维织物的树脂传递模塑(RTM)复合工艺和设备;研制出三维编织预制件表面参数和厚度的测试装置;开展三维编织复合材料的微观结构和力学性能预测以及力学性能测试技术的研究。其中,三维异型整体编织工艺的研究和三维编织设备及织物的研制荣获2001年度国家科学技术进步奖二等奖。

图4-7-6-54 天津工业大学李嘉禄等研制的三维立体异型编织机

2000年,天津工业大学复合材料所完成三维异型整体编织工艺的研究和三维编织设备及织物的研制。此项技术的研制成功使编织工程制件的组合式三维编织机成为可能,其创新点在于多种三维一行整体编织新技术、具有工程应用价值的组合式三维编织机和三维异型整体编织计算机辅助设计系统。

2003年,天津工业大学李嘉禄、陈利、焦亚男等开发出变截面三维多向整体编织技术(均匀移纱减细技术)及计算机辅助设计系统,研制出具有多向加轴纱装置和移纱控制装置的多台联动式三维编织设备,实现具有横截面变化的复合材料结构件的三维多向整体预成型。

2004年,李嘉禄、吴晓青、李晓久等完成表面为不可展开曲面大型机器缝合复合材料的研制,成功改造曲面壳体缝合设备和对接缝合设备,解决缝线张力控制、基步低损伤均匀进给关键技术,解决表面为不可展开曲面课题预制件缝合难题,改造和完善三维五向编织加强筋预制件的编织机和工艺,研制出具有高温控制系统的RTM设备,形成从三维纺织预制件织造到树脂基复合材料制作全过程的研制和生产能力。

2004年,天津工业大学完成先进防热材料用变截面三维多向编织材料的研制。开发出变截面三维多向编织技术,研制出先进固体火箭发动机碳/碳喷管中耐高温连接件的近尺寸三维整体预成型件,保证连接件截面变化处增强纤维的连续性,经CVD渗碳后,连接件具有优良的性能。该项目研究开发出计算机辅助变截面三维多向整体编织技术及三维编织设备,通过对编织纱线运动规律的控制,实现具有横截面变化的复合材料结构件的三维多向整体预成型,是一种新型的高科技纺织技术,具有独创性、先进性和实用性。

2004年,天津工业大学姜亚明完成纬编双轴向多层衬纱织物的成型性研究。该项目自行设计和搭建平面织物面内剪切性能测试装置,研究纬编双轴向多层衬纱织物的结构和几何特性,研究该织物对半球、双半球、圆柱等成型性能,并搭建半球成型模型,揭示纬编双轴向多层沉砂织物对三位曲面的成型特点和成型规件。

2004年,天津工业大学吴晓青、李嘉禄、汪日伟等完成三维编织复合材料树脂充模过程的研究项目。研究三维编织预制件的结构对渗透率的影响规律,主渗透率方向采用数字摄像机提取流动形状,然后用二值化方法提取边缘点,在自行编写的程序中确定方向,提高精度,改善以往只依靠流动前沿形状确定方向的方法。

2004年,天津工业大学陈利、成玲、焦亚男等完成树脂基编织复合材料的粘弹性性能研究,所建立的三维多向结构单胞分析模型为该类材料的力学分析奠定基础,建立的分析方法及计算软件实现树脂基三维编织复合材料的工艺选择、材料性能设计、结构优化等,具有广泛的应用前景。

2004年,李嘉禄、吴晓青、李晓久等完成防科工委大型构件机器缝合复合材料研制课题,重点研究表面为不可展开弧面的大型构件的机器缝合复合材料制件的制作技术。研制成功曲面壳体预制件缝合设备和高性能纤维织物对接缝合设备,解决缝合纱线张力控制、基布低损伤均匀进给等关键技术,适合高性能纤维缝线和高性能基布的缝合。填补国内表面为不可展开弧面壳体缝合复合材料制件制作的空白。

2005年,天津工业大学研制出纬编双轴向衬纱织物与装备。纬编(罗纹结构捆绑)双轴向多层衬纱织物及其制织设备为专有技术,属国内外首创。

2005年9月，天津工业大学焦亚南完成三维编织变截面复合材料的成型设计与优化的研究。该项目从实际应用需求出发，针对异型构件编织过程中涉及的纱线数量增加或减少的问题，对变截面三维编织减纱原理和细观结构以及力学性能进行系统的研究，建立三维编织的计算机表观模拟系统，具有重要的学术意义和工程应用价值。

第八章　环境科学与技术

1983年，南开大学在国内综合性大学中最早成立环境科学系，并承担国内环境科学第一个国家自然科学基金重大项目。以南开大学为主承担的京津渤区域环境综合研究和天津市城市生态系统与污染综合防治研究两个项目，分别于1985年和1987年获国家科学技术进步奖二等奖。

1991～2005年，天津的环境科学研究，南开大学仍是一个重要的方面军，同时，天津大学、天津市环境保护研究院、天津市环境保护局也开展许多有成效的工作。天津关于环境科学与技术的研究水平在国内处于先进。其中，南开大学关于环境化学的研究是国内领先水平，南开大学戴树桂主持并参与的典型化学污染物环境过程机制及生态效应研究荣获2005年度国家自然科学奖二等奖。

第一节　环境化学

20世纪70年代初，天津市汉沽区4.7万亩小麦因受工业污水污染致颗粒无收。为此，1976年，天津市组织南开大学、天津市化工局与中国科学院环境化学研究所等7单位联合进行京津渤区域环境综合研究。南开大学负责研究汞污染、黄磷污染以及DDT、666农药污染问题，成为在国内较早开展有毒化学品对生态环境的作用和影响的研究单位，多项研究成果获奖。1991~2005年间，天津在环境化学研究领域，又取得新的可喜成果。

1994～1998年，南开大学戴树桂、中科院生态环境研究中心徐晓白、中科院动物研究所黄玉瑶共同主持承担国内环境科学领域的重大基金项目“典型化学污染物环境过程机制及生态效应”。南开大学主要承担该项目有机锡化合物为主线的系统研究，参研人员有陈叙龙、陈甫华、黄国兰等。项目组建立可同时测定天然水中6种不同形态的烷基锡化合物的氢化物发生/低温捕集/气相色谱/原子吸收光谱联用方法；研究富里酸（FA），胡敏酸（HA）对无机锡化学甲基化作用及其机理；模拟河口水生生态系统的微宇宙，运用同位素示踪技术，以^{14}C标记的丁基锡氧化物为目标化合物，建立包括食物链在内的多介质环境中的综合数学模型，预测结果与实际采样测定值符合；研究有机锡对藻类、轮虫和罗非鱼的生态毒理效应，探讨组成结构对有机锡毒性影响的规律；基于7种物化和拓扑参数研究一些有机锡化合物对轮虫毒性的定量结构活性相关（QSAR），提出2种新分子连接性指数，并发现由憎水性碎片常数（Hansch常数）和电性常数（Taft常数）作自变量，组成的双参数QSAR模型与有机锡毒性的关系最好，于1998年出版专著《典型化学污染物在环境中的变化及生态效应》。在国内外共发表学术论文200余篇。

1999年1月～2002年12月，南开大学戴树桂与中科院生态环境研究中心叶常明合作，共同主持有毒化学品多元复合体系的多介质环境行为研究项目,南开大学刘广良、金朝晖、张清敏等参加。研究发现:表面活性剂对憎水性有机污染物有增溶作用;涕灭威在土壤中有不可逆吸附行为,并实验测定不可逆吸附量。探索涕灭威在土壤中的吸附机制,认为涕灭威在土壤有机质上的吸附是通过分配作用和化学吸附过程同时进行,并确定氢键是涕灭威与土壤结合的一种重要形式;发现腐殖酸可使涕灭威亚砜和砜的水解速度减慢,FA比同浓度的HA对它们水解的抑制作用更强;阴离子表面活性剂十二烷基苯磺酸钠(SDBS)能够明显促进涕灭威在土壤中的淋溶作用,当模拟降水达705毫米时,可使涕灭威淋溶至130厘米深;SDBS对涕灭威在土壤中的降解有明显促进;建立一种简便、快速检测涕灭威对土壤微生物DNA损伤的方法。结果表明,涕灭威-SDBS复合体系中,二者对土壤微生物的联合作用是拮抗作用。项目首次提出研究环境介质和污染物的双重复合体系问题。在国内外学术刊物和国际学术会议上发表论文30篇。

2003年1月,南开大学戴树桂主持承担黄河兰州段典型污染物迁移转化特性及承纳水平的研究,协作单位有黄河水资源保护科学研究所和黄河流域水环境监管中心,南开大学孙红文、徐建等参与此项工作。项目选择当前国内外特别关注的,而在以往黄河污染物研究中尚未涉及或未深入研究的环芳烃(PAH)和壬基酚(NP)作为典型污染物,基本摸清黄河兰州段中两类有机污染物的污染状况及污染水平,确定污染物质的合理承纳水平;成功应用半透膜采样装置进行水环境中有毒有机污染物的采样,表明发展此技术用于黄河常规监测是可行的;获得黄河中上游水体悬浮颗粒物的各种成分对疏水有机污染物吸附能力和吸附机理的认识;研究壬基酚聚氧乙烯醚在水体中的光降解行为,确定出光降解的主要产物并推断出反应历程;在现场采样分析的基础上,结合源解析的方法,确定黄河兰州段表层沉积物中多环芳烃的来源;首次将马尔柯夫模型(Markor model)用于黄河兰州段水体中多环芳烃环境归趋的研究,获得与专用成熟的逸度模型(Fugacity model)极为相近的效果。在国内外学术刊物上和国际会议及全国性学术会议上发表论文47篇,其中SCI论文13篇,出版专著1部。

2003~2005年,南开大学庄源益、戴树桂、金朝晖等开展沿海城市水环境生态修复基础研究,包括稀土金属和亚硝酸盐对藻类生长的影响、地下水中涕灭威农药的迁移转化和铁粉及纳米铁还原去除地下水中的硝酸盐氮、零价铁去除地下水中偶氮染料和砷、大型蚤对栅藻的摄食行为、载铁球形绵纤维素吸附剂去除地下水As(Ⅲ)、天津市富营养化水体生源要素调查、天津富营养化水体藻类组成及其群落结构的动态变化,以及硅酸盐和硫酸盐对藻类群落结构的影响等。在国内外学术期刊发表学术论文37篇。

第二节 环境的污染与控制

环境的污染,突出表现在水和空气的污染。对环境污染的控制也主要体现在对水和空气污染的治理。1991~2005年,天津的环境保护工作呈现大发展局面,南开大学、天津大学积极发挥作用,天津市环境保护科学研究院等多家环境保护单位发挥各自优势,共同努力为天津市的环境保护工作做出贡献。

一、水污染及其治理

2001年7月,天津市环境保护科学研究院等单位唐运平、邹克华、魏香峰等完成油田采油废水高效生物处理工程技术研究,通过在废水中添加高温优势菌,再辅以生物载体填料,在超常规生物处理温度下不经人工降温直接进行生物处理,使高温采油废水直接生物处理成为可能。经过优势菌处理后的废水,直接达标外排,或进入稳定塘系统,通过塘系统内的微生物的作用,污水最终达标排放。该成果成功用于每日1万立方米规模的采油污水处理,解决采油废水达标排放难题。具有耐高温、耐油、显著提高废水可生化性等优点。

2002年,天津大学张颖、顾平、谭丁开展膜混凝反应器处理轻度污染地表水研究,应用混凝活性炭吸附微滤工艺，处理轻度污染的地表水。该工艺流程简单，停留时间短，设备紧凑，能有效去除水中的浊度和有机物，对氨氮也有一定去除作用。在该工艺中，混凝可有效去除大分子有机物，缓解膜污染；投加粉末活性炭可以改善滤饼层结构，维持膜通量，并对TOC和TTHMPF的去除起到作用；微滤可有效截留悬浮物质，确保出水水质。

2003～2005年，南开大学孙红文、朱琳、刘春光等完成天津市经济技术开发区水环境改善的综合研究，参与工作的还有天津泰达新水源科技开发有限公司、天津市环境保护科学研究院和国家城市给水排水工程技术研究中心。项目首次在天津建造人工景观河道，并利用再生水为唯一水源，利用植物、微生物、水生食物链构成的生态系统的整体功能，实现对环境的修复以及对水质的保持。

2004年4月～2006年6月，天津大学与天津市市政工程建设公司赵新华、孙井梅、黎荣、迟海燕等合作完成排污河道污染沉积物处置与资源化研究。通过在排污河道布点取样和检测，发现在同一断面，重金属含量的最高、最低值均在两侧，分析表明这与两侧沉积物逐渐向中间移动及污水常年由两侧进入河道有关。这一发现为河道治理设计河道断面提供有益的借鉴，即应尽量使用梯形河底。通过冻融试验发现，沉积物的沉积及脱水性能得到提高，泥水明显分离，将上清液滤出后含水率可达到50%～60%。而冻融后沉积物使用压滤机脱水，不需投加任何絮凝剂含水率最低可达到30%。由清淤、脱水、运输和处置可组成4类共32种工艺流程。通过岸边植物物种及植物体内重金属的系统调研，明确植物修复重金属—有机物复合污染的大沽河底泥的方法。使用BP网络技术建立岸边植物体内重金属及附近底泥中重金属含量的相互关系，通过岸边植物体内重金属的测定可初步预测附近底泥中重金属污染情况，避免底泥监测中底泥取样难等问题。该成果用于城市排污河道的环保疏浚和安全处置，降低总工程费用5%，而且使得整个施工过程对周边地区基本没有环境污染的影响，经卫生处置后的底泥，在填埋后不会污染地下水和农作物，具有农用价值。

2005年，南开大学王启山、庄源益、傅学起等研究废水及微污染水的创新处理技术。研究内容包括在消毒之前的各项水处理工艺中尽可能地把水中的有机物去除，避免生成THMs，从而提高供水质量和安全性；水源地有机微污染防治措施及营养盐、藻类的消减技术；有机微污染水的消毒副产物三卤化物等三致物的消减技术；新的强化絮凝技术；强化混凝-气浮工艺去除微污染水中有机污染物；强化絮凝-吸附工艺去除微污染水中有机污染物；强化过滤工艺去除微污染水中的有机污染物；去除微污染水中以干扰素为代表的持久性有机物的强化处理工艺；去除微污染水中有机物、氨氮、藻类及藻毒素的水厂集成工艺。成果明显提高对微污染原水的处理效果，降低自来水中消毒副产物，提高自来水水质，保障人体健康。

2005年，天津城市建设学院熊振湖、马华继、王佳等完成固定化藻菌的脱氮除磷功效用于城市污水处理研究，利用藻菌共生的原理，从优势藻种的培养、藻菌的共固定化和主题反应器的设计、光源的设计和应用等方面着手，从静态和动态两个层面进行实验研究，提出的处理工艺对$NH4^+$-N、P和COD的去除率，分别达到90%、62%和76%。成果应用于天津创业环保股份有限公司3.5万吨/天城市污水处理改造工程，经济和社会效益显著。

2005年12月，天津大学与天津市兴源环境技术工程有限公司、天津工业大学膜天膜工程技术有限公司、军事医学科学院卫生学环境医学研究所顾平、武震、吕晓龙、李君文、孙迎雪、朱高雄等合作完成膜—生物反应器的工程化与应用研究，主要成果是：研制成功高通量、模块化膜组件与膜单元，并投入规模性生产，截至2005年末，销售收入达到8210万元；研制成功膜生物反应器（MBR）本体模块化组件；进一步完善MBR的自控系统，通用性提高，故障率大幅度降低；研制成功MBR远程监控系统，实现对多项工艺参数在线监测，并应用于示范工程；延缓膜污染的物化技术研究取得阶段性成果；研制出MBR快速启动微生物制剂，并确定对于微生物制剂的工业化发酵条件。该项目完成示范工程多项，其中天津市第一中心医院污水处理站处理规模为500立方米/天，应用研究所获得的所有技术稳定运行。

2005年，天津市引滦水资源保护领导小组办公室、天津大学、天津市环境监测中心合作，辛志伟、钟定胜、张宏伟、张继红、张淑英等共同完成天津市水污染物排放总量控制技术与方法的研究。项目对天津市所有水污染源排污开展调查评价，对天津市水环境功能区域现状进行分析评价，开展各水系的水环境质量与水污染物排放总量之间输入响应关系研究，开发符合天津河流特点的河流水质模型和计算软件，并以该课题开发的天津市水环境管理信息系统为平台，为天津市进行第一次系统的地表水环境容量核算，确定各水环境功能区及陆域控制单元的污染物最大允许排放量；根据水环境容量核算结果和水污染管理现状，研究开发全市水污染物总量控制方法和水污染控制指标分配技术，第一次完整系统地开发天津市水污染物容量总量控制技术，并制定整套天津市水污染物排放许可证发放技术及管理办法。

二、空气污染及其治理

1991年，天津环境保护科学研究院郭光焕、阎成芳、刘凤英等完成天津市总悬浮颗粒物总量控制技术研究及应用的研究课题。以天津市城市总体规划为依据，采用系统分析方法，将市区视为一个完整的系统，在大气TSP环境目标值的约束条件下，计算市区大气TSP的区域允许排放总量，并将这个总量分配到排放源，通过控制排放源的允许排放总量确保天津市区环境质量达到所规定的环境目标值。建立一套大气TSP总量控制规划模型系统、模型参数系统和规划方法，编制一套大气污染物总量控制规划信息管理系统软件。

其后，南开大学朱坦、冯银厂、张裕芬等和天津市环境保护局刘洁共同开展天津市大气污染总量控制及分阶段防治技术研究，项目组在国内首次研究并编制开放源类污染源调查技术大纲，在GIS系统上建立开放源类污染源数据库，利用大气颗粒物源解析和大气扩散模型、气象因素相结合的技术方法，制定出“蓝天工程”分阶段方案和环境空气质量分阶段目标值，以及气象因素的影响，环境空气质量分阶段目标值可能的变化范围，为“蓝天工程”提供技术支持。

1999年，天津市环境保护科学研究院孙申、孙广明、蒋伟华等研制成功高效导旋除尘脱硫净化器，采用除尘脱硫一体化装置的结构化设计；除尘脱硫净化器除尘效率大于98%，除SO_2效率大于80%；设备的净化器防腐蚀、耐磨损、耐高温。

2000年，南开大学与天津市环境科学研究院合作，朱坦、郭光焕、白志鹏、王玉秋等完成大气颗粒物源解析技术的开发与应用研究。项目着重于大气颗粒物源解析技术推广应用的能力建设，在受体模型及其算法以及模拟优度的诊断技术、源成分谱和受体化学组成、受体模型应用软件、受体模型用于城市尘污染控制管理等方面进行深入的研究。成果应用于城市环境综合整治、大气颗粒物总量控制等领域，在大气环境资源管理工作中发挥重要作用。

2003年，南开大学和天津环境保护科学研究院朱坦、白志鹏、冯银厂、郭光焕等研究大气污染的源解析技术，提出二重源解析技术，解决颗粒物源解析中一套数据多种结果的诊断问题，并首次在国内研制成功开放源颗粒物再悬浮采样器，解决颗粒物开放源采样的真实性和代表性问题。成果推动颗粒物源解析技术在国内的广泛应用。

2005年，南开大学朱坦、冯银厂、张裕芬等及天津市环保局赵喜梅，共同完成天津市环境空气质量管理与污染控制技术研究。项目组建立大气主要污染物容量总量技术方法，测算天津市大气主要污染物环境容量；建立大气环境容量分配的指标体系，确定不同大气污染源类的基准排放因子和源排放的综合调节系数；并开展容量分配方法研究与排污许可证发放的可行性、可操作性研究，设计出排污许可证发放制度。成果为排污交易制度的设计和施行奠定理论基础。

2005年，南开大学与解放军军事医学科学院卫生学环境医学研究所白志鹏、袭著革、朱坦、戴树桂等合作完成室内空气污染表征与控制技术开发项目，吸收国际研究方法学的先进技术与经验，结合中国国情，以装修的住宅、办公室、会议室等空气中的醛类、苯系物、多环芳烃等几类有毒有害有机污染物及一些无机有害气体气体为典型对象，深入开展室内典型空气污染物检测技术开发、污染物环境化学行为表征及污染控制技术开发等一系列研究，内容包括：以模拟环境舱和室内污染物快速测定技术的开发为重点的能力建设；室内空气污染表征研究；人的时间活动模式及人群对污染物的暴露研究；绿色建材评估体系及相关国家、军队和行业标准研究；室内污染控制技术开发及净化机理研究；室内空气污染的特征分析及污染防治对策等。该项目组率先开展中国室内空气污染的系统化研究，成果为制定室内典型污染物的检测方法、污染控制和环境标准提供翔实的数据支持，为进行环境风险管理提供科学的理论支持，为深入认识和改善国室内环境状况，保护人体健康提供可靠的技术支持。

三、环境生态及其修复

1988~1992年，天津市环境保护科学研究所、天津市水利科学研究所、天津水文总站、天津环境监测中心等单位黄亭、古建国、郭青平、郑裕君、袁秀文、秦保平和龙沛湘共同完成海河（市区段）污染控制技术的研究。项目组系统科学地对海河水环境状况、污染源特性及改善水体水质的治理方案进行全面研究。确认海河的大光明桥、四新桥、柳林、二道闸等河段为富营养型水体，三岔口、三岔口以上河段为中营养型水体。确定海河水体的污染状况及主要污染物的负荷量与各污染来源的负荷比，根据不同阶段海河水源保护的目标和相应的水环境容量，确定各阶段污染物削减量，进而针对海河干流段的实际情况研究市区排水改造、农业排水改造、底泥治理、北运河沿岸生活污染源治理及上游来水优化调度等单元治理措施，在全面分析环境、经济和社会效益的基础上提出分阶段、分目标实施的综合治理方案。成果填补国内封闭性河道水源保护及污染控制研究的空白。

2002~2005年，天津市环境保护研究院、中国环境科学研究院、中国海洋大学、天津大学、国家海洋局第一海洋研究所、天津科技大学共同承担渤海典型海岸带生境修复技术研究，吴伟、吴德星、郑丙辉、李小宁、董双林、陶建华和陈惠彬等参与。课题组针对渤海湾海岸带生境严重退化的实际情况，在技术研究、技术应用示范和管理协调技术三个层面上构建海岸带生境修复技术体系的框架，从生物技术、工程技术和管理技术三个方面进行生境修复技术的研发，最终形成生境修复综合技术体系。课题针对渤海湾的主要海岸带类型（淤泥质海岸带），选择不同的海岸带生境类型（河口、滩涂、人工湿地），从生境退化诊断入手，确定海岸带生境退化的主控因子；筛选适合于渤海淤泥质海岸带不同盐度带的生物种群，开发滩涂生物资源恢复技术，并进行相应的技术示范，开发滩涂人工湿地的水质和低质生境修复技术并进行技术示范；针对渤海入海口海河口受污染与盐分双重胁迫致使生境退化的现状，通过对相关技术的集成实现基地改造，重建退化的河口生态系统，探索一条能够在渤海地区推广的以中度人工干扰结合自然恢复为主导的低成本并能自我持续发展的河口生态重建模式；筛选并确定用于淤泥质海岸带生境退化的生物指示种或种群，建立一套海岸带生境退化的生物指示监测技术；建立淤泥质海岸带生境退化的评估技术及相应的指标体系；结合区域社会经济发展，开展海岸带生境修复与经济协调发展的综合方案。研究取得重要进展，获得多项技术成果，部分成果得到应用与推广。发表论文54篇。

2003年3月，天津科技大学王学魁主持开展渤海湾有害赤潮的生态特征及毒性分析研究。课题组首次系统鉴定渤海天津海域常见的赤潮生物种类33种，监测到在2004年6月和2005年6月渤海湾天津海域发生的大规模有毒赤潮；首次分离纯化天津海域的赤潮原因种普氏棕囊藻，对典型赤潮藻旋链角毛藻、裸甲藻生态学特征进行研究；探讨天津海域赤潮频发的生态学机制，指出水体交换不良、赤潮生物种类繁多、氮和磷等营养盐水平偏高是该海域赤潮频发的潜在因素；提出防止赤潮生物快速增殖、预防和控制有害赤潮发生的途径和有效措施，包括加大海洋生态监控力度、严格污染排放标准及制定海域综合开发利用规划等。

2003~2005年，天津科技大学陈惠彬、刘文铃、刘宪斌等完成渤海海岸带的生物种群筛选及滩涂生物资源恢复技术与示范的研究。课题组应用多学科综合技术及现代生物学、生态学治理技术，对受损的潮间带底栖生态环境、生物缺损现状进行修复，使其有效地促进潮间带生态系统能量的良性循环、改善底质化学、物理特性、增殖生物种群，以恢复受损潮间带的生态平衡；采用种群中度干扰技术和人工投放生物技术，改变潮间带底栖生物优势种群结构，依据生物资源自然增殖规律和生态位理论，建立稳定发展的具有较高规模经济价值的生物优势种群；人工投放修复生物改善底质环境效果最明显，沙蚕实验区对底质起到良好的改善作用，其中底质中的总氮、有机质、石油烃、总汞和砷的含量分别降低18.9%、31.3%、69.2%、27.4%和9.90%，受损生境得到修复；生物优势种群结构发生可喜变化，示范区生物数量增加、种群结构趋向合理、并增添该海区及邻近海区从未出现的高经济价值优良种类，如泥螺。示范区生物物种多样性提高37.5%、滩涂生物资源增长52.42%、主要经济种类的生物量增加103.1%,2004~2005年经济效益达313.6万元。

2004年,天津市环境保护科学研究院包景岭、侯晓珉、黄浩云等完成滨海新区的生态恢复与生态建设方案及示范工程研究。项目组从水资源循环利用与水生态恢复、生态恢复与生态建设、生态工业园建设等方面着手,研究并制定滨海新区生态恢复与建设方案及重点工程——中水利用工程、生态补水梯级利用工程、海水和地下咸水利用工程、湿地生态和河口生态恢复工程、生态走廊和生态绿网建设工程等重点工程,并在此基础上进行北大港湿地自然保护区建设和升级以及经济技术开发区污水回用工程两个示范工程的深入研究。其中水资源梯级利用与循环利用研究,将海水和盐业生产相结合,并重点分析在土地资源方面的效益。研究成果为政府及有关部门指导沿海地区的开发建设、制定中长期建设发展规划提供技术依据,为滨海新区生态建设提供依据。

第三节 环境评价与管理

对环境生态进行综合评价、规划与管理,是走向主动的环境污染的控制与治理,是更高级水平的环境保护工作。在这方面,1991年~2005年,天津市开展大量基础性工作,有些走在全国前列,天津市乡镇工业污染源调查评价及对策研究、水污染物排放总量控制技术与方法的研究、有毒有害气体排放标准的研究以及城市区域环境噪声标准的制定等,是很好的例证。

一、环境评价

1991年,南开大学朱坦为天津方面总负责人,参加完成中德生态学合作计划项目天津城市发展的生态对策研究,对天津城市生态系统结构、功能、动力学机制与调控方法进行系统分析与研究。基于复合生态系统观点,提出生态控制论、生态建设和生态网络理论、泛目标规划方法以及城市生态系统的交互式模拟方法。

2002年,天津大学田一梅、汪泳、迟海燕完成偏最小二乘与灰色模型组合预测城市生活需水量的研究,引入更易于辨识系统信息与噪声的单因变量偏最小二乘回归(PLS1),以克服普通多元回归方法用于中长期预测时自变量多重共线性对拟合模型的干扰。同时,他们将两次拟合等维灰数递补〔DEMGM(1,1)〕模型用于自变量的中长期预测,建立起一套PLS1与DEMGM(1,1)组合预测方法。并且,采用1986~2000年某市生活用水量历史数据,对该方法进行验证。结果表明,平均相对误差仅为1.03%。将该方法引入城市生活需水量研究,预测2005年和2010年某市生活需水量,预测值分别达到0.92×10^9立方米与1.1×10^9立方米。研究成果为该市给水工程规划与决策提供参考依据。

2002年6月,天津大学陶建华和天津市海洋局共同承担渤海综合整治天津方案及其关键基础问题研究,获得重要成果。其渤海综合整治天津方案所开展的基础研究,为今后各项具体整治工程和沿海地区的经济发展做基础理论和技术准备,赢得时间,具有重要的指导意义。

2003年9月,天津市环境监测中心和南开大学合作,秦保平、朱坦、赵立蔚、孙韧等共同完成的大气颗粒物源解析及环境监测信息管理系统通过鉴定。

2005年,南开大学朱坦、徐鹤、吴婧、田丽丽等开展武汉市国民经济和社会发展第十一个五年总体规划纲要战略环境评价,开国内城市国民经济和社会发展规划战略环境评价之先河,研究成果对促进中国战略环境评价实践和管理具有重要的示范和借鉴意义。

二、环境管理

(一)水

1990年6月~1992年6月,天津市环境保护局、天津市乡镇企业局和天津市统计局共同承担,刘文仲、汪丽娟、王海山、赵焕生和韩景明合作完成天津市乡镇工业污染源调查、评价及对策研究。项目全面、系统、定量地调查研究分析天津市乡镇企业环境污染现状，确定主要污染行业、区域和重点污染源。组织1200余人，对12个区（县）228个乡镇2182个污染企业，15个行业进行调查评价，覆盖率100%，获45万多个数据，提供专题报告26篇，建立市、区（县）两级乡镇企业污染源档案，并建立天津市乡镇企业主要污染源环境状况微机数据库。制定天津市乡镇企业环境保护规划，提出确实可行的防治对策和综合整治方案；创造性地制定一套调查研究质量保证体系及技术规范，保证数据科学性、准确性和可靠性；同时，开展外环线两侧、引滦沿线两侧、团泊洼水库、天津电镀行业、小草浆造纸行业等环境污染现状评价及对策研究，紧密与实际应用相结合。促进乡镇企业与环境保护协调、健康发展，获得显著社会、经济与生态环境效益。

1994年，天津市环境保护科学研究所和天津市环境保护局水质管理处合作，陈自强、李桂芳、蒋林燕、孟昭赢共同完成天津市地面水功能区域划分及质量标准的研究。课题组针对中国北方地区水资源短缺，供需矛盾突出的特征，在国内首先提出适合半干旱地区地面水面水功能区域划分的总则、细则、方法及其工作程序。依照北方不同季节降水量差异的特点，对天津市所辖水域环境结合水资源收受，用排功能的各自特色，进行全方位、多层次、分门别类划分功能区域。实施季节动态水环境质量的控制指标，理顺城建、水利、卫生、农业等部门对同一水环境水质的要求，体现清水优先原则，确立高功能高保护的特点。提交严于国家标准的地面水环境质量标准，用于天津地面水水质控制指标，并定量化，提出如色度、气味、浑浊度、硫酸盐、氯化物等考核指标。提交以城市第二水源为源头，建立复合生态系统，改善市区景观河道水质的控制指标和方案。

2000年，天津市地质矿产局地质环境管理处金爱善、傅炳海、林年丰等开展天津滨海新区水资源环境系统综合研究，建立水资源系统评价指标体系，全面考虑地表水、地下水、海水、污水资源化等因素，以实现供需平衡、优水优用，开发利用和环境保护并重为目的。成果为滨海新区水资源规划利用，提供科学依据。

2004年，天津市市政工程质量监督站张宝林、石万同、任家琪等研究制订《城市污水处理厂工程质量验收规范》，总结国内城市污水处理厂工程施工实践经验，综合考虑多种不同的污水处理工艺，当前的技术水平以及今后的发展趋势，真正做到满足工程建设的广泛需要，并充分考虑使用和维修的要求，基本做到安全使用、技术先进、经济合理。成果填补国内城市污水处理厂工程质量验收规范的空白，为保证提高污水处理厂工程质量水平奠定基础。

（二）空气

1993年，天津市环境保护科学研究所石磊、徐金凤、张燕华等完成恶臭排放标准研究。项目组调查1692个居委会、3030封群众来信来访记录，查阅67个恶臭排放物工厂，对4个典型工厂进行环境与排放口的同步测试，获得2000多个数据；对复合恶臭嗅觉实验法——主要是由日本引进的三点比较式嗅袋法进行研究；研究恶臭物质在大气中的扩散规律和计算方法，调研国外恶臭排放标准。综合上述调研结果，制订出符合天津地方实际的恶臭排放标准。

1994年，天津市环境保护科学研究所和天津市环境保护局宫伟、包景岭、叶以文等完成城市环境综合整治定量考核指标体系的研究。课题组从国内城市综合整治定量考核的实际出发，从大气、水、固体废物和噪声四个方面进行指标体系的深入分析和研究，提出合理的指标体系结构，利用系统分析的方法，完成各分类和分项指标的权重，提出包括各分项指标定义解释和评分计算方法的技术规范。评价指标体系具有科学性、实用性和可操作性。该评价指标体系提出的定量考核规划编制技术导则具有较强的实用性，被国家环境保护局采用。

1995年，天津市环境保护科学研究所孙申、阎成芳、陈隆等完成天津市有毒有害气体排放标准的研究。课题结合天津市的环境需要，以扩散模拟计算和治理技术，经济的可行性为基础，制定出18项有毒有害气体的地方排放标准，并颁布实施。对18项有毒有害气体进行毒害性分析，属于Ⅰ类剧毒气体从严控制，属于Ⅱ、Ⅲ类在非人口密集区适当放宽要求，结合地区调解系数确定标准值；利用平原地区利于大气稀释扩散的地理条件，对各种污染物在不同气象条件下，计算出理论控制值；根据治理后污染物的排放量与排放浓度以及设备的投资进行综合效益指标分析，确定达到排放标准的优化治理方案。

2001年，天津环境检测中心与天津市气象科学研究所合作，秦保平、边海、邵莹、王长有等共同完成天津市空气污染预报研究。项目组建立天津市空气污染物排放清单动态数据库，开发与研制天津市污染数据值预报和统计预报系统模型，采用符合天津市实际情况的空气污染动力学数据值预报方法和统计预报方法相结合的方式，建立操作性较强的天津市空气污染预报软件包，研究开展预报工作。

（三）噪声

1992年，天津市环境监测中心陈光华、胡曼华、韩克明等完成天津市城市区域环境噪声标准适用区域划分研究，采用专家咨询和数学模型研究两种方法，从影响噪声区划的19项城市特征指标中，在国内首次优选出4项（①居民、文教、机关；②工业用地；③ 道路用地；④商业用地，作为“噪声区划分类因子”的主要指标）研究出以软分类—ISODATA模糊聚类分析方法为建立噪声功能区划数学模型的区划理论；得出进行噪声功能区划的定量标准；在国内第一个采用定量分析和定性划分相结合的方法完成天津市的噪声功能区划分。为制定天津市的噪声区划标准和城市噪声污染防止与管理提供科学和可靠的依据。

（四）综合

2000年4月～2000年12月，南开大学刘茂和原国家经贸委安全科学技术研究中心合作完成工业危险品公路运输安全管理系统技术研究。通过对工业危险品公路运输过程中的风险分析方法的研究，提出危险品公路运输事故应急救援系统设计和工业危险品公路运输安全管理系统设计，以切实有效地加强危险品运输的安全管理，减少危险品的运输事故的发生；提出危险品运输事故应急方案，及时采取有效措施，防止事故的扩大，把事故的损失减小到最低。

2005年5月～2006年6月，南开大学鞠美庭、冯银厂、李洪远等完成三门峡城市环境保护及环境质量达标规划项目。项目组主要研究城区环境现状和存在问题分析；分析城市工业发展结构的合理性、污染物产生总量对城市环境的影响、城市周边及上下游对城市环境的可能影响；提出和论证环境保护的目标，城市环境污染防治的方针和战略；研究城区环境保护及治理的主要思路和途径、实施方法与步骤，城市环境质量建设指标、改善和保护环境质量的措施；给出各项规划的投资估算；按照环境空气功能区划分标准，提出相应的总量及浓度达标方案；按照地表水功能区划分标准，提出确保地表水达标和水资源保护的具体方案。项目组在土地适宜度分析、能流分析、大气环境容量估算及容量总量控制分析、水环境容量分配与污染物总量控制方案、根据循环经济原则制定固体废物综合整治规划方案、根据循环经济和清洁生产的原理、生态环境保护及建设规划、三门峡市大气颗粒物源解析、三门峡市环境空气质量模拟等方面具有创新性。

第九章 海洋技术

1996年4月，天津市委市政府正式批准成立天津市海洋局，隶属天津市科学技术委员会，2000年划归天津市规划和国土资源局。2002年10月，为加强海洋监测和海洋预报工作，天津市政府批准成立天津市海洋环境监测预报中心。为强化对天津市海岸带、海岛及海域的海洋监察管理，2002年1月，经天津市委市政府批准，建立中国海监天津市总队，为具有行政执法监察职能的处级机构。2005年天津市机构改革，天津市海洋局划归天津市国土和房屋管理局管理。至2005年，天津市有海洋行政管理和科学研究单位40余个，有高级科学技术人员200余名。

天津市海洋局不断加强管理，为天津市海洋事业的发展提供有力保证。1991~2005年，天津市在海洋的调查与开发、海洋资源保护、海洋经济以及海洋观测等各个方面都得到较大的发展，取得一批国际先进和国内领先水平的研究成果。2005年天津市海洋局完成天津市海岸线测量测定工作，走在全国的前列。

第一节 海洋调查

1991~2005年,天津市对海岛与海洋资源以及海洋污染开展多项调查。1992至2005年间,天津海域多次发生赤潮和风暴潮,天津海洋局密切监视与控制。2004年,天津市海洋局牵头组织"全国近海海洋资源综合调查与评价"天津市的任务,全面高质量地完成,撰写出"天津市海洋资源综合调查与评价实施总体方案"。

一、海岛调查

1991年,天津市海洋办公室组织天津市地质矿产局、天津市海岸带开发公司、地矿部华北地质勘测大队、天津市勘察院、国家海洋局情报所、天津大学等单位对天津域内的海岛资源进行调查,结果表明:天津海域唯一具有一定规模的三河岛具有优良的地理环境和优越的地理位置,提出将三河岛建成对外籍人员开放的"水上乐园"的可行性,并对与三河岛毗邻的北塘河口建港通航(千吨级)进行初步评估。

二、海域勘界

2001年,天津市海洋局组织李连增、李国庆、刘菊人等拟订《天津市海域勘界工作方案》,并成立天津市海域勘界工作组开展工作,经广泛搜集历史资料,采用先进仪器的外业调查,认真细致地分析研究,遵循分界界线拐点数最少、继承性、综合性以及完整性等技术原则,完成塘沽—汉沽以及塘沽—大港两条区际海域界线划定草案。

2005年,天津市海洋局完成天津市海岸线的测量测定工作:天津市海岸线为153.2千米,海岛岸线469米,海岸线向海一侧已占用长度为100.35千米,可利用海岸线长度仅剩余52.85千米,潮间带面积为335.99平方千米,已占用潮间带面积为117.71平方千米,可利用潮间带面积仅剩余218.28平方千米。该项海岸线的测量测定工作走在全国前列,

2005年,天津市区际海域勘界工作稳步推进,搜集陆域勘界协议、陆域界限图、区志、地名志、各历史年代行政区划图以及历史沿革、开发现状等相关资料200余份,绘制工作底图5张,完成塘沽—汉沽以及塘沽—大港两条区际海域界限的草案。

三、海洋资源调查

1999年,天津市海洋局组织国家海洋局北海监测中心、交通部天津水运工程科学研究所、国家海洋局塘沽海洋环境监测中心站等单位开展海洋污染现状调查,出海采样20天,完成水环境生态监测5个断面,共设30个站位,获取水文气象数据180个,水质监测项目数据420个,浮游动植物数据120个,获取水环境中底栖生物监测数据60个,增养殖区生物质量监测数据84个。潮间带底栖生物监测5个断面,30个站位,获取底栖生物数据60个。编写《天津海域海洋生物资源现状评价及趋势分析》《海上石油勘探开发和海洋倾废污染海域环境现状评价及趋势分析》《海洋事故与灾害分析》和《天津古海岸与湿地国家级自然保护区现状评价及趋势分析》。

2004年,天津市海洋局牵头组织"全国近海海洋资源综合调查与评价"("908"专项)天津市的任务,交通运输部天津水运工程科学研究所张光玉、天津科技大学王学魁、天津地质矿产研究所王宏、天津市水产研究所李保华任项目负责人。在调研的基础上,项目组完成天津市海洋资源综合调查与评价("908"专项)实施

总体方案，为全面启动“908”专项工作奠定良好的基础。

四、污染基线和污染情况调查

1998年5月和9月，天津市海洋局及所属市海洋监察大队在国家海洋局北海监测中心的配合下，两次在天津和黄骅海域开展海上调查工作。第一次进行水质污染调查，共设水质测站20个，采集水样448个，辅助项目数据198个。第二次进行水质和底质两项调查，设监测站位25个，采集水样500余个，辅助项目数据225个。完成全部样品的实验室分析工作，形成《天津市海洋环境污染基线调查报告》和《天津市海洋环境污染基线调查图集》。

2000年6月，天津市海洋局开展海洋第二次污染基线调查，调查内容分为污染源调查和海域设点观测及取样分析两部分，包括水文气象观测和水质污染调查；部分测站沉积物污染调查，生物残毒与生物学污染指标调查；4条断面的水质、悬浮物、沉积物和生物学污染指标的调查；潮间带底栖生物生态环境调查。完成《天津市海洋第二次污染基线调查总报告》。报告全面反映天津市海域环境污染的基本情况，为制定适应全市海洋经济发展的海洋功能区划、海域环境监测方案提供基础依据。

2005年，天津市海洋局结合国家“908”海洋化学和海洋生态调查项目，将陆源入海排污口监测工作纳入专项调查工作，增设《陆源入海河口污染状况调查与评价》项目，交通运输部天津水运工程科学研究所、天津科技大学、天津地质矿产研究所、天津市水产研究所等11家科研单位、600名科研人员历时6年对全市海洋进行综合调查，对天津海域主要入海河流的河口及河口临近海域进行监测，并对河口区域海洋污染状况进行评估。项目组采集原始数据近59万个，编制完成成果报告和图件，调查成果在全市海洋行政管理、滨海新区开发建设等方面得到广泛应用。

第二节 海洋灾害与监测

1991~2005年，天津市海洋赤潮灾害的发生呈增加与增强趋势，此期间，亦多次发生风暴潮，1992年发生在天津港的风暴潮是1949年以来天津市沿海最严重的一次潮灾，经济损失约4亿人民币。

为保卫经济发展和人民生活，天津市建立海洋灾害监测领导机构和监测网络发挥积极作用。

一、海洋灾害

（一）赤潮

1992年10月，国家海洋局在定期航测飞行时，发现大沽锚地附近有大面积赤潮，分布在大沽灯塔以西约2海里处到大沽灯塔以东5海里处，长7海里、宽1海里、面积约20平方公里，条带状分布、海水呈红色，监测生物种类以星脐圆筛藻、叉分角藻、布代双尾藻为主。

1998年10月，中国海监飞机在距天津港约2公里的海面发现面积约800平方公里的赤潮，天津市海洋局组织进行监视监测，赤潮持续4天，未给天津市渔业资源造成较大损失。

1999年7月，大沽锚地海域发生赤潮，面积为500平方公里。

2000年7月，渤海湾天津所辖海域发生赤潮，天津市海洋局与国家海洋局北海分局密切配合，较好地完成应急监测任务。

2002年，天津市发生两次赤潮，面积为7平方公里，天津市海洋局进行赤潮应急监测，发布8份赤潮通报。

2004年6月，天津近岸海域首次发生有毒赤潮，面积约700平方公里，主要优势藻种为米氏凯伦藻，创下赤潮持续时间最长记录。赤潮发生后，天津市海洋局紧急启动赤潮应急预案，加强赤潮的监视监测和赤潮生物贝毒检测，及时发布9期赤潮通报，保障人民群众的身体健康和生命安全。

2005年6月，天津近岸海域发生有毒赤潮，面积约750平方公里，主要优势藻种为棕囊藻，天津市海洋局启动赤潮应急预案，历时6天，采集水样253个，获取数据460个，发布赤潮通报6份，及时将监测结果报告国家海洋局和天津市政府。

（二）风暴潮

1992年9月1日，强风暴潮袭击天津沿海，塘沽潮位达5.82米，天津港码头2400多个集装箱和大批散杂货被海水淹泡，天津港积水1米多深，沿海海挡潮损严重，经济损失约4个亿，是1949年以来全市沿海最严重的一次潮灾。

1997年，受11号台风影响，全市沿海出现三次超越警戒水位的高潮位，最高潮位达5.46米，形成仅次于1992年以来的第二次强风暴潮。沿海海堤、码头、油井、虾池、原盐等潮损严重，经济损失达1.48亿元。

1999年，全市共出现风暴潮增水超过0.5米27次，其中增水超过1米3次。2000年共出现风暴潮增水超过0.5米20次，其中增水超过1米4次。

2003年10月11日，全市普降暴雨，是天津市近30年来历史同期最大的一场降水。天津市沿海地区出现风暴潮，潮水超过警戒水位（4.9米），达到5.4米。天津市沿海部分渔船、养殖池塘、滩涂贝类资源遭到不同程度的破坏，部分渔民生产生活受到影响，直接经济损失3639万元。

2003年11月25日，由于受偏东大风和天文大潮共同影响，天津市发生风暴潮灾害，风暴潮最高潮位为5.20米。

2005年8月7日，受第九号台风"麦莎"影响，天津地区最高潮位达到5.18米。天津滨海新区遭受风暴潮，以塘沽为最严重，其次是汉沽和大港。

二、海洋灾害监测

1999年，天津市与国家海洋局北海分局共建天津市海洋预报台，2002年更名为天津市海洋环境监测预报中心，该中心与国家海洋局天津海洋环境监测中心站为一个机构两块牌子，负责天津市海洋灾害的监测及变化趋势预测，每天通过媒体发布海温、海浪、潮汐预报，负责发布风暴潮、海冰等海洋灾害的预报警报，开展赤潮灾害应急监视监测工作，发布赤潮监测报告和预报，负责突发性海洋污染事故的调查和对海洋环境影响评估。

2001年，由市海洋局牵头，成立有市防汛指挥部、环保局、海事局、水产局等14个部门和单位组成的天津市赤潮防灾减灾领导小组和天津市赤潮防灾减灾联络小组，建立由海洋行政主管部门、海洋监测机构、重要涉海单位及从事海上生产作业活动的志愿者参加的赤潮监测监视网，及时发现、跟踪观测并通报赤潮现象，为各级领导和政府部门及涉海单位组织防灾减灾和加强海洋综合管理提供重要的信息和决策依据。

2003年，建立赤潮监控区，每年5～10月开展赤潮监控区监测工作，发布赤潮监控区海域监测要素分析及赤潮趋势预测，使渔民能够及时掌握赤潮监控区水质变化情况，合理安排生产。

2003年10月11日、11月25日、2004年9月15日和2005年8月7日天津滨海地区遭受风暴潮，市海洋环境监测预报中心根据国家海洋预报中心发布的风暴潮预报资料和实时监测资料，都准确地发布风暴潮预报和警报，及时启动海洋防灾减灾应急响应系统，通知各有关单位采取有效措施，做好防风暴潮准备，市海洋局每1小时发布1次天文大潮实时速报，为市政府领导决策提供依据，使各单位及时掌握风暴潮情况，最大限度地减少风暴潮造成的经济损失。

第三节 海洋环境保护

1998年1月,天津古海岸与湿地国家级自然保护区管理处正式组建,隶属天津市海洋局,接受国家海洋局业务指导。1999年6月,天津市政府颁布《天津古海岸与湿地国家级自然保护区管理办法》。

1991~2005年,天津市在古海岸与湿地保护方面取得多项全国先进的科研成果。

一、倾废管理

1996年5月,天津市海洋局在国家海洋局海洋技术研究所的支持下,在中国率先安装海洋倾废航行记录仪,实现用现代化手段管理倾废船舶,使疏浚到位率大大提高。

二、古海岸与湿地保护

1992年12月,国务院批准建立天津古海岸与湿地国家级自然保护区,保护对象由贝壳堤扩展为贝壳堤、牡蛎滩和七里海湿地生态系统,整个地区是古海岸变迁的极其珍贵的海洋遗迹。2002年5月,天津古海岸与湿地国家级自然保护区与美国切斯比克湾河口研究保护区签署长期合作意向书,双方在资料、学者交流和科学研究方面开展长期合作。

2002年6月,天津市海洋局启动七里海湿地动物(鸟类)调查及七里海湿地水质监测方法两项科研项目,发现鸟类60余种,其中国家二级鸟类9种,有天鹅(3种)、猛禽等。

2004年,天津古海岸与湿地国家级自然保护区管理处和交通运输部天津水运工程科学研究院汪苏燕、张光玉承担天津古海岸与湿地国家级自然保护区综合科学考察项目。项目组利用先进科技手段,面对保护区全域359平方公里,以核心区和缓冲区为重点考察范围,进行大量的实地调查和监测,查明保护区内存高等植物44科属165种,绝大多数为草本植物,动物资源9大类457种,并对历次科考数据资料进行认真分析和对比,进一步完善保护区本地资源数据库。对保护区生态环境、自然资源保护、保护区管理等方面进行综合评估,形成评价结论和对策建议,为保护区的有效保护、科学管理和资源可持续利用提供科学依据。

2005年10月,保护区处承担《天津古海岸与湿地国家级自然保护区(2006~2015年)保护发展规划》项目,汪苏燕为负责人。整个规划(包括图集)近6万字。规划以保护和恢复七里海湿地自然生态环境为宗旨,兼顾资源可持续利用和当地居民切身利益,将七里海打造成中部区域生态保护网络的重要节点,目标明确,内容全面、布局合理、可操作性强、坚持生态效益和经济效益的统一。对进一步贯彻落实全市"一轴两带"空间战略规划,促进经济社会的和谐发展具有重要意义。

三、综合整治研究

2001~2004年,以天津大学陶建华作为课题负责人,天津市海洋局和天津大学联合开展渤海综合整治天津方案及其关键基础问题研究,该课题建立综合考虑理化和生物学因素的渤海湾生态环境评价指标和灰关联评价方法,对渤海湾水质的富营养化现状进行综合评价;建立空间变异性模型,分析渤海湾水质的空间变异性,得出区域水环境污染的分布特征;对天津近岸海域水环境的承载力进行分析研究;对渤海湾海域海洋浮游细菌的生态特性进行实验室分析,并对不同季节营养盐对浮游植物生消的影响进行实验室研究;建立渤海湾水动力学和生态水动力学数学模型;研究海岸带开发对生态环境的影响,并提出相应对策。共发表论文19篇。该项研究成果对天津海洋经济的发展,指导近岸海域开发建设发挥重要作用。

第四节 海洋资源开发

1995年5月，经国务院批准，天津市成立塘沽海洋高新技术开发区，是国内第一个海洋类型的国家级高新技术产业园区，总体规划面积24平方公里，起步区4.54平方公里，成为天津滨海新区的一个新的经济增长点。

1991~2005年，天津市在制订开发规划与海洋资源开发走在全国的前列。《天津市海洋经济核算方法和统计指标体系研究》为构建天津市海洋统计指标体系和沿海地区国民经济核算体系奠定理论基础，对推进天津市海洋经济的发展具有特殊意义。

一、海洋开发规划

1992年8月，根据国家海洋局关于编制《全国海洋开发规划》的要求，天津市科委和天津市计委成立规划领导小组，10月完成《关于制订天津市海洋开发规划》的编写工作，规划对天津市海洋开发现状、市场需求预测、规划目标以及产业结构和布局都做了较全面的阐述，并将海洋开发环境保护及海洋重大开发利用项目作为独立章节写入该规划中，规划中就海洋的资源开发提出建设性意见和建议。

2000年，天津市海洋局组织制定大比例尺海洋功能区划，使海域使用建立在科学合理的基础上，主要研究人员有李连增、李国庆、胡源等。12月，谢世楞院士主持召开区划项目评审会，专家对天津市大比例尺海洋功能区划给予较高的学术评价，认为达到国内领先水平。2003年7月，天津市政府批准《〈天津市大比例尺海洋功能区划〉修订工作实施方案》。2004年5月，天津市海洋局编写完成《天津市海洋功能区划报告》，2004年11月，进行第二轮征求意见，2004年12月，天津市海洋局主持就《天津市海洋功能区划》召开专家评审会。

二、海洋能源开发

2000年，国家海洋技术中心在国内首次开展波浪能电站研建工作。通过水室摆板机构把波浪能转换成机械能，再利用齿轮柱塞泵把摆板运动的机械能变为液压能，继而用液压马达来驱动发电机转动发电。建成的30千瓦摆式波力电站总体技术指标及性能，对解决边远海岛的缺能少电和开发海岛资源以及国防建设具有积极意义。

三、海洋经济核算方法和统计指标体系研究

2004年9月，天津市海洋局、天津市统计局和国家海洋信息中心共合作完成《天津市海洋经济核算方法和统计指标体系研究》课题，何广顺和王晓惠任负责人。指标体系体现天津开发利用海洋资源形成的产业特点，包括14个门类、23个大类、37个中类、47个小类。按照三次产业范围划分，第一产业主要是海洋渔业；第二产业主要有盐及盐化工业、海洋石油及天然气开采业、海洋石油化工、造船业、海洋水产品加工业、海水利用业等；第三产业有海洋旅游业、海洋运输业及物流业和海洋服务业等。指标体系的建立，全面反映天津海洋经济发展的现状，定期观察、分析、监测海洋经济的发展。建立的海洋经济统计指标体系和核算方法符合国家海洋局行业划分标准，又与国家统计局现行的国民经济行业标准相衔接，使海洋产业统计成为国民经济统计和核算体系的组成部分。该研究课题为构建天津市海洋统计指标体系和沿海地区国民经济核算体系奠定良好的理论基础，对推进天津市海洋经济的发展具有特殊意义。

第五节 海洋观测技术

1991~2005年,天津市在包括岸基观测、船基观测、浮标基观测与天基观测的海洋监测技术,以及监测设备的研究都取得突出的科研成果,在海洋技术方面处于全国领先水平。

一、岸基观测系统

1990年后,国家海洋技术中心在既有的各型海洋水文气象观测系统的技术基础上,先后开展观测自动化、传输自动化、观测组网等研究,并研发相关的台站用海洋观测设备。

1990年后,国家海洋技术中心研制成功SCA6-1型声学水位计,具有不需建静井、安装简单、可在无电地区使用、自动化程度高、又可远传至岸基中心等特点。其性能指标达到同类潮汐(水位)观测仪器的国际先进水平。

1991年,国家海洋技术中心研制成功ZQP1-1型遥测自动观测系统,对水文、气象传感器所测到的资料连续自动采集、处理,每日定时向岸站发报,在台风过境等恶劣气象条件下,能自动加密观测发报时次。在国内首次实现固定站的水文、气象无人观测。

1993年,国家海洋技术中心研制的海滨观测资料处理系统实现中国海洋台站观测资料的自动化整理、编报和记录,经过石岛海洋站的示范运行后,在中国海洋台站逐步进行推广应用。

1994年,国家海洋技术中心针对南沙海域军事气象环境保障需求,研发成功由多个无人自动气象观测站和数据中心接收站组成的海洋水文气象自动观测系统,自动观测风速、风向、气温、湿度、气压等要素,为舰船在该海域作战、训练、航行提供可靠的气象保障。

1994年,国家海洋技术中心开展海洋台站数据通信网络系统建设。系统建成后,将过去一个海洋站资料实时观测数据靠人工传递约需10~20分钟提高到30秒,月报资料由至少3天提高到5分钟。数据传输准确率也大大提高。海洋观测数据传输初步实现自动化,填补国内海洋观测资料有线传输的空白,达到国际同期有线数据传输的先进水平。

2003年,国家海洋技术中心完成CZY1-1型海洋监测站自动监测系统及集成系统的建设,包括56个海洋监测站自动监测系统的生产、系统集成及技术服务任务,其中47个站开展潮汐自动监测,36个站开展海浪自动监测,22个站开展表层水温和盐度自动监测,56个站开展风、气压自动检测,43个站开展气温自动监测,40个站开展湿度和降水量的自动监测。形成的海洋环境监测系统站网实现对中国岸滨海洋环境进行有效监测,为实现海洋环境监测体系的建设奠定坚实基础。

二、船基观测系统

1991年,国家海洋技术中心在国内率先开展多种船基观测技术的研发工作,并成功研制出痕量金属分析采水器、走航式声学多普勒海流剖面仪(ADCP)、高精度CTD剖面测量仪等船基观测设备/系统。

1991年,国家海洋技术中心在国内率先开展走航式声学多普勒海流剖面仪(ADCP)的研制,采用低旁瓣、高灵敏度的换能器,并采用高速信号处理器完成ADCP的控制、数据采集及处理等,能实时显示海流剖面、经纬度、航速、航向、水深等数据,并能实时采集水温数据用以修正声速。

1992年,国家海洋技术中心研制成功QCC10-2型200米痕量金属分析采水器,用于海水痕量金属(Cu、Zn、Pb等)采集。

2001年，国家海洋技术中心研制成功高精度温盐深（CTD）剖面仪及定标检定设备，接近20世纪90年代中期国际先进水平，价格远低于同等水平的进口CTD价格，并具有进口设备无法比拟的技术服务便利条件。

三、浮标基观测系统

海洋浮标因其多参数连续观测能力而在海上现场观测中占据极其重要的地位，是海上观测最直接、最有效的观测手段。国家海洋技术中心是国内最早开展海洋资料浮标、潜标、漂流浮标等浮标的单位。1990年后，在国家"七五"重点科技攻关等重大项目支持的基础上，先后攻克海洋资料浮标、深海测流潜标、浅海测流潜标、漂流浮标等关键技术，并形成产品生产能力。

1991年，国家海洋技术中心攻克深海声学应答释放器、深海海流计、雷达信标机等多项关键技术，完成深海测流潜标系统关键技术及主要部件的研制。该系统在海气相互作用、南海环流及全球大洋环流试验（WOCE）等计划中有良好应用。

1991~1995年，国家海洋技术中心完成海洋资料浮标的研制，该浮标具备16个观测参数、自动化程度高、体积小、造价低、结构灵活、随波性能好、使用维修方便等优势。

1991~1995年，国家海洋技术中心在国内首次开展漂流浮标的研制工作，首次在国内实测绘制连续、大海域的海流流迹图和实时的连续测温数据，为全国海洋工作者提供一种新的海洋环境观测手段，填补国产浮标系列空白。

1992年，国家海洋技术中心完成FSS1-1型浅海潜标系统的研发，适应用于水深300米以浅，具有较强的抗恶劣海况能力，通过将自容式测量仪器或装置挂接在系统不同深度层上，实现长期定点连续多要素同步测量或实验。在海洋资源开发、海洋工程、环境监测及相关海洋科学调查研究与国防建设等诸多领域均有重要应用价值。

从2001年开始，国家海洋技术中心在国内首次开展系缆式剖面测量自动升降平台技术研究，具有自动沿系留缆上下移动的功能，可装载包括温度、盐度、压力传感器、海流计、光度计、荧光计等多种传感器，在移动的过程中进行数据的采集和存储，实现水下定点、连续剖面测量功能。

四、空基观测系统

空基海洋环境观测主要是通过航空遥感设备实现指定海域观测要素的大面积、快速、有效观测。国内海洋航空遥感技术起步较晚、但发展迅速。1991年后，国家海洋技术中心先后研制成功海洋渔场表层温度航空遥感监视和速报系统、航空遥感测冰系统、灾害性海冰航空遥感监测实时传输系统、机载投弃式温盐深浮标等。

1991年，国家海洋技术中心编辑出版国内第一部《渤海航空遥感冰情图集》，为海冰分析预报和科学研究提供重要参考依据，填补国内航空遥感测冰技术的空白。

1991~1995年，国家海洋技术中心开展灾害性海冰航空遥感监测实时传输系统的研究。系统由航空红外辐射计、微波辐射计、航空红外测温仪、高精度GPS等组成，能够快速、大范围地测量冰（水）表层温度、冰厚、机外温度、位置参数等，并实现观测信息的实时传输。同时为国内外卫星应用，建立立体监测网络提供实时可靠的航测信息。该系统填补国内海冰监测传输技术的空白。

1999年，国家海洋技术中心在国内率先开展机载投弃式温盐深浮标技术研究，能够在较短时间内获取同步或准同步大面积海洋温盐剖面资料，直接服务于海洋调查、海洋环境预报、渔业生产等方面，还可快速及时提供海上战场环境参数。

五、天基观测系统

天基海洋环境观测主要是利用海洋卫星实现全球海域的大范围观测。1991年后，国家海洋技术中心围绕海洋卫星数据校正、检验开展相关研究工作，并取得一定的研究成果。

1999年，国家海洋技术中心开展星载遥感数据的真实性检验方案研究，通过将卫星探测所获得的卫星遥感数据产品与其他用独立的方法获得的相应的地球物理量进行比较，评价卫星遥感数据产品的质量。同年，国家海洋技术中心开展SeaWiFS海洋水色遥感应用技术研究，改造SeaWiFS地面接收系统，向国内10个部委25个单位，以及美国、加拿大、日本和德国等国家分发不同等级的SeaWiFS资料。

2003年，国家海洋技术中心建立一个由卫星遥感地面接收处理站、高频地面雷达站、海洋/平台海洋站和其他可利用的监测设备组成的区域性海洋环境立体监测应用系统，能够实时、长期、连续、准确地完成示范区域内的海洋水文、气象、污染/生态等环境要素监测数据的采集、通讯、分析、处理，并有效地向用户提供各种形式的产品分发服务，形成相应的业务化或准业务化系统，并为建立国内全海域的立体监测系统提供示范和相关技术。

六、监测设备研究

1993年，国家海洋技术中心研制SYA2-1型自动盐度计，从定标到测温测盐，完全消除人工调整和查表的工作，给操作人员带来极大方便。

1995年，国家海洋技术中心组织研制具有自动监视倾废船海上倾废作业情况的HYQ-1型海洋倾废航行数据记录仪，它类似于飞机上的“黑匣子”，装在倾废船上可以代替监察人员对其倾废作业进行监视，自动记录倾废航线、倾倒点位置、倾倒时间等参数，准确判断倾废到位情况，计算倾废总航次和总倾废量。HYQ-1型海洋倾废航行数据记录仪的成功研发，填补国内船载海洋倾废监视仪器的空白，为海洋倾废管理提供有效监视手段，投入应用以来，很大程度上规范海洋倾废作业船只的海上作业，并取得很好的经济效益和社会效益。

七、海洋环境监测技术专题总体方案论证

为了从国家层面发展中国海洋高技术研究，从整体上提高中国海洋环境监测、预测和预报的能力，维护国家海洋权益、发展海洋经济、保护海洋环境、减轻海洋灾害造成的损失，1994年，国家海洋局向国家海洋技术中心下达开展海洋高技术项目论证任务，中心组织相关专家对海洋技术领域国内外现状开展详尽分析，制订具体的项目研究建议，于同年底提交《海洋环境监测技术专题总体方案论证报告》，直接推动海洋高技术领域于1996年进入国家“863”计划，成为其八大领域之一。

第十章　生物医学工程

1978年，天津大学开始筹建生物医学工程系，是全国首批获教育部批准成立此专业的三所高校之一，为中国及天津市生物医学工程专业的建设和发展奠定基础。学科创始人王明时得到李曙森校长和天津医学院朱宪彝院长的大力支持，决定由两校合办生物医学工程专业。该系于1980年招收第一届本科学生，由天津大学、天津医学院各选10名学生，共20名学生组成。该系1984年获硕士授权单位，1993年获国家一级学科博士授权点单位，1996年成为全国生物医学工程专业教学指导委员会主任委员单位，2000年设博士后流动站，2002年成为全国生物医学工程专业学位研究生教学指导委员会主任委员（协作组组长）单位，2003年成为天津市级重点学科，2004年获批生物医学检测技术与仪器天津市重点实验室。

该专业在人体信息检测与处理、生物医学信息处理与生理系统建模、医用光电测试技术及医学图像处理、现代光学分析技术与仪器、医学物理及神经工程等多个研究方向开展富有特色的科学研究和技术开发工作，并取得成绩。

1978年,中国医学科学院生物医学工程研究所(以下简称"生物医学工程所")成立。该所是国家级社会公益类非营利性研究机构中唯一的生物医学工程专业研究所,直属于国家卫生部,是国家生物医学工程专业博士、硕士培养点,设有生物医学工程博士后流动站。同时,也是天津市生物医学材料重点实验室的依托单位,是天津市激光医学工程中心的依托单位。该所主要从事生物医学工程新方法、新技术、新材料的研究与开发应用,分为生物医学材料研究和医学工程电子学研究两大领域。生物医学材料的研究与应用属于国内最早的研究单位之一。1991 ~ 2005年期间,在生物热力学与生物电磁学、生物材料与人工器官、医学超声工程等方面取得科研成果,并且在科研成果转化为医学产品方面取得成效。

1986年,天津医学院成立生物医学工程系。其科研范畴涉及医学与工程技术相结合的多重领域,包括生命科学、基础医学、现代生物技术、生物信息学等专业研究方向。1991 ~ 2005年期间,在生物传感器、医学仪器与生物信息处理、神经信息、激光医学等方面取得科研成果。1996年获得生物医学工程硕士学位授予权,2001年与天津大学共建天津市生物医学工程重点学科,2003年获批生物医学工程一级学科博士学位授权点。

1992年,南开大学卢桂章主持国家高技术发展计划("863"计划)课题"微驱动机器人系统及其应用研究",开始研制面向生物医学工程的微操作机器人系统。该系统提供一种重要的新型自动化实验设备。其功能是对微米级生物体进行自动操作,如细胞注射、染色体切割、胚胎样本提取等。该项成果获2002年度国家技术发明二等奖。

2003年,南开大学张建勋主持的"863"课题"机器人辅助显微外科手术系统"通过国家专家组验收。

在天津市工业系统,橡胶研究所在20世纪80年代初就开始研究开发生物医学材料、人体器官替代品及人体组织修复的方法和药物。部分研究成果达到预期目的,具有良好的应用前景。但是,由于体制限制等因素,成果没有推广到临床应用。

第一节 生物医学电子工程

随着现代生物医学研究深入到细胞水平,微操作技术在生物工程中的作用日益重要。对这类微操作实现自动化和提高操作质量的要求也日益迫切,机器人技术的进步为实现这一目标提供了条件。生物微操作主要有微注射与微切割操作两种。微注射是将外源基因注入细胞核,微切割主要是切割染色体。这些操作是生物工程进行转基因和DNA研究的重要环节,也是精度要求最高的环节。当时这些操作都是手动完成,手动操作存在工作效率低,成功率低,操作人员要经长时间训练,有些高难度操作难以完成。南开大学"面向生物医学工程的微操作机器人系统"研究在解决这一问题上取得了突出成绩。南开大学又继续完成了"机器人辅助显微外科手术系统"的研究,该系统满足显微手术操作的运动、稳定度与控制精度的要求。天津大学和生物医学工程研究所的科技人员在电磁场效应对人体的作用上展开研究,并将研究成果用于临床。

一、智能技术应用

(一)用于生物医学工程的微操作机器人系统

1992年12月,南开大学卢桂章主持的国家高技术发展计划("863"计划)课题"微驱动机器人系统及其应用研究",开始研制用于生物工程的微操作机器人系统。1996年研制成功中国第一台用于显微操作的机器人系统。项目建立了一套用于显微操作的微驱动机器人系统。此系统以生物显微镜为基座,配置了三自由度机器人操作手、二自由度电动载物平台、显微视觉及激光测距系统。显微镜、机器人、载物台及CCD摄像机集成为一体,由计算机统一管理。此系统具有自动标定、校准、运动规划和基于视觉的运动伺服能力。

1996年8月,张建勋、张蕾、李庆诚等主持的"863"课题"用于生物工程的微驱动机器人系统样机""生物工程中的微注射操作机器人系统产品样机研制"继续该项目研制;研制了一台面向生物工程操作(注射操作)的计算机控制可自动操作的多自由度的微操作机器人系统。用这一系统,操作人员可通过显微镜视觉观察被操作物以及决定操作进行的策略,并能按照选定的策略通过系统提供的人-机界面和系统进行交互,由系统自动地完成操作。

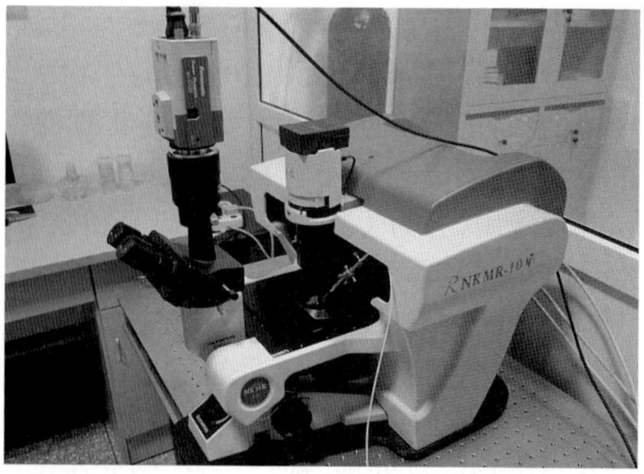
图4-10-1-55 南开大学研制的微操作机器人系统

1998年8月,赵新等主持"面向微操作的关键技术研究"开始微操作关键技术研究。该项目在面向微操作领域的三项关键技术:模块化控制部件的研究,显微图像处理和微操作的拟实环境研究取得了突破性进展,从而推进显微操作机器人系统样机产品化进程。

1999年,获得国内最早的微操作机器人系统整体发明专利"用于生物医学工程的微操作机器人",专利号: ZL 97 1 21702.5,发明人:张建勋、卢桂章、李彬、李庆诚、张蕾、黄亚楼。该发明公开了一种能够在生物医学等领域中完成细微操作的特型机器人系统。该系统主要包括显微镜,操作台,左、右微操作工具,左、右执行机构,微电机组构成的左、右驱动机构,摄象装置和用于控制、规划、管理的计算机。该发明的主要优点是:实现了生物医学工程等需要细微操作领域中的微操作自动化、智能化;系统在微米、亚微米级定位操作精度高,有效操作空间大,目标搜寻快。

2000年,"面向生物医学工程的微操作机器人系统"通过天津市科委组织的鉴定。完成人:卢桂章、张建勋、李彬、赵新、刘景泰、安刚、张蕾、王晓娜。该系统是可用于生物医学工程领域细胞级或亚细胞级操作:它是包含了计算机、自动控制和图像处理技术的一种微操作机器人系统。该系统在显微视觉的引导下,配合计算机控制的微动载物平台以及自动调焦系统,将被操作的生物体调至视野中心;由实验人员通过显微视觉系统在监视器上确定操作点;最后,系统控制多自由度的操作器和捕捉器自动或半自动地完成实验。

2001年,"面向生物医学工程的微操作机器人系统"获2000年度天津市技术发明一等奖。获奖人:卢桂章、张建勋、李彬、赵新、刘景泰、安刚、张蕾。该系统具备:第一,大的操作空间,该系统操作空间为25毫米×25毫米×25毫米,而一般微操作系统操作空间为1毫米×1毫米×1毫米。第二,两个多自由度操作臂可协调工作,普通微操作系统只能同时调节一个自由度。第三,视觉导引,普通微操作系统,实验人员通过显微镜观察工作空间、微操作器和微辅捉器的末端位置,再由手动调节移动微操作器作三维运动,最终实现要求的微操作。该系统由显微视觉图象处理代替人眼观察,来完成目标自动搜索、自动调焦以及目标与操作工具自动定位;并最终引导微操作工具自动或半自动完成给定操作。这是该系统区别于其他任何微操作系统的最本质特征。第四,工具可更换,该系统两个操作臂是通用的,更换相应的工具即可进行不同的微操作实验。

2002年,"面向生物医学工程的微操作机器人系统"获国家技术发明二等奖。获奖人:卢桂章、张建勋、李彬、张蕾。

(二)机器人辅助显微外科手术系统

2003年10月,南开大学张建勋主持的"863"课题"机器人辅助显微外科手术系统"通过国家"863"专家组验收,建立了基于辅助显微外科手术操作的,主-从操作形式的微操作机器人系统的整体体系结构,设计、研制出具有5个运动自由度(三个平动自由度,两个旋转自由度)的,具有高精度定位,低速稳定运动性能的显微手术从动操作机构,设计、研制具有多自由度运动控制功能的,能够有效消除人为操作时因心理条件限制(如长时间操作产生的疲劳抖动等)产生误动作的智能型主动操作机构,建立末端工具的力觉反馈控制系统,主-从系统之间建立双向力反馈系统,使操作者具有力负载感觉。辅助建立显微手术特定操作过程的用力标准,使特定动作过程标准化。验收意见:“课题组开发研制出机器人辅助显微外科手术系统(RAMS)原理样机,样机的主要技术指标达到了合同规定的要求,对动物的显微手术操作实验,表明了机器人系统满足显微手术操作的运动、稳定度与控制精度等技术要求。”

二、电磁场效应研究与应用

(一)磁诱导治疗失眠症

1991年,天津大学王明时在国际上首次将外界物理因子的生物学效应引入到脑科学研究中来,发现了经特殊设计的磁场可以影响人的精神状态,并在细胞水平和神经生物化学方面揭示了其作用机理。据此,研制开发了治疗失眠、调节人精神状态的医疗仪器,并获得睡眠障碍康复仪、电磁波耦合促睡装置、时变磁场促睡装置等3项国家发明专利。其中,“梦神”睡眠器于1994年起批量生产,取得良好社会效益和经济效益。

(二)电磁热疗研究

自1993年起,天津大学万柏坤围绕肿瘤诊治物理技术和脑电非线性动力学特征信息提取与分析两个方向展开了相关研究。与天津肿瘤医院林世寅合作承担并完成国家自然科学基金项目“电容射频温热疗法热区分布计算及深部治癌方案优化研究”(39270218)、国家“八五”科技攻关项目子课题“腔道肿瘤微波热疗热场优化设计”(85-914-02-07)及天津市自然科学基金项目“用于浅表肿瘤热疗的小型超声波加热装置”(963709011)、“腔内肿瘤热疗辐射温度场及治癌方案优化研究”(953610711)。

1999年,万柏坤采用似稳电场模型和有限元数值计算方法对三极板调相式电容射频热疗装置在人体组织中比吸收率和温度分布进行模拟计算和体模实验,发现引入附加内电极可以调控深部热场分布的新技术途径,并因此项研究获得新的国家自然科学基金项目“深部肿瘤热疗有效热区控制新技术研究”(39870237)资助。研究成果在国内核心刊物及国际学术会议上发表论文多篇,并出版专著《现代肿瘤热疗学原理方法与临床》。万柏坤与张力新、田锡惠合作完成天津市自然科学基金“多探头超声热场分布及仪器化研究”(003609111)项目,这种自聚焦超声适合深部肿瘤热疗,为高强度聚焦超声技术(HIFU)的工程设计和临床应用提供了初步理论基础和实验方法,为其技术开发和产品化奠定了前期研究基础。

(三)高频磁刺激研究

1994年,生物医学工程所得到卫生部资助, 开展“脑神经矢量性定位磁刺激技术研究”。该项研究的创新点为:建立了颅内磁感应电场分布数学模型及计算机仿真,进行脑神经及外周神经磁刺激技术研究,提出新型聚焦性磁刺激线圈设计方法。研制成功临床实用性磁刺激治疗仪器样机,对磁刺激线圈周围空间磁场和感应电场分布进行实验测量,为该技术进一步临床应用奠定理论基础。此项研究于1998年完成。

第二节　临床工程

天津市在生物医学工程领域做出成果最多的是用于临床的多种仪器,如:医用传感器、眼科A/B超仪器、内窥镜、激光治疗机、前列腺治疗仪(改进)、智能化多功能针灸治疗仪、骨质疏松治疗系统、负压层流净化病床仪器等。其中王明时研究的“气管插管式传感器”1990年获国家发明四等奖,并批量生产。王延群为课题负责人研制的眼科A/B超仪器获2000年度国家科技进步二等奖,并成功实现产业化。在人体信息分析、检测和处理中,科技人员采用了先进、现代的分析方法和手段,为临床诊断、治疗和康复提供了新途径。

一、传感器

(一)气管插管式传感器

1989年,王明时首创"气管插管式心电、呼吸、体温传感器",可以从气管内壁同时拾取心电、呼吸及体温等生理参数,为实现手术中可同时监护多个生理参数提供了一种方便可靠的新方法。1991年后,该技术完成了产品化设计并投入批量生产。

(二)生物传感器

1989年,天津医科大学生物医学工程系成立传感技术教研室(实验室)。主要进行生物传感器应用基础研究和生物传感器的开发,采用不同载体、不同固化酶的方法制作分子识别元件,创新了以尼龙网为载体的共价键固化酶的方法和流动注入式的测量方法,并在此基础上相继研制葡萄糖传感器、过氧化氢传感器和酶免疫传感器等。以上研究成果在尹立志主持下进行,发表相关研究论文30多篇。

1993年,该系完成天津市基金项目"酶免疫电极法诊断乙型肝炎"的研究,成果被专家评定为具有世界先进水平并获得国家级成果登记,所撰写的文章《尼龙网为载体的薄层流通式酶免疫传感器》(Thin-Layer Flow-Through Enzyme Immunosensor Based on Polycaprolacam Net)被美国化学会收录在Arthur M.Usmani和NaimAkmal编辑的《诊断生物传感器聚合物》(*Dianostic Biosensor Polymers*)一书中。该项研究成果由尹立志主持,邢克礼主要参与。同年,尹立志、邢克礼参加编写的《生物传感器原理及应用》专著,由科技出版社出版,该书是国内首部生物传感器专著。1997年,尹立志作为主编之一,邢克礼参与编写《医用传感器》一书中的化学、生物传感器部分,该书作为医学院校生物医学工程专业的教材使用,曾连续7次印刷,受到读者好评。

2000年,完成"流动注入式乳酸生物传感器的研制",发表相关研究论文5篇,其中的《乳酸生物传感器的临床应用》(Clinical Applications of L-lactate Oxidase-based Biosensor)同时被EI、ISTP收录。该项研究成果及论文由邢克礼主持完成。2003年,邢克礼参与南开大学分子生物所进行免疫吸附剂性能研究,发表论文《IgA肾病免疫吸附剂吸附性能及血液相容性研究》,被EI收录(收录号03317580945)。

二、医学超声技术应用(眼科A/B超仪器)

1992年,生物医学工程所医学超声工程研究室研制成功中国首台眼科超声诊断设备。仪器使用10兆赫兹超声频率,分辨力0.2毫米,定名为眼科A/B型超声诊断仪。其立项目的是为解决中国眼科临床需求,替代国外同类进口产品。该设备专门用于诊断眼科疾病和测量眼的有关参数,A型超声能够准确检测眼角膜厚度、前房深度、晶状体厚度、玻璃体腔深度和眼轴长度,获得其他检查手段无法得到的活体数据,是白内障摘除植入人工晶体复明术的必备仪器。B型超声用于观察眼内组织的形态与结构,在对眼疾病诊断中,对星样玻璃体变性、玻璃体内新鲜积血、视盘下埋藏性玻璃疣、眼球内囊尾幼、眼球内异物、脉络膜脱离、脉络膜骨瘤、脉络膜下出血、晶状体脱位、视网膜囊肿、视网膜脱离、眼内占位性病变等的疾病诊断起着决定性作用。在以上超声诊断仪研究的基础上,又完成国家"十五"科技攻关课题,研制成功中国第一台更高频率的眼科超声生物显微镜,分辨力达到50微米,其应用使中国青光眼病的诊断与治疗有了新的发展和创新。

以王延群为课题负责人研制的眼科A/B型超声诊断仪,定型号为"BME-200眼科超声波诊断仪"。于1997年获得国家五部委颁发的国家重点新产品证书,2000年后,完成天津市科技攻关项目"BME-280白内障超声乳化仪"的研究与开发,2003年获国家重点新产品证书;国家"十五"科技攻关又研究成功中国第一台"BME-300W眼科超声生物显微镜",至此研制成功系列眼科超声诊断仪。2004年,成果转入该研究所参股的天津迈达医学科技有限公司进行成果转化,获得国家技术创新基金资助,形成眼科超声影像诊断设备与治疗系统系列产品,拥有专利和软件著作权十几项,具有全部自主知识产权。占有国内市场60%以上,通过了欧盟CE认证和美国FDA注册,产品出口至几十个国家和地区,不仅实现替代同类进口产品实现全国推广应用的目标,还在国际上形成强有力的竞争局面,创建国产品牌,取得重大的社会效益和经济效益,推动行业的技术进步和产业发展。

三、医用光学测试技术和图像处理(内窥镜)

早在1960年,天津大学即开始"医用光学测试技术和图像处理方向"的研究,1979年,该学科方向的研究并入新成立的生物医学工程专业。该研究方向的创始人虞启琏曾主持和参与筹建6个内窥镜及光学仪器工厂,担任中国仪器仪表学会视听工程学会荣誉副理事长等学术组织负责人及会员。

1991年,虞启琏圆满主持完成国家自然科学基金项目——应用白噪声技术测量液体流变特性的方法研究。1993~1997年,虞启琏负责完成"医用内窥显示系统""耳内窥镜,喉内窥镜""尿道膀胱镜光学设计""尿道膀胱镜""医用硬性内窥镜系列的研究—腹腔镜""医用硬性内窥镜系列的研究—关节镜"等横向项目,由工厂验收合格转入生产并在国内外进行销售。1994年虞启琏完成国家自然科学基金项目——生物血管组织三维形变的测定。1996年主持完成天津市自然科学基金项目——耳鼻咽喉内窥显示技术的研究。

虞启琏获得"一种带保护装置的耳内窥镜(ZL:92231872.7)""多用途双通道光学接口(ZL:92245774.3)""刚性内窥镜转象系统(ZL:94203119.9)""刚性内窥镜棒状镜转象系统(ZL:95216776. X)"等多项专利,掌握了相关关键技术的自主知识产权。在国内外重要期刊和会议上发表论文120多篇,部分被SCI和EI收录。主编《医用光学仪器》(天津科学技术出版社,1988),获天津大学优秀教材奖;主编《医用激光仪器》(天津科学技术出版社,1986)及《验光与配镜》(天津大学出版社,1990);编写《工程光学基础》(机械工业出版社,1988);编写的《计量工程光学》(机械工业出版社,1981);编写《生物医学工程学(基础医学卷)》(黑龙江科学技术出版社,2002)等著作。

四、激光治疗(激光治疗机)

1990~1997年,天津大学刘迎、马世宁、孙虹等开展激光生物研究。其中,将生物散斑作为生物信息的载体用于人体微循环测量和医学成像,研究内容有"动态散斑相关理论及其应用""串级激光散斑统计理论及其在测试技术中的应用""生物组织中超快脉冲时间分辨传播及理论研究",通过对脉冲CCD电子散斑技术用于医学体内活组织成像以及串级生物散斑统计性质的研究,发现一些新现象,受到国际同行重视。在皮肤血流参数与血流分布实时显示和测量研究中,他们对超短脉冲激光在人体皮肤组织中的传播及光计量进行计算机模拟与实验,建立起三层皮肤的物理模型,发表论文3篇。在研究人体组织激光慢相干成像中,采用计算机模拟方法及CCD成像技术,进行人体组织成像实验,建立物理模型,发表相关论文3篇,对激光医学成像临床研究具有指导意义。在开展串级散斑统计性质的研究中,在国内外刊物发表论文6篇。在生物组织中光子迁移的统计性质研究中,他们用光子迁移理论对激光在生物组织中传播的统计性质作理论分析及实验研究,对所设的物理模型的边界条件进行数学假定并且求解有关的数学方程,相关论文9篇发表在《中国激光》等刊物上。

1990年10月,医科大学生物医学工程系开始激光医学方向的研究。1991~1994年,李迎新主持承担天津市基金项目"660纳米激光光动力治疗转移癌研究",提出在肿瘤转移途径上实施光动力治疗,为光动力疗法治疗肿瘤及阻止复发转移提供了一种新的思路和方法。1993年,项目组与天津市中心妇产科医院合作完成自选课题"激光治疗子宫内膜异位症研究及治疗机研制",首次提出用弱激光治疗子宫内膜异位症的方法并完成了专用的激光治疗机。1994年,与天津市希统科技有限公司合作,完成"激光血管内照射治疗仪"的研制,并实现产业化,为推广弱激光血管内照射疗法做出贡献,第二年该公司上交国家利税二十余万元。1996年,与天津大唐光电技术有限公司合作将"子宫内膜异位症激光治疗机"产品化。1997年,与天津市鸣鼎科技有限公司合作,完成"半导体激光体外照射治疗机"的研制开发,首次提出用体外照射血管部位代替血管内照射的疗法,并实施产品化。

1996年1月至2001年10月,由天津大学叶志生、王升平、金贞姬、高惠敏、任国权、张俊林共同完成Q—

开关红宝石激光治疗机，获2001年度天津市科技进步二等奖。Q–开关红宝石激光治疗机由红宝石激光头、激光电源、温度控制的内循环去离子水冷却器、液晶触摸屏微机控制显示器和七关节导光臂组成。整机结构紧凑，性能稳定，操作简单，安全可靠。Q–开关红宝石激光器输出694.3纳米 波长的红色脉冲激光，这种波长的光能被黑色素或深色物质强烈吸收。当用Q–开关红宝石激光照射病变色素组织（太田痣、胎记、痣、老年斑、雀斑等）时，皮肤中的病变色素团块在极短时间内吸收红色激光，使其温度迅速升高气化，进而碎裂成细小颗粒。这些细小颗粒被人体的巨噬细胞吞噬掉，使病变色素组织得到治愈。用Q–开关红宝石激光治疗机治疗时患者痛苦小，治愈后没有疤痕。已广泛地在国内外各医院的皮肤科中得到临床用。

2000年，医科大学建成激光医学重点实验室。为激光医学基础研究、激光医学临床应用研究和新型激光医疗器械研制开发创造了条件。 受上海复旦张江医药公司委托完成“670纳米/690纳米双波长半导体激光治疗机”，为后来研制中国第一台大功率可见光半导体激光治疗机奠定基础。

2001年，李迎新与天津医科大学总医院眼科贺忠江合作完成了天津市基金项目“青光眼滤过激光手术激光机研制”，首次提出激光巩膜切除联合虹膜切除术。与天津市同业科技发展有限公司合作，完成“大功率可见光半导体激光治疗机”项目。同年，与重庆华鼎药业合作，完成了“630纳米/2瓦大功率光动力疗法激光治疗机”的产品化，该产品于2004年获得国家食品药品监督管理局监督管理局的注册许可，是中国第一个可用于光动力疗法的半导体激光治疗机。2005年，与安徽养和医疗器械设备有限公司合作完成“三路输出的630纳米/3瓦半导体激光治疗机”，2006年，获得国家食品药品监督管理局监督管理局的注册许可。这些研究开发工作对于抑制同类进口产品的价格起到积极作用。

2003年，李迎新主持天津市科技攻关项目“高功率半导体激光手术机”，研制开发出一台波长为808纳米的高功率半导体激光手术机样机，激光输出功率为1–50瓦可调，激光输出功率不稳定性小于5%，获得“光敏感光纤连接座”发明专利和“激光手术刀头”实用新型专利。在此基础上，与天津同业科技有限公司合作，完成“全固态532纳米Nd:YAG激光治疗机”的产品化，输出功率15瓦。该机于2008年1月获得国家食品药品监督管理局监督管理局的注册许可，是中国第一个用光动力疗法治疗鲜红斑痣的全固态激光治疗机。

五、生物热力学、电磁学的临床应用（前列腺治疗仪改进）

2002年，生物医学工程所殷涛等承担天津市科技攻关项目“毫米波前列腺治疗仪的改进技术”。前列腺疾病是中老年男性常见病，口服用药难以收到良好效果。利用极高频毫米波的非热效应治疗前列腺疾患收到较好的疗效，治疗急、慢性前列腺炎、前列腺疼痛效果明显，对前列腺肥大可起到较好的非手术改善。弱功率毫米波经直肠照射治疗无创、安全，可提高前列腺疾病治愈率和缩短治疗疗程。该项目创新点为开展毫米波生物效应及对人体作用机理研究，实施毫米波腔内定向辐射技术研究，利用弱功率极高频毫米波的非热效应，产生与细胞组织本振频率相关联的相干激励，有效地改善前列腺局部的血液循环，增强细胞酶活性，激活损伤区域淋巴细胞和巨噬细胞功能。可用于前列腺炎、前列腺增生患者的体内/体外治疗，可替代或辅助药物治疗。该项目2004年底完成，受国家科技部委托，由卫生部科教司组织专家于2005年3月15~16日对前列腺治疗仪的升级改造技术进行专项现场验收。验收小组认为主要技术参数的测试数据符合项目任务书中相应条款的要求。专家组一致认为前列腺治疗仪技术先进、成熟，具有良好的社会效益和经济效益，产业化前景良好。

六、智能化多功能针灸治疗仪

1994年，生物医学工程所殷涛等承担天津市自然科学基金课题“智能化多功能针灸治疗仪的研制”。针对多种针灸仪器存在技术水平低，性能不稳定，安全可靠性低，功能单一的问题，医院需要技术含量高，功能齐全，使患者产生信任感的高档次多功能针灸治疗仪器。及时开发研制系列化智能化的多功能针灸治疗仪成为重要课题。结合针刺手法客观评价方法与评价参数研究、针刺与灸疗的生物物理作用机制研究、灸疗热场分布建模及动态热力学过程研究，进行了智能化多功能中医针灸治疗技术与仪器研究。1999年获得天津市重点科技攻关项目“智能化多功能针灸治疗仪的研制”资助，所研制的BME-50系列中医灸疗仪获得国家专利（专利号ZL95213546.9），仪器自1997年进入市场（津药器监字97第227007号），是当时先进的中医治疗仪器。该项研究综合电刺激治疗技术、频率调制技术和脉冲离子导入技术，开发完成了BME-504A多功能针灸治疗仪产品样机，并在十几家医院进行临床试用，试用表明：该仪器技术先进，设计合理，安全可靠，疗效显著。创新点为可实现电针、体外按摩、药物透入和灸疗等多种治疗效果，具备多路输出、独立调节的功能。该项研究于2002年完成。

七、负压层流净化病床仪器的研制

2003年，生物医学工程所殷涛等承担天津市科委紧急攻关项目，研制成功“针对经空气传播传染病的负压层流净化病床仪器”，立项目的为收集经空气传播的传染病患者周围的污染空气，经紫外线、臭氧联合消毒和HEPA（高效空气过滤器）过滤后将其无害排入大气，净化病房，实现净化消毒隔离防护，保护医护人员，有效控制SARS（非典型肺炎病毒）等呼吸道烈性传染疾病的传播。通过对该负压隔离床的设计原理和实际工作状态的论证、考察、测试，临床效果专家评议组认为：负压隔离床外形与结构设计合理，符合临床上对防护设备的要求；

隔离罩内的负压强度能有效收集患者周围的有害气体，防止其向外扩散；紫外线+臭氧物理消毒系统采用联合消毒方式，可对负压床收集的有害气体进行高强度的消毒，能有效杀灭有害气体中的病原微生物；HEPA高效过滤系统的过滤效率大于95%，可以对经联合消毒后的气体进行过滤。

该项研究解决了负压、高效吸附材料重复使用、紫外+臭氧消毒在该仪器中的联合应用技术。已取得天津市药品监督管理局的市场准入注册证（津药管械2004第2060019号），具有较强的社会效益。2003年底完成此项研究工作。

八、脉冲电磁场骨质疏松治疗系统研制

1994年开始，生物医学工程所在国内率先开展此项课题研究，由屈承端主持。用脉冲电磁场治疗大鼠骨质疏松模型，从骨微细结构、骨密度、骨力学特性和骨细胞活性等证明脉冲电磁场的治疗作用和机理。于1998年，研制出中国第一台脉冲电磁场骨质疏松治疗系统。随后，经安全检测后应用于临床并通过临床使用对治疗系统进行了改进和完善。

该项研究提出以人体最易发生骨质疏松的脊柱和股骨及周围骨骼肌作为治疗靶器官，用仿生脉冲电磁场和床垫式人体形治疗器进行治疗的方法，它同时解决了这一治疗技术遇到的疗效、生物学安全性和全身性治疗效果等难题，使电磁场治疗骨质疏松技术从此进入实用化阶段。

该项研究的创新点为：一是按骨骼的压电特性和生理活动特征设计的仿生脉冲电磁场；二是按人体骨骼结构设计的床垫式人体形治疗器。它们产生的磁力线从人体背部透入，对脊柱和股骨及周围骨骼肌进行仿生的生物物理刺激，对人体胸、腹腔内其他器官基本无干扰，实现安全而有效的治疗。

该项目先后列为天津科委重点攻关项目、科技部重点攻关项目、卫生部科研基金项目和卫生部重点项目。2001年该项科研成果由科技部组织专家验收。2002年该项科研成果由天津市科委组织专家鉴定。2004年被科技部批准为国家重点新产品。临床研究已证明该治疗系统有较好疗效，能减轻和消除骨质疏松引起的疼痛，对多数患者的骨密度有不同程度的改善，降低了骨折发生率。

该项科研成果及时进行科技成果转化，研发出以计算机控制具有治疗方案设计、治疗控制、病人信息记录储存和查询、数据分析的多功能系统；开发了适用于老年患者和骨折患者的床旁移动式治疗等系列产品，实现了产业化。1999年获得天津市药监局颁发的市场准入许可证，投入批量生产，在全国广泛推广应用。已为许多骨质疏松及骨质疏松性骨折患者解除痛苦，获得显著经济效益和社会效益。

九、介入栓塞治疗用微导管和电解脱弹簧圈的研制

1998~2003年，天津大学材料学院常津带领的团队（包括方洞浦、陈贻瑞、吕鸣祥、许晓秋、李润卿、申群英、张爽男、田晓明、于万里）与天津市脑系科中心医院只达石、焦德让、孙瑞发合作，承担天津市重点科技攻关项目“介入治疗微导管的研制”“介入栓塞治疗用电解脱弹簧圈的研制”“介入医学导管及弹簧圈（中试）”。

脑介入微导管与电解脱弹簧圈配套使用，主要用于颅内动脉瘤，颈动脉海绵窦瘘及血管畸形等疾病的介入治疗，对高危险性而无法手术的上述脑血管病变患者具有特殊的应用价值。为打破介入治疗器械完全依赖进口的局面，降低治疗费用并提高诊疗效果，同时降低脑血管疾病的并发症和死亡率，课题组研制出了性能优良的介入治疗微导管和电解脱弹簧圈。动物实验表明，所研制的介入治疗微导管和电解脱弹簧圈能够安全、有效地栓塞动脉瘤模型，为进一步临床应用奠定了坚实的基础。项目组还制定了脑介入治疗微导管和电解脱弹簧圈的企业标准，为标准化和规模化生产提供依据。项目组研制的微导管和电解脱弹簧圈性能已接近或达到国外同类产品水平。由于该项目所研制的微导管费用仅为进口产品的1/4~1/3的价钱，可大大减轻病人的经济负担。

十、人体信息分析、检测与处理

（一）肠鸣音分析

自1990年起，王明时在国际上首次从工程角度利用模式识别技术对人体肠鸣音进行了科学的定量分类，确定了正常音、气过水声、金属音及高调音在时域和频域中的基本特征，从而修订了传统教材上对肠鸣音的定义，使之更具科学性和准确性，从而在肠鸣音客观化分类基础上实现了肠疾患的无损诊断。完成国家自然科学基金和天津市自然科学基金课题，获三项有关科研成果及研制开发出无侵袭肠鸣音诊断系统。

（二）心脑信息处理与建模

天津大学生物医学工程专业，是国内最早从事生物医学信号处理、生理系统建模等相关研究的单位之一。围绕心脑血管疾病发生机制、早期诊断和治疗控制方法，开展了心室晚电位检测、心率变异性（HRV）分析和心脑电信号的非线性动力学分析研究，在心肌缺血的早期诊断、心电信号中高频切迹的产生机理、心电发生的拓扑模型和心率变异性非线性动力学分析方面取得了一系列有创新见解的研究成果。

1994年，吕扬生研发“心室晚电位检测仪”。在此基础上又相继研制了“动态心电图记录系统”等产品。

1995年，吕扬生在国内首次将FPGA技术用于视频图像数据采集、处理和输出控制，成功开发了“B超图像打印仪”，替代了传统胶片打印。

上述的产品成为中国最早的一批具有自主知识产权的医疗仪器产品。所有的产品均获得医疗产品许可证，行销国内百余家医院，并行销海外，至20世纪90年代末，已初具产业规模。

此外，吕扬生主编和参编的《随机信号处理导论》（天津大学出版社，1988）和《生物医学信号的处理和识别》（天津科技翻译出版公司，1997）已成为国内生物医学工程领域本科和研究生教学的经典教材。

（三）神经信息研究

从1991年开始，天津医科大学生物医学工程系田心主持开展神经信息学研究。

1997年，研究神经系统、神经元集群和神经元群三个层次水平上的神经信息处理，以及建模、仿真和控制，认知过程的神经元和神经元集群编码理论和方法，及其在认知机制和神经系统重大疾病机理研究和治疗上的应用。

1998年，承担国家自然科学基金项目“混沌建模和混沌控制在癫痫机理和治疗中的应用”，在该项研究中，针对癫痫中一类至今未知发病机制的重要疑难问题——婴儿痉挛症，从信息学的角度首次提出它的发病机制的新假说：脑干的神经信息传递功能产生障碍，由此引起脑干功能失调，并用混沌学的理论和方法进行验证。

2000年，开展“混沌学在婴儿痉挛症机理研究中的应用”课题研究，在1998年研究成果的基础上，首次在临床上采用无创测取的，能反映脑干神经信息动态特性的脑干听觉诱发响应作为研究脑干功能状态的基本信息，而不是临床上传统采用的失去动态特性的脑干听觉诱发电位的平均值。成功应用脑干听觉诱发响应的相关维数去定量表征脑干神经信息传递的不同功能状态。结果表明婴儿痉挛症患者存在着严重的脑干神经信息传递障碍，验证了婴儿痉挛症发病责任结构是脑干的假说。在以上研究的基础上，在国内外首次提出治疗婴儿痉挛症的新思路：无创刺激脑干中存在神经信息传递障碍的神经元区，“打通”受阻神经传递径路。这个创新思路也能推广应用到其他类型的癫痫的治疗中。

2002年，开展国家自然基金项目“高维混沌系统的研究及在脑电分析中的应用”的研究，创新性地提出用低维混沌的理论和方法研究高维混沌的脑电的弊端，提出并实施了高维混沌的降维分析方法，提出高维相关维数的理论、算法和实施。

2004年，完成的“非线性动力学在难治性癫痫的研究中的应用”获天津市科技进步二等奖，从信息学角度提出，并用混沌学指标验证了难治性癫痫发病责任脑区信息传导障碍发病机制；选用能反映责任脑区功能的动态信息：脑干听觉诱发响应作为适合该研究的特征信号；用混沌指标定量脑干障碍程度；提出并探索用无创经颅磁刺激“打通”障碍，无创治疗难治性癫痫的新途径。

（四）牙病检测

1989~1993年，天津医科大学生物医学工程系刘振宅主持完成天津市基金项目“牙病综合诊断仪的研制”和“牙周袋测量仪的研制”。

1994~1995年，刘振宅与俄罗斯国立莫斯科大学基础医学系和俄罗斯卫生部物理化学医学研究所合作，利用电子自旋共振（ESR）波谱仪测量不同组织中的自由基，对“病理条件下Fe^{2+}在脂质过氧化中作用”进行研究。在此基础上提出利用ESR波谱仪评价血浆抗氧化活性的方法。

2000年，刘振宅等采用膜片钳技术与RT-PCR（逆转录-聚合酶链反应）相结合的方法探讨可溶性Aβ（β-淀粉样蛋白）对大鼠海马CA3区锥体神经元电压门控性钾电流及钾离子通道亚型mRNA（信使RNA）表达的影响，以期揭示可溶性Aβ的神经毒性作用机理及在AD（阿尔茨海默病）发病过程中的作用机制，为AD防治和治疗药物的筛选奠定基础。

第三节 生物材料与人工器官

20世纪80年代开始，天津市工业系统的橡胶研究所开始立项研究生物材料和人工器官。比较成功的有：硅橡胶植入型鼻架（用于医学美容），和天津医科大学第二附属医院合作开展人工膀胱造瘘管研究。该所还和天津儿童医院合作，开展儿童食道修复材料——“食道探子”的研究（该研究针对儿童误食毒药造成食道伤害）。以上研究都取得了预期成果，达到临床应用水平。1990年开始，生物医学工程所立项研究“医用组织引导再生胶原膜”。该项成果为病缺损疾病的治疗提供急需解决的材料，同时为相关领域的发展提供物质基础和可借鉴的思路，具有显著的社会效益。天津大学材料学院在纳米材料的研究与应用中做出贡献，1996年开展的“纳米微球的制备和临床检测”、2001年开展的“新型靶向治疗复合功能性纳米载体系统的研究”都取得了预期的临床应用成果。

一、医用组织引导再生胶原膜

生物医学工程所在“生物材料与人工器官”课题研究方面，取得“医用组织引导再生胶原膜”研究成果。该项目于1990年立项，获得国家自然科学基金、国家火炬计划等的资助，1997年获得药品监督局医疗器械准产注册证。

由意外伤害、恶性肿瘤、生理功能减退等造成的组织缺病损是临床上的常见病和多发病，对该类疾病的治疗一直是临床上急需解决的重大问题。“组织引导再生”是20世纪90年代提出的一个生物学概念，其理论基础是根据不同组织向创口内生长移行的速度不一，通过放置生物隔膜作为物理屏障来阻挡其他组织细胞长入创口，同时为所需组织提供一个空间，保护其增殖，修复创口，从而达到组织修复的目的。其中，人工生物隔膜是实施组织修复技术的关键。针对临床急需，结合引导组织再生性愈合的新理论及新技术，研制具有引导缺病损组织再生功能的生物材料用于组织修复治疗是生物医用材料领域研究的重要方向之一。

选用符合临床要求的胶原为主原料，在研究膜制备工艺、交联剂选择和交联工艺与膜降解时间关系的基础上研制出胶原膜，并对其进行理化和生物学性能研究，建立实验动物病理模型并进行实验研究。建立产品标准，进行临床实验和成果推广。该胶原膜具有显著引导组织再生的效果，生物相容性好，无毒副作用且术后材料能被组织吸收，不需第二次手术取出，病缺损的组织能在该膜的作用下实现功能性/再生性的愈合，恢复原来的健康形态和生理功能，经临床实际应用证明产品质量达到国际发达国家同类产品水平，但价格远低于进口产品。已应用于口腔科、骨科、整形外科、五官科、神经外科及肌腱断裂和脏器穿孔等，尤其是对引导／诱导软组织再生效果更为明显，还可用于组织工程支架和控缓释放药物载体等。

二、纳米生物技术应用

（一）纳米微球的制备和临床检测

1996~1999年，天津大学材料学院常津与天津市中心妇产科医院常青、朱楣光合作，承担天津市自然科学基金项目“孕酮免疫纳米微球的制备和临床检测”。

该项研究采用改进的无乳化剂乳液聚合法制备聚苯乙烯微球，并对聚合反应温度和有机溶剂含量对聚合反应和粒径的影响进行研究；再将合成的聚苯乙烯微球与孕酮抗体反应，结果表明：通过加入少量有机溶剂，提高了聚合反应速度和转化率，制备出粒径可控的单分散聚苯乙烯免疫微球。粒径在200~800纳米之间，微球具有较高的抗体结合容量，且结合后保持了较高的抗体活性。用合成的孕酮免疫胶乳进行免疫凝集实验，观察反应时间，反应温度的影响，确定了免疫反应的基本反应条件，并对临床样品进行检测和验证，为与孕酮激素相关的妇科疾病的诊断提供了新方法。

（二）新型靶向治疗复合功能性纳米载体系统的研究

2001~2005年，天津大学材料学院纳米生物技术研究所常津带领的团队承担国家“973”专项基金项目“TAT介导的新型激发式肿瘤细胞内靶向药物释放体系”，天津市科委应用基础研究重点基金项目“新型靶向激发药物载体系统的研制”和天津市科委重点科技攻关项目“新型靶向治疗载体系统的研究”。

项目以O-羧甲基壳聚糖等8种可生物降解的高分子材料为原料，采用共沉淀、超声乳化、自组装等纳米生物技术优化制备并表征了一系列各具特性的超微载体；并将跨膜肽、药物、基因和抗体等18种不同性质的物质分别与该超微载体系统连接，使其分别或兼具磁性、配体和序列复合靶向功能、跨膜功能和治疗功能。在乳腺癌、胃癌、肠癌、人脑恶性胶质瘤等11种肿瘤细胞系进行了抗体和磁靶向检测、降解和释药行为、肿瘤细胞抑制率、细胞转染过程，细胞原位凋亡及免疫组化、TAT／药物复合物、肝素和鱼精蛋白之间的相互作用等一系列体外实验。并采用荷瘤鼠模型进行抑瘤效果实验。结果表明该载体系统能充分利用TAT独特的跨膜传递功能，有效的介导各类药物尤其是大分子药物和基因杀伤肿瘤细胞，并具有靶向激发的特点，提高了对肿瘤的治疗效果。

2004年，常津及其团队和天津医科大学总医院浦佩玉、康春生合作，承担国家自然科学基金项目“跨血脑屏障基因药物复合功能性超微载体的构建研究”。

脑疾患（如癫痫、脑瘤和帕金森氏病等）已经成为全世界面临的重大医学问题。但是，由于血脑屏障的阻碍，针对脑疾患开发的新药中绝大多数难以达到临床应用。该研究以4种磁性纳米微粒（包括磁性纳米胶束、天然磁小体和两种磁性高分子纳米粒子）、转铁蛋白（或叶酸）、Tat和药物（丙戊酸钠、甲氨喋呤、质粒

DNA 和 siRNA)等为原料,采用一系列纳米生物技术,制备出同时具有跨血脑屏障、磁性和受体介导复合靶向及药物治疗作用的复合功能超微载体系统。通过一系列表征、体外抗肿瘤细胞试验和基因转染试验,证实了该复合功能超微载体系统的成功组装和功能保持。采用同位素锝标记的单光子发射计算机断层成像术(SPECT),在正常和癫痫大鼠模型中证实了4种复合功能性超微载体均能携带药物和基因较大程度的跨越血脑屏障,并定量检测了载体在各脏器的分布。该研究还建立了体外血脑屏障模型,并进行了大鼠癫痫模型治疗实验。经治疗前后脑电图、病理、免疫组化和细胞凋亡等指标检测,证实了该复合功能超微载体系统所携带的抗癫痫药物丙戊酸钠能有效的治疗癫痫发作。该项目的研究成功为解决药物跨越血脑屏障传递这一世界难题提供重要的科学依据。

2002年,由常津为负责人牵头完成的研究项目"纳米生物技术在靶向控释抗癌药物载体系统和医学诊断方面的应用"获得"天津市自然科学三等奖"。

第五篇

工 业 科 技

概 述

1991～2005年，天津作为中国北方重要的工业城市，工业重要行业和重点企业浴火重生，发生深刻变化。面对老工业基地长期形成的老厂房、老设备、老工艺、老产品、老机制等积重难返的局面，1994年，天津市委、市政府决定，经过企业改制、引进外资、调整结构，特别是技术改造和技术创新，用8年左右时间，将国有大中型企业嫁接改造调整一遍，同时大力发展多种经济成分的高科技企业。1999年，全市748户国有大中型企业"嫁改调"提前完成，工业经济的总量、速度和结构发生根本性变化。天津进一步提出"要把技术创新、技术改造与资产调整重组结合起来，实现产业产品结构的优化升级"，市经委发布关于企业技术创新的文件，确定安排200项创新项目，突出抓好1.3升夏利汽车、高效节能工业泵、大型农用胎、高负荷苯酐催化剂、抗酸蚀抗挤毁石油套管、新型传真机、新工艺地塞米松等20个产值超亿元的新产品。2003年，天津进而按照产业发展方向和技术前沿要求，策划一批对产业升级具有重大突破和带动作用的工业技术创新项目，确定做大做强电子信息、汽车、化工、现代冶金、医药、新能源及环保等6大支柱产业，建设好12个技术含量高的产品基地的目标，推进优势产业升级，加大科技投入力度，提升企业创新能力。从1994年实施"嫁改调"到2005年12年间，全市规模以上工业总产值增长5.3倍，年均增长18.5%，在全国31个省市中居第13位，在四个直辖市中居第二位；特别是"十五"期间，工业总产值年均增长23.7%，成为全市经济持续较快发展的主要拉动和支撑力量。技术创新受到各级政府和企业的高度重视，企业技术创新的潜在因素逐步得以发挥。大中型工业企业自主创新的投入力度明显加大，2001～2004年累计投入研发经费69.4亿元，2004年研发经费投入达到24.4亿元，比2003年增长42.69%，成为全市科技研发活动的主体。企业技术改造水平和技术创新能力的提升对于天津工业经济的转型发展起到决定性作用。

一、引进消化和自主创新取得成效。

重视技术装备引进后的消化吸收和国产化。市政府和有关部门鼎力支持夏利汽车的消化吸收，科技立项最多，效果最好，国产化水平达到80%以上，形成具有完全自主知识产权的夏利整车开发和生产平台。夏利轿车单品种销量突破20万辆，获得全国销量冠军和CCTV自主品牌年度大奖。汽车行业进而成功实现与一汽集团的战略重组和与丰田公司的全面合作，形成从1.0～3.0全系列梯型产品结构，汽车生产能力突破40万辆，轿车产量达到32.6万辆，经济型轿车产销量稳居全国第一，进入全新的发展时期。其他如轻工机械、佳能复印机等引进后的国产化也做得好。

培育壮大一批自主创新的品牌产品。国有工业企业多年以科技铸品牌，一批关键工艺和技术取得新的突破。无缝钢管、复方丹参滴丸、皮质激素等成为天津新一代的标志性工业产品。钢管公司石油套管产销量稳居国内第一，跻身世界三强；自主研制开发合金高压耐热无缝钢管，攻克冶炼技术、轧制技术、热处理技术、加工技术等难关，耐高温达到550度，耐高压达到22.5兆帕，达到国际先进水平；通过与世界顶尖企业联合开发三辊在线脱棒连轧技术，使无缝钢管生产装备水平处于世界领先，并开始技术输出。复方丹参滴丸1997年成为国内第一个进入FDA临床试验的心脑血管疾病中药；皮质激素类原料药、地塞米松系列产品生产规模居世界第一。医药集团自主开发的GCLE中间体，打破日本多年的技术垄断，结束天津没有头孢类抗生素的历史。2001年1月，安福隆水针作为世界上第一支"预充式"干扰素成功上市，2002年9月美国SICOR INC公司和中新药业集团追加投资，兴建"华立达生物园"，安福隆销量跃居全国干扰素市场首位。代表医药产业发展方向的华立达生物园、中新药业集团现代中药园相继建成，经过科技部批准，在国内居于领先水平的中药现代化科技产业(天津)基地建立起来。天津清源电动车公司等单位自主研发生产的“幸福使者”纯电动车出口美国市场,为天津电动汽车产业化、参与国际市场竞争奠定基础。大沽化工厂自主开发的PVC优化工艺和“热水入料”新工艺,使产量提高50%以上,在全国推广。手表集团自主开发陀飞轮表,使天津机械手表加工制造达到国际水平,天津“海鸥”为中国手表走向世界打下基础。

图5-0-0-56 清源电动车出口美国市场

二、依靠科技形成重点产业和品牌产品。

坚持技术创新以企业为主体,以效益作为技术创新的目的,所有企业都以市场主导,依据市场需求搞技术创新和新产品开发。特别是“十五”期间,全市工业加快高新技术产业发展和用高新技术及先进适用技术改造传统产业的步伐,围绕重点产业、重点产品组织技术创新项目,共实施工业投资项目1829个,将工业投资的70%投在优势产业,其中电子信息、生物技术与现代医药、新能源、新材料、环保等高新技术项目投资占总投资的38.5%,以促进优势项目自主创新。电子信息、现代冶金、化工成为超千亿元的大产业,天铁冶金、机电、渤海化工、冶金、钢管、医药、建工集团、天钢、一轻等9家企业位列“2005中国500强企业”。

科技创新给天津产业发展方向带来深刻变化。冶金行业通过大规模的技术改造,装备、工艺、技术、产品水平全面提升,无缝钢管产量达到175万吨,为全国第一,钢管公司进入世界同行业四强,海河下游现代冶金基地基本形成。天锻压力机公司开发的半固态金属成型液压机,与传统铸造工艺相比,制件机械性能提高30%,重量轻30%以上,节能35%,生产效率提高9倍;该项目取得专利成果17项,其中发明专利6项,填补国内在液压机技术方面的空白,达到世界先进产品的同类水平。化工行业通过技术改造,百万吨级PVC基地提前一年建成,随着乙烯炼化一体化、天碱搬迁改造项目的开工建设,揭开化学工业快速发展的序幕。长芦汉沽盐场有限责任公司以盐田饱和卤水开发15万吨/年真空精制盐及母液综合利用研究项目,该工艺节省1万公亩结晶区面积,同时节省近20万吨原盐,自主发电能力达到3000千瓦时。天津中药现代化居全国领先水平,医药集团成为全国同行业第四大集团,中新药业、天士力成为全国最大的中药现代化骨干集团,培育出复方丹参滴丸、速效救心丸等销售收入过5亿元的中药和新康泰克、芬必得、寿比山、大输液、皮质激素、干扰素等一批化学原料药与制剂、生物工程药大品种产品。

三、节能减排列为技改重点。

企业把节能减排作为社会责任,努力转变增长方式,把节约能源、降低消耗、消除污染、淘汰落后作为技术改造的重点,依靠科技进步走出一条投入少、产出高、消耗低的新型工业化道路。冶金行业淘汰247万吨落后生产能力;高耗水的造纸行业全部退出;纺织行业淘汰落后设备288台套;碱渣、钢渣、粉煤灰的综合利用率达到100% ,市内昔日的三座废料山变为宝藏。全市海水淡化、中水回用在全国处于领先水平,企业生产多有应用。大港电厂海水淡化成果丰硕。一些主要电厂基本实现污水零排放。石化公司自主开发节水减排综合利用项目,引用多项节水工艺技术,水源回用率达到50%以上,新鲜水用量减少57%,排污水用量减少45%。经过技术改造,“十五”期间,全市工业万元增加值能耗由2.26吨标准煤下降到1.58吨标准煤(2000价),累计下降30.1%,年均下降6.9%。2005年,全市电力弹性系数继续保持在0.88的合理水平;工业万元增加值能耗为1.45吨标准煤(2005价),是全国平均水平的56%,列第三位;工业万元增加值取水29.4立方米,工业用水重复利用率达到91%;固体废弃物综合利用率达到97.3%,几项指标均保持全国领先水平。

四、企业技术创新实力增强。

建立支撑品牌发展的科技创新体系。全市企业技术中心建设形成国家级、市级和企业级三个层次的梯次发展。截至2005年,全市国有工业企业共建立国家级企业技术中心12家,在全国排名第8位;国有工业企业建立市级企业技术中心91家,占全市150家市级企业技术中心的66.6%,居全国第7位。企业技术中心综合能力考评居全国第一,综合创新能力和实力居全国先进行列,从而保证国有企业一批重点自主核心技术取得突破。国家驻津科研院所起到带动作用,诸如核物理所做粮食加工设备项目、707所的焊机项目、机械研究院的新产品研发,乃至驻津军工企业的许多军转民项目,给天津知名品牌配套,促进企业科技实力增强。市属机械、仪表、汽车模具、自行车、轻工、电视、轻化、染料、纺织、造纸等研究所得到市经济综合与科技主管部门的得力支持,与生产一线联系紧密,对企业技改和创新起到积极作用。

企业运用知识产权制度的能力提高。自主知识产权拥有量逐年增加。"十五"期间,全市工业企业共申请专利14959件。2004年企业专利申请量居全国第八位。

制造业信息化水平提升。用高新技术改造提升传统产业,以政府引导、企业投入为主体,建立三个层次的示范应用体系。1991年,在机械、电子仪表和医药3个开展机电一体化的重点局,共开发机电一体化新产品136项。2001年,全市企业信息化技术得到推广,CIMS应用示范启动40余家企业,轻工、模具、服装等行业100家企业开展CAD应用工程,天铁冶金集团和钢管公司开始实施企业信息化工程。通过冶金、汽车等龙头企业开展数字化示范工程,实施5家企业面向产品链集成技术应用;选择25家重点企业开展以ERP、MES、SCM、CRM等技术为代表的企业制造资源管理集成技术示范应用;面向150家中小企业,实施建立以4CP技术部分集成为主的产品创新数字化技术应用,带动500家制造业企业实施信息化。该工程进而带动全市2000多家制造业企业实施信息化,80%以上的重点企业采用计算机辅助设计(CAD)、辅助铸造(CAM),新产品设计能力提高。通过实施中药现代化科技工程,16项中药现代化关键技术在中药企业得到广泛应用。

产学研密切合作。全市围绕优势产业选取高精度数控齿轮传动成套加工装备、现场总线型智能化仪表及主控系统成套产品、中药粉针系列产品、高性能大规格预应力钢绞线、头孢类系列药品及中间体等10项代表产业发展方向、成长性好、拉动作用明显的重大项目,组织产学研联合攻关,促进企业技术中心与大学及科研院所共建研发机构。鼓风机厂与西安交大研究人员合作开展技术研发。天津大学教授帮助锻压机床厂改进工艺,新产品在德国一举中标。天津动力机厂与天津大学合作开发的高压共轨电控燃油系统产业化项目,实现柴油机高压共轨燃油技术和电控单元控制技术,使动力机各项性能指标达到国际先进水平,达到欧Ⅲ排放标准。

第一章 电 力

1991~2005年,天津电力工业技术取得快速发展。其间,建成一大批具有高科技水平的大容量、高参数及超高参数级的发电厂和高电压、超高电压级的输、变电工程,电力工业各种专业技术更加先进、更加环保,电力工业运行更加注重安全、降低能耗、提高效益,科技进步发挥重要的引领作用。电力工业生产调度、综合管理更加注重依靠计算机和信息技术。至2005年底,天津地区的发电厂共30家,总装机容量约为617.892万千瓦。天津电网建成3座500千伏超高压等级的变电站,4条500千伏输电线路,初步形成与华北电网和各主要电源点连接的骨架网络。220千伏系统网络形成一个大"目"字形的双环网和两个三角形的网架,初步实现对天津电网的多路、多方位的安全供电。城市及农村的电网建设、改造工程初步完成,110千伏、35千伏及10千伏电力配电网络遍布城乡,初步实现保证天津地区国民经济快速发展的供电需求。天津电力系统在消化吸收引进技术和高科技装备的基础上,不断进行技术改造和技术创新。据不完全统计,1991~2005年,天津电力工业完成并获得天津地区电力行业科技成果奖的项目有400余项。其中,在"十五"期间获天津市、国家电网公司、华北电网科技进步奖的项目有142项。

第一节 电力工程

1990年后，天津地区发电厂和电力网的建设进入快速发展期。实行多种资金渠道、多家投资办电，发展速度快；按照天津自身能源结构，注重环境保护；采用国内外先进技术与消化吸收、自主创新相结合，科技水平高；改造和新建高电压电网和高参数、大容量发电厂，经济效益和社会效益双提高。

一、发电工程

1991年10月至1992年5月，天津大港电厂实施二期建设改造工程。扩建两台32万千瓦燃煤发电机组（3、4号机组），相继建成投产，成为天津地区第一座百万千瓦级大型发电厂和国内第一座全部利用海水发电（包括海水冷却、海水冲灰和海水淡化后补给锅炉用水）的大型火力发电厂。该工程，锅炉、汽轮机、发电机等主设备，与一期工程相同，均为意大利进口机组，同时引进两套美国ESCO公司设计制造的"盐水再循环多级闪蒸装置"，单台日产3000吨淡水，技术先进，为当时国内首台大型海水淡化装置。1992年后，天津大港电厂经对引进技术设备的消化吸收，实施国产化海水淡化工程的研制开发，由华北电力集团公司科协通过产、学、研结合，组织华北电力大学研究生部及有关专家，与该电厂协作攻关，于1998年完成两台工业施工条件下的海水淡化装置，并投入生产。该国产化装置，造水比为10∶1，提取的淡水含盐量为2～5毫克/升，脱盐率达99.9%，日产2×3000吨淡化水。除满足全厂（包括一、二期）的生产用水和全厂职工的生活用水外，还可部分对外销售桶（瓶）装饮用纯净水。该电厂全部利用海水发电的工程，为国内海水淡化领域的开发提供经验，对干旱少雨缺乏淡水，而又面临大海的天津及环勃海地区的工业、企业建设及经济发展，起到很好的示范作用。该项目1998年获北京市科协金桥工程项目一等奖、华北电管局科技二等奖。

1998年9月18日，天津滨海燃气发电厂（简称燃气电厂）组建成立，是利用伴生油气、环保型的燃气发电厂。渤海湾开采海上石油的伴生天燃气，此前由于不能得到利用，被遗弃点"天灯"，不仅浪费资源，而且污染环境。该厂首期工程，第一套燃气—蒸汽联合循环发电系统于1998年12月完成并正式投产。发电机组总容量为5.6万千瓦，其中燃气发电机组3.8万千瓦，由南京汽轮机厂引进美国GE公司技术和主要部件生产的PG6551B型机组。伴生天燃气先进入燃气机组做功发电后，再将排出的高温烟气（500~600℃）送入一台双压自然循环66.6吨/时余热锅炉（杭州锅炉厂引进荷兰技术），用产生的中温中压蒸汽，推动一台1.8万千瓦抽凝式汽轮发电机组发电，锅炉产生的低压蒸汽供给除氧器加热。该套机组由于采用先进的燃气蒸汽联合循环方式，热效率高，可达46%，技术先进、自动化水平高。由于启动快、不需外部提供启动电源，因此，当发生电网全部瓦解时，还可作为"黑启动电源"。即当电网瓦解时，其最先启动发电，然后按电网调度安排，为恢复发电功能的电厂提供启动电源，这样即可逐步恢复整个电网的正常供电。该机组是天津首台燃气蒸汽联合循环发电机组。

2000年1月，天津市双港垃圾焚烧发电项目启动。同年获国家计委立项批复，2003年工程全面开工。2004年年底，天津市泰达环保有限公司成立研发中心，以垃圾焚烧发电项目为依托，致力于消化吸收国外的先进技术，并进行技术改造与创新，逐步提高关键设备设计和制造的国产化程度，以降低投资成本，提高运营效率。该研发中心通过与高校开展产、学、研合作，及国际技术交流合作，开发具有自主知识产权的前沿技术及装备，取得包括自动擦窗机、自动卸料门、除臭装置、炉渣制砖、飞灰制水泥、飞灰制陶粒共6项科技成果，申报15项国家发明专利，获得天津市科委颁发的科技成果2项，并承担中国光华基金环保发展专项基金项目和天津市科技攻关计划重大科技项目2项。

2005年5月，双港垃圾焚烧发电厂全面建成。日处理生活垃圾1200吨，年处理垃圾约为40万吨，超过天津市城区垃圾产量的1/4。装机有3台400吨/日往复逆推倾斜排式焚烧炉，配3台32吨/时自然循环汽包炉为余热锅炉(4兆帕，400℃)，锅炉及燃烧设备引进日本熊田公司技术，受热面部分由杭州锅炉厂生产，技术先进，可直接燃烧低热值垃圾。配有2台出力12兆瓦(3.8兆帕，395℃)汽轮发电机组，年上网发电量1.2亿千瓦时，相当于每年节约标准煤4.8万吨。采用半干法烟气净化吸收装置加布袋除尘器技术。二恶英及有害金属的去除采用高温分解、活性炭吸附技术等烟气处理方法。处理后的烟气完全符合欧盟和天津市排放标准，具有一定的超前性。燃烧后产生的炉渣可用制作建筑材料，毒性不超标的飞灰可做水泥添加剂，实现资源利用最大化。为避免对环境的二次污染，该厂将垃圾渗出的渗沥收集、回喷到焚烧炉内再燃烧，经850℃左右高温，使有害物质分解。

二、输变电工程

1991~1999年，天津电力设计院自主创新完成具有紧凑布置的二层变电站建筑设计和新型电气主接线的市区35千伏变电站的新型设计。该项目适应天津市区平房改造和城区建设的发展对供电可靠性提出的更高要求，以及市区成为电力负荷集中地区，而市区建筑物密集、土地资源少等特点。至2005年年底，全市已有数十座变电站采用该设计成果并获奖。2000年，天津电力设计院设计的海光寺220千伏变电站工程投产。这是天津市首座建在市中心区的220千伏终端变电站，设计规模为3台15万千伏安变压器、分别由三路220千伏高压电缆供电。同年，该设计成果被评为国家电力公司优秀设计奖。海光寺220千伏变电站是天津市首座高电压等级的无人值班变电站，投运后，除提高运行可靠性外，每年节约运行人员工资指标80万元，具有很好的经济、社会效益。天津电力设计院还将发达国家先进、成熟的“三维”系统技术，成功地在天津电网送变电工程设计中推广应用。至2005年，该设计院在昆纬路、芥园道及白庙等220千伏变电站等工程中，采用三维技术，以多方案的优化技术、逼真的渲染图和三维动画、全方位展示技术，在工程设计投标和提高工程设计质量、效果等方面，均达到国内先进水平。

2002年，天津市电力公司技术中心承担完成“高盐碱含量地质地区接地系统抗腐蚀技术研究”。该课题针对环渤海地区的天津、河北沧州及内陆油田等盐碱地域的发电厂、变电站和输配电线路设施中接触土壤的钢材，当含水量增高，土壤电阻串很低时，接地体受盐碱腐蚀而严重损坏问题，研制出一种抗腐蚀性能优于钢材、新型外包特制混凝土、内裹钢材的抗盐碱接地体，其投资造价低于有色金属接地体。2004年，经国家电力公司主持的技术鉴定认定，该成果最终研制成功的“新型外包特制混凝土内裹钢材的抗盐碱接地体”：①具有较强的耐腐蚀性能，能够满足高盐碱地区对接地网使用寿命(按规程规定30年)的要求；②抗盐碱接地网与热镀锌钢材接地网一次造价基本持平，且能降低运行费用；③与铜地网相比，造价仅为铜的40～50%，使用寿命比铜更长；④能够在高盐碱含量地质地区等各种土壤环境中埋设，耐腐蚀性能稳定；⑤技术便于实施，经济效益显著，推广应用前景广阔。

2005年，天津高压供电公司研究完成“天津市中心220千伏无人值班站相关技术问题的对策”。该项目针对监控中心、220千伏新建无人站和常规站改造等不同情况，总结制订出“220千伏无人值班变电站自动化改造和施工导则”“高压公司无人值班站改造工程新增和更换设备现场运行规程内容增补”(包括10个220千伏无人值班变电站防误闭锁运行规程和计算机监控系统运行规程)、“高压公司防误闭锁装置管理规定”等天津首套220千伏无人站建设、运行管理技术文件，实现技术与管理工作的创新，符合专业管理标准化要求，具有广泛的推广应用价值，促进电网建设的规范管理。至2005年5月，该研究成果指导完成1个监控中心的建设，新建完成4个220千伏无人站和6个220千伏常规站的无人值班改造任务。实现监控中心对10个220千伏无人站的遥测、遥信、遥控、遥调功能和运行管理，为大规模实现220千伏变电站无人值班奠定坚实基础。该项目应用于220千伏无人站的建设，有效节约和降低工程建设投资，提高电力系统安全运行的可靠性，具有重要示范、推广价值。

第二节 发电设备

为保证大容量、高参数发电机组的安全运行，各电厂与科研院所、高等院校合作，围绕稳定满发、节能环保等方面，积极开展研发活动。进一步提高除尘效率和脱硫，在国电第一热电厂、天津大唐国际盘山发电有限责任公司、天津国华盘山发电有限责任公司、天津大港电厂得到应用。一些主要电厂基本实现污水零排放。

一、锅炉系统

1991年，天津第一热电厂与天津电力试验研究所合作研制完成“HG220/100—10型煤粉锅炉浓淡型直流纯体燃烧器”。该燃烧器具有如下功能：①在锅炉额定负荷下运行不结焦，可作为主燃烧器长期连续安全运行；②可节约锅炉点火用油60%～70%；③试验条件下，锅炉出力50%的工况下不投油助燃仍然能稳定燃烧，正常运行锅炉调峰能力增加10%以上；④使锅炉燃烧效率提高1.5%；⑤结构简单，改装一台220吨/时锅炉投资仅约10万元；⑥运行操作方便，检修维护费用低。该项目获1991年度天津市科技进步二等奖。

1992年，天津第一热电厂完成“KBC—1型锅炉灭火保护系统”的研制。该系统主要由C200H可编程控制器、FD—A型火焰检测器及DWER1910系列炉膛压力控制器组成。其安全可靠性强，保护正确动作率100%，火焰检测准确、反应灵敏可靠，显示直观醒目，且系统设备投资少，见效快。

1993年，天津第一热电厂在9号锅炉上进行“TY离子型锅炉除焦、助燃节能素应用性试验”获得成功。对锅炉除垢、防结焦、促燃的效果显著，并能减少烟气中的有害成份。

1994年，天津华能杨柳青发电有限责任公司与天津电力科学研究院合作完成“杨柳青发电厂深度调峰经济性实验”。该实验以正平衡为主、反平衡为辅，达到计量准确，计算精确。对华北电网深度调峰、经济调度，提供可靠数据。确定合理的晚间调峰方式，节约燃料。另外，该厂还完成3号炉集汽联箱寿命损耗微机在线管理系统，加强设备的安全监测和管理。

1995年，天津陈塘庄热电有限责任公司与天津电科院合作完成“提高陈塘庄热电厂电除尘器效率的技术改造”项目。解决锅炉液态排渣加石灰石后粉尘比电阻增加，使除尘效率下降，只能达到约75%的问题，通过改进提高到98.8%，满足环保要求。

同年，天津军粮城发电厂与天津电科院合作，共同完成“200兆瓦机组降低煤耗试验研究及攻关”项目。使该厂200兆瓦机组供电煤耗达到华北网局同类机组先进水平。仅5号、7号机组比1994年降低煤耗7克/千瓦·时，年节标准煤1621吨。1996年，再次联合完成与200兆瓦机组配套的“670吨/时锅炉的高温过热器超温爆管综合治理”，大幅度降低管壁温度，防治锅炉爆管，年创经济效益320万元。同年研究完成的该型锅炉“热风系统改造”，将原有锅炉一次风，改为热风送粉，提高空气预热器利用率，降低排烟温度10℃，提高锅炉效率0.7百分点，年创经济效益34万元。上述两项目均在4台670吨/时锅炉推广应用。2002年和2004年，该厂完成该型锅炉的“深度调峰试验研究”和“锅炉无油启停及助燃方式的研究”，使当时作为天津地区发电主力的4台200兆瓦机组，在安全稳定满发、深度调峰能力和节油、节煤等方面，均创造显著的经济效益和社会效益。

2000年，天津军粮城发电厂和天津第一热电厂、天津电力科学研究院合作完成“锅炉两相流清洗工艺及化学清洗剂的试验研究”项目。清洗工艺在参考国外经验的基础上，对已有的清洗方法进行重大革新。通过大量试验，总结一套当时国内首创的两相流清洗系统和方法，为了使清洗、钝化一次完成，还研究HX—1型化学清洗剂。该工艺节约清洗工时、用水、用药，简化系统，减少大量清洗费用。

二、汽轮机系统

1991年，天津发电检修公司研发完成“不停机带压堵漏技术(含机具改进)”。在不需停机停炉的情况下，在保持压力的管道和压力容器上进行堵漏、消缺，保证安全生产、连续发电。仅1992年和1993年统计，完成114次，减少直接损失3400万元。

1994年，天津军粮城发电厂与天津电科院、西安交通大学、北京计算机中心合作，共同开发完成“军电200兆瓦机组振动在线监测和远距离电话传输诊断系统”。该系统集振动信号分析和智能诊断于一体，应用模糊理论与转子动力学在线分析，能够对振动故障进行综合分析，可对传递、振动、功率、胀差等参数进行监督；对信号进行分析智能诊断，利用电话网络开发计算机远程数据在线传输及反馈处理意见；利用计算机技术开发汽轮机“黑盒子”，能及时记录分析和管理故障信息。该成果2004年获教育部科技进步一等奖。此后，军粮城发电厂又对200兆瓦汽轮发电机进行多项改进：“200兆瓦机组高压加热器随机起停”“200兆瓦机组水处理系统完善化研究及设备系统改进”“200兆瓦机组凝汽器铜管高压水除垢系统”“200兆瓦汽轮发电机氢侧油挡改进”“200兆瓦机组系统稳定装量的研制与应用”“国产200兆瓦汽轮机调节级喷嘴面积优化”“汽轮机组成本在线分析管理系统”以及“提高汽轮机真空严密性测试技术研究”等项目，确保天津电网主力发电机组的安全、稳定运行。

2002年，天津电科院和天津军粮城发电厂共同完成“200兆瓦机组沅江4BP—30型循环泵经济性优化研究”项目。采用新叶型技术和优选水力模型试验相结合，在只更换叶轮不更换其他部件的情况下提高泵效率。采用循环泵大小高效泵配置，开发循环泵经济调度软件，实现计算机在线管理。研究成果适用于大、小容量的所有沅江48P型水泵。经测试：小容量高效水泵提高运行效率达87.67%；大容量高效水泵低速时，最高运行效率达87.44%，流量为13500～18396立方米每时；大容量高效泵高速时，流量可提高到16632～21053立方米每时，提高2000～4800立方米每时。军电200兆瓦机组循环泵，可按不同季节(循环水水温)和不同发电负荷，进行有效地实施最佳经济(成本)调度。同时，这种改进方案投资少，施工简单，经济性强。该项目成果获2000年度天津市技术成果三等奖。

三、发电机系统

1991年，天津军粮城发电厂与天津发电检修公司、天津电力研究所合作完成“水氢气和氢气发电机定子线棒空芯铜线堵塞处理新工艺”。军粮城电厂200兆瓦的5号发电机，因定子引线棒与大联线手包绝缘薄弱，电位外移，发生相间短路后，致使线棒空芯铜线堵塞、深度达80～90毫米以上。该新工艺使用硝酸溶液酸洗发电机定子空芯线，经酸洗疏通后的空芯铜线，仅减薄0.1毫米，流量值达厂家提供值60%以上，不影响安全运行。1992年及1993年，该厂研发完成“ZL—1型发电机氢气除湿器”及“200兆瓦发电机采用冷凝式氢气干燥器”。

1993年，天津华能杨柳青热电厂研制完成“制氢设备防止氢爆控制液位差联锁保护装置”。该成果解决由于压力调整器故障，造成碱液位失常，使氢气中渗入氧气，而发生爆炸危险的可能性。当液位超标时可断电，并有声光报警，提高制氢设备的可靠性。2005年，该厂完成“杨电5号机变组保护改造及故录新增工程”。作为天津市西部电网主力的300兆瓦发电机组，投产时存在的发电机变压器组仍使用原落后的集成电路型保护装置，存在严重事故隐患，也无事故资料的存储功能，威胁该机组的安全稳定运行。该项目完成新微机型发电机变压器组保护，提高设备安全可靠系数，确保主设备稳定运行，防止发生危及天津电网的安全事故。该改造革新工程节约资金80万元。

1997年，天津军粮城电厂与天津电科院、天津大学合作，共同完成“大型汽轮发电机转子及支撑系统非线性振动机理与应用分析软件的研究应用”。课题通过对200兆瓦汽轮发电机组异常振动数据的分析和整理，建立国内第一个非线性振动数据库，提出非线性振动故障产生的原因和防范措施，避免重大事故发生。该成果在军粮城电厂的应用，产生经济效益3088万元，1998年获天津市科技进步二等奖。

2001年，天铁集团热力厂完成新建7.5兆瓦后置发电机组。利用低参数蒸汽发电，实现能源梯级利用，年创经济效益2000万元以上，在国内冶金行业属于首创。该项目获2001年度天津市科技进步三等奖。2002年，该厂完成对1号、2号汽轮发电机组高压加热器回热系统的改造，提高机组热效率，进一步挖掘机组潜力，提高经济效益。2005年3月和9月，该厂先后完成2号、1号汽轮发电机组工艺系统和设备技术开发改造，功率由12兆瓦提升到13兆瓦，热效率提高2%，年创经济效益513万元；同时在机组的原抽汽母管上新增加一条抽汽管道，代替第一锅炉房的减温减压供应焦化厂蒸氨用汽，节约新蒸汽，实现节能降耗和循环经济的要求。

第三节 供电设备

1990年起，天津电网迅速发展，建成一批500千伏和220千伏输、变电项目，增强津电网与华北电网的联接，网架结构更加合理完善，加之实施的城网和农网改造项目的完成，使天津电网的节能环保和供电可靠性得到进一步提高。

1992年，天津市电力工业局供用电处、天津电力试验研究所、汉沽供电局合作研发完成“长效防污闪涂料应用技术”。该成果应用RTV涂料这一防污闪技术措施，可不作任何清扫，在各类污区试运行，设备运行稳定，未发生污闪故障，使设备耐污能力提高1.4～2.0倍。在重污区涂上RTV涂料挂网运行5年多，不作任何清扫，仍运行稳定。经测试，有RTV涂层与无RTV涂层绝缘子雾闪、湿闪电压可分别提高1.6倍和1.3倍，在盐密度相同情况下，起始放电电压可提高1倍。涂有RTV涂层的绝缘子，在干燥状态下，耐受工频电压的能力达到GB775.2-87标准的要求，涂层运行5年不剥落、不龟裂、不起皮，不做完全清除再涂一层，附着力不减。该项目获1997年度华北电管局推广应用技术一等奖。

2003年，天津市电力技术中心(天津电力试验研究所)在长效防污闪RTV涂料基础上，应用纳米级气相二氧化硅技术，开发完成“有色RTV防污闪涂料的研制”。该成果开发出的白色和兰色RTV防污闪涂料，具有良好的电气绝缘性、憎水性、憎水迁移性、抗电蚀性、耐候性和不可燃性，还具有醒目效果，有利于观察，可以提高涂料敷施工质量并避免漏涂，并可避免施工中的火灾危险。该项目获得2003年度天津市科技进步二等奖。

1993年，天津市电力局用电营业处完成“新型脉冲传感器(TDGMC脉冲传感器)”的研制。在电路设计上采用互锁电路，保证摆动时不出现伪脉冲，脉冲数据准确，可靠性高、功率小，各项指标均达到国家标准，获国家专利授权。

1993年，天津电力试验研究所、天津电力局科技处、天津三源电力公司合作研发完成“HB—1型电缆孔洞粉煤灰阻火堵料”。该堵料以粉煤灰为主要原料研制而成，广泛地应用在发电厂和变电站的防火封堵工程中，既环保又防火，年节约费用20余万元。

2002年，天津市电力公司高压供电公司完成“输电线路干字型塔改造”。针对天津地区的110、220千伏输电线路上单回耐张塔多次发生上线吊串撑担及跳线与塔身放电事故，严重威胁电网安全正常运行的情况，该项目对该种塔型的吊串形式进行改造，提高线路的抵御大风能力和健康水平，显著减少故障数量。项目根据天津地区多年来的故障分析，在不破坏原来杆塔的受力结构情况下，通过对杆塔悬点的重新设计，改变挂点形式，将单挂点改为双挂点，将吊串的摆动距离控制在安全范围内，从而提高线路的抗风能力。

2003年，天津市电力公司客户服务中心、用电营销部、科技信息部、生产技术部合作研发完成“天津电力客户服务系统”。该系统将计算机电话集成技术(CTI)、用电MIS、民电MIS系统、车辆GPS、Internet技术以及电网GIS系统集成为一体，涵盖了电力公司对客户的所有用电业务，率先在天津市全市范围内开通了95598

供用电客户服务专线，实现电话、传真、Internet、柜台、触摸屏等多种媒体的受理方式。系统的主要创新点：首次在省级电力公司范围内实现业务流程的规范和统一；在国内首家实现国家电力公司的建设目标，将GPS卫星定位系统应用在电力客户服务中；首次实现网上电力客户服务功能；系统采用工作流程技术和自主开发的中间件软件。该项目成果获2003年度天津市科技进步二等奖。

2003年，天津市电力公司西青供电分公司研究完成“供电企业经营管理决策支持系统”。该系统使用先进的数据库管理及网络资源共享等科技手段，利用数据挖掘技术和企业流程重组技术，对供电企业的业务流程进行再造，实现以信息为中心的供电企业经营管理模式。软件设计根据原有的电力企业主要生产指标之间的逻辑算术关系，建造一系列企业科学化管理的模型。应用C1ient/Server结构，采用人机交互的控制模式，通过对售电量、平均电价、线损率、供电可靠率、固定成本、固定资产6项中间指标的调整与监测，实现了对“利润”的最优控制。在指标的分析过程中，应用了标准比较的评价系统，有效地应用了系统工程的方法，用户可随时进行数据的录入、修改、删除、查询、查看、打印报告书等。同时，通过可靠的理论依据对所输信息及时进行科学的分析，并提供准确的评价及相应的技术方案。该项目获2004年天津市科技进步二等奖。

2005年，天津市电力公司科技信息部、天津市电力公司城东供电分公司合作完成“水树老化XLPE电缆绝缘修复技术研究”。该成果开发电缆修复液和修复液注入系统，主要技术特点：电缆修复液具有成本低、无毒、粘度低、不挥发、难燃、绝缘性能好、与电缆导体及绝缘相容性好等优点；与水聚合反应的生成物为大分子链状聚甲基苯基硅氧烷，是一种绝缘性能良好的硅油类粘稠聚合物；电缆修复液注入系统是一套安全、可靠、易于现场操作和监控、接头工艺简单、施工成本低廉、可带电注液的液体注入系统。电缆修复技术是一种经济、有效和可行的方法，不仅提高了中压XLPE电缆的绝缘水平，延长电缆20年以上的使用寿命，并且可为供电公司省下巨额更换老化电缆的费用。该技术首次对天津市电力公司城东供电分公司一条长为120米，投运超过16年的中压XLPE电缆A相进行了修复。修复液注入全过程用时约3小时，修复半年后对该缆进行了绝缘测试，表明电缆的绝缘水平明显提高。专家评审意见：该成果为延长水树老化XLPE电缆绝缘寿命，提供了实质及突破性的技术方法；实用性强、实施成本低、现场操作简便易行，具有很大的推广潜力。该项成果获得2005年度国家电网公司科技进步三等奖。

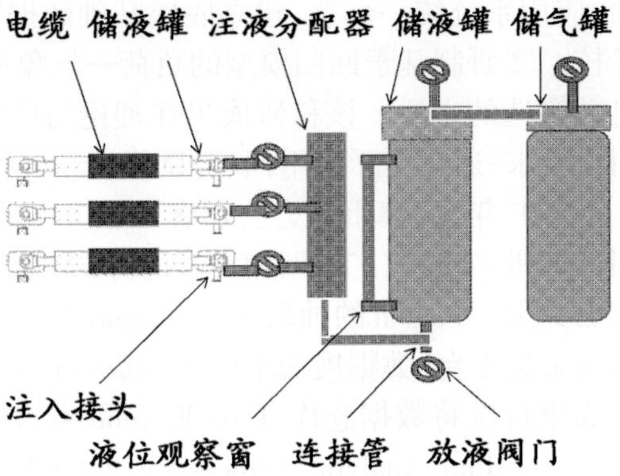

图5-1-3-57 修复液专用装置

第四节 电力管理及调度

1990年后，天津电力局（1989年更名为天津市电力公司）作为天津电网地区电力综合管理部门和电力指挥、调度、监控、协调的调度系统，在电子计算机应用、远动自动化、通讯和继电保护自动装置等方面迈上新的台阶。

一、计算机应用

1991年，天津电力系统开发成功“电力系统在线运行数据引入管理信息系统”。改变计算机的单机应用和专业单项开发的方式，构建起局域网，使MIS的推广使用得到有力支持。1992年，天津电力局MIS系统进一步实现深层次开发和应用,获国务院电力办公室颁发的优秀项目奖。

1993年,天津电力系统生产运行、电网调度,经营管理等各个方面广泛应用计算机,电网经济效益和安全运行水平有效提高。天津电力局的“天津电力物资管理系统”,1993年获得第二届青年科技博览会优秀参展项目奖;“全局联网通讯系统”1994年获华北电管局管理现代化成果三等奖;“发电厂峰谷电量采信系统”1995年获华北电管局管理现代化成果三奖,并获天津市科技成果证书;1996年,在全国首批通过国家电力公司的MIS实用化验收;同年,“生产通用统计软件”获华北电管局现代化管理成果三等奖及天津市科技成果证书,“人事管理软件”获华北电管局现代化管理成果三等奖,“线损管理软件”获华北电管局现代化管理成果三等奖和天津市科技成果证书,“物资管理软件”获华北电管局现代化管理成果三等奖;“电费管理”获1998年天津市科技成果证书;2000年,“无纸化办公系统”“广域网工程”“用电管理系统”“电力故障承询抢修系统”等获天津市电力公司管理创新成果奖。

2005年,天津市电力公司电力营销部和北京清软创新科技有限公司合作研发完成“基于ATM广域网构建电力市场分析预测系统”。该研究以加强和规范电力市场分析预测工作,提高分析水平和预测深度为目标,主要内容包括:①在ATM网络平台上开发电力系统年、月、日负荷预测的一体化系统,采用数据集中存储、应用系统统一部署,建立底层基础数据统一平台;将预测工作分散与集中相结合,对预测管理工作集中考核。②研制基于回归模型的负荷—气象敏感度分析方法。③根据预测对象的特点,研制从预测模型库中自动筛选的方法。该科研成果在理论与应用方面均达到国内领先水平;经过一年多开发和试运行,达到实用化要求;通过实际应用,取得显著的经济和社会效益。

2005年,天津市电力公司客户服务中心研发完成“天津电力客户服务分析、决策支持系统”。该研究采用计算机局域网、广域网相结合的方式,服务器采用UNIX AIX网络操作系统和Oracle9i数据库管理系统,开发工具采用Sagent的抽取工具、Cognos展现工具和门户。客服分析、决策支持系统,由主机系统、备份系统、数据采集平台、数据展现平台等组成,可以实现与各种数据库连接,高速准确地整合各系统数据的功能。研究成果首次将数据仓库(Data Warehouse,DW)技术、数据采集(Extract Transform Load,ETL)技术、联机分析处理(On-Line Analytical Processing,OLAP)技术,应用到电力客户服务分析、决策支持系统中;整合了客服系统、用电MIS系统、民电MIS系统、调度SCADA系统等系统的数据;实现了投诉举报、咨询查询、系统话务、抢修调度、停电信息、居民户表、业扩报装、日常营业、业务费用、客户档案、电量电费、电网运行、系统使用状况、大事记等15项主题功能;每个主题通过即席查询、固定报表或多维分析三种方式来展现;通过系统提供的分析手段,可以发现客户服务生产中的规律,为指导生产提供辅助支持;为天津市电力公司各项客户服务业务的查询、统计、分析等提供了准确、便捷的工具。该系统被推广到天津市电力公司各相关管理部门以及各供电(分)公司。以上研究成果当年获天津市电力公司科技成果一等奖。

二、电力调度及远动自动化

1991年,天津电力局调度处与天津天学合作研发完成“电力监控系统软件(SCADA)”。该软件是基于消化吸收引进的SCADA系统研制出来的,软件规模大(源码5兆字节),定时性强(2至5秒即可反应出电网数据变化并显示画面),可靠性高。整个软件分五大部分:数据采集和预处理;实时数据库;历史数据库;人机界面;外围功能。从而具备各级调度自动化系统的基本功能。继而完成“综合自动化远动装置”(简称“综自”)的研制,将微机通信网络、测量控制等技术融合为一体,可以根据电网的需要,进行不同功能模块的设计组合。与常规的远动装置和继电保护装置相比,不仅具有体积小、性能高等优点,而且能为电网安全运行管理及事故分析提供灵活、可靠的分析手段。从1995年至2005年年底,天津电网调度局自动化处和继电保护处配合“四方公司”“东方电子集团”及“南京南瑞公司”,在天津电网35~500千伏系统中,安装、投运80多套“综自”装置,取得了很好的效果。

1994年,天津城区供电公司研发完成“城区35千伏变电站‘四遥’集控系统”。此系统是集变电站远动化、数据通信自动化、计算机应用技术为一体的系统工程,是为减少变电站值班人员数量,减轻值班人员劳动强度,实现“无人值班”变电站的科技成果。

2005年,天津市电力公司调度中心研发完成“电网调度运行过程管理系统”。该系统充分考虑电网调度运行专业工作要求，引入项目管理思想和图形化的管理工具，利用Cantt图、日历图、网络图、资源图表、文本引擎搜索等工具，对电网异常方式、日志记录、电厂运行等与电网运行管理密切相关的各方面，进行图形化的管理及统计、分析，通过文字、图形和报表等形式，清晰明确地表达和传递出电网运行和管理的信息。

三、继电保护及安全自动装置

1991年，天津电力局继电保护处与杨柳青电厂及南京自动化研究院合作，配合杨柳青发电厂压油工程，开发出具有自适功能的"微机型母线保护(BP—1型)"，获电力部1991年度科技进步二等奖。

1992年，天津电网结合天津无缝钢管工程，在220千伏北民双回线及民钢双回线上，安装12套从英国GEC公司进口的LF—CB—102型数字式分相电流差动保护。通过数字微波、复合架空地线光缆(OPGW)和数字微波和光纤组合的64千比特/秒通道，完成保护数据的传输，使得6条220千伏同杆并架双回线路，实现按相快速跳闸。此项技术在当时全国电网中，属于先进水平。

2005年，天津市电力公司调度通讯中心研发完成"天津电网图形化整定计算软件"。该图形化整定计算软件分为图形建模、故障计算、整定计算、保护定值仿真、数据管理5大功能模块。图形建模(主接线图、电抗图)工具，方便快捷，真正达到工具级水平，在天津电网35千伏以上一次系统图全部绘制完成；故障分析，可以任意设置运行方式，计算速度快，输出数据齐全，结果正确；保护整定，既可手动整定，允许用户参与，处理一些特殊情况，又可自动整定，快速输出全部定值，两者有机结合，提高整定计算工作的效率；仿真功能，可检验保护定值，提高定值的准确性；数据管理功能，包含有各种设备数据，查询方式灵活，能够满足各种要求；仿真功能，可检验保护定值的正确性，提高定值的准确性。

四、电力通讯

1990年后，通信传输技术和交换技术从模拟化向数字化跨越，实现从依靠电力载波、明线载波、电缆载波、音频电缆为手段，发展到以数字微波、光纤为主要传输手段的转变。1991年年底，天津电网建成综合业务城域网，为电力公司和发电、供电、用电部门之间进行数据、图像、信息交换等提供更深更广的服务。

1992年，天津市电力公司承担安装民生村220千伏变电站至无缝钢管厂的光纤通讯系统。该系统为两回复合架空地线光缆(OPGW)，是引进英国BICC公司的光缆产品。1993年，该工程建成投运。通过工程实施，培养设计、施工和管理人才，为以后天津地区光纤通信发展提供技术准备。

1995年，天津市电力公司完成承建盘山发电厂至天津北郊500千伏变电站的500千伏输电线路的建设任务。国内第一条90千米长、无中继OPGW光缆投入运行。

1996年，天津电力公司应用于调度中心机房到调度综合楼22层的622兆比特(STMI)光纤系统建成。该系统从日本富士通公司引进，是天津第一套SDH技术设备，经电力公司调度通信处的配合、安装调试，运行稳定、可靠。该设备速率高、容量大、性能优越，上下电路方便，网络管理先进，设备维护量小。

1998~1999年，城域网完成24个区段、约80余千米的新敷设光缆。至此，天津地区电力通信光缆总数达到1000千米，步入全国电力系统先进行列。

1998~2000年，天津电力系统经过几年的技术准备(选择、引进、安装、调试)，正式完成并投运"ATM数据通信网技术"。实现天津电力系统不同业务的综合利用，在全国电力系统成为最先集用的地区之一。

2000年，天津市电力公司调度中心承担完成"EMS应用软件开发"。该项目是基于国内自主版权的、优秀的CC2000系统软件平台研制开发而成，在该平台上完成实用化的EMS应用软件，在国内是第一家。该成果在原有EMS功能的基础上，增加易于维护的功能，使EMS软件使用有更好的技术支持：①建立网络模型时采用与SCADA系统相同的关键字，以保证数据的唯一性；②所有电力系统设备参数信息，数据源与天津电力调度中心MIS设备参数共享信息；③定义天津电网网络拓扑结构，计算范围包括所有电厂和110千伏以上变电站，实现各种元件与SCADA的描述自动对应功能等几项实用的功能。该项目获得公司科技成果一等奖。

2004年，天津市电力公司调度通信中心研发完成"天津电力调度数据专网建设"项目。该成果使天津电力调度数据专网工程网络设备及网管软件等，全部使用华北公司的产品；建设1个核心点（调度通信中心）、8个骨干点、汇聚其他52个接入节点，实现各供电分公司和调通中心的计算机通信、电量采集数据、调度实时信息、保护故障录波信息的接入；数据专网工程中采用OSPF、BGP、MPLS VPN、QOS等技术和各种有效的网络安全手段，保障和实现数据专网安全、稳定、可靠的运行。数据专网工程具有良好的扩展性，为数据专网的扩展提供良好的基础，并采用网络管理软件，提供完善的网络服务功能。专网采用的MPLS VPN技术，不仅提高网络的传输效率，还加强保密性，网络传输速率也由以往的300比特每秒增加到190千比特每秒以上，成为电网运行重要信息交换的支撑平台。该项目获公司科技成果一等奖。

2005年，天津市城东供电分公司与天津市三源电力设计制造有限公司合作研发完成"基于无线虚拟专网的配电网综合监控系统"。其主要研究内容为：基于GPRS无线虚拟专网的配电网综合监控系统的合理架构；GPRS通信网络的构建和GPRS通信终端产品的开发应用；一次开关设备增加遥测、遥信、遥控的技术改造等。成果包括：研制功能完善、性能可靠、适用于配电网应用的核心设备—SY701型GPRS通信终端1；开发配套的数据中心系统，与GPRS通信终端配合，解决通信可靠性和安全性问题；可以统一实现配电网数据的采集，较好地解决通信实时性问题；统一整合FTU、配电监测仪、台区表、故障指示器等配电网现存的多种监控测量终端，实现信道共享，提高系统的经济性。

第五节　电力信息技术

20世纪90年代后，天津电力信息网络建设得到快速发展，逐渐实现全方位信息服务、信息交流与共享，成为加强科技管理、推动科技进步的重要手段。

1991年，天津电力试验研究所承担完成"天津电力系统图集"的研究。成果获天津电力局情报信息一等奖及天津市最佳科技情报信息三等奖。

1992年，天津汉沽供电局开发完成"汉沽供电局微机网络信息管理系统"。该系统是利用原有计算机资源组成D—LINK网络基础上建立的，投资少，见效快，实用性强，结构简单合理；开发周期短，运行速度快，运行稳定可靠。该系统软件通过微机网络实现"由材料科领料→供电所运行→生技科结算→财务科形成资产"的一条龙资产管理体系。

1992年，天津、北京、河北、山西、内蒙5个电研所共同承担完成"200兆瓦火电机组科技资料专集"项目；1994年共同完成"200兆瓦火电机组故障对策"项目。两项合作成果均获当年华北电管局新技术推广应用一等奖。1996年，上述成果又获国家电力公司三等奖。该两项成果对全国200兆瓦火力发电机组的安全稳定运行和故障诊断、处理及检修均有指导意义，成果报告、资料等向国内各电力部门发行。

1996年，天津市电力公司高压供电公司开发完成"变电运行设备信息网络管理系统"。该成果的创新点在于通过变电站一次主接线图，实现对数据资料的管理，把图形技术和数据库技术有机地结合起来，使用直观、方便、高效。该系统投入运行后，使得固定资产管理、备品备件管理计算机化成为可能。该系统在华北电管局、电力部及直属7个供电单位统一推广使用。

1999年，天津市电力公司人事部、天津市电力公司高压供电公司和天津市电力公司信息中心共同开发完成"天津市电力公司干部人事管理多媒体信息网络系统"。该系统能有效实现人事管理网络化、信息化，使实现人事管理由单机管理向网络化管理转变，由数据分散冗余管理向数据共享转变，由计算机辅助管理向信息化管理转变。

2004年，天津市电力公司技术中心蔡天羽、石枫、徐力等开发完成"信息资源系统完善及安全运行"项目。该成果使面向广域网系统的科技信息资源检索及管理应用更加安全、方便、快捷。配置高速扫描仪和专门识别管理软件，可以将全院的基础数据扫描建库存纳入基础管理，省时省力且规范化，供全局共享。

2005年，天津市电力公司研发完成“关键业务异地容灾系统”。成果技术特点和创新主要体现在：①SAN体系结构的应用简化容灾中心的存储结构，便于存持容量的平滑升级；②充分利用天津电力ATM广域网提供的网络多路径负载均衡功能，为容灾机房提供可靠的链路保证，同时还提供负载均衡的能力，即使在高负载的情况下，也能保证网络的畅通；③采用Oracle数据提供的RAC和DataGuard技术，充分保证业务的连续性。查新的结果表明，该技术是首次在国内实际应用系统中得到使用。DataGuard技术的成功应用，使整个容灾系统可以相对较低的建设成本达到保障数据完整和业务连续的目的；④针对每种不同的业务，提出不同的容灾策略和方法，较好地解决对异构系统和异构数据库进行容灾的技术难题。同年，该公司还研发完成“电力企业知识管理与信息集成平台”项目；与浙江大学快威智能软件有限公司共同研发出“集中生产管理信息系统”。以上成果，均获2005年度电力公司科技一等奖。

2005年，天津市民用电力发展公司开发完成“天津市电力民用电管理信息”。该系统是面向天津市城镇、农村居民用电管理领域的综合性管理平台，业务管理范围涵盖居民户表业务、售电业务、机械表实时收费、低压（10千伏及以下）用户抄核收的管理、台区的管理、工作质量的管理考核等。作为天津市电力公司“数字化企业”建设的重要系统之一，该系统管理全市260.07万用户（城镇、农村），日均实时处理数据11万余条，日均点击量13万余次，系统总体运行效果良好。天津电力民用电管理信息系统作为国内第一个专门面向居民用电管理领域的省级综合业务管理系统，是国内居民用电管理信息化建设的先例。系统在对居民用电管理信息化特点进行深入分析的基础上，结合国际上先进的计算机技术、网络技术、通讯技术和图形技术，以工作流和安全交易为核心，实现天津市居民用电信息的操作自动化、信息资源化、传输网络化、管理科学化。系统依托天津市电力公司的ATM广域网，实现与客服系统、用电MIS系统、计量系统的数据共享，外部实现与中国银行、交通银行、农业银行、工商银行、商业银行、光大银行、招商银行共7家银行、531个收费网点、235个售电网点的实时数据处理，达到数据安全共享、信息及时沟通的目的。

2005年6月，“供电企业资产管理与决策支持信息系统”由天津大学机械学院王洪礼、安德洪、王立春等完成，并通过鉴定。该系统分为工程管理子系统、资产管理子系统和基本信息管理子系统。系统采用C/S模式构建，采用4GL语言与面向对象技术结合，以Microsoft SQL Server 2000作为数据库工具，采用Microsoft ADO相关技术作为数据引擎和基于TCP/IP协议的网络通讯技术。该系统首次重新定义了供电线路资产统计的最小单位，并解决了随之而来的套件自动划归与各种工程费用向资产单位上的合理分摊，保证资产部分变动（如线路频繁的切改、分割）后的准确性与及时性，从而避免了资产虚增和造成的帐、卡、物不一致。该系统将供电企业工程管理纳入资产管理范畴，智能化地记录并控制工程项目从计划申报到决算上帐的资产整个形成过程，克服了分块管理信息孤立的局限性，构筑了资产管理的一体化信息平台。该系统将科学的投资决策方法如模糊综合评判、多目标决策及循环决策过程引入资产形成（项目决策）过程中，提高了项目投资决策的科学性，保证了投入产出比最大化。

2005年底，天津大唐国际盘山发电有限责任公司“信息化盘电”科技与管理创新项目完成。盘电信息化千兆网络设计先进，员工在生活区可以登陆公司信息化平台办公；数据库系统高度统一，采用B/S模式及三层架构；高效的应用系统，率先在全国电力系统实施D7I企业资产管理系统、FMIS财务管理系统，智能燃料系统，实现重要系统间数据流、工作流、信息化、资金流的接口；成功实施SIS系统，并与管理信息系统衔接；建立包括“计算机信息系统运行维护管理标准”“计算机信息系统安全管理标准”“信息化项目管理标准”“WEB综合查询系统管理标准”“D7I应用管理标准”“OA系统管理标准”、电话及视频会议管理标准”的管理标准体系。

第二章　石　油

大港油田勘探范围北起涧河，南至吴桥，西到天津里坦凹陷东缘，东至渤海5米水深线，加上沧县隆起东半部及天津—青县一线，总面积18629平方千米，其中陆地面积16499平方千米，滩海极浅海面积2130平方千米，包括潮涧带面积450平方千米，极浅海面积1680平方千米，海岸线长146千米。20世纪90年代初开始，大港油田勘探工作的部署原则是“深化陆地，加快滩海，积极开拓新领域”，通过推广应用油藏早期描述技术和新的井筒工艺技术，力争有较大的发现和较高的经济效益。1990年至1996年共钻井306口，进尺92.34万米。发现或探明陆地和海域15个含油气构造或油气田，新增石油地质储量19833万吨，天然气地质储量84.36亿立方米。“九五”“十五”期间，老油田开发进入后期，面临越来越大的困难。主要问题是：采出程度高达78%；水淹严重，油田平均含水率高达87.9%；剩余油可采储量的采油速度高达11%；剩余油分布零散，地下油水关系分布异常复杂；自然递减高达17.1%，挖潜难度大，增产措施效果差。针对上述问题，大力强化以“增储稳产、降本增效”为核心的科技创新活动，取得长足进步，高成熟探区精细勘探技术，极浅海勘探开发技术，地质综合评价技术，油气层保护技术，凝析油气藏开发配套技术，复杂断块油田高含水后期精细油藏描述技术，石油工程技术，采油工艺技术，地面工程技术，三次采油技术，油气勘探开发信息应用技术等，均获得很好的应用和完善，为油田稳产增储做出重要贡献。2004年大港油田原油产量突破488万吨，2005年再创历史新高，达到509.95万吨，并生产天然气3.32亿立方米，油气当量达到536.4万吨。

第一节　油气勘测

大港油气勘探工作从油气生成理论出发，充分运用新理论、新技术、新方法，开展油气生成的地质条件、沉积储层评价、油气富集规律、油气成藏机理等多方面的研究。到2005年，大港探区建成具有一定生产规模的大型油气区，在坳陷范围内发现多种油气藏类型。

一、油气地质勘探

（一）生油理论

1991年，勘探开发研究院廖前进等完成“黄骅裂谷盆地油气生成与资源潜力研究”课题。以大量第一手资料为基础，以凹陷为评价单元、分层系研究生油岩的分布规律及有机质丰度、类型和演化，从平面上和剖面上揭示生油岩的一系列特征。建立孔二段、沙三段、沙一段等重点生油层系的综合地球化学演化剖面；分凹陷进行生油层级别的划分和盆地有机质演化阶段的划分；系统总结盆地内多种类型原油、天燃气的地球化学特征；首次发现盆地内存在四种类型未熟、低熟油，提出这四种类型未熟、低熟油的形成分别具有不同的地质条件，在封闭、半封闭的环境下沉积有机质及时保存并经历长时期低温演化作用是其生成的基本地质条件，而生油岩中易于早期演化产烃的特殊有机组分的存在决定其成油类型。从有机质演化机理上完善传统的干酪根晚期热降解成油学说，并深入进行盆地内各凹陷和地区的油源及生油层排烃和运移的研究，明确主力供油层系与潜在的生油层系，总结出油气初次运移是以侧向运移为主和二次运移沿断层作阶梯状侧向运移，确定最新数字化积分计算方法进行资源量预测并提出勘探方向。

1994年，勘探开发研究院廖前进等完成“歧口凹陷偏腐泥型气源岩资源潜力及成藏条件”课题。全面进行包括深层在内的烃源岩演化规律和成烃特征研究，总结歧口凹陷烃源岩成气演化模式，建立偏腐泥型气源岩的判识标准。明确凹陷内天燃气具有多种成因类型，共分布有五大系列八种类型的天燃气。采用二维盆地模拟和数字化积分方法，系统地论证凹陷内分层系、分地区天然气资源及剩余资源分布，并在成藏条件分析的基础上，明确有利勘探目标和有利含气(油)区带，为勘探部署提供依据。

1997年，勘探开发研究院曹延等完成“歧口凹陷北部滩海区上第三系及东营组含油评价与钻探目标评价”课题。从生油、构造、储层方面以大量钻井地质、地震及有机地球化学、沉积储层等多项资料为基础，深入系统地研究歧口凹陷北部滩海区上第三系及东营组的基本石油地质条件，总结已知油气藏特征及富集规律，进行区带评价及圈闭评价。明确东营组下段为好生油岩，具有一定生烃潜力；明确多种圈闭类型提供油气聚集的良好场所；多种断裂组合形式，为油气提供运移通道，断裂活动的多期性，控制油气聚集的阶段性。在对有利区带进行综合含油评价中，优选6个圈闭为近期钻探目标。该项目对在滩海区寻找中浅层油气藏提供重要的地质依据。

1999年，勘探开发研究院廖前进等完成“黄骅坳陷未成熟油-低成熟油成因类型与成藏条件研究”课题。对未熟~低熟油的成因机制、成藏条件及模式进行研究，重点探讨未熟、低熟油成烃机理，论述黄骅坳陷四种未熟~低熟油成因类型的形成特点，解剖孔二段烃源岩层研究其有机岩石学特征、热演化特征，提出自然演化中早期可溶烃类以原生沥青形式由生化和低温热解作用成烃的新认识。应用盆地模拟和化学动力学评价方法，对各地区不同层系烃源岩定量计算未熟、低熟油的生烃量及资源量数据，明确探区内未熟、低熟油四级资源储量(含探明、控制、预测、潜在)，提供可优选的5个重点勘探目标。其勘探成果显著，经济效益突出，对加强浅层未熟、低熟油勘探，开辟找油新领域具有重要的指导意义。

2001年，勘探开发研究院曹延等完成“大港探区南皮、盐山、吴桥生油潜力评价及勘探方向优选”课题。全面系统地开展南皮、盐山、吴桥凹陷基本地质构造特征、地层分布特征研究，明确各凹陷分别属于三种不同类型的沉积凹陷。采用有机岩石学和有机地球化学相结合的方法，建立各凹陷生烃演化模式，明确各凹陷沙河街组具有一定的生烃能力，均属于未熟、低熟生油凹陷。运用多因素油源精细对比技术，总结该地区油气生成条件、成藏条件及油气富集规律，指出油气运移方向，明确孔南地区沙三段原油主要来自孔二段生油层，部分来自沙三段原油混入，孔二段油气运移聚集期晚于圈闭形成期，有利于油气聚集成藏；盐北地区原油具备自生自储能力，油气以短距离运移成藏为主；吴桥凹陷具备油气聚集条件。

2002年，勘探开发研究院何咏梅等完成“黄骅坳陷第三次油气资源评价”课题。完成黄骅坳陷石油地质基础研究、刻度区解剖与参数研究、盆地及区带油气资源综合评价、数据库和图形库建设，实现油气资源评价方法、评价标准、管理模式与国际接轨，提交一套比较符合实际、可信度较高的资源评价结果。进一步深化对大港探区石油地质条件和油气富集规律的研究，建立一套适合大港探区地质条件与国际接轨的资源评价方法体系，形成一套包括成因法、统计法、类比法，适合不同勘探程度区、不同地质需要的油气资源评价方法体系和参数体系，全面落实大港探区的油气资源，并提供一批有利勘探区带和目标，为勘探可持续发展提供决策依据，为油气资源滚动评价奠定基础。

2004年，勘探开发研究院王书香等完成“大港探区中浅层烃源岩评价与资源潜力研究”课题。从油气生成理论出发，运用新理论、新技术、新方法系统地分析中浅层烃源岩有机地球化学和有机岩石学特征，明确东三段~沙一中烃源岩属于优质烃源岩，确定一套有效区分中、浅层及深层各套烃源岩生物标志物等地球化学指标判识标准，建立中浅层生烃演化模式。提出中、浅层有一定烃类生成，其生烃门限随不同区域而发生变化，均属于未熟~低熟演化阶段；总结该区油气生成条件、成藏条件及油气富集规律；对典型油气藏、多油源复合型油气藏进行精细对比，明确中浅层可疑油气及混源油气的油源，确定油气运移方向，合理有效地确定排烃系数，明确中浅层油气资源规模，有利于开辟、扩大找油新领域。

（二）沉积与储层

黄骅坳陷裂谷盆地的演化经历初始裂陷期、裂陷期、裂陷衰减期和坳陷期等4个阶段。其中，盆地裂陷期形成的古近系沙河街组，在黄骅坳陷乃至整个渤海湾盆地一直是油气勘探的重要目的层之一，主要为一套富含烃源岩及湖相砂泥岩组合。经过不断引进新技术、新方法，以不同的研究手段、不同的研究角度，对沉积与储层进行深入探讨，取得多方面的研究成果，为指导黄骅坳陷的油气勘探发挥重要作用。

1991年，勘探开发研究院安文武等完成"黄骅坳陷歧口凹陷海滩~及浅海地区第三系沉积体系和构造特征及含油气评价"课题。重点从地层划分对比，沉积体系展布与储层评价，构造断裂特征及含油气评价等方面进行较系统的论述。对东一段底界划分、沙二段地层统层问题得到统一，趋于合理；地质解释有多个水下扇、三角洲、扇三角洲及网状河流沉积体系，物源来自北、中、南三个方向，且西部沧县隆起物源在北大港构造带占主导因素；岩石类型主要为长石砂岩及岩屑砂岩两类；孔隙类型主要为原生粒间孔和次生溶蚀孔，孔隙结构有粗孔均匀、不均匀，细孔均匀、不均匀，及微细孔不均匀喉道型五种类型交替出现；生长断层是该区的主要断裂，其控制局部构造的形成、发育及沉积体系的展布；构造低部位或凹陷中的水下扇沉积体系发育，是寻找非构造油气藏的有力场所。

1992年，勘探开发研究院郑浚茂等完成"黄骅坳陷中北部沉积与储层评价"课题。从层序地层学的角度对中北区沉积体系进行研究。重点针对板桥~北大港构造带的沉积类型进行分析，指出第三系受北部燕山和西北侧沧县隆起两大物源控制，局部地区受港西古隆起的影响，形成水下扇、重力流水道、三角洲等多种类型的储集体。沙三段沉积时为盆地发育的扩张深陷期，远离物源区，形成浊积扇和浊积水道沉积；沙二段地层不整合于沙三段之上，水体浅，主要发育沿岸滩坝砂沉积；沙一段发育三个沉积层序，主要沉积类型为扇三角洲、滨浅湖和重力流水道沉积。

1996年，勘探开发研究院、石油学校周滨燕等共同完成"大港探区板桥~驴驹河地区细分沉积相与储层特征研究"课题。通过对板桥-驴驹河地区沙一中和沙一下小层砂组的沉积相及砂体分布特征的研究，明确各油组在横向上处在扇中主体亚相的沙体，储集性能好于扇中前缘亚相中砂体。其中重力流水道微相中的砂体储集性能最好；纵向上3500米以内砂体次生孔隙发育，储集性能较好，溶蚀作用是影响储油物性的主要因素，水的溶蚀淋滤作用导致砂岩孔隙度上升；断裂作用使断层附近裂缝发育，从而提高砂岩的渗透性。

1998年，勘探开发研究院张立勤等完成"大港探区前第三系沉积体系与储层评价研究"课题。综合运用新方法，从宏观上描述前第三系主要目的层的沉积体系与储层分布状况，对储层控制因素进行较全面的分析。建立探区内上古生界碎屑岩和下古生界碳酸盐岩的储层划分标准，指出有利目的层组和有利区带；运用高分辨层序地层学新方法，解决难度较大的下石盒子组地层小段划分问题；重新拟订本溪组分层，提出以溶孔为主的储集空间与岩溶发育有一定的关系，明确岩溶具有顺层发育的特点。这一结论为奥陶系风化壳可达上马家沟顶提供依据，同时确定上古生界各组地层的储层分布概况，认为上石盒子组最为有利，山西组次之，太原组和本溪组有利区较为局限。

2002年，勘探开发研究院滑双君等承担完成"黄骅坳陷中北区沙一下碳酸盐岩沉积与储层特征研究"。通过对该区不同油组沉积体系展布，沉积相类型，储层类型特征及主控因素的综合分析，明确老区勘探潜力，指出有利储集相带，为含油综合评价提供地质依据，其主要成果：①利用内源、外源沉积特征相结合的方法，系统地划分沙一下碳酸盐岩沉积相类型，并识别出该区滨湖岸滩亚相的存在；②深入分析湖相碳酸盐岩形成的控制因素，量化沙一下沉积时期地形坡度的计量；③尝试性地建立湖相碳酸盐岩储层评价标准，指出齐家务~孔店西坡可作为继王徐庄、周清庄两个油田之外的有利勘探区。

2004年，勘探开发研究院滑双君等承担完成"黄骅坳陷重点层系沉积体系研究—中北区沙三段沉积体系研究"。以层序地层为起点，建立等时地层格架，在此基础上，研究沉积体系特征，识别沉积相类型，进而完成细分层组沉积相平面展布特征。主要成果：建立古近系高精度层序地层格架体系；明确沙三段沉积时期的物源方向及波及范围；提出辫状河三角洲的相的概念并识别出该区辫状河三角洲的存在及分布范围；提出浅水滑塌体沉积相类型；重新厘定滩砂概念；深入系统地分析储层的影响因素，预测有利储层发育区。

该项研究对勘探有重要的指导意义。

（三）油气富集规律

1991年，勘探开发研究院田克勤等承担完成“黄骅裂谷盆地油气聚集规律及勘探方向”。在构造特征、沉积储层、油气生成、油气分布规律、资源评价等专题研究成果的基础上，重点围绕大港探区资源潜力，今后勘探领域和勘探目标区进行综合研究和综合评价。系统总结黄骅坳陷断陷盆地复式油气区（带）、复式油气藏形成的基本地质条件，综合研究和评价黄骅中南区中生界、沙河街组及滩海区新近系三大领域油藏形成条件和预测有利含油区带，确定重点区带油气富集类型及分布规律，明确黄骅坳陷油气分布在空间上具有南北分区的特点；中北部复式油气藏围绕生油中心，呈向心式环带状分布；孔店南部复式油气区油藏呈雁列式带状分布；纵向上油气藏呈多层楼式结构；提出8个寻找富集区带的有利勘探目标。发现和落实有利圈闭144个，成果陆续应用于油田新增油气储量的需要。

1992年，勘探开发研究院梁复华等承担完成的“黄骅坳陷上第三系油气分布规律及找油方向”，系统地对黄骅坳陷上第三系油藏形成条件及含油特征进行分析。指出长期继承性的深大生油凹陷是形成上第三系油藏的基础；长期发育的同沉积断层是油气运移的主要通道；河道砂体是上第三系油气聚集的良好储集空间；浅层圈闭是油气藏形成的决定因素；明确上第三系油藏以逆牵引背斜油藏及披覆构造油藏为主，具有构造简单、含油规模大、含油井段长储油物性好的特点。明确歧口滩海区是寻找上第三系油藏的重要地区，埕西地区是上第三系新区勘探的主要目标。

1995年，勘探开发研究院付立新等承担完成的“大港滩海区成藏条件研究及重点目标区含油评价”，研究探讨滩海区油气聚集规律、构造样式空间展布规律及主要形成机制。分析认为，多数构造带不具备单一的构造样式，主要表现为不同期次变形叠加的特点，并在滩海区划分出6种主要的构造样式类型；提出滩海地区油气分区聚集及大型断裂侧接段富含油气的规律性认识，逆牵引及带扭性特点的构造组合为区内主要的聚油构造。

图5-2-1-58　中国石油大港油田勘探开发研究院陈松等完成的大港油田南部滩海油气富集规律与预探突破获得2005年度天津市科技进步一等奖

1998年，勘探开发研究院张兵等承担完成“歧口凹陷深层油气富集规律研究与目标优选”。从油气分布现状入手，运用沉积及横向断鼻模式、成岩圈闭、毛细管圈闭模式，分析总结油气藏类型、分布规律及有利成藏条件。明确歧口凹陷下第三系油气资源非常丰富，存在多种油气藏类型；异常高压的存在为深层油气聚集提供有利的储集空间，同时指出同沉积断层下降盘大型背斜及断鼻构造部位油气最为富集；主断层上升盘根部反向断鼻断块构造油气富集；凹陷区及斜坡带砂体发育区油气较为富集，并指出下步勘探方向。

2000年，勘探开发研究院李淑恩等承担完成“白唐马滩海区沙一段油气高产富集规律与勘探部署方案研究”。围绕“寻找油气富集高产区”，以研究区现有地质资料为基础，以精细地层对比、构造精细解释为起点，以储层横向预测技术、压力预测技术、应力场模拟技术为手段，应用地质概念模型的新技术指导油气富集规律的研究。明确白唐马滩海区不同地区、不同层系油气富集高产控制因素，指出白水头、唐家河—马东东地区地质特征不同，造就不同的油气富集高产规律；白水头地区中高产能井均位于构造较高部位；唐家河—马东东地区油气分布主要受储层分布控制。构造控制着油气聚集，而油气的富集高产主要受储层、裂缝、异常高压控制。其后，中国石油大港油田集团有限责任公司进行的“大港油田陆上高成熟探区千米桥潜山大型凝析气藏成藏系统与勘探”项目获得2000年度国家科技进步一等奖。

2001年，勘探开发研究院李红香等承担完成“板桥-北大港地区中浅层油气富集规律与勘探潜力研究”。该项目本着理论联系实际，科研与生产紧密结合的原则，在开展成藏条件及油气富集规律研究基础上，通过对构造、沉积储层、油气藏特征精细研究，明确中浅层油气分布受生油凹陷、油源断层、圈闭、储层分布等因素控制；指出沈清庄~齐家务地区存在三种油气来源；即本地未熟-低熟油气、远距离运移的成熟油气和深大断裂运移的无机成因气。在对浅层目标评价中引入亮点技术，在港西北坡明化镇组发现一类亮点20个；利用全三维地震解释技术开展精细构造解释，在构造重新落实的基础上，部署实施11口井，获工业油气流井9口，高产油气流井2口，成效显著。

2002年，勘探开发研究院李红香等承担完成的“陆上中北区油气富集规律及目标优选”，系统总结油气成藏分布规律和富集高产控制因素。深化油气富集规律的研究，开展油气藏综合评价，发现多个一定规模的油气田和富集高产区块，进一步完善该区中浅层油气分布规律的认识。指出板桥~北大港构造带中浅层油气主要来自于板桥和歧口凹陷，油气分布规律主要表现为：①受同生断层控制，生油凹陷存在内环与外环两个含油带；②油气主要富集在断层发育区及断层形变强烈区；③圈闭类型以背斜圈闭最能富集中浅层油气；④中北区油气具有“东富西贫，南北差异”的特点。

2003年，勘探开发研究院王东林等承担完成“南部油区油气富集规律及目标优选”。从解剖南部油区长期面临的勘探生产难题入手，更新找油模式，深化对中生界沉积储层的研究，系统开展孔一段枣Ⅳ油组成藏特征分析，精细解剖孔西断裂系及断棱带油藏分布特征。明确断棱带油气在平面上沿主断层呈狭长带状分布，纵向上呈多油水系统迭置产出复式聚集的成藏模式，断层转换带是良好的流体泄压区，利于油气成藏。

2004年，勘探开发研究院郝立华等承担完成“歧口凹陷岩性油气藏成藏条件研究与预探目标研究”。重点围绕歧口地区岩性油气藏、成藏条件及油气富集规律，开展歧口地区第三系湖盆结构、斜坡类型和构造演化研究。运用层序地层格架与发育特点，开展沙三段、沙一段、东营组沉积体系与油气运聚规律研究，建立地层岩性圈闭发育样式、成藏模式、4种油气运聚模式，指出歧南西坡、埕北斜坡、歧北西坡为地层岩性油气藏富集的有利区带，油藏以凹陷区供油形成的旁生侧储式为主，油气以断层、不整合面和砂体复式输导为特点，并确定油气运聚的优势方向。

二、地球物理勘探

1991~2005年，是大港油田地球物理勘探技术快速发展的15年。三维地震勘探技术由最初的小道数接收（小于120道）发展到多道接收（大于1500道），过渡带、极浅海地震勘探技术与装备经历起步、发展、完善的阶段，到2005年，综合技术水平达到国际先进水平。同时VSP测井、城区地震采集复杂观测系统设计等地球物理勘探技术也得到全面发展。

（一）资料采集

1991年，大港油田集团地球物理勘探公司（以下简称物探公司）完成首块城区三维地震数据采集，标志着城区复杂地表条件地震采集技术的成熟，同年斜井VSP测井技术应用于油田勘探开发。

1992年，物探公司引进加拿大WATERAFE公司的ARKTOS气枪震源，并于1993年投入生产。1994~2000年先后自主设计建造海豹一号、海豹二号、海豹三号、海豹四号气枪震源船，同时引进气枪震源系统。海豹系列气枪震源船的建造及投入使用，结束极浅海地震采集施工作业过程中采用炸药震源的历史，使得该类地表条件下地震采集作业更安全和环保。同期组建专业滩海地震采集作业队伍，滩海地震勘探装备与技术由起步阶段走向快速发展阶段，达到国内先进水平。由于复杂地表条件下的三维观测系统设计技术的成熟与完善，1994年、1995年先后两次为俄罗斯汉特曼西斯克地球物理公司提供非规则三维地震采集设计技术服务。

2001~2005年，为进一步发展和完善滩浅海地震勘探技术，物探公司先后开展滩浅海地震采集配套装备(放缆艇、钻井艇、压电检波器等)的研制。初至波法检波点二次定位技术研究与软件开发,气枪阵列优化设计及气枪阵列子波技术研究,海上综合导航定位技术开发,推动滩浅海地震采集技术的快速发展,使滩浅海地震勘探综合技术能力达到同期国际先进水平。滩浅海地震采集技术的发展和完善,有效地提高大港油田滩浅海地震勘探的质量,进入沙特、委内瑞拉、尼日利亚等国际滩浅海主流市场。

(二)资料处理

1991年,大港油田引进IBM3083计算机系统,应用软件也从美国的西方地球物理公司的常规处理软件发展到IQ处理软件。大港计算中心在叠前去噪方面一直处于全国计算中心的前列。1991年王秀槐等发表"一种自动剔除地震噪音的新方法",两年后,又研制一种"双向去噪的方法",使参数的自动拾取及去噪功能更加完善,并在全国得到推广。1995年,李国发等把随机噪声的衰减从二维处理推广到三维,提高处理效果。同年开发FK与FX联合道内插技术,FK与FX联合道内插技术的实现使大港油田的道内插水平在全国居领先地位。大港油田在应用叠前资料预测油气方面做了大量的工作,1995年由殷八金等人编写专著"AVO技术的理论与实践"。

1998年,物探公司引进美国的24个节点的SPII并行机和Tensor地震资料处理软件。随着计算机能力的提高,大港油田的地震资料处理能力和技术也得到快速发展,真正实现全三维处理。

2004年初,引进32位128个节点的HP PC机群和法国的CGG处理软件系统,以及专门用于叠前偏移处理的GeoDepth处理系统。叠前时间偏移处理成为常规处理流程,资料的处理精度进一步得到提高。2004年底,引入64位的64个节点的SUN PC机群和Marvel叠前偏移处理系统。

(三)资料解释

1995~2000年,大港油田分阶段引进SUN Solaris工作站,解释软件不断升级,大幅度提高地震解释的精度和速度;地震属性分析日趋成熟,波形聚类技术和测井约束反演技术得到发展,开始利用三维可视化实现解释层面、断层、井轨迹、井曲线等数据的三维空间显示。

2001~2003年,大港油田开始薄储层研究及高分辨及高精度地震资料解释,GeoFrame、Landmark及Jason等多套解释软件相继引入,地震、地质、测井及计算机多学科综合应用能力大幅度提高,大港油田物探公司研究所利用层序地层学、地层切片和地震分频技术在歧南地区实现岩性油气藏突破性进展。

2004年,大港油田利用AVO响应、亮点技术、相干分析等技术识别港东地区明化镇组的河道砂体取得丰硕成果;叠后资料反演实现储层物性反演和识别厚度小于λ/4的岩性体。

第二节　钻井　完井与测井　地质录井

为满足大港油田地面条件复杂地区及滩海地区油气田的勘探开发,大港油田对大位移钻井技术开展重点攻关,先后成功完成港深69×1和张海502FH等一批位移超过3000米的大位移井,其综合技术服务水平在国内处于领先地位。大港油田测井公司拥有齐全配套的测井设备和完善的大斜度井、水平井测井工艺及打捞、解卡工艺,能够优质高效地完成水平井、大斜度井、大位移井、超深井、超高温井及开窗侧钻井等各类复杂井的测井、井壁取心施工任务。除常规测井项目外,还能够完成包括地层倾角、地层测试、介电常数、碳氧比、数字伽玛能谱、井周声波成像、微电阻率扫描成像、核磁共振、交叉式多极阵列声波、高分辨率阵列感应、薄层电阻率、扇区水泥胶结等特殊测井项目的施工作业。

一、钻井及完井

(一)钻井工艺

1. 大位移井钻井技术

1991年,在张巨河地区钻成当时国内水平位移最大的定向井——张17-1井,井深3933.88米,井底位移

2279.38米；

1997年，在洪湖地区钻成国内第一口浅层大位移定向井——红9-1井，水平位移1727.51米，垂深1180.6米，水平位移与垂深之比为1.46:1；

1999年，完成港深69×1井，井深5464.63米，井斜41.42°，水平位移3122.56米，钻井周期144.58天，建井周期160.25天，平均机械钻速5.96米/时。

2002年，为冀东油田完成北堡西3×1井，最大井斜角67.18°，井底位移3049.79米，垂深2452.16米，斜深4189米，位移垂深比1.24:1。

2006年，完成国内陆上水平位移最大的一口侧钻水平——张海502FH井，该井完钻井深5387米，水平位移4128.56米，垂深2845.49米，水平段长602米，最大井斜角96.1°，位移/垂深之比1.45:1。

2. 分支井钻井技术

1998年，为实现"稀井高产、降低油田整体开发成本"，开展分支井钻井技术研究，在大港、冀东油田成功实施一批"鱼骨型水平分支井"。

2004年，在大港油田钻成国内陆上油田第一口鱼骨型水平分支井——家H2，该井设计一个Φ215.9毫米主井眼和两个Φ152.4毫米分支井眼，主井眼采用筛管完井，两个分支井眼采用裸眼完井，同时应用地质导向钻井技术。

3. 深井钻井技术

1998年，钻成板深7井，完钻井深5192米；2000年钻成乌深1井，完钻井深5852米，该井创下Φ311.1毫米井眼钻深5457米、Φ244.5毫米套管下深、Φ311.1米井眼水泥封固段长度和欠平衡钻井深度4项全国记录，达到国际水平。大港油田完成的深井数量在国内东部油田居于首位。

4. 欠衡钻井技术

1997年，应用欠平衡钻井技术发现千米桥潜山油气田后，大港油田快速推广欠平衡钻井技术。拥有3套美国威廉姆斯7100欠平衡装备，其技术和设备可同时满足3口井作业，先后提供欠平衡钻井技术服务20余项。

1998年，完成板深7井是国内欠平衡施工井段最长的一口欠平衡井；乌深1井创下了国内欠平衡钻进井最深的的纪录(井深5852米)；西G2井是国内首次采用油包水钻井液完成的欠平衡井，最低密度为0.84克/立方厘米。

2001年，为吉林油田义51井提供泡沫欠平衡钻井服务。

5. 套管钻井技术

2003年，为满足滩海端岛批钻井的需要，在引进消化国外先进技术的基础上，开展套管钻井技术研究。研制开发具有独立知识产权的套管钻井用驱动器和钻鞋。

6. 液动冲击旋转钻井技术

2004年，为提高硬岩地层机械钻速，开展液动冲击旋转钻井技术研究，成功研制开发具有自主知识产权的射流冲击器计算机辅助设计软件。该技术分别在北京地热井、冀东油田、玉门油田及四川川东等地的6口井中得到应用，机械钻速提高31%~83%。在一些井中，井斜增加的趋势得到有效控制，取得较好的应用效果。

7. 水平井钻井技术

大港油田较早在国内发展和实施了水平井技术，通过大量的研究和不断的实践，在油藏工程研究、钻井工程设计优化、井眼轨迹控制、钻井液体系优选、完井工艺等水平井技术方面都取丰富的经验。1992年，完成当时国内陆上最深、尾管下入最深的长半径水平井——女MH-1井，井深3622.68米，水平段长273.28米，最大井斜92.1°；1993年，钻成中半径水平井——官H1井，井深2347.9米，水平段长208.67米，最大井斜93.4°；1994年，钻成国内第一口短半径水平井——官H2井，井深1847米，水平段长63米，最大井斜95°。

(二)完井工艺技术

1. 固井完井工艺技术

1992年，大港油田解决常规油气井、水平井尾管固井问题。其中女MH1水平井在244.5毫米技术套管中悬挂139.7毫米尾管，悬挂位置为井下2480米，实现悬挂固井一次完成。

2001年，自主研制固井悬挂器等固井工具，能够自主生产应用固井悬挂器、分级箍、浮箍、浮鞋等固井配套工具。

2. 筛管完井工艺技术

1996年，在官H2水平井采用割缝管完井技术，油层上端用裸眼封隔器封隔上部复杂地层，重合段采用悬挂封隔的筛管悬挂器。

1997年，自主研制割缝筛管，并且大量推广应用。

1998年，完成下部筛管上部固井完井技术。

2004年，油气井筛管完井技术打入苏丹国际市场。

3. 特殊井型完井工艺技术

1994年，在西5-14-1K侧钻井中成功应用悬挂筛管完井技术。

1998年，成功开发先期裸眼砾石充填防砂筛管完井技术，在大港港西出砂严重的地区应用5口井，成功率达到100%。

1997年，攻克大位移、水平井完井技术。

2005年，在大港油田第一口水平分支井—家H2井采用悬挂割缝筛管完井技术。该井为三开井，由一个主井眼和两个分支井眼构成。

（三）钻井液

1993～1994年，为解决港东地区沙河街组泥页岩井塌问题，大港油田集团钻井工程公司与石油大学合作优选出有机硅防塌钻井液体系。1993～1994年在港东地区试验15口井，平均井深3397.53米，平均井径扩大率6.87%，平均机械钻速10.48米/时。有机硅钻井液一直是大港油田钻探中深井的常用钻井液体系。

1993～1994年，针对大港油田地质特点，进行屏蔽暂堵保护油层技术应用研究，优选细目碳酸钙、单封等暂堵剂，成为以后现场推广油层保护技术的基本配方。

1994年，在张巨河构造，张海2-2井使用正电胶钻井液，是全国第一口使用正电胶钻井液体系的井。1994年钻探的第一口短半径水平井官H2也使用正电胶钻井液。

1997～1998年，大港油田集团钻采工艺研究院（以下简称钻采院）王小月等研究开发保护油层油溶性暂堵剂。

1999年，在家H2水平井首次应用油包水完井液。

1999～2000年，应用水包油钻井液完成大港油田第一口应用欠平衡钻井技术的生产井西G2井。

2000～2001年，钻采院王小月等研究优选甲酸盐钻井液体系，在滩海地区推广应用。

二、测井

（一）裸眼井测井

2005年，测井公司完成3700测井系统挂接电极系、微电极和连续测斜仪的研究，国产数控测井并测技术的研究，声放磁在组合测井技术的研究，5700测井系统与电极、井径、连斜组合仪的配接等多项研究工作，解决三大系统的组合并测问题。测井公司在14个测井队推广使用研究成果，提高测井成功率，提高测井时效30%以上。

同年，测井公司科研人员完成远探测声波成像测井方法与仪器研究项目，形成具有全部自主知识产权的新型测井技术，填补国内空白。2005年底获“2005年中国石油集团科技十大进展”。该项目共申请专利5项（其中1项发明专利，1项实用新型专利获得国家专利局批准，其余几项正在申请中）；形成专有技术4项；技术成果12项。

（二）生产井测试

同年，测井公司形成注入剖面、产出剖面、工程测井和储层监测四大系列。在注入剖面测井方面，除能完成传统的同位素示踪测井外，还能运用先进的七参数测井仪进行注入剖面测井，对注水层位进行定量解释。能够完成自喷井产出剖面、环空井产出剖面、气举产出剖面、硼-中子寿命测井等生产井测试任务，并且能够进行固井质量、压裂效果、射孔情况及找漏、找串等工程测试和射孔作业。高清晰度的井下超声电视和DDL—V配置的水泥胶结评价、40臂井径和噪声测井能够检查井下套管锈蚀情况、水泥胶结质量和射孔效果。

（三）射孔作业

大港油田测井公司形成过油管射孔、电缆输送射孔和油管输送射孔（TCP）三大工艺技术，以及复合射孔、电缆桥塞、爆炸解卡、切割等施工工艺，可以采用60型、73型、89型、102型、127型、复合射孔等射孔器材实施射孔工程服务，现有的设备和射孔器材能够实施水平井、大位移井、大斜度井、开窗侧钻井及超深超高温井和极浅层井等各类复杂井的射孔施工。TCP射孔成功率达到98%以上，在全国同行业中名列前茅。测井公司大力推广深穿透、大孔径、高孔密射孔技术与地层测试器联作工艺技术，2000年研制成功过油管张开式射孔器，并成功应用于生产，多次完成大斜度井TCP与地层测试器联作施工等作业。

（四）测井资料评价

到2015年，大港油田引进斯伦贝谢GeoFrame、贝克阿特拉斯eXpress测井解释软件包、Forward软件包、Sierre油藏描述软件包，并根据多年解释经验自行开发Cif2000多井评价软件系统、Logview、WLS大港测井软件系统等3个系列20多种解释软件，实现单井数字处理、单井精细解释、多井综合评价。能够进行储层岩性分析、矿物成份分析、物性参数分析、储层液性分析、岩石强度和压力分析，还能进行裂缝类型识别、沉积环境分析、构造类型分析、地应力分析及油藏描述等综合评价。技术人员通过不断的研究攻关，形成一套复杂地质区较完善的单井储层精细评价分析技术，包括常规测井资料的储层评价技术、HDIL储层精细描述分析技术、MRIL-P储层精细描述分析技术、STAR-II储层精细描述分析技术和XMAC气层识别技术，不同程度地解决低孔低渗储层、砂泥岩裂缝储层、岩性低阻油层、钙质砂岩储层（泥质白云质灰岩储层）等测井评价难题。

三、地质录井

（一）常规地质录井

1991年2月，大港油田集团地质录井公司（以下简称录井公司）孙宝绪、王敬田、苏金龙等人与安徽蚌埠自动化研究所合作开发研制成功以单片机为工作核心的DZL-Ⅱ型钻时仪。首次将钻时仪应用于录井现场，结束依靠人为量取深度、卡取钻时的历史。该仪器采用20世纪80年代流行的单片微型计算机技术，其应用程序固化在MCS-51单片机内，通过安装绞车传感器来实现大钩位置的跟踪，以此测量井深，自动记录钻时，减少人为因素的影响。

1997年4月，由录井公司陈宪藻、张鹏研制的全自动岩屑捞洗机投入地质录井作业现场进行试验生产。旨在通过应用该装置摆脱人工捞取清洗岩屑样品的现场工作，从而提高岩屑录井资料的真实性和连续性，为地质录井解释评价和配套技术的有效实施提供条件。全自动岩屑捞洗机由引流器、清洗通道、分离器、岩样接收装置、供水系统、污水回收装置等6部分组成，为岩屑样品采集提出一个创新的思路。

2001年，录井公司张儒勋、杜东莘、宋庆彬等组织论证购置湖北荆鹏软件开发公司生产的35台具有国内先进水平的JP-DZYA地质参数仪。该参数仪应用计算机处理技术，将井深测量与钻井状态判断、钻时计算与循环钻井液迟到时间校准有效结合，使现场地质录井真正达到智能化，同时让手抄填写地质原始资料成为历史，实现地质录井资料整理的标准化、规范化。

2005年4月，录井公司安文武、赵廷生等针对PDC钻头钻井条件下岩屑细碎、捞取困难且不易识别等问题开发研制出岩样观测装置。将岩屑显微成像技术与计算机处理技术、荧光分析技术有机地结合在一起，形成一套解决问题的方法。该装置获国家发明专利。

2005年8月，录井公司熊正祥、陶青龙、甄建、季海林等研制开发出第一台具有自主知识产权的DML地质参数仪。该仪器改变用K系数校正大钩高度的深度计算摸式，采用模拟量多点刻度，消除理论计算和大绳疲劳等因素产生的误差，使井深跟踪更加精确，且仪器符合井场条件下安全等级标准，系统数据库与

WITS相一致，各项技术指标均高于国产仪器，达到国际水平。该仪器随后大量投入录井技术服务现场，一举取代JP-DZYA地质参数仪。

（二）综合录井和气测录井

1993年，录井公司姚汉光、李心刚、刘洁等对TDC综合录井仪软件系统进行汉化改造，相继出台DJ909、DJ936综合录井系统并投入现场进行服务。该汉化系统将TDC综合录井仪计算机处理系统采用的工业控制机更新为通用的微型计算机，使系统更加易于维护，而且界面更适应国内录井技术服务市场习惯和要求。

1995年12月、1999年4月，录井公司两次引进美国HALLIBURTON公司生产的SDL9000综合录井系统4台。该系统为世界先进的综合录井系统，具有DNV安全防爆等级认证，适应于A0区域技术服务，计算机处理系统采用SUN工作站机型，系统管理实现井场网络化，操作系统采用高稳定的UNIX和WINDOWS-NT系统，具有超强功能软件应用系统和录井图绘制系统，色谱分析周期为1.5分钟。由于该系统稳定可靠，符合国际惯例要求，故一直应用于国际反承包和国际综合录井技术服务现场。

1997年12月，录井公司从上海神开公司购进SK-2Q01气测录井仪。彻底淘汰以电子管为仪器组件的SQC701气测录井仪，将气测录井技术提升到与电子计算机技术相同步水平，提高数据采集精度、资料处理速度和参数测量的准确度，实现气测录井的计算机化管理。

1997～1999年，录井公司张儒勋、杜东莘、杜国永、吴明等组织参加与中油总公司徐水物探局、湖北荆鹏软件公司、上海神开公司共同开发10套SLY-6000综合录井仪。实现录井气测数据、钻井液数据、钻井工程数据全部自动采集、计算机处理，实时监测预报，数据、图表打印输出等功能，并实现整机软硬件国产化，其综合技术指标与法国Geoservices公司生产的Geo-6000综合录井仪相当，真正在综合录井系统国产化方面迈出坚实的一步。

1997～2004年，录井公司公司根据企业经营状况、市场需求、综合录井仪器数量及国内外综合录井系统应用状况，购置6台航空航天工业部22所研制生产的SLZ系列综合录井仪，应用到国内及国际反承包录井市场，保证录井市场份额。该综合录井仪以军工产品定制模式、通过吸收国际先进综合录井系统特点，以小型工控机与微型计算机相结合构架现场网络化管理系统，整个采集参数的标定实现智能化。

1999年底到2001年底，录井公司经系统整合，引进8台法国Geoservices公司生产的ALS系列综合录井仪。在保证系统安全防爆等级的基础上，对气体检测分析、数据处理、智能诊断等方面提出要求。同时引进2套快速色谱分析装置，其快速色谱分析周期缩短到42秒，提高录井技术装备的整体水平。定量快速色谱仪在宋庆彬、陈玉新、甄建、王晓成等组成的项目组研究推广下取得良好效果，为后续快速色谱分析的定位奠定基础。

2002年，录井公司引进美国Baker& Hughes公司生产的ADVANTAGE－Ⅱ型综合录井仪1台，满足中油集团在苏丹反承包区块的技术服务需求。

2005年12月，录井公司陶青龙、陈玉新、季海林、孙继森、甄建等组成的项目组，在公司引进加拿大DATALOG公司生产的DATAGLOG—WWMLS综合录井仪的同时，研制开发出德玛气测录井仪。采用微池热导鉴定器（μ-TCD）和微色谱柱技术，使气体分析速度提高到30秒以内。

（三）井场信息远程传输

2003年，录井公司邓建华、宋庆彬等进行井场信息远程传输技术研究。以无线通信方式为媒介，应用数据监听、压缩加密、发送与接收、解密解压、分发与浏览器显示技术，实现现场录井数据的远程实时传输。2004年10月，研究实现电缆测井数据及数字图片的远程传输；2005年12月，研究解决语音及视频图像远程实时传输问题。

（四）录井配套技术

1991年5月，录井公司引进DH910地化录井仪，后将其升级为DH920。该仪器通过对岩屑样品中烃类组分的分析，实现对油气层的解释。2002年7月，引进热解气相色谱仪。2001～2003年，水淹层地化技术在港西、枣园等油田应用，解决水淹层评价的难题，油气层解释符合率达到89.5%，挖潜增产效果明显。

1997年1月，录井公司购置SK-2P01型PK分析仪。该仪器可提供孔隙度和渗透率两个参数，帮助现场对储层性质进行判断。2005年2月，引进RecCore-04型核磁共振岩样分析仪。该仪器可获得比较准确的孔、渗、饱、可动流体等参数，快速对储层做出评价。

1999年，录井公司引进OFA-Ⅱ型荧光分析仪。该仪器利用样品中的荧光物质吸收激发光后发生能量跃迁而发射荧光的原理，实现对油气层的识别，可以克服钻井液添加剂对现场油气识别的干扰，并有利于微弱显示的发现和油气层的定量判断。录井公司安文武、石丰甫、袁保清等基于该技术，研究出钻井液定量荧光录井方法，该研究成果于2004年10月获国家发明专利。2005年，录井公司引进OFA-3DI型石油荧光分析仪，提高油气层识别的准确率。

第三节　油气田开发工程

截至2005年12月底，大港油田投入开发的16个油田（25个开发区）分为6种油藏类型，即中高渗透层注水砂岩油藏、裂缝性碳酸岩油藏、低渗透油藏、复杂断块油藏、天然能量开发油藏和特殊类型油藏。共投产油气水井4677口，其中采油井3223口，注水井1414口。油气井开井2330口，日产油水平14528吨，油田综合含水85.38%，年产油509.95万吨，累积产油1.32321亿吨。

一、油气田开发与开采

（一）油气田开发

1989年至1992年，为改善枣园油田开发效果，由中国石油天然气总公司科技局牵头，以大港油田和石油大学为主，联合国内其他8家科研院所及大学，对枣园油田进行科学研究及开发综合调整，形成一个紧密的“产学研”联合攻关集团。枣园油田年产油由27万吨提高到50万吨。1993年该项目获中国石油天然气总公司科技进步一等奖列当年石油行业10大科技成果之一。

1991年，官104断块实现当年评价，当年全面开发。1990年底官104井获得日产31.2吨的高产油流。为实现勘探开发一体化，尽快建成生产能力，实行整体规划、分块实施、注水先行和高凝油开发的一系列配套工艺措施等正确方针。采用200米井距正方形井网布井，当年建成14.3万吨生产能力。成为大港油田第一个当年发现当年评价当年投入开发整装区块的典范。

1992年8月，完钻当时国内第一口陆地最深的长曲率半径开发水平井—女MH1。井深3623米，水平段长273.28米，投产初期10毫米油嘴自喷日产油80吨，到1995年10月因电泵供液不足而停产，累计产油3.5万吨。

1992年，大港油田开始有组织、有规模的滚动勘探开发。经三维地震资料精细解释，重新落实构造，部署羊G1井。该井于1992年4月开钻，6月份完钻，钻遇馆陶组油层21.8米，试油日产油11.4吨。经计算羊八井断块滚动勘探开发增加含油面积0.6平方千米，增加地质储量170万吨，后钻开发井23口，建产能9.2万吨。

1993年，大港油田第一次规模开展控水稳油综合治理工作。对进入开发中、后期的南北大港上第三系为主的各油田，采取以增加注水井点及改变液流方向为主的综合措施，进行以层系相互利用为主的综合调整。实施后25个有对比条件的开发单元中，有效的有23个，占92%。各开发单元治理后一般综合含水下降1.6%～6.0%；自然递减由1993年的16.75%降到1994年的12.58%，采油速度上升0.2%～1.4%，综合治理效果明显。

1993年2月10日，中国石油天然气勘探开发公司与美国路易斯安那勘探公司（中国）有限公司签定“中华人民共和国渤海湾浅海地区赵东区块石油勘探开发生产合同”，合同自5月1日起生效。合作区面积197平方千米，主要含油目的层为明化镇、馆陶油组。该项目自1993年开始执行，1994年有了初次发现。后经

10年的勘探，成效显著。赵东合作区确定生产面积为27平方千米，2005年生产原油109万吨。

1995年1月16日，中国第一个循环注气开发的大张坨凝析气藏以循环注干气方式投入开发。方案设计注采比0.8，日产井流物40万立方米，日注天然气32万立方米，循环注气7年后衰竭式开采8年共15年，可累积采出凝析油71.6万米立方，天然气10.09亿立方米，凝析油的采收率62.7%，天然气采收率65.1%。至2000年，经过5年的开发有效地减缓地层压降速度，井流物中凝析油含量由630克每立方米下降至450克每立方米。与衰竭式开发相比，凝析油含量减少损失180克每立方米，阶段凝析油采收率提高15.9%。2000年10月大张坨凝析气藏转为北京华油天然气有限责任公司的地下储气库。大张坨凝析油气藏对西气东输，调节天然气供需矛盾，解决京津地区天然气用气调峰具有重大的战略意义。大张坨地下储气库设计最大库容量为17.8亿立方米，日调气量500万立方米，成为国内第一个最大的天然气地下储气库。

1997年，大港油田开始应用难采储量评价技术，规模开发未动储量。优选沈家铺油田的官128断块进行系统评价，开展地质资料重新处理、精细解释、测井储层评价、举升工艺试验、钻评价井、开展井组实验区等一系列工作。1997年部署第一口评价井家37—49井，钻遇油层53.8米，水力喷射泵求产获35.9吨每天的高产。经综合评价，提交1000万吨的优质储量。1998年后全面投入开发，建成产能10万吨/年。

1997年5月，为了探索高含水期油藏微生物驱提高采收率的效果，在港东二区七断块开展微生物驱油现场试验，为国内首例。该断块试验目的层为明三小层，油层温度67℃，综合含水达92.6%。注入井4口，受益油井9口，累计注入原菌液300立方米，7口油井先后见到增油效果。经初步测算累计增油10589吨，提高采收率1.43%。

1998年，大港油田在已开发油田规模实施油藏精细描述技术。立足于老油田，规模开展老油田油藏精细描述工作，重建地质模型，搞清油藏剩余油的分布，为老油田综合调整、挖潜和有效注水，控制含水上升速度和减缓油田递减，提高水驱采收率指明方向。1999年至2003年，完成第一轮精细油藏描述工作，描述20个油气田，描述含油面积325.3平方千米，完成描述储量49702万吨。在20个油田编制93个综合调整方案，预计方案实施后可以增加可采储量1010万吨，提高采收率近2个百分点。随着方案的实施，建成和恢复生产能力110万吨，增产原油139.2万吨，开展过油藏描述的油田，其开发指标都有不同程度的改善，老油田的被动局面有所缓解。

1999年3月，在羊三木油田三断块馆Ⅱ上油组开展碱/聚合物二元复合驱矿场先导性试验，这是全国第一例采用碱+聚合物作为驱替物开展的三次采油现场试验。该试验区共有4口注聚井，18口受益油井，至2003年底累计注入聚合物干粉1040吨，碱干粉5180吨。初步测算试验区增油34000吨。

2001年，在孔店油田二断块油藏开展国内首例本源微生物三次采油现场试验。经生化参数分析和油藏研究，确定周期性注入混气营养液的方案，实施后油井试验有效率68%，显效率41%，统计已累计增油12211吨。

（二）油气田开采

1. 稠油化学降粘吞吐技术

由于大港油田绝大部分稠油区块不适合热采，70%的稠油储量需要依靠冷采技术进行开发。1991年中科院渗流力学研究所开始研究稠油化学吞吐，并于1992年在大港油田进行国内第一口单井化学吞吐试验，随后在官109-1稠油断块规模推广应用获得成功，有效解除井筒近井地带堵塞，达到了启动油层、提高油井产能的目的。

2000年，化学吞吐工艺技术共应用34井次，有效率72.3%，处理后平均日产油7.6吨。尤其是在油层温度条件下原油粘度10000毫帕秒以下的稠油井上应用效果明显，使一批难采地质储量得到了有效动用，为大港油田稠油油藏开采作出了贡献。

2. 稠油油藏自生二氧化碳（CO_2）、化学降粘剂复合吞吐工艺技术

2004年，油田公司采油工艺研究院开展稠油油藏自生CO_2、化学降粘剂复合吞吐工艺技术研究与应用。利用在地层自生CO_2气体，使之在超临界条件下，进入许多溶剂不能进入的空间，起到降低原油粘度和界面张力的作用（CO_2溶于油后，能使油粘度降低30%～60%；溶于水后使水粘度增加20%～30%，水流度降低2～

3倍;使油—水界面张力降低)。同时伴随溶解气驱替原油的作用(标准状态下单位体积产气量可达50~80立方米),有利于剩余油驱替;利用与化学降粘剂复合,降粘和驱替协同效应进一步得到发挥,有效改善稠油在地层中的流动性,适合大港油田油层特点和原油物性。2005年,在采油六厂羊三木和孔店油田现场先导性试验5口井,单井吞吐剂用量在180~250立方米,处理半径在7~8米,单井投入材料费和施工费平均为25万元,5口井共投入125万元。从吞吐效果分析,5口先导试验井均有不同的吞吐效果,其中羊7-13-2、孔1074-1和羊7-13-1效果最显著,单井最高换油率达到了3.4立方米每吨。

3. 三次采油技术

“七五”以来,大港油田针对油田油藏特点开展三次采油提高采收率的研究与矿场试验工作,形成以聚合物驱油为主以微生物驱油为辅的三次采油配套技术,现场应用见到较好效果。截至2005年12月底,累计增油101万吨,当年增油10.25万吨。1986年12月聚合物驱油先导试验在港西油田四区展开,于1995年底见效结束,平均吨聚合物增油514吨,提高原油采收率11.5%;1995年相继在大港开展聚合物驱油扩大试验、工业化推广及污水聚合物驱油技术研究和应用,现场实施区块平均吨聚合物增油157吨,提高采收率7.6%。根据大港南部油田原油酸值较高的特点,1991~2005年在羊三木油田开展碱/聚合物驱油技术研究和现场试验,到2005年底累计增油6.4万吨,展示碱/聚合物驱油技术在酸性油藏的良好应用前景。微生物驱油技术先导试验于1995年10月在原注聚合物驱先导试验井结束后开展,获得每方菌液增油118吨的较好效果。2001年至2005年底,在扩大微生物驱应用规模的基础上,在孔店油田和港西油田开展本源微生物驱油技术研究与试验,累计增油4.3万吨,见效区块提高采收率3.0%,获得增产每桶原油成本为2.5美元的较好效果,形成适合复杂断块油藏应用的低成本三次采油新技术。

4. 调剖技术

1991年,针对大港油田油藏非均质性强,长期注水冲刷导致开发效果变差的问题,开展注水井调剖技术研究试验与应用,研究发展应用以TP-910为主的多种调剖工艺体系,取得显著的增油降水效果。获局级科技进步一等奖,北京国际博览会金奖。

1998~2000年,针对常规调剖效果下降,以北大港油田为先导开展深部调剖技术的系列研究攻关,实现规模化应用,逐步发展成为高含水油田挖潜的主体措施工艺之一。

2001年起至2005年,随着油田开发的不断深入,高含水高采出程度油田挖潜难度的加大,在深部调剖的基础上,研究发展应用深部调驱技术,成功研制疏水型水膨体、新型复合铬离子交联剂和聚氨脂颗粒等调驱剂,研究配套形成适应不同类型油藏条件的调驱系列技术,成为大港及国内东部高含水油田增效开采、提高采收率的主导技术之一。

5. 热采技术

2004年,油藏评价部与辽河油田公司钻采院合作,在孔102井开展两轮次的蒸汽吞吐试验。

2005年,采油三厂和井下作业公司合作,以风险承包的形式开展自21-10、官32-18和家27--52井的蒸汽吞吐施工。

2005年,采油工艺研究院开展枣35区块裂缝性火成岩稠油油藏蒸汽吞吐先导试验方案研究,采油三厂购置2台11.5吨/时的亚临界注汽锅炉,并开展军19-23、自6-14和军25-23井现场先导试验。

(三)油井开采配套措施

1. 压裂

1994年,钻采院程运甫等针对稠油油藏压裂效果差的问题研究成功自生热压裂技术,改善稠油油藏的压裂效果,增油5000吨以上。

1997年,钻采院何志勇等针对压裂失效井的进一步增产、控制含水问题研究成重复压裂及裂缝纵向控制工艺技术,解决裂缝延伸问题,为底水油藏的压裂开辟了新的途径。

2001年,钻采院程运甫等针对高温高压井提高产量问题研究成深井压裂技术,研制高温压裂液和高强度支撑剂,增储5千余万吨。

2002年,钻采院陈紫薇等针对提高压裂效果问题完成无残渣压裂液研制,解决压裂的二次污染问题,增油6000吨以上，压裂效果显著，率先实施海上压裂。

2003年，钻采院程运甫等根据勘探开发的需要研究成超深井压裂技术，形成一套超深井压裂工艺技术。

2. 酸化

1995年，钻采院温晓、任民等针对注水井的堵塞问题研究形成注水井二次酸化防膨增注技术。

2002年，钻采院徐新俊、任民等根据灰岩油藏酸化中存在的问题研究形成灰岩地层易漏失井酸化排液一体化技术，现场实施16井次，累计增油8967吨，平均有效期7个月。

2002年，钻采院贾金辉、徐新俊、任民等针对不同的堵塞类型研究形成油水井解堵综合配套技术，共实施70多井次，累计增油29467吨。

3. 防砂

1992年，钻采院董正海等针对化学防砂问题研究成功CS-1新型固结剂防砂技术，现场实验5口井，累计增油3029.1吨，共创效131万元。

1992年，钻采院陈炳谦等针对机械防砂后处理难度大的问题研究采用双层预充填塑料衬管，现场实验7口井，节约费用364万元。

1995年，钻采院姬晓东等针对化学防砂施工工艺复杂的问题研究成功一次性注入法化学溶液防砂技术，现场实验17口井，恢复井累计产油15008吨。

1998年，钻采院彭鹞等完成割缝管防砂技术的开发与应用，现场实施56口井，恢复产油67100吨。

2002年，钻采院王乐英等针对底水油藏防砂控水问题完成底水油藏防砂工艺技术研究，现场实施32井次，恢复产油68441吨。

二、地面工程

（一）油气集输

1991年，大港油田集团勘探开发设计研究院（以下简称设计院）在王1地区产能建设官二联合站工程中，首次采用油气水三相分离器，缩短工艺流程。

1993年，设计院科研所在马西油站研究并采用密闭容器不停产除砂装置和洗砂装置，成功地解决油田砂害。是年，滨海站进行全面的改造，增加原油稳定装置；之后，官一联、枣一联等联合站在改造过程中，相继增设原油稳定装置，采用正压闪蒸工艺，使稳定后的原油在储存温度下饱和蒸气压低于当地大气压0.7倍；原油稳定装置投产后，油田实现集输和处理过程的全密闭，进一步降低油气损耗。

1994年，大港油田采用循环注气开发方式对大张坨凝析油气田进行进一步开发。根据开发方案和生产特点，大港油田设计院在学习国外先进技术、引进国外管件设备的基础上，采用先进的软件进行模拟和优化，确定适宜的地面工艺流程和参数，不仅满足油田开发的需要，也为国内其他凝析油气田开发提供宝贵的经验。

1999年，大港油田同时在小集联合站和官二联合站脱水流程中试用高效三相分离器。集油气分离、加热、脱水于一体，成功地实现原油一段脱水；2003年在港东联合站推广使用高效三相分离器，大大缩短脱水流程，降低工程投资和运行费用。

2000年，大港油田公司和设计院一起在北大港地区进行双官掺常温水、单管常温集输和单管常温加药集输的室内实验和现场试验并获成功。

2005年，在港西油田彻底改变应用多年的油井进计量站集中计量、双管掺水等传统的集输方式，采用单管常温集输和集输管线串接等技术，简化集输管网，把油田应用多年的三级布站模式改成两级布站模式。取消计量站后，既减少管理环节又节约土地，取得良好的经济效益和社会效益。2005年，设计院科研所在采油三厂典型高凝、高粘区块采用原油改性技术，实现不加热开采和常温集输，取得高凝、高粘原油开采和集输的突破。

（二）油气计量

2004年，在大港油田采油一厂、三厂和五厂，分别建立单井功图法计量试验区，取得较好的效果。2005

年在港西油田油水系统调整中，大面积使用功图法进行单井计量，改变传统的双容积计量方法，提高自动化水平，为油田集输系统全面简化创造条件。

三、滩海工程

为了加快滩海地区的勘探开发，针对渤海湾西部海滩和极浅海区域的海洋环境特点，大港油田从20世纪60年代开始进行海洋环境调查、工程地质钻探、修筑海堤等工作，积累大量的海况资料和滩海工程施工经验。20世纪80年代进行人工岛课题研究。同时，对自升式气垫组合钻井平台的方案进行反复论证和科技攻关。1992年建成“中华第一人工岛”。1998年建成中国第一艘浅吃水自升式钻井平台—“港海一号”。与之相配套的两栖运输装备亦不断进行研制和完善。

(一)海工建设

大港油田为扩大勘探开发领域，寻求油气储量接替区，实现滩海资源量向产量的转化，不断探索海工技术。早在20世纪70年代修筑粘土海堤进行勘探开发，20世纪80年代修筑毛石护坡海堤建岛进行勘探开发，20世纪90年代为解决水浅潮差大、陆上设备下不去、海上装备上不来等问题发展气垫技术。但囿于配套技术不完善，高风险、高投入、低效益始终制约着大港滩海的发展。针对大港滩海的特点，围绕着降低成本，对常规的海堤修筑技术进行优化与创新，引进与研发相结合，进行软基处理、石笼网箱、构件加毛石等新型进海路的试验与研究。特别是庄海2X1进海路采用构件加毛石技术进行先导性试验获得成功，为大港滩海区的勘探开发探索一条新路。在此基础上，通过对进海路及海上人工井场的结构进行优化、改进和完善，设计修建关家堡进海路及人工井场。在南部滩海建成张巨河人工岛、张东海堤和人工井场，庄海2X1进海路及人工井场以及赵东平台。

1. 张巨河人工岛

1991年，利用气垫技术建造张巨河人工岛。从设计、筹备、建岛到岛上第一口探井开钻，历时两年半。该人工岛为桩基、单环、双壁钢沉箱、气垫整体垫升搬移式人工岛。即人工岛的单环、双壁钢沉箱及气垫装置均就近在陆上预制完成，然后，采用气垫技术垫升单环、双壁钢沉箱，靠船拖航就位。岛壁为钢筋混凝土浇注。岛体面积为60×60平方米。至2005年，该岛已无利用的经济价值。

2. 张东海堤和张海2×1人工井场

1992年12月，在张巨河村东侧滩涂区修建张东凸堤2.2千米及堤端海上人工井场100×100平方米，1993年8月底完工。海堤的起点标高工程4.0，终点高程5.0，堤顶宽9米。该工程为大港油田典型的土筑、土工布毛石护坡结构的海堤和人工井场。海堤为凸堤，堤身轴线与波浪方向基本平行。该工程经受1997年10月的百年一遇风暴潮和2003年10月的50年一遇风暴潮的侵袭，海堤结构没有损失，人工井场只是在东南角和东北角局部护坡毛石被波浪冲开。1997年10月进行修复加固，该海堤及井场状况良好，在南部滩海开发过程中利用。

3. 进海路及海上人工井场

两个工程采用对拉板桩技术修建进海路。该技术又称为“构件+毛石”结构，既构件陆上预制，海上组装，桩深扎，梁定位，先构件筑墙，后毛石充填。两条进海路路面黄海高程为1.676米。人工井场采用抛石斜坡堤结构，岛面高程4.0～4.5米。2002年底完成庄海2×1井的钻探。庄海2×1进海路及海上人工井场先导性试验的成功，为滩海开发海工建设打下良好基础。

4. 赵东平台

2003年，赵东平台安装就位、投产。由钻井平台和生产平台组成，中间用栈桥相连，为钻采修一体化平台。平台具有钻井、修井、采油、单井计量、原油脱水、污水处理、注水和原油储存、外输、燃气发电等功能。

(二) 滩海装备

20世纪80年代完成大港管辖地区自然条件、工程地质和海况的调查。认为小于2.5米水深的第一区域带和第二区域带陆上装备下不去，海上常规设备上不来，进行该地区的勘探开发作业必须解决“进得去，站得住，供得上”的难题。确定大港滩海区勘探开发技术路线：在第一区域带采用岸边建井和修建海堤，第二区域带采用气垫运移技术人工岛工程，第三区域带采用自升式钻井平台。

1993年，建成张东海堤及井场。全长2.2千米，由于当时受钻井技术和钻机能力的限制，只是部分地解决第一区域带的钻探评价。同年，气垫运移技术在0米海图水深附近建成张巨河人工岛，到1995年8月完成3口井的钻探实施。1993年起相继研制两艘35吨自航式气垫运输平台，一艘100吨被动式气垫运输平台，一艘10吨牵引两栖拖头等滩海两栖运输装备以及一艘100吨泥撬驳船，2艘小型客用气垫船及研制中的泥里爬两栖作业车、自航和非自航驳船等，形成大港滩海两栖运输装备独有的“飘、爬、浮、滑”特点的浅海运输供应和应急救生保障体系。1996年，由于张东人工岛钻探效果不理想，勘探开发基本处于停顿状态，所研制的装备、设备因闲置、老化及技术原因已全部报废。

1998年10月，国家“八五”重大技术装备攻关项目“港海一号”自升式超浅吃水可移动钻井平台，完成第一口工业性试验井后安全返达天津塘沽南疆码头，成功解决海图水深0～2.5米石油钻探盲区的难题。从1991年初立项起，历时8年，期间得到国家经贸委、中国石油天然气集团公司、中国船舶工业总公、中国船检总局、大港油田集团公司（大港石油管理局）的支持，与中船总708所、大连造船厂、兰石厂、宝鸡石油机械厂、有关大专院校以及油田钻采院、滩海工程公司等单位通力合作。为解决“港海一号”钻井平台海上运输及后勤保障，同年又立项编制520千瓦和2400千瓦两艘浅吃水拖轮，至此形成一套比较完备且适合大港滩海特点的石油钻探装备。

2004年，中国石油天然气集团公司从专业化管理角度，重新整合滩海装备资源，将原隶属辽河、冀东、大港的滩海装备的资产、使用及管理全部划转到新成立的中国石油海洋工程有限公司。“港海一号”平台及520千瓦、2400千瓦两艘拖轮全面服务于渤海湾石油勘探开发生产。

第三章　冶金及金属制品

天津是国家的老钢铁工业基地之一。天津市为解决冶金工业布局分散、结构不合理的问题，20世纪80年代重点抓大无缝工程，90年代抓天津钢厂易地改造工程。随着改革的深入，天津冶金工业形成以天津冶金总公司、天铁冶金集团公司、天钢集团公司、天津钢管公司等四大企业集团齐头并进、争相发展的局面。大无缝钢管工程作为天津钢管公司的前身，1989年以电炉-连续铸锭-MPM轧管机的先进工艺流程开建，通过大规模引进设备和技术，形成以石油套管为特色、品种比较齐全的生产系统，其装备和产品水平进入世界先进行列。1996年投产到2005年，形成年产生铁80万吨、钢坯200万吨、钢材160万吨的综合生产能力。天津钢厂作为天钢集团公司的前身，始建于1935年，是中国最早拥有平炉炼钢、转炉炼钢、电炉炼钢的企业。2001年开工建设高炉-复吹转炉-连续铸锭-轧钢工艺流程的现代化钢铁企业，彻底结束化铁炼钢的历史。2004年在渤海之滨建成跻身国际国内一流的现代化大型企业，形成年产生铁430万吨、钢坯430万吨、钢材400万吨的综合生产能力。始建于1969年8月5日的天津铁厂作为天铁冶金集团公司的前身，多年不断进行配套改造，由单纯的炼铁企业，逐步炼钢轧材，1995年起，钢产量以每年增钢30万吨以上的速度增长，增幅全国领先，同时建成现代化热轧板卷和冷轧薄板工程，至2005年底拥有11个子公司，形成年产生铁350万吨、钢坯350万吨、钢材200万吨的综合生产能力。天津冶金总公司在原冶金局的基础上改制而成，在轧钢和金属制品为主的基础上，逐步形成铁钢材生产系统，2005年有34个生产企业，形成年产生铁200万吨、钢坯200万吨、钢材400万吨、金属制品42万吨的综合生产能力。

第一节 烧 结

20世纪90年代起，国内烧结行业迅速发展，大量新工艺、新技术、新设备陆续推出，跨入世界烧结行业的先进行列。天津铁厂最初作为炼铁为主的企业，在烧结工艺和装备方面取得许多创新成果。

1990年，天铁集团进行酸性精矿参与烧结生产试验攻关取得成功。从此酸性精矿作为主要铁原料，广泛用于烧结生产。同年，132平方米烧结机点火器轻质耐火材料改成高温硫酸盐预制板，延长点火器使用寿命，提高作业率0.1%。

1990～1991年，天铁集团以生石灰取代部分石灰石参与烧结生产，并辅以生石灰配消器，不仅混合料的成球性提高，而且生石灰消化放热还可提高混合料料温，减薄烧结过程中的过湿带，有力促进烧结生产水平提高。

1993年，天铁集团增加一台锤式破碎机和一台熔剂筛，以提高熔剂破碎能力。一烧车间烧结机点火器改造成多缝式点火器，二烧车间点火器改成多缝式烧嘴点火炉，既节约焦炉煤气，又提高表层烧结矿质量。环冷轴流风机完成改造，烧结矿冷却效果明显改善。

1993～1994年，天铁集团进行高品位、高碱度烧结矿生产试验，取得较好效果。通过优化配料结构，调整生产工艺，辅以各种强化措施等，烧结矿品位、碱度不断提高，为高炉增产、节焦作出贡献。

1995～1996年，天铁集团烧结生产推广应用变频调速技术，烧结机、泥辊、配料圆盘、热返矿圆盘、鼓风机等设备的调速电机改为交流电机加变频调速器调速，使电机故障率降低，设备作业率提高，节约电能50%以上，促进设备安全经济运行。

1997年，天铁集团为减少有害漏风率和设备事故，增加烧结矿产量，完成对50平方米烧结机弹性滑道和头部密封系统技术改造。利用可编程控制器代替传统的继电器控制，完成一烧车间PLC改造，进一步提升烧结自动化水平，提高设备作业率2%以上；改造一烧车间多管除尘器，去掉原20余吨的填料，采用专利技术的导向器，旋风子由原铸铁材质改为高铬精铸材质，除尘效率提高到90%以上，除尘器使用寿命延长1倍，达8年之久，高负压转子使用寿命达2年以上；对烧结矿成品系统进行改造，实现烧结矿落地储备，增强烧结生产的主动性，烧结机作业率平均提高3%以上，同年烧结矿产量首次突破300万吨。

同年，天铁集团与天津市冶金新技术开发推广中心共同实施小球烧结新工艺推广项目，在2台50平方米烧结机上应用。原圆筒混合机改为强力混合造球机，采用雾化喷水、固体燃料分加等工艺技术，使混合料粒化成小球，布料时料层合理分布，达到低温原料操作，提高烧结矿的产量和质量。烧结机利用系数提高0.15吨/平方米·时，产量提高10%，节约燃料5千克标煤/吨。

1998年，天铁集团132平方米烧结机应用小球烧结新工艺，采用强制混合料造球技术、新型雾化喷水技术、固体燃料分加技术及偏析布料技术，有效满足精粉条件下的烧结生产要求，烧结料粒级组成趋于合理，粒层透气性明显提高，能耗水平大幅降低，烧结矿产量提高10%。小球烧结新工艺推广应用获1999年度天津市科技进步二等奖。同时，二烧车间还先后完成PC584工业计算机升级改造和集散控制系统改造，设备作业率提高5%以上。

1999年，天铁集团进行低碱度烧结矿生产试验。自主开发烧结自动配料及计算机网络软件，对原料车间操作系统、配料系统等实现远程自动控制和调节，传统的人工手动配料改为微机自动控制配料，配料精度由±5%提高到±0.5%，烧结生产工业自动化水平进一步提高，烧结生产稳定性明显增强。一烧车间一次混合机规格由Φ2.8×6米改为Φ3.0×12米，混合工艺进一步完善，混匀造球效果显著增强。二料场项目建成投产，原料的堆贮、处理能力增强。

2000年,天铁集团自主开发烧结局域网。采集的生产信息数据及时上传至生产服务器,实现生产工艺信息自动采集、传递、统计、管理以及生产管理信息共享,达到生产操作与管理控制一体化。该技术为国内领先水平,获2000年度天津市科技进步三等奖。继一烧车间后,二烧车间也全面实现自动微机配料的智能控制,同时烧结生产心脏设备的主抽风机成功实现计算机远程监控,抽风机安全经济运行水平大为提高。生石灰由气力输送改为机械输送、一烧配料室扩建、精矿仓扩建、一烧混合料上料皮带增宽、抽风机高负压转子等改造项目相继完成,为新建126平方米烧结机投产创造有利条件。原料38平方米和配料25平方米电除尘器建成投产,原料上料系统生产环境显著改善。

2001年,天铁集团126平方米烧结机(6号烧结机)建成投产。其年设计烧结矿生产能力为125万吨。6号烧结机采用国内先进的冷矿、铺底料工艺,技术装备更为先进,自动化水平更高,工艺更加合理完善,多项技术处于国内领先水平。6号机进一步推动烧结生产的发展:采用小球烧结工艺,生产碱度0.7倍、品位61%的酸性烧结矿,有效满足高炉对酸性炉料的生产需求,减少价格昂贵的球团矿使用量,提高入炉矿综合品位和熟料比,炉料结构优化,生产成本降低。

2002年,天铁集团开展管控一体化信息系统建设。采用先进、成熟、可靠的变频调速、PLC可编程序控制器、DCS集散系统、计算机、网络等电子信息技术,实现从过程控制级到管理级的管控一体化信息系统,逐步对一烧操作回路、一烧仪表监控系统、一烧配料系统、二烧操作回路、二烧仪表监控系统、二烧配料系统、原料操作回路、料场操作回路进行改造,并以调度室作为生产信息管理系统中心,完善计算机在生产调度及能源质量方面的应用。126平方米烧结机一次混合机由Φ2.8×6米改为Φ3.0×9米,混匀造球效果提高。成品烧结矿采用自动取样,增强取样的代表性和科学性。

2003年,天铁集团将普通电除尘器改为盲刺式除尘器,提高除尘效率,降低粉尘排放浓度,进一步改善环境,延长风机转子寿命。一次配料实现微机自动配料,提高配料精度,为二次精确配料创造有利条件。开发网络视频监视系统,对一料场、二料场、翻车机、堆取料机、各车间重点岗位等实现实时监控,提高调度效率,管理效益显著。采用进口富粉取代国内富粉组织生产,进口富粉配比逐步加大。为减少高铝进口粉矿对烧结、炼铁生产的不良影响,在烧结料中配加白云石,促进炼铁顺产、高产。

2004年,天铁集团成功进行制粒系统改造。Φ6米造球盘、Φ3.8×18米大型混合机等强化制粒造球设备引入烧结生产,烧结整体工艺技术装备水平大幅提高。由于混匀造球得到强化,混合料物理性能明显改善,混合料中>3毫米粒级含量达到80%以上,烧结料透气性明显提高,低碳厚料烧结真正得以实现,烧结料层平均提高120毫米以上,固体燃耗平均降低10千克/吨矿,转鼓指数提高4.5%,返矿率降低11%,成矿率提高3.5%,烧结各项技术经济指标实现历史性突破,达到同行业先进水平。经济效益和环境效益突出,工序能耗降到70千克标煤/吨矿以下,自主开发将钢泥稀释后在烧结一次混合和制粒系统造球盘喷加的新技术,实现钢泥高效合理回收利用。增建2台4辊破碎机,实现煤、焦分开破碎,燃料粒度合格率达到100%。一烧车间淘汰泥辊加反射板的传统布料工艺,采用"圆辊给料机+4辊布料器"的新型布料技术,克服烧结料不合理的粒度偏析现象,成功实现低温烧结和高氧位烧结新技术,降低工人劳动强度。该混合料制粒系统改造技术是天铁烧结发展史上一次重大的技术革命,技术创新程度很高,达到国内领先水平。该项目获2005年度天津市技术创新一等奖、2005年度天津市科技进步三等奖。

2004年2月20日,天钢公司265平方米烧结系统建成投产。该烧结机有效长度为66.25米,主要为2000立方米高炉生产提供高碱度烧结矿。2005年该机共生产烧结矿215.5万吨,烧结机利用系数达到设计指标,日产烧结矿7000~8000吨。该烧结机吸收国内外投产的最新烧结工艺系统的诸多优点,其采用的一系列新工艺、装备、技术有:小球团烧结技术,厚料层烧结技术(630毫米),偏析布料技术,混合料预热技术,烧结矿整粒技术等。此外,还配备最先进的电除尘装置、余热回收利用系统、污水处理设施及噪声消音器,其废水、废气、噪声均通过天津环保监测中心的测试,达到国家排放标准,被誉为清洁工厂。

2005年,天铁集团一烧车间2号烧结机利用大修期间进行扩容改造。在保持原有生产工艺的基础上,台车规格、星轮、单辊等相关部件作匹配调整处理，使烧结机有效烧结面积由50平方米增加到60平方米，实现年增产烧结矿10万吨以上，为其他烧结机扩容改造积累宝贵经验。托车、压车新技术应用在翻车机系统，翻车机事故率降低。采用石灰竖窑煅烧加工生石灰工艺，生石灰氧化钙含量提高到80%以上，纯白灰烧结得以实施推广。自主开发烧结机新型松料器，改善料层的透气性，提高垂直烧结速度。进厂原料采用自动取样系统，取样更具代表性和科学性。

第二节 炼 焦

1991年，国内的焦炭产量跃居世界第一，成为全球最大的焦炭生产国，炼焦产业进入快速发展期。天津铁厂最初作为炼铁为主的企业，在煤炭焦化工艺和装备方面同样取得许多创新成果。

1992年，天铁集团完成3号焦炉氨水喷洒装置的改造。阻止氨水流入炭化室内，解决由此造成的炉墙损坏及炼焦煤资源浪费的问题，节约维护费用，延长炉体使用寿命。

1993年，天铁集团完成推焦车托压辊及挡辊改造。将推焦车托压辊及挡辊滑动轴承改为滚动轴承，集中润滑改为自动润滑，方便检修维护，降低劳动强度。2003年，推焦移门及平煤机构进而采用液压推动器，其启动、运行速度稳定，容易控制，避免损坏炉门现象的发生，并且延长设备的使用寿命。

1994年，天铁集团增加软水系统。为洗氨塔提供优质软水，提高煤气洗氨效果，降低塔后煤气含氨，防止设备结垢，保证生产的正常进行。2001年，完成高压氨水泵变频控制方式改造，系统采用Momentum PLC及concept组态王软件，通过网络控制技术，用鼓风机监控机做上位机，通过变频控制的PID调节，实现氨水压力的稳定操作，满足生产需求。

1996年，天铁集团投用核子秤自动配煤系统。配煤精度和焦炭的产、质量提高。该项目获2000年度天津市科学技术进步三等奖。1998年引进40千克试验焦炉，通过炼焦配煤试验，对扩大炼焦煤资源、合理指导配煤及稳定提高焦炭质量起到积极作用。2002年备煤预破碎工程完工投用，消除冬季配煤盘堵料现象，提高冬季配煤精度，为生产优质焦炭提供保障。同年，还研制完成并投用焦炭自动采制样系统，实现焦炭采制样自动化，提高取样的代表性和反映焦炭质量的真实性。该系统工艺装备在国内处于领先水平。

1998年，天铁集团引进火焰焊补技术。对焦炉炉墙产生的剥蚀、裂缝、凹坑、掉角、熔洞等进行修补，保证焦炉的正常生产。完成3号、4号焦炉边火道补充加热，使焦炉煤气在边火道内与高炉煤气混合燃烧，从而达到提高边火道温度、改善焦炭质量的目的。2000年完成振动筛改造，将振动筛改成溜筛，解决振动筛检修、维护量大的问题，消除焦炭易堵溜口的事故隐患。同时，改进焦炭挡板式自动放焦装置，变刮板为移动挡板，简化操作，降低粉焦率，在节能、增效方面效果显著，成果获得国家实用新型专利授权；对运焦皮带滚筒进行包皮，延长滚筒的使用寿命，减少维修量；投用焦炉红外线测温系统，使得在测量横排及直行温度时，无需手工记数，数据可以直接储存到测温仪内，然后导入电脑，实现数据的打印统计功能，提高测温准确性。

2000年，天铁集团完成改造焦炉联锁微机监控系统。增强焦炉作业的安全系数，实现推焦电流、推焦时间、装煤量自行记录统计等多种功能，使焦炉操作、维护和管理提高到新水平。2004年研制完成并实施4号焦炉高炉煤气富化加热技术，炉顶空间温度得到有效控制，提高化产品收得率，减缓炉顶空间石墨的生长速度，改善炉顶职工操作环境，提高焦炉纵向加热均匀性，从而提高焦炭质量。由于炉顶空间温度降低，保护炉顶护炉铁件，延长炉龄。

2001年，天铁集团完成备煤皮带系统集控及装卸桥变频控制改造。实现备煤皮带运行的动态监控及粉碎机翻板的自动联锁控制，促进安全生产与管理，降低维护费用，改善职工作业环境。2004年引进皮带热接技术,使得皮带胶接处更加平整,胶接强度大大提高,显著延长皮带的胶接周期和使用寿命。

2002年,天铁集团投用1号、2号熄焦池自动补水系统。实现自动补水,并且能够同时启动报警装置,避免因红焦及漫水而造成的经济损失。同年,煤塔漏嘴、冶金焦仓漏嘴采用液压式自动取煤和放焦,操作方便快捷,降低劳动强度,设备的使用寿命延长。

2003年,天铁集团完成1号、2号粉碎机改造并投入使用。实现锤头最优化排列,且新锤头采用正向旋转无蓖条,待锤头磨损、煤的细度降低后,再采用反向旋转(有蓖条),以延长锤头使用寿命,既满足生产需要,又简化设备、节约备件、减轻劳动强度。同年,采用ZNQY-D型智能汽车煤自动采制样控制系统,采制样过程全部自动控制,实现随机取样,提高取样的代表性并降低劳动强度。

2004年,天铁集团对装煤车气缸改为电液推杆。减小煤车的振动,延长设备使用寿命。2005年,2号推焦车移门机构改为可升降托辊,保证2号大车可同时在4座焦炉上使用,减少职工劳动强度。

第三节 炼 铁

20世纪90年代,天铁集团高炉烧结矿碱度逐步提高到1.7～1.9倍,烧结矿高温冶金性能改善,高炉烧结矿率由65%~70%提高到85%～90%,优化炉料结构,为提升高炉各项技术经济指标奠定良好物质基础。

一、喷煤技术

1991年11月,天铁集团煤粉新喷粉站落成。4台10吨/时球磨机投产。

1997年,天铁集团为推进喷煤产业化进程,空分厂增建15000立方标米/每小时制氧机系统,采用内压缩流程,具有安全系数高、调节裕度大等特点。1998年利用炼钢余氧进行富氧喷煤,并实现全风温操作。1999年5座高炉全部完成单管路加煤粉分配器的喷煤工艺改造,实现高炉的全风口喷煤作业。2000年1号高炉煤比达到172.76千克／吨。该高炉富氧喷煤产业化工程技术项目获2000年度天津市科技进步二等奖。

2003年,天铁集团建成4号空分15000立方标米/每小时制氧机系统。采用外压缩流程,具有氧、氮、氩及液氧、液氮、液氩的生产能力。同年,采用射流式排烟机代替离心式抽油烟对各个油箱排烟进行改造,既避免浪费能源,又降低设备的故障率。该厂还增设一个调压站平衡炼钢、炼铁用氧,实现低压氧气并网,在3号制氧机意外停车时,也可以由1、4号制氧机向高炉提供氧气,供高炉富氧喷吹。

2001年,天铁集团完成对1—4号球磨机的工艺改造。单台球磨机出力由10吨/时提高到20吨/时。

二、设备改造

2002～2003年,天铁集团为解决热风炉燃烧不稳、易灭火问题,对1号、2号热风炉进行改造,将其改造为蓄热式加热炉。

2003年4月,天铁集团为降低炼铁成本,缓解空压风紧张的压力,开始采用氮气代替空压风向高炉输粉,充分利用二次能源,节约一次能源,实现高炉混喷煤粉,为提高喷煤比作出贡献。同年,又实施煤粉浓相输送技术改造,节约用气量和输粉时间。

2003年,天铁集团对制粉1—4号球磨机实施无螺栓衬瓦改造,提高球磨机运行周期。2004年对1号球磨机进行大布袋技术改造,同年10月投产。

2005年,天铁集团对输粉系统进行PLC系统改造。输送煤粉全部实现自动化,大大降低误操作率,保障生产过程稳定和安全。为更好地满足炼铁生产需要,提供清洁优质气源,同年又对原有空压站进行扩容改造，将原5台日立103立方标米/每分钟活塞式空压机改造为6台阿特拉斯100立方标米/每分钟离心式空压机。当年12月底投产2台。

三、技术改造

1992年，天铁集团热风炉助燃风机首次由一炉一机改为集中供风方式。3座热风炉设2台风机，一用一备。同年，引进双腔式风口，淘汰多年应用的空腔风口，以适应冶炼强度提高后对风口性能的要求；在炉役后期高炉生产中引进钒钛渣护炉技术，取得护炉生产成功。

1993年，天铁集团开始在高炉大修中应用炉底自焙炭砖加水冷炉底结构。热风炉为改造型高温内燃式结构，并使用长寿热风阀，喷煤系统改为单管路加分配器浓相输送方式。1997年其3号高炉大修首次由双钟炉顶改为天铁型无料钟设备。到1998年4号高炉大修时，炉底炉缸采用半石墨化低气孔自焙炭砖、复合棕刚玉陶瓷杯结构，炉腹、炉腰采用小块冷却壁，双层水管冷却，炉身采用冷却板和冷却壁相结合的冷却方式，为高强度冶炼条件下的高炉长寿打下基础。2004年开始在高炉大修时铁口周围采用铜冷却壁。2005年又在炉腹、炉腰的薄弱部位引进铸钢冷却壁。

1996年，天铁集团高炉槽下过筛改用琴弦棒条筛。2001年又引进双层棒条式自清理振动筛，过筛效率不断提高。同年对高炉无钟炉顶的关键设备进行改造，使气密箱的使用寿命大大延长；高炉供料的栈桥系统实施电除尘项目，解决栈桥移动收尘和布袋除尘阻力大的难题，改善职工的工作环境。2000年开始开口机由电钻吊挂式开口机逐个改进成为气动凿岩式开铁口机，实现直线开铁口；2003年开始使用无水炮泥，缩短开口时间，确保铁口深度，实现高炉冶练强度提高后的安全生产。

1996年，天铁集团在1号高炉大修中取消二次仪表，应用PLC控制，实现计算机操作的人机控制界面。1997年，天铁集团炼铁厂生产系统完成联网，实现局域网控制。2001年，局域网由100M升级为1G，网络控制技术在国内生产系统中处于领先地位。同年，天铁集团还引进高炉料面红外摄像仪及图像处理系统，打开炉内黑匣子，根据直观的炉内料面和煤气流分布，指导工长调节炉况，促进高炉稳定顺行。2002年，在5号高炉引进工业总线控制技术，成为国内首家在生产中应用该技术的炼铁企业。同年，天铁集团还将雷达料位控制系统和风机变频技术引入高炉生产控制系统中。

1998年，天铁集团对高炉风口区高压水进行改造。水压由392千帕升到784千帕，提高风口冷却强度。同年，在水冲渣设备技术改造中，创新应用虹吸管技术，泄水次数由改造前的4次每年减少到1次每2年，每年可为企业节水5万立方米，并且该项技术获得国家专利。1999年，天铁集团对高炉原料供应系统进行改造，在原转运站不变的情况下，增加一条新皮带及下料流嘴的原料输送系统，实现4条皮带自如切换输送多品种原、燃料，解决炼铁产能提高后原燃料供给能力不足的现状。

1998年，天铁集团首次应用空料线打水停炉操作法，实现安全、快速停炉。并且开炉技术取得突破：第一次应用全烧结矿开炉，避免生矿开炉时石灰石粉化带来顺行差、达产周期长的技术难题，降低材料消耗及劳动强度；应用铁口预埋压缩风管技术，使第一炉铁顺利流出。

2001年开始，天铁集团炼铁厂通过设备改造，高炉炉顶压力大幅度提高，促进高炉节能降耗，生产效率提高。2002年，开发降硅冶炼工艺技术，生铁含硅量逐年下降，高炉增产节焦显著。2003年，开展烧结矿配加氧化镁（MgO）技术攻关，改善炉渣流动性及脱硫效果，铁水一级品率大幅提高。同年，开始进行喷煤系统双系列设备改造，为高炉稳定喷吹和实施混喷技术打下基础。实施热风炉烟气余热回收技术，并采用掺氧烧炉技术，全厂风温水平大幅提高，促进高炉操作技术的整体进步，使得天铁高炉风温、焦比、煤比3项指标在国内同类型高炉中排名前3位，节能降耗成效显著。该厂降硅冶炼工艺技术开发项目获2004年天津市科技进步三等奖；高炉综合应用技术开发项目获2005年天津市科技进步三等奖。

2001年7月1日，天钢公司高炉炼铁工程开工建设。2004年2月29日，2000立方米大型高炉及265平方米带式烧结机、20万平方米大型综合原料场等配套的公辅系统正式建成投产，形成年产140万吨铁的生产能力，彻底淘汰天钢化铁炼钢的落后工艺。2005年，2000立方米高炉共计生产合格生铁141.923万吨。2000立方米高炉的炉底炉缸耐火材料采用大块炭砖炉底、美国UCAR热压小炭砖、陶瓷杯技术。高炉炉顶布料设备引进卢森堡PW公司无料钟炉顶；炉体采用铸铁冷却壁和铜冷却壁结合的薄壁炉衬技术、水渣处理采用新式环保型INBA粒化系统；高炉煤气清洗采用比召夫煤气清洗系统技术；配套高炉煤气余压透平发电机系统（TRT）。为降低焦比节约成本，2000立方米高炉于2005年7月27日采用先进的富氧大喷煤技术，使高炉喷煤比从29.5千克／吨铁增加到135千克／吨铁以上，入炉焦比从喷吹前的560千克／吨铁降至385千克／吨铁。

第四节 炼 钢

天津是国内最早炼钢的地方之一。20世纪90年代初，天津钢厂有100吨平炉2座，20吨转炉3座，3~5吨电炉4座；特殊钢厂有10吨电炉3座；轧钢三厂有30吨电炉1座。随着技术进步和规划调整，这些老设备逐步淘汰或停产。

一、转炉

天钢转炉炼钢厂有20吨转炉三座，能力90万吨，一直是天津的炼钢主力军，由于采用化铁炼钢，工艺落后，能耗高，随着天钢东移而淘汰。1993年5月5日天铁集团增钢工程典礼开工。1994年1月24日天铁集团组建成立炼钢厂。

1994年8月5日天铁集团炼钢厂1号转炉热负荷投料试车成功，结束天铁集团有铁无钢的历史。

1995 ~ 1996年，天铁集团炼钢厂2号、3号转炉相继建成投产。

1997年，天铁集团炼钢厂引进新技术和更新改造设备。1997年3月，溅渣护炉技术应用在转炉上，使转炉炉龄大幅度提高。1998年，采用钢渣磁选工艺，将炉渣中的钢、渣逐级分离并回收利用，变废为宝。1999年3月，开发应用合金烘烤炉，通过预热干燥铁合金，使出钢温降减小，从而降低转炉的出钢温度。1999年7月，改造3号转炉的DCS系统，使下料系统完全实现键盘操作，氧气流量实现真正的PID控制。2000年12月，3号转炉采用音平控渣技术，在降罩条件下实现正常炼钢操作，当年产量达到190万吨。2001年4月13日，重大技改项目"转炉煤气回收工程"，实现设备联动热负荷试车一次成功，转炉煤气实现全量回收，在节约能源、保护环境方面取得重大进步。该项目获2004年度天津市科技进步二等奖。

2001年，天津钢铁有限公司炼钢厂动工建设。1号100吨顶底复合吹炼转炉于2004年3月2日投产，至第一个炉役，炉龄达到12906炉，处于国内领先水平。2号转炉于2005年2月20日投产，3号转炉于2005年5月24日投产。2005年平均炉龄10618炉，最高炉龄达21155炉。天津钢铁有限公司炼钢厂的转炉采用4点啮合全悬挂倾动和扭力杆装置，供氧采用4孔拉瓦尔喷头。转炉配备底吹透气系统，加强钢水搅拌，有利于提高钢的质量，技术装备达到国内先进水平。

二、精炼

1994年，天津钢厂与郑州大学等单位共同开发自排渣法连续脱硫工艺。该工艺实现铁水连续脱硫和渣、铁自动分离、排渣功能，在铁水脱硫方面，属于国内首创，达到国际先进水平。原始铁水中硫在0.04~0.08%范围内，采用混冲工艺，铁水脱硫率可以达到50%以上，采用底部吹气搅拌时，脱硫率可达到80%，可降低综合处理成本60元/吨。该技术解决包衬耐火材料寿命低等技术难点，环境负荷小，在国内有推广条件和应用价值。

2002年，天铁炼钢厂为开发品种钢的需要，新建一座45吨LF钢包精炼炉。2005年第二座LF精炼炉投产，处理钢水量40~50吨/炉。配备钢包喂丝技术。LF炉具有对钢液升温、脱氧、脱硫、脱气、合金微调、吹氩搅拌等功能，使钢液成份和温度更加均匀，可提高钢液质量。LF炉作为转炉和连铸机之间的缓冲设备，保证转炉、连铸匹配生产，实现多炉连浇。

2004年3月3日，天钢公司炼钢厂100吨LF钢包精炼炉投产，处理钢水量70~110吨/炉，处理能力80万吨/年。配备钢包喂丝技术，采用双线喂丝机。LF精炼炉可提高钢液纯净度，均匀成分和温度。通过LF炉精炼，钢水温度可以满足连铸工艺要求；处理时间满足多炉连浇要求并进行成分微调，以保证产品具有合格的成分及实现最低成本控制，并使钢水纯净度满足产品质量要求。

2004年3月3日，天钢公司炼钢厂100吨VD真空精炼炉投产，处理能力80万吨/年。该炉配套包括真空系统、水与介质分配系统、电气设备、基础自动化与监视系统。采用双罐位高架式布置方式及全自动智能型控制方式，额定容量100吨，可以在真空状态下降低有害气体的分压，并在氩气搅拌的作用下，将有害气体除去，技术装备达到国内先进水平。

三、连铸

天津钢厂2台方坯连铸是全国最早全套引进的设备，以此为样板进行消化吸收，形成中国的方坯连铸制造技术。天津钢厂2台板坯连铸机也是全国最早引进技术的样机，为自主研制开发连铸机提供技术资料和经验。

1994年11月，天津钢厂在消化吸收引进板坯连铸机控制系统的基础上，自行开发设计出第二台板坯连铸机控制系统。除实现第一台1—8段二冷水串级调节、二冷水自动起动强冷控制，雾化空气系统自动调节等外，还将原基本拉速配水法改为尾坯吨钢配水控制及拉钢条件逻辑控制等，增加二冷水控制采用一次方程、按工艺条件选择6种配水表以及尾坯处理等功能。该控制系统达到国内领先水平。

1995年1月23日，天铁集团炼钢厂第一台连铸机（2号连铸机）热试成功并投入生产。同年，1号连铸机建成投产。1996年，3#、4#连铸机建成投产，其中1#、4#为5流，2#、3#为4流，可浇注断面为120×120毫米、150×150毫米、160×220毫米、160×250毫米、160×280毫米，浇注半径为R6000毫米。

1996年，天铁集团炼钢厂适应市场需求进行设备改造。2号连铸机断面由150×150毫米方坯改为120×120毫米方坯，1号连铸机由剪切机改为火焰切割机，直流四辊拉矫机改为交流五辊拉矫机。同年年底，天铁集团炼钢厂实现全连铸生产，当年产量达到50万吨。

1999年12月，天铁集团炼钢厂应用小方坯高效连铸改造技术。通过高强度冷却，均匀性好的结晶器振动技术，“二冷”技术，拉矫机技术等技术系统的合成，实现高的拉坯速度、高的作业率、高的连浇率以及高温无缺陷的铸坯；同时引进自动定尺技术，将定尺准确率提高到99.9%，降低工人的劳动强度。

2000年5月，天铁集团炼钢厂成功引进中间包连续测温技术。实现中间包钢水温度的连续测量，提高测量的稳定性和可靠性；同时，将冷床由原来的单侧水平出坯，改造为双侧斜坡出坯，从而将冷床的储坯能力提高3倍。

2003年，天铁集团炼钢厂推行中间包水口快换技术，促进连铸生产的稳定，为炉机匹配工艺的实现奠定基础。

2004年，天铁集团炼钢厂对3#连铸机冷床进行改造。包括连铸机控制设备和液压驱动式步进冷床改造，使生产线具备拉12米钢坯的条件，年底开发应用液面自动控制技术。2005年，为适应市场需要，天铁集团炼钢厂增设一条板坯生产线，年产量达到265万吨。

2004年3月2日，天钢公司炼钢厂1号连铸机热试投产。该铸机为康卡斯特方、圆坯连铸机，6机6流，采用结晶器和末端两极电磁搅拌；结晶器液面自动控制系统；二冷水自动控制；9~16米连续矫直；高拉速，拉坯速度1.7~3.4米/分；浇注时间平均每炉36分钟，可生产150×150毫米、Φ150毫米、Φ160毫米、Φ180毫米、Φ200毫米等断面优质钢坯。

2004年12月9日，天钢公司炼钢厂2号连铸机热试投产。该铸机为全弧形连续矫直方坯连铸机，采用结晶器电磁搅拌;结晶器液面自动控制系统;二冷水自动控制;整体五辊连续矫直式拉矫机;拉坯速度2.4~3.0米/分;可浇铸150×150毫米、160×160毫米等铸坯断面尺寸。

2005年6月28日,天钢公司炼钢厂3号板坯连铸机热试投产。该铸机为直结晶器连续弯曲连续矫直弧形板坯连铸机。连铸机拉速范围0.2 ~ 2.5米/分;设计产量100万吨/年;浇铸断面:180、200、250×1050~1600毫米(100进级)。

2005年12月27日,天钢公司炼钢厂4号板坯连铸机热试投产。该铸机由奥钢联设计制造,为弧型连铸机,直型结晶器,有分段铸流保护装置,连续弯曲/矫直(奥钢联弯曲/矫直技术)。4号连铸机采用结晶器漏钢预报;智能扇形段;动态轻压下新技术,根据品种、规格,拉速控制在1.10~2.00米/分。产量130万吨/年。板坯厚度:180、200毫米和250毫米冷态;板坯宽度范围:1320~2100毫米冷态;技术装备达到国内领先水平。

第五节 轧 钢

天津轧钢企业众多,技术实力雄厚,轧制钢材包括线材、型材、中厚板材、薄板带材、钢管等多个系列。在各种专用无缝钢管和特种管材的生产技术提升和自主研发创新方面成效显著。

一、线材

1995年,天钢集团高速线材厂建成投产。系天津市“八五”重点技术改造项目。该厂引进的高速线材轧机是摩根公司于20世纪90年代向中国提供的第一套高技术的单线无扭控冷线材轧机。设计年产能力35万吨优质光面线材,轧制速度100米/秒。轧机构成为:12架平/立交替的粗轧/中轧机,4架平/立交替的预精轧机,10架V型超重无扭精轧机。设计使用坯料尺寸135×135×16000毫米,成品卷重2~2.2吨,可生产Φ(5.5 ~ 20)毫米共30个产品规格的光面线材,有低、中、高碳钢,低合金钢,焊条钢,弹簧钢,冷镦钢等10余个钢种产品。

2000年,天钢集团高速线材厂引进英国IPL公司的测径仪,即时在线监控盘条外形尺寸,产品的尺寸精度大大提高。

2001年,天钢集团高速线材厂开发出螺纹系列产品,弥补轧机设计初期不能轧制螺纹产品的不足。通过对精轧机内辊环进行重新配置,改进精轧内导卫系统,利用空过架次转速高的优势,改变成品出口架次,提高螺纹钢轧制速度。

2002年,天钢集团高速线材厂为扩大对原料的适应能力,提高产能,对原有摩根孔型系统进行技术改造。设计出轧制120~150毫米断面、新的孔型系统,2002年7月28日完成轧制150方坯的改造工作。

2003年7月,天钢集团高速线材厂将加热炉重油手动燃烧控制系统改造成加热炉计算机人工智能专家控制系统。正常生产情况下,使用专家系统,钢坯开轧温度可控制在工艺要求的±20℃范围内,同轴温差在±25℃范围内,能够满足加热工艺的要求;重油单耗可降低6%~8%,氧化烧损率可降低1‰,具有较好的节能降耗效果。

2003年8月,天钢集团高速线材厂在1架轧机前增加高压水除磷装置。将钢坯表面的氧化铁皮清除掉98%以上,提高产品质量,延长轧辊及导卫使用寿命,同时降低轧件表面氧化铁皮量,降低车间粉尘量,改善职工的作业环境。

二、型材

2002年7日,天铁轧二从意大利波米尼公司引进的全连轧棒材生产线动工,2003年8日投产。采用先进技术和工艺:侧进侧出步进梁蓄热式加热炉;低温轧制技术;轧后余热处理技术;高精度飞剪技术;采用自动计数、自动打包、自动称量等先进技术,生产线全部计算机自动化控制;预留钢坯焊接机位置,将来可实现无头轧制。该工艺技术装备达到国际先进水平。

2004年,天钢集团双棒材生产线开工建设。该生产线为背靠背配置两条全连续式、高架布置生产螺纹钢筋和光面圆钢棒材。生产的钢种有碳素结构钢、优质碳素结构钢、低合金钢及少量合金结构钢、弹簧钢、冷墩钢等。为进一步拓宽产品品种,在1号轧线配置达涅利公司最新发明的大盘卷生产线,可以无扭的方式将Φ(12~32)毫米的棒材卷曲成优质、密实的棒材卷,盘卷最重可达3.5吨;在2号轧线配置两架减定径机组,可以生产Φ(16~70)毫米的高精度优质圆钢。两条生产线均采用LTR-低温轧制技术和QTB-穿水冷却技术,采用达涅利提供的棒材圆钢测径仪,技术装备达到国内领先水平。

三、中厚板材

1994年,天钢中板厂完成重大技术改造。将3辊劳特式轧机拆除,在原地新建一台4辊可逆式粗轧机,率先在全国实现中厚钢板双4辊轧机生产。粗轧机厚度,采用高精度辊缝位置检测仪控制;精轧机安装液压压下AGC。同时,在线配备远红外测温仪,提供每一道次的温度值,以便合理控制道次压下量和终轧温度。在矫直机后,新增一台倍尺剪切机,双倍尺钢板经横断后再进入冷床冷却。为了确保钢板有足够的冷却时间,新建一套滚轮拉钢式冷床设备,延长精整作业线,提高钢板的质量。为提高钢板剪切精度,在2号纵向剪切机上安装微机控制定宽装置,保证钢板剪切的宽度精度;在4号横向剪切机上,安装自行设计的齿条式定长装置,实现3000~12000毫米长度范围内任意定长剪切,提高长度剪切精度。

2002年7月9日,天钢集团中板厂实现钢坯热送。到2004年热装率达到90%以上。钢坯热送、热装的实现,大大降低工序能耗,减少等火时间,提高作业率,并延长加热炉使用周期,降低修炉费用。

2002年11月,天钢集团中板厂对1号加热炉实施内墙粘贴纤维扎块技术,并于2003年2月在该加热炉上应用重油掺水乳化燃烧节能技术,收到良好的节能效果。节油率在5%左右,减少二氧化硫及氮氧化物的排放量。2005年,中板厂继续对加热炉结构、供热制度进行调整,从而提高钢坯的加热能力,改善加热质量,减少等温时间,提高作业率。经过技术改造,该厂成为全国冶金行业生产中厚钢板的重点企业之一。

2004年9月,天钢集团中板厂开始新建3500毫米双四辊可逆中厚板轧机工程。设计生产能力为120万吨/年。该生产线可生产普通碳素结构钢、优质碳素结构钢、低合金高强度钢、压力容器板、锅炉板、造船板、高强度结构钢、汽车大梁板、桥梁板、管线钢板等。生产线主体设备包括:两座蓄热式步进梁加热炉,高压水除鳞系统,3500毫米的粗、精轧可逆式轧机,全液压十一辊强力矫直机,两台63×42米的滚盘式冷床,双边圆盘剪,定尺剪,全自动喷号打标机,厚板火焰切割装置。

四、薄板带材

(一)提高加工技术

1994年10月,天津市冷轧薄板厂与中科院力学研究所合作,开发利用YAG激光技术对冷轧工作辊进行表面加工,成功地轧制出国内首批优质激光毛面冷轧薄板,使中国继比利时、日本、德国之后,成为世界上第四个掌握激光毛化冷轧辊技术并应用于冷轧薄板生产的国家。

1999年,天津冶金第二机械厂与广州富通公司合作成立环通激光技术公司,开发出激光表面改性技术,填补激光加工应用技术空白。其中,70锰铸钢轧辊激光合金化技术,使轧辊单孔过钢量提高80%~120%;开发研制出的激光熔覆、送粉、送丝装置和14种不同成份熔覆材料,对冶金、石化、机械、电力等行业的进口贵重部件可及时进行有效修复。

(二)引进先进工艺

1992年,天津市带钢厂建设Φ280/Φ700×700毫米四辊可逆冷轧机组,并配套意大利米诺公司的AGC系统,实现轧制的张力闭环和厚控闭环控制。生产厚0.2`1.5毫米、宽550毫米的优质中宽冷轧带钢,年产量2万吨。

2004年,天津里碑冷轧板材有限公司投产拉弯矫直重卷机组。系国内自行设计配套的第一条1450毫米宽带拉弯矫直、切边、重卷功能的机组。拉弯矫直重卷机组速度250米/分,年产量25万吨,电气控制是由意大利EDM公司采用西门子全数字交流变频控制系统成套引进,具有延伸率控制精度高、范围广、矫直效果突出,板形可达3I以内。该公司还成功地开发冷轧极薄板、双光镜面板、光面板和酸洗平整板,促进产品结构的调整。

2005年,天津里碑冷轧板材有限公司投资引进意大利米诺公司4辊单机架冷轧机组,使年生产0.2~2.0毫米规格的优质冷轧薄板的能力增至50万吨以上。2005年国内配套电解脱脂清洗线机组等设备。电解脱脂清洗线机组速度240米/分,年产量25万吨,采用全数字西门子交流变频控制系统,清洗表面反射率可达95%以上。其生产设备达到国际先进水平。

(三)开发新产品

2003年,沙摹亚达满公司投入1500万元(占60%)与天津市轧一制钢公司合资成立天津华信制钢有限公司,建设年产8万吨热轧热镀锌带生产线。

2004年,天津市轧一制钢公司利用热轧热镀锌带生产线开发钢结构用热轧热镀锌带产品。产品厚1.5~4.0毫米,宽183~650毫米,镀锌层厚度为100~350克/平方米(双面),常规产品镀锌层厚度为275克/平方米(双面)。冷弯性能、锌层附粘力、表面质量均达到国内先进水平,产品满足冷弯型钢的要求。

2004年,天津市轧一制钢公司与天津市农垦集团公司合资,采用国内领先技术,建设年产15万吨连续热镀锌板生产线。产品厚0.2~1.6毫米,宽700~1250毫米,镀锌层厚度为50~350克每平方米(双面)。产品质量达到国际先进水平,出口美国、欧洲和东南亚等国家。

(四)技术改造

2000年,天钢集团初轧厂利用Φ550×2横列式轧机及附属设备,改造为设计年产量25万吨的带钢生产线。生产线增设推钢式连续加热炉1座、“2立7平”精轧机组、精整区域的两台立式卷取机及附属设备等。产品规格厚度为1.8~4.5毫米,宽度为120~250毫米。为提高产品质量,精轧机组先后增设辊缝仪、在线测宽、上位机、在线测温等新技术。

2001年,天津冶金集团轧一制钢公司通过对已有生产机组的改造,在全国率先开发出厚1.5~2.0毫米,宽196~355毫米的热轧带钢,满足市场以部分热轧带钢替代冷轧带钢产品的需求,满足冷弯型钢用料要求。

2002年,天钢集团初轧厂为降低生产成本,提高产品竞争力,对加热炉实施“油改气”的技术改造项目。由8台Φ2.6米煤气发生炉的煤制气取代重油,并在煤气炉炉体上安装两套测温装置,通过显示温度的变化,测算出煤气炉内煤层和煤灰层的高度、煤灰层的均匀性,在保证煤气产量的前提下最大限度地降低煤耗。

2003年,天钢集团初轧厂在其加热炉纵水管采用孔洞式全热滑轨新技术,消除钢坯在加热过程中的水梁黑印。该技术应用后基本上未出现等温现象,产量提高10吨/时。

2004年,天钢集团带钢厂针对一架Φ550铸钢轧辊孔型磨损严重的问题,采用激光涂敷方法,使轧制吨位由原来的1万吨提高到2万吨。

2005年,天钢集团带钢厂采用先进的无机传热技术进行余热回收。该项目的实施,解决带钢生产和生活用汽问题,既获得经济效益,又获得环保效益,实现循环经济。

同年,天钢集团带钢厂开发带钢新品种。轧制出1.4~1.7毫米薄规格带钢,有效提高带钢经济效益。并实现用150×150×3000毫米钢坯生产厚度为1.4~1.7毫米,宽度145~204毫米的定型产品目标。2005年带钢产量达到53.82万吨,超过设计能力1.15倍。

(五)提高产品质量

2001年1月15日,天铁集团带钢延伸改造工程动工。8月5日热负荷试车成功,生产出第一卷带钢,结束天铁有钢无材的历史。2005年带钢产量达到68万吨。

2002年,天铁集团对轧线导卫系统进行改造。轧线导卫装置的使用周期由原来的1个月提高到2年以上,节约备件材料。

2003年,天铁集团对4辊轧机辊系系统进行改造。将换辊时间由原来的2小时缩短到10分钟,生产作业率提高,带钢质量也得到提高。

2005年,天铁集团的两辊轧机盘车机设计使用,提高轧机的上线率,降低劳动强度。同年,为提高除鳞效果,实施除鳞工艺改造,粗轧采用高压除鳞,中、精轧采用风管除鳞,提高带钢的质量,满足冷轧料的要求。

五、钢管及其他

(一)引进技术

1993年,天津市无缝钢管公司引进具有国际先进水平的德国曼内斯曼.米尔公司的Assel轧机,与从德国KOCKS公司引进的24架张力减径机组形成配套完整的、具有国际先进水平的高精度热轧无缝钢管生产线。重点开发的品种有:高压锅炉管、石油裂化管、石油套管、地质钻探管、汽车半轴套管等。

1995年10月,天津市无缝钢管厂开发空心抽油杆用冷拔高强度无缝钢管。空心抽油杆采油技术是中国首创的先进采油技术,采用空心管材取代普通抽油机上的实心棒材,与实心棒材相比具有强度高、节省钢材等特点。该产品适用于在井下腐蚀性气体环境中长期往复运动,产品在国内处于领先水平。该产品用于国内各大油田,部分产品加工出口,进入国际市场。

1998年5月,天津市无缝钢管厂研制API油管用J55、N80钢级热轧无缝钢管。该项目在国内首先掌握用阿塞尔机组生产油管的技术,并形成一套较完整的适合油管生产的工艺。向大港油田、华北油田提供试制产品,经实际应用证明产品使用性能、质量与进口产品相当,可替代进口产品。

2001年,天津市无缝钢管厂研究开发汽车半轴套管。其产品的外径尺寸、壁厚精度和性能的稳定性等实物质量指标达到或超过国家标准,达到国内先进水平。经国内第一、第二汽车厂等用户使用,完全满足要求。

2001年,天津市无缝钢管厂研制开发船舶用碳钢及碳锰钢无缝钢管。在研制该产品的过程中,结合该厂的装备条件,广泛吸收先进工艺,掌握采用阿塞尔机组和Φ76自动轧管机组生产船舶用碳钢及碳锰钢无缝钢管的技术,并形成一套较为完整的生产船舶用碳钢及碳锰钢无缝钢管的工艺。产品经中港集团天津船舶工程有限公司等用户使用后证明,钢管的性能完全满足用户的使用要求,外径精度、壁厚精度和性能稳定性等实物质量指标达到国内先进水平。

2002年,天津市无缝钢管厂利用Φ76毫米自动轧管机组开发研制穿孔Φ63毫米和Φ68毫米小毛管新工艺。Φ76毫米自动轧管机组原只能穿孔Φ74~85×4.0~12.0毫米的毛管,经过工艺技术开发,现采用Φ70毫米、Φ75毫米管坯通过缩径穿孔、缩径轧制的方式,穿出Φ63毫米和Φ68毫米小毛管,从而降低冷拔成品管的加工成本。

2004年,天津无缝钢管厂通过对轧制工具的改进及工艺参数的优化,在120机组上开发研制成功直径219毫米系列产品。实现在小机组上生产大规格产品的目的。

(二)自主研发高端产品

2002年,天津市轧一制钢公司通过对已有Φ76毫米和Φ219毫米焊管生产机组的改造,在国内率先开发出Φ114毫米、Φ273毫米圆管,100×100毫米、200×200毫米方管,满足钢结构市场的需求。

2003年,天津市冶金材料研究所完成改制后组成天津市天材科技发展有限公司(简称天材公司),实施军工生产线搬迁改造工程后,研究开发航空不锈管材、合金磁性材料系列等新产品。同年,天材公司开发的航空精密无缝不锈钢管,主要应用于军用、民用飞机用精密输送管以及其他精密仪器仪表设备。研究完成的管坯原料冶炼成分的影响及控制、轧制拉拔工艺的影响及控制、内外表面质量控制、晶间腐蚀控制等技术,使晶间腐蚀合格率超过95%,管材超声波探伤合格率超过80%。

2003年,天材公司生产开发出具有自主知识产权的防盗标签用特殊磁性材料,填补国内在这一高新技术领域的空白。同年,该公司开发出镜面钛合金丝材,采用特有的生产工艺技术,与开发生产使用装备相结合,通过冶炼锻轧、关键工模具研制、成品丝材处理工艺,筛选生产高质量钛合金丝材,满足市场需求,取代进口,产品质量达到或超过进口产品实物水平。同年,该公司开发继电器用高矫顽力永磁合金元件,研究开发矫顽力750~850(Oe)磁合金成分;通过实验确定冶炼工艺和锻轧工艺;设计和筛选可以获得高矫顽力的固溶处理工艺温度和时间、可以获得高矫顽力的磁场处理以及稳定化处理的工艺温度和时间。

2004年，天材公司自主研发ASIS446高铬铁素体不锈钢管，并取得发明专利。该产品填补国内空白，产品性能优于国外同类产品，并出口英国。该产品的广泛推广及应用，标志着中国不锈钢产品向高端化发展，节约镍资源，促使不锈钢行业可持续发展。

第六节 金属制品

天津金属制品行业的技术进步，主要表现在采用新工艺和开发高档金属制品两个方面。

一、采用新工艺

1994年，天津市预应力钢丝一厂开发高强度1860兆帕、低松弛（松弛率1000h/2.5）预应力钢绞线。产品强度、屈强比、延伸率、松弛性能，全面达到美国标准ASTMA416-90a的规定，产品达到国际先进水平。

1995年11月，天津市焊丝厂和天津市冶金新技术开发推广中心共同开发线材机械去锈成套技术，建成天津市金属制品行业第一条无酸洗作业线。适用于多钢种（高、中、低碳及低合金钢）和表面质量差线材，处理规格范围大。

1996年至2000年，天津市大成五金厂研制电力输电用铝包钢芯铝绞线产品。采用当代国外先进的连续挤压包覆双金属同步变形工艺，属于国内领先水平；其综合机械性能、导电性能符合技术标准要求，与美标相当，实物质量达到国内领先；具有抗拉强度高、输电效果好、重量轻等特点，使用寿命比普通钢芯铝绞线提高3~6倍，线路维修费用低。经过原机械工业部上海电缆研究所检测，并在惠阳至汕头输变电工程中应用。

1998年12月，天津市大成五金厂开发钢琴配件用钢丝。该产品具有尺寸精度高，综合机械性能适中，弯曲成型不回弹变型，表面光洁度好等特点，达到并优于国外同类产品的实物水平，满足用户要求，可替代进口产品，实现国产化和出口，为天津市高档钢琴生产做出贡献。

二、开发高档金属制品

2002年7月，天津市第一钢丝绳有限公司研制石油用铠缆钢丝绳。该产品解决其内部电缆保护承重、提升等作用，要求改变原抽油杆分节连接状态成为连续状态，钢丝绳长1000 ~ 2000米定尺。为确保石油提升要求抗拉强度≥1870兆帕，钢丝绳破断拉力≥620千牛，钢丝绳不旋转，伸长率不大于15%。通过北京鼎域特种电缆公司使用。

2003年，天津市第二预应力钢丝有限公司与港湾研究所共同研究开发混凝土用缓粘结预应力钢绞线新产品，并制定企业标准。该产品在天津新技术产业园区内的力神电池公司建筑工程中应用。

同年，布顿（天津）钢丝绳有限公司开始研制高速电梯用钢丝绳。2005年7月通过天津市经委组织的鉴定。高速电梯用钢丝绳为钢芯钢丝绳，开发出6种结构7个产品的电梯用钢芯钢丝绳。2004年为张家界观光电梯配制Φ16毫米的高速电梯绳，产品实物质量达到国外著名企业同类产品的先进水平，替代进口。

2004年，天津高力预一预应力钢绞线有限公司研制的主要用于岩土锚固的1×7-Φ17.8毫米，强度1860兆帕级低松弛钢绞线，其破断负荷达到353千牛，在矿井支护工程中得到应用。

第四章 无缝钢管

无缝钢管工程是国家“八五”重点项目。1984年，天津市政府会同国家冶金部、石油部，上报项目建议书。1987年国务院批准可行性报告。1989年6月无缝钢管工程开建。1992年工程主生产线热试成功。1995年，钢管公司技术中心被批准为国家级技术中心；同年12月，无缝钢管工程项目通过国家工程竣工验收。1996年1月1日，天津“大无缝”正式投产。承担无缝钢管工程项目的天津钢管公司（先后于2001年6月和2005年1月改制为天津钢管有限责任公司、天津钢管集团有限公司，简称钢管公司）坚持高水平是财富的理念，不断培育、锤炼原始创新、集成创新和引进消化吸收再创新的能力。至2005年，天津无缝钢管工程建成3套各具特色的轧制机组（即MPM、PQF、ASSEL），其中，PQF机组代表当时世界无缝管轧制技术的顶尖水平。钢管公司开发生产出抗硫化氢、抗挤毁、高强度、热采井、特殊扣等一大批高技术含量、高附加值新品，共达到26个钢级、238个品种、上千种规格，其中60余项科研开发成果填补国内空白；石油套管国内市场占有率达50%，TP140V直连型套管下井6800米，井深达8405米，破亚洲井深纪录；钢坯和无缝钢管年生产能力分别比设计规模扩大3倍，产品出口到80多个国家和地区，其中出口美国的数量占美国进口量的1/3。2005年全年完成钢坯157万吨，钢管140万吨，工业总产值151亿元，销售收入达到200亿元，主要指标增幅均名列天津市工业系统第一。该公司进入国家企业500强、国家制造企业500强和出口500强行列。

第一节 装备技术再创新

钢管公司的炼钢、轧管、管加工等成套技术设备，分别从德国、意大利、美国引进。在对引进技术设备消化吸收的基础上，坚持不断改造和再创新，使工艺装备实现高起步，始终保持国际领先水平。

一、150吨超高功率电弧炉

20世纪90年代初，钢管公司炼钢厂从德国曼内斯曼德马克（后改为西马格德马克）公司引进大型电弧炉，即国内首台150吨超高功率交流电弧炉。该炉采用当时国际上最先进的电弧炉配套技术，包括：①海绵铁/热压块（DRI/HBI）技术；②大容量变压器有载调压技术；③水冷炉壁和水冷炉盖技术；④长弧泡沫渣技术；⑤偏心炉底无渣出钢（留钢留渣）技术等。实行全精炼、全连铸、全过程计算机控制。因此，成为当时国内大型超高功率电弧炉的典型代表。

图5-4-1-59 150吨超高功率电弧炉

2001年5～6月，炼钢厂的宋嘉鹏、姜桂连、张福顺、温德松、张露、高连顺等对150吨超高功率交流电弧炉进行“电弧炉炼钢综合节能技术开发”改造。①增加4支炉壁氧燃烧嘴；②增加3支气雾冷却KT超音速氧枪；③增加2支气雾冷却KT

碳粉喷枪；④增加1套70万立方标米每小时的负压脉冲式布袋除尘系统。改造后，电弧炉冶炼周期由89分钟缩短为67分钟，日最高冶炼炉数由16炉增加到22炉，冶炼电耗由520千瓦·时/吨坯下降到415千瓦·时/吨坯。电弧炉产能增加，烟尘排放达到环保标准要求。

2001年2月20日，钢管公司炼钢厂钢包烘烤器一次点火成功，煤制气正式投入使用。煤制气的投入使用有利于降低生产成本，改善烧重油带来的空气污染，对于改善环境、重造蓝天具有一定的社会效益和经济效益。

2002年10～11月，宋嘉鹏、张福顺、姜桂连、温德松、马全峰、王海东等对电弧炉进行第二次技术改造。电弧炉热装铁水工艺改造包括：①电弧炉跨增加1部75吨天车；②在电弧炉操作平台增加1台兑铁水溜槽小车；③对电弧炉原有的除尘系统（1套70万立方标米/每小时正压反吹式布袋除尘系统）进行改造，扩大其燃烧室容积和数量，延长除尘水冷烟道长度等。同年11月15日，钢管公司技改重点项目——电炉热装铁水试车一次成功，标志着公司炼钢产能进一步扩大，钢水质量进一步改善。改造后，电弧炉冶炼周期由67分钟缩短为54分钟，日最高冶炼炉数由22炉增加到28炉，冶炼电耗由415千瓦·时/吨坯下降到338千瓦·时/吨坯，并提高除尘效果，改善作业环境。经两次改造后，150吨超高功率交流电弧炉冶炼周期缩短至54分钟，冶炼电耗下降到338千瓦·时/吨坯，年产钢能力由原设计的60万吨增长到120万吨。

二、六流弧形连铸机

钢管公司炼钢厂的四流弧形圆坯连铸机于20世纪90年代从德国曼内斯曼德马克（后改为西马格德马克）公司引进。该大规格圆坯连铸机铸坯规格为φ210毫米、φ270毫米和φ310毫米。

2001年9～11月，炼钢厂宋嘉鹏、姜桂连、张再斌、安士亮、时永庄、姚家华等对弧形圆坯连铸机进行高效化改造。改造内容：①扩容中间包和安装控流装置，提高夹杂物去除率；②采用国际上最新型的板簧共振式结晶器振动装置，提高振动精度；③结晶器长度由700毫米调整为800毫米，锥度由单锥度改为抛物线型多锥度；④增加外置式结晶器电磁搅拌装置，改善铸坯凝固组织；⑤配置新型二次冷却系统，合理地选取拉矫机位置及数量。改造后，铸坯拉速提高30%，浇钢周期由75分钟缩短到65分钟，铸坯年产量由55万吨增加到90万吨。

2003年10～11月，宋嘉鹏、温德松、张福顺、张再斌、刘树军、张露等进行第二次技术改造，即弧形圆坯连铸机扩能改造。①在四流连铸机两侧各增加一个铸流，成为六流弧形圆坯连铸机；②相应地将四流中间包扩大改造为六流中间包；③改造接受移送床、1#输出辊道、除鳞机、3#输出辊道等；④浇注跨新增一台75吨天车。改造后，浇钢周期由65分钟缩短到45分钟，铸坯年产量由90万吨增加到120万吨，并且增加一种铸坯φ350毫米规格。经过2001～2003年的技术改造，炼钢厂成为具有国际先进水平的短流程炼钢企业，具备年产120万吨连铸坯的生产能力；连铸圆坯产品的规格增加为φ210毫米、φ270毫米、φ310毫米、φ350毫米等4个；冶炼品种发展到包括中合金钢在内的200余个钢种，产品质量继续保持国内领先、国际先进的水平。

2003年3月13日，钢管公司炼钢厂350毫米铸坯热试成功，成为国内第一家、国际上第二家在弧形半径10.5米的铸机上，拉出350毫米的铸坯。铸坯生产工艺中的350毫米结晶器，由该公司设备中心自主设计、制造，填补国内生产此类结晶器的空白。

三、环形加热炉

1991年6月，钢管公司从意大利皮昂蒂公司引进环形加热炉。该炉以燃油提供热能，中径达到48米，为亚洲最大，炉底采用步进梁式，分预热区、加热区、保温区3段。钢管公司投资4023万元，铺设输气管道6000多米，分阶段、分步骤地对环形加热炉实施“油改气”的技术改造工程。2001年4月24日，钢管公司轧管厂环形炉试用煤气点火一次成功，“油改气”工程正式投产，结束烧油的历史。在管坯加热质量提高、生产成本降低的同时，有效地减少对环境的污染。油改气工程以煤制气替代燃油，投入使用后节省雾化蒸汽3吨／时、空气2850(标准米)3/时,全年可节约计量泵等备件费200万元,年可降低成本2400万元。

四、MPM限动芯棒连轧机组

1991年6月,钢管公司从意大利皮昂蒂公司引进MPM(Multi-stand Pipe Mill,多机架限动芯棒连轧管机)限动芯棒连轧机组(即一套机组)。该连续轧制机组采用7架限动芯棒连轧机,消除浮动芯棒轧制时,钢管制品易出现的“竹节”现象,确保钢管外径和壁厚精度。

2001年起,钢管公司先后组织完成对穿孔后台设备、芯棒冷却设备及电气自动化系统等的技术改造。①由刘千民牵头进行穿孔后台改造,改造5台三辊定心、摆动缸,并由国外进行穿孔后台基本设计,国内设计单位详细设计,相应实施配套加工和土建基础改造。②由范立生牵头进行芯棒循环系统改造,提高辊道电机速度并适当加密;改革冷却站的拨料方式为步进式,增容运输链电机,并配置相应的电气设施。③由刘千民牵头进行增加4#管排锯改造,进口1台管排锯,利用原设计预留位置和方案,在国内配置辊道、回转臂、定尺机和相应电气设施。④由刘锡厚牵头进行限动系统电气改造,将8台384千瓦电机改为400千瓦,并提速,改善电机整流子换向。主传动控制系统DDC改为ANSALDO新型的SPDM系统,同时自动化系统改为AMS等等。上述技改工作从设备工艺上解决制约生产的薄弱环节,使设备能力、可靠性及轧制节奏显著提高。

2002年8月,钢管公司为提升产品质量档次,提高对特殊管材的双探功能,对精整修磨生产线进行大规模改造,调整部分工艺路线,升级改造NDT探伤设备。

2003年,钢管公司由曹五星、唐杰、岳胜主持进行的技术改造,是轧管厂历史上规模最大、技术含量最高的一次。其中,大孔型改造项目共21项,配套改造项目12项,遍及全厂各区域设备,历时21天,使轧制规格最大直径从273毫米扩大到355毫米,与PQF三辊式连轧机组构成完整的产品生产体系。

2005年10月,钢管公司严泽生、张旦天、尹锡泉等承担完成对MPM限动芯棒连轧机组进行孔型优化改造,先后完成轧制工具设计、孔型优化、数学模型编制、连轧和脱管的加工程序设计、轧制工具的改造等任务,全面提升MPM机组的工艺技术水平,使该机组的节奏、质量等各项生产技术指标大幅提高,高附加值品种、新品开发能力显著提升,MPM机组工艺技术保持国内领先水平。

五、PQF三辊式连轧机组

2001年1月,钢管公司与德国西马克米尔公司联合研发世界上第一套PQF三辊式高精度连轧管机组(即第二套机组),对于机组的一些关键设备,采用“点菜式”引进。该机组装备率先采用三辊高精度连轧机,代表国际无缝钢管生产工艺技术的顶尖水平。PQF三辊式连轧机组能轧制高合金管、不锈钢管,其产品的椭圆度、直度、壁厚均匀度及管体质量,均优于限动芯棒连轧机组生产的钢管。与二辊连轧工艺相比,孔型速度差小,轧制稳定,变形均匀。在安装调试过程中,公司技术人员严泽生、刘宏安、刘卫平、朱学强、范立生、李建湘等根据一套机组轧机生产的经验,对原设计提出500余处修改建议,形成具有自主知识产权的工艺操作技术,并与外方签订5年之内不能转让该技术的协议,拥有对PQF技术的独享使用权。在项目建设中,设备总量达11000多吨,钢管公司独立制造其中的7000多吨设备,从而开发形成并具备冶金成套设备的制造能力。

2003年9月4日,第二套机组热试成功。2004年,实现当年投产当年达产。2005年,产量突破50万吨,超过设计能力15万吨。钢管公司通过引进技术,消化、吸收、再创新,使公司无缝钢管生产工艺技术达到世界顶尖水平。

2004年12月24日,168新型钢管厂投产世界最先进的PQF三辊式连轧管机组,在当年实现达产,生产优质无缝钢管35万吨。月产突破4万吨,超过PQF轧管机组设计月产水平。

六、ASSEL连轧机组

2004年10月，ASSEL轧管项目动工。该项目是新建的第三条热轧无缝钢管生产线，以引进德国SMS-MEER公司设计制造的ASSEL轧管机组为核心。与其配置的有意大利LAZZARI公司设计制造的管坯锯、管排锯；德国LOI公司设计，国内制造的21米中径的环形加热炉；德国SMS MEER公司设计制造的锥形穿孔机；德国SMS MEER公司设计，集团公司塞瑞机器公司制造的14架三辊微张力定径机。

2005年2月23日，中径21米的环形加热炉于一次点火成功。3月18日，生产线热负荷试车一次贯通，成功轧制出第一支无缝钢管。下半年，新生产线正式投产，9月即完成年设计月平均产量，实现当年投产、当年达产的奋斗目标。该生产线工艺技术和装备的整体水平达到同类机组国际领先。其工艺特点是，采用国际领先水平的二次斜轧延伸工艺技术，即ASSEL轧管机，是一种带长芯棒轧制的三辊斜轧延伸机，最适宜轧制高精度的中厚壁和厚壁热轧无缝钢管，其壁厚精度可达±(5%~8%)，外径精度可达±0.3%。该机组适用于小批量，多品种，多规格的生产方式，产品规格范围φ(114~219)毫米×(6.0~50)毫米，年生产能力可达16~20万吨。主要品种有：低中压锅炉用无缝钢管、高压锅炉用无缝钢管、结构用无缝钢管、输送流体用无缝钢管、液压支柱用无缝钢管、接箍用无缝钢管、石油钻杆用无缝钢管、车桥用无缝钢管、石油钻铤用无缝钢管、13铬(Cr)、超级13铬(SUP13Cr)石油套管用接箍料、桥箱用无缝钢管等。

七、其他装备

(一)车丝加工线

1992年12月，钢管公司从美国PMC公司引进471管端车丝机4台，1077接箍车丝机4台。该类型车丝机采用刀具旋转方式，可保证丝扣加工精度。

1998年9月，钢管公司王京承担光管线改造项目。从比利时Colinet公司引进NCT7管端车丝机2台，扩大石油套管的产量。

2001年9月，钢管公司对1#、2#套管线的涂漆、喷标系统进行改造；2002年9月，对3#套管线的涂漆、喷标系统进行改造。从而彻底解决产品表面质量问题，使石油套管的外观质量达到国际一流水平。

2003年1月，钢管公司从比利时Colinet公司引进NCC7接箍车丝机2台，ΔLP管端车丝机2台，ΔLC接箍车丝机1台，扩大石油套管的品种，具备特殊螺纹的生产能力。

2004年9月，钢管公司从比利时Colinet公司购买PT5管端车丝机2台。扩大产品品种，提高产量，具备85万吨石油套管的生产能力。

(二)回转窑

1993年11月，钢管公司从英国引进DRI(直接还原铁)厂两座回转窑，每座窑年产量15万吨。1996年11月，DRI工厂建成投产。其实际生产能力达到35万吨，是国内生产规模最大的还原铁厂。钢管公司煤基回转窑直接还原铁厂的技术特点包括：①对原回转窑生产装置的设计进行改进和优化，提高回转窑的生产率；②设计直接还原铁分选系统，有利于提高产品中铁的回收率，保证铁资源的有效利用；③在回转窑烟气系统中，精心设计烟气余热回收锅炉，产出的蒸汽用于热网供热和发电，达到节能和综合利用的目的；④采用高效的布袋除尘设备净化回转窑烟气，使排放到大气的废气含尘量在50毫克每标准立方米以下，由于在工厂的各生产区域均安装除尘设施，并对其除尘效果严密监测，保证工厂环境的洁净；⑤采用自动化领域的新成果(DCS集散控制系统)控制生产过程，确保高的产品质量和劳动生产率。

(三)1000立方米高炉

2004年1月，钢管公司决定由山东省冶金设计院承担设计建设年生产能力80万吨的1000立方米高炉。4月10日高炉工程打桩。10月10日高炉热风炉点火。12月22日高炉烧结系统点火。2005年1月8日，高炉烧结系统生产出合格烧结矿。2005年1月24日，高炉生产出铁水。该高炉技术先进：①优化高炉炉型，加高死铁层高度，可适应强化冶炼、大量喷煤、富氧等需要；②采用PW型串罐无钟炉顶，设备运行可靠，控制灵活，布料无偏析；③采用"卡鲁金"顶燃式热风炉，在全烧高炉煤气的条件下，风温可以达到1200℃；④高炉采用"图拉法"渣处理技术，图拉法渣粒化技术占地少、节水、运行安全、费用低、环保效果好；⑤采用煤气全干法净化技术，流程简单，除尘效率高（净化后的煤气含尘量≤5mg/m3），煤气温度高，热值高，为TRT发电创造有利条件，与湿法除尘相比，该干法除尘节能、节水，还杜绝湿法除尘大量污水的产生，有利于环保；⑥采用高炉煤气差压发电技术（TRT），充分利用高炉炉顶煤气的余压，与煤气干法除尘技术相结合，增强高炉煤气余压发电的效率，节能效果显著；⑦利用剩余的高炉煤气发电，发电机组功率12兆瓦，有效地回收二次能源；⑧高炉喷煤，可以节约焦炭，降低能耗，减少污染，降低生铁成本。

第二节 新产品开发

钢管公司坚持自主创新，通过不断开发新产品，引领企业发展。1997年至2004年，有17个新产品获得国家、天津市和冶金部颁发的20个奖项。其中，"大圆坯连铸用耐火材料的研究与使用"项目获1998年度天津市科技进步二等奖；"高强度抗挤毁石油套管的开发"项目获1999年度天津市科技进步二等奖；"高压气瓶管的开发研究"项目获1999年度天津市科技进步二等奖；"ф250毫米限动芯棒连轧管机ф245孔型系列的开发研究"项目获2000年度天津市科技进步二等奖；"T95抗腐蚀石油套管的开发"项目获2001年度天津市科技进步二等奖，2002年度冶金科技进步二等奖，2002年度国家科技进步二等奖；"TP100H超稠油热采井用石油套管"项目获2002年度天津市科技进步二等奖，2003年度冶金科技进步二等奖；"新型高抗挤套管TP130TT与复合管柱技术"项目获2003年度天津市科技进步一等奖，2003年度冶金科技进步一等奖；"电弧炉炼钢综合节能技术开发"项目获2003年度冶金科技进步一等奖；"高效圆坯连铸机研制"项目获2004年度天津市科技进步一等奖。

一、常规石油套管和油套管

1992年6月27日，钢管公司炼钢连铸系统热负荷试车一次成功。同年12月4日，轧管系统主轧线热负荷试车一次成功，创造10天打通MPM热轧生产线的世界记录。1993年8月管加工系统热负荷试车成功。同年10月、12月，钢管公司炼钢厂、轧管厂相继进入试生产阶段。

1993年12月11日，钢管公司首批试生产的8千米石油套管启运中原油田。1994年1月，首批石油套管产品相继在胜利和中原油田下井成功。

1994年2月8日，钢管公司生产的P110钢级、139.7毫米石油套管在中原石油勘探局卫文79156井下井、固井成功。系该种型号套管在国内首次使用。经国家石油管材质量监督检验测试中心检测，产品质量全部达到国际标准。7月，钢管公司管加工厂进入试生产阶段。7月16日，生产的N80钢级、177.8毫米梯形扣石油套管首次在渤海石油公司使用获得成功。

1996年2月23日，钢管公司成功地完成四川石油管理局委托生产的抗硫化氢耐腐蚀C90石油套管攻关任务，填补国内石油套管生产的一项空白。

1998年9月28日，钢管公司光管线改造工程（光改套）联动负荷试车成功，并通过工程验收，正式投入生产。

2004年2月18日，钢管公司二套管加工热处理线实现热负荷调试、试生产成功。热处理线高温炉升温，加热段至900℃，均热段至890℃，具备常化生产温度，产出的K55、153.7×14毫米接箍料45支钢管，经过几何尺寸测量、性能实验，各项指标全部达到质量要求。11月10日，二套管加工油套管生产线第一根合格的油套管下线，标志着初步具备试生产条件，填补该公司不能生产油管的空白。

二、抗挤毁抗腐蚀石油套管

1998年12月，钢管公司开发的抗挤毁石油套管在四川油田下井深度达到5096米，首次突破井深5000米大关。

1999年10月25日，钢管公司研制开发出用于深井的超高强度抗硫抗挤套管等新品种，填补国内空白。

2000年3月21日，钢管公司生产出ф139.7毫米、ф177.8毫米、ф244.5毫米高抗挤毁石油套管。经专家评审被认定为1999年度国家级新产品，获国家经贸委颁发的“国家级新产品证书”。

2000年12月29日，钢管公司开发研制的152毫米（6英寸）非API标准TP130TT钢级偏梯螺纹套管在中原油田下井成功。该套管是为抗盐岩层研制的特种石油套管，其钢级比P110还要高200000PSI，壁厚为16.9毫米，具有高抗挤毁能力。用来试验的油井井深3991米，在3200～3450米盐岩层使用该套管，其他层面仍使用127毫米（5英寸）P110壁厚10.54毫米长圆螺纹套管，连接处使用钢管公司研制的127毫米P110变扣套管过渡。

2001年5月下旬，钢管公司自主开发的非API系列稠油热采井专用套管TP90H在新疆油田百重七稠油区块顺利下井。标志着该公司开发的稠油热采井专用套管取得新的突破，TP系列套管中增添新的成员。新疆油田每年稠油的产量占其总产量的三分之一，达到300多万吨，每年热采井用套管用量在1.5万吨左右，过去一直选用普通API套管作为热采井套管，套损率较高，特别是2000年该油田在新开发的井深相对较深、稠油粘度较高的百重七区块，由于选用普通N80套管，在首轮注蒸汽的过程中发生多口井套管损坏。钢管公司针对该油田实际，于2001年4月成功开发出适合该油田稠油热采井套管TP90H，首批1000余吨套管在通过各项性能检验及油田商检后，批量下井使用，效果明显，得到普遍好评，迅即在该油田稠油区块推广使用。

2001年9月25日，钢管公司“非API标准规格超高强度抗挤毁TP130TT”套管产品通过天津市经委组织的鉴定。该套管是钢管公司针对普通石油套管难以承受特殊地层高外挤力的情况，独立设计开发的一种非API（American Petroleum Institute，美国石油学会）标准规格、非API标准钢级的，具有钢管公司自主知识产权的高抗挤套管产品，技术水平为国内首创，国际先进。TP130TT超高强度高抗挤毁石油套管产品，凝聚钢管公司的洁净钢冶炼技术、高精度钢管轧制技术、高强高韧钢管处理技术、低残余应力控制技术、套管螺纹抗粘扣加工处理技术等多项科技成果。该产品的研制成功，从根本上解决中原油田盐岩层、盐膏层、射孔段的套管损坏防治的难题，延长套管使用寿命，降低生产成本，产生可观的经济效益和社会效益，标志着钢管公司的石油套管设计开发和生产技术水平达到新的高度。该项目获2004年国家科技进步二等奖。

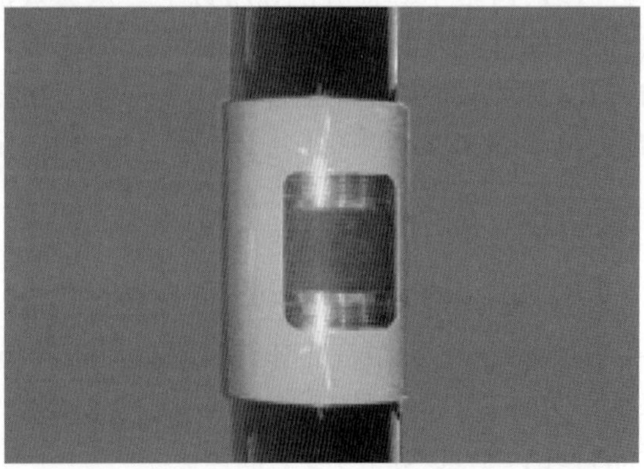

图5-4-2-60　TP130TT超高强度高抗挤毁石油套管产品

2002年12月6日，钢管公司经一年多研制、生产的Φ244.5×11.99毫米偏梯扣TP110TSS高强度抗H_2S套管，在四川东宣汉县黄金镇界内的普光1井顺利下井成功，标志着公司抗硫化氢（H_2S）套管的研制水平迈上新台阶。TP110TSS抗H_2S套管因为强度高，正处于抗H_2S套管强度的拐点位置，产品的开发、研制、生产工艺控制的难度较大。该次下井套管共达320支，下井深度3471.8米。

2003年初，钢管公司为新疆开发出超深井专用超高强度（抗拉、抗挤、高韧性）套管TP140V（Φ127.00×9.50）毫米，并被使用于塔里木油田分公司在新疆阿克苏境内的乌参1井。同年11月，该井喜获高产油气流，日产原油173.22立方米、天然气19.6299万立方米，是国内发现的第一口亿吨级整装挥发性油藏，也是塔里木油田继2000年探明国内最大天然气田——克拉2气田之后，在塔里木盆地的又一重大发现，进一步扩大西气东输的资源基础。该井是地质条件最复杂的一口井，所使用的完井油层TP140V套管，下井深度达

5650～6394米，打破钢管公司套管下井深度的记录。

2003年11月7日，由中石油集团公司科技发展部、吉林油田股份公司勘探与生产分公司共同组织实施重大科研项目全井套管钻井，采用钢管公司最新研制的TP55D钻井专用套管，在吉林油田试验钻进顺利完钻固井。这是中国陆上油田第一口全井套管钻井，标志着中国套管钻井技术及钻井套管的发展进入现场试验应用阶段。套管钻井是世界上先进的钻井技术，摒弃传统的钻杆钻进方式，直接采用套管代替钻杆打井，可有效降低钻井成本，提高钻井效率。9月初，钢管公司接到研制任务后，课题组和有关部门全力以赴，仅用一个月的时间完成从产品设计到生产的全过程，并顺利地通过试验室评价。

2004年5月上旬，由钢管公司设计开发的TP140V(8-1/8")直连型套管在塔里木油田山前构造带的重点勘探井——羊塔克502井顺利下井。套管在穿过复合盐层段后，成功下到设计深度5333米。该套管是专为塔里木油田山前构造带上的勘探井设计的，既可确保有效封堵复合盐层段，又可增加所下套管的层数；也是塔里木油田首次使用内外平直连型套管。钢管公司与油田用户一起设计井场吊装和部分井下使用工具，共同制定详细下套管操作程序，并在下套管过程中进行现场技术服务。该项目标志着钢管公司在开发适合深井、超深井专用套管，以及对于管体性能和丝扣连接形式的研究，取得新突破。

2004年6月9日，钢管公司在辽宁省盘锦市举行稠油热采井专用套管TP120TH阶段总结会，对热采井用套管套损机理、TP120TH套管的设计开发、现场应用及使用评价进行分析总结。辽河油田钻井管理中心、辽河油田特油公司、曙光采油厂、测井公司、石油大学等单位专家一致认为，TP120TH套管的开发与油田的实际需求紧密结合，各项指标均达到或超过设计要求，应用效果明显，经济效益显著，建议扩大推广规模。辽河油田稠油生产量很高，2/3的油井开采稠油，其超稠油油田是世界上油质最稠、开发难度最大的油田之一。稠油井采用高温热采工艺。高温高压蒸汽对套管的反复激励使套管强度大大降低，加之反复热吞吐后造成油井出沙，引起外载荷的不均匀，同时套管射孔后强度的降低，造成套管大量损坏，尤其在射孔井段及附近区域，占整个套损井的80%以上。从失效油井的寿命看，在第2轮即开始发生套变，平均吞吐周期只有4轮，低于油井的设计寿命，造成很大经济损失。钢管公司开发的TP120TH专用套管，系非API标准的新型稠油射孔段耐热高抗挤毁套管，能够解决超稠油热采井的大量损坏问题。2003年1月1日在辽河油田下井成功后，全部11口实验井，平均进入第5轮吞吐，最长的达7轮，井况良好，未出现任何问题。

三、特殊扣石油套管

2000年9月12日，钢管公司与新加坡汉廷一义信公司合资组建的、国家首家特殊扣石油套管生产企业——天津华新特殊扣石油套管有限公司投入负荷试车。该公司开发的特殊扣石油套管2001年11月末在南海油田下井成功，12月16日又首次成功使用于中美合作的渤海油田海上钻井平台。钢管公司特种石油套管产品自此长驱直入国内海上油田。

2003年，钢管公司与长庆油田共同开发的TP-CQ特殊螺纹接头套管在长庆油田成功下井28口。使用结果证明，该套管在上扣控制、下井操作、试压、压裂、试气等方面，使用性能良好，与国外同类特殊螺纹接头套管水平相当。其中，首次使用TP-CQ特殊扣套管下井的G44-4井，成为长庆油田的高产气井。11月6～7日，钢管公司与长庆油田勘探局、中油集团管材研究所、中石化物资装备部、新疆油田开发公司、中原油田物资供应处在西安召开关于TP-CQ特殊扣套管的鉴定评审及技术交流会。专家一致认定，TP-CQ特殊扣套管整体结构设计思想先进，不仅多次上卸不粘扣，而且保证良好的密封性能。该特殊螺纹接头也适用于含有硫化氢和二氧化碳的气井和酸性腐蚀气井。

2004年11月18日，钢管公司承担的天津市科技创新项目“TP-CQ特殊扣套管开发研究”通过市经委组织的验收。由中国工程院院士李鹤林担任主任委员、7位资深油气井及冶金专家组成的验收鉴定委员会一致认定，该产品技术含量高，具有自主知识产权，其接头整体结构设计合理，抗螺纹粘结性能优良，密封结构设计具有独创性。该项目为国内首创，达到国际先进水平。

四、异型管

2000年10月3日，钢管公司热扩管项目顺利试车成功。热扩管机组可使产品外径延伸至720毫米。同年12月16日，轧管厂300孔型试制成功，突破原有的孔型设计极限。

2001年4月8日，钢管公司与美国格兰特钻具有限公司合资组建的天津天管特钻具有限公司成立。该公司在天津经济技术开发区注册登记，主要产品为石油钻井用钻杆料、钻具等。

2001年10月16日，钢管公司轧管厂开发试制出160×160×6.0毫米的方矩型管和2铬13（2Cr13）φ139.7毫米的不锈钢管。产品主要用于建筑施工、结构用材等。用热轧无缝管工艺生产方矩型管，在全国尚属首次，试制获得成功，为批量生产奠定基础。

2002年3月18日，钢管公司完成为三峡工程永久性船闸试制吊杆用钢管的生产项目。157支、345．76吨钢管质量，完全符合用户要求。三峡工程指挥部在国内外寻求厂家，决定由钢管公司试制生产的φ460×25毫米规格钢管，技术含量高，生产难度大，历经7个月试制成功，按合同如期交货，满足三峡工程的急需，在国内尚属首创。

2002年7月1日，钢管公司螺纹试验加工线联动调试一次成功，标志着该公司科研、开发拥有重要手段。技术中心建成中间试验基地，有力地促进新品开发和市场竞争力。

2002年9月30日，钢管公司还原铁厂深加工产品——脱硫剂试生产开工。脱硫剂主要用于城市煤气、焦炉煤气生产中硫化氢气体的脱出。该厂经过探索，用还原铁作为脱硫剂的基料，获取近200多个对比试验数据，取得高于90%的脱硫效果，在国内尚属首例。

2003年8月18日，钢管公司168厂穿孔机热试一次成功。该厂采用Meer公司经过最新改进的锥形辊穿孔机，穿孔效率高，速度快，能穿轧高合金及难变形的金属（不锈钢、镍铬合金等），穿轧出的毛管内部缺陷少、表面质量好、同心度和壁厚均匀性高、外径精度高，可实现大延伸、大扩径量穿孔，有利于扩大产品规格。该热试成功为生产线全面贯通奠定基础。

图5-4-2-61　钢管公司168厂穿孔机热试一次成功

第五章　机　电

天津是国家机械装备制造业的重要生产基地之一。1990年至2005年，天津机械工业系统深化体制改革，推进产业结构和产品结构调整，经历滑坡、启稳、回升、发展的过程。由于依靠技术进步，创新能力增强，外向经济扩大发展，市场能力明显提升。1996年至2000年，围绕市场需求完成新产品开发1716项，投产新产品1420项，机械行业82%的产品实现更新换代，40%的产品达到国际90年代或国内先进水平。2003年，试制投产新产品各350项，企业技术创新能力进一步增强。拥有光机电一体化等3大类62种高新技术产品，工业机器人、加工中心、高速电梯、自动扶梯、平地机、潜油电泵、螺杆泵、蝶阀等一大批产品达到国际国内先进水平。TH6340B模块化加工中心、软密封闸阀、地铁用公共交通型自动扶梯等高技术含量重点新产品研制成功。战略性产业结构和产品结构调整围绕“6大成套设备、10类重点产品”，形成以发电、环保、电梯、输配电、工程机械等成套设备和压缩机、风机、起重设备、工业泵、压力机、数控机床、液压件、减速装置、柴油机、电气传动装置等重点产品为核心的优势产业群。其间，天津工程机械研究院作为国家级科研单位创新发展，发挥行业引领作用。民营企业天津赛象科技股份有限公司依靠科技创新得到长足的发展，其生产的子午线轮胎成套装备开发出十几个系列、几十种关键设备，主要产品具有自主知识产权，技术水平达到或超过国际同类产品的先进水平，产品大量出口。到2005年，机电制造业成为天津经济发展的6个支柱产业之一。

第一节 机床与工具

机床与工具行业内的天津第一机床总厂、天津市第二机床有限公司、天津市磨床总厂、天津市天仪数控机械股份有限公司、天津市异型刃具厂等企业，把优化产品结构作为主要目标，努力转变增长方式，着力增强自主创新能力。通过采用计算机、智能化、机电一体化高新适用技术，加快新产品的开发与研制，多项新产品获得市级科技进步奖，部分新品填补国内空白。

一、齿轮加工机床

1990年至2005年，天津第一机床总厂作为国内生产齿轮加工机床的最大专业生产厂之一，先后研制开发出RE5020数控加工中心、CELL-CON数控镗铣床等。

1992年，该厂研制开发出YKD2250数控弧齿锥齿轮铣齿机，获天津市1995年度科技进步二等奖。同年，研制生产YZX5125插齿机、YZ5125插齿机、YM5150H插齿机。

1993年，该厂研制生产Y9550C锥齿轮滚动检查机、TH6380卧式加工中心、TH6340卧式加工中心、国内第一台XH715GY 5轴联动加工中心和HX715AG 4轴联动加工中心。

1994年，该厂研制生产的YKD2240数控弧齿锥齿轮铣齿机(NC控制)和YKD2140数控弧齿锥齿轮铣齿机(NC控制)，均获得1996年度国家级新产品称号。当年该厂还生产YKD5120数控插齿机(NC控制)、YD9550锥齿轮滚动检查机(PLC控制)、Y9580滚动检查机、XH715C立式加工中心、TH6380A卧式加工中心(FMC多托盘交换)和KD501数控齿扇插齿机。其中，TH6380A卧式加工中心获1996年度国家级新产品称号。

1995年，该厂研制生产YKD2940数控弧齿锥齿轮拉齿机、HMC8000卧式加工中心(FMC)、XH715GY5轴联动加工中心。

1997年，该厂研制生产出YT5120数控插齿机和TH6380B卧式加工中心，获天津市1998年度科技进步二等奖及天津市1998年度技术创新优秀项目一等奖。

1998~2001年，该厂分别研制出TH6340A/1卧式加工中心；YKA5180数控齿扇插齿机、3—HSS数控并联机床、YKD2550数控研齿机、YK51150数控插齿机。

2002年，该厂研制生产YKD2280数控弧齿锥齿轮铣齿机、KJ501数控剃齿刀插齿机、YK5115数控插齿机、YK5150数控插齿机。

2003年，该厂研制生产Y9050淬火压床、YKX5120数控插齿机(静压导轨)、YK9550数控锥齿轮滚动检查机、YK5132数控插齿机、YKW9580A数控万能滚动检查机。

2004年，该厂研制生产YK5150A数控插齿机(翻转工作台)、YK2212数控弧齿锥齿轮铣齿机、YKD2250A数控弧齿锥齿轮铣齿机、YKT2250数控弧齿锥齿轮铣齿机。

2005年，该厂研制生产YK2955数控弧齿锥齿轮拉齿机、YK5180数控插齿机、YK2080G数控弧齿锥齿轮磨齿机。齿轮加工机床基本实现数控化。

图5-5-1-62 YK5132数控插齿机

二、车床

天津市第二机床有限公司(原天津市第二机床厂)1990年开始生产

T2CNC型数控车床。1992年开始对CQ61100型普通车床进行改进设计，改进后产品定型为CT61100型卧式普通车床。1993～2004年，该公司围绕市场和用户需求，先后研制开发T2CNC-3型数控车床、T2-012型专用车床、T2-014型铸管加工专用车床、MC-1、MC-2型球面车磨专机、T2-025型管模专用车床、HGC-6000型烘缸专用车床、T2-019型专用卧式车床。2005年，天津市第二机床有限公司研制开发出MGK1600型立式精密数控磨床，该产品填补国内空白。

三、磨床

（一）成形磨床

1990年，天津市磨床总厂（原天津市机床厂）作为天津市唯一生产磨床的专业厂，研制出的TMCNC11型成形磨床和TMCNC12型数控瓦楞辊成形磨床，分别获国家机械工业部科技进步三等奖和天津市科技进步三等奖。

1993年，该厂研制开发的TMCNC14型龙门数控成形磨床，获天津市科技进步三等奖；同年，研制的MKL7175型数控强力成形磨床，获机械工业部科技进步二等奖和天津市科技进步二等奖、并获天津市奖励基金二等奖。

1994年，该厂研制TMCNC15型数控剪刃磨床，获1996年度天津市科技进步三等奖。

1996年，该厂研制出TMCNC16型数控圆弧剪刃磨床，获天津市科技进步三等奖。

1997年，该厂研制MKL7132/I型数控强力成形磨床。

1998年，该厂研制MKL7132/II型数控强力成形磨床。

2004年，该厂研制出TMCNC17型数控圆弧剪刃磨床、TMCNC型数控龙门瓦楞辊成形磨床。2005年，该厂研制出TMCNC19型龙门式数控剪刃磨床。

（二）平面磨床

1991年，天津市磨床总厂研制开发MBX7480型程控立轴圆台平面磨床。1992年，该厂研制M71100型门式卧轴矩台平面磨床。1995年，该厂研制出M74180型立轴圆台平面磨床。1999年，该厂研制M7120T型卧轴矩台平面磨床。

2000年，天津市磨床总厂转制为天津市津机磨床有限公司，为天津市内燃机厂改制MK1620型数控端面外圆磨床。同年，该公司研制出74系列双头立轴圆台平面磨床，开发大型连杆专用磨床，此系列专用机床达到国内先进水平。2001年，该公司研制出MS74100C（Ⅰ）型半自动双头立轴圆台平面磨床。2002年，该公司开发出M7120型卧轴矩台平面磨床。2003年，该公司研制开发的MK7340型数控卧轴圆台平面磨床，填补国内空白。2004年，该公司研制出M7350E、M7363E型卧轴圆台平面磨床。2005年，该公司研制开发出MT7160×16型卧轴矩台平面磨床。

四、电加工机床

1992年，天津市天仪数控机械股份有限公司（前身是天津市仪表机床厂）研制DK7763大型线切割机床，达到国内领先水平，获天津市1996年度科技进步三等奖。

1994年，该公司研制开发出DK7740D线切割机床。

1998年，该公司研制、开发QTK5620型和QTK5620B型数控砂线切割机，2项产品均填补国内空白。

2001年，该公司研制生产出QTK5620G型数控砂线切割机。

2003年，该公司研制出QTK5640G大型砂线切割机；同年，在原MPM150手动平面磨床的基础上，研制开发出MPM150Y液压自动进给磨床。

五、异型刃具及刀具

1990年，天津市异型刃具厂开始进行新产品设计，有干壁螺钉搓丝板、螺旋槽丝锥、螺旋挤压丝锥、前端正锥螺纹的螺旋槽丝锥、超硬质合金刀具;与天津大学机电分校联合,共同研制开发出干壁螺钉搓丝板。

1992年,该厂扩大磨制丝锥生产线,从瑞士莱斯豪公司、德国格林公司引进CNC控制系统的丝锥生产设备,研制开发出大于M18螺旋丝锥新产品,获天津市1994年度优秀新产品二等奖,其"前端正锥螺纹的螺旋槽丝锥"获国家实用新型专利。

1997年,该厂立项研制"螺旋挤压丝锥",该项目被机械工业部批准,列入1997年机械工业科技发展计划的新产品项目,所研制的螺旋挤压丝锥填补国内空白。

2001年,该厂研制精密成型数控刀具,开发出高精度、高效率、高可靠性和专业化的整体硬质合金刀具,即球头立铣刀、锥度球头立铣刀、R角铣刀、汽轮机叶片叶根铣刀、松塔铣刀、髓腔绞刀等整体硬质合金系列刀具。

第二节 压力加工设备

天津市锻压机床总厂是国内液压机行业的龙头企业之一,技术力量雄厚,建有国家级企业技术中心,全面调整产品结构,加速实施技术创新,开发研制的新产品达到国际先进水平或填补国内空白。其中,申报专利202项;开发研制新产品75种;列为国家级重点新产品项目10个;填补国内空白项目6个。

一、锻压、拉伸液压机

1990年,天津市锻压机床总厂研制开发出YT28-630/1030双动薄板拉伸液压机、HZPU315-2050/1300拉伸液压机,前者在1989年由天津市经委鉴定达到国际先进水平。1991年,该厂研制、开发出THP24-800/1200双动厚板拉伸液压机、YT27-250A单动薄板冲压液压机、YT27-400A单动薄板冲压液压机、YT27-800单动薄板冲压液压机。1992年,研制开发的YT28-630/1030双动薄板拉伸液压机、YT28-800/1300双动薄板拉伸液压机以及YT27-1000A单动薄板冲压液压机,前两种型号的双动薄板拉伸液压机1992年由部级鉴定均达到国际先进水平。

1994年,该厂研制开发出YT12-800快锻液压机、YTA28-800/1300双动试模液压机和YTA98-100模具研配液压机,该两款YTA型的液压机1994年由部级鉴定均达到国际先进水平。同年,研制开发出THP29-2X2000联动纵梁液压机、THP32-3000四柱液压机和THP32-2000A四柱液压机。

1995年,该厂研制开发的THP16-1500液态模锻液压机和THP29-4000纵梁液压机,后者填补国内空白;THP32-1250四柱液压机,处于国内领先水平。同年,研制开发YT27-400B单动冲压液压机,为国内领先水平。1997年,该厂研制开发出的THP29-4000纵梁液压机,属国际先进水平,被列入国家重点新产品。1999年,该厂研制、开发出THP29-3000汽车大梁液压机,获天津市技术创新优秀项目。1998年,该厂研制、开发THP24-2400/3000双动厚板拉伸液压机,填补国内空白,列入国家级重点新产品。1999年,该厂研制、开发出THP29-3000汽车大梁液压机,获天津市技术创新优秀项目。

2002年,该厂研制、开发出的THP34Y-1000移动回转压头框式液压机,被列入当年国家重点新产品和天津市科技发展计划项目;100MN数控钛合金等温锻造液压机和THP34Y-1000移动回转压头框式液压机,均填补国内空白。同年,该厂研制大型高效数控钛合金等温锻造液压机。

二、其他液压机

1990年,天津市锻压机床总厂研制开发出THP72-63磁性材料制品液压机、THP72-100磁性材制品液压机。1991年,该厂研制开发THP98-200研配液压机。1992年,该厂研制开发出THP98-200研配液压机、THP78-1000模料制品液压机,后者为国内先进水平。1995年,该厂研制开发的THP79-630粉末制品液压机在国内领先。1996年,该厂研制开发出THP78-3150磨料制品液压机,填补国内空白。1997年,该厂研制开发的THP78—3150磨料制品液压机为国内领先。

2000年,该厂研制开发大型精密数控液压机,列入重点脱困企业技术创新项目;大型高速高效高精度数控液压机,列入国家重点技术创新项目;THP98C-1000研配试模液压机,填补国内外空白,列入天津市优秀企业技术中心重点项目。

图5-5-2-63 天津市天锻压力机有限公司李森等研制的S-THP61—500+1250+1000温冷挤压液压机生产线,获得2005年度天津市科技进步二等奖

2001年,该厂研制开发THP41-1250单柱校正压装液压机,填补国内空白,列入国家重点新产品;研发制造玻璃钢制品的大型数控系列液压机生产线,列入国家重点技术创新项目;玻璃钢制品的大型数控液压机,处国内先进水平,列入2000工业科技开发基金支持重点技术创新项目;大型数控玻璃钢制品液压机成套装备列入天津市科技发展计划项目。

2002年,该厂研制、开发的THP98C-1000研配试模液压机,被列入2002年国家重点新产品。同年,该公司成为天津市CAD应用示范企业。

第三节 通用机械

天津通用机械工业主要包括泵、阀、减速机、风机、鼓风机、环保机械和电梯等。天津泵业集团有限公司是该行业中的主要企业,1990年至2004年开发和研制多种新产品,分别获得国家级和天津市级的奖项,部分产品申报国家专利,成立市级企业技术中心。天津市减速机股份有限公司以技术创新为主线,研发的部分新产品被列为国家级优秀新产品,获多项成果奖,并获得专利19项。天津市百利二通机械有限公司相继研发一批回转阀门电动装置,部分新品达到国际同类产品水平。天津塘沽瓦特斯阀门有限公司在引进国外技术的基础上,开发研制的多项产品分别获国家级和市级奖项。天津百利阳光环保设备有限公司依靠科技进步,自发研制多项环保设备,获得专利和天津市科技进步奖。作为大型合资企业的天津奥的斯电梯有限公司,技术力量雄厚,通过技术引进开发电梯新品,多项产品通过国家部级和天津市级鉴定,其产品均达到国际同类产品水平,填补国内空白。

一、泵

1990年,天津市泵业机械集团有限公司(原天津市工业泵总厂)研制开发的SNF1300-46、SPF20-40、SNH80-36、SNH440-46、3GR25×4、3GR36×4三杆螺杆泵和2GCS150×2双螺杆泵产品,获机电工业节能产品称号;研制开发的SNH440-46、SNH660-46三螺杆泵产品获国家质量银质奖。同年,该公司还自主研制LGY-6/7型移动式螺杆压缩机。1992年,该公司研制开发出国家级新产品SN系列三螺杆泵。1994年,该公司开发的SM—EY系列高效节能粘稠油三螺杆泵获天津市优秀产品一等奖。1996年,该公司研制开发出SMS210R46E6.7三螺杆泵,该产品获天津市工业设计优秀产品二等奖;CTP牌螺杆泵被天津市政府认定为天津市名牌产品。1997年,该公司研制开发的双螺杆泵获天津市优秀产品一等奖;VSN、ESD系列离心泵获天津市优秀产品二等奖;EH系列单螺杆泵、TMC、EHS船用离心泵获天津市优秀新产品三等奖。1999年,该公司研制开发出的EH系列单螺杆泵和双螺杆造粒机,前者获天津市政府授予的1998年度技术创新优秀项目一等奖,后者获国家专利。同年,该公司自主研制开发出汽液混输双螺杆泵。

1991年,天津电机总厂研发设计生产的潜油电泵获得“第二届北京国际博览会金奖”。20世纪70年代,天津电机总厂生产出国内第一台潜油电泵,改变潜油电泵技术被国外垄断的局面,并于1981年批量生产,在国内各大油田大面积应用。1984年在引进美国REDA公司潜油电泵技术的基础上消化创新,使潜油电泵产品技术及品质有更大的提升,潜油电泵在大庆油田井下运转寿命长达12年。该产品于1994年在全国电机制造行业率先通过国际权威质量认证。

图5-5-3-64 2003年,天津大港油田集团中成机械制造有限公司研制出562(5-5/8″)潜油电泵

1993年,天津市泵业机械集团有限公司研制出4CLG-12J立式海水泵,通过海军装备部专家论证,产品批量生产。1994年,该公司与中国船舶总公司704研究所共同研制出舰船用串联离心泵100CBL-4J和125CBL-6J,产品填补国内空白;研制出SMS210-WJ作为军舰关键输送设备并通过海军部门鉴定。1999年,该公司研制开发的船用离心泵获天津市科技进步三等奖。2000年,该公司研制开发出舰船保障系统用3GC40×12型电动立式三螺杆泵、舰艇用防淋泵ESCE-125MD、MW型汽液集输双螺杆泵。2003年,该公司研制出舰船用2GRY型燃油泵。2005年,该公司研制开发出双流向船工用泵,产品获国家实用专利。

2001年,天津市泵业机械集团有限公司与合肥通用机械共同研制出潜艇用均衡泵;同年,完成科技攻关项目“螺杆膨胀鼓风机组”及“螺杆泵在污泥脱水系统中的应用优化及系统成套项目”的研制任务。2002年,该公司研制开发HW型汽液输双螺杆泵撬装系统及无泄露泵。2003年,该公司研制开发的卧式高压大流量螺杆泵获国家实用新型专利。2004年,该公司研制开发出低噪声主机滑油泵、高压三螺杆泵和法兰连接式齿轮传动三螺杆泵,后者获国家实用新型专利。2005年,该公司研制开发出镶有内套的双螺杆衬套和高压三螺杆泵,产品分别获国家实用专利;同年,研制开发的HW型汽液集输泵撬装系统,被列入国家新产品试产计划。

二、减速机

1997~1998年,天津市减速机股份有限公司(原天津市减速机总厂)创新推出8000系列摆线减速机新系列,使产品更新换代,其传送功率和承载能力提高2~3倍,被列入国家级优秀新产品,获国家机械工业部科技成果二等奖。截至2005年上半年,该公司累计生产76万余台摆线减速机产品供应全国各有关行业。

2000年,该公司相继开发出C型斜齿轮减速级、B型斜齿轮—伞齿轮减速机、P型平行轴斜齿轮减速机和W型斜齿轮—蜗轮蜗杆减速机等4大系列产品,其设计水平、工艺加工制造水平先进,获得19项专利。

到2005年,该公司还研制开发出TJ型油浸式电动滚筒、TDY75油冷式电动滚筒、WD外装式电动滚筒、隔爆电动滚筒、NGW行星齿轮减速机、XMB行星摩擦式无级变速机、硬齿面圆柱齿轮减速机、硬齿面圆锥圆柱齿轮减速机、JZQ圆柱齿轮减速机等系列新产品;研发出由摆线减速机和齿轮减速机派生的专用减速机,包括悬挂式齿轮减速机、塔机回转专用减速机、双卧轴搅拌机专用减速机、沥青搅拌机专用减速机、升降平台专用减速机、升降机专用减速机、包装印刷机械专用蜗轮蜗杆减速机、工业洗衣机用减速机、风力发电偏航齿轮减速机、造纸洗浆机用减速机、石油抽油机用减速机、轧机辊道专用减速机、绞肉机专用减速机、立体停车装置专用减速机和螺旋输送机等。

三、阀 门

1990年，天津市塘沽阀门厂研制的软密封双偏心法兰蝶阀，获天津市技术创新优秀项目三等奖、天津市科技进步三等奖；同年，研制出公称压力1.0Mpa～1.6MPa、公称通径300～1800毫米的微阻缓闭止回阀，该产品获得实用新型专利，并获天津市科技进步奖。1994年，该厂引进美国沃茨的产品，主要用于石油、煤气、化学制品、电力等工业管路截流的理想设备2200-SE公称压力为200PSI，公称通经为51～152毫米的HALE阀。对引进的产品，经过开发研制，使该产品成为出口创汇的主导产品之一，获得天津市科技进步二等奖、天津市技术创新优秀项目二等奖、国家级重点新产品奖和实用新型专利。

1991年，天津市百利二通机械有限公司（原天津市第二通用机械厂，后更名为天津市阀门公司）开发出QA（ZA2/Q60、ZA2/Q120、ZA2/Q250、ZA2/Q500）系列部分回转阀门电动装置，该系列产品具有防爆型，形成引进技术SMC-04/HBC、SMC-03/HBC的互补。1992年，该公司研制QB1小型部分回转阀门电动装置。1993年，该公司研制出QB3、QB4独立式全自动部分回转阀门电动装置。1994年，该公司开发的SMC系列、SMC/HBC系列、QA系列、ZA系列、QB系列电动装置被国家4大部委评为首选产品和优先推荐产品。1994～1995年，该公司消化引进技术研制出ZA2.5、ZA3、ZA4多回转阀门电动装置，其技术水平处于国内领先。1996年，该公司研制出ZA1（ZA1A）、QB5电动装置。1997～1998年，该公司重新设计Q60、Q120、Q500，改型为JA2、JA3，并开发出JA4；改进QB3、QB4、QB5D的设计，型号定为QBR3、QBR4、QBR5，使产品在原QB基础上得到提高。1999～2002年，该公司研制出00M系列多回转阀门电动装置，产品技术水平为国内领先；在吸收国外先进技术基础上研制出QT系列独立式部分回转电动装置，处国内领先水平；研制出的智能化阀门电动装置控制系统，综合性能指标达到国内领先水平和国际同期技术水平。2003～2004年，该公司分别研制出SMC.X.R自动巡检阀门电动装置、K1类核级阀门电动装置，产品达到国际同类产品水平。2005年，该公司研制出ZA1、ZA2专用多回转电动装置。

1994年7月，天津市塘沽阀门厂与美国沃茨工业集团公司共同投资组建天津塘沽瓦特斯阀门有限公司，研制开发中、低压阀门。1995年，该公司引进开发美国沃茨21/50.8毫米-304毫米高性能耐腐蚀蝶阀产品，同时研制、开发出DA型法兰蝶阀及刷镀型的法兰蝶阀。1996年，该公司引进开发美国沃茨21/50.8毫米-304毫米用于水管交叉连接，同时水源需要保护的909回流阀和11/100毫米-406毫米ACV自动控制阀产品，该项系列产品获实用新型专利。1997年，该公司引进开发美国沃茨的公称压力0.6—1.6MPa、公称通经50.8毫米-304毫米D77过滤器，产品获得实用新型专利和天津市科技进步奖；同年，试制完成液动角式蝶型止回阀和弹头式止回阀。1998年，该公司引进开发美国沃茨高性能焊接式耐腐蚀蝶阀和高性能金属密封蝶阀，该产品获天津市技术创新优秀项目三等奖；引进开发美国25.4毫米-76.2毫米（DN25-DN80）31B通用止回阀、JACV自动控制和无销蝶阀，其中用于管端无销的软密封蝶阀获得实用新型专利和天津市科技进步奖。同年，该公司自主开发研制出PN0.6～1.6MPa大口径软密封单偏心法兰蝶阀。1999年，该公司引进开发美国沃茨RW405、RW408橡胶闸阀系列产品，该产品获天津市重大科技攻关项目奖。同年，在开发的JACV自动控制阀的基础上，该公司继续开发出JSACV、JDACV、JJACV等系列自动控制阀产品，自主研制开发成功的三偏心复合圈金属密封蝶阀，获天津市科技进步三等奖、天津市技术创新优秀项目三等奖、国家重点新产品奖和实用新型专利。2000年，该公司引进开发美国沃茨专用消防的公称压力300PS1公称通径63.5毫米-203毫米消防信号卡箍蝶阀；自主开发出压盖式松套伸缩接头和双法兰传动接头。2001年，公司研制开发出公称压力150—200PS1、公称通径DN50—DN750的API594蝶型止回阀和公称压力300PSI、公称通径50.8毫米-304毫米的卡箍蝶阀。2002年，该公司开发出卡箍连接止回阀、DC型法兰式偏心蝶阀和法兰连接中心板式蝶阀，其DC型法兰式偏心蝶阀和法兰连接中心板式蝶阀获得实用新型专利。2003年，该公司研制开发出对夹式无销蝶阀、法兰分离器和卡箍式橡胶闸阀。2004年，该公司开发出球阀、液控止回蝶阀、重锤式液控止回蝶阀、改进型DC法兰式偏心蝶阀、UK衬胶工业蝶阀和609A蝶阀，其中，改进型DC法兰式偏心蝶阀获得实用新型专利，609A蝶阀获得外观设计专利。2005年，该公司研制开发出DN4000电站水利控制阀、球铁系列法兰蝶阀、软密封不锈钢止水给排水闸门和RW409橡胶闸阀。

四、风 机

（一）通风机

1992年，天津市通风机厂研制开发隧道风机92-1 11#和隧道集尘器，产品获得专利。1993年，该厂研制开发隧道风机93-112.5#。1994年研制开发出分卧式、立式罗茨风机。1998年，该厂研制开发出2SZ系列隧道风机。1999年，该厂研制开发出2SZ双速系列隧道风机，研制的"一种双速电机驱动高对旋风机"获得实用新型专利。2001年，该厂与石家庄铁道学院合作研制开发出"高原隧道专用空调机组"，该产品获得实用新型专利。2004年，该厂研制开发变频调速可逆转双系统地铁风机控制柜成套设备，获得国家实用新型专利。

1995年，天津市通风机厂研制开发出射流风机和子午加速轴流风机。1996年投产小型轴流风机。2000年，该厂研制开发出"大型移动式多种动力源垃圾筛分机"，该产品获得实用新型专利；同年，研制投产大型轴流风机。2001年，该厂研制开发出水泥用离心、轴流风机；同年，该厂研制的"水泥窑胴体冷却装置"获得专利。2002年，该厂针对地铁项目研制开发出"变频调速可逆转地铁轴流风机"，产品申请4项实用新型专利，即"防喘振的双向轴流风机""一种有防喘振结构的单向轴流风机""压力回复式出口消声器""压力回复式进口消声器"。2003年，该厂研制开发出"装有弯掠组合叶片的正反向地铁轴流风机"，产品获得实用新型专利。2004年，该厂研制开发投产大型离心风机GY4-73系列单吸双支撑及单吸悬臂支撑，其中"空心轴F式离心风机"获得国家专利。2005年，该厂研制开发出"装有一次性铸造成型叶轮轮毂的射流风机"，获得国家实用新型专利。

（二）鼓风机

1991年，天津市鼓风机总厂研制开发L93WD罗茨鼓风机。该机在原"联合设计"的结构上进行改进，在机体结构、密封结构、齿轮、轴承、冷却、润滑等结构上都积极采用先进技术，机型大，开发加工难度也大。新产品节能、运转平稳可靠、便于维修、寿命长、噪声比同类产品低2~3分贝（A）。1992年5月16日，经天津市机械工业管理局组织的专家鉴定认定：该产品系机电部"七五"期间推广的新产品、节能产品，该厂结合实际改进设计，达到国内先进水平。

1992年，天津市鼓风机总厂自主研制开发MJL系列密集成套型罗茨鼓风机。国内原来罗茨鼓风机只配主机、电机及消声器，MJL系列密集成套型罗茨鼓风机集空气滤清器、进口消声器、主机、出口消声器、止回阀、安全阀、压力表、挠性接头、减振器、整体框架、隔声罩于一体，具有结构紧凑、配套齐全、运转平稳、噪声低等特点。该系列风机共11个规格，分直联及皮带两种传动方式；流量1.01~62.3立方米/分，升压9.8~98千帕；主要用于建材、污水处理、海水养殖、冶炼、石油、化工、食品、轻工等行业的鼓风、气力输送等领域。输送介质为空气。该产品是国内第一个完整的密集型系列，填补国内的空白，结束依赖进口的局面。1993年11月23日，该新产品通过天津市经委组织的产品鉴定，认定该系列风机在国内处于领先地位，在国际处于先进地位。该产品获1996年度天津市科技进步二等奖。

1993年，天津市鼓风机总厂与大连理工大学合作开发TGT42LD罗茨鼓风机项目。采用该厂与大连理工大学联合研制的新型聚四氟乙烯无接触式迷宫式密封（获国家专利），其密封效果与机械密封接近，保证介质的密闭性，满足输送特种介质的要求，但结构简单，具有便于装卸、轴向尺寸小、寿命长等优点。1993年11月23日，天津市科委组织专家鉴定该产品，认定其技术水平在国内处于领先地位，在国际处于先进地位。

1995年，天津市鼓风机总厂与西安交通大学合作开发DC80b单齿鼓风机。其结构与罗茨鼓风机相似，但由于有内压缩过程，所以达到较大压比，一般单级最大压比可达到3，而单级罗茨鼓风机最大压比为2。1996年10月，该成果通过天津市经委组织的鉴定，认定其单齿鼓风机产品技术全新、结构合理，填补国内的空白，性能上接近20世纪90年代国际先进水平。1997年该产品被评为国家科技成果。

1996年，天津市鼓风机总厂在参照国内外先进技术的基础上，自主开发TGD系列双级罗茨鼓风机。该机由两台罗茨鼓风机串联而成，在两台主机间加空气冷却器，使该机实现等温压缩，与同性能的单级罗茨鼓风机相比，有着明显的节能效果。该系列是国内第一个自主开发的产品，具有独立自主的知识产权。1997年12月12日，该成果通过天津市科委组织的鉴定，认定其技术水平达到90年代国际先进。1997年，该产品获天津市科技创新优秀项目三等奖。

1999年，天津市鼓风机总厂与西安交通大学合作开发SL/MJLS系列三叶罗茨鼓风机。该产品与两叶罗茨鼓风机相比，具有明显的节能降噪效果，可用于取代两叶罗茨鼓风机。其采用的主要新技术包括：①转子采用先进的复合型转子型线，起到提高风机容积效率、降低噪声的作用；②壳体上采用先进的逆流降噪技术，起到减少气力脉动、降低噪声、减少冲击力、延长机器寿命的效果；③转子采用球墨铸铁整体结构（国内普遍采用钢轴与灰铸铁叶轮分体结构），提高转子的刚度及强度；④轴承直接装在墙板孔内，减少零件的累计误差，提高装配精度；⑤定位齿轮与轴联接采用胀紧套结构，与传统的齿轮与齿轮毂螺栓连接、齿轮毂与轴联接的结构相比，零件减少，精度提高，方便装拆，齿轮采用5级精度硬齿面，提高精度及寿命。该产品的噪声平均下降5~8分贝（A）；容积效率平均提高3%~5%。由于风机效率提高，使出口气体温度下降；整机精度高，减少各项摩擦损失。当该产品升压到98千帕时，仍不需水冷却，与两叶风机升压超过58千帕时需水冷却相比，属一大突破，为国内首创。该产品共14个规格，分直联及皮带两种传动方式，流量1.01~62.3立方米/分；升压9.8~98千帕。产品广泛用于建材、化工、冶炼、石油、轻工、污水处理、水产养殖等行业。2000年6月14日，该成果通过天津市科委组织的鉴定，认定该产品在叶轮型线、转子结构、齿轮联结等方面为国内首创，综合指标达到20世纪90年代国际同类产品先进水平。2002年，该产品获天津市科技进步二等奖。

2000年，天津市鼓风机总厂与西安交通大学合作开发出GSL系列高正压罗茨鼓风机。这是天津市科学技术发展计划攻关项目。该系列风机有GSL52WD及GSL62WD两个规格。该机采用逆流冷却技术，在风机出口端增加高压回流气体的消声器及空气冷却器，使经过消声及冷却的高压气体返回到机壳与转子形成的基元容积内，使气体的压力脉动减少50%，减少冲击力及噪声，同时使风机的出口温度得以大幅度下降；该机采用先进的三叶复合型转子型线，与原两叶相比，其容积效率平均提高3%~5%、噪声下降5~8分贝（A）。采用上述两项技术，使单级罗茨鼓风机在标准状态下，由原来的最大压比为2提高到2.55，出口最大升压由98千帕提高到156千帕，使原来由2台串级风机才能实现的升压值，在单级罗茨鼓风机得以实现，且机型缩小很多，有着明显的体积小、重量轻、占地面积小的诸多优点。该系列风机于2004年8月24日通过天津市科委组织的验收，认定其噪声比性能相当的双级罗茨鼓风机降低约9分贝（A），可用于取代双级罗茨鼓风机，在技术上取得重大突破，达到国内先进水平。

2002~2005年，天津市鼓风机总厂又开发出MJL250d~350b共6种规格的罗茨鼓风机，性能范围由原来最大流量的62.3立方米/分扩大到155立方米/分。新开发的产品除有原密集型风机特点外，另外采用先进的三叶复合转子型线及逆流降噪技术，使该机与原两叶风机相比，容积效率提高3%~5%，风机噪声下降5~8分贝（A），具有明显的节能降噪效果。至此，天津市鼓风机总厂开发、生产的MJL系列密集成套型罗茨鼓风机，从MJL80c~MJL350b，共达19个规格。

2005年，天津市鼓风机总厂开发出ML83WD罗茨鼓风机。该新产品用以输送煤气、氢气、甲烷、二氧化碳、一氧化碳等特殊介质。该机的最大特点是采用特制机械密封。ML83WD罗茨鼓风机，机型较大，传统方法采用涨圈及氟橡胶骨架油封均有不同程度的泄漏，专为该机设计的机械密封，确保密闭性，满足输送特殊气体介质的要求，且轴向尺寸小，便于装卸，物美价廉，为后来开发同类型产品打下基础。

同年，天津市鼓风机总厂通过引进美国海巴鼓风机有限公司的C系列三叶罗茨鼓风机技术，开发出该系列鼓风机。新产品技术先进，风机转速高、效率高、结构简单、高压时不需水冷却、体积小、成本低，开发的该系列风机共7个规格，分直联及皮带两种传动方式；性能范围，流量4.8~89.2立方米/分，升压28~103千帕。

五、环保机械

2001年，天津百利阳光环保设备有限公司设计研制出城市管道垃圾处理装置，亦称污泥处置设备或污泥快速干燥机。该产品入选中国工业(500项)重大科技产业化成果。同年，该公司设计研制出电池粉碎装置，产品获得专利。2002年，该公司设计研制出大件固体物破碎装置、园林剪切物处理装置、提升输送机、垃圾破袋处理装置，上述开发出的新产品都获得专利授权。2003年，该公司设计研制出日处理250吨城市居民生活垃圾综合处理线。2004年，该公司设计研制出4轴联动破碎机。

第四节　电工器材

电工器材是天津机械制造业的主要行业之一。天津市天变变压器有限公司在技术引进的基础上，开发和研制具有国际领先水平的新产品投放市场。天津百利电气公司从2002年组建当年开始加速新产品的开发与研制，部分新产品达到国际先进水平，多项获得天津市技术创新优秀奖。

一、变压器

1992年，天津市天变变压器有限公司(原天津市变压器总厂)研制出SFSZ7-50000/110三相三绕组油浸风冷有载调压电力变压器。1995年，该公司研发、试制出具有国际领先技术的SH11-315/10非晶合金变压器。1996年研发、试制新S9-630/10节能变压器。1999年研制开发出S9-M-30-1600/10全密封电力变压器。2000年引进新产品——组合式变压器(ZB—315/100)技术，该项目作为天津市科技攻关计划项目立项。2002年投产两台ZGS9-H-500/10组合式变压器、自行开发出11型迭片式铁心节能变压器。2003年引进SG(H)10系列真空压力浸漆干式变压器技术，并试制3台样机：SG(H)10-630/10、SG(H)10-1000/10和SG(H)10-1600/10真空压力浸漆干式变压器。

1999年，合资企业天津市特变电工变压器有限公司组建成立，主要生产干式电力变压器、各种类型整流变压器、接地变压器、消弧线圈、电抗器等特种输变电产品。主导产品有：10kV级SC(B)9、SC(B)10系列环氧树脂浇注干式配电变压器，容量范围30千伏安~2500千伏安；35千伏级SC(B)10系列环氧树脂浇注干式电力变压器，容量范围3150千伏安~25000千伏安。特种变压器产品主要有：城市地铁及轻轨用的ZQSCB系列24脉波牵引整流变压器、ZSCB系列12脉波整流变压器，中压变频调速设备使用的ZTSC系列18中压变频整流变压器，DC9系列27.5千伏级电压等级的单相电气化铁路用变压器、SCB9系列多电压海上平台用特种变压器、DKSC系列接地变压器及XHDC系列干式消弧线圈。同时还研制出非晶合金铁心干式变压器。

二、电气开关

2002年，百利电气公司由天津市低压电器公司和天津电力电子设备公司组建而成，并开始研制开发智能型电器开关。2003年5月，百利电气公司TW30-6300智能型万能式断路器和TM40-160、TM40-250智能型塑壳式断路器通过天津市科委组织的成果鉴定。同年8月，该公司生产的“低字牌”塑料外壳式断路器及万能式断路器两种产品，被授予“天津市名牌产品”称号。同时，该公司生产的产品全部取得强制性认证(3C)。2004年，该公司取得由华信技术检验有限公司颁发的GB/T19001-2000质量管理体认证证书。2004年4月，该公司研制生产的TJ40交流接触器通过3C工厂审查；该公司自主研发的TM40-160、TM40-250塑料外壳式智能型断路器获天津市技术创新优秀项目一等奖；TW30-6300智能型万能式断路器获天津市技术创新优秀项目二等奖。

2005年6月，百利电气公司最新研制的TW40-1600智能型万能式断路器和TJ40系列交流接触器通过市级鉴定。

第五节　工程机械

20世纪90年代开始，工程机械的应用范围快速从传统的土石方施工机械、建筑与筑路机械向国民经济其他领域和部门延伸，在高速铁路建设、市政与园林、物流与超市、建筑物拆迁、水下通讯、陆地与海下管道铺设、地下建筑物与构造物、家庭园艺与绿化等方面广泛使用。与此相适应，天津工程机械研究院（原天津工程机械研究所）与天津工程机械厂、起重设备厂等重组改造，拥有一批经验丰富、技术水平较高的专业技术人才，技术研发平台和研发能力在行业中处于先进水平，具备较强的消化吸收及自主创新能力，主要从事挖掘机械、铲土运输机械、路面与压实机械、陆海管道铺设机械、军民两用机械、焊接技术装备、环保技术装备以及关键零部件的开发、研制、试验，行业标准制修订、科技成果推广应用工作。

一、智能控制研究

（一）在线控制

2001年至2005年，以天津工程机械研究院为项目负责单位，由天津鼎盛工程机械有限公司、天津大学、北京航空航天大学、河北工业大学、天津商学院和唐山公路建设总公司联合完成国家“863”计划“机群智能化工程机械”“工程机械工况监测及质量管理技术研究”“路面施工机械智能化和制造信息化”“智能化平地机的研制与开发”等4项“863”项目。

图5-5-5-65　国家“863”计划项目“机群智能化“

该项目结合国内外前沿技术而开展，其核心技术具有自主知识产权。关键技术为：①基于多智能主体的机群施工调度技术，采用基于多智能控制的分布—分层式树状控制体系，构成基于多智能控制主体的以物流控制为核心的机群施工过程智能化控制系统；②人—机共栖多智能主体控制结构，在建立机群施工过程的各智能主体间完整的信息流基础上，提出人—机共栖智能体结构，提供人机交互人性化界面，改善操作条件，使人机在感知、思维和决策3个层面上实现一体化整合；③智能化路面施工机群的数据通讯方法与数据链协议的制定，涉及由多品种、多数量机械设备组成的施工机群的通讯，在工程机械施工领域创立数据通讯方法与数据链协议，实现机群间在线通讯；④研制机群状态监测与智能故障诊断系统的专家系统，以故障诊断对象为中心组织知识库系统结构，以对象为知识表达的基本单元，将规则、框架、过程等多种单一的知识表达方式，按面向对象的思想组成一种混合模式，即以对象为中心，将其属性、动态行为和处理过程等有关知识封装在对象的结构中，以人机共栖的方式获取机械设备状态信息，实现人机系统功能的最优化分配；⑤基于多目标函数的道路施工机械资源优化配置方法，以质量、成本、施工效率、均衡性生产四者综合形成目标函数，体现人机共栖的特点，既有施工过程中的数学模型的建立、施工参数的判断、机群配置的选型计算，还充分顾及到人的经验的重要性，在经过理论化计算后，加以人工判断，使机群最大限度的满足施工现场的实际要求；⑥研制成功具有自主知识产权的单机智能控制系统，实现单机智能监测、控制、报警、通讯、

GPS定位等功能，硬件采用嵌入式系统设计技术，软件采用实时多任务操作系统，提供人机交互界面，快速响应，提供操作系统API接口，方便用户进行上层开发提升单机协同机群施工整体的综合功能。这些关键技术在“路面施工机械智能化和制造信息化”项目的“机群智能化工程机械”子项目中得到实施。“路面施工机械智能化和制造信息化”项目的“企业信息化工程”子项目，建立并完善计算机网络化支撑环境，主导产品导入物流信息化管理系统，基于PLM的产品协同设计平台也初具规模。

（二）虚拟设计装配

1991年，天津工程机械研究所完成国家机械工业部CAD项目，规模化地使用CAD手段进行产品设计。利用各种CAE软件对产品关键零部件进行结构分析，工作装置铰接点位置优化采用通用优化设计程序；产品和部件总体方案的计算机辅助优化设计；结构件强度和刚度设计用有限元计算；结构件寿命用疲劳计算和寿命预测，建立4C1P协同并行开发平台工艺人员和设计人员网上并行工作，CAPP辅助工艺设计和工艺管理活动，计算机辅助工艺装备设计，计算机辅助工艺定额管理，CAD/CAM辅助模具开发制造等。2001年，开始尝试零部件的全三维CAD造型设计，整机三维CAD虚拟装配。

2002年，天津工程机械研究院使用产品数据管理PDM系统。一方面作为纽带贯穿产品开发的项目管理、流程管理、产品配置管理、图纸文件管理，另一方面作为技术系统与制造系统之间最重要的数据接口，将产品设计BOM以及工艺、工装数据传输给ERP系统。通过产品信息化建设，产品开发和技术管理的全部活动都在网络化协同工作环境中进行。

二、器件材料更新

（一）齿轮、轴类零件材料

1991年，天津工程机械研究所针对齿轮、轴类零件长期使用18CrMnTi、20CrMnTi和30CrMnTi材料的热处理变形大，使用寿命短等缺陷，提出采用20CrMnMo脱气钢替代技术。这种钢淬火变形小，变形规律可掌握，提高传动件的几何精度；这种钢的氧化杂质含量少，可以减少疲劳源，从而提高传动件寿命3～4倍。随着冶炼工艺方法和技术的进步，有效控制轧制比和夹渣水平，传动部件的大小螺旋等主要齿轮件，采用真空脱气工艺冶炼的材料，达到在稳定的热处理工艺下获得淬透性指标100%合格稳定的结果，传动部件的使用寿命进一步提高，反馈率下降50%。1992年，针对半轴等个别关键传动件，开展使用材料及热处理研究，通过采用新材料，改变传统的渗碳层硬化工艺为35CrMo中频感应淬火，提高热处理表面硬化层，解决新式驱动桥的抗扭强度，质量提高，成本降低。

（二）斗齿材料

1991年，天津工程机械研究所针对斗齿用材料的强度和耐磨性均不理想或芯部硬度偏低等原因，与长春精密铸造厂共同研究一种表面和芯部硬度均很高的耐磨材料，斗齿采用低合金钢铸造，具有高硬度、高冲击韧性且更换方便等优点。与日本川崎重工业公司的斗齿装在同一铲斗上进行对比试验，寿命是川崎公司的1.51倍。

1999年，天津工程机械研究院根据引进技术中的斗齿材料的组成成分标准和图纸，进行消化吸收再创新，开展系列齿套新材料铸造、热处理工艺试验。通过装机验证试验，耐磨性提高2倍以上。

（三）销轴衬套材料

1992年，天津工程机械研究院通过消化与吸收引进技术，提出衬套销轴摩擦副改为钢对钢结构，销轴采用中碳钢如40Cr材料，传统的中碳钢高频淬火工艺改为中频感应淬火，以加深淬硬层的深度，延长耐磨性。通过油槽储油润滑衬套销轴摩擦副，提高运动摩擦、挤压、冲击及偏载等磨损失效时效。衬套采用系列新材料和新结构，钢对新型网纹沟槽结构，铜基镶嵌固体润滑材料，高硬度耐磨聚氨酯树脂材料。钢销轴对新型网纹沟槽，优化表面结构，起到接纳和排除硬质颗粒作用，采用激光表面强化处理，提高表面抗磨粒磨损和疲劳磨损性能，采用化学镀Ni-P-PTFE减磨材料提高自润滑性能。采用自润滑性能的衬套铜基镶嵌固体润滑材料，抗磨粒磨损、疲劳磨损和改善润滑。调整垫片采用高硬度耐磨聚氨酯树脂材料，提高调整垫耐磨、耐冲击及抗疲劳性能，使用寿命为钢制调整垫的4倍以上。

三、工程机械及零部件

1991~2005年，天津工程机械研究院承担的国家级和省部级的工程机械重大科研项目，申请专利117项，获得专利117项。19项成果获得省、部级科技进步奖。

（一）工程机械主机

1991年2月12日，天津工程机械研究所牵头，杭州重机厂、沈阳矿山机械厂、大连重机厂、上海彭浦厂、小龙潭煤矿共同承担完成的“1500~2000立方米/时斗轮挖掘机连续开采工艺成套设备研制”项目获国家机电部科技进步二等奖。

1991年1月15日，天津工程机械研究所承担的“轮式装载机CAD系统”科技专项成果参加国家机电部系统CAD成果展览，并被评为一等奖。

1991年，天津工程机械研究所承担国家发改委“八五”重大科技攻关项目“HT7500水泥混凝土滑模式摊铺机关键技术研究”项目，使中国成为亚洲地区完成此项研究的唯一国家。

1992年1月28日，国家机电部“1000万吨级大型露天矿成套设备”项目获1989年国家科技进步特等奖，天津工程机械研究院承担该项目中“320马力推土机关键技术”专项。

图5-5-5-66 WT7500液压稳定土摊铺机

1993年，天津工程机械研究所与山东水利机械厂、泰安起重机械厂合作研制SDZ15装载机。该机采用负荷传感转向系统，使功率利用更合理。该项目获山东省水利科技进步一等奖。

1996年7月至2000年10月，天津工程机械研究院承担天津市重大科技攻关项目“新型稳定土摊铺机”。研制的WT7500、WT9000两种型号稳定土摊铺机，于2000年12月29日通过由天津市科委组织的专家鉴定。2002年12月28日，WTD9500多功能摊铺机、WTB7500型全液压稳定土摊铺机LTY12000全液压沥青摊铺机通过天津市科委组织的专家鉴定。2005年8月29日，“WTD9500多功能摊铺机”项目获天津市2004年科技进步三等奖。2003年10月18日，“WT9500型全液压稳定土摊铺机”项目获2003年度国家工程机械集团科学技术二等奖。2003年06月7日，“WT7500型全液压稳定土摊铺机”项目获2002年度天津市科技进步二等奖。2002年，WT7500摊铺机获国家级重点新产品证书和天津市科技进步二等奖。

图5-5-5-67 新型稳定土拌合机

1997~1999年，天津工程机械研究所完成“WB360全液压稳定土拌和机”研制。该机用于公路、城市道路、机场、码头等稳定基层的就地拌和作业。获1998年度国家机械工业部科技进步二等奖。1998年11月获得科技部、国家税务总局、外经贸部、国家质量技术监督局、国家环保总局联合认证颁发的国家重点新产品证书。

1999年8月4日，天津鼎盛公司和天津工程机械研究院联合开发研制的高性能筑路机械“WS500稳定土厂拌设备”，通过由天津市科委主持召开的新产品鉴定。获天津市1999年科技进步二等奖。2000年6月获得由科技部、国家税务总局、外经贸部、国家质量技术监督局、国家环保总局联合认证颁发的国家重点新产品证书。

（二）工程机械零部件

1991年2月12日，天津工程机械研究所完成的“YJSW315-5a、6a型双涡轮液力变矩器”“结构件应用远程参数控制试验技术”获国家机电部科技进步二等奖。

1992年,天津工程机械研究所与济南液压泵厂、青州液压件厂合作,完成“CBZb型浮动轴式高压齿轮泵系列”的项目。该项目采用“浮动轴式齿轮泵,齿轮马达”专利技术,制造出轴向浮动和径向液压浮动补偿的新型外啮合高压齿轮泵。该系列齿轮泵最高额定压力为25兆帕,排量为160毫升/转。该系列齿轮泵在青州液压件厂及济南液压泵厂投入批量生产,广泛用于各种工程机械。该项目获1995年度国家机电部科技进步二等奖。

1992~1994年,天津工程机械研究所完成“2000万吨级大型露天矿成套设备中关键设备配套液压组件”项目研制。天工所承担研究280马力自行式平地机用多路阀、280马力自行式平地机用轴向柱塞泵、525马力履带式推土机用齿轮泵。其中多路阀项目由四川省机械厅组织鉴定,获得通过并获得四川省科技成果二等奖。

1998年,天津工程机械研究院开展第二代电液控制动力换挡变速器技术研发。

(三)研制实验台

1991年至1995年5月,天津工程机械研究所完成“H/YBT-1型摇摆试验台”项目研制,获1996年国家机械工业部科技进步一等奖和1997年国家科技进步二等奖。1995年11月至1997年10月进行H/YBT-2型摇摆试验台研制、H/YBT-3型摇摆试验台研制。2000年9月1日,天工院鼎成公司承担航天科技集团h/ybt-4型摇摆试验台,动态环境模拟系统国家重点军工项目,完成方案论证和技术设计,立项研制。2005年8月29日,“动态环境模拟系统研制”项目获天津市2004年科技进步二等奖。

四、引领行业发展

(一)解决共性难题和技术保证

2002年,天津工程机械研究院围绕行业亟需解决的技术难题及长远技术发展的要求开展科研,进行共性基础技术和应用技术研究,使得液压液力传动、振动、计算机及自动控制等技术在工程机械产品中得到普遍推广应用,产品的工作性能、安全性和操纵性能提高。2002年,开展远程遥控技术、故障诊断技术、机群控制技术等人工智能化研究,改变传统工作方式,推出新功能产品,使得工程机械产品的可靠性和使用寿命有效提高。

(二)促进科研成果转化

1990年,天津工程机械研究所与有关厂家共同进行的履带推土机行走机构易损件寿命攻关工作,使国产推土机寿命达到日本同类产品的水平,节省钢材和资金。

1990年,天津工程机械研究所研制的CBG2系列高压齿轮泵,工作压力可达30兆帕,采用独特的轴向与径向浮动补偿结构,高温时的容积效率比美国、日本同类产品高4%~8%,使用寿命达4000小时以上,超过美国、日本产品的2500小时,获得国家发明三等奖,使中国工程机械产品的配套水平得到提高。

1995年,天津工程机械研究所对舰用离心水泵课题的研究,创新地系统采用旋流器、副叶片、机械密封和水轴承结构材质的综合防泄漏技术,解决泥砂对离心泵快速磨损而导致漏水的难题,开发出具有防泄漏技术的新水泵系列。

(三)新工艺研究推广

天津工程机械研究所经过生产工艺条件改造,引进技术,消化吸收,创造出一批专用生产设备,促进行业采用新的制造工艺技术。1991年,钢板的预处理、计算机排版下料、机器人焊接、采用加工中心加工零件等工艺,在业内普遍得到应用。1992年,鉴于涂装工艺受到重视,汽车工业涂装工艺经过改造,被移植到工程机械行业。

(四)完善的试验体系

1995年10月,国家机械工业部批准,将设在天津工程机械研究院的三个质检机构合并为一个部级检测中心,全称为机械工业部工程机械及液压件产品质量监督检测中心。该院液压试验室作为国内最早开展中高压液压元件检测试验的单位之一,可完成220马力以下的液压元件的全性能检测试验;柴油机试验室的试验台可进行600马力以下各型柴油机性能检测;土切试验室开展多项煤岩切割阻力试验检测和推土板合理参数的试验分析,为斗轮挖掘机设计、消化引进日本公司技术与自行设计推土机提供依据;自动化试验室的66台试验仪器可承担大型成套自动化设备、试验室台架自动化以及专用仪表和相应的一次传感器生产与研制并进行测试数据的快速处理。

第六节 子午线轮胎成套装备

1989年创立的天津赛象科技股份有限公司(简称赛象公司)通过自主创新,在发达国家的轮胎子午化率达到90%以上,而中国仅为10%左右,高等级子午胎制造设备几乎是空白的情况下,成功地研发出具有自主知识产权的4个系列、70余个品种子午线轮胎关键设备,技术水平达到国内领先、部分产品达到国际同类产品先进水平。到2005年,该公司获得专利33项,其中发明专利2项,软件著作权11项;10个产品列入国家重点新产品计划。"赛象"品牌橡机遍及全国,并出口到法国、美国、日本、英国、意大利等国家的著名轮胎生产企业,在国内橡机行业居于领先地位。

一、关键设备和原材料国产化

1992年,赛象公司张芝泉、张建浩等承担国家经贸委"子午线轮胎关键设备和原材料国产化一条龙"项目中的"六角型钢丝圈缠绕设备"子项目。采用电加热方式对钢丝进行除锈和预热,解决传统酸洗除锈污染环境的问题,钢丝挂胶质量提高。同时,针对以往老设备机械结构不完善、容易造成乱丝形成浪费的问题,设计出先进的钢丝储存装置,保证高速缠绕过程中不乱丝,提高工作效率,减少原材料的浪费。该项目一次开发成功,填补国内空白。1993年获得国家科技进步三等奖,拥有专利5项,其中发明专利1项。

1997年,赛象公司承担并完成国家经贸委"子午线轮胎关键设备和原材料国产化一条龙"项目中的5个子项目。其中,88吋液压硫化机设备项目,主要用于巨型子午线轮胎制造过程中最后的硫化工序,采用先进的液压技术,制造国内首台大口径液压硫化机;轮胎输送线设备项目,用于轮胎半成品/成品的输送,采用机械自动输送方式,解决轮胎生产过程中从上一工序到下工序的自动输送问题;600轮胎胎面生产线和800轮胎胎面生产线项目,是生产子午线轮胎胎面的专用设备,使其具备挤出胎面后进行冷却、裁断、称重等功能;三角胶贴合机设备项目,是用于将子午线轮胎部件三角胶与钢丝圈相联接的专用设备,成功解决钢丝圈与胎体的连接问题。上述设备一次开发成功,替代进口,确立该公司在行业内的信誉与影响力。"轮胎胎面生产线"项目1997年获国家科技进步二等奖;1999年获天津市科技进步一等奖。

2002年,国家经贸委将"载重子午胎成套设备及工程子午胎关键设备研制"列为国家重大技术装备研制项目计划,以满足汽车工业和高速公路的发展需要。赛象公司承担其中13个子项的研制开发,包括密炼机、薄胶片内衬层压延法联动生产线、薄胶片内衬层挤出法联动生产线、0°带束层钢丝帘布生产线、工程胎六角型钢丝圈生产线、铡刀式钢丝帘布裁断机组、90°钢丝帘布裁断机组、Φ150冷/Φ250热双复合挤出机及其联动生产线、三鼓式全钢载重子午胎一次法成型机、工程子午线轮胎成型机、工程子午线轮胎X光检验机、均匀性试验机、检测设备生产线研制等,占全部项目的三分之一以上。开发的产品成为国内轮胎生产企业实现产品升级换代、完成产品结构调整的首选,使轮胎企业能在较短时间内以较少的投入,实现主导产品由传统的斜交轮胎向高等级子午线轮胎的转变,投资减少70%以上。

二、成套设备研发

1997年,赛象公司张芝泉、张建浩、朱伯明等研发"全钢丝载重子午线轮胎一次法成型机"。在产品研发中始终瞄准国际先进水平,应用光机电一体化高新技术,改造和提升中国传统橡机行业的水平,研制成功适用于FIRESTON工艺要求的国产第一台全钢丝载重子午线轮胎一次法成型机。设计制造上具有快速高效、节时省料,降低制造成本的特点,达到90年代初期同类产品国际先进水平。该产品替代进口,每台至少节约投资640万元。2000年,该设备项目获得国家科技进步二等奖。该设备的升级换代产品——“三鼓式全钢丝载重子午线轮胎一次法成型机”项目,被列入国家“十五”科技攻关计划;2005年,该成型机生产出200台套,实现销售收入13亿元人民币,为国家“十五”期间市场急需的载重子午线轮胎的快速发展提供有力的支撑。2004年,“全钢载重子午线轮胎三鼓式一次法成型机”项目获天津市科技进步一等奖。

图5-5-6-68 赛象集团子午线轮胎生产设备

1999年,赛象公司开发的子午线轮胎系列生产设备产品被列入天津市重大高新技术产业化项目计划。该项目产品可满足国家对子午线轮胎生产发展需要,适应汽车工业新的增长要求,并带动相关产业同步发展。项目主要产品“多复合挤出机”用于挤出具有高级使用特性轮胎多复合胎面等橡胶部件的制造,是新型高技术高工艺特性轮胎制造的关键设备;“轮胎胎面复合挤出联动生产线”与“多复合挤出主机”相配套,对挤出的橡胶制品充分冷却、均匀收缩、连续称重、次定长裁断、单条称重、导出分选等工艺处理;全钢丝载重子午线轮胎次法成型机是用于对子午线轮胎胎体进行次成型的关键没备。

2001年,赛象公司开发“轮胎制造专用数控系列设备”项目,列入国家“十五”科技成果重点推广计划。该设备的创新点:一是生产效率高,胎圈直径为22.5″时,每条轮胎的成型时间为7.5～8分,每班可成型轮胎45～50条;二是更换规格省时方便,相同胎圈直径时,更换规格约1个小时,不同胎圈直径时,更换规格约2个小时;三是部件定位精度高,采用滚动导轨,滚动丝杆和三相交流伺服系统控制,内衬层胎侧复合件和胎体帘布均有自动对中装置。

2003年,赛象公司承担国家火炬计划“乘用/轻卡子午线轮胎成型机组”项目,研制成功“一段、二段子午胎成型机组”。该设备能适应的成型子午胎规格范围,达到预定15″~18″钢丝圈直径的指标,特别是二段成型机,可扩大到部分10″口径规格,为扩大轻卡和乘用子午胎生产规模,满足国内外市场需求提供设备保障。设备部件加工精细,组装配合严密,各重点驱动系统均采用伺服控制系统,与国外同类机型的变频系统相比,自动化控制水平提高,对子午胎成型质量起到关键保障作用。由于提高主机转速和与之配合的各工作系统速度,从而使得该设备生产效率提高,能够依据子午胎结构规格不同、成型工艺难度差异等,生产各种规格系列的子午胎,班产能力为80~130条,与国外同类机型相比较,生产率提高约10%左右。2004年10月,该项目通过天津市科委组织的验收。

同年,赛象公司开发“全钢巨型工程子午线轮胎生产关键成套设备”。在没有任何资料可供借鉴的条件下,坚持原始创新,完成该系列项目共9种产品,取得多项创新成果。其核心产品“四鼓式全钢工程子午线轮胎一次法成型机”创新点是:①采用双成型鼓形式,两鼓交替使用,增加工作效率。成型鼓采用双胶囊全反包结构,反包胶囊采用自动调速,保持同步膨胀;成型鼓采用双气缸推动连杆撑快结构,使胎圈锁紧,避免滑移;成型鼓中鼓采用三层薄套结构,定型时薄套缩合。②带束层贴合鼓采用24扇快结构,可调整和改变直径范围,带束层贴合鼓采用伺服电机进行驱动。③气动系统采用精密比例阀控制,电气系统采用工业控制计算机控制伺服系统、交流变频调速电机等,实现夹持环、传递环、成型鼓、贴合鼓、供料系统的精确运行。④滚压装置采用机械手通过计算机控制自动完成工艺动作,保证成型质量,降低操作工的劳动强度。该项目具有自主知识产权,达到国际先进水平,产业化后市场占有率较高,2004年获天津市专利金奖 。

第六章 汽 车

天津是国家重要的汽车生产基地之一。1983年,国家计委和经委依据汽车行业发展规划,确定天津在全国作为轿车的“三小生产基地”之一。以1991年为新起点,天津通过引进国外先进整车生产制造技术,进行消化吸收再创新,开创生产调查当轿车的新阶段;生产的车型,从微型和轻型客车、轻型载货车和多功能乘用车等多系列,逐渐集中为轿车系列。天津汽车工业集团有限公司(简称天汽集团)前身是组建于1970年的天津市第一机械工业局农机汽车工业公司,1993年更名为天津汽车工业总公司,通过走内涵挖潜与引进吸收再创新相结合的发展之路,使夏利轿车和华利微型车迅速成长为天津汽车工业的支柱产品。1997年天津市微型汽车厂、天津内燃机厂、天津汽车研究所共同改制,成立天津汽车夏利股份有限公司(简称天津夏利公司),1999年在深圳证券交易所挂牌上市。天汽集团成为集整车制造、发动机、变速器生产、销售以及科研开发于一体的上市公司,拥有居于国内先进水平的冲压、车身、涂装及装配生产线,整车质量检测线,汽车发动机铸造及机加工生产线,变速器生产线,计算机工作站,检测实验室等,形成夏利系列产品。1995年底,作为国家“八五”重点建设项目、天津市1号重点工程的“夏利轿车15万辆扩建项目”竣工,并于1996年通过国家正式验收,形成年产15万辆20万台发动机的能力。通过“引进—消化—吸收—再创新”的成长之路,夏利产品连续22年蝉联自主品牌微型轿车销量冠军,产品分布全国,远销墨西哥、俄罗斯、伊朗、叙利亚、阿尔及利亚等国家。2003~2005年,天津一汽丰田(夏利与丰田、一汽集团的合资企业)相继推出花冠、卡罗拉、锐志、皇冠、RAV4等系列乘用车。在此期间,由天汽集团、中国汽车技术研究中心、天津力神电池股份有限公司、天津蓝天电源有限公司等四家单位共同投资组建的高新技术企业——天津清源电动车辆有限责任公司(简称清源公司)2001年成立,专门从事电动车辆整车及关键零部件的研究、开发、生产与经营。2005年,清源公司等单位自主研发生产的“幸福使者”纯电动车出口美国市场,标志着天津电动汽车产业化、参与国际市场竞争。

第一节 轿 车

作为国内的轿车重点生产厂家,天津一汽夏利汽车股份有限公司(天津市微型汽车厂)1983年3月以技贸结合方式从日本大发公司引进HIJET(大发)微型厢式客车技术,通过生产微型厢式车起步。1996年,夏利轿车年产15万辆整车;1997年,夏利局部换型车批量投入生产;1998、1999年,相继推出夏利加长型和双燃料轿车;2000年,引进丰田技术的夏利2000型全新轿车投放市场;2001年,夏利推出“静雅”系列两厢电喷自动档轿车。2000年6月,天津汽车夏利股份有限公司与日本丰田公司合资成立天津丰田汽车制造有限公司,引进日本生产技术,生产威弛及其他中高档轿车。2002年6月14日,天汽集团与一汽集团签署重组协议;同年12月26日,天津夏利公司正式更名为“天津一汽夏利汽车股份有限公司”(简称天津一汽),进一步加强与日本丰田公司的合作。2003年5月有,经过156项技术改进的夏利A系列“骏雅”和“绅雅”车型上市。2005年3月,天津一汽生产的具有完全自主知识产权的夏利N3轿车首次大批量出口。同年12月28日,天津一汽夏利新N3 1.3L获选“2005CCTV中国年度汽车自主品牌汽车”。在十几年的时间里,天津夏利公司从CKD来件组装,经过引进技术消化吸收和国产化,逐步自主实施轿车产品设计、工厂改造和生产准备,形成完整的自主创新和自主发展体系,产品制造技术不断提升和发展。特别是20世纪90年代初期和2000年左右实施的技术改造项目,使企业的工艺布局得到优化,持续的新车型投放也有效地拉动冲压、装焊、涂装和总装制造技术的全面提升,确立多品种、大规模、高质量的发展目标。通过采用新的管理技术,优化管理流程,立足挖掘资源潜力,在生产资源基本不变、实际作业面积增加有限的情况下,实现多品种、多车型在装焊、涂装和总装作业的混线生产。截至2005年,天津一汽同时进行两个技术平台轿车产品(夏利、NBC)生产,全面覆盖多个产品系列(威乐、威姿、老夏利、夏利A系列和B系列),多达30余种车型,形成年产20万辆夏利、威乐、威姿品牌轿车的生产能力。

一、设计与制造

(一)车型

1.夏利轿车局部改型

1996年9月,天津市微型汽车厂启动夏利轿车局部换型(Z913)项目。与日本大发公司联合对夏利轿车车身进行局部改进,在376Q发动机和底盘不变的情况下,保持车身中部不变,对二厢和三厢车身进行前后部分变动,增加时尚元素以使车身更加美观、流畅和舒适。同时,产品设计图的转化和绘制均利用计算机完成。1997年8月,该车型投入批量生产,上市销售。

2001年11月,天汽集团对夏利轿车进行7项技术改进,推出"静雅"型两厢电喷自动挡夏利轿车。

2002~2003年,天津市汽车夏利产品开发中心承担天津市科委项目,与天津市传动轴厂合作进行"1.3升夏利轿车底盘功能的提高"项目研究。

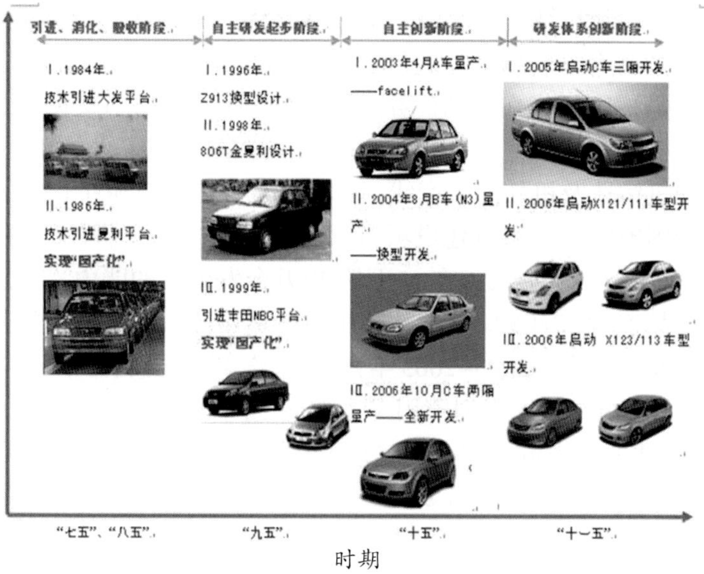

图5-6-1-69 天津汽车产品创新型谱

2.NBC(New Basic Car:新基准轿车)系列产品技术引进与再创新

1999年4月,天津夏利公司组织实施夏利轿车换代车型项目。同年9月,天津夏利公司与日本丰田汽车公司正式签署NBCⅠ和NBCⅡ轿车的技术转让合同。

2000年11月28日,作为夏利换型车的夏利2000型轿车下线。此后经2年匹配及设计,在NBCⅡ平台上完成搭载4AT自动变速器的"雅酷"轿车开发,增加该车型的品种,提高驾驶舒适性;又经过2年,NBCⅡ轿车完成局部换型车开发,车身局部变型、调整前低后高的整车车姿,散热器罩、冲压件、保险杠、安全气囊、驱动轴、仪表板、变速器、空调系统、汽车电子及悬挂系统等部分关键系统实现国产化,并针对中国路况进行设计提升,符合中国人审美习惯和驾乘习惯,全新紧凑型轿车威乐"Vela"成功上市。

2002年12月25日,引进丰田NBCI产品技术开发生产的"威姿"(VIZI)轿车下线。NBC系列产品具有外形紧凑、车内空间大以及安全车身结构等优良性能。天津夏利公司在引进消化吸收过程中,实现重要零部件国产化1057件。其中,与宝钢合作开发的后桥高强度钢板成功实现国产化;前悬臂安全性约束装置以及车身安全性,均达到丰田公司技术标准要求。

2005年7月18日,搭载8A发动机的1.3 L威乐轿车成功下线。该轿车的产品线扩大,得到市场的好评。

3.夏利A系列轿车开发

2001年9月,天津夏利公司启动A系列夏利轿车项目。在引进消化吸收日本大发夏利轿车技术的基础上，充分考虑技术和工艺的继承性，对车身和内饰局部换型设计，产品造型有所突破。同时，对发动机进行满足欧洲Ⅱ号排放标准的技术改造，以满足国家车辆认证和技术法规要求。2003年5月，该系列夏利轿车下线投放市场。

2003年5月14日，夏利二厢和三厢改进型轿车分别命名为“骏雅”和“绅雅”作为A系列2款新车上市。A系列轿车是在原夏利轿车的基础上，对前后保险杠、车灯、前发动机盖、后行李厢盖和车厢内饰、仪表板等部件进行设计，增加安全气囊、ABS、CD音响、电动摇窗机、中控门锁、远程控制电动手动后视镜、电动天线、前后钻石车灯及运动型仪表等配置，对转向系统和空调系统进行设计提升。该2款车共进行156项次的技术与工艺改进，其中重大改进达20多项，内饰与外形方面改变很大，安全性、舒适性、排放性能及整车造型等较原夏利车型有较大提升，符合客户需求。

4. 夏利N3系列轿车开发

2002年10月，天津一汽启动B系列夏利轿车(N3)的产品策划工作。2003年1月，天津一汽实施夏利三厢二次局改项目。该项目被国家经贸委列为第三批国家重点技术改造“双高一优”项目导向计划。2004年7月实施完成。2005年10月通过一汽集团验收。

2004年，天津一汽首次通过自主开发设计方式进行夏利车身改型。本着“省时、省心、省钱”原则共进行150多项技术改进，设计上实现“新造型、新结构、新内饰”，最终成功推出B系列夏利N3轿车。车身改型工作在原夏利轿车的基础上，通过全新的车身和内外饰件设计，实现夏利轿车的2次换型，四门两盖、侧围、顶盖、保险杠、仪表板及内外饰等重新设计，底盘系统改进设计并精心调校，电喷系统欧Ⅲ升级，操控、转向、车灯、车镜及电气系统技术升级，共有129个部件发生变化。该项目开发第一次对钣金件和外饰做改动，初步形成具有自己特色的车身局部换型工作流程，其整车的安全性、可靠性、舒适性及排放性能等大幅提升。

2004年8月，以自主创新支撑的夏利N3投产。8月8日，第100万辆夏利轿车暨全新的夏利N3轿车成功下线。

5. 威志系列轿车开发

2003年年底，全新开发威志轿车项目启动。该车在设计安全技术、节能技术、环保技术及造型技术上取得突破。①安全技术：实施38项主动安全技术、29项被动安全技术，是自主品牌中第1款通过正碰/侧碰/后碰/40%偏置碰撞的车型；装备安全气囊，采用高强度、高刚性车身及可溃式转向柱以增加汽车被动安全性；采用GOA安全车身技术，装备ABS、EBD、动力转向及防侵入式踏板。②全新造型和内饰（自主方案）：造型简洁、时尚、大气，风阻系数低；具有鲜明的时代感，弧形和流线完美结合，配合国际流行的鸣沙金和梦幻绿等涂装色彩；前大灯造型独特，采用国际高档轿车的造型元素，卤素与LED大灯的组合使亮度超强，照射范围更加宽广；内嵌式广角水晶雾灯穿透力强，广角式投射，确保雨雾天气行驶的安全性；车尾灯与前大灯造型相对应，整车充满运动气息；分体式晶钻高透视度组合尾灯，外观新颖，亮度高，后雾灯与倒车灯分别布置在尾灯的两端，分色警示明确，配合尾部造型，美观大方；后部高位刹车灯的安装，保障刹车信号更加清晰明显，利于后部车辆及时掌握刹车意图，提高行驶安全性；前保险杠采用大型包覆式，整车外型圆润饱满。③节能设计：采用丰田系列高品质节能发动机；高效率、优化的传动系统；造型简洁动感，风阻系数0.32；精心匹配的冷却系统和轮胎。④环保技术：排放达国Ⅲ和国Ⅳ(带EOBD)；降低车外内噪声；电磁兼容性；广泛采用环保材料等。⑤舒适性技术应用：对照30多种车型，考虑中国家用特征，后排空间高于平均值7%；经过18个月的内饰色彩设计；NVH仿真模拟；优化的室内通风及空调系统；精心调校的底盘系统，操控稳定性能突出，起步平顺、换挡清晰、高速稳定、转向准确、侧向干扰受控。天津一汽设计分析手段全面提升，CAE分析(模态分析、刚度分析、NVH分析、碰撞分析等)手段贯穿始终。

2005年6月28日，威志轿车首次装车成功，天津一汽第一辆自主研发的轿车诞生。

（二）发动机

1991年4月，TJ376QA发动机产品立项。1992年5月完成产品设计，同年9月完成工艺准备，并试制出样机。TJ376QA发动机为天津华利6350厢式客车配套，满足装用空调对动力配套的需求，并适应燃用低标号汽油，功率较TJ370Q有提升。1994年TJ376QA发动机通过天津市经委组织的新产品生产技术鉴定。1991年TJ370Q发动机获国家机械电子工业部的优质产品称号。1996年9月天内牌TJ370Q和TJ376Q发动机获天津市政府颁发的天津市名牌产品证书。

1991年，TJ376QB发动机同时立项。该发动机是在TJ370Q和TJ376Q汽油机的结构设计基础上，开发研制的变型产品，主要是为提高配套车的动力性能，满足不同客车和轿车等变型车辆配套的需要。1993年上半年，该发动机完成工艺准备和样机小批试制，为上汽集团公司仪征汽车厂和安徽郎溪西雅特汽车制造有限公司等汽车厂家生产的轿车配套。

1996年1~4月，天津市内燃机厂和天津汽车研究所与日本大发公司共同开发设计TJ376QE型发动机。同年6~7月，开始应用共同研制出的EFI系统及相关变更件、新增件和TJ376Q系列产品的通用件。同年9月由天津市经委组织样件鉴定。TJ376QE型汽油机是应用微机控制系统，使燃油喷射、点火装置、怠速装置、废气排放以及故障诊断等项均实现电子控制，提高夏利轿车的动力性、经济性和排气污染控制性能。TJ376QE型汽油机成为天津夏利TJ7100U型轿车配套的动力产品。

1998年初，天津市内燃机厂和天津市汽车研究所共同承担TJ378QE发动机第1阶段试制工作。2000年4月，启动TJ378Q化油器发动机的试制。2001年7~11月，TJ378QE发动机进行装车试验，同年取得新产品新技术鉴定验收证书。该款发动机缸径扩大，由76毫米扩大到78毫米，冲程由73毫米增加到73.4毫米，因此排量由0.993升增大到1.052升，有利于发动机增加外销。

1999年，随着排放法规严格，天津一汽与联合汽车电子有限公司、大陆汽车系统公司、北京德尔福公司不断匹配并联合开发电喷系统，使夏利各车型排放水平从欧Ⅰ标准提升到欧Ⅱ、欧Ⅲ、欧Ⅳ标准，逐步降低污染物的排放。

2003年12月，CA4GB发动机项目启动。2005年6月15日通过产品鉴定。该款发动机采用先进的4气门汽油机技术，双顶置凸轮轴，先进的帐篷形顶置四气门汽油机燃烧室，对称型进排气凸轮；采用正时皮带和无声齿轮驱动配气机构，笔形点火线圈，气缸盖上布置喷油器方式，以及先进的冷却系统布置方式。其动力性和经济型等指标达到丰田A系列发动机的水平。3GA2是TJ376QE的4气门改造，通过一些新技术的应用，各项性能提高。样机试验表明：3GA2的最大功率为48千瓦，最大扭矩为89牛/米，分别比TJ376QE提高23%和16%；油耗小于270克/千瓦·时，比TJ376QE下降7%；排放达到欧Ⅳ标准。每缸四气门，DOHC双凸轮轴直接驱动，提高进气量，并进一步优化燃烧室，燃烧得到改进。燃油控制系统采用"博世"的ME7，使燃油控制和点火时刻更加准确。该款发动机在奥地利AVL公司进行全面技术评审，一次性通过。TA1发动机采用VCT-i智能可变气门正时系统，DOHC双顶置凸轮轴，轻量化镁铝缸盖，硅橡胶合成塑料进气歧管，不锈钢排气歧管，静音正时驱动链条，曲轴偏置设计，笔形点火线圈，电子节气门，无回油燃油系统。功率67千瓦，扭矩120牛/米，排放达国Ⅳ阶段。

（三）变速器

天汽集团所属的天津汽车齿轮厂，有多年生产变速器内的圆柱齿轮及汽车后桥用的螺旋伞齿轮（以下简称后桥主、从动齿轮）的历史，1996年企业转制改称"天津汽车齿轮股份有限公司"（以下简称"汽齿公司"），2004年并入天津一汽，更名为天津一汽夏利变速器分公司。

1997年，汽齿公司启动TJ1010微型汽车用变速器开发工作。该变速器可搭载在华利等微型车厢式车辆上。

2000年，汽齿公司相继开发出给一汽海南马自达配套的CA7130汽车变速器；匹配搭载夏利轿车的3AT100型自动变速器。3AT自动变速器在夏利轿车上的成功搭载，开创国内自主生产微型轿车自动变速器之先河。

2001年，汽齿公司启动为夏利轿车设计的新型变速器5T065的前期准备工作。同年，该厂还组织实施用于皮卡车、SUV车及10人旅行轿车的5T200型汽车变速器开发和生产准备。5T065变速器的开发是在5T063夏利变速器基础上的全面技术升级，新变速器的变速器操作系统改为推拉软轴，离合器操作改为液压系统，具有更大的承载能力和更好的变速换挡性能，驾驶舒适性提高。

2002年9月20日，第1辆顺利下线的"雅酷"轿车在NBCII平台上搭载4AT自动变速器，该车型的驾驶性能提升。

2003年，汽齿公司研制开发换挡性能更好的多锥同步器。该公司在国内首次将该性能更优越的产品结构用于经济型轿车和微型汽车上。

2004年9月，变速器分公司为一汽华利"特锐"配套供应5L063变速器。为夏利N3轿车提供5T063A(4+1)产品和生产准备。开发QR512变速器。

2005年，变速器分公司启动5T070变速器设计。新的变速器主要为1.5升以上发动机排量的车型配套。该变速器齿轮通过改进产品设计和制造工艺，提高变速器承载能力，满足大功率发动机轿车的需要。

二、工艺和装备

(一) 整车

1. 冲压

1990年，为适应从日本大发公司引进的夏利轿车生产要求，通过实施夏利轿车技术改造项目，建成贯通式排列的3条冲压生产线。其中，A线、B线、C线各5台设备。该设备具有传动精度高、闭合高度大、刚性好、台面大的特点，具备左右开出活动工作台、快速换装模具、故障诊断、误操作保护、自动显示、超载保护等功能。冲压作业采用皮带输送机、下料台等辅助设施，冲压线设有的模托起推出机构，加上引进模具的自动化气路装置，实现冲压作业的半自动化生产。改造后使用钢板清洗技术，引进日本帕卡公司钢板清洗机，能自动完成钢板的分层、双张检测、提升、送料、涂油、出料等全部工序操作，提高冲压件表面质量，延长模具使用寿命。生产线和垂直于生产线方向上安装的废料输送线，可将废料直接从模腔滑道或高台滑道滑送到地下废料输送线，最终送往打包间，减少冲压废料对于作业现场的影响，可以满足夏利轿车2种车型(年产5万台)的94种大中型覆盖件的生产需求。冲压生产的模具，除部分直接从日本引进外，大部分按照日本大发汽车公司提供的技术由泰国制造。

1994年，在实施夏利轿车15万辆扩建项目中再次对冲压车间扩建。扩建后，共形成8条生产线(1A、1B、1C、2A、2B、2C、3B、3C)，共有设备114台，其中大型压力机36台，承担夏利轿车、威乐、威姿轿车车型车身覆盖件、关键件等大中型冲压件的生产任务。冲压模具除部分引进外，大部分为国内生产制造。主要采用加工精度高，使用寿命长，冲压工序少的快速换装模具。部分冲压生产采用机械手上下料，普遍使用气动、自动和传感装置，以单动代替双动，实现模具自动卡紧，换模不换气顶杆等技术。

2000年，实施夏利轿车换代车型(NBC)冲压项目国产化。通过从日本引进丰田公司大型冲压件模具，对于整体侧围、顶盖等冲压由5道工序变成4道工序，提高生产效率。由于依赖进口模具势必增加生产准备投入，影响成本改善和对于车身部件生产资源的掌控，因此，在随后实施威姿车身国产化过程中，对于左右侧围外板、左右后车门内外板、背门内外板、顶盖、左右前翼子板、发动机盖内外板、背门口左右角板、左右后轮罩内板、左右后车门外板加强板以及顶盖左右边梁内外板等重要冲压件的模具，选择日本荻原公司在上海的合资企业，其他非主要的冲压件模具则选择国内知名企业进行生产。在冲压材料方面，为摆脱夏利轿车长期依赖日本进口板材的状况，最大限度利用国内资源，在确保整车性能和安全的前提下，自主实施车身材料国产化。在宝钢、鞍钢等板材供应商支持下，经过反复试制、试用和整车结构认证试验等，实现夏利轿车车身材料国产化。

2.装焊

1990年，天津市微型汽车厂实施三厢夏利改造项目后，装焊生产从单一的二厢车型扩展增加三厢车型。对应生产需要，增加三厢专用装焊胎具以及部分国产焊接和悬吊、电气控制等设备。随着新车型生产准备项目增加，对应新车型的装焊工装、夹具、验具设计和制造能力大幅提升，在其后各次夏利换型车改造中，绝大部分选用自主设计自主制造的国产工装、夹具、验具和设备；装焊作业也逐步从刚性生产方式向柔性生产方式过渡，适应多品种、小批量的市场竞争需求。

1998年，夏利轿车的装焊生产通过技术改造形成二、三厢共线。依靠自主创新实施二、三厢夏利混线生产的技术改造，对二厢夏利装焊车间后地板线，主线1、3号位，侧围线、地板总成等相关工位，以及装焊生产控制系统的改造，具备多品种同时混线的生产能力。装焊的设计生产能力为年产15万台夏利轿车。其中，二厢装焊车间年设计产能为8万台，单班产量为132台；三厢装焊车间年设计产能为7万台，其单班产量为116台。

1997年5月，天津夏利公司与天津大学共同承担国家重点科技攻关计划项目的子课题——汽车车身尺寸激光自动检测站项目。该项目通过对车身30~32个关键点误差的自动测定与软件修正技术，可以完成整车自动在线检测，突破传统检测方式，填补将视觉系统用于车身关键尺寸检测的空白。

3.涂装

1996年，通过实施夏利15万辆技术改造项目，涂装生产的设备能力和生产能力得到较大提升，达到国内领先水平。此前涂装车间起步初期的设备、生产能力和工艺水平处于国内一般水平，设备较为简单，前处理采用阳极电泳工艺。

1996年，夏利轿车涂装生产在工艺上采用国际轿车制造通行的3层涂装方式。其中，底漆采用连续浸透阴极电泳处理，中涂和面涂采用往复式自动静电喷涂方式。为适应多品种的多色彩要求，可以提供10种面漆喷涂颜色，并在10秒钟内实现面漆颜色的自动切换。涂装车间的中央控制室可以实时检测整个生产过程的工艺参数、自动喷涂机器人和输送装置运行情况。前处理剂为中日合资生产的国际通用药剂，电泳漆采用国际第4代产品（HB-2000）。

2004年，天津一汽对涂装车间实施以增加产能为目的的技术改造。改造后，生产节拍由原来的1.96分/台提高到1.75分/台，单班增加产能约30台，提高11%。

4. 总装

1991年6月，夏利轿车的总装生产由1983年7月实施的微型汽车一期工程和随后实施的夏利轿车年产3万辆工程，调整为年产5万辆夏利轿车的生产规模。此间，总装生产设备相对简单，通过引进技术形成的技术管理体系和工艺能力逐步培育完善。

1994年3月，实施总投资为22亿元的夏利轿车15万辆扩建项目。在原有生产5万辆夏利轿车的基础上，通过新建10万辆夏利轿车装配车间，使总装生产能力达到年产15万辆的规模，成为继上海大众后的第二条15万辆汽车整车生产线。产能的拉动使得夏利轿车总装设备能力、工艺管理水平进一步完善和提高。

2003年4月，实施夏利轿车检测线改造项目。重点对前轮定位仪、侧滑仪、制动仪、转毂仪、尾气仪、大灯仪等进行维修、更新，同时增加电控系统，以适应国家技术法规和产能增加的需要。改造中新增检测线的计算机控制系统和打印系统，预留ABS系统接口，对下线车辆进行前轮定位、侧滑、车速、制动、大灯、淋雨、排放等安全和环保方面检测。

到2005年，为配合新产品投产和多品种混线生产需要，围绕改进物流和输送系统，对输送台车和吊具进行适应性改造，增置部分工装和工位器具，先后进行技术改造。

（二）发动机

1984~1996年，天津市内燃机厂进行4期（一期、一期填平补齐、二期、二期半）大规模技术改造，发生根本变化。从单一的生产大发厢式货车发动机（TJ370Q），发展为5个品种（TJ370Q、TJ376Q、TJ376QA、TJ376QB、TJ376QE），并引进先进设备和检测设备，有效保证产品质量，满足夏利轿车国产化配套的需要，年生产能力从3.6万台发展到15万台。

1990年，经过历时4年的一期技术改造，采用新工艺、新技术，新建生产线18条，总投资1.045亿元。

1991年，通过一期工程和一期填平补齐工程的技术改造，先后引进为微型厢式货车和夏利轿车配套的发动机制造技术，初步形成具有一定规模的微型汽车发动机生产厂。

1992年，实施新增夏利轿车5万辆技改工程（发动机部分）的任务（简称二期技术改造）。总投资5.096亿元，历时2年。建成生产线29条，形成年产10万台发动机的生产能力。

1993年，进行二期工程改造。采用日本新东公司的砂处理系统成套设备对砂处理系统重新改造。

1994年7月，国家计委批准天津市夏利15万辆扩建项目书，生产纲领为年生产5万辆夏利轿车发动机，生产能力在已批准年产10万台的基础上填平补齐。

1997年2月，受国家计委委托，机械工业部专家组对该项目进行验收，形成年产15万台发动机的生产能力。项目总投资14 806.91万元。

（三）变速器

1991年，汽齿公司仅能生产132变速器总成和轻型货车所需的后桥主、从动齿轮。其圆柱齿轮所采用的工艺，主要为滚、插、剃、热处理表面渗碳及磨削加工，其壳体为铸铁由协作单位供件，基本上是工作台装配，没有装配线及相关的装配机械及设备。后桥齿轮则采用粗开、精切、热处理表面渗碳、研磨、配对等工艺。生产、制造、检测等全过程处于手工作坊式的生产模式。

1992年，汽齿公司作为微型汽车一期填平补齐的企业之一，启动技术改造项目。投资8294万元，增加设备287台。企业迁址前桑园，土地面积增加2倍，厂房面积增加近2000平方米，生产条件有所改善，劳动生产率及产品质量提高。

1993年，天汽集团采取CKD方法，实行引进、消化、吸收，随着设备的调整和工艺的完善，逐步实现国产化，为变速器自给奠定基础。汽齿公司利用世行技术改造项目贷款招标。一是形成12万套5种夏利变速器高精度齿轮配套能力、16万套多种车型后桥齿轮配套能力、20万只出口圆柱齿轮生产能力；二是筹建具备计算机辅助设计系统（CAD/CAE/CAM），计算机生产指挥系统和变速器检测设备等的技术中心。项目实际完成投资19910.11万元。汽齿公司进一步消化吸收TJ7100夏利轿车变速器产品技术，为提高工艺适用性进行部分设计改进。

1994年，汽齿公司为适应夏利15万辆生产项目进一步实施技术改造。新增建筑面积33 000平方米，总建筑面积达到65 000平方米；新增工艺设备263台套，加之一期投入的287台套，达到550台套。引进部分进口高效高精度设备，提高产品工艺性及质量的稳定可靠性。其中，变速器、离合器2个壳体的生产线，引进德国沙曼的立卧两用60把刀库的加工中心12台，并引进物流线、试漏机、浸渗设备等；引进法国滚齿机5台、意大利剃齿机7台、英国搓滚机2台、插齿机1台、意大利剃刀磨1台、法国滚刀磨1台、万能工具磨1台；总装车间引进阿特拉丝16头拧紧机1台，热处理引进法国L1公司的连续炉生产线2台、检测设备SP42 1台，磨工车间引进复合外圆磨等。

1995年，夏利轿车15万辆扩建工程的变速器改造项目与当时启动的世行贷款技术改造项目一并实施。总投资为30042万元。新建齿轮加工、总装、热处理、箱体加工4条生产线。除公用系统外，生产车间、装配试验、壳体加工都按15万台进行规划设计，建成初期形成年产12万台变速器的生产能力，最终形成年产15万台变速器的生产能力，TJ7100夏利轿车变速器国产化率从50%提高到95%。为达到这一要求，汽齿公司通过认真消化吸收日本大发公司产品技术，在实现以CKD方式进行小批量试生产的同时，全面启动TJ7100夏利轿车变速器的国产化工作。1996年，夏利轿车15万辆扩建项目实施完成，夏利轿车、TJ376Q发动机、TJ7100夏利轿车变速器项目相继达到年产15万辆（台）生产规模。

三、安全 节能 环保

1999年开始，为满足国家政策法规的要求，陆续展开TJ7101系列夏利轿车、TJ7131系列夏利轿车和TJ7136U夏利轿车低污染排放，达欧Ⅱ排放标准工作。与国内外有关企业合作，进行台架和道路试验，制定生产一致性保证计划，改造和新增检验试验设备，加强采购资源、生产过程以及最终检验控制。到2004年底，天津一汽在产车型排放指标均提前达到欧Ⅱ排放标准，获得国家给予的低污染排放小汽车减征消费税的优惠政策，累计退税1.37亿元。2005年年底，在产车型全部达到欧Ⅲ排放标准要求，提供性能优良、经济适用、清洁环保的夏利轿车。

2000年，天汽集团充分挖掘技术潜力，在发动机技术升级开发过程中，完成TJ7131、TJ7136系列车型的8

万 km 排放污染控制装置耐久试验，实现低排放车减税的目标。同年，完成 TJ376QE 发动机在夏利 TJ7101、TJ7101UZ 上搭载及试验评价工作。通过对发动机管理系统和排放控制系统的优化和匹配，TJ376QE、3GA2 发动机满足欧Ⅱ、欧Ⅲ排放法规要求，满足欧Ⅳ排放法规要求。在全新 4GA1 发动机开发过程中，充分采用新技术，VCT-i（智能可变气门正时系统）、静音正时驱动链条及曲轴偏置等实现节能和减排目标。

1999~2001 年，天津汽车夏利产品开发中心承担天津市科委项目，与天津市化工研究院合作开发“三元催化转化试验”。2000~2003 年完成“夏利碰撞安全性计算机辅助研究”项目。2001~2002 年完成“夏利轿车燃用含乙醇混合燃料适应性研究”项目。

2005 年，天津一汽自主创新生产的威志轿车在安全、环保、节能方面达到法规标准。设计目标满足法规 GB11551-2000（正撞）、GB27001-2006（侧撞）、GB27002-2006（后撞）；C-NCAP 3 星。设计难点是结构优化和材料优化并降低成本（售价 5 万元）。①保证整车安全性的技术路线。其核心技术是 GOA 车身；主动安全性比被动安全性重要，安全性首先要避免碰撞，整车的操控性、制动性、灯光等是首先需要重点保证的安全项；被动安全系统包括安全带、座椅、车身、气囊、溃式管柱、溃式踏板等部件；通过 CAE 仿真正碰、侧碰、后碰以及实测结果保证整车安全性指标。②保证整车环保指标的技术路线。国Ⅲ/Ⅳ与国Ⅱ相比，NOX、HC、CO 限值加严，测试方法取消前 40 秒怠速，增加 OBD 和-7℃排放要求。EMS 系统提升，后处理使用不锈钢焊接歧管，提升 TWC。冷起动控制是排放控制的关键技术，点燃式发动机冷起动过程对整车 HC 和 CO 的排放贡献量极为突出，约占整车测试过程排放量的 50% 至 80%，因此，冷起动的燃烧优化与排放控制是国Ⅳ排放控制的关键技术之一。对冷起动优化主要通过冷起动过程中的进气量、燃料供给量和点火提前角来实现。③整车节能指标的技术路线。成功研发 VVT，降低整车排放和油耗，搭建 VVT 性能评价试验台。④NVH 噪声源及传递路径研究。⑤试验验证。通过整车性能试验，整车道路可靠性试验，通过最严酷的环境试验——山路、试验场恶路、城市工况、强化腐蚀、湿热（海南）、干冷（漠河）、高原（西藏）、干热（阿拉伯沙漠）等，实现整车道路可靠性试验验证。

第二节 轻型载货车

天汽集团所属的天津市汽车制造厂（后更名为天津华利汽车有限公司、一汽华利[天津]汽车有限公司）主要生产轻型载货汽车。20 世纪 80 年代后期，进行雁牌轻型载货汽车的换型改造项目，包括车身换型、油漆车间改造、新建检测线等。1988 年 11 月，天汽集团与英国 MGA 公司签订“TJ130 汽车车身换型合同”，为确保新车型相应的投产条件，采取车身引进模具与工厂技术改造同步的方法。1990 年年初，英国 MGA 公司向天汽提供的样车到厂。1991 年 7 月，换型改造后新车正式投产。

1990 年，天津市汽车制造厂用于 TJ1041 雁牌轻型载货车引进车身的冲压模具，由日本宫津铁工制作所承制。共完成 180 套冲压模具设计和 120 套冲压模具的制造，110 套装焊胎具的设计和制造，70 套机加工辅具的设计制造。冲压模具水平在当时国内载货车行业属于一流。同年，改进装焊工艺，新增装焊设备 90 台套，承担 TJ1041 雁牌轻型载货车驾驶室总成、车门总成的焊接工作，形成单班年产 3 万辆的生产能力。同时，对油漆车间前处理工序的部分设备进行修正改造，重点对磷化工程改造、新增涂胶泵和喷蜡泵。

1991 年，天津汽车制造厂 TJ1041 雁牌轻型载货车换型改造项目一期工程竣工。TJ1041F 雁牌轻型载货车在原 TJ130 轻型载货车的基础上，引进驾驶室设计，同时引进冲压模具及装焊夹具，使驾驶室在造型、内饰和工艺上达到国内先进水平；匹配新型发动机，功率由 75 马力提高到 85 马力以上，排量 2 升左右，油耗不大于 215 克/马力小时；采用 5 档变速器，最高时速 100 公里/小时左右；其他关键部件同步改造。整车性能达到国际 20 世纪 80 年代初水平。1991 年 6 月 25 日，换型改造后的新车正式投产。该厂还先后开发生产 TJ1041 雁牌双排座、长轴距、柴油动力等轻型载货车，满足市场多样化需求。

第三节　微型客车

1984年3月,天汽集团与日本大发株式会社签署微型客车产品技术转让合同。为扩大天津夏利产能满足市场需求,1992年,天汽集团决定将天津大发微型汽车移至天津市汽车制造厂生产。1995年,天津汽车制造厂更名为天津华利汽车有限公司;天津大发TJ1010微型厢式货车更名为天津华利TJ6320微型客车。2001年,自行研发的微型多功能乘用车"幸福使者"下线。

一、设计与制造

天津微型客车系列是在引进日本大发株式会社HIJET微型汽车车型技术基础上生产的天津大发TJ1010微型厢式货车。在此基础上,先后研制开发出天津华利TJ6320微型客车、天津华利TJ1010微型货车、天津华利TJ6350微型客车、天津华利TJ6320G1半高顶微型客车、天津华利TJ6320G2高顶微型客车。

(一)天津大发微型客车

20世纪80年代中后期,天津大发TJ1010微型厢式货车,采用天津内燃机厂同步引进生产的代表世界微型车发动机最高水平的日本大发3缸发动机,具有造型美观、乘坐舒适、节能省油、噪音小、价格低廉、客货两用等特点,填补国内微型汽车的空白。天津市汽车制造厂因此被国家确定为国内唯一微型汽车大批量生产基地。该微型客车作为国内大中城市第一代出租车的首选用车。

(二)TJ6330G2高顶微型客车

1998年,天津华利汽车公司推出TJ6320G2高顶微型客车。该车系改进型产品,主要部件完全采用从日本大发公司引进的模具制成,车内顶盖加高,增大车内空间,保持空气流通。除颜色、造型更富时代感外,还运用符合国际汽车发展趋势的新技术,在各种微型车中率先装备具有国际水准、符合中国环保法规的燃油蒸发过滤碳罐,碳罐内装活性碳,能过滤汽油在燃烧时带来的有害物质,有效地降低汽车废气排放给空气造成的污染。选用天津内燃机厂引进日本大发技术生产的系列3缸内燃机为动力。采用子午线宽胎。

(三)TJ6350微型客车

1995年,天津华利汽车有限公司推出HUALI TJ6350系列微型客车投放市场。该系列车型是在原天津大发TJ6320微型客车的基础上,通过对车体加长加宽变形而来,俗称"胖大发"。车身设计合理,造型典雅华贵,室内宽敞明亮,可乘座8人。底盘与动力系统匹配合理,选用TJ376QA汽油机,双截面钢板弹簧,加大制动声直径,使其整车动力性、平顺性和制动可靠性更具完美,适合各种道路行驶。HUA LI TJ6350系列微型客车获得天津市1997年名牌产品。

(四)幸福使者

2001年,天津华利汽车有限公司与天津市汽车研究所、中国汽车技术研究中心共同开发"华利.幸福使者"多功能乘用车。该车作为新一代的小型多功能车,参照国外同类最新车型、吸收日本微型多功能车的最新技术,结合中国路况和使用条件;整车全部模具、夹具和验具均由中国台湾制造,关键部件由日本和中国台湾供应;零部件精选外商独资、合资等国内骨干汽车零部件厂家制造。该车是国内"微客与轿车"合而为一的创新之作。

2003年,根据一汽集团总体规划,天津"华利·幸福使者"更名为"一汽佳星·幸福使者",获得国家发改委有关生产的7字头公告和国家环保总局环保目录,完成"CCC"认证。共有CA7100F、CA7100FAI、CA7100FA、CA7110F、CA7110FA5大系列20多个品种,每个系列车型分为普通型、标准型、舒适型和豪华型。

(五)"达路-特锐"小型紧凑多功能车

2003年10月15日,一汽华利(天津)汽车有限公司生产的"DARIOTERIOS特锐"(达路·特锐)小型紧凑多功能车下线。该车型由一汽集团公司与日本丰田汽车公司旗下的大发工业株式会社合作生产，标准型车身长3845毫米，宽1555毫米，高1760毫米，轴距2420毫米，最小离地间隙为195毫米，与传统SUV的厚重外形相比，具有独特时尚的外观，在视觉上更加玲珑和时尚，动感十足。该车搭载1.3升的最新型K3发动机，装备带EBD电控制动力分配系统的4通道ABS，具有高水平的安全性。

2004年6月10日，一汽华利（天津）汽车有限公司设计生产的新装DARIO TERIOS特锐上市。新装特锐CX豪华型，前大灯升级为多重反射卤素4灯式，整体动感活泼，配以车顶尾部扰流板和尾门外置备胎，以及独有的205/70R15宽胎。调整车身颜色，新增更加时尚的红色和蓝色。方向盘改为豪华型，增加镀铬门锁止杆和镀铬内门把手，仪表/中控台换为银色涂装，增加后电动车窗，各车型采用轻松明快的浅色内饰，体现出更强的高品质感和时尚感。

二、工艺与装备

（一）冲压与模具

1994年，TJ6350微型客车冲压件模具由公司自行设计和制造，投资200万元。

1997年，TJ6330G2高顶微型车主要部件完全采用从日本大发公司引进的模具制成，投资1200万元，引进模具23套，具有国内先进水平。

2000年，华利幸福使者全部模具、夹具和验具均由中国台湾制造，关键部件由日本和中国台湾供应，投入1000多万元，在国内处于领先水平。

2003年，特锐小型紧凑多功能车冲压件由日本大发公司提供。

（二）焊装夹具

1997年，TJ6330G2引进设备投资655万元，焊装生产线系引进日本关键设备，自动化程度高、定位准确、工艺先进。

1994年，TJ6350微型客车在原TJ6320微型客车焊装生产线的基础上，自行改进设计，达到国内同类车型领先水平。

2003年，华利幸福使者全部夹具和验具均由中国台湾制造，关键部件由日本和中国台湾供应，投入1000多万元，在国内处于领先水平。

2004年，特锐小型紧凑多功能车主要焊装夹具，以及当时国内不生产或质量不过关的设备，螺栓焊机、涂胶机等，采取引进方法。大总成焊装夹具以气动夹紧为主，中、小总成焊装夹具以手动夹紧为主。

（三）油漆及前处理

1994年，TJ6350微型客车油漆及前处理利用原TJ6320微型客车的油漆及前处理线，略加改造。

1997年，TJ6330G2油漆车间投资2000万元，其中设备投资1000万元，基本能够满足需求。

2000年，华利幸福使者油漆及前处理在天津华夏农用运输车厂油漆及前处理线进行。

2003年，一汽华利（天津）汽车有限公司生产的特锐小型紧凑多功能车完全采用夏利涂装线工艺，利用原夏利涂装线涂装。根据特锐产品要求，采用工件涂层漆、中涂漆和面漆3涂层工艺。底漆使用阴极电泳漆，面漆使用本色和金属闪光漆。油漆车间投资2000万元，其中设备投资1000万元。

第四节　轻型客车

天汽集团所属的天津市客车厂是轻型客车生产企业。1965~1969年开始试制和生产TK-620S旅行车。1974年，在TK-620S的基础上，研制开发TJ-620A型旅行车。1977年，研制开发TJ621型旅行车。1980年，研制开发TJ-620B型旅行车。1982年,产品品牌定名为三峰牌。1983~1988年,研制开发TJ6480B轻型客车及系列产品。1990年,研发生产三峰牌TJ6481A轻型客车系列产品。1992年4月1日,与澳门国恒企业发展有限公司合资,成立天津三峰客车有限公司。

一、设计与制造

(一)三峰牌TJ620B旅行车

1980年,研制开发TJ-620B型旅行车。加装Q492型75马力发动机,3挡变速器;采用蜗杆滚轮式转向机,单管路制动。为非承载式车身。1982年,实现小批量生产。1983年,该车参加全国乘用车展览。

(二)三峰牌TJ6480B轻型客车系列产品

1983~1988年,天津市客车厂对于TJ620B旅行车进行改进并推出TJ6480B轻型客车。采用492QA型85马力发动机,取代TJ620车装Q492型75马力发动机;采用与唐山齿轮厂联合开发的"4T17"型4挡全同步变速器,取代原3挡变速器;采用循环球式转向机,取代原蜗杆滚轮式转向机,传动效率提高;采用双管路制动系统,代替原单管路制动;加装空调。采用自行开发的"TJ621"型承载式车身,取代原TJ620型非承载式车身。

1984年以后,在上述基础上开发厢式货车、公安囚车、运钞车、工程抢险车、救护车等系列产品。还利用该车车身前部,加装货厢,开发出三峰牌TJ123车双排座货车。该车3类底盘TJ6480BY不仅提供给国内改装厂,而且自1996年先后连同散件向菲律宾、越南出口共132台份。三峰牌TJ6480B轻型客车系列产品以结构简单、工作可靠、维修方便、价格低廉,在20世纪90年代一直保持畅销不衰的势头。

(三)三峰牌TJ6481A轻型客车系列产品

1990年4月,天津市客车厂设计完成的三峰牌TJ6481A轻型客车基准型,通过中国汽车工业总公司组织的部级鉴定。该设计样车1988年10月在全国乘用车展评会上获"中华杯"最高荣誉奖。该车型是在自行研制"TJ621" 旅行车底盘基础上,引进英国"I、A、D公司"车身设计、日本"荻原铁工所"提供的车身模具和装焊夹具而生产出的换代产品。该车造型呈流线型,空气阻力系数CD值为0.45(当时轿车CD值为0.30~0.55),其车顶后部呈局部凸起,既可包容后门铰链,又起到分流作用,车辆行驶中可减少车后扬尘。车内宽敞,设11人乘席(含驾驶员),装有冷、暖空调,车身设正、副司机门、推拉式乘客门(中门)和整体式后背门4个门。该车型底盘为该厂自主开发的"TJ621"型底盘,其特点是:前悬架为螺旋弹簧双横臂独立悬架、后悬架为变刚度钢板弹簧;采用液压双管路制动系统(带真空助力器),前、后轮均安装盘式制动器。此外,采用492QA型85马力/3800转/分发动机;采用该厂与唐山齿轮厂联合开发的"4T17"型4挡全同步变速器;采用循环球转向器和750—14型6层及低压子午线轮胎。

1990年,天津市客车厂研制的三峰牌TJ6481AQ3轻型客车通过中汽公司鉴定,并上汽车产品目录投放市场。为进一步提高TJ6481A整车动力性,通过优化设计,选用日本丰田"4Y"型发动机,其最大功率为95.2马力(70千瓦)/4600转/分,最大扭矩为18千克米/3000转/分;安装丰田"DINA"5挡全同步变速器,其最高车速达120公里/小时,最大爬坡度15°,百公里油耗9升,整车动力性、经济性提高。1994年先后出口南美、哥伦比亚。

1993年,天津市客车厂研制的三峰牌TJ6481AQ3轻型客车实现进口动力总成国产化。为降低整车成本,满足用户需求,该厂与四川绵阳、沈阳星光等发动机厂合作开发国产"491Q"发动机,其功能性能可以完全替代进口"4Y"发动机;又与天津汽车齿轮厂合作开发"132D"型5挡全同步变速器,代替日本丰田DINA变速器。通过试验对比,该车动力性经济性完全达到安装进口动力总成水平。为适应不同用户对车辆的不同使用需求,在TJ6481AQ3基础上又开发系列变型车,如公安囚车、救护车、运钞车、工程抢险车产品。

同年,天津市客车厂研制三峰牌TJ6481AQ4轻型客车。该车在TJ6481A基准型基础上,安装瑞典VOLVO公司"B230G型"电喷发动机和"M47型"5挡变速器总成。该发动机功率116马力(85.3千瓦/5400转/分),采用拉线式变速换挡机构,安装液压式准ABS制动防抱死装置,采用205/80SR—14型子午线轮胎。

前轮用盘式、后轮用鼓式制动器。其豪华型安装旋转座椅及高档内饰。

1994年,天津市客车厂与瑞典VOLVO公司退休工程师HOA先生合作开发新型独立悬挂式前桥和助力式转向机构。1995年,进行大量的试制试验,先后在海南试验场和北京交通部试验场进行性能和可靠性试验,并以新产品3辆车参加1998年“中华环保世纪行”活动,从东北的丹东沿海岸线直至广西东兴,现场考查大江河入海口的水质保护情况,行程近2万公里,充分显示新开发产品的优良性能和可靠性。

1995年,天津市客车厂研制三峰牌“6510”轻型客车。为适应国外市场需求,该车在TJ6481AQ3车型基础上,增加一排座椅,改为14座乘席轻型客车。车身为适应增加乘员座椅需要,将中门立柱加宽220毫米,车长由4840增至5060毫米,轴距由2600毫米增至2820毫米。该车前后悬架均采用变刚度钢板弹簧,相应增加传动轴长度,前后制动器均为鼓式制动器。

1996年,天津市客车厂研制三峰牌TJ6481AD轻型客车。该车在TJ6481A基准型基础上,安装493Q型柴油机(功率56.6千瓦)和132D5挡变速器;前、后悬架均采用变刚度钢板弹簧;前后轮均安装鼓式制动器;车内增加一排3人座椅,共设14座席;乘客门分推拉式和折叠式;车顶分平顶、高顶。该车先后出口埃及、阿联酋等国家。

二、技术改造

1980年后,天津市客车厂为提高产能和产品质量,先后进行3次技术改造。1983~1984年,以实现TJ6480B年产3000台为目标,对车身车间、冲压车间进行技术改造。1986~1988年,先后投资1000万美元,与日本狄源铁工所和英国IAD公司技术合作,引进模具、夹具和车身技术,实施TJ6481A车身换型及批量生产的技术改造。1992年,与澳门国恒企业发展有限公司合资成立天津三峰客车有限公司,外方投入1000万美元,占股比26%,与此同时,收购毗邻的公用局自来水铸管厂,新建9000平方米车身车间、6000平方米冲压车间、3.5万千瓦变电站及60吨蒸汽锅炉房,初步形成年产万台的生产能力。

第五节 多功能乘用汽车

天汽集团下属的天津市专用汽车厂是专门进行多功能汽车改装的企业。2003年天汽集团对天津三峰客车有限公司和天津专用汽车厂进行调整重组,与北京佳美亚公司合资组建天津天汽集团美亚汽车制造有限公司,从事汽车整车制造,专门研发轻客、SUV、皮卡等系列产品。2005年10月,美亚汽车制造有限公司重组为天汽集团的全资子公司。

1986年,天津市专用汽车厂在TJ130型载货汽车的基础上,改装成功双驱动TJ1048型载货汽车。该车型爬坡能力强,适用于山区和林区。

1987年,天津市专用汽车厂在TJ1048型载货汽车的基础上改装成功环保沉渣吸排专用车。

1991年,天津市专用汽车厂在TJ1010华利厢式货车和TJ7100夏利轿车基础上改装公安、检察院、法院专用车。

1994~1996年,天津市专用汽车厂在TJ1010华利厢式货车基础上改型设计制造TJ1010L华利长轴距厢式货车,改型设计制造TJ1010SL华利双排座货车和TJ1010SL1华利双排座长轴距厢式货车。

1997~2002年,天津市专用汽车厂在TJ6320华利厢式客车基础上改型设计制造TJ6320G1华利半高顶厢式客车。在TJ1010L华利长轴距厢式货车基础上改型设计制造TJ6350华利平顶加长厢式客车,进而改型设计制造TJ6350A华利半高顶加长厢式客车。对TJ1010华利微型货车改型设计制造TJ5010BX保鲜车和TJ5010BW保温车。

2003年5月,天汽集团美亚公司研制开发TM6500型系列多功能运动车(SUV)。在原三峰客车有限公司研制开发的TJ6460型轻型客车基础上改进,更换前散热器罩、前保险杠、前灯具,扩展为TM6500A、TM6500Q型(汽油发动机)和TM6500D型(柴油发动机)3大系列。此间,进一步研制开发TM1020、TM1021(短轴距、加长轴距)系列皮卡。更换前散热器罩、前保险杠、前灯具,扩展为TM1020A、TM1020AL(汽油发动机)和TM1020AD、TM1020ADL(柴油发动机)型皮卡。研制开发TM6490型系列轻型客车,并在此基础上改变车身高度,扩展为TM6490(平顶)、TM6490(高顶)轻型客车。

2004年,天汽美亚汽车制造有限公司研制开发新品TM6480型城市休闲车(CRV)。并选装前中网、前保险杠、行李架、天窗及脚踏板,扩展为TM6480城市休闲车。

2005年,天汽美亚汽车制造有限公司与北京长城华冠设计公司合作开发具有全部自主知识产权和自主品牌的T3型MPV微型乘用车。该车设计标准符合国家微型车低排放量、节能、环保等各项汽车产业政策,综合性价比优于国内同类产品,从产品类别上填补天津汽车工业整车产品的空白。同年,天汽美亚公司相继自主研发生产天汽美亚牌多功能轻型客车、皮卡多用货车和SUV等整车产品,形成4大系列26个品种,在国内各省市销售,并排量出口南非、中东和南美洲。

第六节 电动汽车

2002年4月,天汽集团作为项目投标单位,联合清源公司及其各投资公司,以及天津大学等共同投标,确定承担国家“863”计划“XL纯电动车开发”项目。该项目研发的纯电动轿车,以夏利2000型为基础,装备镍氢或锂离子高能电池,采用交流异步或磁阻开关电动机,运用最优控制策略,实现制动能量回收,整车性能达到当代电动轿车的先进水平。清源公司等单位从2002年6月起承担一期项目。2003年1月,科技部对项目进行节点检查,6月25日组织专家验收,对项目的完成情况给予较高评价。之后又承担滚动支持的二期项目。项目总共投入3696万元,其中专项资金2146万元。科技人力资源达150人/年,其中有高级工程师以上技术职称68人,博士硕士生52人;取得“电动轿车核心关键技术集成与创新开发”等一批科研成果和多项专利技术、在国内外专业刊物上发表论文30多篇;培养数十名电动汽车技术骨干;建立核心部件和系统集成的研发测试平台。承担的“夏利2000混合动力轿车整车开发”项目也通过天津市科委验收。

一、XL纯电动轿车的开发

2002年6月开始,清源公司等单位组成研发团队研制开发国家“863”项目“XL纯电动车开发” 5辆样车。2003年6月通过国家科技部组织的专家验收。

2003年6月,按照国家“863”项目“XL纯电动车开发”二期滚动项目“XL系列纯电动车开发”要求,开发XL-1和XL-2等两种规格的纯电动轿车,提供满足型式认证要求的样车10辆。二期滚动项目以夏利2000和“威姿”两款轿车为原型开发纯电动轿车,开展整车关键技术、开发平台技术、产业化技术、技术规范及评价、以及示范运行基础条件等方面的科研和攻关工作。以整车轻量化设计、系统一体化设计、整车控制策略优化、电池包均衡及热管理、故障诊断及高压电安全管理、高速数据记录仪及分析系统、GPS定位及基于无线通讯网络的高速数据传输系统、动力总成高速CAN总线分布式控制系统与低速总线车身舒适性控制系统结合的分层网络等作为核心技术攻关重点,在汽车新技术领域实现突破。在开发过程中,建立整车虚拟设计及仿真、动力总成控制系统开发、电机及控制系统开发,动力电池组及管理系统测试标定以及CAN总线控制系统开发等一系列基础研发平台，为整车及核心零部件关键技术的研究提供了高效率的研发手段。

2004年9月起，陆续完成单体电池针刺、挤压、短路、过充电、高空跌落及盐水浸泡、电池组淋水、模拟暴雨、整车涉水、实车碰撞、整车侧翻、操纵稳定性等一系列安全性考核试验。

2005年5月，在天津一汽夏利产品开发中心的转鼓试验台上进行4辆不同配置的纯电动轿车的整车性能匹配试验。优化整车控制策略，并且对不同工况下的一次充电续驶里程、能量消耗率、动力性等性能进行实验室摸底。

图5-6-6-70 电动汽车碰撞试验

2005年6月，委托国家轿车质量监督检验中心，在交通部北京通县汽车试验场，按照国家标准的规定进行新车型定型所需的各项性能及可靠性试验。2005年11月底，试制样车单车运行考核突破20000公里。整车性能完全符合合同任务书的要求，强制性标准检查符合国家有关标准的规定。经受可靠性试验的考验，整车及关键总成的可靠性得到考核，为XL电动轿车的产业化打下较好的基础。

2005年底，该项目通过国家科技部组织的验收。专家认为，开发的纯电动轿车在关键技术集成度、整车动力性、能量利用经济性等方面达到国际先进水平。

二、夏利2000混合动力轿车

2002年，清源公司与天津一汽夏利产品开发中心合作开展天津市科委重大科技攻关项目“夏利2000混合动力轿车整车开发”研制。夏利2000型混合动力轿车整车采用先进的多能源动力总成设计方案，优化混合动力轿车整车的控制策略；采用ISG/IMA的多能源动力总成结构；选用国际流行的混合动力轿车专用的环形电机和动力电池组；开发技术先进、性能可靠的控制系统；实施具有自主知识产权的CAN通讯协议。经过充分的台架试验考验的多能源动力总成匹配在两辆混合动力轿车上，经过环境模拟、转鼓和道路行驶试验，整车性能良好。整车排放达到欧3标准；动力性与原车相当，最高车速160千里/时，爬坡度>25%，节油超过15%。

2003年6月，“夏利2000混合动力轿车整车开发”项目和配套项目“混合动力轿车控制、驱动及电池管理系统开发”同时启动。项目组对整车和发动机进行改进设计，电机及其控制系统、动力系统主控制器、CAN总线系统、电池及其管理系统等关键系统及零部件进行全新设计与开发，各总成部件与发动机和环型电机混合动力总成的联调，样车的装配调试试验。①整车总布置及相关部件的设计。包括前机仓的布置；电池箱的布置；电机控制器的布置；线束的设计。②关键系统及零部件的设计、研发。包括电机及其控制系统的设计开发；动力系统主控制器的开发；CAN总线系统的开发；电池及其管理系统的开发；制动能量回收系统。③样车的试制和试验。包括发动机、环行电机、变速器组合成动力总成；动力总成搭载；发动机进排气、油路、冷却管路的改制安装；电池箱支架的制作，电池箱、电机控制器、主控制器的固定安装；低压线束的改制安装；高压线路的布线安装；功能、动作调试，在转毂试验台上，进行起动模式、急加速助力、最高车速助力的功能调试；排放、油耗试验。

2005年10月，上述两个项目通过天津市科委组织的专家验收。专家认为，混合动力汽车是最接近产业化的车型，研究开发对于节能环保具有现实意义。

三、“幸福使者”纯电动微型客车

“幸福使者”纯电动微型客车是清源公司利用“863”计划“XL系列纯电动车”课题的技术成果，自主开发的。

2002年4月25日，第一辆使用镍氢电池的“幸福使者”纯电动微型客车研制成功。该车型以天津华利汽车有限公司的幸福使者为基础车型，在原型车上进行改装，将传统的动力系统改为电驱动系统，以实现批量生产为目标。研制过程中，样车的开发、车身结构有限元分析、产品的工艺可行性、零部件的可靠性、整车成本、生产布局是关键问题和创新点。①样车的开发。整车结构利用CATIA软件进行总布置和结构设计，充分考虑结构强度、防尘隔噪性能、制造工艺等多种设计要求。利用软件进行装配设计、产品设计、结构设计、曲面设计、工艺设计，做到设计、工艺、加工、试制的同步并行，缩短开发周期，降低开发成本。②部分结构有限元模型建立。其作用是凭借与分析对象实体严格的相似关系，对实体的特征和变化规律做定量模拟，以更深刻更集中地描述对象的主要特征，最大限度地反映整个结构的实际情况。有限元分析的第一步是对研究对象进行合理的简化、建立几何模型，之后将其离散为有限元模型，结构上的受力点和部位用相应的单元代表。结构有限元建模涉及的主要工作有几何模型的简化、材料属性的确定、单元选择及网格划分、有限元模型的连接与装配。结构分析的有限元模型按采用的单元类型，分为板壳单元模型、梁单元模型和板梁结合单元模型3种。梁单元模型在对客车车身骨架结构分析中较常用，而对于现代轿车车身来说，采用板壳单元模型模拟精度较高。根据该车快速计算和精度不用很高的特点，对局部车身结构采用梁单元模拟，也就是板梁结合模型进行有限元分析。③电机及其控制系统设计开发。按照整车要求调整电机参数，根据整车控制策略和动力性、经济性的要求，进行电机控制器的软硬件开发（包括驱动电路开发和控制电路开发），进行控制算法研究、控制策略的仿真等。电机控制器本身进行电磁兼容试验、耐环境试验等考核。④电池及其管理系统的设计开发。对所选用的72V铅酸电池以及电池管理系统进行与整车相匹配的研发，电池管理系统能与CAN总线通讯，具有电池均衡以及各种保护、报警功能等。在台架联合调试、整车匹配试验过程中，针对暴露的新问题多次反复试验，使得系统满足整车的要求。⑤产品的工艺可行性。从样车试制到实现产品的产业化，进行总装和加工工艺的分析，以确保产品的量产化。加工工艺主要侧重于单件和总成的加工，调整加工工艺以降低成本，减少浪费，提高工作效率。总装工艺侧重于生产线总装，根据产量需要，及时调整总装工序、生产节拍、生产线布局、物流配送、人力资源等。

2005年4月，6辆“幸福使者”纯电动微型客车出口美国，开创中国电动汽车产品出口的先河。2005年12月，112辆“幸福使者”纯电动微型客车出口美国。

第七章　船　舶

20世纪90年代，天津船舶工业有较大发展。以天津新港船厂和天津新河船厂为主导力量，民营与合资造修船企业相继成立，不断改革传统的生产工艺和设施，广泛应用高效焊接技术，积极推广计算机在辅助设计和生产、物资、财务、人事管理等方面的应用，实施区域造船、单元组装、预舾装、定置管理、壳舾涂一体化等新技术，进行ISO 9000质量认证，产品质量和生产效率显著提高。造船企业学习国内外现代化船舶设计和生产管理技术，加快转换造船模式，向建造高技术和高附加值船舶发展，2005年造船产量达20万载重吨。修船企业向船舶改装和客滚船、化学品船等高技术船舶修理的方向发展。

第一节　设计与开发

1993年成立的天津新高船舶设计公司（即天津新港船厂设计所）、2002年成立的天津德赛船舶海洋工程有限责任公司以及2003年成立的新河船舶与海洋工程设计公司，主要从事船舶与海洋工程的设计，天津大学船舶与海洋工程教授参与设计工作，设计技术和理念产生根本性变化。造船设计体系由“方案设计—技术设计—施工设计”模式转化为“基本设计—详细设计—生产设计”的模式。要求设计部门提供的图纸由按系统的“施工设计”图转变为按区域的“生产设计”图。计算机辅助设计广泛应用,设计软件的应用和开发,使船舶设计能力和水平得到提高。

1991年,天津新港船厂采用计算机应用于辅助设计,主要用于结构放样、电缆放样、管系放样等数字放样方面,其他图纸设计依然是手工设计、描绘、校对等程序。1996年,在引进结构放样、电缆放样ECPS、管系放样PCPS程序的基础上,逐步开发完善自己特色的放样产品,并利用CAD软件进行部分生产设计绘图。1998年,引进TRIBON软件进行三维立体设计,先后在32500载重吨和35200载重吨船舶生产设计中得到应用。2000年,该厂为设计部门增添计算机、绘图仪和大型智能复印机,利用计算机CAD软件进行设计,完全取代手工绘图,设计质量和速度显著提高,由原先局限于生产设计向详细设计迈进。2002年8月,该厂设计所通过DNVISO 9001:2000版的认证。2005年,该厂从美国PTC公司引进CADDS5软件,建立局域网,并应用CADDS5三维设计软件进行12000载重吨船舶的设计工作。同年6月18日,中船重工船舶设计研究中心以天津新港船厂设计所为主体挂牌成立“中船重工船舶设计研究中心天津分中心”,设计水平提升,业务范围拓展。

2000年,海洋石油工程股份有限公司强化设计手段,采用标准化、规范化设计,提高设计速度和质量。与WORLY公司共同开发的3D设计软件,可在设计中完成配管、设备、结构模型的建立和管线三维设计。同时开发和运用PDS、Intools等设计软件,使各种设计方案得到优化。

2004年,新河船舶与海洋工程设计公司先后引进CCS中国船级社的COMPASS船舶性能计算软件和上海沪东东欣软件公司的船舶舾装设计软件,应用在船体放样、管系放样两个部分,设计的精确度和设计能力提高。

同年,天津德赛船舶海洋工程有限责任公司在船舶设计中用CAD结合“SB3DS”“MASTERSHIP”“SAP5.0ANSYS”等软件,进行受力分析、三维建模、干扰检查、取出另件图、工时定额等工作。

一、运输船舶

(一)货船

1990~1996年,天津新港船厂为上海海运局建造20000、29000载重吨散货船各2艘,为古巴和中国香港建造29000载重吨散货船各2艘,为中国香港建造27000载重吨散货船3艘,为日本建造15000载重吨散货船2艘。2001年,该厂为南非开发建造32500载重吨散货船,船上安装4台起重能力为35吨的克令吊,配备卫星导航,无人机舱,适合远洋承运各种散货。2004年,开发建造35200载重吨大湖型散货船6艘,特别适合于北美五大湖区承运各种散货。2005年,为波兰开发建造37600载重吨散货船。

2005年,天津德赛船舶海洋工程有限责任公司为山东威海东海船厂设计2800载重吨散货船。整条船只有一个大舱口,便于货物的装卸。同年,该公司完成由山海关船厂改装的74000载重吨巴拿马级自卸散货船的生产设计,其5000吨/时的大型自卸装置填补国内的空白。

(二)集装箱船和多用途集装箱船

1997年开始,天津新港船厂为德国建造900箱集装箱船2艘。2001年,该厂成功建造从4900载重吨到7000载重吨的多用途出口船舶。 为德国建造7000吨多用途集装箱重吊船8艘,船上安装2台250吨克令吊,联合起重能力达500吨,配备卫星导航,无人机舱,适合冰区航行,填补国内小吨位大起吊船建造的空白。2005年,该厂为德国建造6500吨多用途集装箱船,配备卫星导航,无人机舱,适合远洋和内河承运各种杂货。同年,开发制造14000吨多用途集装箱船。

(三)其他运输船舶

2001年,天津新河船舶重工有限责任公司为巴哈马建造客货两用的700载重吨客货滚装船。2003年,为韩国制造3400载重吨化学品船。2002~2004年,天津德赛船舶海洋工程有限责任公司为山海关船厂建造的TIV五月花海上透平安装船进行结构与动力装置的生产设计，解决该船液压起升机构的结构设计和推进中压供电系统的关键技术难点。2005年，该公司为韩国三星公司完成70000吨举力的浮船坞的结构生产设计。2005年，天津新港船厂建造"中铁渤海一号"火车渡轮，可装载50节火车箱、50辆卡车、25辆轿车、480名旅客。该轮是国内第一次采用综合全电力推进系统，也是世界上第一次采用第三代电力推进系统的火车滚装船，是当时国内最大、技术最先进、安全性最好、舒适度最佳的客滚船。在建造过程中，成功地完成紧凑式吊舱电力推进的舵桨装置，在船台精确安装，解决高强度材料火车轨道与船板的焊接等技术工艺难题，填补中国建船史上多项空白。该厂设计所还完成广船国际40000载重吨成品油轮、18000载重吨半潜船和原大连造船新厂150000载重吨FPSO储油轮等船舶的生产设计。

图5-7-1-71 "中铁渤海一号"火车渡轮

二、工程船

（一）挖泥船

由天津新河船厂与贻成房地产开发公司、塘沽区资产投资公司2003年共同组建的天津新河船舶重工有限责任公司，主要从事工程船舶的制造。2004年，该公司为比利时JANDENUL疏浚公司制造3700立方米自航式开体泥驳，该船由瑞典FKAB设计院和大连DF-MARINE进行基本设计和详细设计，天津船舶与海洋工程设计公司进行生产设计和船舶建造过程中的技术支持。同年，该公司与业主签订6艘合同的同时，按业主要求，开发建造3700立方米开体耙吸挖泥船，具有吸泥、运输、自卸等综合功能。2004年该公司还建造CSD8060和5553千瓦两种绞吸式挖泥船。2003年，为海河清淤工程，由天津德赛船舶海洋工程有限责任公司设计、杨柳青船厂开发制造80吨半舱泥驳。

（二）特种船舶

2003年，杨柳青船厂开发制造拖带闸门专业的钢质多用途工作船、13米水警巡逻艇、40×15米军用靶船、17.6米双体防汛船。2003~2005年，天津德赛船舶海洋工程有限责任公司开发设计15吨、30吨、45吨抛锚艇，具有起锚、抛锚、修理浮筒、运输货物、接送人员等多种功能，替代以前进口的抛锚艇。2005年，由该公司设计、渤海石油修船公司制造的65米水泥搅拌船，广泛应用于建港施工。同年，该公司为广东大亚湾设计37米浮油回收船。同年，天津新河船舶重工有限责任公司为比利时疏浚工程配套制造DV46工作艇，具有起吊、拖带、油污回收、储藏为一体的多功能艇。还为天津港制造4000HP消防船，具有消防和港口作业拖轮功能。

（三）拖轮

2004年，天津德赛船舶海洋工程有限责任公司为山东石岛港设计2648千瓦港口作业拖轮，采用导管装置代替传统的Z型推进装置，达到港内机动操作目的，为业主节约投资。2004~2005年，天津新河船舶重工有限责任公司为湛江港开发生产5200HP全回转拖轮2艘，为天津港建造5000HP拖轮2艘，为京唐港建造5000HP拖轮1艘，为日照港建造5600HP全回转拖轮2艘。

三、船艇

2001年，主要从事船艇开发生产的杨柳青船厂为天津北运河的配套工程制造4艘游艇。2002年，由天津德赛船舶海洋工程有限责任公司设计，杨柳青船厂制造钢质17米单体游船和20米双体游船、仿"郑和号"外形的54.1×17米仿古船，39.1×11.45米多功能房船，以及90客位钢质游船（该船为集办公、会议、休闲功能为一体的中西合璧式游船）。2003年，杨柳青船厂参照威尼斯"贡朵拉"外形，设计制造7.62米钢质欧式小艇。2004年，天津德赛船舶海洋工程有限责任公司为山海关海上世界开发设计18米半潜式游艇，用于观察水下生物。2005年，杨柳青船厂为北京奥运会青岛分会场帆船比赛制造75米钢质趸船。

四、海洋采油装备

2000年4月，由渤海海洋工程设计院、海洋石油平台厂、海洋石油工程安装工程公司3家合并组建的海洋石油工程股份有限公司，其近海采油设备制造技术达到国内先进水平，同年在上海证券交易所上市，取得对外经济合作经营证书，承揽国外海洋采油工程项目，向深海采油设备制造技术发展。

2002年，海洋石油工程股份有限公司增添蓝疆号起重铺管船，最大起重能力3800吨，可以在水深200米的海域进行吊装和铺管作业。为在水深200米内的海域进行海洋石油工程安装、海管铺设创造条件，也为中国海洋石油开采技术向深海方向发展提供经验。

图5-7-1-72 蓝疆号导管架扶正

2002年，天津德赛船舶海洋工程有限责任公司完成旅大LD10-1/5-2/4-2三个平台生活模块的基本设计和详细设计，为口岸船厂设计半潜载导管架船。同年，天津新港船厂为韩国现代重工设计第5代海洋石油平台，按国际规范，先后承接建造阿帕奇、QK17、QK18-2、NB35-2、PL193的海上石油生活和公共电器模块。

2003年，海洋石油工程股份有限公司打入国际市场。先后承揽韩国石油公司第一个气田DongHae海上安装项目，印度尼西亚SES项目的设计、建造与安装及KODECO项目的有关设计、海上安装和海管铺设。该公司多次获得科麦奇、壳牌、菲利普斯、阿科等国际知名能源公司授予的优质工程、安全施工证书和最佳承包商等荣誉。2001年该公司合作承担完成的“百万吨级海上油田浮式生产储运系统研制与开发”、2002年该公司承担完成的“南海文昌油田工程设计及海上施工安装技术”项目，分别获得2004年中国海洋石油总公司科技进步特等奖、2004年国家科技进步二等奖和总公司科技进步二等奖。该公司在施工中，开发大型结构物称重技术，技术能力达8000吨，重量测量精度<1.5%，全电脑控制，自动化水平高，环境适应性强。设备可安装在一个集装箱内，运输方便，集成度高；用UT代替RT对钢管卷制接长环缝和纵缝检验的新工艺，可快速发现缺陷，提高无损探伤检验效率5~6倍。2005年，研制新长桩起吊技术，采用液压翻转卡具代替旧工艺使用的翻转钩，提高工效，保证安全；全面采用CO_2气体保护焊全位置焊接工艺，同时对壁厚50毫米以上的钢桩接头焊接，采用高性能埋弧焊焊接工艺。海管陆上接长埋弧焊、CO_2气体保护焊焊接工艺和半自动自保护药芯焊拓展、长桩起吊等技术的成功应用与推广，大型结构物称重技术、钢管卷制接长UT代替RT检验工艺等技术开发和创新，显著提高作业质量和效率，降低工程成本和劳动强度。

2004年，该公司自主开发的国产AUT设备在东联和番禺海管项目中成功应用，检验速度提高，成本降低。“水下环氧密闭·干式发泡法兰保护技术”在东联码头项目的成功应用，填补行业和国内空白，为在相关维修专业领域的技术研发与创新拓展思路。

2005年5月，该公司采用Float Over（浮托法）完成位于渤海中部海域南堡35-2油田CEPA组块重达7200余吨的中心平台的海上安装，创造国内采用浮托法安装最大组块的新纪录。标志着该公司海上安装能力从单一的吊装发展到吊装、滑移下水和浮托法安装并举，为海上安装大型平台走出一条新路。该公司开展边际油田开发新模式—“三一模式”（一座简易平台 + 一条海底管道 + 一条海底电缆）的研究。针对锦州20-2凝析气田北高点采用“三一模式”的简易设施，创新地采用独立研发的独腿三桩简易平台形式及具有自主知识产权的单重保温海底管道等多项新技术，使整个工程投资节省约4300万元人民币，内部收益率可由原来的13%上升到20%，有效地降低开发门槛，为低成本开发已探明的众多中小型边际油田开创一条新路。同年，该公司首次完成海上简易无人平台的设计、建造与安装，在单层保温配重管结构的研究和设计，海底管线阳极保护设计等课题中取得实质性的突破，首次完成200米水深桩基式导管架工程设计等。

2005年，该公司完成国家“十五”“863”计划重大专项“渤海大油田勘探开发关键技术”中的3项子课题。

"水下干式管道维修系统"子课题,针对中国渤海海域浑水环境条件,研制开发的60米水深以内、6″~24″管径范围内的单层管配重结构和双层管保温结构海底管道的干式维修作业系统;"海底管道维修的挖沟机"子课题,主要研究和设计一套既能作为水下干式舱系统的配套设备,进行基础开挖,也能作为埋管挖沟的双功能水下作业系统;"海底管线外检测与维修技术总体集成"子课题,集成海底管道外检测装置及其检测技术,形成有效的外检能力,以遥控水下机器人为载体,装备有声、光、激光、电磁、化学等多种高灵敏度、高分辨率的主/被动检测设备,实现对海底非掩埋和掩埋(3米以内)的油气管道的自动/半自动巡检,包括管道走向、管道的位置、管道的埋深、保护电位、管道的悬跨、外部损伤(未渗漏)和渗漏点等状态的监测,并可以对故障点破损状态进行分类和分析。该公司2002年起组织科技人员经过4年多的技术设计、功能实验、陆地建造和安装调试。3项课题在曹妃甸11油田海底电缆检测挖沟复位工程中首次应用获得成功,取得良好的经济效益与社会效益,各项功能均达到预期目标,部分关键技术达到国际领先水平。该系统的研制成功,填补国内海洋石油工程海底管道水下干式维修作业的空白,为沿海海域水下油气管道正常生产和定期检测维修,以及突发泄漏事故提供快速、有效的维修手段。

五、陆用机械

(一)吊机

1990~2002年,天津新港船厂与芬兰柯尼、阿根廷IMPSA、美国TTI、日本三菱、西班牙FPM等著名公司合作,先后为美国、斯里兰卡、泰国、韩国、印度、马来西亚、阿根廷、芬兰以及中国秦皇岛港、天津港、惠州港、盐田港、高栏港、海口港、湄州港、九江电厂等国内外用户建造集装箱吊车、浮吊船、150吨塔吊、116吨港口吊等大型港口吊机100余台套。2002~2003年,该厂为美国乔治亚港建造4台世界上第6代的66吨-141米港口大型集装箱吊车,其自动化程度和制造精度均达到国际先进水平。2005年,渤海石油修船公司制造为海上平台使用的BCOL5吨/12米的吊机。

(二)焦化机械

1993年,天津新港船厂开始制造焦化设备。第一台为北京焦化厂设计制造的4.3米焦化设备,经国家冶金部、化工部、原中国船舶工业总公司专家联合鉴定,认为该产品达到同类产品的先进水平,具备批量生产的条件。到2003年,该厂先后为北京、青岛、天津、广西等近20个地区的钢厂、煤制气企业制造60余台焦化设备。2005年,该厂制造的焦化设备打入国际市场,首次向伊朗出口。

第二节 造修和装备

1990年代,随着航海业的发展和港口扩大改造,船舶的大型化、超大型化成为发展主流。原来造船企业的"小而全"和"大而全"的格局已不适应发展需要,造船企业内取消电镀、酸洗、铸造、热处理等车间,由外单位协作加工物件。1992年,天津新港船厂与塘沽中心桥乡合作建设新中舾装件厂,为天津新港船厂提供舱口、舱盖等舾装件;中钢海洋工程服务公司和天津豪钢机械工程公司除满足天津地区造船企业的舾装件需要外,主要向日本出口舾装件产品。在中国船级社天津分社注册登记的为造船企业提供设备、器材的配套企业有20家。造船企业增添起重设施,提高分段吊装能力,改革工艺流程,逐步向总装造船厂方向发展。

一、大型设施设备

1990年,天津新港船厂随着运输船舶的逐步大型化,为适应29000载重吨船舶的建造,将原来15000吨船台改建成30000载重吨级船台；1994年，将5000吨船台改造成为能建造15000载重吨级船舶的能力；并在两个船台上分别安装150吨和63吨门座式起重机各一台。2005年，该厂将原来15000吨船台进行第二次改造，船台接长到283.7米，使其建造能力达到40000载重吨级。渤海石油修船公司1997年增添195×42×17米的浮船坞一座，用于修理50000载重吨级的船舶和海洋石油平台。

1996～2003年，海洋石油工程股份有限公司先后建设4000吨滑道2台套，8000吨滑道1台套，用于导管架和组块的牵引和移滑；购置250吨履带起重机一台，用于大型结构物的吊装。2002年，该公司增添3800吨蓝疆号起重铺管船一艘，自制与蓝疆号配套的80米水深浮式托管架和150米水深重力式托管架各1套，添置7000吨下水驳船2艘，8000吨导管架下水驳船1艘，DP定位多功能船1艘，395吨和LP1400/1350吨履带起重机各1台。

2004年，杨柳青船厂购置Φ1.2米×9米～Φ2米×15米的多种规格气囊，用于船舶下水。天津新港船厂、海洋石油工程股份有限公司、天津新河船舶重工有限责任公司等企业为便于船体分段、组块和大型钢结构件的运输，均购置液压自走式平板车。

2005年4月，海洋石油工程股份有限公司在青岛市开发区建设亚洲规模最大的海洋石油工程制造基地。总投资17.5亿人民币，主要用于建造国内外海上油气田开发工程所需的桩基式平台、浮式平台和海上油气处理装置总包等相关设施，同时提供海上运输、海上安装工程的配套服务。

二、船舶制造

随着信息化、数字化技术的发展，天津造船业通过消化、吸收成组流水造船、总装造船、精益造船、数字造船、平台造船等5大世界现代船舶先进技术，在造船设计技术、船舶制造、生产流程和生产管理等方面发生重大变化和更新。

（一）现代造船设计

1980年代末，天津新港船厂由于学习日本大岛船厂的先进设计理念，推行生产设计，一直处于国内现代造船设计的先进行列。适应现代造船模式的要求，更新设计理念和内容，船厂设计部门的主要任务，既解决造什么船的功能和结构设计，也提供怎样造船的方案设计，提供合理组织造船生产的造船过程设计。设计部门提供的图纸，由功能/系统/专业划分的施工设计图，转变为按区域/阶段/类型划分的生产设计图。设计阶段的划分相应发生重大改变，从方案设计-技术设计-施工设计转变为合同设计-初步设计-详细设计-生产设计。生产设计不仅包含生产用图，还包含管理工作资料和信息、制作程序、工序要领、托盘表，等等。生产设计的引入，使得造船的生产管理加强，协调工种间的冲突，造船进度加快，造船质量提高。到2005年，天津新港船厂由于设计能力的加强，提升到由专业设计院负责的详细设计阶段。

（二）生产工艺技术

1978年起，天津新港船厂开始研究分段无余量制造技术。推行精度造船，实施分段总组无余量建造。1990年，该厂在船体分段建造中开始实施，并逐步推广应用，提高分段在船台搭载合拢的速度，缩短船舶建造周期，引起国内造船企业的关注。该厂建造的德国4900吨多用途船，其货舱区域有19个分段采用无余量建造，达全船分段总数的45.23%，32500吨货轮舷侧分段总组也实现无余量建造。2004年起，天津新河船舶重工有限责任公司在建造3700立方米泥驳、1600立方米挖泥船、港航挖泥船等船舶中采用该技术，取得明显的经济效益。

1994年，天津新港船厂在船舶制造中，广泛应用光电切割、等离子切割、自动埋弧焊接、二氧化碳焊接、氩弧焊接等现代焊切技术设备和工艺，购置的等离子数控切割机，在水中进行钢板切割，提高工作效率，消除烟尘，达到环保要求。2003年，该厂实现集装箱地脚在分段上预舾装工艺，解决分段建造中集装箱底脚影响管隧舱管系分段预装及密封试验和涂装的矛盾，也解决各工种互相干扰的困难，做到底部分段壳、舾、涂按区域一体化施工，“内底集装箱底脚预装技术”达到国内领先水平。2004年，新河船舶重工有限责任公司为比利时建造的3700立方米自航式开体船舶中，采用“板式电阻加热器”将钢板预热后进行焊接，焊接质量提高。2004年，天津市船厂利用海水潮汐落差，首创起重机臂架无机械动力安装工艺。2005年，杨柳青船厂采用气囊下水工艺，保证2艘75米趸船奥运会项目顺利下水，按时完成建造任务。

（三）生产管理技术

2000年起，天津新港船厂建立计划部负责管理造船部、车间、班组等，自上而下逐级细化4级计划管理体系；贯彻船舶生产三级作业日报制度；实施生产线表、船体、分段、内场、铸锻件订货等标准日程，并与计算机结合，考核计划兑现率，保证生产节拍，理顺建造计划、负荷计划、日程计划之间的逻辑关系；建立标准化的生产计划体系，有效保证生产管理体系正常运行。在造船生产中，建立以分段（中间产品）为导向的生产作业体系。根据区域/阶段/类型组织造船生产的要求，取消原按工种、专业设置的车间，根据中间产品的特性和需要，把多工种专业人员集中在一个生产组织内，成立机装、电装、舾装、甲装等车间，实行壳、舾、涂并行作业，实现工序前移，缩短造船周期。该厂还实现内场、平台、码头等区域壳、舾、涂一体化的分道、定置、流水的标准作业程序。

应用并行工程原理，建立分段壳、舾、涂一体化的设计流程和一体化建造流程。分段实施定置管理，推行中间产品模块化，建立集配中心，有效应用成组技术，将舾装件、设备在集配阶段做组合体，实现工序前移，在前置工序就开始予舾装，提高预舾装率，完善分段完整性。同时，依据“船台完成安装，码头进行调试”的要求，推进工序前移，强化船舶下水完整性。32500吨散货轮的分段预舾装率达90%以上，7000吨多用途船达到80%以上；下水完整性达90%以上，属国内先进水平。船舶建造周期不断缩短，32500吨货船建造周期缩短为10个半月，实现交船前不进坞。该厂把上层建筑总组，整体吊装，提高上层总组预舾装的完整性，作为缩短造船周期最有效的措施之一，其上层建筑总组施工预舾装的完整性达国内最好水平。

（四）信息化技术应用

1990年代，天津新港船厂将计算机应用于船舶生产工艺设计，但还局限于某个部门或某一方面。1994年开发修船管理信息系统（MIS），2002年开发升级为修船决策支持系统（SI-DSS），2003年开发“造船各阶段实际时数与实际物量统计分析系统”“造船建造日程计划管理系统”“造船任务能力S曲线预测系统”，使该厂工程计划管理水平跃上新台阶。2004年，该厂安装局域网，成功引进腾讯通讯软件，为办公自动化建设搭上高速平台。2005年，该厂的“船舶建造标准”计算机查询系统在局域网上正式运行。同年7月，该厂开发的“天津新港船厂造船决策支持系统（SB-DSS）”投入运行，为造船成本目标的制定、执行、过程控制和系统分析，提供有效的信息平台和决策数据参考。同年，天津新河船舶重工有限责任公司建立局域网、用友U8财务电算化系统、OA系统和ERP物流信息系统，以数字化、网络化和数据库技术为手段，以物流系统为核心，建立企业共享信息平台，实现企业资源整合，信息共享。

三、修理

（一）船舶修理

1990年，天津各修船企业在吸收和引进世界先进的修船工艺技术的基础上，与国际修船规范接轨，修船能力和技术水平提高。天津新港船厂修船分厂增设BBC增压器技术服务站、柴油机油头油泵服务站、REXRNTH液压技术服务站、旧件修理服务站等船舶专业技术工程公司。在船舶修理中，采用最高压力达27.46兆帕的高压水除锈、喷砂除锈、无气喷涂、高空作业车等坞修工艺技术和设备；采用微机管理系统，实现修船工艺标准化、技术专业化、坞修机械化，使船舶坞修期处于国内领先水平。2000年把“海龙”号散货船改装成油轮；2001年完成韩国“天仁”号客滚船的改装；2002年把“洪江”号散货船改装为沥青运输船；2005年完成海损严重的“辽海”号修理改装。该厂每年主修和改装国内外货船、客滚船、海上石油钻井平台、挖泥船、液化气船等各类50000载重吨级以下船舶100多艘。

20世纪90年代中期，原天津新河船厂在船舶修理上打入国际市场，先后为俄罗斯、韩国等国家的渔加工船、散货船、沥青化学品船等进行修理和改装。渤海石油修船公司、天津市船厂等企业也承揽国内外货船和各种工程船舶的主机、轴系、货舱、起重机械等项目的修理和改装。

(二)海洋构筑物的修理

1996年,天津新港船厂修船分厂完成滨海512号海洋石油探察船的改装。2001年,海洋石油工程股份有限公司与美国TDW公司合作,采用双封双堵与干式舱相结合的技术,在不停产的情况下进行渤西海管的维修,海管维修能力实现较大突破,开创该公司在高科技领域对外合作的新模式。渤海石油修船公司主要配备海洋石油工程船舶和海上平台的修理,2004年5月至2005年,先后对渤海5号和渤海7号钻井平台、滨海109号工程铺管船以及胜利试采1号平台等海洋平台进行修理,完成700吨起重船船体中间加长、海洋石油298号平台的泥浆舱改造,自立号生活服务平台的住房、发电机房改造等项目。

第八章 电子仪表

天津市电子仪表行业在20世纪80年代技术引进消化吸收的基础上,20世纪90年代国有企业通过嫁接、改造、调整,自主研发和技术创新能力有较大提高,逐步发展成为具有一定规模、门类齐全、领域广泛的电子信息产业服务体系。形成以微小型计算机、显示器、网络产品为核心的信息产业;以光电端机、传真机、军民用移动通讯、导航设备为核心的通信产业;以自动化仪表、电子仪器、电工仪表为核心的仪器仪表产业;以复印机、绘图机和影像设备为核心的办公自动化产业;以微电机、电缆、半导体材料、半导体器件为代表的元器件产业。其中,光缆终端机、计算机键盘、片式瓷介电容、钽电解电容、高压硅堆、区熔硅单晶等产品产量列全国第一位。通过自控系统成套技术的研究、开发、施工,完成数百项知名度较高、水平较高的信息化工程项目。

第一节 元器件与仪表

天津元器件产业发展迅速,半导体器件、电路板、电缆光缆、微电机、仪器仪表、调节阀等产品经过技术创新和引进吸收,技术水平逐步提高,多数产品技术达到国内领先水平,部分技术达到国际先进水平。

一、半导体器件

(一)塑封高压硅堆

1991年,天津中环半导体股份有限公司(简称中环公司)引进的塑封高压硅堆生产线正式投入生产。1993年12月,该公司完成塑封高压硅堆5项新工艺创新及生产线配套技术改造,11项相关设备及20项工装夹具得到改进。产品由原玻璃钝化塑封结构,改进为PI胶钝化塑封结构,产品制造工艺及实物质量均达到20世纪90年代国际先进水平。新工艺产品具有电参数稳定、可靠性高的特点,产品主要电参数水平为:IR1≤8纳安,IR2≤0.6微安。1996年12月,中环公司开发的2CL80系列塑封高压硅堆完成鉴定。该产品反向恢复时间trr小于0.08微秒,主要用于高清晰度电视机、显示器等,打破国外产品垄断的局面。同年,高压硅堆产品打入国际市场。1996年12月,中环公司开发的2CL3509、3512、4509、4512型塑料封装高压硅堆完成鉴定。新产品具有350毫安和450毫安电流及可控雪崩击穿性能,用于微波炉高压整流。1997年,中环公司塑封高压硅堆和超快恢复整流二极管被评为国家级新产品。

1997年12月,中环公司完成2CL70A-74A型塑封高压硅堆和2CLS01-03型双向高压硅堆项目。

2CL70A–74A是2CL70–74塑封高压硅堆的换代产品，为彩色电视机或显示器配套，适应国外对产品微型化的要求。其管体直径2.5毫米，引线直径0.5毫米，具有体积小、性能稳定、可靠性高的特点。新产品性能达到国际先进水平，填补国内空白。为微波炉配套的2CLS01–03型双向高压硅堆，是由两个反向耐压不等的、面对面的高压硅堆（D1和D2）串接而成，并靠D2管的反向可控雪崩特性对微波炉高压变压器起保护作用。新产品性能达到国际先进水平，填补国内空白，打破国外垄断，部分产品随整机出口。

1998年12月，中环公司完成2CL90–93型塑封高压硅堆项目。该产品为高清晰度彩电及显示器回扫变压器配套，其反向恢复时间trr≤0.06微秒，性能达到国际先进水平，产品填补国内空白。

1999年12月，中环半导体股份有限公司完成2CL01–03型超快恢复系列塑封高压硅堆项目。新产品为投影电视、高清晰度电视及频率在1000千赫兹以下的显示器回扫变压器配套，具有硅芯尺寸小（0.52×0.52毫安）和超快恢复（反向恢复时间trr≤0.05微秒）特点，性能达到国际先进水平，填补国内空白。

2002年2月，中环公司为超高清晰度（130千赫兹）显示器回扫变压器配套开发的2CL11–13型超快恢复高压硅堆完成技术鉴定。新产品体内采用新型PI胶钝化材料、环氧树脂封装，采用精致螯合剂作为涂料添加剂改善产品高温性能，具有反向恢复时间trr≤0.045微秒等特点，性能优于2CL70–77、2CL90–93、2CL01–03系列产品，并能替代大部分规格的硅堆用于普通电视上，应用领域广阔。新产品主要技术指标，尤其是反向恢复时间，处于国内领先、国际先进水平，填补国内空白。2004年，天津中环半导体股份有限公司的高压硅堆，历经升级换代、不断开发，其产销量跃居世界第一。

（二）整流二极管与整流器

1993年12月，中环公司开发的玻封、塑封硅整流二极管完成鉴定。该产品生产采用国际先进的纸源扩散技术、硅片双面减薄技术、微晶玻璃钝化封装及PI胶钝化塑料封装等先进技术，有效地控制产品电参数和可靠性，使产品电参数稳定、高温性能好，适用于彩电、显示器等电子设备，做工频、高频整流用。中环公司凭借开发能力强的优势，迅速形成全系列生产能力。产品种类达到60个型号213个规格，芯片全部自制，在国内同行企业二极管生产中居领先地位。

1994年，中环公司引进的硅桥式整流器生产线投入生产。1998年12月，该公司完成T4SB型硅桥式整流器项目，其产品内部采用玻钝芯片，外形模塑封装成型，平均整流输出电流IO=150安，具有高可靠性、高耐压、大浪涌电流、高温特性好等特点，填补国内空白，达到20世纪90年代中期国际先进水平。1999年，硅桥式整流器被评为国家级新产品。

1997年12月，中环公司完成TRU1P等塑封/玻封硅整流二极管项目。该产品各项电参数完全采用国外同类产品电参数指标，产品技术水平国内领先。其中，TRU1P等14种型号硅整流二极管，分别属于反向恢复时间小于0.05～0.1微秒的超快恢复管、反向耐压为1500～2000伏的高反压管和正向电压很小的低损耗管，技术含量高，填补国内空白。

2001年1月，中环公司开发的TH15等快恢复、超快恢复硅整流二极管完成鉴定。该新产品主要为快速、超快速整流电路以及电视机行输出阻尼电路应用配套，瞄准世界先进水平，电性能指标适合高频使用和高可靠性方面的要求，其反向恢复时间国内领先、国际先进。

2001年8月，中环公司T25VB型硅桥式整流器完成鉴定。该产品是为变频空调、充电器及大中功率电源整流配套而自主开发的，技术上瞄准世界先进水平，采用玻钝芯片、外形灌封成型的技术，平均整流输出电流IO=25安，反向最高耐压VR=800伏，正向浪涌电流IFSM=400安，具有大电流、耐潮湿、耐高温、耐浪涌特点。

2004年3月，中环公司研发完成T4KB系列塑封硅桥式整流器。新产品芯片采用该公司自主研制开发的玻璃钝化芯片，各项性能达到国际先进水平。玻璃钝化（电泳法）芯片制造工艺，是将玻璃粉致密均匀地沉积在PN结的表面，再经过高温形成微晶态，起到对PN结表面的保护作用。新产品用芯片平行两列排列，代替传统的"一"字排列，使相同芯片尺寸下引线间距变窄，提高散热效果，确保产品稳定性好、耐高温、耐潮湿、耐浪涌、可靠性高的特点。同年，中环公司的高压二极管、硅整流二极管和硅桥式整流器的产销量达到

12亿支,其中高压二极管的产销量占有世界市场42%的份额,确立该企业在国内外市场竞争中的优势地位。

二、印刷电路板

1966年年初,天津表盘厂(后发展更名为天津东方电子元件厂、天津市元件十九厂、天津市印刷电路板厂、天津普林电路有限公司)的张曾荫和霍树森从当时的国家第七机械工业部引进电路板项目,于1966年底试制出单面电路板。1967年试制出双面电路板。1968年试制出4~6层的多层电路板。该电路板采用人工绘图、玻璃基湿法制版、涂覆感光胶制保护图形、三氯化铁蚀刻、涂覆可剥漆沉铜、高速台钻人工钻孔、工艺导线法电镀等。1969年年初,3类产品生产工艺均已成熟,批量生产的电路板最小线宽/间距达到0.3/0.4毫米,最小金属化孔径为0.7毫米。20世纪70年代初,该厂为中国核试验以及第一台亿次银河计算机批量提供多层电路板。

1985年年初,天津市印刷电路板厂从日本引进单面板的半自动生产线及相关的工艺技术。采用银盐胶片制版,半自动丝印光固油墨制保护图形,氯化铜蚀刻,半自动丝印光固油墨制阻焊图形等工艺。1989年,天津市印刷电路板厂与澳大利亚普林公司合资建立天津普林电路有限公司(简称普林公司),技术水平进一步提升,采用计算机辅助设计,自动化生产,可制成1~14层板,最小线宽/间距为0.12 /0.12毫米,最小金属化孔径0.2毫米。产品达到美国IPC标准,英国BS标准,80%的产品销往欧美市场。

2001年3月,普林公司试制出单面挠性板;2001年8月试制出铝基电路板;2002年5月试制出双面挠性板。2005年1月试制出HDI(高密度互连)板,该HDI板的最小线宽/间距0.075/0.075毫米,最小孔直径为0.15毫米,最小焊盘直径0.25毫米,居世界先进水平。

三、电缆光缆

1991年,天津六〇九电缆有限公司(简称六〇九厂)赵鹏飞等为水下机器人配套研制出中性浮力电缆,为国内首创;王凯等为电话机配套研制出弹簧型电缆组件。两项成果均获得国家机电工业部科技进步三等奖。同年,董华章、李秀琴为航天系统配套研制出的YJ-8系列小型网状电缆,是该公司首次采用电缆组网工艺,新产品具有耐高温、重量轻、集成化的特点,获得国家电子工业部科技进步二等奖。

1992年,六〇九厂研制出为国家重点工程配套的多芯战地野外综合电缆。其结构包括6根SFF-50-1射频电缆和8根AF-200安装线及18对双绞屏蔽线,工作温度在-55℃~+85℃,为一种集多种性能于一体的综合电缆。新产品通过电子工业部组织的科技成果鉴定,达到国内先进水平。

1993年,六〇九厂刘振谦研制出GYTAG嵌槽式光缆、GYTAC型层绞式光缆及GYTAS束管式光缆,并通过市经委组织的设计、生产定型。

1994年,六〇九厂研制开发出为船舶工业配套的CRYP型船用耐温125℃无卤阻燃多芯屏蔽电缆。该产品具有低毒、阻燃、无烟、耐温等级高的特点。通过电子工业部组织的科技成果鉴定,达到国内领先水平,获得1995年国家电子工业部科学技术进步三等奖。同年,该公司还研制出聚氯乙烯绝缘程控电缆系列和尼龙绝缘程控电缆系列,为程控交换机配套。

1996年,六〇九厂杜红杰研制出为国家重点工程配套的WHF型深水电缆。通过国家信息产业部组织的科技成果鉴定,达到国际领先水平。

1997年,六〇九厂进行技术改造,引进奥地利罗森泰公司物理发泡挤出机一台,同时购置其他配套设备多台,建成移动通信系统用馈线生产线,于当年12月投产。同年,该公司电缆二厂研制出SYWY-50-22物理发泡聚乙烯绝缘皱纹铜管外导体射频同轴电缆。成果于1998年1月8日通过天津市科委组织的鉴定,达到国际先进水平,获得天津市1998年度科技进步二等奖,并获得"1998年国家重点新产品"称号,列为天津市技术创新产品,获得天津市技术创新一等奖。该产品特性阻抗为50欧姆,最高工作频率5000兆赫,衰减300兆赫兹时每百米为2.19分贝,2000兆赫兹时每百米为6.46分贝。同年,该厂还开发出多种规格的SYWY系列产品,广泛应用于移动通信领域。

1997年,六〇九厂杨玉萍研制出TGE-712B野战10对音频电缆,为部队提供更新换代产品。成果通过解放军总参通定委和国家信息产业部组织的设计和生产定型鉴定,达到国际领先水平。

1998~1999年,六〇九厂研制出TGE-706芳纶被复线。经国家信息产业部和解放军总参通定委鉴定,达到国际领先水平,为国内首创。新产品每千米重量小于10千克,衰减常数小于等于1.4分贝。该产品具有柔软、重量轻、通话性能好、使用区域广泛的特点,是TGE-701轻型被覆线的换代产品。该产品1999年获得天津市技术创新一等奖,天津市科学技术进步二等奖,并获得国家实用新型专利。2003年,该公司研制出为部队野战配套的TGE-708超轻型被覆线。该产品重量轻、通话性能好,其重量每千米小于等于5.5千克,衰减常数小于等于1.5分贝。成果通过信息产业部科技成果鉴定,达到国际先进水平。

2000~2002年,六〇九厂杨光、杜红杰、李津津、陈志坚等人研制出军用海缆埋设机系缆、HIM-250海缆埋设机漂浮电缆、水喷式埋设机综合电缆和多刀埋设机综合电缆。此类电缆是集光缆、通信电缆、电力电缆、铠装等为一体的大型综合电缆。产品均为国内首创、填补空白,经信息产业部鉴定,达到国际先进水平,获得国家实用新型专利。获天津市科技进步三等奖。

2004~2005年,六〇九厂技术中心研制出为航空系统配套的辐照交联乙烯-四氟乙烯共聚物(XETFE)绝缘电线电缆系列。该系列产品外径小,使用温度在-65℃~200℃,重量轻、抗冲击、抗辐射,适用于航空、航天等领域飞行器上应用。2005年5月,该成果通过国家信息产业部组织的科技成果鉴定,达到国际先进水平,替代进口。

四、微电机

1993年,天津市天虹微电机有限公司(原天津市微电机公司,简称微电机公司)李松森等设计JG120和JG180绞果机用电动机。1994年,该公司张乃信等研制出JG30GS和JG30UL单相电容运转异步电动机。1995年,该公司段卫国设计出JG40单相电容运转异步电动机,郑捷等研制出M系列交流单相双速电容运转电动机,均获天津市1995年度科技进步三等奖。JG系列单相电容运转异步电动机和M系列交流单相双速电容运转电动机,分别取得出口机电产品质量许可证书。

1993年,微电机公司魏春杰等设计开发出2SR250-8型洗衣机用电动机。1995年,段卫国等设计出2SR100A,120A和150A洗衣机用单相电容运转异步电动机。上述产品均出口埃及。1994年陶凤立等设计出RXB150A ,120A和100A洗衣机用单相电容运转异步电动机。1995年,孟庆华等设计开发出ZYR36137-ESC,ZYR36125-SC,ZYR12-36391和ZYR36331永磁直流电动机。1996年,孟庆华等设计开发出ZYR5-36331永磁直流电动机。

1996年,微电机公司段卫国等设计开发出F80,F90和F63系列减速机电机,为日本住友公司配套。同年,微电机公司修杰等设计出为家用电动面条机配套的R5034型单相电容运转异步电动机,1997年获实用新型专利。2003年,微电机公司董立军等设计出R56系列单相电容运转异步电动机,为德国真空设备配套。

1999年,微电机公司邓锐等设计出稀土磁钢无刷直流电动机。结构简单工艺新颖,端盖采用钢板制造,其外观可根据需要喷涂不同颜色。该项目1999年获实用新型专利,2000年获天津市科技进步三等奖。

1999年,微电机公司修杰等设计出YU160S-4型电阻起动异步电动机。用于污水防堵处理机配套。同年,修杰等设计出YYB85-4洗衣机用电动机、YYG25-4甩干机用电动机。2002年,修杰等设计出D-TJ-PSC-6P系列风扇用电动机。产品出口。

2002年,微电机公司齐宗山等设计出S56系列三相转异步电动机。为德国真空设备配套。

2004年,微电机公司张伯元、齐宗山设计出V1030074系列泵电动机。产品出口。

五、流量仪表

（一）水表

1993年，天津市自动化仪表三厂（简称仪表三厂）在引进日本KBMⅡ型干式水表的基础上，从防外磁场干扰设计、材料采用等方面进行改进，研制成功KBMⅡ-20B1型干式数字型水表该产品获得国家专利，被国家经贸委编入国家级新产品“八五”项目表彰名册，于1996年获天津市科技进步三等奖。

1998年，天津仪表集团有限公司（原仪表三厂，以下简称仪表集团）研制出远传冷、热水表。

2000年，仪表集团与丹麦卡姆鲁普公司合作研制生产TAG—15~50型智能热量表。该产品采用超低功耗微处理器技术，适合在集中供热的供暖计量系统中使用。

2003年，仪表集团研制出水表无线抄表系统。该系统包括主控计算机、集中器、采集器、手持机及无线通讯表，辅以管理信息软件。系统无需布线，可靠性高，实现计量、存储、诊断、通讯、管理等功能。

（二）燃气表

1991年，天津市自动化仪表十厂（简称仪表十厂）研制开发出G40工商业燃气表。该表是膜片容积式计量表，适用于煤气、天然气、液化石油气等可燃气体的累积计量。1993年，仪表十厂研制开发出G10、G16、G25、G65、G100系列工商业燃气表，适用于不同流量范围燃气表的计量。1995年，仪表十厂研制开发G4、G6型燃气表。同年又研制开发出“智能卡式燃气表”，顾客通过售气管理系统对智能卡充值，输入到燃气表中，不必入户抄表。

1999年，仪表十厂研制开发出“代码预付费燃气表”。用户持充值卡购气后，输入不同用户代码后对燃气表进行计量。2000年，该厂研制出G1.6、G2.5钢外壳燃气表及远传式燃气表。2002年，该厂研制出带温压补偿型工商业燃气表，解决不同管道压力、温度变化时的准确计量。同年，又研制开发“IC卡式工商业燃气表”。

2003年，仪表十厂研制开发出“无源式预付费燃气表”。该表机械运行不需电源，以避免电磁干扰。2005年，该厂研制开发出G6、G10钢外壳工商业燃气表。

（三）涡街流量计

1991年，仪表三厂为荣获国家科学技术进步奖特等奖的北京正负电子对撞机项目配套流量计。获得由时任国务院总理李鹏签署的证书。1993年，仪表三厂研制出LUGB-2xxx系列涡街流量计，实现对液体、气体和蒸汽流量的准确计量。1994年，仪表三厂张亮等研制的“一种涡街流量传感器”获国家专利。1996年，仪表三厂研制出LUGB-3xxx型插入式涡街流量计系列产品。2002年，仪表集团研制出LU系列智能涡街流量计，单片机组态设定，一体化液晶显示，二线制24伏供电，4～20毫安输出或电池供电。2003年，仪表集团研制出LU-xxxx-B，LUGB xxxx-B系列防爆涡街流量计，可广泛用于石油、化工、纺织、印染等各行业易燃易爆流体介质的测量。同年，仪表集团研制出与跨国公司ABB智能涡街流量转换器配套的传感器产品。2005年，改制后的仪表集团（简称天仪集团）研制出LU型智能一体化稳压补偿，双排液晶显示涡街流量计。

1997年，仪表集团研制出LWY系列智能涡轮流量计。2005年，天仪集团研制出LWY-xxE系列二线制智能涡轮流量计。

1999年，仪表集团研制出LD—25～50B22511型电磁流量计。该流量计为传感器与转换器一体型结构；耐高压、防爆、数字显示；转换器以单片微处理器为核心，实现智能功能；在流量仪表行业首次采用中文界面功能显示。国家经贸委认定该产品为“2000年度国家级新产品”，被列入国家科技成果重点推广计划。同时，该产品获天津市1999年度技术创新优秀项目二等奖。2001年，仪表集团何炳俊等研制的LDZ-Ⅵ型一体化电磁流量转换器产品，获天津市科技进步三等奖。

20世纪80年代，国际上出现现场总线技术。2001年仪表集团开始研制现场总线智能仪表产品。2004年研制出可进行PROFIBUS协议通讯的智能涡街流量变送器产品。2005年，天仪集团整合公司技术力量，通过产学研合作，从电动执行器产品入手，开始全面研制现场总线型智能化仪表。

六、温度仪表

1990年，天津市自动化仪表八厂（简称仪表八厂）研制生产出XMW-10C快速钢水温度数字显示仪。该显示仪与快速热电偶配合，广泛用于炼钢、炼铁、浇铸、玻璃溶液等快速测温场合。1995年，该厂研制生产出XMZ、XMB系列数字式Ⅲ型显示报警仪及ZPE系列电动伺服放大器。

1994年，仪表八厂研制生产出DFQ-2101型自动切换模拟操作器。

1995年，仪表八厂研制出油田专用防爆测温热电偶、热电阻RT-24、RT-64P、RT-84、TC-24、TC-64P。

1996年，仪表八厂研制并生产出XMD-16智能多点巡检控制仪。1997年，该厂研制生产出XMT-100系列智能数字显示控制仪。2000年，仪表八厂重新设计开发出XMT-191、XMT-192型数字温度调节仪。2002年，该厂重新设计开发出XMZ、XMT型数字温度显示调节仪。2002年，仪表八厂研制生产出XMT-800系列准智能数字显示控制仪表。

1998年，仪表八厂邵广义等研制出“TF2××系列太阳能供电器”。该产品既无机械磨损、又无环境污染，且节约能源，是国内环保、能源部门广泛推广和鼓励应用的产品。2000年，该项目被列为国家科技成果重点推广计划项目，纳入国家重点新产品试产计划，并获2000年度国家级新产品证书。

2000年，仪表八厂研制生产出SBWR、SBWZ系列一体化温度变送器模块。2005年研制TC-64、RC-64隔爆型一体化显示模块及XMY-100型一体化内电源液晶显示仪表。

2000～2003年，仪表八厂先后研制出电厂、电站专用的铠装测温热电偶WZPK-01、WZPK-03、WZPK-635和热电阻WZP-001、WZP-014。2004年，研制出WZPSJ-581双金属铂电阻一体化产品。

七、调节阀（控制阀）

调节阀是工业自动化中的执行单元。使用来自系统的控制信号，驱动阀门的动作，达到现场工艺要求的流量、压力、温度等参数。1964年，天津市自动化仪表四厂（原天津市调节阀厂，简称仪表四厂）开始生产仿苏式调节阀4F/FS、5F/FS、8F/FS，应用于石油化工行业。1967年，以仪表四厂总工程师石毓林任组长的全国联合设计组，设计出气动薄膜直通单座/双座调节阀ZMAN、ZMAP系列调节阀，成为中国的第一代调节阀产品，获得天津市优质产品称号。同时联合设计生产气动隔膜阀ZSABT、ZSCDT、ZMABT产品。

1991年，仪表四厂设计生产的气动蝶阀ZSCDW系列，双动隔膜阀A-ES54～58的产品均获得天津市科技进步三等奖。1992年，该厂引进吸收日本KOSO公司技术，生产出的气动执行机构6600RA-W/S和6500RA-W/S系列，以及301K、201C系列球阀产品，获得国家经贸委颁发的国家级新产品奖、机械部颁发的技术进步三等奖，以及天津市优秀项目奖。

1995年，仪表四厂设计生产出高耐腐、高耐磨隔膜阀和电站用大口径隔膜阀系列产品，获得国家经贸委颁发的国家级新产品奖和机械部技术进步三等奖。1998年，该厂设计生产出的气动中线蝶阀6500RA-S-W700系列产品，获天津市优秀设计奖和天津市新产品二等奖。

1999年，仪表四厂针对高压差产品，先后开发出气动薄膜高压差调节阀ZM-B-MX产品及气动高压差球阀301KGY系列产品，成功应用于化工聚丙烯项目。

2001年，仪表四厂自主研制开发出63000RA-W/S系列气动执行机构，成功应用于旋转类阀门驱动。2003年，该厂设计开发出气动偏心旋转阀63000RA-W/S-F系列产品，以及直通隔膜阀KBT、KBEST等产品。

2004年，仪表四厂开发成功并批量生产出PS2智能型电器阀门定位器产品。

2005年，仪表四厂开发生产G系列调节阀产品Z857/867-G。该产品是应用于石油化工、电厂等工矿的高档控制阀产品。同年，开发出K型、KB型气动、手动直通隔膜阀，成功应用于锅炉脱硫项目。

八、电动执行机构

1965年，天津人民仪表厂（即天津市自动化仪表七厂，简称仪表七厂）开始研制工业自动控制系统不可缺少的终端装置——电动执行机构。1968年,研制出第一批DKJ—310输出力矩250牛米的电动执行机构,结束天津不能生产电动执行机构的历史。后经多次全国联合设计和全国技术攻关,使产品历经从Ⅰ型、Ⅱ型到Ⅲ型的发展,成为20世纪80年代末中国各工业自动控制系统的主力装置。1987年底,经国家经委和国家机械工业部批准,仪表七厂引进法国伯纳德公司电动执行机构生产技术,为国内电动调节型执行器第一个引进技术产品。1990年,引进项目建成投入生产。

1991年,仪表七厂消化吸收引进技术,将产品转化为SD系列、A+RS和B+RS角行程电动执行机构。1992年,该厂完成SD系列、A+Z直行程系列的产品转化设计,并投入生产、投入市场,完全替代进口产品,获得国家科委、国家技术监督局、国家劳动部等5部委颁发的国家级新产品证书。1994年,仪表七厂在消化吸收的基础上,自主设计开发出SD系列无触点控制的电动执行机构控制器,并投入生产。

1998年,仪表七厂研制开发成功工作制达100%的SM系列产品。填补国内无100%工作制的空白。2003年,该厂完成SMA+Z直行程系列电动执行机构的研发。

2001年,仪表七厂完成8000~10000牛米大力矩的电动执行机构开发。

2002年,仪表七厂完成的SAQ系列研制,使执行机构手轮具有脱开和电动优先。

2003年,该厂完成智能型电动执行机构的研发。同年完成OAZ小直行程的研发和DY-J一体化的研发,实现老产品的升级。2004年,该厂完成SAQ系列防爆执行机构的开发和研制。

2003年,仪表七厂研发完成SK25NM,用于空调的超小型执行机构。2004年,该厂研发完成DKJ-710以及标准比例调节型技术攻关。同年,该厂完成的具有变频功能执行机构的原理试验,为开创变频产品打下基础。

2005年,仪表七厂完成具有总线型(profibus)电动执行机构开发;同年还完成从单相到三相、完全无触点的智能电动执行机构的开发,产品功能、性能接近或达到国际先进水平。

第二节 文字音像处理设备

天津文字音像处理设备生产,主要是文传机、计算机及图文终端设备、电影放映设备。

一、文传机

1990年,天津光电集团有限公司(国营第754厂,以下简称光电公司)引进国外全套先进生产线及生产工艺技术,开始以CKD(全散装)、SKD(半散装)方式生产传真机。1994年,该公司成立传真机室,开始自主研发传真机。1997年,该公司研制成功国内首款具有全部自主知识产权的"OEF238"传真机。1999年,光电公司研制成功"OEF219"型传真机,并大批量推向市场。该产品获2000年度天津市科技进步三等奖。

2000年,光电公司研制的普及型传真机"OEF116"系列传真机成功投放市场。一举打破国内低端传真机长期被进口产品垄断的历史,销售总数突破10万台。"OEF116"系列传真机获1项国家专利授权,获天津市2003年度科技进步三等奖。2001年,该公司先后有OEF316、OEF616、OEF916等型号传真机推向市场,并填补国内汉字显示传真机的空白。

2002年,光电公司开始多功能传真机研制开发。先后研发成功具有PC打印、PC扫描、PC传真功能的OEF816型传真机;具有GSM无线传真/电话/短信功能的OEF1218无线传真机;具有语音答录、无纸接收等特色功能的OEF519传真机。上述成果共获3项传真机技术国家专利授权,从而使该公司传真机自主研发水平跃上新台阶,被国内业界公认。

2003年,光电公司将研制开发出的OEF1218A无线传真机推向市场,填补国内该领域空白。当年,该公司的OEF系列传真机启用"光电通"品牌,并被评为天津市名牌产品。2004年,该公司把产品研发重点转移到高端及专用市场。先后成功研制出OEF518普通纸传真机;具有双制式来电显示、背光汉显及和弦铃声等特色功能的OEF916A+型传真机和OEF916B+型传真机。其"光电通"传真机被评为天津市50个最具知名度的产品。

2005年,该公司成功研制出国内首款宽带网络传真机和多功能激光普通纸传真机。

二、电影放映设备

1990年,天津市电影机械厂(天津市中环影像设备公司,以下简称中环影像公司)研制出东风FG35Ⅳ型电影放映机。该机采用2千瓦氙灯作光源,内置2千瓦整流器,结构紧凑,工艺先进,广泛用于小厅放映,并出口澳大利亚和英国。同年,该公司在东风FG35B型基础上,完成东风FG35D型电影放映机的研制。该机对东风FG35B型的灯箱进行改进,并增加三镜头转塔,便于镜头更换;增加自动化放映接口,便于连接不同型号的自动放映组件。

1991年,中环影像公司完成东风FG35Ⅳ—B型电影放映机的研制。该机保留东风FG35Ⅳ型电影放映机的特点;设计出弧形片窗,提高画面的稳定性;设计出电动两镜头转塔,片窗和放映物镜可同步自动更换。同时,该机还设计出1800米的供、收片系统。1992年,中环影像公司完成东风FG35E型电影放映机的研制。该机在FG35D型的基础上,对电器系统进行改进,并增加电影放映半自动化系统。

1995年,中环影像公司完成东风FG35Ⅳ-C型电影放映机的研制,采用3千瓦氙灯和内置整流器,使用范围扩大。1996年,中环影像公司完成FG35Ⅳ-D型电影放映机的研制。该机采用5千瓦氙灯和内置整流器,设计光学隔热系统,适用于大放映厅。1997年,中环影像公司完成东风FG35Ⅳ-E型电影放映机的研制,为新一代电影放映机。该机主要特点是:灯箱设计与国际接轨,可与其他国家的灯箱互换;隔仓式风冷,提高氙灯和反光镜的寿命;两镜头转塔,镜头和片窗可同步自动更换;还音系统采用红光LED为光源,后置隙缝模拟/数字立体声还音;微处理器控制自动放映系统;手动与自动放映独立,可以互补等。1999年,该公司在东风FG35Ⅳ-E放映机的基础上,完成东风FG35Ⅳ-ES双片道电影放映机的研制。该机主要用于各电影制片厂作声画编辑使用,并可放映外语或少数民族语言影片。

1994~1995年,中环影像公司完成东风FG35Ⅴ型电影放映机的研制。该机采用2千瓦氙灯,立式点燃,进一步缩小放映机的占地面积;采用弧形片窗,自动转塔,增加放映机的功能,更适合豪华小厅放映。

1998年,中环影像公司研制成东风XP35毫米循环片盘。该产品可以和一台电影放映机联用,实现单机放映。2001年,中环影像公司在国内率先完成红光LED模拟立体声还音系统的国产化,并用于东风牌各型电影放映机中。2002年,该公司完成对美国STRONG公司的TROUPERETTEⅣ舞台追光灯的消化吸收和研制。2003年,该公司研制成东风YP35毫米引片机,作为与东风XP35毫米循环片盘配套使用。2004年,中环影像公司在参考美国样机的基础上研制成3千瓦、4千瓦、5千瓦放映机用整流器。该整流器产品采用漏磁变压器,以降低消耗、提高效率,使效率由一般整流器的50%提高到80%以上。同年,该公司研制成影院、剧场用的调光器,用以控制剧场和舞台的灯光。

1999~2000年,中环影像公司研制成东风FG35Ⅵ型电影放映机。该机采用柜式结构,集灯箱、机座、整流器、电器系统为一体,工艺先进;内置2~5千瓦整流器,采用2~5千瓦氙灯,当使用5千瓦氙灯时,增加光学滤热系统;采用弧形片门和两镜头转塔,镜头和片门可同步自动更换;可变力矩收片,有良好的收片特性;采用红光LED,DOLBY模拟/SR.D数字还音系统,并可安装DTS、SDDS数字还音系统;微处理器控制自动放映和自动切换系统,切换时间可由软件设定;手动与自动独立。

2001年,中环影像公司完成东风FG35毫米3D环幕同步立体放映系统的研制。该公司早在1991年就研制出FG35毫米环幕电影放映系统,由9台电影放映机和一台还音系统组成,由主控制台控制进行同步放映,银幕为360度环形画面,使观众如身临其境。新研制的放映系统可以根据不同的需要,采用2台、4台或6台放映机并配用同步电机和变频器,由主控制台控制完成同步放映,在20分钟内误差不超过1个画格;系统中设有电机收片和自动对片装置,保证再次放映的准确性。与此同时,该公司完成东风PG35毫米循环片柜的研制,作为配套产品。2002年,中环影像公司完成东风FG70毫米水幕电影放映系统的研制。同年,中环影像公司与美国STRONG公司合作开发电影放映机。当年完成美方样机的国产化(除机头箱)试制并返销美国。

2004~2005年,中环影像公司完成东风FG35Ⅶ型电影放映机的研制。该机采用同步带传动的无油机头箱,代替原齿轮传动系统,降低成本,解决国内电影机的漏油问题。该机还采用三镜头电动转塔和带有3种片窗的弧形片门,镜头和片窗可自动更换。该机在原自动放映系统基础上进一步改进:①主控制板由输入、输出为14点增加到34点;②增加液晶显示屏,可随时用汉字显示运行状态或运行故障,便于操作和维修;③主控制板出现故障可手动操作。

第三节 信号传输器件与设备

天津信号传输器件与装备生产的高科技项目是地面导航系统。天津市是国内航空无线电导航地面设备生产基地,其研制和生产航空无线电导航地面设备始于20世纪50年代。20世纪50、60年代,采用电子管线路;20世纪70、80年代,采用电子管与晶体管混合电路;20世纪90年代以后,全部半导体化,采用中、大规模集成电路、应用微处理技术、计算机网络技术,设备实现小型化、智能化。

一、道路交通用反射器及模具

1991年7月,天津市神光新技术开发公司(简称神光公司)成立。该公司集科研、设计、生产、经营为一体,专门研制开发高速公路、城市道路用三角警告标志牌和交通工具(汽车、摩托车、自行车)各系列的反射器模具及其产品,项目纳入国家重点新技术推广示范计划。1993年,该公司持有的塑料光学反射器模具制造方法,获国家发明专利授权。

1994年,神光公司自行车广角型侧后反射器产品、普通型侧反射器产品、小幅条反射器产品、普通型后反射器产品相继研制成功。

1996年,神光公司三角警告标志牌产品、高速公路用轮廓标、梯形轮廓标及突起路标产品研制成功。其中,梯形轮廓标、突起路标分别获实用新型专利授权。1998年,三角警告牌获中国第七届专利新技术、新产品博览会两项金奖。同年2月,经国家公安部、国家交通部、轻工总会和国家经贸委的鉴定,由国家经贸委授予塑料光学反射器产品为国家级新产品称号。后经国家公安部交通安全产品质量监督检测中心、国家交通部工程监理检测中心,国家自行车质量监督检测中心、国家汽车检测中心的技术质量鉴定,以上产品均达到世界同类产品的先进水平。

2000年,神光公司被交通部、公安部、机械局吸收为标准技术委员会委员单位,由神光公司总工程师孙体生执笔起草的“机动车用三角警告牌”国家标准GB19151-2003,于2003年5月23日发布实施。同年,该公司率先建立塑料光学反射器光、色检测实验室。该检测室研究的两项成果,在国家汽车行业协会组织全国汽车检测中心进行反射器光、色检测标准的比对中,被一致认定为,解决行业检测中的共性难题。2001年,国家计量院对神光公司用玻璃微珠反光膜替代反射器作为传递物对逆反射材料光度测试系统的研究,给予较高的评价,并用这种方法,连续3年对神光公司的TR-300检测系统进行标准传递。

2003年,神光公司对三角警告标志牌SG-Q3B-5型进行改型。其特征为顶角部分具有半圆形定位和卡扣装置,获得实用新型专利权。同年,神光公司研制出道路护拦反射器、一种可调节鞋固定角度的滑雪板、超窄形三角警告标志牌、农用车警示反射器、用于道路的突起路标和汽车车身两侧的塑料光学反射器等产品。以上6个产品，均获得实用新型专利授权。

2004年，神光公司研制开发出三角警告标志牌SG-Q3B-3型、载重汽车后反射器SG-Q11型、中小型汽车后反射器SG-Q8型3种新产品，均获国家实用新型专利。同年，三角警告标志牌获天津市科技进步三等奖；SG-Q3B-5型三角警告标志牌获美国发明专利授权。

二、铁道通信

1994年，国营七一二厂（现天津通信广播集团有限公司，以下简称通广公司）研制开发出"TW-42型450MHZ B制式四频组单双工兼容无线列车调度通信系统"。该系统包括：TW-42Uz(4120)车站电台，TW-42Uc(4119)机车电台，调度总机，监测总机，手持台。该系统装备在国内的铁路干线上，用于铁路运输调度指挥，可供行车调度员、车站值班员、列车司机之间进行话音通信。

1997年，通广公司研制开发"TW-43A同异频单工无线列车调度通信系统"。其主要设备包括：TW-43A机车电台（4131、4131G、4131GA)，TW-43A车站电台(4132、4132G、4132GA)，TW-43A调度总机，TW-43A手持台，HY-464监测总机，HY-466入库检测设备，HY—463场强自动检测设备等。装备在国内铁路主干线，通过该无线通信设备实现铁路运输的调度指挥。

2000年，通广公司研制成功"DIMS无线车次号校核系统"。该系统设备主要包括：HY-4401D列车无线调度通行系统车次号机车编码器，HY-4402D列车无线调度通行系统车次号接收解码器等。用于校核实际运行列车车次号，实现对运行列车的实时追踪。

2004年，通广公司研制开发"GSM-R机车综合无线通信设备"。作为新一代列车无线通信系统，具有话音和高速数据传输功能，可用于调度员和列车司机的双向话音通信，还可以在车、地之间进行高速数据传输，将车次号、列车尾部风压数据、车况数据传送到地面，用于指挥列车运行并进行自动防护。

三、地面导航系统

（一）近程中波导航机

1991年，七六四厂研制出国内第一台全固态的K/NGF920(649)型500瓦中波导航机。采用频率合成技术、脉宽调制技术和场效应晶体管宽频带功率合成技术，双机制式，发射机故障自动监测，双机自动转换控制，双线遥控功能，天线自动调谐，全半导体设计，金属柜式结构，重量238千克。同年，该设备获电子工业部科技进步三等奖和天津市科技进步三等奖。1997年，该厂对K/NGF920(649)型500瓦中波导航机的结构设计和天线调谐器进行技术改进，应用单片机技术，研制出车载500瓦中波导航机，获天津市技术创新优秀项目三等奖。2001年，该厂研制出全固态1千瓦中波导航机，该设备在全固态500瓦中波导航机基础上，采用宽频带功率合成技术，双机制式。

1994年，七六四厂研制出国内第一部全固态型200瓦中波导航车。1997年，该厂研制出500瓦中波导航车，车内安装全固态500瓦导航机和晶体管超短波信标发射机，实现半导体化，电力消耗1.5千瓦，获天津市科技进步二等奖。

1995年，七六四厂研制出618型200瓦中波导航机。采用晶体管电路，宽频带功率放大，频率合成，脉宽调制，发射机参数自动监测，双机制式，发射机故障告警自动切换，天线自动调谐，柜式抽屉结构，机动型。

（二）近程空中战术导航系统（塔康）

1997年，七六四厂研制成功全固态航空近程导航系统地面台，采用中大规模集成电路和微处理技术，频率合成技术、晶体管功率合成技术，全半导体化设计，获天津市科技进步二等奖。

（三）近程全向信标/测距设备

1976年，七六四厂研制出国内第一部652(QX00)型全向信标台。采用晶体管，小规模集成电路与电子管混合电路。频率108～118兆赫，输出功率100瓦。系统技术指标达到国际民用航空公约附件10标准有关

VOR(全向信标)规范要求。

1987年,七六四厂研制出国内第一台621型测距设备。采用晶体管、中小规模集成电路与电子管混合电路。频率962～1213兆赫,输出功率1000瓦,末级功放为电子管。系统技术指标达到国际民用航空公约附件10标准有关DME(测距设备)规范要求。

1993～1995年,七六四厂引进技术与国外合作生产澳大利亚DVOR/DME,并于1999年试制出国产化设备。

(四)近程辅助导航设备

2002年,七六四厂研制成功双频段超短波定向机。采用中大规模集成电路、嵌入式PC机,在国内率先实现保密定向功能,获2003年度天津市技术创新优秀项目三等奖。

(五)近着陆引导设备指点信标

1958年,七六四厂试制出国内首部指点信标发射机。于1963年生产定型,被国务院军工产品定型委员会正式命名为63型信标发射机。1976年,该厂研制出背负式646型信标发射机,输出功率6瓦,全部采用晶体管电路设计,单机制式,工作温度条件-40℃～50℃。1983年,该厂研制成功国内第一台半导体化指点信标发射机,于1984年设备定型,命名KDD-645型信标发射机。1988年该厂在645型基础上,改进直流电源、增加遥控功能,研制出645A型信标发射机,技术水平国内领先。

1993年,七六四厂在KDD-645型信标发射机的基础上,减少分立器件,提高电路集成度,减小体积,减轻重量,研制出满足机动导航台装车使用的台式超短波信标发射机。双机制式,重量35千克,体积0.09立方米,仅是KDD-645型的45%。1995年,该厂进一步研制出小型化、适应装小型导航车的新一代信标发射机。该机采用集成一体化75兆赫晶体振荡器,体积0.035立方米,重量16千克。

(六)近着陆引导设备表着陆(盲降)系统

1983年,七六四厂在国内首先采用国际上先进的电子调制技术研制出米波仪表着陆系统航向信标和下滑信标。该设备于1987年设计定型,命名为“HXF-Ⅰ型航向信标发射机”和“XXF-Ⅰ型下滑信标发射机”。技术水平与国外同类产品相当,技术指标达到国际民用航空公约附件10标准Ⅱ类性能。采用晶体管、中、小规模集成电路,全半导体化设计,电子调制,具备完善的监控分系统,航向采用外场监视。双机制式冷备份,设备告警自动切换,遥控距离可达10千米。该设备于1989年获电子工业部科技进步二等奖,1991年获国家科技进步三等奖和天津市科技进步二等奖。

1993年,七六四厂在原米波仪表着陆设备的基础上,经多项重大技术改进,试制出B型设备。采用数字集成电路,提高集成度,简化线路,选用高可靠性元器件、提高设备可靠性,工作温度由0℃～50℃扩展到-10℃～50℃。该设备2005年获国家电子工业部科技进步三等奖,2005年天津市科技进步三等奖。1998～2000年,七六四厂研制出适应不同机场各种地形环境条件的高性能系列化天线系统,为军、民航广泛推广应用。

2003年,七六四厂采用中大规模集成电路、超高频场效应管功率放大,研制成功新型仪表着陆地面设备。新产品应用频率合成技术、微处理技术、计算机网络技术,其系统技术指标符合国际民用航空公约附件10标准Ⅰ类性能,达到国外同类产品先进技术水平,是新一代小型化、智能化设备。该设备2003年获天津市技术创新优秀项目二等奖。

2004年,七六四厂试制出分米波仪表着陆系统,填补国产设备空白。该系统采用大规模集成电路、嵌入式维护计算机、频率合成、微带线功率合成,技术水平国内领先。

第四节　专用仪器设备

天津专用仪器设备生产，包括物流输送设备、热处理设备、全晶体管高频感应加热装置和气象仪器等。

一、物流输送设备

20世纪80年代初，国营建津机器厂（原国营第4508厂）与国家电子工业部第十设计院联合研制工厂物流输送设备和工厂自动化设备，在对引进技术消化吸收和开发创新中，自身技术水平不断提高，产品结构和品质日臻完善。

1991～1995年，建津机器厂为全国各大彩管行业生产各种轻、中、重型悬挂输送设备，地面差速链输送机、地面辊子输送机、地面潜拖传送线、地面反向积放式输送机、地面皮带输送机，智能型积放式输送机、仓储推式悬挂输送机等。

1995～1999年，建津机器厂开发生产彩管工艺设备、电视机组装生产线、洗衣机生产线、冰箱生产线、空调器生产线、螺纹加工设备、电线电缆加工设备、电池生产设备，各种涂漆生产线、塑料喷涂生产线、清洗生产线。

1999年开始，建津机器厂调整产品结构，由电子行业拓展到汽车、摩托车行业以及重工业领域。客户涉及彩管、家电、邮政、食品、橡胶、重工、涂装、摩托车、汽车等。该厂开发生产的悬挂输送机设备远销荷兰、墨西哥、捷克、保加利亚等国家。1999～2002年，建津机器厂为深圳华为生产多种变形组装机柜生产线。

2000～2004年，建津机器厂为重庆宗申集团开发生产出摩托车发动机物流配送系统、总装系统、部装系统积放式输送机、仓储推式悬挂输送机，循环式提升机、往复式提升机，自动仓储设备、自动分拣设备、自动传送包装设备。2004年以后，建津机器厂先后与日资合作生产返来式移载机，旋转机，液压升降机，汽车输送板式链，滑撬，汽车专用提升机等。

二、热处理设备

1993年，天津市高频设备厂研制管桩用高强度凹螺纹钢筋（PC钢棒）热处理生产线成功。该线可对φ7～φ13毫米PC钢棒进行热处理，淬火温度880℃～930℃，回火温度380℃～450℃，线速度25～30米／分（φ9毫米PC钢棒），成品伸直性失高不大于0.05/米。1994年4月，该成果通过天津市经委新产品生产技术鉴定。1997年，该厂研制并生产出全晶体管高频感应加热装置的PC钢棒热处理生产线，比原生产线节约电耗20%。2002年，该厂研制出全晶体管高频感应加热装置的高速PC钢棒热处理生产线。在原有设备功率配置只增加1／3的情况下，通过对加热线圈的改造，使生产线速度达到70米/分，生产效率提高1倍，每吨生产电耗下降近100千瓦时。

2002年，天津市高频设备厂（同年更名为天津市金能电力电子有限公司）李春长、高新华、解洪滨等对原有PC钢棒热处理生产线进行研究，针对PC钢棒的加工特点，提出采用双根PC钢棒同时进行热处理的方案。2003年6月，成功研制出“双线”PC钢棒热处理生产线，使其生产能力达到126米／分（φ9毫米PC钢棒）。该项技术超过国际生产线的加工水平，以“高强度预应力钢棒热处理双线生产设备”的名称，获得国家实用新型专利（专利号：ZL2004 2 0028411.3）。2003年，天津市金能电力电子有限公司根据客户（沈阳培新钢筋有限公司）需求，开发研制拉丝与热处理同时进行加工的PC钢棒热处理“连线”生产线。该生产线自动化程度高，生产人员少。当年完成开发任务，经用户使用后证明，达到进口生产线的产量、质量水平，在节能方面超越进口设备。

2002年，天津市金能电力电子有限公司研制开发成功中国第一条采用全晶体管高频感应加热装置的弹簧钢丝热处理生产线。该生产线可对φ5～φ13毫米弹簧钢丝进行热处理，生产能力为1吨/时。2003年，金能公司再次为该用户研制出可加工φ5～φ17毫米、生产量为1吨/时的弹簧钢丝热处理生产线。

三、全晶体管高频感应加热装置

1991年，高频设备厂承担研制“高效节能的全晶体管高频感应加热装置(75kW/200kHz SIT)”。1993年成功生产出国内第一台全晶体管感应加热装置，填补国家100～200千赫兹频段大功率高频感应加热装置领域电力电子节能应用技术的空白。

1994年9月，天津市高频设备厂试制成功采用国家电子工业部第十三研究所科技攻关成果，生产TS-300D型SIT器件的高频感应加热装置。其启动、调节、保护系统等各项技术性能指标，均达到日本进口的同类设备标准。1995年，该厂先后研制出JSGC50-200、JSGC75-50、JSGC75-100、JSGC100-50、JSGC100-100、JSGC100-200、JSGC150-100等产品，并形成系列化生产，于1995年12月通过天津市经委新产品生产技术鉴定，1996年10月获国家科委颁发的国家“八五”科技攻关重大科技成果奖，同年获天津市人民政府颁发的引进消化吸收科技成果奖，1997年9月被国家科委批准为“国家级科技成果重点推广计划”项目“SIT高频感应加热装置”的技术依托单位。获1997年天津市科技进步三等奖。2004年11月，SIT高频感应加热装置成套设备系列及技术获得天津市科技进步三等奖。

1996年9月，高频设备厂成功研制以IGBT为主逆变器件的250千瓦/15千赫兹高频感应加热装置，填补国内10～50千赫频段大功率高频感应加热装置领域电力电子节能应用技术的空白。先后完成JIGC100-10、JIGC100-20、JIGC100-30、JIGC100-50、JIGC150-10、JIGC150-20、JIGC150-30、JIGC150-50、JIGC200-10、JIGC200-20、JIGC200-30、JIGC200-50、JIGC250-10、JIGC250-20、JIGC250-30、JIGC250-50、JIGC350-10的研制开发工作，形成产品的系列化生产。1997年3月获国家经贸委颁发的“八五”国家技术创新优秀项目奖。2004年1月被天津市科委确认为市级科技成果。

2002年3月，高频设备厂李春长等鉴于新器件MOSFET问世，其性能指标都优于SIT器件的情况，研制以MOSFET为主器件的高频感应加热装置，生产出以MOSFET为主器件的25千瓦/200千赫兹高频感应加热装置。同年10月，生产出75千瓦/200千赫兹高频感应加热装置。2004年12月，金能电力电子有限公司完成120千瓦/200千赫兹高频感应加热装置研制和生产。2005年开始，随着MOSFET器件的完善与更新，该公司进一步推进以MOSFET为主器件的高频感应加热装置的系列化生产。

四、气象仪器

(一)风洞

1994年，天津气象仪器厂(以下简称气象厂)在1986年生产的EDE14型风洞的基础上，成功研制出EDE14A型风洞。该型风洞全长约3米，洞体采用玻璃钢材质，支撑部分为箱体式钢架支撑，采用可控硅控制的1.5千瓦直流电机进行调速和补偿式微差压计风速输出。风速范围为0.4～30米/秒、流场不均匀性小于1.5%、流场不稳定性小于0.3 %。洞体分为大小两个实验段，大实验段尺寸为φ540×500毫米，小实验段尺寸为φ240×380毫米。改进的风洞增加了大实验段，改进了低风速的稳定性，并可对一些较大的风速仪进行检测。2004年该厂开发生产改进型即EDE14A1、A2型风洞，其中EDE14A2型风洞采用变频器控制交流电机进行调速的方式，调速更加直观准确。

2003年10月，气象厂研制成JDF1型直路风洞。该风洞洞体采用木质结构，钢架支撑。全长约19米，分为大小两个实验段。实验段的截面为正方形切圆角，其中大实验段尺寸为：1400×1400×2000毫米、切角R250毫米，小实验段尺寸为：700×700×1400毫米、切角R120毫米。实验段流场特性：气流均匀性相对偏差≤

1%、气流稳定性相对偏差 ≤0.5%、紊流度≤0.5%、气流偏角≤1°。该风洞采用变频器控制交流电机进行调速，调速范围为0.4～45米/秒。具有温度、湿度、压力系数风速修正，电子式微差压计风速采集功能，所有数据均由计算机处理，检测结果可直接打印。

（二）检定箱、观察车

1994年，气象厂研制成DJM10型湿度检定箱。该型湿度检定设备自动化程度较高，与JBB1型数字式标准干湿表配套使用，并通过通讯接口可实现湿度检定箱内湿度的自动调节、控制，其湿度检定数据处理结果可打印。DJM10型湿度箱检测精度高，使用方便，获得1997年度天津市科技进步三等奖。

1998年，气象仪器厂研制成YE-1A型气压检定箱，是各类气压仪器和气压传感器示值检定、校验的专用设备。2001年，该厂进一步开发生产出JDY1型气压检定设备，该设备由温度系数检定箱、示值检定箱和微机控制系统组合而成。

2001年，气象厂研制生产出SDM6A型雨量器。该仪器主要由承水器、储水器、雨量量筒等构成，可用于测定一定时间间隔的大气中降水（雨或雪）量。同年，该厂引进德国技术生产出SL2-1型雨量传感器。

2001年7月，气象厂生产出XCG02型气象观测车。该车具有机动灵活的特点，所搭载的设备精度较高，观测数据准确可靠，可观测高空风速、地面风速风向、地面空气的温度和湿度。转年，气象厂生产出自动气象站计量检定现场校准设施，专门用来现场校准检定自动气象站的气压、湿度、温度、风向、风速、降水、地温、蒸发、日照、太阳辐射等气象要素，解决了大量仪器的送检造成的检测空白，大大缩短了检定时间。该项目获2002年度天津市科技进步三等奖。2003年，气象厂研制出XCJ01型气象检定车，可进行温度检定、气压检定、湿度检定、风速检验、启动风速检验等。整车外形尺寸：5980×2000×2600毫米±50毫米；重量不超过42吨。

（三）自动气象站、探空仪

2002年，气象厂自主研制出最新型的AWSTJ-1型自动气象站。该自动气象站主要包括传感器、采集器和数据处理软件三部分。可根据用户需要任意连接各传感器，包括太阳辐射、CT25K云高仪、超声波蒸发传感器、感雨、日照、FD12P天气传感器、土壤湿度、PMT16气压传感器、PTB220气压传感器、PT100温度、温、湿度传感器、雨量、风速、风向、超声波风等传感器；还可与GPS定位系统、QSE101天气报文编码器、GSM通信和Modem等设备连接；能应用于气象、环保、机场、农林、海洋、水文、军事、仓储、科学研究等领域；可正常运行于各种恶劣的野外环境，甚至一些边远无人的环境极端地区；具有全自动气象数据采集、存储、处理和传送的功能；具有可靠的保护措施，包括可靠的电源控制系统、完善的防雷击、抗干扰等。该自动气象站的硬件和软件，采用模块组合开放式设计，可以灵活组合使用，操作简单，易于掌握。AWSTJ-1型自动气象站具有国际领先水平，适应于中国气象自动站的发展要求，适用于气象台站以及其他业务部门的业务需求。2003年，该厂为建设高密度自动气象站，研制成功新型的DWSZ2型温度雨量站。该站主要由传感器（雨量、温度、风速、风向等组成）、采集处理器、无线传输模块、中心站、中心处理软件等构成。至2005年，气象厂完成观测站的无线通信联网，实现远程管理更多的自动气象站。进一步自主研发出科技含量更高的自动气象站，包括梯度观测的自动气象站、全要素观测气象站等。

2005年，气象厂研制出GTS（U）2-1型数字式电子探空仪。与701型二次测风雷达配合，可完成从地面到高空30千米逐层温度、压力、湿度气象要素的自动采集测量，并实时无线传送到地面站；同时配合测风雷达完成对空间探空仪的定位，通过数据处理输出高空逐层的风向、风速。

第五节 自控 遥控系统

天津生产自控、遥控系统的代表性项目，是工业自动化仪表研究所的工业自控、电视技术研究所的工业电视监控和场所电视监控。

一、工业自控

(一)供热自控

1991年2月,天津市工业自动化仪表研究所李恩洲、张瑞军等为河北省廊坊市热力供应公司研制的"分散型微机控制集中供热锅炉系统",获1991年度河北省科技进步三等奖。1995年2月,该所承接太原烟厂锅炉微机控制系统,在国内较早采用变频器控制锅炉鼓、引风和给煤,有效解决大扰动情况下锅炉蒸汽压力控制不稳的难题,其研制成果成为该所锅炉控制的典型设计。2000年10月,天津市工业自动化仪表研究所王春鸣、于伟、冯艳华等承担完成的"抗大扰动锅炉微机控制系统",获天津市科技进步三等奖。2002年7月,天津市工业自动化仪表研究所承接沈阳惠天股份有限公司沈东热源厂供热锅炉自控系统。沈东热源厂拥有当时亚洲最大的链条式锅炉房,装有90吨热水锅炉6台。该所研制的自控系统当年完成即成功投入沈东热源厂故障调峰运行。

1998年11月,天津市工业自动化仪表研究所中标天津杨柳青电厂热网监控系统,是大型热电联产领域天津市热网自动化水平最高的系统。2000年1月,该所作为天津供热自动控制工程技术总包单位,牵头完成天津市供热工程自动化控制典型设计工作。2000年9月,该所在市八大片集中供热自控工程中承担体院北、建昌道、丁字沽供热站和厂级站、管网站等项目。

(二)生产过程自控

1992年,天津市工业自动化仪表研究所韩明远、吴广芝、孟双成等研制完成的"测量发酵罐中泡沫位置的电容传感器",经国家专利局审核,获国家专利授权。该产品是测量发酵泡沫液位的专用设备,对防止发酵经常出现的逃液、原料染菌,提高自动化管理水平具有关键作用。1994年9月,天津市工业自动化仪表研究所"VC发酵提取过程控制系统",获国家机械工业部科技进步三等奖。

1992年10月,天津市工业自动化仪表研究所完成的"TZCS-9001氮肥厂造气工段集散系统",获国家经委新产品奖。1997年12月,天津市工业自动化仪表研究所沙建庚、姜铁强等承担完成的"巢湖砂轮厂集散型控制系统",获国家机械工业部科技进步三等奖。1998年3月,"巢湖砂轮厂集散型控制系统"获国家机械工业部优秀工程设计二等奖。

1994年2月,天津市工业自动化仪表研究所张为民、沙建庚等承担完成的"瓶罐、器皿燃油玻璃池窑及微机自控系统",获国家轻工部科技进步二等奖。1995年9月,天津市工业自动化仪表研究所中标石家庄宝石集团电子玻管生产自控系统项目,该系统集玻璃窑炉、马弗炉、配料、成型控制为一体,替代进口产品。

1994年10月,天津市工业自动化仪表研究所与渤海石油公司合作,承接海南岛三亚天燃气处理厂自控系统设计、安装、调试工程。该项目是外商承包的国家重点工程。按照国际标准施工,工程顺利通过美国阿科石油公司的验收。1997年10月,该所为石油部装备局投资苏丹的石油管线项目,研制成功石油管道防腐传动控制系统。该系统采用交流变频调速控制,将预热、除锈、吹扫、加热等工艺有机结合在一起,广泛应用于石油、天然气、自来水、污水管道防腐领域,在西气东输等重点工程项目中,该产品市场占有率达80%以上。1998年6月,天津市工业自动化仪表研究所应市政工程局要求,研制成功MF-01-IC车载加油计量管理系统。该系统将油料管理直接延伸到单车,并应用IC卡作为用油计量手段,填补建设工地工程车用油计量管理的空白,获天津市政工程局2000年度施工生产进步三等奖。2000年10月,天津市工业自动化仪表研究所张为民、庞公辅、杨凯等承担完成的"输油管道防腐传动生产线控制系统",获天津市科技进步三等奖;王春鸣、刘红苗、冯艳华等承担完成的"罐区消防水自动喷淋控制系统",获天津市科技进步三等奖。

1996年5月,天津市工业自动化仪表研究所承接天津杨柳青电厂三期扩建化学水处理车间控制系统项目,同年承接太原第一热电厂化学水处理控制系统工程。

1996年10月,天津市工业自动化仪表研究所温锡海、王效国、万德平等承接四川宜宾五粮液酒厂"4.5万吨/年酒精生产自控系统”，单项合同额860万元。研制成果使该厂在糖化、液化、发酵、蒸馏各工段实现全面自动化，酒精生产控制系统的综合技术水平处于国内领先。2000年10月，“4.5万吨/年酒精生产自控系统”获天津市科技进步三等奖。2004年6月，该所承接河南南阳天冠酒厂“30万吨/年燃料乙醇生产自控系统工程”。该项目为国家应对全球石油危机而批准建设的重点工程项目，合同总额1100万元。

1998年6月，天津市工业自动化仪表研究所对天津拓维造纸有限公司产于20世纪30年代的日本纸机进行技术改造。采用西门子变频装置及PLC程序控制器S7-300，利用高速现场总线，实现传动装置的速度链控制，并明显提高软压光水平。

1998年9月，天津市工业自动化仪表研究所于方涛、冯竟等承担完成的“蓟县水泥厂水泥生产自控系统”获天津市科技进步三等奖。

（三）交通、文体及机械制造

1992年10月，天津市工业自动化仪表研究所庞公辅等研制的洛阳火车站列车到发系统获铁道部优质产品称号。1994年9月，该所完成的“火车站列车时刻到发系统”，在7个火车站投入使用，获国家铁道部科技进步三等奖。

1995年，天津市工业自动化仪表研究所任双庆、陈铭等研制的“乒乓球电子计时计分器”在第43届世乒赛上成功应用。得到国际乒联官员、裁判员和运动员高度评价，国际乒联副主席赞誉天津的电子计时计分器超过历届同类产品。当年5月，中共天津市委、天津市政府授予天津市工业自动化仪表研究所为43届世乒赛组织工作先进单位称号，任双庆、陈铭立功受奖。1996年10月，“乒乓球电子计时计分器”获天津市科技进步三等奖。

1995年9月，天津市工业自动化仪表研究所吴玉明、刘东旭等承担完成的“减速机性能试验台微机监测系统”获天津市科技进步三等奖。1998年9月，天津市工业自动化仪表研究所为天津汽车齿轮有限公司研制成功汽车自动变速器过程仿真实验设备，以探求最终经济性、最终动力性换挡规律，为开发研制自动变速器核心部件电子控制单元ECU提供建立数字模型所必需的数据。2000年2月，天津市工业自动化仪表研究所陈宝奎、孟凡中等为天津夏利汽车齿轮厂研制成功夏利汽车变速箱长途路试采集系统。2002年10月，天津市工业自动化仪表研究所承接国家科技攻关项目“汽车电控液力自动变速器智能中央控制单元ECU”。该项目为国内首例。2004年9月“汽车电控液力自动变速器智能中央控制单元ECU”，通过了受国家科技部委托，天津市科委组织，由北京科技大、航天部701所、南大、天大、天津汽车研究所、天津一汽等单位组成的专家组的国家级验收，一致认定，该成果是中国首例具有自主知识产权的ECU，达到同类产品领先水平。2005年6月，该所的“汽车液力自动变速器（AT）电控制单元ECU及AT关键技术研究”“机动车灯具配光性能测试系统”“汽车制动软管挠度疲劳自动试验机”“路灯三遥控制器”4个产品通过天津市科委科技成果鉴定。

1998年10月，该所以厂所结合、产研结合的方式，与天津市仪表八厂合作承担市科委重点攻关项目“虚拟仪器技术在智能化DCS系统产品中的开发应用”，利用国外先进图形编程语言，开发适合中国国情的新一代DCS系统可视化图形编程软件。

2003年2月，天津市工业自动化仪表研究所杜乃成等承担市科技攻关项目“冶金工业与流程工业MES系统”课题的研究。同年8月，该所中标天津钢铁有限公司高炉鼓风机站发电锅炉自控系统。该项目为天钢战略东移项目（市重点工程项目）的一部分，该所承担天钢东移项目累计合同额1000余万元。

二、工业电视与监控系统

1992年6月，由天津市电视技术研究所牵头并完成的国防科工委下达的“电视摄像技术的最新进展及在军事上的应用”调研课题，在网情报成果评审会上获军事情报成果特别奖；“应用电视技术交流会文集”获一等奖。

1992年12月，天津市电视技术研究所刘忠仁等承担完成的“防潮防腐工业电视系统”获中国有色金属工业总公司科技进步三等奖。1992年，天津市电视技术研究所完成的“摄像机防护罩内加热器”“球形扬声器外观设计”获国家专利授权(第86963、第11654)。1993年12月,天津市电视技术研究所陈惠芝、王东江等完成的“高速建材轧机备件国产化与创新”研究成果获国家冶金工业部科技进步一等奖。1993年,该所成果“焊头自动跟踪焊缝的方法装置”获国家专利授权(第21288)。1997年,“针孔型炉内高温电视系统保护装置”获国家专利授权(第270596)。1998年,“视频矩阵切换器”,获国家专利授权(第305226)。2000年,“计算机触摸屏专用机柜”获得实用新型专利证书(第388763)。

1996年6月,天津市电视技术研究所王东江、周秀云等承担,为钢铁、冶金和水泥行业研制,适于工作在700℃~2000℃炉温的“SGB高温工业电视保护装置系列产品”,获天津市科技进步二等奖。1996年12月,“SGB高温工业电视保护装置系列产品”获天津市优秀新产品一等奖。1998~2005年,该所承担完成一系列国内和天津市钢铁、冶金和水泥行业方面的横向课题,分别通过天津市科技成果鉴定。包括1998年的“中宽厚板加热炉内高温电视系统”“低温加热炉内工业电视系统”;2000年的“莱芜钢铁有限公司中型孔钢厂壁炉式高温电视”;2002年的“巢湖东亚水泥厂窑火焰检测电视”“山西三维集团乙炔车间防爆工业电视系统”;2004年的“石家庄钢铁有限责任公司热电锅炉炉内火焰高温工业电视系统”“河北鹿泉东方鼎鑫水泥有限公司水泥窑炉高温工业电视系统”“安阳钢铁股份有限公司90平方烧结机工程高温工业电视系统”“邯钢型棒材厂工业电视”“天钢汽车衡电视监控及红外检测系统”;2005年的“河南宇航化工集团双五工程乙炔车间防爆监视及监听系统”“天津振兴水泥有限公司二线工程工业电视监控系统”和“石家庄钢铁股份有限公司钢包精炼高温工业电视系统”等。

1996年12月,该所杨定军、高玉龙等完成的“ZV-1000广播系统主机”,获天津市优秀新产品三等奖。1998~2005年,该所承担完成国内和天津市其他行业横向课题,并分别通过天津市科技成果鉴定。包括1998年的“山东粮食大厦广播系统”“河南省商丘天宇大酒店广播系统”“铜陵金隆铜业公司音像系统”;2000年的“天津塘沽土地规划管局综合布线系统”“云南运气实业有限公司计算机多媒体电视管理系统”;2001年的“胜利炼油厂调运处光缆传输电视”“莱芜钢铁集团有限责任公司专家楼综合布线系统”“劳动和社会保障局卫星接收系统”“浩天房地产卫星接收系统”;2003年的“山姆士广播呼叫对讲机消防广播系统”等。

三、场所电视监控

1991年12月,天津市电视技术研究所第五研究室单学秋、黎振邦、牛玉芬等为医疗器械公司B超机科研项目配套研制的“YJ23-1型医用监视器”,获得天津市科技进步三等奖。

1995年6月,天津市电视技术研究所一举中标全国铁路最大的监控电视系统“北京西客站客运、行包监控电视系统”工程。1996年12月,“北京西站客运监控电视系统”工程通过验收,受到北京铁路局高度评价。1998年“北京西客站客运电视监控系统”,2001年“北京西站行包电视监控系统”,2004年“北京西站无柱雨棚电视监控系统”,2005年“北京西站客运综治电视监控系统”等,先后通过天津市科技成果鉴定。

1997~2004年,天津市电视技术研究所为国内各行业承担完成公共广播系统的横向课题,并通过天津市科技成果鉴定。包括1997年的“ZV-1000广播系统主机”“济南新客站公共广播系统”“昆明西南商业大厦公共广播系统”“视频矩阵切换器”“许昌亚细亚商场广播系统”“燕园国际饭店广播系统”“微机监控防爆型调度电视”“全天候调度电视系统”;1999年的“BDYIN—1播音系统控制台”;2004年的“天津市热带植物园广播系统”“天津市金元宝服饰商厦改扩建工程中的公共广播系统工程”等。

1997~2005年,天津市电视技术研究所在国内为“场所电视监控”承担完成的横向课题通过天津市科技成果鉴定。包括1997年的“西南商业大厦闭路监控系统”“济南客站电视监控系统”“沈阳新基火炬大厦闭路监控系统”;1998年的“北京建材(集团)有限公司电视监控系统”“铁路徐州站客运电视监控系统”;2000年的“沈阳航空国际邮件交换局多媒体电视监控系统”“热电厂输煤线电视监控系统”“邯郸钢铁集团有限公司工业电视监控系统”“天津市振兴水泥有限公司工业电视监控系统”;2001年的“郑州铁路上编组场电视监控系统”“天津肿瘤医院护病房电视监控对讲系统”;2002年的“滨江国际大饭店电视监控保安系统”“邯郸钢铁集团公安处保安电视监控系统”“内蒙古鹿王羊绒集团保安监控电视系统”;2003年的“安钢第二炼钢厂工业电视监控系统”“大港油田钻井平台电视监控系统”“天津交通广播电台电视监控系统”“宣化火车站保安电视监控系统”;2004年的“海河大桥收费站电视监控系统”“蓟县供电局电视监控系统”“张家口、宣化、沙城火车站保安监控系统”“多米尼加水泥厂工业电视监控系统”“安钢第一炼轧厂工业电视监控系统”“张家口车务段电视监控系统”“泰山水泥有限公司工业电视监控系统”“廊坊车站电视监控系统”;2005年的“天津医科大学第二医院有线电视系统”“轻轨东海路站泰达工交广场LED显示屏系统”“燕宇家园写字楼弱电系统”及“工业对讲机”等。

第六节　精密仪器仪表

在天津精密仪器仪表行业,充分体现出天津大学、天津理工大学等院校专家学者与相关企业实行产学研相结合的创新实力,在光电仪器、光学仪器、压力传感仪器、流量传感仪器、基因脉冲导入仪器等方面取得多项技术创新成果。

一、光电仪器

1991年,天津大学侯文富、缪贵宾、王靖等研制成功ZRS-4智能溶出试验仪,获1991年度天津市科技进步二等奖。仪器采用MCS-51单片机组成控制系统,以计算机软件代替硬件电路;采用新型号电机,与微机构成高精度转速可调系统,取代可控硅直流调速系统及笨重的变速箱。该仪器设计合理,结构紧凑,成本较低,操作方便,易于推广。仪器用于检测药品溶剂或胶囊制剂质量,对温度、转速的控制精度高,具有异常报警、故障自动诊断和自我保护的功能。其主要性能指标达到国际同类产品先进水平。

1992年12月,天津大学、徐州光学仪器总厂张以谟、郁道银、陈晨、李云青等共同完成内窥镜技术研究项目,1995年获国家科技进步三等奖。该项目完成GGN型光纤工业内窥镜系列、NT型内窥镜图像显示仪、GDN型电子工业窥镜三项成果,研制四种不同型号的GGN型光纤工业内窥镜。完成光纤工业内窥镜和电子工业内窥镜的原理设计、样机制造和产品转化,内窥镜图像显示仪器实现医用和工业用光纤内窥镜的双通道观察和图像瞬时记录。项目在国内首创GGN型光纤工业内窥镜系列,并在GGN-Ⅲ型中引入石英传象光纤束元件。在国内首先研制出具有四种不同光学接口装置的内窥镜图像显示仪。并在国内首次将CCD器件作为传象元件应用于内窥镜结构中。该仪器覆盖全国各主要大中型医院,完全替代进口同类仪器,使国内应用的内窥镜不再依赖进口,产生巨大的经济效益和社会效益。

1993年,天津大学孙学珠、陈兴梧、陈本智等研制成功BGCK-1型玻管外径壁厚测控仪,获1995年度天津市科技进步二等奖。项目组提出全反射消光原理同时测量玻管(或其他透明体)外径与壁厚的新方法;开发出由CCD远心光学系统和微机测控系统构成的独具特色的高光敏玻管外径壁厚自动测控技术,解决玻管在高速运动下测控其壁厚尺寸的难题,成果达国际先进水平。

1993年,天津大学于景良、王德福、孙鼎俊等完成全景式(SJ-2)水井检测彩色电视系统的研究项目,获1993年度天津市科技进步一等奖。该系统是一种水井检测仪器,可做全景式观测,能同时看到井四周及下部图像,且无须调焦,远近物体均呈清晰图像,具有直观性,与其他曲线式点测井法相比,其测量结果真实可靠。课题攻克全景式观测、井下高清晰度图像的探测、井下多种信号长距离传输的互相干扰以及开放式光源等一系列技术难关,测试深度可达400米,在最佳条件下观测精度可达0.1毫米,可用于观测水井结构、检查水井故障、指导打捞井中掉落物以及验收水井质量等,成功地解决困扰水文地质工作者几十年的一大难题,是测井技术上的一项重要突破,也使修井成功率大大提高。该系统主要功能和技术性能指标达国际先进水平。

2000年，国家海洋局海洋技术研究所与中国电信集团天津市电信公司刘从信、刘雪堂、林红军、王福苓等研制成功DCC-1型电池电导测试仪。根据自身条件，采用与国外不同的驱动技术，实现对电池电导的测量，具有自主知识产权，性能稳定可靠，电导测量的技术指标达到国际先进水平。该仪器应用于电池生产厂家和电池的使用单位，特别是给电信电力、铁道信号以及一些不允许停电而以蓄电池为后备电源的重要部门，提供一种有效的测试工具。获2000年度天津市技术进步二等奖。

2002年，天津大学高玉成、曲丹丹、贡立青等发明成功GWJ-3型光阻法智能微粒检测仪，获2003年度天津市技术进步二等奖。仪器采用高精度的光阻法传感器设计和闭环稳光电路以及特殊的抗干扰设计，能够准确检测微小粒子的尺寸和计数，采用先进的单片机和128×112点阵液晶显示器使其软件具备极好的扩展性。通过软件对传感器的控制，对故障进行自动判别，采用多功能的传感器进行管路系统的控制，使得液体以恒定流速准确取样计算，通过单片机控制和不同电磁阀的转换实现反冲排堵。仪器提高药品中微粒监测的准确程度，减少人为误差，提高监测效率。操作简单，使用方便，检测精度高，重复性好，其自动化程度和先进性达到国际同类产品水平。

二、光学仪器

1990年，天津大学与天津光学仪器厂合作，方国清，廖志杰，张舒东等共同完成TJ270-30红外分光光度计研究项目，获1992年度天津市科技进步二等奖。仪器首次采用计算机直接比例工作原理，实现硬件工作软件化，提高运算速度和精度。研制出长波红外干涉滤光片、线光型红外光源；采用狭缝变倍和整机增益的自动切换技术。可用于测量并记录物质在4000~400cm~1范围内的红外吸收光谱或反射光谱，可对被测物质进行分子内部结构的分析研究和对物质进行空性鉴别，实现高档次智能化红外分光光度计的自主设计和制造，替代国家对相关产品的进口，具有很大的经济和社会效益。

1991年5月，天津大学毛义、张以谟、李贺桥等研制成功LPS-I型激光粒度仪，获1994年度天津市科技进步二等奖。该仪器可快速准确测量粒径在0.3~168微米范围内的固体粉末或悬浮液的粒度分布。在测量范围内同时使用米氏散射理论和夫琅和费衍射理论，并采用2048相应单元的CCD光电探测阵列，在国内属首创。该仪器可广泛应用于化工、医药、建筑、粉末冶金、轻工及环境保护等部门的生产和科研中遇到的粒度分析问题，并可根据用户需要配置不同的附件，以实现工业上的在线检测与过程控制。

1992年，天津市光学仪器厂谷佩荣、赵振兴、孙宏伟等研制成功WFZ-25型紫外-可见分光光度计，获1992年度天津市科技进步二等奖。该产品最大限度地利用国内的最新科技成果，是国内第一台自行设计的“双光束”微机功能齐全的紫外—可见分光光度计。采用不等比100%T自动平衡原理与高精度的A/D转换和数据处理，仪器在多种数据处理功能及CRT显示、绘图打印输出等功能方面都取得明显进步。

1997年，天津市威德电子有限公司研制成功LAI-3A激光准直测量仪，通过天津市科委组织的技术鉴定，1998年获得国家科委、经委等部门颁发的“国家重点科技新产品”证书。该仪器可远距离、非接触式测量，克服现场阻隔、操作及测量工作的诸多不变；由计算机系统直接给出测量结果，减少人为因素造成的测量误差；直线性好、测量速度快、精确度高；大大降低现场测量人员的劳动强度、缩短工时、节省测量费用。适用于各种大型精密机械、基础建设设施等领域的几何量行位偏差及同轴度、直线度、平行度、垂直度等多项指标的测试与调整。产品应用广泛，获得认可和好评，填补国家空白，取得较好的社会和经济效益。

三、压力传感仪器

1992年，天津市自动化仪表二厂宋焕武、邹本礼、张士良等研制成功YTT-150A差动变压器远传压力表，获1992年度天津市科技进步奖二等奖。该产品既能现场指示压力参数，又可将压力参数转换为0~10毫安标准电流信号输出，可与电动单元组合仪表中的二次仪表、动圈式指示仪表、数字式显示仪表、调节器、计算单元及巡回监测装置组成自动记录、调节控制系统，被广泛用于石油、化工、给水、冶金、电站、轻工业等部门。

2003年，天津理工大学常明、杨保和、曲长庆等研制出金刚石薄膜压力和温度传感器，获2003年度天津市技术发明二等奖。在大面积本征金刚石致密薄膜上图形化选择性沉积掺硼金刚石薄膜，研制出电桥式自补偿温度、压力传感器样件，并进而研制出智能化、双功能（压力、温度）传感器，具有体积小、强度大、介电强度高、精度高，以及便于大量生产等特点。

四、流量传感仪器

1992年，天津市东丽区技术监督局、天津市东丽区环境保护局和天津市东丽区津东水表厂柴寿辰、马连元、刘桂全、陈兴、潘玉亭研制成功LMY明渠流量计，获1992年度天津市科技进步二等奖。采用扩散硅式压力传感器测量帕式槽内液位，用单片机对测量结果进行密度修正，并按设定打印瞬时及日、月累计量值，精度达到1.5级，优于国内其他明渠仪表。精度高、易安装、数据采集自动化，长期稳定性好且价格适中，填补天津在该方面计量器具的空白。

1992年，天津市第三电表厂石怡田、窦俊波、耿玲等研制成功工业用精密三相电度表，获1992年度天津市科技进步二等奖。该产品具有转动防垂量轻的特点，轴与轴承摩擦力矩小，轻载性能好，表柄长、转矩大、受外界附加因素影响小，有较好长年稳定性和可靠性，功率损耗小，节约电能，只相当于国内同类产品有功损耗的1/3，现在功率损耗的1/2，体积小，便于安装，节约材料。

1995年，天津大学、天津市天大泰和自控仪表技术有限公司张涛、徐英、李刚、孙宏军等完成数字式金属浮子流量计的研制，获1995年度天津市科技进步二等奖。项目针对流量传感器、角位移传感器、信号处理单元等仪表的所有重要环节进行全面系统研究，并研制仿真与实流实验平台。仪表的关键技术指标达到浮子流量计的国际主流产品水平。该成果不仅可用于化工、石油、冶金、轻工等领域中低流速流量的测量，还适用于中、高粘度流体的流量测量、水平或垂直安装的大口径管道流量测量，特别适用于环境恶劣的工况和节电要求高的野外作业。

图5-8-6-73　数字式金属浮子流量计

1999年，天津市威德电子有限公司开发成功VID-01 A/B散堆物料体积测量仪器系统，获1995年度天津市科技进步二等奖。仪器的A型为固定式，适用于使用单臂取料机的现场；B型为移动式，适用于龙门式取料机的现场。产品的测量原理基于双目立体视觉成像技术，并将最新数字图像处理、模糊识别处理与测量电视三大技术相结合。测量精度高、速度快、测量不受环境影响，不但可用于煤场的盘煤自动测量工作，也适用于盐场、散装码头、矿山料场等。

五、基因脉冲导入仪器

1996年，天津理工大学徐宝强发明LN-101基因脉冲导入仪，获1996年度天津市技术发明二等奖。该仪器是一种应用于生物工程方面基因转染的仪器，能提供高电压、大电流的尖脉冲，能在等渗生理盐溶液条件下，用于植物、动物和各种微生物细胞的电穿孔，其主要指标达到国外同类产品的先进水平。经过许多用户的使用，性能很好，完全可替代进口产品。该仪器在全国许多国家重点实验室、高等院校、科研单位、医院等单位得到推广应用。

第九章 化学工程与化学工业

1991~2005年,天津化学工业加快技术改造步伐,将大力发展海洋化工摆上重要位置。天津渤海化工集团公司(简称渤海化工集团)作为国家计划单列的企业集团,其紧密层骨干企业、即号称天津"三大化"的国家大型企业天津碱厂、天津化工厂、天津大沽化工厂,以及天津长芦海晶集团有限公司(原塘沽盐场)和天津长芦汉沽盐场,生产工艺技术创新达到新高度。天津化工研究设计院(以下简称"天化院")和国家海洋局天津海水淡化与综合利用研究所(以下简称"海水淡化所")等国家部委驻天津的科研院所充分发挥行业引领作用,在化工技术研发设计和海水化学资源开发方面取得一系列重大科技创新成果。渤海化工集团围绕重点产品生产工艺技术的改进与提高,进行化工新产品、新技术的开发,初步形成多层次的化工科研开发体系,到2005年,所属的10个市级技术中心对于企业发展起到重要技术支撑和保障作用。该集团与天津大学、北京化工大学、清华工业开发研究院等实施产学研合作项目85项,累计获得授权专利109项,形成企业的自主知识产权,提高市场竞争力。天化院作为化工部和中央企业下属的综合性科技开发企业,设有工业水处理、催化剂及载体、无机新材料等专业研发中心,建有新型水处理药剂系列产品、汽车尾气净化三效稀土基催化剂和锂离子电池用六氟磷酸锂等3个国家级高新技术产业化示范基地,集科研开发、生产经营、工程设计、工程承包、技术服务、技术咨询为一体。1991~2005年承担科研项目320余项,授权发明专利43项,获得国家省部级以上科技奖励48项。2005年在滨海新区注册成立天津正达科技有限责任公司,建设1.5万吨级新型水处理药剂及精细化学品装置,标志着在产业化道路上发展到新阶段。其下属的标准理化所,1991~2005年在理化分析和无机化工的国家标准与行业标准的制修订工作中,获得标准类国家及省部级科技进步奖励21项。

第一节 石油化学工程

天津高等院校的石油化学专家长期致力于应用科学研究,特别是天津大学的科研团队具有较强的实力,完成的"炼油分离过程强化研究与关键技术系统集成"项目获2005年度"中国高等学校十大科技进展","炼油分离过程大型化关键技术系统集成与节能"项目获2007年度国家科技进步二等奖。

一、炼油技术

1991年9月至1993年5月,天津大学与中国石油化工总公司九江石化总厂合作,杜英生、郑陵、童仲轩、林学智等共同完成催化裂化吸收稳定系统优化改造研究项目,实现原油二次加工过程的催化裂化,不改反应再生系统和分馏系统。以原吸收稳定系统为基础,应用系统模拟优化技术,探讨各工艺参数对吸收率的影响规律,继而调整工艺流程和参数,根据需要局部采用高效填料和新型内件专门技术,通过优化工艺和强化分离设备,达到增产30%以上,提高C3以上回收率和节能的目的。该项目通过优化改造在技术上取得突破,创造国内同行在相同条件下的高水平、高效益。获1996年度国家教委科技进步二等奖。

1994年5月至2001年12月，天津大学张金利、柴铭、袁兵等合作完成重油加水乳化技术的研究与应用研究。创新点在于：①利用降低界面张力、固体增强膜稳定性、金属离子的定向楔和无机助燃特性，在国内外首次采用天然两亲性生物大分子、超细无机粒子、无机盐和金属有机化合物作为重油乳化剂，燃烧过程中利用"微爆反应"、助燃、降低燃烧温度等原理，提高燃烧效率，降低污染物的排放；②优化重油乳化工艺与设备，建立当时世界上最大的日产3000吨乳化重油的生产线。获2003年度天津市科技进步二等奖。

1995年3月至2001年3月，天津大学张金利、李韡、袁兵等完成柴油冷滤性能改进剂研究与开发项目，成功开发适合高含蜡柴油用的冷滤性能改进剂。通过与油品中蜡的吸附、共晶及分散的作用，以及改变蜡晶的形状、大小及析出量，防止形成三维网状结构和蜡晶沉积，达到既降低凝点又降低冷凝点的作用。该柴油冷滤性能改进剂质量稳定，使用方便，加剂柴油质量可靠，投入使用后取得较高的经济效益。获2001年度天津市科技进步二等奖。

1998年至2005年，天津大学精馏技术国家工程研究中心李鑫钢、姜斌、孙津生等共同完成炼油分离过程强化研究与关键技术系统集成研究。项目围绕建设"千万吨级炼油、百万吨级乙烯"大型化工装置国家能源战略规划和产品工程的重大需求，开展分离过程强化研究及工程化应用，形成关键技术的系统集成。使设备效率大大提高，单位能耗降低，环境污染明显改善。该技术应用于大型炼油减压分离过程中，在广东茂名突破单套装置年炼油能力500万吨的瓶颈，在浙江镇海、上海高桥和金山石化创造800万吨/年炼油能力新记录，并在大连西太平洋首次达到1000万吨/年炼油能力的规模。该项目对于打破国外公司对大型炼油市场的垄断格局，实现中国千万吨级炼油装置零的突破，提升行业的技术水平，解决制约炼油和乙烯分离过程大型化的瓶颈问题，实现国际先进水平的规模效应具有积极的推动作用。获2005年度"中国高等学校十大科技进展"，是教育部当年对中国高校科技进展最高的评价。

1998年8月至2006年1月，天津大学、中国石化工程建设公司、中国石化集团洛阳石油化工工程公司三方合作，李鑫钢、姜斌、蒋荣兴、李和杰、张吕鸿等共同完成炼油分离过程大型化关键技术系统集成与节能研究。针对国内传统炼油技术水平低、能耗高、规模小等突出问题，研究解决炼油分离过程大型化带来的流体分布不均、设备阻力大、能耗高等技术难题和长周期运转带来的装置变形、堵塞等工程实际难题，建立大型蒸馏装置的设计、诊断和技术改造的工程学基础和方法，开发多项专利技术，实现大型炼油分离技术及装备的集成创新与系统节能。标志性成果之一是大连西太平洋石化公司千万吨级炼油项目，使国内单套炼油规模首次突破1000万吨/年，蒸馏强度由原来的3.38吨/平方米·时提高到迄今国内最大的7.96吨/平方米·时，大大强化分离过程，显著降低能耗水平（单耗下降24%），同时减少污染物的排放（SO_2排放量仅为国家标准的1/5）；应用技术还兼备柔性加工能力，适用全球23种原油的加工。标志性成果之二是中石化上海高桥分公司800万吨/年润滑油型减压装置的建设，为迄今国内成功运行的最大填料塔（直径达10.2米）和全球最大的润滑油型原油分离装置之一。该项目应用推广显著推动行业科技进步。获2007年度国家科技进步二等奖。

2003年3月至2004年4月，天津大学与大连西太平洋石油化工有限公司合作，李鑫钢、姜斌、姚元勋、李和杰等共同完成高强度加氢裂化原料减压蒸馏集成技术项目。在保持减压塔壳体不变的条件下对减压塔内件进行改造，采用多折线规整填料、多级全连通式液体分布器、具有捕液吸能作用的双切向挡板进料分布器膨胀补偿集油箱、桁架支撑梁等专利和专有技术，解决减压塔气液负荷变化大、换热量大、塔下部易结焦等技术难题。改造后，使大连西太平洋石油化工有限公司的资产和设施得到充分有效的利用，取得巨大的经济效益。该项目的完成使中国常减压炼油装置首次达到1000万吨/年的生产规模，对国内大型常减压炼油国产化技术具有标志性作用。获2006年度天津市科技进步一等奖。

2003年7月至2005年7月，天津大学与中国石油化工股份有限公司齐鲁分公司胜利炼油厂合作，李鑫钢、杜博华、刘崇洪、孙津生等共同完成稠油炼制减压分离过程大型化关键集成技术及应用项目。针对稠油炼制减压蒸馏大型化过程中的技术难题和设备要求，自主开发、研制和应用ZUPAC规整填料、悬挂式槽式液体分布器、槽盘式气液分布器、通透式填料支撑结构等新型塔内件及技术，提出全塔可视化设计新方法，建立大型蒸馏装置设计、诊断和技术改造的工程学基础和方法，开发出600万吨/年稠油炼制减压蒸馏大型化集成技术。该技术实施后，减压塔进料段的雾沫夹带达到千分之一以下，加氢裂化料中铁离子浓度降到0.3ppm以下；各侧线的产品质量均达到质量控制指标，完全满足加氢裂化原料要求；实现单套装置稠油炼制达到600万吨。天津大学稠油炼制减压分离过程关键集成技术的应用，取得巨大的经济效益。获2007年度中国石油和化学工业协会科技进步二等奖。

二、石油化工技术与装备

（一）石油化工技术

1985年1月至1990年1月，天津大学与华北油田采油一厂合作，刘庆普、哈润华、张余海、刘宏荣等共同完成互穿聚合物网络型堵水剂及堵水工艺项目。开发出能够适应不同地质结构，不同井深条件下的堵水和调剖的“互穿聚合物网络堵水剂”系列产品。其成果是根据聚合物共混改性原理，从化学组成、合成方法等着手，将应用分子设计合成两种以上水溶性高分子，在适宜条件下进行化学交联，制备出的一种互穿网络新型复合聚合物材料。进而解决不同油藏不同含水期，不同缝洞孔发育程度和油井纯油带、过渡带、水淹带的油井堵水工艺。此工艺成果对花岗石变质和灰岩高凝油潜山油藏、砂岩稠油井、含水100%死井堵后均有效。生产1100余吨在99口油井堵水，15口水井调剖，取得显著经济效益。获1991年度天津市科技进步一等奖、1992年度国家科技进步三等奖。

2003年6月至2004年10月，天津大学、中国石化齐鲁股份有限公司烯烃厂、中国石化工程建设公司三方合作，李鑫钢、张秀斌、姜斌等完成大型乙烯装置汽油急冷关键技术的研究。项目基于现代传质理论、计算流体力学、系统分析优化等基本理论和方法，针对大型乙烯装置汽油分馏急冷系统工程放大难题，通过模拟计算、实验研究开发出高效三溢流塔盘技术、低液面梯度技术、气液均匀分布技术、抗堵塞技术等多项关键技术，建立大型乙烯装置汽油分馏急冷塔的工程学方法，实现汽油分馏急冷关键技术集成创新。成功解决齐鲁司烯烃厂汽油分馏急冷塔预原址新建，新建最大塔径只能为9.2米、且要保证乙烯装置由原来的45万吨/年扩至72万吨/年的技术难题。该项目解决束缚中国乙烯急冷装置不能达标的重要难题，形成中国具有自主知识产权的汽油分馏急冷技术品牌。获2006年度教育部科技进步二等奖。

2004年12月至2006年9月，天津大学、中国石化工程建设公司、中国石油化工股份有限公司茂名分公司三方合作，李鑫钢、王子宗、张吕鸿、吴浩、孙希谨等共同完成大型乙烯装置急冷系统关键技术与集成研究。应用现代传质分离理论、计算流体力学、三维图形技术、过程分析与优化方法，建立大型乙烯装置急冷系统的工程学新方法；深入研究大型装置内气液流动与分布规律，开发高强度四溢流塔盘技术、带导向舌孔人字挡板技术、变截面变孔径液体预分布技术、新型分块盘式液体分布技术、重力型液体预分布等关键技术，解决装置大型化带来的放大效应和长周期易堵塞难题。将新开发的关键技术与该课题组已有高流速气体分布技术、热补偿集油箱和塔器桁架支撑梁等专利技术进行集成，开发应用于大型乙烯装置急冷系统的关键技术。装置改造后投料，实现一次开车成功，顺利达到项目控制指标，装置运行平稳，抗风险能力提高，获得良好的经济效益。获2009年度天津市科技进步二等奖和2009年度中国石油化工集团公司科技进步二等奖。

（二）石油化工装备

1993年，天津大学、中国石化总公司济南炼油厂、中国石化总公司北京设计院三方合作，赵汝文、唐清林、杨伯极、金伯英、苏绍清、杜英生、田华明共同完成碳钢渗铝孔板波纹填料与组合式液体分布器的研制与应用项目。开发碳钢渗铝孔板波纹填料和组合式液体分布器两项专利。采用天津大学开发的自分布填料技术，将其置于清洗段格栅填料上端，改善喷淋液初始分布的均匀性，提高洗涤效果。首创槽盘式气液分布器，具有防止雾沫夹带和升膜夹带、抗堵塞、升液位等新功能。获1995年度天津市科技进步二等奖。

第二节 化工系统优化与化工设备

1991至2005年，天津的化工系统不断得到优化，并成功研制新设备，有力地促进社会生产力的持续发展，反映出化学工程与工艺领域科技进步的新面貌。天津大学的高效规整填料及新型塔内件催化分馏技术及化工设备在国内占有很大市场。

一、化工系统优化

(一)填料

1992年9月至1993年3月，天津大学研究人员孙永利、贾绍义、张曾等共同研究新型塔内件和高效规整填料在高压铜洗塔中的应用技术，进行铜洗塔的改造工作。用250Y金属孔板波纹填料代替鲍尔环、矩鞍环等散装填料，并对填料表面进行"软化膜"处理，以增加填料的比表面积和通量，提高传质效率，增加生产能力；用网格式液体分布器代替喷头式液体分布器，以提高操作弹性，减小气体带液量；用溢流式与筛孔式相结合的再分布器代替截锥式再分布器，以改善液体的分布状况，提高传质效率。该技术将新型塔内件和高效规整填料应用于高压铜洗塔的改造，具有创新性，技术路线合理。获2000年度天津市科技进步二等奖。

1998年9月至1999年10月，天津大学与大庆炼化公司合作，由李鑫钢、魏强、徐占武、孙津生等共同完成新型填料集成技术在催化分馏和吸收稳定系统中的开发应用研究。针对林源炼油厂实际运行中出现的生产问题和技术问题，对催化裂化系统进行改进：①首次采用双向波纹填料、不同型号的波纹填料、格栅填料等新型填料技术完全取代板式塔结构，提高分馏效率和处理能力；②设计高弹性液体分布器技术，对其进行相应的彻底改造；③采用新型高效规整填料及塔内件技术对吸收稳定装置的各塔进行改造，包括将解吸塔改为双股进料、对整体工艺实施先进的流程模拟技术获专利14项，其中新型填料技术和双股进料新工艺在国内外属首创。获2004年度科技进步二等奖。

2000年5月至2000年11月，天津大学与锦州石化天元集团公司合作，由陈青松、李鑫钢、李杰、孙津生等共同完成新型填料技术在碳九分离中的应用研究。成果包括：①利用计算机模拟优化技术，在国内首次采用三塔流程，解决碳九芳烃分离装置中存在的装置加工能力低、主要产品偏三甲苯纯度低手收率低以及轻溶剂油过量、均三甲苯损失量大等问题，在此基础上，为装置增加富集均三甲苯产品，为后续流程生产纯偏三甲苯打下良好基础；②三塔流程中各规整丝网填料塔设计时采用大直径丝网填料塔填料盘增强技术、通透式填料支撑结构、填料段初始分布填料、大直径单级槽式气液再分布器等先进填料塔设计技术，解决大直径丝网填料塔中经常出现的填料段上表面中心下沉、消除填料段下部普遍存在的气体涡流和易堵塞倾向、降低分布器在塔内的空间需求，使填料塔处于理想的结构状态，从而确保装置的稳定操作。成果应用范围广、投入产出比小，经济效益显著。获2003年度天津市科技进步二等奖。

2004年12月至2005年4月，天津大学精馏技术国家工程研究中心与山东久泰化工科技股份有限公司合作，孙津生、段永升、田玉峰、王得现等合作完成甲醇精制过程强化研究与品质提升关键技术的开发应用研究。对山东久泰化工科技公司甲醇装置生产中存在的问题进行分析和研究，在不改变塔体的情况下，将预精馏塔中进料口以上塔板及加压塔中部和顶部两段塔板更换为天津大学研究开发的高效、低压降的组合式规整填料，使塔的总理论板数达到合理值；常压塔不采侧线，塔底液沸点降低，从而使原来的高压流程变为低压流程，即加压塔顶蒸汽与常压塔底的温差增大，有利于塔内甲醇的分离，提高甲醇品质；将预精馏塔部分底液与常压塔塔底液汇聚进入补加的回收塔中作进一步处理，提高装置处理量。装置改造后，甲醇精馏塔处理量突破20万吨/年的处理能力，产品质量全部合格。获2006年度中国石油和化学工业协会科技进步二等奖。

（二）造粒

1991年6月至2001年6月，天津大学康仕芳、陈松、赵君等合作研究成功振动喷流造粒技术。对外加振动下射流断裂机理进行研究，建立外加振动下射流断裂的数学模型，并进行实验验证。研究各种操作因素（振动频率、振幅、孔径、射流流速、物料物性、喷嘴结构尺寸、振动方向等）对射流断裂为均匀液滴的影响，得到产生均匀液滴的操作参数范围。进行中试及工业规模的放大实验，研制成功适用于大规模工业化生产、具有自主知识产权的大功率、高温型振动喷流造粒分散装置。与国内外同类技术相比，振动喷流造粒工艺过程简单，设备投资少。该技术成功填补国内空白，技术经济指标达到国际先进水平。获2001年度天津市技术发明奖二等奖。

（三）后处理

2000年，天津渤海化工集团大沽化工厂研究人员刘建文、魏永涛、汤吉彦等完成聚合物后处理技术开发项目。通过对悬浮法聚氯乙烯汽提塔、汽提工艺、干燥器、干燥工艺等后处理技术的攻关，使汽提后聚氯乙烯浆料中含VCM达到国际先进水平，树脂质量明显提高。实现计算机对生产过程的优化控制，达到均衡生产、降低能耗的目的。大沽化工厂PVC分厂后处理三线采用该项攻关技术三年，产品质量稳步提高，能耗逐年降低，特别是树脂残留单体含量降到较低水平，全部达到卫生级树脂的要求。大沽化工厂率先转让给河北宝硕股份有限公司化工分公司4万吨/年规模后处理技术，于2000年5月一次开车成功，各项技术指标符合设计要求。获2000年天津市科技进步二等奖。

二、化工设备研制

1997年10月至1998年11月，天津大学研究人员张卫江、胡金榜、宗润宽等与河北省藁城市聚丙烯厂裴瑞唐、鲍素霞等共同完成均三甲苯生产新工艺技术设备研究。确定利用偏三甲苯常压液相烷基化生产均四甲苯的技术路线联产均三甲苯，工艺路线简单、操作方便、设备投资少、产品质量高。可在一次反应后，经精馏和结晶分离，得到均三甲苯和均四甲苯两种产品。由于该工艺技术和设备先进，产品质量提高，可以稳定地生产纯度≥99%的均三甲苯产品。2001年获天津市科技进步二等奖。

1999年，河北工业大学李春利、李柏青、刘继东等研究开发新型立体传质塔板。具有生产能力大、分离效率高、操作弹性大、能耗低、压降低、抗堵塞以及适宜处理易发泡物料等诸多优点，广泛应用于石化、化工、制药等行业的挖潜改造、节能、环保等项目中，在国内28个省市的大中型企业应用的该塔设备超过1000座，有效地解决生产中的瓶颈难题，对企业产品质量的升级换代具有推动作用。同时，在降低原材料消耗、降低能耗、减少环境污染等方面的社会效益显著。该成果具有自主知识产权，为国际首创，性能达到国际领先水平。获2003年天津市科技进步一等奖。

第三节 催化剂工程

天津在催化剂产品及其装置的研发中，有驻津科研院所的创新成果，也有相关企业和专家学者的研发成果。

一、YS型系列银催化剂的工业开发和应用

1993年，天化院开展“YS型系列银催化剂的工业开发和应用”项目研究，进而注册中国发明专利“乙烯

氧化制环氧乙烷氧乙烷高效银催化剂”，被评为中国专利优秀奖。银催化剂制备是乙烯催化氧化制环氧乙烷的核心技术，是影响EO/EG装置物耗的关键因素。天化院与北京燕山石油化工公司研究院经过多年合作，持续攻关，开发的YS型系列银催化剂适用于SHELL和S.D.等不同工艺的EO/EG装置，其选择性、稳定性和活性逐年不断提高，追踪或达到世界同期工业银催化剂的先进水平。其中，YS-4型银催化剂工业化开发应用，于1991年被评为国家科技进步二等奖。该项目申请中国及国际发明专利，发明涉及乙烯氧化制环氧乙烷的含银催化剂及其载体的制法和用途。该载体经浸渍银化合物和助催化剂溶液，干燥活化后，用于乙烯氧化制环氧乙烷，其选择性高达82~84%。该项发明分别获得欧洲（其指定国为英国、德国、荷兰）、美国、日本和印度的专利权。采用该专利技术生产的YS系列银催化剂占有85%的国内市场，催化剂销售额总计达3亿余元人民币，为国家节省外汇4500余万美元。

1996年，天化院进一步开发YS-6银催化剂。用于国内7套EO/EG装置，催化剂生产获经济效益2080.6万元。由于节约乙烯和增产环氧乙烷，为应用厂家创造的经济效益为23211.6万元；其中扬子、上海、燕山还利用YS-6催化剂适应高负荷运转的特点，在不改变乙烯氧化反应器的前提下，分别对各自装置进行扩能20%~50%的改造，提高环氧乙烷产量和产品的竞争力，对于中国EO/EG行业的技术进步是有力的推动。YS-6银催化剂比国外同类催化剂堆积密度低20%以上，同等情况下可为厂家节约催化剂购置费用。YS-6催化剂覆盖国内70%以上的市场，可用于国内所有EO/EG装置，并可以向国外推广。该项目1998年获中国石化协会科技进步一等奖；1998年获国家科技进步（推广类）二等奖；2001年获国家“九五”科技攻关优秀成果奖。

1999年，天化院接续开发YS-7型银催化剂。平均选择性比YS-6型银催化剂提高一个百分点，初始反应温度低5~10℃，适合于高负荷装置，适用于SHELL和S.D.等不同生产工艺，其性能达到国际最新工业银催化剂先进水平。YS-7银催化剂于2000年上半年成功地应用在辽阳石油化纤公司EO/EG工业装置，考核性能达到国际最新工业银催化剂水平，并显著提高该装置的可操作性。YS-7型银催化剂用于现有装置的扩能改造，为应用厂家提高装置产能，增加经济效益。YS-7银催化剂比国外同类催化剂堆积密度低20%以上，同等情况下可为厂家节约催化剂购置费用。国内EO/EG装置推广应用该催化剂，年节约乙烯达7000吨，价值达2500万元。YS-7型银催化剂于2001年开始应用于天津联化、扬子石化、上海石化、茂名石化和燕化化工一厂，取得显著经济效益。2005年，该项目获中国石化协会科技进步三等奖。

二、顺酐催化剂及装置

（一）苯法顺酐成套生产工艺技术

1995年，中河化工厂在引进美国SD公司1万吨苯法顺酐生产工艺的基础上，通过消化吸收二次开发，研制出国内第一套8800根管的苯氧化反应器，并建成投产。1998年，开发研制国内第一套11000根管的万吨级苯氧化反应器和国内第一套12000吨脱水精制技术，1999年建成投产。2002年，自行开发研制单台套20000吨能力的脱水精制技术，于2003年建成投产。其苯法顺酐成套生产工艺技术达国际先进水平，在全国推广应用。

（二）对顺酐的核心技术—催化剂的攻关

1993年，中河化工厂自行开发的40克苯氧化顺酐固定床催化剂产品技术获得天津市科技进步一等奖。

1999年，中河化工厂在不断提高负荷的基础上，瞄准世界领先的国外公司产品改进配方，自行研制器外活化技术和设备，并申请专利，使催化剂的收率、选择性、寿命等主要性能指标达到或接近国外公司产品水平。

2002年，中河化工厂TH—3B高负荷、高活性顺酐催化剂成功地应用于1.5万吨顺酐生产装置上，每吨催化剂比进口价格低16.5万元，共节约催化剂费用290万元。1993至2005年，中河化工厂共生产顺酐催化剂332吨，创产值6640万元，实现利税1900万元以上。

三、苯酐催化剂及装置

1991年，溶剂厂自行开发60克/立方米苯酐催化剂和生产工艺，成功地应用在自行设计的5000吨/年邻二甲苯法制苯酐生产装置中。突破40克/立方米工艺爆炸极限生产技术的瓶颈，使苯酐60g/m^3生产工艺及装置首次实现国产化。其中，5000吨/年苯酐生产装置及工艺获得化工部科技进步一等奖、国家科技进步三等奖；苯酐60克/立方米催化剂获天津市优秀新产品一等奖。

1995年，溶剂厂逐步开发80克、90克苯酐催化剂和苯酐生产新工艺，其中80克新工艺应用到2万吨/年生产装置之中，居国内领先地位。苯酐反应器设计制造技术由原来的5000吨发展到3万吨，居国内领先水平。

1998年，河北工业大学王延吉等开展应用超临界态合成沸石型超强酸促进催化反应的研究，开发出由甲醇气相氧化羰基化直接合成碳酸二甲酯(DMC)和用DMC代替光气合成甲苯二异氰酸酯(TDI)的催化剂及相应工艺，使DMC和TDI生产更接近于洁净化工生产的要求；并且DMC和TDI合成工艺的耦合可望实现零排放的化工过程。在优化的反应条件下，碳酸二甲酯时空收率为785 g/l-cat.h，实现合成碳酸二甲酯的连续生产工艺，较好地解决其他碳酸二甲酯生产工艺存在的环境不友好等问题。

2002年，河北工业大学王延吉等开展碳酸二甲酯及其系列产品甲苯二异氢酸酯的合成研究。系统研究甲醇气相氧化羰基直接催化合成DMC反应过程，设计制备多相催化剂，其催化合成DMC的空时收率居国内外最高，确定该催化剂失活原因和再生方法。研究由DMC与芳胺合成异氰酸酯的洁净催化反应过程，包括甲苯二氨基甲酸甲酯(TDC)固相催化剂开发、TDC分解制备TDI工艺条件的优化。分别采用两种工艺研究碳酸二苯酯(DPC)的洁净合成，采用苯酚氧化羰基合成DPC，开发新型高效负载型催化剂，DPC收率达到40%，居国内外先进水平；利用DMC与苯酚酯交换反应合成DPC，开发新型高效氧化铅-氧化锌催化剂，DPC收率达到45.6%，在国内外文献中是最高的。该项目通过绿色化学与传统化学工程理论及新材料化学的结合，在国内率先提出"DMC和TDI两个绿色单元过程耦合"以及"DMC与酯交换法合成DPC两个绿色单元过程耦合"，实现"零排放"的化工过程。DMC和TDI两个工艺处于工业放大实验阶段。该成果获2002年天津市技术发明二等奖。

同年，河北工业大学王延吉等开展包覆金属络合物超微细催化剂及碳酸二苯酯洁净合成研究。对苯酚氧化羰基化法和酯交换法合成碳酸二苯酯(DPC)的洁净化工过程进行研究，开发出一种超微细包覆型催化剂Pd-Cu-O/SiO_2。在该催化剂的纳米级颗粒上，贵金属活性中心被包埋或半包埋在载体SiO_2颗粒内，加强贵金属的附着力，因而在反应过程中不易流失，催化活性下降慢，有效延长催化剂寿命，降低生产成本。在有机碳酸酯和异氰酸酯的研究中，王延吉等共发表学术论文70余篇，被SCI、EI收录53篇，获得中国发明专利8项。

四、机动车尾气净化催化剂

2001年，天化院研究人员肖彦、季文璠、薛群山等承担完成的"新型汽车和摩托车尾气净化催化剂研制"课题，通过天津市科委组织的专家鉴定。开发应用于汽车和摩托车尾气污染物净化的催化剂项目，课题研制的LH90型、AX100型两种尾气净化催化剂较好地解决结合强度，具有优良的催化活性和耐老化性能，其配方与制备工艺为国内首创、达到国际先进水平，具有良好的产业化前景。封装成净化器后，在催化剂的作用下，将尾气中的有毒污染物CO、HC在催化剂表面吸附，与表面吸附的氧或气流中的氧发生氧化反应；污染物NOx吸附在催化剂表面，与催化剂表面或气流中的还原剂发生还原反应。其间，自主开发3效催化剂生产的干混预研磨的浆液制备技术、加压密封的预浸渍涂附技术、热气流负压的干燥技术等，具有创新性。开发的夏利轿车用催化剂和催化器，经过相当于80000公里行车试验的强制老化试验后，性能完全达到限值要求。2003年，建设完成50万升汽车尾气净化三效稀土基催化剂产业化项目，被确定为国家级高新技术产业化示范基地。

五、负载型纳米新型催化剂

2001年，南开大学化学学院陶克毅主持承担的"负载型纳米新型催化剂"研究课题纳入天津市重大科技攻关项目。适应纳米科学、纳米材料和纳米技术向各个领域扩展的形势，该课题开展催化剂的纳米化研究和应用，研制负载型纳米载体和负载型纳米非晶态合金新型催化剂与纳米过渡金属氮化物催化剂，以该新型催化材料取代贵金属铂、钯、钌、铑催化剂，取代以骨架镍为加氢催化剂污染环境且安全性差、而其在化学工业中应用广、用量大且长期依赖进口的问题。该课题的前期研究获得国家自然科学基金、教育部科技重点项目、教育部博士点基金、天津市自然科学基金等多项基金的支持，在国内外发表20篇论文，申请（公开或授权）6项发明专利。课题在大量前期基础研究的前提下，开发若干新型纳米载体和负载型纳米催化剂，重点是负载型纳米非晶态合金催化剂和纳米过渡金属氮化物催化剂，在制备方法上形成系列专有技术。

第四节　精细化工

1991至2005年，天津精细化工研究以生产新型精细化学品或改造旧工艺，缩短反应步骤，以达到降低原料消耗，提高产品质量，减少环境污染等为目的，研究开发出能够满足医药、染料及某些特殊行业对特殊精细化学产品需求的多项成果。天津工业大学研制性能优良的多种化学纤维用油剂和助剂，天津大学的2-氰基吡嗪的开发与应用，天津大学与天津双孚精细化工公司、北京燕山石化技术开发设计公司合作开发的树脂法双酚A生产新工艺，天津理工大学研究成功高品质H-酸生产工艺等，达到国内领先水平。

一、化纤油剂与助剂

（一）化纤油剂

20世纪90年代初，天津工业大学王金榜、申兆才、郑帼等研制SL-240涤纶弹力丝后加工油剂。其配方合理，工艺成熟，加工性能良好，经国内十余家化纤厂和五种不同机型编织厂使用，普遍认为各项理化指标和应用性能均达到国外同类先进产品水平。此后，他们研制FSC-168涤纶高速纺油剂，因合成工艺和配方合理，耐热性、平滑性、抗静电性等各项物化指标良好，可纺性好，满足化纤厂生产工艺要求，综合性能达到日本同类产品水平，在国内领先。2000年，该项目获天津市科技进步二等奖。

同期，天津纺织工学院研究人员研制成功NL-250锦纶-66帘子线耐高温纺丝油剂。其主要性能及技术指标能够满足正常纺丝工艺的要求，制成的帘子布、轮胎等产品的各项指标达到和接近配套的国外油剂水平，填补国内锦纶—66FDY耐高温纺丝油剂的空白，减少使用引进成套设备和技术对化工原料的依赖。

20世纪90年代中期，天津工业大学郑帼等研制成功干法腈纶纺丝纺纱油剂，填补国内腈纶干法纺丝纺纱油剂的空白，各项物化指标和性能达到进口的同类油剂产品水平。

2000年，天津工业大学郑帼、魏俊富、刘燕军等完成锦纶高速纺系列油剂的研制与开发。研制生产出锦纶POY油剂、锦纶FDY油剂、锦纶弹力丝DTY油剂3种锦纶高速纺系列油剂。

2002年，天津工业大学郑帼等完成新型涤纶短纤油剂的研制与开发。开发出TDS-2000涤纶短纤油剂，具有高碳醇磷酸酯碳原子数分布合理、单体合成工艺稳定、产品适用范围广等特点，其综合性能达到国际先进水平。

2004年，天津工业大学郑帼等完成“涤纶可分散短纤维助剂”的研制。针对可分散涤纶短纤维国内无专用助剂的现状，根据可分散短纤维对助剂的特殊要求，自行设计合成出高分子量的聚醚和多电荷中心弱阳离子型的表面活性剂作为平滑和抗粘结剂，并对配方进行优化，在国内首次成功研制TFS—90型可分散涤纶短纤维油剂，其整体技术达到国际先进水平。

（二）化纤助剂

1999～2002年，天津工业大学魏俊富等完成高档丙纶细旦纤维纺丝整理剂研究项目。在国内外率先研制出耐硬水、可直接使用自来水配制的短丝整理剂，抗静电性优良。其弹力丝整理剂能够快速退绕，高速纺丝整理剂能解决对聚氨酯摩擦片的溶胀及快速润湿问题。获天津市2002年度科技进步二等奖。

2001年,郑帼等完成干法腈纶造粒剂的研制项目。根据腈纶聚合物造粒原理,从表面活性剂的造粒性能着手,通过对配方和特殊单体的设计研究、优化选择,在国际上率先研制出干法腈纶聚合物造粒剂。同时,郑帼等完成腈纶聚合物造粒剂的研制与开发,在造粒过程中加入表面活性剂,降低水与腈纶聚合物之间的界面张力,使表面活性剂在腈纶聚合物的表面形成吸附膜,从而使水迅速进入聚合物之间,由于水分子的凝聚力使聚合物快速成型,减少水的用量,节约干燥能源,改善粒子的成型,增加粒子强度,减少在烘干过程中聚合物粉末的产生,节约丙烯腈原料,减少安全隐患。获2003年天津市科学技术进步奖二等奖。

二、香料与染料

(一)香料

1992年10月至1993年6月,天津大学孙经武、姚芳连、冯亚凯等研究成功以MTBE法生产对--叔丁基苯酚新工艺。用甲基叔丁基醚(MTBE)代替异丁烯、叔丁醇、卤代烃等做酚类的烷基化剂生产对-叔丁基苯酚是该技术成果的核心,其创新点包括:①为苯酚的烷基化反应创新一种新的烷基化剂;②甲基叔丁基醚(MT-BE)作为烷基化剂代替异丁烯、叔丁醇、卤代烃,生产烷基酚具有成本低、来源广泛、运输方便、简化生产工艺等特点;③采用廉价、运输方便的MTBE取代原工艺中的异丁烯,使得成本降低,利润提高。首次在国内实现较大规模的生产装置,具有一定的国际市场竞争力。获1995年度天津市科技进步二等奖。

1999年11月至2003年8月,天津大学那平、马新宾、黄宗凉、等共同完成黄樟素加氢合成二氢黄樟素的研究与开发项目。使用RaneyNi加氢催化剂在企业已建设的加氢生产装置上完成300吨/年黄樟素加氢合成二氢黄樟素的工作;利用已开发的非晶态镍催化剂,通过技术调优,在原生产装置不变的前提下,生产能力提高到600吨/年;在温和的反应条件下(80℃,0.8MPa)进行加氢反应,产品二氢黄樟素含量≥95%(色谱分析),加氢反应总收率>97%。利用非晶态镍催化剂开展其他相关原料的选择性加氢研究开发,为产业化提供技术储备。成果经企业应用,结果表明工艺路线先进,设计合理,具有流程简单,操作方便,安全稳定等优点,并具有良好的通用性,应用前景广阔。获2003年度天津市科技进步二等奖。

(二)染料

1990年1月至1993年10月,天津大学、沈阳化工研究院与天津染料公司(染料研究所)三方合作,周春隆、张文生、张允中、穆振义、杨鸿敏等共同完成4-氯-2,5-二甲氧基苯胺的合成研究与开发项目。就苯二酚为原料的还原反应等工艺条件,进行中型实验,制备色酚AS-IGR,进一步与3,3-二氯联苯胺反应合成C.I颜料黄83,其中间体达到国外同类产品水平。创新点在于:①合成工艺短,改六步反应为四步反应,工艺简化,设备投资少;②选择特定溶剂及有机类型催化剂,提高氯化反应选择性,使氯化产物不经分离直接进行硝化;③以催化加氢方法替代铁粉还原工艺,显著减少三废排放量,提高氨基纯度。所采用的生产工艺路线合理可行,收效高,技术成熟;具备工业生产条件,且减少“三废”,提高产品质量。该产品填补国内空白。获1997年度国家教委科技进步二等奖。

1997年,天津理工大学李绍武、吕金魁、郑嗣华等研究成功高品质H-酸生产工艺。对传统的工艺进行重大改进,优选工艺条件,有效地控制ω-酸的含量,使之低于1%,同时采用废液套用,工艺中过量的酸、碱和生产中产生的副产物无机盐返回工艺中参加反应,从而形成一条“提高质量、减少污染、降低成本”三者并举的高品质H-酸生产工艺,并于1996年年初成功投入大规模生产,质量得到国际上几家大跨国化工公司认可,出口创汇,取得良好经济效益。获1997年天津市科技进步一等奖。

1999年4至2000年12月,天津大学李韡、王以强、张金利等研究成功高纯2.5-二甲氧基-4-氯苯胺制备新工艺。以苯二酚为起始原料,采用烷氧化、氯化、精密分离、硝化、还原等五步过程,对高纯2.5-二甲氧基-4-氯苯胺制备过程进行优化,获得新工艺,并进行工业实施。用该技术生产的2.5-二甲氧基-4-氯苯胺的纯度≥99%,达到国际先进水平,生产成本低于国外同类产品。获2003年度天津市科技进步二等奖。

2005年,天津理工大学和天津理工产业股份有限公司李绍武、郑嗣华、李梅彤、温同生等完成高档有机着色材料的工艺研究与产业化项目。在高品质中间体（1-萘-8羟基-3,6-二磺酸、1-氨基-4-溴蒽醌-2-磺酸）合成工艺研究并成功实现产业化基础上，致力于项目的终端产品——高档有机着色材料（P.R.179、190、144、177、149，C.I.BK、RD13等）生产工艺的研究开发，成功实现规模化生产。项目利用在中间体合成不同单元反应中引入反应助剂，优化单元操作条件，解决中间体纯度低对产品色差的影响；以固相法替代传统的溶剂法合成功能染料，解决溶剂对环境的污染，形成一条新的合成工艺路线；以水为介质、多烷基卤化胺为相转移催化剂的反应替代溶剂体系，合成高档有机着色材料，提高产品质量和转化率；采用连续分级湿研磨超细化处理工艺进行商品化处理，解决功能性染料在红外伪装迷彩着色分散性能斑点，使产品达到瑞士CIBA质量标准；探究有机着色材料物理特性与应用性能间的规律，添加衍生物，对着色材料实施特殊的表面处理，解决在商品化过程中对物理特性的控制。创建完整的高性能高档有机着色材料系列产品的规模化生产工艺，达到国际先进水平，产品60%出口，累计销售收入1.2亿元，利税4000多万元。获2005年度天津市科技进步一等奖。天津大学等单位张敏华等人完成的“树脂法双酚A生产新工艺”，获得2005年度天津市科技发明一等奖。该技术工获得14项国家发明专利，其中5项核心专利已在主要工业国家获得授权，形成了具有完全自主知识产权的成套树脂法双酚A生产新技术。

图5-9-4-74　高档有机着色材料的工艺研究与产业化

图5-9-4-75　树脂法双酚A生产新工艺

三、活性剂及化学助剂

（一）活性剂

1986年3月至1991年11月，天津大学研究人员谌竟清、宋正孝、姜志新等成功完成离子交换从等电点结晶母液中回收谷氨酸新工艺研究。采用“铵型树脂吸附—调整后工艺料液洗脱”的新工艺流程，克服常规离子交换工艺中铵对谷氨酸的吸附竞争，使谷氨酸的总回收率可提高到90%。酸、碱消耗低，能耗低，水耗低。成果在国内推广使用，具有突出的经济效益与社会效益。获1992年度国家教委科技进步二等奖。

1993年，南开大学研究人员阎虎生、程晓辉、倪爱国、何炳林等研制成功新型大孔弱酸性阳离子交换树脂（D113-Ⅲ）。与之前只有德国的拜耳公司生产的高质量的同类产品（LewatitCNP-80）相比，D113-Ⅲ的产品质量达到、部分指标超过拜耳公司产品，且所用原料易得、价廉。与国内原技术相比，不仅质量提高，而且工艺过程简化，原料成本只相当于原来的60%。该成果于1994年实现产业化，产品广泛用于电力、石化、制药、纺织印染、环保等行业，完全取代进口产品，并出口到20多个国家。获2001年度中国专利优秀奖和2002年度天津市技术发明二等奖。

1998年，天津大学研究人员李永丹、王日杰、李玉敏等完成铁基高温变换催化剂的基础研究项目。开发低铬高活性催化剂设备的专利技术，研究硫与铁催化剂的相互作用，取得成功的机械强度优化方案和可靠性评价方法，提出影响该项国产催化剂质量提高的控制因素，是领先的科学认识，具有实际指导意义。项目执行过程中以实验室新认识为依据，为乌鲁木齐石化总厂化肥厂分析催化剂强度失效原因，并选择可用催化剂，建议的操作方案保证该厂的长期稳定操作。获1998年天津市自然科学二等奖。

2001年，天津师范大学研究人员赵增国历经10年开发研制完成吡啶系列产品工艺。设计的光氯化反应及配套设备结构合理，设置光反射模板及滤波技术，成功地解决反应过程中的聚合、焦油化技术难题，实现光氯化反应的高转化率及高选择性，光氯化反应吡啶转化率达到95%，产品2—氯吡啶的纯度高于98%，氯代吡啶总收率超过80%，以其超过国际上20%的转化率受到宝洁、联合利华等数家跨国公司青睐。

2005年，天津大学和河北华煜化工股份有限公司完成二硝基二苯乙烯二二磺酸新型氧化工艺的开发与应用研究。项目进一步阐明硝基甲苯邻磺酸（NTS）氧化反应机理，建立氧化反应新的动力学模型；将固体微粒技术应用于NTS氧化过程的强化，大幅度降低能耗、提高收率，拓展多相反应技术新的应用领域；开发NTS酸钠非碱制备、碱的回收利用和NTS精制三项关键技术，应用于NTS氧化工艺大大降低碱耗量，降低成本；经过实验室研究、中试放大和工业化试验，相继开发出新型间歇氧化工艺和连续氧化工艺。在河北华煜化工股份有限公司实现工业化生产，2001～2004年累计节支3.74亿元。获2005年度天津市科技进步二等奖。

（二）化学助剂

1990年1月至1992年12月，天津大学研究人员吴锦元，陈宁，何杰等研究成功高浓度二乙烯苯提纯新工艺。立足于国产阻聚剂，对分离技术进行精确电脑模拟计算、测定脱离危险点的新工艺参数、对原有提纯工艺进行改进、进行低压力降塔内件和超大通量波纹填料充填提留段的设计。采用新工艺新设备提纯易聚合的高浓二乙烯苯，并经两年生产验证成功；采用双塔釜式串联流程，巧妙解决釜温过高的问题；采用塔身顶部连续加入阻聚剂的方法，防止堵塔，系该项目独创的关键技术；对进料点以下的提留段，采用特殊制造的超大通量的波纹填料，防止粘性高沸物堵塞填料的可能性，对防止堵塞十分有效。获1994年度国家教委科技进步二等奖。

2001年12月，天化院、冶钢集团黄石无机盐厂的研究人员共同承担完成3000吨/年红矾钠（$Na_2Cr_2O_2 \cdot 2H_2O$）新工艺中试课题。采用添加少量促进剂的造粒焙烧技术，解决有钙焙烧工艺多年未能解决的回转窑炉料结圈难题。无钙造粒焙烧工艺使生产过程粉尘污染小，空气中含尘量减少60%以上。由于返渣作填料和排渣量少，铬矿利用率高，铬矿消耗（以Cr_2O_3=50%标矿计）≤1.20吨／吨产品。与有钙焙烧相比，矿耗降低约10%，可充分利用铬矿资源。无钙造粒焙烧铬铁矿生产红矾钠新工艺，中试试验铬的氧化率比有钙焙烧高5%～10%，提高设备的生产能力，相应地降低能耗和产品成本，对铬盐工业向大型化、集中化方向发展提供有利的技术条件和经济条件。该成果技术上有重大突破，工艺先进合理，获国家发明专利。

2002年，天化院研究人员完成重大科技攻关项目"含示踪剂的阻垢分散剂的研制"项目并实现现场应用。创新点在于，将特定的荧光物与特定的聚合物合成为示踪型阻垢分散剂，可由测定产品荧光强度直接得知药剂浓度。

第五节 聚氯乙烯技术

聚氯乙烯作为渤海化工集团公司的主导产品，经过多年坚持不断地改进与创新，从生产装置、工艺技术到生产品种，在国内处于领先地位。

一、聚氯乙烯新品种研制

1992年，天津化工厂完成高聚合度聚氯乙烯树脂TH—2500型号的工业性试验和TH—4000型高聚合度聚氯乙烯树脂中试，高聚合度聚氯乙烯树脂达到国内领先水平，获得1993年度天津市科技进步一等奖。

1993年，研制成功聚氯乙烯球型树脂，被评为市级优秀新产品。

1994年，在天津化工厂建成聚氯乙烯研究中心和精细化工试验基地，并被国家批准为国家级聚氯乙烯新材料试验基地。利用国产助剂HPMC CRT-50代替日本进口60SH-50，在聚氯乙烯生产中推广应用。同年5月，国家化学工业部在该厂组织聚氯乙烯助剂国产化现场推广会。

1995年，完成TH-4000高聚合度聚氯乙烯树脂采用国产助剂改进配方的中试。

1996年，完成均聚型聚氯乙烯掺混树脂中试，为工业性试验奠定基础。

1997年，采用复合终止剂代替原单一终止剂，使SG-3型聚氯乙烯树脂白度100%达到优级品。

1998年，天津化工厂的氯醋共聚树脂完成30L小釜试验，填补国内空白。

1999年，"系列聚氯乙烯掺混树脂开发与研究"项目被列为国家级技术创新项目，当年完成工试技术的开发，并申请发明专利。

2000年，天津化工厂"高抗冲高流动聚氯乙烯专用树脂开发与应用研究"项目列为市科委重大攻关项目，当年完成小试研究。2001年完成中试技术的开发。2002年1月通过市科委鉴定验收。2002年高抗冲聚氯乙烯树脂被评为国家级新产品。该产品抗冲击强度≥30千焦/平方米，流动性好，适合生产挤出型材和注塑管件，产品技术和性能均达到国内领先水平。

2001年，天津化工厂完成"具有核壳结构的高抗冲聚氯乙烯树脂的研制与开发"和"纳米复合聚氯乙烯抗菌专用料研制与技术开发"两项课题，均为天津市重点科技攻关项目。形成高抗冲聚氯乙烯树脂和高流动聚氯乙烯树脂两个牌号产品，具有抗冲强度高、流动性好的特点，适合生产挤出型材和注塑管件。

2004年，天津化工厂完成消光树脂、氯醋共聚树脂、氯醋共聚掺混树脂、VCM-纳米碳酸钙原位聚合树脂及耐热聚氯乙烯树脂等具有市场潜力的新品种的开发，为聚氯乙烯走上多品种道路提供技术支持。

二、树脂产业化

2001年，天津化工厂通过加大功能型聚氯乙烯树脂向产业化转化的进程，将聚氯乙烯掺混树脂和球型树脂两个国家级技术创新项目实现产业化，2003年6月建成3.5万吨/年生产线，并通过市经委验收，两项目技术均达到国际先进水平。2003年下半年共生产树脂1.25万吨，创产值9875万元，实现利税3500万元。2003年自行开发的用于生产SG-7型和SG-8型的单一聚乙烯醇分散体系配方，在中试成功的基础上，用于大生产，全面提高聚氯乙烯质量，降低成本，当年实现利润89.7万元。聚氯乙烯注塑专用树脂在开发系列品种的同时，逐步实现产业化。2005年生产注塑树脂3.3万吨，销售收入24750万元，实现利税4620万元。

三、原料生产工艺和装置改进

1991~2004年，渤海化工集团聚氯乙烯原料生产工艺发生重大改变。1991年聚氯乙烯生产工艺全部为电石法。1999年以后逐步采用国际先进的乙烯氧氯化法、联合法、进口VCM直接聚合法，使聚氯乙烯生产工艺实现4种路线并存的格局，提高产品原料适应性和产品竞争力。2004年氧氯化法聚氯乙烯达30万吨，占该集团聚氯乙烯总量的29%。2000年，天津渤海化工集团(股份)有限公司、天津大沽化工厂肖卫国、刘建文、李增禄等科研人员完成的"聚合工艺优化与控制"项目成果，获得2000年度天津市科技进步一等奖。该项目在国产30 m^2PVC聚合釜工艺中，首次采用反应中间连续注水工艺，以降低PVC反应过程中浆料黏度，从而提高传热系统，缩短反应周期，并可同时降低水比，提高单釜产量，达到提高生产强度的目的；首次采用反应前期粗料监测技术，从而保证操作人员在反应1.8~2.5小时内判断反应是否正常，降低废品率；首次采用泵出料技术，从而减小因泵出料不净造成的废料增多及因再次聚合造成的产品中含"鱼眼"多的问题；首次将反应后期缩短降压时间应用到大生产中。该项目在天津大沽化工厂整个系统运行后，取得良好的经济效益，在聚氯乙烯行业中起到示范作用，具有很大的推广价值和社会效益。

2003~2004年，大沽化工厂在此基础上开发热水入料新工艺，缩短聚合反应时间，调整水油比，清釜周期由100釜延长至150釜以上，使聚合釜的生产能力进而提高8 %~10 %。2004~2005年大沽化工厂开发全国最大的20万吨PVC后处理装置和相关技术，包括高效节能汽提塔、内热式沸腾干燥床、产品筛分、静态混料及DCS控制系统等，使装置在产质耗等各方面达到国际先进水平，产品竞争能力提高。

第六节 海水与盐化工技术

天津是较早开展海水化学资源综合利用的地区。天津长芦海晶集团有限公司通过产学研合作,开发高纯溴化氢、溴丙烷、二溴甲烷、海水提取硫酸钾和硝酸钾、气态膜溴等新技术、新产品,生产工艺均为国内首创,有的达到国际领先水平。海水淡化所把海水淡化和海水提钾作为重点开发项目,同时也实验研究海水提镁、提碘、提溴等课题,并且逐步具备规模化应用与产业化发展的条件。天化院在无机盐及新材料开发方面取得若干重大创新成果。

一、重质纯碱新技术

1980年,天津碱厂开发研制成功液相水合法生产优质重质纯碱新技术,建成4000吨/年中试生产线,生产出显像管玻壳用的优质重质纯碱,质量达国际先进水平,填补国内此类产品空白,属国内首创。1988年通过市级鉴定。在此基础上,1992年建成5万吨/年优质重质纯碱装置,并使生产实现连续化,产品质量稳定,保证显像管玻壳和高档玻璃工业的需要,不但减少进口,而且开始大量出口创汇。为进一步满足市场需求,经过科技人员的不断创新与改造,又将该技术进一步放大,实现产业化。1993年建成20万吨/年优质重质纯碱装置,取得产业化成果。2002年该项目获天津市科技进步一等奖,天津市技术创新优秀项目一等奖。2005年,重质纯碱产量达到48.21万吨,居国内第一。

图5-9-6-76 天津碱厂开发研制成功液相水合法重质纯碱生产工艺

二、海水化学资源开发

(一)溴素提取

1999年,由海水淡化所承担的"高效低毒农药二溴磷100吨/年中试"课题完成二溴磷的合成技术。继而按照国家规定,连续两年进行两地大田药效试验及原药的毒理、毒力试验,建立一整套分析检测方法,同时完成二溴磷原药和乳油的两项地方技术标准。制备的二溴磷标准品通过质谱、元素分析、核磁共振等诸项检测,填补产品和生产技术双项空白。

2001~2003年,海水淡化所承担的"气态膜法海水(卤水)提溴新技术研究"项目取得较大进展。

2004~2005年,该所完成"气态膜法海水卤水提溴技术与示范研究"课题项目,建成国内最大规模的"气态膜法海水卤水提溴百吨级装置"。

(二)钾盐提取

1994年,海水淡化所为河北省大清河盐场化工厂建成"1万吨/年苦卤与氯化钾制取硫酸钾"生产装置。

1995年,由河北工业大学袁俊生带领的研究团队开展沸石法海水提钾产业化技术研究取得进展。该项目在改性天然沸石离子交换理论研究的基础上,解决钾从海水中高效富集和节能分离的难题,研制成功海水苦卤提取硫酸钾高效节能技术、海水直接提取硝酸钾技术。完成海水苦卤提取硫酸钾300吨/年中试和海水提取硝酸钾200吨/年中试,开发出具有原创性自主知识产权的离子筛法海水提钾高效节能技术。1万吨/

年海水提取硝酸钾示范工程于2005年底建成投产，处于国际领先水平。该成果1996年获中国轻工业科技进步二等奖、1995年获国家海洋局科技进步二等奖、1998年获国家发明三等奖。

1996~2000年，由海水淡化所承担的“海水(卤水)提取硫酸钾技术研究及产业化”课题项目取得进展。形成“1000吨/年钾镁硫肥中试技术”“离子交换法海水卤水直接提取硫酸钾新技术”和“万吨级盐析法苦卤与氯化钾制取硫酸钾技术”等3项科研成果。

2001年，天津长芦海晶集团有限公司与河北工业大学、天津市海发化学工业研究所共同完成200吨“海水提取硝酸钾”中试项目。用该方法生产的硝酸钾在保证质量的前提下，降低产品成本，具有较强的市场竞争力，在海盐同行业具有普遍的推广价值。该技术的开发成功，为解决国内严重的钾资源缺乏问题开辟一条新的渠道，是国际上首次成功应用沸石吸附技术并实现百吨中试结果的项目，技术达到国际领先水平。2004年，1万吨硝酸钾示范工程列入天津市重大高新技术产业化项目，2005年开工建设。

同年，天津科技大学教授马欣华等开展运用相平衡理论建立钾盐提取新技术研究。以丰富的制取海盐后母液——苦卤资源为研究对象，探讨水-盐相图中介稳体系与平衡体系中饱和区域的变化规律，发现在介稳体系中有其不同的成相区，可以从卤水中直接分离出氯化钾，建立具有工艺流程短、节能效果显著等特色的钾盐提取新工艺。以混合溶液相平衡理论为指导，找到在氨液中，硫酸钙与氯化钾反应直接转化为硫酸钾的方法，与国外氨化法相比，具有明显优势。该两项工艺研究成果，开拓海盐苦卤提钾的新技术，在制盐工业和环境保护等方面具有明显的经济效益和社会效益。撰写专著一部，研究成果通过专家鉴定。

图5-9-6-77 海水提取硝酸钾技术设备

(三)镁盐提取

2000年，海水淡化所承担的“盐田卤水提取镁肥、高纯镁系物技术研究及应用开发”项目取得“盐田卤水提取硫酸镁肥中试技术”成果，建成1000吨/年中试装置。2001年，该所又研发出“无机功能材料硼酸镁晶须”，该材料具有成本低廉、性能优越等特点，于2005年启动天津市重点项目“新型功能材料硼酸镁晶须百吨级示范工程研究”。当年，海水淡化所还完成“100吨/年浓海水制取氢氧化镁中试技术”的研究。

图5-9-6-78 氢氧化镁生产设备

三、无机盐及新材料

1991年，天化院研究开发的DBS系列耐高温无机彩色颜料项目获国家发明奖。DBS系列耐高温无机彩色颜料，可分为陶瓷专用、搪瓷专用和耐热涂料专用等3大系列50多个品种，广泛用于日用陶瓷、美术陶瓷、建筑陶瓷、卫生陶瓷、玻瓷玛赛克、人工彩石米、日用搪瓷、美术搪瓷、装饰搪瓷、高温塑料、建筑涂料、高温涂料、防腐涂料等行业。该系列产品采用微晶化包裹技术、晶体晶化稳定技术、矿化催化合成技术和废物清洁化利用等多项先进的工艺技术，具有着色能力高、色调纯正、呈色稳定、釉烧范围宽、耐腐蚀、耐温、耐光、耐候等优良性能。高温大红包裹系列颜料、高温铬锡紫色颜料和翡翠绿系列颜料等产品的制备工艺达到国际先进水平。锆铁红颜料、钒锆蓝颜料、玫瑰红颜料和棕色系列颜料等产品制备工艺达国内先进水平。DBS系列颜料产品质量优良，生产成本低廉，吨产品利润平均约为1.5万元，具有很强的市场竞争力。

1993年，天化院开发研究人员承担的“丙酮缩氨基硫脲”项目被评为化工部科技进步三等奖。丙酮缩氨基硫脲(ATSC)采用硫氰酸铵、水合肼、硫酸与丙酮一步法合成,工艺路线先进合理,填补国内空白,达到国际先进水平。实验表明,该法工艺可靠,设备简单,生产稳定,成本低,收率高达82%。产品中主成分达97%,铁含量<0.001%,熔点172±3℃。经化工部北京化工研究院和国家无机盐检测中心检测,丙酮缩氨基硫脲产品各项技术指标符合Q/SFHJ001-92企业标准所规定的要求,并达到国外同类产品水平。"三废"处理经北京市环保检测中心检测,符合国家排放标准。该产品经多家用户试用,质量稳定,效果好,可代替进口产品,满足引进的聚氯乙烯生产线和国产设备对终止剂丙酮缩氨基硫脲的要求。丙酮缩氨基硫脲的研制,对于扭转终止剂依赖进口而耗用大量外汇的不利局面,促进中国的聚氯乙烯的生产起到重要作用。

1997年,天化院开发研究的"大比表面积造粒白炭黑"项目被评为国家"八五"科技攻关重大成果奖。该项目成果是把粉末白炭黑进行造粒,解决白炭黑粉末飞扬,污染环境及堆密度低的问题,在白炭黑造粒提高密度解决粉尘飞扬的同时,为保证橡胶制品的机械性能,成品粒子在橡胶混炼过程中,必须均匀充分地分散,因此,关键技术是造粒挤压力的调节及干燥器的选择。技术经济指标:技术指标:比表面积:≥180平方米/克;堆密度:≥320立方米/立方厘米;粒度:0.105毫米筛余量3%以下,并满足子午午线轮胎对白炭黑补强性能的要求。每吨产品消耗:耗电760kWh;耗热678万kcal;收率≥97%。与喷雾法干燥白炭黑比较,经测算,造粒品每吨成本比喷雾法低300元,增加效益800元。产品便于输送,能够避免和减少粉尘飞扬,具有环境效益。

同年,天化院开发研究的"预分散颗粒型氧化锌"项目被评为国家"八五"科技攻关重大成果奖。预分散颗粒型氧化锌(ZnO-80)是氧化锌含量为80%的成型产品,是随着子午线轮胎生产线的引进而采用的一种新型橡胶助剂,具有优异的分散性,不起尘,便于运输贮存。该产品选用油酸酯作为分散剂、合成蜡为分散介质。产品质量符合国外公司的标准,指标为:ZnO79%~81%,灼烧减量19%~21%,PbO≤0.25%,Mn≤0.001%,Fe≤0.02%。产品用于子午线轮胎生产可以取代进口同类产品,性能达到国际先进水平。

同年,天化院开发研究的"由固体污染物-含铬铝泥生产磷酸铝铬"项目被评为化工部科技进步三等奖。含铬铝泥是铬盐生产过程排出的固体污染物之一。6价铬含量高,呈胶泥状,很难用水洗出。堆放过程中脱水风化使表面析出铬酸钠,遇雨则溶解后渗入地下或排入河流等水源,对环境造成极大危害。含铬铝泥属于胶性沉淀物,难于过滤,具有对无机盐吸附/夹带严重的特点。该治理技术针对这一难题,找出合适的助滤剂,使胶性氢氧化铝失去吸附活性,使含铬铝泥中的氢氧化铝与铬酸钠达到较高效率的分离。分离后的大部分铬酸钠返回到铬盐生产中的中和工序,使6价铬得到回收,小部分铬酸钠经还原后与氢氧化铝一起溶于磷酸制成磷酸铝铬。该项技术既治理环境污染,又减少大量铬资源的流失,使铝泥变害为利,工艺技术可靠、生产效率高,是有实用价值的新技术。主要技术性能指标:三氧化二铝含量7.9%,三氧化二铬含量4.2%,磷酸盐含量36.7%,密度1.58克/立方厘米。该技术用助滤剂处理铬铝泥,铬铝泥分离率达到98%以上,在处理铝泥方面具有独创性。所得的产品磷酸铝铬,由于耐火温度高达1730℃~1750℃,可作为高温粘结剂用于耐火材料工业、铸造行业,及在高温下使用的金属表面防护涂层。该技术在国内各铬盐厂推广,具有重要经济和环境效益。

2001年,天化院开发研究的"无钙焙烧生产红矾钠新工艺"项目获国家"九五"科技攻关优秀科技成果奖。中国生产红矾钠采用污染环境特别严重的有钙焙烧工艺,生产过程中产生大量铬渣,含6价铬(Cr^(+6))高达1%~2%,还含有1%~2%的致癌物铬酸钙(CaCrO_4)。铬渣解毒成本很高且难以处理,构成严重影响社会和环境的一大公害。该项目是国际上解决红矾钠生产严重污染生态环境问题的新技术,焙烧物料不加任何钙质物作填料,控制工艺技术条件,可用自产铬渣作填料并能循环使用。添加促进剂和造粒剂的造粒焙烧。物料在高温焙烧中不结圈,铬的氧化率和矿的利用率提高10%~15%。排渣量减少65%~70%,渣中污染环境的有毒6价铬离子减少90%~95%。铬渣易解毒达标(Cr^(+6)≤5ppm)排放,还可以综合利用做陶瓷铬黑颜料,有良好的经济效益和环境社会效益。无钙焙烧生产红矾钠新工艺,创造性地解决铬渣不含致癌物铬酸钙(CaCrO_4),铬渣物相组份分选,排除过量杂质硅、铝组份的富集,从而铬渣耐高温,可循环作填料使用。造粒焙烧物料不结圈,提高铬氧化率,熟料易浸取和洗涤,洗渣含Cr^(+6)<0.14%,提高资源

利用率，降低红矾钠产品生产成本。2005年，应用该技术实现产业化的“10kt/a无钙焙烧生产红矾钠新工艺工业性技术开发”项目，获中国石化协会科技进步一等奖。

2002年，天化院研究人员承担的“锂离子电池用六氟磷酸锂及电解液生产技术开发”项目被列入国家“863”攻关计划。六氟磷酸锂及电解液主要应用于锂离子电池制备过程，是锂离子电池的关键材料之一，也是国内锂电池材料中久攻不下的难题之一。项目的主要内容为六氟磷酸锂及电解液产品制备技术的开发、年产80吨六氟磷酸锂及年产600吨电解液产业化装置的建设、电解液产品在锂离子电池生产企业的推广应用。该项目采用国产原料无水氟化锂、五氯化磷、无水氟化氢，经特别精制后，在无水氟化氢溶液中经反应、结晶、分离、干燥得到产品。六氟磷酸锂电解液的制备，是将六氟磷酸锂与有机碳酸酯类混合溶剂按比例配制，通过加入适当的添加剂制备出各种用途的电解液产品。所使用的关键装备具有自主知识产权，不仅做到安全生产，而且产品纯度高，成本低，能够满足锂离子电池电解液的使用要求。该项目获得国家发明专利4项，产品被评为国家级重点新产品。2003年，天化院与河北邢台矿业集团合作，共同出资组建天津金牛电源材料有限责任公司，专门实施该项目的成果转化，建成年产80吨锂离子电池用六氟磷酸锂及年产600吨电解液的生产装置。利用自产的六氟磷酸锂配制的电解液在日本索尼（无锡）电子公司、深圳比克电池股份公司等知名锂离子电池制造企业中大量应用，为中国锂离子电池产业的快速发展作出贡献，取得良好的经济和社会效益。

2003年，天津电力技术中心（天津电力试验研究所）在长效防污闪RTV涂料基础上，应用纳米级气相二氧化硅技术，开发完成“有色RTV防污闪涂料的研制”项目。该成果开发出的白色和蓝色RTV防污闪涂料，具有良好的电器绝缘性、憎水性、憎水迁移性、抗电蚀性、耐侯性和不可燃性，同时具有醒目效果，有利于观察，可提高涂料敷施工质量、避免漏涂，并可避免施工中的火灾危险。该项目获得2003年度天津市科技进步二等奖。

第七节 工业水处理技术

天化院长期开展工业水处理工程技术研究，取得多项科技成果。1998年，国家工业水处理工程技术研究中心通过国家科委组织的验收，该中心的人员、产品技术等依托天化院。2005年，经科技部批准，作为产业化生产基地，依托工业水处理工程技术研究中心建立的天津正达科技有限责任公司整体迁入滨海新区空港物流加工区，该公司以开发和生产工业水处理药剂及石油化工催化剂为主，是集研发、生产、技术服务、技术咨询、技术转让、信息服务和进出口业务于一体的高新技术企业，可年产1.5万吨新型工业水处理药剂、年产3万吨工业节水专用化学品等，为工业企业节水减排提供先进的技术支持和完善的服务。

1993年，天化院研究人员研制的“煤气洗涤循环水阻垢剂TS-611”项目被评为化工部科技进步三等奖。TS-611分散阻垢剂是为防止结垢、维持水质稳定的处理剂，能在高温、高钙硬、高PH值条件下，抑制碳酸钙垢、铁垢、锌垢的沉积，保证高炉、转炉的正常生产。该阻垢剂采用共聚—分离—复配3步间歇法工艺路线和工艺条件，并经1立方米生产装置考核，合成工艺成熟合理，生产操作易于控制，产品质量稳定。其外观、物性指标与日本DP-202阻垢剂基本一致，阻垢性能经实验室评定、现场模拟评价及生产应用考核与日本DP-202相当。 TS-611分散阻垢剂在宝钢高炉和转炉煤气洗涤水系统投放试用6个月，污垢附着温度合格，满足水处理运行工艺要求，可完全替代日本的DP-202阻垢剂，且价格约为日本DP-202的40%~50%，是煤气洗涤水阻垢剂的新品种，具有国内先进水平。煤气洗涤水阻垢动态模拟试验装置及生产监测试验方法测定的洗涤水污垢附着速度切合生产实际，优于国内常用的静态挂片测定方法，具有独创性。

1994年，天化院研究人员承担的"盘锦天然气化工厂循环冷却水处理技术研究及应用"项目被评为辽宁省科技进步三等奖。针对盘锦天然气化工厂年产13万乙烯装置所使用的水质及循环冷却水系统的工况条件，研究人员进行全面分析，开展一系列模拟试验研究，确定免去石灰预处理工序而采用碱性水处理药剂配方的水处理技术。经两年多的开车运行后检查，设备基本无垢，腐蚀轻微。该技术的成功应用，能够保证乙烯装置安全、稳定、长周期、满负荷生产，同时具有节水意义。碳钢腐蚀率<0.02毫米/年，污垢热阻<6.9×10^{-6}平方米·度/千米，达到国际先进水平。该项技术适用于乙烯行业循环冷却水处理装置。全年节约水费2060万元，同时保证乙烯装置安全、稳定、长周期、满负荷生产。

同年，天化院研究人员承担的"TS-809粘泥防止剂的研制及工业应用"课题被化工部评为科技进步二等奖。该成果为国家科委专用化学品专项，适用范围广泛。该品活性组分为3-异噻唑啉酮，属有机硫化合物。具有高效杀菌作用。采用分子加成制备含酯基的巯基化合物，并利用酰胺化反应进一步制成酰胺，该酰胺化合物可在卤素作用下闭环制成异噻唑啉酮。其性能达到国外公司的N-7330指标。外观淡黄-黄绿色液体；气味微：pH值3-5；比重20℃1.030-0.002克/毫升；冻点：-4℃解冻后复原；溶解性：易溶于水和低级醇。巯基丙酸甲酯的合成，国外采用的催化剂为硫化铵，该课题组选用的是氨水，既提高收率（比用硫化铵高2%），又降低生产成本。该产品经济效益可观，为宝钢等企业节约大量费用。由于TS-809粘泥防止剂具有高效、广谱、低毒等优点，在国内工业循环冷却水方面被广泛采用，除取代进口药剂外，还取代国内许多工厂水处理所用的季铵盐、二硫氰基甲烷等药剂。该药剂还成为主要的出口药剂品种之一，开发应用前景广阔。

1996年，天化院研究人员承担的"工业水处理用阻垢分散剂TS-612的研制和应用"项目被评为化工部科技进步三等奖。TS-612是含磺酸盐的多元共聚物，易与磷系药剂复配，适合多种水质不同企业的循环水系统中，生产采用水为溶剂，以过硫酸盐为引发剂的溶液聚合工艺路线，控制容易，技术成熟，产品性能稳定。反应周期短，能耗低，原料易得，生产过程无"三废"污染。TS-612阻垢分散性能良好，特别是对氧化铁垢具有优良的分散性能。应用中试产品3年的结果表明，达到国外同类产品先进水平。

1999年，天化院研究人员承担的"TS系列工业水处理药剂及其技术推广"项目被评为天津市科技进步一等奖，后被推荐评为1999年度国家科技进步二等奖。该项目涉及天化院工业水处理技术领域多年攻关的系列成果，既包括各种药剂的合成、配方的筛选和自控、监测方法，又包括工程设计和设备配套，是化学、物理、生物等多学科技术方法的系统集成，其应用领域包括冶金、化工、发电、石化、轻工、医药、纺织、电子、油田、城建等所有用水的国民经济部门。TS系列工业水处理药剂是在不断研究合成创新药剂的基础上，针对冷却水系统不同的水质及工况条件，组成复合配方及应用技术，在循环冷却水中起到缓蚀、阻垢、分散和杀菌灭藻的作用，保证生产系统长期稳定运行，从而达到节水、节能、减少排污和保护设备的目的；在污水治理方面，针对不同工业废水的污染物特点，对印染废水、新闻纸脱墨废水、钢铁厂集尘水、化肥厂造气废水、高温灰水等，通过化学、物理、生化等多种技术的集成、组成配套的工业废水治理及回用技术，达到减少污染物排放，节约水资源的目的。该项目并且建立多项推广示范工程，达到国内领先和国际先进水平。"TS系列冷却水处理药剂研制及应用"1987年获国家科技进步一等奖，列入"八五""九五"期间国家科技成果重点推广计划；1992年开始列为国家环委会A类最佳实用技术，向全国推广，经济和社会效益显著。

2004年，天化院研究人员承担的"高浓缩倍率工业冷却水处理技术及智能化在线监控系统"研究项目被评为天津市科技进步二等奖。鉴于国内工业冷却水约占工业取水量的60%~70%，循环冷却水浓缩倍率一般只有2~3倍，重复利用率低，单位产品耗水量与国际先进水平存在较大差距的状况，该项技术将中国工业系统普遍运行的浓缩倍率由2～3倍提高到5倍以上，解决循环水水质因提高浓缩倍率而引起的严重结垢及腐蚀问题，从而提高工业用水的重复利用率并最大限度地减少排污量。该技术通过高效阻垢分散剂、缓蚀剂的开发并组成最佳配方，与智能化在线远程监控技术进行有效集成。高浓缩倍率工业冷却水处理及智能化在线远程监控技术开发成功后，首先在天津石化公司乙烯厂建成应用示范工程，结果表明：使循环水系统浓缩倍数从3倍以下提高到5倍以上；控制水中总硬+总碱为1600毫克/升（以$CaCO_3$计），高于国外公司的先进水平（1470毫克/升）；阻垢、缓蚀效果均达到石化公司标准，现场监测平均粘附速率≤15mcm，腐蚀速率≤

0.075毫米/年；应用自动控制装置后，加药和排污全部实现自动化，使得循环水系统运行更加平稳，提高企业的管理水平，取得显著效果，年节水60万吨，直接经济效益300多万元。该技术在化学品性能对比、自动化控制水平及运行费用等方面超过国外相关技术，标志着中国工业水处理技术水平上升到新的高度。

2005年，天化院研究人员参与"关键油田化学品开发与产业化应用"项目研究。"油田化学品产业化开发及应用示范"项目是国家"十五"重点科技攻关项目，以石油大学（华东）为主要技术依托单位，17家企业、300名科研人员参与，进行完井液、油田水处理、调剖堵水、井筒化学处理、3次采油用聚合物、3次采油用表面活性剂、破乳剂等重点技术及油田化学品产业化开发与应用示范和发展战略的研究。天化院研究人员在承担的项目中，成功开发新型油田缓蚀剂、高效杀菌剂、反相破乳净水剂、无污染阻垢分散剂等油田水处理药剂及配套的油田水处理技术，完成中试及产业化建设，形成具有自主知识产权的油田水综合处理技术，获得国家发明专利一项。产品及技术经过2003~2004年两年时间应用，油田生产系统腐蚀率最低控制到1MPY（0.02mm/a）以下；硫酸盐还原菌含量控制在0~10个/毫升，腐生菌和铁细菌含量<10个/毫升；控制高矿化度油田产出水的碳酸盐的阻垢率≥95%，锶钡垢的阻垢率≥90%；净水最终处理效果含油量<5毫克/升，悬浮物含量<1.0mg/L，满足或优于油田水处理控制指标。该研究成果还在南海东部、西部、渤海等海上油田及胜利、吉林等内陆油田建成应用示范点，在渤海、胜利等油田建立实验基地。应用课题成果在海上油田取代跨国水处理公司的产品技术和服务，取得南海油田35%以上的市场份额，为企业节省30%以上的水处理技术和服务费用。课题成果不仅有效地推动国内油田化学品产业化开发和应用示范，也使中国油田水处理技术水平有较大提高。该项目被评为中国石化协会科技进步一等奖。

第八节 橡胶化工技术

天津橡胶化工技术研发，主要是在特种专用橡胶化工和工程轮胎系列化工两个方面。

一、特种专用橡胶化工

1991年，自行车胎厂研制的山地系列自行车胎达到国内领先水平，获天津市科技进步二等奖。

同年，有机化工一厂开发建设中国北方唯一的一套200吨/年促进剂NOBS新产品生产线。1992年开发建设的200吨/年促进剂DPG达到国内领先水平。

1995年，大中华橡胶厂为第43届世乒赛开发的高档运动鞋，受到国家乒乓运动界的好评。

1996年，合成材料研究所开发复印机墨粉用共聚树脂，产品可替代进口。

1997年，有机化工一厂完成400吨/年新产品促进剂TMTD的研究开发项目，填补橡胶助剂品种的空白。1997年建设国内第一套1000吨/年促进剂系列产品造粒生产线装置，2003年又将该技术实现产业化，建成3000吨/年造粒生产线。

1999年，合成材料研究所开发的轿车车身焊缝胶及防石击底胶，获得天津市科技进步二等奖，并被评为国家级新产品。该所自行开发的HA-321纸餐具使用阳离子中性施胶剂，是可降解环保用品的配套产品，1998年获天津市技术创新优秀项目二等奖。

1999年起，力生化工厂重点开发新型系列抗氧剂。当年开发的抗氧剂DSTDP，2000年试制的粒状复合抗氧剂，2001年开发的新型酚类抗氧剂1076#，2003年开发的液体硫代酯类抗氧剂DTDTP等新型抗氧剂系列产品，均属国内领先水平，当年即实现新产品产值。

2002年，天津化工厂与天津大学合作开发聚氯乙烯纳米抗菌专用料，并通过市科委组织的技术鉴定，为调整聚氯乙烯产品结构起到促进作用。

2003年7月,海豚橡胶公司与中国科技大学联合开发“等离子体裂解重油生产导电炭黑新技术”项目通过市科委验收。经过两年的研究试验,使炭黑粒径达到纳米级材料,开辟炭黑生产工艺的新途径。

2005年,橡胶研究所开发的医用硅橡胶制品、声学人工耳、高档乒乓球海绵等新产品,达到国内领先水平,医用硅橡胶制品获天津市科技进步三等奖。该所承担军用特种声学橡胶的研究开发,研制的水雷防污密封透声橡胶和鱼-6原理雷基阵灌注透声橡胶等新产品填补国内空白,为国家水下军事设施建设作出贡献。制品三厂开发的新型汽车胶板替代进口产品,独家为国内奥迪等高档汽车配套,产品性能达国际先进水平,获得天津市技术创新优秀项目二等奖。制品一厂适应造纸业发展需求,淘汰手工粘贴生产工艺,建成600吨高压高速胶轴生产线,在国内较早采用此先进工艺。制品二厂研制成功国内领先的隧道铁路整体道床弹性支承橡胶靴套、铁路提速减震橡胶垫板等橡胶导轨垫系列产品,为地铁、轻轨等城市交通设施配套。

二、工程轮胎系列化工

1996年,国际联合轮胎橡胶有限公司作为20世纪80年代全国唯一引进软件技术和全套装备生产工程轮胎产品,并且高效率地开发新品种,迅速产业化的企业,承担国家“八五”重大科技攻关项目“36.00-51-58PR巨型工程轮胎”的研制开发。通过对轮胎结构、胶料配方、工艺技术条件等进行反复试验,使该产品具有工艺配方先进,结构设计合理,工装设备配套等特点。经过在使用条件最苛刻的本溪铁矿实际使用,达到3万公里的国家攻关目标,填补国内空白,达到国际先进水平,被评为天津市科技进步二等奖。

2002年,该公司开发研制巨型自卸车用轮胎系列、钢丝带束层系列林业胎、全新系列载重机用工程轮胎,并形成10000吨生产能力。其中开发的巨型工程机械轮胎,具备承载能力强、胎体钢度大,抗切割及抗穿刺能力强,连续作业时生热低、气密性好等特点,重点为鞍钢、包钢、首钢等大型矿山配套。开发的钢丝带束层系列林业胎,采用耐切割胎面胶配方和防刺穿的胎侧钢丝带束层,产品达到国际同类产品水平,很快打入北美等国际市场。

2004年,该公司根据国内外市场需求,快速开发出12个规格的超宽断面高漂浮农林业全新系列轮胎,填补国内空白。

2005年,该公司共生产专用工程胎新产品7400吨,创产值1.2亿元,实现利税2000多万元。能够生产12大系列产品,150余个规格,85种花纹类型,1400个品种的工程轮胎,成为国内品种最多、出口量最大的工程轮胎生产企业,产品畅销欧美,用户反映良好。

第十章 石油化工

天津作为国家重要的石油化工基地,天津石化公司是主要的石油化工企业,中国石油大港石化公司(简称大港石化公司)也有部分石化产品。石化企业科研机构与天津大学等高校的科研团队紧密结合,联合攻关,形成较强的技术研发和创新能力。天津石化公司技术中心在消化吸收国外先进技术,调整结构,提高产品附加值,增加企业效益方面发挥重要作用,使化纤差别化率、树脂专用料比例创历史最高水平,2004年被认定为国家级企业技术中心。1991年至2005年底,该公司专业技术人员共完成科研课题556项,获国家和市(部)级科技进步成果奖81项。

第一节　石化原料

天津石化以石脑油为原料,经芳烃加氢、重整、再生、抽提、苯和甲苯分馏、歧化、异构化、酯化,最终产生化纤原料——对苯二甲酸二甲酯(DMT)、精对苯二甲酸(PTA)及其他有机化工原料。DMT、PTA是石油炼制到化纤生产的中间环节,其他产品如乙烯、聚乙烯、聚丙烯、乙二醇、聚醚等则是橡胶、塑料、热塑性树脂以及其他高分子材料的主要原料。化工轻油资源基本实现自给。2005下半年,化工原料综合自供比例达到90%以上,其中重整原料自供比例为95%左右,裂解原料自供比例达到95%左右,化工原料特别是乙烯原料"瓶颈"得到有效缓解。

一、烯烃

2002年,"天津乙烯扩能改造"项目通过竣工验收,使乙烯生产能力从16万吨/年提高到20万吨/年。特别是采用自行开发的诱导冷凝技术,使聚乙烯生产能力从6万吨/年提高到12万吨/年,聚丙烯、环氧乙烷生产能力相应增加,同时合成树脂专用料比例达到60%以上。该项目获得2003年中石化集团公司科技进步二等奖。

2003年,天津石化公司成功开发出高流动性抗冲型共聚聚丙烯注塑专用料系列产品TJPP2027和TJPP2028,填补国内一项空白。同年,专用料TJPP2027获得天津市科技进步三等奖。

2003年,天津石化公司大棚膜专用料线性低密度聚乙烯DFDA-9085项目获得天津市科技进步二等奖。

2004年,大港石化公司建成20万吨/年液化气分离装置。该装置原料为催化装置脱硫后的富丙烯液化石油气,产品为工业用优级丙烯。装置采用先脱乙烷的二塔流程,在丙烯精馏塔中实现丙烯与丙烷及以上馏份的分离,无脱丙烷塔系统、脱乙烷塔和丙烯塔,采用华东理工大学的专利产品,导向浮阀塔板。2005年,MTBE装置投产,MTBE产品纯度达到99%以上,为该公司生产高标号清洁汽油提供保证。

2004年,天津石化公司气相法聚乙烯冷凝技术工业开发项目获全国优秀技术创新成果。微膜级线型低密度聚乙烯专用树脂DFDA-9020项目获得天津市科技进步二等奖。线型低密度聚乙烯(LLDPE)TJDL-9270项目获得天津市科技进步三等奖。

2005年,天津石化公司乙烯装置3号炉技术改造后,不但能够裂解加氢尾油和石脑油,加工能力也由原来的14吨/小时提高到最大21吨/小时,乙烯收率由31.47%提高到33.65%。

2005年,天津石化公司经过多年科研成功地自主开发出高刚性均聚聚丙烯注塑专用料TJPP-M1116。高刚性均聚聚丙烯注塑专用料是具有较高附加值的产品,该类产品的市场主要为国外大型石化公司所占据,价格相对较高。该项目为天津石化创造新的经济增长点,产品填补国内空白。

二、聚醚

1994年,天津石化公司继三石化1993年科研项目"用于涤纶高速纺油剂用特种聚醚合成中间试验"取得成功后,在原三石化厂年产1500吨破乳剂装置的基础上,改造成年产800吨破乳剂及纺织油剂用特种聚醚装置。

1997年4月,天津石化公司1000吨/年乙二醇醚扩建项目投入运行,三石化厂采用新技术提高产品竞争力,使当年的乙二醇醚产品的销量达到历史之最。

2004年,天津石化公司继1997年"3.5万吨/年聚醚改造工程"后,对三石化厂聚醚装置进行改造,使得聚醚综合产能由6万吨/年达到8万吨/年，同比增长17.81%。同年，万吨聚合物多元醇连续化中试项目获得集团公司科技进步三等奖。

2005年，天津石化公司耐温硬泡课题组在多年对聚氨酯原料开发工作基础上，采用从芳环聚酯多元醇和高官能度杂环聚醚多元醇两条路线出发，成功合成两种不同结构的高官能度聚醚多元醇和三种低粘度的聚酯多元醇，并进行试生产。上述聚酯多元醇与聚醚多元醇，无需改变聚氨酯泡沫生产工艺，不增加成本，在天津聚氨酯厂、天津聚星科化工贸有限公司获得应用，产品经用户评价，完全达到质量要求。该项技术具有创新性，达到国内先进水平。

第二节　石化纤维

天津石化公司生产石化纤维的企业芳烃部（化工厂）、聚酯部（化纤厂）注重消化吸收先进技术，改造提升工艺。涤纶短纤维为国优产品；"天仙"牌涤纶短纤维、"大港"牌石油苯、"明珠"牌PTA、"津化"牌聚醚多元醇和聚合物多元醇等产品被评为天津市名牌产品；"天仙"牌涤纶短纤维被评为全国用户满意产品和国家标样产品。

一、原料制备

1991年，天津石化公司"用分步结晶技术分离精制均四甲苯"科研项目通过总公司（部级）技术鉴定，成果为国内首创。

1996年，天津石化公司化工厂DMT扩产改造后，对苯二甲酸二甲酯产量由10万吨/年提高到13万吨/年。同年，为满足DMT装置扩产改造后对原料对二甲苯的需求，提高装置的配套能力和整体效益，对芳烃车间吸附分离和异构化装置进行挖潜改造。改造后芳烃装置每年可多加工混二甲苯2.8万吨，使对二甲苯产量达到8万吨/年，纯度由原来的99.2%上升到99.7%以上，收率大于95%，实现稳产、高产、高纯度，一跃达到国际先进水平。

2004年，天津石化公司继2001年PTA和聚对苯二甲酸乙二醇酯（PET）和PET装置脱瓶颈技术改造后，对芳烃装置进行技术改造。通过更换重整、甲苯歧化及烷基转移高效催化剂，高效分离塔内件等技术创新措施，主要设备没有改动，单位产能投入只有新建的1/5，产能提高33%，使大芳烃重整能力由60万吨/年提高到80万吨/年，PX产能由25万吨/年提高到30万吨/年。

2004年，天津石化公司经过5年科研开发研制出国内唯一的1，4—环已烷二甲醇制备成套技术，生产成本低于国外同类产品，打破外国公司对中国市场的垄断。1，4—环已烷二甲醇是国内外用来开发聚酯新产品最常用的原料之一，此前只有国外几家公司可以生产。

2004年，天津石化公司与华东理工大学合作开发的"三井工艺PX氧化反应过程模型化与操作优化"项目，创建具有自主知识产权的优化PX氧化反应过程的技术与软件包，达到国际先进水平，获得天津市科技进步二等奖。

2005年，由中石化上海石化研究院、天津石化、中石化洛阳分公司共同开发完成的"低氢烃比高空速HLD-001甲苯歧化与烷基转移催化剂研制与工业应用"项目获中石化集团公司2005年科技进步一等奖。工业应用结果表明，该催化剂具有低氢烃比、高空速、起始反应温度低、转化率高和选择性高等特点，催化剂性能及工业应用结果属国际领先水平。

二、涤纶短纤维

1991年，天津石化公司聚酯粉末涂料树脂研制成功。该成果为国内首创，填补国内市场的空白，其产品质量达到国外同类产品水平。

1995年,天津石化公司开发的K—12膜用聚酯切片和香花溶剂油项目被评为天津市优秀新产品一等奖。

2000年,天津石化公司化纤厂生产的“磷系共聚阻燃聚酯切片及短纤维”经中国国际贸易促进会和法国科技质量评价委员会审核,被列为中国进入世界贸易组织WTO推荐产品。

2003年,天津石化公司化纤厂成功进行涤纶异形短纤维的研制,首次建立多孔数异形截面纺丝动力学数学模型、设计制造三叶、正三角及扁平形等异形喷丝板,稳定生产三叶、正三角及扁平形等异形纤维,产品质量指标达到并部分超过国外同类产品水平,总体技术达到国际先进水平。该项目获2004年天津市科技进步二等奖。

2005年,天津石化公司化纤厂在前期研究开发出新型聚酯缩聚催化剂的基础上,成功开发出液态的钛系催化剂,经试验,质量稳定,所产短纤维产品全部为优级品。熔体直纺ECDP短纤维生产技术的开发,实现的边际效益大大超过常规产品;在成功生产毛型ECDP短纤维的基础上,对ECDP丝束进行技术公关,生产的丝束手感和可纺性提高;绵型ECDP成功开发与应用也是新的突破,产品质量稳定。该项目获2005年天津市科技进步三等奖。

同年,天津石化公司与天津工业大学合作研制环保型细旦涤纶高速纺油剂。该产品是细旦涤纶高速纺的专用油剂,可广泛应用于细旦涤纶高速纺的生产和后加工。通过对特殊聚醚单体的合成技术、单体选择及配方设计、生物降解性能以及细旦涤纶高速纺油剂的平滑、润湿、抗静电等性能的研究,解决油剂的生物降解与腐败之间的矛盾,纤维的优级品率达到95%以上,生物降解率达到96%以上。。

同年,天津石化公司在国内首创生产有色正三角截面涤纶短纤维,其技术水平属国内领先。该项目的开发可提高涤纶短纤维的附加值和满足国内纺织业对高档次纤维的需求,具有良好的经济效益和社会效益。

第三节 节能环保技术

天津石化企业重视生产节能与环境保护。为使“三废”的排放标准符合国家的规定要求,大港石化公司不断利用新技术,对污水、废气进行处理,对硫磺进行回收。陆续建成投产柴油碱渣处理装置和综合碱渣的水处理装置,实现对汽油碱渣提取粗酚后废水的处理;对500万吨/年常减压蒸馏装置减顶尾气作为减压炉燃料的流程进行改造和试运,成功实现对减顶尾气恶臭污染的防治;建设5000吨/年硫磺装置,使总硫回收率达到99.8%。

一、污水处理

20世纪70年代开始,大港石化公司的污水处理,采用隔油、一级浮选工艺后进行排放,水质超标时有发生。1985年,设计能力为180吨/时的污水处理场投用,处理工艺为隔油、二级浮选、生化、气浮,外排污水合格率达到95%以上。

1996年,大港石化公司新建500吨/时污水处理场,可以处理含油、含碱、含盐污水。处理工艺为调节、平流隔油池、斜板隔油池、二级浮选、匀质、AO二段生化、沉淀、过滤等八道工艺。1999年,65吨/时污水汽提装置,采用双脱加压汽提工艺,并配有氨回收系统。

2000年,大港石化公司技术部与同济大学、大港油田博士后工作站合作,开展炼化污水处理与回用技术研究。该项目针对炼油厂外排污水的特点,研制开发一种新的污水深度处理回用工艺,采用悬浮载体生物深度处理、无机高分子复盐絮凝、沉淀和石英砂过滤、臭氧部分氧化生物活性炭以及消毒等技术处理外排水，达到研究课题规定的技术指标。处理后的出水水质：COD_{Cr}为30~50毫克/升、BOD_5<10毫克/升、NH_3-N≤5.0毫克/升、浊度<5.0NTU、石油类<1.0毫克/升、细菌总数<103个/毫升。2002年，污水回用生产装置投产，再生水的合格率达到95%以上，污水回收率达到90%以上，吨油耗水率降低到不超过1.1立方米，处理费用低于1.17元/立方米，达到行业先进水平。该项目2004年获中国石油天然气集团公司科技进步二等奖。

2001年，大港石化公司在水处理系统中应用BSOEM01酸碱自动排放系统，可自动控制酸碱性污水中和及排放，减少排放中的人为因素，保证排放合格率。2002年，在水处理改造中应用双室双层浮动床技术，运行速率高，出水水质优于再生离子交换器，再生剂消耗降低。水处理系统改造后，制水率由65.8%上升到87%，吨水耗电量由2.332千瓦时下降到1.525千瓦时。2005年，建成投产年2万吨柴油碱渣处理装置，采用高效生物强化技术，利用特效菌种，以高于传统活性污泥法10倍的容积负荷，将传统生物法难以处理的高浓度、有毒废水比较经济地处理成低浓度、易生化废水的处理工艺。

2005年，天津石化公司完成循环水高浓缩倍数运行及中水综合应用技术的开发，并通过天津市经委组织的成果鉴定。该项目以高碱高硬的宝坻水及水质复杂的工业中水为研究目标，围绕着循环水系统"高浓缩倍数运行"和"中水应用"两大发展方向，自主开发包括高效缓蚀阻垢剂、水质自动化控制系统及在线运行质量检测的成套技术，实现中水补水运行，工业应用中循环水系统运行浓缩倍数达到5.0，达到国内领先水平。

二、废气处理

1982年，大港石化公司沥青装置箱式加热炉改造，对沥青尾气采用高温焚烧技术，减少有毒气体排放。

2003年，天津石化公司乙烯厂"消灭火炬工程"投用，回收燃料气1500吨/年，增效600万元/年，节约能源的同时使环境得到保护。

2005年，大港石化公司对500万吨/年常减压蒸馏装置减顶尾气作为减压炉燃料的流程进行改造和试运。将减顶尾气通过水封罐水洗和减炉低压瓦斯罐切液，引进减压炉作为燃料气燃烧，取消减顶尾气的高点排空，成功实现对减顶尾气恶臭污染的防治。

三、脱硫技术

1986年开始，大港石化公司干气、液化气脱硫采用通过NaOH溶液碱洗的工艺。1996年，采用湿法脱硫的醇胺法脱硫工艺。1997年，建设2000吨/年硫磺回收装置，采用一级热转化加二级催化的克劳斯直通法工艺流程，尾气采用焚烧法处理，硫回收率达到91%以上。2005年，新建5000吨/年硫磺装置，包括硫磺回收，尾气采用加氢还原处理工艺，处理后的尾气送至焚烧炉焚烧，总硫回收率达到99.8%。

四、脱氯技术

2005年，天津石化公司完成降低环丁砜循环系统腐蚀性的研究。该项目采用阴离子交换树脂法净化环丁砜，小试和放大实验表明：在一定的条件下，单位树脂净化量大于300；净化后溶剂的氯含量从原来的5.0毫克/升以上降到1.0毫克/升以下；净化后的贫溶剂腐蚀性明显下降，缓蚀率超过70%；通过对树脂的筛选对比实验，所选用树脂抗有机污染性能和热稳定性能好，用3%的NaOH废液和3%的新NaOH溶液对树脂进行再生后，连续运行6个周期。项目实施过程中未增加新的工业污染，具备工业应用条件。

第十一章　纺　织

天津纺织工业发展历史悠久。但20世纪90年代以后，随着市场变化和产业调整，天津纺织工业设备更新速度慢、初级产品比重大、产品附加值低、市场竞争力差等问题越发显得突出。1994年，天津市按照“利用8年时间对国有大中型企业嫁接、改造、调整一遍”的部署，在国有老纺织企业推行技术改造，对产品结构调整、增强市场竞争力起到明显的作用。1998年，天津市积极实施中央对纺织行业“压锭、减员、重组、改革、创新”的要求，开展纺织改革脱困的“突破口战役”，对一批国有老厂实行兼并、破产、重组和转制等措施，并围绕“科技兴纺”这条主线，加大产品开发力度。此间，天津确立构筑都市纺织框架的基本思路和战略目标。到2000年底，完成扭亏为盈的第一步目标；2002年底，完成改革调整、夯实基础的第二步；2003年开始，迈出科技引领、提速发展、建成框架的第三步，一个用新材料和新技术引领发展，信息技术广泛应用，能够可持续发展的，从绵纺到织布、从印染整理到服装设计加工的完整的产业配套链，在天津空港物流加工区逐步形成。

第一节　绵纺织

随着科技发展，天津绵纺业注重对新型天然纤维的开发，增加纺织新材料，使纺织产品具有多元化、功能化、仿真化和个性化特点。包括天然彩色绵、原竹纤维、麻类新原料；再生纤维素纤维，包括绿色再生纤维素纤维莫代尔、天丝、丽赛、竹浆粘胶纤维；再生蛋白质纤维，包括大豆蛋白质复合纤维及毛类蛋白质再生纤维；新型和功能性合成纤维，包括超细纤维、复合纤维等。纺织面料的科技含量增加，产品档次提升，以满足市场需求。天津第一绵纺织厂（简称绵一，其他绵纺织厂依次简称为绵二、绵三、绵四、绵五）、绵二、绵三、绵四采取自主研发和与大专院校联合攻关的方式，研究多种新型纤维的处理方法，以适应后续加工与各类新产品开发。

一、纤维原料开发

2001年，天津天鼎纺织集团有限公司林明志等人成功开发罗布麻混纺床上用品和服装用纱。针对罗布麻在绵纺设备上的可纺性问题，经反复实践，采用添加助剂、混匀、预开松和定时时效的方法，顺利完成前期处理工作，保证纺纱生产的顺利进行。

2002年，天津天鼎纺织集团有限公司申秀林等人针对新型纤维PTT（低弹改性涤纶短纤）与绵混纺纱线的品种开发，为解决PTT原料静电、梳绵绵网下垂和成纱绵结等问题，选择适合的化学助剂、添加的剂量和处理方法，解决PTT原料的加工难点，通过合理选择梳绵盖板密度，适当加大梳绵、并条张力牵伸等方法，解决生产过程中静电和牵伸不均、色差、绵结等诸多问题，成功开发具有毛感和弹性的针织内衣用纱。

2002年，天津天鼎纺织集团有限公司刘华、尚津生等人开展对天然彩绵纺纱工艺的研究。鉴于人们对绿色环保的追崇，开发多个天然彩绵品种，并在国内最先组织生产，纱线产品畅销河北、广东、山东、江浙等服装产地。“天然彩色绵纱研究及多臂提花装饰布系列产品开发”项目获2006年中国纺织工业协会科学技术奖三等奖。

2004年，天津天鼎纺织集团有限公司（由天津绵三、绵六重组而成）解决麦饭石、远红外、天丝、莫代尔、丽赛等化纤、合纤原料处理方法上的抗静电缠绕问题。采用天津工业大学研制的新型静电防止剂，在原料松包后喷洒在纤维上、闷24小时后进行纺制的方法基础上，创造随机喷洒的新方法。即在抓绵机上方设计安装自动喷静电防止剂液装置，该装置随着抓包不断回转，圆盘上的纤维堆被连续自动均匀地注入油剂，以增加纤维导电率，降低静电，使新型纤维的生产顺利进行。

二、纺纱工艺改进

（一）改进纺纱工艺。

2000年，天津绵纺行业改进传统纺纱工艺，突破强分梳、强打击的传统纺纱理念，实行多梳少打的新工艺原则，针对不同品种采用相应的分梳元件，执行柔和打击、合理分梳的工艺流程。

1．清钢工序

1990年，绵三为控制落率，减少纤维的损伤，将清花A035混开绵机原锯齿刀片打手改为鼻型打手及梳针打手。同年，绵三选用国产A186F梳绵机30台，该机带有变频控制和大卷装，可高速高产。梳绵机滤尘系统由鲁瓦滤尘改为板式滤尘，达到提高真空度和节能目的。绵一的高洪、张兰玉等人对A186F梳绵机进行改造，成功解决因后吸槽内集花堵塞和输绵帘与机器框架间距大而导致轴缠花、帘子跑偏、断裂问题。对A092双绵箱给绵机进行改造，解决A092与A045B凝绵器不配套问题。1994年，绵三引进清钢联合机，缩短工艺流程，提高生条的质量。1995年，绵三与天津再生资源研究所共同研究开发废化纤开松技术及设备，成功研制KS100型废化纤开松机，通过科技成果鉴定。

2．并粗工序

1986年、1992年，绵二分两批引进瑞士E7/5精梳机共计13台，高速并条机RSB-51、2台，D1/2、2台，并条311.303、26台，粗纱454、20台，条并联E5/3、2台，条卷机E4/1a、2台，并卷E2/4a、2台，进口精梳机形成完整的工艺流程，为后来纺制精梳产品打下坚实基础。

3．细纱工序

1990年，绵三为加强细纱前钳口握持力，引进硬度为65°软皮辊，淘汰硬度为75°～80°硬皮辊，在纯绵品种上全部推广使用，效果明显。同年，绵三购进38台FA506V型细纱机，该机为V型牵伸，细纱实现大牵伸倍数纺纱。

2000年，绵一增加两套先进精梳设备，使精梳能力提升到38%；通过更新购置国产倍捻机15台，具备生产股线无接头纱的能力；更新3.8万锭细纱机，使细纱设备达到FA系列国产先进水平；纱场推行较胶辊，使绵纱水平达到乌斯特25%水平。

同年，绵三对80年代的FA502A，FA502MA细纱机进行改进。YJ2—150型摇架更新为YJ2—142型摇架10000锭，该机型中后罗拉传动轴重新设计制造，解决轴易断的问题，新设计的轴使用寿命提高300%。加硅油试验，使细纱锭速由16000转提高到18000转，单产达到历史最好水平。细纱工序以提高单产高效为目标，在电镀钢领基础上进行高渗碳钢领试验，在保养中进行锭子添油。

2004年，天津天鼎纺织集团有限公司引进马佐里DTM129细纱机。采用变频调速、微机自控分段调速先进技术，纺制高支精梳100S纱一次成功，纱线质量进入乌斯特2001公报25%水平以内。

4．后纺工序

1992年，绵三、绵六为提高纱质量，减少纱疵，生产无接头纱，引进日本村田Ⅱ型自动络筒机15台。该机采用自动接头和电脑控制系统。

1995年，绵六率先引进日本喷气纺纱机9台，生产的T/C65/3532S抗起球纱享有很高的信誉和知名度，另可纺制不同类型的花式纱。

2000年，绵一技术人员刘生友在喷气织机上大胆使用国产零部件来替代进口零部件，制作过滤器支架，解决其易损坏问题；通过改变剪刀角度的办法，解决纬停，并延长剪刀的使用寿命；在喷气织机的减震方面，大胆使用汽车减震器，同样收到好的效果，为企业节约资金。

2003~2005年，天津天鼎纺织集团有限公司先后引进日本村田21C型自动络筒机2台，并分别引进毛羽清除装置和异纤清除装置，使纱线质量升档。为提高各种纱线合股水平，分别于2000年、2003年购入倍捻机20台，并纱机3台；2004年购入天津吉田槽筒机1台。

5. 能源动力

1992年，绵三的电水汽能源微机监控管理系统获天津市科技进步三等奖。

1998年，绵四对空调进行溴化锂更新改造，使得制冷效果既保证生产一线的需要，又达到环保节能要求。

（二）新型纺纱技术和产品

1. 竹节纱

2001年，天津天鼎纺织集团有限公司申秀林、张淑萍、张俊芬、王克仁等在细纱机上加装生产竹节纱的纺纱装置，开发竹节纱新品种，获得2004年度天津市技术创新优秀项目二等奖。高峰时达到开锭8160枚，月生产量190余吨，投入生产的不同支数、不同原料、不同风格的竹节纱400余个品种，适用于各种牛仔、梭织和针织布料，织物具有凸凹有致，风格独特，立体感强等特点。在实际生产中摸索出总定量与基纱定量的关系公式，解决织物纬向“刮风”（即一定规律）问题，产品经天津市纺织测试中心检测，各项指标符合国家标准。经过专家鉴定，该产品达到国内先进水平。

2. 非弹力包芯纱装置和超高强涤纶包芯缝纫线

2002年，天津天鼎纺织集团有限公司与天津纺机研究所共同设计、试制，在细纱机上加装非弹力包芯纱装置，实现超高强涤纶包芯缝纫线的产业化。

2004年，绵三按照国产长丝的质量水平可以替代进口的发展趋势，结合所用国产长丝的成型变化，自行设计制造出立式、平式两种非弹力包芯纱装置。从而生产出涤短纤包涤长丝，绵包涤长丝，粘胶包涤长丝，粘胶包锦纶长丝，锦纶短纤包涤长丝，用不同原料，纺包不同支数纱，形成可生产30多种包芯纱，生产规模达到10000多锭。其中，超高强包芯缝纫线具有超高强，低缩率，条干均匀，疵点少等特点，适用于各种高档服装和厚重织物的缝制，经天津纺织工业标准检测中心测试，各项质量指标均达到国家标准。“高强包芯缝纫线技术研究及产品开发”项目获2007年中国纺织工业协会科技进步三等奖。

3. 天丝/绢丝喷气纺纱

2004年，天津天鼎纺织集团有限公司应用MJS纺纱方式，开发天丝与绢丝不同混比的喷气纺纱。天丝纯纺喷气纺纱，利用先进的喷气纺4线双区超大牵伸和高速运转气流双喷嘴特点，对纤维束包缠加捻，构成特种的双重结构纱。该纱线抗起球，抗纬斜，条干均匀，其织物具有抗起球，抗皱透气，悬垂性好，丝质感强等特点。产品经天津市纺织工业标准检测中心测试，各项指标达到国家标准，经国内查新和专家鉴定，达到国内领先水平。

三、织布设备更新

1990年，天津纺织业随着压锭减产、淘汰落后生产力，进入织布设备的更新改造期。通过引进国外新型织造设备，对单浆槽低压浆纱机、窄幅有梭布机进行更新换代，高温高压浆纱机和喷气布机的引进，使布机实现高速、产品品种向高支高密发展，是天津织布业的一次飞跃。

（一）喷气织机引进

1991~1992年，绵一、绵三、绵五引进日本喷气织机320台；1995~2003年，绵一、绵二、绵四先后引进国外各类喷气织机298台；2005年，天纺投资公司引进国外各类喷气织机883台。从而使产品开发由稀薄织物向高支高密织物转移；由单一纤维产品向多元化纤维产品转移；由传统纱布品种向功能性纱布品种转移。天津高新纺织工业园的绵纺织厂成为设备先进的大型绵纺织企业，设备国内一流或国内领先、工艺先进，拥有40万纱锭，2380台无梭织机，以及清梳联、精梳机、紧密纺、喷气纺、自动络筒机、超宽幅无梭织机等，年产绵纱2.7万吨,绵布1.5亿米。

(二)引进设备的消化吸收

1997年,绵二一布厂在片梭织机上研制穿箱机,有效地提高穿箱效率。二布厂喷气织机进口零部件和电气元件用国产替代,节约大量资金。三纺厂用A512粗纱机改纺涤纶缝纫线工程。

2002年,天一公司经过设备改造后,12万锭细纱机全部为FA系列;新增加的24台先进精梳机,使精梳产品覆盖率达到56%;26台倍捻机实现股线无接头和强捻单纱;引进23台自动络筒机实现纱线无接头;引进278台喷气织机后使无梭织机达到506台,无梭布覆盖面达到69.2%。

2003年,天一公司对80台丰田500型双储纬织机进行改造,具备织造异经异纬织物的能力。通过引进设备的消化吸收,完成原品种中粗支平布向高支高密高档服装面料和装饰面料的升级换代。生产能力提高3.5倍,布机效率达到90%以上,绵布入库一等品率达到95%以上。

第二节 毛纺织

二十世纪90年代,毛纺、毛织、毛条企业开始面向市场,企业从大而全向小而精发展,从大批量生产向小批多变过渡,以品牌作为支撑,充分体现企业特色。企业从国外引进先进设备,不断提高原料、工艺、产品的科技含量,使大批新产品投产,满足市场需求。

一、工艺改造

1992年,华欣毛纺织厂陶树宝、耿秀云等为提高TC13068轻型混纺立绒大衣呢的实物质量改进工艺设计。将原2/2斜纹组织变为纬浮线较长的1/3破斜纹组织,使之更有利于纬纱起毛,重新设计经纬密度,调整织造和后整理工艺,使改进后的立绒产品的绒面更加丰满,实物质量稳步提高。1992年6月在全国毛纺产品调研中心举办的"唯尔佳杯"产品大赛中,该产品获得二等奖,成为该厂主要出口和内销品种。

1993年,华欣毛纺织厂在获国家金奖的TC02022纯毛立绒大衣呢的基础上,开展技术攻关,研制开发出市场需求的TC13068轻型混纺立绒大衣呢,使其成为主要出口创汇品种。1996年,该厂研制兔毛大衣呢、台球呢和阿尔巴卡(二八卡)等市场流行的新品种,加大科技含量,取得较好的经济和社会效益。

1996年,恒源毛纺织厂以国产羊毛生产的纯毛高级单面花呢系列产品获1997年天津市政府授予的科技兴市突出贡献奖。

二、改进织机

1994~2003年,天津仁立毛纺厂"仁立"牌舍味呢成为全国著名产品,"仁立"牌的大提花阻燃装饰织物作为航空座椅面料,填补国内空白。其间,1994年,该厂防水防油面料获"中国一绝"奖;1995年,"天马牌"精纺呢绒获天津市场名牌金奖商品称号;同年,全毛阻燃装饰布获"中国国际纺织面料博览会"金奖;1996年,纯毛凡立丁作为奥运会中国体育代表团唯一使用礼服面料;1996年至2002年,"天马牌"精纺毛织品获天津市名牌产品称号;1998年获天津市知名商标称号;2003年精纺毛织品被认定为天津市著名商标。

2004年,恒源毛纺织厂改造织机边撑装置,以通幅撑布代替边撑,消灭边撑痕与刺挂疵点,获2005年天津市职工技术成果优秀奖。

第三节 针 织

天津市针织业具有一定的品牌优势，“梅花”“菲米丽”“双燕”“三花”“丹顶鹤”等在国内外有一定的知名度和影响力。针织企业顺应市场的变化和需求，从设备、工艺及面料等方面进行改革和创新，产品更具有竞争力。

一、设备工艺改进

1991年，针织四厂通过市场调研查找与国外同类产品差距，决定将减小产品缩水作为攻关目标。采取对后整理工序的改进，用国产设备与引进设备相结合，增加湿扩幅，改进4网烘干机超喂，利用海宁尼毯轧光机、“佩斯”烘干机，以及加强操作规程，严肃工艺纪律等措施，使产品各项物理指标均达到国家标准要求，多年的缩水问题得到解决，质量赶上国外同类产品。

1992年，针织二厂改造原有设备，使2+4跑道罗纹绵毛机达到高速，可制造花纹织物，产量提高。该厂研制开发的领口、袖口罗纹机无极装置获国家专利。

1997年，菲森公司对于渔网经编机进行技术改造，将经轴送纱改为纱架送纱，变消极送经为积极送经，以及光电控制的断纱自停，使产品质量提高。2000年，进而将原有的凸轮经编机改造成链杆传动，提高机器转速，降低生产成本和消耗，生产效率、产品质量得以提高。同年，该公司与江苏武进市五洋纺织机械有限公司联合研制的宽幅渔网经编机投产，适合于幅宽2米以上至4米的防风网、宽幅的农业用网、幅宽450目以上至950目的复丝网片生产，填补国内空白。

1999年，天津针织厂对ME—692型呢毯预缩机进行节能的专项改造。由于受针织物毛絮的影响，以及该机调毯汽缸的设计缺失等原因，该机配套的功率为5.5千瓦/时的空压机不能使汽罐动作，而调整呢毯，只起到主机启停作用，造成电能大量浪费，环境噪音大。技术人员对其控制线路进行改造后，在去掉空压机的情况下，对主机启停无任何影响，噪音消除，经实验对产品轧布质量无任何影响，达到提高机台利用率和节能环保目的。

二、产品研发

1991年10月，天津市织袜三厂积极引进项目，技术人员开发出“三花”牌高级绅士袜、女士时装袜、高级男女纯毛袜和毛型女士连裤袜等。其中“三花”牌高级绅士袜中，不仅有单向双罗纹组织，还有为适应脚型穿着舒适的纵横向罗纹组织，产品当时在国内尚属首创。特别是原料选用优等精梳精纺专纺纱，工艺质量标准较高，产品经测试，其强力和条干均达到或超过世界名牌纯绵袜产品剖析检测指标，成为国内袜类产品消费中的佼佼者，实现当年投资、当年引进、当年投产、当年创效益的目标。产品国内畅销，远销东欧，填补该产品的出口空白。先后获得1991年“迎春杯”针织产品设计大奖赛最佳设计奖、天津市优秀新产品三等奖。

1992年6月，针织四厂采用新工艺、新技术，特别是16tex精梳罗纹面料，突破过去只能漂白，只能做内衣的框框，大胆采用流行色，在花色上绣花、补花、转移胶印等先进工艺技术，设计生产的高级色“丽博”体型系列针织衫，就针织品向外衣化、时装化发展作出大胆创新，设计出上百个花色品种。该服装面料手感丰满柔软、弹性好、穿着舒适滑爽，四季适宜，各项技术指标经测试均达到国家标准。在全国第二届“中心杯”评比中获得优秀产品奖，被评为全国纺织行业最畅销产品。

1994年，天津运动衣厂设计开发“菲米丽”牌高档花边内衣系列，睡衣系列、T恤系列、针织休闲装系列及运动系列。"菲米丽"针织内衣系列产品因为具有品质优良、款式新颖和独特设计风格而闻名全国，曾经荣获国家经委国家质量金奖、银奖，商务部国际博览会国际金奖，北京国际博览会金奖，1994年全国纺织新产品展示交易会金奖、银奖，1995年全国纺织新产品展示交易会金奖、银奖，1995年国际名牌服装、服饰博览会内衣类金奖，1995年全国最畅销国产商品展示月天津市场金奖商品等国内多种奖项。

1995年，菲森公司开发、研制生产的经编无结网及网具系列产品，是国内新兴的纺织产业网布产品，广泛应用于水产业、农业、建筑业、体育事业等。产品经天津市有关专家鉴定，获得天津市政府奖及1995年国家级新产品证书。

2000年10月，天津五洋巾毯织物有限公司开发的"双层大提花亚麻凉席"项目，获天津市1999年度技术创新优秀项目三等奖。2001年8月，该公司被天津市政府授予2000年度天津市"技术创新先进企业"称号。同时，该公司开发的"天然彩色绵装饰毯及彩色绵巾被"项目，获天津市2000年度技术创新优秀项目三等奖。

2002年9月，天津五洋巾毯织物有限公司开发的"天然彩色绵多层提花装饰毯及彩色绵巾被"项目获天津市科技进步三等奖。

2003年，天津针织研究所承接国家纺织部大豆蛋白纤维产品试制项目，完成大豆蛋白纤维单面、双面提花，大豆蛋白与氨纶锦纶交织等11种面料的编织染色，以及十几种服装款式的试制工作，还完成珍珠蛋白纤维面料试制。

2003年，有声针织公司开发杜卡美磁性远红外功能系列产品，攻克产品柔软度、磁粉附着牢度等技术难关。经中国计量科学院等机构检测，远红外发射率达94%，穿用20分钟后，人体微循环可增加80%—114.2，血流量增加41.6—60%，能有效提高人体免疫功能。2003年8月申请"远红外磁性织物的制备方法"专利，通过天津市卫生防病中心"保健用品卫生"鉴定。2004年该公司重点开发远红外系列床寝用品，并向配套化发展，除针织内衣，还开发磁疗被、磁疗枕、远红外保健凉席等，使保健功能产品系列化。

第四节 色织与装饰织物

1991～2005年，纺织业中的色织和装饰织物企业是发展最快、也淘汰最快的行业。天津荣泽公司、飞天纺织装饰品有限公司、天津市健龙保健品有限公司、天津市赛远保健品有限公司等以科技引领产品的企业，得到长足的发展。

一、色织

20世纪90年代初，天津色织行业主要产品是涤绵细纺和44寸幅宽的白坯布及弹力牛仔布等。为使产品更新换代，1991~1992年淘汰一部分自动布机，引进意大利的Fast剑杆织机，改变产品结构，织造一些长丝、提花和双轴等产品，产品逐步向高档次转化，质量提高，以外销为主。

2000~2004年，天津荣泽公司自主开发研制出多种原料混纺和交织的产品。利用氨纶包芯纱交织的弹力泡泡纱面料；设计应用天丝、彩绵等原料制造的环保型面料；高支高密全绵面料，经特殊整理，达到仿丝绸效果的面料产品。开发出特氟隆功能整理、吸湿排汗整理、抗菌抗紫外线等功能性整理新技术。自主研发的新产品均被国家信息中心评为"中国流行面料"，企业获"中国流行面料入围企业"称号，并连续获全国印染、绵纺织、色织产品开发年会"优秀创新奖"和"优秀设计奖"。

到2005年，天津市色织行业获国家级新产品10项。部分产品水平在国内同行业处于领先地位。

二、装饰织物

1980年代开始，天津市装饰织物行业通过技术改造和技术引进，拥有国际上较为先进的工艺技术和设备，单一的床单品种向中、高档装饰配套产品方向发展，产品走向世界。

1991年，天津市床单二厂张爱荣、张子富、李多英等研制涤绵涂料轧染工艺成功。提高生产率30%，降低成本15%，工艺革新效益显著。

1992年，赛远保健品有限公司（原天津市麻纺织厂，简称赛远公司）与天津工业大学（原天津纺织工学院）功能纤维研究所合作，在麻纺厂丙纶长丝车间，共同研发试纺成功第一根远红外功能纤维。经检测，远红外性能达到设计要求，其他物化指标均满足要求。

1995年，天津市织物厂（简称织物厂）在全行业率先引进CAD电脑辅助设计、分色系统及荷兰STORK圆网印花机。使织物产品年生产能力达到1000万米，形成包括90英寸印花装饰面料、中高档床上配套用品、保健用品等三大系列产品。吕志高、于晓玲、王伟昭、魏宝林等人研制的涤/绵装饰布系列产品在首届中国国际纺织面料及辅料博览会上获银奖。1996年，该厂飞天系列产品获第二届中国国际纺织面料及辅料博览会金奖。

1997年，织物厂研制开发的“丽丽缎宽幅全绵金粉印花装饰布”“梦娜思工艺床罩件套”“涤/绵宽幅深素色罩印装饰布”，获天津市科技成果三等奖。1999年，“涤/绵宽幅卫生整理装饰布”等飞天产品被中国环境标志产品认证委员会授予中国环境标志产品希望奖，并被天津市人民政府授予天津市名牌产品称号。

1997年，天津市中天纺织有限公司（简称中天家纺）高晓石、程世平、张凤英、张伟等人研制出多色仿浮雕印花绒毯系列新产品，突出花的立体感，改变印花拉绒工艺，在坯布上控制起绒的位置，用粘合剂新配方描边，使纤维粘结，处于干燥状态，在起绒过程中保持原状，达到绒面凹凸浮雕的效果。该项目获天津市优秀新产品一等奖。

1998年，天津市床单厂丁振民、刘智国等人研制开发的远红外线磁性保健羽绒寝具、远红外线磁性保健皮背心，研制开发的“远红外线磁性保健文胸”、远红外线磁性保健护腰和保健鞋垫等产品，分别获得国家发明专利。

1999年，中天家纺的高晓石、程世平、张凤英、张伟等人开发研制出床上用毯类系列新产品。该产品应用FCAD电脑提花设计系统和提花机进行织造，组织结构为单层及纬二重组织和纬三重以上大提花组织。研制过程中，攻克软件应用技术及电脑提花机装造上机工艺参数，操作程序等技术难关，2000年通过天津市科技成果鉴定，达到国内领先水平。同年，开发研制出电热毯专用高档立绒印花毯系列新产品。系由纯绵针织起绒纱织造而成，采用高难工艺设计，技术含量大，其内部结构是一种全新独特效果，整个穿线孔道通过组织变化实现，经过漂染、印花、起绒等高难度深加工后，穿入电器阻件，再经过锁边、缝边等后整理工序。该项目2000年通过天津市科技成果鉴定，2001年被定为国家重点新产品，达到国内领先水平。

2000年，飞天家纺（天津织物厂和天津床单二厂重组，简称飞天家纺）吕志高、王伟昭、张玉震、邓崴等人研制出床上配套产品，获中国国际纺织品博览会床上用品金奖。

2002年，五洋巾毯织物厂“天然彩色绵多层提花装饰毯及彩色绵巾被”项目，获天津市科技进步三等奖。同年，该公司纳米抗菌保健系列–梦中芳草、彩绵制品–世纪宠儿产品，获2002、2003年度流行趋势推荐产品。2003年2月，赛远公司“负离子远红外功能纤维及其制造方法”获得国家发明专利证书；2004年2月，该公司“麦饭石功能纤维及其制造方法”获国家发明专利证书。

2004年，健龙保健品公司丁振民、刘智国等人研制出调节型健康枕、高科技贵族PU健康床垫和“护肤美体无缝健康内衣”产品，经过专家鉴定产品达到国际先进水平，获得国家实用新型专利；研制出的“镶磁亚麻凉席、枕席”产品达到国内领先水平，获得国家实用新型专利。2005年，健龙保健品公司丁振民、刘智国等人研制出绿色天然多功能保健内衣系列产品，是国内第一家将彩绵与多种功能纤维结合的保健内衣，国内第一家采用Oeko–Tex Standard 100认证的功能内衣，国内第一家采用40S纱织造功能保健内衣。突破功能内衣不能采用40S纱的技术难关，纺出不仅具有远红外、负离子、麦饭石保健功能的40S高纱支产品，且做工考究，品质优异。经过专家鉴定产品达到国际先进水平，获得国家实用新型专利。同年，丁振民、刘智国等人研制出“生态拟真隐纺热能床垫”“特级健康床垫”产品达到国际先进水平，获得国家实用新型专利。

第五节 染 整

1991～2005年，天津印染业在重组中不断调整印染产品结构，开发一系列新材料、新技术、新工艺、新产品，使印染业按照“科技兴纺”要求，体现高效、节能、绿色、健康、环保的特点，强化织物的后整理功能。

一、前处理工艺

（一）冷堆工艺广泛应用

1990年起，鉴于印染产品的前处理工序，水、电、蒸汽用量较大，能源耗用、污水排放对环境影响较大，企业生产成本也逐年增大，因而前处理的工艺成为环保和节能的关键。印染产品前处理的冷堆工艺开始推广。

1992年，天津三环纺织印染公司产品前处理的冷堆工艺走向成熟并广泛应用，使清洁生产得到推广。

（二）酶退浆工艺

1990年起，天津三环纺织印染公司在纯化纤织物和粘胶纤维织物的前处理上全面应用酶退浆工艺，用生物酶退浆，减少各类化学助剂在前处理工艺上的应用，是一项绿色环保的工艺。

（三）碱减量处理

1990年，天津三环纺织印染公司从意大利引进减量设备，对纯涤和涤绵产品进行碱减量处理，形成规模生产，使面料的风格发生改变，纯化纤面料更加轻柔，涤绵产品有纯绵的舒适，产品更加丰富。

二、染色工艺改进

（一）一浴法

1999年，天津三环纺织印染公司鉴于T/C织物用分散、活性的染色工艺，以往一般采用二浴法，即先染涤再染绵，工艺流程较长的情况，为了节能，缩短工艺流程，在筛选染化料的基础上，将二浴法改为一浴法。即将分散和活性染料一次浸轧，经过热熔染色机使T/C织物一次完成上染，并确保染色的牢度。

（二）回归反射染色

2003年5月，天津三环纺织印染公司创新工艺，为汽车业发展配套，开发回归反射染色工艺。在染色时将回归反射物同时附着在织物上，手感好，穿着舒适、时尚，从而开发出一种在光照下能够发光，既能起到交通安全提示、又能穿着舒适的外衣，改变以往使用涂层工艺的做法，新增新产品。

（三）印花技术

1．电脑测配色

1991年3月，天津第一印染厂和天津第二印染厂从美国美顿引进电脑测配色设备。天津印染业在测配色手段上更加现代化，测色、配色操作人员从手工操作中解放出来。

2．电子制版

1999年，天津三环纺织印染公司购置杭州开源电脑技术有限公司电脑分色和电子制版系统。彻底抛弃手工描样，提高工作效率，能够当天来样当天制网，适应企业小批多变，保证及时交货，并为企业搭建一个数字化的CAD平台，被天津市经委列为1999年的信息化建设重点项目。

3．精细印花

1992年，天津第二印染厂从德国MBK公司引进圆网印花机。印花系统由电脑自动控制，把天津印染业的精细印花手段提高到新的台阶，为外贸出口装饰布和服装面料提供高精度的花型。

4．特种印花

2005年，天津三环纺织印染公司用平网和圆网印花机进行特种印花的开发。特别是立体特种印花、仿真特种印花技术，在烂绵巴厘纱的基础上，开发出T/C府绸的色彩烂花印花布，在泡泡纱花布基础上开发出条泡烂花布，并且用仿真特种印花技术开发针织布印花。

三、新产品开发

（一）绉布系列

1990年，由天津三环纺织印染公司技术人员杨长福、戴明灼等与天津市第二绵纺厂合作开发纯绵印花的杨柳绉纹布，在国内是第一家。该产品有漂、色、花三大类品种，以花为主，漂、色布为辅。到2000年已发展到纯绵、涤绵、麻绵等多种纤维系列，有涂料工艺、活性印花工艺、分散活性工艺、拔染雕印等多种印花工艺。全绵防印活性绉布工艺1999年被天津市纺织局评为优秀新产品新技术三等奖。

1999年，天津三环纺织印染公司和天津市第二绵纺厂、天津外贸服装进出口公司合作开发凹凸绉布新产品。用绵二生产的C40×4065×56坯布，用进口的日本轧纹机轧纹，经罐练后，用双漂工艺加工而成凹凸绉布。该产品轻薄柔软，穿着舒适，形成漂、色、花系列产品，同时后整理功能也形成系列化，从森林浴到沙滩浴，从清香整理到桑蚕整理，从防菌除臭到凉爽、负离子整理，成为企业的当家产品。成为国内唯一生产此类产品的企业，产品出口日本。

（二）泡泡纱

1999年，天津三环纺织印染公司和天津第一印染厂重组后，利用一印1970年代在北方地区第一家开发的泡泡纱的基础进行开发。主要是泡型的变化和泡形的风格，把过去单纯的碱泡开发成涤泡、规律泡、子母泡，一直到高档次的无甲醛超柔软的涂料印花定位泡泡纱，形成泡泡纱一大系列品种。该产品出口量不断攀升，成为企业的拳头产品。

（三）运动服面料

1999年，天津三环纺织印染公司利用企业的技术优势，开发出柔道布运动装面料，并批量生产。柔道服红白相间、黑白相间、蓝白相间，面料较厚，适应运动员在训练和比赛中出汗量较大的要求，面料的吸湿排汗性能好，特别讲究色牢度考核，生产工艺要求高。2002年，该企业在柔道布生产工艺开发的基础上，相继开发跆拳道布和剑道布等运动服面料，使柔道布、剑道布、跆拳道布生产形成规模，运动服面料系列化。

四、进口设备的改造创新

1993年，天津三环纺织印染公司成立专门技术组织，在对于引进设备进行消化、吸收的基础上，利用国产元件替代进口元件，利用数码技术对进口设备进行改造。这是鉴于天津印染业20世纪80年代开始从国外引进大批设备，随着设备使用期延长，设备故障率上升，进口零部件时间周期长，特别是电子元件三四年后就被淘汰不再生产的情况进行的，保证生产的正常运转。

2002年，天津三环纺织印染公司技术人员何新利用数字电路和模拟电路重新设计制作出简单实用的探边装置。该装置是印染设备中的重要组成部分，在定型机、拉幅机、丝光机等设备上普遍使用，通过光电或机械式传感器识别织物边缘位置，使驱动电机带动大板动作，保持织物边缘位置的准确跟踪，使针板挂针一致，布铗夹布一致，保证设备在高速运行时反应迅速、灵敏，确保产品质量。印染设备所使用的探边和对中装置，有进口和国产的几种型号，出故障后常因维修困难而影响生产。通过该项改进，成功地替代进口探边器，设备投入使用后使企业生产中的难题得到解决。

2005年，天津三环纺织印染公司技术人员何新设计研制用微电脑控制曝光机。该企业原来使用的STORK曝光机是20世纪80年代进口设备，由于电气老化，故障率高，经常出废品，特殊部件损坏后要依赖进口，而办理进口手续繁杂、周期长，经常影响生产，必须对进口设备加以改造。通过工艺条件分析，对设备改造提出要求：要满足使用不同感光材料，适应外界环境温度变化的影响等因素，需要不同的曝光量，可随时调整曝光次数，具有一定的抗干扰能力，并满足可自动和手动的两种操作方式。经反复实验，精简电路硬件，去掉拨码开关，用LED数码管显示曝光次数、设定次数，充分发挥微型计算机逻辑运算功能，体现智能化特点。通过开发元件，增加实用功能，曝光完成后，自动停机，发出声光提示，提醒在暗室的操作者。该控制系统投入使用后效果良好。

同年，天津三环纺织印染公司电气工程师何新用单片机制作意大利MEZZERA卷染机计数器。根据维修经验，针对进口原装计数器的原理进行消化，总结出原电路的优缺点，进而自主开发设计符合实际需要的机型，满足进口设备的需要。在国产常压卷染机、高温高压卷染机上也能使用，投入使用后取得良好的效果。此外，该企业还对圆网印花机回液位控制器、对中装置等进行技术改造。

五、节能环保技术

1999年，天津三环纺织印染公司将T/C染色一浴法作为常规工艺加以推广。前处理的主要工艺手段，应用生物酶和高效短流程等先进技术，使冷堆一步法从源头开始节水节能。在水洗机倒流水水洗法的基础上，加强采集热源机台的冷凝水和部分进口设备的冷却水供水洗机使用，使印染工艺用水进一步节约。加大污水处理后的中水回用，作绳洗机的生产用水，并用于冲厕和锅炉除尘、冲灰。

同年，该公司开发地热资源。冬季将地热井水首先用于居民小区供热，回水经除铁处理后，作为小区居民的生活热水，生活用水回水直接用于水洗机，使水资源得到合理循环利用。

第六节 纺织机械

天津市天寅机电有限公司是隶属天津纺织集团（控股）有限公司的国有独资企业，其前身为天津市纺织机械器材工业公司，授权管理天津纺织机械器材行业。1998年起，该行业对所属企业进行战略性调整和多元参股改制，引入市场机制，形成发展后劲。行业重视整体技术进步，着力开发研制新产品，实施技术改造措施，部分项目利用社会力量，产、学、研结合共同研制。1991~2005年共开发新产品62项，完成5项技术改造和工艺改进。

一、新产品开发

1991年，天津市同拓机电有限公司（简称国际机电公司）作为纺织机械器材研究所改制后的高科技企业，依托研究所的技术优势，主要以纺织机械的两种关键专件、器材——钢领及钢筘的制造设备为主线，研发新产品。为满足钢领制造行业的迫切需要，该公司刘玉凯、王继宗、祁少明等开发设计加工环锭纺纱机钢领专用全自动加工机床。气动及液压控制TCA-1型全自动钢领精车机床，属国内独家研发，生产钢领专用自动机床。TKA-1型全自动钢领轧光机床，在钢领精车后，经过滚轧，使其表面更加光洁。钢领精车机床获天津市经委1992年新产品开发二等奖。

同年，天津市靖隆纺织橡胶有限公司（简称靖隆公司）研制出擦胶工艺及胶料配方，淘汰延用多年的用苯油加乙醇的浸胶工艺，解决重大环保污染问题。每年节约数吨苯和乙醇，生产效率和产品内在质量提高。

同年，天津市玉丰机械有限公司（简称玉丰公司）研制的TJYH-61型空气捻接器，在消化吸收国外同类产品基础上，结合国内纺织工业具体情况，在原理结构上进行创新。其核心部件陶瓷捻接腔于1998年获国家专利（专利号为ZL 97 2 28646.2）。TJYH-61型空气捻接器产品属于国内先进水平。

同年，玉丰公司赵武银、杜绍珊、李铁铮开发研制TJYH-61型空气捻接器。该产品的研制成功填补国内长江以北地区无空气捻接器生产企业的空白。TJHY-61型空气捻接器于1992年10月通过天津市经委、科委组织的中试生产鉴定，1993年获天津市政府科技产品三等奖。

同年，国家纺织器材质量监督中心工程师李大鑫、冯建伟合作研制的JY-28型塑料梭子磨损检测仪项目，通过原天津纺织工业局组织的科技成果鉴定，鉴定结论为国内首创。

1992年，靖隆公司承担天津市经委立项的“法国FM—5型高速粗纱机用涨力皮板”的研制项目。项目完成后通过天津市经济委员会组织的科技成果鉴定。

1993年，靖隆公司在国内率先引进瑞士西赛尔橡胶技术公司冷喂料挤出机加工技术。在充分消化吸收、不断完善设备配置的基础上，生产出国内第一个T/c95—1A、B型高分散度纺绵不处理铝衬套胶辊，被评为“天津市创新优秀项目三等奖”，1998年被评为国家级新产品。

1993年6月，天津市佳可得机电设备科技发展有限公司（前身是天津市第一纺机厂设备技术服务部，简称佳可得公司）受用户厂委托，承接TJGN206型宽幅重型织机及TJZ323型整经机项目。为高水平完成任务，组成以天津工业大学（前身天津纺织工学院）机械系高殿斌、蒋秀明，一纺机厂研究所杨学忠、陈磊为主的项目攻关组。开发国内首台以聚脂单丝为原料用于织造干网的工业织机及配套辅机，织物主要用于建筑、化工、医药、公路、矿山等行业。织物纬密：40~52根/厘米。经过一年时间努力，完成样机任务。1994年12月受厦门工业网带厂委托，在TJGN206型宽幅重型织机基础上改进设计，机型改为TS45型织机，幅宽由4米增至4.5米。

1993年，国家纺织器材质量监督中心工程师刘伟、李伟、余俐合作研制的新型化纤清洗剂项目，通过天津市科委组织的市级科技成果鉴定，达到国外同类产品的技术水平。

1994年，同拓机电公司成功研发新型无梭织机用关键器材—钢筘专用制造装备，全自动编筘机系列产品。由于不断引进国外先进的无梭织机，而国内尚不能制造精密无梭织机关键器材—钢筘，为满足市场需求，节约外汇，该所安排王承健、武砚田、韩晶等多名技术人员，在参考国外先进设备的基础上，设计全自动编筘机。AKB—4000型全自动编筘机，可编制400号平筘（喷水筘及箭杆筘）、异型筘、起毛织物用双层筘，钢筘质量优于行业标准。编筘机研发进而跨出纺织行业，扩展到金属丝网用钢筘制造领域。经反复调研论证，研制成功适合金属丝网用钢筘的DKB—6000型编筘机，可编制350目（公制1400号）钢筘，筘片厚度达0.035mm；并应用先进技术，在编筘机上采用触摸屏输入及显示，PLC实时程序控制全自动编筘机。经鉴定，以上两机型编筘机属国内领先水平。该项目获1996年国家纺织总会科技进步三等奖。该公司还围绕全自动编筘机研发上下游产品。①洗筘机用于清洗织机用钢筘，该机应用超声波技术清洗钢筘，具有节能，环保等特点，清洗洁净度达95%以上。②喷气织机用异型筘气流损失检测仪，与国家纺织器材检测中心共同研制。③FKZT-51型全自动筘片调平机，用于喷气织机用异型筘片调平的专用设备。该机采用4个电机独立传动，触摸屏输入及显示，PLC程序控制，交流变频调速，51根压辊调平，为国内首创。

1994年，靖隆公司张桂开发出HDQ21E-1型和H1000型高速纺化纤导丝胶圈。该产品整圈强度高，运转平稳，具有优良的耐磨性，杰出的运行稳定性、寿命长等特点。

1996年，靖隆公司研制出AL型气鼓式弹性皮辊，俗称“气泡罗拉”，用于引进德国、意大利、法国的及国内的各种毛粗纱机、并条机、针梳机设备。厚度均匀、弹性好，具有良好的抗静电性能，握持纤维能力好，无早期龟裂、不粘缠，使用寿命长，纺纱性能达到国外同类产品水平。通过天津市经委鉴定。

1996年10月，佳可得公司受江苏盐城达阳纺织有限公司委托，研制开发TJGN208提花绒织机，天津市第一纺织机械厂研究所郭忠汉、裴友成、郑天雄、温宗山、张民生共同承担该项任务。TJGN208提花绒织机主要用于织造双革绒、壁毯、地毯、提花毯等，幅宽2米，纬密度50根/厘米，开口为凸轮多臂装置，8片综框。1997年10月完成技术图纸和全部资料，1998年9月完成12台提花绒织机制造任务，填补国内空白，性能结构优于韩国同类设备。1999年获天津市科技创新优秀项目三等奖。

1996年12月，国家纺织器材质量监督中心陈学忠、段继禹、王继忠共同研制JY32型胶圈静摩擦系数测试仪，通过原中国纺织总会组织的部级科研成果鉴定，鉴定结论为国内领先水平。获天津市纺织工业局优秀科技成果奖。

1998年4月，扎努西业公司委托佳可得公司设计制作全自动轴承法兰抛光机，用西门子程控元件实现电子控制，替代人工法兰抛光工序。1998年8月完工，经验收达到自动化要求，达到国内先进水平。

1999年6月，玉丰公司杜绍珊、郝树森、杨凤荣等技术人员研制TJYH-62喷雾式空气捻接器，于2000年10月通过天津市经委鉴定。

1999年11月，佳可得公司受河南中玉有限公司委托，在TJGN208绒织提花机基础上改进设计，进一步提高织机性能及效率。双方同意改动62项设计，幅宽由2米提高到2.5米，由电磁替代机械控制实现张力卷曲机构自动调节，传动中齿轮与轴连接改为三片瓦，滑动轴承改为滚动轴承，增加张力缓冲、电磁刹车装置。项目达到国内先进水平。

1999年，国家纺织器材质量监督中心胡新立、邹继明、张思逊和刘广太共同研制的JY-40型胶圈内周长测试仪和JY-41型胶圈厚度测试仪项目，通过天津市纺织工业总公司组织的局级科技成果鉴定。鉴定结论为：测量精度高，测量数据一致性好，达到国内同类仪器先进水平。

2000年，天津市天宁纺织机械设备有限公司（原天津市一纺机厂，简称天宁公司）鉴于国内布料市场大花型提花织物需求量较大，当时国产提花机只有992针和1480针两种机型，不能满足需要。技术人员刘海华试制出2400针和3000针两种机型，并实现多台机联动，属国产单台针数最多的提花机。该机型满足国内织造大花型提花织物织机的需求，使JK202A提花机系列化。

2000年，靖隆公司开发出TCP76/TCP80日本村田纺纱机专用胶辊。其开车状态、耐磨、耐温性能、回弹性等均达到日本原装进口胶辊的水平，打破外商垄断的局面。技术论文在国家专业期刊“纺织器材”刊登，产品被国家纺织器材协会推荐。

2000年12月，国家纺织器材质量监督中心辛少明、张思逊、胡新立等共同研制的JY-43型喷气织机用钢筘气压值检测仪，通过由中国纺织机械器材工业协会（CTMA）组织的部级科技成果鉴定。鉴定结论为：设计合理，技术先进，测量精度高，填补国内空白，达到国内领先水平。

2001年，天宁公司温宗山、刘海华、郑金奎、杨菊花等设计开发TJGN208型提花绒织机和与其配套的TJGT509型提花机。该机能织造提花挂毯、提花地毯等织物，达到设计指标，结束国产地毯织机不能织造提花型织物的历史。2002年，对该机型又进行优化设计，增加双经提花起毛机构，适用织造宽幅、中厚提花织物。该项目获2002年天津市科技进步三等奖。

2002年，天宁公司完成TJGN202（1000）型重型织机试制。该机型是国内生产的最宽最重织机，幅宽10米，最宽可达20米，主要织造工业用呢、造纸、环保用网，属市级重点项目。当年通过市级鉴定。

2002年，天宁公司裴有成等开发TJGN206型工业织网机。该类织机广泛用于医药、食品、造纸、环保行业，用厚重聚脂类工业网替代不锈钢网或铜网，可节约大量有色金属。

2003年，靖隆公司孙宏维针对纺织用胶圈原材料采用机械高温接枝共混工艺存在的产品质量波动较大、胶圈可靠性相对较差问题，突破传统的配方设计模式，采用NBR/PVC共沉胶为主体材料，设计开发出A-031型新型纺纱胶圈，为共沉胶在国产纺纱胶圈的应用闯出新路。专业论文在“纺织器材”杂志刊登。

2003年，靖隆公司自行开发、自主配方设计拥有自主知识产权的MS-63型和MS-65型纺纯绵免处理软胶辊。该产品在高温、高湿度季节适纺能力强，不需任何处理，不粘缠。经专家鉴定，与进口胶辊处于同一水平，被用户誉为名副其实的免处理胶辊。

2003年3月，天津市纺织集团技术中心委托天津市佳可得公司设计制造拉伸羊毛关键设备。2005年8月完成4台套自动化拉伸羊毛设备，由天津纺织集团立项，属国家科委计划内项目。

二、技术改造和工艺改进

（一）技术改造

1993年6月，天津市纺织针布厂执行新的生产工艺，为使产品升级换代，购置针布冲粹卷生产线成套设备。经检测，用该生产线生产的产品质量显著提高，生产能力稳定上升，产品大批量投放市场。1994年5月，与国内另外两个同类产品上机试验，进行性能对比，一致认定天津市纺织针布厂生产的AC2820X01367型针布分梳效果好，各项指标获第一名。1996年10月该厂根据市场要求，对针布冲淬卷生产线进行技术改造，先后试制出TL-3A型等齿条产品，投放市场后获得较高评价，产品技术优势明显，部分指标达到国内先进水平。1998年，天津市纺织针布厂改制，成立天津市金矛梳理器材有限公司，根据纺织业发展需要，结合针布制造业产品发展方向，选购新型专用设备，使该产品更新换代。

（二）工艺改进

1991年，天津市纺织机械第七配件厂鉴于斜齿罗拉握持纺纱稳定、成纱质量好等优点，为改进生产工艺，组成由杨学孔、孙悟奎、云玉成为主的工艺攻关组，重点解决老机型用直齿罗拉改为新型斜齿罗拉生产工艺问题。通过改进主要工序，更新关键磨具，探索成功直齿罗拉生产工艺改为斜齿工艺。应用新工艺生产的斜齿罗拉，经天津市第一绵纺织厂等用户试纺及天津纺织机械厂研究所认定，均给予充分肯定。经国家纺织机械质量监督检验中心检测，各项指标均达到国家行业标准。

1993年，天津市纺织机械第七配件厂改进罗拉外表面镀硬铬处理。根据国内重点用户天津纺织机械厂要求，企业技术人员与天津纺织机械厂研究所合作，针对表面处理进行研究，从工艺方面多次改进，探讨表面处理方法。经反复试验，罗拉表面镀层牢固，且保持较高硬度，各项指标达到要求。

1995年，天津市纺织机械第七配件厂改进罗拉加工三对齐工艺增加新品种。根据纺织市场需求，研制FA401系列粗纱机用牵伸罗拉。多年延续的三列对齐加工工艺存在许多弊病，主要表现在：基准属粗加工定位不准确；多刀排人工对刀难度大；机械落刀误差较大。改进办法：改用罗拉导柱端面定位，孔中心复位，顶紧后加工；配置主动测量装置，导柱部位精度由Φ+0.005~0.004提高到Φ+0.0025~0.0025；用数控机床替代普通机床。该企业在改进工艺、更新设备，提高质量的同时，产品开发能力增强。

第十二章　轻　工

天津轻工加工业有过辉煌的历史。众多久负盛名的老字号品牌，以精湛技艺和服务体系，形成天津工商业独特而深厚的文化底蕴。在改革开放的进程中，随着经济结构、产业结构和企业布局调整，天津轻工业产品生产经历剧烈变迁，传统的加工产品生产大批转移。面对激烈的市场竞争，天津轻工企业依靠科技自主创新支撑具有比较优势的产品生产，手表、自行车、地毯、体育用品等优势行业则实行知识产权战略，走上标准化高端化发展道路。

第一节　手　表

天津海鸥手表集团公司1992年在天津手表厂基础上组建成立，2003年改组为天津中鸥表业集团有限公司。1991~2005年，其科技自主创新的主要成果有万年历、问表、陀飞轮机械表、ST16系列多功能机械表、ST25系列多功能机械表等。

1997年3月，天津手表厂张兆理、王沄生、李祺研制完成ST16双历自动机械男表机芯的设计并制出样机10只。机芯共由25个部件，173个零件组成，其中与ST6通用的零件55个。ST16机芯技术特点为：①机芯配合直径Φ25.6毫米，厚度5.55毫米，双历加厚0.55毫米，自动加厚1.25毫米；②摆轮振动节拍21600次/时；③走时精度-30~+45秒；④机芯上有22个宝石轴承。结构特点：机芯薄，基础机芯厚度3.75毫米；具有先进的快拨日历和周历3档快拨功能；自动机构可以双向上条，上条效率高；上满发条走时47小时以上；通用性好。

2000年，天津海鸥手表集团公司耿力军、李文平等设计开发多功能自动机械表。到2004年，在ST16基础机芯上，先后设计开发出ST16S、ST16N、ST16Q、ST16L等18个品种的系列多功能自动机械表，具有日历、大日历、周历、月历、年历、星辰、24时、示能显示等多种功能，并相继投放市场。

2001年4月，天津海鸥手表集团公司李文平、张芳、刘连忠、赵国望等研制完成ST17系列薄型自动机械表。该产品的技术特点：机芯直径26毫米，基础机芯厚度3.22毫米；摆轮振动节拍数21600次/时；走时延续时间大于36小时；走时精度-10~+30秒。ST17薄型自动机械男表的传动系统采用直传式二轮输出结构，结构特点：①“一少”，即需要加工的零部件数量少。该产品是企业中采用通用件标准化的典型。整个机芯设计中零部件数为：组件8个，部件21个，零件139个。需要进行新加工的组件为7个，部件为14个，零件46个，其他零部件均与ST6、ST16等产品通用；②“一多”，即花色品种多。ST17薄型自动机械男表将小秒针设计在“6”字位，并可以带有多种功能的附加机构。其附加机构具有可分性，能实现多种不同功能结构的组合，适应市场多花色、小批量的需求。其中，三针分离、能量显示、跳时、大日历、飞返日历、周历、月历、星辰、镂空等机构，形成ST17F、ST17T、ST17V、ST17L、ST17N、ST17TF等20种53个花色的系列产品；③“一薄”，即擒纵叉薄。擒纵叉减薄至0.18毫米，并选择钢材，改变以往产品使用铜材的惯例，克服铜材强度不够容易变形的缺点，满足设计和使用要求。2005年7月，该产品通过由市经委组织的技术鉴定，认为该产品技术工艺水平处于国内领先地位。

2001年5月，天津渤海中鸥表业技术有限公司周文霞、张福云、刘连仲、王云洁等设计研制出ST18薄型日历自动机械男表。机芯共由9个组件、33个部件、170个零件组成，机芯设计符合国际标准。该产品技术参数：机芯最大直径φ26.2毫米（装配直径φ25.6毫米），机芯总厚度3.83毫米，具有3字位日历窗口显示、自动、止秒等功能。该机芯结构特点：①主传动采用先进的偏中心3轮输出传动形式，振动频率为28800次/时，走时精度为-20~+40秒，并且配有微调装置，调整方便准确；②条盒容量较大，延续走时≥42小时；③自动机构设计为整体组合，重锤内嵌滚动轴承；组合换向轮机构可双向上条，提高上条效率；④日历机构埋入主夹板，不增加机芯厚度。

图5-12-1-79 陀飞轮手表

2002年4月，天津渤海中鸥表业技术有限公司江达生、刘连忠、黄子洪等在参考借鉴原“304”机械计时表的基础上，研制开发出ST19计时表机芯。该机芯是一种带有测时机构，可记分、记秒，时、分、秒针指示的5针计时手表，机芯最大直径φ31.3毫米（装配直径φ31毫米），机芯总厚度6.2毫米，19钻，振动频率21600次/时，走时精度-20~+40秒，延续走时≥36小时。此机芯中心位置安装时、分针及测时中心秒针，在3点位安装测时用计分针（量程0~30分），在9点位安装走时小秒针，在6点位可安装12小时（或24小时）指针。机芯及外观采用具有国际水平的精雕镂空、铣花及镀玫瑰金、镀铑等精饰镀饰加工工艺进行处理，大大提高产品附加值。

2002年7月，天津渤海中鸥表业技术有限公司周文霞、刘连仲等研制ST8000陀飞轮机械表。陀飞轮装置是将擒纵调速机构安装在匀速旋转的框架内，使擒纵调速机构在按设计周期工作的同时，又随框架整体公转，提高手表走时精度。该机芯主要技术参数为机芯最大直径Φ30毫米，机芯厚度5.45毫米，摆轮振动频率21600次/时，摆轮采用花摆，直径为Φ8.2毫米，陀飞轮直径为Φ13毫米。该机芯结构特点为：①机芯传动形式采用直接传动式；②整体旋转的擒纵调速装置采用摆轮偏心式；③旋转框架采用下支撑结构，可实现无障碍观察陀飞轮运动;④大直径宝石平面与框架转轴接触,使框架平稳转动,耐磨性好;⑤在表盘面3、9、12点位预留附加机构空间,便于花色品种的增加和变化。⑥采用国际水平的精饰镀饰加工工艺,摆轮设计为螺丝花摆的精调结构,机芯装配面夹板精铣"鱼鳞"纹,背面精铣"日内瓦"条纹,夹板表面全部进行镀铑工艺处理,提升产品档次和附加值。2005年7月,该产品通过市级鉴定,产品的技术及工艺处于国内领先水平。到2005年共研制出具有能量显示、指针日历、雕花镂空等系列陀飞轮机械表共7种。向国家知识产权局申报"手表发条能量显示机构"和"陀飞轮雕花镂空" 两项专利。截至2005年底,累计生产陀飞轮系列机芯3970只,实现产值821万元,利税410万元,产品远销欧美、日本等国家和中国香港地区。2005年3月,玫瑰金陀飞轮手表被天津博物馆收藏;中国嘉德2005钟表相机专场拍卖会上,陀飞轮玫瑰金手表参加竞拍,并以5.2万元拍卖成交,成为中国自行设计的高档机械表中成交价格最高的产品。

2003年9月,天津渤海中鸥表业技术有限公司周文霞、刘连仲等组成设计组设计ST2500多功能机械男表机芯。该产品技术特点:一是增大发条力矩,增大摆轮直径,实现产品多功能储存动力,二是具有良好的工艺性,力求适应多品种的生产。该产品是适应手表市场向多功能复杂机芯方向发展而开发的,产品从设计到样机试制仅用3个月时间。产品技术参数:机芯装配直径φ30毫米,外径φ30.4毫米,机芯总厚5.9毫米,其中自动机构厚2.1毫米,振动节拍21600次/时,走时精度-10~+30秒,延续走时≥40小时,具有自动、止秒、快拨等功能;机芯共有25个部件,173个零件组成,与ST6通用件55个。该产品结构特征:采用偏3轮输出结构,中心时、分、秒针;飞轮在"6"点位显示可作仿陀飞表;在"9"点位预留小秒针;为便于产品的试制投产,设计时采用成熟的机构,擒纵调速采用ST18的擒纵调速机构,手上条与拨针采用ST5结构,自动结构采用ST6C自动机构的传动形式,产品设计达到预期的要求。截至2005年底,共研制开发ST25系列多功能机械表6个品种9个花色。

2004年3月,天津中鸥表业集团有限公司赵国望、黄子洪等组成ST2800项目组,研制开发具有闹铃功能的机芯。该机芯技术特征:机芯直径φ29.4毫米,机芯总厚5.96毫米,振动节拍21600次/时,走时精度-20~+40秒,延续走时≥40小时。该产品结构特点:采用两个原动组件,分别为闹铃条盒和走时条盒;主传动设计为直传结构;擒纵机构使用ST2500的结构;调速器采用ST19的摆轮、游丝;借用ST5机芯的部分结构;分别在机芯的2点位和4点位使用两套前阀结构;并借鉴国外的闹擒纵结构。该机芯具备的功能有:中心4大针,其中最下面的指针是闹铃指针,其他三针为时、分、秒指针;2点位柄轴具有调闹、止闹、闹铃条上弦功能;4点位柄轴具有走时上弦、拨针功能。

第二节　自行车

天津是中国自行车产业的发源地。天津自行车的整套生产制造技术,特别是制管、冲压、金切、焊接、热处理、油漆、电镀等七大关键的工艺,基本上是在20世纪50、60年代通过自力更生、集体攻关逐步形成和发展起来,曾经为国家制定自行车专业技术和质量标准化奠定基础。1991~2005年,天津自行车行业在经历大规模结构调整与改组的同时,生产制造技术也发生质的飞跃。特别是在质量监督检验及其设备的制造,以及电动自行车的研制生产方面,继续走在全国前列。

一、质量检测设备

国家自行车质量监督检验中心(简称自行车质监中心)设在天津市自行车研究所,是首批经国家技术监督局审查认可的国家自行车质量监督检验中心和国家进出口商品检验局审查认可的国家自行车商检实验室。1995年通过中国实验室国家认可委员会审查,成为首批国家认可的检验实验室,同年被国家科委、国家技术监督局认定为科学技术成果检测鉴定国家级检测机构和自行车专用检测设备的归口管理单位。2004年又通过国家实验室项目审查，成为检测/校准实验室。该中心承担自行车、电动自行车国家产品质量监督抽查工作，以及天津市定期质量监督抽查和政府部门委托的专项监督检验工作。

1992年，自行车质监中心设计制造的检测设备“自行车疲劳测试技术的研究及试验机的研制”项目获国家轻工业部科技进步二等奖。1995年，“自行车能量吸收试验机”项目获国家轻工业部科技进步三等奖；“自行车强度检测成套设备”项目获天津市科技进步奖三等奖。1996年，“自行车拨链器振动疲劳试验机”项目获国家轻工业部科技进步三等奖。2004年，该中心完成儿童自行车、电动童车、婴儿学步车、儿童手推车、儿童三轮车的检测设备共计38台套，填补国内童车检测设备的空白，并远销国内外计200多台套。2005年，该中心完成自行车部件疲劳强度试验设备，满足德国标准的车架动态疲劳试验机、满足国际标准的车把疲劳试验机、鞍管疲劳试验机、曲柄组合件疲劳试验机、前叉疲劳试验机。通过行业专家的鉴定，设备达到国际领先水平，销售量达100多台。

二、电动自行车

1992年，天津市飞鸽集团下属企业自行车二厂从德国引进一辆电动自行车，车型的基本配置为摩轮式有刷电机，铬镍电池。在参考引进车型的基础上，该厂组织专业班子，进行电动自行车引进消化再创新的专项研制。该项目由市科委立项，作为自行车行业重点开发的方向性项目拨款予以支持。

1993年，自行车二厂科技人员与社会科研部门相互配合，先后研制出后摩轮式电动自行车和轮毂式电动自行车。初期研制的产品摩轮式电动自行车，电机为有刷电机，功率为100瓦；轮毂式电动自行车，电机为有刷电机，功率为150瓦。以24伏、10安培/小时铅酸电池作为能源。单人骑行续航里程20余千米。1998年产品投入市场。

1998年，天津红旗特种车科技开发有限公司成立，将天津电动自行车推向产业化的道路。在电机方面，鉴于低速无刷轮毂式电机因其不用碳刷而备受关注，就其控制器的技术瓶颈开展研究。在材质方面，天津自行车行业通过深入研究和协调准备，建立镁合金自行车产业化开发机制。

2003年，天津市飞鸽集团自行车三厂技术人员徐庆国、张玉芹等组织专家就镁合金材料（包括铸造合金和挤压合金）在自行车上的应用，开展可行性研究及产地资源考察，并在该厂进行镁合金样车研制和架叉结构优化设计，取得初步成果，开发生产出斯塔特牌电动自行车。该厂技术开发中心与北京首特钢联合开发研制镁合金自行车车架及零部件，同时与哈尔滨光宇集团联合开发磷酸亚铁锂电动自行车专用电池。

2005年，天津市自行车行业生产力促进中心制定“天津市电动自行车用电器部件五项地方标准”。内容包括电动自行车无刷直流电动机、永磁直流电动机、车用控制器、铅酸电池充电器和锂离子电池的技术条件。该标准的制定为国内首创，不仅解决电动自行车只有整车技术标准而没有电器部件技术标准的问题，而且建立电动自行车产品质量新的技术规范。

第三节　家用电器

20世纪90年代，天津家用电器工业迅速发展。1995年天津市二轻集团（控股）有限公司与韩国LG电子株式会社合资，建立乐金电子（天津）电器有限公司，生产空调器、微波炉、吸尘器、空调压缩机、电机及磁控管等产品。通过引进开发和创新，天津家电生产技术水平得到提高。

一、空调器

1992年，天津市空调器公司开发出7000瓦柜式空调器，分体壁挂式空调器。这是天津市首次研制生产壁挂空调器，填补空白。

1998年，乐金电子（天津）电器有限公司开发侧出风柜式空调器。

2000年，乐金电子（天津）电器有限公司开发出等离子空调。等离子技术作为高尖端技术，最初应用于国防科研以及航空航天领域，LG电子第一个把该项技术用于空调。LG等离子空调采用整体空气净化技术，避免能量的虚耗，以生物抗菌过滤层、等离子体过滤层、杀菌过滤层，进行阶段渐进式过滤，彻底清除空气中的各种有害物质，达到净化细菌体、强力除异味、超强除烟除尘的净化效果，把空调空气净化技术提升到新水平。

2002年，乐金电子首次推出电子眼空调。在出风口位置设置的一对电子眼，可以根据人体远近，进行风量和角度的调节。该电子眼系在空调领域首次使用。

同年，康迪空调有限公司开发出小型冷水机组。该产品为家用中央空调，制冷量7.4~64千瓦。适用于80至800平方米。

2003年，乐金电子推出省电双子星系列空调。以使用2-Comp System容量可变型空调来改善冷却及设置空间的四角地带的3D立体制冷的新概念空调的开发。一个室外机拥有一大一小两个压缩机构成，根据负荷的不同启动不同容量组合的压缩机，以达到省电和延长使用寿命的目的。在中国空调容量可变的领域，具有领先优势。

同年，康迪空调有限公司开发出LSQ（R）F24冷水机组。系家用、商用两用中央空调，制冷（热）量24KW。该产品为双系统冷水机组，提高节能效果，控制方便，技术先进。

2004年，乐金电子（天津）电器有限公司开发出商用空调。LG商用空调采用世界先进的数码变频技术，具有节能、环保、设计灵活、操作幅度宽等优点，同时可以选择中央控制、电话控制或互联网控制。自行研究开发出适合四季气候变化的独有的尖端技术，掌握压缩机、线性膨胀阀、过冷凝器、变频控制电路等关键部件的核心技术，进一步提高产品的性能。集中控制功能可同时控制16台室内机。

二、微波炉

1997年，乐金电子（天津）电器有限公司开始生产微波炉

2001年，乐金电子（天津）电器有限公司开发万向转动式烧烤管微波炉。烧烤管旋转加热，解决烧烤不均和速度慢的难题。之后，推出具有国际领先功能的Internet网络大厨微波炉，把微波炉通过数据线与PC机相连，通过Internet网络下载菜谱，尔后把菜谱传送到微波炉，也可远程控制微波炉动作。

2002年，乐金电子（天津）电器有限公司开发温控灵微波炉系列。普通的微波炉根据时间和火力的设定来加热食物，其不足之处是难以把握食物烹调的火候。LG温控灵装有红外感应系统，炉腔内的传感器可以通过食物发出红外线受热产生的能量变化感知其表面温度，通过显示器显示出来，使烹调过程更加直观。

2003年，乐金电子（天津）电器有限公司开发圆胆快速大厨微波炉系列。LG独特的圆形内胆，采用整板一次成型技术，不仅将炉体结构改进更加合理，内部使用空间扩大，而且使微波加热等多方面性能都加以改善，获得国家专利技术认证。其特点为：快速均匀，均匀加热，清洁简便。同年，该公司推出开放式烧烤系统，采用紫晶管加热，料理速度提高30%。

2004年，乐金电子（天津）电器有限公司开发出“蒸神煎霸”微波炉上市。特制的烹饪锅容器，突破微波炉不能蒸、煎、炸的弊端，可以对食物实现蒸，煎，炸等的料理功能。还设置12道左右的自动料理菜单，更大程度上满足消费者料理需求。

同年，纳米抗菌微波炉投放市场。国内率先在微波炉炉体上使用纳米材料，有效杀灭附着在内胆表面的有害细菌，杀菌率高达99.99%，保证饮食健康，不使用的时候也能起到抗菌，杀菌的效果。

2005年，乐金电子（天津）电器有限公司开发的“热风透烤王”系列投放市场。该型号采用后置式热风对流结构，改进自然烤箱原理，保证炉腔内各位置温度完全一致，旋转盘保证食物全方位立体均匀受热，中途不必翻转。特点是：恒温，定温，控温烧烤，可100℃~250℃自由设定温度（每10℃为一档）；特制烹调，热风透烤的料理，给消费者特别享受；还有发酵功能，满足消费者对面食的处理；关注消费者饮食健康的卡路里显

示功能，有利于饮食结构更加合理。

三、吸尘器

2002年，乐金电子（天津）电器有限公司自主开发第一款带有HEPA filter（高效微粒空气过滤器）的吸尘器。HEPA filter是先进有效的灰尘过滤方式，对空气中灰尘的过滤效果可以达到99.5%。

2003年，乐金电子（天津）电器有限公司自主开发第一款立式吸尘器（也称Upright吸尘器）。采用吸嘴与机体一体化设计，吸嘴里带有滚动毛刷。具有使用便利的特点，特别是对地毯的清洁有着其他吸尘器无法比拟的优势。产品畅销北美市场。

2004年，乐金电子（天津）电器有限公司的NANO filter 和 NANO 集尘盒开发成功。NANO filter是利用纳米银离子技术的新型过滤器，能在过滤掉灰尘的同时杀死空气中的细菌，抑制病毒生长。NANO集尘盒对大肠杆菌的有效率达到99.9%。

2005年，乐金电子（天津）电器有限公司采用气旋式集尘方式的Cyking 吸尘器开发成功。气旋式集尘方式采用圆柱形的集尘盒代替传统的集尘袋，把吸入的灰尘在集尘盒里进行旋转，利用离心力分离空气和灰尘，灰尘留在积尘袋里，只排出清洁的空气，所以是不需要积尘袋的新概念的集尘方式，使用便利，易于清洁。产品出口美国和欧盟等国家。

第四节 地 毯

20世纪90年代，中国地毯行业产品结构大幅调整，机制地毯形成显著的发展强势，市场竞争激烈。根据行业加强产品质量管控的需要，天津地毯行业充分发挥天津市地毯研究所在图案设计和新品研制方面的专业技术强项，在突出地毯新图案设计与新品技术研发创新优势的同时，快速拓展标准化和质量检测工作。到2005年，天津市地毯标准化工作和质检机构处在行业科技发展的前沿领地。

1990年，天津市地毯研究所与浙江大学计算机系合作研发的“地毯图案计算机辅助设计系统”在国内地毯行业首开计算机辅助设计图案的先河，成为业内开创性的科技成果。该项目分别获得国家轻工业部科技进步二等奖和天津市科技进步三等奖，以及多项省部级其他奖项。

1992年，以天津市地毯研究所为主，无锡塑料铺地材料厂、北京燕山石化公司化纤地毯厂、威海地毯毛纺厂等单位配合，起草完成的中国首个地毯产品标准GB11746-89“簇绒地毯”，获得国家轻工业部科技进步二等奖和国家技术监督局科技进步三等奖。1993年，该项目获得天津市科技进步三等奖。

1993年，天津市地毯研究所与浙江大学计算机系合作，在“地毯图案计算机辅助设计系统”基础上，研发“壁纸图案CAD辅助设计系统”，为国内壁纸图案设计带来重要的技术革新。该项目获得天津市科技进步三等奖，并于翌年实现技术转让。

1995年，以天津市地毯研究所为主，上海纺织科学院、上海石化总厂实验厂、辽阳石化公司纤维二厂、甘肃无纺织地毯厂等单位配合，起草完成的地毯产品标准GB/T15051-1994“针刺地毯”，获得国家轻工总会科技进步三等奖和天津市科技进步三等奖。

1997年，以天津市地毯研究所为主，北京燕山石化公司化纤地毯厂、浙江美术地毯厂等单位配合，起草完成的地毯产品标准GB/T14252-1993“机织地毯”，获得天津市科技进步三等奖。该标准与“簇绒地毯”“针刺地毯”一并成为中国机制地毯3大类别产品的质量技术法规，为新兴起的机制地毯生产经营提供质量技术规范。

1997年，天津市地毯研究所作为国际标准化组织地毯技术归口单位，代表中国出席在英国举行的第19届国际地毯标准化会议。经过多轮激烈的交涉，最终使中方提案被国际标准采纳，将手工地毯耐人工光源色牢度(氙弧灯)指标由原定的5级改为4级，从而使中国和众多发展中国家合法规避因染料技术水平所限最高只达到4级的瓶颈难题，有效保护地毯出口贸易。

同年，由天津市地毯研究所、国家地毯质量监督检验中心负责，圆满完成香港回归祖国所使用的区旗的全天候耐光色牢度检验测试，展示出自身的质检工作水平与能力。

1998年10月，天津市地毯研究所研发的“现代手绘艺术壁挂”登记为天津市科技成果。该产品为现代室内装饰艺术增加新品，以新、雅、奇、精的艺术特色成为市场上的畅销商品。并于翌年实现技术转让。

2001年，由天津市地毯研究所起草完成的地毯试验方法标准GB/T18044-2000“地毯静电性能评定模拟人体步行试验方法”登记为天津市科技成果。该成果由国家地毯质量监督检验中心出具国内最具权威性的质检报告，被广泛应用于飞机座舱、计算机房、实验室、轮船、车辆和高级宾馆等对静电性能要求高的场所使用地毯的质量监督检验，以保证安全性。

2002年，天津市地毯研究所与天津市卫生防病中心、南开大学、军事医学科学院卫生环境医学研究所，山东威海海马集团等单位配合，起草完成的地毯产品标准GB1858-2001“室内装饰装修材料地毯、地毯衬垫、及地毯胶粘剂有害物质释放限量”，成为中国首个地毯绿色环保检测方法标准。是年7月1日，国家质检总局明令禁止市场销售不符合该国家标准的产品。

同年，天津市地毯研究所检测业务不断扩项，增至31类产品及原材料，280多项技术指标；受检的地毯厂商扩及轻工、纺织、建材、石化、航空航海、商业等诸多行业，遍布全国各地。经过不断创新完善，天津市地毯研究所为中国地毯标准体系的形成和发展做出贡献，促使地毯标准形成涵盖基础标准、产品标准、方法标准3个层面，包容30多项国家标准、行业标准，扩及到200多项相关标准的中国地毯现行有效标准体系。

第五节 体育用品

天津市体育用品主要生产厂家春合体育用品厂和利生体育用品厂，坚持走构建高端化、高质化、高新化产业结构的创新发展之路，在运动器械和皮制球制造方面有较强的技术实力。春合体育用品厂通过与美国波特公司合作，将“中华牌”体育器械打入到国际市场，同时，从引进先进技术，提高产品性能入手，将新品设计与国际接轨，打造优秀的民族品牌。利生体育用品厂(1993年7月更名为天津津港集团有限公司利生运动制品分公司，1996年3月更名为天津南华利生体育用品有限公司，简称南华利生)在发展中注重对整个行业的带动，受国家有关部门委托拟订球类产品的全国行业标准(QB1468-92)，促进行业生产水平提高。南华利生1991年生产的7号篮球获得中华人民共和国金质奖；1992年生产的金杯牌足球获得商业部92最畅销国产商品金桥奖；1993年至1996年生产的“利生”牌篮球、1996年至2004年生产的“利生”牌足球分别被国际篮联和国际足联批准为国际比赛用球。

一、运动器械

(一)产品设计

1995年，天津市春合体育用品厂(简称春合厂)为当年在北京举行的远东及南太平洋残疾人运动会试制生产残疾人专用游泳及跳水升降椅、举重卧推架、立举架、标枪投掷轮椅、田径投掷圈、盲人足球门等6种比赛及辅助训练器械，填补中国残疾人体育运动器械的生产空白。

1999年，春合厂为迎接在天津举办的“第三十四届世界体操锦标赛”，承担为世锦赛研制生产“全套体操器械”共11种体操比赛器械的任务，主要作为国内、国际各类大型比赛使用。经过两年多以创新精神研制生产，产品送交国际体操联合会官方检测机构——德国弗莱堡大学和日本东京工业大学，按照最新国际标准经过静态、动态（模拟机器人）、冲击、震动、稳定性等5种测试系统、使用计算机和现代传感仪器设备检测，连续取得9种比赛器械的国际体联合格认证；其中自由体操场地等6种器械被天津第34届世界体操锦标赛锦赛选用，单杠等5种器械由春合厂与美国AA1公司合作生产，经过20多天120多场次、来自世界72个国家和地区、1400多名中外运动员大运动量的、高密度、超负荷的严格考验，保证大会取得圆满成功，为祖国为天津市人民争得荣誉。

2001年，春合厂借在美国奥兰多举办“春合商品展览”的机会，主动与世界著名的美国波特公司接触，促成合作生产。产品为美国NBA职业篮球比赛系列篮球架以及大量的钢化玻璃篮板产品、手动和电动高度调节器、击球护笼等篮球架系列产品，销售到美国和世界市场。截至2005年，共试制成功由国际篮球联合会（FIBA）认证的Porter牌01235-108、01235-914液压可移动、自动升降的国际比赛篮球架，01535-108、01535-800弹簧助力升降可移动的比赛篮球架，00735-208、00735-200弹簧助力可移动篮球架；研制成功适用于国内比赛和训练的31535-108液压可移动自动升降篮球架，50735、50003支架组装式篮球架，健身工程的地埋式户外训练型篮球架等24种篮球架。同时，研制成功24秒记时器及篮板灯带示分系统，经过美国NBA和在中国的季前赛使用，并为“北京斯坦科维奇杯”世界大型国际比赛使用，获得国际篮球联合会的表彰。

2002年，春合厂与美国全球体育公司合作研制成功各类儿童体操器械。包括儿童小单杠、落地折叠平衡木、跳马平台（获外观设计和实用新型两项国家专利）、儿童助跳板、斜坡垫子、4′×8′折叠垫子、5′×10′5折垫子、6′×12′6折垫子等多种产品，销往美国市场。

2003年，春合厂与德国史必斯公司合作生产跳马平台、德式儿童高低杠、儿童吊环等产品，销往德国市场。

2004年，春合厂研制成功儿童大弹床，出口厄瓜多尔。同时，按照国际标准研制成功比赛用大弹床等产品，满足国内市场需求。

2005年，春合厂与土耳其外贸公司合作开发生产针对欧美人体、适合伊斯兰国家市场的22种户外健身器材，出口土耳其等伊斯兰国家。

（二）产品加工

1999年，春合厂为天津世锦赛研制比赛用“全套体操器械”。研制成功木塑复合材料层压板、自由操场地板、橡胶聚乙烯等8种新材料；研制成功不锈钢单杠杠面热处理工艺、挤拉成型玻璃钢杠面全套模具、助跳板垫扎成型模具等新工艺9种；设计5种新结构产品，使其性能达到国际体联最新标准要求。

（三）产品检测

1997~1999年，春合厂更新改造检测仪器设备，为研制送检产品取得合格认证打下基础。根据国际体联要求，在国际体联举办的世界级大赛中使用的10种比赛器械，必须经过德国和日本官方检测机构，通过动态、静态、冲击、震动、稳定5类测试方法检测，测试精度为1%毫米。而春合厂原有检测设备陈旧、精度低，只有静态和冲击测试两种，频率响应不能达到准确的定量分析目的。为使产品送检前自检结果接近国际标准，春合厂在更新改造检测仪器设备中，采用大规模集成电路技术，研制出静态拉压位移测试系统；为缩小测试误差，将电感式位移传感器更新改造为瑞士奇士乐产的100-5000克的加速度传感器和测试软件；更新计算机，增容加速，提高数据处理能力。通过对被测产品大量的测试和数据分析，指导器材研制，为产品送检取得合格认证奠定基础。

二、皮制球

1994年，南华利生在工艺开发方面技术创新，逐步推广以缠线球代替传统工艺的贴布球。此种缠线工艺与传统的贴布工艺相比，具有强度高，外观美观，机械自动作业，成本经济等特点。从而带动整体行业的球胎制造水平大幅度提高。缠线球工艺推广后，1997年“利生”牌足球产品被评为“武汉97中国体育用品博览会金奖”。1998年“利生”牌皮制球产品被评为“福州98中国体育用品博览会”优秀奖。1997年全国女子甲级复赛联赛WCBA,1998年全国大学生篮球联赛CUBA,首届全国沙滩排球精英赛,均采用“利生”牌产品。

1996年4月,南华利生开发研制橡胶实心球。该种橡胶实心球安全、卫生、耐用。短短几年取代原有的手缝实心球,成为大部分中小学的指定用球。1998年该橡胶实心球申请实用新型专利,于1999年5月获国家专利局授权。

2000年,南华利生研发并推广机贴足球。2002年,推广机贴排球。2003年,南华利生申请“机粘篮球的制作工艺及专用模具”发明专利。2005年,南华利生研制开发机粘篮球及专用模具,大幅提高产品品质和生产效率,降低劳动强度。

2002年9月,南华利生开发研制软式排球。2003年4月,南华利生开发研制手缝软式排球,并获国家实用新型专利。2004年5月,南华利生研制开发新型篮球。

第六节　食品与饮品

天津食品和饮品的生产企业众多。传统的酿酒工艺技术水平提升,反映出诸多企业对于技术进步的追求。天津工业微生物研究所研究人员在食品研发中取得创新成果。

一、酿酒

天津津酒集团在继承酿造技术传统的过程中勇于创新,依靠科技进步开发新品牌产品。其传统产品“直沽牌”直沽高粱酒1998年荣获轻工部优质出口产品银奖;其代表产品“津牌”津酒,作为中国北方地区最早的浓香型低度白酒,2003年4月共有5个系列产品获得国家质检总局颁发的原产地标记注册证书。1999年该企业通过ISO 9001—2000质量管理体系认证,在白酒研究方面取得创新成果,在生产中应用推广新经验。

(一)人工老窖技术

1991年,津酒集团技术人员在对人工老窖泥功能菌、己酸菌的分离、纯化、优选、性能鉴定的基础上,开展固定化细胞新材料研究。主要性能指标:PVA(聚乙烯醇)包埋法与颗粒活性炭吸附法固定己酸菌细胞,两种载体使用次数均在20次以上、发酵液平均产己酸量612毫克/100毫升。与南开大学分析中心合作拍摄了固定化己酸菌细胞、固定化老窖泥功能菌细胞的扫描电子显微镜照片,具有学术资料价值。

1992年,己酸菌扩大培养方式确立。以350千克大缸化学培养基、糟水培养基培养己酸菌、老窖泥。

1993年,窖泥培养新工艺执行,确立培养工艺配方。啤酒干酵母在窖泥培养中的应用,降低窖泥成本、节省资金。

1993~1995年,津酒车间实施全泥窖改造工程。共改造发酵窖池183个。发酵窖池改造后,津酒基础酒中己酸乙酯含量,双轮底基础酒己酸乙酯由2.0克/升达到4.0克/升,大活基础酒己酸乙酯由1.0克/升达到2.0克/升。

(二)传统酿造工艺

1994年,津酒集团挖掘恢复传统酿造工艺生产直沽高粱酒。沿用水泥发酵窖,半机械化生产,续渣双老五甑(回活两甑、大渣四甑、小渣两甑、丢糟两甑),低温发酵,发酵周期12天。2005年9月,“直沽牌”直沽高粱酒被评为天津市名牌产品,出口到东南亚国家、韩国和中国香港地区。以直沽高粱酒为基酒生产的“玉羊牌”玫瑰露酒、滋补保健酒出口到法国、意大利、加拿大和东南亚国家，以及中国香港地区。

（三）勾调理念与创新

1993年，津酒集团技术人员就津酒基础酒进行分析，以白酒勾调新理念为指导，提高白酒质量。开展FFAP（键合石英毛细管柱）白酒毛细管柱直接进样，测定白酒中微量成分定性53个组分，定量26个组分；确定白酒中酸酯含量及平衡性在勾兑中的作用。根据津酒集团基础酒的组成，消费者的口感需求，制定津酒系列酒酒体设计方案。应用四川大学陈益钊教授的理论，创立“白酒酸酯含量平衡勾兑法”，创新白酒勾调理念。努力使技术人员在勾调技术应用实践中，全面掌握从半成品酒到成品酒的各个工艺技术环节，以及相关基本原理、基本技术、基本操作要领。以毛细管气相色谱分析技术分析白酒的香味成分。勾调过程中，首先控制酒的色谱骨架成分，其中酯类是主体香，酸类是味的主体，醇类起调和作用，醛酮起辅佐放香；强调酸酯平衡是勾调出好酒的关键，注重提高基酒质量、调味酒质量、制曲工艺及串蒸工艺；保障储存期，促进酒体发生老熟变化，提高酒质。

1995年，津酒集团立项开展“津牌”珍品津酒的技术研制项目。“津牌”珍品津酒系低度浓香型白酒，产品选用优质高粱为原料，精心勾兑而成。在传统白酒酿造工艺的基础上，采用固定化己酸菌等项现代科学技术，从工艺过程入手，全泥窖发酵容器，双轮底发酵，分层蒸馏，量质摘酒，分级贮存，采用人工和微机勾兑新技术的方法，其工艺路线达到国内先进水平。该产品具有清澈透明，窖香浓郁，口味谐调，醇和绵甜，低而不淡等特点，填补天津市高档酒的空白。“津牌”帝王津酒包装装潢设计新颖，融合中西方的包装特点，具有艺术观赏和收藏价值，属国内首创，1996年度产量10万瓶，创利224万元，税356.4万元，取得较好的经济和社会效益。

2003年，津酒集团开发成功“津牌”龙津酒。该产品属浓郁型、多粮型白酒，选用优质高粱、大麦、小麦、糯米、玉米5种粮食为原料。在传统白酒工艺的基础上，结合现代科学技术，从精选原料开始，优化工艺过程。采用全泥窖容器，双轮底发酵，分层蒸馏，量质摘酒，分级储存，研制成一套具有鲜明特色和专用技术、全新酿造工艺的，其工艺路线达到国内先进水平的“津牌”龙津酒产品，分为38度、52度、55度3种规格。该产品填补天津市高档浓郁型、多粮型白酒的空白。在此基础上，津酒集团研制的“津牌”津酒——龙腾天下，属多种粮食为原料的浓香型高度白酒。其38%vol规格品牌，香气淡爽优雅，入口绵甜，香味谐调，余味爽净，低而不淡，风格突出。52%vol品牌，香气淡爽典雅，入口丰满，醇甜爽净，诸味协调，余味悠长，风格突出。该产品包装设计新颖、大方、独特，瓶中彩色龙船直接接触酒体，获国家知识产权局专利证书。2003年实现产值74.75万元、利税38.76万元。

二、食品研发

1991年10月，天津市工业微生物研究所（以下简称天津工微所）研究人员白耀章、张刚、叶樱等完成天津市科委课题“以大豆为原料生产可可代用品”项目。该新产品开发项目的中试研究是在该课题基础上进行的，经过原料、工艺改进、设备选择和使用，形成产200千克代可可粉生产能力的生产线，所获产品具有可可粉色泽、组成及功能特性，营养成分高于可可粉，在巧克力糖果、冰淇淋、面包、麦乳精等产品上使用，可50%取代市售可可粉。

1991年11月，天津工微所研究人员白耀章、张刚、叶樱、张谦等与蓟县保健植物油厂合作完成“新型老年营养食品——含小麦芽油涂抹食品”项目。该品是适于老年人食用的营养食品，具有低糖，低脂及维生素E高含量的特点，维生素E含量达9~10毫克/每百克，采用全天然成分，不含任何合成食品添加剂。

1991年12月，天津工微所研究人员李淑文、陈国荣、王薇与天津市起士林食品厂柏公芝、李颖新、董涓等人合作完成“双叉乳酸菌在糖果和冰激凌上的应用”项目。该研究将含活性双叉乳酸菌的酸奶粉、酸奶分别应用于糖果和冰激凌生产，制成双叉菌糖果和酸奶冰激凌，具有较高的营养价值和良好的保健效果。由于双叉菌不耐高温，故制成含活性菌的糖果有一定难度，必须提高该菌的耐热性及延长该菌的存活时间。项目成功解决由喷粉干燥剂造粒、烘干及糖果加工中的受热问题，使其适应糖果生产，保证糖果成品中含有一定的活菌数。双叉菌酸奶属国内首创,双叉菌糖果填补国内空白。

1991年11月,项目为天津工微所白耀章、张刚、叶樱、张谦等研究人员与江苏省徐州回民食品厂合作完成“新型营养快餐食品的研制”项目。该品是以乳粉、与糊化谷类粉、蔗糖、大豆蛋白粉以及高效活性钙等原料加工制成的快餐营养粉,不添加任何人工合成原料,用于早餐、加餐,具有营养成分含量高,风味可口的特点,使用方便,经热水冲调后即可食用。技术指标:蛋白质17%~19%,脂肪7%~9%,钙>400毫克/每百克。

1991年11月,天津工微所李红等人完成系列油炸粉的研究项目。该系列产品(椒盐、甜、辣、五香、海鲜味油炸粉)是采用谷物和多种调味料经科学方法精制而成的油炸食品系列专用粉,具有不含传统糊中的明矾,比传统糊使用方便,省油省时,多种口味,易于储存的特点,制成的食品外焦里嫩,香脆可口,营养丰富,口味独特。1992年10月,天津工微所研究人员高学忠、刘敏尧、王建华等人与天津市红旗农场及华海果糖食品厂杜有功、谢青山、松家和合作完成“玉米自然甜化技术研究”项目。自然甜化玉米是以玉米为原料的一种工程食品。经甜化的玉米既保持玉米的营养价值及特性,又具天然的芳香甜味。利用甜化玉米为主要原料,可加工成甜化玉米汁,甜玉米罐头,强化玉米营养粉等系列甜化玉米产品,婴幼儿食品及快餐食品。具有自然甜,易消化吸收的特点,有益人体健康。

1992年9月,天津工微所研究人员庞建华、姜文侠、孙武岳等完成的速食方便米研究项目通过鉴定。该项目是通过一系列物理加工处理后,使大米能在热水浸泡下,很短的时间内又复原成米饭,风味和口感近似一般家庭蒸饭,是居家、旅游,出差、野外作业等的方便食品。研究采用微波脱水技术减少大米营养成分的损失,缩短大米复水时间。其主要技术指标:复水时间≤10分钟,α度≥90%,感观:产品洁白,米粒整齐,无霉味。

1993年10月,天津工微所研究人员高学忠、王建华等完成的甜化玉米(甜化玉米罐头、甜化玉米汁)应用研究项目通过鉴定。项目以普通玉米经生物技术处理制成甜化玉米浆,配合果品原浆,生产甜化玉米饮品,不但保留玉米原有的多种矿物质、维生素、纤维素、蛋白质、脂肪等营养物质,而且含有多种糖类,有利于人体消化吸收,有益于健康。主要技术指标:可溶性固形物≥8.0%不加蔗糖及糖精;外观粒状带糊,色金黄,味甜微带咸鲜味,无杂质存在。用甜化玉米生产罐头,原料来源丰富,不受季节限制,具有广阔前景。

1997年12月,天津工微所研究人员庞志瑞、聂光喻、赵春光、傅亚琴等与加拿大革新食品有限公司合作完成的豆腐香肠研究项目通过验收。该课题是利用易消化吸收的豆腐蛋白质为原料开发灌肠类食品的新品种,以迎合国内外食品消费市场的需要,提供具有保健功能的植物蛋白营养食品。研究成果包括:分析方法的建立,豆腐香肠的配方设计及实验,混合盐和胶原蛋白的研制及应用、豆腐香肠的生产工艺研究、储存实验。2000年1月,天津工微所研究人员程胜利、张谦、鲁德浩等完成的酶水解洋姜生产超高果糖和低聚果糖中试项目通过鉴定。项目筛选的酵母菌产生菊粉酶及水解洋姜中的菊粉的最佳条件,可控制不同工艺条件,分别生产果糖和低聚果糖,作为天然甜味剂。

同年,天津工微所研究人员张刚、蔡永峰等研发完成枣栗子系列食品及其生产方法。该生产方法属于主要含由坚果组成的食品、非酒精饮料及其制备方法。以枣、栗子、低聚糖、白砂糖为主要原料,再加入其他附料,分别制成枣栗子酱,枣栗子饮料,枣栗子羹,枣栗子糊,枣栗子片状食品。该发明产品在营养保健基础上,结合中国传统的民俗与食文化,突出产品的喜庆色彩,赋予更多的“喜”“补”“礼”概念,丰富食品种类。产品原料易得,不需特殊设备,具有工艺简单、能耗低、无环境污染、生产效率高等特点。该项目研究成果申请专利一项:枣栗子系列食品及其生产方法。

2003年6月,天津工微所与天津商学院合作完成的抗冻面包活性干酵母的制备及冷冻面团应用项目通过鉴定,成果为国内领先水平。主要研究人员奚震、李楠、张刚、叶樱等人。苯试验在筛选出LBY-5抗冻酵母的基础上,重点论述面粉的种类、面团的含水量、面团冷冻前发酵时间、冷冻速率与解冻速率,冷冻储藏的温度和时间、解冻方式及添加剂的选择等。

三、饮料研发

1992年12月,天津工微所研究人员赵莉、刘晓红、王薇等完成的乳清发酵饮料的研究项目通过鉴定。研究课题以乳清粉为主要原料,经过配料、发酵科学加工,制成乳清发酵饮料,口感酸甜适口,风味良好,兼有乳酸奶饮料和碳酸饮料的口味，消费对象广泛，是一种新型饮料。

1992年12月，天津工微所研究人员庞志瑞、高学忠、王建华等完成的营养型山楂果肉饮料的研究项目通过鉴定。该饮料选用优质山楂制取果汁和果肉作为主要原料，配以蔗糖、胡萝卜和营养强化剂等辅助材料，经高科技的食品工艺加工而成。

1993年9月，天津工微所研究人员聂光喻、傅亚琴等完成的葵花子奶饮料的研究项目通过鉴定。葵花籽奶是新型的植物蛋白饮料，其原料葵花籽成分中富含维生素E和β族维生素，蛋白质和不饱和脂肪酸的含量也很高。用其制成的饮料营养价值高，经长期饮用，能够补充人体需要的各种营养成分，在保健和抗衰老方面有一定的疗效。1993年9月，天津工微所研究人员赵莉、刘晓红、刘敏尧等完成的果蔬发酵饮料的研制项目通过鉴定。该果蔬发酵饮料以多种果蔬为主要原料，经打浆、榨汁，按一定比例混合，并与多种乳酸菌发酵后调配而成，具有气味清香风味独特，酸味柔和，甜度适中的特点，其营养效价高于果蔬本身，是新型的天然营养保健型饮料。

1994年12月，天津工微所研究人员张谦等完成的嗜哩饮料的研究项目通过鉴定。该品是果蔬汁或蛋白类饮料中含有稳定的冻状颗粒的一种新型饮料，其颗粒在汁中悬浮，且不自溶、不褪色、不含任何人工合成色素。饮料具有天然、口味纯正，形式新颖等特点，分水果型和蔬菜型两种，其颗粒与饮料可同味，也可不同味。

1995年9月，天津工微所研究人员付亚琴、何曼玲、张刚、房鹤鸣等完成的功能性醋酸饮料的研究项目通过鉴定。该项目通过菌种筛选、分离、纯化和选育，从4种活性干酵母中选育出一株酵母菌，具有产酒精含量高(6.5%)，性能稳定之特点。通过基质发酵试验，确定多种原料(谷物、水果、蔬菜、蜂蜜、酒精、蔗糖等)为发酵基质的工艺流程。由此发酵生产出的发酵液调兑成醋酸饮料。产品风味独特，色泽自然(不含人工色素)，果蔬香浓郁，酸爽柔和，营养丰富，对人体具有消除疲劳，增进食欲帮助消化，防治动脉硬化的作用，对治疗肝炎、高血压具有辅助治疗作用，是新型的有多种保健作用的功能性饮料。

2003年6月，天津工微所研究人员叶樱、奚震、姜文侠、庞志瑞、刘然等承担的天津市科委委托的功能性微胶囊绿茶精华素的开发及应用研究项目通过鉴定，成果为国内先进水平。项目主要研究内容：采用低温逆流提取技术进行功能性绿茶精华素的制取，可使浸提工艺连续进行、提高浸出率，保证各项技术指标稳定性，可突破提取率80%的技术难关，能耗低。微胶囊包埋率75%，高度保持绿茶中黄烷醇类、黄酮类、氨基酸、多糖类、生物酶类和维生素类等有效要素的生物活性。

第十三章 制 药

天津是国家重要的制药工业基地之一。1991年至2005年，随着现代制药工程技术迅猛发展，天津制药工业跻身于全市经济发展的6大优势产业之列。天津中药新药的研发和中药现代化，以天津医药集团(以下简称医药集团)、天津中新药业集团股份有限公司(以下简称中新药业)和天津天士力制药股份有限公司(以下简称天士力公司)等为主体，迈出令人瞩目的新步伐。胡锦涛、温家宝、贾庆林等党和国家领导人先后视察现代中药产业园。2004年天津市中药注册品种875个，生产总值占天津医药生产总值三分之一以上。天津西药的生产和研发，集中在天津医药集团和天津金耀集团有限公司(以下简称金耀集团)两大企业集团。全球第一支预填充式a-2b干扰素注射剂，诞生于天津医药集团华立达公司，其基因工程制药技术在国内生物制药领域处于领先地位。金耀集团拥有国内第一支氨基酸输液产品，是国内最大的药用氨基酸原料生产企业，同时是国内皮质激素类药品科研、生产、出口基地和亚洲最大的皮质激素类药物生产企业，设有国家级技术开发中心和国内唯一的甾体药物博士后科研流动站。

第一节 中药制药

天津中药制药工程技术实力雄厚。天津中药集团1994年被批准建立国家级企业技术中心，在进行中成药新产品研制的同时开展中药内在质量的研究。2002年，中新药业在天津经济技术开发区建设现代中药产业园，将天津中新药业研究中心、隆顺榕制药厂、达仁堂制药厂集中于产业园内，使中药的研发、提取、制剂联结成产业链，采用当时先进的中药和植物药提取、浓缩、干燥、制剂技术，成为当年国内最先进、规模最大的植物药生产基地。到2005年，中新药业集团引入一大批仪器设备，科研手段及分析测试水平提高，科研条件得到改善。制剂工艺方面，中成药片剂大多采用薄膜包衣技术，并逐步推广使用水溶性包衣材料，以及干轧制粒、全粉压片、超临界萃取等新技术。天士力公司在中成药新产品、新剂型的研制，推进中药现代化方面，也取得若干创新成果。

一、中药材

1984~1992年，天津市药材公司章臣桂等与上海中医学院合作，针对羚羊角价值昂贵、需求量大等问题，对羚羊角及其骨塞的氮含量、氨基酸含量和微量元素进行药理、临床比较试验，对药用部位和炮制沿革进行考证，确认羚羊角骨塞和羚羊角具有同等疗效。1992年3月该成果得到国家卫生部批准，1995年版“国家药典”据此改为全羚羊角入药，可避免因去掉骨塞而造成的40%原料损失。

1995年，天津市药材集团公司副总工程师李满飞完成“土鳖虫的品种整理和质量研究”课题项目。从两种土鳖虫中分得5种化合物，其中尿囊素、尿嘧啶等经药理试验证明是土鳖虫镇痛的有效成分。1996年该成果获得“国家“八五”科技攻关重大科技成果”证书。

1996年，天津达仁堂制药厂高林善等，针对蜂蜜市场假货泛滥，大多数造假者以C-4植物糖掺入蜂蜜中的手段，采用C13同位素比值技术，利用不同的高等植物在光照下进行光合作用的途径、特别是酶化反应亦不完全相同的原理，对蜂蜜进行真伪优劣鉴别，确保蜂蜜采购的质量。

二、中药饮片

1993年，天津中药饮片厂王学茹等，先后研制成“冷压浸润罐”“隧道式烘干机”“颗粒切制机”等专用设备。其中“颗粒切制机”获得实用新型专利。“冷压浸润罐”集洗、润为一体，让浸润药材药透水尽，有效成分不易流失，避免微生物污染。国家中医药管理局1998年在全国推广使用。通过以塑料袋的小包装取代大包装尼龙袋和牛皮纸袋，对于旋覆花等需要包煎的饮片产品改为机械包装，提高效率5倍以上，成本降低。

1997年，天津市中药饮片厂经过20世纪90年代初期开始的大规模综合性改造，建立化验室、药研室，配置高效液相色谱仪、紫外分光光度仪等设备，检测能力得到提升，被国家医药管理局首批指定为“毒性中药材饮片定点生产企业”。

2002~2005年，天津中药饮片厂针对中药饮片不同品种及影响产品质量的工艺因素，从堆润程度、切制规格、干燥温度、蒸制时间、炒制温度等方面，对制首乌、炒牛蒡子、炒益智、炒槟榔、焦槟榔、蜜炙麻黄、姜厚朴、炙甘草、醋制香附、酒白芍、炒白芍、炒栀子、姜栀子、焦栀子、煅磁石、煅赭石、酒大黄、熟大黄、蜜炙紫菀等20多个品种，确定最佳工艺和可供监测的质量标准。蜜炙甘草，以炒制温度、加蜜量和加蜜方法为重点，用中火炒制，使甘草酸含量不低于2.20%；蜜麻黄，以麻黄碱含量为重点，以60℃干燥，炒制后测得麻黄碱不少于0.40%；醋香附，经反复试验发现，香附在碾串破碎成颗粒后，加20%的食醋拌均闷润4小时，其α-香附酮含量不少于0.11%。

三、中成药

(一)新产品 新剂型

1. 滴丸

1976年开始,天津市中药研究所章臣桂等,通过多种组方及工艺的优选,采取药材与基质加热溶化混匀后滴入不相溶的冷凝液中,收缩制成可被口腔黏膜吸收的滴丸剂“速效救心丸”,1983年在天津市第六中药厂试投产。该品以川芎提取物控制中间体投料,以冰片控制成品含量,率先将含量指标明确写入中成药产品质量标准,1995年被国家科委列为“国家机密级技术项目”。

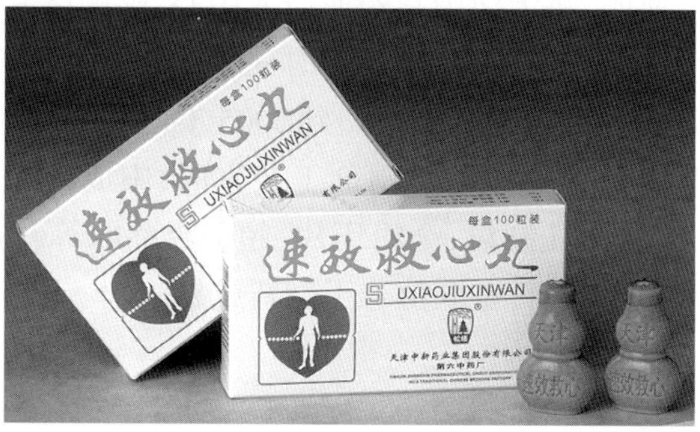

图5-13-1-80 速效救心丸

图5-13-1-81 天士力集团提取车间

1993年,天士力公司研发并拥有自主知识产权的产品“复方丹参滴丸”,被国家卫生部批准作为治疗冠心病、心绞痛的药物上市。该品是根据中医传统理论和现代医药学技术相结合研制的、创新国际量效标准的现代中药滴丸剂,具有多组分、多环节、多靶点保护心血管作用。由丹参、三七、冰片组成,经特殊工艺制成高分散状态的固体分散制剂,其中丹参提取的主要是丹参素为主的水溶性酚酸类物质,三七提取的主要是三七总皂苷。该复方有效成分高,分散均匀,溶出速度快,可直接经粘膜快速吸收入血,提高生物利用度,克服片剂效速度慢、刺激胃黏膜引起胃部不适等弊端。此间,天士力公司探索建立中药提取生产质量管理体系(GEP),自行研制国际领先的滴丸自动生产线,利用计算机在线技术,精确地监控整个生产工艺流程。制定并严格执行内控质量标准24个,率先建立多元化学指纹图谱技术,应用于企业内控标准中,实现从药材、中间体到制剂(GAP-GEP-GMP)的全过程质量控制方法,使重点质量指标高于中国药典标准。围绕该品不断开展基础与临床再研究,先后完成国家级火炬计划,“九五”“十五”“十一五”科技攻关,国家“863”“973”等重点科研项目20多项;与国内外11所大学,17家医院及科研院所合作项目38个;在国外期刊发表学术论文24篇、国内1103篇。获得国际奖项2个,国家级奖项6个,省部级奖项12个;申请相关专利204项。作为现代中药,“复方丹参滴丸”以药品或者处方药品身份在俄罗斯、韩国、越南等国家得到临床应用,截至2005年底,有21个国家批准该药品注册。天士力复方丹参滴丸成为全球首个圆满完成美国FDA三期临床试验的复方中药。

1994年,天津市药材公司章臣桂与天津中药六厂技术人员通过体外抑菌筛选药物,研制成治疗咽喉疾病的“清咽滴丸”。

1999年,天士力公司改进藿香正气的原有剂型,利用现代制剂工艺生产“藿香正气滴丸”。在生产流程中,提取藿香正气中的有效部位,形成固态分子分散体系,使药物分子插入载体骨架中,药物呈分子状态分散,达到最快的溶出速率和最高的溶出度。该药舌下含服可迅速溶解,经舌下粘膜吸收直接进入血液循环,减少肝脏的首过效应,充分发挥药效,提高生物利用度,具有高效、速效和安全的特点。“藿香正气滴丸”使用为水溶性基质,溶点较低,制备方法是固体分散体的熔融法,具有增加溶出、促进吸收的作用。改进后的滴丸剂不含乙醇,溶散快,易于吸收,服用和携带方便。在质量标准上,增加一项含量测定和3项鉴别,有效地控制产品质量。

1999年,天士力公司研制生产的“柴胡滴丸”获得国家卫生部新药证书。该药由北柴胡精制而成,有效成分清楚，药理作用明显。将提取—精馏耦合技术，在线检测和自动控制方法，并将层析技术、脱除重金属技术和标准化指纹图谱分析技术等多项技术综合运用于生产过程，解决现行中药生产工艺薄弱环节的关键问题。国家计委组织的专家评审认为：整个工艺流程中具有多个创新点，在工业化规模生产中，具有创新性和示范性。创新工艺技术的应用使其技术含量得到进一步提升，质量更加可控，能满足患者对中药制剂"3小"（体积小、剂量小、毒副作用小）、"3效"（速效、高效、长效）和"5方便"（贮存、运输、携带、服用等）的要求，避免多数复方中药感冒药存在的处方量大、服用量大，技术含量低、质量可控性差等缺点。

2001年，天津大学科研人员承担的"复方丹参滴丸自动灌装线"项目，获天津市科技进步一等奖。

2004年，天士力公司研制生产的三类中药新药"芪参益气滴丸"获得国家卫生部证书并投产上市。该制剂由黄芪、丹参、三七、降香四味中药组成，具有益气通脉、活血止痛之功，用于治疗冠心病心绞痛，气虚血瘀证之胸痹。2001年10月至2002年8月对其进行Ⅱ期及Ⅲ期临床试验研究，结果证实，"芪参益气滴丸"能明显减少冠心病心绞痛患者的心绞痛发作次数，并能有效地改善胸痛、胸闷、气短、乏力等各项中医症状。其治疗前后各项中医症状改善比较，$P<0.01$，有非常显著性差异。与对照组比较，经统计学分析，胸痛症状比较，有非常显著性差异（$P<0.01$）。该药在2003年12月23日取得SFDA颁发的新药证书。

2004年，天士力公司开发的"穿心莲内酯滴丸"获得国家卫生部中药新药证书。该药是在穿心莲内酯片基础上改制成的滴丸制剂，用于治疗上呼吸道感染（外感风热证）及细菌性痢疾（湿热痢）。由于制备工艺采用固体分散法的熔融法，即将PEG熔融后，加入穿心莲内酯细粉，通过滴管滴入不相混溶的冷凝剂中，通过表面张力的作用使液滴收缩成球状，并冷却凝固而成滴丸。将制成的滴丸与原片剂进行体外溶出速率对比试验，结果表明，滴丸剂溶出速率较片剂快，溶出速率提高。改制后的滴丸剂经薄膜包衣，与空气相对隔绝，药物的稳定性提高。同时苦味得以掩盖，便于服用。滴丸粒小、圆滑，吞咽方便，更便于儿童应用。

2005年，天津市第六中药厂与解放军某部医院合作开发的"舒脑欣滴丸"获准生产。该品将传统古方"芎归汤"采用萃取技术提取有效成分。经"即刻改善脑血流"的实验观察，对血管神经性头痛脑血流异常情况有一定的改善和调节作用，对血瘀血虚头痛、头晕等症显效率达40%以上。中药六厂就此成为生产滴丸的专业化企业。

2. 软胶囊

1979年8月，天津市第五中药厂将药典品种"冠心苏合丸"的大蜜丸改为"冠心苏合胶囊"，因易于服用，起效快，生物利用度高而深得医师和患者青睐，成为全国第一家生产硬胶囊剂型的中药企业。

1989~1991年，天津市药材公司章臣桂与达仁堂制药厂技术人员，针对知名古方处方服用量大、工艺落后等问题，以分离乳化技术制成"藿香正气软胶囊"，使其刺激性减小，患者适用人群扩大，在全国首个将中药大复方制成软胶囊剂型。

1991年末，天津达仁堂制药二厂郝非非、袁雪海等，根据安徽民间祖传秘方研制成功三类新药"痹祺胶囊"，对409例患者由风湿、外伤、劳损所引起的关节、筋骨、腰腿疼痛以及软组织损伤等症的临床有效率达90%以上，其中165名患者病变累及关节和肢体的疼痛明显减轻，关节功能基本恢复。

2002年，中新药业达仁堂制药厂以紫苏子油、芹菜子油等为主要原料，利用CO_2超临界萃取技术，研制成具有改善记忆，克服记忆短路，能明显提高大鼠条件反射正确反应率的"维思得（WISDOM）软胶囊"，2003年获得国家发明专利。同年，该厂开发出藿香正气胶囊（液态），将藿香正气乳化液填充于特定的空心硬胶囊中，工艺稳定，质量可靠。填补国内该剂型的空白。

3. 注射剂

2000年2月，中新药业天津乐仁堂制药厂与法国卢森堡兰花公司合资兴建的"天津华隆医药保健品有限公司"（以下简称华隆公司），采用传统中药生产技术和现代生物技术相结合的方法，提取天然植物的有效成分，生产黄芪多糖粉针剂。2004年8月，由华隆公司改名的天津赛诺制药有限公司，采用多次梯度醇沉、不同等级的分子筛超滤以及凝胶层析等工艺技术，从黄芪中提取分离出有效部位，制成"注射用黄芪多糖"，用于因化疗后白细胞减少、免疫功能低下的肿瘤患者，具有刺激骨髓造血细胞，增强免疫力的功能。该产品可替代进口同类产品，并首个以指纹图谱作为中成药的质量标准，填补天津市中药行业粉针剂生产的空白。同年，以“造血的阿拉伯半乳聚糖组合物”获得国家发明专利，同时在美国、欧盟、澳大利亚等国家和中国香港地区享有专利权。

2004年8月，天津赛诺制药有限公司采用多次梯度醇沉、不同等级的分子筛超滤及凝胶层析等工艺技术，从黄芪中提取分离出有效部位，制成“注射用黄芪多糖”，用于因化疗后白细胞减少，免疫功能低下的肿瘤患者，具有刺激骨髓造血细胞，增强免疫的功能。当年，以“造血的阿拉伯半乳聚糖组合物”获得国家发明专利，同时在美国、欧盟、澳大利亚等国家和中国香港地区享有专利权。

4. 水丸

1988年7月，天津乐仁堂制药厂刘宝生等以天津市第二医院邢震勋多年临床验方研制的“胃肠安丸”，获得“新药证书”，是天津市首个按“新药审批管理办法”规定批准的三类中药新药。经工艺、药理、临床等研究试验，对小儿胃肠道疾病有明显的治疗作用，尤其治疗腹泻效果突出。1993年，该厂以芳香化浊、理气导滞的中医理论为指导，将只限于小儿服用的“胃肠安丸”扩大为成人应用。该品为微丸剂型，剂量小，便于服用和携带。对消化不良，饮食不节引起的急性胃肠炎，显效率达到90%以上；对湿热下注引起的里急后重，湿热重灼肠道，以致气血凝滞，脉络受损化为脓血引起的菌痢，有效率达到83%以上。

1992年，天津药业公司发掘中医药遗产，依照已故著名老中医莫云樵的祖传秘方，结合现代制丸工艺及严格的质量控制标准，将“莫家清宁丸”进行产业化生产，获得天津市卫生局批准上市。2000年该产品被国家药监局列为国家二级中药保护品种，保护期7年。

5. 片剂

1993年，天津市中药制药厂与北京市肿瘤防治所合作，将王代树教授经过10多年的基础研究筛选确定的处方，利用细胞之间的分子转化、调控，将细胞周期失控的癌细胞向正常细胞周期节律转化的作用机理，研制成中药抗肿瘤药“紫龙金片”。2004年，该产品以“治疗肿瘤的药物及其制备方法”获得国家发明专利。

1994年8月，天津同仁堂制药厂根据天津著名中医赵恩俭多年临床验方研制的“肾炎康复片”，获得国家卫生部颁发的新药证书。1999年该厂储玉玲、李永仓、付广振通过肾穿刺证实，“肾炎康复片”具有利尿消肿及改善肾脏组织缺氧作用的物质基础，是该药具有激活‘Na-K-ATP酶’活性，使其在物质转运（主要是钠与钾的转运）、能量转换以及信息传递等方面发挥重要作用的效果，为治疗肾脏类疾病提供依据，达到国内领先水平。

1998年开始，天津市药材集团公司章臣桂与技术中心科研人员，就“乌鸡白凤丸”采取生化酶解法及树脂吸附分离技术进行研究，将20种原料组成的中药大复方，按理化性质分成不同组分处理，去除无效成分，使蛋白质转变成人体易于吸收的氨基酸，制成每片重0.5克的片剂，每次服用2片，与9克重大蜜丸达到同等疗效。该品在中新药业乐仁堂制药厂投入生产，2005年以“治疗气血两虚、月经不调和崩漏带下药物的制备方法”获得国家发明专利。

6. 口服液

1996年，天津乐仁堂制药厂史林等，针对“通脉养心丸”处方中各味中药质地和有效成分溶解性的不同，分别设计提取方法，采取水提醇沉和渗漉水沉等方法，制成可改善心肌缺血，显著抑制ADP诱导的血小板聚集，具有抗血栓形成作用的“通脉养心口服液”，获得国家卫生部颁发的新药证书。

7.颗粒剂

1996年，天士力公司自主研发的以治疗血虚肝亢所致头痛为主的中药新药“养血清脑颗粒”，取得国家级新药证书和生产批件并投入生产。生产工艺方面，采用动态循环提取工艺，提高药材提取率；采用多效蒸发浓缩设备，减少能耗；采用最新喷雾干燥制粒机，实现低糖、小剂量；解决颗粒防潮、肠溶性、药效保持、黏附和结团等问题，颗粒成分均匀、溶出度好、崩解速度快。所有工艺由一台封闭成负压状态的设备完成，污染少，成本低；采用最新全自动包装生产线。产品上市后开展系列研究工作，完成“养血清脑颗粒”降压作用及作用机制的研究，对SHR心肾保护作用及作用机制的研究，对SHR基因表达谱的研究，降压作用的临床研究，包衣技术和球形颗粒的研究，用于降压改善慢性脑供血不足的基础和临床研究等课题。为改善口感，将

“养血清脑颗粒”改制成浓缩丸，降低服用量；制成的微丸圆滑便于吞咽，服用更加方便；改冲服为用水送服，以掩盖药物的不良嗅味；质量标准显著提高，增加川芎的薄层鉴别、马兜铃酸A的检查；制备过程中采用新型辅料和先进的制丸设备，克服传统浓缩丸溶散缓慢的缺点，使之具有与颗粒一致的体外溶出效果。该“养血清脑丸”于2005年12月上市。

8.胶丸

1997年12月，天士力公司研制的中药新药“荆花胃康胶丸”，获卫生部新药证书。该产品是采用现代科学技术和独特的生产工艺，明确稳定的成分指标及可重复的药理和临床应用数据的标准化制剂，具有生产工艺合理，剂量小，质量标准可控，产品稳定、疗效确切、安全性好等优点。该方传统使用为煎剂，由于煎煮时间长短不一，存在挥发成分难于控制、口感差、特殊臭气等不足。现工艺主要按处方比例用水蒸气蒸馏法提挥发性总提取物，从外观和理化性质都符合中国药典要求，临床证实，对胃溃疡患者的治愈率可从原来的70%左右提高到80%~85%。胶丸内的挥发油被包裹，隔绝空气，既防止挥发油被氧化而增加其稳定性，又防止挥发油挥发，同时掩盖挥发油的特异气味，便于服用和携带。该药对HP引起的慢性胃炎等消化道疾病疗效显著，有很好的推广应用价值和市场前景。1998年被评为国家级新产品，获国内专利保护及国家专利保护。

（二）工艺技术

1996~1998年，天津达仁堂制药厂江永萍等为解决软胶囊崩解难题，从软胶囊崩解机理及其影响要素入手研究，发现明胶中有一些官能团在一定的条件下会与内容物发生化学反应，导致明胶变性，影响崩解。通过改进软胶囊明胶皮处方和化胶工艺，使藿香正气软胶囊崩解时间缩短50%以上。

2000年7月，天津中新药业乐仁堂制药厂通过改进工艺，使养阴清肺糖浆降低含醇量。在不影响药效的情况下，减少乙醇刺激性，含醇量由10%~12%，降至1.0%以下，适合儿童、孕妇、司机、酒精过敏者、肝肾功能不健全者服用，得到国内外医患者的好评。

2002年开始，天津中新药业隆顺榕制药厂采取水性薄膜衣工艺，对常年生产的清瘟解毒片、清胃黄连片、桑菊感冒片等产品，用少量安全无毒、物理化学性质稳定的高分子材料加入水为溶剂，增加增塑剂的浓度，逐渐形成均匀透明的水性薄膜衣。比用乙醇做溶媒成本降低，减少溶媒残留，药品生产更加安全。针对中药本身成分复杂，中药成方制剂压片工艺程序繁多的问题，利用喷雾干燥技术，将干压制粒，全粉压片推广使用，逐步替代传统的湿法制粒。以生产“降压避风片”为例，每年可节约工时费用50万元以上。

2004年，天津中新药业研究中心在植物药提取物研究中，利用药材自身酶解技术，将虎杖中富有的白藜芦醇苷转化成白藜芦醇，其纯度达到99%以上，生产成本从原工艺的每千克8000元降低到4500元。

2004年，天津同仁堂制药厂针对普通漂白布橡胶膏剂的裱背易产生皮肤刺激过敏的问题，以具有吸汗透气、富有弹性的纯绵弹性布作为麝香壮骨膏、精制狗皮膏、伤湿祛痛膏等橡胶膏剂裱背材料。贴后关节活动自如、舒适，治疗效果明显。

（三）设备与技术改造

1991年，天津市第六中药厂郭长源等自主设计完成的微机控制滴丸机和滴丸灌装机通过鉴定，以16嘴多头滴丸机代替原8嘴滴丸机，产量提高2.8倍。1994年，研制成第二代集成式模块化中型滴丸机组，达到集中供料、制冷、集中控制，较第一代单片机控制滴丸机组提高生产效率6倍，降低生产成本三分之二。

1992年，天津市第六中药厂投资8000多万元的“滴丸系列产品建设项目”，按照“药品生产质量管理规范”（GMP）标准，建成滴丸制剂生产联合厂房及辅助设施，主要生产工序实现机械化、自动化。1997年底，在全国中药行业率先取得国家GMP认证。

2000~2004年，天津中新药业达仁堂制药厂为解决多年延续的传统中药大蜜丸手工包装给质量和大生产带来的诸多弊病，用5年时间，与北京、上海等制药装备公司合作开发，使大蜜丸产品实现包装机械化，彻底解决手工包装存在的程序繁杂、容易染菌等质量问题。由裸药丸装成大盒一次完成，一条包装生产线可代替包装工人150人，节省人力40倍。该包装形式在国内中药企业被广泛使用。

2004年，天津中新药业提取中心引进德国产低温逆流提取罐组，其具有可低温动态逆流连续提取，单组或多组罐同时使用的特点。该设备用于甘草提取物，比传统设备缩短工时二分之一，不破坏有效成分，且收得率提高18%。德国产板式蒸发浓缩设备，以热交换原理，利用二次蒸发的不凝结气体进行循环使用，使番泻叶提取物的浓缩达到每小时5吨，全年可节约能源近50万元。引进丹麦产喷雾干燥系统，利用其设备内置流化床，以热风循环原理，使黄芪提取物瞬间高温受热，避免落后生产程序多次受热的弊病，有效成分损失降到最低水平，药品质量明显提高。

2005年，天津达仁堂制药厂与青岛大学合作，为确保中药成份的稳定，开发出适用于中药干燥的低能耗、低温真空干燥设备，使六味地黄丸水蜜丸干燥过程中的熊果酸工艺损失由5%下降至2%以下，崩解时限由50分钟下降至30分钟。

第二节　化学制药

天津的化学制药业发展较早。经过20世纪90年代企业改制和产品调整，天津医药集团生产的化学原料药和化学制剂，在抗病毒药物、头孢菌素药物、抗真菌药物、代谢病药物、抗肿瘤药物等门类，具有技术领先优势，形成力生制药股份有限公司、中央药业公司、津康制药等一批在全国享有较高知名度的化学原料药与制剂的生产骨干企业。

一、心脑血管用药

（一）吲达帕胺原料及制剂

1988年，天津力生制药股份有限公司与天津药物研究院从20世纪80年代初开始联合研制开发的二类新药“吲达帕胺原料及其制剂”，取得卫生部颁发的新药证书和试生产批准文号，填补国内空白。由天津药物研究院制药厂生产原料，天津力生制药股份有限公司生产制剂吲达帕胺片。2003年，为满足不断增加的制剂产量的需求，天津力生制药股份有限公司申报吲达帕胺原料药，2004年获得注册批件，实现原料的自主供应。

同年，天津力生制药股份有限公司与天津药物研究院合作开发的二类新药“寿比山牌吲达帕胺片”取得新药证书和生产批准文号。1988年获得全国首届“百病克星”大赛银奖。1990年取得试生产转正批件（90）卫药准字X-105，获得天津市工业科技协作优秀项目三等奖。1993年完成试行质量标准转正。1997年该公司首家开始研制吲达帕胺薄膜衣刻痕片规格。吲达帕胺刻痕片在服用过程中便于剂量的调整，患者可以根据需要掰开服用，灵活调整服药剂量，从而减少副作用。1998年，为提高吲达帕胺片产品质量，该公司对其生产厂房进行GMP改造。1999年通过国家药监局GMP认证，并从意大利引进多台具有预压及能够控制片剂压力、厚度、硬度的压片机，使用新型的高效包衣设备及PTP包装设备，保证片剂高度的均一性及良好的溶出度。成品一次合格率为100%。2000年，吲达帕胺薄膜衣片获得药品生产批件，进入批量生产，所用薄膜包衣材料为世界著名品牌欧巴代，从而实现吲达帕胺片生产工艺技术的升级换代。2002和2005年，寿比山牌吲达帕胺片连续获得天津市名牌产品称号。

2004年，天津力生制药股份有限公司获得吲达帕胺原料药国家药品注册批件。该公司通过吲达帕胺原料GMP认证，完善岗位标准操作规程，对亚硝化—还原合成工艺进行改进，收率提高约10个百分点，含量明显提高。2005年，对吲达帕胺精制工艺进行改进。由于亚硝化-还原合成工艺改进成功，通过缩小精制用溶剂倍数，降低结晶温度，减少活性炭用量等措施，精制收率提高8个百分点。

(二)奥扎格雷原料及制剂

2004年,天津市生物化学制药厂与沈阳东正科技开发有限公司合作开发奥扎格雷钠原料及制剂,完成工艺筛选、质量研究、稳定性试验、药理毒理等工作,向国家食品药品监督管理局申请生产注册,2005年8月22日获得奥扎格雷和注射用奥扎格雷钠的生产批件。奥扎格雷钠是为血栓素合成酶抑制剂,是凝血过程有效抑制剂,药物安全性较高,临床主要用于治疗急性血栓性脑梗塞和脑梗死伴随的运动障碍。由于其治疗效果良好,一上市就抢占此类药品的销售市场,收回投入成本,创造良好的经济和社会效益。

(三)尼莫地平片

1994年,天津市中央制药厂殷志芳等人采用固体分散技术,以PVP为水溶性载体,对原有的尼莫地平片进行工艺改进。该工艺使有效成分以分子状态进入载体网状骨架中,形成非晶体无定性物。药物进入胃肠后,有效成分被迅速溶解、吸收,解决尼莫地平不溶于水、在胃肠中不易被溶解、吸收的问题,使生物利用度得到很大提高。

二、解热镇痛类用药

(一)阿司匹林肠溶胶囊

1997年8月,天津力生制药股份有限公司自主研制的4类新药阿司匹林肠溶胶囊(商品名为益欣雪)获国家新药证书和生产批件。该品采用微丸延迟释放技术,药物以肠溶小球的形式存在于胶囊中,由于小球体积小,很少受到幽门括约肌的阻拦,能随胃的蠕动转运到肠道,释放出阿司匹林,避免局部药物浓度忽高忽低,使其体内血药浓度基于平稳,减少对胃肠道的副作用。该公司采用离心包衣造粒技术制备阿司匹林肠溶微丸工艺,填补国内空白。1999年,益欣雪胶囊被认定为天津市科学技术成果。

(二)洛索洛芬钠片

2003年6月13日,天津新丰制药有限公司取得4类新药洛索洛芬钠片的生产批件,并获国家新药证书。该品种为苯丙酸类非甾体抗炎药,适用于类风湿性关节炎、骨性关节炎、腰痛症、肩周炎、颈肩腕综合症,手术外伤和拔牙后的镇痛和消炎,急性上呼吸道炎的解热和镇痛,具有起效迅速,对胃肠道刺激性小的特点。

(三)酮洛芬凝胶

1995年,天津药业公司科研人员研制成功酮洛芬凝胶,获得国家卫生部颁发的新药证书。酮洛芬是非甾体消炎镇痛药,制成凝胶制剂用于各种骨骼肌损伤的急慢性软组织(肌肉、韧带、筋膜)扭伤、挫伤,以及肌肉劳损所引起的疼痛,也用于骨关节炎的对症治疗。通过透皮吸收给药后,进入整个人体血液循环,减小口服给药引起的胃肠粘膜损害等副作用,耐药性能也得到明显改善。该药因其疗效佳、安全性好,被国家药监局列为乙类非处方药物。

三、呼吸系统用药

硫酸沙丁胺醇缓释片

2005年5月,天津力生制药股份有限公司自主研制的4类新药硫酸沙丁胺醇缓释片(商品名为品川)获得国家新药证书和注册批件。硫酸沙丁胺醇缓释片是利用渗透压原理,采用渗透泵控释技术及激光打孔技术等先进的生产工艺制备而成的缓释制剂,产品质量稳定可控,其制剂工艺处于国内领先水平。硫酸沙丁胺醇缓释片具有零级释药的特征,能够以恒定的释药速率向体内释放出定量的治疗药物,较长时间维持血药浓度处于有效范围,避免普通制剂造成的血药浓度波峰波谷现象,提高用药的安全性、有效性,降低其副作用。

四、抗肿瘤药

盐酸博安霉素原料及粉针剂

1998年,天津太河制药有限公司(1996年由原天津市河北制药厂改制)与中国科学院医药生物技术研究所合作开发研制国家一类新药盐酸博安霉素原料药及粉针剂。原天津市河北制药厂负责生产、工艺研究提供样品及临床药品,承担试制、申报、药检、临床。1990年被批准进行临床,1994年Ⅰ期临床结束,进入Ⅱ期临床。1996年天津太河制药有限公司开始治疗肝癌的专项临床研究,1999年临床结束进行生产报批。该项目在近20年研究开发基础上,按国家Ⅰ类新药申报要求,完成工艺合成、质量标准研究、一般药理学、药效学、毒理学、药代动力学等研究工作,2001年通过专家审核,2004年6月获得国家化学药Ⅰ类新药"新药证书"及生产批文,盐酸博安霉素成为拥有自主知识产权的国家Ⅰ类抗肿瘤新药。

2004年,天津太河制药有限公司获得另一个抗肿瘤药注射用盐酸尼莫司汀生产批文。

五、激素

(一)地塞米松产品系列

1993年,天津药业公司科技人员石俊杰、卢彦昌等人对含氟皮质激素类药物生产工艺进行全面分析,发现"脱氢反应"是其共同的薄弱环节。沿用的传统氧化方法存在很多缺点,反应过程中使用的原材料品种多、消耗高、收率低,影响产品质量和生产成本,同时在生产过程中产生大量有毒有害物质,造成安全防护和环境污染等各类问题。科技人员在选育出新的高效霉菌种的基础上,以"生物脱氢"代替化学脱氢方法,应用于含氟皮质激素药物生产,促使"醋酸曲安缩松""醋酸地塞米松""地塞米松磷酸钠"等多个产品合成工艺路线的改进。同年,天津药业公司石俊杰、武淑婷、袁长东等科技人员承担的"含氟皮质激素类药物的生物脱氢及其化学合成新工艺研究"项目列入国家科委"八五国家科技攻关计划"。1995年,获国家科技进步二等奖和天津市突出贡献奖。

图5-13-2-82 激素合成车间

1997年8月,天津药业公司总工程师卢彦昌等研制成一项新工艺,使"地塞米松"原料成本降低30%~40%,所有质量技术指标全部赶上法国罗素优克拉夫公司的地塞米松,达到国际领先水平,打破同品种产品依赖进口的局面,使含氟皮质激素类药物生物工程技术跃居世界领先水平。

1998年,"地塞米松系列产品新工艺的研究应用"被国家科技部评为火炬计划优秀项目二等奖。2000年,该项目获国家科技进步奖二等奖。

2002年7月,天津大学国家工业结晶技术研究推广中心与天津药业公司合作开发的专利技术"地塞米松磷酸钠的晶型及其结晶制备方法"实现产业化,建成年产60吨地塞米松磷酸钠生产线成功投产。地塞米松磷酸钠结晶新技术的应用,进一步提高产品纯度,有效地控制溶媒残留,晶形完美,产品粒度大且分布均匀,彻底解决原工艺产品粘结问题。该产品历经与多家欧美跨国公司十几年竞争,最终将进口产品挤出中国市场,占领80%的国内市场,全球市场占有率达到40%以上。

(二)曲安西龙系列

1996年8月,天津药业有限公司科研人员在国内首家成功研制出国家级新药曲安西龙原料药和曲安西龙片(阿赛松,强地松的替代产品),曲安西龙片获国家卫生部颁发的新药证书,并于1997年获国家科委等部委联合颁发的"国家重点新产品证书",填补国内空白。曲安西龙是新型肾上腺皮质激素类抗炎药,用于治疗各种变态反应性炎症、各种自身免疫性疾病。由于在分子结构16位上引入羟基,其抗炎作用高于泼尼松、氢化可的松等药物,又因钠潴留等副作用小、生物利用度高等优点,可减轻激素类药物引起浮肿、排钾等副作用,而被临床广泛应用,逐渐成为醋酸泼尼松的换代产品。该产品还因药效好、副作用低等突出特点,被列入国家基本医疗保险药品目录,市场发展前景广阔。

（三）甲泼尼龙系列

2002年，金耀集团科研人员经过多年攻关，成功地研制甲泼尼龙原料药及片剂，质量达到EP版和USP版，为国际先进水平，获国家药监局颁发的新药证书。同年，“甲泼尼龙”被认定为国家重点新产品。在2003年抗击“非典”中，甲泼尼龙片（商品名“尤金”）发挥不可替代的作用。甲泼尼龙系列产品属于促糖类皮质激素类药物，是参与人体的糖、脂肪、蛋白质三大物质代谢的重要激素。自美国Upjohn公司20世纪50年代研制成功以来，在国内外临床上有着广泛的应用，是美国、英国、日本等发达国家药典持续收载的品种。因其疗效确切、安全可靠的特点很快在临床上得到广泛应用。20世纪80年代初开始，国内使用的甲泼尼龙系列药物一直依赖进口，因此该系列药品的国产化成为“九五”期间国家重点科技项目，被国家医药管理局列为皮质激素类药物中急需突破的品种。

2003年，“甲泼尼龙系列产品产业化项目”被认定为天津市重大高新技术产业化项目。该药物被国家卫生部列为国家基本药物目录和国家基本医疗保险药品目录，许多省市也将其收录于公费医疗目录中，有很大的市场潜力。

（四）醋酸氟轻松系列

2005年，金耀集团拥有国内领先水平的生产醋酸氟轻松乳膏的制剂、灌装、包装完美匹配的自动化生产线，醋酸氟轻松乳膏以其质量领先、疗效确切驰名中外，市场销量逐年递增，年产量可达1.5亿支，远销缅甸、柬埔寨、越南、菲律宾等东南亚国家及地区。1994年，醋酸氟轻松获得天津市优秀新产品二等奖。2002年，醋酸氟轻松工艺改进项目获天津市技术创新优秀项目二等奖。2005年，醋酸氟轻松9氟精制工艺改进项目获得天津市技术创新优秀项目二等奖。

（五）丁酸氢化可的松系列

1994年，天津药业公司科研人员研制成功丁酸氢化可的松乳膏（商品名“尤卓尔”），获得国家卫生部颁发的新药证书和生产批件。丁酸氢化可的松是由荷兰Gist-Brocades公司于20世纪70年代中期从众多的甾体17-酯中优选出来的新一代皮质激素类药物。其临床疗效与强效类皮质激素药物相当，又因其化学结构中不含氟，所以较含氟类皮质激素药物毒性低、柯兴氏样症全身反应及局部萎缩等副作用小，安全性高。由于该原料药及制剂产品长期被国外垄断，国内皮肤科临床单位多次提出试制此种外用制剂的要求。天津药业公司吴群城、吕守平等科研人员经过多年研究，成功突破17位酯化合成的瓶颈，研制出丁酸氢化可的松原料药。在此基础上，结合其他乳膏类制剂品种的生产经验重新调整处方，设计专有基质，通过调整乳化剂、增加金属络合剂等手段，制成丁酸氢化可乳膏制剂，成功地填补国内空白，打破同品种药物依赖进口的局面，满足临床需求。丁酸氢化可的松乳膏因其疗效佳、副作用小、安全性好，被列入甲类非处方药物目录、国家基本药物目录和国家基本医疗保险药品目录，成为皮炎、湿疹的首选药物，销售收入过亿元。

（六）哈西奈德涂膜剂

1991年，天津药业公司成功研制哈西奈德涂膜剂，并获得国家卫生部颁发的新药证书。哈西奈德为局部用高效抗炎皮质激素类药物，具有抗炎、抗瘙痒、抗过敏等作用，尤其对牛皮癣有特效，较以往任何含氟皮质激素均好。为进一步提高哈西奈德外用疗效，天津药业公司科研人员在哈西奈德软膏、乳膏等外用剂型的基础上，参考国内外有关涂膜剂资料，潜心研制哈西奈德涂膜剂，用以治疗皮肤过敏性炎症的亚急性或慢性阶段，诸如湿疹、异位性皮炎、接触性皮炎等。该药具有长效、避免感染、涂抹后易形成均匀的弹性薄膜、附着力强等特点，对皮肤损伤有保护封包和延长药效的作用，不污染衣物，使用方便。

（七）注射用氢化可的松琥珀酸钠

2001年，天津市生物化学制药厂科技人员进行重大工艺改进，在全国首家推出自主研制开发的注射用氢化可的松琥珀酸钠。该项目采用水相成盐技术，以注射用水代替丙酮作为反应溶剂，从根本上避免环境污染和有机溶剂残留，工艺一步合成，反应过程平稳，操作简单，产品质量稳定，生产成本降低，同时将收率提高到95%以上。使得注射用氢化可的松琥珀酸钠产品质量达到国际先进水平，大量出口古巴、巴西、智利、伊朗、伊拉克等国家，满足国际市场需求。

2002年,“注射用氢化可的松琥珀酸钠”工艺攻关项目被天津市科委列为火炬攻关项目。2005年,注射用氢化可的松琥珀酸钠工艺研究改进获“天津市技术创新二等奖”。

六、抗生素

1991年,华北制药厂科研人员姚学强、张聚发、巢天浩等承担的“青霉素球状菌氮源代谢的研究及应用”项目获国家科技进步二等奖。

1995年,华北制药厂和北京工业大学科研人员魏志斌、王普、王进秋等承担的“链霉素发酵多模型工艺研究及计算机控制与管理网络系统”项目,获国家科技进步三等奖。同年,中国科学院化工冶金研究所、华北制药厂科研人员刘会洲、韩贵安、陈家镛等承担的“青霉素生产中新型高效破乳剂的研制及开发”项目,获国家科技进步三等奖。

1996年,天津大学和华北制药厂科研人员王静康、韩贵安、薛履中等承担的“青霉素结晶新型技术与设备”项目,获国家科技进步二等奖。

七、避孕用药

(一)壬苯醇醚膜

1989年,天津药业公司健民制药厂成功研发壬苯醇醚膜,用于女性外用短效避孕,填补国内女性外用避孕药的空白。1991年,该药获得国家卫生部颁发的新药证书。经临床研究证明,其杀精作用明显,毒副作用小,安全可靠,是易于广大群众接受的一种外用避孕药剂。该药因其避孕效果佳、安全性好,被国家药监局列为甲类非处方药物,并被国家计生委列为国家免费提供的避孕药物。

(二) 壬苯醇醚栓

1989年,天津药业公司健民制药厂成功研发壬苯醇醚栓,获得国家卫生部颁发的新药证书,填补国内女性外用避孕药又一项空白。该产品采用水溶性聚乙二醇辅以发泡剂的泡腾基质,与液体接触后产生大量泡沫,同时释放高效壬苯醇醚杀精剂,避孕效果明显。另外,采用PVC膜片真空吸塑包装,保证产品内在质量。经体内杀精实验证明,该产品避孕效果好,使用安全、便捷。

第三节 生物制药

天津在抗微生物药物和维生素B2等生物制药的生产与研究方面,医药集团有许多优势产品项目。华立达公司试制的重组人干扰素a2b产品,以及金耀集团研发生产的氨基酸类原料药及制剂,彰显天津生物制药工程技术实力。

一、重组人干扰素a2b

1992年,华立达公司从前苏联国家科学研究院引进基因工程干扰素专利生产技术。经过研究人员近3年探索,1995年华立达公司成功地试制出自己的干扰素a2b产品——安福隆粉针(注射用重组人干扰素a2b)。

1997年,安福隆粉针全部实现国产化,并获得新药证书和生产批件文号(国药准字S10970075/76/77),正式投放市场。重组人干扰素a2b系列剂型为天津华立达生物工程有限公司主要产品。该干扰素具有广谱的抗病毒、抗肿瘤和免疫调节作用，是治疗慢性病毒性肝炎、白血病等疾病的首选药物，还广泛用于治疗其他多种病毒性疾病和肿瘤。华立达公司的安福隆生产技术与国内外其他厂家不同，其整个生产过程不使用任何动物或人血液提取成分，避免制品传播血液病毒的担忧。安福隆粉针的生物学活性和纯度等主要指标均达到或超过欧美进口产品。

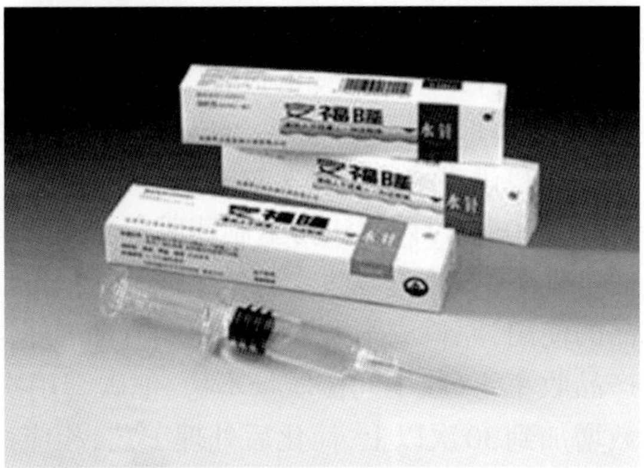
图5-13-3-83　安福隆水针(重组人干扰素2b注射液)

2000年4月，华立达公司的研发人员攻克蛋白质在水溶液中不稳定的技术难题，自行研制开发的安福隆水针(重组人干扰素a2b注射液)，获得新药证书和生产批准文号(国药准字S20000018/19/20)。安福隆水针采用新型预灌装注射器包装，是可以直接注射的干扰素制剂，具有安全、稳定、方便、经济等特点，在提高经济效益的同时创造巨大的社会效益。安福隆水针技术开发及产业化项目，被列为天津市科委支持的重点科技攻关项目和国家级火炬计划项目，拥有自主知识产权，发明专利获得第九届中国专利优秀奖。"稳定的干扰素水溶液"技术在多个国家申请PCT专利并获得授权。2001年安福隆水针获得天津市名牌产品称号和国家重点新产品证书。2002年获得天津市科学技术进步奖二等奖和天津市技术创新优秀项目一等奖。

2003年，华立达公司和天津药物研究院联合开发的捷抚喷雾剂，获得国家新药证书和生产批准文号(国药准字S20030028)，标志着第一支干扰素喷雾剂的面世。安福隆产品的销售遍及国内30个省、直辖市和自治区，产品年销售额上亿元，居国内干扰素市场前茅，并远销欧美等国家，成为国内唯一规模出口的干扰素生产企业。

二、抗微生物药物

(一)马来酸阿奇霉素原料及粉针剂

1999年，天津市生物化学制药厂(简称生化制药厂)与天津市医药集团技术开发有限公司签订技术转让合同，技术开发有限公司将其所开发的国家4类新药注射用马来酸阿奇霉素酸盐、原料及冻干粉针剂转让。同年，生化制药厂成立"马来酸阿奇霉素"课题攻关组并完成改造其配套厂房工程。

2001年，生化制药厂进行4类新药马来酸阿奇霉素和注射用马来酸阿奇霉素生产工艺的摸索、试产、成品检验及包装材料等一系列生产前期的技术准备工作，并向国家食品药品监督管理局提出生产申请。2002年7月19日获得国家药品监督管理局颁发的马来酸阿奇霉素和注射用马来酸阿奇霉素新药证书及批准文号。

2004年，生化制药厂组织科技人员针对马来酸阿奇霉素合成工艺是以乙醇作为溶剂进行马来酸阿奇霉素成盐反应，存在着过程繁琐、操作不便、残留有机溶剂等弊端，经过反复研究试验，采用水相成盐技术生产原料及制剂产品，从根本上解决有机相残留的问题，容易判断反应终点，降低不良反应的机率，增强患者用药安全性。同年，生化制药厂为方便临床医生使用，适应临床重症感染患者和吞服不便患者的需要，经过调研确定开发"马来酸阿奇霉素注射液"，完成工艺研究、确定工艺流程、中试研究、药学研究等工作，产品检验合格。"马来酸阿奇霉素成盐工艺改进"2005年被列为天津市企业技术创新计划项目，并于2005年8月10日获得国家食品药品监督管理局批准。

(二)注射用头孢替唑钠

1995年，天津新丰制药有限公司引进注射用头孢替唑钠，于2002年取得新药证书并成功转化为国产，是国内首家引进该第一代头孢类抗生素品种并成功转化为国产的企业。该项目获得天津市人民政府颁发的"天津市2003年度技术创新优秀项目二等奖"。该品种采用天津新丰制药有限公司张安植等人发明的实用新型专利——药品隔板后，破损率降低。天津新丰制药有限公司生产的其他头孢类粉针剂，还包括注射用头孢唑肟钠、注射用头孢美唑钠、注射用头孢尼西钠、注射用头孢他啶、注射用头孢曲松等，是天津市头孢类粉针剂专业生产厂家。

（三）苯酰甲硝唑胶囊

2001年，原天津河北制药厂自行开发4类新药“苯酰甲硝唑胶囊”，商品名为佳乐宁，并获得新药证书。2002年天津医药集团将该产品内部调整至天津太河制药有限公司生产。

（四）伊曲康唑原料及胶囊剂

2000年2月，天津力生制药股份有限公司获得伊曲康唑原料新药证书和生产批件。2000年开始进行伊曲康唑中试，通过寻找合适的中间体，使该工艺由21步缩为9步，减少设备、人员、工时及许多有毒有害危险品的使用，原料成本大大降低。2001年5月，在小试基础上进行中试研究，除解决设备适应工艺问题外，针对产品收率不稳、中间体质量不稳、钯碳套用次数少、出现中毒等问题，进行重点攻关研究。钯碳套用由10次数增加到30次以上，简化后处理工艺，相应提高中间体的收率和质量，降低原料成本。2005年，进一步改进工艺技术，主要改进合环物的合成工艺，由原工艺路线的三步反应缩减为一步反应，能够从胺基物直接合成合环物，具有显著的优势。工艺更简便，大大提高生产效率，减少“三废”的排放，质量显著提高。“合环物”含量由96%左右提高到99%以上，收率提高8个百分点，原料成本明显下降。

2000年，天津力生制药股份有限公司获得伊曲康唑胶囊（商品名为美扶）新药证书和生产批件。伊曲康唑胶囊采用微丸薄膜包衣技术和药物固体分散技术。 2001年，经过放大试验，利用该公司现有设备，获取离心包衣造粒机技术参数，采用离心包衣造粒工艺生产出合格产品，但工艺仍不十分稳定。2002年，该公司从德国引进胡特林（Huttlin）最新的多功能包衣造粒机和悬浮包衣技术。经过反复试验，完成微丸包衣技术的升级，由离心包衣改进为流化包衣，包衣时间明显缩短，生产效率大幅度提高，微球外观改善，内在质量也更加稳定。2003年，美扶胶囊获天津市2003年度技术创新优秀项目三等奖。2005年，在原工艺的基础上，进行大的工艺改进，调整工艺参数。产品质量明显提高，生产周期大大缩短。产量和收率明显提高，每批单锅产量增加一倍，成品平均收率提高至94%以上。

（五）盐酸环丙沙星

1991年，天津市中央制药厂与中国医学科学院医药生物技术研究所合作承担的国家“七·五”科技攻关项目“盐酸环丙沙星”产品正式投入生产。项目组的张致平、张文忠、刘浚、边其昌等人，以氟氯苯乙酮代替氟氯苯乙酰胺为起始原料，经缩合、醚胺化、环合水解、上哌嗪、成盐精制5步反应，制得盐酸环丙沙星。该工艺具有工艺稳定、操作简便、易于配套、经济技术指标合理，原料成本适中等优点。1991年总收率达40%，原料成本700元/千克。

（六）氯碘羟喹乳膏

1991年，天津药业公司唐德瑄、周吉西、吕守平、薛桂兰等科研人员，参照国内外有关文献报导，及国内著名皮肤科专家提议，研制成功氯碘羟喹乳膏，获得国家卫生部颁发的新药证书。该药由于具有抗细菌、真菌活性，又不同于抗生素类药物易产生耐药性，被广泛用于皮肤感染、伤口感染、溃疡、感染性湿疹样皮炎及各种癣症，为临床医师增添一新的治疗皮肤病的药物。

三、维生素

维生素B2

1992年，天津市河北制药厂从50年代即开始生产的维生素B2，获得国家优质产品和天津市名牌产品称号。当年产量为61吨（其时全国产量130吨）。该厂生产的维生素B2采用生物合成法（即发酵法），生产菌为酵母菌。其产品被称之“天然核黄素”，为绿色品种。

1996年，天津市太河制药有限公司（1996年由原天津市河北制药厂改制）具备微机控制的发酵试验罐，可选育出最佳工艺条件，使研究成果迅速转化为生产力。在提炼方面开展试验，调整部分设备，对沉降、压滤、氧化和热熔转晶等方面工艺改进，使发酵单位提高到6000～6500r/ml（提高1000r/ml以上），总收率由原来的62%提高到65%以上。

1996年，天津市河北制药厂与俄罗斯遗传与育种研究所合作进行基因工程菌生产核黄素项目。经过探索研究,至2004年成功地将维生素B2发酵培养时间由140小时缩短至72小时,发酵单位由6500r/ml提高至7500r/ml,提取收率由62%提高至70%。

2004年10月天津太河制药有限公司与俄罗斯遗传与育种研究所合作改进菌种,2005年成功地将维生素B2发酵单位由7500r/ml提高至18000r/ml,发酵培时72小时,提取收率由70%提高至80%,取得突破性进展。

四、氨基酸类药物

(一)尼莫地平注射液

1987年,天津市氨基酸公司(原和平制药厂)将尼莫地平注射液作为企业重点产品进行自主研发,李钧英、穆俊儒、王淑霞为主创人员,就该产品处方、工艺、质量标准、稳定性及临床等进行大量研究工作。1993年6月,该产品获得国家卫生部的新药证书及生产批件,为4类西药新药,保护期3年。尼莫地平注射液为钙拮抗剂,用于预防蛛网膜下腔出血所引起的脑血管痉挛,治疗急性缺血性脑血管疾病等。

1999年12月,氨基酸公司在原20ml:4mg规格的基础上,申请增加40ml:8mg规格,获国家药品监督管理局仿制药品的批件。新规格改用50ml茶色模具瓶装,采用三通输液器的方法输入,方便医疗用药,满足患者的需求。

(二)替加氟注射液

1991年11月1日,天津市氨基酸公司自主研发的替加氟注射液,经国家卫生部批准同意生产,获得新药证书,为4类西药新药,保护期3年。替加氟注射液原名喃氟啶注射液,其抗瘤谱及作用机制与抗瘤药物氟尿嘧啶相似,但其毒性仅为氟尿嘧啶的1/4—1/7,且治疗指数高,被公认为是有效抗癌药物之一。国内外未见有水针生产。为填补该项空白,温玉麟、李钧英、王淑霞为主创,科研人员研制成功喃氟啶注射液(规格5ml:0.2g)。该品种具有可供静脉及腔内注射给药的优点,是适合于中、晚期腺癌患者应用的有效、低毒的药品,销售市场良好,受到患者好评。

(三)小儿复方氨基酸注射液(18AA-I)

1991年,天津市氨基酸公司为适应婴幼儿代谢的特点,自主研发小儿复方氨基酸注射液(18AA-I),获得国家卫生部颁发的新药证书及生产批件。小儿复方氨基酸注射液(18AA-I)是3类西药新药,适用于小儿因消化系统疾病,不能经胃肠摄取食物者,小儿由各种疾病所引起的低蛋白血症者,小儿受严重创伤、烧伤及败血症等体内氮平衡失调者,难治性腹泻、吸收不良综合症,早产儿、低体重儿的场外营养。该药因其疗效佳、安全性好,被患者广泛使用。

(四)复方盐酸利多卡因注射液

1991年,天津市氨基酸公司生产的复方盐酸利多卡因注射液获得国家卫生部颁发的新药证书,属国家级复方制剂3类新药。1993年经国家卫生部药品审评委员会批准正式投入生产,天津市氨基酸公司也为国内首家投产企业。1994年,获得批准文号:(94)卫药准字X-35号。复方盐酸利多卡因注射液原名为复方薄荷脑注射液,为薄荷脑和盐酸利多卡因的灭菌稀乙醇溶液,是一种长效局部麻醉止痛药,用于肝肠科及外科手术切口部位的局部浸润麻醉、手术麻醉、术后镇痛等。该产品具有强而持久的局部镇痛作用和止痒作用,其麻醉作用比利多卡因稍快,局麻时可出现在作用部位只出现麻木感而不出现麻痹现象。应用该品在肝肠科手术后数日内,既不会出现剧痛,也不会造成末梢神经完全麻醉而影响正常的排便功能,是一种较为理想的局部长效麻醉止痛剂。2000年,复方盐酸利多卡因注射液由国家药品监督管理局批复同意使用商品名"克泽普",其作为新型的肝肠手术的长效局麻止痛剂,在临床上得到充分的验证,并得到广泛应用。

(五)复方氨基酸注射液(18AA-Ⅰ)

1991年1月3日,天安药业公司自主研制开发的复方氨基酸注射液(18AA-Ⅰ)(原名称为"小儿用氨基酸-18注射液")获国家卫生部生产批件。该产品为化药3类药品,其中含有以母乳为基准的8种必需氨基酸和10种非必需氨基酸。在处方上考虑幼儿与成人有不同的代谢,对氨基酸需求量存在差异,调整配方中氨基酸的比例，使其更适合幼儿营养需要。1993年，该品种获得国家医药管理局科学技术进步三等奖。

（六）甘油果糖注射液（商品名“布瑞得”）

1993年4月17日，天津市天安药业公司自主研制开发的甘油果糖注射液获国家药监局生产批件。该产品为化药3类药品，具有先进的配方和独特的生产技术工艺。能有效地消除脑水肿、降低颅内压，是一种安全可靠、使用方便，临床治疗脑水肿的首选药物。该产品为国内首家研制开发，技术水平居于国内领先地位。1998年，获天津市技术创新奖二等奖。2002年，列为天津市火炬项目并通过验收。

（七）复方氨基酸注射液（15-HBC）

复方氨基酸注射液（15-HBC）（原名称：氨复命15-HBC）为天津市天安药业公司在国内首创的化药4类新药。该产品为高浓度的支链氨基酸，用于病人在大面积烧伤、创伤及严重感染等应激状态下肌肉分解代谢亢进，消化系统功能障碍、营养恶化及免疫功能下降病人的营养支持，以及手术后病人改善营养状态。1991年，该产品获天津市优秀产品称号；2004年，获得天津市技术创新优秀项目奖三等奖。

（八）固定化氨基酰化酶拆分D、L-苯丙氨酸

1992年，天津市天安药业公司固定化氨基酰化酶拆分D、L-苯丙氨酸项目，获国家科委颁发的国家科技成果证书。该技术是天安药业公司技术人员在引进俄罗斯菌种的基础上，通过小试、中试等反复试验，摸索确定生产工艺条件，建立优化酶的发酵、提取和固定化技术，应用固定化氨基酰化酶拆分D、L-苯丙氨酸法生产L-苯丙氨酸，并最终实现产业化。

（九）复方氨基酸注射液（3AA）

1993年，天安药业公司自主研发的复方氨基酸注射液（3AA）（原名称“肝病用支链氨基酸-3H注射液”）获国家科委颁发的国家科技成果证书。该药物用于治疗肝昏迷，急性、重症肝炎等。处方为三种支链氨基酸，不经肝脏代谢，不增加肝负担，吸收完全。针对肝病人血浆中缺乏支链氨基酸，该品配成全支链氨基酸输液，降低芳香族氨基酸及色氨酸的浓度，使昏迷状态迅速清醒。

（十）复方氨基酸注射液（18AA-Ⅳ）

1999年，天津市天安药业公司应用国际先进技术自主研制开发的复方氨基酸注射液（18AA-Ⅳ）（商品名“爱欣森”）获国家级新产品称号。该产品是氨基酸含葡萄糖输液，防止氨基酸异化丢失，达到充分利用的目的，临床疗效提高，使应用方便，减少污染。主要用于改善外科手术前后病人的营养状态，适于各种疾病所引起的营养不良，作为节氮疗法补充营养。该产品配方复杂，工艺技术难度大。因为氨基酸和糖在一起共热产生美拉德反应，生成有色物质，影响氨基酸输液的质量。该公司采用独特的先进技术工艺，克服这一难题。

（十一）复方氨基酸注射液（18AA-Ⅲ）

1992年，天津市天安药业公司研制成功复方氨基酸注射液（18AA-Ⅲ）（又名“复合氨基酸注射液18-F”）。该产品为国内首创，属于化药3类新药。产品为高浓度氨基酸输液，适用于消化系统功能障碍，或不能经消化道摄取食物，造成营养不良，低蛋白血症及免疫功能低下的病人；应用于大面积烧伤、大手术、严重感染造成机体高分解代谢蛋白质大量丢失的病人。该品含氨基酸种类最多，由18种结晶氨基酸以生理比例配制的平衡营养型氨基酸输液，其工艺技术复杂，经科研人员不断研制，摸索出最佳的工艺技术路线，产品质量稳定。2005年，该项目获天津市技术创新优秀项目奖三等奖。

（十二）酶法拆分氨基酸（蛋氨酸）医药级L-蛋氨酸

1990年，天津市天安药业公司研究人员研发酶法拆分氨基酸（蛋氨酸）医药级L-蛋氨酸项目技术。该项目引进俄罗斯的实验室技术和放线菌，为实现产业化生产，通过对原料的筛选实现了原料的本地化，完善了菌种的筛选优化和保藏方法；建立和优化菌种发酵过程的控制条件，以及酶提取和固定化技术，并使用生产的固定化酶进行L-甲硫氨酸的制取研究。2001年，该项目获国家重点新产品称号。

(十三)L-苏氨酸新技术新工艺研究及产业化开发

2001年,天安药业公司与天津大学共同合作完成"L-苏氨酸新技术新工艺研究及产业化开发项目"。通过菌种优化、筛选、保藏的研究和发酵、提取工艺的改进优化控制,实现产业化,使产酸率、转化率、提取收率达到规定的要求。对药用级苏氨酸精制结晶过程进行系统工程研究,优化结晶工艺,确定最佳操作时间表,建立柔性氨基酸结晶生产线。该项目技术是引进俄罗斯的菌种,通过对原料的筛选实现原料的本地化,经过结晶工艺的改进产品达到一流品质。2001年,该项目被列入国家"十五"攻关项目计划;同年,被列为天津市重大科技攻关项目,通过验收。

第十四章　建筑材料

1991~2005年,天津市建筑材料集团(控股)有限公司(简称建材集团)及其所属企业,结合生产实际开展技术改造和科研开发,特别是倚重天津市建筑材料科学研究所(简称"建材科研所"),加强自主创新,推进产学研结合,努力使科研成果和产品水平与国内外市场接轨。共完成省部级以上科研成果46项,36项成果转化为现实生产力,社会效益和经济效益较为显著。"澳克"品牌的新型建材产品在天津建筑业有一定影响;"高强灌浆材料""纤维增强复合墙体外保温系统及其配套产品的研究""用于高强高性能混凝土的超细矿物掺合料"等3项成果分别获得2000、2002、2003年度天津市科技进步三等奖。天津水泥工业设计研究院(简称水泥院)是从事水泥工业的技术研究、装备研发及工程设计的综合性甲级设计研究院,对于促进水泥生产的科技进步做出贡献。

第一节　水　泥

天津市水泥行业自20世纪90年代起加快技术进步步伐,新型干法水泥生产成为发展的主导方向,生产技术得到推广。2003年形成570万吨的生产能力,实际产量459万吨,有26家具有生产许可证的企业。其中,新型干法窑3条,设计能力达到150万吨;湿法窑3条,设计能力72万吨;小旋窑2条,设计能力12.8万吨;机立窑17条,设计能力181万吨;水泥粉磨站12个,设计能力154万吨。至2005年,全市水泥年生产能力达到710万吨。

一、干法水泥生产技术

1991年,水泥院全面推广应用新型干法水泥生产技术。从20世纪80年代开展新型干法水泥生产工艺的研究与开发,取得快速发展,使其成为主导技术。该生产技术是以悬浮预热和预分解(窑外分解)技术为核心,应用现代流体力学、燃烧动力学、热工学、流态化学以及粉体工程学等现代科学理论和技术,并利用计算机及其网络信息技术进行水泥工业生产的综合技术。其所涵盖的范围包括,原料矿山计算机控制开采、原料预均化、生料均化、新型节能粉磨、高效预热器和分解炉、新型篦式冷却机、有效的环境保护与除尘装置以及计算、检测、控制等技术。具有高效、优质,节能、节约资源,有利于环境保护和可持续发展的特点。

1996年12月18日,由水泥院设计的日产1000吨水泥熟料的新型干法水泥熟料生产线,在天津水泥股份有限公司投产。通过该生产线，水泥质量得到显著提高。该生产线被誉为“天津新型干法水泥第一线”，标志着天津市水泥工业迈入现代化阶段。

图5-14-1-84 天津市水泥厂1000t/d新型干法水泥熟料生产线

1998年，天津市振兴水泥公司建成具有国际先进水平的日产2000吨水泥熟料生产线。采用国际流行的新型干法生产工艺，制成系统采用辊压机预粉磨与闭路管磨组成的粉磨系统，具有粉磨效率高、电耗低的特点，单位电耗约37.5千瓦时/吨水泥，而球磨系统单位电耗约为44.千瓦时/吨水泥，并可保证水泥产品质量。该公司产品“正通”牌高标号低碱水泥，主要性能达到中热水泥、道路水泥、中抗硫水泥、油井水泥的标准，广泛应用于京津、华北、东北地区生产的预伴混凝土、预制构件，桥梁道路，机场跑道，水利水电、港口码头和地下工程等。

2000年，天津振兴水泥有限公司为应对低品位原燃材料并保证产品质量，在国内率先引进技术先进的英国牛津X射线荧光分析仪加质量控制系统的在线控制方式，使得关键过程产品入窑生料的过程控制能力大大提高，保证熟料和水泥产品的质量稳定。3月，该公司日产2000吨水泥熟料(烧成系统)技术改造项目(即二线技改工程)，列入国家经贸委“国家重点技术改造‘双高一优’项目导向计划”。11月，二线烧成和制成技改项目桩基施工。2003年4月25日，二线烧成系统和水泥制成系统两个技改项目同时开工建设。2004年6月26日，二线技改工程实现全线工艺贯通，生产出合格水泥。到2005年底，该公司拥有两条日产2000吨(实际可达2400吨)新型干法水泥熟料生产线，总生产能力达年产高标号低碱水泥180万吨，成为天津市最大的水泥生产企业。

二、生产工艺改造

1994年，天津市水泥厂对湿法窑系统水泥磨车间单仓泵进行改造。由气动换向阀改为由一单扳机控制的电磁阀，解决故障率高的问题，由改造前平均1次/日达到改造后的2~3次/月，设备运转率提高到95%以上。

图5-14-1-85 远眺天津振兴水泥公司全景

同年12月，由天津水泥设计院设计的日产1000吨熟料新型干法窑外分解生产线在天津市水泥厂厂区内打下第一桩，1995年5月2日破土，1996年12月28日窑系统点火，1997年5月水泥磨投产，建成天津市第一条新型干法窑外分解生产线，并于同年通过鉴定验收。至此，天津市水泥厂具备年产120万吨水泥的生产能力。

1995年，天津市水泥厂对于立窑系统生料磨车间进行改造。废止能耗高、产量低、质量不稳定、污染严重的4台小磨(Φ2.5×3.9M)，用近两年时间，异地改造成为1台(Φ3.4×7.5M)带有计算机配料的闭路循环生料磨，于1995年1月试车投产成功，设计台时产量为53吨，立窑生产线生料制备系统的能力得到稳定与提高。

1996年，天津市水泥厂对湿法回转窑生产线的篦冷机进行改造。篦冷机由第一代横梁篦床改为第二代竖梁篦床，使同步运转率达95%以上；投资45万元对立窑生活区供电系统进行改造，解决立窑生产和生活区线路混乱、不易控制的问题，使综合电耗降至原来的70%，稳定立窑系统的生产、生活供电。

1997年，天津市水泥厂为防止混凝土“碱—骨料反应”，提高混凝土的耐久性，在日产1000吨熟料新型干法窑外分解生产线研制生产低碱水泥获得成功，在京、津、唐地区率先生产出低碱水泥。“利用硅砂尾矿生产硅酸盐系列低碱水泥技术研究”项目获2000年天津市建设系统科技进步二等奖；同年，该项目获天津市政府技术创新一等奖。

2001年，水泥分公司为提高立窑的产质量，对立窑进行小料球煅烧技术综合改造，包括改善腰风、成球盘、预加水、窑体保温等系统。改造后立窑的产质量提高，P.O42.5、P.O32.5及P.S32.5R水泥取得国家“产品质量免检证书”，成为水泥生产免检企业。

2002年起，水泥分公司政策性地关闭立窑。至此，有着45年历史、标志着天津水泥生产起步、一度成为“立窑口径世界之最”、历经10多次技改、曾对天津城市建设做出巨大贡献、共计生产水泥1025万吨的两台立窑成为历史。同年，该公司为提高熟料产量对预分解窑进行改造。投资400多万元增设MFC分解炉，篦冷机改造成为第三代充气梁式篦冷机，喂煤系统由冲板流量计加螺旋泵改为粉研称，使该生产线的熟料生产能力从日产1000吨增至1200吨。

2003年，天津振兴水泥有限公司为进一步提高质量控制的反应速度，由韩晓光、关文涛等组织压片法荧光熟料分析技术攻关。该项攻关成果“利用X射线荧光分析仪提高质控水平”获得2003年度天津市优秀质量攻关成果一等奖。2005年，该公司“改进回转窑冷却机，提质降耗”项目获天津市优秀质量攻关成果一等奖。

2003年，水泥分公司投资20万元对两台湿法回转窑的窑尾喂灰系统进行改造。改气动输送为机械输送，降低装机容量450千瓦。该年节电355万度，节约电费170多万元。该年度水泥分公司共生产水泥154万吨，创历史最高纪录。

三、专业设备研发

(一)节能破碎及粉磨设备

1991~2005年，水泥院为适应大型水泥生产线的需要，推动石灰石破碎工艺技术进步，采用石灰石单段锤式破碎取代两段或三段式破碎。2005年开发的单段锤式破碎机最大产量为1800吨/时，可以为10000吨/天水泥厂配套。此外还有400吨/时大型齿辊式破碎机。

1998~2005年，水泥院鉴于粉磨工艺逐步采用立磨或辊压机代替传统的能耗高的球磨机，采用料床粉磨原理的立磨或辊压机逐步实现国产化的情况，开发原料立式磨。其最大规格为φ5.3米，用于5000吨/天生产线配套。2004年，水泥院开发为10000吨/天配套使用的辊压机。2005年，水泥院开发高效组合式选粉机。同年，水泥院专门用于矿渣粉磨的国产立式磨投入市场。

(二)烧成系统设备

1991~2005年，水泥院将国产烧成系统的低压损预热器和高效分解炉成功地用在各种规模的新型干法生产线中，实现新型干法水泥生产技术的核心——烧成系统的创新。此外，达到国际先进技术经济指标的可控气流篦式冷却机，与预热器、分解炉和回转窑合理匹配，再加上对燃料适应性强和燃烧性能好的多通道燃烧器和低NOx燃烧器，使得烧成系统的整体水平提高。

(三)环保收尘设备

2005年，水泥院将新开发的高浓度高温大型水泥窑窑尾袋收尘器和电收尘器，以及新型行喷脉冲袋式收尘器，成功地应用于多条新型干法水泥生产线中。预热器出口粉尘排放值仅为8.6毫克/Nm^3，低于国家标准GB4915-2004中30毫米/Nm^3限值要求，清洁生产水平提高。

(四)纯低温余热发电技术和设备

1991~2005年，水泥院鉴于国产混压进汽式气轮机的开发成功，大力推广纯低温余热发电技术。该项技术成为国内水泥工业节能降耗的有效途径，既可大量回收350℃以下低温废气余热用于发电，减少水泥生产对环境的废热及粉尘的污染，又可以减少火力发电的燃煤消耗，减少温室气体CO_2的排出量。发电量达到30 kwh/t熟料~35kwh/t熟料。到2005年，国内采用纯低温余热发电的水泥企业有10余家。

(五)生产控制应用软件

2000年，水泥院开发DCS水泥生产控制系统应用软件，可用于各种规模新型干法水泥生产线的集散型控制，在国内外都取得较高评价。

2002年，水泥院开发三维矿床模型开采软件，生料质量控制系统软件，胴体温度扫描监测系统软件，水泥厂生产管理信息系统应用软件等，使水泥生产进入到现代化阶段。

2004年，天津振兴水泥有限公司刘志光、韩晓光等承担天津市建设领域科技发展计划项目“P-MIS系统人工智能化”。采用相对独立于过程控制系统的网络环境，将企业的生产操作、质量控制、维修管理等工作通过信息人工智能化处理，有效地提高操作和控制的工作效率和精准度，并与经营管理、行政管理、办公自动化等有机结合，形成功能强大的信息交流和管理网络，增加辅助分析决策的能力，使企业管理迅捷、准确、互动、高效。项目水平达到国内先进。

第二节 砂浆与混凝土

20世纪90年代，天津逐步实现水泥砂浆与混凝土的工厂化生产。2003年底，天津市预拌混凝土行业有混凝土搅拌站40个，年生产能力达到近4万立方米，实际生产达811万立方米。其中，以合资企业瑞科尔为代表的技术先进型企业，由于采用先进的生产设备和外加剂，其供应的预拌混凝土强度等级最高达到C70（技术储备可达到C100），一次泵送最高纪录达165米，充分显示天津市预拌混凝土施工应用的技术水平。全市混凝土外加剂生产企业32个，品种齐全，年实际生产30万吨。

一、水泥干拌砂浆

1997年11月，建材科研所完成“聚合物刚性防水材料及其施工技术”课题研究。水泥砂浆的抗裂性能和抗渗性能得到显著提高，增强水泥浆体与界面的粘结力，以达到建筑物充分保证防水的需求。该研究项目由殷宝贤、李富山、吴为群等人承担，获得1997年度天津市建委科技成果三等奖、1998年度天津市科技进步三等奖。同年，组织开展“水泥修补砂浆的研究”，该材料用于混凝土建筑物和构件受腐蚀破损后的局部修补，可取得事半功倍的效果。该项目由李富山、诸磊、殷宝贤完成，获1998年度天津市建委科技成果三等奖。

1998年12月，建材科研所组织完成“高强灌浆材料”课题研究。该材料具有流动度大且经时损失小，早强、无收缩、粘结强度高等特点，可广泛用于机器设备基础灌浆、建筑物加固等。该项目由吴为群、诸磊、郭飞等承担，获1998年度市建委科技成果三等奖、2000年度天津市科技进步三等奖。

1999年1月，建材科研所在国内率先进行可再乳化粉状树脂的研发，完成该课题的小试研究。建材科研所认识到，按照国家建设部等4部委关于“鼓励发展预拌混凝土和干混砂浆”的要求，实现商品化、工厂化预拌是建筑科技进步以及保护环境、节约资源的必然趋势，而要实现水泥干拌砂浆的工厂化生产，关键是要制备出可复原的、完全自乳化的聚合物粉状树脂，打破外国公司产品充斥国内市场且价格昂贵的局面。为此，持续开展课题研究与实验。课题由任秀全、柳勇臻承担。2002年9月，柳勇臻、陈鹏、吴为群等完成该课题的中试研究，其成果具有显著的创新性。2004年6月，郭玉清等进行“自乳化粉状树脂产业化与应用技术研究”，产品逐步批量生产。“十五”期间，建材科研所建成年产3万吨的水泥干拌砂浆生产线，生产销售各种功能性水泥干拌砂浆7100吨，满足天津市城乡建设的需求。

2002年12月，建材科研所组织完成“纤维增强高性能水泥基材料”课题研究。成功地抑制水泥基材料早期塑性开裂和后期收缩开裂的严重缺陷，实现水泥基材料的高性能化，产品可广泛用于刚性防水、地下室结构自防水、各种地面材料及建筑修补材料。该项目由郭景强、陈贺新、翟延波等承担。

2004年9月，建材科研所组织完成“干粉砂浆及其生产应用技术”课题研究。共开发技术指标先进、符合国家产业政策的瓷砖粘结剂、内外墙腻子、建筑保温专用砂浆和界面干粉4种新产品。由刘彤、王冬梅、刘凤东等承担。

2004年，水泥分公司总工常玉振经过近两年的研究试验，开发出水泥下游系列产品—干粉砂浆及其稠化粉。投资近300万元改造建设一条年产20万吨的干粉砂浆生产线，同时可年生产干粉砂浆稠化粉1.5万吨，该公司单一生产水泥的传统模式得以改变。

二、高性能混凝土

1999年，建材科研所陈贺新、郭景强、苗伟夫等鉴于应用高性能混凝土是国家建设部确定推广的10项重大技术之一，采用矿物掺合料是高强高性能混凝土的技术特征之一，通常以矿渣为主要原料，而天津市没有矿渣资源，国内矿渣也短缺，故创新提出，将天津有的工业废渣—增钙液态渣用作混凝土掺合料，复合其他成份研制超细矿物掺合料，用其等量替代20%~40%水泥，配制C50~C80高性能混凝土，全面改善新拌混凝土的流变特性，提高混凝土的强度和耐久性。该成果水平为国内领先。2003年9月，屈庆飞、陈贺新、雅菁等又完成超细矿物掺合料生产技术和应用技术的研究。在生产技术方面，通过对磨机的内部结构和外部配置进行系统改造，解决一般设备和工艺难以经济地粉磨超细矿物掺合料的难题，调整优化生产工艺参数，较大幅度降低产品电耗。使该所具有年产3万吨的生产能力，产品性能完全达到Q/12JC3109－2003“用于水泥和混凝土中的矿物超细粉”的要求。在应用技术方面，研究产品细度、掺量对混凝土拌和物工作性能及硬化混凝土性能的影响，使产品在天津市高标号混凝土、立交桥预应力箱梁及混凝土管桩等方面得到广泛的应用，有效改善预拌混凝土的流变性能，提高混凝土强度及耐久性，技术经济效益显著，为发展中的绿色环保型高性能混凝土提供重要原材料。“用于高强、高性能混凝土的超细矿物掺合料”项目成果获得2003年度天津市科技进步三等奖。

2000年，建材科研所刘彤、王冬梅、张继强等在小试成果的基础上完成“PSL低坍落度损失高效减水剂的中试研究”课题。该项研究合成以马来酸肝、苯乙烯、丙烯酸及羟基酯类多元共聚物（即SMAH），作为与水泥具有反应活性的保塑部分，对以β—萘磺酸甲醛缩合钠盐为基本组分的萘系高效减水剂进行改性，通过按合理比例对二者进行复合，研制出低坍落度损失高效减水剂。该减水剂有效地控制和减少拌合物的坍落度损失，不影响混凝土的正常凝结，减水率比萘系高效减水剂有较大幅度的提高，特别是与不同品牌水泥相容性好，是该产品的显著特点。运用该成果形成年产1000吨的生产能力，其中试产品的应用也取得积极效果。

2001年，建材科研所与天津二建建筑工程公司合作，于继光、付金栋、陈贺新、刘元春、郭景强等完成“高性能混凝土及应用技术的研究”课题。批量生产出强度等级C60~C80的免振自密实高性能混凝土，并应用于试点工程、总混凝土量约800立方米，成功地实现钢管混凝土的高抛免振捣施工。该项研究在国内未见文献报导，成果达到国内领先水平。

第三节 墙体材料

天津建材系统在新型墙体材料的研发中起步较早，建材科研所研究人员取得多项创新成果。

1991年，建材科研所、市建材工业局科技处、市建材供应公司陈家龙、李镇、霍祜兴等完成“天津砂资源现状与开发应用研究”课题。通过大量试验，为天津市面临枯竭的砂源，开辟新的途径——利用首都钢铁公司矿业公司尾矿代替优质建筑用砂，对于提高用砂质量，降低工程造价，具有现实和长远意义。该成果达到国内领先水平，获天津市1992年度科技进步三等奖。

1992年，建材科研所王树茜、丁玉华等完成"利用增钙飞灰作混凝土掺合料应用技术研究"课题。利用热电厂立式旋风炉排放的增钙飞灰作混凝土掺合料，取代部分水泥生产水泥制品，效益显著。该项技术属国内首创，成果获得1995年度天津市科技进步三等奖。1993年，作为发明专利第一发明人的边希安，在天津人民建材制品厂参加并完成GRC/陶粒无砂大孔复合墙板的研究开发。该墙板系用作建筑非承重墙或隔断墙的一种预制构件，以玻璃纤维增强水泥作墙板的表层，以粘土陶粒无砂大孔作夹芯制成复合墙板预制构件。

1993年，建材科研所诸磊、孙振芳、殷宝贤等完成"粉煤灰抽孔隔墙板的研制"项目。采用特种水泥、掺入40%湿排粉煤灰作为混合胶凝材料，实现直接湿排灰生产自然养护的新型隔墙板材，材性优良。该项研究成果达到国内领先水平，获得1995年度天津市科技进步三等奖、市建委科技成果三等奖。

1994年，建材科研所王锌、刘彤、陈贺新等在小试成果的基础上完成"YMJ保温系列门的研制及应用"项目。在国内首创向非饲料、非燃料的农作物木杆中内掺阻燃剂制成碎板式木质防火门等系列门。

1997年，建材科研所邹志敏、杨忠华、王树茜等完成列入天津市科技攻关计划的"混凝土小型空心砌块的开发"项目。利用增钙灰渣和粉煤灰生产承重与非承重砌块，效益显著；开发出清水墙承重小砌块，集装饰与承重于一身，利于降低建筑造价。建成年产4万立方米混凝土小砌块生产线，在全市率先批量生产。

2000年，建材科研所王树茜与天津市无机化工研究所李富昌等，在扩大试验的基础上，完成市科委下达的重点攻关计划项目"发泡粉煤灰屋面保温材料的中试研究"项目。该项成果是以热电厂排出的粉煤灰为主要填料，加入适当的建筑胶凝材料和外加剂，经化学发泡而成的一种新型无机保温材料。其中，外加剂和粉煤灰的加入，克服氯氧镁水泥返卤和变形；加入发泡剂，与氯氧镁水泥—粉煤灰—水组成的浆液混合时，立即发生化学反应，放出气体，形成细小气泡被保留在浆液中，硬化后得到独立的泡孔；加入稳泡剂，使产品实现低容量高强度。产品主要用于屋面、墙体、管道等的保温节能。

2003年，建材科研所陈鹏、任秀全、柳勇臻等完成"隔热弹性防水外饰面涂料"项目。该项目被列入天津市2001年度自然科学基金项目计划及天津市建委科技发展计划。项目采用乳液混拼技术，运用涂膜表面状态调节技术，改善涂膜的耐沾污性；使用硼硅酸盐空心玻璃微珠，使涂层具有优良的反射太阳幅射的能力，从而使该涂料隔热、防水、抗开裂及装饰功能实现复合化。其不透水性：0.3MPa、30min不透水；隔热性能：户外照射试验后，涂有该涂料试件的下表面温度比未涂者降低26℃。

第四节　装饰材料

20世纪90年代起，天津建筑材料方面科研人员和专家学者积极开展建筑装饰材料的研发，积极促进新型装饰材料在建筑施工中的运用。

1991年，建材科研所徐宏顺、马玉隽、夏冬等承担完成天津市科委下达的"KI系列水泥地面装饰涂料（中试）"课题。KI系列地面装饰涂料具有耐水、耐油、抗冲击等优良性能，其耐磨性尤为突出，有良好的附着力和硬度，施工干燥周期短，价格适中，装饰效果显著。该中试生产规模为年产300吨，中试产品用于天津市环境装饰协会、天钢二厂、中美天津史克制药有限公司、天津雅玛哈电子乐器有限公司等工程，效果良好。该课题成果获天津市建委1992年度科技成果三等奖。

1992年，建材科研所蒋公泰、张效建等完成"聚丙烯酸酯改性（膨润土）沥青柔性防水涂料"的课题研发。该防水涂料冷施工、无毒无污染，低温柔韧性好，耐老化性能优，适合华北等地区使用，产品分高、中、低系列，该中试装置能年产60吨乳液和600吨防水涂料，中试产品使用效果显著。

1993年,建材科研所苗伟夫、夏冬、陈鹏完成"BR改性沥青耐低温防水卷材"研制项目;同年,徐宏顺、杜学志完成"框架轻板建筑体系外饰面复层装饰涂料的研制"项目;袭著昆、刘明涛、曾宪庭、徐宏顺、杜学志等完成"砂质覆面油毡"研制项目;1994年2月,陶安华完成"耐低温防水卷材粘结剂"研制项目。

1993年,建材科研所陈鹏、夏冬、张庆兴等完成"TJ—518多彩花纹内墙涂料"的研制开发。该涂料以商品硝基漆为主要成膜材料,引入性能优异的改性剂,制成的水包油型多彩涂料的性能达到或超过日本工业标准JISK5667所规定的指标,达到国内领先水平,适用于工民建的中高档室内装饰,效益显著。

1994年,建材科研所陈鹏、夏冬、刘树奇等完成"高强聚合物特种水泥材料的研究",项目被列入市科委1991年自然科学基金计划。采用化学—机械改性方法,使高强聚合物硫铝酸盐水泥材料的抗折强度达125～150MPa,优于聚合物＋OPC体系的强度。该材料浸水、干燥后强度能基本恢复,优于PVA＋HAC体系。该项目在国内率先研究高强度聚合物水泥砂浆材料,并把浸水7天的聚合物水泥净浆材料的湿态强度保持率提高到70%以上,把聚合物水泥砂浆湿态强度保持率提高到90%以上。该项目还探讨材料增强的机理。该项成果水平为国内领先。

1998年,建材科研所张庆兴、任秀全、王冬梅等完成列入市科委科技攻关计划的"中高档建筑防水和密封嵌缝材料"研发项目。该防水涂料采用复合乳化体系,并以丙烯酸酯聚合物改性,技术上有所创新,使防水涂料的低温柔韧性、延伸性、耐老化性能显著提高;研发的彩色屋面防水涂料以丙烯酸酯聚合物为成膜材料,耐老化及防水性能好,可美化建筑物顶层;研发的丙烯酸酯密封膏,施工方便,成膜时间短,硬化后呈橡胶状弹性体,可广泛用于建筑施工中需密封的场所。建成年产600吨生产线,设计合理,一线多用。该项目成果水平为国内先进。

2000年,建材科研所于继光、夏冬、诸磊、郭玉清、陈鹏等完成"柔性聚合物水泥防水卷材"研发项目。该防水卷材以聚合物—水泥互穿网络理论为依据,在国内外率先以60%以上的水硬性水泥与聚合物等共混改性,经捏合、混炼、压延工艺制成彩色、不同规格的防水卷材,技术先进,生产工艺合理,可实现工业化生产。该卷材既有无机类材料的优良耐老化性能,又有橡胶类材料良好的适应基材变形的能力,性能价格比优异,并具有在潮湿基面上施工的突出优点,可用于建筑、市政、水利等工程领域。经专家组评定,该项目成果达到国际领先水平。其后,建材科研所为使该成果转化投产,将专利申请权转让给天津新技术产业园区澳克新技术有限公司。2002年5月,作为该项目的延伸,任秀全、陈鹏、李富山等完成"水泥聚合物弹性防水涂料"研发项目。该涂料属高弹性防水涂料,用于20余万平方米的防水施工,防水效果显著。此外,还研制柔性防水砂浆产品,引入纳米SiO_2改善聚合物,使产品抗拉性能提高20%,断裂延伸提高25%。该成果达到国内领先水平。

2002年10月15日,"年产6万吨水泥基柔性防水复合材料产业化示范"项目在大港区奠基。该项目是由天津新技术产业园区澳克新技术有限公司承担建设,是中加国际投资集团在天津投资的第一个国家级高科技产业化项目。年产6万吨水泥基柔性防水复合材料产业化示范项目技术处于国际领先水平。建成后将加快天津市防水材料的更新换代,带动相关产业的共同发展。

2002年10月,天津城市建设学院研究人员贾堤、费学宁、雅菁等完成"海泡石功能涂料"研究项目。利用海泡石具有大的比表面积和孔道,有效地吸附苯丙乳液中单体化合物的特性,在涂料中加入适量的海泡石,既起到增稠剂的作用,还降低涂料中VOC含量,改善涂料的其他性能。研制的海泡石功能性建筑内墙涂料经生产部门和检测部门检验,不仅各项性能指标均优于国家标准,还具有杀菌、低VOC、高耐擦洗性等优点,具市场推广价值。该项目经天津市科委组织的成果鉴定,为国际先进水平。

2003年3月20日,天津市技术物理所承担完成的天津市科技发展计划项目"高效水泥减水剂的辐射合成研究",通过天津市科委组织的验收和鉴定。该研究从辐射聚合方法入手,在不同剂量率和总剂量下,对聚合反应、化学接枝等进行机理分析研究,得出能指导生产的可靠数据,当减水剂掺量占水泥重量0.5%时,水泥净浆流动度达250毫米,减水率达18%。该项目具有广泛的市场前景,是水泥减水剂的前沿产品,其系列产品可适应不同混凝土施工工艺的要求,广泛应用于民用建筑、工业建筑、水利工程等领域。专家认为该研究成果填补国内辐射法生产水泥减水剂的空白，达到国内领先水平。

2003年10月，天津城市建设学院研究人员承担完成的天津市青年科学基金项目“有机硅改性丙烯酸酯乳液及在建筑乳胶漆中应用”通过专家验收鉴定。有机硅改性丙烯酸酯乳液以硅氧烷键为主键，具有高耐氧化性和低表面能，在应用中表现出特殊的保光性、透气性、抗沾污和耐磨性。该项目选用八甲基环四硅氧烷、乙烯基环四硅氧烷作为有机硅单体，通过本体开环和乳液聚合两种工艺，制备硅油中间体，将硅氧烷链引入到丙烯酸酯分子链上，使极性相差很大的聚合物间形成化学键，化学改性在一定程度上控制有机硅分子链的表面迁移和有机硅微观形态，获得聚硅氧烷/聚丙烯酸酯简单物理共混所没有的种种优良性能。该项目通过对工艺条件、配方的调整，得到性能优良的硅丙乳液，研制的硅丙外墙涂料除达到合成树脂外墙涂料的国家标准外，还具有优良的耐人工老化性和耐沾污性，研究成果具推广价值。

2005年，天津建材科研所王冬梅、殷宝贤、雅菁等完成市科委计划项目“水性环氧树脂改性水泥基建筑粘结剂”课题。该项研究用热固性树脂乳液对水泥材料进行改性，形成三维结构，具有强度高、发展快、性能好的优点。采用水性环氧树脂体系配合硅灰、超细粉等对水泥类材料进行改性，实现有机与无机材料在性能上互补叠加，产品无毒、环保，是对传统溶剂型环氧材料的改进与提升。该成果研发出石材外墙干挂粘结剂、石材拼接粘结剂和高强度界面剂3种新产品，质量全部达到国家行业标准。成果水平为国内领先。

同年，天津建材集团会同水利局、天津大学、市墙改办人员共同完成市科委科技发展项目“利用海泥烧砖技术的研究”。对于海泥砖的脱水、排盐、原料配比、烧成工艺，产品情况环境评价进行试验研究。抗压强度10兆帕海泥砖烧制成功，各项指标基本达到烧结页岩砖标准的要求。经初步测算，海泥砖性能优良，经济实用，有较大的社会效益。项目成果水平达到国内领先。

第五节 节能环保

1991~2005年，天津市建筑节能研究和建材生产的环保技术取得创新成果，对于节能环保和空气质量改善发挥积极作用。

一、建筑节能研究

1999年9月，建材科研所任秀全、李富山、白锡庆等完成“纤维增强复合墙体外保温技术及其配套产品的研究”课题。开发出一整套可靠、实用、经济的外墙外保温技术及其配套产品，并且抓住粘结剂及保护层开发研制这一关键技术取得突破。产品的粘结强度（与砂浆粘结）＞1.5MPa，国外产品实测为1.27兆帕；初期抗裂性，参照GB9779—88测定，该项目产品无裂纹，而进口产品实测0.5小时已出现裂纹；耐候性，相同条件下冻融10次后该项目产品无裂纹，进口产品已出现裂纹；该项目产品还具有明显价格优势。该项目成果水平为国内领先，被天津市科委推荐国家级成果登记。2001年12月，试点工程圆满完成，通过天津市科委的项目验收。从项目产品推广后，该所为200万平方米的外保温施工工程（相当于800万平方米的建筑面积）供料并指导施工，取得较好的经济效益、社会效益。该成果获2002年度天津市科技进步三等奖。

2003年，建材集团杜春礼、谢宁、李福永等完成的“城市住宅建筑节能技术及示范工程”科研项目通过天津市科委组织的验收、鉴定。该项目结合示范工程和砼空心砌块住宅特点，注重对变形缝两侧墙体、外檐门窗洞口侧面、封闭阳台栏板及东西山墙等各围护结构保温、隔热细部构造的研究解决，并为后来南偏东（西）＞450朝向的砼空心砌块住宅隔热做法提供技术依据。经检测分析并通过工程验证，“纤维增强复合墙体外保温技术”其性能指标达到或部分超过国内外同类产品。该项目从淘汰实心粘土砖，发展新型住宅体系的角度，研究与之配套的建筑节能技术，并通过对比分析，编制相应的标准图集及技术规程。适用于砼空心砌块住宅及以轻集料砼空心砌块为填充墙的框轻住宅等新体系。为城市住宅建筑节能，从设计、施工、工程验收等方面提供技术支持和依据。其综合建筑节能技术达到国内领先水平。该项目2005年获天津市科技进步三等奖。

2004年，天津爱舍公司引进德国赫腾公司主机设备，建成一条年产18万m^3加气混凝土砌块和板材生产线，其产品外观精度高，尺寸允许误差仅1~1.5毫米，强度06级的可达到3.5兆帕以上。最大的优点是导热系数小0.11~0.26W/m^2·k，具有良好的保温性能，是唯一可以用单一材料，而不必做复合墙体就能达到“三步节能”的新型材料。

2005年，建材科研所鉴于加气混凝土制品是唯一使用单一材料即可达到“三步节能”的新型墙体材料，必将成为框架结构建筑的首选墙体材料之一，结合爱舍（天津）新型建材有限公司蒸压轻质砂加气混凝土砌块的生产，安排由王冬梅、殷宝贤等在市科委立项，开展“加气混凝土干法施工技术及配套产品的研究”。成功研制出“加气混凝土制品专用粘结剂”以及“专用界面剂”“专用修补材料”“聚合物水泥基腻子”等后续产品，使加气混凝土产品实现薄层砌筑、薄层抹灰，减少抹灰层的空鼓和开裂，效果显著。

二、节能环保技术

1993年，天津市水泥厂投资500万元对立窑生产线的粉尘进行综合治理。增加2台8室LFEF型玻纤袋除尘器处理立窑烟尘并密封处理熟料提升机、破碎机及振动输送等整个系统，使含尘气体浓度小于150毫克/立方米；增加3台4室LFEF玻纤袋除尘器，对烘干机废气排放、水泥磨头仓、混合提升机等扬尘点进行负压密封处理，处理风量5万立方米/时，达到国家排放标准。该项目于1994年首次获得市政府颁发的“市绿化先进单位”奖牌证书。

1998年，天津市水泥厂在全市“蓝天工程”限期治理过程中，投资近300万元，先后对立窑收尘系统、立窑烘干机旋风加电收尘系统、湿法回转窑窑头收尘系统、立窑生产线水泥磨收尘系统、立窑生产线生料磨布袋收尘系统进行改造。改造后效果显著，被天津蓝天工程领导小组授予“天津市2001年实施蓝天工程工作先进集体”奖牌；其间，“治理粉尘的两大措施”项目荣获全国建设建材工会系统职工技协科研技改成果奖。

1999年，天津水泥股份有限公司水泥分公司在天津市建委立项“粉煤灰配料湿法窑煅烧生产硅酸盐系列低碱水泥的应用研究”课题。该项目历经1998、1999年的实验室预配研究后，于2000年1月进行中试，并取得预期效果，各项指标达到国家标准的要求，2002年底通过市建委组织有关专家进行的鉴定。通过研究发现，用粉煤灰和砂岩参与配料（取代粘土），在湿法回转窑生产低碱水泥是完全可行的。该技术在国内领先，属于废物利用的循环经济技术。

2000年，水泥院开展水泥生产过程协同处置废物废渣及副产物的资源化工作。2003年，水泥院受北京金隅集团委托，设计完成一条用水泥窑处理城市工业废弃物的生产线。主要用于处理垃圾焚烧飞灰、垃圾焚烧灰渣、工业污泥、废白土类、乳化剂等液态废弃物以及其他需破碎的固体废弃物等6大类，年处理废弃物量约10万吨。该生产线于2005年投产，成为处置工业废弃物的示范工程，开发和推广对废弃物再循环利用技术，提高可燃废弃物的焚烧技术水平。

2000年，水泥院推行水泥绿色生产技术。包括：①余热利用技术与设备；②水泥窑协同处置废物；③废渣资源化技术与设备；④有害元素的检测与监测。与此相配套，水泥院主编“水泥行业清洁生产评价指标体系”“水泥工业节能设计规范”等，促进国家相关政策和法规的完善。

2000年，天津市振兴水泥有限公司杨泽芬、刘志光、韩晓光等开展的“利用天津市低品位水泥灰岩资源生产高标号低碱水泥的研究”项目通过天津市建委的成果鉴定，成果水平达到国内领先。通过在低品位水泥灰岩生产高性能水泥方面进行研究，使产品除具有低碱、高强特性外，还具有耐磨损、低干缩率、低水化热的特性，有效促进低品位石灰石的利用，提高矿山剥采比，延长矿山使用年限，资源利用率提高。

2002年，水泥分公司开展余热利用项目。共拆除洗浴、采暖用锅炉7台、饮用锅炉38台，利用生产线的余热供给采暖、洗浴，新建一条纯净水生产线供给全厂职工饮水。该项目有效降低环境污染，彻底消除各种锅炉“年检”费用，节约成本，节煤2万吨/年。同年，湿法生产线改造自来水管网，设置中水循环管网，收集生活用水、生产用水、雨水，经过滤，用于设备冷却和生料浆的制备，达到生产过程全部采用中水，该厂共减少自来水用量60%以上，节水85万吨/年。同年，该公司还通过利废技术的攻关，处理各种工业废弃物及危险废物等，至2005年底共计1850.42吨，取得良好的社会和经济效益。

2004年，天津远洋龙达玻璃公司投资1.4亿元在塘沽新建“一窑四线”。日融化量260t玻璃液，年产155万重箱平拉玻璃。采用L型吊墙结构、全窑宽投料技术，设置卡脖深层水包等措施，改进熔窑结构，油耗由过去的16kg/重量箱，下降到12kg/重量箱，单位能耗处于国内平拉工艺生产线领先水平。2005年，该公司以煤焦油为燃料代替重油，进一步节约能源，降低玻璃成本5~6元/重量箱。

2005年，由天津振兴水泥有限公司牛海龙等提出的“二线窑尾高温废气冷却方案”获天津市职工建设节约型社会技术创新成果奖。

第十五章　工业工程设计

1991～2005年，天津形成实力很强的工业工程（成套）设计、建造与检测能力。特别是建国以来国家在天津建立的大型骨干工业设计研究院，通过工程（成套）设计与工艺的技术创新，对于国家和天津市的工业装备水平的提高以及标准化建设，做出重要贡献。

第一节　机械工业工程设计

隶属于中国机械工业集团公司的机械工业第五设计研究院（简称五院）是以工程（成套）设计、总承包为主体业务的综合性甲级设计研究院。承担各类大中型整体工程设计，以及专用设备、生产线、机械化运输装备、工业炉窑的设计和总承包项目。

一、机电工艺与装备

（一）检测与试验

1993年，机械工业第五设计研究院设计研制JCT—2000型微机控制通用荧光磁粉检测线。该线是双回路、全交流、固定式、多功能半自动探伤成套设备，用于汽车、拖拉机及内燃机等行业大批量、多种类、形状复杂的重要零件（亦称保安件）的表面和近表面加工缺陷和疲劳裂纹在线检查和探伤。全线由双回路交流磁化主机、检验转台和输送带式退磁机组成。电磁轭采用高导磁材料的铁芯，连续开机时铁芯不易发热，检测灵敏度高，稳定，交流磁化时间短，退磁容易。主机也可单独使用，采用国外先进的可编程序控制器控制，精度较高，可靠。主要技术特点为：双回路全交流磁化，在复合磁化时可形成旋转磁场，周向磁化电流0~1500安（两路），纵向磁场0～12000安匝；使用美国标准试块，显示清晰、完整、灵敏；当节拍10s/件时，检测能力60.4万件/年；夹持间距≤800毫米。该成果改变“手脚眼并用”的黑磁粉探伤的落后面貌，属国内首创，双回路交流磁化方法达到国际先进水平。该项目获得1995年天津市科技进步奖二等奖。

1999年，五院为西安航空发动机有限公司设计研制YGSTX-1200清洗、荧光渗透检测线。采用荧光渗透方法和后乳化、自乳化工艺检测铝钛合金（如飞机零件）、奥氏体不锈钢件等金属表面开口不连续性的原材料缺陷、加工缺陷和使用中产生的缺陷，同时完成零件的清洗烘干。该线采用的荧光渗透检测技术及微机、PLC等自动控制系统，具有工艺先进、检测灵敏度高、运行稳定可靠、自动化水平高等优点，达到相关的国际荧光渗透标准，在国内航空航天系统首次研制成功。该项目获得2002年中国机械工业科学技术奖三等奖。

（二）汽车制造工艺与装备

1.冲压与模具

1994年，天津微型汽车厂车身冲压新增21台日本小松技术的国产压力机，组织5条生产线。除压力机技术先进外，生产线下地沟中装有废料输送线，能将废料送到车间外的打包间，并在国内首先采用坯料自动送料清洗机，保证冲压件成形质量的稳定。

2.焊接夹具与机械手

1994年，天津微型汽车厂改造扩建二厢装焊车间。利用原装焊线，用轻型悬链把车门总成输送到装门工位，并新增一个5工位的补焊线和24个工位的车身高速线，共形成前后地板、左右侧围、顶盖、车身总成等13条装焊线。生产线采用自动送料、自动夹紧、工序间自动输送，配有多点焊机、自动点焊机和机械手。主要设备及工装从日本大发公司引进，自动化程度高，可靠性强，工艺水平较高，达到8万辆二厢轿车的生产纲领。同时，在原车间的基础上组建三厢装焊车间，对二、三厢共用件的设备和夹具进行复制，并提高自动化水平，自动和多点焊工作量达60%以上，工位之间采用步进式自动输送，车身及零部件用积放式悬挂输送机和轻型链、电动自行小车等输送，达到年产7万辆三厢轿车的生产纲领。改造后的装焊工艺居国内先进水平。

3.油漆

1994年，天津微型汽车厂新建油漆车间，博采英国、日本等国家多家著名公司先进设备，使涂装工艺技术达到国际上90年代水平。油漆前处理采用喷、浸结合方式，并用中日合资生产的药剂，电泳漆HB-2000系世界第四代产品。PUC胶、中涂、面漆采用不同形式的喷枪（杯式或枪式）。自动喷涂机能更换不同的颜色。前处理、电泳采用积放式悬挂输送链和C型吊具；车底胶喷涂采用自行葫芦；各工艺段之间设排空储存段，实现柔性联接。全线工件自动传送，自动转接，中央控制室监控工艺参数及设备运行情况。油漆车间按区划分工艺，实现分区净化。各种设施齐全、先进，废气、废水、废液全部在车间内处理后再排放。配有先进的自动灭火系统，具有自动报警，24小时监控，自动开启功能。前处理UF装置中增添RO装置，使电泳漆利用率更高，超滤功能更好，节省纯水的用量和减少废水处理量，成本降低。喷漆室隔栅设置脱漆皮装置，能处理掉隔栅上黏附的油漆而保持隔栅不变形。小型零件油漆前和粘接前的除锈工艺，采用国内自行研制的超声波清理技术，由于超声波机械作用与化学介质化学作用的结合，大大提高除锈的速度和效率，处理时间仅用3.5分钟。

4.铸造、热处理

1991年，天津汽车发动机厂铸造分厂铁水熔化改进为中频无芯炉→中频无芯炉双联熔炼，以保证获得高温优质铁水。铝合金缸盖铸件采用带CPU加压控制的低压铸造工艺。球墨铸铁凸轮轴桃形表面处理采用重熔硬化工艺。

1994年，天津汽车齿轮厂变速箱齿轮的热处理，引进德国的双排推杆式连续渗碳炉生产线。该线的温度、时间、碳势等工艺参数采用微机控制，碳势可控制在±0.05%，渗碳淬火后，齿轮精度等级下降不到1级，表面硬度误差为±1HRC。该线生产能力为2000吨/年，可同时处理两种不同要求的零件，达到90年代国际水平。

5.机械加工工艺

1994年，天津内燃机厂的曲轴生产线应用新型曲轴内切机床，全线机床PC控制，故障显示，关键工序均配有自动测量装置。

1994年，天津汽车桥厂后制动器制动毂加工，引进德国埃马克公司3台倒立车，车削速度高达700米/分，设备采用先进可靠的数字控制技术，能够实现工件的装卸、加工、测量、补偿等全部自动化。

1994年，天津汽车齿轮厂变速箱壳体、差速器壳体均在引进的加工中心或精镗专机上加工，保证孔的加工精度和位置精度。齿形加工采用高速滚齿、高速插齿工艺，在引进的数控径向剃齿机上剃齿，精度可达6-5-5级。花键轴加工，采用冷轧机搓滚工艺，代替常规的花键铣床。齿轮的外圆精加工，采用数控复合外圆磨床，不同直径的外圆一次磨成。半轴齿轮、行星齿轮的齿形实现冷精锻成形。其他机加工生产线广泛采用CNC机床、机夹不重磨刀具，超硬涂层新材料刀具。

6. 切削加工

1991年，五院为江铃汽车集团发动机厂设计开发并总承包研制TX31-Q型排削及冷却液净化系统。该系统适用于发动机缸体、缸盖等大批量生产的大流量湿式机械加工排除切屑和净化冷却液的成套装置。在金属切削过程中，采用具有一定压力和足够流量的冷却润滑液连续不断地冲洗刀具和工件的加工部位，并及时将切屑全部冲走，含切屑的冷却润滑液经粗、精过滤，将切屑和污物分离后，净化的冷却润滑液再送回机床继续循环工作。其特点是：过滤精度高（<50微米），流量大（可达2000升/分）；系统容量小（130立方米可服务4~7条加工线），压力稳定（0.3~0.4兆帕）；冲刮排屑量大、干净；冷却润滑液增氧除油使用寿命长，用国产液可达11个月；设废水处理站，有害物可达标排放，80%~85%的水可回用；系统运行可靠，自动化程度高，便于管理维修。该技术属国内首创，达到国际同类设备的先进水平，获得1997年国家科技进步奖三等奖和全国第八届优秀工程设计奖铜质奖。1998年进一步完善，为南京跃进集团汽车发动机有限公司承包制造一套。

7. 装配工艺

1994年，天津微型汽车厂新建夏利轿车总装配生产线。主线由6段组成，共150个工位，另有车门、发动机等分装线，全部共22条输送链，总长度7762米，吊具、载具总计1261套。整车总装配工艺达到国际90年代水平。特点是：① 在国内首次采用地面反向积放链用于轿车装配。② 物流系统完善。车间工艺流程呈立体空间布置，各种生产线和输送线共24条，其物流运输形式主要靠悬链，配以叉车、货梯、AGV地面小车等形式，构成以4条主装配线为主体的空间输送网络。③ 生产柔性化。设计中考虑储存段、缓冲段和备用工位，解决生产中的不均匀性。④车门装配工艺先进。在国内首次采用把车门总成离开主装配线进行装配后再回到主线总装，降低总装线上的工作量。⑤尾气排放抽吸装置先进。采用10台空中自行小车组成的环形废气抽吸系统，排放发动机尾气，以减少对车间的污染。⑥储存线上配备识别器。⑦该线对各种液体实现集中供应，管道输送，定量加注，还采用机械手自动涂胶和安装风档等新技术、新设备。

二、工业炉窑

（一）悬挂式曲轴热处理生产线

1995年，五院为南京汽车厂铸造分厂总承包研制，用于铸铁曲轴（约30千克/件）毛坯的正火、回火热处理。由上料台、前室、正火加热炉、喷雾冷却室、回火加热炉、风冷室、下料台、传动系统、控制系统等部分组成。全线采用积放式悬挂输送机传送，工件挂放在输送小车的专用耐热钢吊具上，随小车依次通过各工位进行正火加热、喷雾、回火热处理。其特点和技术参数为：轴垂直加热和冷却，消除变形，提高热处理质量；燃料为轻油，最大燃耗170千克/时；热效率27%；处理工件质量稳定，运行可靠；产量大，可达1～5吨/时。该生产线属国内首创，为提高曲轴等长杆类工件热处理质量，减少变形，提高生产率创出新路，主要技术指标进入国际先进水平行列，经济效益显著。该项目获得1996年国家机械工业部科技进步奖二等奖。

（二）井式内冷光亮球化退火炉

1996年，五院为天津汽车锻件厂承包研制。该项目是周期式热处理炉，适用于等温球化退火工艺的新型炉。其特点为：马弗罐采用薄壁直桶式，结构新颖，不受力，质量减少70%，节省大量耐热钢，炉衬采用全纤维结构，节能30%，能耗指标达到并超过国家一等炉的水平；采用氮气循环冷却系统，解决等温球化退火对速冷工艺的要求，工件在氮基保护气氛中加热、冷却，既保证工件球化和表面质量，又缩短生产周期，经济效益显著；采用PID控温调节系统，炉温稳定性好。等温球化退火工艺为冷锻工艺提供符合德国标准的优质退火毛坯，还广泛应用于标准件、轴承、工模具等行业。该项目获得1999年天津市科技进步奖二等奖。

(三)汽车发动机曲轴热处理生产线

1997年,五院为天津内燃机厂总承包研制。该线将曲轴的正火、急冷、回火、缓冷、卸料、回盘等工序联成一条全自动连续热处理环形生产线,汇集国内外热处理设备的一系列先进技术。采用具有国际先进水平的可控硅模块作为功率元件连续调动,DTL-812带电脑三回路可编程序控温仪,使炉膛温控精度由同类设备的±15℃提高到±5℃。正火炉、回火炉结构新颖,工件温度均匀,高效节能。新型急冷室的冷却速度>60℃/分,急冷速度可调且各工件冷却均匀,确保工件机械性能稳定,偏差小。全线进出料、各炉门启闭、翻料等运转及连锁传动系统,采用PLC可编程序控制器,控制达到国际先进水平。电热元件、料盘等关键耐热配件使用寿命长。该线投资低,产品质量稳定可靠,曲轴热处理生产一次合格率达100%,节电20%。该项目获得1999年天津市科技进步奖二等奖。

(四)超大型台车式热处理炉

1998年,五院为天津通用电气阿尔斯通水电设备有限公司总承包研制。炉膛有效尺寸12.9米×8.7米×6.6米,台车轨距4.5米,台车自重135吨,最大装载量300吨,台车面积12.6米×8.14米×6米,燃料为0-10#轻柴油,最大耗量480千克/时,温控精度±5℃。该炉采用一系列创新技术:柔性自调电动台车、轻型组合式软连接全纤维结构的活动轨道紧压炉门、大跨度浮动式平面全纤维炉顶、高速调温烧嘴的脉冲控制燃烧技术、多区温控、IPTC智能温度程序控制仪进行生产全过程自动控制。该炉是九十年代末国内同类炉型中有效宽、高及台车单体有效面积最大的炉窑,可广泛用于冶金、机械、化工、锅炉、核电站、水电站等行业的大型铸、锻件和焊接结构件的热处理,大型水利工程中的大型水轮发电机组的主体部件——转轮、顶盖、座环、定子机座、转子支架等大型组焊结构件的热处理,处理质量优于美国工程师学会ASME标准,也可更换燃料改为燃气热处理炉。该项目获得2000年天津市科技进步奖一等奖。

三、机械行业改扩建工程

1992年,五院参与天津市政府向世界银行提出的贷款1.5亿美元,改造天津工程机械、机床等5个行业,即"天津工业发展项目"计划的咨询评估,并承担工程机械厂、第一机床厂、动力机厂等企业的设计。总投资达13亿元,总建筑面积7万平方米。大面积地引入先进工艺技术设备及计算机集成制造系统(CIMS)、辅助设计辅助制造(CAD/CAM)、信息管理系统(MRPⅡ)等,改变这些老工业企业的面貌,调整产品结构,实现产品升级换代,增强发展后劲。工程机械厂的平地机和轮式装载机是90年代国际新型产品,总产量新增后达1500台,年产值从1亿元增加到5.5亿元。第一机床厂改造后,生产加工中心及数控齿轮机床精度达到世界当代水平,机电一体化产品达81%。动力机厂引进英国珀金斯柴油机生产制造技术,建立珀金斯(天津)动力有限公司,投资6亿元,新建3万平方米的大柱距螺旋球网架结构厂房,年产1000系列柴油机3万台,生产和经济效益跃上新台阶。

1994年,天津微型汽车厂、内燃机厂、汽车齿轮厂、汽车发动机厂、盘式制动器厂、汽车桥厂、拖拉机厂等7个厂进行扩建和技术改造。共建成25条主要生产线,新增主要生产设备1092台,其中引进310台,主要生产工艺或国内先进,或达到国际90年代水平,1996年建成投产,1997年底天津成为全国4个年产15万辆轿车的生产基地之一。五院设计的天津夏利轿车15万辆扩建项目,获得1999年全国第八届优秀工程设计奖银质奖和国家机械工业部科技进步奖一等奖。

四、行业机械设计

(一)电子仪表

1994年,五院与津京玻壳股份有限公司合作研制新型屏、锥预热及玻壳退火处理线。这是国内第一条自行研制的黑白显象管玻壳后加工处理线,用于电子行业黑白玻壳封接玻屏、玻锥的预热和封接后退火,是玻壳生产中的关键设备。该线包括两台20米×2.16米×1.8米预热炉和两台42米×3米×2米退火炉,燃料为城市煤气。预热炉用燃烧机,集烧嘴、鼓风机、控制装置于一体,既简化结构和控制、占地小,又使燃料燃烧的空燃比得到有效控制,燃烧充分,炉内温差在±10℃以内,可完全消除由于燃烧不完全在产品表面产生的"黑霜";退火炉一改国内外贯用的集中循环模式,采用独特的分段组合式结构,各段炉单独供热,自成系统实现气流上循环,采用温度、热值两个参数独立精确控制炉温,炉膛断面温差小于±5℃,炉温更加均匀,确保产品质量。1995年考核测试玻壳可比单耗平均为740千焦/千克,比JB/T5625-91国家规定的黑白玻壳退火一等炉单耗1287千焦/千克低42.5%,经当时检索,主要技术达到国际先进水平。该线替代进口,降低设备投资,在节约燃料、提高成品率方面,每年为企业取得1000万元的直接经济效益。该项目获得1996年天津市科技进步奖二等奖。

1995年,五院和津京玻壳股份有限公司合作研制完成年产200万只小型黑白显象管玻壳生产热处理成套设备。该套设备除继承前条线的技术外,又采用多台经改造的燃烧机供热,炉温更均匀,温控精度更高,容易实现理想的退火曲线;屏、锥成型后退火采用新型鼠笼式电加热器供热,可按热容量灵活布置,易更换维修;阳极帽封接前预热炉,采用适应工艺特点的大气式引射烧嘴和炉底燃烧机坑道式供热。这些创新把小型黑白玻壳热处理技术推向新水平。该设备较引进技术节省大量资金,经济效益好,并出口美国。该项目填补这一领域的国内空白,获得1998年国家机械工业部科技进步奖二等奖。

(二)食品

1991年,五院为天津市同乐食品厂设计研制TX19-Q型夹心巧克力自动线。该线系将调制好的巧克力浆与心料浆定量浇注、振动、冷却、脱模,并将成品糖块输出的全自动成套设备,由传动装置、浇注头、振动装置、冷却隧道、机架、脱模装置、出料装置、模盘烘烤装置及电气控制等10个部分组成,技术先进,为国内首创。其特点是:能一次浇注成型多品种的夹心和实心巧克力糖;具有适应性强、结构紧凑、重量轻、投资少、占地面积小和对生产厂房无特殊要求等优点。生产节拍3~6秒,班产0.6~2.5吨,制冷量62800~83800千焦/时,总功率5.77千瓦,外形尺寸14米×1.04米×1.8米。该线与国外同类生产线性能和技术指标相似,价格仅为进口设备的1/5左右。其用电量少,不用压缩空气,便于推广。该项目获得1992年天津市科技进步奖二等奖。

(三)生物与制药

1991年,五院与达仁堂制药二厂合作设计京万红系列药品技术改造项目,是中成药行业首次使用的万级洁净厂房。油膏提取由传统手工操作改造成全封闭机械化生产,有效防止内外交叉污染。罐装工序达到1万级洁净度,工艺技术和装备水平处于国内领先地位。经澳、德药政专家检验认定,达到国际GMP标准。该设计获得1993年全国医药优秀工程设计奖三等奖。

1993年,五院为天津市第六中药厂研究设计滴丸剂型系列产品改造项目。建筑面积14866平方米,严格按GMP标准移地改造,净化面积4000平方米,其中2700平方米达到10万级洁净度,形成绿色花园工厂。工艺和生产环境达到国际先进水平,处同行业领先地位,成为国家中药行业按GMP标准建设的明星和样板。该项目获得1998年全国医药优秀工程设计奖三等奖。

2002年,五院与天津泰达药业有限公司合作设计移址新建生产车间。新建面积18000平方米,年产中成药颗粒剂200吨、片剂42240万片、胶囊制剂8360万粒、丸剂26400万粒、糖浆制剂330万瓶。设计增选国内外先进的提取、喷雾干燥、压片、薄膜包衣及包装等固体制剂设备,采用组合式的联合厂房,合理布置工艺流程,夹层暗敷公用管线。按药品GMP规范要求合理布局一般控制区、10万级洁净区。建筑创意美观、气派,受到国家药监局、天津市及开发区主管部门的赞扬。该项目获得2005年国家机械工业优秀工程设计奖二等奖。

同年,五院承担天津中新药业集团股份有限公司物流配送中心网络信息化管理系统技术改造项目。该项目是国家重点技术改造项目(第7批国债专项资金项目)。研究引入国际上先进的物流技术、用市场化的业务流程改造传统产业,使企业生产经营的全过程实现运行的精确化、信息化、数字化、高效化,提升产业水平,使生产企业通过流通创新,进行物流的重新设计整合,赢得分销领域中的利润份额,对促进经济持续发展产生积极影响。该项目获得2003年国家机械工业优秀工程咨询成果奖一等奖。

同年,五院与江苏万邦生化医药股份有限公司联合设计胰岛素与固体制剂异地改造项目。该生化制药工程是国内最大、最先进的糖尿病人用药基地。设计年产10毫升重组人胰岛素和猪胰岛素西林瓶500万瓶、卡式瓶300万瓶；2毫升心先安注射液等三个品种共3500万支；固体制剂2亿片(粒)。引进德国先进技术，使生产技术达到国内领先水平，部分产品达到国际先进水平。投产后经济社会效益显著。

同年，五院承担设计的医学细胞生物制药与液氮深低温自动控制储存库工程，即天津协和干细胞工程产品产业化基地一期工程，是当时建成的亚洲规模最大的脐带血造血干细胞血库。设计规模为：建筑面积46000平方米，投资3亿元，脐血处理能力25万份，冻存库容量50万份，各种基因工程药物95万只。其投入运营后，共保存合格脐带血产品2万余份，其中公共库保存公众捐献脐带血5000多份。在脐血干细胞正常生产的同时，还开发脐血细胞产品，外周血干细胞储存，骨髓干细胞储存等生产项目以及胚胎干细胞储存业务，为社会保存一批重要的生物资源。该项目获得2006年中国机械工业科学技术奖二等奖；2007年中国机械工业优秀设计二等奖。

2005年，五院分别承担天津乐仁堂制药厂中成药出口基地技改项目、天津同仁堂制药厂、天津中央制药厂片剂车间项目、天津怀仁堂制药有限公司、天津第五中药厂、天津中新药业集团股份有限公司达仁堂制药厂、新新制药厂、中国医药保健品进出口总公司美康中药材进出口公司、天津中医学院所属药厂等技术改造项目。工程建设中，改进中药生产工艺和环境，实现机械化自动化生产，达到国际GMP标准，改变中药行业面貌。

(四)新能源

1998年至2004年，五院先后完成天津力神电池股份有限公司锂离子电池一、二、三、四期工程设计。总建筑面积8万平方米，总投资达20亿元。该项工程是以中国电子科技集团公司第十八研究所为依托，引进国外先进的自动化生产设备，在华苑新技术产业园区建成的国内投资规模最大、技术水平最高的锂离子电池产业化重点项目。年产锂离子电池2亿只。

2001年，五院承担设计天津市津能电池科技有限公司非晶硅薄膜太阳能电池产业化示范工程。年生产能力5兆瓦，投资2亿元，建筑面积2.1万平方米。非晶硅薄膜太阳能电池的叠层电池结构优化设计及其制备技术、大面积双玻璃封装技术等的突破，可改变国家光伏产业生产成本高、应用范围小的现状，带动蓄电池、控制器、逆变器、光伏水泵、家用电器、节能灯具等产业的发展。主要车间10万级、局部万级密闭净化，全部用激光切割制造，非晶硅电池用分室连续设备和沉积技术，消除单室技术中反应气体的交叉污染问题。该项目获2002年国家机械工业优秀工程咨询成果奖二等奖。

五、厂房设计

1993年，五院与美国柏克德公司合作设计摩托罗拉电子(中国)公司总部工程。项目总投资3.4亿美元，完成70000平方米的建筑规模。该工程建设引进世界先进电子通讯的带头企业，也在国内工业厂房建筑结构上第一次引进世界一流的美国巴特勒公司轻钢装配式结构体系，从此轻钢装配式结构厂房在国内迅速发展。该建筑宽敞，主厂房、办公楼、动力站房为一体，易合理组织人流、物流，使工艺流程、生产运输、动力供应、管线布置形成最短捷路线，以提高功效和节约能源。建筑设计以人为本，创造舒适美观的工作、生活环境。该项目获得1993年国家机械工业部第三届优秀工程设计奖一等奖。

1994年，五院承担设计天津微型汽车厂装配车间。总长275米，宽105米，高17.8米，两层结构，局部一层，总面积51724平方米。采用轻钢结构厂房，基础采用钢筋混凝土结构，梁和柱采用变截面轻钢等强度设计，屋面采用世界先进技术，保证热胀冷缩时不漏水，维护结构和屋面系统采用彩色压型钢板，中间填充玻璃纤维绵保温。厂房土建8个月如期完成，保证设备安装、调试周期。比采用传统的混凝土结构，工期减少一年半，造价降低。总用钢量3188吨，每平方米用钢量为616.3千克，每平方米造价2213元。车间建筑在当时国内同行业中居领先水平。

1994年，五院承担设计天津微型汽车厂油漆车间。面积27152平方米，局部双层采用排架结构，屋顶为螺旋球网架。同时设计的天津汽车齿轮厂联合厂房面积228287平方米，天津汽车桥厂第二联合厂房面积

10406平方米，天津盘式制动器厂夏利联合厂房7410平方米，以及1995年设计的天津丰田汽车发动机有限公司近3万平方米联合厂房，全部采用排架结构，独立杯型基础，屋顶都为螺旋球网架结构，屋面及维护结构采用新型建筑材料，18×18米大跨度柱网，250~300毫米厚内敷Φ10钢筋网的刚性混凝土地坪，一般设备不设单独基础，水、电、气等管路穿网架空敷设，便于生产设备布置和工艺变化调整又不破坏地面，加上带状窗采光，屋顶采光罩，车间宽敞明亮。这些设计将大跨度柱网螺旋球网架新结构技术较早应用于国内工业厂房建设中。

第二节　电气传动自动化工程设计

1991年至2005年期间，天津电气传动设计研究所（以下简称天传所）承接和完成各类电气传动自动化（成套）设计工程项目1800余项，在设计中努力采用新型的控制方法和控制系统，研制和创新关键的电气传动自动化元件与装置，促进有关工业企业电气传动自动化性能质量和装备水平的提高。

一、电气传动自动化（成套）工程

（一）轧机电气传动

1991年，天传所对武钢冷轧厂1979年由外商调试投产的年生产能力120万吨的冷轧酸洗线电气传动自动化系统实行不停产改造。改造中更换原有从德国BBC公司进口的全套电控设备，采用当时具有国际先进水平的西门子微机直流全数字6RA22共22套，取代原模拟直流调速装置，采用西门子S5-135U双处理器可编程控制器共4套，取代原系统分立元件硬件逻辑单元；改造全线直流传动装置93台、主导值自动化装置27台、操作台箱33个，成套设计及系统集成立足国内。全线设备不停产分期更换，到1993年底投产，共减少停产改造时间101天，可靠性提高。该项目获得1995年国家机械工业部科技进步奖二等奖。

1995年，天传所承担“武钢硅钢扩建工程CA5机组电气自动化系统”项目的核心部分即电气传动的自动化系统。CA5机组是第一条由国内成套、自行设计、制造、调试的高水平的硅钢连续退火处理生产线，系统主要由3台上位机、4套PLC（S5-155U、I/O量5000点）、45台主传动电机交流全数字调速装置（6SE70）、14台炉用风机交流全数字调速装置（6SE70）、14台交流过零触发调功器以及二级通信网络组成。1998年5月，该项目系统投入生产运行，武钢硅钢片厂成为国内高质量硅钢片的核心生产厂。1999年3月国家机械工业部行业管理司组织专家鉴定，认为该项目“是国内最早自行开发设计、目前规模和容量最大、通信功能最先进的全交流化、全数字化、网络化的大型自动化系统；在系统构成、网络通信、动态画面集中监控以及活套控制等方面的性能和水平优于该厂成套引进的1997年投产的同类机组系统，已达到国际先进水平。”系统投产后经济效益显著，系统技术成熟，能代替国外引进的同类系统。1999年，该项成果获得国家机械工业局科技进步奖一等奖。

1997年，天传所承接武钢冷轧厂镀锡线电控系统改造项目。将全部直流电动机改为全封闭的交流异步电动机，把直流调速改为变频调速，同时更新全线的自动控制系统，实现数字化和网络化。该项目的特点是：规模大，全线156台套交流全数字变频调速系统，10余套10千安直流可调电源，4套工业控制计算机；性能高，调速系统涉及6类高性能典型工艺控制，自动控制系统完成全线所有设备的设定、操作、监控、显示和记录，包含多个工艺模型的计算。改造后该线的电控系统处于当时全国先进水平。

2000年，天传所陆续对太原钢铁公司不锈钢热轧厂的热轧中板二辊粗轧机、精轧四辊万能轧机和炉卷轧机等国家早期建设项目的变流机组进行改造。主传动系统原采用直流发电机变流机组传动，直流电动机容量分别为：3500千瓦、5000千瓦及2×3150千瓦。通过改造，采用先进的晶闸管供电数字控制，高精度速度电流双闭环系统。其中,主电路采用大功率晶闸管风冷整流柜12脉波多相整流,减少变流器谐波对电力系统影响;控制系统引进国外多微机通用数字控制器,实现全数字控制;控制功能通过软件编程方法实现,设备紧凑通用性强,功能修改靠刷新程序灵活方便;运行状态和系统信息可通过通讯接口子模块对上位机或现场终端数据交换,人机信息交换可通过操作面板或系统编程设备实现;主传动系统采用多处理器全数字控制先进技术,晶闸管变流器输出功率大,改造后取代变流机组节能效果显著。2002年,该技术改造项目获得天津市科技进步奖二等奖。

2001年,天传所承接河南明泰铝业2000毫米4+1铝板热连轧生产线电气传动自动化工程项目。该项目初轧5.4兆瓦主传动采用交-交变频系统,是国内自行研制的首条热连轧铝板生产线,也是首次将大功率交-交变频系统应用于有色金属生产线。该生产线于2003年投产。

2002~2005年,天传所承接中冶恒通公司1#、2#、3#、4#等4条镀锌生产线工程项目。每条线年产量30万吨,工艺段速度180米/分,入口段、出口段速度250米/分。4条生产线的电气传动自动化控制系统采用全交流、全网络、全数字控制方式,传动系统与上位PLC之间用PROFIBUS-DP通信,均达到当时国内先进水平。

2004年,天传所承接莱钢1500毫米热连轧生产线主传动(8套6兆瓦)工程项目。首次在国内大型热连轧生产线全线采用交-交变频系统。该生产线工程项目于2005年投产。

2005年,天传所承接唐钢1700毫米热连轧生产线工程项目。全线10套大功率主传动全部采用交-交变频系统,最大单机功率达到7.5兆瓦,是在国内承接的最大的大型热连轧生产线。生产线投产后效果良好。

同年,天传所承接中冶恒通公司2#酸连轧生产线工程项目。该酸洗连轧生产线年生产能力为85万吨,是当时生产规模较大的生产线。项目包括计算机二级、一级、传感器和传动全数字控制系统。酸洗部分为全数字交流传动,轧机部分为全数字直流传动。一级自动化酸洗部分,由4套PLC,分别控制入口段、工艺段、出口段和酸液部分,轧机部分用2套PLC,进行轧机区的顺序控制和辅助设备的控制。一级自动化轧机部分,由2套VME总线的高速控制器组成,完成轧机速度控制,AGC控制,轧辊偏心控制,轧制力与位置控制,ATC/张力控制,板型控制,弯辊控制,轧辊冷却控制,焊缝跟踪,轧线速度管理,自动减速控制,油膜补偿等。二级系统完成材料金属学管理和工艺数据的数据库、实施管理任务和数学模型、与一级自动化系统进行通信、实施辅助任务等工作。

(二)高炉电气传动

80年代末,天传所承接攀枝花钢1#高炉(1200立方米)技术改造工程项目。该项目采用美国GE公司系列6高挡PLC,人机接口采用ViewMaster系统和OIT操作员终端等先进技术。项目于1990年成功投产,是国内在高炉自动化控制系统中较早采用上位机人机接画面的成功案例。

1997年,天传所承接天津铁厂4#高炉(700立方米)技术改造工程项目,负责自动化控制系统的研制和设备制造。该项目中成功地采用高炉长寿、精料、高风温、喷吹煤粉、无料钟炉顶、计算机控制等先进技术。该高炉于1998年成功投产。该项目获得2001年天津市科技进步奖三等奖。

2001年,天传所承接天津铁厂5#高炉(400立方米)自动化系统的工程项目。首次在国内采用工业现场总线技术,与PLC系统结合,组成自动化控制系统的方案,大大减少现场电缆的敷设,降低日常生产维护的工作量,使系统综合成本大幅降低。经查阅资料,国际上当时也未发现有将工业现场总线应用于高炉自动化控制的成功先例。同时,还研制采用总线系统控制箱,解决环境(尤其是北方冬天寒冷天气对系统的影响)对系统稳定运行的影响。总线系统采用24伏直流电源分段供电模式,解决低压直流电在长距离供电线路上的损耗问题。该项目于2002年成功投产。

2001年,天传所专门研发适合中小型高炉特点的自动化控制技术方案,针对当时国内民营钢铁企业不断新上小型高炉项目的情况,使得中小型高炉的自动化控制既具有技术上的先进性又有比较低廉的成本。该方案在邢台市德龙钢厂2#高炉(179立方米)自动化系统中得到成功应用,之后在越南太原钢铁公司2#高炉系统中也得到成功应用,促进中小型高炉的自动化控制水平的提高。

2003年,天传所承接天津铁厂2#高炉卷扬电气传动工程项目。在高炉主卷扬和探尺卷扬传动中采用全数字直流调速系统，当时在国内同类项目中是较早应用的。该项目2005年投产。

（三）风洞和试验台传动

1999～2000年，天传所结合航空一集团115厂改造项目，完成603所120千伏安航空发电机测控台研制工作，并首次实现机电总成交钥匙方式。此类试验台是航空工业的重点试验台，采用计算机及全数字控制，产品多年来一直由国外公司垄断，价格很高。天传所技术人员利用掌握的较熟悉的工艺技术，配合先进的全数字调速控制器、数据采集分析系统、精确的负载加载系统和计算机系统，并采用先进的增速机装置及高性能电机，成功开发出国产的高性能航空发电机测控台并通过验收，各项性能指标均达到（部分指标优于）进口产品。天传所在该项目取得成功的基础上，又为航空工业的115厂、125厂、172厂、603所和上海飞机研究所等单位生产配套10多套试验台，产值1300多万元，为航空工业提供优质的实验装置，打破国外产品对市场的垄断。

2002年，天传所承接哈尔滨汽轮机厂320吨高速动平衡试验台电气传动和监控系统的研制任务。该试验台是当时此类试验台中单机容量最大的（4兆瓦/6兆瓦）可控硅供电系统。试验台两台电机轴串联，单台电动机主回路采用天传所研制的RG1B热管系列Φ77大功率晶闸管整流装置12脉动整流，电枢不可逆供电，用励磁可逆实现回馈制动。控制系统采用全数字控制技术，稳速精度达0.02%，动态超调小于1%。采用先进组态软件对整个试验台运行状态实行网络化监控，首次采用触摸屏进行数字化自动操作，操作难度和劳动强度降低。该项目2003年9月投入正式运行，效果良好。

2003年，天传所承接中国空气动力研究与发展中心的Φ5米立式风洞电气传动和监控系统的研制任务。该风洞为亚洲最大立式风洞，风洞实验段圆形截面Φ为5米，高度H为7.5米；风速5~50米/秒。风扇电机额定功率为1.8兆瓦，额定电压为3.3千伏，额定转速360rpm，调速范围1∶15。监控系统完成动力系统的控制与监视，保证动力系统安全可靠运行，采用全数字网络化控制，可编程控制器、变频器、辅助控制系统、高压配电系统、操作计算机和监控管理计算机之间实现网络连接。Φ5米立式风洞项目2003年2月开始设计，2005年9月完成调试正式投入运行。该项目获得2008年国防科技进步奖一等奖。

（四）其他电气传动

1988年，天传所承担秦皇岛煤码头3期工程装卸成套设备电气自动化系统已有设备的后续设计、设备制造、程序软件编制、系统调试、全部中央控制室计算机联网以及管理系统的设计、程序软件编制、系统调试项目。秦皇岛煤码头三期工程是国家重大项目大秦输煤线的配套工程，年输煤能力3000万吨，在工程建设的关键时刻，装卸成套设备国外总包商破产，工程建设被迫中断。天传所在紧迫情况下承接项目，包括2台翻车机、2台堆料机、3台取料机、3台装船机的23台交、直流调速传动系统，以及10台大机的10套PLC（S5-150U、S5-115U）自动控制系统；4个变电站数十台大型皮带运输机4套PLC（S5150U）自动控制系统；中央控制室3台PLC（S5-150U）联网通信和集中监控系统；中央控制室计算机（VAX-8250）管理系统。该项目于1990年通过由国家交通部和国家机械部组织的专家鉴定，认为"该系统满足秦皇岛煤码头三期工程装卸成套设备电气自动化系统的原设计要求，达到同类系统的国际先进水平。"工程于同年通过国家验收。该项目获得1991年国家重大技术装备成果奖一等奖；1991年国家机械电子工业部科技进步奖一等奖；1993年国家科技进步二等奖。

1991年，天传所研制的潜艇主推动电机晶体管励磁调节系统在某潜艇投入运行。在潜艇主推动电机控制上采用晶体管励磁调节系统尚属首次。在研制中，解决系统抗干扰性、低电磁辐射技术难题，具有高可靠性，重量轻，易维护，易操作的特点，电流调节精度±1%，各种保护功能齐全。该励磁系统按照军工产品的质量管理要求，进行严格的产品出厂检验，通过电磁兼容试验，满足军标装艇设备的要求，用于装备某型号系列潜艇，对提高部队战斗力发挥重要作用。该项目获得1993年国家机械工业部科技进步一等奖。

1995年，天传所承接元宝山露天煤矿连续开采工艺成套设备集散控制系统项目。大型露天矿连续和半连续开采工艺设备的集中控制系统研究是国家科技攻关项目，以国家"八五"重点工程、年产原煤500万吨的元宝山大型露天煤矿为依托工程。该工程由德国塔克拉夫公司总承包。天传所负责集散控制系统的组态、硬件配置、数据通信、控制软件与管理软件和适应恶劣环境的成套装置的研制、系统调试。控制对象包括：移动式胶带机4台、固定式半固定式胶带机15台、带分流站的胶带机5台、轮斗挖掘机2台、排土机2台。该系统是“元宝山露天煤矿连续开采工艺成套设备”的子项。元宝山露天煤矿连续开采工艺成套设备集散控制系统，是采用分层网络结构组成的分布式大型自动化系统。根据控制对象分散的特点，采用1个主网和8个子网的通信体系结构，主PLC采用S5155H双机热备技术，24个分站组成8个子网，通过子网的主站与主网相连接。特大型轮斗挖掘机、排土机机上配置多台PLC（S5-115U），亦构成独立子网。该控制系统是当时技术水平高、难度大、可靠性高、功能比较完备的连续和半连续开采工艺成套设备控制系统。该系统于1995年底基本调试完毕，投入运行。1996年11月通过部级专家鉴定，认为该系统达到20世纪90年代初国际先进水平，居国内领先地位。该项目获得1999年国家机械工业局科技进步二等奖。

二、新型电气传动自动化系统设计应用

（一）全数字交直流调速系统

1988年，天传所开展交-直-交变频调速系统的应用研究，在鞍钢1700热连轧机输出辊道，实现模拟控制的晶闸管电流型交-直-交变频调速系统工业运行。该项目成果获得1990年国家科技进步三等奖。

1990年底，天传所在武钢冷轧厂酸洗线改造工程项目中，首先在中小功率直流传动系统中成功应用全数字调速系统，取得经验后，又陆续在棒线材轧机、中宽带轧机等多个工程项目的直流传动系统中，推广全数字调速系统的应用。

1996年，天传所在济南钢铁公司马来西亚中板厂中板轧机2×4000HP主传动中，对系统性能要求更高的大功率直流传动系，应用多处理器模块化的全数字调速系统。取得经验后，又陆续在承德钢铁公司、武汉钢铁公司、天津荣程钢铁公司等十几家工程项目中，在容量大于3000千瓦的轧机直流主传动系统中，推广全数字调速系统的应用，均取得良好效果。

1998年，天传所进一步开展交-直-交变频调速系统的应用研究，在武钢硅钢扩建工程CA5机组电气自动化系统项目中取得实破，实现全数字电压型交-直-交PWM变频调速系统在工业中的成功应用。之后分别在多套轧机及其他工程项目中推广，交-直-交变频调速系统的应用水平提高。

（二）大功率交-交变频调速系统

1993年，天传所通过多年进行大功率交-交变频调速系统的应用研究，研制成功国内第一套兆瓦级模拟控制的矢量控制交-交变频调速系统，应用于长钢一厂300轧机主传动。该项目获得1994年国家机械工业部科技进步二等奖。

1995年，天传所研制成功国内第一套全数字控制的矢量控制交-交变频调速系统，应用于天津市无缝钢管厂轧管机2.5兆瓦主传动。该项目获得1997年国家机械工业部科技进步二等奖。

1997年，天传所成功研制当时国内最大功率的5.4兆瓦矢量控制交-交变频调速系统，并在国内首次将交-交变频系统与TCR型动态无功补偿及谐波吸收系统同步投入运行，应用于武钢大型厂860轧机主传动。该项目获得1999年国家机械工业局科技进步二等奖。

（三）串联叠加高压变频调速系统

2002年，天传所经过2000年4月开始的串联叠加型高压变频调速系统研究，研制成功第一台6千伏、500千瓦样机，投入现场工业运行，成为国内较早实现工业现场安全可靠运行的单位之一。通过该项研究，较好解决次级对称移相多绕组输入变压器、串联叠加PWM多重化输出、高性能双DSP芯片的主从结构、大规模门阵列FPGA、光纤通讯技术、软件模块化设计、系统自诊断、高压单元IGBT的应用以及整体检验和测试技术等一系列关键技术问题。该项目获得2项发明和1项实用新型专利。由中国机械工业联合会组织的专家鉴定结论为：根据科技查新报告，该系统有多处创新，达到国内领先水平。

（四）高速磁浮车辆车载电网系统

2004~2005年，天传所承担“十五”国家“863”高速磁浮交通技术国产化研究重大专项中的“高速磁浮车

辆车载电网系统研制”项目。通过科技攻关，全面掌握高速磁浮车辆车载电网的关键技术，解决在直线发电机频率和电压大幅变化下，获得稳定的440伏主电网能量供出的升压斩波器技术，国产镍氢电池组的充放电及电池管理技术，大功率电源的高频谐振软开关和多单元并联技术，恶劣环境下的电网设备可靠性设计等多项技术，大量采用符合中国国情的新技术方案，用一年多时间将研究开发的产品交付现场，车辆试验运行成功。

（五）自动化系统

1990年，天传所通过多年开展可编程序控制器（PLC）及多微机系统在冶金工厂生产线及轧机基础自动化系统设计的应用研究，在武钢冷轧厂酸洗线电气系统改造工程中，首次应用4套S5-135U，双CPU技术，完成数字给定、垂度调节、位置控制等高性能控制。该项目获得1995年国家机械工业部科技进步二等奖。

1994年，天传所在印度尼西亚金峰集团2000毫米\1+3铝板连轧机电气传动自动化系统成套设备研制中，首次应用2套S5-155U，双CPU、HMI图形控制器、工业以太网（H1网）技术，完成可逆轧机全自动程序控制及精轧机组速度、轧辊定位等控制。

1995年，天传所在武钢硅钢CA5电气自动化系统中，应用4套S5-155U，首次采用二级网络技术，实现与全数字交流传动装置的网络通信及动态画面集中监控。该系统1999年3月通过国家机械工业部行业管理司组织的专家鉴定，认为“在系统构成、网络通信、动态画面集中监控以及活套控制等方面的性能和水平，优于该厂成套引进的1997年投产的同类机组系统，已达到国际先进水平。”该成果获得1999年国家机械工业局科技进步奖一等奖。

1996年，天传所在德国西门子公司对中国市场推出新型S7-400 PLC的情况下，即在泰国伟成发集团双机架中板轧机电气自动化系统中，首次应用2套S7-400，实现可逆轧机程序控制。

1997年，天传所在武钢冷轧厂电镀锡线电控系统改造项目中，实现Modicon Quantum与6SE70交流传动装置的现场总线通信连接。在唐钢二高速线材轧机电控系统项目中，实现GE90-70与6RA70直流传动装置的现场总线通信连接。

2005年，天传所在河北省武安元宝山集团中板可逆热轧机系统中，首次应用西门子公司的SIMATIC TDC多微机系统，其采样时间短，可达100微秒，实现自动化控制系统在单一平台上，能拥有最大数量的接口和最短的循环周期，系统的控制精度及生产效能提高。

三、电气传动自动化装置研制

（一）大功率晶闸管变流装置及通用晶闸管调速装置

1990年起，天传所先后推出ZG、JG系列铝散热器风冷大功率晶闸管系列变流装置。该系列产品采用Φ77毫米国产或进口大功率晶闸管和铝型材散热器；最高输出电压为直流1200V，单柜最大输出额定电流为1400安，并柜后均流系数0.9以上；装置过载能力强，允许200%额定电流过载一分钟；具有标准脉冲接口，可与各种类型控制装置相连接，适用于大容量直流传动及交-交变频传动。该装置的主要技术指标达到国际同类产品的水平。据不完全统计，到2005年已有250台套成功用于各种工业企业现场。

1998年，天传所推出RG系列热管散热器大功率晶闸管系列变流装置。该系列产品采用最新热管散热技术，提高出力约50%；采用Φ77~Φ100毫米国产或进口大功率晶闸管，和工程密封性好的并联风道，各元件均匀冷却；系列产品最高输出电压为直流1200伏，单柜最大输出电流为4000安，并柜后均流系数0.9以上；装置过载能力强，允许200%额定电流过载一分钟；具有电子式导通监视单元可检测出任何原因造成的整流桥缺臂或误导通，也具有标准脉冲接口，可与各种类型控制装置相连接，适用于大容量直流传动及交-交变频传动。该装置的主要技术指标达到国际同类产品的水平。据不完全统计，到2005年已有350台套成功用于各种工业企业现场大容量的传动系统中。

2001年，电传所为适应中小容量直流传动系统的需要，陆续推出ZX系列直流调速装置。该系列装置集微机数字控制和国产晶闸管调速传动技术于一体，具有价格低、性能好、安全可靠、维修简便等优点。系列产品额定输出电压等级从440伏到1200伏，最大输出电流达2000安。过载能力强，允许200%额定电流过载一分钟。主要技术指标达到国际同类产品水平，在中小功率直流传动系统中广泛应用。

（二）晶闸管大容量整流电源

1995年，天传所为山东铝业公司提供3套同相逆并联45千安/500伏晶闸管整流电源，用于电解铝。之后，天传所陆续向中国铝业河南分公司（4套35千安/1150伏）、中国铝业贵州分公司（3套35千安/170伏）、包头稀土院（8套短网10千安/50伏）和中冶恒通冷轧技术有限公司（4套 ±7.5千安/±50伏）等用户提供大容量晶闸管整流电源。该成果达到国际先进的技术指标和工艺水平，获得1997年国家机械工业部科技进步一等奖、1998年国家科技进步二等奖。该整流电源被列为1997年国家级新产品，替代进口设备。

（三）高压大容量静止变频起动装置

1991年，天传所承担宝钢4000立方米高炉48兆瓦鼓风机静止变频起动装置的研制任务。该装置采用交-直-交电流型变频电路，网侧输入电压12千伏，电机侧额定输出电压10千伏，起动装置的额定输出功率达12兆瓦，额定工作时间为30分，过载能力为120% 10分。在30分内可连续起动3台48兆瓦同步电动机驱动的静叶可调轴流式压气机组。每台机组从起动加速到整步并网时间不大于 8.5分。该装置以国产元器件为主，总体性能指标不低于引进国外装置的水平。该项目被列入国家机械电子工业部机械工业科学技术发展计划的新产品试制部分（编号为92169991B）。1994年，按照技术要求完成该装置的研制，并投入工业运行，填补国内大容量静止变频起动装置的空白，替代同类进口设备。该项目获得1996年国家机械工业部科技进步一等奖；1997年国家科技进步三等奖。

1997年，天传所承接安徽省金寨县响洪甸55兆瓦、42兆瓦抽水蓄能电站静止变频起动装置的研制项目。响洪甸抽水蓄能电站两台55兆瓦抽水蓄能机组电机额定电压10.5千伏。静止变频起动装置额定电压10.5千伏，额定输出功率6兆瓦26分，过载能力为120% 10分，在26分内可连续起动3次。该起动装置中，晶闸管采用热管型散热器，控制系统采用全数字控制器，具有与世界发达国家同样的技术水平。2000年，该静止变频起动装置成功投入运行，效果良好。

（四）其他电气传动自动化装置

1991年，天传所“直流传动电控装置微机诊断系统”项目研究，在1989年底完成工业应用研究后，推出诊断系统工业应用产品。产品先后在济钢、太钢、马钢、天钢、本钢、鞍钢、长钢等钢厂，以及印度尼西亚铝厂的轧机主传动的十余套大型电控装置上成功应用，具有开机诊断、在线诊断、故障预报及离线故障分析能力，可完成对传动装置的数据采集、实时监测、故障诊断、故障处理、故障波形再现，按故障出现的顺序显示故障内容等功能。该项研制使国产大中型电气传动装置的可靠性和可维护性提高，填补国内空白，其技术性能达到20世纪80年代中期同类产品的国际先进水平。获得1990年国家机械电子工业部科技进步二等奖。

同年，天传所在总结多年研制直流传动控制系统及消化德国西门子公司SIMADYN-C系统通用控制单元的基础上，研制出一套19英寸通用控制单元，成功用于天传所20世纪90年代初生产的所有大型直流传动和交-交变频装置。该套单元的特点是：采用国际通用的19英寸标准插件结构，可靠性和互换性提高；广泛使用国际通用小规模线性和数字积成电路，集成度和控制性能提高；控制功能更完善，不仅可用于常规直流调速系统，还可用于张力控制系统和矢量控制交流调速系统；引入免调试和少调试功能，单元和系统调试比SIMADYN-C更简便、精确。该控制单元的技术性能达到当时模拟控制单元的国际水平。

2000年，天传所研制加速器用高精度大功率稳流电源，完成1200安晶闸管整流电源1套及300～1000安 IGBT直流电源11套，用于中国科学院近代物理所重离子加速器。特点是电流大，周期脉动，对静态误差，纹波及动态跟踪误差要求极高，均小于10-5。在设备中采用直流有源滤波和电流预控等多项新技术，使电流精度满足上述高要求，系国内首创。

第三节 水泥工业工程设计

1953年建立的天津水泥工业设计研究院(简称水泥院),是以水泥工业的科研开发、工程设计及工程总承包为主体业务的综合性甲级设计研究院,完成各类大中型整体工程设计、总承包项目和专用设备设计。

一、干法水泥生产技术

1991年,水泥院全面推广应用新型干法水泥生产技术。从20世纪80年代开展新型干法水泥生产工艺的研究与开发,取得快速发展,使其成为主导技术。该生产技术是以悬浮预热和预分解(窑外分解)技术为核心,应用现代流体力学、燃烧动力学、热工学、流态化学以及粉体工程学等现代科学理论和技术,并利用计算机及其网络信息技术进行水泥工业生产的综合技术。其所涵盖的范围包括,原料矿山计算机控制开采、原料预均化、生料均化、新型节能粉磨、高效预热器和分解炉、新型篦式冷却机、有效的环境保护与除尘装置以及计算、检测、控制等技术。具有高效、优质,节能、节约资源,有利于环境保护和可持续发展的特点。

1996年12月18日,由水泥院设计的一条日产1000吨水泥熟料的新型干法水泥熟料生产线,在有20多年水泥生产历史的天津水泥股份有限公司投产。通过该生产线,水泥质量得到显著提高。该生产线被誉为"天津新型干法水泥第一线",标志着天津市水泥工业迈入现代化阶段。

同年,天津市最大的水泥企业——天津市振兴水泥公司成立。该公司建成2条具有国际先进水平的水泥生产线。一是1998年7月26日投产的日产2000吨水泥熟料生产线,二是2004年5月26日投产的日产2500吨水泥熟料的生产线,均采用世界流行的新型干法生产工艺,技术经济指标达到20世纪末世界先进水平。该公司的制成系统采用辊压机预粉磨与闭路管磨组成的粉磨系统,具有粉磨效率高、电耗低的特点,单位电耗约37.5千瓦时/吨水泥,而球磨系统单位电耗约为44千瓦时/吨水泥,并可保证水泥产品质量。该公司产品"正通"牌高标号低碱水泥,主要性能达到中热水泥、道路水泥、中抗硫水泥、油井水泥的标准,广泛应用于京津、华北、东北地区生产的预伴混凝土、预制构件,桥梁道路,机场跑道,水利水电、港口码头和地下工程等。

二、水泥专业设备

(一)节能破碎及粉磨设备

1991~2005年,水泥院为适应大型水泥生产线的需要,推动石灰石破碎工艺技术进步,采用石灰石单段锤式破碎取代两段或三段式破碎。2005年开发的单段锤式破碎机最大产量为1800吨/时,可以为10000吨/天水泥厂配套。此外还有400吨/时大型齿辊式破碎机。

1998~2005年,水泥院鉴于粉磨工艺逐步采用立磨或辊压机代替传统的能耗高的球磨机,采用料床粉磨原理的立磨或辊压机逐步实现国产化的情况,开发原料立式磨。其最大规格为φ5.3米,用于5000吨/天生产线配套。2004年,水泥院开发为10000吨/天配套使用的辊压机。2005年,水泥院开发高效组合式选粉机,同年,水泥院专门用于矿渣粉磨的国产立式磨投入市场。

(二)烧成系统设备

1991~2005年,水泥院将国产烧成系统的低压损预热器和高效分解炉成功地用在各种规模的新型干法生产线中,实现新型干法水泥生产技术的核心——烧成系统的创新。此外,达到国际先进技术经济指标的可控气流篦式冷却机,与预热器、分解炉和回转窑合理匹配,再加上对燃料适应性强和燃烧性能好的多通道燃烧器和低NO_x燃烧器,使得烧成系统的整体水平提高。

（三）环保收尘设备

2005年，水泥院将新开发的高浓度高温大型水泥窑窑尾袋收尘器和电收尘器，以及新型行喷脉冲袋式收尘器，成功地应用于多条新型干法水泥生产线中。预热器出口粉尘排放值仅为8.6毫克/千克·立方米，低于国家标准GB4915-2004中30毫克/千克·立方米限值要求，清洁生产水平提高。

（四）纯低温余热发电技术和设备

1991~2005年，水泥院鉴于国产混压进汽式气轮机的开发成功，大力推广纯低温余热发电技术。该项技术成为国内水泥工业节能降耗的有效途径，既可大量回收350℃以下低温废气余热用于发电，又可减少水泥生产对环境的废热及粉尘的污染，还可以减少火力发电的燃煤消耗，减少温室气体CO_2的排出量。发电量达到30千瓦时/吨熟料~35千瓦时/吨熟料。到2005年，国内采用纯低温余热发电的水泥企业有10余家。

（五）生产控制应用软件

2000年，水泥院开发DCS水泥生产控制系统应用软件，可用于各种规模新型干法水泥生产线的集散型控制，在国内外都取得较高评价。

2002年，水泥院开发三维矿床模型开采软件，生料质量控制系统软件，胴体温度扫描监测系统软件，水泥厂生产管理信息系统应用软件等，使水泥生产进入到现代化阶段。

三、节能环保技术

2000年，水泥院开展水泥生产过程协同处置废物废渣及副产物的资源化工作。2003年，受北京金隅集团委托，设计完成一条用水泥窑处理城市工业废弃物的生产线。主要用于处理垃圾焚烧飞灰、垃圾焚烧灰渣、工业污泥、废白土类、乳化剂等液态废弃物以及其他需破碎的固体废弃物等6大类，年处理废弃物量约10万吨。该生产线于2005年投产，成为处置工业废弃物的示范工程，开发和推广对废弃物再循环利用技术，提高可燃废弃物的焚烧技术水平。

2000~2005年，水泥院推行水泥绿色生产技术。包括：①余热利用技术与设备；②水泥窑协同处置废物；③废渣资源化技术与设备；④有害元素的检测与监测。与此相配套，水泥院主编“水泥行业清洁生产评价指标体系”“水泥工业节能设计规范”等，促进国家相关政策和法规的完善。

第六篇

农 业 科 技

概 述

20世纪90年代初，全国改革开放深入、快速发展，经济体制从计划经济转向市场经济，城乡人民生活水平从温饱转向小康。市场对农产品的需求为农业科技的发展提供了更加广阔的空间，同时也提出许多新问题。为适应新形势，科学规划和引导天津农业的发展，天津市科学技术委员会（以下简称“市科委”）和天津市农村工作委员会（以下简称“市农委”）更加重视农业发展战略与对策研究。天津市农业科学院（以下简称“农科院”）农村经济与区划研究所在两委的支持下，联合相关单位开展了一系列软课题研究，为天津农业的科学发展提供了决策支持。

1991年初，天津市政府部署农业后备资源调查和区域开发规划工作。天津市农业区划委员会组织相关人员600多人次调查、分析、并作出规划。当年编发《农业后备资源调查和农业区域开发规划工作要点》《农业区域开发总体规划实用技术教材大纲》。至1992年，完成市及区县农业区域开发总体规划。规划报告对全市农业区域开发条件、潜力进行综合评价和预测分析，提出全市总体及分区、分期开发目标设想，战略措施与合理利用后备资源的建议。1992~1993年，天津市农业区划委员会和天津市农业区划研究所共同编绘出《天津市农业后备资源调查及开发规划图集》。包括概况、农业后备资源、土壤养分、气候资源、水资源、农业区域综合开发六个图集。2004年，市农委立项，由天津市农业资源区划办公室和区划所共同编制“天津市农业资源年度报告（2004年）”，报告收集分析全市开展土地资源、气候资源、水资源、生物资源和农村生态环境方面调查的最新资料和数据，对合理开发和保护农业资源，促进农业和农村可持续发展作出贡献。

1995年，市科委开展农业示范工程，主要包括：种子产业化工程；工厂化农业；向蓟县转移农科院科研成果的院、县合作。经费由1995年的200万元/年增加到2001年的1000万元/年。种子产业化工程的实施大力推进了新品种、新技术向生产应用的转化。农科院在出成果的同时，也形成一支高水平的科研队伍。他们采用高新技术和传统育种技术相结合，培育出水稻、小麦、玉米等粮食作物新品种203个，黄瓜、大白菜、菜花、土豆等蔬菜系列新品种400余个 。这些品种不仅在天津地区推广应用，还辐射到全国。其中，以黄瓜新品种最为突出。天津市黄瓜研究所（以下简称“黄瓜研究所”）的科研人员在侯锋的带领下，围绕建立高效的黄瓜育种技术体系开展育种技术和方法创新研究。他们培育的新品种深受欢迎，在天津成为主栽品种，还推广到全国30个省、直辖市、自治区，占全国黄瓜播种面积的80%。黄瓜品种在全国是唯一没有外国品种打入的蔬菜品种。由于科技体制改革深化的需要，促进了黄瓜研究所由事业单位向企业的转制。侯锋几十年在黄瓜育种方面做出了突出贡献，于1999年当选为中国工程院院士。

专家王炳君经20多年的刻苦攻关，于1989年研制成功马铃薯脱毒微型种薯生产技术。该项技术比当时国内外采用的马铃薯繁种方法提高繁殖系数70倍以上，而亩用种量却由125千克减至7千克，减少了95%，大大减少了马铃薯种薯的储存调运量，且由于进行了脱毒处理，增强了种薯的抗病能力，可使马铃薯亩增产50%以上。该项成果获1994年度天津市科技进步一等奖，1996年获“科技兴市突出贡献奖”。1996年5月14日，此项技术以100万美元向美国转让。这是中国第一个出口的自主知识产权的蔬菜品种。

在种子产业化工程中，天津有一批优良品种走出实验室，并和外省市合作在全国适宜的地区建立种子产业化良繁基地。不仅缩短了种子的繁育周期，而且带动了所在地的经济发展。黄瓜品种在山东、马铃薯在宁夏、花椰菜在云南等地建立了繁育基地。

天津畜牧业在此15年中加大结构调整，猪肉和禽蛋的生产增速放慢，牛羊肉和奶类的发展保持较高水平。畜禽饲养以规模化、集约化为主。随着畜禽繁育技术的发展，在应用人工授精技术和机械化孵化技术的基础上，开始胚胎工程领域的基础和应用研究。2005年，采用胚胎克隆的波尔山羊在天津诞生。天津种子产业化工程中，对畜牧业重点支持了良种猪培育技术的研究与推广。

1995年以后，随着第二代节能日光温室的引进和相关技术的大力推广，天津蔬菜的栽培方式发生了突破性的变化。设施农业提高到一个新的水平，并开始大面积普及。设施农业的耕作方式使喜温果菜的收获季节可以在冬季，有些品种可以一年多次收获。作物品种由最初单一的蔬菜发展到食用菌，花卉，果树等。温室设施的结构和内部装备也在不断优化和完善。设施农业的普及带动了与之相关的育种，农业机械等技术的发展与创新。1996年，天津市投入300万元进行蔬菜大棚示范区招标，市科委和各区县的经费比例是1∶4。在8个涉农区县开展此项工作。示范区落实在津南区，其他7个区县作为附属区，同样得到政府经费支持。各区县的工厂化农业由起步到提升，发展良好。

农科院和蓟县的成果转化合作得到市领导和市科委的大力支持。1996年，市科委给蓟县投入专项经费100万元，副市长曲维枝出席合作签字仪式。为保证工程顺利实施，派出科技副县长。合作转化成果数十项，并对农民进行技术培训。此产业化工程使有优势的科研成果得以实施，还加大了扶贫力度，提升了农民“造血”能力。比较成功的有：黄瓜大棚栽培、食用菌培养技术（数十项）、果树高接换头技术、酒用葡萄栽培等。

20世纪90年代，渤海生态型渔业资源呈大幅下降趋势。天津市在海、淡水渔业资源增值上加大引进、研发力度。严格休渔、禁渔制度，保护渔业资源再生，同时，利用生物育种技术，新型饵料制剂，水处理与循环水技术等高新技术发展海、淡水养殖业。2001年以后，市科委加大了对工厂化养鱼的支持，开展工厂化养殖工程。塘沽、汉沽、大港是海水养殖，西青、北辰是淡水养殖。在海水养殖中，用中草药代替抗生素净化水质，取得良好效果。天津的海水养鱼技术在全国处于先进地位。在和中国科学院海洋研究所的合作中，天津海发海珍品养殖公司承担了国家“863”项目的实验基地。通过实施相关配套技术，达到每立方米水体可产30千克鱼的高水平。

1990~2005年，天津市农业机械化实现了快速发展，农机装备总量、作业水平、作业领域等方面增长幅度较大，全市农业机械总动力由1990年的438.97万千瓦，增加到611.94万千瓦。耕、播、收机械化程度由90%、23%和17%分别达到90.74%、52.56%和23.21%，农机作业领域不断拓宽，由大田向设施农业，由产中向产前产后，由种植业向畜牧业、养殖业和农产品加工业全面发展。

随着农产品的繁荣和增收以及食品安全的需要，对农产品收获后的技术服务成为必需要解决的问题。农科院林果研究所在90年代初开始果茶沙司、全汁发酵果酒等深加工技术的研究，取得良好成果。1996年，在天津市质量技术监督部门的支持下，农科院成立了“天津市农产品农药残留检测站”。1997年，国家科学技术委员会以天津农科院为依托成立“国家农产品保鲜工程技术研究中心（天津）”。该中心研究开发的保鲜技术和产品推广到全国30个省、直辖市、自治区。在保鲜中心的建设中，专家修德仁做出了突出贡献。

2001年，在天津市政府信息化办公室，市科委，市农委的支持下，以农科院信息研究所为依托，开展农业信息技术的研究与应用。2001~2004年，启动农业信息化工程，采用先进可靠的技术和设备，建立农村科技信息综合服务平台，为农业专家系统，远程教育与培训系统提供了网络环境。同时，还建立农村科技信息、农业气象信息等10个特色网站。于2005年建成智能化农业信息处理系统——天津示范区。该系统开发了黄瓜种植，葡萄栽培，生猪、奶牛、对虾、河蟹养殖等6个农业专家决策咨询系统，包括20.4万个数据量的数据库，3210条知识规则的知识库。

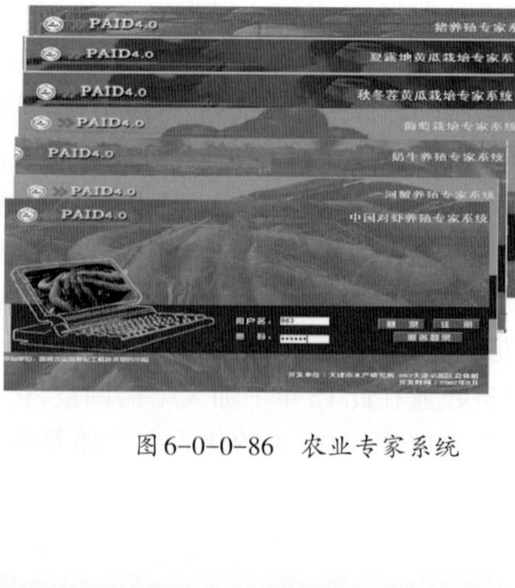

图6-0-0-86 农业专家系统

第一章　种　植

1991～2005年是天津种植业发展较快的时期。在农作物品种选育，耕作栽培方式，植物保护方法，改造土壤和科学施肥等方面都取得一些突破性成果。

天津水稻曾以品质优良闻名全国。1990年以后，农科院利用先进技术培育推广优良水稻品种78个。这些品种抗病丰产，米质优，口感好，不仅在天津地区深受欢迎，还推广到北京、河北、山西、陕西、辽宁、山东等20多个省。从1998年开始，农科院培育出专用强筋小麦系列品种。与此同时，为解决玉米亲本纯度降低，种性退化问题，农科院农作物研究所的科技人员利用杂交育种的方法，采用自交系早代（1～2代）低温条件下筛选、在早代采用高密性增加选择压力、接种病叶营造发病条件、引入热带玉米种质资源、多环境异地鉴定等技术措施，加快品种的区域定位。先后选育成功了2个春玉米、2个夏玉米、1个青贮玉米和4个鲜食玉米新品种。这些玉米新品种耐盐碱、耐瘠薄、适应性强、耐低温能力强。对玉米大小斑病、黑粉病、丝黑穗病、茎基腐病具有较强的抵抗能力，产量高，品质优良，除在天津市大面积种植以外，还推广到东北、新疆、陕西、宁夏等地。

蔬菜育种，在黄瓜、马铃薯、大白菜、花椰菜等品种的培育中继续保持在全国的领先地位。尤其是黄瓜育种，侯锋，吕淑珍带领科研团队主要开展了黄瓜未受精子房培养，黄瓜主要病害抗性基因的分子标记，黄瓜苗期人工接种抗病性鉴定等。在全国首次建立了一套以单倍体技术、分子标记技术、多抗性鉴定技术为核心的黄瓜现代育种技术体系。

1990年以后，天津的蔬菜，瓜果等农作物的栽培方式发生了巨大变化。特别是1995年以后，温室栽培及相关技术的成熟及大力推广，使设施农业得以普及。这种变化逐渐结束了作为北方地区的天津冬季以窖藏蔬菜为主的历史。15年中，棚室结构设计不断优化，设施内部功能不断完善。设施栽培对农作物有特殊要求：耐寒、耐弱光等，农科院蔬菜研究所，黄瓜研究所为满足这一特殊要求研究出系列专用品种。

植物保护，在防治农作物病、虫、草害的过程中，更加突出了环境保护和农产品安全相关技术的研究及成果推广。加强农药残留检测，开展无污染蔬菜基地建设。

在改造盐碱土壤中，天津经济技术开发区园林绿化公司和农科院土壤肥料研究所合作，研究建立了一系列水利、生物、化学等配套技术措施，综合治理盐碱土取得了显著成效，使开发区生态环境大为改观，绿化率，人均绿化面积达到历史最好水平。

施肥，更加注重科学化，研究肥料、作物、土壤的关系。实施定量施肥，肥料配合。开展不同农作物的专用肥料研究与开发，同时，开发有机肥料，生物肥料。

第一节　良种选育

20世纪90年代后，天津市农业科技围绕农业种植结构调整、增加作物产量、提升产品质量，不断拓宽研究领域，采用杂种优势利用、雄性不育、分子标记辅助育种、变性间抗性基因转育、单倍体培养等技术相继研制成功“3优18”“津粳杂2号”“10优18”水稻，“津强系列”小麦，“津春”“津优”系列黄瓜，“津白”“秋绿”系列大白菜,"津品"系列菜花,"蜜龙""碧龙"厚皮甜瓜,"津蜜8号""津蜜20号"西瓜等新品种以及与之配套的栽培技术。这些农作物新品种产量高、品质优、适应性强,除在天津市大面积种植以外,还推广到20多个省、自治区、直辖市。

一、水稻

(一)常规育种

农科院水稻研究所刘瑞符于20世纪80年代育成"津稻1187"。1993年3月12日通过国家农作物品种审定委员会的审定。是年,国家科技部将"津稻1187"确定为国家科技成果重点推广计划项目。到1997年底,"津稻1187"在全国累计种植达53.85万公顷,累计增产稻谷2.6亿千克,成为天津市历史上种植面积最大、为社会创经济效益最高的水稻新品种。水稻品种"津稻1187"推广获1997年度天津市科技进步二等奖。

1986~1992年,农科院水稻研究所王玉玺等用株型紧凑、穗粒数多、千粒重高的"521水稻"做母本,用分蘖力高、抗病性强的"中花8号"水稻做父本进行杂交,经6年5代选育成功"津星1号"。此品种特点是大穗大粒,高产,一般亩产650千克,最高可达760千克。抗倒伏性能好,不早衰,高抗穗颈瘟病。全生育期175天,在京、津、唐等地做一季稻栽培,亦可做麦茬稻栽培。

2000年,农科院水稻研究所牛景用"金珠1号"水稻同一个三系不育系(FH-521A)进行杂交,其杂交后一代再同恢复系"84-11"进行杂交,经8年选育成功"超优1号"。"超优1号"全生育期约145天,对水稻稻瘟病和稻曲病具有较强的抵抗能力。穗大,空秕率低,结实率达91%,以米质优最为突出,米粒蛋青色,有光泽,清香适口。自育成后在天津及国内北方地区大面积推广种植。

同年,农科院水稻研究所刘学军等育成"津稻1007"。该品种用"津稻521"做母本,"武育粳3号"做父本进行杂交,经连续6年选育而成。全生育期约156天,株型紧凑,穗型直立,对水稻稻瘟病有较强的抵抗能力,秆硬抗倒伏,综合抗逆性强。分蘖力中等。灌浆速度快,结实率高,籽粒饱满。米质优良,米饭外观光泽油润,口感黏筋适度,适宜在江苏、安徽北部,山东南部,河南沿黄(河)稻区和陕西关中地区做麦茬稻种植。

1994年后,水稻条纹叶枯病在全国由南向北迅速蔓延,天津水稻该病也呈上升趋势。同时,水稻稻曲病也在中国北方稻区造成较重的病害。1996年开始,牛景等用"C602"水稻做父本,用产自韩国的Hwasung byeo水稻做母本进行杂交,自第二代开始采用花药培养的方法,经7年8代选育,于2002年育成"花育409"。属粳稻中晚熟品种,全生育期170~175天,株高114厘米,穗大粒多,茎秆较强,较抗倒伏,分蘖力较强,对水稻条纹叶枯病和稻曲病具有很强的抵抗能力,耐盐碱。米质优,口感好,食味佳。精米率和整精米率分别为77.6%和77.2%。

(二)杂种优势利用育种技术

1994~1998年,刘学军等用BT型不育系"屉锦A"做母本,"津稻341-2"做父本进行不育系转育,选育出"津稻3412A"不育系,同辽宁省水稻研究所选育的恢复系"C418"配制组合,研制成功"3优18"品种。1998~2000年参加北方稻区品种比较试验和生产试验,3年平均亩产615千克,较对照品种增产9.3%。1999~2000年参加由南京农业大学主持的日本和中国杂交粳稻共同比较试验,在7个参试品种中(日本3个,中国4个),"3优18"水稻亩产达653千克,居参试品种之首。全生育期140~150天,植株生长势强,株高115.3厘米,株型紧凑,茎秆粗壮,穗形较大。对水稻条纹叶枯病、白叶枯病、稻瘟病具有较强的抵抗能力,耐盐碱能力强,抗倒伏,适应范围广。经农业部质量监督检验测试中心检验证实;其糙米率、精米率、粒长、胶稠度、蛋白质含量、支链淀粉含量等9项指标达到国家一级米的标准。2002年被

图6-1-1-87 "3优18"杂交粳稻选育

国家农业部农技推广中心确定为全国唯一的杂交粳稻新品种向全国重点示范推广，2003年被国家科技部确定为“国家科技成果重点推广计划项目”，到2005年年底，已在全国推广种植16.67万公顷。获2005年度天津市科技进步一等奖。

1997～1999年，刘学军等采取“三系法次亚种间杂种优势利用”的方法配制组合成“津粳杂2号”。在连续3年参加天津市组织的区域试验和生产试验中，亩产达657千克，居11个参试品种之首，较对照品种增产19.8%。全生育期165天，株型紧凑，株高约110厘米，结实率达90%，茎秆粗壮，适应性强，对水稻稻瘟病具有较强的抵抗能力，耐盐碱，综合米质好。适宜在京津和冀北、冀东、冀中等地做一季春稻种植，亩产可达700千克，最高可达800千克；亦可在山东、河南做麦茬稻种植，亩产可达650千克。2004年5月被国家科技部确定为“国家科技成果重点推广计划项目”。

2000年，牛景等用遗传差异较大的材料做亲本（母本“341A”，父本“津稻779”），经广泛侧交、筛选育成“津优2003”。全生育期176天，株高115厘米，株型紧凑，根系发达，生长势强，粒椭圆型，茎秆坚硬，抗倒伏能力强，抗稻瘟病，耐盐碱，米质中等。适宜在天津、北京、冀东、冀中等地做一季春稻栽培，亩产可达700～800千克；亦可在河南、山东、江苏北部做麦茬稻栽培，亩产可达700千克。2001年又选育成功“津优29”。该品种用“优—优配组”的技术路线，用“早花2A”做母本，“津稻1129”做父本进行杂交。全生育期160天，株高107厘米，株型紧凑，苗期生长健壮。对水稻稻瘟病、白叶枯病具有较强的抵抗能力，耐盐碱、抗倒伏，稳产性好，米质优。适宜在天津、北京、河北中东部等地做早稻或中稻栽培，亩产可达650～700千克。

2004年，刘学军等用“3412A”（BT型不育系）做母本，用“R148”（“津稻521”×“武育粳2号”）做父本进行杂交育成“10优18”，该品种株高约117.7厘米，全生育期约154天，对水稻稻瘟病、白叶枯病、条纹叶枯病具有较强的抵抗能力，耐旱、耐寒、耐盐碱，产量较高，稳产性较好，米质较优。适宜在天津、北京、河北做春稻种植，也可在江苏北部、山东南部、安徽北部、河南沿黄（河）稻区和陕西关中地区做麦茬稻种植，亩产可达700千克。

二、小麦

强筋小麦 1998年始，农科院农作物研究所将传统的杂交育种和生物技术育种相结合，构建高效育种体系。王继忠等从美国、加拿大和中国黑龙江、甘肃、宁夏、云南等地引进200多份优质春小麦品种资源，进行试种，对其农艺性状、产量和品质进行田间鉴定和室内品质分析，利用图谱分析法筛选出具有优质蛋白亚基的种质资源，择其优良者配制组合，辅助室内测量，通过南繁北育，温室加代等辅助技术，于2001年育成“津强1号”，2004年育成“津强2号”至“津强4号”，2005年育成“津强5号”至“津强6号”小麦。

图6-1-1-88 津强2号强筋小麦

“津强1号”属超强筋类型。株高95厘米左右，全生育期88天，亩产约250千克。“津强2号”株高80～107厘米，全生育期约84天，较抗倒伏，亩产约285千克。“津强3号”早熟，全生育期78～79天，株高78～87厘米，高抗秆锈病，亩产约310千克。“津强4号”全生育期约90天，株高约85厘米，茎秆有弹性，较抗倒伏，高抗小麦条锈病，亩产约340千克。“津强5～6号”株高分别为80厘米和90厘米，抗病性、抗逆性较强。亩产可达370千克，比对照品种亩增产7%～10%。“津强5～6号”的育成解决了天津市和全国小麦生产中长期存在的优质不高产、高产不优质的矛盾。

经农业部谷物品质监督检验测试中心测定，“津强系列”小麦其粗蛋白、湿面筋、沉淀值、吸水率等10多项指标都达到国家一级强筋小麦的标准，极受面粉厂家和食品加工企业的欢迎，用其作原料制做的面包，体积大，孔隙均匀，包心不粘，口感佳。

“津强系列”小麦自2005年起即成为天津市春小麦主栽品种，播种面积占天津市春小麦当年播种面积的90%，在华北地区亦有大面积种植。并给农民和面粉加工企业带来较高的经济效益。农民种植“津强系列”小麦比种植其他品种的小麦亩增收134元。

三、玉米

20世纪90年代初，天津玉米种植的品种不同程度地存在亲本纯度降低、种性退化等现象，生产上难以实现稳定增产。1998年开始，农科院农作物研究所董海合、李凤华等开展高产、抗逆、优质玉米新品种的选育研究。利用杂交育种的方法，采用自交系早代（1至2代）低温条件下筛选、在早代采用高密性增加选择压力、接种病叶营造发病条件、引入热带玉米种质资源、多环境异地鉴定等技术措施，加快品种的区域定位。先后选育出2个春玉米、2个夏玉米、1个青贮玉米和4个鲜食玉米新品种。这些玉米新品种耐盐碱、耐瘠薄、适应性强、耐低温能力强。对玉米大小斑病、黑粉病、丝黑穗病、茎基腐病具有较强的抵抗能力，产量高，品质优良，除在天津市大面积种植以外，还推广到东北、新疆、陕西、宁夏等地。

（一）春玉米

2004年选育成功“津单2号”。该品种用“T7922”玉米自交系做母本，“TJ0618”自交系做父本进行杂交。幼苗拱土能力强，苗期长势整齐一致，株高约300厘米，株型紧凑，生育期约118天，适应性强，品质优良，粗淀粉含量高达74.51%。茎秆含糖量高达12%，在收获粮食以后茎秆还宜做青贮饲料，发展养殖业。适宜在天津及其周边地区种植，亩产可达600千克。2005年又选育成功“津单6号”。该品种用自选系“T1217”做母本，用外引系“598”做父本进行杂交育成。株高269.9厘米，株型半紧凑，生育期约113天。果穗成熟后半下垂，如遇多雨天气，不易烂穗。抗倒伏、抗旱性强，耐瘠薄、耐盐碱，适应性好。籽粒黄色，品质优良，平均亩产602.3千克，适宜在天津及其周边地区春播或夏播种植。

（二）夏玉米

用自选系“JR21”做母本，“Q13”做父本进行杂交，经5年选育于2004年育成“津单8号”。株高约215厘米，株型披散，叶片稀疏，单株叶面积小，通风透光好，适宜密植，生育期约94天。果穗筒型，穗长约20.1厘米，穗轴红色，籽粒黄色，籽粒角质含量高，品质优良，出籽率高达84%，粗淀粉含量为72.9%。适应范围广，丰产性、稳产性好。适宜在天津及华北地区种植，亦可在东北地区中晚熟春玉米区种植，农户在增加玉米产量的同时，茎秆也得到充分利用，推动养殖业发展。使种植玉米的经济效益显著提高。自育成后至2005年已在天津、东北、西北推广种植26.67万公顷。同年还育成.“津单9号”。用外引系“郑58”做母本，用自选系“BWS”做父本进行杂交，株高约274厘米，株型紧凑，单株叶面积小，通风透光好，气生根发达，适宜密植。穗轴白色，籽粒黄色，品质优良，角质含量高，粗淀粉含量高达75%以上。亩产可达740千克，适宜在天津以及华北地区做夏玉米种植，亦可在东北地区中晚熟春玉米区做春玉米种植。自育成后已在天津、吉林等地推广种植3.33万公顷。

（三）青贮玉米

用自选系“340G”做母本，“NDX”做父本进行杂交选育，于2005年育成“津0603”。该品种自出苗至青贮收获期约114天，植株生长势强，株型半紧凑，株高约298厘米，苗期长势整齐一致，对玉米大斑病、小斑病、纹枯病、矮花叶病、丝黑穗病具有较强的抵抗能力。果穗筒型，穗长约23.8厘米，籽粒黄色，近马齿型，秸秆含糖量达11%～15%，籽粒角质含量高，品质优良，出籽率85.9%，适宜做青贮或粮饲兼用。适宜在内蒙古、陕西、宁夏、新疆等地肥水条件较好的地方种植，亩产可达2000千克。自育成后已在天津、内蒙古、宁夏、陕西、新疆、东北地区推广种植1300公顷。

（四）鲜食玉米

2003～2004年，先后选育出“津糯201”“津糯205”“津糯206”等鲜食玉米新品种。此类品种播种期不受时间限制，热量条件允许时，可随时播种。生长期为80多天（82～85天左右），株高226～237厘米。“津糯

图6-1-1-89　彩色糯玉米

201”用“JN1”做母本,“JN2”做父本进行杂交选育。幼苗拱土能力强,易抓苗,苗期长势整齐一致,早发性好,双穗率高。果穗筒形,穗长20.5厘米,大粒,白色糯粒,香糯可口,食用风味佳,青食和保鲜加工均可,品质优良。2005年参加天津市组织的鲜食玉米品种区域试验,平均亩产鲜穗822.8千克,在14个参试品种中列第3位,比对照品种增产12.17%。“津糯205”用自选系“T102M”做母本,自交系“KM946-3”做父本进行杂交。抗病、抗倒伏能力强,适用范围广,品质优。双穗率高达18%。穗粗筒形,种皮薄,粒色紫花,香糯可口,支链淀粉含量达100%,品质1级。青食和保鲜加工均可。平均亩产鲜穗9465千克,比对照品种增产19%。“津糯206”用自选系“JN1”做母本,“J选-2”做父本进行杂交选育。株型半紧凑,穗长筒形,种皮薄,支链淀粉含量达100%,籽粒黄白色,香糯可口,品质1级。适宜在天津及其周边地区种植,亩产可达865千克。鲜食和保鲜加工均可,尤其适合保鲜加工用。

1999～2004年,农科院农作物研究所陈绍慧、杨小玲等承担天津市重点科技攻关项目“超甜型甜玉米新品种开发技术研究”,用由美国引进的超甜玉米品种“NORTHERN×TRASWEET”自交分离6代获得的“7—7—2—3—12”做母本,用“冀承单3号”同从美国引进的超甜玉米“NOVCHEW”杂交后分离选育的自交系“17纯—4—5—2—4”做父本进行杂交,配制组合,选育出“津甜6号”。该品种株型矮、生育期短,适宜密植,株高150厘米,籽粒淡黄色,果实柔嫩,口感甜、嫩、香、脆,鲜食品质佳,货架期长,商品品质好。在京津冀等地种植,每年早春利用地膜覆盖播种,6月初即可采收,亩产1100千克左右。

四、黄瓜

图6-1-1-90　侯锋(右)与吕淑珍

从1976年开始,侯锋、吕淑珍采用杂种一代优势利用的方法选育黄瓜新品种,将不同品种的早熟性、丰产性、抗病性集一体,先后选育成功“津杂1~4号”新品种。其中,“津杂1号”“津杂2号”获1991年度国家科技进步三等奖。在20世纪70、80年代成功研制“津研”“津杂”系列黄瓜品种的基础上,20世纪90年代起,黄瓜研究所侯锋、吕淑珍和哈玉洁、李加旺、杜胜利、李淑菊、马德华等采用常规技术、杂种一代优势利用技术,对国内外黄瓜育种资源及亲本材料进行优势基因的持续聚合,不断拓展科研工作的深度和广度。相继研究成功优质、专用,适于不同栽培方式、不同播种茬口的40多个新品种,并且将选育周期由6~8年缩短为3~4年。

(一)露地栽培

露地栽培的黄瓜品种生育期正值一年最热的季节,故要求其具有较强的耐热性和抗病性。从1987年开始,侯锋、吕淑珍、马德华等采用杂种一代优势利用的技术,用“Jin-90-3”做母本,用“76-2-1-1-6-4”做父本进行杂交,配制组合。1989年～1991年进行区域试验和生产试验,同时,在河北、辽宁、山东、陕西、海南等地进行试种示范及小区比较试验,各地均表现出丰产、抗病、优质等特征。小区试验期间早期产量(亩产)614千克,总产量5583千克,分别比对照品种增加8.40%和47.6%。该品种植株生长势强,抗病性强,在全生育期内可以不施或少施农药。品质优良,商品性状好,育成后即在全国获大面积推广。1994～1995年即在全国推广种植6.67万公顷。1996年,国家科委将“津春4号”黄瓜确定为国家重点科技成果推广计划项目向全国推广。获1995年度天津市科技进步一等奖。“津春系列黄瓜新品种及其推广”1998年获天津市“科技兴市突出贡献奖”。1998年12月获国家科技进步二等奖。

1991年，哈玉洁选育成功腌渍和鲜食兼用的“津春5号”黄瓜。该品种主蔓、侧枝可同时结瓜，瓜条心腔小，肉厚，单瓜重约210克。口感脆嫩，质量符合用于出口的腌渍加工黄瓜的要求，腌渍出菜率高达56.8%（比对照品种高5.2个百分点），是鲜食与出口腌渍加工兼用的优良黄瓜品种，获1996年度天津市科技进步二等奖。

1992～1997年，马德华、吕淑珍、李淑菊等选育出“津绿4号”。该品种耐高温，在夏季36℃～38℃条件下仍能正常生长，主蔓结瓜为主。品质优良，味清香，畸形瓜率低（小于15%）。亩产可达5500千克。获1999年度天津市科技进步一等奖。

1995～1999年，马德华、吕淑珍、霍振荣、李淑菊等育成“津优4号”。该品种适宜在春露地、秋露地栽培，亩产可达5000千克，比对照品种增产8.9%。获2004年度天津市科技进步二等奖。

（二）塑料大棚栽培

利用塑料大棚栽培黄瓜可以改变黄瓜的种植时间，丰富市场供应。1993年，李加旺等选育成功“津春2号”。该品种的育成解决了以往大棚黄瓜种植中长期存在的早熟不抗病，抗病不早熟的难题。早熟性状明显，从播种到采摘仅需65天左右的时间。前期产量比对照品种高约20%。亩产可达5000千克以上。1996～2005年，“津春2号”黄瓜累计在全国推广种植5.33万公顷。获1994年度天津市科技进步二等奖。

1995年，马德华、吕淑珍、李淑菊等研制成功“津优1号”。该品种生育期为60～70天，采收期70～90天。单瓜重约150克，瓜把短，果肉淡绿色，质脆，品质优，商品性状好，亩产达6322千克。选育成功以后迅速获大面积推广，到2005年累计推广16.67万公顷。获1998年度天津市科技进步二等奖。

图6-1-1-91 “津优系列”黄瓜

2000年，哈玉洁等用天津黄瓜“81”做母本，用荷兰黄瓜同中国黄瓜进行杂交后代分离经系统选择而成的“48”做父本进行杂交，配制组合，研制成功“津优10号”。该品种除具有天津黄瓜产量高、抗病性强等特征外，还具有荷兰黄瓜耐低温、瓜条光滑等特点。生长前期耐低温，后期耐高温，亩产在5500千克以上。经菜农使用证实，菜农每种植1亩“津优10号”可比对照品种增加收入700元。获2005年度天津市科技进步二等奖。

（三）日光温室栽培

日光温室栽培的黄瓜，其生长时间正值一年中最寒冷的季节，使用品种须耐低温、耐弱光。1991～1994年，侯锋等选育出一批符合育种目标的自交系和亲本材料，用其配制组合，之后又进行3年品比试验、多点区域试验和生产试验，育成“津春3号”。该品种黄瓜耐低温弱光能力强，在10℃～13℃条件下仍能正常生长，适宜在日光温室做越冬茬种植，亩产达5000千克。1995年被农业部确定为国家科技成果重点推广计划项目，迅速推广到全国15个省、自治区、直辖市，获1997年度天津市科技进步二等奖。

1992年开始，马德华、吕淑珍、李淑菊等将荷兰黄瓜品种同该所黄瓜进行杂交，于1996年育成“津绿3号”。该品种集中荷兰黄瓜耐低温、弱光和中国华北型黄瓜抗病性强的优势，可在冬季12℃～15℃低温条件下正常生长，品质优良。亩产可达6000～8000千克。获1999年度天津市科技进步一等奖。

1987～1996年，李加旺等培育出“津优2号”。该品种是国内第一个利用辐射诱变技术与常规育种相结合育成的。采用钴60γ射线对黄瓜种子进行诱变处理，获得优秀的变异植株，并在其变异后代群体中筛选出综合性状优良的单株，用其做亲本配制成杂种一代黄瓜新品种。该品种早熟性好，从播种到始收65～70天。平均亩产5500千克。1999年被国家科技部确定为农业科技成果重点推广计划项目。获2000年度天津市科技进步二等奖。

1992～1996年，马德华、吕淑珍、霍振荣、李淑菊等育成“津优3号”。该品种早熟性及丰产性好，从播种到采收约65天，采收期80～90天，亩产可达8000千克。1999～2002年累计推广面积达9700公顷，获2002年度天津市科技进步二等奖。

2002～2004年，杜胜利等育成“津优22号”。在育种过程中，取未受精子房进行黄瓜单倍体培养，利用自主研制的黄瓜单倍体技术快速分离纯化获得的具有丰产、抗病、耐低温弱光，质优等特征的高纯度自交系。用其做亲本进行杂交，配制组合。“津优22号”耐低温弱光能力强，成瓜速度快，畸形瓜率低，商品瓜率在90%以上。单瓜重约200克，品质优，亩产可达8000千克。适宜在华北、东北、西北地区日光温室做早春茬栽培，亦可在春大棚中栽培。

五、大白菜

20世纪90年代初，农科院蔬菜研究所丘玉秀等采用杂种一代优势利用的技术选育大白菜新品种，到1996年相继研究出“津绿系列”“津白系列”两个大白菜系列新品种。“津绿系列”（1999年后改称“秋绿系列”）包括“津绿55”和“津绿60”2个早熟品种、“津绿75”和“津绿80”2个中晚熟品种。成熟期分别在55和80天左右，亩产净菜0.4～0.9万千克，从9月下旬起即可陆续成熟上市，丰富秋季蔬菜淡季市场。“津白系列”包括“津白45”“津白56”两个品种。“津白45”生育期45～50天。“津绿”“津白”系列大白菜新品种获1998年度天津市科技进步一等奖。“‘秋绿’‘津白’系列大白菜新品种推广”获2001年度天津市科技进步一等奖。

1995年开始，农科院蔬菜研究所张斌、闻凤英等开展“天津青麻叶大白菜育种技术体系构建及专用型新品种选育”研究，在国内率先开展青麻叶大白菜游离小孢子培养技术与雄性不育系转育技术研究，培育出育种材料，用其配制杂交组合选育大白菜新品种，并运用远缘杂交技术转育耐抽薹基因，突破耐热基因转育等关键技术难点。将常规育种方法育种周期8～10年缩短为2～4年，相继选育成功“春绿1号”“津夏3号”“津秋65”“津秋1号”“津秋2号”“津秋606”“津秋707”“津秋78”等8个具有不同特点，分别适于春夏秋栽培的新品种。这些新品种对大白菜三大病害（霜霉病、软腐病、病毒病）具有较强的抵抗能力，适用范围广，口感甜脆，商品品质好，产量高，一经推出即受到菜农和消费者的欢迎，实现大白菜四季生产和供应。

“春绿1号”为春播品种，耐抽薹性强，在平均气温13℃条件下仍能正常结球。“津夏3号”为夏播早熟品种，耐热、耐湿性强，在35℃高温下能正常结球。“津秋65”“津秋606”为秋播早熟品种，生育期为65天左右。“津秋707”为秋播中熟品种，对大白菜干烧心病具有较强的抵抗能力，生育期约70天，单株重3～3.5千克，亩产可达8000千克。这三个品种具有青麻叶和白麻叶大白菜的杂交特性。“津秋78”生育期75～80天，单株重约4～4.5千克，亩产可达1万千克。2000年～2005年，“津秋78”和“津秋1号”每年在天津市的播种面积超过4000公顷，占天津市秋播大白菜总面积的80%以上。以上新品种选育成功后，除在天津市成为主栽品种以外，还迅速推广到北京、河北、山西等20多个省、自治区、直辖市。

六、马铃薯

20世纪90年代，全国马铃薯种植采用的是块茎无性繁殖技术，种薯繁殖多在高纬度、高海拔的北方或山区进行。南方或低海拔地区需从北方调运种薯。在这种生产方式中，造成种薯退化和病毒感染，严重影响和制约了中国马铃薯生产的发展，也使马铃薯生产的质量和单产在世界处于较低水平。20世纪80年代开始，农科院蔬菜研究所王炳君开展马铃薯种薯生产和栽培技术的研究。20世纪90年代初，发明了用生物技术与无土栽培相结合的马铃薯脱毒微型种薯快繁技术。该技术对种薯生长所需的光、温、水、气、肥等条件进行人工调节，实现了工厂化、规模化生产。每40~60天即可生产一茬优质脱毒微型种薯。在天津市的自然条件下，除七、八两个月受高温限制外，其余10个月都能生产。该种薯每粒重约1~10克，如同一粒蚕豆大小，在每平方米的苗床内可以生产900粒。经田间扩繁后，即可提供大量优质种薯。用此种薯扩繁时，每亩用种量7.5千克，相当于原来用种量的6%，大大减少了储存调运量。由于进行了脱毒处理，增强了种薯的抗病性能，使马铃薯亩增产

图6-1-1-92 王炳君

50%以上。采用此项技术生产的种薯比当时国内外采用的繁殖方法提高繁殖系数70倍以上。1994年,美国威斯康辛州邀请王炳君等人赴美开展学术交流。经对比示范证实,王炳君发明的快繁技术比当时世界上马铃薯研究较为先进的美国的快繁技术提高效率1.43倍。国家科委、国家农业部分别于1991、1993年,将此技术确定为"国家科技成果重点推广计划项目"向全国推广。到2005年,该项科研成果已经推广到黑龙江、吉林、辽宁、河北、山西、内蒙古、陕西、云南、贵州、广西、浙江等23个省、自治区、直辖市。覆盖面积达200万亩,每年为农民增收4亿元。

七、花椰菜

1991~1996年,农科院蔬菜研究所孙德岭等对搜集到的800多份菜花品种资源进行分离、纯化和筛选,采用生物技术进行花粉花药培养,加速育种品种资源的纯化,在分离纯化及抗病性鉴定的基础上,逐代筛选出自交不亲和株系,并根据育种目标选择经济性状优良的株系做亲本配制组合,选育出"夏雪40""夏雪50"等杂种一代菜花新品种。

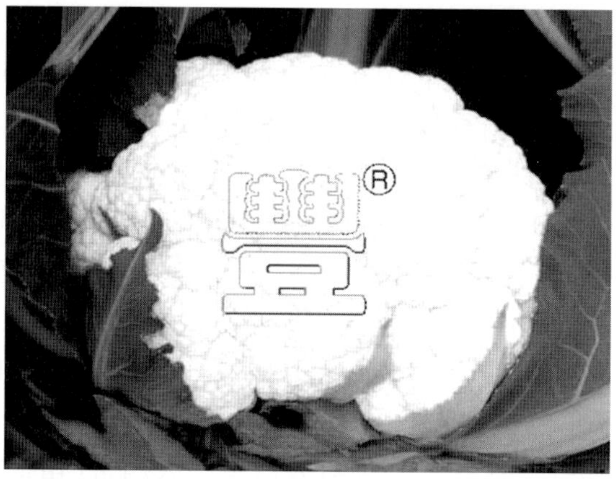

图6-1-1-93 花椰菜"丰花"

1997~2002年,创建和完善菜花游离小孢子培养技术新体系。探索总结出花椰菜游离小孢子培养过程中,花蕾大小、基因型、培养基的组织成分、培养条件等因素对花椰菜、青花菜小孢子胚胎发生的影响,使菜花小孢子出胚率大幅提高(达53%以上),解决了菜花游离小孢子培养中胚胎死亡的技术难题,并获得大量花椰菜的胚胎和再生株,成功地将其应用于菜花新品种选育中。与此同时,还建立和完善雄性不育育种技术体系,经过6代转育,选育出几百个早、中、晚熟期配套的菜花不育系和保持系,丰富育种资源,加快选育速度。到2005年,相继选育出"津雪88""云山1号""丰花60""津品50"等20多个菜花新品种以及与之相配套的栽培管理技术。除在全国20多个省、自治区、直辖市大面积种植外,还出口到日本、韩国、泰国、柬埔寨、菲律宾等十余个国家和地区。"津品50"是国内第一个春季保护地栽培的杂种一代菜花专用品种,成熟期约50天,耐低温、耐高湿、耐弱光,抗病性强,株型紧凑,花球紧实,洁白,单球重0.73~0.82千克,综合性状优良,亩产可达1800~2100千克。"夏雪40"属秋季早熟品种,1996年育成,8月下旬至9月上旬即可成熟上市,该品种耐热、抗病、商品性状好。同年育成的"夏雪50"成熟期约55天。单球重约0.5千克,花球紧实,洁白,亩产可达1850~2280千克。这两个品种一起获1998年度天津市科技进步二等奖。"津雪88"为秋中熟品种,1996年育成,对黑腐病、病毒病具有较强的抵抗能力,花球雪白,高半圆形,极紧实,细嫩。秋季栽培时成熟期约70天,花球单球重1.2~1.7千克,亩产可达3900千克。"津雪88"获1999年度天津市科技进步二等奖,2003年度天津市科技进步奖推广应用一等奖。"丰花60"1998年育成,植株生长势强,抗病性能强,适应性强,成熟期约60天。适宜在天津、北京以及黄河、淮河等平原地区麦收以后种植,冬小麦播种前收获。经济效益较高,农民称之为"麦茬菜花"。自育成后已在农业生产中推广种植2万公顷。获2004年度天津市科技进步二等奖。"津品88"于2003年10月育成,属秋中晚熟品种。成熟期80~85天,对黑腐病、病毒病、霜霉病具有较强的抵抗能力,同时具有较强的耐湿能力。花球呈半球形,花球紧实,球面光滑,雪白,单球重1.1~1.5千克,亩产在3000~5000千克。

八、芹菜

1989~1999年,农科院蔬菜研究所王武台等搜集品种资源,对引进的84个国内外芹菜品种进行试种观察和性状比较,在具有不同优良性状的株系之间进行人工杂交,在国内率先选育出西芹新品种"四季西芹",

一年中可多季栽培。2003年选育成功“赛瑞”“赛星”“赛雪”“赛晶”4个西芹新品种。这些品种实心，粗纤维含量少，维生素含量高，口感脆嫩，商品品质好，不易抽苔，抗病，丰产。“四季西芹”亩产6000～8000千克，食用叶柄48厘米。至2005年，在全国推广种植13.33万公顷。早熟品种“赛瑞”株高达80厘米。中晚熟品种“赛星”单株重1～2千克。“赛雪”叶柄为白色，“赛晶”叶柄为黄绿色。除“赛星”适于保护地种植外，其他都是露地和保护地兼用品种。

九、青椒

2001年开始，农科院蔬菜研究所开展“春保护地甜椒新品种选育及栽培技术的研究”。刘文明等引进、筛选耐低温甜椒和欧洲大果型厚皮甜椒资源，利用远缘杂交技术，通过转育的抗病、耐低温育种材料与高产、耐热育种材料的有性杂交，将抗病、耐寒及高产基因融于一体，于2003年选育出“津椒4号”“津椒5号”甜椒新品种，并总结出适宜天津和中国北方地区甜椒保护地及越夏连秋栽培配套的栽培技术要点及管理方法。

“津椒4号”植株整齐，抗逆性强，植株生长前期耐低温弱光，后期耐高温能力强，在8℃～15℃低温和35℃～38℃高温条件下仍能正常生长。对青椒疫病和病毒病具有较强的抵抗能力。成熟早，连续坐果性好，产量高。果实长方形，外观好，商品性状优良，平均单果重113.7克，最大单果重242.6克，维生素含量高，口感甜脆，适合天津市以及中国北方地区城乡居民的消费习惯。适宜在中国北方春保护地、越夏连秋栽培和南方春、秋露地栽培。在温室和大棚中种植，亩产可达4000千克，越夏连秋栽培，亩产可达5000～5500千克，为天津市青椒的主栽品种，同时还推广到北京、河北、山西、内蒙古等全国10多个省、自治区、直辖市。“津椒5号”抗病、耐热、耐盐碱，果实长方形，果皮薄，表面稍有棱，平均单果重118.4克，最大单果重236克，果味甜，口感脆嫩，坐果率高，前期产量高，适宜早期小棚后期露地种植，亩产可达3500千克以上。

十、菜豆

20世纪80年代中，天津菜豆种植中锈病越来越严重，锈病流行年减产达70%，成为制约菜豆生产的主要障碍。农科院蔬菜研究所岳彬从1990年开始，选择具有抗锈病基因的菜豆品种“12号玉豆”作为抗原亲本，同早熟、优质、丰产的菜豆品种进行杂交，经多次单株选择与混合选择于1996年选育出具有抗锈病特点的系列菜豆新品种“双丰1～3号”菜豆。

“双丰1号、2号”菜豆为早熟品种，适宜春秋两季种植。春季种植时，4月5日播种，55～60天后即可采摘，采摘期30～40天，亩产在2000千克以上。秋季种植时，7月20～30日播种，50～55天即可采摘，亩产可达1500千克。“双丰1号”种子白色，果荚淡绿色，长17～18厘米。“双丰2号”种子棕色，豆荚深绿色，长20厘米。“双丰3号”菜豆为晚熟品种，种子白色，豆荚浅绿色，长20厘米以上，主要用于秋季种植，每年7月15～30日播种，50～55天即可采摘，亩产可达2300～2500千克。“双丰系列”菜豆抗锈病、产量高，适宜双季栽培等特点，深受菜农和消费者的好评。自育成后，除在天津大面积种植以外，还推广到辽宁、山东、广东、广西等地。获1997年度天津市科技进步二等奖。

十一、茄子

2000年以前，天津种植的茄子多为农家品种，在抗病性、产量和商品品质等方面显现的问题日渐增多，育种技术相对滞后。2001年开始，农科院蔬菜研究所井立军、王利英等开展“茄子耐低温材料筛选与新品种选育的研究”，采用杂种一代优势利用技术选育茄子新品种，他们将搜集到的优质茄子品种资源进行耐低温室内鉴定，首次提出以发芽率作为茄子耐低温鉴定指标，并筛选出12个耐低温茄子材料，用其作亲本配制杂交组合，到2005年选育成功了“圆丰1号”“青丰1号”“龙丰1号”3个不同类型的、形态各异的耐低温的茄子新品种。也是天津首次采用杂交一代优势利用技术选育成功的茄子新品种。

“圆丰1号”为紫圆茄。植株生长势强，株型直立，对茄子黄萎病和根腐病具有较强的抵抗能力，耐低温。果实圆球形稍扁，紫色发亮有光泽，果脐小，单果重0.45～0.55千克，果肉洁白，质地细嫩，商品品质好。适宜在天津和华北地区早春保护地和露地栽培，亩产可达5000千克。自育成后，除在天津大面积种植以外，还推广到河北、山东、安徽等地，种植面积达2700公顷。“青丰1号”为绿圆茄，较抗黄萎病、根腐病、绵疫病，早熟。果实浅绿色，卵圆形，光泽明亮，肉质细嫩，单果重0.45～0.55千克，适宜在华北、东北、西北早春塑料大棚、日光温室和春露地栽培，亩产可达6000～7000千克。“龙丰1号”为紫长茄，具有较强的耐低温能力，果实顺直长棒形，顶端钝圆，表皮紫黑色，光泽明亮，单果重0.19～0.22千克，果肉细嫩，商品性状好。适宜在中国东北地区种植，亩产在5000千克以上。

十二、不结球白菜

天津地区种植的不结球白菜（油菜）品种最初都来源于南方，品种混杂、退化现象较为严重。1992年开始，农科院蔬菜研究所张斌等选取出16个类型，30个单株材料进行观察、筛选、纯化，选择出两个遗传特性稳定、纯度高、耐寒性强的自交系材料，用其做亲本配制组合，经过5年选育，到1997年选育成功适宜北方冬春保护地及春露地种植的耐寒性强的杂种一代油菜新品种“寒绿”“冬冠”。这两个新品种产量高、质量好，特别是解决了中国北方地区油菜保护地栽培中存在的先期抽薹的难题。

“寒绿”植株矮壮，叶片油亮深绿，有光泽，叶柄浅绿，叶片数约12片，株型大小适中，单株重约80克，耐寒性强，耐抽薹性强，商品性状好，食用品质佳，亩产可达2600～2800千克。成果累计覆盖面积超过1.53万公顷，获2005年度天津市科技进步二等奖。“冬冠”为束腰型品种，棵型大小适中，叶片深绿亮泽，叶柄鲜绿宽厚，耐寒性强，单株重约120克。在春大棚中种植，定植后约50天即可收获，亩产可达3000～3500千克。到2005年，成果覆盖面积超过2000公顷。以上两个品种自选育成功以后已推广到全国20多个省、自治区、直辖市。

图6-1-1-94 厚皮甜瓜“瑞龙”

十三、厚皮甜瓜

为满足天津果品市场和居民消费的需要，结束厚皮甜瓜种子从国外引进的历史，农科院蔬菜研究所李秀秀、刘莉等从1989年开始，采用变种间抗性基因转育、三交种育种、分子标记辅助育种等技术，到2005年相继选育出“圆首”“瑞龙”“丰雷”“甜9号”“白圆首”“津甜98”“金蜜龙”“瑞龙2号”“蜜龙”“碧龙”等10个厚皮甜瓜新品种。这些品种外观好看，有绿色、黄色、白色，条纹斑点清晰，形态各异。分别适宜于节能型日光温室、塑料大棚、塑料小拱棚栽培，可满足不同地区，不同气候条件下的种植需要，且早、中、晚熟配套，拉开成熟、上市的日期，满足市场需求并给果农带来较高的经济效益。这些新品种抗病性强，产量高，品质优，含糖量高（最高可达17%），口感好，商品性状好，一经育成即显示出广阔的市场前景和竞争优势，受到果农和消费者的欢迎。

瓜的外观可分为光皮和网纹类两种。光皮瓜亩产可在2000～3500千克左右，果肉厚度3.5～4.5厘米，单果重在0.7～2千克，其中，“白圆首”最大单果重2.3千克。网纹类瓜亩产3000～3500千克，“金蜜龙”“蜜龙”亩产可达4000千克。

天津厚皮甜瓜新品种除供应国内市场外，还远销新加坡、俄罗斯等地。

十四、西瓜

天津市种植西瓜历史久远，但普遍存在着优质与裂果连锁，中晚熟品种结籽多、食用不便，适收期短等问题。农科院蔬菜研究所焦定量等以西瓜优质、高产、抗病、耐贮运和少籽、无籽为育种目标，从20世纪90年代开始，开展染色体易位遗传规律及对西瓜结籽性等主要农艺性状的影响、强雌性遗传规律和相关性状分子标记、强雌基因与少籽性状整合以及健康种子生产技术等方面的研究，开拓西瓜育种研究的新领域，在国内率先创建少籽西瓜育种技术体系。到2005年，先后育成“津花4号”（中国第一个少籽西瓜新品种）和“津蜜8号”（中国第一个染色体易位无籽西瓜新品种）等6个优良新品种。这些西瓜新品种食用方便，品质优良，耐贮运，栽培效益显著，并解决了西瓜种植中突出存在的早熟品种优质与裂果之间的矛盾。这些西瓜新品种自育成后，已推广到山东、河南、湖北、陕西等20多个省、自治区、直辖市，分别占同类品种栽培面积的50%。2003～2005年累计推广种植3.33万公顷。

少籽西瓜“津花4号”全生育期90天，单瓜结籽仅有50粒，比普通西瓜减少75%。适宜在小拱棚和露地地膜覆盖栽培，亩产在3500千克以上。“津蜜8号”“津蜜20号”为无籽西瓜品种，抗枯萎病，生育期在105～110天，亩产4000千克，口味好，含糖量12%。“津花魁”“早丰”为适收期长的品种，比一般西瓜可延长10～15天，商品性状好。“津花魁”为中熟品种，适宜在全国各地露地和小拱棚种植，亩产在4000千克以上。“早丰”为中早熟品种，适宜在小拱棚种植，亩产在4500千克以上。“黑橄榄”是一种外形为橄榄状的西瓜新品种。极早熟，全生育期85天。果皮深绿，底隐网纹暗条带，单瓜重3～4千克，红瓤，少籽，单瓜瓜籽数仅为48粒，肉质脆嫩，口感好，中心糖含量达13%以上，货架期长，皮硬，耐贮运。适宜在全国各地露地地膜覆盖和保护地种植，亩产可达2700千克。

十五、食用菌

食用菌在中国东南沿海地区栽培较早，天津因受干燥寒冷的气候条件的制约，且缺少适合天津市栽培的菌种，生产起步较晚，不能满足城乡居民的需求。为改变这一状况，农科院林果研究所王永庄、张志军等经数年研究于1997年相继选育成功“PL72”“津平90”“CR33”等9个优良品种。之后，又选育出杏鲍菇、白灵菇等优质食用菌新品种。这些品种抗逆性强，适应性强，菌丝生长旺盛，朵形好，不易破碎，耐贮运，产量高，商品性状好。经济效益每亩温室的纯收入在1.5万元以上，深受郊县农民和城乡消费者的欢迎。同时，在高效灵芝菌种选育、灵芝多糖高效制备的研究等方面也取得新成绩。建成三级菌种繁育实验室，建有标准化食用菌菌种繁育和栽培示范基地。成为天津市最大的食用菌菌种生产基地和贮存繁育中心，每年为天津市郊县以及天津周边地区的唐山、沧州、衡水、廊坊等地农民提供大批优良菌种，为调整农业种植结构，发展农业经济做出了贡献。每年出口到日本、韩国、美国等国家的菌棒量达300吨。

“津平90”菌株生物学效率高，对光温适应性强，菌丝生长旺盛，生产周期长，产量高，口感鲜美，深受津郊农民和消费者的欢迎。“杏鲍菇PE1”子实体呈保龄球状，菌盖灰棕色，菌柄雪白色，质地脆嫩，味道鲜美，科技人员还利用杏鲍菇菌种“PE1”培育出国内最高纪录（单个子实体重达2.8千克）的杏鲍菇单个子实体。“白灵菇-1”子实体呈手掌状，整个菇体雪白，肉质肥嫩，口感脆滑。高效灵芝菌种株**CT9**综合性状优良，芝形好，红褐色，饱满，菌盖直径8～14厘米，厚0.6～0.9厘米。经天津市质检部门测定，G9灵芝孢子粉多糖含量达13.7%，子实体生物学转化率达10.5%。

第二节 耕作栽培

20世纪90年代始，天津农业的栽培方式和生产技术发生了突破性的变化，以设施农业的发展最为典型。特别是1995年以后，引进第二代节能日光温室及栽培技术并大力推广，使节能型日光温室的结构性能由不尽合理到全面优化,内部可装备各种环境调节装置,有采暖、通风、灌溉、二氧化碳施肥、补充照明等装置,温室性能和栽培技术得到进一步完善。使喜温果菜类收获期提前到春节前后,温室平均亩效益大幅提高。生产作物种类由蔬菜逐渐扩大到食用菌、花卉、果树等园艺类,形成一年四季多茬次、多品种、多覆盖形式相互结合的保护地生产格局。2005年全市拥有设施农业面积2847.3万平方米。

在大面积耕作中也采取了许多新技术新方法,例如:水稻稀植栽培,利用分子标记技术优化葡萄品种纯度等。同时,引进试种成功一批粮食、水果、鲜花等新品种。

一、设施农业

(一)蔬菜设施栽培

1988年,由天津市蔬菜技术推广站孙祥、赵淑明等人组织实施的"塑料棚室蔬菜生产配套技术研究与推广"市级推广项目,主要技术有:选用抗病新品种,多层覆盖,快速育苗,暗管排碱等。使棚室蔬菜生产形成明显的规范化种植格局,带动全市棚室蔬菜生产大发展。1991年,该项目获天津市科技进步奖二等奖。

1992年,天津市蔬菜技术推广站王思恩、薛玉荣等人承担的丰收计划"保护地蔬菜增产技术"项目。在上一项目的基础上增加间种套作,优化种植茬口和棚型结构等技术。较大规模综合推广各类设施蔬菜的生产技术,使保护地蔬菜生产技术水平进一步得到提升。

1992年,天津市蔬菜技术推广站孙书蕴主持的"塑料遮阳网覆盖蔬菜技术效应研究与推广"项目,瞄准夏秋季节蔬菜淡季生产难题,在研究遮阳网技术效应的基础上,大力推广配套技术,为天津及周边地区夏秋蔬菜淡季生产开辟了一条有效途径。

1997年,天津市蔬菜技术推广站关铁炼等在市级推广项目"十万亩蔬菜综合配套技术推广"中,重点以推广蔬菜新品种、大棚多层覆盖提早定植技术、加茬套种技术、遮阳网覆盖栽培技术、配方施肥技术和病虫害综合防治技术等,并将单项技术综合配套进行推广,有效地提高蔬菜综合生产能力,经济效益显著。1997年该项目获天津市科技进步奖二等奖。

1999年,天津市蔬菜技术推广站孙书蕴等在农业部丰收计划项目"远郊县万亩新建温室快速增产技术推广"中,重点把更新改造日光温室结构、推广二代节能温室技术作为重要推广内容。二代温室在采光屋面、墙体结构的设计及材料的应用上都有较大改革。其采光和蓄热保温性能高于一代温室。严冬季节,室内外温差可达30度 以上。

图6-1-2-95 第一代温室实图

图6-1-2-96 第二代温室实图

2000~2001年,天津市蔬菜技术推广站刘振华主持的"保护地蔬菜综合生产技术"和2001~2002年程子林主持的"设施蔬菜节本增效技术"项目,推广了温室间作套种和立体栽培技术,以节水、节肥、节药、节种为核心的节成本增效技术,以及适于日光温室蔬菜生产的机械设备,提高了设施生产的装备水平。

(二)果树设施栽培

2001~2005年,天津农学院王小琼等进行梨、枣、桃、葡萄树种的保护地高效促成栽培,整合多项栽培技术、应用设施栽培示范,总结了具体栽培技术要点,探索出4种果树设施栽培技术模式。选用的新型复合材料组装式环保节能型温室、大棚作为果树栽培设施,成本是钢骨架温室的50%,保温性能提高23度,与露地栽培相比,梨、枣、葡萄提前一个月左右成熟,桃延迟半个月采收,经济效益提高50%左右。项目实施期间示范面积1公顷，推广面积8公顷，节约成本6万元，新增收益200.8万元。

从1995年开始，农科院林果研究所和武清县林业局共同开展了“设施葡萄栽培示范工程”。高献亭等经过3年多实践，发展设施葡萄栽培面积24公顷，亩增经济效益1.5万元，品种优良率达100%，优质果达到95%。为解决设施葡萄栽培中葡萄旺长不结果和不能连续结果的难题，高献亭等探索不同品种葡萄冬季休眠时间，总结出夏季超短梢修剪技术。他们还采用石灰氮处理葡萄冬芽的新技术，使葡萄萌芽时间提前20～25天，从而使葡萄上市时间提前20～25天。同时，还研究出采用单株有主干水平主蔓V形整枝栽培模式，充分利用温室内有限的土地和空间，实现设施葡萄的丰产、优质栽培。到2000年，该技术已在市内一些区县推广267公顷，亩产达1500千克。

二、粮田

（一）稻田

1990～1993年，天津市农业技术推广站张金刚、刘俭等研究推广水稻旱育稀植栽培技术。该技术包括：以集床土调酸、立枯病防治、秧苗化控为一体的水稻旱育秧技术；以稀植少本、依靠分蘖成穗、个体与群体协调发育的水稻种植技术；以前促蘖、中控苗、后攻粒的水稻肥水管理技术。三年累计推广旱育秧面积264公顷，推广稀植面积2.94万公顷，平均亩增产稻谷40.5千克。

2000～2005年，天津市农业技术推广站王景怀针对天津市土壤缺硒的现状，开展富硒农产品生产技术研究并进行富硒水稻生产技术示范。该项技术以优质水稻品种“津原45”为载体，灌浆初期喷施富硒植物营养调节剂，通过水稻植株的生物转化和积累，将稻米的含硒量大幅度提高并稳定于每千克0.2～0.3毫克的范围，为缺硒地区群众补充硒摄入量提供了新的途径，同时也为提高种植业经济效益和农业产业化发展提供了新的途径。富硒植物营养调节剂获得中国发明专利，专利号：ZL01144575.0。

（二）旱田

1.玉米

1995～1997年，天津市农业技术推广站张义林、隋华等引进中国农业大学选育的高油115进行高油玉米开发示范。高油玉米种籽含油率比普通玉米高80%～100%，蛋白质、赖氨酸、维生素、热值等都高于普通玉米。示范从引种、种植示范延伸到玉米加工及畜牧养殖，为天津市玉米生产综合开发进行探索和示范。

2.大豆

2003～2005年，天津市农业技术推广站王瑞卿、郑爱军等引进“科新三号”“科丰14”等高蛋白大豆品种在全市推广，实现了大豆生产的品种更换。研制推广以大豆化学调控、保优防倒、平衡施肥为主要内容的高蛋白大豆保优节本标准化栽培技术，制定出《高蛋白大豆栽培技术规范》天津市地方标准，使大豆产量和品质协同提高。由于高蛋白大豆蛋白含量明显高于普通大豆，在豆制品加工中豆腐产量提高10%，同时提高了豆腐的持水性。

3.红小豆

中国是世界上最大的红小豆生产和出口国，天津红小豆在国内外久享盛誉。长期以来由于生产技术落后，亩产只有50千克左右，且品种混杂、退化、质量下降，为恢复和加强天津红小豆在国内外市场上的竞争能力，天津农学院牟善积等人开展天津红小豆的综合研究：选优提纯天津红小豆良种P85-6，该品种具有较好的典型性、丰产性、适应性，春夏播皆宜，亩产100～150千克，适合在天津及全国各主要红小豆产区种植；制定栽培技术规范，该规范是P85—6品种的配套高产农艺措施；研究提出“天津红小豆选优提纯品种P85—6标准”，该标准是国内提出的第一个红小豆的全面标准；对有关红小豆的基础理论进行了较深入的研究与探讨，撰写出国内第一部红小豆专著《红小豆栽培》，1992年由天津科学技术出版社出版。该成果已在天津、北京、河北等地推广。通过在周边地区推广应用提升了天津红小豆在国内外市场上的竞争能力。

三、果园

1.葡萄

为全面提高茶淀玫瑰香葡萄的品质，突出地方品牌特色优势，农科院林果研究所田淑芬与中国农业大学、汉沽区林业局合作，于2000～2004年开展"利用分子标记技术提高茶淀玫瑰香葡萄优系纯度及标准化栽培技术"的研究。田淑芬等采用国际上较为先进的分子生物标记技术，快速、准确地对玫瑰香葡萄的主要性状、特异性状进行筛选，从理论上说明玫瑰香葡萄遗传背景的共同性和多样性，从分子水平揭示玫瑰香葡萄种性分离的原因，确定玫瑰香葡萄优系的标准基因型，为提高玫瑰香葡萄种性纯度，提高果品质量奠定了基础。同期，田淑芬等通过反复试验，成功研制出调控茶淀玫瑰香葡萄无核、增大果粒、拉长等系列调节剂配方，无核率达100%；开发出茶淀玫瑰香葡萄无核化的调控机制及配套栽培技术，从而使茶淀玫瑰香葡萄特有的穗形整齐、小粒率低、早熟、风味浓郁等优良性状进一步彰显，以品种纯正、品质超群、标准化栽培、规模化生产等特点成为国内的葡萄精品，参与国际竞争。到2005年，该项技术推广面积已超过667公顷，使当地果农增收近亿元。

2.枣

1997～2005年，农学院高梅秀等进行枣优新品种引进、优选及配套栽培技术研究，引入21个枣优新品种在天津市东丽区盐碱地栽培，对各品种树体生长情况、果实产量、果实性状及果实品质进行详细的调查研究，筛选出适宜天津地区栽培的圆丰枣和山东梨枣2个优良鲜食品种，金丝3号、金丝4号和赞皇大枣3个兼用品种。针对所选品种的生物学性状提出了切实可行的栽培技术方案。

3.珠美海棠

1984～1991年，天津农学院赵惠祥等人开展珠美海棠组织培养开发研究，研究适合珠美海棠快速繁殖的培养基和生根培养基配发，使试管苗繁殖率达到8.8，移栽成活率达90%以上，并可周年生产；通过生物学特性研究发现组织培养条件下珠美海棠可耐6‰（0～10厘米）的高含盐量土壤，既可作耐盐碱的绿化优良树种，也可作苹果无毒矮化的砧木；试管苗气孔全开张，根系无根毛，为试管苗移栽提供理论依据。摸索出一套苗木产业化生产程序及在盐碱干旱土壤栽培技术，编入《实用植物组织培养教程》。自1991～1998年该成果在天津、山东等地推广累计创利税2865.80万元。1997～2001年，开展了珠美海棠果实综合利用研究，并于2001年首次加工成果脯、果酱、果汁，生产工艺成熟，产品质量稳定，居国内首创。

第三节 土壤肥料

天津地处九河下梢，东临渤海，土壤盐碱，质地黏重，为农业生产和城市绿化带来很大困难。20世纪90年代，天津农林系统开展土壤调查，并采取暗管排盐、秸秆还田等新技术改造土壤；利用计算机技术实施配方施肥；在保护地蔬菜生产中大面积推广滴灌施肥技术；研制不同农作物的专用肥料等。在上述领域的科学研究和成果推广中取得了新成绩，部分成果推广到全国20多个省、自治区、直辖市。

一、土壤

（一）土壤调查

1.定位监测

天津市土壤肥料工作站（以下简称土肥站）对天津市耕地土壤的养分、生产条件、种植作物、施肥状况进行长期定位监测。监测数据显示，天津市耕地土壤养分含量在不断提高。部分年份的检测数据如下：

1996～1999年、2001～2005年的监测数据(土壤耕层20厘米)统计表

表6-1-3-50

监测年份	有机质(克/千克)	全氮(克/千克)	有效磷(毫克/千克)	速效钾(毫克/千克)
1996	15.0	1.09	38.6	256
1997	16.9	1.19	40.4	255
1998	16.4	1.17	28.4	239
1999	18.8	1.04	13.9	234
2001	18.7	0.92	24.5	225
2002	22.3	1.02	30.4	272
2003	20.0	0.95	47.3	258
2004	23.0	1.09	51.7	318
2005	21.9	1.32	42.5	275

2.地力调查

按照国土资源部和农业部《〈全国基本农田检查工作方案〉的通知》要求,土肥站于2004～2005年对天津市基本农田地力进行调查。地力调查执行农业部制定的《全国耕地地力调查与质量评价技术规程》,全市共取土样3050个,化验pH值、有机质、全氮、有效磷、速效钾等16个项目。利用调查结果建立了天津市耕地资源调查管理数据库。

调查结果显示:土壤酸碱度范围在5.6～9.5之间,平均为8.2,有机质含量16.783克/千克,全氮含量1.095克/千克,有效磷含量30.0毫克/千克,速效钾含量225毫克/千克;微量元素,有效硼为0.29毫克/千克,有效铁为10.9毫克/千克,有效铜为2.53毫克/千克,有效锌为3.68毫克/千克,有效锰为9.7毫克/千克。土壤全盐为1.3克/千克。

(二)土壤改良

1.滨海地区土壤盐碱化防治

天津经济技术开发区所在地原是塘沽盐场三分场,土壤盐分以氯化钠为主。经测定,0～20厘米土层的含盐量为13.9克/千克,地下水矿化度75.4克/升,成为开发区城市绿化和生态环境建设的主要障碍。1994～1996年,天津经济技术开发区总公司园林绿化公司和农科院土壤肥料研究所(以下简称土肥所)合作开展"以开发区为例滨海地区土壤盐碱化及其防治的研究"。科技人员对该区土壤盐渍化现状及其形成原因、滨海盐土和地下水盐分积累过程、化学性质、盐分组成进行系统的研究,首次提出"开发区灌溉频繁的绿地已出现脱盐碱化土壤"的论点。在此基础上,提出治理土壤盐渍化的技术措施:采用客土垫地,抬高地面,降低地下水位;暗管排水排盐,加速土体脱盐;平整土地,深耕深翻,防盐抑盐;大水冲洗,灌溉压盐;增施有机肥料,培肥熟化土壤;化学改良,消除土壤碱(钠)危害;利用粉煤灰等废弃物复垦造林。课题组用磷石膏加有机物和氮素化肥为原料,研制出具有含钙物质和酸性物质两类化学改良剂的优点,并添加有机物质和氮磷钾化肥的碱化土壤改良剂。经过在绿地应用证实,对降低土壤pH值、消除土壤碱(钠)危害、使土壤土质疏松、透水性提高、抑制土壤次生碱化具有良好的效果。1996年开发区绿地养管使用土壤改良剂200多吨,治理面积100多公顷。

2.碱化土壤防治

1995～1997年,土肥所开展"天津地区碱化土壤防治技术的研究",毛建华等对天津滨海地区碱化土壤进行调查,探明碱化土壤的分布特点和形成原因,并首次提出:碱化原因是盐土脱盐过程中的脱盐碱化、苏打型地下水引起的土壤碱化以及碱性水灌溉造成的土壤次生碱化。这些碱化土壤通常呈斑块状插花分布在盐渍土或潮土之中。课题组研制出有机无机相结合,综合含钙物质和酸性物质两类改良剂优点的新型土壤改良剂。提出因地制宜便于推广的施用化学改良剂、增施有机肥和磷肥、咸淡水混合灌溉等农业和水利相结合的综合防治措施。分别在塘沽、汉沽、大港和静海等碱化土壤较为集中的区县共40公顷的土地上进行田间试验。通过综合防治措施的运用,使碱化土壤得到改良,土壤通透性、导水性增强,板结情况减轻,总碱度和钠碱化度明显降低,碱化土壤中的苏打盐消失,耕层土壤中pH值降低0.2~0.4。种植的冬小麦、大白菜增产10%左右,水稻、葡萄增产5%左右,农作物的品质也有明显的提高。

3.秸秆还田

20世纪90年代小麦普遍使用机械收获,农民开始实行小麦秸秆还田。随着玉米机械收获的普及,开始推广玉米秸秆还田技术。1999年国家环保总局发布《秸秆禁烧和综合利用管理办法》,秸秆还田面积迅速扩大。2000年市土肥站在武清、宝坻、蓟县推广小麦高留茬还田和玉米秸秆粉碎还田技术2.8万公顷,每亩秸秆还田量150~250千克,有效增加了土壤有机质含量。

在秸秆还田过程中,土肥站在武清县东蒲洼乡前河淤村开展小麦秸秆堆腐试验。试验表明加入微生物菌剂的秸秆堆肥比传统秸秆堆肥腐熟快,堆后3天温度可以上升到60℃,堆后30天秸秆即可腐熟。秸秆堆肥是优质有机肥料,不仅增加土壤有机质,还可使土壤疏松肥沃。2000~2001年武清区河北屯乡很多菜农使用微生物菌剂制作秸秆堆肥。但是秸秆堆肥劳动强度大,2001年以后使用秸秆堆肥的农户逐渐减少。

二、肥料

(一)施肥

1.肥料定位试验

1978~1998年,土肥所姚炳贵等开展"津郊潮土肥料长期定位试验的研究"。在长达20年的"长期定位"条件下,主要研究:施用化肥、有机肥及其配合对农作物产量和品质的周期影响;高产条件下的定量施肥与肥料配合关系;土壤主要养分演变规律及调控措施,以及施肥、作物和土壤三者间的定量关系等。经研究,取得成果:①肯定小麦、夏玉米连作是天津市旱地农作物主要的高产复种形式。②找出最佳的小麦、夏玉米两季亩产750千克以上的定量施肥和肥料配合指标。③肯定长期施用化肥,只要氮、磷、钾配合就能取得与有机肥和无机肥配合相一致的高产。不能单施氮肥,否则就会破坏地力,造成产量逐年下降。④找出土壤中主要养分变化规律及其调控措施,为培肥土壤提供可靠的途径。⑤明确施肥、农作物与土壤三者磷钾养分间的定量相关关系,为平衡施肥提供准确依据。⑥提出天津市部分壤质潮土地区的缺钾预报。

2.氯化铵使用效果研究

为合理利用氯化铵,土肥所于1987~1991年开展"氯化铵化肥在天津地区使用效果的研究"。陆真元、程奕等在天津市主要土壤类型潮土和盐化潮土上进行数十次田间试验,并配合网室盆栽试验,以标准氮肥硫酸铵或尿素做对照,观测氯化铵在蔬菜中施用对多种蔬菜产量和品质的影响,氯离子在土壤中的去向,同时设立长期定位试验点。在5年时间内以氯化铵为主要原料配制出4个系列14个品种的农作物专用肥。试验结果表明:在茄子、黄瓜等蔬菜中合理施用氯化铵,效果较好,按等氮量施用及合理搭配其他化肥,对蔬菜的田间长势、品质、产量无显著差异。在粮食作物中施用氯化铵可增加谷粒中粗蛋白及氨基酸的含量,长期连续施用氯化铵(连续5年,每亩年施600千克),在0~60厘米土层内,氯离子含量不增加或增加很少,土壤pH值有下降趋势,肥效与等氮量尿素相当。该项成果1988~1991年在天津市各郊县推广应用5.33万公顷,获1992年度天津市科技进步二等奖。

3.钾肥施用技术推广

天津市自20世纪70年代开始,化学氮磷肥料在农田中大量施用,粮食产量大幅度增加,同时也从土壤中挟走大量钾素,造成土壤缺钾现象严重,而传统的钾肥补给来源——农家肥却不断减少,从而导致农田土壤氮磷钾含量比例失调,肥力下降,成为制约农作物增产的一个重要障碍。1990年开始,土肥所周艺敏等深入到天津市12个郊(区)县开展调查研究,采用先进的土壤地理定位信息技术、选择172个有代表性的土壤样点,系统分析土壤中钾素状况、钾素丰缺及土壤供钾能力,在完成天津市土壤营养元素丰缺评价的基础上,1993~1996年连续3年进行了6项水稻、7项玉米、8项小麦田间小区试验,共获取3000多项研究数据,初步找出钾在天津市不同区(县)乡(镇)的施用条件和合理用量;不同钾素含量对主要粮食作物的增产效果、适宜的用钾量及与磷、氮、锰、锌、硫等养分配合施用比例;钾肥在小麦、玉米轮流耕作中的合理分配、施用方法,以及化学钾肥与秸秆还田对土壤钾素平衡的影响,为钾肥的经济有效推广应用提供实用技术和方法。试验结果表明:正确合理地施用钾肥,可使水稻、小麦、玉米分别增产20%、13.5%和14.5%。在小区试验的基础上,还进行小麦、玉米、水稻的大面积示范,并同天津市郊区(县)农业推广部门合作在天津市推广应用1.67万公顷。该项成果获1996年度天津市科技进步二等奖。

4.垃圾堆肥

1992~1997年,土肥所与中国市政华北设计院、天津市河北区环卫局合作开展"提高垃圾堆肥质量及农田应用效果的研究"。毛建华等在两种不同质地的潮土上开展田间长期定位试验。结果表明,垃圾肥能调节土壤PH值,提高土壤肥力,增加有机质和氮磷钾养分含量,改善粘重土壤的不良物理性状。合理使用垃圾肥能提高农作物的产量,提升品质,土壤与农作物中重金属的积累也不会超标。他们还设计出可靠简便的大体积单元式鲜垃圾露天厌氧高温堆肥的式样和结构以及温度测定和气体采集系统,测定各断面的温度和氧气、二氧化碳浓度的变化和堆肥过程中养分与卫生学等指标。试验表明,采用露天厌氧高温堆肥,其堆温、养分及卫生学等各项指标均符合国家标准。该项成果获1999年度天津市科技进步二等奖。

5.无土栽培基质施肥

1998~2001年,土肥所周艺敏等开展"主要蔬菜无土栽培基质和标准化施肥技术的研究"。研制出营养液配方5种,总结出不同配方的栽培基质水肥运移特点(包括持水、保肥性和养分动态变化),研究总结出黄瓜、番茄主要品种在3~4种不同基质栽培条件下、不同生长时期养分吸收规律,提出一套科学施肥的栽培模式。并先后在汉沽区、西青区、津南区、大港区现代化农业科技示范园区进行黄瓜、番茄、樱桃番茄、西芹、生菜、圆白菜、球茎茴香等蔬菜(瓜果)的育苗和栽培试验,对其生长情况、产量、品质进行分析,并同荷兰的无土栽培基质和营养液进行对比,结果证实:与农家常规土壤栽培相比,平均增产60%,可减少农药用量70%,节约灌水70%,平均提前收获15天,产品品质优良,达到无公害蔬菜标准或绿色食品A级标准。该项科研成果基本解决了天津市在引进国外先进的无土栽培技术方面存在的高成本、高投入的问题,为在天津市逐步推广无土栽培技术和蔬菜工厂化生产提供技术支撑。

6.配方施肥

20世纪80年代,天津市开始推广配方施肥技术。1982~1984年推广地力分级法,1984~1985年推广目标产量法,1986年以后推广肥料效应函数法。1989~1991年市土肥站在宝坻和静海两县推广5.35万公顷,比前三年平均产量增产10%以上。1991年以后,随着计算机技术的发展和试验数据的不断积累,配方施肥技术日益完善。2001~2002年市土肥站为宝坻区、静海县制定了土壤养分丰缺评判标准,绘制土壤肥力分级图,应用肥料效应函数方程建立了主要农作物施肥模型,并应用土壤速测技术对推荐施肥方案进行修正。

7.滴灌施肥

2001年,市土肥站在武清区、静海县开展保护地蔬菜滴灌施肥试验。2004年完成滴灌设备与施肥设备的选型配套,制定专用肥配方和施肥方案,在静海县示范推广43公顷。该技术是将滴灌设施与施肥设施有效集成,将肥料按作物不同生育期所需要的养分比例配兑成液肥,然后与灌溉水一起均匀、准确地输送到作物根系土壤。2005年在武清区、宝坻区示范169公顷,主要在茄果类蔬菜和甜瓜、葡萄生产上应用,平均节水50%,节肥42%,增产24%。

(二)肥料加工和专用肥

1.有机肥料加工

有机肥料在农业生产中占有重要地位,但由于有机肥料存在着养分含量低、用量大、施用不便等缺点,不少地区农民已不再重视,任其丢弃堆存,既污染环境,又造成肥源的浪费。1989~1993年,土肥所周艺敏、许前欣等开展"有机肥料科学加工利用的研究",采用先进工艺——微生物接种发酵技术,引进国内外10余种菌剂,分别进行鸡、猪、牛粪等农家肥、作物秸秆接种发酵液肥及堆肥试验,筛选出发酵速度快、养分转化率高、宜于在天津地区推广应用的新型接种菌剂，其发酵速度为：液肥常温下7天完成发酵，堆肥20～30天完成发酵，腐熟率在80%以上。其养分转化率：液肥速效养分提高80%～190%，堆肥由常规的20%提高到50%，时间缩短2～3倍。经试验，研制出直接加工畜禽粪便制造有机液体肥料的生产工艺和有机无机复合型高浓度液肥配方，其有效养分达21%，富含有机质、氮、磷、钾、微量元素、氨基酸等。在3年内共试制液肥40吨，在蔬菜、果树、粮食作物和经济作物中推广应用2000公顷。周艺敏等还利用充氧动态发酵技术研制出有机无机复合颗粒肥，筛选出两种新型配方，总有效养分达25%，有机质含量在20%以上。有机肥料科学加工利用技术的研制成功突破了长期以来国内有机肥料堆放发酵、不便应用、无法实现商品化的应用模式以及单一利用无机化学元素施肥的模式，为有机肥料科学加工开辟了简易、快速、经济、高效的途径。该项研究获1993年度天津市科技进步二等奖。

2.烟草专用肥

1989～1993年，中国农业生产资料公司天津公司与土肥所合作开展“烟草专用肥的应用开发与推广”的研究。崔家璐、姚炳贵等根据不同种植地区烟草的需肥特征，结合土壤养分的丰缺情况以及施肥方法等，确定烟草专用肥的科学配方。采用造粒与混配相结合的生产工艺，并运用两步氨化法，结合控制水分与湿度，从而解决了产品潮解的问题。研制成功的烟草专用肥属中浓度高稳型，养分全，浓度高，氮磷钾养分总量达37%，贮运期长，使用范围广，增产效果显著。经农民使用证实，施用烟草专用肥后，烟叶植株长势较强，叶片大而厚，钾含量高，增加了烟叶的香气。比农民使用的传统的施肥方法可使烟叶增产22.5%，中上等烟叶比例提高5%～10%，深受广大烟农的欢迎。1993～1995年，在河南、陕西、云南等20个省、自治区推广应用达37.6万公顷。该成果获1994年度天津市星火科技一等奖、1996年度国家科技进步三等奖。

3.小麦专用肥

1990～1993年，中国农业生产资料公司天津公司和土肥所合作开展小麦专用肥研制与应用开发研究。李家清、姚炳贵等系统地分析20世纪80年代以后国内肥料研究的进展情况，并结合所在单位小麦施肥和定位试验的科研成果，在试验中通过的检验与统计分析矫正，最后确定在中国北方麦区不同类型土壤与不同土壤肥力条件下小麦专用肥的科学配方。此小麦专用肥养分全、浓度高，各项质量指标均达到国家颁发的标准。其间，该研究分别在天津、山西、山东、江苏、河南、陕西等6省市10个县主要产麦区的20个基点布置52个田间试验与示范区，根据不同土壤肥力水平和不同施肥量的产量结果，摸索出了不同地力水平条件下小麦专用肥合理的施用量与施用技术，为小麦合理施肥提供了科学依据。经北方产麦区农民使用证实，小麦专用肥具有增产效果显著和省工方便等优点，平均比无肥对照增产51%；比农民传统施肥方法增产20%。3年间小麦专用肥在天津、北京、河北、山西等省市累计推广33.8万公顷。研究成果获1992年度天津市星火科技一等奖、1993年度国家星火科技二等奖。

第四节 植物保护

20世纪90年代，随着天津市农村种植结构的不断调整、设施农业的发展和对外开放的扩大，农作物病虫害表现形式及其危害程度发生新的变化，出现新的害虫种群。同时，随着科技进步和社会的发展，对环境的保护和无公害农产品的要求已成为必须考虑的问题。高毒高残留农药不断被高效低毒农药及生物农药所取代，对病虫害提倡综合治理。这些都为植物保护工作的科学研究水平和技术手段提出了新的，更高的要求。为此，天津市农业科技人员根据农业生产的实际需要，针对农作物急需解决的病、虫、草害，组织力量进行研究和成果推广，开展无农药污染蔬菜生产基地建设，筛选成功一批适用的高效低毒农药，加强外来虫害的检疫研究和防控措施。在上述工作中，取得大批行之有效的研究成果。

一、农作物病虫害防治

（一）小麦蚜虫防治

天津市农业局承担的“麦蚜发生规律及防治技术研究”，经三年研究实施，得出小麦蚜虫在相关因素影响下的发生消长规律及对麦田为害特点。掌握最佳防治指标和技术，包括合理用药，精确防治时期。该项研究成果获1992年度天津市科技进步二等奖。

在为害小麦的4种蚜虫中，天津地区以麦二叉蚜和麦长管蚜为主。此2种麦蚜虫在小麦的茎、叶和穗部为害，对苗期和穗期都造成很大影响。麦蚜大发生年份可使小麦减产越过30%。同时可严重影响小麦的品质。以上麦蚜虫以成蚜、若蚜或卵的状态在麦苗、杂草基部或土缝中越冬。次年春，越冬蚜繁殖1—2代后，由有翅蚜迁向麦田，随着气温上升和小麦生长不断扩大种群。麦长管蚜在小麦灌浆乳熟期是繁殖高峰期。小麦拔节至孕穗期，麦二叉蚜繁殖为害达到高峰。小麦蜡熟期，大量产生有翅蚜，陆续飞离麦田，迁向禾本科植物上继续为害和繁殖。秋播麦苗出土后，大部分麦蚜又开始迁回冬麦苗上为害。防治方法：①利用天敌。麦蚜天敌资源非常丰富，如瓢虫科的七星瓢虫等。②农业防治。清除田边杂草寄主；适时冬灌杀伤越冬麦蚜。③药剂防治 。主要使用3种药剂：10%吡虫啉(一遍净)可湿性粉剂2500倍液；50%抗蚜威可湿性粉剂3500～4000倍液；3%啶虫咪乳油100毫升/亩加80%敌敌畏乳油50毫升/亩兑水50千克喷雾。

（二）玉米抗病育种

天津在夏玉米穗腐病流行年份，玉米产量损失比常年高出21%～35%，质量也有明显下降。玉米植株高大，不易用药，各品种对穗腐病的抗病性又有很大差别，因此只有通过抗病育种才能从根本上解决这一病害。1988～1994年，天津市农科院植物保护研究所(以下简称植保所)潘惠康等开展“玉米抗病育种及玉米主要病害综合防治的研究”。经研究，明确玉米穗腐病病害发生与气候条件的关系和穗腐病侵入途径。玉米螟蛀穗是玉米穗腐病的主要媒介。为选育出抗穗腐病强的玉米品种，广泛收集124份具有抗穗腐病特征的玉米品种资源，对其进行抗病性鉴定，从抗病性强、产量高、品质好、适合在天津地区种植的夏玉米品种中向天津地区夏玉米主播品种“黄4早”中导入一个隐性黄顶基因，一个显性抗大斑病基因，并导入抗褐斑病基因，于1991年育成夏玉米自交系“8703”。用该自交系配制成功的夏玉米杂交种“津夏7号”生育期94～96天，对玉米穗腐病、大小斑病、褐斑病具有较强的抵抗能力，果实硬粒型，色泽纯黄，品质好，比对照品种早熟3～5天，比对照品种平均亩增产约100千克。

（三）水稻新病害防治

20世纪90年代，天津水稻产区发生较为严重的水稻细菌性新病害。该病害侵染水稻米粒，病斑环绕米粒腹部呈黑褐色，病斑条状或斑点状，易断裂，露出白色淀粉，病粒瘦小。水稻感染此病造成米质下降。稻农称此病为“蚂蚱口”“黑心病”。1996～1999年，植保所刘水芳等开展天津市农业科技攻关项目“水稻细菌性新病害发生规律及防治技术”。经研究，鉴定出细菌病原菌种为“草生欧文氏菌”，基本搞清病害发生原因和发病规律以及病原菌的侵染循环特症、病害传播途径、菌株侵染途径。筛选出“菌虫清”“浸种净”两种种子消毒剂。在此基础上制订了水稻细菌性新病害的综合防治措施。经津郊稻农实践证实，使用该技术防治效果为85%～99%。1996～2001年，上述综合防治措施在天津市水稻种植区推广应用8.9万公顷。

（四）辣椒疫病防治

20世纪80年代，天津市郊县曾发生大面积辣椒死秧现象，保护地内尤为严重，成为发展辣椒生产的一大障碍。1990～1994年，植保所刘兆敏等开展“辣椒疫病防治技术的研究”。经研究，明确天津地区辣椒疫病病菌为疫霉属辣椒疫霉菌，并验证该疫病的初侵染源为土壤和病残体，水是再侵染的媒介，也是引起田间疫病流行的关键因子。水质、地势、不同的栽培方式与疫病的发生关系密切。同时，总结出“以高垄栽培为基础，改善水质为主导，提高生态防治水平，配合适时化学防治技术”和大面积采用“划片联防联治”的综合防治措施。该技术适用于沿海平原土地盐碱、地下水位高的地区，防治效果在85%以上。1992~1994年在天津市推广应用267公顷，亩增产约30%。

（五）茄子灰霉病防治

到20世纪90年代，天津市茄子保护地栽培面积迅速扩大，由于长期的连作种植，土壤中病原菌大量积累，使得茄子灰霉病连年发生，造成减产或绝收。1994～1999年，植保所王万立等开展“茄子灰霉病防治技术的研究”。主要成果为：①经调查研究，提出造成病害流行的关键因素是温度，当外界低于22℃的最高气温持续时间长的年份，病害会大流行。②从天津市茄子主要产区共分离出122个菌株，并研究其毒性强弱，明确灰霉病菌对多菌灵、乙霉威、速克灵、扑海因等4种常用杀菌剂的抗性关系，为合理用药提供科学依据。③针对茄子灰霉病的病原菌的生物学特征及侵染特点，制订出“闭棚升温”等生态防治措施，控制该病危害程度，利用生态防治，减少用药量。④研制出具有增效作用的、对敏感菌和抗性菌均有极强抑制作用的克抗药剂“45%灰霉威”可湿性粉剂，成本低，效果好。直接控制花后期及幼果期灰霉病的发生，增加门茄和对茄的结果率。上述综合防治措施，防治有效率达80%～90%。可使茄子亩增产19.2%。到2000年该项技术已累计推广1600公顷。

（六）保护地黄瓜、菜豆菌核病防治

菌核病于20世纪90年代中期在天津市逐渐流行，尤其在老菜区保护地黄瓜、菜豆中发病较为普遍，主要危害果实和茎蔓，发病后造成蔬菜产量损失常在30%以上。菌核病成为天津市以致国内北方地区反季节栽培中最严重的低温高湿病害之一。1996～2002年，王万立等开展“保护地黄瓜、菜豆菌核病防治技术研究”，表明天津市保护地黄瓜、菜豆菌核病属于低温高湿病害，造成该病害的病原菌为核盘菌。在天津市可浸染9科24种蔬菜，并详细研究病原菌的生物学特性及侵染特点。首次提出小分生孢子在保护地条件下可以通过气流传播侵染寄主，在发病适期内，累积阴雨日数与当年发病率呈显著正相关关系。在检测病原菌对多菌灵等5种药剂的抗药情况及其之间的交互抗性关系的基础上，复配出克抗药剂45%灰霉威等3组作用方式不同、防效高的杀菌剂配方。提出使土壤菌核腐烂、减少土壤中菌核萌发形成的子囊盘出土、清除病残体、高温闷棚等生态防治措施。并制订生态防治与化学防治相结合的综合防治措施。王万立等研究的防治技术易于操作，防病效果显著，深受农民欢迎。

（七）绿色木霉制剂协控技术

随着天津市设施蔬菜种植面积不断扩大，设施蔬菜病害也逐年加重。其中尤以灰葡萄孢霉引起的灰霉病、茄病镰刀菌引起的根腐病发生较为严重，一般的减产在20%～40%，严重时达60%，甚至绝收。以往防治多采用咪唑类等化学药剂，造成蔬菜农药残留。针对设施蔬菜主要病害抗药性逐渐增强、防治困难以及城乡居民关注的蔬菜农药残留和食品安全食用问题，从1999年开始，植保所王勇等开展绿色木霉制剂化及其协调防控设施蔬菜主要病害的研究，对天津地区设施蔬菜中灰霉病、白粉病、霜霉病、根腐病等病害的状况和发生规律进行系统的调查。明确天津郊县茄病镰刀菌对不同类型杀菌剂抗性水平和交互抗性。通过对具有良好生防潜力的绿色木霉进行筛选、研究、开发，研制出绿色木霉Tr9701制剂，并在国内首次总结出以绿色木霉制剂为主、配合高效低毒的化学药剂协调使用的配方和施用技术。防治效果达77%～85%，蔬菜亩增产6.8%～11.6%，在达到蔬菜病害有效防治的同时，实现生物农药的有效利用与减少或降低化学农药的使用。

（八）绵铃虫综合防治

20世纪90年代初期，绵铃虫在中国北方爆发成灾，造成绵花生产的严重损失。1993～1995年，植保所陈秉恕等开展天津市农业重点科技攻关项目“绵铃虫综合防治技术的研究”，在分析研究绵铃虫爆发成灾原因的基础上，结合天津市绵花生产的特点，根据害虫的发生规律及生物学特征，研究出因地制宜地将农业防治、物理防治、化学防治结合起来的综合防治措施。主要成果为：建立天津市绵田绵铃虫预测预报方法，中长期和近期测报准确率分别达到85%和95%。复配成功药效高、毒性低、价格低廉的“杀虫灵1号”“杀虫灵2号”，用药7天虫口减退率分别达93%～97%和87%～93%；保蕾效果分别为88%～91%和87%～91%。总结出：对绵田进行秋耕冬灌可压低88%的越冬虫口，减轻翌年绵铃虫种群数量。在绵田内种植玉米诱集带诱杀成虫，也可减少20%～22%的二代绵铃虫在绵田的落卵量。经田间示范应用证实，综合防治技术，达到国家规定的综合防治评估标准，比以往的单纯化学防治方法，绵铃虫田间落卵量大幅度降低，亩增产籽绵30~62千克。1995~1996年，上述综合防治措施在天津市5个产绵区县得到较大范围的推广，面积达23.9万公顷。

（九）潜叶蝇协控技术

到20世纪末，随着设施蔬菜种植面积的不断扩大，潜叶蝇成为一类重要害虫，对天津设施黄瓜、番茄、菜豆等蔬菜作物的危害很大。针对以往单纯依靠化学防治，导致害虫抗药性增强、防治困难、环境和农产品污染等问题，植保所白义川等于1999年开始研究设施蔬菜潜叶蝇的多措施协控技术。研究成果：①明确天津郊县蔬菜潜叶蝇有美洲斑潜蝇、南美斑潜蝇、番茄斑潜蝇、葱斑潜蝇和豌豆彩潜蝇5种，潜叶蝇的寄生蜂有19种，优势寄生蜂复合体包括美丽新姬小蜂、潜蛾姬小蜂、底比斯金色姬小蜂。②通过温度对美洲斑潜蝇发育的影响、美洲斑潜蝇的田间消长动态及露地越冬等研究，明确美洲斑潜蝇的发生规律。③明确主要蔬菜上优势寄生蜂的消长动态，设施内自然发生的寄生蜂的越冬情况。④研究优势寄生蜂的繁殖和保存技术，制订优势寄生蜂实验种群饲养流程，明确优势寄生蜂冷藏、滞育诱导和滞育解除条件。⑤提出采用农业和生态防治、物理防治、化学防治和寄生蜂保护利用的设施蔬菜潜叶蝇多措施协控防治技术。该项科研成果为天津市快速发展的设施蔬菜无公害生产提供技术支持。

（十）蝗虫防治技术

20世纪90年代后，受全球气候变暖趋势影响，天津市连年干旱少雨，加快了蝗虫高发年份的频率。1998~2005年，累计发生面积达48.78万公顷。主要发生区集中在北大港水库，独流减河行洪道，子牙新河河道等滨水区域。天津市农业局植保植检站的科技人员对蝗灾进行系统研究并采取防治措施。他们承担的“天津市东亚飞蝗综合治理技术”项目，系统总结分析天津地区蝗虫发生的规律，蝗区类型，天敌种类，以及防治技术。经研究得出东亚飞蝗（天津地区主要蝗虫种类）的特点是：①该虫具有突发、暴发、暴食的特点和群聚、远距离迁飞习性。②该虫以卵在土壤中越冬，并有五个龄期。每个龄期5~7天，5龄内统称蝗蝻，5龄后羽化为成虫，蝗蝻和成虫均可为害，主要取食芦苇和禾本科植物。③在天津地区，该虫可以一年发生两代，5~7月份发生为夏蝗，8~10月份发生为秋蝗。④该虫具有趋向脱水地产卵的习性，因此有“水去蝗来”和“大涝后连旱，蚂蚱成片”的发生特点。蝗灾成因：①环境因素。天津独特的地理环境是蝗虫灾害频繁发生的重要因素之一。天津市境内水库河道众多，干旱年份，水库、河道几近干涸，为蝗虫提供了适宜的生存环境。国有荒地面积大，植被以蝗虫喜食的芦苇为主，为蝗虫提供丰富的食料来源。荒地以盐碱地为主，宜于蝗虫产卵及蝗卵孵化。②气候因素。20世纪90年代后，天津气候多以干旱为主，有利于蝗虫发生。天津冬季气温最低零下10℃~15℃，适合蝗虫越冬，夏、秋季气温有利于蝗虫繁衍发生。若在东亚飞蝗成虫发育、产卵阶段及卵的孵化时期遇到雨水调和的气候，就能提高蝗虫的产卵量、蝗卵的孵化率和蝗蝻成活率。③不宜改造蝗区多。大港区北大港水库、蓟县于桥水库等库区、独流减河行洪道等河道都是不易改造蝗区，在干旱年份便成为蝗虫最好的适生地。防治措施主要采取化学防治与生物防治相结合，飞机和人工防治相结合，取得显著成效。“天津市东亚飞蝗综合治理技术”项目获天津市1998年度科技进步二等奖。

（十一）种子包衣剂

中国开展种子包衣剂研究始于20世纪80年代，以粮食和经济作物为主，蔬菜种子包衣剂的研究尚属薄弱环节。天津市农科院蔬菜研究所马文荷等用产于国内外的无毒杀菌剂、发芽催进剂和多种对蔬菜无毒无害的化学试剂为原料，经单因子和复合因子筛选、室内发芽和田间试验，到1992年研制出包膜型和浸种型两大系列，分别用于大白菜、茄子、菜花、黄瓜、芹菜、西瓜等蔬菜、瓜果品种的种子包衣剂。经各地农业技术部门和菜农使用证实，该包衣剂对蔬菜种子具有杀菌和消毒作用，可使种子发芽率提高10%，并可抵御蔬菜植株的苗期病害，促进幼苗生长发育，使蔬菜亩增产15%。除在天津市使用以外，还推广到全国24个省、自治区、直辖市，并出口到日本、韩国、东南亚等国家和地区。1995年获国家发明专利，获1995年度天津市科技进步二等奖。“蔬菜专用种衣剂的推广应用” 获1998年度天津市科技进步三等奖。到2005年该项科技成果覆盖面积已超过13.33万公顷，使菜农增加收入1.5亿元。

2001~2004年,天津市农业局植保植检站和中国农业大学合作开展"新型药肥复合型种衣剂技术推广应用"项目,谢建军等开发出25%克.福.萎玉米种衣剂和18%咪.多.福水稻种衣剂。两种新型药肥复合型种衣剂经实验、示范,取得理想的效果,对玉米苗期地下害虫、茎基腐病、丝黑穗病和水稻苗期立枯病、恶苗病有很好的控制作用,已大面积推广使用。该项目获天津市2004年度科技进步二等奖。

二、无公害蔬菜生产

(一)无农药污染韭菜生产

1997~2000年,植保所谷希树等开展天津市农业重点攻关项目"无农药污染韭菜生产基地建设及配套技术研究"。对困扰韭菜正常生长的韭蛆危害、造成韭菜产品农药残留超标现象、韭菜中毒事件发生的环节进行调研,重新印证韭菜迟眼蕈蚊生物生态学特性,为不同栽培条件下有针对性地防治韭蛆做技术铺垫;筛选研制出高效、低毒、低残留的两种杀虫剂:20%蛆毙1号乳油、32%蛆毙2号乳油。总体防治效果达90%~95%,施用后农药残留不超标,生产的韭菜产品安全性合格;总结归纳出露地、冷棚、暖棚等不同栽培条件下防蛆技术。对用药时间、用药量、适用药剂品种、禁用药剂做出明确认定,总结归纳出适用于中国北方非污灌区有效治理韭蛆的综合配套技术。并对农业防治的覆土、合理施肥、灌水和清整田园均有明确的阐述。在项目实施过程中,初步建设无农药污染韭菜生产基地7.7公顷,实用技术示范面积867公顷。研究总结的无农药污染韭菜生产基地建设方案、防蛆技术除在天津市大面积应用外,还在北京、河北、山东等省市大面积推广,到2003年累计推广2200公顷。此项研究获2003年度天津市科技进步二等奖。

(二)无公害蔬菜技术应用

2001年,天津市农业局实施农业部丰收计划项目"生物农药在蔬菜上的应用与推广",主要技术内容是:露地菜种植昆虫诱集作物;生物及生物技术的应用;高效、低毒、低残留化学农药技术的合理使用。在实施该项目两年内筛选出齐螨素,稳德、爱诺虫清、菜喜、菌克毒克、苦参素、蔬丹、千胜、螨意、农抗120等生物农药,对蔬菜病虫害有很好的防治效果,为天津市大面积推广无公害蔬菜产品,保障蔬菜不受病虫为害,安全增产提供理想的药剂。

(三)无公害蔬菜绿色防控技术推广

推广蔬菜绿色防控技术,是一项改变单纯依靠化学农药防治蔬菜病虫害的措施。采用生物、物理等方法结合低毒农药控制蔬菜病虫害的发生。2004年,天津市农业局开始引进该项防控技术,2005年在武清区建立20公顷蔬菜害虫色板诱杀技术示范区,示范区作物为棚室黄瓜、蕃茄,示范结果:黄色诱杀板对白粉虱、斑潜蝇、蚜虫的诱杀效果很好。同年在宝坻区建立660公顷蔬菜绿色防控示范区。示范的防控技术为:①频振式杀虫灯诱杀技术。②昆虫性诱剂诱杀技术。③彩色粘虫板诱杀技术。④生物农药"除虫菊素"防治技术。示范区主要为露地蔬菜,采用以上四种综合防治技术,对菜田多种害虫起到很好的控制作用,确保蔬菜的安全生长。

三、新农药研制

(一)夏玉米化学除草剂

1988~1992年,植保所申日升等开展天津市农业科技重点课题"夏玉米化学除草剂(50%丹乙烯乳油)及其应用"的研究,采用破坏杂草的光合系统,使其呈饥饿状态而死亡,达到除去杂草的目的。他先从35种国内外化学药剂中筛选出效果好的作为单剂,复配成64个组合,再从中筛选出药效好、成本低、药源供应有保证、使用方法便捷的9个组合。在温室用盆栽试验做进一步筛选,明确1个最优组合(最佳剂型)参加田间试验,经过4年多的试验,研制成功了夏玉米化学除草剂——50%丹乙烯乳油,并于1992年12月通过专家技术鉴定。夏玉米化学除草剂——50%丹乙烯乳油对一年生单子叶杂草防效可达85%~95%,对双子叶杂草防效可达70%~76%,药效期在45天以上,且对后茬作物如小麦等无副作用。除可清除夏玉米地里的杂草外，也可清除大豆、花生、绵花、芝麻、果树及十字花科、茄科、菊科等蔬菜地内的杂草。经农民使用证实：在夏玉米地内施用，每亩可省工2.5个，增加产量30千克。1991～1996年在天津、河北、山东、江苏、河南等省市推广应用12万公顷。经化工部、农业部批准为新农药品种，取得了“三证”，允许在全国推广应用。

（二）绵花化控制剂研究

1991年始，植保所申日升等开展“绵花化控制剂的研究”，采用单剂筛选与优化复配相结合的方法，并以常规药剂做对照，通过室内筛选、盆栽试验、田间小区试验和生产应用示范等考察试验，于1992年筛选复配出新型植物生长调节剂45%绵花整枝灵水剂。经小区试验和大田示范证实：45%绵花整枝灵内吸性好，药效快，药效期持续长达18～20天，施用后可调节绵花植株体内营养分配，抑制绵花徒长，使植株株形紧凑，果枝短，减少蕾铃脱落，增加伏桃，提高坐果率，保花效果提高1.6倍，保铃效果提高66%以上。绵花全生育期用药两次即可达到全程控制。经整枝灵处理绵株，籽绵亩产可达260千克，比用人工管理的方法亩增产25千克。工艺简单，易于操作，对环境没有污染。该技术自研制成功后，经化工部、农业部批准为新农药品种，取得“三证”，允许在全国推广应用，到1995年推广应用面积6.67万公顷。

四、植物检疫

1990年，天津市相继发现了十余种外来有害生物，对天津农业检疫工作提出新要求。1991年，全市12个涉农区县都成立植保植检站，设专人负责。由天津市植保植检站（以下简称植保站）起草制定《天津市植物检疫办法》，此办法经市政府批准，正式颁布实施。在有害生物的普查监测和防治工作中，植保站的科技人员主要对稻水象甲、黄瓜黑星病、假高粱、美国白蛾、美洲斑潜蝇、蔗扁蛾、番茄溃疡病等十余种病虫害的发生情况进行了调查，并采取了防治措施，取得了良好的效果。

1990年6月，天津首次发现稻水象甲疫情。为控制疫情发展，天津市农林局开展《天津市稻水象甲生物学研究及综合治理工程》项目。经研究，摸清稻水象甲在天津的分布范围、发生规律、生活习性及为害特点。同时，探索出综合防治技术体系。该项目获1994年度天津市科技进步二等奖。调查发现，稻水象甲成虫除为害水稻外，还为害禾本科、莎草科和泽泻科等30多种植物。成虫具有趋光性的特点。越冬代成虫春季表现出明显的趋湿性，秋季新一代成虫则表现出趋干性。该虫在天津一年发生一代，以成虫越冬。翌年5月上旬秧苗长出水面后，在稻田为害。5月下旬至6月上中旬稻田越冬代成虫密度最高。5月下旬成虫开始产卵。产卵期约40天左右，卵经过7~10天开始孵化，6月上旬始见幼虫，6月下旬至7月上旬为新一代幼虫为害高峰期，幼虫经过4个龄期，历期约30~35天。老熟幼虫附着在根部做茧化蛹，蛹经过7~14天羽化成成虫。新一代成虫7月中旬开始出现，7月下旬至8月上旬为新一代成虫高峰期。新一代成虫昼伏夜出，白天潜伏在水稻基部，日落前后爬上叶尖取食或待飞，这时期黑光灯诱虫量最大。8月下旬开始向田间杂草及越冬场所转移，在越冬场所杂草上取食一段时间后进入越冬。1992年后，天津农林局连续7年采用飞机大面积防治，对控制疫情起到重要作用。项目筛选出氯杀威、稻乐丰、来福灵等药剂防治成虫效果均在90%以上，呋喃丹、杀虫双防治幼虫效果较好，均可作为轮换使用药剂。

1996年7月，天津首次发现美洲斑潜蝇。该虫是国家规定的重要植物检疫对象，严重为害蔬菜、瓜类、花卉等多种作物。天津市农林局开展《天津市美洲斑潜蝇生物学及检疫综合防除技术的研究与应用》项目，在组织全市进行大面积疫情普查和防治的同时，对该蝇发生规律进行连续5年的系统研究，摸清该蝇的生物学特性和周年发生消长规律，研究探索出监测调查、预测预报方法和检疫综合防除配套技术，并在全市推广应用，综合控制疫情发展。该项目获1999年度天津市科技进步二等奖。

第二章 畜 牧

1991～2005年，天津畜牧业加大结构调整，猪肉和禽蛋的生产增速放慢，牛羊肉和奶类发展保持较高水平。畜禽饲养以规模化、集约化发展为主。畜禽繁育在应用人工授精和机械孵化技术的基础上，开始胚胎工程的基础和应用研究。同时，从国内外引进优良畜禽品种并培育扩繁。规模蛋鸡饲养场近2万个；瘦肉型猪、蛋鸡、火鸡、瘦肉型鸭、奶牛等商品生产基地已经建成，形成“龙头企业带基地，基地连农户”的贸工一体化的生产经营格局。

在疫病防治中，加强疫苗研究和应用。1996～2000年，良种繁育体系和技术推广服务体系建设日趋完善。形成以乡镇畜牧兽医站为主体，市、县畜牧行政、科研推广、教学等部门为骨干的三级技术服务体系，各级服务组织达300多个；兽医四级防检疫体系（市、县、乡、村）稳定发展。防疫队伍1500余人。

推广科学饲养方法，引进优质饲草，对饲料配方科学化，实现饲料生产产业化。在饲料生产中，调制技术和配合饲料、添加剂得到普遍应用；秸秆青贮、氨化技术推广为发展节粮型畜牧业提供丰富的粗饲料资源。2005年，全市优质饲料产量187万吨，产值达到52亿元。同时，在畜禽饲养的过程中采取措施，加强环境保护。

第一节 品种繁育

1990年以后，天津畜牧品种繁育技术迅速发展，采用了现代的胚胎移植与克隆技术；引进生产抗孕马血清血促性素（PMSG），并研究成功与之配套使用的抗孕马血清促性腺激素（APMSG），取得良好应用效果；在猪、牛、羊、鸡的引种与繁育上取得突破成果。

一、胚胎移植与克隆

（一）胚胎移植

天津从1992年开始应用现代生殖生物学理论结合激素测定方法，进行胚胎移植研究，开展牛的胚胎移植和胚胎的冷冻保存、解冻及移植试验。对黑白花奶牛发情周期血超数排卵试验，超排反应率、可用胚胎数均较高。1992～1995年，由天津市畜牧兽医研究所徐直主持的“牛胚胎移植的研究与应用”取得预期成果。

2001年，天津的胚胎移植技术日趋成熟，首次对育成羊的超数排卵进行研究，平均获可用胚胎11.6枚，与成年供体羊相比差异不显著（$P>0.05$）。将供受体羊的饲养管理、供受体的同期发情、超数排卵、胚胎冷冻、胚胎分割、胚胎移植等技术集成，制定种羊饲养管理、胚胎移植等技术操作规程，形成优质肉羊胚胎产业化配套技术体系。2001～2004年，天津市畜牧兽医研究所冯建忠主持“肉羊胚胎产业化配套技术研究”课题，研制出“抗粘连保护剂”，获2004年度天津市科技进步二等奖。

（二）克隆

天津的克隆技术开始于国际合作，并逐步成熟完善。2002年，天津市畜牧兽医研究所刘海军主持课题

“波尔山羊胚胎克隆技术研究”,该项研究与留美博士刘灵开展国际合作。2005年11月2日,世界首例胚胎克隆的波尔山羊“津生”在天津诞生(英国的Dolly是由体细胞克隆,“津生”由胚胎细胞克隆),标志着天津在动物克隆技术研究领域迈出重要一步,为进一步开展体细胞克隆技术研究奠定了良好基础。

二、血促性素、促性腺激素

1989年,天津实验动物中心(以下简称“动物中心”)从长春生物制品研究所引进抗孕马血清血促性素(PMSG)成果。该项成果引进后,成为动物中心的主营产品。1992年,动物中心在天津市科委支持下成立华孚高新生物技术公司,生产上述产品,行销22个省市,并得到良好反馈。年销售量数万头份,产值数十万元。仅新疆一地就需求用于100万头羊的PMSG量。

由于抗孕马血清促性腺激素(APMSG)是与PMSG配套使用,促进动物繁殖,1992年,动物中心和中国农业科学院畜牧研究所合作承担的农业部国家攻关项目子课题——“抗孕马血清促性腺激素的研究和应用”成果刊登于国家科委科技研究成果公报。同年10月国家科委等五部委颁发给动物中心“兽用抗孕马血清一九九二年度国家级新产品”证书。中试成功后,获1994年度天津市科技进步二等奖。

动物中心陈萸芳等成功制备出高效价抗血清(每毫升含2000个大鼠单位),并建立其活性测定方法。该产品可用于猪、羊等多种动物同期发情及牛的双胎。经临床试用具有专一性强和准确的效价。

三、引种与繁育

(一)种猪

1.引种

1990年,宁河原种猪场被确定为国家级重点种畜禽场。1992年,“五十万头瘦肉型猪推广工程”项目在天津实施,在全市183个乡镇推广优质商品猪饲养技术,为郊县发展规模养猪,减少环境污染找到了科学方法,该项目1994年获天津市科技进步(成果推广)二等奖。1994年开展的“良种猪及配套饲养技术”(农业部“丰收计划”项目之一)利用优良种猪选择最佳杂交组合生产商品猪,推广以氨基酸平衡理论、理想蛋白质模式生产不同生长阶段猪的全价配合饲料等先进、实用技术。1995年,农业部下达“丰收工程”项目——“天津市良种猪饲养及加工技术”。在项目区推广的优良猪种,综合适用技术覆盖面达93%。1995年,市科委、市农委下达的“百万头瘦肉型猪综合技术推广工程”项目,经实施,获1997年度天津市科技进步一等奖。在上述科研成果的研究、开发和推广中,宁河种猪场发挥了重要作用。1999年先后从丹麦引进长白种猪114头、从英国引进大约克种猪60头、从美国引进杜洛克种猪60头,成为当年国内唯一一家同时把世界名种猪全部引进的原种猪场。同时引进种猪活体瘦肉率测定仪2台,ACEMA-64自动化种猪性能测定监测体系12套,ACEMA英文系统软件1套。该场开展生产性试验和杂交组合试验,筛选最佳杂交组合。种猪引进后,利用猪饲料转化率自动测定系统,活体背膘测定仪(B超),采用BLUP(最佳线性无偏预测)方法,在自由状态下自动准确测定、评估种猪生产性能,最大限度地减少人为因素对种猪性能表现的影响。2005年,宁河原种猪场傅润亭主持“天津市种猪良繁体系示范工程”,通过引进15头英系大约克种猪,扩大遗传基因选择强度,建立种猪资源数据库和“育繁推”繁育体系,实现信息共享、科学选种选配。

图6-2-1-97　宁河种猪场

2.繁育

1991年,天津开始白猪育种。引进杂交制种的亲本—东北民猪和加系大约克原种猪,开始正反杂交。

1992年二元杂交后代产生，并进行测定和回交。1993年进行横交。1994年完成天津白猪配套母系的杂交制种研究，拥有回交杂种基础母猪100头，并向社会推广近500头杂交种猪。

1999年，天津市畜牧兽医研究所李千军建立种猪应激综合征（MHS）基因检测的PCR-REFL方法，探索并提出模板DNA的提取、引物设计方法和PCR扩增程序，对扩增产物进行酶切和琼脂糖凝胶电泳图谱分析，检测天津市长白、大约克、杜洛克及皮特兰种猪的MHS基因三种基因型频率和基因频率，为育种工作中猪MHS基因的检测提供准确、简便的方法。

2000年，由市科委批准，宁河原种猪场与天津市畜牧兽医研究所组建“天津市现代畜牧技术工程中心”。2001年，人事部批准成立国内畜牧业唯一一家博士后科研工作站，聘请中国农业大学王楚端教授，开展高分子育种、转基因等高新技术研究。在育种技术上，应用国外先进的遗传标记辅助选择技术，对种猪的恶性高温综合症基因、高产仔数主要基因、毛色基因进行诊断，使核心群种猪全部清除恶性高温综合症基因，提高种猪繁殖力与合格率。2003年，“引进猪种高产仔抗应激分子育种研究”项目，获天津市科技进步二等奖。同年，投资6000万元，采用先进的三区式养猪系统和具有自主知识产权的高产仔抗应激分子育种技术，建设1200头核心群基础母猪、2200头父母代母猪的“天河牌”优质猪配套核心选育场。

2003年，天津市畜牧局开展“猪人工授精技术推广”，成立天津市家畜繁育科技服务中心。实现实施一个项目，熟化一项技术，创立一个品牌，提升一个企业，致富一方农民。此项成果获2005年度天津市科技进步二等奖。

宁河原种猪场积极开展对外交流与合作，2004年10月成功举办了柬埔寨、马来西亚、菲律宾东盟三国养猪技术国际培训班；2005年8月完成中国—柬埔寨种猪示范项目地点的勘察规划和建筑设计。

（二）奶牛

1.引种

1999年天津市奶牛存栏3.34万头，当年市奶牛育种站已拥有母系产奶量8000千克以上的种公牛18头，借助日本援助的当代先进仪器设备，年产细管冷冻精液15万支；2000年市畜牧局从美国、加拿大引进高产种公牛12头，种母牛50头，胚胎329枚。

2.繁育

天津市于20世纪80年代后期引入胚胎移植技术之后，奶牛繁育以胚胎移植和人工授精技术为主。2000年，天津市畜牧局傅润亭主持“奶牛品种及配套技术推广”项目，应用胚胎移植技术，生产牛犊135头，移植妊娠率达51.0%；同时，利用引进体外授精胚胎进行了移植黄牛的试验，共移植14头，其中4头受胎，移植妊娠率为28.57%。通过人工授精技术，推广冷冻细管精液30万支，年总受胎率达到90%，产奶单产量达到6308千克，乳脂率达3.5%。

（三）肉牛

1994年天津市畜牧局、天津市畜牧兽医站和天津市畜牧兽医研究所组织实施“天津市良种肉牛及配套饲养技术”项目，推广肉牛优良品种及杂交牛，利用架子牛进行科学育肥；并利用当地黄牛资源，引进西门塔尔、皮埃蒙特等优良品种、胚胎及冷冻精液生产优质改良牛。到1997年累计改良当地黄牛28120头，生产的西杂一代、夏杂一代表现出较好的生产性能；出栏肉牛38.86万头。

（四）羊

1993年起，天津市畜牧局组织实施优良肉羊品种引进、选育，杂交组合筛选等7个科技项目。引进德国肉用美利奴、澳大利亚陶赛特、英国萨福克及山东小尾寒羊等2926只。1997~1999年武清、大港、蓟县、宝坻、静海等区县，分别引进国内外优良品种种羊10348只，扩繁种羊43800只。2000年9月，天津市农业科学院畜牧兽医研究所从澳大利亚引进世界上最优秀的肉羊品种——纯种波尔山羊39只。

在繁育过程中，天津畜牧业以引进的国外优良品种为主体，开展杂交选育工作，通过人工授精技术、胚胎移植技术，有效地提高了当地肉羊的生产性能。

（五）蛋鸡

1.引种

1998年，为实现养鸡“节本、低耗、高效”，天津市畜牧局引进更新优良海兰白、海兰灰等小型鸡品种16万套，在蓟县、大港饲养；1997~2000年，引进京白939、新红、罗曼、伊莎B380等新品种29万套，在蓟县、宝坻、北辰、宁河等地饲养。到2005年，全市拥有蛋种鸡场11座，存栏成母禽15.2万只。

2. 繁育

1990年以后，天津种鸡繁育完全采用机械化或半机械化方式，种蛋选择、保存和消毒要求严格，蛋库要求隔热性能好；同时普遍采用人工授精方式进行种鸡的繁殖，受精率达到80%以上。人工授精技术的应用提高了公母鸡的比例。同时，可减少疫病传播，降低饲养成本、提高种鸡品质。1999年，天津市兽医站刘克成主持的“天津市家禽优良品种及配套集约化增产技术”项目，推广优良商品蛋鸡536万只，入舍鸡只单产提高1.37千克，产蛋期平均料蛋比达到2.42∶1，节省饲料2554.31万千克。同时，利用生物技术处理鸡粪净化环境，实现产量、质量、效益环保同步提高。

第二节　疫病防控

20世纪90年代后期，通过实施“无规定动物疫病区建设”项目，天津市已基本形成较为健全完善的动物防疫监督、疫情测报、疫病检疫监测和诊断、生物制品冷链、兽药及饲料监察工作体系，使动物防疫及兽药管理基础设施建设水平得到很大提高，动物防疫灭病能力进一步增强。全市猪、禽、大牲畜的病死率分别控制在7%、15%和1%，均低于全国平均水平；猪瘟、鸡新城疫计划免疫率平均达到95%以上，规模饲养场达到100%；出栏生猪的产地检疫率平均达到95%以上，个别区县接近100%；生猪定点屠宰检疫率达到100%。

一、疫苗与兽药

（一）疫苗研究

1991~1994年，天津市畜牧兽医研究所承担的“鸡传染性法氏囊病综合防治规范的研究”在国内首次证实并报道：鸡传染性法氏囊病高毒力强毒是引起全国鸡传染性法氏囊病爆发流行、高死亡率的病因。王文科等采用低母源抗体，三次大剂量中毒力疫苗免疫，缩短免疫低值期，有利于雏鸡主动免疫过程的建立，结合隔离消毒和加强饲养管理，制定综合防治措施。此项研究成果获1993年度天津市科技进步一等奖。1991年天津市禽病诊断培训中心承担“鸡法氏囊病防治技术推广”项目，应用现代先进手段，分离当地TP毒株证实为血清I型，与日本的J毒株为同一亚型。针对这种病株型研制出当地组织灭活苗，建立不同抗体水平的免疫程序，保护率达97.8%，并在国内率先采用福尔马林灭活工艺，开发出高免疫抗体，有效防止病原垂直传播。该中心承担的“鸡传染性法氏囊病免疫及其防治技术”项目，获天津市1995年度科技进步二等奖。

根据家禽疫病动态、疫病流行特点和生产中存在的问题，1996年天津市禽病诊断培训中心组建课题攻关组，开展天津地区家禽系列灭能苗扩大试验研究，在流行病学调查的基础上，对全市流行毒株进行了分离鉴定和特性研究，研制出当地毒株的灭能苗，提出解决鸡场出现变异株的免疫程序，取得良好的免疫效果。

1996~1999年，天津市畜牧兽医研究所丁伯良主持“天津地区主要鸡传染病地方毒菌株的分离及疫苗研制”项目，完成天津地区禽霍乱、传染支气管炎流行病学调查、病原分离及血清学鉴定，筛选出具有良好免疫性的毒菌株，研制成具有地方特色的灭活疫苗，其中禽霍乱疫苗获农业部新兽药证书，提出传染性支气管炎的M_{41}+肾型+腺胃型免疫预防模式，有效控制了禽霍乱与传染性支气管炎的流行。该项目获2000年度天津市科技进步二等奖。

2000~2003年,丁伯良主持“天津地区主要畜禽疫苗的开发研究”。在天津地区首次进行亚单位疫苗研究,研制出大肠杆菌菌毛—外膜蛋白亚单位疫苗、鸡巴氏杆菌荚膜亚单位疫苗,通过田间试验,免疫效果优于普通灭活疫苗。对天津地区鸡传染性鼻炎的病原进行分离、培养及鉴定,并确认了该病病原以C型副鸡嗜血杆菌为主,研制出鸡传染性鼻炎多价油苗,通过田间试验,免疫效果良好。从天津及周边地区共分离到6株H9亚型禽流感病毒,筛选出稳定性好,鸡胚增殖毒价高且具有良好免疫原性的Ss分离株,研制出H9亚型禽流感油乳剂灭活疫苗,在2℃~8℃可保存一年,田间应用3万羽份,免疫保护率达90%,免疫期8个月。应用先进的中空纤维超滤浓缩技术,首次研制成功鸡减蛋性病毒病(ND-IB-EDS-AI)四联油乳剂灭活疫苗,在2℃~8℃可保存一年,田间应用18万羽份,免疫保护率达95%,免疫期6个月。研究出目前生产禽用油乳剂灭活疫苗的最佳乳化条件,使疫苗在2℃~8℃的保存期由6个月延长到12个月。鸡新城疫油乳剂灭活疫苗抗体效价由log28提高到log210。

2000年,天津市畜牧兽医研究所与市农科院共同投资388万元,兴建动物疫苗生产车间,2001年竣工。通过国家农业部验收,取得兽用疫苗生产许可证,成为天津市唯一的动物疫苗生产单位,实现了动物疫苗的产业化生产。

(二)兽药生产

天津市兽药研发生产起步于20世纪80年代,经过不断努力,已成为集科学研发、生产和营销管理于一体的现代兽药产业体系。2005年,全市有兽药生产企业90余个,从业人员5000余人。兽药主要包括粉剂、散剂、预混剂,消毒剂(固体、液体)、最终灭菌小容量注射剂、口服溶液剂、片剂、杀虫剂(固体、液体)、最终灭菌大容量注射剂(静脉注射、非静脉注射)、颗粒剂、粉剂、浇泼剂、细胞毒灭活疫苗、胚毒灭活疫苗、细菌灭活疫苗等18个剂型的1700余个兽药产品,服务于全国各地并远销东南亚、南美等地区。

二、疫病防治

(一)防治技术

从1989年开始,天津市禽病诊断培训中心首次检测出减蛋综合征(EDS)抗体阳性并证实EDS的流行。同年,分离出传染性喉气管(ILT)当地病毒株,该毒株具有较强的致病性,感染鸡群死亡率达30%。1990年传染性法氏囊病(IBD)在全市呈爆发性流行,雏鸡的死亡率高达40%,弱毒苗不能有效地控制该病流行。研制适于当地流行毒株的疫苗是控制IBD流行的关键。1992年肾型传染性支气管炎(IB)传入天津市,该病的特点是除具有呼吸症状外,肾脏病变严重、雏鸡死亡率高并引起产蛋率大幅度下降。

1993年,天津市禽病诊断培训中心承担“家禽主要病毒性传染病免疫防治技术研究”项目,针对天津市养鸡业危害严重的ND(新城疫)、肾型IB、IBD、EDS和ILT的免疫防治进行研究,运用PCR、电镜、核酸探针等技术对所分离的19株病毒的理化特性、生物学特性、抗原性、血清型和免疫原性等进行进一步系统研究。明确天津市流行的IB、IBD野毒与标准的抗原关系,为开发当地毒株灭能苗打下了基础。在天津市首次证实肾型IB、IBD和ILT的感染,建立适用于基层兽医站推广的血清学诊断方法。应用当地毒株研制灭能疫苗,建立新的免疫程序,有效控制ND、IB、IBD、EDS和ILT的流行。该项研究获1997年度天津市科技进步二等奖。

鸡传染性法氏囊病(IBD)是鸡的主要传染病之一,在中国广泛流行。1997年,天津农学院贾英科、马衍忠等承担“鸡传染性法氏囊病中药防治技术的研究”项目,在临床诊断与实验室诊断的基础上,对中药防治进行配方、剂型及生产工艺的研究,提出防治IBD的特效中药配方及药剂配制生产技术、实际应用最佳剂型、用量、疗效及使用方法等,完善了中药防治IBD的成套技术。该药物对自然感染IBD患病鸡群治愈率96%。该项研究获1999年度天津市科技进步二等奖。

2000年,由天津市禽病诊断培训中心承担的“基因测定技术诊断减蛋综合征的研究”项目,进行减蛋综合征(EDS)分子生物学研究,建立EDSV全基因组DNA文库和诊断EDS的PCR标准实验程序,为基层兽医部门对EDS带毒感染的普查,提供了先进、快速、准确、检出率高的技术手段与方法。

猪繁殖与呼吸综合症俗称蓝耳病,是一种严重危害猪的正常生长发育的新传染病,给养猪业带来严重的经济损失。中国在1996年首次发现猪蓝耳病,天津一些猪场也发现了此病。1999年,天津市禽病诊断培训中心首次在天津地区开展大范围的猪繁殖障碍疫情调查,采用分子生物学技术诊断该病,首次分离出猪细小病毒(PPV)、猪伪狂犬病毒(PRV)、猪繁殖与呼吸综合征病毒(PRRSV),针对这些病毒研制成功PPV-PRV-PRRSV三联苗,制定了适于天津市的综合性防治措施,为猪繁殖障碍性疾病的防治提供了可靠的技术保证。

为使城乡居民吃上"放心肉",1995年6月天津市动物检疫站开展"肉品卫生质量检测新技术推广"项目。通过引进、吸收、消化国内外肉品卫生质量检测新技术,综合应用于天津市肉品卫生质量检测工作中,采用便携式定氨器半微量法检测肉品新鲜度技术,测定时间由原来的5小时缩短到40分钟,提高检测符合率46个百分点;引进、扩展、应用MA30红外线水分测定仪检验注水肉技术,比常规法提高工效10倍以上;应用"DTEK免疫棒"法快速鉴别假冒伪劣肉品,提高检测符合率49个百分点。获1998年度天津市科技进步二等奖。

肉鸡腹水症是严重阻碍天津市肉鸡业发展的主要疾病。天津市畜牧兽医研究所丁伯良主持的天津市农业攻关项目"天津市肉鸡腹水症病因与防治的研究"首次确定低温寒冷与高蛋白、高能量日粮是天津市肉鸡腹水症发生的主要直接病因;首次确定以血清总胆固醇含量的变化作为诊断腹水症的早期敏感指标;测定肉鸡血氧饱和度作为诊断腹水症的重要指标;为早期诊断肉鸡腹水症提供重要诊断依据。采用碳酸氢钾饮水法能有效预防腹水症;将中草药与地高辛结合应用于肉鸡腹水症的预防,该研究试验示范鸡33.5万只,中试63万只,肉鸡腹水症发病率控制在5%以下,直接减少经济损失510万元。

(二)防治体系

2000年以来,天津市重大动物疫病防控工作力度进一步加强,预防、控制和扑灭动物疫病的法规制度进一步完善,各级应急指挥系统得到健全,应急工作机制基本建立,依法防治、科学防治、群防群控的局面基本形成。2004年初,及时控制住发生在津南区的高致病性禽流感疫情;2005年成功地防止禽流感、亚洲I型口蹄疫、猪链球菌病的发生。同时,兽医基础设施建设进一步加强,建成市动物疫病诊断监测中心、动物疫情测报中心、2个国家级动物疫情测报站;建成12个公路动物防疫监督检查站和10个检疫卡口;新建了市级兽药、饲料检测实验室;建成市级畜产品检测中心;改造12个区县动物疫病诊断实验室;基本完成57个基层动物防疫中心站建设。更新、补充各类检测仪器设备近千台套,动物防疫体系、检疫监督体系、兽药饲料检测体系、基层防疫体系得到了全面加强,技术手段得到较大改善,检疫、检测能力显著提高。

第三节 饲养与草料

1990年后,天津生猪、蛋鸡、肉鸡养殖均采用专用配合饲料,主要以全价饲料为主,牛、羊饲料发展相对滞后。2005年实施国家农业部奶牛科技入户示范工程,奶牛开始采用全混合日粮(TMR)方法饲喂。随着天津畜禽饲养量的增加,饲料的供应、加工逐渐产业化,日粮配方也逐渐科学化、合理化。为了节约粮食,逐步开发非粮饲料。改进饲喂方法,加强饲养管理,改善生态环境已成为畜牧养殖的中心任务。

一、饲养

(一)生猪

20世纪90年代后,天津的生猪养殖在原来的公母猪分开饲养,仔猪、育肥猪分阶段饲养的基础上加强了饲养管理技术的推广。公猪单栏舍饲,舍外设运动场,提高精液品质;分娩母猪采用定位栏饲养;育肥猪采用全进全出分阶段饲养。进一步完善了养猪配套技术,促进了生猪规范化、集约化饲养。

1992～1994年，天津市畜牧局在“五十万头瘦肉型猪推广工程”项目实施中，深入国营、集体养猪场以及专业户大范围推广优质商品猪饲养技术和粪污处理技术，建造沼气池。提高养猪生产者的技术管理水平。1994～1996年，在蓟县、宝坻、武清、宁河、静海5县推广以氨基酸平衡理论、理想蛋白质模式生产不同生长阶段猪的全价配合饲料和杜洛克、长白、大约克优质种猪，利用优良种猪选择最佳杂交组合，生产优质三元商品猪。自此，确定了生猪饲养的主要品种，全进全出饲养管理技术得到普遍应用。

为推动天津市养猪业上水平，并带动相关产业的发展，天津市畜牧局1995～1998年承担农业部推广项目“天津市良种猪饲养及加工技术”。在屠宰加工厂和规模养猪场推广优良种猪并应用生物技术及疫病防治技术、肉品卫生检疫、检验技术等，实施科学化管理和产业化经营，建设成北方生猪批发市场及12个屠宰加工厂；1995～1997年，实施“百万头瘦肉型猪综合技术推广工程”项目，在全市12个郊区县的12050个养殖场、户推广优良种猪、现代化养猪优化集成技术及经配合力测定的优良杂交组合，生猪性能得到较大提高。如商品猪瘦肉率达57.07%，育肥期料肉比3.38∶1，育肥期死亡率1.5%。该项成果获1997年度天津市科技进步一等奖。

1998年，宁河原种猪场商品猪场，对育肥期商品猪进行微生态制剂——“EM”除臭灭蝇试验示范，试验期40天。经市环保监测中心测定，应用“EM”组猪舍臭味强度下降99.7%，此后普遍推广应用。

2001～2003年，为稳定提高猪肉品质，改善生态环境，刘克成主持完成的“良种瘦肉型(配套系)猪推广”项目，推广从性能测定到饲养管理、疫病防治一套适合天津地区的生猪养殖配套技术。

(二)奶牛

奶业是天津市畜牧业的优势产业之一，“十五”期间，奶牛养殖场、小区发展迅速，奶牛数量由5万头猛增到18万头，导致奶牛质量参差不齐，饲养管理水平跟不上。为解决这些问题，从2000年开始，市畜牧局利用2年时间改良牛群，推广配套技术：①从美国引进50头高产种母奶牛，从加拿大引进母亲产奶量1.2万千克以上的后备公牛12头，利用胚胎移植、克隆和冷冻精液技术，扩增基础牛群；建立奶牛系谱档案，依据DHI测定数据，决定奶牛的选留、淘汰、选种选配，逐步提高牛群整体性能。②普及科学饲料配制、秸秆青贮及微贮技术；推广种植“天农一号”饲用高粱、高油玉米、“中原单32号”等优质牧草，弥补优质干草和青绿饲料的不足。③针对泌乳期、干乳期、围产期不同的营养需要，进行科学饲养管理，规模小的饲养场户实行挂牌饲养，规模较大的饲养场按照不同泌乳阶段实行分群饲养。在落实这些技术措施的同时，也提高了养殖者的管理水平。

2005年，根据全国农业科技入户示范工程总体规划安排和《全国农业科技入户示范工程管理办法(试行)》的有关要求，在1000个奶牛饲养示范户中推广分群饲养管理、TMR(全混合日粮)饲喂、全株玉米种植、核心群奶牛DHI(奶牛生产性能)测定、乳房炎综合防治、奶牛信息化管理技术，促进了示范区生产水平全面提高。初步建立了“科技人员直接到户、良种良法直接到场、技术要领直接到人”的农业技术推广传递模式。

(三)肉羊

1999年，天津市畜牧局将国内外养羊技术组装集成，形成一套适合于天津肉羊生产的技术体系，即“一推四改一化”技术。一推，推广优质肉羊品种，改良本地羊。四改，改革传统放牧形式为半舍饲或全舍饲的饲养方式；改善饲养环境，变敞圈饲养为半封闭饲养；改传统青粗日粮为营养平衡的全混日粮；改粗放管理为科学管理。一化，疫病防治制度化。

(四)蛋鸡

1990年，天津市畜牧局在全市郊县及宝坻种鸡场、华津公司二鸡场、大港油田鸡场、青光养鸡场等鸡场推广优良品种蛋鸡，改进饲养方法，饲喂全价配合饲料，普及最新和有效的防疫灭病等技术；1991年，为进一步提高天津市蛋鸡的良种化程度和饲养管理水平，为市场提供更多的优质鲜蛋，市畜牧局承担了“天津市优良蛋鸡品种及配套技术”研究项目。推广优良蛋鸡品种及综合配套技术，在宝坻县、静海县、清河农场、华津公司养鸡场4个推广区，共推广伊莎褐、京白904、巴布考克B300等优良品种鸡562万只，良种覆盖率达91%。

1997~2000年，天津市畜牧局将蛋鸡饲养技术集成，进行示范推广：①研制一系列禽用高效抗热应激添加剂配方，高温季节可提高产蛋率3%~5%；②在蛋鸡场鸡舍山墙上安装排风扇，进行负压纵向通风，提高舍内空气质量。种鸡场配套运用湿帘技术，使夏季鸡舍小环境得到有效控制；③推广益生素干粉剂和植酸酶制剂，提高产蛋率和降低粪便中磷的含量，减少对环境的污染；④应用生物技术和低能耗无污染环保工艺，对粪便进行无害化处理，制成生物有机肥，实现了能源循环再利用；⑤开发牛油、水草及食品工业副产品等非常规饲料资源，配制营养合理、价格便宜的饲料，降低成本，提高效益。

（五）肉鸡

肉鸡生产虽然在天津起步较晚，但起点高，20世纪90年代初，由两大肉鸡企业带动发展起来。一开始就采用"公司+农户"的模式，由公司为农户统一提供鸡雏、饲料、技术服务及产品回收，发展很快。由于引入竞争机制，同时引进、推广国内几大公司的肉鸡，并注重服务质量的提高，充分发挥各区县畜牧推广部门的协调及组织、服务作用，加强公司与农户之间的沟通与联系，使天津市的肉鸡生产得到长足发展。

1996年，由天津市畜牧兽医站王瑞久主持"天津市良种肉鸡及配套饲养技术"项目，以引智、引技及推广、普及肉鸡优良品种为主线，将国内外先进技术和自有成果组装配套，在武清、静海、大港3个区县的28个乡镇、485个场户推广AA及艾维茵优良品种和网上饲养技术、改进与完善塑膜棚舍、中草药防治疫病技术，示范生物技术；普及全价配合饲料，应用复合酶制剂、多维电解质等新型添加剂和微生态制剂，增强抵抗力，提高成活率；加强管理，在育雏期采用低蛋白育雏料，结合改变光照制度，降低早期生长速度及注意通风、勤换垫草、降低饲养密度、配合中草药等措施，降低猝死症、腹水症等常见病的危害。

（六）肉鸭

天津1989年从英国引进SM1和SM2型樱桃谷父母代种鸭，通过几年生产实践及技术培训，农民掌握了该品种的饲养、繁殖、疾病防治等技术。从1999年开始，推广良种肉鸭及科学饲养管理、疫病防治等集成技术和先进的生产工艺，采用集约化、产业化的经营管理方式组织肉鸭生产，到2001建成樱桃谷种鸭场4座，年供鸭雏能力达300万只；建成年加工能力100万只的肉鸭屠宰加工厂2个和1个羽绒加工厂，形成公司加农户的产、供、销一体化生产模式。

二、饲草饲料

（一）饲草

1.引种

2002年天津市畜牧局引进优良饲草品种55个，其中豆科牧草品种24个，禾本科牧草品种27个，其他牧草品种4个，并在津南区、西青区、大港区、静海县、宁河县试种。通过研究、示范，到2005年，筛选出10个适合天津市的优良饲草品种，并编制出相应的栽培管理规范，推广牧草优良品种种植面积达1420公顷，发展2000亩以上种草企业8个，100亩以上种植户30个，丰富天津优质牧草资源，同时改善土壤生态环境。

为丰富饲草品种，提高饲料蛋白质的含量，天津市积极试种苜蓿、冬牧70黑麦草、苏丹草、墨西哥玉米及鲁梅克斯K-1杂交酸膜等优质牧草获得成功。2005年优质苜蓿种植面积达到2333公顷。

2.储存

2002年由天津市饲草饲料工作站与中国农业大学动物科技学院合作实施的"紫花苜蓿拉伸膜青贮技术推广应用"项目，推广拉伸膜裹包设备和技术、苜蓿半干青贮技术、发酵液特殊青贮技术，引进5个品牌2种裹包形式配套打捆裹包机13台套，解决了雨季苜蓿安全收贮问题。

图6-2-3-98 苜蓿打捆裹包机

3. 利用

①天津畜牧局倡导位于蔬菜生产区的养羊户，将各季节废弃的蔬菜进行收集、洗净，晾晒至含水量45%~50%，铡短与秸秆粉混合饲喂，提高了秸秆的适口性和利用率，还可防止因吃菜过多而引起的腹泻。②位于盛产

芦草的地方，一般在麦收前将大量的青芦草收割、晒干、贮存。可随时与秸秆粉混合饲喂，尤其是冬季干芦草仍保持清香味，营养丰富，适口性好，利用率高，是很好的饲草资源。

（二）饲料

20世纪90年代初，在实施“30万只肉羊生产配套技术”“银羊工程”等7个科技攻关、丰收计划、星火计划项目中，推广对农作物秸秆进行机械揉搓、氨化及青贮技术，示范应用适于母羊、育肥羊不同生长阶段的配合日粮。1998年，天津市畜牧局为解决断乳仔猪采食问题，研制出高效仔猪饲料，并在蓟县第二种猪场进行饲喂试验，在加工中采用膨化技术工艺，有效摒除抗营养因子，提高消化率；采取营养保健配方设计，消除抗菌素，维护仔猪肠道内的微生态平衡；饲喂仔猪增重快、成活率高，明显地提高养猪的经济效益。

开发非常规饲料资源是保持畜牧业持续发展的必要措施。1992～1996年，天津市畜牧兽医研究所王文杰、穆淑琴等开展“非常规饲料资源利用技术研究”，对绵籽饼粕的脱毒方法进行分析选择，开展脱纤维筛分试验，工艺流程设计、氨基酸消化率测定，研制成功专用脱毒、营养强化添加剂产品，为大规模开辟蛋白质饲料资源及利用提出一条有效途径；在国内首次综合运用“理想蛋白质”概念及“电解质平衡、营养免疫、营养调控”等动物营养学理论，研制新型猪日粮配方，从合理利用非常规饲料资源出发，减少鱼粉、大豆饼粕在猪日粮中的用量，对缓解饲料蛋白资源缺乏具有重要意义。该研究成果获1999年度天津市科技进步二等奖。

1998年，天津市畜牧局在部分区县开展饲料添加剂——植酸酶的应用推广。饲料中添加植酸酶即可减少无机磷的用量，同时又可减少磷的排放对水、土壤等资源的污染。

第三章 渔 业

1991～2005年，天津市推行多品种资源增殖放流技术、实施严格的休渔期、禁渔区制度，保护渔业资源再生；利用生物育种技术、新型饵料制剂、水处理与循环水技术等诸多高新技术，发展海淡水养殖业。天津渔业实现从数量型向质量、效益型的转变。至2005年，天津市无公害水产品生产基地108处、总面积3.4万公顷；制定水产标准59项，其中3项国家行业标准；渔业科技社团组织27个、成员5千多人；完成部、市级科研项目151项；获国家农业部科技进步奖1项，国家农牧渔业丰收奖6项，其中“对虾病害综合防治技术”获1998年全国农牧渔业丰收奖一等奖；获天津市科技进步奖33项，天津市星火科技奖7项；获授权专利12项。

第一节 资 源

20世纪90年代的资源调查表明，渤海生态型渔业资源呈大幅下降趋势。1991～2005年，在中国海洋渔业结构实行战略性调整的背景下，天津市在海淡水渔业资源增殖上加大引进、研发力度，开创出一个新局面。

一、资源调查

1991年，天津市水产研究所刘厚义等参加农业部“八五”攻关特立的三省一市（辽宁省、河北省、山东省、天津市）“渤海渔业增养殖技术研究”项目的子课题“渤海对虾资源预报”及“渤海对虾放流技术研究”专题项目。他们依托课题开展天津海区潮间带水域中国对虾仔虾及幼虾行动分布及资源量的调查，摸索出仔虾和幼虾在该水域的行动分布规律，提出潮间带水域是中国对虾仔虾和幼虾生长发育的重要场所，水域环境优劣直接影响仔虾和幼虾的生长与存活。从1991年至1998年，天津市水产研究所每年对天津海区对虾资源进行春、秋两次预报，春季采集对虾卵、秋季捕捞秋虾，预报对虾资源情况，并对放流的对虾苗进行跟踪调查。

1992年和1998年，中国水产科学研究院 黄海水产研究所在渤海进行周年拖网调查，分析渤海主要渔业生物种类资源的变化特征。结果表明，20世纪90年代初期，渤海最重要的对虾、小黄鱼、带鱼资源已严重衰退，而小型中上层鱼类，如：鳀鱼、黄鲫、斑鰶等逐渐成为渤海渔业种类的优势种。到20世纪90年代末期，渤海中各生态型渔业资源都呈大幅度下降趋势，主要种类的生物量下降至历史最低水平。渤海湾近岸部分海域渔业资源的密度仅为80年代末期的1/10。

天津近海渔业可捕到的鱼虾蟹贝类有：黄鲫、斑鰶、银鲳、赤鼻棱鳀、蓝点马鲛、小黄鱼、鳀鱼、梭鱼、棘头梅童鱼、中国对虾、口虾蛄、三疣梭子蟹及多种贝类。捕获量不稳定，贝类占很大比例。其中，1991年，天津海区鱼类捕获量比1990年减产34%，对虾比1990年减产29%，贝类比1990年增产86%；2002年，近海捕捞产量比2001年减幅6.95%；2004年，天津海区捕捞产量比2003年减幅16.35%；2005年，近海捕捞产量比2004年增幅12.17%，其中底栖贝类产量增加1.13倍，但与2002年以前相比还是负增长。另据塘沽区记载，该区2005年近海捕捞产量与1990年对比，鱼类减少45.77%，虾类减少15.62%，蟹类减少79.65%，贝类增加10.28倍，其他减少58.26%。原有的名优海水产品及经济型鱼类资源衰竭，捕捞的主要品种变成为虾蛄。

专家分析，造成渔业资源衰退及种群生物量变化与捕捞强度过大，近海环境污染，入海径流剧减有直接关系。

二、资源增殖

（一）水库增殖放流

1991年，天津市水产研究所王玉佩、天津市农学院倪守明等进行“大银鱼资源保护及人工繁殖技术研究”。课题研究认定天津一些水库中的大银鱼在分类学上属于鲱形总目、胡瓜鱼亚目、银鱼科、新银鱼亚科、大银鱼属、大银鱼；摸清了大银鱼食性、雌雄鱼区别、生长发育、繁殖规律及危害大银鱼生存的凶猛鱼类、栖息水域环境条件等；提出保护与增殖大银鱼资源的技术措施：严格控制捕捞强度；在农田纳水期间，应设置多层网具防止幼鱼流失，确保大银鱼资源再生。课题组一方面采用人工受精技术进行大银鱼的繁殖，即将受精卵移植到水库或在水库中设置孵化箱等。1992年，天津北郊水库、武清县于庄水库、塘沽区黄港一库、黄港二库、蓟县于桥水库都有大银鱼受精卵移植，经一段时间后的检查试捕，均有大银鱼成体出现。其中，以武清县于庄水库回捕率最高，移植效果最好。另一方面，课题组进行大银鱼的成体移植试验，成功后进行推广。1993年冬，塘沽黄港一库从北塘水库移入大银鱼成鱼104.5千克，黄港二库移入221.5千克。1994年4月，发现水库中大银鱼已繁殖出下一代，有4厘米长的大银鱼幼鱼。是年10月，经现场验收预测，两库大银鱼资源量达2.6万千克。“大银鱼资源保护及人工繁殖技术研究”成果，获天津市1995年度科技进步二等奖。

在20世纪90年代，天津大部分水库配置了鱼种繁殖场，如北辰区的水金水库、大兴水库等等，定期向水库投放鱼苗，实现自繁自养。

1993～1994年，蓟县水产局对于桥水库实施增殖放流，投入水库池沼公鱼受精卵4亿粒，大银鱼受精卵1000万粒。1999年，蓟县水产局进一步加大增殖放流力度：确定每年投入40万元用于增殖放流；对水库执行休渔期管理；对捕捞网具做出限制性规定。于是，于桥水库每年5月15日至7月15日封库；捕捞网具只允许使用粘网，且网孔不小于53毫米，其他如拦河网、扣网、扎网、各种网箔等，均不允许使用。

1998年，津南水库试投放匙吻鲟鱼、太湖银鱼、大口胭脂鱼等新品种。利用水库多品种散养开始形成规模。1999～2000年，蓟县水产局除投入于桥水库池沼公鱼受精卵1亿粒外，还投放武昌鱼、草鱼、鲢鳙鱼等大规格鱼种270万尾。2001～2005年，蓟县水产局共投入池沼公鱼受精卵近10亿粒，投放鲂鱼、草鱼、鲢鳙鱼、细鳞斜颌鲴等大规格鱼种近1500万尾。

（二）海区增殖放流

20世纪90年代初期，海区增殖放流以中国对虾苗为主，1991至1993年连续3年放流中国对虾，每年近4000万尾。1998年放流日本对虾苗4000万尾，当年秋汛回捕率达10%。

2003年，天津海区增殖实施多品种放流，放流的鱼类有：红鳍东方豚、梭鱼、牙鲆；虾蟹类有：中国对虾、三疣梭子蟹；贝类有：栉孔扇贝、毛蚶、青蛤、杂色蛤等。

2004年，塘沽区放流红鳍东方豚鱼苗12万尾，汉沽区放流牙鲆20万尾，红鳍东方豚15万尾。2005年，天津市水产局组织实施5次大规模的增殖放流活动，在汉沽区、塘沽区、大港区外海滩涂投放毛蚶、梭鱼、三疣梭子蟹、栉孔扇贝、红鳍东方豚共计1981万尾（粒），并结合落实伏季休渔制度，对贝类增殖生态保护区进行严格管理。

2002年，市农委开始实施滩涂贝类资源养护增殖和开发利用计划。2002～2005年，市农委累计投放经济贝类种苗6.6亿粒，兰蛤12万千克，种苗资金投入124.8万元。2003年，汉沽区外海滩涂建立35平方千米的贝类增殖生态自然保护区，投放栉孔扇贝200万粒，青蛤65万粒，并实行3年休渔。休渔期间禁止任何破坏海域生态环境和采捕贝类资源的渔业活动。2003年，塘沽区等参加国家"863"项目"渤海典型海岸带生态环境修复技术"的课题实施，在塘沽区驴驹河10平方千米的滩涂开辟为增养殖保护区，投放青蛤、文蛤、菲律宾蛤仔、毛蚶、泥螺、沙蚕等经济生物共计2062万尾，设立采捕区、增殖区和养殖区，实行轮捕轮放。2004年，市农委在大港区实施"青蛤人工育苗和增养殖技术示范与推广"项目，划定贝类增殖生态保护区。2005年，塘沽区在驴驹河外海低潮线5米处海域利用92只大小报废渔船沉入海底，建立1.44平方千米的人工鱼礁，建成鱼类产卵、索饵和密集生长的场所。并已在人工鱼礁群区域投放牙鲆鱼苗20万尾，毛蚶10吨。

（三）捕捞结构调整

1999年，中国海洋渔业结构实行战略性调整，首次提出海洋捕捞产量"零增长"目标，后进一步提出"负增长"目标，坚持稳定近海捕捞，积极发展远海、远洋渔业捕捞方针。2002年，天津市启动减船减网、渔民转产转业重大政策。至2005年，全市渔船拆解数量占33.8%，功率减少22.1%，转产渔民938人。全市尚有机动渔船759艘、功率50385千瓦。在稳定近海捕捞方面，加强了渔政执法管理，采取控制近海捕捞船只与处罚海上违规作业等措施。

1993～1995年，天津海洋捕捞公司分别在西非与印度尼西亚（阿拉弗拉海）海域开辟了远洋渔场。以拖网、流刺网为主，捕捞品种主要是带鱼和黄鱼。使用拟饵钓技术捕获鱿鱼、金枪鱼。进入21世纪，天津市远海、远洋捕捞业稳步发展。2001年，中国与韩国签订中韩渔业协定，天津每年约有50艘渔船进入韩国专属经济区水域捕鱼作业，年捕捞量约2000吨。远海、远洋渔业通过引进先进技术与设备，如：超低温冷冻保鲜设备、拟饵鱿鱼钓及灯光诱导捕捞等，捕捞效率提高，效益增加，成为天津市渔业发展中一个主要经济增长点。

第二节 繁育 养殖

天津市依靠科技拓展水产良种繁育，品种多样化、优质化，养殖模式向着工厂化、规模化、集约化、休闲化、无公害化发展。2005年，天津市淡水养殖面积达3.7万公顷，养殖产量近28万吨。其中，有54家工厂化养殖厂（海水34个，淡水20个），总养殖水面达23万平方米。

一、繁育

（一）虾类育苗

1990～1991年，塘沽区水产局刘桂友等承担天津市海水苗种繁育项目"亲虾人工越冬、育苗配套技术研究"，他们选择优质养殖虾作为亲虾，通过专池培育，控制交尾、入室越冬，并经过强化培育，成功地用人工越冬亲虾繁育出对虾早苗。解决海捕亲虾不足、出苗晚等问题。

1993年，流行性虾病波及全国，天津损失惨重，促使对对虾养殖品种结构的调整。1994～1996年，塘沽区水产局承担市科委立项课题“南美白对虾全人工繁育技术研究”。南美白对虾是养殖虾中的优良品种之一。天津市水产技术推广站在天津地区首次从福建及南海沿岸的育苗厂引进南美白对虾种苗，进行养殖试验。2004年，天津农学院孙成渤等在天津警备区八一盐场育苗厂先后引进4000对南美白对虾F2代亲虾，在亲虾培育、交配、产卵、幼体培育及控制水源等方面，采取一系列技术措施，当年人工繁育出虾苗15.1亿尾，成功地在天津首次大规模繁殖南美白对虾。至2005年底，天津对虾育苗产量达到56亿尾，其中南美白对虾苗为46亿尾。

（二）蟹类育苗

1991年，天津市水产研究所马维林等实施“河蟹人工繁养综合技术示范工程”，他们采取调整鲜活饵料品种、控制饵料投喂量，加大换水、清污力度等技术措施，突破河蟹繁殖工厂化育苗难关，首次育出河蟹苗种50多千克。1994年，育出蟹苗达400千克。获1994年度天津市星火科技三等奖。

1993年，塘沽区水产局刘桂友等完成了“河蟹人工控制交尾越冬及育苗试验”项目，该项目采用优选亲蟹、雌雄分养、海水过渡、强化培育、秋季交尾、海水越冬的技术措施，提高了亲蟹的质量。

1995年，天津市农学院水产系顾景龄等针对养殖河蟹个体小、性早熟、抗病能力下降等种质退化问题，开展“河蟹染色体、大颚器官和控制幼蟹性腺早熟”的研究。发现苗种无序交流、频繁南北交叉调运，导致各水系河蟹种质严重混杂，是造成种质退化的主要原因，并提出相应的控制措施。1995～1998年，通过课题成果推广，共实现利税近5000万元。

1995年，天津市塘沽区水产局王振和等进行“三疣梭子蟹全人工繁养技术示范”试验取得成功。从2002~2005年，天津市每年繁育三疣梭子蟹苗种500千克以上。

2000年，天津市水产研究所孙金生等进行“优质河蟹筛选培育技术研究”。他们利用膜片钳技术研究河蟹性早熟的神经内分泌调控机制，揭示出河蟹性早熟形成的原因。通过对海河水系与长江、辽河水系的河蟹进行种群特征比较，确定出判别海河水系河蟹种群形态的特征；利用遗传学原理，采用选择育种方法，结合遗传标记技术，筛选培育出适应天津地区养殖的优质河蟹。

（三）鱼类育苗与引种

天津市淡水鱼人工繁育品种主要有：鲢鳙鱼、草鱼、团头鲂鱼、鲤鱼、彭泽鲫鱼、尼罗罗非鱼、甲鱼、白鲳鱼、湘鲫鱼、斑点叉尾鮰、澳洲宝石鲈及观赏鱼和热带鱼。2005年，天津市生产淡水鱼种苗22.6亿尾，产量为1.6万吨。

海水鱼类人工繁育品种主要有：梭鱼、金头鲷鱼、大菱鲆、褐牙鲆、漠斑牙鲆、大西洋鲷、河豚、石斑鱼、美国红鱼、鲈鱼等。从20世纪90年代开始为适应市场的需求，在人工繁育海水鱼方面，取得了许多新的突破，掌握了一些优质鱼类的繁育技术。

20世纪80年代末期，天津市换新水产良种场的金万昆等研究淡水鱼类杂交技术，用红鲫中的长尾鲫雌鱼和白鲫雄鱼杂交，获得红白长尾鲫。再由红白长尾鲫进行自交繁殖，经12年选育，培育出F5代红白长尾鲫，体色、体型和鳍形等遗传性状稳定在90%以上。蓝花长尾鲫是利用金鱼与彩鲫杂交，经14年培育出F6代，为定向系统选育而成的新品种。墨龙鲤的人工繁育是利用锦鲤混合交配的后代中的黑色个体建立的自交系，再由自交系繁育的黑色个体后代逐代选育至F6代，育成黑色的墨龙鲤。以上3个杂交品种既可观赏，亦可食用，很受养殖户与消费者的欢迎。2002年10月，该研究成果经全国水产原种和良种审定委员会审定、国家农业部批准，确定为国内观赏鱼新品种，获天津市名牌产品。2003年，该成果正式大批量进行人工繁育生产，继而在欧洲和东南亚地区打开市场。

1991～1995年，天津农学院水产科学系董仕等进行“鲤鱼三倍体的诱导及应用研究”，人工诱导三倍体培育的鱼类有不育、生长速度快的特点，不仅可以提高养殖产量，还可避免因近亲杂交而造成的种质退化。该课题获1995年度天津市科技进步二等奖。

1992年，天津市水产技术推广站杨金江、赵嗣宾、刘金全等承担实施“长江原种白鲢鱼的引进和养殖技术推广”。该课题通过养殖引进的长江原种白鲢鱼的水花种苗及成鱼，使天津市白鲢鱼实现良种化。

1993年，天津市水产技术推广站与蓟县水产局引进池沼公鱼受精卵4亿粒，采取网箱保护孵化，自然放流仔鱼苗，投入于桥水库。1995年春，捕捞池沼公鱼22.5万千克，产值达202.5万元。

1998年，农业部水产技术推广总站从俄罗斯引进乌克兰鳞鲤受精卵，由天津市换新水产良种场负责培育，成功后在天津地区推广养殖。乌克兰鳞鲤的优点表现为杂食性、出肉率高、耐低温、生长快、易驯化、易起捕、适宜池塘养殖。

2001年，天津农学院水产科学系从哈萨克斯坦引进丁鱥亲鱼150组，次年又从新疆引进3000尾后备亲鱼进行人工繁殖成功。

塘沽区水产局研究开发“红鳍东方鲀冬季育苗及当年养成”项目，2004年通过验收。该项目通过人工控制生物学密度及性腺发育积温，实现早期繁育。该局于20世纪末期先后从英国、法国引进大菱鲆初孵仔鱼、大西洋王鲷初孵仔鱼，并开展人工育苗。一些优质鱼类如：褐牙鲆、美国红鱼、鲈鱼、漠斑牙鲆等人工育苗也相继取得成功。

汉沽区在2005年培育牙鲆卵7千克，大菱鲆卵4千克，育出牙鲆155万尾，大菱鲆苗26.5万尾。

2005年，天津市海水鱼种苗产量达到800多万尾，主要集中在塘沽区与汉沽区两地。

1991～2005年，天津市水产研究所和天津农学院水产科学系进行30余项人工繁育苗种技术研究，引进20多种优质鱼类品种。

（四）贝类繁育

1991年，天津市水产研究所承担天津市科委“海湾扇贝人工孵化育苗”项目，1994年天津市水产研究所渤海资源增殖站开展海湾扇贝育苗，2000年后，市科委与市农委组织开展贝类育苗技术研究，培育适合天津海区生长的贝类品种。

2004年，大港区承担市科委“青蛤人工育苗和增养殖技术研究与开发”项目，进行室内、室外、土池人工育苗及青蛤增养殖等试验，摸清了天津地区青蛤繁殖期，确定人工培育青蛤种苗适宜的饵料品种、幼体密度及水质状况等因子的指标，取得人工培育青蛤种苗成功经验，当年通过验收。

2004年，天津市水产研究所主持，协同中国水产科学研究院东海水产研究所承担天津市2004年重大农业科技合作项目“青蛤增养殖技术示范”。项目组率先开展青蛤人工促熟技术研究，首次进行青蛤人工促熟诱导排卵试验，并取得成功。人工促熟的青蛤比自然成熟青蛤早1个月成熟产卵，所培育的稚贝规格比同期自然繁殖的大5倍，有利于培育较大规格的苗种。项目组还开展以云微藻为主的开口饵料系列研究，成功解决青蛤幼虫开口饵料品种单一的问题，取得青蛤工厂化育苗技术性突破。

（五）水处理技术

1996年，天津市水产研究所朱福庆等开展“水产品育苗水处理技术”研究，设计出大容量高效率环流混合式双作用臭氧水处理系统，具有处理水量和臭氧投加量连续可调功能。研制的臭氧水处理器在水产养殖与水产育苗中成功解决循环水的净化问题。臭氧是一种强氧化剂，可有效灭杀水中的细菌，脱除水体污染色泽，降低水中生物耗氧量（BOD）和化学耗氧量（COD），使工厂化养殖与育苗生产中的水可以循环使用。

2000年，天津市静海县使用微生态制剂调节水质，在南美白对虾养殖中推广使用。微生态制剂可以用来降解水体中多余的能量，改善水环境，连续使用对养殖的鱼虾有预防疾病的功能。塘沽区、东丽区相继在水产养殖中推广使用微生物制剂，都收到很好效果。常用的微生态制剂有光合细菌、芽孢杆菌、乳酸菌、酵母菌、硝化细菌以及EM复合菌制剂等。

2002年，天津市水产研究所孙广明开始研究臭氧发生器与臭氧水处理装置，4年取得3项实用新型专利和2项发明专利。是年，孙广明与清华大学生物科学与技术系及北京国泉臭氧技术开发中心共同进行“臭氧水处理器在水产品育苗、养殖、与贝类净化中的中试应用”研究，设计研制出双作用循环混合式臭氧水处理装置，首次提出微量臭氧对水产养殖水质净化的机理，设计出微量臭氧净化池塘水质的工艺模式。该研制设备可用于全封闭循环水工厂化育苗、养殖、及鱼虾病害防治，也可在畜禽养殖及蔬菜、水果保鲜等方面推广应用。

二、养殖

（一）对虾、三疣梭子蟹池塘养殖

20世纪90年代初，天津市池塘养殖中国对虾技术已经成熟，池塘海水养虾面积达到4000多公顷，并形成较为完整的对虾养殖产业体系。在此基础上，天津市农委副食处、天津市水产技术推广站、天津农学院等单位，在大港、汉沽等区实施“降低成本的养虾综合技术示范工程”，推广面积1393公顷，通过对对虾基础饵料的培养、对虾苗种的中间培育、养殖水质监测、人工配合饵料的使用及虾鱼、虾贝套养等技术研究，两年总产对虾424.914万千克，每千克虾降低成本4元。研究成果获1991年度天津市星火科技二等奖。

1993年，塘沽区驴驹河首次利用1.47公顷土池试养三疣梭子蟹。1995年，在三疣梭子蟹育苗取得突破的基础上，梭子蟹与对虾混养取得成功。2001年塘沽、汉沽两区总养殖面积已达1220公顷。

1995年，天津市汉沽区杨家泊镇与天津市农学院水产科学系荣长宽等在杨家泊进行“中国对虾全封闭养殖技术研究”，3年累计获得利税达3870.60万元。研究成果获1997年度天津市科技进步二等奖。

2000年，天津市水产技术推广站和汉沽、塘沽区水产技术推广站张勤、李连同、刘宗豹等根据国家农业部“对虾精养健康养成技术规范”，在汉沽区杨家泊镇与塘沽区宁车沽乡的347公顷水面上进行了“对虾健康养殖技术”试验，采取改造虾池，建立封闭或半封闭的养虾循环系统，用小面积、高水位、高盐度海水配兑淡水，抽取地下半咸水、沉淀海水等技术措施，进行对虾精养。2000～2001年两年合计总产对虾382.15万千克，总利润为5921.96万元。

2000年，天津市水产技术推广站和津南、北辰、塘沽区水产技术推广站张勤、张福芸、赵明、刘宗豹等进行“名优虾类品种引进及培育淡化养殖技术研究”。引进新品种南美白对虾、刀额新对虾进行养殖试验，摸索出虾苗淡化的最佳时期、虾苗淡化过程中对盐度的敏感指标及盐度随时间下降幅度指标、淡化用水的物化指标及淡化时间与虾苗投放的最佳时机；同时成功研究出混养、二茬养殖等技术模式，并制定出海虾淡养综合防病技术措施。该项目获2001年度天津市科技进步二等奖。

2001年，在海水养殖业继续稳定在中国对虾精养高产模式的基础上，天津市水产技术推广站和汉沽、塘沽、大港区水产技术推广站张勤、刘宗豹、张学彬、夏德庆等进行“海水名特优水产品养殖技术推广”，养殖方式为三疣梭子蟹与对虾混养、红鳍东方鲀与对虾混养、日本对虾两茬养殖。推广面积为1533公顷，采取池塘改造、增加暂养区、池塘清淤消毒及肥水、种苗暂养、水质调控、翻耕疏松池底、病害防治等技术措施，产三疣梭子蟹49.05万千克，红鳍东方鲀22.8万千克，中国对虾36.86万千克，日本对虾22.5万千克。总产量131.24万千克，总利润2613.34万元。改变了过去海水养殖单一的“一条虾”养殖模式，获2003年度天津市科技进步二等奖。

随着淡水养殖南美白对虾获得成功，养殖技术迅速推广，掀起天津市内陆淡水池塘养虾热潮。2001年，天津市淡水养殖南美白对虾面积为533公顷，产量633吨。到2005年天津市淡水养殖南美白对虾养殖面积超过6667公顷，产量达到2.2万吨，南美白对虾养殖成为天津市调整水产养殖品种结构的典范。

2001年，天津市宁河县天祥水产有限公司进行“在膜覆盖生态系统中南美白对虾优质、高效养殖技术的研究”，借鉴海南地区的养虾模式并加以创新，将大池塘改为0.3～0.4公顷的小池塘，采用土工膜覆盖，配备贮水池、养成池、沉淀池、生物净化池，设置排污系统，构成膜覆盖生态系统，有效地控制高密度养虾易产生水质污染的问题。其结果平均亩产1208千克，最高单产1510千克，平均亩效益12080元。2002年，对此大面积推广。

（二）河蟹池塘养殖

1992年，天津市水产技术推广站周希明、时建伟等对“天津市鱼蟹混养综合增产技术”进行研究，并在天津市的静海、汉沽、宁河、西青、大港、东丽、北辰等区县进行推广性试验，当年推广1673公顷，1993年推广1707公顷，两年向市场提供鲜鱼664.28万千克，活蟹59.31万千克。

1993年，“河蟹精养配套技术的研究”历经7年实施结出硕果，其蟹苗大面积暂养成活率达到70%，最高达到90%，蟹苗亩产165千克，成蟹亩产175千克，该项目由天津市宁河县与天津农学院顾景龄等合作完成。

1994年，天津市水产局时建伟、张勤、赵嗣宾等实施“天津市十万亩河蟹增养殖技术推广”项目，运用河蟹增养殖技术，推广池塘、洼淀鱼蟹混养；稻田培养蟹种；池塘精养蟹种；水库河蟹增殖等增养殖生产模式，达到增加河蟹产量，提高经济效益的目的。1994～1995年，该项目在天津市的9个区县推广河蟹养殖面积达12280公顷，共产成蟹75.47万千克，蟹种47.56万千克，增加利润5787.83万元；鲜鱼1211.30万千克；稻谷404.50万千克。总产值17478.95万元，利润8976.03万元。该项目获1995年度天津市科技进步二等奖。

1994年，宁河县水产技术推广站承担“天津市十万亩河蟹增养殖技术推广”项目的子课题。该县七里海地区是天津河蟹的主要产区，1991年，其河蟹养殖面积达到1333公顷。1992年，该县水产技术推广站承担“天津市鱼蟹混养综合增产技术”项目子课题，开发稻田养蟹、池塘精养、大水面粗养等模式。2000年，该县推广大规模生态养殖模式，池塘精养河蟹最高亩产量达到201千克。2002年，七里海河蟹被评为“天津市名牌农产品”，钓河蟹的休闲渔业迅速发展起来。2005年，其垂钓面积达33公顷，创造可观的经济、社会效益。是年，宁河县畜牧水产局从河蟹种质入手与天津市水产研究所共同实施“七里海优质河蟹繁养技术研究与示范”项目。

（三）鱼类池塘养殖

20世纪90年代初期，天津市水产局科教处、天津市水产技术推广站、市农委副食处、天津农学院水产系吕祖哲、吾福荣、杨金江等进行了“天津市鱼禽结合生态养鱼技术开发”研究。通过鱼与畜禽的生物结构，合理配置优化组合养殖，实现能量和物质的合理流动，构成鱼与畜禽养殖系统的良性循环。1991年推广试验1640公顷，1992年推广试验6053公顷。该项目获1992年度天津市星火科技二等奖。

1992年，市农委副食处、天津市水产技术推广站、天津农学院水产科学系、塘沽区水产局等共同进行“鲫鱼大面积高产及混养技术开发”研究，提出“一年两季，两年三茬”以及反季节商品鱼养殖模式。鲫鱼高产面积达910公顷，新增效益705.59万元，鲫鱼混养面积达2057公顷，新增效益406.08万元。该项目获1994年度天津市星火科技二等奖。

1994年，由天津市水产局主持，杨金江、支宗伟、缴建华等实施“十万亩名特优水产品增养殖技术推广”，利用已成功的名特优水产品增养殖技术，大范围推广淡水白鲳、革胡子鲶、梭鱼、加州鲈鱼、斑点叉尾鮰、鳜鱼等的池塘套养和大水面增殖技术，池沼公鱼水库移植技术。1994～1995年推广面积1.95万公顷，产鱼4134.41万千克，名特优水产品总产量214.94万千克。该项目获1995年度天津市科学技术进步二等奖。

1995年，由天津市水产局主持，郑广友、赵凤武、刘金全等进行的“大水面网栏养鱼技术”研究，成功地开发出：网栏结构、混养鱼种类、品种比例、饲养管理、鱼病综合防治及捕捞等技术。在天津市北大港水库设网栏，养殖面积达133公顷，取得亩产168.94千克，亩利润827.70元，总产值223.24万元的效益。

1996～1998年，天津市水产技术推广站张勤、缴建华等进行“天津市名特优水产品增养殖综合技术推广”，推广淡水名特优品种有良种异育银鲫、方正鲫、彭泽鲫、革胡子鲶、大口鲶、斑点叉尾鮰、鳜鱼、大银鱼等，海水名特优品种有中国对虾、三疣梭子蟹、河鲀、鲈鱼、梭鱼。采用池塘主套养技术、大水面“三网”的主套养技术、大水面增养殖技术、稻田养鱼蟹技术。3年推广养殖面积达12.13万公顷，产量达95585.13吨、经济效益达60086.70万元。该项目获1999年度天津市科学技术进步二等奖。

1997年，由天津市水产局主持，缴建华、郑广友、田金国等承担完成“池塘主养鲂鱼高产技术推广”项目，以鲂鱼占80%的比例进行饲养，使用淡水枝角类和海淡水鱼虾等代替鱼粉、配制低成本的人工配合颗粒饲料，采取中西医结合防治鱼病技术。推广面积186.7公顷，产鱼305.16万千克，其中鲂鱼224.97万千克。

1998年，由天津市水产技术推广站的缴建华、包海岩等完成"淡水池塘80:20养鱼模式高产高效技术"推广项目，该项目是农业部渔业局丰收计划项目，推广内容以收获时主、配鱼比例为80:20设计鱼种的投放数量，同时研制鲫鱼、鲂鱼的低成本优质颗粒饲料，健康养殖、综合防治及日常饲养管理技术等等。推广面积2886.7公顷，2年累计总产量2893.49万千克，总产值27784.27万元，总效益7263.64万元。

1999年，天津市水产技术推广站缴建华、包海岩、张勤等对"低洼盐碱地连片池塘高产养鱼技术"进行研究，利用2年的时间，在天津市武清、静海两个县的低洼盐碱地连片池塘上，共计1755.2公顷，采取降低池水盐碱程度的综合调控技术：保持池塘高水位、选择适宜的清塘药物、定期补调池水、施基肥和追施化肥、使用药物及吸附剂调节水质、定期水质监测等；改进养殖模式：根据水质状况选择放养或套养种类及放养密度、精选优质大规模鱼种；选用优质颗粒饲料、科学投饵；坚持预防为主，防治结合的原则，综合防治鱼病。2年的总产量达到1587.62万千克，平均亩产为603.02千克。同年，天津市水产技术推广站张勤等进行"天津市淡水养殖开发新区综合配套技术推广"，采取选择适宜低洼盐碱地池塘养殖的鱼类、结合鱼病综合防治技术、全价人工颗粒饲料的配制及投喂、水质调控等技术。至2002年累计推广面积6364公顷，总产量65046.9吨。该项目获2002年度天津市科学技术进步二等奖。

（四）甲鱼集约化养殖

1996年，天津农学院邢克智等与天津市西青区小南河养殖公司、天津市蓟县水产局共同完成了"中华鳖（甲鱼）集约化养殖技术的研究"。该项目确定出一种新的鳖卵孵化介质和鳖卵孵化生态因子的适宜范围；根据鳖在各个生长阶段对营养的需求，研制出系列饵料配方及添加剂预混料和能够提高鳖非特异性抗病能力的中草药添加剂，以及其他具有生物活性的物质。商品化生产的鳖生产周期从3～4年缩短到1年，亩产量从500千克提高到3000千克，达到高产、高效、优质、无公害的效果，被列为天津市名牌产品。该项目获1996年度天津市科技进步二等奖。

（五）工厂化养殖

1995年，天津市西青区德仁水产养殖中心建成。该淡水工厂化养殖厂建有微流水养殖车间1.2万平方米，平均深度2.0至2.5米。养殖品种有埃及革胡子鲶、乌鳢鱼、罗非鱼、淡水白鲳、美国嘎鱼（云斑鮰鱼）、长江杂交鲶等8个品种，以革胡子鲶为主养鱼，最高产量可达2000千克每平方米。2004年产革胡子鲶400多万千克，效益200多万元。

图6-3-2-99　工厂化养鱼实用技术研究

1996年，天津市精武水产种业有限公司建设其繁育养殖工厂化基地。2000年，该养殖厂内建成12座设施化养殖车间，总面积2.7万平方米，引进鲟鱼进行规模养殖。2001年，从新疆引进丁岁鱼3400尾，亲鱼30尾，从广州引进条纹鲈3500尾，从宁河引进加州鲈1000组进行繁育养殖。

1998年，天津市水产研究所李文抗等承担天津市重点攻关项目"工厂化养鱼实用技术研究"，在静海天津市水产引育种中心设计建成1000平方米车间、160立方米水体的工厂化养殖的专用设施。该设施有封闭式循环水处理设备，自主设计、研制的臭氧发生器及混合装置，用于水体净化、灭菌；采用生物菌种提取、扩增计量接种等技术，降解水中氮、磷；自主设计的监视监测系统，可以及时观察与获取水质监测数据；自动投饵设备，可以控制投饵时间、次数及数量，提高饲料的利用率。整套设施投资大大低于国内其他同类设施。试验结果折合一年三茬，每立方米产量达到：奥尼罗非鱼226.6千克，白鲳246.6千克；每亩产值达到：奥尼罗非鱼166.1万元，白鲳128万元。

2000年，天津市海发珍品有限公司海水工厂化养殖厂投入使用。该厂设施先进，养殖水面16000平方米，建有高效内循环水养殖系统，总循环量为每小时7040立方米，110分钟就可将养殖用水全部循环一次，平均产量为30千克每平方米。在水处理方面，具有液态纯氮、臭氧灭菌、高效内循环和水质监控等配套设施，可以在全封闭、内循环条件下进行高密度生产。在生物净化技术方面，采用接种活菌制剂的方法降解和转化水中的氨氮，除去氨氮的效率可达80%以上。

至2005年，天津市有54家工厂化养殖厂，其中海水养殖厂34个，淡水养殖厂20个，总养殖水面达23万平方米。海水养殖品种主要有：牙鲆、石斑鱼、大菱鲆、大西洋鲷、金鲳鱼、条纹鲈、黑鲷等。淡水养殖品种主要有：鲟鱼、鲈鱼、斑点叉尾鮰、淡水黑鲷、鳜鱼、美国红鱼、罗非鱼、鲶鱼、白鲳鱼、热带鱼、观赏鱼等。具有一定规模的海水养殖厂有：天津市诺恩水产技术发展有限公司、天津市汉沽欣亿达养殖有限公司、天津市汉沽恒孚水产技术开发有限公司天津市西青区兴旺水产公司。

（六）水产养殖机械化

1996～1997年，市农机部门实施的国家农业部丰收计划项目，“天津市池塘养鱼机械化配套技术推广”项目，完成养殖池塘的池体环境改造机械化设计，高效节能水体溶氧机械化设计，全价饲养配料制、抛投机械化设计，重点推广了自动投饵机械化技术和鱼病综合防治技术。

至2005年，天津市水产养殖机械保有量发展到1.234万台。期间，1990年，渔用机动船794艘，增氧机1632台，饵料机202台，投饵机67台，合计2695台；1999年，渔用机动船1562艘，增氧机8591台，池塘挖掘机1183台，合计1.13台，2000～2004年，养鱼机械化设备基本稳定在1.04万台左右。

第三节 饲料 病害防治与安全保障

1991～2005年，天津市开发出多种饲料添加剂、中草药制剂、中西药物复合剂等，在后期开始实施无公害水产品行动计划。

一、饲料、药物

（一）饲料

天津市水产研究所李立真等根据国外资料报道，研发成功“FA-101”饲料添加剂。至1993年，经5年多推广试用表明，该添加剂对鲤鱼、鲑鱼、虹鳟等鱼类生长发育有显著促进作用，并能提高幼鱼成活率、增强免疫力及鱼肉鲜美度。

1996年，天津市水产研究所王玉佩等进行“鱼用饲料有毒有害成分及控制技术的研究”。提出饲料中“毒绵酚”的安全限量，研发出可转化“毒绵酚”的添加剂。

2000年，天津农学院水产系白东清、乔秀亭等开展复合酶和植酸酶研究，开发出多种新型非营养性鱼用饲料添加剂。发表《复合酶制剂对鲤氮磷钙利用率的影响》《植酸酶对鲤肠、肝胰脏蛋白酶活性的影响》等多篇论文。该非营养性添加剂系指微生态制剂、酶制剂与中草药制剂等，可提高饲料营养物质利用率与减少氨氮的排放，具有安全环保功能。

2003年，天津市水产研究所、天津市水产技术推广站、天津市无公害水产品管理办公室共同实施天津市农业科技重点项目“无公害鱼用配合饲料、药物应用技术推广”。在133公顷养殖面积中，使用无公害鱼用配合饲料2600吨，生产无公害彭泽鲫9万千克，经农业部天津渔业环境质量监督检验站抽测，产品符合无公害水产品鲫鱼质量标准。

2004年，天津农学院水产系的乔秀亭、白东清、邢克智等发明一项专利“虾复合预混料”，该产品主要成分有多种维生素、矿物质、氯化胆碱及离子掩蔽剂，具有提高饵料利用率和改善水质的作用。离子掩蔽剂既能掩蔽饵料中某些金属离子对消化酶的抑止，又不影响虾对这些离子的吸收，使虾的生长速度提高10%以上。

（二）药物

1991年，天津市水产研究所王云祥、王玉佩等承担市科委"水产系列药物研究"课题，设计、研制出鱼用高效广谱抗菌内服药"鱼服宁"。鱼服宁的西药成分具有抗菌、阻断细菌蛋白质的合成，干扰细菌早期阶段的糖代谢，起到抑制灭杀细菌作用；中药成分可以消炎、止血、收敛、增进免疫、促进病愈。鱼服宁在天津、河北、山西、内蒙古等地的池塘、网箱养殖上推广试用，效果显著。至1995年，池塘应用已累计达8000公顷，网箱应用达16公顷，有效率为100%，治愈率达70%以上。是年，鱼服宁产品制定出质量标准，天津市药政部门颁发了生产许可证和兽药生产批号。

1995年，天津市水产研究所在"鱼类粘孢子虫病防治技术研究"项目中，筛选研制出抗鱼类粘孢子虫病的中西药复合制剂"鱼服宁2#"。

20世纪90年代末，塘沽区、东丽区开始在水产养殖中推广使用微生物制剂。2000年以后大力推广芽孢杆菌、硝化细菌、EM复合菌、噬菌体等有益微生物制剂，不仅改良了水质，也预防水产品病害的发生。

2002年，天津市水产技术推广站的张勤等在"南美白对虾淡水养殖技术"项目的病害防治研究中，使用微生态制剂——益生菌类调控水质，改善养殖环境，控制疾病发生。在津南区、北辰区、宁河县、汉沽区、静海县推广，使用面积633公顷，总产量252.15万千克，总利润2736.81万元；每亩产量265.42千克，每亩利润2880.85元；其投入产出比为1:2。

2002年，天津农学院水产科学系邢克智等主持承担天津市农业重点攻关项目"南美白对虾人工配合饵料及虾用中草药的研究"。他们通过研究"黄柏对南美白对虾抗氧化及部分免疫活性的影响""枳实对南美白对虾健康的影响""微生态制剂对水产养殖动物的抗病和促长机理的研究进展"，筛选出一些具有诱食效果的中草药和提高鱼虾机体免疫力的中草药。用鲤鱼、鲢鳙鱼、南美白对虾进行试验，效果显著，特别在鲢鳙鱼、鲤鱼出血病防治中发挥了独到的作用。

2004年，天津市水产技术推广站承担了天津市水产局"中草药防治虾病试验"项目，利用传统中医药理论，结合现代中医药研究成果，配制出纯中药制剂。该药不含任何抗生素和激素类药物，无毒副作用，无刺激性，无残留，不产生抗药性。利用水族箱进行实验，对细菌性虾病预防率达80%以上，治疗率70%以上。

二、鱼、虾病害防治

（一）鱼病防治

1989年，全国暴发了淡水鱼类传染性鱼病。受波及，天津市1991年发病面积达4513公顷，占淡水养殖总面积的20.5%，损失产量2344吨。1991年，国家科委将"暴发性鱼病防治技术研究" 立为"八五"科技攻关项目，由浙江省淡水水产研究所和中国科学院水生生物研究所主持，天津市水产研究所王玉佩等负责天津市暴发性鱼病防治技术研究。课题采取定点和随机取样调查相结合的方法对天津市重点发病鱼池进行系统研究，发现暴发性鱼病主要是通过水环境传播，水质恶劣是导致暴发性鱼病的主要原因。课题通过用物理、化学及药物处理养殖用水，并提出免疫预防、药物防治和生态控制等有效易行的多种防治措施。

是年，天津农学院水产科学系的刘茂春、米瑞芙、邢克智等分别对鲢鳙鱼暴发性出血病、白鲢鱼急性出血症及鲤鱼出血性腐败病进行研究，提出综合防治技术，将万亩水面发病率控制在15%以内，发病池鱼的死亡率降到20%以内，试验池塘发病率控制在2%以下，治疗有效率达100%，治愈率达90%以上。1995年"鲤鱼出血性腐败病的研究"获天津市星火科技二等奖。

1995年，天津市水产研究所王玉佩等完成"鱼类粘孢子虫病防治技术"研究。课题对天津地区鲤、鲫鱼类粘孢子虫病病原、流行病学、发病率、死亡率进行系统调查；对鲤、鲫粘孢子虫病的组织病理及血液学进行全面分析、化验，研究了鱼类粘孢子虫病的发病机制及致死的原因；从增强体质、延缓衰竭、杀灭病原体的角度抑制病原感染，研究出了该病的诊断和治疗方法。

2000～2005年，天津农学院水产科学系对天津地区鱼虾病害进行了多方面研究，如：感染疱疹病毒大菱鲆的细胞病理学研究，患肠炎病大菱鲆的组织病理学研究，正常牙鲆与腹水病牙鲆血液生理指标的比较研究，河蟹土池育苗中的敌害——利氏才女虫的防治等。该学院水产科学系蔡中华等对鲑鳟科鱼类的肿瘤坏死因子进行研究，包括该基因的克隆、体外重组、表达与纯化等。

（二）虾病防治

1993年，全国暴发流行性虾病，天津市发病面积高达90%以上，绝收面积占发病面积30%，天津市水产研究所王云祥等承担"对虾暴发性流行病防治及控制技术研究"。课题采用生物学、病理学等方法，首次发现寄生在对虾肝胰脏细胞质内的"对虾立克次氏小体"新病原；提出综合防治方法；，研制出中西药物复合剂"对虾抗毒灵"。

1994～1995年，天津市水产研究所张勤、刘洪锁、李洪光、李连同等在调查天津市沿海地区暴发流行性虾病过程中发现汉沽区杨家泊地区利用高盐度海水兑淡水养殖的对虾发病晚或不发病。据此，进行系统调查研究，认为高盐度海水兑淡水作为养殖水源，隔离了病原传染，是发病晚或不发病的主要原因。1996年，天津水产研究所承担农业部渔业局的全国农牧渔业丰收计划项目"对虾病害综合防治技术"。总结杨家泊地区养殖经验，采取小面积、高水位、精养、混养结合等技术措施，取得显著效果。1996～1997年，该项技术推广面积达402.2公顷，总产量达到70.15万千克。经全国水产技术推广总站审定，天津市汉沽区被评为全国经济技术指标及组织管理工作较好的7个示范区中的第一名。

2000年，天津农学院水产科学系完成《患蓝色肝病的中国对虾的组织与细胞病理学研究》。

养虾池赤潮也是对虾养殖业的主要灾害之一，2003～2005年塘沽区水产局刘桂友等与天津市水产研究所张勤等合作，承担了市科委的"虾池赤潮综合防治及示范工程"项目。

2004年，天津市水产技术推广站张勤等承担"进京水产品标准化生产技术研究"，为保证水产品质量，使用微生态制剂及中草药，保证养殖水环境稳定及鱼虾健康生长，做到在无公害水产品养殖生产中不用药或不用违禁药。示范区的水质状况经农业部渔业环境及水产品质量监督检验测试中心（天津）的测定，均达到无公害养殖用水水质标准。示范区生产的南美白对虾、鲤鱼、鲫鱼、草鱼、梭鱼、花白鲢、褐牙鲆、大菱鲆、石斑鱼经农业部渔业环境及水产品质量监督检验测试中心（天津）的测定，均达到无公害水产品质量标准。

三、病害防治监测

1995年，天津市成立天津市水产养殖病害防治中心。该机构承担水生动物防疫检疫和水产养殖病害防治、水产养殖病害防治技术科研及技术推广、咨询等工作，为天津市及周边地区水产养殖业服务。2000年，全国沿海省市开展了水产养殖病害测报工作试点，天津市作为沿海试点省市之一，由天津市水产养殖病害防治中心承担天津区域水产养殖病害测报工作。到2005年，天津市已建立测报点40个，测报面积达2.7万公顷，占天津市水产养殖总面积的60%以上。每月定期向国家农业部报送测报结果，每年定期撰写工作及病害情况分析报告。根据天津市水产养殖病害防治中心测报，2005年天津市鱼虾病害种类为55种，测报品种有鱼类13种、甲壳类2种。

1995年，天津市水产研究所成立天津市渔业环境监测站。1996年天津市渔业环境监测站加入全国渔业环境监测网，按照全国渔业环境监测网的要求对天津市渔业环境进行检测，1999年完成了渤海湾水生动物的产卵场及洄游通道的常规水化学指标与资源状况的监测。1999年开始筹建"农业部渔业环境及水产品质量监督检验测试中心（天津）"（以下简称"测试中心"）。2002年"农业部渔业环境及水产品质量监督检验测试中心（天津）"通过国家农业部计量认证和农业部实验室机构审查认可。2003年，经天津市技术监督局的计量认证和机构授权成立"天津市质量监督检验站第23站"。2004年，原天津市渔业环境监测站更名为天津市渔业生态环境监测中心，具有渔业生态环境监测、渔业资源监测、微生物及生物病害监测、污染评估及水产品质量监测资质。

2002年，配合无公害水产品行动计划，天津市开始加大水生动物检疫力度，指定天津市水产养殖病害防治中心进驻天津滨海国际机场对进出天津市的水产苗种进行检疫，严把苗种质量关。是年，天津市水产养殖病害防治中心检验检疫全市苗种场17个,检验检疫进出天津市的苗种100批次、16个品种、12亿尾。2004年检疫苗种42亿尾。

2004年,天津市水产养殖业开展了HACCP体系应用,该体系是一种危害控制预防体系,通过对生产全过程进行危害分析和在生产过程中关键环节上的有效控制,保护食品在生产过程中不受危害。2005年,天津市按照HACCP质量保证体系建立了40处无公害水产品生产基地,31个单位取得了《天津市出口水产品产地注册证》,全市4个无公害水产品生产基地生产的南美白对虾和日本对虾获得全国统一标志的无公害水产品认定。2005年,全市新建无公害水产品生产基地108处、总面积3.4万公顷,其中养殖池塘无公害基地面积1万公顷。水库滩涂增殖基地面积2.4万公顷。

四、无公害水产品行动计划

2002年,天津市实施无公害水产品行动计划,组建水产品质量监督检验测试中心,农业部渔业环境及水产品质量监督检验测试中心(天津),并通过农业部计量认证和农业部实验室机构审查认可。该中心可检测水产品21种。2002~2003年。测试中心引进高压液相色谱仪、气相色谱仪、酶标仪等仪器,增加对激素类、抗菌素类物质的检测。2005年,该中心通过农业部扩项评审,检测参数增至181项。

是年,由天津市水产研究所制定相关水产品品种无公害食品标准,制定《淡水池塘养殖水质标准》《无公害水产品养殖基地建设规范》等养殖技术规范。由天津市宁河县制定七里海河蟹养殖、工厂化育苗、养殖环境、醉蟹、河蟹贮存等系列地方标准。2003年,市农委颁布《天津市无公害水产品标志管理办法》(试行),《天津市无公害水产品产地认证程序》与《天津市无公害水产品认证程序》。

2003~2005年,天津市每年开展无公害水产品技术培训与宣传,每年培训相关人员数以千计,发放相关技术资料数以万计。期间全市累计认定无公害水产品产地188处,总面积50910.92公顷,认定养殖面积约占全市统计在册总养殖面积的50%以上。其中,普通养殖面积20604.98公顷,工厂化养殖面积13.01公顷,温棚养殖面积10.13公顷,增殖面积(指水域及滩涂)30282.80公顷。全市累计认证无公害水产品254个,产量12.13万吨,约占全市水产品总产量的38%。

2005年,市农委批准开展无公害生产技术示范,批准项目包括"臭氧技术在养殖业上的应用示范""无公害水产品养殖投入品控制技术"。对无公害水产品养殖基地产地安全管理,包括产地环境、投入品、生产过程管理。养殖用水需达到《无公害食品 淡水养殖用水水质》《无公害食品海水养殖用水水质》两项行业标准。投入品要达到《无公害食品 渔用药物使用准则》《无公害食品渔用配合饲料安全限量》等行业标准。测试中心负责对全市渔业生态环境和水产品质量安全状况实施定期与不定期检测。2005年春节,全市水产品质量安全检测,安排产地、市场、超市36批次的水产品抽样;品种有对虾、牙鲆、鲫鱼、罗非鱼、甲鱼等,检测合格率为100%。

第四章 农业机械化

1990~2005年,天津市农业机械化水平大幅提高:拖拉机由3.606万台增加到4.562万台,联合收获机械由92台增加到2720台;农用运输车由1.953万辆增加到13.94万辆;百亩耕地拥有机械动力83.49千瓦。15年间,天津市农机局组织实施了"农业机械化示范园区建设" "保护性耕作示范""农作物秸秆还田及综合利用""农用航空站建设"等重大农业机械化工程建设项目。完成市农委科技工程关于机械化精播、化肥深施、稻麦连作、秸秆氨化、肉牛饲养、旱作农业等6个重点项目。集成推广技术体系的建设和应用,主要有:保护性耕作机械化、旱地耕作蓄水保墒、秸秆饲料化工程、绿色无害化蔬菜生产综合、新型节能日光温室综合配套、鱼虾养殖机械化配套技术等技术体系。组织实施和推广：稻麦连作机械化综合增产，玉米收获机械化、夏玉米免耕覆盖精量播种机械化、绵花生产机械化、蔬菜保护地机械化、膜下滴灌、鸡粪发酵烘干处理技术等一批农业机械化科技项目。先后研制出：小麦与玉米免耕施肥播种机、全幅玉米联合收割机、绵花拔秆机、葡萄藤掩埋机、温室卷帘机、畜禽废弃物资源化处理设备等机具设备。

第一节 机械化种植

从20世纪80年代起，天津市已经推进粮食作物的全程机械化。1990～2005年，通过机械化旱作节水农业示范区建设和膜下滴灌技术示范工程的实施，推广机械化土壤深耕、深松、小麦机械化免耕播种、机械化秸秆粉碎还田、机械化镇压保墒技术、膜下滴灌技术等农机化新技术。1993年，天津市小麦生产综合机械化水平达到70%。2005年，小麦耕、播、收机械化程度均达到98%以上，实现了全过程机械化。水稻作为天津市三大主要粮食作物之一，种植面积随水资源由丰裕到紧缺，从1998年的56千公顷减少至2005年的13.3千公顷。1991年，天津市水稻播种面积55.06千公顷，机收面积1千公顷，机收水平2%，机具以割晒机为主；2005年，全市稻麦联合收割机159 0台，机收面积4.48千公顷，机收水平为30.5%。玉米是天津市种植面积最大的农作物，但生产过程机械化水平却十分低下。20世纪80年代初，只有西青、宝坻等区县一些集体农场引进北京生产的自走式联合收获机和黑龙江生产的4YW-2型牵引式玉米收获机，数量很少。天津市通过机具补贴、扶持重点企业等方式，促进玉米收获机械化技术的推广应用，玉米生产机械化水平有所提高。天津设施农业在1978年以前是简易落后的状况，没有专用的农机具，到1990年发生了较大的变化，以后逐步提高完善。设施农业生产机械化从2000年起进入快速发展期。2000年，全市拥有温室180.73万平方米，田园管理机500台。2005年，全市拥有2847.3万平方米，田园管理机980台。

一、大田耕作

（一）水田

1990年，水稻收获因国内成熟机型较少，具有防陷装置的小型割晒机仍为水稻收获的首选机型。KC-070型联合收割机和1065型收割机加装履带，也可用于水稻全喂入收获。

1991～1993年，天津市农业机械研究所承担市科委攻关项目“水稻割前脱粒收割机的研制”。张景岐等研制出水稻割前脱粒收割机一台。样机采用割前脱粒收获方式，利用谷物在田间的自然状态，直接将穗头送入脱粒器脱粒，茎秆不进入脱粒器，省去逐篙器和夹持输送装置，以纹秆带式脱粒器取代弓齿式脱粒器，提高了生产率。

1998年，天津市农业机械试验鉴定推广站（以下简称天津农机鉴定推广站）引进日本洋马水稻半喂入收割机。当年水稻半喂入收割机的保有量增至20台，以洋马Ce-1（35马力）、久保田PR0488型两大品牌为主。洋马Ce-1型半喂入收割机配置直喷式柴油发动机，排气量大、功率高、油耗低。采用快速二次脱粒和二次清选系统，脱粒后的谷物和茎秆分别经专用通道，在排尘口副滚筒中再次分离，降低含杂率。久保田PR0488型半喂入收割机加长脱粒筒、扩大清选室，通过再筛选螺旋杆齿对谷物进行二次处理，破碎率低，与主、副脱粒筒二次脱粒方式相比，脱净率高，谷物品质提高。

1999年，天津水稻半喂入收割机保有量为50台，加之引进的跨区作业机具共300台，机收面积40千公顷，机收水平为71%。

天津农机鉴定推广站于1999年承担国家农业部丰收计划项目“天津市稻麦连作机械化综合增产技术推

广”项目，重点推广水稻联合机收技术及稻茬秋麦旋耕播种技术，并在水稻机收、电场种子处理、全方位深松、秸秆还田等多项技术的应用方面取得突破。累计推广稻麦连作机械化种植面积16.6千公顷。

水稻机械化插秧技术的引进示范始于1999年，天津农机鉴定推广站引进两台高速插秧机，在宝坻区八门城镇召开大型现场演示会进行示范推广。两台机具中，一台为日本产洋马6行高速插秧机，另一台为延吉产2行插秧机，由于育秧技术不配套，机械化插秧技术的推广受到制约。

（二）旱田

1.小麦

随着小麦机收跨区作业的开展，机收面积由1990年的94.64千公顷增加到2005年的108千公顷，其中跨区13.87千公顷。小麦收获机械由以割晒机为主，发展到以联合收获机械为主。1990年全市联合收割机73台，机动收割机156台，割晒机4031台，机收水平66%，到2005年自走式联合收割机保有量达2430台，割晒机100台，机收水平增至98%。

1991年，天津农机鉴定推广站在全市大面积推广应用带种肥分施的小麦半精播、小麦沟播机械化技术。即：在秋季耕整地后，使用沟播机一次完成开沟、施肥、播种、覆土、镇压等作业，该技术有利于小麦出苗，使其生长健壮，安全越冬，麦苗分蘖率也明显高于常规播种方式。通过沟播机的推广应用，小麦半精播面积达万亩，提高了小麦播种机械化水平。

1994～1995年，天津市农业机械研究所实施化肥深施机具改进项目，对702A单体播种机进行了改制。课题组变原来单一的楔式开沟器为复合式开沟器，在开沟器底托板上方，安装具有较大前倾角的导肥板，改进后的播种机达到种肥分施的农艺要求，肥深6～8厘米，种深4～4.5厘米，无露种现象，种肥左右水平距离3～4厘米，垂直2～4厘米。

1999～2001年，天津农业机械推广站在实施农业部丰收计划项目“天津市旱地耕作蓄水保墒机械化技术推广”过程中，孙岩等重点推广机械化土壤深耕、深松、机械化秸秆粉碎还田、机械化镇压保墒技术等农机化新技术，使项目区深耕深松推广度达80%，精播30%，半精播60%，机械化秸秆粉碎还田技术达60%。深松作业采用了ISO-2.5型深松联合作业机和ISO-250型全方位深松机。ISO-2.5型深松联合作业机具有深松、浅松和碎土功能，作业后可形成虚实并存的犁底层。ISO-250型全方位深松机松土范围大，碎土效果好，作业同时在深松部件底部形成鼠道，兼有排涝功能。这两种机型配套动力均为东方红75/802拖拉机。机械化镇压不仅能压碎坷粒、封闭裂隙、防止汽态水蒸发，而且可使土粒紧密结合，使土壤水份上升，起到保墒提墒作用。机械化秸秆粉碎还田作业是利用JQ-150型和JQ-180型秸秆还田机将直立作物秸秆切碎后，均匀抛撒于地表，再通过深耕埋入土壤底层，起到改善土壤理化性状，培肥地力，增强土壤蓄水抗旱能力的作用。

2001～2003年，天津市农业机械推广总站实施“天津市机械化旱作节水农业示范区”项目，高宝成等在项目示范区推广旱作节水灌溉机械化技术、保护性耕作机械化技术。重点推广新疆-2型稻麦联合收获机、2BQM-40气吸式免耕精量播种机、秸秆打捆机、3WM-650机动喷雾机、YJP-63×220中型移动卷盘式喷灌机、1GQN-180型旋耕机、2BY-3F小麦播种机、小丰600N型微耕机。示范区旱地种植机械化作业率达到95%，灌溉节水率达到60%。该项目通过综合运用农业工程技术，提升了示范园区示范样板功能和农机化装备水平，为天津市探索“华北滨海半湿润偏旱农业区”机械化旱作节水农业的新途径提供了经验。

2004～2005年，天津市农业机械推广总站以膜下滴灌技术示范工程项目为依托，以滴灌工程规划设计及安装、滴灌管路机械化铺设、机械化铺膜、毛管及塑料残膜回收、作物所需的化肥和农药与水一起滴灌施用等技术为重点，对绵花播种机滴灌带铺设装置进行改进，对温室膜下滴灌技术进行滴灌带横向布置试验。温室膜下滴灌技术的应用，降低农业灌溉成本，提高土地和水资源的利

图6-4-1-100 移动式卷管喷灌机

用率，并有效地提高农作物的产量和品质，增加效益增强市场竞争力，降低自然灾害的风险。

2.玉米

1990年，玉米机播面积30.49千公顷，作业水平20%，机收面积0.81千公顷，机收水平0.5%。2005年，玉米机播面积155.65千公顷，机播水平52.56%，机收面积3.45千公顷，机收水平达1.16%。

1995年，武清县津武玉米收获机厂成立，从河北农业大学引进技术，开始生产与11~12.5千瓦四轮拖拉机配套的4YW-1型单行背负式玉米收获机。该机生产效率达0.13~0.20公顷/小时，水平当时处于领先状态。该机型的特点是结构简单，操作方便，适于中小地块作业，不存在行距适应性问题。1996年产量达到100台，产品销往天津、河北、宁夏、甘肃等地。

1999年，天津富康农业开发有限公司研制出4YW-3型背负式玉米收获机，该机一次可收获3行玉米。2001年，富康公司根据国家科学技术部《关于下达2000年度国家科技计划的通知》要求，在4YW-3型的基础上，开发出4YW-Q型全幅玉米收获机。4YW-Q型全幅玉米收获机的前割台采用独创的摘穗辊式三链型摘穗单体，实现了玉米收获机割台任意行数的配置。在总体设计上，将玉米割台由传统的拉秸秆被动喂入，改变为主动拨禾强制喂入，加置了扶禾装置的辅助配合，提高了摘穗单体的可收获效果。结构配置比传统的收获机更为简单，比原来的3行、4行收获机减少了1～2组摘穗装置，既降低了机具成本，又实现了玉米任意种植行距的全幅收获，解决了传统式玉米收获机必须对行收获，适应性差、效率低、损失率高的难题。4YW-Q型全幅玉米收获机配套动力为40千瓦以上轮式拖拉机，收获幅宽为2.1米，适应任意行距，实现不对行收获。生产率达到8～12亩/小时，籽粒损失率<1.5%，果穗损失率<2%，籽粒破碎率<1%。该机2002年投入批量生产，其产品除在天津销售外，已推广到河北、山东、内蒙、辽宁、河南、新疆、安徽等省市自治区。2003年被评为天津市第三届农业名牌，富康公司成为中国玉米收获机主要生产企业之一。

到2005年，全市玉米收获机械保有量达50余台，玉米机播种面积155.65千公顷，机播水平52.56%，机收面积3.45千公顷，机收水平1.16%，低于全国平均水平。

（三）保护性作业

2002年开始，天津组织实施国家农业部保护性耕作示范推广项目。示范推广小麦玉米两茬平作保护性耕作技术模式，示范区玉米免耕播种作业面积达到实施面积的100%，小麦免耕播种面积达到实施面积的84%，秸秆还田面积达到实施面积的95%。玉米秸秆粉碎长度5厘米以下，机械深松深度26厘米，表土作业深度10厘米。较项目实施前增产6.2%，减少作业工序，降低作业成本10%。制订出小麦玉米两茬平作保护性耕作技术规范，开发研制出小麦免耕播种施肥机具，对引进的保护性耕作机具进行质量跟踪检测。到2005年末，全市共有蓟县、宝坻、武清等7个区县的72个乡镇512个自然村示范推广这一新的耕作技术，国家累积投资690万元，建设核心示范区面积22.7千公顷，推广实施保护性耕作机械化作业面积48千公顷。2002～2005年，投入机具共计9210台套，其中新增各类机具2432台套。

图6-4-1-101 全幅玉米收获机

二、设施耕作

1996～1998年，天津农机推广站实施市科委攻关计划项目“日光温室优化设计及环境控制技术”，刘宝利等完成日光温室结构的优化设计、温室二氧化碳增施技术的研究及温室耕整地机械设备的应用研究。采用先进有限元计算机程序对温室结构进行分析、优化，其建造技术先进。项目实施过程中建造新型日光温室102栋。

1997～1998年，天津农机推广站实施的农业部丰收计划项目“天津市新型日光温室及机械化综合配套技术推广”。胡伟等重点推广三种适合天津自然及经济条件下使用的新型节能日光温室。制定温室设备配备方案，开发研制的绳拉式、爬坡式、侧置摆杆式三种卷帘机，研制出多功能田园管理机。该机配套动力4马力，旋耕深度3～23厘米，单铧犁效率1～2亩/小时，锄草效率1～2亩/小时，播种效率1.5～3亩/小时。解决了天津市蔬菜反季节生产存在的设施陈旧、机械设备配套不齐，机械化作业水平较低等问题，促进全市蔬菜保护地向温室建筑标准化、温室配套设备完善化，温室栽培规范化，温室主要生产环节机械化方向发展，提高蔬菜生产抵御自然灾害能力，实现增产增收目标。

同时，市政府蔬菜办公室与天津市农机推广站联合实施“新型节能日光温室综合配套技术示范推广项目”，赵秀萍等研究设计出天津型日光温室，示范、推广有机无土基质栽培技术、酵素菌腐热有机肥制作与施用技术及温室应急加热设备，使栽培制度由冬春一茬发展到周年生产，提高设备利用率和蔬菜整体设施生产水平。推广新型日光温室面积4.42千公顷，推广温室配套机具6430台套。

1997～1999年，为解决日光温室覆盖材料的整体机械卷铺问题，天津农机推广站组织实施市科委农业攻关项目“蔬菜工厂化生产设施设备及技术示范”，谢敏等重点进行保温被、草帘的整体卷铺设计，卷帘机中电动机和减速机的合理配置及减速机的开发研制。研制出五种形式的卷帘机和一种减速机，首次提出简单且行之有效的同轴不同步挂钩式双层草帘的整体卷铺方式，采用卷铺保温被的侧置摆杆支架卷铺草帘，并开发出2K-H-D型温室卷帘机专用减速机。

2000～2001年，天津农机推广站实施市科委攻关项目“LPG温室增温及二氧化碳发生兼用设备的研制与开发”，史业滕等研制出液化气增温及增施二氧化碳设备，开展液化气增温设备在不同温室内的升温效果、增施二氧化碳的效果和对作物产量影响的研究。研制的YRQ-100W型液化气增温设备采用室内直燃的燃烧方式，液化石油气通过燃烧产生二氧化碳和水，应用液化气增温设备进行二氧化碳增施。该设备具有自动点火和熄火保护装置，使用安全可靠。采用脉冲连续放电点火，放电时间长，点火效率高。当火源一旦熄灭，感应针就会感应到控制气路使电磁阀马上关断，防止气体外溢，起到安全保护作用。该设备具有定时功能，加温功能、温检功能。用半导体，线性温度PN结检测，经可调设定温度比较器指示和控制可控硅开关燃气阀，温控范围为15～25度，温度达到设定值后，控制燃气阀自动关闭，低于设定温度，自动启动。该设备二氧化碳排放量1.16立方米/小时，一氧化碳排放浓度为0.018%。气密性：压力4.2千帕条件下稳压1分钟漏气量<0.07升/小时。该项技术在天津市不同类型的日光温室内做过应用效果研究，产品已经有100台在温室中得以应用。

2000～2001年，天津农机推广站实施农业部丰收计划项目“天津市蔬菜保护地机械化技术推广”，蒲小平等重点推广二代节能日光温室和自主设计的天津型节能日光温室。在耕整机械化技术推广应用中，引进、试验、开发、推广了6种温室用耕地机：上海产“小牛”600N型6马力微耕机（汽油机）、山东潍坊产“杰农”6马力多功能微耕机、广西柳州产6马力微耕机、青岛产5马力多功能微耕机、天津静海兴盛机械厂生产的“禾丰”4马力多功能微耕机、天津北辰区农机局研发的2马力多功能微耕机（IGZ-2型和DGZ-5型）。这些机具的特点是：体积小，操作灵活，可在狭窄地块作业，不留残耕。扶手可作360度转动，垂直方向可作30度调整，速度适中，旋耕碎土性好，耕深可调，最深可达30厘米，工作效率每小时耕地0.8亩，油耗0.3～0.5千克/亩。课题组还推广北京产的渗灌、天津产的滴灌及河北产的小管灌设备，并进行重力滴灌设备的试验。推广3种实用的二氧化碳气肥增施设备：碳铵与硫酸反应式二氧化碳发生器，燃烧式二氧化碳气肥增旋装置，二氧化碳发生剂。推广土暖加热技术和燃煤热风炉技术。采用的石家庄产日光温室蔬菜补光灯，紫光波长范围在400～500毫微米，红光波长范围在600～1000毫微米，紫外线波长范围在300～400毫微米，这些波段的光都能被蔬菜吸收，参与光合作用，促使蔬菜正常地生长发育。推广补光灯160台套。项目实施两年，推广面积6.97千公顷，新增经济效益达5650.3万元。

2001～2003年，天津农机推广站实施市农委农业重点技术推广项目“设施蔬菜生产规范化技术推广”，蒲小平等引进推广微耕机、热风炉、卷帘机、二氧化碳增施等设备1600台套。通过对设施设备和生产技术的规范，将设施结构的更新、品种换代及无害化生产技术有机结合起来进行推广和普及，示范推广面积2.61公顷。

2003～2005年，天津农机推广站实施市科委科研攻关培育项目"新型日光温室复合材料开发研究"过程中，蒲小平等进行新型日光温室复合材料开发及应用研究、新型温室保温被研制及应用研究和设施养殖业废弃物处理设备开发研究。建成一个日光温室复合材料专业生产厂和一个新型温室保温被专业生产厂。实现年产值1200万元，利润150万元。研制的新型复合材料是将三维纤维材料经骨架浇铸机浇铸而成，由它制成的温室骨架及纵拉杆，外敷玻璃钢涂层，具有防腐、防潮、使用寿命长、不损伤塑料薄膜、可拆卸的特点。保温墙体采用新型聚苯砌块砖轻材质，替代传统粘土砖、珍珠岩结构墙体，材质轻，具有环保、节省土地资源、增加保温效果的特点。研制的新型温室保温被是由特选PE膜制成，取代普遍采用的防水布，具有耐高、低温，抗老化、耐疲劳，耐横向纵向拉力的特点，通过采用非缝合制被工艺，将特选PE膜和毛毡直接压合在一起，克服了缝制工艺中针脚渗水的难题。

第二节 机械化养殖

1990年以后，天津机械养殖技术主要有："肉牛饲养配套农机化综合技术推广""肉用北京鸭旱养机械化综合技术推广"；饲料种植、收获、加工机械和设备的研制、改进及推广应用；对畜禽粪便的机械化处理。

一、饲养

1990年，天津市机动挤奶器保有量41套，到2005年增至170套，机械化挤奶仍在低水平徘徊。

1994～1995年，为解决肉牛粗饲料不足的问题，降低肉牛饲养成本，天津市农机推广站开展"肉牛饲养配套农机化综合技术推广"项目，采用氨化技术、绵籽饼脱毒技术和工业废弃物养殖肉牛，使肉牛育肥期缩短到100～120天，日均增重1.5千克，每千克增重精料消耗在2～3千克以内。课题组推广以煤作燃料、蒸汽加热、传热的新型氨化炉10座，秸秆打捆机、铡草机、粉碎机、搅拌机50台套，制定出肉牛养殖配套农机化综合技术规范，形成年出栏肉牛1000头的生产开发示范基地。

1995～1996年，天津农机推广站实施农业部丰收计划项目"肉用北京鸭旱养机械化综合技术推广"。主要技术为：网床养鸭、塑料暖棚机械化养鸭、配合饲料育肥、疫病综合防治技术等。上述技术适合天津市各养鸭饲养场使用，与传统的地面饲养相比，具有鸭子增重快、减少污染、降低鸭子死亡率、改善鸭舍环境等优点。通过项目实施，肉鸭在饲养49天后，平均体重即可达3千克以上，且网上养鸭死亡率仅为2%。

1996年1月~1997年12月，池塘养鱼机械化配套技术推广等项目的示范推广，取得较显著的经济和社会效益。

二、饲料加工

1990年，全市饲料粉碎机保有量3788台，牧草收割机508台，到2005年饲料粉碎机109万台，牧草播种机103万台，牧草收割机104万台，牧草翻晒机106万台，草籽收获机105万台，青贮饲料收获机108万台。

1992～1994年，天津市农业机械试验鉴定推广站开展"秸秆氨化设备改进研究"，对以煤代电，利用蒸汽加热、余氨回收装置用于各种农作物秸秆的快速氨化处理设备进行研究，研制的9AL-50Z型蒸汽氨化炉，碳铵分解快，氨化时间短；采用氨气回收装置，不污染环境，节省氨源；采用上下对流空气循环装置，秸秆氨化质量稳定可靠。炉体设计水平先进。

1992～1995年，天津市农业机械试验鉴定推广站开展"秸秆氨化设备推广"，研制和推广电加热氨化炉、压力蒸汽加热氨化炉、茶炉加热氨化炉、热风加热氨化炉等不同类型的氨化设备,完成不同秸秆处理量的氨化炉设计、制造及利用地热建设大型秸秆氨化站的研究设计工作,满足大、中、小型养殖场和养牛专业户的需求。建成各种类型的秸秆氨化炉70座,年处理秸秆能力达到9750吨以上。

1995～1998年,天津市农业机械试验鉴定推广站实施市科委攻关计划项目"秸秆机械化微贮及利用技术开发研究",戴冠英等进行秸秆微生物发酵菌剂研制及微贮效果研究,秸秆微贮配套工程设施,设备及处理工艺研究,以及秸秆机械化微贮技术在实际生产中的应用研究。项目实施过程中,在国内首次研制开发出用于秸秆微贮的微生物菌剂和适合大规模机械化作业的液体菌剂,并开发出双缸隔膜泵液体菌剂喷洒设备,提出奶牛、肉牛饲喂微贮秸秆的营养供给量推荐标准。开发的双缸隔膜泵液体菌剂喷洒设备,采用将隔膜泵及配套电机安装在可移动的车架上,加装两级过滤装置,压力高、流量大、喷射距离远,可一机多用,具有结构紧凑、移动方便、减少阻塞故障等特点。该项目实施期间,共生产复合菌种5000千克,直接生产菌剂效益40万元,1998年获天津市科学技术进步二等奖。

三、粪便处理

天津市畜禽粪便已成为农业面源污染的主要来源。全市用畜禽粪便作肥料、饲料和燃料的三种方式均有应用,但所占比例很低。由于资金及技术等问题,粪便无害化与资源化以及商品化处理率不足1%。

(一)制肥

天津将畜禽粪便用作肥料的主要做法有:粪尿撒施、自然堆肥、好氧发酵制肥三种方式。其中,自然堆肥约占60%、自然干燥占1%;塑料大棚日光自然干燥为0.1%。随着天津市有机食品和绿色食品的发展,有机肥料的需求量不断增加。

1990年以来,许多养殖专业户采用快速烘干工艺生产有机肥,取得良好效益,减轻畜禽粪便对环境的污染。东丽区粪便处理设备厂曾生产此类设备,主要用于鸡粪处理,但由于烘干机排出的臭气会产生二次污染,政府强制关闭了一些鸡粪烘干厂,养殖户不再采用此方式进行粪便处理。

1998年,天津市农业机械研究所实施市农委"鸡粪工厂化无公害处理技术及有机复合肥工程"项目期间,高宝成等在宝坻、大港等区县建立4个示范点,推广好氧发酵干燥处理技术及9JG-6型鸡粪干燥处理成套设备。在塑料大棚内,采用具有搬运功能的短轴搅拌器翻动湿鸡粪,利用鸡粪中的微生物进行好氧发酵,把有机污染物转化成动植物营养,除去有害成分,并通过发酵产生的热量(温度50～70度)杀死病菌虫卵,同时蒸发水分,除去臭味,经深加工制成颗粒状复合有机肥或专用肥。设备造价10～18万元/套,年产量1600吨。项目结束后,宝坻示范点生产有机肥已具规模。

2001年,宁河种猪场以中德合资的方式投入资金300万元,建成有机肥生产厂,年生产有机肥8000吨,是天津市最早生产复合有机肥的企业之一。粪便由送料器送进发酵槽,经深槽好氧发酵,螺旋搅拌器搅拌推进,烘干、制粒、装袋,包装出售。

2005年,天津农机推广站引进的可移动式畜禽粪便固液分离机,将粪水输送、固液分离、干物质装袋、输送,作为一个整体的系统,在设计理念上领先一步。其产品具有很强的市场竞争力,受到业内人士的普遍关注。该设备的推广应用提升了畜禽养殖场粪污治理的技术水平,其作业方式灵活,易形成专业化、规模化生产,并可大幅度减少设备投资。

(二)制燃料

天津农村使用沼气始于1985年。2000年,天津市启动生态家园富民工程,沼气建设进入新的发展阶段。2005年,全市文明生态村共建沼气池800座。新建户用沼气池2514座,全市沼气池饱有量5000座,处理量约占畜禽粪便产生量的1%。其中,蓟县、宝坻和武清是沼气发展较快的地区。

2005年,天津农机推广站完成天津市科委科研攻关培育项目"设施养殖业废弃物处理技术及设备研究"项目,在北辰区红旗养牛场试制安装了日处理量0.6吨的高架钢结构高温厌氧沼气发酵罐、在东丽区世纪星养猪场安装日处理量3.0吨的设备，并增置沼气储气罐、脱硫装置，制定工艺流程。解决了北方地区，冬季低温产气量少的问题，产气效率明显提高，实现边排放、边回收、边资源化利用。

天津市水蓝畜牧养殖有限公司以股份制形式投资7000万元建造华北地区最具规模的养猪场。该公司自2001年开始筹建废弃物处理设施，建成全市最大的沼气工程，所产沼气用于发电，日处理粪水600吨，日产干粪30～40吨。

第三节 机械 设备与设施

1990年以后，天津相关单位研究制造出一批拥有自主知识产权的农业机械和设备，引进示范了一批机械和设备。2002年开始启动天津塘沽农用航空站。

一、机械、设备

1990年开始，农业机械化进入以市场为导向的发展阶段。天津市农机企业和科研机构面向市场需要，开发适合小生产规模、适合农村购买力、适合国情的农机产品，形成一批具有自主知识产权的农机产品。与此同时，先后从国内、外引进推广先进农业机械、设备。

见下表：

1991～2005年自主研发的农业机械及设备一览表

表6-4-3-51

序号	研制时间	机具、设备名称及型号	研制单位	专利情况
1	1991～1993	水稻割前脱粒收割机	天津市农机研究所	—
2	1992～1994	9AL-50Z型蒸汽氨化炉	天津市农机鉴定推广站	—
3	1995	4YW-1型单行背负式玉米收获机	武清县津武玉米收获机厂	—
4	1997～1998	WJ100型自动卷帘机	天津市秋明农渔机电有限公司	—
5	1997～1998	多功能园田耕整机	天津兴盛食品机械厂	—
6	1998～2000	9JG-6型鸡粪发酵干燥设备	天津市农机研究所	—
7	1999	4YW-3型背负式玉米收获机	天津富康农业开发有限公司	—
8	2000～2003	M200-2型葡萄埋藤机	天津市农机研究所	20062000263135
9	2000～2003	3WG-350型葡萄风送喷雾机	天津市农机研究所	—
10	2000～2001	CO_2增施设备	天津市农机鉴定推广站	—
11	2001	4YW-Q型全幅玉米收获机	天津富康农业开发有限公司	—
12	2003～2004	2BMFS-10型小麦免耕施肥播种机	天津市农机研究所	—
13	2003～2005	高温厌氧沼气发酵罐	天津市农机试验鉴定站	—

1996～2005年引进示范的农业机械及设备一览表

表6-4-3-52

序号	引进示范时间	机具、设备名称及型号	引进示范单位	示范推广规模
1	1996～2004	自动投饵机	天津市农机鉴定推广站	5150台
2	1997～2003	卷帘机	天津市农机鉴定推广站	1682台
3	2000～2003	微耕机	天津市农机鉴定推广站	3656台
4	2000～2003	热风炉	天津市农机鉴定推广站	688台
5	1999～2001	深松机	天津市农机鉴定推广站	50台
6	1999～2001	气吸式玉米免耕播种机	天津市农机鉴定推广站	24台
7	1999～2001	秸秆粉碎还田机	天津市农机鉴定推广站	170台
	1999～2001	小型半精量免耕播种机	天津市农机鉴定推广站	680台
8	1999～2001	CO_2增施设备	天津市农机鉴定推广站	800台(套)
9	2002～2004	湿冷式保鲜贮藏技术及设备	天津市农机试验鉴定站	1套
10	1998	洋马Ce-1型、久保田PR0488型半喂入水稻收割机	天津市农机试验鉴定站	20台
11	2005	可移动式畜禽粪便固液分离机	天津市农机试验鉴定站	10台
12	2004.4～2005.12	膜下滴灌设备	天津市农机推广总站	5套

二、设施

天津塘沽农用航空站于2002年4月启动，2005年8月正式投入运行。该农用航空站是经国家农业部批准立项的全国五个农用航空站之一，总投资4338.3万元，其中农业部投入扶持资金2000万元，塘沽区政府及联建企业自筹2338.3万元。2005年8月，3架5-B(D型)多用途飞机，着陆在塘沽农用机场，天津农用航空站正式启用。天津塘沽航空站的建成极大地提升了农机装备水平，对农业生产抵御农作物病虫害、森林防火等发挥重要作用。

第五章　农业生物技术

20世纪90年代，天津农业生物技术在微生物、植物病毒病理、生物农药和助剂等方面进行深入地研究与开发。先后开发成功光合细菌培养、秸秆发酵、植物病毒检测与脱毒、无病毒优质苗木选育、快繁等新技术；研制出防治绵铃虫新生物农药、菊脂类农药植物型增效剂、新型高效复合植物生长调节剂等新产品。上述科研成果在动物饲料、畜禽水产养殖、农作物种植与植物保护、环境保护等领域得到广泛的应用，并取得良好效果。

第一节　微生物

微生物开发利用主要成果是开展光合细菌的培养、中试及推广，用于净化有机废水；研制出秸秆发酵生物添加剂，提升秸秆饲料的品质。

一、光合细菌应用

为了有效地净化有机废水，改善海、淡水养殖生态环境，1989～1997年，天津市农业生物技术研究中心（以下简称“生物中心”）陈秀为等开展光合细菌的培养、中试及推广应用研究。该项目研制出液体和固体两种剂型的水质净化剂和饲料添加剂。液体产品为多菌株复合菌液，经生物工程发酵技术制成，产品呈红色或紫红色，略黏稠，活菌体含量超过40亿/毫升。菌体粗蛋白含量达67.10%，常温下可保质6个月。固体产品为固体材料吸附后经低温烘干制得，含水量在10%以下，常温下可保质18个月。菌体对人畜无毒无害，其蛋白质含量达60%以上，并富含维生素B和其他生理活性物质。该项科研成果主要应用于水产养殖、畜禽养殖、农业生产和环境保护等领域。在水产养殖中应用，可以净化水质，防治鱼虾病害，还可作为鱼虾蟹贝类育苗开口饵料，增强幼苗抗病能力，提高成活率，在畜禽养殖中应用，可促进动物生长，提高蛋鸡产蛋率。

“光合细菌生产及应用技术中试”的主要成果是研制成功一套比较先进的光合细菌规模生产工艺及配套装置，通过200亩人工养殖对虾应用光合细菌的生产性试验，改善养虾池水质，明显延缓对虾暴发性流行病的暴发期。同时还研制出应用振动流化床干燥吸附于载体的光合细菌固体物料的先进工艺。1996～1997年，进一步开展“光合细菌在水产及畜禽养殖上的应用及推广”，完善菌剂4级生产程序，改进外照明槽式培养装置及生产工艺，使光合细菌的生产规模扩大，技术更加完善，较好地解决菌种更新复壮问题，使菌剂保质期由原来的10℃～15℃保存3～5月、25℃～30℃保存15天分别增加到1年和6个月。同时，使光合细菌的应用范围更加扩大，由初期主要在河蟹、对虾育苗，养殖期净化水质等方面应用，扩展到淡水养殖、南方名贵鱼大棚越冬、观赏鱼养殖、肉鸡生产等方面，并取得了好的效果。他们还制订出“光合细菌菌剂使用技术规范”。该项成果已推广到天津、河北、山西、等10多个省、自治区、直辖市。

二、秸秆发酵

为了解决采用传统青贮方法贮存秸秆易发生霉变以及秸秆含水量低，纤维老化，作饲料适口性不好的问题，1995～1997年，生物中心陈秀为等研制出秸秆发酵生物添加剂。该添加剂由6株秸秆发酵菌经科学配伍，通过生物工程技术发酵制得，其浓度达到每克含有效菌数60亿，除含有促进秸秆发酵复合有益微生物外，还含有多种酶、维生素、脂肪酸和微量元素，是一种复合秸秆发酵生物添加剂。将秸秆用机械加工处理后，按比例加入复合微生物发酵剂、辅料和水，放入密封的设施中10～15天，经微生物发酵后，干黄秸秆即变为质地柔软、湿润蓬松、气味酸香、适口性好的饲料。反刍家畜食用后，对增加食欲、改善代谢功能、增加抗病能力都有明显的效果。同时，该项技术易于操作，农民使用水泥窖、土窖、大缸都可制作。制作好的发酵秸秆（青贮饲料）发酵效果好，不产生霉变，随取随喂，一般可保存1年的时间，且制作成本低廉。使用该添加剂，不仅比自然青贮饲料质量好，还可以减少20%～30%的霉变损失，使秸秆利用率达90%以上。“秸秆机械化微贮及利用技术开发研究”获1998年度天津市科技进步二等奖。2000年该项技术被确定为天津市农业重点推广计划项目。2000年12月1日获国家发明专利证书。到2001年该项技术已推广到全国30个省、自治区、直辖市。利用该项技术不仅解决牲畜的饲草问题，还避免由于焚烧秸秆造成的环境污染。2002年4月，应朝鲜民主主义人民共和国大圣公司之邀，科研人员赴朝，在1个国营农场、1个部队农场做了500吨稻草发酵示范，效果好，受到朝方欢迎。“秸秆发酵生物添加剂及其配制方法”获2005年度天津市技术发明三等奖。在此基础上，陈秀为等开展“秸秆资源饲料化技术研究”，使秸秆通过生物处理后达到降解木质纤维素、增加蛋白质的效果，除可用于饲喂反刍动物外，还可用来饲喂鸡、鸭、鹅、猪等单胃动物。

第二节　植物病毒研究

为了解决葡萄栽培过程中易感染病毒的问题,生物中心开展了一系列的研究。1992年开展“天津地区葡萄主要病毒检测及脱毒技术的研究”,1993年开展“无病毒优质葡萄苗木选育和配套技术模式的研究”,1997年开展“葡萄组培苗脱毒快繁技术的研究”,上述研究应用于生产实际,取得预期效果。

一、病毒检测及脱毒

由于葡萄苗木属于无性繁殖,一旦感染病毒,便终生带毒,并通过繁殖材料传给后代,造成严重病害。因此,有效的检测手段和脱毒技术是急需解决的问题,1992年,生物中心曹为玉、郑燕棠主持开展的“天津地区葡萄主要病毒检测及脱毒技术的研究”,查清天津地区葡萄病毒的主要种类为葡萄卷叶病毒(GLRV)和葡萄扇叶病毒(GFV)。在国内首次采用酶标记免疫吸附测定法(ELISA)检测出葡萄卷叶病毒,并利用生物学方法分离鉴定出烟草花叶病毒(TMV)、黄瓜花叶病毒(CMV)、葡萄扇叶病毒(GFV)以及两个待测的葡萄病毒分离物(即同所有葡萄和蔬菜病毒抗血清不产生阳性反应)。在葡萄病毒病脱毒技术的研究中,总结出利用热处理箱脱毒和茎尖脱毒相结合的脱毒技术,使葡萄卷叶病毒、葡萄扇叶病毒脱毒率分别达84%和87%。在国内首先提出和建立培养无毒优质葡萄苗木的配套技术模式,包括田间取样或引进、检测、脱毒、快繁、驯化、选育、入园等程序,为实现工厂化育苗、建立无毒化优质葡萄繁育基地提供了科技支撑。

二、无病毒苗木选育

1993～1996年,生物中心与市科委蓟县翠屏湖科学园、天津市中法合营王朝葡萄酿酒有限公司合作,共同开展“无病毒优质葡萄苗木选育和配套技术模式的研究”。科研人员研究总结出以血清跟踪检测病毒为中心,结合生物学鉴定,以脱毒处理和组织培养为基础,杜绝病毒再侵染的配套技术措施:选择和繁育无毒苗木。经检测凡不带有当地葡萄主要病毒的单株,经单芽或绿枝扦插等育苗方法扩大繁殖;选择符合种植无病毒葡萄苗木的地块做无病毒母株园。具体条件是:30年未曾种植过葡萄的地块,有独立的水源并不经过其他葡萄园,间隔和葡萄病毒有关作物如桃树、茄科作物等10米以上。确保母株园带毒率在10%以下;实施以血清跟踪进行病毒检测。利用葡萄卷叶病毒和扇叶病毒抗血清,采用ELISA(酶标记免疫吸附测定法)检测母株,凡是呈阴性反应的编号繁殖。每年5～6月和9～10月,按品种分别采集叶片和成熟叶柄或枝条,进行葡萄扇叶病毒和卷叶病毒的检测,发现阳性反应及时拔除病株,并处理株穴土壤。他们在蓟县建立10亩无毒葡萄母株园。落地葡萄苗经病毒检测全无毒,根系发达,枝叶茁壮,果实丰收。该项研究为无病毒葡萄苗木生产提供配套技术模式,方法和经验。

三、组培苗脱毒快繁

20世纪90年代中期,葡萄酿酒业迅速发展,对优质酒用葡萄需求量大增,酿酒葡萄生产基地紧缺无病毒苗木。1997～2001年,生物中心张福庆等开展“葡萄组培苗脱毒快繁技术的研究”。研究确定酒用葡萄病毒主要有3种:扇叶病毒、卷叶病毒和番茄环斑病毒。根据各种病毒在田间的发生规律和症状,1997年春、秋两季在葡萄园进行赤霞珠、霞多丽、黑比诺、梅鹿辄等品种无病毒症状表现的植株筛选,对所选植株进行农业生产特性观察和营养系选择,确定营养系选择方法的基础位置。1998～2000年,经过大量筛选,得出各葡萄品种最适培养基,进行组培试管苗的茎尖热处理脱毒技术研究,脱毒效果达到百分之百。确定脱毒有效途径，即：营养系选择＋试管苗茎尖培养＋热处理＋试管苗茎尖培养。在这基础上，将检测无病毒的各葡萄品种营养系在其相应的最适营养基上培养，采用组培驯化苗小茎段扦插育苗技术和盆栽葡萄绿枝扦插技术进行快繁，建立和完善葡萄无病毒苗木工厂化生产技术体系。

组培驯化苗单芽带叶小茎段扦插育苗技术与最佳培养基的筛选研究加快了苗木繁殖速度，所育苗木生长健壮、整齐一致。1998～1999年蓟县五百户乡应用该技术建立赤霞珠葡萄生产园，葡萄生长状况达到预期效果。该项技术的研制成功为天津市高质量酿酒用葡萄园的建立和发展奠定基础。

第三节 生物农药与植物调节剂研发

为了解决绵铃虫化学杀虫剂对环境造成的污染，生物中心开展"绵铃虫致病微生物的分离培养和应用效果研究"；为了减少农药用量，保护环境，开展"菊脂类农药植物型增效剂的研制"；为促进植物生长和提高座果率，开展"新型高效复合植物生长调节剂的研究"。上述研究经推广应用，取得良好效果。

一、生物农药

20世纪90年代，绵铃虫害在全国呈逐年加重的趋势。绵农防治绵铃虫多采用化学杀虫剂，虽防治效果明显，但造成环境污染。采用对人畜无害、在环境中无残留的、安全、有效、经济的生物农药防治各种农作物害虫已经成为农业科研领域的新课题。1996～2000年，生物中心陈秀为主持开展"绵铃虫致病微生物的分离培养和应用效果研究"。科研人员从自然死亡的绵铃虫虫体上分离出一种新的昆虫病原菌——肠杆菌科沙雷氏菌属粘质沙雷氏菌。该菌对绵铃虫、菜青虫、甜菜夜蛾有明显的毒杀作用，并能用人工方法培养。他们对该菌进行生理、生化特性研究，确定其分类位置，并研究其致病机理。通过人工方法培养出微生物菌剂，并在田间试验。在绵田中使用5天后，绵铃虫虫口减退率达66%；在白菜地中使用48小时后，菜青虫虫口减退率达80%以上。2000～2002年，在天津市武清区、宝坻区应用面积7万亩，使绵铃虫和菜青虫达到有效早期控制。同时，由于减少化学农药的使用量，对提高农产品品质，保护环境起到重要作用。

二、农药增效剂

以往城乡居民使用的灭蚊蝇药多为菊脂类，但由于蚊蝇抗药性的产生，使施药浓度不得不连年增加，加重对环境的危害。为解决上述问题，1990~1996年，生物中心同北京农业大学合作，开展"菊脂类农药植物型增效剂的研制"。生物中心徐金生等从十几种野生植物中筛选出不仅有直接杀灭蚊蝇效果，而且对菊脂类农药有增效作用的天然药用植物C，以选定植物的提取液作为增效剂，加入不同浓度的菊脂类农药，观察药用植物提取液的增效效果，并对配方进行初选，从筛选出对杀灭蚊蝇有较好效果的几个配方中分别进行室内、室外空间的药效试验，将获得满意结果的配方初步定名为卫生杀虫剂A，又称"室内净"。从1994年开始对中选配方的药液制剂进行毒性试验和毒力测定，同时进行热贮稳定性试验，以考察配方的合理性。测定结果表明，此卫生用药具有低毒、安全、持效长等特点。在天津、北京等地对药效进行进一步的验证，分别在笼养条件下和室内外空间中进行，结果表明，该药对蚊蝇、蟑螂都有较好的杀灭效果，尤其对具抗药性家蝇效果更好。10天以内杀灭率达100%，20天以内过夜家蝇均死亡，有效期持续30天以上。经市科委组织的专家鉴定，认为该增效剂高效、低毒。

三、植物调节剂

1993~1997年，徐金生主持开展"新型高效复合植物生长调节剂的研究"。经研究试验，成功研制出一种复合植物生长调节剂——45%多效三灵水剂。该制剂由两种激素组成：一种是抑制激素，能促进根系及生殖生长，增加作物的叶绿素含量；另一种是促进型激素，能促进细胞分裂。两种激素的效果是提高座果率。他们将最佳配方用清水分别作200倍、300倍、500倍、800倍和1000倍稀释，在葡萄开花前15天全株喷洒，找出最佳使用浓度。在最佳浓度使用中，再分别在开花前15天、10天、盛花期及盛花后期10天喷洒，测定单穗的坐果率，找出最佳使用时期。结果表明：45%多效三灵水剂在葡萄上使用具有明显的增产作用，将该制剂稀释800倍，在葡萄开花前8~10天全株喷洒，可缩短葡萄果柄、明显增加叶片内叶绿素含量和果实糖度，提高坐果率，葡萄平均单穗增产率达20%~30%。在花生上使用也有明显的增产作用，试验证明，将该制剂稀释3000倍，分别在花芽分化始期（播种后约25天）和始花期（播种后约45天）两次喷施，可促进花生根系生长，花生产量可提高20%~30%。该制剂稳定性好，对环境无污染，对人畜安全。1994~1997年，在天津市、河北省、山东省的16个县推广应用20万亩。

第六章　农产品保鲜技术

20世纪90年代开始，天津农业快速发展，农产品种类丰富，产量大增。对农产品贮存保鲜的需求越来越明显。天津市在深化农产品采后生理研究的基础上，抓住保鲜温度、湿度、气体和防腐四要素，提出以微型节能保鲜冷库、MA（自发气调贮藏技术）保鲜膜和绿色保鲜剂相结合的保鲜配套技术体系。并以此为指导，开展技术研究和配套物化成果的研制，开发出具有自主知识产权的物化成果四大系列——保鲜剂、保鲜膜、保鲜设备、果实袋。研究成功农产品保鲜综合控制技术，形成物理、化学、生物的产后保鲜综合控制体系。把现代制冷技术、气调技术、真空减压技术、生物涂被技术、空气放电技术、微胶囊技术、辐射技术、光电子技术和计算机控制技术应用于农产品产后保鲜中。在农产品保鲜理论、设施、材料和保鲜工程技术的研究与创新，以及在技术集成、成果转化等方面都取得显著成效。1997年，国家科学技术委员会以农科院为依托，成立"国家农产品保鲜工程技术研究中心（天津）"（以下简称"保鲜中心"）。从此，天津承担起全国农产品保鲜技术的研究、开发和成果推广工作。1998~2002年，保鲜中心开展天津市农业科技重点推广项目"果蔬保鲜新技术推广"（该项目于1999和2000年分别被国家科技部确定为国家重点科技推广项目和国家重点星火项目）。建立"微型保鲜冷库＋自发气调小包装＋无公害保鲜剂"的工程技术模式和产地"公司＋微型保鲜冷库＋农户"的技术推广模式，带动中国果蔬产地贮藏的产业化发展。科技人员深入华北、东北、西北等地区，研究推广不同气候条件下葡萄无公害标准化栽培技术（直接示范面积300亩，辐射带动面积20余万亩），使上述地区采收的葡萄最大限度地符合贮藏保鲜要求，玫瑰香、巨峰、红提等葡萄品种保鲜时间达6~7个月，好果率达96.4%。形成果蔬产、贮、销一条龙技术模式，推动果蔬产地保鲜技术标准化、产业化，创立技术推广信息化网络。该技术在全国26个省、自治区、直辖市推广应用，4年间，新建微

图6-6-0-102　国家农产品保鲜工程技术研究中心（天津）

型保鲜冷库1836座，辐射全国15620座，开发果蔬保鲜膜1200吨，果蔬总贮量达7.9万吨。该项目获2002年度天津市科技进步一等奖。到2005年，天津的科研成果推广到全国近30个省、自治区、直辖市 。使用该中心的研发成果贮藏保鲜的农产品，包括果品、蔬菜、粮食三大类，共80个品种。

第一节 冷 藏

1996年，农科院林果研究所（以下简称“林果所”）开展“农产品微型节能冷库应用”的研究，成果获得专利，并推广应用。2001年，保鲜中心开展“便携式微型节能保鲜冷库”的研究，成果获专利，并批量生产。同时，保鲜中心开展“果品减压贮藏技术研究”，成果在全国推广。

一、冷藏设施

1996～1998年，林果所开展“农产品微型节能冷库应用”的研究。该项目1997年被天津市科委列为星火计划项目，1998年被国家科技部列为国家星火计划项目。李喜宏等研制成功的微型节能冷库可因地制宜，就地取材，农户院中空地、废弃房屋、土窖等均可利用。低投资、低能耗，高效益，适合中国国情，深受农民欢迎。冷库温度在-5℃～15℃，可随意调节，自动控温、测温，温差＜±0.5℃。能源来自机械制冷、自然冷源、生物能等。通过调节贮藏环境温度，利用自发气调及相关辅助技术，延缓农产品衰老，达到果蔬保鲜。以巨峰葡萄为例：贮藏192天，好果率达98.6%；贮藏220天，好果率达95%。提出微型节能冷库分类、库体设计与工艺、设备选型与匹配、温度与设备控制、使用管理与农产品保鲜工程技术等5项技术标准。该项成果获1998年度天津市科技进步二等奖，2003年5月获国家发明专利证书。

2001～2003年，保鲜中心关文强、李喜宏等开展“便携式微型节能保鲜冷库”的研究。该项研究分别于2002年、2003年被天津市科委和国家科技部确定为星火计划项目。项目对3种柔性聚烯烃发泡保温材料的导热性能、热物理参数及导热的理论模型进行系统研究。以PEF（交联聚乙烯）、EPE（非交联聚乙烯）、NBR/PVC（橡塑海绵）3类专用发泡复合保温材料为主，设计出3种类型热流值小于10瓦/平方米的库体材料，形成“便携式库体＋专用设备＋温度语音在线管理系统”的便携式微型节能保鲜冷库。该项成果经中试后，建成1000平方米的厂房、配备专用设备和中试生产线，年产可达500台（套）。

二、减压冷藏技术

1998～2002年，保鲜中心承担农业部“九五”重点科研项目——“果品减压贮藏技术研究”。张平等以物理、植物生理生化等学科为理论基础，成功研制出微型减压贮藏保鲜设施。同时，研究减压条件对易腐难贮果品贮藏生理生化效应及品质的影响。该设施可贮存果品1.5万～2万千克，日耗电25度，真空度可在0～0.09兆帕范围内调控。利用该设施研究出贮藏保鲜大枣、桃、樱桃等果品的配套工艺技术。该设施与配套工艺的使用，使保鲜效果明显优于薄膜小包装气调冷藏技术，尤其是在不加湿的情况下，果品失重率轻微。应用0.06～0.08兆帕最佳真空度，冬枣贮存保鲜期可比普通冷藏延长30天以上，贮存期100天的冬枣保脆率可达90%以上。采用0.07～0.09兆帕真空度，桃的贮存期可比普通贮存技术延长贮期1个月，并明显降低桃的果肉和果心褐变，在一定程度上保持果肉的硬度和桃的风味。该设施投资少、耗能小、操作简单，适合于广大农村果蔬产地应用。把微型减压贮藏设施与微型节能冷库组合使用，取得更加良好效果。2004年7月，获科技部、商务部、质检总局、环保总局颁发的“国家重点新产品证书”。

2005年5月，保鲜中心开始实施天津市星火计划项目——“果蔬微型减压保鲜设备生产中试及贮藏示范”。科技人员对果蔬微型减压设备进行优化设计、性能改进，实现真空度在0～0.095兆帕范围内任意调节与全自动控制；生产出优化的微型减压容器系统与自控机组；建成生产车间；建立质量检测与控制体系；确定生产工艺流程和产品配套使用技术，具备年产220台（套）的能力。同时，将研究成果推广到全国10余个省市。

第二节　制剂保鲜

1997年开始，保鲜中心开展了多项保鲜化学制剂的研究，主要针对水果和蔬菜。其中“新型果蔬保鲜剂的研制与应用”获天津市科技进步二等奖，并获专利。1999年后，保鲜中心与农科院植物保护研究所共同开展生物保鲜制剂研究，为果蔬采后病害防治提供了新方法。同时，保鲜中心进一步开展了“化学防腐保鲜剂对果蔬伤害机理及调控技术的研究”，探究保鲜剂的应用效果及调控方法。

一、保鲜剂研发

（一）化学制剂

1997～2000年，保鲜中心开展天津市农业重大科技攻关项目“新型果蔬保鲜剂的研制与应用”。张华云等就二氧化硫对果蔬伤害机理以及果蔬对不同保鲜剂的敏感性进行深入研究。数十人的科研团队经近10年攻关，研制成功3种亚硫酸盐类葡萄保鲜剂：CT-2葡萄保鲜剂。具有释放速度适中、有效期长等特点，能使巨峰葡萄在冷藏条件下贮存7个月，好果率达97%以上，果实无明显漂白现象；双重释放复合型葡萄保鲜剂。能使红地球、红宝石等葡萄品种贮藏6个月，好果率达97%以上，使红地球等高档葡萄在贮藏过程中容易腐烂和漂白严重的难题得到解决；两段释放葡萄保鲜剂。具有快速释放与缓慢释放相结合的特点，能使玫瑰香、龙眼葡萄以及南方多雨省份生产的葡萄的贮藏期延长1～2个月。上述3种葡萄保鲜剂应用后，贮藏的葡萄中二氧化硫残留量小于国家规定的标准，是国内唯一获得A级绿色食品生产资料证书的保鲜剂。同时，还研制出仲丁胺类及复配保鲜剂10种，其中包括果蔬运输保鲜剂2种，果蔬液体复配保鲜剂4种，果蔬烟剂2种，库房消毒烟剂2种。并研究总结出20多种果蔬保鲜剂的配套保鲜技术。他们采取研究与开发同步进行的方法，在全国建立73个县级示范区，使该保鲜剂在26个省、自治区、直辖市推广应用。建成葡萄保鲜剂生产线一条，年生产能力达6亿片。“新型果蔬保鲜剂的研制与应用”获2000年度天津市科技进步二等奖。“CT-2亚硫酸盐葡萄保鲜剂”2001年12月被科技部、外经贸部、税务总局、质检总局、环保总局确定为国家重点新产品。“葡萄保鲜剂和生产方法”2003年获国家发明专利证书。

2002～2003年，保鲜中心开展国家农业科技成果转化资金项目“无二氧化硫伤害的葡萄保鲜剂中试”。王文生等经研究实验，针对不同葡萄品种对二氧化硫的忍耐性差异，改进完善保鲜剂的配方和生产工艺，并制定配套的贮藏技术。该保鲜剂用于葡萄保鲜时能够缓慢而均匀地可控释放，保鲜效果好。经中试，具备工业化生产的条件。该成果在天津、河北、山西、辽宁、山东、新疆等地的葡萄产区进行产地中试和批量贮藏，效果良好。

2002～2004年，保鲜中心开展农业科技成果转化资金项目“多元果蔬液体防腐保鲜剂生产中试”，王莉等经2年多努力，取得预期成果。建成中试车间和半自动化生产线，设计编制出操作规程及工艺流程，建立质量保障体系，形成年产40吨的生产能力，使该保鲜剂具备工业化生产的基本条件。同时，进一步完善多元果蔬液体防腐保鲜剂的配方，产品质量稳定，澄清透明，稀释液无析出物，在54（±2）℃下14天，活性物质的总分解率小于5%，无结晶现象。产品最大使用量低于国家关于食品添加剂使用标准的允许使用量，卫生安全性高。由于溶液的pH(酸碱)值可以根据不同的果蔬进行调节，而且抑菌谱广，不但对灰霉菌有抑制作用，而且对青霉、根霉、黑曲霉以及某些细菌所引起的病害都有显著的抑制作用，因此适用果蔬范围广泛。该成果在16个省、自治区、直辖市进行产地中试和批量贮藏。应用该保鲜剂可使冬枣贮藏3～4个月，好果率达95%；可使蒜薹贮藏10个月，薹稍仍为绿色。

(二)生物制剂

1999～2002年，保鲜中心与农科院植物保护研究所共同开展天津市重点科技攻关项目“果蔬生物涂被保鲜剂的研究”。张平等将生防酵母菌与涂被保鲜剂有机地结合在一起，进行果蔬采后病害的生物防治，是有机保鲜果蔬的新方法。他们针对农产品的不同需要，对涂被剂进行系列的专用化和多功能化研制。根据涂被剂的理化特性和果蔬的生物学特性，研制成功增亮型、护绿型、防腐型、防褐型4种生物涂被保鲜剂。增亮型涂被保鲜剂主要用于苹果、脐橙等果品，可增强其表面光泽；护绿型涂被保鲜剂主要用于西洋梨系列，可抑制其叶绿素损失，有效地保护果皮原有的绿色；防褐型涂被保鲜剂主要用于莲藕、蒜米等，使之洁白、不褐变；防腐型涂被保鲜剂主要用于草莓、黄瓜等易腐果品，延长其货架期。

二、保鲜剂应用研究

1998～2000年，保鲜中心开展天津市重点自然基金项目“化学防腐保鲜剂对果蔬伤害机理及调控技术的研究”。张华云、王文生等利用生物化学测定、电子显微镜检测方法，通过不同剂量化学防腐保鲜剂对果蔬处理，测定对不同果蔬的超微结构、过氧化系统包括各种酶及抗氧化物质、主要生理生化代谢及营养物质的影响，确定其伤害机理，根据伤害机理采取调控技术措施。经过研究，揭示出细胞汁液pH值(酸碱度)缓冲容量、抗氧化系统是决定葡萄对二氧化硫敏感性的主控因子。通过细胞学的研究，揭示出葡萄伤害果皮蜡质结构的变化；提出葡萄表面蜡质结构与耐二氧化硫程度的关系。为不耐二氧化硫伤害的葡萄保鲜剂的研制及贮藏技术的研究提供依据。通过对葡萄品种在常温和低温下急性伤害阈值和低温下慢性伤害的研究，提出现有葡萄品种对二氧化硫敏感性可归纳为3种类型：即以红宝石、红地球葡萄为代表的二氧化硫敏感型，以秋黑、牛奶葡萄为代表的二氧化硫中等敏感型和以龙眼、玫瑰香葡萄为代表的二氧化硫忍耐型，为葡萄及其他果蔬合理应用保鲜剂起到重要的指导作用，实现葡萄品种与葡萄防腐保鲜剂应用的统一。科技人员还通过对采前因素、果蔬本身和贮藏条件对果蔬贮藏品质影响的研究，提出避免或减少果蔬贮藏化学伤害的调控技术。即根据果蔬种类、品种对化学保鲜剂的敏感性，选择最佳的保鲜剂及其用量；根据果蔬的环境条件确定保鲜剂用量；通过采前套袋、喷钙等措施提高果蔬品质，增加其对化学保鲜剂的忍耐性。

第三节　膜保鲜

将纳米材料加入保鲜膜中会出现特殊优良性能，2002年，保鲜中心开展“纳米保鲜膜气调防腐机理及效应的研究”，研制出纳米保鲜膜，成果获专利。根据需要保鲜的不同食物的特性，保鲜中心和林果所研制出不同的专用保鲜膜，并推广应用。

一、纳米材料应用

常规聚氯乙烯(PVC)、聚乙烯(PE)保鲜膜中加入纳米材料后，会表现出特殊优良的物理、化学性能。通过向PVC、PE塑料添加纳米材料，改变氧气和二氧化碳渗透特性、路径，调节极性分子、水的扩散速度，发挥纳米材料防霉、抗静电、增强的特性，使其既具有常规保鲜膜的气调、保湿功能，又具有普通药剂的防霉功能，具有十分重要的意义。2002~2005年，保鲜中心李喜宏、关文强等开展天津市自然科学基金科研项目"纳米保鲜膜气调防腐机理及效应的研究"，将纳米这一高新技术应用于果蔬自发气调保鲜领域，研究出具有优良自发气调效果的纳米保鲜膜。他们利用钛、银、钙、粘土等纳米材料为添加剂，通过纳米粒子处理、配方、工艺技术研究，研制出银系聚乙烯、钛系聚氯乙稀、碳酸钙聚乙烯等3种纳米保鲜膜。含4%W/W（重量/重量）银系纳米材料保鲜膜对葡萄灰霉菌的抑菌效应为67.9%，0.12毫米厚银系纳米保鲜膜试样较常规保鲜膜阻氧效应提高79%。经国家包装测试中心测定，钛系PVC纳米富士苹果保鲜膜纵向拉伸强度提高36%，透氧率降低18%，透湿率降低10%，二氧化碳渗透率仅变化1.5%。用银系纳米保鲜膜在0℃下贮藏富士苹果208天，果肉硬度7.57千克/平方厘米，无二氧化碳伤害。经研究得出不同$CaCO_3$（碳酸钙）添加量对PE/$CaCO_3$（碳酸钙聚乙烯）纳米保鲜膜透气性能及物理强度的影响规律。$CaCO_3$经铝酸脂交联处理，随加入量增加，膜透氧率呈抛物线型增加。PE/$CaCO_3$纳米保鲜膜用于菜花、青椒、蒜薹、桃等果蔬保鲜效果优于常规保鲜膜。"添加纳米材料保鲜膜"2003年10月获国家知识产权局颁发的"发明专利证书"。

二、专用保鲜膜研发

（一）果蔬专用

1996年3月～1999年10月，林果所李喜宏、陈丽等开展"果蔬专用保鲜膜的研制与应用"的研究。他们根据膜材料不同，其透气、透湿性能不同的原理，依靠果蔬采后自身呼吸代谢降低贮藏环境中的氧气，提高二氧化碳，反过来自发地调节、抑制自身呼吸代谢，拮抗乙烯等衰老激素的催熟作用，减少自身养分消耗，达到延长自身寿命的保鲜目的。经过攻关试验，研制成功果蔬专用保鲜膜共24种类型，32个品种，47种实用规格。确定果蔬专用保鲜膜的新配方、成型工艺与技术标准。明确富士苹果、葡萄、猕猴桃、蒜薹等20多种果蔬专用保鲜技术工艺与方法。该保鲜膜气调指标稳定、透湿性稳定、低温下柔软、透明度好。除在天津市大量应用外，还推广到全国26个省、自治区、直辖市。该研究成果获1999年度天津市科技进步二等奖。2003年10月获国家发明专利证书。

2002～2004年，保鲜中心李家庆、李喜宏等承担国家科技部农业科技成果转化资金项目——"多功能果蔬保鲜膜中试"。经3年多的努力，建成1600平方米的保鲜膜中试车间，2条生产线及相关仪器设备；确定保鲜膜的生产、工艺技术参数和产品质量标准，并形成年产1000吨的生产能力。研制出新型系列果蔬保鲜膜PVC和PE两大系列40多个品种。新型系列果蔬保鲜膜在低温下柔软，防结露，气调效果好而稳定。它通过对透过气体的选择吸附和交换方式，调节袋内气体成分，具有微孔调气、调湿、防雾、纳米抗菌、增强、阻隔等功能。3年间中试生产多功能果蔬保鲜膜864吨，研究成果在全国20多个省、自治区、直辖市推广应用。

2003～2005年，保鲜中心陈丽、李喜宏等开展国家科技攻关计划项目"果蔬自发气调保鲜关键技术研究"。自发气调保鲜技术是利用保鲜膜的选择透气性能，适度控制膜内的氧气、二氧化碳和湿度，达到适合不同果蔬要求的保鲜环境。他们以果蔬采后生理参数和数学模型为基础，以聚乙烯（PE）、聚氯乙稀（PVC）树脂为基材，通过改进保鲜膜加工设备参数、生产工艺、配方设计等手段，结合物理机械性能测试和生物贮藏试验，研制和筛选适用于不同果蔬品种的专用保鲜膜。经2年多研究和试验，确定苹果、蒜薹、葡萄等10余种果蔬、20多个品种的果蔬自发气调贮藏保鲜指标，包括最佳温度、湿度、透气比和贮藏期。研究果蔬采后病害发生机理并提出防治措施。研制成功新型果蔬防雾保鲜膜4种、微孔保鲜膜3种和纳米保鲜膜1种，保鲜和防霉效果显著。

（二）粮食专用

1999年1月～2003年12月，保鲜中心开展天津市星火计划项目"粮食保鲜膜与大米保鲜技术研究"。该科研项目2000年被国家科技部列为国家重点星火计划项目。陈丽、李喜宏等用天津市水稻研究所提供的天津小站稻3个品种为研究对象，研究大米采后生理生化变化规律，包括大米的呼吸强度、脂肪酸、总酸、还原糖、粘度值等生理指标变化规律，研究大米等粮食自发气调保鲜指标，明确大米保鲜阈值，为确定大米自发气调专用保鲜膜的特性提供依据。研制成功大米专用微囊化辣素缓释防霉保鲜剂2种、保鲜膜专用纳米防霉母料2种，开发筛选出防霉、防潮、防陈化专用聚乙烯、聚氯乙稀保鲜膜5种，并确定专用膜的生产工艺和技术参数。专用微囊化辣素缓释防霉保鲜剂对灰霉菌、青霉菌、黑曲霉菌等抑菌效应大于69%，银系聚乙烯防霉保鲜膜防霉效应大于60%。通过研究，确定大米在不同温度条件下聚乙烯、聚氯乙稀专用保鲜膜自发气调保鲜技术参数及其氧和二氧化碳变化规律。在常温条件下对含水量为14.5%的大米自发气调包装(MAP)保鲜7个月，无虫、霉变现象，总损耗小于1%。该粮食保鲜膜和大米保鲜技术的研究首次将具有防霉、驱避、抑菌的纳米膜技术与自发气调进行组合，达到粮食常温保鲜功能，应用范围广泛。

第七篇

医药卫生
科技

概　述

天津医药卫生科技领域学科门类齐全，基础深厚，部分学科历史上在全国一直处于领先地位。20世纪90年代后，随着改革开放，新技术的引进，发展更加迅速，在一些学科领域取得突破性成果。

天津基础医学主要在天津医科大学（1994年以前为天津医学院和天津第二医学院），学科门类涉及人体解剖与组织胚胎学、免疫学、病原微生物学、病理与病理生理学、人体寄生虫学、医学生理学、生物化学等。1991—2005年间，各学科加强基础研究，承担数十项国家级和省部级科研项目，取得一批高水平的研究成果，突破一些关键技术。1991年，天津第二医学院许屏等将荧光染色技术应用于医学研究中，成果获得该年度国家科技发明四等奖。1994年起，天津医科大学孙保存等开始研究大肠癌发生中细胞增殖与凋亡及基因调控。取得优异成果。

临床医学在此15年间快速发展，在内、外科，肿瘤，妇产与儿科，神经病与精神病，眼科，耳鼻咽喉科，口腔科，影像医学与核医学，放射治疗，麻醉，医学检验，护理学等方面都做出一定成绩。

天津的内分泌学科在全国具有领先地位和重要影响。重点在甲状腺疾病，代谢性骨病，糖尿病等疾病的研究与临床中取得多项成果。天津在心血管疾病的研究与治疗中也有一定的基础和成果。专家石毓澍主编《临床心律学》，全面系统地介绍心律学的基本理论，诊断方法等专业知识。天津医科大学总医院，天津医科大学第二医院，天津市胸科医院的医务人员在对心脏病的治疗中提出一些新方法，推出一批新成果。坐落在天津的中国医学科学院血液病医院（血液学研究所）是全国最大的国家级科研型血液病医疗机构。15年间，不断取得新成果。2002年，韩忠朝等在国际上首创了自体外周血干细胞移植治疗下肢缺血性病患者的新技术，有效降低了溃疡面积和截肢率。此项技术的成功实践为加强干细胞的基础研究和进一步拓展临床应用奠定了基础。21世纪初，中国医学科学院血液学研究所创建了技术先进，世界上规模最大的脐带血造血干细胞存储公共库和自体库，成为全国首批通过执业验收的脐血库之一。"脐带血造血干细胞库的建设和相关技术研究"获2003年度天津市科技进步一等奖。

外科领域，科研能力和临床水平在全国处于领先地位的学科有：神经外科、移植外科、泌尿外科等。生物技术、腔镜技术、血液净化、器官移植、放射介入等五项应用技术研究促进临床外科发展，一些高端技术从引进阶段进入快速发展，创新阶段。15年来，在神经外科的颅内肿瘤，颅脑损伤；泌尿外科的膀胱肿瘤，微创手术，下尿路功能障碍性疾病，泌尿器官替代；骨科的骨创伤，骨及软组织病变，创伤急救，骨关节病，脊柱外科，手显微外科，小儿骨科和骨科基础研究等方面取得了一批科研成果和临床治疗方法的突破。在普通外科，20世纪90年代初，天津市南开医院率先引进腹腔镜技术，开展技术创新，很快发展到多学科联合和复杂大器官手术阶段。腔镜微创技术在临床应用中取得良好效果。天津市第三中心医院肝胆外科成功进行肝细胞分离培养，包埋，移植的动物实验，开展生物型人工肝的研究，用于治疗急性肝功能衰竭，取得圆满成果。1997年，天津市第三中心医院经国家卫生部批准，成立"卫生部人工细胞工程技术研究中心"。在移植外科，天津医科大学总医院在小肠移植的研究中取得研究成果。1991年后，天津市第一中心医院开展肝移植临床研究。1998年，该院成立移植外科，是国内第一个器官移植专业科室。2001年后，该院在肝肾、肝胰、胰肾等多器官联合移植获得成功。

1991至2005年，肿瘤学的发展较为突出，不仅在临床医疗上进步较快，在肿瘤流行病学、肿瘤病因学、病理学等学科上都有突破性进展。在临床上，头颈部肿瘤、脑瘤、乳腺肿瘤、泌尿系统肿瘤等是天津医疗技术的强项，其诊断、治疗技术多有创新。多项研究在细胞水平、分子水平上有新进展。肿瘤的生物学技术及物理疗法达到新高度。天津在国内率先采用干细胞移植治疗乳腺癌，并从分子层面揭示肿瘤转移抑制基因，找到一些肿瘤基因治疗的新靶点。专家郝希山在肿瘤临床治疗中取得多项突破性科研成果，获得多项国家和天津市科技进步奖及科技发明奖。郝希山于2003年当选为中国工程院院士。

20世纪90年代，天津市妇科开创显微手术；对子宫内膜异位症的诊疗技术首创了新概念；体外受精等一系列辅助生殖技术获得突破性进展；出版《妇产科内分泌学》，率先将祖国医学运用到内分泌领域；进行子宫内膜癌、卵巢癌的临床及实验室研究，并对某些妇科术式提出改良。围产医学多项研究为减少难产，降低母儿患病率和死亡率以达优生优育的目的取得良好效果。儿科临床治疗中有多项突破性进展，例如：心脏介入治疗代替多年依赖开胸手术的传统治疗。PKU(苯丙酮尿症)杂合子筛查，结合基因分析有可能阻止有胎PKU患儿的出生。在国内率先创建小儿微创外科，首次将腹腔镜技术应用于小儿外科领域。

天津市精神卫生服务机构从1990年的十余所至2005年发展为60所，医护人员增长一倍。服务内容有门诊，住院治疗及心理咨询，心理测量等。卫生资源和医疗水平处于全国领先地位。在神经系统疾病中，对治疗脑血管障碍、痴呆、癫痫等方面取得较好的科研成果。

20世纪90年代初，天津眼科在白内障的治疗中取得了突破性的进步。由海外友人捐助，在天津医学院建立世界人工晶体中国天津培训中心，在国内率先采用超声乳化白内障吸除术和人工晶体植入术，为白内障的治疗开创了一条新途径，提高到一个新水平，并取得良好效果。此后，医务人员还针对这一技术展开相关研究，使其更加完善。例如：折叠人工晶体植入、黄色晶体应用、小切口不缝合技术、人工晶体植入与糖尿病视网膜病变的研究等。1998年，袁佳琴编写相关学术著作，指导该项技术的临床应用。眼眶肿瘤诊断和治疗也是天津眼科的优势学科。天津医科大学第二医院于1999年成立天津市眼眶病研究所。至2005年，积累病例1万余例，手术5000余例。影响波及国内外。研究成果获1999年度国家科技进步二等奖。耳鼻喉科的突出成就在于结合头颈肿瘤开展诊断，手术及重建。天津市第一中心医院在全国率先将螺旋CT投入临床应用。口腔科在口腔生物力学，口腔修复工艺及技术，下颌关节重建术，生物隔膜技术应用，遗传性乳光牙本质的致病基因研究等方面做出了成绩。

图7-0-0-103 由新加坡捐赠的天津医科大学人工晶体中心

1985年，天津医学院总医院学科带头人吴恩惠主编《头部CT诊断学》，这是国内第一部头部CT专著，书中收入多项创新成果，为天津乃至全国医学临床的头部疾病CT诊断提供了理论基础。该项成果获1998年度国家科技进步三等奖。此后，天津医科大学总医院、天津市第一中心医院、天津市环湖医院等单位取得了多项关于头部影像学的天津市科技进步二等奖，推动该领域的科技发展。与此同时，在骨放射、胸腹部放射等方面也取得一定成果。在临床治疗的放射介入领域，吴恩惠和他的团队也做出了突出贡献：1994至2005年间先后主编出版《介入性治疗学》《中华影像医学——介入放射学卷》、翻译出版《介入性磁共振成像》。上述著作在国内有较大影响和学术价值。

1994年，天津医科大学成立公共卫生学院。2000年后，天津市卫生系统将相关单位合并，成立天津市卫生防病中心，并于2003年扩建。随着时代的发展，疾病防控的内容出现了许多新变化，不仅要控制老传染病的复发，还要应对新的突发性传染病。尤其是2003年在全国爆发的传染性非典型肺炎(SARS)，死亡率高，对社会危害大。市领导高度重视，组织相关医院和市防病中心进行指导和救治，并开展SARS流行病学研究。天津疫情达到在全球流行期最短，解除“禁区”最快的地区。相关研究成果获2005年度天津市科技进步一等奖。对于非传染病的防控，逐渐从老四病转向新四病，尤其是对发展较快的糖尿病进行重点研究，在针对糖尿病的研究中取得多项成果。

在中医领域，随着改革开放的深入，加强学术交流，大量引进现代科技方法和医疗设备用于中医理论研究和临床实践。同时,对中药汤剂剂型进行改革,广泛采用冲剂、颗粒剂、胶囊等。天津的针灸科在全国一直处于领先地位,改革开放以后,加强国际交流,在国外也产生了较大影响。针灸研究取得多项高水平科研成果。2004年组建的天津市重点实验室为天津市科学技术委员会和天津市教育委员会首批确定的天津市重点实验室。针灸学科带头人石学敏于1999年当选为中国工程院院士。专家张伯礼在中医诊治脑血管病及中药现代化中做出贡献,于2005年当选为中国工程院院士。

天津市中西医结合的科学研究及临床应用历史长,涉及学科门类广。早在1963年,天津市南开医院就被卫生部确定为全国首个中西医结合临床研究基地。此后,不断有中西医结合的专科研究机构相继建立。学科门类由急腹症,骨伤发展到外科,内科,妇科,皮肤科等多学科,并取得良好的临床效果和多项研究成果。1982年,世界卫生组织把中西医结合治疗急腹症,骨折确认为中国5项世界领先的医学项目。进入20世纪90年代后,天津的中西医结合在高层次上快速发展。在中西医结合治疗急腹症做出突出贡献的学科带头人吴咸中于1996年当选为中国工程院院士。1998年,建立天津市中西医结合研究院。2003年,"通里攻下法在腹部外科疾病中的应用与基础研究"获国家科技进步二等奖。

图7-0-0-104　吴咸中(右)带领的科研团队进行通里攻下法在腹部外科疾病中的研究与应用

1991至2005年,天津药学领域科技水平发展迅速,在药理、药剂、生药、药物分析、新药研发及制药新工艺等方面的研究与开发中取得众多成果,为天津和全国医药行业提供了重要的技术支持,做出了显著贡献。为了给药物研究提供基础条件,大力加强实验室建设。其中,天津药物研究院就承担了6个国家级或部级重点实验室、检测中心建设。药代动力学学科带头人刘昌孝于2003年当选为中国工程院院士。

第一章　基础医学

1991年前,天津基础医学研究成果多产于天津医学院基础医学部。1994年,天津医学院与天津第二医学院合并组建天津医科大学后,更名为基础医学院(以下简称"医大基础院")。该院的研究领域涉及人体解剖与组织胚胎、病原生物与寄生虫、免疫学、病理与病理生理、生理、生物化学、药理学等学科。2000年,病原生物学与免疫学科和病理与病生理学科列入国家"211工程"重点建设学科。2005年,该院基础医学学科被批准为一级学科博士学位授权点。随着不断加大对基础医学科学研究的支持力度,该院先后完成国家"973""863"项目,国家自然科学基金项目、省部级科研项目等数十项成果,其中有的取得突破性进展,达到国际领先或国际先进水平。

第一节 人体解剖与组织胚胎学

1991年以后，天津医科大学（以下简称“医科大学”）在临床应用解剖学和神经解剖学研究的基础上研发火绵胶薄层化切片技术。应用该技术方法取得多项成果，对临床诊断治疗提供全新的研究思路与方法，从而该校建立起神经生物学实验室和断层解剖学实验室。该校在组织与胚胎学方面，着重研究碘缺乏病机理与碘过量对人脑发育的影响以及脑缺血发病机理。

一、人体解剖学

1991～1995年，医大基础院陈仲欣等完成脊髓动脉的应用解剖学研究，观测国人标本60例，对前、后根髓动脉的起源和分布脊髓节段以及颈膨大动脉、腰膨大动脉和脊髓前正中动脉的形成进行统计分析，对临床选择脊髓动脉造影具有重要的参考价值。

1992～1996年，该院郭守祥、李云生完成“雌性激素对小鼠脑发育和抗衰老的影响”研究。研究证实雌激素替代疗法和孕酮联合治疗，促进鼠脑微管蛋白合成及大脑皮质运动神经元多聚核糖体的增加，并能延缓小鼠寿命。

1997年起，医大基础院李云生等将研发的火绵胶断层解剖切片技术，广泛应用于颅底、眼眶、四肢及盆腔等断层解剖研究。2000年，该技术方法在《中国临床解剖学杂志》首次发表。此后，应用该技术方法与天津医科大学总医院（以下简称“总医院”）合作完成“海绵窦断层解剖及CT、MRI研究”。2001年，该院吴樾等在大体解剖学的基础上，开展了前颅底形态学研究与新手术入路探讨，展示了该区域复杂的解剖关系，为传统手术、显微外科手术、眶颅相关外科学等交叉学科以及影像学诊断治疗提供以立体的形态学为基础的全新研究方法与研究思路。2003年，该院李云生等在“直肠癌直肠系膜切除术的应用基础研究”中，应用火绵胶薄层化切片和电镜技术，提供该区域神经、筋膜和直肠肌间神经丛等丰富的形态学资料，为开展以火绵胶断层解剖切片技术为特色的临床形态学研究奠定了基础。

二、组织学与胚胎学

1991年，天津第二医学院许屏等将荧光染色技术应用于医学研究中，这一“显示分化程度不同的细胞的荧光染色法”获1992年度国家技术发明四等奖。

1991年后，天津医学院陈雪娴进行碘缺乏病发病机理的研究。经对大鼠甲状腺的超氧化物歧化酶免疫组化和免疫研究，证实碘缺乏对甲状腺的损害，并对脑垂体的激素分泌细胞进行免疫组化研究，表明碘缺乏可通过反馈作用，引起脑垂体的激素分泌细胞的异常改变，为探讨碘缺乏病的发病机理提供实验依据。1994年，医大基础院陈雪娴等建立低碘大鼠脾的动物模型并发表“阐述碘缺乏造成甲状腺功能低下可以对脾的形态学产生影响”的论著。1999年，完成碘缺乏大鼠脾脏的超微结构研究，证实碘缺乏大鼠脾脏免疫细胞出现微细结构的改变，从而证实甲状腺和免疫系统之间的关系，甲状腺激素作用于免疫系统，免疫系统的改变可以进一步影响甲状腺乃至整个神经内分泌系统。2003年，医大基础院刘皓等研究碘过量对胸腺的形态学影响。结果表明碘过量可以通过影响甲状腺和垂体的功能，进而影响胸腺的生长发育，进一步佐证神经内分泌系统和免疫系统之间可相互调节，相互影响。

1994年后，医大基础院王世忠等在“雄性大鼠生殖器官形态结构的研究”中，对睾丸生精小管和附睾内碱性磷酸酶分布进行研究，并通过荧光染色等技术探讨不同发育阶段生精细胞内碱性磷酸酶的分布。1998

年，王世忠等进行“脑缺血动物模型复制及发病机理的研究”，参与大鼠局灶性脑缺血动物模型的复制，并通过血管灌注等方法显示大鼠脑缺血区的变化，探讨中药白术颗粒对局灶性脑缺血的病理学影响。2002年，进而研究大鼠脑干超早期病理学变化及其对血流的影响。从中观察到大鼠脑干早期不同时间段的病理损伤，神经细胞核酸含量降低，并发现脑干局部血流量减少。

1999～2002年，医大基础院梁玉等与天津大学合作，开展“镍钛记忆合金生物相容性研究”。用兔子作动物模型，研究镍钛合金种植前后骨骼骨折的愈合情况，表明镍钛合金具有良好的组织相容性，为镍钛合金用于临床治疗骨骼提供实验依据。

2003年，该院刘皓进行碘过量对脑发育的影响的研究，对大脑、小脑、海马和垂体进行形态学研究，结果表明低浓度碘过量对脑发育未产生明显影响，而高浓度碘过量（生理剂量的50和100倍）则可对脑发育产生一定的影响。经对碘过量胸腺进行了免疫组化和电镜研究，表明低浓度碘过量未造成明显影响，而高浓度碘过量则可以导致胸腺形态结构改变。

第二节　免疫学

天津在医学免疫学科的研究领域主要涉及机体内外环境平衡、机体防御机制、肿瘤发生与发展等重要生命科学问题，其学术成果多涉及当今重大医学问题，为肿瘤、器官移植、过敏性疾病、自身免疫性疾病及免疫缺陷等疾病的诊断、治疗与预防提供重要的理论指导和技术支撑。1991年后，在免疫分子与免疫微环境、免疫细胞信号传导通路调控、感染性疾病的分子免疫学方面开展研究，不少成果达到国际先进水平，其论文发表在国际一流杂志，被科学引文索引（SCI）收入论文130余篇。到2005年，以上几方面研究，都已深入到分子研究领域。

一、免疫分子与免疫微环境

1994年，医科大学姚智等开展细胞因子与疾病方面的研究工作。结合细胞因子半衰期短的特点，针对具有临床应用前景的细胞因子，开展细胞因子修饰方面的研究，以期延长细胞因子在体内的半衰期。该院联合相关企业，对干扰素α2b、白细胞介素-6（IL-6）及白细胞介素-11等具有临床应用前景的细胞因子进行修饰研究，使其在体内的半衰期得以延长，更好的发挥生物学效应。2002年，又完成“长效人重组白细胞介素-6的研制”，该产物是由T细胞、B细胞、单核巨噬细胞、成纤维细胞等分泌的一种细胞因子，其作用靶细胞种类繁多，在细胞因子网络中发挥着多种生物学功能，其分泌异常往往会导致一些免疫异常性疾病的发生。但IL-6又具有抗肿瘤等多种作用，为此对其进行了深入研究，使其更好的发挥其抗肿瘤等生物学效应。该成果获2002年度天津市科技进步二等奖。

2000年，医大基础院免疫学科与美国耶鲁大学合作成功分离出数十个具有生物学活性的免疫多肽单体。此后，又联合北京大学、中国药科大学及临床药理基地，经过人工合成、体内外抗肿瘤药效的筛选、毒理药代研究及临床研究，于2005年研制出具有自主知识产权的抗肿瘤Ⅰ类新药。同期还开展骨肿瘤骨转移方面的研究，建成活体肿瘤实时检测方法，从中发现一种新型与肿瘤转移密切相关的肿瘤转移抑制蛋白。

二、免疫细胞信号传导通路调控机制

2003年起，医大基础院王金龙进行“性激素与自身免疫病关系的研究”，发现雌性激素对甲状腺炎、系统

性红斑狼疮发生、发展具有重要作用。

2004年,该院杨洁从有关STAT6信号传导通路调控机制的研究及过敏性疾病治疗方面开展免疫细胞信号传导通路调控机制的研究。结果表明JAK-STAT6传导通路的异常与过敏性疾病密切相关;并且利用分子生物学技术建立IL-4/STAT6细胞水平高通量筛选模型——工程细胞株,在上海国家新药筛选中心进行抗哮喘新药筛选,从1600个化合物中筛选出3个对JAK-STAT6通路有显著抑制作用。

三、感染性疾病的分子免疫学机制

2001年,医大基础院白虹进行沙眼衣原体小鼠肺炎的易感性差异以及免疫学发生机制方面的研究。发现中性粒细胞趋化作用相关的趋化因子及其受体(CXC/CXCR2,CC/CCR-1,2)的表达在遗传背景不同的小鼠中存在显著性差异。利用中性粒细胞趋化因子受体CXCR2基因敲除小鼠,证明了中性粒细胞在宿主抗衣原体感染中发挥重要的免疫防御的作用。

第三节 病原微生物学

1991~2005年,医大基础院病原微生物学科以分子微生物学为主攻方向,包括分子细菌学、分子病毒学、临床病毒学和肿瘤基因治疗等。在国内率先开展"反义技术阻抑病毒基因表达的研究",成功构建HBV(乙型肝炎病毒)的HBsec质粒并获得表达,为研制HBV的高效疫苗提供新抗原。建立起单克隆抗体的方法,进行多项临床诊断和基础研究。

一、分子细菌学

1991年,天津医学院陈恩临对志贺菌致病机制开展研究,提取、纯化出志贺菌外膜蛋白。1994年,对志贺菌外膜蛋白和O抗原多糖进行致病作用的分析,发现二者在该菌致病过程中缺一不可。同年,该院陈锦英在致肾盂肾炎大肠杆菌(UPEC)鉴定方法的研究中,建立适合国情的血清学和分子生物学等多种鉴定方法,并在临床菌株的分离鉴定中应用,效果良好。1995年,医大基础院陈锦英对致肾盂肾炎大肠杆菌粘附特性及其DNA多态性进行研究。采用分子遗传学和免疫学相结合的方法,建立用于国内分离UPEC菌株分型鉴定的ELISA方法和papA PCR法,并通过斑点杂交,RFLP(限制片段长度多态性)和Southern杂交,确定其优势基因型和菌株的多态性,同时,选其代表株UPEC132,对其黏附基因克隆和序列分析,证实其为papAF13+papG2,与国外同类菌株存在差异,构建papA DNA疫苗并开展中药抑制的UPEC黏附,进行UPEC感染防治的研究,上述结果为该领域进一步深入研究奠定基础。该成果获2001年度天津市科技进步二等奖。1999年,陈锦英在对"荚膜糖蛋白新药的制备及其免疫调节作用研究"中,在国内成功筛选出一株肺炎克雷伯菌Kp9,建立和优化了细菌培养、发酵和荚膜糖蛋白的提取和纯化的方法,并用提取的荚膜糖蛋白经实验证实具有很强的刺激细胞免疫和体液免疫的作用,动物实验证实对金黄色葡萄球菌和大肠杆菌的感染具有保护作用。2000年,陈锦英从多种细菌中提取出完整肽聚糖,发现该混合细菌裂解物可有效提高细胞免疫、体液免疫,并显示出一定的抗瘤活性。

1998年,医大基础院钟启平在"致腹泻肠杆菌内毒素及其亚单位分子特异性的致病的研究"中,发现福氏志贺菌、大肠埃希菌O29的O抗原成分在体内外均有毒性作用,其单独毒性作用与完整LPS分子不同。2003年,钟启平又进行"医院感染细菌全核心LPS脂质体的制备及免疫效应分析",提出用脂质体包裹医院感染常见革兰阴性细菌LPS,以作为非特异性免疫增强剂,以期提高特定人群机体免疫力。该研究已经证实,用脂质体包裹的LPS免疫动物,可致动物对内毒素休克、腹水瘤、实体瘤均有显著抗性。

二、分子病毒学

1994年,医大基础院李冬田以杆状病毒、烟草花叶病病毒等为载体,如携带丙型肝炎病毒抗原(Ag)基因,并获高效表达,产生对HCV的特异性免疫效果。同年,该院訾自强在"对人小肠粘膜细胞表面轮状病毒受体的研究"基础上,建立轮状病毒受体的纯化方法,阐明该受体的理化性状、生物学活性、组织细胞的表面定位,进一步研制受体疫苗、抗病毒制剂以及对轮状病毒性腹泻的特异性诊断提供理论基础。2001年,訾自强在对反义硫代脱氧寡核苷酸(AODN)及黄芪体外抑制柯萨奇病毒B组(CVB)持续感染作用的研究中,成功建立CVB3和CVB5的持续感染细胞模型,并在两个模型中进行了AODN及黄芪的药效试验。

2001年,医科大学实验动物部出现普通绵耳绒猴大批死亡。医大基础院李晓眠等在死亡动物体内分离出了一株尚未被归于任何种属的新型副粘病毒,并基本完成测序。在流行病学调查中,发现该病毒可能与幼儿下呼吸道感染有关。

三、临床病毒学

1991年,天津医学院李秋香等在对乙型肝炎的治疗研究中,制备出乙肝特异性转移因子,用铬(^{51}Cr)白细胞黏附抑制试验证实其对乙肝的特异性,结果表明对乙肝表面抗原的消除率高达30%以上。同年,该院任中原等开展应用反义RNA对乙型肝炎病毒基因表达调控作用的研究,并对丙型、乙型肝炎病毒的cDNA进行克隆,建立相关表达系统。1994年,该院李晓眠等在对柯萨奇B组病毒(CVB)感染诊断方法的研究中,首创间接ELISA法检测试剂盒,用于临床诊断具有快速、敏感、特异等特点。2001年,李晓眠在对单纯疱疹病毒(HSV)新型检测方法的研究中,在国内首次用HSV重组蛋白gG1和gG2建立HSV-Ⅰ和HSV-Ⅱ的分析方法,为HSV感染临床诊断提供一种新型分型检测方法。

2003年,医大基础院李梅开展SARS早期诊断方法研究。制备出严重急性呼吸综合症相关病毒(SARS-CoV)的纤突蛋白、核蛋白单克隆抗体,并将双抗体夹心法用于SARS的早期诊断。

四、肿瘤基因治疗

1997年,医大基础院李冬田、李秋香等进行多种单一和融合自杀基因对肿瘤治疗的体内、外实验和对放疗增敏作用的研究,取得较单一自杀基因更好的杀瘤效果。2000年,李秋香等完成含HSV-TK基因重组腺病毒的构建及其对肿瘤抑制作用的研究。成功构建含HSV-TK基因重组腺病毒,证实对多种肿瘤细胞有抑制作用且有旁杀伤效应。在动物肺癌模型中,证实对肿瘤细胞的抑制作用。2001年,该院李冬田等完成含胞嘧啶脱氨酶(CD)基因重组腺病毒的构建及其单独或联合AdTK对恶性肿瘤抑制作用的研究。成功构建含CD基因重组腺病毒,证实对多种肿瘤细胞有抑制作用且有旁杀伤效应,在动物肺癌模型中,证实对肿瘤细胞的抑制作用。2001年,李冬田等完成内皮抑素基因(ES)的获取及其分泌型质粒构建的研究。从人肝癌组织中提取总RNA逆转录扩增内皮抑素基因,再构建含内皮抑素基因的重组分泌型质粒,该重组分泌型质粒可成功分泌表达内皮抑素。2002年,李秋香等完成血管抑素(AS)基因克隆及其在E.coli DH5α的表达研究。从人肝癌组织中提取总RNA,经RT-PCR获得AS与K1-5两片段并进行序列分析,成功构建分泌型重组融合表达载体pEZZ18-AS并在E.coli DH5α中进行蛋白表达,确定生物活性。同年,李冬田等完成含CD和ES融合基因重组腺病毒的构建和体外抑瘤作用的研究。成功构建含CD和ES融合基因重组腺病毒rAd-CDglyES,证实对多种肿瘤细胞有抑制作用且表达产物有ES活性和放射治疗的增敏效果。2004年,李冬田等完成细菌内同源重组法构建含融合自杀基因CDglyTK的重组腺病毒。成功构建含融合自杀基因CDglyTK的重组腺病毒。在国内外首次构建成功的含双杀伤功能基因——胞嘧啶脱氨酶基因和内皮抑素基因的复制缺陷性腺病毒,并证实其发挥相应独立的生物学活性,对放射治疗亦有增敏效果。

第四节 病理与病理生理学

20世纪90年代，天津医学院针对国内外病理学发展现状，开始专科病理的分工，逐步形成了内分泌病理学、消化系病理学、心血管病理学等研究方向，建立一支在病理诊断与研究的专业梯队，对重要疾病的发病机理在分子水平上开展研究。2001年，医大基础医学院病理学与病理生理学科被列入国家“十五”“211工程”重点建设学科，确定肿瘤发病机理的分子生物学研究；细胞凋亡的基因及肿瘤血管生成调控机制；甲状腺疾病和代谢性骨病发病机理三个主要研究方向。建立细胞遗传学，分子生物学、细胞生物学，形态计量学等新的实验室。引进荧光原位杂交，比较基因组学、聚合酶链反应（PCR）、显微图像分析、基因芯片、组织芯片等技术方法，开展多项分子病理学研究。肿瘤血管生成，细胞凋亡调控、大肠癌、肺癌的发病机理，自身免疫性甲状腺疾病和代谢性骨病的发病机理等研究处于国内前列。

一、病理学

（一）内分泌病理

1996年，医大基础院谭郁彬等利用大鼠骨质疏松症的动物模型研究细胞因子在骨质疏松症发病中的作用，提出相关防治策略。2000年，该院江昌新、谭郁彬等完成的“六种内分泌和非内分泌器官肿瘤组织的多种神经内分泌表达与肿瘤生物学行为相关性研究”，从多脏器、多肿瘤的角度阐明内分泌和非内分泌器官肿瘤与肿瘤生物学行为密切相关，提示神经内分泌表达在肿瘤发生、分化、生长过程中的调节作用。同时观察到自身免疫性甲状腺疾病中细胞粘附分子和免疫活性细胞的变化。同年，该院林建韶、孙保存等经观察神经内分泌免疫网络在炎性肠病发病中的作用，提出T淋巴细胞、肥大细胞、肽能神经纤维相互联系，相互作用，共同参与克隆病和溃疡性结肠炎的发病过程。

（二）消化系病理

自1994年起，医大基础院孙保存等经研究大肠癌发生中细胞增殖与凋亡及其基因调控，提出大肠上皮癌变中存在“细胞选择性增殖”现象，证明“Fas抵抗”和“Fas反击机制逃逸细胞凋亡”，参与大肠癌的发病。1996年，孙保存等利用二甲肼诱发的小鼠实验性大肠癌模型，观察非甾体抗炎药舒林酸对大肠癌的防治作用，证实该类药物可通过诱导癌前病变和癌细胞的凋亡发挥有效的防治效果，且预防优于治疗，并在基因水平上探讨该药的作用机制。还利用细胞培养和大肠癌移植瘤模型观察细胞趋化因子及其实体在大肠癌器官特异性定向转移中的作用机制，证实趋化因子受体拮抗剂可在体内外抑制肿瘤细胞迁移、浸润，对大肠癌肝转移发挥抑制作用。上述研究对阐述大肠癌的发病机理和寻找新的预防措施和治疗策略具有重要的意义。1998年，医大基础院张乃鑫等利用肿瘤细胞系观察绿茶的抗肿瘤作用，证实其有效成分茶多酚具有抑制细胞增殖，诱导细胞调控的作用。

（三）肿瘤病理

1995年，医大基础院张维铭等针对E_6、E_7的DNA序列而研制成人乳头瘤病毒16型聚合酶链反应检测试剂盒，该试剂盒可以通过特异性引物扩增E_6、E_7序列，准确诊断$HPV_{16、18}$（人乳头瘤病毒）型的存在。经总医院、天津市第一中心医院（以下简称“一中心医院”）、天津中心妇产科医院等试用，效果很好。同年，该院谭郁彬、江昌新、惠京等经观察非小细胞肿瘤，卵巢癌等6种肿瘤中的神经内分泌细胞，提出多种肿瘤细胞可向神经内分泌细胞分化的见解，并进一步证实肿瘤异质化现象。张维铭等观察到端粒酶再活化在肺癌发生中的作用，并利用反义核酸技术抑制肺癌细胞的增殖，为基因治疗提供新线索。同时，还利用基因差异显示技术筛选出胃肠发病的相关基因。2000年开始，该院孙保存等开展对肿瘤的血管生成拟态研究，证实恶性黑色素瘤、滑膜肉瘤、间皮肉瘤、上皮样肉瘤、横纹肌肉瘤等双向分化恶性肿瘤中存在这种特殊的微循环模式，具有血管生成拟态的肿瘤，恶性度高，易血管转移，预后差；此外利用细胞培养黑色素瘤移植模型和鸡胚移植瘤模型研究血管生成拟态的分子机制，提出间充质干细胞参与肿瘤血管生成的观点，丰富肿瘤血管生成理论。

(四)心血管病理

1994年，医大基础院邱近明等在“前列腺素E2对动脉粥样硬化影响和机理的实验研究”中，开展修饰脂蛋白与血管壁细胞相互影响对动脉粥样硬化的作用研究，利用组织培养和动物模型观察前列腺素E2抑制动脉粥样硬化的作用及其分子机制。该项目获1996年度天津市科技进步二等奖。

(五)呼吸病理

2003年，医大基础院孙保存等在抗“非典”一线，进行天津市第一例“SARS”尸体解剖工作，为抗击“SARS”获得宝贵资料。同年，该院王新允等观察到肺癌细胞周期调控及细胞凋亡的变化，为肺癌发病提供依据。马鸿达利用形态学计量方法观察吸烟对小气道结构的破坏，使形态计量学方法在病理研究中得到应用。

二、病理生理学

1991年，天津医学院首次从“甲亢”“甲低”病人血清中分离出TSH(促甲状腺激素)受体的兴奋性抗体(TSI、TGI)及抑制性抗体(TSII、TGII)，据此建立TSH受体抗体(TRA b)酶标免疫药盒，为甲亢的诊治和预后提供技术指标，并在全国17个省市推广应用。与此同时，还制备出具有特异、灵敏、易于掌握的甲状腺刺激抗体(TSI)单克隆抗体，经对自身免疫性甲亢患者血清TST(甲状腺刺激免疫球蛋白)的临床检测，效果满意。

自1995年，对Graves′(格雷夫斯)病的研究从细胞水平转向分子水平，开始反义肽抗体治疗Graves′病进行实验研究。从1996~2005年间，医大基础院陆凤先获得天津市及国家多项科研基金资助，进一步探讨人工合成反义肽核酸(asPNA)对Graves′病可能的治疗作用，该研究成果可为基因治疗的理论根据。

2000年，为在国内消除碘缺乏病，实施全民食盐加碘干预措施，并于1995年在全国开展碘营养监测工作。天津医科大学被指定为主要参加碘营养监测单位，对新疆、内蒙、贵州、四川、陕西、江苏、广东、大连市等地区进行碘营养调查。在1995、1997、1999和2002年四次全国范围的碘缺乏病的调查中，天津医科大学作为全国控制碘缺乏病专家组成员单位之一，参与全民食盐加碘实施后对儿童智力和精神运动改善的评估、尿碘新测试方法的研制、碘盐浓度标准的制定等各项工作。到2000年全国已基本达到消除碘缺乏病的目标。

第五节 人体寄生虫学

1987年，天津医学院基础医学系建立的弓形虫实验室是全国最早组建的弓形虫研究室。1990年后，该院寄生虫学教研室在弓形虫、隐孢子虫、卡氏肺孢子虫，华支睾吸虫，猪囊虫，旋毛虫等方面的研究均取得多项成果，对弓形虫的研究尤为突出。

一、弓形虫

1990年，天津医学院刘佩梅等建立检测弓形虫循环抗原(CAg)的Dot-ELISA方法，对其方法的特异性，敏感性进行研究。结果显示：该方法特异性强，敏感性高，重复性好。1992年，该院佟小莺等用Dot-ELISA方法检测人工感染不同量的RH株和PP株弓形虫家兔血清中的CAg，结果发现：血清CAg动态与弓形虫虫株毒力密切相关。同年，该院武苏平等用间接血凝实验(IHA)、间接荧光实验(IgG-IFA)与斑点酶联免疫吸附实验(Dot-ELISA)对202例进行抗癌治疗的患者进行弓形虫抗体的血清学调查。其阳性率分别为13.37%(27/202),14.85%(30/202)和19.8%(40/202),经统计学处理,三种方法的检出率无显著性差异(P>0.05)。

1994年,医大基础院吴增强等用IHA法对肿瘤和糖尿病患者进行弓形虫抗体检测,结果阳性率分别为12.62%(27/214),10.25%(33/322)。性别和年龄组间均无显著性差异。对照组弓形虫抗体阳性率为4.20%(31/738)。同年,该院吴增强经观察弓形虫RH株速殖子对HeLa细胞和小鼠腹腔细胞的侵入形态,显示出虫体侵入细胞是一主动过程;并对弓形虫顶端复合物的细胞器及其间的关系给出进一步描述。

1996年,医大基础院刘佩梅等用纤维素粉(CF-11)过滤法、微孔滤膜过滤法和淋巴细胞分离液密度梯度离心法对弓形虫速殖子纯化方法进行比较。结果显示:平均回收率和细胞清除率分别为:CF-11法:34%和89%,微孔滤膜法:11%和85%,淋巴细胞分离液密度梯度离心法:25%和100%。

1997年,该院杨秀珍等首次报道弓形虫RH株速殖子在HeLa细胞内可以形成包囊样结构。弓形虫PP株、SH1速殖子在HeLa细胞上均可成囊,其成囊现象与速殖子接种量及培养基pH值有关,并显示一定的虫株间差异。同年,对国内分离的3株弓形虫在HeLa细胞内生长动态进行了观察,并与国际标准RH株进行比较。结果显示:3株弓形虫中,国内分离的CN株对HeLa细胞的侵入力和增殖力与RH株最接近。3株弓形虫速殖子的体外培养收集速殖子研究发现,接种后6天速殖子的累积收获量存在差异性,其中以SH1株收获量大,RH株次之,PP株最少,接种量为10^5时,收获量大,10^4次之,10^3最少。在培养基pH为6.5时的收获量大,pH7.0次之,pH8.0最少。显示出pH6.5的培养条件较适于试验的3株弓形虫速殖子体外增殖,同时,弓形虫的体外增殖也与接种量及不同弓形虫分离株有关。

2000年,刘佩梅等制备出SPA(金黄色葡萄球菌A蛋白)—ELISA弓形虫抗体诊断试剂盒。该试剂盒在4℃可保存3个月,-20℃保存半年,其活性不变。检测了50份孕妇及可疑病例血清或脑脊液,阳性率为4%,与HIA检测结果一致。同年,该院朱云娟等制备出抗弓形虫速殖子单克隆抗体(McAb),并对其特性进行分析。结果发现:McAb属IgG1亚类。通过SDS-PAGE(聚丙烯酰胺电泳)和Western blot分析所识别的抗原分子量为16.5和24KD,竞争抑制试验显示50%抑制率时抗原浓度为40微克/毫升。将RH株速殖子与McAb腹水进行孵育后接种于小鼠腹腔,并不能延长小鼠的平均死亡时间。用McAb-ELISA法检测人工溶于PBS和正常人血清中的弓形虫RH株速殖子抗原,最小检出量为0.78微克/毫升和1.5微克/毫升。用RH株速殖子10^3/只感染小鼠,分别于第6天和第8天能检出循环抗原。同年,该院刘俊燕建立间接免疫酶法,并用此法观察弓形虫RH株感染的急性病变及虫体在主要脏器的动态分布。结果发现:经腹腔感染小鼠时,虫体首先侵入腹腔内的器官,再通过血液循环播散,最后通过血脑屏障到达脑。2001年,刘俊燕等进行弓形虫慢性感染鼠形成包囊的实验研究。结果提示,接种包囊或速殖子是影响成囊的重要因素,感染包囊小鼠脑内易形成包囊。2002年,杨秀珍等为检测组织内弓形虫感染建立敏感、特异、快速的聚合酶链反应(PCR)技术,该技术灵敏度能达到检测出一个虫体的DNA,且特异性强。以PCR法检测实验鼠肝、血中DNA的动态变化,结果显示:PCR技术可用于诊断血和肝脏组织内的弓形虫。同年,刘佩梅研究了小鼠感染RH株弓形虫后脾细胞的IFN-r(r-干扰素)、IL-2(白介素-2)活性动态变化。结果显示:感染后第2天、第5天、第7天小鼠脾细胞IFN-r活性虽有升高,但各组均值与感染前比较均无显著性升高(P>0.05),感染与未感染小鼠的IFN-r活性无显著性改变(P>0.05)。鼠脾细胞IL-2活性在感染前、后有显著性变化(P<0.05)。感染后第3天、第4天较第2天、第5天、第7天显著性下降(P<0.05),至感染后第9天感染鼠全部死亡。说明RH株弓形虫感染宿主后刺激宿主产生的内源性IFN-r和高活性的IL-2不能引起有效的保护性免疫,致使虫体大量繁殖,小鼠死亡。

2003年,刘佩梅等用PCR技术评价大蒜素及其与复方磺胺甲基异恶唑(SMZco)治疗小鼠弓形虫病的疗效。结果显示,大蒜素与SMZco联合应用治疗弓形虫病具有协同作用,大蒜素单药治疗作用不明显。

2005年,刘俊燕等分别以腹腔、皮下和口服3种不同途径感染Fukaya株弓形虫速殖子,观察弓形虫感染小鼠慢性期病变特点及虫体在脑内的成囊过程,统计脑内虫体数量及形成包囊情况。结果显示:3种感染途径的腹腔含虫数均为腹腔感染>皮下感染>经口感染。比较小鼠脑内虫体分布:腹腔感染组,第28天的脑内虫体达到高峰，此时脑内包囊最多。皮下感染组，第21天的脑内虫体最多，脑内包囊也多。经口感染组，第21天脑内虫体最多，但脑内偶见包囊。经口感染Fukaya株速殖子似不易成囊。经腹腔、皮下和口服感染虫体的小鼠存活率在第42天分别为100%、66%、80%。结果提示：弓形虫感染慢性期小鼠脑多被累及。腹腔与皮下感染弓形虫Fukaya株速殖子比口服易成囊。经腹腔感染方式建立弓形虫慢性感染动物模型较稳定。

二、隐孢子虫

1991年，医大基础院纪伟华等对天津市儿童医院（以下简称“儿童医院”）腹泻患儿开展隐孢子虫流行病学调查，结果显示：天津市隐孢子虫在腹泻儿童中的感染率为0.4%左右。2003年，对天津市内4个养老院的老年人进行肠道寄生虫感染情况调查。结果表明，老年人容易感染蓝氏贾第鞭毛虫和隐孢子虫，感染率高于一般人群水平。

三、卡氏肺孢子虫

1997年，医大基础院佟小莺通过大鼠高蛋白食物，皮下注射醋酸考的松及其饮水中加入四环素的方法，建立卡氏肺孢子虫大鼠模型。与传统方法比较，证明该方法能使动物模型的病死率降低，成活率提高和寿命延长。2002年，佟小莺等研究卡氏肺孢子虫包囊抗原的纯化方法。采用肌肉注射地塞米松诱发大鼠卡氏肺孢子虫肺炎，瑞—姬氏染液复合染色法检获肺组织中的肺孢子虫包囊，用改进的胶原酶消化法、Percoll不连续密度梯度离心分离、超声粉碎纯化卡氏肺孢子虫包囊抗原，获得相对纯净而完整的卡氏肺孢子虫包囊抗原。同年，采用瑞—姬氏染液复合染色法制作出颜色鲜明，结构清晰，易于观察的卡氏肺孢子虫包囊和滋养体染色标本。2004年，佟小莺探讨SPA-ELISA检测卡氏肺孢子虫抗原对诊断卡氏肺孢子虫肺炎的价值，并与病原学检查进行比较。结果表明SPA-ELISA检测痰液和肺泡灌洗液抗原比病原学检查敏感性高，而检测血清抗原不适用于诊断卡氏肺孢子虫肺炎。

四、华支睾吸虫

2001年，医大基础院纪伟华等对天津市18个区县多条河流进行华支睾吸虫囊蚴感染情况调查。调查发现，天津市北部的州河、翠屏湖及东部的部分河流受到了华支睾吸虫的污染，海河也出现了阳性结果。

五、带绦虫

1999年，医大基础院纪伟华对带绦虫妊娠节片进行12种染料不同染色方法的筛选，从中筛选出的孔雀绿染色法能制作出结构清晰、易于观察、颜色鲜亮的带绦虫妊娠节片。随后，佟小莺等将此法扩展到对细粒棘球绦虫原头蚴染色的研究，制作出染色效果理想的原头蚴标本，并找到该染色方法的最佳条件。

六、猪囊虫

1992年，天津医学院孙贵珍等用猪囊虫囊液抗原免疫BALB/c小鼠与SP2/0细胞融合，成功制备出抗猪囊虫单克隆抗体。1993年，该院安桂珍等用单克隆抗体建立了检测猪囊虫循环抗原（CAg）的双单抗夹心ELISA方法。1994年，安桂珍观察测定血清猪囊虫特异性抗体及CAg的临床价值。结果显示：同时测定血清抗体和CAg，可作为诊断活动期囊虫病的可靠方法。1995年，对症状性癫痫患者进行脑囊虫病血清学调查研究后发现，测定CAg不但可为症状性癫痫患者提供病因诊断，而且能协助判定囊虫病是否处于活动期，为进一步进行临床治疗提供依据。1996年，通过对38例囊虫病例进行分析，发现天津地区囊虫病有上升趋势，随即开始囊虫病诊断试剂盒的研制。2000年，囊虫病快速ELISA诊断试剂盒研制成功，并应用于临床。

七、旋毛虫

1992年，天津医学院朱静和、谢醒民等对旋毛虫幼虫ES(排谢分泌抗原)抗原及S_3(杆细胞颗粒相关)抗原诱发小鼠保护性免疫进行研究。实验证明，ES和S_3抗原免疫接种后，可诱导小鼠产生较强的保护性免疫力，攻击感染后成虫和幼虫数量显著减少，抗体水平明显升高，嗜酸性粒细胞数量增多，幼虫囊包周围炎细胞大量浸润，巨噬细胞吞噬功能增强。

2001年，医大基础院安桂珍、杨树森等比较旋毛虫成虫虫体抗原、新生幼虫抗原和肌幼虫抗原接种小鼠诱导产生的保护性免疫。结果表明，三种抗原均可激发特异性体液免疫和细胞免疫，诱导小鼠对攻击感染产生保护性。其中，成虫抗原、新生幼虫抗原显示出更好的免疫原性。2004年，安桂珍等比较旋毛虫成虫虫体抗原、排泄分泌抗原和表面抗原对小鼠产生的免疫保护作用。结果显示：成虫虫体抗原、排泄分泌抗原和表面抗原免疫组的成虫减虫率分别为84.48%、89.98%和85.16%；肌幼虫减虫率分别为69.82%、78.80%和73.94%。3种抗原免疫组小鼠血中的嗜酸性粒细胞(EOS)数明显增多，血清中IgG抗体滴度明显升高，IgG抗体的几何平均倒数滴度(GMRT)分别是未免疫组的6.96、7.99和6.06倍。实验证明，旋毛虫成虫虫体抗原、排泄分泌抗原和表面抗原均能诱导宿主产生较强的抗攻击感染保护力，且可激发特异性体液免疫和细胞免疫。成虫的排泄分泌抗原显示出更强的免疫原性。2005年，安桂珍等制备出分泌抗旋毛虫肌幼虫排泄分泌(ES)抗原的单克隆抗体(McAb)杂交瘤细胞，并对其及分泌的McAb进行了鉴定。结果：获得2株抗旋毛虫肌幼虫ES抗原杂交瘤细胞，均能稳定分泌高滴度、特异性的IgM类McAb，并识别不同的抗原决定簇，为研制旋毛虫病诊断试剂盒和制备基因工程抗体奠定了基础。

第六节 医学生理学

20世纪90年代以来，天津市在医学生理学研究方面，主要开展应用生理学和电生理学研究。特别是低氧生理、运动生理、睡眠生理、神经递质与调质、中西医结合等方面的基础研究。同时采用睡眠多导图、离体脑片、多管微电极微电泳、离子敏感电极等电生理技术及分子生物学技术，开展急腹症、癫痫、呼吸暂停综合症、老年性痴呆、心脑血管疾病等研究。从中建立起实验性急腹症、癫痫、老年性痴呆、应激性消化道溃疡等动物模型。

一、电生理学

1993年，医大基础院刘人杰等开展“中药治疗急性胰腺炎的细胞及通道电生理研究”，应用离体胰片灌流技术和分子生物学方法，探讨中药清胰汤治疗急性胰腺炎的细胞和分子机制，制备出三种不同程度急性胰腺炎模型。研究表明：在急性坏死性胰腺炎大鼠模型中，胰腺外分泌部存在坏死和凋亡两种细胞死亡方式；清胰汤治疗急性胰腺炎可能是通过抑制M、ß受体和多巴胺受体实现的；DCL-2基因中度表达可能与抑制细胞凋亡有关；hsp70基因表达与抑制胰酶激活有关。同时还建立起胰腺细胞分离和培养方法，研究胰腺外分泌细胞对细胞外钙离子(Ca^{2+})的依赖时程，研究结果提示无Ca^{2+}介质使胰腺腺泡细胞对乙酰胆碱(Ach)的敏感性降低，高钙则增加胰腺细胞对Ach的敏感性。

1995年，该院王卫国在“牛磺酸对丘脑痛觉整合功能调制作用的电生理学机制”研究中，证实牛磺酸对大鼠丘脑腹后外侧区痛敏神经元单位放电活动可产生压抑与易化两方面的影响，说明牛磺酸对丘脑痛敏神经元活动有一定调制作用。

1996年，该院孙兵在“理气开郁药调节睡眠节律的电生理机理研究”中，经对睡眠脑机制及递质调节的实验研究，提示出神经递质失调导致失眠以及中药在调整中枢神经递质改善睡眠节律方面的良好效果。

1997年，医大基础院徐淑梅等在“癫痫发病机制的研究”及“理气开郁药与转移因子对癫痫的调制实验研究”中，建立海马内注射毛果芸香碱制备慢性家兔癫痫模型的方法，并采用离体脑片技术、脑电技术等探讨癫痫发作及中西药结合治疗的神经电生理机制，研究表明柴胡、桂枝、钩藤和郁金能够抑制癫痫模型的大脑皮层放电和中枢神经突触传递过程，使癫痫的发作次数、持续时间减少，间隔时间延长，其作用可能与其对钙离子(Ca^{2+})内流和Ca^{2+}释放及一氧化氮的抑制作用有关；而转移因子通过增强机体免疫力在与理气开郁药联合治疗癫痫方面起到协同作用，研究结果提示柴胡、钩藤、郁金、桂枝等中药制剂具有抗癫痫作用。

1998年，该院张际国等在“活血化瘀药调制实验性急腹症综合电生理研究”中，建立实验性急腹症动物模型，揭示出中药治疗急腹症的电生理机制。同年，张际国等在“关于神经元调制中的综合电生理研究”的研究中，证实理气开郁药参与大脑皮层高级神经活动的调制作用。同年，张际国在“睡眠二号胶囊对力竭性运动后睡眠的调制评价”研究中，表明睡眠二号胶囊通过调节力竭性运动后脑睡眠调节相关递质发挥作用。继而开展与人体运动康复和健康促进的某些整体生理学、医学及其方法学应用问题研究，研究表明整体运动康复治疗对神经系统疾病、冠心病和代谢紊乱综合征等具有显著预防和改善作用。

1999年，医大基础院仇晓菁、姜如岗进行“银杏叶提取物对大鼠海马缺氧损伤的保护作用”等研究，探讨低氧条件下的神经电生理机制，证实银杏叶提取物对缺氧大鼠海马神经元损伤具有预防和保护作用。同年，在低氧生理学研究领域，姜如冈等在海拔5000米高山现场观察人体神经系统的急性和慢性低氧适应并自行研制设计电脑软件分析低氧适应过程的神经反射，利用离体脑片电生理系统探讨急性低氧适应时神经递质的作用。同年，该院张文霞等开展“电化学疗法对小鼠B细胞淋巴瘤的干预”的研究，提示电磁结合化学疗法对小鼠B细胞淋巴瘤具有显著的抑制和治疗效果。

2002年，该院田德润等开展电针对食源性肥胖大鼠模型和饥饿大鼠模型体重及摄食量的影响研究，并探讨其中枢神经化学机制。结果显示：不论对于肥胖大鼠模型还是饥饿大鼠模型，电针均使摄食量和体重明显降低。电针降低体重的作用对于饥饿大鼠同样有效，这可能与电针下调神经肽Y，降低饥饿感有关，而不是通过促进能量输出来实现。电针可能是通过调节多种神经肽的变化从而使机体能量调定点达到新的稳态。

二、应用生理学

1999年，医大基础院姜如岗、孙兵等开展“调心滋肾组方调治老年性痴呆机理的基础”研究，对滋肾组方抗痴呆的作用进行探讨，结果证实滋肾组方可以提高大鼠海马组织中胆碱酯酶活性，降低大鼠海马组织中单胺氧化酶活性，从而提高衰老大鼠学习记忆能力，具有一定抗痴呆作用。

2001年，该院金学隆等在“脑外伤时的应激性消化道出血的先兆性微循环的指征探究”“脑干出血时的应激性消化道出血的先兆性微循环的指征探究”和“内囊出血的应激性消化道出血的先兆性微循环的指征探究”等研究中，就内囊出血发生后多发的颅压高进行分析，探讨其单一颅压高动物模型的建立方法，进一步明确单纯的持续颅压亢进可以导致消化道黏膜血流改变，结果表明内囊出血—颅压高—迷走神经放电增强—消化道黏膜微循环障碍—出血形成的一系列病理生理过程。

2002年，该院王学瑞等对“生理状态大鼠对不同应激原慢性应激的适应性反应”进行研究，通过慢性应激的不同方式验证应激反应的生物学特性之一：诱导交叉性适应和对诱导适应的干预效应，并在此基础上分析研究下丘脑、垂体和肾上腺皮质在慢性应激反应中神经递质及其相关调质与激素适应性反应的特征及其干预效应，为探讨生理学整体水平功能整合适应特征及其可干预性研究奠定基础。2003年，王学瑞等对“逍遥散干预非垂体中介性肾上腺皮质功能调节”进行研究，结果表明逍遥散煎剂可以有效降低生理和病理慢性应激刺激引发的血浆皮质酮水平的增加。

2003年，该院王玲等开展“Ⅱ型糖尿病及其慢性并发症发病机制的研究”。制备出糖尿病大鼠模型，检测糖尿病不同时期各组织的氧化应激以及氧化应激与细胞凋亡和某些细胞因子的关系，并探讨氧化应激在糖尿病及慢性并发症中的作用，结果表明在糖尿病早期各组织存在明显的氧化应激，氧化应激在糖尿病慢性并发症的发生发展中起重要作用。

2004年，该院孙兵等在“电磁对癫痫大鼠模型的影响”研究中，通过实验证实在匹罗卡品点燃癫痫模型中，低频经颅磁刺激可以延迟匹罗卡品点燃的形成，抑制点燃后的癫痫发作过程；神经细胞凋亡研究显示，低频经颅磁刺激可明显降低匹罗卡品致痫大鼠海马各区细胞凋亡数量，表明调心滋肾组方具有显著的抗痫作用。同年，开展的“血管机能及高血压发病机制的相关研究”，通过观察多种血管活性物质、酶、蛋白和相关信号分子对血管机能的调节，从细胞和分子水平研究血管组织（如血管内皮和平滑肌）损伤和修复的机制及与心血管疾病的相关性，探索实现血管正常功能的生理基础，阐明高血压的发病机理与防治对策。

第七节　生物化学

1991~2005年，医大基础院主要围绕2型糖尿病、心血管病、老年痴呆、肥胖、肿瘤等疾病开展发病机理研究。其研究内容包括：胰岛素及其相关受体的基因序列分析、基因克隆及表达研究；载脂蛋白的结构与功能，脂质代谢酶的结构与功能，脂蛋白的相关受体结构与功能等脂质代谢的分子生物学研究；钙通道及信号传导途径研究；肿瘤蛋白基因结构、蛋白质结构与功能，肿瘤蛋白免疫抑制功能及抗原决定簇的综合分析研究。

一、胰岛素受体

自20世纪80年代开始，医大基础院汤新之等在研究激素受体及受体后信号传导系统生化与分子生物学的基础上，对2型糖尿病发病机理、基因诊断、疾病预测以及和肥胖等疾病的关系进行研究。在进行“2型糖尿病胰岛素受体基因突变及受体酪氨酸激酶域自身磷酸化研究“中，发现受体结合域2，3，6外显子和受体激酶17-21外显子存在静止突变，并经测序予以证实；自身磷酸化程度与胰岛素浓度及受体状态密切相关。为观察2型糖尿病与可能致病候选基因之间的关系，该研究采用SSCP及RELP方法对天津久居汉族人群及家系进行候选基因多态性分析，发现当地2型糖尿病患者某些基因型频率和等位基因频率具有明显特点。汤新之等在对核DNA基因突变进行研究的同时，对中国2型糖尿病人群线粒体基因突变热点区域进行筛查，所发现的点突变可能是2型糖尿病的易感基因，从而建立起临床基因诊断技术。在2型糖尿病的研究中，发现胰岛素与其受体并介导信号传递步骤至关重要。通过对2型糖尿病人群及家系、高蔗糖饮食诱发胰岛素抵抗等实验，采用受体结合动力学分析方法，发现不同程度的2型糖尿病患者及肥胖因素对胰岛素受体结合点数及亲和力有不同的影响。该研究探讨糖尿病的基因治疗，提出人工智能胰岛构建设想，进行胰岛素克隆及原核表达工作及胰岛素重要效应分子—葡萄糖转运蛋白的活性测定等研究。对2型糖尿病发病机理、基因诊断及治疗研究，具有广阔前景和重要意义。

二、脂代谢分子生物学

1994年，医大基础院解用虹等开展“载脂蛋白E基因型测定的研究”。以往所用超速离心、等电聚焦电泳测定方法，不仅要求血样量大，而且需要长时间的超速离心和等电聚焦电泳，成为开展相关研究的瓶颈。而解用虹等建立的载脂蛋白E基因多态性测定新方法所需资金、时间和血样均低于原测定方法的十分之一。经对121名新生儿（使用脐带血）和数百名老人在内的近千人载脂蛋白E基因型的测定和相关研究，进一步证实载脂蛋白E基因型与血胆固醇血症和老年痴呆的内在关系，此法可为早早期确定易患人群，开展早期防治提供试验数据。

严重的高甘油三酯血症与冠心病、急性胰腺炎、不孕、先兆流产和子癫等多种疾病存在内在联系，脂蛋白脂肪酶结构和功能是影响血脂水平，特别是甘油三酯水平的重要因素。2002年，解用虹等建立起应用聚合酶链反应—单链构象多态性结合DNA测序筛查脂蛋白脂肪酶基因突变的技术方法，继而开展包括高甘油三酯血症患者在内400余名人群脂蛋白脂肪酶10个外显子和部分内含子基因突变的筛查，同时研究和探讨其与血脂水平的内在联系。研究发现并报告1例LPL基因外显子3（Leu103→Leu）C562→T同义突变杂合子；完成1例跟踪十余年严重高甘油三酯血症患者脂蛋白脂肪酶基因突变的筛查，并依据家系调查和脂蛋白脂肪酶活性测定，确定其发病原因为外显子5（Pro207→Leu）C875→T基因突变杂合子；检出报告3例内含子3的3'—受位剪接位点（3'-ass）上游6bp的C→T转换的突变杂合子，该基因携带者多为高甘油三酯血症患者；还确定Ser447→Stop是中国人群常见的单核苷酸多态性位点，是影响血甘油三酯水平和脑血管疾病的重要因素，为进一步开展相关研究提供基础数据和检测技术与方法。在此期间，解用虹等完成小鼠和人载脂蛋白CII的基因克隆和基因工程表达与纯化，为制备抗体和应用于检测奠定基础。

三、钙通道

2001年，医大基础院于公元等开展"建立钙通道及信号传导途径研究"。钙离子（Ca^{2+}）在细胞内的超负荷直接造成细胞的损伤并以间接形式参与细胞内传导路径的修饰。钙离子在细胞内的自动平衡的调节，介导细胞信号转道以及细胞在不同状态下受损伤的分子学机理的研究。受体/离子通道变异引发Ca^{2+}分布异常已经在心脏病理过程中，如缺血，增生，失代偿，组织损伤中已经得到证实。Ca^{2+}在细胞内的超负荷直接造成细胞的损伤并以间接形式参与细胞内传导路径的修饰。组织的缺血导致细胞内游离Ca^{2+}浓度的上升被认为是导致组织不可逆损伤的主要因素。包括老年痴呆和其他一些神经病理状态均涉及异常细胞内钙自动平衡调节障碍。Ca^{2+}作为细胞内重要的信使在信号转导过程正逐步得到深入的认识，该研究建立起模拟离体心脏的前期筛选方法、配体—受体结合测定方法以及相关的分子生物学的研究方法。生物膜与离子通道的研究与疾病发生、信号调节和药物作用机理密切关联。

四、肿瘤蛋白

2003年，医大基础院康英姿等开展肿瘤标记-甲胎蛋白（AFP）的蛋白质结构与功能的研究，对甲胎蛋白三大功能及抗原决定簇的综合分析，成功构建抗原图谱；借助转基因小鼠证明甲胎蛋白具有极强的免疫抑制作用。2005年，该课题组进行线粒体氧压应激相关基因DJ-1的基因克隆以及蛋白表达，分析DJ-1蛋白抗氧化功能的结构，为探讨肿瘤以及线粒体相关疾病分子水平的发病机理，为今后征服疾病提供重要的理论基础。

第二章　临床医学

1991～2005年，天津在内科、外科、肿瘤、妇产与儿科、神经病与精神病、眼科、耳鼻咽喉、口腔、影像与核医学、放射治疗、麻醉、医学检验、护理等临床医学科技方面取得较大发展。20世纪90年代初期，天津在全国率先提出科技兴医的卫生发展战略。巨核细胞与血小板的系统、亚低温治疗重度颅脑损伤、功能性间置空肠代胃术、中国女性分娩问题产科生理常数、眼眶肿瘤诊断和治疗等诸多临床与基础研究取得突破性进展。

内科学方面，天津在国内率先开展消化道激素研究；重点建设内分泌学科并成立内分泌代谢病研究中心，同时，干细胞的应用研究方面取得多项成果。外科学方面，20世纪90年代天津相继成立肝胆、泌尿、神经、器官移植等十多个外科研究所，依托研究所重点发展使外科整体科研能力和临床水平居国内领先。以腹腔镜和消化内镜为优势的腹部外科微创技术；肝、小肠移植的实验与临床研究；新型吸附剂、血液净化装置、微囊化肝细胞和人工肝的实验和临床研究；脑血管介入性治疗、亚低温治疗重度颅脑损伤、微侵袭技术、神经营养因子及神经干细胞的基础与临床研究；泌尿系统肿瘤、内分泌及肾替代研究等形成一定优势，取得一批标志性成果。骨外科在骨折愈合机理、微波原位热疗保肢技术、显微修复技术及软组织损伤和感染创面用药等技术项目达到国内领先水平，此外复杂骨关节置换、脊柱畸形和脊髓损伤、关节镜诊疗技术、烧伤代谢营养支持、吸入性损伤诊疗具有明显诊疗优势。总医院神经外科是国内第一个建设的独立神经外科专业科室（1952年），也是当时国内唯一在临床科室内附设有独立的神经病理、神经生理及神经生化研究室。肿瘤诊治方面，天津有骄人的进步。科研整体水平有较大提高，多项研究在细胞水平、分子水平上有新进展。在国内率先采用干细胞移植治疗乳腺癌。在肿瘤流行病学、肿瘤病因学、病理学等学科成就突出。头颈部、乳腺、腹部等肿瘤临床诊断和治疗技术也多有创新。

妇产科学方面，20世纪90年代天津开创妇科显微手术；对子宫内膜异位症的诊疗技术首创了新概念；体外受精等一系列辅助生殖技术获得突破性进展；出版《妇产科内分泌学》率先将祖国医学运用到内分泌领域；进行子宫内膜癌、卵巢癌的临床及实验室研究，并对某些妇科术式提出改良。围产医学多项研究为减少难产，降低母儿患病率和死亡率以达优生优育目的取得良好效果。儿科学方面，小儿内科的介入治疗、PKU杂合子筛查、钾通道激动剂等技术方面得到较好成果。新生儿科、小儿外科等专业不断细分，其治疗技术不断进步。在精神学与神经病学方面，天津在中枢和周围神经系统疾病治疗脑血管障碍、痴呆、癫痫，以及强制医疗、药物依赖、精神病司法鉴定等诊疗技术发展较好。

眼科学方面，天津在眼部疾病诊疗的相关研究中取得快速发展，在斜视与儿童弱视、玻璃体视网膜病和眼科屈光学等眼科学领域得到加强，在国内形成一定的技术优势。耳鼻咽喉科学方面，天津在临床诊治技术取得较大进步，并将多项研究成果和新技术应用于临床应用。同时，开展喉狭窄治疗新方法研究。口腔医学方面，各口腔医院研制的新设备、新技术、新剂型等科研成果广泛应用于临床，改善治疗效果。

影像与核医学方面，由传统放射学迅速向医学影像学转化；由模拟图像向数字化图像、网络化发展；由单纯影像诊断向诊断与介入治疗并重发展；由解剖形态学成像向功能成像、分子影像学成像发展；同时建立起神经、胸部、腹部、骨、介入等放射学专业分支。科研方向以血管病的影像诊断及介入治疗、肿瘤影像诊断与基础研究、脑胶质瘤基因治疗影像学研究、老年人及相关疾病骨矿量影像学研究为重点。其中，国内第一部头部CT专著在天津诞生。其神经放射学、骨放射、腹部放射等方面技术发展较好。超声医学从仪器设备到超声医师队伍及其医学学术水平迅速发展。同期，天津在放射治疗、医学检验、麻醉、护理学等临床技术和科研方面取得不同程度的进步。

第一节 内科学

1991～2005年，天津在内分泌与代谢、心血管、血液、消化、呼吸、感染等内科系统疾病的检验和治疗技术方面进步较快。20世纪90年代，天津在干细胞的应用研究方面取得多项成果。干细胞技术已趋成熟，逐步走向规模化。此外，在巨核细胞与血小板的系统研究中取得突破性进展，并完成全国范围内白血病流行病学调查等。总医院在国内率先开展消化道激素研究。对缺碘性甲状腺疾病的研究为国家制定全民食盐加碘政策做出决定性贡献。1996年，“内分泌学科”被列入天津医科大学“211工程”重点建设行列。1997年，卫生部在天津建立"激素与发育重点实验室"。2003年,天津成立"天津市内分泌与代谢病重点实验室"。2004年,天津医科大学代谢病医院与天津市内分泌研究所实行院所合一管理体制,进一步加强基础与临床研究的紧密结合,是国内从事内分泌代谢病研究中心之一。在临床治疗高血压方面,国内首次建立起一种利用反向遗传学方法及原理研究常见重要疾病的工作程序及管理典范。研究成果增进对医院感染多重耐药菌耐药及播散机制的认识。

一、内分泌与代谢系统

(一)甲状腺疾病

1.检测

1992年,天津市内分泌研究所、天津医学院附属医院方佩华、赵学勤、刘福臣等在"甲状腺激素方法学科研成果推广应用及转化药盒生产"研究中,制备出各种甲状腺激素的多克隆抗体,用^{125}碘标记T3、rT3、T4,制备标记抗原,组装成甲状腺激素四种放免试剂盒向全国推广。获1992年度天津市科技进步二等奖。

1994年,天津医科大学代谢病医院内分泌研究所(以下简称"医大内分泌所")张天庚等在"酶联免疫吸附法测定促甲状腺受体抗体(TRAb)及临床应用"研究中,用酶联免疫吸附法测定自身免疫性甲状腺疾病患者体内TRAb含量,可作为诊断、治疗效果及预测复发等方面的免疫学指标。

1998年,医大内分泌所田恩江等在"甲状腺轴系激素微管固相放免分析的研究"中,建立三碘甲状腺原氨酸(T3)、四碘甲状腺原氨酸(T4)、促甲状腺激素(TSH)、微管固相放射免疫分析(RIA)方法。实验结果表明:第一抗体用量较少,而且能较长时间地保持其抗体的生物活性。操作简洁,灵敏度高,简单实用,同位素污染的范围小。

1999年,医大内分泌所赵学琴等在"血清甲状腺激素(T3、T4)酶免固相方法学建立及试剂盒研制"中,建立的β半乳糖苷酶标记T3、T4固相抗体方法。其灵敏度、特异性、精确度、健全性等各项方法学指标达到并超过放免法。

1999年,医大内分泌所陆凤仙等在"催产素、加压素反义肽的研究"中,应用固相催产素反义肽亲和层析,分别分离纯化催产素、加压素反义肽及其受体复合物,所测得的催产素、加压素受体蛋白分子量与其他方法得到的分子量相同。该项研究还对反义肽识别特性的机理及普遍性进行探讨,为"分子识别"理论提出实验依据。

2001年,总医院方佩华、何红鹏、吕枚等完成"hTPO抗原决定簇基因的克隆和表达及其产物的临床应用"研究。在国内首次克隆人体甲状腺过氧化物酶(hTPO)抗原决定簇基因,并在原核系统表达,利用基因工程产品做抗原建立检测TPOAb的酶联免疫吸附测定方法。该项目获2001年度天津市科技进步二等奖。

2001年,医大内分泌所阎玉芹等组织国内5家实验室完成国家尿碘测定方法的标准工作,"尿碘的砷铈催化分光光度测定方法"在全国31个省、市、自治区各级相关实验室普遍应用,使全国尿碘测定方法得到统一,明显提高尿碘检测质量,保证国内人群碘营养监测结果的可信性和可比性。

2.治疗

1998年,总医院谭建等对"天津市食盐加碘后居民甲状腺肿与碘营养状况的调查研究"表明:天津3年的食盐加碘防治,居民的碘营养状况得到根本改变。首次提出应严格控制碘盐碘含量上限,上限不应超过60毫克每千克。居民碘营养的总体状况表明:碘缺乏情况已得到控制。

1999年,医大内分泌所陈祖培等在"碘及自由基对甲状腺疾病发病机理的实验研究"中,证实缺碘人群广泛存在自由基生成过多而致的过氧化损伤,并伴有自家免疫活动增强;缺碘或高碘导致的过氧化损伤及其诱发的自家免疫机制是甲状腺进一步受损和萎缩趋势的发病机理。

1999年,医大内分泌所王栋等在"联合型瑞文测验中国常模(CRT-C2)的再修订"研究中,从防治碘缺乏病(IDD)的实际需要出发,利用瑞文推理测验(SPM)的标准型和彩色型图形编制出联合型瑞文测验(CRT),使整个测题的适用范围上下限延伸,可扩大到5~70岁。为此,该项研究按心理测量学要求完成中国农村儿童、中国城市儿童和中国成人三个智商常模，是国内唯一的再修订版。

2002年，医大内分泌所李兰英在“甲状腺激素与脑发育的研究”中，首次报告人TRa3，基因序列已提交美国国立生物信息中心（NCBI）的基因库（Genebank）。提示不同碘水平对体外培养神经细胞生长的影响，表明碘对神经细胞的生长和分化没有直接作用，碘营养失衡对神经系统的损伤主要是由于碘缺乏使甲状腺激素合成不足所致。

2003年，医大内分泌所陈祖培等完成“轻度缺碘地区全民食盐加碘后（USI）甲状腺疾病谱的变化及碘过量对人群危害和疾病谱的调查研究”。结果表明：碘缺乏对人体的危害远大于碘过量，机体对碘过量有较强的代偿能力，人体对碘的可耐受最高摄入量为推荐摄入量的6.5倍，现用食盐加碘浓度是安全的。

2005年，医大内分泌所完成的“全国部分低碘地区食盐加碘后儿童智商测定研究结果分析”，表明低碘地区儿童智商由补碘前的90提高到103。证实食盐加碘已使危害全国下一代脑发育落后的状况得到彻底纠正。

（二）代谢性骨病

1991年，天津医学院内分泌研究所庞智玲等完成“人胎大脑神经细胞成骨细胞无血液原代培养模型的建立与应用”研究。该方法可用于激素、生长因子、微量元素等方面的细胞、分子水平的分析研究和某些嗜神经病毒的检测。提示T3对神经细胞存活、分化以及神经特异性烯醇化酶（NSE）和微管相关蛋白（MAP2）表达均有促进作用，与体内骨形成有关，不同剂量的氟对成骨细胞生长和分化呈双相作用。该成果获1991年度天津市科技进步二等奖。

1995年，总医院邱明才等在“氟中毒的骨形态计量学系列研究”中发现：低剂量（百万分之五）可以增加骨体积，而高剂量（百万分之二十五）则可以抑制骨形成，并据此结果提出氟中毒的阈值理论。氟中毒病人骨活检的结果表明，骨组织仅有很少量的四环素荧光标记，覆盖在骨小梁表面的类骨质所占比例增加，平均类骨质宽度增加，表明骨软化的存在。病人间的骨体积差异很大，但所有病人均有网织骨形成，其中包埋有增大的骨细胞。适当补充维生素D和钙剂有助于治疗氟中毒合并的骨软化。该项目获1995年度天津市科技进步二等奖。

1997年，总医院、天津市内分泌研究所邱明才、杨宝恩、王觉英等完成“髂骨正常计量参数的检测和几种代谢性骨病的系列研究”。该研究用国产材料制备国内第一张不脱钙骨切片，应用四环素双标记的方法开展骨动力学研究，把中国的骨代谢研究提高到一个新水平；自筹资金建立中国第一个骨计量学实验室并使其国产化、现代化；第一个报告大样本（248人）正常人髂骨形态和动力学参数的正常值；第一个在临床上开展骨活检检查，为代谢性骨病的诊断提供病理学基础。在原发性甲旁亢的研究中首先发现并证明软骨病和骨矿化障碍不均一性的存在，为预防病人术后出现的低钙抽搐提供理论依据；在国际上首先发现破骨细胞吸收类骨质的现象，对传统的破骨细胞只吸收矿骨化的理论提出挑战；首次用SPA测定正常人、甲亢和糖尿病病人的骨矿物质含量；在地方性氟中毒的研究中第一个在国际上提出氟中毒阈值理论，氟是一种潜在的致软骨病因子和细胞毒的观点。该研究获1997年度国家科技进步三等奖。

（三）糖尿病

1992年，天津第二医学院及其附属第一中心医院任铁生、于国宁、蔺静等完成“天津市区糖尿病流行病学及其危险因素研究”。该研究通过对天津市市区62577人进行的糖尿病（DM）及糖耐量低下（IGT）的流行病学调查，揭示出天津市DM的患病率为11.53%、IGT的发生率为16.23%，分别探讨其人群（年龄、性别、民族、职业等）与地区分布的特征。

1996年，天津市急腹症研究所和天津市南开医院（以下简称“南开医院”）李方儒、何清宇、袁恒达、曹泽伟等完成“糖尿病胆石形成因素的实验及临床研究”。临床资料证实：糖尿病人群胆石症检出率是常人的2～3倍，与糖尿病长期未得理想控制有关。

2000年，总医院于德民、刘铭、何庆等在“大鼠胰岛细胞和小鼠βTc3凋亡相关基因及转染的研究”中表明：在长期高糖体外培养条件下，大鼠胰岛细胞中bc1-xL/bcl-xS比率显著降低，而这一比率的变化可能在高糖所致的β细胞凋亡中起着重要的作用；在国内建立过表达bcl-2基因的β细胞克隆。

2001年，总医院冯凭等开展“瘦素、脂肪酸与胰岛细胞功能的相关研究”，将重组瘦素作为治疗药物应用于肥胖动物，阐明肥胖症对人体的危害以及与糖尿病之间的关联。

2001年，冯凭等开展的“血清瘦素及相关因素的研究”，采用较大样本对天津地区人群血清瘦素水平及影响因素进行研究，对血清瘦素水平与性别、体重、体脂、年龄等因素关系作出详细报道。对瘦素的生理作用及其机制，瘦素对于人体代谢及其他功能的影响都有重要意义。

2002年，总医院薛承锐、梁泉、赵战朝等完成“植物性神经对肝脏葡萄糖代谢影响的机理研究”。该项目模拟损伤原因建立动物模型，建立一种去肝脏胆碱能神经动物模型，在此基础上对糖代谢的影响变化进行初步探讨，为深入研究植物性神经对肝脏葡萄糖代谢的作用奠定基础。

2003年，总医院冯凭、崔景秋、强桂芬等完成“PGE对糖尿病性动脉粥样硬化内皮功能氧化应激及病理形态学的影响”的研究，证实PGE1和大剂量PGE2可减少糖尿病(DM)性动脉粥样硬化(AS)家兔主动脉内皮细胞损伤、抑制平滑肌细胞(SMC)增生，减少病变面积，减轻病变程度。

2004年，总医院朱铁虹等完成“胰淀素与2型糖尿病发病、磺脲类降糖药继发失效相关性及对策研究”，研究表明：胰淀素抑制胰岛素分泌与作为胰岛B细胞内胰岛素信号传递因子Ca++含量和/或cAMP聚集量减少有关，并首次观察到磺脲类降糖药继发失效患者血浆胰淀素水平与胰岛素分泌的相关性。

(四)甲状旁腺疾病

1994年，医大内分泌所陈昆明等在国内率先建立人血清降钙素(h-CT)放射免疫测定法，为钙磷代谢的临床和科研提供重要手段，对甲状腺疾病、甲状旁腺疾病、钙磷代谢研究，对肿瘤的诊断，监测均有重要意义。

1995年，总医院邱明才等完成“甲状旁腺机能亢进症髂骨形态和动力学病变的研究”。结果发现甲状旁腺机能亢进(PHPT)病人的骨小梁表面存在着骨矿化障碍不均一性，即同一髂骨部位，不同骨小梁表面的矿化障碍不同。骨形态和动力学参数测量的结果表明，病人合并有不同程度的软骨病，而软骨病则是PHPT患者血钙正常的主要原因。

2001年，医大内分泌所张镜宇等在“重组人甲状旁腺(PTH)激素高效表达系统”研究中，完成重组人PTH1-84在大肠杆菌中的高效表达。动物实验表明，所制备的重组人PTH1-84(rhPTH1-84)可使骨质疏松大鼠的骨密度得以显著的恢复，并提高骨的力学强度，具有治疗骨质疏松症的临床应用前景。

2005年，医大内分泌所郭刚等在“高表达量且具有生物活性的PTHrP(1-86)和PTHrP(1-141)重组蛋白制备方法的建立”研究。证明重组的PTHrP可使骨转换加快，促进新骨生成，使骨的力学性能提高，抗弯曲强度高，抗变形能力增强，韧性增高，脆性降低，不易发生断裂。

二、心血管系统

(一)冠心病

1992年，天津医科大学第二医院(以下简称“医大二院”)姜铁民、李志坚、李广平等在全市首次采用经皮冠状动脉介入术(PCI)治疗冠心病取得成功。

1993年，天津市胸科医院(以下简称“胸科医院”)屈大展、霍森、刘寅等率先应用经皮冠状动脉成形术(PTCA)治疗急性心肌梗死(AMI)患者，研究者对2例急性心肌梗死6小时内患者行冠状动脉造影，经造影导管向闭塞的冠状动脉缓注尿激酶，溶栓治疗再通后，对残留狭窄在90%者立即行PTCA，使其减少至20%左右，康复过程明显缩短。

1995年，胸科医院屈大展、赵炳让、刘寅等在采用PTCA治疗AMI基础上，应用冠状动脉内支架成形术治疗2例AMI，术后随访患者症状及心电图在内的各项指标均有明显改进。

1997年，胸科医院吴建国、赵茹、田青平等进行“直接冠脉支架治疗急性心肌梗死及川芎嗪防治冠脉介入治疗后再狭窄”的研究。该项目在国内首先将川芎嗪应用于临床防治冠脉介入后再狭窄的治疗，证实川芎嗪在降低再狭窄率和提高完全无症状生存率优于传统的治疗方法。

2000年，胸科医院和天津市心血管病研究所张我素、刘柏年、杨桂铭、张燕杰等完成“粒细胞发光在急性心肌梗塞溶栓再灌注中的研究”。观察到缺血再灌注时，PMN氧化活性增加；PMN-CL峰值及吞噬指数高峰前移可作为AMI溶栓再通又一指标。

同年，总医院万征等在“单纯和复加切割球囊术治疗冠心病研究”中，证实切割球囊术对血管弥漫病变、严重钙化病变、开口处病变、分叉病变、小血管病变及支架内再狭窄病变的治疗安全有效，特别对支架内再狭窄病变的疗效优于单纯的球囊导管扩张术。

2001年，总医院万征等完成“声学密度技术在冠心病诊断和介入治疗的应用研究”。该技术以超声背向散射积分为基础，通过分析二维图像取样容积内背向散射信号的强弱，观察心肌超微组织结构的病理变化，证实声学密度技术能够早期、准确地反映出正常、缺血、梗死和再灌注心肌的组织特性。

同年，胸科医院和天津市心血管病研究所毛用敏、崔让庄、陈倩等完成“载脂蛋白AI基因变异与冠心病的关系”研究。表明血浆ApoAI含量与冠心病的发病呈负相关，ApoAI含量与基因变异有关。冠心病级P2等位基因的患者ApoAI含量明显低于P1患者。ApoAI启动子变异基因也与ApoAI含量有关。

2002年，胸科医院、医科大学和天津市塘沽医院冯津萍、卢奕、陈书中、赵炳让、梁伯平等完成“缺血再灌注心肌细胞凋亡机制及防治的研究”。研究证实再灌注时可出现炎症细胞因子升高，bax高表达和bcl-2的低表达，出现心肌细胞凋亡。

2003年，胸科医院许静、付乃宽、卢凤民等引进经皮穿刺桡动脉冠状动脉腔内成形术和支架术，临床治疗10例成功率为90%，与常规经股动脉途径相比，具有损伤小、血管并发症少、止血方便、恢复快、不影响抗凝或溶栓药物连续使用之优点。

同年，总医院黄灿亮在“多普勒组织显像技术测量心肌运动指数评价心绞痛患者总体心功能的临床研究”中，利用超声多普勒组织显像（DTI）技术在同一幅图像中完成心肌运动指数测量，避免生理性心率变异引起的误差，使心肌运动指数测量更简便，结果更精确。

2004年，胸科医院刘寅等进行“^{32}P放射性球囊血管内照射防治血管成形术后再狭窄的研究”。研究证实放射性液态球囊行血管内照射安全、有效、可行，能减少靶血管再次血运重建次数，对冠状动脉血管成形术后再狭窄防治具有临床治疗意义。

同年，总医院万征进行“药物洗脱支架在冠心病介入治疗（PCI）中的临床应用”研究，通过抑制炎症反应和细胞增殖、延缓血管内皮化，使PCI术后的支架再狭窄率从普通支架的约30%降至10%以下。

2005年，总医院黄灿亮在“背向散射技术定量分析颈动脉斑块评价冠心病发病类型的临床研究”中，利用背向散射参数值在不同组织或同一组织不同病生理状态下会因组织超微结构的不同而发生变化鉴别组织结构的变化，区分不同的组织成分。

同年，总医院黄灿亮、万征、袁文利等完成“声学密度定量技术在冠心病及心包疾病研究中的应用”研究。采用声学密度定量鉴别心包积液和心包脂肪，可鉴别常规超声无法鉴别的心包积液和脂肪，提出检测急性心肌缺血方面与单光子发射计算机断层成像术（SPECT）具有良好的一致性。

是年，一中心医院李志军、刘剑虹、陈洁等完成“序贯治疗不稳定型冠状动脉疾病的实验及临床研究”。该研究在家兔动脉粥样硬化的基础上耳缘静脉注射垂体后叶素诱发急性心肌缺血，建立不稳定型冠状动脉疾病（UCAD）动物模型。并证实UCAD的发生与炎症反应密切相关。该项目获2005年度天津市科技进步二等奖。

（二）心律失常

1991年，医大二院李忠诚、李广平等在全市进行首例室上性心动过速的射频消融术。

1994～1995年，胸科医院信庭文、王惠中、董其克等完成6例7条右侧旁路的射频消融，该法使用大头导管自右股静脉置入至二尖瓣环房侧标测，消融。患者采取透视体位左前斜位45°，显性旁路在窦律时标测心室最早激动点，隐匿性旁路在心室起搏或心动过速发作时，标测心房最早激动点，作为射频靶点。消融后心动过速均不能被程序刺激诱发，显性旁路△波消失，且无并发症。

1996年，医大二院石毓澍主编的《临床心律学》，全面系统地介绍心律学的概念，详实地论述心律失常的基本理论、诊断手段、药物治疗和介入治疗方法，并结合病例资料，对心律失常治疗的策略进行详细推理和论证，对心律失常的诊断和治疗具有指南意义。该书获1996年度天津市科技进步（著作）二等奖。

1998年，胸科医院信庭文、许静等应用双大头导管射频消融技术治疗阵发性房性心动过速；许静、吴尚勤等应用射频消融双向阻滞法治疗阵发房扑均获得成功。

2000年，胸科医院陈元禄等进行“加味炙甘草汤注射液治疗病态窦房结综合征的电生理研究”，提示加味炙甘草汤注射液对窦房结损伤的兔窦房结自律性的恢复有促进作用，对窦房传导功能无明显的影响。同时表明，加味炙甘草汤可延缓部分病窦征患者的病情发展。

2003年，医大二院李广平等经对“阵发房颤电重构的实验研究”，证实电重构是心房颤动，乃至心律失常的普遍现象，并对逆向电重构的作用进行研究，提出心脏电学顿抑的概念。

（三）高血压

1995年，总医院贺能树、曹喜才、吴恩惠等完成“肾动脉狭窄性高血压的影像学研究”。该研究首先提出在中国大动脉炎（TAKAYASA病）是肾动脉狭窄性高血压的主要病因。观察JGA（肾小球旁器）超微结构，阐述PTRA后血压下降的机制。对血管成形术后管径增大的机制提出“反向平衡”的假说。该项目获1995年度天津市科技进步二等奖。

1997年，中国人民武装警察部队医学院（以下简称“武警医学院”）李玉明、刘治全、杨鼎颐等完成“盐敏感性高血压的钠代谢障碍与钠泵α1亚单位基因突变及遗传特性”研究。研究发现高血压病患者的盐敏感性个体在盐负荷后有“低减”与“增强”型两种肾排钠反应；提出“低减”型盐敏感者减弱的肾排钠反应系钠泵的Ouabain抵抗现象所致；证实“低减”型排钠盐敏感者的Ouabain抵抗现象系钠泵α1亚单位基因118及129位密码子的点突变所致；同时发现该种突变以常染色体显性方式遗传。项目研究明确高钠作为高血压病危险因素的具体致病环节，并在国内首次建立起一种利用反向遗传学方法及原理研究常见重要疾病的工作程序及管理典范。该项目获1998年度国家科技进步三等奖。

2000年，医大二院周长钰等在“高血压钙代谢异常及钙剂、钙拮抗剂的降压机制研究”中，证实自发性高血压大鼠及原发性高血压患者，其红细胞膜三磷酸腺苷（ATP）酶活性均降低。提出以补钙前的基础红细胞膜Na+-k+-ATP酶及Ca2+-ATP酶活性为指标的判断函数。

2002年，总医院贺能树、田俊芝、孙健中等完成“肾动脉狭窄性高血压介入治疗的临床与实验研究”。通过介入治疗肾动脉狭窄性高血压38例，提出球囊血管成形术可作为治疗肾动脉狭窄性高血压的首选治疗方法。

2005年，医大二院王林、李玉明、郭宏等在“单纯收缩期高血压（ISH）同型半胱氨酸（HCY）遗传及代谢因子的研究”中采用生化分析和DNA提取、基因测定等分子生物学技术，对ISH发病与HCY水平的改变及相关因素的关系进行多方位的探讨，为ISH的筛查及预防提供理论依据。

（四）心包和胸腔积液

1995年，胸科医院吴建国、裴诚民、耿庆国等在国内首创“经皮血管镜直视心包活检引流灌洗术”。该方法利用介入技术以塞林格方法放入止血鞘，放光积液后，使用血管镜技术，经皮通过鞘内行心包直视检查。该项目获1996年度天津市科技进步二等奖。

1997年，胸科医院李月川、林燕萍、李文全等研制成功“多功能胸腔穿刺活检针、细导管引流装置”并应用于临床。

1999年，胸科医院和天津市心血管病研究所李月川、李树花、李建等开展“凝集块对恶性胸腔和心包积液诊断价值的研究”，提高了病理诊断阳性率。

三、血液系统

（一）巨核细胞与血小板

中国医学科学院血液学研究所（以下简称“血研所”）韩忠朝等自1984年起对巨核细胞与血小板进行系

统的研究。1989年,经研究证明巨核细胞和血小板的生成受许多刺激因子的调节,除TPO(血小板生成素)和一些白介素(IL-3、IL-6和IL-11)外,还受一些非造血因子(FGF-1、FGF-22、IL-13)和糖胺聚糖类物质的刺激。其中,糖胺聚糖有刺激巨核细胞与血小板生成的作用。1990~1992年,研究证明对巨核细胞系有相对特异性的抑制因子是血小板衍生的PF4。ß-TG和CTAP-111等因子及血小板反应蛋白(TSP)对巨核细胞的生成也有抑制作用。1992年,实验证实巨核细胞系的分化增殖是一个连续的多阶段细胞和生物学过程。证实巨核细胞与红细胞有一个共同祖细胞的推测。1993年,在国际上最早系统归纳出巨核细胞和血管内皮细胞在结构上有许多共性,许多巨核细胞调节因子对血管皮细胞有类似调节作用,许多血管因子对巨核细胞也有调节作用。在骨髓增殖性疾病中,血小板有自发性聚集的特点,其巨核细胞也有自发性增殖的特点,这些特点在疾病缓解后不存在。1996年观察到巨核细胞系白血病细胞对三氧化二砷的敏感性比正常造血干祖细胞大,三氧化二砷在对正常造血干祖细胞的增殖不起作用的低浓度时能诱发巨核细胞系白血病细胞凋亡。血研究所韩忠朝、宋玉华等完成的"巨核细胞和血小板的病理生理学特征及其生长调节"项目获2001年度国家自然科学二等奖。

(二)双功能抗体

1998年,血研所杨纯正、朱祯平等在微型双功能抗体(Diabody)研究中,获得具有中国自主产权的抗CD3和抗CD20单克隆抗体轻、重链可变区基因的DNA序列。同时,基于该序列构建的抗CD20/抗CD3 Diabody在大肠杆菌中获得高效可溶性表达。实验结果显示,抗CD3/抗CD3 Diabody在Raji细胞移植瘤部位富集,并介导人T淋巴细胞杀伤Raji细胞,明显延长裸鼠生存期,60%的裸鼠长期存活。该项研究在国内外首次证明抗CD3/抗CD20 Diabody体内有效性,"抗CD3和抗CD20双功能抗体的研制"项目获2001年度天津市科技进步二等奖。

(三)趋化因子

1999年,血研所韩忠朝等在"趋化因子调节细胞生长和耐药反应"的研究中,发现趋化因子(CKs)之一的血小板第四因子PF4能抑制造血,特别是对巨核细胞系造血的抑制。同时,发现PF4生物活性受肝素等糖胺聚糖的影响,肝素等糖胺聚糖有中和PF4的活性和结合细胞的能力。证明PF4等CXC-CKs抑制血细胞增殖的活性位于其中部区域,与CK结合糖胺聚糖的能力无直接关系。进而发现PF4还显著减低骨髓细胞对多种化疗药物的敏感性。动物实现表明:PF4及其相关多肽可加速化疗后造血前体细胞的恢复。由于PF4等CKs只调节正常造血细胞的耐药反应,对肿瘤和白血病细胞不起作用,因此可望用以治疗肿瘤和白血病化疗诱发的骨髓抑制。该项研究在国际上首次证明PF4能促进致死量照射后造血干细胞(LTC-IC)的存活和增殖。该项目获2003年度天津市自然科学二等奖。

(四)干细胞及干细胞因子

1999年,血研所开展"脐带血造血干细胞库的建设和相关技术研究",该项目建立"天津市脐带血造血干细胞库标准技术操作规程、质量标准和管理规程";开发出一套"脐带血库文件管理与数据库系统"软件,实现脐带血生产全程自动化和电子化。在国内率先创立公共脐带血库与自体脐带血库共营的运行模式。到2003年各项技术成熟稳定,广泛应用于干细胞及组织器官临床移植、干细胞组织工程等领域。该成果获2003年度天津市科技进步一等奖。

2000年,血研所与上海望春花公司、北京华银公司联合组建"协和干细胞基因工程有限公司"。该公司先后建立干细胞库、干细胞移植中心免疫及基因诊断以及基因工程药物基地。2001年,血研所与天津经济技术开发区合作,组建中国医学科学院血液学研究所泰达生物技术中心。该中心主要从事干细胞应用基础研究(包括干细胞的扩增、分离纯化、鉴别及干细胞相关基因调控等)和干细胞相关治疗产品的研制。

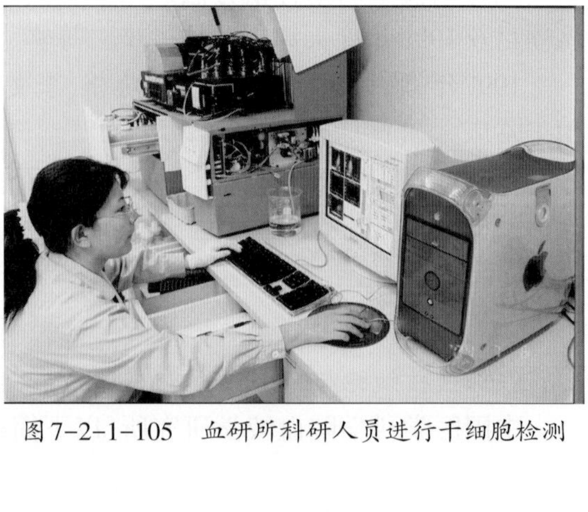

图7-2-1-105 血研所科研人员进行干细胞检测

2002年，血研所韩忠朝等从再障贫血病人的尿中分离出一种新的干细胞因子，命名为血液血管细胞生成素（HAPO）。其既可促进血液血管共同的干细胞的增殖，又可通过刺激血管新生治疗血栓栓塞性心、脑及周围血管性疾病，还可用于细胞治疗产品的生产。经氨基酸和cDNA序列查证，HAPO是一个前未报道的新型干细胞因子。采用高密度发酵技术，适于工业化生产。在临床前动物实验中发现，重组的HAPO对造血干祖细胞与血管内皮细胞具有促增殖作用。以同位素半致死量照射后，小鼠为实验模型，用HAPO治疗，能提高其生存率，加速骨髓重建。

（五）血液病治疗

1994年，血研所全年完成20例造血干细胞移植（治疗急慢性白血病19例，多发性骨髓瘤1例），其中，骨髓移植：异体11例、自体7例；外周血干细胞移植：异体、个体各1例。2004年，血液病医院全年完成干细胞移植71例，所有患者均获造血重建，无患者发生早期移植相关死亡，其中包括8例无血缘关系供者造血干细胞移植。对急性白血病的治疗，完全缓解率达85%～90%，难治性急性白血病的完全缓解率达60%左右；干细胞移植治疗外周血管病13人次，有效率达100%。

2000年，血研所邵宗鸿、陈桂彬、郝玉书等完成“骨髓增生异常综合征恶性造血克隆鉴别的研究”。从细胞形态学、细胞免疫学、细胞生物学及分子生物学等方面分析骨髓增生异常综合征（MDS）的恶性造血特征，研究发现：MDS可有典型的病态造血、也可无病态造血；溶血性贫血、营养性贫血及其他继发性血液系统疾病也可见难与MDS病态造血区别的形态学异常。单以形态学指标诊断MDS欠灵敏，不特异。MDS骨髓细胞髓系早期抗原表达增高，粒单核细胞系抗原表达错位，CD117表达增高。MDS多见染色体核型异常。同正常对照组相比，MDS造血干祖细胞体外培养CFU-GM集落产率明显减少，分化障碍；而CFU-E、BFU-E集落产率明显增高。细胞周期延长。MDS成熟中性粒细胞超氧阴离子及中性内肽酶水平减低。Evil及MDS1-Evil基因在MDS骨髓细胞过度表达且与预后有关。并建立MDS综合性诊断标准，提高MDS诊断的准确性。该项目获2000年度天津市科技学进步二等奖。

同年，血研所赵春华、尤胜国、唐佩弦等完成“慢性粒细胞白血病发病机理及实验治疗研究”。该研究在深入探讨慢粒发生分子机制基础上，建立人慢性粒细胞的原代细胞模型，提出慢粒白血病耐药、凋亡延迟以及异常增殖多因素致病学说，并论证生物治疗慢粒白血病综合方案，为临床治疗提供以生物治疗为主的综合治愈慢粒的新途径。该成果获2000年度天津市自然科学二等奖。

2001年，血研所宋玉华、马小彤、李戈等完成“新型疱疹病毒感染与病态造血”研究。发现成人慢性特发性血小板减少性紫癜的HHV-6检出率尤高，其血小板IgG抗体升高与HHV- 6感染有关。对HHV-6感染与造血干细胞移植疗效的关系研究结果表明：受者出现HHV-6活动性感染，但是HHV-6的活化与延迟造血干细胞植活无明显相关。从一例白血病患者的骨髓测出新型疱疹病毒HHV-8DNA。这一国内外首例报道的白血病患者感染HHV-8，为临床治疗和实验提供新思路和新方法。

2002年，血研所韩明哲、冯四洲、邱录贵等完成“自体骨髓移植治疗急性白血病”研究。将传统的预处理方案改为全身放疗/环磷酰胺，提高患者对放疗的耐受性，自行设计的联合化疗预处理方案，具有用药时间短、对白血病细胞杀伤力强的特点，对急性非淋巴细胞白血病（ANLL）的疗效与经典的预处理方案相等；探索研究白细胞介素-2与干扰素- a 联合激活骨髓对白血病细胞的净化作用，降低移植后白血病的复发。通过对111例急性白血病患者进行自体骨髓移植，ANLL与急性淋巴细胞白血病首次缓解期移植者5年无病生存率分别达55%与65%，有效地解决国内患者因独生子女多难以找到匹配的同胞骨髓供者的难题，而骨髓移植疗效相当，同时具有节省治疗费和提高疗效的特点。该项目获2002年度天津市科技进步二等奖。

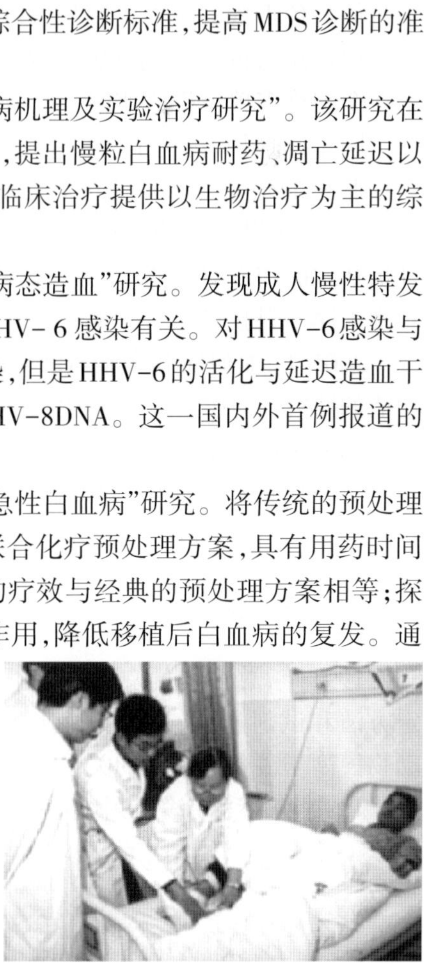
图7-2-1-106 杨崇礼（右2）查看病人

2002年，血研所王建祥、卞寿庚、杨崇礼等完成“白血病流行病学、发病机理与治疗方法的研究”。通过调查全国范围内白血病流行病学，明确国内白血病的发病率、分布规律及危险因素。研究发现治疗慢性粒细胞白血病的有效药物——靛玉红,使患者病情得到缓解,长期存活。提出治疗急性髓系白血病的高效诱导方案,建立多药耐药性髓细胞白血病的治疗方法。发现的AML-M2b分子标志用于AML-M2b诊断、鉴别诊断及微量残留白血病的监测,有益于个体化治疗及预后。该项目获2002年度天津市科技进步一等奖。

2003年,血研所韩忠朝等首次采用动员后的外周血干细胞移植,成功地治疗一例严重动脉硬化下肢闭塞性脉管炎。同年,韩忠朝等又运用外周血干细胞移植治疗糖尿病下肢坏疽,患者下肢血流明显改善,溃疡面未再发展。外周血干细胞移植可避免大剂量抽取骨髓的痛苦,任何年龄的患者都可从外周血获得生长血管的干细胞,这是治疗血管疾病方法上的突破。"血液干细胞移植治疗肢体缺血的基础和临床研究"获2004年度天津市科技进步二等奖。

同年,血研所和泰达生命科学技术研究中心韩忠朝、李妍涵、何睿、丁顺利等完成"恶性肿瘤抗血管新生治疗新方法"研究。发现白血病细胞表达血管内皮生长因子(VEGF)及其受体mRNA,患者血浆VEGF升高,其水平影响化疗疗效;研制出病毒载体介导血小板第四因子(PF4)及其活性片段p17-70病毒载体治疗组合物的体内基因治疗技术;应用腺病毒载体携带凝血酶敏感蛋白(TSP-1)抗血管新生活性区段到靶细胞,在患处产生持续高浓度的多肽;研究肝细胞生长因子HGF/c-met系统在血管生成中作用;建立基因治疗动物模型。该项目获2003年度天津市自然科学二等奖。

2004年,血研所肖志坚、郝玉书、刘世和等完成"髓系肿瘤染色体核型的研究"。该项目通过大系列病例研究查明中国髓系肿瘤患者染色体核型异常的特点,提供国内该领域的基础数据。在国内最先证实染色体核型异常是髓系肿瘤诊断和分型以及独立亚型确认的重要依据,据此可制定指导患者个体化治疗的策略,在此基础上对国内急性髓系白血病最常见的t(8;21)染色体易位进行深入研究,在国际上首次阐明t(8;21)染色体易位形成的主要机制是通过非同源染色体DNA断裂的修复。在国际上首次证实部分t(8;21)急性髓系白血病患者的白血病细胞起源于胎儿期。以细胞遗传学作为主要依据的髓系肿瘤患者的个体化治疗方法在全国许多单位推广使用。该项目获2004年度天津市自然科学二等奖。

同年,血研所杨纯正、熊冬生、许元富等完成"血液肿瘤耐药机制及克服耐药研究"。该项目完成一株耐药细胞株的建立及其耐药机制的研究;发现4个基因与细胞耐药有关,并确证sorcin基因与白血病耐药相关;发现一个肿瘤耐药逆转剂咯萘啶和一种抗耐药肿瘤药物PHⅡ—7;制备出抗Pgp单抗;设计和制备出一种抗Pgp/抗CD3双功能小抗体;设计并完成国内首例白血病患者临床耐药逆转的实验研究。该成果获2004年度天津市科技进步一等奖。

2005年,血研所和实验血液学国家重点实验室吴克复、郑国光、马小彤饶青等完成"白血病细胞性质和功能的研究"。用分子、细胞生物学和免疫学方法对肿瘤细胞性质和功能,尤其是炎症与肿瘤相关的细胞因子IL-18、mM-CSF、LL-37以及离子通道P2X7在白血病细胞中的作用和意义进行研究,证实细胞因子和信号分子在白血病细胞中的作用除了影响增殖、分化调控外,同时还能明显地改变白血病细胞的其他性质和功能。该项目获2005年度天津市自然科学二等奖。

四、消化系统

1991年,总医院黄象谦、杜宝恒、黄乃侠等完成"消化道激素的研究"。该研究应用于自行建立的VIP测定方法和试剂盒,以及应用放射免疫、组织化学,层析分析等方法研究正常人和胎儿,以及消化道疾病及其动物模型与消化道激素的关系。

1992年,天津市第三中心医院(以下简称"三中心医院")钱绍诚、李涛、吕洪敏等在"耐热性肝再生刺激因子的研究"中,研制出耐热又不含蛋白质的促肝因子。证明耐热性肝再生刺激因子能促进成熟肝细胞的再生。

1995年,三中心医院钱绍诚、韩涛、吕洪敏等经"柴胡合剂抗肝纤维化作用的动物实验及临床研究"证实,该药具有抑制胶原纤维等细胞外基质形成的作用,同时还发现该药具有保护肝细胞,调整氨基酸代谢紊乱，改善肝功能的作用。

1999年，三中心医院韩涛、钱绍诚、王宝恩等在“星状细胞培养应用于抗肝纤维化中药作用机理研究”中，观察中药复方及其组成的单味药对胶原合成与降解的基因表达及蛋白质分泌水平的影响。从复方中药中，筛选出抗肝纤维化作用最为突出的几种单味药，且证实复方中药的抗纤维化效果优于单味药。

1999年，三中心医院吕洪敏、张瑞红、张文等在“已酮可可碱抗肝纤维化作用的实验研究”中，发现使用已酮可可碱治疗肝纤维化，能有效降低反应肝纤维化程度的透明质酸、层粘蛋白、Ⅳ型胶原的水平，可使肿大的脾脏回缩，血小板回升。

五、呼吸系统

1993年，总医院朱宝玉、徐升茂、雷露茜等在“肺功能参数微机自动分析研究”中，研制出肺功能仪与微机接口插件及数据传输软件和肺功能参数自动分析软件。对临床诊断具有重要意义。

1998年，总医院朱宝玉、尤一鸣、曹洁等在“运动心肺功能无氧阈自动分析方法”研究中，确立呼吸与血流动力学模型，以呼吸和循环联合研究开辟一条新途径。

2000年，天津市肺科医院和天津医科大学张玉环、白景文、杨海贤、柳仓生等完成“咳嗽变异型哮喘病人支气管超微病理及干预措施”研究通过进行支气管镜检查，及其黏膜活检、灌洗，经超微病理形态学观察，显示出尽管是早期哮喘患者亦具备哮喘的诊断的指标。

2004年，医科大学总医院朱宝玉、冯靖、郭美南等完成“慢性阻塞性肺疾病患者‘早期（临界）呼吸衰竭’的研究”。定义动脉血气分析中“动脉血氧分压≥60毫米汞柱且＜72毫米汞柱”这一区间为“临界呼吸衰竭”状态，在国内外首先提出慢性早期（临界）呼吸衰竭这一概念。

六、感染系统

2003年，医大二院宋诗铎等在“医院多重耐药细菌感染的基础和临床研究”中，应用分子流行病学检测手段，对医院感染多重耐药菌进行目标检测，从而获得当年的天津市病原菌抗菌谱变迁的资料并掌握多重耐药菌的播散规律。同时，对市内免疫功能异常的多重耐药医院感染病人进行危险性评估，建立以危险程度不同为依据的治疗和预防策略。研究临床分离的多重耐药细菌的耐药机制及播散机制，从耐药性水平和垂直两个播散方向，研究表型和基因型的变化，整合子在细菌耐药性播散中的作用，增进对医院感染多重耐药菌耐药及播散机制的认识。该项目获2004年度天津市科技进步二等奖。

第二节　外科学

1991～2005年，天津应用生物技术、腔镜技术、血液净化、器官移植、放射介入等技术研究促进普通、肝胆、神经、心胸、血管、泌尿、骨、烧伤、移植等外科学发展，一些高端技术从引进阶段进入快速发展、创新阶段。20世纪90年代初期，天津相继成立肝胆、泌尿（1979年）、神经（1993年）、肛肠（1996年）、普通（1998年）、脊柱、器官移植（1998年）和血管等外科研究所，并以研究所为依托充实相应的重点发展学科，神经外科、移植外科、泌尿外科等重点学科在科研能力和临床整体水平上均处于国内领先地位。20世纪90年代，胃肠外科专业发生革命性变化。1996年，总医院普通外科被市卫生局批准为天津市重点学科。1998年，成立“天津普通外科研究所”，是全国为数不多，以普通外科疾病为研究目标的基础与临床研究机构。

总医院神经外科是国内第一个建设的独立神经外科专业科室，于1952年成立，也是当时国内唯一在临床科室内附设有独立的神经病理、神经生理及神经生化研究室。总医院赵以成等举办全国首届神经外科进修医师培训班，为全国各地培养国神经外科奠基者与学术带头人，此后每年举办神经外科医师进修班，为各地培养诸多神经外科医师。1980年在原有研究室的基础上，建立天津市神经病学研究所。20世纪90年代后期，已设有神经创伤、神经病理、神经肿瘤、神经生化、神经内分泌及神经流行病学等6个研究室，神经外科先后被评为国家211工程重点建设学科、国家级重点学科，并获准建立天津市神经损伤变异与再生重点实验室与教育部中枢神经创伤重点实验室。

1991年，南开医院率先引进腹腔镜技术，开展技术创新很快发展到多学科联合和复杂大器官手术阶段。截至2005年可通过腹腔镜微创技术治疗肝囊肿、结肠癌、肾上腺肿瘤等多种疾病，期间完成各类腹腔镜手术25000余例，经十二指肠镜微创诊断和治疗胆胰疾病31000余例。1998年，首创肠梗阻、肠粘连松解术及腹腔镜、12指肠镜、术中胆道镜三镜联合治疗复杂性胆结石新方法。同期，应用腹腔镜行胆囊结石和胆管结石手术治愈率为98.26%和99.6%。

1991年后，天津市在微囊化肝细胞、人工肝等研究领域取得阶段性成果。三中心医院肝胆外科于1996年被市卫生局批准为天津市重点学科。1997年，经国家卫生部批准，成立“卫生部人工细胞工程技术研究中心”。2005年，以干细胞、肿瘤生物治疗、细胞生物工程技术为主要研究方向组建“天津市再生医学疾病生物治疗研究中心”，2005年被列入天津市重大高新技术产业化项目。天津市肿瘤医院（以下简称“肿瘤医院”）和三中心医院在肝癌外科治疗系列工作形成天津市肝外科治疗的特色。

同期，天津应用神经导航系统、间质内放射治疗、微波热疗等对颅内病变和胶质瘤进行临床治疗，制订出以CT等影像学检查脑垂体腺瘤的早期诊断标准，在国内建立当时唯一的儿童期髓母细胞瘤体外细胞系。在颅脑损伤方面，率先在国内建立亚低温监护病房，并确立一整套急性重型颅脑创伤病人亚低温治疗和护理规范等。

天津引进各种先进诊断和治疗骨外伤器械，临床诊治水平有大幅度提高。伴随高暴力损伤成倍的增长，全市创伤骨科对多发骨折和累及关节内的骨折治疗水平迅速提升。脊柱外科引进国内外先进技术，治疗各种脊柱畸形、椎管狭窄等疾病取得长足进展。微创脊柱外科技术从无到有。小儿骨科治疗儿童发育各种畸形，一直保持国内领先水平。手外科与显微外科断肢、断指再植成活率提高。用各种带血管皮瓣治疗大面积软组织缺损，使需要截肢肢体得以保存。骨与软组织肿瘤，引进国外对肿瘤分型，并主要由天津肿瘤医院与天津市天津医院（以下简称“天津医院”）开展对肢体恶性肿瘤保肢手术。1996年，天津医院建立关节置换中心，人工关节置换开始用于治疗髋关节强直、股骨头坏死、膝关节退行性关节炎。市医大附属医院、市各中心医院、人民医院、中国人民武装警察部队医学院附属医院（以下简称“武警医学院附属医院”）等关节置换水平均已跻身于国内前列。

一、普通外科

（一）肝胆外科

三中心医院宋继昌、李涛、孙多先等完成生物型人工肝—ACA微囊肝细胞及人工细胞膜壳聚糖的研究，成功地进行肝细胞分离培养、包埋、移植的动物实验，并建立各项技术指标。海藻酸钠-壳聚糖-海藻酸钠（ACA）微囊肝细胞用于治疗急性肝功能衰竭，发挥人工肝辅助功能。“生物型人工肝-ACA微囊肝细胞实验研究”项目获1993年度天津市科技进步二等奖。

2000年，三中心医院杜智、李涛、陆伟等完成“微囊生物细胞移植研究”。通过对大动物的胰岛、肝细胞和肾上腺髓质细胞进行微囊化，分别用于糖尿病、急性肝衰和晚期癌症疼痛的治疗研究。全面系统进行微囊牛肾上腺髓质细胞移植治疗晚期恶性肿瘤，有效缓解患者疼痛，减少吗啡类药物的使用。首次进行适合胰岛移植的猪种筛选并比较全面地进行微囊大鼠和猪胰岛的体外体内研究。该项目获2005年度天津市科技进步二等奖。

2004年，该院杜智、李涛、舒桂明等完成“微囊肝细胞的安全性及疗效研究”，将海藻酸钠—聚赖氨酸—

海藻酸钠(APA)微囊肝细胞植入正常SD大鼠腹腔三个月,结果显示白细胞介素—2、T细胞亚群、肝肾功能、电解质、蛋白质等生化指标和组织学检查均无明显变化,经形态学检查显示微囊肝细胞在三个月内有较高存活率。将APA微囊肝细胞植入由氨基半乳糖诱发的FHF大鼠腹腔,结果显示能改善肝功能,提高存活率,延长存活时间。该研究为急性肝功能衰竭提供一种安全有效的治疗方法。

2005年,该院杜智、高英堂、王毅军等完成"肝癌治疗技术的研究",该项目应用抑制性消减杂交技术、基因芯片、RT-PCR和组织芯片等技术从基因和蛋白质水平对肝癌的分子切缘进行初步的研究,从多个基因和蛋白质分子水平观察癌内和癌旁组织的表达差异,为进一步精确定位肝癌分子切缘及寻找新的肝癌诊断、预后标志物和治疗靶点奠定基础,对肝癌的诊治预防具有重要意义。该项目采用术中超声引导荷瘤门静脉染色及切缘冷冻的治疗方法,在最大限度地保护正常肝脏的同时,提高治愈率并有效地减少术后局部复发,取得较好临床治疗效果。

(二)胃肠道外科

1996年,针对因肠系膜血管栓塞发生全小肠坏死、影响患者生存,总医院开展临床研究,建立肠系膜动脉栓塞诊疗程序,力求早期发现、早期治疗。在手术中采用肠系膜上动脉气囊导管取栓手术挽救临迫坏死肠管生机,使用计划性再开腹或断端肠管外置方法观察肠壁存活情况,以此减少肠管切除长度,最大限度维持病人营养状态。

1998年,天津市第三医院(以下简称"第三医院")张淑堃、哈智华、刘继会等完成"细胞因子与老年急腹及其多脏器功能障碍关系的临床研究"。该项目首次观察纳络酮治疗与多种细胞因子的关系,发现其可降低细胞因子活性,应用后TNF a 、IL-6活性水平下降,与对照组差异显著。研究结果表明外周血单个核细胞分泌的TNF a 、IL-6活性水平是感染过程中的主要调节因子,它们的过度释放是触发多器官功能障碍综合征的关键因子之一,是评价病情及预后的敏感指标。

1999年,总医院刘彤等借鉴国外经验,按照国际标准开展胃癌、结直肠癌的标准化区域淋巴结清扫,强调解剖学标志暴露,进行个体化消化道功能性重建,提高天津市胃肠道恶性肿瘤的手术治疗水平。2000年,总医院开展结直肠癌肝转移的临床应用研究,通过超声检查对左、右门脉汇合类型进行研究,发现肠癌肝转移的易发因素。

(三)腔镜微创技术

1991~1998年,南开医院秦鸣放、鲁焕章、张晓东等应用腔镜微创技术治疗1500例胆石症,研究证实应用腹腔镜胆囊切除术治疗复杂性胆囊结石是可行的;对胆囊结石合并胆管结石者采用十二指肠镜、子母胆道镜及腹腔镜联合治疗,治愈率90%以上,该技术与传统的开腹外科手术相比具有损伤小、痛苦少、恢复快的优点。1998年,开展经胆管液电碎石术治疗胆管结石,经内镜快速治疗胆总管结石,经内镜胆管金属支架治疗恶性胆管狭窄和内镜联合中药治疗急性化脓性胆管炎等临床研究。

1998年,南开医院范君度、鲁焕章和高德宝等完成"经内镜快速治疗胆总管结石的临床研究"。该研究在内镜室增加带监视系统的X光机,对B超初步诊断为总管结石的患者行内镜逆行性胰胆管造影,一经确诊即行内镜乳头括约肌切开,并在X线监视下取石或碎石。经临床100例治疗与手术对比,黄疸消退时间,住院时间及手术残余结石发生率均明显优于手术治疗组,痊愈率98%,且损伤小、恢复快、不行剖腹,经济简便。

1998年,南开医院秦鸣放、邹富胜、李文等在国内首创三镜联合治疗复杂性肝外胆管结石的新术式——"三镜联合胆总管探查术"即在十二指肠镜下进行经内镜逆行胰胆管造影,根据十二指肠乳头的解剖情况进行经十二指肠镜乳头括约肌切开术,而后行内镜鼻胆管引流,缓解胆道压力,确保无残余结石。该术式既完善腹腔镜、内镜联合治疗胆总管结石的适应症和禁忌症,又扩展腹腔镜微创手术的治疗范围。并在国内36家医疗单位推广应用。"三镜联合治疗复杂性肝外胆管结石的临床研究"项目获2003年度天津市科技进步二等奖。

(四)疝和腹壁外科

1998年,天津市天和医院(以下简称"天和医院")刘胜利、三中心医院孙惠军等在天津市率先开展"疝环充填式无张力疝修补术”。1999年，天津市人民医院王西墨、王荫龙在天津市率先开展平片“Lichtenstein(利希腾斯坦)无张力疝修补术”。1999年，中华外科学会外科分会成立疝和腹壁外科学组。2000～2003年，天津的三级医院普通外科已将疝环充填式和Lichtenstein列为最基本的疝修补手术。仅天津市人民医院就完成Lichtenstein无张力手术500余例。

2004年，天津市人民医院正式成立独立于普外科的疝和腹壁外科，成为国内最早的疝外科专业科室。在国内推广腹外疝治疗“专业化”和“规范化”理念，开展并推广“平片、局麻、日间”新模式。2005年，天津市人民医院邀请时任美国疝学会主席、Lichtenstein无张力疝修补术发明人之一Amid博士到天津交流并定期举办国内研讨会和培训班，成为国内Lichtenstein无张力疝修补术的培训基地。

2005年，针对国内缺乏有关腹股沟疝流行病学数据，天津市人民医院王西墨、王荫龙在全市开展对自然人的腹股沟疝流行病学调查，填补全市该项空白。为普及“无张力疝修补”理念和方法、提高该技术的社会效益，2005年天津市人民医院江涛主持与天津市慈善协会合作开展“关爱孤老、低保家庭疝气患者大型公益活动”，为逾百位患者免费实施手术。

二、神经外科

(一)颅内肿瘤

1991年，总医院杨树源等根据患者血清激素水平、对脑垂体腺瘤按功能进行分类，并以CT等影像学检查制订出脑垂体腺瘤的早期诊断标准，从而使40例垂体瘤在不足1厘米大小的微腺瘤期得以早期诊断。此后，在国内首先开展经筛、蝶窦显微外科手术治疗脑垂体腺瘤100余例，术后经半年至6年的随访，视功能改善率达87.3%，术后激素恢复正常率为61.43%，其中微腺瘤为75.76%。闭经妇女术后53.66%恢复正常月经，其中微腺瘤为80%，不孕妇女术后29.27%怀孕并正常分娩，其中微腺瘤为53.3%。

同年，总医院浦佩玉等在“初发及复发恶性星形细胞瘤体外细胞系TJ8510与TJ861的建立及其特征比较”研究中，建立同一病例、相同部位的初发及复发恶性星形细胞瘤体外细胞系TJ8510及TJ861，进行形态学、DNA倍性测定，染色体核型分析，胶质纤维酸性蛋白(GFAP)等多项生化标志检测，卡氮芥(BCNU)的药物敏感试验、异种动物移植等诸多特征鉴定并进行比较。结果发现两者同样具备恶性星形细胞瘤的基本特征，其不同处在于TJ861细胞表面结构更复杂，具有更多微绒毛和球状纤维足，提示其侵袭力更强；细胞群体中S期比例及集落形成率更高；并有一11/1q标记染色体，且有显著抗药性，虽经高达50微克/毫升BCNU处理后仍可存活；说明复发瘤的干细胞株起于初发瘤中侵袭力更强、更具生长优势、且有显著抗药性的细胞。1992年，浦佩玉等在国内建立当时唯一的儿童期髓母细胞瘤体外细胞系，进行形态学，细胞生物学，染色体核型，生物化学，异种动物移植等特征鉴定。该研究对于探讨髓母细胞瘤生物学特性，建立动物模型，研究病因，改进治疗手段均有一定价值。获1992年度天津市科技进步二等奖。

1992年，天津市第二中心医院(以下简称“二中心医院”)王兆铭、刘令仪、李维廉等研制出聚四氟乙烯脑瘤术中微波热疗辐射器，对脑胶质瘤和脑转移瘤手术摘除后的瘤床进行微波热疗。经光、电镜检查结果证实，该装置对残留肿瘤细胞具有选择性杀伤作用，临床治疗30例取得较好疗效。同年，天津市环湖医院(以下简称“环湖医院”)和二中心医院的赵克明、贡雁行、任智英完成卡氮芥明胶海绵脑恶性肿瘤残腔铺置化疗的临床研究。该研究在脑胶质瘤切除术后用明胶海绵吸附高浓度的卡氮芥，贴附于肿瘤残腔的创面上，通过渗透作用以杀死残腔壁上浸润的非肉眼可见的瘤细胞，以达到延长患者生存期的目的，并可消灭个别瘤细胞的蛛网膜下腔种植，临床应用结果显示，患者的中位生存期比美国BTSG疗法明显延长。“明胶海绵吸附卡氮芥局部化疗治疗脑恶性肿瘤”项目获1996年度天津市科技进步二等奖。

1993年，二中心医院李建文、梁振文和李维廉等完成“遥控后装高剂量率铱-192间质放疗治疗脑胶质瘤的临床研究”，该方法具有对脑组织放射损伤小、肿瘤部位治疗剂量高、无头皮损伤、较少出现脑水肿等优点。经临床随访观察，较常规疗法的效果明显提高。

1994年，环湖医院焦德让等应用自制弹簧圈进行颅内动脉瘤的血管内栓塞，应用电解可脱弹簧圈栓塞治疗颅内动脉瘤。

1995年，总医院浦佩玉等对胶质瘤的生物学特性进行比较全面系统的综合研究。先后发现胶质瘤对化疗药物敏感性的异质性与其染色体数目有关，胶质瘤患者免疫功能低下主要与胶质瘤细胞自分泌转化生长因子β2有关。并发现在胶质瘤患者血浆中，与免疫调控有关的神经递质去甲肾上腺素及肾上腺素显著降低，进而提出胶质瘤患者免疫功能低下的机制之一是神经免疫网络调控紊乱。1997年，浦佩玉等完成"脑胶质瘤微波加热治疗的基础及临床研究"，该研究试用天津大学自动化工程系研制的微波热疗仪（2450MHZ）对脑体膜，离体猪脑，活体兔脑进行加热试验；观察热场分布及有效温度范围，引起脑组织损伤的临界温度和时间及其毒副作用；同时通过加热对体外培养胶质瘤细胞的生长抑制作用探讨有效的加热剂量。在此基础上对30例胶质瘤患者进行临床Ⅰ/Ⅱ期试验，通过病理组织学、超微结构检查、DNA含量、多胺含量及酶化学检查等确定局部加热治疗胶质瘤的加热剂量、效应及作用机制。根据肿瘤切除程度及其与周围脑组织距离，提出加热温度以43℃~45℃，20分钟为宜，且无不良反应及毒副作用。

1997年，环湖医院成立微侵袭神经外科研究室，首次利用神经导航系统治疗颅内胶质瘤等病变的研究。1998年，该院只达石、李建国、崔世民等在"应用无框架神经外科导航系统治疗颅内病变的研究"中，以显微镜、支架和计算机工作站组成的无框架神经外科导航系统，根据立体定向的原理指导外科医生进行手术操作，使医师能更好地理解解剖结构与病变的关系，选择最佳手术入路，准确达到靶病灶。临床应用20例颅内病变的治疗，取得良好的效果，该项目获1999年度天津市科技进步二等奖。

1998年，总医院江德华等采用生化、病理、免疫组化等方法对热应激状态下热休克蛋白70（HSP70）基因表达与调节因素进行研究，探讨胶质瘤细胞在加热或加热并用相关因素处理情况下，hsp70mRNA与HSP70表达水平的比较，提出HSP70不能与hsp70mRNA同步表达是细胞严重损伤、难以存活的分子标志。

2000年，总医院浦佩玉等在"脑胶质瘤表皮生长因子（EGF）/表皮生长因子受体（EGFR）基因表达和EG-FR反义RNA抑瘤作用的研究"中，采用细胞生物学和分子生物学等实验技术，同步研究50例胶质瘤EGFR及其两个配体EGF和转化生长因子α（TGF-α），以及与EGFR相关基因C-erbB2的表达，发现胶质瘤中前述基因均有不同程度表达，尤以EGFR最突出，提示EGF/EGFR在肿瘤发生、发展中起重要作用；其表达阳性率及表达水平与肿瘤恶性程度及增殖活性明显相关。胶质瘤患者尿液内EGF含量突出升高，术后其含量与肿瘤切除程度及近期预后显著相关。反义EGFR基因转导入胶质瘤细胞，不仅在体外逆转人脑及鼠脑胶质瘤细胞的恶性表型，抑制细胞增殖，诱导细胞凋亡，而且体内致瘤性丧失。对鼠脑内已形成瘤灶者应用反义EGFR基因治疗，治疗后大部分动物肿瘤消失，生存期大大延长，从而为反义EGFR基因治疗胶质瘤提供实验依据。

2002年，总医院杨学军等在"自杀基因治疗恶性胶质瘤的研究"中，应用基因工程技术构建携带HSV-tk基因的逆转录病毒与腺病毒载体及其对应的包装细胞系，并应用上述两种病毒载体及GCV和ACV两种自杀基因底物，系统进行人脑胶质瘤与鼠脑胶质瘤的自杀基因体内外治疗实验；使用核磁共振成像全程动态监测脑胶质瘤基因治疗的全过程；通过透射电镜直接观察到HSV-tk阴性肿瘤细胞吞噬凋亡囊泡并导致自身凋亡现象，并发现向肿瘤细胞中导入Cx43基因可增强肿瘤细胞的间隙连接通讯，加强旁效应。该项目获2002年度天津市科技进步二等奖。

2002年，一中心医院王金环、总医院浦佩玉、李牧等完成"脑膜瘤和胶质瘤bFGF基因表达及bFGF反义寡核苷酸抑瘤作用的研究"。研究发现bFGF表达随脑膜瘤及胶质瘤恶性程度增加而增加，证实其对瘤细胞增殖起促进作用；胶质瘤细胞的凋亡与bFGF基因表达呈负相关；bFGF具有促进血管增生作用且与胶质瘤恶性进展有关；bFGF反义寡核苷酸对bFGF基因表达有明显抑制作用。同步检测脑膜瘤、胶质瘤bFGF基因及相关基因的表达，并发现bFGF的表达程度可作为判断肿瘤恶性程度及预后的标准，自行设计bFGF反义寡核苷酸抑瘤实验，效果良好。

2003年，总医院申长虹等在"松果体区肿瘤术式改良"研究中，从最初的大体解剖到显微外科解剖，进而成功应用于临床，取得良好的手术效果，并在业内得到推广。将传统的侧卧位时手术侧向上改为手术侧向下，利用重力作用使手术侧的脑组织自然下垂，从而减少牵拉脑组织所产生的诸多弊端，同时又利用大脑镰自然挡住对侧脑组织的下垂。结果表明该术式显著增加手术野的自然显露，最大限度地减少对脑组织的牵拉，提高手术的安全性。

2004年，中国人民解放军第二五四医院和中国人民解放军海军总医院江荣才、于新、刘宗惠、李士月等完成“立体定向治疗囊性颅咽管瘤的基础临床与研究”。该项目对颅咽管瘤的相关基础进行研究，在国内外率先应用CT-引导立体定向囊内注射放射性同位素治疗囊性颅咽管瘤并进行系统总结，发展联合化放疗、γ刀治疗、术后激素替代治疗等疗法。其肿瘤消失率超过72%，控制率接近90%，许多患者长期存活。使用该疗法，比开颅切除手术，大幅节省费用和人力物力。该疗法具有微创、疗效确实、并发症少、适用范围广等特点，多家单位已应用。该项目获2004年度天津市科技进步二等奖。

2004年，总医院杨树源等在脑膜瘤PDGF-VEGF基因表达及反义核苷酸体外抑瘤作用的研究中，建立脑膜瘤体外培养的方法，通过检测人脑膜瘤组织和细胞中血小板源性生长因子（PDGF-B）和血管内皮生长因子（VEGF）mRNA及其蛋白表达。通过用反义寡核苷酸（ODN）抑制瘤细胞PDGF-B和VEGF的表达，探讨脑膜瘤基因治疗的可能途径。研究发现非典型性脑膜瘤PDGFB链及PDGFβ受体表达明显高于良性脑膜瘤。二者表达与人脑膜瘤增殖活性及恶性程度相关。应用PDGFB链反义寡核苷酸可在体外抑制脑膜瘤培养细胞生长，提出PDGFB链可以作为反意基因治疗脑膜瘤的优选靶向。研究项目还报告了PDGFB链反义寡核苷酸可以在体内抑制脑膜瘤培养细胞生长；人脑膜瘤雄激素受体、表皮生长因子受体mRNA及蛋白高表达。人脑膜瘤雄激素受体与表皮生长因子受体表达呈正相关关系；IFN-α、5-FU在体外对脑膜瘤培养细胞的生长有抑制作用；IFN-α与5-FU联合应用可提高疗效。“脑膜瘤PDGF- B和VEGF基因表达及反义核酸体外抑瘤作用的研究”获2004年度天津市科技进步二等奖。

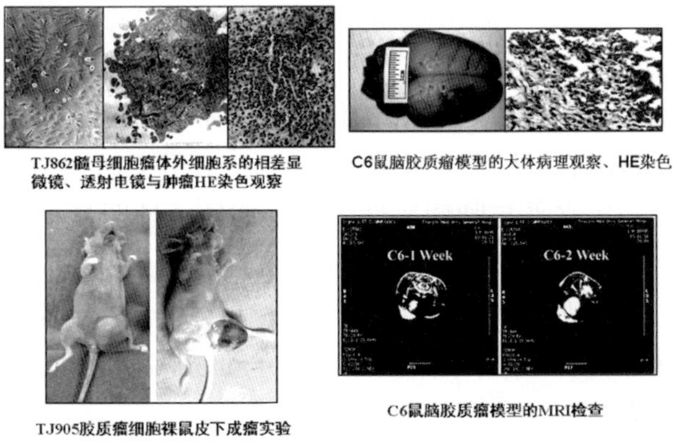

图7-2-2-107 总医院浦佩玉等完成人脑胶质瘤基础与临床研究

2005年，总医院浦佩玉、康春生、于士柱等完成“人脑胶质瘤的基础与临床研究”。在分子病理学的研究部分对系列重要生长因子及其受体在胶质瘤中的异常表达进行了相应的研究；对多种抑瘤基因的缺失、突变与甲基化进行研究。尤其发现与国外报告不同的是国人低恶度胶质瘤中很少出现p53基因突变而EGFR过表达并不少见，原发性胶质母细胞瘤中EGFR扩增及过表达率高而p53突变率也高的研究结果，提示在国人胶质瘤发生发展过程中两者并存而不相互排斥。该项目经对胶质瘤基因表达谱的研究，发现一批未被全面研究的重要的相关靶基因如隔蛋白7（SEPT7），Wnt/β连接素和Notch等，采用纳米技术改进基因转导载体，建立RNA干涉治疗胶质瘤的新技术；摸索出联合基因治疗的新方法，进而提高胶质瘤的治疗效果。该项目获2005年度天津市科技进步一等奖。

2005年，总医院张建宁、朱涛、杨树源等完成“脑垂体腺瘤生物学特征与临床诊治的研究”。在国内外首先采用大鼠肝细胞膜PRL受体为测定工具，对腺瘤患者PRL分子量不均一性、免疫活性与生物活性不一致性进行综合研究。首先应用银染PCR-SSCP方法进行GH腺瘤患者gsp基因突变的研究；在国内率先提出DNA半定量测定及细胞周期分析可作为判断肿瘤生长速度、侵袭性生长程度及恶性度客观指标；首先研究垂体腺瘤雌激素受体mRNA的表达。该项目获2005年度天津市科技进步二等奖。

（二）颅脑损伤

1993年，天津医学院附属医院杨树源等从多方面对重型颅脑外伤急性期的病理生理变化进行广泛研究，累计使用临床病例548份，检测各类指标42种。结果表明，重型颅脑损伤急性期神经递质、神经内分泌、血流变学、多种生化指标及神经电生理活动均有改变，且与脑外伤的病情及预后有关，可作为判断伤情及预后的指标。其中有关脑乳酸中毒、低氧血症、儿茶酚胺类递质的变化在脑外伤后的病理生理变化中占有重要地位。儿茶酚胺类神经递质及激素类变化表明二者是脑外伤后影响治疗,预后的重要病理生理变化。“重型颅脑损伤的临床及病理生理研究”项目获1993年度天津市科技进步二等奖。

1994年,环湖医院只达石、张赛、刘敬业等在亚低温治疗重度颅脑损伤的临床研究中,创建和应用亚低温单元,不但可及时控制颅脑创伤后急性期的高颅压、高热和脑内外一系列应激性变化,还可保护全脑,尤其是创伤边缘区脑细胞的存活以及减少伤后脑细胞凋亡等变化。该技术的建立使重度颅脑损伤临床死亡率下降为25.8%,恢复良好率达40.1%。通过研究建立一个亚低温单元,确立一整套急性重型颅脑创伤病人亚低温治疗和护理规范。“亚低温治疗急性重型颅脑损伤临床及基础研究”项目获2001年度天津市科技进步一等奖。“亚低温治疗急性重型颅脑创伤的临床及实验研究“项目获2004年度国家科技进步二等奖。

1996年,总医院杨树源在“重型颅脑损伤中弥漫性脑损害的临床及病理生理研究”中,重点探讨脑弥漫性轴索损伤(DAI)的诊断及重型脑损伤后急性期低氧血症的临床及病理生理问题。首先建立DAI动物模型,对DAI的脑水肿进行磁共振波谱学研究;对临床患DAI的病人进行血清及脑脊液髓鞘碱蛋白测定,探讨其诊断意义。通过对重型脑外伤病人急性期血儿茶酚鞍的测定、经心导管血流动力学的监测、肺动静分流的测定等手段,对低氧血症的发生机制进行研究。并在国际上首次对重型脑外伤进行肺活检,探讨其急性期交感神经系统活动亢进,引起儿茶酚胺的过度释放,所造成的肺功能障碍及低氧血症等一系列理论,揭示低氧血症的发生机制。该成果经28所医院推广应用,一致认为该项成果对认识DAI这种特殊类型脑外伤有很大意义,有助于DAI的临床诊断。该项目获1996年度天津市科技进步二等奖。

1998年,第三医院张淑堃和医科大学姚智、华勇等完成“细胞因子网络及mRNA表达在中枢神经损伤、修复过程中作用的临床研究”。应用细胞生物学、分子生物学方法,从基因、分子水平研究细胞因子(CKs)网络中关键的细胞因子-肿瘤坏死因子(TNF a)、白细胞介素1(IL-1)、白细胞介素6(IL-6)与mRNA表达水平在CNC损伤、修复过程中的动态变化及应用糖皮质激素对CKs的影响。

2000年,总医院高永中等完成的“用‘T’型管行脊髓空洞-腹腔分流术的疗效观察”,应用显微外科技术和“T”管分流装置,对脊髓空洞内的脑脊液进行成功分流,共治疗病人22例,对围手术期进行系统的监测和管理,同时用B超加MRI结合临床检查随访半年至五年,对脊髓空洞症治疗有效率近100%。

2001年,总医院杨树源等在“颅脑损伤后bFGF基因表达及外源性bFGF的治疗作用”研究中,建立两种急性脑创伤的动物模型,采用分子生物学实验技术,对碱性成纤维细胞生长因子在脑组织中的表达、分泌变化以及与脑创伤严重程度之间的关系进行观察和分析,验证外源性碱性成纤维细胞生长因子对脑创伤的治疗作用。建立重物落体弥漫性脑创伤模型;报告急性颅脑创伤后检测大鼠脑组织神经元bFGF表达;检测重物落体弥漫性脑创伤模型脑组织神经元bFGF表达;提出急性颅脑创伤后脑组织神经元中内源性bFGF相对表达不足的概念,验证了外源性bFGF的治疗作用;为临床应用bFGF治疗急性颅脑创伤提供理论依据。该项目获2001年度天津市科技进步二等奖。同年,杨树源等在“实验性脑创伤后IL-1β基因表达及IL-1受体拮抗剂治疗究”中,建立了两种急性脑创伤的动物模型,采用分子生物学实验技术,对白介素-1在脑组织中的表达、分泌变化以及与脑创伤严重程度之间的关系进行了观察和分析,并验证了白介素-1受体拮抗剂对脑创伤的治疗作用。建立重物落体弥漫性脑创伤模型;报道实验性脑创伤后IL-1β、TNFα的蛋白及基因表达情况;利用原位杂交的方法观察脑创伤后IL-1β和TNFα在脑组织中的表达情况;报道重组白细胞介素-1受体拮抗剂对脑创伤的治疗作用;发现脑室内注射重组IL-1ra可以有效减轻创伤后脑水肿。2003年,杨树源等在“急性脑创伤后迟发性神经元死亡分子机制的研究及其治疗方法”研究中,建立急性脑创伤的动物模型,获取脑创伤内减压手术中废弃的人脑组织、神经元体外培养;采用分子生物学、细胞生物学、超微病理学等实验技术,对脑创伤后神经元损伤的病理改变、凋亡相关基因p53、bcl-2、bcl-xL、bax、caspase3的表达和作用、细胞内钙离子超载情况等进行观察和分析,并验证p53、bax反义寡核苷酸对脑创伤的治疗作用,对未来开发新药物,临床抢救急性脑创伤病例具有理论指导意义和实用开发价值。该检测人急性脑创伤后基因p53、bcl-2、bcl-xL、bax、caspase3的表达、激活和对神经元凋亡的作用,提出以上基因是导致神经元凋亡的重要原因。该成果获2003年度天津市科技进步二等奖。

2003年，环湖医院黄慧玲、只达石、张琳瑛等完成“常温和亚低温下针刺法治疗颅脑损伤的临床和实验研究”。首次研究常温和亚低温下针刺法对颅脑损伤患者的颅内压、血糖、尿素氮等指标的影响；应用微透析技术动态研究针刺疗法对颅脑损伤大鼠脑代谢生化指标的变化；针刺治疗对脑外伤大鼠神经元型NOS、诱导型NOS、神经元特异性烯醇化酶、热休克蛋白70蛋白表达的影响。针刺治疗颅脑观察结果表明：期良好恢复率为亚低温治疗组（58.5%）＞亚低温针刺组（57.2%）＞常温针刺组（47.5%）＞常温西医治疗（37.8%）。病死率按以上顺序分别为：29.3%、25.7%、27.5%、36.6%。

2005年，总医院和血研所杨树源、刘辉、张建宁、王宁等完成“神经干细胞移植治疗颅脑损伤的研究”。通过对胎鼠、胎儿海马神经干细胞分离培养、综合应用相关技术检验海马神经干细胞的nestin表达。使用人胎儿神经干细胞、骨髓间充质干细胞治疗大鼠弥漫颅脑损伤后的神经功能缺失，均明显改善受损大鼠神经功能。并报告胎儿骨髓间充质干细胞在大鼠颅内的神经分化。将含有白介素12的质粒pcDNA3.1-scIL12转染到人胎儿海马NSCs，应用转染IL-12的人胎儿海马神经干细胞免疫基因治疗大鼠颅内C6胶质瘤，可见明显的肿瘤消退。该成果获2005年度天津市科技进步二等奖。

三、心胸外科

1985年，胸科医院在中国香港大学何其成教授的帮助和指导下完成天津市首例成冠状动脉搭桥术并取得成功，此后，澳大利亚圣文森特医院方斯沃斯教授多次来胸科医院进行技术指导和交流。1992年，胸科医院李庆和、郭志刚和文其祥等独立完成冠状动脉搭桥术16例，同时还与澳大利亚圣文森特医院协作完成5例（共21例），共搭桥62支，其中19例患者心绞痛完全消失。2003年冠脉搭桥手术年手术例数达530例，手术量位居全国先进行列。

1997年起，胸科医院戴继民、李庆和姜楠等引进Bentall手术根治Marfan氏综合征及主动脉根部疾患，截至2002年完成手术110例，成功率达96%以上，取得良好疗效，使众多危重患者得到及时救治。填补天津市医疗卫生新技术空白，在心脏大血管外科领域跻身全国领先行列

2003年，总医院张鹏等在“新辅助化疗治疗局部晚期非小细胞肺癌（NSCLC）的临床研究”中，对58例局部晚期NSCLC的患者随机分组，以97国际肺癌分期为基准、以铂制剂为基础进行新辅助化疗的前瞻性随机对照研究，并对新辅助化疗后肿瘤细胞耐药相关因子GST-π进行研究。结果表明：铂制剂为主的新辅助化疗能够使局部晚期NSCLC的原发灶和淋巴结降期，提高手术切除率；能够较早控制全身潜在的微小转移灶，潜在延长无病生存期，提高总体生存率；新辅助化疗对凋亡蛋白caspase-3具有诱导增加作用；可使肺癌铂类相关耐药蛋白GST-π表达水平有所升高，但是并没有产生明显的继发性耐药现象。

2004年，胸科医院姜楠、徐栋、王强等对三个瓣膜联合置换术中三尖瓣处理方法进行研究，对临床上风湿性心瓣膜病合并重度三尖瓣关闭不全的患者，在行二尖瓣和主动脉瓣置换的同时行三尖瓣置换术。其疗效优于三尖瓣成形术，患者生活质量明显改善。

四、血管外科

1991年，一中心医院血管外科主要治疗病种为陈旧性缺血性脑梗塞，其方法为颈动脉内膜剥脱术。其他治疗的病种包括急性下肢动脉栓塞、大隐静脉曲张、下肢深静脉血栓形成、血栓闭塞性脉管炎、周围血管损伤、肝硬化门脉高压症。

1992年，血管外科整体迁入天和医院，开展腹主动脉瘤及下肢动脉硬化闭塞症的腔内治疗，对传统的大隐静脉曲张术式进行改进，将原来的大切口分段剥脱改为小切口点式剥脱术。扩大颈动脉内膜剥脱术的手术适应症，由原来以治疗陈旧性缺血性脑梗塞为主要适应症扩大至严重的颈动脉狭窄合并有TIA或其他脑缺血症状的患者，以预防脑卒中为目标，完成颈动脉内膜剥脱术300余例。

1995年，天和医院成立天津市血管外科研究室。同年，中华医学会外科学会血管外科学组和天和医院

血管外科联合成功举办第三届全国血管外科学术会议，邀请欧洲著名血管外科专家对大血管疾病进行病例讲座及手术示范，就大血管、周围血管疾病的诊断、治疗、腔内治疗及基础研究进行深入广泛的讨论。1996年，天和医院血管外科被批准为天津市卫生系统14个重点发展学科之一。

1996年，天和医院栗力等完成“反转加强前壁颈静脉成形术治疗颈静脉瘤样扩张”的研究，在国内首次应用自体颈内静脉成形治疗颈静脉瘤样扩张，避免使用人工血管移植术引发的相关并发症。1997年，栗力等完成“球囊PTA治疗动脉短段狭窄的临床研究”。通过微创治疗动脉病变，使血管损伤具有可控性。1998年，胸科医院栗力在天津市首先开展腹主动脉瘤腔内覆膜支架移植术，完成“重症头臂型大动脉炎的外科术式改进”，对重症大动脉炎头臂干三支病变患者原有手术方式进行改进，为无流出道之供脑血管建立，为国内首创。同年，又完成“腔-肠-房国产人工血管移植治疗长段下腔静脉阻塞技术”研究，为治疗布-加氏综合征提供新的手术方式，在降低门静脉压力的同时降低下腔静脉压力。

1998年，天和医院于国涛在全市首先应用人工血管建立血液透析患者的血管通路，其“人造血管通路的建立及在血液净化中的应用”研究，对于长期血液透析，因自身血管条件差、不能行自体动静脉瘘的患者开创了崭新的血液透析通路。

1998年，环湖医院姚鑫、李牧、尹龙等完成“椎基底动脉的显微外科解剖”研究。选取25例成人尸头标本，经解剖后行双侧颈内动脉和椎动脉插管，在双人双目手术显微镜下观察、测量椎基底动脉的管腔直径和长度，同时描绘血管走行、侧支循环、供血范围及与周围组织的关系。该成果对临床补充后循环血管解剖知识，提高临床手术技能。

2001年，胸科医院栗力、周宁、董双忠等完成“血管镜引导下取栓与溶栓治疗”研究。通过对具体病例操作，研究在连续动脉血流状态下，应用血管镜清楚显示动脉局部轮廓及病变的效果。在不阻断血流条件下，对动脉栓塞取栓的整体性及溶栓的疗效进行评价。

2003年，胸科医院栗力、董双忠、崔若昱等完成“颈内动脉残端指数测定在颈动脉内膜切除术中的应用研究”。该研究采用核磁血管成像（MRA）准确反映颅外段颈动脉、椎基底动脉、willis环有无病变与病变的程度，术前MRA检查结合术中SI测定，对评估供脑血管病变与程度、颈动脉被阻断后侧支血供代偿状况。纠正颈动脉残端压测量的弊端，达到预防不可逆缺血性脑卒中的发生，提高手术安全性。

2003年，天津市人民医院成立血管科，开展血管腔内微创技术治疗血管疾病，在全市首先开展颈内动脉支架治疗颈动脉狭窄的新技术，同时普遍开展下肢动脉硬化症的腔内微创治疗及肾动脉狭窄的腔内微创治疗。

2004年，天津市人民医院开展布加氏综合征的手术治疗，成功完成2例布加氏综合征腔-肠-房人工血管搭桥手术、胸腹主动脉夹层及假性动脉瘤的腔内隔绝术。2005年，完成各种术式血液透析血管通路手术2000余例。同年，于国涛、栗力、刘洪等完成“建立临时转流预防颈动脉内膜剥脱术中脑缺血”研究，通过大量临床手术经验总结，研究在颈动脉内膜剥脱术中应用转流管避免阻断脑供血，对脑组织具有明显保护作用，降低术中脑缺血及术后脑再灌注损伤引发的围手术期死亡率及卒中率，具有重大的临床意义。

五、泌尿外科

天津市在泌尿系统肿瘤基础与临床研究方面1991～2005年取得较大进步。在国际上首次提出“两类移行上皮癌”的概念，改进早期发现膀胱癌的尿脱落细胞学方法，在国内首创利用阴茎腹侧面斜形带蒂皮条翻转埋藏法治疗尿道下裂一次成型术，设计研制成功隔膜型人工膀胱等。

（一）肾盂和膀胱肿瘤

1992年，天津医学院第二附属医院、天津市泌尿外科研究所畅继武、随志方、马腾骧等完成的“建立经EB病毒转化人-B淋巴细胞生产人源性单克隆抗核抗体系列”项目获1992年度天津市科技进步二等奖。在国内首先建立人肾盂移行细胞癌TPC-1细胞系，传60余代。在建系的同时建立新的培养方法，使原代培养成活率达84%以上，超过当时国内外34%成活率，为临床抗癌药物药敏实验提供新的技术手段。

1993年，天津医学院第二附属医院韩瑞发等完成膀胱内灌注BCG抗肿瘤作用机制的研究。该项目采用病理组织学，单克隆抗体免疫组化等方法及液相色谱放免及电镜扫描分析测定，首次发现卡介苗（BCG）灌注对癌及上皮HLA、DR抗原的表达与细胞介导的免疫反应的关系。揭示BCG增强原性与免疫易感性的机制，建立测定尿中多胺可作为评价BCG抗肿瘤效果，监视肿瘤复发探讨生物反应调节剂抗肿瘤作用机制的主要生物学标记物与指标。

1993年，天津医学院附属医院虞颂庭、吴明明、李黎明等完成预测膀胱肿瘤预后的研究——膀胱肿瘤标记物的探讨研究。证明：患者的ABO抗原及T抗原阴性者，癌细胞的恶性度及浸润能力均高于阳性者，病人的复发率也随之增高；病人外周血淋巴细胞及癌细胞染色体的畸变率高于对照组所患癌症的浸润性大，术后复发率随之增高；癌细胞的DNA/FCN异倍体率大于对照组则恶性度高、浸润能力强。“膀胱癌标记物、异质性、病因与治疗、预后的关系”项目获1993年度天津市科技进步二等奖。

1999年，医大二院赵耀瑞等在“膀胱组织中转化生长因子（TGF-β1）的定量分析及其对LAK细胞的影响”实验研究中发现，TGF-β1可抑制淋巴因子激活杀伤（LAK）细胞的增殖和溶瘤活性，这种抑制作用可被TGF-β1单克隆抗体拮抗，抑制LAK细胞的分化，揭示出膀胱癌细胞大量分泌的TGF-β1可能是影响膀胱癌免疫治疗效果的主要因素，并作为判断膀胱癌预后的重要指标。

1999年，总医院林毅等完成“端粒酶活性在泌尿系统肿瘤中的检测和应用”研究，以聚合酶链式反应（PCR）为基础的高特异性、高敏感性的同位素标记方法，测定端粒酶活性技术，检测端粒酶在膀胱癌和前列腺癌组织中的表达，并应用该技术对前列腺活检标本进行检测。定性地分析端粒酶活性在膀胱癌前列腺癌中的表达，半定量地测定端粒酶的活性。在膀胱癌和前列腺癌组织中，端粒酶的相对活性与肿瘤细胞的病理分级、临床分期有明显的相关性。癌转移灶（淋巴和骨转移）的端粒酶活性也高于原发病变。在检测端粒酶的同时，加入内标ITAS（Internal telomerase assay standard），可防止假阴性的产生。

1999年，畅继武等在“两类移行上皮癌早期病变与基因表达产物的研究”中，提出两类移行上皮癌发生发展的途径，对多种癌与抑癌基因衍变进行研究，对两类移行上皮癌端粒酶活性用高压液相进行半定量检测。结果表明两类移行上皮癌端粒酶活性有显著差异。

2000年，医大二院马腾骧、畅继武、徐勇等完成“膀胱移行上皮癌诊断治疗的应用基础研究”，在诊断治疗方面完善移行上皮“内翻性肿瘤”的分类原则，并在国际上首次提出“两类移行上皮癌”的概念，由此建立起对膀胱癌的诊断与治疗更有指导意义的更完整的分类方法。在国内首先建成膀胱移行上皮癌细胞系，随后建立培养正常移行上皮的高效方法。同时，改进早期发现膀胱癌的尿脱落细胞学方法，将诊断的阳性符合率由以往HE染色的36%提高到86%。对两类膀胱癌的分子生物学机制的研究中，发现两类癌之间存在着多种基因表达差别，这些差别决定两类癌的不同生物学特性。在对BCG抗膀胱癌的作用机理研究方面，提出检测HLA、DR抗原可作为免疫效应与判断预后的重要生物指标。发现不同分化程度的膀胱癌细胞其纤维结合蛋白（FN）表达具有明显的差别，低表达FN可能是BCG抗膀胱癌疗效差的重要原因之一。该项目提出的“纤维粘连蛋白介导BCG抗膀胱癌”的观点有助于膀胱癌治疗。该研究历经20年，获2000年度国家科技进步二等奖。

图7-2-2-108　马腾骧（前）课题组正在进行项目研究

同年，医大二院韩瑞发等在“泌尿系统肿瘤MDR1基因的表达及抗药性的逆转”研究中，在国内首先对人膀胱癌初发病、再发病，抑癌基因（MDR-1）、PGP170（编码是糖蛋白）的表达，抗药表型特征进行研究，阐明肿瘤抗药机制；提出MDR-1、P53、RASP21基因的共同表达是膀胱癌复发与腔内化疗失败的主要原因与机制；采用基因转导建立膀胱癌抗药细胞系，为研究膀胱癌抗药逆转提供模拟人天然抗药的生物工具和治疗的新靶点；在国内首次应用并博定逆转膀胱癌细胞抗药性，为化疗药物与抗药逆转剂的联合应用预防膀胱肿瘤开创新靶点。

2001年，医大二院张淑敏等完成"移行细胞外源性野生型P53对膀胱癌基因治疗的研究"，利用外源性野生型P53对膀胱肿瘤进行基因治疗的探索，利用Lipofectamine将外源性野生型p53基因导入人膀胱移行细胞癌TBC-1和MBST739细胞系中，通过该P53的表达，检测多项生物学指标如细胞生长曲线、细胞周期、凋亡指数、软琼脂克隆率及T739小鼠接种等，多项研究结果表明被转染的细胞系在体外标准条件下，生物学活性有所改变，代表肿瘤增殖能力的指标明显下降，说明Wt-p53-cDNA转染肿瘤细胞得到表达后，P53起到了关卡作用，显示较好的抗肿瘤作用。通过研究为肿瘤的治疗寻找新靶点，制定新的肿瘤治疗策略。研究进一步阐明膀胱肿瘤的发生、发展以及治疗的机理，特别是与化疗的联合将使分子生物学技术和理论从实验走向临床，是一种新的治疗方法，多个单位采用上述两个细胞系用于实验取得良好效果。

2003年，医大二院畅继武等在"高恶性膀胱癌移行上皮癌与相应正常移性上皮差异表达基因的分子克隆及功能的研究"中，为阐明移行上皮癌发生发展的分子途径，利用抑制、削减杂交与斑点印记杂交技术，从中筛选出高恶性移行上皮癌差异表达基因片段，发现5个与高恶移行上皮癌有关的未知新基因。对其中一个新基因进行差异分析、用免疫杂交荧光技术进行全长克隆、染色体定位和结构分析，结果表明：BQ135232是与膀胱癌发生密切相关的新基因。该基因与高恶性移行上皮癌的生长、增殖、凋亡密切相关，为诊断与治疗高恶性膀胱移行上皮癌提供新依据。经市科委组织专家鉴定，认为该项成果达到国际领先水平。

2004年，医大二院韩瑞发等完成"基因重组BCG的实验研究"等项重大科技攻关课题，首次应用基因重组技术成功构建分泌型表达载体"phIFN-α-2b"和"重组IFN-alpha-2b-BCG"菌苗；首次证实重组BCG分泌的IFN-α-2b具有增强人外周血免疫细胞钟样蛋白受体的表达与活性，提出TLR是重组BCG免疫细胞介导的抗肿瘤作用新机制；首次建立制备冻干重组BCG菌苗真空与冷冻干燥参数与流程。成功的制备出重组hIFN-α-2b冻干BCG菌苗；证实冻干后重组hIFN-α-2b-BCG菌苗，外源质粒、插入基因、遗传、cfu/ml、形态特征、hIFN-α-2b的表达、生物免疫活性功能及抗肿瘤效应，不受低温冷冻与真空干燥过程的影响。

2005年，天津市泌尿外科研究所畅继武等完成"强化树突状细胞转化特异性CTL治疗肿瘤的基础及临床应用研究"。该研究建立起一条完整的从实体肿瘤中提取、纯化-肽复合物和体外定向培养、扩增DC与XTL的技术路线；构建成GPI-B7-pcDNA3表达质粒；获得高效、持久表达GPI-B7-1的二氢叶酸缺欠性CHO细胞株；构建成双刺激信号肿瘤疫苗与功能检测。在LAK细胞治疗基础上，成功利用DC+CTL代替或联合LAK细胞治疗肿瘤，对200多例患者进行治疗，取得10%有效，80%显效，5%无效，5%其他的治疗效果，该成果完善肿瘤生物学治疗完整的技术体系，为中国肿瘤生物学治疗开发出一条切实可行的技术路线，此技术推广到天津多家大型医院。该项目获2005年度天津市科技进步二等奖。

（二）微创治疗

1989年，天津医学院第二附属医院建立天津市首个碎石中心。首次在国内开展单一超声定位压电式碎石，日均治疗患者30人左右，从治疗病人数量到治疗效果都达到国内外领先水平。1994年引进瑞士气压弹道碎石机，U100双频激光和科威中钬激光碎石机，并在国内较早开展输尿管镜、经皮肾镜等微创碎石技术，开展泌尿外科介入超声诊断、超声定位体外碎石和泌尿系介入超声诊疗工作。2003年，被天津市卫生局批准成为天津医科大学第二医院尿石症治疗中心。同时中心又引进三代超声气压弹道碎石机，科以人钬激光碎石机，高端彩色超声诊断仪，经皮肾镜，输尿管软、硬镜。

2004年，总医院李黎明等在"应用腹腔镜微创手术治疗肾上腺疾病的临床研究"中，共开展各类腹腔镜肾上腺手术400余例，手术例数、成功率全国领先。报道3例既往有肾脏或肾上腺手术史者再行腹腔镜肾上腺切除术取得成功，进一步扩大了腹腔镜手术的适应症。行后腹腔镜嗜铬细胞瘤切除手术31例，手术例数及成功率居全国领先地位，其中应用腹腔镜成功切除1例腹主动脉旁异位嗜铬细胞瘤为国内首例报道。探索对肥胖患者行腹腔镜肾上腺手术，并进行手术方法的改进，取得良好临床效果。该项目获2004年度天津市科技进步二等奖。

2005年，医大二院徐勇等完成"微创手术在泌尿系统肿瘤治疗中的作用" 研究，探讨多极射频消融对小肾癌和前列腺癌治疗的可行性；研究腹腔镜与膀胱镜联合应用治疗膀胱特殊部位肿瘤的可行性，证明该方法是膀胱肿瘤微创治疗TURBT技术的扩展与进步；腔镜手术与开放手术的多种形式结合增加微创手术技术在泌尿系统肿瘤治疗中的使用率。通过动物实验以及临床应用研究，并结合相关病理学分析，对各种泌尿系统肿瘤的微创治疗方法进行客观评价，使多种微创手术治疗方法的实验研究在临床得到应用与普及。该项目获2005年度天津市科技进步二等奖。

（三）下尿路功能障碍性疾病

1990年，二中心医院陈彦明在国内首创利用阴茎腹侧面斜形带蒂皮条翻转埋藏法治疗尿道下裂一次成型术。经动物实验及临床应用证明，该技术操作简便，术后感染、尿瘘等发生率低，手术成功率达85%以上。阴茎矫正满意，尿道外口为正位或冠状沟，无尿瘘，排尿畅。阴茎斜形带蒂皮条翻转埋藏法治疗尿道下裂一期成形术，手术简单，成功率高，不受尿道缺损长度的限制，适用于各种类型的尿道下裂。该项目获1991年度天津市科技进步二等奖。

1999年，总医院崔喆等率先开展尿动力学检查工作。2005年，该院崔喆、李黎明、强万明等完成“下尿路梗阻性疾病尿动力学及超微结构研究”。通过透视电镜观察逼尿肌超微结构和神经轴突的改变。国内首次利用膀胱-尿道同步测压诊断膀胱逼尿肌与尿道外括约肌协调功能。较早率先利用压力-流率测定对老年男性排尿困难患者和女性下尿路症状患者做出诊断，正确选择手术适应症。并应用尿动力学检查对糖尿病膀胱进行评估并做相关超微结构基础研究。

压力性尿失禁、女性盆腔脏器脱垂、女性尿道及尿道周围疾患，女性排尿障碍、膀胱尿道阴道瘘等女性下尿路疾患严重影响女性患者的生活质量。1999年，医大二院方平在天津率先开展女性压力性尿失禁、盆底疾病的科学研究及临床治疗工作，填补天津市空白。共完成女性压力性尿失禁手术近一千五百例，患者年龄从23岁至82岁，经过严格术后疗效观察及长期随访，治愈率达98%，满意率接近100%。方平在国内率先引进“SPARC微创无张力吊带术”及“TOT尿道无张力吊带术”治疗女性压力性尿失禁，治愈率居国际领先水平，同时独创改良盆底修复联合TOT吊带术，较于其他网片治疗盆底脱垂的术式具有疗效可靠、微创、经济、并发症少等优势，使伴有盆底脱垂的女性压力性尿失禁患者治愈疾病，提高生活质量。

（四）人工泌尿器官和异种排异反应

1997年，医大二院王广有等完成的“可控性体内植入式人工膀胱研制与应用”研究，该项目以医用级硅橡胶为材料，设计研制成功隔膜型人工膀胱，研究制定出相应的植入手术方法，并进行人工膀胱流体力学性能的测试，人体盆腔有关径线的测量等。该项目满意解决国内外研究中仍未解决的肾积水、上尿路感染、输尿管及尿道吻合的剥离、假体被包裹组织压缩等问题。该人工膀胱植入体内后无需佩戴外接集尿袋、留置导尿管或插管导尿，保持正常排尿习惯，解决肾积水等一系列阻碍人工膀胱应用于临床的关键性问题。

1999年，医大二院顾汉卿等开展“复合式人工肾的研究”，将血液透析与血液灌流等新技术结合起来研制一种新型人工肾血液净化装置。在国内首次合成一种以聚苯乙烯为骨架的球形碳质树脂，可以满足复合式人工肾用灌流器的使用要求。在国内外首次合成聚乙烯醇衍生物的接枝共聚物作球形活性碳的微囊材料，具有高渗透与抗凝血的特点。制备成复合式人工肾用血液灌流器完成动物实验和临床研究，已开发使用。2005年，顾汉卿等完成的“九五”“十五”攻关项目成果与天津泰达创业中心共同开发研究医用气囊导尿管/医用导尿包、医用储液袋等项科研成果，推动国内生物医学工程研究的成果转化。

2004年，医大二院马腾骧、王广有、李胜芝等完成“人衰变加速因子（DAF）和膜反应性溶解抑制物（CD59）基因转移及表达的研究”，确定多基因转移抗异种排斥的较好基因组合方式。该研究针对国际上对建立转基因抗异种排斥问题，采用三基因显微注射技术、联合注射策略，建立转HT/CD95与DAF基因鼠/转基因猪之后，建成人HT（α-1，2岩藻糖苷转移酶）和人补体调节蛋白三基因基因鼠模型，为建立联合转基因猪实现异种移植奠定基础。

六、骨外科

天津新世纪骨科学会于2002年成立，每年召开全市骨科学术研讨会，交流诊疗经验，邀请国内外专家讲座，培养中青年骨科医生，成为天津市医学会中最活跃的学术团体。天津医院承办《中华骨科》杂志，在戴祥祺等努力下进行重组，邀请国内各省市专家为编委，此杂志已成为中国骨科学核心期刊。

(一)创伤骨科和创伤急救

1.创伤骨科

天津医院张铁良研究“跟骨骨折综合治疗”技术是治疗跟骨骨折微创技术，当时国内外骨科对跟骨关节内骨折多采用切开复位钢板内固定方法。因跟骨两侧皮肤薄，切开复位并发症是7%~15%患者术后皮肤边缘可能发生坏死，继发感染，新技术是利用骨圆针经皮将塌陷的骨折块撬起，配合闭合复位手法恢复跟骨宽度，术后用跟骨固定靴外固定，利用弹性踏轮，患者可早期练习功能活动，从而减少小腿肌肉萎缩及足部小关节粘连，靴内配合鞋垫，患者可早日扶双拐下地步行。不仅减少切开复位内固定带来的合并症，也无需再次手术取钢板，明显降低医疗费用。该项目获1987年度国家发明二等奖。

1992年，天津医院骨伤科学研究所辛景义、张铁良研制三维踝钳复位器，藉助器械三维方向调节功能治疗踝关节内翻型骨折，在三个平面、四个方向进行营利调节，对移位的内踝、外踝骨折施力使骨折块归位，并保持固定直至愈合，免除患者接受开刀之苦，取得良好疗效，“三维踝关节复位固定器”项目获1993年度国家发明三等奖。

1992年，天津医院骨伤科学研究所吴英华、张铁良首次引进国际治疗四肢骨折的“AO”治疗原则。AO是1960年由瑞士发起的骨折治疗组织，提倡“骨折绝对解剖对位，骨折块坚强内固定，早期功能活动及保护血运”四项原则。首次与国际对骨折的分型、治疗原则接轨。1995年，改进“AO”发展为“BO”治疗原则。

1996年，张铁良、韩慧等完成“肱骨上端骨折治疗及肌动力学研究”。首创俯卧式闭合复位方法，此种方法使患者接受闭合复位时的体位，由仰卧位改为俯卧位。减轻医生复位时牵引，巧妙的利用杠杆力量，解决旧式复位方法难以纠正的骨折远近段前后重叠或前后成角移位的难题，此技术已在全国推广。

1996年，天津医院顾云五、于顺禄、赵春英完成“加压外固定器治疗关节内骨折生物力学与组织学研究”，结果显示抗压力强度及骨愈合速度在第4、8周明显高于对照组，为外固定器治疗关节内骨折提供理论依据。

同年，张铁良首次引进国外带锁髓内钉治疗股骨干、肱骨干、胫骨干长管状骨折，在全市各家医院已成为治疗这些部位的主要技术，并与国际治疗上述部位骨折接轨。

是年，天津医院马毅、王小同、李延宏完成“肩锁、锁骨外固定器治疗肩锁关节脱位锁骨骨折”研究，取代传统用石膏或切开复位内固定的治疗方法，用于275例患者，优良率为96.5%，获1996年度天津市科技进步二等奖。

1998年，天津医院尹双波、张铁良完成“应用三相截骨和距跟关节融合术治疗陈旧性跟骨骨析”研究。针对陈旧性跟骨骨折常遗留下后足畸形和距跟关节创伤性关节炎等症，实施“三相截骨和距跟关节融合术”，减少骨折畸形引起的后足疼痛和功能障碍。

同年，天津医院金鸿宾、万春友、姚辉等设计“三维可调骨折外固定支架”治疗胫腓骨骨折，具有固定合理、组织损伤少、可及时换药等优点。

是年，天津医院辛景义、张铁良、赵欣等完成“抗遮挡桥形钢板及可吸收垫圈的研制”，可减少接骨板固定后由于应力遮挡而引起骨断端不愈合。

2004年，天津医院张铁良、尹双波、张建国等完成“改善骨折断端力学环境促进骨折愈合的研究”。为解决内固定器械(钢板、髓内钉)在设计上未能达到德国医学博士沃尔夫提出的wollf定律要求，以致骨折不愈合或迟缓愈合屡屡发生的问题。该研究以长椭圆孔细髓内钉作内固定，与可调节压力的外固定器连接，可随时调节骨折断端纵向压力。经动物实验和生物力学测试及数十例临床小腿骨折患者试用均取得优良效果。该项目获2004年度天津市科技进步二等奖。

2005年，天津医院吴英华、张铁良、金硕等设计出“经尺骨鹰嘴关节外斜形截骨入路治疗肱骨髁间骨折”，术中不损伤鹰嘴关节面软骨，有利于肘关节功能早日恢复。经鹰嘴关节外单平面斜行截骨的手术方式，减少鹰嘴关节面半月曲度改变及关节面不平等关节紊乱的发生。使截骨面积加大，优化力学性能，缩短截骨端骨愈合时间，经26例临床病例治疗证实，治疗效果满意。

2.创伤急救

1998年，天津医院王基、金鸿宾、金晓琴等完成“创伤急救的VIP程序”研究。该程序针对创伤早期致死的三个主要矛盾以逆转和边治疗边诊断的观念加快抢救的节奏。提出“快、足、稀”的扩容抗休克技术，可操作性强，易于掌握，经血液动力学测定显示，程序对复苏危重创伤是有效的。经十几年的临床实践使严重多发伤成活率从84%提高到95%以上。

（二）骨及软组织病

1991年，天津医院姚树源、于建华、尚天裕等“应用带旋髂深血管蒂髂骨植骨治疗成人早期股骨头坏死”。其术式在清除股骨颈病故的基础上，植入带旋髂深血管蒂髂骨，该术式可使股骨头重获血运，带血管蒂髂骨块能促进股骨头修复。对早期股骨头坏死治疗，经3~8.5年随访优良率88.5%，X线片显示塌陷的股骨头有所塑性与髋臼相应。

1993年，天津医院朱式仪、石忠琪、李汉民等用“人工桡骨头置换治疗粉碎性桡骨头骨折”。该研究采用医用高分子量聚乙烯材料制成九种规格的人工桡骨头假体，经对25例桡骨头粉碎性骨折的治疗应用，证明假体生物力学和组织相容性良好，恢复肘关节功能疗效优良率为88%。

1998年，天津医院马宝通、李秀兰等利用细胞分离技术进行“自体皮肤细胞移植治疗创伤感染创面的临床研究”，不需要大面积切取自身皮肤，依靠皮肤细胞繁殖创面，为骨科感染创面治疗开辟新途径。

2000年，一中心医院刘宗礼和天津市医药科学研究所宋宏良、杨学琪、刘爱恒等完成“自体骨髓与生物陶瓷复合移植治疗骨缺损”研究。采用自体骨髓与由羟基磷灰石、磷酸三钙组成的双相陶瓷进行骨缺损的动物实验治疗，证明此复合移植物兼有骨诱导、骨传导作用。

2003年，天津医院舒衡生、张铁良、马宝通等在“腓肠神经和隐身经营养血管逆行岛状皮瓣的临床应用研究”中，创新设计的隐神经皮瓣，蒂部保留1.5厘米宽的皮桥，使皮瓣蒂部的血运更能得到保障，使皮瓣切取和成法面积更大。解决国内外关于外踝后上方5厘米处存在皮肤软组织缺损时能否应用腓肠神经皮瓣的困难。

2005年，一中心医院姚树源，姜文学及天津医院马宝通等完成随意髂骨皮瓣临床和实验研究，该项目在髂部设计随意型髂骨皮瓣，具有丰富血供，应用此法临床治疗前臂挠（尺）骨缺损性骨不连18例，皮瓣全部成活。

（三）关节疾病

1991年，天津市大港医院张如明等完成膝关节囊外髌骨钻孔术治疗髌股骨退变性骨关节病的临床研究，该研究基于关节囊等软组织退行性改变损害髌骨静脉回流引起髌骨内静脉郁滞和骨内高压的机理，设计膝关节囊外髌骨钻孔的术式，创造用脑压表测骨内压的新方法。临床应用40例（61个关节），取得87.5%临床症状减轻的效果。该项目获1991年度天津市科技进步二等奖。

1995年，天津医院高志国、汪锡纯等完成“应用几何形人工膝关节治疗晚期类风湿性关节炎”研究；1999年，天津医院张福江等引进“高屈曲度旋转平台全膝人工关节并应用临床”，两项目分别获1995年和2004年填补天津市医学空白。2002年，天津医院于建华等引进的“髋臼旋转截骨治疗成人髋臼发育不良”技术，可以恢复髋关节生物力学结构，对髋臼发育不良青壮年患者可避免或推迟人工髋关节置换。2003年，于建华等引进的“全髋关节置换治疗成人发育性髋关节脱位”技术与常规全髋关节置换相比手术具有一定的复杂性和特殊性。应用该技术治疗患者60余例，取得良好的临床效果。

2000年起，天津医院引进腕、肘、肩、踝及髋关节镜手术。2002年，天津医院赵力、黄竞敏和费起礼等引进腕关节镜技术诊治病因不明性腕关节疾病，镜下探查并用刨削器及器械清理、修整病灶组织。优良率达91.67%。2004年，天津医院黄竞敏引进的“关节镜下松解术治疗肘关节功能障碍”，该技术填补天津市空白。2002年，天津医院建立“人工关节置换中心”，成为天津市及全国治疗关节病的重点科室，带动了天津市人工关节置换技术的发展。

(四)脊柱骨科

1990年,天津市红十字会医院张学利、江毅、田成瑞等,由日本引进桐田式掀盖椎板切除减压术,治疗各种类型的颈胸椎管狭窄症。该术式具有脊髓神经暴露充分,能有效地分解硬膜粘连,同时止血彻底,避免术后迟发血肿造成脊髓神经二次受压而影响疗效的优点。经155例患者随访观察,治疗效果良好。其临床有效率为94%,患者术后功能改善率为76.8%。1992年,该院赵春风、田成瑞、江毅等利用机械力学旋转自行推进的原理研制出"ZDS-旋转推进式颈椎椎体间盘切除器"。该研究依靠导向丝锥的稳定作用,将切除钻通过连接帽与其机纹吻合,可使切除器沿导向丝锥螺纹自动上下行切除椎体或间盘。经40例临床应用效果满意,具有消除脊髓震荡、安全系数大、骨块不折断等优点。

1994年,天津医院赵合元等设计新操作方法为"颈椎管内侵入方式",减少操作器械因素造成的脊髓再损伤,提高手术疗效。

1996年,天津市红十字会医院江毅、张学利和江汉等为防止和治疗腰椎伤病时发生失稳,进行腰椎失稳与椎间梭型镶嵌植骨的研究。该项研究对正常腰椎模拟各种不同术式破坏腰椎解剖结构,观察腰椎不同部位位移变化和引起失稳的规律,对40例腰椎间盘脱出、椎管狭窄手术行全板切除间盘,髓核摘除的同时,进行椎间梭型镶嵌植骨,提高手术疗效,有效预防由于间盘及后部结构切除造成的腰椎失稳。

1998年,天津医院邓树才、孙志明、赵合元等完成"应用椎弓根螺钉内固定器加椎间植骨融合器治疗腰椎滑脱症"研究,利用椎弓根螺钉的提拉,将滑脱椎体复位,加以Cage的椎间植骨使相邻椎体融合,保证远期疗效,解决以往滑脱复位不佳及容易折钉和滑脱复发的问题。

1999年,天津医院贾占华等完成"脊柱肿瘤切除人工椎体置换术治疗脊柱肿瘤及合并截瘫"研究。使用脊柱钛网,前路钢板内固定技术,有效减少术中因损伤而致截瘫发生。

2000年,天津医院胡永成等在国内率先开展脊柱肿瘤全切的基础及临床研究。对四肢肿瘤配合微波热疗,应用大段骨移植进行保肢,最大限度保留肿瘤患者肢体功能。

同年,天津医院徐宝山率先在国内开展椎体成形术的微创技术,治疗老年人衰竭性椎体骨折和脊柱肿瘤取得良好疗效。

2002年,天津医院邓树才、马毅等引进Halo-vest架治疗颈椎损伤,解决对于上颈椎损伤后非手术治疗长期卧床的问题很好的避免卧床所致的并发症,对于颈椎骨折脱位应用Halo-vest架可以大大提高复位的比例,从而对颈脊髓损伤的手术治疗和康复创造有力条件。

同年,天津医院孙志明、赵合元和邓树才等引进CD-Horizon系统,对15例上胸椎外伤性骨折脱位的患者行上胸段后路内固定手术,术后有14例完全复位,1例由完全脱位成为Ⅰ度脱位。2003年,再次用于治疗下腰椎多节段椎管狭窄,对患者在三维空间上矫正、固定,同时结合植骨融合,使患者症状明显改善,证实该系统具有较好的脊椎内固定作用。

2003年,三中心医院江毅完成"严重先天性脊柱侧凸前路截骨后路三维矫形的临床研究"。通过前路多节段截骨,切除半椎体、截断骨桥及对脊柱侧凸彻底松解;以及后路用椎弓根钉,钉棒系统矫形,明显提高矫正率。临床应用15例,矫正率平均为62.5%,最高达87.5%。

同年,马毅,赵合元,邓树才等应用solis椎间融合器治疗退变性颈椎间盘突出和颈椎失稳,保留患者术后颈椎椎间高度生理曲度,解决单纯取植骨造成椎间高度丢失的问题。2004年,马毅"应用椎弓根技术治疗下颈椎损伤"——经颈椎椎弓根螺钉固定,能同时解决颈椎三柱稳定问题。2004年,夏群等引进齿状突骨折空心螺钉内固定术及胸骨柄到肋二水平倒"T"形胸骨劈开入路治疗颈胸接合部脊髓压迫症新技术。

2005年,天津医院邓树才等针对老年人骨质疏松所致衰竭骨折,引进kyphon球囊椎体成形微创手术,解决高龄患者骨折延迟愈合甚至不愈合的问题。

（五）手外科

1.皮瓣修复创面

1994年，天津医院阚世廉以付神经、肩胛上神经、膈神经代替肌皮神经。以肋间神经代替正中神经，以尺神经部分束代肱二头肌肌支，恢复屈肘功能。1994年，天津医院金风华完成“应用腹部‘S’超薄双皮瓣治疗手部大面积脱套伤”研究。1998年，天津医院陈克俊采用带血管蒂背阔肌修复肱二头肌或三角肌瘫痪恢复患者上肢主要功能。陈克俊应用多种带血管蒂皮瓣、肌皮瓣转移或移植术，修复小腿或足部外伤后软组织及皮肤缺损，减少骨因暴露而发生感染，此项技术获2008年度天津市科技进步二等奖。1999年，天津医院宫可同应用腓神经，小隐静脉为蒂的新型皮瓣修复小腿及足踝部位的创面获得成功。2002年，天津医院詹海华完成“尺动脉上皮支皮瓣的临床应用”研究。

2.周围神经损伤修复

1994年，天津医院阚世廉总结“神经移位治疗臂丛根性撕脱伤”的病例填补天津市的空白。

3.手外科基本工作

1994年，天津医院费起礼的第一腕掌关节创伤性半脱位韧带重建。2001年，天津医院鲁毅军的Sauve-Kapanelji手术治疗下尺桡关节脱位。2001年，天津医院周佩兰的新型外固定支架治疗闭合性锤状指分别填补全市的空白。

（六）小儿骨科

1992年，天津医院朱玉奎、陈宗源和汉沽医院苏士海等完成双功能支架固定治疗幼儿先天性髋脱位研究，该支架由带固定带的半圆形大腿圈和半圆形小腿圈、连接板及可调节的长短横杆组成，为国内首创，临床应用155例，优良率94.1%。

1994年，儿童医院谷继卿、刘远峰、王继龙等设计研制出胸骨压迫器治疗小儿鸡胸，该器械分左右两叶，背侧以合页连接，胸侧有伸缩性接头、螺旋顶杆、压板，该压迫器科产生4~8千克垂直压力，经72例临床应用总有效率为82%。

1997年，天津医院杨建平率先在国内开展闭合复位、经皮克氏针固定治疗Gartland Ⅱ、Ⅲ型肱骨髁上骨折属于微创技术，术后肘关节功能好；防止复位后的再次移位导致的畸形愈合及肘内翻发生。1999年，杨建平通过多螺旋三维CT重建探讨先天性马蹄内翻足的病理变化，在国内外首次提出独立行走后的病理改变是足内侧柱与外侧柱失平衡的理论，建立重建足内、外侧柱平衡、恢复胫距、距舟、跟骰关节正常解剖序列的手术技术。2000年，杨建平率先在国内开展应用Ponseti技术治疗出生后2周～3个月的先天性马蹄内翻足，通过手法矫正、连续石膏固定，使其在5～8周内即可获得满意的矫正，避免手术治疗。2001年，杨建平率先在国内开展早期一期手术治疗发育性髋脱位，把传统的3岁后才能手术治疗提前至1.5岁。建立规范化、精细化手术操作的6项原则，明显降低手术创伤和术中出血；通过股骨短缩截骨有效地降低术后股骨头坏死的发生率。

2001年，天津医院任秀智在国内早期开展多段截骨髓内固定治疗儿童成骨不全症。建立对成骨不全症的规范治疗体系。预防再次骨折，并恢复患儿的行走功能。2002年，天津医院龚仁钰开展Pemberton骨盆截骨术。杨建平开展Dega骨盆截骨术矫正小儿髋关节发育不良，尤其适于神经肌肉型髋关节发育不良，有积极的临床效果。2003年，天津医院龚仁钰在国内率先开展应用90°直角钢板技术治疗神经肌肉型髋关节疾患及发育性髋脱位后残余的股骨近端外翻畸形，重建下肢的机械轴线，最大限度的避免畸形复发。2003年，天津医院蔡少华在国内开展闭合复位、弹性髓内钉治疗儿童长骨骨折技术，属于微创技术，利于骨折的早期愈合，能早期下地活动，减少长时间卧床骨牵引的痛苦。2004年，天津医院杨红军、曾裴在国内先期开展应用可延长棒技术矫正幼儿脊柱侧凸畸形。2005年，天津医院任秀智在国内率先开展运用牵拉成骨原理，采用Ilizarov外固定支架一期矫正儿童下肢成角伴短缩畸形，与传统的先手术矫正成角畸形再次手术肢体延长相比，手术微创、治疗周期短、重建下肢机械轴线、能最大限度的避免畸形复发以及早发骨性关节病。

（七）骨科基础研究

1995年，天津医院李秀兰等开展的“偎脓长肉作用机制的研究”，证明中药是良好的免疫促进剂，它促使创面产生大量有益脓，它是一种来自局部微血管的营养液，富含大量的免疫活性细胞和免疫活性因子，它们相互调节，进而促进局部组织细胞的抗感染和组织修复。2004年，李秀兰等还开展自体皮肤细胞移植修复感染性难愈创面的研究，将细胞工程技术与外用中药应用相结合，建立细胞移植在感染创面应用的技术平台，在动物实验研究的基础上进行了临床研究。研究感染性损伤和溃疡及合并骨折、肌腱损伤、烧伤、冻伤等30余例，创面修复速度提高≥30%，修复组织瘢痕松软。

同年，天津医院于顺禄等应用不脱钙塑料包埋骨制片技术开展的试验动物骨折愈合过程的骨计量学模型建立及观察研究，为骨折研究提供提供一组标准的骨折愈合组织形态计量参数指标及愈合时间曲线图形，同时也为进一步观察和研究各种药物和骨折治疗方法的疗效奠定基础。

1997年，天津医院金鸿宾、费起礼和林鸿培等编著的《急症骨科学》，该书共16章，内容涉及各种急性感染、疼痛及软组织损伤等疾患，对手外科、足外科、关节镜外科、脊柱外科及运动医学等重点介绍，该书介绍的创伤急救程序，符合中国的骨科急诊规范模式，获1997年度天津市科技著作二等奖。

同年，总医院郭世绂主编的《临床骨科解剖学》，该书分为躯干、上肢、下肢三篇，包括各部位骨骼解剖特点，重点描述骨关节结构，并广泛联系有关神经、血管及脏器病变。全书约150万字，千余幅图，供临床、教学及科研参考使用。获1997年度天津市科技著作二等奖。

是年，天津医院李瑞宗主编的《骨肿瘤诊断图谱》获1997年度天津市科技著作二等奖。该书刊出四百余幅彩色病理资料照片和几十幅X光照片。全面详实地介绍了各种骨与关节（包括腱鞘、滑囊）肿瘤，及各种瘤样病变的病理组织学图谱。同时，为了与肿瘤进行鉴别，还附带列出一些常见骨病的图谱。各幅图均附有诊断要点及简要说明，具有很高的学术价值。

2004年，总医院冯世庆等发现神经营养因子（NTFs）在脊髓损伤再生中的整合机制后，转入对多种NTFs促进脊髓神经组织不断再生的研究。将NTFs转基因技术和胚胎脊髓移植、外周神经移植等结合起来，使局部释放的NTFs不断刺激和引导宿主纤维与移植物的整合和联系，促进脊髓损伤的修复。同时，对可降解的生物材料——壳聚糖和转基因脊髓生物相容性的研究，发现壳聚糖能够促进转基因的脊髓生长，并能够逐渐被降解，而且其降解速度和程度是可调控的。

七、烧伤外科

天津市第四医院（以下简称“第四医院”）、天津市烧伤研究所在1991～2005年间共收治住院的各类烧伤病人10238例，治愈率99.1%，LA50（半数死亡率面积）的综合分析统计93.4%。该院创立大面积烧伤病人早期创面切痂+异体皮+微粒皮覆盖创面的技术。可一次性切除Ⅲ度创面达60%左右，用极少的正常皮肤覆盖创面，解决供皮区少的难题。采用脱细胞+薄断层自体皮技术用于烧伤后瘢痕切除创面的修复，术后外观接近正常皮肤的优点，既解决供皮区的缺乏又减轻新瘢痕的形成。同期该院在吸入性烧伤、烧伤患者营养支持进行较深入的研究。

1992年，第四医院邓诗林、索经轩、刘庚祥等完成磨痂术用于深Ⅱ度烧伤的早期手术治疗的临床研究，该项研究采用高速自动磨皮机，根据不同程度的烧伤创面选择磨头，通过在烧伤痂皮表面的高速运转，磨去坏死组织，以保证制皮的成活。该疗法具有出血量少、时间短、愈合快等优点，为深Ⅱ度烧伤的早期治疗提供一种新术式。

1994年，一中心医院高兰兴、王其芳和金宏等完成严重烧伤后维生素A、E、C代谢特点及补充适宜剂量研究。发现严重烧伤后维生素A、E、C明显下降，脂质过氧化物（LPO）显著升高，提出烧伤后补给维生素A、E、C分别为各自正常需要量的4倍、10倍和12倍即能得到良好的临床效果。

1997年，第四医院苏东、秦志刚、张学英等完成“阴沟肠杆菌的质粒分析在烧伤感染中的分子生物学研究”。研究显示粪便可作为烧伤感染的贮菌源形成粪便——伤口二重感染途径；提出阴沟肠杆菌的氨基糖甙类抗菌药物耐药性基因位于质粒上并具有可传递性；在检测到耐氨基糖甙类抗菌药物阴沟肠杆菌的同时应避免使用氨基糖甙类抗菌药物治疗其他革兰氏阴性杆菌的感染。该研究从流行病学、院内感染、耐药菌株方面为指导临床合理使用抗菌药物提供实验室依据。

1998年，第四医院刘群、邓诗林和王玉莲等完成“经纤维支气管镜吸入性损伤诊断和治疗的临床研究”，该研究通过对54例严重烧伤合并吸入性损伤患者应用纤维支气管镜进行动态检查，观察气管粘膜的组织形态改变，提出喉头以上损伤为轻度，气管隆突以上病变为中度，气管隆突以下充血水肿型为重度，支气管有坏死溃疡为特重度损伤的三级四分分类标准。同时借助支气管镜对吸入性损伤后进行痰液取样和包括吸引、刷洗、灌洗、局部抗菌治疗、止血与溶蛋白酶类等药物治疗，达到有效治疗效果。该研究不仅提出吸入性损伤的分度和分期标准，也总结出纤维支气管镜对吸入性损伤的一系列有效治疗方法。

1999年，该院曹丽萍、邓诗林、王玉莲等完成“烧伤病人的能量代谢规律及合理营养支持的研究”，该项目应用计算机控制的间接测热仪，对65例测量烧伤病人进行静息能量消耗测量，并结合血氨基酸谱、血浆激素、非蛋白呼吸商、蛋白质氧化率等项监测，研究发现烧伤后能耗立即增加；研究还对疾病的严重程度、病程、合并症及手术等因素进行观察，提出变异系数；提出无严重合并症的大面积烧伤患者以1.2 REE为总能量摄入量对烧伤患者进行营养支持是合理的。该成果为临床开展能量代谢研究和指导对危重者合理营养支持提供理论依据和实践经验。

2002年，第四医院高志刚、邓诗琳、王玉莲等完成“早期重组生长激素强化肠内营养对烧伤衙高代谢反应调节作用的研究”。对46例严重烧伤病人随机分组观察，证实严重烧伤病人伤后尽早开始肠内营养并适时应用重组人生长激素可调节高代谢反应，促进蛋白质合成，改善营养状况。

2003年，第四医院王玉莲等完成“早期重组生长激素对强代肠内营养对烧伤后高代谢反应、调节作用的研究”，应用间接测热仪监测烧伤病人能量消耗、呼吸商，并将重组人生长激素早期应用于重度烧伤病人的抢救、严重创面和外科大手术后病人的治疗，可促进蛋白合成，改善营养状况，促进创面愈合，降低高代谢反应从而对多脏器功能不全的产生具有预防作用。

八、移植外科

（一）小肠移植

1990年，总医院王鹏志开始小肠移植相关基础与临床研究工作。在以探讨小肠移植排斥反应为主线的基础研究中，采用细胞生物学、分子生物学方法探讨众多分子在排斥反应前期的变化规律，为排斥反应的分子治疗奠定实验基础。同年，该院王鹏志等在“实验性小肠移植技术与排斥反应研究”中，利用显微外科技术制作大鼠小肠移植模型以研究其排斥反应，施行实验性大鼠小肠移植240次，发现未予免疫抑制剂组大鼠平均存活9天，封闭群内移植者较封闭群间移植者的平均生存时间显著延长，进行免疫抑制治疗组大鼠大多存活28天以上。受体外周血和移植物浸润T淋巴细胞亚群等免疫组化检查可较早地发现移植免疫反应的迹象，虽病理检查仍是诊断移植免疫反应的可靠指标，对移植免疫反应进行多参数的综合分析和评估有助于小肠移植后免疫反应的早期诊断。此后，小肠移植研究不断深入，先后建立大鼠、小鼠和猪等稳定的动物小肠移植模型，创建肠系膜血管对端吻合式小肠移植。以细胞生物学、分子生物学方法探讨众多分子在排斥反应前期的变化规律，指出排斥反应中多分子参与的可能性，为排斥反应的分子生物学治疗奠定实验基础。多项基础研究经成果鉴定达国内领先和国际先进水平。在小肠移植临床研究中使用快速整块切取方法成功获取无心跳尸体供肠，先后完成小肠移植手术2例（当时全国仅4例），并对病人术后出现的严重排斥反应和多源性感染的控制方法进行有益的尝试。1997年，经世界小肠移植登记处予以确认，为全球31个小肠移植中心的第22个单位。“同种异体小肠移植的基础与临床研究”项目获1999年度天津市科技进步二等奖。

（二）肝移植

1991年以后，一中心医院沈中阳带领下，开展器官移植的临床研究。1994年5月，由日本专家协助完成首例原位肝移植，术后生存11年，创造并保持当时的中国肝移植最长生存记录。1998年9月，该院成立移植外科，是国内第一个含移植外科、麻醉、ICU、组织配型等多学科协作的器官移植专业科室。9月底，2天完成4例肝脏移植，是当时连续开展肝移植例数最多的纪录。2000年12月该院移植外科被市卫生局命名为天津市器官移植中心，2001年2月确认为天津市医药卫生重点学科。2001年成立天津市器官移植研究所，2003年12月更名为东方器官移植中心。该中心是集移植外科、移植内科、移植手术室、移植ICU、移植实验室、移植B超、腔镜室等多学科协作的专业化器官移植中心。2005年，肿瘤医院李强完成天津市首例亲体肝移植获得成功。

1998～2005年，一中心医院共完成肝癌肝移植手术1088例，占全部肝移植病例的46.8%，其中符合Milan标准的病例共321例。该院针对肝癌肝移植术后肿瘤复发问题重点研究肝癌微转移的分子生物学诊断，证实术中肿瘤微转移的主要是经肺动脉途径。同时，研究各种临床与病理因素对肝癌肝移植术后生存的影响，国内率先总结出肝硬化合并偶然癌的临床病理特点。探讨了多种免疫抑制剂对体外培养的不同生物学性状肝癌细胞系影响的作用途径和分子生物学机制，纠正和提高了对现有免疫抑制剂的认识。

1999年，一中心医院针对肝移植术后乙肝复发率高的难题。在国内率先使用更昔洛韦、乏昔洛韦、干扰素抗病毒治疗预防移植术后乙肝复发；同年，该院试用国产乙肝免疫球蛋白（HBIG），及"拉米夫丁+HBIG联合用药方案"。采用该方案后患者术后一年乙肝复发率降至3%以下。是年，该院沈中阳、陈宝公、谷川等完成"肝脏移植治疗终末期乙型肝炎肝硬化"。该研究利用肝移植与肝炎抗病毒治疗的最新成果将原位肝移植技术用于终末期乙型肝炎后肝硬化的治疗，采用经门脉插管、UW液灌注、快速供肝切取及动脉吻合中的分支补片技术，该术式可缩短供肝热缺血时间，保证肝动脉血运，减少术后肝动脉栓塞发生。该项目获1999年度天津市科技进步二等奖。2001年7月，中华医学会器官移植分会召开"肝移植术后预防乙肝复发专题研讨会"，该会制定肝移植术后乙肝复发和HBV再感染的诊断标准，所提出的联合用药预防方案被称为天津方案，已被国内多家器官移植中心采用。

2001年以后，一中心医院在肝肾、肝胰、胰肾等多器官联合移植获得成功。同时，改良背驮式肝移植、减体积、劈裂式肝移植等新术式，应用于临床。2003年度完成器官移植手术400余例，其中肝移植手术253例次。2004年，肝脏移植总例数达507例，肾脏移植总例数达367例，肝移植、肾移植年度例数均居国内首位，肝移植手术例数连续8年居全国第一，截至2005年，该中心共完成肝移植手术近4000例次。年度肝移植例数跃居世界第一，一年生存率、3年生存率、5年生存率分别达90%、72%、51%，达到国际先进水平。

第三节　肿瘤学

1991～2005年，天津在肿瘤临床诊断和治疗技术上多有创新，在国内率先采用干细胞移植治疗乳腺癌，并从分子层面上揭示肿瘤转移抑制基因，找到一些肿瘤基因治疗的新靶点。科研整体水平提高，多项进入到细胞水平和分子水平，肿瘤的生物治疗及物理治疗技术有新进展。1994年，肿瘤医院变更隶属关系，改为天津医科大学附属肿瘤医院（以下简称"肿瘤医院"）。1996年，肿瘤学被列入国家"211工程"重点建设学科。1998年，肿瘤医院被卫生部批准为临床药理基地，并被教育部批准为博士学位授权点。肿瘤医院张天泽等编著的《肿瘤学》，获1998年天津市科技进步（著作）一等奖。2002年，肿瘤学被批准为国家重点学科。同年，该院建立分子诊断实验室，开展肿瘤细胞的遗传学研究。2004年，该院被批准为教育部乳腺癌防治重点实验室和天津市肿瘤防治重点实验室。天津对肿瘤学科的基础与临床研究，涉及面广、单位多，成就大。有关脑肿瘤、泌尿系统肿瘤、眼眶肿瘤等可参见该书外科学等相关章节。

一、肿瘤流行病学和病因学

（一）肿瘤流行病学

1990年，天津市肿瘤登记报告中心已建成40万人群试验性肿瘤预防保健网，被世界卫生组织（WHO）肿瘤登记报告协会(IARC)接纳为正式成员。1996年,天津参与由全国14个市、县合作承担的国家项目"常见恶性肿瘤的发病、死亡及危险因素监测方法的研究"。建立全国肿瘤发病、死亡登记、逐级报告的方法及全国肿瘤发病、死亡资料数据库,为中国制定肿瘤防治策略提供依据。1996年,天津医科大学(以下简称"医科大学")王庆生等在"社区恶性肿瘤二级预防的方法学评价及前瞻性研究"中,经对12万人群的乳腺癌发病普查,提出中国乳腺癌具有与欧美不同的生物学行为,乳腺癌发病率快速上升,发病年轻化、高峰年龄下降及多原发癌比率低等特点。同时采用社区调查及宣教培训等方法,建立一套适合国情、民情的肿瘤预防体系,开发出"肿瘤个体危险度评价系统"软件。2004年,肿瘤医院郝希山等在"天津城市居民恶性肿瘤流行趋势分析及预防的研究"中,对1981～2000年天津市区370万人口恶性肿瘤发病、死亡资料进行统计分析,研究证实天津市恶性肿瘤发病率的变化趋势与人口年龄变化趋同,人口老龄化是导致恶性肿瘤总体发病率上升的主导因素。推测出天津城市人口未来10年恶性肿瘤发病率以及癌谱的变化规律。提出中国当前常见癌谱兼具发达国家与发展中国家癌谱的双重特征,报告全人群59种恶性肿瘤5年总体生存率提高80%,即由1981～1985年的19.81%提高到1996～2000年的35.64%,为20多年来恶性肿瘤的防治效果评估提供依据。该项目获2004年度天津市科技进步一等奖。

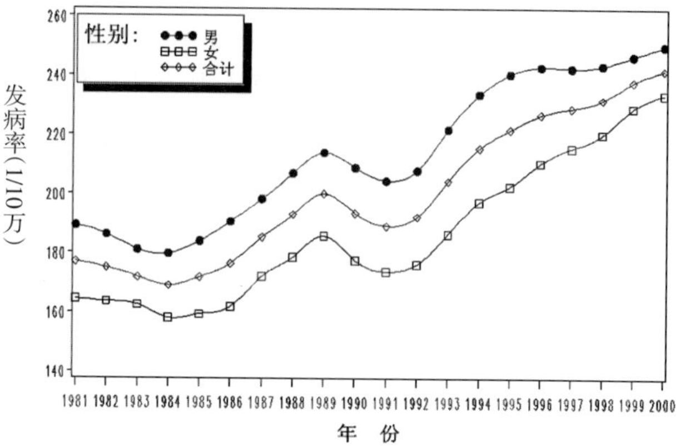

图7-2-3-109　天津市恶性肿瘤发病率(1981~2000)

图7-2-3-110　天津医科大学郝希山(中)讲话

2001年,医科大学陈可欣对天津市儿童白血病的流行趋势以及相关危险因素进行多层次、多角度、单因素和多变量的统计分析,首次发现儿童白血病的发生与父母文化水平密切相关。2003年,天津市肿瘤研究所王培忠在"天津市肿瘤病人生存质量的评价"研究中,应用SF-36生活质量调查量表对2004年8～12月医科大肿瘤医院对就诊的乳腺癌患者的生活质量进行调查,对影响乳腺癌患者生活质量的主要因素进行分析。结果发现高龄和低龄患者,受教育程度低,家庭收入低、离异或丧偶、有吸烟史及不了解自己病情的患者生活质量相对较差。为此,对预防措施的制定应更有针对性。

(二)肿瘤病因学

1990年,医科大学王庆生等在"天津市女性肺癌病因因素研究"中,对天津市女性肺癌高发的病因因素进行统计分析,发现体块指数小,吸烟,做饭油烟大、次数多、饮食中钠和硫胺素摄入多以及维生素C和E摄入过少均为女性肺癌独立危险因素。1996年,天津对1996～1998年市区1000例乳腺癌患者家族史进行调查。采用遗传流行病和分子流行病学方法对32个高危遗传家系的外周血标本进行乳腺癌易感基因(BRCA)和BRCA2基因突变的检测分析。初步得到年龄、家族史、乳腺癌易感基因突变,均与乳腺癌的发生相关。同时还发现两个国内外尚未见报道的易感基因突变位点的改变,即首次发现中国乳腺癌家系BRCA1第11外显子上的1584位点上发生突变。2001年,医科大学钱碧云在"毒物代谢酶基因多态与肺癌遗传易感性研究"中发现,携带特异的毒物代谢酶基因个体可能与吸烟协同增加患肺癌的风险。2005年,医科大学组建分子流行病室,开展人群基因多态性与肿瘤易感性关系的研究,包括甾体激素代谢通路相关基因多态性、致癌物代谢通路相关基因多态性、DNA损伤修复相关基因多态性及XPD基因多态性等。

二、肿瘤病理学

（一）临床病理

1992年，肿瘤医院引进嗜银核仁组成区（AgNOR）技术，制定AgNOR颗粒的分型和计数辅助细胞学的良性和恶性判断的标准，在全国率先引入细胞学诊断。1999年引进细胞采集器技术，解决多年来胸腹水制片欠清晰和富集细胞少的难题，提高了阅片效率及一次检查的阳性率，并在国内迅速传播。

1999年，肿瘤医院张连郁等用免疫组化方法检测89例原发于淋巴结内非霍奇金淋巴瘤（NHL）中BCL2和BCL6蛋白的表达情况，发现BCL2和BCL6表达在NHL各组织类型之间有明显差异，且B细胞来源者明显高于T细胞来源者。研究证明，BCL2是弥漫性大B细胞淋巴瘤（DLBCL）中可作为独立判断预后的生物学指标，而BCL6则可能与生长的生存时间有关。该项目首次研究了BCL2和BCL6蛋白表达与NHL病理发生和预后的相关性，并在国内率先提出两种基因在蛋白水平的协同表达对DLBCL的临床亚组的划分，初诊时检测DLBCL患者两种蛋白的表达，对预后判断，为临床化疗提供个体化方案具有重要的意义。

（二）乳腺病理

1992年，肿瘤医院傅西林等在“我国女性乳腺癌多原发灶的前瞻性病理学研究”中，首次在国内应用全乳腺次连续大切片技术，对236例女性乳腺癌根治术标本的多原发病灶病变进行研究后，在国内首次提出中国女性乳腺癌的多原发灶发生率为19.9%，多原发灶的70%只累及一个象限，83%均分布于主原发癌相邻或相同的象限。为中国乳腺癌的病理学研究及手术术式的改进提供了具有重要参考价值的资料。1996年，傅西林等开展的“乳腺癌前病变与乳腺癌相关的多指标病理学研究”在国内首次应用全乳腺大切片技术结合癌胚抗原（CEA）、c-erbB-2癌基因产物免疫组化检测及流式细胞术（FCM）测定DNA含量、s期细胞比率（SPF）和细胞增殖指数（PT），并对393例乳腺癌标本，进行癌旁和癌前病变与乳腺癌相关性的多指标前瞻性综合研究。研究证实，对癌前病变特别是导管上皮重度不典型增生和重读乳头状瘤病进行CEA、c-erbB-2癌基因及FCM分析等多项指标检测，有利于发现早期乳腺癌。

1998年，肿瘤医院牛昀等在“腋淋巴结阴性乳腺癌转移潜能相关癌基因及其蛋白表达临床病理学研究”中，对196例病例进行5年随访后，采用免疫组化法和原位杂交法，结合临床病理学指标，通过多因素logistic回归分析，提出简便可靠的预测转移参考指标数据和数学模型。该研究成果为腋淋巴结阴性乳腺癌病人的个体化治疗提供重要的参考数据。2000年，牛昀等在“细胞周期调控因子与乳腺细胞癌变的相关性研究”中，进行两对细胞周期调控因子蛋白水平和基因水平的联合检测，提出细胞周期素D1（Cyclin D1）等4种调控因子与乳腺癌的发生发展过程有密切的相关性。研究结果进一步明确乳腺细胞癌变的分子机制和发展规律，为乳腺癌前病变的基因治疗提示靶点实验室依据，对筛选高危病例提供客观性辅助指标。该成果获2002年度天津市科技进步二等奖。

2003年，肿瘤医院于泳等在“乳腺导管内癌特性的形态学及分子生物学研究”中，明确不同亚型导管内癌的生物学特性，探讨乳腺癌发生发展规律，提出以癌细胞核为主的新分型方法。该方法为实现导管内癌的个体化治疗方案提供理论和实践依据，并在国内各省市应用。2004年，该院付丽等在“乳腺浸润性微小乳头状癌（IMPC）生物学行为研究及应用”中，针对临床上具有特别不良生物学行为、预后极差的乳腺浸润性微小乳头状癌进行研究，发现IMPC的细胞具有“集团性生长、侵袭、转移等”形态学特性。该研究为IMPC的诊断及鉴别诊断提供指标。该成果已被国内外多家医院应用。2005年，牛昀等在乳腺癌前病变与导管内癌的克隆性研究中针对乳腺癌发生机制早期诊断这一热点问题采用女性X染色体失活嵌合性A2位点的克隆性分析技术，探讨各种增生性病变及导管内癌的克隆性起源，为从癌前病变中筛选高危病例提供理论依据和辅助检测方法，并进一步证实外周型乳头状瘤伴不典型增生是乳腺的一种癌前病变。2005年，肿瘤医院只向成、郝希山、史玉荣等完成“乳腺癌易感基因在国人乳腺癌家族中突变的研究”。通过PCR，杂合性双链分析以及DNA测序，对BRCA1和BRCA2全部外显子进行突变检测和分析，阐明BRCA在国人中突变规律。率先发现BRCA1中两个新的与疾病相关的突变位点；在国人中发现BRCA2中一个西方人群中的突变位点；建立国人筛查BRCA突变的方法等。该项目获2005年度天津市科技进步二等奖。

（三）分子病理学

2002年，肿瘤医院建立分子诊断实验室，开展肿瘤细胞的遗传学研究。2004年，该院孙保存等在"双向分化恶性肿瘤血管生成拟态分子机制的研究"中，提出：在双向分化恶性肿瘤组织中，存在血管生成拟态这一独特的肿瘤血液供应模式；肿瘤的生长过程中可能存在不同的肿瘤血液供应模式间彼此过度的"三阶段假说"；双向分化恶性肿瘤细胞自身可以分泌PAS阳性物质、CD31蛋白、Ⅳ型胶原等物质可作为血管生成拟态形成的物质基础等一系列重要的科研论断。该研究通过对肿瘤组织具有血管生成拟态的患者进行早期诊断、治疗、抑制肿瘤的血道转移，可以提高其生存率，并找到一些肿瘤基因治疗的新靶点。

2005年，肿瘤医院孙保存在"FLIP干扰性小RNA阻断大肠癌细胞免疫逃逸的体外试验研究"中，首次提出大肠癌发生中存在凋亡受抑制为特征的"细胞选择性增殖"现象，并提出舒林酸的预防效果优于治疗效果及Fas/FasL系统参与凋亡诱导机制的观点，证实大肠癌中存在"Fas抵抗"和"Fas反击"现象，通过基因干预手段可以部分解除对细胞凋亡的抑制，发挥促进癌细胞凋亡的作用，提出CXCL12-CXCR4系统与基质金属蛋白酶系统间相互协同，共同促进大肠癌细胞的侵袭和器官特异性转移。研究成果对提供大肠癌预后评估指标和预防癌前病变、器官特异性肝转移的基因治疗靶点，制定大肠癌及其癌前病变药物和基因治疗策略奠定基础。

三、肿瘤临床

（一）头颈部肿瘤

1991年后，天津在以甲状腺癌为重点的头颈部肿瘤保留功能切除术、转移及预后的研究中，首次提出人的颈动脉仅保留一侧即可保障大脑供血的论点。同时，利用复合皮瓣、骨肌皮瓣整形修复中晚期头颈部肿瘤患者的头颈部缺损，使患者得到功能与外形的恢复。其中，肿瘤医院李树玲等完成颈动脉分歧部切除术后脑血流代偿机制的血流动力学和影像学研究，"不进行血管重建的颈动脉分歧部切除术后脑血流代偿机制血流动力学研究"项目获1996年度天津市科技进步二等奖。

1993年，李树玲主编的《头颈肿瘤学》获1996年度天津市科技进步（著作）二等奖。

2003年，一中心医院、天津市塘沽医院和天和医院杨宝琦、王景和、谢刚等完成"上颌窦癌临床治疗研究"。当时，国内外治疗上颌窦癌的方式较多，但缺乏有效的系统治疗。该研究将手术、放疗、冷冻、介入等疗法联合应用系统治疗。在10年中观察27例，其治愈生存率一年为100%，二年为80%，三年为63%，五年为29.6%。

2005年，肿瘤医院高明等在"降钙素及其基因相关肽在甲状腺髓样癌诊疗中的规律性研究"中，首次阐明甲状腺髓样癌术后血清中降钙素基因相关肽的变化规律；术后1周时血清中降钙素的水平可以作为判断疗效和预后的指标；提出1000皮克/毫升为临界参考值，大于该值时应采取综合治疗；血清降钙素基因相关肽水平可以作为术前降钙素水平正常的甲状腺髓样癌患者的辅助性肿瘤标记物。

（二）乳腺癌

20世纪90年代初期，肿瘤医院石松魁、郎义方开展乳腺癌改良根治术后一期乳房再造，即将国产人工硅胶假体植入胸肌后，使切除乳房部位重新隆起，且保留乳头、乳晕使患侧与健侧乳房对称。2001年，该院张学慧等进行乳腺癌根治术后，应用上蒂横行腹直肌肌皮瓣进行Ⅰ、Ⅱ期乳房再造及乳头、乳晕再造的研究。经过70余例手术观察，患者满意度达98%，达到既根治肿瘤，又可重塑新乳房，弥补患者的形体缺陷和精神创伤。

90年代中期，郝希山等在"1千例乳腺癌多参数分子标记预测预后并提高疗效的回顾及前瞻性研究"中，利用免疫组化、原位杂交对695例已知预后结果的病例进行16种肿瘤相关基因检测，筛选出8种与乳腺癌转移有关的预后因子，并首次利用数学模型预测转移。在国内率先开展"干细胞移植治疗乳腺癌的研究"，制定出适合中国的干细胞动员、采集、程序冷冻、复苏、生物检测及超剂量化疗、放疗等实体瘤规范治疗方案。完成国内最大组治疗病例（131例），创零移植相关死亡率，为国际最低。其高危复发乳腺癌3年无病生存率移植组达87.6%，对照组58.4%。

1999～2001年，肿瘤医院方志沂、刘君等应用染料法（专利蓝）对临床腋淋巴结阴性乳腺癌进行检测，对照改良根治术后的腋淋巴结病理检查，探前哨淋巴结活检技术（SLNB）的应用前景。研究结果显示SLNB技术推测乳腺癌腋窝淋巴结转移状态的准确率为97.1%，对34例T1乳腺癌的准确率达100%。该成果提示使用SLND获取乳腺ALN病理资料具有损伤小、并发症少，可最大限度地满足患者的形体需要。同时，针对前哨淋巴结检测中的假阴性问题，采用次连续切片和免疫组化技术，对37例患者常规病理切片阴性的乳腺癌腋淋巴结（SLN）进一步检查，结果发现4例（10.8%）存在微转移灶，提示使用次连续切片和免疫组化方法可进一步提高应用SLNB的可靠性。

2002年，肿瘤医院刘佩芳、鲍润贤、牛昀等完成“乳腺良、恶性病变动态增强MRI表现特征与血管生成相关性研究”。该项目首次将乳腺良恶性病变动态增强MR早期增强率、强化峰值和时间—信号强度曲线类型3项指标与应用免疫组化测定的病变组织MVD和VEGF表达水平2项指标间的相互关系分别进行详尽的相关性研究。首次提出MVD和VEGF是影响乳腺病变MR早期强化率、曲线类型的主要因素。提出乳腺动态增强MRI作为一种客观、无创且在活体上可实施的检查技术，有助于乳腺癌早期诊断并在一定程度上对判断肿瘤预后具有潜在作用，该成果获2002年度天津市科技进步二等奖。

2003年，肿瘤医院在采用大剂量化疗医治乳腺癌时，用自体外周血造血干细胞移植作支持，并用标准剂量化疗作对照，结果表明大剂量化疗联合干细胞移植治疗术后的高危乳腺癌可以提高患者的5年总生存率，优于标准剂量化疗，但并不能改善患者的无病生存率

2004年，肿瘤医院刘君等在“乳腺癌保乳手术安全范围的分子病理学及临床研究”中，通过对48例切缘阴性象限切除标本行次连续大切片检查，观察乳腺内原发癌及癌旁病变情况；对62例乳腺癌全乳腺切除标本采用常规病理、免疫组化及分子生物学方法，分析癌瘤向周边浸润及周围组织癌变趋向的规律；以及保乳手术后切缘阳性和切缘阴性两组病例的对照分析。证实保乳手术安全切除范围为肿瘤边缘外2厘米，远离乳头端可缩小至瘤缘1厘米，达到既能根治肿瘤又能保持乳房良好外形的目的。同期，肿瘤医院李丽庆等在靶向药物赫塞汀（Herceptin）联合紫杉类药物的随机对照研究中，证实细胞毒药物联合分子靶向治疗可显著提高乳腺癌患者的有效率及生存期。

（三）胸部肿瘤

1999年，肿瘤医院尤健等在“肺癌细胞凝血酶敏感蛋白-1和CD44基因表达与肿瘤发展的关系”中，应用免疫组化法和RT-PCR法检测例肺癌组织中CD44和TSP-1表达，探讨其与患者预后的关系。结果显示TSP—1在肺腺癌中的表达分别明显高于鳞癌和小细胞癌，$CD44_H$在肺腺癌中的表达高于鳞癌，$CD44_V$在肺鳞癌中的表达明显高于腺癌，同时用免疫组化法及RT-PCR法检测TSP-1表达，两法符合率为84%。研究结果证实肺癌的TSP-1、cD44lH及$CD44_V$表达均有一定的病理学特异性。肺腺癌中TSP-1可能与患者的预后有关。2000年，该院王长利等在“非小细胞肺癌患者淋巴结转移规律及预后的研究”中，通过对318例肺癌根治术患者淋巴结的转移特点和范围、胸部淋巴结转移规律的分析研究，提出：上叶肺癌应常规清扫肺隆突下及上纵隔；无隆突下淋巴结转移可不清扫八区、九区；下叶及右中叶肺癌，无论有无肺门或隆突下淋巴结转移，均应广泛清扫上下纵隔淋巴结。术前胸部CT的结果不能作为淋巴结清扫的依据。

2001年，医科大学王新允、张乃鑫、李玉浩等完成“人肺癌细胞周期调控因子与凋亡关系的研究”。该项目应用免疫组织化学技术检测NSCLC、SCLC和正常肺组织中细胞周期调控因子CyclinD1、P53、P16、p21、RB、c-fos及nm23基因蛋白、表皮生长因子受体、耐药因子Pgp等的表达，并进行增殖细胞核抗原的检测。同时应用流式细胞术定量分析NSCLC和正常肺组织的DNA指数、增殖指数、凋亡率及bcl-2、c-myc基因表达，为细胞凋亡的研究开辟新途径。2002年，医科大学张维铭、徐垚、梅玫等完成“人原癌基因扩增抑癌基因异常及端粒酶活化及肺癌诊断相关性研究”。该项研究利用分子杂交技术对肺癌的K-ras、c-myc、erbB-2基因激活进行分析比较，证实K-ras突变为肺腺癌特有，而鳞癌主要表现为erbB-2的扩增。

（四）腹部肿瘤

1.胃肠道肿瘤

肿瘤医院郝希山等自1985年历经十几年，从解剖学、病理学、肿瘤学和消化道学等多学科角度，将基础研究与临床应用紧密结合，从代胃空肠的神经传导、运动生理、消化液与消化道激素分泌以及对495例术后患者的消化功能与营养状态诸方面进行研究。肿瘤医院郝希山、李强、王家仓等完成“功能性间置空肠代胃术的临床与基础研究”，该研究为胃癌全胃切除术将保留神经运动功能的空肠两端适度结扎后吻合于食管与十二指肠断端之间，构建一个代胃，使全胃切除术后并发症大幅度减少，在消化道外科术式研究中获得突破性进展。该成果获2001年度国家科技进步二等奖。在全胃切除重建术中采用功能性间置空肠代胃并创建适度结扎技术，称为“郝氏法”。与六种不同全胃切除术后消化道重建术的比较证实：功能性间置空肠代胃术是最符合生理要求的代胃术式，通过国内外22家大中型医院推广应用300余例均取得良好的效果。

1992年，肿瘤医院李晓璘、张熙曾研制成功新型食管胃吻合口扩张器，为食管癌、贲门癌术后吻合口狭窄的患者解决进食困难的痛苦。1994年，医科大学张熙曾、李晓璘对食管常规使用的直形手术刀予以改进，设计并制成双面刃“食管气管用曲形手术刀”，以适应胸部深在手术野，一次完成食管或气管的切割，且切缘整齐。1999年该院姜宏景等完成的“食管癌、贲门癌端粒酶活性的研究”，提示端粒酶是一种很好的肿瘤标志物，对于肿瘤的早期诊断、疗效判断有重要意义。2000年，该院梁寒开展的活性碳吸附丝裂霉素C腹腔化疗的临床和实验研究，结果显示应用该方法3年、5年生存率分别为70.16% ，44.51%，比常规静脉化疗组的3、5年生存率分别提高43.07%及30.06%，证实活性碳吸附MMC腹腔化疗能提高进展期胃癌根治性手术后无瘤生存率，适用于经根治手术的高危患者。梁寒还对进展期大肠癌患者手术中进行热疗及热化疗，使C期大肠癌的3年生存率由59.65%提高到80.12%。

1994年，肿瘤医院郝希山、李强等完成新型袢式胆肠吻合术研究，该术式对无法切除的梗阻性黄疸内引流病例选择空肠Treitz韧带60厘米处于结肠前与胆囊或胆总管吻合，距吻合口2厘米处行7号丝线结扎输入支将肠腔闭合，再距吻合口输入支15~20厘米，输出支25~30厘米，行空肠及空肠侧侧吻合，该术式设计合理，简便易行，适用于中晚期肿瘤引起的胆道梗阻患者。该项目获1996年度天津市科技进步二等奖。

2002年，中国人民解放军第二五四医院及第三军医大学第一附属医院王东旭、房殿春、刘为纹等完成“胃癌及癌前病变组织中多种肿瘤相关基因异常的研究”。该项研究利用人体和动物模型标本运用分子生物学技术及免疫组化方法系统分析胃癌及癌前病变——不同类型肠化生、异型增生组织中抑癌基因p73等失活；癌基因K-ras等激活；细胞粘附分子CD44和基质蛋白TN异常表达，探讨抑癌基因失活与幽门螺杆菌感染、端粒酶活化、微卫星DNA不稳定性的关系。其成果可用于胃癌早期诊断、预后判断或基因治疗的分子指标。同年，一中心医院闫旭、祁吉、沈文等完成“多层螺旋CT仿真胃镜及三维成像在胃肿瘤诊断中的应用研究”结果表明：CT仿真胃镜等技术完全适用于胃肿瘤的临床检查；综合运用该技术，在对胃肿瘤的检出、定位、分期等方面可发挥较大作用。

2.肝胆胰肿瘤

1991年，肿瘤医院郝希山等在“天然胡萝卜素对癌前病变的化学干预研究”中，利用具有高分泌甲胎蛋白功能的人肝细胞癌裸小鼠模型，观察β-胡萝卜素与阿霉素联用对宿主存活期的影响，结果表明β-胡萝卜素与化疗药物联用具有协同抗癌作用，显著缓解化疗产生的毒副作用，提高宿主对大剂量化疗的耐受性。

1999年，肿瘤医院李强、郝希山、郝继辉在“巨块型肝癌的分型及其生物学行为的临床与实验研究”中，首先依据肉眼形态和预后不同提出巨块型肝癌不同亚型的观点。观察两型肝癌的大体与生物学特点，并在此基础上提出分型的依据。从分子生物学，特别是肿瘤血管生成及端粒酶活性角度论述两型肝癌的生物学行为差异，对两型肝癌采用免疫组化、RT-PCR病理大切片、端粒酶等进行比较研究，结果两型大体形态不同的肝癌在临床资料、病理组织学分级、血管生成、端粒酶检测等方面存在显著差异。为临床工作中及时准确地对肝癌估计预后，制定治疗方案，奠定理论基础。该研究获2001年度天津市科技进步二等奖。

2000年，肿瘤医院李强等完成“肝血管肝外确认、肝内处理切肝术式的临床研究”。该研究合理地运用肝解剖的特点，提出肝血管的2、4、5、6、7点确认法，使之肝内血管处理标准、规范、肝切除边界清楚，收到比传统切肝术式更好的效果。2005年，李强、郝继辉、史玉荣等完成“肝癌血管形成与其临床特征及生物学行为研究”。从肝癌的临床特征和生物学行为角度，创新性地对肝癌复发方式和规律进行分类。从大体形态对肝癌的生物学行为作出预判，指导治疗。在临床工作结合分子生物学水平阐述外在差异的内在机理，从宏观、微观等多角度阐述肝癌的生物学行为特点，并首次提出肝癌外科手术切缘的理论。

2002年，天津市大港医院和总医院王绍山、齐清会、张倜等完成“三氧化二砷治疗肝癌的实验研究”。在国内外首次对As_2O_3在大鼠体内诱导原发性肝癌细胞凋亡的作用机理进行研究。证明经腹腔内途径给As_2O_3治疗大鼠体内原发性肝癌有效。

2005年，肿瘤医院刘方等对“原发性肝癌根治术后选择性肝动脉化疗栓塞（TACE）对预防复发疗效评价”的研究，结果表明：将TACE作为长期治疗方法，维持到术后两年，覆盖整个复发高峰期，可以显著降低高复发因素肝癌根治术后的1、2年复发率，即由30%与53.3%降到6.7%与16.7%。同时，对小于10厘米微小肝癌病灶（隐匿性肝癌）采用16层螺旋CT扫描与选择性血管技术联合应用血管CT成像（Angio-CT）进行检查，结果表明：Angio-CT的图像后处理技术可以清晰显示肝脏肿瘤的特点、供血血管与毗邻结构关系，有助于诊断肝内转移的微小病灶。

（五）盆腔肿瘤

1991年，肿瘤医院王鸿本、李文录等研制成具有14种监护功能的“膀胱尿流自动监护仪”，可用于尿道、膀胱留置尿管和耻骨上造瘘术前、术后患者。经临床验证基本上能代替人工监护。1993年，该院贾炜莹等在“膀胱癌手术中粘膜美蓝染色法检查切除原位癌临床应用的研究”中，将美蓝只能使肿瘤部位着色的特性，应用于膀胱癌手术中，能发现用肉眼无法发现的残留病灶并切除。对提高膀胱肿瘤手术切除率，降低术后复发率具有重要作用。2001年，姚欣与郝权完成“内源性TGFβ1对人膀胱癌生长作用机制的研究”“人膀胱癌相关基因cDNA片段的克隆与初步鉴定”的研究，为膀胱癌的基因诊断和治疗提供理论依据。提出TGFβ1（转移生长因子β1）是膀胱癌基因治疗的理想靶基因，转染含TGFβ1反义RNA的复制缺陷型逆转录病毒载体，有可能成为膀胱癌临床治疗的新方法。同时验证Cu.Zn-SOD、TBX3、CI.Ca4基因与膀胱癌具有相关性，发现并命名的3个新基因YHHQ1、XHL、LHX，并初步认定为新的膀胱癌相关基因。

（六）骨与软组织肿瘤

1992年，肿瘤医院张如明等在肢体软组织肉瘤切除后，以邻近肌肉为动力，将邻近正常肌腱转位于患区，替代已损毁的功能，最后用显微外科的皮瓣或肌皮瓣移植或转位覆盖缺损区创面。经临床实践证实，该方法可以使患者免于致残，并可减轻患者的心理压力和生活负担。1994年又研制成功肋骨固定型人工全肩关节（PF型假体）以解决肩部肿瘤切除后，胸上肢肌残留，重建肩关节功能的问题，疗效明显优于传统方法。功能重建后，肩关节功能已达到外展90度，前屈70度，后伸40度，内外旋超过30度明显提高患者生存质量。1997年张如明等开展“股二头肌或比目鱼肌蒂腓骨转位治疗膝部肿瘤性骨缺损研究”，临床应用15例，骨愈合征最早8周，获得随访的10例全部骨性愈合。

2001年后，肿瘤医院宋金钢等将负瘤骨灭活再植技术与带血管蒂的自体骨移植联合应用进行肱骨近端恶性骨肿瘤保肢重建，克服了灭活骨回植后易发生吸收、骨折不愈合、再骨折的缺陷。杨蕴等进行的“顺铂热灌注治疗肢体恶性肿瘤的药代动力学及临床研究”，为保肢创造有利的局部条件，使肢体热药灌注成为肢体恶性肿瘤保肢手术的重要辅助治疗手段。

四、肿瘤生物治疗

1991年，肿瘤医院黄建英等在“抗人乳腺癌特异糖蛋白单克隆体的研制及临床应用研究”中，采用生化及固相免疫吸收法使乳腺癌特异抗原浓度相对增加，使用细胞融合技术获得能分泌高效价单抗的抗乳腺癌特异糖蛋白的细胞系M3G4。同年，黄建英等鉴于组织型纤溶酶原激活因子（tPA）具有血栓定位和溶栓作用，可作为肿瘤化疗的增效剂。采用细胞工程法制备tPA，用一步法从黑色素瘤细胞系Bowes的条件培养上清液中纯化tPA，并制成药盒提供临床应用。1992年，该院牛瑞芳在“肿瘤标志物α1酸性糖蛋白（α1AGP）的血清激光散射浊度法测定”研究中，成功的制备出单价抗血清。其性能比火箭电泳法更简单、快速、准确、稳定性高，可适用于更大面积人群的肿瘤普查。同年，郝希山等在“自体脾LAK细胞（淋巴因子激活的杀伤细胞）/rIL-2（重组白细胞介素-2）经肝动脉插管输注治疗原发性肝癌的研究”中观察到脾LAK细胞表型为T细胞表型，并从实验和临床应用两个方面研究自体脾LAK细胞的生物学特点，电泳特征及对瘤细胞的体外杀伤功能，该研究为肝癌的防治提供一种新方法。1993年，该院毛慧生等在“基因重组人白细胞介素Ⅱ的制备”研究中，建立起一套独特的IL-2分离纯化方法，比常规方法省时、简便、成本低、活性高。1996年，黄建英、李树玲等针对抗肿瘤药物对肿瘤细胞缺乏足够的选择性杀伤作用的特点，在“抗人乳腺癌单抗免疫磁性药物毫微粒的体外抑瘤及体内定位显像实验研究”中，成功制备出磁微粒。该微粒能显著增加药物浓度，经体外抑瘤实验证实，抑瘤率达90%~100%。1997年，牛瑞芳等在“NAG酶（N-乙酰一-D·氨基已糖酶）荧光比色测定细胞毒方法的建立及其应用研究”中，所建立的测定细胞毒方法，最少可检出100个细胞，灵敏度高，并避免使用放射性同位素的缺点，较之乳酸脱氢酶（LDH）释放法操作简单，结果稳定，不易受环境影响、重复性好。

1998年，肿瘤医院刘红等鉴于nm23基因是被实验证实的肿瘤转移抑制基因，在“nm23基因表达与乳腺癌远处转移及预后相关性的研究”中，揭示出nm23基因与原处转移呈显著负相关，可作为一个独立的预后因素应用于临床，从而为临床预后判断提供一个新指标。1998年，郝希山等完成“自体外周血干细胞移植联合大剂量放化疗治疗实体瘤的实验与研究”，使肿瘤的生物治疗进入一个新的阶段。外周血干细胞移植后造血恢复较快，比以往的骨髓抑制造血重建早3~10天，且移植无相关死亡，近期疗效良好。35例乳腺癌患者随访48个月，其中27例高危患者生存良好，仅1例于移植后14个月复发，平均无病生存期19个月，无病生存两年以上者8例，无病生存率达到68.7%。该项目获1998年度天津市科技进步二等奖。

2000年，郝希山等在耐药逆转与干细胞治疗实体瘤的临床应用基础研究中，成功地建立应用逆转录-聚合酶链反应（RT-PCR）方法监测乳腺癌等实体瘤多药耐药基因（MDRI）及谷胱甘肽S-转移酶（GST-π）两种耐药基因的实验体系，并对该两种耐药基因与临床资料的相关性进行研究，在国际上首次提出加温联合干扰素α（IFNα）及异搏定的逆转效果最佳。采用自体外周血干细胞移植治疗实体瘤，解决了放化疗由于对骨髓的毒副作用限制而不能加大应用剂量，使疗效难以提高的难题。另一方面为清除术后、放化疗后仍残留的微小病灶，在国内首先开展了MAGE/CEA肽疫苗冲击树突状细胞诱导特异性杀伤性T淋巴细胞治疗实体瘤的研究，该方法能提高患者自身细胞对毒性T淋巴细胞（CTL）的特异性杀伤力，且无任何毒副作用。此项研究在实体瘤干细胞移植方面取得成功，尤其能降低移植相关死亡率。“耐药逆转与干细胞及树突状细胞治疗实体瘤的应用基础研究”项目获2000年度天津市科技进步一等奖。

2001年，郝希山等在“乳腺癌转移预报基因芯片的研究”中，利用人表达谱基因芯片筛选乳腺癌转移预后相关基因群，用于乳腺癌患者的转移和预后预测，指导临床实施个体化治疗。制备的“乳腺癌转移预报基因芯片”经大样本临床病例验证后，用于乳腺癌患者的转移危险度评估，并可指导临床个体化治疗。2002年，肿瘤医院冯玉梅等在“乳腺癌隐匿转移基因诊断方法的优化及临床应用”研究中，对以CK19（细胞角蛋白19）为标志的乳腺隐匿转移癌基因检测方法进行优化，对方法的灵敏性和可靠性进行实验验证，既可避免假基因的干扰，又提高检测灵敏度。该方法可检测到常规病理学和影像学不能查出的乳腺癌淋巴结和血行转移的隐匿转移，还适用于上皮性肿瘤淋巴结、外周血和骨髓隐匿微转移诊断、良恶性胸腹水的鉴别诊断及治疗疗效的动态监测。

2002年，肿瘤医院任秀宝等开展“野生型P53转染树突状细胞（DC）诱导特异性抗肺癌免疫应答的实验研究”，研究用携带整个野生型P53 OORE的质粒转染DC使其在细胞内表达，生成多个表位，成为诱导特异性免疫反应的有效抗原，诱导强大的CTL（细胞毒性T淋巴细胞），而且不存在MHC（主要组织相容性复合体）限制性。此方法为开辟一条肿瘤免疫治疗新途径提供重要的依据。

2003年，肿瘤医院郝希山以MUC1、MUC1/Y DNA疫苗体外修饰抗原递呈能力最强的树突状细胞，成功诱导出肿瘤杀伤细胞，有效地杀伤了特异性肿瘤细胞。该方法作为一种肿瘤生物治疗，具有低毒、高效的特点，可以在不同角度和层面上发挥抗肿瘤的协同作用。“MUC1、MUC1/Y体外修饰DC诱导特异性抗肿瘤免疫应答”项目获2003年度天津市科技进步二等奖。同年，该院王华庆等在“人参皂苷Rg3促进自体外周血干细胞移植后免疫重建的基础与临床研究”中，将免疫治疗的新方法进一步推广应用到造血干细胞移植的临床实践中，发挥中医药在免疫重建中的作用，提高自体外周血干细胞移植后的生存率、降低复发率。同年，该院于泳、傅西林、牛昀等在“乳腺导管内癌特性的形态学及分子生物学研究”中，针对乳腺癌诊疗研究提出新的分型方法，共治疗乳腺导管内癌147例，在导管内癌的个体化治疗方案制定方面确有实用价值。

2005年，郝希山等在“恶性肿瘤异基因造血干细胞移植生物治疗研究”中，所建立的非清髓性异基因造血干细胞移植联合个体化生物治疗的新方案，能明显提高晚期化疗抵抗性实体肿瘤患者的临床治疗效果，延长患者生存并提高生存质量。不仅进一步扩大造血干细胞治疗实体肿瘤的适应症，而且显著降低大剂量放化疗导致的严重毒副作用，尤其对体况较差的高龄患者，有明显的治疗优势。

五、肿瘤物理治疗

(一)肿瘤消融治疗

1990年，天津市肿瘤研究所林世寅、于世起等研制成功“肿瘤热疗用多点测温技术及仪器”，解决肿瘤热疗、电磁波介质加热中急需解决的单管多点探头的无扰测温问题。在强磁场下和35℃~50℃范围内，测温、控温准确，精确度达0.2℃，可在不停机连续加热的同时进行瘤内测温。该成果获1992年度国家发明三等奖。同期，林世寅、李丰彤等又成功完成“腔道肿瘤温控热疗机”研制，该机可分别对宫腔、宫颈、阴道、直肠、食道等多种腔道肿瘤进行治疗。辐射器上可粘附无扰多点测温探头，测温、控温准确，所获治疗数据可自动显示、存储、记录并打印。该研究获1991年度国家发明三等奖。

1998年，李丰彤先后中标卫生部与国家自然科学基金课题各一项，分别为“恶性肿瘤组织间电化学加热综合疗法的建立与应用研究”和“肿瘤热疗生物活体仿真动态模型的建立及热场分布研究”。两项研究针对人体生物组织电磁特性，建立射频电磁辐射场下生物组织的物理模型与数学模型；在引入血管直径及血液灌流的条件下，建立仿真动态的热物理模型；获得了能准确反映电磁场衰减特性的生物组织吸收电磁波能量沉积分布；以及血管热“缺失”效应的非稳态模型瞬态温度分布；采用分子生物学技术对人宫颈癌Hela细胞株受热后随温度变化的热致死机理进行研究，给出Hela细胞凋亡程度和坏死程度的分析；DNA损伤程度分析；以及热休克蛋白HSP70和E-cal钙粘蛋白的表达等结果，为肿瘤热疗临床实践提供理论依据。

(二)肿瘤放射治疗

1991年后，肿瘤医院邓满国等为解决Leibinger头刀定位系统对口腔及颈部区域的肿瘤不能定位和治疗的问题，研制口腔及颈部立体适形放射治疗定位仪，该项研究系采用三维适形治疗计划系统取代传统的二维治疗模式，使定位系统板与三维坐标系统一体结构使定位更加准确，从而可提高肿瘤局部控制率，降低周围正常组织并发症的发生率。该院王伟等又对胸部肿瘤适形放疗技术与剂量学进行研究，达到在提高肿瘤治愈率和控制率的同时，不增加或减少放疗不良反应的目的。并摆脱了传统模式可能造成的肿瘤靶区的漏照射、欠剂量以及邻近危及器官和组织的过量照射。

1999年，肿瘤医院王平等研制出“常规放射治疗辅助定位装置”。经临床应用表明，该装置装卸方便、安全可靠，可提高放疗质量，降低肿瘤局部复发可能性。2000年，引进瑞典全数字化电子直线加速器技术，开展全身立体定向放疗。2001年，该院李智华等针对乳腺癌术后放疗摆位精度和重复性检查的问题，进行乳腺癌全野半野切线照射技术对肺照射体积的定量分析研究，制定出一套从模拟机定位-CT扫描-加速器摆位的程序，并将等中心技术、乳腺定位架、激光定位技术应用其中，解决对肺部照射剂量的量化分析的问题。

2001年，肿瘤医院王平、李瑞英、朱莉等完成“鼻咽癌腔内近距离治疗双管一体施源器的研制及临床临用”研究。该器可用于鼻咽癌外照射后腔内残留或放疗后腔内复发的治疗，具有造价低、应用简便、无毒副作用、可长期携带、适宜分割放射治疗及腔内热疗等优点。可使鼻咽顶剂量增加134.5%，后壁增加60.7%，侧壁增加23.3%~40.0%，软腭剂量降低75.1%，减少伤害。效果满意，并发症减少。该项目获2001年度天津市科技进步二等奖。

2004年，肿瘤医院朱莉等自行研制成功的鼻咽癌腔内热疗辐射器，有效加热温度可以控制在41℃~42℃，相应的热电偶测温装置，直径0.05毫米超细热偶丝制成的测温探头，实现实时测温，精度±0.5℃。经临床应用取得较好的效果。在热疗的同时联合放疗能够提高鼻咽肿瘤的完全缓解率及有效率，热增强比分别为1.68和1.39，解决了辐射器操作复杂、固定性差、软腭及周围组织易受损伤和给患者带来的难以忍受的痛苦等弊端。同年，刘莉等研制出放疗定位模板，用以解决患者在定、摆位过程中体位重复性和准确性的问题。

第四节 妇产科学与儿科学

20世纪90年代初，天津首次提出以子宫内膜异位症的症状、体征为依据进行临床分期，并将李-张术式应用于临床手术治疗；俞蔼峰主编的《妇产科内分泌学》出版；子宫内膜癌、卵巢癌的相关研究，子宫全切术式的改良；产科生理常数等围产医学多项相关研究均取得可喜的进展。1997年，建立天津市中心妇产科医院（以下简称“中心妇产医院”）生殖医学中心，先后取得体外授精胚胎移植、卵胞浆内单精子显微注射、冻融胚胎移植、多胎妊娠减胎术等一系列辅助生殖技术，在天津市的首例体外授精妊娠分娩成功。2005年，该中心通过卫生部“体外授精胚胎移植技术”的准入审查，成为天津市第一家具有此资质的医疗研究机构。2001年，中心妇产医院成立全国首家子宫内膜异位症诊疗中心。

1991 ~ 2005年，天津在儿科学临床治疗方面取得进步，小儿内科、新生儿科、小儿外科等专业不断细分，其治疗技术取得不断发展进步。

一、妇产科

（一）妇科学

1. 子宫内膜异位症术式

1988年，中心妇产医院、天津市妇女保健所、天津市滨江医院岳琏、李宝森、张殿文等针对重度直肠子宫内膜异位症、直肠、乙状结肠受累的患者，采用李-张氏术式切除子宫内膜异位病变。采取直肠低位前切术及直、结肠套式吻合术，术后无肠腔及肠吻合口瘘发生，效果满意。1993年，又改进李-张氏术式应用于临床。其特点是清除盆腔脏器病变既干净、彻底，避免肠吻合口瘘的发生，同时操作较简单，便于掌握。根据子宫内膜异位症多侵及直肠前壁，而肠吻合口瘘则多发生在直肠后壁这一特性，设计出仅切除直肠前壁病变，保留直肠后壁。为加强直肠后壁，防止肠吻合口瘘的发生，先剔出直肠后壁粘膜层，并行直肠后壁肌层折叠缝合术，再行端——端吻合术。该术式因保留直肠后壁肌层及直肠、乙状结肠系膜，所以直肠上动脉未受到破坏，从而保障肠管两断端供血良好，避免肠吻合口瘘的发生。李—张氏术式曾在三中心医院、工人医院、汉沽医院等多家医院推广应用，经随访效果满意，无复发。“李—张氏术式切除直肠子宫内膜异位病变的研究”项目获1996年度天津市科技进步二等奖。

2. 子宫内膜异位症诊疗

1991年，中心妇产医院岳琏、李宝森等在国内外首次提出以子宫内膜异位症的症状、体征为依据的临床分期，对重度患者依病情与需求实施手术治疗，术中按国际采用的R-AFS分期，确立保守手术、半根治手术、根治手术及附加手术等一系列手术治疗方案，使手术个别化、系统化。并将大网膜移植术、前腹壁子宫悬吊术、子宫次广泛切除术及直肠端——端套式吻合术应用于子宫内膜异位症手术中，手术强调采用锐性分离脏器组织。临床应用手术切净率达100%,术后妊娠率高达41.2%,复发率低至3.3%。该项目获1991年度天津市科技进步二等奖。

3. 子宫全切术式

1996年,二中心医院周荣庆、石春玲、郭晓荣等根据临床经验总结设计一种不钳夹宫颈旁组织,又去除宫颈的全切子宫的新术式—经腹宫颈剔出法全子宫切除术。该术式在断扎子宫血管后,不再行任何宫颈旁钳夹,只是上提子宫,将宫颈剔出,所余创面缝合止血即可。经临床52例观察随访,手术时间与失血量均优于对照组,术后阴道顶端肉芽发生率明显减少。

4. 妇科内分泌学

总医院俞蔼峰主编的《妇产科内分泌学》,书中介绍该领域的理论及研究成果,并附有具体临床病例,基础与临床密切结合。在某些章节中有中西结合内容,率先将祖国医学运用到内分泌领域。该书获1998年度天津市科技著作二等奖。2002年,一中心医院和总医院宿爱琴、糜若然、涂持坤等完成"子宫内膜细胞外培养及间质细胞分泌功能与调控的研究"。实验设计同时研究三种激素的交互作用,将子宫内膜间质细胞和腺上皮细胞成功进行分离、纯化及原代培养,建立人子宫内膜间质细胞体外蜕膜化模型,证实睾酮能刺激ESC增殖、分化和凋亡,与雌孕激素合用抑制细胞增殖;ISC能分泌E2、PRL,LHRH、FSH、HCG能直接作用于子宫内膜细胞,阐明下丘脑、垂体、卵巢激素对子宫内膜细胞的分泌功能有直接调控作用。

5. 子宫内膜癌症

1999年,总医院薛凤霞等完成"影响子宫内膜癌预后的多因素研究",在不同层次、不同水平上对影响子宫内膜癌预后的相关因素进行单因素及多因素研究。提出手术分期、脉管浸润、核分裂指数、腹腔细胞学、S期细胞比例(SPF)、增殖细胞核抗原(PCNA)是影响预后的重要指标。对术前可得到的8个指标进行多因素预后分析,发现病理分级、SPF及P53表达情况是影响子宫内膜癌预后的最重要因素。在对术后可得到的包括DNA、SPF、Her-2/neu、P53、PCNA等生物学指标在内的12个预后指标进行多因素分析,发现与预后关系密切的3个指标:手术分期、SPF及P53表达情况。该项目获1999年度天津市科技进步二等奖。2000年,薛凤霞等在"Ⅰ、Ⅱ型子宫内膜癌临床病理特征及CyclinD1、bcl-2基因表达的研究"中,从两个部分对两种病理类型的子宫内膜癌在临床病理特征的差异以及反应增生及凋亡的基因表达方面的差异进行研究。对Ⅰ、Ⅱ两型子宫内膜癌临床病理特征进行系统观察,发现Ⅱ型子宫内膜癌病理类型以浆液性乳头状腺癌及透明细胞癌多见,分级以Ⅱ、Ⅲ级多见,易出现深肌层浸润、分期晚、淋巴结转移率高。报道正常子宫内膜周期以及子宫内膜增生的CyclinD1表达情况。经对子宫内膜癌中CyclinD1、bcl-2表达情况与Ⅰ、Ⅱ两型之间的关系进行相关研究,发现Ⅰ型子宫内膜癌的CyclinD1表达明显高于Ⅱ型,CyclinD1可能参与雌激素的致癌作用。bcl-2可能与子宫内膜癌发生的早期有关,与Ⅰ、Ⅱ两型的关系不明显。该项目获2000年度天津市科技进步二等奖。

6. 卵巢癌症

2001年,中心妇产医院和总医院曲芃芃、焦书竹、高企贤、朱颖军等完成"CD44基因表达与卵巢癌转移的相关性研究"。研究表明CD44H基因表达与卵巢上皮性肿瘤的进展有关;CD44H参与卵巢种植转移过程;CD44HmRNA表达量是估计卵巢癌预后的指标之一;血中可溶性CD44H表达的测定可作为预后、复发及评价疗效的监测指标之一。2004年,总医院瞿全新等在"卵巢上皮癌中端粒酶激活与顺铂化疗敏感性的基础与临床研究"中,首先探讨端粒酶与卵巢上皮性癌顺铂化疗敏感性的关系,在此基础上进一步探索以端粒酶反义基因治疗增强顺铂敏感性的可行性,为临床开发低毒高效的化疗增敏剂奠定实验基础。探讨端粒酶活性与卵巢上皮性癌化疗敏感性关系,从体外到动物体内系统地观察端粒酶反义脱氧寡核苷酸治疗对卵巢上皮性癌顺铂(CDDP)敏感性的影响。

(二)产科学

1. 产科生理常数

1992年,中心妇产医院岳琏、王淑雯和南开大学吴荣、王公恕等针对中国女性分娩问题进行产科生理常数的研究,首次对全国20个民族的6835例女性骨盆进行系统研究,分别从骨盆、新生儿头颈线和产程三个方面进行。经骨盆临床测量、X线测量和相互对照，建立中国女性骨盆的正常生理径线尺度及型态，并对20个民族分别建立个自女性骨盆正常径线及型态。经统计对比提出各地区、各民族间的差异；应用统计聚类法对20个民族女性骨盆进行聚类分析，分为10类。研究创造回归方程骨盆测量法，开辟骨盆测量新途径，为分娩的骨产道问题提供可靠的科学数据，有重要理论意义及实用价值。同时，出版《中国女性骨盆的研究》专著。在中国新生儿头径研究中，建立中国各民族各地区足月新生儿头径、臀径、肩径共16条径线及身长、体重的生理常数。胎儿体重每增加200克，胎头各径线增加0.1厘米，周径增加0.3～0.5厘米，并提出胎头与骨盆径线的关系，骨盆任何一条径线小于9.5～10厘米，应引起注意。在中国妇女产程研究中，对国内6个民族初产妇2778例的产程进行研究，观察中国妇女产程的时限、产程各阶段宫口扩张的速度，以及每扩张1厘米所需时间，同时对产程进展过程中各阶段胎头下降的位置及下降的速度进行统计分析，分别建立标准数值及产程中宫口扩张曲线与胎头下降曲线。研究建立中国妇女产程时限和产程各阶段数值，总结出产程预警线、异常线及警戒区数值，主要提示处理分娩的时间观念的重要性，对基层及农村接生人员提供一个处理分娩与时间关系，应用该研究改进的产程图监护产程非常科学，只用一张图纸，标出5条产程进展曲线，即可反映产程全过程。胎儿在宫内情况一旦出现异常能及时发现、及时处理，可减少难产及母婴合并症。该研究所确立的代表中国妇女产程生理常数填补多民族初产妇产程时间研究的空白，对指导提高产科医疗质量有重要的科学意义和实用价值。该项目获1995年度国家科技进步三等奖。1994年，天津市妇女保健所苏玉梅、赵世省、郑力明等完成“天津地区围产儿死亡及畸形儿的监测与研究”。选择天津地区有代表性的医院，建立完善的监测网络，研究天津地区城乡孕28周至出生一周围产儿的死亡率、畸形儿发生率及死因病谱的流行病学特征。对围产儿死亡及畸形儿发生的危险因素进行回归分析，提出与围产儿死亡有关的主要因素是胎位异常、产次，妊高症等；与畸形儿发生有关的主要因素为孕早期接触化学物质、孕早期流感、孕早期服药等。在监测同时还进行干预研究，采取多种妊产保健措施，对降低出生缺陷发生率有明显效果。

2. 羊水过少治疗

1994年，中心妇产医院、天津市妇产科研究所王懿贤、周曰序、刘润环等提出“单味黄芪治疗中期妊娠”取得明显效果。由于孕期羊水过少的发病率呈上升趋势，其造成新生儿并发症发生率高达49.9%，而国内外尚无有效的治疗措施，应用黄芪治疗可调节与改善母体的胎儿与胎盘间的液体交换，从而维持正常的生理调节机制，使羊水量恢复并保持正常，降低患病率而达到优生优育的目的。

3. 女性病理骨盆

1998年，中心妇产医院王淑雯、岳琏、刘勃晨等针对积累的164例女性病理骨盆，以人体形态像和X线骨盆像对照并结合病因分析，研究发生病理骨盆和骨盆变形的规律，观察、总结病理骨盆患者体表的特征及其X线骨盆像的特点，揭示女性病理骨盆诊断要点以及病理骨盆对分娩的影响。是人类学研究的历史档案，也是中国女性骨盆研究的补充，为骨盆研究和教学开创新的视点，提供了珍贵的资料。对产科的科研、教学及提高临床医生辨认与处理难产的水平以保障母儿的安全与健康都有重大的意义与价值。

4. 女性尸骨骨盆

1999年，中心妇产医院王淑雯、岳琏、刘勃晨等对天津地区151具女性尸骨骨盆，2具新生儿骨盆，3具新生儿头颅的研究。归纳分析骨盆形态、结构特征，新生儿骨盆及头颅的特点，并通过直观的分析，阐明各类骨盆、儿头入盆的变异与分娩的关系及导致难产的机制。确定出多种罕见的发育性骨盆的变异类型及病理骨盆类型。该研究实体骨盆资料，从50年代挖掘、制作与研究，是产科学及人类学史上稀有的宝贵财富。该研究1999年获天津市科技进步二等奖。

5. 产前监护与适时分娩

2005年，中心妇产医院王淑雯等完成“产前监护的研究”。通过自孕16周开始系统、连续、动态的监护资料，总结中心妇产医院1207例孕妇，其中931例正常妊娠，276例异常妊娠，各孕周体重、宫高、腹围、血压、平均动脉压的均值、生理界限数值、异常界限数值并绘制相应的妊娠曲线图。通过对异常妊娠276例妊娠图的观察，创造性地对比妊高征、巨大儿、低体重儿各孕周各指标妊娠曲线图与正常妊娠图的不同表现。该研究首创正常妊娠曲线标准对照图表，临床医生可将孕妇每次检查时所绘出的妊娠图及时对照，一目了然、方便快捷地发现异常，及时处理。同时进行适时分娩系统工程研究，阐明孕产期子宫收缩与适时分娩的关系，并设立头位分娩专家系统辅助判定分娩方式，减少难产率与母儿患病率。

二、儿科学

（一）小儿内科

1.介入治疗

1990年，儿童医院范崇济创建儿童心导管室，开展先天性心脏病右心导管及心血管造影。1995年，在国内率先开展儿童心肌炎并心律失常的电生理研究和儿童急性病毒性心肌炎并Ⅲ度房室传导阻滞阿斯综合症心内临时起搏器治疗。2001年，范崇济、刘扬等开展先天性心脏病动脉导管未闭、肺动脉瓣狭窄的介入治疗。2004年，张宏艳等在国内率先开展先天性心脏病室间隔缺损、房间隔缺损的介入治疗，代替多年依赖开胸手术的传统治疗。

2.呼吸疾病

1996年，医大二院、天津市医药科学研究所韩忠、宋宏良、刘长山等完成“小儿哮喘氯喹非松疗法的抗炎机理”研究。率先采用氯喹非松疗法治疗小儿哮喘。经对52例患者进行一年治疗，一年追踪，其显效率达94.23%，好转率100%，达到满意的临床治疗效果，并在国内多家医院推广。特别是通过豚鼠模型建立及药物实验，经组织学及超微结构研究，进一步证实该疗法有控制炎症及抗纤维化的作用。1999年，医大二院刘长山等开展天津市儿童哮喘流行病学调查、哮喘的诊断、雾化吸入疗法治疗哮喘等小儿呼吸道疾病的研究，调查显示天津市区小儿哮喘的患病率2000年为1.49%，高于1990年的0.79%近1倍。2001年，天津市在国内最先开展射流式雾化吸入疗法治疗哮喘及毛细支气管等呼吸道疾病，效果良好，并在全市推广。2002年，儿童医院万莉雅、张琴、范永琛等通过总结不同年龄脉冲振荡呼吸阻抗变化规律及特点，建立天津市3～14岁儿童脉冲振荡法呼吸阻抗正常参考值及其方程式，广泛应用于哮喘病、慢性咳嗽、间质性肺炎等呼吸系统疾病的鉴别诊断。

3.PKU杂合子筛查

1997年，儿童医院宋力、徐凤铎、孟英韬等对婚孕群体进行苯丙酮尿症（PKU）杂合子筛查的研究，该研究首先建立并完善高效液相色谱快速检测血浆苯丙氨酸、酪氨酸的简便方法，并应用此法对2000余例婚孕妇女和101例PKU患者父母进行血浆检测，筛查出可疑的PKU致病基因携带者，对检出的可疑杂合子用PCR-SSCP和DNA序列分析法进行突变基因分析，总符合率为94.1%。研究证实，血浆苯丙氨酸浓度、苯丙氨酸/酪氨酸、苯丙氨酸2/酪氨酸比值可作为PKU杂合子的初选方法，结合基因分析有可能阻止有胎PKU患儿的出生。该研究在优生和遗传学研究中有重要的应用价值。2005年，儿童医院、天津市儿科研究所宋力、孟英韬、党利亨等，利用已获取的样本资源，对苯丙酮尿症杂合子高危人群的基因型进行研究。采用分子生物学方法进行苯丙氨酸羟化酶突变基因分析，验证上述生化方法的可行性。通过与天津地区已知PKU杂合子的突变基因频率进行比较，初步摸清天津地区该病致病基因的遗传特点。该成果为开展的产前基因诊断提供基础，为普遍开展PKU杂合子的人群筛查，为制定防止PKU患儿出生的策略提供科学依据。

4.心脏病

2002年，儿童医院张宏艳等完成“钾通道激动剂对瞬间内向电流及触发活动的调节”研究。采用心肌细胞膜片钳技术，通过在离体豚鼠心室肌细胞药物制备心肌细胞触发激动模型，对钾通道激动剂（PCA）对瞬间内向电流及触发活动的调节进行研究，首次观察到PCA可以开放KATP，增加K^+外流，明显抑制Iti及Ica-L，中止触发活动，使动作电位时程缩短，具有内源性钙通道阻滞剂作用，对心室细胞具有保护作用。率先将尼可地尔（Nicorandil）及中药康心宁临床应用于特发性室性心动过速，心电图Q-T段延长综合征并室性心动过速的治疗。治疗前后患儿心功能明显改善，有效率分别为65%及86%，病死率降低。该方法简便，其治疗方法已被儿童医院列为临床治疗常规，并向全国推广。该成果为相关中药的开发研制奠定理论基础并获

2002年度天津市科技进步二等奖。

5.内分泌

2002年，儿童医院孙桂香、高文英、吕玲等完成“先天性肾上腺皮质增生症21羟化酶基因突变的研究”。用PCR方法直接检测32例21-OHD患儿CYP21第3、第6外显子300bp、600bp缺失。用PCR-ACRS检测32例21-OHD患儿及其父母，检测出3例患儿CYP21第2内含子656位点突变，2例第4外显子CD172点突变，3例第8外显子CD356点突变，8例点突变被证实。方法新颖、简便，结果可靠，检测中不使用同位素，填补国内对该基因检测的空白。2005年，儿童医院孙桂香、武光林、谷奕等完成“天津市儿童单纯性肥胖发病及其影响因素的研究”。该项目通过天津市2～16岁儿童中单纯性肥胖发病情况的流行病学抽样调查，应用体重指数法计算发病率。按同年龄、同性别、同学校配比进行研究，显示其发病率：BMI≥25标准的发病率6.4%，男7.7%，女6.2%，城市7.7%，农村6.2%。BMI≥24标准的发病率9.4%，男11%，女8%。男多于女，城市高于农村。其危险因素依次为父母肥胖、运动强度、蛋白质摄入量、出生体重、看电视时间、进餐速度、维生素C摄入量、碳水化合物摄入量、学习成绩和脂肪摄入量。肥胖度和血压、血糖、果糖胺、胰岛素、C肽、血脂成正相关，与HDL和APOA呈负相关。

6.肾病

2002年，儿童医院、一中心医院张碧丽、李志军、宋兰云、周红等完成“局灶节段性肾小球硬化模型的建立及中西医结合治疗的实验研究”。研究采用小剂量分次阿霉素-间羟胺-高脂饮料法，建立大鼠局灶节段性肾小球硬化（FSGS）模型，结果提示造模成功。参麦-肝素-苯那普利联合治疗FSGS可起到多靶位协同治疗的良好疗效，临床应用该研究方法治疗激素耐药性肾病综合征取得满意疗效。

7.血液病

2003年，肿瘤医院和医科大学陈可欣、武光林、钱碧云、何敏等完成“天津市儿童白血病的流行状况和危险因素研究”。利用天津市1981～2000年肿瘤报病资料，对天津市儿童白血病20年的流行状况和危险因素进行全面、系统分析研究，首次发现儿童白血病的发生与父母文化水平密切相关。

（二）新生儿科

1991年，儿童医院、天津儿童保健所、医大二院周秦玉、顾红娟、刘瑞霞、赵蓓、常迈莉等完成“天津市早产儿低体重儿发生率及有关因素研究”。对23707名产妇、990例活产单胎早产儿、低体重儿童采取等比例匹配正常足月儿进行多因素对照研究，经计算分析结果表明，天津市的早产儿、低体重儿的总发生率为4.18%，其中早产儿为2.36%，低体重儿为1.82%。影响其发生的主要因素为孕母年龄过大或过小，身高、体重、文化程度、妊高症、孕妇被动吸烟、产前因素（过累、性交）、早破水等。为降低新生儿病列率和远期伤残率，并据此研究提出预防和宣教措施。

1994年，医大二院刘瑞霞等在“北方八地区低出生体重儿发生率的发生因素的调查研究”中，调查产妇26941例，新生儿体重低的发生率为5%，发生因素中母亲疾病较社会因素重要。并在国内外首次报告母孕期父吸烟≥10支/日、母每日被动吸烟≥8小时，胎儿体重下降465克，身长下降2.1厘米。

1996年，儿童医院张巧芳、范崇济、张宏艳等完成“婴儿急性重症病毒性心肌炎致泵及呼吸衰竭的治疗研究”。该研究在国内率先在该症治疗中首选正性肌力药多巴胺与血管扩张剂硝普钠联合应用，治疗0.5～2小时血压逐渐恢复，休克得以纠正，其后予以地高辛及利尿剂。对休克好转后再次出现呼吸急促发绀的患儿，及早使用CPAP鼻塞给氧，平均治疗24小时救治成功。经10年临床应用，取得满意疗效，病死率由65%降为11.6%。该抢救方案层次分明，易于掌握。

2002年，医大二院郑军等开展应用无创辅助通气装置（Infant Flow System）结合肺泡表面活性物质肺内灌注治疗早产儿呼吸窘迫综合症（RDS）技术项目，提高RDS早产儿的抢救成功率，使胎龄<32周的早产极低体重儿成活率达90%以上。与秦皇岛市共同完成早产儿尿渗透压及肾溶质负荷与液体疗法课题研究，提出动态监测早产儿尿渗透压及肾溶质负荷变化来调整液体疗法，为指导早产儿的液体疗法提供有效可行的理论依据。

2003年，儿童医院陈悦、黄敬孚、张桦等完成“间接免疫光法检测CMV感染细胞中早期蛋白方法的研究”。研究建立一种检测婴幼儿感染CMV的方法，并可判断该病人是否在近期存在有CMV感染。该方法敏感、稳定、快速、简便，适用于新生儿的检查，可检出病人血清中的抗病毒早期抗原抗体。

2004年，总医院初桂兰等开展“新生儿缺氧缺血性脑病神经损伤相关分子机制探讨及临床干预的研究”。该项目对其发病机制及其治疗进行系统的研究：建立新生鼠缺氧缺血性脑损伤模型，探讨缺氧缺血性脑损伤的发病机制，同评估神经元型一氧化氮合酶和环氧化酶-2特异性抑制剂7-硝基吲唑、NS398以及1，6-二磷酸果糖的脑保护作用；研究环氧化酶-2、半胱氨酸蛋白酶-1、白细胞介素-18、血管内皮生长因子对未成熟脑组织神经损伤和修复的影响。

（三）小儿外科

1999年，儿童医院崔华雷、包国强、谷继卿在国内率先创建小儿微创外科，首次将腹腔镜技术应用于小儿外科领域。2001年，崔华雷等将治疗范围扩展到小儿外科的大部分领域，突破严重的腹膜粘连、肠回转不全、胸腔及腹腔肿瘤、巨大脾、腹膜炎、阑尾周围脓肿、肝部分切除、胆囊及胆道穿孔等多被认定为腔镜手术的相对或绝对禁忌症，治疗病种达30余种，成为国内小儿微创手术例数、治疗书段、积累经验最多的单位之一。2003年，儿童医院用腹腔镜治疗罕见的儿童胃部疾患。一例生后 8 个月患胃幽门窦部隔膜的8岁女童，用腹腔镜为其治疗，开 4 个 3 毫米的小孔切除一山脊样的隔膜，从此开展幽门窦部隔膜微创手术。

第四医院应用国际先进技术配合早期整形手术，摸索出一套符合小儿生理、心理特点的治疗方式，在治疗小儿烧伤方面取得突破性进展。到2002年，该院救治的数千例烧伤患儿中，包括600多例中、重度烧伤和300余例严重大面积烧伤患儿，治愈率达100%，烧伤致残率大幅降低，极大地提高患儿愈后生活质量。

2005年，儿童医院嵴华雷、谷继卿、王晓晔等完成“分阶段综合疗法防治腹膜粘连的研究”。通过体内、外实验，完成大鼠术后腹膜粘连机制过程的动态观察、中药分阶段防防治大鼠腹膜粘连的正交研究。深入探讨腹腔粘连的机制，证实腹膜粘连的形成存在着腹膜损伤、腹腔内感染及炎症反应-纤维蛋白渗出、纤维蛋白基质形成-成纤维细胞迁移、机化的时间顺序；提出腹腔镜手术结合序贯制药防治腹膜粘连的新观点。

第五节 神经病学与精神病学

1991～2005年，天津在治疗中枢和周围神经系统疾病及精神分裂症、心身疾病、中毒性精神障碍等精神疾病技术方面取得进步。其中，利用非线性动力学研究治疗难治性癫痫成效突出。1990年，天津市精神卫生服务机构共有14所，从事精神卫生服务的医护人员约千余人。历经十数年的发展，经对全市18个区县365家医疗机构的调查显示，截止2005年年底，天津市有60家医疗机构提供精神卫生服务，从业人员共2209人，表明天津市精神卫生服务能力有很大提高。所提供的精神卫生服务包括住院、门诊、精神病学联络会诊、心理咨询或治疗（心理门诊）、心理测量、心理热线、家庭访视以及心理健康教育或网络咨询等。提供住院治疗的医疗机构共21家。与全国相比，天津市精神卫生资源处于国内较高水平，仅低于上海市和北京市。1992年，经天津市政府批准依托天津市公安局安康医院（以下简称“安康医院”）成立天津市戒毒所。开展二氢埃托菲替代疗法治疗海洛因等药物依赖，1996年，天津引进美沙酮疗法替代上述方法，填补该项空白。2000年，安康医院柳振清等编辑出版《精神科实用手册》；2001年，安士慧主编的《实用精神科整体护理手册》为提高诊疗和护理质量发挥重要作用。

一、神经疾病

（一）中枢神经系统疾病

1993年，天津市安定医院（以下简称“安定医院”）郭恩元、虞珏茹、于殿卿完成“阿尔采莫氏痴呆诊断与防治的研究”。痴呆程度量表复核排除假性痴呆；应用痴呆鉴别诊断量表，排除非阿尔采莫氏痴呆和血管性或混合性痴呆；结合神经系统意识方面无障碍、认识能力有障碍、认知和记忆进行性衰退，行为模式改变等临床表现及头颅CT显示脑萎缩无梗塞灶影像学特征，作为临床诊断的依据。

同年，儿童医院和天津市儿科研究所王晓云、刘芬、高文英、吴海等共同完成“小儿先天性智力低下染色体脆点表达结构及临床意义的探讨”。该研究通过对智力低下（MR）组65例与智力（MN）60例染色体脆性位点（FS）表达频率、分布及排列的研究及应用显微扫描技术对FS结构的研究，不仅从理论上，而且在临床上对FS的形成机制，FS与MR的关系及其临床意义，MR的发病机理等进行阐述。研究显示：MR组FS表达频率显著高于MN组；脆点表达不受性别，年龄影响，3p14及新发现的1p31、1p36、2p13及7p22五个脆点与先天性MR有关，对脆点结构变化提出依据。FS的发生率可作为MR诊断及病因研究的依据。

1995年，天津市脑系科中心医院张楷文、王媛、孙瑞发等在颅脑损伤后脑积水进行外科治疗的研究中，采用自制硅橡胶腰大池——腹腔（L-P）分流管治疗外伤性交通性脑积水30例，术后患者腰椎穿刺压力较术前下降，脑室内压力降低，脑室壁所承受的压力下降，脑室逐渐变小，脑室额角周围低密度消失，患者症状体征改善。一次手术成功率90%。

1996年，儿童医院和天津南开大学医学院高文英、朱天慧、陈悦、刘芬等完成“18对引物检测亿DMD基因缺乏及6对重复双核苷酸序列多态性检测DMD携带者”研究。该研究采用18对检测假肥大型肌营养不良症（DMD）缺乏的聚合酶链反应（PCR）引物，应用多重PCR技术对37例DMD患者进行基因缺失率及基因缺失区域的研究，发现19例（51.4%）有不同基因片段缺失，17例缺失患者中，有13例缺失45-52号外显子（76.4%），缺失48号外显子者占61.5%。同时采用6对重复序列多态性检测DMD携带者，为临床建立全面、准确、简便的检测DMD方法。该方法在优生及临床医学中有重要的应用价值。

1997年，天津港口医院苏明秋、王宝仁、陈乐明等完成“颈部动脉激光照射对缺血性脑病TCD BEAM血流变影响的研究”。该项目对缺血性脑病采用颈动脉体外激光照射治疗，激光功率20毫瓦，波长803纳米，能量密度10焦/厘米，功率衰减<0.5毫瓦/厘米。治疗后，动脉血液峰速降低或增高，血管基本正常，血流速度增块，伴涡流或湍流血管基本消失或明显改善，血管杂音消失，频谱形态改善，S/D\PI\RI指数降低。脑电活动地形图显示脑功能状态改善，表明该技术能够改善脑供血不足患者的生活质量，有预防或推迟脑中风发作的作用。

同年，环湖医院只达石、宋建良、秦进喜等完成“强脑因子治疗急性脑梗塞和急性颅脑损伤临床作用研究”。以乳猪脑组织为原料制备强脑因子，经高液相色谱（HPLC）检测强脑因子所含小分子肽为72.1%，明显高于进口脑活素（58.7%），其总氨基酸中所含的必须氨基酸的含量均超过脑活素。动物实验研究结果显示，强脑因子可显著提高老化鼠抗自由基能力。经临床对急性脑梗死、急性颅脑损伤应用证实强脑因子有与脑活素等同的明显疗效。此外，其对SOD和MDA的影响提示其在抗衰老方面也有临床治疗价值。

是年，医大二院张哲成、李新、沈世鑫等完成“抗磷脂抗体对缺血性脑卒中前期血栓及高凝状态影响的研究”。该研究采用国际标准设计，建立酶联免疫吸附试验定量检测226例缺血性脑血管患者血清抗心磷脂抗体（aCL），并与147例健康者相对照。研究表明缺血性脑血管病（ICVD）组aCL阳性率（23.3%）明显高于对照组的4.76%（ $p<0.01$ ），且IgG型aCL比IgM型aCL的阳性率明显升高（ $p<0.01$ ），提示aCL特别是IgG型与ICVD密切相关。表明aCL可做为ICVD危险性增加的一项指标，检测aCL对解释病原、估计预后、指导预防和治疗具有重要临床意义。1999年，该院王纪佐、李新、张哲成等在上述研究基础上完成“脑梗塞中抗磷脂抗体的致病作用及其新治疗的研究”。研究结果显示，ICVD组蛋白C；抗原、总蛋白S及游离蛋白S降低阳性率为17%、26.6%和23.4%，明显高于对照组（ $p<0.05$ ）。综合分析发现aCL水平与蛋白C、总蛋白S及游离蛋白S水平呈负相关。对年经有反复发作史和原因不清的ICVD的治疗和预防提出有价值的指导方向。

1998年，天津市港口医院张志强、王宝仁、陈乐明等完成“急性脑梗塞血浆AT-Ⅲ、PC、PS活性变化研究”。利用发色底物法、凝固法测定急性脑梗塞不同时间血浆AT-Ⅲ、PC、PS三种抗凝蛋白活性。经临床60例监测，证实三种抗凝蛋白活性在脑梗塞急性期均下降，且在大多数情况下呈一致性改变，其中AT-Ⅲ活性下降较为明显。1998年，总医院杨树源、环湖医院杨玉山、一中心医院刘成铮等完成“血管内溶栓治疗急性脑梗塞”研究。该研究对37例急性脑梗死患者进行经血管内接触性溶栓的前瞻性观察，研究者在动脉造影后，将导管导入临近梗死的部位，注入溶栓剂尿激酶或精制蝮蛇抗栓酶。研究结果证实急性期溶栓后，59.5%症状明显好转，21.6%好转，总有效率达81.0%。经术后脑血管造影证实，溶栓后栓塞血管再通者占25.0%，血循环改善、侧枝循环开放者占48.6%，合计达74.3%，未见严重并发症及药物不良反应。

1999年，总医院江德华等经对脑缺血后神经元继发损伤的研究，采用活体微透析技术、立体定位、高压液相色谱及放免技术，应用局灶性脑缺血动物模型，并结合临床脑梗塞患者的抗氧化剂应用双相观察。结果显示：脑缺血早期纹状体缺血部位大量多巴胺（DA）溢出，同时其代谢产物二羟苯乙酸（DOPAC）及高香草酸（HVA）明显降低，表明过氧化氢产生过程主要发生在神经元内；缺血时脑组织自由基明显增多及氧自由基清除酶活力下降。实验证实，缺血同时脑组织兴奋性氨基酸递质谷氨酸的合成减少，降解加速并释放于细胞外液增多，从而发挥N-甲基-D-天冬氨酸（NMDA）所介导的神经细胞毒作用；研究还证实脑缺血时r-氨基丁酸（GABA）及P物质（SP）拮抗剂对缺血的纹状体有保护作用。研究结果支持给予小剂量甘露醇，大剂量维生素C是治疗脑血管病的有效方法。

同年，总医院杨露春等完成“血液流变学对脑血栓形成的作用机理”的研究。经对脑梗塞和短暂性脑缺血病人血液粘度、血小板聚集性、血浆纤维蛋白原含量及红细胞变形性进行检测，结合头部CT检查，观察血液流变学指标变化与脑缺血部位的关系，发现大动脉的梗塞与小血管闭塞发生机理不同，全血粘度和血球压积的增高与大血管闭塞密切相关；血小板聚集性的增高与深穿支的缺血有关；老年普遍性脑萎缩者红细胞变形能力下降可能与老年普遍性脑萎缩有关。杨露春等研制出“BL88-C型红细胞变形激光衍射仪”用于红细胞变形性的检测和研究。

2003年，医科大学田心、陈世畯、陶华英等完成“非线性动力学在难治性癫痫研究中的应用”。该研究用信息学和混沌学的理论、方法，通过婴儿痉挛症（IS）组、局限性癫痫和正常组的脑干听觉诱发响应（BAER）的相关维数定量脑干障碍程度，创新应用高维混沌降维和混沌特性的定量鉴别方法验证其发病机制——脑干信息传导障碍，提出和探索用无创经颅磁刺激“打通”障碍。该项目获2003年度天津市科技进步二等奖。

2005年，环湖医院黄楹、孙梅、陈悦达等完成“经额外侧入路手术治疗鞍区中线病变的临床研究”。该研究结合微创的概念，设计一种全新的手术入路，额外侧入路体现锁孔手术入路，创伤小，出血少，恢复快的部分优点，又具有常规翼点入路显微手术视野大、操作便利及运用成熟的优点。成功治疗鞍区病变128例，效果良好。

（二）周围神经系统疾病

1992年，儿童医院黄敬孚、杨宝昌、张慧等完成“小儿重症格林——巴利综合症全血交换疗法的临床应用研究”。该研究采用全血交换疗法治疗重症患儿27例，均在急性进展期换血。与对照组比较，换血组进展期明显缩短，进入恢复期的时间明显提前，植物神经受累减少，可降低病死率。该疗法不仅清除血浆中的免疫致病成分，还可清除致敏淋巴细胞，并可能改善红细胞免疫状况，清除补体抑制素CT，补充纤维连接蛋白，有利于机体的恢复，与血浆置换法比较，不需昂贵的设备，不需要管道循环血量，更适合小儿。

二、精神病学

（一）精神分裂症

1993年，安康医院引进眼动仪。同时，该院陈静医与上海市精神卫生中心合作进行“眼球活动与精神疾病”研究。通过对近5000例患者的观察，精神分裂症诊断复合率为83.5%。

1996年，安康医院周思等完成“暴力行为的精神分裂症遗传病因学研究”，从遗传学角度对精神分裂症病因进行研究，采取家系调查和细胞遗传学的方法，其一、二级亲属患病率为42.4%远高于一般群体患病率。暴力行为精神分裂症患者染色体分析显示，男性患者中大Y染色体出现率18.8%，明显高于正常男性大Y染色体出现率1.43%，研究证实遗传因素是精神分裂症发病的主要因素，大Y染色体与精神分裂症发生有一定相关性，该成果为临床诊治、社会治安防控、司法精神病鉴定提供基础理论支撑。

1998年，安康医院周慧完成"女性精神分裂症血清雌二醇水平的观察研究"，从生物学角度探明雌激素含量与女性精神分裂症之间的关联性。研究结果表明女性精神分裂症患者血清雌二醇水平明显低于正常人。对有精神病家族史的女性进行雌二醇监测，做到早期预防，对临床观察病情及治疗有一定的指导意义。同年，安定医院刘建勋、冯志颖、田红军等完成"精神分裂症患者几种细胞因子单个核细胞分泌水平的研究"。该研究用生物学方法从四个方面检测比较分裂症外周血单个核细胞培养上清液白细胞介素-1β（IL-1β）、白细胞介素-2（IL-2）、白细胞介素-6（IL-6）、肿瘤坏死因子α（TNFα）、干扰素γ（TFNγ）的分泌水平。发现除TFNγ外，其他四项均明显升高。Ⅰ、Ⅱ混合型间血清水平也有明显差异；随病情好转除IL-2显著升高，IFNr无明显变化外，其他三项均明显下降；患病期水平异常与服药无明显相关性，而与病情严重程度有关。2002年，安定医院刘建勋等在"精神分裂症相关易感基因的研究"中，通过基因扩增症限制性片段长度多态性技术发现精神分裂症与Xp11区域Hsu93305基因座相关联，提示该染色体区域可能存在精神分裂症的易感基因，该发现对精神分裂症的病因学及其治疗有广泛的应用价值。

1999年，安定医院冯志颖在精神疾病患者性染色质频率研究的基础上，将口腔粘膜性染色质检查用于伴有第二性征特异的精神疾病患者，该法有助于筛查性染色体异常所致的精神障碍病例。且方法简便、费用低廉、实用价值高，使很多曾多次住院均被误诊为精神分裂症或情感性精神障碍的性染色体异常的病例明确诊断，有利于社会康复和避免社会隔离；研究还据此提出男性多1条X染色体和女性少1条X染色体易于伴发精神障碍的观点，对于纯化精神疾病的诊断、减少误诊具有重要临床意义。

2000年，天津市内分泌研究所王栋、钱明、滕瑞涛等完成"津医精神运动成套测验（JPB）的研制及其实证研究"，由于采用选择应时、划消数字、符号记入、视觉保持、连接数字和转动插棒等多项测验加以组合对个体进行一级测验，可从多方面反映心理功能。采用标准分数的原理处理各项测验成绩，使成套测验可获得一个总成绩。JPB为评估脑的精神运动功能障碍提供新的测试方法。

（二）情感性精神病

1991年，安定医院购置设备建立音乐治疗室，也开展音乐治疗，作为精神疾病恢复期和轻性精神障碍的辅助治疗，为不同情绪状态的病人选取不同的乐曲进行治疗。2002年，一中心医院心理科在原有普通音乐治疗的基础上，引进多感音乐治疗系统。该系统为富含低频、中频或高频并以正弦波为主的治疗性乐曲，配以相应情节的动态视频信号或画面，并刺激治疗对象的躯干，使其随音乐同步震动，同时观察、测量并记录其脑电波频谱成分的变化，不断调整音乐处方，直至取得预期疗效。适用于各类轻性精神障碍、抑郁症、焦虑症、神经性摄食障碍、儿童注意缺陷与多动障碍以及各种情绪问题等。

2000年，安定医院刘建勋等在"芬氟拉明对抑郁性障碍血浆催乳素、皮质醇及生长激素影响"研究中，采用激发实验（FCT）对30例抑郁症和抑郁性神经官能症患者进行了血浆催乳素（PRL）、皮质醇、和生长激素测定，发现抑郁症患者PRL明显低于正常对照组，抑郁症组PRL也明显低于抑郁性神经官能症组，证实上述患者中5-羟色胺水平降低是导致临床症状的主要原因。研究者认为FCT可作为抑郁症和精神分裂症进行鉴别诊断的辅助手段。抑郁性障碍患者的自杀意念与其PRL对FCT△值呈极显著负相关，提示PRL对FCT反应低下是反映抑郁症中枢5-HT功能不足的生物学指标。2004年，刘建勋等在"应用光疗技术治疗抑郁失眠症的研究"中，依照时间生物原理在不同时间内通过不同的光照参数治疗抑郁症、睡眠觉醒障碍、倒班作业及时差综合征。经对30例抑郁症患者和20例睡眠障碍患者及50例对照者进行光照治疗，发现模拟血型500lux，1000lux，1500lux，2000lux，2500lux，较为有效，以2500lux效果最佳。模拟晨光以250lux，500lux，1000lux较为有效，以1000lux效果最为显著。

2003年，天津中医学院第一附属医院（以下简称"中医一附院"）杜元灏、李桂平、颜红和安定医院张新军等完成"针刺治疗郁证的基础和临床研究"。该研究首次提出郁证的发病机理为"脑神失调，肝失疏泄"，确立治则及"调神疏肝针法"，并从神经内分泌免疫网络角度揭示调神疏肝针法治疗郁证的内在机理。通过对110例郁证患者的临床疗效观察，证实其总有效率为98.0%。经对6000余名患者治疗，治愈率达70%以上。

（三）心身疾病

1993年，天津市心理卫生专科医院、中国人民解放军第271医院和中心妇产医院陈复平、吴永红、李宝森等完成“冠心病等疾病心理症状心理干预的临床研究”。该研究对冠心病、高血压和子宫内膜异位症等疾病的心理症状采用综合心理干预并进行心理量表评估，结果显示，通过心理干预患者的心理健康水平有显著提高。该成果提出和创立综合心理干预氛围的技术，拓宽治疗各类疾病的手段和思路。

1995年，安康医院陆佩云等完成“中国人个性测查表（警察版）的研究”，为所招对象适应警察这一特殊工作，为提高招警质量，从性格和心理特征方面提供科学的依据。此成果公安部在天津办培训班向全国推广。

1997年，安康医院邵胜利等完成“自杀危险程度计算机评估系统—自杀高危人群筛选版”，为自杀的预防提供一个量化的、较为满意的、实用的评估工具，经天津市公安局组织专家鉴定：国内尚属首创。该系统编写的条目简明易懂，综合性强，信度和效度经四组人群的检验，评估结果与日常观察具有较高的一致性，该系统检索快捷准确，操作简便，对快速筛查有自杀意念的高危人群提供方法，并由计算机自动分析处理。

2000年，天津市实验中学赵子声、张红、于学兰和天津市安定医院张嫦等完成“中学生心理发展过程中易出现的心理卫生问题及防范措施的研究与实验”，对培养中学生良好个性心理品质进行探索。

2005年，安康医院张艳等完成“心理防预制对二型糖尿病患者血糖的影响”的研究，对预防糖尿病发生和对其治疗发挥指导作用。

（四）儿童期精神障碍

1996年，儿童医院将感觉统合训练治疗应用于儿童注意缺陷与多动障碍，提高注意力；对学习技能发育障碍和学习困难儿童，促进全面发育和平衡左右脑发育。2004～2005年，将感觉统合训练作为综合康复计划之一应用于儿童孤独症和3～10岁精神发育迟滞儿童的康复训练治疗中，使他们的各项能力得到全面发展和提高。

2002年，儿童医院成立儿童孤独症康复训练中心，并引进美国“应用行为分析（ABA）”的方法和“听力统合”治疗，用于儿童孤独症的结构化课程式训练，为儿童孤独症的治疗增加了新的康复手段。

2003年，中医一附院李宝珍、李少川、刘昌孝等完成“多动合剂治疗多动综合征生化基础的实验及临床研究”。该研究提出小儿多动综合征的病机为脾虚肝旺，痰热动风。首创豁痰镇惊、和阳熄风治疗原则，运用该法研制有效复议多动合剂。建立动物模型，证实该方是通过对单胺类神经递质失衡的生化作用机制。

（五）中毒性精神障碍

1992年经市政府批准安康医院成立天津市戒毒所。同期开展二氢埃托菲替代疗法治疗海洛因等药物依赖，1996年该院张广福等引进美沙酮替代疗法，填补天津市该项空白。

2001年，安康医院肖瑞森等根据滤过器的性能指标及灌流的特点，设计血液虑过灌流疗法，用高压液相色谱仪进行吗啡定量检测，用吗啡依赖犬进行滤过灌流模拟实验的方法，完成“血液吸附净化戒毒疗法的实验研究”，该疗法不存在依赖问题，疗程短，效果好。通过测定治疗前、后白细胞、红细胞、血小板、总蛋白、白蛋白数值变化，评价该疗法对血液的影响，证实该疗法不存在血液相容性。

第六节 眼科学

1991～2005年，天津在斜视弱视与小儿眼病、白内障、青光眼、屈光不正、眼底、眼眶等方面疾病的诊疗技术快速发展。20世纪90年代，天津市眼科医院（以下简称“市眼科医院”）成立准分子激光治疗中心，先后开展不同的激光矫正屈光不正技术，并进行一系列具有开创性、前沿性的相关临床和基础研究。市眼科医院在低视力的鉴别诊断标准、结合神经影像学及遗传学特征开展复杂性斜视术式创新、眼科微创手术技术的标准化与规范化、遗传性眼病的发病机制及快速筛查技术等方面也取得较大进步。2001年，市眼科医院通过ISO 9002国际质量管理体系认证，在华北地区卫生行业尚属首家，成为当时全国通过认证的10所医院之一，标志着该院在管理上已与国际接轨。

20世纪90年代初，由新加坡知名眼科专家林少明捐并募款，在天津医科大学创建世界人工晶体中国天津培训中心。在国内率先采用超声乳化白内障吸除术和人工晶体植入术，使白内障手术进入一个新时期。1997年又相继开展角膜屈光手术、后部玻璃体切割术。同年，林少明获国家科学技术委员会颁发的“国际科学术技合作奖”。1999年，该中心增名为天津医科大学眼科中心（以下简称“医大眼科中心”）。

一、白内障

1997年，医大眼科中心张红采用透明角膜切口超声乳化白内障吸除并植入折叠人工晶体，使手术时间缩短。1998年，该中心袁朝旭使用Lotmar视力仪预测白内障术后最佳矫正视力效果显著。该中心汤欣采用改良巩膜隧道小切口不缝合白内障超声乳化术取得成功。张红对严重晶体不全脱位实施自闭性小切口囊袋内吸除术及囊间法超声乳化术获得良好的效果。该中心孙慧敏对黄色人工晶体植入后的对比敏感度和色觉进行研究，黄色晶体作为一种新型人工晶体，植入白内障患者眼内，比以往常规人工晶体提高人眼的视功能，为黄色晶体的应用提供依据。2000年，该中心季建研究的“新式非超声乳化不缝合白内障摘除术”，被全国多家医院采用，该术式适应症广泛，手术中组织创伤小，并发症少，简化手术过程，术后视力恢复快，同时具有手术费用低，方法简单，容易掌握，操作方便等特点。同年，汤欣将传统巩膜隧道改良为“L”型巩膜隧道切口，减少手术性散光。2001年，该中心徐延山首创无虹膜眼的带虹膜人工晶体植入术。汤欣植入新型多焦点人工晶状体，提高人工晶体眼的视觉质量。2004年，汤欣使用新型人工晶状体推送器，缩小手术切口，减少术后散光。该中心李筱荣应用软壳技术完成超声乳化手术，减少手术损伤。

1998年，医大眼科中心袁佳琴编写的《人工晶体植入术图谱》。该书从眼科显微手术基础开始，详细介绍超声乳化手术和折叠人工晶体植入式，并有国内外小切口非超声乳化白内障摘除术专家多年手术方法的经验介绍。2000年，袁佳琴及其博士研究生王桂琴等在“多种新型表面修饰人工晶体的实验研究”中采用载能离子束联合低温等离子体技术对聚甲基丙烯酸甲酯（PMMA）IOL进行氟离子处理联合肝素表面修饰，并植入猕猴眼内；采用低温等离子体联合离子束技术对硅凝胶软性IOL表面进行碳、钛及氮化钛修饰，进行表面特性检测及体内外实验，以提高人工晶状体的生物相容性。

2000年，第三医院引进全电脑白内障超声乳化等设备，为白内障复明工程奠定基础。请国内著名超声乳化人工晶体植入专家操刀手术，为患者提供免费咨询服务。

2001年，中国医学科学院放射医学研究所贾德林、孙凯完成“《X、γ、β射线和电子束所致眼晶体剂量估算规范》研究和制定”。该标准统一眼晶体的正确表示最值和表达方式，给出科学、规范的剂量估算方法。采用公式化的表达方式，简化各种复杂的眼晶体剂量估算问题，提高其准确性和可操作性。首先推算得到由经常使用的量值计算眼晶体剂量的系数表。创造性的给出非能光子所致眼晶体剂量的估算方法和相应的计算公式。

总医院应世灏在以往“采用天然甲状腺素治疗白内障的研究”基础上，从动物甲状腺中提取甲状腺素，制成内障清眼药水。1975年曾用于白内障治疗，获中、美、英发明专利证书。2002年获国家二类新药证书，并于2005年上市。在治疗机理研究中，发现该激素能增加和保护酶活性，从而改善钠泵功能，保护-SH基，使动物模型眼体征好转，患者临床体征好转，且光镜、电镜下病变减轻。结合裂隙灯立体摄影长期观察早、中、中晚期皮质性白内障的疗效，发现该药物能长期提高或稳定视力，减轻病变和推迟病变发展达10年以上，推迟或免除手术治疗。

2004年，医大眼科中心李筱荣等完成“超声乳化囊袋内人工晶体植入联合玻璃体切割术治疗增殖性糖尿病视网膜病变”研究，改进常用的晶体切割术，保留晶体后囊膜，既降低糖尿病眼前节并发症的进展，又植入高质量可折叠人工晶体，对糖尿病患者术后的有效视力有很大提高和维护。2005年，李筱荣完成“靶向抑制人工晶状体植入术后上皮细胞增殖”项目，该研究将抗人晶状体上皮细胞单克隆抗体和抗代谢药物5-FU，以可生物降解的天然高分子为载体材料，采用先进的纳米（毫微粒）制备技术，制备出具有靶向性的控释毫微粒复合物，并将靶向、控释技术融为一体，成功培养人晶状体上皮细胞，国内首次制备抗人晶状体上皮细胞单克隆抗体。2005年，李筱荣、张红开展“应用25G玻璃体切割系统实施手术”，采用25G小口径手术设备，无需巩膜切口缝线，减少手术时间、手术创伤和术后散光。

2005年，医大眼科中心孙慧敏在“先天性遗传性白内障相关基因定位的研究”中，成功构建一组已知白内障致病基因的微卫星标记库，便于以后遗传性白内障的研究和防治。致病基因GJA8新突变点的发现丰富GJA8基因资料，为晶状体缝隙连接蛋白（Cx50）的功能研究提供依据。

二、屈光不正

1991年，市眼科医院谢天钧、李碧珊等与天津市合成工业研究所共同开发研制成功透气性硬角膜接触镜，应用于屈光不正人群，性能达到国际同类产品水平。

1994年，市眼科医院王雁、赵堪兴等开展屈光性角膜切削术（PRK）。在此基础上发现国内该技术在治疗超高度近视受限并发症易出现等技术难点，采用多区切削法进行治疗，减少组织切削30%、明显减少角膜下雾状混浊等并发症。

1997年，医大眼科中心赵少贞开展屈光性角膜切削术（PRK）。1998年，市眼科医院王雁等开展准分子激光角膜原位磨镶术（LASIK），提高手术的安全性及精确性，极大缩短手术时间。此后，通过结合PRK手术与LASIK手术的各自优势，利用稀释的乙醇松解角膜上皮，取代原来PRK机械法去除上皮的方法。2000年，医大眼科中心赵少贞开展准分子原位角膜磨镶术（LASIK），可使大量普通近视及高度近视眼患者摘掉眼镜，有效提高患者的生活质量。2005年，采用角膜热成形术治疗远视及老视，国内率先对高度远视和老视进行手术治疗，使用透热疗法摘除老花镜，并保持手术效果至少1年以上。

1999年，市眼科医院王雁等针对PRK、LASIK手术进行一系列术后安全性研究，主要围绕术后散光、高度近视术式选择、手术对眼底视盘的影响、超微结构变化的影响分析等，与澳大利亚学者的共同发现角膜屈光手术术后并发症的组织病理学基础，是准分子激光对角膜组织的特异性生物组织反应。

2002年，医大眼科中心赵少贞等完成的“PRK术后泪液中上皮生长因子（EGF）、转化生长因子β1（TGF-β1）和白细胞介素1α（IL-1α）含量变化及其主要受体在角膜上皮细胞的表达的研究”，检测EGF、-TGF-β1和IL-1α在泪液中的变化规律，证实上述主要受体在角膜上皮细胞的表达，并从临床角度分析当这三种因子增加时，上皮细胞分化与增殖明显，使近视回退。

2003年，市眼科医院王雁等开展乙醇法准分子激光上皮瓣下角膜磨镶术（LASEK），并进行LASEK手术相关伤口愈合的基础研究。2005年，王雁等尝试使用机械刀制作上皮瓣，开展机械法准分子激光上皮瓣下角膜磨镶术（Epi-LASIK），扩大角膜屈光手术矫正屈光不正的适应症，尤其是对于角膜厚度偏薄的患者。同年，该院引入Intralase飞秒激光仪，开展飞秒激光辅助的LASIK（FS-LASIK）手术动物实验研究，显著降低机械刀制作角膜瓣术中的并发症，角膜屈光手术进入全激光治疗时代。

同年，市眼科医院王雁、赵堪兴等针对眼科临床的视觉现象，结合临床开始对人眼和近视眼的波前像差特点进行观察。2004年，开始与南开大学母国光院士团队结合现代物理光学方法和理论进行长达20余年的临床研究，建立各种基于个性化的人眼光学模型，为临床提供重要的新观察方法和手段。同时，为解决临床视觉难点，控制手术并发症，提高手术的安全性起到重要作用。

三、眼底病

1995年，市眼科医院魏景文主编完成《临床眼底病彩色图谱》。该图谱采用编著者多年积累的大量眼底病彩色图片，并对特殊疑难病例附有大量荧光造影对照超声和病理图像，以证实诊断的正确。具有资料丰富、病种全面系统、内容新颖、图文并茂、文字传述准确等特点。

同年，市眼科医院陈松等完成“早期老年黄斑变性（AMD）长期临床追踪观察”研究。在流行病学调查的基础上，率先采用Humphrey视野分析仪黄斑阈值程序进行黄斑光敏度短期波动及颜色明度敏感性检测，应用FM100-色调实验仪、对比敏感度检查仪、暗适应检查仪及Amsler表对早期AMD进行多项视功能检测，同时显示出上述方法为AMD的早期诊断最价值的方法，提出对视力正常而眼底、眼底荧光血管造影及视功能检测有异常者，应诊断早期AMD的新概念，该研究对AMD早期诊断和预后具有重要价值。该成果获1998年度天津市科技进步二等奖。

1996年，市眼科医院赵秉水、张金华等试制并采用C_2F_6气体作为填充物应用于治疗玻璃体视网膜相关疾病的手术治疗，并进行一系列相关研究，国内玻璃体视网膜手术一直在延用此项技术。

1997年，医大眼科中心开始进行玻璃体视网膜手术并加强眼底疾病的诊断治疗水平研究。2001年，徐延山等开展“氪黄绿激光眼底光凝治疗糖尿病视网膜病变”研究，使用多波长氪激光光凝虹膜周边部以开放房角，有效降低眼压，是非手术有效治疗原发性闭角性青光眼的有效方法，可使一些早期病例病情得到控制，甚至提高视力，而且使一些伴发早期白内障、玻璃体混浊的糖尿病视网膜病变得到积极治疗。

2001年，市眼科医院赵堪兴等首次成功地检测出国人视网膜色素变性病人致病基因突变谱。在两个视网膜色素变性家系、数十人的血中分离出脱氧核糖核酸（DNA），并采用分子生物学分析技术进行基因分析，同时与100名正常、无亲缘关系的志愿者进行比较，发现一常染色体显性遗传家系视网膜色素变性病人的视紫红质光受体341位谷氨酸残基的基因密码子，由GAG（谷氨酸）突变为TAG（终止密码），致使光受体短缺，功能失常。该研究还发现一X一性联锁遗传视网膜色素变性家系光传导中GTP酶调节因子（PRGP）基因缺失28个碱基，致使PRGR失去功能。这两个发现均为国际首次报道的视网膜色素变性致病基因突变谱。

同年，市眼科医院赵堪兴、王乐今、李宁东、王擎等完成“中国人视网膜色素变性分子遗传学研究”。通过致病基因定位克隆，从分子水平探究导致中国人视网膜色素变性的发病原因和发病机制，研究基因突变与视网膜色素变性临床表型之间的关系，进一步揭示视网膜色素变性发病的物质基础，该研究成功检测出国人群视网膜色素变性病人致病基因突变谱，为基因治疗、产前诊断、优化人口质量提供依据。该项目获2005年度天津市自然科学二等奖。

2002年，市眼科医院陈松、韩梅、王兰惠等完成“共焦激光扫描系统对老年黄斑变性检查及激光治疗评价的研究”。率先对不同类型老年黄斑变性（AMD）的患者进行图像分析，提出早期老年黄斑变性发生脉络膜血管充盈时间延长、脉络膜循环异常和黄斑部视网膜局部结构的异常改变。同时在ICGA指导下光凝治疗AMD的脉络膜新生血管，为老年黄斑变性的诊治提供有价值的研究方法。老年黄斑变性的发病机理、早期诊治和视功能检测方法在全国得到推广应用。

2005年，市眼科医院陈松、关禹博、林锦镛等完成“全氟萘浣液在眼内应用的实验与临床研究”。研究发现全氟萘烷液（PFDL）引起的病理改变严重程度与PFDL在眼内存留时间呈正向关系，并且与PFDL量和纯度有关。

四、青光眼

1991年，市眼科医院林锦镛等开展先天性青光眼房角组织的超微结构观察，发现小梁发育异常、小梁板基质内胶原纤维产生过多、睫状肌纤维向前推移及房角区间叶组织残留是先天性青光眼的主要原发病理改变，对青光眼的治疗方法选择和发病机理研究具有重要实用价值。

1995年，总医院贺忠江与中国人民解放军装甲兵工程学院等单位合作研制“中心视野体积计量法和中心视野立体分析仪”，根据国际视野学会主席Greve的有关理论，创立可供计算机存储的中心视野分区命名法，权衡视野范围和光阈敏感度两类参数的关系，发明用“总灰度值”评估中心视野体积计量法，属国际首创。该项目获1996年度国家科技发明三等奖

2001年，医大眼科中心季建完成“非穿透小梁切除术治疗开角型青光眼”，改良非穿透手术，达到抗瘢痕化的目的。同年，该中心徐延山采用氪激光周边虹膜成形术治疗原发性闭角型青光眼。该技术可在门诊进

行，操作简便，并发症少。2003年，该中心邢小丽引进半导体激光经巩膜睫状体光凝术治疗青光眼。

五、眼眶病

1999年，医大二院建立天津市眼眶病研究所。该院宋国祥等历时几十年进行"眼眶肿瘤诊断和治疗的研究"，探索眼眶肿瘤的临床综合治疗方法，改良几种眼眶肿瘤的手术方法，系统开发眼眶影像诊断技术，对提高眼眶肿瘤的诊断水平及加速中国眼眶病学的发展起到积极的推动作用。该项研究积累眼眶肿瘤病历10000余例，完成手术5000余例，居世界首位。吸引全国各省、市、自治区及国外大量患者前来就诊。该研究获1999年度国家科技进步二等奖。

2000年，医大二院唐东润等在"应用F-VEP进行术中视力监护的临床研究"中，对将视觉电生理检查应用于眼眶手术中视力监护、预防视力丧失发生的实用性进行探讨，在视觉电生理仪主机基础上改进研制成适合于手术中使用的术中监护仪。在动物实验取得经验后，广泛应用于临床的眼眶肿瘤手术中，可及时发现手术操作对视神经的影响程度，提示手术医师权衡利与弊，减少失明率，提高患者的生存质量。2002年，该院唐东润、宋国祥、赵红等在"眼眶血管瘤介入性治疗的研究"中，采用介入性方法治疗眼眶血管瘤，在B型超声引导下应用平阳霉素进行瘤内注射，使注射更准确、安全、直观，为难治性血管瘤探索一条新的治疗途径。

2002年，医大二院何彦津等在"泪腺上皮性肿瘤临床病理及分子生物学研究"中，对泪腺原发上皮性肿瘤的发病机制及生物学特征等方面从病理及分子生物学角度进行系统研究，使泪腺肿瘤的诊断提高到一个新的水平，运用病理学、免疫学及分子生物学技术，从细胞蛋白和分子水平探讨泪腺肿瘤的发生发展规律，对泪腺肿瘤的临床诊断、病情监测、彻底治疗及预后判断具有十分重要的指导意义。

六、斜视、弱视与小儿眼病

1991年，市眼科医院杜翠琴等研发的用于治疗先天性第三对颅神经麻痹所致重度斜视系列手术，采用外直肌超长量退后与内直肌超常量缩短配合上、下斜肌移位的方法以解决该手术治疗中的重大难点。

同年，市眼科医院张安琦、赵堪兴等引进并应用选择观看法（PL）幼儿视力检查仪进行检测，取得1620只眼婴幼儿视力均值及正常视力动态观察数据，为早期诊断婴幼儿视力发育迟缓、先天性遗传性眼病、术后视力变化情况及单眼弱视的诊断提供依据。

是年，赵堪兴等在国内首创拮抗肌同时减弱矫治Duane眼球后退综合症的手术方法，取得较好的临床效果。研究开发16导VEP拓谱图采集处理系统，开展无创伤性儿童斜视性弱视发病机制的研究，探讨弱视多导诱发电位空间分布特征。

1993年，市眼科医院赵堪兴、李丽华、蒋虹亮等开展动态随机点立体图形刺激所印发的立体视觉诱发电位的研究，临床应用于30例正常人双眼及单眼观察动态随机点立体图时的立体视觉诱发电位变化，将立体视觉的检查由主观性转变为客观性，排除儿童心理、智力发育等因素对检查的影响。

1999年，市眼科医院王乐今、赵堪兴等通过探讨单眼视觉剥夺后，在视觉发育障碍形成弱视的不同时期，c-fos、c-jun、egr1、bcl-2表达特性动态变化，以及F-VEP的变化规律。结果表明：弱视猫两侧视皮层部分基因表达不平衡，剥夺时间的长短与抑制细胞凋亡基因bcl-2有关，对于认识弱视的发病机制和指导弱视诊断治疗具有重要意义。

同年，市眼科医院赫雨时、赵堪兴、张开伯等编著的《斜视》，获得1999年度天津市科技进步著作类二等奖。该著作依据长年的临床实践，融入斜视弱视诊疗新技术，特别是异常视网膜对应和弱视训练技术、麻痹性斜视的临床分型手术设计手术技巧、先天性特发性眼球震颤的矫治技术等，被同行公认为当时斜视领域最具权威性的著作。

2001年，市眼科医院岳以英、赵堪兴、郭新等完成"先天性冲动性眼球震颤二个反方向中间带治疗的研究”。采用三棱镜中和两侧代偿头位扭转角的方法,对头位改善且不转向另一侧者按最大代偿头位扭转角设计并实施手术。在国内最先开展眼球震颤“中间带”转移手术矫治特发性眼球震颤引起的代偿头位,提高主要视野的视功能。对有斜视的眼球震颤患者设计先在主导眼手术矫正头位。应用斜肌直视手术矫治复杂难治斜视,为双眼上斜的患者提供新的治疗途径。

2005年,总医院颜华等完成“2001年中国0~6岁残疾儿童抽样调查”,通过流行病学调查,摸清当时全国残疾儿童的数量、分布、结构和生存状况,发现全国0~6岁视力残疾儿童主要的原因为先天性白内障、视神经萎缩、先天性青光眼、先天性脉络膜缺损以及眼内肿瘤等。对国家有关残疾人和残疾人事业的计划、政策的制定、实施、评估提供可靠依据。

七、低视力

1991年,市眼科医院王思慧等开展儿童低视力病因以及助视器应用研究,并依据研究结果设立低视力门诊,出版专著《实用低视力处理》指导临床诊治,并指导建立国内首家低视力学校。

1993年,市眼科医院赵堪兴、张安琦、王思慧等致力于治疗儿童低视力的系列研究,揭示儿童弱视、斜视、低视力相关疾患的致病机理、诊断方法及预防方法,研制成功“低视力专用视力表”并获得国家专利。

1998年,市眼科医院王雁、王思慧等通过对视残和低视力患儿的视野、对比敏感度、双眼视、色觉等视功能的筛查和评估,针对其特点确立视残和低视力患儿视功能检查规范,并应用于诊断和视功能康复治疗,取得良好效果。

八、眼外伤

2004年,总医院颜华等在“严重眼外伤的临床与实验研究”中,以实验研究为基础,选择最佳手术治疗时机,充分发挥联合手术的优势治疗严重眼外伤,包括玻璃体切除手术联合角巩膜缘切口治疗眼内巨大异物及眼内炎,临时人工角膜下玻璃体切除联合角膜移植治疗角膜血染无光感眼和眼内炎,玻璃体切除手术联合眼内填充物治疗严重眼外伤导致的复杂视网膜脉络膜脱离等,克服以往治疗方法的局限性,提高治疗效果。该项目获2004年度天津市科技进步二等奖。

九、角膜眼表病

1991年,市眼科医院武桂芳等在临床开展应用自体纯角膜上皮移植治疗翼状胬肉技术。该技术解决传统手术方式排斥反应、瘢痕以及复发率高等问题,该成果获1991年度天津市科技进步二等奖。

1993年,市眼科医院崔文治、王思慧、寇鹤然等研制的中药“复明冲剂”应用于治疗急性全葡萄膜炎,避免全身应用激素治疗产生的副作用及激素禁忌症患者的治疗问题。

2005年,医大眼科中心张晓敏完成“角膜缘干细胞培养体系的建立”研究,提出在角膜缘上皮细胞培养中,细胞悬液培养法优于组织块培养法。

第七节　耳鼻咽喉科学

1991~2005年,天津在耳、鼻咽、喉等方面的临床诊疗技术和基础科研工作取得较大进步。一中心医院、天津市第四中心医院(以下简称“四中心医院”)、环湖医院,总医院、肿瘤医院、天津医科大学第三医院(原韶山医院,以下简称“医大第三医院”)等单位将多项研究成果和新技术应用于临床应用。

一、耳科

一中心医院周祥宁、宋明明、马元煦等自1990年开展内耳器官培养和神经生物学研究，先后进行内耳感受器官对位听节神经元体外发育的诱导作用、听觉前庭系统和嗅觉系统的神经生物学研究、哺乳动物靶组织对位听神经节神经元在体外存活与分化的影响等系列研究，证实了碱性成纤维细胞生长因子(bFGF)对鸡胚延脑的听觉前庭核神经元在体外发育早期的显著刺激作用及bFGF直接作用于神经元的机理。周祥宁完成的“哺乳动物靶组织对位听神经节神经主元体外存活与分化的影响”研究获1995年度天津市科技进步二等奖。

1992年，一中心医院周祥宁、林必锦、任群等采用现代显微外科技术，行颈、胸交感神经显微切除术治疗对侧型迟发性内淋巴积水，使手术操作在明视下进行，防止损伤颈、胸交感神经周围的血管、重要神经和胸膜，且不损伤耳蜗及前庭功能，为迟发性内淋巴积水的治疗提供一条新途径。

1993年，天津第二医学院附属韶山医院任明中等在“窄带噪声耳鸣掩蔽器的研制及临床应用”研究中，以高科技电子技术选择与患者耳鸣频率和强度相近的窄带噪声对耳鸣产生掩蔽，可起到临床治疗作用。1994年，该院任明中、李崇谦等完成国人乙状窦后内耳道进路解剖学和手术的研究，对国人的乙状窦后手术的解剖学进行实验研究，明确开颅窗标志线及适宜的部位。同时把前庭神经切断术的手术适应症扩大到耳蜗神经切断术，用以治疗单侧全聋患者的严重神经性耳鸣。1997年，任明中等在“面神经梳理术的机理研究”中，从病理生理及病理组织学角度分析研究手术近远期疗效的机理。通过神经梳理不同刀数的结果差异证明梳理平面多少对于临床疗效的影响，并自神经梳理后3个月超微形态的动态变化结果，探讨术后复发与预防问题。

1999年，一中心医院陈太生开展耳石复位治疗良性阵发性位置性眩晕(BPPV，又称耳石症)研究。2004年天津市卫生局授权一中心医院眩晕诊疗中心开展耳石复位治疗BPPV。该技术首先对耳石责任半规管定位，然后通过床旁手法转换患者头位及体位，使异位到半规管的耳石回归椭圆囊而即刻解除眩晕。同年，该院陈太生引进视频眼震图技术，使眩晕前庭功能评定从眼震电图提升到视频眼震图，提高前庭功能检测精度和效率；2005年，在国内率先引进前庭自旋转试验(VAT)技术，发现中枢性眩晕患者的VAT高增益特征，为中枢与周围性眩晕鉴别提供客观手段，奠定一中心医院眩晕诊疗在国内的领先地位。

2000年，总医院隋秀丽等设计出“外耳道带蒂转移皮瓣+自体颞肌筋膜”进行鼓膜成型的术式，既可解决移植膜固定困难、易形成钝角愈合的问题，又可保证移植膜的血液供应，明显提高手术的成功率。该治疗法经临床应用及长期随访，表明移植膜成活率高，穿孔闭和率达100%，并无移植物钝角愈合、变薄、萎缩及再穿孔等。病人手术后听力均获提高，其中53%手术后听力恢复至正常使用水平，手术后3个月阻抗测听检查鼓室压图为“A”型。

二、鼻咽

20世纪90年代，环湖医院赵绰然第一次将鼻内镜技术应用于临床检查，并逐渐进行鼻内镜鼻腔鼻窦手术。

1991年，一中心医院张玉庚，杨宝琦创建“间接显微咽喉手术”，进行各种咽喉部疾病的手术治疗。可以在局部麻醉下完成，临床应用范围广。并在全市及国内推广应用。1993年，该院张玉庚、杨宝琦创建“下鼻甲骨折移位术”治疗慢性肥大性鼻炎的新型手术方法。该术式扩大中鼻道和总鼻道，改善鼻腔通气功能，不损伤或极少损伤鼻粘膜，保护粘膜的湿热调节和清洁保护功能，被誉为生理性鼻科手术。此术操作简便，效果良好，至2000年已成为临床治疗慢性肥大性鼻炎的常规手术。

1995年，环湖医院刘钢在国内率先开展经鼻内镜脑脊液鼻漏修补术，经鼻蝶垂体瘤切除术，斜坡肿瘤切除术，经口咽入路处理颅颈交界区病变，鼻眶肿瘤及视神经减压手术等，成功完成相关手术数百例。内镜经鼻入路脑脊液鼻漏修补术，术后恢复好，避免开颅手术的诸多并发症。1998年，刘钢对内镜下EC耳脑胶修补脑脊液鼻漏、功能性鼻内镜手术临床经验进行总结。2001年在天津成立全国唯一的鼻病诊疗专科机构。

2005年，环湖医院赵金城、刘纲等编译出版《颅底显微手术学》。

1995年，一中心医院、天和医院、河北邢台眼科医院等单位的张玉庚、黄永旺、王春华等完成“软硬腭后移鼻咽缩窄术治疗儿童开放性鼻音的研究”。该研究设计鼻咽缩窄术，采用软硬腭后移延长软腭长度以增加其活动度，使发音时缩小鼻咽的前后径，再将翼内板劈开内移以缩小鼻咽左右横径。缩窄鼻咽腔改善鼻口声气分流比率，并利用术后语言训练，把发音的共鸣点引向硬腭前部，减少气流发音时过多地进入鼻咽部，从面矫正吐字不清开放性鼻音。手术前后采用放射线，鼻流计，语图频谱等对共鸣位置的分析作为手术病例选择和疗效判断标准，取得满意的效果。

2000年，一中心医院张玉庚开展阻塞性睡眠呼吸暂停综合症（OSAHS）研究，制定国人首个咽解剖关系指数，进一步根据咽部解剖生物力学原理，提出OSAHS的病生理特征是“腭咽关闭-开放力平衡失调”的观点，促进了悬雍垂腭咽成形术的手术切口、软腭切除范围和操作流程标准化，并在全国推广应用。

2001年，肿瘤医院王平、李瑞英、朱莉等完成“鼻咽癌腔内近距离治疗双管一体施源器的研制及临床应用”。该施源器可保证将软腭等正常组织推开，同时使放射源贴近靶区，从根本上改善剂量分布。与鼻咽腔调形态高度一致，适形性好，能紧密镶嵌于鼻咽腔内，固定性好，位置重复性好，减少系统误差和随机误差，提高治疗精度，为临床开展超分割放射治疗及鼻咽腔内热疗工作提供设备。施源器造价低廉，应用简便，减轻患者痛苦。该项目获2001年度天津市科技进步二等奖。

三、喉

四中心医院金国威长期致力于喉癌治疗的系列研究，在喉癌的早期诊断、手术、发音重建与术后声学分析、嗅觉功能、味觉功能的评估与恢复、头颈部大面积软组织缺损修复、术后生活质量分析等方面提出独特的新方法，最大程度地保留、重建患者的喉功能，提高患者的生存质量，并将这些研究成果应用于临床。1992年，天津铁路分局天津铁路中心医院金国威采用气管食管裂隙状瘘发音重建术对喉全切除术后患者行二期发音重建术，手术可在局部麻醉下施行，操作简单，手术仅需30分钟左右，术后患者即刻发声讲话，音色较浑厚，响度大，连贯性好，术后较少出现误咽。“全喉切除术后Ⅱ期发音重建术”获1992年度天津市科技进步二等奖。1993年，该院金国威、李少诚、石继红等在动态喉镜下进行喉部疾病的诊断治疗过程中，发现早期喉癌声带黏膜僵硬及声带黏膜波波动消失的改变，从而为喉癌的早期诊断提供一种新的诊断方法。根据喉癌病变的不同范围和程度，创新不同手术方式，扩大手术适应症。尤其是对晚期喉癌及复发癌术后大面积组织缺损的修复，可减轻病人的痛苦，延长其寿命。发音重建术的实施，提高了病人的生存质量和生活信心。该院近20年采用该方法治疗喉癌病人413例，术后均能发音讲话，音质、音量均达生理常态，病人生活正常。该成果已向全国推广，各地数十家医院应用该技术治疗喉癌病人约800例，效果明显。“喉癌的早期诊断与手术新方法”项目获2001年度天津市科技进步二等奖。2001年，金国威等采用声学分析方法对全喉切除术后发音重建的发音效果进行客观分析，以声强、声时、基频、共振峰的频率及能量、频率微扰和振幅微扰为基本测试项目，进行客观评价，并应用于临床对发音重建手术进行改进与规范。其首创的喉癌患者全喉切除后人造声门（气管食管裂隙状瘘）发音重建术，已成功地使300余名因喉癌全喉切除后无喉病人重新几乎像正常人一样说话交流，其音调、音色接近生理常态。这一新术式，已在全国临床上广泛推广应用，很好地恢复无喉患者的语言功能，显著提高他们的生存质量。2004年，金国威等对喉全切除术后患者的嗅觉进行全面综合分析包括鼻腔大体结构及嗅上皮超微结构的观察，嗅觉功能的测试，分析找出造成嗅觉减退或丧失的主要原因，对喉全切除术后患者及早给予简单而有效的闭口鼻腔呼气法干预，以维持患者正常的嗅觉功能或恢复其减退的嗅觉功能。

1994年，一中心医院杨宝琦和医大第三医院黄永旺在“动态声门图像分析仪的研制及临床应用研究”中，利用频闪喉镜将声带的动作记录下来，进行计算机处理，研制出动态声门图像分析仪，得出数据形式和数据内容。利用比值关系分析声门运动，为一些难诊断的喉疾病提供定量指标及诊断依据。

同年，一中心医院、天津市耳鼻喉科研究所、医大第三医院杨宝琦、张玉庚、熊允谷、刘桂莲等开展的喉狭窄治疗新方法研究，该项目根据成喉的理论指导设计新的手术方法，对声门上狭窄以会厌切除法治疗；对声门狭窄应用声带错位法治疗，会厌下降至声门间，使声门呈倒三角；对声门下狭窄采用开放伤口换药法，使瘢痕不能形成环状收缩；气管狭窄则以甲状腺峡作桥墩，翻转皮瓣搭桥术治疗。并采用中药活血化瘀法，促进伤口愈合，减少感染和瘢痕形成。该项目获1995年度天津市科技进步二等奖。

是年，医大第三医院黄永旺等在“多导频谱同步分析用于共鸣腔的研究”中，指出歌唱者声部不同取决于共鸣腔的共振，进而提出声部划分原则，对于鉴别声音质量给出客观评价指标，提出临床病理性声音嘶哑新的分类方法，用于研究生理病理多种发音特点，诊断矫治各种发音障碍。1997年，黄永旺等在“嗓音源与声带振动及应用研究”中，利用数字检测和数字信号处理的方法，借助微机系统进行声带振动的研究，提出新的声门图分析参数及新的方法。该系统实时采集多路嗓音源信号，并应用LPC和FFT方法进行分析，计算出声带振动参数，应用于喉科研究、嗓音研究及喉科临床检查。

1995年，一中心医院杨宝琦、林鹏、牛兆林等开展声门癌功能性手术新方法的研究，该项目在充分研究声门癌解剖学、组织学及病理学的基础上，提出以甲状软骨内膜为声门癌T1、T2切除的标志界限，对于声门缺损，采用带蒂浅筋膜转移移植进行修复的新方法，较好地保留喉的发音功能，提高治愈率，五年无瘤生存率达96.7%。

1996年，一中心医院林鹏、杨宝琦、杨硕郎引进并开展喉全切除术后气管造口成型术和BlomSinger发音重建术，使90%以上的病人获得流畅的发音，使众多无喉患者从不能说话的痛苦中解脱出来，并掌握多种发音重建的手术和方法，如食道语、气动式人工喉（小喇叭）和电子喉的方法，是国内开展发音重建方法最多、最全的科室。

1997年，一中心医院刘吉祥、杨宝琦、杜建群等完成“功能性发音障碍临床矫治研究”，首次提出两级中枢言语控制理论。“两级中枢”理论即人的言语发音是受皮质及皮质下中枢双重控制的，从而解释各种功能性语言障碍的形成原因及治疗机理。发现功能性发音障碍不仅是功能性失音一种，还包括青春期假声、痉挛性发音障碍等。该项目应用动态喉镜诊断功能性失音，发现声带粘膜波消失，而治愈粘膜即恢复正常。同时，用发音法进行矫治，经230例临床应用获成功，且方法简便，实用性强。2001年，杨宝琦等完成“两极中枢理论指导下各种言语障碍的系列矫治”的研究，设计一整套矫治方法。使矫治变得相对简单，在其指导下制定出的各种发音法，用很简单的语言训练可使认为很复杂的问题得到解决。

1998年，一中心医院刘吉祥、杨宝琦、杜建群等完成间接显微喉动态镜手术临床研究，该手术方法使患者喉部基本保持原生理状态，术者可根据声带的振动、黏膜波情况来确定需切除的病变组织范围，最大程度改变发音效果，适用于不宜行直达喉镜手术的患者，手术效果明显高于常规手术方法，临床进行50例手术，成功率达94%。2004年，刘吉祥等应用记波扫描声带振动图像的自动分析系统，对声带振动功能实现客观、定量分析，记波扫描，可使声音嘶哑患者很快找到病因并得到及时治疗。

1999年，一中心医院林鹏、杨宝琦、杨硕郎开展显微支撑喉镜下CO_2激光微创手术切除肿瘤，成功地完成400多例，收到满意的效果。同期，在全市率先开展早期喉癌保留喉功能的显微喉镜下CO_2激光喉肿瘤切除术，保留了患者的喉功能，患者恢复快，减少并发症的发生。

2003年，一中心医院李丽、林鹏等完成“代谢酶基因多态性与喉癌发病、临床预后关系的研究”。该研究建立基因检测代谢酶活性失衡的方法，可应用于高危人群筛查，进一步阐明喉癌的发生、发展及转归的规律，对于预防喉癌具有较大应用价值。采用微量血白细胞直接进行PCR基因检测，打破以往提取DNA后再进行PCR基因检测的方法，更加简便、省时、经济。同时，可用于喉癌患者的临床预后的评估，提高其生存率。

第八节 口腔医学

1991～2005年，天津的口腔医学在口腔生物力学、口腔材料学、口腔修复工艺及技术等方面取得快速发展，天津医科大学口腔医院（以下简称“医大口腔医院”）研制的复合消毒剂、包埋料、高温高压清洗机、精密附着体、纯中药制备的空管药物新剂型、新型气管插管钳、有可伸缩波纹管的气管导管、铸钛修复体化学抛光技术、电磁感应加热技术等降低治疗成本，改善治疗效果。口腔生物力学分析扩大了倾斜基牙固定义齿的适应范围，三维有限元模型的建立，使口腔修复效果更符合生理要求。首次发现遗传性乳光牙本质的致病基因DSPP的基因突变位点。

一、口腔修复

1993年，医大口腔医院史书俊、董旭东等以2%戊二醛为主体配以多种成分，研制出新型高效复合消毒剂，该消毒剂可用于医院器械消毒、餐饮业、旅游业等。其对乙肝病毒、白葡萄球菌、白念芽胞杆菌灭活效果优于其他消毒液，尤其对金属医疗仪器及光学镜头无腐蚀性，可缩短杀菌时间，提高使用戊二醛的安全性，降低消毒成本。1999年，该院史书俊、侯小明等完成倾斜牙作为临床修复用基牙的可行性研究。为解决曾认为应将牙齿缺失后邻牙倾斜和下颌第三磨牙的倾斜牙拔除，结果导致临床因缺少基牙而修复困难的问题。首先在确定统一的基准面基础上提出测量牙体倾斜角度的新方法，用全口曲面断层X线进行测量，使测量数据更准确，克服国内外传统测量方法的不足。其次通过三维光弹法、贴片云纹干涉法及三维应变技术对不同程度的倾斜基牙进行固定义齿修复前后基牙牙周组织应力的定性和定量分析，揭示出应力—倾斜角度之间的变化规律，得出极限倾斜角度为70°的磨牙选做固定桥基牙时，其牙周组织应力分布仍然在生理限度内的重要结论，扩大其适应范围。“倾斜基牙固定义齿修复的实验研究及临床应用”项目获1999年度天津市科技进步二等奖。2000年，为解决原有国产包埋料不能进行固定修复问题，促进国产钛在口腔修复领域广泛应用，史书俊等先对国内外有代表性的四种铸钛包埋材料的技术指标进行对比分析，优化出包埋料各项性能的理想指标，探索出包埋料总膨胀与钛铸件精度之间的量变规律，并在此基础上研制出口腔铸钛专用包埋料。

1999年，医大口腔医院张连云、李长义、刘亚林等与天津市精工医疗设备技术有限公司合作研制出用于清除口腔修复体表面污物的高温高压清洗机，该设备通过高温高压双重作用，能够完全祛除修复体表面上的粉尘、残蜡、油污等，增强不同材料之间的结合强度，减少义齿表面色素沉着及菌斑的聚集，增加义齿的美感，经与临床普通清洗方法效果对比观察证明：该设备储水量大、升温快、压力大，并设有多层自动保护装置。2001年，医大口腔医院张连云、杨贤金、李长义等完成“口腔铸钛修复体化学抛光的实验研究”。在借鉴工业化学抛光的理论和技术的基础上，通过纯钛铸件化学抛光液成分、比例组分配制研究，经过对抛光件表面性能、机械性能测试和临床抛光效果评价，探寻出一种全新的钛义齿化学抛光模式，用以改变传统的物理抛光方法。该抛光液的研制成功，可提高工作效率、降低劳动强度，解决以往抛光过程对环境的污染和制约钛修复体临床广泛应用的瓶颈问题。该成果获2001年度天津市科技进步二等奖。2005年，医大口腔医院、天津大学张连云、崔振铎、刘亚林、胡欣等完成“齿科激光焊接技术实验与应用研究”。项目应用Nd-YAG激光器进行齿科CoCr-NiCr异种合金激光焊接，通过组织结构和机械性能测试分析优化焊接工艺参数，考察热处理过程对焊件机械性能、组织结构及成分的影响，进行焊件耐腐蚀性和生物学性能研究，将优化工艺参数应用于临床修复体制作，通过随访观察评价焊接效果。简化义齿制作工艺，提高义齿修复质量，丰富和完善齿科异种金属焊接理论。

2000年，教育部、卫生部面向全国各大医学院、医疗单位公开招标——编辑《全口义齿》视听教材，医大口腔医院在激烈竞争中成功中标。李长福运用全口义齿修复学理论，总结归纳国内外最新研究成果，将自己数十年修复、教学经验融入教材的编辑工作中。该教材通过临床示范将难于掌握的操作进行详细的说明，并运用动画形式将难于理解的理论进行形象化演示，取得了良好效果。该教材已成为医学院校、临床医学工作者口腔修复的辅助教学和业务提高的工具。2003年10月，《全口义齿》教材荣获全国第八届优秀科技音像制品培训和技术类二等奖，为天津市科技音像制品的最高奖项。

2002年，医大口腔医院刘亚林、张连云等采用全自动高频电磁感应加热技术替代传统酒精灯为热源的加热方式，研制出齿科电磁感应加热器。经与进口同类样机对比测试并在多家医院临床应用证明：该设备在操作安全性，加热温度、速度、能效等方面与进口产品等同。2003年，该院李长义、张连云、刘亚林等在“口腔精密附着体的开发研制及临床应用研究”中，采用精加工技术，加工研制出精密附着体成品预成件，改变以往国内均为半精密附着体义齿或半成品预成件的现状和国外传统附着体义齿加工方法。在制作工艺上，将异种激光焊接引进齿科修复领域，使制作工艺更加简化，成本较引进品低，便于普及应用。经临床试用，其附着体精度高，力学性能良好，所用材料对人体无毒害无腐蚀，美观、稳定性好、固位力强、咀嚼效能高、患者感觉舒适，义齿焊接区未见断裂、开焊、变形及腐蚀变色现象。

2002年，中国石化集团天津石油化工公司陈继贡、单振顺、周素贞等完成“复方口腔溃疡复合膜的研制与应用”。该项目成膜材料PVA17-99具有黏膜附着力强，在唾液中不易溶解的特点。药膜成膜材料PVA05-88d黏膜分泌物作用下可迅速溶解，将药物单向缓释放到病灶，使药物在病灶区起效快，作用时间长。中药冰片与甲硝唑等配伍可使病灶迅速愈合，经临床116例观察总有效率达98.3%。

2004年，医大口腔医院高平、周晖、李长义等采用三维有限元的方法，建立三维有限元模型。该模型不仅包括复杂的上下颌骨，还具有精细牙合 面结构的全牙列，而且上下牙列之间具有牙尖交错位的咬合关系。该模型可使上下颌骨之间通过相互运动，模拟上下牙之间的功能性咬合接触状态并进行动态分析，使应力分析更接近于口腔实际功能状态。这种三维有限元模型，可以按照患者的实际髁导斜度、切导斜度进行功能性咬合模拟，为口腔修复体的设计提供理论依据，使口腔疾病患者的修复效果更符合生理要求。

二、口腔内科

1994年，医大口腔医院郭翰敏、苑诚等对空管中药治疗实证型根尖周炎进行临床研究，用中草药制成酊糊剂，探讨纯中药制剂治疗根尖周炎的疗效。结果表明此药具有其他空管药物同等疗效，操作简便，药源广泛，价格低廉，安全性好。

1999年，医大口腔医学院赵军与中国医学科学院基础医学研究所沈岩合作，利用定位候选克隆致病基因的策略，对天津塘沽区的一个遗传性乳光牙本质家系进行研究，发现患者的牙本质涎磷蛋白(DSPP)基因的DSP区外显子3的3658位核苷酸发生C→T无义突变。该研究首次发现遗传性乳光牙本质的致病基因DSPP的基因突变位点，并于2001年在《自然遗传》上报道此致病基因。该刊的评论文章指出：“这篇第一流文章的发表，表明定位克隆取得成功的故事已不再是西方科学界的专利了”。“遗传性乳光牙本质致病基因的研究”获2002年度国家自然科学二等奖。

2002年，医大口腔医院仝健等与中国医学科学院放射医学研究所等单位合作完成“牙齿颌骨钙利用实验研究”。该研究将放射示踪技术应用于口腔医学中牙齿及颌骨的钙代谢，发现牙齿颌骨的钙利用几乎与胸骨和股骨相当，且成年牙齿颌骨仍有较高的钙代谢能力，牙齿及颌骨钙含量的增加规律与血液中钙的涨落一致，不同钙源制剂中的在体内钙利用的程度有差别，有机钙优于无机钙等等。该研究成果为口腔临床医学及预防保健提供基础依据，并获2002年度天津市科技进步二等奖。

三、口腔颌面外科

1990年，天津市口腔医院田奉宸、庞晓纲、濮礼臣等应用显微外科技术，在国内首创自体带有神经血管的第二跖趾关节游离移植进行颞下颌关节重建术。临床治疗10例,成功9例,经颈动脉造影,99mTC同位素扫描和3-5年的随访,全部病例无关节器质性改变。该术式被专业教科书收录。

1992年,口腔医院田奉宸、濮礼臣、庞晓纲等采用吻合臀上血管深上支的肌髂骨瓣移植修复大型骨缺损,移植骨块即刻与受区血管吻合,进而有效地保证移植骨成活。临床使用该法修复下颌骨肿瘤切除后缺损8例,修复先天性下颌骨发育不全3例,均获成功。该成果在解剖学与临床应用于治疗先天性下颌骨发育不全方面属国内外首创。

1994年,天津市口腔医院姚晖、司胜军与中国医学科学院生物工程研究所张其清等进行生物隔膜技术引导牙周组织再生的实验研究与临床研究,该项目首次采用牛腱中提取的胶原蛋白为基本材料,用涂复法制成胶原膜,再将此膜用醛类交联后制成适用于组织引导再生的胶原膜材料,并在动物实验的基础上,临床应用于牙周组织再生术治疗60颗牙,有效率达100%。

2002年,医大口腔医院李彦秋、刘长兰、杜咏梅等在利用微生物纤维的基础上配合甲硝唑用于拔牙创口,并进行相关动物实验与临床应用研究,结果证实微生物纤维—甲硝唑有良好的通气性,可起到抑制带入牙窝内的厌氧菌生存的作用,其降解后的产物能促进成纤维细胞增殖,加速肉芽组织生长和血凝块的机化,诱导新骨形成,加速创口愈合,经多家协作临床医院应用表明其使用方法简便,易于保存,对环境无污染,且患者容易接受,不论在临床效果还是在使用安全性、造价等方面都有优势。

第九节 影像医学与核医学

1991~2005年,影像医学与核医学由传统放射学迅速向医学影像学转化。天津建立起神经放射学、胸部放射学、腹部放射学、骨放射学、介入放射学等专业分支。科研方向以血管病的影像诊断及介入治疗、肿瘤影像诊断与基础研究、脑胶质瘤基因治疗影像学研究、老年人及相关疾病骨矿量影像学研究为重点。同时,在放射介入治疗肝癌、肺癌及肾动脉狭窄性高血压等方面取得较大发展。

20世纪90年代以来,天津超声医学学科发展很快,从仪器设备到超声医师队伍,超声医学的学术水平不断提高,诊断的内容不断拓展,其技术应用领域涉及全身各个脏器与组织结构。随着彩色多普勒超声仪器的广泛应用,其技术迅速普及到腹部(肝胆胰脾)、泌尿系、胃肠、妇产科、心脏、小器官、外周血管、颅脑以及肌骨超声等各个学科领域。介入性超声诊断与治疗已经成为肿瘤等疾病介入治疗的手段之一。超声诊疗技术已成为临床各学科不可或缺的检查及治疗监测手段。

一、影像医学

影像医学在与计算机、生物医学工程学结合的研究基础上,由模拟图像向数字化图像、网络化发展;由重叠二维图像向二维断层图像和三维、四维图像发展;由单纯影像诊断向诊断与介入治疗并重发展;由解剖形态学成像向功能成像、分子影像学成像发展。

(一)影像诊断

1. 放射诊断

(1)神经系统

国内第一部头部CT专著是1985年,由总医院吴恩惠主编的《头部CT诊断学》。1995年,出版第二版。该书首次报导中国人脑室正常值;提出脑内血肿周围环状强化与肉芽组织形成和消失有关的观点;报告正常中国人脊髓与硬膜囊径线值与比值,并与欧洲人正常颈髓比较,具有不同特点;提出椎体许莫氏结节CT表现与病理的关系及发生机理;报告一氧化碳中毒的CT表现动态演变过程及与临床预后的关系。该专著获1998年度国家科技进步三等奖。

1998年，吴恩惠、张文波等进行“正常成人及颞叶癫痫病人MR（磁共振）体积测量及MR表现的研究”，发表国内第一篇有关颞叶癫痫的MRI（磁共振成像）研究文献。其中，报告正常国人海马结构的测量方法、体积的正常值范围以及信号强度的正常值范围，从而为MRI检查判断颞叶癫痫的异常提供可靠依据。

2000年，一中心医院刘筠、祁吉、张文波等完成“颅神经的MR成像”研究。通过大体解剖、断层解剖与磁共振影像相对照，系统研究12对颅神经各段的颅内位置、行程和毗邻关系；通过比较成像参数，改良扫描方法，优化并建立适用于大多数MR机型的12对颅神经的MR检查方法。使用结果显示：该技术简单、易掌握，并提高颅神经的显示率和颅神经病变检查的阳性率，为临床诊治提供客观依据。该项目获2000年度天津市科技进步二等奖。

2001年，总医院吴恩惠、王振常、张云亭等完成“眶尖断层解剖及CT、MRI研究”。首次用火绵胶包埋法、组织切片机行尸头眶尖连续切片，观察其细微断层解剖结构和眶尖脂肪分布，证实其与海绵窦脂肪相连续，分析脂肪改变对眶尖病变的鉴别诊断及临床意义；首次描述经眶尖走行的颅神经的显示情况；提出影像学可显示眶尖内总腱环；系统研究不同病变累及眶尖影像学表现，探讨其构成规律、影像学特点及诊断价值，确立诊断及鉴别诊断标准。

同年，环湖医院刘梅丽、崔世民、张蕾莉等完成“磁共振弥散灌注成像在超急性期脑梗死影像半暗带的研究”。研究显示发病后最初2～6小时CT及常规的磁共振检查是正常的，而弥散加权成像诊断为脑梗死，这就为超早治疗赢得时间；研究还采取年轮状方式选择几十个点由外向中心测定病灶ADC值，判定缺血性影像半暗带可被挽救组织ADC的拟值为$(6.507\pm1.046)\times10^{-4}$毫米^2/秒，此带是濒临死亡的组织，为损伤可逆与否提供更为科学的依据。

2002年，总医院张云亭在“脑缺血性半暗带影像学检查方法实验与临床研究”中，对超早期脑梗死动脉溶栓治疗病人进行动态观察，表明脑梗死的超早期时缺血性半暗带并非为“带”状，而呈“星芒”状；应用免疫组化HSP72染色定性分析，显示在急性期脑缺血半暗带呈散在或点状分布；缺血性半暗带的形态和存在范围随缺血时间的不同，其表现形式可不同。同年，张云亭在“脑梗死后短T1信号—MRI（磁共振血管成像）演变和病理机制的研究”中提出：短T1信号产生的病理基础，血管再通及侧枝循环的建立所致的出血性转变是产生的主要机制。

是年，总医院于铁链等完成“正常国人Willis环的MRA[3]形态及其与缺血性脑血管病相关性实验和临床研究”，对国人正常Willis环（大脑动脉环）进行分型，并得出各类型的发生率；提出并初步证实缺血性脑血管病发病危险性与Willis环的形态类型有关。

是年，一中心医院祁吉等完成“侧颅底神经血管区：多层面CT和高场强MR影像解剖学研究”。该研究从影像解剖角度出发，了解侧颅底结构和彼此间的相互关系，使这一区域病变的影像诊断有了定位基础；规范并优化该区各个结构的影像学检查方法，明确其影像表现及检查限度，对外科制订手术入路和临床治疗具有重要意义。

2003年，总医院张云亭等利用CT灌注成像技术评价星形细胞肿瘤的活性、进行术前分级及监测放射治疗疗效。经研究证明CT灌注所得结果与肿瘤微血管密度呈线性正相关，CT灌注可准确反映肿瘤的活性；并发现CT灌注可准确监测肿瘤放射治疗后的疗效；研究还显示CT灌注可明显提高术前对星形细胞肿瘤分级的准确性。

2005年，一中心医院祁吉等完成“老年性痴呆的实验性病理——影像学研究”。通过建立Aβ（1-40）海马注射AD大鼠模型，观察AD早期脑组织的形态学改变及海马的功能异常。首次发现AD大鼠模型早期MI/Cr的改变与多种因素有关。发现AD临床前期的影像学特征，使老年性痴呆的影像诊断拓展到代谢领域，用于指导AD的早期预防与治疗。该项目获2005年度天津市科技进步二等奖。

同年，环湖医院和总医院崔世民、韩彤、刘力、张云亭等完成“弥散张量和功能MR成像对皮质脊髓束与肌力相关性的研究”。通过研究发明一种联合成像方法，即将皮质脊髓束、皮质功能区和病变同时显示在一幅图像上，替代临床医师靠解剖学层面和经验对脑功能区定位的传统方法。该项目获2005年度天津市科技进步二等奖。

（2）肌骨系统

1993年，总医院李景学等完成“单能定量CT测量骨矿含量（BMC）的研究”，自制定量计算机体层摄影术（QCT）校准体模，可与现有CT机配套用于BMC测量。经与骨组织计量学及骨灰化对照分析，证实单能定量CT（SEQCT）测量的准确性。国人男女两性最大骨量分别在25～40岁及20～35岁之间。40岁以前，男女两性BMC无大差别；40岁以后女性骨量减少明显快于男性。以椎骨BMC 95毫克/厘米^{2}作为骨质疏松性骨折阈值是适宜的。2000年，总医院蔡跃增、李景学等采用骨矿定性与定量相结合的检查方法，研究老年人骨矿分布和丢失的特点，测量部位的准确性和测量价值，为临床诊断和随访骨质疏松提供较理想的检测部位。并提出退行性脊椎病的老年人单纯以双能X射线吸收测量法（DEXA）测量腰椎正位骨矿密度（BMD），诊断骨质疏松是不精确的，必须做多部位测量，综合分析才能得出正确的诊断。

1997年，总医院李景学主编的《骨关节X线诊断学》获1997年度天津市科技著作二等奖。该著作为国内第一部有关骨关节疾患放射诊断专业参考书，首次提出脊椎结核等病的分期、分型。

1999年，医大二院廉宗澂等在“磁共振成像（MRI）对骨肿瘤范围确定的可靠性评估”研究中，对30例四肢原发性骨肿瘤手术前的MRI、CT和X线平片的检查和病理所见进行对照观察，结果表明MRI是确定肿瘤范围的最佳影像学技术，可为保肢性手术方案的制定提供重要参考。

2000年，廉宗澂等对“月骨无菌性坏死演化中舟月韧带撕裂的作用”进行临床—影像学研究和动物实验。经对大量月骨无菌性坏死病例的临床资料分析，发现患者均无明显的外伤史，且均伴有舟骨与月骨分离，证实舟月韧带撕裂引发月骨无菌性坏死的假设成立。动物实验证实韧带切断引发的骨坏死是不可逆的，骨内无再建血管。从而揭示出多年来悬而未决的舟月韧带撕裂与月骨无菌性坏死的因果关系，使月骨坏死的早期诊断和治疗成为可能。2001年，廉宗澂等在“骨骺部位损伤的影像—病理动态研究”中，建立高度稳定可靠的动物实验模型，分别从骺板直接损伤、间接损伤、干骺端损伤三个方面进行研究。结果表明MRI能显示X线不能显示的隐匿性损伤和小的线样骨桥，还可早期准确显示骨骺缺血性改变，从而为临床制定合理治疗计划提供信息，以避免畸形的发生及发展。2002年，廉宗澂等在“正常膝关节中小韧带和肌腱的解剖及MRI研究”中，对40侧尸膝进行大体解剖学观测，明确膝关节中小韧带的形态学特点；确定骨性标志及各结构的长轴与骨性标志所成的角度，并据此制订MRI斜位扫描方案；优化出显示膝中小韧带的脉冲序列、各结构的最佳显示方案及其MRI表现，并在国内外首次报道一套能完整显示膝关节中小韧带长轴的定位方法。

（3）心血管系统

1995年，总医院贺能树等在“肾动脉狭窄性高血压的影像学研究”中，提出国内肾动脉狭窄的主要病因是大动脉炎，而不是动脉粥样硬化，纤维肌增生也较少见；大动脉炎所致的肾动脉狭窄多见于年青女性；在血管造影上，肾动脉狭窄程度必须在70%以上才具有血液动力学意义；实验研究表明：肾动脉狭窄后球旁细胞增多，其来源为极垫细胞、平滑肌细胞，可来自血管外周细胞。该成果获1995年度天津市科技进步二等奖。

（4）内分泌系统

2002年，总医院吴恩惠等在“肾上腺CT检查的系列研究”中，确立肾上腺CT检查方法，使其标准化；确立国人正常肾上腺CT表现及正常值，为判断肾上腺病变，特别是增生提供可靠依据；得出功能性肾上腺病变的CT表现、诊断标准，以及CT诊断价值和限度等结论。2004年，总医院白人驹等在“肾上腺肿瘤MR反相位成像的表现与研究”中，建立反相位实验模型，深入研究反相位成像表现与组织脂肪含量的关系；测定肿物标本脂肪总量和脂肪成分的差异，分析其与反相位成像表现的相关性，证明肾上腺肿物的脂肪含量在一定范围内与其反相位成像的信号下降程度成直线相关；并提出冰冻切片脂肪染色结合图像分析法进行肾上腺肿物脂肪含量半定量的分析方法，证明其较以往应用的组织病理方法更直接和准确。

2003年，总医院白人驹、张云亭等主编国内第一部内分泌影像专著《内分泌疾病影像学诊断》。该书规范化了各种内分泌腺的CT、MRI检查技术；首次提出甲状旁腺腺瘤的动态增强CT表现；研究并明确胰腺各种功能性神经内分泌肿瘤的影像表现，强调MRI的检查价值；系统研究肾上腺腺瘤与非腺瘤的影像表现差异，指明MRI同、反相位检查和CT、MRI动态增强检查的重要性；提出肾上腺偶发瘤的临床处理程序。该书对于推动国内内分泌疾病影像诊断的发展具有重要意义。

2.超声诊断

第三医院任焕忠1990年率先在天津开展颅脑超声诊断，开展心血管病与脑血管病联合诊断的研究，着重探讨老年人脑血流速度与左室功能的关系，为临床在心脑血管疾病进行综合诊断、治疗及疗效评价上提供重要参考价值。同时，为天津市及外省市培养了超声专业技术人才。

中心妇产医院吴钟瑜主编的国内第一本妇产科超声专著《实用妇产科超声诊断学》，于1990年出版。同年，中心妇产科医院吴钟瑜、宗芷萍、杜梓柏等完成"B型超声波对诊断早期先天性胎儿畸形的研究"。该研究有效地提高B超对胎儿先天性畸形的早期诊断，及时终止妊娠，降低围产儿死亡率，减少出生缺陷。经临床结果核实，诊断符合率达98%以上，对各种畸形的早期诊断提出明确的依据。1996～2003年，对此进一步深入研究，在行彩色超声产前检查的孕妇1297例中，检出胎儿心脏异常99例，占7.6%：包括结构异常51例，心律失常54例，其中结构异常合并心律失常6例。该研究确定产科超声检查中筛查胎儿心脏异常的方法和途径；总结常见类型的胎儿复杂性先心病的声像图表现；分析胎儿先心病从发现到诊断和处理的复杂、多样性；提高先天性心脏病的产前诊断和围生期诊断水平。

1992年，中心妇产医院吴钟瑜、张国英、吴银莲等完成"应用超声推测卵巢肿瘤的种类和性质的研究"。对406例卵巢肿瘤的超声声像图特点与手术治疗、大体标本形态及镜下病理诊断等方面的对照分析，将临床常见的卵巢肿瘤声像图分为浆液性囊腺瘤及囊腺癌、粘液性囊腺瘤及囊腺癌、畸胎瘤（良、恶性）、实性或偏实性卵巢肿瘤和转移性卵巢肿瘤等五类，诊断符合率达96.8%。该研究利用声像图与卵巢肿瘤大体标本物理特征的良好相关性，总结出不同卵巢肿瘤声像图的特点和病理之间的关系，为超声检查推断卵巢肿瘤的种类及性质提供有价值的资料和诊断依据。

同期，南开医院开展胃十二指肠溃疡及溃疡病急性穿孔、不同病理类型的胃肠道肿瘤、各类型肠梗阻、不同病理类型的急性阑尾炎以及胃肠道的炎性和缺血性病变的超声诊断等胃肠疾病的超声诊断。

1995年，中心妇产医院吴钟瑜、周敏、王晓莉等完成"彩超与二维超声在滋养细胞疾患分类诊断和化疗监测中应用研究"。该研究应用二维超声观察479例滋养细胞瘤病灶形态、范围及内回声，对其中175例应用彩色多普勒观察病变处血流的分布、流量及动力学改变。样本数量大，首次提出良、恶性滋养细胞疾患的早期诊断依据和恶性滋养细胞疾患发展各阶段分类及诊断依据；并首次提出应用超声诊断宫旁侵犯的声像学依据及应用超声在化疗中评价该病的转归指标。

1997年，中心妇产医院吴钟瑜、周宏、张家锦等完成"二维彩色超声对各种类型异位妊娠声像图的研究"。应用二维彩色超声对种植在输卵管壶腹部、卵巢、腹腔等十个不同部位的异位妊娠进行子宫大小、宫腔等情况的观察。全面、清楚地阐述十个部位异位妊娠超声图像特征和鉴别诊断依据，从声像学角度提出子宫外异位妊娠及宫内异位妊娠的异位妊娠新分类法，及髂窝三角在诊断异位妊娠内出血的几项具体措施，并将超声影像、血流频谱学与临床生理病理相结合，实现异位妊娠的早期诊断和正确处理，其诊断总符合率达94.2%。中心妇产科医院吴钟瑜编写的《实用妇产科超声彩色图谱》《实用妇产科超声诊断学》《妇产科超声鉴别诊断图谱》分别于1997年、2000年和2003年出版，为提高妇产科超声诊断水平做出重要贡献。

（二）介入治疗

1. 放射介入治疗

1994年，总医院吴恩惠、贺能树主编出版中国首部《介入性治疗学》。2002年，贺能树、张云亭、白人驹主译出版全国首部《介入性磁共振成像》。2005年，由贺能树、吴恩惠主编的《中华影像医学—介入放射学卷》。上述著作在国内均有较大影响与学术价值。

（1）肝癌

1999年，总医院曹喜才、贺能树等在“^{90}钇玻璃微球治疗肝癌的临床研究”中，根据肝癌血供特点，首次提出含有^{90}钇玻璃微球的“三明治”疗法，即首先经导管注入^{90}钇和超液化碘油悬浮液，然后注入三种化疗药，最后用明胶海绵颗粒适量栓塞肿瘤周围血管。并对部分病人采用经皮腹动脉药盒导管系统（PCS）植入术，为肝癌介入治疗建立永久新通道，随时可选择最佳给药时机和给药剂量。治疗后获得较好的临床效果，平均生存期19.5个月，比单纯TAI治疗明显延长，生存质量显著提高。2003年肿瘤医院郭志等开展肿瘤氦氖刀靶向治疗，应用介入序贯氩氦冷冻治疗原发性巨块型肝癌取得较好效果，在短期内即可明显降低肿瘤体积，为治疗原发性巨块型肝癌提供一种安全、有效的治疗方法。并首次提出影响治疗效果主要因素是肿瘤血管“热池效应”，而经导管行肝动脉化疗栓塞（TACE）是抑制“热池效应”的有效方法，对序贯物理消融的疗效有重要临床推广应用价值。2004年，总医院曹喜才等在“^{32}P和化疗药、栓塞剂配伍介入治疗肝癌研究”中，采用改良式Seldinger技术，经肝动脉灌注^{32}P-GMS、超液化碘油和化疗药混悬液治疗30例肝癌病人。探讨^{32}P-GMS+TACE治疗肝癌的优越性和安全性；参考分区模型，估计肿瘤和非瘤肝组织的吸收剂量，评估量效关系；观察近期疗效和相关因素之间的关系及远期随访结果。经实际应用，表明该方法具有较高的临床实用价值。

（2）肺癌

1991年开始，肿瘤医院张俊义等开展肺癌支气管动脉灌注治疗等介入疗法，至1995年病例数增至200例/年，并于1997年后开展中晚期肺癌支气管动脉化疗与放疗的联合治疗。2002年，总医院和胸科医院曹喜才、徐乃勋、杨海贤等完成“支气管肺癌介入治疗的临床研究”。该项目采用三明治方法介入治疗肺癌，临床有效率由52%提高到80%，其治疗间隔时间由4周延长到8-10周。

（3）肾动脉狭窄

2002年，总医院贺能树等在“肾动脉狭窄性高血压介入治疗的临床和实验研究”中，用肿瘤坏死因子（TNF）和干扰素（IFN）于肾动脉壁内注射形成大动脉炎样病理改变，建成家兔大动脉炎模型；发现大动脉炎动物模型的血管壁中膜增殖、平滑肌细胞的凋亡；发现雌激素有拮抗TNF并减轻TNF造成的血管壁增厚的作用。临床通过介入治疗肾动脉狭窄性高血压38例，研究探讨经皮血管成形术治疗肾动脉狭窄性高血压的临床应用价值，比较球囊血管成形术与血管内支架成形术治疗大动脉炎的临床效果和远期疗效。研究结果表明：球囊血管成形术是治疗肾动脉狭窄性高血压的有效手段，可作为首选治疗方法；血管内支架成形术主要适用于球囊血管成形术失败及闭塞再通后的患者；大动脉炎活动期不宜进行介入治疗，但大动脉炎对球囊成形术反应良好；肾动脉开口以上的腹主动脉狭窄改变，也可造成肾血管性高血压，应首选介入治疗。

（4）肺结核空洞和肺气肿

1992年，天津市肺科医院范勇等首次将纤维支气镜与放射介入结合进行肺结核空洞的介入治疗，使耐多药肺结核的空洞闭合率达25.9%，痰菌阴转率达81.8%；随即推广至全国22个省市自治区。2003年范勇等人在国内率先开展四期肺气肿的介入治疗，使用自主研发的单向活瓣肺减容支架完成国内首例拥有自主知识产权的经纤维支气管镜微创肺减容术，为临床治疗重症慢性阻塞性肺疾病提供一种微创、经济的治疗方法。

2. 超声介入治疗

1998年，三中心医院率先在天津开展术中超声技术，用于病灶的检出及定性、定位诊断及辅助制定治疗方案，更改了近20%肝癌患者术前拟定的手术方案，成为肝癌切除术中不可或缺的辅助检查方法。

1999年，三中心医院经翔等率先在天津成立介入超声治疗室并临床开展超声引导下多种介入诊疗工作，奠定天津介入超声的发展基础。同年，三中心医院最早引入高强度聚焦超声（HIFU）技术，三中心医院经翔等完成天津首例肝癌患者的HIFU治疗，此后，引进射频消融及微波消融等多种局部热消融治疗技术，用微创开展早期肝癌患者的局部消融治疗，有效提高患者生存期，对符合米兰标准的肝癌患者，超声造影引导下热消融治疗1、3、5年生存率分别达到92.9%、74.7%和58.1%。

2005年,三中心医院超声科在全市最早引进超声造影检查技术,用于肝硬化背景下小肝癌的早期诊断及肝癌患者局部热消融治疗前评估、治疗中、后疗效监测。首次提出超声造影检查即刻评价热消融疗效的具体时间和方法,作为行业内热消融后疗效评价的标准方法。

二、核医学

1991年,天津医学院附属医院和北京师范大学刘金玲、胡自正、李玉琦、田美荣等完成“^{125}碘标记睾酮(直接法)放射免疫测定方法的建立及临床应用”研究。采用高浓度反应液一步合成法,组装试剂药盒稳定可靠,成本低廉,易于推广,优于国内当时引进的同类产品。

2000年,中国医学科学院放射医学研究所郑钧正和卢正福研究制定出《临床核医学中患者的放射卫生防护标准》,其强制性国家标准GB16361-1996已推广应用覆盖全国各地。

2005年,总医院方佩华、吕枚、李宁等在“重组人ICAM—1膜外片段蛋白和建立人血清slCAM—1RIA技术及临床应用”研究中,应用基因工程技术,在国内外率先在原核表达系统大量获取含有人ICAM-1膜外Ⅰ、Ⅱ、Ⅲ功能区基因的融和蛋白,产率达35毫克/升培养基,该产物具有免疫活性。在国内外首次将此融和蛋白作为抗原,从免疫家兔获取抗体,成功建立人血清sICAM-1 RIA。进一步应用此放免技术在国内率先开展较大规模的血样sICAM—1检测用于临床,结果提示sICAM—1能可靠反映格雷夫斯病(Graves′)患者的机体免疫状态,可作一项新的免疫学指标。该成果获2005年度天津市科技进步二等奖。

第十节 放射治疗学

1991～2005年,天津在立体定向放射治疗、肿瘤组织间三维立体放射治疗、放射性疾病诊断标准等放射诊疗方面有一定的进步。

2001年,总医院和中国医学科学院放射医学研究所曹永珍、姜恩海、吕仲虹、杨天恩等完成“立体定向放射治疗中脏器动度的实验与临床研究”。在国内首次进行肺呼吸动度及膈肌动度的测量,得出国人肺及肝脏肿瘤随着呼吸动度的动度范围。首次确定立体定向放射治疗安全边界问题和CT扫描每一层组织的时间与呼吸运动周期时间的关系,为位于胸腹腔肿瘤行立体定向放射治疗奠定理论与临床基础。

2005年,医大二院柴树德、毛玉权、郑广鈞等完成“应用TPS三维立体种植放射性^{125}I粒子近距离治疗晚期肺癌”的研究。探讨应用肿瘤组织间三维立体定向放射治疗计划系统(TPS),CT引导下经皮穿刺和纤维支气管镜直视下肿瘤内种植放射性^{125}I粒子近距离内照射治疗晚期非小细胞肺癌的方法、疗效及并发症的处理。完整的粒子植入的治疗程序,特别是确定肺癌治疗最佳剂量。发明专用于大气管内瘤体粒子植入的嵌入导管和导丝。根据“巴黎原则”及放射性^{125}I粒子的剂量学特点,利用植入模板同时将多排、多根植入针刺入瘤体,确保放射剂量。该项目获2005年度天津市科技进步二等奖。

2005年,中国医学科学院放射医学研究所、总医院、天津市民族医院姜恩海、王知权、曹永珍、江波、王晓光等完成“放射性口腔疾病诊断及生物剂量估算标准研究”。该研究研制定出中国放射性口腔疾病诊断及生物剂量估算标准,把ICRP有关受照器官剂量,强化累积剂量融先进性、科学性和实用性于标准条款中。明确规定放射性口腔疾病临床分期、诊治原则,应用荧光原位杂交法和G-显带分析稳定性染色体畸变特点估算生物剂量。有效指导放射性口腔疾病诊治、规范放射工作人员和放射事故受照人员的生物剂量重建。

第十一节 麻醉学

1991～2005年，天津在麻醉药氯胺酮在超前镇痛作用机理和强迫振荡肺功能测定技术应用于麻醉学等临床研究取得一定进步。

2000年，胸科医院和天津市心血管病研究所吕学思、赵彤、魏浩成、王惠芬等完成“强迫振荡肺功能测定在心脏外科围麻醉期的应用研究”。该研究将强迫振荡肺功能测定技术应用于麻醉学、呼吸生理学与心脏外科学的跨学科研究。提出成人心内直视手术围麻醉期振荡法呼吸力学参数值的变化范围及规律、不同频率相位角回归预计值方程。建立围麻醉期呼吸力学研究和评价的新方法，该方法除适用于心脏外科围麻醉期的肺保护研究和常规监测外，尚可应用于危重病和各种需要进行呼吸功能评价的场合。该方法操作简单、设备费用低廉、对病人无任何伤害，可以量化评价气道、肺和胸部组织的粘性、弹性和惯性阻力的瞬间变化，并直接指示病变关键部位，特别是对小气道病变和肺充血的早期诊断有明显的优点。2001年，胸科医院和天津市心血管病研究所赵连云、王惠芬、魏浩成、张国春等运用强迫振荡阻力测定法于临床的肺功能检测。首先提出阻塞性呼吸系统疾病气道阻塞部位，肺组织顺应性变化的典型频谱表现；哮喘疾病的诊断及疗效评估优于传统方法；胸腔内外肿物导致上气道阻力与胸廓惯性阻力的独特频谱表现；限制性疾病气道阻力及顺应性典型表现；心外手术围麻醉期肺保护评估指标及预计回归方程；儿童呼吸道疾病鉴别诊断。该技术操作简便、快速，无禁忌症。

2004年，总医院王国林等在“氯胺酮作用机理及临床应用新途径研究”中，对传统的静脉麻醉药氯胺酮在超前镇痛的临床和药代动力学、药物相互作用及抗炎作用等方面的机制进行较为深入的研究。从细胞水平研究发现25微摩尔/升以上氯胺酮对脂多糖（LPS）刺激内皮细胞黏附分子-1（ICAM-1）表达和核转录因子-κB（NF-κB）易位、甲酰甲硫氨酰-亮氨酰-苯丙氨酸（FMLP）刺激白细胞CD11b表达和白细胞与内皮细胞黏附具有抑制作用，而N-甲基天门冬氨酸非特异性拮抗剂（代号MK-801）不具备上述抗炎作用，即氯胺酮在内皮细胞、白细胞及其相互作用水平发挥抗炎作用，且该作用并非由N-甲基天门冬氨酸（NMDA）受体介导。对佐剂关节炎大鼠模型观察证明氯胺酮可降低大鼠热痛敏，抑制关节炎引发的下丘脑和脑干一氧化氮/鸟苷酸环化酶（cGMP）含量增高，干预NO/cGMP信号转导。临床观察中，等辐射分析法显示氯胺酮和异丙酚在麻醉诱导的催眠、麻醉末点呈相加作用，复合应用后血流动力学更加稳定。术前静脉或硬膜外应用亚麻醉剂量氯胺酮明显增加术中、术后镇痛效果，减少阿片类药物用量，降低术后视觉模拟评分（VAS）评分，具有明确的超前镇痛作用，硬膜外给药效果明显优于静脉给药。药代动力学测定证实，亚麻醉剂量氯胺酮硬膜外给药血药有效浓度维持时间长，延长其消除半衰期，为超前镇痛提供理论依据。该项目获2004年度天津市科技进步二等奖。

第十二节 医学检验学

1991～2005年，天津在新型细胞因子研制、大肠杆菌中的高效表达、采用国产试剂建立酶法测定尿酸的新技术等临床医学检验方面取得进步。天津第二医学院医学检验系创建于1984年，是国内第一批成立检验系的院校之一。1994年，原天津第二医学院医学检验系更名为医科大学医学检验学系。

1992年，天津市医药科学所和天津市临床检验中心李明润、帅真、李明和温庭民等完成“尿酸酶制备及其在尿酸测定中的应用”。该研究采用国产试剂建立酶法测定尿酸的新技术，首先以猪肝为原料运用现代生物化学的分离方法，提取出具有生物活性的尿酸酶，对其动力学性质进行研究。同时，对用自制尿酸酶建立酶法测定尿酸的标准化进行考证，结果显示用此酶制成的尿酸测定试剂盒其准确性、精密度、批内与批间变异均满意，经临床应用准确可靠。

1995年，医科大学医学检验学系姚智等利用原核表达系统成功表达人IL-6，并对IL-6进行中试研究，对IL-6、IL-11及INFα2b等细胞因子进行修饰，开展新型细胞因子研制的工作。同时研制10余种细胞因子的单克隆抗体，并在此基础上建立生物学方法，检测体液内或细胞所分泌的细胞因子生物活性。1996年，姚智等完成的“关于经点突变及3’端非编码区修饰的人IL-6基因在大肠杆菌中的高效表达”，该课题从人外周血单个核细胞中克隆出人IL-6cDNA，经过其3’端非编码区修饰后构建hIL-6的表达质粒，并获得大肠杆菌中的高效表达，其表达量、纯化后的纯度、生物学活性等指标均高于国内外水平。

1997年，一中心医院王学谦、吴胜群、张雅敏等完成“反相高效液相色变法测定人血血小板活化因子方法学的研究”。该研究建立的反相高效液相色谱法（RHPLC）测定血小板活化因子（PAF），为临床PAF研究提供分析途径。其RAF标准工作曲线，线性关系良好，相关系数R=0.9997，同一浓度样品批内变异系数CV=1.9%，低、中、高三个浓度PAF平均回收率为81.5%、83.2%、83.8%，与生物经典法对照，测定结果有较好的相关性（r=0.9079）。研究解决RHPLC测定人血PAF实验条件最佳化和确立方法学质量参数等问题，且具有快速、准确、灵敏、重复性好及操作简便等优点。

2000年，天津市内分泌研究所和湖北、福建等省卫生防疫站阎玉芹、刘列钧、张亚平、赵文德等完成“尿碘的砷铈催化分光光度测定方法”的研究。该方法简化尿样消化条件并减少有害物质的释放污染。通过优选测试条件，拓宽检测范围，提高检测的精密度、准确度和灵敏度，使最低检测浓度达到5微克/升，检出碘量为1纳克。同时，提高方法的抗干扰能力，该方法已在全国广泛应用。

第十三节 护理学

1991～2005年，天津积极致力于护理学的科学研究，加强国际护理研究的合作和探索，在儿童护理、老年护理、妇产科护理、社区护理、护理教育和肿瘤护理等方面不断取得进展。医科大学（原天津医学院）于1983年在全国解放后首先恢复五年制本科高等护理教育，建立护理学院。1994年，医科大学护理学院在全国首批获得硕士学位授予权。1996年，国家教育部批准成立中国高等护理教育学会，医科大学护理学院为常设机构。

1991年，天津医学院护理学院马荫楠、李淑文等对儿童医院血液科门诊一例白血病患儿病情恶化后进行临终关怀。该患儿在治疗4年半的时间后，病情恶化，研究者对该患儿及其父母进行临终关怀。该个案报告是临终关怀引入国内后，对一例患儿及其家庭进行具体实施临终关怀而取得的宝贵经验的总结。

1991～1993年，天津医学院护理学院马荫楠、李淑文等与美国加州大学护理学院马丁森合作，对肿瘤医院儿科病房一例13岁晚期卵巢癌患儿及其父母进行临终关怀，研究忧伤辅导在学龄儿童临终前提高生存质量的作用以及独生子女临终关怀中家庭解组与重组。其研究结果受到马丁森的高度评价，马丁森推荐了马荫楠参加东南亚地区临终关怀会议。

1996年,医科大学护理学院(以下简称"医大护理院")李文霞等完成"儿童社会生活能力及其影响因素的研究"。结果表明儿童社会生活能力的发展不平衡,与家庭,尤其父母的素质和教养方式对儿童社会生活能力的形成与发展有重大影响。

1996年,医大护理院王春梅等完成中加合作项目"天津市初级卫生保健人员工作情况调查与分析"。结果显示全市初级卫生保健人员的基本情况和工作状况,并对未来初级卫生保健人员的培养和发展提出建设性意见。同年,王席伟等在完成"中国孕产妇围产期教育的研究"中,对天津地区孕产妇围产期教育现状进行调查,该研究结果表明孕产妇围产期教育可以提高孕妇自我预防、自我保健的意识和围产期保健指标。

1999~2000年,医大护理院王席伟完成"妇女围绝经期身心护理研究"。对天津市新兴街600名40~60岁妇女绝经及其影响因素进行调查,结果表明围绝经期症状与年龄、职业、教育程度、月经初潮有关;对绝经期妇女进行以健康教育为主的护理干预措施,研究结果表明对围绝经期妇女实施护理干预可减轻其心理问题和躯体症状,并且确定在社区开展围绝经期干预的可行性,为妇女保健工作提出指导性意见。

2002年,医大护理院王春梅在完成"Neuman系统模式在社区护理工作中的应用"研究中,对天津市和平区354名老年人生活质量调查分析,阐述社区卫生服务的重点,建立和完善老年人医疗保健和社会养老保障体系,把提高和改善社区老年人生活质量作为社区卫生服务的主要目标。

2002年,医大护理院商澄、孙荣、张清等在"护理干预对提高哮喘患儿家庭管理能力作用的研究"中,该研究以寻求护理干预对提高哮喘患儿家庭管理能力的作用为目的,研究结果显示:采用适当的护理干预对哮喘患儿家庭管理能力的提高具有十分重要的意义。

2003年,医大护理院王席伟开展"对城市居民健康相关行为进行研究"。采用调查问卷方法对天津市和平区新兴街600名城市居民进行调查。掌握城市居民健康相关行为现状,调查表明危险行为广泛存在,必须引起高度重视,对城市居民健康促进工作提供科学依据。

2003年,医科大学与日本早稻田大学合作开展"中国社区老年健康教育干预效果研究",医大护理院刘纯艳等在王顶堤社区医院等单位开展健康普查和问卷调查,采用预防医学手段,提高社区老年人的自我保健意识,省去一些高额的医疗费用,受到社区老年人的欢迎。同年,刘纯艳主持与美国密执根大学在"SUSAN G. KOMEN乳腺癌基金会"的支持下进行"通过国际合作性护理干预促进中国妇女乳腺癌的早期发现"项目的研究。该项目以讲课、模型训练等方式对目标人群进行干预,显著提高妇女的乳腺自检意识。

第三章 预防医学与公共卫生

1991~2005年,天津市卫生防病体制进行两次重大改革。1994年,天津医学院与天津第二医学院合并组建医科大学,并成立医科大学公共卫生学院。2000年起,按照国家卫生监督与防病体制改革的要求,天津市卫生防病中心、天津市食品卫生监督检验所、天津市劳动卫生职业病研究所、天津市职业病防治院、天津市结核病控制中心、天津市健康教育所等6单位先后合并,组建新的天津市卫生防病中心(以下简称"市防病中心")。2003年,经天津市"非典"防治领导小组第22次会议和23次市长办公会批准,总投资1.6亿元的市防病中心扩建工程立项并施工,其扩建后的总建筑面积3.9万平方米。

天津市预防医学取得令人瞩目的成就。在传染病的防控上,不仅对复发的"老传染病"研究出新的防控与治疗措施和方法,而且对新出现的甚至是突发性的传染病也得到及时控制与有效治疗。对非传染病的防控研究范围进一步扩大,由"老四病"发展到"新四病",其防控方法亦有新发现,尤其对糖尿病的研究取得多项成果。

这一时期，天津市对公共卫生研究的广度与深度都有提升。在劳动卫生、饮水卫生、少儿妇幼卫生、卫生检验方法与标准，以及病媒与消毒、健康教育等方面，都有既十分重要又与日常生活息息相关的科技成果呈现。对营养与食品卫生的研究是天津市预防医学发展中的重要特色。不仅关注居民的营养与健康状况，还将食物中微量物质对人体的作用与需求量进行深入研究，对一些应限量的物质给出其合理的摄入量，对某些食物的营养机制研究，从细胞层次到分子层次寻根溯源，探究营养物的作用机理。

第一节 传染病防控

20世纪80年代后期，肺结核、性病、乙型及丙型病毒性肝炎等这些在天津已被控制的传染病病种又呈发展趋势。90年代，天津先后发现或证实的新发传染病或病原体有艾滋病、传染性非典型肺炎、军团菌病、禽流感、庚型肝炎、猫抓病、莱姆病等，传染病的预防和控制形势十分严峻。1999年，天津首次从病人和水产品中监测出O_{139}群霍乱弧菌。2001年，天津又从牛、羊肉和其粪便中监测出O_{157}:H_7出血性大肠杆菌。

市防病中心郝洪起、杜殿军、冯洪友等完成“传染病发病趋势预测预报方法的研究”。该方法实用性、科学性强，准确性高。该成果达到国际先进水平，获1991年度天津市科技进步二等奖。

天津市于20世纪60年代初开始儿童疫苗的免疫接种工作，20世纪70年代末制定《天津市预防接种实施细则》，全面实行计划免疫，并将流脑、乙脑疫苗纳入计划免疫。20世纪80年代，开展脊髓灰质炎强化免疫活动，同时开展疫苗质量、免疫效果和人群免疫状况的监测，并建立常规免疫、麻疹、新生儿破伤风、儿童乙肝等监测系统。90年代，制定《天津市计划免疫督导方案》，组织专业人员定期对基层卫生院和区县卫生防病站开展计划免疫督导检查。1998年制定《天津市计划免疫档案管理要求》，促进各级计划免疫工作规范管理。同年结合天津市乙型肝炎和风疹流行状况，将乙肝疫苗和风疹疫苗纳入计划免疫管理。1999年，天津市将甲肝、流感、流行性出血热疫苗作为重点人群接种的疫苗，其后又在全市推广使用流行性腮腺炎疫苗、水痘疫苗、流感嗜血杆菌疫苗(Hib)等安全、有效的疫苗。2002年10月1日，乙肝疫苗正式纳入儿童计划免疫，成为首批将乙肝疫苗正式纳入儿童计划免疫的省市。通过开展计划免疫，减少了传染病的发生、致残和死亡，疫苗相关传染病的控制工作取得显著成绩。

一、结核病防控

天津市结核病防治所成立于1955年，1993年更名为天津市结核病控制中心。2002年，该中心又整建制并入天津市疾病预防控制中心。经过几代结核病防治专业人员的不懈努力，不断研究并采用先进的结核病控制技术和措施，使全市结核病防控取得优异成绩。

1993年，天津市结核病控制中心王撷秀等完成“天津市结核病控制工作模式的研究”，创造“专家技术策划、领导行政推动、机构组织实施、社会人群参与”的工作模式，首次提出结核病防治工作的技术性、行政性和社会性，并将此三性有机结合，为天津市结核病控制在全国保持领先水平做出贡献。该项研究于1998年获国际结核病与肺部疾病联合会(IUATLD)颁发的国际贡献奖证书。1993年，王撷秀等研发出“天津市结核病控制微机网络管理系统”，对全市结核病进行微机控制，实现信息的快速录入、查询、检索、统计分析，可节省手工成本，消除手工统计的误差。

1996年，王撷秀完成“农村地区初级卫生保健与现代结核病控制实施性研究”，明确提出农村结核病有新的发展趋势，将农村地区结核病控制工作纳入初级卫生保健，创建一整套标准化、规范化、制度化的工作体系。此后，天津市各级政府开始把初级保健与结核病防治工作纳入政府工作日程。

2000年，天津市和国际结核病与肺部疾病联合会合作完成“肺结核间歇化疗方案的研究(studyA)”，在国内首次将两种间歇化疗方案的治疗效果同国内现有的化疗方案治疗效果进行对照，研究表明间歇化疗方案可减少肺结核病人治疗过程中的药物副作用，降低治疗费用。2001年，市防病中心成为IUATLD在中国设立的第一家合作临床研究中心。2002年和2004年，王撷秀先后当选为亚洲第一位IUATLD副主席和主席。天津市逐步走向结核病控制的国际舞台。

二、性病与艾滋病防控

1993年，市防病中心朱效科、徐桂华、沈宗林等与市公安局科研人员合作，开展对收教的卖淫嫖娼人群进行性病和艾滋病检测、监测和诊治。1994年，市防病中心朱效科、张辉与中国预防医学科学院郑锡文等合作，在天津完成中国第一个艾滋病哨点监测，探索艾滋病高危人群的哨点监测模式。卫生部于1995年向全国推广并实施开展艾滋病的哨点监测。1994～1995年，朱效科等多次到河北省廊坊地区，对天津市血液中心和一中心医院等单位报告的艾滋病病毒(HIV)感染者进行现场流行病学调查，并采血进行复核和确认。首次发现农民商业献血人员中HIV的感染者，并完成现场流行病学的诊断报告，为国家对艾滋病防治提供了重要的决策依据。1995年，市防病中心朱效科、陈宝起、孔立等与市戒毒所张广福等合作，开展对戒毒人群的HIV和梅毒的不定期监测和检测，对戒毒人群的性病、艾滋病防治提供了重要依据。

1995年，由国家艾滋病参比实验室批准的天津市第一家艾滋病确认中心实验室成立。该实验室由政府投资、世界卫生组织及欧盟资助近300万元，其硬件设施处于国内同行业领先地位，接近发达国家同级实验室规模，其出具的检测报告得到卫生部及世界卫生组织专业部门认可。1997年，市委、市政府批准组建的全市第一个性病艾滋病预防和控制机构——天津市性传播疾病控制中心成立。其负责全市艾滋病性病监测、防治及与控制有关政策的制定实施，以及全市有关部门与医疗单位的艾滋病及重点性传播疾病技术鉴定等。1998年，由世界卫生组织资助、卫生部认定的天津市性病艾滋病咨询热线由联合国艾滋病规划署和世界卫生组织向全球公布，每年接待咨询电话5000余次，成为对外普及艾滋病知识和开展宣传教育的一个重要窗口。1998年12月1日，天津市性传播疾病控制中心门诊开诊，对求医者开展诊断治疗。

2000年，市防病中心郑钟洁、朱效科与天津市工人医院科技人员合作完成“女性下腹痛征处理的研究”。该研究发现，性病病原体是引起盆腔炎的重要病原体，淋病双球菌、沙眼衣原体、人型支原体和厌氧菌均为导致盆腔炎的病原体，因此治疗盆腔炎不应使用单一抗生素，而要使用广谱抗生素联合疗法。这为缺少实验室检测的地区治疗盆腔炎提供了一个有效的治疗方案。2002年，该中心艾滋病性病实验室通过国家实验室认可，开展关于衣原体培养试验、HIV病毒载量试验的探索。2003年，该中心朱效科、董笑月、宁铁琳等组织实施全市性病门诊就诊患者的HIV流行病学调查和血清监测，并开展对吸毒人群HIV流行情况的专项调查和检测。同时，宁铁琳在全市首次开展对艾滋病人的CD4/CD8淋巴细胞亚群的检测项目，参与并接受美国和中国国家实验室提供标准样品的比对试验，并通过考核。2004年，该中心在全市范围内开展艾滋病防控工作现状评估，约1080个城乡居民接收该项评估调查，并参与起草、制定包括艾滋病免费检测和免费抗病毒治疗等一系列具体的方案措施。同时，市防病中心开展对吸毒人群HIV流行情况及行为学的系统调查，初步掌握全市吸毒人群HIV流行现状和特点，为开展有针对性的控制措施提供了科学依据。

2005年，该中心起草《天津市〈艾滋病疫情网络专报〉实施补充规定》，全市艾滋病网络直报全面启动。年内，起草《天津市艾滋病病毒感染者和艾滋病病人管理意见》《天津市艾滋病职业暴露应急预案》《天津市艾滋病抗病毒治疗和自愿咨询检测实施方案》等一系列艾滋病防治工作的相关文件，为全市的艾滋病防治工作提供了依据。同年，朱效科、王栩冬、刘东等完成以“以高危人群为主，严把采供血关”的50万人群监测工作。建立10个市级“哨点”对性病门诊就诊者、暗娼、吸毒者、结核病人、孕产妇、远洋船员、术前输血患者等7类人群开展HIV哨点监测工作。在和平区、塘沽区、东丽区和汉沽区开展对商业性工作者的行为学干预试点工作，对其开展宣传教育、发放安全套等干预工作，提高该人群的自我保护意识。

三、肝炎防控

1988年，天津医学院卫生系来则民等通过对1200名献血人员乙型肝炎病毒感染状态进行研究，发现其抗-HBs乙肝阳性率为29.08%，研究结果建议尽快使用敏感性高、特异性强的酶联免疫吸附法或放射免疫测定法等检测技术代替反向间接血凝法，以减少经输血后传播乙型肝炎的危险；通过对天津地区乙肝病人和HbsAg(乙肝表面抗源)携带者HDV(丁型肝炎病毒感染者)首次进行血清学研究，发现其抗-HDV阳性率为9.73%，研究结果表明HDV感染的发生与年龄、性别无关，在人群中呈散发和均匀分布，且感染市区高于农村，鉴于天津市有较高的HDV感染率，应引起有关方面的高度重视；通过对3269名大学新生的乙型肝炎Ⅱ型(HB_2)感染情况进行调查，结果发现HBV_2感染率为1.5%，并首次报告中国HBV_2在HBsAg携带者中的比例为18.3%，研究发现HBV_2阳性率与当地人群HBsAg阳性率呈显著正相关，而与当地人群抗-HBs阳性率无关，该结果为进一步研究HBV_2的发生对乙型肝炎病毒的传播以及乙肝疫苗的效果评价具有重要的指导意义。

20世纪90年代初期，天津市病毒性肝炎疫情实行分型报告管理，在甲、乙和非甲非乙型肝炎的基础上，增加丙型和戊型肝炎。1997年，市防病中心范殿英等采用国际标准试剂对乙型肝炎Ⅱ型病毒(HBV2)进行流行病学及临床研究，在国内首次发现HBV2可引起输血后肝炎，并发现乙型肝炎表面抗体阳性不能阻断HBV2。

1996～1998年，市防病中心单爱兰等对重组酵母基因乙肝疫苗在不同人群中血清学免疫效果进行研究。结果显示，在阻断乙肝母婴垂直传播方面，5微克和10微克疫苗的免疫保护率分别为72.22%和88.63%，5微克疫苗对HBsAg(乙肝病毒表面抗原)阴性母亲所生新生儿的免疫应答：抗—HBs(乙肝病毒表面抗体)阳性率90.6%，高中(职专)学生的抗—HBs阳性率为100%。同期，单爱兰等对甲肝疫苗接种人群的甲肝抗体水平进行现状调查。经36573人年观察，结果表明：全市儿童甲肝疫苗接种率10岁以下(不包括10岁)达45%左右，10～19岁组16.5%，20岁以上各年龄组近于零；抗—HAVIgG(甲肝病毒中和抗体)阳性率分别为30.66%、49.40%和82.01%，仍然显现出抗—HAVIgG阳性率随年龄的增高而增加的规律；而19岁以下的儿童甲肝人年发病率为14.90/10万，明显低于20～29岁组(28.79/10万)。

2005年，单爱兰等经对1～59岁人群乙肝感染指标的血清流行病学监测，表明全人群抗-HBs携带率为2.61%，5岁以下儿童为0.95%，从血清学角度体现出天津市对乙肝的控制措施有力，效果佳。同年，全市甲型肝炎报告发病率为0.87/10万，首次低于1/10万以下，为全国最低，可望得以持续。

四、非典型肺炎防控

2003年，传染性非典型肺炎(SARS)传入天津。一个月内，确诊175例SARS病患者，死亡严重，对社会威胁极大。市防病中心及时封锁集中收治SARS病例的武警医学院附属医院，市防病中心主任王撷秀亲临现场进行专业指挥、指导，并组织开展SARS的流行病学研究。天津市疫情成为流行期最短、解除“禁区”最快的地区。

2003年8月至2004年10月，天津市卫生局局长张愈主持，由市卫生局、武警医学院附属医院、市传染病医院、市海河医院、市防病中心、天津中医学院及市胸科医院等单位田惠光、李玉明、曹武奎、张伯礼、王撷秀等共同进行“天津市SARS患者流行病学回顾性调查和健康随访与干预试验研究”。该研究分三期对SARS患者进行SARS-CoV特异性抗体免疫球蛋白G检测(IgG)，发现原临床确诊患者中抗体阳性率为99.34%，临床疑似者中抗体阳性率为87.5%，临床观察病例为45.95%，抗体总阳

图7-3-1-111 天津市SARS患者流行病学回顾性调查和随访研究成果

性率为88.64%。三期随访的抗体动态检查发现，IgG抗体水平出现下降趋势，并且个别患者抗体开始转阴。在随访研究中，对随访患者的生理、病理和心理及体征变化等进行跟踪和评价，建立随访的数据库，为SARS的深入研究提供了有价值的信息资源。该项研究获2005年度天津市科技进步一等奖。

五、流感防控

2001年，市防病中心作为中国-WHO流感（H1N1）监测项目主要完成单位之一，在儿童医院和二中心医院设立国家级流感监测点，开展流行季的流行病学和病原学监测。2003年和2004年又先后增设三中心医院、南开区黄河道医院和津南区咸水沽医院，并于2004年率先在中国北方片区开展全年监测，逐步建立健全区级监测点，形成以哨点医院为基础，覆盖天津各区县的流感监测网络。该网络在检测流感的流行毒株、掌握流感疫情动态、监测毒株活动变化规律、防控人禽流感扩散等方面起到重要作用。

2005年，市防病中心孔梅等在天津地区流感病毒分子流行病学和致病性的研究中，对所分离的流感病毒进行HA（血凝素）基因变异分析及流感病毒对MDCK（狗肾传代细胞）、Hela细胞毒性分析，首次从分子水平揭示出天津市流感病毒的变异特点和规律，建立SSCP（单链构象多态性分析）方法，用于筛查流感病毒代表株，并证实天津市2003～2004年流行的甲3亚型流感病毒抗原性发生变异，其致MDCK细胞凋亡能力强于乙型流感病毒。

六、恙虫病防控

1996年，市防病中心张之伦、丁建清、郝连义在天津市恙虫病研究中，采用细胞分离培养、恙螨鉴定、荧光抗体等技术，从天津不同地理环境鼠体表面采集螨类并进行病原分离和鉴定，研究结果为恙虫病自然疫源性变迁由中国长江以南至长江以北提供了依据，否定了传染病学教科书所说的恙虫病系长江以南地区发生的自然疫源性疾病的论点，揭示出中国恙虫病疫源地的变迁趋势。同时，经对自然疫源地调查，首次摸清天津恙虫病的传播途径是通过病媒昆虫叮咬传播，证明天津存在恙虫病。

七、出血热防控

2005年，市防病中心丁建清、田永琴、王书梅等在天津市媒介动物自然感染肾综合征出血热病毒的研究中，首次从社鼠中分离到出血热病毒，并揭示出雌雄鼠类、季节、鼠种与出血热发病的关系。

第二节　非传染病防控

1991年前，天津市对非传染性疾病进行群防群治，尤其对高血压、冠心病、脑卒中、恶性肿瘤（简称“老四病”）开展大量防控与实验研究。1991年起，天津市重点在高血压、脑卒中的控制与干预以及糖尿病发病危险因素研究等方面取得进展。1989～1998年，天津市卫生局等单位对慢性病防治项目进行卫生经济学评价研究。根据卫生资源、人力投入、健康生存年及患者年医疗费用的关系计算投入产出比，结果显示在天津市慢性病防治工作中投入1元可产生4.7元的经济效益。2000年起，天津市将非传染病防控研究深入到基因层次，从分子水平探究肿瘤细胞凋亡机制，探讨糖尿病发病的危险因素。

2004年，市防病中心对天津地区疾病谱进行分析，确定将糖尿病、精神疾病、意外伤害和肝硬化（简称“新四病”）纳入全市疾病监测体系之中。2005年1月，市防病中心将其营养与食品卫生学部、慢性病预防与控制学部、学校卫生学部整合，成立非传染性疾病预防控制研究所。同年6月，开始对全市“新四病”发病情况进行监测。

一、高血压与脑卒中防控

1991年，市卫生局组织天津市卫生防病中心、市心血管病研究所于世北、宋桂德、崔荣慧等，对“老四病”人群开展健康户口动态监测，每两年进行一次居民食盐摄入量调查，并在部分社区开展控制高血压、预防脑卒中的干预活动，结果显示控制血压可显著降低脑卒中的死亡率。

1991年起，天津市劳动卫生研究所王援相等在非传染四病与职业因素的关系研究中，对塘沽盐厂职工进行高钠膳食人群与高血压关系的研究，对同一地区两个人群9570名职工高血压患病率进行调查，并通过现岗、离岗工人死亡回顾调查和膳食调查，探索高钠膳食与高血压的关系。同时，进行限制高血压病例及正常血压者食盐摄入量试验。这是在国内高钠膳食盐业工人中进行的首次食盐干预试验。结果提示，露天作业重体力盐工的酱油、咸菜及食盐三者每日食盐总摄入量在10克以下，可以达到降压效果。

二、肿瘤防控

2000年，市防病中心宋桂德、黄浩云、李芮等开展以肿瘤为代表的流行病学地理信息系统研究，在天津市死亡统计资料和环境地理信息系统的基础上，将天津市2000年的肿瘤死亡数据应用地理信息系统（GIS），对肿瘤死亡的流行状况按街道进行数字化地理信息分析，建立起一套可应用的计算方法和直观的肿瘤地理流行病学图像，能被广泛应用在疫情发布、卫生信息分析工作中。该研究也为开展其他慢性病地理流行病学研究奠定了基础。

2004年，医科大学公共卫生学院俞鸣在“肿瘤细胞对肿瘤坏死因子相关凋亡诱导配体（TRAIL）的耐药机制”研究中，发现低浓度凋亡相关蛋白（Bcl-2）抑制剂虽然本身无法诱发凋亡，但可起到线粒体呼吸链解偶联作用，从而协同TRAIL诱导凋亡的作用。BH3结构域拟似物（BH3I-2'）、Bcl-2小分子配体2-乙基-6氨基-4-溴（1-氰-2-乙氧-2表乙）-4-色原烯-3酸（HA14-1）具有与经典解偶联剂羰基氰化物间氯苯腙（CCCP）相似的功能，即消耗线粒体跨膜电位、产生活性氧（ROS）、增加氧消耗、抑制ATP的合成等。这种解偶联作用可通过线粒体途径协同TRAIL诱导耐药细胞凋亡的作用，并当半胱氨酸蛋白水解酶（Caspase）被抑制后，可引起细胞坏死现象的出现。该研究首次发现解偶联作用可有效克服细胞对TRAIL诱导凋亡的抵抗。

三、糖尿病防控

1997年，医科大学公共卫生学院焦振山等进行“复合元素酵母防治糖尿病及高脂血症的研究”，通过动物实验，探讨复合铬、锌、硒元素的酵母对糖尿病及高脂血症的作用。研究结果发现，复合元素酵母对糖尿病、高脂血症有明显的预防和治疗作用，其可降低空腹及餐后血糖水平，并明显降低血清胆固醇及甘油三酯水平。

1998年，该院王建华等在“二型糖尿病及其常见并发症的危险因素研究”中，发现20余个危险因素，如高血压、不良应激事件、肥胖和高血脂等，并计算出各因素的相对危险度和归因危险度。同年，该院马骏等完成“非胰岛素依赖型糖尿病继发冠心病的社会心理因素研究”，对非胰岛素依赖型糖尿病（NIDDM）继发冠心病（CHD）病例进行配比病例对照研究，探讨社会心理因素与糖尿病继发冠心病的关系。通过条件Logistic回归分析，发现不良应激事件可增加患者继发的危险性，建议保持良好的心理平衡，对生活中不可避免的一些应激事件采取积极应付策略，对NIDDM继发CHD及其他心身疾病的预防和控制都有积极意义。2001年，马骏对按WHO诊断标准确诊的102例二型糖尿病病人进行1:1配比病例对照研究，采用logistic回归分析方法处理资料。结果显示，胰岛素抵抗与二型糖尿病发病有关，是二型糖尿病发病的独立危险因素。

1999年，医科大学焦振山在“糖尿病膳食指南和个体饮食计划的研究”中，测定常见单一及混合食物的血糖生成指数，通过血糖指数来指导糖尿病人合理地选择食物，建立个性化饮食方案，避免因食物选择不合理而造成血糖控制不利。

2001年，医科大学吴蕴棠等开展“锌铬硒对糖尿病大鼠相关基因表达影响的研究”，结果表明：糖尿病大鼠糖、脂代谢紊乱，氧化与抗氧化系统平衡失调及基因表达发生改变。经补充锌、铬、硒后，使糖尿病大鼠糖、脂代谢紊乱得到改善，提高抗氧化能力，而且锌和硒的作用优于铬，三者之间未见明显协同作用。应用信使核糖核酸(mRNA)差异显示技术，分离到差异显示的互补脱氧核糖核酸(cDNA)片段，提示锌、铬、硒对糖尿病大鼠某些基因的表达产生诱导或抑制作用，其可能与糖尿病大鼠代谢紊乱有关。

2002年，王建华在国家自然科学基金项目“妊娠糖尿病的筛查及其危险因素和易感基因研究”中，了解到天津市和河北省承德地区的妊娠糖尿病(GDM)发病率，探讨GDM的危险因素及其对母婴的影响，运用聚合酶链反应—单链构象多态性分析(PCR-SSCP)和聚合酶链反应-限制性片断长度多态性(PCR-RFLP)技术检测葡萄糖基酶(GCK)基因和细胞毒性T淋巴细胞抗原(CTLA-4)基因突变情况，通过巢式病例对照研究方法，探讨基因突变与GDM之间的联系。这在当时属国内大样本、大范围的GDM发病情况的流行病学比较研究。结果发现：初孕年龄大、有经产史和糖尿病家族史、孕前BMI(身高体重指数)高是GDM的独立危险因素；并阐明CTLA-4外显子1和启动子核苷酸变异、GCK外显子7突变均增加GDM发生的危险。此项研究达到国际先进水平。2005年，王建华等在“天津市二型糖尿病、常见并发症及其分类的流行病学特点研究”中，总结出天津市二型糖尿病并发肺结核病近10余年的发展变化趋势，糖尿病并发肺结核病的危险因素，包括环境因素和遗传因素以及两种因素的交互作用，为糖尿病和肺结核病的预防和控制提供了科学依据。

2005年，医科大学齐秀英承担国家自然科学基金项目“成人隐匿性自身免疫性糖尿病人群患病率及危险因素研究”。该项目研究对象共8109人，二型糖尿病(T2DM)498人，患病率为6.14%，其中成人隐匿性自身免疫性糖尿病(LADA)46人，患病率为0.57%，LADA在T2DM患者中比例为9.24%。LADA与T2DM临床特点分析显示：LADA患者注射胰岛素的比例高于T2DM患者，LADA患者平均收缩压和极低密度脂蛋白胆固醇水平均低于T2DM患者。危险因素分析结果表明：年龄、腰臀比、糖尿病家族史、不按时三餐和精神创伤是LADA发生的危险因素，而鱼类摄入是LADA发生的保护因素。1∶2配比病例对照研究，未发现血清柯萨奇B组病毒(CBV)IgM抗体和IgG抗体与LADA之间有统计学联系。LADA患者的CTLA-4基因启动子318位点C-T变异和外显子1第49位点A-G变异的频率高于T2DM对照和非DM对照；分别与T2DM对照和非DM对照比较，logistic回归分析结果显示，CTLA-4基因启动子318位点C-T变异和外显子1第49位点A-G变异均增加发生LADA的危险性。

是年，吴蕴棠等在“锌、硒调节糖尿病糖、脂代谢紊乱的分子机制”的研究中发现，与糖尿病对照组相比，硒可分别上调、下调糖尿病大鼠蛋白磷酸酶2A(PP2A)、磷脂酶D (PLD)的mRNA表达水平，锌可上调PP2A的mRNA表达水平，受锌、硒调控的两个外源基因在肝细胞内表达后，对糖代谢某些关键酶的蛋白表达产生不同影响。研究结果提示，锌、硒对于糖尿病糖、脂代谢紊乱的调节机制之一可能是以PP2A、PLD为介导，通过作用于胰岛素信号传导途径来完成。另一机制可能是作用于胰岛素信号传导体系之外的生物学靶点，以调节糖代谢中某些关键酶的蛋白表达水平来完成。该研究结果为利用营养素预防和控制二型糖尿病的发生与发展提供了理论依据和实验基础，为进一步研究营养素与糖尿病的关系提供了有益线索和研究新思路。

是年，医科大学俞鸣等在“糖尿病肢端神经微血管病变分子流行病学研究”中，指出影响糖尿病肢端神经微血管并发症发生的危险因素，发现血管内皮生长因子(VEGF)及神经生长因子(NGF)等生长因子在该并发症发生、发展过程中的重要作用，即VEGF在糖尿病肢端神经微血管并发症早期表达增加，而NGF表达减少。该研究还明确复合元素酵母对于糖尿病肢端神经微血管病变的防治作用和可能的机理，为控制或延缓糖尿病肢端神经微血管并发症的发生，控制或减少危险因素，并监控患者体内VEGF、NGF等生长因子的水平，对该病的早期发现及延缓发生有指导意义。

第三节 卫生学

1991～2005年，天津市在卫生学的研究方面取得进展。劳动卫生方面，侧重对在劳动中引起相关疾病的职业性危害因素——铅、磷、二噁英、放射线等进行相关研究，并取得可喜成绩；饮水卫生方面，侧重对饮用水水质监测、消毒、降氟、限铝等问题的研究，成效显著；针对儿童、少年生长发育及其常见病防治、学习环境监测开展研究，不断提高儿童、少年卫生水平；产妇卫生方面，着重对弓形虫问题及产后抑郁症的预防对策开展研究；卫生毒理方面，探讨牛磺酸抗癌作用机理、发现骨髓造血干细胞对铅的敏感性；在卫生检验方法研究中，建立e抗体检测、二噁英生物检测体系等；为防止职业病的发生，制定出多项职业卫生标准；在杀灭苍蝇、蚊子、跳蚤等病媒及消毒杀菌作用的研究上取得新进展；通过对健康教育的研究与知识普及，提高健康理念，降低脑卒中病死率及一些职业危害因素对健康造成的损害。

一、劳动卫生

(一)铅

1991年，天津医学院卫生系刘志敏等应用维生素B_1驱铅实验方法，观察到维生素B_1有驱铅作用。1991年后，天津市劳动卫生研究所(以下简称“市劳研所”)刘昶庭、周启玲等针对有害职业因素对女性生殖机能及子代健康影响进行研究。在铅作业产妇血铅浓度与胎儿水平关系的研究中，通过研究18例铅作业女工及胎儿不同组织部位中铅的水平，并1:1与对照组配对分析比较，结果表明：铅对女工及子代确有影响，铅不仅能通过胎盘传递给胎儿，并在胎盘组织中有一定的蓄积。

1996年，市劳研所在“铅对仔鼠行为功能影响的实验研究”中，见到母鼠血铅水平低于50微克/分升的情况下，仔鼠发生行为功能异常。经电镜超微结构显示，仔鼠中枢神经系统损伤是行为异常的病理基础。

(二)磷

2004年，由国家环保总局和卫生部牵头，市劳研所王延让、杨雪莹、李建国等获得世界银行加拿大信托基金支持项目，主要研究滴滴涕对中国妇女儿童健康的影响，通过流行病学调查和实验室检测相结合的方法，了解到企业生产及企业附近儿童及其母的状况，同时检测环境样品和生物样品中DDT的蓄积水平。首次在国内外建立生物样品中微量DDT的测定，初步评估DDT对中国妇女和儿童健康的影响，为国家履行《斯德哥尔摩公约》而制定国家实施方案提供了参考依据。该项目研究结论由中国政府向世界公布。

(三)二噁英

1998年，医科大学公共卫生学院曹树义等在“职业接触二噁英人群健康效应的研究”中，通过检测接触二噁英人群的皮肤、尿、免疫功能、神经行为功能及车间二噁英浓度，在国内首次较全面地评价职业接触二噁英人群的健康效应，为厂矿、环保部门提供了可靠的数据和方法。

2005年，该院汤乃军等在国家自然科学基金项目“职业暴露二噁英致氯痤疮发病机理探索性研究”中，初步探讨可能在氯痤疮发病过程中发挥重要作用的AhR、CYP1A1、GSTA1、c-fos和TGF-α mRNA等基因的表达状态，蛋白磷酸化信号转导途径中酪氨酸激酶、有丝分裂原激活蛋白激酶活性的表达，以及角蛋白17、角质形成细胞转谷氨酰酶在表皮层表达分布和表达量的改变，研究指标在氯痤疮组和对照组间差别显著，为二噁英诱发氯痤疮发病机制的研究提供了理论依据。

(四)放射线

2002年，市防病中心商迎庆等在“天津海关集装箱和检查系统放射防护评价研究”中，以国际公认的辐射防护三原则为基准，对天津海关的集装箱检查系统进行放射防护设计与评价，在国内首次提出的防护设计和评价方法,可作为制订标准和法规的重要依据,对海关建立相应检查系统具有参考价值。

2005年,该中心张继勉等在"介入放射学中的辐射剂量控制与应用研究"中,参照国际公认的指标,对临床实行较多且所致辐射剂量较大的冠状动脉造影术及经皮穿刺腔内冠状动脉形成术介入操作中的辐射剂量进行测量,并对影响辐射剂量的相关因素加以分析,建立心血管介入手术剂量系统数据库,达到国内领先水平。

二、环境卫生

(一)饮水卫生

1990年起,天津市对部分区县每年都参加全国农村饮水普查监测。由于天津市农村人口以饮用深井水为主,到2005年,经检测其细菌总数合格率90.20%,大肠菌群合格率为95%。

从1991年开始,市卫生防病中心监测高层建筑二次供水质量,要求每年高层水箱至少要清洗消毒一次,并由取得卫生许可证的专业清洗消毒企业来完成。同时,对市区4大自来水厂每年在枯水期和丰水期对出厂水水质进行监测,项目为全分析。监测结果表明,高层建筑二次供水水质合格率由1991年的85%上升到2000年的98%以上。

1992年,天津医学院刘凤珍等研制出"活性氧化镁降氟剂"。经实验研究表明,其有降低饮水中氟化物的作用。同年,刘凤珍等在"国人铝日允许摄入量"和"饮水铝卫生标准"的研究中,发现铝的过量摄入可引起多方面的损害,包括:铝的蓄积性可引起小鼠脑病理改变,对动物行为造成损害,诱发精子畸形等,建议饮水铝卫生标准为0.2毫克/升。该成果获1992年度天津市科技进步二等奖。

到1995年,天津市仍有11000余人,集中在蓟县北部山区5乡32村)饮用地窖水,水质差且水质波动大。为此,市防病中心刘洪亮等于1996年开展"天津市地窖饮用水卫生现状与对策研究",并研制出简易持续饮水消毒器,用以处理地窖饮用水,使水质合格率由23%提高到100%。

1998年,刘洪亮等开展"引滦水源病原微生物消长规律与控制对策研究",通过调查引滦入津的水污染状况,检测水中细菌、f2噬菌体和隐孢子虫,并分析其变化规律。调查发现,引滦工程明渠受到生活污染,几处倒虹闸在丰水期会出现污水倒灌。此后,天津将引滦工程明渠改为暗渠输水,并重修或改建倒虹闸,基本解决了天津市民饮水污染问题。

2001年,市防病中心刘洪亮等开展"嗜肺军团杆菌的分布规律和分子鉴定技术研究",建立细菌培养后血清学鉴定与半套式聚合酶链式反应技术双阳鉴定用于军团菌的鉴定分型,并以天津为现场,系统研究自然环境和生活环境中嗜肺军团菌的时间、空间分布规律。结果表明,自然水体和空调冷却水军团菌检出率较高,而且在淋浴喷头及喷泉水等与人群生活密切相关水体中均有检出,提示嗜肺军团菌分布广泛,应尽快采取防控措施。

天津市通过改水降氟工程建设,饮水型氟中毒病情明显好转。静海县西翟庄乡东尚码头村8~12岁儿童氟斑牙指数从1991的1.19下降至1999年的0.81,特别是8岁儿童氟斑牙指数从1.22降至0.63,氟斑牙检出率从53.1%降至26.7%。2005年,市防病中心对饮用水氟和降氟改水工程的监测表明,农村地区饮用水氟浓度仍然较高,降氟改水工程的质量中报废工程比例较高,正常或间歇运转工程的主要改水类型是打深井和理化降氟。

(二)食盐加碘工程

1995年起,在全国开展的碘营养监测工作中,医科大学被指定为主要参加碘营养监测单位,对新疆、内蒙、贵州、四川、陕西、江苏、广东、大连市等省市进行碘营养调查。在1995年、1997年、1999年和2002年四次全国范围的碘缺乏病的调查中,医科大学作为全国控制碘缺乏病专家组成员单位之一,参与全民食盐加碘实施后对儿童智力和精神运动改善的评估、尿碘新测试方法的研制、碘盐浓度标准的制定等各项工作。到2000年,全国基本达到消除碘缺乏病的目标。1996年,全国开始实施"全民食盐加碘工程"。天津经过10年5次18个区县的碘缺乏病监测,每次调查涉及30所小学,1200名学生),结果表明:8~10岁儿童甲状腺肿率由1995年32.6%降至2005年1.8%,证明食盐加碘后居民碘营养水平得到普遍提高。监测人群合格碘盐食用率自2002年一直保持在90%以上,达到国家《碘缺乏病消除标准》。天津市8~10岁儿童甲状腺肿率由1995年(干预前)的32.2%降至2005年的1.8%,达到国家控制标准以下;8~10岁儿童尿碘中位数由1995年(干预前)的96.1微克/升,提高至2005年的228.1微克/升,防治效果显著。

天津市经过30多年对地方病的基础防治,特别是2005年经过对"天津市水源性高碘"和"天津市饮用水高氟水源筛查和降氟改水工程质量监督、检测"调查研究,对地方病病种、地区分布、病区类型划分以及基础防治方法、手段与效果都有较明确和深入的了解,积累了大量地方病防治调查监测工作数据。天津市水源性高碘危害调查发现,静海县的14个乡、镇和大港区的1个镇存在水源性高碘问题,涉及人口约43万人,结合地理分布特征及时向政府有关部门建议,向这些地区居民供应食用"非加碘盐"。

三、少儿卫生

(一)生长发育研究

1990年起,天津市每5年参加一次全国性的学生体质调研。数据表明,天津市少年儿童的各项生长发育指标在全国处于中上等水平,各年龄组每10年平均身高增加4.83厘米,体重增加5.35千克,胸围增加1.65厘米,生长发育长期加速现象有加剧的趋势。

1998年,医科大学阎佩琦等开展"天津市小学生儿童多动综合症的调查和干预研究"。该项研究发现母孕期母亲患病史、儿童头部外伤史及不良的家庭教育环境为危险因素,还发现多动综合症的学生身体发育与正常儿童无差异。这是天津较早进行的较大规模的儿童神经行为发育研究。

自2004起,市防病中心每年在全市范围内开展学生生长发育情况监测,及时了解发育状况及其变化规律,逐步加强对盲聋哑等残疾少年儿童生长发育和心理发育的调查。

(二)常见病防治

1992年起,天津市认真贯彻落实卫生部、教育部联合颁布的"学生常见病综合防治规划",以沙眼、视力低下、龋齿、营养不良、肥胖、贫血、蛔虫感染为重点,并按照"全国学生常见病综合防治技术方案"的有关规定,在全市范围内加大对学生常见病的防治力度,开展学生常见病的筛查、诊断和防治,采取有效措施,取得明显成效,多种常见病患病率显著下降。但视力低下仍然是学生中最为高发的常见疾病,在市区和农村均位居第一,且呈快速上升趋势,明确提出应重点加强对学生视力低下的防治,在积极开展用眼卫生宣传、推广眼睛保健操和定期调整学生座位的同时,还应更换可调式课桌椅,改善教室采光照明条件,改造学校教室硬件条件,优化学习环境。

(三)学习环境监测

1991年始,天津市市区各卫生防病站均开展对学生学习生活环境的卫生监测,监测内容包括建筑设施、环境噪声、室内微小气候、采光、照明以及黑板、课桌椅等的设置,通过监测发现不利于学生健康或不符合卫生标准的情况,及时反馈教育行政部门加以改善,以利于促进学生身心的健康发育。根据监测结果及反馈意见,学校对不符合规定之处进行改善,使学生的学习生活环境更科学更合理。2005年监测结果显示,学校环境监测合格率达到80%以上。

四、妇幼卫生

1991年,天津医学院卫生系鲁春起等在承担国家自然科学基金项目"天津地区弓形虫与围产医学的关系"研究中,采用血清学方法调查天津地区产妇弓形虫的感染情况。结果表明,产妇弓形虫感染后存在发生异常孕产(流产、早产、死胎、畸形等)的高度危险性。

2005年,医科大学张欣等在"产后抑郁症的流行病学和预防对策研究"中,提出给产妇的丈夫一定的"产假",鼓励患产后抑郁症的妇女在产后6个月后适当恢复工作等多项产后抑郁症预防的对策,有利于产后抑郁症状的缓解。

五、卫生毒理

1991年成立的天津市化学品毒性检定所，于1997年被农业部首批认证为农药1～2阶段毒性检测单位，2000年并入市防病中心并设立毒理学部。毒理学部是市防病中心下设的学科，主要承担政府、监督部门及客户委托的工业化学品、新化学物质、农药、食品、食品添加剂、转基因食品、化妆品、药类等毒理学检测和评价，以及保健食品和保健用品的安全性与功能性评价工作，同时承担突发事件应急处理中毒物中毒分析及相关毒理学检测等任务。2000年起，毒理学部与南开大学环境科学与环境工程学院合作，对城市回用水进行雌激素活性及致突变性等研究，还承担多项国家、市级和局级科研课题研究，完成多项新技术、新方法的引进与应用。

20世纪90年代初，天津医学院田庆伟等在"稀土在农牧养殖业中应用的安全性毒理学评价"研究中，证实活性氯化稀土、碳酸稀土、氨基酸稀土等稀土新剂型的安全性，对稀土在食品、药品和农业、畜牧养殖业中的应用安全性提供了科学依据。

2002年，医科大学公共卫生学院田庆伟等在"牛磺酸抗诱变抗肿瘤作用及其机理研究"中，着重探讨牛磺酸或高脂饲料对二甲基苯蒽诱发大鼠乳腺癌的影响。结果表明：膳食中补充5%牛磺酸对诱发肿瘤的生长具有一定的抑制作用，并在一定程度上有对抗高脂膳食的促癌作用。该作用可能是通过调节免疫功能、增强抗氧化能力及调节脂代谢等多种途径实现。

2005年，该院杨昆等在"铅对骨髓干细胞的损伤作用及其机理的研究"中，应用体内和体外实验，研究醋酸铅对大、小鼠骨髓造血干细胞增殖、分化调控的影响，从干细胞损伤的角度，探讨铅的血液毒性作用机制，研究发现骨髓造血干细胞对铅较为敏感，铅染毒小鼠外周血变化不明显时，已引起骨髓生长障碍，且随浓度增加抑制作用增强，呈明显的剂量—效应关系，进而为在干细胞水平上采取相应措施防治铅对外周血的损伤提供依据。

2005年，医科大学公共卫生学院李袭丽、白成江、田庆伟等对甜菊甙、富马酸二甲酯等多种食品添加剂的安全性进行研究，证实三价铬酵母的Ames试验、枯草杆菌重组试验、SOS显色试验均呈阴性；通过对甜菊甙、富马酸二甲酯毒代动力学、慢性毒性及致癌性研究，证实甜菊甙为安全的天然甜味剂。

六、卫生检验

1991年起，市劳卫所刘黛莉、李志华、王延让等通过对"空气中两种状态共存的对硝基苯胺采样方法的研究"，深入探索不同状态共存于空气中的同一种污染物的采集方法，受到国内同行关注；刘黛莉、李志华、李建国等开展"尿中有机磷农药代谢产物分析方法研究"和刘黛莉、李志华、王延让等开展"尿甲酚作为甲苯生物监测指标的研究"中，使生物监测方法研究由80年代以尿汞、尿铅、尿砷、尿尼古丁测定发展到监测对象进入人体代谢产物的分析研究，使研究的深度与难度较80年代有显著提高；刘黛莉、李志华、王延让等深入进行有机磷农药杀螟松、消斑灵，有机氮农药丙溴磷，有机氯农药溴氢菊酯、氯氢菊酯在作物、土壤、水及食品中残留量分析等方法的研究与应用。

1995年，市防病中心范殿英采用基因表达的乙型肝炎e抗原作为免疫源，首次运用电融合与PEG（聚乙二醇）技术，一次融合成功克隆出成活的杂交瘤细胞，建立e抗体检测方法。该成果获1996年度天津市科技进步二等奖。

1995～2005年，医科大学公共卫生学院郝俊、何莉萍等建立起头发中铝、铜、铁等的检验方法及乳制品中蛋白质、钙等的测定方法，并建立阶导数单扫描极谱法测定食品中凯氏氮含量测定方法。所建方法检出限低、重现性好，结果准确可靠，分析时间缩短，测量简便、快速。

2003年，市防病中心丁建清、王书梅、田永琴等在国内率先利用霍乱外膜蛋白（OMPW）合成引物对天津市保留的霍乱弧菌进行检测，并与毒素基因引物（ctxA）合用开展双重引物PCR检测，以区分产毒和非产毒霍乱。该成果被国内多家疾病控制部门采用。

检测二噁英类化学物质通常多用高效气相色谱-质谱联用技术，过程复杂、要求高，成本大。2003年，医科大学公共卫生学院张万起等利用分子生物学方法与技术，构建基于AhR和ARNT的二噁英生物检测体系，发现随二噁英剂量的增加二者的结合程度也相应增加，当两种蛋白足量时，最低可以检测到0.25皮摩尔二恶英，检测下限为匹克级，达到对二噁英类化学物质进行检测的目的，为进一步建立低成本、高效率的痕量二噁英生物检测方法提供了研究基础和依据。

2003年起，市劳卫所开展一系列作业场所空气中有毒有害物质测定方法的研究。其中，王延让、张昊、李浩等承担的“工作场所空气中过氧化氢的长时间采样检测方法的研究”，赵淑岚、张健等承担的“工作场所空气中四种无机酸离子色谱法的研究”，均通过市科委组织的科技成果鉴定。

七、卫生标准

1989年起，市劳卫所徐佳等开展“车间空气中对硝基苯胺（PNA）卫生标准（引进）研究”。经过两年现场调查，空气中PNA浓度均在0.2mg/m^{3}以下，工人皮肤污染严重，并有工种之间差异，体检未观察到任何与接触PNA有关的阳性结果，结合国外标准和中国实际情况进行综合分析，提出最高容许浓度3mg/m^3（皮）的建议。该标准于1996年被卫生部批准为国家卫生标准。该所徐佳、陆丽敏、杨杰等在“车间空气中考地松卫生标准研究”中，经毒理学实验观察，小鼠LD50和大鼠经皮LD50均属中等毒性，有明显蓄积性，亚慢性实验毒性家鼠与大鼠两种动物大剂量组均出现生长抑制、甘油三酯显著升高。经综合分析，建议在目前条件下，考地松车间空气中卫生标准最高容许浓度3mg/m^3。该标准于1996年被卫生部和国家技术监督局批准为国家卫生标准并颁布实施。

2004年，天津市疾病预防控制中心王延让、杨雪莹、刘静等承担科技部课题“职业卫生标准制定”。该课题由中国疾病预防控制中心职业卫生与中毒控制所组织进行，天津市承担“职业接触五氯酚的生物限值”的研究。该课题的立项意义是，建立一种职业人群接触五氯酚的生物限值，检测工作场所的五氯酚浓度对工人尿样中五氯酚的浓度的影响，验证空气五氯酚测定方法的准确性，从而更有力地保护职业接触五氯酚的职业人群。该项标准于2006年被卫生部和国家技术监督局批准为国家卫生标准并颁布实施。

八、病媒与消毒

（一）病媒

1992年，天津市卫生防病中心孙晨熹与天津三环气雾剂厂合作完成新药剂——速灭灵高效气雾杀虫剂的开发，以拟除虫菊酯类药物与S1（增效醚）进行混配，其机理是通过抑制害虫神经系统的Na-K-ATPase，调控细胞膜Na离子的瞬间通透性使其中毒死亡，主要用于杀灭蚊、蝇、蟑等。该制剂具有用药量少、效果好、污染小、对人畜无害、使用方便等特点，在全国范围内推广。

是年，该中心孙晨熹与农业部农药检定所合作，首次以国标形式颁布实施“农药登记用卫生杀虫剂室内药效试验方法”。该标准的出台，对统一国内检测方法，规范农药登记制度，防止国外不合格产品进入国内市场，促进中国卫生杀虫药剂产品的研制开发，具有重要意义。1994年，孙晨熹等首次对日本产电热蚊香滴加液单剂及混剂对成蚊药效进行评价，对比电热蚊香片加入不同药剂和不同比例药剂混用对成蚊的击倒效果，为厂家科学合理地使用滴加液提供了依据。

2000年，该中心曹晓梅、孙晨熹等开始研究家蝇抗药性。2001年，在“家蝇击倒抗性para基因钠离子通道cDNA突变区的研究”中，发现新的基因片断，并申请到美国NCBI的GenBank（基因银行）核苷酸序列库登陆号。2002年，又在“家蝇抗药性的分子检测方法的研究”中，揭示出家蝇对拟除虫菊酯抗药性产生的机理。该研究于2005年通过市科委组织的专家鉴定，达到国际先进水平。

2004年，张咏梅、孙晨熹等对天津市野外家蝇抗药性及其谷胱苷肽s转移酶、乙酰胆碱酯酶、羧酸酯酶、多功能氧化酶进行生物、生化测定，对阿维菌素、吡虫磷等药剂对抗性家蝇的毒力进行初探。通过生物学及生化测定的试验，得到相关药物对家蝇抗性的具体数据，并从动物的机体酶指标对抗性进行的识别，为药物的选择提供了重要依据。通过交互抗性的研究，为新药剂的选用和混配提供了数据，为延缓抗药性的发展提供重要依据。

2005年，孙晨熹、李今越等引进印鼠客蚤并进行8种药剂对成蚤杀灭试验，筛选出最佳的药剂及使用剂量，可为阻断鼠疫传播提供科技支持。同年，孙晨熹、李今越等首次在天津蓟县捕获骚扰阿蚊。此蚊系大型蚊虫，叮咬力强，是流行性乙型脑炎的重要传播媒介。这一蚊种的捕获，为控制流行性乙型脑炎的研究提供了条件。

（二）消毒

1994年，医科大学战威等选择天津地区不同污染程度的20个天然水源水样，对其有机污染指标与氯消毒后三卤甲烷形成的相关性进行研究，发现用液氯消毒饮用水后产生的三卤甲烷量与原水中的有机污染程度呈正比，实验证明三卤甲烷具有强烈的毒性和致癌性。1999年，战威等建立的水中隐孢子虫卵囊的检验方法，操作快速、简易，回收率高。2000年，战威为寻找一种较好的饮用水消毒方法，研究氯胺和二氧化氯协同对水中大肠杆菌和f2噬菌体的灭活作用。结果表明，协同消毒效果显著提高，而且在相当长的时间内在水中保持着大于0.30毫克/升的余氯量，作用1小时可将再污染的大肠杆菌全部杀灭，从而有效地控制了水质的再污染，与传统的氯消毒相比，此项技术优势显著。2001年，战威等将氯胺和二氧化氯协同对饮用水消毒方法应用于天津市引滦河水系中隐孢子虫污染率的调查。历时12个月的监测结果表明，在多数监测点隐孢子虫存在较多，且多发于春季。调查结果为预防隐孢子虫病的大规模流行和政府部门制定引滦水源保护措施提供了科学依据。

1997年，市防病中心沈芃、李景芹、王惠芬等通过试验在国内第一次证明，2、4、4′-三氯-2′-羟基-二苯醚消毒剂具有杀菌作用。1999年，该中心邱立军所研制的口腔器械戊二醛消毒盒对保证口腔器械消毒质量，防止血源性医院感染的发生具有积极作用。

2002年，市防病中心李强等制定的天津市地方标准——色谱法检验溶液中戊二醛浓度，比化学滴定法方法简便，结果准确。此方法为防止医疗系统使用不合格的戊二醛对手术器械等进行消毒，控制医院感染起到积极作用。

2005年，市防病中心沈芃、徐文体通过试验证明，酸化水内镜清洗消毒机对内镜消毒具有良好效果，为内镜消毒提供了新的选择。同年，沈芃、徐文体、丁津华等经试验证明，双氧水雾化加臭氧消毒装置对呼吸机等复杂内部结构医疗器械具有良好消毒效果。是年，沈芃、徐文体、宁培勇等对胸科医院手术用品进行广泛监测，在手术器械中检出细菌，并用法国梅里埃EPI细菌鉴定试剂对检出细菌进行鉴定，针对发现的问题提出改进措施，对控制医院术后伤口感染起到重要作用。

九、健康教育

1991年起，天津市健康教育所积极开展社区健康教育、学校健康教育、农村健康教育、控烟宣传等工作及相关的研究，制作健康宣传材料300余种，累计印发各种资料2000多万份，举办各种规模的健康教育培训班200余期，组织大型健康教育公益宣传活动50余场次，并与电视台开办健康教育系列节目等。

1992年，以城市卫生检查为契机，健康教育纳入各级政府目标责任制范畴。制定出社区健康教育规范、学校健康教育规范、医院健康教育规范，每年按规范要求对18个区县进行“达标”考核验收，进一步推动、规范全市健康教育工作。

1996年，天津市健康教育所承担世界银行贷款卫生Ⅶ项目健康促进子项目中的健康教育干预任务，开展社区健康教育、控烟工作等相关研究，社区慢性病健康教育的研究取得成效，创办出“天津模式”。其中，天津市城区居民脑卒中社区干预效果的研究显示：干预社区标化发病率、标化死亡率及病死率分别为214.52/10万、46.95/10万、21.88%，比非干预社区分别低26.45%、49.90%、31.65%。干预社区平均发病年龄、平均死亡年龄分别为68.4岁和72.2岁，较非干预社区分别推迟6.0岁和7.6岁。是年，天津市出台第一个控烟法规《天津市公共场所禁止吸烟条例》。

2000年，受卫生部委托，天津市健康教育所作为项目牵头单位，主持、策划并实施在全国152个试点城市开展的社区健康教育现状调查项目。

2002年，依据天津市卫生资源重组规划，将建所51年的天津市健康教育研究所整体并入天津市卫生防病中心，担负起全市18个区、县的健康教育指导任务。

2005年，天津市公安交通管理局与市防病中心合作完成"天津市公安交警健康状况与健康促进调查研究"课题。当年通过由市科委组织的科技成果鉴定，达到国际先进水平"。

第四节 营养与食品卫生

20世纪90年代，天津市对营养与食品卫生的研究，侧重于膳食营养的干预。实验证实，铝是生活环境中促成或导致机体衰老的因素之一，并给出日允许摄入量。2000年起，天津市对营养机制的研究较为深入，在细胞水平或分子水平上，研究木瓜、大豆异黄酮、叶酸、锌、硒等对大脑、神经、内皮等细胞的保护作用或免疫调节作用；在食品卫生方面，着重研究农药残留、食品添加剂等问题，并制定出相关的政策与检测方法。

一、营养调查

2002年，卫生部、科技部和国家统计局组织开展的"居民营养与健康状况的调查"中，天津市河西区、武清区4000余人接受调查。

2003～2005年，市防病中心江国虹、李静、常改等开展"天津居民营养与健康状况调查研究"。通过对以上调查情况进行分析，结果显示：天津居民蔬菜、水果、豆奶类摄入量严重不足，而油脂类摄入严重超标；膳食纤维、维生素A、钙、锌营养素缺乏者高达60%以上；平均膳食脂肪供能比达46.5%。分析过程中，还对脂肪供能比、水果蔬菜摄入量、膳食纤维摄入量与多种慢性疾病间的关系进行探讨，为开展宣教及慢性病预防控制提供了理论依据。

二、膳食营养干预

1993年，天津医学院卫生系徐格晟等选取天津64种食物，测定其铝的含量，结果发现不同的食物铝含量差别很大，大多数天然食物铝的含量在10毫克/千克以下，其中植物性食物中铝的水平要高于动物食品。据此估计，天津人平均每天从天然食物中摄入的铝大约为3.79毫克，若考虑各种来源的铝，大多数天津人每日摄入3～10毫克铝。1995年，徐格晟研究天津城乡居民常用食物铝的含量与居民摄入量，居民对含铝添加剂及药物摄入量，血铝水平与疾病、衰老的关系，结果证实铝是生活环境中促成或致机体衰老的因素，提出：铝日允许摄入量为0～0.7毫克/千克体重；老年性痴呆及慢性肾功能不全患者应限制高铝食品摄入量；建议在食品加工中限制使用硫酸铝钾。

1997年，医科大学公共卫生学院黄国伟主持完成"氟铝联合对人体脑细胞和骨细胞毒作用的研究"。结果表明：氟铝联合对人大脑神经细胞和成骨细胞的作用不同；对大脑神经细胞，低剂量铝即可产生不利影响，且随铝剂量的增加而增强，加入一定量氟并未对铝的毒作用产生明显的影响，说明该研究剂量氟铝对大脑神经细胞不存在拮抗或协同作用；而对于成骨细胞，高剂量铝才能产生毒作用，一定量的氟对铝的毒作用有抑制作用。该研究结果为铝或氟中毒相关疾病的深入研究提供了依据，并确定铝盐降氟的应用前景，同时也为防治饮水及食物中氟铝共存地区所存在的危害提供了科学依据。

2003～2004年，市防病中心江国虹、常改、杨溢等对膳食纤维干预改善便秘进行研究。结果显示：高膳食纤维组排便形状、排便次数都显著好于对照组，证实膳食纤维干预改善便秘的效果及应用于社区干预的可行性。2005年，他们又研究五味袋泡茶对高脂血症降血脂的干预效果。结果显示：经过30天干预，受试人群血脂下降总有效率88.46%，其中总胆固醇、血清甘油三脂下降有效率分别为84.62%和67.13%，为广泛开展社区慢性病干预提供了依据。

2004年，医科大学张万起在"制定全国不同人群膳食中碘的可耐受最高摄入量的研究"中，选择健康志愿者，分别接受不同剂量的碘，通过补碘前后甲状腺激素水平等相关指标的比较，观察不同补碘水平对甲状腺功能的影响，发现中国成人在接受500微克/天碘补充剂时即可出现亚临床甲状腺功能减退的个体，而国外人群在接受这一水平的补碘剂量时人群的甲状腺功能正常。该研究结果表明，中国人群对高碘耐受的能力与国外人群试验的结果存在差别，因此在建立中国人群碘安全摄入量的同时，应该立足于中国人群的碘营养水平，建立适合中国人群的碘安全摄入量范围。该研究结果为人群合理补碘，避免由于碘过量引发危害，使人群的碘营养水平保持在一个安全范围内提供了理论依据。

三、营养机制

2001～2002年，医科大学公共卫生学院黄国伟等完成中日合作项目"木瓜粉对体外鼠胚大脑神经细胞缺氧损伤保护作用的研究""木瓜粉对小鼠免疫功能调节作用的实验研究"和"木瓜粉对缺血性脑梗塞患者临床治疗效果的研究"等3项研究。第一项研究采用无血清体外培养鼠胚大脑神经细胞，将神经细胞造成缺氧损伤，在无血清培养液中加入不同剂量的木瓜粉，观察木瓜粉对缺氧损伤的保护作用。结果显示：缺氧0.1毫克木瓜粉/毫升组的神经细胞MTT及NSE活性均高于缺氧对照组，并有显著性差别（$P<0.05$）；形态学观察结果也显示缺氧0.1毫克木瓜粉/毫升和0.5毫克木瓜粉/毫升组的神经细胞缺氧损伤后恢复明显好于缺氧对照组；木瓜粉对大脑神经细胞缺氧损伤恢复具有明显的促进作用。第二项研究选用BALB/C纯系小白鼠分成3批共144只，随机分为对照、低剂量、中剂量和高剂量4个剂量组。结果显示：低、中、高剂量组小鼠胸腺/体重比值和脾脏/体重比值均高于对照组，$P<0.05$）；3个剂量组小鼠脾淋巴细胞增殖力均高于对照组，其中高剂量组小鼠脾淋巴细胞增殖力高于对照组，$P<0.05$）；绵羊红细胞诱导小鼠DTH试验，低、中、高剂量小鼠24h、48h足趾增厚均高于对照组，$P<0.05$）；中剂量和高剂量BN组NK细胞活性高于对照组，$P<0.05$）；木瓜粉具有免疫调节作用。第三项研究显示，木瓜粉能够增加急性期、恢复期缺血性脑梗塞病人血中超氧化物岐化酶（SOD）、谷胱甘肽过氧化物酶（GSH—PX）、总抗氧化物（TAC）活性，可降低急性期病人丙二醛（MDA）的量；能够改善急性期、恢复期缺血性脑梗塞病人肢体功能、记忆功能和智能；病人的自觉症状有明显改善。

2002年，该院张万起等用离子交换色谱法和亲和吸附的方法研究"人T细胞中核酸结合亲环素（hCyP33）与使核糖核酸（mRNA）结合的特异性"，证实hCyP33同具有结构的mRNA特异性结合，在mRNA跨核膜。2003年，张万起等在大肠杆菌中克隆表达并纯化小鼠FK506结合蛋白23（FKBP23）与谷胱甘肽转硫酶（GST）的融合蛋白GST-FKBP23及内质网体中热激蛋白70（Hsp70）的成员免疫球蛋白结合蛋白（BiP）的融合蛋白GST-BiP，并用Factor Xa因子酶切制备游离的FKBP23及BiP，将结合在还原型谷胱甘肽-Sepharose 4B凝胶上的两种融合蛋白分别交叉地亲和吸附克隆制备的两种游离蛋白，经免疫印迹证实FKBP23与BiP特异性结合，进一步证实FKBP23可与内质网体中天然的BiP结合，发现哺乳动物内质网体中肽脯氨酰顺反异构酶的家族成员与分子伴侣（molecular chaperone）的主要成员Hsp70具有相互结合的作用。

2004年，该院黄国伟在"大豆异黄酮对体外血管内皮细胞ox—LDL损伤的保护作用"研究中，采用氧化低密度脂蛋白（ox-LDL）诱导血管内皮细胞（VEC）损伤，建立VEC氧化损伤模型，观察大豆异黄酮（SI）对氧化损伤VEC的保护作用，并探讨其机制。结果显示：ox-LDL可诱导VEC损伤，且其内MDA含量不同，对VEC的损伤程度不同；ox-LDL中MDA含量为1.0nmol/mL时为适合实验研究的损伤浓度；SI可增强VEC自身抗氧化能力，可抑制LDL氧化，但对ox-LDL无逆转作用；SI可降低氧化损伤VEC细胞MDA含量及LDH释放百分比，增强SOD、GSH-PX活性，增加一氧化氮（NO）含量，并可降低氧化损伤VEC内皮细胞-单核细胞粘附率,减少凋亡细胞的出现,改善VEC氧化损伤后的形态;同浓度SI与维生素E对氧化损伤VEC起到相似的保护作用;SI可能通过其抗氧化作用保护VEC免受ox-LDL损伤,从而预防动脉粥样硬化的发生。2004年,该院常红在“大豆异黄酮对大鼠脑缺血损伤作用的影响”研究中,通过建立大鼠脑缺血损伤模型,采用RT-PCR(逆转录-聚合酶链反应)测定脑组织原血红加氧酵素-1(HO-1)、HO-2和血中淋巴细胞HO-1 mRNA的表达水平,测定血液及脑组织中抗氧化生化指标、神经细胞凋亡、神经功能缺损评分、病理检查等。结果显示:大豆异黄酮可以提高脑缺血大鼠学习记忆能力、血清及脑组织SOD和GSH-PX活性、血淋巴细胞及脑组织HO-1和HO-2 mRNA表达水平以及6h时各兴趣区rADC、rDCavg、rFA值;降低血清及脑组织MDA含量、血浆同型半胱氨酸水平;减轻脑缺血大鼠脑组织的病理改变以及超微结构改变,其作用机理为大豆异黄酮可通过提高机体抗氧化能力,降低血浆Hcy浓度,提高HO-1和HO-2mRNA表达水平对缺血性大脑损伤起到一定的保护作用。

2005年,黄国伟在“关于大鼠脑细胞同型半胱氨酸的合成与转运的研究”中,发现儿茶酚甲基转移酶(COMT)的底物—3,4双羟基苯甲酸选择性地增加胶质细胞中同型半胱氨酸的排出,而对于神经元并无作用。同样,COMT的底物多巴胺、槲皮素也可诱导胶质细胞输出同型半胱氨酸,并且此作用可被COMT的抑制剂所抑制。同型半胱氨酸排出的增加可能是由于COMT活化后,同型半胱氨酸合成的增加。因此,该研究结论为COMT的激活诱导胶质细胞持续合成同型半胱氨酸,并向神经元转运。同年,黄国伟在国家自然科学基金项目“叶酸对神经干细胞增殖分化调控机制的研究”中,通过体外培养胎鼠、新生鼠大脑神经干细胞(NSCs)和大鼠大脑中动脉栓塞(MCAO)模型,研究显示:叶酸可通过Notch和丝裂原活化蛋白激酶(MAPK)信号通路两条途径,促进体内和体外NSCs的增殖分化,叶酸可上调Notch信号通路中Notch1、Hes1/Hes5 mRNA表达水平,同时促进相应的蛋白表达量,下调Mash1 mRNA及蛋白表达量;可促进NSCs、MAPK信号通路中磷酸化细胞外信号调节激酶1/2(pERK1/2)蛋白表达量。在正常条件和缺氧条件下,叶酸可促进NSCs增殖,且具有一定的剂量效应;在分化期,体外研究显示叶酸可促进NSCs向星型胶质细胞分化,但对NSCs向神经元分化作用不明显,体内研究显示叶酸可促进NSCs同时向星型胶质细胞和神经元分化。叶酸可降低MCAO大鼠血浆和体外培养NSCs同型半胱氨酸(Hcy)含量,抑制体外NSCs和体内神经细胞凋亡。叶酸可提高MCAO大鼠机体的抗氧化能力,改善学习记忆功能和病理改变,促进机体的功能恢复。该研究显示叶酸对NSCs另一作用机制为,叶酸可降低Hcy含量和抑制Hcy导致的氧化应激,从而促进NSCs的增殖分化,抑制神经细胞凋亡。

2005年,该院孙忠对补硒糖尿病大鼠与糖尿病对照组之间差异显示的基因片段进行克隆、测序、同源性分析,发现有5个基因片段:Se-2、Se-6、Se-10、Se-14、Se-18,在基因库(GenBank)中未找到高同源性的序列,为新的EST片段,其中4个基因片段(Se-2、Se-10、Se-14、Se-18)在糖尿病对照组、糖尿病补硒组肝脏中的表达量均低于正常对照组,糖尿病补硒组的表达量高于糖尿病对照组;在大鼠多种组织中表达水平也不甚相同,4个新基因片段被Genbank收录。结果显示:分离并克隆的4条与补硒有关的糖尿病大鼠差异显示的新基因片段,可能与硒改善糖尿病糖脂代谢紊乱有一定关系。

是年,该院吴蕴棠进行“补充锌硒糖尿病大鼠差示基因片段的克隆鉴定”的研究,对前期研究中分离到的不同处理组间cDNA差异片段进行克隆、测序及基因序列的同源性比较。12个基因片段中有10个在GenBank上找到与之同源性较高的序列,而另外2个(2#、6#)未找到与之同源性较高的序列,为新的基因片段,均已在Genbank上成功登录。逆转录-聚合酶链式反应(RT—PCR)验证结果显示,锌、硒均可上调糖尿病大鼠未知基因2# mRNA的表达,锌同时可上调糖尿病大鼠未知基因6# mRNA的表达。

四、食品卫生

1991年,天津医学院王笃圣等根据3年天津市营养调查成果,针对儿童最易缺乏的营养素——维生素A、D、B_1、B_2、C以及铁、锌等,开展“多维奶片和补血强力奶片的研制与儿童食用效果”研究。此两种奶片由天津市食品卫生监督检验所、天津市乳品食品监测中心检验,质量符合营养及食品卫生标准。经100例学龄前儿童食用效果观察表明，有明显的补血、消除维生素缺乏症、增进儿童食欲的良好作用，无不良反应。同年，王笃圣等与天津体育科学研究所合作开展“儿童少年运动员营养补充食品研究”，针对生长发育期的儿童少年运动员的生理特点及对营养素的特定需要，研制出口感较佳、服用方便、原料来源容易、生产工艺较简便、价格适中的全营养补充食品。经少年体校队员100天的食用，通过营养调查以及生化（血、尿中蛋白质、维生素和矿物质等）检难和身体发育、技能、身体素质等指标，进行身高、体重、胸围及速度、爆发力、大小肌群力量和耐力等的观察，发现营养状况明显改善，对预防贫血和消除维生素A、B_2缺乏症均有明显效果。同时，该食品可增强儿童少年运动员的身体发育和健康，并对提高内脏机能水平和身体运动素质全面发展产生良好的作用。

1992年，王笃圣针对儿童少年营养问题进行“儿童营养食品研究”，研制出合理的营养食品，包括补铁食品、补钙与核黄素食品、补维生素A、D食品和补赖氨酸食品等四类。通过对小学与学前儿童进行65～70天食用观察，采用膳食调查、体格检查、生化检验等各项指标综合评价，表明儿童营养强化食品优于普通加餐食品，对于儿童生长发育，预防贫血以及维生素A、B_2等营养素缺乏，提高蛋白质营养水平均取得预期效果。

1994年，医科大学公共卫生学院徐格晟、张万起等参加修订的国家卫生标准在全国实施。在新标准基础上，徐格晟等开展“煎炸油与煎炸食品的卫生学研究”。根据煎炸油的卫生状况、平均极性组份含量、煎炸油的劣变规律和市售煎炸食品的吸油率，以居民经常食用的煎炸食品为研究对象，进行不同种类煎炸食品和煎炸油卫生状况的研究及安全评价，提出居民日常食用的不同种类煎炸食品的安全摄入量。结合煎炸试验及10年间煎炸油的卫生状况对比，研究探讨煎炸油的劣变规律，提出“筛选并指定适宜煎炸的优良油种为煎炸油、减少重复煎炸、降低煎炸油温、适当增加煎炸中期新油的添加比例”等改善煎炸油工艺的具体措施。为推动新标准的实施，1998年医科大学与和平区卫生防病站合作，积极进行新国极性组分（PC）测定方法的应用与推广工作。

随着农药残留问题的日见突显，2000年起，市防病中心江国虹、霍飞、李静等开展“天津地区果蔬农药施用与残留状况的调查及控制措施的研究”，并建立天津市果蔬农药动态检测系统。经调查，天津地区自1998年以后津郊菜农、果农施用农药的种类和数量，并采样检测部分市售蔬菜、水果农药残留量，比较5种不同去除农残的洗涤方法的效果。此项研究为政府部门制定相应政策、指导农民合理用药、指导居民科学清洗蔬菜水果等提供了有力依据。

2002年，市防病中心针对甲醛在水发货、粉丝、白糖等食品中作为防腐和增白剂的滥用问题，开展食品中甲醛含量的监测，全年共监测样品84份，并对比性的检测出二氧化硫、过氧化氢，分析污染环节和残留水平，为制定相关标准奠定了基础。

2002年，针对居民喜饮豆浆的膳食特点，该中心开展豆浆中蛋白质等营养成分以及脲酶等抗营养因子的监测，为制定豆浆卫生标准和开展转基因大豆的营养质量评价提供了数据资料。

第四章　中医学

1991～2005年，天津在中医理论与临床研究方面引入大量现代科技研究手段与方法，使中医学步入现代科技发展轨道。特别是进入21世纪前后，各中医教学、科研、医疗单位广泛开展实验科学研究。临床诊断广泛应用现代化验技术，并大量采用血流变学等生化指标，中医诊断给出量化标准。在医疗上，广泛采用现代医疗设备，临床工作更趋规范化。从临床上筛选出的有效方剂，一方面进入到实验研究阶段，探究方药作用机制；另一方面中药汤剂的剂型改革悄然兴起，冲剂、颗粒剂、胶囊等被广泛采用。针灸作为天津中医在全国的领军地位亦在不断提高，对针灸的作用机理、量化标准、经络实质及临床应用研究等都取得关键性进展。1999年，天津中医学院第一附属医院石学敏当选为中国工程院院士。2004年组建的天津市针灸学重点实验室，成为市科委和市教委首批确定的天津市重点实验室。

2004年，天津市中医药研究学院及其附属医院、市长征医院、市中医医院、市医药科学研究所等5个单位整合重新组建天津市中医药研究院，天津市中医学研究步入新阶段。2005年，天津中医学院张伯礼当选为中国工程院院士。

第一节　中医基础理论研究

天津在中医学基础理论的研究方面，以往多有建树。1991年后，除继续对中医典籍进行训诂考证，阐明发微之外，还针对临床出现的新病种及经典医书中存在的老问题，以现代科学理念及实验研究方法进行探究，提出新的论点、论据，阐明理论实质，从而使古老的中医学基础理论崭露生机。

一、歧黄发微

1991年，天津中医学院（以下简称“中医学院”）郭霭春对《黄帝内经·素问》著作年代进行考证，得出其全书不是同时代产物，而是由战国至西汉时期不同医家撰述、编辑整理而成。同年，中医学院杨毓隽从阴阳、形神、升降、肾气等四方面对“内经”的生命观进行系统探讨，阐述中医生命观的宏观科学性。2000年，中医学院肖延龄、杜元灏对“内经”中“六腑之气街”提出质疑，经考据应理解为“六经之气街”，突出了气血运行的作用，提示了针灸治疗原理，同时也是俞募等穴能治脏腑疾病的机理之所在。2001年，天津中医学院第一附属医院（以下简称“中医一附院”）周莲菊通过对“内经”研究，发现其中蕴涵丰富的情志医学思想，在病因、治则、预防各方面涉及广而具体，奠定了中国古代情志医学思想。同年，周莲菊、赵敏等研制《黄帝内经》计算机检索系统，符合中医分类规律和中医理念。

2002年，中医学院于铁成从歧伯、雷公所处的文化背景探讨“内经”的医学流派，提出以岐伯为代表的文化地域是以药物治疗为主要手段，而雷公为代表的东部文化反映在医学上是以针刺为主，在经络方面发展了经络诊断，使后来的各派中医逐渐融合渗透。2003年，中医学院王玉兴针对历来认为虚里为胃之大络的观点，结合“内经”从多途径进行探讨，提出“虚里乃胃之大络的起点”的观点。2004年，天津市公安消防部队医院王淼提出“内经”的养生思想是在吸取道家思想的基础上发展起来的，顺应自然为养生的重要原则，调神为重要措施，重视正气在养生中的指导原则。2005年，中医一附院傅立新认为“神明所主”观点至今无定论，提出“脑主脏而不奉脏”的观点，强调脑为神府，明确脑对人体的主宰作用，心神在脑神总摄下发挥作用。

二、仲景探源

1991年，中医学院张有俊通过研究“伤寒”“金匮”，对张仲景温中之法进行归纳，其温胃、温脾、强心温中、补肾温中、暖肝温中和温补肺胃诸法，对后世温补学说产生影响。1995年，中医一附院牛元起对《伤寒论》设计主导思想进行研究，从其选材、体例、文法、文字着手，认为其以“辨”为主线，依“辨”定取舍，一切从辨证出发，实为中医方法学典范。1995年，天津市塘沽医院刘芳荣分析《伤寒论》中113方中保津存阴的25方及兼治阴伤的45方，提出阴津在张仲景学说中的重要性，《伤寒论》为后世养阴学说奠定基础。1996年，天津市铁路中心医院廖辉对《伤寒论》中针灸的施用规律进行探讨，得出三阳宜针、三阴宜灸的观点，取穴法则为循经取穴，注重辨证灵活、随证治之。

由于历来对少阳位置有争议，2000年，总医院柳少青通过对古籍和临床研究，认为少阳当位阳明之后，太阴之前，与《伤寒论》原旨一致，对辨证用药有指导意义。2000年，中医学院阚湘苓提出《伤寒论》之风寒外袭的太阳病是营卫不和证之一，营卫不和见外感亦见内伤，其专方桂枝汤全方位兼顾营卫化源、运行、布散各环节而达治疗目的。2003年，中医学院叶桂兴对太阳与阳明合病提出其并非两经症状简单相加的观点，其病中心仍在太阳，故治疗上仍从太阳入手，重在发表，兼及阳明。

2004年，中医学院张国骏、王东强、史丽萍观察《伤寒论》中的四逆散对肝脏损害的保护作用，发现四逆散能降低石胆酸灌胃造成肝损害小鼠谷丙转氨酶、谷草转氨酶升高水平，对肝脏具有一定保护作用。同年，中医学院方玲对《伤寒论》中“阳去入阴”句结合该条方证，综合归纳古今医家不同认识，层层剖析，提出该句应为“离少阳，入少阴或厥阴”的观点。是年，中医学院年莉对《伤寒论》吴茱萸汤原书叙症过简的问题，通过病案进行方证学调查，发现本方证当发秋冬，以耳源性眩晕和血管性头痛多见。

2005年，中医学院刘公望对《伤寒论》中合方进行系统研究，认为合方非简单叠加，而是具协同、扩大作用，既为临床用药提供新思路，亦系仲景学术思想之延伸。同年，张国骏对阳明病的后世注家分类方法提出异议，认为仲景本意无此，其共性特征是胃家实，当明确发病性质、证侯分类来理解《伤寒论》辨证体系。同年，中医学院刘思顺、马晓峰、范英昌对《金匮要略》大黄甘遂汤进行研究，指出其可抑制贮脂细胞的激活和转化，减少成纤维细胞生成，为治疗肝纤维化良方。同年，马晓峰提出《金匮要略》中“气分”一证乃后世之心下痞、肝脾肿大、胃下垂，皆宗气不能正常运转，水聚不散而致，故利湿宣散当收到良好效果。

三、医籍求真

1991年，中医学院郭洪耀、张海凌对唐朝开元时期医书《广济方》进行辑复工作，以《外台秘要》刊本为主，参考《医心方》等十数种医籍，将《广济方》辑复而成，对本草、方剂、治疗及唐宋医史的研究有重要意义。1993年，中医一附院石学敏、周继曾、邵文虎主编《中医纲目》选临床各科以纲目分列，较全面地吸收同时代的中医新成果、新技术，特别是在癌症的治疗方面收载多种治疗方案，为临床医生提供方便。1994年，中医学院李桂兰对《难经》中针灸学术思想进行探佚求真，认为其所阐述原穴、俞募穴、五俞穴及母子补泻手法，对后世影响较大，奠定了针灸学理论基础。

1995年，中医学院朱广仁针对中医教材对“肺阳虚”弃而不载或以“肺气虚”代权“肺阳虚”现象，从经典医籍及肺之生理病理多方面考证，认为“肺阳虚”当存在，并对临床有一定指导意义。1996年，中医学院张国霞对《温病条辨》中神昏治法进行探佚求真，发现其实质为泻热以醒神，其中泻阳明法最为出色，其发展仲景之说故创清心开窍、清营透热、除湿开窍、养阴复脉之法。2003年，中医学院肖照岑针对多年来传染病有不断新生之势，运用温病学理论进行探究，提出温病学说对传染病有较大的治疗优势，运用温病学提供了新的医疗途径。2004年，马晓峰对《医宗必读》进行研究，发现其内伤病证的病名确立、脉证表现突出脏腑辨证，为后世病名的确立及证型划分奠定了基础。同年，中医学院杨雪梅、王玉兴对《素问玄机原病式》进行研究，发现其论述始终未离五脏六腑，从取类比象归类脏腑病证、亢害承制论述脏腑病机、六气病因到六气病机的转化加以探讨，从发病机制方面完善了脏腑辨证理论。2005年，中医学院张炳立针对在温病的治疗史上以药物为主的现象，依据文献及结合临床，初步概括了温病卫气营血针法施治规律，补充了温病治疗学。

四、中医新论

1999年，一中心医院郑於敏继承郑静侯的广西针派手法，运用灵龟八法并配以与本穴相应的交会穴增加疗效，对中风、痹证效果显著。2001年，正道中医咨询中心运用天津师范大学王志田“子午流注”和“药对岁物药品”理论，用时间天体医学辅助运算系统，使中医治疗更加规范。

2001年，天津市中西医结合急腹症研究所田在善与医科大学方步武提出腹腔丛、骨盆丛可能是古代医学家认定的中焦、下焦部位基础，心丛、肺丛可能是上焦的基础，三焦实体是自主神经中几个较大的神经丛或神经结构。

2003年，中医学院秦玉龙对中医证侯规范化、标准化进行研究，指出当时的研究误区，提出建立中医信息系统，区分专用字词程度等级、专用字词规范方案。

21世纪初，中医学院张伯礼等开展“方剂组分配伍关键科学问题的基础研究”，发现在药效物质和作用机理基本清楚基础上，组分配伍研制现代中药的模式在多个关键技术取得突破，搭建了相应的技术平台，初步阐明方剂的作用在于整合调节的理论实质。该成果获2005年度天津市自然科学一等奖。

图7-4-1-112 张伯礼(右)与科研人员进行学术讨论

第二节 针灸研究与临床

20世纪80年代起，中医一附院石学敏首创针刺治疗中风的“醒脑开窍”法，观察门诊上万人次，住院4千人次，显效率达85%。1991年开展其作用机制研究，通过动物实验证实该法可明显改善脑血流、脑代谢，并可改善高脂血、高粘血症，通过349例大样本与传统针法比较，优于传统针法，该方法影响国内外针灸同行。此后，天津的针灸技术在脑卒中痛证、糖尿病、癫痫、老年痴呆、抑郁症、甲亢、不孕不育、视网膜及视力疾病的临床治疗中均取得较大进展。2003年“石氏中风单元疗法”经9000余例验证，其疗效居国内领先水平。

一、实验研究

(一)针刺机制研究

1991年，中医学院徐汤苹开展“十二井穴刺络放血实验”研究，发现该刺法可改善脑血肿大兔的硬膜外脑血流图，抑制脑中胆碱能M受体，兴奋肾腺α受体和β受体，使脑血管扩张，脑血流量增加。

1997年，中医一附院石学敏、韩景献、温廷益、邢来君等开展“针刺对快速老化鼠活性基因影响的实验研究”，首次在国内采用国际公认与老年痴呆病症最为接近的自然老化动物模型，取人中、内关、太冲为主穴，对快速老化鼠脑、肝细胞核活性基因转录、调控水平方面的影响进行研究，提示出针刺抗衰老的分子生物学机理。该成果获1997年度天津市科技进步二等奖。

2000年，中医一附院石学敏、韩景献、李平等开展“针灸治疗大动脉炎(头臂动脉型)的临床及实验研究”。该针法可明显调节患者肢体及颅内血流量，改善血液循环及能量代谢，加速机体自身修复，居国内领先水平。该项目获2000年度天津市科技进步二等奖。

2000年，石学敏、韩景献、李平等开展“衰老相关基因的筛选及针刺干预作用的实验研究”。该项目以日本快速老化脑萎缩模型为对象，发现以“调神益智，平肝通络”针法对靶点基因有调节作用，并发现eIF3基因可能与衰老相关，获2000年度天津市科技进步二等奖。2002年，石学敏、温廷益等利用基因表达谱芯片筛选出老年痴呆相关的异常表达基因，对该病早期诊断筛选药物和针刺取穴的研究打下基础。该成果获2002年度天津市科技进步二等奖。

图7-4-2-113 石学敏开展针刺机制研究

2004年,市中医医院薛莉、吉学群、于颂华等探讨针刺对Ⅱ型糖尿病的作用机制,采用Ⅱ型糖尿病大鼠模型针刺中脘、曲池等穴,发现大鼠血糖明显下降,说明针刺可抵抗胰岛素逆转。

(二)经络实质

1991年,中医学院郭义等开展"家兔经穴钙离子特异性"的实验研究,针刺时可使穴位点钙离子升高,经穴外钙离子浓度下降,提示钙离子参与了经络活动。1995年,郭义、张艳军以钙离子在经穴上的变化为研究对象,通过针刺实验动物,测定钙离子的变化规律,表明钙离子是经穴与脏腑相关的重要环节,亦是针刺效应产生的关键,对经络实质的提示具有重要启发作用。

2005年,中医学院韩煜、王津生等通过对人体经络原穴进行阶跃脉冲响应的测量,将原穴量化,发现已存在或还在潜伏的疾病,对诊断和治疗有重要意义。

(三)针刺手法

1991年,天津市中医院(以下简称"市中医院")张智龙以意气行针法,即以意念产生经气运行,以意鼓动人体促进气血运行而不强调外在刺激的一种针法。用此法治疗癫痫,使经气直达病灶,两年内未复发者达71.43%。1994年,石学敏、芦绍强、罗利对病态窦房结综合征采用多组穴位进行治疗,为难治之症提供最佳的治疗方针及理论依据,总结出系列穴位最佳组合。1996年,中医一附院王舒等采用风池穴常用四种针法,对动物椎基底动脉供血不足者进行施治,并以颅底血流动力学动态监测,提示不同手法的作用机制亦不相同,为临床上根据病情制定治则提供依据。2000年,东丽医院陈树岷就针灸中的子午流注的纳甲法、纳子法是以治疗疾病的即日为标准而疾病却没有当时发作时间规律特性问题,创纳时法补充子午流注,简单易学,疗效可靠。

二、针灸临床

(一)脑卒中

1991年,中医学院韩静文根据大脑皮层功能定位原理,以头针高速捻转加电兴奋治疗中风后遗症皮层性尿频、尿失禁,有效率91.76%。同年,中医二附院王欣于舌下金津、玉液两穴放血治疗舌喑,给病邪以出路,较一般针灸奏效迅速。1992年,市中医院郑艳霞采用维生素B_1、B_{12}、加蓝他敏穴位注射,取穴以阳明经为主,治疗肌肉萎缩,使中风患者在肢体恢复方面痊愈26.5%,总有效率98.1%,体现治萎"独取阳明"的学术思想。1992年,中医一附院杨兆钢提出脑病中假球麻痹其病机关键在于关窍阻闭,神气失导,因而制定调神导气、滋补三阴、通关利窍针刺法则,临床治愈率68.92%,总有效率98.05%。

1995年,市中医院韩禅虚、张智龙在以针刺治疗脑梗塞病人的同时,开展"复脑膳"食疗的观察研究,每日晚餐加用由黑木耳、核桃仁、海带、芹菜组成的"复脑膳"200克,通过200例病人观察,不仅在近期可改善血液流变和凝血指标,而且远期疗效亦佳。其间还开展针刺治疗胰岛素依赖型糖尿病合并脑梗塞的临床研究,取调理脾胃之穴,意在升清降浊、健脾运胃,使胰岛分泌增多,改善脂质代谢和高粘血症,提高脑梗塞的治愈率。

1998年,中医二附院张青云对脑血管疾病中肢体麻木者采用十二井穴刺血法,通滞调气,祛瘀散结,使微循环得以改善,导致身体产生应激反应,从而影响神经调节。1999年,一中心医院郑於敏继承郑静侯的广西针派,运用灵龟八法并与相应的交会穴配合,使中风患者疗效增加。2001年,三中心医院侯婷婷、李晓华等从夹脊穴是知觉神经和运动神经交会的枢纽出发,针刺夹脊穴配合曲池、合谷、三阴交、阳陵泉等穴治疗中风后遗症,探试治疗此症的新方法,有效率93.75%。2003年,中医学院郭义、王彦云等观察十二井穴刺络放血对中风初期患者意识状态的影响,按病情分为大面积、中面积、小面积三组,该手法对唤醒患者意识有一定效果,特别是对患者小面积意识状态有明显改善。2003年,石学敏研制的"石氏中风单元疗法",以醒脑开窍针刺和丹芪偏瘫胶囊为主,配以康复、饮食、运动、心理及护理疗法,经9005例患者验证,该疗法可降低致残率,缩短病程,改善生存质量,并在理论方面形成一套治疗系统。

（二）痛证

1991年，中国人民解放军第272医院（以下简称“272医院”）李连生以梅花针为主治疗顽固性头痛，叩击疼痛处至多个血滴为度，并针刺风池穴，有效率97.26%。通过研究表明，该法可改善大脑供血，针灸兼有双向调节作用。同年，南开医院李方儒、徐杰民、杨松年等对胃脘痛患者采取埋线疗法，用大号弯针自脾俞穿入，从同侧胃俞穿出，将1号羊肠线双根带入皮下。该法可调动机体抗病能力，特别对消化性溃疡疗效甚好。1994年，干部疗养院吴世谦以芒针治疗腰椎间盘突出症，运用迎随补泻手法和飞经走气手法，通过经络作用使腰椎间盘复位，马尾神经自然还纳。2000年，宝坻县中医院王贯民以齐刺之法针刺后顶穴治疗椎动脉型颈椎病，激发督脉经气，祛瘀通痹，使椎—基底动脉血流速度明显增加。2003年，中医一附院王舒、石学敏以经筋刺法治疗周围性神经麻痹，疗效优于传统针法，改善了神经功能和局部血液微循环。2003年，四中心医院廖辉采用互动式针刺手法治疗肩周炎，其效优于传统肩三针手法，使骨关节粘连得以较快松解。同年，和平中医院卓华以“烧山火”针刺手法治疗腰椎间盘突出症，该手法使病位周围血管扩张、微循环改善，起到活血止痛目的。同年，中研院附院韩秋艳对胃脘痛取中脘、足三里、内关、膻中等穴，以电针治疗，可健脾益气，温中和胃，调节胃肠运动。2005年，武警医学院附属医院吴名在治疗颈椎病时，依据“经脉所过，主治所在”，突破以局部取穴的方法，大量采用远端取穴方法，收到满意效果。

（三）戒毒

1995年，中医一附院仝桂兰、罗利等对滥用二氢埃妥啡所致戒断反应综合征以调神法针刺人中、阴陵泉等穴，有效率达100%，证实针刺可以通过在脑内释放吗啡样物内啡呔而起作用。1998年，中医学院徐立针刺耳穴肺、气管、内分泌及四关穴用于戒烟，成功率80%，并证实针刺耳穴可以激发吗啡样物质或吗啡样因子，可降低或消除吸烟欲望，针四关穴具有行气开闭、镇静安神作用。

（四）灸疗

2002年，南开中医院张秀国用雀啄灸法温灸督脉治疗侧索硬化症，使督脉通调，阳明气血充盈，四肢得以濡养，收到一定疗效。2003年，市中医院宫军以灸法治疗Ⅱ型糖尿病，将艾柱在穴位点燃，每穴5~10壮，每次6穴，通过观察血糖可知灸艾可使胰岛分泌增强，改善症状。

第三节 中医内科

近现代，在天津的中医中擅长内科疾病者，名医荟萃，成就卓著。1991年起，天津中医对血液循环系统、神经系统、泌尿生殖系统以及老年病、传染病等多种疾病开展广泛深入的研究，尤其在老年痴呆、肾病、脑卒中的治疗方面取得进展。不仅临床上疗效骄人，还在实验研究上有所突破，成功建立多种动物模型，并在进行基因筛选、探究药物作用机制、总结疾病演变规律等方面取得成果。1997 ~ 2005年，共获市级科技进步奖一等奖1项、二等奖6项。

一、传染病

（一）流感

1992年，天津市中医药研究院附属医院（以下简称“中研院附院”）张曾譻等在研究历代治疗外感的基础上，自拟荆防解毒合剂治疗流行性感冒，经1144例观察，证实该药具有疏风散寒、宣肺止咳、解毒清热的作用。1995年，天津市中医研究所（以下简称“中医研究所”）蒋连泓开创中药雾化吸入抗病毒、抗细菌治疗上呼吸道感染新方法，有效率达95.72%，优于西药雾化吸入剂疗效。同年，天津市和平中医院（以下简称“和平中医院”）冀瑞铎以《证治准绳》中外感方为基础，研制感冒灵口服液，在与康泰克、天津感冒片、抗病毒口服液为对照组的比较中，在起效速度、适应证范围方面有明显优势。1997年，中医学院李慧吉研制出具有清热、泻火、解毒、抑菌的清热灵汤剂，治疗各种流感发热效果良好。该院章顺意、夏蓉西通过实验证实，该药可提高巨噬细胞和T淋巴细胞的吞噬能力。2000年，中医一附院赵建国、卞金玲、韩力等开展“板青液预防脑卒中患者医院感染的临床研究”，研制出具有清热解毒、凉血化瘀、凉血利咽的板青合剂，对预防医院感染，特别是对脑卒中患者可明显降低医院感染率，增强人体免疫力，达到阴阳调和目的，优于常规中药治疗及抗生素治疗组。该成果获2001年度天津市科技进步二等奖。

（二）非典型性肺炎

2003年，中医学院张伯礼、张军平、杨树人等首次开展急性烈性传染病的中医学现场流行病学调查，提出“非典”的六个基本证侯，为提高中医救治水平提供了科学依据。同年，总医院陈津生提出非典型性肺炎属于中医“寒疫”范畴，研制出“抗萨1、2号”方剂，取得良好的退热效果，并可快速消除临床症状。同时，针对极期、恢复期以及后遗症，制定出中药治疗方案。经体外病毒药效学实验证实，“抗萨1号和2号”对SARS病毒具有有效抑制作用，最小有效浓度是46微克/毫升。该院研制的实验药剂“抗萨1号和2号”，以成果的形式转让给天津天士力药业集团，商品名为“安体威颗粒”获天津市药品监督管理局“中药制剂B类”进入临床。其“中医药抗SARS病毒的基础与临床研究”成果，获2005年度天津市科技进步二等奖。同年，天津市传染病医院（以下简称“传染病医院”）贾建伟等对非典型肺炎在西医对症支持基础上，以藿朴夏苓汤化裁组成“非典Ⅱ号”用于中期病人，12例患者全部出院。该院杨树人、朱理珉等对“非典”严重急性呼吸综合征在西医对症治疗、吸氧等基础上早期以白虎加苍术汤或三仁汤加味，恢复期以清暑益气汤加味，收到较好效果，并可防止激素减量后的复发。天津中医学院第二附属医院（以下简称“中医二附院”）杜瑞斌、白慧梅、赵英强等以清暑益气汤合沙参麦冬汤治疗“非典”在恢复期便秘症状，有效率达90%，使腑气通则肺气降，从而改善肺功能。2004年，中医二附院魏葆林、孙增涛等以益气活血法为主治疗“非典”恢复期病人，缓解不适症状，胸片及功能指标获得明显改善。

（三）乙型肝炎

1997年，传染病医院郑淑文以清热解毒、活血化瘀、扶正祛邪之中药治疗慢性乙型肝炎，治疗效果显著，并发现该组中药能够部分阻止病毒变异。2000年，天津市肝病研究所施伯安、张俊富、崔丽安等以抗乙肝免疫核糖核酸和中药复方“仙灵脾冲剂”治疗慢性乙型肝炎，收到较好效果。

二、循环系统疾病

（一）心律异常

1991年，中医学院王立斌对阮士怡研制的益肾健脾、涤痰复脉方药组合开展抗心律失常的实验研究，发现该方有加速钠离子向心肌细胞的内流促进细胞膜的去极化，提高心肌细胞自动除极的效果。1999年，中医一附院王竹瑛、王化良等以益气养血、熄风复脉法研制“脉安宁”制剂，治疗室性心律失常，能较好地消除室性早搏，改善心肌供血，优于心律平治疗并可改善血流变指标。2000年，天津市红桥中医院傅津治疗病态窦房结综合征，以益气温阳、滋阴复脉立法拟“增脉灵”方，温阳使缓慢心率增加，滋阴使阴中求阳，又防阳之太燥。

（二）冠心病

1991年，市中医院马连珍对寒凝瘀滞之心绞痛采用以细辛、乳香、没药为主药制成“心痛膏”，其症状改善率97%，心电图改善75%。1996年，中医学院范英昌、徐东琴等观察中药“心复康”对心肌梗塞过程中细胞生物学的影响进行研究，证实“心复康”具有有效防治心肌梗塞作用。1997年，中医一附院胡国强、田菲等通过观察300例冠心病患者，证实不同型的冠心病存在客观指标的差异，并指出证型间的变化规律。2000年，何海菊、傅娟等对张洪义依据清代王清任的诸活血汤化裁而来的“逐瘀生新方”进行研究。该方可保护血管内皮细胞及其凝血免疫物质转运和生物活性物质释放等多种生理功能，为治疗冠心病血瘀证的有效方剂。

（三）心衰

1991年，中医一附院阮士怡、王化良以软坚涤痰、强心复脉法研制“新生脉片”治疗慢性充血性心力衰竭，总有效率为96.9%，明显改善心功能状态，效果优于对照组。1996年，中医二附院孙兰军、田芬兰等运用“强心冲剂”治疗充血性心力衰竭，症状明显改善。经实验研究，该药可改善心衰血液动力及心脏内分泌激素水平。至2003年，孙兰军、赵英强等对“强心冲剂”的实验研究，得出该药可保护心肌功能、改善心肌收缩水平。2003年，中医一附院段可杰、郭利平等对院制剂“新生脉片”开展实验研究，观察多项指标，证实该药具有抗心室失常的重塑作用。2005年，天津市静海县中医院姜英采取商陆、附子为末调糊敷神阙穴治疗充血性心力衰竭，为简易有效方法。

（四）肺心病

1991年，272医院胡国华、苏满祥以地黄、附子、汉防已为主药研制“强心冲剂”，治疗肺心病心功能不全收到良好效果，并通过实验研究证实，该冲剂能提高心肌功能，增强免疫能力，是防治肺心病之理想方剂。

1999年，医科大学第三附属医院姚熙慧自拟平喘补身汤治疗慢性肺源性心脏病，纠正了其氨基酸代谢紊乱，提高免疫功能，改善肺通气换气功能，缓解了病情。

（五）动脉硬化症

1997年，中医一附院张军平等在防治动脉样硬化症“益气软脉方”实验研究的基础上，观察到该方的主要成方红芪多糖可显著抑制高脂血清培养下的平滑肌细胞增殖，有良好的清除自由基作用。1996年，中医学院范英昌、阮士怡等通过实验，探讨动脉硬化的发病机制及中医疏肝活血方法治理该病的机理，提示该法具有防治动脉硬化病的前景广阔。1999年，中医一附院黄文政、李艳梅采用“血瘀逐瘀丸”治疗动脉硬化症，疗效确定，并研究该方对动脉硬化症的作用机制及该症的危险因素。2002年，阮士怡创“补肾复脉方”治疗动脉粥样硬化疾病，临床上有效的研究结果显示，“补肾复脉方”具有补肾化痰、软坚散结功能，对缺氧内皮细胞有明显的保护作用。

（六）高血压

1992年，中医研究所李自然、李立祥根据中医辨证论治原则创立气功的降压功法，通过调息静观、督任运气方法，使血压趋于平稳，特别是对收缩压下降明显，作用独到，起到群体防治该病的作用。1994年，天津市河西医院李泓、张静、刘宗蔚等开展垂体—性腺轴激素水平与原发性高血压及中医辨证分型的关系研究，发现阳亢型、阴虚阳亢型及阴阳两虚型性腺水平下降，为高血压的治疗提供依据。1995年，南开医院赵悦惠、王平等研制“舒心降压片”以防已、女贞子为君，治疗原发性高血压，经测定血清内源性类洋地黄物质降低，维持内环境稳定。1998年，中研院附院李泓自拟降压中药“舒脉灵”冲剂治疗高血压收效良好，并开展实验研究，发现其可调整植物神经功能，抑制肾素—血管紧张素—醛固酮系统，调节内分泌水平。2002年，中医学院郑林、王学岭开展高血压肝阳上亢证与血瘀病机的相关研究，得出高血压肝阳上亢证多伴有血瘀病机，在辨证治疗时应注意活血药物的应用，可增加其疗效。

三、呼吸系统疾病

1996年，中医二附院董国立自拟具有宣肺平喘、化瘀止咳之功的“杏贝宁喘汤”治疗哮喘，收到良好效果。经研究，该方可提高哮喘患者肺通气功能，提高肺活量，气道反应均有不同程度降低。同年，该院孙增涛在系统整理治咳喘临床经验的基础上，观察宣肺中药对哮喘豚鼠气道炎的影响，提示宣肺中药有拮抗炎性介质变化的作用。1997年，中医研究所邢淑丽认为慢性阻塞性肺病感染期病机为本虚标实，痰瘀伏肺，拟定活血清热化痰方剂，临床收效。通过动物实验证实，该药能增强活力中性白细胞和巨噬细胞的吞噬能力，提高非特异性免疫力。1998年，中医一附院田乃姮、张超等运用中药“敏喘平”治疗支气管哮喘，效果良好，对于激素依赖的哮喘患者可作为替代品。2003年，该院刘贵颖、刘玉庆以“咳喘灵”治疗哮喘，经实验研究显示，该方是通过上调Fas蛋白在嗜酸细胞的表达而完成。2004年，刘贵颖、吕英、朱振刚等运用该院制剂“咳喘口服液”治疗支气管哮喘，以泼尼松为对照组，在肺功能改善方面优于对照组，无不良反应。

四、消化系统疾病

（一）脾胃病

1991年，中医二附院邵祖燕、刘福林等以鸡胚粉为主要原料制成鸡胚冲剂治疗脾虚证，总有效率94.83%，并经实验证实鸡胚确有健脾强身作用。1994年，南开医院赵家驹采取敷脐疗法治疗脾肾两虚病人，以肉桂、白芷、茴香、雄黄为末，上盖以艾绒，胶布固定，对增强体质、改善脾胃虚弱病人的症状有效，简单易行。1994年，邵祖燕，刘福林、刘永珍等研制具有温阳散寒、理气活血作用的胃速安散治疗消化性溃疡，证实有明显的镇痛作用，总有效率达95.25%。1995年，中医学院高金亮、徐东琴等在治疗脾气虚型慢性萎缩型胃炎研制“胃炎克方”，通过实验观察，其方可明显减轻模型动物胃粘膜炎细胞浸润程度，增加胃粘膜厚度，说明该方有修复慢性胃炎对胃的损害作用。1997年，中研院高金亮首创益气养阴行消法治疗术后殘胃炎，总有效率达94.3%，显效率65.9%。同年，高金亮、庞树玲在国内首创健脾益胃、清热化湿、活血化瘀综合治疗消化性溃疡，其一年复发率和二年复发率仅为6.18%和10.62%。1999年，该院王金贵运用腹部推拿手法治疗胃下垂，通过腹部伏冲之脉直接影响冲、任、督、胃四脉，促进经气循行流通，调节脾胃升降功能，显效率95.5%。2004年，天津市武清中医院陈宝贵对胃脘痛强调谨守病机，各司其属，以疏肝和胃、养阴益胃、健脾温胃、化滞开胃、泄热清胃、祛湿健胃、化瘀调胃、开窍醒胃八法，综合该病治则系统。

2004年，总医院唐芳等在“藿香及其制剂肠屏障保护及促进吸收功能的临床与实验研究”中，以缺血—再灌注大鼠为研究对象，通过观察藿香水提成份和挥发油成分及经典处方有效成分在大鼠肠机械屏障、免疫屏障损伤时对细胞因子、NO、细胞膜流动性、组织学和超微结构变化的观察，结果证实：藿香水提液和挥发油与藿香正气制剂保护肠屏障功能的作用，是通过抑制细胞因子TNF-α的合成，降低血清中TNF-α水平，维持血中NO正常浓度及细胞膜流动性等多方位的综合性肠上皮细胞的结构和功能的保护而实现的。但藿香不同成分作用靶点及部位侧重各异，藿香复方的肠屏障保护作用优于中药单品。该研究较全面地揭示了芳香类中药及复方肠粘膜保护作用机理。

（二）胃癌前期病变

1995年，中国人民解放军空军天津医院马连生研制复方制剂“胃细胞逆转丸”，治疗萎缩性胃炎、胃十二指肠溃疡3000例，临床症状痊愈率97.1%。1999年，中医一附院陈大权、王文仲以软坚活血、清热解毒的“胃神口服液”治疗胃癌前期病变，证实该药可抑制增殖，增强免疫功能。2002年，中医学院雒明池以黄芪、党参、丹参组成具有益气活血作用的“胃2号冲剂”治疗胃癌前期病变，在临床上取得一定疗效，发现该方可以使胃粘膜腺体的萎缩及肠上皮化生、不典型增生的程度明显减轻，从而对胃癌前期病变有阻断作用。2003年，该院袁红霞、代二庆提出气阴两虚是胃癌前期病变的病机，以中药“善胃方”治疗该病，对胃粘膜细胞增殖有抑制作用。2005年，中医二附院李慧臻以具有健脾活血理气作用的制剂“胃安散”治疗该病，较好地改善了临床症状及抑制腺体萎缩、肠上皮化生、异型增生作用。

（三）肝硬化

1994年，中医二附院董国立在治疗肝病时总结四法，即清热解毒、活血利湿；疏肝解郁、健脾养胃；滋阴柔肝、软坚化痰；益气化瘀，气水并治，临床疗效确切，影响后来临床医生。1997年，中医一附院汤毅、章伟与香港福康医药有限公司研制的泰一口服液，具有扶正固本、益气养阴等功效，使肝硬化患者的血浆蛋白得到明显改善，白蛋白与球蛋白比值恢复正常。2000年，传染病医院胡东胜、钱静运用具有较大毒性之中药大戟、甘遂、商陆等组成“消臌散”敷脐治疗肝硬化腹水，通过神阙穴局部吸收，毒性变小，安全可靠，使腹胀症状明显改善，腹水消退。

(四)胆石症

1996年,第一医院吕宗勃、王子云采取耳穴电冲击方法治疗胆石症,达到病人自觉耳部发热胀为宜,排石者部分可当天排石,有效率达80%,排空率8.3%。

五、泌尿生殖系统疾病

(一)肾病

1991年,市中医院肾病研究室张大宁等对慢性肾功能衰竭概括为"虚、瘀、湿、逆"四大病机,提出补虚活血为本,祛湿降逆为标的治则,创制肾衰系列方剂,包括补肾扶正胶囊、活血化瘀胶囊、肾衰灌肠方等。经临床和实验研究,该系列方能够降低血尿素氮、血肌酐,改善肾血流量,提高免疫力。同年,中医一附院柴彭年以益肾软坚、通利排石为治则,筛选高效低毒药物组成"结石通一号"治疗泌尿系结石,对肾结石有效率达88.75%,显示该药对结石有很好的排石、溶石双重作用。1992年,中医学院张洪义、曹式丽等以补肾活血之生晒参、首乌、丹参、大黄等并用低蛋白饮食治疗肾性贫血,总有效率74.36%。1992年,曹式丽、何永生等采取祛瘀生新法治疗慢性肾功能不全,从血证论治慢性肾功能衰竭疾患,改善肾小球血流动力学指标,对延缓该病进展有较大意义。同年,中医一附院黄文政、柴彭年依据慢性肾衰的正虚邪实之本质,提出脾肾气血、阴阳虚损和湿浊毒邪、瘀血内阻为病机关键,应用和中降浊、扶肾补虚、活血化瘀法研制中药口服液"扶肾液1、2号",总有效率81.76%。1995年,该院张云秀、郝文洁以扶正祛邪法组中药黄芪、仙茅、仙灵脾、紫草等,治疗乙肝病毒相关性肾炎,有效率达90%。1997年,中医二附院王耀光、田麒等以温阳益肾、泻浊活血法治疗肾小球肾炎。经研究证实,该方法具有活血化瘀、抗纤维化、保护细胞膜、恢复抗氧化能力等方面作用。1999年,中医一附院郭利平、张军平运用血清药理学新方法观察益肾健脾、活血利水方药对肾小球系膜细胞抑制增殖的影响,证实该方药在此方面有较好的作用。该药可明显抑制肾小球系膜细胞增殖及其细膜外基质成分纤维连接蛋白和IV型胶原的产生,显示出良好的肾小球硬化拮抗效应。

2000年,南开医院赵恩俭在治疗尿毒症时选用益气健脾、补肾利水、降浊解毒、活血化瘀之药治疗该病,使水湿之症得到缓解,延长患者生命。同年,中医一附院黄文政、曹式丽等进行"肾炎3号方治疗慢性肾炎临床及实验研究",依据中医"少阳主枢"理论,结合慢性肾炎本虚标实的病机,创立以疏利少阳为主,兼益气养阴、活血化瘀的治疗原则,研制出"肾炎3号"复方口服液,观察256例患者,完全缓解32%,总有效率87%。该方在降低蛋白尿、减少血尿、提高血浆蛋白、改善脂质代谢、调节免疫功能、改善高凝状态和改善肾功能等方面具有良好的作用。在实验中,成功地进行了大鼠肾小球系膜细胞体外培养,采用血清药理学的方法,观察该方对系膜细胞增殖和相关性细胞因子及基因表达的影响。该项目获2000年度天津市科技进步二等奖。2002年,中医学院李燕林、李慧敏在应用具有泻浊化湿、活血解毒作用的妙慈方治疗肾功能衰竭的基础上进行实验研究,发现经治疗后的肾小管、集合管坏死数明显降低,减轻了肾小管阻塞程度。2005年,林燕、曹式丽等将肾性血尿分为外感风湿、湿热壅盛、阴虚内热、瘀血阻络4型,临床以中医证侯定性与实验室指标定位相结合,规范了诊断过程和治疗方法。

(二)前列腺疾病

1991年,中医一附院刘鸿玺、王哲、刘庆忠以直肠内用中药活血化瘀、通络解毒之"前列腺1号"电离导入法治疗慢性前列腺炎,通过实验观察该药可提高血清吞噬细胞功能,促进前列腺炎痊愈。1994年,中医学院朱理璎等研制"癃淋安康"治疗老年性前列腺增生,显效率达73.5%,并通过实验证实该药对内分泌起到正性调节作用,提高内分泌系统的应激能力。1997年,中医一附院杨兆钢以芒针治疗慢性前列腺炎,通过调节神经血管功能、抗菌消炎、缓急止痛等作用效果明显。2001年,中医学院王慧生、王志华认为前列腺增生乃湿热毒邪与滞气败血瘀阻水腑而成,研制前列安冲剂,消除前列腺感染后造成的腺泡和腺腔内的炎性分泌物,并可减轻其增生程度,最终通过毒去瘀散使体内邪去正安。

（三）生殖器炎症

1994年，中医研究所高纪和、王志华对外生殖器官炎症选用具有清热解毒、燥湿杀虫功效的中药研制成“百乐净特效洁阴宝”。该药具有广谱抗菌性，行销部分省市。1999年，高纪和、王志华根据祖国医学理论和历代经验，研制清热燥湿方治疗外生殖器官疾患，临床观察优于西药组，效果显著。2004年，中医研究院附院赵宝忠经临床筛选药物和试用研制消炎复春汤治疗精囊炎，其效优于复方新诺明片治疗该病，且无副作用，远期疗效好。

（四）功能性障碍

1991年，中医研究所高纪和主编《中国男科证治类萃》。该书是国内外第一部系统整理祖国医学领域中防治男科疾病的大型学术著作，从散在历代医学著作中挖掘而成，提供男科的深化研究。同年，天津市河西医院张越林以海马、郁金、蜈蚣等中药研制“起萎冲剂”治疗阳萎，滋肾填精、疏肝通络、提高血中睾酮含量。1995年，天津市医药科学研究所赵泰、王玉芬等以白芍、蜈蚣为主研制健脾冲剂。该药具有养血益精、舒肝通络、调理阴阳作用，用于男性性功能低下、不育症的治疗，效果满意。

（五）不育症

1992年，中医研究所高纪和、孟庆辉以补肾壮阳法研制鱼鹿生精汤治疗特发性少精症，有效率达93%，精浆中锌、钙含量较治疗前明显提高，对精浆中微量元素的异常状态有一定调节作用。1994年，中医一附院王兢、刘红潮、王玉香以补肾填精、益气养血、化瘀通络、清热利湿为治则，制成“育灵1号”膏剂治疗不育症，提高受孕率，并证实该药有雄性激素样作用，提高性功能。1997年，天和医院张越林针刺肾俞、太溪、命门、关元等穴治疗男性少精症，发现该法能促进下丘脑—垂体分泌和调节促性腺激素作用，有效率达80.8%。2000年，南开中医院赵宝忠以补肾益精、补气养血、助孕赞育为法，研制“益乾赞育丸”治疗不育症，提高了精子的数量和质量，疏通精液通道的梗阻，防治生殖系统的感染，提高孕育成功率。2003年，其以利湿化痰、祛瘀散寒法拟化精赞育汤治疗精液不液化症，有效率达95%。

六、血液病

（一）贫血

1991年，中医学院陈通开展“肾主骨生髓”的实验研究，以“补肾方”对大白鼠实验性白细胞减少症的周围血液白细胞作用及对骨髓造血功能的影响，发现补肾方对两者皆有升高作用。该“补肾方”可改善白细胞减少症。1992年，该院戴锡孟、杨学爽等以补肾活血法，重用血肉有情之品研制“贫血丸”治疗再障性贫血，与八种治疗该病的其他方法比较，“贫血丸”具有疗效好、无毒副作用的优势。同年，市中医院孟智宏、刘大功等对再生障碍性贫血病人舌象进行微观观察，该组病人舌象明显区别正常组。通过舌象观察，认为其多存在瘀血、精血亏损及水湿障碍，为临床提供诊断依据。1993年，中医学院杨学爽、范宝印等以“大黄正血灵”治疗鼻衄，总有效率为94.5%。通过实验发现该药有类似去甲肾上腺素收缩血管的作用，效果好且安全，还可免除由填塞带来的呼吸困难和继发性感染。

1993年，中医一附院杨文华、万增智在补肾活血法治疗再生障碍性贫血取得较好临床效果的同时，对其机理进行研究，发现该法可刺激造血干细胞生长，改善骨髓造血微环境，增强免疫功能。2002年，该院史哲新以健脾补肾法结合叶酸、维生素B_{12}治疗巨幼红细胞性贫血，近期疗效及远期疗效优于西药组和单纯中药组，并能明显缩短疗程，防止恶化。1994年，市中医医院孟智宏、赵宝安对再生障碍性贫血患者舌蕈状乳头进行观察，发现该病患者舌蕈状乳头萎缩，是判断精血亏损程度较为灵敏的一个诊断指标。

（二）白血病

1998年，戴锡孟、杨学爽等应用传统中成药六神丸和梅花点舌丹治疗白血病，经证实该药可杀伤白血病细胞，减轻对脏器的损害。该成果获1998年度天津市科技进步二等奖。同年，戴锡孟针对白血病化疗后引起骨髓抑制、血象下降，研制中药免疫合剂减轻化疗反应，实验发现该药有益气养血、滋阴补肾、减轻骨髓抑制，促进造血功能。同年，杨学爽、杨文华把急性白血病分为热毒炽盛、热毒血瘀、气血双亏三型辨证，收到一定效果，显示出较大治疗优势。2002年，万增智、杨文华在运用全蝎治疗白血病时，发现其可使HL—60细胞凋亡。2004年，开展益气养阴、活血化瘀法治疗微小残留白血病细胞凋亡机制的研究，发现该药主要作用于细胞的DNA合成后期以及有丝分裂期，可抑制白血病细胞的生长代谢，使白血病细胞快速凋亡。

（三）白细胞减少症

1992年，中医一附院隋卓琴以现代医学腹部按摩法治疗白细胞减少症。该手法具有疏通任脉、宣通气血、调和阴阳作用，有效率达100%，治愈率71.8%。

七、内分泌代谢疾病

（一）糖尿病

1993年，天津市河东医院柴润芳、卢思森、张桂芬等对具有益气养阴、活血滋肾作用的“胰活散”进行实验研究，发现其可降低空腹血糖、果糖胺、胆固醇浓度，对胰岛细胞有一定修复作用及增加细胞分泌颗粒作用。2000年，第三中心医院张桂芬、侯婷婷、卢思森继续研究“胰活散”的降糖作用，发现该药对胰岛β细胞的损伤有修复和增加细胞分泌颗粒的作用，起到增加活性、达到降糖效果。

1996年，天津市第一医院张柏林、苏文弟、陈劲松等完成“中药糖复康对非胰岛素依赖型糖尿病的临床及实验研究”。通过对413例非胰岛素依赖型糖尿病患者证型分布调查和运用中医理论进行症状学分析，提出“阴阳（气阴）俱虚是糖尿病（消渴）的基本病生理变化，阳（气）虚是启动因素”的观点符合临床情况。在此基础上研制出中药糖复康胶囊，临床有效率为86.78%。药效学实验显示：在同等剂量下糖复康的降糖效果优于降糖灵和金芪降糖片，并改善胰岛素分泌和脂蛋白代谢，减轻微量蛋白尿。

1997年，中医一附院牛元起、袁益君等以“舟楫饮”治疗糖尿病，临床效果良好。经实验证实，该药对胰岛结构有明显的保护和修复作用。1998年，总医院王作成、曲竹秋对具有良好降糖作用的“糖尿停”浓缩液进行实验研究，证实该药有良好的改善糖耐量、降血脂、阻止肥胖发生以及降低外周血清胰岛素水平作用。

1998年，天津市第一医院张柏林、陈劲松以补肾扶阳、益气生津之法研制的“糖复康”用于治疗糖尿病，优于降糖灵和金芪降糖片，通过实验发现对Ⅱ型糖尿病更有疗效，表明该药可下调尿蛋白排泄率，与西药苯那普利作用相似并下调肾皮质蛋白质非酶糖化终产物。至2001年，以“糖复康”治疗糖尿病肾病，从细胞活性物质表达环节入手，对该药的作用机理进行系统研究，丰富了中医治疗糖尿病、肾病的理论。

（二）高脂血、高粘血病

1996年，中医学院张仲一对药食兼用的保健饮品“降脂饮”进行降脂实验研究，发现其能明显降低血清胆固醇、甘油三脂，改善血流变，优于西药安妥明。1997年，第三医院赵景华将益气活血、行气破瘀之中药组成“降粘防栓灵”冲剂治疗高粘血症，能明显降低全血粘度及血浆粘度，改善全血触变性，增加红细胞变形性。同年，中医一附院阮士怡、王竹瑛采用补肾软坚方法防治肾虚型动脉硬化症，该法能显著改善患者的脂质代谢紊乱和血流变异常。1998年，第三医院张春玲、韩国英采用院制剂“释凝降粘胶囊”治疗高粘血症和缺血性脑血管病，以藻酸双脂钠为对照组，在改善血流变指标和干扰血栓形成方面优于西药。

1999年，中医学院张伯礼、高秀梅等采用高胆固醇血症家兔模型观察自然恢复和降脂中药对该症的影响，确定了中药降脂的临床意义。2000年，该院范英昌、陆一竹等开展调肝导浊中药对脂蛋白代谢及主动脉平滑肌细胞增殖调控的影响进行研究，证实其可有效调整脂代谢，防止动脉硬化的发生。至2001年，针对动脉硬化症气滞痰阻病机，系统研究了调肝导浊中药通过多靶点、多途径对动脉硬化的调控作用。

2000年，中医学院刘俊荣、李俊杰观察健身八段锦可以降低低密度脂蛋白和提高高密度脂蛋白，其功法集调心、调息、调形于一体，调动人体内在潜能，提高机体对物质的吸收、代谢、转化和排出功能。1996～2001年，该院石学敏、周素琴针对高粘滞血症，研制成“精制化瘀通脉复合汤剂”，内含丹参、川芎、降香等。通过实验研究，证实该药为抗高粘滞血症的理想药，对预防心脑血管疾病有应用价值。2003年，天津市河西中医院王文波以院制剂通脉降脂胶囊治疗高脂血症，能够纠正血液流变学各项指标，改善临床症状，具有多重防治心血管疾病的作用。

（三）甲状腺疾病

1995年，总医院曲竹秋、王士相、王宏镛等完成“消瘿冲剂治疗甲状腺机能亢进临床及实验研究”。该研究确立“从肝论治”的治疗原则。提出以酸泻肝木为主治疗甲亢的六法并将六法融于一方，研制成治疗甲亢的新型中成药——消瘿冲剂。经临床试验取得满意的疗效。该项目获1995年度国家中医药科技进步奖。

1997年，中研院附院张曾譻、唐方、王振立确立了甲状腺机能亢进的病因为精明失养，当以健脑宁心、柔肝滋肾之法研制“甲安口服液”，明显降低T3、T4水平及脑细胞耗氧量。2002年，天津市北辰中医院采取综合疗法——内服养阴舒肝中药，针刺内关、合关等穴，并以软坚散结中药局部离子透入治疗甲状腺机能亢进症，疗效较好，特别适宜不能接受西药治疗者。

八、风湿类疾病

1992年，天津市中西医结合津华医院王兆铭对风湿类疾病提出祛风散寒、利湿通络，意在驱除侵入人体的风寒湿邪；解毒消肿、活血化瘀，意在解决关节周围炎症；补肾坚骨、扶正固本，意在改善骨质疏松，修复骨腐蚀，调节免疫功能，并研制出“类强炎”冲剂和“消肿散结”冲剂治疗风湿类疾病，在10万患者中筛选资料齐全的800例进行统计，其有效率达98%。1996年，中医学院陆肇中以扶正固本、搜风化瘀、活血通痹为法，研制出“陆氏顽痹冲剂”治疗类风湿关节炎，可减轻患者痛苦，降低发病率。2001年，中医一附院左芳、刘维、王慧采取针刺大椎、华佗夹脊联合中药活血通络治疗强直性脊柱炎，能较好地改善脊柱功能，缓解腰背疼痛，起到疏通经络、扶正祛邪的作用。同时，以白虎加桂汤合四妙散治疗痛风性关节炎，以西药别嘌呤醇为对照，效果优于西药，改善机体嘌呤代谢，增加尿酸排出。同年，该院风湿科运用中医分型理论，吸收现代医学新知识、新技术，制定系列治疗方案，提出类风湿关节炎量化评估系统，对风湿病的诊断及治疗评价有重要意义。2004年，中医二附院杨玉兰、高常柏认为类风湿关节炎发病根本因素为正气不足，在治疗上运用益气养血、调和营卫、补肾壮骨、活血涤痰、健脾益胃、清热利湿等复方复法，多途径、多层次联合用药，避免因用西药所引起的毒副作用，达到治疗目的。2005年，中医一附院刘维运用该院治疗类风湿协定处方“清痹片”治疗类风湿关节炎，其疗效与甲氨喋呤作用相当，可有效控制病情进展，且无不良反应。同年，该院曹克光、臧力学、唐丽等认为痛风因为浊毒瘀滞，以清热利湿解毒、活血化瘀为法，拟“痛风合剂”治疗痛风及高尿酸血症，可缓解症状，防止反复发作。

九、神经与精神病

（一）脑卒中

1999年，中医学院张伯礼、宋其云对中风危险因素及相关证侯进行流行病学调查，总结出中风病基本证类特点和演变规律，建立了中风先兆症诊断标准，并进行治疗方案优化研究，同时还就天津地区中风病危险因素及证侯开展调查研究，收集1524例病历，危险因素依次为高血压、冠心病、荤食、吸烟、饮白酒、暴怒、口咸等。该项目获1999年度天津市科技进步二等奖。2002年，第三中心医院林书珩以祛风通络、活血化瘀中药电离子导入治疗脑隙性梗塞后肢体活动障碍，总改善率为96.2%，对基底节区及丘脑区梗塞疗效较佳。2003年，中医一附院付立新、赵建国等对急性脑卒中引发心脏病损伤采取针刺治疗，可改善患者异常心电图及生化指标，提示该治疗方法对心肌具有保护作用。

（二）抑郁症

1996年，天津市安定医院林虹对产后精神障碍抑郁型患者，采取电针治疗，取神门、本神等穴，优于单纯毫针刺法。2000年，该院宋文水、周正保在中医治疗各类精神病多采取逍遥散或二陈之类舒肝祛痰之法的情况下，而采取疏肝镇静、清热解毒法并研制“舒心乐”浓缩剂治疗，显效率为88%。2002年，中医一附院武连仲依据舌与经络脏腑关系、舌与神明关系，采取点刺舌部穴位治疗抑郁症，使精神性失语患者获得痊愈。同年，一中心医院白炳清根据英国心理学家艾森克“人格理论”五型和中医将人格分为阴阳25种人的“五态人”进行对照研究，得出两者内涵有异、又相互联系的论点，为临床辨证提供理论依据。同年，中医二附院侯冬芬以“五态人”为人格分型依据，对精神病患者和心理正常者对照研究，得出精神病患者以“偏阳”者多，正常人中以“偏阴”者多的结论。2003年，该院杜元灏、李桂平以调神疏肝针法治疗抑郁症，该针法优于传统针法，取得与西药百忧解的相同疗效。

（三）焦虑症

1996年，安定医院刘正学以疏肝理气、活血化瘀、养血安神法，自拟“焦虑宁”冲剂治疗焦虑症，有效率达87%。又因该药副反应少，适于中老年患者。1997年，中医一附院邵文虎以交泰丸为主方加减自制“安眠足浴液”，治疗由焦虑所引起的失眠症，起到引火归源、水火相济、阳入于阴的作用。2002年，滨江医院傅谧亚认为溃疡性结肠炎患者情绪稳定性差，好焦虑，在一定程度上影响该病恶化，故采取心理疗法包括心理、认知、情绪、行为干预治疗该病，提高了近期治愈率。2004年，中医一附院颜红采用中药祛烦益聪汤配合心理疗法治疗考试焦虑证，总有效率达90%，使学生社会功能得以恢复。2005年，安定医院崔金波以电针加心理疗法治疗焦虑症，激活网状结构与大脑皮层觉醒，又可降低过度激活，收到良好效果。同年，该院王志凌、李育红以清热开窍、调整气机、宁心安神为法，针刺任、督、心、脾经穴治疗广泛性焦虑，收到较药物治疗更佳的效果，并且避免了药物不良反应。

（四）痴呆

1991年，中医一附院王学美对阮士怡所创“降脂软脉灵”抗衰老作用进行研究，表明该方可降低肝中氧化脂质及心肌褐素的含量，对老年性痴呆亦有作用，该药具有抗氧化作用。1997年，张伯礼等承担国家“九五”攻关课题“多发梗塞性痴呆大鼠模型的实验研究和中药拮抗作用的观察”，在进行血管性痴呆的流行病学调查和中医证侯学调查基础上，研制“健脑益智冲剂”，临床有效率达80%，实验研究成功地改进多发梗塞性痴呆的大鼠模型，从行为学、形态学观察并从脑内P物质、中枢神经递质等方面进行发病机制及中药治疗机制的研究。该项目获1997年度天津市科技进步二等奖。1999年，中医学院、中医一附院张伯礼、张军平、梅健勋、李苓等开展“清脑益智方对体外培养胚胎大脑神经细胞生物学影响”研究，从保护神经细胞的角度，采取离体实验手段观察中药对神经元兴奋毒性损伤的保护作用，寻求中药作用靶点，进而探讨该方对体外培养的人胚和鼠胚大脑神经细胞和胶质细胞的影响。该研究表明，该方可多途径保护受损伤的脑神经细胞，初级作用点是在星形胶质细胞，还可保护血管壁细胞，起到对血管性痴呆的防治。该项目获2000年度天津市科技进步一等奖。

2000年，中医学院杨幼新、赵亚莉、张世林认为人之脏器功能衰退从脾肾开始，故以培补温养脾肾之先、后天之本来延缓衰老，研制“补肾健脾冲剂”，实验证实可改善细胞代谢，使自由基减少并清除。2002年，该院林云、陆小佐等以填精补髓、醒神开窍、化瘀逐瘀法研制“抗痴呆1号”，治疗老年大脑功能不全，并且和清宫寿桃丸、洗心汤、补阳还五汤、知柏地黄丸、还少丹进行比较，发现该药效果最好，尤其对境界性痴呆的治疗效果更佳。同年，武清中医医院陈宝贵对老年期血管性痴呆进行研究，认为治疗上需补益五脏之精气，兼以化痰祛痰，开窍通络，创“回神丹”颗粒剂治疗该病，对轻中度痴呆疗效显著且持久。2003年，市中医医院张大宁、张宗礼、车树强针对老年期肾虚血瘀、浊毒内停等特征，采用补肾活血降浊通利疗法，研制“补肾活血胶囊”对老年痴呆证进行治疗，为中医治疗提出新的治疗途径。

十、肿瘤

1993年，胸科医院宋傧对恶性肿瘤化疗后的毒副作用施以补肺、健肝、温肾法减轻化疗药物的毒副作用，以化疗祛邪，中药扶正达到祛邪而不伤正的目的。1995年，空军天津医院李金文、张瑞阳、史重华等研制“抗癌化瘀止痛膏”，依发病脏腑敷在其经络主要穴位上，较三阶梯止痛方法效果明显，同时发现一些转移到皮肤上的肿瘤包块，外敷后包块变软、缩小，说明该药存在抗癌作用。1999年，肿瘤医院王毓敏对放射疗法所致口腔炎以滋阴清热合剂治疗，有效率达83%，可减轻痛苦，保证放疗顺利完成。同年，北辰中医医院马国海以该院验方“溶岩胶囊”治疗肝癌，该胶囊由藏红花、三七、麝香、半边莲等组成，改善了临床症状，对提高巨噬细胞活性，提高生活质量，延长生存期有一定作用。2001年，胸科医院李桂武、史东升以扶正培本、益气养阴、清热解毒为法，研制了抗癌中药“宁肺片”治疗肺癌，效果接近化疗效果，但无毒副作用。同年，中研院附院刘华一、王蓉等开展由人仙草、壁虎等组成的“仙碧方”对肿瘤治疗机理的研究，通过实验发现该药对荷瘤小鼠红细胞粘附肿瘤细胞能力有增强作用，提高免疫能力，可应用于肿瘤的二级防治用药。2002年，中医学院陈通采用补肾益髓方药治疗癌症化疗后引起的白细胞减少症，使患者白细胞数目有所提高，改善造血机能，长期服用未出现肾上腺皮质激素样副作用，证实肾主骨生髓的中医理论。

2002年，中医一附院贾英杰、田菲等提出肺癌机理为毒瘀并存的观点，以解毒祛瘀法治疗该病，通过实验证实，该药确可阻滞癌细胞生长。同年，以木鳖子、姜黄、莪术、冰片自制外用膜剂治疗中度癌痛，该膜剂具有活血止痛、解毒散结作用，可局部诱发肿瘤细胞凋亡和破坏肿瘤血管形成，抑制肿瘤增生，缓解对周围组织及神经的侵润压迫。同年，中医一附院周正华、方桢等对失去手术机会的中晚期食管癌患者，采取内镜下微波平扫的方法清除坏死组织并局部化疗药物，予滋阴降浊、益气养血中药，短期内收到疗效。2004年，贾英杰以祛瘀解毒、扶正抗癌为原则研制中药“化坚丸”和“消岩汤”治疗各种肿瘤，在化疗配合下，既使癌细胞凋亡，又提高生活质量，延长生存期。

第四节 中医外科与骨伤科

1991～2005年，天津中医在治疗外科疾病方面未见重大成果出现，仅在创伤、疮疡、脉管炎、肛肠疾病等方面小有进展。有的将中药与现代成膜技术结合起来，更便于外用；有的扩大传统疗法的应用范围，提高治愈率；也有的以中医治则研制出新的中成药，取得较好疗效。

天津中医对骨伤病的治疗上，多见于传统的推拿、按摩、刮痧、走罐等治法上。1991年后，操作上多有改进，有的是多种疗法结合应用，有的还配合药物治疗，还有的研制出腰椎复位牵引机治疗腰部疾患，均获得较好疗效。

一、中医外科

（一）创伤

1995年，中医研究所高纪和、王慧生、王志华将中药与现代成膜技术融为一体，研制成不透气和疏水性的中药外用涂膜新剂型，治疗创伤，具有加速愈合、不妨洗浴和近水作业的特点。1999年，该所王志华、万寿玲对软组织损伤采取由川芎、丹参、乳香、没药等十几味中药制成的“舒通酊”治疗，实验发现该药有良好的透皮吸收功能，可加速血液循环，促进组织代谢，由于有温热疏通作用，也可起到止痛效果。

（二）疮疡

1991年，中医二附院王锡荣继承津门已故名医于东川的外科经验，自制“提毒散”和“拔毒生肌散”，治疗淋巴结核和胸壁结核，71例病人全部治愈。且自拟“清热解肌汤”治疗下肢丹毒，疗效极好，以此为基础治疗多种感染疾病而具有发热症状者，每每收效。2000年，中医一附院张庚扬、王军等在中医辨证论治的基础上，运用“丹黄消炎液”外治中药治疗糖尿病足坏疽，治愈率提高到63.5%，使原来12%截肢率下降为5.6%。2001年，中医一附院刘宝生、魏子冬、张庚扬等治疗急性坏死性筋膜炎，外治采用清创引流术、中药换药、点状植皮，并分热毒炽盛、阴液不足、气血两虚三型辨证施治，治愈率90.7%。2003年，天津市公安医院李岩利用火针点刺缠腰火毒、丹毒、手癣等症，扩大了火针在以往只用于排脓的作用范围，在点刺处复以火罐拔出败血，达到以热攻热的目的。2005年，张庚扬将糖尿病足坏疽分为气阴两虚、湿热毒盛、气血两虚三型，并研制消疽系列汤剂，同时采用西药降糖、控感染方法，对局部创面注重气血外荣，祛腐生肌，变逆为顺。

（三）脉管炎

1997年，中医一附院张庚扬、杜钰生以活血、疏通、祛湿为法制成“通脉散”，治疗静脉血栓，有效率为89%。2005年，中国医学科学院血液病研究所李尚珠以痹祺胶囊治疗血栓性浅静脉炎，达到温经通络活血的作用，有效率为95%。

（四）肛肠疾病

1996年，中医一附院杜克礼、张丽芬对溃疡性结肠炎采取“肠炎灵Ⅰ号”灌肠治疗，对充血、水肿、糜烂及溃疡有良好疗效。1997年，中医二附院朱士达、窦和勤以自拟中药大黄、附子、黄连等保留灌肠治疗慢性溃疡性结肠炎，治愈的患者较西药对照组平均时间缩短，且无不良反应。同年，中医一附院中医外科以切开挂线法治疗高位复杂性肛瘘，与国外单线切开及腹部造肛门等手术比较，具有疗效高、疗程短、远期疗效好等特点，无完全性肛门失禁症。同年，总医院周云岩以三棱针挑刺背部有效点治疗肛门部疾患，使湿热外泄，清泻血中之瘀滞，不致下迫肛门，对神经—体液系统有良好的调整作用。

二、中医骨伤科

（一）颈椎病

1998年，中医学院朱鹏飞采用一指禅推法沿督脉、足太阳膀胱经自上而下反复推之治疗颈椎病及其他脊椎病，刺激俞穴，推动经气，改变了机体的神经生物电及神经介质的信息活动，达到治疗目的。2001年，中医一附院陈元成鉴于刮痧走罐在临床应用范围大，而市售润滑液效果不明显，遂以黄芪、丹参、红花为主于花生油中浸泡后炸焦滤液备用，在治疗颈椎病上收到很好效果。同年，该院纪君时、苏玉亭在按摩治疗颈椎病的同时，观察患者椎动脉血流量等方面的改变，发现按摩颈椎可改变上行头部的血流量，总结出按摩最佳部位和手法的结合。2005年，该院孙庆、董桦采取通脉调气推拿手法治疗并观察患者血浆内皮素和5—羟色胺有明显改善，使颈椎病得以明显改善，疼痛缓解，为按摩治疗脑病及颈椎病提供了依据。

（二）肩周炎

1997年，急腹症研究所郑文郁、邹英杰以刮痧、按摩、拔罐三法结合治疗肩周炎，使代谢产物得以排泄，周围炎症消失，简便易行。2004年，中医一附院董桦运用推拿手法配合服用独活寄生汤及中药熏蒸治疗肩周炎，以药力与热力的作用改善局部血液循环，促进炎性物质的吸收，达到镇痛、松解粘连、滑利关节的作用。2005年，中医学院韩顺平将传统治疗肩周炎的暴力牵拉和轻揉两种治疗方法结合起来，形成点拔揉运推拿法治疗肩周炎，相得益彰。

（三）腰椎间盘突出症

1995年，中医一附院孔令勤研制腰椎复位牵引机治疗腰部疾患，使腰椎间盘突出症在按摩的配合下，缩短疗程。该牵引机获国家专利。2001年，该院王平、古思鹏在按摩名家叶希贤所创治疗手法的基础上，加以改进，采取十步正骨法治疗腰椎间盘突出症，在效果上优于叶氏传统手法对照组，并缩短了治愈时间。

（四）股骨头坏死

2002年，中医一附院谭涛以腹部推拿手法治疗股骨头坏死，同时配合理筋手法及口服股骨头康复片，通过直接按压腹主动脉，提高血流速度，改善股骨头血供，起到活血通络作用，有效率达94.59%。

（五）骨折

2002年，河西骨科医院陈桂珍以血竭、乳香、没药、水蛭等组成接骨散，对骨折病人结合固定敷于患处，起到促进愈合、舒筋活血、消肿止痛的作用。2004年，武清中医院王光辉对于骨不连及骨延迟愈合在内外固定的基础上，采用“坚骨壮筋膏”外敷，达到瘀祛、新生、加速骨折愈合的目的。

（六）骨质疏松

1995年，天和医院张越林开展老年骨质疏松与中医肾虚证的关系研究，对该病采取天然中药“胎盘粉”

胶囊治疗，使该病缓解，部分病人骨度值增加，证实肾虚是老年骨质疏松的重要病机，亦说明肾主骨的正确性。1997年，中医学院崔洪英、张柏丽开展补肾中药对骨质疏松大鼠骨形态影响的研究，发现该药对与雌激素治疗骨质疏松有同等疗效，且毒副作用小。

第五节 中医妇科

天津中医在治疗妇科疾病方面，历史上名家荟萃，成绩斐然。进入20世纪90年代，老一辈妇科名中医渐出，代之而起的有市中医院王宝书、中医二附院韩冰、中心妇产医院张丽蓉等。至2005年，在治疗月经不调、妇科炎症、功能性子宫出血，不孕症、子宫肌瘤、囊肿以及更年期综合症等多种妇科病方面均小有建树。

一、月经不调

1993年，市中医医院王宝书、范春茹、车胜男对闭经、稀发月经症根据中医常见证型，研制出补阳、补阴、解郁、化瘀系列调经胶囊，疗效可靠，特别是远期疗效优于西医治疗。1995年，中医二附院韩冰、萧美茹等对子宫内膜异位症提出“瘀久挟痰，渐成癥瘕”的病机，确立了活血化瘀、软坚散结之法，研制“妇痛宁”颗粒冲剂，疗效确切，并可调经助孕。1999年，中医研究所刘永志自拟“环宁汤”治疗宫内节育所致月经异常，运用活血化瘀、清热凉血、益气止血之法，减少经期出血量和经期出血时间，并改善了子宫内膜浅表溃疡及慢性炎症。同年，中医学院李灵芝、李桂华采用自拟“龟鹿调经方”治疗高泌乳素血症，全方共奏滋肝补肾、生精血、解郁调经助育之功，使闭经得以治愈，与西医常用药溴隐停比较，疗效无差异，但无副作用。

2002年，中医二附院赵志梅开展子宫内膜异位症病机研究，经临床和动物实验得出子宫内膜异位症虽以血瘀为本，但病程长，常发生久病及肾的后果，故其病机应为肾虚血瘀。该成果获2002年度国家中医药管理局科技进步奖二等奖。

2003年，安定医院张新军对精神病患者因服药所致闭经采取健脾祛痰、解郁行气之法治疗，总有效率达75%，且作用持久，优于其他方法。

二、妇科炎症

1994年，天津市水阁医院刘毓敏以“子宫丸”为基本方，研粉纳入宫颈治疗子宫颈糜烂，总有效率为94%，较西医常用外治疗法减轻创伤刺激。1996年，第三中心医院李建文配制“抗宫炎片”治疗宫颈糜烂。该药具有止血散瘀、消炎之功效，抑制杀灭致病菌，安全可靠，治愈率92.1%，有效率达100%。1997年，中医研究所刘永志利用紫草油治疗老年性阴道炎，疗效良好，共奏清热燥湿、解毒生肌作用，解决了口服中药不易接受、外洗疗效差的问题。

1998年，中医研究所哈孝贤以中药提取物质与现代工艺相结合，研究出“阴道泡腾片”治疗宫颈糜烂，具有高效、经济、方便等特点。2002年，该所胡晓蕙采用该所自制内含蛇床子、苦参等药的“外用Ⅱ号”治疗阴道炎、宫颈炎，并通过实验证实该药具有清热燥湿、解毒消肿、祛腐生肌之功效，提高了中性粒细胞吞噬功能，对炎症的过度持续反应具有抑制和治疗作用。2004年，中医一附院夏阳以中药“治带方”和“内洗方”治疗细菌性阴道疾病，对厌氧菌的杀灭作用较强，疗效优于甲硝唑，无副作用，复发率较低。

三、功能性子宫出血

1997年，中医一附院夏阳、朱颖以固冲汤加减治疗无排卵型功能性子宫出血，肯定疗效后，进而探讨其治疗机理在于增加凝血机制和调节人体激素水平。2000年，该院张吉金采用益肾软坚法治疗子宫内膜囊腺型增生性功血症，研制"二甲丸"，显效率达85%。2001年，中医学院王玲以"功血宁Ⅰ、Ⅱ号"治疗功能性子宫出血症，该方集前人及当代经验之长，效果优于其他疗法。

四、不孕症

1991年，市中医医院王宝书、车胜男、张新玲以补肾化瘀法选仙灵脾、桑寄生、菟丝子组成"仙灵脾汤"治疗不孕症。该方对不孕症患者既起到调经补血、补肾强身的作用，又能起到促进受孕机制的作用，受孕者达50%。1992年，中医学院沙明荣对黄体功能不全所致不孕自拟具有促排卵、健黄体之功效的"助黄汤"治疗，经观察大多基础体温双相，70%受孕。1995年，中心妇产医院张丽蓉对习惯性流产采取补肾方法，自拟"安胎饮"为主方，治愈率达82%，提示该病主要病机为肾气虚损。1998年，中医一附院王惠津、韩桂茹对输卵管阻塞性不孕在通液术实施基础上，内服中药"通塞汤"，外敷"通塞包"，并予中药灌肠离子导入，针刺关元、中极等穴，妊娠率达91%。

五、子宫肌瘤

1991年，中医学院吴高媛治疗子宫肌瘤在采取辨证治疗的基础上，加用二氧化碳激光局部经络穴位照射，增强活血化瘀、消炎止痛目的，优于单纯中药组。1992年，中医研究所哈孝贤、董淑芹等以补益脾肾、软坚化瘀为法治疗子宫肌瘤，研制成"肌瘤丸"，总有效率达94.27%。1994年，市中医院王宝书、车胜男、李桂华以行气活血、除湿祛痰之法研制"化肌瘤丸"，对12厘米直径以下肌瘤效果尤为明显，并观察到该药可使患者血中雌二醇水平下降。1996年，哈孝贤、王玲在治疗子宫肌瘤400人次基础上，发现其普遍意义的证型，筛选有效方剂，研制成新一代制剂"肌瘤丸"，具有益脾肾、化坚结、破瘀血、除痰湿的作用，临床收到显著疗效。2003年，李灵芝以活血化瘀、温经通脉、散结消肿为法，自拟"散结消瘤汤"治疗子宫肌瘤，通过实验发现该药可抑制结缔组织增生，改善微循环，改善血流变异常。

六、囊肿

1999年，中医研究所哈孝贤、刘永志对卵巢囊肿突破中医关于瘀血积结的传统认识，指出该病应属于痰积夹瘀的观点，故以涤痰通络、破瘀消癥为法制成"卵巢囊肿冲剂"，临床有效率达94.91%，使患者避免了手术之苦。2001年，张丽蓉根据《医学衷中参西录》拟消结汤口服，及中药保留灌肠、宫腔注药治疗子宫内膜异位囊肿，该方起到破瘀消癥的作用。

七、更年期综合征

1996年，中医学院张柏丽、安秀玲开展补肾中药对更年期骨质疏松症的实验研究，显示该药能增加骨质疏松大鼠的骨量和骨强度，用于临床可避免应用雌激素的副作用。2000年，南开医院左芳将妇女更年期综合征分型辨证，阴虚阳亢型以六味地黄汤加减，气滞血瘀型用血府逐瘀汤加减，痰湿内阻型用温胆汤加减，并施以针灸，总有效率达92%。2002年，中医学院吴高媛、刘宏艳开展针刺治疗更年期综合征的实验研究，选取足三里、三阴交、太冲穴治疗，取得很好疗效。实验发现通过机体复杂的自稳调节系统以激发经气，调动机体产生抗御病邪的功能，升高雌激素水平，降低促激素水平。同年，中医一附院石学敏、沈晓明等认为更年期综合征为肾精亏虚、脑肾失济，采用调神益智针法治疗，显效率达80%，基础研究表明该针法可稳定平稳神经——内分泌中枢环境。

第六节 中医儿科

近现代的天津,也曾有过一些名望较高的儿科中医师。迨至当代,小儿有疾多找西医就诊,中医儿科日渐衰落。1991~2005年,天津研制出一些新制剂、新疗法,用于治疗小儿心肌炎、小儿癫痫、多动症、小儿肾病以及积症等疾病,并通过实验,验证其药物作用机理,进而提高疗效。

一、心肌炎

2000年,中医一附院陈宝义、刘虹运用通脉口服药治疗小儿病毒性心肌炎,总有效率达91.85%,并通过实验证实,该药具有抗病毒、抗脂质过氧化、改善心脏血液循环的作用。2002年,该院陈宝义、乔卫平、尹成望等对小儿迁延性心肌炎期前收缩的病机认为热毒损伤心体之后造成的心脉瘀阻、血虚风动,研制安心律胶囊以养血复脉、潜阳熄风,副作用小,解决了该病用西药毒副作用大的问题。2005年,中医学院王卉针对迁延性心肌炎病情反复波动的问题,采用黄芪注射液足三里穴位注射,提高患儿免疫力,避免反复呼吸道感染,减少病情波动。

二、小儿癫痫

1995年,中医一附院李少川、陈宝义、马融等认为小儿癫痫是脾虚痰伏、气逆风动,提出健脾顺气、豁痰熄风法为治则,研制出"抗痫胶囊",显效率53.44%,总有效率81.18%。1997年,李少川治疗该病注重益气安神,并顺势利导,以柔制刚,既消除致痫之痰,又重视脏腑阴阳的调理,使疗效在原基础上得以提高。2002年,马融提出小儿癫痫发作的病机为肾虚精亏、风痰闭阻,治疗宜用益肾填精、豁痰熄风之法,并研制出"熄风胶囊"治疗该病,疗效颇佳。

三、多动症

1995年,中医一附院李少川、李宝珍将儿童多动综合征分为"痰热内动、虚火妄动、阴虚水亏"三型辨证论治,分别以清痰除热、抑阳助阴、填精补阴法治之,收到较好疗效。至2003年,在此基础上研制"多动合剂",通过实验研究证实该药具有改善调节神经递质的功能并与调节单胺类神经递质失衡有关。2004年,马融对儿童多动症又提出肾阴不足、肝阳偏旺为病机,益肾填精为大法,研制"益智宁神颗粒冲剂"治疗该病,效果又有所提高。

四、小儿肾病

20世纪80年代,中医一附院李少川研制出"小儿肾病合剂",在临床上运用收到较好的效果。至1991年,中医一附院何绚为探讨其治病机制对该药进行实验研究,结果表明该药具有改善机体免疫功能、保护和促进肾上腺皮质功能、修复肾病大鼠肾小球病变的作用。至1999年,中医一附院李新民扩大"小儿肾病合剂"治病范围,并在治疗阿霉素肾病的基础上,开展实验研究,对肝白蛋白mRNA表达进行观察,并证明它与肾病的相关性,提示中医药在肾病治疗中具有修复改善病理组织的作用。2000年,马融、李新民根据小儿肾病综合征特点,结合少阳主枢理论,提出疏解清化、健脾利湿方法,并研制出新一代"肾病合剂",临床有效率达97.6%,减少复发。

五、积症

1994年,中医学院王惠玲将小儿脘腹痛分为积滞型与虚寒型,分别以“消积散”“温中散”敷脐,效果显著,方法简单,患儿家属乐于接受。2003年,蓟县中医医院王会东对婴幼儿腹泻积滞采取肉桂、干姜、吴茱萸等研末调醋敷脐的方法治疗,使药物容易通过脐部吸收,直达病所,患儿易于接受。

第七节　中医眼鼻喉科

天津中医治疗眼疾以往多以针刺为主。1991年起,以针刺加中药治疗视网膜疾病;针刺治疗青光眼,可增加房水排出,加用泻肺平肝药可降低眼压;针刺治疗近视眼可使视力恢复。

一、眼疾

(一)视网膜疾病

1991年,市眼科医院夏淑珍以针刺睛明、球后、承泣、健明等穴治疗视网膜阻塞,疏理眼部经气,使视力得以恢复,较活血化瘀中药治疗效果好。1995年,中研院附院孙超以补肝肾之中药结合针刺风池、翳风、睛明等穴治疗原发性视网膜色素变性,优于单纯中药或单纯针灸疗效。

2002年,中医一附院杨光在治疗顽固性视神经萎缩时采取先通后补法,先予脉通液、复方丹参液、口服血府逐瘀汤,用强手法针刺,然后予以能量合剂,黄芪注射液、自制益明汤,用小手法针刺,该方法效果显著。同年,该院赵君菁采取活血化瘀、滋补肝肾之中药,配合针刺太阳、风池、攒竹、四白等穴及离子导入综合疗法治疗陈旧性视网膜静脉阻塞,对提高视力确有一定疗效。同年,宁河县医院王淑玲对视神经萎缩采取针刺风池、翳风、太阳等穴,中药用杞菊地黄汤、丹栀逍遥散加减,配合西药脑活素治疗,共奏调和气血、通经活络、去疾明目之功。2005年,南开中医院崔建华提出糖尿病视网膜病变病机为气阴亏损、瘀血阻滞贯穿始终,自拟糖网宁煎剂治疗该病,总有效率达71.25%。

(二)青光眼疾病

1995年,中医一附院杨光以针刺治疗青光眼观察近千例病人,分析多项生化指标,验证针刺治疗青光眼的作用机理是通过疏肝理气、泻肺利水针法使房水流量加快,减少眼压,并使房水得到良性循环。1998年,该院张广庆、李志勇运用平肝降逆、通络明目针法治疗青光眼及视网膜疾病,通过实验证明该针法有增加房水排出、保护视网膜的作用。2002年,张海翔、杨光等开展量化针刺对房水流量控制的研究,通过204只眼及家兔针刺后的生化分析,得出量化针刺能够控制房水流量,是防治青光眼的有效方法之一。2005年,张广庆、李志勇以泻肺平肝、利水化瘀法自拟“三子平降散”治疗慢性青光眼,可明显降低眼内压,改善眼部血液循环。

(三)视力疾病

1991年,中医一附院杨光以针刺太阳、四白、攒竹、手三里穴治疗青少年近视眼,改善眶区血流,解除睫状肌疲劳和痉挛,使视力有不同程度的恢复,有效率达95.5%。1999年,中医学院万焕对小儿近视、远视等小儿眼科疾病采取疏筋理气、柔筋缓急、调节筋脉按摩手法,达到外呼内应的作用,使气血流通、肌肉强健,达到治疗目的。同年,中医二附院宋雪锦对视力疲劳采取具有清热舒肝、散风通络作用的“眼适汤”,并用毫针刺攒竹、四白、太阳、风池穴，总有效率达96%。

二、鼻病

1999年，南开医院何芙莉、闫姝采用该院制剂“复方苍耳滴鼻液”治疗过敏性鼻炎，临床效果肯定，实验发现其可使鼻黏膜上皮层小血管内嗜酸性白细胞明显减少。2003年，中医二附院王军以曲安萘德于迎香穴封闭治疗季节性变态性鼻炎，较肌肉注射无副作用，用量小，并疏通于阳明经气，清泄肺热。

2003年，南开医院沈啸洪、陈洁、林文森等完成“补气固表治疗变态反应性鼻炎机理的研究与临床应用”。经过对900多病例研究，提出该病的病机是肺气虚表不固，用补气固表方法，远期疗效达87%。在国内首先进行中药复方制剂治疗该病，证实该药剂具有多靶点、多环节、双向调节及稳定性的药效优势。临床研究证实，该补气固表方剂能够调理机体体液免疫和细胞免疫，可抑制皮肤被动过敏反应，改善鼻黏膜上皮细胞和亚细胞，抑制环核酸的合成，抑制炎症细胞浸润，并具有免疫调节作用。

三、喉病

2002年，第三中心医院姜法祥、杨存礼、李连安采用冰硼散、锡类散、牛黄散三散混合外涂的方法治疗口腔及咽喉溃疡，配合P—转移因子口服液，效果确定。2004年，中研院张大宁、张勉之依据金水相生之理用滋补肺肾之阴，兼清火热之邪的方法创“润嗓冲剂”治疗咽干、咽痛、音哑者，对语言职业者意义更大。2005年，该院朱愉等认为变态反应性咽炎同属中医“喉痹”范畴，从症状、体征等方面拟定客观化诊断标准，在治疗上以祛风利咽、消肿止咳为法创“咽炎2号”方，效果显著。

第八节　中医皮肤科

中医治疗皮肤病主要见于天津长征医院、中研院附院、中医学院等单位，在以内服中药或自行研制的中药冲剂治疗痤疮、皮炎、白癜风以及银屑病等顽固性皮肤病等方面，取得疗效。

一、痤疮

1997年，长征医院边天羽、毛舒和、蒋秀彩采用边天羽所创“舒肝冲剂”治疗痤疮，收效良好。通过实验证实，该冲剂有疏肝清热、活血化瘀的作用。同年，中研院附院张容自拟清热活血的“平痤欣”糊剂倒膜治疗聚合型囊状痤疮，通过检测证实该药结合面膜所发挥的物理渗透效应有抑脂制菌作用。2000年，中医一附院隋亚汶、马彩茗对面部痤疮采取中药面膜加点刺放血、排脓之法。此法具有消炎、活血化瘀、祛湿之功，轻、中度5～8天痊愈，重症15天痊愈。

二、皮炎

1991年，长征医院毛舒和、乔树芳在临床有效方剂凉血消风汤的基础上，研制出“皮炎2号冲剂”治疗常见皮肤病，尤其对感染性皮肤病有针对治疗作用。2001年，该院王雷等以黄芩提取物——黄芩总黄酮治疗荨麻疹，并进行免疫学及药物动力学研究，证实该药具有抗变态反应及抗组织胺作用。2002年，该院张玉环、孙晓慧、陈保疆等以健脾利湿法异病同治异位性皮炎和支气管哮喘。研究表明，该法通过调理脾胃可提升机体免疫力，优于单一西药治疗效果。2002年，市中医医院翟金莹以梅花针局部叩刺、酒精灸配合走罐治疗带状疱疹，消除脾经湿热和肝经炎热之邪。

三、白癜风

1991年，长征医院边天羽、刘世明、齐建文在“清肝消白汤”的基础上，研制出“白斑冲剂”治疗白癜风，有效率达91.1%。1994年，该院齐建文、王世贤、丁素先采用中药研制“白斑一号”糖浆，有效率达98%，显效和痊愈率达66%，电子光镜下观察，黑色素明显增加。2000年，该院马铁牛、李维云对儿童活动期白癜风患者不能做自皮移植者，采取健脾祛寒法治疗，应用“白斑冲剂”和“胃苓冲剂”有效率达69%。2003年，该院乔树芳等开展疏肝活血颗粒对黑素细胞及黑素代谢的影响的研究，发现疏肝活血药物可改善黑素细胞的生成，为中药对黑素细胞调控提供了可行方法。2005年，程林医院王冠红以调和气血、疏通经络、活血化瘀之中药，配合梅花针治疗儿童白癜风，总有效率70.6%。

四、银屑病

1993年，中医学院杜志坚对银屑病采取中医内治法治疗，分血热毒盛、血瘀热壅、湿热郁遏、血燥失润等四型辨证论治，有效率达95%，并不易复发。同年，和平中医专科门诊部以针刺神道、灵台等穴治疗牛皮癣，总有效率达95%。该针法经气传感，直接作用于心肺感应区，宣气疏表，提高人体免疫机能，达到扶正祛邪的作用。1998年，中医一附院姜相德、李进等根据中医治则，筛选大黄、土大黄等，制成“银屑灵涂膜剂”治疗银屑病，总有效率达96%，显效率44.5%。2003年，和平中医院王秀玲、张竞民以圆利针刺督脉为主的穴位，兼局部围针疗法治疗银屑病，总有效率95%，痊愈率60%。

第五章　中西医结合

天津市中西医结合研究在全国各省市中名列前茅。1963年，南开医院被卫生部确定为全国首家中西医结合临床研究基地。1975年，天津建立国内第一个中西医结合研究机构——天津市中西医结合急腹症研究所。此后，天津市中西医结合骨折研究所（1977年）、天津市急救医学研究所（1985年）及天津市中西医结合皮肤病研究所（1987年）相继建立。天津中西医结合研究由20世纪60、70年代的探索阶段，发展到20世纪70、80年代初的逐步深入阶段。1982年世界卫生组织把中西医结合治疗急腹症、中西医结合治疗骨折确认为中国5项世界领先的医学项目。自20世纪80年代中期开始，天津中西医结合研究走向高层次发展阶段。在临床诊治上，把西医辨病与中医辨证结合起来，充分发挥中西医两法互参互补优势，疗效高于单用西医或中医疗法；在“难病”治疗上，提高治愈率，降低病死率；在治疗的病种上，由急腹症、骨伤发展到外科、内科、骨科、妇科、皮肤科等多学科，形成多病种全面开花；在医学理论研究上，对中医“证”与治则的研究有所突破，实验研究硕果累累。中西医结合方面的学术论文数以千计，著述颇丰，仅急腹症方面的专著就有15部之多。此外，1996年，长征医院边天羽、丁素先、刘世明等主编的第二版《中西医结合治疗皮肤病学》，成为全国中西医皮肤病医生的工具书。1997年，津华医院王兆铭主编的《中西医结合实用风湿病学》，集中全国著名老中医治疗风湿病的经验，是一部以中西医结合体系系统介绍风湿病治疗的专著。

1991～2005年，是天津中西医结合研究在高层次发展阶段上的快速发展时期，出现“交叉兼容”“优势互补”“结合创新”三种中西医结合形式共同发展的新局面。1996年，吴咸中当选为中国工程院（医药卫生学部）院士。1998年，天津市中西医结合研究院建立。2003年，“通里攻下法在腹部外科疾病中的应用与基础研究”获国家科技进步二等奖。2005年8月28日，中国工程院院长徐匡迪向吴咸中80华诞发来贺函，在评价其学术成就时指出："通过长期实践逐步形成和不断完善规范的治疗原则与方法，在博取两法之长的基础上，建立中西医结合治疗急腹症的新体系。"

第一节 急腹症

20世纪60、70年代，天津在中西医结合治疗急腹症方面主要是摸索手术与非手术疗法的适应证，研究中西医两种诊断与治疗方法的合理结合，以求扩大非手术疗法的范围，代表著作有：《中西医结合治疗急腹症手册》(1970)、《中西医结合治疗急腹症》(1972)、《新急腹症学》(1978)。20世纪70年代后期到80年代，对几种常见急腹症的分期、分型不断完善，手术与非手术疗法的选择更趋合理，对急腹症治疗机制的研究初步展开，对中药剂型的改革取得进展，代表著作有：《急腹症方药新解》(1981)、《中西医结合治疗常见急腹症》(1981)、《急腹症研究》(1988)、《脾虚证的现代研究》(1992)。20世纪90年代以后，对急腹症的研究进入高层次发展阶段，诊断更为精确，辨证的客观指标相继建立，对几种疑难急腹症的治疗取得较大进展。在实验研究上获得一批高水平成果。90年代，腹腔镜技术引入中国，腹部外科出现药物疗法、手术疗法与微创技术三者的完美结合。这一阶段的代表著作有：《腹部外科实践》(1990、1993和2004共3版)、《中国急腹症治疗学》(1996)、《证与治则的现代研究》(1999)、《急腹症方药诠释》(2001)、《中西医结合普外手册》(2001)。

一、临床医疗

(一)急性肠梗阻

1961年起，吴咸中等以"六腑以通为用"的理论为指导治疗急性肠梗阻，通过大样本、多中心观察，疗效不断提高。该项研究对传统治疗方案进行重大改进，从而改变了国内外急性肠梗阻治疗的模式。据南开医院2003年统计，1978～2000年手术率和中转手术率明显下降，非手术率明显提高。该法被《黄家驷外科学》等多种权威著作收入。

1961～2000年南开医院急性肠梗阻治疗结果统计表

表7-5-1-53

		手术治疗		非手术治疗	病死率
年代	例数(例)	早期手术数(%)	中转手术数(%)	例数(%)	例数(%)
1961～1978	3800	680(17.9)	594(15.6)	2526(66.5)	144(3.8)
1979～2000	1484	179(12.0)	106(7.2)	1199(80.8)	41(2.8)

(二)重型急性胰腺炎

20世纪80年代中期，国内外对重型急性胰腺炎(SAP)的病理生理认识不一，疗法各异，曾一度纷纷进行"规则性胰腺切除"或早期实行"腐胰组织清除术"，但均未能改变治疗效果，病死率都在30%以上。从1993年到1998年，天津市中西医结合急腹症研究所(以下简称"市急腹症所")吴咸中、崔乃强等采用前瞻性研究方法，进行中医辨证分期论治。初期重用通里攻下，以大承气汤或柴胡陷胸汤为主；进展期以清热解毒、活血化瘀为主，辅以通里攻下，代表方剂为清胰汤或清胰承气汤。据南开医院1993～1996年145例重型急性胰腺炎中西医结合临床研究结果显示：初期死亡9例，占6.2%；进展期死亡15例，占10.3%，病死率显著下降。与国内外同期治疗结果比较，疗效显著。1992年，"经内镜对胆胰疾病的诊治观察和实验研究"获天津市科技进步二等奖。此外，市急腹症所赵连根、伍孝先、吴咸中等还对治疗急性胰腺炎有效中药进行筛选及实验研究，从病因学和发病学的角度，筛选出抑制胰酶的最佳中药元胡与活血化瘀最佳中药桃仁，并应用其注射液进行实验治疗。实验结果表明，两种注射液联合应用使家兔重型胰腺炎病情明显减轻，存活时间延长，死亡率降低，血清淀粉酶及白细胞介素-6水平下降，胰腺微循环改善，胰组织氧供增加，提示中医药对重型急性胰腺炎具有较好的治疗作用。

（三）急性重症胆管炎

1983年前，天津对急性重症胆管炎（ACST）的治疗以急症手术引流为主，病死率10%～20%。1983～1990年，南开医院、天津医学院附属医院（以下简称"津医附院"）等单位共治疗ACST 270例，其中鼻胆管引流及中药联合治疗200例，手术及其他治疗70例。结果ENBD加中药组死亡率3例，病死率下降为1.5%；对照组死亡10例，病死率为14.3%，全组共死亡13例，死亡率为4.8%。1992年初到1995年10月，临床上根据该病的发展过程，将该病分为急性期、缓解期和恢复期，并根据中医辨证和临床表现制定分期治疗方案，调整中药处方，改进剂型。初期选用大承气汤冲剂治疗，缓解期以内服活血清解冲剂为主，恢复期则根据引发急性重症胆管炎的病因进行治本治疗。在治疗的213例ACST中，36例手术治疗，4例术后死亡，177例完成鼻胆管引流加中药分期治疗，2例死亡，占1.1%。全组共死亡6例，病死率为2.8%，较同期国内外报告之病死率显著下降。急性重症胆管炎病死率由80年代后5年的4.8%下降到90年代前5年的2.8%。

（四）肠源性内毒素血症

1993年起，吴咸中、崔乃强等多次选择处于全身性炎症反应综合征不同发展阶段的病人，观察其血中内毒素、细胞因子及炎症介质的变化，以及大承气汤和承气合剂对其影响。观察结果较一致地显示，经过承气类方剂治疗，除少数病例外，上述观察指示均在治疗3～7天后明显下降。1998～2001年，对245例腹腔感染病人进行观察，结果表明，中药治疗组从第1天内毒素及TNFα水平开始下降，第3、7天下降更明显，已接近正常，对照组则居高不下，说明通里攻下中药对肠源性内毒素血症有肯定的疗效。

（五）重型脓毒症

2005年，总医院于泳浩等在"重型脓毒症状态下的免疫失衡与中药的调节作用"研究中，通过临床研究发现，重型脓毒症病人发病早期的下丘脑-垂体-肾上腺（HPA）轴过度活化、2型T辅助细胞（Th2）型免疫反应优势与病人不良预后相关。中药大承气颗粒可促进免疫平衡和神经内分泌恢复。分子水平和动物模型的研究发现，单核细胞分泌能力改变是脓毒症免疫平衡变化的基础，HPA轴激素对免疫平衡的改变具有重要作用，中药大黄素具有双相免疫调节作用，参脉则呈免疫刺激。早期予以免疫刺激或中药治疗，可提高重型腹膜炎存活率。该项目是在中西医结合急腹症研究的基础上，采用现代理论和研究手段对重型脓毒症的发病机理进行深入研究，并从免疫平衡和神经内分泌调节等新的角度观察中药的治疗作用。在此基础上，对临床近百例腹腔内感染和大手术后重型脓毒症病人发病早期采用中药治疗，取得良好疗效。

二、证与治则

（一）证

1961年，南开医院吴咸中、许树朴在急腹症临床治疗中，对该病按中医分期分型进行探索，以八纲为主，结合病机分为气、血、寒、热、湿、食、虫等七类。1991年前后，齐清会、吴咸中在临床观察到急腹症后期和腹部大手术后，患者常出现一过性脾虚证和胃阴虚证，血瘀证更常贯穿于该病全过程，胃阴虚患者血浆内毒素水平高于正常，免疫病理反应异常等与中医的"燥热病邪耗伤胃阴""热去津伤"有相似之处。同期，该院还对脾虚证进行研究。结果表明，当处于一过性脾虚证候时患者可出现消化道运动功能障碍，消化吸收功能减弱，胃肠激素、内分泌功能、免疫功能低下等多方面改变，而急腹症的常见症状腹痛、炎性包块或痛性包块、内毒素休克、DIC出现的瘀斑、微循环障碍等无不与血瘀症相关。南开医院以活血化瘀法应用于腹膜炎、肠粘连的防治研究具有突破性意义。

1985～1997年，天津医学院的硕士、博士研究生在吴咸中、崔乃强等导师的指导下，建成20个腹部外科疾病动物模型，包括腹膜炎和腹腔脓肿，急性肠硬阻和急性肠扩张，急性胆道疾患和胆石症，急性胰腺炎以及多器官功能不全综合征(MODS)等动物病理膜型。这些模型为研究急腹症的证与治则提供了必要的技术支撑。1999年,总医院齐清会、吴咸中等建立"腹部外科胃阴虚证诊断标准",设计出养阴益胃汤治疗急腹症过程中胃阴虚证,以保急腹症尽快痊愈。同年,对证与治则的大量研究成果集成《证与治则的现代研究——急性腹部疾病》一书在天津出版。

(二)治则

治则的研究起始于20世纪60年代初期,以代表方剂为研究对象,探讨治则的作用机理。吴咸中认为,中医的理、法、方、药是一个有机整体,治则即法。1973年,吴咸中首倡"以'法'为突破口,抓'法'求'理'"的研究思路。在这一思路的指导下,天津市医疗科研单位对吴咸中所指出的治疗急腹症"八法"(即通里攻下法、活血化瘀法、清热解毒法、理气开郁法、清热利湿法、健脾和胃法、补气养血法、温中散寒法)代表方剂和药组进行长期实验研究。其中,又以通里攻下法为根本大法,大承气汤为该法的代表方剂。

1993~1997年,医科大学、南开大学、市急腹症所等单位承担的市科委课题"中西医结合治疗急腹症机制研究",其子课题由7个增至11个。1993~1996年,市急腹症所田在善、吴咸中等承担的"肠源性内毒素血症引发的肝、肺损伤及大承气汤的保护效应"研究,是在以往30年间两轮实验研究后的第三轮研究,是在证实大承气汤能明显增强肠道的推进功能,揭示大承气汤具有提高肠平滑肌电兴奋性的作用基础上,进一步探究大承气汤的抗肠道内毒素(LPS)移位效应。实验表明,大承气汤对肠道的排毒、灭毒、减小内毒素池,增强肝脏对从肠道吸收的LPS的灭活处理能力,可能在抗肠道LPS移位作用上具有重要意义。

同期,南开大学杨文修等从离子机制角度探讨清胰汤、单味中药及其单体的药理作用。实验证明钙离子及氢离子细胞内流的调节,可能是中药治疗胰腺炎作用机制之一。津医大与市急腹症所合作从机械、生物、化学及免疫等四个方面研究通理攻下法对肠屏障功能的保护作用,并从细胞水平和分子水平上证明大承气汤与主药大黄以及大黄的有效成分均对肠屏障有保护作用。同时,该药对肠源性内毒素对肝、肺的操作亦有保护作用。

1994年,总医院秦鸣放、王鹏志等在"内毒素诱生细胞因子的实验与临床研究"中,从分子水平阐述G-细菌感染状态下如何控制内毒素血症的发生规律,从分子生物学和细胞生物学角度对内毒素、巨噬细胞和某些细胞因子分阶段进行研究,从而证实中药组方"承气合剂"在体内外均具有明显的拮抗内毒素诱生巨噬细胞分泌肿瘤坏死因子的作用。提出对腹腔内感染患者实行两阶段中西医结合治疗的方法和原则,研究还证实该方法有明显提高机体抗感染能力、增强免疫功能、减少并发症等作用;"大承气冲剂""承气合剂"对G-菌内毒素和其诱发的细胞因子具有强烈的拮抗作用。

20世纪90年代后5年,吴咸中等承担科技部攻关课题"优质高效复方中药的示范开发研究——大承气颗粒",对通里攻下法代表方剂大承气汤进行剂型改革,最终形成优质高效的大承气颗粒,并得到临床验证。对通里攻下法的研究揭示其"胃肠效应""腹腔效应"和"整体效应"的作用机理,证明此法具有调整胃肠运动功能、清除肠道菌毒、缩小内毒素池、保护肠屏障、抑制过度炎性反应、调节神经-内分泌-免疫功能等综合作用,从而可防治肠源性内毒素血症,进而防治多脏器功能不全综合征。这不仅使传统医学的经典方剂为防治危重症提供了可能,同时揭示出中医"釜底抽薪、急下存阴"的科学内涵,丰富了祖国医学"肺与大肠相表里"等学说。

在急性重症胆管炎实验研究中,通过动物实验,在整体、器官、细胞和分子水平上研究急性重症胆管炎的病理生理机制及中药对急性重症胆管炎大鼠肠、肝、肺功能损害的保护作用和中药对急性重症胆管炎大鼠免疫功能的调节。

2003年,天津市中西医结合急腹症研究所、医科大学、南开大学、总医院等单位吴咸中、崔乃强、何清宇、田在善、林秀珍等开展"通里攻下法在腹部外科疾病中的应用与基础研究",表明该法具有调整胃肠运动、改善腹腔脏器血运、清洁肠道、保护肠屏障、调节免疫及保护脏器等作用;承气类方剂具有多种药理活性成分,其最基本的靶位在胃肠道,特别是在出现"胃家实"阶段,应用该方剂有利于病情的控制及转复;建立并不断完善急性肠梗阻、重症急性胰腺炎、急性重症胆管炎、急性腹膜炎及多脏器功能障碍综合症等病种的“通里攻下法”治疗常规，取得明显的临床疗效。该项目获2003年度国家科技进步二等奖。

1996年，南开医院田在善、李东华、沈长虹等提出大承气汤对重要器官功能障碍或衰竭作用和肠道微生物移位相符合，并通过实验证明大承气汤具有减少肠源性内毒血症的作用。1997年，总医院尤胜义、周维平等研究通里攻下法的代表方剂大承气汤对胃肠激素的影响，证明可能是增强肠运动的作用。1998年，第三中心医院杜智等首创用中药腹腔灌注结合NK—107树脂血液灌流的综合疗法治疗急性重症胰腺炎，取得较好效果。

2001年，总医院齐清会等经对腹部外科胃阴虚证和治疗的研究表明：特定条件下的胃阴虚症呈多种病理性改变，且包括甲状腺、肾上腺皮质功能低下，消化道分泌功能减退以及胃黏膜形态学改变，与中医的“燥热病邪耗伤胃阴”或在温热病后期出现的“热去伤津”有相似之处。根据中医辨证使用养阴益胃汤，可有效改善因腹部手术后或急腹症造成的胃阴虚症状，明显改善胃阴虚证的病生理变化，促进患者顺利度过康复期。

2002年，对难治性黄疸，杜智等采用中药制剂“利胆膏”和西药激素、舒胆通治疗，提示利胆膏可改变血管壁纤维化程度，降低门脉压力，使肝内血循环改善，肝细胞再生。2002年，南开医院殷铭在治疗急性肠梗阻时应用中药攻下通里、活血化瘀解除梗阻后择期手术，可降低手术危险性、减少并发症发生、提高远期疗效。2004年，急腹症所刘洪斌、崔乃强、李东华等开展中药清胰汤对重型胰腺大鼠的影响研究，证实清胰汤对水肿型胰腺炎具有良好疗效，可抑制磷脂酶A_2活性、降低NF—KB表达、减少细胞因子产生。

第二节　多器官功能障碍综合征

20世纪70年代中期，一中心医院在临床对急性多器官功能障碍综合症（MODS），开始以中西医两种理论与方法进行研究。到20世纪80年代后期，提出并证实内毒素是感染性MODS的始动原因。1991年，研制出用于菌毒并治的新中成药“血必净”，在临床治疗中采用辨证施治。2001年对MODS的治疗，由“三证三法”发展为“四证四法”，并建立起一套中西医结合综合治疗MODS方案，疗效明显。

在治疗机理研究上，20世纪90年代证实活血化瘀法能降低患者的血内毒素水平，起到免疫调节作用。通里攻下法能保护肠屏障，减少细菌及内毒素移位，并增加胆汁分泌，起到保护肝脏功能的作用，证实通里攻下法治疗MODS的重要价值。

一、临床治疗

20世纪80年代后期，天津市第一中心医院急救医学研究所（以下简称“市急救医学所”）崔乃杰、宗育杉等在该所证实内毒素是感染性MODS始动原因和“菌毒并治”新理论的基础上，进行菌毒并治及防治感染性多系统脏器衰竭的研究。经体内外实验研究，证实抗毒和解毒疗法可以减轻或纠正因内毒素引起的形态、酶化学、微循环、血管活性物的释放等损伤，并能提高实验动物的成活率。通过临床治疗与对照各98例观察，病死率由传统疗法的78.6%下降为26.5%，四个脏器以上衰竭者病死率由国外的100%降至50%～40%。该项目获1991年度天津市科技进步一等奖。同期，研制出有针对性的拮抗内毒素中药“神农33号”，临床治疗效果明显，经进一步研究被认定为治疗脓毒症菌毒炎并治的国家二类中药“血必净”，2003年开始在全国各大医院广泛使用，为脓毒症、多脏器功能衰竭综合征提供了有效的治疗药物。同时，还筛选出具有明确拮抗和破坏内毒素作用的单味中药——连翘，可按需清除循环中不同分子量“毒”性物质。此外，还研制出用于“中药血液净化”的床旁多功能血液净化机。

同期，市急救医学所崔乃杰、傅强等在MODS、脓毒症研究中归纳和总结出“三证三法”的基础上，又进行

“感染性多脏器功能失常综合症发病机制及中西医结合防治研究”，发现内外源性细菌内毒素血症、弥漫性血管内凝血（DIC）、免疫功能麻痹是该综合征的3个重要发病关键。在西医药治疗的基础上，辨证应用“清热解毒”“活血化瘀”和“扶正固本”三大中医治则，使感染性MODS 3个以上脏器受累者的治愈率达50%。该项研究获2001年中华医学科技奖二等奖。同期，曹书华、崔乃杰、王勇强等进一步完善MODS的中医证候分型，对瘀血证、腑气不通证、毒热证、急性虚证，分别采用活血化瘀法、通里攻下法、清热解毒法、扶正固本法进行辨证治疗，同时对中药保护内皮细胞，减轻炎症的机理进行实验研究，开创出以“四证四法”对MODS进行辨证施治的原则，并建立起一套较完整的中西医结合综合治疗MODS方案，临床治疗中使MODS患者病死率明显降低。

二、疗法机制

20世纪90年代，市急救医学所曹书华、王今达、任新生等进行活血化瘀法对MODS防治作用机制的研究，证实活血化瘀疗法确有改善MODS预后、降低病死率的作用。研究结果显示，活血化瘀法可降低MODS患者血内毒素水平，达到“菌毒并治”的作用；降低MODS患者血浆血小板激活因子水平，从而起到脏器保护作用；降低MODS患者血清及组织氧化氢水平，抑制组织iNOS mRNA的表达，减轻组织损伤；对促炎细胞因子、肿瘤坏死因子α、白介素-6有明显的下调作用，阻断过度炎症反应；对血管内皮细胞有明显的保护作用；可提升血浆活化蛋白C水平，改善MODS患者的凝血机能紊乱；提高人类白细胞抗原（HLA-DR）水平，缓解免疫麻痹，起到免疫调节作用。

1992年，吴咸中指导外地博士生在天津研究建成非细菌性多器官功能不全综合征的动物模型。该模型用酵母多糖给SD大鼠腹腔注射，不引入外源性细菌而造成多个脏器形变，酷似临床MODS，且伴有内毒素血症和炎症介质。该成果为研究MODS机制和实验治疗提供了条件。

1996年，市急腹症研究所崔乃强、赵琪、葛智慧等在通里攻下法治疗急腹症所致MODS的疗效观察研究中，揭示出通里攻下法所用的大承气汤有保护肠屏障、减少细菌及内毒素移位的作用，可缓解腹胀及肠屏障，由此对改善心肺功能极为有利，在相当程度上可缓解和改善心率和心律的状态。研究还证明，大承气汤能显著增加严重腹内感染大鼠模型的肝血流量，增加胆汁分泌，从而起到保护肝脏的作用。

1998年，南开医院赵琪、崔乃强、李继坤等研究证明，大承气汤能抑制MODS发病时TNFα（细胞活性因子的一种）、IL－1及IL－6（白细胞介素1及6）的活性表达，因此能部分抑制各种病因所致过度免疫反应及过度炎症反应，从而对组织脏器具有保护作用，这可能是通里攻下法治疗MODS的机制之一。同年，他们还揭示出大承气汤能使MODS患者及模型大鼠血清急性期蛋白（APP）水平降低，并阻碍大鼠肝细胞体外合成分泌APP，表明该中药方剂具有提高MODS发病时机体防御能力倾向和增强免疫调控因子的作用，使机体迅速由急性反应相过渡到下一时相，以利调整机体免疫功能，对抗病原微生物对宿主的直接侵害及肠道细菌或毒素的移位。2003年，吴咸中、崔乃强、邓诗林、曹书华、金鸿宾等完成“多脏器功能障碍综合征发病机理及中西医结合治疗的深入研究”。该研究以创伤外科、腹部外科、大面积烧伤及内科急性危重病等不同的病种为研究对象，系统观察不同病因病理所致的肠源性内毒素血症、全身性炎症反应综合征及多器官功能障碍综合征的发生、发展规律，比较4种疾病中的异同，从局部及整体水平上阐明通里攻下法对脏器的保护作用，证实通里攻下法在治疗腹内感染所致MODS中的重要价值，为MODS的中西医结合规范化治疗和深入研究提出了依据。该成果获2005年度天津市科技进步一等奖。

图7-5-2-114 天津市南开医院吴咸中（右）等完成“多脏器功能障碍综合征发病机理及中西医结合治疗的深入研究”

第三节 内科病

1991～2005年，天津市在中西医结合治疗内科疾病方面，较多的采用中西医结合的理念和中西医两类药物及治疗方法相结合的医治方案。其中，以中西医结合辨证分型治疗乳腺癌；以中医分型，中西药联合或西医常规结合刺络拔罐治疗肺心病；建立动物模型，以分子生物学理论与实验方法研究植物神经对肝脏葡萄糖代谢的影响机理等等，从而使内科疾病在临床及部分治疗机制的研究上提高到一个新水平。

一、肺心病

90年代初，胸科医院马凤英、陶宗玲将病窦综合征按中医分心肾阳虚、气滞血瘀、气虚、气阴两虚等四型，以益气助阳、活血化瘀为基础，并配合扩冠、抗心律失常药物治疗，疗效显著，同时对不能安装起搏器者可起到维持生命的作用。1995年，天津市中医药研究院附属医院刘振永对慢性肺心病急性发作期以清热化痰祛瘀行水为法联合抗生素、扩张支气管药及祛痰剂治疗，以弥补不足之处，效果较单用西药有所提高。同年，该院张志铭、王佩华对肺心病呼吸衰竭病人针对急则治标原则，采取调气、消痰、化瘀诸法研制出"肺胀Ⅰ号"口服液，并联合西药常规治疗，临床上收到较好效果。

1996年，南开医院朱简、杨燕生等对急性心肌梗塞采取西药极化液、硝酸甘油等常规治疗的同时，应用中成药健心片或益气活血药后，出现心电图改善、心肌酶降至正常的效果。2000年，天津市中医药研究院第二附属医院在治疗支气管哮喘急性发作时，采取肺俞、膈俞拔罐法联合西药常规治疗，起到宣泄风寒、通畅气血的作用。2001年，该院郭家奎、王立存、王满利等对急性脑梗塞采取调神通络法针刺，联合尿激酶及活血化瘀中药制剂静脉滴注治疗，24小时后70%患者得到控制。该法取中西医优势互补，可降低病死率及病残率。2002年，三中心医院刘金芝、王士泳对慢性肺源性心脏病发作期在西药常规作用下，采取具有清热化痰、止咳平喘、利水消肿作用的"肺心合剂"治疗，收效显著，改善了病人的心肺功能。2003年，天津市肺科医院叶祖明对哮喘患者在西医常规治疗下，采用刺络拔罐方法治疗，可明显改善症状和氧分压、二氧化碳分压状况。

二、肝胆疾病

1998年，一中心医院李跃汉、王广舜、宋迎春在治疗有机磷中毒时，注重肝肠循环为闭合增毒路径，采用中医疏肝利胆法与胆汁引流相结合的方法，对中毒后的肝脏具有明显的保护作用。1998年，天津市第一医院和传染病医院联合以中西医结合方法治疗肝炎后肝硬化，在抗肝纤维化研究方面取得进展，获1998年度国家中医药管理局科技进步二等奖。2000年，肝病研究所张俊富、程镭对肝硬化食道静脉曲张症，在西药保肝方法基础上，加用具有活血化瘀功效的抗纤软坚冲剂，血瘀证好转，食管曲张改善，说明两者之间存在内在联系。2003年，该所对肝硬化合并上消化道出血在西医常规治疗基础上，用中药乌药、降香、五倍子煎汤加葡萄糖酸钙灌胃取得迅速止血效果。

2002年，总医院薛承锐等在"植物神经对肝脏葡萄糖代谢影响的机理研究"中，建立起充分游离的肝脏去神经支配的动物模型，从而在以往单纯的迷走神经切除手术基础上，解决交感神经不能被完全去除的问题。同时，应用抗VAChT单克隆抗体，从形态学上证实肝脏去神经之完全和充分，以及监测在实验期间神经没有再生现象，对肝脏去神经程度和有否神经再生的问题做出判断。从而发现：游离肝脏去胆碱能神经支配动物，存在由胰岛素及胰高血糖素介导的肝糖原合成障碍；去迷走神经肝脏肝细胞胰岛素信号传导蛋白IR、Glut2表达减弱。初步明确迷走神经对肝细胞胰岛素信号转导基因水平影响的作用机理，发现肝脏葡萄糖代谢新的作用机制，为进一步研究植物性神经对于肝脏其他功能的影响奠定基础。

三、神经、精神疾病

1999年，天津市脑系科中心医院刘桂双对脑梗塞病人分痰热瘀结和气虚血瘀两型分别予中风1、2号治疗，并每日针灸；西医点滴血塞通、脑活素，口服脑通片及降压治疗，有效率达97.5%，比单用西药效果佳。2002年，红桥医院王光明对血管性痴呆采取西药胞二磷胆碱、脑复康联合中药补肾填精豁痰化瘀中药治疗，收效较好。该法可激活脑代谢、改善智能、控制发展。

四、泌尿生殖疾病

1994年，天津医学院第二附属医院崔金才对肾脏移植后采取辨证论治，推陈出新，纠正免疫抑制之副作用，效果优于单纯西药组。1998年，医科大学第三医院姚熙慧、贺玉珍采用"肾炎康得片"配合激素治疗成人原发性肾病综合征，该中药可降低毛细血管通透性，抗炎消肿，提高激素在体内发挥作用，改善长期大量使用激素而加重的高凝状态，从而进一步保护肾功能。2001年，一中心医院李春荣、邵凤珍对小儿乙肝相关肾炎，采用口服中医协定处方"肾病合剂"，结合激素、免疫抑制剂、抗病毒、干扰素等治疗，提高治愈好转率。同年，第三中心医院薛钧尘自拟泌尿排石汤，以清热利湿、排石通淋为主，结合黄体酮肌肉注射，治疗泌尿结石，总有效率86.8%。同年，第一医院曹乃文、侯美娟、谢莹等对儿童原发性肾病在采取激素、环磷酰胺治疗基础上，应用中药五皮饮及六味地黄丸加减治疗，可提高血浆皮质醇基础水平，减少复发。2003年，四中心医院赵连玉以血府逐瘀汤联合西药常规治疗成人原发性肾病综合征，提高疗效，降低副作用发生。

2001年，中医二附院陈嘉兴自拟"化浊利湿汤"合霉素或克拉霉素等抗生素治疗非淋菌性尿道炎，疗效肯定，优于单用西药或中药。2002年，第三中心医院孙淑梅对生殖道尖锐湿疣采取"爱宝疗液"局部治疗的基础上，结合调理气血、清除湿热中药，有效率100%，复发率降低。

五、内分泌和代谢疾病

1992年，中医二附院刘惠敏对糖尿病坏疽采取中西医结合治疗，自拟"四虫散"和清湿毒中药口服，用西药脉通、川芎嗪静滴，配合手术，治愈率86%，截肢率下降至7%。2002年，天和医院张越林认为甲状腺功能减退患者泌乳素升高病机为脾肾阳虚、命门火衰，自拟"抑乳汤"联合甲状腺素片治疗，收效良好。2003年，第三中心医院邸阜生以益气活血中药"糖肾清浓缩液"加开博通治疗糖尿病肾病，疗效优于西药基础治疗，并可降低胆固醇及甘油三酯。2004年，中医学院王惠君、邢海涛对原发性高尿酸血症，将其分为湿热痹阻、瘀血痹阻、脾肾亏虚、湿热下注、脾肾虚衰等5型辨证论治，配合西药，并将治疗系统规范化。

六、肿瘤

1999年，肿瘤医院张瑾在吴咸中、李特指导下，完成对乳腺癌中西医结合辨证分型研究。结果表明：早期乳腺癌以气滞型和血瘀型为多见。早期患者多存在气血功能失运，但未影响正气；晚期患者以阴血虚型和阳气虚型多见，全身症状明显，表现为本虚标实，阴阳及气血的平衡失调。2000年，肿瘤医院李雅玲在西医化疗基础上采取健脾理气法治疗原发性肝癌，抑制和延缓肿瘤生长转移，通过实验证明健脾理气药在改善全身情况和延长生存率方面有一定作用。2001年，该院对晚期乳腺癌病人在化疗及内分泌治疗基础上加扶正祛邪中药，辨证与辨病相结合，具有免疫促进作用，可提高治疗效果，延长生存期。

七、高脂血症

1997年，天津铁路中心医院瘳辉、焦茂对高脂血症采取XL—200型血液辐射治疗仪，抽200毫升血液经紫外线辐射及高氧合处理后合并丹参注射液回输，降脂显著，疗程短。

第四节　骨科病

1991年前，天津在中西结合治疗骨科疾病方面一直走在全国前列；1991年起，从理论到临床都有创新。在深入开展临床力学研究中，创造出一批新型的骨折固定器和器材；从骨折后的血液循环研究入手，揭示出骨微循环与骨折愈合的关系；从对柳木夹板局部外固定的力学测试和分析中，提出“粘弹性固定理论”；从“偎脓长肉”作用机制的研究中，发现外用中药的抗感染作用不是抑菌，而在于提高机体的免疫功能，骨折创面所产生的“脓”与西医所指的“脓”有本质区别，等等，从而使天津在中西医结合治疗骨科疾病上又向前推进一步。

一、骨折

1994年，天津医院赵文宽在“应用镍钛记忆合金螺丝钉治疗新鲜股骨颈骨折”研究中，从材料与生物力学研究入手，选用具有良好生物相容性、耐腐性，而且在抗应力、抗旋转扭力加压等力学性能方面均符合力学设计要求，并优于传统材料的镍钛记忆合金作为内固定器材。经临床应用107例，随访观察2年无骨不连接，未发现股骨头坏死，无滑钉及折断，表明内固定可靠，遂在各级医院推广应用。其主要作用机制是：它可以改善股骨头的应力分布状态，减小拉应力，并变拉应力为压应力，从而使压应力增强，在股骨距处表现最为突出。这表明记忆合金螺丝钉不但可以固定骨折，还可防止股骨头塌陷等重大合并症。

1995年，天津医院顾云五在“中西医结合治疗骨折的微循环研究”中，总结出在骨折愈合过程中受多种因素影响，其中在骨折修复中肌肉与骨的微循环不可分割。同时，通过对小夹板固定治疗骨折时全身血液循环超微结构的观察，首次建立包括软组织损伤因素的兔骨折愈合模型，对比分析骨折后的微循环变化和骨修复的超微结构改变，阐述骨微循环与骨折愈合之间的关系。实验结果表明：对照组的微循环改变主要为血管增生扩张；对照组1至4周出现血管增生扩张，5至8周后微循环开始改善并逐渐接近对照组水平；处理组邻近骨折线、骨皮质、骨细胞变性、坏死较对照组明显；形成骨痂的主要细胞是成骨细胞；处理组该细胞呈区域性变性，出现胶原合成障碍，对骨痂形成不良，骨折愈合相对延缓。

2003年，天津医院王志彬等在“柳木夹板局部外固定的力学测试和分析”研究中提出，采用布带、纸压垫、夹板等植物性材料，其外固定系统力学性能不稳定，会给骨折的临床治疗效果带来一些不确定因素。通过对小夹板外固定系统的力学测试，提出小夹板外固定系统治疗骨折的“一个杠杆、两个约束条件”的粘弹性固定理论，同时也为小夹板的改革发展提出科学的理论依据和力学参数。2005年，王志彬等研制的可调式骨伤塑料夹板采用铸塑工艺制成。其结构与性能特征是变直板为符合肢体外形的并带有透气孔的弧形板，具有舒适、美观的特性。尤其是选材以塑代木、生产规范、制作方便，便于推广应用，获得国家新型实用专利。同时，该研究为解决传统小夹板，因绑缚在直边夹板上的绵质固定带很容易松脱，松紧度难于把握等问题，还研制出一种可调式骨伤塑料夹板，可垂直夹板轴线将其绑缚在肢体上。

2005年，天津医院在“抗应力遮挡内固定钢板的有限元分析”研究中，以三维有限元法（FEM）适于内固定钢板并将其改为中心外凸形状进行应力和变形分析。有限元分析中采用1223个节点、763个八节点六面体等参与和3564个自由度。改进后的内固定钢板比原来的内固定钢板在正向力、弯矩My和Mz的作用下，柔度分别增加60.1%、30.8%、61.2%。改进后的钢板刚度和应力替代作用被降低，符合生物力学。

二、骨组织损伤修复

1964年，天津市人民医院李瑞宗与方先之在国内首次发表用动物活体进行骨折愈合模型的研究，提出骨折愈合的骨痂分期方法。同时,对中西医结合治疗骨折的骨愈合机制开展理论研究,对完善小夹板治疗骨折的“动静结合”“筋骨并重”等原则给出实验依据。

1991年,天津医院于顺禄等在“实验动物骨折愈合过程的骨计量学模型建立及观察”研究中,引进开发骨组织不脱钙切片、骨组织形态计量学技术,创建从整体实验设计、活体标记技术、临床实验动物取材方法到标本的制备、各项骨计量方法的观测、统计学处理与分析等一套完整体系。由于骨计量学的开展而获取骨细胞水平、组织水平以及器官水平上的活体信息,实验采用四环素活体标记技术,研究骨修复与骨重建的骨计量学的指标,是揭示骨的生理机能与病理改变之间关系研究的一种新方法。

1996年,天津中医药研究院高金亮、张伯礼,天津医院徐澄、于顺禄等在国家中医药管理局“九五”重点攻关课题“中医药治疗原发性骨质疏松症的临床与实验研究”中,采用骨组织形态计量学的动力学指标,通过活体四环素双标记的办法,利用四环素能与钙特异性结合并沉积在骨矿化前沿(Minaralization front)的特性,把时间因素标记在骨的重建过程中,测定多组骨动力学组织学指标参数,求得骨矿化沉积率、单标四环素表面、双标四环素表面及单、双标四环素表面比、矿化延迟时间、骨再建单位时间和纠正矿化沉积率等多项骨动力学指标,以获取骨细胞水平、组织水平以及器官水平上的活体信息。

三、“偎脓长肉”作用机制

“偎脓长肉”是中医外科传统的疗疮愈伤法则,也是生肌膏等外用中药得以治愈一般西药难以奏效的感染创面和感染性开放骨折的根本原因。20世纪90年代中期,天津医院李秀兰、南开大学徐尔真等用现代科学手段和动态观察方法,从整体、器官和功能层次上,从细胞和分子水平上进行一系列研究,解决了外用中药“偎脓长肉”的抗感染途径、“脓”的来源、“脓”的细胞成份、功能状态及其作用以及“脓”的免疫活性因子和对创面的调节作用等难题。发现:①外用中药的抗感染作用与西药和抗生素不同,它不直接抑菌,而在于提高机体的免疫功能。②生肌膏等外用中药是良好的免疫促进剂,可使创面产生大量的有益“脓”。这种脓与西医所指的脓有本质的不同,它是一种多来自于局部微血管的营养液,富含免疫活性细胞和免疫活性因子,构成中药—细胞—细胞因子—细菌之间的动态平衡网络体系,可以有效地调节创面组织细胞功能,从而起到抗感染和促进组织愈合的作用。这是“偎脓长肉”作用机理的实质。③纤维结合蛋白是脓液中最重要的活性因子,纤维结合蛋白与生肌膏联合作用于感染创面,发挥“偎脓长肉”高效免疫促进和纤维结合蛋白促有丝分裂两大作用优势,进而加速感染创面修复进程达20%,是一条修复感染创面简便而快捷的新途径。实验研究过程中,在揭示外用中药“偎脓长肉”作用机制的同时,创新多项实验技术:标准“偎脓长肉”动物造模;创面渗出液和创面细胞的收集、分离和纯化技术;创面微血管通透性定量检测;肉芽FBS株建立和无血清培养技术等。李秀兰、徐尔真等1987年开展的“生肌膏等外用中药偎脓长肉作用机理的研究”,李秀兰、师宜健等1993年开展的“纤维结合蛋白加速感染创面修复作用的研究”及2000年开展“偎脓长肉加速感染创面修复作用机制研究”,为外用中药的开发和中医基础理论研究开辟了新途径,促进了外用中药的临床应用,提高了感染创面和感染性开放骨折的治愈率。

四、皮肤和骨缺损修复

1998年,天津医院马宝通、李秀兰等利用细胞分离技术,开展“自体皮肤细胞移植治疗创伤感染创面的临床研究”,为骨科感染创面的治疗开辟了新途径。2000年,李秀兰、白人骁等开展的“皮肤和骨缺损修复技术的研究”,分为组织工程皮肤和组织工程骨两部分。其创新点:①研制和优化作为诱导因子的中药生肌液,证实其具有对皮肤细胞和成骨潜能细胞增殖和分化的调节功能;且安全、高效、价廉、易贮存,为研究新一代细胞因子打下基础。②发明表皮细胞、成纤维细胞和骨髓基质细胞快速分离、扩增技术,从而证实优化的生肌液作为诱导剂对皮肤和骨种子细胞的表皮细胞、成纤维细胞和骨髓基质细胞在促进其增殖抑制凋亡和调控表型表达中的作用,培养出具有抗炎活性的皮肤种子细胞,实现了中药诱导因子对骨髓基质细胞成骨诱导。2005年首次发现成纤维细胞在中药诱导因子作用下成骨表达，又因成纤维细胞来源丰富、获取方便、诱导分化趋向稳定，可作为骨种子细胞的新来源。③研制出具有良好仿生化的壳聚糖—明胶皮肤载体和壳聚糖—明胶—酸三钙骨修复微孔载体，含中药的载体复合物，对皮肤细胞和载体复合物进行生物学评价，并通过小动物和大动物实验考察，实现在体内外与目标细胞的融合和功能表达，提高抗感染能力和组织修复速率。④创立皮肤细胞在感染创面的移植技术。中药与组织工程技术结合，突破感染环境下细胞和组织移植禁区。对临床感染性难愈合创面实施18例，成功率100%；创面收缩率提高20%~30%，且瘢痕组织松软，不易发生水疱，深受医患欢迎。也证实经优化的中药诱导剂有望成为安全、可靠的新型骨诱导因子。

1999年，天津医院金鸿宾等参与吴咸中主持的国家"九五"攻关项目"多脏器功能障碍综合症发病机理及中西医结合治疗的深入研究"，其中严重多发伤成活率从84%提高到95%以上。

第五节 皮肤病及妇科病

1991~2005年，天津在中西医结合治疗皮肤病的研究上，对一些重型系统性疾病进行深入研究，建立起红斑狼疮动态信息数据库，对脓疮性银屑病，结合性痒疹等均取得较好疗效。1996年，《中西医结合治疗皮肤病学》的出版，标志着对皮肤病的系统研究达到新水平。

同期，天津在中西医结合治疗妇科病方面也取得一些新进展，对外阴白斑、宫颈炎、更年期综合征、功能性子宫出血、宫颈糜烂等常见妇科病的治疗，取得较显著的效果。

一、皮肤病

1993年，天津市长征医院边天羽、丁素先、陈效勤等在积累大量系统性红斑狼疮病例基础上，建立该病动态信息数据库系统，在治疗上采取中药"凉血消风汤"和"狼二号"加疏肝活血汤配合皮质激素及免疫抑制剂的中西医结合方法最有优势。1997年，该院毛舒和、匡朴、吴泓等对泛发性湿疹属血热型的病人采取中药皮炎2号颗粒口服与外用K霜治疗，实验证实此方法有较大优势且安全可靠。同年，该院王志珍、李颖奎、寿建中利用全血培养法，观察"凉血皮炎2号"对细胞内毒素诱导人外周白细胞产生肿瘤环死因子的影响，该药能明显抑制肿瘤环死因子的产生。2000年，津南区中医门诊部冯桂丽治疗顽固性荨麻疹采用西咪替丁、扑尔敏、维生素C加上祛风和营止痒中药口服，较单纯西药效果好。2001年，长征医院齐云对脓疮型银屑病在西药激素、环磷酰按、迪银片治疗基础上，自拟扶正凉血解毒汤和活血理湿解毒汤，可调节免疫力，避免不良反应。2002年，乔树芳以清热解毒中药"痒疹冲剂"联合西药免疫抑制剂治疗结节性痒疹，总有效率达62.5%。

二、妇科病

1991年，中心妇产医院张丽蓉、王丽芳等对外阴白斑采取中药外洗，内服"六仙汤"及外涂氯氟舒松软膏或丙酸倍氯软膏、生肌橡皮膏，有效率达94.2%，对促进组织祛旧生新、萎缩组织恢复、色素代谢的恢复具有独到之处。1992年，该院王桂芬、邢建华针对子宫颈炎电烙后出血较多、恢复慢等问题，在电烙后采用"上皮安"中药软膏局部外敷，起到祛腐生新作用。

1998年，该院韩林飞对更年期综合征在用西药肾上腺素能阻止剂、调节植物神经功能及心理治疗基础上，采用中药辨证治疗，取得效果。同年，南开医院曹保利将功能失调性子宫出血分为血热妄行、气滞血瘀、肾虚、脾虚、气血两虚型等进行辨证论治，并以激素、止血药物维生素K等西药治疗，效果显著，降低了复发率。同年，韩林飞对慢性盆腔炎采取西药抗菌素和中医辨证论治方法，将该症分为湿热瘀结及寒凝气滞治之，优于西药组。2003年，该院郭金荣、唐政平采用多功能红外治疗仪，配合自制中药“蛤雄散”治疗宫颈糜烂，可促进组织再生修复，加速愈合，有显著远期效果。

第六章 药 学

1991~2005年，天津药学领域大力加强实验室建设，为科研提供基础条件。天津药物研究院承担了6个国家(或部级)重点实验室、检测中心的建设，包括：中华人民共和国医药管理局制药用原料(中间体)、辅料标准化技术归口单位实验室，中华人民共和国医药管理局新药研究管理中心天津高血压药理研究室，联合国人口基金避孕药质量保证中心，中华人民共和国医药管理局新药研究管理中心天津药代动力学与临床药理研究室，天津药物研究院天津市新药安全评价研究中心，天津药代动力学和药效动力学省部共建国家重点实验室。这6个实验室在天津市和全国医药行业的新药研究中发挥了重要作用。天津医科大学(以下简称“医科大学”)药学院药理学科确立了心血管药理学、药物代谢与药物动力学、中西医结合(消化)药理学和抗炎免疫药理学4个研究方向，并建立相关实验室。2003年，天津中医学院中药药理实验室、细胞生物学实验室获批中华人民共和国中医药管理局三级科研实验室。2004年，中药药理学实验室经天津市科学技术委员会(以下简称“市科委”)、天津市教育委员会(以下简称“市教委”)认定为首批天津市重点实验室。

科研与开发：天津药物研究院以新药研究与开发为主，同时开展基础研究，15年中，每年新开研发课题几十项，按药物用途和治疗作用划分，涉及8个领域，包括：防治心脑血管疾病药物，防治精神与神经系统疾病药物，防治呼吸系统疾病药物，防治消化系统疾病药物，防治内分泌系统疾病药物和抗骨质疏松症药物，合成抗菌药及抗真菌药物，防治泌尿和生殖系统疾病药物，其他类药物；按项目性质可划分为7大类型，包括创新药物的筛选，中药的药材及植物化学研究，化学合成药物的新产品、新工艺研究，药物新制剂研究，药物分析研究，药理、毒理和药代动力学研究，重大药物中间体及新工艺研究。

该院在这一时期开展研究课题近700项，共获得国家和天津市各级科技奖励48项。在完成的研究课题中，有164项取得新药证书，在天津市和全国推广生产，为临床用药提供更多更好的选择，其药品研发的质量和数量，在天津市和全国都位于前列。授权专利11件，2005年年底被授予天津市专利示范企业称号。

医科大学15年间共完成20余项国家及省市级科研项目，共获得国家和省部级奖6项。科研成果促进、提升了教学水平，加强了人才培养的能力。

天津中医学院中药研究领域从弱到强实现了快速发展，并取得一批重要成果。15年间共完成国家级课题12项，省部级课题19项。荣获国家级奖励1项、省部级一、二等奖励8项。

第一节 药 理

1991年后，天津药理研究与应用有了快速、深入的发展，开拓了许多新领域。主要在临床药理、心脑血管药理、中西医结合药理、肿瘤药理、药物毒理方面做出了新成就。“国家医药管理局天津药代动力学与临床药理研究室”是国内首家从事药物代谢动力学研究的实验室，做了大量开创性的工作。医科大学加强基础建设，建立了细胞培养、分子与生化、电生理与血流动力学、化学分析、重量分析、光谱分析、色谱分析等实验室。

一、临床药理

1995年12月26日，中华人民共和国医药管理局批准在天津药物研究院成立“国家医药管理局天津药代动力学与临床药理研究室”，该室的研究重点为药物代谢动力学和药物制剂的生物利用度及生物等效性研究。

图7-6-1-115　刘昌孝在药代重点实验室

1997年建立的17项实验规范和17种标准操作规程，同年通过卫生部临床药理基地专家组的考核，得到好评。该室配备大量先进的仪器设备，在学科带头人刘昌孝的带领下，1996～2000年，完成药代动力学研究100多项，其中：国家新药基金项目9项，国家“七五”至“九五”科技攻关项目15项，军内攻关项目3项；一类新药8项。“前体药物的药代动力学规范研究”和“生物技术药物的药代规范研究”为科技部“九五”科技攻关“重中之重”项目，2001年1月按计划提前完成研究，通过专家验收。“前体药物和生物技术药物的临床前药物动力学规范研究”获2001年度天津市科技进步二等奖。“药物动力学数学模型与新药的药物动力学研究”获2003年度天津市科技进步一等奖。该项目在药物动力学模型的数学分析中应用多发展药物动力学的数学模型和衍化复杂的数学模型的分析等方面有创新。其《药物动力学概论》在模型分析上有独到之处，公式推算突破了旧框框，提出了一些精炼准确的计算公式和方法，出版药物动力学中英文版专著7本，在国内外学术期刊发表药物动力学学术论文165篇，论文论著引用共256次。该项目对于药物评价，临床应用和药物设计及新药发现均具有理论和应用价值。

该室在完成国家重点攻关课题的同时，积极为天津市新药临床研究提供技术支持。1997年和2000年分别与医科大学总医院和天津医药科学研究所合作，开展临床药理研究和采用同位素技术开展药物代谢动力学研究。1997年还与医科大学总医院联合建立临床药理基地，并顺利通过卫生部临床药理基地专家组的考核。该室重点完成药物制剂的生物利用度和生物等效性研究，已发展成为国内药物代谢动力学最具研究实力的实验室之一。

该室为天津企业新药研发提供技术支持，开展药物代谢动力学研究。曾先后为天津力生药厂、天津中药六厂、天津中央制药厂、天津中美史克公司等10余家企业申报新药提供药物代谢动力学研究报告，提升天津市药物研发质量，推动天津市医药行业的科技进步。1999年2月，“肿瘤坏死因子的动物药代动力学研究”获得泰国世界医学金象奖，2000年10月“小檗胺的研发”获得世界综合医学大会（香港）紫荆花创新医学金奖，刘昌孝被授予“紫荆花医学成就奖”。

2003年1月，科技部批准天津市和科技部共同创建“天津药代动力学和药效动力学省部共建国家重点实验室”，该室以天津药物研究院为依托，是国家启动的首批29个省部共建重点实验室中唯一建立在转制企业的重点实验室。实验室建立6个相关实验室研究单元，即新药发现研究、药代动力学研究、药效动力学研究、生物技术药物研究、毒代动力学研究和临床药理研究。该室自成立到2005年，申请了12项具有自主知识产权的候选化合物国家发明专利，均获授权（见列表）。“临床前新药的药物动力学”技术平台，于2003年获得国

2003～2005年药代重点实验室申报的专利情况一览表

表7-6-1-54

专利申请号	专利名称	申请日期	发明人	授权日期
CN200310106663.3	杞芪口服液及其制备方法	2003.10.17	刘昌孝　刘风玉　顾以保　魏广力	2006.8.30
CN200510016205.X	噻吩并吡啶取代的乙酰肼衍生物	2005.2.23	刘登科　王平保　赵专友　蒋庆峰	2007.5.30
CN03153585.2	黄芪冻干粉针剂及其制备工艺	2003.8.18	韩英梅　王亚静　赵娜夏　赵专友	2007.12.19
CN200310107201.3	一种含活性成分阿德福韦或其盐的经注射给药的制剂及其制备方法	2003.12.5	徐为人　任晓文　马　晋	2008.4.30
CN200510015371.8	甘草次酸-30-酰胺类衍生物及其用途	2005.10.14	王建武　徐为人　雍建平　汤立达	2009.5.20
CN200510014971.2	一种黄芪甲苷注射液及其制备方法	2005.9.2	韩英梅　王亚静　赵专友　赵娜夏	2009.9.2
CN200510015103.6	艾拉莫德微粉化及口服速释制剂	2005.9.16	王杏林　高　晶　梅林雨　刘昌孝	2010.5.12
CN200510015340.2	艾拉莫德结晶形态及其组合物	2005.10.9	梅林雨　梁忠信　王杏林　高　晶	2011.5.4
CN201010236615.6	艾拉莫德结晶形态及其组合物	2005.10.9	梅林雨　梁忠信　王杏林　高　晶	2012.5.23
CN201010236636.8	艾拉莫德结晶形态及其组合物	2005.10.9	梅林雨　梁忠信　王杏林　高　晶	2012.5.23
CN201010236651.2	艾拉莫德结晶形态及其组合物	2005.10.9	梅林雨　梁忠信　王杏林　高　晶	2012.5.23
CN200510015288.0	噁唑烷酮类化合物	2005.9.30	刘登科　徐为人　黄长江	2012.11.21

家重大科技项目"863"计划中"创新药物和中药现代研究"的子项目立项，2005年年底超额完成计划目标并通过国家验收。截止2005年年底，该室已完成10个创新药物的临床前药物动力学研究；作为合作单位完成国家"863"项目的"创新药物研究的临床前药物动力学研究"中8个课题和国家"973"项目"基于功能基因组学的创新药物研究"中的"建立ADME/T快速研究筛选系统"（2004CB518902）的研究、"方剂配伍规律研究：中药组分配伍作用模式的基础研究"（2005CB523404）。

二、心脑血管药理

1991年9月，中华人民共和国医药管理局批准成立"国家医药管理局新药研究管理中心天津高血压药理研究室"。该室以天津药物研究院为依托，旨在提高抗高血压药药效学的研究水平，为国内抗高血压药的新药筛选和药效学评价提供技术支持。1991～1995年，该室以合作或委托方式先后为中国科学院、中国医学科学院、中国军事医学科学院、中国医科大学及其他医药科研单位完成的各类抗高血压药物药效学研究项目中，一类新药5项，二类新药22项，三类新药9项。1996～2000年，相继为全国科研院所完成新药药效学研究项目70多项，其中一类新药19项。在抗高血压新药药效学研究方面，是全国同行中接受项目最多，完成质量最好的实验室之一。在抗心脑缺血新药的评价中建立了多个心脑缺血模型，形成一整套抗心脑缺血新药的实验操作规程。在溶栓新药药效学研究中，特别针对基因工程制品药效学试验技术含量高、难度大的特点，利用包括同位素跟踪技术在内的多种方法，成功建立多种体内外血栓形成及栓塞病理模型，对推动国内基因工程类溶栓药的研究具有重要作用。在抗慢性心衰药药效学研究中，建立犬心脏起搏心动过速和下腔静脉狭窄方法形成的两种稳定的慢性心衰模型，在全国抗慢性心衰药物的开发及心衰的基础性研究中发挥重要作用。在该室研究、评价的项目中，有4个一类新药通过审评。为表彰该室在新药开发中做出的突出贡献，1997年12月，中华人民共和国医药管理局授予该室新药研制特别奖。

1991年，天津医学院基础医学院王国祥等开始研究牛磺酸及联合用药抗心律失常作用，其结果显示牛磺酸及牛磺酸与钙拮抗剂、肾上腺受体阻滞剂等合用对多种实验性心律失常动物模型有防治作用。同年，王国祥应邀参加美国阿拉巴马大学召开的国际牛磺酸学术会议，出版英文版的牛磺酸学术专著。1994年，完成"牛磺酸的心肌电药理学研究"项目，发现牛磺酸具有广谱抗心律失常作用，与其他抗心律失常药合用，能减少其他抗心律失常药的剂量（因大部分抗心律失常药都具有致心律失常作用）。在此基础上，课题组提出以牛磺酸为母体构架，与痕量金属离子结合形成新的高效配合物，该配合物具有显著抗心律失常作用。

1995年，医科大学基础医学院刘艳霞对缺血、缺血再灌注、缺血预适应时心肌形态和功能的改变，以及黄芪甙Ⅳ等药物对心肌的保护作用进行研究。经蛋白组学的研究发现三磷酸腺苷(ATP)合酶在缺血预适应中的作用及寡霉素敏感相关蛋白(OSCP)可作为新药靶标,相关研究论文在国际学术刊物上发表,被SCI收录。

1997年,医科大学基础医学院娄建石等完成"无创性测定药物对心功能血流动力学的调节作用的研究"。该项目采用自主研发的阻抗法测定体表心电信号,并转换为血流动力学指标,成为清醒动物测定心功能的新方法。2001~2005年,娄建石主持完成"新药牛磺酸镁的研制及主要药效学研究"及"新药牛磺酸镁主要药效学研究"。牛磺酸镁是积十几年研究,在天然氨基酸基础上,进行化学修饰产生的新的抗心律失常化合物。牛磺酸与二价阳离子进行配位结合形成新的配合物,在国际上属首次提出,并陆续发现该配合物具有很好的心肌保护和抗心律失常作用。

1999年,天津中医学院张伯礼、高秀梅等与中国中医研究院、清华大学共同承担"973"项目——"复方丹参方药效物质及作用机理研究",该研究在基本搞清方剂药效物质基础及作用原理的基础上,提出由组分配伍组建现代中药的研究模式和筛选方法,强化主效应,兼顾次效应,减少副效应,优选出最佳配伍比例,建立以组分配伍优化设计现代中药的新模式,并研制了两个以组分配伍的新药,使中药研制由经验组方过渡到在经验基础上结合实验研究的优化设计组方,同时探索由经验组方过渡到在经验的基础上依靠科学实验依据指导组方的方法,为"名特优"小复方中药的二次开发开创了一种新模式。该项研究获2004年度国家科技进步二等奖。

三、中西医结合药理

1994年,医科大学基础医学院林秀珍主持国家自然科学基金资助项目"大黄及大黄有效成分对细胞内游离钙浓度的影响"研究;主持市科委项目"通里攻下法对肠屏障功能保护作用的研究"。通过十余年的研究,建立中药治疗急腹症的4种屏障保护作用学说:肠道机械屏障、生物屏障、化学屏障和免疫屏障,完善大承气汤及其君药大黄的"通里攻下""清热解毒""活血化淤""攻防兼备"的药理作用和机制的新观点,为中西医结合治疗急腹症,防治肠源性内毒素血症等方面提供了现代医学的新理论。

1997年,医科大学基础医学院方步武开始从事抗炎免疫药理和抗肝纤维化药理研究。提出以肿瘤坏死因子α(TNFα)和白介素-6(IL-6)判断急腹症伴发全身炎症反应综合征(SIRS)及多器官功能障碍综合征(MODS)的参考值,以白介素-6(IL-6)和新喋呤判断烧伤脓毒症的预后,提出急腹症内毒素血症期的概念,以及大承气颗粒和清胆灵在不同原发病所致的不同程度的全身炎症反应中的用药方案并揭示其药理作用基础,证实了中西医结合分阶段早期防治全身炎症反应的可行性、必要性和有效性。1998年,建立外周血和细胞培养上清液中亚硝酸盐的新测定方法——荧光分光光度测定法。开始抗肝纤维化药理研究,首创牛血清白蛋白制备肝纤维化动物模型。2002年,提出并采用四氯化碳(CCl_4)复合因素所致肝纤维化模型,证实青蒿琥酯具有抗肝纤维化的作用,并采用肝星状细胞($HSC-T_6$)揭示青蒿琥酯抗肝纤维化的作用机理。

2001年,医科大学基础医学院孟林等从事中药抗腹泻药东北鹤虱的研究与开发。以药理活性为导向的活性成分的分离、提取和分析,从整体、器官、细胞和分子水平上,应用现代药理学分析方法,探讨药物效应的机制,同时进行该药物的制剂学研究,制备了东北鹤虱胶囊剂。经实验证实,东北鹤虱胶囊能够缓解腹泻症状,并具有明显的抗炎、镇痛及抗菌作用。

四、肿瘤药理与毒理

1994年,医科大学基础医学院何景华主持的抗肿瘤药理研究工作,采用先进的偶联技术将核素(99m锝、111铟、113铟)与抗体连接制得肿瘤导向和预定位诊断药物,用于肿瘤的早期和定位诊断。"肿瘤的放射免疫显像新技术的建立及其临床应用"于1996年获得天津市技术发明二等奖。

1999年2月,天津药物研究院组建"新药安全评价中心",旨在建立一个符合国家GLP(实验室管理规范)规范要求的药物安全性评价实验室。该实验室先后承担国家"九五""十五"攻关项目,"863"项目,卫生部、中华人民共和国医药管理局、天津市等各类项目新药的药理、毒性研究，完成几百项包括大鼠、恒河猴、家犬、比格犬长期毒性、特殊毒性等安全性研究，积累了丰富的经验，并起草、执行了几百份标准操作规程。这些工作使该室成为天津市首家按GLP要求开展研究的新药安全评价实验室，对缩短新药开发时间，降低成本，增强市场竞争力，推动天津市中药现代化、国际化，加快现代医药产业化发展，打造天津医药品牌，发挥重要作用。

天津中医学院马红梅、张伯礼等通过毒理物质和机制研究发现，关木通真正的毒性成分可能是马兜铃酸体内代谢产物马兜铃酰胺；肾毒性不局限于肾小管上皮细胞。研究结果上报中华人民共和国药监局和药典会，并被2000年版药典采用。

20世纪70年代初，天津市医药科学研究所在中草药一药多筛的基础上，从马蔺子种皮中分离出马蔺子甲素等化学成分进行系统的药学研究，并确定其抗癌作用。1976年始，进行了马蔺子素胶囊的临床抗癌作用观察，证明其对肺癌，肝癌，胃癌，食管癌及急性白血病有效。1978年，在进行马蔺子素抗癌临床观察中，发现该药与放疗合用有放射增敏作用。针对这一作用扩大临床观察，证明疗效。1984年马蔺子素的肿瘤放射增敏作用研究被列入国家 "六五"重点攻关项目。在此期间，向卫生部申报新药，并被批准进行新药临床研究。1993~1995年卫生部指定广州中山医科大学肿瘤医院组织全国多家医院进行临床研究。总结Ⅱ、Ⅲ期临床4009例的有效率统计，与单放疗相比，服用马蔺子素可使肺癌、宫颈癌放疗的肿瘤消失率提高两倍以上，使食管癌，头颈部肿瘤的肿瘤消失率提高一倍以上，使骨转移癌的显效率提高一倍以上，使肺癌，食管癌和头颈部肿瘤的5年生存率显著提高。研究成果“一种新型苯醌化合物，其制备方法及含该化合物的放射增敏剂”为发明专利，于1990年公开，1994年9月14日被中国专利局授于发明专利证书（专利号：ZL88109119.7）。该项目发明人为李德华、吴寿金、王士贤、匡朴、许兢兢等。马蔺子素放射增敏研究，1997年获得天津市科技进步二等奖。马蔺子素胶囊剂于1998年9月经国家批准正式生产，转让山东新华制药厂上市推广应用。

第二节 药 剂

20世纪90年代初，天津医学院，天津药物研究院开展药剂研究，取得专利成果，并和生产实际相结合，开发新产品。主要有：“具有阻滞作用的栓剂”“含有微囊的栓剂”“麻仁软胶囊”“一种新型pH依赖型结肠定位释药系统”等。

一、栓剂、滴眼液

1990年，天津医学院药学院叶咏年、冯喜增等对新型栓剂进行研究，先后获得“具有阻滞作用的栓剂”（专利号90100148.1）、“含有微囊的栓剂”（专利号92112395.7）两个专利；1994年，叶咏年、黄欣完成“麦迪霉素栓剂及其含微囊长效栓剂研究”，获中华人民共和国科学技术委员会颁发的国家科技成果证书。1998年，叶咏年和张湘雯获得“盐酸洛美沙星滴眼液”新药证书。

二、麻仁软胶囊

1992年，天津药物研究院与天津中央制药二厂合作研究开发麻仁软胶囊。当时，全国中药制剂没有软胶囊剂型，此项研究是一个创新。华伟义、于丽云等以传统中药麻仁丸为基础，运用先进的工艺和现代制药技术，对处方成分进行科学提取，通过药理、药效和制剂等方面的研究，成功研制成麻仁软胶囊，于1994年取得新药证书。新剂型与原剂型相比，具有服用更方便，起效更快的优点。该项目在研制过程中注重科学研究与企业生产的密切配合,成为产研结合的突出范例。

三、定位释药系统

1996年以来,医科大学药学院房志仲等进行血栓溶解酶药效学及剂型研究;完成芬必得空心胶囊的质量研究,解决了芬必得的稳定性问题;复方5—单硝酸异山梨酯缓释胶囊的研究,为配合天津市太和药厂申报新药完成了实验研究资料。罗达灵通胶囊和蚊王胶囊急性毒性、长期毒性、初步药效学及定性试验研究;芪连消渴胶囊对正常大鼠血糖及对大鼠24小时尿量影响的试验研究;糖肾康对抗试验性肾损伤及糖微平对动物微循环影响的试验研究;胰达康2号的急性毒性和慢性毒性试验研究等,为配合天津市华博医院申报医院制剂完成了实验研究资料。获得“一种新型pH依赖型结肠定位释药系统”发明专利;舒芬太尼复合丙泊酚靶控输注的药代动力学研究,为临床合理用药提供理论依据;研究建立家兔口腔溃疡模型和幽门狭窄大鼠模型,为新药研究提供新的试验方法。

第三节 生药与药物分析

1991~2005年,天津在生药领域主要开展了资源调查、药材品种整理和质量研究,并将现代技术应用于生药研究中。同时,在药物分析领域医科大学采用近现代色谱技术、光谱技术和生物学手段,将多维色谱、胶束色谱、电色谱、毛细管电泳分析技术、色谱工作站技术及紫外、红外,气—质联用、液—质联用等手段建立微量物质自动化定量检测系统,对中、西药进行多元化研究。

一、生药

医科大学药学院的生药学科15年间坚持发掘天津市的中药和天然药物资源,特别是在蓟县八仙山地区开展大量的植物资源调查工作,而且在天津特有的生药资源的现代研究与应用方面,展开一系列研究。1991年,天津医学院药学院建立标本室,开展该地区品种调查、生药外形鉴别及组织形态鉴别方法等,同时结合中药质量检验的需要,进行中药材混乱品种及真伪优劣的研究。

天津药物研究院参加国家“七五”攻关课题(课题延续到“八五”),获得丰硕成果。常用药材品种整理和质量研究(党参、防风等68个专题)为解决中药材规范的国家标准问题。“七五”期间,中华人民共和国科学技术委员会、中华人民共和国计划委员会和财政部确定了“完成100种常用药材的品种整理和质量研究”的攻关目标,北方组由北京医科大学药学院楼之岑负责,多所大学、科研单位共同参加完成。天津药物研究院作为参研单位,此项目由“七五”延续到“八五”。由张树花、袁毓湘等参加完成了三棱、决明子、刘寄奴、冬葵子、瞿麦等(7种,分别为三棱类、刘寄奴类、决明子类、冬葵子类、瞿麦类、白药子类、萱草根类)药材整理,进行新药形态、性状、组织学研究,开展组分测定、药理药效和化学研究,如期完成国家验收和成果鉴定。该课题1992年11月获国家科技进步一等奖。

自1997年起,医科大学段宏泉等针对尚无质量控制标准的有毒中药雷公藤及其制剂,开展“有毒中药雷公藤药效物质基础及有效部位的色谱指纹图谱研究”,在系统阐明雷公藤药效成分的基础上,建立了有效化学成分组成明确的色谱指纹图谱,提出以雷公藤红素和雷公藤甲素的含量控制结合有效成分色谱指纹图谱控制雷公藤制剂的质量。其中,在雷公藤属药用植物的药效成分研究中获得重要研究进展,利用各种色谱分离技术结合各种有机波谱解析、X–射线单晶衍射和化学衍生合成,从雷公藤及其制剂中分离鉴定了210种有机化学成分,其中文献未见报道的化合物109种,结合药物筛选技术,阐明中药雷公藤抗炎免疫抑制作用的化学物质基础,发表18篇SCI收录的论文,他人引用226次。该研究不仅为有毒中药雷公藤及其制剂提供了更加合理可靠的质量控制方法，解决了有毒中药质量控制的难题，而且雷公藤药效成分的阐明为临床合理用药提供了理论依据。

2003年，段宏泉、周晔等将现代化学分析和生物技术手段引入生药学，在中药质量控制上应用指纹图谱技术、PCR技术即聚合酶链式反应（polymerase chain reaction, PCR）、RAPD（Random Amplified Polymorphic DNA，随机扩增多态性DNA）技术和PCR-RFLP（RFLP即限制性片断长度多态性restriction fragment length polymorphism）技术等，对中药的质量加以控制。在生药资源方面，以分子生物学手段建立黄精和玉竹的鉴别方法。在中药现代化研究中，以各种现代色谱分析技术，包括高效液相-质谱联用技术，建立现代化的质量控制和标准。

二、药物分析

1991~2005年，医科大学药学院李惠芬采用近现代色谱技术、光谱技术和生物学手段，将多维色谱、胶束色谱、电色谱、毛细管电泳分析技术、色谱工作站技术及紫外、红外，气-质联用、液-质联用等手段建立微量物质自动化定量检测系统，对中、西药进行多元化研究。其采用离子对色谱技术同时分离测定生物碱三种有效成分。同时运用现代化手段对中、西药进行质控的科学化、规范化研究。先后完成卫生部药典委员会“天仙子质控标准的研究”，教育部课题“紫杉醇分离纯化研究”，三类新药胆必清颗粒剂的质量标准研究及四类新药牛黄冠心丸、胃肠寒痛胶囊的质量标准等研究工作。王润玲研发的四类新药精氨酸布洛芬及其糖浆剂的质量标准已经通过中华人民共和国食品药品监督管理局审批，并于2003年获得精氨酸布洛芬盐及其糖浆剂的新药证书。

2003年7月，医科大学药学院实验中心被中华人民共和国中药管理局批准为中药分析三级重点科研实验室。

第四节 新药研发与新工艺

天津市在新药研究与开发中，涉及8个领域、7大类型，参加了国家各个时期相关重点攻关项目的研究，1991-2005年，为天津市医药产业提供36个新药证书，这些新药在国内或首次上市、或独家生产，成为天津市制药行业的重点拳头产品。在制药新工艺中，主要进行了“环丙氟哌酸新工艺的研究”“3,4,5-三甲氧苯甲酸甲酯合成新工艺研究”“常用中药饮片研究”“马齿苋胶囊的制备工艺研究”“养血清脑颗粒二次开发研究”等。

一、新药研发

（一）盐酸丁丙诺啡及其制剂的研究开发

盐酸丁丙诺啡是吗啡、蒂巴因类衍生物，1982年载入英国马丁大药典，作为英国医院首选的镇痛药，在美、法、德、印度等国普遍用于临床。国家医药管理局于20世纪80年代将其列入科研试制计划，要求按国家二类新药列题仿制。天津药物研究院张丽云等于1985年完成药物合成研究，1990年11月获得新药证书，1991年获生产文号，1992年6月正式推广生产。该药品以蒂巴因为起始原料，经九步反应制得，总收率高于文献报道，原料立足国内，工艺路线合理，原料及注射液质量达到国外同类产品水平。在此基础上，1994年又进行新剂型舌下含片的研制，1997年12月获得新药证书。该药品的注射液及舌下含片成为中国临床镇痛一线用药。其注射液的生产企业——国家麻醉药品定点生产企业：天津药物研究院药业有限责任公司，在天津市仅此一家，在全国只有两家，对发展天津市麻醉镇痛药品生产具有重要意义。盐酸丁丙诺啡及其制剂的研究于1996年获国家科技进步三等奖。

（二）新型心脑血管系统药物苯磺酸氨氯地平的研究

1996年，天津药物研究院开始苯磺酸氨氯地平及片剂的研制。罗振福、张丽云、靳朝东等选择以邻苯二甲酸酐和乙醇胺为起始原料的制备工艺，攻克4个关键技术难题：改变低温反应操作工艺提高了收率；设计合成苯磺酸，解决了原材料问题；反复实验研究，确定主要杂质的结构和来源并自制样品；通过对中间体的精制，除去杂质提高产品质量。经过一系列研究、改进，使操作简便，适合工业化生产。2002年取得新药证书，当年由宁波制药厂投入生产。取得良好经济效益和社会效益。

（三）头孢菌素药物重要中间体GCLE的研究

新型头孢菌素中间体7-苯乙酰胺基-3-氯甲基头孢烷酸对甲氧基苄酯（GCLE）作为国家“九五”攻关项目和天津市重大科技攻关项目，于1996年由天津药物研究院投入开发研究并率先在国内研制成功。2000年通过国家验收，2003年通过市科委组织的科技成果鉴定，荣获2005年度天津市科技进步二等奖。孟红、赵平、王学知等研究出的GCLE合成工艺具有反应条件温和、操作简单、原料廉价易得、适合于大规模生产的特点。该项研究打破日本产品在中国的垄断，为进一步发展头孢药物打下良好的基础。此项研究成果于2002年成功转让给天津市中央药业有限公司，2005年在天津市新建的头孢类药物基地——天津市津康制药有限公司规模化生产，产品行销海外，创造了良好的经济效益和社会效益。GCLE的研制成功同时带动了下游第三、四代头孢菌素新药的开发，由该院研制的第三代口服头孢菌素新药头孢地尼，已率先在全国独家获得新药证书并获得国家发明专利授权。GCLE作为头孢菌素药物的重要中间体，为提高中国头孢菌素这一大类药物的研发和生产水平具有重大意义。

（四）脑卒中急性期治疗药阿加曲班的研究

阿加曲班为凝血酶抑制剂，可直接选择性地作用于凝血酶活性部位，不产生抗原和变态反应，对进展性、皮质性脑血栓有显著疗效，是世界上批准用于脑卒中急性期治疗的第一个合成药物。天津药物研究院于1999年3月开始立项研究，在周英、周学福、刘尚才的带领下，2002年4月完成合成工艺等临床前研究，取得临床批件。2005年取得新药证书，同年5月产品获准上市，由该院所属泰普药品科技发展有限公司、药业有限责任公司国内独家生产。该课题2001年列为市科委重大科技攻关项目，2003年列入国家“863”计划，2004年确立为“创新药物和中药现代化”重大专项课题滚动项目，并被评为2004年度国家重点新产品；该项目的产业化推动还被列入2004年度国家“863”计划引导项目。阿加曲班的研制成功为临床脑卒中急性期治疗开拓了新的局面，也为天津市医药产业结构调整和医药经济增长做出贡献。

（五）抗乙肝病毒新药阿德福韦酯的研究

阿德福韦酯是一种新型核苷类抗乙型病毒性肝炎药物。该药为腺嘌呤磷酸酯化合物阿德福韦的前药，在体内转化为阿德福韦有效地抑制HBV DNA（乙肝病毒基因）发挥抗病毒作用，而且对拉米夫定耐药的变异株也有明显的抑制作用。天津药物研究院于2000年9月开始立项研究。张殿镇、徐莉、赵健等研究出具有自主知识产权的新晶形阿德福韦酯，于2003年7月取得临床批件，2005年4月取得国家一类新药证书和生产批文，并于同年5月在国内率先上市。该课题被列为市科委重大科技攻关项目，仅用一年多的时间在国内率先按一类新药的要求完成了阿德福韦酯片用于拉米夫定耐药病人的安全性和有效性评价。

二、新工艺

（一）环丙氟哌酸新工艺的研究

环丙氟哌酸（环丙沙星）为国家重要的氟喹诺酮抗菌药物，1986年由太原制药厂研制成功并投产，国内相继又有十余家药厂生产，但因收率低、成本高，严重制约国内生产规模的扩大和市场供应。1987年，天津药物研究院徐嘉彦带领研究团队着手对其进行新工艺研究，最终成功地以氟氯苯胺为起始原料，以6–氟–7–氯–4–氧–1，4–双氢–喹啉–3–羧酸乙酯、1–乙基–6–氟–7–氯–4–氧–1，4–双氢–喹啉–3–羧酸乙酯、1–乙基–6–氟–7–氯–4–氧–1，4–双氢–喹啉–3–羧酸–硼–双（乙氧基）酸酯等中间体与无水哌嗪缩合制备氟哌酸，对氟氯苯胺计算的总收率达到62%，降低了成本，使中国环丙氟哌酸生产的工艺水平得到提高。1991年9月，承担该项目的课题组获得中华人民共和国计划委员会、中华人民共和国科学技术委员会、财政部联合颁发的“七五”国家科技攻关集体荣誉证书。

（二）3，4，5-三甲氧苯甲酸甲酯合成新工艺研究

该产品为抗菌增效剂甲氧苄啶（TMP）的前体物，是一关键中间体。天津药物研究院徐嘉彦在上世纪80年代末开始研究，做了大量开创性的工作，取得技术、工艺上的突破，完成该中间体的研制。该产品推动了中国抗菌增效剂的工业化生产，此项研究工作于1991年获国家发明三等奖。

（三）常用中药饮片研究

该课题被列为国家“八五”重大科技攻关项目。1991年，天津药物研究院张铁军等根据历史沿革在传统炮制工艺的基础上运用现代科技手段，通过化学、药理及毒理研究，对常用中药天南星、地黄等的炮制工艺展开研究，确定最佳炮制工艺并制定了饮片质量标准，对实现中药饮片炮制生产规范化、饮片质量标准化及保证临床疗效具有重大意义。该项目于1996年通过国家成果鉴定，同年获得中华人民共和国计划委员会、中华人民共和国科学技术委员会、财政部颁发的国家“八五”科技攻关重大科技成果证书。

（四）马齿苋胶囊等药的制备工艺研究

1992年，医科大学在中药制剂提取工艺与质量标准化研究方面做了大量工作。李崇芳、周晶研制的“降低卷烟焦油量的植物制剂的研制方法”获得专利（专利号为89103114.6）。周晶等完成的三类新药“心脑安口服液”的临床前研究，“马齿苋胶囊的制备工艺研究”获首届国际老年临床医学学术会议优秀论文奖。

（五）养血清脑颗粒二次开发研究

为保护中医药资源和产权优势，推动国内中药行业现代化、产业化发展，2004年，天津中医学院张伯礼首先提出“中药大品种二次开发”理念，着手于临床安全、疗效显著的名优中成药产品，提出以科技创造效益，以基础研究成果带动市场销售的市场营销策略，培育年销售额过亿元的“中药大品种”，形成大品种群，推动国内制药行业整体产业化进程。2005年，天津中医学院率先与企业合作，开展了“养血清脑颗粒二次开发研究”。明确养血清脑颗粒降压作用的特色和优势，为临床用药提供依据，并探索中成药二次开发的新途径，为其他已上市中药的再开发做了示范性研究。

第八篇

城市建设科技

概　述

1986年起，天津市以国务院印发的《关于天津市城市总体规划方案的批复》为指导，城市建设发生日新月异的变化。1993年，天津市人民政府（以下简称“市政府”）对天津的城市性质做出重要调整，强调商贸、金融等第三产业的发展，突出经济中心的功能，将中环线以内划定为城市中心区，并建成天津市体育中心及奥林匹克运动员村，之后成功举办第43届世界乒乓球锦标赛、世界体操锦标赛等赛事。1994年3月，中共天津市委员会（以下简称“市委”）、市政府正式确定全面建设滨海新区，其定位为“以天津港为依托，公用设施统一配套的国际先进的综合性工业基地，具有自由港功能的高度开放的现代化经济新区”。1999年，国务院对天津城市总体规划的批复中，确立天津新的城市发展目标：天津是环渤海地区的经济中心，要努力建设成为经济繁荣、社会文明、科教发达、设施完善和环境优美的现代化港口城市和中国北方重要的经济中心。2002年10月，天津市开始实施综合开发海河两岸规划，通过建设若干个不同类型的功能性区域，将海河市区段形成独具特色的服务经济带、文化带和景观带。20世纪末及21世纪初相继建成周邓纪念馆、平津战役纪念馆、科技馆、自然博物馆、天津博物馆及银河公园等一系列现代化的爱国主义教育基地，成为群众性的学习、休闲、娱乐场所。2005年10月，天津滨海新区的开发开放正式纳入国家整体发展战略规划，滨海新区建设取得快速发展。

1991～2005年，城市建设系统按照天津城市总体规划确定的发展目标，不断加强科研院所建设，加大科技经费的投入，完成一大批科研课题，科技成果的转化率不断提高，在新技术、新工艺、新材料、新设备的应用和推广上取得重大突破，并创建一批高难度、高质量、高科技的工程，为提高城市建设的整体水平和提升城市形象发挥积极作用。天津市在对城市的规划设计与勘察测绘工作中，积极推进“城市数字化”建设，逐步实现“3S”技术、计算机网络技术、数据库技术与仿真技术等一系列新技术，并不断扩大推广新技术的应用领域。

天津市政公路工程技术瞄准国内外先进水平，在科学研究、新技术推广、科技管理和人才培养等方面，积极组织科技攻关和新技术推广应用，取得一批创新性科技成果。1991～1995年，以京津塘高速公路建设为主要标志，天津的城市道路与公路工程技术得到长足发展。依托京津塘高速公路工程，研究开发一批新技术、新工艺，施工机械化水平迅速提升，软土路基处理技术、水泥稳定碎石基层技术和沥青路面摊铺自动找平工艺等一整套高速公路施工技术在国内居领先地位。1996～2005年，高速公路和城市快速路设计施工技术继续发展，软土地基综合加固技术和软土路基沉降控制方法的研究达到国内领先水平；城市立交工程随着八里台立交桥、中山门立交桥的建成，桥梁设计与施工技术逐步向轻质、高强、大跨度、桥型多样化和预制装配化方向发展，建成一批构思独特、造型新颖、桥型多样的斜拉桥、悬索桥、拱桥、梁桥等，成为天津城市形象的重要标志；先后研制和引进一批先进的科研设备和施工设备，道路养护技术水平不断提高；城市排水管网功能不断完善，新型塑料排水管材不断涌现并推广。

天津市在建筑科学技术领域不断取得进步。建筑科学方面，以天津大学为代表的科研团队在建筑学研究、土木工程研究和水利水电工程研究等方面取得一系列达到国际先进水平的科研成果，其中多项成果获得国家或天津市科技奖励，并在诸多建筑工程中得到成功应用。随着城市建设的发展，高层建筑和大体量建筑成为天津市主要建设项目，天津市又是一个软土地基典型的城市，深基坑技术的发展直接关系到建筑物的质量与安全。多年来，建筑科研机构与建筑施工企业相结合，在建筑工程施工中研发出大量技术创新型成果。在深基坑支护技术应用上有很大的发展，比较突出的有工具式钢管支撑符合支护体系、三道混凝土环梁支护技术、地下钢筋混凝土连续墙、超深超厚地下墙连续施工技术。在深基坑基础施工中，土方开挖施工采用半逆施工法、全逆施工法、岛式和对称、分层开挖等技术，地下水排放采用锚拉钢桩帷幕止水、承压水层的盖挖逆作施工期间的地下降水施工技术等。高层、超高层建筑的日益增多，对基础的承载力要求越来越高，桩基础运用愈来愈广泛，天津市自主研发的高喷插芯组合桩、劲性搅拌桩等桩型在地基处理方面得到成功的应用，并编制了沉降控制桩基础技术规程、劲性搅拌桩技术规程、高喷插芯组合桩技术规程等地方标准。随着钻孔灌注桩的大范围使用，基桩的动测技术得到发展，出现了声波透射法、桩身内力测试及成孔检测技术。针对建筑物高度和体量的不断增加，各种新的结构体系不断涌现，并促进施工工艺的不断创新。在高层、超高层钢结构领域，钢结构技术的研究取得一定进展，并建立较完整的高层钢结构分析理论，形成高层钢结构成套技术，钢结构施工技术也达到国际先进水平，具有相当的钢结构加工、制作及安装能力，初步形成钢结构加工、制作及安装等施工的专业化设备及队伍。

天津市公用事业工程技术的发展，主要体现在城市供水、供气和供热上，其共同点是解决好来源、储配和节能等方面的问题。在供水方面，发明一种全部采用国产材料的EDL膜堆和暗道式无回路淡室隔板，开发出高纯水生产工艺设备；开发出从水源、水厂净化工艺到管网末稍全过程的技术集成系统，建立完善的饮用水水质安全保障体系；采用先进的气浮技术和气水反冲技术，解决了高藻水问题，提高了芥园水厂的水质；完成“膜技术处理饮用水成套技术及装置的研究”，生产出第三代净水器；开发出膜生物反应器、污水处理药剂、监控技术等中水处理的技术和设备，并在部分企业和新建的居民小区推广。在供气方面，90年代初天津民用燃气以煤制气、液化石油气、天然气三种气源并用，90年代后期天然气逐渐取代煤制气，燃气工程技术研究由制气研究转向以输配及储气研究为主，在管道施工、维修管理等方面的技术都有较大提高。2000年以后，科研重点转向对燃气的开发应用上，燃气的应用空间更加广阔。在供热方面，1990年以前全市居民集中供热普及率仅为11.39%，供热方式以中小锅炉及小煤炉为主。90年代，天津拆除一批能耗大、污染重的小锅炉，并入运行效率较高的集中供热锅炉和热电联产供热管网，逐步形成地热、热电联产和大型锅炉供热三种热源并举的局面，科研重点转向节能保温和计量供热等方面并取得一定成效。2001年起，天津市加大对清洁能源与再生能源供热的研究及应用力度，重点推广地热供热技术并取得实效。

1991年起，天津市更加重视园林绿化科技工作，培育出一批适于天津地域生长的草种、树种和花卉，全市绿化水平不断提高。1996年，天津市出台园林科技发展“九五”计划和2010年长期规划，先后颁布一系列技术规程或地方标准，园林绿化科技工作更加规范化、科学化。在虫害的防治研究方面取得突破性进展，大量放飞人工规模化繁育的周氏啮小蜂防治美国白蛾，以虫治虫，使市树——绒毛白蜡得到更有效的保护。经过对花卉的长期研究，筛选、培育出芳香化系列仙客来、藤本月季、彩色马蹄莲等30余个新品种，把市容装扮得更加美丽。天津动物园先后对食草类、灵长类、鸟类等动物由圈养、笼养改为散放，开创了动物园建设的第三种模式。天津经济技术开发区（以下简称“天津开发区”）成功利用海湾泥、粉煤灰和碱渣配成种植土营造出大片海防林，并采用排盐洗碱的新方法，将制碱废料堆成的碱渣山改建成公园。至2005年，全市每年新建绿地面积由1995年的100万平方米提高到2000万平方米以上，人均公共绿地由2.19平方米提高到8.38平方米。园林绿化技术的进步，促进了全市绿化程度的提高。

第一章 城市规划与勘测技术

1986年8月4日，国务院印发《关于天津市城市总体规划方案的批复》，是天津市第一次经国务院批复的城市总体规划方案，规划年限至2000年，以此指导城市各项建设。1996年，天津市规划局参照《天津市城市总体规划方案》，编制《天津市城市总体规划纲要（1996～2010年）》，并于1999年8月经国务院批准实施。新一轮规划按照建设北方重要经济中心的要求，强化天津作为环渤海乃至整个北方地区的区域经济中心的地位和作用，对城市人口规模、用地规模、城市布局、基础设施等进行调整，突出中心城区和滨海城区的协调发展。

在此期间，科学技术对城市规划的编制起到积极的促进作用。在对城市的规划设计与勘察测绘工作中，积极推进"城市数字化"建设，逐步实现"3S"技术、计算机网络技术、数据库技术与仿真技术等一系列新技术。不断扩大推广新技术的应用领域，从城市规划管理向勘察、测量、设计及研究、开发扩散。据对1992～2005年统计，城市规划系统共获国家级和省部级科技进步奖和勘察设计成果奖158项次。到2005年底，全市拥有规划设计资质的单位30家，获得建设部和市级优秀规划设计奖94项。

第一节　城市规划

根据《天津市城市总体规划》，市规划局于1994年编制完成"滨海新区总体规划"。1997年和2001年，先后编制出"海河东岸南站地区概念性规划"和"海河两岸规划咨询方案"。同期，根据天津市区域经济地位及城市规划布局，道路交通路网结构呈现出"双港"（海港、空港）"双高"（高速铁路段、高速公路）"双快"（快速路、快速轨道）的特点，编制了公共、公用设施规划以及历史文化风貌保护与文体设施建设规划。市规划局还针对中心城区的土地资源配置与产业结构调整做出规划，并于1996年开始实施。

一、总体规划

1994～1996年，为适应社会主义市场经济体制的转变和不断增多的经济社会发展新因素，天津市对《天津市城市总体规划方案（1986～2000年）》进行适应性调整和修订，规划期限为1996～2010年。1999年，国务院在对天津城市总体规划的批复中，确立天津新的城市发展目标：天津是环渤海地区的经济中心，要努力建设成为经济繁荣、社会文明、科教发达、设施完善和环境优美的现代化港口城市和中国北方重要的经济中心。

该规划不单从市域范围来考虑天津的发展，而是放眼于京、冀、环渤海和整个北方地区；城市规划范围不局限于城区，而是扩展到乡村，包括行政辖区11919.7平方千米。总体规划紧紧围绕天津新的城市定位进一步充实完善，增强区域观念，突出强调"三港（海港、空港和信息港）、二心（中心商务区和中心商业区）"，大力发展第三产业，努力改善城市环境，充分发挥天津在环渤海地区的作用，增强服务功能，向世界展示天津良好的城市形象。规划确定到2010年，天津成为全国率先基本实现现代化的地区之一。为使规划有较强的适应能力，给城市留有一定的更长远发展的余地和空间，确定在中心城区（外环绿化带围合的范围）外围建设军粮城、新立村、杨柳青、大寺、咸水沽、双街、双港和小淀等8个城镇组团。同时，对城市规模进行调整，确定2000年全市常住人口为1000万人，其中由中心城区、滨海新区及8个组团组成的中心城市实际居住人口540万人，城市建设用地440平方千米；2010年全市常住人口为1100万人，流动人口250万人左右，其中中心城市实际居住人口660万人，城市建设用地556平方千米。

该规划在继续深化和完善"一条扁担挑两头"的城市布局结构的基础上，形成以海河和京津塘高速公路为轴线，由中心城区和滨海新区及多个组团组成的中心城市。中心城市调整为多中心、组团式布局结构。滨海城区的布局结构则以塘沽城区为重点，向外辐射汉沽区、大港城区和海河下游工业区构成。沿京津塘高速公路和海河至天津港方向作为城市发展主轴，其余中小城镇均采取主要交通走廊分布，形成放射型城镇网络，构建由中心城市、县城、中心城镇和一般建制镇构成的四级城镇体系。

根据城市总体规划和分区规划，1999～2000年对外环绿化带以内的中心城区进行控制性详细规划，设置176个控制性规划单元。控制性规划的编制由以往委托开发商的做法改为全部由政府统筹安排，加强规划编制的公平性、合法性和权威性。通过利用新的规划工具和技术，每个控制性规划单元的规划都由计算机技术自动生成三维动画，实现规划设计的智能化飞跃。其规划成果均采用统一的技术规范，改变原“一事一议”的做法，将不同控制性规划单元有机地联系在一起，整体性得到加强。

2004年，为达到与北京市、河北省等周边地区总体规划的衔接和结合，组织编制了《天津市城市总体规划纲要（2004～2020年）》。在此基础上，编制完成《天津市城市总体规划（2005～2020年）》，内容包括区域协调、城市性质与发展规模、城市空间布局、城市综合交通、城市水资源与环境保护、历史文化名城保护等方面。

二、滨海新区规划

1994年3月，市委、市政府正式确定全面建设滨海新区，并计划用10年左右的时间基本建成。根据《天津市城市总体规划（1996～2010年）》，编制了《天津市滨海新区总体规划（1996～2010年）》。新区规划面积350平方千米，由塘沽地区（包括塘沽城区、天津开发区、天津港、天津港保税区）、汉沽城区、大港城区和海河下游工业区（包括东丽区和津南区的部分土地）组成，形成“一心三点”组合型城市布局结构。滨海新区定位为“以天津港为依托，公用设施统一配套的国际先进的综合性工业基地，具有自由港功能的高度开放的现代化经济新区”。

2005年6月，天津市编制完成《天津滨海新区国民经济和社会发展第十一个五年规划纲要》，确定滨海新区的规划面积为2270平方千米，总体布局为“T”型结构：沿津塘高速公路和海河建设“高新技术产业发展轴”，沿海岸线和海滨大道建设“海洋经济发展带”。在“轴”与“带”交汇处，建设国际港口大都市标志区和生态宜居的滨海新城，构成滨海新区的核心区。同时，规划建设先进制造业产业区、滨海高新技术产业区、滨海化工区、滨海新区中心商务商业区、海港物流区、临空产业区、滨海休闲旅游区等七个主要产业功能区，形成“服务环渤海，辐射‘三北’（华北、东北和西北），面向东北亚的现代化制造研发基地、中国北方国际航运中心和国际物流中心”。

2005年10月，在《中共中央关于制定国民经济和社会发展第十一个五年规划的建议》中，将天津滨海新区的开发开放正式纳入国家整体发展战略规划。天津市按照国家“推进天津滨海新区开发开放”要求，依据国务院批复的《天津市城市总体规划（2005～2020年）》，一方面组织编修滨海新区总体规划，另一方面积极落实滨海新区发展定位、发展目标、用地空间布局、综合交通及生态发展等，将滨海新区建设成为中国北方对外开放的门户、高水平的现代制造业和研发转化基地、北方国际航运中心和国际物流中心，以及宜居生态型新城区。

三、海河两岸发展规划

1991年，根据国务院批准的《天津市城市总体规划方案（1986～2000年）》对海河性质的定位，着手编制海河两岸发展规划，对两岸的工业、仓储等用地进行调整。

1994～1996年，在《天津市城市总体规划（2005～2020年）》修编中，注重自然生态和人文生态结合，规划出海河沿线中心商业区、中心商务区及历史风貌建筑保护区和几处大型绿化用地，为海河两岸综合开发奠定了基础，并运用新的方法和技术手段编制海河两岸地区控制性详细规划，对河岸沿线的土地性质、开发强度、建筑高度、绿化率等做出明确规定。为吸收国内外城市规划的先进理论和经验，于1997年和2001年，分别同澳大利亚和法国的城市规划专家合作，先后编制出《天津市海河东岸南站地区概念性规划》和《天津市海河两岸规划咨询方案》。

2002年10月，市委、市政府决定正式实施综合开发海河两岸规划，并提出用5年时间，通过建设若干不同类型的功能性区域，将海河市区段建设成“以旅游、景观功能为主，兼有排沥、防洪、航运等功能的一条生活性河道”，最终形成独具特色的服务经济带、文化带和景观带。海河综合开发地段始于三岔河口，终于海河与东外环线交汇处，全长约16千米。规划注入经营城市和市场化开发理念，突出规划暨策划的思想，逐步把海河沿岸现有的工业、仓储用地调整为商贸、金融、旅游和绿化用地。在实施水体治理、堤岸改造、道路交通、桥梁隧道、通航、绿化广场、环境工程、灯光夜景、公共建筑和整修置换等十大基础工程的同时，将海河两岸开发区域划分为若干个节点。根据节点不同的位置、历史背景、经济和文化底蕴等因素，采用城市设计的方法进行规划设计，以突出海河的区域形象和标识性。

2003年，红桥区三岔口运河经济文化商贸区、河北区大悲院文化商贸区、南开区古文化街海河楼商贸区、和平区和平广场中心商业区、河东区南站中心商务区、河西区海河水上运动世界等海河6个节点重点项目启动。同时，开展有国内外著名规划设计单位参加的规划设计方案竞标活动，海河两岸规划建设拉开序幕。

四、公共与公用设施规划

（一）城市道路交通与路网结构

根据《天津市城市总体规划（1996～2010年）》中综合交通规划，天津港在现有基础上于2010年将建成现代化国际深水大港，面向东北亚、辐射中西亚的国际集装箱枢纽港，届时港口货物吞吐量达3亿吨，集装箱达1000万标箱。天津滨海国际机场将建成为国内主要枢纽机场和国际定期航班机场，并将发展为中国北方航空货运中心。海港和空港的建设构成天津地区对外交通的主要枢纽。

规划确定高速铁路着手新建京沪、津秦、京哈等天津铁路段及京津、津唐、津保等城际铁路天津段，拟建黄万铁路、津蓟与北环铁路联络线等运输通道，形成环形放射式铁路网络结构。

按照国家和区域干线网规划，在京津塘高速公路基础上，相继建成津滨高速、津保高速、津蓟高速、津福高速（天津段），并拟建津汕、津沪等高速公路天津段及京沪高速公路延伸线、津唐高速公路延伸线和国道112高速公路天津段。“双高”的建成将成为天津市对外交通的基础。

在中心城区和滨海城区之间，以原有的京津塘高速公路和津塘、津港快速公路为基础，相继建设津滨高速、津沽二线、杨北公路、津沽公路和津塘二线等公路，密切中心城区与滨海城区之间的交通联系。

中心城区在“三环十四射”基础道路网络上，形成以地面、地下和立交相结合的立体化城市道路交通体系。2003年起，陆续投资建设全长145千米、平均时速60～80千米的快速路网，包括两条快速环路、两条横向通道、两条纵向通道和三条快速射线。两条快速环路——东南半环和西北半环，总长48.9千米，建成后将在中环线以外形成一个新的环路，加上两横、两纵、三条快速射线，整个快速路系统覆盖天津城区，形成绿化、景观、智能交通、综合服务、道路桥梁五位一体的快速道路体系。同时完善包括主干路、次干路、支路在内的道路系统，构成结构合理、等级清晰、高效便捷的四级道路网络。

（二）历史文化风貌建筑保护与文体设施建设

天津是国家级历史文化名城，特别是在近、现代的发展历程中，孕育着丰富的历史文化底蕴，有“百年中国看天津”的历史文化特色。

2004～2005年，在海河周边恢复性整修中，规划遵循对历史风貌建筑修旧如旧、注重新旧建筑协调等原则，将西式建筑群，含历史名人故居，建成新的文化旅游资源区。同时，对和平路、赤峰道及“五大道”等地区的西式建筑小洋楼群，含革命烈士等名人故居及近代军阀、清末遗老遗少故居，进行修建、保护，注重保持天津著名文化旅游胜地的原有风格。

海河上的解放桥、金汤桥、金钢桥等桥梁，具有悠久的历史和特殊意义，是经典的建筑杰作和宝贵的历史文化遗产，要在恢复历史原貌的基础上加以保护。其中，金汤桥曾是1949年解放天津时的胜利会师地，因年久失修，无法承担通车负荷。其桥身部件经整修，于2005年10月1日重新开放，仅供参观游览。

20世纪末及21世纪初相继建成周邓纪念馆、平津战役纪念馆、科技馆、自然博物馆、天津博物馆及银河公园等一系列现代化的爱国主义教育基地，成为群众性的学习、休闲、娱乐场地。

天津市西南部形成体育中心。该地区北临水上公园，西接堆山公园。1993年建成天津市体育中心及奥林匹克运动员村，并于1995年举办第43届世界乒乓球锦标赛、1999年世界体操锦标赛等国际竞赛活动。为迎接2008年奥林匹克运动会在北京召开，天津市作为协办城市，决定在该地区建设更大型的奥林匹克运动场馆及相应配套设施。

五、土地资源配置与产业结构调整

由于历史原因，天津市大量的工厂、仓库建设在城市中心的黄金区位上，仅中环线以内就有各类企业1600多家，占地5000万平方米。这些企业不仅自身经营不景气，污染扰民，而且造成城市用地结构和经济结构的不合理，影响城市功能的发挥。1993年，市政府对天津的城市性质做出重要调整，强调商贸、金融第三产业的发展，突出经济中心的功能，并将中环线以内划定为城市中心区。由此，市规划土地局提出新的思路——实施“双优化工程”（土地资源配置和产业结构调整双重优化）。在进行的初期，先作为“调整城市功能布局，提高城市中心区土地使用价值”的软科学课题研究。尔后，由于研究成果在技术、经济、法律以及操作等的可行性方面达到较高水平，有利于促进城市功能布局的完善，改善城市面貌和生态环境，最终形成市政府的决策。

截止1996年6月底，市区共有52个企业实施搬迁、改造、嫁接、跳产等，调整土地面积683.69万平方米。“双优化工程”的实施与成效，引起社会各界的关注。国家体制改革委员会天津调查组对此高度评价：“双优化工程”是使天津走出“钱少、人多、产业结构调整难”困境的一个“突破口”，为老工业城市的新生提供一条现实并极具综合治理意义的出路。

随着对可持续发展认识的不断深入，城市中心区1600多家企业逐步实施“双优化工程”。市政府在深化实施中，相继制定和出台《天津市实施“双优化工程”土地资产管理的暂行规定》等各项配套法规，强化城市规划的实施，有力地促进了天津市“工业东移”战略和“三五八十”宏伟目标的实现。

第二节　规划实用技术

1991年前，天津市在城市测绘与工程勘察中开始使用计算机及激光测距技术。1991年开始应用计算机编制规划。1995年，在城市测绘中开始应用地形图数字化技术。1999年，开展地理信息系统技术（GIS）。2004年，引进遥感（RS）及航空摄影技术。同年，应用全球定位系统（GPS）技术建立天津市地理空间信息基准框架。到2005年底，3S技术与CAD技术在全市规划设计、测绘工作中广泛应用。由于在数字环境下3S与CAD的结合应用，最终建立“天津市规划和国土资源业务管理系统”。

一、规划设计技术

1991年，天津市城乡规划设计院首次利用计算机技术为海口市编制三条景观带规划。1992年，天津市规划设计单位规划设计CAD出图率20%，1995年天津规划设计单位规划设计CAD出图率达到25%，1998年设计人员每人一机，CAD出图率100%。2000年，天津市规划设计单位大多提升计算机设备档次，实现计算机仿真模拟城市实时漫游，利用三维动画技术的表现手法，突破规划设计传统的图纸和文本的表现形式，利用数据库、仿真等技术，进行多方案比较。

1998年，天津开始采用公众意向、公众评议等多种社会参与方式，并利用网络、报刊、电视、广播等多种宣传方式，对规划成果进行公示或展示，提升规划成果的透明度，提高广大群众的城市规划意识和法制观念，引导群众关注规划方案。2002年，控制性详细规划在城市中心区实现全面覆盖。

2002年以后，天津市规划设计单位建立局域网、国际互联网，成功注册互联网域名并推出院网页，初步建成公共信息系统，实现网上办公、绘图、基础资料共享和成果图网上发布等，为采用开门修编规划设计方案创造有利条件。通过招标和委托等方式进行专题研究和规划方案的修编,并邀请国内知名专家、学者组成专家咨询组和评审组,对规划进行指导和咨询,规划成果的质量进一步提高。

2003年8月,为加强城市规划重大问题研究,组织开展“天津市城市空间发展战略研究”,重点研究城市定位、发展目标、空间布局和重大基础设施建设等战略问题,为城市总体规划修编奠定了基础。2004年5月,在修编《天津市城市总体规划(2005~2020)》工作中,通过招标确定一批专业研究单位,开展对天津市城市总体规划方案环境影响评价等18项专题研究,为规划修编方案提供了理论和技术支持。

二、城市测绘技术

1995年底,天津市测绘院以世界银行“建立城市地下管网数据库”贷款项目为契机,开始对地形图数字化工作进行研究。1997年,该院完成“天津市外环线以内6913幅1:500比例尺数字化地形图”,并将1:500比例尺地形图缩编为1:2000比例尺地形图。

1998年,该院开始研发数字影像制作技术,当年底完成“天津市1:10000比例尺彩红外正射影像图”数据制作,并于1999年完成“天津市外环以内1:2000比例尺真彩色正射影像图”数据制作,建立0.2米分辨率真彩色数字影像库。

1999年10月,天津市成立基础地理信息中心,专门负责基础地理信息的数据管理、分发服务、系统开发及建库工作。21世纪初,该中心具备数字化采集和生产地形图、管线图、地籍图、影像图等多图种的能力,能够对各类数据建库并管理、维护和提供使用。随着GIS的开发,实现“以基础地理信息为依托,向社会提供多种服务”的目标,并以GIS为卫生局提供120急救系统,为消防局提供119报警系统,为公安局制作110报警系统等。

2004年,市测绘院引进当时世界上最先进、高精度数字航空遥感系统。应用该技术生产出的数字影像具有清晰度高、生产周期短、后期处理便捷等优点,产品出现供不应求的情况。同年,天津市基础地理信息中心应用GPS技术逐步建立“天津市地理空间信息基准框架”,包括天津市空间坐标基准框架、天津市高程基准框架和天津市重力基准框架。当年5月完成框架的方案论证与详细技术设计。到2005年底,3S技术和CAD技术在全市规划设计与城市测绘工作中得到广泛采用。

三、工程勘察技术

(一)工程地质钻探

20世纪80年代,天津在兴建高层、超高层建筑和大型工业建筑中,钻探设备采用北京DPP—100型汽车钻机,钻探深度达100米。到90年代,天津市勘察院(以下简称“市勘察院”)对该钻机动力传动系统和提升系统进行改造和完善,在欧加华大厦及“津塔”写字楼工程中,钻探深度达150米,破历史记录。

(二)现场原位测试

1.载荷试验

20世纪90年代以前,多采用为浅层平板载荷试验,深层平板载荷试验则因天津地下水位浅不能应用。为准确确定深层地基土承载力,1995年市勘察院开发出深层螺旋板试验,用以估算天然地基平均沉降量,不仅能简单、准确确定地基土承载力,还可提供地基土的变形模量等力学指标。

2.标准贯入试验

其现场勘探工作基本沿袭常规做法,但对其成果利用有所发展,即用标准贯入成果估算桩基础的最终沉降量。

3.触探测试

通常应用的静力触探多为双桥,即同时测得探头的锥尖阻力和侧壁摩阻力,测试深度一般不超过40米。1984年,铁道部第三勘察设计院(以下简称“铁三院”)第一次引进德国与荷兰合作生产的触探设备,测试深度可达80米以上,其成果利用除选择桩基持力层、估算单桩承载力外,还用于估算桩基础最终沉降量。

1998年,市勘察院在原静力触探的基础上,将双桥探头改为三桥探头,可同时测得锥尖阻力,侧壁摩阻力及孔隙水压力,在天津经济技术开发区、保税区等沿海地区取得成功的经验。

4.土样试验

1998年,市勘察院建立与常规勘探取土样试验的力学指标间的相关关系,在沈阳地铁岩土工程详细勘察中采用扁铲侧胀试验,用于判别土类,确定静止侧压力系数与水平基床系数,效果良好。

(三)土工试验

1998年,市勘察院在压缩试验中,以气压加荷替代人工砝码加荷,并应用电脑控制的自动加荷及试验数据的全自动采集。在物理试验中,称重的电子天平与电脑相接,含水量试验、密度试验、液限试验、塑限试验均由电脑采集,计算数据准确、可靠。颗粒分析试验中,均改由电脑自动进行计算、绘图,有效地缩短了试验时间,提高了数据的准确度。

(四)地基与桩基处理

1991年,市勘察院为解决复杂体型建筑物沉降与均匀沉降等难题,开展桩土相互作用、D-P模型有限方法、Geddes法、地基—基础—上部结构共同作用的研究,初步解决了沉降可能性判断的难题,使天津市地基土性质的测评更为科学。1993年,该院在浅层土图系的基础上编制出"天津市区深基坑工程、地质特性及桩基工程地质图系"。1998年,重力式水泥土挡墙、悬臂桩、内支撑、双排桩等技术研究成果推广应用到软土地区深基。

2001年,市勘察院对刚性桩复合地基、沉降控制桩基础技术进行深入研究,提出广义桩土相互作用理论,并在多层建筑地基处理以及高层建筑桩基础中推广应用。2003年,天津应用高密度电法测试手段,使山区等特殊土层勘察检测获得技术保障。

(五)数字规划

20世纪90年代,天津的"数字规划"进入启蒙阶段。1999年,在开展GIS应用研究基础上,开发出文档管理、图形管理和信息发布相互独立的三大板块应用系统。2000年,天津"数字规划"开始向图文一体化的计算机网络信息系统发展,实现城市规划信息的输入、设计、存储、更新、查询检索、统计分析,以致业务管理办公自动化。同时,触摸屏技术有所发展,可更方便群众看到各类城市规划信息和业务案件办理过程的进展。2002年,市规划和国土资源局进一步"以数字规划为核心,实现Internet上的GIS"的研究与开发。在继承原有业务办公自动化的基础上扩展范围与功能,实现业务管理人员实时带图作业及多源、多样海量图文信息快速浏览和互查互访。在数字环境下,利用地理信息系统技术、遥感技术、计算机网络技术、数据库技术和办公自动化技术,对城市规划管理范围内的业务可进行原子式解析和组件式构造,其方案达到较高水平。在详细设计中,将基于工作流的行政事务结构化审批,以及城市规划信息、城市建设过程和政府审批信息的集成化管理与动态更新汇集一体,最终建立起"天津市规划和国土资源业务管理信息系统",从而实现城市规划和土地管理信息的采集、传输、整合、作业、存储、统计分析的数字化,随时为市政府和各级管理部门提供及时、准确、动态、权威的信息服务,辅助领导分析与决策。当年5月,由国家基础地理信息中心、欧亚科学院、南开大学等单位组成的鉴定小组对该系统作出鉴定,认为该成果达到国内领先水平,很有推广价值。

第二章 市政公路工程技术

1991年起,天津市加快高速公路和城区快速路建设,城市道路交通网络逐渐完善。至2005年底,天津共建成高速公路11条(段),总里程达到603千米;建成主跨100米以上特大桥7座,总长1000米以上的跨河桥、高架道路桥15座,立交桥102座。道路设计和施工中,研究开发出一批新技术、新工艺,施工机械化水平迅速提升,达到国内领先水平。桥梁设计与施工技术逐步向轻质、高强、大跨度、桥型多样化和预制装配化的方向发展,桥梁养护管理的技术水平进一步提高。城市排水管网功能不断完善,新型塑料排水管材不断涌现并得到推广应用,排水管网与泵站工艺设计技术、排水管道顶管施工技术、质量检验技术、养护维修技术取得突破。

1991～2005年，天津市政公路工程技术瞄准国内、国际先进水平，在科研、新技术推广、科技管理和人才培养等方面，积极组织科技攻关和新技术推广应用，取得科技成果316项，其中达到国内领先及以上水平的成果125项，占成果总量的40%；61项成果获得省部级科学技术奖励。

第一节 道路工程技术

1991～1995年，天津市依托京津塘高速公路工程，研究开发一批新技术、新工艺，施工机械化水平得到迅速提升，软土路基处理技术、水泥稳定碎石基层技术和沥青路面摊铺自动找平工艺等一整套高速公路施工技术得到应用。

1996～2005年，天津市道路工程设计与施工技术水平快速发展，并开发推广一批新技术和新材料，其中软土地基综合加固技术和软土路基沉降控制方法研究达到国内领先水平。随着八里台立交桥、中山门立交桥等城市立交工程的建成，天津市在立交设计理论、立交造型、交通分析、方案评价等方面处于国内领先水平，先后研制和引进一批先进的科研设备和施工设备，开发出城市道路计算机辅助设计系统，研发推广沥青路面冷再生技术、改性乳化沥青稀浆封层技术、沥青路面封缝技术等新技术，编制完成城市道路、快速路及高速公路等养护技术规程，建立养路费征收微机联网及高速公路远程办公等信息管理系统，初步形成科学化养护管理体系。

一、规划与建设

（一）公路网规划

1991年，天津市政工程设计研究院（以下简称"市政设计院"）李孝圭等根据交通部编制《1991~2020年全国公路网规划》的部署，于1994年完成《天津市公路网规划》的编制。该规划于1995年9月通过审查并报交通部核查备案。2001年结合天津市国民经济的快速发展，将该规划中的公路网总里程调整为15000千米。

2003年4月，天津市公路网规划发展目标再次调整为："以中心城区和滨海新区为双核心，辐射东北、西北、华北腹地，沟通华东、华南，连接周边大中城市、交通枢纽，通达市域11个新城，覆盖重要中心城镇"的高速公路网络，形成"3∶3∶10"的天津市干线公路网格局，即京沪、京沈、唐津等3条国家干线高速公路，京津塘、京津二通道、京津三通道等3条高速公路，以中心城区及滨海新区为中心向周围省市及市属区、县的10条射线高速公路。

（二）工程建设

1、高速公路 1993年9月，京津塘高速公路全线通车。该公路建设以软基处理、水泥稳定级配碎石基层施工、沥青混合料配合比设计与质量控制、沥青路面大型机械化施工等成套施工技术，获1997年国家科学技术进步一等奖。1993～2005年，天津市共建成高速公路11条（段），共计603千米。

2、城市快速路 2003年，天津市中心城区快速路全线开工建设。中心城区快速路系统由两条快速环路、两横两纵快速通道和两条快速联络线组成，全长约220千米。快速路规划为双向六至八车道，设计速度60～80千米/时，设置互通式立交31座，分离式立交20座，下穿地道10座。快速路两侧设置辅路，供慢速交通使用并设置10～30米宽绿化带，具有生态绿化景观效果。到2005年，天津建设的快速路有铁东路、东南半环等，其中立交工程12座。

二、工程设计

(一)工程设计规范标准

2000年前,天津的城市道路设计采用国家标准"城市道路设计规范"。天津市市政工程局结合天津特点,制定《天津市城市道路及公路工程设计技术暂行规定》。该规定于2000年7月由天津市建设管理委员会(以下简称"市建委")批准颁布施行。

2005年5月和7月,经市建委批准,天津市开始施行由市政设计院王晓华等编制的《天津市城市快速路设计标准》和由市政设计院编制的《天津市市政工程设计文件编制标准》两项地方工程建设标准。同年,市政设计院刘润有等完成《国家建筑标准设计图集》中《城市道路—水泥混凝土路面(05MR202)》《城市道路—软土地基处理(05MR301)》和《城市道路—无障碍设计(05MR501)》的编制任务,并经全国工程建设标准设计专家委员会审定、建设部批准出版发行。

(二)路面结构设计

1996年,天津市市政工程研究院(以下简称"市政研究院")赵可、市政设计院王玉秀等研究出"碾压混凝土复合式路面成套技术"。该技术在RCC板上加铺沥青混凝土形成复合式路面(AC—RCC),在唐津高速公路单幅路上做900米试验路,为复合式路面推广积累了经验。

1998年,天津市国腾公路工程监理咨询有限公司(以下简称"国腾公司")研究超载轴与回弹弯沉的相互关系,在津围公路改造工程中做了大量不同轴载的弯沉测定,得到轴载换算关系式 $\frac{N}{N_1}=\left(\frac{p'}{p}\right)^{6.3}$ 。该成果应用于津围公路改造工程的路面结构设计。

2001年,市政设计院王新岐等从天津交通特性与现状路面结构调查入手,通过理论分析,结合室内外试验,对设计参数选用和结构组合设计等方面进行综合研究,提出沥青路面设计参数的取值方法和一整套系统化、程序化的结构设计方法。

(三)路基处理技术

20世纪80年代,在京津塘高速公路建设中,针对滨海地区软土地基的特点,采用抛石挤淤、填土预压和路面分期修建的浅层处理技术,取得节省路基处理费用、缩短施工周期的效果。同时还开展排水固结法等深层处理技术研究,通车多年证明,路面平整度可满足高速公路行车要求,取得预期效果。

1992年,在塘沽区新北路跨线桥引路工程中,采用粉体搅拌桩处理技术。经处理后搅拌桩和地基土形成复合地基,可提高软土地基强度,满足设计的路基沉降要求。1996年,市政设计院朱兆芳与西安公路交通大学折学森等,在"软土路基沉降控制设计新方法"研究中,提出"软土路基沉降计算方法",经在唐津高速公路试验段进行实测对比试验表明,该方法具有良好的工程适应性,能反映软土地基沉降的一般规律。

1998年,市政设计院马承祖等在总结多项天津地区软土地基加固技术设计、施工经验的基础上,完成"天津市软土路基加固处理技术的研究"课题,所提出的主要指标在路基设计中得到广泛应用。2000年,该院朱晓东等与天津市第五市政公路工程有限公司合作,研究"软土地基强度随固结变形增长"的规律,建立软土地基三维固结微分方程组和相应的求解公式,并编制软土地基沉降和固结度计算程序,初步探索出软土地基强度随固结变形增长的规律,对软土地基处理设计、施工均有借鉴作用。2002年,该院刘润有等开展复合地基设计方法的研究,利用粒料桩(碎石桩、砂桩)、加固土桩(水泥搅拌桩、粉喷桩、旋喷桩)以及水泥粉煤灰碎石桩等对高填土路段地基进行处理,桩土构成复合地基,以减少地基工后沉降,提高地基承载力。通过研究,将刚性基础下的复合地基理论应用到柔性基础,扩展为"桩+桩间土+桩顶柔性垫层+刚性垫层"复合地基。此法广泛运用到高速公路桥头路基处理中。

(四)立交工程设计

1990年,市政设计院赵建伟等在完成的适用于微型计算机定线程序中,增加计算绘图程序,并在上海杨高路立交工程中应用。1992年,赵建伟等承担"城市道路立交计算机辅助设计(CAD系统)"的研制开发。其开发的软件功能丰富,广泛用于立交工程的方案设计,可提高工效10倍以上,具有自主知识产权,获1998年度天津市科技进步二等奖。

1993年,市政设计院邱志明、朱兆芳、王玉秀等在上海莘庄立交工程设计中,运用立交交通分析法,采用20个流向的定向匝道加苜蓿叶四层组合型立交方案,解决了六叉路口30个流向的98%交通量,得到评审专家的一致好评。1998年,该项成果在天津市金狮立交桥和顺驰立交桥等设计中推广应用。

三、道路工程材料

(一)改性沥青

20世纪90年代后期,天津市公路管理局(以下简称"市公路局")、天津市道路桥梁管理处(以下简称"市道桥处")、市政研究院等单位积极开展SBS改性沥青的生产技术研究并取得突破性进展,在重要交通、景观道路上得到推广应用。为探索解决沥青面层的高温稳定性,2001年起,引进特立尼达和多巴哥湖沥青(天然沥青)作为掺配剂,以大于20%的掺配量来提高混合料的动稳定度,并在津晋公路上试验,通车3年未出现车辙,路况良好。

2002年,通过室内试验和试验路,成功应用SEAM(一种掺入硫磺的颗粒)生产的改性沥青用于津沽公路。配制的AC—20I型混合料的马氏稳定度达137千牛,动稳定度7389次/毫米,均高于重交沥青的指标。生产、施工过程中硫蒸汽对环境的影响在环保控制范围内,在二级公路及重载公路上应用。

2004年和2005年,市公路局和天津滨海发展投资控股有限公司分别对胶粉沥青混凝土进行试验研究,并在顺驰立交辅路及大沽南路上试验,路用性能良好。

(二)沥青玛蹄脂碎石混合料

2002年,市政研究院在沥青玛蹄脂碎石混合料(SMA)配合比设计、路用性能、施工技术等方面取得突破。其压实成型采用旋转试验机,级配优化以加配重振实方式确定粗集料的骨架间隙率方法和以最小骨架间隙率进行,用动态剪切流变试验和弯曲流变试验研究胶泥的组成设计。课题还对SMA面层的施工技术进行研究,试验证明振动压路机和轮胎压路机均可用于SMA面层施工。其分段碾压,波浪式推进的合理碾压方式具有实用价值,并在津晋高速公路上完成8千米(单幅)SMA示范工程。2005年,在市区成都道、永安道等工程中应用,效果良好。

(三)高性能沥青混凝土

2004年,国腾公司和天津市公路建设发展公司合作研究"高性能沥青混合料设计及应用",将美国Superpave技术国产化。该成果在津蓟高速公路建设中推广应用。用旋转压实仪成型试件设计目标配合比,现场用马歇尔方法控制生产配合比的做法,实践证明是可行的。试验路工程的压实度大于98%,突破沥青混合料压实度长期维持在96%的低水平,路面施工质量有所提高。

(四)彩色沥青混凝土

20世纪50年代,天津市在中心广场修建砖红色沥青路面,但未广泛推广。21世纪初,天津市第一市政公路工程有限公司重新开发彩色沥青路面技术,采用沈阳生产的脱色沥青为基质沥青,掺加矿物颜料和彩色集料,生产红色沥青混合料,并在天津开发区管委会办公楼前及海河东路工程中应用。

(五)工业废渣

1978年,天津在城市道路工程中开始应用粉煤灰。1994年起,市政工程院对粒化增钙渣的路用性能进行长达3年的系统试验研究。研究表明,石灰增钙渣混合料早期强度高、后期强度增长迅速、抗冻能力强、收缩性小、疲劳寿命长、造价较低,是一种优良的筑路材料,可用于高等级道路的基层、底基层。1996年,该院完成国家行业标准"粉煤灰类道路基层施工及验收规范"的编制,并颁布施行。2000年,该院对大沽化工厂排放的皂化渣路用性能进行研究。由于材料的水稳定性良好,干缩较小,适合用作高液限粘土的稳定材料。可用作各级公路、城市道路的垫层和底基层,也可用作轻质路基材料。皂化渣替代石灰,可使废渣资源化,减少环境污染,降低工程造价,经济与环境效益显著。此后,市公路局还开发应用甩干电石灰。

（六）土工合成材料

20世纪90年代，市政工程院等单位研究应用土工合成材料控制沥青路面的反射裂缝和软土地基处理。经对不同材料的对比试验，提出控制沥青路面反射裂缝的材质要求及施工工艺，可较好改善路面的不均匀沉降。

（七）沥青混合料配合比设计

2002年，市政工程院赵可等依据级配设计理论和沥青混合料性能研究，提出新的连续级配范围，用旋转试验机（GTM）作为配合比优化的手段，进行采用GTM的沥青混合料配合比设计方法研究。课题成果应用于京珠高速公路军山长江大桥桥面铺装、103国道天津段改造工程和津晋高速公路天津东段工程，设计采用的混合料路用性能良好，工程质量得到提高。

21世纪初，为适应新技术、新材料不断涌现的形势，先后对《天津市市政工程质量检验评定标准》《天津市市政工程施工技术规程》进行修订，并分别于2003年10月1日和2004年10月1日颁布施行。

四、道路维修与养护

（一）维修技术

1999年，天津市公路建设发展公司、市政设计院及市公路局对旧路材料再生利用进行研究，分析不同级配、不同添加剂对冷再生混合料的抗压强度、抗压模量及劈裂强度的影响，确定现场冷再生的设计参数，并完善设计方法，为推广应用冷再生技术提供了科学依据。2004年，市公路局在工程实践的基础上编写出《公路沥青路面基层冷再生设计与施工技术规程》，经市建委批准作为天津市地方工程建设标准，自2004年12月施行。

2000年，市公路局刘真岩、张永明等对“改性乳化沥青及稀浆封层技术”进行研究，利用进口沥青加工设备，研制出性能优良的乳化沥青。通过试验，验证改性乳化沥青稀浆封层混合料的高温稳定性、低温抗裂性和耐久性等性能优于普通乳化沥青稀浆封层混合料，掺入玻纤丝或加设玻纤布可改善稀浆封层的弯拉强度，增强抗裂抗渗能力。通过津汉公路、新津杨公路、104及103国道铺筑的试验路，证明改性乳化沥青稀浆封层具有较高的路用性能，适用于交通量大的沥青路面表面层维修养护。与使用热沥青相比，可节省能耗30～50%，节省沥青10～20%，延长可施工时间1～2个月。

2002年，市公路局引进热再生工艺的“修路王”设备，改变传统的旧路挖补工艺。新的修补工艺是利用“修路王”将病害部位用红外线加热软化，加入沥青活化剂和新的混合料，就地拌和，碾压成型，得到没有接缝的新路面。2003年，市公路局研究用沥青路面封缝技术维修路面裂缝，能将裂缝完全封闭，使病害不再发展，其材料成本仅为进口材料的三分之二。2005年，市公路局编写出《公路沥青路面裂缝密封施工技术规程》，经市建委批准作为天津市地方工程建设标准颁布施行。

（二）养护技术

1991年，市道桥处邹南昌等研制完成路面养护管理决策系统，可提供道路的种种状态信息，提出养护处治方法，预测路况变化，编制维修计划，获1992年度天津市科技进步二等奖。1993年，市公路局开发出具有收费、路政、劳资等管理功能的“高速公路行政管理系统”。

2003年，市道桥处编制的“天津市城市道路养护技术规程”，经市建委审定并批准为天津市工程建设标准，于2003年8月1日施行。2005年12月，市道桥处编制的《天津市城市快速路养护技术实施细则》及天津市公路设计院与天津市公路建设发展公司合作编制的《天津市高速公路养护技术规范》经市建委批准，成为天津市地方工程建设标准。

（三）养护维修机械

1991年，市道桥处机修厂孙雄等研制成功“WBI—250自行式稳定土拌合机”，获1992年度天津市科技进步二等奖。该设备是国内大功率、中间置式筑路拌和机械，主要性能指标达到国际先进水平，性能稳定，使用安全可靠，作业效率高，拌和质量好，与进口设备相比，每台可节约100万元以上。1995年，该处耿波等研制的“道路养护工程车”，可减轻劳动强度，提高工作效率。2001年，市公路局引进冲击压实机械，利用大功率牵引车带动三棱型或五棱型钢碾，以其产生的2500千牛冲击力对密实性差的路基和拓宽路基进行追加压实，解决了路基不均匀沉降难题。2004年，市道桥处完成LX1200A全液压铣刨机的研制，其整机方案设计采用国际通用标准。该机械行走装置为轮胎式，四轮驱动，全液压转向。

（四）检测技术

20世纪90年代以前，道路弯沉测定采用贝克曼梁式弯沉仪，因其精度较低，仅测得静态汽车荷载作用下路面的（最大）回弹弯沉值，对路面结构性能评价不够充分。90年代初，市政工程局引进交通部研制的自动弯沉测定车可进行连续测定。该车在检测路段时以一定速度行驶，弯沉通过位移传感器等装置被自动记录下来，周而复始地向前连续测定，通过计算机输出弯沉检测的结果是总弯沉，且测试速度快。

2000年，天津市市政工程质量监督站引进落锤式弯沉仪。该仪器通过计算机控制系统对路面施加脉冲荷载，能准确测定弯沉盆，为路面结构层模量反算提供数据。其特点不仅是测速快、精度高，还能较好地模拟行车荷载对路面的动力作用。通过对落锤式弯沉仪和贝克曼梁测弯法进行回归分析，在国内首次建立地方性回归模型。天津市参加交通部组织的全国公路网普查，使用该仪器对总长10121千米的16条公路进行弯沉检测与评价，为交通部提供重要的地方公路信息。

第二节 桥梁工程技术

1991～2005年，是天津市桥梁建设史上技术发展又好又快的时期，共建成主跨100米以上特大桥7座（其中主跨300米以上特大桥2座），总长1000米以上的特大桥15座（含跨河桥10座，高架道路桥5座），立交桥102座。桥梁建设技术总体上向轻质、高强、大跨度、桥型多样化和预制装配化的方向发展，处于国内先进或领先水平，从而促进了桥梁设计、施工、养护管理以及桥梁工程质量水平的提高。

这一时期，天津建成首座主桥为钢与混凝土结合梁独塔斜拉桥（1991年），全市最大跨度的钢管拱桥（1998年）和预应力混凝土连续箱梁桥，在国内首次将轻集料混凝土应用于引桥（2000年），并建成当时国内最大跨度的独塔斜拉桥（2001年）和双塔双索面混凝土斜拉桥以及自锚式悬索桥（2003年），首次采用大悬臂脊骨梁新桥型结构（2004年），建成构思独特、造型新颖的不对称拱桥（2005年）。其间研究应用的“先简支、后连续”预应力混凝土小箱梁新型结构，对提高桥梁结构的耐久性和使用功能取得明显效果，并在建造桥梁结构技术上有较大进步。

一、桥型

（一）梁式桥

梁式桥是天津在桥梁建造中最多的一种桥型结构。1991年，市政设计院张洪海、李玉泽在唐津高速公路的桥梁设计中，率先采用跨径为30米预应力混凝土小箱梁桥型结构。1994年，市政设计院李光新主持设计建成的开发区滨海大桥，桥梁全长1375米，是天津首次采用变径胶囊成型的跨径为25米后张预应力混凝土空心板梁桥，获1998年天津市优秀设计二等奖。2000年建成的唐津高速公路永定新河大桥，由市政设计研究院孙运国等设计，市政工程院曹诚等研究，其引桥首次成功采用轻集料混凝土。同年，该院黄思勇、赵国勇等结合滨海立交工程设计，通过试验研究完成25米预制后张预应力混凝土小箱梁研制，与同等跨径的预应力空心板梁相比，可较大的降低工程造价。此后，“先简支、后连续”施工工艺，广泛应用在高速公路和城市快速路的桥梁建设中。

2002年，市政设计院孙运国、冯克岩主持设计建成的快速路东南半环海津大桥，主桥为3孔×55米，预应力混凝土曲线等高连续箱梁桥，平面曲线半径为490米，是天津唯一的跨越海河系的大跨度曲线箱梁桥。该桥突破传统施工方法，成功采用MSS造桥机施工工艺，在大跨径和弯桥施工技术上达到国内领先水平。2004年建成的北运河大桥，主桥为(40＋60＋40)米的三跨预应力钢—混凝土结合连续梁。最大特点是40度的大斜度和变截面。市政设计院康莉、刘旭锴等对其大斜度钢—混凝土组合梁设计与施工技术进行研究，较好地解决了钢桥线形和构造细节设计难题。同年，该院吴云、黄思勇在塘沽国防路高架桥工程中，设计采用脊骨梁桥结构形式，由箱梁、两侧悬臂肋梁和桥面板三部分组成，桥下净空大，外形美观，使用功能好。

（二）拱桥

金钢桥为1924年修建的立转开启桥，由于钢结构锈蚀严重，桥面狭窄，承载能力低，不适应交通发展的需要。1996年改建成双层桥。市政设计院刘旭锴、张振学负责设计，上层桥主桥为跨径(25+101+25)米三孔中承式钢管混凝土拱桥，是天津首次采用的大跨径钢管混凝土拱桥新桥型，具有体轻、跨大、建筑高度低、经济指标好、施工工艺简捷等优点，桥面净宽15米，专供机动车行驶。工程中开发并应用钢管拱安装控制精度工艺、钢管混凝土浇筑工艺等14项成果，总体水平达到国内领先。

1998年建成通车的永定新河彩虹大桥，由铁三院周四思主持设计，主桥为(164.7+168.0+164.7)米三孔下承式钢管混凝土系杆拱桥，桥面总宽29.0米，矢跨比1/5，拱肋由两根直径1500毫米钢管焊成哑铃形截面组成，高度3.75米。2004年在开发区西区建成的钢筋混凝土斜立柱肋双铰型上承式拱桥，分别跨越唐津高速公路、津滨高速公路和京津塘高速公路三座跨线桥。其桥梁中线与相交公路斜交。主桥桥型均为跨径62米钢筋混凝土肋拱桥，矢跨比为1/7.05。每幅桥上部构造由三片拱肋和拱上建筑组成拱架，现浇桥面板和拱梁联结成整体，拱脚处设置有系杆。同年，建成通车的下承式无风撑钢拱桥——快速环路东南半环友谊路桥，主桥跨径为85.0米，矢跨比1:9.23，桥面总宽34.4米，采用无风撑体系，横桥向由三片箱形拱肋组成，桥面系采用钢与混凝土结合梁板结构。由市政设计院谢斌、李宏祥负责设计，天津第五市政工程公司施工。在该工程中完成“整体桥梁结构静力、动力特性分析研究”与“三片拱肋的无风撑钢坦拱桥稳定性有限元分析”等理论研究成果。

2005年建成的不对称斜式钢拱桥——大沽桥，由美籍华人邓文中院士构思设计，寓意“日月生辉”，是海河上的一座标志性建筑，也是一座科技含量高、文化品位高的精品桥。跨径为(24+106+24)米，由两个不对称斜式拱肋组成，大拱肋矢高39米，小拱肋矢高19米。车行道宽24米，人行道宽度由桥头的3.0米按曲线分别渐变到桥中观景台的8.5米(小拱侧)和11.5米(大拱侧)，拱肋截面为梯形钢箱，桥面系为正交异性板钢箱梁结构。2006年该桥获世界著名桥梁大奖——尤金·菲戈奖。

图8-2-2-116 大沽桥

（三）斜拉桥

1991年，市政设计院徐履平主持设计的海河刘庄桥在原浮桥旧址改建而成，跨径为(32.0+71.85+12.04)米，桥宽17.2米，主梁采用“I”形钢板梁与钢筋混凝土桥面板组成结合梁，梁高1.0米，主塔为钢筋混凝土“H”型塔，斜拉索为扇形双索面，结构为漂浮体系。该工程设计获1993年天津市优秀设计一等奖。

2001年，塘沽海防路海河大桥建成通车。主桥为跨径310米+190(3×48.0+46.0)米钢与混凝土混合型独塔斜拉桥，引桥为预应力混凝土梁式桥，桥梁全长2220米，桥面宽23.0米。主跨采用正交异性钢箱梁结构，边跨采用预应力混凝土箱梁结构，边跨与主跨之比为0.613，梁高为3.0米。主塔为钢筋混凝土“A”型塔，塔高167.3米(桥面以上126.0米)，塔高与主跨之比为1/2.46，塔柱采用矩形空心截面。斜拉索为双面扇形索，索距主跨为16.0米，边跨为8.0米，结构为纵向半飘浮体系。由

图8-2-2-117 刘庄斜拉桥

市政设计院刘旭锴、韩振勇、施颖负责设计，2004年获国家优秀设计银质奖。

2003年建成的滨海大桥，是丹拉高速公路跨越海河的一座特大双塔双索面钢筋混凝土斜拉桥。由市政设计院刘旭锴、丁雪松、谢斌等设计，其主桥跨径（152+364+152）米，是中国北方跨度最大的混凝土斜拉桥，桥宽30.9米，主桥采用预应力混凝土肋板式梁结构，飘浮结构体系，梁肋高2.0米，宽1.7米，菱形塔，塔高140.12米（桥面以上高度100米），塔墩为钢筋混凝土灌注桩基础，扇形索索距为4.6～6.8米。

（四）悬索桥

2003年建成的咸阳路子牙河桥（后定名西河桥）由市政设计院刘文江等设计。主桥为跨径（48.05+115.0+48.05）米自锚式悬索桥，桥面全宽42.0米。引桥采用预应力混凝土连续箱梁桥结构。主桥采用正交异性板分离式连续钢箱梁结构，梁高2.5米。主缆采用直径5毫米高强镀锌平行钢丝，每根主缆由19股127丝组成，直径为270毫米，截面为正六边形，矢高为19米，矢跨比1/6，塔高32米（桥面以上21.5米），桥塔采用钢筋混凝土门形塔柱，吊索采用直径7毫米高强镀锌平行钢丝成品索，索距4米。

（五）高架桥、立交桥

1991～2005年，天津市修建的高架桥、立交桥量大面广。建造中多因地制宜，根据地形地物变化，采用40米～82米之间的特殊跨径，建成具有弯坡斜异结构特点和不同层次的立交桥。

2003年，天津市建成最长的高架桥，即快速路东南半环富民路到程林庄路北高架桥，先后跨越津塘公路、张贵庄路、先锋路、程林庄路和京山铁路，全长5300米，由市政设计院王艳宁等设计。2004年建成的卫津南路立交桥，是天津市规模最大、最高的立交桥。其桥梁面积为14万平方米，共四层，第四层桥面距地面27.0米。该桥由市政设计院张洪海等设计。2005年建成的最大跨径高架桥，为地铁1号线南段高架桥78号～81号墩段，位于半径429米的曲线上，最大跨径为82米，跨径和结构难度在同类型桥梁中为天津市第一，全国第二。该桥由市政设计院冯克岩、陈明贵设计，中铁山海关桥梁厂加工，第二市政工程公司承建。

二、结构设计与施工

（一）设计理论与计算

天津市在桥梁设计中，自1985年以来一直沿用极限状态理论，2004年全面执行以可靠度理论为基础的概率极限状态设计理论，确立设计基准期概念，确定桥梁结构的设计基准期为100年。同时，完善桥梁耐久性设计理论，强调桥梁设计在完成规定内容的计算分析外，还应全面满足构造和工艺方面的要求。

20世纪90年代，天津市公路和道路网桥梁建设发展很快，原有的设计理论与计算方法多不能满足桥梁建设的需要。1991年，市政设计院和西南交通大学周绍烈、张汝亮、陈孟达等开始进行“中小桥计算机辅助设计（简称LQCAD）软件系统”的开发研究。该软件系统适用于中小跨度公路梁（板）桥设计，其简支梁桥软件具有国内先进水平，下部结构设计达到国内领先水平，获1996年度天津市科技进步二等奖。

1998年，市政设计院王淑训、刘旭锴、张振学等结合立交桥梁结构中预应力混凝土曲线箱梁和异形箱梁结构完成“预应力混凝土曲线箱梁研究”。其对曲线箱梁和异形箱梁计算分析的方法，具有选取单元模型合理、更真实反映曲线箱梁和异形箱梁的受力特性、计算准确方便、输出结果明确等特点，在天津顺驰立交桥等工程中成功应用。

从2000年起，桥梁结构计算分析方法在常用桥梁结构计算软件“桥梁博士”“同济大学平面杆系”的基础上，又相继引进美、韩等国空间有限元软件，并广泛应用于工程设计。

（二）桥梁抗震

天津市在桥梁的抗震设计中，一般按基本裂度设计，重要桥梁设计按基本裂度，提高一度设防，并进行抗震动力稳定与验算分析。在桥梁的结构型式上，多为现浇普通钢筋混凝土连续箱梁和预应力混凝土连续箱梁。进入21世纪，预制的“T”型梁和小箱梁，采取“先简支、后连续”的做法较多。这期间，按照设计规范的强制性条文规定，各种形式的桥梁都应采取相应的抗震设施，“T”型梁在梁端间设有抗震栓、侧面设有抗震挡，板梁和箱梁在梁端纵向设抗震栓、侧面设抗震挡，抗震挡内侧粘贴橡胶板。2001年建成的滨海新区塘沽海河独塔斜拉桥，除结构采用漂浮体系外，在主桥的主塔柱与主梁之间设置横向限位支座，主梁侧面相应位置设有支撑垫石并铺设四氟板式橡胶支座，是一项有效的减震措施。2003年建成的丹拉高速公路滨海大桥，按着“小震不坏、中震能修、大震不倒”的分级设计理念，利用桥梁结构能力设计的方法和减震消震的桥梁设计手段进行抗震设计，结构上采取漂浮体系，主桥主梁在塔柱两侧，边墩设置纵横向限位及减震装置。

（三）预应力技术

预应力混凝土结构的混凝土强度通常用C50级。2001年修建的红旗路西青道立交桥预应力混凝土箱梁首次采用C60级。

预应力筋的材料通常用1860兆帕级。2003年修建的东南半环海津大桥，第一次采用2000兆帕级高强度低松驰钢铰线，使预应力体系应力水平提高7.5%，梁体断面尺寸削减10%左右，梁体自重减轻，钢铰线材料用量减少，提高桥梁整体性能并降低工程造价。

2003年，在快速路东南半环高架桥工程R线中，天津首次将体外预应力技术应用于混凝土箱梁，钢铰线用环氧全装无粘结筋。

（四）轻集料混凝土

1999年，市政研究院曹诚等在“桥用高强轻集料混凝土应用技术研究”中，提出适合中国轻集料特点的高强轻集料混凝土设计方法。经对高强轻集料混凝土性能的系统研究，制定出相应的施工工艺和质量控制方案。同期。市政设计院孙运国、何铭等针对唐津高速公路永定新河大桥的特点，首次将CL40级轻集料混凝土应用于该桥引桥的主要受力结构上，实际强度水平达到CL50级。此成果获2001年度天津市科技进步二等奖，并在东南半环海津大桥的桥面铺装中予以推广。2004年，曹诚等编制完成“桥用轻集料混凝土应用技术规程”。当年，经市建委批准，作为天津市地方工程建设标准颁布执行。

（五）斜拉桥施工

1993年，市政设计院黄大健、韩振勇、周立志等完成“大跨度预应力混凝土斜拉桥牵索式长挂蓝施工技术”，在国内首次应用，其综合技术水平达到国内领先，获1995年度天津市科技进步二等奖。此后，在全国广泛应用，对推进斜拉桥技术发展具有重要意义。同时，该院黄大健、韩振勇、钱永龄等完成“斜拉桥施工控制系统”，对斜拉桥成桥理想状态下内力优化进行计算，充分发挥斜拉桥塔、梁、索结构各部分的受力特性；完善斜拉桥设计计算分析软件和施工控制分析软件，对施工实测结果能及时分析识别，提出对策并自动修正，起到指导施工的作用。该成果获1997年度天津市科技进步二等奖，在吉林市临江门大桥工程应用并取得较好效果。

1998年，在天津站人行天桥工程中，市政设计院赵国勇、刘旭锴、黄思勇等完成“悬拼工艺及测控技术”及“动力分析及测试试验”两项科研成果。天津市道路桥梁管理处崔毅等完成“天津站人行天桥安装控制动力分析及施工工艺研究”。以上研究成果成功应用于工程建设中，结合天津站区的地理特点和特殊要求，辅跨采用拖拉法施工，主跨采用自行研制的悬臂吊机设备，实施单侧悬臂拼装施工工艺。

（六）移动模架施工

2003年，市政工程局在快速路东南半环海河大桥工程的主桥施工中，采用自挪威引进的移动模架逐孔架设施工技术（简称MSS造桥机施工工艺）。这种移动模架施工技术在国内尚属首次应用。经消化吸收后，其中造桥机由天佳设备安装公司制造。该机造桥的最大跨径可达66米，也是当时国内造桥施工技术中跨度最大的设备，在大跨径和弯桥施工方面达到国内领先水平。

三、附属设施

（一）桥梁支座

在桥梁建设中，20米以上跨径的“T”型梁、10米以上跨径的板梁、20米以上跨径的小箱梁等不同跨径的连续箱梁，以往多采用矩形和圆形板式橡胶支座以及四氟板式橡胶支座，支座反力较大的墩柱采用盆式橡胶支座，在桥梁的纵坡上采用坡式橡胶支座，由于桥梁的结构型式的不断发展，也要求不同的支座型式与之相匹配。2002年，在快速路东南半环海津大桥施工中，天津首次应用22500千牛和12500千牛大吨位盆式抗震支座。2003年，在丹拉高速公路滨海大桥施工中，设计采用橡胶隔震支座，这种支座利用夹层橡胶的隔震技术，具有双线性滞回特性的橡胶（铅芯）隔震支座，能起到减震隔震作用，是21世纪初研究并推广的新技术。

（二）桥梁伸缩缝

20世纪80年代，天津在建永和斜拉桥时，引进国外伸缩装置技术。此后，天津开始研制与生产桥梁伸缩装置。1992年，天津市公路局研制出三维伸缩装置（后称模数式伸缩装置），当年在中环线西青道立交桥施工中首次应用。20世纪90年代末期，一般的跨河桥梁，立交的主桥、引桥、匝道桥的伸缩缝大多采用模数式伸缩装置，依据结构长度和安装温度确定伸缩量，多为80型、160型、240型和320型。1998年，市公路局研制出弹性体改性沥青桥梁伸缩缝，它适用于旧桥伸缩缝改造和新建中小桥等伸缩变位小于5厘米的结构伸缩缝。2001年，市政研究院又研制出埋置式桥梁伸缩缝，在桥梁的渐变段和立交匝道的异形段得到应用。至2005年，天津的桥梁伸缩缝安装工艺日臻成熟。

（三）桥面防水及铺装层

20世纪90年代初，混凝土桥面铺装层，一般为6~10厘米C30防水混凝土或纤维网混凝土（抗渗等级W6），在其中布设一层或两层钢筋网片，桥面铺装层上再施做防水层。90年代中期，桥面防水采用“两布六涂”工艺，由于铺涂工序多、工期长、施工过程易损坏，且玻璃纤维布易老化，未推广使用。此后，在高速公路或城市快速路桥梁上，采用聚合物防水涂料和桥梁用APP改性沥青防水卷材施做防水层，效果较好。2002年，在海津大桥的主梁顶面采用水泥基渗透结晶型防水材料作防水层，既可提高混凝土本身的防水性，又不影响主梁混凝土与桥面铺装混凝土的连接强度。

进入21世纪初，天津的钢桥修建增多，围绕提高钢桥面铺装的高温稳定、低温抗裂性及增强铺装层与钢桥面之间的粘结力，市政行业组织联合攻关。2004年，在子牙河自锚式悬索桥（西河桥）桥面上铺筑浇注式改性沥青混凝土面层达到预期效果。2005年，海河大沽桥钢桥面又成功地应用环氧沥青混凝土作面层，从而使天津在钢桥面铺装技术上处于国内先进水平。

（四）桥梁景观与照明

20世纪90年代初期，桥梁的功能照明基本上延续以往做法，只是更加注重景观效果、自动控制和降低能耗。此后，在城市的跨河桥梁和城市的立交桥以及特大型的斜拉桥、悬索桥的景观照明上，进步很快。1996年在金钢桥改建工程中，市政设计院潘中敏、谢金友、王守义第一次成功地将泛光照明和世界先进的光纤照明技术应用到该桥的夜间景观照明上，既少有污染，节约能源，又符合绿色照明要求。21世纪初，在城市立交桥的地袱栏杆上各种色彩的轮廓照明，在桥梁侧面的上翼缘和腹板以及墩柱上都做有各种投光照明，将立交桥夜间装扮得更加壮丽。滨海新区塘沽海河上的独塔斜拉桥，桥上有功能照明，对桥塔和斜拉索有投光照明，在塔顶四周有障碍照明，并且采取时控开关，随着日出、日落而自动控制。

四、管理与维修

（一）桥梁管理

1994年，市道桥处研制出“天津市城市桥梁管理系统”，初步奠定城市桥梁管理科学化基础。2004年2月，该处又编制出“天津市城市桥梁养护技术规程”，用以指导和规范桥梁设施的养护工作。当年12月，该处又制订“天津市城市桥梁养护操作技术规程”，作为天津市地方标准颁布实施。

1995年，市公路局参加交通部组织的“公路桥梁管理系统”研究，获1996年度国家科技进步二等奖。1996年，该局实行“桥梁管理工程师制度”，保证桥梁的管理到位，安全畅通。2003年，该局试行“公路桥梁标准化养护制度”，注重桥梁的耐久性，可延长桥梁使用期限。

（二）桥梁养护

对桥梁钢筋的锈蚀情况和混凝土裂缝，过去主要靠目测或破损检查。1995年，先后引进钢筋锈蚀仪、裂缝观测仪、混凝土碳化测试仪等设备，用无损检测方法，准确地判断、定量地描述病害情况，并在东堤头桥、张贵庄立交桥、永和斜拉桥等桥梁应用。为防止水对混凝土的损害，提高桥梁的耐久性，自1998年起，先后引进涂料和卷材等沥青基桥面防水材料。为避免和减少环境对混凝土的影响，2001年引进渗透结晶型防水材料及硅烷类、氟碳类材料，用于当杨路当城桥和宝平路田场立交桥等。此类材料可渗透到混凝土体内3毫米以上，能抑制水及有害离子侵入混凝土内部，而且可以透气，不改变混凝土外观。2002年引进弹性成模型保护材料，在八里台立交桥维修工程中应用。

（三）桥梁维修

2001年，在八里台立交桥维修工程中引进水泥基钢筋防锈材料和聚合物修补砂浆，可用于不断交的桥梁混凝土结构修补。此后在旧桥改造中，“T”型梁横隔板的连接、板梁的绞缝以及混凝土的修补进一步得到应用，使桥梁钢筋混凝土结构修复技术得到提高。

在混凝土裂缝处理上，1998年开始引进弹塑体聚合物沥青伸缩缝材料，应用于小变位的桥梁伸缩，具有高粘性和高弹性，施工完工即可放行交通。2000年，引进有一定延度的聚合物成膜型弹性涂装材料、丙烯酸酯防水涂料、柔性水泥基成膜涂装材料（弹性水泥）等，用于小于0.2毫米的混凝土裂缝修补；大于0.2毫米的裂缝，可用同类型的腻子处理，然后再涂涂料。这类涂料因具有一定的弹性，其主要作用是防水、抗氧气和二氧化碳的渗透。同时引进“闭可注”法，即自压力注胶法。当裂缝大于0.3毫米且已不再发展时，可将裂缝清理干净后注入补缝胶，对裂缝进行封闭。京津公路引河桥、永和斜拉桥、东堤头桥等均应用这些技术。同年，市政研究院赵可、宋晓燕研制出新型国产材料，在八里台立交桥、中山门立交桥等处应用，效果良好。同年在西青道立交桥等处应用SCM高强无收缩混凝土抢修桥梁伸缩装置，6小时覆盖钢板后即可开放交通。2004年在外环张贵庄立交桥引进树脂沥青混凝土代替水泥混凝土锚固伸缩装置，可在施工后两小时达到使用强度，开放交通。2005年，市公路局张永明研制出国产化树脂沥青混凝土，被普遍采用。这些技术的应用，使天津市的桥梁伸缩装置快速更换技术得以发展。

（四）桥梁加固改造

1.桥面铺装层加固改造

1998年，市公路局刘真岩提出，对“T”型梁桥面铺装层的加固，应将预制焊接形式改为现浇刚接形式，将原焊接连接的部位切开凿除，用现浇形式重新连成整体，避免应力集中引起的病害，并先后改造西流城大桥、普济河道立交桥等几十座桥梁，加固效果好，简便易行、投资较少。2002年改造的东风大桥，处于海淡水混合处，桥长1062米，上、下部结构均有比较严重的病害，经采用此工艺加固后，功能恢复。

2.综合加固技术

1985年建的八里台立交桥，由于水侵害造成部分结构严重损坏。2000年上半年，市道桥处杨渡主持对该桥进行加固改造。用碳纤维材料对现浇板梁、“T”梁、墩柱等部位进行结构补强；用“H”型高强免振灌浆料解决墩柱、帽梁的扩体超薄混凝土（5～10厘米）浇注难及与普通混凝土粘接力差的问题；用聚合物修补砂浆解决大面积混凝土用普通材料维修易损坏的难题。综合整修桥梁栏杆、景观照明，不仅使八里台立交桥的各种病害得到根治，还增加了景观效果。

3.顶升纠偏

1982年建的十一经路立交桥，其东引桥为弯坡斜的曲线连续箱梁。由于交通量、车辆载重量增加以及环境等因素的影响，使东引桥的一联曲线连续箱梁产生纵向滑移和水平横移，影响桥梁的安全。2000年，市政局杨玉淮和市道桥处杨渡、崔毅等实施“天津市十一经路立交桥连续箱梁纠偏复位工程”。在工程中采用顶升复位工艺和监控技术结合，对桥墩和主梁的应力变化量及钢支架的梁柱应力状况进行有效的监测控制，成功地解决多支点、大吨位、四跨连续箱梁的同步顶升难题。纠偏中将同步精度控制在15毫米以内，达到同步顶升的目的和效果，确保连续箱梁顶升复位的安全。

4.顶升抬高

2004年和2005年市城建集团韩振勇等先后主持北安桥和狮子林桥顶升抬高工程。该工程利用PLC控制液压同步顶升技术，实现力和位移控制、操作闭锁、过程显示、故障报警等多种功能。全自动完成纵向整体同步顶升、横向分别同步顶升，达到预期目的，取得良好效果。

5.墩台基础加固

从1995年开始，天津对大庆桥、八道沽桥等多座桥梁出现贯通裂缝的墩柱，采用钢筋混凝土围带或钢箍进行加固。2002年,对当城桥采用旋喷注浆法加固基础,取得成功。在原桥墩周围按矩形布置旋喷桩,桩长10米,桩径60厘米,咬合15厘米,桩内插直径25毫米钢筋。旋喷桩顶部现浇一圈钢筋混凝土梁,在原灌注桩位置顺桥向做斜撑,周围用水泥土加固。

第三节　排水工程技术

1991~2005年,天津市排水工程技术取得突破性进展。排水管道工程以实现排水管道工艺改革一体化为标志,在沿用混凝土管平口抹带工艺的基础上,改为钢筋混凝土承插口、砂基础排水管道的新工艺,形成一套完整的排水管道工艺体系,居国内领先水平。随着新型塑料管材的发展,天津对各种塑料管材在排水管道工程中的应用技术进行研究,编制出相应的工程建设标准;聚氯乙烯管、硬聚氯乙烯(UPVC)双壁波纹管、增强聚丙烯(FRPP)塑料排水管、玻璃钢夹砂管、高密度聚乙烯中空肋壁缠绕管等一批新型管材得到推广应用;排水管道不开槽施工技术取得显著进步;机械顶管先后引进泥水平衡和土压平衡顶管技术并在工程中成功应用,一次顶进距离不断延长;排水管道施工质量检验技术,由闭水试验发展为闭气试验,既便于操作又可提高施工质量和检验速度;对排水管道的养护维修,大量研究与应用非开挖管道修复技术。在管网与泵站工艺设计中,针对沿海平坦地区排水特点,研究与推广使用低压管道长距离排水。修建大型地下泵站、卵型护壁合一分层逆作泵站、地下连续墙护壁合一泵站等,泵站土建结构形式发生变化。开展泵站无人值守运行的研究,完成示范工程建设,泵站维护管理水平得到提高。

一、管道工程

(一)管材

1992年,市政工程局高复栋、盛应光等进行"排水管道改革一体化"研究,经对排水管道工程采用承插口钢筋混凝土管及相应的接口、基础研究,形成一套钢筋混凝土承插口排水管道完整的工艺体系,从而使天津排水管道工程技术取得突破性进展。该项研究获1993年度天津市科技进步二等奖。此后,市政研究院高复栋、马永安等进一步研究新型塑料管材的应用。1995年经对聚氯乙烯塑料管作排水管道全面系统研究,揭示出塑料管用于排水管道在埋地条件下的工作特性。1996年写出《UPVC排水管道设计、施工及验收技术规程》。1997年,市政研究院与市政二公司、市政工程建设公司合作,在广开四马路施工中应用硬聚氯乙烯双壁波纹管材,并在施工现场有针对性地进行专题模拟试验,编制出《UPVC排水管道施工预算定额》。这一塑料管用作排水管道技术,对排水管道施工工艺带来重大改革。

2002年,市政研究院又在南开二纬路排水工程中进行FRPP塑料排水管材应用技术研究,解决了在浅覆土条件下,既保证路基施工压实要求,又保证管道安全承载性能的问题。同年,制定出FRPP塑料管材用于排水工程的设计通用图和施工验收技术规程及DN800~1000毫米FRPP大口径塑料管材用于排水工程的预算基价,为天津推广应用塑料管材提供了理论依据。2004年,该院编制完成《增强聚丙烯室外排水管道工程技术规程》,经市建委批准,作为天津市地方工程建设标准颁布施行。

2003年,创业环保公司等编制的《埋地玻璃纤维增强塑料加砂(RPM)排水管道技术规程》,用以指导、规范和促进RPM管在天津排水工程中的应用。在东郊污水处理厂进水管道工程中,采用DN1800~2000毫米玻璃纤维增强塑料管。此后,天津大量使用RPM管材。2004年,在地铁一号线旧排水管道切改工程中,用管径DN1600毫米的RPM管进行顶管施工。同年,市政工程建设公司、市政研究院完成"高密度聚乙烯(HDPE)中空肋壁缠绕管材应用技术",编制出《埋地聚乙烯(PE)排水管道工程技术规程》。

（二）设计与施工

1.管网设计

随着城市建设的发展和环保标准的提高，雨水、污水往往需要经过长距离输送才能排到允许受纳的水体。1990年起，市政设计院研究压力排水系统，利用给水管道压力输送的基础及下水管道排水的特点，突破重力流的束缚，提出“压力排水系统”设计方法及工程保证措施。该成果在多项市政排水工程中应用。

1993年，市政设计院胡大卫、卢心虹、杨晓杰等在天津无缝钢管总厂排水工程中，对管道设计采用压力流标准选择管材、路由、水力坡度、埋设深度及防腐、放气、泄水等技术措施，并解决缓解开、停泵水锤关键技术问题。即：对低压系统，在水泵出口设置高型敞开式出水池，池内安装可调高度的溢流堰；对高压系统，不能采用高型出水池，改用并联管路时，采用“出水闸门液压缓动、开泵瞬间回流缓冲、泵闸启闭控制时差、系统运转压力自控”等方法，从而使无缝钢管总厂的压力排水系统达到平稳、安全运行。

1995年，市政设计院王志林、苏功军、赫雷等在绍兴道污水外排工程中，开发压力排水管道技术，对长50千米、直径1.2米的长距离输送污水管道，共设八座接力提升泵站，自动联网控制，在国内首次实现长距离、大口径压力输送污水系统技术。

2001年，市政设计院承担天津市“津河”整治改造工程设计，使河道断面，新颖合理；桥梁造型，各具特色；泵站建筑，节地经济，达到截污整治，净化水体的目标。此后，相继对月牙河、陈台子河、南运河、四化河等进行河道整治改造。

2003年，市政工程局、市政设计院杨玉淮、张大群等编制《天津市城市排水工程设计技术规定》，内容涉及排水管道及泵站工艺、城镇生活污水处理厂工艺、排水结构工程、排水电气与控制等设计技术以及排水专用机械设备设计及造型技术等，经市建委批准，自2003年9月1日起施行。

2.顶管技术

1993年，天津市政二公司（以下简称“市政二公司”）张多马、杨万楼、孙秀英等开展“加长顶管一次顶进距离”研究。通过多顶点、分压环、改善后背受力情况、增设中继间接力顶进等方法，使长距离顶管一次顶管距离不断创新记录。1994年，在友谊路排水管道工程施工中，D2000毫米混凝土管一次顶距由80年代的25~30米，增加到65米。1995年，在金钟河大街排水管道工程中，D2200毫米混凝土管一次顶进78米。1997年，在苏州工业园区，D2200毫米混凝土管道在一次顶距达到103米的基础上，通过研究顶管减摩、膨润土润滑配比，再次创下一次顶进145米的记录。

1996年前，天津多采用人工顶管方法。1996年引入平衡式顶管施工技术。市政二公司在引进的泥水平衡式顶管主机上，自行研制配套设备。1997年，先后在保定道、二宫利用该技术穿越中环线。2001年，在张贵庄立交桥旁用泥水平衡顶管一次性穿越外环路、外环河，在河底仅2米浅覆土条件下，河道不截流断水，并且保证外环线交通不断行，圆满完成110米顶管任务。

1999年，顶管技术从泥水平衡发展为土压平衡，同样不需要降低地下水位，而土压平衡工艺排出的渣土比泥水平衡法所排出的泥浆水容易处理，并可连续出土。是年，市政二公司在货厂大街排水工程中为保证建国道两侧建筑的安全，采用土压平衡法将直径2400毫米混凝土管顶进长度达290米。至此，天津在土压平衡和注浆减阻控制地面沉降等方面达到国内先进水平，在长距离大口径管道平衡式顶管施工技术上已经成熟。

（三）质量检验

1985年，天津在混凝土管道施工质量检验中，开始用闭气法代替过去的闭水试验法。1987年制定出《混凝土排水管道工程闭气检验标准》，于1993年颁布实施。2002年，市政研究院在此基础上编制的新标准，将原标准最大管径由1200毫米扩大到2200毫米。2003年12月，又在京、津两地进行不同管径闭气、闭水检验对比，证明新标准均能满足管道施工质量检验要求。经天津市建委批准，作为地方工程建设标准于2004年

12月颁布施行。2005年,市政研究院又在国内首次编制出塑料排水管道工程闭气检验标准。

(四)养护维修

1997年,天津市排水管理处研制成袖珍式超声多普勒污水流量计,安装在纪庄子排水系统6座泵站的20多个出水管上,为采集管网动态变化数据提供便利条件。此后,该产品得到广泛推广应用。2000年该处开发的"天津市排水管理地理信息系统",实现排水设施信息资料的查询、检索和信息共享等,为排水设施的养护、排水监控、市区防汛调度等搭建了技术平台。

2005年,市排水管理处首次采用非开挖管道修复技术,应用德国非开挖全内衬玻璃纤维内管修复方法,对友谊路46年前修建的混凝土管道进行修复。该管道全长1102米,管径为1000毫米,管道埋深为3.9~5.0米。施工前先进行高效清洗,用地下管道电视监测车载系统进行摄像机检查,对局部管道破损点先行修复,然后将玻璃纤维软管送入到要修补的管道,吹胀后用蒸汽保持180~200分钟,待树脂固化后牢固覆在原下水道内壁上,几个小时后即可重新投入使用。

二、泵站工程

(一)泵站设计

1991年起,天津市政泵站建设中的新技术开发应用取得长足进步,主要有"多站合一"的新型泵站、大型多功能市政泵站、压力排水泵站、全地下式和半地下式潜水泵站及新颖的卵型泵站等,泵站的自动化水平、市政泵站的集中监测和调度技术在国内产生很大影响。

1995年,天津经济技术开发区建成的二期雨水、污水泵站,是一座综合性大型泵站,雨水流量26.52立方米/秒,污水流量3.96立方米/秒。该站选用国内外居领先水平的水泵、格栅清污机等设备,包括首次引进大型潜污泵和大型混流泵,在泵站的工艺布局、结构形式、电气自控以及运行管理水平等方面都更为现代化。同年,市政设计院设计的开发区东海路雨水泵站,排水能力32立方米/秒,是在软土地基上建设的一座超大规模的压力排水泵站。该院胡大卫、尹富荣、纪正国等首创卵型泵站工艺,将平面布置成蛋型,进水以小角度扩散,保持进水流态平稳均匀,出水用较大角度收缩,达到平滑、顺畅,卵型结构受力均匀,承受不均匀沉降的能力较强,达到技术先进、经济合理的目标。

2003年,天津市九河设计公司在海河沿岸综合开发工程中,将大沽路、七马路、会师广场三座泵站设计成集多功能于一体的全地下式排水泵站,将格栅井、沉砂池、集水池、出水池、变配电间、自动控制室合建在地下,地上仅设置必要的人员出入通道口、通风孔、设备吊装孔。为防止因突然停电,溢水淹泡泵房,在进水闸井处设置在15秒内快速关闭的速闭闸门,并设有通风系统和除湿及除臭设备。由于采用编程控制器可根据格栅后的液位信号开停车,自动调节,适应来水流量的变化。

2004年,市政设计院齐欣等编制的《天津市城市排水泵站建设标准》,市建委批准为地方工程建设标准,当年10月1日颁布施行。

(二)施工工艺

1993年,市政二公司在西园道雨水泵站工程施工中,因距沉井不足16米处有6层高的居民住宅楼,采用水泥搅拌桩作为止水帷幕用于深基坑维护,并用一系列监测手段观测沉降量及围幕内外水位差,使挖土不引起房屋破损,以保护周边建筑安全。

1995年,市政设计院在天津经济技术开发区东海路大型雨水泵站采用"卵形工艺布置"和"护壁结合,分层逆作"施工方法。其利用旋喷桩和灌注桩组成深基坑支护和止水帷幕,再加以内衬成为防渗结构层护壁合一,并以多道环梁使中间容积分成三层进行逆作施工,随开挖随逐层向下建成。

2003年,市九河设计公司设计的全地下式雨水泵站,下部结构采用地下连续墙、护壁合一的作法,建在海河岸边的景观带内,距海河最近而池深接近12米的深池泵站。

第三章 建筑科学技术

1991～2005年，天津市在建筑科学技术领域不断取得进步，理论上有新突破，技术上有新发展。在建筑科学方面，主要反映在关于建筑学研究、土木工程研究和水利工程研究中取得多项科研成果，并获国家或天津市科技成果奖励。在建筑工程施工技术方面的进步多表现在技术引进后的再创新上，特别是在建筑物的地基基础工程、钢筋与模板工程、混凝土工程、钢结构工程等施工方面研发出大量技术创新型成果，对提高工程质量和节能、降耗等发挥重要作用。

第一节 建筑科学

1991～2005年，天津大学等科研团队在建筑科学研究中取得一系列科研成果，其中多项成果获国家或天津市科技进步奖。在建筑理论研究方面，提出当前中国建筑的创作方向和影响天津建筑风格的因素与特性，并提出中国现代建筑史的起始期。在建筑物抗震降噪研究方面，完成"提高钢筋混凝土高层建筑抗震性能的分体柱技术""天津轻轨工程抗震分析与减震降噪研究"等多项成果，达到国际领先或先进水平。在建筑物光环境研究中，完成灯光可视化设计和测试系统等项目，提高了灯光和测试评价的技术水平。在建筑设计理论研究方面，开发出一套完整、具有完全版权的网格结构设计系统软件；完成"深基坑支护理论的研究""钢筋混凝土超高层建筑结构试验研究"和"天津博物馆建筑结构及关键技术研究"等项目，并在国内首次对北方沿海地区钢筋混凝土高层超长无缝结构进行温度场的全过程系统研究。

一、建筑学研究

1982年起，天津大学建筑学院教授邹德侬与建设部龚德顺、窦以德一起开始中国现代建筑史的研究，由此奠定天津大学建筑学院中国现代建筑史研究的基础。至2005年，邹德侬等先后完成《中国现代建筑史》《中国现代建筑论集》等十余部著作，发表论文70余篇。其中有些研究成果填补该领域的空白，受到国内外同行专家的高度评价，引起广泛关注。在邹德侬的指导下，培养造就一批该领域的研究学者，形成比较完整的学术体系和研究梯队。

（一）建筑史研究

1986年1月至2000年12月，天津大学邹德侬、曾坚、刘丛红等完成"中国当代建筑创作理论研究与应用"项目。该项目是老中青教师团队历时10余年，在国家自然科学基金和教育部、建设部、国家新闻出版署等支持下，结合30余个建筑创作项目以及大量教学成果组成。具体内容包括：中国当代建筑创作演进研究；西方当代建筑理论对中国建筑创作的影响；亚洲现代建筑与中国现代建筑的比较研究；全球化环境下中国建筑创作方向研究；将理论成果应用于建筑设计和建筑教育，取得显著成果。该项研究具有系统性、开拓性、时效性、实践性等特征，是在建筑学基本理论平台上，系统、开拓性地研究建国以来建筑创作的曲折进程，澄清了许多理论难点，解决了许多方向性问题，并长期、大力应用于建筑设计和教育。项目成果用于建筑创作

30余项，获奖5项，其中天津大学建筑系馆、王学仲艺术研究所、山东艺术学院教学实习综合楼、枣庄农业银行、天津市武清县石各庄镇建设等项目已经建成，受到用户好评；发表论文70余篇，专著8部，其中10篇论文受到省、部级奖励；用于教学新开课9门，指导国际、国家级设计和论文竞赛等，获得重要社会效益。该成果获2001年度天津市科技进步二等奖。

1991年1月至2001年12月，天津大学建筑学院邹德侬、曾坚、路红等完成“中国现代建筑史研究”项目。中国现代建筑史研究为一级学科“建筑学学科”所属的二级学科“建筑历史及其理论”。课题组对中华人民共和国成立50年余年的中国建筑发展历程、经验教训以及若干热点问题进行系统和创造性的研究，取得以《中国现代建筑史》为代表的重大成果，填补一项学术空白。关于中国现代建筑史起始期的确定，现行的起始期是1949年，该课题组论证为1920年代末；将1920年代以来的发展史分为7个时期，并对其背景、发展特点、经验教训和热点问题详加论述分析得出相应的科学结论；提出国家性建筑和国际性建筑的概念，论证二者是特殊性和普遍性的关系，提出中国是国际现代建筑运动的组成部分，中国建筑和国际建筑不是对立的关系；针对苏联建筑对中国现代建筑的影响和留下的许多悬案，从西方现代艺术史的高度，对俄国十月革命以来建筑的复杂演变以及波及中国的详情做了全面研究和分析，解决了一些悬案；针对改革开放后在引进西方现代建筑理论的误区进行正本清源；提出引进建筑理论应“可知”“可行”“进行双向研究”；全面总结改革开放以来中国现代建筑的成就和存在的问题，为今后的发展提出前瞻性的见解。以专著《中国现代建筑史》为代表的研究成果，全面拓展了中国现代建筑研究的新领域，结束了建国50余年来没有完整建筑历史的状况，对建筑教育有重大意义，有助于了解中国现代建筑的现状。《中国现代建筑史》获第十三届中国图书奖（2002），“中国现代建筑史研究”获2002年度教育部自然科学一等奖。

1992～1996年，天津大学邹德侬、曾坚、路红等完成“中国当代建筑史（1949~1989）”研究。该项目通过对中国现代建筑与近代建筑之间的关系研究，对中国现代建筑所做的历史分期和对现代建筑实例的收集、整理，为中国现代建筑发展方向提供借鉴，对中国现代建筑的保护有重要意义。其创新点包括：提出中国现代建筑史的起始期为1920年末；提出“国际性建筑”和“国家性建筑”的概念；对中国现代建筑理论的发展线索进行考证和分析；提出中国现代建筑文化遗产保护问题。该课题取得的成果在建筑学教学、建筑设计和城市规划、城市管理以及国家宏观管理部门得到广泛应用，有效地指导了建筑设计和城市规划实践，对中国现代建筑遗迹的保护有现实意义和社会效益。该项成果具有很高的理论价值和指导价值，为培养更多更好的优秀建筑人才提供了理论依据，达到国际先进水平。

1998年8月至2001年9月，天津大学与天津市规划和国土资源局、天津市城市建设学院、天津市建筑设计院、天津市房屋鉴定勘测设计院滕绍华、荆其敏、刘景梁、洪再生、路红等合作完成“天津建筑风格研究及设计应用”项目。该项研究深入探讨天津市建筑历史和文化的深邃性背景，研究天津建筑风格逐步形成的复杂性与独特性，并通过其与设计实践的结合以及具体应用，力求在现代天津的城市设计与建筑设计中充分把握和体现天津的城市特色，提出影响天津建筑风格的主要因素、天津建筑风格的特性、天津建筑风格设计和管理的应用导则等。该项目首次对天津建筑风格进行明确、清晰地定义，并将天津建筑风格的研究成果在设计实践中进行创造性的应用。该项成果对于展示天津市的城市建筑风格研究水平，引导相关理论及应用研究向纵深发展具有十分重要的意义，对其他城市风貌建设也具有参考借鉴作用，主要应用于城市规划、城市设计、建筑设计及城市建设管理等部门。该成果获2001年度天津市科技进步二等奖。

（二）建筑光环境研究

天津大学教授沈天行早在20世纪50年代师从著名物理学家钱伟长并完成研究生学习，在母校天津大学创立建筑物理专业，成为国内建筑技术学科的重要开创人之一。在后来50多年里，沈天行致力于建筑光环境研究，先后发明“灯光可视化设计及测试系统”“日照现场测量系统”“采用图像处理技术测试光环境的系统”等光环境测试系统。这些发明成果达到国际领先水平，推动中国建筑物理学科的发展。同时，在她的指导下，培养、造就一批年轻有为的学者和学科高端人才，马剑是其中杰出代表。天津大学教授马剑作为国内建筑技术科学重点学科带头人，开创中国照明光生态研究、中国古建筑油饰彩画人工光照保护研究的先河，在该领域达到国际领先水平。

1995年10月至1997年12月，天津大学沈天行、马剑、王立雄等完成“灯光可视化设计及测试系统”的研究。该项目根据光色及物体色进行色度计算，不但能逼真地显示灯光实际的静态效果，而且能用动画方式显示动态效果，为艺术创造提供先进的科学设计手段。该系统解决了高大建筑立面照明不便、测试照度不能瞬时测定亮度分布的问题，提高了灯光和测试评价的技术水平。该项成果创新点包括：首次使灯光设计可根据灯的配光、功率、光效、灯的位置、投射方向等算出目标物的照度分布及亮度分布；可提供设计方案的灯型、功率、灯位、投射方向，为照明工程的施工和调试带来便利；创造性地利用摄影立体测量的原理，使没有建筑图纸的旧建筑也能应用该系统进行灯光设计。该成果作为应用系统在灯光可视化设计及测试中具有很大优势，达到国际先进水平，获1998年度天津市科技进步二等奖。

2001年2月至2002年6月，天津大学沈天行、袁磊研究开发“日照现场测量系统”。该系统利用配有鱼眼镜头的数码相机及指南针，在现场的待测点向上（天空）拍摄180℃的鱼眼图像，并定出正南方向，输入拍摄地的城市名，用所编的程序就能很方便的看出该点受遮挡影响的周围物体。其创新点包括：利用数码成像及图形处理等先进技术，结合太阳运动的规律，可现场操作，快速、方便；所编软件覆盖了全国东西南北中各代表城市，可适用于全国；操作时不受时间和天气的限制，无需提供环境设计的原始数据或图纸。该系统的设备简单，操作方便，高效快捷，不受时间和天气的限制，可用于解决居民为“争取阳光权”时面临的取证难问题，也可帮助购房者选择满足日照要求的房屋，并能方便确定太阳能传感器或集热器的合理位置，具有较大的实用价值和较高的经济社会效益。该成果获2004年度天津市技术发明二等奖。

二、土木工程研究

天津大学建工学院土木工程专业创建于建校之初的1895年，具有悠久的办学历史和深厚的学术积淀。设有结构工程研究所、防灾减灾与防护工程研究所、桥梁与结构工程研究所、地下工程研究所、钢结构工程研究所和土木工程检测中心。土木工程专业主要的优势研究方向包括：大开间体系研究，软土地基与结构相互作用，工程结构可靠性与耐久性，工程结构设计理论，高层建筑深基础、基坑工程、软土地基处理，工程防灾、减灾体系理论与应用，大型结构系统可靠性，空间钢结构、住宅钢结构研究，结构检测、加固与补强，新型建筑材料等。

（一）提高钢筋混凝土高层建筑抗震性能的分体柱技术

1988年9月至2002年11月，天津大学建筑工程学院李忠献和北京市建筑设计研究院郝永昶牵头，胡庆昌、徐云扉、赵艳静、康谷贻合作完成该项目。其通过采用隔板将钢筋混凝土高层建筑中的短柱，劈成四根截面相同且独立配筋的“长”柱思想，以提高钢筋混凝土高层建筑中短柱，特别是超短柱的抗震性能；采用分体柱技术提高钢筋混凝土高层建筑抗震性能的试验与理论研究，编制钢筋混凝土分体柱框架非线性有限元分析的计算程序；针对工程应用问题，进行足尺寸分体柱的隔板材料和施工工艺的试验，总结提出钢筋混凝土分体柱及分体柱框架抗震设计的设计建设，为分体柱技术在钢筋混凝土高层建筑抗震设计中的工程应用提供可靠的理论基础和详实的试验依据，达到国际领先水平。该成果获2002年度天津市科技进步一等奖。

图8-3-1-118 钢筋混凝土高层建筑抗震分体柱

（二）结构半主动-智能控制理论及其技术原理

1989年1月至2001年10月，天津大学何玉敖、何琦、郭婷等完成该项目。该项研究横跨结构工程学、现代控制工程学与智能理论的交叉领域，提出半主动-智能控制理论及其技术原理。其创新点包括：不需要外部能源的提供与安装复杂的作动器系统，易于建筑结构工程实用；以智能理论与方法取代常规的振动控制理论与方法，从而确保达到在线控制的实际技术要求，做到投资少而获益大。该成果获2002年度天津市自然科学二等奖。

（三）深基坑支护理论的研究

1994年8月至1998年12月，天津大学建筑工程学院陆培毅、郑刚、严驰等完成该项目。在基坑工程中，普遍采用柔性的挡土支护结构、弹性抗力法，这是分析结构受力的主要方法。该项研究完善和发展了该种方法，编制出平面和空间有限元抗力弹性发程序，提高了计算精确度。其创新点包括：首次将支护、支撑体系作为整体，进行空间有限元分析；首次进行双排桩支护的程序编制；在基坑稳定分析中首次将承压水、渗流水的作用考虑进去，并提出分析方法；首次采用系统技术进行深坑支护的研究，是天津市岩土工程技术的提高和总结。所得结论为天津地区深基坑开挖技术规范，提供可靠的理论根据和计算方法。该成果获1999年度天津市科技进步二等奖。

（四）基于并行设计思想的网格结构设计系统及其程序的研究与开发

1996年1月至1998年12月，天津大学建筑工程学院龚景海、刘锡良、邱国志完成该项目。其针对中国网格结构设计中存在的问题及国内外计算机在建筑工程中应用现状及发展趋势，提出采用面向对象数据建模方法建立建筑工程统一标准的数据模型及相关理论与方法，开发一套完整的、具有完全版权的网格结构设计系统软件。其创新点包括：采用面向对象数据建模方法建立建筑工程统一标准的数据模型及相关理论与方法；提出建筑工程并行设计子循环的概念，合理组织设计进程；提出网格结构面向对象数据模型的表达形式；提出采用遗传算法进行网格结构杆件下料优化。通过网络实施建筑工程并行设计是建筑工程设计技术发展趋势，对以后的工程实际有很高的参考价值。开发的软件功能强大、计算可靠、使用灵活、方便操作，相关理论与方法具有国际先进水平。该成果获1999年度天津市科技进步二等奖。

（五）弦支结构体系关键技术研究

1999年3月至2008年3月，天津大学陈志华、韩庆华、尹越等完成该项目。其属于大跨度空间钢结构领域，主要研究弦支穹顶及各种弦支结构体系的各项关键技术，研究成果也可应用于其他大跨度结构体系中。其创新点包括：弦支穹顶结构体系分类方法研究及新型弦支结构体系的提出，其中研发的弦支筒壳结构体系、弦支混凝土集成楼盖结构申报国家发明专利；通过推导空间索单元刚度计算公式和环索预应力设定的基本公式，提出确定放样态张拉控制值的方法；对弦支穹顶结构动力性能的研究，建立弦支穹顶有限模型；研究弦支穹顶结构的索夹节点力学性能，研发的预应力钢结构滚动式张拉索节点，申报国家发明专利。该成果成功应用于天津市保税区商务中心屋盖弦支穹顶结构、天津博物馆贵宾厅弦支穹顶屋盖、山东茌平体育馆等多项工程中，相继在国内外核心期刊上发表30多篇论文，研究成果被列入《预应力钢结构技术规程》和《天津市空间网络结构技术规程》。

（六）高层钢管混凝土建筑抗震性能实验与理论研究

2001年1月至2003年12月，天津大学李忠献、丁阳、王成博等完成该项目。之前国内外对钢管混凝土结构的研究多集中于力学行为，较少对框架结构的工作性能展开研究。该项研究的创新点：建立钢管混凝土框架结构抗震性能的模型，并进行低周反复荷载作用下的试验研究；建立适用于反复荷载作用下钢管混凝土结构材料的本构关系，对其受力性能进行了有限元分析，与模型试验吻合很好。通过对一座三层钢管混凝土建筑的抗震性能进行系统的实验与理论研究分析，表明钢管混凝土结构能保证钢与混凝土的协同工作，充分发挥两种材料的强度和刚度特性，其抗震性能优于钢筋混凝土结构和钢结构，成果具有重要的理论意义，可广泛应用在高层建筑尤其是住宅建筑中，具有较大的社会效益和经济效益。该成果获2004年度天津市科技进步二等奖。

（七）天津博物馆建筑结构及关键技术研究

2001年4月至2004年4月，由天津大学、天津六建建筑工程有限公司陈志华、王小盾、余建星、陈质枫等完成该项目。为建造政治文化中心区域标志性建筑物的天津博物馆，研究人员在很多关键技术上开展创新性研究。创新点包括：利用建筑仿生学原理，博物馆整体设计为天鹅造型及入口大厅的羽毛状斜墙；大空间可呼吸体系通过巧妙的结构布置，实现了温度应力释放和抵抗结构外力的和谐统一；弦支穹顶结构体系节省钢材，造价低，降低施工难度，大大提高结构的稳定性能；新型镀瓷铝板的使用，提高耐久性，使设计的展翅飞翔的天鹅建筑造型得以实现，增强建筑物造型的表现力及整体美感，反映天津的城市特点，为天津市的风貌增添一份独特的文化气息。该项目多项技术设计先进，具有推广应用价值，获2004年度天津市科技进步一等奖。

图8-3-1-119 天津博物馆

（八）钢筋混凝土超高层建筑结构试验研究

2001年，天津市政工程设计研究所、天津大学、天津市地震工程研究所毕继成、佟景伟、赵素敏、颜莓、王承春等完成该项研究。该项目在超高层建筑中应用基础研究理论，完成钢筋混凝土超高层建筑结构受力模型试验研究；完成双塔楼超高层建筑风洞试验研究；完成场地动力特性测定及结构地震反应分析试验研究；完成不同混凝土登记框架梁柱节点模型试验研究；完成天津市鸿吉商贸中心工程基础底板、土压力和钢筋应力及沉降观测测试研究；完成天津市鸿吉商贸中心工程北洋钢铁大厦超高层建筑结构温度应力的有限元分析。该成果为制定钢筋混凝土高层超高层建筑结构设计技术规范提供了依据，获2001年度天津市科技进步二等奖。

（九）天津轻轨工程抗震分析与减震降噪研究

2002年1月至2003年12月，天津大学建工学院与天津滨海快速交通发展有限公司合作，李忠献、丁阳、王成博、张金立等完成该项目。其对天津轻轨工程的抗震安全性分析及减震措施、车桥系统耦合振动分析及基础变形和地震作用的影响以及噪声分析和降噪措施等进行系统的研究，进行相应的抗震、隔震设计，并采取措施降低噪音。创新点包括：提出一种考虑SSI效应的车桥系统耦合振动的分析方法，建立了三维空间模型；采用隔声式声屏障起到了良好的降噪效果；将研制的复SMA（形状记忆合金）智能减震器用于天津轻轨工程，降低桥墩的内力和墩顶位移，为保证天津轻轨工程的建设和运营的安全性提供了可靠的理论依据，具有重要的理论意义和巨大的工程价值。研究成果在天津市区—滨海新区快速轨道交通工程中成功应用，具有推广应用前景，达到国际先进水平。该成果获2004年度天津市科技进步一等奖。

（十）天津地区高层建筑超长结构无缝设计与施工全过程控制研究

2003年，中铁十八局集团有限公司与天津大学合作，顾谓建、张兴彦、李素清、刘海兰等完成该项目。课题组利用现代传热学理论和有限元力学分析技术，对超长无缝结构进行从建筑材料的导热计算到结构整体的温度场的内力与变形计算，总结温度场作用下超长结构的变形与应力的基本规律；在国内首次对北方沿海地区钢筋混凝土高层超长无缝结构进行温度场的全过程系统研究，在设计与施工全过程控制中提出综合集成技术和方式建筑物产生裂缝的各种措施，对超长无缝结构整个施工过程中的温度效应进行有效控制，最大限度地发挥各种建筑材料的作用。该成果获2003年度天津市科技进步二等奖。

（十一）体育中心大跨度空间结构抗风抗震安全性与损伤监测研究

2005年1月至2008年1月，天津大学丁阳、李忠献、王成博等完成该项目。其系统地开展大跨度空间结构的抗风抗震、智能控制、损伤识别以及施工过程仿真研究。创新点包括：确定适于大跨度空间结构风速时程模拟的数值方法，提出了考虑屋面板自振效应和流固耦合效应的大跨度空间结构风荷载计算方法；研究地震动场的模拟和地震动场输入参数的合理选取问题；提出多维多点平稳及非平稳地震输入下大跨度空间结构随机地震反应分析方法；确定适于大跨度空间结构损伤定位的损伤参数，提出适于大跨度空间结构的两步损伤定位法。项目研究成果全部应用于天津奥林匹克中心体育场大跨度空间结构，通过不同施工方案的仿真确定了合理的支撑卸载方案。为保证体育场大跨度空间结构的抗风抗震安全性与长期健康监测性提供了可靠的理论依据和技术支撑。大跨度空间结构随机地震反应分析方法研究成果在2008年北京奥运会田径训练馆、北京体育大学国家队训练基地田径训练中心综合训练馆、天津站无站台柱雨篷等大跨度结构工程中得到进一步推广和应用。该项目成果弥补中国《建筑结构荷载规范》规定的风振系数不完全适于大跨度空间结构风荷载计算的不足，修正了中国《建筑抗震设计规范》采用的地震反应分析方法基于一致地震输入假定的不完善之处，为相关设计标准的制订和修订提供了可靠的理论依据和工程实践应用范例。

（十二）矩形钢管混凝土柱及梁柱节点关键技术研究

2005年1月至2008年4月，天津大学陈志华、杨强跃、姜忻良等完成该项目。其在对国内外现有矩形钢管混凝土柱计算理论比较分析的基础上，提出矩形钢管混凝土柱计算的叠加理论；进行矩形钢管混凝土柱的超声波检测试验、剖切试验、钢管与混凝土粘结状态有限元分析，证实叠加理论的科学性；编制用于工程实际的可视化计算程序；针对内隔板节点等的不足之处，研究提出外肋环板节点与隔板贯通式节点，分析其受力机理及承载力计算理论，进行这两种节点的有限元分析、静力试验、拟静力试验，研究这两种节点的破坏形态和特点以及延性、耗能能力等抗震性能，并提出外肋环板节点与隔板贯通式节点梁翼缘受拉模型的节点承载力计算公式。创新点包括：提出新的计算理论，依据超声波和剖切试验验证矩形钢管混凝土柱叠加理论；提出外肋环板节点与隔板贯通式节点，并编制天津市钢结构住宅设计规程和天津市矩形钢管混凝土节点技术规程，提出六项专利技术。该项研究成果中的叠加理论被天津市钢结构住宅设计规程采用，并稳定应用于工程设计中；外肋环板节点与隔板贯通式节点也成功地应用于大量的实际工程中；编制的天津市矩形钢管混凝土节点技术规程增加了这两种新型节点形式及相关内容，具有系统性、先进性、可操作性，有关矩形钢管混凝土柱的计算理论及梁柱节点的六项专利技术有着广阔的应用前景。

三、水利工程研究

天津大学水利工程系始建于1933年。经过半个多世纪的发展，天津大学水利工程学科已经形成一套完整的和有特色的学科体系，为中国的水利、水电、水运行业培养大批优秀技术和管理人才，为国内高等院校相关学科培养大批优秀教师，为国家和地区经济建设、国防建设做出突出贡献，成为中国水利工程学科领域重要的人才培养和科研基地，完成多项国家重大科研、生产建设项目和技术创新、研发项目。

（一）高水头大流量泄洪结构脉动荷载与流激振动研究

1980年至1995年9月，天津大学崔广涛、林继镛、彭新民等完成该项目。课题组为揭示特大型水利水电工程（二滩、小湾、构皮滩）泄洪引起的随机动水荷载及其诱发水工结构振动规律，改进并完善其消能防冲、抗振的水力设计理论和计算方法，可及时应用并转化为生产力，进行高水头大流量泄洪结构脉动荷载与流激振动研究。其创新点包括：用频谱分析方法研究挑跌流对河床或护坦的随机荷载特性，提出了脉动压力是构成基础上的块体失去稳定的主要荷载之一和存在泄流诱发薄拱坝振动的可能性；首次推导出预报射流作用河床和过孔板水流在轴对称曲面上的脉动壁压幅值；采用了大型加重橡胶坝体模型；探索出一套预报水流诱发结构振动的技术路线和方法。研究成果在总体上属国内领先水平，在水弹模型试验方面达到国际先进水平，成果在国内水利水电工程广泛推广使用。

（二）波流与淤泥质底床的相互作用

1980年1月至1997年12月，天津大学建筑工程学院赵子丹、练继建、张庆河等完成该项目。课题组以研究淤泥质河口海岸的波浪水流运动和泥沙输移的规律为目标，提出一套更完整的理论模型，从更深层次揭示了淤泥质海岸波流和泥沙运动规律。创新点包括：根据连续性假设，由泥层中的轨迹速度导出泥层中的质量输送公式；对底泥为塑性流体运动的分析，采用二元不定常运动条件下的剪应力-剪应变率关系式；对不规则波作用情况，采用组成波方法求解；把泥床物质作为整体考虑，建立粘性泥沙悬扬起动的动力分析模型。该项研究对于发展淤泥质海岸河口动力学，弥补理论上的空白，用于指导实践产生巨大的经济、环境和社会效益。该成果先后获国际水力学会议亚洲太平洋会议最杰出论文奖（1988）、钱宁泥沙科学奖和1998年度天津市科技进步二等奖。

其后，天津大学练继建、崔广涛、杨敏等进行“水利枢纽厂坝隔（导）墙流激振动与结构优化研究”。导墙结构流激振动响应往往是其结构设计的控制条件，其结构的安全和结构优化设计与流激振动响应关系密切。但单纯的水力模拟和数值计算难以正确确定导墙流激振动的响应。该项目采用泄洪激振的水弹性实验模拟很好地解决问题，建立相应的理论计算模型，开展原型观测，提出导墙结构安全评价的指标以及安全监测、健康振动的理论分析方法，并通过原型观测来验证。该课题在现场原型观测试验和水弹性模型试验的基础上，采用流激振动正反分析方法通过实测有限点的响应特征，回归出整个位移场和动应力场，得到最大动力响应值；提出导墙结构泄洪振动位移及应力响应的安全评估指标。虽然这些指标是针对三峡工程导墙（挑流消能区导墙）提出的，但由于结构参数中采用了无量纲形式并考虑了水头因素，因而对其他工程也有参考价值和适用性。该成果获得2005年度天津市科技进步一等奖。

图8-3-1-120 水利枢纽厂坝隔（导）墙流激振动与结构优化研究成果展示

（三）海岸波浪场新型模式理论

1995年8月至2001年6月，天津大学、华东师范大学、上海大学承担，黄虎、周锡礽、丁平兴、吕秀红等完成该项目。该研究多角度、多层次地对波浪传播模型理论进行广泛、深入研究和探索，取得一批较为系统、创新的理论新成果。简述为：发现并修正在Liu-Dingemans三阶演化方程中存在的若干错误，据此建立一种新的非线性抛物型波浪方程和波—流相互作用方程，同时经过简化寻找到波群解，最后推演出四阶演化方程，确定了具有某些重要稳定性和显示边带非对称增长性的四阶项；建立了波浪从深水向浅水传播的非线性水波统一方程；面对影响波、流和海底沉积结构相互作用的众多因素，运用分叉和混沌动力学的观点、方法进行分析和处理，揭示出这一动力系统深层次结构潜在的丰富变化特性；充分考虑近岸波浪传播介质的复杂多变性，建立波浪在近岸水域传播的“广义缓坡方程”，可包含更为丰富和完整的近岸动力场信息；有效地给出两层海洋流体波—流相互作用的Hamilton描述；较为全面、深刻地归纳、分析和总结了国内外海岸波浪场模型的研究进展，由此阐明其思想、原理和各种建模手段。该成果有多篇论文在国内外重要刊物上发表。

（四）水利工程仿真基础理论与方法研究

1995年10月至2003年7月，天津大学钟登华、白玉川、曹志先等完成该项目。课题组以大型水利工程复杂施工、多沙河流及淤泥质河口海岸的泥沙运动、流域洪涝灾害等问题为主要研究背景，结合国内大型水利工程建设及海河流域治理与规划特点，对涉及的问题的机理进行深入分析与探索，建立水利工程模拟仿真的基础理论与方法体系。根据具体的水利工程及河流海岸的实际情况，采用数学模型方法与计算机动态仿真技术相结合的方式，模拟其运动过程的规律。创新点包括：针对大型水利工程复杂施工问题，结合地下洞室群施工、大坝施工、施工导流以及施工总布置等应用领域，重点研究水利工程施工全过程动态仿真的理论方法，并研究结合地理信息系统（GIS）的可视化仿真方法；针对粘性泥沙起动与输移、紊流拟序结构演化与掀沙过程、稳流拟序结构与床面形态的相互作用等方面，开展对河流海岸动力过程模拟的基础理论研究，建立水流底边界层拟序结构的演化规律、掀沙机理及床面形态发展非线性动力学机制模拟的基础理论，并深入研究水流泥沙数学模型及其在工程中的应用方法；深入研究流域水文过程模拟的理论与方法，提出多支流河道洪水演进过程的模拟方法，研究水文过程模拟下的洪水风险计算方法，并结合海河流域的特点进行应用研究。该项目的研究不仅为设计、规划与决策提供科学依据，而且用逼真形象的动态演示为决策提供直观的辅助手段。在国内外重要学术刊物上发表论文50余篇，被SCI和EI核心版检索20余篇。该成果对推动水利工程基础学科向数字化、可视化、智能化方向发展，对“数字水利”建设和发展有重大理论和现实意义，在多项工程中成功应用，取得显著的社会和经济效益。该成果获2004年度天津市自然科学一等奖。

（五）大型地下洞室群施工系统仿真理论方法及其工程应用研究

1996年6月至2003年6月，天津大学与国家电力公司中南勘测设计研究院合作，钟登华、王忠耀、刘东海、冯树荣等完成该项目。该研究集循环网络仿真系统、网络计划分析与优化系统、GIS技术、可视化技术等先进技术于一体，为复杂地下洞室群施工系统提供了一整套科学研究思路、技术路线和实现手段。提出的创新点包括：基于GIS的地下洞室群施工三维动态可视化仿真理论与方法；地下洞室群施工通风动态仿真分析方法；基于NURSB技术的复杂地质三位重建及可视化分析方法等。这是一项推动水电工程设计和管理向数字化、可视化、智能化方向发展的开拓性研究，可为地下洞室群施工组织设计、管理和决策提供科学有效的分析手段，极大提高了工程设计和施工管理的现代化水平，有显著的社会和经济效益。

（六）可视化仿真技术及其在水利水电工程中的应用研究

1997年4月至2001年12月，天津大学与国家电力公司成都勘测设计研究院合作，钟登华、张社荣、刘东海、李景茹等完成该项目。可视化仿真技术是计算机可视化技术和系统仿真技术相结合的一种新型仿真技术。课题组在深入研究基础上，结合工程应用，研制出可视化仿真软件，为复杂大型工程施工组织设计提供了科学的理论方法和先进技术手段，提高了设计管理水平。创新点包括：提出基于GIS的三维动态可视化仿真技术；提出复杂地下洞室群施工系统可视化仿真理论与方法，并开发出相应软件（ESAS）；提出水利水电工程施工导截流三维动态可视化理论与方法，并开发相应软件（CDMIS）。该研究是一项推动水电工程设计和管理向数字化、可视化、智能化方向发展的开拓性工作，在龙滩、溪洛渡、三峡、拉西瓦等水利水电工程中得到成功应用，取得显著的社会和经济效益。

（七）大型水利水电工程可视化仿真技术及其工程应用

1997年4月至2004年6月，天津大学与国家电力公司成都勘测设计研究院、国家电力公司中南勘测设计研究院、国家电力公司昆明勘测设计研究院和中国水利水电第十四工程局合作，钟登华、张社荣、刘东海、肖白云、何有忠等15人共同完成该项目。该项研究针对大型水利水电工程设计和施工管理的特点，创造性地提出采用可视化仿真技术，研究复杂工程系统的内部机理和运行规律，从而解决了其中存在的技术难题。在此基础上，该项目还深入研究基于GIS的三维动态可视化仿真技术，实现工程全过程仿真建模、仿真计算过程及成果的可视化。该项目同时研究复杂地下洞群施工可视化仿真与优化方法、混凝土坝施工三维动态可视化仿真与优化方法、施工导截流三维动态可视化仿真方法和施工总布置可视化仿真方法，研制开发了相应的可视化仿真软件，在具体工程中展开应用研究。该项研究总体上达到国际领先水平，共发表相关论文90余篇，其中SCI收录2篇，EI收录15篇，出版著作3部，初步形成完整的理论体系，对水利水电工程设计与施工管理向数字化、可视化、智能化方向发展具有推动作用，对水利水电工程“设计革命”和学科发展具有重大的理论意义和现实意义。该研究成果在溪洛渡、三峡等20项大型水利水电工程中成功应用，取得显著社会效益和经济效益，具有广阔地应用前景。该成果获2005年度天津市科技进步二等奖。

（八）海河口清淤泥沙运动规律及三维数学模拟的工程应用研究

1999年1月至2001年12月，天津大学白玉川、白志刚、邢焕政等完成该项目。其针对海河口清淤，尤其是拖淤搅动所引起的泥沙扩散范围、涨落潮流引起的泥沙回淤强度、清淤及拖淤的工程效益问题，进行预测和评估研究。一是结合海河河口的泥沙特征及河口各种清淤方式，对海河口粘性泥沙的运动规律进行研究，研制和建立针对淤泥质河口（如海河口）的三维泥沙数学模型及相应流场含沙量变化的动态演示系统；二是通过与实际测量结果的对比，较准确地反映了海河口泥沙的运动规律及河口淤积状况。该项研究为天津市三大河口（海河河口、独流减河河口、永定新河河口）的治理规划提供了科学依据。同时还撰写了《海河口拖淤泥沙运动规律数学模型及拖淤工程效益的研究》《海河口淤泥起动规律的实验研究》《独流减河口清淤方案及河口导堤工程方案优化》《河口泥沙运动动态演示系统及实践》等研究报告，完成海河水利委员会河口治理规划项目，研究报告被海河水利委员会制定《河口规划报告》时采用。该成果获2002年度天津市科技进步二等奖。

（九）地震作用下穿越管道的安全可靠性研究

2000年8月至2001年10月，天津大学、天津市水利局引滦入港工程管理处承担，景悦、余建星、刘瑞深、詹强等完成该项目。该项研究在5个方面展开。基本理论探讨：地震作用下结构与土的相互作用，灰色关联分析及新理论模型，灰色关联模式识别方法，离散多目标灰色决策方法；管道沿线地质分析研究：基于灰色理论的地震作用下砂土液化研究，场地类别判定的灰色模式识别方法，地面位移对管道的影响研究，地面变形对管道的影响研究，砂土液化实验研究；地震作用下管线的可靠性研究：安全裕度方程研究，非线性动态方程研究，结构地震动力可靠性分析技术研究，简化动态响应方程的建立；引滦入港穿越管道的可靠性分析：剩余强度的计算，基于灰色理论的地震波作用下管道可靠性分析方法，地面位移（断层）下穿越管道可靠性分析，砂土液化下穿越管道可靠性分析方法；穿越管道防抢预案：将灰色可靠性引入穿越管道抗震领域，被专事管道管理单位应用于输水管道管理，为管道管理单位提供决策性意见。该项研究成果的运用，可为国家节省大量的投资，获2002年度天津市科技进步二等奖。

（十）城市智能型防洪减灾决策支持系统研究

2001年8月至2003年8月，天津大学钟登华、冯平、阎俊爱等完成该项目。中国城市的发展，需要设计减免洪灾损失、城市防洪等措施的决策系统。该项成果能为决策者提供当前和一定预见期内的水文气象、洪水等有关信息，帮助决策者做出正确的决策。创新点包括：将人工智能中的专家系统、人工神经网络和地理信息系统应用在城市防洪减灾DSS中；研制开发了城市智能型防洪减灾决策支持系统的数据库及管理系统；提出基于遗传算法的神经网络洪水径流的预测模型。这是一项城市防洪减灾的非工程措施系统，运用后可以显著提高城市防洪减灾的决策效率和效能，是通过地图式查询，实现信息的可视化管理，从而为决策者提供快捷直观的动态信息支持，应用前景十分广阔，具有重要的社会和经济效益。该成果获2003年度天津市科技进步二等奖。

第二节 建筑工程技术

1991～2005年，天津经济快速发展，新建的居住小区、公用大厦鳞次栉比，城市面貌大大改观。大体量的钢筋混凝土建筑达到新高度，软弱土中的基坑开挖达到新深度，大型钢结构造型优美、新颖，充分体现科技进步。在地基基础工程施工中，完成粉煤灰作为结构填方和软土地基处理技术等试验研究，并在建筑工程中得到应用。随着基坑深度的加深和基坑体积的加大，促进深基坑施工技术的发展。深基坑施工中，在提高深基坑支护技术的同时，还积极做好土方开挖和地下水排放。在钢筋与模板工程施工中，研发出钢筋套管挤压接头一次成型工艺技术，达到一次性同步完成几道压痕的钢筋连接，并完成新型多功能爬架提模工艺和高层建筑外墙清水混凝土滑框倒模施工工艺。在混凝土工程施工中，研发出一系列混凝土外加剂、混凝土掺合料、自密实混凝土自密实混凝土等，并得到广泛应用。在钢结构工程施工中，采用大跨度球冠形网壳、螺栓球节点网壳和钢—混凝土组合梁等结构，并使用计算机建立三维模型和空中倒钩等技术，在天津体育中心、天津博物馆等工程中得到应用。

一、地基基础施工技术

（一）土方工程

在城市建筑中，黄土的用量大、成本高。1994年，天津市建筑科学研究所（以下简称“市建科所”，1997年改为天津市建筑科学研究院,简称"市建科院")在"粉煤灰作为结构填方的试验研究"中,与天津机械施工公司共同完成天津海绵铁厂(天津钢管公司下属分厂)两个堆料场填方工程。其地基承载力分别达到30吨每平方米和15吨每平方米,工程使用粉煤灰12.7万立方米,节约投资142万元。此后,该成果还用于房心填土、大面积回填土、堆场地坪处理及道路修筑等工程。2000年,在大港区挖湖堆山工程中采用粉煤灰填方,堆山高度约50米。

(二)桩基础工程

1992年,天津市第一建筑工程有限公司(以下简称"市一建公司",其他各建筑工程公司均相应简称为"市二建公司""市三建公司"等)完成的紫金花园工程(坐落河西区紫金山路与宾水道交口),地下3层,采用桩径1600毫米大截面梅花形灌注桩,桩长50米。市二建公司1994年承建的百货大楼新厦扩建工程和1995年承建的天远国航大厦工程(坐落河东区机场路),均采用直径800~1600毫米大直径灌注桩,桩长达61.5米。1998年,万隆公寓工程(坐落河北区狮子林大街与金纬路交口,又称金海湾公寓)采用支盘桩(三支盘),桩径650毫米,盘径1400~1600毫米,桩长25米。同年,市勘察院和天津大学建工学院主编完成《天津市挤扩灌注桩技术规程》,使桩基础施工有所遵循。

2001年,天津市建筑构件工程公司(以下简称"市构件公司")建成年产20万延米的预应力混凝土管桩生产线,并与市建科院等单位编制完成地方标准《先张法预应力混凝土管桩》《先张法预应力混凝土薄壁管桩》。2004年,市构件公司等单位批量生产先张法预应力混凝土管桩和薄壁管桩,并应用在天津市奥林匹克体育中心(以下简称"市奥体中心")、河北工业大学新教学楼等工程。

(三)地基处理

1998年,市建科院和天津大学岩土工程研究所、天津港湾研究所、市勘察院等单位完成"软土地基处理技术试验研究"。其多项成果在真空加堆载联合预压加固吹填土软弱地基、碱渣作为工程土用来造陆和回填地基、粉喷水泥桩技术加固软弱地基和波速综合法检测复合地基承载力、静载荷试验的快速校正法、粉煤灰作为结构填方以及双灰桩处理加固软弱地基等建筑工程中得到应用,并取得良好的工程效果和社会经济效益。该研究成果纳入天津市地方标准"岩土工程技术规范"。水泥深层搅拌桩湿法复合地基适用于6~8层民用建筑,可减少土体孔隙率,增大土体强度,提高基础承载力,在深基坑支护防渗和其他工程中得到应用。1999年建成的新城小区(坐落河西区大沽南路)和中嘉花园(坐落红桥区西沽)、2000年建成的御河公寓(坐落红桥区三条石)、2001年建成的水云花园(坐落南开区水上西路)等工程,均采用该项技术。2001~2005年,在荣华园(坐落河西区陈塘庄,现称世芳园)、瑞江花园梅苑(坐落河西区解放南路)、奥林匹克花园(坐落红桥区丁字沽三号路)等工程中,采用水泥粉煤灰碎石桩(CFG桩),施工面积接近800万平方米。

(四)检测

1、桩基检测 在桩基工程施工中,通常应用动测法和声波透射法、桩身钻芯法等抽样检测工程桩质量。1991年,市建科所完成"桩基动荷载检测方法的研究",使低应变基桩检测技术更加完善。1994年,该所引进用于基桩检测的"FET-B高应变桩基动测分析系统",并根据天津市270根桩的静动对比数据,给出适合天津地区高应变CASE法动阻尼系数Jc值的取值范围及建议值。2002年,市勘察院等单位编制完成《建筑基桩检测技术规程》。

2、地基检测 确定地基承载力以往多以静载试验为主。1994年,河北工业大学土建学院与天津市地质工程勘察院对水泥深层搅拌桩及碎石桩复合地基检测方法进行研究,一致认为采用波速综合法可以较全面地进行复合地基承载力及其质量综合评价与判断,是一种比较精确可靠的检测方法。该方法使用方便、快捷,覆盖面积大,可弥补静载试验点少的不足。同年,该学院在总结常规检测方法的基础上,提出快速法检测水泥深层搅拌桩复合地基的方法,其中包括静载荷快压校正法。

二、深基坑施工技术

1991年起,高层建筑成为天津城市建设的主要建设项目,尤其在中心城区高层建筑的高度不断增加,基础的埋深和桩的长度也不断增加,还有一些大空间的建筑物,如体育馆、展览馆和大型工业厂房的体量也越来越大,基础的埋深也很大。城市高层建筑工程和大体量建筑工程的施工都需要开挖深基坑。深基坑技术的发展直接关系到建筑物的质量与安全。深基坑技术是一门综合性、复杂性并具有危险性的高难度技术,涉及工程地质、土力学、基础工程、结构力学、岩土工程等各学科和技术要点。天津市是一个软土地基典型的城市。长期以来,从事建筑工程、市政工程的科研院所、高等学校和施工企业的专家们悉心研究深基坑技术,并与实践相结合,取得显著的成效。

深基坑在施工时首先要防止基坑周边发生塌陷,因此深基坑的支护是深基坑施工的重要措施。随着基坑深度的加深和基坑体积的加大,深基坑支护的难度也加大,促进深基坑支护技术的发展。1995年,天津市建委对全市深基坑支护设计要求进行规范,规定开挖深度超过6米的基坑工程支护设计方案必须经天津市建委技术顾问委员会专家论证。实践中,天津市在深基坑支护技术应用上有了很大的发展,比较突出的有工具式钢管支撑符合支护体系、三道混凝土环梁支护技术、地下钢筋混凝土连续墙、超深超厚地下墙连续施工技术等。2005年,开展软土地基深基础工具式钢支撑复合支护体系研究与应用,形成标准化程度高的深基坑支护体系施工技术,应用于软土地基深基坑支护技术,并可替代地连墙转抵达边梁技术、零层板加固的支顶柱等,具有较强的技术辐射能力。

天津市在深基坑施工中除做好支护外,还做好土方开挖和地下水排放。在土方开挖施工中,采用半逆施工法、全逆施工法、岛式和对称、分层开挖等技术。在地下水排放方面,采用锚拉钢桩帷幕止水、承压水层的盖挖逆作施工期间的地下降水施工技术等。代表性的工程有劝业场新厦工程(坐落和平区滨江道与和平路交口)、万科中心商厦工程(坐落河北区中山路)等。桩基础具有承载力高、稳定性好、沉降均匀以及良好的抗震性等特点,因此在各类建筑工程中得到广泛应用,尤其适用于建造在软地基上的各类建筑物。随着高层、超高层建筑的日益增多,对基础的承载力要求越来越高,桩基础运用愈来愈广泛。由天津市相关单位自主研发的高喷插芯组合桩、劲性搅拌桩等桩型在地基处理方面得到成功的应用。在此基础上,天津市编制出《沉降控制桩基础技术规程》《劲性搅拌桩技术规程》《高喷插芯组合桩技术规程》等地方标准。随着钻孔灌注桩的大范围使用,基桩的动测技术得到发展,出现声波透射法、桩身内力测试及成孔检测技术。

(一)悬臂桩与内支撑

1994年,市三建公司承建的河川大厦(坐落和平区南京路235号),坑深10米和6米,采用槽边退台、深坑用密排悬臂灌注桩、浅坑用隔栅式水泥土搅拌桩综合支护等技术。1995年,市一建公司等单位设计施工的泰达大厦(坐落河西区解放南路),基坑呈矩形,面积3900平方米,深7米和4.4米,分别采用非密排灌注桩和水泥土搅拌桩,较深的坑四角加角撑的支护技术。2004年,在城基中心大厦(坐落和平区南京路)施工中,其基坑为A、B两坑连体,坑深11米,采用大直径灌注桩围护,坑内用一道混凝土平面结构支撑。

(二)混凝土内支撑环梁

1994年,市一建公司承建的奥东大厦,基坑深9.20米,呈长方形,采用椭圆环梁于长边坡中间用钢支撑对顶。同年,市六建公司针对今晚报大厦(坐落南京路358号)深基坑的多边形形状,把环梁直径加大到64米,并将工程上钢管混凝土柱的钢管先用于支护放射梁,把环梁与边坡的压顶梁连成一体,成功地解决约1万平方米、坑深9.3米的大型基坑支护技术。1995年,市三建公司在金皇大厦(坐落河西区南京路)施工中,采用深基础地下连续墙围护,因主楼基坑深达14.5米,故分三层环梁进行支撑,首层环梁还部分利用楼板作为支护。1998年,市一建公司设计施工的津汇广场(坐落和平区南京路),深基坑呈三角形,面积约1.2万平方米,坑深13.5米,地连墙围护,内支撑设两道3个格构环梁,并与楼板共同支护形成逆支正施工艺。2000年,市一建公司等单位承建的开发区金融街,基坑呈三角形,面积约2万平方米,深6.80米,是灌注桩围护大型基坑。施工单位应用“深基坑环梁支护结构设计与施工成套技术”,并根据基坑形状采用直径为120米、80米两个格构环梁和直径为45米、30米两个单环梁共4个环梁作支护。

(三)钢支撑技术

1994年,市三建公司承建的移通大厦(坐落和平区荣吉大街16号),基坑深9米,地下连续墙围护,采用直径325毫米的钢管作内支撑支护。1996年,市一建公司设计并施工的立达公寓工程(坐落南开区卫津南路),基坑呈方形长方形,深6.4米,采用灌注桩围护,内支撑采用角钢焊制的格构梁支于角部,边坡中部加强加密围护结构加宽压顶梁。2004年,市一建公司将钢格构支撑构件形成标准化和节点件通用化,编制出标准图集,并应用于万顺国际公寓的基坑支撑。

(四)逆作法支护

1992年,市二建公司承建的劝业场新厦工程,基坑深7米,一侧紧贴老楼,采用全逆作法支护技术。1997年,在华联商厦(坐落和平区滨江道)二期扩建工程施工中,深基础结合逆作法与明开挖两种方式的优点,采用半逆作法支护技术。同年,市一建公司等单位设计施工的紫金花园工程(坐落河西区紫金山路与宾水道交口),基坑呈近似长方形,坑深14.1米,施工中以地下连续墙围护兼作地下室外墙,以灌注桩端插入钢格构柱为中间支承柱,用工程结构梁板做坑内水平撑的全逆施工方法。1996年,天津市建工集团(控股)有限公司(以下简称"市建工集团")将"深基坑环梁支护结构设计与施工成套技术"和"深基坑支护逆支正施施工工艺" 两项成果,应用于市一建公司承建的津汇广场(坐落和平区南京路)深基础工程。该工程围护结构用地下连续墙,厚1米,深25.8米,在负二层和负三层楼板标高,设两道水平支撑,并采用"地连墙环梁与工程楼板联合支护体系逆支正施"施工工艺,使基坑变形小于设计允许值,可确保基坑周围的建筑物、构筑物、地下管道、道路等安全和正常使用,而且提前工期12%,日挖运土方5000~9000立方米,节省资金1000多万元。

(五)锚杆支护及预制地连墙

1992年,市二建公司承建的天津日报大厦(坐落河西区围堤道)业务综合楼工程,坑深9.5米,施工中采用钢板桩围护、坑外土层锚杆支护技术。1994年,市六建公司在信达广场(坐落和平区曲阜道与解放北路交口)土建施工中,为保证基坑安全,采用预应力土层锚杆支护技术。该工程的塔楼共51层,总高度达238米,塔楼基坑深度14.5米。1997年,市建工集团完成地上31层、地下2层、总建筑面积42630平方米的天津奥林匹克大厦工程(坐落和平区成都道与昆明路交口)。该工程为框架剪力墙结构,主楼采用桩基,基坑周长259米,主楼基坑深9米。施工中,采用预制混凝土地下连续墙,每5块板为一个单元槽段,用泥浆护壁成槽,预制墙板两侧预留八字榫槽,墙板就位后灌细石混凝土,顶部用冠梁将墙板连成整体。通过测试墙板顶部水平位移和平面支撑应力,周围居民楼的沉降控制在1.1~7.3毫米。

三、钢筋与模板工程技术

(一)钢筋工程

1992年,市建科所在原钢筋套管挤压接头技术的基础上,研发出"钢筋套管挤压接头一次成型工艺技术",达到一次性同步完成几道压痕的钢筋连接。该项技术在天津市程控交换机厂主厂房等工程中用于1万多个接头,效果良好。1993年,市六建公司在天宇大酒店(坐落和平区电台道)工程中应用粗直径钢筋锥螺纹接头技术,共使用锥螺纹接头2100个,合格率100%。同年,市建科所又重点对不同直径(相差一级)钢筋套管挤压连接中的工艺技术参数的确定进行攻关,同时改进机具设备,实现工艺配套和技术系列化。在天津科技馆等工程中应用1.7万多个接头。1994年,该技术工法被评定为天津市市级工法。

21世纪初期,锥螺纹钢筋接头技术逐渐被直罗纹钢筋接头代替。2002年,天津开始应用力学性能更好的新Ⅲ级钢(HRB400)钢筋,并分别在天津外商投资企业活动中心、总医院医学中心等工程中应用,不仅节约钢材、降低造价,还便于施工。

(二)模板工程

1992年起,市二建公司先后研发出1570级钢绞线后张法无粘结预应力无梁楼盖结构等新技术,并在天津百货大楼新厦等大跨度楼盖结构施工中应用,提高了楼板的抗裂性能及房屋净空高度,便于模板工程施工。1993年,市二建公司在万科中心商厦(坐落河北区中山路)工程施工中,采用提架倒模工艺。该工艺易于控制模板标高,模板体系有较好的应变能力,模板的每层垂直运输不用塔吊或其他机械,速度快、效率高,外围架体用电动提升,工效提高3~5倍。同年,该公司参与研制的"康瑞模板早拆支撑系统"投入使用。该系统在丝杠顶撑上加双螺旋调节手柄及双翼型支托,安置在直径48毫米钢管顶端用以支撑混凝土楼板及模板。1995年，市一建公司通过对大跨度无梁楼盖塑料模壳支模早拆体系研究，编制出施工工艺标准化手册，在大胡同小商品商场三期工程中应用。同年，市三建公司在188米的金皇大厦（坐落河西区南京路18号）主体工程施工中，采用导轨式滑车升降模架技术，把传统的爬模工艺和爬升脚手架技术有机的结合为一体。

2002年，市建科院完成“新型多功能爬架提模工艺”，改变“工具柱与大模板互为支撑，交替爬升的方法”，在爬架上增加“滑动支座”实现爬架自升，在没有墙板（即无模板）的高层建筑结构上可同样应用。同年，市一建公司通过对高层建筑施工中的混凝土模板设计与施工进行系统研究，编制出高层建筑外墙清水混凝土滑框倒模施工工艺。

四、混凝土工程技术

（一）商品混凝土

1994年，市一建公司与市建科所合作完成“商品混凝土合理配合比及质量控制研究”，为商品混凝土提供C10～C40强度等级的泵送、非泵送混凝土配合比技术，成为天津市Ⅲ级粉煤灰在商品混凝土中应用的技术基础。

（二）混凝土外加剂

1991年起，市建科所研发的12个系列混凝土外加剂在建筑施工中得到广泛应用，包括YND系列混凝土防冻剂、全天候系列混凝土泵送剂、用于高性能混凝土的外加剂、抗裂减缩剂、早强剂、膨胀剂、阻锈剂、防腐剂、预拌砂浆专用外加剂等。1994年，市二建公司自主研制成功ZJ-7混凝土抗冻剂、ZJ-8缓凝早强减水剂、ZJ-9、ZJ-10混凝土泵送剂等，并在百货大楼扩建工程、天远国航大厦、天星河畔广场（坐落河东区十一经路）、邮电网管大厦（坐落和平区新兴路）等超高层建筑施工中应用，技术效果显著。1998年，市建科院黄靖、黎春海、曹鸿海等完成“用于高性能混凝土外加剂的研究与应用”，掺用UNF-5S系列外加剂，并辅以优质的掺合料，可配制高流态、高保塑性的高性能混凝土，减水率达29.6%～43.2%，且可进行泵送施工，技术效益和经济效益显著。该成果获1999年度天津市科技进步二等奖。2002年，市建科院研发出一种用缓凝材料代替常规使用的油脂填充在钢绞线和塑料护套之间的新技术，使用这种缓凝材料，既可满足施工期间的工艺要求，又使钢绞线和混凝土粘结成一体共同受力，结构更加安全耐久。2004年，市六建公司将该项技术应用在天津市力神电池有限公司锂离子电池主厂房扩建等多项预应力混凝土工程中。

（三）混凝土掺合料

1992年，市建科所先后完成“立式旋风炉增钙灰和液态渣掺于砂浆”“增钙粉煤灰作普通钢筋混凝土掺合料”“Ⅲ级原状粉煤灰在蒸养混凝土构件中应用”等3项研究。1998年，市三建公司对混凝土预拌系统进行改造，在设备上增加掺加超细矿粉的储料罐、掺料口及计量器，在混凝土生产中应用磨细矿粉。同时，该公司与天津市建筑材料科学研究所（以下简称“市建材所”）、天津市城建学院合作完成用于高强、高性能混凝土的超细矿物掺合料，并于2005年出版天津市地方规程《混凝土用矿物掺合料应用技术规程》。2001年，市建科院完成“增钙灰在商品混凝土中的应用研究”，并于2004年编制出天津市地方标准《增钙粉煤灰在预拌混凝土中应用技术规程》。

（四）自密实混凝土

2001年，市二建公司与市建材所合作进行高性能混凝土及应用技术研究，研发出自流平免振捣混凝土，并在罗马花园住宅小区（坐落河西区）等钢—混凝土组合结构工程中应用，施工性能良好。2002年，市建科院试验研究采用常用材料，强度等级C30～C60的自密实混凝土配制技术，可满足泵送要求，具有良好的抗分离性和间隙通过性，采用泵送高抛免振成型施工工艺，可一次浇筑高达12米的钢管混凝土。2003年，该成果在天津滨海新区泰达国际会展中心工程中得到进一步应用，混凝土一次性抛落最大高度35米。超声波检测表明，混凝土结构均匀密实，无质量缺陷。

（五）清水混凝土

2001年，市二建公司在天津理工学院高层住宅楼外檐混凝土施工中，应用清水混凝土施工技术，取消在混凝土表面抹灰，只刮腻子刷涂料，效果良好。同年，市六建公司在天津博物馆空间异型混凝土柱施工中，采用跳仓分段浇筑等技术措施，达到清水混凝土柱表面平整光洁的预期效果。2005年，市构件公司在天津奥林匹克中心（坐落南开区宾水西道）体育场预制清水混凝土看台板的研制和生产中，采用反打工艺预制清水混凝土看台板，并在大港区体育中心看台工程的观礼台板上应用。这一施工技术也适于预应力桥面梁、墙板或挂板等预制清水混凝土构件。

（六）混凝土耐久性

1997年，市建科院完成"天津市混凝土碱—集料反应的研究"。该项目通过对蓟县石矿采石场现场的取样并分析测定，发现蓟县开采的部分岩石具有碱活性，有的具有碱—硅酸反应，有的具有碱—碳酸盐反应。同时，证实秦皇岛地区和蓟县的砂子属非活性集料，还查明天津所用水泥基本上属于高碱水泥，含碱外加剂的使用也相当普遍。课题组在调研天津部分立交桥因碱—集料反应发生裂缝受损的情况，表明天津是碱—集料反应的多发性地区，研究出几种掺合料可对混凝土碱—集料反应起到抑制作用，并于2000年编制出《天津市预防混凝土碱集料反应技术管理规定》（试行）。2005年，市建科院完成"抑制混凝土碱集料反应技术措施"研究，并将"试行本"修订为《天津市预防混凝土碱—集料反应技术规程》。

（七）混凝土施工工艺

1995年，在市三建公司承建的金皇大厦工程中，要对9200立方米基础进行大体积混凝土浇筑。该工程基坑深14.5米，地下室三层，底板厚2.9米，地梁高3.25米。该公司选用C45混凝土，采取缓凝、斜面分层、搭设暖棚等工艺措施浇筑，效果良好。1996年，在杨村国家粮食储备库建设工程中，市三建公司等单位应用18米跨先张法预应力拱板屋架现场预制工艺。该工艺结合现场场地情况，对传统的张拉平台、张拉墩等设施进行改进，可降低预制成本，避免大型预制构件远途运输。2000年起，天津市大部分工程采用现浇的实心混凝土楼板，替代了沿用30多年的预制空心楼板。2005年，市二建公司在铜锣湾广场（坐落和平区东马路与南马路交汇处）二期工程地下车库楼盖施工中，采用现浇空心楼板结构。该结构为无梁式楼盖，底面平整，可提高楼层净空，且便于模板施工。

五、钢结构工程技术

1991年起，天津市在高层、超高层建筑的钢结构施工技术达到国际先进水平，具有相当的钢结构加工、制作及安装能力，初步形成钢结构加工、制作及安装等施工的专业化设备及队伍。在钢结构加工制作技术方面，实现施工详图设计电脑化、材料管理程序化、加工工艺和焊接工艺自动化。在钢结构安装方面，采用各种安装策略，完成一批复杂的大型现代空间结构的安装。在施工组织管理技术方面，发展了总体施工规划技术、异常情况应急处理技术及安全管理技术等。在复杂钢结构施工分析方面，建立一系列复杂钢结构施工跟踪分析策略与实用方法。代表性工程有金皇大厦、天津万顺国际公寓、天津奥林匹克中心体育场等。

（一）空间钢结构

1992～1994年，市三建公司承建天津市奥林匹克体育中心主馆工程。该工程屋顶结构采用跨度108米的球冠形网壳，支撑结构为48根18米高的钢筋混凝土柱，柱上设有环梁，屋面钢结构共96个支点，分别处于柱顶及环梁上，网架冠顶标高35米，钢网架总重620吨。该公司在施工中采取冠周小单元预制、高空环形拼接、冠顶整体吊装等方法，屋顶钢结构仅用85天完成安装。经市建科院测试，屋顶钢结构满足荷载作用下的使用要求。该项目获1995年度天津市科技进步二等奖和国家建筑工程鲁班奖。

2001～2004年，市六建公司承建天津博物馆工程。该工程建筑面积约3.4万平方米，屋盖采用螺栓球节点网壳结构。为实现天鹅造型当中脊背与长颈过渡使用弦长79米、弦高11.5米的箱型断面梁，梁的线条既有上下弯曲又有左右扭曲。施工中，使用计算机建立三维模型，吊装时使用立体胎膜和空中倒钩等技术，安装过程中对3250个三维坐标点严格控制,确保安装精度,完成造型优美的曲面结构。该工程获2005年詹天佑土木工程奖。

(二)组合结构

1994年,市一建公司在泰达大厦施工中,采用钢—混凝土组合梁结构。这种组合结构把混凝土和钢材(如H型钢和钢管等)结合在一起,充分发挥不同材料的性能特点,提高了建筑结构的使用性能。同年,市六建公司承建的今晚报大厦工程中,采用钢管混凝土柱结构,抗水平力结构采用钢筋混凝土核心筒体及钢管柱—板体系,其中钢管混凝土柱的最大外直径尺寸为1120毫米。2001年,市建工集团、市二建公司等单位联合开发"钢—混凝土组合结构住宅体系",并在2002年丽苑小区彩丽园(坐落河东区鲁山道)11层住宅工程中应用。该体系由钢管混凝土柱、钢—混凝土组合梁、抗侧力支撑以及节能复合外墙板组成。其科研成果获2003年度天津市科技进步二等奖。此后,该成果在天津及外省市多项工程推广应用,其中天津罗马花园达30层。2003年,市建科院开展超声波法检测中小直径钢管混凝土方法研究,实现中小尺寸截面钢管混凝土常规缺陷的定性测量。至2005年,完成天津市泰达国际会展中心及天津市奥林匹克体育中心等十余项建筑工程的钢管混凝土质量检测。

(三)焊接施工工艺

1991年,市机电公司在石化公司6.4千米DN250毫米输油管线施工中,首次使用钨极氩弧焊打底加手工电弧焊盖面焊接技术,质量合格率达99%,使工期缩短并成本降低。1993年,该公司在承建14万吨乙烯工程中,对两台200立方米球形气罐进行现场组焊,其组焊和整体组装质量优良。2001年,市机电公司在松下电子厂房工程的箱型钢柱焊接中,应用熔嘴电渣焊焊接技术,完成钢柱内隔板与腹板接触面焊接施工,焊丝的消耗量比埋弧焊减少50%,电能消耗量减少35%。2005年,该公司为德国洛伊公司淬火炉体制造加工时,使用全自动专家型振动时效装置,以消除钢构件焊后残余应力,比传统的热时效处理节约能源90%,节约成本80%,且工期缩短,不产生时效氧化皮,无环境污染。

第四章 公用事业工程技术

天津市公用事业工程技术的发展,主要体现在城市供水(自来水)、供气(燃气)和供热(集中供热)上,其共同点是解决好来源、储配和节能三方面的问题。自引滦入津工程建成后,水源问题大为缓解,研究方向转向水质的提高上。2000年后,供水技术研究除常规净水技术外,还完成电去离子技术和膜技术。净水厂处理后的水质达到欧共体水质标准和高纯水、药用水和电子一级水。2002年,有4路天然气源进市,煤制气渐被取代。20世纪90年代天津基本形成地热、热电联产和大型锅炉供热三种热源并举的局面,科研重点转向节能保温和计量供热的研究上。

管道施工修建往往成为技术发展的关键。2004年,天津创下2880毫米混凝土管成功穿越永定新河,在14米深处一次顶进340米的新纪录。供气的重点在调峰,提高储气技术水平则成为重中之重,建造5000立方米高压球罐的完全国产化是世纪之交储气技术的重大突破。这一时期,在供热技术上天津大力推广应用水源热泵、地源热泵和污水热泵。

在节能方面,天津开发与利用并举。在供水上,泥中取水、污水处理、中水利用、抄表到户等方面都有科技创新。在燃气上,2000年后科研重点转向开发用气的新途径,从民用到生产,进而用作交通燃料,既扩大了应用范围又利于环保,燃气科技进入新领域。在供热上,采用双膜法制备锅炉用水和供热网补水。

第一节　供水工程技术

自“引滦入津”工程完成以后，天津城市用水有了稳定的水源，为加速发展供水事业提供了条件。1991～2005年，天津在产水、输水、节水以及用水管理上，都有较大发展，供水科技有长足进步。在产水技术上着力于质量的提高，力求达到直接饮用水标准，供水量不断增加。2005年，全市供水管网长度4320千米，供水范围涉及市内六区及部分新四区，供水面积480平方千米，供水人口近500万人。但天津仍是个缺水严重的城市，节水问题成为水科技的当务之急。开发新水源，从产水工艺中节水，开发中水、废水代净水等，天津正在走向节水型城市。由于信息技术的普及，在用水管理上信息化程度也在不断提高。

一、产水

（一）集约化制水

为了更有效地利用水资源，便于将“引江、引黄、引滦”三水源切换互补，2003年天津启动津滨水厂建设工程。该厂与天津现有的常规净水厂相比，增设预处理工艺，并引进法国、德国利满高密度Densadeg澄清池和“V”型滤池技术，强化常规处理工艺。该工程的消毒工艺，采用“北方地区安全饮用水保障技术”中的消毒工艺成果——短时游离氯后转氯胺的顺序消毒工艺，确保出厂水浊度在0.3NTU以下，高于国家颁布的《城市供水水质标准》。在水的深加工上，全部采用臭氧——生物活性炭深度处理，水质的生物和化学稳定性更高。该水厂是中国北方现有大型净水厂中唯一全部采用臭氧——生物活性炭深度处理的净水厂，经处理后的水质，达到欧共体水质标准。

（二）处理高藻水

20世纪末，天津市的源水，夏季高藻水问题日益突出。以往处理高藻水只能依靠成倍地投加混凝药剂和消毒剂。2002年，天津的百年老水厂——芥园水厂与美国泰科地球公司合作建成天津泰科水务有限公司，并在老厂改造中，利用国际先进的气浮技术和气水反冲技术，处理水中杂质，解决了高藻水问题，提高了出厂水质。

（三）水质安全保障

2002年，科技部首次将供水领域研究列入“863”计划，公开招标。天津市自来水集团有限公司（以下简称“市自来水公司”）联合哈尔滨工业大学等五所大学成功中标“北方地区安全饮用水保障技术”课题。该课题针对以天津水源为代表的中国北方地区水源水质特点，开发涵盖从水源、水厂净化工艺到管网末稍全过程的技术集成系统，建立完善的饮用水水质安全保障体系，有效地解决了北方地区饮用水的安全问题。该项研究包括7个方面的技术问题，即：水源水质改善工程技术；安全预处理技术；去除微量有机物、氨氮、藻和藻毒素技术；新型安全消毒法与消毒二次污染的控制技术；出厂水二次污染控制与安全输配技术；饮用水及其净化技术的安全评价方法；示范工程建设与系统化的技术方案等。天津市针对原水藻类高发的特点，充分发挥气浮技术在去除藻类方面的优势，结合安全预处理技术、强化常规技术，以及短时游离氯后转氯胺的安全氯化消毒工艺，形成优化组合的最佳示范工程工艺方案，并付诸实施，有效地保障了出水水质。

（四）制备高纯水

2001年3月，中国军事医学科学院卫生装备研究所龚承元、刘红斌、苏建勇等完成“电去离子技术和反渗透——电去离子高纯水设备的研究”，获2002年度天津市科技进步一等奖。电去离子（以下称EDL）是20世纪90年代发展起来的新型膜分离技术，可用于连续生产纯水、高纯水，是中国工业用纯水设备的升级换代产品。该项研究，发明一种全部采用国产材料的EDL膜堆和暗道式无回路淡室隔板，以解决膜堆内窜水与树脂泄漏，改善水力学状态，同时确定国产EDL膜堆的运行参数，实现膜堆长期稳定运行，进而开发出RO—EDL高纯水生产工艺设备，所产水质达到国家药用水标准及电子水一级标准。

（五）膜技术制水

1979年，天津大学北洋公司、天津大学环境工程系安鼎年等开展纳滤膜制水工艺研究。2002年初，研制出以纳滤膜为核心，集其他膜技术、分离技术、吸附、氧化等高科技手段为一体的"净化水产生装置"。该装置首次将微絮凝过滤技术应用于纳滤膜的预处理，并在预处理中建立"微絮凝过滤—吸附—紫外线消毒—精滤—超滤"的组合处理工艺，其所产之纳滤水，既除去水中微量有机污染物，又可保留人体所必需的矿物质，各种离子配比符合健康所需的最佳含量。经市科委组织专家鉴定，该制水工艺及出水质量指标达到国际先进水平。2003年3月，天津大学完成"膜技术处理饮用水成套技术及装置的研究"，生产出第三代净水器，主要用于军队后勤保障及农业等领域。

二、输水

（一）管道施工

1999年，市政二公司在排水工程中采用土压平衡施工工艺，其顶管纪录是将管径2400毫米的混凝土管，一次顶进290米。2004年，天津市管道工程集团有限公司在穿越永定新河顶管工程中，将潮白新河水通过引潮三泵站直达北塘水库。该工程采用多刀盘土压平衡掘进机施工，将外径2880毫米的混凝土管，一次顶进长度为340米，管道深度14米，创下天津顶管施工的新纪录。这也是华北地区穿越河流管径最大、覆土最深、一次顶进距离最长，而且成本最低的顶管工程。

（二）管网改造

天津市自来水事业有100多年历史。一些老旧供水管道因其老化严重，经常出现破损漏水。2003年，市自来水公司实施小区旧管网改造工程，对市内六区超期服役及腐蚀严重的老旧管道改换为球墨管、PE管（埋地聚乙烯管）和免维护直埋闸等新型管材管件，达到无漏水、无水质污染、无水压低问题。至2004年底，共改造旧管道124千米，142片小区60万人口受益。

2004年，该公司在供水管网内装置内窥镜，在管网运行状态下可清晰地观测到管网内部及其附属设施的运行状态，为管网安全稳定运行及其附属设施的维修、维护、更换提供了科学依据。该装置采用不锈钢、有机玻璃套筒等密封材质防水，用可调焦摄像装置及冷光源拍摄管道内图像，再用视频连接将图像输出，用涡轮涡杆在地面上调焦，用丝杆传递克服管网压力，从而实现在不停水状态下对供水管网的监测。这种供水管道带压检测在国内尚属首例。2006年1月17日，该项目通过市建委鉴定，成果达到国内领先水平。

（三）二次供水

据2005年调查，天津市有1183处高层建筑二次供水设施不合格，居民饮用水的水质、水压不达标，严重影响居民的日常生活。当年，市自来水公司与各区及国土房管部门实施二次供水设施改造工程。由于历史遗留下的二次供水问题很多，许多高层建筑普遍存在着原设计落后，材质低劣、设施老化，维护保养不到位，水质、水压无保证，严重渗漏等问题。市自来水公司分别采用工频、变频、增设消毒设备等技术手段，对某些小区旧管网进行改造，在支管加装管道泵、地泵加压等多种方式，从而解决了六层以上居民的饮水问题。2005年，共完成115处高层建筑二次供水设施改造项目，4458户居民约1.5万人受益。

三、节水

（一）泥中取水

通常自来水厂在净水工艺中产生的滤池反冲洗排水和沉淀池排泥水均排入河中，既污染环境又浪费水源。2005年，市自来水公司启动水厂污泥处理项目。其中新开河水厂建成包括两座高密度沉淀池和一座污泥均衡池和投加药系统及离心系统的污泥处理车间，沉淀池的上清液可回收，每天节水量可达到水厂日供水量的1.5%～3%。该项目运行后，日产污泥92.18吨，不仅可充分利用水资源，也进一步提高了新开河河道的通航及行洪排涝能力。

（二）废水利用

1997年，天津市商业委员会柴寿武研制出“废水替代净水冲厕自控装置”，可节水20%以上，在第46届尤里卡世界发明博览会上获得金奖。

四、用水管理

20世纪90年代，天津市对居民用水多按居住区分片管理，各片设置总表，单元房内安装分表，非单元住房户无表，水费则依据总表数由各户均摊，造成水资源的浪费流失。2002年初，天津市启动自来水抄表到户改造工程，到2004年11月结束。市内六区与新四区的居民住宅生活用水，共进行入户转换140万户，改造户内水表167.8万具，其中：安装无线远传水表53.3万户，60.8万具，占安装总量的38%；安装IC卡水表12万户，12.5万具，占8.57%；改造户内管道37万户，提前实现市政府提出的三年完成全市自来水抄表到户改造工程的预期目标。2005年，市自来水公司实现营业抄收服务工作的电子化。

2005年5月，市自来水公司津南水务有限公司与北京工业大学联合承担的市建委项目“基于GIS技术的小城镇供水实时监控管理系统的开发与应用”通过鉴定，达到国际先进水平。该项目以津南区供水系统为研究对象，经对其调研分析，开发出适合中国小城镇管理特点的基于GIS技术的小城镇供水实时监控管理系统的软硬件工艺方案，将GIS技术和供水科学化管理技术结合起来，针对小城镇发展和管理需求，综合利用视频、地理信息系统、自控、网络通讯等数字化技术，成功地开发出适合小城镇供水特点的现代化管理系统，实现对小城镇供水系统的信息化集成管理。该成果具有很强的适用性。

第二节 供气工程技术

20世纪80年代中期，天津以煤制气技术为主要研究方向。1984～1987年，天津市实施“三年气化工程”，由引进后的消化、吸收到自行设计制造，形成100万立方米的制气能力。到90年代初期，天津民用燃气形成煤制气、液化石油气、天然气三种气源并用的格局。90年代中后期随着渤西天然气在天津登陆（1997年），陕气进津（1998年），华北油田向津供气（2002年），加上原有的大港油田（1974年），供气形成四个天然气气源。90年代后期煤制气渐被取代，燃气工程技术研究也由制气转向以输配气及储气为主。到2005年底，天津地下燃气管道总长度达6700千米，管道最高设计压力由0.8兆帕提高到4.0兆帕。在管道施工、维修管理等方面的技术都有较大进步。5000立方米的高压球罐制造技术从引进到国产化，再到相继投产运行，天津的储气能力迅速提高。由于天然气气质优良、气量充足，2000年以后，科研重点转向对燃气的开发应用，燃气由生活用气到工农业生产，以至用作汽车燃料，燃气的应用空间更加广阔。

一、煤制气

天津市有三个煤制气厂。天津市第一煤气厂于1984年建成投产；1999年气源转换为天然气，2000年停产。天津市第二煤气厂（以下简称“二煤气厂”）于1991年引进的变频调速装置用于焦炉高压氨水泵上，对焦炉操作管理和环境保护起到很大作用，不仅可降低设备故障率，节约电能，而且对改善环境效果显著。天津市第三煤气厂仅为企业内部生产提供气源。

1998年，二煤气厂自行设计改造3号、4号锅炉使用混烧煤气。2003年，该厂又进行2号锅炉改造，可以纯烧煤气，既节约动力煤，又能减少多余煤气排放造成的环境污染。

2002年下半年，二煤气厂在原料煤中配入大同弱粘煤生产冶金焦的试验，提出四套原料煤配比试验方案。2005年，该厂为进一步解决配比的准确性及配煤系统的可靠性，采用JGC—40I型带式称重给料机对配煤系统进行改造，从而保证各单种煤按配比准确配合，既可保证焦炭质量，又可提供煤制气。

2003年，为将处理后的污水综合利用，二煤气厂改造澄清池连续加药系统，对多种药剂进行选型筛选实验，确定适合的药剂，进行污水加药澄清处理，提高污水排放的质量，并使回用污水完全达到熄焦工艺要求。同年，净化系统引进压滤机替代三法离心机，可节约维修费用和电能。

2004年初，该厂对煤气净化所需终冷水由原连续补充新水，改造为循环水补水，使终冷水质得到改善，减少设备腐蚀，节水效益显著。同年，对净化洗苯系统进行改造，更换新型填料——碳钢孔板波纹规整填料，使填料表面积增加近3倍，吸收效率高。

随着天然气的广泛应用，出于环境保护的需要，继第一煤气厂全部停产，二煤气厂也于2006年停止运行，煤制气也随之退出气源行列。

二、燃气输配

1997年4月，陕甘宁至北京天然气干线天津支线工程（“陕气进津”的气源管线）动工，管线起点为河北省永清门站，终点到达天津市第一煤气厂，全长67千米，管径400毫米，设计压力2.0兆帕，年输送能力4亿立方米。管线采用S360钢材，焊接工艺采用当时比较先进的下向焊接，钢管外部采用聚乙烯三层复合结构防腐，外加电流阴极保护。1998年7月管线竣工，陕甘宁天然气顺利引入天津。在该项工程中，首次采用水平定向穿越技术成功穿越子牙河，穿越距离463米，钢管管径400毫米。其后，又成功穿越海河下游、永定河、蓟运河等多条河流，最大管径600毫米，最大穿越距离1500米。

1998年1月至1999年12月，为适应城市环保和城市建设发展需要，节省土地资源，天然气公司开展“无公害智能型地下调压装置”的研究与应用。该项目重点对地下调压技术从方案确定、工艺设计、设备造型等方面着手，结合国内天然气输配工艺的特点，在输配压力级制、管网工艺系统、管网最低点积水问题及安全控制等方面进行研究与创新。该成果获得国家专利。

2000年1月至2001年11月，由天津市燃气集团有限公司（以下简称“燃气集团”）、天津大学环境学院合作完成“天津市燃气输配系统优化调度”的研究。该项研究运用时间序列、数学模拟、系统优化的理论和方法，建立输配管网工况模拟仿真系统，其运算速度、精度达到实用要求。同时，建立城市燃气输配系统优化调度模型，设计编制求解程序，能够提高燃气输配系统安全稳定供气的程度和输配气的效率及效益。成果应用后，较好地解决了燃气管网的用气负荷量预测问题，为制定生产供气计划及设备管道的抢修、维修方案等方面提供了准确的科学依据，增强了供气系统的安全性及可靠性。

2005年9月开始，燃气集团对原燃气调度系统进行升级改造，主要是将燃气现场气源站、储气罐站、高压调压站、中压调压站、工业大用户等站点的压力、流量、温度等参数，合计440多条数据，通过多种无线传输技术传输到调度中心，并利用工控组态软件实现气源站、储配站等站点的现场工艺图及实时数据的显示，通过棒图、趋势图等不同形式显示现场运行参数，对各种报警信号能够及时做出响应，使调度人员能够实时了解整个城市燃气的使用分布以及生产运行情况，对各种突发事件做出快速反应，达到合理调配燃气资源。

三、储气设施

1996年，二煤气厂建成全市首座大型干式低压储气柜，储气量10万立方米。相对于浮动罐顶、用水密封的湿式气柜而言，干式气柜是固定罐顶、用油密封的储气设施，罐体更加安全可靠，同时使运行成本降低，维护费用减少，且由于储气量的增加，对全市煤制气的用气调峰起到关键作用。

1998年，天津市引进日本的大型球罐设计制造技术。这种高压球形储罐，在储存相同体积燃气的容器中结构最合理,钢材消耗最少,占地面积最小。全市第一座高压球罐站在陕津天然气输配公司建成,共建有5台5000立方米高压球罐,设计储气能力30万立方米,设计调峰能力23万立方米。

2000年12月,天津市渤西油田天然气利用工程指挥部、天津市煤气工程设计院合作完成"国产化5000立方米高压天然气球罐技术研究"。该项研究主要围绕整体结构及工艺结构、钢材选用、科学计算、科学配置球罐数量及单罐容积4个重大技术难题,并在配气工艺技术、球罐结构形式、球罐安全性能、球罐材料选择等方面进行优化和创新。采用该项技术建造球罐获得成功,并在国内首次实现在设计、材料、制造和安装方面的完全国产化。2001年10月29日,该项研究通过市科委组织的成果鉴定,居国内领先水平。该成果获2001年度天津市科技进步二等奖。

利用该项技术,滨海电厂高压储配站在2000年建成6台5000立方米高压球罐,设计储气能力20万立方米,设计调峰能力10万立方米,主要供滨海电厂发电使用。同样利用该项技术,津沽高压储配站于2002年6月建成8台5000立方米高压球罐,设计储气能力30万立方米,设计调峰能力20万立方米,成为渤西、陕北、大港三种天然气气源的交汇枢纽站,从而实现了三种天然气气源的互补及合理调配。

四、管网维护

(一)燃气管网区域计量

2000年12月,燃气集团完成"燃气管网区域计量"的研究。该项目在不变动燃气管网的前提下,采用先进实用技术,在各区域交界处DN500毫米管道上安装插入式流量计与原有门站和调压站计量仪表形成计量系统,实现区域计量。研究插入式仪表在复杂工况下运行情况,解决了双向流计量、高低峰流速悬殊计量、不停气下的安装维护、燃气气质和仪表环境对精度的影响等,用数据分析流量规律。采用该技术后,可实观对区域用气量的客观分析,找出供销差率过大的原因。该技术对降低燃气行业供销差率及推动计量管理工作有指导作用。

(二)燃气管网地理信息系统

2002年8月至2004年8月,燃气集团又完成"天津市燃气管网地理信息系统的研究"。该项研究是针对燃气行业管网运行管理实际,为提高燃气管网的管理水平,及时处理管网事故,为管网的更新改造、重点监护提供决策依据进行的研究。该项目采用1:500地形图作为燃气管网地理信息系统底图,提高标注、查询的准确性,将图形与属性信息以空间对应关系方式进行管理,除三维空间关系外,还有时间、权属、类别等多维要素,形成多层面立体管理模式,增强管理功能,提高管理效率,加大辅助决策与分析作用,在大量数据的支持下,提供燃气管网隐患预测、报警及旧管网改造项目生成等。

该系统克服以往燃气行业地理信息系统的缺陷,形成有自主知识产权,功能完备,并对实际管理工作具有很强实用性的专业地理信息系统,在燃气管网规划、事故抢修和气源转换中起到关键作用。该项研究于2004年12月通过市建委组织的成果鉴定,居国内领先水平。该成果获2005年度天津市科技进步二等奖。

(三)燃气管网检漏

2004年6月,燃气集团第三销售分公司引进德国先进的气体监测智能仪器,并对气体监测信息管理软件进行改进,创建中文版,增加数据分析曲线功能。该技术广泛应用于管网的燃气置换中,操作人员可以清楚地掌握管道中燃气浓度和氧气浓度的变化,准确测出燃气浓度达到标准的时间,可为管网的可靠、安全运行提供基础数据。

(四)检修状态下供气

2003年9月,天津市陕津天然气集输有限公司、燃气集团完成"故障或检修状态下天然气供气方式的研究"。该项目针对单条气源管线供气,一旦发生故障只能中断供气的问题进行研究,确定车载压缩天然气作为临时气源,以应对供气管线运行中出现的突发情况,确保向各类用户稳定供气。该项目研发的移动式撬装调压站占地小、重量轻、操作灵活方便、无污染,进出口压力可调节范围大,能提供多种压力级制的输出适合长输管线故障状态或检修状态下的临时供气及不具备管道供气条件的用户应用天然气,既解决了故障或检修状态下用户停气问题,又可弥补单线供气方式的不足,保证安全稳定供气。该项研究于2005年1月通过市建委组织的成果鉴定，达到国内领先水平。

（五）新材料应用

在2002年的旧管网改造工程中，采用免开挖修复新技术，即管道内衬（管中管）技术，可减少路面破坏，降低工程成本，有的地区还采用聚乙烯管材取代钢管，可增强管道防腐性能，延长管道寿命。

2003年5～12月，燃气集团第三销售分公司成功应用燃气金属软管连接户内燃气用具。该管材连接牢固、耐腐蚀、柔韧性好、密封性强，可避免橡胶管易老化、脱落和弯曲易阻气等缺点，是防止室内燃气泄漏爆燃的一种新型金属软管。

五、燃气应用

（一）用于空调

1996年，燃气公司成立天然气集中空调推广应用小组，通过调研与分析，确定使用燃气空调的可能性。1997年6月，开始安装配套风道系统和直燃机主机，铺设燃气管道，调试空调设备。1998年2月点火运行，天津市第一台天然气集中空调应用成功，从而拓宽了天然气的应用领域，为减少季节用气量的差异提供了新路子。

2003年4月，燃气集团开始“燃气区域空调三联供”的应用研究。实施供暖、制冷、热水三联供的燃气应用模式，不仅拓宽了天然气的应用领域，还有效削减了燃气季节用气量的差异，最主要的是应用燃气替代煤，可大幅度降低空气污染。

（二）用于供热

2002年4月，燃气集团、中国市政工程华北设计院合作完成“燃气锅炉智能与优化控制系统”的研究。其主要作用是根据环境条件及历史数据建立模型，进行燃气负荷预测控制，并利用变频技术，比例调节空气燃气配比，进行温炉过程控制，进而提高锅炉效率，降低燃气消耗。采用该技术，燃气消耗可降低5%至10%，节电20%以上。该成果获2002年度天津市科技进步二等奖。

（三）用于农业生产

1998年11月至2001年10月，天津市液化气有限公司、天津市农机试验鉴定推广站完成“温室液化气加温增二氧化碳设备”的研究。该项目是以液化气为能源，燃烧释放热量，同时产生二氧化碳和水，为温室作物生长提供所需的温度、湿度条件及二氧化碳，具有为温室补充二氧化碳及增温的双重功能，可减少环境污染，提高温室作物的产量和质量。该设备具有脉冲连续放电自动点火、熄火保护、自动温检、精确可调等特点，实现了整机国产化。2001年10月，经市科委鉴定，达到国内领先水平，并获国家专利。

1998年10月至2001年3月，由天津市液化气有限公司、天津市农村能源办公室联合研究完成“液化石油气粮食烘干技术及其成套设备”。该项目是研究以液化石油气为燃料的粮食烘干技术和设备，在消化、吸收国外先进技术设备的基础上进行创新，实现整机国产化。该技术是采用液化石油气燃烧后产生的热烟气，通过与鼓风机鼓入的空气混合后再与干燥塔内不断循环的粮食进行热交换，进行干燥。该项目于2001年3月通过市科委组织的鉴定，研究成果达到国内领先水平，获得国家专利。

（四）用于汽车燃料

2003年3月，燃气集团与中国石油天然气总公司共同投资建设的天津市首座天然气加气母站投入使用。其加气规模、技术设备居国际领先水平，每日可提供压缩天然气3.2万立方米，可供1000部公交车和3000部出租汽车运行。该项目的投入运行，标志着天然气在天津的应用范围由工业和民用的能源动力，拓展到交通燃料这一全新的领域。同时，该站可作为车载天然气气源，向尚未通管道的周边区域提供天然气，实现除管道输送天然气之外的另一种运输方式。

六、信息化管理

1991年，二煤气厂开始进行监控管理一体化调度系统的开发研究，并与中科院沈阳自动化研究所合作完成“基金会现场总线分布工业控制系统开发应用”。该项目来源于国家“九五”科技攻关重点项目(97—756)“新一代全分布式控制系统研究与开发”,2000年通过科技部、中国科学院组织的成果鉴定,并获2001年度中科院科技进步一等奖、2002年度国家科技进步二等奖。开发的“现场总线分布控制系统系列软件”,拥有国内自主版权,并在二煤气厂实现第一个应用工程,企业生产过程控制的自动化程度和可靠性有所提高,焦炉的安全生产和产品质量得以保证。2000年4月,燃气集团完成“天然气收费管理计算机网络系统”的研究。该系统采用局域网分层架构采用流行的视窗语言编程,界面友好,易扩展。其共设8个子系统:收费录入、统计查询各种信息、报表处理、用户数据管理、数据备份、初始化、地址代码字典、图形查询输出,可解决天然气收费效率低、易出差错等问题,进一步规范运营管理,提高工作效率,改善服务质量。

2004年8月,燃气集团完成“燃气集团电子收费及信息管理系统”的研究,使电子收费系统升级。该系统不仅能完成电子收费划帐功能,而且可完成与燃气相关的报修、维修、服务、违章等安全普查管理功能,将原来的人工管理全部实现电子信息化。其客户服务子系统共享户籍和收费信息并拥有完善的数据管理和分析功能,具有完善的数据管理和全面的权责划分,使各级管理人员掌握不同的数据;科学的分析功能,为掌握供销数据及市场预测可提供管理决策依据。

2005年3月,燃气集团完成“天津市燃气集团流量计计量远程采集管理系统”。该系统进一步利用计算机技术、通信技术和网络技术,实现对大型工商用户流量计量数据直读远程采集、传输;实现远程实时动态管理和历史数据分析,并可与实时运行的调度系统、营业收费管理系统、客户服务系统链接,实现数据共享;同时能保证计量系统在较恶劣的环境下长期稳定运行,使供气企业能及时动态掌握用户的用气状况,确保安全稳定供气,计量准确。2005年7月,该项目在燃气集团投入应用,并于2006年1月通过市建委组织的成果鉴定,达到国内领先水平。

第三节　供热工程技术

天津市集中供热事业起步于20世纪80年代。起步虽晚,发展却较快,到90年代初具规模。但由于供热体制及技术条件的限制,出现前所未有的困难。供热收费率逐年下滑,能耗过高,质量下降,供热单位负担过重,难以为继。节能成为供热体制改革中的重中之重,而降低能耗的关键在于加快“科技兴热”的步伐。为此,天津在热源、输配、计量三个方面进行体制改革和供热技术的改造与提高。

一、热源

1990年底,全市居民集中供热面积578.28万平方米,普及率仅为11.39%。供热方式以中小锅炉及小煤炉为主,能耗大,污染重。

1998年,天津市供热办公室(以下简称“市供热办”)开始组织高等院校、科研院所开展包括计量供热系统特性、热计量装置、技术标准、热价制定及管理方法等一系列供热技术专题研究。2001~2004年,天津市陆续出台《集中供热住宅计量供热设计规程》《集中供热住宅计量供热施工质量验收规程》《低温热水地板辐射供暖技术规程》《电热辐射供暖技术规程》等地方标准。2005年,市建委又下发《供热计量示范工程技术指导意见》。这些技术标准与文件对供热系统设计、施工、运行等各方面提出强制性要求,具体到必须安装散热器温控阀、管网水平平衡设备、变频调速设备等,构成一个较为完善的供热系统节能标准体系,也为开发热源作好政策和技术上的准备。

同期,天津拆除并网一批热效率低、能耗大的小锅炉,将这些小锅炉供热用户并入运行效率较高的集中供热锅炉和热电联产供热管网。2001~2005年,全市完成拆除并网小锅炉房共计426座,不仅降低能耗,而且有效地减少了污染。

为了提高锅炉供暖的运行效率，2001年后，市供热办对全市的锅炉房提出具体节能改造要求与目标，要求新建的大型锅炉房一律安装节能系统装置，全部采用计算机自动控制系统，按室外气温变化控制锅炉的供热，水泵与鼓风机实行变频控制。同时，加大对清洁能源与再生能源供热的研究及应用力度，重点推广地热供热技术。2005年，全市有115眼地热井用于供热，供热面积947万平方米，其中居民供热面积达290万平方米，每年可节约燃煤7.7万吨标煤；公建供热面积657万平方米，年节煤19.7万吨标煤。此外，还因地制宜开发并推广应用水源热泵、地源热泵和污水源热泵技术，共实现22个项目的34万平方米地源热泵、水源热泵供热。2005年，实现污水源热泵供热。

2004年，市供热办组织相关单位完成“双膜法处理二级出水回用于供热系统成套装置“的研发。该装置利用污水厂的再生水（中水）替代自来水或地下水，用膜法替代传统离子交换法制备锅炉用水和供热管网补水，使再生水处理后达到锅炉和供热管网用水的水质标准。

二、输配

2001年，天津市管道工程集团有限公司建成国内第一条以环戊烷为聚氨酯发泡剂的预制直埋式保温管生产线。该公司杨宁、邵丽方、刘津强等经对其保温管性能研究，证实环戊烷是氟里昂的最佳替代物。同时，对该生产线的关键设备，即由国外引进的高压发泡机进行改造，研制出适宜国内生产的配套设备，并对其生产工艺与安全系统进行研究、开发与设计，可确保生产及储运过程中的安全。该成果属国内领先水平，获2002年度天津市科技进步二等奖。

2001年，市计量所刘巍、田生亮、曹文洪等在“供热计量仪表检定装置”研究中，根据建设部提出的“集中供暖的民用建筑逐步实施按供热量计量收费”的要求，为正式开展的供热计量仪表强制检定工作提供了计量检测专用设备。2002年6月，该项目通过国家检验检疫总局组织的成果鉴定，其成果获得实用新型发明国家专利，并在国内计量检测机构广泛推广。

2004年，天津市管道工程集团有限公司保温管厂严忠辰、张裕民、方晓光等进行“无补偿直埋保温管的热风预热技术研究”，通过以空气作为预热介质，在无补偿直埋保温管的热敷设中，提高预热质量，减少预热时间。该保温管厂在国内首次对水和空气通过传热性能及热物性分析研究，比较在不同风温、风速下的预热结果，选择预热工艺参数及设备选型，编制预热操作规程。该技术的创新点在于，采用合适的工艺和工装保证空气加热到预定的温度，并能在管道内流动通畅。这种无补偿预热直埋敷设方式具有管网造价低、施工周期短、管网寿命长、维修工作量小等优点。

三、计量

2001年，市计量所刘巍、田生亮、曹文洪等完成“供热计量仪表检定装置”研究。该项目根据建设部提出的“集中供暖的民用建筑逐步实施按供热量计量收费”的要求，为正式开展的供热计量仪表强制检定工作，提供计量检测专用装备。2002年6月，该项目通过国家检验检疫总局组织的成果鉴定，其成果获得实用新型发明国家专利，并在国内计量检测机构推广。

第五章　园林绿化技术

20世纪90年代初，天津市加大对园林绿化科技工作的力度，大力引进草种、树种和名贵花卉，筛选并培育出适于天津地域生长的植物,注重对病虫害的防治和园林养护技术的研究。1996年,天津市出台园林科技发展“九五”计划和2010年长期规划。同时,市政府先后颁布“城镇绿化养护”“草坪建植管理”“大树移植”“古树名木保护与复壮”等一系列技术规程或地方标准,使园林绿化科技工作走上规范化、科学化道路。2000年起,天津动物园先后对食草类、灵长类、鸟类等动物由圈养、笼养改为散放,被国内同行称为动物园建设的第三种模式。

2001年,天津开发区利用海湾泥、粉煤灰、碱渣配成种植土,营造海防林获得成功,并创新排盐洗碱的新方法,将近代遗留下来的制盐用卤化池和由制碱废料堆成的碱渣山改建成风景秀丽的公园。

随着园林绿化科技的发展,全市绿化进度进一步加快。1995年起,每年新建绿地面积都在100万平方米以上。2003年后,每年新建绿地面积达2000万平方米以上。1990～2005年,全市建成区绿化覆盖率由11.5%提高到36.40%,建成区绿地率达到28.51%;人均公共绿地由2.19平方米提高到8.38平方米;全市拥有大小公园由115处增加到203处,公园面积由1851.56公顷增加到2699.11公顷。

1991～2005年,天津市园林绿化局完成局级以上的科研项目100余项,其中27项获国家和省部级科技进步奖。

第一节 城市绿化技术

1994年3月,市委、市政府正式确定全面建设滨海新区。由于滨海新区多为重盐碱地区,土地含盐碱量很高,土壤粘度大,不适宜草木生长,新区的绿化建设成为天津城市绿化的重点与科技攻关的难点。

1996年,天津市颁布“城镇绿化技术规程”,绿化技术更加规范。同年,天津经济技术开发区(以下简称“天津开发区”)在原长芦盐场的卤化池上,采用一系列排盐、播种、布局等创新技术,建成泰丰中心公园。1998年,对滨海地区园林植物适应性选择及配置技术进行研究,为滨海地区的园林绿化和植物配置提供了技术依据。2000年,滨海新区又利用海湾泥、废碱渣和粉煤灰按科学配比作为绿化种植土,并采用工程措施,营造海防林,使树木成活率和保存率达到90%,使盐碱地的绿化技术提高到一个新水平。同期,继完成津河河岸绿化后,又相继完成月牙河、复兴河、四化河、北塘排水河等多项沿河造绿工程。2004年,将天津碱厂多年堆积的碱渣山恢复生态,建成紫云公园,突显出天津“以废造绿”的绿化科技特色。

一、盐碱地造绿

1996年,天津开发区在长芦盐场卤化池上建成15298平方米的泰丰中心公园。该园原土壤物理性能差,质地紧密,含盐量高达10%。建园工程首先沿起伏地形表面敷设鱼骨状三级排盐系统,草坪播种选用混播技术,并在大土方造型上以(50×50)米的方格网划分区域,人工湖采用钢性防水。

1998年,天津市园林绿化研究所(以下简称“园林绿化所”)谭唯广、周洪义等完成“天津滨海地区园林植物适应性选择及配置技术的研究”。滨海地区地势低洼,土壤瘠薄、粘度大、含盐量及地下水矿化度均高,地下水位在1米左右,年降雨量不足600毫米,植被种类少,尤其是能适应该区的木本植物更少。该项研究提出首先进行土壤改良,对地下实施隔离排碱、洗盐,实施结果使盐碱土明显改善。同时,经对滨海地区植物适应性选择及配置的调查研究,筛选出白蜡、国槐、洋槐、馒头柳、侧柏、紫穗槐等40种适应性强的园林植物和毛白杨、栾树、龙柏、碧桃、凌霄等42种适应性较强的园林植物,为滨海地区园林绿化和植物配置提供了技术依据。

1999年,天津开发区绿化公司提出滨海新区的绿化模式。该区东侧沿海挡建防护、游览一体化的生态圈;海挡至东海路东侧和与塘沽、北塘接壤的西、北两侧的地区为盐生植被保护圈;沿开发区边界建成环城调气、防污、美化生态圈,形成点、线、面、片、立体的绿化网络。

2004年，塘沽区园林局对原天津碱厂碱渣堆放地进行绿化。通过人工塑山、铺设隔离淋水层、排盐碱管线、客土绿化、铺设供水系统等工程措施，将其改造成一座占地33万平方米，堆山30米高，栽植乔灌木、常绿树和种草共45万平方米的紫云公园，成为塘沽一处景点。此外，塘沽区的森林公园和植物园都是利用重盐碱废土、堆通过高淋水排盐改造土壤，达到种树绿化的标准，使昔日只长草、不长树的盐碱滩，变成绿树成荫的园林。

二、"新土源"造绿

天津沿海为淤泥质海岸，土壤含盐碱量高、地下水位高、蒸发量大、土壤黏度大、风沙大，防护林建设需要进行土壤改换。同时，天津开发区正处在滨海重盐碱地区、且地势低洼，绿化建设需要大量客土抬高地面，但挖取客土不仅破坏供土地区的生态环境，且成本昂贵。2000年，天津开发区绿化公司吸收借鉴前人成果，利用港口清淤海湾泥、碱厂的废渣和电厂的粉煤灰，按一定比例混合，形成"新土源"，在天津渤海淤泥质海岸带营造出宽4米、长8.1千米的东海路海防林带。2001年，天津开发区又利用这种"新土源"作为绿化种植土，同时采用工程措施，使树木成活率和保存率达到90%以上，继而在开发区规模利用，实现废弃物的资源化，产生可观的环境效益和经济效益。当年，经市科委组织专家鉴定，认为该研究独创性显著，达到国际先进水平。

三、废弃地造绿

2002年，大港区利用废弃物堆山挖湖，形成新的园林景观。挖湖堆山占地面积77公顷，其中山体面积10.28公顷，主体山高30米，堆山总土方量110万立方米，采用当地电厂36万立方米粉煤灰和挖湖盐碱粘土混合填筑，表层为种植客土，粉煤灰和挖湖盐碱粘土混合改善土壤物理结构，有利于土壤脱盐。同时，挖湖堆山实现了废物的资源化，开辟了水面，改善了生态环境。

2005年，天津市利用市区拆迁的工程废土在体育中心西南侧红旗南路和宾水西道原废弃坑洼水塘地堆山绿化，堆成高50米、面积12公顷的山体，三座山峰相连，整体面积达30余公顷，栽植乔木、花灌木6000余株，使昔日一片水洼地变成绿草如茵、花木成林、水塘清澈见底的花园。

四、河岸绿化

1999年，天津市完成津河改造园林绿化项目规划。改造河段自解放南路（湘江道）至三岔河口，横跨河西、和平、南开、红桥等四区，全长18.5千米，对河岸两侧38万平方米空地进行绿化规划，7万平方米的旧绿地实施调整改造；根据不同地段的环境特色，沿河两岸以植物造景为主，强调季相变化，栽植70余种树木；两岸绿地分别以"人与环境""人与文化" "人与历史"为主题，注意新旧绿地的结合，使校园绿地和河道融为一体；为解决河岸护堤与道路高差大的问题，绿化大量采用挡土墙设计。

2002年，天津市进行月牙河和复兴河绿化改造工程。"两河"改造以生态为本，围绕"水"做文章，创意突出地域特色，强调生态环境艺术个性，因地制宜，将生态景观与文化内涵有机地融入河道的总体设计。

2003年，天津市又进行月牙河二期和四化河、北塘排污河等改造景观建设。主要施工技术是将园路、广场铺装成形式多样的景观，讲求植物配置，使植物栽植的自然生态性、生物多样性更趋合理，河道绿化更突出人性化。

第二节 园林养护技术

1991～2000年，天津园林在防治虫害方面取得多项成果。在防治国槐叶柄小蛾、遏制白蜡吉丁虫、摸清三种蚧虫的生活史及发生规律、规模化繁育周氏啮小蜂等技术上都有较大突破，从而对市树绒毛白蜡及国槐等多种园林树种起到有效的防治害虫作用。

1996年起，天津市先后颁布“城镇绿化养护”“园林植物保护”“草坪建植管理”以及“大树移植”“古树名木保护与复壮”等一系列地方标准，又对域内的古树名木进行普查、建档、输入计算机，并采取有针对性的复壮措施。天津的园林养护走上法制化、科学化管理轨道。

2001年，天津市开始采用性引诱剂，诱杀小木蠹蛾雌成虫。2005年，又针对5种钻蛀害虫提出防治措施，对多种树木可持续有效地防治虫害。

一、虫害防治

1992～1994年，红桥区园林局周云等采用综合防治方法，防治国槐叶柄小蛾获得成功。1992年，市园林绿化所张良玉等应用综合防治技术遏制白蜡吉丁虫虫害，为天津市树——绒毛白蜡防治虫害提供了新技术。2000年，市园林绿化所胡文华、张淑萍等完成“天津市园林树木几种主要蚧虫防治技术的研究”，摸清槐坚蚧、白蜡绵粉蚧和日本龟蜡蚧的生活史及发生规律，归纳出3种蚧虫共有21种寄主植物，并筛选出适宜的药剂，给出适时防治的最佳方法。

1997年，美国白蛾天敌周氏啮小蜂在塘沽区放飞。1999年，天津部分地区开始大规模放飞人工繁育的美国白蛾天敌周氏啮小蜂，共放飞4亿头，对美国白蛾的防治取得良好的防治效果。同年，市园林绿化所庞建军等经过3年研究，对周氏啮小蜂人工规模化繁育技术获得突破，一举解决蜂种采集和保存、替代寄主获得和保存、蜂种扩繁、规模繁蜂、人工控制定期出蜂及放蜂等技术问题。2000年，市园林绿化所张连生、周洪义等通过对美国白蛾生活史的观察，摸清其造成危害的习性和防治的最佳时期，查清其寄主植物的种类和数量，并成功地完成对该小蜂大量繁殖的研究，同时筛选出7种无公害农药，形成由人工防治、无公害药剂防治和以虫治虫生物防治三部分组成的美国白蛾生物防治系统工程技术，并在全国范围内进行推广。此外，还完成人工繁育周氏啮小蜂的规模生产技术研究。

图8-5-2-121 天津市园林绿化研究所采用树干钉茧放蜂技术防治虫害

2000年，市园林绿化所张淑萍、胡文华等完成“选用低、无毒农药防治花灌木刺吸口器害虫研究”。该项目针对天津市碧桃、山桃、西府海棠、木槿、花石榴等五种主要园林花灌木，年年出现严重的蚜、螨危害情况，筛选出低毒、无毒农药若干种。使用后，既减少了打药次数，又收到良好防治效果。同年，市园林绿化所刘金英、庞建军等完成“天津市园林植物几种主要害虫可持续性防治技术的研究”，总结出国槐尺蛾、桑白盾蚧等5种害虫发生规律及最佳防治时期，并筛选出高效、无公害、来源方便、价格较低的几种药剂（齐螨素、烟参碱等）及槐小卷蛾性引诱剂。

2001年，市园林绿化所庞建军等采用人工模拟合成性引诱剂，诱杀小木蠹蛾雄成虫，降低雄成虫数量，使小木蠹蛾雌成虫绝大部分不能交配，不能产出有效卵繁育后代，达到持续有效地防治小木蠹蛾危害绒毛白蜡树的目的。

2005年，市园林绿化所、红桥区园林局张淑萍、周云等针对新传入的六星黑点豹蠹蛾、云斑天牛、双斑锦天牛及原严重发生的光肩星天牛和臭椿沟眶象等5种钻蛀害虫，探索其发生危害规律，提出防治措施，其中有关六星黑点豹蠹蛾、云斑天牛、双斑锦天牛等3种害虫在天津地区发生危害的规律和防治措施的研究尚属首次。

二、绿化养护

1996年，天津市颁布《天津市城镇绿化养护技术规程》。2002年，颁布《天津市园林植物保护技术规程》《天津市草坪建植管理技术规程》。

2000年，天津市园林绿化工程开始推行监理制度，全市首家园林监理公司——天津市方正园林监理公司成立。是年，市园林绿化所杨瑞兴等完成“天津市城市园林树木物候观测的研究”。经过对市区的主要园林树木进行连续18年的观测，在其中17年资料基础上进行统计、分析、总结，对原天津市区四季的划分予以修订，重新编制出自然历，确定天津主要园林树木的绿色期、开花期、秋色叶树的观叶天数以及历月园林生产要事。

2001年，天津开发区开始用中水灌溉园林绿地。

三、古树名木保护

从1996年开始，天津市开展古树资源普查。通过实地观测、访问乡里百姓、查找史料，确定古树名木，对确定的古树进行编号、登记、照像、测量、评定生长势，对普查清楚的720株古树名木建立档案，记录其学名、科属、树龄、胸径、冠幅、生长势、病虫害情况，并保存古树的冬态、夏态照片。天津古树中最多的为油松，占全部古树的60.3%，最高树龄的为蓟县许家台村的编号为A0080的国槐，树龄为1380年，胸径2米；最稀有的是编号为A0082的槐榆，树龄为1380年，胸径2.65米，槐树上长出榆树。

从2000年开始，天津市每年为古树施用“古树专用肥”，并使用害虫天敌进行古树病虫害防治，对濒危古树采用埋设渗水管降低地下水位和盐分法、挖环沟设竖井透气法、设鉄篦透气砖和打孔透气法、叶面施肥法、修补树洞法等，对80多株古树进行复壮。

2001年起，天津古树名木保护获得新进展，开发出“天津市古树名木管理数据库”软件，将古树名木全部输入计算机管理。针对造成古树衰弱濒危的原因，提出古树复壮的技术措施，通过降低地下水位、排盐、开发施用古树专用肥、增加根部透气性、调整根冠比、防治病虫害等多项措施，复壮濒危古树。

第三节 园林植物技术

1991年起，天津市园林植物科研重点主要体现在对草坪草、树木、花卉的引进新品种，从中筛选出适宜盐碱土地生长的新草种，适应天津地区生长的抗旱、抗寒、耐盐碱的新树种，以及经引进、筛选并培育出名贵花卉的新品种，尤其对仙客来进行全面系统研究，不仅培育出芳香化系列品种，还找出其退化原因，提出保持良种优势的技术措施。

1996年，天津市编制出园林树种规划，并制定出一整套园林植物保护管理的技术规程，园林植物管理更加科学化。

2005年，天津市应用生物技术培育花卉，建立起快繁育苗综合技术，实现花卉生产的规模化。

一、草坪

1996年，市园林绿化所在大港油田含盐量0.56%～0.71%的土壤中，播种3500平方米高羊茅获得成功，使天津耐盐碱地区又增添一个优良新草种。1998年，天津市绿化工程处康新民、陈周羡等从引进的3种41个草坪草品种中筛选并应用推广13个品种，总结出在草坪卷生产中直播建植、铺设建植及养护管理的技术要点，制定出冷季型草坪建植与养护质量标准。2000年，市园林绿化所汤巧香、马小军等完成"天津市滨海地区草坪耐盐性鉴定及引种研究"，引进草种9个属46个种，经过严格筛选和耐盐性鉴定，筛选推出4个属12个品种，确定矮生型高羊茅和草坪型黑麦草为现阶段天津市的主栽品种。至2005年，天津共有草坪5578.32万平方米，比1990年增加4239.33万平方米。

二、树木

1996年，完成"天津市城市环境与园林树种规划的研究"，编写出《天津城市园林树种规划》。该规划是天津园林第一个树种规划，以引进成功树种为主，同时充分选用乡土树种，以保持天津树种特色。该规划考虑到天津的自然条件，规划树种以落叶树种为主，尽可能地选用常绿树种，形成冬季见绿的园林景观；积极发展可观花的藤本树种、木本地被，使天津城市树种多样化；树种规划分为骨干树、观赏树、特定用途树、值得推广树等4类。

三、花卉

（一）引种保质

1996年，市园林绿化所付新生、质慧等引进仙客来优良品种，并采用杂合基因型繁种，培育出有特色的新品种，从繁种技术改进、营养控制、筛选基质及选择播种期、提高苗期的营养及植保水平入手，提供生产壮苗的技术措施。2000年，该所付新生、姜世平等进行"仙客来彩云系列芳香化育种研究"，培育出彩云芳香化系列品种，获全国第三届花博会金奖。同年，姜世平、卢李红等研究仙客来良种优势保持技术，确定仙客来良种应具备的条件，找到仙客来良种退化原因，提出保持良种优势的技术措施，从而延长仙客来良种优势保持期。

1997年，市园林绿化所王和祥、么秀文引进木本地被植物40种（含变种），从中筛选出8种适应天津地区生长的木本地被植物。1999年，该所么秀文、王和祥等共引种鸢尾属植物40余个，通过耐盐性、耐荫性、耐寒性等抗逆性试验，筛选出优良品种10余种。

2005年，市园林绿化所姜世平等完成"名贵花卉新品种选育与开发技术的研究"。通过研究，筛选出适合天津地区生长的丽格海棠品种6个、鹤望兰品种3个、口红花2个等新品种。通过组织培养、营养繁殖等手段，取得丽格海棠和口红花的优质组培苗；采取叶插法生产的丽格海棠小苗，质量达到甚至超过进口小苗的标准；实现年产鹤望兰种苗2.5万粒（株）切花4万支，成品花0.5万盆的生产规模；年产口红花4.2万株；年产丽格海棠苗12万株。

（二）新品种繁育

1998年，市园林绿化所杨奎姝、张和琴等从国内外引进三季花藤本月季14种，彩色马蹄莲及大叶花烛16种，从中优选出9种，并提出在冬季适当喷涂植物保温剂能有效防止月季抽条。在此基础上，通过组培和常规繁殖方法相结合，培育试管苗2.4万株；在彩色马蹄莲继代培养基发明跟踪国内有关研究成果，完成"一步成苗"试验，可简化培养程序，降低成本；大叶花烛试管苗组培，利用液体培养基替代固体培养基进行，达到快繁种苗效果。同年，该所么秀文、张和琴等从国内外共引种藤本植物39种（含品种），并对引进的品种进行抗旱、抗寒、耐盐碱等抗逆性试验,推广藤本植物10种2.5万株,总结出优良的观花藤本植物的繁殖方法和养管要点。2001年,市园林局在西青区建成7200平方米的智能型全光温室,继而建立天津花卉生产示范中心,生产安祖花等花卉新品种。

2005年,市园林绿化所杨奎姝、刘亮梅等将组织培养生物技术与分株及扦插等常规繁殖技术相结合,建立一套快繁育苗综合技术,选用可适合多倍体萱草、黄天人菊、亚菊等新品种试管苗的繁殖和生根的通用培养基,使成本降低,为组培快繁技术的应用开辟一条经济、方便、可行的途径,使该成果快速进入市场。同年,由天津市农业生物技术研究中心和园林绿化所共同完成的市科委应用基础研究重点项目"应用生物技术培育花卉和番茄新品种",经过三年努力,成功地推出两个改变花色的仙客来新品种。这是在国内首次采用原位生殖系统导入法——花粉管通道法对仙客来进行遗传转化,成功地得到仙客来转化种子4400余粒,播种后,其中8株白色植株花瓣出现黄斑或略显黄色,个别花瓣变成黄色花瓣;3株白花植物的个别花瓣出现桃红色条带,甚至整个花朵完全变成桃红色。

(三)土壤肥料

2000年,市园林绿化所韩国英、肖广尧等完成"花苗圃生产性圃地土壤养分分析及改进技术的研究"。通过对市区绿地土壤肥力的调查分析和动态监测,进行施肥试验,找出一个合理施肥方法,以达到保持土壤肥力和充分利用现有土壤资源的目的。

2004年,市园林绿化所肖学斌等在对园林长效(缓释)复合肥的研究中,提出长效复合肥的配比原则,进行复合肥的成型造粒试验,确定工艺流程,并通过控释方法与材料的研究,获得以C包膜作为复合肥的包膜材料,缓释效果好,3个月释放95%,有利于植物营养的吸收,减少有效成分的流失。

第四节 园林动物技术

1991~2005年,园林动物的饲养和繁殖技术不断发展,科技设备有所改善,野生动物饲养管理更加规范。

1996年冬,将长颈鹿运抵海口市,创下陆路运输长颈鹿的最长距离纪录。2000~2002年,先后将食草动物、灵长类动物和禽类由圈养、笼养均改为散养,实现饲养方式上一次重大变革,饲养技术获得全面提高。

2000年,天津首次繁殖成功白颊长臂猿,并全人工育幼成活。2001年,首次进行人工孵化与育雏东方白鹳获得成功。天津的动物繁育技术取得较大进展。

一、饲料配制

1997年7月,天津动物园建成占地1660平方米的新配餐室。该室根据动物食性不同划分为:杂食动物饲料配制间、肉食动物饲料配制间、颗粒饲料制做间等功能区,同时配有冷冻、保鲜等专用库房,从而使动物饲料配方的制定、制做更加科学规范。

1999年,天津动物园李明君、陈会艳等经过两年的积极工作,完成配餐室效能监察,根据季节变化,分别制定出肉食动物、草食动物、杂食动物和鸟类的饲料配方,保证不同种类的动物营养合理化,使动物营养配餐在科学化、规范化方面向前迈进一步。

1999年,天津动物园陈会艳等制定出大熊猫专用窝头配方,改变大熊猫长期饲喂杂食动物窝头配方的传统方法,并针对大熊猫喜食甜食的特点,在配方中添加白糖,通过补充带壳鸡蛋提高配方中的蛋白含量,使大熊猫摄入的营养价值更加全面,适口性更好,采食量增加。

二、饲养

1995年12月，天津市濒危动物繁殖中心在天津动物园建立。这是全市第一个野生动物繁殖、实验及科普机构。其设有生化室、医疗室、电子监控室、孵化室以及杂食动物、肉食动物、灵长类动物、涉禽动物等动物的饲养区，为野生动物繁殖研究提供了有利条件。

1996年12月，天津动物园李宝忠、张泽殿、柴恭春等将一雌性2岁长颈鹿用加装帆布篷顶的货柜汽车，经过5天6夜运抵海南岛，行程3000多千米，在国内创下冬季陆路运输神经质动物——长颈鹿的最长距离纪录。2000年8月底，天津动物园草食动物大型散放区——三洽园建成并投入使用。该区总面积9.6万平方米，内设7个小区14座兽舍，及各种功能小亭26个。小区内散放混养草食动物共20种300多只，实现游客与动物在自然环境中的和谐相处，是野生动物展出模式由笼舍到场景式乃至浸入式转变的一种尝试，为游客从环境生态学、物种行为学和物种保存的层次上了解动物，增长知识，陶冶情操提供了条件。

2001年5月8日，天津动物园灵长类动物"猕猴"散放饲养区——灵峪建成并对游人开放。该园占地13320平方米，内有假山6座，最高峰9.6米，人工瀑布2处，园中心有一条由山石塑成的水渠把6座山相连。园内放养猕猴108只，游客能入园近距离无障碍参观猕猴。因灵峪模拟灵长类动物栖息建造，既可满足猕猴天性活泼的需要，又适应它们回归自然的生态需求。

2002年5月1日，天津动物园鸟类动物散放饲养区——鸟语林建成并对游客开放。鸟语林共占地6000平方米，内设有小山1座，小渠2条，涉禽湖、游禽湖共2处，亭台小榭栈道各1处，并利用原有绿化基础，整个区域用钢结构支撑大面积尼龙网罩，游客身临其境，仿佛置身于鸟语花香的动物世界。

三、繁殖

1994年3月，日本赠送天津的大型动物——长颈鹿，经天津动物园张泽殿、李斌等研究在天津首次繁殖成功。

1995年，天津动物园卢宝泉、张丽敏、王俊莉等与天津师范大学生物系合作，对小熊猫粪便中甾类激素变化与繁殖行为的关系进行研究。研究结果表明，雌性小熊猫的粪中的雌二醇和孕酮的含量变化在非繁殖期和繁殖期具明显的规律性，只有咩叫次数同这两种粪中甾类激素含量的变化相关显著，粪中甾类激素的峰值可用于推测小熊猫的发情和排卵日期，从繁殖生理上解决了排卵监测和妊娠诊断等重大问题，为类似其他珍稀动物在不伤害动物的情况下，安全、准确监测生殖期内分泌机制提供了科学方法，对笼养下繁殖濒危动物具有重要研究意义。

1996年3月6日，日本神户王子动物园赠送天津动物园的一对黑猩猩在先后多次怀孕流产后，首次繁殖一雄性小猩猩，因母猩猩身体原因，不能自然育仔。天津动物园高建国、张可晶、李博伟等在天津市儿童医院帮助下，进行人工育幼成功。不论黑猩猩的繁殖，还是人工育幼，在津均属首次。

2000年，天津动物园一对白颊长臂猿繁殖成功，并由高建国、皮云涛、王俊莉等进行全人工育幼成活。白颊长臂猿繁殖成功并全人工育幼成活，均属天津首次。

2001年，天津动物园张丽敏、孙肃反等首次对国家二级保护动物东方白鹳进行人工孵化与育雏研究，并取得成功。

四、医疗

1994年5月，天津动物园柴恭春、屈大水等采用化学安定剂——氯胺酮，麻醉东北虎，进行因外伤所致东北虎峰窝织炎治疗并取得成功。

1995年，该园王杰、柴恭春、屈大水等对园内水禽湖散养水禽夏秋季大群发病死亡原因进行专项研究，查明水禽湖散养水禽大群发病死亡的原因是肉毒梭菌毒素中毒所致。

第九篇

社会发展
科技

概　述

科学技术的进步促进天津经济社会发展日新月异。天津市地处环渤海的中心，特殊的地理环境与气候，使其较早成为中国北方重要的经济中心。天津作为直辖市，是中国北方最大的综合性港口城市，拥有世界等级最高的人工深水港——天津港。1991～2005年，随着天津市经济总量的增长，全市环境保护、水务、气象、灾害预防、水运、交通、航空、邮电、广播电视、计量标准与质量监督检验检疫等社会发展科技水平快速提升。科技与行业紧密结合，普遍采用新技术、新工艺、新设备，或引进消化吸收再创新，或研发改造或原始创新，科技创新能力逐步增强，科技实力有了质的飞跃。

天津环境保护、水务、气象和灾害预防科技进步有效地为全市生产、生活提供技术支撑。天津环境保护科技以气水臭固污染防治、农业环境污染防治、环境监测等为重点开展科学研究。1993年，天津引进先进的工艺技术设备等建成当时全国处理规模最大的城镇污水处理厂。十多项国家级科研成果使天津在污水处理技术上处于国内领先地位。1993年，国家科技部在天津挂牌成立全国唯一的国家给水排水技术研究中心及其试验基地。1995年，建成第一座生活垃圾卫生填埋处理场。2002年，成立国内唯一专门从事恶臭污染研究的国家环境保护恶臭污染控制重点实验室。2003年，建成第一座应用连续微滤膜过滤—反渗透膜过滤的污水再生水厂。同年，完成两项具有国际水平国家级的污水再生水示范工程。天津港针对油和化学污水、煤尘、煤雨水造成的污染及生活污水等进行治理。面对全市水资源短缺和水环境恶化的状况，重点开展城市水源、非常规水及其供需平衡和优化配置等水资源研究。水利工程建设中研究解决软基加固施工技术、新型护坡材料、水工材料快速检测等多项技术问题。农村水务开展节水灌溉和农田排涝等技术研究，以保证全市农业旱涝丰收。防洪减灾重点开展洪水预报、实时调度、风险图制作等研究，成果得到应用。天津气象科技十五年间发展很快。20世纪90年代天津气象观测基本上仍延用传统设备人工观测。之后，雷达探测发展为多普勒天气雷达，人工接收短波气象传真信号发展为以遥感为主的“3S”技术（GPS-全球定位系统、GIS-地理信息系统、RS-遥感技术），卫星云图接收和雷达探测等设备更新，全市基本实现气象探测自动化。同时，开展酸雨、大气边界层梯度及花粉浓度等特种观测。气象通讯技术的传输介质不断升级，由无线电高频到集团话路专线，再到卫星数据通信、宽带网传输，从局域网到广域网再到因特网。气象探测与通讯技术的提高，促进气象预报时效扩大，内容扩展，精度不断提高。天气预报产品多样，质量较稳定。海上大风、风暴潮出现的时间及潮位等海洋气象预报，是天津气象预报的重要特色。专项气象预报服务于全市的多种行业和部门。应用气候预测技术使预测和分析天津气候变化更加科学。天津在国内首先将全球定位系统引入地形变测量中。1992年，建成当时全国最大的GPS地震监测网——“华北地形变监测网”。同期，应用大地形变测量技术监测市内地面沉降和地铁、大型工程等施工的地形变。至2005年，防震监测技术向网络化、自动化、数字化迈进，其监测网点已覆盖全市。

天津水运工程、铁路和城市轨道交通及航空科技高速发展。天津港港口吞吐量以每年平均17.8%的速度递增，2005年超过2.4亿吨/年；集装箱吞吐量为480.1万标准箱。航道设计中边坡坡度优化取得突破性进展，建成15万吨级航道。实施老码头改造，加大航道疏浚力度，创新回淤治理方法，创造出在淤泥质海滩建设深水港的奇迹。运用创新软基加固技术，低成本高速度地扩展港区面积。板桩码头结构有较大突破。引进专业生产、水文测验、测绘工程和地质勘察等设备，使天津港装备始终保持国内领先水平。同时，研制重型、机械化施工设备，为水运工程建筑物向“大型、深水”发展提供保障。2000年起以“适航水深应用”技术为核心，开发水深动态维护保养新模式。2000年后，挖泥船的设计与建造、疏浚仪表和挖泥机具的研制，以及老旧挖泥船改造等均取得重大进展。港口现代化、信息化亦排在全国前列。伴随中国铁路多次提速,建设标准不断提高,天津在既有铁路提速改造、重载铁路、客运专线和城市轨道交通勘察设计、施工手段与技术水平得到前所未有的大发展。勘察测绘设计人员攻克多项关键技术难题,在国家重大铁路项目中,特别是长大艰险隧道、新特型桥梁、高等级铁路施工中均有重大技术突破,成绩斐然。铁路和城市轨道交通相继采用数字化测绘、3S技术、航测技术、测绘新仪器、综合勘探方法等勘察设计手段。破解在路基、桥涵、通信、信号、接触网设计等方面关键技术难题,开创客运专线无碴轨道设计和一次铺设跨区间无缝线路之先河。1997年,首次采用掘进机法(TBM)施工,开创中国长大铁路隧道施工划时代的局面。2000年,技术创新解决集深基、群桩、高墩、大跨、长联于一体的特大桥施工难题。2001~2004年,津滨轻轨工程抗震分析与减震降噪技术、松软土地基轻轨超长高架桥设计、施工控制技术研究取得重大进展。2002年,天津地铁工程突破标准化设计模式。天津航空不断更新飞行保障系统和服务设施等设备,不断改进和提升民航的安全运营和保障服务能力。同时,随着空中交通流量的持续增加,民航机务维修、空中交通管理、机场通信导航、航空经济与运输、航空安全管理等方面科学技术研究取得较大进步。"飞行品质监控和飞行图形仿真系统"与"民航发动机可靠性研究"成绩显著。2002年,建立国内首个省部级"民航地面特种设备研究基地"。2003年,建立"航空运输经济与管理科学研究基地"。2005年,在津成立"民航机务维修工程研究基地"。

天津邮电和广播电视科技处于快速发展期。天津邮政由机械化向电子化发展,信件、报刊、特快专递、金融、集邮等计算机网络相继建成使用。电话应用技术引进与创新并举,电讯技术有长足进步。1993年天津电话网实现程控化;1997年,国内首创"增强型双局号平稳过渡法",在国内多地电话号码升位中发挥重要作用。电报被不断扩大的电话功能所取代,汉字显示寻呼机(BP机)曾风靡一时,1998年后,逐渐被手机取代,移动电话迅速普及。2001年天津建设通用无线分组(GPRS)网络,年底关闭模拟移动通信,向数字移动通信转化。2003年,建成宽带城域网,使天津信息基础设施建设实现跨越式发展。2004年,国内首创基于ITIL的电信运维管理平台。20世纪90年代初期以立体声直播为主。随后,逐步引进高科技、高质量的技术设备;大量采用计算机控制、网络、数字存储等新技术,实现由模拟向数字化转轨。在节目制作、播出,传输、发射等方面质量和现代化程度得以提高。1996年,开始接收卫星信号转播节目。1998年,实现全数字化播出。2003年,建成天津人民广播电台互联网广播系统。2004年,电视卫星节目完成从KU波段转到C波段播出的整体平移。2005年,天津市级广播电视系统基本实现数字化播出。年底,具备数字高清节目的制作能力,形成以有线、无线传输为主要手段,涉及光缆、微波、卫星等多项传输技术的传输体系发射技术实现由模拟向数字的转变;同时,全市实施有线电视数字化。

天津计量标准与质量监督检验检疫的整体科技水平不断提升。1991年后,天津为满足市场经济发展需要,加快筹建新的最高计量标准装置,启动实施代码条码技术。1997年,全面快速推进标准化工作,出台《天津市地方标准管理办法》,制订数百项地方标准。同时,以滨海新区开发开放为契机,把具有自主知识产权和优势产业的技术标准上升为国际标准、国家标准。截至2005年年底,天津在十大类计量领域建立最高社会公用计量标准231项,标准化技术上走在全国前列。1991~2005年,天津产品质量检测技术是引进与自主创新相结合,批量引进仪器设备,同时自主创新研制出各种用于产品检验的仪器、仪表、机具、装置等,开发出检验管理和鉴定的系统软件等。在危险品检测、致病菌检测基因芯片研制以及转基因研究等尖端科技方面有创新。大量产品质量标准的制定,检验方法的创新,为提高产品质量提供技术保证。

第一章　环境保护

1991～2005年，天津随着经济总量的快速提升和城市化水平的提高，环境保护工作更加需要依靠科技进步增强自主创新能力。天津市环保科技紧密围绕"创建国家环境保护模范城市"和"创建生态城市"等重点环保工作，组织开展气水臭固污染防治、农业环境污染防治、环境监测等科学研究。1993年，天津成立全国唯一的国家给水排水技术研究中心及其试验基地，成为城镇污水处理行业科学研究与工程实践的核心与前沿。同年，国内首个地方恶臭标准《天津市恶臭污染排放标准》正式颁布实施。2002年，依托于天津市环境保护科学研究院建设的国内唯一专门从事恶臭污染研究的国家环境保护恶臭污染控制重点实验室正式挂牌成立。2004年天津建立由多要素、多参数相结合的天津市环境监测动态信息库。

20世纪90年代前，天津建成全国第一座规模最大、配套齐全的26万吨/日纪庄子污水处理厂。1993年，引进法国缺氧/好氧工艺、计算机监控系统和沼气发电设备及技术，建成当时全国处理规模最大40万吨/日的东郊污水处理厂。在两厂建设和运行中，市政工程局又相继承担国家及天津市"八五"、"九五"科技攻关课题：厌氧/好氧、厌氧/缺氧/好氧、序批式活性污泥法、污水生物除磷脱氮工艺、污泥中温消化技术、污泥高温堆肥、污水再生利用等10多项国家级攻关科研成果，从而奠定天津在全国污水处理技术上的领先地位。1995年天津市建立第一座生活垃圾处理场—双口生活垃圾卫生填埋场，垃圾渗滤液采用上向流污泥厌氧床和序批式活性污泥法的变法连续—间歇复合新技术。2003年，先后完成两项具有国际水平的国家级污水再生水示范工程。十五年间，天津港建成生活污水处理厂，油、化学污水处理中心，以及对煤雨水造成的污染进行治理等。煤尘治理主要通过防风网、人工造雪等方法控制煤尘污染。采用防污屏解决疏浚中的环保问题，同时为解决草海污染内源问题对国内湖泊环保疏浚进行研究，疏挖区草海水质得到明显改观。

第一节　环境监测与防治

1991～2005年，天津在环境保护方面对大气环境、水环境、恶臭、噪音污染监测与防治控制取得较好进展。在农业环境污染治理方面，针对农田土壤、蔬菜镉及其他元素、重金属、有机污染物、氮素等污染及控制开展研究，同时，研究提出湿地生态保护与恢复重建的途径与方法。

一、大气环境监测与保护

2000年，天津市环境监测中心（以下简称"市监测中心"）和天津市气象科学研究所秦保平、边海、邵莹、王长友等完成"天津市空气污染预报研究"。该项目研究城市空气污染状况，开展空气污染预报的探索，通过对历年空气污染监测数据和相应气象条件的分析，建立城市空气污染数值预报和统计预报模式，为全国开展空气污染预报业务提供可借鉴的模式。该项目获2001年度天津市科技进步二等奖。

同年，市监测中心孙韧、刘伟、王长友等完成"空气质量预报方法在滨海地区的应用研究"。该项目通过对天津滨海地区多年空气污染源状况、污染气象条件、空气质量监测数据的收集与分析，掌握滨海地区空气污染特征，即以二氧化硫、可吸入颗粒物为代表的煤烟型污染，采暖期的空气污染明显重于非采暖期。运用数理统计方法将多种数据相互间规律性关系实施定量表征，构建可模拟污染物时空分布规律空气污染统计预报方程，并应用于空气质量的预报，提高空气预报时效和预报精度。

2003年，市监测中心孙韧、刘伟等完成“天津市臭氧污染水平、防治对策”研究，摸清全市近地层臭氧的污染现状、时空污染特征及分布规律。2005年，该中心袁倩、刘伟等在“天津市空气污染风险评估预警预报系统研究”中，重点研究污染源类别对空气质量贡献比例及建立污染源解析模型，完善空气污染预警预报技术。

2004年，市监测中心秦保平，南开大学朱坦等在“大气颗粒物源解析及环境监测信息管理系统”研究中，应用“二重源解析”技术，定量计算出1996～2000年总悬浮颗粒物和可吸入颗粒物中各类污染源的贡献率和分担率，指出空气污染的重点治理区域，并提出以控制城市扬尘、煤烟尘、机动车尾气尘为主的空气污染防治措施。首次建立由多要素、多参数相结合的天津市环境监测动态信息库，实现全市环境监测数据共享及动态管理。该项目获2004年度天津市科技进步二等奖。

二、水环境监测与保护

1997～2000年，市监测中心和北京大学殷红、王迎等完成“天津市养鱼水质监控系统的研究”。为摸清污水养殖对水生生态系统带来的污染和影响，该项目对淡水养殖的水质进行研究，指出鱼外周血微核率报警浓度，污养鱼塘特征水质指标的含量范围及不同月份的变化趋势，筛选和确定污水鱼塘水质监控指标和鱼体监控指标，建立监控体系和警情报告制度，从技术和管理上对污染加以控制，从而保护淡水养殖，生态健康和公众食用水产品的安全性。

2002年，市监测中心王德龙、张玉惠等完成“水质生化需氧量测定微生物传感器快速测定法”研究。该项目为快速、准确测定生化需氧量，及时反映水体水质状况，就生化需氧量这一反映水体状况的重要监测指标进行研究，制定水质生化需氧量微生物传感器快速测定方法，该方法可以满足对环境监测快速、准确的需要，及时对地表水，生活污水和工业废水排放进行监控，尤其对环境污染事故的污染程度能及时报告检测结果。该项目2002年经国家环保总局认可，其所制订的标准于2002年7月1日起实施，同时被纳入环境科学出版社出版的《水和废水监测分析方法》第四版和增补版中，被广泛应用。

同年，市监测中心曹喆、梅鹏蔚等完成国家环保总局项目“天津市湿地生态环境现状及演变研究”。该项目采用遥感、地理信息系统、全球定位系统技术对天津市湿地进行全面调研，通过对天津近一个世纪以来的湿地演变轨迹研究发现：天然湿地不断减少，人工湿地逐渐增多，湿地减少是自然因素与人为因素共同作用的结果，城市拓展、石油开发、工农业发展占用、水污染等对湿地环境构成较大威胁，湿地的许多生态功能已经消失，研究提出湿地保护与恢复重建的途径与方法。

是年，市监测中心秦保平、张震与南开大学、气象研究所协作完成“引滦输水工程流域生态环境状况及污染防治对策研究”。该项目对引滦输水工程起点——隧洞出口至终点共234千米输水河道、水库的水生生态环境进行调查，并对引滦输水工程流域的水体、底质、水生生物进行系统研究，定量提出于桥水库营养盐的来源和比例，同时应用遥感技术对引滦上游及于桥水库周边土地利用状况进行定量分析，科学地评价于桥水库的富营养化水平，建立于桥水库径流模型，为防治引滦输水工程流域水污染提供技术支持。

2003年，为制订饮用水的污染防治措施和确保水源安全，市监测中心秦保平、张震等开展“天津市于桥水库饮用水安全研究”。该项目以于桥水库为中心，对汇入水库的河流、地表径流、地下水、水库底泥释放等污染负荷进行调研，分析水质、底质变化趋势，利用污染负荷评估模型对各类污染贡献率进行计算，提出各类污染源的防治和消减措施，针对流域管理提出一套完整的管理方案，提供技术支持。

2004年，为深入了解市区景观河道水生生态环境质量，市监测中心孙韧等在“城市景观河道水生生态环境的维护与管理”研究中，就降雨径流对河道的影响进行实际监测，研究表明，城市不同功能区地表径流的污染状况随降雨时长、季节更替呈现显著动态变化，降雨径流强烈的冲刷机制将累积在地面的各种污染物带入河流，造成景观河道营养盐污染严重，而建立植被缓冲带修复、水资源再生、雨水综合利用与控制等工程可改善景观河道的生态环境。

三、恶臭监测与控制

1990年，天津市环境保护科学研究院（以下简称“天津环科院”）作为主要参加单位编制《国家恶臭污染物排放标准》，1993年8月标准正式颁布实施。

1992年，天津环科院组织编制全国14个省市、自治区恶臭污染状况及污染源的调查汇总报告。对国内的恶臭污染现状和污染特征进行全面掌握，为中国恶臭污染管理政策、法规标准的制订提供科学依据和技术支持。

1993年3月20日由天津环科院编制的国内首个地方恶臭标准—《天津市恶臭污染排放标准》正式颁布实施。1995年天津环科院对原有的标准进行修订并于1995年颁布，1996年1月1日实施。该项目获1996年度天津市科技进步标准化成果二等奖。

1999年，天津环科院组建国家环境保护恶臭污染控制重点实验室（以下简称“恶臭控制实验室”）。2002年7月通过原国家环保总局验收，9月正式成立。该室是国内唯一专门从事恶臭污染研究的实验室，为国内各级环境管理部门进行恶臭污染环境治理提供决策的知识基础和科学依据，也为企业和公众提供最佳恶臭防治和控制技术及咨询服务等。

2002年，恶臭控制实验室开发研制恶臭污染嗅觉测定的三点比较式臭袋法的配套仪器设备，使恶臭污染的嗅觉测试方法更加规范、科学，有利地推动恶臭污染测试技术的发展。2002～2005年该实验室先后在江苏、浙江、广东、河北、北京、上海等省市推广恶臭污染控制标准及分析测试方法，促进国内恶臭污染防治的发展。这期间该实验室通过恶臭污染测试技术研究，对全国40余家企业恶臭工艺废气及居住环境空气质量进行测试、评价，为各地环境管理部门提供科学依据。

2003年，恶臭控制实验室开发研制出面源采样器的实用技术与方法，设计开发臭氧氧化、固体吸附、生物滴滤等多台套脱臭设备，并通过现场调试与运营，解决部分企业存在的恶臭污染问题。

2004年，恶臭控制实验室从澳大利亚引进国内第一套动态嗅觉计。该嗅觉计是欧美普遍采用的恶臭嗅觉测试仪器，与所用的三点比较式臭袋法相比可进行气体自动稀释，提高配气过程的精度与准确度，实现嗅觉测试的自动化、智能化。

四、噪声监测与控制

1999年，市监测中心陈光华、陈向党等完成“环境噪声监测优化布点研究”。该项目就天津市环境噪声达标区监测中存在的监测网格偏多、监测工作量过大等问题进行探讨，对1991～1996年环境噪声“达标区”监测数据进行分析，提出在区域面积小于10平方千米情况下，区域环境噪声监测网格数调整至不少于30个，区域环境声级所反映的环境噪声时空分布规律及声源构成特性基本不变，布点的测量误差一般不大于1分贝（A），且形状越规整误差越趋于减小，进而优化区域环境噪声监测点位。

2004年，天津港对5艘同型号拖轮进行噪声污染治理。对拖轮机舱内噪声源的分布特点和轮机工活动范围进行分析，采用隔离噪声的技术措施对仪表台及轮机工操作位进行封闭，建立一个隔阻声源的集中控制室。封闭材料选用两层钢板，钢板间距1.2厘米，中间装入超细玻璃绵，吸声系数为1.9。治理前拖轮机舱工作操作位的Leq在100分贝以上，最高达到106分贝，超过卫生标准20分贝之多治理后的隔声集中控制室，噪声为72～76分贝，达到《工业企业噪声设计控制范围》的要求。

五、农业环境监测与防治

1994～1998年，市监测中心沈伟然、殷红等完成“天津市近郊农田镉污染及控制对策研究”，该项目根据农田土壤、蔬菜镉污染较严重的状况，对天津市近郊农田土壤镉的临界含量以及土壤、蔬菜、生态系统中镉及其他元素污染的相关关系进行研究，提出严格控制污泥农业利用，合理规划使用污泥，控制磷肥的使用和北塘排污河铜、锌污染,建立完善的输水系统等措施。

1998~2001年,市监测中心殷红、王迎等完成“天津市农业环境污染影响及对策研究”。该项目针对天津市农业环境中重金属、有机污染物及氮素等主要环境污染因子的污染状况,全面分析天津市农业环境污染影响因素,研究有机污染在土壤及农产品中的残留状况,确定以农药和多环芳烃为代表的农业有机污染类型。

2001年,市监测中心和北京大学秦保平、陶澍、刘伟、张枝涣等完成“天津市近郊农业有机污染危害及其治理对策研究”。该项目通过筛选天津农业生态环境介质,较系统地研究土壤、植物、河流水质及沉积物、养殖鱼塘生态系统、大气降尘等多介质中多环芳烃、有机氯农药、滴滴涕的污染状况与分布特征,模拟1952~2020年间天津地区农业有机污染物的迁移、分布动态变化,针对天津市农业环境有机物污染存在的突出问题,提出改善农业环境的管理方法和技术措施。

第二节 城市污水及垃圾处理

1991~2005年,天津陆续设计建成东郊、开发区、咸阳路、北仓污水处理厂并完成纪庄子污水处理厂的改扩建工程。市政工程局取得国家及天津市“八五”“九五”等10多项污水污泥处理工艺技术国家级攻关科研成果,处理技术的集成,带动处理关键设备、除臭技术的开发,污泥带式压滤机、旋转式滗水器等在全国占有一定市场份额。先后完成两项具有国际水平的国家级污水再生水示范工程,在国内首次大规模将再生水用于住宅区居民冲厕杂用及工业高端用水。污水处理厂施工方面,相继研究应用曝气池水工大模板混凝土浇注工艺、预应力绕丝等施工技术,均系国内首创。1995年,天津建立第一座生活垃圾处理场—双口生活垃圾卫生填埋场,垃圾渗滤液采用先进的复合新技术。

一、污水

1992年,经国家科委批准,天津依托中国市政工程华北设计研究院(以下简称“华北设计院”)建立国家给水排水工程技术研究中心。纪庄子污水处理厂和天津市污水处理研究所(以下简称“市污水所”)成为全国唯一的国家给水排水工程技术研究中心试验基地。同年,为解决城市工业高有机浓度废水的预处理,市污水所赵丽君、候景树、马文杰等完成“悬浮载体曝气工艺的生产应用”研究,在曝气池中投加焦炭颗粒,利用三相流化床原理,有效提高污泥负荷,从而提高废水中污染物的去除效率。在天津中药六厂、天津中美史克制药有限公司废水处理中应用。该项目获1993年度天津市科技进步二等奖。

1993年,天津又一座40万吨/日的大型污水处理厂——东郊污水处理厂建成投入运行,是天津市第一次利用国外政府贷款,解决天津市水环境和渤海湾污染的一项重要工程。该厂采用传统活性污泥法,对部分污水进行生物脱氮处理,用污泥进行厌氧消化。引进先进优质设备,工艺与设备均位于国内先进行列。天津市市政工程设计研究院(以下简称“市政设计院”)冯生华、周雹等在东郊污水处理厂设计中,开发出前置缺氧脱氮工艺、沼气发电与市电并网等多项新技术,获1997年度天津市科技进步二等奖。

1999年,市政设计院张大群、王秀朵等在“城市中小型高效、简易污水处理厂工艺及装备的研究”中,采用的序批式活性污泥法(SBR)的变法,连续-间歇复合新技术(DAT-IAT),使流程简化,造价大幅降低,在开发区污水处理厂应用。该成果对国内中小城镇的污水处理厂建设很有意义,该项目获2000年度天津市科技进步二等奖。同时“连续间歇曝气序批式活性污泥污水处理方法”在全国受到极大关注。2002年,DAT-IAT

技术推广到抚顺市、本溪市的污水处理厂。

2000年，华北设计院阚薇莉、刘龙志等设计的纪庄子污水处理厂实施改扩建工程。日处理规模由26万吨/日扩建至54万吨/日。扩建后污水处理工艺由传统活性污泥法改为部分采用厌氧/好氧生物处理工艺，部分采用厌氧/缺氧/好氧工艺。2004年年底，新建系统试运行达标。

2005年，天津建成咸阳路污水处理厂，日处理能力45万吨。市政设计院郭淑琴、卢心虹、胡大卫、姚念民等在国内大型污水厂设计中首次采用优化A/O生物除磷、硝化脱氮、化学法降解尾水余磷等新工艺，以改进型的初沉池，能量分布器、螺旋刮刀等新设备提高沉淀出泥效果。采用优化多座旋流沉砂池工艺布局，将六座沉砂池巧妙地布置成梅花型解决配水不均匀问题。同时，成功引进周进周出沉淀池技术，该项目获2005年度天津市优秀设计一等奖。

二、污泥

1991～1995年，由华北设计院、市污水所、同济大学李成江、赵丽君、高廷耀等完成国家“八五”科技攻关项目“城市污水污泥处理技术”研究，对提高污泥消化效率、污泥高温堆肥、污泥热能综合利用与回收和沼气脱硫技术进行研究。所提出的高温酸化—中温甲烷化两相厌氧消化工艺，可解决生产性厌氧消化池运行中的技术难点；提出的气提筒式沼气搅拌器和沼气射流搅拌两种低能耗搅拌技术国内均属首次使用；通过将沼气用于发电、动力鼓风机和锅炉的研究，提出可靠的技术参数，使热能利用率达到75%以上；针对依托工程干法脱硫问题，增加脱硫工序，提高脱硫剂硫容，降低脱硫中硫化氢浓度。

1992年，市污水所和农业部环保科学标准研究所赵丽君、赵子定等在“城市污泥高温堆肥及园林绿地应用技术的研究”中，全面研究污泥堆肥产品的质量和肥效，对堆肥场环境影响进行初步评价，给出污泥高温堆肥的工艺路线和技术参数，特别是在污泥堆肥极限含水率的控制及不投加外加剂直接堆肥工艺等关键技术上有所突破。

1992年，市监测中心沈伟然、殷红、张文具等完成国家“八五”科技攻关环保项目“城市污水污泥土地处理技术研究”。该项目就天津市两大污水处理厂产生的大量污泥用于农业造成污染的问题进行研究，对1992～1995年污泥林地中的重金属负荷、氮负荷、卫生学指标、地下水影响、树木生长等进行综合性研究，确定处理限制性设计参数，提出城市污水污泥的土地处理技术工程设计方法，并在天津开发区盐碱地城市绿化防护林建立3000平方米的污泥林地处理应用工程，从而确定天津市污泥林地处理的安全使用量。该项目获1998年度天津市科技进步二等奖。

1995年，市污水所李强、侯景树等对生物肥料精加工技术进行研究，以城市污水处理厂脱水污泥堆肥后的散装污泥肥料为原料，精加工成颗粒产品，加工工艺简单可靠，密实度适中，肥份缓释、长效，并具有一定的溶散性。

1996年，华北设计院、市污水所赵丽君、李成江等在国内首次研究污泥高效厌氧消化技术、污泥两相厌氧消化技术、污泥生物能综合利用技术、利用城市污泥生产有机复合肥及颗粒肥料等，成果用于深圳污泥生产有机复合肥示范工程，形成商品化。在青岛海泊河污水处理厂应用污泥生物能综合利用技术，取得良好的社会、环境、经济效益。

2000年，天津水工业工程设备有限公司（以下简称“天津水工业公司”）、天津珀金斯配套有限公司、天津开发区污水处理厂赵丽君、项佩琳、石风林等共同完成“中小型高效污水处理及污泥后处理工艺及设备”项目研究，在全国首次利用自主研制的TBP—WN—B型污泥处理机，采用高性能的活性石灰稳定快速干燥处置技术，建立10吨/日干泥生产线。示范工程表明，经过快速干燥的污泥，可用于工程用土、发电厂原料掺合料以及垃圾填埋场覆盖土。

三、设备

20世纪90年代，纪庄子污水处理厂和市政机械厂朱雁伯、石凤林、邓伯燎等研制出与国外同类压滤机同等水平的国产化污泥带式压滤机。由于在价格上与进口脱水机相比有较大优越性，及重大推广价值，遂形成系列产品，销售全国。

1998年，天津水工业公司、市政设计院、华北设计院张大群、张悦、金宏、张文利、耿耀海等完成“城市污水处理技术和关键设备的开发”。该项目将科研、设计制造、产品销售、示范工程融为一体攻关的成套性研究开发方式，为环保产业的跨越式发展开创新途径。所研制开发的七项产品，结构新颖、实用性强、效率高、能耗低。其中大流量旋转式滗水器、后置步进式阶梯格栅、驱动与清污一体机构的爬行格栅、蓄能式液压污水速闭闸门四种产品为国内首创。

2001年，天津市百阳环保设备有限责任公司研发的旋转式滗水器，荣获第二届太平洋经济合作理事会国际贸易投资博览会金奖。2002年，国家科技部批准为“国家科技成果重点推广计划”项目，为国内上百家大型SBR工艺污水处理厂配套使用。

四、除臭

1996年，市污水所、市政设计院在辽河油田污水处理厂应用土壤脱臭技术，有效地解决该厂主要构筑物的异味。

2000年，天津水工业公司、天津康诺科技实业有限公司赵丽君、辛毅等在进行污水处理厂除臭的生产性研究中，引进高能离子空气净化技术，有效地清除空气中的细菌、可吸入颗粒物、硫化氢、有机污染物等有害物质。试验表明，高能离子空气净化系统不但除臭效果好，且简便灵活，可按需开停。尤其是运行成本低廉、节能，每净化一个立方米臭气仅耗电0.01千瓦时。2002年，在天津南丰路雨水泵站工程中，首次采用高能离子除臭技术及设备。2003年，市政设计院在长江三峡水环境保护项目—湖北省宜昌市夷陵区污水处理厂工程设计中，应用此项技术，对硫化氢、甲烷、氨的去除率高达81.5%~100%，取得显著的环境效益。

2003年，天津市西南角雨污水泵站工程，是全市第一座采用生物除臭技术及设备的城市雨水泵站，有效解决排水泵站散发恶臭气体污染周边环境问题。

五、施工

1991年，天津第二市政公路工程有限公司赵子良、李恩成、杨立生等引进消化吸收钢膜施工技术，并结合实际自行加工制造，形成独特的SZ系列模板工艺。首次应用于东郊污水处理厂大型曝气池施工建设中。实践证明：该项技术实用可靠、加快进度、保证质量。

同年，天津第三市政公路工程有限公司在国内首次将污泥消化池滑模施工技术和无粘结后张预应力钢筋砼工艺应用于青岛海泊河污水处理厂建设。1995年后，该公司相继研究应用导流墙施工安装工艺、曝气池水工大模板浇注工艺、大型构筑物预应力绕丝技术、地下工程大体积抗渗混凝土整体浇注技术，这些工艺技术均属国内首创。

六、污水再生水

1993年，天津市环保所、天津大学环境工程研究所、天津市纪庄子污水处理厂于锡忱、安鼎年、唐鸿德、赵丽君、朱肇源等完成国家“七五”科技攻关项目“城市污水资源化”，以硝化和反硝化技术为核心，解决污水脱磷脱氮技术；应用高效脱色去浊、消毒的过滤深度净化工艺；以回用于工业为主要目标的水回用技术，以及回用于市政杂用等5项成套污水处理及回用技术；建成污水回用3项示范工程。

1995年，市政工程局陈福明、市污水所赵丽君等完成国家“八五”科技攻关项目“城市污水回用于工业工艺用水成套技术”研究，采用常规活性污泥法与生物膜相结合的A/O（缺氧/好氧）强化工艺，在低温低碳氮比的条件下，氨氮平均去除90%，总氮去除70%以上；利用河道作为回用水的输配水渠道的开放循环研究，为污水回用提供可行途径；课题还对纤维球过滤技术、竖向逆流气浮池和生物接触滤池复合深度工艺、聚砜中空超滤膜技术、TK-1活性炭下向流固定床补充处理、陶粒固定床好氧生物膜等速过滤技术等进行研究。开发出新型璜酸盐阻垢分散剂，首次选用气钠型离子交换树脂对再生水软化等，取得实用性参数和经验。课题还完成污水回用于工业工艺用水的效益评估及数据库、图文库等；某些成果已用于天津市乙烯工程污水回用。

1999年，市政设计院、天津水工业公司针对天津开发区污水二级处理的出水中高盐量的特点，提出污水反渗透脱盐这一关键深度处理工艺方案。2003年，由华北设计院设计，天津建成第一座应用连续微滤膜过滤—反渗透膜过滤（CMF—RO）即双膜工艺的开发区污水再生水厂，设计能力3.0万吨/日，同时铺设枝状输配水管网28千米，分质处理的再生水回用目标是景观用水和工业高端用水。2004年，该项目被国家建设部确定为全国再生水示范工程。

1999～2001年，天津制定《天津市中心城区再生水资源利用规划》，并申请国家再生水示范工程项目——建设纪庄子再生水厂。规划明确指出：天津市再生水主要服务方向为工业冷却水、景观水体用水、生活杂用水、农业用水等。2004年，天津市市政工程局规划处、中水公司与南开大学等，针对再生水处理工艺的关键技术进行实验研究。以卫国道中水处理站为实验基地，进行10个流程，8个氮、磷等水质分析指标的测试，包括引入紫外吸光度UV254作为一项综合性水质指标，从而完成“天津市再生水资源利用方案的修正稿”。

华北设计院李金河、焦兆明等设计，2003年建成投产的纪庄子污水回用工程，是国内规模最大、工艺最先进的工程，是以纪庄子污水处理厂二级出水为水源，建成的日处理能力5万吨的再生水厂。该厂引进法国连续微滤（CMF）作为核心设备，处理工艺采用混凝—沉淀—CMF—臭氧，所产之水回用于梅江居住区内公建和居民冲厕、园林绿化、道路喷洒、景观水体补充和周边工业区循环冷却锅炉补充水等，梅江成为全国首次将再生水大规模回用的居民住宅区。

2004年，天津水工业公司和市政设计院张大群等编制完成国家污水再生利用系列标准之一《城市污水再生水回用于工业用水标准》，为污水资源化的实施提供设计依据。

七、城市生活垃圾

2001年，市政设计院张大群、金宏、王立彤等完成天津首座生活垃圾填埋场的工程设计，建成的2700吨/日第一座生活垃圾处理场—双口生活垃圾卫生填埋场，总库容量达850万立方米，属当时亚洲最大规模，300吨/日垃圾渗滤液，采用上向流污泥厌氧床（UASB）和序批式活性污泥法（SBR）的变法连续—间歇（DAT-IAT）复合新技术处理。

第三节　港口污染治理

1991～2005年，天津港建成生活污水处理厂和油、化学污水处理中心。对煤雨水造成的污染进行治理，煤尘治理主要通过防风网、人工造雪等方法控制。采用防污屏解决疏浚环保问题，同时研究国内湖泊环保疏浚解决草海污染内源问题。

一、港口污水

1992年，天津港引进全部设施，建成处理能力2000吨的生活污水处理厂并投入运行。该厂采用生物氧化法，全程自动控制，出水指标全部达标。1998年，天津港建成南疆处理能力为150吨/小时的污水处理中心，主要处理南疆到港油轮的船舶压舱水和油库区作业过程中发生的含油废水。2000年，天津港建成南疆处理能力为600立方米/天的生活污水处理中心。2001年，南疆污水处理中心又分别设立6个分散的生活污水处理设施点，处理工艺选用序批式活性污泥法。设施投入使用后，南疆港区的污水治理率达到100%，全部达标排放。

2001年,天津港建成化学污水处理设施。该设施污水处理能力为70吨/小时,工艺采用序批式活性污泥法。

同年,南疆港为治理煤雨水造成的港区水体污染,配套建成南疆煤雨水处理能力为100吨/小时的处理中心。

2003年,天津港港口医院建设污水处理设施,采用厌氧生物污水处理技术,实际处理能力达到100吨/天。

二、煤尘治理

（一）防风网

1997年,天津港和交通部天津水运工程科学研究所合作进行防风网控制煤尘污染的研究,结合天津港的自然环境条件,通过降低风速、风能,最大限度地损失来流风的动能,避免其明显涡流,减小风的湍流度从而减少起尘。1999年,通过数次风洞试验成功研制出用于港区内煤炭堆场区适用的防风网,并建成于天津港煤炭堆场,经塘沽环保局监测站监测试验证明其防风率达到80%,具有明显的抑尘效果,在国内尚属首例。2002年,该所张光玉等应用空气动力学原理,研究用防风网技术,防护港口的煤炭粉尘,并将其应用于工程设计。

（二）苫盖网

2004年,天津港对各煤炭、矿石作业区内的堆场采用专业的苫盖网进行苫盖,以加强对港区煤炭、矿石粉尘污染的控制。苫盖网采用透水、透气的网状材料,有一定的耐拉强度,可保证苫盖的整体景观效果,同时又有利于煤炭货垛的通风及散热。

（三）覆盖剂

2005年,为解决港区内煤垛静态扬尘问题,天津港煤码头公司试用德国抑尘剂PS-07(统称覆盖剂)。经试验最终选用1:400配比,其防尘效果符合要求,且添加覆盖剂的煤仍能正常使用。其后,覆盖剂的使用实行标准化,煤垛扬尘得以控制,同时节省大量喷淋用水。

（四）人工造雪

焦炭码头公司于2004和2005年分别购置2台造雪机,运用洒雪的方法来抑制煤炭起尘。在冬季洒雪过程中,可以净化空气中的扬尘;雪覆盖在煤炭表面上,较长期存放可形成薄壳,起到苫盖抑尘作用。通过洒雪喷淋设备的实际应用,抑尘效果显著,还能弥补港区内冬季采用其他抑尘、除尘技术的缺陷。

（五）冬季喷淋

2004年,第二港埠公司煤炭堆场喷淋防尘设施建成并投入使用。该喷淋防尘设施由泵房、蓄水池、地下管网和货场喷洒点组成,共埋设地下管道1500米,在该货场内均匀分布15个喷洒点,共安装20部喷枪。喷淋采用PLC程控技术自动控制,可实现24小时全货场循环或定点、定时自动喷洒。

三、环保疏浚

为减小疏浚工程对环境的影响,防污屏装置有效地将施工水域同外界隔离开来,从而防止混浊水的扩散,保护周围水域生态环境免遭破坏。1996年起,中交天津航道局有限公司(以下简称"天航局")开始对防污屏进行研究,其结构为上部分为浮体,中间部分为设加强带的帘布,下部分为配重,用锚定位。2000年秦秀华、王立强等首次将防污屏应用于青岛李村河疏浚工程中,防污屏布设于吹填工程围堰泄水口处,经现场跟踪检测,三类海水水域悬浮物人为增加量为0～12.4毫克/升,四类海水水域悬浮物人为增加量为1.4～27毫克/升。实践证明防污屏装置发挥其应有的作用和功能,有效地防止污泥扩散。该成果相继在秦皇岛港西港区集装箱码头改造疏浚工程、大连大窑湾疏浚工程应用。

1997年,天津航道勘察设计研究院承担国内首例湖泊环保疏浚示范工程的设计—"滇池草海污染底泥疏挖处置工程设计"。该工程是中国"三湖污染治理"重点项目之一,目的是清除污染底泥,解决草海污染内源问题,为水体生态恢复创造条件。在项目设计中,根据污染底泥的特性,提出合理的污染底泥疏浚方案和堆场外泄余水及底泥处置方案,工程实施后,疏挖区草海水质得到明显改观,达到预期的效果,为国内湖泊环保疏浚起到示范作用。该成果获1999年度天津市科技进步二等奖。该成果在安徽巢湖、无锡太湖、杭州西湖、温州温瑞塘河等多项湖泊与河流的污染底泥疏挖与处置工程应用。

第二章 水务科技

1991~2005年,天津市水务部门面对全市水资源短缺、防洪任务重和水环境恶化的状况,以“发展大都市水利,建设节水型社会”和“构建供水、防洪排涝、节水和水生态四大体系”为目标,围绕水资源、水利工程与管理、水灾防治、农田水利等重点领域展开科学研究,为天津科学发展提供技术支撑。

水资源研究方面,重点开展包括污染物调查、防治及保护措施等城市水源研究,雨洪水、微咸水、污水、海水等非常规水的研究,水资源供需平衡研究和优化配置研究等,并取得一批科研成果。这些成果的应用,保证全市供水安全,为生活、生产、生态用水提供水资源保障。

水利工程建设管理研究方面,重点开展新型护坡材料、软基加固施工技术、水工材料快速检测技术等多项研究。成功研发出联锁板、绿色混凝土、植物护坡等一批护坡技术,改变传统河道护砌方式。发明的低位抽真空软土地基加固技术,两次被国家科技部列为重点推广项目,应用于沿海吹填造陆及地基加固工程中。开发出输水工程自动监测系统,可及时了解输水水文、水力要素,保证输水安全和建筑物安全。

农田水利方面,重点开展节水灌溉和农田排涝研究,包括渠灌区管道输水节水灌溉、设施农业灌溉、水稻节水灌溉、排涝泵站现场测试技术。其中,渠灌区管道节水灌溉和温室滴灌施肥智能化控制系统两项成果被国家科技部列为农业科技成果转化项目,保证全市农业旱涝丰收。

水灾防治研究方面,重点开展洪水预报、实时调度、风险图制作等研究,研究成果得到应用,减少自然灾害对生命财产的损失。

第一节 水资源

1991~2005年,天津通过开发微咸水、雨水、海水等非常规水源试验,增加可利用水量。在水资源配置方面,开展天津市水资源供需平衡分析研究,大气水、地上水、地下水联合调度运用研究,以及缺水条件下各行业用水优化配置研究。在水资源保护方面,重点对于桥水库开展湖流特性、引滦输水水质对该库水质的影响研究,并对水库流域污染源调查与防治等进行研究。同时,对北大港水库水质保护措施、城市水环境改善与水源保护示范、地下水水质与地表水污染关系分析、地下水污染物分布规律及形成机理等进行研究。

一、水源开发

(一)淡水

2002年,天津市引滦工程于桥水库管理处(以下简称“于桥处”)陈振飞、杜学君、黄艳菊等对于桥水库以上流域水资源现状评价及径流量预测模型进行研究,利用泰森多边形原理,计算流域平均雨量,建立降水—径流模型、水位—渗漏量模型、水位—蒸发量模型及水位—水库损失量模型,同时采用模糊数学综合评价方法，把反映各种环境问题的实测值转化为反映地质环境质量优劣程度的质量值，建立函数关系，掌握其变化趋势，查清于桥水库流域自1960年建库40多年来的天然年径流量及其变化规律，掌握现状条件下的水资源状况，为于桥水库科学调度，充分利用自产资源，合理适时引调滦河水提供依据。

2002～2003年，天津市水文水资源勘测管理中心（以下简称“水文水资源中心”）和天津市城市节约用水办公室（以下简称“市节水办”）杨国彬等，为合理管理地下水开采，开发出“天津市机井工程管理信息系统”。该系统为一套具有管理和直观分析天津市地下水开采功能的软件。使用ArcView地理信息系统管理机井工程信息，使系统对信息的处理和表现能力更加丰富，能满足管理人员对各类信息交叉查询的需求。

2004年，天津市水利局农田水利处（以下简称“农水处”）及天津市水利科学研究所（以下简称“水科所”）李东丽、王贵珠、李桐等进行库容量测新技术在中小型水库推广应用，分别在新地河水库、津南水库、鸭淀水库应用，测量总面积25平方千米，该成果可准确地确定水库水下地形，对水库的清淤疏浚、水库周边农业灌溉、春季的抗旱调水和汛期以蓄代排具有指导作用。

2005年，水科所张存民、罗莎、董立新等进行梅江居住区、华苑产业区雨水控制、利用试验研究。通过对1970～2004年天津市降雨量分析，摸清城区多年平均降雨量和雨水资源量，并根据市区下垫面现状，确定城区径流系数和城区可利用雨水资源量，对雨水处理后的水质检测可达到灌溉用水标准。据统计，仅梅江居住区两年收集雨水160万立方米，用于绿化灌溉，每年可节约资金60万元。

（二）海水

1.海水淡化

天津市是较早发展海水淡化与综合利用的地区。至20世纪90年代，天津市海水利用技术已具备规模化应用与产业化发展的条件。2003年6月，天津市科委组织专家论证，确定天津市1000吨/日反渗透海水淡化示范工程建设方案，由国家海洋局天津海水淡化与综合利用研究所（以下简称“海水淡化研究所”）、天津科技大学、天津大有海水资源技术开发有限公司等分别承担工程设计与系统集成、海水预处理、海水深度预处理和基础设施建设。工程于同年12月建成投产，是天津市第一个反渗透海水淡化工程。2004年，又进行二期项目——海水淡化产业链的研究，为按照循环经济理念建设万吨级以上海水淡化示范基地奠定基础。

图9-2-1-122 天津市反渗透海水淡化示范工程

2.海水直接利用

1992年，天津大港电厂二期工程四台机组全部采用海水直流冷却技术，年利用海水量17亿立方米，年节约淡水6000万立方米。

1999年，海水淡化研究所在天津碱厂建成中国首例100立方米/小时海水循环冷却工业试验装置。该装置在中国首次实现用海水代替淡水作为工业循环冷却水，并首次采用普通碳钢换热器材实现海水循环冷却技术，在SW9800系列海水缓蚀剂、阻垢分散剂、菌藻杀生剂和海水冷却塔等关键技术上取得重大突破，形成成套生产和水处理技术（产品），有效地控制海水腐蚀、结垢和生物附着问题。

2000年，由海水淡化研究所承担“海水直流冷却技术研究”完成海水管道金属和有机覆盖层防腐蚀技术、电化学防腐蚀生物附着双防技术和防除海水管道内生物附着技术的研究，同时编写完成《海水直流冷却实用技术指南》，为制定海水直流冷却设计规范提供技术依据。

2004年，海水淡化研究所与天津碱厂合作建成2500立方米/小时海水循环冷却技术示范工程。该工程是中国首个千吨级海水循环冷却工业化示范工程，是中国首例具有独立自主知识产权的海水循环冷却工业装置。通过将海水循环应用于纯碱生产系统中吸氨塔和真空吸收塔替代淡水循环冷却，每年可节约淡水资源63万立方米，年节约资金149.9万元，工程的综合运行成本较淡水循环冷却可降低50%。

图9-2-1-123　天津碱厂海水循环冷却示范工程项目

同年，海水淡化研究所为深圳福华德电厂建成具有全部自主知识产权的1.4万立方米/小时海水循环冷却技术产业化示范工程，2005年，完成二期1.4万立方米/小时海水循环冷却工程。这是中国第一个在电力系统较大规模应用海水循环冷却技术的工程，突破万吨级（配套）海水冷却塔、万吨级工程示范等多项关键技术，形成海水循环冷却集成技术，实现海水循环冷却产业化技术突破。工程运行结果表明，采用海水循环冷却年节约淡水约300万立方米，综合运行成本较淡水循环冷却降低50%～75%，热排水量比海水直流冷却降低95%以上，经济指标优于淡水循环冷却。

二、优化配置

1995年，天津市水文总站进行水资源宏观战略研究，论证当地水资源与外调水资源量，并根据天津用水情况，进行水资源供需平衡分析，预测出2000年、2010年、2020年天津市用水量。

1996年，水科所南鸿飞、王大光、张福山等进行天津北部平原区“三水（大气水、地表水和地下水）”优化运用研究。选取典型试验区，结合农业生态需要对试区进行节水型水利工程技术改造，进行“三水”优化调度和联合应用、建立以浅层地下水资源最大开采量为目标函数的“三水”优化调度、运用数学模型，并提出经济合理、符合当地实际的技术指标，使“三水”利用达到良性循环。

同年，水科所罗世纲、王立新、钟水清等对引滦入津（天津段）调度运用及水量合理利用进行研究。根据系统分析及反馈控制模拟的技术原理，建立引滦入津输水工程优化模拟模型，结合现代数据库管理技术，建立大中型输水工程调度管理软件系统。该项成果可用于短时实时调度及长期规划，实际应用表明，自优化模型可比常规经验决策节水9%左右。

1999年，水科所郭青平等对南水北调实施前天津城市供水措施和对策进行研究，以引黄济津为重点，制定可行的应急调水措施和方案，并对挖潜水库死库容、超采地下水、挤压农业用水、工业用水优化配置政策性节水和限水等方面进行研究，提出在不同干旱程度时适应天津实际情况的强制节水和强化保水措施。

2002年，于桥处黄艳菊等进行州河流域库群联合调度研究，通过建立水资源优化调度模型，合理规划、制定出一套完整的风险共担、效益共享的优化调度方案。在保证水库本身工程安全、满足下游防洪标准的前提下，合理调度，充分利用该流域水资源；蓄泄得当，使于桥水库多蓄水，发挥流域整体的经济效益。

三、水质保护

1991年，针对引滦沿线水质保护问题，为防止水生植物阻塞过水建筑物，水科所张存民在原有捞草机的基础上，研究捞草机的捞草及卸草形式，通过做模型对捞草及卸草形式进行模拟实验，得出能在引滦上适用的捞草机的方案。该方案能节省大量人力、物力，不但适用于引滦工程，也适用于其他泵站、排灌站、电站等。

1993年，农水处许树国等进行天津地下水水质调查评价与地表水污染关系分析研究，将水质与水量相结合，地表水与地下水相结合，系统地评估全市地下水资源的质量状况及其分布，探讨地下水污染的主要来源、污染变化规律和趋势，调查不合理开发利用地下水资源对生态环境的影响，提出预防与治理的措施。

同年，水科所高慧颖、徐启昆、宋玉香等进行武清县北京排污河的两侧和污灌区农业环境污染调查及防治途径的研究，将地上部分通过土柱试验与地下水研究有机结合起来，并运用模糊数学与内梅罗污染指数法综合评价北京排污河河水及污灌区土壤、作物和地下水的污染状况，并提出切实可行的防治措施。

1994年，水文水资源中心刘德友进行引滦输水十年水质评价及趋势分析研究，摸清引滦水质状况，水质水量变化规律以及水库对水质的影响作用，进而做出水质预测，为保护引滦水资源提供可靠依据。

同年，水文水资源中心郑裕君、刘德友、杜士江等进行海河干流（二道闸以上）水文水质分析，深入研究海河干流区段的暴雨特性、汇水区域下垫面状况，汇流及排涝特性、各种水文要素的变异趋势，水质监控的措施及相应的冲污实例。同年，水科所郭青平、江浩、张芳等进行海河河道水流特性及其在改善水质方面的应用研究，分析海河污染物的扩散问题，并根据海河的流动特点建立一维和二维数学模型，进行引滦补水的一些冲污方案的研究和该系调水冲污方案的研究，给出海河最佳冲污方案。

是年，天津市水文总站郑裕君、康金栓、杜士江等对天津市入河排污口进行调查评价，以水资源、水系分区及市属行政分区为框架，全面了解全市各类污水排污口门的产污量、排污途径、纳污水量及污染物量等多种情况，选择典型的排污口门和重点河道进行实时跟踪监测，从而摸清全市主要河道的污染现状，为全市污染源的综合、重点清理和加强水资源管理提供依据。

1995年，天津市水文总站朱秀成等进行引滦输水水质水量监测监控一体化系统研究及规划，对引滦自1983年通水十年来的水质、水量、泵站系统分析评价、统计计算、调研论证、实测率定、深入探索和扩展广泛研究，基本摸清引滦输水工程的输水水质水量和与之相匹配的水文系统工程的现状和问题。通过十年资料的分析检索、研究，掌握引、产、输、供水资源的变化规律，提出充实、完善和提高的方案。

同年，水科所宋玉香针对染化工厂的废水进行污水资源化措施可行性试验研究。通过试验，首先采用除硫，之后用微电解加絮凝的方案，使废水达到易于生物降解的要求，最终通过土柱渗滤的作用，使降解废水达到排放标准或农灌标准的大部分指标。同年，天津市蓟县水利局胡晓光、张凤林、于宏斌等对天津市蓟县山区水土流失及以小流域为单元综合治理模式进行研究，从分析山区水土流失现状入手，探索适合蓟县山区特点的小流域综合治理模式，立足于合理开发利用水土资源，坚持因地制宜科学配置水土保持措施，达到生态上协调、经济上高效、总体功能最佳的水流域标准式样，是天津首次对山区水土流失的研究成果。

1996年，水科所郭青平、周潮洪、于凤良等进行南水北调北大港水库水质保护措施研究。通过研究调水入库的基本调度模式、入库时期的流动特点、库区底泥释放、蒸发、渗漏规律，探讨最佳入库、出库方式，及口门的最佳规模、位置，对比研究分库与不分库之间的差异，研究探讨南水北调合理调度工程方案，提出南水北调工程中北大港水库水质保护工程措施。

2004年，天津市水利局王宏江、张国立、陈振飞等进行于桥水库流域及州河下游段污染源调查与防治措施研究，利用水量、水质同步检测的技术手段，探索水库以上流域内入库河流跨流域调水的水污染负荷变化规律，掌握工厂、企业、城市污水的排放规律及各种污染物的排放总量，确定治理重点。同时利用前置库水生植物净化措施和汛期洪水、引滦输水的优化调度方案，大幅度削减污染物负荷的入库量，有效地提高水库的水质，并对水库底质现状提出治理方案。

同年，为解决天津水资源和水环境面临的污染问题，提高市区河道生态和景观功能，水科所刘学功、李金中、江浩等承担天津市重大科技攻关项目“城市水环境改善与水源保护示范工程”研究。示范工程以人工湿地技术为核心，结合人工浮床、人工沉床、喷泉曝气增氧、人工投菌等多项生物—生态水体净化技术的联

图9-2-2-124 生物生态技术景观效果（植物为茭白）

图9-2-2-125 生物生态技术景观效果（植物为梭鱼草）

合运用，对外环河水环境进行治理。工程占地面积约32000平方米，其中潜流湿地系统占地25000平方米，人工沉床和浮床系统占地4000平方米，水体净化能力达到每天4000～8000立方米，出水主要水质指标达到地表水Ⅳ类标准。系统管理维护方便、运行成本低、出水水质好，克服冬季运行的技术难题。工程建设与城市景观紧密结合，在实现水体净化的同时，达到美化城市的目的。

是年，水文水资源中心康金栓等采用原子荧光光度法测定水中砷、硒、铅、汞的含量，为制定水利行业相关标准提供依据。该测定法技术成熟，操作简单，易于实现分析过程自动化，运行成本较低，在水环境监测领域有很高的实用价值。

2005年，水文水资源中心闫学军、张伟、张国立等进行天津市地下水主要污染物分布规律及形成机理研究，采用水文地质分析、数理分析、热力学分析、室内和现场试验、数学模拟综合研究技术路线，设计并完成5个野外原状土样的氨氮垂向入渗试验，建立氨氮一维迁移数值模型，模拟研究氨氮从地表灌溉水到潜水再到第Ⅱ组承压水的迁移过程，为防治地下水氨氮污染提供理论依据，同时探索出一种综合研究技术路线研究地下水污染物分布规律及形成机理。

四、城市节水

（一）工业

1992年，市节水办孙本习、孙菁，天津哥罗化学工业有限公司张为，天津市经纬针织厂窦克文等，为提高天津洗染行业的水利用率，研究“洗染废水处理回用于印染全工艺”。经混凝、气浮、砂滤吸附处理后的洗染废水，水质达到纺织工业纯绵和化纤织物的印染生产用水标准，其COD去除率平均达到86%，色度去除率平均达到99%以上。用处理后的废水染布，产品质量各项指标达到出厂标准。

2001~2002年，市节水办刘志达、李华茂、赵树林等，为解决在城市建筑中开采应用地热源灌采比偏低问题，开展“管井灌采地下水应用于冷暖空调的试验研究”。针对第四系粉细砂层特点，设计、开凿出具有双滤层的灌采二用井（冬夏互为灌采使用），研制出规范的井口及管道密封系统，建立负压回灌工艺方法，达到灌采平衡。2001年11月至2002年8月（冬夏两季），经采用低温差、大流量进行的真空回灌试验，确定平均回灌量冬季每小时45.3立方米和夏季每小时55.78立方米，最大灌采量每小时67.1立方米，单位回灌量与单位出水量之比为0.504∶1，单井自身采灌比为0.74∶1，比单独使用的回灌井的灌采比提高二倍以上。互为灌采并能疏通井内各种形式堵塞，可防止涌砂现象，使井的寿命延长。

（二）民用

2000~2003年，市节水办刘国安、刘志达，天津开发区桑马科技开发有限公司仇之瑞等，为解决公共场所用水浪费严重的问题，开展“智能型节水控制系统”研究。该系统由计算机及配套控制管理软件和安装在冷热供水管路各个给水部位上的智能型节水给水器组成，以用户卡为媒介实现用户登记、甄别、注册编码，用户卡加密、充值，用水量记录、付费情况记录、统计，用水量、用水时间、用水次数设定，超限额用水加价处理，用水记录显示、查询、提示，非法身份报警等用水控制与管理。该系统蕴含多项国内外先进设计思路与方法，给水器部分机电一体化，结构新颖，可以像普通水龙头一样安装在供水管路上，系国内首创，控制部分采用单片机进行运算处理，使用“函数计算”方式，设计合理，外型精巧。用户卡内为多重运算加密，智能型节水给水器防水、防盗，防恶意破坏，防电磁干扰，一卡多用，使用方便，安全可靠，便于推广。安装该系统后，实测节水率达30%以上，节水效果显著。在南开大学、天津财经大学等6所高等院校和21所大专院校推广应用，综合节水效益达35%以上，节水300万立方米，减少排污量360万立方米。

第二节　水利工程

1990～2005年，天津市先后进行海河干流治理、北运河综合治理、引滦水源保护、海挡治理、外环河整治、海河堤岸改造等重点工程，并建成城市防洪圈，使天津市防洪能力基本达到50年一遇标准。针对工程建设中遇到的技术问题，在施工技术、护坡材料、软基加固等方面开展一系列研究工作，研制水下整坡机、环保型河道清淤设备、轻型插板机等先进施工设备，用于生产施工。取得联锁板、植物护坡、环保绿色植被混凝土等科研成果，并在工程建设中大规模推广。在软基处理及地基加固方面，发明低位抽真空技术，广泛应用于沿海吹填造陆及地基加固工程中。

一、工程建设

（一）清淤

1998年，水科所张存民等根据海湾泥吹填疏干的工作需要，研制出一种轻型插板机。该设备便于拆装和运输，可在表面承载力每平方米1吨的泥场中作业，最大插深8米，单根排水板插设时间小于5秒，机身平移每秒8米，滚移每秒2米，下插每秒3米，提升每秒7米，适应稀、软土地插板要求。

2002年，天津市水利工程有限公司娄景悦等研制成用于清淤的全套工程机械设备。包括浮船式液压抓斗机，半舱式泥驳，全封闭易抓净液压双面抓斗等。可用该设备集装、运、卸为一体，水中提升过程不泄漏，清淤开挖过程对河底淤泥土质不扰动。

（二）护坡

1997年，水科所李振等在引进混凝土联锁板技术后，先后开发出两类四种混凝土联锁板，可部分替代浆砌石护坡及普通预制混凝土板护坡。1999年该所又对混凝土联锁护坡技术应用开发推广，据统计1999～2000年生产的90万块混凝土联锁板比采用浆砌石护坡节省投资337.5万元。

1998年，水科所闫海新、王银生等为改善天津海岸生态环境，进行海堤植物护坡试验，筛选护坡植物，并提出适合不同海岸条件的合理结构型式，使海堤建设与生态环境改善有机结合起来，形成绿色环保型海堤。与无护面土堤坝海挡相比，每千米长可减少土体损失5005立方米，节省维修费用约30万元。经四年试验，互花米草可在潮间带种植，柽柳适合在土壤含盐量1.2%～2.0%时种植，碱茅可在土壤含盐量2.24%的盐土上种植，可有效保护坡面土体的稳定。

2000年，天津市河道闸站管理总所杨秀富等鉴于现有闸门的腐蚀情况，采用纳米碳纤维技术，研制出现代无金属水工闸门，耐腐蚀，运行效果好。

2001～2003年，水科所孙永军等为改变水利工程护坡形式功能单一的局限性，利用无砂大孔混凝土的特点，通过改善混凝土孔隙内部的碱环境，解决其本身强度和孔隙率的矛盾，实现在混凝土上长草的目标，从而研制出环保型绿色植被混凝土。既可加固堤防，防止水土流失，又能恢复水系周边的生态环境。

（三）软基处理

1991～1992年，水科所曹大正等进行低位抽真空加固

图9-2-2-126　软基加固处理技术

吹填土及其下地基研究。该研究系在吹填前预做加固工程，采用独特分离式排水造压方式，在吹填土层底部连续获得80千帕以上真空度。吹填后利用吹填土自身做封闭层，在吹填土底部造真空，利用大气压能、太阳能、风能使吹填土在100天左右可使渤海湾淤泥达到80%固结度，加固后垂向控制厚度为1.2~1.5米，最小控制单元面积45000平方米。加固系统与垂向塑料板桩复式连接，在完成吹填加固同时，完成其下地基80千帕以上承载加固，比传统真空加固法节省工程投资40%，缩短工期200天以上。1997~2005年先后用于市内吹填造陆工程、生态护坡、吹填筑挡、淤背固堤等多项示范工程。该成果获1997年度天津市科技进步二等奖。

1999年，水科所孙永军等将电渗法加固软土地基与吹填沙袋坝两种技术结合起来，把传统电渗法的电极布置形式由垂向插设改为水平方向布置，开发一种新型围海围堰充填泥袋坝。充填泥袋坝用渤海湾滩地淤泥替代吹填袋坝中的砂，造价较吹填砂袋坝降低20%以上，同一种土体达到相同固结度电渗法加固软土较真空预压法时间缩短5~10倍。

二、监控

(一)质量检测

1997年，水科所薛元贵等针对天津市水利建设工程存在的混凝土、砂浆强度严重超出或达不到设计要求问题，提出天津市水利建设工程混凝土、砂浆质量控制适宜的快速检测方法，并进行大量试件试验，成果应用于海河干流治理等大型水利建设工程质量检测中。其中，砂浆强度快速检测技术系在国内首次应用。

1999年，水科所张建华等对已有水泥强度快速检测方法进行分析比较，利用水泥早期强度，推求28天水泥强度的快速检测方法，建立相应的关系曲线和经验方程，同时结合水泥强度检验新标准(ISO法)，对水泥强度快速检测方法的部分条款进行调整，使该方法更适应ISO法的特点要求。

2000年，水科所李广智等针对传统的标准试件抗压强度在某些情况下不能代表结构混凝土的真实状态和性能的情况，分别对回弹、超声、超声回弹、核子密度、射钉、钻芯等各种检测方法的测强的影响因素进行分析研究，确定各种方法的研究重点，结合天津市水利工程实际，制定出适用性良好的混凝土结构测强曲线，并确定各种测强曲线的适用范围，以提高混凝土结构检测的精确度。

同年，水科所王守霆针对环刀法检测堤防筑土压实度制约工程进度，采用核子法快速检测，通过室内及现场进行大量的试验、分析，对比得出适应天津土质特点的操作程序及试验方法。用该法检测可提高工效20倍以上，并最大限度地减少施工过程中机械设备及人员的无效投入，确保工程质量，加快工程进度。

2001年，天津市水利局基建处马树军、闫海新、李广智等针对水泥搅拌土防渗墙无损检测无规范标准，对天津市五类典型土质的水泥搅拌土不同配比，建立水泥搅拌土强度、波速、渗透系数等指标与其影响因素之间的数学回归模型和人工神经网络模型，两模型互相支持、验证，可以预测水泥搅拌土的灰土比和强度。对现场模型墙进行高密度震动映像纵波与瑞利面波现场测试，重点解决测试中传感器、偏移距、震源的选择和测试信息的反演技术。建立水泥土防渗墙无损检测技术的标准流程，从测试波速、不均匀系数、强度等指标上对防渗墙的施工质量从量上进行判定。

(二)优化运行

1996年，天津市引滦工程管理处王宏江等，为准确地反映引滦沿线各测站的水情数据，进行“引滦沿线水情传输与自动显示系统的方案研究”。该系统能定时传输各测站的水情数据，随时召测各测站的水情数据，对全部水情数据进行预处理，时实数据的更换间隔可任意设定、全部水情数据均可直接传送到水调中心。

1997年，水科所聂荣智、于子明等结合引滦输水工程的运行，针对不同类型水工建筑物输水流量计量方法进行研究，探讨将水工建筑物测流技术应用于大型专用输水工程流量计量的特点及实施方法。由于采用水工建筑物测流，其断面固定，变化很小，测量方便，数据精确。

1999年，天津市引滦工程尔王庄管理处（以下简称“尔王庄处”）刘尚为等根据引滦入津尔王庄引供水枢纽工程的实际运行情况，采用大系统递阶分析和逐次收紧约束的自适应目标控制模拟技术，以尔王庄暗渠泵站能耗最小，输水保证率以100%为目标，建立尔王庄引供水枢纽工程优化调度数学模型。应用该成果可合理安排泵站开机台数，正确调节水泵叶角，使各泵站机电设备和输水建筑物达到最佳运行状态，实现枢纽工程的计算机辅助管理和优化调度。

同年，天津市引滦工程宜兴埠管理处王志强等为寻找一种简捷的闸门运行测控手段，对光电感应器在闸门保护中的应用进行研究。选用可全天候工作并将检测与控制集成在一起的红外光电感应器替代传统的旋转式机械限位装置，以提高保护系统的可靠性和灵敏度，保证水闸的安全运行。该装置结构小巧，安装位置灵活，适用于各种类型的水闸及同类运行要求的设施。

是年，于桥处周军、王立林等，为监测、掌握盘山电厂用水量，设计开发“盘山电厂取水口计量数据自动采集系统”。该系统通过无线电台调制成音频号，发往中心站，通过专门软件进行数据处理，流量信号采用脉冲信号，保证传输数据与源流量计误差为零。利用雨量、水位遥测技术，把流量转化为数字编码存储在数传仪芯片中，保证数据在掉电后不丢失。

2000年，水科所田世炀等针对尔王庄明渠泵站低扬程、大流量、短流道的特点，确定水泵机组开停过程中的最佳闸门预开和预关高度等控制参数。建立起液压闸门自动控制系统，以保证控制机组开停机过程中泵站出口液压闸门的准确启闭，有效地解决以往用人工手动控制时存在的水泵机组开停过程中闸门阻水和后池水倒灌问题。

同年，尔王庄处陈振飞、于子明等用超声波流量计采集流量数据，并将数据传到工业控制机，通过TH—2000闸门监控装置实现按实测流量或按闸门开度与过水流量进行闸门的自动控制。实现按给定输水量自动控制暗渠两孔闸门开启高度，按量供水，并能进行实时监测，与已完成的尔王庄引供水枢纽工程优化调度系统相融合，达到对暗渠输水量控制的要求。同期，于子明等还引进高集成度微处理器C8051F021，开发出SW-2000系列水位计、闸位计，进而提高闸位的起降精度，更精确地控制其流量。

2003年，天津市引滦工程潮白河管理处周建玉、闫凤新，水科所杨春长等在“潮白河泵站优化运行与自动监控系统研究”中，通过建立泵站自动监控系统，实现泵站运行和管理的实时监控；在不顶托明渠两岸农田条件下确定泵站前池最高运行水位为1.75米；建立自流道输水数学模型，确定自流道在安全输水条件下的最大过流能力为每秒30立方米；通过研究泵站机组的运行规律，建立泵站运行数学模型。确定泵站机组在高效率、低能耗运行条件下的泵站前池最低运行水位为1.45米；优化运行系统以输水流量每秒30立方米为分界值做出判断，当上游来量小于该值时，选择自流道输水；当上游来量大于该值时选择泵站开机输水。

2004年，天津市引滦工程工程潮白河管理处闫凤新等在原电动机润滑系统上加装自动化元件，利用中控室工控机实现潮白河泵站7台机组14个油槽润滑油补给的自动控制。

（三）安全监测

1998年，水科所杨春长、刘学功等针对引滦入港输水管道漏水问题，建立自动监测系统。该系统采集数据准确，其水量月累积相对误差为万分之三，水位误差最大值为4.8%，测站数据采用定时自报及中心站实时召测方式，有测站与中心站两个报警系统，无论测站或管道出现问题，都可及时发现并报警，以保工程安全运行。

1999年，尔王庄处刘尚为等研制开发出新一代微机励磁装置，在国内同步电动机装置中首次采用16位单片机和高集成度可编程系统器件，实现全数字化，速度快，功能多，抗干扰力强，采用三相五线式高效阻容系统和热管散热器，三相全控桥晶闸管采用热管散热器，具有顺向励磁和后备励磁投入功能，确保电机可靠平稳起动，具备失励失步保护、带励失步保护及带载自动再整步等功能，系统开放性好，运行参数可在线显示，用户可在线修改参数，便于运行管理。具有多种数字通讯接口，便于实现厂站的计算机监控。

同年，尔王庄处刘尚为等开发“引滦尔王庄引供水枢纽工程自动监测系统”，综合运用计算机技术、传感技术和自动化技术，对尔王庄引供水各工程均可自动采集参数，建立自动监测调度中心，形成局域网，预留广域网接口,实现优化调度运用,确保安全输水。

2001年,尔王庄处王志高等针对泵站机组运行中冷却水和润滑水示流器经常出现误动作及信号丢失问题,研制出适合该暗渠泵站运行参数的智能示流器。该装置采用的涡轮传感器具有低流速工作特性,能满足尔王庄暗渠泵站电机冷却水示流器低水压的工作环境。

2003年,于桥处黄燕菊等针对于桥水库工程缺乏完善的监测手段,研究提出于桥水库大坝安全监测系统的总体框架模式,制定工程安全监测和网络通讯方案,开发测量控制单元和大坝安全信息管理系统,进行水库大坝安全监测传感器及视频监视系统设备的选型和应用。运行表明,该系统对水库大坝安全起到监测作用。

三、除险加固

(一)隐患探测

1997年,水科所汪长余对引滦入港地下输水钢管阴极保护现状及治理方法进行研究,选择检测管道电位,土壤电阻率及土壤理化指数等指标,勘察南干线,穿越河流、公路及用钢管材料的区域现场的地质环境,采用近参比法和远参比法相结合的方法检测管地电位。并根据土壤对钢铁腐蚀影响因素及评价指数进行取样,对土质化验结果及现场检测资料进行综合对比分析,摸清规律,总结出一套行之有效的钢管阴极保护方法。

1999年,水科所田世炀等研究堤防隐患综合探测技术,力求定量检测堤防质量及存在的隐患,给出土壤物理力学指标与测试参数的函数关系,为定量分析堤防隐患提供依据。

2001年,水科所汪长余等利用多点瞬态面波法的波速与土堤防渗系数和孔隙率反比的变化规律,为定性检测评判河道堤防质量、检测灌浆加固堤防效果提供科学依据。该法可连续检测,且操作简单、准确可靠。

(二)病害防治

1989年,天津市水利科技情报中心站张金鹏等采用数理统计及巴雷特图分析水工建筑物病害主次关系的方法,对天津市水工建筑物病害现状进行研究,阐明天津水工建筑物的病害现状和存在的主要问题 。并对建筑物中混凝土裂缝、碳化及钢筋锈蚀,冻融破坏,环境水侵蚀、水工钢闸门锈蚀原因等病害的成因进行分析提出防治措施。

1992年,水科所刘奕森、刘学功等以实用鉴定法与可靠性鉴定法对水工混凝土建筑物进行诊断评估,并将多种提高耐久性能的复合材料和施工工艺组合应用于治理各种混凝土建筑物病害。

1995年,水科所闫海新对混凝土建筑物老化宏观评估方法和现场检测技术进行研究。建立以层次分析为基础,以结构耐久性为重点的水工混凝土建筑物老化实时评估系统,并在模型中引入神经网络技术对系统进行分析判断。通过对典型建筑物现场检测,分析各种检测方法的可靠性,并引入贯入阻力法检测混凝土强度提高检测可靠性,降低检测对结构的损伤。

(三)安全评估

1997年,水科所汪长余等在"引滦入港地下输水管线检测方法"研究中,借助浅震仪进行地质勘探及柱基测试技术探测地下掩埋体的损坏状况。经对八种不同地质环境产生的不同波形进行分析、比较,总结地下掩埋体的变化规律。应用表明:该技术操作简单、检测结果准确、费用较低。

2000年,天津市水利局引滦工程管理处陈振飞等在永定新河输水钢管剩余寿命评估及可靠性研究中,得出影响其使用寿命和使用可靠性的主要因素是腐蚀和地震。经对永定新河倒虹吸的查勘分析、现场测量,对腐蚀状态的描述,腐蚀面积的计算导出剩余强度计算公式,计算出剩余强度及剩余寿命。经对地震作用下永定新河倒虹吸钢管可靠性分析,找出其最弱部位及管段。

同年,天津市水利局引滦入港工程管理处景悦和天津大学余建星等对地震作用下穿越管道安全可靠性进行研究。经对管道和地震动力作用下的可靠性分析,研究判断在砂土液化时、地震位移时和地面变形时穿越管道的安全可靠程度。从而找出输水管道系统的薄弱环节,提出在这些环节进行抗震加固。该项目获2002年度天津市科技进步二等奖。

(四)堤防加固

2001年,尔王庄处于子明等在尔王庄水库(平原水库)大坝高喷灌浆防渗加固工程中,采取粘土中添加膨润土,使粘土塑性指数Ip由10提高到17达到设计要求。同时利用膨润土的特性,调节和改善防渗体的力学性能和抗渗性能,使防渗体变得柔软,以适应由于地基不均匀沉降对防渗体所造成的压力。另在防渗体内加入适量的膨润土,使所配制的浆液具有流动性、均匀性、可泵性与浆液颗粒分散性均好的特点。由于防渗加固工程中水库围堤的抗渗性能得到提高,防渗加固实验段内的坝体和坝基局部部位渗透系数,由每秒0.001厘米降低到平均每秒5.84×0.0000001厘米;渗透水力坡降由0.054下降到平均0.023。

2003年,尔王庄处樊世明针对天津市尔王庄水库堤基内存在的粉土及粉砂层的液化可能性、孔隙水压力的消散等问题进行水库大坝地基基础地震液化及加固处理措施研究,成果表明尔王庄水库堤基中的粉土、粉砂层在7度地震烈度下,整体土层发生液化的可能性不大。在动荷载作用下孔压累积具有一定规律性。当粉土、粉砂累积孔压达到围压60%以上时,土体有发生循环流动的可能,但仍符合双幅应变的液化标准。尔王庄水库围堤堤基最有可能发生液化的区域出现在背水坡的坡脚或围堤的正下方。据此提出防震措施,供水库加固设计与施工应用。

(五)隧洞补强

2000年,天津市引滦工程隧洞管理处朱永庚针对隧洞出口埋管段混凝土骨料软化,白色斑点发展迅速,混凝土强度分布不均等问题进行综合检测。通过对各种新材料、新施工工艺的实验,提出混凝土补强处理方案,采用化学灌浆法,注入水溶性聚氨酯堵漏剂用以处理确保隧洞洞室安全。

(六)管道防漏

2001年,水科所汪长余在"输水管道渗漏快速封堵技术研究"中,采用自压封堵原理,将密封胶套在管内打开,对所要封堵的承插口(漏水处)覆盖,水压越大,封堵效果越好。结果表明,采用胶套止水的柔性封堵方法,不但能封堵漏水,而且还有适应管道再次沉降变形的能力。经查新自压封堵法,属国内首创。

第三节 农田水利

20世纪80年代天津推广应用"井灌区低压管道输水灌溉技术"及"暗管排咸技术",高效开发地下水,改造低洼易涝中低产田使农田旱涝保收。然而,渠灌区输水灌溉和设施农业灌溉的落后方式还没有根本改变。1991~2005年,天津市水务部门重点开展地表水农田节水、设施农业灌溉施肥一体化、非充分灌溉、泵站更新改造前后评估等技术研究,取得渠灌区管道输水灌溉、温室滴灌施肥智能化控制系统、微咸水灌溉以及泵站现场测试,水稻浅、湿、晒灌水技术等一批灌溉排涝实用技术。前两项被国家科技部列为农业科技成果转化项目,在全国推广应用。

一、常规水灌溉

(一)节水灌溉工程

1.井灌区管灌

井灌区低压管道输水灌溉技术是天津市20世纪80年代末期的研究成果,多年来不断完善,技术日臻成熟。地表采用塑料软管将水直接送到田间,灌溉水的利用系数达0.8以上,节水效果明显。1994年,农水处、水科所及相关区县水利局承担的"十万亩低压管道输水灌溉技术推广"项目是市农委1994年科教兴农"百万"工程之一。到1996年共推广6867万平方米,铺设低压管道654千米。推广中注重管道输水与机井测试改造的有机结合,还研制出管道可调进排气阀,效益显著。三年累计节水1548万立方米,节电172万度,节地112万平方米，灌溉直接增产效益542万元，总效益1402万元。

2.渠灌区管灌

1996年，水科所万日明、杨万龙等承担并完成天津市科委农业攻关项目“渠灌区管道灌溉系统关键技术研究”。该项目针对天津市渠灌区面积大、水的利用率(40%～50%)低、农业水资源严重短缺等状况，经试验研究，提出渠灌区采用大口径低压管道输水灌溉节水工程模式，探索出从系统的规划设计，管材、管件，施工工艺到运行管理等一套成熟技术，应用该技术可使灌溉水利用系数提高到0.8，与土渠输水相比亩均年节水达100立方米以上，节地5%，粮食增产20%，工程使用寿命在30年以上。

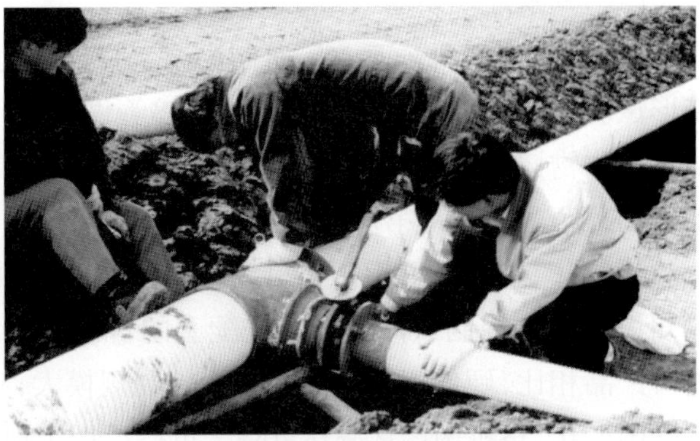
图9-2-3-127　干支管连接

2000年，天津市水利局完成的“渠灌区管道输水灌溉节水技术推广应用”项目，引入变频技术，实现恒压变流量供水，更加适合多种作物的灌溉要求；研制出管沟开挖机械，提高施工效率和质量，降低工程成本；扩大灌溉控制范围，单系统控制规模增大到66.7万平方米，管径加大到315毫米，灌溉水源拓展为地上、地下水联合运用的多水源，提高灌溉保证率。该项目建立起比较完整的规划设计、施工工艺、安全保护、运行管理等技术规程和四级推广体系。

2002年，市水利局水科所、农水处和科技处共同承担国家科技部农业科技成果转化资金项目“渠灌区管道输水节水灌溉工程技术生产性试验”。该项目由万日明主持研制出直径400毫米、500毫米大口径管材和玻璃钢配套管件，工作压力0.2兆帕，开发多功能给水栓，采用恒压变频供水技术，将单系统控制规模扩大到133.3万平方米，推广田间闸管技术和小畦灌溉技术；建成2个恒压变频供水示范工程和49.8平方千米渠灌区管道输水节水灌溉工程；编写”渠灌区低压管道输水灌溉工程技术规范”。通过多项创新和改进，完善和发展渠灌区管灌技术成果。为改善农田水利基础设施薄弱状况，促进节水型社会的发展提供技术支撑。

图9-2-3-128　给水栓和田间软管

3.微灌

1991年，水科所葛淑芳等开展“微灌技术在蔬菜种植业中的应用研究 ”，通过建设1.27万平方米试验示范工程，对国内常用几种滴头和相关设备进行田间应用试验，显示出各种设备在当地的使用特性，为用户选择适宜的滴灌设备提供重要参数。开展滴灌对蔬菜生长环境影响试验，结果显示滴灌技术对促进保护地蔬菜生产有显著增产效益。

图9-2-3-129　蔬菜滴灌

1997年，水科所杨万龙针对温室及水土资源特点，围绕规模化温室微灌系统的规划设计方法，灌排系统的工程模式，施肥装置，蔬菜微灌灌溉制度等开展攻关研究，在全光现代温室，引进国外最先进的灌溉施肥自动化控制系统和自动冲洗过滤器。通过该项技术的研究与示范，完善和发展规模化温室微灌系统的规划设计方法，开发出微灌系统的优化设计软件；建成适宜滨海盐碱地持续利用的灌排系统工程模式；开发SF型低差压施肥器和DSF型多功能施肥器；制定蔬菜的灌溉制度。试验证明,设施农业采用微灌技术可节水60%,节能50%,增产20%。

(二)节水灌溉设备

1994年,水科所杨万龙等研制出温室自动移动式微喷设备。其主机运行轨道,通过室内4米跨度的挠度变形试验,确定采用管径19毫米的镀锌管做导轨,既可满足主机运行要求,又节省资金。同时,根据温室的结构及作物情况,进行系统的水力设计和水力设备选型,并完成现场安装调试。该设备经天津市西郊菜篮子工程的蔬菜生产基地第六埠蔬菜场高级玻璃育苗、养花温室使用,系统运行良好,达到设计要求。

2000年,杨万龙等承担市科委重大科技攻关项目"温室滴灌施肥智能化控制系统"。首次研制出具有自主知识产权的控制软件及与系统配套的自冲洗过滤器、文丘里注肥器、pH-EC监测仪等关键仪器设备。与进口产品相比,硬件配置高、功能多、控制规模大,实用性强,价格比进口产品低30%~40%,产品关键技术设备已国产化,整机国产化率达70%。可广泛用于现代温室、日光温室、塑料大棚的花卉、蔬菜等作物不同栽培模式的灌溉施肥自动化控制,具有节水、节肥、省工、增产增效和环保的综合效益。至2005年,生产组装的10台样机,已在天津、上海等7个示范区内应用。

图9-2-3-130 FICS-1型现代温室滴灌施肥智能化控制系统

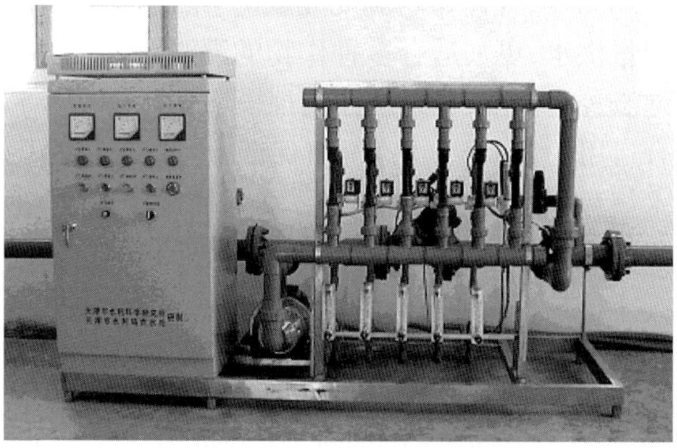

图9-2-3-131 FICS-2型日光温室滴灌施肥智能化控制系统

(三)节水灌溉制度

1.水稻浅湿晒

1995年,水科所王善昌等针对天津市在水稻种植中严重浪费灌溉水问题,进行"控制灌""浅湿灌""浅水灌"及"深水淹灌"四种灌水模式对比试验,提出适用于天津市的"控制灌"和"浅湿灌"灌水模式。与传统的深水淹灌相比,浅湿灌溉具多项优点,每万平方米土地可减少灌水量3345立方米,省水29.4%,减少灌溉用电283千瓦时,省电29%,每公顷增产稻谷1707千克,增产11%;灌溉水生产效率达到每立方米1.08千克。1997年,农水处开始对水稻浅、湿、晒节水灌溉技术进行大面积推广应用。由1997年的5333万平方米,到1999年推广面积达2.13亿平方米,实现每公顷节水3000立方米,万平方米均节电96度,每公顷增产525千克。

2.作物耗水

1996年,水科所以水稻为试验品开展非充分灌溉的作物耗水规律及优化配水模型的试验研究。从中摸清受旱条件下水稻的耗水规律,拟合得出用Jensen模型表示的水稻水分生产函数表达式,在此基础上建立优化配水模型、编制操作软件,并提出实施优化灌溉制度需要的技术和管理措施。

2002年,水科所赵世敏等在津南节水灌溉试验中心日光温室内,分别采用筒测法和田测法,得出黄瓜、辣椒、苦瓜、油菜、生菜等蔬菜的需水量、需水规律;制定出各种蔬菜的灌溉制度;给出日光温室内土壤、植物蒸散发经验公式。研究表明不同品种的瓜果类或叶类蔬菜,其日均需水量和生育期需水总量均不相同,为科学灌溉提供依据。

3.农业用水定额

2002年,天津市节约用水事务管理中心组织编制"农业用水定额",水科所赵世敏等经调查统计,摸清天津市农业用水的基本情况。以理论计算法和调查法的分析比较为基础，确定最终的灌溉定额。“农业用水定额”涵盖粮食、油料、蔬菜、果树、牧草五大类30种主要农作物以及农村生活用水和鱼塘补水，涉及到63种用水定额，2003年9月将其作为天津市地方标准，由市质量技术监督局发布、执行。

二、非常规水灌溉

（一）再生水

1998年，水科所宋玉香等承担“高效持续利用污水灌溉新技术研究”。该项目在传统的污水土地处理技术和污水灌溉技术基础上，克服原有的污水土地处理技术处理能力低、处理效果差、不具有可持续性、受季节影响大以及对用于污水处理和污水灌溉的土地的土质要求高等不足，其总磷和总氮的去除率分别达到98%和85%，悬浮物和化学耗氧量的去除率分别达到95%和70%。

2002年，天津市农业环境保护管理监测站在武清区东浦洼乡后河淤村实施天津市城市再生水用于农田灌溉的试点工程。依托武清区第一污水处理厂，通过储存塘净化等技术措施，进行2000亩大田作物的灌溉试验。2004~2005年，与农业部环保所和天津市水利科学研究所协作完成“城市再生水灌溉农田安全技术体系”研究。该项目建立由储存塘净化工程、快速生物监测技术、再生水农田灌溉水质标准、再生水农田灌溉制度以及农田环境定点监测、定期评价制度等组成的“城市再生水灌溉农田安全技术体系”，制定天津地区《城市再生水农田灌溉水质标准》（DB12/T264-2006）、天津市主要农作物（小麦、玉米）的城市再生水农田灌溉制度，以麦穗鱼作为监测生物的城市再生水生物监测技术等。再生水灌溉产出的农产品符合国家食品卫生标准；节省淡水资源360立方米/年·亩。年亩均节电80度和节省电费48元，节支66.7%，两年来项目区节支总额达到19.2万元。小麦平均增产10.65%，夏播玉米平均增产26.8%，两年新增利润达到81.1万元。

（二）微咸水

1998年，水科所朱利贞、汪绍盛、薛霞等针对天津干旱地区水源问题，以建农田节水灌溉工程为手段，加大水管理力度，进行地下咸水及地上淡水的开发利用研究，摸清各层地下水水质、水量变化情况，建设混水工程控制咸淡水混合比例，结合节水工程技术和农艺措施实施微咸水优化灌溉制度，达到节水增产的目的。

天津市浅层地下咸水分布面积占全市总面积2/3以上。其中，全盐量每升3克以内微咸水资源量1.02亿立方米，量大面广。2003年，水文水资源中心、水科所、农水处等完成“微咸水农田灌溉综合利用技术研究”。水科所严晔端等以安全灌溉和资源化开发利用为目标，合理开发浅层微咸水并制定一系列综合技术措施。针对氯离子浓度高的微咸水水质特征和因氯离子引发土壤渗透值增高而形成对作物危害的问题，解决在浅位粘重土壤条件下，利用高氯离子浓度的3～5克每升微咸水进行农田直接灌溉的技术难点，实现增产和土壤安全的双重目标。在研究过程中，探索出浅层咸水其含水介质以粘性土为主的钻井工艺和井型结构，有效增大单井出水量。为确保微咸水安全灌溉和可持续利用，研发出新型土壤改良剂和科学施肥技术及合理作物种植形式，并采用科学的灌溉制度，达到安全、增产、高效的效果。经5年的灌溉试验，证明在一定条件下采用每升5克以内的咸水实施小麦灌溉是可行的。

三、除涝

1995年水科所万日明、杨万龙等在“天津市灌排泵站节能测试技术研究”中对泵站的流量、功率、扬程及转速诸参数的测试方法、测试设备以及测试精度的评估等进行研究。研制出ZN3—64D型测流仪、ZN4—Ⅱ测压仪等多种测试仪表设备。研究成果应用于各种不同用途的泵站技术改造前后的水泵机组装置效率的现场测试，或新建泵站工程验收及泵站运行日常监测。测试精度满足

图9-2-3-132 流速仪法测流现场

《泵站现场测试规程》SD140-85规定的指标。

2001年,农水处针对天津市大部分扬水站设施严重老化,农田排涝沟渠淤积严重,除涝体系减灾能力降低的情况,开展"天津市农田除涝区防灾减灾系统"研究。采用降雨径流相关图法,重新分析计算径流量,以数学模型方法分析印证,并依据重新修订的排涝模数,计算测定各排涝小区的排涝能力。根据确定排涝标准的不同,提出四个农田排涝改造方案,从中优化出推荐方案。进而修订《天津市平原区农田除涝水文手册》,开发出天津市市除涝信息系统,直观反映出天津农田除涝系统基本情况。

第四节 水灾防治

天津市地势低洼,较低处距海平面约1米,加之河道冲沙水量大幅度减少,地面、堤防严重下沉,防洪工程年久失修,险工多,河道行洪能力已严重衰减,防汛一直是一项重要任务。为提高天津市防洪除涝抗灾能力,使防洪工作逐步达到科学决策与调度。自1990年起,天津着力开展与防汛有关的计算机硬、软件的基本建设。先后建成防汛大屏幕会商系统、卫星云图接收处理系统、雷达图像显示系统、广域网实时水情显示系统、防汛计算机局域网、水文基本数据库、防汛实时水情调度信息电子显示屏等。此外,还研制永定河蓄滞洪区地理信息系统、大清河洪水演进系统、部分河系的洪水预报系统。2001～2005年,进行城市防洪信息系统工程建设,包括水文信息采集、数据传输及移动通讯、计算机网络和防汛决策支持系统四个子系统。

一、防洪

(一)洪水调度与管理

20世纪90年代,水科所开展对天津市各大水系的洪水灾害管理研究。该所魏玉琴等对大清河系洪水在一维河道和二维蓄滞洪区(洼淀)的演进情况进行数值模拟,研制直观的图像显示方法,并对洪灾风险进行评估。水科所周潮洪等对天津市十三个蓄滞洪区不同蓄滞洪水位下面积、蓄量及淹没损失进行计算分析。2005年,天津市在城市防洪决策支持系统的开发中,引进丹麦水力学研究所的河网建模软件包和国内相关模型,建立蓟运河实时洪水预报调度系统。

1991年,水科所魏玉琴、贾福慧、张胜利等开展大清河洪水灾害研究,应用一维和二维不恒定流数值模拟技术,研究洪水灾害及河道行洪能力。研制用于多个洼淀联合滞洪逻辑控制软件系统,可在任意节点加入或分出流量的计算模式。其彩色图象显示软件直观动态地反映出洪水演进及形成灾害的过程,绘制出动态风险图。

1996年,天津市水利局朱志强等,开发"天津市防汛调度资料数据库系统"。该系统以实时水情、雨情等有关信息为基础,参照天津市水系图、海河流域水系图、防汛调度示意图,选择地显示相应站点的水文要素、随时过程、重要水情、灾情以及调度信息等。通过该系统可以及时、直观、全面地解行洪河道现状并可在微机上实现对主要河系、主要闸站洪水过程的查询、求值计算、绘制过程曲线等,当河道、水库、洼淀、闸站超过控制标准时,具有自动报警功能。

同年,水科所魏玉琴、贾福慧等,在大清河超标准洪水研究中,采用二维不恒定流数值模拟技术对大清河水系建立"五洼"联用抵御洪水的数学模型,对100年、200年、500年一遇的洪水进行多方案模拟计算,绘制出风险图及动态风险图。采用计算网格1平方千米为单元进行统计分析,并绘制出泛区内社会经济结构分布及洪灾损失分布图,提出不同频率洪水灾害信息统计及分析的有关数据。

1997年,由于永定新河的泄流能力已远低于原设计水平,天津对永定新河进行减灾可行性分析。水科所周潮洪等通过建立复杂河网洪水调度模型,二维洪水演进模式,损失评估模型,结合地理信息系统,开发永定河现状泄流能力计算,不同频率洪水现状调度方案计算,指出存在问题,提出减灾措施。

1999年,天津市水利局朱芳清、水科所周潮洪等通过建立复杂河网洪水调度数学模型、二维洪水演进数学模型、洪水评估模型及成果分析综合系统,完成永定河(卢沟桥以下)实时洪水调度系统。鉴于河网的结构、边界条件、控制条件的多样性,把众多的控制条件、可变参数、成果分析等简化到可视化界面中,方便实用、计算速度快,适应永定河防汛调度的要求。该系统被国家防汛抗旱办公室、海河流域防汛抗旱办公室和天津市防汛抗旱办公室应用,成果获2001年度天津市科技进步二等奖。

2002年,水科所聂荣智、夏中华等,采用ARCGIS地理信息系统软件,建立"天津市行洪河道堤防信息管理系统"。该系统对天津市19条一级行洪河道、西部防线及海挡的地图扫描数字化,建立天津市行洪河道及主要堤防的基础电子地图,并采用Geodatabase格式建立行洪河道地理空间信息数据库。建立以webGIS为平台的行洪河道信息查询系统。建立行洪河道属性数据信息管理系统,实现数据更新维护和管理功能。

2003年,水科所夏中华、周潮洪等采用水文、水力两种模型相结合的方法,建立蓟运河实时洪水预报调度系统,适用于中国北方地区的实时洪水预报和调度。该系统可实时洪水预报及洪水演进分析,对不同的调度方案进行仿真计算,实现洪、涝、潮一体化实时预报。同年,夏中华等开发的"天津市城市防洪信息系统工程决策支持系统",首次在天津市比较系统地建成从信息接收处理、数据存储、信息查询到洪水预报和调度仿真的多种防汛应用系统。

2004年,天津市引滦工程黎河管理处沈爱生等进行黎河流域产汇流基本特征研究,通过对暴雨洪水资料的统计分析,查清黎河流域的暴雨和洪水特征及产、汇流的基本规律,合理确定主要产流参数及流域蒸发能力,建立洪水预报模型—新安江模型,经检验和误差评定,预报模型具有较高的合格率,可以进行实时洪水预报。

(二)河口清淤

1996年,天津市水文总站郑裕君等在永定新河泥沙运动情况研究中,对1993~1995年永定新河相关断面连续实测大量水文资料的分析,总结出永定新河潮汐水流和输沙基本特征,河道对潮水波形的影响及潮波变形特点,以及沿河长潮汐变形、泥沙输移、河道淤积的现状及发展趋势。

2002年,水科所周潮洪等开展淤泥质河道清淤效果分析及工程泥沙问题研究。开发出清淤设计及综合分析系统,可通过界面操作完成基础资料的分析、淤积规律研究、泄洪能力计算、清淤效果分析、多方案比较等工作,设计并显现出永定新河清淤方案效果。

二、防潮

1996年,天津市水文总站谢润起在天津近海风暴潮研究中,以北炮台、海河闸实测潮位90年代的资料为基础,运用统计学方法对历史风暴潮的发生机率进行分析,提出不同频率年、月和汛期的极值潮位。建立不同风、风程、风暴潮增水的数值模型,最高潮位预报准确度96%。

2002年,水科所郭青平等对天津市滨海近岸流浪潮特性及工程应用研究,通过资料分析、现场观测、模型实验等手段,对天津滨海近岸的海流、波浪、潮汐的特性进行研究与分析,得出不同标准下的潮位、各种波高以及海流特性,并依次推算天津海挡的顶高程。在原有资料和实地观测资料的基础上,利用虚拟流动法建立数学模型,对不同标准下天津近海岸的潮汐进行计算分析,并根据实验结果和泥沙理论,对天津近海几个不同岸段首次进行冲刷、淤积分析,得到的结论与实际情况吻合。

第三章 气象科技

1991～2005年是天津气象科技发展历程中的快速发展时期。在气象探测技术上，由传统的人工方法向应用仪器自动探测转变，气象探测自动化由市区县向乡镇推进。对气象信号的接收，也由人工接收短波气象传真信号发展为以遥感为主的“3S”技术，一套设备接收多颗卫星数据，接收稳定、图像清晰。雷达探测发展为多普勒天气雷达。气象通讯技术的传输介质不断更新，从无线电高频到集团话路专线，又到卫星数据通信和宽带网传输，从局域网到广域网再到因特网。气象探测与通讯技术的提高，促进气象预报在时效上、内容上不断扩展，精度不断提高。天气预报产品质量较稳定、品种多样，海洋气象预报是天津气象预报的重要特色，气象科技的发展使天津气象台及时、准确地预报海上大风、风暴潮出现的时间及潮位，减少经济损失。同时，专项气象预报为全市的多种行业和部门提供服务，尤其对空气污染浓度及污染指数级别的专项气象预报，准确度达75%左右。在国内首创动态再现或预测城市中暴雨形成的沥涝积水演进过程。随着气候预测技术的发展，对天津的气候变化给出科学的预测和分析。农业气象方面重点开展资源分析与兴农网建设。人工影响天气方面开发智能化人工增雨和防雹。

第一节 气象探测

20世纪90年代末及21世纪初，天津市气象局（以下简称“市气象局”）在全市各区县共建成20余个自动气象观测站，对雷达探测和卫星云图接收等气象探测设备进行更新，提高探测和接收的质量，开展酸雨、紫外线强度及花粉浓度等特种观测。

一、自动气象站观测

天津市气象观测站在1991年前开始使用PC-1500计算器编报气象观测数据，录制地面气象记录月报报表，并向中国气象局上报数据磁带。在20世纪90年代基本上仍延用传统气象观测设备，进行人工气象观测。1991年，天津各区县气象站分期分批采用PC-1500计算器编报及录制地面气象记录月报表数据，并上报数据磁带。1997年，全市各气象台站采用磁盘录制地面气象记录月报表数据。

1999年，在人工观测的同时，天津市建成1个6要素（气温、湿度、气压、风向、风速、雨量）中心观测站（以下简称“中心站”）和9个自动雨量站组成的自动观测站网，气象探测开始整体由传统人工方法向仪器自动探测转变。2002年，陆续建成塘沽、西青和渤海A平台3个自动气象观测站。其中，塘沽站为8要素观测，较中心站增加地温、蒸发的观测；西青站为9要素观测，较塘沽站又增加太阳辐射的观测；渤海A平台为7要素观测，较中心站增加海水温度的观测。2003年，在蓟县、宝坻、武清、宁河、汉沽、大港、静海、北辰、东丽、津南气象局建成7要素自动气象观测站，均较中心站增加对地温的观测。同年12月，在天津市区建成6个5要素自动气象观测站，较中心站少测气压一项。

2004年1月1日，全市各区县气象观测业务实现人工观测与自动气象站观测双轨运行。2005年7月，蓟县许家台乡和盘山风景区建成2个自动气象观测站。气象探测自动化由市区县向乡镇推进。

二、遥感与遥测

（一）卫星云图接收

1991年前，天津市气象台（以下简称“市气象台”）配备117型传真机，与56型短波接收机配合，人工接收中国北京与日本东京发射的短波气象传真信号，通过电化学湿纸方式记录并产生各种天气图和数值天气预报图；后来接收气象传真图片逐渐改为用短波接收机、79型定频机以及全晶体管化加小规模集成电路设计的123型传真机，提供相关气象信息。

1991年，市气象局建成极轨气象卫星接收站。JSZ—9C极轨卫星接收系统及与之配套的386微型计算机构成的图像处理系统，可接收中国风云1号卫星信号和美国诺阿（NOAA）卫星云图。1992年，市气象台淘汰卫星云图接收设备和人工冲洗、烘干照片方法，改用微型计算机自动接收处理卫星云图照片，可接收高分辨率宽幅云图，显示在计算机屏幕上，使用方便，数据存储量提高。1994年，气象台应用计算机建立天气预报图形、图像工作站。1998年，对接收机、图形处理系统、伺服系统进行全面升级改造，由齿轮传动改为步进电机传动，一套设备可接收多颗卫星数据，使接收更稳定，图像更清晰。2001年安装极轨气象卫星接收处理系统VSAT次站和小站，开展以遥感为主的“3S”技术（即GPS-全球定位系统、GIS-地理信息系统、RS-遥感技术）研究及应用服务。

（二）雷达探测

1985年，西郊区气象站引进美国WSR—81S十公分数字化天气雷达。1992年，完成对该雷达发射机磁控管、接收机本振等国产化改造，降低其使用成本；加强对回波强度、移向、移速、回波顶高、回波的水汽分布等要素数字化观测，以及雷达联防重要灾害性降雨、冰雹天气数字化观测。1999年，再次对十公分雷达设备进行异地改造，实现由市气象台微机发出指令，经过无线信道传输至西郊区气象站，微机接收命令后，控制雷达设备做开机和回波观测扫描等操作。2000年，多普勒天气雷达在天津滨海新区气象预警中心使用。

三、特种观测

（一）大气边界层梯度观测

1986年，在265.2米高的气象专用铁塔上，按照大气边界层气象对数廓线的特点，设置15层梯度观测层，在各层安装温度、风向、风速传感器，分别进行全天候自动观测，成为全国首例观测项目。1995年，在20、120、250米高度处分别增加设置湿度传感器，对大气边界层梯度观测，获取第一手数据，为环境评价、防治城市污染等提供资料。

（二）酸雨观测

1992年，天津市采用PHS型PH计、DDS型电导率仪等开始观测酸雨。记录降水过程中的气象要素，测量水样的PH值和电导率（K）值，化验水样中的化学成分等。

（三）花粉浓度观测

1999年，天津市采用Leica GALEN-Ⅲ/TV三目电视生物显微镜、花粉采集器等仪器开始观测花粉浓度。全市共建4个花粉采集点，观测时间为每年3～10月。在此期间，每天在一定范围内发布24小时花粉浓度观测实况数据。

第二节　气象通信

1990年后，在天津市气象通信技术中，通信传输介质不断更新，从无线电高频到集团话路专线，再到卫星通讯、地面宽带网。传输内容不断增多，从单纯语音信息，到有文本格式的常规气象信息，再发展到卫星通讯阶段。

1991年，信息网络采用只能连接几台机器的3+网，后诺威勒网络实现各办公室间网络连接，市气象局内所有用户单位都能在局域网上共享资源。2003年，网络设备全面更新，桌面达到100兆，关键业务服务器可到千兆连接。随着因特网的发展，传输介质的不断升级，带宽由0.064兆增加到2005年的100兆线路共享。

一、数据通信

（一）无线数据通信

1990～1994年，市气象局与各区县气象台站间的通信一直采用400兆赫特高频电话通信系统，各种气象预报指导产品是由预报员利用高频电话口述给各气象台站人员。

1994年10月，市气象局与北京邮电部数据所合作，对高频电台进行无线数据传输改造，配备微机和无线数传调制解调卡，实现基于高频电话通信系统的无线数据通信网。1995年，该网基本建成并试运行，同时开展区县气象预报工作站软件的研究，完善无线数据通讯系统。该系统硬件部分由无线信道网络和微机通信系统组成，系统无线中继台设置在天津电视塔274米处的机房内，通讯范围覆盖全市，达到全天候、高质量通讯。设计人员将自行设计并研制的电台与调制解调器之间的适配器，改造为高频电台，既可用于通话又可传输数据。区县气象台站无线数据通信网的软件由通信软件和应用软件组成。该项无线数据通信系统的研制、使用将各区县气象台站以高频无线数据通信网淘汰原有的气象传真图接收机。从此，气象传真图及市气象台的各种气象预报均可通过该数据通信网以图形和文本信息方式传至各区县气象台站。

（二）地面电话数据通信

1993年前，市气象局与中国气象局间数据传输利用“四报一话”（在一条线路上划分为一段话路和四段报路）线路，可传输一定常规气象观测和普通语音信息。1993年，市气象局淘汰一类传真机、电传机、实时库和填图微机外接口等通信和数据处理设备，建成“全话路”地面数据通信专线，利用地面长途电话专线和通信用计算机实现与中国气象局间的数据传输，速率为9600波特，同年9月升为19200波特。

1998年，市气象局建设“169接入网工程”，在其局域网上配置远程拨号访问服务系统，区县气象台站与市气象局气象资料的传输质量得以提高。

1999年，区县气象台站升级远程访问服务系统，提高气象数据的传输速率和质量，将电话拨号线路由169电话线路改为4路集团电话线路，能接受4个拨号用户的同时访问。扩展后的远程访问服务系统替代原有的高频无线数据通信网。2000年，区县台站研制气象报文自动收编、转发系统，实现其地面观测记录的计算机发报。2002年，通过采用拨号联选器等手段使远程访问服务系统得到完善，使其成为市气象局与各区县气象局间数据通信的主要手段。

（三）卫星数据通信

1995年，市气象局筹建“气象卫星综合应用业务系统”（以下简称“9210”系统）。1996年10月，安装省级小型卫星通信地球站，开通话音地球站和数据地球站，11月安装调试省级网络系统，完成“9210”系统，并与网络设备、话音地球站及数据地球站连接，构成广域网。省级网络采用总线型拓扑结构，实现双机热备份。

1997年，塘沽气象局建成小型卫星地球站及配套设施。“9210”系统正式运行后，市气象局和塘沽气象局将中国气象局的地面电话数据传输改为卫星线路传输，中国气象局的各种气象信息和预报产品也改用卫星广播接收软件进行接收。

二、信息网络

（一）局域网

1993年，市气象局建成诺威勒（Novell）局域网络系统代替原有的3+网，网络速度达到10兆波特。

1997年4月，实现“9210”系统小型机与诺威勒网的互联。1998年，市气象局改造局域网，用星型网络代替总线型网络，网络带宽为共享100兆。通过对用户的分组，划分成不同的IP地址段，实现用户联网，并对上网计算机进行统一管理。1999年，市气象局内所有用户单位都能够在局域网上共享资源。2003年，建成新的网络系统，局域网在设备、带宽和功能上进一步加强。其网络拓扑结构选择树型结构，网络主干和关键业务服务器实现千兆连接。利用核心交换机Catalyst 6509的路由交换功能实现虚拟局域网的划分及外部虚拟局域网的路由设置，并在网络中利用访问控制列表设置相应的访问策略，以提高数据访问的安全性。2004年，局域网设置防病毒服务器，安装赛门铁克网络防病毒系统，解决局域网的计算机病毒防范问题。

（二）气象专用广域网

2003年，市气象局建成气象专用广域网。该网由市气象局局端设备和各区县局设备以及连接两端的2兆同步数字体系的光纤线路组成。市气象局用华为Quidway 3680E路由器可提供16个2兆接口，用于从光纤上提取16个2兆电路。区县局网络设备为华为Quidway 1760路由器，同时在路由器AUX端口连接调制解调器，利用电话线实现对光纤线路的自动拨号备份。

2004年，市气象局逐步建立与市防汛抗旱指挥部、地质环境监测总站、市环境监测中心、飞机场、市农业局等同城用户间的2兆SDH光纤广域网连接，将各同城用户纳入到气象专用广域网中，部分单位利用网络连接实现气象预报服务与天气会商。

（三）因特网

1997年，市气象局利用“9210”系统的卫星通信、小型机网络，通过数据通信局提供的64K数据专线与基带调制解调器开通169气象信息专线——“天津热线”，实现气象信息在因特网上的发布。

2002年，市气象局通过ADSL线路实现局域网接入因特网。其线路由2兆铜缆、ADSL调制解调器和路由设备构成，最终接入局域网交换机。

2003年，市气象局在数据局设立托管服务器，建立市气象局门户网站，逐步开通专业气象服务网站、兴农网网站等气象特色网站，实现政务公开。同年，市气象局连接ADSL线路的路由器改为思科防火墙，提高访问因特网的安全性。

2004年，市气象局为增加局域网接入因特网的途径，采用移动公司2兆光纤线路。2005年，市气象局完成局域网接入因特网的100兆共享线路建设。

第三节 天气预报

1991～2005年，天津在气象预报技术、科研方面发展很快。不仅在常规气象预报上时效扩大，内容扩展，数值天气预报释用技术不断更新，理论研究逐渐深化，而且在工业、农业、城建、环保、能源等多方面开展专项气象预报服务。“短期气象预报业务流程”投入使用，短期预报精度和预报产品的质量有所提高。同时，对海洋气象预报进行多项研究。对海雾成因、次级环流对当地天气的影响，以及海洋气象中尺度数值预报进行系统研究。

一、常规气象预报

（一）时效与内容

1、时效

1991年前，市气象台每天发布24小时气象预报、48小时天气趋势预报，还定期发布中期天气趋势预报和长期气候趋势预报。1991年1月 1日开始，增加发布48小时气象预报。1999年7月，试发布短时3小时气象预报，2001年12月正式发布。2003年3月，在天津电视台天气预报节目中发布72小时气象预报。2003年

6月1日开始，通过广播、电视等媒体向公众发布6小时气象预报。

2、预报内容

1997年前，气象预报内容主要有天气现象、风向风力和温度三项，1997年1月1日开始增加发布降水概率预报。1998年4月1日制作分县的天气预报，并通过高频电话网及169信息网发布。

2000年，市气象台开发海河流域面雨量预报方法，2000年7月，每天早晨7:00计算和试发布该流域面雨量预报。2002年，正式向海河流域所在各省气象部门、中国气象局和海河水利委员会发送该流域面雨量预报，为海河流域防汛抗旱工作提供气象信息。

2004年，为做好地质灾害预报预警工作，市气象台于9月14日首次发布地质灾害预警并获得成功。

为做好防灾减灾和突发性气象灾害的防范工作，提高气象灾害预警信息使用效率，2005年1月1日，市气象台对公众发布“灾害性天气预警信号”。2005年汛期，该预警信号信息以滚动字幕形式在天津市电视台电视节目中播出。

（二）数值天气预报

1991年6月15日，市气象台接收并应用中国气象局中期数值天气预报业务（以下简称“T42”）的预报产品制作当地中期气象预报。随该局中期数值天气预报业务的不断更新，市气象台先后使用其T63（1993年）、T106（2000年）、T213（2002年）等中期数值天气预报产品指导制作当地中期气象预报。

1992年，第二代中尺度数值天气预报模式在天津投入业务使用；1994年、2001年先后投入使用第四、第五代中尺度数值天气预报模式。

1993～1997年，天津市气象科学研究所（以下简称“市气科所”）解以扬、林枚等承担中国气象局应用开发项目，对天津地区强对流天气的气候特征及成因、大尺度概念模型、中尺度系统诊断分析、数值试验及预报进行研究，建立强对流天气档案库及大尺度概念模型相似识别、多尺度多要素物理量诊断分析、区域数值预报业务、卫星数字化云图与多尺度物理量场结合估算降水等系统，以提高强对流天气预报的准确率。

1999～2003年，为深入分析250米低层大气风、温梯度结构变化规律，市气科所解以扬、刘学军、朱玉强等承担中国气象局“低层大气风、温廓线预报方法研究”项目，利用天津市气象铁塔测得的大量观测事实，开展对低层大气风、温廓线预报方法的研究，建立可投入预报业务使用的250米低层大气风、温廓线的定量预报方法。

2005年，为提高天气预报的时效和精度，市气科所解以扬、孟冬梅等引进中国气象科学研究院开发的“大气非静力多尺度天气预报数值模式”，利用南开大学‘南开之星’高性能计算机建立天津地区高时空分辨率的中尺度数值预报系统。探索将气象卫星、多普勒雷达探测资料与常规地面探测资料、高空探测资料进行融合分析，产生出精细的数值预报初始场，使天津地区数值预报的准确程度得到提高。

（三）可视化天气会商

2002年，市气象台开展电视远程可视天气会商系统建设，当年实现与塘沽区气象台电视远程天气会商。2003年，市气象台对可视天气会商系统的部分硬件设备进行更新和升级，使可视天气会商系统得到进一步完善。

2004年，市气象台与全市5个区县气象站开通可视化天气会商，制定并执行《与区县台站可视化预报会商内容及会商流程规范》。2004年6月，完成可视天气会商系统影视墙大屏幕项目建设，在每日天气会商和监视天气变化中发挥作用。2005年汛期前，气象台与全市所有各区县气象台站均实现可视化天气会商。

（四）短期气象预报

1994年，市气象台建立天气预报图形、图像工作站，具有处理、显示、储存实时气象资料和数值天气预报产品，以及图像迭加、分屏显示及剖面显示等功能，同时取消欧洲数值预报中心数值预报图的人工绘图工作，提高气象信息的使用效率。1998年4月1日，市气象台增发对各区县站的短期天气预报，同年5月，在天气会商室内建立预报领班、主班、副班席位制，解决预报人员利用计算机调看天气图拥挤的问题。是年，“气象信息综合分析处理系统”开通使用，短期数值预报信息及各层次天气分析图、更多的气象信息等均可通过计算机在该系统上调用。

2000年，市气象台刘盎然、刘娟、杨德江等研制完成“天津市气象决策服务系统”，并于2001年投入气象业务运行，包括气象预报、重要天气报告、气候预测、气象情报、灾情收集评估等。同年，实现与天津市政府网的连网和气象资料上网传送。根据政府部门需求制定决策气象服务方案、服务周年大纲等，进一步完善天津的决策气象服务工作。

2003年，沙尘暴客观预报方法在常规天气预报中应用。同年，市气象台开发“短期预报自动评分软件”并投入使用。2004年，该台利用中国气象局及日本、欧洲数值预报中心的数值天气预报产品开发当地降水概率、温度、夏季大雨以上降水等预报应用软件，纳入短期气象预报业务流程。

2003年，市气象台刘盎然、张志云等参加水利部项目“于桥水库应急调度分析系统——于桥水库汛限水位动态控制应用研究”，对于桥水库地区汛期、主汛期进行划分，指出影响水库地区暴雨天气的七种环流类型，并对降水综合预报方法进行研究，给出于桥水库地区三天的短期降水预报方法。

（五）中期气象预报

20世纪70年代后期，天津市气象台开始制作、发布全市中期天气预报，包括3～5天天气预报、旬天气趋势预报等，为市领导部门以及有关单位提供预报服务。

1988～1991年，市气象台周鸣盛、刘娟等研究天津初冬寒潮引发初冰冻的中期预报方法，得出引起初冬初冰冻天气的三种典型大气环流模型及中期预报指标。使用该方法制作天津初冬初冰冻中期天气预报，收到较好效果。

1993～1995年，市气象台刘娟、闫雅珍等对“影响天津农业生产的灾害性天气，干热风、倒春寒的中期预报方法”进行研究，提出当地中期预报方法，应用于预报服务。

1986～1996年，中期天气预报人员使用数值预报产品，包括中国T106产品，欧洲中心数值预报产品和日本数值预报产品，结合实际预报经验、长波理论、天气动力学理论及其他统计学方法，使中期趋势预报的水平逐步提高，质量稳定。

（六）短时气象预报

1992～1995年，为提高灾害性天气的预报准确率，市气科所王炜、石学军、解以扬等完成“雷达探测结合中尺度数值预报对雹暴的预测”，利用雷达探测结合中尺度数值预报，开展对雹暴的预测研究，研究成果可在冰雹云到来1～2小时前，对其发生、发展、移动路径及落区作出较为准确的预报。

2000年，塘沽滨海新区预警中心引进多普勒数字化天气雷达。2001年，市气象台开始建设短时气象预警工作站。2002年，市气象台安装多普勒数字化天气雷达终端显示器，及时接收该天气雷达探测信息，用以制作短时天气预报。之后，气象卫星和多普勒天气雷达、闪电定位仪等特种观测设备和观测资料在短时气象预报中发挥作用。2004年，利用第五代中尺度天气预报模式（即MM5）和多普勒数字化天气雷达资料研发短时降水预报和温度预报软件，提高短时天气预报水平。市气象台利用精细天气预报业务方法和短时预报预警业务方法及时发布3~6小时滚动气象预报和0～3小时订正气象信息，为专业气象用户提供短时预报，为人工影响天气防雹、增雨作业提供短时预报和跟踪预报服务。

（七）开通气象专线

2004年，市气象台与水利部海河水利委员会（以下简称“海委”）间开通2兆的通信专线，每天向海委提供所需的各种气象资料、雷达回波图象及海河流域面雨量预报，派出预报业务人员参加海委天气水文会商。

2005年汛期，开通市气象台与海委间的可视化天气会商渠道。同时，市气象台与市防汛指挥部开通2兆专线通信网，向市防汛部门及时提供多普勒数字化天气雷达回波图象、卫星云图等气象资料和各类气象预报，做好天津安全渡汛的气象服务。

二、海洋气象预报

（一）风暴潮预报预警

1991年，市气象台荣艳淑等对“天津市塘沽风暴潮灾害的物理机制及预报方法”进行研究，提出塘沽风暴潮灾害预报指标，并应用在气象预报中，对2005年8月9日台风“麦莎”引起的渤海风暴潮预报起到作用。

1992年9月1日受台风影响，塘沽出现强风暴潮，市气象台在风暴潮发生之前多次向市防汛指挥部防潮分部、天津沿海各工矿企业及有关单位发布风暴潮预报，使受灾损失得以减低。

1994年、1996年、1997年，天津沿海都出现5米以上高潮位强风暴潮，市气象台及时准确地预报出风暴潮出现时间、潮位，为国家减少数亿元的经济损失。

(二)海区预报

1991年，市气象台开始发布中国沿海12个海区天气和风浪预报，为海上实施作业的用户提供针对性气象预报服务。1994年，预报范围扩展到中国和日本沿海的30个海区。

1992～1993年，市气象台与天津大学联合开发“海洋预报录入系统”。应用该系统，预报人员可方便地将预报结论输入计算机，并自动生成预报文本，通过自动传真发送到用户。同时该系统还可以在DOS环境下将预报的文字转化为语音，利用警报器广播系统向用户广播。

1995年，市气科所王淑芬、解以扬、李培彦等完成“利用数值模拟开展渤海湾西部、边界层次级环流的研究”，分析不同气流经过海岸线附近引起的次级环流及垂直运动情况，以及对天气的影响。指出次级环流可以触发中尺度对流活动，既可使该地区天气系统得以维持和发展，又易产生灾害性天气。

1998年开始，市专业气象台选派技术人员随海上运输和海洋石油作业船出海，根据海洋施工作业需要，现场制作有针对性的气象预报，提供服务。

2002～2004年，市气科所解以扬、孟冬梅等承担科技部社会公益项目“渤海海洋气象中尺度数值预报试验系统研究”，开展渤海大风天气的数值试验、大雾灾害的模拟能力检验和数值试验、海冰的预测等研究，建立渤海地区非静力中尺度数值预报系统。该系统根据当地的地形高程、土地利用状况等，对模式的参数进行修正，建立模式产品的动力统计解释应用方法，有助于改善数值模式预报风速偏小的弱点。

三、专项气象预报

市气象台在开展专项气象预报时，注重满足与气象密切相关的行业需求。1993年，市气象台对纺织行业中空气湿度与产品质量控制的关系进行研究。纺织行业可根据该台提供的湿度预报采取不同的通风、降温、抽湿等措施，以达到节能降耗目的。

1995年，市气象台魏华等研究“冬季采暖节能气象预报方法”，根据冬季采暖期室内温度、供暖系统给、回水温度的关系，针对不同天气状况、温度、风向，对供暖企业控制给、回水温度进行指导，达到既保温又节能的目的。

1995～1997年，市气科所与市电力局合作完成“气象灾害对电力设施的影响及服务研究”，对气象灾害给电力输、变、送电及电力设施造成的灾害进行调查与评估，研究不同性质的大雾与输电线路事故的关系及预防措施，建立起电力气象服务系统。

1998年，为实时预测、动态评估城市中强降水内涝灾害的风险变化，市气科所解以扬、夏祥鳌等承担的中国气象局“气象灾害(强降水)评估及对策研究”项目，利用城市暴雨沥涝仿真模型，建立内涝灾害风险区划，可为合理制定减灾对策提供依据，并提高城市强降水灾害的风险分析评估水平。

1998年，市气科所与中国水利水电研究院合作，共同开展“天津市城区暴雨沥涝监测预警系统开发研究”，在城市洪涝灾害仿真模型基础上，结合天津市城区沥涝的具体特点和服务要求，采用具有时空变化特征的实时降水信息和降水的数值预报结果，动态再现或预测城市中暴雨形成的沥涝积水演进过程。在城市排水管网系统的模拟方法上实现地面与地下管网水体相结合的模拟计算，计算精度有所提高，进而探索气象、水利与城建领域相结合的新路。

1999年，市气科所白玉荣等与市胸科医院等单位合作，共同参加中国气象局应用开发项目“花粉浓度潜势预报”，分析花粉的季节、区域分布特征，对气温、风、降水、积温等气象要素与花粉浓度的关系进行较深入地探讨，给出花粉症的临床特征与花粉症的防治措施。

2002～2005年，市气科所解以扬等联合天津大学建工学院、江苏省气象台、江苏省气象科学研究所等单位共同承担中国气象局预测减灾应用技术开发项目“城区暴雨内涝仿真系统技术推广”，开发出城市暴雨内涝仿真系统。该系统以平面二维非恒定流基本控制方程为骨架，以城市地表与明渠河道水流运动为主要模拟对象，考虑到城市的地形地貌特征和排水系统特点，依托地理信息系统（GIS）进行信息预处理和后处理，可监测和预测暴雨造成的城市内涝灾害，也可对不同重现期的内涝灾害进行风险评估。

第四节　气候预测

20世纪90年代，短期气候趋势预测在以往统计分析方法的基础上，注重对前期强信号因子的分析，应用动力和统计预报相结合的方法，开展短期气候预测工作对天津的气候变化给出科学的分析与评价。

一、短期气候预测

1991年，市气科所闫孝时等对天津地区雨季的起止时间、大气环流特征及其在雨季中随时间的变化情况进行统计分析。其统计预报方法以多因子资料序列为依据，选取最佳因子拟合得到预报方程，可预报天津地区雨季结束时间。

1992年，市气象台梁平德等采用人工智能方法，以“机器学习”的归纳与观察方式，在微机上实现时间序列历史演变预报，并将实践经验和“机器学习”的功能发展为周期性、持续性、相似性和一般化等四种预报模型。1994年，梁平德等根据500百帕月平均高度数据计算1951～1990年40年间1月份平均地转风场，分析冬季亚洲急流与中国东部主要季节降水的关系。研究表明南支急流（25°～30°北纬，70°～115°东经范围内）强（弱），随之长江以南春季雨量偏多（少），华北夏季雨量偏多（偏少）的变化规律。同时研究得出印度夏季风雨量与华北夏季降水、长江以南春季降水显著相关。

1994～1996年，市气科所周鸣盛等承担中国气象局科研项目“华北干旱研究进展”，从近百年华北地区降水的变化入手，分析研究华北干旱形成的原因，对以往华北地区干旱、洪涝的研究加以总结提炼，建立天津降水、温度数据库及华北旱涝预测人工智能系统。1997年，市气候服务中心刘爱霞等分析研究天津市近百年降水变化规律，开展旱涝成因研究。从气候、大气等方面研究天津旱涝发生的背景，在认识旱涝长期天气过程的基础上，探讨短期气候预测前期强信号，并对以往的数理统计气候预测方法进行检验，建立天津市旱涝短期气候预测及服务系统。

2001年，市气象台刘蕴然等通过对初夏大气环流的分析，揭示天津盛夏旱涝与初夏环流间的物理关系，指出中国华北初夏500百帕出现正高度差中心时，天津盛夏容易出现干旱；反之，出现负高度差中心时，易出现多雨。

2003年，市气候服务中心段丽瑶等通过分析天津春季沙尘天气的气候背景以及历史演变规律，研究影响其前期各种气候和环流因子，建立相关气候预测概念模型。2004年，市气候服务中心周慧等根据500百帕高度因子、赤道中东太平洋海温特征等对海河流域夏季降水的影响，制作海河流域夏季降水预报。同年，市气科所韩素芹等参加“EOS/MODIS卫星资料在渤海海冰监测中的应用研究”，利用组件式GIS技术实现对渤海海冰的发生、发展趋势进行动态监测和实时预测功能。

二、气候分析

1989年，为摸清外环线绿化林带对天津生态环境的影响，天津市气候应用所陈凤贤等应用数理统计方法，对1990～1992年天津的气候及变化进行研究。指出自绿化带建成后，天津城区的热岛现象趋于减弱，空气相对湿度增加，平均风速与风沙日降低，气温和降水趋向稳定。

1991年，天津市气候应用所冀文萍等在研制的“气候诊断评价资料分析软件”中，对气候要素的周期、阶段、异常状况、演变过程、相似时段等分析，资料均可用于各类气候分析、气候预测研究及专业服务。

1997～1998年，天津市气候服务中心陈凤贤等在天津30年历史气象资料整编基础上，撰写《天津城市气候》一书，首次从城市热岛、温度、湿度、降水、风、辐射和热量平衡等方面论述天津城市气候特征及大气污染环境状况、城市气象灾害及防御等。

2002年，天津市气候服务中心郭军等根据气候业务需要以及政府决策部门的需求，开展天津地区旱涝变化状况的实时监测工作，实现对实时资料进行自动采集、检索和判别，为政府决策部门提供天津旱涝灾害的各类信息。

2004年，在“全国第三次风能资源普查”工作中，为摸清天津市风能资源的拥有数量及分布状况，受天津市发展和改革委员会委托，天津市气候服务中心刘娟、郭军等应用数学计算方法，对天津15个气象台站1971～2000年测风数据进行风能资源多项参数计算，并对天津地区风能资源进行评价，给出天津市风能资源的分布状况、变化特点、风能资源总储量和技术可开发量。根据风能资源优劣分布、变化特征，结合地形、地貌特点和建设条件，提出天津市风能资源可开发区域建议，为天津市风电发展规划和风电场工程规划提供有力的技术支持。

第五节 农业气象

1991～2005年，农业气象在推进现代化建设、提高服务针对性和时效性等方面取得较大的发展，特别是利用计算机、网络、3S技术等手段，开展农业气象情报预报、农业遥感、农业气候资源及灾害监测评估等业务服务工作取得较显著的社会和经济效益。

一、资源分析

1995年，市气科所宛公展等完成“天津市农业气候资源评价与开发利用研究”，对天津市热量、水和光能资源及农业气象灾害进行综合评价与分析，建立农业气候资源数据库与计算机检索咨询系统，分析决策系统。

1997年，市气科所黎贞发等完成天津市津南区水稻遥感动态监测及估产方法研究，利用地理信息系统和遥感技术进行水稻种植面积估算，精度超过90%；研制出遥感估产综合模式；同时建立一套气象卫星水稻遥感资料处理系统。

2001年，该所黎贞发、孙治贵等完成“天津市主要粮食作物管理信息系统开发研究”，依托“3S”技术，完成信息标准化、数据采集处理及数据库建设、遥感资料的处理与应用、信息同化处理及复合、系统功能二次开发集成等技术。

2001～2003年，该所黎贞发、孙治贵等完成“天津市农业信息化工程”，开发智能化农业决策系统气象数据库、基于webgis下运行的农业基础地理信息系统、农业气象特色网站等，完成农业基础地理数据库，农业气象数据在黄瓜、葡萄、猪、水产等种植、养殖业专家咨询网络系统中得到应用。

2005年，市气科所黎贞发、韩素芹等完成“天津市农业气候区划”和“蓟县气候资源调查及利用评价”项目。对天津市12个区县1971～2000年气象观测资料进行农业气候资源和灾害分析、评价，采用地理信息系统和数字地形图资料，编制全市农业气候状况统计报表和图集；制作蓟县山区500米小网格精细气候资源分布图；完成葡萄、苹果种植的气候规划。

二、硬件设备

1999年9月，对极轨卫星接收处理设备进行升级改造，成为新一代极轨气象卫星接收处理系统，设备运转全天候无人值守。

2005年，安装卫星数据广播应用系统（DVB-S），接收国家气象卫星中心主站广播的EOS/MODIS和NOAA/FY-1卫星资料，星下点分辨率由原来1.1X1.1平方千米提高到250X250平方米，同一地点同一天多次卫星扫描覆盖，资料数据可用于农作物长势监测、作物产量预报及干旱、洪涝、湿地、海冰、沙尘暴等农业和生态环境监测，监测手段从地面扩展到大面积遥感监测。

三、软件开发

1993～1995年，市气科所姚奎元等建立天津市农业气象业务服务系统，实现农业气象情报、预报业务由手工制作向计算机自动制作的转变。1998～1999年，市气科所黎贞发等开发天津区县气象台站农业气象服务综合系统，包含通信、信息处理浏览及分析、预报产品制作及分发、客户服务等，适合区县气象局使用。

2001年，市气候服务中心刘爱霞、高鹰等完成“农业气象记录质量控制与可视化报表”软件，解决历史农业气象资料从纸质到电子版的转化及信息查询输出和农业气象资料电子化难题，并在全国气象系统推广使用。同时，编写中华人民共和国气象行业标准《农业气象观测记录年报数据文件格式》。

2002年，市气科所完成天津市农业气象信息网站的开发建设，利用互联网为广大农民提供农业气象信息。2003年，建设天津兴农网，内容包括气象预报、农业气候、农业气象情报以及农业生产管理、农业新品种、农业科技等方面信息。

第六节 人工影响天气

1991～2005年，天津地区旱情日重，雹情频频。天津市人工影响天气办公室（以下简称“市人影办”）先后采用歼击机发射催化剂火箭弹、气球携带碘化银、火箭与高炮联合以及智能化人工增雨等多种增雨措施，开发空中水资源，并根据不同类型的冰雹云采用多种射击方法进行人工消雹，作业区内没有出现重大雹灾。

一、增雨

1991年后，天津地区严重干旱，天津市政府要求采取多种措施在全市范围内进行大规模抗旱节水工作，人工影响天气是措施之一。1996年，市人影办在空军杨村机场部门的配合下，应用歼击机向云层内发射催化剂火箭弹的方式进行人工增雨试验。1997年，市人影办采用气球携带碘化银焰弹对空中层状云和夏季利用高炮对积状云进行增雨的试验工作。2000年，天津市委、市政府把人工增雨、开发空中水资源列为天津市抗旱节水的五项措施之一。市人影办进行火箭、高炮联合增雨试验，效果比较显著。2002年，市人影办与河北省人工影响天气办公室联合在天津市实施飞机人工增雨作业。

2003年，市人影办靳瑞军等完成天津市科委的攻关培育项目“智能化人工增雨技术研究”，通过多普勒天气雷达、卫星云图、探空等大气探测技术，以及对云和降水的观测，结合数值模拟和外场试验，对天津市火箭人工增雨作业云系的演变规律、降水特征以及人工增雨作业技术进行研究。通过研究确定出适合火箭人工增雨作业云系的宏观监测、识别技术和判别指标，整合气象信息综合分析处理系统、多普勒雷达产品和火箭、高炮增雨防雹作业催化剂扩散模拟系统，建立火箭人工增雨作业指挥系统，实现指定区域内火箭高炮作业方案设计及效果评估。

2005年，为增加山区降雪和做好森林防火，市人影办配合蓟县林业部门，在蓟县盘山、八仙山、九山顶安装三部碘化银燃烧炉，开展以针对降低森林火险等级和增加林区降雪为目的的高山地基人工增雨（雪）工作。冬季，在碘化银焰炉中燃烧碘化银烟条，使催化剂直接进入积雨云层中，实施人工增雪作业。

二、防雹

天津是中国北方冰雹灾害多发地区之一，每年大约有50多万亩农田遭受冰雹灾害。1991年后，市人影办开展人工防雹工作，对空中积雨云进行人工消雹作业。经调查，作业有效区内没有出现重大雹灾，防雹保护面积累计达到1万余平方千米。消雹多用炮击，根据冰雹云的不同种类，确定不同的作业部位和作业用药弹数量。作业方法采用前倾梯形、垂直梯度、水平射击法、同心圆射击法、扇形点射、侧向射击等。全市9个区县设立防雹炮站44处，其中17处为高炮站。天津警备区调拨“三七”高炮24门用于人工防雹或增雨。

2005年，市、区县两级财政共同投资800多万元，对全市52个人工影响天气作业炮站基础设施进行改造，新建改建炮库、炮台、弹药库、值班室等，弹药库安装避雷装置，加装防盗设施，配备防火设施，新建通讯铁塔，改善通讯质量。同年，更新双管“三七”高炮57门，购置火箭发射设备17部。

第四章 地质灾害预防

1991年，中国地震局第一监测中心（原国家地震局测量大队和原国家地震局第一地形变监测中心，以下均简称“一测中心”），首先将GPS技术引入地形变测量中，建立国内首个全球定位系统（GPS）试验网——京津地区GPS试验网。同期，天津市应用大地形变测量技术监测市内地面沉降，并不断拓宽地形变测量监测和研究领域，进行地铁、大型工程等施工的地形变监测。在防震监测技术上向网络化、自动化、数字化迈进，至2005年，天津防震监测网点已覆盖全市。

第一节 大地形变监测

1991～2005年，天津在大地形变监测技术上的进展，主要体现在对水平形变和垂直形变监测技术的引进、开发和利用方面，取得丰硕成果。其中，一测中心在国内首次将GPS应用于地形变观测与地震活动研究。该中心先后获国家科学进步奖二等奖1项（1991年），中国地震局科技进步一等奖2项、二等奖8项，获国家测绘局测绘科技进步一等奖1项（2005年）。

一、水平形变监测

（一）建网与观测

一测中心作为主要承担、实施单位，参与多项工程的建设和观测。其中，在1990年完成监测网设计、勘选和标石埋设的基础上，1992年建成当时全国最大的GPS地震监测网——“华北地形变监测网”，该网共选建42个观测点，最短边长30千米，最长边长362千米，平均141千米，布设在东经107°～122°，北纬33.5°～42°的区域内。将GPS观测点沿华北的主要活动构造带布设，以有效监测华北地区地壳运动和大震的发生，力争控制主要的地震活动带和重点地震监视区。

1994～1996年，建设“首都圈地形变监测网”。1998年参与“首都圈防震减灾示范区系统工程”和“中国地壳运动观测网络工程”的建设。其中“首都圈地形变监测网”覆盖北京、天津两个直辖市及石家庄、张家口、承德等十多个城市。重点监测京、津、石三大交通枢纽及密云、官厅、陡河三个水库。

1994～1998年，一测中心对“首都圈地形变监测网”进行改建，对GPS观测网采用分层布局的网点布设技术创新方案，全网由93个测站(点)组成，观测点优先选址在地震活动区以及块体活动边界。第一层首都圈，由57个测站组成，点距平均为50～100千米。在主要活动断裂两侧点距缩短，测站加密，并和原有国家三角点联合，两个观测站之间距离可缩短到20～30千米。第二层首都圈外围，华北地区GPS监测网站距离大，密度低，共有30个站。第三层为利用全国布设的上海、长春、天津、西安、乌鲁木齐、海口6个跟踪站。另外，新选建4个GPS站。1998年，国家计委组织对该网进行验收，结论是:超过原有设计指标的精度要求。

早期的GPS测量是利用原有的三角测量所使用的三角点，利用光学或重锤对中方法，测量结果误差较大。20世纪90年代中期开始，一测中心在建设GPS网时由最初的三角点改为水泥观测墩(包括土层墩、基岩墩)，墩高约1.2米，顶部安装专用的三心一致(目标、标石、仪器三个中心)的不锈钢归心盘，观测误差可控制在0.5毫米之内。同时，把GPS观测由昼测夜停改为24小时连续观测，以后又改为96小时连续观测，观测资料连续可靠。在此后的国家重点项目——中国地壳运动观测网络工程及福建省、山西省、天津市GPS观测网建设中都采用首都圈GPS地形变监测网观测墩的强制归心装置技术。

(二)探测与数据分析

1.块体边界运动及形变

20世纪90年代，一测中心利用积累的GPS观测数据，研究板块边界的变形，并建立板块刚体运动模型，中国大陆构造块体的现今活动和变形与模型。2003年，一测中心黄立人完成的“中国大陆块体的现今活动和变形”、李延兴等完成国家重点基础研究项目“中国大陆现今地壳运动与活动地块及其边界运动学研究”和2004年完成的“由GPS结果研究中国大陆应变—应力场的特征及动力学问题”等项研究，发现不仅板块边界变形，板内也有变形。他们在研究中建立起活动块体整体旋转均匀应变和块体整体旋转线性应变弹性运动方程和中国大陆水平形变场、应变场和全国地壳运动速度场，以及中国大陆地壳运动的动力学模型。

2.气象探测

1998年，一测中心李延兴等开展GPS测量大气折射模型、GPS测量大气折射改正、应用地基GPS技术遥感大气柱水汽量等试验研究。在理论上证明利用地基GPS观测探测大气可降水量的可能性，改进并完善利用地基GPS观测探测大气可降水量的软件系统，提高实时数值天气预报的准确性。

3.地震预测

2004年，一测中心对“中国地壳运动观测网络工程”三期复测的全部GPS数据进行统一处理，结果被用于当年的1～3年中国大陆地震大形势判定和年度会商，并在2005年度震情趋势判定中给出新疆乌什附近地震危险区的预测，2005年2月15日发生的乌什6.2级地震就发生在该危险区内。

4.GPS数据处理

1996年，一测中心杨国华等利用GPS的最新测量成果分析中国大陆GPS基准站观测误差的时序特征、误差分布及垂直形变特征，以及GPS基准站时序水平位移特征，均取得新的成果。

二、垂直形变监测

(一)形变信息提取

20世纪90年代初期，一测中心开展形变信息提取方法的研究。1996年，该中心薄万举提出单项异常变化信息提取的新方法——多点组信息法。这种方法给出标准化信息流，有利于合成多项不同量纲的异常信息，建立四点组斜率法线性数学模型。1999年，他又提出新的形变前兆的提取方法—斜率差信息法。这种方法能有效地提取短临异常变化的信息，包括突变转折阶跃趋势消失或减弱等各种类型的异常信号。

(二)中长期地震预测

1999年，一测中心谢觉民在地壳形变方法对地震中期趋势的判定研究中，以华北地区研究为实例，提出中期地震危险区划分的地壳垂直速率梯度标准，并提出垂直形变尺度特征是预测地震危险性的重要指标。

同年，一测中心薄万举等在建立大地形变测量指标体系中给出15种指标并指出：在均衡基准下垂直形变高速率上升区与下降区的交界处、高形变梯度带转弯处、出现明显的隆起区且形变等值线呈四象限分布、水平剪应变高值区、面收缩较明显的区域、形变异常活跃的断层带的端点和拐弯处或相互交汇处等区域，是容易孕育发生中等以上强烈地震的区域。该研究成果从历史地震中给出较好的对应结果，从现实地震中得到较好的验证。

2001年，一测中心薄万举等用大面积水准资料研究全国大地形变场，全国垂直形变梯度场、梯度信息和地震活动关系，发现中国大陆地壳升降活动呈北西向条带的分布特征，并且由西南向东北有逐步减弱的趋势。

（三）“坝体决口”的孕震模式假说

一测中心薄万举长期开展以断层形变寻找块体活动边界的研究，通过断层活动量级的空间分布给出华北地区活动块体的划分。在大地形变测量中短期前兆指标体系的建立和检验统计分析的基础上，2001年提出“坝体决口”的孕震模式假说，该假说能较好的解释地震前兆分布的时空范围常常大得难以置信，某些前兆（如地下水）常能对应数百千米以外的地震的这种现象。

三、工程中形变监测应用

1991年，一测中心自主研制开发的自动垂直形变仪，由传感器探头、计算机采集系统等组成，可在2分钟内连续自动采集多路形变数据，实时反馈空间形变信息指导施工。该系统成功用于天津市地铁一号线的施工。2003～2004年，地铁一号线小白楼至下瓦房盾构施工区间，穿越天津市重点保护建筑——名人王中山故居，其建筑内安装该垂直形变监测系统。

1991年，天津广播电视塔建成后，为掌握电视塔在日照、风等自然外界荷载条件下，发生塔身中心位移、塔身挠曲等变形数据，一测中心根据委托承担对天津广播电视塔微形变的监测研究。该中心自行研制的电子倾角仪（DQY）安装于塔身的三个不同高度位置，对塔身进行自动连续监测获取数据，可以清楚地观测到塔身的变形情况。1995年的监测结果表明，天塔的热变形和风荷载下的变形都很明显，监测到由于太阳方向的不同造成天塔各处吸收的热量不同，使得天塔在一天之中呈现出有规律的倾斜变化，但其变化量未超出设计要求，表明天塔运行是正常的。

1994年，一测中心自主研制的CZY-Ⅰ型垂直形变监测仪，在上海香港广场灌注桩加压施工中，通过样机比测试验。该仪器应用水连通液面平衡原理和传感技术、电子技术、计算机控制技术等，实现隧道或地面构筑物等被测目标相对垂直形变的智能化自动监测。该仪器的技术关键通过高精度位移传感器实现物理量与电学量的线形变换，设计承载位移传感器磁感部件运动浮子的几何形状与物理特性，提高对液面变化及传感器静摩擦力的分辨率。应用计算机技术设计数据采集接口电路，线性放大电路，实现目标判别、自动巡回采集、数据处理等。“CZY—Ⅰ、Ⅱ型垂直形变监测仪”先后应用于上海、广州、深圳和天津地铁施工形变监测，天津高层建筑深基坑开挖过程中支护系统形变监测，天津地面沉降分层研究的大直沽地下分层标垂直形变监测等。

2002年，在天津地铁一号线用盾构机施工中，首次采用地形变监测。南楼至土城盾构区间段全长882.43米。盾构机沿线穿越土质结构松散，地下水较丰富，地下管线繁多，并随着盾构机的掘进，周围土体应力产生变化，使沿线地面及建筑物随之变形。经一测中心采用各种大地形变动态监测为该地下施工提供准确方位、高程和变形数据，确保施工安全与工程质量。

2003年，一测中心采用二等精密水准测量方法，对天津地铁一号线隧道施工进行垂直变形监测。为保证隧道环片拼装后两周内隧道垂直变形相对稳定，在隧道的环片上部每隔5米布设一个监测点，正常掘进段每隔20~30米布设一个监测点，每次测量都从隧道外稳定点起测，监测周期为2周，垂直变形小于0.01毫米/天停止观测。

建筑物微形变监测技术于1991~2005年间应用于金皇大厦、今晚报大厦等十多处天津大型建筑物应用，还在鲁、沪、深、穗、宁等省市广泛应用。

图9-4-1-133 “挖掘高手”盾构机

第二节 地面沉降

1991年前，天津市建立的地面沉降水准监测网主要采用精密水准水测量的监测方法。1995年将GPS技术应用于地面沉降监测。天津市控制地面沉降工作办公室（以下简称“天津控沉办”）和一测中心等单位在天津陆续建立一批带有强制归心装置的连续GPS观测站，运用现代空间测量技术，开展地面沉降监测的可行性试验研究。同期，在相关区、县建立监测网站，开展观测与分析。21世纪初期，天津开始对地面沉降规律、预警评价的指标体系、海河两岸地面沉降的现状和机理进行研究，并提出有效控沉对策。2005年，实施“渤海潜在淹没区”监测。

一、沉降监测

天津市处于新构造沉降区，加上过量开采地下水造成的人为地面沉降灾害，引起市相关部门密切关注。1985～1995年，一测中心获得大量观测数据，为天津市采取控制地面沉降措施和研究提供科学依据。天津市地面沉降监测网一等精密水准路线，由最初的22条线1000余千米，逐渐扩大至2005年的1400余千米，覆盖面积约1万平方千米。1991～2005年，一测中心施测一等水准年平均观测量为1161.36千米。2004～2005年实施海河流域GPS点水准联测。

1995年，一测中心建成由13个连续GPS观测站组成的天津市滨海新区地面变形GPS监测网。为研究地面变形，配合地面沉降的精密水准测量，又建一批GPS观测站，分布在市内以及蓟县、大港区等区县，GPS监测网覆盖全市区域。同年，对天津市滨海新区地面变形GPS监测网进行首次观测，此后每年在同一时期进行复测。2005年完成66个站的观测任务。根据2005年天津市水文水资源勘测管理中心任立生、一测中心黄立人等的研究，天津GPS沉降监测的十年（1995～2004年），GPS测得的全部370个地面沉降点的大地高结果与水准测量的正常高的结果，比较试验结果表明：用GPS所测定的大地高变化来监测地面沉降可以达到当时天津市监测地面沉降测量（水准）正常高变化的精度，采用GPS方法监测天津市地面沉降，可避免因天津市水准原点的变动对沉降结果影响。

1997年，天津控沉办匡绍君、董国凤等开展“GPS技术在天津市地面沉降监测中的应用研究”。由于天津地处滨海沉积区，地面沉降监测的高程基准点远离监测目标区，每年需动用70人、耗时一个半月、投入100多万元经费来传递高程基准，才能完成对地面微量沉降的监测。而利用GPS技术取代水准联测，把高程基准直接传到沉降区内任意点，监测精度高，减少测量时间和经费。负责沉降监测的天津市测绘院等单位，应用该技术将宝坻基岩点高程基准，传递到天津市区和滨海新区，只需用工20人次、用时10天、投资约10万元的费用便可完成。

2000年，天津控沉办匡绍君、董国凤、路旭等开展“利用INSAR测量天津市地面沉降应用研究”。该研究利用合成孔径雷达干涉INSAR测量技术对天津地面沉降进行监测，其结果可以与水准测量结果相结合，更加准确、真实、客观地反映沉降情况，发现新的沉降漏斗，修正等值线勾绘错误。该成果广泛应用于地面沉降控制测量，道路、桥梁、坝的垂直形变监测等。根据当时的雷达影像资料价格与地面常规水准测量所需费用比较，预期在达到相同精度前提下，经费可比传统方法节省50%以上。

2004年，天津控沉办董克刚、于强等在海河两岸地面沉降监测与控沉研究中，以GPS-RTK技术为平台，建立海河两岸地面沉降的综合监测系统，实时快速准确地监测出两岸各地段的地面沉降和两岸重点大型高层建筑及桥梁的沉降变形，并结合土体分层沉降监测、土层孔隙水压力监测及海河两岸的水位地质资料，综合研究海河两岸地面沉降的现状和机理，为海河经济重大举措提供强有力的技术支撑。该成果对于防治海河地面沉降灾害,确保海河两岸基础设施的安全、海河的泄洪能力及抵御海水入侵、遏制地下水资源环境恶化有着重大的战略意义。采用GPS-RTK技术,可节省监测费40%~70%,并可借鉴推广到国内其他类似城市的地面沉降监测中。

2005年,一测中心受天津控沉办的委托,实施“渤海潜在淹没区”项目的监测任务。把做好的标石埋设在潜在淹没区,并把它作为控制点来测量其点位的GPS坐标。控制网建成后,采用Trimble5700动态测量系统,2005年12月完成塘沽、汉沽两个区的高程点加密工作,完成3172个高程点加密。在此次潜在淹没区监测中,使用二等精密水准测量规范,施测成果达到规范要求,为天津市政府实施控沉决策提供准确的下沉标高依据。

二、沉降控制

1993年,天津地质学会完成天津地面沉降与对策研究。研究报告在概述国内外控制地面沉降的基础上,重点研讨天津地沉的特点。在区域自然条件及地质构造背景的制约中,讨论因人为开采地下水引起地沉的定量分析,揭示天津地沉的历史发展、空间展布和演变的客观规律。对控制地面沉降的制约条件、技术可行性,提出相应的调整地下水开采层次与地区,提高人工回灌效益等对策措施。

1998年,天津控沉办匡绍君、姚忠杰等开展“天津和邻近地区构造沉降及控沉远景问题的研究”。该研究主要运用地质学方法,结合地震、地壳形变、地球物理测深和GIS等计算机技术,确定天津及邻近主要活动断层的活动特征,进而对地面沉降的基本特征、分区和分类特征进行深入研究。其沉降区的主要特征等成果对研究和分析天津及相关城市发展规划,基本建设和防灾减灾均具有重要作用。

2000年,天津控沉办匡绍君、路旭,天津港务局张凤展等开展“天津港港区地面沉降规律研究”。该研究结合水文地质资料和地下水开采资料,以及地基处理情况进行系统研究,总结出不同基础的港口设施与地面沉降的基本规律,预测沉降趋势,提出现有沉降观测网改造和高程基准点选择的原则,以及相应的控沉措施。该成果对于滨海新区建设中克服软土地基的弱点,降低成本,具有重要价值。

同年,天津控沉办杨建图、姜衍祥等开展“深基坑变形不均匀沉降及监测方法的研究”。该研究应用自行编制的三维有限元程序分析天津市深基坑开挖引起地面变形的规律,通过对典型工程进行系统的内力和变形理论分析,结合实际工程经验对理论分析结果进行验证,总结出适合天津市深基坑工程的开挖变形与地面不均匀沉降的估算方法,并提出深基坑工程变形控制的规定及必须的监测项目。该成果为进一步研究天津市深基坑设计、施工、监测,以及深基坑开挖与周边地区沉降控制,制定相关的地方性标准和规程具有重要参考和应用价值。

2001年,天津控沉办姜衍祥等采用线性规划模型和地下水力模型耦合的方法,建立确定地下水开采量的最优化模型,用以解决地下水开采与地下水水位下降的关系、水位降与地面沉降的关系问题,进而确定各用水单位地下水合理开采量的总体原则和控制指标,包括水文水资源控制指标、地质指标、环境控制指标、社会经济指标等。同时,以控制地面沉降为目标,建立最优化数学模型,确定用户地下水最佳开采量。该研究成果成为水资源管理部门制定全市各用水单位地下水开采指标、实施计划用水的重要依据。

2003年,天津控沉办杨建图、姜衍祥、路旭等利用地面沉降地理信息系统建立地面沉降预警评价的指标体系及其评价的基本方法和流程;建立基于地理信息系统的地面沉降空间数据库;利用MAPGIS二次开发工具与VB开发语言建立地面沉降预警分析系统;采用数据库、图形库、模型方法库三库合一技术等为科学控制地面沉降提供依据。信息系统建设对地面沉降的防治进行科学管理,为地下水资源合理开发利用及监督管理提供决策信息,成为控制地面沉降工作中信息处理、查询和分析的先进工具,具有显著的社会效益。

同年,水科所、天津控沉办和天津市水利工程基建管理处周潮洪、杨建图、王守斌、董树龙、刘波等在“天津市地面沉降对水利工程的影响研究”中,提出:地面沉降对水利工程影响程度的评价指标和评价方法,建立GIS评价系统;水利工程沉降灾害经济损失评估的原则和方法,建立评估系统;建立基于GM(1,2,M,N)的地面沉降预测模型,使之能模拟地面沉降对地下水开采量的滞后现象和非线性关系。研究成果提高决策部门对地面沉降危害性的认识,有利于把握总体情况,以便在规划建设中趋利避害,积极采取控沉措施,避免和减少地面沉降带来的损失,节约工程投资。

2004年,天津控沉办杨建图、姜衍祥、路旭等对地面沉降预警预测系统进行研究。该项目采用水力学、水文地质学、环境科学及人工智能的技术与方法,通过分析研究区域地下水开采量及水位埋深与地面沉降之间的定量关系,建立地面沉降预测的神经网络模型,实现沉降过程的预测。课题应用所建模型对研究区域的背景沉降量、地下水开采层次、开采强度、水位动态及分层影响强度等进行研究,模拟并分析地下水开采总量和层次分布以及地下水水位埋深等因素对塘沽区地面沉降过程的影响,研究成果为该区部署控沉工作的重点提供可靠依据。

第三节　地　震

1991～2005年,天津市在地震监测预报、地震灾害预防、地震应急与救援防震减灾三大体系建设方面,取得重要进展。天津市地震监测台网基本实现数字化、网络化,地震应急指挥系统纳入中国地震应急指挥技术系统,地震预测预报与震灾预防基础性应用科学技术研究水平都有所提高。研究工作涉及地震地质、地球物理、地球化学、地震学、水文地质、大地形变测量等有关学科领域。

在此期间,天津市地震局(以下简称“市地震局”)先后完成省部级地震科学技术研究项目79项,其中包括中国地震局地震科学联合基金、天津市自然科学基金项目25项,中国地震局或天津市科委等省部级科学技术研究项目54项。在国内外各类刊物上发表学术论文253篇。

一、监测与预报

(一)监测

1991年起,天津市地震监测台网经过多次调整、优化组合,至1995年年底建成包括有天津市地震遥测台网、地下流体动态监测网和市地震局无线通信网在内的3网8台,一些地震监测设备陈旧,资料管理不够规范和出现突发地震时,地震部门通讯方式落后等有所改善。

自1996年起,天津市参与国家地震局组织实施的“数字化遥测地震台网和地震前兆台网改造工程”“首都圈防震减灾示范区系统工程”,2001年年底完成天津市数字化遥测地震台网、强震台网和地震前兆台网建设。

天津市遥测地震台网经过全面数字化改造和建设,台网布局的合理性得到改善,监测方式实现数字化、综合化和网络化。台网中心可接收到天津市行政区内28个子台84道地震信号(18个台使用DDN专线,10个台使用卫星通讯传输)。台网对本区地震监控能力由原来的M_L2.5级提高到M_L1.0～1.5级;5分钟内可提供自动处理的地震三要素结果,10分钟内提供复核后的地震速报参数;定位精度小于5千米;每天产出数据500多兆。

建成的天津市数字化强震台网拥有强震台34个,其中包括新建的实时传输数字强震台14个,拨号数字强震台16个,强震台网中心1个等。该台网可与数字遥测地震台网观测结合,实施对微震到中、强地震的全面监测;所构成的天津市地震烈度速报网,可直接获得烈度≥Ⅳ度以上地震的烈度分布情况,进而为地震预报、科学研究、工程结构抗震设计提供基础资料。

在数字化地震前兆台网建设中,改造和扩建数字化地震前兆台站11个。前兆台网实现自动获取观测数据和网络传输;前兆数据由模拟记录变为数字记录,便于分析预报人员直接应用。

2002年起,市地震局组织、实施“天津市中国数字地震观测网络项目”。在地震观测台网建设方面,新建3个井下数字测震台,80个烈度速报台,30个固定强震动台。在地震前兆观测方面,新增10个观测项目,涉及6个台站。

天津市在地震台网的改造建设中,应用通讯、网络、数据处理等现代科学技术,建成覆盖全市的地震观测网点,形成全市统一、数据共享的数字地震观测网络,可获取大量地球物理、地球化学、地球动力学等方面的高精度、高时空分辨率的基础数据。

(二)预测预报

1.理论与方法

1992年,市地震局聂永安等与南开大学等单位合作承担"地震波理论与计算在地震研究中的应用"。从理论上对震源距不为零情况下尾波散射问题进行研究。为提高计算速度和精度,通过含贝塞尔函数的数值积分方法的研究,提出相应的算法。应用地震波资料开展地震分析预报方面,考虑拾震器摆位海拔和地震波震相清晰度的情况下,提出提高地震定位精度的方法。同时,针对强震迁移现象,提出构造活动波概念并根据中国几大块体的Q结构,给出华北及西南部份地区的Q结构。该成果获国家地震局1995年度科技进步奖二等奖。

1993年,市地震局龚绍京等在国内首次系统地对一系列地磁短周期变化物理量及其与地震的关系进行研究,发现地磁短周期变化的明显异常的时空规律,特别是异常的周期效应,证实地震的发生确实伴有深部电导率的变化,揭示出用这些参量进行地震预报的前景。同年完成的"地磁短周期变化研究"成果获1994年度国家地震局科技进步二等奖。

2000年,市地震局完成天津及邻近地区地下流体地震预报技术研究。该项工作以水动态、水化学、油井动态、热流体等地下流体观测项目为主,以强震预测技术为重点,开展地下流体异常信息提取方法的无量纲化研究,实现地下流体异常信息的时、空动态图像演化。在深入研究唐山7.8级、大同6.1级、5.8级、包头6.4级和张北6.2级等地震前后地下流体动态演化与强震关系的基础上,建立地下流体"异常迁移模型",提出地震危险区判定的5个标志和3个步骤,并据此对天津及邻近地区危险性进行综合预测。成果在天津实际应用,并在山东、上海等地推广应用。

2.实用技术

1991~2000年,市地震局先后参加并完成中国地震局组织的"地震短临预报方法及其物理基础的研究""强地震预测预报技术研究"等项目的研究,完成以强地震中短期预报研究为主的省部级科技项目47项;先后开展以《年度地震短临跟踪方案》为指导的震情短临跟踪研究、首都圈震情短临跟踪判定、地震大形势预测等方面的研究工作。研究成果大多直接应用于天津市日常地震监测预报工作,其中相继建立并不断完善中期震情判定指标、中强地震短临预报指标及决策和中等地震短临预报指标体系,使地震预报由经验性的预测向指标化判定方向迈出重要一步。1999年随着"首都圈分析预报技术系统示范工程"的实施,天津市地震局建设集计算室、会商室、数据库系统和远程会商系统为一体的现代化地震分析会商技术系统。从2000年开始实现分析预测和震情会商的微机网络化和多媒体化。

2001年,市地震局刘连柱、赵根模、陈宇坤等完成天津海河隐伏断裂活动性定量分析研究。该项目采用多种物探、化探、钻探和3S技术对天津海河断裂进行了全面的研究,明确提出海河断裂全长约330千米,西起太行山山前断裂带的涿县附近,向东经天津市区抵达塘沽入渤海。海河断裂天津段长度约85千米,西起武清区、东至塘沽区。基本查明它的空间位置、倾向、倾角、上断点、滑动速率、断层应力场等几何学、运动学参数,确定断层最新活动年代、地震危险地段、最大可能震级、峰值加速度影响带范围等主要参数。研究报告还对天津市城市防震减灾和建设提出对策和建议。该项成果为城市规划和重大工程项目选址提供依据,已应用于天津市地震监测、预报及部份重大工程项目建设。该成果获2001年度天津市科技进步二等奖。

2001~2005年,市地震局开展以强地震中短期预报为主的科学技术研究,先后完成省部级项目10项。结合天津区域的地震、地质环境特点,建成"天津市地震预测基础信息库",筛选出适合天津市地震中短期预测的异常指标,建立天津市中短期地震预测综合指标体系,建成天津市地震中短期预测模型,并在日常震情信息的分析与处理工作中,开始应用地震分析预报系统软件。同时,在加强地震序列快速判定分析软件研制的基础上,对天津市及邻近地区的地震活动特点及其分类的特征做出分析与判定。

上述研究成果已主要应用于天津市及邻近地区的地震预测预报。市地震局根据1991～2005年的年度震情趋势判断意见的结果统计,除个别年份对震情的估计偏高外,多数年份对地震活动水平的年度趋势判断意见与实际情况有较好的一致性。

二、应急指挥技术系统

1995年建成的天津市地震局地震无线通信网,是以移动通信为特色、兼顾定点通信、基本复盖全市、可24小时工作的地震专用超高频无线电话语音通信网络,网络的基站设在市地震局。

1997年2月市地震局建成的天津市地震快速反应系统,以计算机网络为依托,将地震速报、趋势判断、前兆数据报送、异常分析处理及地震应急指挥查询等工作相互联通、形成一个有机的地震快速反应系统,实现地震数据采集、传输、处理的自动化和网络化。应用结果表明,这一系统可提高地震分析预报工作的效率和可靠性,为在地震突发事件情况下,可及时了解地震异常变化、快速反应为领导快速决策提供必要的技术支撑。

2001年完成的"天津市地震应急指挥系统"(以下简称"应急系统")是"首都圈防震减灾示范区系统工程"项目的组成部分,由地震应急指挥技术系统、震害快速评估与辅助决策系统、地震现场震情及灾情获取系统三部分组成,应急系统的指挥大厅设在天津市地震局。应急系统的技术装备有海事卫星观测、数字影像、视频图像实时采集、远程视频实时传输、地震现场灾害损失评估及信息快速传输设备等。应急系统的现场通信网络,可保证地震现场与天津市地震应急指挥中心和天津市抗震救灾指挥部的通信联络,做到以最快的速度将现场的震情、灾情信息及图像迅速传递,为天津市领导和指挥决策部门的应急指挥提供决策信息。

2002年9月21日,天津市防灾应急指挥中心建成天津市防灾应急指挥系统,并投入应用 。

2004年,市地震局起动"中国数字地震观测网络—天津市地震应急指挥技术系统"的建设任务。

三、工程性震灾预防

1990～1997年,市地震局先后完成塘沽区地震危险性分析、天津经济技术开发区地震小区划以及震害预测、大港油田震害预测工作。1998年3月1日,《中华人民共和国防震减灾法》实施以后,市地震局完成天津电视塔、奥林匹克中心体育馆和水上运动中心、京沪高速公路、津滨轻轨、北疆发电厂等100余项重大或重点工程的地震安全性评价。2005年,完成"A320空中客车组装厂拟选场址地震构造环境及地震活动"的研究,认为场址所在地区在地质构造环境上相对稳定地块,区域地震对这一地区的最大影响烈度为Ⅶ度;根据历史地震综合分析,近场区在50年内的地震活动水平不会太高。研究成果为A320空中客车组装厂选址工作提供客观翔实的资料基础。

1998年,市地震局和天津市塘沽区地震办公室牟光迅、郭效民、付仲生、张昱等完成天津市地震快速反应系统建设。系统以计算机网络为依托,将地震速报、趋势判断、前兆数据的报送、异常分析处理及应急指挥查询等工作内容相互联通,形成一个有机的地震快速反应系统,实现数据信息采、传输、处理的自动化和网络化。系统包括地震快速定位系统、震后早期趋势估计系统、地震前兆分析管理系统、地震快速反应指挥查询系统、计算机网络系统建设。该系统是地震快速反应系统应用程序的运行平台,着重解决各系统的网络互联、联机联调和多种通讯方式的入网等问题,为地震快速反应系统整体功能的实现,提供强有力的技术支持。该项目获1998年天津市科技进步二等奖。

1999～2005年,市地震局开展"天津海河隐伏断裂活动性定量评价""天津市活断层探测与地震危险性评价"研究。"海河断层"是华北地区横跨天津市的区域性规模较大断层。2001年完成的"天津海河隐伏断裂活动性定量评价",基本查明该断层在天津市行政区内的空间分布状况,分段活动性和地震危险性。

2002年启动的"天津市活断层探测与地震危险性评价"工程项目是天津市首次从区域地壳稳定性角度、对天津断层和沧东断层开展的专题研究。到2005年年底,已完成这两条断层的区域探查、试验探测与断层活动性初步鉴定工作。

第五章 水运工程

天津港是一个货运种类多，外贸吞吐量大的综合性港口。1990年全港完成吞吐量2063.3万吨，其后15年，港口吞吐量以每年平均17.8%的速度递增，2005年港口吞吐量超过2.4亿吨/年，在中国沿海港口中排名第4位。天津港装卸转运的货物以集装箱、大宗散货、液体散货以及件杂货为主。天津港港口装卸能力强大、工艺模式全面、装卸系统复杂、技术先进，尤以集装箱码头行业领先。2001～2005年，天津港先后竣工10万、15万吨级航道工程，航道水深从底标高-12.0米到-17.5米，宽度从180米到234米，提高了大吨位船舶的通航能力和港口竞争力。创造出在淤泥质海滩建设深水港的先例，跻身国际深水港之列。

1991～2005年，天津港在全国沿海港口率先完成对老码头的改造，加大航道疏浚力度，创新回淤治理方法，相继完成5万吨级、10万吨级和15万吨级航道建设，创造出在淤泥质海滩建设深水港的奇迹。运用创新软基加固技术，低成本、高速度地扩展港区面积，拓宽发展空间。天津港引进集装箱、煤炭、矿石和石油化工产品等先进专业生产设备，装备水平始终保持国内领先地位。港口的总体布置由小港池窄突堤向宽港池长顺岸发展。码头结构向深水化、大型化发展。在工程结构方面，高桩码头结构朝长桩大跨方向发展。桩型上向多样化、大截面、长桩发展。板桩码头结构有较大突破，从上世纪只能建设千吨级至3.5万吨级泊位的状况发展到可建设10万吨级以上的大型深水泊位。重力式码头最大水深达30米以上；预制后的沉箱连同附属设施重量从上世纪几百吨发展到2万吨的钢筋混凝土沉箱。水运工程建筑物在向“大型、深水”发展中得益于重型、机械化施工设备的研制。2000年后，在航道工程方面，对挖泥船的设计及建造、疏浚仪表与自动化的研制、疏浚挖泥机具的研制以及老旧挖泥船改造上均取得重大成绩。航道设计中边坡坡度优化有突破性进展。建设复式航道方案，创新航道建设设计理念。到2005年，天津港拥有专业化集装箱泊位16个，泊位规模为2~10万吨级；天津港集装箱码头泊位数和码头长度拥有量居全国第四位，2005年集装箱吞吐量480.1万标准箱，在世界集装箱大港排名第16位。

第一节 勘 察

1991～2005年，天津在水文测验、测绘工程、地质勘察等方面的设备更新主要以引进为主，其中波浪、海流、潮位测、水温、含沙量等观测；控制、地形量、水深、导航定位、适航水深、计算机辅助等测量；地质勘探、土工试验、原位测试等方面的技术装备有所改进。

一、水文测验

20世纪90年代初，中交第一航务工程勘察设计院有限公司（以下简称“一航院”）观测海流沿用SLC9-2型直读海流计，可显示、存储海流的流速、流向，并可将数据直接记录在电脑中。潮位观测采用sw-40型水位计；表层水温观测采用SWL1-1型表层水温表，中、底层水温观测采用SWC1-1型闭端颠倒温度表；含沙量观测采用过滤称重方法观测海水含沙量。

1995年，一航院水温观测引进WTR-1a型高精度数字水温仪；引入光电测沙仪，结合率定曲线，确定海水含沙量。1997年，潮位观测采用SCA6-1型声学水位计；2002年临时验潮站采用hyc-01b型自容式便携验潮仪。2005年，该站采用TGR-2050型自容验潮仪，长期验潮站采用加拿大TGR-1050 HT实时无井潮位仪。同年，水温观测采用加拿大TGR-2050潮位计；一航院引进挪威NORTEK公司的声学多普勒波浪剖面流速测量系统。

2004年，天津水运工程勘察设计院引进加拿大RBR自容验潮仪XR-420-TU进行临时潮位观测。同年，引进挪威NORTEK公司的声学多普勒测量仪“阔龙”进行剖面流速自动测量；引进小“威龙”进行单点流速自动监测；引进“浪龙”进行剖面流速及波浪测量；引进美国RDI公司的走航式声学多普勒流速仪WHS horse进行剖面流速、流量测量。2005年，引进美国浊度仪OBS-3A进行含沙量测验。

二、测绘工程

20世纪90年代，天津开始使用全站仪进行地形测量，实现数字化测图。20世纪90年代中期，应用水深测量定位导航及测深软件，可获得所需各种测量数据，适时显示测量轨迹图形，并能使定位与测深同步进行；在现场就可发现缺测和漏测，随时补测，可解决传统水深测量定位点和测深点不一致问题。2000年开始使用实时动态差分RTK GPS测图和进行大比例尺水深测量，大幅提高定位精度。并使用GPS系统，引进美国5700型RTK GPS进行控制测量。

1997年7月21日，天津港建立接收GPS卫星信号的信标台，可全天候接收卫星导航数据，并发射差分修正信号，为中国沿海及近海船舶导航。定位精度一般可达2～5米，距离较近(50千米以内)且天气好时，定位精度可达1米以内。使测量范围无限扩大，定位数据和测深数据同步采集，实现数字化水深测量。2001年，天津水运工程勘察设计院引进荷兰“Silas走航式适航水深测量系统”。同年引进高精度多波束测深系统RESON SEABAT 8125。2004年，地球物理探测开始引进英国CM2型旁侧声纳和加拿大SeaSPY海洋磁力仪。

三、地质勘察

20世纪90年代，一航院引进试验室数据自动采集系统进行土工试验，提高试验效率，减少人为因素对试验结果的影响。原位测试采用sws型地层剖面探测系统。

第二节　水运建筑工程

1991～2005年，天津港在码头结构、防波堤和护岸、仓库、造陆、试验检测、回淤治理以及船坞等方面的工程技术均取得长足进步。高桩码头采用斜顶桩与板桩墙组合的承台结构。遮帘式板桩码头和分离卸荷式板桩码头新结构使深水板桩码头的应用付诸现实。板桩码头开发出地下连续墙结构、“HZ”组合型钢板桩及“BOX”型组合钢板桩等前墙新结构形式，“T”型地下连续墙结构等新形式也得到应用。一航院设计的某核电工程建设15～20吨钩连块体作护面、结构断面设有防渗隔热柔性地连墙的抛石斜坡堤新结构；在几个港口工程中采用宽肩台斜坡堤新结构；创新开发出半圆型防波堤轻型结构、半圆型混合堤轻型结构、箱筒型基础防波堤新结构，以及“双联”型人工块体新护面结构。一航局研制出具有国际领先水平的坐底式水下基床抛石整平船、软体排铺设船、振动砂桩船和水上插板船等设备。天津港务局等单位联合研究，论证得出天津港属“轻淤港”。

一、码头结构

(一)桩基码头

1992年，一航院设计建成天津港南疆港区石化码头(南1～4号)为天津第一座液体化工码头，设计最大靠泊能力为15万吨级,为该港区第一座碟型布置的高桩墩式码头,首次采用钢管桩,直径为700～800毫米。

同年,在一航院任福延、郭莲清设计的天津港东突堤工程中,东突堤北侧通用杂货码头,首次采用海上水泥深层拌和法(CDM工法)加固地基的重力式沉箱码头结构,该成果获1999年全国第八届优秀工程设计银奖。1995年海上深层水泥搅拌加固软基技术纳入国家"九五"国家重点科技攻关项目,一航院进行计算方法的研究,2002年经交通部专家委员会评审为国际领先水平。

1992年,交通部第一航务工程局(以下简称"一航局")引进全站仪,并研制开发微波定位和GPS三维定位打桩定位技术,应用于桩位控制。2002年该局开发海上GPS打桩定位技术,解决夜间施工中桩基工程外海定位的难题。

1993年,一航局引进日本"打桩12号",该船桩架高65米,配备当时国内最大的D-80型柴油打桩锤。2003年该局引进"天威"号全回转起重/打桩船,打桩桩架最大高度90米,配备荷兰S-280和SC-250液压打桩锤各1台,在国内首次使用D-160柴油锤,可施打直径2.5米超常桩。

1998年,天津港打桩开始采用水冲沉桩工艺,一般采用内冲内排法。水冲沉桩采用的射水压力和用水量根据不同土质条件取用。水冲沉桩常辅以高压空气喷射排碴,空气压力300～800千帕,最高可达1000千帕。2004年,建成20万吨级散货码头,为当时最大吨级的深水泊位。

2005年,一航院对天津港的高桩梁板码头结构进行研究,总结出合理的码头结构排架间距,充分发挥大直径钢管桩的承载力,优化出合理的梁板尺寸,并兼顾施工中现浇混凝土的潮位要求,这一研究成果为天津港码头工程建设提供经济合理的设计方案。

(二)板桩码头

2000年,天津深基工程有限公司研制出"双钻抱管"技术,克服"单钻抱管"成槽易偏斜及宽度受限制等诸多缺陷,工程质量和施工效率得以提高,成为地连墙板桩码头特有的成熟的成槽施工方法。

2001年,一航院刘永绣、吴荔丹、李元音等设计出半遮帘式板桩码头新结构型式,建成当时世界最大吨级的地连墙板桩码头。2003年,采用此结构在唐山港京唐港区建成中国第一座5万吨级板桩码头,该工程为自主首创的新码头结构型式。2003年,刘永绣、吴荔丹等创新设计出全遮帘式板桩新结构,建成世界最大的10万吨级的地连墙板桩码头和国内外第一个遮帘式钢板桩码头。两结构均获国家专利授权,并实现板桩码头大型化、深水化发展的突破。同时,建立两结构的设计理论,并首次提出码头新结构的实用简化计算方法。2005年,刘永绣、吴荔丹、刘进生等首创设计出遮帘式组合HZ型钢板桩码头新结构型式,在唐山港曹妃甸港区煤码头工程中使用,成为当时世界最大的第一座10万吨级遮帘式钢板桩码头。

2001年,一航院开始设计半遮帘式、全遮帘式板桩码头新结构型式。2004年,为提高遮帘桩等矩形、方形断面桩的抗弯能力,天津深基工程有限公司在原有反循环成槽工艺的基础上,研发出矩形方、方形灌注桩成孔组合钻具。该技术使整个成孔速度较以往钻进与切削分步完成的速度提高30%~50%,成孔质量提高。

(三)重力式码头

1992年,一航院吴荔丹等在烟台港西港池二期工程中设计采用重力式小沉箱结构,沉箱重不超过500吨。基础处理采用海上水泥深层拌和法(CDM工法)。采用海上水泥深层拌和法加固海底软土地基,形成重力式码头基础。1996年年底竣工投产。

二、防波堤和护岸

(一)斜坡堤

1992年,天津港在南疆东部港区围埝工程中首次使用充灌模袋。1993年,天津港开始进行模袋混凝土护面施工技术的应用研究和大型充灌袋施工技术应用研究。1994年,一航院设计采用大型充填袋筑堤和土工织物泸层及软体排护底等防护措施,取代传统的抛石堤心的斜坡式堤,在天津港北大围堰和北大防波堤围海造陆等国内多项工程中广泛应用。2004年,天津港建设公司在北大防波堤一期西内堤工程中采用的"大型充灌砂土袋堤心和模袋混凝土护面"新技术获得成功,该工艺与传统的抛石筑堤和草袋筑堤相比,围埝整体稳定性好，在天津港地基软弱且砂石料缺乏的自然条件下尤为适宜。

1994年，一航院谢世楞、祝世华等首次参与设计核电站海域工程防波堤等取、排水构筑物，并在广东岭澳核电站海域工程中成功实施。该取排水防波堤采用15～20钩连块体作护面的抛石斜坡堤，结构断面设有防渗隔热的柔性地连墙。施工中对堤内隔堤、泵房等水工构筑物采用干式施工方案抽干约60公顷水域的水。该工程荣获2003年全国第十届优秀工程设计铜奖。

1995年，一航院设计大连北良粮食码头，建成国内第一座宽肩台全抛石斜坡堤，堤长385米，泥面标高为-14.0米，-23.0米以上清除软土泥，以下5.0米采取抛石挤淤处理；外坡采用300～2500千克块石护面；陆上推进法施工。该堤外坡容许在波浪作用下发生变形，直至形成"动态平衡"剖面；护面块石重量比常规斜坡堤轻，施工简便，进度快；造价约为常规式的70%；在特大波浪作用下的损坏较轻。

20世纪90年代，常用的随机安放型的块体多为"扭王字"和"扭工字"型，规则摆放的块体多为"四脚空心方块"型和"栅栏板"。1999年，一航院王美茹等在分析研究国外一百多种形状各异的块体基础上研制成功"双联"型人工块体，它具有消浪性能好和稳定性高等优点，更适用于水深和波浪相对较大的地区。

（二）软基防波堤

1994年，一航院引进日本半圆型防波堤轻型结构，该结构由带底板的半圆形拱圈空心构件和抛石基床组成。与传统的直立式防波堤相比，具有抗滑稳定性能好，堤身断面经济；地基应力分布均匀且构件轻型地基应力较小；可抵御大浪的袭击，无后续工序，施工简便。尤适用于软弱地基和砂石料来源缺乏的地区。1995年始，该院经物理模型试验验证，对出水堤（和潜堤）、堤内外侧及半圆空腔里侧波浪作用下的半圆堤。同时，该院谢世楞等研发出半圆型堤断面尺度优化、半圆形堤波压力数模分析和弹性地基上半圆型构件内力等计算软件。

1997年，一航院王美茹、谢善文、李元音等针对天津港水浅、波浪不太大，软基较厚，砂石来源缺乏，设计出半圆型混合堤轻型结构，并首次实施于天津港五期围埝工程。该堤身为半圆型拱圈和底板组成的预制钢筋混凝土构件，坐落在抛石基床上。具有波浪作用力小，断面经济，地基应力均匀，圆拱结构受力性能好，安放后无后续的填石、现浇混凝土等工序，施工简便。施工工艺采用平躺预制，具有模板支拆难度小，有利于混凝土的浇注和震捣等。在天津港东疆港区围海造陆建设北大防波堤和南北防波堤延长等多项工程中，其主体工程多采用半圆形堤型结构，工程造价降低，工期缩短。1998年始，谢世楞、谢善文、李元音等设计应用半圆型（含半圆型沉箱）混合堤结构在长江口深水航道治理一、二期工程中得到推广应用，并创造前所未有的高质量和高速度；该一期工程2005年获全国第十一届优秀工程设计金奖。

天津港海底表层及浅层土为淤泥和淤泥质粘土，土体的物理力学指标较差，原采用的抛石堤和半圆体混合堤不能完全适应水深和软土地基的要求。2001年，由天津港集团公司、天津大学、中交一航局和一航院共同开展对箱筒型基础防波堤结构的研究和工程试验工作。天津港（集团）有限公司李伟和天津大学别社安提出箱筒型基础直立堤的新结构，该结构是一种全新的水工结构型式，由安装在水下土中的基础部分和其上的挡浪结构两部分组成，并作为一个整体进行预制、下水、浮运和下沉安装。基础部分为一倒扣的箱体，在箱体中设有十字隔板；上部挡浪结构有直立墙、直立圆筒、横卧半圆筒等多种形式。具有易于满足结构的稳定性，结构自身即可解决基础处理，可分体或整体预制及在水上气浮运输安装等特点，该结构能够满足天津港深水区建造大量的永久性或临时性防波堤围埝工程的需要。具有工程造价低和建造速度快等特点，适用于砂石料紧缺的地区及软土地基。该结构所采用的气浮拖运及定位，抽负压下沉等施工工艺和方法属国内首创。2004年初建成试验段并首先应用于天津港北大防波堤海底标高-4.0～6.0米堤段。其后，箱筒型基础结构大规模应用于天津港的防波堤建设。

2002年，一航院在长江口深水航道治理二期工程设计中，在水最深、浪最大、地基条件最差的北导堤区段由谢世楞提出一种新型空心方块斜坡堤。该堤由空隙率63.3%和14.4吨/块的大自重空心方块筑成，其堤身空隙率达78%，自重仅为等高抛石堤重的30%。该堤于2004年12月完工，空心方块斜坡堤成功地解决在恶劣自然条件下"导流、挡沙"和软基承载能力及整体稳定性等重大技术难题。

（三）护岸

1997年，一航院在厦门国际会展中心前埔路堤首次设计和成功实施“天力消浪块”景观护岸并成为旅游亮点之一。该院王美茹等自主研发的“双柱型消浪块”，先后被推广应用于厦门、烟台及威海等多项景观与护岸工程。该设计用于烟台滨海北路的景观工程，获2005年国家优质工程银质奖。

1998年1月交通部第一航务工程局更名为中港第一航务工程局（以下简称“一航局”）。2002年，一航局建造的“长建1号”基床抛石整平船，该船可以在风力≤7级、波高≤1.5米、流速≤2.0米/秒时进行抛石、整平作业，10级以下大风可就地抗风浪。该船可使基床抛石、整平和质量检测三道工序合并施工，精度和基床密实度均明显优于传统的人工整平，在国内首次实现抛石、整平工序的机械化和信息化施工。同年，该局建造“安定1号”大型箱桶型基础组件定位安装船，将其中复杂的人工作业转化为水上机械化操作，减轻劳动强度。经配备一航局自行开发的GPS海上施工定位系统，可全天候作业，提高箱桶型基础组件安装效率。该船采用的坐底就位作业方式和先进的安装软件，提高船舶抗风浪能力和沉箱定位的稳定性，及海上施工、安装的精确度。

三、仓库设计

1991年，一航院设计的烟台17号泊位散装化肥库，采用54米跨两铰钢门式刚架结构，高25米，顶部架设皮带输送机廊道，基础采用斜桩和直桩组合结构，面积为7550平方米，达到国内领先水平。1992年后，该院引进和设计大跨度轻型钢门式刚架结构，在天津等沿海港口设计建造多栋，长度120~160米的件杂货库、集装箱交接库，屋面和墙体均采用彩色压型钢板结构。2001年，该院为秦皇岛港设计18000平方米散装化肥库，高29.7米，顶部架设皮带输送机廊道，采用抽柱式大跨度钢门式刚架结构，最大跨度为77米，中托架跨度21米，钢门式刚架结构，分别支撑在基础和中托架上，达到国内领先水平。2002年，该院为秦皇岛港八公司设计60米跨度，长度120米仓库，采用变截面钢筋混凝土柱，屋面采用柱面网壳结构，屋面和墙体均采用彩色压型钢板结构仓库，基础采用斜桩和直桩组合结构，面积为12000平方米。2005年，该院为锦州港设计80米跨度仓库，采用直接交汇节点大跨度钢管桁架，格构式钢柱，屋面和墙体均采用彩色压型钢板结构，达到国内领先水平。

四、造陆工程

1997年，天津港在南疆五期围埝工程中首次试用半圆体结构围埝。1997年代后，码头、护岸倒滤层由土工织物滤层替代原采用的粒料倒滤层，以防止漏砂现象。大型充灌袋堤心结构使用的土工布是一种新型合成材料，具有倒滤、排水、加筋、隔离、防渗和防护六大功能。2000年天津港在南疆南部开发一种大型充砂袋堤心围埝。施工时，在部分砂垫层完成后，用打设排水板和铺设土工布软体排的方法进行软基处理，然后充灌大型充灌袋形成堤心，以块石或混凝土块为护面。该围埝结构简单，施工效率高，费用低，在天津港北大防波堤、东疆港及南疆港区广泛应用。

21世纪初，土工合成材料应用范围不仅为一般护坡和浅层护体，而且发展用到工程结构主体，涉及工程安全寿命等技术领域。调查统计资料表明，使用土工合成材料与采用传统材料相比，可综合降低工程造价10%～40%，其中沉排护底降低5%～30%；充填袋筑堤降低15%～40%；土工织物加筋垫层降低10%～25%；直立加筋土岸壁降低15%～40%；模袋混凝土护坡降低24%～29%，而且明显降低工人劳动强度，加快施工进度。建埝和吹填的施工，天津港采用一埝多级吹填，逐层加高和多埝（大埝、子埝共2～3道）分层吹填，逐层建埝，效果良好。

五、试验检测

（一）结构试验与测试

20世纪90年代，为改进防波堤、护岸及码头结构的型式，天津港东突堤南侧码头的部分东护岸进行钢筋混凝土大圈结构试验。

2004年，天津港完成"围海造陆工程中和技术应用研究"，通过采用室内试验、现场试验与施工等多种手段，在海堤充填材料、整体稳定、地基固结沉降等方面取得重要理论成果。2005年，天津港于汝民、黄力军、李伟等完成"插入式箱筒形基础防波堤结构研究与应用"项目。该结构稳定性好，受力合理，重量轻、可以整体预知，在水上可以气浮运输，现场安装方便，结构可搬移重复利用，工程费用低，建造速度快，适用于软土地基。

（二）地基工程测试技术

1996～2000年，一航局建立一套完整的深层水泥搅拌法（CDM）工法设计计算方法。研制一套适合于不同龄期、不同强度的搅拌体取样设备，制定出一套完整的CDM现场取样与强度试验规程。在搅拌土工程特性的研究中无侧限抗压强度与水泥掺量、养护条件、龄期、水泥品种、水灰比等参数的关系，归纳于国内主要港口水泥强度发展的共同规律，并在实际工程中得到验证。同期，该局对CDM拌和体取样技术、室内和现场强度测试技术进行研究，规范取样和现场测试方法，改进施工质量监控技术，提出一套输浆、搅拌、提升、定位和调平等自动测试技术。2000年，经交通部组织专家鉴定，基本计算理论与设计方法研究为国际领先水平，填补国内空白；现场取样技术研究成果为国内领先水平；搅拌土工程特性研究成果为国际先进水平。

六、回淤治理

交通运输部天津水运工程科学研究所（以下简称"交通部天科所"）、国家海洋局一所、国家原子能院等单位联合，于1988年在天津港首次进行"中子活化示踪沙技术"的试验研究获得成功，在抛泥区泥沙运动研究中得到应用。1992年，交通部天科所曹祖德等研发出三维潮流数学模型，在天津港等沿海港口航道泥沙淤积治理中应用，该项目获1992年度国家科技进步二等奖。

20世纪90年代，天津港与交通部天科所进行维护疏浚工程与回淤规律等研究，经确定维护土方的合理计算方法，分析天津港抗强淤能力。研究认为强淤对20至25万吨级航道、港池与泊位建成后的天津港整体上不构成大的威胁，在天津港不存在骤淤碍航现象。

1998年，天津港主航道宽度已达180米，水深-12.0米，航道平均淤强下降至0.6米左右，与1973年相比，航道平均淤强下降近70%。天津港的浮泥运动曾是入港泥沙的一种主要运移形式，90年代后期浮泥在短期内对港口的影响基本消失。海河入港含沙量下降到0.18千克/立方米。2000年起，交通部天科所根据天津港细颗粒泥沙运动特性，提出一系列航道淤积计算公式，应用在天津港15至30万吨级及复式航道的建设中。

2000～2002年，天津港及天津市海亿海洋工程技术开发有限公司完成适航水深的一系列研究，确定天津港适航水深淤泥重度值为1.20～1.30吨/立方米。从提高船舶航行安全考虑，天津港适航水深标准重度取1.25吨/立方米较合适。2002年，天津港全面开始使用适航水深后，提高维护疏浚效率；增加码头使用率；增加大型船舶趁乘潮延时。2005年，交通部天科所编制完成行业技术标准《淤泥质海港适航水深应用技术规范》。

2001年12月，天津港务局和天津市海慧海洋工程研究所共同完成"15至25万吨级航道开挖与泥沙回淤评价研究"。该项目对天津近海条件，开挖15到25万吨级航道的可挖性、边坡稳定性与泥沙回淤进行深入分析，确定了建设深水航道的可行性。2003年，交通部天科所、中交一航院、天津大学等单位联合完成"天津港15万吨级航道工程泥沙问题研究"，解决底部粉沙层的泥沙运移扩散、边坡稳定性与泥沙回淤规律等问题。

2004年，交通部天科所开发出海岸河口数值模拟软件"TK-2D"和引进MIKE21、DELFT3D数学模型软件，在天津港建设工程研究中广泛应用。并利用整体波浪潮流泥沙物理模型试验研究，分别对"天津港防波堤延伸工程方案""天津港东海岸一期工程""海河口防洪与综合利用开发""天津港总体布局规划"等重大工程进行试验研究,依据模型实验研究成果,对水工建筑物布置和防淤等工程措施予以优化。

七、船坞工程

20世纪70年代,一航院设计建成天津新港船厂2.5万吨级修船坞,为桩基式船坞结构,首次设计气控式卧倒坞门;同期一航院设计建成青岛原红星船厂(现名北海船厂)1.5和2.5万吨级1号、2号修船坞,首次设计锚拉式船坞结构;同期一航院设计建成山海关船厂1.5和5万吨级的1号、2号修船坞,首次设计在风化岩地基上的排水减压式船坞结构型式和虹吸排水系统,其中2号修船坞为当时国内最大的修船坞。1997年,经一航院设计建成的大连中远港口船坞基地为6万吨级船坞,该船坞工程首次设计为升浆混凝土坞底、沉箱式坞墙和坞口结构,采用湿法施工,经全国优秀工程勘察设计评审委员会评审认定结构型式为国内外首创。该工程设计获2000年度国家优秀设计铜奖。

第三节 港口总平面布置和工艺

2001~2005年,天津建成的东突堤工程,是从小港池窄突堤发展成宽港池长顺岸的转折点。同时,改变了对正向门口的设计理念。装卸工艺与设备方面,在天津港东突堤北侧改扩建的集装箱码头工程设计中,为解决堆场容量不足的矛盾,首次大批量采用轨道式集装箱龙门起重机(RMG)的装卸工艺方案,取得显著效益。在国内率先研制成功集装箱装卸岸桥和场桥都能同时起吊2个20呎标准箱的操作工艺以及双箱作业吊具,实现国内集装箱装卸运输的重大突破。随着煤炭运量的快速增长,天津港确定实施"南散北集"和"黑白分家"的港口建设部署,建成天津港南疆专业化煤炭码头、环保型焦炭专业码头,采用连续作业的焦炭装卸工艺,实现无扬尘作业。装卸设备方面研制出新型坛式六瓣散货抓斗、液压抓斗等,焦炭公司研制出焦炭防破碎高效自卸装船属具——专用簸萁,成功开发出可拆换斗尖的多瓣抓斗。天津港对散粮专业接卸设备进行全系统改造,使散粮疏运实现全封闭无污染运行。一航院设计的大连北良粮食码头工程,港内散粮输送采用全皮带机、全封闭无污染的工艺方案。

一、总平面布置

(一)港口总体布置

随着船舶大型化,泊位吞吐量的提高,陆域堆场面积需求加大,操船要求水域扩大,同时由于集装箱码头和散货码头的建设,窄突堤已不能适应吞吐量增长的需要,港口的总体布置由小港池窄突堤向宽港池长顺岸发展。1993年,一航院任福延、赵智帮、郭莲清等设计建成的天津港东突堤工程,是从小港池窄突堤发展成宽港池长顺岸的转折点。

天津港东突堤工程采用深层水泥拌和法加固码头基础、软土岸坡和接岸结构,在软土地区建成重力式沉箱码头;用氧化沟方法处理港口生活污水;供电设施中总变电所和各分所之间采用遥控、遥信、遥测等技术。此外,在一个工程项目中建设12个泊位;建设的突堤码头陆域面积之大,刚吹填完的突堤堤心全部采用真空预压,面积约80万平方米;堆场面层大面积铺设高强混凝土联锁砌块约70万平方米,在国内均属首次。该项目1999年获国家优秀设计银奖;2002年获第二届詹天佑土木工程大奖。

(二)正向口门布置

1991年前,港口工程设计认为正向口门布置航道起着导浪作用,恶化港内泊稳条件。1991年,一航院赵智帮等在烟台港西港池二期工程和大连港大窑湾散粮码头工程方案设计中,均发现主浪向和航道夹角较小,属正向口门,航道边坡对波浪的折射作用非常明显。由于航道边坡的折射作用,使航道内波浪发散波高减小,则进入港内的波能减少,港内泊稳条件得到改善,改变了正向口门的设计理念。但折射出的波浪和航道外波浪叠加,使防波堤堤头某些部位波高加大,设计时尚需认真研究。

1997年,国家计划委员会将"深水航道对波浪传播影响规律研究"专题纳入国家"九五"攻关计划重点科技项目。一航院等单位联合攻关,研究得出航道对波浪作用的规律,国内外尚属首次。该研究对确定浚深航道后产生的波浪传播影响及采取相应的工程措施有指导意义。据此理论2003年开始建设的天津临港工业区和2005年开始启动的临港产业区,均采用正向口门,港内均取得良好的泊稳条件。

(三)粉砂质海岸建港

1991～2005年,一航院设计并建成多个粉砂质海岸港口,总结出港区粉砂质海岸建港经验:港区尽量采用环抱式全封闭港池;在强淤区应用防沙堤掩护;尽量利用天然水深布置航道减少航道开挖;减少港池水域面积;防止沿堤流冲刷及其对港池航道的淤积;建开敞式码头应预留出足够的备淤备冲深度等。

(四)复杂地形建港

1993年,一航院赵智帮、刘永绣、魏恒州等设计大连北良粮食有限公司码头,该码头一次建设3个泊位,最大船型为8万吨级,码头年设计吞吐能力910万吨。其陆域为高山,海边为海蚀陡崖,开山弃石填海得到大片陆域,其中部分块石用于建设宽肩台式防波堤和铁路大堤,可谓一举两得。为减少开山工程量,陆域按台阶式布置。港内铁路车场设在柳柴沟山谷中,两侧高山,经整平山谷可以布置铁路车场,牵出线延伸至铁路大堤和防波堤上。在狭窄陆域上布置如此规模的大型散粮码头、技术工艺之先进,创造当时中国乃至世界建港和粮食流通史上的八个第一;并成为复杂地形条件下成功建设港口的典范和国内散粮码头的标志性工程。

(五)进港船舶最大吃水

2003年,一航院在天津港30万吨级原油码头总平面设计中,为准确地确定码头设计水深,赵智帮等研究渤海水深问题。研究发现,自老铁山水道至天津港4#锚地的航路中有2处浅段,共约75千米长,其海底高程均浅于-24.5米。按照欧洲引航协会的标准计算,进出天津港最大船舶只能航行20米左右吃水的船。按照现行海港总平面设计规范,30万吨级油轮,最小吃水18.9米,最大吃水为23.2米。因此进出天津港的只有一部分吃水较小的30万吨级船可以航行。此论点提出后立即引起上级部门重视,并责成有关部门进一步研究。

二、装卸工艺与设备

(一)集装箱

1991年前,天津港率先建成由一航院开发设计的中国第一座专业化的集装箱码头。码头装卸船采用集装箱装卸桥,水平运输采用集装箱拖挂车,堆场作业引进轮胎式集装箱龙门起重机(RTG)装卸工艺模式。1991年后,该院设计的天津港三港池集装箱码头、东方海陆集装箱码头、营口港和锦州港等集装箱码头,也均采用RTG装卸工艺模式。随着原油价格不断上涨,导致堆场装卸作业主要设备RTG的营运成本也在不断提高。同时为适应集装箱运输系统的高效装卸作业和逐步全面自动化的需要,传统的RTG由于受柴油机适合的安装功率的限制,其操作速度无法提高,以及其运行轨迹不规则难以实现全面自动化。2002年,该院在天津港东突堤北侧改扩建的集装箱码头工程设计中,为解决堆场容量不足的矛盾,首次大批量采用轨道式集装箱龙门起重机(RMG)的装卸工艺方案。经试运转显示出RMG的诸多优点,与RTG设备比较,RMG具有堆场面积利用率高,跨度大,是RTG集装箱堆场的1.3倍;装卸效率高,而RTG则需2～3台;不需定时换轮胎,且由电力驱动,不用柴油机,故障率很低,设备完好率几乎是100%,维修成本很低;能耗小,营运成本低;易于实现集装箱码头装卸工艺的全面自动化;以电为动力,运行中无高音噪声、烟等污染。2005年天津五洲国际集装箱码头投产第二年完成集装箱吞吐量112万标准箱。由一航院设计的烟台港三期集装箱码头、青岛招商国际集装箱码头等均采用RMG装卸工艺。

天津港由于第六代超巴拿马型以及超大型集装箱船的出现,要求码头装卸作业高速高效,加大码头前沿装卸作业区域。2001年和2003年相继改造27、28、29段集装箱码头和东突堤北侧码头，加大码头前方装卸船作业区域宽度，分别在码头前沿增加40米和52米的新建码头承台，将其宽度增加到70~80米。其中，集装箱装卸桥海侧轨至码头前沿线的距离分别确定为7.5米和3.5米，均大于《海港总平面设计规范》JTJ211-99规定的3米。2001年，天津港集装箱码头公司在改造升级的27、28、29段集装箱码头上配备由上海振华港机公司制造的当时国内最大的超大型集装箱装卸桥。装卸桥额定起重量为吊具下61吨，吊钩下69吨，轨距30米，外伸距63米。同年，天津港在国内率先研制成功集装箱装卸岸桥和场桥都能同时起吊2个20呎标准箱的操作工艺以及双箱作业吊具，实现国内集装箱装卸运输的重大突破。2004年天津五洲国际集装箱码头有限公司购置规格为65吨——66米超大型集装箱装卸桥。其起重能力大，对20英尺的集装箱可进行双箱吊运装卸，按天津港到港远洋航线集装箱标准箱折算系数1.5计算，其装卸船速度可以提高33%；外伸距大，可对船宽60米、甲板上堆箱24列的特超大型集装箱船进行装卸作业。

20世纪80、90年代由天津港从日本和韩国引进轮胎式集装箱龙门起重机（RTG），其吊具下额定起重量30.5吨和35吨，跨距23.47米，堆箱高度"堆3过4层"和"堆4过5层"；2000年后采用由上海振华制造的RTG，其吊具下额定起重量40.5吨，跨距23.47米，堆箱高度"堆4过5层"。2002年在天津五洲国际集装箱码头采用24台轨道式集装箱龙门起重机（RMG），其吊具下额定起重量60吨，轨距33米，堆箱高度"堆4过5层"，跨内堆箱9列+1车道。

（二）大宗散货

1.煤炭

2000年前，天津港没有专业化的煤炭码头，煤炭业务主要安排在杂货码头，采用门机—抓斗直取装卸工艺进行装船作业，效率低，占用多个泊位，污染港口。随着煤炭运量的快速增长，天津港断然决定实施"南散北集"和"黑白分家"的港口建设部署，于2000年年底建成天津港南疆专业化煤炭码头，共有4个泊位，码头长度1110米。一航院设计的散货装卸工艺采用国外"C"型转子双翻翻车机，最大卸车效率可达4300吨/小时，装船采用单台效率6700吨/小时的大型移动式装船机，堆场设有相应的堆料机/斗轮取料机，系统由高效的带式输送机连接，形成一套完整的现代化散货装卸系统工程，设计吞吐能力为4300万吨/年。2001年后，该院设计的秦皇岛港煤四期工程煤炭卸火车采用"O"型三翻转子式翻车机，卸车效率达5600吨/小时，装船机额定能力为6000吨/小时，设计总通过能力达4500万吨/年。

2000年初，天津港在南疆开始建设散货物流中心堆场，该堆场作为煤炭和焦炭的集散中心承担储存、中转任务。煤和焦炭由散货物流中心堆场通过长廊式胶带连续输送机（简称"皮带长廊"）运往前方码头，煤的皮带长廊长10.4千米、宽1.8米、线速度为5.6米/秒；焦炭皮带长廊长9.1千米、宽1.6米、线速度为3.6米/秒。

2.焦炭

焦炭由焦炭码头堆场或散货物流中心堆场装船，完全采用自动化的斗轮取料机、胶带输送机、转接塔等设备自动完成。天津港环保型焦炭专业码头于1999年建成投产，有2个7万吨级深水泊位，码头长度684米，前沿水深-13.8米，10万平方米焦炭堆场，货物吞吐量达1800万吨/年以上。该码头由一航院设计，采用连续作业的焦炭装卸工艺。装卸设备为悬臂式斗轮堆/取料机，堆料高度17米，额定堆/取能力1800吨/小时；移动伸缩臂架式装船机，额定能力1800吨/小时，机头溜筒具有伸缩旋转和柔性布料功能，降低焦炭在装船过程中的破碎率。环保设备由湿式除尘系统和干式除尘器两大部分组成，干式除尘器安装在各转接机房的皮带机转接点，湿式除尘器系统遍布于各堆场和卸车坑周围，实现无扬尘作业。控制系统由中控室计算机和PLC组成，可实现工艺流程及整个系统运行作业的自动控制，同时对系统的安全运行实施动态监控。此套连续输送设备为国内唯一的焦炭专业化连续输送装卸设备，该引进设备达到国际领先水平。

焦炭破碎是影响装船的困难问题。2001年，天津港焦炭码头公司自行研制改造，将原接触式料位检测改用射线非接触式自动检测；将内置式自动控制斗门改成外置式自动控制，解决焦炭经常堵塞问题。2003

年，天津港在“焦炭专业化装卸设备防破碎技术研究”中，研制出新型坛式六瓣散货抓斗、液压抓斗等，以减小抓斗自重，提高抓取比。提高连续输送装卸作业质量，降低破损率。2004年，天津港焦炭码头公司研制焦炭防破碎高效自卸装船属具——专用簸萁，应用于南5号泊位门机、抓斗作业线。2004年，天津港成功开发出可拆换斗尖的多瓣抓斗，提高散货抓斗的耐用性，降低抓斗磨损。通过快速拆换磨损最严重的抓斗斗尖，显著降低抓斗维修成本与维修时间。

3.散粮

20世纪90年代，在散粮船舶到港密度大或专用卸船设备维修时，天津港用门座起重机与抓斗配合进行卸船作业。散粮码头同时停泊两艘散粮船时，还采取移动式连续卸船机系统和原“门机—抓斗”两套工艺流程同时作业的方式卸船和装车，以减少船舶在港停泊时间。1991年前，天津港建成的散粮码头是由件杂货码头改造而成，是国内首次引进英国西蒙公司散粮成套装卸系统设备的专业化码头。后经再次改造，采用相邻泊位的门座起重机/抓斗代替原配的吸粮机进行清舱作业。码头规模3.5万吨级，设计通过能力350万吨/年。1998年，天津港对散粮专业接卸设备进行全系统改造，使散粮疏运实现全封闭无污染运行，并提高作业效率。20世纪90年代后期，一航院设计大连北良粮食码头工程，码头设计通过能力910万吨/年。装船采用2台2000吨/小时的移动式连续装船机；卸船采用2台1000吨/小时的机械连续式卸船机。港内散粮输送设备采用全皮带机工艺方案，整个散粮中转设施系统流畅、操作灵活、能力匹配。

同期，天津港采用轻型卷板式薄钢板圆筒仓——港口中转库，筒仓直径20米，单仓容量4300吨，筒仓独立布置。一航院在秦皇岛、营口和大连等地设计的粮食码头均采用钢筋混凝土圆筒仓，组成连体群仓布置，筒仓直径为6～12米，单仓容量800～3000吨，筒仓排列分为正交和60°斜交两种形式。2000年起，根据粮食市场变化，部分港口散粮码头建设一批周转期较长的大直径圆筒仓，单仓容量在1~3万吨之间，通常作为储存仓使用。大连北良国家粮食储备库总容量60万吨，包括20个直径35米，单仓容量3万吨的大直径钢筋混凝土圆筒仓，呈两列独立布置。2005年一航院设计的天津临港佳悦粮油码头一期工程大豆储存库总容量12万吨，形成12个直径26米，单仓容量1万吨，成组独立布置的钢筋混凝土圆筒仓。

（三）件杂货

随着进、出口件杂货物集装箱化率的提高，通用杂货在全港吞吐量中所占比例不断减小。1991年后，天津港件杂货码头由船上吊（船吊）装、卸船作业，逐步发展为门座起重机（门机）和船吊联合装卸船作业。2000年后，随着货种的变化和船型的加大，门机的能力也逐步加大，钢杂泊位采用25吨、40吨门机配合下舱叉车进行钢材装卸船作业。通用散杂货泊位采用40吨-43米、轨距12米的大型门机配备散料抓斗进行大宗散货矿石等接卸作业。件杂货码头堆场装卸车及拆码垛作业采用轮胎式起重机（轮胎吊）及叉车。水平搬运机械采用牵引平板车，运距超过150米时采用载重汽车运输。2005年，一航院设计的北港池件杂货码头堆场作业采用电力的轨道式龙门起重机（轨道吊）和双动力轮胎吊（电、油两用）进行堆场作业。

2000年前后，进口散装铁矿石运量速增。天津港研制出专用料斗（大型漏斗），装卸工艺改为门机、抓斗将矿石卸入料斗，并通过料斗直接装自卸卡车。由于专用料斗容积比抓斗大，可以储存矿石，实现门机连续作业，充分发挥门机效率；同时，料斗卸料可以控制，装车时可一次装满，既安全、高效又防止撒漏。

（四）石油化工

1992年，一航院在天津港石油化工码头设计中采用直径400毫米的装卸臂，单台装卸效率可达3600立方米/小时。装卸臂与油船集油口的连接方式也由传统的螺栓连接改为手动或液动型快速连接器，减轻现场劳动强度，缩短船舶作业时间。2000年后，该院设计的天津港30万吨级原油码头装载臂都配带紧急脱离装置（ERS），可与码头快速脱缆装置联合动作，为紧急情况下船舶与码头快速脱离提供可能。2005年，该院设计的天津临港佳悦粮油码头采用轨道式移动装卸臂，进行食用油装卸船作业，提高设备使用的灵活性，有利于码头总体布置。

1993年建成的天津港唯一从事散装液体货物装卸的大型石化专业化码头，所采用的装卸工艺是应用混油装卸系统，消防安全和装卸操作管理均采用微机控制。可同时进行原油和成品油装卸作业，码头前沿分别安装效率为1225立方米/小时和1750立方米/小时的大型输油臂4台,装卸作业时,完全实现自动化操作。为适应到港船舶燃油供给的需要,至2005年末,天津港已建有20座各类油品储油罐,罐存油量共四个等级,最高为万吨。

20世纪90年代,一航院设计石油化工码头的卸船作业主要利用船泵压力接卸,将所载油品直接送入港区储罐。对于液化天然气码头,因介质汽化、管线投资等接卸罐区距码头一般不超过1千米,船泵扬程满足不了输送要求时进行二次加压接力输送。装船作业采用港区设置高位储罐,重力流装船或设置装船泵,将储罐内油品泵送至船舱。随着环保和节能要求的提高,利用油气回收法降低油品装卸过程的蒸发损耗的技术日趋成熟。装卸工艺改为直接装运到预先靠泊的空载油船内的"船—船直取"作业。码头工艺管线吹扫放空,较多采用自流排空加泵抽吸工艺,或按照油品的火灾危险等级采用惰性气体、压缩空气、水等介质进行吹扫置换。随着码头管线种类和公用管线的增多,逐步采用管道清管器吹扫新工艺,实现设备和管道的有效利用。

第四节 港口配套工程技术

1991~2005年,在天津港区的电力、控制、通信、节能等方面大量应用先进技术并开发创新,总体达到全国港口领先水平。天津港建设数字化港口和国际互联网服务网站。生产业务应用系统方面,集装箱码头和杂货码头管理系统、调度指挥系统均得以完善,同时,配煤工艺和节煤技术方面得以改进。

一、供电、照明和控制

(一)供电系统

1991年,天津港建成的110千伏变电站,装机容量为2×16000千伏安,电压为110千伏/6千伏。该站是全国港口第一座具有80年代国际水平的变电站,该站采用计算机实时监控110千伏变、配电系统的运行,取代传统的人工巡视。采用遥信、遥测、遥控等技术,通过计算机和电站自动控制设备实现远方变电所开关开闭状态的信号传递、远方变电所各种电量数值信号传递和远方变电所开关的遥控。高、低压电器及控制电器均采用当时世界一流技术的产品。整个110千伏变配电系统运行状态通过模拟屏显示,其设备和技术在国内同类变电站中达到一流水平。

1993~1994年,天津港对原有的35千伏供电系统实施改造,建成系统性能与110千伏变电站系统相匹配的一、二号2座6千伏配电站,开口容量均达到8000千伏安,并首次实现站与站之间的网络联络。

到2005年末,港区供电范围近50平方千米,供电线路已近1500千米;1990年年供电量为2647万千瓦时,到2005年年供电量达21000万千瓦时。

(二)电气设备

1990年后,天津港在6千伏电压等级中采用自动和人工手动控制无功功率补偿,在400伏电压等级中采用自动跟踪补偿装置。2002年,为减少电网中谐波影响,在低压无功功率补偿设备中开始选用具有谐波治理功能的MV系列动态无功功率补偿装置,该装置改变过去单一无功补偿的功能,可实现无功动态补偿与消除高次谐波综合控制功能,从而达到降低供电系统损耗、提高系统利用率、稳定系统网压、降低谐波电流对系统的破坏作用的效果。

2000年以后,断路器的保护和控制系统大多采用集保护、测量、控制信号、闭锁、自动化和通信于一体的综合保护装置,由微机控制,系统和开关所有控制操作、测量值的读取、信号的检测和功能参数的设立均能通过人机接口进行。

2005年建成投运的北港池110千伏变电站,在6千伏电压等级中采用"电压、无功综合控制及电能质量管理系统装置",该装置通过对有载调压变压器和并联电容器组进行自动综合优化控制来抑制港区大型机械起动时瞬时产生的冲击性无功负荷的影响，从而保证电网供电质量。

（三）控制系统

1991年投运的北疆110千伏变电站、6千伏配电站及其下属的7个6千伏变电所首次采用计算机实时监控系统，应用计算机技术和通信技术在主控制中心通过遥测、遥信、遥控对远方的设备运行状态进行监视、控制，实现变电所无人值守管理。

1996年，天津港电力调度中心建成投运，该中心采用RD-800调度系统，将港区内的全部电力信息均接入计算机系统，使港区的任何区域的任何开关的状态信息都能够及时准确地在2～5秒钟内发送到主站，并进行设备位置变位及声光报警，同时进行全部信息的存储归档，调度人员可以直观地了解到任何时刻的系统运行状况，确保及时下达调度命令。

截止到2005年，天津港供电系统变电站（所）的运行管理全部采用计算机实时监控，通过遥信、遥测和遥控对该站及远方系统实施实时监控管理。

二、信息与通信

（一）网络建设

1993年天津港成立信息中心。1997年天津港首先在机关大楼内部各部室与信息中心之间采用局域网技术。1999年开始使用ATM交换机，机关大楼各层的以太网交换机，通过光纤与ATM交换机相连，实现局域网内的通信。该核心交换机的带宽为155兆。1998年10月开通天津港国际互联网服务网站。之后，服务网站两度提速，提供从静态信息的查询到动态信息的发布，从天津港主页的建设到各基层公司主页的链接。

2002年年底建成天津港光缆基础网络，采用千兆以太网技术作为主干结构。天津港通过设置带宽控制设备为各公司分配不同的带宽，实现信息中心为全港唯一的互联网出口。在光缆基础网络建成后，先后与天津海关、天津海事局等港口相关单位实现光纤连接。2002年10月，天津港通过VPN（虚拟专用网）技术实现远程系统。此后，全港的船代公司和货主码头安装VPN，可实时使用天津港生产调度系统。2005年，以天津港信息中心为核心，全港30多家主要生产业务单位为二级节点的光缆基础网络已全面调通。2004年，天津港无线备份网络基本建成，无线网络与光缆基础网络共同使用。

（二）电子数据交换技术

1994年，国内第一艘第四代集装箱船中远“珍河”轮首航，第一个关于船图的数据文件用中远格式发至香港，开通天津港的港航电子数据交换系统。1997年，天津港口电子数据交换（EDI）中心为国家“九五”重点科技攻关项目，在全国港航系统中首家建成，率先实现国际集装箱运输信息交换方式。2001年，天津港EDI报文统一到部标报文和国际标准报文，实现舱单、船图的电子数据在船代、码头、理货、海关等单位间的多向流转；开通与外国船公司EDI业务，开通在互联网上为用户提供服务的功能，实现集装箱运输业务与国际接轨。2002年随着天津港光缆网建设完成，港区内的公司与EDI中心服务器实现光纤通信。

（三）应用系统的研发

1. 生产业务应用系统

1998年，天津港开发完成天津港船舶调度管理信息系统、决策支持系统、生产业务应用系统。其中，天津港船舶调度管理信息系统采用AMT技术，将EDP与EDI紧密集成，实现船舶调度的无纸化办公，满足港口调度业务和货运管理的实时性要求。

2003年，天津港进行全面的信息资源规划和系统开发。2004年，在现代通信、计算机网络和中心数据库环境基础上整合生产调度信息系统。该系统建立全港统一的信息资源管理基础标准，统一管理天津港生产业务系统的数据。2005年10月货运系统投入运行。

2. 集装箱码头管理系统

1996年，天津港引进美国IBM RISC/6000 J40双机系统作为服务器，采用C/S结构，应用ORACLE数据库系统，由PC机作为前端机。集装箱码头生产管理系统是由大连海事大学管理学院和天津港共同开发的，应用于船舶配载、电子数据交换、泊位管理、装卸船、业务计收费、货运站和堆场管理等。2002年,天津港进行集装箱码头第四次计算机系统的全面升级改造工程,引进由比利时COSMOS研制的集装箱码头操作管理软件和功能强大的计算机服务器群、千兆有线网络和无线网络系统,实现实时现场作业控制和全面办公自动化。

2004年,天津港黄力军、李宝元、马平文等在“天津港集装箱网络自动化操作管理系统”研究中,采用双箱装卸工艺,集成计算机网络、无线通信、视频与互联网技术,覆盖从集装箱进场、装箱、报价、出场、装卸船等过程,基本实现对集装箱动态数据的实时监控和管理,实现港口集装箱堆场无人数字化管理与生产要素的动态配置管理。该项目获2005年度天津市科技进步二等奖。

2005年,天津港集装箱码头有限公司在该公司3C(Computer、Communication、Control)生产体系的基础上,将全球卫星定位(GPS)、地理信息(GIS)技术引入港口集装箱行业,成功研发出具有自主知识产权的“集装箱码头生产过程控制可视化管理系统”。该系统将计算机、通讯、自控、GIS、GPS、多媒体、DLP大屏幕等技术融入COSMOS集装箱操作系统、AS400计算机网络系统、TEK无线数据传输系统、多种装卸机械电控系统,实现对码头、堆场、集装箱、装卸桥、轮胎吊、叉车、集卡生产数据的动态跟踪、自动采集、精确定位、生产过程精细化过程控制、三维可视化管理。有效地解决集装箱码头司机操作的任意性、生产信息的滞后性、安全生产和特殊自然环境对生产的制约等国际性行业难题。该项目创建独特的集装箱码头3C2S[2]生产体系,打破国外公司在该领域的技术垄断。

3.杂货码头管理系统

2002年,天津港开发库场计算机图形格式化系统,应用图形模式进行库场管理,能够及时、准确地在计算机上反映库场货物堆存的实际情况,对港口货运系统科学高效地进行场地货物管理发挥重要作用。2004年,天津港石化码头管理信息系统、煤码头管理信息系统正式运行。

为更好地规划生产信息资源,达到调度货运信息的共享、信息分析的目的,促进业务流程的整合,提高业务工作人员的工作效率和工作质量, 2005年8月,天津港完成该系统的升级开发,成为综合生产管理系统。

4.调度指挥系统

2005年,天津港调度指挥中心建成,实现对天津港全港运营状况信息系统的集中监控管理和自动化操作,引入新的信息管理方式,借助大屏幕展示方式,实现信息系统管理效率和管理质量的同步提升。

在发挥原有生产业务系统、船舶自动识别系统(AIS)、卫星测时测距导航/全球定位系统(GPS)功能的基础上,又建立天津港船舶交通管理系统(VTS)、智能交通系统、现场监控系统。通过指挥中心网络和大屏幕系统将各系统的功能整合起来,统一进行管理。能够更快的响应、解决问题,提高管理效率和质量。同时指挥中心内各个不同部门业务上互相协作,信息上实现资源共享。通过调度指挥中心的视频会议系统实现天津港集团可视会议的召开,对企业相关资源进行统一调度,最大化的利用资源,从而节约成本、提高效率。

三、港口节能技术

1990年交通部认定天津港为国家级节能一级企业。1991年,天津港开发“天津港能源管理信息系统”,并在使用中不断改进,使节能工作更为科学、规范。

(一)节电技术

1.应用变频调速技术

1996年,天津港一公司在10吨—30米门机上开始应用变频调速技术,在门机旋转、变幅机构驱动系统中安装日本安川公司的G3、G5系列变频器。通过变频器可平滑改变电源输出频率从而平滑调节电机转速,实现平滑的无级调速。其特点是调速平稳和范围宽、机械特性好、运行平稳安全可靠,在生产过程中能获得最佳速度参数。门机应用变频调速技术后,能节电30%。

1999年,天津港焦炭码头公司在全港引进大吨位全变频门机,均采用PLC控制,起升、变幅、旋转、走行四大机构全部采用变频技术。

2.应用能量回馈装置

1999年,焦炭码头公司在引进的40吨门机上率先应用电能回馈技术。电能回馈技术可使门机4个运行机构实现在直流端的能源共享,将门机各机构运行时产生的位能负载能量和制动能量回馈到直流公共端,其回馈能量可供其他机构设备使用。

3.货场、道路照明节电技术

1998年,天津港一公司在天津港首次应用光控、遥控技术开发新一代货场照明光控、遥控智能化控制装置,实现货场照明控制智能化。原有货场照明采用人工开、关灯,由于不同场地照明条件的要求不同,灯杆的分布较广,开、关过程长,形成电能浪费。运用无线遥控技术,实现远程控制开关和自动检查。每间隔一小时对照明设施进行自检,掌握运行状况以便及时采取相应措施。为避免照明设施启动、关闭时对电网的瞬时起伏冲击,在开启和关闭时采用延时技术,达到顺序起动或关闭。该装置还加入光控节电自动开关,能够根据现场照度情况,实施自动开、关灯。当现场照度低于设定值时可自动开灯,现场照度高于设定值时自动关灯。

2005年,天津港四公司应用货场照明系统节电器进行货场照明节电试验,获得成功。此项技术本身不产生谐波,可直接启动负载,对负载电流浪涌系数无限制,而且其输入网络呈高阻态,能较好地抑制输入电压、电流的瞬变。节电器可随时调节供电电压,使供电电压稳定在220伏左右,节电率达到10%以上。

4.电网谐波治理技术

2000年,天津港电力公司开始使用无源型滤波器,进行谐波治理。在港区新一号、三号等多个变电所安装无源型滤波器,这种滤波器能就近吸收门机所产生的谐波电流,精确控制电容器组的投切时间,减少投切时的冲击电流和操作过电压,同时可根据负荷大小自动调节无功补偿,减少无功损耗。经天津电力科学研究院谐波监理站检验测试,达到预期效果。治理后,天津港电网运行的电能质量指标满足GB/T14549-93电能质量公用网谐波国家标准,使负载产生的谐波得到了有效控制,年线路损耗电能减少70211千瓦时,变压器损耗电能减少19780千瓦时,年供电能力增加约140万千瓦时。还避免由于谐波引起的变压器、电抗器、电容器等设备的损坏。

5.零空闲变速操作技术

2003年,焦炭码头公司采用斗轮机"零空闲变速操作技术",解决斗轮臂架在不同位置时效率变化大的问题,使整个取料工步的流量相对恒定,有效提高生产效率。焦炭斗轮机取料作业的生产效率比原来提高30%以上,平均每月节电10792千瓦时。

6.超级电容储能装置

2004年,集装箱码头公司为了降低轮胎式起重机的能耗,提高能源利用效率,在轮胎式集装箱场桥上安装超级电容储能装置。逆变电源工作于在线方式,其直流输入从超级电容器组正负极接入,当处于柴油机组发电工作状态时,直流能量由发电机组供电的整流器组提供;当柴油机组停机时,由超级电容器组提供后备直流电能,经逆变器向交流负载提供稳定可靠的交流工作电源,超级电容储能装置节电率达10%左右。

7.改进配煤工艺

传统的配煤工艺是由两条生产作业线共同来完成配煤作业,而取料机、堆取料机(取料)和皮带机的装机容量较大,取料机功率为891千瓦,堆取料机(取料)功率为915千瓦,皮带机功率为945千瓦,存在严重的大马拉小车现象,影响装卸生产效率和设备有效利用率。2005年,煤码头公司自行开发生产配煤小皮带机,改变原配煤工艺。新型配煤工艺中,配煤小皮带机的额定功率只有15千瓦,能耗大减。

(二)节煤技术

1.太阳能集热器

2001年,天津港生活服务中心在四公司后方浴室选用太阳能集热器、燃油炉辅助热补的装置,代替原燃煤锅炉供热水洗浴方式。该装置用76平方米太阳能集热器和1台15万大卡燃油炉辅助加热,可供每天200人次洗浴。

天津港生活服务中心在一公司后方浴室安装太阳能集热器300平方米和1台20万大卡燃油炉辅助加

热，可供每天600人次洗浴。太阳能集热器节能效果良好，与单用电加热方式比较年节约能耗成本40多万元；与单用燃油炉加热方式比较年节约能耗成本10多万元。

2.地源热泵空调系统

2003年，天津港一公司在七米检查桥使用地源热泵空调系统，取代原来冬天用电热板加热取暖、夏天用空调制冷的方式，使室内温度得到有效调整，满足冬季室温在20℃±2℃，夏季室温26℃±2℃国家标准要求。地源热泵空调系统耗电量少，运行费用低，达到节能降耗要求。

地源热泵空调系统利用冬夏地下与大气的温度差，不使用地下水资源，而是通过导管内特殊介质循环取得地下能量，通过主机工作置换进行取暖和制冷，夏季能效比为1∶5.4，冬季为1∶3.8。地源热泵系统采取特殊的换热方式，它通过地表能交换实现制冷和制热的双功能温度调节，不受室外温差影响，能达到最佳的室温效果。

3.凝结水回收技术

2001～2003年，天津港生活服务中心先后在集团公司机关锅炉房、四分公司前方和后方锅炉房、五分公司后方换热站、四港池换热站加装自行设计的凝结水回收再利用设施。该设施主要解决冷凝水回收利用及凝结水回收系统汽蚀及腐蚀等问题。其工艺流程为：锅炉→换热器→凝结水回收器→凝结水箱→锅炉，该设施每小时可回收温度60℃～80℃的凝结水28吨，实现能源再利用。

第五节　航道工程

20世纪90年代，中交天津航道局有限公司的疏浚技术装备——挖泥船大部分设备老化。疏浚装备方面开始应用疏浚工程（耙吸挖泥船）电子图形监控系统、购进大型和超大型自航耙吸挖泥船、大型绞吸挖泥船、大型链斗挖泥船、抓斗挖泥船等。同时，天航局加强对老旧自航耙吸挖泥船的改造，并先后研制出“自航耙吸挖泥船耙头位置监控系统”和“自航耙吸挖泥船装载监测系统”“高精度绞刀深度监控系统”“绞吸挖泥船计算机辅助决策系统”“双金属复合绞刀”和“绞吸挖泥船环保绞刀头”等。天津港在导助航设施中增加卫星定位助航系统（DGPS），使船舶进出航道的可靠性得以提高。至2005年年底，天航局拥有各类疏浚船舶77艘，其中挖泥船28艘，拖轮7艘，锚艇15艘，泥驳18艘，其他辅助船9艘，总装机功率14.9万千瓦。

1995年，航道设计中边坡坡度优化取得突破性进展。1997年，天津港进行航道整治，将第五代集装箱船靠泊码头以东主航道浚深至-12.0米，拓宽至180米，形成天津港主航道，总长21.5千米。2005年，一航院提出复式航道设计理念。航道施工技术方面，天航局开发出“三锚五缆施工法”。以“适航水深应用”技术为核心进行“天津港深水航道、港池、泊位适航水深应用与水深动态维护研究”；天津港又联合天津市海亿海洋工程技术有限公司开展“天津港水深维护动态管理”研究等，均取得可喜成果。

一、航道设计

（一）边坡坡度优化

为满足天津港吞吐量快速增长的需要，解决港口深水化问题。1995年，一航院赵智帮等在设计天津港5万吨级航道扩建工程时，对航道边坡坡度优化进行研究，港内、外航道两侧边坡坡度均采用1∶5，改变过去港外航道边坡坡度1∶10～1∶20太缓的设计。1998年航道开挖工程取得成功，表明采用该比例是正确的。2001年，该院在天津港10万吨级航道工程设计中，航道边坡坡度全部采用1∶5。由于边坡坡度变陡，挖方量减少1730万立方米，节省资金数亿元。2002年，天津港航道优化设计引起交通部重视，组织有关单位对《海港总平面设计规范》（JTJ211-99）中的航道边坡坡度部分进行修订，促进在全国航道设计中，选用更加合理的边坡坡度。

（二）复式航道

2001年后，天津港吞吐量大量增加，致使进出港船舶剧增，航道非常紧张，船舶待泊时间增加和货船不能按时离港，制约港口发展。根据天津港多年统计，1万吨级及其以下小船占进出港船舶总数的70%以上，影响天津港航道通过能力的主要因素是小船占用大航道。2005年，一航院赵智帮提出复式航道设计理念，以解决船流密度过大和小船占用大航道问题。为此，在主航道南北两侧各挖一条平行于主航道的万吨级以下船舶单向航道，北进南出，使大小船分流，各行其道，主航道可万吨级以上船舶双向航行，主航道与南北两侧的万吨级航道构成复式航道。其优点：主航道只有占到港船舶总数30%的万吨级以上船舶双向航行，大幅度减轻主航道的通行密度；大小船分道航行，大船航速提高，万吨级以下船没有对遇，增强航道的通行能力；为避免进港上航道的船舶和出港船舶的交叉，调整锚地的布置，将进港锚地布置在航道北侧。万吨级以上船舶：在灯塔以东适宜的水深处由航道北侧上主航道或由航道南侧离开主航道。万吨级以下船舶：进港的在灯塔以西上北侧万吨级航道，出港的走南侧万吨级航道，这样进出港船舶在港外没有交叉。主航道宽420米，底标高-19.5米。万吨级以下小船航道宽100米，底标高-9.0米，南北两条万吨级航道估算挖泥量约为800万立方米，挖泥量较小施工容易。据国内外调查，在人工航道中天津港复式航道尚属首创。

二、导助航设施工程

2001年，天津港在导助航设施中增加卫星定位助航系统（DGPS），该系统具有定位精度高，系统简单，技术成熟，设备使用灵活、方便等特点，不受地理环境和气候变化的影响。天津北塘RBN/DGPS站已于1997年正式建成并开通使用。它包括基准台、播发台、完善性监控台和监控中心。信号覆盖范围大于300平方千米，完全能满足引航使用要求。只要选择相兼容的GPS接收机即可使用。在导助航设施中增加DGPS卫星定位系统，船舶进出航道的可靠性提高。

三、疏浚装备

（一）自航耙吸挖泥船

1991年后，天津港开始应用“疏浚工程（耙吸挖泥船）电子图形监控系统”。该系统由航迹仪自动导航定位和耙头自动跟踪显示两个子系统组成。具有编制施工图形，实时定位及航迹显示、标绘功能，并可随船位自动切换、显示设计断面和平面图形及耙头水下动态位置，监控导航及施工定位作业，能将施工参数和航迹贮存再现和绘制水深图，系统并可与DGPS定位系统连接使用。随着全球卫星定位系统（GPS）迅速发展，天津港大中型挖泥船施工和水深测量广泛用DGPS系统及计算机图形处理技术，把DGPS定位信息与电子海图背景有机结合起来，可实时显示船位、航迹和周围地理情况，达到全天候定位和导航作业，定位精度可达米级或亚米级，提高挖泥效率和时间利用率。交通部在沿海地区无线电指向标站上，建立DGPS系统差分台，供导航使用，挖泥船只要装设接收机即可实现DGPS定位，精度可达1～5米。

1994年，天航局自荷兰购进自航耙吸挖泥船—“通力”，该船是国内首次引进的具有艏吹装置的，兼有挖抛和挖吹两种功能的自航耙吸挖泥船，其船型为大型宽、小吃水，泥舱容量5400立方米，装有耙头高压冲水系统，可调节式泥舱溢流系统、深舱装舱系统使其具有较高的生产率，又配以DGPS定位系统，功能齐全的测深系统、挖泥操作的显示和监视系统。2003年天航局购进的挖泥船—“通坦”，其自动监控系统要比“通力”更加先进。同期，天航局加强对老旧自航耙吸挖泥船的改造，分别将津航浚105、107、108三艘自航耙吸挖泥船加大挖深，安装自行设计的主动耙头具有高压冲水功能和耙头对地角度调节功能，可提高对工程的适用性和挖掘能力，延长使用寿命。在自航耙吸挖泥船疏浚仪表与自动化的研制方面，该局李金贵、王勇、费牗公等于1998年和2000年先后研制出“自航耙吸挖泥船耙头位置监控系统”和“自航耙吸挖泥船装载监测系统”。2003年，天津港首次引进舱容为33000立方米超大型自航耙吸挖泥船，应用于十五万吨级航道二期工程中，大幅提高挖泥效率。

(二)绞吸挖泥船

为适应江河湖泊环保治理事业的发展和港口经济建设、沿海滩涂资源的开发,2000年天航局购进海狸1200型绞吸挖泥船“浚江”和“浚湖”,为分体式,整船拆装方便,适合陆路运输,吃水1米多,公称生产率450立方米/时,最大挖深10米,设计排距1500米,适用于内河、湖泊的清淤工程。“浚湖”船属于环保型,配有可防止污染淤泥扩散环保绞刀头、监视污染土可能扩散的混浊度检测仪、用于提高挖泥精度和生产量的钢桩台车装置、生产测量系统、提高挖泥船深度指示器精度的桥梁下放深度电子指示系统、移锚吊杆装置、符合欧洲Ⅱ级环保标准的EUI电喷式发动机。2004年天航局购进美国造的“津航浚221”“津航浚222”两艘绞吸挖泥船,公称生产率1900立方米/时,最大挖深21米,设计排距3000米。在绞吸挖泥船疏浚仪表与自动化的研制方面,自行合作研制出“高精度绞刀深度监控系统”“绞吸挖泥船计算机辅助决策系统”。天航局张庆海、杨建华、刘俸林等于1994年和2000年先后研制出“双金属复合绞刀”和“绞吸挖泥船环保绞刀头”并分别获得了国家发明专利和国家实用新型专利。至2005年年底,天航局拥有绞吸挖泥船12艘。

(三)链斗挖泥船

2004年,天航局引进1989年德国造自航链斗挖泥船“津航浚306”,航速6.5节[1节(kn)=1海里/时],最大挖深24米,斗容0.75立方米/只,泥斗数量可以根据挖深调整,最多可安装63个斗,桥梁有一加长段可根据挖深拆装,自航时双车推进,动力为柴油机,两台主发电机可根据挖掘土质选用其中一台,船形为流线型,总装机功率1926千瓦,公称生产量750立方米/时。该船是当时国内最大的链斗挖泥船。

(四)抓斗挖泥船

天航局于2003年和2004年先后从日本购进1988和1989年建造的非自航抓斗挖泥船“津航浚405”“津航浚406”,这两艘挖泥船均以柴油机为动力。“津航浚405”配有18立方米抓斗一只,6立方米抓斗一只;“津航浚406”配有20立方米抓斗一只,13立方米抓斗一只。两船均可做浮吊使用,最大挖深50米,公称生产量800立方米/时。

四、施工技术

(一)施工工法

1998年,天航局刘德来、董保顺在标准的“三缆施工法(五锚五缆)”基础上通过创新改进,开发出“三锚五缆施工法”,其特点是弃用左右两口定位边锚由横移锚代替,除降低移锚、倒收台车的工作量外,还大幅降低施工船对施工水域的占用,从而也使该类挖泥船的适用范围大大拓宽。与常规“三缆施工法”相比:少两口边锚,节约边锚移锚时间,减少移船时间,挖泥时间利用率提高3%左右;少占用水域,消除对挖槽两侧水域的水深要求,使不能施工的变为可能,提高设备利用率;减少施工干扰,提高时间利用率。此工法在特殊工况或定位钢桩出现故障的情况下,仍能使施工船正常施工。2001年津航浚215船在苏丹工程开挖珊瑚礁时,船艉水深达200米,不能使用钢桩;2003年在天津港北港池疏浚工程中因淤泥土层厚,钢桩漏桩严重,钢桩起升困难,均采用“三锚五缆”法施工,皆保证工程顺利实施。

(二)施工监控技术

20世纪90年代,天航局引进DGPS定位系统,可全天候进行挖泥导航施工,并可提高挖泥船的平面定位精度;同时,为使挖泥船施工时能够及时掌握潮位的变化以控制挖深,减少施工超深,还自行开发出“潮位自动遥报系统”,该系统将采集的潮位数据传送到挖泥船上,显示并打印出潮位值,其传输距离可达35千米,精度±2厘米,

2000年,天航局引进一套GeoSwath条带测深系统,其扫测宽度可达水深的10倍左右,大幅提高水深测量效率和精度。在此之前,水深测量采用单波束回声测深仪,其效率约为GeoSwath条带测深系统的20%。

五、维护疏浚

2000年起,天津港黄力军、丁乃庆、刘富强等以“适航水深应用”技术为核心进行“天津港深水航道、港

池、泊位适航水深应用与水深动态维护研究”。将可航行浮泥计入航深；采用人工手段将大于适航水深浮泥容重临界值（天津港为1.30吨/米^3）的淤泥搅稀，使之达到适航要求，增加航深；迅速处理局部水深浅点区海底泥沙，提高整个水域的通航水深标准。这些新技术，不间断地实施于两次维护疏浚之间，以延长维护疏浚周期。水深维护保养新模式，由两大部分组成，先是在前次维护疏浚后，在水深逐渐变浅的过程中，全天候实施非疏浚的水深保养手段（适航水深应用、适航增深与水深浅点处理等），增加航深，延续维护疏浚周期，这阶段工作称为“水深保养”；当适航浮泥资源全部用尽后，再实施随后的维护疏浚，称为“水深维护”。“水深保养”与“水深维护”两个阶段工作有机结合，构成“水深维护保养”工作的全过程。该项目获2005年度国家科技进步二等奖。

2002年起，天津港联合天津市海亿海洋工程技术有限公司开展“天津港水深维护动态管理”研究。先后开发出“抓吸疏浚”“气吸疏浚”“环保疏浚”等专项施工工艺，以及“适航增深”“水深浅点处理”“复合适航增深”等维护技术。从单一的静态水深维护管理转为复合的动态水深维护管理体系，并成功解决“天津港北疆无吹泥地”“港口生产与维护施工的矛盾”“三十万吨级满载油轮安全靠港作业”等诸多难题，为天津港提供优质的水深条件，为港口生产与发展需求提供有效支撑。同年，该公司章大初等研制成功卧式吸泥泵船。卧式吸泥泵排泥浓度可达40%，满足装驳外运的要求，所组建的“卧式吸泥泵”船队，成为天津港北疆诸泊位与部分港池维护疏浚主力。局部清淤采用深水移泥法。当大吃水船进出港，而局部水深不足时，采用深水移泥装置，可在短时间内将浅点泥沙移至四周深水区，保证大吃水船只进出。

第六章　轨道交通

20世纪90年代，中国铁路步入快速发展和大提速时期，铁路建设标准不断提高，路网规划日趋完善。铁道第三勘察设计院集团有限公司在既有铁路提速改造、重载铁路、客运专线的建设中，不断改进勘察设计手段，3S技术、数字化测绘、航测技术、测绘新仪器、综合勘探方法等广泛应用于铁路和城市轨道交通勘察测绘。先后完成京九、朔黄、哈大、秦沈等客运专线，天津港1000万吨煤下海工程、大秦线年运量一亿吨配套工程、津滨轻轨等铁路和城市轨道交通的勘察设计。铁三院在秦沈客运专线关键技术研究中，实现新建铁路一次铺设跨区间无缝线路、桥上无碴轨道，破解在路基、桥涵、通信、信号、接触网设计等方面的关键技术难题，开创客运专线无碴轨道设计和一次铺设跨区间无缝线路之先河，并创造中国铁路第一时速321.5千米/小时的试验速度。

21世纪初，全国铁路施工机械化水平快速提升，最具代表的是全断面硬岩掘进机在长大隧道中的运用。驻津的中铁十八局集团有限公司（以下简称“中铁十八局”）在国家重大铁路项目的建设上，尤其是在长大艰险隧道、新特型桥梁、高等级铁路施工中均有重大技术突破。1996年，南昆铁路八渡南盘江特大桥施工中解决当时世界上最高的V型支撑铁路桥梁技术难题；1997年，西康铁路秦岭特长隧道在中国铁路隧道中首次采用掘进机法（TBM）施工，开创长大铁路隧道施工划时代的局面；2000年，中铁十八局经技术创新，解决集深基、群桩、高墩、大跨、长联于一体的内昆李子沟特大桥施工难题。2002年，渝怀铁路彭水隧道这一西南山区典型复杂地质铁路隧道工程施工中，创造出在不良地质条件下，掘进速度快，生产安全无事故的范例。

1999年，天津市区至滨海新区快速轨道交通工程（以下简称“津滨轻轨”）启动，2001年试验段开工。2005年5月1日正式投入运营。津滨轻轨由铁三院设计、天津滨海快速交通发展有限公司建设，为国内首条最高时速可达100千米/小时的城市轨道交通项目，采用一次性铺设无缝线路技术，减少振动和噪音，提高列车平稳、舒适程度，延长钢轨安全使用寿命，通信传输系统采用开放式传输网络OTN系统，信号采用列车自动控制ATC系统，在国内的轨道交通工程中，均属于当时最为先进的控制技术。2001~2004年，津滨轻轨工程抗震分析与减震降噪技术、松软土地基轻轨超长高架桥设计、施工控制技术研究取得重大进展。

2000年前，地下铁道管理处负责天津地铁生产运营的工作，地铁安全运营15年。2000年10月，天津市地下铁道总公司（以下简称"地铁总公司"）成立，承担天津地铁1号线工程建设。2002年11月该线全面动工，全线采用地下、高架、地面等多种敷设方式，车站及区间结构型式多样，集中地铁设计的全部形式，突破标准化设计模式。特别是天津西站至新华路既有线改建技术、半高安全门系统、DV750V钢铝复合接触轨、电阻再生能量吸收装置等均为国内首创。2001~2005年，地铁总公司获得省部级科技进步奖2项，制定出5个天津市地方标准。

第一节 勘察设计

铁三院承担着全国乃至世界一些地区的铁路勘察设计任务。1991~2005年，其勘察设计任务与技术手段、技术水平得到前所未有的发展。在既有铁路提速改造、客运专线的建设中，不断改进勘察设计手段，采用新技术、新设备、新工艺。15年间，铁三院获国家级优秀勘察、设计、软件、标准、咨询等各类奖项共46项，其中国家科技进步奖3项；省部、市级奖共193项。

一、勘察

1993年，铁三院正式使用GPS技术施测深圳地铁一期工程的控制测量。1995年，GPS技术开始应用于秦沈客运专线项目航空摄影测量的像控点联测，此后在航测项目中得到广泛应用，替代常规的航测导线测量。1998年，该院用航测方法内业测绘大比例尺工点图和横断面图；2001年，该院韩祖杰等自主研发的"铁路通用数字地图编辑软件包"，可快速实现采集数据的自动批量转换和地形图整饰，在特征提取、三维建模和模型分析方面为铁路设计提供必要的基础数据。该软件获2004年度国家优秀软件铜质奖。

铁三院在大秦铁路桑干河峡谷区工程地质选线中，采用综合勘探方法，重点利用航测遥感技术，进行大面积地质调绘填图，重点工程地段进行必要的物探，关键部位进行钻探，查明重点工程地质和水文地质条件，为方案比选提供可靠的地质依据。1993年获国家优秀工程勘察金奖。

1997年，铁三院在朔黄铁路恒山越岭地段工程地质勘察中采用遥感（航片、卫片判释、航测地质成图等）、综合物探（地震折射法、直流电阻法的高密度电法、联合剖面法、电测深法、综合测井法和室内岩芯测试）、钻探（最深孔达286.1米）和外业调查（其中大面积测绘454平方千米）相结合的方法，查明地层、岩性、地质构造、工程地质及水文地质特征、煤矿采空区等不良地质现象。朔黄铁路恒山越岭地段工程地质勘察2002年获全国优秀勘察铜奖。

1997~2000年，铁三院辛民高、白恒恒、樊五星等在朔黄线长梁山隧道为载体的长大隧道施工超前地质信息预报研究中，采用岩体工程地质力学分析、相关性分析、长期水文地质观测等综合研究技术，提出围岩分类判别标准，提出相应措施建议。在国内首次采用节理相关性分析推断软弱夹层、断层在洞内的出现里程位置；在铁路行业首次引入地下水在含水带和裂隙壁间运动的概念，为铁路长大隧道施工防止涌水、失水预测预报工作提供经验。该成果获2001年度天津市科技进步二等奖。

1998~2000年，铁三院在胶州~新沂铁路主干断裂活动性和全新世断陷构造及场地岩土条件的基础上对沂沭断裂带进行地壳稳定性分区。对9条线路方案进行地质条件和造价估算方面的比选，最后选定莒县北方案。该院发现第四纪最新活动的板泉新断陷和莒县新断陷，制定出胶新铁路选线原则，对工程地质稳定性分区评价，为国家决策胶新铁路建设提供科学依据。

1998～2003年，铁三院在朔黄铁路特殊岩土工程地质勘察中，地质调绘的基础上采用钻探、静力触探和原位测试等综合勘探方法，查明软土的分布和工程特性。

二、设计

（一）轨道

铁三院承担勘测设计的秦沈客运专线是国内第一条自行设计、施工，行车速度达到200千米/小时以上的双线电气化客运专线铁路，全长404.65千米。1999～2001年，铁三院李树德、闫红亮等在秦沈客运专线轨道设计中成功解决新建铁路一次铺设跨区间无缝线路及新型桥上无碴轨道结构设计等技术难题，在国内首次研究确定不同轨道结构过渡段设计以及路基、桥梁等线下工程技术参数，在沙河、狗河及跨双河公路3座特大桥上成功设计、铺设具有自主知识产权的桥上长枕埋入式和板式无碴轨道，联合开发CA砂浆和充填式垫板等关键技术，跨区间无缝线路最长轨条达200.918千米。新建客运专线轨道设计技术研究获2005年度天津市科技进步二等奖。

图9-6-1-134 中国首条时速160公里以上的快速铁路——秦沈客运专线

（二）桥涵

1992年建成通车的大准铁路黄河特大桥，主跨96+132+96米三跨连续栓焊钢桁梁，铁三院在国内铁路钢桥中首次采用节间距12米的无竖杆三角桁架，132米中跨桁架上，以柔拱肋加劲，既增强刚度又节约钢材。铁三院在1995年建成通车的北京铁路西站丰台路立交桥主桥16+36+16米预应力混凝土连续梁设计中，对孔用两片钢筋混凝土拱肋予以加劲，形成一种拱梁组合结构，拱梁之间用网状吊杆联系。该桥结构新颖、外型美观，增大中孔跨越能力。

1999～2001年，铁三院李凤芹、王召祜、陈后军等完成秦沈客运专线斜交刚构连续梁桥设计。该设计减少桥梁支座数量，降低养护维修费用，且桥梁整体性能强、结构刚度大、抗震性能好；边墩和桥台用活动支座与梁部相连接，使结构在温度跨度较大的边墩和桥台处不受温度力的影响，改善结构的受力状况。该桥具有较好的动力性能，特别适合在客运专线上使用。由于刚构连续梁桥的梁、墩、台均可斜做，铁路能以任何角度跨越既有道路、河流等，桥下道路顺畅，因此桥梁和两侧路基高度显著降低，桥梁长度显著减小，从而使总体工程造价降低。

2001～2002年，铁三院施新宇、王召祜、宋毓澜等依托秦沈线开展移动模架拼架法客运专线32米预应力混凝土双线单箱筒支梁研究。客运专线跨度32米双线整孔预应力混凝土简支箱梁，梁重750吨，由于其自重大，受国内架桥机条件的限制，无法整孔架设，采用移动模架造桥机实现逐孔原位现浇，逐孔制造，成功解决这种箱梁的施工应用问题。该梁是对铁路常规跨度简支圬工梁一次升级与跨越，研究成果提出的在小支点距条件下桥位现浇和节段拼装设计属国内首创，经中国铁路工程总公司组织评审，该成果达到国内领先水平。

2003年，铁三院孙树礼、王召祜、王桢等结合青藏铁路拉萨河特大桥所处的特殊地理气候条件及抗震要求（8度震区）研制开发铰轴滑板钢支座。该支座结构紧凑，传力途径明确，主要传力部件之间采用面接触，接触应力较小且均匀，从根本上解决由于接触应力大、材料强度及硬度不足而引起的运营病害；在构造上增设可更换摩擦幅，使摩擦幅抽换方便；具有良好的滑动和转动性能，对梁部的变形约束小；材料用量较传统辊轴钢支座少，制造、运输、安装、养护和维修方便。铰轴滑板钢支座成功应用于青藏铁路拉萨河特大桥的建设中。

2004年，铁三院王召祜、宋顺忱、李义兵等研制开发的双曲面调高支座，具有受力均匀、横向可以转动、纵向转动灵活，同时还具有减震调高的功能。同年，王召祜、宋顺忱、李义兵等研制开发的调高测力盆式橡胶支座，集调高、减震、测力3种功能为一体，可以测试各支座受力情况，以避免整孔箱梁出现三条腿现象。上述两支座均适用于软土地区、无碴轨道或磁悬浮铁路的桥梁及要求内力调整的超静定结构，对客运专线、高速铁路的建设起到积极作用。

（三）隧道设计

20世纪90年代，铁三院在朔黄线长梁山隧道、寺铺尖隧道、水泉湾隧道设计中首次采用复合衬砌施工工艺。朔黄线隧道围岩破碎、含水的软岩地段设计采用钻、注、锚三为一体的自进式锚杆，以解决普通的砂浆锚杆坍孔及注浆不饱满的难题。该隧道洞身冲沟与断层相交处有地下水自断层渗流，为当地居民用水来源，为防止隧道施工引起水位大幅度下降，设计采用帷幕注浆，超前15米加固围岩，防止地下水渗漏及保护环境。长梁山隧道采用超前地质预报技术，以地面地质调查为基础，台车钻速测试为辅，长期和短期地质预报相结合的方法，根据预报结果及时调整设计工法。支护采用湿喷混凝土工法，在国内建筑业中很少大规模的使用，特别是采用国产转子活塞式湿喷机（TK—961）尚属首例。坍方段设计采用局部拱部进行网喷补强，局部拱脚和拱腰处加密锚杆，网喷厚度不小于0.20米，以增强初期支护，遏制坍方蔓延。

北京地铁“复八线”西单站地处繁华闹市区，在不影响地面生活、交通及安全的情况下，在地面6米以下采用浅埋暗挖法修建一个长258.8米、宽25.88米、高13.16米三拱两柱双层大跨度车站，其工程规模、施工难度和工程风险之大，在国内乃至世界地铁车站暗挖施工领域罕见。1990年，铁三院首次在松散地层中采用“双眼镜法”的浅埋暗挖施工工艺，实现历史性突破。

铁三院张佩竹等编制的城市轨道交通设计调线调坡集成系统应用软件，输入实测竣工后的有关数据，可自动生成城市轨道交通调线调坡的线路平面图、纵断面图、放大纵断面图、结构横断面图、铺轨综合图。该软件于2004年首次在天津地铁1号线设计中应用。

（四）路基

1998年，铁三院屈晓辉、崔俊杰、宋绪国等依托秦沈客运专线，研究新建铁路客运专线路基设计技术，采用将路基作为土工结构物设计理念，研究高速列车动应力的传递和衰减规律。通过弹性变形和动强度控制，确定客运专线路基强化结构形式；通过对过渡段的结构综合刚度分析，在路桥、路涵、堤堑连接处设置过渡段，保证路基横向及纵向刚度的均匀过渡；突破传统设计模式，对软土、松软土地基加固处理进行动态设计，有效控制软土、松软土路基工后沉降、沉降速率；通过对填料的静、动力特性研究，对填料进行适用性判别和以动强度控制，以静强度为标准进行填料化学改良，提出一套适合新建铁路客运专线路基的系统设计技术。该成果获2003年度天津市科技进步一等奖。

（五）枢纽与站场

1999年，铁三院完成标准设计叁站（99）8080 60千克钢轨道岔组合布置图集，图集组合型式多，覆盖面广，通用性强，利于制造，便于铺设。标准设计内分有道岔组合布置形式32种。车站设计中采用本道岔组合布置，能缩短车站咽喉区长度，使车站平面布置紧凑，布局合理，节省铺轨、土方、用地，降低工程造价。若地形困难，地面建筑物多，人口密集，站坪短的大站改扩建设计中使用更显示本图集优越性。获国家第六届优秀工程建设标准设计银质奖。

2001年，铁三院设计的哈大线电气化改造工程，其大连枢纽，新建双向二级四场站型金州编组站。该站根据车流特点，站址选择正确，车站布置图型选择合理，车站设备规模满足运输需要，驼峰设计首次在编发线连挂区布设新型的TDJ303BM型（双向慢回程）减速顶调速设备，与相邻编组站及枢纽内其他技术作业站分工合理。哈尔滨枢纽哈尔滨南编组站由单向三级四场扩建为双向三级六场，日解编能力达1.8万辆；该站作为枢纽技术作业站，设计布局合理，确定的枢纽改造工程和电化范围满足运输能力的需要，车站设计方案正确，站型选择经济合理，调车场尾部首次采用TDJT-101型停车顶，哈大铁路电气化引入哈尔滨枢纽工程设计。

2002年，铁三院完成的《区段站咽喉区布置图集》叁站（02）图形型式多，覆盖面广，通用性强。在区段站实际设计过程中具有较强的指导作用，新建区段站可根据设计规模和型式直接采用本图集对应图形，改造既有区段站可参考相应图形灵活运用，并获2004年度国家优秀工程建设标准设计银奖。

铁三院主持编制的《铁路驼峰及调车场设计规范》《工业站、港湾站设计规范》《铁路集装箱结点站设计暂行规定》，分别于1999年、2001年和2003年由铁道部发布实施。

2005年，铁三院完成丰台西编组站下行系统驼峰调速系统自动化技术改造，设计出点连式调速系统，以解决点式驼峰调速系统控制精度不高的问题，属国内首创。

（六）给排水

2000年，铁三院在秦皇岛至沈阳客运专线和胶州至新沂铁路工程中采用新型聚乙烯给水管材，球墨铸铁管、聚乙烯管代替给水铸铁管，塑料给水管、排水管在设计中广泛使用。秦沈客运专线葫芦岛北站设计使用新型钢结构水塔，采用钢支筒，不锈钢水箱，使用与观赏功能相结合，造型独特别致。

2004年，铁三院贺占民、薛林海、石玉川等开发的“客运工具的清污装置”，利用重力排污，设置在箱体内，中水软管中的水自吸回流到自动回水阀的排泄口，地漏排除，避免软管中水到处洒落；可放在列车整备厂或指定站点的场所使用。上下水接口设计合理，上水管内存积水，排入排水管道排放，不影响铁路路基，管道使用寿命长，场地整洁卫生。该设备结构简单，节省能源。

（七）供电

1998年，铁三院在大秦线年运量一亿吨配套工程（秦皇岛、山海关地区电气化改造）中，国内首次采用110千伏单相变压器供电技术。2001年11月正式开通的哈尔滨至大连电气化改造工程中，该院系统引进德国的设计方法、运营管理模式、变电、接触网技术和装备，是国内引进的第一条电气化工程项目。全线采用单相220千伏全并联供电方式和柱上分区所设计技术。在消化吸收德国设计标准体系Re200c的基础上，采用接触网新型交叉线岔的设计原则和各种典型道岔的新型交叉线岔平面布置、接触悬挂降高技术等，均属国内首创。在供电可靠性、降低牵引网损耗和节省运营成本、提高接触网受流质量和减少弓网事故、减少对跨线建筑物改造等方面，与国内外同类设计相比，具有明显的优势，该项设计获2004年全国优秀工程设计银奖。其工程获2004年第四届詹天佑土木工程奖。

2003年，铁三院设计的秦沈客运专线开通运营，时速200千米/小时，采用220千伏单相变压器供电，在国内自行设计的电气化铁路中尚属首例。牵引变电所采用安全监控及综合自动化系统，接触网采用精确道岔布置技术和CATMOS接触网-受电弓动态模拟仿真系统等技术和设计手段。

（八）通信

20世纪90年代，铁三院首次提出客运管理信息系统，并开发研制“列车到发微机通告系统”，该系统可将车站值班员或行车指挥中心掌握的列车到发时刻信息及时、准确地传递给该站其他相关值班人员，以便迅速地为旅客提供乘降车及其他服务，同时也是旅客车站通告显示网的信息源点，在天津站首次应用。1996年，该院开发研制电子售检票系统并首次应用于北京西客站工程中。2003年在秦沈铁路中，该院采用通告显示综合信息网络，以列车到发通告系统为主导，由列车到发通告、旅客引导显示、客运广播、电视监视子系统构成，采用两级网络结构，全线构成以专线网为主，分组交换网为辅的综合信息管理广域网。从而首次在铁路实现全程联网信息共享、全程集中图像监控、全程集中广播等功能，并为拓展办公自动化、多媒体查询等新业务提供综合信息处理平台。获2004年中国铁路工程总公司优秀设计一等奖。

1993～1997年，铁三院在京九铁路工程北京至商丘段中采用20芯G.652光纤单模充油松套管层绞单元式直埋型光缆，光纤的传输衰耗窗口采用双波长窗口（1.31微米/1.55微米）；首次开通SDH STM-4及SDH STM-1光同步数字通信传输系统及网管系统，实现传输网的数字化及集中维护管理，获1999年国家优秀工程设计金奖。1999年在京九铁路传输通道扩容工程中，首次开通密集波分复用（16波）光传送系统；2001年在中国铁通西北环传送网工程中，开通密集波分复用（40波）光传送系统。

1999～2003年，铁三院在秦沈铁路工程中首次采用20芯（16芯G.652光纤、4芯G.655光纤及16芯G.652光纤）两条单模充油松套管层绞单元式直埋型光缆，建成不同径路的双光缆通信环路及光纤集中监测系统，开通用于干局线通道的SDH STM-4及用于区间车站通道的SDH STM-1光同步数字通信传输及接入系统，并利用SDH STM-1系统在相邻两车站间构成二纤双向通道自愈环，提高光缆线路及传输系统的可靠性。

（九）信号

1997～2001年，铁三院设计建设的哈大线哈尔滨站车站联锁设备采用TYJL-Ⅱ型计算机联锁，联锁道岔338组，为当时全国最大的分布式计算机联锁车站。系统具备双套联锁软件、双机热备、多微处理、计算机监测、远程诊断等功能。

1999～2001年，铁三院设计建设的哈大线沈阳编组站等驼峰设备具有进路和速度控制、驼峰无线机车信号和遥控等自动化功能。系统具备的双推双溜、无线遥控等技术性能。

1999～2003年，铁三院设计建设的秦沈客运专线行车指挥系统，具备列车及调车进路控制、列车运行跟踪、列车运行图管理、运行统计报表、信号设备集中报警等功能。

第二节　施　工

1991～2005年，中铁十八局在国内轨道交通领域承担西康、渝怀、南昆等铁路、秦沈客专、津滨轻轨等多项著名工程。在中国轨道交通快速发展及设计标准不断提高的环境下，及相关施工机械设备大发展的促进下，开展技术研发，尤其在长大铁路隧道、铁路新特型桥梁、客运专线等领域技术创新贡献明显，极大地推动国内轨道交通整体施工技术水平的提升。15年间，该集团共获国家级科技进步奖5项，省部级科技进步奖27项；国家级工法7项，省部级工法16项。

天津滨海快速交通发展有限公司（以下简称“滨海快速公司“）于2001年1月18日成立，负责津滨轻轨工程建设和运营。津滨轻轨是当时国内已建和在建最长的一条城市轨道交通工程，全线分东、西两段建设，线路长52.9千米，共设车站19座，设车辆段、停车场和控制中心各一处。

2000年前，地下铁道管理处为解决地铁的重大隐患，先后完成全线轨线的维修及设备更新，通讯系统改造，25辆机车大修，地铁调度中心改扩建，引进ADtranz微机连锁系统，改造信号系统等。经三年设备改造，地铁安全运营。2001年10月西站至新华路既有线停止运营，地铁总公司对地铁1号线进行改、扩建。新地铁1号线总长度为26.188千米，共设22站，35千伏主变电所4座等，保留穿越中心商业区的既有线区间。2001～2004年，地铁总公司成功组织完成大规模既有线综合改建工程，开创国内地铁既有线改建的先河，创造新模式并突破工程中的多项技术难点。同期，天津地铁1号线地下结构采用明挖法等多项施工方法，其中SMW工法、盾构法、暗挖法、冻结法在天津地区轨道交通工程中首次应用。

一、隧道

（一）开挖

1995年开工建设的西康铁路秦岭Ⅱ线隧道先期采用钻爆法进行平导施工，中铁十八局彭道富、李洪奇、陆晓辉等对硬岩、岩爆、高温和涌水等进行研究。施工中克服高达28520立方米日涌水量和高达38℃的洞内施工高温，安全顺利地通过27条断层带和3200米长的强烈岩爆区，创造出口独头掘进8.9千米，月均掘进236米、最高月掘进426米的成绩，总结出“秦岭硬岩特长隧道平导钻爆法快速施工技术”。该技术解决长大隧道平导快速施工的开挖爆破、机械化配套、控制测量、反坡排水、通风、通讯、ITC312挖掘装载机技术改进等综合施工问题。

1997年，中铁十八局在西康铁路秦岭Ⅰ线隧道施工中，首次采用隧道掘进机，安全顺利地完成隧道掘进机进场、组装、调试和一系列配套工程。1998年2～5月进洞施工，完成1000米的试掘进。Ⅰ线隧道单口平均月进尺338.7米，创造最高月掘进509米、日掘进35.2米的全国记录。西康铁路秦岭隧道实现中国铁路隧道施工从风钻风镐、凿岩台车及钻爆法到TBM的技术跨越。“秦岭特长铁路隧道修建技术”获2003年度国家科技进步一等奖，“长大隧道全断面岩石掘进机掘进技术研究与应用”，获2005年国家科技进步二等奖。“TB880E型隧道掘进机（TBM）施工系列工法”于2001年获国家级工法。

2002年建成的渝怀铁路彭水隧道，全长9028米，隧道穿越长达近700米的四条断层破碎带，300多米的岩溶极发育地段，汇集涌水、突泥、暗河、岩溶、瓦斯、顺层滑坡、岩爆等众多地质灾害，施工难度大。中铁十八局雷升祥、张番琦、冯涛等研究开发出复杂地质条件下彭水隧道综合施工技术，提出临时中柱法、中导洞先行台阶扩挖方案，成功地解决复杂地质浅埋、大跨、顺层滑坡等重大工程地质问题；提出的不良地质综合整治、钻爆法快速施工、施工防水及充分利用平导斜井辅助导坑等综合技术，解决施工中地下超量涌水等难题，施工中平导的利用率达到87.8%，斜井的利用率达到147%；全隧实现光面爆破，推广应用全断面光面爆破、超近间距隧道光面爆破、预留光爆层的光面爆破、大跨段软弱围岩微震光面爆破等新技术；首次研究提出施工安全风险预测、规避理论与方法，有效地预测和防止施工过程中的涌水、瓦斯、塌方等地质灾害，创造出在不良地质条件下，掘进速度快，生产安全无事故的范例。

（二）支护

1990年，中铁十八局廖金福、赵文轩、王廷元等在国内首创STC型喷射混凝土粘稠剂。该产品具有无毒、无异味、无腐蚀、不易燃烧和爆炸的特性，对人体和钢筋均无害，适应于国产的各式干喷机和各种水泥的无机高分子类喷射混凝土外加剂。据此编写的“掺STC粘稠剂半湿式喷混凝土工法”于1991年获国家级工法。“STC型喷射混凝土粘稠剂”获1995年国家科技进步三等奖。

（三）衬砌

1994年，中铁十八局刘宗云、谈梦进等研制成单线隧道电控机动钢模衬砌台车。该车由行走机构、车架、钢模板、模板垂直升降机构和侧向伸收机构、操作台及电控装置六部分组成，与传统衬砌台车比较，加大模板主骨架；配置自行研制的曲线隧道加宽衬砌调整装置；车架用工字钢做主干架件，纵向里面桁架焊接成四片组成；采用电器控制、机械传动的支收模机构，性能可靠，收支模时间短，使用人力少、造价低。

1995年，该局廖金福、张明泉等研发的隧道混凝土抗软水侵蚀技术，在岐岭隧道混凝土衬砌施工中，掺加粉煤灰、减水剂，采用最佳掺量有效阻止环境水的侵蚀，达到设计强度和抗渗性能要求。同年，该局康秀江、廖金福等研发的侯月铁路桃坪隧道衬砌裂缝整治技术，施工中采用拱部回填注浆；嵌钢拱架；立模回填钢拱架槽；边墙回填压浆；裂缝化学注浆；边墙基础注浆加固。通过隧道衬砌收敛量测，混凝土本身抗拉强度提高3～4倍，使隧道衬砌混凝土裂缝得以整修，质量达到设计要求。

（四）辅助施工

1990年，中铁十八局康秀江、刘朝祯等对隧道施工过程中的通风、防尘、防毒、净化、个人防护技术进行研究，研制的1.2米刚性风管，其百米漏风率低于2%，可解决隧道开挖空气质量恶劣的问题，形成隧洞通风防尘净化治理技术。该局编写的“隧道施工降尘净毒综合治理工法”于1991年获国家级工法。1994年，该局唐燕生、赵恩金、单家琪等研制的地下工程净化机，可解决隧道地下施工空气质量恶劣的问题，用于地下工程降尘净毒和工厂车间产生粉尘、烟尘、纤维尘、油烟、氮、氧化物有害气体的净化。尤其在隧道开挖施工中降尘净毒，提高能见度，改善空气质量方面效果好、能耗低。放炮后，作业人员可提前一小时进洞，使出碴时间缩短。1998年，该局参与研制2DT64-12.5型动叶可调对旋轴流式隧道通风机。在该风机的设计研究中应用综合技术性能优化设计方法和风机CAD技术，采用三元扭曲叶片，运用合理的流型，建立设计计算数学模型及CAD程序，优化结构参数、气动参数及制造工艺，采用包覆式消声降噪结构，设计新颖、实用；风机的叶片可在停机状态下调节，结构简单实用，安全可靠；风机风压高、风量大、体积小，尤其适用于长隧道管路通风，为国外同类产品价格的1/3～1/4。

2001年，中铁十八局在东秦岭特长隧道出口段平导开挖施工中，研究开发平导快速施工综合技术。该技术涵盖长大隧道分阶段通风、超前地质预报、平导快速掘进机械化配套、光面爆破等相关技术。分阶段通风技术采用小断面特长平导分段压、抽混合通风方式，并在风管选材和管路的安装、使用、管理上总结出一整套防漏降阻的方法，使管路平均百米漏风率低于1%，使平导工作面和正洞多工作面爆破的通风排烟难题得以解决，为洞内作业创造良好环境，保证平导快速施工。“特长隧道平导有轨运输施工工法”获2002年铁道部优秀工法。

（五）整体道床技术

2001年，中铁十八局以西康线秦岭隧道为载体进行弹性整体道床技术研究，从根本上解决特长隧道内轨道结构在运营中的维护问题。在国内首次采用橡胶套靴式弹性支承块整体道床开发技术，应用后施工速度快、工程质量好、确保安全，各项指标均达到设计规范要求，“弹性支撑块整体道床施工工法”于2003年获评为国家级工法。

二、铁路桥梁

1996年，中铁十八局建成的南昆铁路八渡南盘江特大桥，最大高度115.6米，其中5、6、7号墩采用V型支撑，为世界上最高的V型支撑铁路桥梁，施工难度极大。该局赵广发、张番琦等研究开发的八渡南盘江特大桥V型支撑连续梁施工技术，通过设置临时支座，同时在V肢、墩顶之间施加预应力，保证V型支撑、盖梁施工的全过程稳定；通过设置水平预应力拉杆施加预应力抵消水平分力的方式，解决在V型支撑两个斜肢混凝土未形成倒三角之前，下步施工荷载极易造成两肢交接处内侧混凝土拉裂的问题；通过合理选择施工平台和V型盖梁施工支撑体系，满足在高墩上修建V型支撑的安全性要求；创新采用斜向爬模，灵活、方便，机械化程度高，解决V肢外侧仰面立模难的问题，降低劳动强度；采用静动态应力应变仪进行施工监测，高精度地控制住高空中盖梁施工的线型。“在高墩上修建V型支撑施工工法”于1999年获评为国家级工法，“铁路高墩V型支撑连续梁桥施工技术”获2000年度天津市科技进步二等奖。

1996年，中铁十八局张番琦、句鹏、张斌梁等研究开发DPM型高墩爬模及应用技术，其设计以空心墩内井架为承力主体，采用固定大模、活动模板、舌模组成可调模板，拼组简便、爬升方便，施工速度快，较好地解决桥墩变坡、变曲率的问题。

1998年，中铁十八局兰远均、吴登银、王廷元等研究八渡南盘江特大桥空心高墩液压自升平台式翻模施工技术，在施工中采用自升平台翻模，并进行墩壁留孔插管升台法；扶杆法——纠偏纠扭；抽杆割导管灌孔法；收坡提升支架与吊架分离法等技术改造。据此编写的“高墩液压自升平台翻模施工工法” 获1998年铁道部级工法。

2000年，中铁十八局建成的内昆铁路重点控制工程李子沟特大桥，主桥设计为(72+3×128+72)米五跨一联预应力混凝土刚构－连续组合梁，主墩为弧端变坡高墩，高度分别为107米、103米、96米、70米。该桥在国内首次采用预应力混凝土多跨刚构连续梁结构体系、弧端变坡超百米高墩、大型群桩基础，其工程量和施工难度大。该局张番琦、彭道富、吴登银等研究开发出李子沟高墩大跨长联刚构-连续组合梁桥快速施工成套技术，解决在复杂地质条件下大型群桩快速施工技术难题，单墩月成桩达1020米；研制的大型弧端变坡高墩液压提升平台式翻模，结构合理，操作简单，抗风、抗扭能力强，可连续提升，有效解决超百米高墩墩身边坡和弧形端面施工技术难题；解决高墩上多跨连续钢构合拢难、梁体悬灌线性控制难、承台大体积混凝土防开裂难等一系列问题，保障百米高墩大跨桥梁施工的安全性。该技术获2002年度天津市科技进步一等奖。

三、高速铁路

（一）路基施工技术

1999年开工建设的秦沈客运专线，是国内第一条运行速度200千米/小时的快速铁路客运专线，中铁十八局承担的辽河特大桥沈台路桥过渡段位于辽河河床中，路基填筑高度12.47米。该段地处辽河冲积平原，地基承载力低，沉降量大，由于过渡段位置的特殊性，大型压实设备难以靠近桥台，而秦沈客专要求工后沉降在一般地段不得大于15厘米，路桥过渡段处不得大于8厘米，施工难度很大。中铁十八局和石家庄铁道学院联合对秦沈客运专线震动液化区路桥过渡段高填方路基的施工进行研究，提出干振碎石桩处理震动液化区地基的信息化施工技术，并总结施工质量控制标准；桥台台后过渡段级配碎石的施工工艺及水平测斜仪全断面沉降测量新技术；碎石土路基的施工工艺及质量控制；以控制临界动应力和累计塑性变形及弹性变形为目的的、以动态特征为主要内容的基床底层改良土的试验方法及施工工艺；级配碎石基床表层施工工艺及质量控制标准等，综合解决由于铁路路基建设战线特别长，造成的A、B组填料严重缺乏的问题。

（二）大跨度梁预制技术

2001年，中铁十八局在秦沈客运专线B28～3标段114孔跨度24米单线箱梁施工中，研究开发出“秦沈客运专线跨度24米单线箱梁现场预制技术”，形成现场制梁场址的选择及梁场规模确定的系统理论；研制成功半自动化液压内模，制梁速度达到单套模板每3天预制一榀，效率提高50%；设计成功整体拆装行走式外模的模板设备和钢筋绑扎台座，定位准确，操作方便；自行设计加工的大吨位大跨度万能杆件龙门吊，机械化程度高，安全性好；研制加工30吨行程1米液压水平千斤顶移梁，保证移梁的安全便捷。该技术解决大跨度大吨位箱梁预制难的问题，“铁路客运专线24米后张单线箱梁现场预制工法”获2002年铁道部级优秀工法。

四、津滨轻轨

（一）设计施工技术

津滨轻轨是天津市重大建设工程之一。津滨轻轨全线桥梁总长占线路总长的87%，工程桥梁规模大、工程技术条件复杂，为解决一系列难题，保证津滨轻轨高架桥优质高效的建成需进行专题研究。2001～2004年，由铁三计院、滨海快速公司、中铁十八局、天津大学李小江、张金立、高应钦、孙树礼、张兴彦、孙衍福等完成“松软土地基轻轨超长高架桥设计施工”研究。在津滨轻轨高架桥设计中解决预应力混凝土箱梁的徐变上拱、特长桥梁无缝线路固定区、伸缩区的合理桥梁结构型式、桥墩设计受力和合理联长等问题，以及无碴轨道连续梁桥沉降控制小于1厘米的难题。提出多项耐久性措施，满足桥梁耐久性设计要求。在国内轨道交通高架桥中首次采用50米钢—混凝土简支结合梁、交角为25.9°的22米斜简支钢—混凝土结合梁和钢横梁—混凝土墩柱组合框架墩等复杂结构形式。在二跨津塘公路和跨新港四号路时采用两座四跨预应力混凝土连续刚构桥，针对结构特点按照各种振型叠加反应谱法和时程分析法对其进行地震反应分析，为设计多跨连续刚构桥抗震和保证结构安全提供依据。该研究在国内轨道交通高架桥中首次采用一系列复杂结构型式，确定的桥梁结构型式，施工管理模式、快速施工控制技术最大程度地提高建设效率。该项目获2004年度天津市科技进步奖一等奖。

图9-6-2-135 试运营的津滨轻轨

2002～2004年，滨海快速公司、铁三院和中铁十八局完成“津滨轻轨桥梁徐变和桥面线形控制及其长期监测试验研究”。该成果关于桥梁徐变发展规律长期观测与理论计算分析结果为正确确定桥上整体道床承轨台的混凝土浇注时间提供合理建议。通过控制徐变确定承轨台混凝土的合理浇注时间，为合理组织施工工序确保工程质量加快施工进度起到重要作用，具有较大的推广应用价值。

2004年，滨海快速公司参与完成“天津轻轨工程抗震分析与减震降噪研究”。对列车运营噪声的原因和传播机理进行分析，进一步探索降低轻轨铁路列车运营噪声的措施。同时，有效解决轻轨工程抗震设计中所存在的抗震安全性难以保证的问题，确保工程建设的质量。详情参见第八篇第三章。

(二)车辆

津滨轻轨车辆在国内首次采用轻量化不锈钢车体。动车长19500毫米,拖车长19000毫米,四辆编组列车长度79080毫米,车辆宽度2800毫米。

(三)通信、信号及列控系统

津滨轻轨正线和试车线信号系统采用列车运行自动控制系统系统,包括传输、调度专用通信、综合数据处理、通信电源及接地等十几个子系统。借助美国USSI公司的信号系统,列车具有自动防护、自动驾驶功能。其中,通信传输系统采用开放式传输网络OTN系统,信号采用列车自动控制ATC系统,在当时国内轨道交通工程中均属于最为先进的控制技术。通信传输系统采用开放式传输网络OTN系统,信号采用列车自动控制ATC系统,在国内的轨道交通工程中,均属于当时最为先进的控制技术。

(四)轨道

采用一次性铺设无缝线路技术,减少振动和噪音,提高列车平稳、舒适程度,延长钢轨安全使用寿命;线路采用支承块式整体道床,减少养护维修工作量,设置声屏障,其中在市区一些地段采用微穿孔技术,设置透明声屏障,在国内轨道交通工程中首次采用。

(五)防灾报警系统

津滨轻轨防灾报警系统(简称"FAS")是以火灾报警系统为主兼顾对其他灾害的报警。FAS系统实行两级管理,在控制中心楼内设防灾控制中心(主控级),在各车站及车辆段、停车场、主变电所等设防灾控制室(分控级)。全线FAS系统以各分控级独立检测、报警、控制为主,控制中心主控级接收显示分控级的信息,不对各分控级的现场设备进行直接控制。

五、地铁

(一)既有线改建

2001~2003年,地铁总公司组织设计从车站平面布置、竖向交通、无障碍设施、导向系统等均营造舒适的空间,达到车站的功能要求及使用标准,以解决改建车站底部和顶部标高受到区间轨面高程和路面高程限制的难题。2002~2004年,采用既有洞体断面测量、限界检测、中线座标高程高精度测量和线路中线三维动态拟合的方法解决新旧洞体的精确衔接问题,并创造性提出既有区间采用设备限界作为限界检测的标准,解决既有区间净空不能满足建筑限界的问题。同期,在调线和调坡设计中,研究解决钢轨拆除时现状平面测绘问题和新建线路与既有线路顺接方案,控制侵入限界问题的发生。2003~2004年,地铁总公司在国内首次引入模块化设计理念,实现整车的模块化设计、组装,制造出国内城轨车中尺寸最小的B型车辆,通过采用模块化地铁列车,车辆的总装配速度加快,设备发生故障的检修周期缩短,解决隧道内车顶空间小,设备体积大,无法布置的难题,成功处理设计的车辆限界问题。

2002~2004年,地铁总公司通过使用液压锤完成既有线旧结构大规模钢筋混凝土箱体拆除施工,提出一系列新旧结构差异沉降控制措施,以解决既有结构拆除、新旧结构连接处地下水封堵和差异沉降、新旧结构防水连接等多项技术难题。

同期,地铁总公司在既有线环控通风系统中,采用上送下回的气流组织形式,火灾时送风机逆转排烟,送风设备及管道兼做排烟的运行模式,以解决既有结构空间小、风道布设困难的技术难题。既有线站台横向通风空调的技术解决方案,成功地解决既有线车站站台空调送回风问题,节省工程投资,并在国内首次提出地铁采用变频控制变风量空调通风方案。该技术成果对地铁运行具有很好的节能效果。

(二)地下结构工程

2003~2004年,地铁总公司在西南角、二纬路、营口道等车站的风道及出入口处围护结构施工中,引进劲性水泥土搅拌桩(SMW工法),在水泥搅拌桩内插入型钢,起到支护作用,止水效果好。采用该工法施工速度快、抗渗效果好、污染少、噪音低、节省投资。

2003～2004年，地铁总公司在西站、西南角站等基坑围护结构施工中引进钻孔咬合桩，采用全套管钻机钻孔成桩，即一根桩为钢筋笼，一根桩为素混凝土，先施工素混凝土桩，再施工钢筋混凝土桩，互相咬合，咬合量为桩径1/3～1/4。有效解决既有线改建施工中由于既有结构周边回填碎石屑、混凝土块等建筑垃圾造成的基坑围护结构钻孔桩施工困难，搅拌桩成桩质量不高，无法保证止水效果的问题，降低成本、缩短维护结构施工工期，基坑开挖过程中未发现渗漏水现象，保证基坑安全。

2003～2005年，地铁总公司在小白楼-下瓦房-南楼-土城沿大沽南路区间段，采用盾构法施工。该线路沿线有滨江购物中心、凯旋门大厦、天津日报社大厦等建筑，埋深8～17米，采用该工法可连续作业，施工周期短，投资少；对交通和环境影响小。

2004～2005年，地铁总公司在小白楼车站-下瓦房车站区间隧道的联络通道施工中，采用"隧道内水平冻结加固土体，隧道内开挖构筑"的全隧道内施工方案，在隧道内采用冻结法加固地层，使联络通道外围土体冻结，形成强度高，封闭性好的冻土帷幕，在冻土帷幕中采用矿山法进行通道及集水井的开挖构筑施工。由于施工不占用地面，冻结和开挖引起的地表沉降容易控制在规范要求之内，冻土帷幕均匀性好且与隧道管片结合严密，解决区间隧道的联络通道因土层土质松软、结构松散、孔隙比大、含水丰富、承载力低、容易压缩、在动力作用下易流变特性而造成的开挖后天然土体本身难以自稳的难题。

2005年，地铁总公司在天津地铁1号线工程部分出入口、风道工程采用暗挖法施工，形成一整套天津地铁暗挖施工方法，即淤泥质及粉质粘土地层预加固技术、超浅埋、平顶直墙、大断面分部、分层开挖技术、大断面隧道分部开挖施工支护及主体结构施工技术、用FLAC3D进行隧道结构计算及稳定性分析技术、矩形断面隧道结构防水技术、大断面隧道结构变形及内力监测技术。成功解决天津地铁既有区间风道因位于天津市主要交通干道下，采用明挖法施工，对地面交通影响大，且需要大量切改管线的难题。

（三）钢混叠合梁

2003～2004年，天津地铁1号线高架车站复兴门车站位于五岔路口，地铁总公司在施工中采用45+82+45米钢混叠合梁方案，在立交桥引桥及大沽南路路口之间的曲线段布设复兴门车站，车站大里程侧在300米半径的曲线段采用82米主跨的连续钢混叠合梁桥跨越大沽南路，成功地解决工程跨越复兴河、郁江道及大沽南路的难题，这是当时国内城市轨道交通中跨度最大的连续钢混叠合梁桥结构。

（四）钢铝复合接触轨

2004年，地铁总公司在天津地铁1号线全线三轨施工中采用钢铝复合接触轨供电技术，与低碳钢普通接触轨相比，复合轨的重量轻，利于施工安装；单位电阻较小，牵引网的压损和电能损耗均明显降低，可减少牵引变电所的数目和土建工程量，压缩车站的规模和降低运营费用；在地下区间段采用该技术向地铁车辆受流后，可减少三轨发热量，降低隧道内的温度，对改善隧道内温度升高有较大作用；复合轨的不锈钢带接触面非常平整和光滑，可避免接触轨与受流器间产生电弧和减少两者的磨耗，延长其使用寿命。

（五）再生电能回收

2004年，地铁总公司在天津地铁1号线的牵引供电系统中应用电阻型再生电能吸收装置。在轨道交通车辆运行过程中，由于站间距较短和列车起制动频繁，其再生制动能量是相当可观的。采用该技术降低隧道及车站内温度，提高沿线环境空气质量，有效降低车辆自重与耗能，减少运营维护工作量及成本。

（六）轨道减振降噪

2003年，地铁总公司在天津地铁1号线全线轨道系统中，采用新Ⅱ型高弹性减振扣件、新型弹性短轨枕、减振夹板及新型轨下垫层等轨道减振降噪技术，即在环境振动敏感地段采用新Ⅱ型高弹性钢轨扣件和弹性套靴式整体道床轨道结构，有效降低轨道振动；采用无缝线路铺设技术，减少轨缝冲击；在不能铺设无缝线路地段采用钢轨减振接头夹板，有效降低车轮对轨头的撞击；在高架轨道地段采用新型减振弹性垫板，有效缓冲轨道振动向基础的透入。通过采用多项减振技术，使轨道降噪效果在不引进国外技术的基础上达到较高水平，降低工程造价。

（七）安全门与售检票系统

2005年，天津地铁1号线在国内率先采用自动售检票（AFC）系统，并与全线同期开通，节省人力资源，实现车站的自动化管理。同年，天津地铁1号线全线各站在国内地铁建设中首次使用半高安全门系统，人性化的配置，保证乘客的安全，方便站台管理。

图9-6-2-136 地铁1号线安全门

（八）标准

2003年，天津市市政质量监督站与地铁总公司联合编制《城市地下铁道工程质量检验标准》（DB29-54-2003），该项标准用于检验天津地铁1号线工程质量。2005年，地铁总公司与天津第三市政公路工程有限公司联合编制《天津市地下铁道深基坑施工技术规程》（DB/T29-143-2005），该标准用于天津地铁深基坑施工的质量检验。同年，该公司与天津第二市政公路工程有限公司联合编制《天津市地下铁道盾构法隧道工程施工技术规程》（DB/T29-144-2005），该标准用于天津地铁盾构法施工的质量检验。是年，该公司与天津大学联合编制《天津市地下铁道SMW施工技术规程》（DB/T29-145-2005），该标准用于天津地铁基坑支护采用SMW工法施工的质量检验。2005年，该公司与中铁隧道集团有限公司联合编制《天津市地下铁道暗挖法隧道工程施工技术规程》（DB/T29-146-2005），该标准用于天津地铁暗挖法施工的质量检验。

第七章 航空科技

1991～2005年，天津民用航空事业处于快速发展阶段。飞行保障系统和服务设施设备不断更新，民航的安全运营和保障服务能力不断提高。1996年，坐落在天津机场的中国民航天津市管理局航管站与通信管理站合并为航务管理中心2001年，该中心更名为民航天津空中交通管理站（以下简称“天津空管站”），成为隶属民航总局的驻津单位。

随着天津机场建设朝着国际机场方向发展，15年间天津在民航机务维修、空中交通管理、机场通信导航、航空经济与运输、航空安全管理等方面研究取得较大进展。2002年，驻津的中国民航学院（以下简称“民航学院”）建立“民航地面特种设备研究基地”，这是中国民航建立的第一个省部级科研基地。2003年，建立“航空运输经济与管理科学研究基地”。2005年，由民航学院牵头负责依托中国航空集团公司并联合南京航空航天大学建立中国民航总局规模最大的省部级科研基地“民航机务维修工程研究基地”。

2003年10月，民航学院和中航商用飞机有限公司联合组建中航商用飞机有限公司客户服务技术支持中心，该中心的成立标志着中国国产的具有独立知识产权的商用飞机有了本土化的客户服务技术保障和科研基础。2005年，中国民航产业化基地正式列入天津航空城和滨海新区总体规划。

第一节 机务维修养护

民航机务维修养护对民航飞行安全至关重要。20世纪90年代以来，民航每年都发生多起发动机空中停车，对飞行安全构成威胁，经过航空公司、民航总局、设备生产厂家的努力，空中停车率逐年下降，但换发率逐年上升。综合民航安全和效益因素，发动机使用可靠性研究的重要性和必要性突显。

1996年11月，由欧盟、中国民航总局、欧洲宇航工业联合会和空中客车工业公司联合主办的适航、维修研讨会在民航学院召开。1999年，民航学院建成"中国民航机务维护模拟机培训中心"。该中心引进加拿大波音737机务维护模拟机，专门用于民航机务人员培训和开展科研工作。2002年，民航学院成立"民航机务维修人员资格培训及考试管理中心"，作为民航总局在民航机务维修人员执照管理方面的技术服务机构。同年10月，该中心更名为"民用航空器维修人员执照考试管理中心"。2004年，民航学院与新加坡明康宇航集团签署合作协议，在民航机务维修、飞机机型及民航资源服务等领域开展合作

一、发动机故障诊断

天津民用航空运输起步较晚，航空产业十分落后，客机全部需要进口，特别是航空发动机全部依赖引进。1992年，民航学院范作民等对"航空发动机状态监控和故障诊断系统"进行研究，通过检测发动机的状态，对发动机进行参数趋势、气路和发动机振动分析，寻找发动机故障，确定故障的原因、部位、程度和趋势，编制出相应的检查计划和维修程度的综合技术。1998年，范作民等对该系统实际应用数据特别是对发动机各类故障的分布概率进行统计，对"航空发动机故障诊断分析系统"中各类发动机故障原因和故障征兆进行统计分析，从理论上开展深层次研究，给出以主因子模型为中心的发动机故障诊断学的一个新的理论体系，并成功解决机载记录数据的处理和传输问题，建成一个完整的由机载记录数据到地面译码和计算分析的状态监控和故障诊断系统，提高数据的可靠性和准确性，获1998年度国家自然科学基金资助。

2000年，民航学院许春生等完成"民航发动机可靠性研究"，该项目根据发动机性能衰退情况对拆发时间分阶段计算做出预测，设计性能排序软件，建立发动机各项监控值或警戒值，对发动机试车数据、适航信息进行分析，对发动机性能进行加权评估及发动机机群科学管理。该研究能够及时预报大量故障隐患，避免多起空中停车，对提高发动机使用可靠性，显著降低发动机的换发率。

二、维护模拟机

2004年，民航学院官颂、杨国庆等完成"B737飞机常见故障的统计分析及在模拟机上的实施"研究，该项目基于人工智能理论，设计出B737单机版和网络版机务维护专家系统（BMES），该系统采用规则对象、框架对象及实体对象，并用面向对象的编码方法实现对不同对象的调用，完成通用故障推理、框架推理及层间推理，知识库维护程序具有开放性和可扩展性，减少航材的误拆误换率。

三、执照考管系统

2004年，民航学院任仁良等完成"民用航空器维修人员执照考试和管理系统"研究，该系统实时运行在Internet上，是国内实用的Web下基于J2ee跨平台在线考试系统，采用数据库与应用程序分离模式，确保数据安全；IC卡身份识别技术，可有效防止替、代考现象；使用计算机进行口试评估，提高考试的公正性；应用Web压缩技术加快数据传输速度，为实现网上实时在线考试创造条件。该成果获2004年度中国民航总局科技进步二等奖。

第二节 空中交通管理

1991年前，天津机场没有明确规定指挥区域，只是根据塔台特高频无线电台的有效通讯距离，尽早、尽远地与飞机沟通并保持联络，实施程序管制。随着空中交通流量的持续增加，可用空域资源相对有限，以保证飞行安全为主要目标的空中交通管制系统越来越不能满足各个航空公司的需求。1995年，天津机场的指挥区域经过多次调整，重新确定天津机场飞行区域。2001年，成立进近管制指挥室。2002年，升级为雷达管制。

一、空中管制

1995年12月22日，北京军区空军(1995)司航字第528号文件，重新确定天津机场飞行区域。2001年8月9日零时，天津空管站进近管制指挥室正式成立并投入运行，这是实现提高天津空中交通综合保证能力的一次飞跃。2002年3月21日零时，天津近进管制由程序管制升级为雷达管制。管制间隔标准为雷达管制间隔标准：顺向为20公里，逆向为30公里。

二、空中流量监控

20世纪90年代，由于飞机数量少，航班飞行频度低，空中交通流量规模小，流量监控没有提到日程上来。21世纪以来，随着飞机数量增多，飞行频度大幅度提高，空中流量监控引起管理部门高度重视。2002年，中国民航总局“民航空中交通管理研究基地”在民航学院建立，研究用先进技术与设备对空中流量进行监视与控制，引导飞机在规定的航路上有序飞行，避免拥挤与撞机。民航学院徐肖豪等完成“空中交通流量监控网络系统”研究，该系统从空中交通监视雷达、航空电信网等运行系统中获取空中交通动态数据，并参照航班数据、结合预达模式和位置算法而综合成空中交通活动轨迹，并能够对指定的管制区域的空中交通流量数据进行预测、统计和显示。该系统通过对进离场航班排序、预测，对密集航班进行预先调配，从而缓解空中矛盾，对保证飞行安全、减少航班延误、加速空中交通流量，提高航班正点率有明显作用，有效地解决由于流量控制而导致的航班延误频发的问题。

三、空域管理评估

随着民用航空运输快速发展，如何解决空域拥挤现象，将有限的空域进行有序管理，已刻不容缓。2005年，为提高民航的空域管理能力，中国民航总局空管局苏兰根与民航学院徐肖豪等合作完成“空域管理与评估系统”研究，该系统采用国际民航组织的标准，结合国内实际情况，实现空域数据和资料的科学管理、空中交通流量的统计和预测、空域规划设计方案的技术评估和空域容量的准确估算。

四、导航

1996年，民航学院吴仁彪等承担国家自然科学基金项目“阵列方向图的自适应综合方法与控制方法研究”。该研究揭示出一般自适应阵列和机载雷达空时二维自适应滤波中方向图畸变的机理，指出常用对角加载波束保形方法的局限性和性能极限，并首次提出一种能精确控制自适应阵列方向图峰值副瓣电平的方法，能同时克服干扰协方差矩阵估计误差、阵列和通道幅相失配误差引起的方向图畸变。在方向图综合方面，从自适应阵列“功率倒置”原理出发，巧妙地利用干扰谱结构引起的自适应方向图畸变，提出一种适用于任意阵列结构的方向图综合方法，可以设计出具有任意形状的方向图，被成功地推广应用到某复杂水听器体积阵宽容波束形成，以克服结构遮挡和散射引起的方向图畸变。该项目1999年通过国家自然科学基金委验收，评价结果为特优。

2000年，民航学院吴仁彪、苏志刚等承担国家"863"项目"基于曲线孔径的三维高分辨率合成孔径雷达成像技术研究"。该项目研究两种前沿微波对地观测技术，基于曲线孔径和机载双天线合成孔径雷达（SAR）的三维高分辨率雷达成像技术，提出一种通用的自聚焦和超分辨率成像新方法，适用于聚束式曲线合成孔径雷达SAR、干涉SAR、逆合成孔径雷达（ISAR）和常规二维SAR成像系统，其稳健性得到大量仿真和实测数据的验证。可应用在需要对人造目标和局部观测区域进行超分辨率雷达成像的新一代战场感知系统、城市规划、城市地震后破坏性评估等各种场合。

2003年，民航学院吴仁彪、韩萍等完成国家自然科学基金项目"地面运动目标检测、成像与识别中的关键技术研究"。该研究提出一种基于一维高距离分辨率（HRR）雷达像的自动目标识别（ATR）新方法，系统地研究幂变换对ATR性能的影响，并提出一种幂变换系数的自适应预处理新方法，可大幅提高ATR的性能。同时还开展基于SAR像的目标识别和高距离分辨率雷达地杂波抑制研究，可应用于高空无人侦察机信号处理当中。

2004年，民航学院吴仁彪等完成"稳健阵列信号处理新方法及其应用"研究，该项目在"阵列方向图的自适应综合方法与控制方法研究"成果基础上进行深入研究，根据实验数据对主要研究内容指标进行统计分析和测试验证，从理论上归纳总结，获得稳健阵列信号处理新方法并将其应用，获2004年度天津市自然科学二等奖。

第三节 机场特种设备

随着民航航班密度的增大，对机场特种设备需求增加，对除冰效率提出更高的要求，需要大量即热式飞机除冰车，而国产化替代价格昂贵的进口产品趋势形成。2004年，中国民航总局"民航机场工程研究基地"在民航学院建立。2005年，民航学院与天津工程机械研究院签署"发展民航科技产业技术"合作协议，双方主要在航空特种车辆、航空检测设备、航空特种机器人技术、航空模拟仿真技术、特种机务设备等领域的研究与开发方面进行全面合作。

一、跑道测试车

1999年，民航学院王立文等对"机场跑道摩擦系数测试车"进行研究，采用定滑溜比后桥单向差速三排链传动系统、测量臂传动机构、洒水系统、液压保压和吸振系统等，实现在各种道面和干态、雨天、雪天条件下，进行摩擦系数测量，可用于民用、军用机场跑道，也可用于高速公路道面摩擦系数测量。

1999年，民航学院王立文、孙毅刚等研制出"机场跑道摩擦系数测试车自动标定装置"。该装置采用专用控制器作为计算控制核心，步进电机为执行器件，高精度传感器为测量一次传感元件，系统构成可靠且严谨，机械上采用三点托架滚动滑盘结构，将垂直和水平力的测量集成在一个框架中，保证两个力的测量相互独立，互不干扰，可完成稳定的高精度的磨擦系数车的水平和垂直力的标定任务。该器具替代人工加载，减少人为干预，提高精度。

二、飞机除冰车

早期中国民用机场使用的飞机除冰车基本上依靠进口，且绝大部分是工作效率低、能源浪费较大的老式飞机除冰车。随着航班业务繁忙，通过车载燃油热交换器循环加热方式的老式飞机除冰车已不能满足作业要求而趋于淘汰。1991年以来，中国民用机场和航空公司已引进10多台即热式飞机除冰车，但价格十分昂贵。2004年，民航学院王立文等完成“即热式飞机除冰液加热装置与控制系统研究”，采用并联式燃烧器喷射柴油对除冰液进行加热，计算机控制燃烧器输出功率，实现根据不同流量和温差自动控制除冰液的温度，具有自适应能力，流动开关、流量传感器、温度传感器对除冰液加热过程的流动状态及温度进行监控，具有自动保护功能，使加热系统可靠性高。该成果解决即热式飞机除冰车的关键技术问题，为取代进口、开发出具有自主知识产权的国产即热式飞机除冰车和集中式除冰设备提供技术支撑。2005年，民航学院王立文等将即热式加热系统应用于飞机集中式除冰系统，设计制作出“飞机集中除冰车”产品，通过首都机场股份公司验收并投入使用。针对首都机场的实际需求，在国内首次对飞机集中除冰系统进行深入研究，为飞机除冰过程的集中管理以及除冰液的再生回用奠定基础。该系统将温度、能源、液压、机械等多种成熟控制技术应用到机场除冰系统，实现高效快速除冰功能，完成飞机除冰产品的国产化。

三、消防模拟系统

2004年，民航学院王立文等研制出“消防应急救援模拟系统”，该系统采用计算机、电子及控制技术，设计应急救援模拟系统，系统设置分多个等级，可以满足各类人员的训练需求，为民航消防应急救援方面的研究提供技术平台，具有环境可调、红外探测及烟雾发生能力，指挥室可对现场情况进行实时监控，实现在紧急情况下障碍穿越、方向识别及路径判断等能力训练。该系统模拟民航运行中的隐患和事故，以及严重或恶劣的场景氛围，具有真实火情的设置、控制和异常情况下报警功能，用于灭火训练，同时逃生训练能够训练在异常情况下的逃生能力和心理素质，以提高相关人员的消防意识、消防技能以及消防应急救援能力。

第四节 航空安全管理

1998～2001年，民航学院孙瑞山等先后完成“航空公司安全评估系统”“民用机场航空安全评估系统”和“空中交通服务安全评估系统”的研究，这三个系统基本覆盖民航全行业，是中国民航安全管理工作的重要组成部分。

1999年，航空危险品运输实验室在民航学院建成，它是中国第一个专门航空危险品运输实验科研机构。2003年，中国民航总局“航空运输经济与管理科学研究基地”在民航学院建立。2005年，民航学院与中国科学院自动化研究所联合成立“民航安全智能监控与识别联合实验室”。

一、飞机程序设计

1991年，民航学院朱邦旭、都业富等完成“民用飞机选型程序研究”，针对中国民航引进和购置飞机机型多的特点，在对飞机技术性和经济性进行评估的基础上，运用综合的评估方法，研制出一整套适用于较复杂的多目标决策评估软件系统，获得适合某一航线或航线网的机型排序，为飞机选型提供科学依据。该项目获1994年度国家科技进步三等奖。

二、飞行品质监控

1999年，中国民航总局安全技术中心陶亦渊与民航学院陈治怀等共同完成“飞行操纵品质监控分析工程”，从理论上提出监控标准的确定原则，总结译码数据的处理方法，并规范飞行品质的监控模型和算法，为中国民航飞行品质监控工作的开展提供理论依据。

同年，中国民航总局安全技术中心谢孜楠、陶亦渊与民航学院陈治怀等共同完成“飞行品质监控和飞行图形仿真系统”，该系统在上述研究的基础上，将航空电子技术、计算机仿真技术和风险控制理论有机结合，成功地应用于航空安全管理领域，中国民航90%以上的航班受到飞行品质监控，降低飞行事故率，提高安全管理水平。该项目获2000年度国家科技进步二等奖。

三、航空安全

2003年，民航学院孙瑞山等完成“航空公司信息管理系统”，该系统采用PB开发工具和ORACLE大型数据库平台，符合未来对数据管理要求，满足高等级系统安全和数据安全的要求，给出航空公司安全信息收集、分析和利用的综合解决方案。系统具有收集、综合分析安全信息、自动告警、飞行技术评估以及安全法规查询等功能，在安全数据分析上，采用偏差分布和方差综合分析方法，分析操作偏差，可以对飞行参数给定偏差进行预测。

2003年，民航学院孙瑞山等参与完成“民用航空人为因素研究及应用”，该项目深入研究国际航空人为因素的发展历程和理论成果，根据中国国情和文化特点，及民航行业的特殊性，第一次全面、深入地在民用航空的机组、机务维修、空中交通管制和安全管理系统中开展人为因素的调查与研究。民航学院负责该项目中人为因素事件分析方法研究和数据库研究开发工作，通过对中国民航近十年的不安全事件和事故分析、研究，基本查清国内民用航空运输中的主要人为因素问题、形式和特征。找到影响民用航空运输飞行安全的主要人为因素，提出解决长期困扰航空安全的人为差错问题的解决措施，研究制订出具有纠正和预防措施闭环审计的调查程序和差错调查表并在系统内实施，取得明显效果。

2005年，民航学院孙瑞山等完成“民用航空安全评估系统”研究，该系统应用“人、机、环境”系统科学理论和现代管理学思想，在分析大量的民航典型事件的基础上，采用“基元事件分析方法”“事故树分析法”以及“层次分析法”等，根据中国民用航空运输业的结构和运行模式，采用管理安全度、显示安全度和综合隐患指数三个总指标，建立分层的评估模型及关联关系计算民航系统的安全状况，系统中各层次的权重由层次分析法和事故/事件统计方法相结合的方法确定，及时发现不安全隐患和薄弱环节，引导安全行为，能够客观评估民用航空运输业安全保障能力和安全工作状况。

第五节 飞行保障系统

1991～2005年，天津机场通讯导航、夜航灯光配置、气象保障、安全检查、情报服务等方面，不断改进设备，提高飞行保障能力。

一、导航工程

（一）导航台

1993年，天津机场北近台使用764厂生产的615型100瓦归航机（NDB），有效距离大于100海里。1996年，南、北远台更新安装764厂生产的618型200瓦NDB，有效距离大于100海里；北远台使用644型指点标。1998年，北远台增加安装一部645B型指点标。1998年和2002年，超远台分别更新为645B和645A新型设备，作为定点提供跑道入口端距离的设备，其顶空辐射宽度为600米±200米。2003年，南远台新增加一部

618型200瓦NDB设备。

1994年，滦县和泊头导航台使用新63型NDB，后因2000年校飞不合格，由北京机场调拨使用649型500瓦NDB，有效距离大于100海里。

1994年，天津机场引进澳大利亚AWA公司的VRB-51D/LDB-101型多普勒特高频全方向测距装置/测距系统(DVOR/DME)，有效距离大于100海里。1995年滦县和泊头导航台完成上述设备安装调试。

(二)助航灯光

1996年，天津机场南进近系统淘汰环视灯，安装顺序闪光灯，提高助航保障能力。1997年8月，天津机场购置的恒流调光器投入使用，改变此前使用手动调整电流来改变灯光回路亮度，手动调整电流操作难度大，电流不稳，恒流调光器按使用光级自动调整输出电流，电流平稳，灯光回路亮度一致性较好，从此天津机场大量使用恒流调光器。

2002年，北坡度灯投入使用，淘汰"T"字灯。同年，引进灯光监控系统，实现助航灯光的开启与监控由计算机操作。

(三)进近设备

1992年，天津机场二次雷达站建于塔台四楼，引进意大利Alenia常规航管二次雷达。1999年，老塔台三楼安装意大利Alenia多雷达处理系统，并于2001年正式运营南京28所生产的多雷达处理系统，用于对北京传输来的MP1、MP2进行格式和坐标转换，供Alenia多雷达处理系统融合使用，其有效距离大于300千米。

1992年，天津机场建立16号仪表着陆系统(ILS)，引进挪威NM3500型仪表着陆系统，使天津机场达到双向Ⅰ类盲降进近标准，其有效距离在航道线10°和35°范围内分别为25和17千米。1996年，引进意大利FSD-40型DME与16号ILS设备配套使用，安装在北下滑台，后与南下滑台的FSD-10型DME进行互换，DME的有效距离大于100海里。1997年，天津机场引进意大利ALCATEL公司的新型SN-400型仪表着陆系统，对原34号ILS设备进行更新，其有效距离与NM3500型ILS相同。1997年5月，该34号ILS设备获准开放使用，经民航总局批准，天津机场达到国际Ⅰ类气象条件开放标准。

2002年，导航技术室李刚等完成"雷达录象录放性能的改造"。该项目提高雷达信号录象的存储能力，改善录象重放质量，使录象重放以多途径操作来实现，提高雷达管制下录象资料的分析能力。

二、通讯工程

(一)地空通信

1993年和1997年，天津机场引进美国STANCIL 16和英国RACAL WORDSAFE MAXIMA 32通道记录仪，用于地空通信、重要电话、热线的实施录音和飞行信息的实施录象，后者增加记录雷达录象的功能。1997年，16通道记录仪作为RACAL设备的备份，以保证各类飞行的如实记录。

1994年和1999年，天津引进意大利OTE收发信机和德国BECKER便携式收发信机，用于塔台陆空通话，使地面管制员和飞机之间的通讯手段得到改善，保证地空联络的不间断性。同时完成塔台特高频、多声道录音机、中西文终端(电传机)等设备的安装调试，使管制指挥通信保障能力得以提高。

(二)报文发布

1994年，天津机场完成ZB-32路自动转报机的安装，可自动收、转、存电报，解决以往人工通信所造成的速度慢、不准确的弊端，保证天津机场的信息传递畅通。1995年，TP8分组交换设备投入运营，它与卫星地面站共同发挥作用，使电报传输速率大幅提高，有线、无线互为备用。2000年，天津机场完成DMHS-M转报系统的安装，报文处理量和设备稳定性大幅提高，可提供多种通信接口，以拓展业务空间。

(三)内话系统

1991年，天津机场安装北京启名星公司内话系统，有16路有线和8路无线信道，实现无线、有线内部通信集一体的通信方式。1997年，引进意大利SITTL公司的M600/19型内话系统，有24路无线和48路有线信道，6个席位。同年，天津机场使用美国MOTOLORA模拟800兆智能集群无线通信系统，有10个信道机。该系统用于机场地面各单位之间的通信联系，与有线语音通信形成互补，覆盖天津机场东、西两个航站区，使机场地面指挥能力得以提高。

1994年，天津机场成立民航蓝天无线寻呼台。1995年，引进DID专线技术，并增设"490"局，全面实现局内通话、局间通话的自动接续。同时用光纤代替原电话电缆作为中继线。1997年，490局升级为2490局。2002年，启用北电M1型电话程控交换机，装机容量为4000多门，并在局间采用1号信令进行传递，可接收电话的反极信号，使电话接续的速度及通话质量得以提高。

1995年，天津机场安装TES通讯卫星系统，用于话音传输和数据传输，卫星地面站的开通，实现民航卫星会议电话及调度卫星电话入网，同时实现与北京机场雷达联网、自动转报联网、航空波道联网；1996年初，完成PES通讯卫星系统的安装，为气象部门全国联网提供可靠保证。

1996年，天津机场安装民航二所开发的航班信息系统，该系统在自动转报系统的基础上，进行报文信息分解、自动显示和处理。提供准备的飞行实时信息，用于站调、塔台、现场、商调、安检等十几个部门。1999年，由于"千年虫"问题通信部门对航班信息系统进行更新，采用民航数据公司的航班信息系统。

三、航空气象

（一）气象观测

1991年，民航天津市局航管站气象台综合技术室邢绍伟完成"气象观测报表自动统计系统"的研制，该系统对气象原始观测资料进行分析处理，能自动生成气象所需的各种气象报告和统计报表，观测报告准确率提高，大幅降低观测员劳动强度，研究成果在全国部分机场推广，收到良好的经济效益。

1995年，天津民航气象启用气象自动观测（AWOS）系统。该系统自动测量风向风速、能见度、跑道视程、温度、湿度、气压及云高、降水量等气象要素值，避免人工观测数据处理过程中人为因素的影响，气象资料的准确性和连续性得以提高，使气象资料的积累更加丰富和完善。

1995年，民航天津市局航管站气象台付连江等完成"气象电报自动接收处理系统"，通过汇总分类保存全国各机场气象台的气象情报资料，以便随时调用，并能拍发天津机场的各种气象报告，缓解劳动力紧张和纸张浪费的问题。

1997年7月1日，天津机场气象观测实施半小时观测。在每日北京时间04:00～24:00整点观测期间增加半点观测。包括云、有效能见度、垂直能见度、风向风速、露点、温度、气压等观测项目。

2002年，民航天津空管站气象台高宇、何征斌、王晋宁等完成"自动观测系统应用软件改造"项目。该系统实现自动观测系统数据规范化处理，并在华北各机场推广。

（二）气象设备

1991年，天津机场气象台购置振筒气压仪，用于测量该站气压值。

1994年，天津机场气象台购置气象卫星云图接收处理系统，用于接收处理气象卫星探测到的全球天气资料，为航路飞行提供及时、准确、可靠的云系分布情况；提供云顶高度、温度及云的厚度的实况资料。

1995年，天津机场航行情报自动通播系统开始启用，主要用于自动播放航行气象情报信息，便于飞机随时接收机场航行情报。同年8月，714C气象雷达系统投入使用。该设备用于天气探测，随时监测机场对流性天气的发生、发展及演变情况，提供对流性天气回波的测量及分析处理结果，为飞行人员选择最佳起飞、降落时机和航空器安全绕飞、选择最佳航线提供服务。

1998年，天津机场购置美国05103/06206型风向风速仪。2001年，更新振筒气压仪，用于自动观测系统的备份手段，同时投入运行。同年，组织安装MICAPS气象信息综合分析处理系统，用于收集处理气象局的数值产品资料。

（三）气象服务

1997年，天津机场气象台在华北空管局立项研制的《天津机场气候志》于1998年完成并通过民航总局有关部门验收，其水平达到国际民航气象组织的编写规定及要求，并于9月获准在全国民航机场推广。

1999年，天津机场气象台正式启用卫星广播传真系统，用于接收处理气象资料，为飞行员提供大范围的高空风、温度、云状等气象要素值、锋面的移动方向及速度的预报值，随时提供最新的航路、航站气象资料，使飞行员能及时掌握最新的天气资料及天气演变情况。同年，天津机场气象预报开始发布趋势着陆预报。

2001年，气象局域网投入运行。该系统能收集处理所有的气象资料，为驻机场各个航空公司提供及时、准确、可靠地查询服务。

四、安全检查设备

1995年，天津机场采用可穿透力12毫米钢板的SMEX—D8380HH型X光机，增强图像边缘处理，图像呈现相对清晰；同时，采用02PN8 HI-PE/PH-TR-600型金属探测门，具有对接收信号过滤功能的数字信号处理分析，可通过RS-232C系列接口实现所有参数由终端、调制解调器或计算机完成操作控制，探测速度达15米/秒。1997年，采用DTF-1型钟控定时装置探测器，对可疑物品进行时钟探测，查找可疑物品中的钟控定时引爆装置，并根据X光机图像进行综合分析。1999年，航站楼建立安检信息管理系统，可通过该系统随时查看安检现场，以及存储联网X光机的扫描图像和安检现场监控录像。2001年，开始使用METOR 200型—METOR 250型金属探测门，通过脉冲磁场探测线圈感应区域中的金属物体，经控制器处理后，当信号超过报警界限时，金属物体就被探测到，并可通过门两侧的指示灯上看出金属所在位置。2002年，采用HI-SCAN16580型、HI-SCAN6040i型和HI-SCAN6046si型X光机，均通过线扫描对包裹进行检查，不断增强图像边缘处理，剔除有机物或无机物，具有放大图像和翻转图像的功能，提高危险物品识别度。2004年，采用IONSCAN400B型毒品炸药探测器，该探测器是通过离子迁移光谱原理技术，分析被检测物品，能很快检测出炸药及毒品的成分。

五、航行情报

1990年，天津机场航行情报室增设电传机，航行情报员开始自行收发航行通告（NOTAM），改变原来由电台负责收发NOTAM，从而能及时、准确地提供NOTAM。1993年引进民航二所研制的航行通告处理系统，实现航行情报工作的自动化。1998年"航行通告自动处理系统"投入使用，使本机场的航行情报工作基本与国际民航组织的要求接轨。

1998年，天津机场完成34号跑道和16号跑道NDB仪表飞行优化设计。2002年完成东航天津分公司塘沽基地仪表飞行程序设计，2003年完成中信海直塘沽直升机机场的仪表飞行程序设计，为两个通用航空机场的按时开放并投入运营奠定基础。

第六节 服务设施与设备

1991～2005年，天津机场服务设施和设备逐步得到改善，航班运营管理逐步实现自动化。2001年，天津机场完成候机楼改扩建工程。2003年6月完成原候机楼A区流程合理化改造。改造和新增面积共6900平方米，改建后的国际区面积达到12600余平方米。值机柜台增至15个，边检通道增至8个，安检通道增为4个，满足高峰600人次/小时的流量，建设后的候机楼形成一个完善的服务体系。贷物存放与运输不断发展。随着离港需求的不断加大，设备不断更新，2005年实施离港改造工程。

一、离港系统

1990年以前，天津机场主要采用手写机票以及手写登机牌的纯手工方式为旅客办理乘机手续。1990年天津机场离港系统（DCS）投入使用，该系统采用数字数据网（DDN）专线与中国民航信息网络股份有限公司北京计算中心主机相连，使用通用通信处理机（UCP）统一接收并处理天津地区的值机、配载、订票等离港数据信息。值机柜台、配载等航站楼内终端设备通过电话线同UCP处理机连接。售票终端使用Model连接DDN专线，实现同UCP处理机的数据连通。当时使用的终端设备为全英文终端，无法实现汉字与拼音的输入、输出。

1996年，由于UCP处理机容量过小、处理速度较慢、维护复杂等原因，天津机场离港系统核心处理设备升级为分布式通信处理机（DCP），终端机升级为智能终端，实现汉字拼音的输入、输出功能，但终端操作指令仍为全英文。

2005年，天津机场离港改造工程使离港系统与售票系统完全分离，售票系统采用通用网络前端平台（Eterm）方式，通过因特网络直接访问中航信售票系统主机，实现代理、网络等多种售票模式。离港系统则采用小型机、服务器模式，通过DDN与虚拟专用网（VPN）网络双模式与中航信北京主机相连，其中一种模式断网，自动启用另一种模式，大量降低因连接线路中断而造成的系统故障。离港系统终端升级为普通PC机，大幅降低后期维护成本。操作系统使用中国民航信息网络股份有限公司自主研发的新一代离港前端系统，实现操作界面全部汉化，缩短办理值机手续的时间。

二、航班运营管理系统

1990年以前，天津机场值机、登机、到达、行李提取等引导服务全部采用人工方式，由工作人员现场悬挂手写指示牌，楼内信息播报完全依靠服务人员呼喊。1990年，由渤海无线电厂设计的信息系统投入使用，实现天津机场航站楼内航班显示、广播的电子化。该系统包括航班显示、客运广播、消防广播和闭路电视等系统。此后，通过不断的自主研发、测试实现航班录入的自动化，根据提前存储的季度航班时刻表，比对次日航班计划自动生成次日航班信息。2000年，由民航第二设计所研制的计算机综合信息管理系统投入使用，该系统由计算机网络系统、主机集群系统、应用系统、信息发布系统、广播系统和时钟系统七部分构成。

三、货物装卸与货运中心

1997年天津机场组建天津滨海国际机场民航客货中心。1999年迁入新库区，仓库面积6000多平方米，其中海关监管库5000平方米，并设有冷冻库、保鲜库、贵重物品库、载货集装器存放等功能区域，配置叉车、拖头车、拖盘、拖板等专项设备，年货物吞吐能力达5万吨。2001年，成立天津机场海关快件监管中心，对天津机场区域内的航空快件运输业务进行专项监管。2005年9月天津机场与北京空港航空地面服务有限公司合资成立专业化公司—天津空港货运有限公司，设备设施齐全。

第八章　邮电科技

20世纪90年代，天津通讯发展迅速，技术不断更新换代。邮政由机械化向电子化发展。信件、报刊、特快专递、金融、保险、网上增值等相继建成计算机网络并投入运行。在电讯技术上，电话功能不断扩大，方便实用，遂取代电报。1995年启用移动电话并迅速在全市普及。1996年，天津在国内率先开通全球通讯系统。汉字显示寻呼机（BP机）出现后，虽曾迅速风靡，但1998年后，渐被手机取代。

同期，邮电系统不断进行体制改革。1999年1月天津市邮政局（简称“天津邮政”）从天津市邮电管理局（简称“天津邮电”）中分离出来，邮、电开始分立。同年，天津移动通信局（简称“天津移动”）从天津邮电中独立出来，形成移、固分营。2000年，天津成立“中国电信集团天津市电信公司（简称“天津电信”），而天津邮电仍为行政管理部门，实行政、企分开。到2002年，天津电信更名为“中国网通集团天津通信公司”（简称“天津通信”)实现南北分拆重组。同期,天津相继建立联通、铁通、卫通。

通讯体制的与时俱进既扩展业务范围,又加速通讯技术深入发展。天津早期研发的“双局号平稳过渡法”在电话号码升位工作中发挥出重要作用。天津移动经过4次扩容,大幅度提高天津通讯普及率。据对4家电信运营商电话普及率的统计,几项主要指标均大幅度超出全国平均指标。2003年天津移动研制的“移动会议电话系统”可实现250人与会通话,在“非典”期间发挥重要作用。同年,建成宽带城域网使天津信息基础设施建设实现跨越式发展。光缆覆盖全市,宽带无线微波覆盖市区。到2005年年底,天津移动交换机容量达450万门,载频总数达19000个。技术上从模拟移动通讯向数字化通讯转化。

第一节 邮 政

1990年后,天津邮政逐步形成“科技兴邮”局面,成功引进信函自动分拣机,基本实现邮件处理机械化。天津邮政的运能、运力得到发展。邮政金融计算机网络(绿卡工程)、报刊发行计算机系统、特快专递计算机系统、邮政电子化支局系统、集邮计算机网络系统等相继建成投产,计算机应用渗透到邮政所有行业。1999年,全国邮、电分立后,天津邮政独立运营,进一步推进科技现代化建设。2004年天津在全国首先实现全部邮政电子化网点统版升级改造。新版本上线,天津邮政发展空间更大、服务更到位。

一、邮件传递

(一)邮件处理

1993年5月,邮政广告公司商业信函微机自动处理系统投产使用。该系统采用微机系统三套,并有多路控制器、票据打印机设备、自动封装机、自动过戳机等全套设备,自行移植开发软件,形成可在全国各省、市、县80多万个企业单位信息库中根据用户需要自动提取所要发函单位,完成商函排版、印刷、打印、封装、过戳等成套智能服务系统。每小时可完成2500件以上商业信函的印刷处理。

1994年,天津东楼邮局采用北京研制的邮政综合业务处理计算机系统。该系统应用微机局域网络将各营业台席工作站通过网络服务器联网,各工作站都具有函、包、汇邮政综合营业功能。投递收发工作站可将进口汇票、包裹、挂刷数据键入后为窗口投交使用,并能生成投递清单、减少营业汇检工序。该系统按业务划分组成函包收寄、速递国际、大宗收寄、出口封班等10个模块。

1999~2001年,天津邮政开始建设综合计算机网络。该工程于2001年10月10日前分别完成机房基础设施建设、广域网和局域网单项设备安装的验收。该网络集服务、生产、管理、决策等功能于一体,与全国236个中心城市信息中心联接成为中国邮政骨干网络。该网络广泛应用于邮政生产、经营、管理和对外服务等各个环节,并通过“183”电子邮政网站、“185”客户服务中心等与公用电话网和公用数据通信网互联。天津邮政投入运行的应用系统包括:邮政储蓄、支局电子化、邮资票品管理、报刊发行系统、特快专递邮件跟踪查询、电子汇兑、电视电话会议、电子邮政、邮政量收、邮政物流等系统。其中,速递跟踪查询新系统(EMS)的站点覆盖天津近290个速递业务开办局,并面向用户开通跟踪查询服务。速递跟踪查询系统具有辅助速递邮件处理功能,三率统计功能(邮件处理信息上网率,邮件处理信息上网及时率和N日投递率),当地和全网业务量与生产作业质量统计分析功能,以及与万国邮联交换数据的功能,可满足邮联速递业务的技术要求。

2001年9月,天津在国家计委立项,实施天津邮件处理中心工艺设备安装工程,同年各项设备全部安装完毕。2002年1月对该中心工艺配套工程项目进行全面测试,重点对各设备系统单元的安装质量和安全设施、系统性能等进行检测,结果表明各系统安装质量优良。是年6月18日天津邮件处理中心进行投产使用。

2003年,天津邮政进行邮政综合业务平台建设,利用建成的邮政综合网的网络资源,整合邮政营业网点系统、绿卡系统的设备资源,实现信息的高度共享。从而搭建起以客户为中心、三网合一的信息网络,最终实现统一服务、统一路由、统一处理、统一对外、统一清算。

天津邮政电子化支局系统统一版本工作于2004年12月完成。在全国第一家实现全部邮政电子化网点统版升级改造。新版本上线运行后,实现业务数据应用集中管理,最大限度的降低系统维护难度,提高邮政速递邮件收寄信息和封发信息上传精确度,提高国际邮政合作业务信息上网的及时率和准确率。同时,统一版本的运行为经营管理、大客户管理、欠费管理、资费稽核提供基础数据,实现与速递子系统封发数据的传输。

2005年8月完成与国家邮政局OA系统的互联互通。11月完成“邮政短信接入系统”,率先完成“短信业务接入系统”。

(二)集邮与报刊

1993年4月24日,天津邮政和天津电话设备厂联合开发的集邮预定取票系统投入使用。该系统采取预付款方式,以卡带证自动计费,并有防跳取、漏取功能,工作时将磁卡片插入,由磁卡机读出用户信息,经微机处理后,信息指令送回磁卡机以完成各项操作。预订取票系统使用后,操作工序由七道变为一道。

2001年,天津市邮政局启用报刊发行计算机处理系统。该系统涵盖发行专业的多个生产环节,并利用中国电信的PSTN拨号线路使全局40多个部门定点及塘沽局与市发行局计算机中心联网。该系统主要功能是将市内36个投发部及报刊零售公司的报刊收订点与市内发行计算机中心联网,各收订窗口每天将数据通过电子化支局网络向报刊发行计算机中心传输,并通过邮政综合计算机网向全国省际网、报刊社、全市邮政分发部门、各营业网点传输相关信息,发挥互订功能,使业务处理时限大大提前。

二、储汇信息传递

(一)储蓄

1991年,天津邮政研究所开发研制“代发工资业务微机处理系统”投入使用。该系统将代发工资12万余人的数据输入微机中。在中国邮政储蓄系统中属于首创。

1992年,天津解放北路邮电支局邮政储蓄,率先使用微机处理活期、整存整取、礼金卷等6种储蓄业务,使用后,查询迅速、缩短用户等候时间。

同年,天津邮政局实施邮政储蓄电子化工程。该局与机电部十五所签定协议,使用太极专用金融终端(TFS--9000)系统组建天津邮政储蓄电子化网点,先后在解放北路等15个邮电支局开通使用。该系统在市邮政储汇局设立邮政金融处理中心与各网点金融终端联网,以集中方式提供各类金融服务。网点终端(储蓄营业窗口)具备处理各类业务功能,中心对终端网络使用市话专线,点对点构成信息传递通道。中心业务处理子系统有移行处理、日终处理等,终端柜员系统有系统控制、交易处理等功能。

1995~2002年,天津邮政储蓄计算机系统进行三次升级改造,1998年、2001年绿卡一、二期工程和2002年绿卡三期工程。此改造解决主机处理能力不足问题,也为中间业务发展提供极大的空间。2003年初,该系统开通运行的业务有:当地定、活期储蓄和储蓄卡业务,活期储蓄和绿卡异地通存通兑业务,波河机消费业务,并支持各种代收、代付等。经过参与银行卡联网联合改造,现在用户可以持邮政绿卡在天津及外地邮政储蓄网点或全国100个实现跨行交易的城市方便、快捷地进行交易。

天津储蓄统一版本工程的建设始于2003年6月,2004年11月9日系统切换上线。在此期间先后完成设备选型,标准数据准备,会计初始化准备,人员培训,网络改造,前端外设验证,数据移植,外围系统测试(包括ATMP/POSP,支付网关,综合服务平台,银联),主机系统安装调试,切换测试,切换预演,压力测试,凭证发放,正式切换方案及切换流程的制定等一系列工作。建成邮政储蓄业务处理,会计核算,资金清算,事后监督,信息管理,代理保险,代理开放式基金等系统。各项指标运行良好,异地开户方系统成功率由上线前的95.15%上升到98.38%,银联开户方交易成功率由上线前的87.47%提高到92.65%,行内异地交易日均对帐不符由上线前的14笔左右下降到8笔左右。现帐务主机日终处理平均30分钟,较切换前效率有较大提高。

(二)汇兑

2002年年底,天津电子汇兑系统联网建设实现突破,联网网点达到214个。使用电子汇兑业务后,网点之间汇兑信息全部通过电子汇兑系统传输和处理,使单笔汇款业务的到达时限由原来的几天缩短为24小时。同时,全国范围内开通2小时到账的电子汇兑业务。2003年根据用户的需求,增加实时到帐业务,用户可在几分钟内即可收到对方来款。

2005年国家局确定实施汇兑网和储蓄网互通工程,实现邮政跨业务种类、跨业务环节的集成。电子汇兑可在已有的现金—现金汇款业务基础上,为客户提供现金—账户、账户—现金、账户—账户三类汇款,优化汇兑业务处理流程。

2005年4月,天津市邮政局在各储蓄和营业柜台开通193台POS机,启动银联移动支付业务。用户持银联卡在POS机上将银行卡卡号与手机号码进行绑定后,用手机编辑短信就可以实现自助缴纳手机话费和账户余额查询等功能。天津局此项业务的开办,实现移动和联通两公司手机话费的绿卡代缴功能。

天津局作为全国邮政储蓄外币系统第一批上线省份,于2005年完成应用软件系统5个试运行网点、三个区县中心软件、储汇局省中心业务、清算、会计控制管理软件的安装、各机构的标准数据整理和确认、网络路由与全国外币中心的导通等,弥补多年来邮政储蓄业务服务币种单一的缺陷。

(三)代交代付

1997年天津邮政局同中国邮电部数据所共同开发"绿卡工程"代收话费"一单结"计算机应用系统。该系统以前置机的方式将电话局的SQL数据库服务器与"绿卡"数据库相连接,利用"绿卡"网点实现当即报号,当即打印收据。全市"绿卡"网点均可交费,且长途、市话、移动电话三种费用"一单结",改变用户分别交费和交费难的局面。

2005年1月,天津邮政信息局完成的代理保险、代理基金系统在三个邮政储蓄窗口试点成功。天津邮政代理保险系统成功完成中国人寿、泰康人寿、太平洋人寿等保险公司实时出单、续期缴费等业务功能的测试。代理基金系统完成基金的开户、申购、查询等测试交易。

2005年8月,国家邮政局推广的"网汇通"业务计算机处理系统在天津局投入使用。"网汇通"可为用户在40余家网站购物提供资金支付的便利服务。用户可采取购买网汇通卡、在网上注册网汇通汇户号、"网汇通充值汇款"等三种方式办理"网汇通"业务。

第二节 电 信

20世纪90年代,天津在电报应用技术上没有大的发展,而在电话应用技术上,边引进,边创新,有长足进步。1990年天津开办可视电话。1993年天津电话网实现程控化,同时,在国内首创双局号平稳过渡升位技术及增强型升位技术,天津的电话号码由6位安然升至8位,这一技术被全国许多地区采用。1995年,天津又在国内首先开通全球移动通信系统。此后,邮电系统进行体制改革,邮、电分立,移、固分营,天津电讯技术更加迅速发展。2001年天津开始建设通用无线分组交换技术网络。是年12月31日午夜全部关闭模拟移动通信,进入"数字时代"。此后,不断提高通信网络质量,降低网络成本,开发出"移动动态资料管理系统",2004年首创"基于ITIL的电信运维管理平台,实现运维管理流程的规范化、信息化和自动化。

一、电报

1992年天津市津科电子有限公司,市邮政局,市长途电信局联合研制开发出"电报网质量监督系统"。

该系统利用公众交换机构成质量监督系统，可对所辖支局随时进行质量动态监督检查，经过试用，其性能良好，功能稳定，操作简便。

二、固定电话

(一)程控化

早在1985年天津就引进第一部程控电子交换机。到1989年天津的程控交换机占市内电话交换机总容量的73.5%。但直到1991年，天津部分电话网仍沿用步进制或纵横制。1993年，天津市电话网包括武清、静海、宝坻、宁河、蓟县等五个县(区)、32个农村电话支局以及长途自动交换机全部实现程控交换和数字传输，在全国居邮电先进行列。

1995年1月14日长途局113台开始使用人工长途智能系统，具备自动存储排队等待功能。

(二)升位

1993年前，国内外电话号码升位多采用单局号升位法。此法在升位过程中易出现长时间现行号码停呼及短时通信中断。1993年12月，天津市邮电管理局升位办公室郭绍生、王安平、刘德宝等研发的"双局号平稳过渡升位法"，设置为新、旧局号并存于程控交换机的局数据设置中，在实施过程中均可做为程序运行数据。即在一定时限内新旧局号均可使用，从而使在升位调试时间内不停机，不中断通话。该成果在天津电话号码由六位升七位时成功采用，获1994年度天津市科技进步二等奖。

1997年，天津市邮电管理局在制定电话网升八位总体技术方案时，考虑到全市电话网总装机容量达到150万门，通信网中有4种制式共6种机型，升位工程涉及面广、技术性强，时间紧、风险大。该局滕勇、王安平、薄今纲等又在原双局号升位法的基础上创新，制定出"增强型双局号平稳过渡升位技术方案"。该方案既涵盖在国内各城市普遍安装的6种交换机型可同时进行号码置换完成升位，又避免升位过程中可能产生的瞬间中断，妥善地解决在特大城市电话网中交换设备多制式、多机型、多种自动特服系统和七号信令环境下平稳升位的问题，成功运用于全国各地电话网的电话号码六位升七位和七位升八位工程中，先后获1997年度天津市科技进步二等奖和1998年度国家科技发明三等奖。

(三)可视电话

1991年5月17日天津市长途电信局在全市首次开办可视电话业务。1994年9月长途局电视会议电话室开通。1995年10月28日邮电公网电视电话会议业务对社会开放。

1996年10月30日天津市邮电管理局与美国全视通公司(Picture Tel)签署协议，建设天津会议电视网。该会议电视系统采用高清晰度编解码压缩技术，将16Mb/s信号压缩为2Mb/s，再通过传输设备的SDH2Mb/s端口进行点对点的专线方式进行传输，其中包括市委、市政府各一个节点。该系统于1997年建成，常年使用，运行良好。

1996年2月15日天津卫星通信地球站向"亚洲二号"通信卫星传输中央电视台第四套电视节目信号。8月25日天津至香港的第一条卫星数据专线电路开通。

2001年，根据国家邮政局统一部署，开发全国邮政会议电视业务。国家邮政局和全国31个省、自治区、直辖市邮政局，共计32个点都可充分利用全国邮电综合网资源。

2005年，天津市邮政局利用天津市邮政信息网资源，对"国家局电视电话系统"进行升级，延伸其功能。实现点对点、一点对多点、多点对多点的对话，并具备实时视频会议、远程教学及数据传输等功能的会议电视系统，可以达到即时、互动的远程沟通。它的投入使用可利用邮政信息网资源和信息化手段提高运行效率、节约运行成本。

会议电视信号的传输基于邮政综合网的广域网平台，由新桥公司的自动柜员机交换机提供512K的电路仿真。国家邮政局负责会议电视系统的引进与安装调试。各省市负责机房装修和配套设备置备工作。该系统包含1个会议中心及市各区局、郊县等14个分会场，并可与全国会议电视系统实现互联互通。

（四）公用电话

1992年4月10日CN型磁卡公用电话机在天津电话设备厂投入生产。10月天津对日本、美国、意大利、韩国、新加坡、加拿大等国和中国香港的108直拨受话人付费电话全部开通。

1995年11月26日汉沽区及五县的人工长途台关闭。天津市各区、县长途电话全部实现自动化、程控化。

2003年10月29日天津通信首台安装在公交巴士上的无线公话正式开通，实现固定公话移动打，为公交乘客提供方便的通信服务。天津通信市场部与公交部门合作推出的这一新举措，开创公话业务新模式。

三、移动电话

1988年12月，天津市长途电信局引进瑞典爱立信公司移动通信系统，建立能覆盖天津全市各区、县的移动电话网，即B网，属于第一代移动通讯技术。该B网容量1500户，有9个基站，114个信道，1990年11月投入运行。1992年9月，移动电话B网进行第一次扩容，其容量达5060户。1993年5月，B网进行第二次扩容，其通信能力增至可容纳25060个用户。同年5月1日，移动电话号码由6位升至7位，原90局改为901局。6月17日，移动电话903局开通。1994年3月21日，移动电话905局开通，号码资源增加2万个。同年10月1日，移动电话障碍台开始对外服务，受理用户遇到的各种问题。

1990年9月15日，天津市邮电管理局与香港CSL公司签订人工漫游协议，规定天津、香港两地用户携机到达对方地区，均可使用移动电话通话。1993年4月1日，天津、上海、广州3城市与全国20余个城市、自治区，同时签订实施移动电话人工漫游合同。1993年9月8日，京津间900兆移动电话自动漫游业务区正式开通，这是国内首次实现移动电话跨区自动联网。1994年7月1日，天津市移动电话系统与河北省石家庄、秦皇岛、唐山、廊坊、沧州、保定、邯郸、邢台、衡水等9个城市移动电话系统B网联网，从而实现京、津、冀地区的移动电话用户自动漫游。

1993年10月11日香港—塘沽摩托罗拉64千比特/秒高速数据电路开通。1994年7月，天津市投资2.58亿元兴建移动电话A网，其一期工程908局于同年9月28日开通，增加容量2万户。二期工程906局、904局分别于1994年12月13日和1995年1月26日接纳用户。1995年8月18日，A网工程全部开通，共增容5万户。A网和B网均属模拟式移动电话。

1995年1月1日，A网和B网在各自系统中实现全国自动漫游试运行，同年6月28日，两网自动漫游正式投入运行。9月23日零时，天津模拟移动电话号码由7位升至8位，是继北京之后第2个移动电话升8位的城市。同年，模拟移动电话先后开通900、902、904、906、907、9086、9088等7个局。

1994年，国家启动移动通信第二代技术，数字移动电话网（GSM）。该网具有进行国际、国内自动漫游，智能卡计费，保密性能好，抗干扰能力强，可开发多种新业务等诸多优点。天津投资1.45亿元兴建GSM数字移动电话网。1995年3月31日，数字移动电话“全球通”部分基站开通，该系统容量3万户，可覆盖全市大部分地区。同年7月17日，数字全球通实现京津间人工漫游。11月28日实现京、津、冀（共33个市县）地区的自动漫游。1996年1月，实现全国15个省市联网自动漫游。天津是国内第一个开通GSM业务的地区。

1999年8月，天津移动通信有限责任公司成立。2000年网络规模达120万户左右。截至2001年年底，天津移动通信完成GSM的7次扩容，网络容量达到230万户，拥有无线基站820个，建成82套微蜂窝和直放站，网络覆盖率达99%。同时，为提高网络质量，解决传输资源缺乏矛盾，该公司加大传输网的建设和全网优化的工作，使网络质量更加精细化，达到无缝覆盖。2002年，公司开展“打造精品网”活动，减少“盲区”，提高话务承载能力和通话的质量。天津移动通信网络在20多次全国评比中名列第一。

2001年2月，天津移动的通用无线分组业务开始建设GPRS网络。这是一种基于GSM系统的无线分组交换技术，从提供端到端的、广域的无线IP连接。GPRS依靠高速数据处理技术，以“分组”的形式，传送资料到用户手上。GPRS作为GSM网络向第三代移动通信演变的过渡技术（2.5G），有接入迅速、永远在线、流量计费等多方面优势，特别适合于频发小数据量的实时传输。截至2005年年底，天津移动通信先后经过4期扩容，系统容量达到120万户，连接激活成功率（PDP）高达99%以上。此外，GPRS为天津市信息化建设提供全方位整体解决方案。横向以移动标准化产品为核心，实现产品覆盖和捆绑，纵向加快步伐为成熟行业应用提供高可靠性服务。GPRS开通的WAP上网浏览、笔记本无线接入互联网、私有专网等服务，都有效地应用在政府、公安、交通、金融、证券等行业。其中超大规模的集团客户如海关、电力、水文、警务、物流等，均使用天津移动量身定做的直连+VPMN、短信、GPRS等业务。天津移动成为物流行业移动信息化建设的全国示范基地，实现无缝覆盖并全国漫游，从而带动更多物流企业提升自身信息化水平，提高企业运转效率。随着互联网技术与移动通信技术的融合，天津移动通信正逐步从传统的语音业务服务商向信息服务提供商转变。

2001年12月31日，根据中国信息产业部《关于中国移动通信集团公司停止使用模拟移动通信业务频率的通知》精神，天津模拟移动通信网于午夜24时全面关闭。至此，天津移动通信全面进入“数字时代”。到2005年年底，天津移动交换机容量达450万门；载频总数达到19000个；全网基站总数达到1700多个；传输网络初具规模。

四、信息管理

1998年3月27日天津邮电“九七工程”（全国范围内实现电话营业计算机综合系统）在当地网内开通使用，电话营业实现传递工单电子化，以计算机数据库代替卡片管理。

1999年，天津移动公司李跃、辛凡非、闫五四等研制的“天津移动客服短消息中心系统”，把客户服务中心和短消息服务两大业务整合在一起，通过一个综合的智能业务平台完成各项功能。该成果有效地提高接续效率和系统设备的利用率，减少初期投资成本和后期运营成本，促进统一服务，统一维护和管理。利用该系统平台开发的“全球呼”、话费查询、话费预警、短信秘书服务、股票信息点播等服务项目，经济和社会效益显著。其中“全球呼”的推出在短消息应用领域是一个创新，市场潜力很大，并在全国推广。

2000年3月22日天津网通（即当时的天津电信）与联通移动通信局合作，向联通130手机用户开通天津电信当地IP电话（网络电话）业务。

2001年，天津移动闫五四、阚建杰、李永春等完成“天津移动动态资料管理系统”的研究，其成果是基于计算机与通信网络管理技术的一种综合信息管理系统，该系统通过计算机软件功能，帮助用户科学有效地管理通信网络和用于通信网络的日常维护生产、网络优化、网络规划、建设和决策等，研究成果为提高通信网络质量、降低通信网络成本提供行之有效的解决方案。系统开发应用，提高资源的利用率与工作效率，保护基础投资，完善资料维护手段，缩短障碍处理时间，提高客户的满意度，取得重要的社会效益。该成果获2002年度天津市科技进步二等奖。

2002年8月2日天津通信VDSL业务开通暨现场装机在天津开发区“阳光新干线”商住小区举行，天津通信首批VDSL业务正式投入商用。

2002年，天津移动公司张学红、薄今纲、闫五四等承担完成的“天津移动会议电话系统”，其成果为用户提供随时、随地、随意实现多方同时通话的新技术、新业务。特别是在2003年“非典”期间，该成果为社会正常开展工作发挥巨大作用。这种移动会议电话系统组网简单，在不改变现有基础网络结构条件下，最多可实现250人与会通话。该系统与固定电话相比，具有更大的灵活性，可方便地召开电话会议。呼入式的交互式会议电话保密性能好，操作简便，特别适合临时性的紧急会议，以及分布在不同地点的公司企业内部召开会议、布置工作、汇报情况、交流经验等，是一种省时、方便、经济的会议新方式。

2003年，天津移动闫五四、阚建杰、李荣盛等完成“交换机智能巡检系统”。该成果利用计算机网络技术和数据库技术，通过首创的智能分析引擎，实现对交换机报告的智能分析；采用设备代理引擎，实现与多种设备接口的交互；采用队列控制器，保证交换机巡检任务的有序进行，提供对设备监控的多种方式；采用独创的“插件式软件体系结构”，保证系统功能的平滑扩展。研究成果独创6项移动通信网交换机智能检测的软件核心技术为该系统的开发应用可提高网络监控维护人员工作效率3倍以上，完善监控维护手段，缩短障碍处理时间，提高客户满意度，具有显著经济、社会效益。2003年，天津移动徐波、郭强、陈奇志等研制完成“多功能无线系统维护优化支撑系统”。该成果集成BSS负荷预警和话务模型分析、性能指标综合分析及优化、无线频率资源管理及系统参数检查、障碍检查和故障处理等重要功能。可采用图形、曲线、表格等多种格式表达。可对MSI PLANET、MOTOROLA GI（规划软件、摩托罗拉优化软件）所需无线网络数据实时采集，准确校对，从而做到与MSI PLANET、MOTOROLA GI的无缝连接，成为使用MSI PLANET、MOTOROLA GI必不可少的支撑系统。该系统采用计算机程序设计技术，通过与GSM技术理论和MOTOROLA无线网络设备原理相结合，解决GSM网络优化和维护工作中设备负荷管理、局数据管理、性能统计分析、网络设计规划等诸多难题，实现无线核心设备预警功能、话务模型提取功能、无线网络维护、优化支撑功能。对其开发应用可提高网络优化和网络维护的工作效率与劳动生产率，保证无线核心设备的安全运行，为网络规划提供重要依据，最大限度地保护企业的投资。

2004年，天津移动张学红、闫五四、阚建杰首创国内第一个基于ITIL的电信运维管理平台。该平台基于成熟的ITIL引擎进行构架，利用IT网络作为通道，通过独创的7项核心技术，将流程管理、工单管理、值班管理、维护作业计划管理、短信通知及工单受理、SLA受理超时提醒及受理级别的提升、信息发布系统、业务论坛、资料管理、知识库、系统管理、网管告警自动派单、工单报表统计、流程管理等功能有机的组织起来，形成一套有效的网络生产运行维护的统一指挥、调度、管理、监督的运维支撑平台，实现运维管理流程的规范化、信息化和自动化，达到业务流程的可监控、可管理和可优化，实现客户投诉快速反应机制，缩短故障的处理时限，提高天津移动的服务品质和业务管理水平，树立企业工作高效化、管理科学化，增强企业竞争力。

图9-8-2-137 集管理、指挥、调度为一身的天津移动网络集中管理中心

五、网络技术及管网铺设

1995年12月16日 天津在市话管网建设中，破路113.5沟公里，埋设管道1602孔公里，数量和速度居全国城市之首。

1997年5月1日 邮电智能网300业务向公众开放，并实现全国联网。11月26日天津开通当地ATM宽带业务网，同时开通远程医疗、数学系统。同年7月28日天津市数据通信局营业厅对外营业。7月31日市重点建设项目“信息港”工程应用系统之一“天津热线”开通。

1998年7月23日 天津当地网交换网管系统投入运行。

1999年6月 市政府召开“政府上网工程”启动大会。天津邮电管理局提供“天津热线”作为其政务公开的主平台，并提供免费或优惠专线服务等一系列政策。12月10日天津邮电管理局牵头，中国电信天津电信网、中国移动通信天津移动网、中国联通天津通信网等进行2000年全市时钟网间在线联网测试。测试结果表明，计费系统、通信系统、网络设备均正常无误，天津通信网跨入2000年准备工作基本就绪。

2000年6月15日，天津市数据通信局对第三届“电子商务国际论坛”进行网上直播。

2001年9月6日天津市教委成人教育信息资源网与天津热线合作开通网络大专教学。

2002年5月16日，天津开通“视听新干线”业务，作为国内首家内容应用捆绑接入统一计费平台，为内容应用业务的拓展进行积极的探索。9月28日 天津市通信公司无线市话网（俗称“小灵通”）投入试运行，公司内部业务及外部试用业务开通。无线市话网络的建成，解决固定电话不能移动、覆盖范围受有线连接限制的问题，对固定电话网络起到有效的补充作用，让固定电话“移动起来”。

2003年3月3日天津通信与天津电信网间互联传输和交换工程的测试工作结束，实现网间互联互通。从而解决两个网络中用户的当地业务互通，方便用户使用。

2004年6月15日天津通信流媒体平台测试开通，与视听新干线成功对接。实现二者的内容存储和用户计费统一管理，既利用视听新干线对用户计费，又利用流媒体对ICP(互联网内容提供商)视频数据进行集中存储，有效实现对天津宽带客户的统一受理和视频发布。同年7月20日由天津通信组建的天津市通信业首套电信级商用视频会议系统二期扩容工程投入试用。扩容后的视频会议系统可以提供ADSL(非对称数字用户线路)、IP(IP接入网)、ISDN(综合业务数字网)等多种接入，客户可以通过以上方式实现单独或混合组网。

第九章　广播电视

20世纪90年代以来，天津市广播电视系统强化项目建设，加大数字化、自动化、网络化设备的引进力度。在节目制作、播出，传输、发射等方面科技现代化程度明显提升，节目制作和播出质量进一步提高。截至2005年年底市级广播电台设有新闻、经济、交通、生活、文艺、音乐、滨海7个系列台，为中波、调频播出，共有16个频率。4套节目上传亚洲2号卫星播出；10套节目实现有线广播电视网播出，其中4套专供；所有节目均在因特网上直播。市级电视自办节目13套。天津卫视节目卫星覆盖进一步扩大，并在全国29个省会城市或直辖市、1个计划单列市及27个地级市播出。天津人民广播电台(以下简称"天津电台")的录制、播出、总控和音频工作站系统的设备数字化程度达到94.58%，系统数字化程度为96.63%。天津电视台电视中心总体数字化率为90%以上，单个节目现场制作系统的数字化率为95.84%，单个频道播控系统的数字化率为97%以上。数字有线电视、数字移动电视实现试播出。1991～2005年，天津市广播电视系统获部、省级科技进步奖3项。

第一节　播控技术

20世纪90年代初期主要以立体声直播为主。1991年开始由模拟向数字化转轨，逐步采用计算机控制、网络、数字存储等技术。到2005年，天津市级广播电视系统基本实现数字化播出。

一、广播播控

1991年3月，天津电台经济台立体声直播室正式投入使用。直播室的设备便于主持人操作，嘉宾席设在主持人对面，双方容易沟通；热线电话不仅听众能与主持人通话，听众之间也可以直接对话，通过长途线路还可与外省市及国外电台进行联播。

1994年年底，天津电台基本完成广播播控中心的技术改造，实现新闻、文艺、交通、教育、音乐等台6套节目全部由主持人直播或以立体声播出。数字音频工作站是以计算机控制的大容量硬磁盘为主要载体的数字音频处理系统，是电台数字化播出的基础和核心组成部分，年内天津电台建成数字化播控中心。1998年10月，该台交通频道使用音频工作站完成日常节目制作及自动播出。

2001年7月1日，天津电台完成数字化播控中心的设备安装调试，实现全套系统由模拟向数字技术跨越。新广播中心的广播工艺系统全面实现广播节目采编、录制、播出及管理系统数字化、网络化,使电台的节目制作能力和播出质量明显提高。该工艺系统由总控制室、播出、录制、音频工作站——自动播出系统网络、录音棚、信息管理系统网络及交通台视频监控路况播报等7个系统组成。广播中心通过建立数字音频矩阵及两大计算机网络实现数字音频信号可交换,网上资源共享。自动播出网络采用在一个网络上按频道分域、分服务器/阵列柜管理的结构,以提高服务器的响应速度和磁盘阵列数据响应速度,电台节目制作能力和播出质量明显提高。同年9月1日投入使用。是年,交通台研制的由主要路口的视频路况监视系统、出租车移动路况采集系统和基于电子地图智能化路况辅助播报软件系统三部分组成的天津路况信息地图化辅助播报系统,使用后起到利用电台广播疏导交通的作用。

2003年5月,天津电台建成天津人民广播电台互联网广播系统。该系统由采集制作、媒体管理、流媒体服务三部分构成,工作流程明晰、高度自动化,具备实施远程监控功能,技术含量高、运行成本低。截至2005年,该系统在线直播9套节目,录播80多个栏目节目,每个栏目保留节目约两个月。

2004年下半年,天津电台开始对广播中心进行数字化、网络化改造。对采编网和自动播出系统进行升级,对网络机房进行改造,实现广播中心采编、制作、播出及管理全系统数字化、网络化和自动化。其中自动播出系统的升级改造使其应急切换能力更强,更加稳定,进一步提高节目制作能力和播出质量。采编网升级改造后实现多媒体采、编、播一体化,具有更强大的管理和编辑功能。2005年完成电台启动数字卫星转播车工程项目,天津首次将现场节目由制作到播出全套设备集于一车,实现电台台外现场直播和异地节目的传输,成为全国广播界首辆功能完备、具有较高数字化水平的卫星转播车。该项目与国内同类系统比较,具有多功能、高可靠、结构合理、经济实用等特点。

天津电台的数字音频资料库建设到2005年年底除硬件改造外,完成1.2万盘的转储任务,抢救并保留大量资料,为资源共享、节目交换,发挥数字化、网络化播出系统的优势。

二、电视播控

1991年及1993年,天津电视台将自行研制的电视节目自动播控系统(APS-905系统)先后应用于原29、23两频道。此时,天津电视台三套自办电视节目均实现播控自动化,在全国省级电视台名列榜首。

1997年开始的第二次电视中心改造,正处在电视设备由模拟方式向数字化转化时期。当时,已有的数字设备还不够成熟,系统改造又没有方案可供借鉴,天津电视台采用音频嵌入新技术,实行微机网络化管理,自动控制电视节目播出和国内外地区间的联播。新电视中心于1998年10月1日启用,实现全数字化播出。

1998年11月28日,中国电视技术学会组织的有国家广电总局科技司、电视专家学者参加的"全数字电视播出中心研讨会",在天津电视台播出中心举行。该会对天津电视台实施的数字化改造工程给予充分肯定。同年12月28日,天津电视台通过亚洲2号卫星向亚太地区转播发送电视节目。

1999年,天津电视台根据电视节目播出的实际和需要,改进电视剧插播广告节目的制作和播出流程,在播出中心建立广告节目的上载编辑机房。2000年4月3日在天津电视台第二套节目投入使用。是年6月21日,连同天津卫视和第一套节目,3个频道全面实现电视广告节目硬盘自动播出。

2003年8月将原有线电视频道并入C区播出中心,并对总控部分进行改造。建成拥有9个频道的硬盘播出中心。

2004年,天津电视台采用数字存储技术、网络技术、媒体资产管理技术、网络化非编技术、多频道DVB(可查阅的数字视频广播)TS流播控技术等,解决以往电视台在制播过程牵扯环节、标准、素材格式过多,造成频道增加、系统扩充、成本过高的问题。截至2005年年底,通过中央和天津广播电视网络有限公司的集成平台播出4套数字电视节目,开展数字电视业务,实现全市乃至全国范围内自办数字电视付费频道节目的播出。

第二节　制作技术

制作广播与电视节目涉及到摄像、录音、节目后期制作、演播室、录音棚、转播车等多项技术。20世纪90年代，天津电台与电视台注重引进高质量、高科技的技术设备，保证1995年与1999年两次在津举办的世界性体育大赛的完美播出。此后，随着广电节目制作技术的不断发展，数字化、网络化等新技术被大量采用，天津广播电视节目制作水平有较大提高，到2005年年底，天津具备数字高清节目的制作能力。

一、广播节目制作

1991年，天津电台引进瑞士产高质量A807型录音机替代国产635型录音机。1994年开始使用数字音频磁带机（DAT）。1998年开始使用迷你光盘（MD）。

1999年年底16号录音棚全套录音设备更新被列入到广播工艺系统项目之中。其构建原则和技术要求符合数字音频技术和设备发展的最新水平，能满足录制高水平大型音乐、戏剧节目的要求。

2001年建成天津电台广播中心语言文艺录制系统，包括11个语言文艺录音室的设备均配置全数字专业调音台、数字磁带录音机、CD和MD机、卡座机。新的设备与天津电台的播出系统联网，实现全自动化数字播出。同时，通过数据格式转换，可以进入非线性自动播出网络，用于节目播出。录音室与广播中心通讯网络直通，录制人员可与总控室及直播室人员对话，还可通过调音台的内置话筒及监听，与演播人员交流。录音室与总控室间设有双向数字音频信号通道。录音室既可随录总控室来的各种节目源，又可将播音室的实时播音、音频工作站、卡座、CD、DAT等不同的节目源传到总控室直接播出，成为一个备用直播室。新建成的广播中心的核心设备全部数字化，功能齐全实用，操作简单快捷，录制水平全面提高。同期，天津电台还相继改造采编系统，实现记者远程文字和音频采编和主持人播报网络读屏；建成记者采访电话回传系统，突现广播的快捷并提高时效性。

二、电视节目制作

1990年，天津电视台利用演播室和插播间建立一条龙式的新闻节目制作中心。同年又引进6讯道彩色电视转播车。

1995年第43届世界乒乓球锦标赛期间，天津电视台利用美国GVG16×16矩阵开关，完成台内外电视信号的切换调度，实现实况转播和节目包装交替进行。参加场馆转播任务的两部彩色电视转播车的节目输出视频信号和包括国际声及现场解说混合声的音频信号，通过微波和光缆送至设在天津电视台的“世乒赛演播室”中心机房，经信号处理、分配调度，分别送往节目制作有关机房统一安排播出，或经邮电微波电路，送往中央电视台。同年天津电视台引进模拟分量设备。1996年又引进Thomson公司摄像机、SONY公司切换台和SP系列录像机等设备从而提高天津电视台节目制作质量。

1999年第34届世界体操锦标赛期间，天津电视台运用电视转播车等设备，在场馆建立一个数字二级切换调度中心，数字输出信号向国内外传送。同年，该台在演播室的数字化改造中，引进数字摄像机、数字切换台、数字录像机等设备并通过数字光端机与播出中心相连，接收和传送的数字音频嵌入视频信号，实现电视节目信号共享。是年，该台还建成数字录音棚。

2000年天津电视台筹建虚拟演播室，2001年投入使用。该虚拟演播室为全数字三机位系统，采用两维半虚拟技术，使用特殊的数字信号处理方式，把图象放大四倍仍保持很高的图象质量，并且场景一般是一张特别大的广角位图，通过有效的插值算法，保证镜头推拉、俯仰、平摇过程中背景的平稳变化，加之丰富的大屏幕切换特技、无限蓝箱、深度键等实用功能，基本满足节目制作需求，投资成本大幅度下降。

2003年3月，天津电视台完成的虚拟演播室升级改造项目从根本上改变原嵌入式体系结构，使硬件的通用性、处理能力有很大提高。采用先进的标准配置，硬件运转安全可靠，图形处理大大提升。所有的制作和控制功能都通过一个三维实时虚拟引擎来实现，增强人性化设计，具有即看即所得的实时观看修改效果。整体场景与节目制作系统采用网络连接，资源共享。运行稳定、可靠、操作性强，便于调整，达到该室改造目标。虚拟场景，免除栏目景片的制作，节省经费。

2003年，天津电视台引进高端合成设备，以解决复杂的高质量片头制作问题。2004年对后期制作设备进行大幅度更新换代，用系列数字设备替代模拟设备。为满足高标清电视节目制作和存储的需要，同年，将800平方大演播室改建成高/标清兼容演播室，并投入使用。该室在视频系统方面，配置7台LDK-6000高清晰度电视摄像机，高清信号切换台和高清矩阵具备高清晰度电视节目的直接制作能力。天津电视台拥有大量标清节目素材，在系统中又增加高/标清视频信号上、下变换功能，并为解决在上、下变换过程中出现的视频延迟现象，标清节目录制采用音频嵌入方式，保证声画同步。同时，还配有高清度录像机HDCAM和标准清晰度录像机IMX，可以根据需要进行高、标清节目的录制。在音频系统方面，高/标清兼容演播室采用全数字系统，立体声工作方式进行音频节目制作，并为制作5.1声道环绕声节目预留接口。该系统的建成使天津电视台成为全国第一个拥有高/标清兼容演播室的电视台，在全国同行业中处于领先水平。2005年，天津电视台完成5个演播室的标清数字化改造，拥有14个电视演播室，配有相应的电视节目制作设备和演播制作环境，能够完成台内各种节目的制作。

第三节 传输技术

1991年，天津采用全数字多路视频、音频光缆传输设备，建成广播电视节目数字信号传输系统。同年利用热线电话转接器进行现场实况转播。

1996年，天津开始接收卫星信号转播节目。1998年，天津建成卫星地面接收站，开始上卫星播出。2000年天津电视台购置卫星车传送电视节目，并于2001年首次用于新闻直播采访。

2002年，天津电视台进一步更新广播节目传输手段。2003年该台在天津有线电视网中播出节目。2004年数字广播节目传输系统更加完善，天津广播电视卫星节目完成从KU波段播出转到C波段播出的整体平移。2005年，天津北方移动电视节目开播。到年底，天津广电系统形成以有线、无线传输为主要手段，涉及光缆、微波、卫星等多项传输技术的传输体系，新技术的采用成为广播电视的有效技术保障。

一、有线传输

（一）热线

1991年，天津电台开始利用热线电话转接器进行现场实况转播。2000年天津电台播控中心与音乐台安装综合业务数字网线路。2001年，天津电台启用新一代有线数字传输设备，利用ISDN专用数据电话线路传输高质量音频信号进行现场转播。它利用APT-XTM编码技术来实现无损压缩，利用两条ISDN线路（4个B通道），以256千比特/秒传输速率实现22千赫兹音频带宽（或2×15千赫兹的立体声），提供CD（激光唱片）级的音频质量。

2003年天津电台充分利用有线广播电视网的调频广播频率资源，开办多套面向不同受众群的专业化、特色有线调频广播频道，不断提高广播的整体收听率。是年5月23日7个频道节目在因特网上开通，6月中旬分别开通戏曲台和古典音乐台,除在线直播外,还有88个录播栏目在因特网上播出。为广播节目在天津有线电视网中播出,年内还建成从传输机房到天津有线电视网前端机房的信号传输系统。到2005年天津共有10套立体声广播节目在有线电视网播出。

(二) 光纤光缆

1991年建成的,自天津广播电视局至电视塔的数字信号传输系统,就采用光纤传输。该系统应用全数字多路视频、音频光缆传输设备并以“树型”结构集中传输方式和迂回双路由互为备份,打破传统的点对点、一对一分散传输方式,实现微机控制与自动化管理。

1998年10月,天津市广播电视局在传输信息部机房架设12芯多模光缆,实现天津电台各机房间的联网用于节目传输。同年天津电视台利用电缆传送数字电视节目信号,作为光缆传送的备用通道确保线路传输畅通安全。利用电缆传送电视台 GPS 统一时间和总控的黑场台主锁相信号,以保证电视台内不同楼宇各系统间的协调一致。

2001年,天津电台完成广播节目信号传输通道的数字化改造。广播节目信号从数字播出中心采用AES / EBU 音频标准传送到传输机房,采用数字光传输设备,将7套调频广播节目和6套中波广播节目分别传送到天塔、杨柳青和四号各发射机房。

2004年,天津电台将播出中心的AES / EBU 数字音频主、备路信号分别传送到传输机房,经信号分配后,采用数字光传输设备,将主、备路数字信号分别独立传输到天塔、杨柳青等发射机房。从此天津市具备主、备独立的广播电视节目数字信号传输和调度能力。同年,天津电台上传卫星播出的立体声节目数量增加到5套,其主用信号采用加拿大的数字光缆传输设备。经两路迂回光缆路由,传送到杨柳青卫星地球站,另两路备份信号采用数字微波设备和数字光缆传输设备。

2005年,天津北方移动电视节目开播,电视节目增加到3套,将编码、复用后的压缩码流用数字光缆传输设备,经两路迂回光缆路由,传送到天塔发射塔,作为天津移动电视节目发射的主、备用信号;至此,天津地区可移动接收多套电视节目。

二、无线传输

(一)微波

1993年前,天津电台利用微波抛物面天线和原电视发射塔上的无源反射板将节目信号直接发送到杨柳青发射台。是年,天津电台对传送到杨柳青发射台的微波设备进行改造,将两个直径2米的抛物面天线安装在电视天线塔上,6G和8G微波于同年启用。1995年世乒赛广播节目的传输以STL(演播室到发射机传输环路)无线传输为主,调频发射为辅,信号接收后分送天津电台直播室和北京的中央电台、国际电台(英语)、国际电台(朝语)。三路信号均经调制成超群信号,再经同轴电缆传至中央电台、国际电台播出。1996年,天津电台对节目传输微波进行更新。在1997年世界体操锦标赛、迎香港、澳门回归等大型现场转播中STL微波均发挥作用。2002年和2003年广播节目传输备份更加完善,形成由传输机房到杨柳青机房,光缆与微波互为主、备;由传输机房到塘沽机房,卫星与微波互为主、备安全可靠的广播节目传输系统。

(二)卫星

1996年1月,天津电台接收卫星信号转播中央电台节目。1998年12月,天津电台建成卫星地面接收站,安装中央电台卫星接收机,接收亚太2号卫星ku波段中央电台和国际电台的节目并转播。同时,天津电台的节目也上卫星播出。同年,在天津广播电视卫星地球站工程中,建立天津上星信号压缩、编码、处理和信号光传输、微波传输系统。采用数字光缆传输设备,传送到天津卫星地球站,作为上星节目的主用信号。同时采用7G、8G数字微波传输设备,作为上星节目的备用信号。既满足上星节目的高质量要求,又确保传输的高可靠性。

2000年,天津电视台利用调制合成方式,在电视台内部传送相关的境外电视节目。同年,天津电视台购置SWE—DISH 150KM 卫星车传送电视节目,扩大电视新闻异地采访和实况转播范围。2001年12月引进卫星上行车,首次用于新闻直播采访。2002年天津电视台的现场直播节目从天津扩大到全国。

第四节 发射技术

20世纪90年代,广电发射技术经历由模拟到数字的转变。到2005年,天津广播电视发射系统设备日臻完善,实现中波、调频、模拟、数字电视的发射,覆盖范围进一步扩大。

一、中波发射

1993年天津电台进行频率调整。将4个中波广播频率分别调整为:909千赫,1071千赫,1386千赫,567千赫。1994年,天津电台引进大功率全固态数字调制中波广播发射机,省去大型电子管的更换,整机效率高出电子管发射机整机效率的20%左右。

2001年杨柳青发射台从法国引进6部全固态数字调制中波发射机,全面更换原电子管发射机,加强与改善对天津及周边地区广播节目信号的覆盖与质量,大幅降低费用。使天津中波发射系统的技术水平在全国同行业中处于领先地位。到2002年12月天津广播的发射机全部更新为数字全固态发射机。

2003年4月天津广播电视电影集团技术中心中波机房并机系统进行改造,采用90度并机相移网络,在并机网络中采用易于控制,响应速度快,工作寿命较长的真空继电器,并采用工控机对并机网络及发射机进行控制。经运行说明此网络不但隔离度高,且工作稳定、可靠,可确保安全播出。

2004年,天津广播电视电影集团技术中心设计并完成"中波广播频率的选频"投入使用。该项目通过对中波频率规划和周边中波频率环境因素的分析,确定中波广播频率选频原则。据此选定666千赫兹作为天津电台新的广播频率,并经国家广电总局批准。使用效果良好,无临频干扰现象。

2005年9月,天津广播电视电影集团技术中心开始进行DRM数字中波发射和接收试验,该试验包括闭路试验和开路发射试验两个阶段,通过试验不仅得到大量的试验数据,还为开展数字中波广播积累经验。其优越的音质和灵活的业务模式使人们对中波广播刮目相待。

2005年天津广播电视电影集团技术中心全面启动中波发射机改造工程。进一步改善中波广播的覆盖和收听效果,扩大天津广播的实力和影响力。

二、调频发射

1991年,天津广播电视塔竣工,塔上装有高382米6层背腔式圆极化天线供发射调频和电视广播。是年年底,完成设备安装调试、开播。同时,天津电台的调频立体声广播移至天塔发射。

1998年12月,从国外引进全固态调频广播发射机。2000年,天津的六套中波广播节目全部实现与调频广播并播,中波广播节目全部上调频广播。

2003年下半年,天津广播电视电影集团开始建设调频同步网,在采用调频同步广播发射系统后,有效地解决调频广播移动收听、减少信号交迭区干扰,从而提高广播收听质量、节约频率资源和加快广播专业化。天津广播电视电影集团根据天津的具体情况,确定一期工程以天塔—塘沽为发射站点组建同步网。在调频同步方式上采用卫星信号做信号源,通过设置卫星接收机的PCR(节目时钟参考),使两地卫星接收机的解码时钟与上星TS流包头中的时钟信息锁定,从而消除音频解码环节产生的随机偏差,保证两地的卫星信号有确定的时间差。到2005年,相干区的调试仍在进行。

三、电视发射

1991年,天津广播电视塔采用进口全固态发射机。年底,天津市无线电视发射覆盖任务全部转移到天塔。

1994 年启用天塔管理中心与中国广电部设计院联合制定的“天津广播电视塔分布式计算机监控系统工程方案”。

1996年从国外引进多路微波分配系统(MMDS),用于微波频道,将天津有线电视台和中央台节目传送到天津四郊五县。

1999~2000年,天塔与天津计算机研究所合作对五套电视发射机和三套调频发射机进行实时监控改造。2001年,天津广播电视局对天塔实时监控系统工程进行验收,认为该系统具备对电视和调频发射机自动开关机、自动巡检、故障自动倒机、自动抄表和信息自动存储等多种监测和控制功能。先进性、可靠性、稳定,增色达到设计要求。

2004年3月,天津广播电影电视集团与清华大学合作开发天津数字电视地面广播,可在时速120千米的交通工具上接收电视节目,且图像稳定、清晰,音质好。同年开始对清华DMB-T标准做单点发射、移动接收的开路试验,结果表明在天津广播电视塔使用DMB-T制式的数字电视发射机对天津地区进行数字电视信号覆盖完全可行。

四、卫星地球站

1998年,天津市广播电视局进行广播电视卫星地球站建设,选定杨柳青发射台为站址。广电局李汝勤、邓卉、李广全等负责方案设计,组织系统集成、安装、调试。同年12月18日天津广播电视卫星地球站通过亚洲卫星公司的入网测试,投入试运行播出。12月28日6时55分天津广播电视卫星节目向全国和东南亚的部分地区播出。国内首家实现从节目播出到卫星接收的全数字广播电视节目传输和利用中波发射台建设卫星地球站;在国内广播电视卫星地球站系统中,首家采用ku波段固态功率放大器,获2000年度天津市科技进步二等奖。

2004年天津卫星地球站完成Ku转C波段改造项目建设。天津卫视节目由使用亚洲3S卫星Ku波段转发器传输,转为使用C波段转发器传输,同年实现两套卫视节目在C波段播出。从而解决Ku波段雨衰造成的信号衰落,提高“天津卫视”节目的接收质量,适应节目24小时不间断播出的需要。该项目于2005年2月完成入网测试。

第五节 有线电视

天津有线电视专用网是一个能覆盖全市,技术先进、性能完善、安全可靠,能与国内、国际接轨,与现代化大都市相适应的广播电视和信息传输网,为天津市信息化建设提供功能强大、运行可靠的基础网络。有线电视网络实施的广播电视“村村通”工程,全部解决山区行政村和20户以上的自然村有线电视“村村通”,可以接收32套电视和收听3套广播节目收视问题。到2005年年底,天津仅有6个20户以下自然村84户农民尚未解决看电视听广播问题。天津电视台通过有线频道收转中央电视台和全国各省市电视台上星节目40余套,入网总数增到170万户。同时,在全市实施有线电视数字化。

一、山区电视工程

1999年12月蓟县山区“村村通”广播电视一期工程启动，2000年6月底全面竣工。该工程采用有线广播电视网为主、部分小前端补点的方案。即主干线采用二级光缆传输，个别光缆难以架设到的村建设卫星接收小前端，通过电缆分配网入户。

2004年8月30日全国“村村通”广播电视工作电视电话会议后，天津市按照“因地制宜，注重实效”的原则，把蓟县山区“村村通”广播电视二期工程的目标锁定在20户以上自然村，并在原“村村通”光纤网的基础上进行改造，延伸光缆到村。到2005年5月，安装有线电视用户868户，平均入户率76.6%，全部解决山区行政村和20户以上的自然村有线电视“村村通”，可以接收32套电视和收听3套广播节目。

二、电视专用网

天津广电局按照“天津市有线广播电视专用网技术方案”，于2000年实施天津有线广播电视专用网B平台（宽带数据业务的管理平台）一期工程，建设市区一级环网，为网络所覆盖的用户提供与Internet、天津信息港、网通、广电干线网的连接端口和宽带接入。

2001年又完成天津有线广播电视专用网B平台二期工程建设，包括天津市区数据平台二级环网和天津市所辖区、县数据骨干网络的建设。构成较为完整的天津市城域范围内的宽带数据交换平台。

2002年实施的三期工程，进行接入网改造，全市建设近600个光节点，接入模式根据实际情况采用双绞线或电缆调试解调器（Cable-Modem）方式。

三、电视网络

2002年，天津市网络公司完成的“天津市广播电视网络有限公司NOC（网络运行管理中心）项目”投入使用。NOC是全市网络通讯管理、监控和维护，解决网络问题、路由管理、性能监视的主要部门。NOC主要由网络管理系统和安全系统组成，用以解决全市网络的隐患，减少网络发生故障时的经济损失。

2003年，天津广播电视网络电视有限公司“利用HFC双向网的空余资源实现多点监控系统的技术方案”投入使用。该方案包括解决图象传输、控制信号传输、多点分控等方面的具体问题。同年7月该公司完成“应用于网络电视的大规模流媒体点播平台”建设。其核心技术——大规模流媒体点播平台，是以网络服务、应用服务、数据存储三层体系为架构，以SAN和流媒体服务集群为硬件核心，并引入负载均衡技术对大规模、高强度流媒体点播进行控制和引导，使设备集群可以达到支持一万个并发流媒体点播的能力。当月，该公司还建成网络运行中心信息管理系统，集信息检索、查询、记录、整理、输出打印为一体，实现文档、单据无纸化。

2004年，该公司又完成数字电视集成平台建设。该平台是唯一能为天津市行政区内用户提供端到端数字电视业务服务机构，可播出84套数字电视节目和10套数字广播节目，播出容量相当于45套模拟电视节目，广电总局SDH网络传输的39套数字电视节目，约占用14个模拟频道。最终根据节目的增加播出系统容量将扩容到150套数字电视，使用25个模拟频道。另外安排2-3个模拟频道播出数据广播，安排相应频道播出NVOD。是年年底，全市建成1550光纤系统为骨干的有线电视模拟传输网（A平台），系统设计带宽862千赫兹，网络用户达到180万。建设全市骨干数据网（B平台），骨干带宽622兆比特/秒。全市骨干网络结构为3环1线。全市共建立核心机房2个，一级分中心机房19个，二级分中心机房18个。市区建成600个光节点工程，每个光节点平均覆盖2000有线电视用户，共120万用户。

四、有线数字电视

从2002年开始，天津广播电视网络有限公司进行有线数字电视试验，拟用8个模拟频道传输有线数字电视试验节目。其中3个模拟频道传输中央广播式VOD节目，1个模拟频道传输中央电视台6套数字电视节目，其他4个模拟频道传输自办数字电视节目，包括8套境外节目、12套境内卫星节目以及股票、游戏、电视杂志等。

2002年10月，天津有线数字电视播出系统建成并投入使用。天津数字有线电视播出系统一期建成后，实现节目源自由切换和调度，该系统充分利用Motorola设备特性，实现1+1备份和原距离的光传输。

2005年，天津市有线电视实现网络整合，做到一市一网，为有线电视的数字化过渡和网络多功能开发提供条件，并在一些小区进行有线数字电视试验，制定有线数字电视整体平移计划。

第六节　监测与动力保障

自1992年起，天津广播电视系统设专门技术部门对播出效果进行监听、监看和监测。为领导和播出部门提供第一手的科学监测数据，以先进的技术手段保证播出安全。

截至2005年，天津市广播电视电影集团的变配电系统形成9座电站、26台变压器，运行总容量13575千伏安的供电规模。其中8个10千伏站：卫津路变电室、天津广播电视塔和杨柳青发射台3处都是3路电源供电。先进的动力保障技术成为优质播出的有效保障。

一、监测

1992年，天津市广播电视局维护处建成小型监测系统。对天线、接收、监测和信号控制各子系统调整，增加监测屏幕墙和信号控制台。

2000年6月，实施“广播电视监测系统技术改造方案”。同年10月，应用计算机实施科学、自动管理的广播电视监测。此次改造规模较大，更新全部监测设备，实行对广播、电视播出效果的全方位全天候的自动监测。既可依靠DAS—2000分布式广播音频数字记录系统，进行硬盘录音（备查），又可通过局域网实现远端查询。值班员还可通过广播中心、中波发射、调频发射的三个途径的信号迅速判断故障环节。实时记录故障现象，并可通过局内网络随时查询。

是年，天津广电局王世良、张志英、裘毓勤等完成“自动化网络化广播电视监测系统”。广播、电视信号的载波监测是取自广播调谐器和电视机的AGC直流电平信号，将其送至MAVD型多通道峰值电平图示仪，该仪器具有载波越限报警、记录和彩色光柱直观显示的功能。

2003年，天津广电局再次对监测系统进行更新改造，试用具有大容量计算机硬盘记录功能的电视自动监测系统，实现对四套电视播出内容进行全天候的监测和随录。其监测功能包括彩底、彩条、无视频、无伴音等。其具有便捷的网络查询和灵活友好的显示界面，随录的内容可保留三天。是年，全国有线广播电视监测网天津有线监测分中心建成并投入运行。该中心担负着天津市有线广播电视网络播出的监测任务。其监测规模更大，并通过超大容量的计算机硬盘系统随录各个频道的节目内容，以备查考。

二、动力保障

1991年，天塔变电站共安装6台干式变压器，3390千伏安。3路10千伏电源供电，高压自投，“全主全备”运行方式，合同容量10170千伏安，成为广播电视局第一座3电源和唯一的“全主全备”站。

1995年1月，天津市广播电视国际新闻中心变电站建成启用。该站安装主变八台，总容量6325千伏安，是广播电视局第一座容量超过6000千伏安的变电站，是原有容量1700千伏安的3.72倍。单位建筑面积供电能力达61.8伏安/平方米(6325千伏安/10.2318万平方米),是原37.5伏安/平方米(1700千伏安/4.5318万平方米)的1.65倍。被称为“华北第一站”。该站由三路10千伏电源供电,运行方式为“二主一备,备用自投”。站内电气设备,高压系统选用手车式真空开关柜,干式变压器,低压系统设备为多米诺开关柜。天津市广播电视国际新闻中心变电站低压系统属“双主变暗备用”的供电方式,重要负荷均在用户末端低压自投,用户侧且配置UPS电源,供电可靠性高。

1997年10月,天津广电局与天津大学自动化学院合作研制成变电室微机管理实时检测系统,随后又完成微机管理电量计费一期工程,2002年完成二期工程,并接入局内局域网运行。

2001年12月,在广电系统变电站内使用天津广播电视电影集团与天津大学电器与自动化学院联合研制的“智能化电能量实时检测与结算系统”,使广电系统内各用户电能自动准确计量,电费的分类、分时段计费以及电力负荷的实时监测和负荷的科学管理。该系统具有模块化、通用化和网络化的技术特点,同时具有B/S、C/S的网络集成。截至2004年,该系统安全运行两年多,完全达到设计要求,功能齐全、运行稳定、计量准确、数据可靠,使天津广电系统在电能计量、计费及负荷管理上实现计量自动化、管理信息化、决策科学化;既保证系统内部节能增效,又确保广播电视的安全播出。

2005年,完成天塔变配电系统改造。其综保系统的结构采用总线型、模块化的开放性系统,各采集单元均为智能化设备,与上位计算机共同完成遥测、遥控和现场测控,并与其他智能设备通讯并做集成。它可以对用电系统进行自动化管理,高压遥测测量相电压、线电压、三相电流、零序电流、有功功率、无功功率;低压进线及各出线回路能测量三相相电压、线电压、三相电流、零序电流、有功功率、无功功率、功率因数、三相不平衡度、谐波含量,保护开关动作,开关变位状态及报警;温度测量:对变电室内的变压器进行温度监测,并能报警和提供多种报警信号和报警处理。

第十章 计量与标准

1991年后,由于市场经济建设发展和滨海新区开发建设需要,天津市加快筹建新的最高计量标准装置的速度。1991~2005年,天津采用国际标准和国外先进标准(以下简称“采标”)数量(种)共922项;标志数量361项。2005年年底,天津在几何量、温度、力学、电磁学、电子、时间频率、电离辐射、光学、声学、标准物质等十大类计量领域共建立最高社会公用计量标准231项,其中千克砝码工作基准装置、克砝码工作基准装置、活塞式压力计工作基准装置三项标准为国家工作计量基准。

1991~2005年,天津的标准化技术发展大体可分三个阶段。1991~1996年工业采标以六大支柱产业为重点,农业开始推行标准化示范工程。代码条码技术刚刚起步。1997年后,以滨海新区开发开放为契机,天津的重点行业的主要产品全部采用国际标准组织生产。农业以副食品为主的产品建立地方标准体系。天津开发出组织机构代码网络管理系统和条码商品信息服务系统。2001年后,六大支柱产业普遍采标,全面开花。农业标准化围绕三个体系建设,实施农产品标准监督。组织代码与商品条码技术普遍应用。

第一节 计 量

1991~2005年,天津市新建计量标准共76项。针对工业、财贸、卫生等方面的实际需要和完善国家计量检定规程的要求,研究开发出长度、温度、力学、理化等各类计量检定、检测用仪器装置,天津的计量检定检测水平进一步提升。1991年9月6日"国家计量先进单位颁证大会"在津举行。天津市有58个企业荣获国家计量先进单位。2004年,天津与河南、广东合作完成国家质检总局项目"测量边界允许误差单向性理论及其应用研究",提出测量边界允许误差单向性理论,对制定产品标准、计量检定规程和规范等工作具有指导意义。

一、计量标准

自1991年至2005年,天津市新建计量标准共76项。1991年,天津建立滚轮式皮带秤、悬臂式电子皮带秤两项力学检定装置及一氧化碳和二氧化碳红外线气体分析仪、汽车排放气体测试仪、色散型红外分光光度计、荧光分光光度计、原子吸收分光光度计、火焰光度计、粉尘采样器等7项理化类检定装置。1992年建立医用超声源1项声学类检定装置。1993年建立高绝缘电阻测量仪、绝缘电阻表及脑电图仪等3项检定装置。1994年没有新的计量检定或校准装置建立。1995年建立木直(折)尺检定器、一等金属量器、二等金属量器、压力(差压)变送器等标准及铯原子频率标准装置和公用电话计费器检定装置。5年间,天津市计量检定所共建立市级计量标准19项。

1996年,天津建立水泥胶砂搅拌机、水泥胶砂振动台、水泥净浆搅拌机和耐电压测试仪、交流数字功率表、心电监护仪6项检定装置和直流比较仪式电位差计、超声波探伤仪等2项标准装置。1997年,又建立质量流量计、饮用量器等2项检定装置。1998年未建标。1999年是历年来天津建立计量标准最多的一年,有温度计量类工作用辐射温度计检定装置,长度计量类三坐标测量机检定装置,力学计量类数字压力计、轴(轮)重仪、定量包装机、液态物料定量灌装机、心脑电图机检定仪等检定装置,电磁计量类检定直流低电阻表、指针式频率表、交流电能表及交流电能表检定装置等,还有光学类电脑验光仪检定装置和理化类生化分析仪检定装置。全年建标13项。2000年,只有热量表标准器组一项。1996~2000年,5年间总计建标24项。

2001年,建立力学计量标准9项,即转速表、水表、立式计量罐、卧式计量罐、球形计量罐、水泥罐、汽车罐、船舱检定装置及钟罩式气体流量标准装置。电磁计量标准2项,即电流互感器和电压互感器检定装置。2002年,建立力学类标准动平衡机、扭矩扳子、滑板式汽车测滑检验台及摩托车轮偏检测仪、滚筒式车速表检验台、滚筒反力式制动检验台等5项,理化类标准建有二等标准酒精计、二等标准密度计及(CT)X射线辐射源、液相色谱仪检定装置,还有光学类汽车前照灯检测仪检定装置共10项。2003年仅4项,长度类水准仪和经纬仪检定装置,力学类的回弹仪和IC卡电话计时计费检定装置。2004年未建标。2005年力学类建有液位计与可燃气体检测报警器检定装置、气体流量与液体流量标准装置和咪表检定装置,光学类阿贝折射仪、医用激光源及理化类的气体氧分析仪检定装置。2001~2005年,5年间总计建标33项。

二、计量检定检测

(一)长度计量

1996年,天津市计量技术研究所(以下简称"市计量所")赵一党、郭维哲、田耀光等采用光栅技术开发研制出"KJY-300型光栅数显式卡尺检测仪",使卡尺检定实现数字显示连续测量,为企业提高生产的卡尺产品质量,提供更为科学的技术检测手段,为计量量值的统一提供技术保证。该技术在国内已推广应用。2005年,该所田勇、路瑞军、孙建华等完成"光滑极限量规检定装置控制系统"的研制。光滑极限量规检定装置原为英国20世纪60年代产品,自动化测量程度低,其电控部分为电子管元件组成的电路,且因部分元器件损坏已无备件维修,装置处于待报废状态,但其机械部分性能尚完好。该项研制通过采用集成电路实现高精度信号放大、滤波电控箱及计算机控制系统,选配新型回转检测传感器替代原控制系统,实现测量信号的自动采集、处理、自动输出测量结果。旧设备更新改造,提高工作效率。

(二)温度计量

1995年,市计量所贾瑞华、季可、杨全喜等研制出体温计校准装置。该装置通过对高纯有机物质的选择与提纯内装置的研究,研制玻璃三相点池并建立高纯物质密封装填系统和抽空系统,研制一套体温计校准装置并已用于医疗机构。1999年，该所高勇、刘巍、王超英等完成“超长恒温区立式温度检定装置”的研制。该项目为保证温度计量检定的准确可靠，检定过程中必须具有恒定稳定达标的温场，经大量试验，研制出恒温区域：200毫米～250毫米，温度范围：300℃～600℃，水平温场：0.2℃，垂直温场：0.5℃的超长恒温区立式温度检定装置，可满足长感温区的温度仪表计量检测需求。2001年，该所王立新、尚世声、王美华等完成“表面温度计综合检定装置”的研制。通过采用一套检定装置，实现对接触式和非接触式两类表面温度计的检定。2003年，该所王立新、侯明锋、蒋静等完成“一、二等铂电阻温度计标准装置”的研制。该项研究通过利用新技术对整套标准装置进行改造，使其在自动化水平、控温准确度、环保等方面技术水平有显著提高。

（三）力学计量

1990年，市计量所刘景利、宫风顺完成“DS-1型模拟科氏音发生器研制”。模拟科氏音发生器是检定电子血压计的必备设备，通过该设备模拟产生人体脉动信号、即科氏音信号，以其为标准信号，实现对电子血压计的计量检定。该设备具有准确度高、性能稳定、操作方便。同年，市计量所与天津市纺织工业研究所合作研制成“电动单元组合仪表检定装置”。该装置能检测温度、压力、电参数等多项检测内容，具有功能齐全、性能稳定、读数直观、操作安全、使用范围广等特点。1992年，市计量所刘景利、王立新、宫风顺等开发研究“膨胀法真空检定装置微机控制和检测”。使真空检定装置通过微机控制实现人机对话，全面实现对真空系统的控制、检测、计算和打印功能，可满足真空计检定、校准的工作要求。

1993年，市计量所张大建、张伟、尚家甫等完成四屏显示出租车里程计价表的研究。因当时国内城市出租汽车行业发展很快，原有的“分立元件”“一屏显示”“时距分离”计价及干簧管接触测量转数的技术产品，急需新产品取代。该成果采用集成电路、微电脑技术，研制出能及时显示“行驶距离”“等候时间累积”“收费金额”和“时间”的四屏显示、时距并进及应用霍尔元件非接触测量车轮转数，具有抗干扰能力强和防作弊能力强的第一代多功能集成电路的出租车里程计价表。该研究成果为国内出租汽车里程计价表技术换代提供技术支撑，获1995年度天津市科技进步二等奖。1997年该所张斌、宁书岩、刘勇等研制的“计价器综合测试仪”，是针对当时国内尚无该种专用测试仪的情况，研制出的适应性广、成本低的实用型专用测试仪。使用该仪器后，在出租汽车计价和维修过程中，可迅速查找出影响正常计量中各参数的误差及损坏部位程度，缩短计价器维修时间，提高维修工作效率和质量。2000年，该所张斌、戚英、刘勇等又完成“出租车计价器检定专用红外线遥控器”的研制。通过研制一种高可靠性、高安全性的出租车计价器检定装置专用的红外线遥控器，实现对原有计价器检定装置从有线控制到无线控制，减少人为操作误差，提高检定工作效率15%～20%，并保证控制的安全性。

1996年，市计量所和天津市玻璃器皿厂陈兴、李长生、郭胜利、闫盛海等完成“啤酒量杯”的研制。当时，在国内啤酒销售中使用以“扎”为单位进行计量，造成计量单位制的混乱，为保证国家计量单位制的统一，禁止制造非法定单位的量器，天津在国内率先制造推广以升为单位的“啤酒量杯”。同年，该所张抗美、马增润、高森林等研制开发出“LD系列智能防腐流量计”。该流量计适用于任何导电液态的流量计量，尤其适用于强酸强碱腐蚀性介质流量的计量，可提高化工生产流量计量耐腐蚀能力，延长使用寿命，保证生产的连续性。该项成果已应用到天津盐厂、天津硫酸厂等企业。1997年，市计量所刘景利、郭维哲、唐永珍等研制的“燃气调压站微压记录仪”，是具有时间、压力可随时采集、储存（可以储存15天内的压力随时间变化的信息）、传输功能的微压记录仪。若与测试点微机联网，可实现对管网的燃气压力统一调控。测量范围0～5000帕、测量精度±1.5%FS（满量程）（测量精度fs=full scale最大误差仪表满里程），最小分辨率10帕。1999年市计量所杨金奇、王凤海、高茜等和天津第一市政公路工程有限公司第二机械站杨志明共同完成“意大利进口混凝土搅拌站称重系统挖潜改造”项目。该项目是在进口机械设备因损坏已无法使用的情况下，通过改变其结构并将原称重系统提高一个准确度等级，使该套进口设备重新投入国家重点工程施工中，继续发挥其重要作用。该成果广泛应用于市政、建筑等行业。

2003年，市计量所陈兴、田生亮、张大建等完成“天然气自动计量系统”的研究。该项目通过采用多种国际领先的新设备、新工艺，配合自行设计的测量软件，解决对大宗天然气的自动精确计量问题，并最终解决长期困扰天津市燃气公司和大港油田的天然气计量问题。2004年，该所陈兴、刘振中、李晓仲等完成“加油机计量自动检测装置”的研制。该项目针对在加油机上作弊，坑害消费者的问题。以高准确度液位、温度采集系统、专用标准量器、智检仪及数据处理等技术手段及措施，实现车载“暗访式”加油机计量监测装置。该装置为计量执法现场检定提供科学公正数据，使利用计量器具作弊的不法行为受到遏制。2005年，该所韩胜利、王立新、王凤海等完成“钢砼电子汽车衡”的研制。该项研究因采用钢砼与钢纤维复合型台面，其电子汽车衡准确度高，具有防腐、防静电功能，并降低成本、节约能源。

(四)理化计量

1991年，市计量所张大建、贾瑞华、张斌等研制成“气相色谱仪检定装置”。该装置采用双积分原理数字测量技术，由Z80系列芯片组成，系国家计量检定规程所需的检定装置。经国家技术监督局评定其成果属国内首创，在全国计量检测单位广泛应用。1994年该所贾瑞华、季可、杨全喜等完成温度定点装置研究。通过研制高纯度物质、温度恒温槽及微机自控系统，建立高纯度物质密封装填系统和抽空系统，研制出温度定点装置。可作为温度次级标准，广泛用于生产、科研及计量部门。1996年该所张大建、张伟、张艳等研制的“色谱仪检定专用测量仪B型”，解决“色谱仪检定专用测量仪A型”所涉及不到的检定项目的检测技术问题，两者配套使用可实现对色谱仪所需检定的全部技术指标。该仪器的研制成功，实现对色谱仪的自动检测，进一步提高量值传递的可靠性。该成果已在国内计量检定机构广泛应用。2000年，该所贾瑞华、张大建、季可等研制成功“高精度低温凝固点下降测量装置”。该装置是通过将Smit装置改进应用于低温，用计算机控制温度并记录完整的凝固曲线，可准确确定凝固点和高纯有机物质的纯度。2003年该所张志宏、魏桂华、何霞等研制出“精密温湿度发生器”。该设备温度调节范围是5℃～50℃，不确定度是±0.5℃，湿度调节范围10～95%RH，不确定度±2%RH，是计量部门对温湿度表进行计量检定必备的标准设备。

第二节 标 准

1991～2005年，天津采标数量(种)共922项；标志数量为361项。1997年1月8日天津市第十二届人民代表大会常务委员会通过《天津市实施〈中国人民共和国标准化法〉办法》，全面推进标准化工作的开展。先后出台《天津市地方标准管理办法》等地方性法规，制订“商品房面积计量”“蔬菜中农药残留最高限量”“卫生湿巾”等数百项地方标准。天津标准化工作步入健康发展的快车道。2003年，天津市质量技术监督局被国家标准委授予“2003年度全国标准化工作先进单位”。

1990年前后，随着国民经济信息化与国际接轨的步伐加快，天津开始推行组织机构代码标识制度，并启动条码技术的实施。1999年前后，天津开发出“天津商品信息服务系统——条码软件”和“天津市组织机构网络管理系统——代码软件”。2004年，相继完成对全市所有组织机构代码历史档的电子扫描，天津在代码、条码技术上走在全国前列。

一、采标

1991年，天津市按照国务院《产品质量振兴纲要》确定的目标，瞄准重点产品，推动企业采用国际标准或国外先进标准。同时，结合改革和开放的形势，对技术引进、技术改造项目，要求必须采用国际标准和国外先进标准，以使产品质量达到国际水平。并在企业采用国际标准申请贷款、政府贴息、项目纳入科技成果评定以及评选地方名牌产品等方面给予政策支持。各区县政府、市各有关部门也都将“采标”工作纳入自己的计划，进行考核认定，推动全市采标工作深入发展。

1991～1993年，贯彻落实国家技术监督局《全国技术监督工作纲要》《天津市“八五”期间管理现代化发展规划》，制定天津市采标验收及管理办法。

1994年，天津将所确定的重点采标项目上报35项，争取列入国家级重点新产品试制鉴定计划。经国家技术监督局批复14项享受“增值税先征后返”等减免税政策，8项享受“增值税先征后返”政策。

1998年，贯彻国务院“质量振兴纲要”，突出基础元器件和重大技术装备产品的采标比重。同时，启动区街和乡镇企业采标工作。有2项采标重点产品被纳入国家级重点新产品试制鉴定计划，获得国家5个部委颁发的国家级新产品证书。

2000年后，围绕天津经济工作抓好结构调整、技术创新、扩大开放，积极研究WTO/TBT规则，完成“贸易技术壁垒对天津经贸发展的影响及其对策”的研究。将采标工作的着眼点放到如何适应中国加入世贸组织后的新形势，引导和帮助企业熟悉和掌握WTO/TBT规则，积极应对技术贸易壁垒影响，扩大国际市场。2005年，对涉及天津经济发展中六大支柱产业的537家企业，1556种产品的采标情况进行调查研究，有635种采用国际标准，803种采用国外先进标准，综合采标率达到92%，1556种产品实现的工业总产值达到全市工业总产值的60%，出口创汇近百亿。

二、标准化

（一）企业标准化

1991年3月4日天津颁发“天津市企业标准化管理办法”。1992年5月5日又颁发“天津市产品执行标准登记证书管理办法”。1997年公布实施《天津市实施〈中国人民共和国标准化法〉办法》。天津钢管公司、渤海化工集团、汽车公司的主要产品全部按照国际标准组织生产，加速支柱产业、重点行业与国际惯例的接轨，提高企业技术进步和市场竞争力。

2004年开展和推广工业企业标准化良好行为活动，经企业自愿申请，确定4个国家级试点企业和20个市级试点企业。2005年天津市4个国家级试点企业通过国家标准委组织的AAA级确认验收，4个企业通过天津市质量技术监督局组织的AA级确认验收，12月8日召开全市“创建标准化良好行为企业推进工作会”。

（二）农业标准化

1.标准化示范工程

1992～1993年天津在蓟县推行瘦肉型猪标准化示范工作；在西青区王稳庄乡推行淡水养鱼标准化示范工作；在西青区上辛口乡推行蔬菜基地标准化示范工作。1994年确定武清县为粮食作物综合标准化示范县试点，宁河县为瘦肉型猪综合标准化示范县试点。1995年，蓟县、宝坻、宁河瘦肉型猪标准化示范工作列入国家1995年至1998年农业标准化工程计划。1996年新增塘沽区人工养殖虾标准化示范工程。

2.地方标准体系

1997年制定“无公害蔬菜”等评价性农业地方标准，提高农业科技成果转化生产力的速度和在农业经济增长中的份额。1998年完成瘦肉型猪国家示范项目和武清县林果市级示范项目的验收。制定并组织实施“绿色食品基地农药使用准则”。1999年组织开展无公害蔬菜生产示范工程，全面实施《蔬菜农残最高限量及测定方法》。2000年，汉沽区葡萄标准化示范区通过国家技术监督局验收。同年，天津市质量技术监督局被授予全国“农业标准化先进单位”称号。该局以加快提高农产品品质为重点，实施农业标准化体系建设，承担《农产品安全质量无公害蔬菜安全要求》《农产品安全质量无公害蔬菜产地环境要求》两项国家标准的起草工作。补充完善150项农业地方标准，组织制定50项农业地方标准。2004年贯彻全国农业标准化会议精神，围绕农业标准化三个体系：（标准体系、检测体系、监督体系建设），加强对农产品标准实施的监督。

三、代码与条码

（一）代码

为了对中国境内依法成立的机关、企业、事业单位、社会团体和民办非企业单位等机构赋予一个在全国范围内唯一的、永久不变的法定代码标识。天津市作为全国首批四个试点省市之一，于1989年推行组织机构代码标识制度。1993年，按照全国统一颁发代码证书的要求，天津建立以各行政区域管理为原则的代码证书发放体系。

1997年，国务院决定推行组织机构代码标识制度，并制订新的强制性国家标准。同年12月，出台强制性国家标准GB 11714-1997《全国组织机构代码编制规则》。1998年，根据国家要求，天津开始进行组织机构代码新版证书的更换和发放。1999年，进行组织机构代码证书年检及发放组织机构代码IC卡。

2000年，天津市技术监督信息研究所王金海、冯连景、左庆普研究开发出"天津市组织机构代码网络管理系统"，并在全国首次采用网络化两级管理、实行集中赋码的新方法。从而自根本上解决组织机构代码重名重码问题，并广泛应用于银行、税务、统计、公安等部门，显示出代码的准确性与唯一性。由此使天津市组织机构代码数据质量发生质的飞跃。

同年，该所王家祥、由方岚、陆钧开等利用计算机对信息的采集加工整理，对外提供服务从传统的信息服务向电子服务的转变，开发出"电子信息服务系统"。该系统具有界面友好，操作简单，信息采集规范化，存储安全，达到人机结合提高工作效率的目标，并实现信息网上交流功能，大幅提高工作效率。是年，陆钧等又开发出"组织机构代码IC卡与CA合一网络安全应用系统"。该项目成功地将现实社会中的组织机构的身份证——组织机构代码证与虚拟网络社会中的身份安全证明——CA证书合为一体，确保在电子政务和电子商务活动中，数字信息传输时的安全性、完整性、准确性和不可抵赖性。用以保证组织机构在现实社会和虚拟的网络社会中，从事社会活动时，身份的一致性、合法性、真实性，实现多卡合一、信息资源共享。

2001年天津市技术监督信息研究所更名为天津市质量技术监督信息研究所。该所王金海、王雨、王家祥研制出"天津市组织机构代码名录"软件系统。该系统利用天津市组织机构代码信息库的信息，在信息化建设不完善的阶段，通过对企业基础信息的加工，为社会提供天津市组织机构的基本信息。系统采用广域网络化管理，通过利用国家经济行业分类标准，对数据进行分类，并利用组织机构代码的信息采集点进行信息采集。将所采集的信息经系统加工后，以电子图书或印刷品向社会发行。

2003年，天津市人民政府颁布1号令"天津市组织机构代码代表管理办法"于同年7月10日起施行。2004年，天津进行组织机构代码档案的电子化扫描，相继完成全市所有组织机构代码历史档案的电子扫描。

（二）条码

利用光电扫描设备实现机器自动识别商品，以达到自动化管理的商品条码技术在中国起步较晚但起点较高。1991年4月，中国加入国际物品编码协会（EAN）。此后，条码技术快速发展。到1995年年底，加入国际物品编码协会的中国企业已有21813家，位居世界第四位，国内采用条码标识的产品超过80万种。

1996～1997年，天津市技术监督信息研究所张含光、杨奎发、王磊在"条码技术在商业流通领域应用的研究"中，分析了天津商业自动化管理系统的现状，提出提高全市商业自动化程度的对策与建议。继而对商贸EDI——电子数据交换在天津开发应用的可行性进行研究，提出在全市推广实施商贸EDI以及建立天津市条码胶片制作中心的可行性方案及对策。1998～1999年，该所张然、王磊、杨奎发开发出"天津市条码商品信息服务系统"。该系统对天津市带有条码标识商品的企业生产信息、商品条码使用信息和运输包装条码使用情况的配销信息进行分析加工，为天津工商业提供产品的相关信息服务，为保证条码的真实性和唯一性，为建立国家条码商品信息网奠定基础。该系统结构设计合理，功能设置完善，具有较强的实用性、先进性和可操作性。该系统的建立，加快国民经济信息化和与国际接轨的步伐，为政府的宏观调控提供动态依据，同时还维护商品条码的真实性，避免假冒商品条码及"一物多码""多物一码"现象的发生。

2001年10月，天津市质量技术监督信息研究所王金海、陆钧、左庆普编著《现代条码技术与应用》一书，详细介绍国内外条码技术的发展史，阐明国际上常见条码码制的编码规则、特点、符号技术、识读、印刷和应用技术以及中国有关条码方面的规定和技术标准，便于条码技术的普及与应用。同时，该所陆钧、王磊、杨奎发完成"推广应用物流条码的可行性研究"，对物流条码和商品条码进行对比研究。从物流条码的标准体系、国内外物流条码的应用典型以及天津应用物流条码的可行性等方面予以阐述，有助于物流条码的推广。

第十一章 质量监督检验检疫

1991～2005年，天津市产品质量检测技术得到较快发展。机构体制的改革，进一步理顺领导关系，加强领导力量。一些检验技术单位整合升格为院，使产品质量检验技术力量相对集中，为技术发展提供组织保证。硬件设备的批量引进与自主创新使现代检验技术进一步普及推广，一些质量检验管理系统软件的开发为检验技术的发展提供物质保证。同时，大量产品质量标准的制定和一些检验方法的创新，进一步促进检验技术的能力与水平的提升，为提高产品质量提供技术保证。工业产品质量监督检测十分复杂。品种多，涉及到生活用品与生产用品等；目的多，涉及到质量安全、卫生执法、商贸等方面；方法多，涉及到尖端技术与适用技术等。

这一时期，天津的产品检测技术发展特点是：技术引进与自主创新相结合，以引进仪器设备为主，加速赶世界先进水平，以适应市场经济发展需求。在技术创新上，硬件与软件并举，既研制出各种用于产品检验的仪器、仪表、机具、装置等，又开发出用于检验管理和鉴定的系统软件，众多数据库、数学模型相应建立。在检测方法研究中，开展尖端学科交叉技术研究。检测技术，由常量发展到微量、痕量，建立起新型、超灵敏度的分析方法。

天津是口岸城市，负有进出口商品检验、进出境动植物检验检疫、出入境卫生检疫和食品卫生监督检验任务。1999年前，上述任务分别由天津进出口商品检验局、天津进出境动植物检疫局和天津出入境卫生检疫局承担。1999年8月根据国家检验检疫局的总体部署，以上三局合并组成天津出入境检验检疫局(以下简称“天津检验检疫局”)。该局肩负着既要为国家把关，又要促进外贸发展的重任。截止到2005年，该局已建有7个国家质检总局的国家级重点实验室，6个区域性实验室，共完成国家标准104项、行业标准77项，获国家科技进步奖1项、天津市科技进步奖10项、国家商检总局科技进步奖10项、国家质检总局“科技兴检”奖16项。在危险品检测、致病菌检测基因芯片研制以及转基因研究等尖端科技方面有重大创新。

第一节 产品质量检测

1991～2005年，天津在食品、药品、纤维品、电器、珠宝以及印刷、石化、建材、特种设备等工业产品质量检验技术不断取得进步。中药材、中成药检验技术的发展，使大批中药材、中成药有了定性、定量的检验方法、检验标准和标准品。光电纤维成分，含量检测仪器的成功研制，对纤维品成分、质量的检验方法更加准确、便捷。“门式液压可变幅式起重吊运系统”的研制，为天津市在超大型起重设备的检验提供静载荷试验的可行性与实用性。

随着农业产业结构的调整及城乡居民生活质量的不断提高，农业生产从单纯追求数量到注重农产品的数量与质量并重。中国加入世界贸易组织后，农产品直接参与国际竞争，天津市出口的农产品输往全球137个国家和地区，对农产品检测技术要求提高。农药残留量从分类检测发展到多残留检测；重金属检测由常量种类增加并发展到微量、痕量致病微生物检测，由聚合酶链式反应发展为多重聚合酶链式反应，可同时检测多种病菌；同时，研发出快速、精准和高通量检测转基因技术。

一、食品药品

（一）食品检测

1992年，天津市产品质量监督检验所杨家琮等在果汁饮料黄岩桔原汁的含量测定研究中，针对国内果汁饮料尚无检测原汁含量的指标和检测标准，对果汁和果汁饮料内在质量检验无可行依据，产品质量难以控制等问题，研究出以质量监督为目的的多参数测定方法，并提出参数的标准值和变动范围，建立起果汁含量对应参数的数学模型。是年，该所孟宪钟等采用气相色谱法对白酒中主要香气成分进行完全分离定量，并用白酒标准样品与实际酒样进行对比鉴定，为鉴别白酒的真优伪劣提供准确、快速的可靠方法，具有很好的实用性。1999年，该所李旗等在“人参保健食品鉴别及营养成分检测方法的研究”中，通过高效液相色谱法对人参主要成分进行分析，确定人参保健食品主要成分的鉴别及分析方法。成果推广应用后为人参保健品检测提供一种快速、简便、准确的实用技术及鉴别真伪的手段，居于国内领先水平。2001年前，国内检测碳酸饮料多用二氧化碳容积倍数法，测试手段笨重、落后。2001年，天津市武清区产品质量监督检验所与天津市纺织工业研究所根据国家标准共同研制出智能二氧化碳测试仪，获国家发明专利。2005年，天津市产品质量监督检测技术研究院高亦军等完成“天津市食品行业生产技术现状分析及提高质量安全水平的研究”。该研究通过对调味品、肉制品、冷冻饮品生产企业的规模、产值、设备、设施、产品质量、检验能力等情况进行调查和数据统计分析，建立数学模型，提出天津市食品企业生产技术现状、存在的主要问题和产生原因，以及提高天津市食品安全水平的建议。成果推广应用后，有效提高天津市食品行业质量安全水平。

（二）药品检验

1.设备与装置

1991年后，天津市人民政府支持天津市药品检验所（以下简称“市药检所”）申请的“中日技术合作项目”。该所通过日本国际协力事业团渠道，于1993年获得日方提供5.26亿日元的合作经费，用于购进日本现代分析检验仪器与对技术人员的培训。市药检所在硬件设备技术上跃居国内一流水平。该项目的引进为更新药品检验技术，特别是为中药与中成药的检验提供现代化技术方法。

1992年，市药检所与中国药品生物制品检定所合作，开发出“天津药品检验及药品质量监督管理系统”软件。为该所实施业务管理智能化创造条件。同年，该所宫作铭等研制出“YB-1型药物熔点仪”。该仪器采用真空玻璃杯，硅油传温液、电磁搅拌，程序设计完全符合中国、欧洲等国药典对熔点测定的要求。程序设计合理，升温准确，且可将被测样品在其熔点的前10度放入仪器中等待，测样时升温速率任意设定，并设有高温过温保护。该仪器的研制使国内在药品的熔点测定，得以统一化、规范化、标准化。当年被国家科委等单位评为国家级新产品。1993年，该所杨泽生等针对市场无上开盖带窥视镜便于观察样品变化的干燥箱，开发研制出“YB-1型真空恒温干燥箱”。该仪器设计原理采用双层样品架、真空压强自动调节，将单向自动保护阀、微型放气阀等集于一体。该成果转让给天津大学精密仪器系投产。

1998年，市药检所刘树春在“栓剂溶出度测定方法的研究”中，通过对几种不同装置的设计与实验比较，研制出横置旋转渗透池栓剂溶出度测定装置。在用于栓剂的溶出度测定时，运动过程平稳，缓慢，可产生类似肠蠕动效果。在栓剂融化之后，仍与内溶出液有一个反方向运动，使栓剂自由吸附在渗透膜上，达到完全溶出的目的，可满足药品质量控制所要求的高重现性，适于栓剂类药品的质量控制。

2.方法与标准

1991年，市药检所在参加卫生部制定“进口药材质量标准与检验方法”的项目研究中，吸取传统中药经验鉴别的精华，结合生物来源查找并提取有效成分，采用现代检测技术，制定出符合中国用药习惯的检验方法与质量标准。其中，采用气相色谱法鉴别豆蔻、麝香；红外光谱鉴定天然牛黄；薄层色谱法检定熊胆、西洋参；紫外分光光度法测定血竭吸收度及天然牛黄中的胆酸、胆红素含量；显微鉴别犀角、羚羊角等。同年，该项目获国家科技进步二等奖。上述进口药材的检验方法收载于《进口药材质量标准》中。

同年，市药检所完成卫生部组织的“澄清中药材混乱品种”项目研究任务。重点对市售的8种贯众进行分析。其中，分离出绵马贯众的活性成分，并采用薄层层析法和薄层扫描法进行含量测定。该项目获1991年度国家科技进步三等奖。1992年，该检验方法收载于《中国药典1995年版一部》。

1993年，市药检所金智珠在中药材香附的气相色谱保留指数研究中，采用毛细管气相色谱法，比较不同产地、不同品种的香附挥发油色谱图，并对香附中含量较高组分的保留指数进行编谱。结果表明：不同产地的香附，其色谱图与保留指数一致。不同品种的香附中，竹节香附与香附的谱图与指数不同，而大香附则有望成为新的药材资源。该项研究所建立的香附挥发性成分标准气相色谱图与保留指数谱，可用于鉴别香附的真伪与混乱品种。该检验方法简便易行，可比性强，是一项新的药材鉴定方法。

同年，该所吕归宝等对中药及中成药制剂中活性成分测定方法进行研究。该研究采用高效液相色谱法先后测定甘草中的甘草酸、藤黄中的藤黄酸、香加皮中的4-甲基水杨醛、藿香正气水中厚朴酚和厚朴酸等活性成分。同时，对上述中药中的单体活性成分进行结构鉴定，制定对照品，从而制定出检测此类中药的质量标准。该检测方法分别收载于《中国药典1995年版一部》和《进口药材质量标准》。

1999年，市药检所高元泰等主编的《实用中药鉴别大典》一书经由天津市科技出版社发行，为生产、科研、临床等基层药检人员提供一部实用参考书。

2001年，南开大学生命科学院白刚与市药检所等单位共同完成天津市科委自然科学基金项目“植物超灵敏度免疫分析法研究”。该项目利用生药中的特异性抗原物质，制成特异性抗体，根据抗原与抗体的免疫学反应原理，对一些尚无测定方法的常用生药进行分析。先后对植物性生药甘草、人参、天花粉、茯苓、半夏及动物性生药麝香、牛黄、地龙等共十几种生药进行研究。从中筛选出特异性抗原物质，并将其制成单克隆和多克隆抗体，从而建立起新型、超灵敏的酶免疫分析法。

2002年，天津在市药检所内建立“天津市药品包装材料检测中心”，并在全市首次开展对药品包装材料的检测。检测范围从塑料、玻璃、陶瓷类药瓶扩展到包装用铝箔、聚氯乙烯硬片，以及胶塞类、复合膜类、输液袋类等。同时，研究检测方法，制定检验标准，使包装材料检测纳入药品质量检验规范。

中药对照品的研制一直是制约中药现代化发展的瓶颈。国家科技部把中国药典2000年版收载的对照品研制难度较大的70种中药列为“九五”攻关项目。莲子心对照品研究为其中之一，由市药检所寿国香等承担。该项研究采用制备色谱、树脂吸附、凝胶过滤等分离纯化技术研制出对照品。再以紫外、红外、核磁、质谱以及元素分析等方法测定对照品莲心碱高氯酸盐含量。同时，以离子对反相高效液相色谱法测定莲子心的有效成分——莲子心碱的含量，制定出其质量标准。该方法被载入中国药典2005年版，对进一步提升新版药典的科技含量和其在国际上的地位提供依据。

（三）纤维品检验

天津市对纺织纤维产品的检验多由天津市纺织纤维检验所（以下简称“市纤检所”）承担。该所始建于1950年，到1991年仅设有绵花、化纤、毛麻3个专业科室，纤维检验技术多沿用传统方法。1994年11月，该所由纺织局全建制划归天津市技术监督局管理，变更隶属关系。1997年，市纤检所的性质定为具有行政执法职能的事业单位。其主要职能是：纤维、纤维制品质量监督检验及行政执法工作，从而加速纤维产品检验技术的发展。

1998年，市纤检所刘宝礼、安志泉、冉祥凤等研制成功JFX-Ⅰ型便携式绵花品级实物标准压实仪。该仪器专用于绵花品级实物标准制作过程中的压实工序。使用该仪器可将绵花品级实物标准压实过程由原来的60天缩短为2天，压力可控、可调，从而改变以往沿用的以砖头等重物压实方法。该仪器可避免绵花品级实物在标准制作过程中被污染的弊端，实现制作过程仪器化。该压实仪可缩短实物标准制作周期，其压实绵花实物标准为首创。同年，该所安志泉、冉祥凤、吴晓晨研制开发出JFX-Ⅰ纤维、纤维制品检验证书及报告计算机管理系统。采用数据库编程软件完成检验证书及报告的编辑录入、编辑、修改、统计、打印等程序。由原来的手工出证变为计算机出证及计算机统计汇总。实现检验证书的计算机管理，该管理系统推广到全国16个省市，80多个单位应用。

判断纤维成分、检测纤维质量，通常主要靠手摸、眼看、火烧分析燃后灰的状态，而用化学方法进行检测确定纤维的成分和含量，则需要时间很长。用物理方法检验纤维的物理性能，用计数与修正系数校正纤维成分含量百分数，误差在±10%。2001年，市纤检所刘宝礼、安志泉、程明等研制出JFX-Ⅱ型微型光电纤维成份、含量检测仪，采用200倍光学镜和相应的结构组成，是一种现场使用的快速、便携式纤维成份、含量检测仪器。

（四）电器质量检测

1994年，天津市产品质量监督检验所（以下简称“市质监所”）苏一弓等完成“多功能耐压试验装置”研究。该装置采用交流可控调压、直流倍压整流、定时控制、零位过流保护、声光报警等技术，可用于产品的耐压、绝缘电阻、漏电流性能的测试。具有功能多，体积小，便于携带，适合现场检测等特点。1997年市质监所张存礼等完成“通用型电池容量放电性能测试系统”，该系统采用单片机循环检测，在控制单元和测量单元之间采用光电隔离技术，使电压测量精度重复性达到0.5%，具有测试方便、自动记录和输出，在国内首次实现对通用型电池容量测试仪器的自动化检测。1999年该所栗志成等完成“电热水器试验装置”研究，该装置测量范围涵盖GB4706.12-1995的内容，可对贮水式电热水器、水箱式电热水器、出口敞式热水器、开口式电热水器性能进行测试，电源部分采用稳压及高温绝缘性能的电力隔离技术，既保证测量精度及标准要求，又可根据需要选用采温点，自动运算出温升、温度等指标，实现自动化控制。该成果推广应用后对有效监管相关产品质量，保证应用者安全，提供有效的检测设备。2000年，市质监所张存礼等研制成“锌银扣式电池自动放电检测仪”，该仪器采用单片机控制，电路采用软件抗干扰措施，保证电压测量精度，在放电过程中对电池电压进行巡回扫描，使电压测量精度重复性和一致性达到0.5%。同时，测试方便、省时省力，测试工作科学有效，该仪器可满足GB/T7168-1996和IEC60086-2标准要求，该成果推广应用后更便于对锌银扣式电池产品质量监管。

（五）珠宝质量检测

1992年，市质检所李大勇等研制的“黄金饰品压延机”，该机达到国家标准GB9288-88黄金含量分析方法中仪器和设备的要求，并具有体积小、重量轻和噪声低等优点。1996年，该所曹维宇等建立“珠宝玉石辅助鉴定信息系统”，该系统将计算机技术科学地运用到珠宝玉石的鉴定中，突破以往鉴定，在较大程度上依赖个人经验的局限，提高鉴定工作的客观性和可靠性。其所采用的数据库技术，用户可以不断丰富，又具有开放性，可为珠宝鉴定、教学和商贸提供应用。同年，曹维宇完成“宝石鉴定记录系统”，该鉴定记录系统是应用Foxbase数据库技术开发的应用软件，在宝石鉴定中具有快速输入、输出、查询和统计功能，可提高宝石检验工作效率，规范宝石鉴定用语。经市技监局组织的专家鉴定认为：该成果居于国内领先水平。2001年曹维宇等还完成“珠宝玉石检验信息管理系统”，该系统安全、可靠、稳定优化，能充分利用实验室检测资源，保证检测数据的准确性，使实验室检测的管理水平有所提高。

（六）印刷品检测

1996年前，国内用于油墨检验的相关仪器多系体积大，荷载压力不符合标准GB5211.19-88中规定的技术指标。市质监所苏传健等研制成功的“MJ-PM180平板研磨机”，其技术指标可满足上述标准要求，使油墨检验更加规范。2005年苏传健等研制成防伪全息产品特性指标检测仪，该检测仪采用具有稳定输出功率的氦—氖激光器，以保证测量精度；采用光机电一体化设计以使整体结构紧凑，可用于不同场合；采用自动扫描技术可使测量更加简便、快捷、准确。该项目的研究成功为印刷品防伪提供一种能满足防伪技术要求和符合管理规范的检测仪器。

（七）石化产品检测

20世纪90年代，天津的汽车保有量迅速增加，车用汽油、柴油消耗量不断增长，对车用石化产品质量检测技术创新要求迫切。1998年，市质监所蒲宏业等完成“汽车制动液模拟试验台”研究。该模拟试验台符合国标GB12981-91的技术要求，可按该项标准要求进行汽车制动液行程模拟试验，该试验台的研制成功，对提高国内汽车制动液的质量水平，确保行驶安全具有重要作用。

同期，由于石化产业增长速度加快，城市机动车燃油消耗量增加，排气污染日趋突出。在车用汽油中加入具有节能和清净效果的添加剂可以消除积碳，提高燃油的使用效率，改善机动车尾气排放。但必须加速制定出完善的石化产品质量标准，从源头控制机动车排气污染和节约能源的有效措施。2005年，天津质检院杨佳玲等研究制定出《含燃油添加剂车用汽油》《含燃油添加剂车用柴油》两项天津市地方标准。这两项标准是在GB17930的基础上增加燃油经济性、尾气排放污染物及清净性指标，对燃油品质和燃油添加剂品质的提升和天津市“蓝天工程”的有效实施起到重要作用，有效促进该市石化产业的发展。

（八）建材产品检测

2001年，市质监所孟少蒲等完成“陶瓷片密封水嘴测试系统”研究，完成的各项指标符合GB/T18145-2000技术指标要求，可按标准要求完成试验项目，项目在二冲程调节技术和多工位双层同心罗盘技术的应用方面具有创新，执行机构机械手由摆动汽缸和直线汽缸组合而成。该系统构思巧妙、新颖，具有环保、节水、集成化特点。

（九）特种设备检验

1980年，天津市锅炉压力容器技术检验所（以下简称“市锅检所”）成立。1991年设立天津市职业安全卫生检测检验所。1993年建立天津市锅炉水处理技术开发公司。2001年，上述三个单位均整体划转到天津市质量技术监督局，为其直属事业单位。随后，天津市锅炉水处理技术开发公司更名为天津市锅炉水质监测中心。天津市职业安全卫生检测检验所更名为天津市特种设备监督检验所（以下简称“市特检所”）。

2003年，市锅检所王泽军在“柱状圆筒超标径向开孔工程比对方法研究”中，从直接工程应用视角，针对锅炉、压力容器、压力管道中经常遇到的超标开孔结构及影响开孔结构强度的诸多几何因素进行分析，从而建立起完善的具有数值稳定性的开孔结构有限元应力分析模型，并在大规模系列计算的基础上建立起柱状圆筒超标径向开孔强度分析基础数据库。同时，给出在内压作用下，柱状圆筒超标径向开孔强度分析工程比对方法并开发出专用分析系统。该系统的应用，可使未掌握复杂有限元应力分析技术的技术人员快速对超标开孔结构进行强度评价，评价时间从5～7工作日下降到10分钟之内，取得明显的社会经济效益。

2004年，市锅检所、市特检所、天津市锅炉水质监测中心，三家单位组合建成天津市特种设备监督检验技术研究院（以下简称“市特检院”）。担负天津市特种设备（含锅炉、压力容器、压力管道、电梯、起重机械、游乐设施等）的监督检验、定期检验、型式试验、锅炉水质监测及相关的技术咨询、技术服务工作。

2005年，市特检院王泽军在“大型球形容器局部消应力热处理效果评价与参数优化”的研究中，采用数值模拟和试验相结合的方法，分析局部热处理的机理，对影响其效果的十种因素进行分析与归类，得出球形容器体积、壁厚、加热区域弧长半径和恒温温度是影响局部消应力热处理效果主要因素的结论，提出球形容器局部消应力热处理加热区域弧长半径的推荐准则。该项目研究解决大型球形容器局部热处理的机理及参数优化选择问题，研究成果有广泛的应用前景，对保障大型球形容器安全使用具有重要意义。

同年，市特检院郑质璞在“超大吨位起重机负荷试验检测技术研究”中，针对吊装能力最大负荷2500吨的门式液压可变幅式起重吊运系统无法采用常规起重机载荷试验方案的难题，依据检验规程，采用全高直立上下对拉加载，吊点处安装测力传感器控制，加载量的方式进行静载荷试验，载荷动力由设备自身的提升机构提供，载荷值的大小由测力装置监测、显示。经过实际操作起重载荷真实可信，数据计量准确，能保证设备的法定验收检验，能使相应机构和受力部件的承载能力得到检验证实。该技术的研制成功，为超大载荷试验开创了一种全新的思路和方法。

二、农产品检测

（一）农药残留检测

1998年，农科院植物保护研究所同天津市产品质量监督检验所、天津市乳品食品检测中心共同制定国内第一个地方性蔬菜农药残留标准——《蔬菜中农药最高残留限量和测定方法》（地方标准），经天津市技术监督局批准发布，在天津市范围内组织实施。该标准对天津市蔬菜种植中经常使用的57种农药的最高残留限量做出规定，其中马拉硫磷、对硫磷（1605）、甲拌磷、甲胺磷、久效磷、克百威、涕灭威等7种高毒农药在蔬菜种植中禁止使用,在蔬菜产品中不得检出;其余50种农药在蔬菜产品中的残留量不得高出地方标准规定的农药残留最大限量。同时,还规定市场与田间检测蔬菜农药残留情况的抽样规程和产品判定规则以及该标准的使用范围,为开展蔬菜产品中农药残留检测提供依据。

2002年,农科院中心实验室程奕、郭永泽等与日本杂贺技术研究所合作研究"农产品农药多残留检测技术"。该项目在引进、消化、吸收日本农药残留检测技术的基础上发展、创新,建立适应中国农产品出口需要的农药残留检测技术体系。到2003年共检测水果、蔬菜、油脂类、果汁类、腌渍类等不同农产品中62种农药残留量;到2004年,检测的残留农药种类扩大到80种;到2005年扩大到205种以上,包括拟除虫菊酯类11种、有机磷类52种、有机氯类18种、氨基甲酸酯类11种,以及其他杀虫剂18种、除草剂59种、植物生长调解剂2种、杀菌剂40种、杀螨剂10种。全部农药品种方法加标回收率达70%以上,3天即可提交检测报告,方法检出限和定量限达到多残留分析的要求。采用固相萃取净化技术和气质联用技术,通用性和实用性较强,具有方法先进、高效准确、快速实用等特点。固相萃取技术用于农产品中农药残留检测时,利用高效、高选择性的吸附剂将样品中的目标农药吸附,并与样品基体和干扰化合物分离,然后再用洗脱液洗脱,从而达到分离和富集目标农药的目的,其特点是不需要大量互不相溶的有机溶剂,处理过程中不会产生乳化现象。

农产品中农药多残留(200种以上)检测技术的研制成功及其应用较之以前的农药残留检测技术,工作效率有较大提高,检测一种农产品的205种农药残留,采用常规方法分类检测至少需要4人/7日,而应用农科院研制成功的检测技术只需2人/3日,提高工作效率90%,降低检测成本30%。

2001~2005年,郭永泽、张玉婷等结合天津市农业生产和城乡居民消费需求以及农产品出口外销的实际情况制定出"蔬菜水果""葱姜蒜"两大类农产品中205种农药多残留检测方法和"腌渍菜""果汁""花生大豆"三大类农产品中62种农药多残留检测方法纳入《天津市地方标准》,并经天津市主管部门颁布实施。《天津市地方标准》对五大类农产品中农药残留多组份测定方法之测定范围、测定步骤、定性(定量)测定、最低检出浓度、准确度和精确度作出具体详细的规定,为天津市这一领域的工作提出规范性行动指南。

(二)重金属检测技术

20世纪90年代,农科院中心实验室孟兆芳等开展农产品和食品中重金属检测的研究。先后采用紫外可见光光度法、原子吸收光谱法、原子荧光法、电感耦合等离子体质谱法等微量、痕量分析技术对农产品中重金属含量进行检测。可检测铅、镉、汞、砷、锑、铋、硒、碲、锡、锗、锌等11种重金属。2004年,孟兆芳等制定出《农产品中砷、汞联合快速测定法》(天津市地方标准),和指导全市各行业、和部门开展农产品中砷、汞的快速测定,对推动天津市农产品检测技术的发展起到重要作用。

(三)致病微生物检测技术

2003年,天津农业部门对传统的致病菌检测采用聚合酶链式反应法(PCR)。该方法操作繁琐,一般一次只能同时扩增检测少数几种微生物。2005年,农科院中心实验室王永等在"农产品及加工品中致病微生物快速检测的研究"中,按照分子生物学和生物信息学理论,对致病菌毒力岛靶基因保守性分析,研制出检测沙门氏菌、单核细胞增生李斯特菌、金黄色葡萄球菌和蜡样芽胞杆菌同步富集培养基配方。进一步研究出多重聚合酶链式反应技术。从而达到多种致病菌快速鉴定的目的。具有高效性、系统性、经济简便等特点。检测时间由几天、几个星期缩短到16小时,其敏感性、特异性明显高于传统的方法,检测成本降低80%以上。通过对82份样品进行检测,并与国际通用检测方法比较,其阳性符合率为100%。

(四)转基因检测技术

20世纪90年代,转基因农作物的食品安全问题已引起国人关切。2002年,王永等在国内率先开展农产品转基因快速、精准和高通量检测技术研究,开发出快速检测试纸(或试剂盒)技术,利用免疫层析的原理,将抗原或抗体固定在层析介质上,相应的抗原或抗体通过毛细泳动,与特异性物质结合后即滞留在该位区,根据显色反应即可作出判断。转基因快速检测技术具有快速、易于操作、使用方便、灵敏度高、检测费用低等特点。可在5~10分钟内检出0.1%的转基因成分。该技术研制开发成功,为食品加工企业验收原料提供技术服务,并为转基因农产品的市场标识和出入境大宗转基因农产品的检测提供技术保障,打破国外对该项技术的垄断,检测量每年达数百批次,为转基因农产品安全管理提供技术支撑。

2004年,王永等结合天津市农产品和食品转基因检测工作的实际情况,制定《鲜番茄及番茄制品中转基因成分的定性检测方法》和《以大豆为原料的酱油等发酵产品中转基因成分的定性检测方法》两部天津市地方标准,对鲜番茄及番茄制品中转基因成分和以大豆为原料的酱油等发酵产品中转基因成分的检测范围等内容作出详细规定。

第二节　出入境检验检疫

1991～2005年,天津食品安全、动植物检验检疫、危险品、卫生检疫等技术不断创新发展。1992～1997年,天津首创烟草双霉病的检疫标准,证明在天津地区可诱发小麦矮化腥黑穗病,从而严禁疫区小麦输入。2001年,天津对进口原木及木质包装的检疫除害处理技术有所创新,并找到能替代溴甲烷的检疫除害药剂。同期,在检测技术上解决植物转基因检测、家禽体内药物代谢残留量测定及饮料中多种抗氧剂的测定。2001年后,天津在食品出入境安全检测技术上,对果蔬着重包装、储运中的安全及农药残留量的检验方法研究;对肉类侧重加热终点检测及同化性激素残留检测。同时,研究开发出食源性致病菌检测基因芯片及聚合酶链式反应(PCR)检测方法,实现进出口食品安全监测与预警自动化。对危险化学品的检验主要从包装、储运管理标准及性能测试等方面进行研究。在安全理论及标准体系上均有所创新,建立起完整的危险化学品分类与方法标准体系及符合中国国情的安全评估理论体系和检验鉴定方法体系。此外,还对出口打火机安全性能进行研究,提出检验标准。

一、食品安全

(一)果蔬

2002年,天津检验检疫局王利兵、赵国庆、尚为等承担食品安全重大科技专项"食品储藏、包装与运输过程中安全关键技术研究"。在国内首次建立创新性果蔬保鲜技术体系,开发出特异性的基因诱导调控技术产品,并改善其耐贮性,推迟果蔬成熟、衰败,延长了货架期。在研究中,建立起一种基于HACCP原理,既适应国际上对食品安全控制技术的发展趋势,又符合中国实际,并可用来指导国内食品生产企业进行科学的安全加工、储运和包装。即具有中国特色的"食品加工、储藏、包装和运输的安全评估及危害控制"模式、规范、体系及其法规。该项目总投资2100万元,共获得国家专利15项,完成国家标准58项、行业标准58项。参与此项研究的有中国农大、卫生部、浙江大学、江南大学、荷兰瓦赫宁根大学等国内外研究机构的100多名研究人员。2004年,该局许泓、林安清、唐丹舟等对果蔬中107种农药残留量进行系统的检验研究。应用同一的提取、净化及GC-MS测定程序,确定最佳GC-MS的EI-SIM检测方法及107种农药的选择离子,既可用于筛选检测又可用于确证。研究中,在国内首次应用快速漩流浓缩技术,提高低沸点农药的回收率;首次应用MS No-vent快速切换技术,实现质谱不破坏真空更换色谱柱,避免基质中杂质的干扰。其方法操作简便、快速,定性定量准确,首次在国内实现果蔬中百种以上农药残留的同时测定,应用领域广泛。

(二)肉类

2005年,天津检验检疫局郑文杰、刘煊、贺艳等研制畜肉热加工终点温度检测试剂盒。该课题利用蛋白质组学最新研究成果,针对畜肉及其制品在蛋白质加热过程中所发生的变化开展比较研究,寻找牛、羊、猪肉及其制品加热终点温度指示蛋白质,建立加热终点温度的检测方法及检测试剂盒。同年,该局许泓、林安清、古珑等对动物源性食品中多种同化性激素残留的检验方法进行研究。该课题采用生物酶对试样进行酶解,提高检测结果的真实性;采用同位素标记物作内标,提高测定结果的准确性;采用高效率的固相萃取柱或凝胶渗透色谱净化手段，改善方法检出限；采用先进的LC-MS-MS技术，提高分析方法的效率，做到一次测定10种以上的激素。该课题所监测的项目基本满足进出口国家对动物源性食品检测标准的要求，为动物源性食品进出口安全快速检测与确证提供可靠方法。

（三）致病菌检测

2005年，天津检验检疫局王利兵、杨金良、郑文杰等参与完成国家"863"重大科研项目"食源性致病菌检测基因芯片的研制"。该课题以致病菌中合成表面抗原的基因及其他可能的特异基因为靶基因，筛选特异DNA探针，进行拥有自主知识产权的食源性致病菌检测用基因芯片产品的研发，探索常见重要食源性致病菌的芯片检测技术，应用于出入境检验检疫及其他领域，灵敏度达102-3cfu/ml，6-8小时完成检测。该产品克服传统方法的灵敏度低、耗时长、低通量的不足，可检测出当时检验检疫中尚无有效检测技术的大肠杆菌O26和O85等强致病菌株，为国家设立进出口贸易技术措施提供科学依据，为食品安全领域芯片检测技术的应用奠定基础。同年，该局张宏伟、郑文杰、唐丹舟等承担国家质检总局课题"食源性致病菌多重实时荧光PCR检测方法研究"。该课题建立起大肠埃希氏杆菌、产肠毒素大肠埃希氏杆菌、大肠埃希氏杆菌O157：H7、志贺氏菌属、沙门氏菌属、小肠结肠炎耶尔森氏菌、副溶血性弧菌、单增李斯特氏菌、金黄色葡萄球菌等常见食源性致病菌的多重实时荧光PCR检测方法，对反应条件相近的菌进行组合，利用不同的荧光标记，可在同一体系中同时检测多种食源性致病菌。该研究成果应用于临床检测、食物中毒监控、环境监测、进出口食品及国内食品的监督检验等方面，可减少检验工作量，缩短检验流程。

（四）安全监测

2002年，天津检验检疫局唐丹舟、穆乃强承担国家"十五"重大科技攻关项目"食品安全关键技术"中的子课题"进出口食品安全监测预警与风险控制技术研究"。该课题基于国际食品法典委员会（CAC）的理论框架，结合中国实际，对进出口食品安全检测数据实时收集、汇总、处理，自动发现存在的对正常状态的偏离情况，实现进出口食品安全监测与预警的自动化，进而实现对进出口食品安全状态、安全趋势的科学评估与预测，为建立中国合理的技术性贸易措施，防止境外不安全食品进入国内，保证食品质量，保护全国广大出口食品加工、经营企业的利益提供科学依据。

二、动植物检验检疫

（一）动物

2002年，天津检验检疫局王云凤、常春艳、古珑等承担国家质检总局项目"高效液相色谱-质谱法测定家禽药物代谢物残留量"研究，解决了家禽中4种硝基呋喃类药物代谢物残留量检测技术问题，为破解国外对中国出口动物源性食品所设置的技术壁垒提出应对方法，促进中国动物源性食品出口，同时，对国内设立技术保护措施提供技术支持。

2003年，该局唐丹舟、林安清、张曼等承担的"饲料中多种抗氧化剂检测系统方法研究"是国家"十五"课题"食品安全关键技术——食品添加剂、饲料添加剂和违禁化学品检验技术的研究"的子课题。该课题采用自动固相萃取样品前处理技术，大幅提高对复杂饲料样品的净化效率；首次建立饲料中8种抗氧化剂HPLC同时检测，HPLC-MS-MS确证的方法；所建立的检测方法的精密度、准确度及检出限等性能指标均可满足对饲料中抗氧化剂检测的要求，具有高效、灵敏、准确和可靠的特点，易于掌握和推广，为食品安全的监督管理和监控提供有效的技术保证。

2005年，天津检验检疫局黄庆林、刘永胜、楼旭日等承担国家质检总局课题"氧硫化碳在检疫除害处理中的应用研究"。该项研究选用代表性有害生物林木害虫或仓储害虫等为实验材料，测试不同温度、不同药剂剂量下对有害生物的熏蒸处理效果，提出不同条件下杀灭目标有害生物药剂浓度检测值以及适宜的氧硫化碳使用标准，研究氧硫化碳在口岸检疫除害处理中的应用，为在溴甲烷禁用后提供一种新的检疫处理技术方法。

（二）植物

1992年，天津检验检疫局杨维长、王学令、张树德等采用干叶粉碎法、冰冻匀浆法、蔗糖密度梯度提取法分离提取烟草霜霉病卵孢子取得成功，为进行卵孢子活性检测、病害侵染和烟草霜霉病的检疫技术标准化研究提供技术支撑，并有效防止烟草霜霉病的传入。该项目实用性强，属国内外首创，获1997年度天津市科技进步二等奖。1996年，该局杨维长、王学令、李振秀等完成“小麦矮化腥黑穗病（TCK）在天津地区定殖可能性的研究”。研究证明，中国北方冬麦区的秋冬和早春低温及低温期累计长度若结合适宜的土壤相对持水量，在一定条件下，可以诱发TCK发生，确定天津地区是TCK可发生区。由于天津港所处的重要地位，加强检疫管理，严禁疫区小麦输入中国，是降低TCK传入风险的必要措施。该研究成果为防止TCK从天津口岸传入提供技术支持，获2000年度天津市科技进步二等奖。

2001年，天津检验检疫局郑文杰、刘煊、唐丹舟等完成“国家转基因植物产品检测实验室及检测技术体系的建立”研究。该课题主要是建立转基因产品检测实验室体系、检测方法体系、检测标准体系，进而建立转基因产品检测信息库，并完成转基因抗虫绵检测技术研究。该局根据研究成果，制定发布了7项国家标准、12项行业标准，研制4项ISO国际标准，同时研制生产14种检测试剂盒，覆盖当时国际上已商品化的转基因作物、品系及其加工产品的56种外源基因，为全国每年约300亿人民币进出口相关农产品提供转基因检测的技术支撑和管理依据，具有实际应用价值。同年，该局黄庆林、刘永胜、楼旭日完成“进口原木检疫除害处理技术研究”，系统地进行淡水、海水及海水加药剂浸泡原木的实验，首次提出溴甲烷熏蒸处理原木的技术指标和安全熏蒸范围，明确溴甲烷为处理原木的最佳熏蒸剂。该研究成果具有重要推广应用价值。在同类研究中达到国际先进水平。获2004年度国家质检总局“科技兴检”二等奖。

2004年，天津检验检疫局黄庆林、刘永胜、楼旭日完成“木质包装检疫除害处理技术研究”。该项研究，适应了进出口贸易对木质包装检疫除害处理技术及相关标准制定的迫切需要，并有创新性突破，属国内领先水平，达到同类研究国际先进水平。研究成果已在国内出口货物木质包装检疫除害处理中得到实际应用，为制定国际货物贸易木质包装检疫措施标准提供了依据，可有效减少溴甲烷的使用量，保护生态环境和自然资源。获2004年度国家质检总局“科技兴检”二等奖。

三、危险品

（一）储运标准

2001年，为保证危险品的储运安全，天津出入境检验检疫局王利兵、刘金凤、李宁涛等经对危险货物中散包装的深入研究，制定出《出口危险货物中型散装货物包装容器性能检验规程》其中包括总则、复合中型散装货箱、刚性中型散装货箱、木质中型散装货箱、柔性中型散装货箱、纤维板中型散装货箱、金属中型散装货箱等7项危险货物包装中散系列检验标准。在制定标准过程中按照联合国《关于危险货物运输建议书》的试验要求，进行堆码试验、跌落试验、顶部提升试验、扯裂试验、倾覆试验和复原试验，对试验数据均参照国际现行标准来确定并提出一些技术创新点，同时对危险品中散包装进行准确、高效检验鉴定和研究，实现对危险品包装安全性能的准确评估。为出口危险货物中型散装货物包装容器的检验提供依据，为保证危险货物的顺利出口、改变出口危险货物中型散装容器的现状提供技术保证。

2002年，天津检验检疫局王利兵、赵国庆、尚为等承担国家“十五”重大标准科技专项“危险化学品包装、储运和管理标准研究”。创建中国危险化学品安全理论及方法体系，实现危险化学品安全评价技术理论的创新；首次建立中国的危险化学品国家标准体系；开展危险化学品水生生物毒性分级研究，并制定相应的国家标准；开展国内危险品化学品的分类和标签系统研究，并制定相应的国家标准；首次制定中国危险化学品安全领域的强制性国家标准104项（已发布）、行业标准22项；获国家专利10项。该项目建立的标准体系完全与国际接轨，有效打破发达国家设立的技术贸易壁垒，维护国家利益，为国内生产、储运及包装危险化学品的生产企业提供统一标准，危险化学品的包装、贮运、销售等环节的质量迅速提高，大幅降低各种安全事故的发生，。该系列标准实施一年来，为国内企业带来的直接和间接经济效益20亿元。

2005年，王利兵、李宁涛、高伟平等承担的国家质检总局项目“进出口危险品安全关键技术研究”。该课题主要进行危险化学品分类技术与方法、危险化学品及包装技术标准体系和试验方法、危险化学品便携式数据查询处理系统的研究以及危险化学品、包装试验设备的研制，建立和完善危险化学品的基础标准体系，逐步建立一套完整的危险化学品分类与方法标准体系，形成符合中国国情的危险化学品安全评估理论体系和检验鉴定方法体系，最大限度地保证危险化学品的运输安全，保护国家和人民的生命财产安全、生态环境，具有重大的实际应用价值。

（二）性能测试

2004年针对欧盟发布打火机CR法规的设限，受国家商务部委托，天津检验检疫局王利兵、李宁涛、李晶等根据《国际危规》《联合国关于危险货物运输建议书》及《出口危险品打火机检验标准》的要求，在五个月内，进行数百次试验，获得五万多个数据，完成80余万字的《中国出口打火机安全性能研究》，为中国打破欧盟技术壁垒提供有力的技术支持。“打火机试验方法及设备的研究”用于测试打火机的安全性能，安全可靠，实用性强，同年，他们还完成“危险品遇水放出易燃气体物质试验仪”研究。在国内首次实现对危险品遇水放气物质的定性和定量分析，为危险品的安全储运提供大量数据。

四、卫生检疫

2002年，天津检验检疫局开展“检验检疫标准体系研究”。该研究是检验检疫标准化建设项目，是集法律法规（含WTO规则、国际惯例、国外技术壁垒）、标准管理机制、标准技术及体系结构为一体的综合性科学研究课题。该局王利兵、冯智劼承担危险品、包装检验及鉴定专业标准体系研究，毕玉国、关淳承担卫检专业标准体系研究。该课题在进行检验检疫标准体系基础理论研究、检验检疫标准化管理运行机制研究的基础上，建立一套动态的、前瞻性、预见性的检验检疫标准体系表，并将现行的检验检疫标准和使用的国家标准、国际标准及其他行业标准进行清理、分类，通过分析和归纳，将仍然适用的标准纳入体系，对需要修订、废止或者需整合的标准提出处理建议，为全国进出口企业、管理者和使用者提供技术指导，规范技术要求，对促进检验检疫和对外经济贸易发展具有重要意义。

2003年，应控制疫情之急需，市计量所张大建、王立新、刘巍等研制成“红外辐射温度计检定校准装置”。该项目以单片机控制黑体空腔温度，形成均匀温场，实现对测量人体温度用红外辐射温度计的检定校准。“非典”期间使用该装置完成对全市各海、陆、空口岸所需测量人体温度红外辐射温度计的计量检定，并获2003年度天津市科技进步一等奖。

2004年，天津检验检疫局毕玉国、关淳等完成“国境卫生检疫标准编写基本规则”。该课题涵盖国境卫生检疫标准体系内所涉及的全部内容，构建了国境卫生检疫标准编写的总体框架，已成为国境卫生检疫行业标准编写的指南性文件，对规范卫检标准编写、提高编写质量具有重要意义。

第十篇

科 技 人 物

第一章　已故院士传略

（以出生年月为序）

至2005年，在天津（含曾在天津工作过）的中国科学院和中国工程院院士中，先后有10人逝世。已故院士按出生年月先后依次为：侯德榜，茅以升，杨石先，王曰伦，高振衡，陈省身，史绍熙，严志达，陈荣悌，孙大中。

一、侯德榜

图10-1-1-138　侯德榜

侯德榜（1890年8月9日～1974年8月26日），化学家，“侯氏制碱法”创始人。出生于福建省闽侯县。中共党员。1955年当选中国科学院技术科学部学部委员（院士）。

（一）*主要履历*

1910年，上海闽皖铁路学堂毕业，在英资津浦铁路实习；1913年，北京清华留美预备学堂毕业，保送入美国麻省理工学院化工科学习；1916年，美国麻省理工学院化工科毕业，获学士学位；1918年，美国纽约普拉特专科学院毕业，获制革化学师证书；1918～1921年，在美国哥伦比亚大学研究院研究制革，1919年获硕士学位；1921年，以《铁盐鞣革》论文获哥伦比亚大学博士学位；1921年，应范旭东聘请回国，入其开办的塘沽碱厂；1923年起，任塘沽碱厂技师长（即总工程师）兼制造长，并兼任北洋大学教授；1927年起，在永利化学工业公司任总工程师兼塘沽碱厂厂长；1936年，兼南京铔厂总工程师；1938年，兼永利川厂厂长、总工程师；1945年，任永利化学工业公司总经理；1949年起，当选中国人民政治协商会议全国委员会委员，第二、三、四届全国委员会常委；1950年，当选中华全国自然科学联合会副主席；1952年，任中央财经委员会委员、重工业部技术顾问；1952年，任公私合营永利化学工业公司总经理；1953年，参加中国民主建国会，先后当选为第一、二届中央委员会常委；1954年起，当选第一、二、三届全国人民代表大会代表；1957年，加入中国共产党；1958年，任化学工业部副部长，当选中国科学技术协会副主席；1974年8月26日，在北京病逝。

（二）*主要科技成就*

1921年，侯德榜应化工实业家范旭东之邀，回国投身永利碱厂。经过潜心研究，于1926年成功研制出“红三角”牌优质纯碱，先后荣获美国费城万国博览会和比利时工商博览会金奖，被誉为“中国工业进步的象征”。

1933年，侯德榜撰写的专著《纯碱制造》（英文版）公布于众，打破了苏尔维集团的技术垄断，被各国化工界公认为制碱工业的权威专著，相继译成多种文字出版，对世界制碱工业的发展起到重要作用。1934年，他受命全面主持南京永利硫酸铔厂的建设，仅用30个月，建成中国第一座大型化工联合企业，为中国化学工业的发展奠定了基础。

1940年2月，试验成功新的制碱方法，被称为“侯氏制碱法”，在世界制碱技术史上开创了新的一页。1943年10月22日，他被英国皇家学会化工学会授予名誉会员。同年，受巴西政府和印度塔塔公司邀请，协助勘察厂址，改进方法，开创中国制碱技术输出先河。

1953年7月1日，“侯氏制碱法”被授予新中国第一号专利证书。后经侯德榜提议，“侯氏制碱法”更名为“联合制碱法”，生产规模越来越大，为新中国化工事业发展做出重大贡献。

侯德榜晚年为发展中国小化肥工业做出贡献。他倡议用碳化法制取碳酸氢铵，亲自带队到上海化工研究院，与技术人员一道，使碳化法氮肥生产新流程获得成功。侯德榜是这一技术的首席发明人。

二、茅以升

茅以升（1896年1月9日～1989年11月12日），桥梁学家、土木工程学家、教育家、社会活动家。出生于江苏省镇江市。1955年当选中国科学院学部委员、技术科学部副主任。1982年当选美国国家工程科学院外籍院士。1984年为加拿大土木工程协会荣誉会员。中共党员。

图10-1-2-139 茅以升

（一）主要履历

1916年，毕业于唐山路矿学堂（现西南交通大学），被清华学堂官费保送赴美国留学；1917年，获美国康奈尔大学土木专业硕士学位；1919年，获美国卡内基·梅隆大学理工学院工学博士学位。其博士论文《桥梁桁架的次应力》的科学创见被称为"茅氏定律"，获卡内基理工学院颁发的金质研究奖章，同时获康奈尔大学优秀研究生"斐蒂士"金质研究奖章；1919年12月，回国，先后任唐山工业专门学校教授，南京东南大学工科教授兼主任，河海工科大学校长，天津北洋工学院院长兼教授，江苏省水利局局长，交通部中国桥梁公司总经理兼总工程师，北方中国交通大学校长等职；1933～1937年，任钱塘江大桥工程处处长，主持修建中国第一座公路铁路兼用的现代化大桥——钱塘江大桥；1943年，当选教育部部聘教授；1948年，当选中央研究院院士；1949年，任北方交通大学校长；1950年，任铁道技术研究所所长，后更名为铁道部科学研究院，任院长；1955～1957年，出任武汉长江大桥技术顾问委员会主任委员；1979年，应邀访问卡内基—梅隆大学，获"卓越校友"奖章；1982年，当选美国国家工程院外籍院士；1982年，被美国国家科学院授予外籍院士称号；1987年10月，加入中国共产党；1989年11月12日，在北京逝世。

（二）主要科技成就

20世纪30年代，茅以升领导设计并修建杭州钱塘江大桥，成为中国第一座自主设计建造的铁路、公路两用桥。他采用"射水法""沉箱法""浮运法"等，解决建桥中的一个个技术难题。该桥于1937年9月26日建成通车。同年12月23日，为了阻断敌人，茅以升受命炸断亲手建造的大桥。抗战胜利后，茅以升又主持修复了大桥。钱塘江大桥铸就了茅以升作为中国现代桥梁工程学奠基人与开拓者的地位。

20世纪50年代，在武汉长江大桥建设过程中，茅以升担任由中外专家组成的技术顾问委员会的主任委员，解决大桥建设中14个难题。该桥为铁路、公路两用的双层钢桁梁桥，于1957年9月建成，比原计划提前15个月，成为中国大陆贯穿南北的交通大动脉。

茅以升是最早从事科普事业的科学家之一。1950年，当选为中华全国科学技术普及协会副主席。他积极倡导科普教育，在200多篇论著中，《桥话》《中国石拱桥》《桥梁次应力》《钱塘江桥》《中国的古桥与新桥》等科普论著约占三分之一，其中《没有不能造的桥》1981年获全国新长征科普创作一等奖，1962年发表在《人民日报》上的《中国石拱桥》被选入初中语文课本并一直沿用。其先后率团访问捷克、苏联、意大利、瑞士、法国等国，并作学术报告，加强国际科技交流。他在华侨知识分子中从事大统一、大团结工作，号召两岸科技工作者为祖国统一"大桥"各修一座"引桥"。

茅以升作为一名教育家，在教育界工作20余年，当过5所学校的教授、2所大学校长、2所学院院长，为国家培养出一大批科学技术人才。他长期担任学会领导工作，是中国工程学术团体的创建人之一。2006年1月9日，中国科学院国家天文台将一颗由中国科学家发现的小行星命名为"茅以升星"。

三、杨石先

杨石先（1897年1月8日～1985年2月19日），蒙古族。化学家，农药化学和元素有机化学的奠基人和开拓者。出生于浙江省杭州市。中共党员。1955年当选中国科学院化学部学部委员（院士）、化学组组长。

（一）主要履历

图 10-1-3-140　杨石先

1910～1918年，就读于清华学校；1918～1923年，美国康奈尔大学学习，先后获应用化学学士学位和有机化学硕士学位；1923～1928年，任南开大学化学系教授。1928年，兼任南开大学理学院院长；1929～1931年，任美国耶鲁大学研究院研究员。1931年，获有机化学博士学位；1931～1937年，任南开大学教授，兼理学院院长；1937～1938年，任长沙临时大学化学系教授，兼化学系主任；1938～1945年，任昆明西南联合大学化学系教授，兼化学系主任，并兼昆明师范学院理化系主任。并于1941～1946年任北平中央研究院通讯研究员，1943年兼任西南联合大学教务长；1945～1947年，任美国印第安那大学访问教授兼研究员。1947年，选为美国"化学荣誉学会"会员；1948～1985年，任南开大学教授、代理校长（1948年）、副校长（1952～1957年）、校长（1957～1980年）、名誉校长（1980～1985年）；　1951～1982年，当选中国化学会第十七届至二十届理事会常务理事，并当选第十八届与第二十届理事会理事长；1957年，任国务院科学规划委员会化学组组长；1962年，创建南开大学元素有机化学研究所，并任所长。同年，兼任中国科学院化学研究所学术委员会委员；1978年，任国家科委化学学科组名誉组长；1980年，当选中国科学技术协会第二届全国委员会副主席、常务委员；1985年2月19日，在天津病故。

（二）主要科技成就

20世纪40年代，杨石先对植物生长调节剂（植物激素）进行大量的文献普查，并写出《植物生长激素》书稿，为开展植物生长调节剂研究奠定基础。

50年代初，合成出中国独特的植物生长调节剂，并进行有机磷化学的研究，成为中国农药化学的奠基人。1956年2月，他以国务院科学规划委员会委员、化学专家综合小组组长的身份参加由周恩来总理主持的《中国十二年科学技术远景规划》编制工作，并在周总理关怀下，开展农药化学的研究。1957年11月，以专家顾问的身份参加中国科学技术访苏代表团，并开始系统地开展元素有机化学研究。

1962年，杨石先以国家科委化学专业组组长和农药、农械专业组副组长的身份参加国家10年科学技术规划会议，向中央领导递交《关于我国农药生产，特别是磷有机农药生产的几点意见》，针对磷有机农药一般毒性大的特点，提出选择毒性较低的几个品种优先进行生产。同年，受周总理委托，筹建南开大学元素有机化学研究所，继续开展有机磷化学研究，又进行有机氟、有机硅、有机硼、金属有机化学等新领域研究，填补国内化学学科中一个空白。经过数以百计的实验，先后研制出杀虫剂（久效磷、螟铃畏）、除草剂（除草剂一号、燕麦敌、除草剂十六号）、杀菌剂（灭锈一号、叶枯净、克菌壮）、植物生长调节剂（7104、矮健素）等多种新农药，并培养一大批科学研究人才。

1978年，杨石先获全国科学大会先进工作者称号，其主持的10项研究成果受到全国科学大会表彰。他们研制的8种除草剂、杀菌剂、杀虫剂在各地农药厂正式生产，试制成功的"胺草磷"把农药研制工作推向新的水平。1988年8月，杨石先等在有机磷生物活性物质与有机磷化学方面的成果获1987年度国家自然科学二等奖。

杨石先摘录农药资料卡片10余万张，发表学术论文97篇，主编、撰写一系列有关有机磷化学、有机农药化学方面的著作，并主持编辑《世界农药进展》等期刊。他既重视应用科学，也重视基础研究，积极支持人工合成胰岛素和核糖核酸等纯理论性的基础研究，亲自主持评审这类重大科研成果。

杨石先先后担任全国人民代表大会第一至五届的代表，全国政治协商会议常务委员会委员，中国科学技术协会第二届全国委员会副主席、常务委员，中国科学院数理化学部委员，中国化学会第十七至二十届理事会理事长、常务理事，天津市科协主席，天津市文教委员会副主席，河北省政协副主席，河北省科委副主任，中国科学院河北省分院院长，中国民主促进会第四至六届中央委员会委员和第七届中央委员会顾问等职。为纪念这位著名的科学家和教育家，并鼓励年轻的大学生、研究生在化学方面做出成绩，南开大学设立"杨石先教授奖学金"。

图 10-1-4-141　王曰伦

四、王曰伦

王曰伦（1903年1月23日～1981年7月20日），地质学家，区域地质学家、地层学家。出生于山东省泰安市。中共党员。1980年当选中国科学院地学部学部委员（院士）。

（一）主要履历

1927年，毕业于山西大学工学院采矿科；1927～1929年，任瑞华地质调查研究会技术员；1929～1934年，任北平农矿部（实业部）地质调查所调查员；1935～1937年，在贵阳地质处工作；1938～1941年，任经济部中央地质调查所昆明办事处主任；1942年5月，任甘肃地质矿产调查队队长；1943～1949年，任中央地质调查所西北分所所长；1949～1950年，任兰州地质调查所所长、甘肃省企业厅地质师；1951～1953年，任北京地质调查所、地质部普查委员会工程师，地质部221勘探队副队长；1956年，任地质部地质矿产研究所矿床室副主任；1957～1963年，任地质部地质研究所前寒武纪地质及变质岩研究室副主任；1963～1981年，任地质部天津地质矿产研究所所长、名誉所长、研究员；1981年7月20日，在天津病逝。

（二）主要科技成就

20世纪30年代，王曰伦在云南省奠定中国前寒武地层层序及其底界。1937年，其发现黔东震旦系冰碛层，为地层对比找到可靠依据。

20世纪40年代，他组织并参与对甘肃、陕西、宁夏、青海和新疆等地区的煤、石油、石膏、铁、铜、钨资源调查，3次组织考察队对祁连山、白银厂、六盘山地区的矿产资源进行全面调查，填制1/20万地质图18幅（每幅经宽一度纬高40分），区域地质图9幅，详测矿区图14幅，概测矿区图34幅，甘肃省1/50万地质图一幅。编写岩矿专著16种，地质及其他50余种，煤矿汇报1册，并发现铁、铬、硫磺、重晶石矿、煤田、油田多处，为新中国成立后全面开展西北地质工作奠定基础，为开发西北各省矿产资源、加速西北地区建设起到重要作用。

50年代，他改正和厘定了五台山区变质地层的层序。与贾兰坡在周口店地区进行地质考察，认定周口店第四纪冰川有3期，证明北京猿人和山顶洞人产生于间冰期内，首次把猿人文化与第四纪冰期、间冰期联系起来，使长期争论的问题由此取得一致意见。所著《周口店第四纪冰川现象的观察》，得到李四光的高度赞誉。此后，中外学者对该地区动物化石研究以及对土壤所做孢粉研究，均证实王曰伦等的发现。

60年代，其组织、参加华北前寒武纪及第四纪地质研究，主编全国中、晚元古界对比划分专著，代表作有《中国海相火山—沉积成矿理论及相关地质问题》《对中国寒武纪以前古老沉积岩划分的意见》和《全国震旦系对比线索》。其研究成果“中国震旦亚界（晚前寒武系）”获1982年度国家自然科学三等奖。

王曰伦50年代在五台山区进行古老岩系中的铁矿资源调查时，注意到花岗岩、闪长岩（或玄武岩）与大理岩、片岩及石英岩等相间出现的现象。1956～1965年，在天津蓟县震旦系中的串岭沟组、大红峪组及其他地层中注意到层状的中基性、碱性的火山岩。1966年，在四川拉拉山铜矿和云南大红山铁矿发现有火山岩。1970～1971年，在研究山西平顺西安里铁矿时，在其围岩奥陶系灰岩中发现很多海相海底火山喷发物，在邯邢铁矿中也见有海相火山岩成矿证据，提出海相火山成矿理论观点。

王日伦的研究领域十分广泛，在地质科学基础理论研究中，以前寒武纪地质研究造诣最深，同时对区域地质、矿床地质，地层古生物、石油地质、煤田地质、第四纪地质等学科也有较深研究，且有独到见解，先后发表论文、著作和报告百余篇。

五、高振衡

高振衡（1911年6月21日～1989年11月14日），有机化学家和化学教育家。出生于北京市。中共党员，中国民主同盟盟员。1980年11月当选中国科学院化学部学部委员（院士）。

图 10-1-5-142 高振衡

（一）主要履历

1930～1934年，在清华大学化学系学习；1934～1940年，在清华大学、西南联合大学化学系任助教；1940～1941年，在清华大学农业研究所任助教；1942～1946年，赴美国哈佛大学留学，获博士学位。1946年回国；1946～1949年，任南开大学化学系教授；1949～1971年，任南开大学化学系副主任；1972～1980年，任南开大学化学系主任；1978～1989年，当选为中国化学会第二十届、二十一届、二十二届理事会理事；1980年，任《高等学校化学学报》编辑委员会副主编；1989年11月14日，在天津病逝。

（二）主要科技成就

20世纪50年代初到60年代初，高振衡将量子化学计算应用于有机分子结构与性能关系的研究，处理了芳基汞、氯乙烯基氯化汞等化合物的结构，根据计算得到π电荷分布及π-键序，首次指出在上述化合物分子中由于汞原子的空p轨道的参与形成大π键。通过分析氯乙烯基氯化汞和双氯乙烯基汞的反应性质，提出在顺式氯乙烯基氯化汞的结构中存在一个新型的化学键——四电子三中心键。在探讨烃基氯化硫对不饱和键的加成反应机理的研究过程中，确定加成的位置及立体化学，揭示反应的离子性特点。

70年代起，开始有机闪烁剂和有机激光染料的研究，对五元杂氮氧化合物——恶唑、恶二唑类杂环化合物的有机荧光分子在合成、结构与光性能测试、溶剂效应及其量子化学处理等方面取得进展，开发出优良性能的有机闪烁剂及激光染料。至80年代，合成出30多个系列700多种恶唑、恶二唑、苯并恶唑类化合物，并从中筛选出多种新型紫外光谱区激光染料。此后，又试制成功IBOP等，性能优于国外同波段的激光染料，1978年获全国科学大会奖。1980年8月，参加国际纯粹与应用化学联合会在美国举办的第五届物理有机化学讨论会，发表《2,6-二取代苯并二恶唑的研究》论文，受到与会者的重视。1979年起，连续承担国家科委“六五”、“七五”科技攻关项目，通过国家鉴定研究成功的新激光染料30多种，先后获得天津市科技成果奖、国家自然科学奖、国家发明奖和国家教委科技进步奖等奖项。

高振衡还开展仿生有机化学反应、有机光化学、卡宾化学及天然丰度氘核磁共振法研究有机化学反应、有机负碳离子及有机正离子基化学等方面的研究，为中国有机化学研究接近和赶上世界先进水平做出长期不懈的努力。至1990年1月，在《中国科学》《化学学报》和《高等学校化学学报》等刊物发表论文100多篇。其60年代编著的《有机化学结构理论》，长期为高等学校所使用；80年代初编著的《有机光化学》，是国内在该领域的重要著作；《物理有机化学》（上、下册），被许多高等学校用作大学本科生和研究生的教材，获国家教育委员会优秀教材一等奖。

六、陈省身

图 10-1-6-143 陈省身

陈省身（1911年10月28日～2004年12月3日），美籍华人，国际数学大师、著名教育家。出生于浙江省嘉兴市秀水县。1961年当选美国科学院院士，并入美国国籍。1988年当选意大利林琴科学院外籍院士。1989年当选法国科学院外籍院士。1995年当选中国科学院首批外籍院士。2009年，国际数学联盟正式宣布设立“陈省身奖”。

（一）主要履历

1930年，南开大学毕业，到清华大学任助教并就读清华大学研究生；1934年，清华大学研究生院毕业，赴德国汉堡大学留学；1936年9月，到巴黎大学做学术访问；1937年，聘为清华大学教授；1943年7月，在美国普林斯顿大学开展大范围微分几何研究，发表数篇独具创见的微分几何论文；1948年，任中央研究院数学研究所代理所长，入选中央研究院第一届院士；1949年，任芝加哥大学几何学正教授。10年中，拓展了美国的微分几何，形成美国的微分几何学派；1960年，迁往加州大学伯克利分校，一直工作到退休；1972年9月，首次偕夫人回国，与中科院院长郭沫若等会见；1975年，获美国国家科学奖；1981年，退休后出任美国数学科学所第一任所长，任期3年，后任名誉所长；1984年5月，获得世界数学最高奖项——沃尔夫奖；1984年8月25日，邓小平在北京接见陈省身夫妇。其后，1989年、1996年、1999年，3次受到江泽民接见；1984年，受中华人民共和国教育部之聘，担任南开大学数学研究所所长，1992年起任名誉所长；1998年，捐出100万美元建立"陈省身基金"；2000年，定居天津市；2004年9月，获得首届邵逸夫奖；2004年12月3日，在天津因病逝世。

（二）主要科技成就

陈省身的数学研究范围广，包括微分几何、拓扑学、微分方程、代数、几何、李群和几何学等多方面。他是创立现代微分几何学的大师。20世纪40年代，他结合微分几何与拓扑学的方法，完成黎曼流形的高斯—博内一般形式和埃尔米特流形的示性类论。他首次将纤维丛概念应用于微分几何的研究，引进后来通称的陈氏示性类（简称陈类），为大范围微分几何提供了不可缺少的工具。他引入的一些概念、方法和工具，远远超过微分几何与拓扑学的范围，成为整个现代数学中的重要组成部分。

陈省身是一位杰出的教育家，培养出大批优秀的博士生。特别是退休后，每年回南开大学指导数学研究工作，并于1985年创建南开大学数学研究所，亲任所长。

鉴于其取得的一系列杰出成就，获得许多荣誉和奖励。其中，1975年获美国总统颁发的美国国家科学奖，1984年获数学界最高荣誉沃尔夫奖，被国际数学界尊为"微分几何之父"。他是美国国家科学院院士，美国艺术科学学院院士，英国皇家学会外籍会员，意大利Lincei科学院外籍院士，法国科学院外籍院士，第三世界科学院创始者，巴西科学院的通讯院士。2004年11月2日，经国际天文学联合会小天体命名委员会讨论通过，将一颗编号为1998CS2的小行星命名为"陈省身星"，以表彰他对全人类的贡献。

七、史绍熙

图10-1-7-144 史绍熙

史绍熙（1916年8月19日～2000年9月16日），工程热物理学家、燃烧学家。出生于江苏省宜兴市。中共党员。1980年当选中国科学院技术科学部学部委员（院士）。

（一）主要履历

1939年，北洋大学机械系毕业，获学士学位；1949年，获英国曼彻斯特大学博士学位；1951年，回国，任天津大学教授；1952年，在天津大学建立内燃机专业，任内燃机教研室主任；1956年，任国内首批研究生导师；1958年，任天津大学第二机械系主任，并创建天津内燃机研究室；1960年，在教育部支持下将天津内燃机研究室扩建为天津内燃机研究所，任所长；1979年，任天津大学副校长兼热物理工程系主任，创立工程热物理专业，筹建热能研究所，兼任所长；1981年，评选为国内首批博士研究生导师，并出任天津大学校长；1984年，聘为美国世界开放大学研究生指导教授；1987年，主持建成国内第一个内燃机燃烧学国家重点实验室，任实验室主任和学术委员会主任，同时建立国内唯一的内燃机学科博士后科研流动站；1989年，组织召开世界第18届国际内燃机会议（CIMAC）并担任大会主席；2000年9月16日，在天津病故。

（二）主要科技成就

20世纪50年代末至60年代初，提出一种全新的燃烧方式，定名为复合式燃烧过程。经过近4年的试验研究获得成功，1963年通过鉴定，并于1982年获国家发明二等奖。

在燃烧室内空气运动与粒子运动的研究中，提出粒子在旋转气流中的运动转迹新方程；在直喷式柴油机压缩过程湍流场变化规律的研究中，发现在上止点附近燃烧室不同部位湍流强度的变化规律；在发动机充气过程的研究中，提出在进气终结时缸内涡流比的计算公式。同时开展燃料喷雾特性的研究，并取得重要成果。

1957年，发表《关于内燃机空气消耗量的测定法》论文，并首次把粒子示踪法应用于缸内流动测量。1987年，在英国机械工程学会组织的国际会议上发表论文《内燃机气缸内压力测量的数值仿真及数字信号处理的研究》，首次成功地把数字信号处理和数字滤波技术应用于内燃机缸内压力测量，并发展3种数字滤波法，取得良好效果。1987年，成功地研究出应用激光衍射原理的柴油机喷雾场自动分析测量系统，达国际先进水平。1988年,研究成功光电调制反馈激光多普勒测速仪,获得国家专利。

1980年,在国内首先进行柴油机燃用甲醇的研究,并在第15、16届国际内燃机燃烧学术会议上先后发表论文《甲醇作为柴油机代用燃料的研究》和《双燃法燃用甲醇的研究》。在第八届国际醇类燃料会议上发表《在柴油机上用双燃料法燃用甲醇的燃料控制系统的研究》论文。1988年,在492Q型汽油机上进行燃用纯甲醇(M100)研究并取得成功,燃油消耗率达到国际先进水平。1989年,完成"柴油机用热表面点火法燃用纯甲醇(M100)的研究",热效率比原柴油机提高4%,功率增加9.6%。

史绍熙在国内外学术刊物上发表70多篇论文。1983年创办《内燃机学报》,成为中国内燃机行业唯一的高级学术刊物。他还主编《燃烧科学与技术》杂志,并兼任《工程热物理学报》副主编和《中国科学》与《科学通报》编委。1984年,主编的380多万字《柴油机设计手册》由中国农业机械出版社出版,具有较高的实用价值和学术价值。1992年,其主编的300多万字《内燃机设计手册》由机械工业出版社作为重点科技图书出版。

八、严志达

图10-1-8-145　严志达

严志达(1917年11月1日~1999年4月30日),数学家。出生于江苏省南通市。1993年当选中国科学院数理学部院士。

(一)主要履历

1936~1941年,考入清华大学物理系,后转入数学系;1941~1946年,任昆明云南大学助教,1946年考取中法交换生留学;1947~1949年,在法国斯特拉斯堡大学攻读博士学位,1949年获法国国家博士学位;1949~1952年,任法国国家科学中心助理研究员;1952~1985年,任南开大学数学系教授;1985~1999年,任南开大学数学研究所教授;1980~1985年,任中国数学会第三届、第四届理事会理事;1993年,当选中国科学院院士;1999年4月30日,在天津病故。

(二)主要科技成就

严志达长期从事李(Lie)群、李代数以及微分几何领域的研究,在特殊李群的拓扑,实半单李代数的分类理论等方面获重要成果,在把微分几何理论应用于研究齿轮啮合问题方面颇有建树。20世纪40年代末,严志达致力于特殊李群的拓扑研究,成功地算出特殊李群的贝蒂(Betti)数,从而在李群拓扑的研究上获得重大突破,在国际数学界引起很大反响。1952年回国后,他致力于实半单李代数分类理论的研究。至50年代末期,找到用角图来刻划分类的方法,使分类理论极大简化。在此期间,严志达还开展实半单李代数的自同构问题及相关几何问题的研究,并把这些结果总结起来,先后写成专著《李群与微分几何》《半单纯李群李代数表示论》,于60年代出版。之后,其在实半单李代数实表示理论上获得很好的结果,美国《数学评论》对此颇有好评。1954~1966年,在南开大学主持"李群与微分几何"讨论班,为国家培养一批活跃在该领域的优秀人才,获得一系列引人注目的科研成果。其中,1956年、1962年先后到复旦大学、中国科学院、北京大学等讲学;1958年赴罗马尼亚出席国际几何会议,并访问莫斯科大学。1972年开始,对啮合理论进行系统研究,奠定其数学基础。1981年,先后访问美国普林斯顿高等研究所和法国。

几何学是严志达的一个重点研究方向。在上大学期间,在陈省身的指导下,合作求出积分几何的运动基本形式,被称为陈—严公式。该研究成果至今仍被人们引用。留学法国期间,其从事曲面丛几何研究并获得若干成果,关于二次外微分型等价问题研究,成为东欧不少数学家研究工作的基础。20世纪50年代至60年代,重点研究几何学上的对称空间理论。60年代初,运用他关于实单李代数分类的新方法,成功地解决了仿射对称空间的局部分类问题。

严志达在齿轮啮合理论的数学基础论文,是用微分几何工具建立的一套有效解决齿轮啮合所遇到各种问题的方法。他明确提出两类界限点、诱导法曲率等许多重要概念,导出齿面间的曲率关系,即诱导法曲率公式。该成果被选为1978年全国科学大会重要成果,并获得天津市科学进步一等奖。

九、陈荣悌

图10-1-9-146 陈荣悌

陈荣悌(1919年11月7日~2001年11月15日),化学家。出生于四川省垫江县峡云乡。致公党党员。1980年当选为中国科学院化学部学部委员(院士)。

(一)主要履历

1941年,四川大学化学系毕业,到资源委员会犍为焦油厂任工务员;1942年,考入武汉大学研究生院;1944年,武汉大学研究生院毕业,任中央大学化学系助教;1945年,任中国石油公司助理工程师;1947年,赴美国学习及工作;1952年,获美国印第安纳大学博士学位后,先后在美国西北大学做博士后和芝加哥大学任研究员;1954年,回国,任南开大学化学系教授,从事热力学、动力学、配位化学及络合催化方面的教学和研究工作;1979年,代表中国首次参加第20届国际配位化学会议,并被选为该会执行委员;1982~1990年 当选为中国化学会第二十一届、二十二届理事会理事;1988年,任美国斯瓦斯摩尔(Swarthmore)学院特约讲座教授;2001年11月15日,在天津病故。

(二)主要科技成就

陈荣悌是国际上研究溶液中配合物化学的早期科研工作者之一。在科研方面,对配合物在溶液中的组成和稳定性研究及实验方法上都有所发展(如折光法)。提出了配合物化学中的线性热力学函数关系,对工业上选择催化剂有理论指导意义,引起国际化学界的高度重视。多年从事热力学和热化学、动力学及反应机理、结构和配合物理论,络合催化理论和应用等方面的研究。1973年起,开始从事无汞催化剂的研制工作,较好地解决了国内氯碱厂生产聚氯乙烯所用汞催化剂的汞污染问题。1979年,陈荣悌参加在印度召开的第20届国际配位化学会议,宣读关于直线自由能关系的实验研究论文,居国际领先水平。1983年,筛选出一种既有助催化作用,又有溶解高聚物能力的液相络合催化剂,并一次试车成功,经济效益十分显著。20世纪80年代,用大量实验数据证明直线自由能关系和直线焓关系在配位化学中的存在。至90年代,将配位化学中的直线自由能关系发展成为更普遍的"线性热力学函数关系"。

陈荣悌发表论文280余篇,专译著3部。获国家发明三等奖1项,国家教委优秀科技成果二等奖2项。他在配合物化学领域的卓越成就得到国际化学界的高度评价和赞誉。1987年获苏联科学院丘加耶夫奖状和奖章。自1979年起,历次代表中国参加国际配合物化学会议。在教学方面,共培养出硕士生30余人、博士生20余人。

十、孙大中

图10-1-10-147 孙大中

孙大中(1932年6月20日~1997年5月1日),地质学家。出生于山东省威海市。九三学社成员。1991年当选为中国科学院地学部院士。

(一)主要履历

1955年,毕业于北京地质学院;1955~1964年1月,在合肥工业大学任教;1964年,调入地矿部天津地质矿产研究所工作。1980年3月任副研究员。1981年6月任研究室副主任。1987年4月任研究员。1987年5月任研究室主任;1992年11月,调入中国科学院广州地球化学研究所工作,任研究员;1997年5月1日,因病在广州市逝世。

(二)主要科技成就

孙大中长期从事前寒武纪地质、地球化学等研究。其在对中条山前寒武纪地质和深部地质研究中,用综合年代学方法建立了新型的年代构造格架,提出火成岩年代—地球化学作为岩石圈"探针"的新方法,并建立年代地壳结构模式,重新解剖中条山前寒武纪重大地质事件和铜矿成矿历史,在理论和方法上都有突破。他对冀东的构造格架、地层划分、岩石演变和成矿规律进行总结,建立一个较完整的冀东早前寒武纪地壳演化模式,对部分麻粒岩成因提出新论点。

在对华北克拉通的研究中,他提出太古宙地壳成熟度高,富大半径亲石元素和亏损高强场元素,以大面积底板垫托作用形成的高级变质区为主,同时指出元古为垂直增长的网点位置的底板垫托模式,并指出中国大陆地壳,特别是华北克拉通的前寒武纪基底的地球化学性状、增长方式和主要增长时段等,在全球有其时空特殊性。

他著有7部专著(或合著),约120篇中英文学术论文,其代表作有《冀东早前寒武地质》和《中条山前寒武纪年代构造格架和地壳结构模式》。其研究成果获得1978年全国科学大会奖、国家自然科学二等奖和部级科技成果一、二、三等奖项共8次。

第二章　优秀科技人才

在社会主义现代化建设中,涌现出一大批优秀科技人才。建国后,至2005年,在天津工作或曾在天津工作的42名专家教授当选为中国科学院和中国工程院院士。在中共中央组织部、国家人事部、中国科协、国家知识产权局等组织的评选优秀科技人才活动中,天津市有31人受到各种表彰与奖励,其中13人获中国青年科技奖称号,10人获全国优秀科技工作者称号,2人获全国杰出专业技术人才奖称号,2人获新世纪巾帼发明家称号,4人获中国青少年科技创新奖称号。230名优秀科技人才获得天津市各种表彰与奖励,其中166人获得天津青年科技奖称号,50人获得天津市优秀科技工作者称号,4人获天津市科技重大成就奖,4人获天津市国际科技合作奖,5人获天津市巾帼发明家称号。

第一节　天津两院院士

至2005年,在天津工作或曾在天津工作的42名中国科学院和中国工程院院士中,中国科学院院士有23人,中国工程院院士有19人。1991～2005年,天津市有31人当选为中国科学院和中国工程院院士,其中,中国科学院院士12人,中国工程院院士19人。

一、中国科学院院士

至2005年,天津市共有中国科学院院士23人,其中,1991～2005年当选的有12人,南开大学数学研究所所长、著名数学家陈省身于1994年当选为中国科学院首批外籍院士。至2005年,先后有10名中国科学院院士因病逝世,1名院士调离天津,实际在天津工作的中国科学院院士有12人。

中国科学院院士名录

(按当选年份排序,同年份的按出生年月排序)

表10-2-1-55

姓名	性别	生卒年月	工作单位及行政职务	专业技术职务	隶属学部	当选年份
侯德榜	男	1890.8～1974.8	曾任塘沽碱厂总工程师兼北洋大学教授、永利化学工业公司总工程师兼塘沽碱厂厂长,1958年调任化学工业部副部长、中国科学技术协会副主席等职	总工程师	技术科学部	1955
茅以升	男	1896.1～1989.11	曾任天津北洋工学院院长,1950年调任铁道部科学研究院院长等职	教授	技术科学部	1955
杨石先	男	1897.1～1985.2	南开大学校长、名誉校长	教授	化学部	1955

续表 10-2-1-55

姓名	性别	生卒年月	工作单位及行政职务	专业技术职务	隶属学部	当选年份
王曰伦	男	1903.1 ~ 1981.7	天津地质矿产研究所所长、名誉所长	研究员	地学部	1980
高振衡	男	1911.6 ~ 1989.11	南开大学化学系副主任、主任	教授	化学部	1980
史绍熙	男	1916.8 ~ 2000.9	天津大学校长兼热物理工程系主任和热能研究所所长	教授	技术科学部	1980
申泮文	男	1916.9 ~ 2017.7	南开大学	教授	化学部	1980
何炳林	男	1918.8 ~ 2007.7	在南开大学历任高分子教研室主任、化学系主任、高分子化学研究所所长等职	教授	化学部	1980
陈茹玉	女	1919.9 ~ 2012.3	南开大学	教授	化学部	1980
陈荣悌	男	1919.11 ~ 2001.11	南开大学	教授	化学部	1980
徐叙瑢	男	1922.4 ~	天津理工学院（1997 年调北方交通大学）	教授	数学物理学部	1980
余国琮	男	1922.11 ~	天津大学	教授	化学部	1991
刘广均	男	1929.7 ~	核工业理化工程研究院	正高级工程师	技术科学部	1991
母国光	男	1931.1 ~ 2012.4	南开大学	教授	信息技术科学部	1991
孙大中	男	1932.6 ~ 1997.5	天津地质矿产研究所（1992 年调中国科学院广州地球化学研究所）	研究员	地学部	1991
严志达	男	1917.11 ~ 1999.4	南开大学	教授	数学物理学	1993
周　恒	男	1929.11 ~	天津大学	教授	数学物理学部	1993
陈省身	男	1911.10 ~ 2004.12	南开大学数学研究所所长、名誉所长	教授	外籍院士	1994
彭一刚	男	1932.9 ~	天津大学	教授	技术科学部	1995
张春霆	男	1936.9 ~	天津大学	教授	生命科学和医学学部	1995
姚建铨	男	1939.1 ~	天津大学	教授	信息技术科学部	1997
程津培	男	1948.6 ~	南开大学 国家科技部	教授 副部长	化学部	2001
葛墨林	男	1938.12 ~	南开大学	教授	数学物理学部	2003

二、中国工程院院士

1994 年起，天津市参加中国工程院院士遴选工作。1994 年，1 人当选为中国工程院院士。至 2005 年，在天津工作的中国工程院院士共有 19 人。

中国工程院院士名录

（按当选年份排序，同年份的按出生年月排序）

表 10-2-1-56

姓名	性别	生卒年月	工作单位	专业技术职务	隶属学部	当选年份
钱皋韵	男	1927.3~	核工业理化工程研究院	研究员	能源与矿业工程学部	1994
李正名	男	1931.1~	南开大学	教授	化学、冶金与材料工程学部	1995
汪顺亭	男	1935.1~	中国船舶总公司第七0七研究所	研究员	机械与运载工程学部	1995
吴咸中	男	1925.8~	天津医科大学	教授	医药卫生学部	1996

续表10-2-1-56

姓名	性别	生卒年月	工作单位	专业技术职务	隶属学部	当选年份
沈家祥	男	1921.11~2015.7	天津大学	教授	医药卫生学部	1999
曹楚生	男	1926.6~2017.11	水利部天津水利水电勘测设计研究院	正高级工程师	土木、水利与建筑工程学部	1999
侯　锋	男	1928.2~	天津市农业科学院	教授、名誉院长	农业学部	1999
谢世楞	男	1935.5~	交通部第一航务工程勘察设计院	正高级工程师	土木、水利与建筑工程学部	1999
王静康	女	1938.4~	天津大学	教授	化学、冶金与材料工程学部	1999
石学敏	男	1938.6~	天津中医学院第一附属医院	教授院长	医药卫生学部	1999
李猷嘉	男	1932.11~	天津华北设计院	正高级工程师	土木、水利与建筑工程学部	2001
叶声华	男	1934.6~	天津大学	教授	信息与电子工程学部	2003
王玉明	男	1941.1~	天津新技术产业园区鼎名密封有限公司	正高级工程师	机械与运载工程学部	2003
刘昌孝	男	1942.4~	天津药物研究院	研究员	医药卫生学部	2003
郝希山	男	1945.9~	天津医科大学	教授	医药卫生学部	2003
陈予恕	男	1931.3~	天津大学	教授	机械与运载工程学部	2005
余贻鑫	男	1936.11~	天津大学	教授	能源与矿业工程学部	2005
陈念念	男	1941.10~	天津核工业理化工程研究院	研究员	能源与矿业工程学部	2005
张伯礼	男	1948.2~	天津中医学院	教授	医药卫生学部	2005

第二节　获全国优秀科技人才称号人员

在中共中央组织部、国家人事部、中国科协等组织的评选优秀科技人才活动中，天津市有30余名科技人员分别受到表彰与奖励。其中，13人获中国青年科技奖，10人获全国优秀科技工作者称号，2人获全国杰出专业技术人才称号，2人获新世纪巾帼发明家称号，4人获中国青少年科技创新奖。

一、中国青年科技奖获得者

1988年起，天津市参加中共中央组织部、国家人事部和中国科协设立的中国青年科技奖评选活动。至2005年，天津市共有13人获得中国青年科技奖称号。

获得中国青年科技奖名录

表10-2-2-57

姓名	性别	工作单位	获奖年份	届别
李　昌	男	中国民用航空学院无线电系	1988	第一届
王振华	男	中国海洋渤海石油公司计算中心	1990	第三届
陈志敏	男	天津大学数学学院	1992	第四届
翟京生	男	海军海洋测绘研究所	1994	第五届
陈永川	男	南开大学组合数学研究中心	1998	第六届
王春峰	男	天津大学系统工程研究所		
李喜宏	男	中国(天津)农产品保鲜工程技术研究中心	2000	第七届
邓运华	男	中国海洋石油渤海公司		
赵春华	男	中国医学科学院造血干细胞和基因工程中心		

续表10-2-2-57

姓名	性别	工作单位	获奖年份	届别
吕晓龙	男	天津大学膜科学与技术研究所	2004	第八届
许京军	男	南开大学物理科学学院		
吴文清	男	天津石化公司乙烯厂		
钟登华	男	天津大学研究生院		

二、全国优秀科技工作者获得者

1997年，天津市参加由中共中央组织部、国家人事部和中国科协开展的“全国优秀科技工作者”评选活动。至2005年，天津市共有10人获得全国优秀科技工作者称号。

获得全国优秀科技工作者称号名录

表10-2-2-58

姓名	性别	工作单位	获奖年份
陈永川	男	南开大学数学研究所	1997
姚建铨	男	天津大学激光与光电子研究所	1997
张其清	男	中国医学科学院生物医学工程研究所	1997
王撷秀	女	天津市结核病控制中心	2000
闫希军	男	天津天士力集团有限公司	2000
杜　智	男	天津市第三中心医院	2000
吴永平	男	中国石油天然气股份有限公司大港油田分公司	2000
张万钧	男	天津市经济开发区园林绿化公司	2000
张伯礼	男	天津市中医学院	2000
陈光星	男	天津市宝坻县袁罗庄科协	2000

三、全国杰出专业技术人才奖获得者

1999年起，天津市参加国家人事部组织的“全国杰出专业技术人才”的选拔推荐工作。至2005年，天津市先后有2人获得“全国杰出专业技术人才”称号。

获得全国杰出专业技术人才奖名录

表10-2-2-59

姓名	工作单位	职称(职务)	获奖年份
陆　芸	天津医院	副主任医师、副院长	1999
张伯礼	天津市中医学院	教授	2002

四、新世纪巾帼发明家获得者

2002年起，天津市参加由中华全国妇女联合会、国家知识产权局、中国发明协会共同主办的“新世纪巾帼发明家”评选活动。至2005年，天津市先后有2人获此称号。

获得新世纪巾帼发明家名录

表10-2-2-60

姓名	性别	工作单位	职务(职称)	获奖年份
王静康	女	天津大学化工学院国家工业结晶技术研究推广中心	主任、教授、中国工程院院士	2002
陈　丽	女	国家(天津)农产品保鲜工程技术研究中心	材料工程部副部长、研究员	2004

五、中国青少年科技创新奖获得者

2004年8月24日，在北京举行的首届中国青少年科技创新奖颁奖大会上，天津市有4人获此奖项。

获得中国青少年科技创新奖名录

表10-2-2-61

姓名	所在院校及年级	获奖年份	届别
张昕楠	天津大学建筑学院1999级本科生	2004	首届
易　龙	南开大学化学学院2000级本科生	2004	首届
孙　涛	天津医科大学基础医学学院2000级本科生	2004	首届
柴恭泉	天津市实验中学学生	2004	首届

第三节　获天津市优秀科技人才称号人员

在天津市组织的评选优秀科技人才活动中，有200余名科技工作者受到表彰与奖励。其中，4人获天津市科技重大成就奖，3人获天津市国际科技合作奖，5人获天津市巾帼发明家称号，166人(其中2人分别2次当选)获天津青年科技奖，50人获得天津市优秀科技工作者称号。

一、天津青年科技奖获得者

1990年，中共天津市委组织部、市人事局、市科协设立天津青年科技奖。该奖项面向全市广大青年科技工作者设立，旨在造就一批进入世界科技前沿的青年学术和技术带头人，表彰奖励在经济发展、社会进步和科技创新中做出突出成就的青年科技人才，激励青年科技工作者为加快社会主义现代化建设做出新贡献。至2005年，共举办7届，表彰168名优秀青年科技工作者，其中1990年25人，1992年34人，1994年21人，1996年20人，1998年23人，2001年24人，2004年21人。

获得天津青年科技奖称号名录

表10-2-3-62

姓名	性别	工作单位	获奖年份
王　俐	女	南开大学高分子化学所	1990年(第一届)
王连生	男	环境保护科学研究所	1990年(第一届)
戈小云	女	机械部第五设计院	1990年(第一届)
朱　东	男	天津航空机电公司技术处	1990年(第一届)
吕　旗	男	天津大学物理系	1990年(第一届)

续表10-2-3-62

姓名	性别	工作单位	获奖年份
闫新文	男	天津肿瘤研究所	1990年(第一届)
刘柱庭	男	铁路局电子计算所	1990年(第一届)
刘深厚	男	天津大学机械系	1990年(第一届)
汲　勇	男	天津理工学院机械系	1990年(第一届)
宋文芹	女	南开大学生物系	1990年(第一届)
何秀坤	男	电子部第四十六研究所	1990年(第一届)
李纪扣	男	天津轻工业学院自动化系	1990年(第一届)
国占昌	男	天津铝合金厂	1990年(第一届)
张立新	男	天津大学土木工程系	1990年(第一届)
张守余	男	天津市政工程勘测设计院	1990年(第一届)
张素勤	女	天津大学材料系	1990年(第一届)
张越林	女	天津河西医院	1990年(第一届)
赵　忠	男	天津大学机械系	1990年(第一届)
郭保平	男	天津经济技术开发区计划统计局	1990年(第一届)
顾洪恩	女	天津大学物理系	1990年(第一届)
康利文	男	青光养鸡总场	1990年(第一届)
黄森忠	男	南开大学数学系	1990年(第一届)
彭道富	男	铁道部十八局施技处	1990年(第一届)
廖　明	男	南开大学数学系	1990年(第一届)
戴凤岩	男	地质部天津地矿所	1990年(第一届)
王振华	男	渤海石油公司计算中心	1992年(第二届)
张　维	男	天津大学系统工程研究所	1992年(第二届)
张其清	男	中国医学科学院生物医学工程研究所	1992年(第二届)
陈超英	男	天津大学电力及自动化系	1992年(第二届)
汤美华	女	中国医学科学院血液学研究所	1992年(第二届)
李茂祥	男	天津市禽病诊断培训中心	1992年(第二届)
李绍忠	男	天津市第一建筑工程公司	1992年(第二届)
边润强	男	天津理工学院自动化系	1992年(第二届)
陈　悝	男	中建六局安装公司	1992年(第二届)
曾小平	男	天津钢厂第二炼钢厂	1992年(第二届)
王立才	男	机电部第十八所	1992年(第二届)
丘　毅	男	机电部天津工程机械研究所	1992年(第二届)
徐晓辉	男	河北工学院电气工程系	1992年(第二届)
顾永治	男	总后车船研究所	1992年(第二届)
彭　翔	男	天津大学精仪系	1992年(第二届)
张　民	男	天津针织十一厂	1992年(第二届)
刘卫民	男	交通部天津水运工程研究所	1992年(第二届)

续表10-2-3-62

姓名	性别	工作单位	获奖年份
张守余	男	天津市政工程勘测设计院	1992年(第二届)
马冬青	女	天津农科院林业果树研究所	1992年(第二届)
王文杰	男	天津畜牧兽医研究所	1992年(第二届)
孙贵宝	男	天津国营农场管理局	1992年(第二届)
杨恩辉	男	南开大学数学系	1992年(第二届)
张金忠	男	南开大学生物系	1992年(第二届)
马建标	男	南开大学高分子研究所	1992年(第二届)
王昌禄	男	天津轻工业学院食品工程系	1992年(第二届)
刘玉军	男	天津轻工业学院机械系	1992年(第二届)
李　涛	男	天津二医附属河东医院	1992年(第二届)
刘玉琐	男	天津制革公司第一制革厂	1992年(第二届)
龙　晓	男	天津大学精仪系	1992年(第二届)
张承民	男	河北工学院数理教研室	1992年(第二届)
崔得良	男	天津理工学院材料物理所	1992年(第二届)
丁秀珍	女	空军天津医院内一科	1992年(第二届)
周永旭	男	天津工业泵总厂	1992年(第二届)
陈学书	男	前进日用化学厂	1992年(第二届)
李朝兴	男	南开大学高分子化学研究所	1994年(第三届)
袁　直	女	南开大学高分子化学研究所	1994年(第三届)
陈志敏	男	天津大学数学系	1994年(第三届)
郑兴灿	男	中国市政工程华北地区设计院	1994年(第三届)
周玉明	男	天津市勘察院	1994年(第三届)
李　军	男	中国水利水电基础工程局科研所	1994年(第三届)
翟国君	男	海军海洋测绘研究所	1994年(第三届)
陈晓波	男	南开大学物理系	1994年(第三届)
纪承军	男	天津市气象局技术装备处	1994年(第三届)
林恩平	男	中国石油天然气总公司工程技术研究所	1994年(第三届)
陈周羡	男	天津市园林管理局绿化处程林苗圃管理所	1994年(第三届)
刘景泰	男	南开大学计算机系	1994年(第三届)
林　彬	男	天津大学机械系CAD/CAM及精密加工教研室	1994年(第三届)
李秀苒	女	电子部第四十六研究所	1994年(第三届)
冯远明	男	天津大学精密仪器工程系	1994年(第三届)
唐　英	女	天津机械涂层研究所	1994年(第三届)
夏庆龙	男	渤海石油公司计算中心	1994年(第三届)
严　云	男	中国石化第四建设公司衬里公司	1994年(第三届)
薛树津	男	天津市电子线缆公司	1994年(第三届)
王成山	男	天津大学电力及自动化系	1994年(第三届)

续表10-2-3-62

姓名	性别	工作单位	获奖年份
季　民	男	天津大学土木工程系	1994年(第三届)
王　强	男	河北工业大学化学工程系	1996年(第四届)
王玉新	男	天津大学机械系	1996年(第四届)
王中胜	男	天津大学系统工程研究所	1996年(第四届)
白　刚	男	南开大学计算机与系统科学系	1996年(第四届)
卢宝泉	男	天津动物园	1996年(第四届)
孙德岭	男	天津市蔬菜研究所	1996年(第四届)
孙绪江	男	天津石化公司研究所	1996年(第四届)
孙建军	男	电子工业部第四十六研究所	1996年(第四届)
张铁军	男	天津药物研究院	1996年(第四届)
陈永川	男	南开大学数学研究所	1996年(第四届)
邹　哲	男	天津市规划设计管理局	1996年(第四届)
吴厚政	男	天津大学材料科学与工程系	1996年(第四届)
罗德强	男	天津动力机厂研究所	1996年(第四届)
钟登华	男	天津大学水资源与港湾工程系	1996年(第四届)
姚　智	男	天津医科大学检验系	1996年(第四届)
夏振海	男	河北工业大学材料与工程系	1996年(第四届)
颜炳文	男	南开大学元素有机化学研究所	1996年(第四届)
韩振勇	男	天津市市政工程设计研究院道桥设计一所	1996年(第四届)
翟京生	男	海军海洋测绘研究所	1996年(第四届)
樊明祥	男	天津中环三津公司	1996年(第四届)
卜显和	男	南开大学化学系	1998年(第五届)
马德华	男	天津市黄瓜研究所	1998年(第五届)
王春峰	男	天津大学系统工程研究所	1998年(第五届)
王树新	男	天津大学机械学院机械工程系	1998年(第五届)
元英进	男	天津大学化工学院生化工程系	1998年(第五届)
卢彦昌	男	天津市药业有限公司	1998年(第五届)
李广平	男	天津医科大学第二医院	1998年(第五届)
李永丹	男	天津大学化工学院催化科学与工程系	1998年(第五届)
李明智	男	南开大学允公集团	1998年(第五届)
李春成	男	天津市科学学研究所	1998年(第五届)
李俊建	男	地矿部天津地质矿产研究所	1998年(第五届)
张伟平	男	南开大学数学研究所	1998年(第五届)
张传友	男	天津钢管公司钢管研究所	1998年(第五届)
张华庆	男	交通部天津水运工程科学研究所	1998年(第五届)
张军平	男	天津中医学院第一附属医院	1998年(第五届)
张建树	男	天津市蔬菜技术推广站	1998年(第五届)
陈永川	男	南开大学组合数学研究中心	1998年(第五届)

续表10-2-3-62

姓名	性别	工作单位	获奖年份
郝建民	男	电子工业部第四十六所	1998年(第五届)
胡　珂	男	天津市测绘院	1998年(第五届)
倪建和	男	机械工业部天津工程机械研究所	1998年(第五届)
唐万生	男	天津大学系统工程研究所	1998年(第五届)
黄亚楼	男	南开大学计算机与系统科学系	1998年(第五届)
董世华	男	机械工业部天津电气传动设计研究所	1998年(第五届)
马军海	男	天津财经学院管理系	2001年(第六届)
王东江	男	天津市电视技术研究所	2001年(第六届)
牛瑞芳	女	天津医科大学肿瘤学中心实验室	2001年(第六届)
申　虹	女	南开大学物理科学学院	2001年(第六届)
邓运华	男	中国海洋石油渤海公司	2001年(第六届)
白海力	男	天津大学理学院	2001年(第六届)
朱铁麟	男	天津市建筑设计院	2001年(第六届)
沈中阳	男	天津市第一中心医院	2001年(第六届)
沈鑫基	男	天津市锻压机床厂	2001年(第六届)
李敏强	男	天津大学系统工程研究所	2001年(第六届)
李喜宏	男	中国农产品保鲜工程技术研究中心	2001年(第六届)
李鑫钢	男	天津大学化工学院	2001年(第六届)
杨　膺	男	天津液压机械(集团)有限公司	2001年(第六届)
杨愚鲁	男	南开大学信息技术与科学学院	2001年(第六届)
张兴彦	男	中铁第十八工程局科研设计院	2001年(第六届)
练继建	男	天津大学建筑工程学院	2001年(第六届)
胡　伟	男	天津市农机发展服务中心	2001年(第六届)
赵春华	男	中国医学科学院造血细胞和基因工程中心	2001年(第六届)
姜铁强	男	天津市工业自动化仪表研究所	2001年(第六届)
赵　巍	男	天津国际联合轮胎橡胶有限公司	2001年(第六届)
徐立军	男	天津大学自动化系	2001年(第六届)
高秀梅	女	天津中医学院中医工程研究所	2001年(第六届)
黄积涛	男	天津理工学院化工系	2001年(第六届)
廖前进	男	大港油田公司油气勘探开发技术研究中心	2001年(第六届)
王　舒	男	天津中医学院第一附属医院	2004年(第七届)
方复全	男	南开大学数学研究所	2004年(第七届)
丛培金	男	中环半导体有限公司	2004年(第七届)
吕晓龙	男	天津大学膜科学与技术研究所	2004年(第七届)
刘旭锴	男	天津市市政工程设计研究院	2004年(第七届)
许京军	男	南开大学物理科学学院	2004年(第七届)
阮国岭	男	国家海洋局天津海水淡化与综合利用研究所	2004年(第七届)
李　靖	男	南开大学化学学院	2004年(第七届)

续表10-2-3-62

姓名	性别	工作单位	获奖年份
李耀荣	男	天津宝成机械集团有限公司	2004年(第七届)
杨学军	男	天津医科大学总医院	2004年(第七届)
吴文清	男	天津石化公司乙烯厂	2004年(第七届)
张　健	男	国家计算机病毒应急处理中心	2004年(第七届)
张　磊	男	天津华立达生物工程有限公司	2004年(第七届)
陈立文	男	河北工业大学管理学院	2004年(第七届)
陈秋双	女	南开大学信息技术学院	2004年(第七届)
胡云凌	男	天津市建筑设计院三所	2004年(第七届)
钟登华	男	天津大学研究生院	2004年(第七届)
段发阶	男	天津大学精仪学院	2004年(第七届)
闻凤英	女	天津科润蔬菜研究所	2004年(第七届)
贾有良	男	天津市测绘院	2004年(第七届)
舒歌群	男	天津大学科技处	2004年(第七届)

二、天津市优秀科技工作者

1997年,市人事局、市科协共同设立“天津市优秀科技工作者”荣誉称号,并组织开展评选、表彰工作,旨在激励广大科技工作者积极投身“科教兴国”事业,为发展科技事业、促进经济繁荣、推动社会进步做出更大贡献。至2005年,共有50人获得天津市优秀科技工作者称号,其中2000年21人,2005年29人。

获得天津市优秀科技工作者称号名录

表10-2-3-63

姓名	性别	工作单位	获奖年份
聂永安	男	天津市地震局地震研究室	2000
温和平	男	天津市聚氨酯塑料制品厂	2000
朱　龙	男	天津市第二预应力钢丝有限公司	2000
张　勤	女	天津市水产研究所	2000
邢克智	男	天津农学院	2000
李嘉禄	男	天津纺织工学院	2000
申泮文	男	南开大学化学系	2000
何翠花	女	天津福津木业有限公司	2000
陆锡蕾	女	新型建材建筑设计研究院	2000
李国良	男	天津自然博物馆	2000
李浙东	男	交通部天津水工所	2000
唐宗成	男	天津市汉沽区茶淀乡人民政府	2000
王莉莉	女	天津市大港区建设工程质量监督站	2000
张伯良	男	天津市东丽区新立镇政府	2000
张继波	男	天津市津南区双港镇农科站	2000
高永新	男	天津市武清县农业局	2000
吴咸中	男	天津医科大学	2000

续表 10-2-3-63

姓名	性别	工作单位	获奖年份
王　宏	男	天津地质矿产研究所	2000
沈鑫基	男	天津液压机床总厂	2000
沈中阳	男	天津市第一中心医院	2000
李明智	男	天津戈德防伪识别有限公司	2000
王玉明	男	天津新技术产业园区鼎名密封有限公司	2005
刘昌孝	男	天津药物研究院	2005
张芝泉	男	天津赛象科技股份有限公司	2005
龙以明	男	南开大学数学所	2005
陈予恕	男	天津大学力学系	2005
张军平	男	天津中医学院	2005
丛培金	男	天津市中环半导体有限公司	2005
缴建华	男	天津市水产研究所	2005
万日明	男	天津市水利科学研究所	2005
乔东明	男	天津市种子管理站	2005
只达石	男	天津市环糊医院	2005
黄　靖	男	天津市建筑科学研究所	2005
张永明	男	天津市公路管理局	2005
李洪峰	男	天津港务局	2005
詹隽青	男	军事交通学院	2005
李若新	男	军事医学院卫生装备研究所	2005
张民杰	男	天津市国家安全局	2005
畅继武	男	天津市医大二院天津市泌尿外科研究所	2005
朱可能	男	天津市电力公司技术中心	2005
周四思	男	铁道第三勘察设计院	2005
胡　伟	男	天津市农业机械发展服务中心	2005
郭庆秋	男	天津市特变电工变压器有限公司	2005
张福芸	女	天津市津南区畜牧水产局水产技术推广站	2005
吕铁宏	男	天津有容蒂康通讯技术有限公司	2005
王　辰	男	天津市晨光化工有限公司	2005
辛乃宏	男	中盐制盐工程技术研究所	2005
刘庆廉	男	燕化集团天津润滑油脂有限公司	2005
董在成	男	宁河县蔬菜技术推广中心	2005
刘　勋	男	蓟县畜牧局技术服务中心	2005

三、天津市科技重大成就奖获得者

2000年，天津市设立科技重大成就奖。至2005年，共有4人获此殊荣。详见“获奖科技成果”。

四、天津市国际科技合作奖获得者

2000年,天津市设立国际科技合作奖。至2005年,3人获得天津市国际科技合作奖。详见“获奖科技成果”。

五、天津市巾帼发明家获得者

2005年,天津市知识产权局与市妇联开展天津市首届“巾帼发明家”评选活动,其中5人获得天津市首届“巾帼发明家”称号,5人获天津市首届“巾帼发明家”提名奖。

天津市首届“巾帼发明家”名录

表10-2-3-64

姓名	工作单位	职务(职称)	获奖年份
冯亚青	天津大学化工学院	教授、博士生导师	2005
许根慧	天津大学化工学院	教授、博士生导师	2005
宋存先	中国医学科学院生物医学工程研究所	研究员、博士生导师	2005
陈　虹	中国人民武装警察部队医学院	教授、硕士生导师	2005
王秀朵	天津市市政工程设计研究院	专业总工程师兼院副总工程师	2005

天津市首届“巾帼发明家”提名奖名录

表10-2-3-65

姓名	工作单位	职务(职称)	获奖年份
叶丽虹	南开大学	教授、博士生导师	2005
赵国防	天津农学院	教授	2005
胡　珂	天津工程机械研究院	高级工程师	2005
崔玉霞	天津渤天化工有限责任公司	高级工程师	2005
张瑛瑛	天津市塘沽区鑫宇环保科技有限公司	总工程师	2005

附　　录

重要讲话

天津市副市长梁肃
在全市技术创新工作会议上的讲话
（摘要）

（1999年12月29日）

一、深刻理解全面上水平的重要意义，努力提高加强科技进步和技术创新重要性、紧迫性的认识

今年10月，江总书记、朱总理在天津考察工作期间，视察了天津科技企业，听取了科技工作的汇报并做了重要指示。这使得科技战线干部群众受到了巨大鼓舞和激励，进一步增强了我们做好工作的信心。刚刚闭幕的市委七届五次全体会议，是在世纪之交的关键时刻召开的一次重要会议。当前，科技战线的一项重要任务，就是要把江总书记、朱总理对科技工作的指示和市委七届五次全会的精神学习好、贯彻好，在认清形势、把握基调、明确肩负职责的基础上，增强全市工作全面上水平，科技工作要率先上水平的紧迫感，用科技工作整体上水平来确保全市全面上水平。

（一）加深对技术创新重要意义的理解，进一步明确科技工作上水平的任务。

今年8月，中央召开全国技术创新大会，并作出了《中共中央、国务院关于加强技术创新，发展高科技，实现产业化的决定》，这是我国科技发展史上一个具有里程碑意义的盛会。江泽民总书记、朱镕基总理、李岚清副总理分别作了重要讲话。江泽民总书记在讲话中指出，“全面实施科教兴国战略，大力推动科技进步，加强科技创新，是事关祖国富强和民族振兴的大事。”《中共中央、国务院关于加强技术创新，发展高科技，实现产业化的决定》，是实施科教兴国和可持续发展战略的一项重大举措，是科技工作今后一个时期的纲领性文件。

在新形势下，加深理解全国技术创新大会和中央《决定》的精神，有利于我们进一步明确科技工作率先上水平所肩负的历史责任。这就是，(1)必须走有中国特色的技术跨越式发展道路，把实现技术跨越作为加强技术创新和科技成果产业化的重要目标。(2)促进企业成为技术创新的主体，成为科技成果转化的主力。建立健全企业技术创新机制，全面提高企业技术创新能力。(3)发展高科技，实现产业化。这不仅是科技与经济结合的关键点，而且也是国民经济发展的着力点。

（二）深刻领会市委全会精神，进一步提高技术创新的自觉性。

市委七届五次全体会议，确定了“乘势而上，开拓创新，全面上水平”的工作基调。提出，天津已经进入全面追求上水平的年代。全面上水平，是时代的要求、历史的责任、人民的愿望。

全市工作全面上水平，核心是经济工作整体上水平。经济工作整体上水平的主要任务是抓好结构调整、技术创新和对外开放三件大事。这三件大事，事事都与科技进步密切相关，因此，经济工作整体上水平，科技工作必须要率先上水平，科技界要承担起这一光荣而艰巨的历史使命。

这次全会审议并通过的《中共天津市委关于加速科技进步和技术创新的若干意见》，是市委面向新世纪，抓住机遇，迎接挑战的重大决策，对今后本市科技事业的发展具有重要的指导意义，对21世纪本市经济和社会各项事业的发展也将产生深远影响。《若干意见》深刻阐述了依靠科技进步，加强技术创新的重要意

义，提出了主要任务和目标，全市科技工作上水平，就是要围绕《若干意见》提出的目标，全面落实各项任务。对此，我们一定要增强做好科技工作的自觉性，抓住机遇，发挥优势，横下一条心，迎着困难上，用5年左右时间，使科技工作的水平得到整体和全面提高，为全市经济发展做出新的贡献。

（三）抓住机遇，迎接挑战，进一步增强责任感和紧迫感。

本市经济已经连续5年高于全国平均增长水平，位居全国发展较快地区的行列，形成了自己的特色和优势。如何巩固和发展天津的特色和优势，如何在保持经济良性运行的同时加快发展，这是我们面临的严峻挑战和考验。目前，知识和科技的更新速度越来越快，科技成果商品化、产业化的周期大大缩短，新科技革命的浪潮来势凶猛。作为重要因素参与经济竞争的同时，科技进步各个领域本身的竞争也日趋激烈。如果我们不紧紧跟上科技进步的时代潮流，不在技术创新上大踏步前进，就会陷入极为被动的境地。作为老工业基地，作为沿海开放城市，我们既有累积多年的深层次矛盾需要解决，又有国际经济一体化趋势对我们更直接的影响需要应战。这几年，我们虽然发展很快，但与世界发达国家和国内先进地区相比，仍然有很大差距。据统计，去年天津市国内生产总值人均占有1700美元，这个水平高于全国平均水平一倍多，而同期欧美、日本等国则达3万美元左右。不缩小这个差距，我们参与国际竞争就难于取胜。经济上的差距，是科技实力差距的反映。提高科技整体实力，必须要解决好科技工作不适应经济和社会发展需要的薄弱环节。包括：(1)能够拉动全市国民经济发展的、市场前景好、能较快形成经济规模、拥有自主知识产权的高水平重大项目不多。(2)企业还没有真正成为科技进步的主体。大部分科技资源集中在独立的科研机构中，游离于企业之外，不适应产业化的要求。科技体制改革还需要进一步加快。(3)促进科技成果产业化的市场机制还不够健全，科技投入不足。(4)培养和吸引大批高水平人才，仍然是科技进步事业发展中的突出问题。解决好这些问题，是形势的需要，是发展的需要。因此，全面上水平不是想不想上，要不要上的问题，是形势逼着我们要上水平，跨世纪的发展目标要求我们必须上水平。对此我们一定要增强加快发展的紧迫感和危机感。

二、技术创新和高新技术产业化为科技上水平奠定了良好的基础和条件

首先，市委、市政府科技发展的指导思想清楚，路子明确。1995年，市委、市政府召开天津市科学技术大会，提出了实施“科教兴市”战略，并制定了《关于贯彻全国科学技术大会精神加速科学技术进步的实施意见》。当时，立昌同志在大会讲话中强调指出，天津已经进入全面追求科技进步的年代，经济发展必须要走科技路，吃科技饭，新上项目要把住“病从口入”关，低水平重复建设的项目一个都能不上，宁肯少上项目也绝不再欠科技帐。在此之后，又对科技工作提出了高人一筹，领先一步的要求，本市科技事业进入了大发展的时期。市委、市政府审时度势，从本市的实际出发，在市第七次党代会和市十三届人大一次会议上，进一步明确了天津经济建设从根本上“必须走出一条依靠科技进步、提高整体素质，实现加快发展、增强经济实力的路子。”从全面追求科技进步的年代，到全面追求上水平的年代，天津已经进入了一个新的发展阶段。正是因为我们坚定不移地在全市范围内不断加大“科教兴市”战略实施力度，我们才具备了今天加强技术创新，发展高科技，实现产业化的初步基础和上水平的条件。

其次，高新技术产业迅速发展，重点领域初具规模。几年来，通过实施“科技百亿工程”“重大科技产业化工程”和制定实施《天津市高新技术产业发展规划》，出台了一批配套支持的政策，一批以高新技术为特征的新兴产业初具规模，高新技术产业在经济总量中的比重稳步提高，据统计，1999年全市高新技术产品产值将达570亿元，占工业总产值的比重达20%。电子信息、生物技术与现代医药、新能源三个领域占高新技术产品产值的70%。重大产业化工程20个项目今年预计产值增幅达两倍多。锂离子电池、镍氢电池、α-2b干扰素等一批高新技术项目正在形成产业规模，并显示出良好的发展前景。天士力公司的复方丹参滴丸以药品的形式通过美国FDA临床用药申请，已直接进入二、三期临床验证阶段，成为国产中药进入美国正规药品市场的先行者。

第三、科技进步带动了传统产业的发展。在传统产业改造中，本市坚持引进国外先进技术与自主创新相结合，大力推动企业技术创新工作，促进企业成为技术创新的主体。在突出抓好对国外先进技术消化吸

收的同时,注重新产品开发和在传统产业中推广CAD、CIMS等共性高新技术,使工业系统新产品产值率达到22.5%。传统产业大量应用现代高新技术,使许多企业再次焕发生机。汽车公司应用新技术生产的环保型夏利汽车,在北京等大城市受到青睐。药业公司大胆革新地塞米松生产工艺,多次大幅度降低产品成本,在与国外著名公司的竞争中取得了初步胜利。

第四、坚持引进与自主创新并重的方针,初步摸索出一条具有天津特色的发展高新技术产业经验。一批国外知名企业落户津门,一批民族高科技企业迅速壮大,一批重点高科技产品已经具有较强的市场竞争能力。天大天财公司股票上市并实现配股、南开戈德公司借壳上市,一些高新技术企业开始着手海外融资,发展高科技实现产业化的资金渠道进一步拓宽,带动了高新技术企业的发展。经济技术开发区和新技术产业园区已初步成为本市高新技术产业的发展基地。高新技术产品出口迅速增长,高新技术产品出口额占全市出口额的比重已达23.8%。

第五、科技体制改革使科研单位增强了适应市场的能力。一批科研院所开始向企业化转制,推动了科技资源的合理配置。民营科技企业达到5200家,预计今年技工贸总收入达230亿元,增长幅度达15%。信息港建设加快了全市信息化进程,提高了城市功能。科技计划项目引进市场竞争机制,实施招投标制度、评估制度等,取得了好的效果。

第六、综合科技实力和科技创新能力显著提高。本市综合科技实力在全国各省市中的排名,由1993年度的第七位,跃升至1998年度的第三位。在国家"九五"科技攻关重中之重的51个项目中,本市独立承担或参与的项目就达17项。一批优秀科技成果获得国家级奖励,获奖数量、级别等都达到近年最好水平,地方申报项目的获奖数量在全国各省市中排第二位。在今年中国科学院和工程院院士遴选中,本市有5位专家当选中国工程院院士,是历次遴选新增院士人数最多的一次,这不仅是五位院士的荣誉,也是天津科技事业发展进程中一件值得庆贺的大事。

我们要充分利用好这些基础和条件,乘势而上,开拓创新,全面推进科技工作整体率先上水平。

三、以技术创新为突破口,促进科技工作率先上水平

科技进步和技术创新是生产力发展的决定因素,是经济和社会发展的主导力量。天津经济工作上水平,科学技术必须首先上水平。

实现科学技术上水平,必须要坚定不移地走好"依靠科技进步,提高整体素质,实现加快发展,增强经济实力"的路子。如何走好这条路子,科技工作要以技术创新为突破口,在提高传统产业技术水平、促进高新技术产业化、增强技术储备三个方面抓出成效。

市委《若干意见》明确了全市科技上水平的方向和主要任务。我们要以全面落实《若干意见》为目标,在2000年从6个方面抓好技术创新工作。

(一)提高技术创新能力,运用高新技术改造传统产业。

江泽民同志指出,"技术创新,主要是企业应用新的知识和新技术、新工艺,采用新的生产方式和经营管理模式,提高产品质量,开发新的产品,增强市场竞争的能力和抵御风险的能力。"

企业作为市场竞争的主体,只有抢占技术制高点,才能跳出低水平竞争的圈子,在激烈的市场竞争中立于不败之地。目前,天津市部分企业技术创新机制还不适应形势发展的要求,表现在科技投入方面,差距明显。据统计,本市企业科技研究开发的经费投入占销售收入的比重仅为1%左右,而世界发达国家的大企业达到5%以上。本市企业的技术装备水平大大落后于国际水平,已过折旧年限仍在使用的设备高达35%,六、七十年的设备占60%。一些企业的生产工艺也是相当陈旧。要改变这种状况,必须要从改革机制入手,增强创新意识,使企业真正成为技术创新的主体。

今年全市国民经济继续保持良好发展态势,国内生产总值预计增长10%以上,工业生产摆脱了徘徊局面,实现了快速发展,成为拉动经济增长的主要因素。我们要抓住有利时机,加快技术创新和运用先进技术改造传统产业的步伐,一方面利用国家增量资金,加大技改投入,对落后的工艺进行一次根本性的革命;另

一方面积极推广应用CAD. CAPP. CAM. CAE. CIMS、RP、虚拟制造技术等先进共性技术，提高企业自主开发能力、快速适应市场能力，提高产品技术附加值和产品质量，促使传统产业实现升级，获得新的发展。

农业技术创新是全市技术创新的重要组成部分，农业科技产业化也是全市科技进步的重要标志。要进一步加强农业科技开发，加快农业技术创新，促进信息技术、生物技术等先进技术与传统农业技术的结合，加大农业先进技术推广力度，建设一批高标准农业科技示范区和示范项目，促进农业加快科技产业化、实现现代化。

（二）加快高新技术产业化步伐，塑造新世纪的支柱产业。

国际科技发展动态显示，高新技术及其产业自80年代以来，一直保持着强劲的发展势头，已经成为经济增长最重要的源泉。过去10年中，主要发达国家高新技术产业在制造业中的比重翻了一番，目前这一趋势还在加快。本市高新技术产业的发展已有一定的基础，并在某些领域形成了相对优势。但是从天津的产业结构看，高新技术产业产值占工业总产值的比重、高新技术产品出口占全市出口的比重，这两项指标都还不高。按照全面上水平来要求，我们要在四个方面努力实现高新技术产业发展上水平。一是发展速度实现上水平。我们要以面向21世纪的战略眼光和气魄，着眼长远，狠抓当前，整体推进，重点突破，力争经过几年的努力，到2005年，使本市高新技术产业产值占工业总产值的比重达到25%以上，初步形成高新技术支柱产业，使本市产业结构有一个根本性的变化。二是发展规模实现上水平。现在实施的20项重大高新技术产业化项目到2002年计划总产值达到121亿元，规模还不大。要选择一批有产业前景、有人才资源、有技术储备的重大项目和重点领域，有针对性地加强政策支持和工作推动，加大投入，加快进度，努力形成一批有天津特色、能够达到100亿元产值规模的高新技术产业，成为经济发展新的支柱行业。三是机制创新实现上水平。全面引进市场与竞争机制，通过资产重组和科研机构与企业跨部门、跨行业联合，促进科技资源的优化组合。积极推行招投标制度，建立科学公正的科技评估体系。以市场为导向，以产品为龙头，采用现代企业运行机制，促进产业结构调整。四是基地建设实现上水平。新技术产业园区和经济技术开发区要努力建设成为本市高新技术的孵化基地和产业化基地。要以全国一流水平为目标，强化科技成果产业化的服务功能，成为本市高新技术产业发展的示范区。

（三）加大研究与开发力度，搞好技术和项目的储备。

我们要实现跨世纪发展目标，就必须在一些关键产业和重点领域形成足够的技术支撑能力。这样，才能真正做到高人一筹，领先一步。

一是要跟踪世界科技发展趋势，结合国情和市情，深入开展科技发展战略研究。结合制定本市科技发展“十五”规划，选择重点领域，做好战略性技术储备的计划，选准应用基础研究和战略性高技术研究的突破口。当前要重点抓好电子信息、生物技术与现代医药、新能源等重点领域的科研开发，尽快建立具有战略性、前瞻性的技术储备“项目库”，每年向重大高新技术产业化计划提供3至5个成熟项目。

二是大力培育科技项目资源，开发一批具有自主知识产权的科技成果，为天津市高新技术产业和新兴支柱产业的发展提供知识源泉和技术储备。以数字化技术、光电子技术、纳米技术、新药创制技术等高新技术领域为重点，以达到中试水平为标准，积极开展重大科技攻关，并力争跻身国家级计划，为产业化提供较为成熟的项目资源。要进一步强化知识产权意识，努力开发拥有自主知识产权的项目和产品。在某些战略性、基础性的重点领域，我们必须要坚持自主创新，要有自主的知识产权。

三是要进一步开阔视野、广辟渠道，积极吸纳国内外高科技资源，增加高新技术项目储备。充分挖掘高等院校、本市和驻津科研单位的科技成果，筛选出一批有产业化潜力和市场前景的项目，组织力量进行二次开发。进一步加强与中国科学院、工程院以及国内著名大学、科研单位的科技合作，有针对性地吸纳重点领域的科研成果，积极争取把国家“863”成果引入本市进行中试和产业化。大力吸引国外跨国公司在天津设立研发机构。围绕重点领域进一步加强引进国外智力工作，推动本市与国外著名科研机构的科技交流，建立项目协作关系。举办高水平学术论坛，积极支持重点领域的学术交流活动，使天津在若干学科成为全国、乃至世界的学术交流中心。

(四)加快信息港工程建设,推动经济与社会信息化进程。

要进一步加快信息产业发展,不断完善信息化建设体系。把天津市建设成为全国主要的信息中心和重要的信息装备与产品制造基地。2000年,要基本完成信息港工程总体规划第一阶段的建设任务,完成“2119工程”基本构架。大力推动电子商务等新兴服务业的发展,努力提高第三产业的科技含量。启动国有企业上网工程,推动企业上网。加快实施政府上网工程,完善交互网建设。加强信息资源建设. 大力发展软件产业。

(五)进一步深化科技体制改革,构建新型技术创新体系。

要按照加速技术创新和科技成果产业化的要求,深化科技体制改革,转变运行机制,把科技人员的聪明才智和潜能充分发挥出来,把现有科研设施的能力进行合理配置和充分利用。要重点做好四个方面的工作。一是加快科研院所转制步伐,2000年上半年要完成市属开发型科研院所企业化转制。同时,要积极吸引和鼓励驻津科研院所转制属地化,进一步加强这些具有较高水平的科技资源与本市经济发展的融合。二是加强科技创新体系建设。2000年,新建2至3个科学研究中心、8至10个工程技术中心。到2002年,要建成10个科学研究中心、20个工程技术研究中心和50个企业技术开发中心,使其成为全市科技创新体系的骨干。三是进一步加强科技服务体系建设。发挥技术市场、科技咨询、科技信息、专利服务、生产力促进中心、科技创业中心等科技服务机构的功能,在市场开拓、技术开发、信息咨询、人才培训等方面提高服务功能和水平。四是大力推动民营科技企业发展。要为民营科技企业创造平等竞争的环境,积极帮助民营科技企业解决实际困难,扶持其加快发展。

(六)进一步创造有利于技术创新和科技成果产业化的社会环境。

加强技术创新,发展高科技,实现产业化,是跨越科技和经济两大领域,涉及诸多环节的工作,必须依靠和集中全社会的力量,共同推进。在这方面,要重点解决好三个问题。

一是人才问题。要把人才建设和重点领域建设、基地建设结合起来,培养造就一支高素质人才队伍。对科技人员,在注重培养学术研究能力的同时,要加强对创新和创业能力的培养。努力造就一批有科技头脑的经营管理人才。通过充分发挥两院在津院士及本市中青年授衔专家作用,在高等院校、科研院所、重点行业、优势学科和重点高新技术领域,选拔一批具有国内先进水平的优秀科技人才进行重点培养,努力造就一大批德才兼备、能够站在国内和世界科学技术前沿的学术带头人和尖子人才,抓紧建立和完善高层次的“人才库”。积极吸引国内外杰出科技人才来津工作,鼓励他们以各种方式参与本市经济建设。要积极创造条件,不断改善科技骨干的工作和生活条件。

二是机制问题。进一步健全科技发展和科技成果转化的激励机制,落实和完善鼓励技术创新、发展高新技术产业的有关政策措施。《若干意见》中确定了一些相关政策和措施,在资金、税收、技术入股、聚拢人才等方面有很大的突破。比如,允许和鼓励技术、管理等生产要素参与收益分配;以高新技术向企业出资入股的,其作价金额可由提供技术与资金的各方协商决定,科技成果占股权的比例不受限制,等等。各有关部门要制定具体实施细则,把《若干意见》和有关政策、措施落到实处。要改革本市科学技术奖励制度,鼓励和规范社会力量对各种科学技术的奖励,精简奖项和获奖数量,加大奖励力度。

三是资金问题。要进一步拓宽高新技术产业发展资金渠道,努力提高全社会科技投入水平。企业要尽快成为科技投入的主体,高新技术企业每年用于研究开发的经费要达到年销售额的5%以上,国有大中型企业要达到2%至3%,一般工业企业不低于1%。要确保每年财政科技投入增长高于财政经常性收入的增长幅度。同时要积极吸纳社会各类资金用于科技事业的发展,建设多渠道、社会化的科技投入体系。对社会力量资助本市科研机构及高等院校的科研开发经费,按照国家有关规定给予税收优惠。积极建立风险投资机制,推动高技术企业上市融资,通过资本运作迅速壮大规模。

政策法规

中共天津市委、天津市人民政府《关于依靠科技进步，加快经济发展的若干意见》

（津党发〔1992〕17号　1992年8月8日）

（略）

天津市技术市场管理条例

（天津市第十二届人民代表大会常务委员会第三次会议通过　1993年10月28日公布实施）

第一章　总　则

第一条　为繁荣技术贸易，完善技术市场管理，推动科学技术为经济建设服务，根据国家有关法律、法规，结合本市实际情况，制定本条例。

第二条　凡符合国家产业政策和技术政策，促进经济建设、技术进步和社会发展的技术，都可以作为商品进行交易，但国家另有规定的除外。

第三条　各级人民政府应当对技术市场实行放开、搞活、扶植、引导的方针，鼓励开展多层次、多渠道、多形式的技术贸易活动。

第四条　从事技术贸易活动，应当遵循自愿平等、互利有偿、诚实信用的原则。

第五条　鼓励公民、法人和其他组织参与技术市场交易活动，其知识产权和其他合法权益受法律保护。

第六条　在本市行政区域内从事技术贸易活动，应当遵守本条例。

第二章　管理机构

第七条　市人民政府科学技术管理部门是全市技术市场的主管部门。区、县人民政府科学技术管理部门负责本地区的技术市场管理工作。其他有关行政管理部门负责本系统的技术市场管理工作。

第八条　技术市场行政主管部门的职责是：（一）贯彻、实施有关技术市场的法律、法规；（二）审核、管理技术贸易机构，核发《技术贸易证书》；（三）管理技术合同的认定登记，进行技术市场的统计分析；（四）负责技术市场管理和经营人员的培训、考核工作；（五）组织交流技术市场信息，协调和监督技术贸易活动；（六）对在技术市场工作中做出成绩的人员进行表彰和奖励；（七）会同或者协同有关部门对技术贸易活动中违反本条例的行为进行检查处理；（八）负责技术市场的其他管理工作。

第九条　各级工商、财政、税务、物价、统计等部门，应当按照各自的职责，协同技术市场行政主管部门对技术市场进行管理。

第三章　技术贸易机构

第十条　公民、法人设立技术贸易机构，应当具备下列条件：（一）有机构的名称和场所；（二）有技术商品的经营范围；（三）有与业务范围相适应的专业技术人员；（四）有与业务范围相适应并能独立支配的财产和资金。

第十一条 设立技术贸易机构,应当经技术市场行政主管部门审核合格后,向工商和税务行政管理部门办理注册登记手续。

第十二条 技术贸易机构分立、合并、迁移、撤销或者变更其他注册项目的,应当到技术市场、工商和税务行政管理部门办理变更或者注销登记手续。

第四章 技术贸易活动

第十三条 订立技术合同,应当符合技术合同法及其实施条例的规定。合同的标的可以是专利技术,也可以是非专利技术,以及实现这些技术的物质载体。

第十四条 技术贸易机构在工商行政管理部门核准的经营范围内,可以从事下列活动:(一)进行技术开发、技术转让、技术咨询和技术服务等技术贸易活动;(二)生产或者经销科研中试产品和科技新产品;(三)组织和开展技术成果的推广和应用;(四)符合开展中介业务条件的,可以进行技术中介服务;(五)具备法人资格的,可以创办或者领办技、工(农)、贸一体化的科技开发实体;(六)其他技术贸易活动。

第十五条 涉及国家安全或者重大利益需要保密的技术,国家实行许可证制度的技术,在进行交易时,按照国家有关规定办理。

第十六条 技术中介机构和技术经纪人的合法活动和收入,受法律保护。

第十七条 科技人员在完成本职工作和不侵犯所在单位技术权益的条件下,从事技术贸易活动的合法收入,受法律保护。科技人员参与技术贸易活动,应当遵守法律、法规的有关规定。

第五章 技术合同认定登记

第十八条 技术合同的认定登记,由市技术市场行政主管部门设立的技术合同登记机构,按照国家有关部门的规定进行,并实行一次性登记制度。经认定登记的技术合同,可以享受技术市场优惠政策。

第十九条 技术合同登记机构,应当审查当事人订立的合同是否真实、合法,对于真实、合法的,应当发给登记证明并核定技术性收入。技术合同登记机构,应当自接到申请之日起三十日内,做出认定结论,并书面通知申请人。

第二十条 从事技术合同认定登记的工作人员,应当具备专业技术知识,并经考核合格后,方可从事认定登记工作。

第二十一条 通过招标确定的技术项目,应当依照技术合同法的规定,由当事人订立委托开发合同。该合同经技术市场登记机构认定登记,可以享受技术市场优惠政策。

第二十二条 技术合同登记机构对申请认定登记的合同,按合同成交额的千分之一至千分之二收取认定登记费。

第二十三条 技术市场行政主管部门和技术合同登记机构,应当按照国家有关部门的规定,做好统计工作。

第六章 财税管理和收益分配

第二十四条 技术的价款、报酬或者使用费,由当事人根据技术成果的经济效益和社会效益、研究开发技术的成本、技术成果的工业化开发程度、智力劳动强度以及当事人享有的权益和承担的责任协商议定。技术的价款、报酬或者使用费中包含非技术性款项的,应当分项计算,不得将非技术性收入计入技术性收入。

第二十五条 企业单位支付的技术价款、报酬或者使用费,可以一次或者分期摊入成本。事业单位支付技术价款、报酬或者使用费,可以在事业费包干结余或者预算外收入中列支;没有事业费包干结余和预算外收入的,可以在事业费中列支。

第二十六条 法人和其他组织从事技术贸易的收入，应当纳入本单位的财务管理。

第二十七条 技术合同当事人凭技术合同登记机构的认定登记证明，可以向税务部门办理减免税手续。

第二十八条 从事技术贸易活动的技术供方凭技术合同的登记证明，可以从技术性纯收入中提取20%至40%的金额，用于奖励有关人员。购入新技术的企业，可以从采用新技术而增加利润之日起一年内，从新增利润中一次性提取一定的金额，用于奖励有关人员。必要时，市人民政府可以制定具体奖励办法。

第二十九条 各级人民政府应当筹建技术市场发展基金，用于技术成果商品化、产业化以及加速技术成果的推广应用。

第三十条 企业事业单位从事技术贸易活动的收入不超过免税额度的，免征所得税。新开办的集体性质的技术贸易机构，从取得第一笔收入的月份起，免征所得税一年。免税期满纳税确有困难的，经税务部门批准，可以减免所得税。企业事业单位和个人从事技术贸易活动的收入，按照国家有关规定，享受减免营业税优惠。

第三十一条 税务部门对公民个人从事技术开发、技术转让的技术性收入征税时，按照技术成果的实际开发时间确定征税基数。

第七章 奖励和处罚

第三十二条 各级人民政府及其有关主管部门，应当对在技术市场和技术贸易工作中做出显著成绩的单位、集体和个人，给予表彰和奖励。

第三十三条 技术合同登记机构擅自提高合同登记费标准或者违反规定进行认定登记的，由技术市场行政主管部门，对其进行通报批评，责令限期整顿；情节严重的，取消其登记权。

第三十四条 技术市场行政主管部门和技术合同登记机构的工作人员玩忽职守、营私舞弊的，由所在单位对其进行批评教育或者给予行政处分；构成犯罪的，由司法机关依法追究刑事责任。

第三十五条 在技术贸易活动中违反国家保密规定，泄露国家技术机密的，由所在单位给予行政处分；构成犯罪的，由司法机关依法追究刑事责任。

第三十六条 在技术贸易活动中，侵害公民、法人或者其他组织合法权益的，依法承担民事责任；构成犯罪的，由司法机关依法追究刑事责任。

第三十七条 当事人对技术市场行政主管部门及其他行政管理部门做出的决定不服的，可以在接到决定书之日起十五日内，向其上级行政机关或者法律、法规规定的行政机关申请复议，也可以依法向人民法院提起诉讼。

第三十八条 发生技术合同争议的当事人，可以通过协商或者调解解决。当事人不愿协商、调解或者协商调解不成的，可以依据合同约定的仲裁条款或者事后达成的书面仲裁协议，向技术合同仲裁机构或者经济合同仲裁机构申请仲裁。当事人一方在规定期限内，不履行仲裁决定的，另一方可以申请人民法院强制执行。当事人未在合同中订立仲裁条款，事后又没有达成书面仲裁协议的，可以向人民法院起诉。

第八章 附 则

第三十九条 本条例自公布之日起施行。

天津市实施《中华人民共和国科学技术进步法》办法

（天津市第十二届人民代表大会常务委员会第五次会议通过　1994年1月26日公布实施）

第一条　为了发挥科学技术第一生产力的作用，促进科学技术进步，推动科学技术为经济建设服务，加速本市经济、社会的发展，根据《中华人民共和国科学技术进步法》，结合本市实际情况，制定本办法。

第二条　各级人民政府应当保障科学研究的自由，鼓励科学探索和技术创新，鼓励自然科学研究与社会科学研究相结合，保护知识产权，促进科技成果转化为现实生产力。

第三条　全社会都应当尊重知识，尊重人才，增强科学技术意识，注重普及科学技术知识，切实提高公民的科学文化水平，推动科学技术进步。

第四条　各级人民政府和有关主管部门，应当采取有效措施，鼓励科学研究和技术开发，推广应用科学技术成果，改造传统产业，发展高新技术产业以及应用科学技术为经济建设和社会发展服务的活动。

第五条　市人民政府领导全市科学技术工作，根据经济建设和社会发展的目标，组织制定全市科学技术发展规划和计划，制定相应的技术政策。区、县人民政府领导本区、县的科学技术工作，根据本区、县的实际情况，采取措施，推进科学技术进步工作。

第六条　市人民政府科学技术行政管理部门，负责全市科学技术工作的宏观管理与统筹协调，编制科学研究发展计划方案。市人民政府其他有关行政管理部门，在市人民政府规定的职责范围内，管理科学技术进步工作。

第七条　市人民政府应当采取措施，推进科学技术进步，使本市经济增长中科学技术进步因素所占比重逐年提高，其增长的幅度要高于全国平均增长水平。

第八条　市和区、县人民政府，应当建立和发展技术市场，运用市场机制，对科学技术成果进行推广和应用。

第九条　有农业的区、县人民政府，应当根据全市农业科学技术规划，编制本地区的农业科学技术进步规划，逐步建立区域性农业科学技术成果推广实验区和种养业品种改良繁育基地，发展高产、优质、高效的现代化农业。

第十条　市和有农业的区、县、乡、镇人民政府，应当采取措施，保障和改善农业技术推广机构的工作条件，支持建立农民科学技术协会、专业技术研究会和其他群众性科学技术推广服务组织。农业技术推广机构和群众性科学技术推广服务组织，可以依法进行农业技术承包和农业技术推广服务活动。

第十一条　农业科学研究机构、高等院校和科学技术工作者，可以与农业技术推广机构建立多种形式的科学技术经济合作组织，其中对农业提供技术服务的，享受国家在税收、信贷等方面给予的支持。

第十二条　各级科学技术行政管理部门和行业主管部门，应当支持乡镇企业和城市集体企业的科学技术进步，鼓励大中型企业、科学研究开发机构、高等院校和社会团体以各种方式为乡镇企业和城市集体企业提供技术服务。

第十三条　企业应当根据行业特点，制定实现科学技术进步的目标，并采取措施，推进企业科学技术进步。企业应当充分发挥总工程师或者技术负责人在科学技术进步工作中的作用，实行技术工作责任制。

第十四条　工业企业进行技术改造，从国外引进先进技术和设备，应当经过咨询论证，贯彻国家的产业政策和技术政策。

第十五条　企业应当逐步推广和采用国际标准，完善企业技术标准和质量、计量规范管理。

第十六条　企业应当按照国家和本市有关规定，建立健全管理人员、科学技术工作者和工人的技术培训制度，不断提高职工的科学技术水平。

第十七条 本市建立新技术产业园区，对区内企业在税收、信贷、人才流动、进出口贸易等方面实行优惠政策，鼓励高新技术产品的开发和生产，促进高新技术成果的商品化、产业化，支持高新技术企业参与国际竞争。企业、科学研究开发机构和高等院校，在新技术产业园区内，可以创办或者联办高新技术企业，并享受国家和本市规定的优惠政策。

第十八条 市人民政府应当采取措施，保障基础研究和应用基础研究的发展。重点基础性研究课题，由市科学技术行政管理部门按照计划组织实施。各有关主管部门应当支持和加强基础性研究及重点实验室的建设。

第十九条 本市设立自然科学基金和青年科学基金，资助基础研究和应用基础研究，扶持优秀青年的科学研究活动。

第二十条 市科学技术行政管理部门应当会同有关部门，本着集中优势、重点发展、择优支持的原则，对独立科学研究开发机构实行宏观管理。

第二十一条 鼓励公民、法人或者其他组织依法创办民营科学研究开发机构，其合法权益受法律保护。对其中从事高新技术研究开发的机构和做出突出贡献的个人，应当同样享受国家和本市规定的有关优惠政策。

第二十二条 市人民政府应当对于从事基础研究、高技术研究、重大工程项目研究、重大科学技术攻关项目研究、重大社会公益项目研究的科学研究开发机构，根据实际需要按项目每年为其拨付一定经费。用以改善科学研究条件和更新实验手段。

第二十三条 各级人民政府和企业事业组织，应当提高包括优秀技术工人在内的科学技术工作者的社会地位，逐步改善其工作、生活条件，对在工作中应用科学技术做出显著成绩的，给予优厚待遇。

第二十四条 本市逐步实行科学技术工作者和用人单位双向选择的聘用合同制，健全人才交流中介服务组织，为人才合理流动创造条件。

第二十五条 科学技术工作者有依法创办或者参加科学技术团体的权利和接受继续教育的权利与义务。各级科学技术协会和学术团体，应当在组织科学技术工作者参加学术和技术交流，参与科学技术重大项目的决策论证，普及科学技术知识，开展咨询服务，以及维护科学技术工作者合法权益等方面发挥作用。

第二十六条 科学技术工作者在完成本职工作和不侵犯本单位技术权益的前提下，经所在聘用单位同意，可以在企业事业单位或者其他组织兼职，其合法收入受法律保护。科学技术工作者从事兼职活动，应当遵守法律、法规的规定。

第二十七条 有关单位或者组织对科学技术工作者完成职务技术成果，或者履行技术开发、技术转让、技术咨询、技术服务合同的，应当从所获得的技术性纯收入中，按照规定提取奖酬金予以奖励。

第二十八条 出国留学人员以外币向本市企业投资进行技术开发或者实行技术入股的，依照国家和本市的规定享受优惠政策。

第二十九条 市和区、县人民政府应当制定措施，吸引国内外科学技术工作者来本市工作；对来本市工作的出国留学、进修人员，本着来去自由的原则，为其提供方便，并在解决住房、医疗保健、配偶和子女进市户口等方面给予照顾。

第三十条 具有高级职称的科学技术工作者根据工作需要、本人意愿和健康状况，经批准可以按照国家规定延长离休、退休年龄。

第三十一条 离休、退休的科学技术工作者，可以创办、领办科学研究开发机构和科学技术企业。各级人民政府和企业事业单位，应当为离休、退休的科学技术工作者从事科学技术活动创造条件，提供方便。

第三十二条 市和区、县人民政府在财政预算中用于科学技术的经费应当逐年有所增加，其增长幅度应当高于财政经常性收入的增长幅度。任何单位和个人不得挪用、克扣、截留财政用于科学技术的经费。

第三十三条 全市科学技术研究开发的经费与国民生产总值的比例应当逐年提高，并逐步达到全国先进水平，具体比例由市人民政府规定。

第三十四条 企业应当逐步增加研究开发和技术创新的投入,其技术开发费按实际发生额计入成本费用。企业技术开发费的使用列入企业年终审计。

第三十五条 金融机构应当设立专项科学技术开发项目贷款,根据需要逐年增加贷款数额,并优先发放。

第三十六条 企业和具备企业法人资格的科学研究开发机构,根据国家有关规定,可以通过发行债券、股票等方式,向社会筹集科学技术开发资金。

第三十七条 本市建立科学技术投资风险基金,支持科学技术成果的商品化、产业化。

第三十八条 市和区、县人民政府,应当鼓励公民、法人或者其他组织开展国际科学技术交流与合作。本市企业事业单位或者个人,可以依法与境外的科学技术界开展科学技术合作,举办科学技术研讨会、展示会、展览会等活动。

第三十九条 市和区、县人民政府,应当鼓励企业引进技术,扩大出口,推动双向技术交流。其中为发展高新技术需要进口的设备及其零部件,以及出口高新技术产品,按照国家规定享受优惠政策。

第四十条 参与国际科学技术合作交流的单位和个人,必须保守国家秘密,维护国家利益。对属于国家严格控制的珍贵生物种质资源的出境,必须按照国家有关规定经有关部门批准。

第四十一条 境内外的组织和个人来本市投资进行科学研究和技术开发,可以采取合资、合作或者国家准许的其他形式,其合法权益受法律保护。

第四十二条 各级人民政府对在科学技术进步活动中做出贡献的单位和个人,应当给予表彰和奖励。具体奖励办法,由市人民政府规定。

第四十三条 各级科学技术行政管理部门,对违反本办法的组织和个人,有权进行检查、督促,并向其上级主管部门提出处理建议。对违法情节严重的组织和个人,或者应当作出处理而拒不处理的有关主管部门,报请同级人民政府予以处理。

第四十四条 违反本办法规定,有下列行为之一的,依法承担民事责任或者行政责任;构成犯罪的,依法追究刑事责任:(一)玩忽职守或者滥用职权作出错误科学技术决策造成重大经济损失的;(二)侵犯科学技术研究开发机构自主权,干扰科学研究和技术开发正常活动的;(三)挪用或者克扣科学技术经费的;(四)压制发明创造,打击迫害科学技术工作者的;(五)侵害科学技术工作者的发明权、专利权、著作权或者其他科学技术成果权,扣发科学技术工作者应得的荣誉证书、奖金或者报酬的;(六)在科学技术活动中,弄虚作假,骗取优惠待遇或者奖励的;(七)非法窃取或者泄露科学技术秘密的。

第四十五条 本办法自公布之日起施行。

中共天津市委　天津市人民政府
《关于贯彻全国科技大会精神，加速科学技术进步的实施意见》

（津党发〔1995〕23号　1995年8月16日）

（略）

天津市科学技术普及条例

（天津市十二届人民代表大会常务委员会第三十三次会议通过　1997年6月18日公布实施）

第一章　总　则

第一条　为了加强科学技术普及工作，提高本市公民的科学文化素质，促进社会主义物质文明和精神文明建设，根据《中华人民共和国科学技术进步法》和有关法律、法规，结合本市实际情况，制定本条例。

第二条　本条例所称科学技术普及(以下简称科普)，是指用公众易于理解和接受的方式，将科学知识、科学思想和科学方法向公众传播推广的行为。

第三条　科普工作是国家基础建设、基础教育和科学技术工作的重要组成部分，是一项社会公益事业。

第四条　科普工作应当坚持普及与提高相结合，具有针对性、趣味性和通俗性，符合实际，注重实效。

第五条　科普工作应当有利于社会主义物质文明和精神文明建设。科普工作应当反对迷信、愚昧和反科学、伪科学行为；不得以科普为名宣传不健康、不文明的生活方式和有损社会公共利益的内容。

第六条　科普工作应当坚持科学态度，不得将尚无科学定论、违背科学原则和科学精神的主张或者意见，作为科普知识传播和推广。

第七条　市和区、县人民政府应当加强对科普工作的领导，将科普工作纳入国民经济和社会发展以及科学技术发展的规划，作为精神文明建设的考核内容。乡、镇人民政府和街道办事处应当做好本辖区的科普工作。

第八条　市和区、县科学技术行政管理部门是科普工作的主管部门，负责本行政区的科普工作。

第九条　全社会应当尊重科普工作者的劳动成果，支持他们的工作，保障其合法权益。

第二章　重点、形式和内容

第十条　科普工作应当提高全体公民的科学文化素质，其重点是：(一)增强青少年对科学技术的兴趣和爱好，培养他们的观察能力、思维能力、实践能力和创造能力，使其树立科学的世界观和人生观；(二)向农民传播先进的种植、养殖和加工技术，提高农业综合效益；(三)提高工人的生产技能和技术创新、技术发明能力，提高产品质量和产量，增加企业经济效益；(四)提高国家机关领导人员和企业事业单位负责人员的科学决策能力和科学管理能力。

第十一条　科普工作可以采取下列形式：(一)举行科普讲座、专题报告、研讨会和科普作品展示会；(二)举办科学技术咨询、服务、信息发布和示范活动；(三)在中学、小学中开设科技活动课；(四)在学校中开展科技发明、制作，撰写科技论文和组织科学考察等课外活动；(五)组织科学技术下厂下乡，开展科学技术兴工兴农活动；(六)组织科学技术培训和岗位技术培训，举办技术、技能竞赛；(七)编写、制作、出版科普读物和科普影视作品;(八)设立科普画廊(橱窗),展示科普图片、模型或者实物;(九)参观科学技术场馆,阅读科普图书、报刊,观看科普电影、录像,收听收看广播、电视中的科普专题节目;(十)开展科学技术周活动;(十一)其他形式。

第十二条 科普工作的内容:(一)介绍当代科学技术发展动向、前景、问题和对策等方面的知识,以及当代科学技术的新思想、新理论、新方法、新成果;(二)推广先进适用的新技术、新工艺、新材料、新产品;(三)普及有关计划生育、环境保护、资源合理开发利用和抵御自然灾害等方面的科学知识;(四)普及有关卫生、保健、婚姻、殡葬、商品使用等日常生活中的科学知识,倡导科学、文明、健康的生活方式;(五)宣传科学方法,介绍运用唯物辩证法和现代科技手段解决实际问题的知识;(六)普及科学思想,介绍科学对人类社会发展的引导和促进作用,树立正确的科学价值观和科学技术是第一生产力的观念;(七)其他有关内容。

第三章 组织和管理

第十三条 本市建立有科学技术行政管理部门和其他有关部门、社会团体参加的科普工作联席会议制度,统筹协调和组织全市的科普工作。

第十四条 市科学技术行政管理部门负责制定全市科普工作的总体规划和工作计划,实行政策引导,实施监督检查。

第十五条 市科学技术协会参与制定全市科普工作的总体规划和工作计划,组织开展日常性、群众性的科普活动。

第十六条 教育行政管理部门应当会同有关部门、社会团体制定青少年科普工作计划并组织实施。

第十七条 卫生、体育、计划生育和环境保护行政管理部门应当结合爱国卫生、健康教育、全民健身运动、计划生育和环境保护做好科普工作。

第十八条 旅游和文物行政管理部门应当提高工作人员的科学文化素质,利用自然和人文景观、科普场所和旅游设施做好科普宣传工作。

第十九条 民政行政管理部门应当结合婚姻登记和殡葬管理做好科普工作。

第二十条 商业和技术监督行政管理部门应当结合商品性能的宣传和产品质量监督检查做好科普工作。

第二十一条 工业和农业行政管理部门应当结合生产、保障劳动者的身心健康、维护劳动者的合法权益做好科普工作。

第二十二条 人事行政管理部门应当加强对国家机关工作人员和企业事业单位负责人员的科普教育,制定计划,组织实施,定期考核。

第二十三条 文化、新闻出版、广播电视、工商、公安以及其他有关行政管理部门应当根据各自的职责,做好科普工作。

第四章 社会责任

第二十四条 普及科学技术是全社会的共同责任。社会各界应当支持和组织开展科普工作。

第二十五条 报纸、刊物应当加强科普宣传,刊登科普文章;广播电台、电视台应当开设科普节目;影视制作、发行放映单位应当保证科普影视作品的制作、发行和放映;街头电子屏幕应当有科普宣传内容。出版单位应当加强科普书籍和科普音像制品的出版。

第二十六条 各类学校应当结合学生特点制定科普工作计划并组织实施。

第二十七条 区、县、乡、镇农业技术推广机构和农业技术研究会应当通过技术培训,普及先进实用的技术以及有关安全生产的知识,提高农业综合效益。

第二十八条 企业应当向职工普及与生产经营、职业卫生、安全防护等有关的科学技术知识,提高职工的科学技术水平。

第二十九条 商业、服务业机构应当结合商品销售和服务工作做好科普工作。

第三十条 医疗、卫生和计划生育机构应当结合医疗保健和计划生育工作做好科普工作。

第三十一条 工会、共青团、妇联应当结合职工、青年、妇女的特点开展群众性科普活动。

第三十二条 科研机构、企业和学校应当支持科技人员和教师参加科普活动。

第三十三条 科研机构、高等学校的实验室和企业的生产车间,能够对外开放的,可以有组织地向青少年开放。

第三十四条 教育、科技、新闻工作者,国家机关工作人员和企业事业单位管理人员,应当结合本职工作积极参与科普工作。

第三十五条 在住宿、餐饮、文化、体育、商业等公共活动场所不得进行封建迷信活动。新闻媒介不得对迷信、愚昧和反科学、伪科学行为以及不健康、不文明的生活方式,作正面肯定性的宣传和报导。

第五章 科普组织和场所

第三十六条 科技馆、博物馆、天文馆、图书馆、青少年科技中心(宫)是专业科普活动场所。国家投资兴建的科普场所不得挪作他用。

第三十七条 科普组织和科普场所在开展科普工作中享有以下权利:(一)获得活动经费;(二)接受合法捐赠;(三)申请科普专题项目;(四)享受有关财税优惠政策;(五)兴办经济实体,开展有偿服务,所得收入用于科普工作;(六)获得名誉、荣誉、奖励和有关知识产权;(七)为加强和改进科普工作,向有关部门提出批评和建议;(八)法律、法规规定的其他权利。

第三十八条 科普组织和科普场所有下列义务:(一)改进科普工作的形式和内容,提高科普工作质量;(二)面向公众的科普活动,不得以营利为目的;(三)科普场所应当向社会公众开放,并优先、优惠向青少年开放;(四)抵制伪科学、反科学和封建迷信的活动;(五)遵守本条例有关科普工作的规定;(六)法律、法规规定的其他义务。

第六章 科普工作者

第三十九条 在科普场所中从事科普工作的人员和中学、小学专设的科技辅导员为专业科普工作者。其他从事科普工作的人员为非专业科普工作者。

第四十条 科普工作者享有下列权利:(一)依法创办或者参加科普组织,自主开展活动;(二)申请科普项目经费;(三)接受专业技术培训,提高工作水平;(四)向有关部门就科普工作提出批评、意见和建议;(五)法律、法规规定的其他权利。

第四十一条 科普工作者应当履行下列义务:(一)开展或者参加科普活动,传播普及科学技术知识,推广应用科学技术成果;(二)学习新知识、新技术,提高科学文化素质,增强工作能力;(三)遵守本条例规定的科普工作原则;(四)法律、法规规定的其他义务。

第四十二条 专业科普工作者按照国家和本市有关规定参加相应系列的专业技术职务评审时,其科普著作、论文、直接参与指导的科普竞赛成绩和开展科普工作的其他优秀成绩,应当作为晋升专业技术职称的依据。非专业科普工作者的科普著作、论文、直接参与指导的科普竞赛成绩,可以作为晋升专业技术职务或者其他职务的参考条件。

第七章 保障措施

第四十三条 各级人民政府应当保证对科普经费的投入,并随着经济的增长每年有所提高。科普经费应当列入同级财政预算,及时划拨,专款专用。

第四十四条 各级人民政府应当将科普设施建设纳入当地市政、文化建设规划和社会主义精神文明建设计划,并保障科普设施的正常运行。

第四十五条 有关部门、社会团体和企业事业单位应当安排必要的人力、物力、财力用于科普工作。

第四十六条 本市鼓励下列活动:(一)采用先进技术开展科普活动;(二)境内外组织和个人捐款、捐物,兴办或者联办科普设施,发展科普事业;(三)境内外组织和个人捐助建立科普基金;(四)开展国际间、地区间的科普交流活动。

第四十七条 科普组织和场所按照国家有关规定享受减免税收的优惠待遇,税收的免除部分用于发展科普事业。

第四十八条 出版、发行科普图书、报纸、期刊和音像制品,根据国家有关规定享受优惠待遇。

第四十九条 在街头设立科普画廊(橱窗),有关部门应当按照国家规定减免各项费用。

第五十条 各级人民政府和有关部门应当逐步改善科普工作者的工作和生活条件。

第八章 奖励与处罚

第五十一条 市人民政府设立科普奖励项目,制定奖励标准和管理办法。

第五十二条 各级人民政府对在科普工作中做出突出贡献或者捐资数额较大的集体和个人,应当给予表彰或者奖励。

第五十三条 市教育、科技等有关行政管理部门对在市级以上青少年科学技术竞赛活动中取得优异成绩的在校学生和指导教师,应当给予奖励。

第五十四条 有关部门、单位和团体可以设立科普奖励项目,表彰科普先进集体或者先进个人。

第五十五条 国家机关工作人员和企业事业单位有关人员玩忽职守给科普事业造成重大损失,或者滥用职权,侵犯科普工作人员合法权益的,由其所在单位或者上级机关给予行政处分;构成犯罪的,依法追究刑事责任。

第五十六条 国家机关工作人员或者科普工作者参加封建迷信活动或者反科学、伪科学活动,影响恶劣或者造成重大损失的,由其所在单位或者上级机关给予行政处分。

第五十七条 破坏科普设施,擅自改变科普场所和设施用途,挪用科普经费,转移科普单位财产的,由其所在单位或者上级机关给予行政处分;责令其恢复原来场所和设施的用途,交回被挪用的经费和被转移的财产,赔偿由此所造成的经济损失;构成犯罪的,依法追究刑事责任。

第五十八条 进行反科学、伪科学活动并扰乱社会秩序或者骗取财物的个人或者组织,由公安部门依照《中华人民共和国治安管理处罚条例》予以处罚;构成犯罪的,依法追究刑事责任。

第五十九条 各级科学技术行政管理部门,对违反本条例的单位和个人,有权进行监督检查,并向其上级主管部门或者所在单位提出处理意见。有关上级主管部门和单位应当作出处理。

第九章 附 则

第六十条 本条例自公布之日起施行。

天津市促进民营科技企业发展的若干规定

（津政发〔1998〕21号 1998年2月12日公布实施）

民营科技企业是我国经济体制和科技体制改革的产物，也是推动科技事业和经济发展的一支有生力量。大力发展民营科技企业，对于加快实施科教兴市战略，实现经济体制和经济增长方式的根本性转变，推动经济、社会发展，具有十分重要的意义。各级人民政府要进一步解放思想，更新观念，真正把发展民营科技企业列入重要议事日程，关心、支持民营科技企业发展，帮助他们解决实际困难和问题，促进天津市民营科技企业再上新台阶。为此，特作如下规定。

一、民营科技企业是指以科技人员为主体，从事科学研究、技术开发、技术转让、技术服务、技术咨询和高新技术产品研制、生产、销售，以科技成果商品化为主要内容，以市场为导向，实行自筹资金、自愿组合、自主经营、自负盈亏、自我发展、自我约束的知识密集型经济实体。

二、加强政府对民营科技企业的指导。市科委要会同有关部门做好对全市民营科技企业的统筹规划、服务、协调、监督等工作。民营科技企业的资格认定，在天津新技术产业园区之外注册的企业，由市科委或市科委授权各区、县科委、天津经济技术开发区科技局负责；在天津新技术产业园区之内注册的企业，由天津新技术产业园区管理委员会负责。经认定的民营科技企业，可享受有关优惠政策。要充分发挥民营科技企业家协会的桥梁和纽带作用，积极支持他们协助各级政府做好有关行业服务和行业自律工作。

三、将民营科技企业发展纳入全市经济发展的总体规划，鼓励民营科技企业按照国家产业政策、技术政策进行研究开发和生产经营，加速科技成果转化，扩大产业规模。重点扶持一批骨干企业，对技术含量高、科技成果多、市场前景好、年技工贸总收入超过亿元的民营科技企业集团，经市政府有关部门认定后，可享受天津市扶持大型企业集团的有关政策；支持并鼓励优秀民营科技企业通过平等竞争，承担市级及其以上的技术开发和新产品试制项目，在科研项目立项、贷款、科技三项费使用、科技成果鉴定、开展国际科技合作等方面，可享受国有企业的同等政策。

四、从文件下发之日起新开办的天津新技术产业园区外注册的民营科技企业，其所得税实行5年内先征后返，前两年100%返还，后3年50%返还。在新技术产业园区内注册在区外经营并被认定为高新技术企业的民营科技企业，可享受新技术产业园区的优惠政策。

五、要采取多种形式，拓宽融资渠道，对具备条件的民营科技企业，经有关部门批准，可优先安排发行企业债券、股票及上市。对具有一定规模、科技含量高、经济效益好、市场前景好的大中型民营科技企业，支持其向股份公司转化。

六、民营科技企业年技工贸总收入达3000万元以上的，经有关部门批准，可以取得或扩大自营进出口权；经批准可享受外贸公司的同等政策。

七、民营科技企业投资建设的固定资产投资项目，凡符合国家及本市产业政策，用于科研、生产的，可适用固定资产投资方向调节税零税率，以鼓励民营科技企业扩大规模。

八、在国家、市政府批准建立的国家、市、区县级开发区内，可以以优惠的出让价格将土地使用权出让给民营科技企业。

九、鼓励民营科技企业的科技人员以技术、资本等投资入股。创建公司制民营科技企业或进行公司制改造、可以高新技术成果作价入股，其比例最高可占注册资本的35%。民营科技企业在进行公司制改造时，可将无形资产的30%作为创业奖励股，奖励在企业创业和发展中起着不可替代作用的科技人员和管理人员。

十、完善民营科技企业的分配方式,坚持按劳分配为主体,多种分配方式并存的分配制度。内部分配可按照工资总额的增长幅度低于经济效益的增长幅度,职工实际平均工资增长幅度低于本企业劳动生产率增长幅度的原则进行。

十一、民营科技企业的科技人员,可以按照国家和本市职称工作的政策规定,参加本市专业技术职称评定,所取得的专业技术资格与其他国有企业、科研单位的专业技术人员同等对待。

十二、民营科技企业特别是国有民营科技企业应按照建立现代企业制度的方向积极进行转制工作,在转制过程中,可享受天津市现代企业制度试点的有关优惠政策。国有民营科技企业改制为股份合作制的,可参照市人民政府办公厅《转发市体改委(关于放开放活国有小型企业的实施意见)》(津政办发【1996]34号)及市体改委等五部门《印发(关于放开放活国有小型企业的实施意见的补充意见)的通知》(津体改委发[1996】34号)的有关政策执行。

十三、积极鼓励民营科技企业参与国有资产的结构调整与重组,对有条件兼并、承包、租赁、收购国有中小企业的,经批准可享受优化资本结构试点城市的有关政策。

十四、从1998年起,对于民营科技企业上缴的所得税,各级财政部门按照实际上缴额,每年至少集中50%作为本地区科技发展基金,用于民营科技企业的贷款、担保等,支持民营科技企业发展。

十五、鼓励和支持民营科技企业进行技术创新。其当年直接用于研究开发新产品、新技术、新工艺所发生的费用,按照财政部、国家税务总局关于促进企业技术进步有关财政税收问题的规定,实行税前扣除。民营科技企业进行技术改造和新产品开发购置的测试仪器、设备等固定资产,经批准可实行快速折旧。

十六、民营科技企业开发的新产品,自售出之日起,经有关部门审核,可按国家级产品3年内、市级产品2年内,将所得税新增部分,全部留给企业,用于生产和经营。同科研单位、大专院校进行技术合作,购买技术专利、引进国内外先进技术所发生的费用可分期摊人成本。

十七、支持并鼓励民营科技企业按照《中华人民共和国公司法》建立母子公司体制,符合条件的可组建科技企业集团。

十八、鼓励民营科技企业安置国有企业或城镇集体企业下岗职工。当年安置下岗职工占民营科技企业全部职工总数60%以上的,经批准,免征企业所得税3年;免税期满后,当年新安置下岗职工占原从业人数30%以上的,经批准,可减半征收企业所得税两年。

十九、外地和留学归国的高级专业技术人员来天津市创办民营科技企业,经有关部门批准,可优先办理调入落户手续;个人投资200万元以上并拥有可供转产的高新技术成果的,优先办理本人及家属落户手续。留学归国人员兴办科技企业,优先安排科研开发基金的使用。

二十、把民营科技企业人才列入全市人才资源管理与开发规划。市及各区县人事局及其所属人才服务机构要认真做好这些企业存档人员的人事代理工作,并采取有效措施,为民营科技企业发展提供各类专业人才。

二十一、免收民营科技企业的工商和科技行政管理费;天津市科技贸易街管理委员会对驻街企业收取管理费的标准由原来不高于营业额的5‰降至3‰。

二十二、民营科技企业集团的核心层企业,在名称中可以不反映行业特点;设立非公司企业,注册资本在10万元以上的,企业名称允许直冠市级名称;设立公司的按公司法规定办理。自然人投资的民营科技企业的注册资金最低标准为1万元。

二十三、各级政府应定期表彰先进的民营科技企业、企业经营者、民营科技企业管理部门和个人,并给予奖励。

二十四、由市科委根据本规定制定天津市民营科技企业管理办法。

天津市民营科技企业管理办法

（津科发政字〔1998〕049号 1998年2月24日公布实施）

第一章 总则

第一条 为发展民营科技事业、保障科技企业的合法权益和加强监督管理，进一步促进天津市经济发展和科技进步，制定本办法。

第二条 本办法所称民营科技企业是指以科技人员为主体，从事科学研究、技术开发、技术转让、技术服务、技术咨询和高新技术产品研制、生产、销售为主要业务，实行自筹资金、自愿组合、自主经营、自负盈亏、自我约束、自我发展的不要国家编制的具有新型运行机制和经营方式的科技型经济组织。包括采用集体经济、合作经济、股份制经济和私营经济的民有民营科技企业和国有科研院所、大专院校、大中型企业创办的并明确划清产权关系后实行国有民营的科技企业。

第三条 民营科技企业依法取得企业法人资格。民营科技企业应遵守国家的法律、法规和规章。

第四条 科技、经济、工商、财税、金融、劳动人事等管理部门及公检法等执法部门应采取积极措施和扶持政策，推动民营科技企业的发展，保护其合法权益。

第二章 民营科技企业的设立、变更和终止

第五条 鼓励和支持下列人员创办民营科技企业或到民营科技企业工作：

1.大中专毕业生、研究生和留学归国人员；2.经所在单位批准的科技人员；3.离休、退休、辞职、待业的科技人员；4.外省市来津的科技人员；5.其他非在职的科技人员。

鼓励和支持各企、事业单位、大专院校、社会团体等法人办国有民营或集体、股份合作制民营科技企业。

第六条 申办民营科技企业应具备下列条件：1.有企业的专有名称、组织机构和企业章程；2.有与技术开发、生产经营和服务规模相适应的资金、场地和科技人员；3.有固定的科研、生产、经营场所和明确的经营范围。

第七条 法人投资创办民营科技企业时，必须制定协议书，在章程中明确下列事项：1.产权关系；2.投资方式及资产收益方式；3.新办企业领导人的产生方法；4.投资者与经营音之间的权利、义务和风险责任；5.利用国有资产创办民营科技企业，必须保证国有资产的保值与增值。

第八条 民营科技企业可以采取以下组织形式：1.集体企业；2.私营企业；3.合伙企业；4.合资企业；5.有限责任公司；6.股份有限公司；7.股份合作制企业；8.国有民营企业。

第九条 申请开办民营科技企业必须持“第六条”规定条件证明材料向企业所在地的区、县科学技术委员会或开发区、科技管理部门办理资格审批手续后向同级工商行政管理部门申办企业登记，经核准发给营业执照后，始得营业。

第十条 凡从事国家规定的特殊专业的民营科技企业必须报请专业主管部门审批。

第十一条 民营科技企业的分立、合并、转让、迁移及改变经营范围等，应经原认定的科学技术委员会或开发、保税区、新技术产业园区科技管理部门重新认定，并向工商行政管理部门办理变更登记或者重新登记。

第十二条 民营科技企业在解散、破产、被撤消或因其他原因终止时，应依法进行清算，并向工商行政管理部门办理注销登记，报原审批所在地科学技术委员会或开发区、保税区、新技术产业园区科技管理部门备案。

第三章 民营科技企业的权利与义务

第十三条 民营科技企业依照国家法律法规和产业政策的规定．有权自主决定科研、生产经营范围、机构设置、聘用或辞退职工、工资制度和利润分配形式，享受国家、市有关鼓励企业科技进步的优惠政策。

第十四条 民营科技企业可以向所在区、县政府或开发区、保税区和新技术产业园区职称主管部门申报专业技术职务，按照本市职称评审的有关规定，评定相应的专业技术职务，已按本市职称主管部门的有关规定评定专业技术职称的人员应聘到民营科技企业工作的，其职务和待遇，由聘用单位自行确定。

第十五条 民营科技企业在承担科技计划任务、接受委托科研项目、科技成果鉴定与登记、申报科技奖励、申请科技贷款、评定专业技术职务及在评选授衔专家等方面有与国有科研院所同等权利。

第十六条 民营科技企业所需特殊生产资料和设施，可向政府有关主管部门申请供应。

第十七条 民营科技企业可以按照有关规定开展国际科技合作、引进国外智力、参加境外培训、同外国公司、企业和其他经济组织或个人举办国际科技交流活动、兴办中外合资（合作）研究开发经营机构（企业）。民营科技企业可以依法在国外投资，设立分支机构、销售网点。

第十八条 民营科技企业在境内召开国际会议或其职工因业务需要出国（出境），由原审批（认定）所在地科学技术委员会或开发区、保税区、新技术产业园区科技管理部门依据有关规定审查后报有关部门办理审批手续。

第十九条 民营科技企业职工依法组织工会，职工的合法权益受国家法律保护。

第二十条 民营科技企业可以组织成立民营科技企业协会等社会团体组织。

第二十一条 除国家法律、法规规定，任何单位不得以任何方式要求民营科技企业无偿提供财务、物力、信息、人力。民营科技企业有权拒绝摊派。科学技术主管部门和工商行政管理部门有权制止对民营科技企业的摊派。

第二十二条 民营科技企业必须按国家规定在金融机构开设账户。民营科技企业必须按照国家财务会计法规和税务部门的规定，健全财务会计制度、配备财会人员、建立会计财薄、报送财务报表。严格履行纳税义务，接受税务部门的监督检查。

第二十三条 民营科技企业必须按照国家统计法规和统计部门、科学技术委员会的规定，报送科技统计报表，接受统计部门、科学技术委员会的监督检查。

第二十四条 民营科技企业应加强职工的思想政治工作，依照国家劳动法律保障职工合法权益和福利待遇，改善职工劳动条件，保障职工安全与健康。

第二十五条 应届大中专毕业生、研究生，到民营科技企业工作的，由用人单位直接与毕业生所在院校联系，经用人单位主管部门（私营科技型企业由所在地区科委）同意并征得毕业生分配主管部门批准，可列入毕业生分配计划。非本市户口的应届本科生、研究生或专业急需人员，按有关规定应聘到天津市民营科技企业工作的，可将档案交市或区、县政府人事部门所属的人才交流服务机构管理。本市全民所有制干部应聘到营科技企业工作的，其档案、人事、工资关系可放在政府人事部门所属的人才交流服务机构管理。

第二十六条 鼓励新成立的民营科技企业实行各种形式的股份制；鼓励现有民营科技企业在界定产权的基础上实行股份制改造。

第二十七条 各区、县应利用科技发展基金为民营科技企业建立生产中试基地，委托金融机构发放流动资金贷款。

第二十八条 鼓励民营科技企业从事技术进出口工作。符合规定条件的，可以向有关部门申请自营进出口权。

对外贸易机构要积极为民营科技企业承办代理进出口业务。鼓励外贸企业与民营科技企业相互投资或参股,组成技工贸、农贸企业集团。要根据民营科技企业的发展需要,为民营科技企业引进外国专家,组织民营科技实业家到国外培训。

第四章 管理与监督

第二十九条 各级政府科学技术委员会和开发区、保税区、新技术产业园区科技管理部门是民营科技企业的业务归口管理部门,要协同有关部门,加强对民营科技企业的指导、管理、统计和服务,统筹协调企业登记、认定、人员培训、专业技术职称资格评审、科技成果鉴定等项工作;协助办理科技人员出境、技术出口、贷款申报等有关手续;推动民营科技企业的股份制改造;进一步优化民营科技企业发展的外部条件和内在机制;逐步完善规章制度。

第三十条 民营科技企业职工的失业、养老、医疗等社会保障工作应纳入社会化管理。

第三十一条 各级政府科学技术委员会和开发区、保税区、新技术产业园区科技管理部门对已登记注册的民营科技企业,每年在工商执照年检前进行一次认定,不符合本办法规定的及年技术性收入低于技工贸总收入20%、用于科技开发经费低于企业总支出5%、科技人员比例低于从业人员30%的企业,不再按民营科技企业管理,不享受相关优惠政策与权利。

第三十二条 各级管理部门工作人员违反本办法规定,滥用职权、徇私舞弊、收受贿赂或者侵害民营科技企业合法权益的,有关主管机关应当根据情节给予行政处分、经济处罚;触犯刑律的,依法追究刑事责任。

第五章 附则

第三十三条 本办法由天津市科学技术委员会负责解释。

第三十四条 本办法自公布之日起施行。

天津市促进科技成果转化条例

(天津市第十二届人民代表大会常务委员会第四十一次会议通过 1998年4月14日公布实施)

第一章 总 则

第一条 为促进科技成果向现实生产力转化,维护科技成果转化各方的合法权益,加速科学技术进步,推动经济建设和社会发展,根据《中华人民共和国促进科技成果转化法》和其他有关法律、法规,结合本市实际情况,制定本条例。

第二条 科技成果转化活动应当注重经济效益和社会效益,遵循自愿、互利、公平、诚实信用的原则,依法维护从事转化活动当事人的合法权益,维护国家和社会公共利益。

第三条 市和区、县人民政府管理、指导和协调本行政区域内的科技成果转化工作。市和区、县科学技术行政部门、计划部门、经济综合管理部门和其他有关行政部门按照同级人民政府规定的职责范围,管理、指导和协调科技成果转化工作。

第四条 本市鼓励和支持企业从事科研、开发和技术改造,使企业成为科技成果转化的主体。

第五条 各级人民政府对在科技成果转化工作中做出突出贡献的单位和个人给予奖励。

第二章 组织管理

第六条 各级人民政府应当将科技成果转化工作纳入国民经济和社会发展计划,推动建立科技成果转化市场机制,健全科技成果转化体系,鼓励和支持公民、法人和其他组织转化科技成果,促进科技成果的商品化、产业化和国际化。

第七条 市科学技术行政部门会同市计划部门、经济综合管理部门和其他有关行政部门编制本市重大高新技术产业化工程项目计划,经市人民政府批准后,按照各自职责负责组织实施。

第八条 各级人民政府应当优先安排和重点扶持下列科技成果转化项目:(一)对经济的发展和行业技术进步有明显促进作用的;(二)能形成一定规模效益并且在国内、国际市场具有竞争力的;(三)有利于资源的合理开发利用,节约能源,降低消耗,保护生态环境,防止污染,改善劳动条件的;(四)技术含量高、市场容量大,对形成高新技术产业或者开发出口产品有明显效果的;(五)采用国内外先进技术、工艺和装备,改造落后技术、工艺和装备的;(六)促进高产、优质、高效农业和其他农村经济发展的;(七)有利于贫困地区经济和社会发展,有效发挥当地资源优势的;(八)有利于教育、文化、卫生、计划生育等事业发展及其他具有显著社会效益的。

第九条 各级人民政府应当扶持发展技术市场、科技信息市场,鼓励开展技术开发、技术转让、技术咨询、技术服务、技术承包、技术入股等活动,促进科技成果转化。

第三章 转化实施

第十条 科技成果转化项目可以公开招标,择优确定中标单位。

第十一条 科技成果完成单位、科技成果转化实施单位和科技成果转化投资单位合作转化科技成果的,应当依法签订合同,约定各方享有的权利和承担的风险。

第十二条 本市鼓励农业科研机构、农业试验示范单位独立或者与其他单位合作,实施农业科技成果转化,为农业生产提供产前、产中、产后综合配套技术服务。农业科研机构可以依法经营其独立研究开发或者与其他单位合作研究开发并经过审定的优良品种。

第十三条 以高新技术成果作价向有限责任公司或者非公司制科技开发型企业入股,其高新技术成果必须经评估机构评估和市科学技术行政部门认定,作价总金额可以超过公司或者企业注册资本的百分之二十,但不得超过百分之三十五。

第十四条 职务科技成果权属单位及其科技成果完成人和参加人应当促进职务科技成果转化。国家设立的科研机构、高等学校取得的具有实用价值的职务科技成果,本单位未能适时地实施转化的,科技成果完成人和参加人在不变更职务科技成果权属的前提下,可以根据与本单位签订的协议进行该项科技成果的转化,并享有协议规定的权益。科技成果完成人或者课题负责人,不得阻碍职务科技成果的转化,不得将职务科技成果及其技术资料和数据占为己有,侵犯单位的合法权益。

第十五条 对国家利益或者社会公共利益具有重大意义的科技成果需要尽快推广使用的,按照国家有关规定办理。

第十六条 经国家和本市认定的大中型企业或者企业集团的技术中心,其财务实行独立核算的,享受独立科研机构的优惠政策。

第十七条 本市鼓励和支持科研机构转为科技企业或者成为企业化管理的研究开发机构。本市鼓励和支持科研机构进入企业或者企业集团,成为企业的技术开发机构,或者依法通过联营投资、参股、控股、兼并等方式与企业联合,促进科技成果转化。转为企业和进入企业或者企业集团的科研机构三年内可以保留事业单位法人地位,享受国家和本市的优惠政策。

第十八条 科技成果检测机构和评估机构应当按照国家有关规定取得执业资格;在科技成果转化活动中对科技成果进行检测和价值评估,必须遵循公正、客观的原则,如实提供检测结果和评估证明。

第十九条 本市鼓励和支持依法取得资格证书的技术经纪人建立技术中介机构，在依法领取营业执照后从事科技成果转化的代理或者居间等中介活动，其合法权益受法律保护。

第四章 促进措施

第二十条 各级人民政府应当逐年增加科技成果转化的投入，主要用于下列方面：（一）列入市科技发展重大项目的科技成果转化投资；（二）中间试验、工业性试验、示范性生产线以及农业试验示范工程等；（三）重大科技成果转化贷款的贴息；（四）科技成果转化的引导资金；（五）社会公益性的重大科技成果转化项目的补助资金；（六）风险投资；（七）其他促进科技成果转化的资金。科技成果转化资金必须专款专用，任何单位和个人不得挪用或者截留。

第二十一条 本市鼓励设立科技成果转化基金或者风险基金，其资金来源由政府、企业事业单位以及其他组织和个人提供，主要用于支持重点科技成果转化项目的实施。

第二十二条 金融机构应当根据国家产业政策和国家信贷政策，逐年增加对科技成果转化的贷款；对重大科技成果转化的贷款项目，应当优先安排。

第二十三条 保险机构应当本着自愿的原则，为科技成果转化提供保险服务。

第二十四条 企业研究开发新产品、新技术、新工艺所发生的各项费用，按照国家规定计入成本；为开发新技术、研制新产品所购置的试制用关键设备、测试仪器，单台价值在十万元以下的，可以一次或者分次摊入管理费用，其中达到固定资产标准的，应当单独管理，不再提取折旧。企业技术开发费年增幅在百分之十以上的，按照国家规定以实际发生额的百分之五十抵扣应税所得额。

第二十五条 列入市级试制新产品计划的新产品所实现的利润，第一年免征所得税，第二年减半征收所得税。经市科学技术行政部门会同有关部门认定的中间试验产品，享受市级新产品优惠政策。

第二十六条 企业的科研机构直接用于科学研究、科学试验的进口仪器、设备、化学试剂和技术资料，按照国家有关规定免征增值税，并享受减免关税的优惠政策。

第二十七条 企业为实现科技成果转化而进行中间试验，报经财税部门批准，中间试验设备的折旧年限可以在国家规定的基础上缩短百分之三十至百分之五十。

第二十八条 科研机构（含已转为企业的科研机构），在技术转让、技术开发过程中取得的技术培训、技术咨询、技术服务收入，按照国家有关规定免征营业税。科研机构和高等学校从事技术开发和技术转让，进行技术培训、技术咨询、技术服务、技术承包、技术入股所取得的技术性收入免征所得税。

第二十九条 企业事业单位进行技术出口、技术转让，或者在技术转让中发生的与技术转让有关的技术咨询、技术服务、技术培训所得年净收入，经财税部门批准，免征所得税。

第三十条 新开办的独立核算的科技创业服务中心和科技成果检测、评估、咨询、信息机构以及其他技术服务机构，经财税部门批准，自开办之日起第一年至第二年免征所得税。

第五章 技术权益保护

第三十一条 科技成果完成单位将其职务科技成果转让给他人的，单位应当从转让该项职务科技成果所取得的净收入中，按照百分之二十至百分之四十的比例提取资金，对完成该项科技成果及其转化做出重要贡献的人员给予奖励。

第三十二条 企业事业单位独立研究开发或者与其他单位合作研究开发的科技成果实施转化成功投产后，单位应当连续三至五年从实施该项科技成果新增留利中按照不低于百分之五的比例提取资金，对完成该项科技成果及其转化做出重要贡献的人员给予奖励。

第三十三条 合作进行科技成果转化的各方，应当就保守技术秘密达成协议。当事人不得违反协议或者违反权利人有关保守技术秘密的要求,披露或者允许他人使用该项技术。技术交易机构或者中介机构对其在从事代理或者居间服务中知悉的有关科技成果的秘密负有保密义务。

第六章　法律责任

第三十四条　违反本条例第十四条第三款规定的,由所在单位给予行政处分;造成经济损失的,依法承担民事赔偿责任;构成犯罪的,依法追究刑事责任。

第三十五条　违反本条例第十八条规定的,由科学技术行政部门责令改正,没收违法所得,处以违法所得一倍以上三倍以下的罚款;情节严重的,依法由有关行政部门吊销营业执照和资格证书;造成经济损失的,依法承担民事赔偿责任;构成犯罪的,依法追究刑事责任。

第三十六条　违反本条例第二十条第二款规定的,由其所在单位或者上级主管部门责令改正,并对责任人给予行政处分;构成犯罪的,依法追究刑事责任。

第三十七条　违反本条例第三十三条规定的,按照《中华人民共和国技术合同法》和其他有关法律、法规处理。

第三十八条　在科技成果转化工作中滥用职权、玩忽职守、徇私舞弊的,由其所在单位或者上级主管部门给予行政处分;构成犯罪的,依法追究刑事责任。

第七章　附则

第三十九条　天津经济技术开发区、天津港保税区、天津新技术产业园区参照本条例,具体负责所辖区域内的促进科技成果转化工作。

第四十条　本条例自公布之日起施行。

关于促进高新技术产业化的意见

(津政办发〔1999〕12号　1999年3月10日公布实施)

为加快实施科教兴市战略,促进科技成果向现实生产力转化,进一步扶持高新技术产业,使其逐步成为天津市国民经济发展的重要力量,根据《关于印发(天津市高新技术产业发展规划)的通知》(津政发[1999]3号),现就促进天津市高新技术产业化提出如下意见。

一、实行高新技术产业化项目认定制度。由市高新技术产业发展规划实施办公室(以下简称市规划实施办)按照《天津市高新技术产业发展规划》,根据项目的科技水平、市场前景与风险、经济效益及其他有关事宜进行认定。具体认定办法由市规划实施办另行制定。高新技术企业的认定仍按现行有关规定和程序办理。

二、设立天津市科技发展资金。1999年至2000年(2001年及其以后另定),市财政每年安排5000万元科技发展资金,主要用于重大高新技术产业化项目的补助和一定期限内的贷款贴息及吸引人才等。具体实施管理办法由市财政部门和市规划实施办制定,报市人民政府批准后实施。

三、根据国家产业政策和扶优扶强的原则,政府在投资上将支持高新技术产业化项目发展。

四、本市具有政府投资职能的投资公司,今后原则上每年都要将一定比例的资金投入到经认定的高新技术产业化项目中去,由市规划实施办负责监督实施。

五、支持本市各类投资公司进行资本重组,具备条件的投资公司可单独成建制改组为国有独资的高新技术风险投资有限公司,也可联合组成多元投资主体的高新技术风险投资有限公司,专门从事对高新技术产业的投资。鼓励社会各类法人依法投资于高新技术产业，支持其单独或共同设立高新技术投资公司，从事高新技术产业投资。拓宽高新技术产业引资渠道，鼓励各方面力量积极争取国内外其他资金投入高新技术产业。

六、在同等情况下，优先推荐承担高新技术产业化项目的股份有限公司上市。

七、承担重大高新技术产业化项目的企业，由市财政部门连续三年每年从企业新增增值税地方分成部分中提取50%，充实市科技发展资金，主要用于企业开发技术、吸引人才和奖励企业家。具体实施管理办法和资助额度由市财政部门会同市规划实施办另行制定。

八、经高新技术企业认定机构重新认定，坐落在新技术产业园区外的高新技术企业，其所得税地方部分可比照园区企业的政策执行。

九、从1999年起，本市各类投资公司向本市重大高新技术产业化项目的投资额占被投资企业资本金20%以上的，经市财政部门会同市规划实施办认定，对其该项股权分利免征企业所得税。

十、重大高新技术产业化项目建设过程中的供排水、煤气增容和大配套费，项目单位可以提出减免申请，由市规划实施办会同市建委及有关收费部门，采取一事一议的办法，酌情给予一定幅度的减免。

十一、市房管部门对高新技术产业化项目，减半收取购置生产经营用房的交易手续费和产权登记费，其他合法收费按现有规定最低标准掌握。

十二、国有独资重大高新技术产业化项目，经市土地管理部门批准，可以划拨方式取得土地使用权。

十三、承担高新技术产业化项目的企业，兼并连续三年亏损企业或困难企业作为生产用地的，其兼并原企业的房产，可按规定的程序，向其所在地地方税务部门提出减免房产税的申请，财税部门酌情给予减免。

十四、高等院校、科研院所将高新技术成果转让给坐落在本市的企业，经财税部门认定，一次性转让的收益免征所得税地方部分。

十五、政府有关部门资助的应用性高新技术研究项目，其成果在鉴定后一年内实施转让的，成果完成人可享受不低于200%的转让收益。一年内未实现转让的，由政府有关部门负责向社会公开转让。

十六、法人或自然人的高新技术成果，作为无形资产参与产业化项目投资共同设立公司的，经市科技管理部门批准，其成果价值占注册资本的比例最高可按35%掌握。其中职务成果（含政府或部门资助的高新技术项目成果），从项目转化实施起三年内，成果主要完成人可享受不低于所占股权60%的股权收益；第四年至第六年可享受不低于40%的股权收益。经公司股东会批准，成果完成人的股权收益可作为个人股份投资入股。

十七、高新技术成果研究人员的股权收益（股息、红利），其收益率在银行同期存款利率上浮两个百分点以下的部分，免征个人所得税；若直接投资于高新技术成果转化项目的，全部免征个人所得税。转让股权的所得收入照章纳税。

十八、中央各部委、外省市企业和海外留学生带高新技术成果来津实施产业化的项目，经市规划实施办认定，可享受市科技发展资金的补助和贷款贴息优惠。

十九、外省市科技人员带高新技术成果来津实施转化的项目，经有关部门批准，本人、配偶和未成年子女的户口可迁入本市；成批成建制迁入本市的科研机构中具有高级技术职称的专业人员，可免交城市基础设施增容费。

二十、允许企事业科技人员在不影响本职工作和不侵犯本单位技术权益的情况下，兼职从事高新技术研究与成果转化工作。

二十一、天津市工程技术新学科专业高级资格评审委员会和天津市高级工程师（正高级）评审委员会，对促进高新技术成果转化的人员，可以其经营和转化科技成果业绩为主要参评条件，评定相应的专业技术职务任职资格。贡献突出者可不受学历、资历和岗位职数等条件的限制,破格评定相应的专业技术职务任职资格。

二十二、在评定市科教兴市杰出人才奖、向国家推荐享受政府特殊津贴人员或有突出贡献的中青年专家、评选市中青年授衔专家时,优先考虑在高新技术产业化工作中取得显著成绩的科技人员。

二十三、企业可按高新技术成果转化利润的一定比例,提取奖励资金,用于奖励积极促进高新技术成果转化并有贡献的经营者(非成果拥有者)和高新技术企业的主要经营管理人员(非成果拥有者),该奖励资金可在企业成本中列支。

二十四、社会团体和个人,利用各种合法渠道引进国内外资金投入到高新技术企业的,该企业应按一定比例予以奖励。

中共天津市委《关于加速科技进步和创新的若干意见》

(津党发〔1999〕39号 1999年12月16日)

(略)

天津市促进技术交易条例

(天津市第十三届人民代表大会常务委员会第24号公告 2004年11月12日实施)

第一章 总则

第一条 为了保障技术交易当事人的合法权益,促进技术交易,加速科技成果的转化,促进科技进步和经济发展,根据国家有关法律、法规,结合本市实际情况,制定本条例。

第二条 自然人、法人和其他组织在本市行政区域内从事技术交易的活动,适用本条例。涉外以及涉港澳台技术交易,按照国家和本市有关规定办理。

第三条 本条例所称技术交易是指技术开发、技术转让、技术咨询、技术服务等交易活动。

第四条 政府通过制定政策,加强服务,鼓励、支持开展有益于经济建设、社会发展和科技进步的技术交易。技术交易活动不受地区、行业、隶属关系、经济性质和专业范围的限制。

第五条 市科学技术行政部门负责本市行政区域内技术交易活动的规划、协调和管理工作。区、县人民政府和天津经济技术开发区、天津港保税区、天津新技术产业园区管委会的科学技术行政部门负责本地区技术交易活动的管理工作。工商、财政、税务等部门,在各自的职责范围内,共同做好与技术交易相关的工作。

第六条 各级人民政府对在技术交易活动中做出显著成绩的单位和个人,给予表彰和奖励。

第二章 技术交易

第七条 技术交易活动应当遵守法律、法规和有关规定,不得损害国家利益和社会公共利益。技术交易当事人应当按照平等、自愿、公平、诚实信用的原则进行技术交易。

第八条 技术交易活动可以采取举办技术交易会、洽谈会、信息发布会、科技集市、常设技术市场以及技术中介服务等多种渠道,以技术招标、技术承包、技术入股、技术拍卖以及组织科研生产联合等方式进行。

第九条 政府鼓励以招标、投标方式进行技术交易。招标投标活动应当遵循公开、公平、公正和诚实信用的原则。各级科技计划项目均可进入技术市场公开招标。

第十条 政府采取措施,支持和保护科研单位和科研人员以技术入股方式完成技术交易。经认定以技术入股方式完成的交易,属于技术开发、技术转让和与之相关的技术咨询、技术服务的部分,可以享受本条例规定的有关优惠待遇。

第十一条 以承包方式订立的合同,根据其实质内容认定为技术开发、技术转让和与之相关的技术咨询、技术服务合同的部分,可以享受本条例规定的有关优惠待遇。

第十二条 为技术交易提供技术商品的单位和个人,应当保证该技术的合法性、可靠性和真实性,其在技术交易中的合法权益受法律保护。任何单位和个人未经他人允许,不得以他人的技术成果进行交易。当事人一方明知或者应知另一方非法占有他人技术成果与之进行技术交易,视为侵害他人技术权益。

第十三条 技术交易项目的价款、使用费用或者报酬,由当事人商定;也可以经无形资产评估机构评估后,由当事人议定。

第十四条 技术商品的广告必须符合国家法律、法规有关广告管理的规定,技术项目的拥有者委托他人设计、制作、发布广告必须与有关技术文件、技术鉴定证书等证明材料一致。广告的经营者和发布者不得设计、制作、代理和发布内容不实、证明文件不全的技术商品广告。

第十五条 在技术交易活动中,禁止下列行为:(一)侵犯他人知识产权、技术权益;(二)窃取他人技术秘密;(三)假冒专利技术;(四)做虚假广告、宣传;(五)串通招标、投标;(六)以欺骗、胁迫等手段签订技术合同;(七)国家法律、法规禁止的其他行为。

第十六条 从事技术交易的,应当按照《中华人民共和国合同法》的规定订立技术合同。

第十七条 技术合同签订后,当事人可以向科学技术行政部门申请认定登记。科学技术行政部门应当按照国家的《技术合同登记管理办法》和本条例的有关规定确定是否予以登记。

第十八条 市科学技术行政部门主管全市技术合同认定登记工作。区、县人民政府和天津经济技术开发区、天津港保税区、天津新技术产业园区科学技术行政部门的技术合同登记机构,具体负责办理技术合同的认定登记工作。

第十九条 技术合同认定登记实行按地域一次登记制度。技术合同成立后需要进行认定登记的,技术开发合同的研究开发人、技术转让合同的让与人、技术咨询和技术服务合同的受托人应当向所在地的技术合同登记机关提出认定登记申请。

第二十条 当事人申请技术合同认定登记,应当提交真实、完整的书面合同文件和相关附件。当事人应当将认定后的技术合同及有关证明材料,报送主管税务机关备查。

第二十一条 技术合同登记机关应当自受理认定登记申请之日起十日内,情况复杂的最迟不超过三十日内完成认定登记事项,对经认定符合登记条件的,发给技术合同登记证明,并载明经核定的技术性收入额。对认定为非技术合同或者不符合《技术合同登记管理办法》和本条例规定登记条件的合同,应当不予登记,并在合同文本上注明“未予登记”字样,退还当事人。

第二十二条 技术合同认定登记除收取经物价部门核定的合同登记工本费外,不得收取管理费和其他额外费用。

第二十三条 当事人对技术合同登记机关的认定结论有异议的,可以按照《中华人民共和国行政复议法》的规定申请行政复议。

第三章 技术交易服务

第二十四条 本条例所称技术交易服务是指提供技术交易场所服务、技术交易经纪服务、技术交易咨询服务、技术交易法律服务、技术评估服务、技术信息服务等活动。

第二十五条 从事技术交易服务活动,应当遵循公正、公平和客观、真实、科学的原则。

第二十六条 设立技术交易服务机构,应当具备下列条件:(一)有组织章程和服务规范;(二)有与服务范围、规模相适应的专业技术人员和管理人员;(三)有固定的场所和必需的资金、设施;(四)法律、法规规定的其他必须具备的条件。技术交易服务机构从事中介服务的,其从业人员应当依据有关规定接受培训,取得资格证书。

第二十七条 技术交易服务机构应当以促进技术成果商品化为目的,在工商行政管理部门核准的范围内,从事技术交易服务活动。

第二十八条 政府鼓励技术经纪人依法开展业务活动,并依法保护技术经纪人的合法权益。技术经纪人应当依法取得资格和执业证书。

第四章 技术交易鼓励措施

第二十九条 企业单位支付的技术价款、报酬或者使用费,可以一次或者分期摊入成本。事业单位支付技术价款、报酬或者使用费,可以在事业费包干结余或者预算外收入中列支;没有事业费包干结余和预算外收入的,可以在事业费中列支。

第三十条 从事技术交易的技术供方凭技术合同的登记证明,可以从技术性纯收入中提取百分之二十至百分之四十的金额,用于奖励有关人员。购入新技术的企业,可以从采用新技术而增加利润之日起一年内,从新增利润中一次性提取百分之十至百分之三十的金额,用于奖励有关人员。

第三十一条 从事技术交易活动的当事人,签订的技术合同经认定登记证明后,可以享受国家规定的税收优惠。

第五章 法律责任

第三十二条 违反本条例第十二条规定,在技术交易活动中提供虚假技术或者侵占他人技术成果的,应当依照《中华人民共和国合同法》、《中华人民共和国专利法》的规定承担赔偿责任。

第三十三条 违反本条例第十四条规定,设计、制作、代理和发布内容不实、证明材料不全的技术商品广告的,由工商行政管理部门依法予以处罚。

第三十四条 违反本条例第十五条规定的,由有关部门依照法律、法规规定予以处理;构成犯罪的,由司法机关依法追究刑事责任。

第三十五条 违反本条例第二十条规定,伪造、骗取技术合同登记证明的,由科学技术行政部门撤销登记,并处五千元以下罚款;有违法所得的,没收违法所得;涉及税务违法的,由税务机关依法处理;构成犯罪的,由司法机关依法追究刑事责任。

第三十六条 当事人对行政机关所给予的行政处罚不服的,可以依法申请行政复议或者提起行政诉讼。

第三十七条 行政机关工作人员或者技术合同登记机构管理人员玩忽职守、滥用职权、徇私舞弊的,由其所在单位或者上级主管部门给予行政处分;构成犯罪的,由司法机关依法追究刑事责任。

第六章 附则

第三十八条 自然人、法人和其他组织在本市行政区域内依法订立技术培训合同、技术中介合同的，可以参照本条例的规定申请认定登记，并享受有关优惠待遇。

第三十九条 本条例自公布之日起施行。1993年10月28日天津市第十二届人民代表大会常务委员会第三次会议通过的《天津市技术市场管理条例》同时废止。

《天津市科学技术奖励办法》实施细则

（津政发〔2005〕43号 2005年6月3日发布）

第一章 总则

第一条 为做好天津市科学技术奖励工作，提高天津市科学技术奖的评审质量，保证奖励的科学性、公正性和权威性，根据《天津市科学技术奖励办法》(2000年市人民政府令第33号，以下简称《奖励办法》)，制定本细则。

第二条 本细则适用于天津市科学技术奖所包括的科技重大成就奖、自然科学奖、技术发明奖、科学技术进步奖、国际科学技术合作奖的推荐、评审、授奖等各项活动。

第三条 本市行政区域内的个人或组织完成的涉及国防、国家安全并由于国家安全和保密不能公开的项目，可向国防科学技术工业委员会、公安部、国家安全部推荐。除此之外的项目均可推荐天津市科学技术奖。

第四条 天津市科学技术奖励贯彻尊重劳动、尊重知识、尊重人才、尊重创造的方针，鼓励团结协作、联合攻关，鼓励自主创新，促进科学研究、技术开发与经济、社会发展紧密结合，加速实现科技成果的商品化和产业化。

第五条 天津市科学技术奖的推荐、评审和授予遵循公开、公平、公正原则，建立科学的评价指标，严格规范推荐、评审和授奖程序，不受任何组织或者个人的干涉。

第六条 天津市科学技术奖授予在科学发现、技术发明和促进科技进步等方面做出创造性贡献的个人或者组织，并对同一项目授奖的公民、组织按照贡献大小排序。在科学研究、技术开发项目中仅从事组织管理和辅助服务的工作人员，不得作为天津市科学技术奖的候选人。第一完成人完成的项目，同年度最多申报两项。

第七条 天津市科学技术奖是本市授予个人或者组织的荣誉，授奖证书不作为确定科学技术成果权属的直接依据。

第八条 由市科委主管本市科学技术奖励工作，负责天津市科学技术奖评审的组织工作，并依据国家有关规定，管理社会力量设立的面向本市的科学技术奖。

第二章　奖励范围、条件和评审标准

第一节　科技重大成就奖

第九条　《奖励办法》第九条第一款(一)所称“在当代科学技术前沿取得重大突破或者在科学技术发展中卓有建树”,是指候选人在基础研究、应用基础研究方面取得系列或者重大发现,丰富和拓展了学科的理论,引起该学科或者相关学科领域的突破性发展,为国内外同行所公认,培养出一支学术队伍,使得该学科处于国内领先地位并进入国际先进行列。

第十条　《奖励办法》第九条第一款(二)所称“在科学技术创新、科学技术成果转化和高技术产业化中,创造重大经济效益或者社会效益”,是指候选人在科学技术活动中,特别是在高新技术领域取得系列或者重大科技成果,并以市场为导向,积极推动科技成果转化,实现产业化,引起该领域技术的跨越发展,促进了产业结构的变革,为本市创造了重大的经济效益或者社会效益。

第十一条　科技重大成就奖候选人应当具备下列基本条件:

(一)热爱祖国,具有良好的科学道德。

(二)长期从事科学研究或者技术开发工作,曾主持完成不少于五项国家、省部级基础研究和科技攻关项目或重大企事业技术研发项目。

(三)仍活跃在当代科学技术前沿,正在主持国家、省部级科技计划项目或合同金额不少于100万元的企事业技术研发项目。

同时应符合下列条件之一:

(一)领衔完成的基础研究、应用基础研究系列成果中至少有一项获得国家自然科学奖一等奖或两项获得国家自然科学奖二等奖。

(二)领衔完成的基础性研究和技术创新系列成果中至少有一项获得国家技术发明奖一等奖,或有两项获得国家自然科学奖或国家技术发明奖二等奖,在本市应用并创造明显经济效益或社会效益。

(三)领衔完成的基础性研究、技术创新和产业化系列成果中至少有一项获得国家科学技术进步奖一等奖,或有两项获得国家科学技术奖二等奖(不限奖种),在本市应用并为本市创造显著经济效益,以利税计,近三年累计不少于1000万元。

(四)领衔完成的基础性研究、技术创新和产业化系列成果中至少有一项获得国家科学技术奖二等奖(不限奖种),或者至少有两项获得省部级科学技术奖一等奖(不限奖种),在本市应用并为本市产生重大的经济效益,以利税计,近三年每年不少于1000万元。

属于社会公益类成果且无法以经济效益来考核应用效果的,主要考核该成果形成的社会效益,且该成果必须在本市应用,并相应地为本市产生特别显著的社会效益。

第十二条　科技重大成就奖每年度授奖人数不超过2人。

第二节　自然科学奖

第十三条　《奖励办法》第十条第二款(一)所称“前人尚未发现或者尚未阐明”,是指该项自然科学发现为国内外首次提出,或者其科学理论在国内外首次阐明,且主要论著为国内外首次发表。

第十四条　《奖励办法》第十条第二款(二)所称“具有重要科学价值”,是指:

(一)该发现在科学理论、学说上有创见,或者在研究方法、手段上有创新。

(二)在学术上处于国内领先水平以上。

(三)对于推动学科发展有重要意义,或者对于经济建设和社会发展具有重要影响。

第十五条　《奖励办法》第十条第二款(三)所称“得到国内外自然科学界公认”是指主要论著已在国内

外公开发行的学术刊物上发表或者作为学术专著出版一年以上，其重要科学结论已为国内外同行在重要国际学术会议、公开发行的学术刊物，尤其是重要学术刊物以及学术专著所正面引用或者应用。

第十六条　自然科学奖候选人应当是相关科学技术论著的主要作者，并具备下列条件之一：

（一）提出总体学术思路、研究方案。

（二）发现重要科学现象、特性和规律，并阐明科学理论和学说。

（三）提出研究方法和手段，解决关键性学术疑难问题或者实验技术难点，以及对重要基础数据的系统收集和综合分析等。

第十七条　自然科学奖授奖等级根据候选人所做出的科学发现进行综合评定，评定标准如下：

（一）在科学上取得重要进展，发现的自然现象、揭示的科学规律、提出的学术观点为学术界所公认和广泛引用，推动了本学科或者相关学科的发展，或者对经济建设、社会发展有重大影响的，可以评为一等奖。

（二）在科学上取得较大进展，发现的自然现象、揭示的科学规律、提出的学术观点为学术界所公认和引用，推动了本学科或其分支学科的发展，或者对经济建设、社会发展有重要影响的，可以评为二等奖。

（三）在科学上取得了一定进展，发现的自然现象、揭示的科学规律、提出的学术观点为学术界所公认和引用，对学科的发展有一定影响，或者对经济建设、社会发展有较大作用的，可以评为三等奖。

第三节　技术发明奖

第十八条　《奖励办法》第十一条第一款所称的“产品”包括各种仪器、设备、器械、工具、零部件以及生物新品种等；“工艺”包括农业、工业、医疗卫生等领域的各种技术方法；“材料”包括用各种技术方法获得的新物质等；“系统”是指产品、工艺和材料的技术综合。

第十九条　技术发明奖的授奖范围不包括仅依赖个人经验和技能、技巧又不可重复实现的技术。

第二十条　《奖励办法》第十一条第二款(一)所称“前人尚未发明或者尚未公开”，是指该项技术发明为国内外首创，或者虽然国内外已有但主要技术内容尚未在国内外各种公开出版物、媒体及各种公众信息渠道上发表或者公开，也未曾公开使用。推荐技术发明奖的项目一般应获得发明专利。

第二十一条　《奖励办法》第十一条第二款(二)所称“具有先进性和创造性”，是指该项技术发明与国内外已有同类技术相比较，其技术思路、技术原理或者技术方法有创新，技术上有实质性的特点和显著的进步，主要性能(性状)、技术经济指标、科学技术水平及其促进科学技术进步的作用和意义等方面综合优于同类技术。

第二十二条　《奖励办法》第十一条第二款(三)所称“经实施，创造显著经济效益或者社会效益”，是指该项技术发明成熟，并实施应用一年以上，取得显著的效益。

第二十三条　技术发明奖候选人应当是该项技术发明的全部或者部分创造性技术内容的独立完成人。

第二十四条　技术发明奖授奖等级根据候选人所做出的技术发明进行综合评定，评定标准如下：

（一）属国内外首创，或者国内外虽已有但尚未公开的重要技术发明，技术思路、技术原理或者技术方法有很大创新，关键技术上有很大进步，主要技术经济指标达到了同类技术的国际先进水平，对本领域的技术进步有显著的推动作用，并产生了很好的经济效益或者社会效益的，可以评为一等奖。

（二）属国内外首创，或者国内外虽已有但尚未公开的重要技术发明，技术思路、技术原理或者技术方法有较大创新，关键技术上有较大进步，主要技术经济指标达到了同类技术的国际水平，对本领域的技术进步有推动作用，并产生了较好的经济效益或者社会效益的，可以评为二等奖。

（三）属已有先进技术组合，技术思路、技术原理或者技术方法有明显创新，主要技术经济指标达到了同类技术的国际水平，对相关领域的技术进步有一定的推动作用，并产生了一定的经济效益或者社会效益的，可以评为三等奖。

第四节　科学技术进步奖

第二十五条　《奖励办法》第十二条第一款(一)所称“技术开发项目”,是指在科学研究和技术开发活动中,完成具有重要市场价值的产品、技术、工艺、材料、设计和生物品种及其应用推广。经济效益以年度利税计不低于50万元。

第二十六条　《奖励办法》第十二条第一款(二)所称“社会公益项目”是指在下列社会公益性科学技术事业中取得的重要成果及其应用推广:

(一)标准、计量、科技信息、科技档案、科技管理、科学技术普及等科学技术基础性工作。

(二)环境保护、医疗卫生、自然资源调查和合理利用、自然灾害监测预报和防治等。

第二十七条　《奖励办法》第十二条第一款(三)所称“在推广实施已有科技成果中,做出技术创新,取得显著经济效益和社会效益”,是指在实施被列入市级及以上政府推广计划的成果中有技术创新和工作创新,取得显著的经济效益和社会效益并通过验收,推广覆盖率一般不低于30%,能够以经济效益体现的项目,其年利税连续二年不低于500万元;或在实施被列入国家级推广计划指南的成果中,有技术创新和工作创新并通过市级验收,为本单位或本系统产业结构调整、优化、升级和技术进步发挥了重要的作用,创造出显著的经济效益和社会效益,以年利税计连续二年不低于200万元。

第二十八条　《奖励办法》第十二条第一款(四)所称“重大工程项目”,是指列入市级以上(含市级)国民经济和社会发展计划的重大综合性基本建设工程、科学技术工程等。

第二十九条　科学技术进步奖中重大工程项目的奖励仅授予组织。在完成重大工程中做出科学发现、技术发明的个人,符合《奖励办法》和本细则规定条件的,可另行推荐自然科学奖或技术发明奖。

第三十条　科学技术进步奖候选人应当具备下列条件之一:(一)在设计项目的总体技术方案上做出重要贡献。(二)在关键技术和疑难问题的解决中做出重要技术创新。(三)在成果转化和推广应用过程中做出创造性贡献。(四)在高技术产业化方面做出重要贡献。

第三十一条　科学技术进步奖候选单位应当是在项目研制、开发、投产、应用和推广过程中提供技术、设备和人员等条件,对项目的完成起到组织、管理和协调作用的主要完成单位。各级政府部门一般不得作为科学技术进步奖的候选单位。

第三十二条　科学技术进步奖授奖等级根据候选人或候选单位所完成的项目进行综合评定,标准如下:(一)技术创新程度大,技术难度大,总体技术水平和主要技术经济指标达到国内领先或国际先进水平,创造出很大的经济效益或社会效益,对行业的技术进步和产业结构调整或对科技发展和社会进步有重大意义的,可以评为一等奖。(二)技术创新程度较大,技术难度较大,总体技术水平、主要技术经济指标达到国内先进水平并接近国际先进水平,创造出较大的经济效益或社会效益,对行业的技术进步和产业结构调整或对科技发展和社会进步有较大意义的,可以评为二等奖。(三)技术创新程度明显,有一定的技术难度,总体技术水平、主要技术经济指标达到国内先进水平,创造出一定的经济效益或社会效益,对行业的技术进步和产业结构调整或对科技发展和社会进步有一定意义的,可以评为三等奖。对于拥有自主知识产权的高新技术成果产业化项目,评审时,应给予加权分。

第五节　国际科学技术合作奖

第三十三条　《奖励办法》第十三条所称“外国人或者外国组织”,是指在双边或者多边国际科技合作中对本市科学技术事业做出显著贡献的外国科学家、工程技术人员、科技管理人员或科学技术研究、开发、管理等组织,以及资助本市科技事业的发展并做出显著贡献的外国人或外国组织。

第三十四条　国际科学技术合作奖每年授奖数额不超过5个。

第三章　评审机构

第三十五条　由市科委负责全市科学技术奖评审的组织工作、科学技术奖评审专家库建立工作及科学技术奖评审委员会组建等工作。市科委科技成果管理部门具体负责评审的日常工作。

第三十六条　天津市科学技术奖评审委员会的主要职责是:(一)负责天津市科学技术奖的评审工作。(二)向市科委报告评审结果。(三)为完善天津市科学技术奖励工作提供政策性意见和建议。(四)研究、解决天津市科学技术奖评审工作中出现的其他重要问题。

第三十七条　天津市科学技术奖评审委员会由10至15人组成。主任委员由市科委主任担任,设副主任委员2至4人、秘书长1人。评审委员会委员由科技、教育、经济等领域的专家、学者和有关行政部门领导组成。

第三十八条　天津市科学技术奖评审委员会可以根据评审工作需要,设立若干学科(专业)评审组,负责各学科(专业)的初评工作。学科(专业)评审组设组长1人、副组长1人,成员若干人。成员根据每年推荐的候选人的具体情况,从天津市科学技术奖评审专家库中选聘。

第三十九条　天津市科学技术奖评审委员会及其学科(专业)评审组的成员和相关的工作人员应当对候选人和候选单位所完成项目的技术内容及评审情况严格保守秘密。

第四章　推荐、评审、异议及其处理

第四十条　天津市科学技术奖候选人可由下列单位推荐:(一)各区、县人民政府。(二)市人民政府各有关部门。(三)各高等院校、市人民政府直属单位,各控股公司、集团公司,各驻津科研单位,以及其他经市科委认定、符合推荐条件的单位。除前款所列推荐单位之外,科技重大成就奖候选人还可由3名同行业的中国科学院院士、中国工程院院士、天津市科技重大成就奖获奖人联合推荐;上述推荐人每年度只可推荐1名候选人。

第四十一条　推荐单位应负责对推荐的项目进行初审,并根据同行专家意见在推荐书上签署包括推荐奖类、奖级的具体意见。两个以上(含两个)单位共同完成的项目,一般由第一完成单位的上级主管部门负责推荐并组织初审,亦应根据同行专家意见在推荐书上签署包括推荐奖类、奖级的具体意见。个人完成的项目,应由其居住地的区县科委负责推荐并组织初审。

第四十二条　推荐单位和推荐人推荐天津市科学技术奖的候选人、候选单位,应当征得候选人和候选单位的同意,并填写由市科委制作的统一格式的推荐书,提供符合要求的鉴定证书、评估证书、验收证书、国家法定专门机构颁发的批准文件和其他必要的评价材料与证明材料,且应以近十年的为主。推荐书及有关材料应当完整、真实、可靠。申报项目的主要科学研究及技术开发工作,应是以申报单位名义完成的为主。推荐科技重大成就奖、技术发明奖一等奖和科学技术进步奖一等奖的候选人,应根据具体情况提供审计部门出具的财务审计报告。前款所提"必要的评价材料"是指:(一)符合要求的鉴定证书、评估证书、验收证书;(二)国家法定专门机构颁发的批准文件;(三)其他需提供的评价材料。

第四十三条　推荐自然科学奖、技术发明奖和科学技术进步奖的候选人或候选单位所完成的成果,应是按照国家有关规定办理完科技成果登记手续的,否则不予受理。

第四十四条　天津市科学技术奖单项授奖人数和授奖单位数实行限额。一等奖人数不超过12人,单位不超过7个;二等奖人数不超过8人,单位不超过5个;三等奖人数不超过5人,单位不超过3个。科学技术进步奖中实施推广项目的授奖人数可增加1至3人,授奖单位可增加1至2个。

第四十五条　同一技术内容不得在同一年度重复推荐参加自然科学奖、技术发明奖和科学技术进步奖的评审。

第四十六条　凡存在知识产权以及有关完成单位、完成人员等方面争议的,在争议未解决前不得推荐参加天津市科学技术奖评审。

第四十七条 按照法律、行政法规规定必须取得有关许可证且直接关系到人身和社会安全、公共利益的项目,如动植物新品种、食品、药品、医药器械、农药、基因工程技术和产品等,在未获得主管行政机关批准之前,不得推荐参加天津市科学技术奖评审。

第四十八条 本细则规定的推荐单位和推荐人,应当在规定的时间内向市科委科技成果管理部门提交推荐书及相关材料,并由市科委科技成果管理部门对推荐材料进行审查。对不符合规定的推荐材料,可以要求推荐单位和推荐人在规定的时间内补正,逾期不补正或者经补正仍不符合要求的,不提交专家评审。

第四十九条 对经审查合格的推荐材料,由市科委科技成果管理部门提交相应的学科(专业)评审组或者组织具有评审资格的同行专家依照评审规则进行初评。初评可采用会议评审、专家独立评审和网络评审等方式。初评结果的确定应当遵循以下原则:(一)等级优先原则,即优先遵循评审专家建议的等级,量化排序。(二)评分排序原则,即相同建议等级评分按照评分从高到低的顺序排序。(三)学科平衡原则,即不同学科(专业)组的获奖率保持相对平衡。获奖与否及其等级的确定必须得到半数以上专家同意,最后将初评结果提交评审委员会审议。科技重大成就奖通过初评的人选要征求在津两院院士、同行业权威专家以及已获得过天津市科技重大成就奖人员的意见,并将该意见提交评审委员会。

第五十条 评审委员会审议初评结果并做出评审决议。对科技重大成就奖、国际科学技术合作奖,以及自然科学奖、技术发明奖和科学技术进步奖一等奖进行复审。复审一等奖项目采用差额方式,差额率为20%至30%。复审采用投票表决方式产生评审结果,获得三分之二多数(含三分之二)的方能通过。

第五十一条 天津市科学技术奖评审实行回避制度。推荐单位、推荐人认为有关专家和相关工作人员参加评审可能会影响公正的,可书面提出理由及相关的证明材料要求其回避。科学技术奖候选人及其直系亲属和存有直接利害关系的人员应回避,有关工作人员可以视实际情况予以回避。

第五十二条 市科委主任办公会对评审委员会做出的决议进行审核,并向社会公告,接受社会监督。

第五十三条 公告异议期为30天。有异议者,应当在异议期内向市科委科技成果管理部门提出,逾期不予受理。

第五十四条 提出异议的单位、个人应当提供书面异议材料和必要的证明材料并表明其真实身份,否则不予受理。

第五十五条 异议分为实质性异议和非实质性异议。凡对涉及候选人、候选单位所完成项目的创新性、先进性、实用性等方面,以及推荐材料不实所提的异议为实质性异议;对候选人、候选单位排序的异议,为非实质性异议。项目的完成人、完成单位及该项目的推荐单位或推荐人对评审等级的意见,不属于异议范围。

第五十六条 市科委科技成果管理部门在接到异议材料后,应当对异议内容进行审查,如果异议内容属于本细则第五十四条和第五十五条所述情况,并有充分依据的,应予受理,并应在30天内处理完毕。

第五十七条 实质性异议由市科委科技成果管理部门负责协调,由有关推荐单位或推荐人协助。涉及异议的任何一方应当积极配合,不得推诿和延误。推荐单位或推荐人接到异议通知后,应当在一周内核实异议材料,并将调查、核实的书面材料及时报送市科委科技成果管理部门。必要时,市科委科技成果管理部门可以组织评审委员及专家进行调查,提出处理意见。

非实质性异议由推荐单位负责协调,提出初步处理意见报送市科委科技成果管理部门审核。涉及跨部门的异议处理,由市科委科技成果管理部门负责协调,相关推荐单位或推荐人协助,其处理程序参照前款办理。异议在规定的期限内处理完毕的,提交本年度评审,否则不提交本年度评审。异议处理应保护异议人的正当合法权益。

第五十八条 异议处理结果应经市科委主任办公会审议通过。

第五章 授奖

第五十九条 市科委将天津市科学技术奖的获奖人选、项目及等级等情况报市人民政府批准。

第六十条 天津市科学技术奖每年度授奖项目不超过300项。

第六十一条 天津市科技重大成就奖由市长签署证书并颁发证书和奖金;自然科学奖、技术发明奖、科学技术进步奖由市人民政府颁发证书和奖金;国际科学技术合作奖由市长签署并颁发证书和奖牌。

第六十二条 天津市科技重大成就奖每项奖金数额为50万元;自然科学奖、技术发明奖、科学技术进步奖每项奖金数额分别为:一等奖8万元,二等奖3万元,三等奖1万元。

天津市科学技术奖励经费每年不低于500万元,由市财政列支。科技重大成就奖的奖金根据每年评审情况据实拨付。

第六章 附则

第六十三条 符合国家科学技术奖励条件的,由市科委负责按照国家下达的推荐限额数量择优推荐。已经获得国家和省部级科学技术奖的,除被列入推广项目外,不得再申报天津市科学技术奖。

第六十四条 本细则自发布之日起施行,原《天津市科学技术奖励办法实施细则》(津政发〔2001〕52号)废止。

关于进一步实施科技兴贸战略的意见

(津政发〔2004〕43号 2004年4月3日公布实施)

为深入贯彻落实《国务院办公厅转发商务部等部门关于进一步实施科技兴贸战略的若干意见的通知》(国办发〔2003〕92号)和全国科技兴贸大会精神,把实施科技兴贸战略作为促进对外贸易工作的主线,推动天津市高新技术产业和外贸出口向更高水平发展,特提出如下实施意见:

一、实施科技兴贸战略的指导思想和工作目标

以党的十六大关于坚持走新型工业化道路的要求为指针,大力支持和鼓励具有自主知识产权的高新技术产品出口,加快出口促进体系建设,着力优化出口商品结构,加大研发和引进国外先进技术及关键设备的力度,积极运用高新技术改造传统产业,加速实现出口方式的根本转变。

通过实施科技兴贸战略,把促进高新技术产品出口同提高传统商品的技术含量和附加值结合起来,促进外贸出口实现由粗放型向集约型的根本转变。用3至5年时间,力争培育一批出口达上亿美元的高新技术重点出口企业和重点商品,培育一批具有自主知识产权和知名度的自创品牌产品。2004年,天津市高新技术产品出口力争达到65亿美元,2010年力争达到150亿美元,年均增长20%以上,占全市外贸出口总额的比重达到50%左右。

二、强化联合工作机制,全面推动科技兴贸工作

加强对科技兴贸工作的领导,健全市科技兴贸领导机构,制定全市鼓励高新技术产品出口的政策规划,进一步发挥科技兴贸联合工作机制的作用,定期研究、协调解决高新技术产品出口中遇到的问题,全面推动科技兴贸工作。

各区、县外经贸部门要根据市科技兴贸领导小组制定的鼓励政策和计划,结合各自区域经济发展规划和产业优势,制定本区域实施科技兴贸工作的方案,加大对高新技术企业的支持力度,促进高新技术企业的快速发展。在全市形成市、区两级工作推动机制，上下联动、整体推进，形成全方位、多层次支持高新技术产品出口的工作格局。

2004年6月底前编制完成《天津市高新技术产品出口企业名录》，以后每年修订一次，对进入高新技术产品出口企业名录的企业给予重点政策扶持和定期跟踪服务。

三、大力扶持优势产业，支持高新技术产品出口

根据全市产业分布和高新技术产品出口的现状，确定天津市电子信息、生物制药、新材料、新能源、环保、汽车零部件等作为重点扶持的领域。

（一）大力扶持进入高新技术出口商品名录的企业。对注册资金50万元以上的高新技术生产企业、注册资金100万元以上的高新技术流通企业，帮助办理进出口资格登记。

（二）进一步加大科技兴贸资金支持力度。鼓励出口企业技术创新，增强高新技术产品研发能力。在天津市科技攻关计划中增设科技兴贸专项，支持出口企业高新技术产品研发、加强知识产权保护、建立技术标准、建立完善为高新技术产品出口服务的中介服务体系、培训技术人员、促进与国外技术交流等，对科技型企业实施“走出去”战略给予一定扶持和资助。对高新技术产品出口采取立项资助、贷款贴息等多种形式予以支持。加大对列入国家级或市级火炬计划的高新技术出口产品的贷款贴息力度。优选天津市高新技术出口产品申报国家科技兴贸行动计划。

（三）建立中小高新技术企业走向国际市场帮扶机制。由市外经贸服务中心联合有关大专院校和天津市优秀外贸企业、中小高新技术产品出口企业，建立走向国际市场帮扶机制，帮助缺乏国际市场信息的高新技术产品出口企业开拓国际市场。

（四）扩大高新技术产品出口企业和高新技术产品参加广交会的比例。以第90届全国出口商品交易会（广交会）摊位为基数，再新增摊位优先用于支持高新技术产品出口企业。对新提出申请参加广交会的高新技术产品生产经营企业优先安排；对出口规模快速增长的高新技术产品出口企业优先安排；对扩大经营高新技术产品的进出口企业优先安排。

（五）积极鼓励高新技术企业开拓国际市场。2004年要集中安排部分市外贸发展资金和中小企业国际市场开拓资金，支持高新技术企业开拓国际市场活动。重点安排12项开拓国际市场计划，帮助高新技术企业、集体民营企业和新获进出口经营权的企业走出去。充分发挥天津市在比利时常驻机构的作用，帮助企业开拓欧洲市场。以长兴国际贸易（比利时）有限公司为窗口，建立天津出口商品常年展示洽谈中心和分拨中心，将天津市的出口产品由比利时向欧盟其他国家辐射。组织高新技术企业参加欧盟国家举办的国际博览会，促进与法国北加莱、里尔地区的经贸合作，扩大对欧洲市场出口。以保税区在美国南卡州建立的“中国天津商贸工业园”为平台，鼓励企业走出去设点，促进外贸服务和生产加工向境外延伸，带动对美贸易的发展。

（六）积极落实2004年国家高新技术产品技术更新改造项目贷款贴息计划。在认真进行调研摸底的基础上，确定重点项目积极向商务部推荐，争取更多的高新技术企业享受贴息政策，促进全市高新技术产品出口。

（七）实施品牌战略，支持具有自主知识产权的高新技术产品出口。抓住世界高新技术产业转移的时机，制定各项优惠政策，加大招商力度，努力争取一批世界著名跨国公司在津建立研发中心和高新技术生产基地。吸引并扶持国际一流人才在津创办科技型企业和研发机构。注重引进高科技产品的核心技术和尖端技术，提高天津市高新技术产品的实力和水平，带动天津市传统产业改造。培育一批在电子信息、生物制药、新材料、新能源、环保等领域的高新技术企业集群。2004年力争使一批具有自主知识产权的高新技术产品进入国家重点出口名牌商品目录。

（八）大力扶持科技型企业实施“走出去”战略。在继续吸引外资投向高新技术产业的同时，积极实施“走出去”战略，支持和推动有条件的科技型企业到境外建立营销网络或设立分支机构、研发中心。充分利用当地的信息、人才、资金，开拓国际市场，培育跨国经营的高新技术产品出口企业。

（九）建立高新技术产品出口企业绿色通道。在天津市已有36家出口企业享受便捷通关优惠政策的基础上，进一步扩大便捷通关适用范围。对2003年出口1000万美元以上的高新技术产品出口企业实行便捷通关，创造优质快捷的通关环境。扩大高新技术出口企业分类管理范围，积极推行高新技术产品加工复出口3C免检措施，实行不定期抽检，实现快速通关。对高新技术产品出口企业优先核准出口退税，保证及时足额退付。

（十）支持加工贸易企业与海关联网。积极鼓励加工贸易企业与海关实行联网，用市外贸发展资金对实行加工贸易联网的高新技术产品出口企业给予适度资助。

四、推动天津市国家级软件出口基地建设

为促进软件出口工作，以科技兴贸领导小组成员单位为基础共同建立软件出口联席会制度，定期研究、协调解决软件出口工作中的问题。

（一）积极扩大软件出口规模。坚持理念创新、资源整合、管理改革、环境重构的原则，以软件产品出口为导向，以软件出口企业为主体，以软件出口基地为依托，聚合全市人才、技术和管理资源，突出重点，形成特色，有效地促进软件出口规模不断扩大。积极扩大对日本、韩国的软件外包业务；根据天津市电子信息产业优势，努力发展通讯领域和消费类电子领域的嵌入式软件配套出口；逐步培育欧美市场。2004年全市软件出口力争达到1亿美元，2006年软件出口力争达到2.5亿美元。

（二）设立天津市软件出口奖励基金。自今年起对软件出口企业进行专项奖励，安排专项资金支持软件出口服务体系建设和具有自主知识产权的软件产品研发。对进入国家出口基地的软件出口企业，加大资金支持力度。

五、加快高新技术产品出口促进体系建设

努力建设高新技术产品出口促进支撑体系，从项目研发、技术改造、资金、贸易便利、市场开拓、人员出入境、信息服务等方面对高新技术产品出口给予政策支持和中介服务。搞好科技兴贸战略研究，为高新技术产品出口创造良好的政策环境。

（一）建立完善高新技术产品出口信贷资金支持体系。在外汇管理上，对高新技术产品的出口企业，予以政策支持。加强对高新技术企业融资服务工作。优先向政策性银行和商业银行推荐重点高新技术出口企业进行信贷授信，加大金融支持力度，解决出口企业资金困难，推动高新技术产品出口。发挥出口信用保险对扩大高新技术产品出口的积极作用，加大对高新技术企业投保出口信用保险的支持力度。在国家资助的基础上，市外贸发展资金对出口信用保险保费贴补率增加到30%，为企业提供信用保险项下的融资便利。充分发挥政府资金投入的示范效应，吸引和利用社会资金、风险投资，支持高新技术产品的生产和出口。利用出口信息网络平台等形式，组织金融、创业投资公司、高新技术企业、中介服务机构以及政府有关服务部门进行洽谈，为科技兴贸工作搭建融资、合作与信息交流平台。

（二）加强培训交流工作，促进高新技术企业发展。对天津市科技兴贸所需国际型、高层次的管理和专业人才采取引进和培养并重的方式，研究制定人才实施计划。有计划地采取国内和国外、请进来和走出去相结合的方式，为高新技术企业进行外贸政策、业务知识和市场开拓等方面的培训。同时举办软件出口、汽车国际化标准、现代物流、跨国公司全球采购等系列讲座与培训。对高新技术企业人员的培训费用给予一定资助。

（三）建设完善的科技兴贸中介服务体系。2004年重点建设一批国际化的生产力促进中心，为行业及高新技术产品出口服务。大力扶持与国际接轨的高水平科技兴贸中介机构，发挥南开大学、天津大学、财经学院等院校及有关咨询机构在科技与国际经贸方面的学科优势、国外合作关系和信息渠道，为天津市科技兴贸提供多方面咨询服务，并开展知识产权管理和保护、国际标准认证、技术性贸易措施等相关方面的调研和战略研究。

（四）建设基础信息服务体系。依托科技服务中介机构，建立和完善高新技术产品出口信息服务体系和《高新技术产品对外交易项目库》。

天津市科普税收优惠政策实施细则

（津科社〔2004〕223号　2004年12月9日公布实施）

第一章　总则

第一条　目的和依据　为保障国家科普税收优惠政策的实施，根据《关于鼓励科普事业发展税收优惠政策问题的通知》〔财税（2003）55号〕（以下简称《通知》）和《科普税收优惠政策实施办法》〔国科发政字（2003）416号〕（以下简称《实施办法》），结合本市实际，制定本实施细则。

第二条　适用范围　本实施细则适用于本市综合类科技报纸、科普基地、进口科普影视作品、科普活动、科普捐赠等事项的认定和政策管理工作。凡符合本实施细则有关规定的企事业单位、社会团体，党委、政府及其工作部门以及科协、工会、妇联、共青团组织可以向相关管理部门申请认定，经审核批准后享受税收优惠政策。

第三条　管理部门与职责　天津市科学技术委员会（以下简称市科委）负责协调管理和统计，以及科普基地、科普活动的认定；天津市新闻出版局负责综合类科技报纸的认定；天津市财政局、天津市国家税务局、天津市地方税务局、天津海关按各自职责予以核准落实税收优惠政策。

第二章　科技类报纸和音像制品的认定和管理

第四条　认定范围　综合类科技报纸和科技音像制品是指以普及科学知识、倡导科学方法、传播科学思想、弘扬科学精神为宗旨，经批准正式出版的报纸和音像制品。

第五条　认定标准　综合科技类报纸在报纸批准登记时按分类标准进行认定。科技音像制品由天津市新闻出版局按照中国标准音像制品编码分类代码（ISRC）中的A—马克思主义、列宁主义、毛泽东思想，B—哲学，D—政治、法律，E—军事，F—经济，K—历史、地理，N—自然科学总论，O—数理科学和化学，P—天文学、地球科学，Q—生物科学，R—医药、卫生，S—农业科学，T—工业技术，U—交通运输，V—航空、航天，X—环境科学、劳动保护科学等类别进行认定。

第六条　惩戒措施　违规出版物和多次出现违规的出版社、报社不得享受税收优惠政策。

第三章　科普基地的认定和管理

第七条　认定范围　科技馆、自然博物馆、对公众开放的天文馆（站、台）、气象台（站）、地震台（站）及高校和科研机构对公众开放的科普场馆（场所）可以申请认定，其中：（一）科技类场馆是指科技博物馆（含科技馆）、青少年科技站（馆、中心）等科学技术类的科普教育场馆（场所）；（二）自然科学类博物馆是指展出生物活体或标本、以研究物种资源为主要功能的自然科学类科普场馆（场所）；（三）高校和科研机构对公众开放的科普基地是指高校和科研机构内设的植物园、标本馆、陈列馆等科普场所。

第八条　认定条件　申请认定的科普基地必须同时具备以下条件：（一）申请认定科普基地的单位，必须专门从事面向公众的科普活动，有开展科普活动的科普专职人员、场所、设施、工作经费等条件；（二）面向公众从事《科普法》所规定的科普活动，有稳定的科普经费来源；（三）有适合常年向公众开放的一定的科普展教设施、器材和固定场所；（四）累计每年开放时间不少于200天；且每年免费开放累计不少于20天（含法定节假日）；（五）有常设的内部科普工作机构，并配备3名以上专职科普工作人员；（六）有明确的科普工作规划或年度科普工作计划；（七）有关科普项目的资金单独核算。

第九条 认定程序 科普基地按照下列程序认定:(一)符合以上认定条件的科普基地可以提出认定申请,填写认定申请表并附相关材料于当年第一季度、第三季度内向所在区(县)科委申请认定;(二)区(县)科委收到申请后先行预审,应在十个工作日之内将通过预审的相关材料和预审意见报送市科委审批;(三)市科委在收到区(县)科委的预审报告后,应在十五个工作日内作出认定或不予认定的决定,并通知相关区(县)科委和被认定的科普基地单位;(四)市科委认定科普基地单位后于一个月内向天津市财政局、天津市国家税务局、天津市地方税务局和国家科技部备案。

第十条 年度管理 科普基地应于每年年底向所在区(县)科委提交年度报告,内容包括报告当年科普基地工作情况(说明参观对象、人数、开放天数等),并填妥相关统计表格;报告翌年科普工作计划;报告有关科普活动投入及经费使用情况等。区(县)科委初审后,将审理意见报告市科委。市科委根据区(县)科委初审意见,作出次年是否继续认定的决定。

第四章 进口科普影视作品的认定和管理

第十一条 认定条件 进口科普影视作品申请认定应符合下列条件:(一)由经认定的科普基地自行进口或委托进口的;(二)属于《通知》附件2所列税号范围;(三)必须是为其自用,不得进行商业销售或挪作他用。

第十二条 申请和审批 符合条件的科普基地可以向所在区(县)科委提出申请,并附带进口影视作品的合同、协议(含中文译本)和相关资料。区(县)科委收到申请后先行预审,应在十个工作日之内将通过预审的相关材料和预审意见报送市科委审批;市科委在收到区(县)科委的预审报告后,应会同天津市新闻出版局在十五个工作日内做出认定或不予认定的决定,并通知相关区(县)科委和科普基地单位;市科委认定进口科普影视作品后于一个月内向天津市财政局、国家科技部和新闻出版总署备案。

第五章 科普活动的认定和管理

第十三条 认定范围 市和区(县)的党委、政府及其工作部门以及科协、工会、妇联、共青团等组织开展科普活动可以申请认定。

第十四条 认定条件 申请认定科普活动的,必须同时具备下列条件:(一)必须是符合《科普法》规定,以普及科学知识、倡导科学方法、传播科学思想、弘扬科学精神为宗旨的社会性、群众性科普活动。票价设定必须面向普通市民;(二)必须是由地方党委、政府及其工作部门和科协、工会、妇联、共青团主办的;(三)必须有具体的科普活动方案;(四)设置有专门的科普活动组织工作机构,有完备的组织管理、财务管理等制度。

第十五条 申请 符合条件的主办者按下列规定申请认定:(一)主办单位应在科普活动举办前一个月提出申请,申请书中应包括科普活动批件、科普活动方案(指主办单位、承办单位、活动目的、活动规模、请示核定的门票价格等内容);(二)区(县)级科普活动向所在地区(县)科委提出申请;市级科普活动向市科委提出申请;(三)跨市或区举办的科普活动向获得门票核定所在地的政府科技管理部门提出申请,不得重复申请认定。

第十六条 审核 区(县)级科普活动结束后一个月内,主办单位应将科普活动总结报告及相关证明材料、资料报经所在地区(县)审核同意后,由市科委审批。市级科普活动结束后一个月内,将科普活动总结报告及相关证明材料、资料报市科委审批。市科委审核同意后一个月内向天津市财政局、税务局和国家科技部备案。

第六章 科普税收优惠政策及实施

第十七条 科普税收优惠政策适用期限 科普税收优惠政策自2003年6月1日起执行。各类科普事项经认定后,可以享受科普税收优惠政策。

第十八条 科技类报纸、音像制品优惠政策 2003年6月1日~2005年12月31日,综合类科技报纸和科技音像制品在出版环节的发行收入，实行增值税先征后退办法。

第十九条 科普基地优惠政策 科普基地的门票收入免征营业税。2003年6月1日～2005年12月31日，科普基地从境外购买自用科普影视作品播映权而进口的拷贝、工作带免征关税，不征进口环节增值税，免征对境外单位转让上述播映权等无形资产应代扣(缴)的营业税；以其他形式进口的自用影视作品，免征关税和进口环节增值税。

第二十条 科普活动优惠政策 科普活动的门票收入免征营业税。

第二十一条 对科普基地捐赠优惠政策 企事业单位、社会团体按照《捐赠法》的规定，通过中国境内非营利的社会团体、国家机关对科普基地的捐赠，符合《中华人民共和国企业所得税暂行条例实施细则》第十二条规定的，在年度应纳税所得额的10%以内的部分，准予扣除。

第二十二条 减免办理 被市科委认定科普基地、科普活动的单位，须携带认定批文及营业执照、税务登记证原件及复印件等相关文件，到主管税务部门办理免税等手续。

第二十三条 海关办理免税手续 对经认定的进口科普影视作品拷贝、工作带申请享受税收优惠时，科普基地须持进口科普影视作品批准文件、其他证明文件以及海关要求的其他材料，在科普影视作品进口前向天津海关提出申请。天津海关按规定办理减免税手续。

第七章 附则

第二十四条 应用解释 本实施细则的具体应用问题，由市科委会同有关部门解释。

第二十五条 生效日期 本实施细则自颁布之日起施行。

关于促进天津市科技企业孵化器建设与发展的意见

（津政发〔2005〕12号 2005年2月8日公布实施）

为加速天津市科技创新体系建设，构筑和完善科技孵育体系，促进科技成果转化和高新技术产业化，推动科技与经济的有效结合，培育新的经济增长点，根据有关法律法规和天津市实际情况，现就促进天津市科技企业孵化器建设与发展，提出如下意见。

一、指导思想

天津市孵化器建设的指导思想是：深入贯彻落实党的十六届四中全会和市委八届七次全会精神，全面落实科学发展观，以提高科技持续创新、创业能力为主线，以构筑创新创业环境为重点，把孵化器建设纳入天津市科技发展的整体战略中，按照优化布局、突出重点、机制创新、整体带动的思路，通过优化结构布局和运行机制，充分发挥孵化器的孵化和辐射作用。集中目标，整合资源，聚集人才，加强引导，带动全社会的投入，建设国内一流、布局合理的创业孵育体系，进一步完善高新技术成果转化和推广应用的支撑环境，提高天津市高新技术产业的持续创新能力，培育科技型中小企业。

不断完善适合天津市高新技术转化和产业培育的发展环境和整体布局。在改造提升综合型孵化器服务功能、服务水平和服务业绩的同时，突出高新技术产业特点，重点发展专业型孵化器和区域特色产业孵化器，引导孵化器向集约化、专业化、多元化、网络化、功能化的科技服务业发展。

二、发展目标与原则

（一）天津市孵化器建设的总体目标是：通过政府引导，整合社会资源，提高天津市现有孵化器的服务功能与服务水平；建立面向高新技术领域的专业孵化器群和面向区域经济的特色产业孵化器群。重点建设公共技术支撑服务体系，积极推进科技成果转化和产业化，为高新技术企业提供先进、开放、配套的技术支撑平台，为高新技术企业营造良好的发展环境；围绕创新、创业，提供优良的服务。帮助在孵高新技术企业提高技术水平、管理能力和综合素质;结合天津市经济发展和产业布局,充分运用风险投资机制,培养一批高新技术企业,加大科技对经济发展的贡献。

(二)天津市孵化器建设的原则是:以支撑体系为重点,环境建设为基础,鼓励创新为宗旨,人才培养为杠杆,中介服务为纽带,风险资金为后盾,产业发展为方向,实行政府引导,市场运作,需求拉动,多元投资,突出特色,协调发展。坚持系统规划、分类指导、层次推进、资源整合、规范运作的原则。积极提倡孵化器投资主体多元化、运作市场化、发展专业化和国际化。

在宏观布局上,重点引导电子信息、生物医药、新材料、新能源等高新技术领域,石化、汽车、冶金等优势产业,面向各区县特色经济的各类孵化器建设和发展,充分利用国内外两个市场和两种资源,聚集技术创新及产业化过程的各种资源,推动科技型企业不断创新创业。抓住天津市高新技术产业发展中的新兴产业,完善产业链,加速产业化和集群化。

三、孵化器的主要任务

科技企业孵化器是以促进科技成果转化和高新技术产业化、培养高新技术企业和企业家为宗旨,连接技术创新源头和高新技术企业的重要社会经济组织,是科技创新体系的重要组成部分。政府支持和鼓励各类组织、企业以及个人创办孵化器,引导和带动科技创新、创业孵育体系的形成和发展。

市科技主管部门负责对全市的孵化器进行宏观管理和业务指导,制定全市孵化器发展规划和管理办法,并择优支持。符合条件的孵化器可自愿申请认定为市级科技企业孵化器。各类孵化器,要通过全方位的优质服务降低创业企业的创业风险和创业成本,为社会培养成功的科技企业和企业家,为全市经济发展创造新的经济增长点,促进区域经济的更快发展。

孵化器应当发挥社会中介机构的作用,吸引科技服务机构入驻,为在孵企业提供良好的服务。要突出与高校、科研院所等技术创新源头的紧密联系,并广泛建立与社会相关组织的联系网络。引入风险投资和社会融资机制,加快孵化基金、担保基金等多种形式投融资体系的建设。

孵化器要建立适应社会主义市场经济的运行机制,不断提高和完善自身的服务功能,提高运行质量。聚合孵化资源,增强孵化综合能力。在提供高质量服务的同时,实现自收自支、自主经营、自我约束、自我发展的良性循环。

要促进孵化器的国际化进程,鼓励开展国际交流与合作、管理人员的培训和经验交流等;通过建立与国外科学园区、孵化器的伙伴关系,推动孵化器、科技型中小企业和科技创新活动与国际接轨,促进科技兴贸的发展。

充分利用现有资源创办孵化器,盘活现有房产、仪器、设备等物业资源以及已建的科研中心、工程中心及公共条件平台等科技资源,形成开放格局和共享机制,面向中小企业服务,充分发挥资源的放大效应。

四、政策措施

(一)市科技主管部门设立支持孵化器建设和发展的引导资金,重点支持符合天津市孵化器建设总体布局和与天津市重点支柱产业结合紧密的孵化器公共服务平台、信息网络等共享设施的建设。

统筹科技资金,集中财力对孵化能力强、政策鼓励范围内的孵化器给予重点资金支持。对经市有关部门认定和年度考核合格的孵化器,3年内给予税收扶持政策,即对孵化器自身缴纳的营业税和企业所得税地方分享部分,由孵化器所在区县财政部门予以返还,所需资金由市财政和区县财政按财政体制规定分别负担;设立市科技企业孵化器贷款担保代偿金,在孵企业发生还贷风险时,可由市有关部门给予部分风险代偿补贴(具体管理办法另行制定)。

(二)符合市总体布局要求并经专家论证通过的新建孵化器,市科技主管部门给予一定的启动资金支持;对于区县建立的特色产业孵化器,实施市、区两级共建,即在区县政府对孵化器予以政策和资金支持的基础上,市科技主管部门给予一定的启动资金支持。

(三)对于符合企业登记条件的孵化器应依法向工商行政管理部门申请登记注册,其主要经营范围核定为“科技企业孵化器”,注册名称中可使用“孵化器”字样,以体现行业特点,但不能作为企业组织形式使用。

对于经认定的市级孵化器，市科技主管部门赋予其对在孵企业申报市科技发展计划的初审受理权。同时对于在孵企业申报的项目，同等条件下可优先考虑立项。对于在孵企业获得国家有关计划资助的，将优先予以匹配资助。

（四）孵化器内的在孵企业经认定可享受天津市高新技术企业有关优惠政策；孵化器内的软件企业经认定可享受天津市软件企业有关优惠政策。

（五）孵化器通过各种形式，定期发布在孵企业优秀项目，吸引金融资本进入，帮助在孵企业畅通融资渠道。在孵企业毕业以后，市科技主管部门择优对其承担的科技项目予以支持，并帮助协调投融资和信贷支持。要引导研究院所、高校、相关企业、跨国公司的技术中心或实验室进驻孵化器，形成先进的技术开发、实验和检测平台，帮助高新技术企业提高在技术研究和开发方面的创新能力，降低开发成本。

（六）建立市孵化器行业协会，加强孵化器行业自律，定期举办孵化器行业发展论坛，促进孵化器经验与信息交流、合作与发展。充分利用天津市高校及科研院所的优势，组织对孵化器经营管理人才的培训，提高孵化器管理水平。

启动天津市孵化器综合服务信息网络的建设，形成综合服务信息网络，以信息化促进孵化器快速发展，建立各孵化器和相关服务机构网页，为孵化企业提供便捷的信息服务，把孵化器建成信息平台、创新平台和服务平台。

关于进一步促进高新技术成果转化的暂行办法

（津政发〔2005〕19号　2005年3月22日公布实施）

第一条　为加快实施科教兴市战略，规范高新技术成果转化活动，根据《中华人民共和国促进科技成果转化法》、《天津市促进科技成果转化条例》等政策法规，结合天津市实际，制定本办法。

第二条　本办法所称高新技术成果转化是指为提高生产力水平而对科学研究与技术开发所产生的具有实用价值的高新技术成果进行的后续试验、开发、应用、推广直至形成新产品、新工艺、新材料，发展新产业等活动。凡在本市实施高新技术成果转化项目的法人或自然人均可以按照由市发展改革委、市科委联合编制的《天津市当前优先发展的高新技术产业化重点领域指南》，申请高新技术成果转化项目的认定。凡经认定的高新技术成果转化项目，可适用本办法。

第三条　实行高新技术成果转化项目认定制度。成立由市科委、市发展改革委、市财政局、市经委、市知识产权局组成的天津市高新技术成果转化项目认定办公室（以下简称项目认定办公室），负责本市高新技术成果转化项目的认定工作，并由天津市高新技术成果转化中心负责组织对在津开发的或引进国内外高新技术成果转化项目进行技术等级、市场前景、项目风险和知识产权等方面的认定。经国家和本市市级有关部门批准的项目及获得科技型中小企业技术创新资金资助的项目可简化认定程序。

第四条　市政府设立高新技术成果转化专项资金（以下简称专项资金），促进高新技术成果项目转化。经认定的高新技术成果转化项目，使用专项资金给予适当扶持，并可给予贷款贴息等扶持；经认定的拥有自主知识产权的高新技术成果转化项目，使用专项资金优先予以扶持。

第五条　由项目认定办公室负责向有关机构推荐经认定的转化项目，对符合银行贷款条件的，商业性银行可优先予以贷款。项目单位可凭专利权到开展质押业务的银行申请质押贷款，科技担保机构予以担保。并优先推荐承担高新技术成果转化项目的企业上市。在同类商品中，政府优先采购高新技术成果转化的产品。

第六条　承担高新技术成果转化项目的企业，经认定后，兼并连续3年亏损企业或困难企业的房产作为生产用房的，其兼并原企业的房产，可按规定的程序向所在地地方税务局提出减免房地产税申请，财税部门按照有关政策给予减免。

第七条 在境外取得长期居留证的从事高新技术成果转化的海外留学生在津取得的工薪收入，可视同境外收入，在计算个人应纳所得税额时，减除规定费用后，并可适用附加减除费用的规定。

第八条 对单位和个人从事转化项目的技术转让、技术开发和与之相关的技术咨询、技术服务获得的收入，免征营业税。

第九条 申报认定的高新技术成果转化项目，凡具备专利条件，适合用专利加以保护的，应及时申请专利。对本市企事业单位和个人申请国内外专利，市知识产权局按照有关规定给予资助。

第十条 在本市注册并缴纳所得税的企业，企业税后利润投资于经认定的高新技术成果转化项目，形成或增加企业的资本金，且投资合同期超过5年的，与该投资额对应的已征企业所得税地方收入部分，从专项资金中给予适当扶持。

第十一条 高新技术成果可作为无形资产参与转化项目投资。高新技术成果作为无形资产的价值占注册资本比例可达35%。合作各方另有约定的，从其约定。高新技术成果作为无形资产投资的价值，须经具有资质的评估机构评估，并经市科技主管部门予以认定。

第十二条 中央各部委、外省市和海外留学生及国外专家带高新技术成果来津实施转化的项目，以及具有自主知识产权的高新技术成果转化项目，经认定后，可享受专项资金资助、贷款贴息。

第十三条 鼓励技术、管理等生产要素参与收益分配。在部分高新技术企业（国有独资）中进行试点，在实施公司制改制时，经国有资产管理部门批准，可将前3年国有净资产增值（不包括房地产增值部分）中拿出一定比例作为股份，奖励有贡献的职工特别是科技人员和经营管理人员。

第十四条 企业、科研机构、高等院校转化职务科技成果，应当根据不同的转化方式，依法对研究开发该项科技成果的职务科技成果完成人和为成果转化做出重要贡献的其他人员给予奖励。奖励形式可采取现金、实股或期权等方式。

（一）以技术转让方式将成果提供给他人实施转化的，成果主要完成人应享有不低于转让所得的税后净收入20%的收益。以股权投入方式进行转化的，成果主要完成人应享有不低于该项目成果所占股份的20%的股权，该持股人依据其所持股份分享收益。其他成果完成人和为成果转化做出重要贡献的人员应取得相应的股权或受益。

（二）企业、科研机构、高等院校自行实施转化或以合作方式实施转化的单位，应在项目成功投产后3至5年内，每年从实施该项成果所得的税后净利润中提取不低于5%的比例，对完成该项科技成果及其转化做出重要贡献的人员给予奖励。企业通过实施成果转化来改造传统产业的，在科技成果投产后连续5至10年内，每年应从新增税后净利润中提取不低于5%比例的资金，对转化该项科技成果做出重要贡献的人员给予奖励。

（三）企业自主开发的非本企业主导经营领域的成果，自行转化实施的，在项目盈利后3至5年内，每年应从实施该项成果的税后净利润中提取不低于10%比例的资金，对完成该项科技成果及其转化做出重要贡献的人员给予奖励。

上述奖励中，成果主要完成人所得奖励份额应不低于奖励总额的50%。该项奖励资金可在企业成本中列支。

第十五条 鼓励大专院校、科研院所的科技人员兼职办科技企业，兼职从事高新技术成果的转化工作，所在单位应继续为科技人员从事应用研究开发提供科研实验条件。

大专院校、科研院所的科技人员和管理人员离岗办科技企业或从事高新技术成果转化工作，允许其在3年内保留与原单位的工作关系。3年内回原单位工作的，应提前一个月向原单位提出申请，单位应予接收，并按离岗前职级安排适当工作岗位。3年内达到法定退休年龄的，由原单位办理退休手续。离岗期间，离岗人员停止享受原单位工资福利待遇，但养老保险、医疗保险、失业保险及住房公积金仍按原渠道交纳，工龄连续计算，遇工资正常晋升或国家调整机关事业单位工资时，如没有违法违纪行为，原单位应按相关政策调整其档案工资，并与原单位在职人员同样享受天津市住房货币分配政策。

科技人员和管理人员兼职或离岗办科技企业，从事高新技术成果转化工作，应遵守与原单位的约定，保守原单位的商业秘密和技术秘密；使用原单位或他人商业秘密和技术秘密的，应与原单位或他人签订许可或转让协议。

第十六条 鼓励外商在津投资创业、转化高新技术成果。

（一）鼓励外商在本市投资高新技术产业、设立研究开发机构和转让先进技术。在津注册的外商投资企业，在本市新研发的具有自主知识产权的高新技术成果转化项目，从专项资金中予以扶持。

（二）鼓励外商投资企业加强技术开发活动，外商投资企业当年发生的技术开发费比上年增长10%以上（含10%）的，经税务部门批准，允许再按技术开发费实际发生额的50%抵扣当年度的应纳税所得额。经认定的外商投资技术密集型、知识密集型企业，报税务部门批准，减按15%的税率缴纳企业所得税。

（三）外商投资设立的研究开发中心，在投资总额内进口国内不能生产或性能不能满足需要的自用设备及其配套技术、配件、备件，可按规定免征关税和进口环节增值税。对其转让技术，比照国内科研机构免征营业税。鼓励外商投资设立的研究开发中心参与国内产、学、研合作。

（四）外商投资企业、外商投资设立的研究开发中心、外国企业和外籍人士向本市转让技术，可持本市技术转让合同登记证明，按规定向税务部门申请，免征营业税。鼓励企业和研究开发机构聘用外籍专家，其薪金可列入成本。

第十七条 市科委负责本市高新技术企业认定工作。市科委委托市高新区管委会、市开发区管委会、保税区管委会负责受理及认定各自区域内注册的高新技术企业，并报市科委备案，由市科委颁发高新技术企业证书。经认定的高新技术企业可享受国家和本市有关高新技术企业的政策。

第十八条 鼓励境内外各类资本（包括民间资本）建立创业投资机构。经批准成立的创业投资公司，可用其全额资本金进行投资。在本市注册的创业投资机构，其投资于经认定的高新技术成果转化项目、高新技术企业或政府支持的科技计划及产业化项目的资金，累计超过其对外投资总额70%的，自获利年度起3年内，返还企业所得税地方分成部分。

第十九条 充分发挥天津技术产权交易机构为技术产权流动、股权交易的服务功能。建立科技成果转化和科技型企业成长提供创业风险投融资的进入和退出机制，促进创业资本的良性循环。

第二十条 凡政府资助的产品开发研究项目，在规定期限内未认真开展转化工作的，暂停对该项目组和项目执行人的政府资助。凡发现经认定的高新技术成果转化项目执行情况与项目转化计划有严重不符或两年内未实施转化的，撤销该项目的认定资格。

第二十一条 本办法自下发之日起施行。

天津市科技创新专项资金管理办法

（津政办发〔2005〕35号　2005年6月3日公布实施）

第一章　总则

第一条 为促进科技成果转化和高级人才引进，全面发挥科技进步对于经济社会全面、协调、可持续发展的核心引领和支撑作用，根据《国务院办公厅转发科学技术部财政部关于科技型中小企业技术创新基金的暂行规定的通知》（国办发〔1999〕47号）精神及财政财务制度的有关规定，结合天津市实际情况，制定本办法。

第二条 天津市科技创新专项资金是市人民政府设立的用于引导本市企业及科研单位吸引优秀人才、引进具有国际先进水平高新技术和支持自主知识产权重大科技成果转化的专项资金。

第三条 天津市科技创新专项资金的管理和使用，应遵照国家的有关法律、法规规定，符合国家及天津市产业政策。遵循诚实申请、公开受理、择优支持、目标管理、专款专用的原则，确保天津市科技创新专项资金规范、安全和高效使用。

第四条　天津市科技创新专项资金的来源主要有：（一）财政预算安排的天津市科技创新专项资金；（二）天津市科技创新专项资金的银行存款利息；（三）天津市科技创新专项资金投资回收的资金；（四）其他资金。天津市科技创新专项资金当年未安排的资金结转下年，滚动使用。

第五条　由市人民政府主管科技和财政的领导同志以及市有关部门主要负责人组成天津市科技创新专项资金领导小组，负责确定年度工作重点和审批立项等重大事项。

第六条　由市科委、市财政局等部门组成天津市科技创新专项资金领导小组办公室（以下简称“办公室”），办公室设在市科委。负责受理项目申报、项目初选和提出评估项目名单，组织天津市科技创新专项资金专家咨询委员会对申报项目的技术水平和经济效益进行评估论证，提出资助经费建议，进行日常管理、检查验收和综合统计等事项。

第七条　由天津市相关领域知名专家组成天津市科技创新专项资金专家咨询委员会，负责申报项目的整体技术经济评价、立项建议和执行情况、年度评估等咨询工作。

第二章　支持范围、方式与额度

第八条　天津市科技创新专项资金主要用于以下方面：（一）支持具有国际先进水平、拥有自主知识产权的重大科技创新成果转化，支持农业高科技成果转化；（二）支持国内外拔尖人才、优秀团队和知名科研机构携带技术、资金来津创业；（三）支持资源、环保、卫生等重大社会公益性科技工程的应用基础研究和技术开发；（四）支持购买先进技术、引进高级人才以及科技成果转化过程中支出的聘请专家、委托中介机构等费用。

第九条　根据申报项目特点，从天津市科技创新专项资金中分别以无偿资助、贷款贴息、资本金投入等方式给予资助。原则上一个申报项目只能申请一种资助方式。资助额度一般为500至1000万元，对提升天津市科技竞争能力和产业升级有重大意义的申报项目上不封顶。（一）无偿资助：主要用于技术购买费、工程咨询设计费、人员费、试验运行费、大型仪器设备费、科技基建费、国际合作费等的补贴；（二）贷款贴息：原则上按不低于银行贷款年利息的50%给予补贴；（三）资本金投入：经天津市科技创新专项资金领导小组批准的资本金投入项目，可由天津市科技创新专项资金领导小组明确委托有关国有资产授权经营公司进行管理。

第三章　项目申请、审批与资金拨付

第十条　凡符合天津市科技创新专项资金支持条件的申报项目，由项目承担单位向办公室提交立项建议书；初步审查符合要求的申报项目，经局级（或区县）主管部门审查后，向办公室正式提出立项申请。办公室随时受理申请，进行形式审查，出具受理通知书。

第十一条　正式受理的申报项目，应向办公室提交以下材料：（一）《天津市科技创新专项资金项目申请书》；（二）《天津市科技创新专项资金项目可行性研究报告》及有关证明材料（包括成果来源和权益证明、企业法人营业执照、专利证明、高新技术企业认定证书、经审计的年度会计报表等）；（三）局级（或区县）主管部门出具的《推荐意见书》。

第十二条　天津市科技创新专项资金专家咨询委员会对受理项目的市场前景、技术创新性、技术可行性、风险性、效益性、申报单位的经营管理水平等进行客观评估、论证，并提出立项建议。办公室审核汇总后报请天津市科技创新专项资金领导小组审批，一般每季度审批一次。

第十三条　按规定需要招标的受理项目，通过招标方式确定承担单位。

第十四条　经天津市科技创新专项资金领导小组批准的支持项目，由办公室向项目承担单位和局级

（或区县）主管部门下达立项通知和天津市科技创新专项资金计划，并与承担单位签订《天津市科技创新专项资金项目执行合同书》。

第十五条 市财政局按照天津市科技创新专项资金领导小组批复的资金使用计划，将天津市科技创新专项资金及时拨付至项目单位，并负责天津市科技创新专项资金的使用管理与监督。

第四章 项目管理与监督

第十六条 天津市科技创新专项资金项目承担单位应按照《天津市科技创新专项资金项目执行合同书》的有关条款，实行目标责任制管理，项目法人、首席专家分别承担实施、技术管理职责。引入中介机构推行项目监理制。

第十七条 天津市科技创新专项资金项目承担单位要自觉接受办公室和监理机构对项目实施过程的监督、检查，并按半年和年度向办公室报送项目进展和资金使用情况。

第十八条 天津市科技创新专项资金支持项目完成后，由承担单位和各责任人作出工作总结报告、技术报告、绩效分析报告和经费决算报告，办公室组织天津市科技创新专项资金专家咨询委员会或监理机构对项目进行验收，验收时可对承担单位使用天津市科技创新专项资金情况进行必要的审计。通过验收的项目由办公室出具验收合格通知书。

验收的主要内容包括：（一）合同计划进度执行情况；（二）经济、技术指标完成情况；（三）研究开发取得的成效情况；（四）资金落实与使用情况；（五）实施前后，承担单位的整体发展变化情况。

第十九条 因客观原因，项目承担单位需对项目目标、进度和经费进行调整或撤销时，应提出书面申请，经办公室审核并报天津市科技创新专项资金领导小组批准后执行。

第二十条 如发现承担单位有严重违约行为，办公室将依据项目合同书的有关条款撤销或中止项目执行合同。对撤销或中止的项目，承担单位应进行财务清算，将已拨付的天津市科技创新专项资金上缴市财政局。

第二十一条 办公室对有关机构、有关人员在项目申报、实施、管理中弄虚作假、玩忽职守、以权谋私者，提出行政处分建议，情节严重构成犯罪的，依法追究其法律责任。

第二十二条 对项目执行好、经济社会效益显著、社会影响良好的承担单位和个人，办公室上报天津市科技创新专项资金领导小组同意后，以天津市科技创新专项资金领导小组名义给予表彰。

第二十三条 办公室每年年底前，综合天津市科技创新专项资金支持项目的执行情况和使用情况，编制年度执行报告，上报天津市科技创新专项资金领导小组。

第五章 附则

第二十四条 本办法自公布之日起试行。

天津市科技计划项目资金管理办法

（津科财〔2005〕76号 2005年6月23日公布实施）

第一章 总则

第一条 为加强天津市科技计划项目资金（以下简称“科技项目资金”）的管理，统筹安排各项科技项目资金，提高资金使用效益，根据国家有关财务规定，按照部门预算管理、国家科研计划实施课题制管理等要求,结合天津市的实际情况,制定本办法。

第二条 科技项目资金,是指天津市人大审议批准的、市财政拨款用于天津市科技计划和科技创新体系建设等的资金,由市财政局和市科委共同管理。本着促进天津市科技和经济加速发展的原则,科技项目资金用于支持科技计划项目(以下简称“科技项目”)的研究开发以及科技创新体系建设,主要包括:科技创新研究与开发计划、科技成果转化与产业化推动计划、科技发展战略研究计划和科技创新能力与环境建设计划等方面。

第三条 科技项目资金的支持对象,主要是具有独立法人资格的企事业单位。优先支持具有较强自主研究开发能力、具备较好科研条件的科研机构、高等院校和企业。

第四条 科技项目资金的使用根据科技项目类型、课题规模及管理工作的需要,对科技项目按照成本补偿式和定额补助式两种方式给予不同额度的资助。科技项目资金主要用于:设备购置费、能源材料费、试验费等。同时,承担单位必须根据科技项目研究开发和科技创新体系建设的需要,根据不同单位性质和不同情况,落实一定比例的配套资金。为发挥政府资金的引导作用,对于部分使用银行贷款的科技项目,可以采取贴息或者实行事后补贴的资助方式。

第五条 科技项目资金的管理分为直接管理和委托管理两种方式。直接管理,是指科技项目承担单位直接管理科技项目资金的使用。委托管理,是指对于部分重大科技项目和科技创新体系建设,可委托有资质的专业机构或管理机构以投资等形式进行管理。

第六条 市科委每年根据科技工作安排,确定科技项目资金支持的方向和重点,并按照市财政局的统一要求,负责编制科技项目资金的部门预算。

第七条 科技项目资金的预算管理,坚持公开、公正、公平原则,实行专家论证、中介机构评估和政府决策相结合的立项审批机制;科技项目资金的安排,实行优化资源、突出重点、合理安排、效益优先的原则;科技项目资金的决算管理,坚持实事求是、严谨认真的原则,严格实行科技项目资金验收制度。

第八条 市科委要按照财政科技项目支出预算管理的有关要求建立科技项目库,加强对科技项目资金的管理。

第二章 科技项目资金管理职责

第九条 科技项目资金管理各方的职责与权限:

(一)市财政局

1.负责核批年度科技项目资金总预算及各计划年度科技项目资金预算;2.负责核批计划管理费预算;3.会同市科委审定并下达年度科技项目资金预算;4.监督检查科技项目资金的管理和使用情况;5.负责审批年度决算。

(二)市科委

1.负责提出年度科技项目资金总预算建议;2.负责组织科技项目资金预算的申报和评审(评估);3.负责编制计划管理费预算,并具体管理计划管理费;4.负责安排年度科技项目资金预算并会同市财政局下达预算;5.会同市财政局监督检查科技项目资金的管理和使用情况。

(三)科技项目组织单位及受托管理部门

1.负责组织科技项目申报单位编报科技项目资金预算;2.组织科技项目承担单位按科技项目实施进度执行预算,监督落实科技项目约定支付的匹配资金及其他配套条件;3.按照市财政局、市科委的要求汇总报送科技项目资金预算执行情况;4.受市财政局、市科委委托,对专项资金的管理和使用情况进行监督检查。

(四)科技项目承担单位

1.负责编制科技项目资金预算;2.落实科技项目约定支付的匹配资金及其他配套条件;3.负责科技项目资金的财务管理和会计核算;4.接受上级有关部门和市科委的监督检查,并按要求提供科技项目资金预算执行情况和有关财务资料。

第三章　科技项目资金开支范围

第十条　科技项目资金开支范围包括：科技项目研究开发、科技创新体系建设资金以及计划管理费。

第十一条　科技项目研究开发、科技创新体系建设资金，指与科技项目研究开发或科技创新体系建设有关的所有直接费用和间接费用，包括人员费、设备费、能源材料费、试验外协费、租赁费、信息费、差旅费、会议费、国际科技合作与交流费、贷款贴息费、管理费、其他费用和期初运行费。

人员费，指直接参加科技项目研究开发或科技创新体系建设研究人员支出的工资性费用。列入的人员要与项目合同中确定的参加人员（数）一致。科技项目组成员所在单位有事业费拨款的，由所在单位按照国家规定的标准从事业费中及时足额支付给科技项目组成员，并按规定在科技项目资金预算的相关科目中列示，不得在政府资助的科技项目资金中重复列支。国家另有规定的，按照有关规定执行。

设备费，指科技项目研究开发或科技创新体系建设过程中所必需的专用仪器、设备的购置和维修费用；样品、样机购置费及设备试制费。科技项目资金所购置和试制的单台价值在5万元以上（含5万元）的仪器设备（含样机）需单独列示。单台价值在5万元以上（含5万元）的仪器设备优先通过协作共用的方式解决，如确需购买，由市科委批准。

能源材料费，指科技项目研究开发或科技创新体系建设过程中所支付的原材料、燃料动力、低值易耗品的购置等费用。一次购置但可重复使用（使用寿命在一年以下）且单台价值在1万元以下（不含1万元）的各类仪器设备，在能源材料费项下列支。

试验外协费，指科技项目研究开发或科技创新体系建设过程中发生的试验、加工、测试等费用或带料外加工费用及因委托外单位或合作单位进行的试验、加工、测试等发生的费用。发生试验外协费超过该科技项目资金预算的20%或单项外协费超过1万元（包括1万元）时，必须与协作单位签订相关的合同书。

租赁费，指科技项目研究开发或科技创新体系建设过程中租赁专用仪器、设备、场地、试验基地等所发生的费用。

信息费，指科技项目研究开发或科技创新体系建设过程中发生的信息检索费、论文版面费、数据调查费和上机费等。

差旅费，指在科技项目研究开发或科技创新体系建设过程中，为科技项目研究开发或科技创新体系建设而进行国内调研考察、现场试验等工作所发生的交通、住宿等费用。出境（含港澳台）差旅费只能通过申请国际科技合作与交流计划项目列支。

会议费，指科技项目研究开发或科技创新体系建设过程中组织召开的与科技项目研究开发或科技创新体系建设有关的专题技术、学术会议的费用。

国际科技合作与交流费，指用于市科委列入科技计划的国际科技合作与交流计划项目的费用。

贷款贴息费，指市科委给予使用银行贷款的计划项目实行贷款贴息的补助资金。

管理费，指科技项目承担单位及受托管理单位为组织管理科技项目而支出的相关费用。包括现有仪器设备和房屋使用费或折旧、直接管理人员费用和其他相关管理支出。科技项目承担单位及受托管理单位所提取的管理费一般不得超过科技项目财政拨款额的5%。

其他费用，指除上述费用之外与科技项目研究开发或科技创新体系建设有关的其他费用。

期初运行费，指科技创新平台建设初期（一般不超过两年）正常启动运行所需的人员费、办公设备费、专利技术引进费等相关一次性费用。此费用仅限于科技创新体系建设项目中列支。

第十二条　计划管理费，指市科委为组织科技项目及科技创新体系建设，开展科技项目及科技创新体系建设的论证、招投标、预算评估、科技项目管理、审计及绩效考评等工作所发生的费用。计划管理费由市科委负责具体管理，年度预算每年报市财政局核定。

第十三条　有关科技项目的前期预研所发生的费用，由科技项目承担单位自筹解决。

第四章 预算的申报、审批和执行

第十四条 科技项目分组织申报、招标、自由申报三种方式进行，其中：组织申报是指市科委组织实施的科技项目；招标是指通过招投标方式确定的科技项目；自由申报是指申报单位每年根据市科委发布的下一年度选题指南申报的科技项目。

市科委组织有关专家或委托中介机构，对组织申报、招标、自由申报的科技项目进行论证和评估，对审核确定立项的科技项目，将会同市财政局审批科技项目资金的预算。

第十五条 科技计划项目的管理。市科委每年对科技计划项目执行情况进行抽查，同时组织对重大科技项目实施情况的检查及验收，并在每年末，根据当年科技项目的执行情况编制年度科技项目的执行报告。

第十六条 科技项目申报单位在编报《天津市科技计划项目申请书》或编写《天津市科技计划项目投标书》时，应严格遵守目标相关、政策相符、实事求是的原则，认真填报科技项目资金预算，并按要求提供相关资料。科技项目资金预算要求同时编制来源预算和支出预算，不得编制赤字预算。科技项目资金来源预算，包括用于同一科技项目或科技创新体系建设的各种不同渠道的科技项目资金；科技项目资金支出预算，包括与科技项目或科技创新体系建设有关的所有直接费用和间接费用。同时须按照科技项目和科技创新体系建设的具体进度编制年度或阶段用款计划。

第十七条 市科委组织有关专家或择优遴选有关中介机构委托其组织专家，对拟组织实施的科技项目或科技创新体系建设项目资金进行预算评审或评估。需采用招投标方式，确定承担单位及其科技项目资金预算的，按市科委科技计划招投标管理的有关规定执行。

第十八条 市科委，根据论证及预算评审或评估意见，综合平衡后，会同市财政局审定并批复科技项目或科技创新体系建设资金预算。经批准的科技项目或科技创新体系建设资金预算一般不作调整。确有必要调整时，应按照预算审批程序重新报批。

第十九条 科技项目资金，按照财政集中支付的原则直接拨付到科技项目或任务承担单位或受托管理单位指定账户，并按照市科委、市财政局和有关金融机构关于科技项目资金结算的规定进行支出管理。

第二十条 市科委，按照科技计划管理的有关规定与科技项目或任务承担单位或受托管理单位签订任务合同书，并按任务合同书约定的用款计划拨付科技项目资金。科技项目或任务承担单位应按照合同的约定，落实配套资金、资产及其他配套条件，并严格执行科技项目或科技创新体系建设资金预算。

第二十一条 科技项目资金形成的资产（包括固定资产和无形资产等），应按照国家有关规定进行管理。

第二十二条 科技项目或科技创新体系建设，因故中止未完成的，科技项目或任务承担单位，应当按照有关管理程序报经市科委批准后，将剩余科技项目资金归还原渠道，剩余资产按照国家有关规定处置。

第五章 决算的编制和验收

第二十三条 科技项目或任务承担单位及受托管理单位须按以下规定编报科技项目资金决算。对于一个年度内资助的科技项目或科技创新体系建设，只在结题验收前编制科技项目资金总决算表，不编制年度科技项目资金决算表，直接报送市科委。对于分年度资助的科技项目或科技创新体系建设，应当编制年度科技项目资金决算表，并于每年的二月十五日前向市科委报送上一年度科技项目资金决算表。同时，在结题验收前编制科技项目资金总决算表。

第二十四条 科技项目或科技创新体系建设在结题验收前，市科委，需组织有关专家或委托中介机构，对其进行科技项目资金检查或审计。并根据检查结果或审计报告，签署科技项目资金验收的意见。

第二十五条 科技项目或科技创新体系建设验收由市科委负责。在验收时，科技项目或任务承担单位及受托管理单位除提供工作报告和技术报告外，还需提供科技项目资金使用情况报告（含科技项目资金决算表）。验收委员会成员中，除技术专家、管理专家外，还应包括财务专家。

第二十六条 在研科技项目或科技创新体系建设的年度结余科技项目资金，结转下一年度继续使用；

已完成并通过验收的科技项目或科技创新体系建设结余的科技项目资金，经市科委批准后，用于补助单位研究与开发项目支出。计划管理费年度结余，纳入下一年度预算计划，继续按规定用途使用。

第二十七条 科技项目或科技创新体系建设验收后，所取得的科技成果均应到市科技成果登记机构进行成果登记，科技项目全套技术档案须报送市科委备案。

第六章 监督与检查

第二十八条 科技项目或任务承担单位及受托管理单位要严格执行国家有关财务制度，并按照合同的约定严格执行科技项目资金预算，加强对科技项目资金的监督和管理，并对科技项目资金实行专户管理、单独核算。

第二十九条 市科委、市财政局组织有关专家或委托有关中介机构，对科技项目资金的管理和使用，进行科技项目资金检查或委托审计，并逐步建立科技项目资金支出绩效考评制度，考评结果将作为科技项目或任务承担单位及受托管理单位以后年度申报科技项目和委托管理资格审查的重要依据。

第三十条 市科委、市财政局，对科技项目或任务承担单位及受托管理单位在申报、管理和实施过程中，存在弄虚作假、截留、挪用、挤占科技项目资金等违反财经纪律的行为，可根据情况采取通报批评、停止拨款、取消申报资格、追回科技项目资金等措施予以相应的处罚，同时要求所在单位或者其上级主管部门按照有关规定对主要负责人给予行政处分；情节严重，构成犯罪的，依法追究刑事责任。

第三十一条 市科委、市财政局，对受委托中介机构在科技项目资金预算评估、中期评估和验收工作中，存在弄虚作假、隐瞒真相、同科技项目或任务承担单位或受托管理单位串通作弊等行为的，取消其继续承担科技项目资金预算评估、中期评估和验收工作的资格；情节严重，构成犯罪的，依法追究刑事责任。

第七章 附则

第三十二条 其他科技专项资金可参照本办法制订相应的科技计划项目资金管理办法。

第三十三条 本办法由天津市科委、天津市财政局负责解释。

第三十四条 本办法自二○○五年七月一日起施行。

《天津市科技创新专项资金管理办法》实施细则

（津科财〔2005〕197号 2005年11月28日公布实施）

第一章 总则

第一条 为了加强对“天津市科技创新专项资金”（以下简称“专项资金”）的管理，提高资金使用效益，根据国家有关财政财务制度和《天津市科技创新专项资金管理办法》(津政办发[2005]035号)，制定本实施细则。

第二条 专项资金纳入市财政局预算管理，实行专款专用。专项资金根据资助项目特点，分别以无偿资助、贷款贴息、资本金投入等方式给予资助。对无偿资助项目，除天津市科技创新专项资金领导小组（以下简称“市领导小组”）批准的引进人才项目，资助资金一般不高于资助项目总投资的30%。对贷款贴息项目，按照项目承担单位申请项目贷款额年利息的50—100%确定贴息额度。对资本金投入项目，专项资金投入数额一般不超过企业注册资本的20%（不控股），并指定有资质的国有资产授权经营公司进行管理。

第三条 天津市科技创新专项资金领导小组办公室（以下简称“办公室”）负责管理专项资金，每年根据市领导小组确定的专项资金支持方向和重点，编制年度专项资金使用计划。

第四条 专项资金的使用,坚持公开、公正、公平原则,实行专家论证、中介机构评估和政府决策相结合的立项审批制度;专项资金的安排,实行优化资源、突出重点、合理安排、效益优先的原则。

第二章 专项资金开支范围

第五条 专项资金开支范围:指与执行项目有关的所有直接费用和间接费用。具体包括技术购买费、工程咨询设计费、人员费、试验运行费、大型仪器设备费、科技基建费、国际科技合作与交流费、贷款利息及其他费用。

技术购买费,指经批准用于购买具有国际先进水平高新技术的使用权或所有权所支付的相关费用。

工程咨询设计费,指经批准用于实施引进技术和项目所必须支出的设计、调研、咨询、论证、评估等费用。

人员费,指经批准的引进科技人才的费用及直接参加项目实施人员支出的费用。项目组成员所在单位有事业费拨款的,由所在单位按照国家规定的标准从事业费中及时足额支付给项目组成员,并按规定在项目预算的相关科目中列示,不得在政府资助的项目经费中重复列支。国家另有规定的,按照有关规定执行。

试验运行费,指重大社会公益性科技工程项目实施初期(一般不超过两年)正常启动运行所需的专用仪器、设备、样机等进行生产试验、设备调试、运行维护等费用。

大型仪器设备费,指项目实施过程中所必须的无法实行协作共用的专用仪器、设备购置费或租赁费。项目所购置和试制的单台价值在20万元以上(含20万元)的仪器设备(含样机)需单独列示。

科技基建费,指为保障引进技术的实施所必须发生的车间(实验室)、工程及附属配套设施等方面的土建支出。

国际科技合作与交流费,指项目实施过程中用于国际科技合作与交流工作的费用。

贷款利息,指专项资金项目发生的贷款利息支出。

其他费用,指除上述费用之外与项目实施有关的费用。

第六条 有关项目的前期预研所发生的费用,由项目承担单位自筹解决。

第三章 专项资金申报、审批和拨付

第七条 项目申报单位应遵照实事求是的原则,认真填报《天津市科技创新专项资金项目申请书》,并按要求提供相关资料。申报的项目资金预算应包括与项目实施有关的所有直接费用和间接费用,同时须按照项目的具体进度编制年度或阶段用款计划。

第八条 办公室组织有关专家,或择优遴选有关中介机构对拟实施的项目资金预算进行评估或评审。

第九条 根据专家论证意见及项目资金预算评估或评审结果,办公室审核立项建议,并提出专项资金资助使用计划安排,在报请市领导小组审批后,给予正式立项。

项目承担单位因项目执行需要,确需对项目资金预算(包括单个科目预算)进行调整的,应将调整后的资金预算报送办公室备案。但对项目资金预算(包括单个科目预算)调整幅度超过15%以上的,项目承担单位应提出书面申请,经办公室审核批准后执行。

第十条 对批准的项目,办公室将委托市科委按照有关规定与项目承担单位或受托管理单位签订合同,市财政局根据项目的用款计划和完成进度拨付资金。项目承担单位应按照合同的有关规定,落实配套资金、资产及其他配套条件,并严格执行项目资金预算。

第十一条 项目承担单位应在办公室指定的金融机构开立账户,实行专户管理,单独核算。按照《天津市科技创新专项资金项目执行合同书》和财务制度的规定使用项目资金,并接受办公室对项目资金使用情况的跟踪管理、检查和审计。

第十二条 项目完成后,项目承担单位须及时进行财务结算,对属于按规定准予核销的部分,经办公室批准后予以核销,其余部分在资本公积金中单独反映。

第十三条 项目因故撤销或中止的,项目承担单位应及时提出书面申请,经办公室审核并报市领导小组批准后，将剩余的专项资金上缴市财政局，项目实施过程中形成的资产按照国家有关规定处置。对发现项目承担单位有严重违约行为的，办公室将中止执行合同，停止拨款。项目承担单位应进行财务清算，将已拨付的专项资金上缴市财政局，剩余的资产按照国家有关规定处置。

第四章　决算的编制和验收

第十四条　项目承担单位及受托管理单位应按规定编报项目资金决算报告。对于一个年度内资助并完成的项目，应在项目验收前编制项目资金决算报告；对于分年度资助的项目，应在每年7月15日和1月15日前向办公室报送项目资金使用情况报告，在项目验收前编制项目资金决算报告。

第十五条　项目承担单位应在合同到期后的二个月内，向办公室提出验收申请，并提供与项目实施相关的工作报告、技术报告、资金使用报告以及有关资料。

第十六条　办公室负责组织专家咨询委员会（包括资金评审专家）及中介机构对项目实施情况进行检查和审计，并根据检查结果和审计报告出具项目验收意见。

第十七条　在研（未完）项目的年度结余专项资金，结转下一年度继续使用；已完成并通过验收的项目结余专项资金，经办公室批准后，用于原项目承担单位科技研究与开发工作的支出。

第十八条　项目验收后，所取得的科技成果均应到市科技成果登记机构进行成果登记，凭成果登记表办理验收结题手续。

第五章　监督与检查

第十九条　项目承担单位要自觉严格执行国家有关财务制度，并按照合同约定严格执行项目资金预算，加强对专项资金的监督和管理。

第二十条　在项目执行中及完成后的一年内，办公室要组织有关专家或委托有关中介机构对项目承担单位承诺的配套条件、自筹资金和专项资金的到位及使用情况进行检查或审计，并逐步建立专项资金使用的诚信及绩效考评制度，考评结果将作为项目承担单位以后年度申报项目资格审查的重要依据。

第二十一条　对项目承担单位在申报、管理和实施过程中，存在弄虚作假、截留、挪用、挤占专项资金等违反财经纪律的行为，办公室将依据项目合同书的有关条款撤销或中止项目合同，并根据情况采取通报批评、停止拨款、取消申报资格、追回专项资金等措施予以相应的处罚，同时要求所在单位或者其上级主管部门按照有关规定对主要负责人给予行政处分；情节严重，构成犯罪的，依法追究刑事责任。

第二十二条　对受委托中介机构在专项资金预算评估、中期评估和验收工作中，存在弄虚作假、隐瞒真相、同项目承担单位串通作弊等行为的，办公室将取消其继续承担专项资金预算评估、中期检查和验收工作的资格；情节严重，构成犯罪的，依法追究刑事责任。

第六章　附则

第二十三条　本办法由市财政局、市科委负责解释。

第二十四条　本办法自公布之日起试行。

获奖科技成果

表1 获国家自然科学奖项目

序号	项目名称	获奖单位	获奖人	获奖等级	获奖年份
1	DNA分子的结构、动力学和序列的理论研究	天津大学	张春霆	二等奖	1997
2	若干生物医学高分子的研究	南开大学、北京大学、武汉大学、南京大学	冯新德 何炳林 卓仁禧 林思聪 马建标	三等奖	1999
3	微尺度大气运动中气溶胶物理过程的研究	南开大学、中国科学院安徽光学精密机械研究所	温景嵩 朱珍华 曾宗泳 马成胜	三等奖	1999
4	巨核细胞和血小板的病理生理学特征及其生长调节	中国医学科学院血液学研究所	韩忠朝 宋玉华 沈志祥 吕联煌 王振义	二等奖	2001
5	分子磁性的基础研究	南开大学	廖代正 王耕霖 姜宗慧 阎世平 程 鹏	二等奖	2003
6	中国主要植物染色体研究	南开大学	陈瑞阳 宋文芹 李秀兰 李懋学 林盛华 梁国鲁	二等奖	2003
7	复杂非线性系统的动力学理论与应用	天津大学	陈予恕 陆启韶 褚福磊 徐健学 吴志强	二等奖	2003
8	辛道路的指标理论与在非线性哈密顿系统中的应用	南开大学	龙以明 朱朝锋 刘春根 胡锡俊	二等奖	2004
9	Atiyah-Singer指标理论的若干研究	南开大学	张伟平	二等奖	2005
10	光折变新效应、机理与器件的研究	南开大学	许京军 张光寅 刘思敏 张国权 孔勇发	二等奖	2005

表2 获国家技术发明奖项目

序号	项目名称	获奖单位	获奖人	获奖等级	获奖年份
1	翡翠绿系列颜料的制造方法	化工部天津化工研究院	张登高 纪 柱 董保生 李 火 张彦玲 徐金平	三等奖	1991
2	肿瘤热疗用多点测温技术及仪器	天津市肿瘤研究所	林世寅 于世起 李丰彤 左春刚 李瑞英	三等奖	1991
3	电子衍射测定未知晶体点阵新方法	天津大学、太原机械学院	陈玉如 李会军 刘文西 王建邦 杨治安	三等奖	1991
4	电子元器件稳定易焊锡基复合材料	天津大学	唐致远 郭鹤桐 张 栋	三等奖	1991
5	树脂砂增强防潮剂	天津大学、盖县化工厂	张永年 林秀森 徐永梅	四等奖	1991
6	悬挂式加固抽油泵	天津市大港石油管理局第一采油厂	郑 勇 徐玉德 马士俊 乔来庆	四等奖	1991
7	具有自适应共振系统的新型振动机械	天津大学	王义昌 陈绍洪 穆成栋 袁剑平 石 红	三等奖	1992

续表2 获国家技术发明奖项目

序号	项目名称	获奖单位	获奖人	获奖等级	获奖年份
8	电加热菱镁矿石生产二氧化碳气体的方法及设备	机械电子工业部第五设计研究院	李君爱　刘志强	三等奖	1992
9	干电池电解液快速净化的电化学工程方法	天津大学、张家口市电池厂	谷林瑛　王嘉启　毕又澄　秦尔华　谷雅丽	三等奖	1992
10	一种生长异形红宝石的技术	天津市硅酸盐研究所	王崇鲁	四等奖	1992
11	乙苯和乙醇合成对二乙苯催化剂及制备方法	南开大学	潘履让　刘述全　李赫咺	四等奖	1992
12	吸附型硅藻土助滤剂	天津大学	钟顺和　尚秀芬　赵　静	四等奖	1992
13	显示分化程度不同的细胞的荧光染色法	天津第二医学院组织胚胎教研室	许　屏	四等奖	1992
14	三维踝关节复位固定器	天津医院骨伤科学研究所	辛景义　张铁良　韩　慧	三等奖	1993
15	鲜食玉米新品种津鲜一号	天津市农作物研究所	邵景坡　张巧云	三等奖	1993
16	山楂蜜汁饮料加工技术	天津市林业果树研究所	马冬青　李永力	三等奖	1993
17	聚乙烯醇缩丁醛的辐射降解工艺	天津市有机化工实验厂、天津技术物理研究所、中国科学院、长春应用化学研究所	王德印　杨文英　臧智慧　张自成	四等奖	1993
18	从等电点结晶母液中回收谷氨酸的离子交换工艺	天津大学	谌竞清　宋正孝　姜志新　牛文泰	四等奖	1993
19	组合式液体分布器	天津化学工程研究所、天津大学化工分离技术及新型填料开发中心	赵汝文	四等奖	1993
20	N型热电偶用补偿导线的合金丝	天津市电工合金厂	陈鸿德	四等奖	1993
21	石英钟模拟日照规律的自动开关	天津市电力工业局路灯管理处	王伟仁	四等奖	1993
22	无底浮式系统及水下大型刚性基础起浮搬迁技术	中海石油工程设计(塘沽)公司	王钦健　李丕德	三等奖	1995
23	中心视野体积计量法和中心视野立体分析仪	天津医科大学总医院、中国人民解放军装甲兵工程学院、天津市内分泌研究所	贺忠江　王精业　王　沛　吴映虹　袁佳琴　陈春良	三等奖	1995
24	直拉硅片缺陷的控制与利用	河北工学院、中国原子能科学研究院反应堆研究设计所	徐岳生　张维连　任丙彦　鞠玉林　陈炳贤　高秀清	四等奖	1995
25	连杆式子午胎成型鼓及其型综合权函数方法	天津大学	王玉新　陆锡年　祝毓琥	四等奖	1995
26	碳酸锶的制造方法	化工部天津化工研究所	熊尚彬　林　录　程　宏　陈秀珍　李绍文　曾令聪	四等奖	1995
27	塔式液膜结晶器	天津大学	王静康　杨志勇　薛履中　王玉德　尹秋响	三等奖	1996
28	八字型螺旋槽段面密封气系统及试验装置	天津市机械密封件厂、天津市克兰密封有限公司	王玉明	四等奖	1996
29	汽油机射流燃烧技术	天津大学	刘友钧　尚秀镜　李志雄	三等奖	1997

续表2 获国家技术发明奖项目

序号	项目名称	获奖单位	获奖人	获奖等级	获奖年份
30	铁基形状记忆合金连接管道系列技术	天津大学、天津滨海新技术产业集团股份有限公司	刘文西 刘道志 陈金铭 张清玉 许连文 王红新	四等奖	1997
31	电话网双局号平稳过渡升位法	天津市邮电管理局	郭绍生 王安平 滕 勇 陈克艺 吴承英 李南枝	三等奖	1998
32	苦卤综合利用制取硫酸钾新技术	国家海洋局，天津海水淡水与综合利用研究所……	吴观泉 吴宗生 袁俊生 李三兴 宋来堂 刘华军	三等奖	1998
33	用化学方法提高固体表面光洁度的研究及应用	河北工业大学	刘玉岭 徐晓辉 李湘都 王永滨 张德臣 张志花	三等奖	1999
34	血沉曲线检测分析方法及仪器研制	天津中医学院、天津大学	张伯礼 戴品忠 刘正光 高秀梅 徐宗佩 王津生	四等奖	1999
35	面向生物医学工程的微操作机器人系统	南开大学	卢桂章 张建勋 李 彬 张 蕾	二等奖	2002
36	先进制造中空间几何尺寸测量的现场校准方法和装置	天津大学	叶声华 殷纯永 郑继贵 曲兴华 郭继华 杨学友	二等奖	2004
37	新型离子筛的研制及其应用	天津大学	王榕树 王林双 那 平 赵丽丽 张裕卿 孙 岩	二等奖	2004
38	螺旋式浮环密封装置	天津鼎名密封公司	王玉明	二等奖	2005

表3 获国家科技进步奖项目

序号	项目名称	获奖单位	获奖人	获奖等级	获奖年份
1	骨水泥固定及珍珠面无骨水泥固定人工关节的实验及临床的系列研究	中国人民解放军总医院、北京钢铁研究总院、天津市合成材料工业研究所	卢世璧 王继芳 孙燕群 徐英忱 童衍传	一等奖	1991
2	稀土优化综合处理在电工铝导体中的应用研究	机械电子工业部上海电缆研究所，上海交通大学、长通电缆厂、赤峰市电线电缆厂、南宁电线电缆厂、沈阳电缆厂、天津市电缆厂	黄崇棋 丁关森 沈建华 陈秀琴 方莲华 夏明通 李守忠 狄家良 林锐思	二等奖	1991
3	乙烯氧化制环氧乙烷YS－4型催化剂工业试生产和工业试用	燕山石化总公司研究院、天津化工研究院、燕山石化公司化工一厂	金积铨 金国权 商连弟 徐 勇 祝石华 周兆瀛 高士乔 程绍福 赵西明	二等奖	1991
4	进口药材质量标准制订与检验方法研究	中国药品生物制品检定所、天津市药品检验所、上海市药品检验所、广州市药品检验所、北京市药品检验所	秦祥林 贾宗才 谢培山 朱孝芸 周富荣	二等奖	1991
5	青霉素球状菌氮源代谢的研究及应用	华北制药厂	姚学强 张聚发 巢天浩 杨增展 任金生 李东玖 刘文富 王民卫 杨文晴	二等奖	1991
6	塑料棚蔬菜生产配套技术推广	全国农业技术推广总站二处、辽宁省农牧厅园艺处、江苏省农林园艺处、山东省农业技术推广总站、北京市农业技术推广总站、天津市蔬菜工作站、上海市蔬菜技术推广站	张真和 魏克武 赵红玉 赵山普 赵淑明 郁樊敏 董玉昌 齐 波 王 玮	二等奖	1991
7	混凝土结构设计规范GBJ10-89	中国建筑科学研究院、清华大学、天津大学、上海城市建设学院、铁道部北京铁路局堪测设计院、北京有色冶金设计研究总院	李明顺 白生翔 胡德忻 腾智明 车宏亚 陆竹卿 沙志国 周起敬 孙慧中	二等奖	1991
8	低亚管道输水灌溉技术研究和推广	水利水电科学研究院、水利部农田灌溉研究所、山东省水科所、北京市水科所、天津市水利科学研究所、河北省衡水地区水利局、济南市水利局	金永堂 杜泉楷 朱利贞 胡树森 张兰亭 李龙昌 焦恒民 余 玲 周福国	二等奖	1991

续表3 获国家科技进步奖项目

序号	项目名称	获奖单位	获奖人	获奖等级	获奖年份
9	北方冬小麦气象卫星动态监测及估产系统	国家气象局气象科学研究院、国家气象局卫星气象中心、北京市农林科学院、河北省气象局、天津市气象局、河南省气象局、江苏省气象局	李郁竹 肖乾广 刘国祥 阎宜玲 孟宪钺 史定珊 汤志成 刘笃慧 王稳成	二等奖	1991
10	铁路泥石流沟判别、警报、防治、机理的研究	铁路部科学研究院(西南所、铁建所)、铁道部专业设计院、铁道部兰州铁路局、铁道部成都铁路局、西南交通大学、铁道部第二勘测设计院、铁道部第三勘测设计院	谭炳炎 潘仲仁 李鸿科 荆绍华 沈寿长 徐永良 靳 蕃 王宇丰 廖有南	二等奖	1991
11	全国工业污染源调查评价与研究	中国环境监测总站、天津市环境监测中心站、江苏省环境监测站、辽宁省环境监测站、青岛市环境监测站	刘全义 徐伯麟 李斯复 周桂玲 何兆德 安德亮 陈仰胜 徐鸿楷 高秀兰	二等奖	1991
12	400兆赫单工无线列调系统设备及甚高频单工调频无线电台	国营712厂	钱祥宝 李毓彬 郑 敏 曹监恒 刘树林	三等奖	1991
13	外循环式复极(单极)氯酸盐电解槽	化工部天津化工研究院、广西贺县光明化工厂	于培贞 叶绪莘 凌培元 刘佑镜 王 玲	三等奖	1991
14	新型高固色率KE型活性染料—藏青R和艳红7B的研制	天津市染料化学七厂	林长祥 苏继长 阴振英 王素娜 苏长湘	三等奖	1991
15	NK—P植物营养素(钛微肥)	南开大学	范秀菊 冯 霄 王积涛 程远允 孟桂兰	三等奖	1991
16	N—去甲基万古霉素的开发研究	华北制药厂、中国药品生物制品检定所	贺秉坤 陈 杰 刘玉芬 张胜利 陈曙曦	三等奖	1991
17	津杂1、2号黄瓜新品种	天津市黄瓜研究所	吕淑珍 侯 锋 霍振荣 哈玉洁 李家旺	三等奖	1991
18	木质湿法超薄型硬质纤维板生产技术研究	天津市木材工业研究所、天津市木材五厂	贾广盈 胡新龙 王春生 刘 毅 刘宝平	三等奖	1991
19	机械舞台自动控制系统	天津舞台科学技术研究所	周省如 何锡扬 闫 瑛 范洪光 刘 震	三等奖	1991
20	三维潮流数学模型及其应用	交通部	曹祖德 王桂芬 张英平 陈声亮 冯玉林 张 浩 王荣贵	二等奖	1992
21	互穿聚合物网络型堵水剂及堵水工艺技术	天津大学	刘庆普 哈润华 张余海 刘宏荣 孙凤明	三等奖	1992
22	大型制碱碳化过程计算机控制系统	化工部推荐	韩建勋 李九龙 袁树滋 刘醒福 刘汝江	三等奖	1992
23	ZWF-4型注射液微粒分析仪	总后勤部推荐	胡子平 吴克钗 陈惠发 刘向健 李成彬	三等奖	1992
24	舞台防火幕传动阻尼装置	文化部推荐	周省如	三等奖	1992
25	秦皇岛煤码头三期工程装卸成套设备电气自动化控制系统	机械电子部天津电气传动设计所	马 戎 皮壮行 屠基俊 洪传文 仲明振 朱光华 谢保侠 谷 岭 周瑞娟	二等奖	1993
26	铁道车辆滚动轴承Ⅱ型润滑脂	铁道部科学研究院、天津汉沽石油化学厂、成都铁路局、哈尔滨铁路局	蒋秋芝 刘庆廉 嵇启兰 阎 鹏 王胜民 张 念 曹德厚 史炳连 刘家安	二等奖	1993
27	GB10066.1—88《电热设备的试验方法通用部分》和GB10066.4—88《间接电阻炉》	机电部西安电炉研究所、上海电炉厂、江西电炉厂、天津市电炉制造总厂、上海实验电炉厂、西安重型电炉厂	蒋聪吉 葛华山 郭健全 袁 溶 邱松根 刘西萍 毛润辉 柴凤山 张万淳	二等奖	1993
28	原子法激光浓缩铀宏观量收集试验	核工业总公司理化工程研究院、中科院上海光机所	潘文杰 诸旭辉 王之江 徐品方 汤星里 邱 成 林福成 张立原 洪清汉	二等奖	1993

续表3　　　　获国家科技进步奖项目

序号	项目名称	获奖单位	获奖人	获奖等级	获奖年份
29	TX S—LL电加热钢丝圈挤出联动生产线	天津橡塑机械厂	张芝泉　李建志　姚　栋	三等奖	1993
30	年产五千吨邻二甲苯法制苯酐六十克工艺生产装置	天津溶剂厂、化工部第六设计院、北京化工研究院、华南理工大学	张铁城　钟道迪　梁育德 张琮麟　裴德余	三等奖	1993
31	ZJL5型横管连续蒸煮器(50T/D漂白苇浆)	天津轻工业机械厂	王广维　陈松涛　张力宏 黄成希　王　宣	三等奖	1993
32	包醛氧淀粉的研制及开发的研究	天津大学	田汝川　陈炎泉　于九皋 刘景林　杨洪顺	三等奖	1993
33	三门峡大坝观测资料分析与安全评价研究	水利部能源部天津堪测设计院、水利部三门峡水利枢纽管理局	赵志仁　朱化广　吴百进	三等奖	1993
34	粉尘爆炸泄压研究	公安部天津消防科学研究所	王宝兴　张银花　马克辛	三等奖	1993
35	仔猪大肠菌腹泻基因工程多价疫苗	军事医学科学院生物工程研究所	黄翠芬　陈添弥　黄培堂 张林元　李丰生　于公义 张兆山　王叙甫　赵立权 方门忠　陈惠珠　李淑琴 徐秀英　冯书章　孟　枋	一等奖	1995
36	东风4C型内燃机车	大连机车车辆厂、永济电机厂、天津机车车辆机械厂、沈阳铁路局	赵燠南　周西敏　白福全 杨产兴　孙兆祥　陈吉庆 徐振东　张常义　吴昭平	二等奖	1995
37	MSB和MS可逆式六辊冷轧机研制与应用	冶金部钢铁研究总院、山海关冷轧带钢厂、苏州冶金机械厂、天津轧钢一厂	杜海英　张树堂　韩旭中 曹　前　李泽全　刘洪范 杨　斌　董炳军　马九如	二等奖	1995
38	我国四种预分解窑型分析研究与改进	武汉工业大学北京研究生部、天津水泥工业设计研究院、南京化工学院、冀东水泥厂、宁国水泥厂、柳州水泥厂、江西水泥厂	陈全德　高长明　王师尹 胡道和　刘寿绵　汪　澜 李昌勇　崔素萍　兰明彰	二等奖	1995
39	含氟皮质激素类药物的生物脱氢及其化学合成新工艺	天津药业公司	石俊杰　武淑婷　袁长车 郭长兴　李金禄　张恩民 吴雅林　李昭瑜　杨风洪	二等奖	1995
40	《素问》整理研究	天津中医学院	郭霭春　吴仕骥　高文柱 郭洪耀　韩　冰　郑恩泽	二等奖	1995
41	中国控制系统计算机辅助设计(CADCSC)软件系统	南开大学、中国科学院系统科学所、北京大学、中国科技大学、北京理工大学	王治宝　韩京清　许可康 叶庆凯　庞国仲	三等奖	1995
42	内窥镜技术研究	天津大学、徐州光学仪器总厂	张以谟　郁道银　陈　晨 李云青　齐　龙	三等奖	1995
43	TH系列高性能防腐涂料的研制及其推广应用	国家海洋局天津海水淡化与综合利用研究所	唐功麒　黄　鑫　李金山 吴伟鑫　闫明久	三等奖	1995
44	STC型喷射混凝土粘稠剂	铁道部第十八工程局	廖金福　赵文轩　邓晋宏 杜永碧　黄思盛	三等奖	1995
45	中医舌诊客观化研究	天津中医学院中医工程研究所、天津大学	张伯礼　徐宗佩　高秀梅 诸　凯　王益民	三等奖	1995
46	产科生理常数研究 1、中国女性骨盆,2、中国新生儿头径,3、中国妇女产程	天津市中心妇产科医院、南开大学数学系	岳　琏　王淑雯　吴　荣 王公恕　左义欣	三等奖	1995
47	“醒脑开窍”针刺法治疗中风病临床及实验研究	天津中医学院第一附属医院	石学敏　周继曾　韩景献 张存生　卞金铃	三等奖	1995
48	链霉素发酵多模型工艺研究及计算机控制与管理网络系统	华北制药厂、北京工业大学	魏志斌　王　普　王进秋 姜宏铎　刘文富	三等奖	1995
49	QJX型高效空气除菌过滤系统	核工业理化工程研究院、华北制药厂	吴文政　崔贤民　于长江 李宗塘　王民卫	三等奖	1995

续表3 **获国家科技进步奖项目**

序号	项目名称	获奖单位	获奖人	获奖等级	获奖年份
50	ABT生根粉系列的推广	中国林业科学研究院、北京市农林科学院、黑龙江省农技推广总站、吉林省白山市科协、山西省林学会、昆明市农科所、内蒙古海拉尔农牧场管理局植保公司、广西林业厅林技推广站、河南省林业厅林技推广站、青海省农林厅林技推广站、天津市农林局、湖南省林业厅林技推广站、辽宁省林业厅、陕西省林业厅林技推广站、江西省林业厅林技推广站、解放军总后农技推广站、云南省大理州科委、中国农科院品种资源所、北京大学、上海市农科院作物所	王　涛　陈国平　原德琨 于龙生　齐德恩　金佩华 晋宗道　蔡世英　梁桂芝 李仕臣　陈良玉　倪宏兴 农韧刚　栾　双　张桐先 刘兆华　林睦就　黄品龙 张　仁　薄淑芬　唐明鑫 黄文思　李更新　叶昌淳 黄亨履　高崇明　吴惠民	特等	1996
51	塔里木沙漠石油公路工程技术研究	塔里木石油勘探开发指挥部、中科院兰州沙漠所、中国石油天然气总公司工程技术研究院、中科院新疆生物土壤沙漠研究所、中国石油天然气总公司长庆筑路公司、铁道部科学研究院建筑所、新疆交通科学研究所、新疆综合勘察院、新疆石油学院、天津大学		一等奖	1996
52	105m燃油蓄热式显像管玻壳玻璃池炉	中国电子工程设计院、天津津京玻壳股份有限公司	华中令　李玉峰　黄宗范 赵建刚　曾厚礼　褚少立 王化煦　梁玉良　贾　路	二等奖	1996
53	微机重力坝CAD系统	水利部电力工业部天津勘测设计研究院	莘志宏　邱　浩　张梅琳 赵有鑫　刘聪凝　陈靖齐 林元旦　杨宝山　杨志河	二等奖	1996
54	年产24万吨磷铵国产化装置	南京化学工业(集团)公司设计院、江西贵溪化肥厂、江苏省化工设备制造安装公司、三门峡化工机械厂、北京市橡胶制品设计研究院、中国航天工业总公司11所、天津橡胶制品一厂	韩云阁　葛祖元　宋文练 金明友　郭　洁　林振澄 于铁成　魏国贤　谢　珍	二等奖	1996
55	LCS7催化裂化催化剂研制与应用和RHZ200、CC14重油催化裂化催化剂	中国石油化工总公司石油化工科学研究院、兰州炼油化工总厂、齐鲁石化公司催化剂厂、抚顺石油化工公司石油二厂、齐鲁石化公司胜利炼油厂、天津石化公司炼油厂、巴陵石化公司长岭炼油化工总厂	范中碧　周素静　王颜明 黄大智　梁文坚　张有祥 潘　煜　曲令多　刘清林	二等奖	1996
56	青霉素结晶新型技术与设备	天津大学、华北制药厂	王静康　韩贵安　薛履中 平志存　张美景　王玉德 李改存　刘世昌　王永莉	二等奖	1996
57	王朝全汁干型葡萄酒规模化生产工艺技术	中法合营王朝葡萄酿酒有限公司	徐文恒　宋正祥　王志芹 刘建华　张春娅	三等奖	1996
58	中浓度高稳型烟草专用肥及其应用技术	中国农业生产资料天津公司、天津市土壤肥料研究所	崔家璐　李风山　李家清 姚炳贵　蒋顺发	三等奖	1996
59	石油水平井钻井成套技术	胜利石油管理局……大港石油管理局……		一等奖	1997
60	京津塘高速公路工程建设成套技术	京津塘高速公路联合公司……天津市第五市政工程公司、天津市第一市政工程公司……天津市道路桥梁工程监理公司……		一等奖	1997
61	LM-X850,600轮胎胎面复合挤出联动生产线	天津市橡塑机械联合有限公司、	张芝泉　汤　静　张建浩 张志谦　林文泉　徐伦高 董哲锦　王云飞　薛友强	二等奖	1997
62	染料工业废水综合治理技术与工艺	清华大学、天津市环境保护科学研究所……		二等奖	1997
63	马钢300平方米烧结成套设备	西安重型机械研究所……天津重型机械厂……		二等奖	1997

续表3　　获国家科技进步奖项目

序号	项目名称	获奖单位	获奖人	获奖等级	获奖年份
64	全国海岛资源综合调查与开发试验	全国海岛资源综合调查领导小组办公室…… 天津市海岛资源综合调查领导小组办公室……		二等奖	1997
65	年产二万吨复极式离子膜法烧碱国产化装置	河北沧州化工实业(集团)公司……天津大沽化工厂……		二等奖	1997
66	涤纶仿真丝乔其立绒技术及产品	天津丝绸集团公司丝绒厂、中国纺织科学研究院	孙惠菊　潘菊芳　李国桂　卫世文　杨文芳	三等奖	1997
67	髌骨正常计量参数的检测和几种代谢性骨病的系列研究	天津医科大学总医院、天津市内分泌研究所	邱明才　杨宝恩　王觉英　陈兴源　白成江	三等奖	1997
68	氯碱生产过程优化控制系统	渤海化工(集团)股份有限公司、天津大沽化工厂	肖卫国　王志明　张珍妹　于现军　冯圣文	三等奖	1997
69	宝钢高炉鼓风机静止变频启动装置	天津电器传动设计研究所	叶澄中　仲明振　张春喜　吕明伟　董世华	三等奖	1997
70	TX31 Q 型排屑及冷却液净化系统	机械部第五设计院……	王守业……	三等奖	1997
71	盐酸丁丙诺啡及其制剂的研究开发	国家医药局天津药研院……	张丽云……	三等奖	1997
72	水电站地面厂房微机CAD系统	水利部电力工业部天津勘测设计研究院	陆宗磐　段祝龄　朱凤娟　耿振云　许志强	三等奖	1997
73	关于抑制搪瓷制品鳞爆的5020#与907#瓷釉的研究及应用	天津进出口商品检验局、天津市搪瓷厂	冯润中　刘金鉞	三等奖	1997
74	杨子地台周边及其邻区优质锰矿成矿规律及资源评价	冶金工业部西南地质勘查局,冶金工业部天津地质研究院……	侯宗林　薛友智　黄金水　刘红军　姚敬劬　林友焕　王六明　李色篆　余中平	二等奖	1998
75	同相逆并联45KA/500V晶闸管整流电源	机械工业部天津电气传动设计研究所,山东铝业公司	竺子芳　李凯芃　葛和德　徐清书　李考勇　孟宪臣　孙立锦　黄　嘉　周立新	二等奖	1998
76	津春系列黄瓜新品种推广(推广类)	天津市黄瓜研究所		二等奖	1998
77	准直技术及应用	天津大学	叶声华　朱鸿锡　蒋诚志　曲兴华　刘文卿	三等奖	1998
78	中国人手腕骨发育标准CHN法	天津体育学院……	黄耕培　张绍岩　杨士增　邵伟东　欧建华	三等奖	1998
79	WYD系列一体化及DN3系列分体式悬挂点焊机的研制	天津市陆华科技公司……	江　涛　李振山　季江生　魏　毅　陈　成	三等奖	1998
80	1600T/h抓斗卸船机	交通部水运科学研究所……	虞守仁　戚再强　林大伟　王跃忠　丁方明	三等奖	1998
81	重载列车用MT-2、MT-3型缓冲器及16、17号转动和固定车钩	天津机车车辆机械厂……	樊连波　王　金　瞿孝文　傅殿武　王凤洲	三等奖	1998
82	大型、高温袋式除尘系统——在北京水泥厂的应用	国家建材局天津水泥工业设计研究所……	胡　南　林　宏　石建良　王作杰　杨盛林	三等奖	1998
83	《头部CT诊断学》	天津医科大学、人民卫生出版社	吴恩惠　张云亭　白人驹　王　兵	三等奖	1998
84	视觉检测技术及应用	天津大学	叶声华　王　仲　杨学友　郏继贵　段发阶　王春和　麦继平　周富强　孙长库	二等奖	1999
85	TS系列工业水处理药剂及技术推广	化学工业部天津化工研究设计院	周连江　李裕芳　郑书忠　方燕萍　李玉祥　冯　豪　滕厚开　衣龙欣　张宜莓	二等奖	1999
86	滨海浅潜水地区综合治理、规模绿化技术的研究	天津经济技术开发区园林绿化公司	张万钧　郭育文　王斗天　杨永利　王树生　周洪义　陈铁明　张民胜　王　英	二等奖	1999
87	眼眶肿瘤的诊断和治疗的研究	天津医科大学第二医院	宋国祥　田文芳　孙丰源　肖利华　何彦津　唐东润　张　虹　赵慧芳　周晓冬	二等奖	1999

续表3 **获国家科技进步奖项目**

序号	项目名称	获奖单位	获奖人	获奖等级	获奖年份
88	飞秒激光技术的研究	天津大学	王清月 邢岐荣 张伟力 章若冰 戴建明 向望华 柴 路	二等奖	1999
89	新型工业结晶技术与设备	天津大学	王静康 薛履中 张美景 王玉德 尹秋响 王永莉 侯宝红 徐 昭 李桂芝	二等奖	1999
90	渤海的快速钻井技术及其应用	中国海洋石油渤海公司、中国石油技术服务塘沽分公司、中海石油北方钻进公司、中国海洋石油测井公司塘沽分公司	王家祥 周守为 曹式敬 方长伟 王爱国 王长利 李 勇 董星亮 李自立	二等奖	1999
91	土地处理系统—城市污水处理革新/替代技术研究	中国科学院沈阳应用生态研究所……天津市环境保护科学研究院……	孙铁珩 王绍堂 郑学海 李培军 周思毅 丁庭华 李万庆 区自清 刘忠翰	二等奖	1999
92	东亚飞蝗蝗区勘查及可持续控制技术的研究与应用	全国农业技术推广服务中心……天津市植保植检站……	朱恩林 常兆芝 吕国强 姜瑞中 王贵生 于志宣 谢长举 刘举鹏 王向荣	二等奖	1999
93	软(硬)质湿法造粒炭墨技术的研发及新品种研制	天津海豚炭黑有限公司	刘克明 刘俊才 杨士福 仇祯祥 王景禹	三等奖	1999
94	复方丹参滴丸现代药学系列研究	天津天士力制药集团有限公司、解放军第二五四医院	闫希军 吴乃峰 郭治昕 叶正良 杨伟钦	三等奖	1999
95	NK-U防伪印油(墨)及密码识别系统	天津戈德防伪识别有限公司	李明智 赵启正 张志光 董铁望 王淑芳	三等奖	1999
96	渤海西部自营探区近期油气体系勘控研究与实践	中国海洋石油渤海公司	曹文贤 邓运华 于 水 焦 博 王志君	三等奖	1999
97	松花江三姓浅滩航道整治关键技术研究	交通部天津水运工程科学研究所	王益良 王义安 刘 臣 赵连白 王永成	三等奖	1999
98	“风云二号”气象卫星电源分系统	电子工业部第十八研究所	黄才勇 钱成喜 蒋钦琳 黄金盘 曹 阳	三等奖	1999
99	大港油田陆上高成熟探区千米桥潜山大型凝析气藏成藏系统与勘探	中国石油大港油田集团有限责任公司		一等奖	2000
100	曙光计算机应用示范(天津)工程	天津天大天财股份有限公司、南开大学、天津市计算中心、天津市科学技术信息研究所、天津市计算机研究所、天津市对外经济贸易委员会计算中心、曙光信息产业公司	寇纪淞 马其慧 韩维桓 李宝纯 孙富元 王俊铁 张洪奎 周石悌 万家泰 郝淳海	二等奖	2000
101	全钢丝载重子午线轮胎一次法成型机	天津市橡塑机械联合有限公司	张芝泉 朱伯明 张建浩 汤 静 毛小馨 张 晨 王东海 曾志清 陈英铸 姚 昆	二等奖	2000
102	低压电器可靠性设计及检测技术	河北工业大学、苏州高新技术产业开发区电器技术研究所、国家继电器质量监督检验中心	陆俭国 李志刚 王景芹 苏秀苹 李 奎 骆燕燕 杜太行 胡德霖 韩 青 刘教民	二等奖	2000
103	膀胱移行上皮癌诊断治疗及应用基础研究	天津市泌尿外科研究所	马腾骧 畅继武 徐 勇 韩瑞发 王广有 张广建	二等奖	2000
104	地塞米松系列产品新工艺的研究与应用	天津药业有限公司	卢彦昌 袁长东 杨 凤	二等奖	2000
105	锂离子蓄电池研制及应用技术研究	信息产业部电子第十八研究所		二等奖	2000
106	BME—200眼科超声波诊断仪	中国医学科学院生物医学工程研究所		二等奖	2000
107	武钢硅钢扩建工程CA5机组电气自动化系统	天津电气传动设计研究所		二等奖	2000
108	全国水中长期供求计划研究	水利部南京水文水资源研究所……水利部海河水利委员会……		二等奖	2000
109	澳门国际机场人工岛工程建设成套技术	中国港湾建设(集团)总公司……天津港湾工程研究所……		二等奖	2000

续表3 获国家科技进步奖项目

序号	项目名称	获奖单位	获奖人	获奖等级	获奖年份
110	卡托普利对急性心肌梗塞病死率及并发症影响的多中心随机临床研究	中国医学科学院心血管病研究所、天津胸科医院……		二等奖	2000
111	飞行品质监控和飞行图形传真系统研究	中国民用航空总局航空安全技术中心、中国民航学院……		二等奖	2000
112	渤海海域上第三系大油田群的发现	中海石油研究中心渤海研究院、中海石油(中国)有限公司天津分公司、中海石油研究中心勘探研究院	龚再升 茹　克 邓运华 朱伟林 曹文贤 周德湘 韩庆炳 周　毅 米立军 马前贵	二等奖	2001
113	高档干红葡萄酒酿造技术与原料设备保障体系的研制与开发	中法合营王朝葡萄酿酒有限公司	王树生 张春娅 李　巍 刘建华 田凤英 尹吉泰 王　方 田卫东 张福庆 徐作滨	二等奖	2001
114	三维异型整体编织工艺的研究和三维编织设备及织物的研制	天津工业大学	李嘉禄 韩其睿 李晓久 陈　利 姚承照 管　国 李学明 焦亚男 孟广泉 王晓生	二等奖	2001
115	气相法聚乙烯冷凝技术工业开发	天津联合化学有限公司等	吴文清 韩国栋 李　邦 张显峰 郝　报 葛生林 寇承杰 莫惠林 马洪涛 谢会林	二等奖	2001
116	民航发动机使用可靠性研究	中国民航学院等	许春生 王泰伦 孟惠民 倪继良 李光辉 曾学锋 李书明 叶德金 马乾绰 侯跃环	二等奖	2001
117	压力容器极限与安定性分析及体积型缺陷安全评估工程方法研究	国家质量技术监督局锅炉压力容器检测研究中心、清华大学、合肥通用机械研究所、南京化工大学、天津大学材料科学与工程学院	陈　钢 徐秉业 陈学东 沈士明 岑章志 杨铁成 刘应华 石智豪 霍立兴 谢铁军	二等奖	2001
118	功能性间置空肠代胃术的临床与基础研究	天津医科大学附属肿瘤医院	郝希山 李　强 王家仓 柳建中 王殿昌	二等奖	2001
119	油气田地层特性与钻井液、完井液技术研究	大港石油集团有限责任公司……	徐同台 张玉士 洪培云 李建成 赵玉娟 王行愚 范维庆 张兰英 薛　芸 雷耀州	二等奖	2002
120	低压电器试验技术与检测技术的研究	河北工业大学……	陆俭国 刘教民 李志刚 魏世泽 赵小英 杜太行 王景芹 刘帼巾 孙壮志 胡德霖	二等奖	2002
121	干式气体密封	天津新技术产业园区鼎名密封有限公司……	王玉明 李德刚 杨　桦 舒浩华 朱国俊 何仲思 段雪梅 蔡彩玉 王海宁 刘艳梅	二等奖	2002
122	三种固体废弃物应用技术研究	天津市泰达盐碱地绿化研究中心	张万钧 郭育文 黄明勇 王斗天 张民胜 金成甲 刘桂茹 王建新 马作国 曹大正	二等奖	2002
123	T95高强度抗硫化氢套管的研制	天津钢管有限责任公司	关永生 关大新 陈为民 付继成 孙开明 徐　华 刘怀刚 许文妍 文海明 赵晓林	二等奖	2002
124	海上中深层高分辨率地震勘探技术	中海石油研究中心勘探研究院、中海石油地球物理勘探公司……	何汉漪 徐光周 温书亮 张洪昌 张学工 胡天跃 刘永江 张云鹏 邵启群 何樵登	二等奖	2002

续表3 获国家科技进步奖项目

序号	项目名称	获奖单位	获奖人	获奖等级	获奖年份
125	益肾化浊法治疗老年期血管性痴呆的研究	天津中医学院等	张伯礼 王永炎 刘金生 唐启盛 张允岭 徐秋萍 曹晓岚 陈汝兴 赵建军 王荫华	二等奖	2002
126	深水防波堤新型结构形式研究和斜向波堤与直立式防波堤相互作用研究	中交水运规化设计院、大连理工大学、交通部天津水运工程科学研究所、大连港务局、中港第一航务工程局三工程公司	牛恩宗 毛 铠 邓 磊 马德堂 李玉成 陈汉宝 文 立 孙昭晨 赵 军 曹香光	二等奖	2002
127	现场总线分布控制系统开发及应用	……天津市第二煤气厂……	王天然 于海斌 王 宏 邹益仁 张广川 张彦武 赵海燕 范 宇 赵志家 李令奇	二等奖	2002
128	云南半细毛羊培育	……天津市畜牧兽医研究所……	高源汉 杨春荣 黄光璧 浦 勇 付 昭 卜新亚 陆德文 阳留贵 李高荣 陶万忠	二等奖	2002
129	秦岭特长铁路隧道修建技术	铁道第一勘察设计院、中国铁路工程总公司、中国铁道建筑总公司、中铁隧道集团有限公司、中铁十八局集团有限公司、中铁一局集团有限公司、铁道科学研究院、中铁西南科学研究院、西南交通大学、石家庄铁道学院		一等奖	2003
130	中低焓地热工程建设技术	天津大学、中国地质大学(北京)、天津市地热管理处、天津地热勘查开发设计院、黑龙江科技学院	何满潮 李春华 朱家玲 徐能雄 姚磊华 张百鸣 刘 斌 张 伟 王 坤 景海河	二等奖	2003
131	通里攻下法在腹部外科疾病中的应用与基础研究	天津市中西医结合急腹症研究所、天津医科大学基础医学院、南开大学、天津医科大学总医院	吴咸中 崔乃强 何清宇 田在善 林秀珍 杨文修 齐清会 伍孝先 解基良 郭世铎	二等奖	2003
132	新型干法水泥生产关键技术与装备开发及工程化应用	天津水泥工业设计研究院	刘志江 侯宝荣 宋寿顺 郭文叁 胡芝娟 陈庆十 余 彪 狄东仁 林修文 隋明洁	二等奖	2003
133	煤层气勘探技术研究与试验	中国石油勘探开发科学研究院廊坊分院、华北石油管理局、中国石油长庆油田公司勘探开发研究院、大港油田集团钻采工艺研究院	赵庆波 吴国干 李景明 李五忠 张建博 王红岩 姚 超 李安启 单文文 李文阳	二等奖	2003
134	数字高清晰度电视系统关键技术与设备	上海交通大学、浙江大学、天津大学、西安电子科技大学、北京北广电子集团有限责任公司、国家广电总局广播科学研究院、中国电子科技集团公司电子科学研究院	张文军 郭 柯 杨 杰 方向忠 孙 军 余松煜 王 匡 李 华 葛建华 卢江浩	二等奖	2003
135	资源环境、区域经济空间信息共享应用网络	中国科学院遥感应用研究所、国家信息中心、国家计委宏观经济研究院信息咨询中心、中国水利水电科学研究院、国家林业部信息中心、国土资源部信息中心、国家海洋信息中心	阎守邕 徐 枫 曾 澜 陈宣庆 王世新 庄大方 李浩川 陈蓓玉 王庆杰 杨丽沛	二等奖	2003
136	钢筋混凝土多层及高层异形柱框架结构成套技术	河北工业大学、北京工业大学、天津市轻工业设计院	曹万林 曹泽润 霍 达 魏文湘 吴建有 胡国振 周明杰 郝春森 王绍英 曲英华	二等奖	2003
137	公路工程灾害预防与治理综合技术研究及工程应用	山东省交通厅公路局、北京科技大学、洛阳至三门峡高速公路建设指挥部、中铁十八局集团有限公司、山西祁临高速公路有限责任公司	王松根 高永涛 田鲁泉 马 飞 张玉宏 吴顺川 王春江 王金安 姚惠发 杨绍波	二等奖	2003

续表3 获国家科技进步奖项目

序号	项目名称	获奖单位	获奖人	获奖等级	获奖年份
138	镧系元素时间分辨荧光分析技术及仪器的配套研究	解放军第二军医大学、上海新波生物技术有限公司、解放军总医院、中国医学科学院放射医学研究所	韩 玲 吴冠英 李振甲 陈 杞 赵启仁 戴长生 李美佳 唐晓燕 陈泮藻 游冬青	二等奖	2003
139	海洋平台结构检测维修、安全评定与实时监测系统	哈尔滨工业大学、中海石油(中国)有限公司天津分公司、海洋石汕工程股份有限公司维修分公司、清华大学、石油大学(华东)、大连理工大学、上海交通大学	欧进萍 张兴才 员彩芬 肖仪清 程保荣 陈国明 王全增 顾永宁 赵 强 牛世广	二等奖	2003
140	城市电网规划理论、模型、方法的研究与工程应用	天津大学、天津新技术产业园区天大求实电力新技术有限公司	余贻鑫 王成山 黄纯华 葛少云 肖 俊 严雪飞 贾宏杰 刘 昱 王 辛	二等奖	2004
141	复方丹参方药效物质及作用机理研究	天津中医学院……	张伯礼 高秀梅 商洪才 孙有富 王义明 李 梢 胡利民 潘桂湘 王 怡 郭利平	二等奖	2004
142	亚低温治疗急性重型颅脑创伤的临床及实验研究	天津市环湖医院	只达石 张 赛 黄慧玲 林 欣 李增惠 张琳瑛 尚彦国 陈荷红 苏晨方 肖绪林	二等奖	2004
143	长江三峡二期上游围堰防渗墙施工技术研究与工程实践	中国水利水电基础工程局	蒋振中 胡迪煜 宗敦峰 李 军 刘克华 高永康 解同芬 胡 斌 郭宏波 鲁志军	二等奖	2004
144	米非司酮用于紧急避孕、黄体期避孕及催经的研究	国家计划生育委员会科学技术研究所……天津市计划生育研究所……	肖碧莲 吴尚纯 翁梨驹 程利南 贺昌海 赵 珩 雷贞武 曹晓明 梅庆明 倪风贤	二等奖	2004
145	高效规整填料精馏塔技术及应用	天津大学	余国琮 张鹏飞 许春建 朱慧铭 李凭力 田华明 周 明 袁希钢 杨志才 冯惠生	二等奖	2005
146	大型旋转机械和振动机械重大振动故障治理与非线性动力学设计技术	天津大学……	陈予恕 黄文虎 闻邦椿 朱 均 武际可 薛禹胜 张 文 曹树谦 吕和祥 丁 千	二等奖	2005
147	大型水利水电工程可视化仿真技术及其工程应用	天津大学……	钟登华 张社荣 刘东海 肖白云 何有忠 黄 河 郑家祥 王忠耀 崔广涛 张宗亮	二等奖	2005
148	井下工具检测技术及试验平台的研究与开发	天津大学……	胡小唐 刘 合 刘喜林 王凤山 杨乃群 徐世民 傅 星 胡晓东 裴晓含 王金友	二等奖	2005
149	天津港深水航道、港池、泊位适航水深应用与水深动态维护研究	天津港(集团)有限公司	黄力军 丁乃庆 刘富强 胡 宁 张建国 钱平生 孙建鹏 王承刚 李进军 刘树东	二等奖	2005
150	新型高抗挤套管与复合管柱技术	天津钢管集团有限公司……	高德利 严泽生 刘一江 张传友 徐志谦 王 京 李铁成 付继成 李 飞 张建设	二等奖	2005
151	长大隧道全断面岩石掘进机掘进技术研究与应用	……中铁十八局集团有限公司……	杜彦良 刘 春 彭道富 崔 原 杜立杰 沙明元 徐明新 孙 谋 万治昌 房炳杰	二等奖	2005
152	牵引供电自动化系统成套技术及应用	……铁道第二勘察设计院……	陈小川 高仕斌 王 韧 徐志根 蒋先国 蒋 勇 熊列彬 郭勤俭 陈德明 李 岗	二等奖	2005

续表3 获国家科技进步奖项目

序号	项目名称	获奖单位	获奖人	获奖等级	获奖年份
153	镍氢电池、电池组及相关材料产业化关键技术的研究与系统集成	南开大学	吴　锋　单忠强　方世璧　陈　实　石力开　高学平　毛立彩　曲金秋　王国庆　宋德瑛	二等奖	2005
154	中国海岸带环境遥感监测与信息系统技术集成及其应用	……国家海洋信息中心……	周成虎　蒋兴伟　侯一筠　工钦敏　陈述彭　陈介中　王　宏　恽才兴　杨晓梅　苏奋振	二等奖	2005
155	大型精对苯二甲酸生产过程智能建模、控制与优化技术	中国石化集团天津石油化工公司	钱　锋　钱积新　邢建良　郑国栋　冷家厂　颜学峰　赵　均　王振新　杜文莉　王行愚	二等奖	2005

表4 国家级和天津市级国际科技合作奖获得者名录

姓名	国籍	出生年份	获国家级奖年份	获天津市级奖年份
陈省身	美国	1911	1995	——
林少明	新加坡	1934	1997	——
毛焕宇	加拿大籍华人	1951	2001	2000
罗伯特·迪盖特	法国	1927	2002	2001
乔丹·M·菲利普斯	美国	1923	——	2002

表5 天津市科技重大成就奖获得者名录

姓名	工作单位	职称(职务)	年度
侯　锋	天津市农业科学院	中国工程院院士、名誉院长	2000(首届)
张芝泉	天津赛象科技股份有限公司	总经理兼总工程师	2002
余国琮	天津大学化工学院	中国科学院院士、教授	2003
何炳林	南开大学	中国科学院院士、教授	2004

表6 获天津市科学技术奖(一、二等奖)项目

序号	项目名称	获奖单位	获奖人	获奖等级	获奖年份
1	高强预应力钢丝的研制	冶金部建筑研究总院	邹春明　袁贞义　王世勋　吴汝霖　翟巧玲　殷冬生　张秀凤　陶树人	一等奖	1991
2	菌毒并治—防治感染性多系统脏器衰竭的研究	天津市急救医学研究所	王今达　崔乃杰　宗育杉　李荣成　李志军	一等奖	1991
3	培育冬小麦新品种津麦2号	蓟县农业技术推广中心	王继光　邢树萍　李广全　王廷芳　汪俊峰	一等奖	1991
4	天津广播电视塔	天津广播电视局、天津市建委、广播电影电视部设计院、中国建筑第三工程局、天津规划局、中国人民解放军第五七一四厂、中国机械工业第三安装工程公司	胡晓槐　杜文志　王全来　汪祖培　周正一　石文华　肖永琪　李恩久　肖励生	一等奖	1991
5	SC400、SC1100型B超声显像仪	天津市医疗电子仪器公司	段宗文　孔宪利　甄家义　张渝生　王金龙	一等奖	1991
6	于桥水库富营养化及防治研究	天津市环境保护科学研究所、天津市水利科学研究所、天津市水文总站、天津师范大学、南开大学、北京大学、北京环境保护科学研究所	朱　萱　边金钟　王运洪　李思明　赵金福　高文娟　王建华　陈庆男　李明德	二等奖	1991
7	地热开发利用研究	天津大学(天津地热研究培训中心)	蔡义汉　陈　松　齐金生　陈　平　段志强	二等奖	1991

续表6 **获天津市科学技术奖(一、二等奖)项目**

序号	项目名称	获奖单位	获奖人	获奖等级	获奖年份
8	华山参滴丸	天津市第六中药厂	潘力加 佟永岭 郭长源 任福纯 阎振江	二等奖	1991
9	氟哌酸新工艺	中国药科大学、天津市中央制药厂	王尔华 刘文起 田文报 杨伟饮 赵陆华	二等奖	1991
10	TJ270-30红外分光光度计	天津光学仪器厂、天津大学电力及自动化工程系	方国清 廖志杰 孙 波 刁东红 张舒东 李晓明 刘 婕	二等奖	1991
11	自撑式双排抗浮桩护壁工艺研究	天津市第一建筑工程公司	杜有亮 高嘉和 李建军 贾建平 秦序柱	二等奖	1991
12	高温(120℃)铅护套潜油泵电缆	天津市电缆总厂	奚仲波 赵辛庄 韩宝华 马俊江 杨玉秀	二等奖	1991
13	益肾健脾,涤痰散结法补肾抗衰片延缓衰老的临床及实验研究	天津市中医一附院	阮士怡 王竹英 王化良 范英昌 马广信	二等奖	1991
14	SY/00型电子游戏机	机械工业部46研究所	邱瑞琪	二等奖	1991
15	HG220/100-10型煤粉锅炉浓淡型直流钝体燃烧器	天津市第一热点厂 天津电力试验研究所	吴大鹏 刘昌印 陈荣华 汤金生 李曙光	二等奖	1991
16	玉米前重型栽培技术体系的研究	天津市农业技术推广站、天津市北郊区南王平乡人民政府、蓟县农业技术推广中心、宝坻县农业技术推广中心、武清县农业技术推广中心	张义林 徐志孝 隋 华 刘宝山 刘振江 张泽明 钟有龙	二等奖	1991
17	“醒脑开窍”针刺法对中风病疗效的实验研究	天津市中医学院一附院	石学敏 胡国强 周继曾 张存生 韩景献	二等奖	1991
18	ZRS-4智能溶出试验仪	天津大学无线电厂	侯文富 缪贵宾 王 靖 刘 锁 武金键	二等奖	1991
19	天津市中型水面对虾养殖配套技术研究	天津市农村工作委员会、天津农学院	荣长宽 宋绍奎 梁素秀 陈秀为 张起印 陈六林	二等奖	1991
20	腔道肿瘤温控热疗饥	天津市肿瘤研究所	林室寅 李丰彤 于室起 李瑞英 王海磐	二等奖	1991
21	芥末油提取工艺研究	天津市调味品研究所	李美华 陈树生 倪金玲	二等奖	1991
22	热锻压模具材料研究	天津大学力学系、天津市硬质合金研究所	王洪礼 迟仲玉 孙 景 王尚志 伊克甫 陈尔仪	二等奖	1991
23	区域污水回用技术方案优化分析	天津市环境保护科学研究所	孙孝然 李宪法 葛 剑 叶树义 张 翔	二等奖	1991
24	鲜食玉米新品种津鲜一号	天津市农作物所	邵景坡 李洪安 李福中 李凤台	二等奖	1991
25	重度子宫内膜异位症手术治疗研究	天津市中心妇产科医院	岳 琏 李宝森 张殿文 于桂荣	二等奖	1991
26	传染病趋势预测预报方法的研究	天津市卫生防病中心	郝洪起 杜殿军 冯洪友 刘 军 朱 凯	二等奖	1991
27	稳定塘处理天津市城市污水系统研究	天津市环境保护研究所	边嘉敏 张春生 谭步云 阎玉荣 雷公民	二等奖	1991
28	淋巴系统恶性肿瘤的基因诊断	天津市第二医学院	朱 平 刘乐宇 张洪清 杨湘龙 刘志萍	二等奖	1991
29	TM-8/4可调工位玻璃器皿压机	天津市轻工业学院、天津市玻璃器皿厂	张建国 吴祈明 徐洪福 王 榕 王健康 任立选 姚树仁	二等奖	1991
30	天津站地区道路交通规划设计	天津市城乡规划设计院	冯 容 李宝书 邹 哲 肖连望 张肖峰	二等奖	1991
31	膝关节囊外髌骨钻孔术治疗髌股退变性骨关节病	天津市大港医院	张如明	二等奖	1991
32	潮白河双层橡胶坝技术研究	天津市水利科学研究所、宁河县水利局	柴 珣 曹永龙 刘洪达 秦春萱 薄连顺 惠 应 叶以同	二等奖	1991

续表6 获天津市科学技术奖(一、二等奖)项目

序号	项目名称	获奖单位	获奖人	获奖等级	获奖年份
33	HG8011机车性能及在线工况参数测量处理系统	天津市中环科学仪器公司	孙志国 聂广满 杨宏熠 赵丕广 吴福和	二等奖	1991
34	阴茎斜形带蒂皮条翻转埋藏法治疗尿道下裂一次成型术	天津市第二中心医院	陈彦明	二等奖	1991
35	自体纯角膜上皮移植术在翼状胬肉手术中的应用	天津市眼科医院	武桂芳 韩 梅 林锦镛 穆祥云	二等奖	1991
36	全可控电子制动装置	天津市华光电器控制设备厂、天津市发电设备总产	翟风翥 李桂芬 郭殿荣 张玉山 刘洪禄 徐起顺	二等奖	1991
37	TJ862髓母细胞瘤体外细胞系的建立及其特征	天津市医学院附属医院、天津市神经病医学研究所	傅佩玉 钟 跃 王淑兰 李 萍 王广秀	二等奖	1991
38	真皮下血管网超薄皮瓣及快速断蒂的实验和临床应用研究	中国人民解放军第254医院、天津第二医学院、天津第二医学院附属第一中心医院	王业江 魏志达 王其芳 张凤起 陈万芳	二等奖	1991
39	双气浮综合净水技术	天津市纺织工业设计院工程	刘兴华 张乃平 沈学良 宋巧立	二等奖	1991
40	汽车位置光电自动测量系统	天津大学精密仪器工程系、天津市公安局车辆管理所	王春和 梁和争 叶声华 孙 琪 赵金元 李建新	二等奖	1991
41	21寸平面直角彩电外壳模具CAD/CAM	天津市计算中心、天津长城电子公司、天津大学机械制造工程系、天津轻工业学院、天津市塑料制品模具厂	薛大中 陈 亿 崔文林 李洪林 杜君文 倪士俊 柴玉海	二等奖	1991
42	TS-B型通用电工实验台	天津师范大学物理系、天津师范大学校办工厂	常向荣 庞大勇 徐钧津 董春鹏 刘家冀 胡会来	二等奖	1991
43	TX19-Q型夹心巧克力自动线	机械电子工业部第五设计研究院、天津市永兴食品机械厂	张集明 王守业 罗禄琼 姚明理 李维军	二等奖	1991
44	TXS-LL电加热钢丝圈挤出联动生产线	天津市橡塑机械厂	张之泉 李建志 姚 栋	二等奖	1991
45	扑克牌自动生产流水线	天津市第四印刷厂、天津市机械设计院包装研究所	孟三良 丁治勤 焦学勇 张绍良 舒嘉宾 王培娥 陈丙治	二等奖	1991
46	优化配方施肥技术的研究与推广	天津市土壤肥料工作站、静海县农业局土壤肥料工作站、宝坻县土肥站、武清县农林局土肥站、宁河县农林技术推广中心 蓟县农业局土肥站	曲自新 刘志杰 曲玉琢 罗伟忠 荣庆武 李又富 陈子学 张洪利 杨连志 李欣然 梁万成 徐庭梅	二等奖	1991
47	万亩低产池塘和网箱养鱼综合技术开发	天津市农村工作委员会、天津市水产局、天津市农学院、天津市水产技术推广站	吕祖哲 宁书正 刘茂春 吾福荣 杨仲斌 杨金江 陈 秀 赵开伦 时建伟 董景川 霍士俐 杨 晓	二等奖	1991
48	TS系列水质稳定剂新技术的应用	天津钢厂氧气厂、化工部天津化工研究院	白永忠 阎家华 刘文利 史木林 孙国胜 孙铁宗 郭玉玲 方燕平 姜翠云 霍建彭 王博厚 张绪清	二等奖	1991
49	宇宙牌XNY-1型太阳能热水器推广应用	津西农村能源办公室	陈俊奎 姚占明 高向忠 黄金岭 高 乐 房秀芬 王凤祥 高庆成	二等奖	1991
50	天津市商品瘦肉型猪配套技术开发及推广	天津市农村工作委员会、天津市畜牧局	叶月皎 樊航奇 李绍兴 周广森 李天相 李澍田 王文杰 董思政 王继兴 张淑芳 王民双 于桂元	二等奖	1991
51	天津市工业产业与产品结构研究	天津市科技情报研究所、南开大学经济研究所、天津大学技术经济系统工程系、天津市计划委员会工业计划处、天津市计委信息中心	杨日初 唐 杰 和金生 樊月龙 杨秀静	二等奖	1991
52	DB/1200-B21-81-85天津市蔬菜种子分级标准	天津市种子管理站	杨淑惠 邢彦霞 纪荣印 阎富英 杜生礼	二等奖	1991
53	GBU281-87外照射慢性放射病诊断标准及处理原则	中国医学科学院放射医学研究所、四川省劳动卫生职业病防治研究所、卫生部工业卫生实验所	刘力群 王敬英 贾德林 徐秀凤	二等奖	1991
54	天津市土壤环境背景值研究	天津市环境监测中心	薛亚珍 沈伟然 王金英 张若兰 张文具	二等奖	1991

续表6　　获天津市科学技术奖(一、二等奖)项目

序号	项目名称	获奖单位	获奖人	获奖等级	获奖年份
55	用高效液相色谱法测定长春花细胞培养物中阿吗碱和蛇根碱的方法研究	天津市农科院中心实验室	王　萍　常冬至　王　欣	二等奖	1991
56	TS型密封三维桥梁伸缩装置	天津市市政工程研究所、天津公路管理局、天津市市政工程勘探设计院	马云生　元世华　于淮祥　徐家俊　王莲英	二等奖	1991
57	SR-10-24型热烟熏蒸煮设备	天津市肉类联合加工厂	严志祥　宋志生　陈　扬　王树新　赵庆余	二等奖	1991
58	ZB125L、ZB200L斩拌机	天津市肉类联合加工厂	陈　扬　严志祥　赵建峰　潘玉玲　张廷贵　李蕴璞　朱绍刚	二等奖	1991
59	塘沽地热供暖试验研究	天津市塘沽区政府热化办公室、天津市塘沽区政府咨询委渤海石油公司、天津市塘沽区重点工程指挥部、天津市塘沽区供热管理处	曹金荣　张初阳　井开域　董风元　苑秉新	二等奖	1991
60	科技成果推广工作奖	天津市种子管理站	严光磊　魏阳生　周宗濂　孟昭旭　姜秀华　张兆芬　陈启元　杨淑惠　王国春　王友助　赵　明　李　琦	二等奖	1991
61	推广技术项目	天津市南郊区科学技术委员会	孟凡龙　王文德　赵树元　许惠定　戴世昌　何洪梁　史宝江　章春海　陶长才	二等奖	1991
62	推广技术项目	天津市植物保护研究所	冯　樾　陈恩选　张宝仁　夏志红　孙克荣　申日升　陈秉恕　杨崇实　刘兆敏　石守良　陈增建　姚丽竹	二等奖	1991
63	卫星用太阳电池空间辐射损伤模拟试验研究	天津市技术物理研究所、机械电子工业部第十八研究所	李　浩　徐寿岩　黄才勇　杨瑞霞　唐　军　刘全民　黄家驹	一等奖	1992
64	高转化率醋酸泼泥松生产菌株BY-2-13-51的选育及应用	天津轻工业学院、天津市天津药业公司	杜连祥　路福平　鲁梅芳　王昌禄　武淑婷　庞俊陆　石俊杰	一等奖	1992
65	Z13-30名色环氧聚酯水性浸涂漆	化工部涂料工业研究所、天津市丽华色彩总厂	刘跃奎　余新利　吴英昌　王世玲　张寿多	一等奖	1992
66	山楂蜜汁饮料加工技术	天津市林业果树研究所	马冬青　李永力　姜　彪　雷　霞　王丽英	一等奖	1992
67	津鲜一号鲜食玉米生产技术开发研究	天津市农作物研究所、武清县种子管理站	邵景坡　高同生　张巧云　傅从贵　李树清　杨宝民　栾文斗	二等奖	1992
68	碱性玫瑰精6GDN(桃红精6GDN)	天津市津西北方福利化工厂	李彤年　毕湘樵　高孟贤　孙绍友　高仲贤	二等奖	1992
69	天然高粱红色素生产技术及产品	天津师范大学、天津师范大学天然色素厂	集体	二等奖	1992
70	YB41硬盒小包包装机及YB56透明纸包装机	天津市第二轻工机械厂、天津市轻工业机械研究所	张国维　马桂芸　李鸿环　程金台　王自起　刘万轩　张春哲　杨善玲	二等奖	1992
71	亚硫酸镁盐制浆蒸煮废液板式蒸发器用清洗剂及清洗工艺的研究	天津市轻工业化学研究所、天津造纸厂	陈　健　许　蕴　曲振衡　孙经烈　周翼轮	二等奖	1992
72	(玻璃器皿烘口)低压鼓风燃烧系统	天津轻工业学院、天津市玻璃器皿厂	张建国　马肖玲　陆文秀　曾孝宇　任立选　吴祈明　祝清华	二等奖	1992
73	天财通用会计网络软件	天津大学信息与控制研究所、天津市财政局	寇纪淞　王中胜　杭建民　张　汀　沈福章　叶春圃　倪　锐	二等奖	1992
74	WBI-250自行式稳定土拌和机	天津市道路桥梁管理处机械修理厂	孙　雄　耿　波　朱金明　刘　伟　沈海燕	二等奖	1992
75	林丹高浓度悬浮制剂	天津理工学院	杨志生　萧如亭　李炎章	二等奖	1992
76	氯化铵化肥在天津地区使用效果的研究	天津市土壤肥料研究所、天津市农村生产资料公司	陆真元　程　奕　刘恭燕　张仲国　李玉华　石文靖　王敬海	二等奖	1992

续表6　　获天津市科学技术奖(一、二等奖)项目

序号	项目名称	获奖单位	获奖人	获奖等级	获奖年份
77	眼眶深部海绵状血管瘤超声,CT定性定位诊断及手术方法	天津医学院第二附属医院	宋国祥　田文芳　肖利华　孙丰源　张　虹	二等奖	1992
78	SM系列平面直角单色显示器	天津市显示器厂	刘宝贵　王　巍　于子均　张立华　刘正齐　李景山	二等奖	1992
79	四乙基米氏酮	天津市南星科技开发公司	高秀彬　萧耀民　王家宏　古风才	二等奖	1992
80	双氧水生产用SR-芳烃溶剂的研制	天津石油化工公司研究所、天津市大港化工实验厂	张　竞　么树荃　张俊民　潘玉凤　张　平	二等奖	1992
81	天津丹系长白猪选育研究	天津市畜牧局、北京农业大学、天津市宁河县畜牧水产局	陈清明　李绍兴　范全太　王立先　王凤来　杨铁民　李振宽	二等奖	1992
82	全喉切除术后Ⅱ期发音重建术	天津市铁路分局天津铁路中心医院	金国威	二等奖	1992
83	LH-T型新系列电动葫芦双梁起重机	天津市起重设备总厂研究所	雷克平　马士强　门玉林　娄兴华　商建民	二等奖	1992
84	牛结核检疫中非特异性反应研究	天津市农场管理局、吉林农业大学	李忠全　何昭阳　胡希荣　张允茂　李德生　李卯年　高　晶	二等奖	1992
85	CGO-6型重氮复印机	天津市中环复印绘图机械公司	张占昆　刘润林　葛德津　李明华	二等奖	1992
86	天津市城市干道沥青路面养护管理系统	天津道路桥梁管理处	邹南昌　黄宝玉　宋光元　杨海英　陈少青	二等奖	1992
87	建立经EB病毒转化人-B淋巴细胞生产人源性单克隆抗核抗体系列	天津医学院第二附属医院、天津市泌尿外科研究所	畅继武　随志方　马腾骧　李邱玲　张淑敏	二等奖	1992
88	神油	天津达仁堂制药二厂	陶　智　袁雪海　郝非非　王书文	二等奖	1992
89	新型垂直筛板(NewVST)性能及应用研究	河北工学院	杜佩衡　王庆瑶　于文奎	二等奖	1992
90	双螺杆泵系列产品开发研究	天津市工业泵总厂	周永旭　刘彤贤　胡　刚　张清泰　宋鼎康	二等奖	1992
91	TRI近交系大鼠的培育及其生物学特性的研究	天津医学院实验肿瘤研究室	林炳永　张玉英　窦桂荣　王东茂　多文星	二等奖	1992
92	FM650C复膜机	天津市轻工装潢机械厂	任德华　吴风启　李恒政　陆景桥　马　杰	二等奖	1992
93	$6QA_{60}S$(N50Z)铅酸蓄电池	天津市蓄电池厂	张其煦　万建平　高　崴　赵克祥　马玉宝	二等奖	1992
94	HYA、HYA C铜芯聚烯烃绝缘铝塑综合护层市内通信电缆	天津市电缆总厂	王宗仁　张令宜　董慧娟　吴　颖　李　川　张迎春　张俊华	二等奖	1992
95	GYJ系列液体灌装机	天津市食品包装机械厂、天津市宝坻县农机监理站	高文生　王建华　徐天禄　冯银波　王玉山　吴文元　陈跃道	二等奖	1992
96	液化石油气成套灌装输送设备	天津市长龙链式输送机厂	王建国　赵海军　兰成学　李勤生　边少增	二等奖	1992
97	TG型锅炉除烟垢清烟节能素	天津理工学院、天津师范大学	厉时成　谈启明	二等奖	1992
98	"醒脑开窍"针法形态及组织化学实验研究	天津中医学院第一附属医院	石学敏　翟　娜　李　萍　刘煦欣　胡国强　路秀芬　赵立荣	二等奖	1992
99	经内镜对胆胰疾病的诊治观察和实验研究	天津市南开医院、天津市中西医结合急腹症研究所	鲁焕章　徐东琴　范君度　富光华　高德宝　许　峰	二等奖	1992
100	高粘度树脂	天津市油墨科学技术研究所	贾和春　周金泉　于金凯	二等奖	1992

续表 6

获天津市科学技术奖(一、二等奖)项目

序号	项目名称	获奖单位	获奖人	获奖等级	获奖年份
101	电解盐水微机控制系统	天津大沽化工厂	张珍妹　于现军　杨广鑫　李宝利　程殿彬	二等奖	1992
102	盐酸环丙沙星及其片剂的研制	中国医学科学院医药生物技术研究所、天津市中央制药厂	张致平　张文忠　刘　浚　边其昌　李家泰　史淑珍　郭惠元	二等奖	1992
103	电力半导体器件用散热器挤压型材	天津市铝合金厂	国占昌　王　刚　刘德新　周永顺　姚　伟	二等奖	1992
104	SL-240涤纶弹力丝后加工油剂	天津纺织工学院、天津石油化工公司长丝厂	王金榜　申兆才　郑　帼　蒋富宝　马怡静　张春玲　王家惠	二等奖	1992
105	WFZ-25型紫外-可见分光光度计	天津市光学仪器厂	谷佩荣　赵振兴　孙宏伟　秦　方　刘　捷	二等奖	1992
106	机床电磁离合器零件激光热处理生产应用成套工艺设备研究	天津市机床电器总厂、北京机床研究所	赵　杰　张魁武　黄竹修　常晓惠　杜昭山　邵宝茹　于浦源	二等奖	1992
107	异种网互联涉外信息网络系统	天津市公安局十五处、天津大学计算机工程与科学系	徐汉申　许林英　李　建　滑建忠　刘国庆　杨学长　李希荃	二等奖	1992
108	国人铝日允许摄入量的研究	天津医学院卫生学系	刘凤贞　于德奎　吕　严　徐格晟　黄国伟	二等奖	1992
109	天津市中低产小麦技术开发示范工程	天津市农林局	王嘉秀　姚振凡　陈同植　刘训江　王瑞卿　杨书峰　杨怀芳　马秀生　薛玉森　王　岭　韩铁军　李忠良	二等奖	1992
110	天津市中低产玉米技术开发示范工程	天津市农林局	徐志孝　张义林　隋　华　韩树婷　陈增付　李瑞丛　王　荷　金　英　张树森　吕建继　杨　春　邱荣学	二等奖	1992
111	麦蚜发生规律及防治技术研究	天津市植保植检站、静海县植保植检站、宝坻县植保植检站、大港区植保植检站	陈晓文　郑世清　张宝恕　钱聚荫　李秀玲　王秀英　孙振华　兰卫东　陆建高　朱永生　唐玉琴　申洪利	二等奖	1992
112	甲状腺素方法学科研成果推广应用及转化药盒生产	天津市内分泌研究所、天津医学院附属医院	方佩华　赵学勤　刘福臣　宋建良　黄乃萍　戴连起　侯秉璋　刘嘉玉　杨立昌　王　绮　张镜宇　周荫保	二等奖	1992
113	蛋鸡综合配套技术推广	天津市畜牧局	叶月皎　彰春和　傅润亭　刘庆丰　刘成理　罗会仁　王文杰　王宪立　王学玲　黄秀奇　郑　磊　杨铁民	二等奖	1992
114	格列齐特(达美康)产品及工艺	天津市新新制药厂	刑汝文　刘恩顺　张重文　王桂荣　许玉坤　刘建丰　周　武　刘凤君　朱起林	二等奖	1992
115	天津市社会经济科技的投入产出分析	天津市统计局、天津市科学技术情报研究所	杨宝民　任庆文　高　峰　于忠义	二等奖	1992
116	关于提高天津市经济效益的政策与管理研究	天津市计划经济研究所、天津市科学技术情报研究所、天津市科学学研究所	马献林　秦广生　任庆文　孙兰玉　陈德隆　张秀章	二等奖	1992
117	天津市城市区域环境噪声标准	天津市环境监测中心等	陈光华　胡曼华　韩克明　陈向党　石丽娜	二等奖	1992
118	DS310-1型0.5级三相有功电能表 AN31K型1.0级三相有功电能表 AS31型2.0级三相无功电能表	天津市第三电表厂	石怡田　窦俊波　耿　玲　陈正玲　李忠文	二等奖	1992
119	一级标准物质-苯的研制	天津市计量技术研究所	贾瑞华　贾桂荣　张大建　杨全喜　邓芝英	二等奖	1992
120	引进洗衣粉生产装置的消化、吸收	天津市合成洗涤剂厂	孙惠芳　吴顺发　张家荣　吴桂明　刘业明	二等奖	1992

续表6 获天津市科学技术奖(一、二等奖)项目

序号	项目名称	获奖单位	获奖人	获奖等级	获奖年份
121	中型高炉喷吹煤粉技术	天津铁厂	赵之泉 李朝金 范广泉 杨士云 王中杰	一等奖	1993
122	一体化及分体式悬挂点焊机	天津市陆华科技公司、重庆长安机器制造厂	江 涛 李振山 季江生 魏 毅等	一等奖	1993
123	高聚合度PVC树脂	天津化工厂	戈文章 宗永兴 廖世铿 张建达 常 江	一等奖	1993
124	全景式(SJ-2)水井检测彩色电视系统的研究	天津大学电子工程系	于景良 王德福 孙鼎俊 孙嘉纲	一等奖	1993
125	鸡传染性法氏囊病综合防治规范	天津市畜牧兽医研究所、天津市畜牧兽医站、中国农业科学院哈尔滨兽医研究所	王文科 王景德 陈冠春 张 健 王文旗 王建华 王笑梅	一等奖	1993
126	天津市吨粮田技术开发示范工程	天津市农林局	陈同植 王 树 姚振凡 张义林 马秀生	一等奖	1993
127	6130ZG型柴油机	天津动力机厂	罗德强 郎国生 周逢源 田 远 高凯顺	二等奖	1993
128	选育柠檬酸优良产生菌研究	天津市工业微生物研究所	于云岭 刘桂芳 蔡永峰 孙武岳	二等奖	1993
129	高参数密封试验台	天津克兰密封有限公司、沈阳鼓风机厂、天津市自动化仪表成套设计所	王玉明 杨肃清 柏均佳 邱 海 王 强 贾培起 王志安 李 鉴	二等奖	1993
130	平炉微机热工自动控制炼钢的研究	天津钢厂第一炼钢厂、天津钢厂钢铁研究所	赵大力 马绍明 杨增诗 路久范 李元民 堵亚光 傅晓平	二等奖	1993
131	包装印刷品表面油墨耐摩擦材料及其印刷工艺技术	天津环球磁卡公司	裴绍立 郝连玖 李德奎 刘光亭 赵学斌	二等奖	1993
132	蓝天六必治牙膏	天津牙膏厂	潘 超 梁玉树 卢秀文	二等奖	1993
133	SG-5球形PVC树脂	天津化工厂、化工部锦西化工研究院	刘东升 李新祥	二等奖	1993
134	金芪降糖片的生产工艺	天津市中药制药厂	谢克明 郑 宁 马德明 高 庆 韩海岭	二等奖	1993
135	塑料槽蓄电池装配线研制	天津市蓄电池厂	李俊明 李葆谦 陈泽明 刘振民 侯庆战	二等奖	1993
136	用声发射技术对多层型氢气瓶的可靠性分析	天津石油化工公司机械研究所、天津石油化工公司化工厂	刘 印 李建国 蒋仕良 何秉富 胡庆华 董恩久 王淑芬	二等奖	1993
137	FG型医用X线胶片	天津感光材料公司	谭庆珍 劳 菲 刘宝孝 张邦彦 鲍子兴	二等奖	1993
138	地热深井潜水电泵	天津大学地热中心、天津市潜水电机厂、天津市水泵厂、天津市潜水泵厂	张 启 齐金生 徐金明 马恩成 陈文启 刘金华 梁 军	二等奖	1993
139	投料曝气法-悬浮载体曝气工艺	天津市污水处理研究所	赵利君 侯景树 马文杰 陈双星	二等奖	1993
140	GYIAS束管式单模光缆	天津电子线缆公司	任庆政 薛澍津 刘振谦 漆光临 冯 春	二等奖	1993
141	低碳低磷粒铁	天津铁厂、北京科技大学	赵之泉 陆春明 张大维 李朝金 冯士根 秦民生 张建良	二等奖	1993
142	厚壁长筒管开缝加工技术	天津城市建设学院	杨贺来 巩万安 孙善平	二等奖	1993
143	天津城市污水湿地处理系统研究	天津市环境保护科学研究所、天津市水利科学研究所、天津市环境监测中心	张建文 米瑞兰 李万庆 严晔端 殷 红 邱汉文 杨筱曼	二等奖	1993

续表6 **获天津市科学技术奖(一、二等奖)项目**

序号	项目名称	获奖单位	获奖人	获奖等级	获奖年份
144	四辊轧机液压压下计算机自动设定轧钢系统	天津市中板厂、冶金部钢铁研究总院	张进之 刘雅娴 孟繁城 刘起龙 白埃民 石辅祥	二等奖	1993
145	SM1418平面直角单色显示器	天津显示器厂	王永安 曹玉瑛 薛来平 夏德祥 陈凤岭	二等奖	1993
146	隔声防火玻璃的研制	公安部天津消防科学研究所	王志远 吴颖捷	二等奖	1993
147	N-Ⅲ型工业射线胶片	天津感光材料公司	王惠洁 杨学敏 吕淑英 顾振明 刘书强	二等奖	1993
148	平阳霉素提取新工艺	中国医学科学院医药生物技术研究所、天津市河北制药厂	计鸿章 戴丽华 张秀荣 陈幼鲁 鞠京五	二等奖	1993
149	500KV铝包钢绞线良导体地线	天津市大成五金厂	吴典斌 孙东平 莫 璋 顾乃健 孟昭茹	二等奖	1993
150	促进剂系列产品	天津市有机化工一厂	肖熙荣 高殿秀 李汉融 刘文会 邹燕燕 方守军	二等奖	1993
151	IGS-1型工程钻机	天津探矿机械总厂	吴元成 王 毅 何宝龙 刘永刚 王维忠	二等奖	1993
152	天津市稻水象甲生物学研究及封锁除治综合治理工程	天津市植保植检站	郑世清 李秀文 张宝恕 许桂芳 军 农	二等奖	1993
153	排水管道改革一体化	天津市市政工程研究所、天津市市政工程勘测设计院、天津市市政工程局	高复栋 李合旦 盛应光 张鸿梁 刘连琴 陈 洪 丰景华	二等奖	1993
154	新型高耐磨锌合金及其应用(代青铜)研究	天津理工学院一分院	彭日升 刘 杰 刘智勇 张程勇 张厚奎	二等奖	1993
155	ZL型锌系金属表面磷化处理剂	天津理工学院、天津市昆仑磷化材料厂	励时成 李长吉 王锡珍 宫 延 王培璋 王德发	二等奖	1993
156	720号滤油滤料	天津美纶股份有限公司	郭亚华 段锦英 于庆王 李仲阳 任福来	二等奖	1993
157	搞高连铸比攻关	天津钢厂	曾小平 林英权 凌遵峰 刘立志 刘维明	二等奖	1993
158	膀胱癌标记物、异质性、病因与治疗、预后的关系	天津医学院附属医院	虞颂庭 吴明明 李黎明 韩树楠 王建宇	二等奖	1993
159	有机肥料科学加工利用的研究	天津市农科院土壤肥料研究所、蓟县土肥工作站	周艺敏 许前欣 张金盛 王正祥 翁丽萍 王铁民 徐庭梅	二等奖	1993
160	管带式散热器翅片刀具设备研制	天津市工具研究所	杨锡宫 黎金铭 栾培军 卢凤梧 许勋扬	二等奖	1993
161	国产HI系列单克隆抗体白血病免疫分型诊断试剂盒研制	中国医学科学院血液学研究所	沈德诚 汤美华 张金香 白金芬 陈 璋	二等奖	1993
162	MZ-12A型强力煤电钻	天津煤矿专用设备厂	任廷连 王殿弼 赵 磊 鲁乱子 范钦亚	二等奖	1993
163	天津市乡镇工业污染源调查、评价及对策研究	天津市环境保护局、天津市乡镇企业管理局	刘文仲 汪丽娟 王海山 赵焕生 韩景明	二等奖	1993
164	高产抗病辣椒新品种-津椒3号	天津市蔬菜研究所	魏乃荣 陆长萍 李云华 刘文明 李素文	二等奖	1993
165	离子膜法制烧碱用螯合树脂生产应用技术	南开大学	张政朴 李贺先 张 华 王 瑛 陈洪彬	二等奖	1993
166	MS(VC)-6C-650六辊可逆轧机液压系统	天津市液压件二厂、冶金部钢铁研究总院	何书正 杜梅英 杨少泉 丁 淳 于国敏 梅扶长 张登峰	二等奖	1993
167	重型颅脑损伤的临床及病理生理的研究	天津医学院附属医院神经外科、天津神经病学研究所	杨树源 王明璐 李庆彬 薛庆澄 马景鑑	二等奖	1993

续表6 获天津市科学技术奖(一、二等奖)项目

序号	项目名称	获奖单位	获奖人	获奖等级	获奖年份
168	补肾活血法治疗慢性再生障碍性贫血临床观察及实验研究	天津中医学院	戴锡孟 杨学爽 杨文华 孙平旺 贾志杰	二等奖	1993
169	农村能源综合开发技术试点的研究	天津市农村能源办公室、天津市津南区新能源办公室	任志强 杜金华 王沛 田玉达 杨爱萍 牛馨菊 孙桂珍	二等奖	1993
170	LMJ-1型沥青混合料级配、计量微机控制系统	天津轻工业学院、天津市塘沽市政工程公司、天津市第二沥青厂	范树礼 杨玉良 刘文岑 张金铭 刘均正	二等奖	1993
171	产科生理常数的研究	天津市中心妇产科医院、南开大学	岳琏 王淑雯 吴荣 王公恕 左义欣 周凤阁 李庆熙	二等奖	1993
172	LPS-1型激光粒度仪	天津大学现代光学仪器研究所	毛义 张以谟 李贺桥 刘铁根 张登臣	二等奖	1993
173	生物型人工肝-ACA微囊肝细胞及人工细胞膜壳聚糖的研究	天津市第三中心医院肝胆研究所	宋继昌 李涛 孙多先 杜智 崔润海 高茹 吴永珠	二等奖	1993
174	天津钢铁炉料交易市场综合管理系统	天津市电子计算研究所	王世钧 赵永坚 朱虎威 肖力 张群	二等奖	1993
175	多聚酶链式反应技术(PCR)诊断病毒性心肌炎	天津市胸科医院心血管研究所	张志尧 沈作浮 聂晓红 王晓维 吴尚勤	二等奖	1993
176	果蔬沙司新产品研制	天津市林业果树研究所	马冬青 李永力 胡云峰 韩建新 饶佳柳	二等奖	1993
177	万亩水稻机械化农业综合示范工程	天津市津南区农机局、天津市津南区农林局、天津市农机局科教处、天津市汉沽区农机局	杨丕显 郑清林 林玉柱 李家国 戴冠英 邵曰芬 韩金华	二等奖	1993
178	城市道路CAD系统	天津市市政工程勘测设计院	李孝圭 朱晓东 徐建平 赵建伟 范广利	二等奖	1993
179	水稻旱育稀植栽培技术的研究与推广	天津市农业技术推广站	张金钢 刘俭 郑爱军 陈怀东 郑宗富 张玉华 袁廷成 李庭贵 贾子玉 邵曰芬 时迎春 史淑华	二等奖	1993
180	天津市低产低质果园改造技术示范与推广	天津市林业工作站	赵万明 邢昌琪 杜长城 侯明 于长年 齐金生 赵广年 马润生 张富民 刘志明 孟玉霞 谢洪俊	二等奖	1993
181	配套应用新技术改善枣园油田开发效果	大港石油管理局采油三厂、石油大学	王德明 郦福新 谢良尊 边增凯 常斌 姚素贞 姚世明 邢振义 刘小芳 王贺林 李瑞青 张一伟	二等奖	1993
182	天津市工业技术发展分析与对策研究	天津市科技信息研究所	雷风徐 陈悦 徐铭 李殿林 戴木权 周孝其 王晶垣	二等奖	1993
183	天津市科技发展若干重大问题研究	天津市科学学研究所、天津大学管理工程系、天津市高等学校软科学学科组、河北工学院工业管理工程系	陈爱珍 吴育华 张庆华 李浩志 殷亮 孙宪义	二等奖	1993
184	天津市全社会对科技投入调查与研究	天津市科学学研究所、南开大学会计系	冯燕奇 唐洁 邢红红 张保生 张健华 盛刚	二等奖	1993
185	恶臭排放标准研究	天津市环境保护科学研究所	石磊 徐金凤 张燕华 李秀荣 袁秀文	二等奖	1993
186	LZZ型金属管转子流量计	天津市东丽区技术监督局、天津市宇光仪表研究所	柴寿辰 宁文涛 陈兴 刘仕远 石万元 邵再鹏	二等奖	1993
187	科技成果推广工作奖	天津市农村工作委员会	张树明 倪守明 张宝成 刘维林 吕福旭 陈秀 杨吕喜 宋绍奎 郝淑敏 孙盛图 赵萍	二等奖	1993

续表6　　获天津市科学技术奖(一、二等奖)项目

序号	项目名称	获奖单位	获奖人	获奖等级	获奖年份
188	C14MP55P-系列单色显示管	天津中环三津有限公司	张文铭　冯志存　胡小试　顾时来　陈亚方	一等奖	1994
189	脱氢硫代对甲苯胺双磺酸及其工艺	天津市先达化工公司	凌嵩云　尹秀亭　赵智田　迟丽荣　王秀文	一等奖	1994
190	马铃薯脱毒微型种薯的开发研究	天津市农业科院蔬菜研究所	王炳君　刘晓辉　李戌彤　王鲁野　居玉玲	一等奖	1994
191	软(硬)质炭黑湿法造粒	天津炭黑厂	刘俊才　刘克明　杨士福　仇祯祥　刘彦伯　刘代浩　王景禹	一等奖	1994
192	城市电网规划计算机辅助决策系统——模型研究与软件开发	天津大学、天津电力工业局	余贻鑫　肖　健　黄纯化　周　义　王成山　葛少云　戴宏伟	二等奖	1994
193	黑色金属计算机网络交易系统	天津师范大学天师高新技术发展总公司	金家瑞　刘　强　张　斌　张　芃　张彦兵	二等奖	1994
194	采用ASME压力容器规范的研究	天津石化机械制造安装工程公司	赵　武　丁　静　窦克贤　于甲辰　梁云忠	二等奖	1994
195	果实采后软化机理及其控制	天津市林业果树研究所	吕昌文　齐　灵　修德仁　杨汉祥　马　筠	二等奖	1994
196	以MTBE法生产对-叔丁基苯酚新工艺	天津大学应用化学系、天津市福达化工厂	孙经武　姚芳连　冯亚凯　李海平　孟继红　曹永发	二等奖	1994
197	籼、粳亚种间杂交选育中、晚稻新品种研究	天津水稻研究所、天津市植物保护研究所	牛　景　张奎敏　李艳萍　朴钟泽　陈增建　张兆芬	二等奖	1994
198	针刺治疗病态窦房结综合征的临床与电生理实验研究	天津中医院第一附属医院	石学敏　芦绍强　罗　利　蒋戈利　马津全	二等奖	1994
199	石油炼制污水净化场空气中有害物质对人体健康影响的研究	天津石油化工公司职业病防治所、北京燕山石油化工公司职业病防治研究所	宁文生　张宗雁　郝进枝　刘　炎　王永定　蒋培青　李凤琴	二等奖	1994
200	天津本地电话网号码六位升七位相关技术的研究	天津市邮电管理局、天津市市内电话局、天津市长途电信局	刘德宝　郭绍生　王安平　滕　勇　陈克艺　吴承英　李南枝	二等奖	1994
201	五种专用型控制电缆	天津德塔控制系统有限公司	陈金城　张启禄　王　凯　王自成　兰志成	二等奖	1994
202	普兰娜电脑艺术化妆品	天津市化妆品科学技术研究所	李小和　郝　政　藏路一　谢培新　束效先	二等奖	1994
203	数控曲线齿锥齿轮铣齿机YKD2250A	天津第一机床总厂	王保强　陈晓鹏　肖绪才　黄玉玺　刘　峰	二等奖	1994
204	城市环境综合整治定量考核指标体系的研究	天津市环境保护局、天津市环境保护研究所	宫　伟　包景岭　叶以文　侯晓珉　王连生	二等奖	1994
205	不锈钢餐具成套技术装备(60万打/年)	天津市不锈钢制品研究所、天津市斯特轻工技术装备开发公司	杨廷寿　王雅琪　李玉珍　李柏林　于万铭　王福森　刘继斌	二等奖	1994
206	抗血清性促性腺激素(APMSG)的研究及中间试验	天津实验动物中心、中国农业科学院畜牧研究所	张春礼　唐蔚东　陈萸芳　罗应荣　张一玲　刘恩柱　史光华	二等奖	1994
207	处理工业废水用塑料微型孔过滤装置	天津市华光过滤器材厂	李秀敏　王恒明　王建光	二等奖	1994
208	35KV及以下交联聚乙烯绝缘电力电缆	天津市电缆总厂	佟　辉　单继先　席会陵　卢玮琦　姚　剑	二等奖	1994
209	复合维生素、复合微量元素食品强化剂的研究	军事医学科学院卫生学环境医学研究所	王喜生　杨生奎　闫　志　刘继鹏　杨奎修	二等奖	1994
210	放射工作人员外照射个人剂量监测、评价及其质量控制体系的研究	中国医学科学院放射医学研究所	张良安　张文艺　苑淑渝　常贺新　宋世均	二等奖	1994

续表6 获天津市科学技术奖(一、二等奖)项目

序号	项目名称	获奖单位	获奖人	获奖等级	获奖年份
211	MKL7175型精密数控强力成型磨床	天津磨床总厂	王冬梅 朱炎文 王学军 赵红岩 吴彦月	二等奖	1994
212	天津市公安局人像数据库管理系统	天津市创远电脑系统发展公司、天津市公安局人口信息计算机管理系统工程领导小组	谢睦南 甘建仁 刘文胜 曹新国 李向华 李明军	二等奖	1994
213	玻璃器皿成型自控系统节能优化设计	天津轻工学院、天津市玻璃器皿厂	张建国 曾孝宇 徐洪福 任立选 艾高烈 刘玉松 刘玉珊	二等奖	1994
214	本质安全防暴电路用集散型、电动型仪表信号电缆	天津安琪尔特种线缆有限公司	王怀善 李洪志 王彦 李琪 韩家友	二等奖	1994
215	津春二号黄瓜新产品	天津市黄瓜研究所	李加旺 李光	二等奖	1994
216	BGCK-I型玻管外径壁厚测控仪	天津大学精密仪器系、天津市宝成电子玻璃厂	孙学珠 陈兴梧 陈本智 何在新 杨贺林 苗长彬 王锡颖	二等奖	1994
217	空调器生产线	天津市轻工装备研究所	邓学孟 高士森 曲和平 王林 马守智	二等奖	1994
218	JCT-2000微机控制通用荧光磁粉检测线	机械工业部第五设计研究院、天津市第六机床厂	朱德金 谭鑫 段继红 袁惠清 刘儒安 朱趁龙 许玲	二等奖	1994
219	PXB系列消声器	天津市长城过滤设备厂	赵宽 王建立 李恩怀 王守印 刘四合	二等奖	1994
220	五十万亩水稻综合技术推广工程	天津市农林局	张金刚 刘俭 孙连祥 张鹏至 贾子玉 田广元 裴家林 王印来 李树清 陈怀东 张宝成 钱聚荫	二等奖	1994
221	五十万头瘦肉型猪推广工程	天津市畜牧局、天津市畜牧兽医站、天津市畜牧兽医研究所	叶月皎 樊航奇 秦守愚 周礼贤 王文杰 李绍兴 孙玉淑 倪守明 齐宗佑 王子伦 董恩政 李会生	二等奖	1994
222	应用导热油节能技术	天津市油毡厂	薛德生 耿凤祥 孙树勋 杜正 陈立新 郭芳	二等奖	1994
223	蓟县农业高产高效益综合技术示范工程	天津市蓟县人民政府、天津市农业科学院	蒋如生 周连荣 曹兴瑞 刘燕方 侯明 李千军 张旭 田广元 蒋振国 沈欣 孙国兴 王景禄	二等奖	1994
224	京津塘高速公路高新技术产业带(天津段)发展研究	天津市规划局、南开大学、天津师范大学、天津市新技术产业园区管委会、天津市科学学所、天津市科技信息所	穆学明 薛敬孝 谭作顺 张志超 楚义芳 宋大铭 虞泰年	一等奖	1994
225	九十年代天津农业的基本思路与对策研究	天津市科学技术信息研究所	王虎权 申凌田 毛科军 李春成	二等奖	1994
226	天津园林生态经济发展战略研究	天津市园林管理局、天津市和平区城建局	贺振 徐金祥 徐恒醇	二等奖	1994
227	华北地区冬小麦公顷产量4500至5250kg栽培技术规程指定与推广	天津市农业技术推广站、天津市技术临督局、武清县农业技术推广中心、宝坻县农业技术推广中心等	姚振凡 王瑞卿 武秀兰 李杰 于长来 汪俊峰 董山	二等奖	1994
228	天津市地面水功能区域划分及环境质量标准的研究	天津市环境保护科学研究所、天津市环境保护局水质管理处	陈自强 李桂芳 蒋林燕 孟昭赢	二等奖	1994
229	科技成果推广优秀工作奖	天津市东丽区科学技术委员会	王天春 刘湘会 郭庆明 张红卫	二等奖	1994
230	科技成果推广优秀工作奖	天津市农业科学院科研管理处	马克俭 崔永兹 蒲长光 陈益山 李家庆 田学敏 张要武 郭郢 凌喆 刘雪玲 霍文娟	二等奖	1994
231	高负荷苯氧化制顺酐固定床催化剂的技术开发	天津市中河化工厂	姚少华 霍玉 黎吉非 武学军 张建刚	一等奖	1995

续表6 获天津市科学技术奖(一、二等奖)项目

序号	项目名称	获奖单位	获奖人	获奖等级	获奖年份
232	基于动态特性的数控机床研究与开发	天津大学、天津第一机床总厂、天津市天动数控专用设备技术开发公司	刘又午 王树新 吴建华 王树勋 柴宝连 李文富 周秉勇	一等奖	1995
233	津春四号黄瓜新品种选育	天津市黄瓜研究所	吕淑珍 霍振荣 陈正武 沈文云 马德华	一等奖	1995
234	蔬菜种子通用包衣剂的研制及应用	天津市蔬菜研究所	马文荷 刘 莉 孙德岭 于莹娟 张宝珍	二等奖	1995
235	预应力混凝土用低松弛钢绞线	天津市预应力钢丝一厂	邹春明 张秀凤 金庆波 翟巧玲 徐 昕	二等奖	1995
236	新型屏、锥预热及玻壳退火处理线研制	机械部第五设计研究院、津京玻壳股份有限公司	张金声 岳云鄂 赵建刚 司国炯 张 伟 高 祥 尚德志	二等奖	1995
237	鲤鱼出血性腐败病的研究	天津农学院	邢克智 蔡中华 刘茂春 陈成勋 郭永军	二等奖	1995
238	中国北方人才市场人才智力信息系统	中国北方人才市场、北京伟仕公司天津分公司	王强岱 李 新 朱骁勇 贺英凯 李继成 张 鑫	二等奖	1995
239	正常国人髂骨形态计量参数的研究	天津医科大学总医院、天津市内分泌研究所	邱明才 杨宝恩 王觉英 李玉坤 朱 梅	二等奖	1995
240	芬必得缓释胶囊生产工艺	中美天津史克制药有限公司	黄 斐 徐海潮 魏洪君 刘益明 张卫华	二等奖	1995
241	天津大银鱼的增殖、移植及人工繁殖技术研究	天津市农村工作委员会、天津农学院、天津市水产研究所	倪守明 荣长宽 王玉佩 张洪贵 岳丙宜 周瑞莲 杨 祯	二等奖	1995
242	高能量摩托车用全密闭免维护铅酸蓄电池	天津市斯诺旅通电器技术有限公司	陈有孝 梁高俊 胡风翔 徐志金	二等奖	1995
243	鲤鱼三倍体的诱导及应用的研究	天津农学院	董 仕 陶炳春 乔秀亭 刘茂春 谢宝华	二等奖	1995
244	哺乳动物靶组织对位听神经节神经元体外存活与分化的影响	天津市第一中心医院	周祥宁	二等奖	1995
245	第43届世乒赛计算机系统	天津市电子计算机研究所	郑 平 沈大龙 蔡连忠 戴晓萍 刘俊伶	二等奖	1995
246	四屏显示出租汽车里程计价表的研制	天津市计量技术研究所	张大建 张 伟 尚家甫 艾学璞 邸雅军	二等奖	1995
247	中小桥CAD(LQCAD)系统	天津市市政工程设计研究院、西南交通大学	张汝亮 周绍烈 陈孟达 张 强 刘元久 许庭华 郑和平	二等奖	1995
248	智能局域网研究	南开大学计算机与系统科学系	吴功宜 曹 勇 徐敬东 韩毅刚 周 乐	二等奖	1995
249	小麦制粉粉间设备及工艺自控系统	核工业理化工程研究院	李文洪 田肇生 朱志贤 徐家驹 郭本余	二等奖	1995
250	小尾寒羊的引进选育及其利用	天津农学院、天津市警备区青光农场	王学玲 周广森 杨晋怀 孙新平 盛广宏 王燕生 曹风歧	二等奖	1995
251	针刺对快速老化痴呆模型小白鼠(ASM-P/8)脑功能影响的实验研究	天津中医学院第一附属医院	石学敏 韩景献 李 平 赵俊宏 刘庆忠	二等奖	1995
252	SGB高温工业电视系统保护装置系列产品	天津市电视技术研究所	李月国 王东江 周秀云 韩 洪 陈惠芝	二等奖	1995
253	天津市蔬菜生产现代综合技术的应用	天津市蔬菜研究所、天津市西青区农林局、天津市水利科学研究所、天津市农业机械研究所	刘俊云 任锡俊 阎德来 刘国宁 葛淑芳 王文琴 李志邈	二等奖	1995
254	氟中毒的骨形态计量学系列研究	天津医科大学总医院、天津市内分泌研究所	邱明才 陈兴源 白成江 张 鑫 齐全乐	二等奖	1995

续表6 获天津市科学技术奖(一、二等奖)项目

序号	项目名称	获奖单位	获奖人	获奖等级	获奖年份
255	肾动脉狭窄性高血压的影像学研究	天津医科大学总医院	贺能树 曹喜才 吴恩惠 白景文 杨海贤	二等奖	1995
256	复方丹参滴丸	天津市天使力联合制药公司	阎希军 吴乃峰 杨伟钦 张利 张国民	二等奖	1995
257	津青50、60天大白菜新品种选育	天津市津北蔬菜研究所	范贵明 施瑞和 边学孔 范玉杰 王贵森	二等奖	1995
258	微血管压力直接测量方法及其应用的研究	天津市心血管病研究所、天津市胸科医院	金正根 王乃欣 张化新	二等奖	1995
259	海河(市区段)污染控制技术的研究	天津市环境保护科学研究所、天津市水利科学研究所、天津市水文总站、天津市环境监测中心、农业部环境保护检测所	黄亭 古建国 郭青平 郑裕君 袁秀文 秦宝平 龙沛湘	二等奖	1995
260	膜式分步结晶法生产均四甲苯技术研究	天津石油化工公司研究所	孙绪江 张俊民 王同舜 张军 齐彦伟	二等奖	1995
261	乙肝单克隆抗体细胞标的建立及其产品化	南开大学、天津市卫生防病中心	汪和睦 范殿英 鲁玉瓦 于素文 汪洲 韩风文 刘勇	二等奖	1995
262	优质涤纶仿真丝绸技术及产品研究	天津丝绸集团公司丝绒厂、中国纺织科学研究院	孙惠菊 潘菊芳 李国桂 卫世文 杨文芳 杨计军 柳景明	二等奖	1995
263	十万亩名特优水产品增养殖技术推广	天津市水产技术推广站、天津市水产局养殖处	杨金江 支宗伟 缴建华 刘金全 董景川 沈晓红 霍仕俐 金文生 孙龙仪 吴士顺 张洪选 刘国祥	二等奖	1995
264	天津市十万亩河蟹增养殖技术推广	天津市水产技术推广站、天津市水产局养殖处	时建伟 张勤 赵嗣宾 霍仕俐 刘国祥 张希才 潘秀义 王化明 李新丽 张毅 孙龙仪 杨殿臣	二等奖	1995
265	鸡传染性法氏囊病防治技术推广	天津禽病诊断中心	张森瑞 李茂祥 王瑞久 何宏虎 刘毅 曹少清 高国森 王淑英 宋宝霞 庞淑英 杨亚东 齐秀芬	二等奖	1995
266	盐滩绿化技术的推广应用	天津经济技术开发区管理委员会、天津经济技术开发区绿化委员会、天津经济技术开发区规划建设管理局	张万钧 吴凤起 高亭 王建华 周洪文 王树生 马家勇 陈铁明 王英 李秉奎 刘立民 刘桂茹	二等奖	1995
267	天津市津南区农村能源综合建设	天津市津南区农村能源综合建设办公室	孙希英 杨学义 杜金华 薛克伦 杨爱平 赵世昌 田家綮 王沛 王绍梧 任万山 潘巨泉 房式彬	二等奖	1995
268	大跨度P.C斜拉桥牵索式长挂篮施工新技术	天津市市政工程设计研究院、铁道部第三工程局、同济大学	黄大健 陈克济 赵智 陈德伟 韩振勇 李栓虎	二等奖	1995
269	天津市水资源管理和决策支持系统	天津市水资源项目研究管理中心、天津市经济发展研究所、南开大学管理系、天津市科技信息研究所、天津市环境保护研究所	周年生等集体奖	二等奖	1995
270	天津市跨世纪经济发展的关键技术	天津市科学技术评价中心、天津市计划委员会科技处	雷风徐 任庆文 王振鹏 余学林 常冬至 何芳荣 陈悦	二等奖	1995
271	北方技术交易市场建立与运作研究	河北工业大学、天津市技术市场协会、天津市专利管理局、中国技术市场报社、天津市科学技术信息研究所	张贤模 赵景洲 宋祖祺 张乃玺 李浩志 冯国梧 赵敬	二等奖	1995
272	天津市有毒有害气体排放标准的研究	天津市环境保护科学研究所	孙申 阎成芳 陈隆 黄平沙 单景芬	二等奖	1995
273	食品中放射性物质限制浓度和检验方法两项国家标准的研究和制定	中国医学科学院放射医学研究所、甘肃省放射卫生监督监测所、中国辐射防护研究院	诸洪达 韩佩珍 雷尊成 黄星辉 沙边茂	二等奖	1995

续表6 获天津市科学技术奖(一、二等奖)项目

序号	项目名称	获奖单位	获奖人	获奖等级	获奖年份
274	针织内衣表面疵点彩色样照	天津市针织技术研究所……	徐桂兰 邢志贵 刘凤荣 张勤学 王作民 郭卫民 崔 征	二等奖	1995
275	科技成果推广工作优秀奖	天津农林局科教处	贾玉生 王 树 王瑞卿 王 斌 袁淑欣 徐士珠 姚庆云 杨 林 王福玉 韩树婷 刘守愚 王家武	二等奖	1995
276	科技成果推广工作优秀奖	天津市畜牧局科教处	祝培瑜 杨铁民 闫恩泽 吴汝毅 毛育才	二等奖	1995
277	热网络及综合用能技术	天津石油化工公司涤纶厂、国家环保局南京环境科学研究所	阎尔平 续治敏 张国利 张晓弟 陈双基 付连臣 王百富	一等奖	1996
278	科技成果推广工作优秀奖	天津市蔬菜研究所	张国梁 运广荣 于莹娟 张大方 张恩瑾 任光辉 丁仲凡 史永华 赵景芝 覃圣雷 李卫民 张光源 吕敬刚 徐晨英 蒋玉梅	一等奖	1996
279	津春系列黄瓜新品种推广	天津市黄瓜研究所	侯 锋 吕淑珍 高象昶 哈玉洁 马德华 李加旺 陈正武 邹志毅 李 光 霍振荣 杨 森 李淑菊 王 全 任双亮 孙忠魁	一等奖	1996
280	大开间消能抗震轻型建筑新体系研究	天津市新型建材建筑设计研究院、天津大学土木工程系	陆锡蕾 严士起 张 方 谷 贻 陈云霞 曹祖同 王 燕	二等奖	1996
281	超高层建筑钢管砼柱板结构体系应用技术研究	天津市第六建筑工程公司、天津美新建筑设计有限公司	王学旺 张佩生 何玉泉 廖勋海 葛志义 韩世明 许伯珊	二等奖	1996
282	高品质溴氨酸生产工艺	天津理工学院	李绍武 吕金魁 郑嗣华 刘金文 温同生	二等奖	1996
283	聚氨酯软泡淘汰氟里昂技术	天津市聚氨酯塑料制品厂	温和平 刘桂芬 韩 敏 赵家柱 王 丽	二等奖	1996
284	中华鳖(甲鱼)集约化养殖技术的研究	天津农学院、天津市西青区小南河养殖公司、天津市蓟县水产局	邢克智 蔡中华 乔秀亭 刘茂春 郭永军 马敬福 张光羽	二等奖	1996
285	交变湿热室智能控制及试验系统	天津大学	郝久玉 李惠敏 许中昌 范金生 王吉林	二等奖	1996
286	TCZ-510型野战猝发汉字终端	天津通信广播公司、中国人民解放军总参谋部通信部驻天津市军事代表室	陈风云 高 瑛 刘 岩 李相东 秦宝连 马学迎 马 严	二等奖	1996
287	NB系列无触点式CO_2/MAG弧焊机	天津市电焊机总厂	褚 华 周建中 梁国强 张 楠 张洪元	二等奖	1996
288	经皮血管镜直视心包活检引流灌洗术	天津市胸科医院、天津市心血管病研究所	吴建国 裴诚民 耿庆国 张志尧 张我素 梁爽林 程津新	二等奖	1996
289	N115炭黑	天津海豚炭黑有限公司	刘俊才 仇祯祥 唐金利 张宝明 刘克明	二等奖	1996
290	航测解析数字化成图	天津市测绘院	胡 珂 王 伟 周 奎 张晓东 张 慧	二等奖	1996
291	CS-100水溶性透明漆	天津化学试剂五厂、中国人民解放军防化研究院技术开发部三部	董淑香 张 建 吴相洪 韩舒琴 黄宝菊 张柏良 吴嘉生	二等奖	1996

续表6 获天津市科学技术奖(一、二等奖)项目

序号	项目名称	获奖单位	获奖人	获奖等级	获奖年份
292	重型颅脑损伤中弥漫性脑损害的临床及病理生理研究	天津医科大学总医院	杨树源 王明璐 张赛 温智勇 杨学军	二等奖	1996
293	夏利轿车前、后减震器总成	天津市汽车减震器厂	赵凡 王作元 刘宝山 高士来 冯会生	二等奖	1996
294	36.00-51-58层级无内胎巨型工程机械轮胎	天津国际联合轮胎橡胶有限公司	郝力 李佩琦 赵巍 李强 戴永良	二等奖	1996
295	玻璃器皿压制生产线的研制	天津轻工业学院、天津市玻璃器皿厂	徐洪福 张建国 曾孝宇 陈浩 刘玉松 刘玉珊 李双月	二等奖	1996
296	稳定塘工程及风能曝气技术研究	天津市汉沽区环境保护局、天津市环境保护科学研究所	边嘉敏 张建生 阎玉荣 张金鸿 蒋林燕 刘启荣 谭步云	二等奖	1996
297	钾肥对主要作物增产作用的研究	天津市农科院土壤肥料研究所	周艺敏 景海春 朱静华 兰跃龙 翁莉萍	二等奖	1996
298	汽车胶工业性试验	天津光电通信公司、三友(天津)高分子技术有限公司	李士学 戴岩军 高芝香 姜继艳 李建武 王军 张连仙	二等奖	1996
299	检测乳腺导管液肿瘤标志物诊断早期乳腺癌的研究	天津市肿瘤医院	李树玲 张瑾 国爱英 方志沂 郎义方	二等奖	1996
300	鸡肾脏型传染性支气管炎预防的研究	天津市北辰区青光养鸡总场	康立文 黄秀齐 甘孟侯 朱广明 刘兴龙	二等奖	1996
301	烟草霜霉病卵孢子提取方法研究	中华人民共和国天津动植物检疫局、中华人民共和国动植物检疫局	章正 杨维长 王学令 张树德 崔铁军 魏亚东 罗加凤	二等奖	1996
302	前列腺素E2对动脉粥样硬化影响和机理的实验研究	天津医科大学基础医学院	邱近明 宋文静 赵庆伟 徐东波 刘术娟	二等奖	1996
303	聚氯乙烯绝缘聚氯乙烯护套数字设备电缆	天津有容通讯线缆有限公司	吕铁宏 张惠敏 王美怡 刘士龙 范有孚	二等奖	1996
304	加工、兼用型黄瓜新品种津春五号	天津市黄瓜研究所	哈玉洁 王全 赵国芸	二等奖	1996
305	MJL系列密集成套型罗茨鼓风机	天津市鼓风机总厂	冯育棠 杨光 李文英 赵学录 孟庆伟	二等奖	1996
306	毛精纺休闲西装面料	天津市仁立毛纺织厂	曹汝红 怀森平 蔡琴 姚明珠 陈伟	二等奖	1996
307	天津口岸推广国际集装箱运输系统(多式联运)工业性试验成果项目	天津市交通委员会、天津港务局	冯房柱 刘明哲 于汝民 康群网 王茜东 高文禄 范广春 王泽之 牟承云 徐英 耿靖献 丁彩英	二等奖	1996
308	十万头肉牛饲养技术推广	天津市畜牧局、天津市农机局	叶月皎 戴冠英 樊航奇 周礼贤 王文杰 王玉柱 祝培瑜 王子伦 王玉柱 薄小平 董恩政 金程顺	二等奖	1996
309	利用余热热载体加热等综合节能新技术生产优质石墨电极	天津市碳素厂	任建疆 毕道敏 张宝田 孙继江 陈秀敏	二等奖	1996
310	关于“双优化工程”的研究	天津市规划设计管理局、天津市土地管理局、天津市城市规划设计研究院	赵友华 蔡云鹏 张志升 霍兵 张志强 白艳霞 蔡胜任	二等奖	1996
311	天津市三十万辆轿车发展战略研究	天津市计划委员会、天津市科学技术协会、天津汽车工业(集团)有限公司、中国汽车技术研究中心、机械工业部第五设计研究院	汪声銮 冯超 张道成 王耀明 张正智 柴志安 王淑琴	二等奖	1996
312	H/YB-1型摇摆台台体同轴度误差测量及安装基准给定系统	天津大学、机械部天津工程机械研究所	叶声华 朱鸿锡 孟青伟 陶国智 陈长江 王仲 张晓捷	二等奖	1996

续表6 获天津市科学技术奖(一、二等奖)项目

序号	项目名称	获奖单位	获奖人	获奖等级	获奖年份
313	75kwaSIT高频感应加热装置	天津市高频设备厂、天津市金能电力电子有限公司	姜士林 赵长汉 李家骥 姜钰明 张永发 安文彬 陈 莉	二等奖	1996
314	新型吸附材料–碳分子筛	天津市京津中船吸附材料厂、北京中船气体工程开发公司	姚庆瑞 杨宝文 林成永 刘学麾 李 辅	二等奖	1996
315	李—张氏术式切除直肠子宫内膜异位病变的研究	天津市妇女保健所、天津市滨江医院、天津市塘沽区肛肠医院	李宝森 张殿文	二等奖	1996
316	红细胞沉降动态研究及血沉曲线分析记录仪的研制	天津中医学院、天津大学	张柏礼 戴品忠 刘正光 高秀梅 徐宗佩	二等奖	1996
317	不进行血管重建的颈动脉分歧部切除术后脑血流代偿机制血流动力学研究	天津市肿瘤医院、天津市肿瘤研究所	李树玲 高 明 颜宪秋 刘经祖	二等奖	1996
318	肩锁、锁骨外固定器治疗肩锁关节脱位锁骨骨折	天津市天津医院	马 毅 王小同 李延宏	二等奖	1996
319	FA／O高纯多功能界面活性剂的研究及在微电子中应用	河北工业大学	刘玉岭 徐晓辉 李相都 庄 天	二等奖	1996
320	明胶海绵吸附卡氮芥局部化疗治疗脑恶性肿瘤	天津市环湖医院、天津市第二中心医院、中国人民解放军271医院	赵克明 贡雁衍	二等奖	1996
321	肿瘤的放射免疫显像新技术的建立及其临床应用	天津市肿瘤医院	庞 雁 何景华 牛瑞芳 王殿昌 高 硕	二等奖	1996
322	LN–101基因脉冲导入仪	天津理工学院	徐宝强	二等奖	1996
323	新型袢式胆肠吻合术的研究	天津市肿瘤医院、天津市肿瘤研究所	郝希山 李 强 顾 林 王殿昌	二等奖	1996
324	《中国含油气盆地油田水》	大港油田集团有限责任公司	高锡兴 李俊军	二等奖	1996
325	《腹部外科实践》	天津医科大学总医院、天津医科大学第一中心、医院中国医药科技出版社	吴咸中 黄耀权 于素芝	二等奖	1996
326	《头颈肿瘤学》	天津市肿瘤医院、中国医科大学附属第一医院、上海第二医科大学附属第九人民医院、北京医科院肿瘤医院、天津科学技术出版社	李树玲 费声重 邱蔚六 屠规益 刘经组 葛正津 于素芝	二等奖	1996
327	《临床心律学》	天津市医科大学第二医院、天津科学技术出版社	石毓澍 郝俊利	二等奖	1996
328	《临床皮肤病鉴别诊断学》	天津医科大学总医院、中国医药科技出版社	傅志宜 于素芝	二等奖	1996
329	《妇产科病理学》	天津市第一中心医院、天津市科学技术出版社	林 崧 于素芝	二等奖	1996
330	《中西医结合皮肤病学》	天津市长征医院、天津科学技术出版社	边天羽 丁素先 刘世明 毛舒和 马 洪	二等奖	1996
331	《中医纲目》	天津中医学院第一附属医院	石学敏 周继曾 邵文虎 牛元起	二等奖	1996
332	27.00–49–48层级E3、B4型无内胎巨型工程机械轮胎	天津国际联合轮胎橡胶有限公司	赵 巍 戴永良 李 强 张文怡 张巨光	一等奖	1997
333	高品质H–酸生产工艺	天津理工学院	李绍武 吕金魁 郑嗣华 曹玉臣 闫绍柏	一等奖	1997
334	东方红3号广播通信卫星太阳能电池阵(8010太阳电池阵)	电子工业部第十八研究所	唐 军 黄才勇 施增模 徐寿岩 薛祖铭	一等奖	1997
335	百万头瘦肉型猪综合技术推广工程	天津市畜牧局、天津市畜牧兽医站	叶月皎 史迎春 樊航奇 王文杰 马丽荣 王子伦 孙玉淑 董恩政 王建民 祝培瑜 刘德永 王凤双 李振宽 王德恩 祁金栋	一等奖	1997

续表6　　获天津市科学技术奖(一、二等奖)项目

序号	项目名称	获奖单位	获奖人	获奖等级	获奖年份
336	津春三号黄瓜新品种选育	天津市黄瓜研究所	侯　锋　吕淑珍　马德华　霍振荣　李淑菊	二等奖	1997
337	大型火电机组非线性振动事故机理分析及应用研究	天津大学、天津市电力科学研究院、天津军粮城发电厂	陈予恕　金宗武　田家玉　丁　千　张　宁　赵　凯　曹树谦	二等奖	1997
338	低位抽真空加固吹填土及其地下基础研究	天津市水利科学研究所	曹大正　宋士良　马淑玲　张文清　王守霆	二等奖	1997
339	电工产品有限元逆问题及优化设计	河北工业大学	汪友华　张惠娟　饶利芸　彭玉清　颜威利	二等奖	1997
340	杨家泊中国对虾全封闭养殖技术研究	天津市汉沽区杨家泊镇人民政府、天津农学院	荣长宽　李桂杰　郑术本　刘堂凤　陶广龙　杨宗东　郭海利	二等奖	1997
341	多发梗塞性痴呆大鼠模型的实验研究和中药拮抗作用的观察	天津中医学院、北京中医药大学	张伯礼　王永炎　张云岭　梅建勋　王同胜　刘金生　徐宗佩	二等奖	1997
342	菜豆锈病菌生理小种鉴定及抗锈病育种	天津市蔬菜研究所	岳　彬　孙立全　李国红　王郁铨　徐晨英	二等奖	1997
343	现代化草坪草卷生产与建植工艺	天津农工商总公司、天津红港绿茵花草有限公司	张殿京　孙克泰　李悦生　孙国庆　白智生　李德增　周之杭	二等奖	1997
344	PY160C、PY180平地机	天津市天工工程机械有限公司	邢全清　吴光朗　孙孝安　尹金凯　周培昌	二等奖	1997
345	天津港维护疏浚工程与回淤规律的研究	交通部天津水运工程科学研究所、渤海石油港口建设工程公司	蒋睢耀　温令平　冯学英　凌光懋　钱平生　徐金山　何荣福	二等奖	1997
346	三维动态模拟试验系统与试验技术	中国汽车技术研究中心、长春汽车研究所、航空工业总公司609所	张维纶　施光涛　潘星辰　朱　旗　丁　昕	二等奖	1997
347	大园坯连铸用耐火材料的研究与应用	天津钢管公司炼钢厂、洛阳耐火材料研究院、南苑耐火材料有限公司	孙兆宽　周川生　景重阳　于　青　陈　超　陈　鹏　邹立新	二等奖	1997
348	家禽主要病毒性传染病免疫防治技术研究	天津市禽病诊断培训中心	李茂祥　田仁位　段印祥　何宏虎　刘　毅	二等奖	1997
349	马蔺子素放射增敏研究	天津市医药科学研究所	李德华　吴寿金　王士贤　匡　朴　许竞竞	二等奖	1997
350	基于曙光机的天财税收征管系统	天津大学、天津天大天财股份公司、天津市国家税务局、天津市地方税务局	王以真　周时悌　雒明山　王中胜　马玉彤　杨新子　王爱民	二等奖	1997
351	150t高功率电炉合理供电曲线研究	天津钢管公司、北京科技大学	邹文正　李士琦　姜桂年　孙开明　姚如松　周国平　谷力功	二等奖	1997
352	电话号码七位升八位技术方案研制与实施	天津市邮电管理局、天津市电话局	滕　勇　王安平　薄今纲　刘克康　傅彦生　孙秀亭　吴宇辰	二等奖	1997
353	城市污泥土地处理技术研究	天津市环境监测中心、天津市经济技术开发区总公司园林绿化公司、天津市环境保护科学研究院	沈伟然　殷　红　张文具　党秀芳　王秀珍　张万钧　赵景林	二等奖	1997
354	电梯导轨型钢及工艺	天津峰利电梯轨有限公司	刘京礼　杜连峰　韩文勇　吴红利	二等奖	1997
355	针刺对快速老化痴呆模型鼠活性基因作用机制与临床关系的研究	天津中医学院第一附属医院、南开大学微生物学系、全国针灸临床研究中心	石学敏　韩景献　温廷益　邢来君　王　舒　李　平　蔡刚强	二等奖	1997
356	眼眶肿瘤B超,CT,MRI定性诊断及眶内容切除后眶腔修复的研究	天津医科大学第二医院	宋国祥　孙丰源　肖利华　何彦津　唐东润	二等奖	1997
357	天津联科信息网络系统研究	天津市科学技术信息研究所	余学林　刘文成　万家泰　顾建成　徐肖君	二等奖	1997

续表6 获天津市科学技术奖(一、二等奖)项目

序号	项目名称	获奖单位	获奖人	获奖等级	获奖年份
358	重复压裂及裂缝纵向控制工艺技术	大港油田集团有限责任公司	李延美 何志勇 程运甫 邹 剑 张胜传	二等奖	1997
359	瘦肉型皮特兰猪的引进与杂交利用的研究	天津市津南区畜牧水产局、天津市畜牧兽医研究所、天津市津南区咸水沽镇四里沽村四联养殖厂、天津市津南区咸水沽镇克俭猪场	祁金栋 刘国恒 李千军 刘树华 李忠友	二等奖	1997
360	节粮型日粮快速羔羊肥育技术的研究	天津农学院	王学玲 周广森 张学炜 王子伦 王洪凤	二等奖	1997
361	易染型仿毛短纤维的研究-阳离子染料常压沸染聚酯短纤维(ECDP)	天津市化学纤维研究所、济南合成纤维厂	陈淑珍 范 钧 田毅生 郁成礼 高健中 尉鹏飞 孙 曼	二等奖	1997
362	船舶柴油机运行状态连续无孔监测仪	天津大学机械工程学院、天津远洋运输公司	郝志勇 王永福 舒歌群 李正国 张殿昌 汤春祥 薛 远	二等奖	1997
363	超大规模本地电话网综合测量与维护系统	天津市电话局 、天津市威望计算机通信公司	滕 勇 薄今纲 徐 江 王 芸 李雪刚 李烨勃 国立园	二等奖	1997
364	静海县十万亩旱作农业综合技术推广示范	静海县人民政府、天津市农业机械局科教处、天津市农科院中心实验室、天津市土壤肥料工作站	袁大恒 戴冠英 谷跃琴 金 红 唐玉柱 王文玲 黄世江	二等奖	1997
365	新型高效杀螨杀虫剂"哒螨灵"中试	天津市新农药技术开发研究中心、天津市京津农药厂	王学礼 邢玉安 申日升	二等奖	1997
366	ZB43型硬盒硬条包装机组	天津市华特包装机械有限责任公司第一分公司	张国维 李 梅 王自起 刘万轩 孟宪伍	二等奖	1997
367	JX2005半自动叶轮型面粗精铣机床	天津市机械研究所、天津市鼓风机总厂	邢长元 马庆双 姜 云 蒋 丽 刘 平 郑家燧 李悦来	二等奖	1997
368	SJ-9608多通道通讯记录仪	天津市科华新技术开发公司、中国科学技术大学科技实业总公司	冯佑璋 王仁华 任旭光 戴礼荣 张淑敏 徐 超 王学强	二等奖	1997
369	地下连续墙多层锚杆深基坑支护正逆结合施工研究与应用	天津市第二建筑工程有限公司	韩日君 顾晓鲁 付金栋 郭金星 张国良	二等奖	1997
370	十万亩蔬菜综合配套技术推广	天津市蔬菜技术推广站、天津市人民政府蔬菜办公室	关铁炼 赵秀萍 孙书蕴 张建树 李庆寨 王玉仿 乔永久 潘巨泉 张秀莲 程瑞明 王洪月 王永强	二等奖	1997
371	水稻品种"津稻1187"推广	天津市水稻研究所、天津市种子管理站	刘瑞符 陈秀琴 张兆芬 刘振华 谷守贤 刘学军 陆之田 刘 建 马忠友 张 旭 金洪英 王 立	二等奖	1997
372	王朝葡萄酒酿造品种优质丰产栽培技术的开发与推广	天津农垦集团总公司、天津市林业果树研究所、中法合营王朝葡萄酿酒有限公司	胡承宏 齐思儒 修德仁 田卫东 高献亭 李 巍 程瑞平	二等奖	1997
373	天津市东郊污水处理厂新技术开发与应用	天津市市政工程设计研究院	冯生华 周 霆 沈云法 张大群 郝振明	二等奖	1997
374	金钢桥改造工程新技术开发与应用	天津市市政工程设计研究所、天津市第一市政工程公司、天津市市政工程研究院	王淑训 王顺来 刘旭锴 徐耀宇 李运舟 张振学 王立军	二等奖	1997
375	斜拉桥施工控制系统	天津市市政工程设计研究院、同济大学	黄大健 韩振勇 钱永龄 陈德伟 何 铭 周立志	二等奖	1997
376	天津海域污海洋处置和环境管理信息系统研究	天津大学机械工程学院、天津市环境保护局海洋环境保护办公室、天津市环境监测中心	陶建华 王德龙 辛志伟 张亦泳 安 敦 王泽良 曾庆云	二等奖	1997

续表6 **获天津市科学技术奖(一、二等奖)项目**

序号	项目名称	获奖单位	获奖人	获奖等级	获奖年份
377	天津市通信与电子信息产业发展战略研究	天津市计划委员会、天津市科学技术协会、天津市电子仪表工业总公司、天津市邮电管理局、中国联通天津分公司、天津市海慧海洋工程研究所	吴咏诗 杨恩泽 卢桂章 丁润涛 陈树春 周剑琴 张建和	二等奖	1997
378	汽车维护工艺规范	天津市交通局科学技术研究所、天津市长途汽车公司、天津市汽车运输五场、天津市汽车运输六场	游治国 何 昭 王玉宽 张骏发 张士群 马学高 孔宪鹏	二等奖	1997
379	科技成果推广工作优秀奖	天津市人民政府农业办公室	张树明 倪守明 郝淑敏 宋绍奎 吕福旭 孙盛图 刘宝成 赵 萍 张宝成 杨昌熹	二等奖	1997
380	科技成果推广工作优秀奖	天津市畜牧局	周礼贤 祝培瑜 隋 苗 王瑞久 倪守鹏 刘永成 沈建业 董恩政 张永跃 李至林 贺明宽 张建华	二等奖	1997
381	科技成果推广工作优秀奖	天津市农业机械局科教处	王润卿 戴冠英 胡 伟 邓树奎 陈 芳 张宝苓	二等奖	1997
382	八千亩河堤经济林综合开发示范工程(滨海盐碱地苹果密植速生丰产栽培技术研究)	天津市大港区科学技术委员会、天津市大港区农林畜牧局	张世启 李乃惠 周永辉 张富民 窦洪树 王希江 于宝恒	二等奖	1997
383	3.4–二氯苯胺	天津兴水化工有限公司	刘百里 肖水生 张天永 张会清 任立福	二等奖	1997
384	十万只羊肉综合技术开发	天津市东丽区畜牧水产局	刘景文 卢玉明 刘明坤 杨永凯 赵海东	二等奖	1997
385	抗AIDS药物筛选新模型	南开大学	耿运琪 陈启民 刘淑红 陈家童 梁 栋	二等奖	1997
386	全方位视觉灯光自动引导系统	天津理工学院	曹作良 张立明	二等奖	1997
387	《石学敏针灸学》	天津中医学院第一附属医院、天津科学技术出版社	石学敏 卞金玲 李 岩 吴玉兰 于伯海 张慧勇 周继曾	二等奖	1997
388	《X线诊断学基本功》	天津医科大学第二医院、天津医科大学总医院、天津科学技术出版社	廉宗澄 贺能树 于荣溥 刘阴棣 吴复扬 魏津生 郝俊立	二等奖	1997
389	《骨关节X线诊断学》	天津医科大学总医院、天津市天津医院、人民卫生出版社	李景学 孙鼎元 王 兵	二等奖	1997
390	《卵巢临床与病理》	天津市第二中心医院、天津科学技术出版社	范郎娣 张慧英 王开伟 袁向远 王丽华	二等奖	1997
391	《临床骨科解剖学》	天津医科大学总医院、天津科学技术出版社	郭世绂 陈金铨 郝俊利	二等奖	1997
392	《骨肿瘤诊断图谱》	天津市天津医院、天津科技翻译出版公司	李瑞宗 李兰萍 卞昭汉 徐 瑾 袁 泳	二等奖	1997
393	《急症骨科学》	天津市天津医院、北京科学技术出版社	金鸿宾 费起礼 林鸿培 徐利明 赵尔弘	二等奖	1997
394	采油微生物产品的研究和应用	南开大学、大港油田集团有限责任公司	刘如林 陈智宇 梁凤来 刘金峰 刁虎欣 杨怀军 张心平	一等奖	1998
395	“津白、津绿”系列大白菜新品种选育	天津市蔬菜研究所	丘玉秀 张 斌 宋连久 王玉龙 闻凤英	一等奖	1998
396	超高压大电流线路阻波器	水力部电力工业部机电研究所	朱梦熊 韩荫奇 张彦停 侯春明 杨泽明	一等奖	1998
397	工业冷却水处理药剂及应用技术推广	化学工业部天津化工研究设计院	郑书忠 方燕平 孙中哲 李红兵 孟淑贤 张秀玲 李俊文 滕厚开 汪 棣 赵卫东 张光辉 崔金圣 陈 军 肖 勃 李卫丽	一等奖	1998

续表6　获天津市科学技术奖(一、二等奖)项目

序号	项目名称	获奖单位	获奖人	获奖等级	获奖年份
398	掺钛蓝宝石飞秒激光器及自相关器	天津大学精密仪器与光电子工程学院	张伟力　柴　路　邢岐荣　王清月　戴建明　章若冰	一等奖	1998
399	《肿瘤学》	天津市肿瘤医院、北京医科大学临床肿瘤学院、天津科学技术出版社	张天泽　徐光炜　吴孟超　吴秉铨　闵华庆　李树玲　马　洪	一等奖	1998
400	磁性配合物功能材料的基础研究	南开大学	廖代正　姜宗慧　阎世平　王耕霖	一等奖	1998
401	TH6380B卧式加工中心	天津第一机床总厂	吴　胜　胡光曦　杨　威　门志春　魏淑英	二等奖	1998
402	继电器、接触器可靠性检测技术的研究	河北工业大学、苏州高新技术产业开发区电器技术研究所	陆剑国　李志刚　李　奎　燕　燕　胡德霖	二等奖	1998
403	城市立交CAD系统	天津市市政工程设计研究院	赵建伟　孙继承　李传宪　朱兆芳　李孝圭	二等奖	1998
404	常见果树病害数值诊断法研究	天津市农学院　天津市林业局	赵国防　陈德芬　高德明　赵大顺　姜立强　柴慈江　李伍宝	二等奖	1998
405	空间用高效大面积长寿命硅太阳电池	电子工业部第十八研究所	徐寿岩　李兴华　杜永超　杜梦水　孙　竞	二等奖	1998
406	大面积激光涂敷系统及工业应用	天津纺织工学院、吉林省乾安镭射冶金工具厂、天津市东丽区天宝机械制造厂	杨洗陈　王云山　赵　新　姜连发　熊华业　王宝琦	二等奖	1998
407	TEC1-12707致冷组件	电子工业部第十八研究所	李光正　王泽深　王凤跃　余秀法　张　红	二等奖	1998
408	免疫促进剂的开发与利用	天津农学院	李富桂　张文生　徐学辉　王红宝　冯玉臣	二等奖	1998
409	酒用葡萄优质丰产栽培技术	天津市林业果树研究所	高献亭　修德仁　齐思儒　程瑞平　田卫东	二等奖	1998
410	汽车发动机曲轴连续热处理生产线	机械工业部第五设计研究院、天津汽车夏利股份有限公司内燃机制造分公司	凌云鸿　姚明理　戈小云　吴祥霈　殷继红　朱　钦　王金城	二等奖	1998
411	H-1三盐基硫酸铅	天津市红星化工厂	张志英　王玉春　付连义　陈国良	二等奖	1998
412	以国产试剂为基础的时间分辨荧光免疫分析的研究和应用	中国医学科学院放射医学研究所	赵启仁　李美佳　张福华　陈　艾　庄湘链	二等奖	1998
413	201校园卡系统	天津市电话局、深证市华为技术有限公司	滕　勇　薄今纲　陈洪文　国立园　李烨勃　刘　骏　吴宇辰	二等奖	1998
414	配电网运行与改造决策支持系统	天津大学电气自动化与能源工程学院	余贻鑫　王成山　肖　峻　黄纯华　贾宏杰	二等奖	1998
415	金属表面耐蚀涂层的研究	河北工业大学、天津开发区特涂层技术有限公司	阎殿然　何继宁　李香芝　武建军　葛汇业　刘艳改　刘立顺	二等奖	1998
416	井式内冷光亮球化退火炉研究	机械工业部第五设计研究院、天津汽车锻造有限公司	戴兰生　冯建国　唐　静　王立存　高　翔　王　瑜　王玉辉	二等奖	1998
417	高压气瓶管的开发研究	天津钢管公司	严泽生　杨效勇　张永厚　缪　明　庄　钢	二等奖	1998
418	模拟火山岩浆及喷发流动系统的开发研制	天津莱声机电科贸公司、国家地震局火山与地震景观建设办公室	李玉翔　吴宁远　吴荣辉　傅保罗　郑筱春　李文璋　运焕然	二等奖	1998
419	秋早熟菜花新品种-夏雪40、夏雪50	天津市蔬菜研究所	孙德岭　李素文　张宝珍　方文惠　刘奎彬	二等奖	1998
420	通里攻下法对肠源性内毒素血症防治研究	天津市中西结合急腹症研究所、天津市南开医院	吴咸中　崔乃强　葛智慧　赵　琪　刘　竞	二等奖	1998

续表6 获天津市科学技术奖(一、二等奖)项目

序号	项目名称	获奖单位	获奖人	获奖等级	获奖年份
421	早期老年黄斑变性长期临床追踪观察	天津市眼科医院、天津市眼科研究所、湖南医科大学附属二院	陈　松　聂爱光　谭家铨 姜德咏　唐朝诊	二等奖	1998
422	天津市地震快速反应系统建设	天津市地震局、天津市塘沽区地震办公室	牟光迅　郭效民　付仲生 张　昱　田　山　王俊国 崔晓峰	二等奖	1998
423	秸秆机械化微贮及利用技术开发研究	天津市农业机械试验鉴定推广站、天津市农业生物工程研究中心、天津市畜牧兽医研究所	戴冠英　蒲小平　陈秀为 王文杰　张　哲　张宝乾 穆淑琴	二等奖	1998
424	东亚飞蝗综合治理技术的研究与应用	天津市植保植检站、天津市大港区农林畜牧局植保植检站	于志宣　栗振华　窦　峰 谢建军　官宏义　谢志庚 李顺功	二等奖	1998
425	灯光可视化设计及测试系统	天津大学建筑学院	沈天行　马　剑　王立雄 袁景玉　孟　涛	二等奖	1998
426	腈纶干法纺丝纺纱油剂的研制	天津纺织工学院	王金榜　郑　帼　杨洪祥 马正敏　解　炜	二等奖	1998
427	高强度高抗挤毁石油套管的开发	天津钢管公司、西安管材研究所	邹文正　傅继成　张　毅 张传友　庄　钢　杨　勇 刘怀刚	二等奖	1998
428	热水锅炉间接供暖量调节方式的研究	天津市房产供热公司	吕　跃　姚永笑　孙如川 蒋　涛　张　莉	二等奖	1998
429	天津移动电话网系统	天津市长途电信局	周　珊　阚建杰　徐　波 余　晖　张永东	二等奖	1998
430	新城疫-传染性支气管炎-减蛋综合症三联油乳剂苗的研究	天津农学院	张安国　马衍忠　霍鸿度 杨友民　左　颖	二等奖	1998
431	新型500瓦中波导航车	国营第七六四厂	李长生　吴　伟　郑云鹏 居邵清　王　建	二等奖	1998
432	体外溶栓放射分析	中国医学科学院放射医学研究所	牛惠生　李怀芬　杨　熠 赵专友　王映兰	二等奖	1998
433	车载数据采集与处理系统	中国汽车技术研究中心	陈　弘　郑　宏　李宏光 朱西产　袁　健	二等奖	1998
434	中医药治疗白血病的临床及实验研究	天津中医学院	戴锡孟　杨学爽　杨文华 孙平旺　戴锡珍	二等奖	1998
435	津优1号黄瓜新品种选育	天津市黄瓜研究所	马德华　吕淑珍　霍振荣 李淑菊　庞金安	二等奖	1998
436	2CL80-87、2CL3509塑封高压硅堆	天津市中环半导体公司	张贵武　丛培金　魏庆忠 李　萍　郝润萍	二等奖	1998
437	API油管用J55、N80钢级热轧无缝钢管研制	天津市无缝钢管厂	钟锡弟　郭凤滨　李培达 吴印岭　陶学智	二等奖	1998
438	双环带螺旋槽端面密封的研制及工业应用	天津新技术产业园区鼎名密封有限公司、齐鲁石油化工公司橡胶厂	王玉明　桑立中　田淑芹 李晋鲁　王竹青　梁冠金 杜　辉	二等奖	1998
439	自体外周血干细胞移植联合大剂量放化治疗实体瘤的实验与研究	天津医科大学附属肿瘤医院	郝希山　邵　莹　佟仲生 崔秀珍　任宝柱	二等奖	1998
440	啤酒糖化发酵过程DCS集散控制系统	天津市华云自动化成套设备有限公司	朱一白　潘运军　韩增军 刘卫平	二等奖	1998
441	聚氨酯软泡垂直发泡CFC替代快速熟化装置	天津市轻工装备研究所、天津市轻工新技术开发公司、天津市聚氨酯塑料制品厂	邓学孟　高世森　曲和平 郭志强　王从众　温和平 张一鸣	二等奖	1998
442	C80级高性能耐蚀泵送重混凝土研究与应用	铁道部第十八工程局	廖金福　雷升祥　张兴彦 刘金良　农升河	二等奖	1998
443	MZQ-Ⅱ型分色光纤冷光源	天津市刑事科学技术研究所、天津市银成新技术有限公司	秦明伟　曹新华　张之愈 张怀志	二等奖	1998

续表6　　获天津市科学技术奖(一、二等奖)项目

序号	项目名称	获奖单位	获奖人	获奖等级	获奖年份
444	全固态Ⅱ型近程导航地面台	国营第七六四厂	张贤成　冯忠和　朱全德 胡伯泰　杨荣花	二等奖	1998
445	天津市蓟县库区科技扶贫工程	蓟县人民政府	孟庆田　刘素侠　李　银 高布凤　纪金旺　胡春明 刘贺学　耿宗长　李春生 赵士海　李甜华　孔宪波	二等奖	1998
446	热管节能系列产品推广	天津华能集团能源设备厂	张俊如　高振华　吴志祥 赵春生　尹淑芹　吴志军 周永强　朱华东　王瑞广 井连庆　李　兴　陈　民	二等奖	1998
447	农产品微型节能冷库应用	天津市林业果树研究所	李喜宏　陈　丽　修德仁 刘建华　董凤香　王善广 李丽秀　张　平　王春生 冯建华　胡云峰　郭　郢	二等奖	1998
448	肉品卫生质量检测新技术推广	天津市动物检疫站	张建华　高福奎　王志成 丰玉珍　刘子芝　徐振起 马丽荣　庄振江　林兆年 骆　维　刘子玉　刘　莹	二等奖	1998
449	高产高效温室蔬菜生产试验示范	天津市蔬菜研究所、武清县农业委员会	李卫民　钟有龙　石岩岭 杨景秋　谢继存　肖庆居 张秀链　诸葛昌江 曹　强　蒋文喜	二等奖	1998
450	天津市启动信息港建设的思路与对策研究	天津市科学技术评价中心、天津市人民政府研究室、天津市信息化工作领导小组办公室、天津市发展计划委员会	张峻屹等集体奖	二等奖	1998
451	天津新技术产业园区发展战略研究	中共天津市委研究室、天津新技术产业园区管理委员会	曹达宝　李大亚　张世玮 冯卫华　虞一平　戎鹏举 韩书君	二等奖	1998
452	IGM型智能卡燃气表	天津市贺博电子工业有限公司	丛跃进　杜忻育　杨海峰 冯　艳　梁海涛	二等奖	1998
453	夏利轿车引进自动喷漆生产线关键设备的故障诊断与自行维修技术	天津大学机械工程学院、天津夏利汽车股份有限公司汽车制造分公司	黄　田　张大卫　倪雁冰 宋永明　林君智　韩鸿志 周立华	二等奖	1998
454	科技成果推广工作优秀奖	天津市农林局	贾玉生　袁淑欣　隋玉柱 官宏义　王福玉　牛馨菊 王　树　王瑞卿　杨　林 邱宝林　刘志芬　王　晨	二等奖	1998
455	科技成果推广工作优秀奖	天津农垦集团总公司	李德增　栾志华　张　哲 祁继和　白福琴　于　林	二等奖	1998
456	优质小站稻研究及综合开发	天津市优质小站稻开发公司、天津市津南区农业委员会	徐庆海　盛宏达　杨学义 孙希英　郑宝福　王　溟 尹玉江	二等奖	1998
457	效益型水产养殖综合技术开发	天津市东丽区畜牧水产局	刘景文　廉宗成　苏作龙 马树敏　信世花	二等奖	1998
458	津奥啉(SC2053)小麦化学杂交新技术	天津市农作物研究所	肖建国　梁　毅　陈绍慧 石斯发　冯　刚　王继忠	二等奖	1998
459	超亲核催化剂高分子化及酶模拟	天津理工学院	黄积涛　郑嗣华　张嘉琪 孙经武　王　强　曹爱丽	二等奖	1998
460	金刚石微粉制造的新工艺-SDZ法	天津广播电视大学、天津超硬磨料研究中心	张书达　朱瑶华　王有起 刘建萍　张　军	二等奖	1998
461	电池内压测试新方法及DNY-1型电池内压测试仪	天津大学化工学院、国家高技术新型贮能材料工程开发中心	陈延禧　韩佐青　田建华 单忠强　俞　涛　洪　涸	二等奖	1998
462	《非线性光学频率变换及激光调谐技术》	天津大学精密仪器与光电子工程学院科学出版社	姚建铨　马长芳	二等奖	1998
463	《临床妇科学》	天津市中心妇产科医院、天津科学技术出版社	柯应夔　杜梓伯　岳　琏 李庆熙　郝俊利　邢风达	二等奖	1998

续表6　　获天津市科学技术奖(一、二等奖)项目

序号	项目名称	获奖单位	获奖人	获奖等级	获奖年份
464	《妇产科内分泌学》	天津医科大学总医院、上海第二医科大学附属瑞金医院、上海科学技术出版社	俞蔼峰　吴一鹗　葛秦生　翟瞻粲　胡自正　石　萍　方婷媛	二等奖	1998
465	弱光非线性的机理、测量及应用	南开大学	田建国　张春平　张光寅　许京军	二等奖	1998
466	新型功能性大环多胺化合物的研究	南开大学	卜显和　张智慧　张若桦　安道利　陈荣悌	二等奖	1998
467	生物合理方法设计合成新农药及其构效关系研究	南开大学	杨华铮　刘华银　邹小毛　谭惠芬　程慕如	二等奖	1998
468	波流与淤泥质底床的相互作用	天津大学建筑工程学院	赵子丹　练继建　张庆河　洪柔嘉　李贺青	二等奖	1998
469	铁基高温变换催化剂的基础研究	天津大学化工学院	李永丹　王日杰　李玉敏　张继炎　张　鎏	二等奖	1998
470	新型铁基磁性薄膜的结构与磁性研究	天津大学	姜恩永　王忠杰　孙多春　白海力　吴　萍	二等奖	1998
471	巴拿赫空间上的算子理论	南开大学	定光桂	二等奖	1998
472	金属离子对植物根细胞毒害作用的研究	天津师范大学化学与生命科学学院	刘东华　蒋悟生　王　威　王春利	二等奖	1998
473	XJL-THD-50型全钢丝载重子午线轮一次法成型机	天津市橡塑机械联合有限公司	张芝泉　朱伯明　张建浩　张　晨　毛小新	一等奖	1999
474	潘家口重力坝迎水面水平裂缝水下封堵等综合处理设计	水利部天津水利水电勘测设计研究院、水利部海河水利委员会引滦工程管理局	曹楚生　武永新　高晓梅　张克忠　杜雷功　孙继栋　丁建敏	一等奖	1999
475	超大型台式热处理炉的研制	机械工业部第五设计研究所、天津阿尔斯通水电设备有限公司	司国炯　凌云鸿　胡筱筎　程柯文　陈贵环　李　玉　张会义	一等奖	1999
476	白光信息处理用于航空彩色摄影的光学/数字新技术及设备	南天大学、长春光学精密机械研究所、中国人民解放军总参谋部第55研究所、中国人民解放军第5311工厂	母国光　方志良　赵长祥　翁志成　刘福来　李金祐　丛小杰	一等奖	1999
477	耐热黄瓜品种津绿4号、耐寒黄瓜品种津绿3号的选育	天津市黄瓜研究所	马德华　吕淑珍　霍振荣　李淑菊　庞金安	一等奖	1999
478	多孔大跨度钢管砼无推力系杆拱桥—彩虹大桥施工技术	铁道部第十八工程局、铁道部第十八工程局第五工程处	范成国　张兴彦　冯希民　童顺军　王克太　王存江　冯焕富	一等奖	1999
479	新型高性能掺杂KNSBN晶体自泵浦相位共轭器的研究	南开大学物理科学学院	张光寅　许京军　刘思敏	一等奖	1999
480	趋化因子PF4调节造血和血管内皮细胞增殖以及放化疗反应的研究	中国医学科学院血液学研究所	韩忠朝　马月霞　蔡英林　郭　娟　顾　洁	一等奖	1999
481	物理发泡聚乙烯绝缘皱纹铜管外导体射频同轴电缆SYWY-50-22(7/8″)	天津六〇九电缆有限公司	庞瑞林　马连国　徐长丽　李金花　徐晓川	二等奖	1999
482	防伪自动售货机	天津戈德防伪识别有限公司、天津南开戈德电子有限公司	李明智　张志光　沈世镒　高世森　王春露　张永泓　王淑芳	二等奖	1999
483	高效气浮技术与成套设备	天津市环境保护科学研究所、天津大学建筑工程学院	范凤申　张宏伟　王连生　辛志伟　宋秋萍　孙铁夫　李江华	二等奖	1999

续表 6 获天津市科学技术奖(一、二等奖)项目

序号	项目名称	获奖单位	获奖人	获奖等级	获奖年份
484	喹禾灵(禾草克)右旋光学化工艺技术	南开大学元素有机化学研究所	陈 彬 刘凤萍 杨华铮 谭惠芬 杨秀凤	二等奖	1999
485	P(G)JD2&XJD1 型无功功率动态补偿装置	机械工业部天津电气传动设计研究所	宋 斌 王玉华 王 阳 朱德林 王剑元	二等奖	1999
486	药芯焊丝成套生产装备与技术	天津大学、天津市三英焊业有限责任公司	陈邦固 张 智 刘继元 吴爱国 粟卓新 王秀文 李柏林	二等奖	1999
487	天津市重金属污染物资源化工艺、设备和工程研究	天津市环境保护科学研究院、地质矿产部天津地质矿产研究所、天津大学化工学院	丁 洪 王伟济 金凤鸣 段旭川 刘淑兰 王连卿 张春生	二等奖	1999
488	WB360 全液压稳定土拌和机	机械工业部天津工程机械研究所	张金兴 吴国祥 孙云富 陈胜奇 王 彬	二等奖	1999
489	小麦矮化腥黑穗病在天津地区定殖可能性的研究	中华人民共和国天津出入境检验检疫局、国家出入境检验检疫局科技与国际合作司	杨维长 章 正 姚文国 王学令 李振秀 罗加凤 崔铁军	二等奖	1999
490	151 具女性尸骨骨盆研究	天津市中心妇产科医院	王淑雯 岳 琏 刘勃晨 岳天浮 姜月萍	二等奖	1999
491	GT3D 便携式快速定位定向装置	中国船舶重工集团公司第七研究院第七〇七研究所、中国人民解放军总装备部炮兵装备技术研究所	张子剑 张若玉 赵国华 郭建钢 于 敏 刘嘉倬 肖宏德	二等奖	1999
492	选择性树脂吸附法银杏叶提取物及生产工艺	南开大学高分子化学研究所、天津市阳成高科技天然制品有限公司	何炳林 史作清 许名成 路延龄 施荣富 金晓农 欧阳绍江	二等奖	1999
493	"津雪 88"菜花(花椰菜)新品种选育	天津市蔬菜研究所	孙德岭 李素文 张宝珍 葛长鹏 刘奎彬	二等奖	1999
494	复杂地区地震勘探技术攻关与应用	大港油田集团地球物理勘探公司	王其华 王长春 陈水兴 徐开静 叶苑权	二等奖	1999
495	家用洗衣机壳体阴极电泳涂装生产线	中国船舶重工集团公司第七研究院第七〇七研究所	冯修礼 门连通 卢修泉 顾建民 易红雯	二等奖	1999
496	CR17330 型锂-二氧化锰电池	信息产业部电子第十八研究所	潘凯红 石全利 张 晶 刘 靖 张 莹	二等奖	1999
497	中国参考人研究	中国医学科学院放射医学研究所、中国辐射防护研究院生命科学研究所	王继先 陈如松 诸洪达 李本孝 赵永昌 徐 钧 尹协瑜	二等奖	1999
498	同种异体小肠移植的基础与临床研究	天津医科大学总医院	王鹏志 朱理玮 李克敏 刘 彤 罗宇东	二等奖	1999
499	高效导旋除尘脱硫净化器	天津市环境保护科学研究院	孙 申 孙广明 蒋伟华 贾志东 韩树新	二等奖	1999
500	TGE-706 芳纶被复线	天津六〇九电缆有限公司	杨玉萍 秦宝连 杨 光 宋在旭 王景海	二等奖	1999
501	电器现代设计方法研究	河北工业大学	陆俭国 苏秀苹 李 奎 张乃宽 骆燕燕	二等奖	1999
502	天津美洲斑潜蝇生物学及检疫综合防除技术的研究与应用	天津市植保植检站、宁河县农业技术推广中心	李秀文 李 崴 栗振华 郭文英 王凤珩 兰洪霞 杜慧勤	二等奖	1999
503	氧化抑制剂—高纯氯乙烷的制备	天津联合化学有限公司	陈 锚 潘正律 吴会清 杨新叶 苗嘉宗	二等奖	1999
504	7JPC486N、7JPC586N 型加固便携式笔记本微机	中国船舶重工集团公司第七研究院第七〇七研究所	郭景川 曹 晖 周墨龙 高树先 江 勇	二等奖	1999
505	GZS1 全数字程控直流柜	机械工业部天津电气传动设计研究所	陈雪梅 袁吉也 詹 云 范 磊 陈 刚	二等奖	1999
506	非常规饲料资源利用技术研究	天津市畜牧兽医研究所	王文杰 穆淑琴 李千军 郑成江 马 墉	二等奖	1999

续表6　　**获天津市科学技术奖(一、二等奖)项目**

序号	项目名称	获奖单位	获奖人	获奖等级	获奖年份
507	滇池草海污染底泥疏挖处置工程设计	天津航道勘察设计研究院	刘文生　李进军　丁金惠　杨建华　刘　景	二等奖	1999
508	深基坑支护理论的研究	天津大学建筑工程学院	陆培毅　郑　刚　严　驰　顾晓鲁	二等奖	1999
509	WS500稳定土厂拌设备	天津鼎盛工程机械有限公司、机械工业部天津工程机械研究所	闫维佳　孙云富　贾建中　张　浩　杨懋伦	二等奖	1999
510	远红外功能母粒、纤维及制品	天津市麻纺织厂	孙　治　栾凤祥　张金凤　王　玉　赵健民	二等奖	1999
511	分布式虚拟现实系统技术与建筑设计应用系统的研究	天津大学电子信息工程学院	孙济州　邢昌玉　车　明　张新荣　李晓红	二等奖	1999
512	黄骅坳陷未成熟油-低成熟油成藏条件及勘探目标评价	中国石油大港油田地质勘探开发研究院、大港油田集团勘探公司	吴永平　廖前进　于俊利　周立宏　李　军　曹来勇　曹　延	二等奖	1999
513	用于高性能混凝土的外加剂的研究与应用	天津建筑科学研究院	黄　靖　黎春海　曹鸿翔　杨继延　张鸿毓	二等奖	1999
514	基于并行设计思想的网格结构设计系统的研究与开发	天津大学建筑工程学院	龚景海　刘锡良　邱国志	二等奖	1999
515	改善建筑铝型材构件焊接性工艺技术研究	天津市焊接研究所	白津生　刘光春　韩春兰	二等奖	1999
516	远程教育系统	天津天财网络软件有限公司、天津有线电视台	王廷梁　寇纪淞　董建新　梁　琼　宋应伟	二等奖	1999
517	针刺对快速老化脑萎缩型小鼠SAM-P/10脑、肝抗氧化酶活性及其基因表达水平影响的实验	天津中医学院第一附属医院、南开大学生命科学院	石学敏　牛淑敏　赵俊宏　韩景献　李　平　刘一凡　王　舒	二等奖	1999
518	天津八仙山国家级自然保护区动植物种质资源保护与开发应用的	天津市林业局	许　宁　唐廷贵　林兰泉　杨竹舫　刘国卿	二等奖	1999
519	鸡传染性法氏囊病中药防治技术的研究	天津农学院	贾英科　马衍忠　霍鸿渡　马文芝　刘田生	二等奖	1999
520	脑脓肿的基础实验与临床研究	天津医科大学总医院	杨树源　张建宁　赵春生　赵以成　方　都	二等奖	1999
521	中医中风病危险因素及证候调查研究	天津中医学院	张伯礼　宋其云　徐宗佩　高秀梅　王同胜	二等奖	1999
522	提高垃圾堆肥质量及农田应用效果研究	天津市土壤肥料研究所、中国市政工程华北设计研究院、天津市河北区环境卫生管理局	毛建华　孟繁雨　陆文龙　潘　洁　张宝祥　郭秀芳　李秀文	二等奖	1999
523	黄瓜苗期人工接种抗病性鉴定技术	天津市黄瓜研究所、中国农业科学院蔬菜花卉研究所、黑龙江省农业科学院园艺研究所、山东省农业科学院蔬菜研究所、广东省农业科学院植物保护研究所	李淑菊　冯东昕　关钟燕　张光明　朱天圣　李宝栋　夏秋雨	二等奖	1999
524	全数字控制同步发电机可控硅励磁系统	天津理工学院	赵　辉　王红君　赵　刚　陈在平　王树森	二等奖	1999
525	影响子宫内膜癌预后的多因素研究	天津医科大学总医院	薛凤霞　焦书竹　赵凤喜　糜若然　岳天孚	二等奖	1999
526	轿车车身焊缝胶及防石击底涂胶技术开发	天津市合成材料工业研究所	陈晓康　张惠芳　高俊玲　曹明刚　郭鸿飞	二等奖	1999
527	辐照交联聚烯烃绝缘机车车辆用电缆	天津市电线总厂	邢太文　邵国旺　刘元臣　孙腊梅　郑国俊	二等奖	1999
528	果蔬专用保鲜膜的研制与应用	天津市林业果树研究所、天津市农产品保鲜研究中心	李喜宏　陈　丽　修德仁　温桂书　蒲长光　王铁英　胡云峰	二等奖	1999

续表6 获天津市科学技术奖(一、二等奖)项目

序号	项目名称	获奖单位	获奖人	获奖等级	获奖年份
529	GD系列辊道用三相异步电动机	天津市起重电机厂、天津市特种电机研究所	潘立国 李桂莲 王学强 彭树程 李树学 付华荣 陶德琴	二等奖	1999
530	LC-98A智能微功耗便携电阻焊测试仪	天津市陆华科技公司	徐明 姚丽芝 成海晖 鲍吉麟 王文富	二等奖	1999
531	港池蛇形造波机的研制	交通部天津水运工程科学研究所、天津理工学院	张福然 赵连瑞 孙精石 孟昭林 陈汉宝 李俊义 赵军	二等奖	1999
532	全铜无价质高频焊接工艺及热水器集热板	天津天马线缆实业总公司	黄新华	二等奖	1999
533	FSC-168涤纶高速纺油剂	天津纺织工学院、中国石化集团天津石油化工公司	葛启 崔永芳 魏俊富 葛继均 郑帼 张继梅 吕新建	二等奖	1999
534	肝移植治疗终末期乙型肝炎肝硬化	天津市第一中心医院	沈中阳 陈宝公 谷川 郝明利 刘振文	二等奖	1999
535	通译英汉、汉英科技翻译软件	天津市大通通译计算机软件研究所	陈光火 屈奋雄 肖永茂 沈名星 郭鑫	二等奖	1999
536	应用无框架神经外科导航系统治疗颅内病变的研究	天津市环湖医院	只达石 李建国 崔世民 杨玉山 姜炜	二等奖	1999
537	倾斜基牙固定义齿修复的实验研究及临床应用	天津医科大学口腔医学院、天津医科大学口腔医院	史书俊 侯小明 赵学锋 李长义 刘金鼎 邓嘉胤	二等奖	1999
538	天津市名特优水产品增养殖综合技术推广	天津市水产技术推广站、天津市水产局养殖处、天津市西青区水产技术推广站、天津市汉沽区水产技术推广站、天津市津南区水产技术推广站、静海县水产技术推广站、天津市塘沽区水产技术推广站、天津市东丽区水产技术推广站	张勤 缴建华 王智毅 李连同 肖培弘 高树权 沈晓红 孙志景 廉宗成 赵仕海 靳家栋 张力	二等奖	1999
539	天津地区万亩酒用葡萄优质丰产栽培技术推广	中法合营王朝葡萄酿酒有限公司、中国玫瑰香葡萄研究中心、蓟县林业局	李巍 田卫东 齐思儒 张福庆 李英明 徐梦月 周兰 唐宗成 王增明 解景山 贾爱军 张文举	二等奖	1999
540	小球烧结新工艺推广应用	天津铁厂	刘玉全 李海禄 龙平 张兵 张陆伟 时秉旭 张文东 崔辉 韩海金 姜辉明 李泓 朱培生	二等奖	1999
541	科技成果推广工作优秀奖	天津市卫生局	苑淑玲 宋哲民 赵克正 张愈 刘宝珠 陈洁 张荣江 熊智 杜学武 杨智 李万林 徐同起	二等奖	1999
542	科技成果推广工作优秀奖	天津市农业科学研究院	李家庆 路凯旋 马克俭 陈益山 刘书亭 赵玉洁 霍文娟 郭郢 陈绍慧 凌哲 李吉生 谷荣祥	二等奖	1999
543	科技成果推广工作优秀奖	天津铁路分局科学技术委员会办公室	李述武 王晓光 赵立文 吴长厚 乔延洪 沈勇 王文玲 宋金瑛 赵凤云 朱志武 陈禧平 张捷	二等奖	1999
544	机场专用新型清扫车	天津扫地王专用汽车有限公司	刘运成 武镪 张俊鹤 任正勇 严信德	二等奖	1999
545	VID-01 A/B散堆物料体积测量仪器系统	天津市威德电子系统有限公司	武长贵 李生良 张玉明 曾峦 周辉	二等奖	1999
546	小麦玉米秸杆切碎灭茬机	河北农业大学、天津富康农业开发有限公司	王文忠 黄克平 郭玉富 马洪亮 张世芳 胡伟 刘建国	二等奖	1999

续表6 **获天津市科学技术奖(一、二等奖)项目**

序号	项目名称	获奖单位	获奖人	获奖等级	获奖年份
547	滨海地区绿化新土源的研究	天津市泰达盐碱地绿化研究中心	张万钧 郭育文 杨永利 王斗天 张民胜 黄明勇	一等奖	1999
548	制备电池用氧化亚钴(CoO)的新方法	南开大学新能源材料化学研究所	阎 杰 王登国 周 震 许光惠 高 峰	二等奖	1999
549	《影响图理论方法与应用》	天津大学管理学院、天津大学出版社	詹原瑞 孙维善 张质文	二等奖	1999
550	《斜视》	天津市眼科医院、天津市科学技术出版社	郝雨时 赵堪兴 张开伯 王云祥 李恩江 刘学淑	二等奖	1999
551	P-N结击穿电压蠕变的研究	天津大学电子工程信息学院	郭维廉 郑丽滋 宋永淳 于彩虹	二等奖	1999
552	马氏体相变晶体学、形态学研究及应用	河北工业大学	谷南驹 宋晓艳 王宝奇 彭会芬 马晓莉	二等奖	1999
553	积分方程、积分-微分方程及相关方程的高效有限元方法	天津商学院	张书华 林 群 严宁宁	二等奖	1999
554	酶的结构、稳定性及应用基础研究	天津大学	何志敏 张子丁 吴金川 何明霞 冯耀宇 姚传义 郭从容 张 峻	自然科学一等奖	2000
555	新型抗癌抗病毒活性磷脂-核苷缀合物及α-氨基磷酸衍生物研究	南开大学	陈茹玉 戴 庆 周 嘉 张成祥 李惠英 黄君珉 迟国臣 陈焕明	自然科学一等奖	2000
556	合成受体的分子识别	南开大学	刘 育 尤长城 厉 斌 陈荣悌	自然科学一等奖	2000
557	制造系统理论与优化方法的研究	南开大学	涂奉生 陈秋霜 贾春福	自然科学二等奖	2000
558	慢性粒细胞白血病发病机理及实验治疗研究	中国医学科学院血液学研究所	赵春华 尤胜国 唐佩弦 范尔进 李 牧 陈 卫 何学鹏 陈一鸣	自然科学二等奖	2000
559	基于电学敏感原理的过程层析成像技术的研究	天津大学	徐苓安 徐立军 熊汉亮 董 峰 董琰婷 马艺馨 邓红梅	自然科学二等奖	2000
560	系统建模与辨识	南开大学	王秀峰 李 波 卢桂章 王治宝 劳育红 乞敬换	自然科学二等奖	2000
561	机械加工系统的声振识别与动态测控技术	天津大学	王太勇 郭红旗 张纪锁 朱梦周 张 策	自然科学二等奖	2000
562	生化反应系统中的非线性动力学研究	天津大学	王洪礼 元英进 张琪昌 郭树起 孙 景 苗志奇 谭 欣	自然科学二等奖	2000
563	氧载体强化传氧及载体生化反应器的研究	天津轻工业学院	贾士儒 李 波 张恺瑞 袁玉华 陈贵斌	自然科学三等奖	2000
564	用生物物理技术对下法药物治疗急腹症机理的研究	南开大学	杨文修 李俊英 金正根 许文胜 于海鹰	自然科学三等奖	2000
565	大鼠胰岛细胞和小βTc3凋亡相关基因及转染的研究	天津医科大学	于德民 刘 铭 何 庆 吴 锐 尹 潍	自然科学三等奖	2000
566	泌尿系统肿瘤MDR1基因的表达及抗药性的逆转	天津医科大学	韩瑞发 张广建 吴长利 马腾骧 吴 海	自然科学三等奖	2000

续表6 获天津市科学技术奖(一、二等奖)项目

序号	项目名称	获奖单位	获奖人	获奖等级	获奖年份
567	功能化液晶高聚物改性环氧树脂热固性材料	南开大学	张保龙 石可瑜 由英才 何尚锦 杨克莲	自然科学三等奖	2000
568	聚合物共混增容作用的研究	南开大学	张邦华 宋谋道 周庆业 余海斌 李春刚	自然科学三等奖	2000
569	HLA-Ⅱ类抗原和DC等IAC在AITD和SAT发病中作用的病理形态研究应用	天津医科大学	江昌新 谭郁彬 方佩华 刘岩 赵天如	自然科学三等奖	2000
570	等离子体温室气体化学转化基础理论研究	天津大学	刘昌俊 许根慧 姜涛 李阳 张月萍	自然科学三等奖	2000
571	多组分聚合物相结构及其光散射的研究	天津大学	盛京 沈宁祥 原续波 袁晓燕 刘文耀	自然科学三等奖	2000
572	广义系统理论与方法研究	天津大学	李光泉 唐万生 高志伟 郑丕谔	自然科学三等奖	2000
573	汽车非线性乘坐动力学基础理论研究	河北工业大学	檀润华 陈鹰 苑彩云 杨灿军 张瑞红	自然科学三等奖	2000
574	面向生物医学工程的微操作机器人系统	南开大学	卢桂章 张建勋 李彬 赵新 刘景泰 安刚 张蕾	技术发明一等奖	2000
575	螺环类光致变色防伪材料	南开大学	李明智 孟继本 王淑芳 董铁望 王永梅 张志光 施志华 刘俊勇	技术发明二等奖	2000
576	络合精馏技术及其在高纯甲萘胺制备中的应用	天津理工学院	肖如亭 李乃瑄 董庆洁 孙有光 谢秀荣	技术发明三等奖	2000
577	废水高效厌氧污泥床处理技术及成套设备	南开大学	张振家	技术发明三等奖	2000
578	聚合工艺优化与控制	渤海化工(集团)股份有限公司、天津大沽化工厂	肖卫国 刘建文 李增禄 魏永涛 汤吉彦 陈树泉 刘继龙 李宝利 王建兵 郭海军 魏以峰 许居庆	科技进步一等奖	2000
579	大跨度下承式钢管混凝土筒支拱桥的设计研究	铁道部第三勘测设计院、天津经济技术开发区总公司市政公司	周四思 孔繁昌 彭道富 孙树礼 孙树林 张璠琦 王召祜 刘全景 杜殿锁 陈后军 高成云 李凤芹	科技进步一等奖	2000
580	耐药逆转与干细胞及树突状细胞治疗实体瘤的应用基础研究	天津医科大学附属肿瘤医院	郝希山 邵莹 任秀宝 刘洪隐 冯玉梅 佟仲生 李慧 刘虹 崔秀珍 任宝柱 徐琪 牛瑞芳	科技进步一等奖	2000
581	干式气体密封	天津新技术产业园区鼎名密封有限公司、中国石化股份公司巴陵分公司鹰山石油化工厂	王玉明 李德刚 杨桦 舒浩华 朱国俊 何仲思 段雪梅 蔡彩玉 王海宁 刘艳梅	科技进步一等奖	2000
582	建立天津市交通控制指挥系统的研究	天津市交通工程科学研究所	武长顺 吕克逊 田建坤 聂方 杨爱学 章竞秋 徐志言 王亮 刘彦 刘宝靖 王宏宾 李广林	科技进步一等奖	2000
583	清脑益智方对神经细胞保护作用及机制研究——脑脊液药理学建立及应用	天津中医学院、天津中医学院第一附属医院	张伯礼 张军平 梅健勋 李苓 陈晓玉 高秀梅 徐宗佩	科技进步一等奖	2000
584	王朝高档干红葡萄酒的开发	中法合营王朝葡萄酿酒有限公司	王树生 张春娅 尹吉泰 王方 李巍 徐作滨 田卫东 张福庆 刘建华 吴军 李春和 王岩	科技进步一等奖	2000
585	电器试验数据高速采集与处理技术的研究	河北工业大学、苏州高新技术产业开发区电器技术研究所	陆俭国 刘教民 杜太行 赵小英 刘志刚 胡德霖 王晓宏 孙壮志	科技进步二等奖	2000

续表6 获天津市科学技术奖(一、二等奖)项目

序号	项目名称	获奖单位	获奖人	获奖等级	获奖年份
586	均三甲苯生产工艺技术	天津大学、河北省藁城市聚丙烯厂	张卫江 白 鹏 裴瑞唐 马友光 胡金榜 鲍素霞 宗润宽 陈印聪	科技进步二等奖	2000
587	大港地层矿物质组分和理化性能及钻井液技术研究	大港油田集团钻井工程公司泥浆技术服务公司	张玉士 陈远数 王鲁坤 宗瑞国 徐军献 王思友 吕宝军 马运庆	科技进步二等奖	2000
588	大港复杂断块油藏聚合物驱完善配套技术研究和应用	中国石油大港油田油气勘探开发技术研究中心、中国石油天然气股份有限公司大港油田公司技术发展处、中国石油大港油田第二采油作业区	张幸福 狄连城 陈智宇 李玉萍 马立军 邵定波 杨怀军 闫云贵	科技进步二等奖	2000
589	电磁式扭振实验台	天津大学	郝志勇 黎家玲 舒歌群 刘昌文 薛向党 高文志	科技进步二等奖	2000
590	衰老相关基因的筛选及针刺干预作用的实验研究	天津中医学院第一附属医院	石学敏 韩景献 李 平 温廷益 于建春 王 舒 杨增瑞 刘庆忠	科技进步二等奖	2000
591	坐底式基床抛石整平船	中港第一航务工程局	吕以同 赵子平 姜玉田 马方婷 魏安琪 徐元锡 向 阳 徐大光	科技进步二等奖	2000
592	功能性聚醚的研制与开发	天津纺织工学院高新技术实业公司	郑 幗 孙荣生 杨洪祥 魏俊富 刘燕军 周 存 姜 虹 徐进云	科技进步二等奖	2000
593	T95高强度抗硫化氢套管的研制	天津钢管公司	关永生 关大新 陈为民 付继成 孙开明 徐 华 刘怀刚 阎应龙	科技进步二等奖	2000
594	针灸治疗大动脉炎(头臂动脉型)的临床及实验研究	天津中医学院第一附属医院	高其芳 石学敏 李 平 卞金玲 李 岩 郑健刚 韩 艾 远慧茹	科技进步二等奖	2000
595	新型塔内件和高校规整填料在高压铜洗塔中的应用	天津大学	孙永利 贾绍义 张 曾 赵沧燕 王玉洁 刘 涛 王天民 郝国廷	科技进步二等奖	2000
596	聚合物后处理技术开发	渤海化工(集团)股份有限公司天津大沽化工厂	刘建文 魏永涛 汤吉彦 刘继龙 郭艳芬 倪 巍 李武文 杨广鑫	科技进步二等奖	2000
597	新型果蔬保鲜剂研制与应用	国家农产品保鲜工程技术研究中心(天津)	张华云 修德仁 王世军 张 平 王善广 李喜宏 胡云峰 刘 俊	科技进步二等奖	2000
598	宽带多媒体城域网分配与接入技术	天津市南开区信息网络中心	韩树森 刘秋平 王建国 田春苗 陈 立 刘学智 鹿凯宁 罗续业	科技进步二等奖	2000
599	大港油田滚动勘探开发技术研究及应用	中国石油大港油田油气勘探开发技术研究中心	王德明 石占中 刘海富 刘树明 王怀忠 王华崇 任宝生 彭红珍	科技进步二等奖	2000
600	京沪高速公路高陡路堑边坡加固综合技术研究	中铁第十八工程局、北京科技大学	高永涛 张兴彦 崔长俊 王英祖 陈广平 王志杰 吴顺川 徐德亮	科技进步二等奖	2000
601	大气颗粒物源解析技术的开发与应用研究	南开大学、天津市环境保护科学研究院	朱 坦 郭光焕 白志鹏 刘凤英 孙玉香 朱先磊 冯银厂 阎玉虎	科技进步二等奖	2000
602	天津市深部基岩地热资源开发潜力研究	天津市地质矿产局	李明朗 赵维明 李春华 陈炳晖 韩砚奎	科技进步二等奖	2000
603	铁路高墩V形支撑连续梁桥施工技术研究	中铁第十八工程局	赵广发 张璠琦 兰远均 吴登银 黄 健 陈 野 韩立民 付兆岗	科技进步二等奖	2000

续表6 获天津市科学技术奖(一、二等奖)项目

序号	项目名称	获奖单位	获奖人	获奖等级	获奖年份
604	氢化可的松转化新工艺的研究	天津轻工业学院、天津市津津制药厂	杜连祥 王 敏 王春霞 路福平 庞俊陆 袁东超 张 军	科技进步二等奖	2000
605	天津广播电视卫星地球站系统	天津广播电视局	李汝勤 邓 卉 李广全 蔡中兴 苗云峰 杨雨祥 杨红杰 周敬波	科技进步二等奖	2000
606	原油集输系统卧式容器密闭清砂工艺技术试验研究和实际应用	大港油田集团勘察设计研究院	穆向谦 田中玮 韩 专 张 芃 徐正芹 金雄耀 张劲松 高述生	科技进步二等奖	2000
607	RTV硅橡胶涂料应用技术	中国华北电力集团公司、天津市电力公司、清华大学	关志成 朱可能 袁泽领 赵 辅 李同喜 薛家琪 王黎明 贾志东	科技进步二等奖	2000
608	城市中小型高效、简易污水处理厂工艺及装备的研究	天津市市政工程设计研究院、天津水工业工程设备有限公司、天津市祥森环境工程设备开发有限公司	张大群 王秀朵 郭 静 王守明 宋启元 张述超 李 建 韩小清	科技进步二等奖	2000
609	日光温室冬春茬花专用黄瓜新品种津优2号的选育	天津市黄瓜研究所	李加旺 孙忠魁 张文珠 李 光	科技进步二等奖	2000
610	肾炎3号方治疗慢性肾炎的临床及实验研究	天津中医学院第一附属医院	黄文政 曹式丽 陈志强 何永生 杨洪涛 朱小棣 黄怀鹏 姜德训	科技进步二等奖	2000
611	天津地区主要鸡传染病地方毒(菌)株的分离及疫苗研制	天津市畜牧兽医研究所	丁伯良 王英珍 黄金海 鄢明华 张 健 白朋勋 张建良 赵殿齐 郭 鲁 孟红星	科技进步二等奖	2000
612	津江MEP润滑脂	燕化集团天津润滑油脂有限公司	王洪卫 曹玉发 刘庆廉 高艳青 王以胜 刘清华 解建平 张 爽	科技进步二等奖	2000
613	药芯焊丝工艺润滑剂研究及开发	天津大学、天津市电焊条公司	张韵慧 张则甠 李 芃 张红军 魏建强 尹淑梅 李之唐	科技进步二等奖	2000
614	Ⅰ、Ⅱ型子宫内膜癌临床病理特征及CyclinD1、bc1-2基因表达的研究	天津医科大学总医院	薛凤霞 李 卉 焦书竹 朱元喜 韩玉昆	科技进步二等奖	2000
615	龙潭路住宅建筑节能成套技术研究	天津市津墙房地产开发有限公司、天津市广厦建筑设计院、天津市建设工程质量监督管理总站、天津市人民政府供热办公室、天津市房产住宅科学研究所	滕绍华 林彩富 刘向东 王旭光 沈 建 崔志强 张中一 董 静	科技进步二等奖	2000
616	天津长途电信帐务与综合营业系统	天津市长途电信局	周 珊 袁 洪 赵 勇 韩 燕 姜 莹 张 晖 高建国 李 梅	科技进步二等奖	2000
617	骨髓增生异常综合征恶性造血克隆鉴别的研究	中国医学科学院中国协和医科大学血液学研究所血液病医院	邵宗鸿 陈桂彬 郝玉书 宋玉华 法祥光 冯宝章 刘 鸿 施 均	科技进步二等奖	2000
618	工厂化农业技术研究与示范区建设	天津港田集团公司、天津市津南区科学技术委员会、天津市新河集团公司、天津市武清区东赵庄村	集体	科技进步二等奖	2000
619	高炉富氧喷煤产业化工程	天津天铁冶金集团有限公司	刘志嘉 刘玉全 龙 平 马建国 吕春风 林士光 黄庆富 韩以楠	科技进步二等奖	2000
620	颅神经的MR成像	天津市第一中心医院	刘 筠 祁 吉 张文波 李吉龙 倪红艳 李 鹏	科技进步二等奖	2000
621	天津市给水管网信息管理及分析系统研究	天津市自来水集团有限公司、天津市公用事业设计研究所、哈尔滨工业大学市政环境工程学院	郭 智 赵洪宾 袁伟康 何文杰 郑 毅 韩宏大 魏宝成 袁一星	科技进步二等奖	2000

续表6 获天津市科学技术奖(一、二等奖)项目

序号	项目名称	获奖单位	获奖人	获奖等级	获奖年份
622	GDT系列固定封闭式交流低压配电柜	机械工业部天津电气传动设计研究所	陈 彪 王 博 孔振宇 蔡 维 韩东明 王昕煜 尹贵君 田秀珍	科技进步二等奖	2000
623	三维异型整体编织工艺的研究和三维编织设备及织物的研制	天津工业大学	李嘉禄 韩其睿 李晓久 陈 利 姚承照 管 国 李学明 焦亚男	科技进步二等奖	2000
624	DCC-1型电池电导测试仪	国家海洋局海洋技术研究所、中国电信集团天津市电信公司	刘从信 刘雪堂 林红军 王福苓 王艳萍 阎云祥 陈 钢 尹东彦	科技进步二等奖	2000
625	WNS型系列燃油(气)蒸汽锅炉	天津市宝成集团有限公司	李耀荣 杨文利 李凤丽 董黎明 吴振平 陈永娟 于运学	科技进步二等奖	2000
626	复杂非线性系统的动力学理论与方法	天津大学……	陈予恕 陆启韶 唐 云 徐健学 褚福磊 吴志强 徐 鉴 孙政策 丁 千 甘春标 陈芳启	自然科学一等奖	2001
627	三维光折变存储材料及其存储器的研究	南开大学	许京军 孙 骞 张光寅 张心正 孔勇发 黄 晖 刘思敏 张国权 乔海军 陈晓军 李冠告 丁大同	自然科学一等奖	2001
628	精馏过程中若干基础理论问题研究	天津大学	余国琮 袁希钢 杨志才 刘春江 马友光 曾爱武 黄 洁 王树楹	自然科学一等奖	2001
629	功能性有机-无机杂化材料的组装与性质研究	南开大学	程 鹏 杨光明 刘 欣 李立存 王文珍 寇会忠	自然科学一等奖	2001
630	超分子金属有机化学研究	南开大学……	张正之 麦松威 支志明 匡善明 徐凤波 李庆山 宋海斌	自然科学一等奖	2001
631	几何量光电在线测量新原理方法研究	天津大学	叶声华 褚继贵 段发阶 曲兴华 孙长库 杨学友 王 仲 卢荣胜	自然科学二等奖	2001
632	新型化合物软X射线光学多层膜的制备及其结构稳定性研究	天津大学	姜恩永 白海力 王存达 田仁玉	自然科学二等奖	2001
633	光纤光栅、全光纤集成光子器件与系统研究	南开大学	董孝义 袁树忠 开桂云 刘志国 盛秋琴 吕福云 吕可诚 赵启大	自然科学二等奖	2001
634	去壁低渗法(WDH法)及其在我国植物染色体研究中的应用	南开大学	陈瑞阳 宋文芹 李秀兰 安祝平 陈成彬 祁仲夏 纵微星 刘 松	自然科学二等奖	2001
635	针刺治疗中风病的研究	天津中医学院第一附属医院	石学敏 韩景献 李 平 王 舒 卞金玲 杜元灏 赵建国 李 岩	自然科学二等奖	2001
636	现代非线性动力学理论及在机械系统中的应用	天津大学	王洪礼 张 伟 张琪昌 孙 景 郝淑英 牛西泽 张新生 刘 晟	自然科学二等奖	2001
637	血液净化生物材料研究	南开大学、天津市第三中心医院	俞耀庭 陈长治 杨 彦 蔺恩富 何炳林 宋继昌 钱绍诚	自然科学二等奖	2001
638	红豆杉细胞培养生产紫杉醇的新方法	天津大学	元英进 葛志强 李景川 胡宗定 胡国武	自然科学三等奖	2001
639	壁湍流相干结构综合检测技术的实验研究	天津大学	姜 楠 王振东 舒 玮	自然科学三等奖	2001

续表 6 获天津市科学技术奖(一、二等奖)项目

序号	项目名称	获奖单位	获奖人	获奖等级	获奖年份
640	模拟纳米晶体原子分布及其X射线散射理论图谱	天津理工学院	常 明 白 明 孙 伟 杨保和	自然科学三等奖	2001
641	焊接电弧光谱信息及其在过程测控中应用	天津大学	李俊岳 李 桓 宋永伦 柳 刚 杨运强	自然科学三等奖	2001
642	混沌时序非线性动力系统重构、预测及其控制技术	天津大学	马军海 盛昭瀚 王 宁	自然科学三等奖	2001
643	系统中非线性、非均衡建模理论和方法研究	天津大学	张世英 钟登华 高仁祥 袁学民	自然科学三等奖	2001
644	人前列腺平滑肌细胞的培养及前列腺基质增生诱因的研究	南开大学	张 琚	自然科学三等奖	2001
645	α-组态核碰撞粗共振结构的核分子轨道深势模型研究	南开大学	高成群 杨宝胜	自然科学三等奖	2001
646	智能系统和系统辨识若干问题研究	天津大学	王正欧 张建平 林 燕 朱 涛 林 晨	自然科学三等奖	2001
647	生物医用材料的离子束技术表面优化	天津师范大学	李德军 赵 杰 顾汉卿 崔福斋 牛丽芳	自然科学三等奖	2001
648	超大规模集成电路纳米磨料化学机械全局平面化新技术	河北工业大学	刘玉岭 王 新 檀柏梅 刘 钠 张楷亮 曹 阳 于 广 张德臣	技术发明一等奖	2001
649	几何量计量仪器自标定、现场标定新技术	天津大学	叶声华 曲兴华 郑继贵 付敬业	技术发明一等奖	2001
650	新型稀土镍基储氢合金(AB_5)电极材料及其制备方法	南开大学	吴 锋 宋德瑛 袁华堂 张允什 曲金秋 高学平 汪根时 周作祥	技术发明二等奖	2001
651	先进柴油机共轨式电控燃油系统及其相关应用技术	天津大学……	苏万华 汪 洋 谢 辉 李绍安 佟德辉 林铁坚	技术发明二等奖	2001
652	振动喷流造粒技术	天津大学	康仕芳 陈 松 赵 珺 辛振林 沈国宏 赵思源 张 猛	技术发明二等奖	2001
653	万吨级汽液固三相流化床卤水蒸发装置的关键技术研究	天津大学、天津长芦汉沽盐场有限责任公司	李修伦 林瑞泰 张利斌	技术发明二等奖	2001
654	3-HSS型并联机床关键技术与产品	天津大学	黄 田 倪雁冰 张大卫 曾子平 林汉元	技术发明二等奖	2001
655	镍氢二次电池负极残片中合金粉的回收及失效电池负极合金粉的再生	南开大学、天津和平海湾电源集团有限公司	阎 杰 王 荣 阎德意 周 震 邓 斌	技术发明三等奖	2001
656	激光有机光导材料制备技术	天津市先立新技术有限公司	李祥高 李兴民 周笑非 董淑芬 赵玉棠	技术发明三等奖	2001
657	天津碱厂低盐份优质量质纯碱工程	天津渤海化工有限责任公司天津碱厂	集体	科技进步一等奖	2001
658	复方丹参滴丸自动灌装线	天津大学、天津天士力集团有限公司	王宝光 杨德燕 耿世钧 柴天达 门大春 王冬生 张国雄 陈林才 呼英俊 贺忠海 刘 鹏 郝金钟	科技进步一等奖	2001
659	亚低温治疗急性重型颅脑损伤临床及基础研究	天津市环湖医院	只达石 张 赛 陈荷红 黄慧玲 肖绪林 苏晨方 林 欣 黄丽君 毛 瑞 庞心元 王 颖 王 辰	科技进步一等奖	2001
660	秋绿、津白系列大白菜新品种推广	天津市蔬菜研究所	闻凤英 王玉龙 刘晓晖 宋连久 赵 冰 丘玉秀 徐晨英	科技进步一等奖	2001
661	李子沟高墩大跨刚构-连续组合梁桥快速施工成套技术	中铁十八局集团有限公司	赵之义 张璠琦 彭道富 吴登银 黄健杜 洪 举 陈 野 刘治德 申传胜 苏在林 黄 俊 翁卫军	科技进步一等奖	2001

续表6 获天津市科学技术奖(一、二等奖)项目

序号	项目名称	获奖单位	获奖人	获奖等级	获奖年份
662	天津市地热资源开发利用集约化技术研究及工程应用	天津大学、中国地质大学(北京)、天津市地热管理处、天津地热勘查开发设计院、黑龙江科技学院	何满潮 李春华 朱家玲 徐能雄 姚磊华 张百鸣 任红艳 张伟 韩砚奎 徐平 王坤 刘斌	科技进步一等奖	2001
663	黄瓜杂交制种技术及繁育体系研究	天津市黄瓜研究所	吕淑珍 高象昶 李光 陈正武 杨森 任双亮	科技进步一等奖	2001
664	长大隧道施工超前地质信息预报研究	铁道第三勘察设计院	辛民高 白恒恒 樊五星 屈晓辉 荆志东 邢文宝 许再良 刘振田	科技进步二等奖	2001
665	血管性痴呆的临床和实验研究	天津中医学院	张伯礼 王永炎 张允岭 宫涛 陈汝兴 谢颖珍 梅建勋 张军平	科技进步二等奖	2001
666	二维码加密识别技术及其应用	天津南开戈德集团有限公司、天津南开戈德股份有限公司	李明智 沈世镒 吴忠华 施志华 张则年 安树森 王淑芳 晏振宇	科技进步二等奖	2001
667	"预充式"重组人干扰素α-2b注射液(产品名称:安福隆水针)	天津华立达生物工程有限公司	张磊 许玉昆 邓杰 田莉 吕津 谢皖 吴伯冬 于骏	科技进步二等奖	2001
668	致肾盂肾炎大肠杆菌(UPEC)粘附特性的研究	天津医科大学	陈锦英 李方涛 李宝艳 何健民 康宁 苏琦华 郑铃 何庆	科技进步二等奖	2001
669	大型焦炉固液燃料烘炉技术	天津市第三煤气厂……	美辉明 左树行 高兴锁 贾连起 戴成武 王保国 马兴翼 仝树涵	科技进步二等奖	2001
670	主跨175m钢管拱桥连续液压竖向转体等同步控制技术研究与应用	中铁十八局集团有限公司	张播琦 吴登银 钟启宾 胡瑞海 韩利民 李继平 彭道富 韩学勤	科技进步二等奖	2001
671	TP10OH超稠油热采井用石油套管	天津市钢管有限责任公司	胡秉仁 卢小庆 邹文正 刘怀刚 方华 张宝利 杨效勇 严泽生	科技进步二等奖	2001
672	柴油冷滤性能改进剂研究与开发	天津大学	张金利 李韦华 袁兵 郭翠梨 王一平 陆红	科技进步二等奖	2001
673	王朝香槟工艺酒酿造技术的研究	中法合营王朝葡萄酿酒有限公司	王树生 徐秀玲 尹吉泰 田卫东	科技进步二等奖	2001
674	前体药物和生物技术药物的临床前药物动力学规范研究	国家药品监督管理局天津药物研究院	刘昌孝 魏广力 李全胜 陈拯民 蔡永明 肖淑华 高连用 曾勇	科技进步二等奖	2001
675	鼻咽癌腔内近距离治疗双管一体施源器的研制及临床应用	天津医科大学附属肿瘤医院	王平 李瑞英 朱莉 王佩国 齐洁	科技进步二等奖	2001
676	聚偏氟乙烯中空纤维微孔膜及成套装置	天津膜天膜工程技术有限公司	吕晓龙 李新民 刘建立 陈智 石君 周友志 许以农 张彬	科技进步二等奖	2001
677	J422等碳钢焊条性能提高	天津市金桥焊材有限公司	侯立尊	科技进步二等奖	2001
678	蓝天六必治生物酶牙膏	天津蓝天集团股份有限公司	梁玉树 孙群 黄强 范美华 卢秀文 黄磊 潘超	科技进步二等奖	2001
679	WT7500型全液压稳定土摊铺机	天津鼎盛工程机械有限公司、天津工程机械研究院	张金兴 陈胜奇 孙云富 闫维佳 吴国祥 贾建中 胡莹 孙朝晖	科技进步二等奖	2001
680	巨块型肝癌的分型及其生物学行为的临床与实验研究	天津医科大学附属肿瘤医院	李强 郝希山 郝继辉 郭晓静 陈华 郑红	科技进步二等奖	2001
681	国产化5000m³高压天然气球罐技术研究	天津市渤西油田天然气利用工程指挥部、天津市煤气工程设计院	金建平 李金亭 黄立民 黄红祥 胡茂杰 田大栓 李大川 高秀民	科技进步二等奖	2001

续表6 获天津市科学技术奖(一、二等奖)项目

序号	项目名称	获奖单位	获奖人	获奖等级	获奖年份
682	天津建筑风格研究及设计应用	天津大学、天津市规划和国土资源局、天津城市建设学院、天津市建筑设计院、天津市房屋鉴定勘测设计院	滕绍华 荆其敏 刘景梁 洪再生 路 红 夏 青 陈 天 周长林	科技进步二等奖	2001
683	桥用高强轻集料混凝土应用技术研究	天津市市政工程研究院、天津市公路建设发展公司、天津市市政工程设计研究院、天津第三市政公路工程有限公司、天津第一市政公路工程有限公司	曹 诚 吕大镛 刘兰强 孙运国 王春阳 魏宏云 郑铁柱 刘润楠	科技进步二等奖	2001
684	电力系统暂态稳定性裕度分析新算法研究及其应用系统开发	天津大学、天津市电力公司调度通信中心	房大中 王守东 刘明志 宋文南 孙景强 胡晓馨 龚成虎 张 尧	科技进步二等奖	2001
685	抗CD3和抗CD20双功能抗体的研制	中国医学科学院血液学研究所	杨纯正 朱祯平 熊冬生 许元富 彭 晖 刘汉艺 邵晓枫 范冬梅	科技进步二等奖	2001
686	沥青及沥青混合料改性研究	天津市市政工程研究院	赵 可 魏如喜 杜月宗 原建安 李海聪 商耀祥 罗东花 吴立勇	科技进步二等奖	2001
687	板青液预防脑卒中患者医院感染的临床研究	天津中医学院第一附属医院	赵建国 卞金玲 韩 力 程 宇 杨桂生	科技进步二等奖	2001
688	天津市空气污染预报研究	天津市环境监测中心、天津市气象科学研究所	秦保平 边 海 邵 莹 王长友 刘彩霞 朱玉强 房玉梅 冯建秋	科技进步二等奖	2001
689	口腔铸钛修复体化学抛光的实验研究	天津医科大学口腔医院	张连云 杨贤金 李长义 崔振铎 吴海树 韩素丽 邓嘉胤 曾 东	科技进步二等奖	2001
690	颅脑损伤后bFGF基因表达及外源性bFGF的治疗作用	天津医科大学总医院	杨树源 杨新宇 崔建忠 雪 亮 张建宁 高俊玲 王丽蕙	科技进步二等奖	2001
691	钢筋混凝土超高层建筑结构试验研究	天津市政工程设计研究院、天津大学、天津市地震工程研究所、南京航空航天大学	毕继成 佟景伟 赵素敏 颜 莓 王承春 李江河 董 雪 李鸿琦	科技进步二等奖	2001
692	中国当代建筑创作理论研究及应用	天津大学	邹德侬 曾 坚 刘丛红 运迎霞 赵建波 戴 路	科技进步二等奖	2001
693	大口径直缝焊管全自动数控液动飞锯机	天津理工学院	张玉华 柴晓艳 刘福生 靳希敏 温殿英 周鸿翻	科技进步二等奖	2001
694	中空纤维膜生物反应器污水处理系列装置研究与开发	天津大学	杨造燕 顾 平 李 力 朱文亭 吕小龙 刘锦霞 田淑媛 齐庚申	科技进步二等奖	2001
695	基于分布式数据处理及数据迁移技术的边检综合管理系统	中华人民共和国天津出入境边防检查总站、天津市思嘉科技发展有限公司	张亚平 陈 健 贾 欣 秦彦刚 宋庆维 李桂锁 刘长山 曾春海	科技进步二等奖	2001
696	喉癌的早期诊断与手术新方法	天津市第四中心医院	金国威 李少诚 石继红 郭晓力	科技进步二等奖	2001
697	天津市海河隐伏断裂活动性定量评价	天津市地震局	刘连柱 赵根模 陈宇坤 陈化然 赵国敏 刘晓年 聂永安 卫鹏飞	科技进步二等奖	2001
698	天津市塘沽区地热流体回灌研究	天津市地质矿产局	李明朗 付炳海 陈炳晖 久建新 张惠生	科技进步二等奖	2001
699	大港探区陆上第三系石油地质综合研究与勘探实践	中国石油大港油田油气勘探开发技术研究中心	吴永平 杨池银 韦阿娟 李洪香 廖前进 王振升 祝文亮 肖敦清	科技进步二等奖	2001
700	hTPO抗原决定簇基因的克隆和表达及其产物的临床应用	天津医科大学总医院	方佩华 何红鹏 吕 枚 谭 建 江昌新 肖 茜 李 进 姬永丽	科技进步二等奖	2001

续表6 获天津市科学技术奖(一、二等奖)项目

序号	项目名称	获奖单位	获奖人	获奖等级	获奖年份
701	160水冷柴油机设计、研究与开发	天津大学、湘潭柴油机厂	康秀玲 付光琦 祖炳锋 徐玉梁 张厚晚 杨又鑫 李朝阳 沈海秋	科技进步二等奖	2001
702	电力电子式多微机控制大功率直流传动系统及应用	天津电气传动设计研究所	李冬梅 俞智斌 郭谅 候伟 王春武 戴薇 石来润 乔聪明	科技进步二等奖	2001
703	燃气汽车技术规范研究及专用装置检测设备	中国汽车技术研究中心	张红卫 吴志薪 马宗华 赵春明 亓玉梅 顾严平	科技进步二等奖	2001
704	人民币智能检测仪研究及其应用	天津南开戈德集团有限公司、天津中钞戈德智能技术有限公司	李明智 沈世镒 张则年 吴忠华 安树森 符雪涛 陈春生 张庆生	科技进步二等奖	2001
705	Q-开关红宝石激光治疗机	天津大学	叶志生 王升平 金贞姬 高慧敏 任国权 张俊林	科技进步二等奖	2001
706	多复合挤击机联动生产线	天津赛象科技股份有限公司	张芝泉 张建浩 朱伯明 陈定康 唐国梁 汤静 张晨 施政敏	科技进步二等奖	2001
707	冶金型钢厂计算机集成制造系统	天津市轧三制钢有限公司、清华大学、北京科技大学	徐鸿章 梁雨锋 丁文一 万秋伟 张贺利 钟约先 鹿守理 常剑峰	科技进步二等奖	2001
708	SL MJLS系列三叶罗茨鼓风机	天津市鼓风机总厂、西安交通大学	杨光 冯育棠 彰学院 李文英 赵学录 刘凯 张翠平 孟庆伟	科技进步二等奖	2001
709	复杂断块油田特高含水期剩余油分布研究及实施效果分析	中国石油大港油田油气勘探开发技术研究中心	任宝生 益立新 芦风明 王华崇 钱迎春 窦松江 史长林 田秀霞	科技进步二等奖	2001
710	半刚性太阳电池板电路研究	信息产业部电子第十八研究所	邹庆云 徐寿岩 谈宝宁 孙彦锋 金海雯 吕伟 程保义 赵颖	科技进步二等奖	2001
711	新型全自动多用燃气(油)锅炉	河北工业大学、天津宝成集团有限公司	俞颐秦 齐承英 曹惠玲 李耀荣 吴晋湘 韩伟 闫运忠 董黎明	科技进步二等奖	2001
712	通信光纤自动切换系统	中国电信集团天津市电信公司长途线务局	张国柱 曹俊忠 刘明忠 董普选 明世君 张玉岭 贾绍良 刘玉生	科技进步二等奖	2001
713	南开太阳结算管理系统(NKTY256P)	天津市南开太阳高技术发展有限公司	刘景泰 安刚 卢桂章 王孝喜 张蕾 姚世春 鹿明 杨涛	科技进步二等奖	2001
714	低成本高效砷化镓/锗太阳电池研究	信息产业部电子第十八研究所	杜福生 陈文浚 孙强 肖志斌 乔在祥 郭爱萍 傅云龙 李春燕	科技进步二等奖	2001
715	名优虾类品种引进及培育淡化养殖技术研究	天津市水产技术推广站、天津市津南区水产技术推广站、天津市北辰区水产技术推广站、天津市塘沽区水产技术推广站	张勤 张福芸 赵明 刘宗豹 张振奎 韩世华 刘保中 骆凤权	科技进步二等奖	2001
716	永定河防汛调度系统的建立与应用	天津市水利科学研究所、天津市水利局水源调度处	朱芳清 周潮洪 郭书英 张长青 刘哲 常守权 杜津媛 魏素清	科技进步二等奖	2001
717	啶虫脒农药合成的新工艺	天津大学	闻建平 黄琳 朱智勇 邵泽才 金明辉 万龙岩 李增彦 刘春生	科技进步二等奖	2001
718	天津市公安车管业务互联网系统	天津市公安局车辆管理所	武长顺 邵元和 袁丁 范权 单祥群 陈兆捷 任平生 李永武	科技进步二等奖	2001
719	电力大系统安全性与稳定性的理论与方法	天津大学	余贻鑫 王成山 贾宏杰	自然科学一等奖	2002

续表6 获天津市科学技术奖(一、二等奖)项目

序号	项目名称	获奖单位	获奖人	获奖等级	获奖年份
720	功能高级有序结构分子聚集体研究	南开大学	卜显和 杜 淼 张若桦 陈 巍 刘 河	自然科学一等奖	2002
721	星系相互作用和并合过程与星系形成和演化关系的多波段观测和研究	天津师范大学……	夏晓阳 吴 宏 邓祖淦 邹振隆 薛随建	自然科学一等奖	2002
722	壳聚糖基仿生高分子凝胶	天津大学	姚康德 刘文广 尹玉姬 赵 峰	自然科学一等奖	2002
723	有机锡化合物的合成结构及其应用	南开大学	谢庆兰 李 靖 徐效华 郑健禺 张招贵 孙丽娟	自然科学二等奖	2002
724	临界参数及其他化工数据测定与研究	天津大学	马沛生 梁英华 夏淑倩 李 平 刘耘畦 夏 清	自然科学二等奖	2002
725	计及柔性的机械多体系统动力学理论与应用研究	天津大学	王树新 章 青 张大钧 张海根	自然科学二等奖	2002
726	CO_2活化与反应固体催化剂分子设计	天津大学	钟顺和 王建伟 高 健 黎汉生 李 青 王希涛 肖秀芬 邵 宇	自然科学二等奖	2002
727	结构半主动-智能控制理论及其技术原理	天津大学	何玉敖 何 琦 郭 婷 吴建军 何亚东 冯德平 李忠献 王元战	自然科学二等奖	2002
728	改善动力学特性的智能化机构的理论与实验研究	天津大学	张 策 马文贵 宋轶民 刘建琴 姚燕安 常宗瑜 唐力伟 杨玉虎	自然科学二等奖	2002
729	金属材料多轴低周疲劳寿命预测	天津大学	陈 旭 许爽燕 高 红 安 柯 田 涛	自然科学三等奖	2002
730	半导体微腔激光器自发发射、瞬态响应和模式特性的研究	河北工业大学……	赵红东 沈光地 张存善	自然科学三等奖	2002
731	原癌基因Lmo2的果蝇同源基因克隆及其功能研究	南开大学	朱天慧	自然科学三等奖	2002
732	植物染色体微分析技术及其应用	南开大学	李秀兰 陈成彬 许文胜 宋文芹 陈瑞阳	自然科学三等奖	2002
733	内燃机声振信号测量及其对工作过程识别的研究	天津大学	舒歌群 郝志勇 薛 远 林建生 刘维馨	自然科学三等奖	2002
734	纳米生物技术在靶向控释抗癌药物载体系统和医学诊断方面的应用	天津大学	常 津 常 青 姚康德 魏 民 毛津淑	自然科学三等奖	2002
735	阅读不耗电类纸电子书	天津津科电子有限公司	李庆诚 刘全礼 王计会	技术发明一等奖	2002
736	弱酸性阳离子交换树脂	南开大学	阎虎生 程晓辉 何炳林	技术发明二等奖	2002
737	组合式螺旋浮环密封	天津新技术产业园区鼎名密封有限公司	王玉明	技术发明二等奖	2002
738	碳酸二甲酯及其系列产品甲苯二异氰酸酯的合成	河北工业大学	王延吉 赵新强 姜瑞霞 李 芳 王淑芳	技术发明二等奖	2002
739	高速公路汽车防撞系统	天津理工学院	徐宝强 袁其平 李 骥 王德会 童峥嵘	技术发明三等奖	2002
740	复方丹参方药效物质及作用机理研究	天津中医学院	张伯礼 王永炎 高秀梅 商洪才 潘桂湘 王 怡 郭利平 孙有富 刘密新 张 萌 胡利民 秦彩玲	科技进步一等奖	2002
741	电去离子技术和反渗透-电去离子高纯水设备的研究	中国人民解放军军事医学科学院卫生装备研究所	龚承元 刘红斌 苏建勇 朱孟府 马 军 张西正	科技进步一等奖	2002

续表6　　获天津市科学技术奖(一、二等奖)项目

序号	项目名称	获奖单位	获奖人	获奖等级	获奖年份
742	白血病流行病学、发病机理与治疗方法的研究	中国医学科学院血液学研究所	王建祥　卞寿庚　杨崇礼　钱林生　郝玉书　李幼升　肖志坚　杨天楹　薛艳萍　齐淑玲　林泽嬉　王志澄	科技进步一等奖	2002
743	铁基耐液锌腐蚀材料及热镀锌内加热技术	河北工业大学、天津市工大镀锌设备有限公司	曹晓明　姜信昌　温　鸣　许长庆　武建军　谷南驹　齐洪林	科技进步一等奖	2002
744	提高钢筋混凝土高层建筑抗震性能的分体柱技术	天津大学……	李忠献　郝永昶　胡庆昌　徐云扉　赵艳静　康谷贻	科技进步一等奖	2002
745	果蔬保鲜新技术推广	国家农产品保鲜工程技术研究中心(天津)	李善宏　陈　丽　许向路　胡云峰　修德仁　关文强　成国祥　冯晓元	科技进步一等奖	2002
746	新型高抗挤套管(TP130TT)与复合管柱技术	天津钢管有限责任公司……	严泽生　高德利　刘一江　邱　锋　宋　明　王　京　李铁成　付继成　李　飞　张建设　张传友　覃成锦	科技进步一等奖	2002
747	数字高清晰度电视机顶盒技术	天津大学……	国澄明　俞斯乐　黄建峰　陈　珊　李　华　野锦德　国狄非　张　涛　许辉福　李　坚　林志浩　陈全中	科技进步一等奖	2002
748	甲氨基阿维菌素苯甲酸盐合成技术	南开大学	徐风波　张正之　解　放　贺水济　毕富春	科技进步二等奖	2002
749	小型断路器可靠性技术的研究	河北工业大学……	陆俭国　骆燕燕　李志刚　王景芹　唐春潮　李文华　王海涛	科技进步二等奖	2002
750	滞洪、分洪区铁路选线设计研究	铁道第三勘察设计院	张红旭　屈晓辉　崔显付　白宝英　陈德江　于兴义　王守端　邢文宝	科技进步二等奖	2002
751	大港不同类型油藏精细油藏描述及实施效果评价	中国石油大港油田油气勘探开发技术研究中心、中国石油大港油田第二采油作业区	赵平起　王　羽　芦凤明　郑振英　庞洪汾　陈善勇　郭宝玺　班艳华	科技进步二等奖	2002
752	戈德印章治安管理信息系统	天津南开大学戈德防伪技术有限公司	李明智　董铁望　张忠锋　初　春　商荣庆　孙　阳　阎　东　张毅硕	科技进步二等奖	2002
753	1000吨单氟磷酸钠生产线的研发设计与调试达产	核工业理化工程研究院	马玉芳　杜贡生　鲁　继　李其轩　陈金铨　王茂林　胡惠兴　刘训芝	科技进步二等奖	2002
754	保护地黄瓜新品种“津优3号”的选育	天津科润农业科技股份有限公司	马德华　吕淑珍　霍振荣　李淑菊　庞金安	科技进步二等奖	2002
755	果树病害数值诊断法推广应用	天津农学院、天津市林业局、静海县林业局、天津市北辰区农林局、天津市汉沽区林果技术推广站、蓟县林业局、天津市西青区农业技术推广服务中心	赵国防　陈德芬　高德明　张素芬　王兆毅　赵大顺　张金海　姜立强　李俊柱　李　银　文丽华	科技进步二等奖	2002
756	北大港构造带油气精细勘探研究及高效储量区块发现	中国石油大港油田油气勘探开发技术研究中心、中国石油大港油田勘探事业部	杨池银　李洪香　周建生　曹来勇　刘玉梅　祝文亮　马建英　黄国平	科技进步二等奖	2002
757	长效人重组白细胞介素-6的研制	天津医科大学	姚　智　卢　奕　李会强　朱智彤　郁春艳　帅建华　李鸿钊　李　昕	科技进步二等奖	2002
758	OTIS3000微机控制交流变频变压调速乘客电梯	中国天津奥的斯电梯有限公司	沈　言　王亚军　张世参　张新伟　刘　涛　行根超　高岩光　邢金海	科技进步二等奖	2002
759	组合绝缘数字同轴射频电缆	天津有容蒂康通讯技术有限公司	吕铁宏　焦　建　唐丽洁　李金龙　刘士龙　王美怡　宋百江	科技进步二等奖	2002

续表6　　获天津市科学技术奖(一、二等奖)项目

序号	项目名称	获奖单位	获奖人	获奖等级	获奖年份
760	西瓜育种方法创新及系列新品种选育	天津科润农业科技股份有限公司	焦定量　段爱民　王　鸣　李长缨　张艳宁　李秀秀　吕敬刚　刘　莉	科技进步二等奖	2002
761	大港滩海油气富集规律与勘探	中国石油大港油田油气勘探开发技术研究中心、中国石油大港油田滩海勘探开发公司	廖前进　王光奇　袁淑琴　李淑恩　王振升　孙晓明　韩品龙　张绍辉	科技进步二等奖	2002
762	羊三木疏松砂岩稠油底水油藏综合配套技术研究与应用	中国石油大港油田油气勘探开发技术研究中心、中国石油大港油田油气开发事业部	吴永平　邵定波　马先平　韩启清　王丽荣　赵　晓　邢金生　刘存林	科技进步二等奖	2002
763	活性石灰气烧矩形竖窑新技术的研制与开发	天津天铁冶金集团有限公司	肖宝明　陈志强　韩以楠　甄新占　李和太　王景玉　商晓郁　马金邦	科技进步二等奖	2002
764	新型填料技术在碳九分离中的应用	天津大学……	陈青松　李鑫钢　李　杰　孙津生　刘　岗　于爱华　刘　杰　姜　斌	科技进步二等奖	2002
765	钾通道激动剂对瞬间内向电流及触发活动的调节	天津市儿童医院	张宏艳　范崇济　李小梅　张巧芳　石　军　任自文　陈　森	科技进步二等奖	2002
766	大中口径油气管线自动焊设备及工艺	中国石油集团工程技术研究院	唐德渝　冯　标　李春润　张建护　谷　侠　张田利	科技进步二等奖	2002
767	奶牛高产高效新技术研究	天津农垦集团总公司、天津市奶牛研究所、天津市畜牧兽医研究所、天津市工农联盟农场、天津市红光农场	张允茂　徐　直　王文杰　田雨泽　贾福德　刘　壮　张　喆　李德生	科技进步二等奖	2002
768	高清晰度显示器用超快恢复系列塑封高压硅堆	天津市中环半导体有限公司	丛培金　李　萍　刘长蔚　王旭萍　张鑫慧　孙建伟　陈玉勇　张贵武	科技进步二等奖	2002
769	海河口清淤泥沙运动规律及三维数学模拟的工程应用研究	天津大学	白玉川　白志刚　邢焕政　朱保粮　顾元棪　张效先　王尚毅　姜乃申	科技进步二等奖	2002
770	JGW型心理试验台	天津市师范大学	阴国恩　吴晓荣　董春鹏　刘家骥　王国钧　谷　午　沈德立	科技进步二等奖	2002
771	天津市淡水养殖开发新区综合配套技术推广	天津市水产技术推广站、天津市武清区水产技术推广站、静海县水产技术推广站、天津市西青区水产技术推广站、宝坻县畜牧水产局水产技术推广站、天津市津南区水产技术推广站、蓟县水产技术推广站	张　勤　缴建华　张立民　东世民　刘维汉　张　力　张福芸　赵仕海　孙志景　包海岩　樊丙新	科技进步二等奖	2002
772	GWJ-3型光阻法智能微粒检测仪	天津大学	高玉成　曲丹丹　贡立青　薛剑英　周鑫玲　罗诗金	科技进步二等奖	2002
773	辐射抗性小鼠IRM-2的培育与应用研究	中国医学科学院放射医学研究所	周继文　王月英　岳井银　吴红英　李　进　穆传杰　王汝勤　赵忠萍	科技进步二等奖	2002
774	地震作用下穿越管道的安全可靠性研究	天津大学、天津市水利局引滦入港工程管理处	景　悦　余建星　刘瑞深　詹　强　任秀萍　石江水　姚青岭　罗延生	科技进步二等奖	2002
775	天津移动通信动态资料管理系统	天津移动通信有限责任公司	阎五四　阚建杰　李永春　黄　涛　周奕瑾　王　真　李荣盛　高淑芬	科技进步二等奖	2002
776	“吸交法”提取柠檬酸新工艺工业化生产技术	天津科技大学……	高年发　杨　枫　付华廷　林繁震　梁仕仁	科技进步二等奖	2002
777	燃气汽车闭环电控系统的研究开发	中国汽车技术研究中心、河北工业大学、天津市汽车研究所	吴志新　黎　苏　赵春明　苏　琴　陈　嵩　高洪林　马宗华　顾严平	科技进步二等奖	2002
778	聚丙烯给电子体DCPDMS产品开发及应用	天津京凯精细化工有限公司……	李必刚　赵起超　赵丽梅　马良兴　韩华良　沈国华	科技进步二等奖	2002

续表6 获天津市科学技术奖(一、二等奖)项目

序号	项目名称	获奖单位	获奖人	获奖等级	获奖年份
779	老年性痴呆异常表达基因的筛选及芯片的研制	天津中医学院第一附属医院	石学敏 温廷益 壮元灏 韩景献 李 平 樊小农 王 舒 刘庆忠	科技进步二等奖	2002
780	计算机网络高速光互连技术及应用	天津大学	井文才 张以谟 周 革 刘文耀 刘铁根 葛宝臻 黄战华 蔡怀宇	科技进步二等奖	2002
781	钢-混凝土组合结构住宅建筑体系	天津市建工集团(控股)有限公司、中国建筑科学研究院、天津二建建筑工程有限公司、天津建工集团建筑设计有限公司	张佩生 耿立新 付金栋 张克明 冯兆民 曹立国 刘元春 张洪雾	科技进步二等奖	2002
782	非接触IC卡系统终端	天津环球磁卡股份有限公司	刘兴刚 纪鸿舜	科技进步二等奖	2002
783	零坍落度混凝土振捣密实和碾压混凝土坝设计研究	水利部天津水利水电勘测设计研究院	曹楚生 王宏斌 武永新 朱健慰 高晓梅 苏广新 杜雷功 李成乾	科技进步二等奖	2002
784	以环戊烷为聚氨酯发泡剂的预制直埋式保温管生产	天津市管道工程集团有限公司	杨 宁 邵丽云 刘津祥 陈宝强 周曰从 赵 峰 英 杰 于桂霞	科技进步二等奖	2002
785	牙齿颌骨钙利用实验研究	天津医科大学口腔医院、中国医学科学院放射医学研究所、中国人民解放军第二五四医院	仝 健 刘士有 李怀芬 李志勤 赵广军 牛惠生 李耀玲	科技进步二等奖	2002
786	巴豆酸生产工艺研究	天津市捷鑫化学工业有限公司	刘秉奇 丁永平 杨春禄 张 东 刘翠华	科技进步二等奖	2002
787	燃气锅炉智能与优化控制系统	天津市燃气集团有限公司第一销售分公司、中国市政工程华北设计研究院	孟 红 项友谦 李维光 张 平 张 涛 刘 明 王柏森 贾光金	科技进步二等奖	2002
788	利用高温盐制取一水硫酸镁和工业盐技术	天津市昌昊化工股份合作公司、天津长芦海晶集团有限公司	牛自得 魏炳举 李 臻 刘文斌 王宗玉 张德强 姚占力 祝宝举	科技进步二等奖	2002
789	自体骨髓移植治疗急性白血病	中国医学科学院血液学研究所	韩明哲 冯四洲 邱录贵 严文伟 韩俊领 赵英新 李海燕 韩忠朝	科技进步二等奖	2002
790	自杀基因治疗恶性胶质瘤的研究	天津医科大学总医院	杨学军 黄 强 浦佩玉 王广秀 王春艳	科技进步二等奖	2002
791	落锤式弯沉仪(FWD)应用技术研究	天津市市政工程质量监督站、河北工业大学	张宝林 樊兆强 杨 辉 王云明 攸 颖 刘晓宇 孟 赟 孙建华	科技进步二等奖	2002
792	XBZ1系列智能型XBJ1系列紧凑型箱式变电站	天津电动传动设计研究所	张卫东 崔 静 何凌峰 王 阳 蔡心一 吕元华 尤俊强 陈恭珏	科技进步二等奖	2002
793	天津草坪病虫害诊断及综合防治技术的研究与应用	天津市植保植检站、中国农业大学、天津市塘沽区植保植检站	李 崴 李秀文 栗振华 石会平 赵美琦 王印来 张美蓉 王海旺	科技进步二等奖	2002
794	高档丙纶细旦纤维纺丝整理剂	天津工业大学	魏俊富 郑 帼 葛 启 徐进云 周 存 孙波泉 刘燕军 姜 虹	科技进步二等奖	2002
795	乳腺良、恶性病变动态增强MRI表现特征与血管生成相关性研究	天津医科大学附属肿瘤医院	刘佩芳 鲍润贤 牛 昀 于 泳 宁连胜 肖渤翰 杨建梅 汪 沁	科技进步二等奖	2002
796	SC系列自动洗胃机	天津市同业科技发展有限公司	翟贵生 刘凤岗 万智存 王子梁	科技进步二等奖	2002
797	引进猪种高产仔抗应激分子育种研究	天津市宁河原种猪场	李振宽 赵宏志 王爱国 李士金 周伟良 李俊奇 韩玉环 付金恋	科技进步二等奖	2002

续表6 **获天津市科学技术奖(一、二等奖)项目**

序号	项目名称	获奖单位	获奖人	获奖等级	获奖年份
798	SC(SCB)10-30~2500/10系列树脂浇注干式变压器	天津市特变电工变压器有限公司	郭共文 陈 杰 龙 巍 郑立伟 郑绍忠 庄 华 秦 琦 凌 良	科技进步二等奖	2002
799	天津数字化前兆台网建设工程	天津市地震局	付仲生 刘连柱 赵国敏 邓守琴 韩润泉 董洪军 张有昌 吴玉田	科技进步二等奖	2002
800	MPEG-4流媒体数字编码机	天津七所信息技术有限公司	戴永康 崔宝英 吴俊杰 李 军 温 山 段智魁 王繁珍 李 中	科技进步二等奖	2002
801	细胞周期调控因子与乳腺细胞癌变的相关性研究	天津医科大学附属肿瘤医院	牛 昀 傅西林 于 泳 刘铁菊 吕阿娟 冯玉梅 牛瑞芳 李 妤	科技进步二等奖	2002
802	猪血"功能性肽-Fe"中试生产技术	天津科技大学、天津市顺利实业发展有限公司	刘安军 曹小红 王稳航 林兆辉 王丽霞 张 莉 范意芳 郭顺利	科技进步二等奖	2002
803	湍流及其控制	天津大学	周 恒 罗纪生 姜 楠 舒 玮 曹 伟	自然科学一等奖	2003
804	Seiberg-Witten理论与四维拓扑	南开大学	方复全	自然科学一等奖	2003
805	蛋白质分离复性方法和理论研究	天津大学	孙 彦 董晓燕 白 姝 史清洪 甘一如	自然科学一等奖	2003
806	"自由基—金属"配合物及多自旋体系的基础研究	南开大学	姜宗慧 阎世平 赵琦华	自然科学二等奖	2003
807	光互连及其检测技术的理论与实验研究	天津大学	井文才 张以谟 周 革 刘铁根 刘文耀 唐 锋 李海峰 张红霞	自然科学二等奖	2003
808	分叉、混沌理论及其应用	天津大学、北京工业大学、石家庄铁道学院	王洪礼 张 伟 杨绍普 张琪昌 苏文利 竺致文 沈 菲 胡 斌	自然科学二等奖	2003
809	富勒烯化学的理论研究	南开大学	赵学庄 尚贞锋 潘荫明 王贵昌	自然科学二等奖	2003
810	金属氢化物—镍电池关键材料研究	南开大学	高学平 阎 杰 王先友 周 震 刘 剑 叶世海 宋德瑛	自然科学二等奖	2003
811	稳健阵列信号处理新方法及其应用	中国民用航空学院 、西北工业大学	吴仁彪 苏志刚 马远良 韩 萍	自然科学二等奖	2003
812	高性能纤维结构与性能研究	天津工业大学	肖长发 张宇峰 安树林 贾广霞 吴世臻	自然科学二等奖	2003
813	介入性血管内药物和基因的靶向投递和控释体系	中国医学科学院生物医学工程研究所、中国医学科学院北京协和医院	宋存先 杨 菁 孙洪范 朱文玲 崔秀敏	自然科学二等奖	2003
814	恶性肿瘤抗血管新生治疗新方法	中国医学科学院血液学研究所、泰达生命科学技术研究中心	韩忠朝 李妍涵 何 睿 丁顺利 刘 澎 徐 斌 杨仁池 吴立华	自然科学二等奖	2003
815	非晶硅(a-Si)基薄膜功能集成器件和技术的研究	南开大学	熊绍珍 赵 颖 吴春亚 孟志国 代永平 张延忻 王宗畔 耿新华	自然科学二等奖	2003
816	大型发电机组机电耦联与磁固耦合振动问题研究	天津大学	邱家俊 杨志安 李文兰 牛西泽 邱 宇	自然科学三等奖	2003
817	钴基纳米金属多层膜的微结构与磁性研究	天津大学	姜恩永 吴 萍 白海力 王合英 王存达	自然科学三等奖	2003

续表6 获天津市科学技术奖(一、二等奖)项目

序号	项目名称	获奖单位	获奖人	获奖等级	获奖年份
818	低维SiC材料的制备及相关性质研究	天津理工学院	刘技文　谢仿卿	自然科学三等奖	2003
819	一种基于离散/小波变换的医学影像信息传输算法设计	天津医科大学	康晓东	自然科学三等奖	2003
820	光纤光栅传感技术与应用	南开大学	董孝义　开桂云　袁树忠　张伟刚　盛秋琴　刘志国	技术发明一等奖	2003
821	变截面三维多向编织技术	天津工业大学	李嘉禄　陈　利　焦亚男　陈光伟　吴晓青　张国利　余　勤　陈　迎　周　清　李学明	技术发明一等奖	2003
822	金刚石薄膜压力和温度传感器研制	天津理工学院	常　明　杨保和　曲长庆　潘　鹏	技术发明二等奖	2003
823	高弯曲弹性回复性共聚酯纤维的研制	天津石油化工公司研究院	杨瑞玲　黄象安　李文刚　马国玉　陆建忠	技术发明三等奖	2003
824	粮食聚烯烃基保鲜膜的研制与应用	国家农产品保鲜工程技术研究中心(天津)	李喜宏　陈　丽　胡云峰　关文强　邢福保	技术发明三等奖	2003
825	高效圆坯连铸机研制	天津钢管有限责任公司、东北大学、钢铁研究总院	宋嘉鹏　朱苗勇　姜桂连　胡坤太　李广田　张再斌　张兴中　杜成武　安士亮　杨玉兵　郑学然　郑淑国	科技进步一等奖	2003
826	新建铁路客运专线路基设计技术研究	铁道第三勘察设计院	屈晓辉　崔俊杰　宋绪国　彭泽仁　崔维孝　常杰峰　吴连海　刘远锋　杨明雨　郭绍影　荆志东　崔尚彦	科技进步一等奖	2003
827	新型立体传质塔板开发应用	河北工业大学	李春利　李柏春　刘继东　吕建华　张文林　杨振生　王志英　于文奎　王福宽　宋志英　王志生　陈华艳	科技进步一等奖	2003
828	多段塞复合凝胶体系调驱技术研究与配套应用	中国石油大港油田油气勘探开发技术研究中心	陈美华　张生富　文先哲　胡　静　吴国会　杜树勋　王学民　陆　斌　胡洪亮　李雅光	科技进步一等奖	2003
829	高效精馏塔技术及应用	天津大学	余国琮　张鹏飞　许春建　朱慧铭　李凭力　田华明　周　明　袁希钢　杨志才　冯惠生　崔现宝　俞旭峰	科技进步一等奖	2003
830	药物动力学数学模型与新药的药物动力学研究	天津药物研究院	刘昌孝　刘定远　魏广力　李全胜　肖淑华　黄玉荣　顾以保　高连用　余志凌　陆　榕　高　晶　只德广	科技进步一等奖	2003
831	天津港十万吨级航道、港池、泊位适航水深应用与维护措施研究	天津港(集团)有限公司	黄力军　丁乃庆　刘富强　钱平生　胡　宁　张建国　孙建鹏　王承刚　李宝元　余厚新　周宇辉　李长茂	科技进步一等奖	2003
832	“津雪88”菜花新品种推广	天津科润农业科技股份有限公司	孙德岭　方文惠　赵前程　张宝珍　孙立全　赵宗武　蔡荣旗　李素文	科技进步一等奖	2003
833	脐带血造血干细胞库的建设和相关技术研究	中国医学科学院血液学研究所、协和干细胞基因工程有限公司	韩忠朝　邱录贵　韩俊领　陆　敏　李　茜　闫凤英　应红光　肖志坚　杨丛林　宋开宇　赵英新　梁晓岚	科技进步一等奖	2003
834	急性脑创伤后迟发性神经元死亡分子机制的研究及其治疗方法	天津医科大学总医院	杨树源　杨新宇　雪　亮　张建宁　白景文　于士柱　张庆瑜　胡　震	科技进步二等奖	2003

续表6 获天津市科学技术奖(一、二等奖)项目

序号	项目名称	获奖单位	获奖人	获奖等级	获奖年份
835	天津电力客户服务系统	中国华北电力集团公司天津市电力公司	胡玉海 刘学智 王志刚 韩 强 刘 勇 陈风辉 金生明 周一路	科技进步二等奖	2003
836	智能化农业信息技术应用示范工程	天津市农业技术推广站、天津市科润农业科技股份有限公司黄瓜研究所、天津市农业科学院信息研究所、天津市气象科学研究所、天津市农业信息中心	刘克祥 崔洪宇 田云臣 李 杰 郑爱军 隋 华 黎贞发 仇家山	科技进步二等奖	2003
837	高浓缩倍率工业冷却水处理技术及智能化在线(远程)监控系统	天津化工研究设计院	郑书忠 彭树森 程 峰 孙元杰 王恩祥 郭亚新 聂常明 李俊文	科技进步二等奖	2003
838	复杂地质条件下特大断面导流隧洞综合施工技术	中铁十八局集团有限公司	张璠琦 李生宏 崔连友 苏 睿 张 勇 宫志群 孟祥义 刘金良	科技进步二等奖	2003
839	特长输水隧洞群贯通测量技术研究与实践	水利部天津水利水电勘测设计研究院	伍志刚 王卫国 张国良 王庆玉 白玉春 丁浩清 曹催晨 李江深	科技进步二等奖	2003
840	红葡萄酒稳定性的技术研究	中法合营王朝葡萄酿酒有限公司	王树生 张春娅 尹吉泰 王 方 刘建华 李 巍 吴 军 邢 凯	科技进步二等奖	2003
841	KZJ-系列全数字(防爆、高压)型交流电动机软起动器	河北工业大学 天津开发区正泰电器有限公司	刘子胥 张福民 凌跃胜 刘宏勋 杜 江 李双会 王利辉 权 全	科技进步二等奖	2003
842	固相有机合成载体树脂	天津南开和成科技有限公司、南开大学	史作清 路延龄 范云鸽 施荣富 阎虎生 马玉新 丁 杰 杨益忠	科技进步二等奖	2003
843	电子海图显示信息系统	中国船舶重工集团公司第七〇七研究所	杨功流 陈超英 何河通 张崇猛 谢 英 王夙歆 宁作福 侯全新	科技进步二等奖	2003
844	凝析油气藏可采储量标定方法及开发后期提高采收率研究	中国石油大港油田油气勘探开发技术研究中心、中国石油大港油田第八采油作业区	何 鲜 刘树明 杨广荣 安振月 李国江 余元洲 李庆国 马 乔	科技进步二等奖	2003
845	气调贮藏设备技术开发	天津市森罗科技发展有限责任公司	郭晓光 宋传铭 李百荣 管大勇 刘吟笙 张子剑 邓映峰 顾传庆	科技进步二等奖	2003
846	针刺治疗老年期痴呆的临床及基础研究	天津中医学院第一附属医院	石学敏 韩景献 李 平 王 舒 刘庆忠 来丽萍 樊小农 于建春	科技进步二等奖	2003
847	天津房地产系统分析与应用研究	天津大学、天津市建设管理委员会	赵黎明 刘翠乔 李 波 王文红 徐青青 全怀周 欧阳效辉 孔繁昌	科技进步二等奖	2003
848	数控YAG激光焊接机	天津大学	张国顺 李荷芬 任志华 孙攀峰 张 健 黄复清 许宝忠 李 梅	科技进步二等奖	2003
849	供电企业经营管理决策支持系统	天津市电力公司西青供电分公司	安德洪 王立春 马义秀 李慧清 孙树和 李德民 李 鹏 陈朝霞	科技进步二等奖	2003
850	津优黄瓜新品种推广	天津科润农业科技股份有限公司	王艳飞 李怀智 孟攀奇 孙玉河 付海鹏 陈正武 李 光 赵国云 王 全 杨 森 张庆栋	科技进步二等奖	2003
851	5ZL165X7Y、5LZ172X7Y螺杆钻具的研制	大港油田集团中成机械制造有限公司	吴爱民 李明谦 张西江 杨 阳 夏秀文 袁洪涛 王春阳 吴 越	科技进步二等奖	2003
852	城市智能型防洪减灾决策支持系统研究	天津大学	钟登华 冯 平 阎俊爱 崔广涛 张社荣 刘东海 熊开智 宋 洋	科技进步二等奖	2003

续表6 获天津市科学技术奖(一、二等奖)项目

序号	项目名称	获奖单位	获奖人	获奖等级	获奖年份
853	大型汽轮发电机组轴系扭振危害及其控制的研究	天津大学、天津军粮城发电厂	郝志勇 张俊红 高文志 张其显 付鲁华 胡益章 张亚平 郭军华	科技进步二等奖	2003
854	商务安全支撑平台的研究及其在戈德协同商务办公系统中的应用	南开大学 天津南开大学戈德防伪技术有限公司	邵秀丽 刘 璟 董铁望 张忠锋 雷建军 延 峰 阎仲璞 阎 东	科技进步二等奖	2003
855	FA491型粗纱机	天津宏大纺织机械有限公司	陈谷人 祝宪民 高秀满 刘广喜 刘敦平 李向杰 王学俊 冯广轩	科技进步二等奖	2003
856	免疫调节剂胞肽生物预防畜禽疫病的研究	天津市润拓生物技术有限公司	李守军 鲍恩东 李旭东 梁 武 牛文海 刘爱玲	科技进步二等奖	2003
857	海洋一号卫星太阳电池阵模拟供电及检测设备	中国电子科技集团公司第十八研究所	王保平 张文超 李 萍 王 朴 付增英 陈 琳 刘贵庚 赵春阳	科技进步二等奖	2003
858	海上油田浅层气固井技术的研究与应用	天津中油渤星工程科技股份有限公司、中海油田服务股份有限公司	吕光明 王同有 聂 臻 王永松 王建东 蔡久能 裴 燕 陈宗江	科技进步二等奖	2003
859	QNY$_1$G106碱性蓄电池	中国电子科技集团公司第十八研究所	檀立新 胡树清 鲁文东 辛宇光 李永利 张越青 周亦龙 刘 娜	科技进步二等奖	2003
860	MUC1、MUC1/Y体外修饰DC诱导特异性抗肿瘤免疫应答	天津医科大学附属肿瘤医院	郝希山 刘 虹 邵 莹 任秀宝 魏 枫 李 慧 李 峥 张乃宁	科技进步二等奖	2003
861	高校节水综合示范工程研究	天津大学	张宏伟 朱文亭 邢国平 孙宝盛 田 林 赵新华 杨建江 刘洪波	科技进步二等奖	2003
862	防水式坚固型计算机	中国船舶重工集团公司第七〇七研究所	张 军 曹 晖 严丽峰 戴 然 耿蔚明 陶婷华 杜建华 王 戈	科技进步二等奖	2003
863	转炉烟气净化回收与综合利用技术	天津天铁冶金集团有限公司	罗永生 刘玉全 杨廷强 吴作成 宋海旺 闻义才 邢金泉 王振营	科技进步二等奖	2003
864	高龄焦炉维护技术的研究开发	天津天铁冶金集团有限公司	龙 平 刘超英 平金山 张 平 赵洪武 欧阳中然 林艳敏 哨洪臣	科技进步二等奖	2003
865	套管内侧钻工艺技术研究与应用	大港油田集团井下作业公司、大港油田集团钻采工艺研究院	郭继岩 胡永雄 贾正发 张 恒 黄德辉 罗永庆 于成水 常 青	科技进步二等奖	2003
866	大棚膜专用料线型低密度聚乙烯DFDA-9085	天津石油化工公司乙烯厂	李希宏 吴文清 张 英 寇承杰 李 邦 孙洪霞 韩国栋 赵文胜	科技进步二等奖	2003
867	无位置传感器永磁无刷直流电机及其微机控制系统	天津大学	夏长亮 史婷娜 王太勇 王 娟 陈 炜 李 斌 郑云祥 文 德	科技进步二等奖	2003
868	笔记本电脑电池全自动检测线	天津市升茂经贸科技开发中心、摩托罗拉(中国)电子有限公司	陈晓东 张 萌 马庆双 赵希军 刘 悦	科技进步二等奖	2003
869	重油加水乳化技术的研究与应用	天津大学	张金利 柴 铭 袁 兵 李红梅 王一平 李韦华 李 禄 张东利	科技进步二等奖	2003
870	现代草坪卷生产及应用推广	天津农垦集团总公司、天津红港绿茵花草有限公司	孙克泰 白智生 李悦生 孙国庆 郭继霞 张传胜 赵 龙 云宝庆 袁爱民 张介亮 卞学龙	科技进步二等奖	2003

续表6 **获天津市科学技术奖(一、二等奖)项目**

序号	项目名称	获奖单位	获奖人	获奖等级	获奖年份
871	熄风胶囊治疗小儿癫痫强直—阵挛性发作的研究	天津中医学院第一附属医院	马　融　李新民　魏小维　张喜莲　杨常泉　熊　杰　孙希焕　刘玉珍	科技进步二等奖	2003
872	黄樟素加氢合成二氢黄樟素的研究与开发	天津大学	那　平　马新宾　黄宗凉　李良龙　董　勇　赵沧燕　余延栋　马妙玲	科技进步二等奖	2003
873	层压型专业制卡带胶膜	天津博苑高新材料有限公司	鹿秀山　李增勇　李春刚　敬得发　孙　鹏　牛海梅　武海东　王建强	科技进步二等奖	2003
874	海水名特优水产品养殖技术推广	天津市水产技术推广站、天津市塘沽区水产局、天津市汉沽区水产技术推广站、天津市大港区水产技术推广站	张　勤　刘宗豹　张学彬　夏德庆　林春友　刘德永　武宝岭　袁金红　蔡　琰　张景增　郭富节	科技进步二等奖	2003
875	天津地区高层建筑超长结构无缝设计与施工全过程控制研究	中铁十八局集团有限公司、天津大学	顾谓建　张兴彦　李素清　刘海兰　洪　武　刘金林　娄汉国　葛志忠	科技进步二等奖	2003
876	高纯2,5—二甲氧基-4-氯苯胺制备新工艺	天津大学、天津市染料工业研究所	李　铧　王以强　张金利　张允中　方志平　张宝幸　王一平　赵沧燕	科技进步二等奖	2003
877	成品油销售及测控系统	天津大学、中国石油天然气股份有限公司华北石化分公司	刘宝坤　张景涛　童　刚　杨立峰　刘存柱　申亚芳　苏文利　余　斌	科技进步二等奖	2003
878	PY200大功率平地机	中外建发展股份有限公司	肖红路　许红旗　董志广　刘清华　薛玉玲　曹凤新　石学军　朱德江	科技进步二等奖	2003
879	腈纶聚合物造粒剂的研制与开发	天津工大高新技术实业公司	郑　帼　刘燕军　周　存　徐进云　魏俊富　孙波泉　姜　虹	科技进步二等奖	2003
880	职业性放射性疾病诊断标准(总则)及外照射慢性放射病诊断标准研制	中国医学科学院放射医学研究所	姜恩海　陈子齐　贾德林	科技进步二等奖	2003
881	高档有机颜料红179生产工艺	天津理工学院	李绍武　郑嗣华　李梅彤　温同生　于景明　吕金魁　马成先　闫绍柏	科技进步二等奖	2003
882	三镜联合治疗复杂性肝外胆管结石的临床研究	天津市南开医院	秦鸣放　邹富胜　李　文　王　庆　勾承月　李　宁　杨嫒蓉	科技进步二等奖	2003
883	无公害韭菜基地生产配套技术示范及推广	天津市植物保护研究所	谷希树　白义川　胡学雄　张永田　杨红军　陈俊荣　徐维红　夏金明　魏　军　朱荣芹	科技进步二等奖	2003
884	非线性动力学在难治性癫痫研究中的应用	天津医科大学	田　心　陈世畯　陶华英　宋毅军　王兆月　宋　莹　耿新玲	科技进步二等奖	2003
885	膜与膜过程基础研究	天津大学	王世昌　王　志　王宇新　李凭力　徐世昌　王纪孝　郝继华　李金通　张　颖	自然科学一等奖	2004
886	水利工程仿真基础理论与方法研究	天津大学	钟登华　白玉川　曹志先　冯　平	自然科学一等奖	2004
887	新型过渡金属有机化合物的合成、反应、结构和性质研究	南开大学	宋礼成、胡青眉、范洪涛、路国梁	自然科学一等奖	2004
888	焊接结构延寿中的超声波及相变应力作用研究	天津大学	霍立兴　王东坡　王文先　张玉凤　荆洪阳	自然科学一等奖	2004

续表6 获天津市科学技术奖(一、二等奖)项目

序号	项目名称	获奖单位	获奖人	获奖等级	获奖年份
889	髓系肿瘤染色体核型的研究	中国医学科学院中国协和医科大学血液学研究所血液病医院、实验血液学国家重点实验室	肖志坚 郝玉书 刘世和 李建波 卞寿庚 钱林生 薛艳萍	自然科学二等奖	2004
890	智能预测自适应控制理论与应用研究	南开大学、天津工程师范学院	陈增强 袁著祉 孙青林 张兴会 刘忠信 李 翔	自然科学二等奖	2004
891	有机光电薄膜的制备及相关器件性能研究	天津理工大学、南开大学	华玉林 印寿根 程晓曼	自然科学二等奖	2004
892	纳米新催化材料的制备及其在环保中的应用基础研究	南开大学	关乃佳 章福祥 陈继新 高文亮	自然科学二等奖	2004
893	固体激光器及其谐振腔	南开大学	张光寅 宋 峰 颜彩繁 焦忠勇 张包铮	自然科学二等奖	2004
894	铣削过程动力学建模、物理仿真与控制理论	天津大学	张大卫 黄 田 杨志永 徐安平 闫 兵	自然科学三等奖	2004
895	双向分化恶性肿瘤血管生成拟态分子机制的研究	天津医科大学附属肿瘤医院	孙保存 郝希山 张诗武 赵秀兰 邱志强	自然科学三等奖	2004
896	环糊精聚合物固体相光度法的研究	天津商学院	李 荣 姜子涛	自然科学三等奖	2004
897	胰淀素与2型糖尿病发病、磺脲类降糖药继发失效相关性及对策研究	天津医科大学总医院	朱铁虹 尹 潍 张卫华 高淑玮	自然科学三等奖	2004
898	非晶与纳米软磁材料的研究	天津理工大学	王 治 何开元 张雅静 贺淑莉	自然科学三等奖	2004
899	针刺干预脑梗塞的微血管机制研究	天津中医学院第一附属医院	杜元灏 翟 娜 关 玲 石学敏 李 谈	自然科学三等奖	2004
900	对环境友好的超高效除草剂的创制和开发研究	南开大学	李正名 王玲秀 贾国锋 黑中一 王素华 王建国 王红学 赵卫光 李永红 寇俊杰 范志金	技术发明一等奖	2004
901	直拉区熔(CFZ)硅单晶的研制	天津市环欧半导体材料技术有限公司	沈浩平 李 翔 汪雨田 刘为钢 高福林 胡元庆 郭丽华 高树良	技术发明二等奖	2004
902	影像板用新型光激励发光材料	天津理工大学	熊光楠 娄素云	技术发明二等奖	2004
903	用于食品安全评价与环境污染检测的生物芯片研究与应用	中国人民解放军军事医学科学院卫生学环境医学研究所	李君文 高志贤 靳连群 王红勇 王新为 晁福寰 金 敏 王 涛	技术发明二等奖	2004
904	与小麦中未知抗白粉病基因紧密连锁分子标记的筛选与利用	天津师范大学	王振英 彭永康 陈 宏 王景安	技术发明二等奖	2004
905	日照现场检测系统	天津大学	沈天行 袁 磊	技术发明二等奖	2004
906	乳酸芽孢杆菌粉剂的生产方法与应用	天津科技大学、天津市新星兽药厂	杜连祥 戚 薇 陈 莹 路福平 王建玲 吕学敏 魏建军	技术发明二等奖	2004
907	增益平坦的超宽带光纤放大器	南开大学	袁树忠 刘艳格 董孝义 开桂云 张伟刚 张 昊 蒙红云 于 岭	技术发明二等奖	2004
908	FA/O半导体材料切削剂及技术	河北工业大学	刘玉岭 檀柏梅 周建伟 王胜利 李薇薇	技术发明二等奖	2004
909	SY-120型日光温室卷帘机	天津市三元机电设备厂	赵世昌 范宝琴 孙洪安	技术发明三等奖	2004

续表6 获天津市科学技术奖(一、二等奖)项目

序号	项目名称	获奖单位	获奖人	获奖等级	获奖年份
910	共振筛动力学性能分析与调整技术	天津大学、平顶山天安煤业股份有限公司田庄选煤厂	陈予恕 高亚平 曹树谦 林 建 张文德 卢安民 郎作贵 郑和平 王志林	科技进步一等奖	2004
911	大港陆上油田提高开发水平地质技术研究及应用	中国石油天然气股份有限公司大港油田公司油气开发处	周嘉玺 赵平起 王华崇 倪天禄 赵 明 蔡明俊 徐世银 赵郁文 何 鲜 王大兴 王世军 陈智宇	科技进步一等奖	2004
912	天津轻轨工程抗震分析与减震降噪研究	天津大学、天津滨海快速交通发展有限公司	李忠献 丁 阳 王成博 张金立 张兴彦 高应钦 黄 健 樊素英 张智新 张爱华 韩圣章 于泳湖	科技进步一等奖	2004
913	河流、海洋和水环境数值模拟技术及其应用	天津大学	陶建华 袁德奎 刘长根 李清雪 姜国强 孙 涛 谢伟松 韩 光 宋文筠 何 磊 孙 健 杨祖声	科技进步一等奖	2004
914	TST-LCZ-3-80全钢载重子午线轮胎三鼓式一次法成型机	天津赛象科技股份有限公司	张芝泉 张建浩 朱伯明 王东海 毛小馨 张 晨 陈英铸 廖万辉 蒋富林 叶 健	科技进步一等奖	2004
915	松软土地基轻轨超长高架桥设计、施工控制技术研究	铁道第三勘察设计院、天津滨海快速交通发展有限公司、中铁十八局集团有限公司、天津大学	李小江 张金立 高应钦 孙树礼 张兴彦 孙衍福 张智新 李义兵 杨春立 郑永红 杨少玉 李 黎	科技进步一等奖	2004
916	血液肿瘤耐药机制及克服耐药研究	中国医学科学院中国协和医科大学血液学研究所血液病医院、实验血液学国家重点实验室	杨纯正 熊冬生 许元富 齐 静 高瀛岱 谭耀红 邵晓枫 杨 铭 范冬梅 彭 晖 薛艳萍 刘汉芝	科技进步一等奖	2004
917	赋形缓冲减振坐垫设计及其制造模具研制	天津大学、天津市天大银泰科技有限公司	崔国起 陈光辉 刘建军 周 昱 窦连贵 李林安 刘炳坤 刘洪涛 刁 海 杨 莉 赵 咏 闫建勇	科技进步一等奖	2004
918	天津城市居民恶性肿瘤流行趋势分析及预防的研究	天津医科大学附属肿瘤医院	郝希山 陈可欣 宋丰举 钱碧云 何 敏 于世北 王培忠 董淑芬 只向成 王继芳	科技进步一等奖	2004
919	天津博物馆建筑结构及施工关键技术研究	天津大学、天津六建建筑工程有限公司	陈志华 王小盾 余建星 陈质枫 严定中 张忠秀 肖广福 刘 杰 吴松年 李 阳 史 杰 张跃亭	科技进步一等奖	2004
920	蓟县山区综合技术开发与示范	蓟县山区综合开发有限责任公司	赵国明 李森阳 王铁锤 李 银 付志鸿 杜长城 王学珍 付立红	科技进步二等奖	2004
921	系列生物防护技术与装备	中国人民解放军军事医学科学院卫生装备研究所	陈世谦 孙景工 朱孟府 王南林 王永烈 刘圣军 杨荆泉 龚承元	科技进步二等奖	2004
922	复方丹参滴丸指纹图谱分析与质量控制技术	浙江大学、中国药品生物制品检定所、天津天士力集团有限公司	程翼宇 林瑞超 叶正良 钱忠直 范骁辉 刘 燕 王 毅 吴永江	科技进步二等奖	2004
923	三井工艺PX氧化反应过程模型化与操作优化	中国石化集团天津石油化工公司、华东理工大学	钱 锋 王铭松 颜学峰 李克明 杜文莉 杨 军 冯少辉 冯 利	科技进步二等奖	2004
924	肉羊胚胎产业化配套技术研究	天津市畜牧兽医研究所、天津吉盛畜牧业有限责任公司、天津市中敖畜牧业有限公司	冯建忠 刘海军 张金龙 杨 昇 刘玉堂 吴德国 阎振富 张效生	科技进步二等奖	2004

续表6 获天津市科学技术奖(一、二等奖)项目

序号	项目名称	获奖单位	获奖人	获奖等级	获奖年份
925	“丰花60”花椰菜(菜花)新品种选育	天津科润农业科技股份有限公司	孙德岭 李素文 张宝珍 赵前程 刘奎彬 蔡荣旗 方文惠	科技进步二等奖	2004
926	无公害蔬菜全程监测高产栽培技术示范与推广	天津市农业高新技术示范园区管理中心	王隆清 陈绍慧 杨小玲 王 萱 马洪英 杨振山 程 奕 乔志利 赵仁顺	科技进步二等奖	2004
927	大型泵站柱板式机墩动力分析、共振研究和应用	中水北方勘测设计研究有限责任公司	仇德彪 谢熙曦 贾伟智 闵家驹 洪慧俊 刘 群 门乃姣 刘冰营	科技进步二等奖	2004
928	玫瑰香汉沽产地葡萄酒的开发	中法合营王朝葡萄酿酒有限公司	高孝德 王树生 李 巍 张春娅 张福庆 尹吉泰 田凤英 刘建华	科技进步二等奖	2004
929	电弧炉炼钢综合节能技术开发	天津钢管有限责任公司、北京科技大学、钢铁研究总院	宋嘉鹏 李士琦 姜桂连 刘润藻 郭 征 张再斌 李京社 韩进山	科技进步二等奖	2004
930	Φ6〃区熔硅单晶的研制	天津市环欧半导体材料技术有限公司	沈浩平 李 翔 汪雨田 刘为钢 高福林 郭丽华 高树良 咎兴利	科技进步二等奖	2004
931	血液干细胞移植治疗肢体缺血的基础和临床研究	中国医学科学院中国协和医科大学血液学研究所血液病医院、实验血液学国家重点实验室、国家干细胞工程技术研究中心	韩忠朝 黄平平 李尚珠 韩明哲 肖志坚 杨仁池 邱录贵 冯四洲	科技进步二等奖	2004
932	食品安全快速检测方法与装备研究	中国人民解放军军事医学科学院卫生学环境医学研究所	高志贤 王红勇 李凤琴 房彦军 周焕英 李君文 计 融 宁保安	科技进步二等奖	2004
933	动态环境模拟系统研制	天津鼎成高新技术产业有限公司	张国胜 鲁士军 王四新 沈延康 罗学惠 林其生 胡 珂 田魁岳	科技进步二等奖	2004
934	天津天铁冶金集团有限公司CIMS工程	天津天铁冶金集团有限公司	刘玉全 龙 平 吕春风 王春常 韩金玉 王向东 魏 涛 徐 平	科技进步二等奖	2004
935	脑膜瘤PDGF-B和VEGF基因表达及反义核酸体外抑瘤作用的研究	天津医科大学总医院	杨树源 雪 亮 徐广明 周阅昌 林 瑜 杨新宇 张建宁	科技进步二等奖	2004
936	医院多重耐药细菌感染的基础和临床研究	天津医科大学第二医院	宋诗铎 祁 伟 魏殿军 刘德梦 薛艳萍 巩 路 郝邯生 何 屏	科技进步二等奖	2004
937	新型填料集成技术在催化分馏和吸收稳定系统中的开发应用	天津大学、中国石油天然气股份有限公司大庆炼化分公司	李鑫钢 魏 强 徐占武 孙津生 王义东 张吕鸿 王功祥 姜 斌	科技进步二等奖	2004
938	丙烯酸树脂骨水泥	天津市合成材料工业研究所	窦宏仪 王 磊 徐士清 刘 沛 刘 振	科技进步二等奖	2004
939	改善骨折断端力学环境促进骨折愈合的研究	天津市天津医院	张铁良 尹双波 张建国 林枫松	科技进步二等奖	2004
940	勘测设计协同作业系统研究及应用	铁道第三勘察设计院	郑致平 李华良 高春梅 罗法水 时 瑞 于 炀 侯继伟 陈志军	科技进步二等奖	2004
941	益气活血软脉方药对老年动脉硬化影响的临床与实验研究	天津中医学院、天津中医学院第一附属医院	张军平 张伯礼 郭利平 陈晓玉 阮士怡 张志尧 高秀梅	科技进步二等奖	2004
942	电气化铁路牵引供电系统新型成套设计技术研究	铁道第三勘察设计院	蒋先国 崔校玉 陈学光 侯树清 杨振龙 张兴昭 周 凡 张洪涛	科技进步二等奖	2004
943	高层钢管混凝土建筑抗震性能试验与理论研究	天津大学	李忠献 丁 阳 王成博 田 力 张爱华 许成样 卢海林 郝水昶	科技进步二等奖	2004

续表6 **获天津市科学技术奖(一、二等奖)项目**

序号	项目名称	获奖单位	获奖人	获奖等级	获奖年份
944	凝析油气田型地下储气库地面工艺技术研究	天津大港油田集团石油工程有限责任公司	孟凡彬 刘科慧 王　峰 周学深 陈雪松 胡　颖 李力秀 高述生	科技进步二等奖	2004
945	健康生态型氧气发生器的研制	河北工业大学	梁广川 梁金生 欧秀芹 李昌隆 陈忠南	科技进步二等奖	2004
946	行波型超声波电机及其控制系统研究与应用	天津大学	夏长亮 史婷娜 王太勇 徐绍辉 李　斌 郑云祥 郑　尧 杨　荣	科技进步二等奖	2004
947	新型药肥复合型种衣剂技术推广应用	天津市植保植检站、中国农业大学种衣剂应用化学技术研究发展中心、天津科润北方种衣剂有限公司、天津市宝坻区农业技术推广服务中心、宁河县农业技术推广中心	谢建军 刘西莉 张志武 马淑慧 哈德卿 曹玉霞 杨红军 王红梅 王秀英 史滟濒 史继宝	科技进步二等奖	2004
948	新型涤纶短纤油剂的研制与开发	天津工业大学、中国石化集团天津石油化工公司	郑　帼 陈卡佳 葛　启 刘燕军 陈伯夫 周　存 徐进云 王建中	科技进步二等奖	2004
949	天津市机动车安全检验多媒体网络信息资源管理系统	天津市公安局车辆管理所、天津市天源检测设备技术服务有限公司	武长顺 黄全利 薛俊友 陈和平 黄全有 李贺伟 谢　刚 尤文平	科技进步二等奖	2004
950	半导体封装集成质量控制计算机辅助管理系统研究与开发	天津大学	齐二石 何曙光 聂　斌 张勋仁 简祯富 刘洪涛 李中阳 魏红美	科技进步二等奖	2004
951	泰达开发区生态型水源地的系统构建技术和工程应用	中国科学院生态环境研究中心、天津泰达自来水公司	曲久辉 张广云 尹澄清 冯文清 刘俊新 仲　志 陈耀东 王新兵	科技进步二等奖	2004
952	大气颗粒物源解析及环境监测信息管理系统	天津市环境监测中心、南开大学	秦保平 朱　坦 赵立蔚 孙　韧 刘　伟 解　辉 白志鹏 张　赞	科技进步二等奖	2004
953	城市污水处理厂工程质量验收规范	天津市市政工程质量监督站	张宝林 石万同 任家琪 樊兆强 张多马 韩风桐 林文波 杨玉淮	科技进步二等奖	2004
954	低位抽真空吹填土及其下软土地基加固技术	天津市水利科学研究所	曹大正 顾立军 刘学功 闫海新 冯伟骞 史庆生 孙永军 费守明	科技进步二等奖	2004
955	内镜、腹腔镜联合治疗肝外胆管结石方法研究及临床应用	天津市南开医院、天津市中西医结合医院、天津市中西医结合急腹症研究所	秦鸣放 赵宏志 邹富胜 王　庆 勾承月 李　宁 王震宇 王　洁	科技进步二等奖	2004
956	徽膜级线型低密度聚乙烯专用树脂DFDA-9020	天津石油化工公司乙烯厂	彭树森 吴文清 孙洪霞 孙彤杰 张　英 李　邦 寇承杰 马洪涛	科技进步二等奖	2004
957	氯代羟基二苯醚类化合物的生产工艺	天津理工大学	卢俊瑞 张桂芝 吕振波 尹　宁 李　平 鲍秀荣 张　昱	科技进步二等奖	2004
958	枣园低流度复杂断块油藏稳产技术研究及应用	中国石油大港油田南部油气开发公司	李晓良 张家良 王庆魁 夏国朝 张学才 郭旭耀 王学立 倪金忠	科技进步二等奖	2004
959	黄骅凹陷隐蔽油气藏成藏规律研究与勘探实践	中国石油大港油田油气勘探开发技术研究中心	吴水平 郝立华 王　听 周育文 刘淑芝 王玉善 廉　梅 任彩云	科技进步二等奖	2004
960	针刺治疗呆症的临床及分子机理研究	天津中医学院第一附属医院	韩景献 李　平 于建春 刘庆忠 于　涛 丁晓蓉	科技进步二等奖	2004
961	活血化瘀软坚散结法对EMS神经—内分泌—免疫网络的整体调节作用	天津中医学院第二附属医院	韩　冰 萧美茹 李同玺 马平仲 赵志梅 曹立幸 卫爱武 许丽芬	科技进步二等奖	2004

续表6　　获天津市科学技术奖(一、二等奖)项目

序号	项目名称	获奖单位	获奖人	获奖等级	获奖年份
962	涤纶异形短纤维的研制	中国石油化工股份有限公司天津分公司化纤厂、东华大学	王建中 王华平 张勇 杨崇倡 肖刚 朱方亮 张玉梅 周天	科技进步二等奖	2004
963	4102增压中冷车用柴油机关键技术的研究及应用	天津大学、东风朝阳柴油机有限责任公司	宋崇林 王守元 高文志 贾贵起 张延峰 赵昌普 贺兆欣 庞华廷	科技进步二等奖	2004
964	应用腹腔镜微创手术治疗肾上腺疾病的临床研究	天津医科大学总医院	李黎明 林毅 朱军 强万明 刘桂彬	科技进步二等奖	2004
965	IMDS系统研究与应用	中国网通集团天津市通信公司	滕勇 刘克康 孙雄 梅冬 林伟 李淑婷 倪晓峻 何凯	科技进步二等奖	2004
966	立体定向治疗囊性颅咽管瘤的基础研究与临床应用	中国人民解放军第二五四医院、中国人民解放军海军总医院	江荣才 于新 刘宗惠 李士月 陈琳 于君 郭阳 修波	科技进步二等奖	2004
967	THP10—10000100000千牛数控等温锻造液压机	天津市天锻压力机有限公司	卢志永 冯永平 田永康 刘玉民 陈福祥 毕大森 隋岩 芦震	科技进步二等奖	2004
968	复杂地质条件下彭水长隧道综合施工技术	中铁十八局集团有限公司	雷升祥 冯涛 马民 崔永杰 高扬 张守同 梁双宝 徐纪永	科技进步二等奖	2004
969	严重眼外伤的临床与实验研究	天津医科大学总医院	颜华 许瀛海 史秀茹 王秀芳 于金国 王鑫	科技进步二等奖	2004
970	天津港集装箱网络自动化操作管理系统	天津港集装箱码头有限公司	李宝元 薛翎森 马全胜 刘宝合 刘振鹏 李悦军 王鲲 阎武	科技进步二等奖	2004
971	越夏栽培黄瓜新品种"津优4号"的选育	天津科润农业科技股份有限公司	马德华 吕淑珍 霍振荣 李淑菊 庞金安	科技进步二等奖	2004
972	新型智能电阻焊控制器及焊机集中控制联网管理系统	天津七所高科技有限公司	张益民 邵丽 成海晖 郭锦华 卢修泉 徐建辉 尉学森 何为	科技进步二等奖	2004
973	大港潜山深层钻井技术研究与应用	大港油田集团钻采工艺研究院	路继臣 李洪俊 何卫滨 高彦香 王长在 徐学军 龚雅明 马金山	科技进步二等奖	2004
974	氯胺酮作用机理及临床应用新途径研究	天津医科大学总医院	王国林 于泳浩 谢虹 王海云 陈鸿 崔薇 任书琴	科技进步二等奖	2004
975	表面为不可展开曲面大型机器缝合复合材料制件的研制	天津工业大学	李嘉禄 吴晓青 李晓久 焦亚男 陈利 张国利 万振凯 周清	科技进步二等奖	2004
976	天津市大气污染总量控制及分阶段防治技术研究	南开大学、天津市环境保护局	朱坦 刘洁 冯银厂 张裕芬 徐宏辉 王帅杰 吴建会 白志鹏	科技进步二等奖	2004
977	基于合成受体的分子识别及其纳米超分子体系的构筑	南开大学	刘育 张衡益 陈勇	自然科学一等奖	2005
978	方剂组分配伍关键科学问题的基础研究	天津中医学院、中国中医科学院、浙江大学、中国人民解放军军事医学科学院毒物药物研究所、清华大学、中国科学院大连化学物理研究所、北京中医药大学	张伯礼 王永炎 程翼宇 李澎涛 梁鑫森 罗国安 张永祥 高秀梅 乔延江 商洪才 史大卓 郭利平	自然科学一等奖	2005
979	代数组合学中的组合变换	南开大学	陈永川	自然科学一等奖	2005
980	分子模板——分子识别联用的基础研究和应用	南开大学	何锡文 陈朗星 李文友 李一峻	自然科学二等奖	2005

续表6 获天津市科学技术奖(一、二等奖)项目

序号	项目名称	获奖单位	获奖人	获奖等级	获奖年份
981	细胞代谢信息与次生产物合成的基础研究	天津大学	元英进 马红武 葛志强 赵学明 李春	自然科学二等奖	2005
982	中国人视网膜色素变性分子遗传学研究	天津医科大学、天津市眼科医院	赵堪兴 王乐今 李宁东 王擎 赵晨 陆莎莎 王立 熊世红	自然科学二等奖	2005
983	白血病细胞性质和功能的研究	中国医学科学院血液学研究所、实验血液学国家重点实验室	吴克复 郑国光 马小彤 饶青 林永敏 张斌 杨应华 张秀军	自然科学二等奖	2005
984	生物及结构复合材料原位自生复合机制的基础研究	河北工业大学、上海交通大学	崔春翔 申玉田 孙继兵 李艳春 徐艳姬 王如 刘双进 吴人洁	自然科学二等奖	2005
985	新型有机功能化合物设计、合成及性能研究	南开大学	孟继本 李金亮 徐黎立 吉保明 李小六 王永梅	自然科学二等奖	2005
986	大型海岸工程结构物稳定性分析理论与方法	天津大学	王元战 闫澍旺 李炎保 杨树耕 刘建起 郑斌 华雷娜	自然科学二等奖	2005
987	光、电化学生物传感技术理论研究	南开大学	陈强 史海滨 吴宝艳 李静 黄加栋	自然科学二等奖	2005
988	不对称合成中新型手性磷、氮试剂的设计、合成和应用研究	南开大学	唐除痴 周正洪 赵国锋 李康应	自然科学三等奖	2005
989	运动性疲劳的线粒体膜分子机制运动氧化应激及其调控研究	天津体育学院	张勇 刘树森 文立 聂金雷	自然科学三等奖	2005
990	激光快速凝固TiC-Ni复合涂层的微观结构和耐磨性研究	天津工业大学	孙荣禄 王云山 唐英 杨洗陈	自然科学三等奖	2005
991	树脂法双酚A生产新工艺	天津大学、天津双孚精细化工有限公司、北京燕山石化技术开发设计公司	张敏华 洪定一 谈遒 秦金来 刘宗章 周继东 董秀芹 钱胜华 朱洪涛 张宗礼 刘成 李复生	技术发明一等奖	2005
992	固体表面高精密加工技术及专用纳米材料	河北工业大学	刘玉岭 檀柏梅 李薇薇 王娟 牛新环 张西慧 张建新 刘钠	技术发明二等奖	2005
993	大尺寸光学级铌酸锂晶体	南开大学	孔勇发 许京军 孙军 孙骞 张光寅	技术发明二等奖	2005
994	2.5GHzSiO_2/ZnO/IDT/金刚石膜SAW滤波器的研究	天津理工大学	杨保和 陈希明 吴小国 熊瑛 常明 孙杰	技术发明二等奖	2005
995	用于发酵液分离与精制的中空纤维膜双向流技术	天津工业大学、天津膜天膜工程技术有限公司	吕晓龙 郭振友 马世虎 李先锋	技术发明二等奖	2005
996	一种腈纶聚合物造粒剂、制造方法及其应用	天津工大高新技术实业公司	郑帼 刘燕军 周存 徐进云 孙波泉 姜虹 辛丽霞	技术发明二等奖	2005
997	显微外科手术机器人系统	天津大学、南开大学、天津市天津医院	王树新 张建勋 韩宝平 负今天 李群智 丁杰男	技术发明二等奖	2005
998	氟硅酸钠氨化生产高补强白炭黑	天津化工研究设计院、多氟多化工股份有限公司	宁延生 朱春雨 侯红军 张富山 马慧斌 陈宏伟	技术发明二等奖	2005
999	产生高Y-亚麻酸含量的转基因大豆的方法	南开大学	邢来君 李明春 卜云萍 财音青格尔	技术发明二等奖	2005
1000	紫外荧光防伪纤维	天津南开戈德集团有限公司、天津南开大学戈德防伪技术有限公司	李伯平 王淑芳 董铁望 王旭	技术发明二等奖	2005
1001	锂离子电池负极材料中间相炭微球的研制	天津大学、天津市铁诚电池材料有限公司	王成扬 贾永平 郑嘉明 高林汉 张毅民 刘国强	技术发明二等奖	2005

续表6　　获天津市科学技术奖(一、二等奖)项目

序号	项目名称	获奖单位	获奖人	获奖等级	获奖年份
1002	高效环保型制冷剂及优化匹配新技术	天津大学	杨　昭　马一太　李　汛　苏维诚　李丽新　李敏霞　刘圣春	技术发明二等奖	2005
1003	智能中空纤维分离膜及其应用研究	天津工业大学、天津膜天膜工程技术有限公司	肖长发　安树林　贾广霞　封　严　李先锋　刘　亚　张宇峰　杜启云	技术发明二等奖	2005
1004	秸秆发酵生物添加剂及其配制方法	天津市农业生物技术研究中心	陈秀为　沈　庆	技术发明三等奖	2005
1005	中药浸取液三相流化床高效防垢蒸发浓缩技术及装置	天津大学、天津中新药业集团股份有限公司乐仁堂制药厂	刘明言　聂万达　李修伦　凌宁生　林瑞泰	技术发明三等奖	2005
1006	新型聚酯缩聚催化剂的研制	中国石化集团天津石油化工公司	郭灵通　臧国强　李明玉　张　媛　马颖涛	技术发明三等奖	2005
1007	生物降解塑料聚3—羟基丁酸酯(PHB)发泡材料加工技术	中国民用航空学院、天津市一轻集团(控股)有限公司	李　梅　李志强　张　楠　霍晓燕　李志新	技术发明三等奖	2005
1008	天津市SARS患者流行病学回顾性调查和健康随访与干预试验研究	天津市卫生局、中国人民武装警察部队医学院附属医院、天津市传染病医院、天津市海河医院、天津市卫生防病中心、天津中医学院、天津市胸科医院	张　愈　田惠光　李玉明　曹武奎　张伯礼　王撷秀　张玉环　只达石　程津新　焦振山　曹　茜　王世鑫	科技进步一等奖	2005
1009	水利枢纽厂坝隔(导)墙流激振动与结构优化研究	天津大学	练继建　崔广涛　杨　敏　彭新民　安　刚　马　斌　黄锦林　白俊光　张　蕊　黄津明	科技进步一等奖	2005
1010	人脑胶质瘤的基础与临床研究	天津医科大学总医院	浦佩玉　康春生　于士柱　王金环　黄　强　王广秀　江荣才　钟　跃　董　伦　夏之柏　尤永平　李彦和	科技进步一等奖	2005
1011	农业专家系统(黄瓜、葡萄、猪、奶牛、对虾、河蟹)开发与应用	天津市农科院信息研究所、天津市水产研究所、天津农学院、天津市畜牧兽医研究所、天津市林业果树研究所、天津科润农业科技股份有限公司黄瓜研究所、北京农业信息技术研究中心	陆文龙　宋文平　李千军　张树林　田淑芬　张学炜　崔洪宇　宋治文　马享优　傅志茹　马　墉　赵先健	科技进步一等奖	2005
1012	多脏器功能障碍综合征发病机理及中西医结合治疗的深入研究	天津市中西医结合急腹症研究所、天津市第一中心医院、天津市天津医院、天津市烧伤研究所、南开大学、天津医科大学	吴咸中　崔乃强　邓诗琳　曹书华　金鸿宾　方步武　杨文修　傅　强　于泳浩　崔克亮	科技进步一等奖	2005
1013	高产多抗杂交粳稻新品种“3优18”的选育	天津市水稻研究所	刘学军　马忠友　孙林静　苏京平　刘俊云　郭　郢	科技进步一等奖	2005
1014	高档有机着色材料的工艺研究与产业化	天津理工大学、天津理工产业股份有限公司	李绍武　郑嗣华　李梅彤　温同生　马成先　栾寿海　闫绍柏　吕金魁　曹玉臣　吴志东　张金来　郑伯旭	科技进步一等奖	2005
1015	基于模糊小生境遗传算法优化的电机设计技术研究与应用	天津大学、扎努西电气机械天津压缩机有限公司	夏长亮　史婷娜　陈　炜　王太勇　万淑敏　甄洪滨　宋国兰　李　斌　修　杰　方红伟　薛　梅　李洪凤	科技进步一等奖	2005
1016	大港油田南部滩海油气富集规律与预探突破	中国石油大港油田勘探开发研究院	陈　松　段润梅　何　滨　汪勤学　刘　福　于　平　袁淑琴　肖建玲　苏俊青　王桂芝　于长华　张　兵	科技进步一等奖	2005
1017	数字式金属浮子流量计的研制	天津大学、天津市天大泰和自控仪表技术有限公司	张　涛　徐　英　李　刚　孙宏军　李巧真　李宏锁　倪晋铨　苏　锋	科技进步一等奖	2005
1018	室内空气污染表征与控制技术开发	南开大学、中国人民解放军军事医学科学院卫生学环境医学研究所	白志鹏　袭著革　朱　坦　戴树桂　张华山　杨丹凤　董永春　姬亚芹	科技进步二等奖	2005

续表6 获天津市科学技术奖(一、二等奖)项目

序号	项目名称	获奖单位	获奖人	获奖等级	获奖年份
1019	二硝基二苯乙烯二磺酸新型氧化工艺的开发与应用	天津大学、河北华煜化工股份有限公司	张凤宝 张国亮 戈建华 覃志忠 段卫东 宫占胜 赵永江 王淑兰	科技进步二等奖	2005
1020	应激对心肌的损伤作用及防护措施的研究	中国人民解放军军事医学科学院卫生学环境医学研究所	钱令嘉 弓景波 赵 云 杨发青 吴淑庆 胥 达 易 丹 王新兴	科技进步二等奖	2005
1021	针刺治疗郁证疗效评价及对神经内分泌、免疫等相关因素的影响	天津中医学院第一附医院	石学敏 侯 庆 王 舒 杜元灏 申鹏飞 阎 莉 刘 健 仝桂兰	科技进步二等奖	2005
1022	"益气调血,扶本培元"针法治疗老年期痴呆的研究	天津中医学院第一附属医院	韩景献 于建春 于 涛 丁晓蓉 刘存志 王 彤 张雪竹 孟迎春	科技进步二等奖	2005
1023	机群智能化工程机械	天津工程机械研究院、天津鼎盛工程机械有限公司、北京航空航天大学、河北工业大学、天津大学	郑尚龙 李学忠 王福山 吴国祥 张明路 魏洪兴 王振刚 钱明刚	科技进步二等奖	2005
1024	水泥工业与民用空间网格结构关键技术研究	天津大学、天津水泥工业设计研究院	陈志华 王小盾 刘锡良 郑水田 靖 华 韩庆华 尹 越 闫翔宇	科技进步二等奖	2005
1025	集装箱码头生产过程控制可视化管理系统	天津港集装箱码头有限公司	黄力军 李宝元 马平文 薛翎森 马全胜 刘振鹏 周儒欣 秦加法	科技进步二等奖	2005
1026	新建客运专线轨道设计技术研究	铁道第三勘察设计院	李树德 闫红亮 齐春雨 李秉涛 刘林平 仇 湘 胡叙洪 高福康	科技进步二等奖	2005
1027	高磨蚀性和粘湿性混合料的破碎工艺研究与设备的开发	中天仕名科技集团有限公司	廖正光 彭海兰 潘新庆 王自清 祁俊尧 陶 峰	科技进步二等奖	2005
1028	SARS中医证候学及中西医结合疗效分析研究	天津中医学院、天津中医学院第一附属医院、天津市传染病医院、天津中医学院第二附属医院	张伯礼 张军平 梁树人 工泓午 马 融 孙增涛 高秀梅 贾彦涛	科技进步二等奖	2005
1029	补肾活血法在肾间质纤维化上的应用研究	天津市中医药研究院、天津市公安医院、天津医科大学	张大宁 张勉之 张敏英 多秀瀛 王 莹 刘树松	科技进步二等奖	2005
1030	重组人ICAM—1膜外片段蛋白和建立人血清sICAM—1RIA技术及临床应用	天津医科大学总医院	方佩华 吕 枚 李 宁 张志友 孟召伟 高 硕	科技进步二等奖	2005
1031	国内外名特优新蔬菜品种的引进与推广	天津科润农业科技股份有限公司、天津市农业高新技术示范园区管理中心、天津市园艺工程研究所	孙德岭 李洪安 管长志 吴 峰 高国训 李成彤 鲁福成 王利英 王 萱 马洪英 王 莅	科技进步二等奖	2005
1032	天津电力民用电管理信息系统	天津市民用电力发展公司	戴祝英 刘学智 刘 东 刘 君 刘占东 冯 涛 刘 佳 王 延	科技进步二等奖	2005
1033	高转化率氢化可的松生产菌株蓝色梨头霉JY-2#的选育与应用	天津科技大学、天津市津津药业有限公司	杜连祥 王 敏 路福平 庞俊陆 袁东超 董艳苓 别松涛 只莹莹	科技进步二等奖	2005
1034	汽车电控液力自动变速器(AT)电控单元ECU及AT关键技术研究	天津市工业自动化仪表研究所、天津市天派工业自动化技术有限公司、天津一汽夏利汽车股份有限公司变速器分公司	陈宝奎 徐滨宽 孟繁中 秦克景 史小贤 孙崇炎 张 建 刘 莹	科技进步二等奖	2005
1035	新混凝土防碳化技术研究及应用	中水北方勘测设计研究有限责任公司	武永新 吴正桥 于玉森 耿振云 李秀明 许煜忠 时长波 于海江	科技进步二等奖	2005
1036	脑外科无框架立体定向仪	天津市华志计算机应用有限公司	关 伟 王荣军 陈国良	科技进步二等奖	2005

续表6 获天津市科学技术奖(一、二等奖)项目

序号	项目名称	获奖单位	获奖人	获奖等级	获奖年份
1037	千吨级海水循环冷却技术研究与工程示范	国家海洋局天津海水淡化与综合利用研究所、天津渤海化工有限责任公司天津碱厂	侯纯扬 赖振国 武杰 吴芸芳 王维珍 高良富 李亚红 刘春艳	科技进步二等奖	2005
1038	TP-CQ特殊扣套管开发研究	天津钢管集团有限公司	王京 刘硕琼 李强 徐志谦 扬博 白仁昭 张军 孙宇	科技进步二等奖	2005
1039	脑垂体腺瘤生物学特征与临床诊治的研究	天津医科大学总医院	张建宁 朱涛 杨树源 李萍 佟晓光 朱士广 刘兵 张云亭	科技进步二等奖	2005
1040	插齿加工机床数控化关键技术研究	天津大学、天津第一机床总厂	王树新 柴宝连 喻宏波 王威 方沂 李彦征 贺琼义	科技进步二等奖	2005
1041	农药多残留快速检测试剂盒的研制和开发	天津科技大学	王硕 曹小红 张燕 王俊平 段振娟	科技进步二等奖	2005
1042	淡水鱼类工厂化育苗技术的研究	天津农学院、天津市西青区精武水产良种场、天津市换新水产良种场	邢克智 郭永军 蔡中华 陈成勋 陶秉春 马敬福 金万昆 张美婷	科技进步二等奖	2005
1043	水工闸门水动力及其流激振动特性研究与工程应用	天津大学	练继建 杨敏 彭新民 李火坤 安刚 林继镛 王丽娟 白俊光	科技进步二等奖	2005
1044	机电设备智能诊断与动态测控系统	天津大学	王太勇 夏长亮 秦旭达 土国锋 万淑敏 邓学欣 彭永胜	科技进步二等奖	2005
1045	天津市水污染物排放总量控制技术与方法研究	天津市引滦水资源保护领导小组办公室、天津大学、天津市环境监测中心	辛志伟 钟定胜 张宏伟 张继红 张淑英 杨桂玲 孙韧	科技进步二等奖	2005
1046	转基因产品检测方法的研究	中华人民共和国天津出入境检验检疫局	郑文杰 刘烜 赵卫东 刘伟 唐丹舟 贺艳 刘辉 高晓敏	科技进步二等奖	2005
1047	MCl00型摩托车测试用交流底盘测功机的研制	天津大学、天津市天波科达科技有限公司	陶俊卫 任泽牛 任立环 张坤良 李志宏 庞晓伟 丁至珠 李建兴	科技进步二等奖	2005
1048	绞吸挖泥船计算机辅助决策系统	天津航道局、上海交大东伟科技有限公司	周泉生 田俊峰 顾明 刘瑞祥 朱小明 丁树友 李金贵 李瑞祥	科技进步二等奖	2005
1049	微创手术在泌尿系统肿瘤治疗中的作用	天津市泌尿外科研究所	徐勇 牛远杰 赵耀瑞 许淑华 刘春雨 畅继武 陆志强 马宝杰	科技进步二等奖	2005
1050	S-THP61—500+1250+1000温冷挤压液压机生产线	天津市天锻压力机有限公司	李森 毕大森 吴爱国 隋岩 李海军 李凤岚 郭金宝 商玉锦	科技进步二等奖	2005
1051	先行“协同办公、目录服务及资源应用平台”软件包	天津市电子计算机研究所	徐梦苏 刘彦凯 王家超 边学海 边文奎 屈凤荣 王晶晶 马振贵	科技进步二等奖	2005
1052	猪人工授精技术推广	天津市畜牧局、天津市畜牧兽医站、天津市家畜繁育科技服务中心	隋茁 赵祥增 莫会松 杜淑清 周友明 杨占明 李凯 王德恩 李振宽 刘同藻 王祖昌	科技进步二等奖	2005
1053	神经干细胞移植治疗颅脑损伤的研究	天津医科大学总医院、中国医学科学院血液学研究所血液病医院	杨树源 刘辉 张建宁 王宁 林欣 卓杰 韩忠朝 刘斌	科技进步二等奖	2005
1054	天津市燃气管网地理信息系统的研究	天津市燃气集团有限公司	张天华 孙伯全 金建平 张全雨 于文霞 高秀民 包彬 费学欣	科技进步二等奖	2005

续表6 获天津市科学技术奖(一、二等奖)项目

序号	项目名称	获奖单位	获奖人	获奖等级	获奖年份
1055	沿海多功能航标工作船	中华人民共和国天津海事局、中国船舶工业集团公司第七〇八研究所、中港集团天津船舶工程有限公司	赵业兴 陈英俊 孟淑媛 焦修明 葛明奎 李含苹 王如政 王先建	科技进步二等奖	2005
1056	中医药抗SARS病毒的基础与临床研究	天津医科大学总医院	陈津生 李 彬 唐 方 张京玲 孙 忻 王 安 李正祥 刘 弘	科技进步二等奖	2005
1057	水泥窑尾新型行喷脉冲袋收尘器的开发与应用	中天仕名科技集团有限公司	王作杰 李志军 李继海 李 勇 季永利 戴 浚 王国有 李明飞	科技进步二等奖	2005
1058	强化树突状细胞转化特异性CTL治疗肿瘤的基础及临床应用研究	天津市泌尿外科研究所	畅继武 李振莉 隋志方 汤 洋 庞志宇 张淑敏 马富玲 张淑敏	科技进步二等奖	2005
1059	液动冲击旋转钻井技术研究	大港油田集团钻采工艺研究院	胡国清 张文华 桑 路 工 雷 徐学军 张永忠 谈献英 泰建民	科技进步二等奖	2005
1060	压裂充填防砂工艺技术研究	大港油田集团有限责任公司钻采工艺技术开发服务中心	李怀文 王绍刚 陈桂和 董正海 马德中 党 伟 何志勇 槐春生	科技进步二等奖	2005
1061	耐寒性不结球白菜资源引进及杂交新品种“寒绿”选育	天津科润农业科技股份有限公司	张 斌 宋连久 刘晓晖 闻凤英 赵 冰 丘玉秀 王玉龙 罗智敏	科技进步二等奖	2005
1062	《纳米生物技术》	天津大学	姜忠义 成国祥	科技进步二等奖	2005
1063	优质春大棚黄瓜新品种津优10号	天津科润农业科技股份有限公司	王 全 哈玉洁 杨瑞环 刘殿林	科技进步二等奖	2005
1064	节能高速玻璃器皿压制生产线的推广	天津科技大学	张建国 朱根土 秦 诚 傅 旻 白瑞祥 张峻霞 李茂廷 胡 军 苏海龙 陈 浩 刘 卉	科技进步二等奖	2005
1065	天铁工业用水综合处理技术开发	天津天铁冶金集团有限公司	吕春风 韩金玉 吴作成 尹世谦 凌兵善 杨作清 王南山 张 辉	科技进步二等奖	2005
1066	ABS道路试验方法及JA50型ABS测试仪的研究与开发	中国汽车技术研究中心、上海耐思科技有限公司	刘 地 曹 伟 赵义瑜 许志光 吴节灵 尚庆福 岑文远	科技进步二等奖	2005
1067	汽油机塑料进气歧管的开发	天津大学、重庆宗申汽车进气系统制造有限公司	刘德新 蒋中林	科技进步二等奖	2005
1068	PWM可逆大功率电池测试系统	天津理工大学	魏克新 赵 钢 黄孙伟 万仁君 张书军	科技进步二等奖	2005
1069	微囊生物细胞移植研究	天津市第三中心医院	杜 智 李 涛 陆 伟 邵新华 方淑昌 朱争艳	科技进步二等奖	2005
1070	头孢菌素药物中间体(GCLE)	天津药物研究院	孟 红 赵 平 王学知 刘志友 徐 莉 蒋婉琳 曹 光	科技进步二等奖	2005
1071	老年性痴呆的实验性病理一影像学研究	天津市第一中心医院	祁 吉 宋 焱 尹建忠 刘 筠 叶 静	科技进步二等奖	2005
1072	应用TPS三维立体种植放射性^{125}I粒子近距离治疗晚期肺癌	天津医科大学第二医院	柴树德 毛玉权 郑广钧 闫卫亮 杨景魁 梁吉祥 石树远 田美荣	科技进步二等奖	2005

央广播事业局参加“全国彩色电视制式检验与经验交流会”,进行工作汇报。在全国汇报会上,虽然看到国家彩电的从无到有,但全国未有任何一个自主研究的彩电制式能胜出。

1971年,天津大学为了加强在国家彩电制式攻关方面的理论研究和实验研究工作,成立由俞斯乐任技术负责人的彩色电视科研组,成员包括:陈容之、王兆华、张春田、李桂苓、野锦德、丁润涛、黄元、潘一匡、郭福云、李华、李惠敏、许树檀、李文元等。他们通过对国外三种制式进行分析研究与比较,选定以PAL制为突破方向。为了能通晓PAL制,掌握其设计思想与特点、电路工作原理和研制编解码器,彩电科研组于1971年3月,通过国防工业出版社出版国内第一本以PAL制为主线讲述彩色电视原理和设备的书籍《彩色电视技术》。实际内容是翻译德文期刊《RUNDFUNK-TECHNISCHE MITTEILUNGEN》(1966-1967)上连载的PAL制讲座文章,再经编辑而成。

此后九年(1971至1979),由俞斯乐任技术负责人天津大学彩色电视科研组相继开展制式研究专用设备研制、PAL超声延迟线研究、相位逐行对换的正交平衡调幅制(换相制)研究以及制式攻关收尾等工作,在全国彩色电视大会战留下重彩浓笔的一页。

1971~1976年,为了能对PAL制及新制式进行实验研究,彩电组以李桂苓、野锦德等为主,投入不少人力自行研制供制式研究专用的编解码器等设备。研制从提高国内专业工厂生产的PAL编码器开始。首先在平衡性上进行改进,并将其做成具有切换功能;另外又在彩色副载频附加半场频(25Hz)偏置的方法上也有所改变,使其也能在加与不加之间进行切换。这样,就可以适应做两种不同制式性能比较实验的需要。研制换相制编码器的主要难点是在预制换相副载波和提高平衡调幅器的平衡性。为此,设计精确正交和逐行轮换副载波电路,并成功地把载波泄漏限制到远低于7毫伏。而为了对比PAL制和换相制在图像细节信号互串方面的性能,专门设计整数倍行频信号发生器和窄彩条信号发生器;为验证两种制式在色同步信号功能上有所不同,又特地研制能检验这些功能的解码器。另外,为使对编解码图像质量的主观评价的结果可靠,还专门研制可将PAL制和换相制信号合成、并能同时同屏解码显示的主观评价系统。彩电组的自制设备,除组内自用外,还曾在1972年全国彩色电视接收机集中设计会议上,为开展工作提供所需的各种信号。
1972~1976年,有关文献都提到,PALD解码器采用由PAL超声延迟线和直通均衡网络及加、减法器组成的梳状滤波器,可以完善分离色度信号的两个分量U、V,因而它是PAL电视机克服NTSC制相位敏感性的核心部件。但是此前国内外文献大都只强调了延迟时间应为色副载波半周期的整数倍(例如,63.943微秒),而没有明确指出这是相延时,而群延时仍应为行周期(64微秒)。为此,俞斯乐主持彩电组对PAL超声延迟线的相频特性不能通过坐标原点的问题展开深入的研讨。并由李桂苓等通过专门实验,验证若忽视群延时的57毫微秒差异,就会造成色度信号两分量的高次边频分量的串色,引起图像上的“边缘爬行”现象,影响图像质量。为解决这个问题,由张春田等开展专门的研究。此项研究对PAL超声延迟线的传输特性,包括玻璃延迟体及粘贴层的声传播特性、压电换能器的机电转换特性进行深入解剖分析。利用压电换能器机电等效电路进行的分析计算表明:尽管在玻璃延迟体和粘贴层内的声传播是非色散的,但由于换能器的复杂谐振结构,电机和机电转换过程具有不容忽视的色散性质,因而延迟线的群、相延时差可达上百毫微秒。只要正确选择换能器材料参数和精细调整端接电路及直通均衡网络,PAL制对群、相延时的不同要求可以同时满足,梳状滤波器可以完善分离色度信号。实验检验表明,理论预测与实验结果十分吻合。从而纠正此前电视界中存在的忽视PAL超声延迟线的色散特性的问题。

几乎同期, 1972年,彩电组在完成和、差色差信号行轮换平衡调幅制的研究之后,集中力量对王兆华提出的换相制进行理论与实验研究攻关。换相制也是基于彩色相序交变原理来克服NTSC制的相位敏感性缺点。但它采用逐行对换色度信号两分量相位的技术措施;而不像PAL制那样把两色度信号分量之一的相位逐行倒置。PALD解码器为了完善分离两个色度信号分量,采用色散特性延迟线;而换相制解码器用非色散特性延迟线(即群、相延时均为64.000微秒)就可以实现完善分离。而且设置的色同步信号的功能比PAL制的多。是年4月,在北京又召开一次全国电视专业会议。会上讨论试播台的建设问题,对设备提出要搞集中设计,全部国产化;而对制式提出暂行PAL制的建议。但同时仍明确还要继续自主研究,并“决定天津大学制式攻关组承担国家彩色电视新制式研究任务”。经过进一步的提高工作，到1975年12月，在中央广播事业局同意下，由电视办在天津市就换相制召开“彩色电视制式研究协作会议”。会上有人提出“换相制与PAL制数学模型等效”的观点，故会议未对换相制能否选定为国家制式作出明确结论。而是规定要继续进行多径接收、开路试验等工作。1976年5月又召开有天大、成电、上科大、北邮 、广研所等近10个单位参加“换相制理论分析问题座谈会”。会上天大代表汇报了对两种制式在数学上等效问题的分析结果(即换相制的色度矢量可以等效于基准镜相轴旋转450后的PAL制色度矢量)；会上代表还一致认为“应加速专利分析工作”。会后，俞斯乐面对现实，向天津市领导彩电会战的“三电办公室”表明不宜将换相制定为国家制式的态度。天大彩电组的换相制研究至此结束。

1977年1月，上海科技大学彩色电视制式研究组编写出版了一本《科技资料(彩色电视专辑)》。在其第63页上，有如下一段叙述：“自75年12月天津电视会议后，根据国家计委、四机部、中央广播事业局、邮电部的广电字(76)095号文件精伸，在天津、北京、上海、成都等地对换相制进行一系列的性能试验和理论研究工作。就目前情况来看，在设备条件等同情况下，换相制与PAL制具有同等技术水平，但有关换相制是否是个独立的彩电制式，尚有不同看法，有所谓PAL论和换相论之分。”这正是对换相制研究结局的真实记录。

此后，天大彩电组有秩序地进入制式攻关收尾，为避免“数学模型等效”之嫌，俞斯乐提出一种采用两个逐行反向调相90o的正交副载波分量来形成色度信号的“对转制”，其副载频无需偏置也能保证亮、色频谱的交错。但由于时机已失，只进行理论研究工作。另外，针对采用PAL制而其延迟线在色散特性上有严格要求的问题，俞斯乐与李文元合作，又研究一种矩阵分离PAL解码方案(PALMS)。它通过梳状滤波器的锯状相频特性转变色度信号，再由矩阵电路实现两分量的分离，而不依赖梳状幅频特性的分离作用，使延迟线只有群延时一个要求，容易实现。论文在第9届国标广播会议(英国Brighton)发表，为EI所收录。

经过近十年的科研实践磨练，彩电组的一些主力，从“彩电盲”成长为可在国家彩电科技进步中大有用武之地的专家。1978年，为1977年恢复高考后第一届大学生用的统编教材《电视原理》的编写任务下达到天大，天大彩电组的人员承担此重任。同年，陈容之、俞斯乐成为首批“通信与电子系统”专业硕士生导师，开始招生经学校申报，教育部批准于1979年建立以俞斯乐任主任电视研究室。

彩电组的一些主力，后来成为天大电子信息领域第一个博士点的前几名博导；并在电子信息工程学院的学科建设中发挥重要作用。现在使用的《电视原理》已是第6版，它在20多年的电视科技人才培养中建立了功勋。

DJS-153和DJS-155小型电子计算机

DJS-153小型电子计算机是原天津市无线电研究所(后改名为天津市电子计算机研究所)于1980年引进消化吸收再创新的产品，被电子工业部定位为100系列机。DJS-153机总设计师是童宣明。全部部件采用国产化设计，包括各板块逻辑图和印制板的设计、印制板国内加工、元器件指标指定与采购，以及各部件的调试及整机系统调试。DJS-153机在国内首次采用NMOS存储器，该机的设计完成代表当时国内小型计算机的先进水平，获得电子部科技成果一等奖。DJS-153小型电子计算机设计完成后，技术转移给天津电子仪器设备厂、北京无线电三厂和苏州无线电厂等单位

项目小组进行开发研究

生产。

1983年,在DJS-153的基础上,天津市无线电研究所设计完成DJS-155加固型双机双工小型计算机。项目负责人是付园明和张奎元。该机型为适用于特殊条件的加固型双机双工小型电子计算机,重点解决双机双工技术。设计为双机双工的I/O(输入和输出板),是为解决各部件耐高温,耐低温,抗震等特殊的要求,在电路设计和结构件设计上都进行了较大改进,并严格进行元器件筛选。该系统为中国国内小型机首次采用双机双工系统和CMOS存储器。成果获电子工业部科技成果二等奖。

DJS-155加固型双机双工小型计算机设计完成后转移给云南计算机厂投入生产。

天津计算机工业小区建立和发展

20世纪80年代,大量国外计算机产品拥进中国市场,国产计算机产业受到严重冲击,在何去何从的关键时刻,天津市政府果断做出建立天津计算机工业小区的决定。1984年时任市长的李瑞环主持技改领导小组会议,讨论到天津计算机厂迁扩建项目时说:不要只看是一个厂的迁扩建,要从长远看,计算机是一个朝阳产业,要按一个计算机工业小区规划,征地不要留尾巴,160亩一次性征齐。1985年2月完成小区规划设计,11月第一期土建奠基,虽然当年资金紧张,仍列为市重点工程。1986年,第一座厂房楼的钢筋混凝土框架完成。1987年市技改办现场调度,要求力争年内竣工。此时国家电子工业部制订的发展计算机产业的太极计划正待启动,天津建设计算机工业小区的举措正逢其时。经部、市协商,联合启动天津市发展计算机产业方案形成,并于1988年4月联合发文,项目总投资一亿五千万元。天津计算机工业小区建设从此纳入计划,天津计算机公司与天津计算机厂合并成天津中环计算机公司进驻小区,成为天津发展计算机产业新的起点。

经电子部推荐,1988年美国CST公司与天津合资成立天津计算机系统设备公司,第一个进驻小区,由刘尤本、刘连棣任中方经理。1989年引进VAX高挡小型机应用软件技术,先后开发上百套应用系统,有地形测控系统、自动化系统、财务系统、电力系统、公安系统等,取得高挡小型机应用系统开发多项成果,并得到高端市场的应用。

经电子部推荐,1989天津爱普生公司进驻小区,1990年开业。引进生产针式打印机关键部件打印头和喷墨打印机部件。从而促进天津红星工厂打印机国产化设计与制造。

经电子部推荐,IBM公司在考察后于1990年进驻小区,合资成立天津先进系统设备公司(英文缩写TAIPC)。引进生产IBM公司的PS-2准32位小型机、商用终端机和存折打印机,并与天津中环计算机公司的安泰公司联手开发应用系统。

天津NEC于1992年成立,并于当年在小区建厂房,生产NEC数字程序控制交换机,推出61E品种,建立100万线生产体系。开设了应用软件培训基地,为用户进行系统应用的培训。

计算机工业小区的建立,吸引国内外和本市一批IT产业的聚集,除整机厂外,一些电子元器件产品、网络产品纷纷在小区内落户。因为该小区技术设施配套较好并可以享受天津高新技术产业园区的优惠政策,所以筑巢引凤的效应凸显。

天津纬度站的建立与撤销

现代意义的天津天文学的发端，启于天津纬度站的建立。天津纬度站全称为中国科学院北京天文台天津国际纬度站。

20世纪50年代，中国科学发展十二年远景规划提出的有关纬度变化研究工作立项。经中国科学院批准，中国科学院紫金山天文台派邹仪新等筹建天津纬度站，并由她出任天津纬度站首任站长。1957年4月，该站于天津市西郊曹庄子开建，翌年建成天顶仪观测室等，该站是天津历史上最早的配置精密观察测量设施的天文台，开展纬度、极移等方面的观测研究，以及人造卫星观测工作。

纬度观测研究属天体测量学及天文地球动力学范畴。天津纬度站建立后，邹仪新和科研人员共同完成了大量开创性的工作，利用天顶仪、照相天顶筒等天文观测设备，精密测量纬度、经度（时间），精密测算地极坐标，其观测研究成果供国内有关科学研究部门、测绘部门等使用。也为国际纬度服务中央局和国际极移服务中央局提供了具有世界先进水平的测纬和极移坐标值。

天津纬度站

1964年，由朱永和、裔培荣先后牵头的极移服务与研究组，利用天津纬度站高质量的纬度观测资料，测算并提供地极坐标，研究地极坐标的变化规律，研究与极移有关的地球物理问题，1979年开始使用上海、北京、陕西、云南、武昌等5个天文台站的纬度观测结果，测算并每半个月发布一次地极坐标内插值、外插值，其“中国的综合地极坐标系统”被国内授时、测绘等有关单位正式采用。之后，该组又和南京大学等单位合作，采用分布于世界各地的43架测纬、测时天文望远镜的观测结果，建立以1968.0年平北极为原点的地极坐标系统。该系统精度高，正式通过中国科学院鉴定，成为中国极移服务的常规工作，得到有关单位正式采用和好评。

1957年10月，人类第一颗人造地球卫星上天，应苏联科学院要求，中国科学院组建人造卫星地面跟踪观测站网，在紫金山天文台设立的人造卫星光学观测办公室下12个观测站里，天津站即是其中之一。该站设于南开大学，由中科院河北分院领导，站长吴大任，业务负责人是母国光和庄威风。初期使用AT—1型广角望远镜等对苏联发射的卫星进行光学观测，观测数据分别发送至苏联“宇宙”计算中心和南京紫金山天文台。1960～1961年，在南开大学物理系帮助下，该站开展卫星无线电观测。1961年该站迁至郊区曹庄子天津纬度站。1961年，中国科学院首台MX-1502双频积分多普勒接收机安装在天津纬度站，厉国青、裔培荣使用该仪器对美国海军导航卫星系统的卫星进行无线电观测，测定地心坐标，试图用人造卫星多普勒观测方法确定比经典的时间纬度观测手段更精确的地极坐标。1962年8月，中国科学院对人造卫星地面跟踪观测站网进行调整，天津人卫站归并至北京天文台。

天津纬度站还开展其他相关天文研究工作。1974年开始，厉国青、裔培荣和中科院地理所纽仲勋等承担地理经纬度和子午线实测的沿革研究课题，发表论文8篇。对于元朝著名科学家郭守敬主持的大规模测量进行研究，挖掘的《四海测验》历史资料、有关学术论文及上报的内部报告，引起外交部的重视，被作为中国对南海诸岛拥有主权的重要证据。另，对元朝纬度测量的探究和1978年厉国青等的“我国地理经度概念的提出”一文在《中国20世纪学术大典》《清代台湾地图的演变》等多种书刊中被引载。

20世纪70年代，陈淑贤等在天津师范大学开始高等院校天文教学工作，同期，赵生等筹建天津天文馆。80年代，厉国青等开展人造地球卫星测地工作。

1989年中国科学院决定天津纬度站撤销。但天津的天文学事业还在发展，并取得新成绩。天津师范大学在星系相互作用和并合过程与星系形成和演化关系的多波段观测和研究方面获得一定成果。

索　　引

附　　录

1.该索引包括重大科技事项索引、单位名称索引和人名索引;
2.该索引按各字汉语拼音音序排列;
3.索引后的数字表示内容所在的页码。

重大科技事项索引

第一篇　科技队伍与机构

第二篇　科技管理与服务

第三篇　基础科学

第四篇 高新技术及其产业化

第五篇 工业科技

第六篇 农业科技

第七篇 医药卫生科技

12. 亚低温治疗重度颅脑损伤
13. 膀胱移行上皮癌诊断治疗的应用基础研究
14. 跟骨骨折综合治疗
15. 天津市城市居民恶性肿瘤流行趋势分析及预防研究
16. 研究发现胶质瘤化疗敏感性与染色体数目有关
17. 设计完成一种新型连续性空肠间置代胃术式
18. 肿瘤热疗用无扰测温技术及仪器
19. 产科生理常数的研究
20. 成立天津市戒毒所
21. 非线性动力学在难治性癫痫研究中的应用
22. 系统开发眼眶影像诊断技术
23. 首次发现遗传性乳光牙本质的致病基因DSPP的基因突变位点
24. 中心视野体积计量法和中心视野立体分析仪
25.《全口义齿》视听教材
26. 创建世界人工晶体中国天津培训中心
27. 建立天津市中西医结合研究院
28. 通里攻下法在腹部外科疾病中的应用与基础研究
29. 菌毒并治防治感染性多系统脏器衰竭的研究
30. 多脏器功能障碍综合征发病机理及中西医结合治疗研究
31. 常用中药材品种整理和质量研究
32. 复方丹参方药效物质及作用机理研究
33. 天津药代动力学和药效动力学国家重点实验室

第八篇 城市建设科技

1. 市委、市政府确定全面建设滨海新区
2. 实施综合开发海河两岸规划
3. 实施历史文化风貌建筑保护与文体设施建设
4. 天津市成立基础地理信息中心
5. 京津塘高速公路全线通车
6. 中心城区快速路网全线开工建设
7. 快速轨道——津滨轻轨全线运营
8. 滨海新区的开发开放正式纳入国家整体发展战略规划
9. 地铁一号线主体完工并试通车
10. 道路立交计算机辅助设计（天津市科技进步二等奖）
11. 海河大桥建成通车（国家优秀设计银质奖）
12. 大跨度预应力混凝土斜拉桥牵索式长挂蓝施工技术（天津市科技进步奖二等奖）
13. 不对称斜式钢拱桥——大沽桥建成（获世界著名桥梁大奖——尤金·菲戈奖）
14. 排水管道改革一体化研究（天津市科技进步二等奖）
15. 中国当代建筑史研究（国家科学技术奖自然科学奖一等奖）
16. 天津轻轨工程抗震分析与减震降噪研究（国家科技进步奖二等奖）
17. 可视化仿真技术及其在水利水电工程中的应用研究（国家科技进步奖一等奖）
18. 水利工程仿真基础理论与方法研究（天津市科学技术奖自然科学一等奖）
19. 北方地区安全饮用水保障技术研究（天津市科技进步二等奖）
20. 国产化5000立方米高压天然气球罐技术研究（天津市科技进步二等奖）
21. 建成以环戊烷为聚氨酯发泡剂的预制直埋式保温管生产线（天津市科技进步二等奖）

第九篇 社会发展科技

1. 国家环境保护恶臭污染控制重点实验室
2. 国家给水排水工程技术研究中心试验基地
3. 建成40万吨/日的东郊污水处理厂
4. 华北地形变监测网
5. 天津港老码头改造
6. 天津港东突堤工程
7. 应用双膜工艺建成第一座开发区污水再生水厂
8. 城市污水资源化
9. 天津市空气污染预报
10. 秦岭特长铁路隧道修建技术
11. 长大隧道全断面岩石掘进机掘进技术
12. 民航发动机可靠性研究
13. 飞行品质监控和飞行图形仿真系统
14. 增强型双局号平稳过渡升位技术方案
15. 建成天津人民广播电台互联网广播系统
16. 广播电视卫星地球站建设
17. 进口药材质量标准与检验方法

单位名称索引

人名索引

姓　名　页码

姓　名	页码

编后记

天津市科技史志编修办公室(以下简称"科技史志办")自1986年成立以来,始终坚持实事求是的思想路线,发扬艰苦奋斗、不断创新的精神,1998年完成首轮《天津通志·科学技术志》的编纂工作之后,即着手对首轮科技志编纂工作进行经验总结。1999年完成天津市科委软科学研究项目"中国地方科技志编纂理论与方法研究",2005年又与北京市科技史志办公室共同完成北京市科委立项的软科学研究项目"科技志编纂若干理论与方法的研究"。1999～2001年,科技史志办在担任全国科技史志研究会理事长单位期间,编辑完成6期《科技史志》杂志,组织多次全国科技史志学术交流与研讨活动。2000年,科技史志办完成市科委软科学研究项目"关于编纂科技大事记的研究",并于2003年出版《天津科学技术大事记(～2000年)》。科技史志办在编修《天津科学技术志》的同时,一直关注着"地方科技年鉴"的编纂出版,并于2004年出版《天津科技年鉴(创始卷)》,其后,《天津科技年鉴》作为年刊逐年编辑出版,并多次获得国家级奖励。科技史志办这些软科学研究成果和专著、刊物等,为进行第二轮科技志编纂做好了理论储备和资料积累。

根据中国地方志指导小组对于续修地方志提出的要求,天津市地方志编修委员会选定天津市科委为第二轮修志试点单位。2005年,天津市科委全面启动二轮《天津市志·科学技术志》编修工作。至2018年,历时13年,二轮《天津市志·科学技术志》终于编纂成书,与读者见面。

二轮《天津市志·科学技术志》全书共设10篇,76章,200余万字,记述的时间断限为1991～2005年。二轮科技志编修工作紧紧围绕天津市科技发展"八五""九五""十五"规划的实施,力求全面反映这一历史时期科技发展的突出成就和重要历程,系统记述从基础科学、高新技术到各个行业领域的科技发展和创新成果,特别是科学技术在促进经济社会发展中取得的主要成效,以及深化科技体制改革、优化科技创新环境等方面采取的重大举措。全书在内容上横跨诸多学科和诸多行业,覆盖面广,为了突出科技发展主线,在纵向上力求理清15年间各个领域科技发展的脉络。本书记述的历史时期,正值天津市机构改革与企业转制的关键时期,许多系统和单位面临领导班子换届,人员更迭,资料散失,增加了组稿的难度。由于撰稿人多是从本单位的工作出发提供资料,科技史志办为了使来稿达到志体要求,通常要经过培训、面谈、Email和电话等方式反复与撰稿人进行交流,每个章节的志稿都须经过十几次甚至几十次的修改、查询、补充、审评,如此等等。可见本书编修工作经历的难度非常之大。

在编修二轮科技志过程中,我们坚持走"政府主持,众手修志和专家修志"相结合的路子,经历了组织发动、稿件征集、分纂总纂、评审定稿的编纂过程。2018年3月9日,书稿通过市地方志办组织的专家复审,并给予很高评价,认为该书观点正确,视野开阔;内容丰富,资料翔实;体例完备,结构严谨;行文规范,语言洗练。体现了时代特点,突出了地方特色和专业特色,做到了思想性、科学性和资料性的统一;具有很强的存史、资政、教化价值,是一部精心编纂的合格志书。

本书的编纂过程伴随着的是编辑人员在繁重与默默无闻的工作业态下的代代相续,体现的是编辑人员对修志事业的执着和对科技事业的感念与情怀。在科学思想的指导下,在与各单位的交流、与专家学者研讨过程中,考订成果、著述史实,科技史志办编辑人员的编辑能力、团队协作能力得到提升,整体编纂出版水平实现了跃升。

天津市科委历来十分重视科技史志的编修工作,历届科委主任对修志工作都给予过具体的批示,天津市科学学研究所在人员配置和办公条件上给予了保障。同时,本书的编纂工作,得到中国地方志指导小组的具体指导,得到天津市地方志办公室的大力推动,得到天津市各有关委办局、企业集团、高等院校、科研院所和各区县科委等单位的大力支持，天津市科学技术信息研究所也为该书的编写工作提供了很大的帮助，在此表示感谢。

同时，衷心感谢参与本书编纂工作的专家学者、组稿人、撰稿人。因为你们的辛勤付出，成就了这部跨越各职能部门管理范围的综合性科技资料文献。感谢国内、市内各级有关领导给予的关注与支持，特别是本书得到了原天津市委常委、市人大副主任王成怀，天津市原副市长、市人大副主任梁肃等的关心和指导，在此谨致谢意！

求实为本成大业，集思广益著华章。在此，向已故天津科技史志主编李树夫表示深深的怀念。

天津市科技史志编修办公室
2018年7月

组稿与撰稿人员

（姓氏笔画为序）

丁宏宏	于 谧	于彩虹	万日明	马 昱	马 骏
马元威	马玉隽	王 戈	王 兰	王 冰	王 宏
王 萍	王 琥	王玉荣	王生田	王立新	王兆军
王延群	王宇珍	王纪晨	王明时	王明忠	王秉成
王学凤	王学政	王学铮	王承刚	王建设	王建新
王项南	王春常	王美茹	王颖奇	王满华	历国青
毛铁伦	尹德山	孔宪波	邓文瑞	石 群	白玉娟
艾淑华	卢海宏	卢梅奎	田 军	田在善	丛继坤
冯 培	冯绍峰	宁晓梅	江 涛	邢 卓	邢淑颖
曲远芳	毕 玲	曲爱丽	朱 洁	朱子平	庄淑梅
刘 平	刘 红	刘 虹	刘 桐	刘 娟	刘 维
刘长山	刘文安	刘玉飞	刘立存	刘永绣	刘亚平
刘茂生	刘学功	刘树清	刘爱平	刘晓年	刘晓玲
刘润田	刘淑云	刘淑静	刘景泰	齐 勇	齐玉梅
安丽丽	祁 伟	孙文敏	孙玉林	孙永军	孙百顺
孙春水	孙家琦	苏燕舞	杜 珺	李 华	李 芮
李 悦	李 娟	李 晶	李广行	李广智	李文颖
李龙顺	李向上	李会娟	李庆斌	李亚丽	李进军
李来库	李宏捷	李佑强	李国建	李明琪	李宝成
李春成	李珍萍	李贵生	李新明	李慧芝	杨 昕

杨　荣	杨　翊	杨　斌	杨　瑾	杨万龙	杨卫红
杨文宝	杨文艳	杨志红	杨晓刚	杨晓菊	杨耀锡
吴　肖	吴志诚	吴晓古	何　峰	何灵均	谷建军
汪长余	汪新霞	沈　文	沈天桔	宋　芳	余　知
张　乐	张　军	张　振	张　圆	张　娟	张　雁
张　辉	张　慧	张士琦	张亚楠	张丽红	张利刚
张启俊	张国庆	张建亭	张贵生	张铁良	张家明
张海河	张景成	张韫菁	张新升	张静楷	陈子强
陈云红	陈可欣	陈申阳	陈志远	陈国廷	陈萸芳
陈翠荣	陈晓明	邹　立	邵守良	苗玉成	宗建新
武玉峰	卓玉生	周　蕊	周　璐	周天慈	周长钰
周文琴	周志华	周树良	周晓冬	周琳生	周智华
孟玉环	孟胜煦	赵　政	赵凤华	赵文华	赵玉秀
赵世敏	赵冲久	赵苏民	赵学铭	赵洪亮	赵智帮
郝金才	郝雅梅	相俊红	钟　翔	段炳柱	侯庆春
侯军儒	俞崇新	姚晨辉	秦　月	贾晓慧	夏中华
徐　勇	徐一凡	徐慧明	奚　洋	高　旭	高　杰
郭士明	郭青平	郭金奎	郭建辉	诸葛涛	袁根正
康　莉	黄　欣	黄　河	黄泉河	戚　红	常　津
常　琳	寇　颐	寇绍荣	董　怡	董　敏	董昊悦
韩仲琦	韩宝玲	韩晓明	韩瑞发	韩瑞洁	程宏美
傅晓晖	谢　宁	靳海燕	楼关寿	蔡光耀	蔡钰馨
管学富	廖建炜	潘　润	薛元贵	戴永锋	魏恒州

英文翻译　天津外国语大学高级翻译学院　李　晶